BUSINESS LAW

TEXT AND CASES IN THE LEGAL ENVIRONMENT

Sixth Edition

Business Law

Text and Cases in the Legal Environment

Sixth Edition

John R. Allison
University of Texas at Austin

Robert A. Prentice
University of Texas at Austin

The Dryden Press
Harcourt Brace College Publishers

Fort Worth   Philadelphia   San Diego   New York   Orlando   Austin   San Antonio
Toronto   Montreal   London   Sydney   Tokyo

Publisher	Liz Widdicombe
Acquisitions Editor	Scott Isenberg
Developmental Editor	Glenn Martin
Text Designer	Bill Brammer
Copy Editor	Cindy Simpson
Indexer	Leslie Leland Frank
Compositor	G&S Typesetters
Production Services	Seaside Publishing Services, San Diego
Text Type	10.5/12 New Caledonia
Cover Image	© Mark Humphries

Address for Editorial Correspondence
The Dryden Press, 301 Commerce Street, Suite 3700, Fort Worth, TX 76102

Address for Orders
The Dryden Press, 6277 Sea Harbor Drive, Orlando, FL 32887
1-800-782-4479, or 1-800-433-0001 (in Florida)

ACKNOWLEDGMENTS: Chapter 1 Legal Focus International Box: Excerpts from *The Wall Street Journal,* October 20, 1992, B7 Col. 1. Reprinted by permission of *The Wall Street Journal,* © 1992 Dow Jones & Company, Inc. All rights reserved worldwide. **Box 11-1:** Wayne Green, "Ruling May Hurt Lender-Liability Suits," *The Wall Street Journal,* June 30, 1992, B7. Reprinted by permission of *The Wall Street Journal,* © 1992 Dow Jones & Company, Inc. All rights reserved worldwide. **Box 12-1:** Kirk A. Pasich, "Beware the 'Creeping Contract'," as published in the *National Law Journal,* March 2, 1992, p. 25, by permission of Kirk A. Pasich, Hill, Wynne, Troop & Meisinger, Los Angeles. **Box 14-2:** Meredith Wadan, "More Firms Restrict Departing Workers," *The Wall Street Journal,* June 26, 1992, B1. Reprinted by permission of *The Wall Street Journal,* © 1992 Dow Jones & Company, Inc. All rights reserved worldwide. **Box 16-1:** Ellen J. Pollack and Richard Gibson, "Written Confirmation of Deals is Upheld," *The Wall Street Journal,* April 2, 1991, B2. Reprinted by permission of *The Wall Street Journal,* © 1991 Dow Jones & Company, Inc. All rights reserved worldwide. **Box 34-1:** Eric J. Wallach, "Businesses Fear Case May Bring Courts into Partnership Matters," as published in the *National Law Journal,* September 24, 1992, p. 18, courtesy of Eric J. Wallach, Esq., Rosenman & Collin, New York. **Box 36-1:** Ann Monroe, "Pitfalls for Partnership Investors May Lurk in That Seemingly Insignificant Fine Print," *The Wall Street Journal,* February 13, 1987, 23. Reprinted by permission of *The Wall Street Journal,* © 1987 Dow Jones & Company, Inc. All rights reserved worldwide. **Box 37-1:** Jefferey Tannenbaum, "Partnership, Corporation Aren't Only Ways to Start Out," *The Wall Street Journal,* May 14, 1991, B2. Reprinted by permission of *The Wall Street Journal,* © 1992 Dow Jones & Company, Inc. All rights reserved worldwide. **Box 38-1:** Avery D. Foreman, "Redefining Close Corporations," ABA Journal, March 1992, reprinted by permission of the ABA Journal. **Box 51-1:** Michele Galen, "Getting the Kinks out of Your Credit Report," reprinted from the May 25, 1992 issue of *Business Week* by special permission copyright © 1992 by McGraw-Hill, Inc.

ISBN: 0-03-097733-9
Library of Congress Catalog Number: 93-072829
Printed in the United States of America
3 4 5 6 7 8 9 0 1 2   016   9 8 7 6 5 4 3 2 1

The Dryden Press
Harcourt Brace College Publishers

THE DRYDEN PRESS SERIES IN BUSINESS LAW

Allison and Prentice
The Legal Environment of Business
Fourth Edition

Allison, Prentice, and Howell
Business Law: Text and Cases
Sixth Edition

Allison, Prentice, and Howell
Business Law: Text and Cases
Alternate Fifth Edition

Estey
The Unions

Lieberman and Siedel
Business Law and the Legal Environment
Third Edition

Lieberman and Siedel
The Legal Environment of Business

Maurer
Business Law: Text and Cases
Second Edition

Spiro and Houghtelling
The Dynamics of Law
Third Edition

Warner
The Legal Environment of Business

THE HARCOURT BRACE COLLEGE OUTLINE SERIES

Webb
Business Law

Preface

We have had but one goal in preparing the sixth edition of *Business Law: Text and Cases in the Legal Environment*—to make the text a more useful vehicle for the study of Business Law by future business managers at both graduate and undergraduate levels in our colleges and universities. In striving to attain this goal, we rejected the temptation merely to fine-tune the prior edition and have developed a number of new features that will be highlighted later in the preface.

This edition, nonetheless, retains the basic strengths of earlier editions, which can be described as follows:

First, we have continued to use a lucid, conversational writing style. In addition, we have tried to illuminate legal principles by frequent use of examples to show how these rules apply to "real world" situations.

Second, illustrative court cases are interspersed throughout the text materials, rather than relegated to chapter ends. As in previous editions, each case begins with a presentation of the facts by the authors so that students will not be confused by the sometimes difficult terminology used by the courts. The opinions of the courts, on the other hand, are carefully edited but retain the courts' own language. This approach ensures that the students first have a clear idea of the elements of the controversy that are relevant to the text discussion and then gives them a feel for the way the court resolved. it. It allows students to see how the court weighed conflicting evidence in deciding what the facts were, how it viewed particular facts as relevant or irrelevant to the issue at hand, and how it selected the legal principles that it felt to be dispositive of those issues.

CHANGES IN THIS EDITION

The most significant changes and additions are the following:

- Boxed inserts in each chapter highlight and explain current events related to the relevant legal topic (The Law at Work), relevant international applications (Legal Focus: International), and relevant ethical principles (Legal Focus: Ethics).
- A new chapter on Environmental Protection Law, Chapter 50, has been included.
- Chapter 2, Court Systems and Jurisdiction, has been almost completely rewritten.
- Chapter 3, Litigation and Alternative Methods of Dispute Resolution, has been expanded and completely rewritten, with much greater coverage of alternative dispute resolution.
- Chapter 5, Constitutional Law, has been completely rewritten.
- Chapter 9, Business Torts, and Chapter 22, Sales: Warranties and Products Liability, have benefited from substantial rewriting.
- Chapters 24–28 on Commercial Paper have been completely rewritten, and now include coverage of revised Articles 3 and 4 of the UCC.
- Chapters 33–40 on Business Organizations have been substantially rewritten, and now include coverage of revisions to the RMBCA, RULPA, RUPA, and the recent legislative creation in many states of LLCs (limited liability companies).
- Chapter 41, Securities Regulation, and Chapter 42, Legal Liability of Accountants, have been substantially updated.
- Chapter 49, Employment Law, has been substantially updated and rewritten.
- Chapter 52, The Legal Environment of International Business, has been substantially rewritten.
- The remainder of the book has been updated where necessary and includes almost 100 new cases.

ANCILLARY MATERIALS

Business Law: Text and Cases in the Legal Environment, sixth edition, is supported by a comprehensive ancillary package which includes an *Instructor's Manual and Transparency Masters,* a *Test Bank,* a set of preprinted tests, a *Computerized Test Bank*, and a *Study Guide*.

Each instructor has his or her own unique approach to the teaching of Business Law. Our *Instructor's Manual* is a tool that assists the instructor in integrating his or her style with the approach taken by the book. Each chapter includes helpful authors' suggestions for teaching the chapter. Chapter outlines have been added to assist the instructor in organizing lecture notes. Succinct case briefs are included for each case in the book. We have also added an annotated list of additional cases so that the instructor can easily supplement the cases found in the text. Each chapter in the *Instructor's Manual* ends with answers to end-of-chapter questions and problems.

The *Test Bank* contains over 2,000 multiple-choice and true-false questions. We have added numerous essay questions for the instructor to choose from.

A *Computerized Test Bank* is also available for this edition for use on the IBM PC®.

A comprehensive *Study Guide* provides additional review and reinforcement of all topics covered in the text. Each chapter of the guide, which has traditionally been well received by students and instructors, begins with a chapter summary. The key term and matching exercises also provide an excellent review for students. The purpose of these two sections is to test the student's basic mastery of the concepts, laws, and rulings discussed in the text. Multiple-choice and true-false questions are provided, as well as case analysis problems which provide fact-patterns to which the student is asked to respond. All three types of questions will test the student's comprehension of the material in an examination setting. The questions are similar in format and type to those included in the *Test Bank*.

Another feature of the *Study Guide* is the inclusion of legal forms. We include these forms to give the student a good idea of how legal concepts are employed in the business world.

ACKNOWLEDGMENTS

As with any major undertaking, this text owes its existence to the efforts of many individuals. We wish to thank Luis Rodriguez at Arkansas State University for his preparation of the *Test Bank*, and Ellen Harshman at St. Louis University for the *Study Guide* for this edition. The reviewers who read the manuscript for this edition provided valuable suggestions, and we wish to acknowledge them here. They are John McGee (Southwest Texas State University), Charles Wyzanski (Boston University), Diane Hathaway (University of Cincinnati), John Norwood (University of Arkansas), and Laurel Boone (Webster University). Additionally, we would like to thank all the past reviewers who have contributed to the formation of this book: Peter A. Alces (University of Alabama), William Burke (University of Lowell), Thomas Giordano (St. John's University), William Halm (Ferris State University), Don Hoy (Des Moines Area Community College), Avi Liveson (Hunter College), Gene A. Marsh (University of Alabama), John Patrick McConnell (Washington State University), Patricia Nunley (Baylor University), Robert Peace (North Carolina State University), Daniel Reynolds (Middle Tennessee State University), John Sherry (Cornell University), and Ronald L. Taylor (Metropolitan State College).

We also wish to thank our editors at The Dryden Press, Scott Isenberg (Acquisitions Editor), Glenn E. Martin (Developmental Editor), and our Production Manager, Diane Southworth, for their continued support.

In addition, we are grateful to our students for keeping us fresh and fully challenged, and to our families for their continued support.

John R. Allison, *Austin, Texas*
Robert A. Prentice, *Austin, Texas*

To the Student

Welcome to the study of Business Law. Among our goals is the desire to help you learn (1) to understand how the legal system interacts with and to a large extent shapes business activity in this country; (2) to recognize specific legal concepts that will be useful in any business career; (3) to become comfortable with the interplay between legal and ethical principles so that you may better analyze the "musts" as well as the "shoulds" of conduct in a civilized society; and (4) to master the process of legal analysis which is, basically, an important form of problem solving that can be helpful in resolving any type of problem that might arise. Legal problems are, after all, only another type of business problem.

We have written this book to challenge you. Many legal concepts are complicated. They lose their meaning and relevance if they are oversimplified. This book is designed to allow you to learn as much as possible and not to shortchange the hard-working student with a thirst for knowledge. At the same time, the book contains a number of features to enhance learning which have enabled thousands of students using earlier editions to master the important concepts being presented. Do not be intimidated! The law is interesting, it is fun, and it is generally based on common sense.

Among the helpful pedagogical features of this book are (1) key terms defined in the glossary and highlighted in boldface type in the text; (2) chapter summaries designed to emphasize the key points in each chapter; and (3) questions and problems at the end of the chapters provided to illustrate key concepts and to give you an opportunity to apply the principles that you have learned from reading the text.

CASE ANALYSIS

This textbook will familiarize you with basic legal concepts, enable you to avoid legal problems in the course of your business activities, help you decide when it is necessary to call an attorney, and make it easier to deal with your attorney. The book is not designed to make you a lawyer or to give you all of the legal reasoning skills that law school would impart. Nonetheless, you will definitely learn some of the techniques of legal analysis in reading this text, and one of the most important is the ability to "brief" a case.

The study of law is, to a large extent, the study of the written opinions of the judges who decide legal cases. The essence of legal reasoning has been said to be the ability to reason analogically among these opinions. Indeed, a law school textbook is often filled with cases, supplemented by a few questions but very little explanatory material. The students must analyze the cases, extract the key principles, and construct their own syntheses of the legal rules in that field of study.

The aim of a business law text is somewhat more modest. As you examine this book, you will see that it consists primarily of explanatory material that sets forth basic legal principles and then explains them with the aid of examples. Although the chapters are primarily textual, they typically contain several opinions from real cases to illustrate the most significant principles. The importance of these cases cannot be overstated. They put the abstract principles into a concrete, useful, and often interesting context.

Your professor will likely urge you to "brief" these illustrative cases as a way of familiarizing you with the basics of legal reasoning. This is a tried-and-true method of studying the law and, with practice, is easy to master because the briefing process is not complicated. A brief is to a case simply what a book report is to a book—your summary of the principal points of the court's opinion. If you analyze the court's opinion and summarize that analysis in your own words, you will more readily understand and retain its key points.

There is no one correct form for a brief, but a typical brief might contain these elements:

1. Name of the Case. The title of a case, e.g., *Smith v. Jones,* indicates the parties to the suit. When a case is first filed, a title of Smith v. (versus) Jones usually tells us that Smith is the *plaintiff,* the part who seeks relief in court against the *defendant,* Jones. Note, however, that many of the cases contained in this text are opinions not of the trial court but of appellate courts. If the judgment of the trial court is appealed, the rule followed by most states is that the title of the case remains *Smith v. Jones* in the appellate court no matter which party is the *appellant* (the one bringing the appeal). In the federal courts, on the other hand, the appellant's name appears first. Under this rule, if Jones (defendant) loses in a U.S. district court and appeals to a U.S. court of appeals, the title of the case will become *Jones v. Smith* in the higher court. For this reason, when one sees a case in a federal appellate court (and in some state appellate courts), one cannot assume that Jones was the plaintiff in the suit simply because his or her name is listed first. The facts of the case must be read carefully to determine who brought the suit.

2. Citation. It is not important for you to master the legal citation system. Nonetheless, your professor may wish you to have a passing familiarity with it. The heading of the cases in this text will not only give the case name but also will specifically indicate which state or federal court rendered the decision. The major case in the first chapter, for example, is titled: *Soldano v. O'Daniels,* California Court of Appeal, 190 Cal. Rptr. 310 (1983). The California Court of Appeal is an intermediate appellate court in the California state system. (You will study the structure of the state and federal court systems in Chapter 2.) The rest of the citation tells us that this opinion may be found in a law library in Volume 190 of the California Reporter, at page 310, and that the decision was rendered in 1983. All important state and federal appellate court opinions are contained in bound volumes to which these citations refer. Recent innovations in computerized legal research have, in fact, led to an entirely new supplementary system of citation.

3. Facts. Lawsuits are filed because things have happened to people. Contracts have been breached. Products have exploded. Trade secrets have been stolen. Legal principles are "fact sensitive." To do justice in a particular case, legal principles must be tailored to the specific facts involved. In a trial, those facts are adduced in the form of testimony of witnesses and submission of documents. When an appellate court hears a case on appeal, the judges read a transcript of the important testimony given at the trial level. When any court issues its opinion, it will summarize the facts as it understands them from the testimony and documents presented by the parties. A typical legal opinion will begin with such a summary.

Your authors have taken the court's summaries of the relevant facts and further winnowed them down. You will note that each major case in this chapter begins with a factual summary printed in boldface. That summary will tell you what happened that led to a lawsuit being filed, what lawsuit was filed, and what if any action was taken before the case reached the court whose opinion is quoted. Some briefs contain the trial court ruling as a separate section rather than including it in a summary of the facts. In briefing the case, be sure to put the facts into your own words. The authors' summary can usually be boiled down even further, and it is helpful to your understanding of the case to go to this effort.

4. Issue. Judicial opinions are written largely to answer legal questions that are raised in the litigation. The cases that have been selected for inclusion in this text were chosen to illustrate particular legal principles. Each case answers one or two key legal questions. Detecting the issue in a case is sometimes the most difficult part of writing a brief. Sometimes the court will come right out and phrase the issue itself. (The *Soldano* opinion does this in the first sentence.) More commonly, you must decide the issue for yourself after reading the opinion. The issue often revolves around the question of what should be the content of a particular legal rule.

5. Holding. This is simply the legal answer provided to the issue presented to the court.

6. Rationale. The most important part of an opinion is the judge's explanation for why they have ruled as they have. Their reasoning is contained in the rationale of the opinion. Our text presents excerpts from the judges' own reasoning that explains why they decided the cases as they did. Again, the best way for you to understand the judges' reasoning is to read the opinions carefully and then summarize that reasoning in your own words. A good brief is, in fact, brief. It contains the essence of the judges' reasons for ruling as they did, but no more.

SAMPLE BRIEF

If you took the *Soldano v. O'Daniels* case in Chapter 1 to 25 law professors and asked them to brief it, all their briefs would be similar, but no two would be alike. As in book reports, there is no absolute "right" or "wrong" brief in terms of either structure or content. We have included a sample brief of the *Soldano* case, however, to give you some indication of what a brief might look like.

NAME: **Soldano v. O'Daniels**

CITATION: **California Court of Appeal, 190 Cal. Rptr. 310 (1983)**

FACTS: Plaintiff's father was killed in Happy Jack's Saloon by a gunman after a bystander had gone to summon help at the Circle Inn. The bartender at the Circle Inn refused to call the police or to allow the bystander to do so. Plaintiff sued the bartender and the bar's owner. The trial judge granted summary judgment for defendants, ruling that they had no legal duty to help plaintiff's father in any way.

ISSUE: "Does a business establishment incur liability for negligence (thus requiring it to pay money damages to a close relative under the state's wrongful death statute) if it denies use of its telephone to a Good Samaritan who explains an emergency situation occurring without and wishes to call the police?"

HOLDING: Yes. The trial court's ruling is reversed.

RATIONALE: Although it has been criticized, the general rule is that citizens have no *legal* duty to help their fellow man in peril. The law has imposed some exceptions, such as where there exists a special relationship (for example, psychiatrist–patient), but these exceptions do not apply here.

Nonetheless, public policy supporting crime prevention demands creation of a new, limited exception in cases such as this. Although the law should not impose a duty on these defendants to actively assist the plaintiff's father or on anyone to allow someone claiming an emergency to enter their homes, there should be a duty not to obstruct the efforts of a Good Samaritan who wishes to call the police from a public establishment, where a response to the request involves little, if any, cost or risk.

Brief Contents

Table of Contents

BUSINESS LAW

TEXT AND CASES IN THE LEGAL ENVIRONMENT

Sixth Edition

PART I

THE LEGAL ENVIRONMENT OF BUSINESS

PART I OF THIS TEXT consists of 10 chapters that are devoted to matters that cut across or substantially affect all areas of law. Its purpose is to lay the groundwork for an understanding of the somewhat narrower substantive bodies of law, such as the law of contracts and corporation law, that are covered in the parts of the text that follow.

These introductory matters are largely concerned with structures, processes, and analyses—the structure of our existing laws and court systems, the legal processes by which laws are made and applied to actual controversies, and analysis of the historical reasons responsible for these structures and processes.

Chapter 1 examines the nature and purpose of legal rules—the special characteristics that set these rules apart from other societal rules and the characteristics these rules must possess if they are to remain an effective part of the legal system.

Chapter 2 provides familiarity with the structure and jurisdiction of the federal and state courts, and Chapter 3 examines the roles of the trial and appellate courts in the resolution of real controversies. We examine these "adjudicatory processes" of the law in these chapters so that actual court cases can be utilized in the text as early and effectively as possible. Chapter 3 also discusses alternative dispute resolution—means by which disputes are resolved without court litigation.

Chapters 4 through 6 deal with the most important *sources* of legal principles and processes. Chapter 4 explains the difference between *common law*—law that is made by judges in the courts—and *statutory law*—law which originates in the legislatures. In Chapter 5, our paramount source of law—the Constitution—is explored; particular attention is paid to the role played by the Constitution in empowering and limiting the actions of government in regulating business activities. Chapter 6 discusses the role of federal and state administrative agencies as makers, interpreters, and enforcers of law through rule-making and decision-making activities.

Chapters 7 through 9 examine the various kinds of "wrongs" that our legal system must deal with. Chapter 7 briefly looks at the basic nature of criminal law and procedure, and then devotes most of its attention to "white collar crime"—that is, crime in business. Chapter 8 provides a broad overview of the law of torts, or civil wrongs, which are those kinds of wrongful conduct (such as negligence or defamation) that may be encountered in both business and nonbusiness settings. Chapter 9 then looks at *business torts,* a term we use to describe torts that occur almost exclusively in the course of competition among business firms. Tort actions arising out of the sale of defective products, however, are reserved for later discussion in Chapter 22 when we study the law of sales transactions.

Chapter 10 concludes Part I with an examination of the ethical questions and moral obligations that permeate business life. The chapter pays special attention to the relationship between law and ethics, and the ethical problems that often run as undercurrents beneath legal problems.⚖

Chapter 1

Nature and Sources of Law

Law as a Subject of Study
What Is the Law?
Rules and Processes
Requisites of a Legal System
Some Classifications of Law
Legal Misconceptions
Law, Justice, and Morals

A. P. Herbert once wrote: "The general mass, if they consider the law at all, regard it as they regard some monster in the zoo. It is odd, it is extraordinary; but there it is, they have known it all their lives, they suppose that there must be some good reason for it, and accept it as inevitable and natural."[1]

LAW AS A SUBJECT OF STUDY

Although the law is not nearly as odd or extraordinary as many persons believe, it is undeniably "there"—an integral part of the environment that has been a source of great interest, even fascination, for centuries.

Considering the pervasiveness of the law, this is hardly surprising. Almost all human activity is affected by it in one manner or another, and this alone is adequate explanation for such widespread interest. Certainly, anyone contemplating a business transaction of any magnitude today realizes that he or she must consider not only the physical and financial effort it will entail but—to some extent, at least—the legal ramifications as well. And beyond the practical effect law has on individual conduct in specific situations, it possesses additional characteristics that make its study uniquely rewarding.

First, although the law is by no means an occult language understood only by lawyers, it clearly is a subject that is *academically stimulating*. For students to get any real benefit from a course in law, they must at the very least learn to recognize precise legal issues, understand the reasoning of the courts as set forth in their decisions, and subject this reasoning to critical analysis. These activities involve varying degrees of mental exercise; and although this is not always pleasurable, it fosters a degree of mental discipline that is not easily acquired elsewhere.

Second, students should have the opportunity to consider the law as a *societal institution*—to see how it has affected conduct and thought and how it has been influenced by them in return. Whatever the law is, it certainly is not static, and it certainly does not exist in a vacuum.

This approach, which emphasizes the impact of social and economic changes on the law, gives the subject a liberal arts flavor. When viewed in this light, the law and its processes become rewarding to anyone having even a passing interest in economics, sociology, and political science.

WHAT IS THE LAW?

Ever since the law began to take form, scholars have spent impressive amounts of time and thought analyzing its purposes and defining what it is and what it ought to be—in short, fitting it into a philosophic scheme of one form or another. Although space does not permit inclusion of even the major essays in which these philosophers defend their respective views, their conclusions provide us with useful observations about the nature of law. Consider, for example, the following:

We have been told by Plato that law is a form of social control, an instrument of the good life, the way to the discovery of reality, the true reality of the social structure; by Aristotle that it is a rule of conduct, a contract, an ideal of reason, a rule of decision, a form of order; by Cicero that it is the agreement of reason and nature, the distinction between the just and the unjust, a command or prohibition; by Aquinas that it is an ordinance of reason for the common good, made by him who has care of the community, and promulgated [thereby]; by Bacon that certainty is the prime necessity of law; by Hobbes that law is the command of the sovereign; by Spinoza that it is a plan of life; by Leibniz that its character is determined by the structure of society; by Locke that it is a norm established by the commonwealth; by Hume that it is a body of precepts; by Kant that it is a harmonizing of wills by means of universal rules in the interests of freedom; by Fichte that it is a relation between human beings; by Hegel that it is an unfolding or realizing of the idea of right.[2]

Although these early writers substantially agree as to the general *purpose* of law—the ensuring of orderliness to all human activity—their *definitions* of the term vary considerably. Today there is still no definition of *law* that has universal approval, even in legal circles—a fact that is no doubt attributable to its inherent breadth. One can understand how very broad the law is by considering just these few widely

[1]*Uncommon Law,* 1936.

[2]Huntington Cairns, *Legal Philosophy from Plato to Hegel* (Baltimore: Johns Hopkins University Press, 1949).

varying matters with which the law must deal: (1) the standards of care required of a surgeon in the operating room, (2) the determination of whether an "exclusive dealing" provision in a motion picture distributor's contracts constitutes an unfair method of competition under federal law, and (3) the propriety of a witness's testimony when it is challenged as constituting "hearsay" under the rules of evidence.

A brief comment about *sources* of law is in order at this early point. In our legal system (and in most others throughout the world), there are *primary* and *secondary* sources. Primary sources, which contain legally binding rules and procedures, include federal and state constitutions, statutes (legislative enactments), administrative agency regulations, and court decisions; also included are federal treaties and city ordinances. Secondary sources summarize and explain the law, and sometimes criticize and suggest changes in it. Such sources are not legally binding, but are frequently referred to and used by courts, administrative agencies, legislative staff members, and practicing attorneys as aids in determining what the law is or should be. Secondary sources include research articles in academic legal periodicals, restatements (which consist of summaries of and commentary on specific subject areas of law by experts in those areas), legal texts and encyclopedias, and others.

RULES AND PROCESSES

At the risk of oversimplification, it can be said that two major approaches to the teaching and study of law exist today. The *rule-oriented approach* views the law as consisting of the rules that are in effect within a state or nation at a given time. This is very likely what practicing attorneys have in mind when they speak about the law, and it is a perfectly respectable view. Witness the following definition adopted by the American Law Institute: "[Law] is the body of principles, standards and rules which the courts . . . apply in the decision of controversies brought before them."[3]

The *process-oriented approach* sees the law in a broader light: The *processes by which the rules and principles are formulated* (rather than the rules and principles themselves) constitute the major element of law. Because law is necessitated solely by human

activity, those who emphasize process contend that the ever-changing problems resulting from this activity and *the ways in which the law attempts to solve them* must receive primary emphasis if one is to gain a proper insight into the subject. The following definition expresses this view: "Law is a dynamic process, a system of regularized, institutionalized procedures for the orderly decision of social questions, including the settlement of disputes."[4]

Obviously, the law is both rule and process. Each approach to the teaching and study of law is legitimate; indeed, each is essential and inevitable. The only difference is in emphasis. In this text, process is emphasized in the first few chapters, and rules in many of the later chapters. Our discussion of rules and principles, however, always includes related legal processes.

REQUISITES OF A LEGAL SYSTEM

For a legal system to function properly, particularly within a democratic government such as ours, it must command the respect of the great majority of people governed by it. To do so, the legal rules that compose it must, as a practical matter, possess certain characteristics. They must be (1) relatively certain, (2) relatively flexible, (3) known or knowable, and (4) apparently reasonable.

In the following chapters we consider these requirements more fully and determine the extent to which our legal system satisfies them. For the moment, we give brief descriptions of each of the four.

Certainty

One essential element of a stable society is reasonable certainty about its laws, not only at a given moment but over long periods of time. Many of our activities, particularly business activities, are based on the assumption that legal principles will remain stable into the foreseeable future. If this were not so, chaos would result. For example, no television network would enter into a contract with a professional football league, under which it is to pay millions of dollars for the right to televise league games, if it were not reasonably sure that the law would compel the league to live up to its contractual obligations or

---

[3]*Restatement, Conflict of Laws 2d*, §4. The American Law Institute, 1971.

[4]James I. Houghteling, Jr., *The Dynamics of Law* (New York: Harcourt Brace Jovanovich, 1963).

to pay damages if it did not. And no lawyer would advise a client on a contemplated course of action without similar assurances.

Because of these considerations, the courts (and to a lesser extent the legislatures) are generally reluctant to overturn principles that have been part of the law for any appreciable length of time. This is not to say, of course, that the law is static. Many areas of American law are dramatically different than they were 50 or even 25 years ago. However, most of these changes resulted from a series of modifications of existing principles rather than from an abrupt reversal of them. The *Soldano v. O'Daniels* case later in this chapter illustrates one such modification.

Flexibility

In any nation, particularly a highly industrialized one such as the United States, societal changes occur with accelerating (almost dismaying) rapidity. Each change presents new legal problems that must be resolved without undue delay. This necessity was recognized by Justice Cardozo when he wrote that "the law, like the traveler, must be ready for the morrow."[5]

Some problems are simply the result of scientific and technological advances. Before Orville and Wilbur Wright's day, for example, it was a well-established principle that landowners had unlimited rights to the airspace above their property, any invasion of which constituted a *trespass*—a wrongful entry. But when the courts became convinced that the flying machine was here to stay, the utter impracticality of this view became apparent and owners' rights were subsequently limited to a "reasonable use" of their airspace.

Other novel problems result from changing methods of doing business or from shifting attitudes and moral views. Recent examples of the former are the proliferating use of the business franchise and of the general credit card. Attitudinal changes involve such questions as the proper ends of government, the propriety of Sunday sales, and the circumstances in which abortions should be permitted.

Some of these problems, of course, require solutions that are more political than legal in nature. This is particularly true where large numbers of the citizenry are faced with a common problem, such as the many difficulties faced by disabled persons in overcoming stereotypical attitudes and physical barriers, and where the alleviation of the problem may well be thought to constitute a legitimate function of either the state or federal government. The passage by Congress of the Americans with Disabilities Act of 1990 is an example of an attempted solution at the federal level of this particular problem.

Regardless of political considerations, however, many problems (particularly those involving disputes between individuals) can be settled only through the judicial process—that is, by one of the parties instituting legal action against the other. The duty to arrive at a final solution in all such cases falls squarely on the courts, no matter how novel or varied the issues. It is to their credit, but it is also their curse, that Americans increasingly turn to the courts for dispute resolution, and not to the churches, schools, or other institutions that are available.

Knowability

One of the basic assumptions underlying a democracy—and, in fact, almost every form of government—is that the great majority of its citizens are going to obey its laws voluntarily. It hardly need be said that obedience requires a certain knowledge of the rules, or at least a reasonable means of acquiring this knowledge, on the part of the governed. No one, not even a lawyer, "knows" all the law or all the rules that make up a single branch of law; that could never be required. But it is necessary for persons who need legal advice to have access to experts on the rules—lawyers. It is equally necessary that the law be in such form that lawyers can determine their clients' positions with reasonable certainty to recommend the most advantageous courses of action.

Reasonableness

Most citizens abide by the law. Many do so even when they are not in sympathy with a particular rule, out of a sense of responsibility, a feeling that it is their civic duty, like it or not; others, no doubt, do so simply through fear of getting caught if they do not. But by and large the rules have to appear reasonable to the great majority of the people if they are going to be obeyed for long. The so-called Prohibition Amendment, which met with such wholesale violation that it was repealed in 1933, is the classic example of a rule lacking widespread acceptance. Closely allied with the idea of reasonableness is the

---

[5]Benjamin N. Cardozo, *The Growth of the Law* (New Haven: Yale University Press, 1924), pp. 19–20.

requirement that the rules reflect, and adapt to, changing views of morality and justice. Figure 1.1 summarizes the qualities a legal system must possess to function properly.

SOME CLASSIFICATIONS OF LAW

Although the lawmaking and adjudicatory processes are the major concern in Part I, the products that result from the lawmaking process— the rules themselves and the bodies of law that they makeup—must not be overlooked. At the outset, particularly, it is useful to recognize some of the more important *classifications of law*.

Subject Matter

One way of classifying all the law in the United States is on the basis of the *subject matter* to which it relates. Fifteen or 20 branches or subjects are of particular importance, among them

- Administrative law
- Agency
- Commercial paper
- Constitutional law
- Contracts
- Corporation law
- Criminal law
- Domestic relations
- Evidence
- Partnerships
- Personal property
- Real property
- Sales
- Taxation
- Torts
- Wills and estates

Two observations can be made about this classification:

1. The subjects of agency, contracts, and torts are essentially *common law* in nature, whereas the subjects of corporation law, criminal law, sales, and taxation are governed by *statute*. Most of the remaining subjects, particularly evidence and property, are mixed in nature.

2. Several of these subjects obviously have a much closer relationship to the world of business than the others; these are the topics that fall within the usual business law or legal environment courses of a business school curriculum. Agency, contracts, corporation law, and sales are typical examples.

Federal and State Law

Another way of categorizing all law in this country is on the basis of the governmental unit from which it arises. On this basis, all law may be said to be either *federal law* or *state law*. Although there are some very important areas of federal law, as we shall see later, the

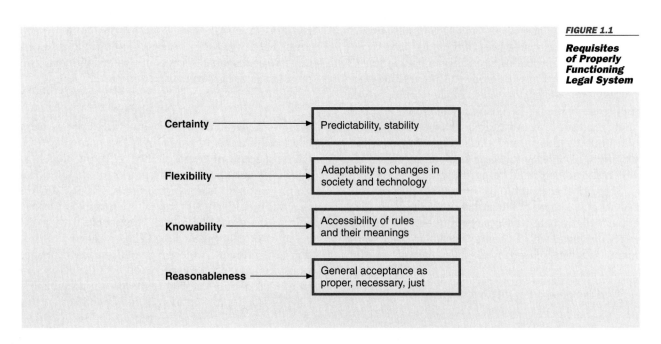

FIGURE 1.1

Requisites of Properly Functioning Legal System

great bulk of our law is state (or "local") law. Virtually all the subjects in the preceding list, for example, are within the jurisdiction of the individual states. Thus it is correct to say that there are 50 bodies of contract law in the United States, 50 bodies of corporation law, and so on. But this is not as bewildering as it appears, because the rules that constitute a given branch of law in each state substantially parallel those that exist in the other states—particularly in regard to common-law subjects.

Common Law (Case Law) and Statutory Law

The term **common law** has several different meanings. It sometimes is used to refer only to the judge-made rules in effect in England at an early time —the "ancient unwritten law of England." It sometimes is also used to refer only to those judge-made rules of England that were subsequently adopted by the states in this country. In this text, however, we define the term more broadly to mean *all the rules and principles currently existing in any state, regardless of their historical origin, that result from judicial decisions in those areas of law where legislatures have not enacted comprehensive statutes*. This type of law, examined further in Chapter 4, is frequently referred to as case law, judge-made law, or unwritten law.

The term **statutory law,** by contrast, is generally used to refer to the state and federal *statutes* in effect at a given time—that is, rules that have been formally adopted by legislative bodies rather than by the courts. When *statutory law* is used in contrast to *common law*, it also comprises state and federal constitutions, municipal ordinances, and even treaties. Statutory law is frequently referred to as *written law* in the sense that once a statute or constitutional provision is adopted, its exact wording is set forth in the final text as passed—although the precise meaning, we should recall, is still subject to interpretation by the courts. The subjects of statutory law and judicial interpretation are also covered in Chapter 4.

Civil and Criminal Law

Civil Law

The most common types of controversies are civil actions—that is, actions in which the parties bringing the suits (the **plaintiffs**) are seeking to enforce private obligations or duties against the other parties (the **defendants**). **Civil laws,** then, are all those laws that spell out the rights and duties existing among individuals, business firms, and sometimes even government agencies. Contract law, tort law, and sales law all fall within the civil category.

The usual remedy that the plaintiff is seeking in a civil suit is *damages*—a sum of money roughly equivalent to the loss that he or she has suffered as a result of the defendant's wrong. Another civil remedy is the *injunction*—a court degree ordering the defendant to do or not to do some particular thing.

Criminal Law

Criminal law, in contrast to civil law, comprises those statutes by which a state or the federal government prohibits specified kinds of conduct and which additionally provide for the imposition of *fines* or *imprisonment* on persons convicted of violating them. Criminal suits are always brought by the government whose law has allegedly been violated. In enacting criminal statutes, a legislature is saying that certain activities are so inherently inimical to the public good that they constitute wrongs against organized society as a whole.

In addition to the nature of the liability imposed, criminal suits also differ from civil suits in another significant respect. In a criminal action it is necessary that the government's case be proved "beyond a reasonable doubt," whereas in civil actions the plaintiff—the person bringing the suit—need prove his or her allegations only by "a preponderance of the evidence."

Crimes are either *felonies* or *misdemeanors*, depending on the severity of the penalty that the statute prescribes. A **felony,** the most serious of the two, is usually defined as crime for which the legislature has provided a maximum penalty of either imprisonment for more than one year or death, as in the cases of murder, arson, or rape. **Misdemeanors** are all crimes carrying lesser penalties, for example, most traffic offenses.

Finally, it should be noted that some wrongful acts are of a dual nature, subjecting the wrongdoer to both criminal and civil penalties. For example, if X steals Y's car, the state could bring a criminal action against X, and Y could also bring a civil action to recover damages arising from the theft.

Public and Private Law

Some branches of law deal more directly with the relationship between the government and the individual than do others. On the basis of the degree to which this relationship is involved, law is occasionally classified as *public law* or *private law*.

When an area of law is directly concerned with the government–individual (or government–business) relationship, it falls within the *public law* designation. Subjects that are most clearly of this nature are criminal law, constitutional law, and administrative law. Because *criminal laws* deal with acts that are prohibited by a government itself, the violation of which is a "wrong against the state," such laws more directly affect the government–individual relationship than do any of the other laws. To the extent that our federal Constitution contains provisions substantially guaranteeing that certain rights of the individual or business cannot be invaded by federal and state government activities, the subject of *constitutional law* falls within the same category. *Administrative law*—comprising the principles that govern the procedures and activities of government boards and commissions—is of similar nature, in that such agencies are also concerned with the enforcement of certain state and federal statutes (and regulations promulgated thereunder) against individual citizens and businesses.

Many other areas of law, which are primarily concerned with the creation and enforcement of the rights of one individual against another, fall within the *private law* category. Although a state is indeed concerned that all its laws be properly enforced, even when individuals' or business firms' rights alone are being adjudicated, the concern in these areas is distinctly secondary to the interests of the parties themselves. There also are many areas of law that are of a mixed public-private nature; examples include state or federal statutes that regulate business activities and also create rights and obligations that individuals and businesses themselves may enforce.

LEGAL MISCONCEPTIONS

Before proceeding to the more substantive areas of law, we will reflect briefly on two widely held misconceptions about our legal system.

Myth of the One Right Answer

It is widely believed that there is one "correct" legal answer to any legal controversy. This is true in some situations but certainly not as often as many persons believe. The chief reasons for divergent legal opinions are quite explainable:

1. Many rules are expressed in rather general terms to fit varying situations. Consequently, they afford the courts considerable latitude in deciding how they should be applied to specific situations.

2. The ultimate legal processes are in the hands of people, the judges, whose application of rules is always subject, to some extent, to their individual economic and political philosophies and personal moral beliefs. The law, therefore, is not an exact science and never will be.

3. The nature of most legal problems is such that something can be said in behalf of both litigants. The ordinary controversy does not present a clear-cut case of a "good" person suing a "bad" one. In some cases, each party has acted in good faith; in others, each is guilty of some degree of wrong. Additionally, there are some "legal collision" situations, in which one general principle of law may lead to one result while a second will lead to a different result. In such instances each principle will probably have to undergo some modification when applied to particular cases, with results that are not always harmonious.

Myth of Judicial Eccentricity

The feeling is sometimes expressed that the law is not based on common sense—that its rules are so esoteric and arbitrary, and the judges and lawyers so preoccupied with them, that the results are not in keeping with reality or with what a reasonable person would expect. This indictment, in very large measure, is false. Cases invariably present practical problems for the courts, and the courts keep the practical considerations in mind in choosing the rules that apply.

Take, for example, this situation: C, a contractor, agrees to build a house according to certain specifications for O, the owner, for $60,000. When the house is completed, by which time O has paid $36,000, O discovers that the family room is 10 inches shorter than the plans specified. O refuses to make further payments for this reason, whereupon C brings suit to recover the balance of $24,000.

Now, as far as contract law is concerned, the principle is well established that a person who breaches a contract is not permitted to recover anything from the other party. The question here is, should that rule be applicable to this specific situation, where that would mean that C would not recover any of the balance? The practical person might well say, "I wouldn't think so—where the defect is so slight, it would seem unfair for C to suffer a loss of $24,000." The law reaches the same conclusion: under a view known as the *doctrine of substantial performance,* a person in C's position is usually permitted to recover most of the unpaid balance (even though C did, technically, breach the contract).

The foregoing does not mean, of course, that the law is perfect or that startling or unfair decisions never occur. They do. But by and large the unreasonable result occurs with much less frequency than reports in the news media would indicate; and even in such cases, the possibility usually exists that an appellate court will subsequently repair much of the damage.

LAW, JUSTICE, AND MORALS
Law and Justice

There is a close relationship between law and justice, but the terms are not equivalent. Most results of the application of legal rules are "just"—fair and reasonable. Where this is not so to any degree, the rules are usually changed. Yet it must be recognized that results occasionally "are not fair." Without attempting to defend the law in all such instances, some cautions should nevertheless be voiced.

First, there is never complete agreement as to what is just; there are always some decisions that seem just to some people but not to others. And even if there were unanimity of opinion—a perfect justice, so to speak—the facts in many cases are such that it is simply impossible to attain this end.

In some situations, for example, a legal controversy may arise between two honest persons who dealt with each other in good faith, as sometimes occurs in the area of "mutual mistake." Take this case: P contracts to sell land to G for $40,000, both parties mistakenly believing that a General Motors plant will be built on adjoining land. When G learns that the plant will not be built, he refuses to go through with the deal. If a court rules that the mistake frees G of his contractual obligations, the result might be quite unjust as far as P is concerned. And if it rules otherwise, the decision might seem quite unfair to G. Yet a decision must be made, one way or the other.

Second, in some instances it is fairly clear who is right and who is wrong, but the situation has progressed to the point where it is impossible, either physically or legally, to put the "good" person back into the original position. These "bad check" cases will illustrate: A buys a television from Z, giving Z her personal check in payment. If the check bounces, it is

clear that Z should be allowed to recover the set. But what if the television has been destroyed by fire while in A's hands? Here the most the law can do is give Z a *judgment* against A—an order requiring A to pay a sum of money to Z equal to the amount of the check, which A may or may not be financially able to do. Or suppose that A had resold the television to X before Z learned that the check had bounced. Would it not be unfair to permit Z to retake the set from X, an innocent third party?

Because of these considerations, and others to be discussed later, the most the law can seek to accomplish is *substantial* justice in the greatest possible number of cases that come before it.

Law and Morals

Although the terms *law* and *morals* are not synonymous, legal standards and moral standards parallel one another more closely than many people believe. For example, criminal statutes prohibit certain kinds of conduct that are clearly "morally wrong"—murder, theft, arson, and the like. And other rules of law impose civil liability for similar kinds of conduct that, although not crimes, are also generally felt to be wrongful in nature—such as negligence, breach of contract, and fraud. To illustrate: S, in negotiating the sale of a race horse to B, tells B that the horse has run an eighth of a mile in 15 seconds on several occasions within the past month. In fact, the animal has never been clocked under 18 seconds, and S knows this. B, believing the statement to be true, purchases the horse. In such a case, S's intentional misstatement constitutes the tort of *fraud,* and B—assuming he can prove these facts in a legal action brought against S—has the right to set aside the transaction, returning the horse and recovering the price he has paid.

Why, then, are the terms *law* and *morals* not precisely synonymous? First, in some situations moral standards are higher than those imposed by law. For example, a person who has promised to keep an offer open for a stated period of time generally has the legal right to withdraw the offer before the given time has elapsed (for reasons appearing in a later chapter). Yet many persons who make such offers feel morally compelled to keep their offers open as promised, even though the law does not require this. Second, sometimes the law imposes higher standards than do our morals. For example, no religions or philosophies feature the 65-mile-per-hour speed limit as a major tenet, yet it is illegal to drive faster.

Third, many rules of law and court decisions are based on statutory or practical requirements that have little or no relationship to moral considerations. For example, in the area of minors' contracts, we will see later that most courts feel, on balance, that it is sound public policy to permit minors to disaffirm (cancel) their contracts until they reach the age of majority, even though the contracts were otherwise perfectly valid and even though the persons with whom the minors dealt did not overreach or take advantage of them in any way. These observations notwithstanding, a society's moral standards will always heavily influence its legal standards. The relationship between legal standards and moral standards, as well as many related questions, is explored thoroughly in Chapter 10.

The interplay between law and morality is illustrated in the following case. Because the study of law involves to a very great extent the ability to reason from cases, students must have some familiarity with court procedures and jurisdiction. For this reason, major emphasis on cases will begin in the following chapter. The case below is our first, and therefore requires a few prefatory comments:

1. This is a *wrongful death* action authorized by statute to allow close relatives of deceased persons to sue those whose wrongful acts have caused a death. Without such statutes, we could be held liable for carelessly or intentionally injuring someone but could escape civil liability if we killed him or her. Under a state wrongful death statute, the *wrongful* act must be a *tort,* such as negligence or assault and battery, for which the deceased could have filed suit if only injury and not death had occurred. In this case, the basis for the wrongful death action is a

claim by the *plaintiff* that the *defendant* committed the tort of negligence. The subject of torts is discussed in Chapters 8, 9, and 22. In addition, the plaintiff is seeking to hold both the bartender and his employer legally responsible for damages. Although it is only the bartender's conduct that is in question, under the law of *agency* the bartender's employer also can be held liable if the bartender was acting within the *scope of his employment* at the time of the incident. The bartender clearly was acting within the scope of his employment in this case. If the court finds the bartender liable and the employer pays the judgment to the plaintiff, the employer will have a legal right to reimbursement from the bartender. As a practical matter, however, employers seldom exercise this right. The law of agency is discussed in Chapters 31 and 32.

2. In a civil case, the jury is normally the "judge of the *facts.*" The trial judge decides the *law.* However, a judge, for reasons of judicial efficiency, can grant a summary judgment, terminating the case before it is ever tried. Summary judgment is appropriately granted if the evidence in the case so clearly indicates that factually one side or the other is entitled to prevail that a trial would be a waste of time. Only if the judge can conclude that there is "no genuine issue of material fact" should a summary judgment be granted on this ground. The following case involves a situation in which the trial judge had granted a summary judgment for the defendant.

3. If a trial court does grant a summary judgment motion, the losing party can always seek review in an appellate court. If the appellate court finds that the ruling was in error, the case will be returned to the trial court with instructions for a trial on the issue.

Soldano v. O'Daniels

California Court of Appeal, 190 Cal. Rptr. 310 (1983)

Case

On August 9, 1977, Villanueva pulled a gun and threatened the life of Soldano at Happy Jack's Saloon. A patron of Happy Jack's ran across the street to the Circle Inn and informed the bartender of the threat, asking the bartender either to

call the police or allow him to use the phone to call the police. The bartender refused both requests. Soon thereafter, Villanueva shot Soldano to death. The plaintiff in this wrongful death action is Soldano's child. The defendants are the bartender and his employer. The trial judge dismissed the claim in response to

the defendants' motion for summary judgment. Plaintiff appeals.

Andreen, Associate Justice:

Does a business establishment incur liability for wrongful death if it denies use of its telephone to a Good Samaritan who explains an emergency situation

(continues)

SOLDANO V. O'DANIELS

(handwritten: the Issue) *(handwritten: Conclusion)*

(continued from previous page)
occurring without and wishes to call the police?

. . . There is a distinction, well rooted in the common law, between action and inaction. It has found its way into the prestigious Restatement Second of Torts, which provides in section 314:

The fact that the actor realizes or should realize that action on his part is necessary for another's aid or protection does not of itself impose upon him a duty to take such action.

The distinction between malfeasance and nonfeasance, between active misconduct working positive injury and failure to act to prevent mischief not brought on by the defendant, is founded on "that attitude of extreme individualism so typical of Anglo-Saxon legal thought." (Bohlen, *The Moral Duty to Aid Others as a Basis of Tort Liability,* part I (1908) 56 U.Pa.L. Rev.217, 219-220.)

Defendant argues that the request that its employee call the police [or permit the requestor to make the call] is a request that it do something. He points to the established rule that one who has not created peril ordinarily does not have a duty to take affirmative action to assist an imperiled person. . . .

The refusal of the law to recognize the moral obligation of one to aid another when he is in peril and when such aid may be given without danger and at little cost in effort has been roundly criticized. Prosser describes the case law sanctioning such inaction as a "refus[al] to recognize the moral obligation of common decency and common humanity" and characterizes some of these decisions as "revolting to any moral sense." (Prosser, *Law of Torts* (4th ed. 1971) §56.)

As noted in *Tarasoff v. Regents of University of California,* 131 Cal. Rptr. 14 (1976), the courts have increased the instances in which affirmative duties are imposed not by direct rejection of the common law rule, but by expanding the list of special relationships which will justify departure from that

rule. . . . In *Tarasoff,* a therapist was told by his patient that he intended to kill Tatiana Tarasoff. The therapist and his supervisors predicted the patient presented a serious danger of violence. In fact he did, for he carried out his threat. The court held the patient–therapist relationship was enough to create a duty to exercise reasonable care to protect others from the foreseeable result of the patient's illness.

. . . Here there was no special relationship between the defendant and the deceased. But this does not end the matter.

It is time to re-examine the common law rule of nonliability for nonfeasance in the special circumstances of the instant case.

Besides well-publicized actions taken to increase the severity of punishments for criminal offenses, the Legislature has expressed a social imperative to diminish criminal action. [The court then referred to laws passed to compensate citizens for injuries sustained in crime suppression efforts, to make it a misdemeanor to refuse to relinquish a party line when informed that it is needed to call the police, and to establish an emergency '911' telephone system.]

The above statutes . . . demonstrate that "that attitude of extreme individualism so typical of Anglo-Saxon legal thought" may need limited re-examination in light of current societal conditions and the facts of this case to determine whether the defendant owed a duty to the deceased to permit the use of the telephone. . . .

As the [California] Supreme Court has noted, the reluctance of the law to impose liability for nonfeasance, as distinguished from misfeasance, is in part due to the difficulties in setting standards and of making rules workable [citing *Tarasoff*]. Many citizens simply "don't want to get involved." No rule should be adopted which would require a citizen to open up his or her house to a stranger so that the latter may use the telephone to call for emergency assistance. As Mrs. Alexander in Anthony Burgess' *A Clockwork Orange*

learned to her horror, such an action may be fraught with danger. It does not follow, however, that use of a telephone in a public portion of a business should be refused for a legitimate emergency call. Imposing liability for such a refusal would not subject innocent citizens to possible attack by the "Good Samaritan," for it would be limited to an establishment open to the public during times when it is open to business, and to places within the establishment ordinarily accessible to the public.

. . . We conclude that the bartender owed a duty to the plaintiff's decedent to permit the patron from Happy Jack's to place a call to the police or to place the call himself.

It bears emphasizing that the duty in this case does not require that one must go to the aid of another. That is not the issue here. The employee was not the Good Samaritan intent on aiding another. The patron was.

It would not be appropriate to await legislative action in this area. The rule was fashioned in the common law tradition, as were the exceptions to the rule. . . . The courts have a special responsibility to reshape, refine and guide legal doctrine they have created.

The words of the Supreme Court [in *Rodriguez v. Bethlehem Steel Corp.,* 115 Cal. Rptr. 765 (1974)] on the role of the courts in a common law system are well suited to our obligation here:

The inherent capacity of the common law for growth and change is its most significant feature. Its development has been determined by the social needs of the community which it serves. It is constantly expanding and developing in keeping with advancing civilization and the new conditions and progress of society, and adapting itself to the gradual change of trade, commerce, arts, inventions, and the needs of the country. . . .

In short, as the United States Supreme Court has aptly said, "This flexibility and capacity for growth and adaptation is the peculiar boast and excellence of the common law." [Citation omitted].

The possible imposition of liability on the defendant in this case is not a

(continues)

Soldano v. O'Daniels

(continued from previous page)
global change in the law. It is but a slight departure from the "morally questionable" rule of nonliability for inaction absent a special relationship. It is a logical extension of Restatement section 327 which imposes liability for negligent interference with a third person who the defendant knows is attempting to render necessary aid. However small it may be, it is a step which should be taken.

We conclude there are sufficient justiciable issues to permit the case to go to trial and therefore reverse.🙪

Comment

1. As this is our first case, a few comments about the mechanics of case reporting are in order:

   a. The opinion, written by Justice Andreen, is that of an intermediate appellate court in a state system. It hears appeals from California state trial courts, and its decisions can be appealed to the California State Supreme Court.
   b. The ellipsis points (. . .) appearing in the opinion indicate portions that have been deleted by the authors of this text. Deletions are made to eliminate redundancy or exclude issues irrelevant to points that the case has been selected to illustrate.
   c. When a general principle of law is stated in a decision, the court will frequently *cite* (refer to) earlier cases in which that principle has been established. Here, for example, the court has referred to *Tarasoff v. Regents of University of California* for such a purpose. To facilitate the reading of opinions, the authors have generally omitted such references except where the cited case is heavily relied on to support the decision.

2. A word of caution: It is imperative for readers to acquire the ability *to determine the precise issue of a case*, so they will not leap to unwarranted general conclusions. Could we say, for example, that the instant case establishes the principle that on seeing one person attack another with a knife, a bystander has the legal duty to personally intervene to save the victim? Not at all. This court was very careful in stating the issue narrowly and emphasizing that it was only creating a small exception to the traditional rule.

SELECTING AND USING ATTORNEYS

Choosing an attorney can be as important as choosing one's clergy, banker, or doctor . . . and more difficult.

Individuals

Individuals frequently require an attorney's services for their business matters as well as for their personal affairs. As sole proprietors of or partners in a business enterprise, individuals facing (or seeking to avoid) legal problems must select an attorney. This is no easy task.

Now that the Supreme Court has made advertising by lawyers permissible,[6] at least a little more information about attorneys is publicly available than was formerly the case. Still, much investigation and consultation may be required before a selection is made, in part because most attorneys (especially successful ones) choose not to advertise. In addition, much attorney advertising is not very informational.

If friends or business associates have had similar problems in the past, their advice may be particularly helpful. If their experience with a specific attorney was quite favorable, that attorney can be contacted. Professionals in the area of concern are also valuable resources. For example, if the legal problem is financial in nature, an individual's banker might provide valuable insight regarding lawyers with experience in that type of case. A call to a nearby law school permits consultation with a professor who specializes in the problem area and who will probably know local attorneys who practice that type of law. A trip to a library to consult the *Martindale-Hubbell Law Directory*, which gives significant background information on attorneys and their specialties (and even rates them), can be beneficial. Finally, the Yellow Pages will list

---

[6]*Bates v. State Bar of Ariz,* 433 U.S. 350 (1977).

local attorneys and contain the number of a lawyers' referral service sponsored by the local bar association.

An individual consulting an attorney must not be hesitant to ask questions, including: How much will I be charged for an initial consultation? Do you frequently handle this type of case? Will my case receive the attention of an experienced lawyer in the firm? How will the fee be structured? How much is your representation likely to cost for the total case?

The matter of fees is a delicate subject, but the client should demand that all specifics be spelled out before hiring an attorney. For many types of cases, lawyers work for an *hourly fee.* The rate charged varies with the geographic area, type of firm, and type of case. Unless the client investigates thoroughly, "comparison shopping" will be impossible. Some types of cases, particularly plaintiffs' personal injury cases, are handled on a *contingency fee* basis. That is, the lawyer's compensation is a percentage of the plaintiff's recovery, *if any.* No recovery usually means no fee for the attorney. Sometimes contingency fees are set on a sliding scale where the attorney receives an agreed percentage if the case is settled out of court, a larger percentage if the case is settled after suit is filed, and a still larger percentage (usually around 33 percent, but sometimes as high as 50 percent) if the case must be tried.

Once a relationship is established, clients must be completely open with their attorneys. Only if attorneys are given all relevant information by their clients can they provide effective counsel. Clients should trust their lawyers unless there is specific evidence of unethical practices, overbilling, or the like. The attorneys are being paid to provide advice, and that advice should normally be trusted just as a patient trusts a surgeon's advice. However, clients should always remember that it is *their case* that is the basis of the relationship. The attorney works for and is paid by the client, not vice versa. Matters of strategy are in the attorney's discretion, but the client has the ultimate choice of whether to file suit, whether to accept a settlement offer, and whether to take an appeal. An attorney who refuses to follow a client's instructions should be discharged.

Corporations

Corporations are even more dependent on attorneys than individuals. As fictional entities, corporations must appear in court through a licensed attorney. That is, whereas individuals have the right (although

it is not usually the sensible thing to do) to represent themselves in court, corporations do not. Not even the president of the corporation can represent it in court if the president is not an attorney. Much of what was said about selection and use of attorneys by individuals is also applicable to corporations.

Many corporations have "in-house" counsel—lawyers who work for the corporation full time. Other corporations farm out all their legal work to law firms that represent a number of other clients as well. Many larger corporations combine these approaches, with routine matters handled by in-house counsel and litigation and specialty matters handled by outside counsel.

The high cost of litigation, particularly attorneys' fees, is a major concern for corporations. The average manufacturing company spends about 1 percent of its revenues on legal services. Some corporations have reacted to this problem by increasing their reliance on in-house counsel. Others have put their legal business up for competitive bid by law firms. Still others have instituted "legal audits" in which experienced attorneys evaluate a company's practices to detect potential legal troublespots. These troublespots might not be illegal practices, but only activities that might invite litigation or inhibit success should litigation ensue. Such "preventive law" is being hailed, much as is preventive medicine. An attorney who can keep the client out of court altogether is probably more valuable than one who can win a case in court.

Corporations, like individuals, must cooperate with their attorneys. Obviously corporations can act only through their employees. Those employees must also be open and cooperative. The Supreme Court has recognized this, holding that the attorney–client privilege applies to communications made by corporate employees to the corporation's attorneys.[7]

SUMMARY

The law pervades our lives, both business and personal. Philosophers have characterized the law in an endless variety of ways, but two major approaches are the *rule-oriented* and the *process-oriented.* The former sees the law as a set of rules and standards the courts use to resolve cases; the latter views the law more as a dynamic process for resolution of social questions.

[7]*Upjohn Co. v. United States,* 449 U.S. 383 (1981).

LEGAL FOCUS

International

As the world's economy becomes more integrated and less limited by national boundaries, the services of lawyers who specialize in international trade law are more in demand. One fact that surprises many multinational companies is that the hourly rates of American lawyers specializing in international trade are considerably lower than the rates of similar specialists in many other nations. The average hourly rate for experienced international law specialists in theUnited States was recently found by the *Wall Street Journal* to be in the $210–$350 range. In contrast, the rates for similar lawyers in Germany were $340–$680; in Japan, $230–$470; in Hong Kong, $260–$390; in the United Kingdom, $480–$690; and in Saudi Arabia, $275–$350. Sometimes these variations are a bit deceptive, however, because international law firms competing for business in some of these nations, such as Japan, commonly agree to a cap on the total fee for a job even if it ultimately requires more hours than originally anticipated.

Although many factors probably contribute to the higher fees for international law specialists in a number of other nations, such as the current weakness of the dollar against other currencies, one important reason may be that American lawyers are more accustomed to competing vigorously for business than those in many other nations. Many people claim today that there are too many lawyers in the United States. While this assertion certainly might contain a substantial element of truth, one benefit could be increased competition for business and thus lower fees than in countries with far fewer lawyers per capita. ◊◊

Source: *Wall Street Journal*, Oct. 20, 1992, B7, col. 1.

An effective legal system must provide certainty, yet be flexible so it can adjust to changed circumstances. It must be knowable so that people realize what is generally expected of them, and it must generally be considered reasonable.

Our multifaceted law can be classified in many ways. Each law will fit into a particular subject-matter category—contract law, corporate law, tax law, and the like. At the same time it will be either a federal or a state law, a court-made rule or a statute, a civil or a criminal law, and a public or a private law. As in any field of study, mastery of the proper labels for concepts can facilitate understanding.

The untutored are likely to have various misconceptions about how the legal system operates. Because the law has so many human factors, there is no one right answer to legal questions. Witnesses perceive "facts" in different ways. Lawyers will view "the law" in various ways, depending on policy considerations and their own feelings of justice. You cannot simply feed the facts and the law into a computer and produce *the* right answer. Although it is generally helpful to have as much money as possible when facing a legal struggle, the ability to hire the best lawyers does not guarantee anyone absolute immunity from the restraints and punishments of the law. Finally, although judges do not always make the best decisions, their conclusions are seldom based on pure whim. Many judicial actions that seem ludicrous when summarized in the newspaper are really quite reasonable when understood in context.

One important purpose of law is to produce justice. Unfortunately, this is an amorphous concept. Because not all people can agree on what is just, not everyone will agree on whether our law is producing justice. The law is heavily influenced by society's moral convictions, though practical considerations cannot be ignored in making legal rules.

Finally, hiring a lawyer is likely to be a difficult task for individuals and corporations alike. Substantial investigation and careful reflection are advised.

KEY TERMS

Common law
Statutory law
Plaintiff
Defendant
Civil law
Criminal law
Felony
Misdemeanor

QUESTIONS AND PROBLEMS

1. In two cases reaching the U.S. Supreme Court in 1985, the executive branch of the United States government—through action by the Solicitor General—asked the court to overrule its controversial 1973 decision in *Roe v. Wade,* 410 U.S. 113. (In that case the court held that a Texas statute making it a crime for anyone to have an abortion within the state except to save the mother's life violated the implicit right to privacy in the U.S. Constitution.) In effect, this controversial ruling "legalized" abortion to the extent that it gave pregnant women the absolute right to an abortion during the first trimester of their pregnancies.

Leaving aside the precise constitutional question that is raised, do you generally agree or disagree with the 1985 position of the executive branch? In other words, do you feel—because of religious beliefs or moral principles—that state law (as the Reagan administration argued in 1985) or each individual woman (as the Supreme Court held in 1973) should determine the question of abortion? Discuss.

2. Although there is no universal agreement as to what law is when viewed in the abstract, there seems to be substantial agreement among philosophers as to what the *primary purpose* of law is.

   a. How would you describe this purpose?
   b. Identify the specific passage or clause in each of the philosophers' quoted observations that substantiates your conclusion.

3. Briefly summarize the main factors that require a nation's legal rules to be flexible and somewhat changing.

4. If X and Y make a contract and X later refuses to go through with the deal, without any legal excuse, we say that X's conduct is a *wrong* but it is not a *crime.* Why is it not a crime?

5. For some years the Washington Interscholastic Activities Association had a rule that prohibited girls from participating on high school football teams in the state. When this rule was challenged by parents of two girls who wanted to go out for football, the Supreme Court of Washington had to decide whether the rule violated the state constitution (*Darrin v. Gould,* 540 P.2d 882, 1975). Leaving aside the precise legal question that was posed, do you think that such a rule is a good one? Discuss.

6. In 1884, a ship sank 1600 miles from shore. Dudley, Stephens, Brooks, and a 17-year-old boy, Richard Parker, scrambled into a life boat with only two pounds of turnips to eat and no fresh water. They caught a turtle, but by their 12th day in the raft the provisions were completely consumed. Soon thereafter Dudley and Stephens proposed killing the boy for food, but Brooks resisted the idea. Finally, on the 20th day after the shipwreck as the boy lay almost dead, Dudley and Stephens slit his throat and Brooks joined them in eating him. Four days later a passing ship picked up the three survivors. They were returned to England where Dudley and Stephens were charged with murder. Assume that you are the judge in this case. Assume further that the evidence shows (a) all four men would have been dead by the 24th day had Parker not been eaten and (b) the mandatory penalty for murder is death. What will you do? (*Regina v. Dudley & Stephens,* [1884] L.R., Q.B. 61.)

7. A minor child and its mother brought a paternity action against defendant. Defendant admitted that he was the father of the child and agreed to pay child support but filed a counterclaim against the mother claiming (a) she had falsely represented that she was taking birth control pills, (b) defendant had engaged in sexual intercourse with her in reliance on the misrepresentation, and (c) as a direct result of the birth he had been injured in the form of mental agony and distress and creation of an obligation to support the child financially. The mother moved to dismiss the counterclaim, arguing that even if the facts alleged by defendant were true, he should not be allowed recover money damages. Discuss. (*Lasher v. Kleinberg,* 164 Cal. Rptr. 618, Cal. App. 1980.)

8. A wooden bridge crossing a canal was destroyed by a fire of unknown origin one afternoon. McCarthy soon learned of the fire; he attempted to contact the county commissioners but failed. Simpson also learned of the fire and told another traveler, Ramos, that he would notify somebody about the fire, but he did not do so. At 6:30 the next morning, Roberson drove off the bridge in the dark and was killed. No barricades or any type of warning devices were at the site of the burned-out bridge. Roberson's wife brought a wrongful death action against McCarthy and Simpson. Should she prevail? Discuss. (*Roberson v. McCarthy,* 620 S.W.2d 912, Tex. Civ. App. 1981.)

Court Systems

Problems of Jurisdiction

Law, Equity, and Remedies

LEGAL RULES AND principles take on vitality and meaning only when they are applied to real-life controversies between real persons, when the rules are *applied to facts*—when, for example, a particular plaintiff is successful or unsuccessful in his or her attempt to recover a specific piece of land from a particular defendant, or where one company is successful or unsuccessful in recovering damages from another company as a result of an alleged breach of contract on the latter company's part. But the fitting of rules to facts—the settlings of legal controversies—does not occur automatically. This process, which we call **adjudication,** has to be in somebody's hands. Traditionally that "somebody" has been the state and federal courts that hear thousands of cases each year.[1] As Figure 2.1 indicates, rules and facts come together in the adjudication process, leading to a decision.

The primary reason, then, for looking at the courts and the work that they do is to gain an overall awareness of this important legal process. There is, however, another reason for doing so. In the following chapters many actual cases are presented. The reader is given the basic facts of a particular controversy, the judgment entered by the trial court on the basis of those facts, and excerpts of the appellate court's decision in affirming or reversing the trial court's judgment. Obviously, some familiarity

with court systems and the judicial process will facilitate one's understanding of the legal significance of each step in these proceedings.

In this chapter, then, we take a brief look at the state and federal court systems and at some problems of jurisdic-tion arising in those systems. We also examine some additional matters, such as venue, conflict of laws, and the law–equity distinction. In Chapter 3, we will study the litigation process, focusing on the functions of the trial and appellate courts, and then we will discuss some alternative methods of dispute resolution.

COURT SYSTEMS

As a result of our federal system of government, we live under two distinct, and essentially separate, sovereign types of government—the state governments and the federal government. Each has its own laws and its own court system. For this reason, it is necessary to study both systems to acquire an adequate knowledge of the court structures within which controversies are settled.

The Typical State System
Although court systems vary somewhat from state to state, most state courts fall into three general categories. In ascending order, they are (1) courts

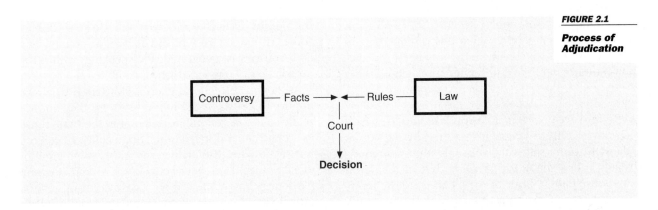

FIGURE 2.1

Process of Adjudication

[1] In addition to the state and federal trial courts, many administrative agencies (such as the Federal Trade Commission) also hear certain kinds of controversies—usually those in which the agency is contending that a company has violated the agency's own rules or regulations. (The general subject of administrative agencies, including the role that they play in the adjudicatory process, is covered in Chapter 6.)

of limited jurisdiction, (2) general trial courts, and (3) appellate courts (which frequently exist at two levels).

Courts of Limited Jurisdiction

Every state has trial courts that are limited as to the kinds of cases they can hear and are thus called **courts of limited jurisdiction.** Examples include justice of the peace courts, municipal courts, traffic courts, probate courts (hearing matters of wills and decedents' estates), and domestic relations courts (handling divorce, custody, and child support cases). Numerically speaking, these courts hear most cases that come to trial. However, they need not be discussed in detail here because many of the matters they hear are relatively minor in nature (such as traffic violations) and others involve very specialized subject matter (such as a dispute over a deceased person's estate).

General Trial Courts

The most important cases involving state law, and the ones we will be most concerned with hereafter, commence in the **general trial courts.** These are courts of "general jurisdiction"; they are empowered to hear all cases except those expressly assigned by statute to the courts of limited jurisdiction. Virtually all important cases involving contract law, criminal law, and corporation law, for example, originate in the general trial courts. In some states these courts are called *district courts*, in others *common plea courts*, and in still others *superior courts*. Whatever the specific name, one or more such courts normally exist in every county of every state. Throughout the remainder of the text, we will sometimes refer to these general trial courts simply as *state trial courts* to distinguish them from federal trial courts. When this is done, we are referring to the state trial courts of general jurisdiction rather than to those of limited jurisdiction.

Appellate Courts

All states have one or more **appellate courts,** which hear appeals from judgments entered by the courts below. In some states there is only one such court, usually called the *supreme court,* but in the more populous states a layer of appellate courts is interposed between the trial courts and the supreme court. Such courts decide legal questions; they do not hear testimony of witnesses or otherwise entertain new evidence.

The Federal Court System

Article III, Section 1 of the U.S. Constitution provides that "the judicial power of the United States shall be vested in one Supreme Court, and in such inferior courts as the Congress may from time to time ordain and establish." The numerous federal courts that exist today by virtue of this section can, at the risk of oversimplification, be placed into three main categories similar to those of the state courts: (1) specialized trial courts, (2) U.S. district courts, and (3) appellate courts—the courts of appeal and the Supreme Court.

Specialized U.S. Courts

Some federal courts have very specialized subject matter jurisdiction. Examples include the U.S. Tax Court, which hears only federal tax cases, and the U.S. Claims Court, which hears only claims against the U.S. government. These and other specialized federal courts are somewhat analogous to the courts of limited jurisdiction in state court systems.

U.S. District Courts

The basic trial courts within the federal system are the *U.S. district courts,* sometimes called *federal district courts.* Most federal cases originate in these courts.

Congress has created 94 judicial districts, each of which covers all or part of a state or a U.S. territory. The federal districts, with the exceptions noted above, essentially are based on state lines. The less populated states have only one federal district court within their boundaries, whereas most of the remaining states have two, and a few states have three or four. U.S. territories such as Puerto Rico, Guam, and the Virgin Islands each have one federal district court. Every square foot of land in this country and its territories is, geographically speaking, within the jurisdiction of one U.S. district court.

Although the federal district courts are the most important courts in the federal system, they are not really courts of general jurisdiction in the same sense as are the general state courts. State courts of general jurisdiction are essentially a repository of general judicial power; if no other court has jurisdiction over a particular type of case, then a state court of general jurisdiction has power to hear the case. Federal courts, however, are part of the federal government, and the federal government is a government of limited powers under our Constitution. Thus, as we will

FIGURE 2.2

Federal and State Court Systems

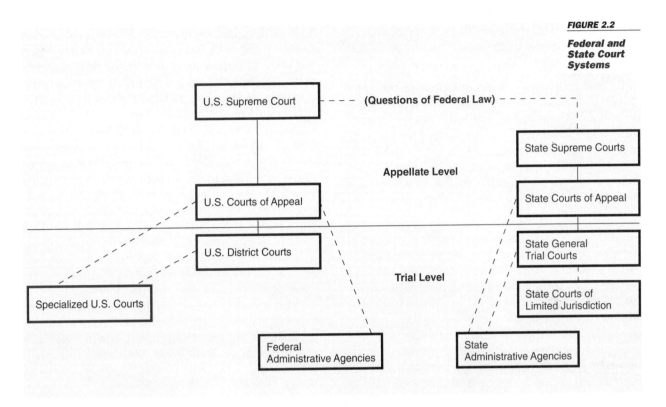

see shortly, even our most important federal trial courts—the U.S. district courts—have power to hear only those cases that have been specifically placed within their jurisdiction by the Constitution and federal statutory enactments.

Appellate Courts

Above the district courts are two levels of *federal appellate courts*—the U.S. courts of appeal and, above them, the U.S. Supreme Court. There are 13 U.S. courts of appeal. Eleven of these, located in "circuits" across the country, have jurisdiction to hear appeals from the district courts located in the states within their respective boundaries. For example, the U.S. Court of Appeals for the Ninth Circuit in San Francisco hears appeals from decisions of district courts within the states of Alaska, Arizona, California, Hawaii, Idaho, Montana, Nevada, Oregon, and Washington. Each of these 11 appellate courts also hears appeals from the rulings of federal administrative agencies.

The jurisdiction of the remaining two appellate courts is somewhat different from that of the others. The U.S. Court of Appeals for the District of Columbia hears appeals from the federal district court located in the District, as well as appeals from rulings of federal

agencies that are issued there. The other appellate court is the U.S. Court of Appeals for the Federal Circuit, which hears all patent appeals from Patent and Trademark Office boards throughout the country and appeals from decisions of the U.S. Claims Court.

Appeals from judgments of the U.S. courts of appeal, like appeals from judgments of the state supreme courts that present federal questions, can be taken to the U.S. Supreme Court. In most cases, however, these appeals are not a matter of right. Rather, the parties who seek review must petition the Supreme Court for a *writ of certiorari,* and the Court has absolute discretion in deciding which of these cases are sufficiently important to warrant the granting of certiorari.[2] In a typical year the Court can hear only about 150 of the approximately 4500 appeals that are made.

Some Observations

The typical state court system and the federal system can be diagrammed as in Figure 2.2. Several general comments can be made about this diagram.

---

[2] A *writ of certiorari* is an order of a higher court requiring a lower court to forward to it the records and proceedings of a particular case.

1. The basic trial courts are the U.S. district courts and the state general trial courts; all courts above this level are appellate courts.

2. Trial courts must settle questions of both *fact* and *law,* whereas appellate courts rule on questions of law only. Questions of fact are "what happened" questions: for instance, did the defendant corporations expressly or implicitly agree not to sell goods to the plaintiff? Questions of law, by contrast, are "what is the rule applicable to the facts?" (Much more is said about the fact/law distinction in the next chapter.)

3. Although most decisions of the trial courts are not appealed, a substantial number are. Hereafter we are concerned primarily with the *decisions of the appellate courts.* There are several basic reasons for this. First, state trial courts usually enter a judgment without writing a formal opinion as to their reasoning; and, even if there is such an opinion, it is normally not reported (published). Appellate courts, however, normally do write opinions that are reported, and access to them is available to anyone wishing to look up the rulings of law involved. Second, appellate courts have more opportunity to delineate the legal issues in their opinions for the benefit of lawyers and others who may read them. Third, if the appellate court disagrees with the result reached by the trial court, the appellate court's decision is, of course, controlling.

4. Once a case is initiated within a given court system, it will normally stay within that system until a final judgment is reached. Thus, if a case is properly commenced in a state court of general jurisdiction, any appeal from the trial court's judgment must be made to the next higher state court rather than to a federal appellate court. And if a case reaches the highest court in the state, its judgment is usually final. In other words, on matters of state law, state supreme courts are indeed supreme.[3] However, should a state supreme court rule on a case that turns on interpretation of a federal statute or a provision of the U.S. Constitution, an appeal could be taken to the U.S. Supreme Court, which has the final word on matters of *federal law.*

5. With regard to the "title" of an appealed case, the state and federal courts follow somewhat different rules. In most state courts, the original plaintiff's name appears first—just as it did in the trial court. Suppose, for example, that Pink (plaintiff) sues Doe (defendant) in a state trial court, where the case is obviously *Pink v. Doe.* If the judgment of the trial court is appealed, the rule followed by most state courts is that the title of the case remains *Pink v. Doe* in the appellate courts, no matter which party is the *appellant* (the one bringing the appeal). In the federal courts and in a few states, however, the appellant's name appears first. Under this rule, if Doe (defendant) loses in a U.S. district court and appeals to a U.S. court of appeals, the title of the case will be *Doe v. Pink* in the higher court. For this reason, when one sees a case in a federal appellate court so entitled, one cannot assume that Doe was the party who originated the action in the trial court. That determination must be made by referring to the facts of the case as set forth in the decision of the appellate court.

PROBLEMS OF JURISDICTION

In a general sense, the term **jurisdiction** refers to the legal power of a governmental body or official to take some type of action. With respect to courts, jurisdiction means the power to adjudicate, that is, to hear and decide a case and render a judgment that is legally binding on the parties. A court normally has such power only if it has both **subject matter jurisdiction** and **personal jurisdiction.** Any action taken by a court without complete jurisdiction has no legal effect.

Subject Matter Jurisdiction

Subject matter jurisdiction consists of the power to hear a particular kind of case. In each of our states, provisions in the state constitution specify which types of cases are within the subject matter jurisdiction of which types of courts. Typically, state legislative enactments then provide more detail on the subject matter jurisdiction of particular state courts. As we have already seen, some state courts have very limited jurisdiction, and one set of state courts will have more general jurisdiction. In the federal system, the U.S. Constitution specifies in general terms the kinds of cases that are within the subject matter jurisdiction of the federal courts, and federal statutes

---

[3]The normal terminology is being used here. In a few states, however, the "supreme court" label is given to an intermediate appellate court, with the highest court in the state bearing some other name. The court of last resort in the state of New York, for example, is the Court of Appeals of New York.

provide more detail. The federal courts themselves have also added more detail to the jurisdictional rules through their interpretations of the relevant constitutional and statutory provisions.

Subject Matter Jurisdiction of the Federal Courts

As we have already seen, the federal courts have subject matter jurisdiction over only those kinds of cases that are designated by the U.S. Constitution and federal statutes.

Criminal Cases

Federal courts have jurisdiction over criminal cases in which a violation of a federal criminal statute is alleged. There is a large body of federal criminal law, including statutes making it a crime to smuggle drugs into the United States, hijack an airplane, commit securities fraud, threaten the president, cross state lines after having committed a state law crime, and so on. Some federal statutes, such as the securities and antitrust laws, include both civil liability and criminal penalty provisions. Congress has power to pass criminal laws, like noncriminal ones, only if there is some basis in the Constitution authorizing it to do so. Many federal criminal laws are based on the constitutional provision that empowers Congress to pass laws regulating interstate commerce, but others are enacted under the power granted by different constitutional provisions.

Civil Cases

We are primarily concerned about the jurisdiction and functions of courts in civil cases. Most of the time it will be obvious whether a particular civil case can be heard by a federal court, but sometimes there are difficult questions. These questions may arise when a plaintiff's attorney thinks it would be in the client's best interest to have the case decided by a federal rather than a state court, but where some of the facts relating to the jurisdictional question are not clear. There can be many reasons why a plaintiff's attorney might prefer to file a case in federal court. For example, if the case has to be filed in a state where the attorney normally does not practice, the attorney may be unfamiliar with the procedures of that state's courts and thus may be more comfortable in a federal court in that state, where the procedures are basically the same as in federal courts in other states. Likewise, if a plaintiff has filed in a state court where the defen-

dant's attorney usually does not practice, the latter might attempt to have the case moved to a federal court for the same reason. Sometimes a question about federal versus state court jurisdiction can arise because the plaintiff has filed a case in federal court but the defendant's attorney sees some strategic advantage in having the case decided by a state court. There are two general categories of civil cases that the Constitution and federal statutes have placed within the subject matter jurisdiction of the federal courts.

Federal Question Cases. Federal courts have subject matter jurisdiction over any civil case in which the plaintiff's claim arises from either the U.S. Constitution, a federal statute, or a federal treaty. For example, if a group of environmentally concerned citizens sues a corporation alleging that it was polluting a stream in violation of the federal Clean Water Act, there would be a **federal question.** The plaintiff's claim must directly raise a question of federal law; if the plaintiff's claim does not raise a federal question, the defendant cannot create federal subject matter jurisdiction by raising a federal question in a defense or counterclaim.

It is common for a plaintiff to assert two or more legal claims based on the same set of factual circumstances. If one of these claims raises a federal question and thereby creates federal subject matter jurisdiction, the federal court also has subject matter jurisdiction over any other claim arising out of the same facts, even if the other claim is based on state law rather than federal law. This type of federal subject matter jurisdiction is called *pendent* or *ancillary* jurisdiction and represents a pragmatic attempt to avoid multiple lawsuits.

Federal jurisdiction based on a federal question may be either *exclusive* or *concurrent*. A claim arising under the U.S. Constitution creates concurrent federal–state jurisdiction, which means that it can be heard by either a federal or state court. A claim arising under a federal statute usually creates concurrent federal–state jurisdiction unless the statute itself says otherwise. A number of federal statutes, such as the patent, copyright, antitrust, and securities laws, specifically provide for exclusive federal court jurisdiction; claims thereunder can be filed only in a federal court.

If a federal question case is taken to a federal court, it is normally done at the outset, in one of the federal district courts. However, if (1) a particular federal question case is characterized by concurrent federal–state jurisdiction, (2) the plaintiff chooses to file the case in a *state* court, and (3) the case proceeds through the state court system until all avenues of appeal in that system are exhausted, either party may ask the U.S. Supreme Court to review the case because of the presence of the federal question. In this situation, as in most others, the U.S. Supreme Court has discretion to hear or not hear the case.

Diversity of Citizenship Cases.   Diversity of citizenship creates federal subject matter jurisdiction only if the amount in controversy is greater than $50,000. When federal jurisdiction exists because of **diversity of citizenship,** it is always concurrent federal–state jurisdiction, and the plaintiff has a choice of filing in a federal court. If the plaintiff chooses state court and the case is heard in the state court system, there can be no appeal to the U.S. Supreme Court or any other federal court. (Thus, the situation is different with a diversity case filed in state court than with a federal question case filed in state court.)

In the case of an individual, citizenship in a state for federal jurisdiction purposes means U.S. citizenship plus residency in that state. The phrase *diversity of citizenship* encompasses several different situations. By far the most important situation included within the phrase is one in which the plaintiff and defendant are citizens of different states. Diversity of citizenship also exists when one party is a citizen of a state in the United States and the other is a citizen of another nation.

In several ways, federal courts have interpreted the diversity of citizenship concept rather narrowly to exclude some kinds of cases that logically might have been included. For example, if a case involves multiple plaintiffs or multiple defendants, diversity of citizenship exists only if there is *no common state citizenship on opposite sides of the case.* Thus if P1, a citizen of Nebraska, and P2, a citizen of Kansas, join in a suit against D1, a citizen of New York, and D2, a citizen of Kansas, there is no diversity of citizenship.

If a corporation is a plaintiff or defendant, it is considered to be a citizen of the state where it was *incorporated;* in addition, if it has its *principal place of business* in another state, it is viewed as a citizen of that state as well. Thus, for the purpose of determining whether a federal court has jurisdiction on the basis of diversity of citizenship, it is possible for a corporation to be a citizen of two states. Neither Congress nor the U.S. Supreme Court has defined the term *principal place of business.* Most lower federal courts have held that the state where a company has its headquarters is its principal place of business. Suppose that P, a citizen of New York, sues D Corporation, which was incorporated in Delaware and has its principal place of business in New York. Because there is common state citizenship on opposite sides of the case (New York), a federal court would not have subject matter jurisdiction on the basis of diversity of citizenship.

The original reason for permitting diversity of citizenship cases to be heard by federal courts was to guard against "hometown verdicts"—decisions by juries or judges that are biased against an out-of-state party. If this ever was a problem, there is little if any evidence that it is still a problem. In any event, if there is such a problem, it is unclear how placing these cases in a federal trial court can solve it. Juries in federal courts are taken from the local population just as they are in state courts, and federal judges are almost always from the state where they serve. For these reasons, and also because diversity of citizenship cases involve questions of state law, bills have been introduced in Congress a number of times over the years to eliminate diversity of citizenship as a basis for federal subject matter jurisdiction. No such bill has passed, however.

Removal from State to Federal Court

When concurrent federal–state jurisdiction exists, the plaintiff has the initial choice of filing in state or federal court. If the plaintiff chooses state court, however, the defendant may have a **right of removal.** This means that, within a short time after the plaintiff files the case in state court, the defendant may have the case moved to a federal district court in the same geographic area.

The defendant has a right of removal in any federal question case, so that if the defendant chooses he or she can always have a federal court rule on claims against him or her that are based on federal law. The right also exists in diversity of citizenship cases, except in the situation where the plaintiff filed the suit in the state where the defendant is a citizen.

Personal Jurisdiction

In the great majority of cases, a court must have *personal jurisdiction* in addition to subject matter jurisdiction. Personal jurisdiction is the court's jurisdiction over the parties to the case. In a civil lawsuit, the plaintiff submits to the court's personal jurisdiction by filing the case; thus, any question about personal jurisdiction relates to the defendant.[4] Personal jurisdiction over the defendant is a requirement in so-called **in personam** cases, in which the plaintiff seeks a judgment that will be legally binding against the defendant (whether an individual, corporation, government agency, or other entity). The judgment might be an award of money damages that the defendant has to pay or some other remedy such as an injunction requiring the defendant to take or refrain from taking some particular action. Most cases are of the *in personam* variety. The other type of case is an *in rem* action, which will be discussed after this section on personal jurisdiction. In our legal system, personal jurisdiction is a concept that arises only in civil cases, not in criminal ones, because in a criminal case the defendant must be arrested and bodily brought before the court before he or she can be tried.

Although the rules for a court's acquisition of personal jurisdiction over a defendant vary somewhat from state to state, these rules all have the same objective: compliance with the constitutional requirement of *procedural due process*. We will study due process in some detail in Chapter 5, Constitutional Law. What is basically required by procedural due process, however, is (1) adequate notice, (2) a meaningful opportunity to be heard (that is, a hearing), (3) an impartial decision maker, and (4) in court actions, some significant contact between the defendant and the *forum state* (the state where the lawsuit has been filed).

Appearance

As we will see, some of the methods for obtaining personal jurisdiction differ depending on whether the defendant is a *resident* of the forum state or a *nonresident*. However, regardless of the residency of the defendant, the defendant automatically submits to the court's personal jurisdiction if he or she makes an **appearance.** In this context, the word *appearance* is a term of art. It does not refer to an actual physical presence in court; instead the term refers to the taking of any formal steps to defend the case. Thus if the defendant, normally acting through an attorney, files a motion to dismiss, an answer to the plaintiff's complaint, or almost any other court papers aimed at defending against the claim, the defendant has made an appearance. Once this has happened, the trial court has personal jurisdiction and the defendant cannot thereafter challenge the existence of

such jurisdiction. Therefore, if the defendant wishes to contest the court's personal jurisdiction, this must be completed before taking any other action that would constitute an appearance.

The major exception to this rule is the *special appearance*—a motion or other formal action taken by the defendant solely for the purpose of challenging the court's personal jurisdiction. If the only action the defendant takes is to challenge the court's personal jurisdiction, this action does not give the court jurisdiction. If the defendant properly makes the special appearance before taking any other formal action in the case but the trial court denies the challenge to its personal jurisdiction, the defendant can then defend the case on its merits without losing the right later to have an appellate court rule on the personal jurisdiction question.

Service of Summons

If the defendant has not made an appearance, the plaintiff must see to it that the court acquires personal jurisdiction. Whether the defendant is a resident or nonresident, the preferred method is *personal service of summons*. The **summons** is the formal notice of the lawsuit.[5] A copy of the plaintiff's complaint is usually attached to the summons. *Personal service* means delivery to the defendant in person while the defendant is physically within the forum state. Traditionally, an officer such as a sheriff, marshal, deputy sheriff or marshal, or constable was always used to deliver the summons. In recent years, however, the rules in many places have been changed to permit other persons, such as the plaintiff's attorney, to deliver a summons. In the federal district courts, for example, the rules were changed in the past few years to place responsibility on the plaintiff's attorney for seeing that the summons is served; the actual delivery of the summons to the defendant can be performed by any person at least 18 years old who is not a party to the lawsuit (such as a clerk in the office of the plaintiff's attorney). Whoever attempts to deliver a summons must make a sworn statement to the court as to whether the attempt was successful or unsuccessful.

In the case of a resident defendant, there are several alternatives to personal service of summons, including (1) permitting the authorized summons-server to leave the summons at the defendant's

---

[4] It should be mentioned in the interest of accuracy that a court does have to obtain personal jurisdiction over a plaintiff with respect to a defendant's counterclaim, but this would rarely present any problem.

[5] In some places, other terms, such as *process* or *citation*, are used instead of the term *summons*. Sometimes the term *service of process* is used in a general sense to describe delivery of any legal papers in a lawsuit, including a summons, a subpoena to testify, and other papers.

residence with someone older than a specified age (such as 16 or 18 years), (2) permitting the server to leave the summons at the defendant's regular place of business, or (3) permitting the server or the court clerk to mail the summons to the defendant's residence or business. In the latter case, registered or certified mail is required in some places, but only first class mail is required in others. In some states, it is required that personal service first be attempted before one of these alternatives can be used; in other places this is not required.

Corporate Defendants

Although many of the rules for acquiring personal jurisdiction over a corporation are the same as for an individual, some are a bit different because of the nature of a corporate entity. The rules regarding the making of an appearance are the same for a corporation as for an individual.

If there is no appearance, there are several possible means for serving summons on a corporation. First, if the corporation has a *registered agent* in the forum state, service on that agent is sufficient. This service may be by personal delivery or by some alternative method permitted in that particular court system. A corporation is supposed to have a registered agent for receiving summonses and other legal notices in the state where it is incorporated and in any other state where it does business. In this regard, *doing business* usually means having some physical presence in the state, not just advertising or receiving mail or telephone orders. In most places, service of summons also may be accomplished by delivering it to an *officer* of the corporation if one is located within the forum state.

Long-Arm Statutes and Due Process

As a general rule, a summons is effective to give a court personal jurisdiction only if it is served on the defendant within the forum state. Thus if P files a suit for breach of contract against D in a state or federal court in Michigan, a summons issued normally must be served on D within Michigan to give the court personal jurisdiction. This requirement presents little problem if D is a resident of Michigan. Not only will it usually be possible personally to deliver the summons to a resident defendant but, as we have already seen, various alternatives are available for accomplishing service of summons to someone who is a resident of the forum state. Also, if a corporate defendant has either its headquarters or a registered

agent in the forum state, the requirement is not difficult to meet.

However, if an individual defendant is a resident of some other state or nation or if the corporation has no registered agent in the forum state, serving a summons becomes more difficult. The defendant in such a case is not likely to "hang around" in the forum state so that a summons can be served. If personal jurisdiction cannot be obtained, the plaintiff is faced with the prospect of filing suit in a state (or nation) where personal jurisdiction can be obtained; unless the claim is quite large, the substantial extra expense could mean that pursuing the claim is not economically feasible.

There are certain circumstances in which it is possible for a court to gain personal jurisdiction over a defendant even though that defendant has not made an appearance and has not been served with a summons within the forum state. The procedural due process guarantee in the Constitution is essentially aimed at ensuring basic fairness. A number of years ago, the U.S. Supreme Court decided that the due process requirement of basic fairness is satisfied if a nonresident defendant has had significant prior contact with the forum state. (The Court used the term *minimal* contact, but *significant* better describes the concept as it has been applied over the years.) In addition to the contact requirement, the Supreme Court said that a particular state had to have a statutory procedure for making sure that a summons was actually forwarded to the nonresident defendant at its out-of-state address.

In response to this Supreme Court decision, every state has adopted a so-called **long-arm statute** specifying such a procedure. In many states, the long-arm statute specifies that personal jurisdiction can be acquired over a nonresident defendant who has "done business" or committed a "tort" (that is, wrongful conduct for which civil liability can be imposed) within the forum state. In other states, the statute simply provides that jurisdiction can be acquired in any circumstances in which the defendant's prior contact with the state is sufficient to comply with the fairness requirement of due process. Even if the state statute specifies certain kinds of contact, such as doing business, the application of the statute in a particular case is still subject to court review for compliance with procedural due process.

Long-arm statutes provide that, when the evidence shows that the defendant has had sufficient contact with the forum state, the summons is to be sent to a central office in the forum state. In most states, this is the secretary of state's office. The official in charge of that office then has the responsibility to send the summons to the defendant at its out-of-state address.

The courts have divided the due process requirement of significant contacts into two categories. First, suppose that the lawsuit arises from a specific contact that the nonresident defendant had with the forum state. For instance, the defendant may have driven his or her car into the forum state, where he or she had an accident that is now the basis for the lawsuit. Or the plaintiff's complaint may be based on some specific business he or she and the defendant conducted within the forum state. In such a situation, the defendant's contact is sufficient for that particular lawsuit even if it was the defendant's only contact with that state. Second, suppose that the lawsuit arises from actions of the defendant that occurred in some place other than the forum state. In such a case, the long-arm statute can be used to acquire personal jurisdiction against the nonresident defendant only if the defendant's prior contacts with the forum state were of a substantial and continuous nature. The reason for this distinction is, again, basic fairness. When a nonresident defendant has had substantial and continuous contacts with a particular state, the courts believe that it is fair to require the defendant to defend against lawsuits in that state even if the facts leading to the lawsuit arose somewhere else. However, the courts have concluded that it is not fair to haul a nonresident defendant into court if his or her only contact with the state has been of an isolated or insubstantial nature, except in the situation where the lawsuit actually involves the specific actions of the defendant within that state.

Before leaving the discussion of personal jurisdiction, we must make an observation about enforcing court judgments. Suppose that D, a resident of Wisconsin, drove his car to Tennessee for a vacation. While there, he had a collision with a car driven by P, a resident of Tennessee. If P files a lawsuit against D in a Tennessee court, the Tennessee long-arm statute is used to acquire personal jurisdiction over D, and if P wins a judgment for damages, D cannot just go home to Wisconsin and ignore the judgment. If D has "nonexempt" assets back home, P will be able to get the Wisconsin authorities to enforce the Tennessee judgment by seizing D's assets in Wisconsin. More will be said about enforcing court judgments in the next chapter.

The following case illustrates some of the principles we discussed concerning the requirement that a nonresident defendant have had significant contacts with the forum state.

Helicopteros Nacionales de Colombia v. Hall

United States Supreme Court, 466 U.S. 408 (1984)

Petitioner "Helicol," a Colombian corporation, entered into a contract to provide helicopter transportation for Consorcio/WSH, a Peruvian company closely connected to a joint venture headquartered in Houston, Texas, during the company's construction of a pipeline in Peru. One of the helicopters crashed in Peru, killing four U.S. citizens. Respondents, survivors and representatives of the four decedents, filed this suit in Texas state court in Houston.

At the request of Consorcio/WSH, Helicol's chief executive officer had flown to Houston to negotiate the contract; the agreement was signed in Peru. During the years 1970–1977, Helicol also purchased helicopters, spare parts, and accessories for more than $4,000,000 from a Fort Worth, Texas, company. Helicol had sent prospective pilots to Fort Worth for training and to ferry the helicopters back to South America and also sent some management and maintenance personnel there for technical consultation. Helicol received into its New York and Florida bank accounts more than $5,000,000 in payments from Consorcio/WSH drawn on a Houston bank.

However, Helicol has never been authorized to do business in Texas and never had an agent for service of summons there. Nor has it ever performed helicopter operations, sold products, solicited business, signed contracts, based employees, recruited employees, owned property, maintained an office or records, or had shareholders in Texas.

Helicol filed a special appearance in the trial court and moved to dismiss for lack of personal jurisdiction. The trial court denied the motion and, after a jury trial, entered a $1,141,200 judgment against Helicol. The Texas Court of Civil Appeals reversed for lack of

(continues)

HELICOPTEROS NACIONALES DE COLOMBIA

(continued from previous page) *personal jurisdiction, but the Texas Supreme Court later reinstated the verdict. Helicol then appealed to the U.S. Supreme Court.*

Blackmun, Justice:

The Texas Supreme Court first held that the State's long-arm statute reaches as far as the Due Process Clause of the Fourteenth Amendment permits. Thus, the only question remaining for the court to decide was whether it was consistent with the Due Process Clause for Texas courts to assert *in personam* jurisdiction over Helicol.

The Due Process Clause of the Fourteenth Amendment operates to limit the power of a State to assert *in personam* jurisdiction over a nonresident defendant. Due process requirements are satisfied when *in personam* jurisdiction is asserted over a nonresident corporate defendant that has "certain minimum contacts with [the forum] such that the maintenance of the suit does not offend 'traditional notions of fair play and substantial justice.'" *International Shoe Co. v. Washington,* 326 U.S. 310 (1945). When a controversy is related to or "arises out of" a defendant's contacts with the forum, the Court has said that a "relationship among the defendant, the forum, and the litigation" is the essential foundation of *in personam* jurisdiction. *Shaffer v. Heitner,* 433 U.S. 186 (1977).

Even when the cause of action does not arise out of or relate to the foreign corporation's activities in the forum State, due process is not offended by a State's subjecting the corporation to its *in personam* jurisdiction when there are sufficient contacts between the State and the foreign [out-of-state] corporation. *Perkins v. Benguet Consolidated Mining Co.,* 342 U.S. 437 (1952). In *Perkins,* the Court addressed a situation

in which state courts had asserted general jurisdiction over a defendant foreign corporation. During the Japanese occupation of the Philippine Islands, the president and general manager of a Philippine mining corporation maintained an office in Ohio from which he conducted activities on behalf of the company. He kept company files and held directors' meetings in the office, carried on correspondence relating to the business, distributed salary checks drawn on two active Ohio bank accounts, engaged an Ohio bank to act as transfer agent, and supervised policies dealing with the rehabilitation of the corporation's properties in the Philippines. In short, the foreign corporation, through its president, "ha[d] been carrying on in Ohio a continuous and systematic, but limited, part of its general business," and the exercise of general jurisdiction over the Philippine corporation by an Ohio court was "reasonable and just."

All parties to the present case concede that respondents' claims against Helicol did not "arise out of," and are not related to, Helicol's activities within Texas. We thus must explore the nature of Helicol's contacts with the State of Texas to determine whether they constitute the kind of continuous and systematic general business contacts the Court found to exist in *Perkins.* We hold that they do not.

It is undisputed that Helicol does not have a place of business in Texas and never has been licensed to do business in the State. Basically, Helicol's contacts with Texas consisted of sending its chief executive officer to Houston for a contract-negotiation session; accepting into its New York bank account checks payable on a Houston bank; purchasing helicopters, equipment, and training services from Bell Helicopter for substantial sums; and sending personnel to Bell's

facilities in Fort Worth for training.

The one trip to Houston by Helicol's chief executive officer for the purpose of negotiating the transportation-services contract with Consorcio/WSH cannot be described or regarded as a contact of a "continuous and systematic" nature, and thus cannot support an assertion of *in personam* jurisdiction over Helicol by a Texas court. Similarly, Helicol's acceptance from Consorcio/WSH of checks drawn on a Texas bank is of negligible significance. Common sense and everyday experience suggest that, absent unusual circumstances, the bank on which a check is drawn is generally of little consequence to the payee and is a matter left to the discretion of the drawer. Such unilateral activity of another party or a third person is not an appropriate consideration when determining whether a defendant has sufficient contacts with a forum State to justify an assertion of jurisdiction.

The Texas Supreme Court focused on the purchases and related training trips in finding contacts sufficient to support an assertion of jurisdiction. We do not agree with that assessment, for the Court's opinion in *Rosenberg Bros. & Co. v. Curtis Brown Co.,* 260 U.S. 516 (1923) makes clear that purchases and related trips, standing alone, are not a sufficient basis for a State's assertion of jurisdiction.

Nor can we conclude that the fact that Helicol sent personnel into Texas for training in connection with the purchase of helicopters and equipment in that State in any way enhanced the nature of Helicol's contacts with Texas. The brief presence of Helicol employees in Texas for the purpose of attending the training sessions is no more a significant contact than were the trips to New York made by the buyer for the [defendant] retail store in *Rosenberg.*

[Reversed.] ⬡

Comment The result in this case would have been the same if Helicol, the defendant, had been headquartered in Oklahoma rather than the nation of Colombia. In addition, we will see very shortly that the analysis of the personal jurisdiction issue, and the ultimate result, would have been the same if the plaintiff had filed the suit in a *federal* court in Houston rather than a state court there. (A federal court probably would have had subject matter jurisdiction on the basis of diversity of citizenship.)

Foul-Ups in Service of Summons

We should note that although it is rather unusual, occasionally something can go wrong in the summons-serving process. This can happen in the case of either a resident or a nonresident defendant. Suppose that the rules for serving a summons have been complied with, but for some reason the defendant did not actually receive it. For instance, the summons may have been properly left at the defendant's residence with a friend or family member who lost it and forgot to tell the defendant. Suppose also that the defendant did not know about the lawsuit and thus did not answer the plaintiff's complaint and that the plaintiff then received a default judgment against the defendant because of the latter's failure to respond.

Within a certain period of time thereafter (such as a year or two, depending on the state), the defendant may ask the court to set aside the default judgment and give the defendant a chance to defend against the complaint. The trial judge will do so if convinced that the defendant really did not receive the summons, had no actual knowledge that the lawsuit had been filed, and has some plausible rebuttal or defense to the complaint.

Note—Personal Jurisdiction in Federal Courts

As a general rule, a federal court in a particular state faces the same constraints on its ability to acquire personal jurisdiction as would a state court in that state. Most of the time, a summons issue by a federal district court is effective only if served within the state where the court is located. The federal court can, however, make use of the state's long-arm statute to obtain personal jurisdiction over a nonresident defendant in the same circumstances in which a state court could do so. There are certain exceptional situations in which a federal court summons has a wider reach than one issued by a state court; in a few types of federal question cases, the federal statute that forms the basis of the plaintiff's claim includes a specific provision permitting nationwide service of summons. One example of this is found in the federal laws regulating the issuance and trading of securities in interstate commerce.

In Rem Cases

As mentioned earlier, a court usually must have personal jurisdiction over a defendant because most lawsuits are of the *in personam* variety. However, if the plaintiff's case is characterized as **in rem,** rather than in personam, the court is not required to have personal jurisdiction over a particular party. (It still must have subject matter jurisdiction, however.) A case is an in rem one if the plaintiff's objective is to obtain a judgment of the court against some item of *property,* rather than against a particular defendant.

Suppose, for example, that D borrowed money from Bank B and executed a document giving B a mortgage on a home or other piece of real estate. The mortgage makes the real estate collateral for the loan and gives B a right to take ownership and possession of the property if D fails to repay the loan on its agreed terms. If D defaults, B will exercise its right by filing a *mortgage foreclosure* action in court. The object of the action is not D, but instead is the acquisition of the title to the property. This is an in rem case, and it is not required that the court have personal jurisdiction over D. B can simply have a notice published in a local newspaper, which is not sufficient notice for personal jurisdiction but is sufficient for an in rem case to proceed. As a practical matter, if it is possible to get personal jurisdiction over D, B will usually see to it that the court obtains it, so that B can also get an in personam "deficiency judgment" against D; this is a judgment for any amount of the loan that may remain unpaid if the proceeds from the sale of the property are inadequate.

Other examples of in rem cases include court actions to establish ownership to lost or abandoned property or to give the government title over property that has been forfeited because it was used in connection with certain crimes such as drug dealing.

Related Matters

If we assume that the court has both subject matter and personal jurisdiction, there still may be other preliminary matters to consider. These other matters might include questions regarding venue, *forum non conveniens*, and conflict of laws.

Venue

If a state district court in Texas has subject matter and personal jurisdiction in a case filed by P, *every* district court in Texas has such jurisdiction. The question of where within the state the lawsuit should be heard is a question of **venue.** Every state has statutes that specify which counties are the appropriate venue. Typically, venue is appropriate in either the county where the defendant resides or where the accident or transaction took place. Sometimes venue may lie in other places; if the case involves real estate, the appropriate venue may be the county where the land is located. If there are two or more permissible venues, the plaintiff normally may choose among them when filing the lawsuit. In the federal court system, federal statutes specify which federal districts are the appropriate venues.

Although venue is not the same as jurisdiction, the rules governing venue questions have some of the same ultimate objectives as the rules pertaining to personal jurisdiction. The main objective is fairness, and a secondary one is efficiency.

Forum Non Conveniens

A court with both subject matter and personal jurisdiction may decline to exercise them if another court, more conveniently connected to the suit, also has both types of jurisdiction. Under the doctrine of **forum non conveniens,** the court may choose to transfer the suit or even dismiss it, forcing the plaintiff to file in the more convenient court.

For example, in one case arising out of a defendant's agent carelessly causing a fire in the plaintiff's warehouse in Virginia, the plaintiff sued 400 miles away in New York City where the state court had subject matter jurisdiction over the simple tort case and personal jurisdiction because of the defendant corporation's many business contacts in New York. However, the New York court declined to exercise its jurisdiction on grounds that the suit was more conveniently brought in Virginia where the plaintiff and all witnesses were located and where the accident had occurred. The only justification the plaintiff gave for filing in New York—that a New York jury was likely to give a bigger verdict—was inadequate.[6]

In determining the most convenient forum, courts will consider private interest factors such as ease of access to sources of proof, costs of obtaining witnesses' attendance, the possibility of a view of the site of the accident, and the convenience of the parties. Public factors to be considered include the imposition of jury service on residents of the community, the congestion of court dockets, and the interest in having local controversies decided at home.

The *forum non conveniens* doctrine can also be applied internationally. For example, a U.S. court of appeals affirmed a decision of the U.S. district court in New York City that used the doctrine as a basis for transferring a case from that federal court in New York to a court in India. The case involved claims against Union Carbide Corporation arising from the tragic leak of toxic gases from a chemical factory that killed more than 2000 people in Bhopal, India. The federal trial judge took this action only after being convinced that Indian law and procedure were designed to handle such claims and provide substantial justice and that an Indian court would take jurisdiction over the claims. The court also conditioned its dismissal in favor of the Indian courts on Union Carbide's consent to the jurisdiction of the Indian courts and its waiver of any statute of limitations defense.[7] (A statute of limitations specifies a time limit for filing a lawsuit.)

It should be noted that although the term *venue* is not used, the doctrine of *forum non conveniens* actually involves a very specialized and somewhat ad hoc type of venue question.

Conflict of Laws

Assume D Corporation, formed in Delaware with its principal place of business in Colorado, hires P from California to do subcontracting work on D's condominiums in New Mexico. The contract is negotiated in California, Colorado, and New Mexico before being signed in Colorado. When New Mexico officials ordered P to stop work because he did not have a license to do such work in New Mexico, D fired him. P sued in Colorado to recover for the work he had performed before being stopped. Several states' laws are potentially applicable to this case. If they all lead to the same result, it does not matter which state's rules are applied. However, in this case, New Mexico law bars P from recovery because he had no license. Colorado and California law would allow him to recover despite the lack of a license. Thus, there is a *conflict of laws*. To determine which state's laws to apply, we must resort to *choice of law* rules, which are designed to prevent a plaintiff with multiple jurisdictions from which to choose (because all have subject matter and personal jurisdiction) from "forum shopping" for the jurisdiction with the laws most favorable to him or her.

---

[6]*Gulf Oil Corp. v. Gilbert,* 330 U.S. 401 (1947).

[7]*In re Union Carbide Corp. Gas Plant Disaster at Bhopal, India in Dec. 1984,* 809 F.2d 195 (2d. Cir. 1987).

Conflict of laws questions also can arise in international disputes. Recall for a moment the example of the case against Union Carbide that was transferred from a federal court in New York to a court in India under the doctrine of *forum non conveniens*. The federal court could have retained jurisdiction and decided the case. If so, it probably would have applied the law of India to decide the case; to do so, the court obviously would have to call on experts in Indian law.

Contract Cases. If the parties stipulate in the contract that, for example, "California law will govern any disputes arising out of this contract," the courts will normally respect that choice if it was fairly bargained and California has at least a passing connection to the parties or the transaction. It is especially desirable for the parties to an international transaction to negotiate and include a clause in their contract specifying which nation's law should be applied to any dispute arising from the deal.

Absent a choice by the parties, the traditional view was to apply the law of the state in which the contract was made to any litigation about the validity of the contract and to apply the law of the state in which the contract was to be performed to any litigation about the performance of the contract. The strong modern trend, however, is to use an *interest analysis.*

Using an interest analysis to determine which state's law to apply, courts would consider such factors as the relevant policies of the forum and of other interested states, the protection of justified expectations (that is, which state's laws did the parties assume would apply), certainty, predictability, ease of determination of the law to be applied, and uniformity of result.

In contract cases specifically, most modern courts attempt to determine the state with the "most significant relationship" to the parties and the transaction, considering such factors as (1) the place of contracting; (2) the place of negotiation; (3) the place of performance; (4) the location of the subject matter of the contract; and (5) the domicile, residence, nationality, place of incorporation, and place of business of the parties.

In the factual situation outlined previously, the Colorado Supreme Court applied New Mexico's law,

---

LEGAL FOCUS

International

There are always many things to think about when negotiating a substantial contract. Parties should attempt to anticipate and provide in the contract for as many contingencies as possible. As we will see in the next chapter, one of the events that the parties should plan for in advance is a possible future dispute arising out of the transaction. Including a clause in the contract that specifies some type of nonlitigation dispute resolution procedure, such as arbitration, is something the parties should at least consider carefully. Even if they do not agree in advance to resolve future disputes outside the courts, however, there are still some other dispute-related matters they might try to resolve at the outset.

Although such agreements are almost always important, their significance is even greater when the transaction involves companies from different countries. It is possible and often desirable, for example, to agree where any later lawsuit should be heard. Such a "forum selection" clause will usually be upheld by courts in the United States and other countries so long as the place selected in advance has some connection with the parties or the transaction and the clause is not the product of fraud or an extreme abuse of bargaining power by one party.

A forum selection clause not only constitutes an agreement in advance about where any subsequent lawsuit will be heard, but also serves as consent to the personal jurisdiction of the court in the chosen location. Thus, the parties to a business transaction usually can waive the right to contest a court's personal jurisdiction. Likewise, the parties can agree that a particular state's or nation's law should apply to any future dispute. They also can resolve venue questions in advance. One thing that contracting parties cannot do, however, either in advance or after a dispute has arisen, is create subject matter jurisdiction in a court that does not have it otherwise. Subject matter jurisdiction, whether in a state or federal court in the United States or a court in another country, is a matter of governmental power, and cannot be created by private parties. ◢

reasoning that New Mexico's interest in protecting its citizens from substandard construction by unlicensed subcontractors outweighed Colorado's interest in validating agreements and protecting parties' expectations.[8]

Tort Cases. Assume that a husband and wife from New Mexico are killed when a plane the husband is piloting crashes in Texas. The parties intended to return to New Mexico and had no other contacts with Texas. The estate of the wife filed suit against the husband's estate in state court in Texas. Texas's doctrine of interspousal immunity would not allow the suit. New Mexico has no such doctrine; its law would allow the suit. Which state's law should apply? The traditional view is to apply the law of the place of the tort—Texas. But why would Texas courts care whether a New Mexico wife's estate can recover from a New Mexico husband's estate? Again, the strong modern trend is to move away from an automatic choice of the law of the place of the tort to an interest analysis. Modern courts often use the following factors in deciding which state has the most significant relationship to the occurrence and the parties: (1) the place where the injury occurred; (2) the place where the conduct causing the injury occurred; (3) the domicile, residence, nationality, place of incorporation, and place of business of the parties; and (4) the place where the relationship, if any, between the parties is centered. In this case, New Mexico law was applied.[9]

LAW, EQUITY, AND REMEDIES

In the next chapter we will examine the major steps in the process of adjudication, paying particular attention to the roles played by the trial and appellate courts in that process. We will see that in all legal controversies the plaintiff is asking for a **remedy**—an order addressed to the defendant, requiring that person either to pay money or to do (or not to do) a particular act. A remedy, then, is "the means by which a plaintiff's right is enforced or the violation of a right is prevented, redressed, or compensated."[10] All remedies are either "legal" or "equitable" in nature, a fact that can be explained only by a brief glimpse at the development of the early court systems in England.

Courts of Law

Some 900 years ago, the first Norman kings of England established a system of courts by designating individuals throughout the country to be their personal representatives in the settling of certain kinds of legal disputes. These representatives could grant only very limited types of relief: (1) money damages, (2) possession of real estate, or (3) possession of personal property.

In settling disputes, the courts made up their own rules as they went along, based largely on the customs and moral standards then prevailing, plus their own ideas of "justice" in particular situations. The formulation of rules in this manner, a process that continues today in some branches of law, gave birth to the *common law* (which we will study in more detail in Chapter 4). The royal courts ultimately became known as **courts of law,** and the remedies that they granted were *remedies at law.*

Courts of Equity

When plaintiffs needed relief other than what the courts of law could grant, they often petitioned the king. Such petitions were frequently decided by the king's chancellor, who granted relief when he thought the claim was a fair one. Out of the rulings of successive chancellors arose a new body of "chancery" rules and remedies for cases outside the jurisdiction of the courts of law. This developed eventually into a system of *courts of equity,* as distinct from the courts of law.

A plaintiff who wanted a legal remedy, such as money damages, would bring an **action at law** in a court of law. A plaintiff wanting some other relief, such as an **injunction** (for example, an order forcing D to stop grazing cattle on land belonging to P) or a **decree of specific performance** (for example, an order commanding D to live up to a contract to sell land to P), brought an **action in equity** in an equity court. Other common equitable actions, in addition to those asking for injunctions and decrees of specific performance, include (1) divorce actions, (2) mortgage foreclosure suits, and (3) actions for an accounting, brought by one member of a partnership against another.

The Present Scene

Although the distinction between legal and equitable remedies as diagrammed in Figure 2.3 persists today, there has been a fusion of law and equity courts in

[8]*Wood Bros. Homes, Inc. v. Walker Adjustment Bureau,* 601 P.2d 1369 (Colo. 1979).
[9]*Robertson v. McKnight,* 609 S.W.2d 534 (Tex. 1980).
[10]*Black's Law Dictionary,* Fifth Edition, Copyright 1979 by West Publishing Co.

FIGURE 2.3

Major Differences Between Law and Equity

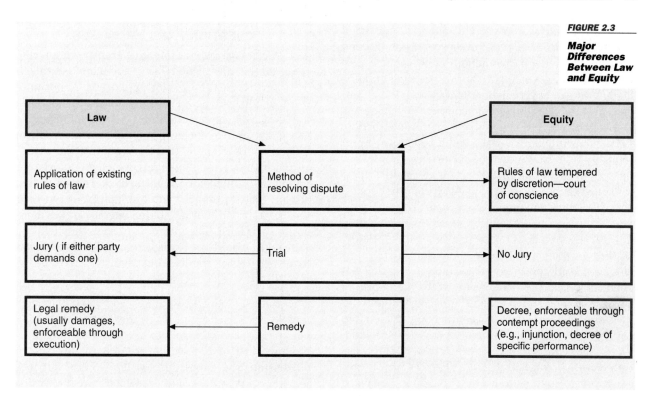

virtually all states. This means that separate courts of law and equity, as such, have been eliminated. Instead, the basic trial courts in the state and federal systems are empowered to hear both legal and equitable actions.

Today, the basic distinctions between the two kinds of actions are these:

1. Whether an action is one at law or in equity depends solely on the *nature of the remedy* that the plaintiff is seeking.

2. There is *no jury* in an equitable action. Questions of both fact and law are decided by the court, that is, the trial judge.

3. Proceedings in equitable actions are *less formal* than those at law, particularly in regard to the order in which witnesses' testimony can be presented and the determination of admissibility of their evidence.

4. Equitable remedies are considered to be exceptional. Therefore, when determining whether to grant an equitable remedy, a court considers certain factors that it would not consider in a typical money damage suit. For example, even if the plaintiff has proved that the defendant has violated the plaintiff's legal rights,

a court may refuse to grant an injunction or other equitable remedy in any of the following situations: (1) The plaintiff does not have "clean hands"—that is, has been guilty of unfair conduct in his or her dealings with the defendant; (2) an award of money damages—a "remedy at law"—would adequately redress the harm done to the plaintiff, so that an equitable remedy is not necessary; or (3) the granting of an equitable remedy might interfere substantially with the rights of some third party who is not involved in the case.

SUMMARY

Both the state and the federal court systems are organized similarly. At the first level are general trial courts, supplemented by specialized courts of limited jurisdiction. Appeals from the judgments of these courts are heard by appellate courts. In some states and in the federal system, there is an intermediate appellate court as well as a supreme court for a final appeal.

Federal courts can hear only the types of cases specified in the Constitution, primarily cases turning on federal questions and cases where a citizen of one state is suing the citizen of another for more than

$50,000. State trial courts can hear almost any type of case, except for a few categories specifically limited for exclusive federal jurisdiction. However, if a case with federal subject matter jurisdiction potential is filed in state court, it might not stay there; the defendant may remove it to federal court.

Every court must have subject matter jurisdiction. Personal jurisdiction over the defendant is also a prerequisite to a valid judgment. Courts frequently use the long-arm statute of their state to establish personal jurisdiction over defendants from other states, consistent with due process, of course. The establishment of subject matter and personal jurisdiction does not end the inquiry as to where a case will be tried—matters of venue and *forum non conveniens* must also be considered. A court deciding a case that has contacts with many states will have to use choice of law rules to determine which state's law to apply.

Historically, common law courts were divided into courts of law, which rendered mostly damage judgments, and courts of equity, which could grant more varied forms of relief. Though there are no longer two separate court systems, the procedures in a court may vary depending on whether the plaintiff asks for damages or injunctive relief.

KEY TERMS

Adjudication
Courts of limited jurisdiction
General trial courts
Appellate courts
Jurisdiction
Subject matter jurisdiction
Personal jurisdiction
Federal question
Diversity of citizenship
Right of removal
In personam
Appearance
Summons
Long-arm statute
In rem
Venue
Forum non conveniens
Remedy
Courts of law
Action at law
Injunction
Decree of specific performance
Action in equity

QUESTIONS AND PROBLEMS

1. A Michigan Department of Transportation rule required that all railroads have "adequate toilet facilities" for the health of their employees. About one-third of plaintiff CSXT's locomotives did not have toilets. CSXT protested, and a state administrative law judge upheld the rule. CSXT then filed suit in federal court, claiming that the state rule was inconsistent with federal regulations, which do not require toilets. The Michigan Department of Transportation argued that the federal court should refuse to hear the case (abstain) because of the ongoing proceedings at the state level. The question arose as to whether a state court would have jurisdiction to decide a lawsuit involving federal statutes and regulations. Would it? (*CSXT, Inc. v. Pitz*, 883 F.2d 468, 6th Cir. 1989.)

2. Rate, a Georgia lawyer, is owed $55,000 in legal fees by Jackson, a Florida resident. Although Rate could have brought suit to recover the debt in a federal court in Florida on grounds of diversity of citizenship, she chose, instead, to file her suit in a Florida court in the county in which Jackson lives. If Jackson now asks that the suit be transferred to a federal court, will his request have to be granted? Explain.

3. While walking across Gomez's property one evening, North is injured when she falls into an unguarded excavation. When North brings a negligence action against Gomez in the proper state court to recover damages, that court applies the rule that a trespasser cannot hold a landowner liable even if he or she is guilty of negligence, and the court dismisses the action. North appeals the decision to the state supreme court, which affirms the rule of nonliability. In this case, is the ruling of the state supreme court final? (If North were to appeal to the U.S. Supreme Court, would it refuse to consider the case?) Why or why not?

4. On December 21, 1985, an Arrow Air Corp. charter plane carrying 248 soldiers from active duty in the Middle East back to Fort Campbell, Kentucky, crashed in Newfoundland, killing all aboard. Relatives of the victims sued Arrow in Kentucky. Arrow moved to dismiss for lack of personal jurisdiction. Evidence showed that Arrow was incorporated in Delaware with its main office in Florida. Arrow hangared an aircraft in Kentucky in 1983, flying five cargo flights per week. It also made flights into Kentucky for the Military Airlift Command in 1984–

1985, earning more than $2 million in charter revenue. The crash in question was Arrow's second flight into Fort Campbell. Arrow had no bank accounts or phone number in Kentucky. Does a Kentucky court have personal jurisdiction? (*In re Air Crash Disaster at Gander, Newfoundland*, 660 F. Supp. 1202, W.D. Ky. 1987.)

5. Plaintiffs bought an Audi automobile in New York. Later, while moving to Arizona, they were involved in a serious collision in Oklahoma when the Audi caught fire after being struck from behind. Filing in Oklahoma, plaintiffs sued the New York retailer from whom they had purchased the car and the wholesaler who had provided the car to the retailer. These defendants claimed that because they only sold cars in New York, an Oklahoma court had no personal jurisdiction over them. Does the Oklahoma long-arm statute reach this far? Discuss. (*World-Wide Volkswagen Corp. v. Woodson*, 444 U.S. 286, 1981.)

6. Dennis married Francie in West Virginia in 1976. They spent their married life in New Jersey, where their children were born. In July 1987, they decided to separate. Francie moved herself and the children to San Francisco. Dennis visited Los Angeles on a business trip and then went to San Francisco to see the kids. When he arrived, Francie had him served with a summons and a divorce petition. Dennis went back to New Jersey and had his lawyer file a special appearance in California—a motion to dismiss the California suit for lack of personal jurisdiction. Should the motion be granted, given Dennis's lack of contacts with California? Discuss. (*Burnham v. Superior Court of California*, 110 S. Ct. 2105, 1990.)

7. The plaintiff corporation, incorporated in Michigan, hired the defendant from Florida to operate a helicopter to spray agricultural chemicals on fields in Ohio. In a contract written and signed by the plaintiff in Michigan and later signed by the defendant in Florida, the defendant agreed that if he left the plaintiff's employ he would not enter into a competing business. After two years, the defendant left plaintiff's employ and did begin a competing business in Ohio. The plaintiff sued in Ohio to enforce the convenant not to compete. Such a covenant is void under Michigan law but enforceable if reasonable under the laws of Florida and Ohio. Which state's law should be applied by the Ohio court? Discuss. (*S&S Chopper Service, Inc. v. Scripter*, 394 N.E.2d 1011, Ohio App. 1977.)

8. The defendant airline, a Delaware corporation headquartered in New York, invited several Illinois travel agents to take an expense-paid vacation to Mexico. While in Mexico, one of the travel agents was killed by unknown assailants. His wife, the plaintiff, sued the airline in Illinois, claiming that its Illinois employees knew at the time of the invitation that portions of Mexico near the trip site were overrun with bands of armed guerrillas, yet they negligently failed to take precautions for the safety of her husband. Mexico's law would allow recovery on the plaintiff's theory; Illinois law would not. Which law should apply? Discuss. (*Semmelroth v. American Airlines*, 448 F. Supp. 730, E.D. Ill. 1978.)

9. Durant was left paralyzed from the waist down when his tractor struck the defendant's guide wire. Durant sued the defendant on a theory of negligent maintenance, filing the suit in Lee County, South Carolina. The defendant filed a motion to change the suit's venue to Sumter County on grounds of convenience to witnesses. Nine of defendant's employees, who would also be witnesses, filed affidavits stating that they would have to travel 23 miles to the Lee County Courthouse. The plaintiff responded with an affidavit indicating that because of his paralysis it was difficult for him to move and that the Lee County rescue squad had agreed to transport him to and from the Lee County Courthouse but no further. Should the court grant the motion to change venue on *forum non conveniens* grounds? Discuss. *See Durant v. Black River Electric Cooperative, Inc.*, 248 S.E.2d 264 (S.C. 1978.)

Chapter 3

Litigation and Alternative Methods of Dispute Resolution

The Adversarial System

Litigation: Pretrial Proceedings

Litigation: Trial Proceedings

Litigation: The Appellate Courts

Note on Performance of Judges

Alternative Dispute Resolution

M ANY AMERICAN NOVELS, movies, and television programs feature courtroom scenes to produce dramatic tension for readers and viewers. This is appropriate, because courtroom battles can produce high drama. Nothing quite matches the tension that litigants and attorneys feel when a jury verdict is about to be announced in open court.

This chapter will look at the litigation process, from the initiation of a civil suit through the trial process all the way to final appeal. After this examination, you will be better able to appreciate the context in which these few dramatic moments occur. You will also understand that litigation can be extremely complicated, expensive, and time-consuming. Indeed, litigation is usually something to be avoided. But when you cannot avoid litigation, it pays to understand the process.

Our discussion focuses on procedures in civil lawsuits rather than in criminal prosecutions. Although many of the procedures in the two types of proceedings are the same, there also are a number of important differences. Some of these differences are noted in Chapter 7, Criminal Law and Business. In addition, a few differences between civil and criminal procedures will be mentioned in this chapter.

After we have studied the civil litigation process, we will explore some other ways of resolving disputes, especially those that arise in business. These other methods, which are sometimes grouped together under the name *alternative dispute resolution,* include arbitration, mediation, and other techniques. Such methods are being used with greater frequency today in an effort to resolve disputes more quickly, less expensively, and without destroying valuable relationships.

THE ADVERSARIAL SYSTEM

Before studying the process of civil litigation, it is important to note that both civil and criminal proceedings in the United States are based on the so-called **adversarial system.** This approach to litigation is one of the key features of American law inherited from England.[1] The term *adversarial* has a very spe-

cialized meaning in this context. Even in a nation that does not use the adversarial system, the parties to a lawsuit or a criminal prosecution obviously are adversaries. However, when we use the term *adversarial* to describe the English/American approach to litigation, we are referring primarily to the amount of control that the parties and their attorneys have over the procedure.

Under the adversarial system, the parties themselves (acting through their attorneys) research the law and develop the facts. They decide which issues are going to be presented, which legal arguments are going to be made, what evidence should be gathered and presented, and how the evidence is to be introduced in court. The trial judge does not make these decisions; indeed, the judge normally takes no action unless a party specifically requests it. For example, if one party's attorney attempts to introduce testimony or physical evidence that is not legally admissible, the judge usually will not keep the evidence out unless the other party's attorney makes an objection. If an attorney overlooks a relevant legal argument and fails to make it, the judge normally will not take the initiative to include that argument in the legal analysis of the case.

Although the parties and their attorneys have primary control over the issues and evidence, the trial judge obviously has the duty to exercise ultimate supervisory authority over the entire process. In addition, within the adversarial framework the rules relating to control over issues and evidence can vary somewhat from one court system to another. For example, in some states in the United States, as well as in the federal district courts, trial judges may sometimes ask questions of witnesses if they believe that an attorney's questioning is not eliciting certain important testimony. Similarly, in some states and in the federal courts, trial judges can "comment on the weight of the evidence"—make comments to the jury about the strength of particular testimony or other evidence. In other states, judges cannot do these things. Finally, as case loads and delays increase, more trial judges in the adversarial system probably

---

[1]Although America derives its adversarial system from England, today the American courts typically use a more extreme version of the adversarial system than do the English courts; in other words, the degree of party control (rather than judge control) over the litigation process is usually even greater in the United States than in England.

will take a greater degree of control over the process in the future than they usually have in the past. However, the general idea that the parties and their attorneys should have primary control is so firmly embedded that it will undoubtedly continue as a fundamental element in our system of litigation.

The adversarial system can be contrasted with the so-called **inquisitorial system** of litigation used in European nations and, indeed, in most other parts of the world that did not inherit the English legal system. In general, the trial judge (or panel of judges)[2] in the inquisitorial system has much more control over the process, and the parties have much less than in the adversarial system. The judge often will have the authority to decide which issues will be addressed, although the parties certainly will provide important input. The judges are usually in charge of the investigation and gathering of evidence; they do not do this personally but have investigators who answer directly to them. Judges make rulings and take various other actions on their own initiative rather than merely responding to the parties' requests for action.[3] It should be noted, finally, that there is significant variation in procedural details among the many countries that use the inquisitorial system, just as there is variation within the adversarial system.

There are good and bad points about both of these systems. The adversarial system requires fewer judges and more lawyers than the inquisitorial system. The inquisitorial system requires that more of the time and energy devoted to a case be expended by public officials (judges and investigators) than by the parties and attorneys. Thus, the adversarial system shifts more of the cost to the private sector, whereas the inquisitorial system places more of the cost in the public sector. The adversarial system also puts primary responsibility for developing the facts in the hands of those (parties and their attorneys) who have a natural incentive to do a more thorough job. However, putting this responsibility in the hands of the parties and their attorneys also means that the

fact-gathering process may be aimed more at seeking strategic advantage than finding the truth.

LITIGATION: PRETRIAL PROCEEDINGS

Pretrial proceedings consist of two stages, the **pleading stage** and the **discovery stage.** We will look at each of these steps briefly.

The Pleading Stage

The typical suit is commenced by the plaintiff, through an attorney, filing a **complaint** (or petition) with the court having jurisdiction of the case. At the same time, the plaintiff asks the court to issue a summons to the defendant.

After receiving the summons, the defendant has a prescribed period of time in which to file a response of some sort, normally an **answer,** to the complaint. After that has been completed, the plaintiff can file a **reply** to the answer. The complaint, answer, and reply make up the *pleadings* of a case, the main purpose of which is to permit the court and the parties to ascertain the actual points in issue.

The Complaint

The *complaint* sets forth the plaintiff's version of the facts and ends with a "prayer" (request) for a certain remedy based on these facts. The plaintiff alleges those facts that, if ultimately proved by the evidence, will establish a legally recognized claim against the defendant. Suppose, for example, that the plaintiff bought a boat from the defendant, a dealer. The plaintiff claims that the boat leaks badly. After the two parties are unable to resolve their differences, the plaintiff institutes a lawsuit by filing a complaint. The complaint may allege that the parties made an agreement for the sale of the boat on a particular date for a particular price, the price was paid and the boat delivered, the plaintiff used the boat and found that it leaked, the defective condition of the boat is in violation of a warranty made by the dealer, and the plaintiff has suffered economic harm because the boat is worth far less in its defective condition than it would have been worth if not defective. If these facts are ultimately proved, the plaintiff has a good claim against the defendant for breach of warranty. However, the plaintiff might also allege that the defendant intentionally lied about the condition of the boat, thus committing the tort of fraud or perhaps violating a state deceptive trade practice statute.

---

[2]In many other countries, it is more common to have a panel of three or more trial judges in significant cases, rather than the single trial judge that typically presides over a trial in the United States.

[3]There are other differences in the two systems that cannot be discussed here in detail. For example, in many countries that use the inquisitorial system, the trial in a civil lawsuit is not a single, highly intensive event. Instead, it may consist of a series of several conferences among the judges, parties, and attorneys. The process of investigation and evidence gathering takes place not only before the first conference but also between later conferences. Each meeting brings the case closer to a conclusion. This kind of process can work in these countries because juries of citizens are not used.

In most complaints, the remedy requested by the plaintiff is an award of money damages to be paid by the defendant to compensate the plaintiff for his or her loss. If the plaintiff seeks some other remedy, such as an injunction, it will be requested in the complaint. Sometimes the plaintiff's complaint may request multiple remedies, such as damages for past harm and an injunction to prevent future harm. In the boat example, the plaintiff might request money damages for breach of warranty or perhaps fraud. This is not the type of case in which the plaintiff would seek an injunction. The plaintiff might, however, request the equitable remedy of *rescission,* an order of the court cancelling the contract, along with *restitution,* a return of the purchase price.

The Answer

The defendant usually responds to the complaint by filing an *answer.* The answer may include several components. One thing it always contains is a *denial* of the plaintiff's allegations. In some places, the defendant is permitted to make a *general denial,* which simply denies all the plaintiff's allegations together. In other court systems, the rules require a defendant to deny each allegation individually; any allegation not denied is deemed to be admitted. The rules in some systems permit a general denial in most cases, but require specific denials of certain types of allegations. Regardless of the form, a denial is essentially a formality that places the plaintiff's allegations in issue and places the burden on the plaintiff to prove the assertions he or she has made.

It must be remembered that the plaintiff in a civil lawsuit (and the prosecution in a criminal case) bears the overall burden of proof. In other words, if the plaintiff does not ultimately produce evidence that convinces the jury (or judge if there is no jury) of the correctness of the allegations in the complaint, the plaintiff loses. Although the defendant must respond with an answer, he or she is not obligated to *prove* anything. Nevertheless, if a defendant believes that the facts create a legally recognized **defense** (sometimes called an *affirmative defense*) against the plaintiff's claim, he or she will assert the defense in the answer after the denial. A defense defeats the plaintiff's claim *even if the plaintiff is able to prove those facts that establish all the elements of his or her claim.* Asserting a defense consists of alleging those facts that, if ultimately proved by the defendant, will establish a legally recognized defense against the plaintiff's claim. For

virtually every type of civil claim, the law recognizes one or more defenses. In the boat example, the defendant might allege as a defense to the breach of warranty claim that there was a *disclaimer* in the sale contract stating clearly and conspicuously that the boat was a reconditioned one and was being sold on an "as is" basis. If proved, this allegation would defeat the plaintiff's breach of warranty claim. Such a defense would not defeat a fraud claim, however. (In criminal cases, there are also legally recognized defenses against virtually all types of criminal charges.)

When asserting a defense, the defendant does not make a claim or request a remedy but simply tries to defeat the plaintiff's claim. Sometimes, however, the defendant may wish to assert a claim against the defendant in the form of a **counterclaim.** The defendant will allege facts that, if proved by the defendant, will establish a legally recognized claim against the plaintiff, and the defendant will ask for money damages or some other remedy. Either party alone might prevail on its claim, or both may prevail; in the latter event, the amount of the smaller judgment will be subtracted from the amount of the larger judgment.

Most counterclaims arise from the same set of circumstances that led to the plaintiff's claim (a so-called *compulsory* counterclaim). In such a case, the rules in most court systems require that the defendant assert the claim in this case as a counterclaim if it is to be asserted at all; he or she cannot keep quiet about it now and later sue the plaintiff (with their roles and names obviously reversed) on the claim. However, if the defendant's claim against the plaintiff arises from an unrelated set of circumstances, it is a so-called *permissive* counterclaim, and the defendant has a choice of asserting a counterclaim in the present case or suing separately.

In the boat example, the defendant might assert a counterclaim alleging that the plaintiff had not paid all the boat's purchase price, in violation of the sale contract, and request damages in the amount of the unpaid portion. It is not a rare occurrence for a plaintiff to have the tables turned by a counterclaim and to regret that he or she ever filed a lawsuit. The existence of a potential counterclaim sometimes may persuade a plaintiff not to file a complaint in the first place; at the very least, a realistic possibility that the other party may be able to prove a counterclaim can dramatically affect the bargaining positions of the parties as they attempt to negotiate a settlement.

The Reply

If the defendant raises new matter—additional facts—in the answer, the plaintiff must file a reply. In this pleading, the plaintiff will either deny or admit the new facts alleged in the answer.

Motion to Dismiss

Although technically not part of the pleadings, the **motion to dismiss**[4] must be mentioned at this point. The defendant will file such a motion instead of an answer if he or she believes that the plaintiff has no claim even if all the allegations in the complaint are true. In this motion, the defendant asserts that the plaintiff has not even stated a "cause of action"—that is, that even if the plaintiff's allegations are true (which the defendant is not admitting), the law does not recognize such a claim. The motion does not refer any evidence but merely takes aim at the allegations made in the plaintiff's complaint. Suppose, for example, that Ralph, the owner of a retail store in Milwaukee, is upset about some of the business practices of a competing retailer in town. In a private conversation between Ralph and George, the president of the other retailer, Ralph says, "You and your people are liars and cutthroats; you screw your customers whenever you think you can get away with it; you have the morals of a gutter rat." The conversation is not overheard by anyone else, and Ralph does not repeat any of it to anyone. If George sues Ralph for the tort of defamation, alleging these facts, Ralph will probably file a motion to dismiss and the court will grant it. Even if what Ralph said about George and his company was false, the tort of defamation (slander or libel) can occur only if false defamatory statements about someone are *communicated* to a third party. Thus, George and his company have no claim against Ralph even if events were exactly as George described in his complaint.

If the court grants the motion to dismiss, the plaintiff will be given an opportunity to amend the complaint. If the problem cannot be corrected by an amendment to the complaint, the court will dismiss the plaintiff's case. However, if the court denies the defendant's motion to dismiss, the defendant will then file an answer.

---

[4]The terminology used in referring to this particular type of motion to dismiss follows the rules of procedure that have, in recent years, been adopted by many states. The earlier name for this same pleading device—the *demurrer*—continues to be used in a few states, however. In such states, what has been said here in regard to the motion to dismiss applies with equal force to the demurrer.

Like other actions of a trial judge, a ruling on a motion to dismiss can be appealed to a higher court. The plaintiff can begin such an appeal immediately if the trial court grants the motion to dismiss, because this results in a final determination of the case at that level. However, if the trial judge denies the motion to dismiss, the defendant must wait until the case ends at the trial level before appealing; in this situation, the trial judge's ruling on the motion to dismiss probably will be only one of several grounds for the appeal.

The motion to dismiss is the first of several types of motions that give the trial judge an opportunity to end the litigation early when he or she is convinced that there is no doubt about the outcome and thus no reason to continue.

Defendant's Failure to Respond

Assuming that the court has jurisdiction, the defendant must respond within a specified time period by filing either a motion to dismiss or an answer. This time period is 20 days in the federal district courts and about the same amount of time in most state courts. The clock starts ticking when the defendant receives the summons and complaint. If the defendant does not respond during this period, the court may grant a **default judgment** against the defendant. By failing to respond, the defendant has given up the right to contest liability. The only issue to be determined is the amount of money damages to which the plaintiff is entitled, or the appropriateness of some other remedy the plaintiff may be seeking. The court will conduct a hearing at which the plaintiff presents evidence on the question of damages or other requested remedy.

The Discovery Stage

In early years, cases moved directly from the pleading stage to the trial stage. This meant that each party, going into the trial, had little information as to the specific evidence that the other party would rely on in presenting his or her case. Trial proceedings, as a result, often became what was commonly described as a "cat and mouse" game, with the parties often bringing in evidence that surprised their opponents. This situation was a natural outgrowth of the control parties have over evidence gathering and presentation in the adversarial system.

The undesirability of these proceedings was finally perceived by lawyers and judges, with the result that the Federal Rules of Civil Procedure, adopted in 1938, provided means (called *discovery proceedings*) by which much of the evidence that each party was going to rely on in proving his or her version of the facts would be fully disclosed to the other party before the case came to trial. The most common discovery tools recognized by these federal rules, which have now been essentially adopted by the states, are *depositions, interrogatories,* and *requests for production of documents.*

A deposition is testimony of a witness that is taken outside of court. Such testimony is given under oath, and both parties to the case must be notified so that they can be present when the testimony is given and thus have the opportunity to cross-examine the witness. Depositions are taken for these reasons: (1) to learn what the key witnesses know about the case, (2) to gain leads that will help obtain additional information, (3) to preserve the testimony of witnesses who might die or disappear, and (4) to establish a foundation for cross-examination of witnesses who might later change their stories.

Interrogatories are written questions submitted by one party to the other, which must be answered under oath. Use of this device is a primary way by which the questioning party may gain access to evidence that otherwise would be solely in the possession of his or her adversary.

A demand for documents permits a party to gain access to those kinds of evidence—such as business records, letters, and hospital bills—that are in the possession of the other party. Under modern rules of civil procedure, the party seeking the documents has the right to obtain them for purposes of inspection and copying.

A party must make a good faith effort to comply with the other party's legitimate discovery request. The court can impose various sanctions on parties and attorneys who do not make such an effort. These penalties may include the assessment of discovery costs, attorney's fees, or monetary penalties. In cases of flagrant disregard of legitimate discovery requests, the court can even dismiss a claim or defense or grant a default judgment against the offending party. The following case provides an example of such a situation.

Profile Gear Corp. v. Foundry Allied Industries, Inc.

U.S. Seventh Circuit Court of Appeals, 937 F.2D 351 (1991)

Case

Profile Gear Corp. manufactures and sells gears, gear assemblies, and various machine tool products. Under a contract with the U.S. government, Profile supplied replacement final drive assemblies for the Bradley fighting vehicle. Profile entered a contract with Foundry Allied Industries, under which Foundry was to supply Profile with aluminum castings that were a major component part of Profile's final drive assemblies. A dispute arose between Profile and Foundry over the contract terms. Profile claimed that all the contract terms were in a purchase order and other forms it sent to Foundry, and these terms obligated Foundry to supply 2434 sets of castings at a fixed price of $455 per set. Foundry claimed, however, that

the contract included the terms and conditions contained in a quotation that Foundry sent to Profile. One of these terms permitted Foundry to raise the price as the cost of aluminum increased. Profile refused to pay for castings it received after Foundry raised the price. Profile filed suit for breach of contract in federal district court (there was diversity of citizenship), claiming damages of $120,000. Foundry asserted a counterclaim for breach of contract, claiming damages of $320,000.

During pretrial, Profile and its attorney repeatedly refused to make various documents available in response to legitimate discovery requests by Foundry. In addition, Profile and its attorney lied to Foundry's attorney and to the district judge on several occasions about the nonexistence of documents or about its in-

ability to find or obtain them. On four different occasions, the district judge levied monetary penalties against Profile and its attorney for this behavior. The conduct continued, however; ultimately, the district judge gave Profile notice that default judgment would be entered against Profile on Foundry's counterclaim if Profile did not immediately comply with various discovery requests. Profile did not do so, and the court granted default judgment for Foundry on its counterclaim in an amount of $360,000 (damages plus interest).

Eschbach, Circuit Judge:

"For a long time courts were reluctant to enter default judgments, and appellate courts were reluctant to sustain

(continues)

PROFILE GEAR CORP. V. FOUNDRY ALLIED INDUSTRIES, INC.

(continued from previous page)
those that were entered. . . . Those times are gone." *Metropolitan Life Insurance Co. v. Estate of Cammon*, 929 F.2d 1120 (7th Cir. 1991). . . . The story begins with Profile Gear's response to interrogatories that the defendant Foundry served on July 28, 1989. Instead of answering the interrogatories, Profile responded "See Complaint" and "See Documents Produced," which the District Court properly characterized as evasive conduct. [On September 14,] the District Court imposed a sanction of $250, and ordered Profile to "respond to all outstanding discovery requests by September 25, 1989." . . .

Meanwhile, Profile [moved for sanctions against Foundry.] Its motion stated that Foundry had offered to produce certain documents for Profile's Chicago counsel only in Racine, Wisconsin. In fact, this problem had been resolved and the documents offered in Chicago. At a September 19 hearing, the District Court asked, "You told me in your motion that you have to go to Racine to see the documents. That is not the fact, is it?" To which Profile's counsel answered, "No, no, your Honor." The District Court issued a second sanction of $250 against Profile's counsel "for pursuing this motion when he knew the representations were not true."

The District Court issued more substantial sanctions four months later, on January 17, 1990. At this point, Profile had been caught in a clear lie. Profile had responded "none" in answer to re-

quests for documents concerning other disputes involving the contract language at issue in this case. Yet, in depositions, a Profile employee admitted the existence of such a dispute. And when documents were finally produced, they showed that Profile's counsel sent and received letters regarding this dispute just one month before stating that no documents existed. . . .

Two other incidents were similar. As of January 17, 1990, Profile admitted receiving at least three quotations for aluminum castings. Profile claimed that these quotations were missing from its files, but offered essentially no explanation for their absence. So too, Profile failed to produce a two page statement that it had asked a former employee to prepare. The statement was mailed to Profile, but Profile's counsel denied receiving it. The District Court concluded that, "in a strict credibility contest, [Profile's counsel] would not prevail over the reliability of the United States mail."

In addition, Profile refused to disclose the minutes of meetings of its own board of directors because "they are not within the immediate control of Profile's officers or counsel," and it refused to disclose monthly and quarterly financial reports because they concerned a "unique defense" that was otherwise unspecified. . . . This conduct led to a third set of sanctions. [On January 17, 1990,] the District Court ordered Profile to pay various of Foundry's attorneys' fees and "to immediately engage in a thorough search for all documents

described in Foundry's document request that remain undisclosed. . . . These documents shall be produced by February 1, 1990." The District Court also warned, "Should Profile fail to fully comply with this order, the court will determine whether to enter [default] judgment in favor of Foundry." . . .

Instead of complying, Profile for the first time claimed that it had 100,000 documents to produce, and this volume of material would take 30 days to assemble. This failure by Profile to meet another firm deadline led to a fourth sanction. . . . [T]he District Court ordered Profile to pose a bond by March 1, 1990 in the amount of Foundry's counterclaim, and warned that a default judgment would be entered if the bond was not posted. [Profile did not post the bond.]

The District Court's findings of intentional delay and repeated dishonesty are adequately supported [by evidence in the record]. . . . [T]he District Court did not abuse its discretion in entering a default judgment. For comparison, we note that this Court [that is, the Court of Appeals] has stated that a district court need not impose any lesser sanctions prior to entering the sanction of default judgment. . . . A district court is not required to fire a warning shot prior to issuing a default judgment as a sanction. And even absent a finding of dishonesty, we have affirmed numerous default judgments due to dilatory tactics. . . .

[Affirmed.] ⚖

Comment

1. It should be emphasized that, as punishment for Profile, the trial court granted a default judgment to Foundry on its counterclaim without regard to whether Foundry had proved this claim. Thus the court's action was very different from the action of a court in granting a summary judgment, which will be discussed shortly.

2. Although Profile's attorney was guilty of substantial misconduct in the case, Profile probably would not have a good malpractice claim against its attorney, because the evidence strongly suggested that Profile's management either directed or at least knew about and agreed to most of this conduct. Profile had a different attorney on appeal.

Abuse of the Discovery Process

Almost everyone who is knowledgeable about the American litigation process agrees that it is better to permit pretrial discovery than to have "trial by ambush." Most of them also admit, however, that the discovery process is plagued by frequent abuses. Discovery can be misused for the purpose of causing delay or confusion or imposing extra costs on the other party. One party may flood the other with voluminous and unnecessary interrogatories, take far more depositions than necessary, conduct depositions in an inefficient and wasteful manner, ask for a much larger volume of documents than necessary, respond to the other party's request for documents with truckloads of material when a few boxes would do, and engage in other tactics intended to wear the other party down. Just as the original need for pretrial discovery was an outgrowth of the adversarial system, so too are these abuses of discovery.

Trial judges generally possess the same power to punish parties and their attorneys for abusing the discovery process as they have to punish them for failing to comply with legitimate discovery requests. Traditionally, however, too few trial judges have exercised adequate supervisory control over pretrial discovery. This failure probably often has been attributable to the fact that they simply have had too many cases on their dockets. Although an increasingly heavy case load may cause a judge to have less time to supervise the pretrial proceedings in each case, it also makes it even more important that the judge exercise tighter control over all aspects of every case. Many judges are finding that they have to be good managers as well as good judges. In recent years, necessity has been leading more and more trial judges to exercise tighter control over the pretrial discovery process and other aspects of litigation. This is especially evident in the federal district courts, where it is becoming commonplace for judges to hold pretrial conferences with the attorneys, at which schedules and deadlines are established for conducting discovery and dealing with other pretrial matters. It also is becoming more common for trial judges, particularly federal district judges, to impose various penalties on parties and their attorneys for abuse of discovery. In the federal system, as well as in some state court systems, *magistrates* are increasingly used as judicial assistants to perform various tasks including supervision of pretrial discovery. As has happened in other matters over the years, it is likely that many state courts will follow the lead of the federal courts in supervising discovery more closely and punishing abuses of discovery more severely. Indeed, courts in some states have already begun to do so. There still is much room for improvement, however.

Summary Judgment

At or near the end of discovery, one party or the other (and occasionally both) may file a motion for **summary judgment** as to one or more of the issues in the lawsuit. In filing such a motion a party is arguing to the judge, in essence, that the evidence produced by discovery makes it so clear that the moving party is legally entitled to prevail that a trial would be a waste of time. A judge should grant such a motion only if a thorough review of the evidence obtained through discovery indicates that there is "no genuine issue as to any material fact"—that is, that there is no real question as to any important factual matter. Although summary judgment can be granted against either party, the fact that the plaintiff has the burden of proof means that summary judgments for the defendant are more common than for the plaintiff. Thus, if a defendant files a motion for summary judgment, it will be granted unless the plaintiff has presented at least enough evidence during discovery to create a genuine issue on all the required elements of its claim. However, if a plaintiff files the motion, the court will grant it only if (1) the plaintiff has produced enough evidence to prove the elements of its claim, (2) the defendant has failed to present evidence that creates doubt about any of these elements, and (3) the defendant also has failed to present evidence sufficient to create a genuine issue regarding an affirmative defense.

Judges traditionally have been reluctant to grant summary judgment motions, especially when a jury trial has been requested. In recent years, however, the U.S. Supreme Court has urged the federal district courts to make more use of summary judgment when there really does not seem to be much doubt about the ultimate outcome. In *Celotex Corp. v. Catrett*, 477 U.S. 317 (1986), the Court stated that "summary judgment procedure is properly regarded not as a disfavored procedural shortcut, but rather as an integral part of the Federal Rules [of Civil Procedure], which are designed to 'secure the just, speedy and inexpensive determination of every action.' " Not only are federal courts making increasing use of summary judgment, but it is very likely that more state courts also will do so as heavier case loads put greater pressure on judicial resources.

LITIGATION: TRIAL PROCEEDINGS

The Trial Stage

Unless a lawsuit is settled out of court or disposed of by the granting of a motion to dismiss or motion for summary judgment, it will eventually come up for trial. In the **trial stage** a jury may be impaneled, evidence presented, a verdict returned, and a judgment entered in favor of one of the parties.

Trial by Jury

In most civil lawsuits in which the plaintiff is seeking a so-called remedy at law, there is a constitutional right to jury trial. Because most lawsuits involve claims for money damages, such a right usually exists. In the federal courts, the right to trial by jury in civil cases is guaranteed by the Seventh Amendment of the U.S. Constitution. (For federal criminal cases, the right to jury trial is found in the Sixth Amendment.) Almost all state constitutions provide similar guarantees for cases tried in state courts.

When there is a right to jury trial, a jury will be impaneled if either party formally requests one. Failure to demand a jury trial constitutes a waiver of the right to one. The jury is a fact-finding body; its function is to consider all of the evidence and determine to the best of its ability what really happened. The jury determines whether particular testimony or other evidence is believable ("credible") and how much strength it seems to have as proof of the alleged facts. The jury is required to follow the judge's instructions as to the applicable legal principles. If neither party requests a jury, the trial judge performs the fact-finding role in addition to the judicial function. When there is no jury, the trial judge usually is required to prepare formal written "Findings of Fact" and "Conclusions of Law" after hearing the case. Although it is increasingly common today for both parties to waive a jury trial, especially in business disputes, there are still a great many jury trials. Most of the discussion in the remainder of this chapter assumes that there is a jury.

The use of juries drawn randomly from the local population is another unique feature of litigation inherited from the English system.[5] The jury system is sometimes criticized as being inefficient and unpredictable. Critics offer several arguments to support the claim that the jury system is an inferior method for resolving disputes, including the following:

1. Jurors do not have to meet any particular educational requirements.

2. Jurors do not have the experience or training to sift through substantial amounts of evidence, weigh it, and make carefully reasoned decisions.

3. Untrained and inexperienced decision makers are likely to be influenced too easily by irrelevant sympathies or by the rhetoric of a highly skillful attorney.

4. Many of the rules of procedure and evidence that lengthen and complicate lawsuits exist only to accommodate an untrained and inexperienced fact-finding body.

Supporters of the jury system counter with a number of their own arguments, such as the following:

1. General experience in "living" is more important for deciding the average case than is any kind of specialized training or experience.

2. Juries serve as a limited but valuable check on the power of the judicial branch of government.

3. Juries provide a means for direct, continuous input of community values into the legal system.

Impaneling a Jury

However one may feel about the jury as an institution, it will no doubt continue to be an integral part of our legal system for a long time to come. When a jury is to be impaneled, names of prospective jurors are drawn from a list of those who have been randomly selected from public records (such as voter registration or driver license) for possible duty during the term. Each prospective juror is questioned in an effort to make sure that the jury will be as impartial as possible. This questioning is conducted by the plaintiff's and defendant's attorneys, by a judge, or by all three, depending on the practice in the particular court system. This preliminary questioning of prospective jurors is called the *voir dire* examination. (*Voir dire,* from the French, means "to speak the truth.")

If questioning indicates that a particular person probably would not be capable of making an impartial decision, the judge will excuse the person by granting a **challenge for cause** made by one of the

---

[5]Although juries are no longer used extensively in civil lawsuits in England, they continue to be used there in criminal cases.

attorneys. A challenge for cause may be granted, for example, if it is shown that a prospective juror has a close friendship, family relationship, or business association with one of the parties or attorneys, a financial interest in the case, or a clear bias resulting from any other aspect of the action.

The attorney for each party also has a limited number of **peremptory challenges** (or *strikes*). Such challenges permit the attorney to have a prospective juror removed without giving any reason for doing so. The U.S. Supreme Court has ruled, however, that attorneys in civil or criminal cases, or government prosecutors in criminal cases, violate the *equal protection clause* of the U.S. Constitution if they exclude jurors because of their race. Proving this, of course, may be very difficult.

Once the number of prospective jurors who have survived both kinds of challenges reaches the number required by law to hear the case, they are sworn in and the case proceeds. Traditionally the number of jurors has been 12, but in recent years courts in quite a few states and in the federal system have reduced the number of jurors in civil cases, with eight being a common number.

Presentation of Evidence

After the attorneys for both sides have made opening statements outlining their cases, the plaintiff begins to present its case. As we have seen, the plaintiff has the *burden of proof*—the duty to prove the facts alleged in the complaint. In a normal civil case, the plaintiff must convince the fact-finder of the truth of the allegations by a preponderance of the evidence—in other words, the plaintiff has to tilt the scales somewhat in its favor on each of the alleged facts. The plaintiff attempts to meet this burden by presenting evidence to support his or her version of the facts. This evidence may consist of the sworn testimony of witnesses, as well as physical evidence such as documents, photographs, and so on. When an item of physical evidence is introduced in court, it is usually required that a witness with personal knowledge about the item give sworn testimony about its authenticity. A witness who gives false testimony while under oath may be convicted of the crime of *perjury*.

The testimony of a witness is normally elicited by questions from an attorney. When a witness is called to testify in court by the plaintiff's attorney, that attorney questions the witness first. This is called the *direct examination*. As a general rule, an attorney cannot ask *leading questions* during the direct examination. The attorney for the other side must object, however, before the judge will order the attorney to stop asking leading questions. A leading question is one that suggests its own answer, that is, it "puts words into the witness's mouth." "You saw the defendant's car smash into the plaintiff's car while the defendant was going at a high rate of speed, didn't you?" is a leading question. If the attorney calls an *adverse witness*, however, the rule against leading questions does not apply. An adverse witness is either the opposing party to the case or some other witness for the other side. After each of the plaintiff's witnesses testifies, the defendant's attorney has an opportunity to conduct a *cross-examination* of that witness. The attorney is permitted to ask leading questions in cross-examination. The purpose of cross-examination is to discredit or cast doubt on the witness's testimony. For example, a cross-examination might divulge that (1) pertinent facts in the direct examination were omitted, (2) a witness's powers of observation were poor, (3) the witness made a statement in the past (such as in a deposition) that is inconsistent with his or her present testimony, thus creating doubt about his or her credibility, or (4) the witness is not completely disinterested because he or she stands to gain or lose something from the outcome of the case. At the judge's discretion, the plaintiff's attorney may then have a chance to conduct a *redirect examination* to deal with any new matters that might have developed during cross-examination. The judge similarly has discretion to permit another cross-examination after the redirect, but this is unusual.

After the plaintiff has completed its presentation of evidence, the defendant then has the same opportunity. The defendant's purpose will be to offer evidence tending to show that the plaintiff's allegations are not correct. If the defendant has asserted a defense or counterclaim, he or she also will offer evidence to meet the burden of proof on those allegations. The procedures and rules are the same when the defendant presents evidence as when the plaintiff was doing so, except that the roles obviously are reversed on direct, cross-, and redirect examination.

Rules of Evidence

Before going on, a brief mention of the **rules of evidence** is necessary. These rules attempt to ensure that the evidence presented in a court of law is relevant to the issues and is as accurate and reliable as

These days, many suggestions are being put forth for improving our system of civil litigation, some of which consist of ideas borrowed from other nations. One of the changes being proposed is adoption of the so-called "English rule," or "loser pays" rule. The gist of this proposal is that the United States should borrow from England the rule that whoever loses a civil lawsuit is responsible not only for his or her own attorney fees but also for the other party's attorney fees. Under current U.S. federal and state law, with very few exceptions each party is responsible for its own attorney fees, regardless of who wins the case. Thus, a defendant can run up huge legal bills even if he or she ultimately wins. It is argued by some observers that the current U.S. practice encour-

ages frivolous claims, especially when combined with the fact that many cases are taken by plaintiffs' attorneys on a contingency basis, the plaintiff owing the attorney a fee only if the case is won.

One must always recognize, however, that any such change involves trade-offs. The current U.S. practice did not develop accidentally; it represents a social policy choice in favor of keeping the courts as available as possible to those who have at least arguable claims. There is no doubt that the loser pays rule discourages the filing of lawsuits. In England, however, those who are relatively poor have much better access to publicly funded legal counsel than in the United States. Large companies and wealthy individuals can afford to take the risks involved in filing a lawsuit under the loser pays system. In addition, trade unions in England usually finance litigation on behalf of their members. Thus, those who are most

strongly discouraged from filing lawsuits, even when they have good claims, are the many members of the middle class who do not belong to trade unions.

Some argue that a better solution for the United States is to make trial lawyers more responsible to the court and less responsible to their clients. For example, monetary penalties against plaintiffs' lawyers who file claims that have little factual foundation, and more frequent granting of summary judgments against plaintiffs with weak cases, might serve as solutions that are more narrowly tailored to fit the problem than adopting a loser pays rule. One difficulty with any major change in American litigation that some other nations do not face, however, is that our legal system consists of 51 separate jurisdictions. To accomplish substantial change, rules must be altered in the federal courts and in the courts of 50 different states.

possible. The rules of evidence apply whether there is a jury performing the fact-finding role or whether the trial judge is doing so. The rules are more important, however, and are often applied more strictly in a trial before a jury than in one before a judge. As mentioned earlier, even if evidence is inadmissible under the rules of evidence, it will be excluded only if the attorney for the other side objects. Such an objection is made during the trial when an attempt is made to introduce the evidence. Before trial, however, if an attorney can identify inadmissible evidence that the other side probably will try to present in court and can convince the judge that the other side may be able to "sneak in" some of this evidence before the attorney has a chance to object, the judge may grant a motion ordering the other side not to make the attempt.

Although the rules of evidence are so numerous and complex that a complete treatment is impossible here, we can provide a flavor of them by discussing

three kinds of evidence that are commonly excluded by the rules.[6]

Irrelevant Evidence. If a witness is asked a question that can have no possible bearing on any of the disputed facts, the opposing attorney may object on the basis that the answer would constitute **irrelevant evidence.** In a personal injury suit arising from an accident, for example, such matters as the defendant's religious beliefs or the fact that he or she was convicted of a charge of reckless driving several years earlier would have no bearing on the present case. Objections to such evidence would sustained by the court. Documents or other physical evidence can also be excluded on grounds of irrelevancy.

[6]Cases brought in the federal courts are governed by the Federal Rules of Evidence, which Congress adopted in 1975. The rules of evidence applied in state courts are adopted by the various state legislatures or by state supreme courts (under authority delegated by the state legislature). The state rules vary somewhat but are generally uniform on the major points. The federal rules of evidence are widely acknowledged as representing the most modern view of evidentiary rules, and are increasingly being adopted at the state level.

Hearsay. In our common experience, we all know that second-hand information is usually not as reliable as first-hand information. The law takes this fact into account by holding that, in general, **hearsay evidence** is not admissible in court. Hearsay evidence may take the form of oral testimony by a witness, or it may consist of a statement in a written document that is offered as evidence. Oral or written evidence is hearsay if (1) it consists of a statement made by some person who is not testifying personally in court and (2) the evidence is offered in court for the purpose of proving the truth of that statement. Thus if an issue in a particular case is whether a trucker delivered a shipment of goods to the X Company on a certain day, witness W (a jogger in the vicinity at the time) could testify that she saw packages being unloaded from a truck on the day in question. But neither W nor any other witness would normally be allowed to testify that she was *told by a third party,* Z, that Z saw goods being unloaded on the day in question. In the latter situation, W's testimony would be inadmissible hearsay because it related a statement of Z, who is not testifying in person, and the evidence is being offered for the purpose of proving the content of Z's statement.

There are many situations in which second-hand statements can be placed into evidence because they are not offered for the purpose of proving the truth of the statements. In a breach of contract case, for example, the plaintiff or some other witness may testify in court that the defendant (D) said "I will sell you my car for $10,000." This would not be hearsay, because the witness's testimony is not being offered for the purpose of proving that the internal content of D's statement is true. Indeed, D's statement cannot be characterized as true or false; there may be a question about whether D actually said it, but there can be no issue about the truth or falsity of the statement's content. Sometimes such a statement is called a *verbal act.* Another example would be, in a defamation case brought by P against D, the statement allegedly made by D that "P is a thief, a liar, and a cheat." A witness's testimony in court that D said this would be offered for the purpose of proving that D actually said such a thing and not for the purpose of proving the content of D's statement as a factual matter.

Even if evidence constitutes hearsay, sometimes it is nevertheless admissible under an exception to the hearsay rule. Exceptions exist for situations in which, despite being within the definition of hearsay, partic-

ular kinds of evidence are likely to possess a relatively high degree of reliability. For example, a ledger or other business record includes "statements" of the person who made the entry in the record; these statements relate to the factual details of particular actions or business transactions. If the person who made the entry is not testifying personally about his or her recollection of a certain transaction, but instead the business record is offered to prove particular facts about the transaction, the business record is hearsay. There is, however, a well-established exception for business records. Such records are usually made with care because the business firm relies on them for many important purposes. The exception usually applies if a witness in custody of the records can testify under oath that the record was made "in the usual course of business" and was made at or near the time of the act or transaction being recorded.

Opinion. Sometimes a witness is asked for or volunteers information that he or she believes to be true but that is not based on the witness's personal knowledge. As a general rule, such **opinion evidence,** whether in oral or written form, is not legally admissible. For example, in an auto accident case, a witness properly could testify that he or she had observed the defendant's car weaving back and forth on a highway shortly before the accident. On the basis of this observation, however, the witness could not testify that the defendant was "obviously drunk." Evidence normally is supposed to take the form of information based on direct observation; the drawing of inferences, the forming of opinions, and the reaching of conclusions are tasks for the jury (or the judge if there is no jury).

Opinion evidence is not always excluded. On technical matters that lie outside the knowledge of ordinary jurors, it is frequently necessary that qualified experts be permitted to state their opinions as an aid to the jury's or judge's determination of what facts probably occurred. Thus a physician may give an opinion as to cause of death or as to whether a particular course of medical treatment is generally accepted within the medical community. Similarly, a civil engineer may give an opinion as to the likely cause of a bridge collapsing. Unless the attorney for one party agrees (*stipulates*) that a particular witness called by the other party is qualified to testify as an expert, the judge must make a ruling on whether the witness is so qualified. In the average situation, a person called as an expert witness is stipulated as such by the other side.

Motion for Directed Verdict

After all the plaintiff's evidence has been presented, the defendant's attorney often makes a **motion for directed verdict.** This motion makes the same assertion as the earlier motion for summary judgment, except that the motion for directed verdict is based on more evidence, including the personal testimony of witnesses in court. The motion asserts that the plaintiff's evidence on one or more of the required elements of its case is either nonexistent or so weak that there is no genuine issue of disputed fact. Thus, "reasonable minds could not differ" on the factual question, and the judge should decide the case "as a matter of law" instead of sending it to the jury. Sometimes it is said that the motion raises the issue of whether there is a "jury question."

If the defendant's motion for directed verdict is denied, the defendant then presents its case as discussed earlier. At the close of the defendant's case, the plaintiff can make a motion for directed verdict. The motion contends that the plaintiff's evidence on the required elements of its claim is so overwhelming and the defendant's rebuttal evidence is so weak that reasonable minds could not differ in the conclusion that the plaintiff has met its burden of proof. Again, the motion asks the judge to decide the case as a matter of law and not send it to the jury. The defendant can also make a motion for directed verdict at this time, regardless of whether he or she had earlier made one after presentation of the plaintiff's case. Motions for directed verdict are denied in most cases, because once a case has progressed this far there usually are genuine issues of fact that must be resolved.

Instructions to the Jury

When a case is submitted to the jury, the judge provides instructions to guide the jury in its deliberations. These instructions are often read aloud to the jury in open court; in some states, a written copy of these instructions is then given to the jury before they begin their deliberations. The instructions typically contain several parts, including (1) general rules of conduct, such as requirements that the jurors (a) refrain from discussing the case with anyone except other jurors in formal deliberations until the case is over and they are discharged and (b) not speculate about the effect that insurance coverage or attorney fees might have on the ultimate judgment; (2) definitions of certain relevant legal terms; and (3) the court's *charge* to the jury.

The charge is the core of the instructions and gives the jury a legal framework for performing its job. A charge may be *general* or *special* or a combination of the two types, depending on the court system. In the same system, different types of charges may be used in different types of cases; in a particular state, for instance, a special charge might be used in civil cases and a general charge in criminal ones. Although the general charge is most common, mixed special–general charges are increasing in usage. A general charge outlines and explains the relevant legal principles for the jury; it then asks them to decide the relevant facts and reach a verdict either for the plaintiff or for the defendant. (In a criminal case, the charge would ask for a verdict of guilty or acquittal.) A special charge is a series of questions to the jury; each question relates to a disputed fact and asks for a yes or no answer. If a special charge is used in a typical money damage case, there will be a final question about damages that asks for an answer in the form of a dollar amount, assuming that previous questions have been answered favorably to the plaintiff.

The following case illustrates the critical importance of the judge's instructions to the jury.

RILEY V. WILLIS

Court of Appeal of Florida, 585 So. 2d 1024 (1991)

Juanita Willis, a minor, and her sister were walking along the side of Highway 50 in Brooksville with their dog between them. The dog was not on a leash. Juanita walked closest to the road. Joseph Riley was driving on Highway 50, which he used every day to travel to and from work. Just as Riley's truck pulled even with the girls, the dog darted toward the road. Juanita leaned into the road and was struck by the front of Riley's truck. Juanita, plaintiff, filed suit against Riley, defendant, alleging that Riley's negligence was the cause of her injuries. (See Chapter 8 for a discussion of the tort of negligence.) Riley raised the defense of contributory negligence. Under Florida law, as in most states today, if the jury finds that both the plaintiff

(continues)

RILEY V. WILLIS

(continued from previous page)
and the defendant are negligent, the plaintiff's damages are reduced by the percentage that his or her negligence contributed to the occurrence. However, if the plaintiff's negligence contributed more to the occurrence than did the defendant's, the plaintiff cannot receive any money damages.

In the trial, Riley testified that he saw the two girls and slowed from 45 mph to about 35 mph as he approached but did not sound his horn or move to the left of his lane. He also stated that after his truck pulled alongside the girls, he lost sight of them and did not see the dog bolt or Juanita bend into the road.

At the close of the evidence, the trial judge gave the jury instructions about what a plaintiff has to prove to establish a claim of negligence against the defendant and what a defendant has to prove to establish a defense of contributory negligence. In addition, the court included an instruction setting forth a Florida statute detailing the special duty of a motorist to avoid "obstructions" in the roadway by moving to the left of the center of the highway. This instruction had been requested by Juanita's attorney. However, the judge refused to include an instruction, requested by Riley's attorney, concerning a county ordinance that required people to keep their dogs on a leash. The jury found that the plaintiff's negligence contributed 40 percent to the incident and the defendant's 60 percent. The trial judge entered judgment requiring defendant to pay 60 percent of the amount of damages found by the jury to have been suffered by the plaintiff.

Riley appealed on the following grounds: (1) The trial judge should not have included the jury instruction about a motorist's special duty to avoid obstructions. (2) The trial judge should have included the jury instruction about the county ordinance requiring an owner to keep his or her dog on a leash, because

Juanita's dog was not on a leash and this contributed substantially to the accident.

Goshorn, Judge:

Riley asserts that an instruction governing a motorist's duty to avoid an obstacle was improperly given. The instruction contained section 316.081 (1) (b), Florida Statutes (1987), which provides in relevant part: "(1) Upon all roadways of sufficient width, a vehicle shall be driven upon the right half of the roadway, except as follows: (b) When an obstruction exists making it necessary to drive to the left of the center of the highway; provided any person so doing shall yield the right-of-way to vehicles traveling in the proper direction upon the unobstructed portion of the highway within such distance as to constitute an immediate hazard. . . ."

The controversy surrounding the instruction concerns the word "obstruction" and whether evidence of an obstruction hindering Riley was presented at trial. The term "obstruction" is not defined by Chapter 316. Black's Law Dictionary 972 (rev. 5th ed. 1979) defines "obstruction" as "a hindrance, obstacle or barrier." The evidence presented at trial is unrefuted that at the time of the accident Riley's view was unobstructed and the road was clear. It is also unrefuted that Juanita did not bend into the path of Riley's oncoming truck until the truck was practically upon her. Prior to that moment, Juanita and Ebony [her sister] were walking along the side of the road. The obvious inference from the instruction is that Juanita herself was an obstacle that Riley was statutorily obligated to avoid. Yet no testimony or other evidence was presented that Juanita posed an obstacle to the oncoming truck, making it necessary for Riley to drive to the left of the center of the highway.

Jury instructions must be supported by facts in evidence and an instruction not founded upon evidence adduced at trial constitutes error. Whether that error requires reversal depends on

whether the improper instruction in some manner affected the jury's deliberations by misleading or confusing it. . . . The instruction at issue in [this case] quite likely confused and misled the jury by creating the erroneous impression that Riley was obligated to somehow avoid Juanita when she reached out into the road and became an "obstacle" simultaneously with Riley's passing. The giving of the improper instruction requires reversal.

Riley also appeals the trial court's refusal to instruct the jury on Hernando County Ordinance 86-2, section 6-5, the local leash law: "The owner, harborer, keeper or person having custody or care of an animal shall ensure that: (1) All dogs, except police dogs on active duty, shall be kept under physical restraint by a responsible person at all times while off the premises of the owner, harborer or keeper." The trial court refused to grant the instruction because no evidence was presented that Juanita owned the dog. However, the ordinance is also applicable to a person who is a "harborer, keeper or person having custody or care of an animal." The record is undisputed that the dog was walking unleashed between Juanita and Ebony until it darted toward the road and Juanita tried to grab it. . . .

A party is entitled to have the jury instructed upon its theory of the case when there is evidence to support the theory. In *Orange County v. Piper,* 523 So. 2d 196 (Fla. 5th DCA) this court set forth three elements that must be met in order to establish that failure to give a requested jury instruction constitutes reversible error: (1) The requested instruction accurately states the applicable law, (2) The facts in the case support giving the instruction, and (3) The instruction was necessary to allow the jury to properly resolve all issues in the case. [The requested instruction met these requirements.] Riley's theory of the case attempted to show that, but for the girls' failure to walk the dog on a leash, the dog would

(continues)

RILEY V. WILLIS

(continued from previous page)
not have darted toward the road and Juanita would not have lunged into Riley's oncoming truck. Riley's requested instruction sought to bolster his claim that Juanita's own negligence resulted in the accident; her failure to comply with the local leash law was a direct and proximate cause of her accident. Indeed, violation of a municipal ordinance is prima facie evidence of negligence. The failure to give the requested instruction was reversible error. [Reversed and remanded for a new trial.] ⚖

After the Verdict

After the jury has reached its verdict, the court usually enters a judgment in conformity with it. Occasionally this does not happen, however, because the losing party still has an opportunity to make two additional types of motions. One is the **motion for judgment notwithstanding the verdict** (or *motion for judgment N.O.V.*, an abbreviation for the Latin equivalent, *non obstante veredicto*). This motion makes the same contention earlier made in the motion for directed verdict; it essentially asserts that the judge earlier should have granted a directed verdict in favor of the movant and should not have let the case go to the jury because the evidence was so one-sided in the movant's favor. Although a judge rarely grants this motion, it does provide the judge with something of a "safety valve" if a jury goes completely against the evidence.

The other post-verdict motion that may be filed by the party who suffered an adverse jury verdict is the **motion for new trial.** This motion alleges that the trial judge committed one or more errors in the trial that probably affected the outcome. The errors alleged in such a motion may include erroneous rulings on objections to evidence, erroneous wording of the instructions that misstated the applicable law, and so on. A motion for new trial is usually a prerequisite for appeal; a party normally must give a trial judge the opportunity to correct his or her own mistakes by granting a new trial before the party can complain about these mistakes to an appellate court.

The following case illustrates the reasoning employed by a court in ruling on a motion for judgment notwithstanding the verdict.

BEEBE-OWEN V. WESTERN OHIO PIZZA, INC.

Court of Appeals of Ohio, 1991 Ohio App. Lexis 3034 (1991)

Case

Sharon Beebe-Owen, the plaintiff, had worked for Western Ohio Pizza for seven years as the director of management information services, managing various computer systems. (Hereafter, the last name Owen will be used, because the appeals court used the shortened version in its decision.) As a result of an incident between Sharon Owen and Eric Marcus, another employee of Western Ohio Pizza, she filed a lawsuit against Marcus and Western.

On April 4, 1988, Sharon Owen, Eric Marcus, and six other employees traveled in a van from their place of work in Dayton, Ohio, to Cincinnati to watch a Cincinnati Reds baseball game. In the lawsuit, the evidence established that Eric and Sharon drank beer at the ball game although she denied becoming intoxicated. The evidence also established that Eric at various times during the day kissed and hugged Sharon. Sharon testified that Eric kissed her after the game— "he just reached out and pulled me by the shoulders and embraced me."

In cross-examination, she testified: "He hugged me at the ballpark, he kissed me at the ballpark, he hugged me a couple of times in the van, he kissed me a couple of times in the van. He tried to unsnap my bra in the van when I asked him not to. Sure, he had his hands on me more than that." After the game the group returned to Dayton and went to the Olive Garden Restaurant. Sharon testified that while she was walking toward the restaurant she heard footsteps and Eric threw his arms around her shoulders "and hit me

(continues)

BEEBE-OWEN V. WESTERN OHIO PIZZA, INC.

(continued from previous page)
really hard and just pushed me to the ground and ended up falling on my leg." However, Eric testified to a different version of the incident, saying that he "put his arms around her to give her a hug and she stumbled and we fell in a heap."

Phyllis Phillips, a secretary at Western Ohio and one of the eight who attended the baseball game, gave the following testimony: She had nothing to drink that day. She sat with three other employees in a different part of the ballpark from Sharon and Eric; when the game ended she went over to where Sharon and Eric were seated and saw Sharon with her arm around Eric and she was kissing his ear. Sharon was staggering when she got up to leave her seat, and she was loud and her speech was slurred. While they were standing by a souvenir stand she observed Sharon go up to Eric and put her arm around him and hug and kiss him. Sharon had her arm around Eric in the van on the return trip and was kissing him. She did not see Sharon and Eric fall in the restaurant parking lot but heard something and saw them lying on the ground laughing.

Janet Heitman, research coordinator for Western Ohio, was the "designated driver" for the trip to the ball game and also did not drink alcohol that day. Her testimony about the conduct of Eric and Sharon during the trip was practically identical to that of Phyllis Phillips. She also stated that both Sharon and Eric appeared to be under the influence of alcohol and that on the way back five people were "smashed into the back seat" and were engaged in horseplay. She stated she did not see Eric and Sharon fall in the parking lot but saw Eric kneeling over her and Sharon was laughing. She said Sharon could not get up. Sharon was taken by ambulance to a hospital, where she underwent surgery for a severe knee

injury and remained hospitalized for ten days.

The defendant also introduced into evidence the written notes made by a nurse when Sharon was admitted to the hospital; the notes were made as a regular part of the admission process. One of the nurse's statements in the notes was that Sharon had told her that she had been hurt while "playing with a friend, who had tackled her." The plaintiff's attorney did not challenge the notes as hearsay evidence, so the court made no ruling on this point; however, it is likely that the notes were within an exception to the hearsay rule.

Sharon worked three days in June, from mid-July until November 7, 1988, and two weeks in December 1988. She applied for workers' compensation medical benefits and Western Ohio certified her claim on June 16, 1988; she received these benefits. Her full salary was continued by Western until March 12, 1989. Western asked her to obtain information from her physician as to when she could return to full employment. When she failed to provide the requested medical information to her supervisor, her salary was discontinued.

On March 30, 1989, Sharon Owen and her husband filed this lawsuit, asserting various claims against Eric Marcus and Western Ohio Pizza. Shortly thereafter, both she and her husband, who also worked for Western, were terminated. The trial judge granted summary judgment in favor of Western on all claims, and in favor of Eric on most of the claims. The claims of Sharon's husband also did not survive summary judgment. However, Sharon's claim against Eric for the tort of assault and battery remained alive and went to trial. A mixed general–special charge was used in the jury instructions. In response to specific questions, the jury found that Eric had been negligent but that he had not committed the

intentional tort of assault and battery, because the jury concluded that Eric was not guilty of an "intentional offensive physical contact without consent" as required by the law for an assault and battery claim.

The jury rendered a general verdict against Eric for $41,000 in damages.

Both sides filed motions for judgment notwithstanding the verdict. Eric's motion asserted that he could not be held liable at all for simple negligence, because he was a co-employee, this was a work outing, and workers' compensation benefits were Sharon's only legal remedy. Sharon's motion argued that the jury's finding that Eric was guilty of only negligence, and not assault and battery, was so contrary to the overwhelming evidence that Eric should have been found guilty of assault and battery by the judge as a matter of law. The trial judge granted Eric's motion and denied Sharon's and entered judgment in favor of Eric. Sharon appealed.

Brogan, Judge:

[First, the appellate court agreed with the trial court's decision to grant Eric's motion for judgment notwithstanding the verdict. This was a work outing, and Sharon and Eric were within the scope of their employment at the time. In such a situation, an employee has no legal claim against the employer or a fellow employee for mere negligence; the benefits provided under state workers' compensation law are the only remedy. The employee can maintain a claim for an intentional wrong such as assault and battery, if it can be proved. The jury was properly instructed on these matters but apparently did not adequately understand the instructions and found Eric liable for damages after finding that he was only negligent. Thus, the trial court was correct to grant Eric's motion for judgment N.O.V.]

(continues)

BEEBE-OWEN V. WESTERN OHIO PIZZA, INC.

(continued from previous page)

[Turning to Sharon's claim that the trial court should have granted her motion for judgment N.O.V. because the evidence overwhelmingly proved assault and battery on Eric's part, the court of appeals stated:] The test to be applied by a trial court in ruling on a motion for judgment notwithstanding a verdict is the same as that for a motion for a directed verdict. The evidence must be construed most strongly in favor of the party against whom the motion is made, and where there is substantial evidence to support his side of the case, upon which reasonable minds may reach different conclusions, the motion must be denied. The jury could have reasonably believed Marcus' version of the incident where he fell on Mrs. Owen. The trial court appropriately denied the motion [and submitted this question to the jury]. . . . The judgment will be affirmed. ⚖

LITIGATION: THE APPELLATE COURTS

Nature and Role of Appellate Courts

If a party is dissatisfied with the outcome in the trial court, and his or her attorney believes that legally material errors may have been committed in the trial, the party may wish to appeal the trial court's decision to a higher court.

The function of an *appellate court* is very different from that of a trial court. An appellate court does not hear evidence or make any factual determinations; instead the court seeks to determine whether material errors were committed by the trial court. A material error is one that probably affected the outcome. If a case is appealed to the highest court in a particular system after having been heard by an intermediate level appellate court, the high court essentially "reviews the review" of the intermediate appellate court.

In most appellate courts, the party who is appealing is usually referred to as the *appellant;* the other party is the *appellee.* Sometimes different terms are used, such as *petitioner* and *respondent.* When an appellate court writes its opinion in a case, it normally uses either of these sets of terms to refer to the parties. Occasionally, however, the court's opinion will refer to the parties by their original trial court designations—plaintiff and defendant.

An appellate court always includes at least 3 judges, and often more. When the court has more than 3 members, it sometimes expands its capacity for work by dividing into panels of 3 judges for each case. When this is done, the entire membership of the court has the authority to review the decision of the 3-judge panel, although it usually does not do so.

For example, the various U.S. courts of appeal, which have from 6 to 28 judges, usually divide into 3-member panels to hear cases, and only rarely does the entire membership of one of these courts review a panel decision. The U.S. Supreme Court, however, does not divide into panels; all nine of its justices participate in deciding each case.

The Process of Appeal

The Record

The appellant's attorney begins the appeal by filing a notice of appeal and by requesting that the clerk of the trial court prepare the *record* of the case and send it to the appellate court. There is a fee for preparation of the record. The most important part of the record is the *transcript* of the trial. During the trial, an official court reporter was recording every word of the proceedings, including all the attorneys' questions, witnesses' answers, attorneys' objections, and the judge's rulings. The transcript is a typewritten copy of this verbatim account. Copies of the pleadings, motions, jury instructions, and other official papers in the case also are included in the record if they are relevant to some point being raised on appeal. In addition, the record may include items of physical evidence that were introduced and considered in the trial court; such items might include a written contract, business records, or a map or photograph.

Written Briefs

The appellant's attorney prepares an *appellant's brief* and files it with the appellate court. The brief sets forth errors that the appellant claims were made by the trial judge. These alleged errors usually relate to the trial judge's actions in (1) ruling on motions, (2) ruling on objections to evidence, or (3) stating the relevant law in the jury instructions. The remainder of the brief then presents arguments, based on applicable legal principles, that the cited actions of the trial judge amounted to material errors. The appellee's attorney then responds with the *appellee's brief* (or *reply brief*), in which it is argued that under applicable law the trial judge's actions were correct (or even if erroneous, the errors did not affect the outcome and were "harmless").

Oral Arguments

Appellate courts usually schedule several periods of time during the year in which the parties to appeals are permitted to make *oral arguments.* During one two-week period, for example, an appellate court might hear oral arguments in 50 or so cases. In each case, the attorney for each side will have a brief period (typically from 30 to 60 minutes) to clarify and emphasize the most important points in the written briefs and to give the appellate court judges an opportunity to ask questions.

Appellate Court's Decision

As was mentioned earlier, an appellate court serves a very different role from that of a trial court. The court studies the record, considers the legal points made in the briefs and oral arguments, does legal research, and decides whether one or more material errors occurred in the trial.

Review of Trial Court's Factual Determinations

Some of the points raised by the appellant may require the appellate court to study the evidence that appears in the record, such as the transcript of witnesses' testimony and physical evidence that has been included in the record. For example, if the appellant claims that the trial judge erred in ruling on a motion for summary judgment, directed verdict, or judgment N.O.V., the appellate court must determine whether the evidence in the record created a genuine fact issue or whether it was overwhelming in the other direction. The court does not, however, decide what the facts are; fact-finding is a trial court function. Indeed, even if the judges on the appellate court believe that they might have reached a different conclusion had they been performing the fact-finding task in the trial court, they normally will not overturn the trial court's (jury's or trial judge's) factual determinations so long as there is any substantial evidence in the record to support those conclusions. Appellate court judges recognize that the jury or judge that performed the fact-finding role was in a better position to assess the evidence, especially when key evidence took the form of testimony from witnesses who testified and were cross-examined in person. Moreover, in any multilevel decision-making system, it makes very little sense to redo everything at successive levels.

Review of Trial Court's Legal Determinations

Much of the appellate court's attention is focused on pure legal questions, that is, reviewing the trial judge's rulings on legal questions. For example, when the trial judge rules on a motion to dismiss or frames the instructions to the jury, he or she makes decisions as to what the applicable legal principles are. In some cases, especially when there is no jury, the trial judge makes formal written *conclusions of law.* These legal principles may derive from precedents (prior decisions in other cases—see Chapter 4), federal or state statutes, administrative agency regulations, or constitutional provisions. In response to the appellant's contentions on appeal, the appellate court decides whether the trial court's interpretations and applications of these legal principles were correct. An appellate court is not so reluctant to overturn the trial court's legal determinations as it is to reverse factual determinations.

Decision Making

The appellate court judges deliberate individually on a case and consult with each other. They decide the case by majority vote. If the majority concludes that no material errors occurred, it *affirms* the lower court's decision, usually sending the case back to the trial court for appropriate action to enforce the judgment. If the court decides that some material error was committed, it *reverses* the lower court's decision. (Sometimes the terms *vacate* or *set aside* are used instead of *reverse.*) Occasionally an appellate court may reverse the decision outright and order a contrary judgment. In most cases of reversal, however, the appellate court *remands* the case to the lower court, where some type of further proceeding will be conducted in accordance with the appellate court's opinion. The further proceeding in the lower court may be of a very limited nature, such as merely requiring the trial judge to reconsider some portion of the decision by applying a slightly different legal standard to the already-established facts. Sometimes, however, the additional proceeding necessary to correct the error after remand may be a completely new trial.

Appellate Court's Opinion

One of the judges is assigned the primary responsibility for writing the court's formal opinion; however, the key language of the opinion is the product of agreement among the judges in the majority. If a judge does not agree with some of the reasoning or language of the opinion but still agrees with the overall result, he or she may wish to write a separate concurring opinion setting forth areas of disagreement. If the decision is not unanimous, a judge who disagrees with the majority decision has the opportunity to write a dissenting opinion setting forth his or her

views. Although a dissenting opinion has no effect on the outcome of that case, a persuasive dissent on a close and controversial issue may provide "ammunition" for continuing debate on the question in future cases (or in future legislative debates).

As we have already mentioned, an appellate court usually upholds a jury's or a trial judge's factual findings but is not so reluctant to reverse on the basis of errors of law committed by the trial judge. The following case presents an interesting example of this proposition. Technically, the error asserted by the appellant is that one of the important factual findings of the jury was not supported by any substantial evidence in the record. In reversing the decision, however, the appeals court actually does so on the basis of the trial judge's erroneous interpretation of the law in submitting a particular issue to the jury. Things are not always (or even usually) neat and tidy.

LEHR V. VANCE

Court of Appeals of Ohio, 1991 Ohio App. Lexis 3922 (1991)

At the time of the incident that led to this lawsuit, Delores Lehr and John Vance were married but separated. They owned two vehicles, a 1986 Ford van and a 1986 Honda Prelude. The evidence in the case did not indicate whose name or names were on the titles of the vehicles, and because there had not yet been a divorce there was no court judgment splitting up their property. After their separation, Delores, the plaintiff, took possession of the 1986 Honda Prelude, and John, the defendant, kept the van. Each of them apparently had keys to both vehicles.

In the trial John testified that shortly after they separated, he received an anonymous telephone call informing him that the Honda Prelude would be returned to him if he put the keys to the vehicle and $100 in his mailbox. The caller said that the car could then be recovered at a bowling alley parking lot at the intersection of Route 161 and Cleveland Avenue. John did as the caller sug-

gested and acquired possession of the Honda. After the Honda was taken from her possession, Delores took the Ford van from John's residence, apparently stating to either the defendant or the police that she needed some form of transportation. John testified in court that later the same day, he received a second telephone call, again from an unidentified caller, informing him if he wanted to have the van returned to him, he should place $100 and the keys to the van in his mailbox.

John testified that he believed that the anonymous calls were from an agent of his wife for the purpose of extorting money from him in exchange for the return of the automobiles. He said that he based his belief on a prior incident in which Delores had taken his clothing and required him to "buy" the clothes back from her. He had no other evidence to support this belief, however. John testified that he asked the caller if Delores was responsible for the proposed exchange, which the caller denied.

A short while later, Delores was at her parents' home when her mother noticed someone entering the Ford van, which was parked in the driveway next to the home. Delores testified in court that she approached the vehicle and stepped onto the running board inquiring as to who the person was and what he was doing. This individual's identity was never established in court. Delores said that as she attempted to question this person, he suddenly drove the van from the driveway and proceeded onto the street with her still standing on the running board holding on to the side of the van. She stated that the driver ignored her pleas to stop and drove at a high rate of speed, keeping her from safely stepping from the van. Then the driver of the van suddenly applied the brake, throwing Delores from the van onto the roadway.

As a result of being thrown from the van, Delores received serious injuries. She sued John, claiming that the driver was acting as John's agent in trying to seize the van, and that John was thus liable for the driver's

(continues)

LEHR V. VANCE

(continued from previous page)
recklessness. John responded by claiming that Delores caused her own injury by jumping on the running board of the van as the driver was trying to leave; he also asserted that the driver was not his agent but was someone Delores was using to help with a scheme to extort money from John. The jury rendered a verdict in favor of John on the basis that Delores's own negligence contributed more than 50 percent to her injuries; under the law of Ohio (and most other states), this meant that she lost the case. The jury thus made no finding on the question of who the driver was working for. Delores appealed, claiming that the verdict was contrary to the overwhelming evidence and that the trial judge should have granted either a judgment N.O.V. or a new trial.

Strausbaugh, Judge:

[The appeals court drew an analogy from statutes and case law in Ohio that concern the right of a "secured creditor" to act on its own, without court action, to seize the collateral held by a debtor who has defaulted on the debt. A secured creditor is one owning a security interest in a specific item of personal property that serves as collateral for a debt. Under the law of Ohio and most other states, the secured creditor has the right to use "self-help"—to seize the property on its own, without court action—only if the creditor can

do so without a "breach of the peace." The court recognized that the present case did not involve a seizure of collateral by a secured creditor, but it did involve a seizure of property by one claiming a legal interest in it. The court stated that the situation was analogous, and the same basic rules should apply; the one claiming a right to the property could not seize it if doing so involved a breach of the peace. A breach of the peace is an intentional or reckless act and is not simple negligence. Thus, if a breach of the peace occurred, any contributory negligence on Delores's part was not a defense against her claim; contributory negligence is a defense only against a claim of simple negligence. Elaborating, and quoting from a prior decision of the Ohio Supreme Court, the appeals court stated:]

Fundamental public policy requires the discouragement of extrajudicial conduct which is fraught with the likelihood of resulting violence. . . . Breach of the peace . . . includes an act which is likely to produce violence, which reasonably tends to provoke or excite others to break the peace and which is not performed under judicial process. . . . Where a creditor legally enters upon the private premises of his debtor for the purpose of repossessing collateral security kept thereon and is (1) physically confronted by one in charge of such premises, (2) told to desist his efforts at repossession, and (3) instructed to depart from the premises, the refusal by the creditor to heed such commands constitutes a breach of the

peace . . . and such creditor thereafter stands as would any other person who unlawfully refuses to depart from the land of another.

We find the policy emanating from the foregoing decision [of the Ohio Supreme Court] to be sound and equally applicable herein. Given the clearly wanton and reckless conduct of the unidentified driver of the van, we find that contributory negligence is not a defense in the present case. [Thus, the trial court should not have submitted a contributory negligence issue to the jury.] When first confronted by plaintiff, the driver should have ended his efforts to take possession of the van. When he instead sped away with plaintiff holding on to the side of the van and then suddenly stopped, the driver should have known that his conduct would likely injure plaintiff. Defendant would therefore be . . . responsible for all of the acts of the driver during his efforts to take the van if it is determined that the driver was acting as defendant's agent. However, [the defendant will not be liable if it is found that the driver was not acting as his agent. When the case is reheard, the only issue will be whether the driver was the defendant's agent. If he was, the trial court should then] allow the jury to determine the amount of damages to which plaintiff is entitled. The judgment of the trial court is hereby reversed and the cause is remanded for further proceedings consistent with the law and this opinion. ⚖

Enforcement of Judgments

If a judgment for the plaintiff survives the appellate process (or if no appeal was ever taken), the plaintiff may still have to worry about enforcing the judgment. In the relatively unusual case in which the court's judgment grants an injunction or other equitable remedy, the court will enforce the judgment by fining

or jailing the defendant for *contempt of court* if the defendant fails to comply. In the typical case, however, the judgment awards an amount of money damages to the plaintiff. If the defendant is financially well-off, is well-insured for this type of claim, or is a corporation with adequate assets, enforcement of a money judgment will probably present no major obstacles. It can be very difficult, however, to collect a judgment from some people. Indeed, the probable collectability of any judgment is one of the things a party often must take into account in deciding whether to file a lawsuit in the first place.

If the defendant refuses to pay a valid judgment, the plaintiff will ask the court to issue a **writ of execution.** This writ empowers a law enforcement official to seize defendant's nonexempt property and sell it at auction until enough money is raised to satisfy the judgment.

Another procedure is a **writ of garnishment,** which orders a third party holding property belonging to the defendant to deliver the property to the custody of the court. In most cases, the third party is a bank, stock broker, or other entity holding funds or securities belonging to the defendant. A writ of garnishment may also be issued against a third party who owes a debt to the defendant, ordering the third party to pay the debt to the plaintiff instead of the defendant. If the writ of garnishment targets some type of property other than money, a law enforcement officer will sell the property at auction and the proceeds will be applied to pay the judgment. Many (but not all) states even allow garnishment of wages—a court order to the defendant's employer to pay a specified percentage of the defendant's wages or salary to the plaintiff every week or month until the judgment is fully paid. As we will see in Chapter 51, federal law places a limit on the portion of a person's wages that can be taken by garnishment.

In speaking of *nonexempt* assets, we are referring to the fact that all states have *exemption laws* specifying that certain types of property cannot be seized for the purpose of satisfying a court judgment. The laws vary quite a bit among the states, some states having very liberal statutes exempting much valuable property and others having extremely limited statutes exempting very little. The most common type of property protected by exemption laws is an individual's *homestead,* or residence; however, many states provide for such an exemption only up to a limited dollar amount.

In the discussion of personal jurisdiction, we mentioned that a nonresident defendant cannot just go back to his or her home state and ignore a judgment. If a defendant has no nonexempt assets in the forum state, the plaintiff can have the judgment enforced by execution or garnishment in any other state where the defendant has such assets. As long as the court that issued the judgment had subject matter and personal jurisdiction, the authorities in other states are required by the U.S. Constitution's *full faith and credit clause* to enforce the judgment. Although it is more difficult to enforce a judgment by trying to seize assets located in another nation, it often can be performed if such assets can be identified. The United States is a party to bilateral and multilateral treaties with many countries that obligate each nation to honor the valid court judgments of the other country or countries that have signed the treaty.

Regardless of whether a plaintiff can collect a judgment—in fact, regardless of whether the plaintiff wins or loses the lawsuit—once a case is finally concluded, the plaintiff is finished. The doctrine of *res judicata* ("the thing has been adjudicated") specifies that a plaintiff cannot start over by filing another claim against the defendant based on the same general facts. The plaintiff is barred from reasserting not only the same claim, but also any other claim that he or she reasonably could have asserted the first time around. If the later claim arises from the same general events as the earlier claim, the doctrine of *res judicata* applies even if the plaintiff has come up with new evidence. Figure 3.1 pictures the entire process of civil litigation by means of a flow chart.

NOTE ON PERFORMANCE OF JUDGES

The overall performance of a legal system obviously depends to a great extent on the character and competence of its judges. For this reason, particularly, it is distressing to note that the judges of this country have, as a class, come in for rather heavy criticism over the years. Although much of this criticism may be unjustified, there is cause for concern.

Three factors are chiefly responsible. First, judges' salaries are often lower than the income that can be earned in private practice by good attorneys. Second, in the United States, persons who aspire to a career in the judiciary are not required to take special training or to go through an apprenticeship of a year or two, as is the case in many countries. Third, the judges of our state courts have traditionally been elected. This has frequently resulted in the nomination of candidates by the political parties on the basis of their party service and loyalty, rather than on ability and experience. And, once elected, incumbent judges have not easily been dislodged even when their performance has been mediocre or worse.

In recent years, in an effort to alleviate the short-comings resulting from the election of judges, more than 30 states and the District of Columbia have adopted some form of "merit plan" selection of judges. Although these plans vary to some extent, they all are based on the idea that when a judicial vacancy occurs, a judicial nominating commission develops a list of three to five persons whom they feel to be the best qualified for the job. (These commissions are nonpartisan in nature and are usually composed equally of lawyers and nonlawyers.) The list of names is submitted to the governor, who selects one person to fill the vacancy. Thereafter, appointees must indicate before their terms of office expire whether they wish to stand for another term. If so, the appointee runs unopposed in the next general election, with the voters simply indicating whether they are satisfied with the performance rendered during the first term

FIGURE 3.1

Litigation Flow Chart

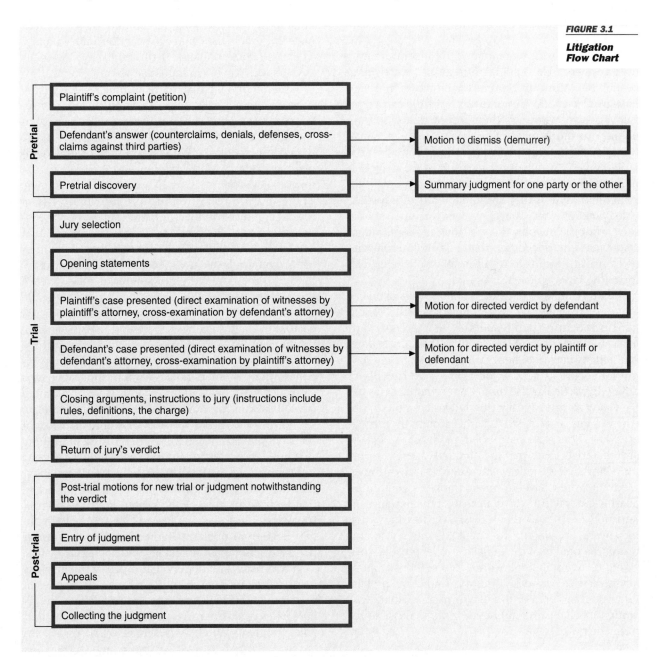

of office. If the appointee loses on this vote, the appointive process then begins anew.

Generally speaking, there has been less criticism of federal judges than state judges. Most criticism of federal judges tends to be based on their ideological slant rather than on their competence. Although there are a great many very fine state court judges and some federal court judges who are not as capable as we might wish, on a nationwide basis the average federal court judge is probably somewhat more able than the average state judge. This is true at both the trial and appellate court levels.

Federal judges are nominated for appointment by the president. The Federal Bureau of Investigation (under the Attorney General) conducts a thorough background check on nominees, and the American Bar Association reviews their records and issues an opinion to the Attorney General on their qualifications to serve. This information is available to the U.S. Senate, which must confirm the president's nominations. If confirmed, federal judges have lifetime tenure unless they are found guilty of impeachable conduct by Congress. The nature of the selection process, plus the fact that a federal judgeship carries more prestige than a position on a state court, usually seems to result in relatively high quality on the federal bench.

Whether in the state or federal courts, being a judge is becoming an increasingly stressful occupation in modern times, especially at the trial court level. In many parts of the country, state and federal trial judges face such heavy case loads that they simply cannot do as good a job as they are capable of doing. In particular, the number of criminal cases has increased so dramatically that judges are able to devote less and less time to the civil cases on their dockets. The constitutional requirement of a speedy criminal trial means that the criminal cases get priority. Many federal judges, for example, have discovered that they have to spend most of their time hearing federal drug cases, instead of the far more interesting civil cases they envisioned hearing when they were appointed. To maintain, much less improve, the quality of the judiciary, relief must be provided in a number of forms. More judges, more magistrates to supervise discovery and other pretrial processes, and greater use of alternative dispute resolution mechanisms are but a few of the possible reforms that may help.

ALTERNATIVE DISPUTE RESOLUTION

We have already noted some of the criticisms directed at the American legal system, as well as some of the responses from the supporters of the system. There can be no question that in the United States, there is an enormous amount of litigation that consumes tremendous resources. Many people, particularly in the business community, argue that Americans are too eager to sue, there are too many lawsuits of questionable merit, and these lawsuits take too much time and cost far too much money. They also commonly assert that there are too many lawyers with too much influence.

Others contend that there is much value in the way we traditionally have resolved many controversies in the United States. One can argue, for instance, that we tend to use formal litigation more than people in most other countries for several legitimate reasons: (1) We are the most heterogeneous, diffuse, and open society the world has ever known. These characteristics tend to produce more use of formal adjudication than in more homogeneous, static societies. (2) We place great value on the "rule of law," rather than the "rule of individuals," another factor that tends to cause people to look to courts for the interpretation and enforcement of rules. (3) We are not, nor would we want to be, a passive people who accept wrongs with fatalistic resignation as is the custom in some societies. (4) One of the strong legal traditions we inherited from England is the attitude that the courts have authority to formulate legal principles when there is no legislation applicable to a case. Because courts in our system have this limited type of lawmaking power, we naturally use them to set norms of behavior for society to a greater extent than people do in nations with a different system. (5) Our legal profession is much better educated than in most nations, with attorneys being more independent and more readily available to people who feel that their rights have been violated. In some parts of the world, the scarcity of lawyers leads people to obtain help from organized crime syndicates (such as the Yakuza in Japan) in making and collecting claims.

It also bears mentioning that much of the increase in litigation rates in recent years is not the result of greedy individuals trying to "make a killing" by filing claims against businesses, but instead is attributable to greatly increased filings of cases (1) by corporations against other corporations as a strategic business maneuver and (2) by and against government agencies.

Although there is much disagreement about whether there really are *too many* lawsuits in the United States, most knowledgeable observers agree that the litigation process is not nearly as efficient as it should be—lawsuits commonly take far too much time and money. In addition, in the case of disputes between business firms, lawsuits tend to decrease the chances that they will be able to maintain a valuable commercial relationship with each other. Although litigation is sometimes necessary and courts will always play a central role in dispute resolution in this country, recent times have witnessed widespread efforts to use other methods.

These other methods are frequently referred to as **alternative dispute resolution** (ADR) techniques. Although these methods do not always work and certainly are not a cure-all for society's problems, they often enable the parties to a dispute to lessen the "sharpness" of the adversarial system, replacing it with an increased emphasis on trust, respect, and win–win solutions.

Negotiated Settlement

Before we address specific methods of ADR, it is important first to point out that most disputes never get to the courtroom. Sometimes a person or business will just "lump it," that is, take a loss rather than pursue a claim. A corporation may do this to keep a valued customer or supplier, perhaps thinking that this particular problem is a one-time occurrence. Also, people sometimes do not pursue claims because they decide that it is not worth it; the perceived likelihood of winning or the size of the claim may lead to a conclusion that pressing a claim will be more trouble and expense than it is worth. Sometimes, instead of lumping it, a party may be able to reach a compromise with the other without ever going to court.

Even when lawsuits are filed, at least 90 percent of them are resolved without a trial. Some of these are disposed of by some pretrial action of the judge, such as the granting of summary judgment. A large percentage of claims filed in court are resolved by a negotiated out-of-court settlement, with part of the agreement being the dropping of all claims and counterclaims.

The problem with the traditional practice of filing

suit and then ultimately settling it out of court is that it usually has been performed very inefficiently. Parties and their attorneys generally have not started thinking seriously about settlement talks until the trial date is very near, thousands of dollars and many months (or years) having already been spent on pretrial discovery and strategic maneuvering. It seems that parties and their attorneys often have felt that they just were not "ready" to talk settlement until just before trial. Thus, enormous time and money traditionally have been spent preparing for an event (the trial) that usually does not happen. In addition, spending so much time, money, and energy battling each other during a lengthy pretrial process tends to make the parties harden their positions, escalating the intensity of the conflict.

Arbitration

Arbitration is a very old method for resolving disputes that in recent years has become increasingly popular. In arbitration, the parties select an arbitrator (or a panel of three arbitrators), submit very brief pleadings, and present evidence and arguments to the arbitrator. The arbitrator makes a decision, usually called an *award,* which is legally enforceable like a court judgment if the parties had agreed beforehand that it would be binding. Thus, arbitration resembles litigation in that there is actually an adjudication by a third party whose decision is binding.

Despite this superficial resemblance to litigation, arbitration is quite different in many ways. Most of these differences translate into cheaper, faster, and less painful dispute resolution. These differences also increase the chances that the parties can walk away from the process with a commercial relationship still intact. The parties have the ability to control the entire process. They select the decision maker, who may be an expert in the subject matter of the dispute. They also can decide what rules and procedures to use. Unlike litigation, the proceeding can be kept entirely private, which often may be very important to the disputants. There is no required pretrial discovery, although the parties do frequently agree to exchange documents before the arbitration hearing. The parties can decide whether the arbitrator is required to strictly follow particular rules of law and evidence; they usually do not, in which case the arbitrator's duty is just to do justice between the parties. There is essentially no appeal from an arbitrator's award, and a court will not review the arbitrator's factual or legal determinations. A court normally will set aside an arbitration award and require a new arbitration hearing only if the evidence shows that the award was affected by fraud or collusion or if there was some serious procedural error such as lack of notice to one of the parties. Although arbitration has a number of advantages over litigation, one can readily see that there are also some important trade-offs that the parties should know about before agreeing to arbitrate.

Arbitration is generally categorized as either *labor arbitration* or *commercial arbitration*. Labor arbitration involves the resolving of disputes within the labor–management context, usually when the particular group of employees is represented by a union. The relationship between the company and unionized employees is based primarily on a collective bargaining agreement. Almost all collective bargaining agreements include a multistage process for resolving workplace disputes, with legally binding arbitration as the last step. Most of these disputes involve claims by employees that they have been fired or otherwise disciplined without the adequate justification the contract requires. The federal Taft-Hartley Act makes collective bargaining agreements, including arbitration provisions, legally binding.

The term *commercial arbitration* is usually used to describe almost all other forms of arbitration.[7] It includes the use of arbitration to resolve disputes arising from almost any kind of business transaction, including construction contracts, agreements for the sale of goods (such as supplies or equipment), insurance arrangements, joint ventures, and many others. In the United States, the Federal Arbitration Act (FAA) makes commercial arbitration agreements and arbitrator awards legally enforceable if the underlying business transaction affected interstate commerce. If there is no significant effect on interstate commerce, state arbitration statutes in every state usually make the arbitration agreement and award enforceable, although some of these state laws are less "friendly" to arbitration than the FAA.

In addition, most of the world's significant trading nations are parties to one or more multilateral treaties under which they agree to enforce arbitration agreements and awards in international commercial transactions involving citizens of other nations that signed the particular treaty. The most important of these treaties is the 1958 United Nations Convention on the Enforcement of Arbitral Awards.

Most commercial arbitration agreements (domestic or international) are of the *predispute* variety (or *future disputes*); this is a clause in some types of commercial contracts by which the parties agree that if there is any future dispute arising from the transaction, they will submit that dispute to legally binding arbitration. It is also possible for parties to make an agreement to arbitrate after a dispute has already occurred, but this is not usually what happens.

Although the parties to an arbitration agreement can agree as they wish, they usually specify that the arbitration will be coordinated and supervised by an established arbitration organization. In domestic commercial arbitration, the oldest and most frequently used organization is the American Arbitration Association (AAA), which handles about 55,000 commercial arbitration cases per year. In international commercial arbitration, there are several important sponsoring organizations, including the AAA, the International Chamber of Commerce in Paris, and the London Court of Arbitration (which is not a court despite its name).

Although most arbitration is still voluntary, the trial courts in more than 20 states and 20 federal districts have adopted *court-annexed arbitration*. These programs generally apply to cases involving money damage claims below certain amounts, which range from a few thousand dollars to $150,000 (and a few state programs have no limits). In this form of arbitration, shortly after the lawsuit is filed, the trial judge refers the case to arbitration, with a panel of local attorneys serving as arbitrators. The parties must participate in the arbitration, but the award is not legally binding if either party formally demands a regular trial within a short time after the award (usually 30 days).

Mediation

Other forms of ADR are quite different from arbitration. The various other types do not produce a decision that is legally binding on the parties. Instead, these methods are aimed at facilitating agreed settlements by (1) creating a structure that encourages the parties to get together and seriously negotiate much earlier, before they have hardened their positions and spent so much time and money, (2) trying to build

---

[7]Even when the dispute is between employer and employee, if no union or collective bargaining agreement is involved the arbitration is commonly classified as commercial.

trust and respect between the parties, (3) making the parties more realistic about the weaknesses of their positions and the strengths of the other side's positions before the dispute has escalated very far, and (4) creating an environment in which the parties are more likely to think of creative solutions to their problems that can benefit both sides rather than thinking about the dispute only in legalistic and dollar terms.

The most important version of this type of ADR is **mediation**, another old method being used much more in recent years. Like ADR generally, most mediation is entirely voluntary; it is created and controlled by the parties. The third party chosen by the disputants to help them find a solution to their differences is called a *mediator*. A mediator does not impose a solution but tries to help the parties themselves achieve one. Various approaches are used in mediation, depending on the wishes of the parties, the nature of the dispute, and the skill and personality of the mediator. The mediator may do as little as persuade the parties to talk to each other. Going further, he or she might help the parties agree on an agenda for a meeting and provide a suitable environment for negotiation. The mediator might point out that particular proposals are unrealistic, help the parties formulate their own proposals, and even make proposals for them to consider. In some situations, the mediator may try very hard to persuade them to accept a settlement he or she believes is reasonable.

Mediation has facilitated resolution of a wide range of disputes, such as many kinds of business disputes, international political conflicts, labor disputes, landlord–tenant disagreements, disputes between divorcing spouses, and multi-party controversies over environmental protections. It also can be very useful in combination with some other form of ADR, such as arbitration. For example, when IBM claimed that Fujitsu had illegally copied the former's mainframe operating system software, they spent several years and a great deal of time, money, and energy unsuccessfully trying to negotiate a settlement. They reached certain settlement agreements, but disagreements continued to break out, largely because of the technical complexity of the problem. The parties agreed to arbitration by a law professor experienced in dispute resolution and a retired computer industry executive. (The use of a two-member panel was unusual.) The arbitrators recognized that the controversy presented factual disputes about past copying

that would be almost impossible to resolve. They focused primarily on the future, ordering Fujitsu to provide a complete accounting of its use of programs under the earlier settlement agreement and requiring the parties to participate in mediation regarding programs falling outside the earlier agreement. The arbitrators became mediators; through mediation, new agreements were reached, after which the professor and executive resumed their roles as arbitrators and incorporated the new agreements into a binding arbitration order.

Although most mediation is voluntary, a number of states and a few federal districts are using court-annexed mediation, in which a trial judge refers the parties to mediation shortly after the case is filed. Although participation in this type of mediation is required, the mediator still does not impose an outcome on the parties.

Summary Jury Trial

Unlike most ADR techniques, the **summary jury trial** (SJT) can be used only after a lawsuit has been filed. The trial judge usually selects cases for SJT that he or she thinks (1) are unlikely to be settled by the parties through normal negotiation and (2) will probably require substantial trial time. Either the parties have performed some amount of pretrial discovery already, or if not, they are given an opportunity to conduct limited discovery before the SJT. A small (such as six-member) jury is selected in the same way that regular juries are chosen. To ensure that the jurors take their responsibility seriously, they are not informed that their decision is nonbinding.

The parties are then given a few hours to summarize their positions and their evidence (sometimes including key portions of videotaped deposition testimony) and to give closing arguments. After the jury renders a verdict, the parties are urged to negotiate a settlement based on the additional guidance that the jury's reaction to the case provides. Despite the fact that difficult cases are usually chosen for SJT, it has generally enjoyed a very high success rate, with most of the cases settling shortly after the SJT. The procedure tends to puncture inflated expectations and make parties choose more realistic settlement positions.

Minitrial

The **minitrial**, which has been used almost exclusively in disputes between corporations, involves summary presentations of evidence and arguments (similar to the presentations in an SJT) by opposing attorneys to a panel consisting of a neutral advisor and high-ranking executives from each company. The company representatives, who should have settlement authority, retire for direct settlement negotiations shortly after the presentations. They may seek the opinion of the neutral advisor before beginning settlement talks or only after negotiations have stalled. The exact design of the procedure, like the decision to use it in the first place, depends on the agreement of the parties. The minitrial has had a number of notable successes in complex, difficult disputes involving some of America's largest and best known companies. For example, almost immediately after a minitrial, Allied Corporation and Shell Oil settled a contract dispute that had been dragging on for almost ten years, including four years of expensive litigation.

Regulatory Negotiation

Regulatory negotiation, sometimes called *reg-neg* or *negotiated rule making,* has been a reasonably successful alternative to traditional administrative agency rule making. Agency regulations are often challenged in court, commonly taking years finally to receive court approval or disapproval. A number of federal and state agencies have avoided such litigation through a process in which the agency meets with representatives from interested groups to negotiate the content of regulations before they are formally proposed. The negotiations frequently involve a neutral third party acting as a mediator. The scope and validity of a rule produced through this process is much less likely to be challenged; in fact, the procedure sometimes produces both an agreed-on regulation *and* an agreement not to file a lawsuit challenging the regulation. The Environmental Protection Agency has been one of the leaders among federal agencies in using regulatory negotiation for new water and air quality regulations.

Future of ADR

Other forms of ADR have been used, often consisting of variations or hybrids of the methods we have discussed. Given the time and expense associated with traditional litigation and non-ADR negotiation, the use of ADR is likely to increase. In Texas, for example, the legislature stated in a recent law that "it is the policy of the State to encourage the peaceable resolution of disputes . . . and the early settlement of pending litigation through voluntary settlement procedures." The law charges the courts of the state with the responsibility to carry out that policy by encouraging use of arbitration, mediation, SJTs, minitrials, and the like.

SUMMARY

The basic phases of litigation are (1) the pleadings phase, in which the parties set forth their claims on paper; (2) the discovery phase, where investigation discloses evidence to support the parties' positions; (3) the trial phase, which includes the impaneling of a jury, presentation of proof by the parties in accordance with the rules of evidence, various motions made by the parties, instructions by the judge to the jury, and finally, deliberation by the jury. Often, there is (4) the appellate phase, where parties unhappy with the jury's verdict seek reversal or a new trial order from a higher court on the grounds of a legal error made by the trial judge or because the jury's verdict was not based on any substantial evidence.

This litigation system is as controversial as it is important. Reforms of the adversary system and our methods of selecting judges are continuously being debated.

Because of the time and expense involved in litigation, there has been a growing trend toward the use of alternative methods of dispute resolution, including arbitration, mediation, minitrials, summary jury trials, and regulatory negotiation. That trend is likely to continue to accelerate.

KEY TERMS

Adversarial system
Inquisitorial system
Pleading stage
Discovery stage
Complaint
Answer
Reply
Defense
Counterclaim
Motion to dismiss
Default judgment
Summary judgment
Trial stage
Challenge for cause
Peremptory challenge

Rules of evidence
Irrelevant evidence
Hearsay evidence
Opinion evidence
Motion for directed verdict
Motion for judgment notwithstanding
the verdict
Motion for new trial
Writ of execution
Writ of garnishment
Alternative dispute resolution
Arbitration
Mediation
Summary jury trial
Minitrial

QUESTIONS AND PROBLEMS

1. After 10 years of litigation, a federal antitrust case was submitted to a formally summoned jury. However, the attorneys were given only a half-day in which to present their case and the decision of the jury was not binding. Why would such a procedure be undertaken?

2. Wydel Associates, a partnership, sued Thermasol, Ltd., on a breach of contract claim. Thermasol moved to dismiss the lawsuit because the contract contained a clause stating that any dispute should be arbitrated in New York rather than litigated. Wydel argued that the arbitration clause was not binding because the law of the state in which its partnership was formed provided that any partnership agreement to submit a claim to arbitration must be signed by *all* the partners. This contract had been signed by only one Wydel partner. Should the court dismiss the suit? (*Wydel Associates v. Thermasol Ltd.,* 452 F.Supp. 739, W.D. Tex. 1978.)

3. The Brockton Bank sued First United, a broker-dealer, after the defendant induced the bank to purchase a 90-day $1 million CD from a bank (Penn Square) that failed. In discovery, Brockton sought to determine how much research First United had performed before making the recommendation to purchase. Four times during discovery, the defendant made untimely and only partial responses to court orders to produce documents. After arguing unsuccessfully for months that certain documents should be protected from discovery, the defendant claimed that the documents had been discarded long before. Sus-

pecting the documents had been destroyed, the trial judge ordered the defendant's president to appear in court. The president did not appear, his attorney stating, "My client chooses not to obey." What should the court do? (*Brockton Sav. Bank v. Peat, Marwick & Mitchell,* 771 F.2d 5, 1st Cir. 1985.)

4. In a report on the plaintiff's business, the defendant television station reported, "[W]e spoke to Judge Rissman . . . he says they've [customers of the plaintiff] got a good case." The plaintiff sued for defamation, claiming that this conversation never took place. The defendant moved to dismiss the suit on grounds that the conversation did take place and that it was just one man's opinion, anyway. Should the court dismiss? (*Action Repair, Inc. v. American Broadcasting Co.,* 776 F.2d 143, 7th Cir. 1985.)

5. The defendant company built a swimming pool for Denault. On January 9, 1978, the defendant's president was served with a summons in a lawsuit filed by Denault. Denault claimed the defendant's sloppy building of the pool forced her to spend $2000 on repairs. Under the court rules, an answer was due from the defendant on January 29. The defendant tried to answer on January 31, but the court refused to accept the filing because it was untimely. The court entered a default judgment against the defendant and set a hearing to establish damages. The defendant moved to set aside the default judgment on grounds of "excusable neglect," pointing out that its president had received two summonses in the same week and thought Denault's had been served at the same time as the other summons, on January 13. Should the judge set aside the default judgment? (*Denault v. Holloway Builders, Inc.,* 248 S.E.2d 265, S.C. 1978.)

6. Under a kickback scheme devised by Moore, a purchasing agent, one of the bidders on a construction project submitted several price sheets; the purchasing agent read that bidder's price list last, choosing the highest one that was still low enough to get the bid. On discovering the extra sheets, Moore's secretary, Marren, exclaimed: "I've found the evidence I've been waiting for for a long time!" Marszalek overheard this statement. At Moore's criminal trial, Marszalek was asked about this statement because Marren died before trial. Should Marszalek be allowed to testify about the statement? (*United States v. Moore,* 791 F.2d 566, 7th Cir. 1986.)

7. On behalf of her children who had heart valve problems, Fontenot sued Upjohn Company, claiming that a drug Upjohn manufactured caused the defects. During discovery, the plaintiff was asked which experts she would call to testify that the drug had actually caused the defects. She responded, "Unknown at the present time." After more time for discovery, Upjohn moved for summary judgment on grounds that the plaintiff had produced no evidence to indicate that the drug had caused the heart defects. The plaintiff responded by pointing out that Upjohn had produced no evidence showing that the drug did *not* cause the defects and by arguing that the question of causation is inherently a jury question and inappropriate for resolution on a summary judgment motion. Should Upjohn's motion be granted? (*Fontenot v. Upjohn Co.*, 780 F.2d 1190, 5th Cir. 1986.)

8. A plane owned by Douglas landed at the Los Angeles airport and received permission from the tower to enter runway 22. Because of the shape of his plane, the Douglas pilot was not in a position to see clearly ahead, so he zigzagged the plane at 15-degree angles as he taxied to improve his forward vision. However, the plane collided with a P-51 owned by the government, which was parked along the side of runway 22.

The pilot of the government plane, which was painted a brown camouflaged Army color, said after the accident: "I am sorry. I had no business being there. I have been here for about 10 minutes. I called for a truck and they haven't come after me yet." The government sued Douglas for negligence; Douglas raised a contributory negligence defense. At the close of the evidence, the government moved for a directed verdict in its favor on the questions of respective negligence. The judge denied the motion and the jury found for Douglas. On appeal, the government argued that the judge erred in failing to grant its directed verdict motion. Discuss. (*United States v. Douglas Aircraft Co.*, 169 F.2d 755, 9th Cir. 1948.)

9. According to one court, "Lawsuits have become particularly inappropriate devices for resolving minor disputes. They are clumsy, noisy, unwieldy and notoriously inefficient. Fueled by bad feelings, they generate much heat and friction, yet produce little that is of any use. Worst of all, once set in motion, they are well-nigh impossible to bring to a halt." Is this a fair assessment? Does it help explain the trend toward use of alternative methods of dispute resolution? (*Blackburn v. Goettel-Blanton*, 898 F.2d 95, 9th Cir. 1990.)

THERE ARE SEVERAL BASIC processes by which law is made: (1) the formulation of rules by the courts—the judges—in deciding cases coming before them in those areas of law in which no statutes apply; (2) the enactment and interpretation of statutes; (3) the interpretation and application of constitutional provisions; and (4) the promulgation of rules and regulations by administrative agencies. In this chapter we look at the first and second of these law-making processes. First we show how *common law* (or *case law*) is formed by the courts. Then we turn our attention to the enactment and interpretation of statutory law.

ORIGIN OF COMMON LAW

As we described in Chapter 2, the early king's courts in England largely made up the law on a case-by-case basis. If, for example, a plaintiff asked for damages for breach of contract in a situation in which the defendant denied that a contract ever existed, the court had to spell out the nature of a contract—that is, specify the minimum elements that the court felt must exist for it to impose contractual liability on the defendant. Similarly, if a defendant admitted making the contract in question but sought to escape liability for reasons of illness or military service, the court had to decide what kinds of defenses ought to be legally recognizable—defenses that should free the defendant from his or her contractual obligations.

Over a period of time, as more and more cases were settled, a rudimentary body of contract law came into being. Thereafter, when other cases arose involving contractual matters, the courts quite naturally looked to the earlier cases to see what principles of law had been established. The same procedure was followed in many other branches of law, and the legal rules that arose in this manner constituted the common law, or **case law,** of England.

The common-law rules that had developed in England became the law of our early colonies. When those colonies achieved statehood, they adopted those rules as a major part of their respective bodies of law. As the territories became states, they followed suit so that at one time the major portion of the law of all states (with the exception of Louisiana) was common law in nature.[1]

The Current Scene

Gradually, the state legislatures began to pass increasing numbers of statutes, with the result that today most branches of the law are statutory in nature. For example, all states now have comprehensive statutes governing the areas of corporation law, criminal law, tax law, municipal corporations, and commercial law. Some of these statutes have been based largely on the common-law principles that were in effect earlier. Others, however, have been passed to create bodies of rules that did not exist previously or that expressly overrule common-law principles.

Despite the ever-increasing amount of statutory law in this country (which we examine in some detail later in this chapter), several branches of law today are still essentially common law in nature in 49 states—particularly the subjects of *contracts, torts,* and *agency.* In these areas, in which the legislatures have not seen fit to enact comprehensive statutes, the courts still settle controversies on the basis of judge-made or *case law*—the rules formulated by the courts in deciding earlier cases over the years, as illustrated in Figure 4.1. (Although many of these rules had their origin in England, as has been indicated, our definition of common law also includes those additional rules that have originated in the state courts in this country.)

In deciding each case, judges bear the twin burden of attempting to provide "justice" for the case at hand while at the same time setting a precedent that will serve the greater interests of society when applied in future cases. The common-law rules, like legislative statutes, must serve public policy interests—the "community common sense and common conscience." Therefore, courts have laid great stress on the customs, morals, and forms of conduct that

---

[1]Louisiana continues to be governed by the *civil-law* (as distinguished from common-law) system. Under such a system, adopted by most European countries, virtually all law is *codified*—that is, statutory.

FIGURE 4.1

Common Law

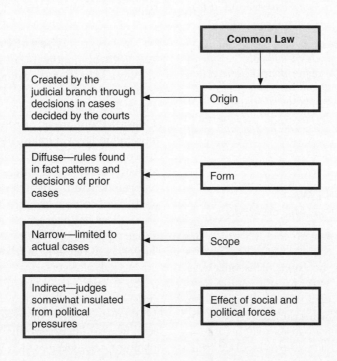

are generally prevailing in the community at the time of decision. There is no doubt that occasionally the judge's personal feelings as to what kinds of conduct are just and fair, what rule would best serve societal interests, and simply what is "right" or "wrong" enter the picture.

Role of the Judge

Benjamin N. Cardozo, an associate justice of the U.S. Supreme Court, contended that four "directive forces" shaped the law, and especially the common law, as follows: (1) philosophy (logic), (2) history, (3) custom, and (4) social welfare (or sociology).

In a lecture on the role of philosophy in the law, Cardozo briefly commented on the special tasks of the judge in interpreting statutes and constitutions, and then continued:

We reach the land of mystery when constitution and statute are silent, and the judge must look to the common law for the rule that fits the case. . . . The first thing he does is to compare the case before him with the precedents,
whether stored in his mind or hidden in the books. . . . Back of precedents are the basic juridical conceptions which are the postulates of judicial reasoning, and farther back are the habits of life, the institutions of society, in which those conceptions had their origin, and which, by a process of interaction, they have modified in turn. . . . If [precedents] are plain and to the point, there may be need of nothing more. Stare decisis *is at least the everyday working rule of the law. . . .*[2]

Early in that same lecture, however, Cardozo cautioned that the finding of **precedent** was only part of the judge's job and indicated how the law must grow beyond the early precedents:

The rules and principles of case law have never been treated as final truths, but as working hypotheses, continually retested in those great laboratories of the law, the courts of justice. . . . In [the] perpetual flux [of the law,] the problem which confronts the judge is in reality a twofold one: he first must extract from the precedents the

---

[2]*Stare decisis* means literally "to stand by decisions."

underlying principle, the ratio decidendi [the ground of decision]; he must then determine the path or direction along which the principle is to move and develop, if it is not to wither and die. . . .

The directive force of a principle may be exerted along the line of logical progression; this I will call the rule of analogy or the method of philosophy; along the line of historical development; this I will call the method of evolution; along the line of the customs of the community; this I will call the method of tradition; along the lines of justice, morals and social welfare, the mores of the day; and this I will call the method of sociology. . . .[3]

COMMON LAW—
THE DOCTRINE OF *STARE DECISIS*

The heart of the common-law process lies in the inclination of the courts generally to follow precedent—to stand by existing decisions. This policy, as we were told by Cardozo, is referred to as the doctrine of *stare decisis.* Under this approach, when the fact pattern of a particular controversy is established, the attorneys for both parties search for earlier cases involving similar fact patterns in an effort to determine whether applicable principles of law have been established. If this research produces a number of similar cases (or even one) within the state where a rule has been applied by the appellate courts, the trial court will ordinarily feel constrained to follow the same rule in settling the current controversy. (But, as we will see later, this does not mean that the

[3]Benjamin N. Cardozo, *The Nature of the Judicial Process* (1921). Excerpts are used by permission of the Yale University Press.

courts are reluctant to abandon a precedent if it produces clear injustice under "contemporary conditions.")

Types of Precedent

Authority originating in courts above the trial court in the appellate chain is called **mandatory authority.** The judge must follow it. Thus, a state trial judge in Ohio will follow the rulings of the Ohio Supreme Court if there are any precedents from this court; if not, the judge will follow the prior decisions of Ohio's intermediate appellate courts. The intermediate appellate courts will do the same thing, and the Ohio Supreme Court will follow its own precedents. In matters of federal law, the Ohio Supreme Court will follow the holdings of the U.S. Supreme Court. A judge who does not follow mandatory authority is not impeached or shot at dawn but certainly runs a strong risk of reversal.

So strong is the hold of mandatory authority that judges will usually follow it even though they violently disagree with its reasoning and result. The following case illustrates this fact. The case involves a claim of *negligence,* which we shall study in detail in Chapter 8. It means simply that the defendant was more careless than a reasonable person would have been under the circumstances and should be liable for injuries that result. The case also involves a defense of governmental immunity, which stems from the ancient English doctrine that the King (or in this case the government) "can do no wrong" and therefore cannot be sued absent his consent. The decision is by a Michigan intermediate appellate court, sitting between the trial court and the Michigan Supreme Court in the appellate chain.

EDWARDS V. CLINTON VALLEY CENTER

Court of Appeals of Michigan, 360 N.W.2d 606 (1984)

Case

The plaintiff is the estate of Jean Edwards, who was fatally stabbed by a former mental patient. The defendant is a government mental hospital that refused to admit the killer after she was brought to *the facility by police when she threatened to "kill someone." The plaintiff alleges that the defendant's refusal to admit the killer was negligent. The trial judge dismissed the suit on a purely legal ground—governmental immunity. The plaintiff appealed.*

Bronson, Presiding Judge:

Under the rule of *stare decisis,* this Court is bound to follow decisions of the Michigan Supreme Court, even if we disagree with them. The rule of *stare decisis,* founded on considerations of expediency and sound

(continues)

EDWARDS V. CLINTON VALLEY CENTER

(continued from previous page)
principles of public policy, operates to preserve harmony, certainty, and stability in the law. However, the rule "was never intended to perpetuate error or to prevent the consideration of rules of law to be applied to the ever-changing business, economic, and political life of a community." *Parker v. Port Huron Hospital,* 105 N.W.2d 1 (1960).

In *Perry v. Kalamazoo State Hospital,* 273 N.W.2d 421 (1978), the majority of the Supreme Court held that governmental immunity for tort liability extends to the day-to-day care public mental hospitals provide. An attempt to distinguish the instant case from *Perry* could not possibly withstand logical or honest analysis. As a member of the Court of Appeals, I am obligated to follow the decisions of our higher court. For that reason, and that reason alone, the order of summary judgment is affirmed.

I feel compelled, however, to register my fundamental disagreement with the result adopted by the *Perry* majority. I am much more inclined to follow the narrow interpretation of governmental immunity advanced by the dissenters, because the operation of a mental hospital is not an activity which can be done only by the government, it is not a governmental function within the meaning of [the Michigan statutes establishing governmental immunity], and, therefore, a mental hospital should not be immune from liability for its torts.

If ever a factual situation invited reconsideration of the wisdom of a broad interpretation of what is, in the first place, an archaic doctrine, it is presented in the instant case. The Pontiac police bring Wilma Gilmore to the state-operated Clinton Valley Center. Gilmore threatens to kill someone. Gilmore had been previously institutionalized at the center. The center

refuses to admit Gilmore. Four days later, Gilmore once again goes to the police and repeats her homicidal threats. She is told to leave. Two days later, Gilmore enters the apartment of Jean Edwards and fatally stabs her in the arms, throat, and abdomen. Of note is that nowhere in the record does the center offer a reason for its refusal to admit Gilmore.

I fail to see how summarily relieving the hospital of responsibility for such obvious gross negligence, without requiring of it even the slightest explanation, serves any viable public interest or protects the people of our state. Instead, it harshly imposes the entire risk of the center's negligence on Jean Edwards and her family. The time has come for either the Legislature or our Supreme Court to preserve and promote justice by modifying the doctrine of governmental immunity.

Affirmed. ◊◊

What if a trial judge searches the law books and discovers that there is no precedent in the state on the legal question presented? In such a case, the judge may examine the decisions of courts of other states. For example, assume a state trial judge in Oregon is faced with the question of whether a landlord who did not attempt to lease an apartment after a tenant moved out in the middle of a lease should be barred from suing the tenant for damages. No Oregon cases address the issue, and the only case "on point" was rendered by the Alabama Supreme Court. Must the Oregon judge follow the Alabama precedent? No. Because the Oregon judge's decision cannot be appealed to the Alabama Supreme Court, the latter's rulings are not mandatory authority.

The Alabama decision would constitute **persuasive authority.** That is, the Oregon judge can study the Alabama decision and, on finding it persuasive, may choose to follow it. However, if the judge finds the decision not to be persuasive, the judge need not apply its rationale in Oregon.

What if there are two existing precedents, that of the Alabama Supreme Court and one from the North Dakota Supreme Court, that reach diametrically opposed results on the same issue? Again, they are both only persuasive authority for the Oregon judge who can study them and follow the one that seems more reasonable. Of course, the judge can also reject both persuasive precedents and create yet a third approach to the issue. Despite the importance of stability to the law, the majesty of the common law lies in its flexibility and adaptability. Although judges revere stability, they will change a rule when they become convinced that it was wrongly established and never served society's interests or that, although it was a good rule when established, changing social, moral, economic, or technological factors have rendered it outmoded. If no valid reason supports a common-law rule, no matter how long it has been established, the judges should and usually will change it.

Sometimes common-law rules change slowly. Exceptions or qualifications to a rule will slowly appear in the case law. Most of the history of the common law is of a slow evolution as the law keeps pace with a changing society. Refer back to *Soldano v. O'Daniels* in Chapter 1. That case not only illustrates a minor change in the slow evolution of the law regarding our duties to our fellow citizens, but it also contains some eloquent language extolling the virtues of our flexible common law.

Sometimes the law will change dramatically, as when modern judges decide an established rule no longer serves society and must be scrapped, as the following case illustrates.

FLAGIELLO V. PENNSYLVANIA HOSPITAL

Supreme Court of Pennsylvania, 208 A.2d 193 (1965)

Mrs. Flagiello, a patient in the Pennsylvania Hospital in Philadelphia, fell and broke an ankle while being moved by two of its employees. She brought this action against the hospital to recover damages, alleging that the employees were guilty of negligence. The defendant hospital moved for a judgment on the pleadings, contending that under the case law of Pennsylvania, it was well established that a charitable institution was not responsible for the wrongs of its employees. The trial court sustained this motion and entered judgment for the defendant. The plaintiff appealed to the Supreme Court of Pennsylvania.

Musmanno, Justice:

. . . The hospital has not denied that its negligence caused Mrs. Flagiello's injuries. It merely announces that it is an eleemosynary institution, and, therefore, owed no duty of care to its patient. It declares in effect that it can do wrong and still not be liable in damages to the person it has wronged. It thus urges a momentous exception to the generic proposition that in law there is no wrong without a remedy. From the earliest days of organized society it became apparent to man that society could never become a success unless the collectivity of mankind guaranteed to every member of society a remedy for a palpable wrong inflicted on him by another member of that society. In 1844 Justice Storrs of the Supreme Court of Connecticut crystallized into epigrammatic language that wise concept, as follows: "An injury is a wrong; and for the redress of every wrong there is a remedy; a wrong is a violation of one's right; and for the vindication of every right there is a remedy." *Parker v. Griswold,* 17 Conn. 288.

[The court addressed itself to several specific arguments advanced by the defendant to support its contention that charitable institutions were not, and should not be, subject to the general rule stated above. One of these arguments was that, on economic grounds alone, the imposition of liability on charitable institutions would be financially ruinous to them. The court rejected this argument, noting first that, as a general rule, a defendant is never permitted to escape liability as to valid claims solely on the ground that an entry of a judgment against the defendant would be financially burdensome, or might even force the defendant into bankruptcy. The court also noted that the rule of immunity as to charitable institutions originated in this country at a time when most of their patients paid nothing for the services they received and that the rule was an effort by the courts to preserve the meager assets of such institutions. Judge Musmanno further observed that conditions have now changed; that so-called charitable hospitals operate on the same basis as ordinary business establishments; that in 1963 "the fees received from patients in the still designated charitable hospitals in Pennsylvania constituted 90.92 percent of the total income of such hospitals," and the plaintiff did, in fact, pay the defendant $24.50 a day for services rendered her.

On these facts, the court rejected defendant's claim of immunity based on financial considerations. The court then turned to the remaining major contention of the defendant, specifically, that the rule of immunity as to charitable hospitals was so firmly established in the case law of Pennsylvania, including cases decided by the Pennsylvania Supreme Court, that, under the doctrine of *stare decisis,* the rule could not now be abandoned by the courts. In that regard Judge Musmanno, in a lengthy examination of cases, concluded that the immunity doctrine originated in an early English case that was soon overruled there, that the American courts seemed to adopt the rule of that case blindly, without examining the validity of the reasons ostensibly underlying it, and further noted that approximately half the states in this country have now rejected the doctrine of immunity. The court then continued:]

Failing to hold back both the overwhelming reasons of rudimentary justice for abolishing the doctrine, and the rising tide of out-of-state repudiation of the doctrine, the defendant hospital and the Hospital Association of Pennsylvania fall back for defense to the bastion of *stare decisis.* It is inevitable and proper that they should do so. Without *stare decisis,* there would be no stability in our system of jurisprudence.

Stare decisis channels the law. It erects lighthouses and flies the signals of safety. The ships of jurisprudence must follow that well-defined channel which, over the years, has been proved to be secure and trustworthy. But it

(continues)

FLAGIELLO V. PENNSYLVANIA HOSPITAL

(continued from previous page)

would not comport with wisdom to insist that, should shoals rise in a heretofore safe course and rocks emerge to encumber the passage, the ship should nonetheless pursue the original course, merely because it presented no hazard in the past. The principle of *stare decisis* does not demand that we follow precedents which shipwreck justice. . . .

There is nothing in the records of the courts, the biographies of great jurists, or the writings of eminent legal authorities which offers the slightest encouragement to the notion that time petrifies into unchanging jurisprudence a palpable fallacy. [Emphasis added.] As years can give no sturdiness to a decayed tree, so the passing decades can add no convincing flavor to the withered apple of sophistry clinging to the limb of demonstrated wrong. There are, of course, principles and precepts sanctified by age, and no one would think of changing them, but their inviolability derives not from longevity but from their universal appeal to the reason, the conscience and the experience of mankind. No one, for

instance, would think of challenging what was written in Magna Charta, the Habeas Corpus Act or the Bill of Rights of the Constitution of the United States. . . .

While age adds venerableness to moral principles and some physical objects, it occasionally becomes necessary, and it is not sacrilegious to do so, to scrape away the moss of the years to study closely the thing which is being accepted as authoritative, inviolable, and untouchable. The Supreme Court of Michigan said sagaciously in the case of *Williams v. City of Detroit*, 364 Mich. 231, that "it is the peculiar genius of the common law that no legal rule is mandated by the doctrine of *stare decisis* when that rule was conceived in error or when the times and circumstances have so changed as to render it an instrument of injustice."

The charitable immunity rule proves itself an instrument of injustice and nothing presented by the defendant shows it to be otherwise. In fact, the longer the argument for its preservation the more convincing is the proof that it long ago outlived its purpose if,

indeed, it ever had a purpose consonant with sound law. "Ordinarily, when a court decides to modify or abandon a court-made rule of long standing, it starts out by saying that the reason for the rule no longer exists. In this case, it is correct to say that the 'reason' originally given for the rule of immunity never did exist." *Pierce v. Yakima Valley Hospital Ass'n*, 260 P.2d 765.

A rule that has become insolvent has no place in the active market of current enterprise. *When a rule offends against reason, when it is at odds with every precept of natural justice, and when it cannot be defended on its own merits, but has to depend alone on a discredited genealogy, courts not only possess the inherent power to repudiate, but, indeed, it is required, by the very nature of judicial function, to abolish such a rule.* [Emphasis added.]

We, therefore, overrule *Michael v. Habnemann*, 404 Pa. 424, and all other decisions of identical effect, and hold that the hospital's liability must be governed by the same principles of law as apply to other employers. . . .

Reversed and remanded. ⚖

PROFILE OF OUR FEDERAL AND STATE STATUTORY LAW

Although a significant portion of our law is still common law in nature, most of our federal and state law today results from the enactment of **statutes** by legislative bodies. These are the formally adopted rules that constitute our *statutory law*, the second of the major sources of law.[4] All states, for example, have comprehensive statutes governing such subjects as banking law, criminal law, education, consumer sales, and motor vehicle law.

Similarly, at the federal level, sweeping statutes in

the areas of antitrust law, labor law, food and drug regulation, and securities law have long been in effect. Newer (and usually narrower) statutes are added every year, including, for example, the Consumer Product Safety Act of 1972, the Bankruptcy Reform Act of 1978, and the Trademark Counterfeiting Act of 1984. Figure 4.2 summarizes the origin, form, scope, and effect of statutory law.

In this section our first objectives are to look at the reasons for the existence of statutory law, to become acquainted with the basic rules that delineate the jurisdictions of the federal and state governments, and to note the contrasts between statutory and common law. We then turn our attention to the closely related area of statutory interpretation—the process by which the courts spell out the precise meaning of statutes that are applicable to the particular cases coming before them—and conclude with a summary

---

[4]The term *statutory law*, when broadly used in contrast to *common law*, includes not only laws passed by legislative bodies but, additionally, U.S. treaties, the federal and state constitutions, and municipal ordinances. In this chapter, however, the term is used in its more customary sense, referring only to acts of the state legislatures and of Congress.

FIGURE 4.2

Statutory Law

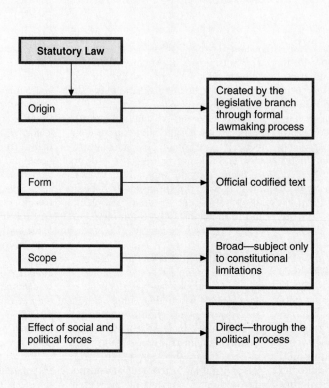

of selected state statutes that are of special significance to the business community.[5] As a backdrop for a better understanding of the issues that are addressed in this chapter, however, a brief description of the vast scope of our statutory law is first in order.

STATUTORY LAW—THE RATIONALE

There are many reasons for the existence of statutory law, three of which deserve special mention.

1. One of the primary functions of any legislative body is to adopt measures having to do with the *structure and day-to-day operation* of the government of which it is a part. Thus many federal statutes are of the "nuts and bolts" variety, relating to such matters as the operation of the federal court system, the Internal Revenue Service, and the administration and employment rules of the U.S. Civil Service Commission. In a similar vein, many state statutes relate

to such matters as the property tax laws, the operation of school systems, and the setting forth of powers of municipalities within their borders.

2. Many activities are of such a nature that *they can hardly be regulated by common-law principles* and the judicial processes. In the area of criminal law, for example, it is absolutely essential for the general populace to know what acts are punishable by fine and imprisonment; the only sure way to set forth the elements of specific crimes is through the enactment of federal and state criminal statutes. Similarly, the activities of corporations are so complex and so varied that they do not lend themselves to judicial regulation. Few judges, for example, have either the expertise to deal with such questions as the conditions under which the payment of corporate dividends should be permitted or the time to deal with the spelling out of such conditions on a case-by-case basis. Thus the only practical way to deal with these and other problems is by the drafting of detailed statutes, which, in total, make up the comprehensive corporation laws of the states.

---

[5]Many federal statutes, as well as some state enactments, are discussed in later chapters on topics such as employment law, securities regulation, and environmental protection.

3. A third function of a legislature is to change expressly (or even overrule) common-law rules when it believes such modifications are necessary, and—even more commonly—to enact statutes to *remedy new problems* to which common-law rules do not apply. Thus a state legislature might pass a statute making nonprofit corporations (such as hospitals) liable for the wrongs of their employees to the same extent as are profit-making corporations, thereby reversing the early common-law rule of nonliability for such employers. Or a legislature, aware of increasing purchases of its farmlands by foreign citizens—a situation not covered by common-law rules—might react to this perceived evil by passing a statute placing limits on the number of acres aliens may own or inherit. (More than 20 states today have such statutes, and approximately 10 have passed laws that prohibit aliens who live outside the United States from owning *any* farmlands within these states' borders.)

LIMITATIONS ON LEGISLATIVE BODIES

Procedural Requirements

All state constitutions (and, to a lesser extent, the federal Constitution) contain provisions about the manner in which statutes shall be enacted. As a general rule, acts that do not conform to these requirements are void. For example, virtually all state constitutions provide that revenue bills "shall originate in the House of Representatives," a requirement that also appears in the federal Constitution. Typical state constitutions also contain provisions (1) restricting the enactment of "special" or "local" laws that affect only a portion of the citizenry, (2) requiring that the subject of every act be set forth in its title, and (3) prohibiting a statute from embracing more than one subject. Additionally, all constitutions prescribe certain formalities in regard to the enactment processes themselves, such as specific limitations on the time and place of the introduction of bills, limitations on the amendment of bills, and the requirement that bills have three separate readings before final passage.

These kinds of provisions, although appearing to be unduly technical, actually serve meritorious purposes. For example, although legislatures normally strive to pass statutes of general application, it is necessary that some laws operate only on certain classes of persons or in certain localities of a state. Such special or local laws are valid only if the basis of their classification is reasonable; two of the purposes of the constitutional provisions just mentioned are to ensure such reasonableness and to guarantee that the classes of persons covered be given notice of the consideration of the bill before its passage. Similarly, the purpose of requiring that the subject of an act be expressed in its title is to ensure that legislators voting on a bill are fully apprised as to its subject, thereby guarding against the enactment of "surprise" legislation. And the purpose of the requirement that a bill contain one subject is to prevent the passage of omnibus bills (those that bring together entirely unrelated, or incongruous, matters).

Requirement of Certainty

All statutes are subject to the general principle of constitutional law that they be "reasonably definite and certain." Although the Constitution itself does not expressly contain such a provision, the courts have long taken the view that if the wording of a statute is such that persons of ordinary intelligence cannot understand its meaning, the statute violates the due process clause of the Constitution and is thus invalid.[6] In such instances, it is said that the statute is "unconstitutionally vague."

As a practical matter, most statutes that are challenged on the ground of vagueness or uncertainty are upheld by the courts. This is because most statutes are, in fact, drafted carefully and because the courts are extremely reluctant to declare a statute unconstitutional if they can avoid doing so. Thus, if the wording of a statute is subject to two possible but conflicting interpretations, one of which satisfies constitutional requirements and the other of which does not, the former interpretation will be accepted by the courts if they can reasonably do so.

An application of the vagueness analysis in a criminal case occurred in *Kolender v. Lawson*, 461 U.S. 352 (1983), in which the U.S. Supreme Court struck down, on the ground of vagueness, a California statute that required persons who loitered or wandered on the streets to provide "credible and reliable" identification and to account for their presence when requested to do so by a peace officer. The court, speaking through Justice Sandra Day O'Connor, said, "It is clear that the full discretion accorded to the police whether the suspect has provided a

---

[6]*State v. Jay J. Garfield Bldg. Co.*, 3 P.2d 983 (Ariz. 1931).

'credible and reliable' identification necessarily entrusts lawmaking to the moment-to-moment judgment of the policeman on his beat," and "furnishes a convenient tool for harsh and discriminatory enforcement by local prosecuting officials against particular groups deemed to merit their displeasure."

In a case involving regulation of business, rather than criminal charges, the courts will not be as demanding in applying the vagueness test, as the next case illustrates.

U.S. V. SUN AND SAND

U.S. Second Circuit Court of Appeals, 725 F.2d 184 (1984)

The Consumer Products Safety Commission (CPSC) issued an administrative complaint charging that Sun and Sand Imports had imported and transported in interstate commerce flammable children's sleepwear in violation of the Flammable Fabrics Act (FFA). The garments in question are sold in sizes that fit infants and toddlers, are made of soft stretchable fabric with no trim, have attached feet and a front zipper running from neck to crotch, and are, admittedly, made of flammable fabric. The trial judge enjoined importation of the garments pending conclusion of CPSC administrative proceedings.

Sun and Sand appealed, arguing that the regulatory definition of sleepwear is void for vagueness under the due process clause of the Fifth Amendment.

Timbers, Circuit Judge:

Children's sleepwear is defined in a regulation promulgated under the FFA as

any product of wearing apparel up to and including size 6X, such as nightgowns, pajamas, or similar or related items, such as robes, intended to be worn primarily for sleeping or activities relating to sleeping. Diapers and underwear are excluded from this definition.

In addition, the CPSC uses the following factors to determine whether an item of children's clothing is sleepwear within the meaning of the regulation: the nature of the product and its suit-

ability for use by children for sleeping or activities related to sleeping; the manner in which the product is distributed and promoted; and the likelihood that the product will be used by children primarily for sleeping or activities related to sleeping in a substantial number of cases.

Before turning to the merits of Sun and Sand's vagueness challenge, we must determine what standard to apply. A provision is void for vagueness if it is so vague that it gives no warning to the challenger that his conduct is prohibited. In *Village of Hoffman Estates v. The Flipside, Hoffman Estates, Inc.*, 455 U.S. 489 (1982), the Supreme Court held that a more relaxed standard is to be applied to economic regulations which do not implicate fundamental rights and provide only for civil penalties. The instant case involves an economic regulation. Sun and Sand argues that the more restrictive standard should apply because the FFA provides criminal penalties for willful violations. The critical distinction is that criminal penalties are imposed only for *willful* violations of the FFA. A scienter requirement may mitigate the vagueness of a law.°

Moreover, the CPSC here sought only a cease and desist order. Sun and Sand remains free to assert a vagueness defense in any criminal action which may ensue.

We hold that the definition of children's sleepwear set forth in the regulation promulgated under the FFA is sufficiently specific. Moreover, the CPSC's criteria for determining

°"Scienter" indicates an intent to violate the law.

whether an article of clothing is primarily sleepwear provide guidance to the manufacturer, as do the examples provided by the cease and desist orders published in the *Federal Register*. In addition, the agency is willing to give pre-enforcement advice to manufacturers concerned with the applicability of the FFA to their products. We find these factors persuasive. We decline Sun and Sand's invitation to require an unworkable level of specificity. In *Boyce Motor Lines, Inc. v. United States*, 342 U.S. 337, 340 (1952), the Supreme Court recognized that because "few words possess the precision of mathematical symbols, most statutes must deal with untold and unforeseen variations in factual situations, and the practical necessities of discharging the business of government inevitably limit the specificity with which legislators can spell out prohibitions."

Sun and Sand focuses upon a 1978 memorandum by a compliance officer to the CPSC stating that "[d]ifferences between CPSC and firms regarding particular garments may then be litigated, as necessary, to resolve differences of opinion as to the intended use of the garments and to establish case precedents." Statutes and regulations, however, are not impermissibly vague simply because it may be difficult to determine whether marginal cases fall within their scope. *United States v. National Dairy Products Corp.*, 372 U.S. 29, 32 (1963). The burden upon a manufacturer of defending a cease and desist proceeding in a marginal case does not render the standard vague. It is not unfair to require that "one who
(continues)

U.S. v. SUN AND SAND

(continued from previous page) deliberately goes perilously close to an area of proscribed conduct shall take the risk that he may cross the line." *Boyce Motor Lines, supra.* Only a reasonable degree of certainty is necessary. We hold that that requirement has been complied with here.

[The court then concluded that the trial court had properly held Sun and Sand's products to be within the statute because, *inter alia:* (1) they had the same characteristics as infant sleepwear, especially the attached feet; (2) Sun and Sand does not promote them as playwear; (3) customers in several stores were shown Sun and Sand's garments when they asked for sleepwear; (4) Sun and Sand's garments were intermingled with sleepwear in many stores; and (5) the garments bore a "striking similarity" to classic sleepwear garments.]

Affirmed. ☙

STATUTORY LAW AND COMMON LAW— A CONTRAST

Statutory law and common law differ in several significant respects. The most obvious of these are the *processes* by which each comes into being and the *form* of each after it becomes operative.

Processes and Form

Legislative acts become law only after passing through certain formal steps in both houses of the state legislatures (or of Congress) and, normally, by subsequent approval of the governor (or the president). The usual steps are (1) introduction of a bill in the house or senate by one or more members of that body; (2) referral of the bill to the appropriate legislative committee, where hearings are held; (3) approval of the bill by that committee and perhaps others; (4) approval of the bill by the house and senate after full debate; and (5) signing of the bill by the executive (or legislative vote overriding an executive veto). At each of these stages the opponents of the bill are given considerable opportunity to raise objections, with the result that the bill may be voted down or may pass only after being substantially amended. *Common-law rules*, by contrast, are creatures of the judicial branch of government; they are adopted by the courts for settling controversies involving points of law on which the legislature has not spoken.

In addition to these obvious contrasts between the two types of law, others are equally significant. We note these briefly.

Social and Political Forces

The social and political forces within a state have a greater and more evident impact on statutory law than on common law. Judges are somewhat more insulated from such pressures than are legislatures. Additionally, the steps required in the enactment of statutes enable representatives of vocal special-interest groups (who are frequently at odds with one another) to attract considerable publicity to their causes. And, of course, the raw political power that each is able to exert on the legislators plays a significant, although not always controlling, part in the final disposition of a bill.

In addition to the political and financial pressures that have always been wielded by lobbyists, the past 20 years have seen an enormous increase in the activities of political action committees (PACs). Whereas lobbyists' activities are intended to sway the votes of lawmakers, PACs direct their efforts to raising funds for the election of candidates who will support their particular causes. A hint of the power of PACs can be gained from just three statistics: (1) more than 4000 PACs are registered with the Federal Elections Commission, representing virtually every business, union, and special interest group imaginable; (2) spending by PACs for the 1990 elections was estimated to be more than $150 million, even though there was no presidential race that year; and (3) about 95 percent of the incumbents in the U.S. House of Representatives win reelection every term, a statistic that many attribute in large part to the fact that PACs tend to support incumbents.

Legislative Options

Although judges are required to settle controversies that come before them, legislatures generally have no duty to enact legislation. Thus legislatures have the option of refraining from the passage of laws when there is little public sentiment for them or when competing groups are so powerful that inaction is, politically, the better part of valor.

Legislative Scope

Subject only to the relatively few constitutional limitations placed on it, the legislative power to act is very broad. Thus legislatures are not only free to enact statutes when case law is nonexistent, but they also can pass statutes that expressly overrule common-law principles. Examples of the latter are those statutes involving the legality of married women's contracts. Under English and early American common law, it was firmly established that married women lacked the capacity—the legal ability—to contract, and thus any agreements they entered into while married had no effect. Today, all states have enacted statutes that give married women the same rights to contract as those enjoyed by other citizens.

As for jurisdictional scope, legislatures have the power to pass broad statutes encompassing all aspects of a given subject, whereas the courts can "make law" only in deciding the cases that come before them. Every state, for example, has comprehensive corporation acts, in which virtually all aspects of corporate activities, from incorporation procedures to dissolution procedures, are specified in detail. Similarly, every state has an all-encompassing criminal code, within which the criminal offenses in the state are defined.

STATUTORY INTERPRETATION

We have seen that legislative bodies make law whenever they enact statutes. By doing so, they formally state what kinds of conduct they are requiring or prohibiting in specified situations and what results they expect from the passage of these laws on the rights and duties of affected parties.

But the true scope and meaning of a particular statute is never known with precision until it is formally construed by the courts in settling actual disputes arising under it. This search for legislative intent, which usually necessitates a *statutory interpretation*, is thus another major source of our law. **Interpretation** is the process by which a court determines the precise legal meaning of a statute as it applies to a particular controversy.

Interpretation: A Necessary Evil?

Whenever a dispute arises in which either of the parties is basing his or her case on the wording of a par-

ticular statute, one might think that the court's job would be mechanical in nature; that is, once the facts were established, a careful reading of the statute would make it clear what result the legislature intended in such a situation. Although this is often true, there are many instances in which it is not.

To bring the nature of the problem into sharper focus, consider the following situation. X flies a stolen airplane from one state to another and is convicted under a U.S. statute that makes the interstate movement of stolen motor vehicles a federal crime. In this statute, a motor vehicle is defined as "an automobile, automobile truck, automobile wagon, motorcycle, or any other self-propelled vehicle not designed for running on rails." Is an airplane a "motor vehicle" under this law? The problem is that the words of the statute are broad enough to embrace aircraft if they are given a literal interpretation; yet it is at least arguable that Congress did not really intend such a result. (The U.S. Supreme Court answered no to the question, with Justice Holmes saying that the term *vehicle* is "commonly understood as something that moves or runs on land, not something which flies in the air"— although he did admit that "etymologically the term might be considered broad enough to cover a conveyance propelled in the air."[7])

Plain Meaning Rule

The primary source of legislative intent is, of course, the language that makes up the statute itself. In the relatively rare case when a court feels that the wording of an act is so clear as to dictate but one result and that the result is not "patently absurd," the consideration of other factors is unnecessary. If, for example, a state statute provides that "every applicant for examination and registration as a pharmacist shall be a citizen of the United States," a state pharmacy board would have to refuse to process the application of an alien even though he or she may have *applied for* U.S. citizenship as of the date of the pharmaceutical examination.[8] In cases of this sort (and occasionally in others in which the language is somewhat less precise), the courts say that the statute possesses a **plain meaning** and that interpretation is thus unnecessary.

Aids To Interpretation

Many statutes, however, do not easily lend themselves to the plain meaning rule. There are

---

[7]*McBoyle v. United States*, 283 U.S. 25 (1931).
[8]*State v. Dame*, 249 P.2d 156 (Wyo. 1952).

several reasons why courts frequently must interpret statutes before applying them, including the following: (1) Legislatures sometimes draft statutes with an element of "deliberate imprecision," intentionally giving courts a degree of latitude in applying the statute. They may do this because they legitimately recognize the difficulty of defining certain concepts in the abstract or because they want to avoid making a specific decision on a controversial political issue. (2) Even if a legislature tries to define all the key elements of a statute with great precision, the effort sometimes fails because some concepts are extremely difficult to define without reference to a specific set of facts. (3) The complex process of amendment and deletion as a bill goes through the legislature sometimes leads to a product that is less clear than the originally introduced bill. (4) The choice of particular language may have been the result of compromise among factions in the legislature, which sometimes leads to a lack of clarity. (5) At its best, language is imperfect, and few words are susceptible to but one meaning.

Therefore, in many cases a court must interpret a statute before using it as a basis for deciding a case. Even when a court asserts that a statute has a plain meaning, it often bolsters its conclusion by resorting to various interpretive aids. The aids or devices used by a court to ascertain the legislative intent may be grouped into several categories.

First, a court sometimes refers to a dictionary or other standard reference source. It is presumed that legislative bodies use words in their common, or-dinary sense, and a standard dictionary may be the best starting point to determine common English usage. If anyone claims that the legislature used a word in an unusual or technical sense, that party has the burden of proving it. General rules of grammar and punctuation are also usually followed unless there is a clear indication that the legislature in-tended otherwise.

Second, the court will examine the law's **textual context,** which involves reading the statute as a whole rather than concentrating solely on the language in question. Sometimes other language in that section of the statute, or perhaps similar language in another section of the same statute, may provide a clue as to what the legislature intended. This is simply an appli-cation of one of the cardinal principles of communica-tion—do not take words out of their context.

Third, a court might examine the statute's **legisla-tive history.** Comprehensive legislative histories are available for federal statutes, and less comprehensive histories are available for the statutory enactments of several states. A statute's legislative history may con-sist of several components. All bills are considered by one or more committees of the legislature, which hold hearings on the bill at which testimony and other evidence is presented by proponents and oppo-nents of particular positions. Sometimes a verbatim *transcript* of all the oral testimony, written state-ments, and other evidence is published. After the committee has held hearings and deliberated, it will vote on whether to send the bill to the full body (house or senate) with a favorable or unfavorable recommendation. The committee often prepares a written report to accompany its recommendation. Dissenting committee members may also write a mi-nority report. These *committee reports* are also part of the legislative history. Finally, the transcript of the *floor debates* when the entire body considers the bill forms part of the legislative history, as well. In the case of federal legislation, these transcripts are pub-lished in the *Congressional Record.* The legislative history, especially the hearing transcripts and com-mittee reports, can provide a wealth of information about the background and purpose of the law, the reasons for using particular language, how and why amendments and deletions were made, and other relevant matters.

Fourth, the statute's **circumstantial context** may be taken into account by a court seeking to discern the meaning of legislative language. This term simply describes the conditions or social problem that led the legislature to act. If, for example, the law was passed to fight organized crime, the courts will con-strue ambiguous language to help achieve that pur-pose. Evidence of the circumstantial context may be derived from several sources, including the legisla-tive history.

Fifth, a court will consider *precedent* when inter-preting a statute. Thus, prior judicial interpretations of the same statute, or of similar language in another statute, may be taken into account.

Regardless of the reason why a particular statute needs to be interpreted, and regardless of the partic-ular interpretive aids employed, the court's sole task is to do the best it can to determine the legislative in-tent. The court's job is not to improve on what the legislature said or to make the statute mean what the court thinks it *should* mean. Even though determin-ing what the legislature meant can be an elusive goal, the courts must do the best they can.

Box 4.1
The Law
at Work

As seen in the *Sedima* case in this chapter, Congress passed the federal racketeering law (the Racketeering Influenced and Corrupt Organizations Act, or RICO) for the purpose of providing better legal weapons against organized crime's infiltration into legitimate business. It includes extreme penalties both in criminal cases prosecuted by the U.S. Justice Department and in civil cases initiated by private parties claiming harm as a result of the defendant's RICO violation. To draft an effective law, however, the subject matter of the law must be reasonably definable. Organized criminal activity, using legitimate business as a front, has proved to be very difficult to

define. Because of definitional problems, the law has been used very little against "mobsters" but has been used extensively against truly legitimate businesses that arguably have violated some other state or federal law, such as the disclosure provisions of the federal securities laws.

Many bills have been introduced in Congress to solve the problems courts have had in attempting to interpret RICO. The content of these bills, none of which has passed so far, often reveals just how difficult it is to define organized criminal operations. For example, one recent bill proposed to adopt a so-called "gatekeeper" approach, which would empower the federal district judge to make several initial factual determinations before RICO could be applied. Under this bill, before RICO could be used, the

federal judge would have to reach a conclusion that the "magnitude" of harm caused by the alleged violation was great enough to make use of RICO "appropriate." The law could be used only against "major participants" in "egregious" unlawful behavior. Such a bill, like many others aimed at fixing RICO, would almost certainly create more problems of statutory interpretation than it would solve. RICO is one of those laws that focused on a serious problem and had admirable goals, but that turned out to be something of a "Frankenstein monster." The law may not be repairable, and may need to be repealed. Will most members of Congress be willing, however, to take the political risk of repealing a law that the public views as being targeted at mobsters? Only time will tell. 🔖

A final comment on statutory interpretation relates to the concept of *implied repeal.* Sometimes a party to a case will contend that some provision of a statute was implicitly repealed by later action of the same legislative body. The courts operate from a strong presumption against implied repeal; a court will find that a legislature intended to amend, repeal, or make an exception to an earlier statute only if the evidence of such intent is very clear. For example, in *Tennessee Valley Authority v. Hill,* 437 U.S. 153 (1978), the TVA, a federal government-owned corporation, was 80 percent finished with the construction of a major dam project on the Little Tennessee River when an ichthyologist from the University of Tennessee discovered a previously unknown species of "snail darter" in the river. At the time, this was the only known habitat of the fish, and there was no way of knowing whether efforts to transplant the species to another habitat would be successful. In accord with the federal Endangered Species Act, the Secretary of the Interior placed the snail darter on the

endangered species list. This statute required all federal agencies and departments to take all "action necessary to insure" that their programs and activities would not jeopardize endangered species or damage their critical habitats. A lawsuit was brought in federal district court seeking an injunction that would prohibit the TVA from completing the project because it would destroy the snail darter's habitat. The TVA claimed that Congress, by appropriating funds to the project for several years, had implicitly created an exception to the Endangered Species Act for "substantially completed federal projects." The Supreme Court invoked the presumption against implied repeal and held that if Congress wanted to create an exception to the Endangered Species Act it had to express its intent clearly. Applying the statute exactly as it was written, the Court affirmed the lower court's decision granting an injunction against the TVA. Not long afterward, Congress passed legislation specifically giving TVA permission to complete the project.

The next case, which involves the federal Racketeering Influenced and Corrupt Organizations Act (RICO), provides an example of a statute that has proved to be very difficult to interpret. Part of the reason for this difficulty is that the target of the statute, organized crime, cannot be defined easily. There is no doubt that the statute was aimed primarily at the infiltration of legitimate business by the Mafia and other organized criminal operations. However, in more than 90 percent of the cases in which RICO's civil liability provisions have been used, the defendants were legitimate businesses, including stock brokerage firms such as Merrill Lynch and Dean Witter, CPA firms such as Arthur Andersen and Price Waterhouse, banks such as Citibank and Continental Illinois, and manufacturers such as Boeing and Miller Brewing. The problem is that the severe civil penalties in RICO, including the automatic tripling of damage awards, were probably intended by Congress to be used only against "mobsters." To slow down the spate of RICO lawsuits, some federal courts interpreted RICO's provisions to require that plaintiffs show that defendants had been previously *convicted* of certain specified "racketeering acts." The U.S. Supreme Court was called on to resolve the meaning of the statute. As you read the opinion, identify which interpretative aids the Court uses. Also, take note of the Court's effort to not stray very far from the specific language that Congress used. In this case, as in a number of others, the Court is essentially saying, "This is what the actual language of the statute seems to say; if this isn't what the legislature really intended, we wish they would change the law and tell us exactly what they do mean."

Sedima v. Imrex Co., Inc.

U.S. Supreme Court, 105 S.Ct. 3275 (1985)

Case

Plaintiff Sedima entered into a joint venture with the defendant Imrex Co. to provide electronic components to a Belgian firm. The buyer was to order parts through Sedima; Imrex was to obtain the parts in America and ship them to Europe. Sedima and Imrex were to split the net proceeds. After Imrex filled $8 million in orders, Sedima became convinced that Imrex was inflating bills, cheating Sedima out of a portion of its proceeds by collecting for nonexistent expenses.

Sedima sued Imrex and two of its officers under the Racketeering Influenced and Corrupt Organizations Act (RICO). RICO contains both criminal provisions and the civil provisions that Sedima invoked. Sedima claimed that Imrex had by its presentation of inflated, fraudulent bills committed mail and wire fraud, which are "racketeering" acts within the meaning of RICO.

The trial court dismissed the RICO claims, and the Court of Appeals affirmed for the reason, among others, that the complaint was defective for failing to allege that the defendants had been convicted of mail and wire fraud. Sedima appealed.

White, Justice:

RICO takes aim at "racketeering activity," which it defines as any act "chargeable" under several generically described state criminal laws, any act "indictable" under numerous specific federal criminal provisions, including mail and wire fraud, and any "offense" involving bankruptcy or securities fraud or drug-related activity that is "punishable" under federal law. Section 1962, entitled "Prohibited Activities," outlaws the use of income derived from a "pattern of racketeering activity" to acquire an interest in or establish an enterprise engaged in or affecting interstate commerce; the acquisition or maintenance of any interest in an enterprise "through a pattern of racketeering activity"; conducting or participating in the conduct of an enterprise through a pattern of racketeering activity; and conspiring to violate any of these provisions.

Congress provided criminal penalties. In addition, it set out a far-reaching civil enforcement scheme, §1964, including the following provision for private suits:

Any person injured in his business or property by reason of a violation of section 1962 of this chapter may sue therefor in any appropriate United States district court and shall recover threefold the damages he sustains and the cost of the suit, including a reasonable attorney's fee. §1964(c).

The Court of Appeals found the complaint defective for not alleging that the defendants had already been criminally convicted of the predicate acts of mail and wire fraud, or of a RICO violation. This element of the civil cause of action was inferred from §1964(c)'s reference to a "violation" of §1962, the court also observing that its prior conviction requirement would avoid serious constitutional difficulties, the danger of unfair stigmatization, and problems regarding the

(continues)

SEDIMA V. IMREX CO., INC.

(continued from previous page)
standard by which the predicate acts were to be proved. . . .

As a preliminary matter, it is worth briefly reviewing the legislative history of the private treble damages action. The civil remedies in the bill passed by the Senate, S. 30, were limited to injunctive actions by the United States. . . .

During hearings on S. 30 before the House Judiciary Committee, Representative Steiger proposed the addition of a private treble damages action "similar to the private damage remedy found in the antitrust laws. . . . [T]hose who have been wronged by organized crime should at least be given access to a legal remedy. In addition, the availability of such a remedy would enhance the effectiveness of [RICO's] prohibitions." The American Bar Association also proposed an amendment "based upon the concept of Section 4 of the Clayton Act [i.e., the treble (triple) damage provision in the federal antitrust laws]."

Over the dissent of three members, who feared the treble damages provision would be used for malicious harassment of business competitors, the Committee approved the amendment. . . .

The Senate did not seek a conference and adopted the bill as amended in the House. The treble damages provision had been drawn to its attention while the legislation was still in the House, and had received the endorsement of Senator McClellan, the sponsor of S. 30, who was of the view that the provision would be "a major new tool in extirpating the baneful influence of organized crime in our economic life."

The language of RICO gives no obvious indication that a civil action can proceed only after a criminal conviction. The word "conviction" does not appear in any relevant portion of the statute. To the contrary, the predicate acts involve conduct that is "chargeable" or "indictable," and "offense[s]" that are "punishable," under various criminal statutes. As defined in the statute, racketeering activity consists not of acts for which the defendant has been convicted, but of acts for which he could be. Thus, a prior conviction requirement cannot be found in the definition of "racketeering activity." Nor can it be found in §1962, which sets out the statute's substantive provisions. Indeed, if either §1961 or §1962 did contain such a requirement, a prior conviction would also be a prerequisite, nonsensically, for a criminal prosecution, or for a civil action by the government to enjoin violations that had not yet occurred.

The Court of Appeals purported to discover its prior conviction requirement in the term "violation" in §1964(c). However, even if that term were read to refer to a criminal conviction, it would require a conviction under RICO, not of the predicate offenses. That aside, the term "violation" does not imply a criminal conviction. It refers only to a failure to adhere to legal requirements. This is its indisputable meaning elsewhere in the statute. Section 1962 renders certain conduct "unlawful"; §1963 and §1964 impose consequences, criminal and civil, for "violations" of §1962. We should not lightly infer that Congress intended the term to have wholly different meanings in neighboring subsections.

The legislative history also undercuts the reading of the court below. The clearest current in that history is the reliance on the Clayton Act model, under which private and governmental actions are entirely distinct. The only specific reference in the legislative history to prior convictions of which we are aware is an objection that the treble damages provision is too broad precisely because "there need *not* be a conviction under any of these laws for it to be racketeering." 116 Cong. Rec. 35342 (1970) (emphasis added). The history is otherwise silent on this point and contains nothing to contradict the import of the language appearing in the statute. Had Congress intended to impose this novel requirement, there would have been at least some mention of it in the legislative history, even if not in the statute.

Finally, we note that a prior conviction requirement would be inconsistent with Congress' underlying policy concerns. Such a rule would severely handicap potential plaintiffs. A guilty party may escape conviction for any number of reasons—not least among them the possibility that the Government itself may choose to pursue only civil remedies. Private attorney general provisions such as §1964(c) are in part designed to fill prosecutorial gaps. This purpose would be largely defeated, and the need for treble damages as an incentive to litigate unjustified, if private suits could be maintained only against those already brought to justice.

Underlying the Court of Appeals' holding was its distress at the "extraordinary, if not outrageous," uses to which civil RICO has been put. Instead of being used against mobsters and organized criminals, it has become a tool for everyday fraud cases brought against "respected and legitimate 'enterprises.'" Yet Congress wanted to reach both "legitimate" and "illegitimate" enterprises. The former enjoy neither an inherent incapacity for criminal activity nor immunity from its consequences. The fact that §1964(c) is used against respected businesses allegedly engaged in a pattern of specifically identified criminal conduct is hardly a sufficient reason for assuming that the provision is being misconstrued.

It is true that private civil actions under the statute are being brought almost solely against such defendants, rather than against the archetypal, intimidating mobster. Yet this defect—if defect it is—is inherent in the statute as written, and its correction must lie with Congress. It is not for the judiciary to eliminate the private action in situations where Congress has provided it simply because plaintiffs are not taking advantage of it in its more difficult applications.

[Reversed.] ◌◌

SELECTED STATE STATUTES

Before leaving the subject of statutory law, several widely adopted state statutes deserve brief mention.

Uniform Commercial Code

The **Uniform Commercial Code** (UCC) is especially significant to businesspersons because (1) it is a dramatic illustration of one way changes in law can occur in response to shortcomings that exist in prior law; (2) it governs numerous commercial law subjects; and (3) it has been adopted with little variation by all states except Louisiana (which has adopted only Articles 1, 3, 4, and 5).

Historical Background

At the beginning of this century, the growth in interstate commercial activity was hobbled by great variation in the commercial laws of the various states. This caused substantial planning problems for merchants and raised legal expenses as a cost of doing business to unnecessarily high levels. In 1941, the National Conference of Commissioners on Uniform State Laws and the American Law Institute joined forces to draft a single "modern, comprehensive, commercial code, applicable through the country." Most states have adopted the official 1962 version of the UCC, along with amendments in 1972 and 1978.

Coverage

The UCC consists of 11 "articles," or chapters. The 9 substantive areas of law covered by the code are found in Articles 2 through 9. (Articles 1 and 10 are merely introductory and procedural.)

Article 2, Sales, consists of 104 sections that govern virtually all aspects of the law of the sale of goods. Many provisions from the various articles of the UCC are discussed at pertinent points throughout this text. Article 2A, the first new article added to the UCC since 1962, regulates leases of goods. As of this writing, 9 states have adopted Article 2A. Wider adoption is expected to come in the near future.

Article 3, Commercial Paper, includes sections governing such matters as the rights and obligations of the makers of notes and the drawers of checks and drafts and the rights and duties of holders and endorsers of all types of negotiable instruments.

Articles 4 through 8 deal with more specialized situations, such as the duties that exist between depositary and collecting banks and the resolution of problems resulting from the issuance and transfer of bills of lading and other documents of title. Article 9 covers all kinds of secured transactions, which arise when creditors seek to retain a security interest in goods physically in the possession of a debtor.

Deceptive Trade Practices Acts

Most states have **deceptive trade practices acts,** which specifically forbid specified kinds of business misconduct. The typical act, for example, prohibits merchants from "passing off" (representing and selling) their goods or services as those of another; from representing used goods as being new; and from disparaging the goods or services of their competitors by false representations of fact. Additionally, the typical statute also prohibits such practices as advertising goods or services with the intent not to sell them as advertised, and the making of false statements concerning the reasons for, or the amounts of, price reductions. Such acts will be discussed in Chapter 9.

Business Organization Acts

All states have comprehensive statutes that control the formation, operation, and dissolution of various forms of business organizations. These will be studied in Chapters 33–40. For now it is sufficient to make just a few observations about these laws. In the area of general partnerships, there is substantial uniformity from state to state because virtually all states have adopted versions of the Uniform Partnership Act (UPA). The UPA has successfully accomplished the uniformity for partnership law that the UCC was meant to create for commercial transactions.

There is less uniformity for limited partnership law because some states' laws are based heavily on the Uniform Limited Partnership Act (ULPA) of 1916, others are based on the Revised Uniform Limited Partnership Act (RULPA) of 1976, and still others have adopted portions of a 1985 amended version of RULPA. Still, the states' laws are generally similar and moving in the same direction.

There is even less uniformity, however, in the states' laws governing corporations. Here, there is no *uniform* act, only two versions of a *model* act, the Model Business Corporation Act (MBCA) and the Revised Model Business Corporation Act (RMBCA). Many states pattern their laws after one of these two model acts, but most have felt free to introduce their own variations. Furthermore, many states pattern their corporate codes not on some version of the MBCA but on the Delaware Corporate Code. Delaware is the leading corporate law jurisdiction in the nation.

SUMMARY

Judge-made or common law is not as pervasive in the American legal system as it once was, but it still dominates several important subject areas. As cases in these areas are decided over the years, a substantial body of precedent builds up. A judge who finds relevant decisions from courts above him or her in the appellate chain should follow that mandatory authority. If the only existing precedents come from courts that could not review the judge's decision, they need only be followed if the judge finds them persuasive.

The heart of the common law is the doctrine of *stare decisis*, which provides that relevant precedents from earlier cases should normally be followed so that the law will have stability and predictability. However, the common law is also flexible; it can be adapted to changing societal conditions. Therefore, if the policy reasons underlying a particular common law rule have evaporated, that rule can be changed. The need to correct an injustice outweighs the need for stability.

In recent years statutory law has become increasingly dominant in most areas of our legal system. The Constitution specifies the areas in which the federal Congress can legislate, and reserves the other areas for the states. If the proper procedures are followed and the laws passed are not so vague that citizens are unable to conform their actions to the law's requirements, the courts will enforce those laws. The courts may also be required to interpret the laws, for a legislature can never foresee all the circumstances that might arise. Then the courts must discover the legislative intent and construe the laws in such a way as to attain the legislative purpose. To achieve this the court will use various analytic techniques, including a close examination of the textual context, the stated purpose of the law, and its legislative history.

KEY TERMS

Case law
Precedent
Stare decisis
Mandatory authority
Persuasive authority
Statute
Interpretation
Plain meaning rule

Textual context
Legislative history
Circumstantial context
Uniform Commercial Code
Deceptive trade practices acts

QUESTIONS AND PROBLEMS

1. Dissenting in *Taylor v. Allen,* 151 La. 82 (1921), Justice O'Neill wrote: "I have heard that lawyers in one of the Western states [say that a] precedent is a 'goose case.' The expression arose from the perplexity of a so-called 'case lawyer,' who was unprepared to advise his client whether he was liable in damages because his geese had trespassed on his neighbor's lawn. The lawyer said he had found several cases where the owners were held liable because their horses, cows, sheep, goats, or dogs had committed acts of trespass; but he could not find a 'goose case.' The distinction which he observed was that his 'goose case' was not 'on all fours.'" Explain what constitutes a "goose case." How does one avoid the problems of the perplexed lawyer in Justice O'Neill's story?

2. Maddux was injured when the car she was riding in was struck by a car driven by Donaldson, and almost immediately thereafter, by a second car driven by Bryie. When Maddux sued the two negligent drivers, the facts of the case were such that it was impossible to determine which of her injuries were caused by the first collision and which by the second collision. At the time of the suit, the Michigan common-law rule was that, in such a case, neither defendant could be held liable for any damages; accordingly, the trial court dismissed Maddux's action. She then appealed to the Supreme Court of Michigan, claiming that the rule of nonrecovery was too unfair to an injured plaintiff. Do you agree with this contention? If so, what do you think a better rule would be? (*Maddux v. Donaldson,* 108 N.W.2d 33, 1961.)

3. In a number of cases, the Supreme Court of State X had adopted the rule that a seller of land who overstated the *value of the land* to a prospective buyer was not guilty of fraud, even if he or she knew that the true market value of the land was much lower than the figure that he or she stated to the buyer. (In these cases, the reasoning of the court was that the value of any property is merely a matter of

opinion and that the buyer should realize this.) Suppose that a new case reaches the Supreme Court in which the buyer of land claims that the seller was guilty of fraud when the seller intentionally misrepresented the *rental value* of the property (seller told buyer, an out-of-state resident who had never seen the land, that "it can readily be rented for $100 a month," a statement that proved to be false). If the Supreme Court felt that the seller in such a case should be made to pay damages on the theory that he *was* guilty of fraud, would the court have to overrule the prior decisions, or do you think the facts of the new case are sufficiently different to permit the court simply to apply a different rule to it? Explain your reasoning. (*Cahill v. Readon,* 273 P. 653, 1928.)

4. A student demonstrator and four labor pickets were convicted in the Hamilton County Municipal Court, Ohio, of violating a Cincinnati ordinance making it a criminal offense for three or more persons to assemble on a sidewalk "and there conduct themselves in a manner annoying to persons passing by." On appeal to the U.S. Supreme Court, the five contended that the ordinance was unconstitutionally vague (that it was so vague that it violated the due process clause). Do you agree with this contention? Discuss. (*Coates v. Cincinnati,* 402 U.S. 611, 1971.)

5. The City of Petersburg had maintained a cemetery for more than 100 years when it decided to move some of the bodies onto a 1.1-acre tract adjacent to the cemetery so that a road running in front of the cemetery could be widened. The Temples owned a home directly across the street from the 1.1-acre tract. They sued to prevent the bodies from being moved onto the tract, citing a state statute which said: "No cemetery shall be hereafter established within the corporate limits of any town; nor shall any cemetery be established within 250 yards of any residence without the consent of the owner of such residence." Can the city take the proposed action? Discuss. (*Temple v. City of Petersburg,* 29 S.E.2d 357, Va. 1944.)

6. Johnson, a teenage boy living in North Carolina, owned a motorcycle. After the motorcycle's original headlight became very weak, he and a friend taped a five-cell flashlight to the handlebars, and that evening, with both boys on the motorcycle, they had a collision with an automobile. In ensuing litigation, the car owner pointed out that a North Carolina statute required every motorcycle to have a "headlamp," and he contended that the flashlight was not a headlamp. If you were a judge on the North Carolina Supreme Court hearing the case on appeal, what steps would you take in deciding whether the flashlight was a headlamp under the statute? What would be the result? (*Bigelow v. Johnson,* 277 S.E.2d 347, 1981.)

7. In 1885 Congress passed a statute which provided: "[I]t shall be unlawful for any person, company, partnership, or corporation, in any manner whatsoever, to prepay the transportation, or in any way assist or encourage the importation or migration of any alien or aliens . . . into the United States . . . under contract or agreement . . . made previous to the importation or migration of such alien or aliens, . . . to perform labor or service of any kind in the United States." In 1887 the Holy Trinity Church of New York City made a contract with Warren, a pastor then living in England, under the terms of which he was employed to serve as its pastor. Pursuant to that contract, Warren immigrated to the United States and assumed his pastoral duties. The church was soon charged with violating the quoted statute. Did Congress intend the statute to cover this case? Discuss. (*Holy Trinity Church v. United States,* 143 U.S. 457, 1892.)

8. A city ordinance required that operators of coin-operated amusement machines be licensed and provided that the chief of police was to determine whether an applicant had any "connections with criminal elements." The city manager, after receiving the report of the chief of police and reports from the building inspector and the city planner, would then decide whether to issue the license. (If the application was denied, the applicant could then petition the city council for a license.) In a legal case brought by a rejected applicant, the contention was made that the licensing ordinance was *unconstitutionally vague* because of the "connections with criminal elements" language. Do you think this contention is correct? Why or why not? (*City of Mesquite v. Aladdin's Castle, Inc.,* 102 S.Ct. 1070, 1982.)

Chapter 5

Constitutional Law

Organization of the Federal Government

Authority of Federal and State Governments

Protecting Basic Rights

THE MOST IMPORTANT SINGLE document in the United States and, arguably, the world, is the U.S. Constitution. This document is the foundation of our democratic system of government and the basis of our many freedoms. Although drafted in a simpler time, the Constitution has evolved over the past 200 years to keep pace with changes in American society. Partly through amendment, but more importantly through flexible Supreme Court interpretations, the Constitution has remained as vital and timely as it was when originally written.

Few areas of the law can be studied without reference to the Constitution. For example, Chapter 2 discussed the structure of the federal court system, which is established in the Constitution, as well as the exercise of personal jurisdiction by state and federal courts, which is constrained by the Constitution's due process provisions. The Constitution governs the ability of the government to intervene in business activities; for example, Chapter 6 points out that the government's power to conduct inspections and searches of business firms is limited by the Fourth Amendment of the Constitution. The Constitution contains several protections for defendants charged with crimes, as discussed in Chapter 7. The Constitutional right to freedom of speech affects the principles of defamation law discussed in Chapter 8 and the rules of trademark and copyright law discussed in Chapter 9. Although not everyone realizes this fact, the Constitution has at least as much relevance to the operation of business enterprises as it does to the personal affairs of individuals. Our discussion of constitutional law in this chapter is fairly broad, but it will emphasize the role the Constitution plays in both empowering the government to regulate business and placing limits on the exercise of these regulatory powers.

Before turning to a discussion of the U.S. Constitution, it bears mentioning that every state in this country also has a constitution. These documents include many provisions similar to those found in the federal Constitution, such as those separating state governments into three branches and protecting fundamental liberties. Most state constitutions are much more detailed than the U.S. Constitution. A state constitutional provision is the supreme law within that state, unless it conflicts with the U.S. Constitution or some other federal law.

The U.S. Constitution contains three general categories of provision:

1. It prescribes the basic organization of the federal government into legislative, executive, and judicial branches.

2. It delineates the authority of the federal government, in contrast with the states, by granting specific powers to the three branches of the federal government.

3. It protects certain basic rights of individuals and businesses by placing limitations on federal and state governmental power.

ORGANIZATION OF THE FEDERAL GOVERNMENT

One major function of the Constitution is to establish the basic organization of the federal government into legislative, executive, and judicial branches. The essential function of the legislative branch, Congress, is to make laws, as well as to collect revenue and appropriate funds for carrying out those laws.

The main function of the executive branch is to enforce these laws; however, the executive branch also plays the primary role in conducting foreign relations and directing our military forces. The basic task of the judicial branch is to decide how particular laws should be applied to actual disputed cases.

Separation of Powers

As a general proposition, each branch of the federal government is supposed to exercise only those types of powers expressly given to it by the Constitution. Stated somewhat differently, one branch generally is not supposed to encroach on the powers of another branch. The doctrine of **separation of powers** is, however, a flexible one that is subject to various exceptions based on practicality.

Checks and Balances

To begin with, the Constitution expressly provides for a number of "checks and balances" to insure against any single branch of government developing an excessive degree of power. Examples include the requirement that the president sign legislation passed by Congress (the executive veto power) and the ability of Congress to override a presidential veto by a two-thirds vote in both houses.

Judicial Review

Another type of permissible interplay among the three branches of government is *judicial review*. Although this could be characterized as another form of "check and balance," the concept of judicial review is not expressed in the Constitution. During the early days of the Republic, the question of which branch had ultimate authority to determine constitutional issues was unsettled. In *Marbury v. Madison*, 5 U.S. 137 (1803), the U.S. Supreme Court assumed this power for the judicial branch of government. Because of the practicality and logic of placing this task in the hands of the federal courts and because of the stature of Chief Justice John Marshall, the author of the opinion in *Marbury*, the doctrine of judicial review is generally accepted without question today. Under the principle of judicial review, the federal courts have the final say in deciding whether the Constitution has been violated by a congressional law or executive action. It is no exaggeration to say that "the Constitution means what the Supreme Court says it means." (Although not involving a federal separation of powers question, it also should be noted that the doctrine of judicial review later expanded to include the power of the federal courts to determine whether actions of *state* courts, legislatures, and executive officials violate the U.S. Constitution.[1])

Reasonable Overlap of Functions

It is sometimes necessary for one branch of government to engage in an activity that closely resembles the type of function that the Constitution has assigned to another branch of government. For example, in providing for the implementation of many of its regulatory laws, Congress has found it necessary to give judicial-like powers to government agencies that are not part of the federal judiciary. These agencies may be part of the executive branch, such as the Social Security Administration (part of the Department of Health and Human Services), or they may be relatively independent of the executive branch, such as the Securities and Exchange Commission. In any event, such an agency frequently performs an adjudicative type of function, that is, deciding whether an individual meets the requirements for Social Security disability benefits or whether a corporation has made misleading statements in connection with the issuance of stocks or bonds. Similarly, Congress sometimes has to exercise investigative powers that traditionally have been considered executive in nature. Also, the federal courts engage in a form of "lawmaking" when they interpret provisions of the Constitution and federal statutes.

There are many other examples of situations in which one branch, to effectively carry out its primary role, may find it necessary to perform tasks similar to those of another branch. Performing such a "borrowed" function is permissible under the separation of powers doctrine so long as (1) it is reasonably necessary and incidental to the primary functions of that branch of government, and (2) the power of one branch is not substantially enlarged at the expense of another branch.

Especially in recent years, the U.S. Supreme Court has not seemed to be greatly concerned about most exercises of judicial-like powers by Congress or the executive branch, so long as they are based on good reasons and are reasonably limited. However, the court has tended to scrutinize legislative–executive overlaps more closely. For example, in *Bowsher v. Synar*, 478 U.S. 714 (1986), the Supreme Court decided a legal challenge brought against the so-called Gramm-Rudman Act of 1985, which established an automatic process for reducing the federal budget deficit. Under the statute, after a rather complex process the Comptroller General essentially determined the amount to be cut from the next year's budget. The Comptroller General is an employee of Congress and thus is part of the legislative branch. The Supreme Court concluded that this aspect of the Gramm-Rudman Act violated the separation of powers doctrine because budget execution is an executive power. This was not an appropriation of funds, which is a congressional power; to be valid exercise of the legislative appropriation power, the action would have had to go through the normal voting process in

---

[1] In a similar vein, it also has come to be an accepted principle in our law that state courts have the power to determine whether state legislative or executive actions are valid under that particular state's constitution. Moreover, state courts have power to review state legislative and executive actions for conformity to the U.S. Constitution, subject only to possible ultimate review by the U.S. Supreme Court. This power of state courts to apply the U.S. Constitution to state legislature and executive actions, is, of course, an example of concurrent state–federal subject matter jurisdiction, as discussed in Chapter 2.

both houses of Congress. The Court was of the opinion that there was too great an encroachment by Congress on the power of the executive branch. (Congress later amended the law to place the budget reduction power in the executive branch.)

Delegation of Powers

The final category of exception to the separation of powers doctrine is found in the principle that Congress may expressly delegate legislative powers to the other two branches. Congress often delegates rule-making powers, for example, to federal administrative agencies that are outside the legislative branch. For example, in the Securities Exchange Act of 1934, Congress prohibited fraudulent and deceptive practices in connection with the sale of securities and delegated to the Securities and Exchange Commission the power to make rules specifying in more detail the types of conduct that would violate this prohibition. Congress also has delegated certain rule-making powers to the federal courts, namely, the limited power to prescribe rules of procedure and evidence. Express delegations of legislative power are normally valid so long as Congress (1) indicates the basic policy objectives it is seeking to achieve and (2) provides some degree of guidance as to how the power is to be exercised.[2]

AUTHORITY OF FEDERAL AND STATE GOVERNMENTS

A second major function of the U.S. Constitution is to delineate the authority of the federal government, in contrast with that of the states. In our dual system of sovereignty, there are 51 primary governments—the federal government and the 50 state governments. When the original 13 colonies ratified the Constitution, they agreed to cede certain important sovereign powers to the federal government; as other states were added they similarly agreed. Under our system of federalism, the federal government has those powers that are specifically given to it in the Constitution—the so-called **delegated powers** (or *enumerated powers*). Those powers not granted to the federal government continue to reside with the states—the so-called **reserved powers.**

Our discussion of federal authority will focus on

the power of Congress and primarily on the power of that federal legislative body to regulate business activities. Article I, section 8 of the Constitution spells out the powers of the U.S. Congress, the most important of which include the power:

To lay and collect Taxes, Duties, Imposts and Excises, to pay the Debts and provide for the common Defense and general Welfare of the United States; . . .

To borrow Money on the Credit of the United States;

To regulate Commerce with foreign Nations, and among the several States, and with the Indian Tribes;

To establish an uniform rule of Naturalization, and uniform Laws on the subject of Bankruptcies throughout the United States;

To coin Money, regulate the Value thereof, and of foreign Coin, and fix the Standard of Weights and Measures; . . .

To establish Post Offices and post Roads;

To promote the Progress of Science and useful Arts, by securing for limited Times to Authors and Inventors the exclusive right to their respective Writings and Discoveries;

To constitute Tribunals inferior to the Supreme Court; . . .

To declare War, grant Letters of Marque and Reprisal, and make Rules concerning Captures on Land and Water;

To raise and support Armies, but no Appropriation of Money to that Use shall be for a longer Term than two Years;

To provide and maintain a Navy;

To make Rules for the Government and Regulation of the land and naval forces;

To provide for calling forth the Militia to execute the Laws of the Union, suppress Insurrections and repel Invasions;

To provide for organizing, arming, and disciplining the Militia, and . . .

To make all Laws which shall be necessary and proper for carrying into Execution the foregoing Powers, and all other Powers vested by this Constitution in the Government of the United States, or in any Department or Officer thereof.

State Police Power

In most circumstances, the lines of demarcation between the authority of the federal and state governments are quite clear. Most of the legislative powers delegated to the federal government under article I, section 8—such as the power to operate post offices and to maintain the various armed forces—involve such obviously federal powers that no state reasonably could claim to possess any regulatory authority over them.

By the same token, the powers reserved to the states are also relatively clear and well established.

---

[2]At the state government level, the same general principles typically are applied to the separation of powers doctrine and its exceptions.

Virtually all the powers of a particular state derive from the **state police power**—a term referring to the inherent governmental power to regulate the health, safety, morality, and general welfare of its people. Statutes relating to the operation of motor vehicles, the manufacture and sale of alcoholic beverages, and the regulation of crime obviously fall within the police power, because they are directly involved with matters of health, safety, and morals. Typical state laws based on the "general welfare" component of the police power are those that regulate such matters as marriage and divorce, the inheritance of property, and landlord–tenant relationships.

The power to enact zoning laws specifying restrictions on the use of real estate also falls within the state police power, but state legislatures normally delegate this power to their cities; thus, most zoning regulations are actually found in city ordinances or the regulations of city zoning commissions. In fact, state legislatures may delegate any part of the police power to local political subdivisions such as cities or counties. They also sometimes delegate very limited police powers to specialized political subdivisions of the state, such as port authorities, flood control districts, school districts, water supply and conservation districts, hospital districts, and so forth. Later, when we discuss limits that the U.S. Constitution places on state governmental powers, it should be understood that these limits are the same whether the state power is exercised directly by the state or is delegated to a local government entity.

Federal Power—The Commerce Clause

In examining the authority of the federal government, we are primarily concerned here with the power to regulate business. Although in many areas there is a clear delineation between the powers of the federal government on one hand and the state governments on the other, one area presents difficult problems—regulation of commercial activities. Despite the fact that the federal power to regulate commerce is very broad, the states also have a substantial amount of regulatory power over commerce. The dual nature of the power to regulate commerce has created many instances of state–federal friction. Seldom does a year go by in which the U.S. Supreme Court does not decide an important case bearing on the respective spheres of authority to regulate commerce.

Federal Regulation of Interstate Commerce

Article I, section 8 of the U.S. Constitution grants to Congress the power "to regulate Commerce with foreign Nations, and among the several States." Many provisions of the Constitution were aimed at preventing various kinds of provincialism and thus at making the United States truly "united." By giving Congress the primary authority to regulate interstate commerce, the **commerce clause** was intended to make the United States a common market, with the many economic advantages of trade that is unhindered by state boundaries. Before the adoption of the Constitution, economic "Balkanization" had plagued trade relations among the Colonies under the Articles of Confederation, the Colonies having erected various barriers to free trade among themselves.

By giving Congress the power to regulate trade with foreign nations, the framers of the Constitution recognized that the nation could not join the international trading community unless it could speak with one voice in maintaining international trade relations.

Until the late 1930s, the Supreme Court interpreted the commerce clause very narrowly with respect to the power of Congress over interstate and foreign commerce. The Court took the view that Congress could regulate a commercial activity only to the extent that it actually occurred *in the course of* interstate or foreign commerce. To the extent that an activity took place within the borders of a particular state, Congress could not normally regulate it, no matter how great the activity's ultimate effect on interstate or foreign commerce might be. Thus, under this older interpretation, Congress had no constitutional power to regulate manufacturing or other productive activities within a state; for example, it could not regulate wages, hours, or working conditions of manufacturing employees.

Beginning in the late 1930s, the Supreme Court took an almost 180-degree turn in its interpretation of the commerce clause. Since that time, the power of Congress in this area has been interpreted very broadly. It is still true that any commercial activity that actually crosses state or national boundaries is within the scope of the commerce clause. In addition, the regulatory power of Congress today extends to any activity that has "any appreciable effect" on interstate or foreign commerce, even though the activity took place solely within a particular state.

In the increasingly interdependent national and

international economy in which we find ourselves, most significant commercial activities have an "appreciable" (that is, meaningful or significant) effect on either interstate or foreign commerce. Today, most of our federal regulatory laws have been passed by Congress under this expanded commerce clause power. Examples include the federal laws regulating securities markets, workplace safety, wages and hours, and competition (antitrust laws). Indeed, Congress often uses the commerce clause as a constitutional foundation for enacting legislation even when its primary goal is not an economic one. Examples of this include laws aimed at protecting the environment and prohibiting employment discrimination.

"Commerce" includes almost anything remotely related to an economic activity, including manufacturing, advertising, contracting, sales and sales financing, transportation, capital-raising, and so on. Because the federal regulatory power encompasses *intrastate* commercial activity that affects interstate or foreign commerce, few local businesses can escape the reach of the federal government. For example, in *Wickard v. Filburn*, 317 U.S. 111 (1942), an Ohio farmer was limited by federal law to raising 11.1 acres of wheat. Farmer Filburn ignored the limitation and planted 23 acres. He fought a penalty assessed by the government by arguing that because he used much of the wheat he grew right on his own farm and sold the rest at an elevator a few miles away, he was not engaged in interstate commerce. But the Supreme Court held that the power to regulate interstate commerce includes the power to regulate prices. The purpose of the law in question was to support agricultural prices by limiting production. If all small farmers such as Filburn were viewed as beyond the reach of the act, the supply of wheat would no doubt increase and appreciably *affect* the price of wheat selling in interstate commerce. Congressional authority extended to Filburn.

More recently, in *McLain v. Real Estate Board of New Orleans*, 444 U.S. 232 (1980), a question arose whether a number of New Orleans real estate firms and trade associations had violated the federal antitrust laws by entering into several price-fixing contracts. The lower courts dismissed the action, ruling that the defendants' actions, which involved sales of land in New Orleans, were "purely local" in nature and thus not subject to federal law. The Supreme Court reversed, finding that the indirect effects of the defendants' activities were sufficiently related to

interstate commerce to justify application of federal law. This finding of sufficient effect—a "not insubstantial effect"—was based primarily on the fact that (1) significant amounts of money lent by local banks to finance real estate purchases came from out-of-state banks, and (2) most of the mortgages taken by the local banks were "physically traded" by them to financial institutions in other states.

Although there are very few businesses today whose activities are so completely local (intrastate) in nature as to be outside the power of Congress to regulate, it is important to note that Congress has not exercised all its regulatory power. The fact that an activity affects, or even directly involves, interstate or foreign commerce does not necessarily mean that Congress has chosen to regulate the activity. The power granted by the commerce clause, as interpreted by the Supreme Court, can be viewed as a reservoir of law-making power. In any given situation, Congress may or may not have drawn from that reservoir to enact legislation. The same is true of other powers granted by the Constitution.

In addition, when Congress decides to regulate a particular commercial activity, it sometimes chooses to exercise less than its full constitutional authority. For example, Congress might choose to include within a particular law only certain activities that actually cross state or national boundaries, even though it could regulate activities not crossing these boundaries because of their effect on interstate or foreign commerce. For instance, Congress has expressly exempted "intrastate offerings" of stocks and bonds from many of the document-filing requirements of the federal Securities Act of 1933, leaving the regulation of intrastate sales of new securities to the discretion of the particular state. Congress may choose to exempt certain activities in other ways, as well. Thus, the employment discrimination prohibitions found in Title VII of the 1964 Civil Rights Act apply only to employers whose businesses affect interstate commerce *and* who have 15 or more employees, thus exempting employers with a smaller number of workers. Similarly, other laws might expressly exclude from coverage businesses with assets below a certain value or transactions below a stated amount.

State Regulation of Commerce

Despite the dominant federal role, the states retain substantial authority to regulate commercial activities.

A state's police power permits it to protect the health, safety, and general welfare of its citizens. This power includes the authority to regulate commercial activities within the state, even if those activities have a substantial effect on interstate or foreign commerce and even if they originated outside the state. To give effect to the primary power of the federal government in these areas, however, the courts have developed several principles that limit the power of the states. These include preemption, discrimination against interstate commerce, and unduly burdening interstate commerce. Although different, all these concepts are closely related, and more than one of them may sometimes be at issue in the same case. (These principles also apply to state laws that affect foreign commerce—that is, international trade. Unless we say otherwise in this discussion, international commerce will be included within the term *interstate commerce*.)

Federal Preemption. The concept of **federal preemption** is a general principle of constitutional law that applies to any state–federal conflict. The doctrine of preemption is relevant regardless of whether a particular federal power comes from the commerce clause or from some other provision of the Constitution. However, we discuss the preemption doctrine in the context of the federal commerce clause power because it is in this context that most of the issues arise.

If a particular governmental power is exclusively federal, we say that there is federal preemption of this field of government activity. Federal preemption may be either express or implied, or it may result from a direct conflict between state and federal law. As we mentioned in the previous section, some federal powers in the Constitution are obviously of an exclusively federal nature, such as conducting foreign affairs, maintaining an army, and establishing a monetary system. The state governments have no power to act in such matters. In the case of other powers granted to the federal government, however, it may not be so obvious that the power is exclusively federal. When the Constitution gives the federal government a certain type of authority and a state attempts to exercise a similar or related power, the courts may have to determine whether there actually is federal preemption.

Express Preemption. When a preemption question arises, we begin with one basic proposition: the **supremacy clause** found in article VI, section 1 of the Constitution makes federal law the "supreme law of the land." The supremacy clause applies regardless of the specific source of the state or local law and regardless of the specific source of the federal law. The supremacy clause means, among other things, that if the Constitution gives a power to the federal government, the federal government also has the authority to prohibit the states from exercising a similar power. For example, the Constitution specifically gives Congress the power to enact patent laws that protect the creative work of inventors. When using this power to pass patent legislation, Congress can engage in *express preemption* by specifying in the legislation that the states have no power to adopt similar laws. If Congress exercises its authority expressly to preempt the states, no state can adopt a law that provides to inventors any legal protection for their inventions that is basically the same as the protection provided by the federal patent laws.

Although Congress has this power of express preemption, it usually does not use it. In fact, when passing a law, Congress often provides expressly that states retain the power to adopt similar or related laws so long as those laws do not conflict with or hinder the objectives of the federal law.

Implied Preemption. When Congress has chosen to regulate some activity but has said nothing about whether the states do or do not have power to pass related laws, a question of *implied preemption* may arise. For example, Congress has extensively regulated labor–management relations, as discussed in Chapter 49. Federal law establishes a framework within which groups of employees may fairly and democratically decide whether they want to form a union and, if so, which labor organization they wish to represent them in negotiating with the employer about wages, hours, and working conditions. The conduct of both employers and unions is closely regulated during this process. Once a group of employees decides to be represented by a particular union and the union is officially certified, the employer is under a legal obligation to bargain with the union in good faith. The objective of the regulated negotiation process is to achieve a collective bargaining agreement governing the rights and responsibilities of the employer and employees during the term of the contract. Suppose that, in State X, there has been a history of labor strife in a particular industry that is important to the state's economy. Strikes by employees and lockouts by employers have sometimes resulted, causing economic harm to the state. In response, State X's legislature passes a statute authorizing the state governor to issue an executive order ending a strike or lockout in that industry after a stated time period if the governor finds that serious harm is being done to the state's economy. Assume that, when the governor later exercises this power, a union or employer challenges the validity of the state law under which the governor acted. Because the federal labor–management relations laws say nothing about state authority to engage in similar regulation, a challenge to the state law is likely to be based on a claim of implied preemption. (The employer or union might also claim that the law places an undue burden on interstate commerce—this concept will be discussed shortly.)

When a claim of implied preemption is made, the one challenging the state law is asking the court to draw an inference about the intent of Congress—in other words, that party tries to prove that Congress implicitly intended to preempt the regulation of this general area. The challenger usually must prove two conditions before a court will conclude that implied preemption exists. First, it must be shown that the federal regulation is relatively *comprehensive*. In other words, the court must be convinced that Congress attempted to impose a fairly complete regulatory structure on this type of activity. Otherwise, it makes no sense to infer a preemptive intent on the part of Congress. This first condition is clearly met in the case of federal labor–management relations laws.

Second, it also must be shown that there is a very strong need for a uniform national regulatory policy in this area, so that individual state laws of this type are likely to interfere with the objectives of the federal regulatory effort. Most unions represent employees in several states, and many of the employers that negotiate with unions also operate in more than one state. Moreover, a group of employers may negotiate with one large union, and sometimes one large employer must negotiate with several unions. In other words, relationships between companies and unions generally transcend state boundaries, but the objective of a particular negotiation is a single contract. If these often-sensitive negotiations had to be conducted within a framework of several different sets of state regulations, it would be extremely difficult for the parties ever to achieve a collective bargaining agreement, and the collective bargaining agreement is the cornerstone of federal regulation in this area.

Thus, the second condition for implied preemption also exists. Because both conditions are met, the Supreme Court has concluded that the states are preempted from adopting laws dealing with the company–union relationship.

It should be noted that, even in a situation in which there is implied federal preemption, states still may protect important state interests by passing laws that are only peripherally related to the federally regulated area and that are not likely to interfere with the federal regulatory objectives. For example, despite implied preemption, an employee may be punished under state criminal or tort law for assault and battery or property destruction even though the wrongful conduct occurred during the course of a union-sponsored strike.

Direct Conflict. A much narrower form of preemption occurs when a specific state law is in *direct conflict* with a specific provision of federal law. In the labor–management relations setting, recall that there is no express federal preemption. For the sake of illustration, now let us also assume that either (or both) of the requirements for implied preemption were not met. What this would mean is that there is no federal preemption of this general field of regulatory activity, and the states could enact laws regulating company–union relations. However, if a particular state provision comes into direct conflict with a federal law, the state law is void to the extent of the conflict. Suppose that, even if there is no express or implied federal preemption, there is a specific federal statute that empowers the U.S. president to seek a federal court injunction ending a strike or lockout under certain carefully prescribed conditions. In such a case, the law in State X authorizing its governor to halt strikes or lockouts might very well be void because of a direct conflict with the federal law.

A state law is not void because of direct conflict just because the state provision deals with the same type of activity. Moreover, the mere fact that a state law is more stringent than a similar federal law does not make the state law void. For example, the fact that California law places stricter pollution control standards on automobiles does not mean that this state law is in conflict with federal auto emission control regulations. A state law is void because of direct conflict in only two situations. First, there is a direct conflict if it is impossible to comply with both the state and federal laws. An example of this would be a state law *requiring* wholesalers to grant quantity discounts to retailers in the state even in circumstances in which the discounts are not justified by any lower costs of selling in larger quantities. This state law would require conduct that violates the federal Robinson-Patman Act's prohibition of price discrimination.

Second, even if it is literally possible to comply with both laws, there nevertheless is a direct conflict if the state law substantially interferes with the purpose of the federal law. For example, suppose that when Congress passed the law giving the president authority to stop strikes or lockouts in certain carefully defined situations, it clearly indicated an intent to permit government interference in company–union confrontations only when national defense is threatened or when a national economic emergency exists. In such a case, the hypothetical law giving the governor of State X the power to stop strikes when economic injury to the state is threatened might be void for direct conflict because it interferes with objectives of the federal law.

It should be reemphasized that either type of direct conflict is really just a narrower form of implied preemption, with the preemption applying only to a specific state law and a specific federal law rather than to an entire field of regulated activity.

One final note on the concept of preemption is worth mentioning. In this country, there is a presumption *against* preemption. Thus, a court will normally find federal preemption only if Congress or a federal agency clearly expressed that intent or if the evidence of implied preemption or direct conflict is very strong. In the European Economic Community (EEC), however, the presumption is reversed. When the EEC adopts a regulation of some kind, there is a presumption that this law was intended to preempt related laws of member nations.

The following case illustrates the concept of implied preemption in the case of a federal regulatory system aimed at encouraging the use of American ports in international trade.

XEROX CORP. V. HARRIS COUNTY

U.S. Supreme Court, 459 U.S. 145 (1982)

 Pursuant to its powers under the commerce clause, Congress established a comprehensive customs system aimed at placing certain controls on the flow of goods into and out of the country, while at the same time encouraging international trade between the United States and other countries. For many years, federal customs law has provided for a system of "customs bonded warehouses" at various U.S. ports of entry. These warehouses are owned and run by private operators but are under the continuous control and supervision of the federal customs officials at that port. Ordinarily, imported goods are subject to a federal tax known as a "duty." However, under certain conditions federal customs law permits goods to be imported duty-free if they are stored in a customs bonded warehouse. The owner of imported goods is permitted

to store them in such a warehouse when they are intended for ultimate sale somewhere outside the United States—in other words, when the United States is just a stopover for goods that are destined for sale in some other country. Such goods can remain duty-free in the customs bonded warehouse for up to five years. If they are stored for more than five years or if the owner changes its plans and markets the goods within the United States, an import duty must be paid. Congress established this system for the purpose of encouraging the use of American ports as a stopover for goods in international trade when the owner finds it efficient to do so.

Increased use of American ports produces more economic activity in the vicinity of those ports.

Xerox Corporation manufactured parts for copying machines in Colorado and New York. These parts were then shipped to Mexico for

assembly. After assembly, the copiers were imported into the United States and stored in a customs bonded warehouse in Houston, Texas, while awaiting shipment to various destinations in Latin America. The copiers were designed especially for sale in the Latin American market; the machines operated on an electric current of 50 cycles per second as is common in Central and South America, rather than the 60 cycles per second that is standard in the United States. In addition, all printing on the machines and instructions was in either Spanish or Portuguese; thus there was no question about Xerox's claim that the goods were not intended for sale in the United States. (Until 1974, Xerox had shipped its Mexican-assembled copiers to the Free Trade Zone of Panama, where they were stored tax-free. In 1974, rising anti-American sentiment in Panama caused Xerox to look for another storage facility. It decided on

(continues)

XEROX CORP. V. HARRIS COUNTY

(continued from previous page)
the Houston customs bonded ware-house because of the excellent port facilities at Houston and its proximity to Latin America.)

Beginning in 1977, Harris County (where Houston is located) assessed local property taxes on Xerox's copiers in the customs bonded ware-house. (The city and school district also levied these taxes.) The taxes were nondiscriminatory—they applied to all goods in described categories for the period of time they were physically located within the county, regardless of where the goods originated or where they came from. The county did not place a tax directly on imports or exports as the goods entered or exited but instead based the tax on the physical location of the goods within the county for the duration of their stay. Thus, the local property tax was not automatically void under the constitutional prohibition against state or local taxes on imports or exports. Xerox filed suit in a state trial court in Houston, alleging that the tax measure was unconstitutional because it was impliedly preempted by the federal regulations setting up the system of customs bonded warehouses. The trial court ruled for Xerox, but the intermediate level state appellate court reversed and upheld the tax. The Texas Supreme Court refused to review the decision, and the U.S. Supreme Court agreed to hear Xerox's appeal of the federal constitutional question.

Burger, Chief Justice:

Government regulated, bonded warehouses have been a link in the chain of foreign commerce since "a very early period in our history." *Fabbri v. Murphy,* 95 U.S. 191, 197 (1877). A forerunner of the present statute was the Warehousing Act of 1846, ch. 84, 9 Stat. 53 (1846). A major objective of the warehousing system was to allow importers to defer payment of duty until the goods entered the domestic market or were exported. The legislative history explains that Congress sought to reinstate:

"the sound though long neglected maxim of Adam Smith, 'that every tax ought to be levied at the time and in the manner most convenient for the contributor to pay it;' [by providing] that the tax shall only be paid when the imports are entered for consumption . . ." H.R. Rep. No. 411, 26th Cong., 1st Sess. 3 (1846).

The Act stimulated foreign commerce by allowing goods in transit in foreign commerce to remain in secure storage, duty free, until they resumed their journey in export. The geographic location of the country made it a convenient place for transshipment of goods within the Western Hemisphere and across both the Atlantic and the Pacific. A consequence of making the United States a center of world commerce was that:

". . . our carrying trade would be vastly increased; that shipbuilding would be stimulated; that many foreign markets would be supplied, wholly or in part, by us with merchandise now furnished from the warehouses of Europe; that the industry of our seaports would be put in greater activity; [and] that the commercial transactions of the country would be facilitated. . . ." App. to Cong. Globe, 29th Cong., 1st Sess. 792 (1846) (remarks of Sen. Dix).

To these ends, Congress was willing to waive all duty on goods that were reexported from the warehouse, and to defer, for a prescribed period, the duty on goods destined for American consumption. This was no small sacrifice at a time when customs duties made up the greater part of federal revenues, but its objective was to stimulate business for American industry and work for Americans.

In short, Congress created secure and duty free enclaves under federal control in order to encourage merchants here and abroad to make use of American ports. The question is whether it would be compatible with the comprehensive scheme Congress enacted to effect these goals if the states were free to tax such goods while they were lodged temporarily in government regulated bonded storage in this country.

In *McGoldrick v. Gulf Oil Co.,* 309 U.S. 414 (1939), the City of New York sought to impose a sales tax on imported petroleum that was refined into fuel oil in New York and sold as ships' stores to vessels bound abroad. The crude oil was imported under bond and refined in a customs bonded manufacturing warehouse and was free from all duties. We struck down the state tax, finding it preempted by the Congressional scheme.

The Court determined that the purpose of the exemption from the tax normally laid upon importation of crude petroleum was "to encourage importation of the crude oil for [refinement into ships' stores] and thus to enable American refiners to meet foreign competition and to recover trade which has been lost by the imposition of the tax." The Court went on to note that, in furtherance of this purpose,

"Congress provided for the segregation of the imported merchandise from the mass of goods within the state, prescribed the procedure to insure its use for the intended purpose, and by reference confirmed and adopted customs regulations prescribing that the merchandise, while in customs bonded warehouse, should be free from state taxation."

The Court concluded that

"the purpose of the Congressional regulation of commerce would fail if the state were free to impose a tax which would lessen the competitive advantage conferred on the importer by Congress, and which might equal or exceed the remitted import duty." . . .

The analysis in *McGoldrick* applies with full force here. First, Congress sought, in the statutory scheme reviewed in *McGoldrick,* to benefit American industry by remitting duties otherwise due. The import tax on crude oil was remitted to benefit oil refiners
(continues)

XEROX CORP. v. HARRIS COUNTY

(continued from previous page)
employing labor at refineries within the United States, whose products would not be sold in domestic commerce. Here, the remission of duties benefited those shippers using American ports as transshipment centers. Second, the system of customs regulation is as pervasive for the stored goods in the present case as it was in *McGoldrick* for the refined petroleum. In both cases, the imported goods were segregated in warehouses under continual federal custody and supervision. Finally, the state tax was large enough in each case to offset substantially the very benefits Congress intended to confer by remitting the duty. In short, freedom from state taxation is as necessary to the Congressional scheme here as it was in *McGoldrick.*

Although there are factual distinctions between this case and *Mc-Goldrick*, they are distinctions without a legal difference. We can discern no relevance to the issue of Congressional intent in the fact that the fuel oil in *McGoldrick* could be sold only as ships' stores whereas Xerox had the option to pay the duty and withdraw the copiers for domestic sale, or that in *McGoldrick* the City sought to impose a sales tax and here appellees assessed a property tax. . . .

[The state appeals court decision is reversed; the tax is unconstitutional and thus void. Because of this holding, there is no need to address the additional argument of Xerox that the tax is, in practical effect, a constitutionally prohibited tax on imports.] ⚖

Discrimination Against Interstate Commerce.
Even when there is no preemption of any kind, a state cannot pass a law that discriminates against interstate commerce (or international commerce). Such discrimination interferes with the primary authority of Congress over interstate and foreign commerce, and thus violates the supremacy clause. States may not, for example, shelter their own industries from competition emanating from other states or nations.[3] Although states may act to preserve their own natural resources, they cannot do so by discriminating against out-of-state buyers. They also cannot require that business operations that could be conducted more efficiently elsewhere take place within the state. For example, a state could not require that shellfish caught off its shores be processed in-state before being shipped elsewhere for sale.

A state's intent to discriminate might be explicit or it might be inferred from surrounding circumstances. For example, in *Philadelphia v. New Jersey*, 437 U.S. 617 (1978), the state legislature of New Jersey explicitly prohibited garbage from being imported into the state. Operators of several landfills in New Jersey, as well as several cities from other states that had agreements with these landfill operators for waste disposal, challenged the law. The Supreme Court held that the law unconstitutionally discriminated against in-

terstate commerce; even a desire on the part of New Jersey to conserve landfill space was not a strong enough state interest to justify an explicit discrimination against the interstate transportation of solid waste. In its opinion the Court also distinguished the so-called quarantine cases, in which state quarantine laws had been upheld. The Court said that these laws, which forbade the transportation of diseased livestock or plants, had been held to be constitutional because they were aimed primarily at the act of moving the livestock or plants from one place to another, whether the movement was totally within the state or into it from another state.

Sometimes the circumstances may lead a court to conclude that a state intended to discriminate against interstate commerce even though the intent was not made explicit. As with any question of intent in the law, the court attempts to draw the most logical inference from surrounding circumstances. An example is *Hunt v. Washington State Apple Advertising Commission*, 432 U.S. 333 (1977), which involved a North Carolina law, unique in the 50 states, that required all apples sold in the state to have only the applicable grade under U.S. Department of Agriculture grading standards stamped on the crates; state grades were expressly prohibited. For many years all apples shipped from the state of Washington had been stamped with grades under that state's grading system. In all cases, Washington state grades were superior to the comparable federal ones. The state of

---

[3]Although it often may be unwise to do so, Congress does have the power to shield business in the United States from international competition.

Washington and its apple industry had spent decades developing the quality and national reputation of its apples. If they still wanted to sell apples in North Carolina, Washington apple growers would have to segregate apples intended for shipment there and package them differently, in addition to losing the competitive advantage of being able to use their well-known grading standards. North Carolina asserted that the law was adopted to protect consumers in the state from deception and confusion caused by multiple grading systems. The evidence was very convincing, however, that North Carolina was really engaging in economic protectionism by placing Washington apples at a disadvantage in the North Carolina market. The factors indicating an intent to discriminate against interstate commerce included (1) the complete lack of evidence that any consumers in North Carolina had ever been confused or deceived by multiple apple grading standards, (2) the fact that customers do not normally buy apples in the crates on which grades are stamped, and (3) the fact that the local North Carolina apple industry would clearly benefit from the Washington apple industry's increased costs of selling in North Carolina and its inability to use its highly reputed grading system. The law was found unconstitutional.

When a court concludes that a state has intentionally discriminated against interstate commerce, the state action is almost always void. It would be a rare case indeed in which a state could prove a sufficiently important state interest to justify such discrimination, because the interest could almost always be promoted by less restrictive means that do not discriminate in this way.

Most questions about state power over commerce involve attempts by a state to regulate the activities of business firms. However, if the state government itself actually becomes a *participant* in the market, the state has much more latitude. In fact, the Supreme Court has held that the general rule prohibiting discrimination against interstate commerce does not apply when a state or local government is a seller or buyer. For example, when a state or a city makes contracts for the purchase of goods or services, it may grant preferences to in-state companies or individuals. The same exception applies when the state is a seller. For example, in *Reeves, Inc. v. Stake*, 447 U.S. 429 (1980), the state of South Dakota owned a large cement factory, and during times of short supply state law required that a preference be given to in-state buyers over those from outside the state. The Supreme Court upheld the state's discriminatory policy.

Unduly Burdening Interstate Commerce. Another restriction on the power of the states to regulate commercial activities is that they may not unduly burden the free flow of interstate or international commerce. The concept we just discussed, discrimination against interstate commerce, involves a question of intent, whereas the concept of unduly burdening involves a question of impact. The two concepts are closely related, often both being raised by a challenger in the same case. Some of the same information will often be relevant to both types of claims. Despite their close relationship, however, the two concepts provide separate grounds for invalidating a state regulatory measure.

If a state law challenged on this basis is shown to hinder the free flow of interstate commerce in some way, the court uses a balancing analysis to determine whether the law is constitutional. The analysis is very similar to the balancing of competing interests that takes place throughout constitutional law and, indeed, throughout the law generally. To determine whether there is an undue burdening of interstate commerce, the court balances the local interest being furthered by the state law against the degree of burden it places on interstate commerce. In general, the stronger the state interest, the greater will be the burden that can be tolerated under the Constitution. Purely economic interests of a state are certainly legitimate, but such interests typically do not weigh as heavily as a state's interest in protecting the safety and health of its citizens or protecting them against fraudulent or other wrongful practices. In addition, some economic interests are stronger than others; thus, a state law aimed at preventing the spread of a citrus fruit disease that could wipe out a major industry in the state could permissibly burden interstate commerce to a greater extent than one aimed at protecting an economic interest of less magnitude.

The *Hunt* case discussed in the previous section also illustrates the undue burdening concept. There, the local interest did not weigh very heavily in the balancing process because there was no evidence to indicate that consumers actually had been deceived or confused by multiple apple grading standards, and the regulation would not have solved such a problem if there had been one. On the other side, the evidence demonstrated that the North Carolina law would impose substantial economic inefficiency on the selling of Washington apples in North Carolina. The Washington apple industry had developed substantial economies of scale in packaging, storing, and shipping its apples, and compliance with the North Carolina law would destroy much of these scale economies. In the *Hunt* case, the Supreme Court ultimately struck down the statute because it unduly burdened interstate commerce. Even though there was ample evidence to infer intentional discrimination against interstate commerce, the Court said that it was not necessary to make a ruling on that separate contention.

Another example is *Kassell v. Consolidated Freightways Corp.*, 450 U.S. 662 (1981), which involved an Iowa law that prohibited the use of 65-foot double-trailer trucks on its highways, while allowing 55-foot single trailers and 60-foot double trailers. States around Iowa all allowed 65-foot double trailers, but Iowa claimed that the law was a safety measure. However, statistics showed no relationship between truck length and accident rates. Instead, studies showed a strong positive correlation between mileage driven and truck accident rates. Thus, the evidence of a legitimate state interest was quite weak; in fact, the law actually worked against safety interests by requiring use of smaller trucks that would have to travel more total miles to deliver the same amount of cargo. However, interstate commerce was substantially burdened because trucks with the more efficient 65-foot double trailers either had to go around the state or unload onto smaller trucks when reaching the Iowa border. The law was found unconstitutional.[4]

Finally, many of the cases involving the undue burdening concept have challenged various state and local taxes on property items used in interstate commerce. Examples include state road use taxes on trucks used in interstate transportation, and state or local property taxes on items such as railroad cars, airplanes, barges on inland waterways, and shipping containers. As we saw in the *Xerox* case, a local prop-

erty tax was found unconstitutional because it was preempted by the federal law setting up a system of customs bonded warehouses. Usually, however, there is no federal regulatory scheme that preempts state or local taxes on the instrumentalities of interstate commerce. In most cases, state and local government entities do have the right to tax such items located or used within their jurisdiction. It usually is only fair that the owners should pay some type of tax to contribute to the cost of police and fire protection and other services they receive within the taxing jurisdiction.

Such a tax must be carefully designed, however, to avoid being stricken down by the courts. First, it is obvious that the tax must not discriminate against interstate commerce by being higher for items used in interstate commerce than for items used only within the state. Assuming that the tax is nondiscriminatory, the Supreme Court has held that such a tax must meet three additional requirements to avoid being invalid under the undue burdening theory. The tax (1) can only be applied to property or activities that have a substantial "nexus" (that is, connection) with the taxing jurisdiction, (2) must be reasonably related to the services provided by the taxing jurisdiction, and (3) must be "apportioned" so that the item is not subjected to multiple taxation in the various places in which it is used or located. This last condition, the requirement of apportionment, has been an issue in a great many cases. It basically requires a formula that bases the tax only on the degree of connection the item has with the particular taxing jurisdiction. For example, a state might apportion a property tax on railroad cars by taxing only a fraction of the value of the cars that corresponds to the average fraction of a tax year the cars are located in the state.

Regarding taxation, in *Japan Line, Ltd. v. County of Los Angeles*, 441 U.S. 434 (1979), the Supreme Court held that a local property tax could not be levied on an item owned by a *foreign* company or individual and used exclusively in foreign commerce. The items in question were modular shipping containers owned by a Japanese corporation. The nondiscriminatory property tax imposed by Los Angeles County was based on only the time the containers spent in that county and would have been valid if the containers were used in interstate rather than international commerce. For two reasons, however, the Supreme Court concluded that the tax unduly burdened international commerce and was thus

---

[4]After the *Kassell* case, Congress stepped in to provide a degree of national uniformity to the regulation of truck-trailer lengths on interstate highways and on other "primary" highways built or maintained with any federal funds. The congressional enactment, which applies to about 42,000 miles of interstate highways and 140,000 miles of other highways, requires states to permit double-trailer rigs with each trailer having a length up to 28 feet, an approximate total rig length of 65 feet. The law also requires states to permit such rigs to have a width up to 102 inches, with exceptions for particular highways specifically found to be too narrow for rigs of such width to operate safely.

unconstitutional. First, in the case of property owned by a foreign citizen, U.S. courts have no power to require the foreign jurisdiction to apportion its own taxation of the item; consequently, permitting a state or local property tax in this country would create a risk of subjecting the property to taxation on more than its total value. Second, such a tax might interfere with the ability of the United States to "speak with one voice" in matters of international trade.

Other State Limitations

At this point, two other constitutional limitations on the discretion of states are appropriately mentioned—the full faith and credit clause, and the contract clause.

Article IV, section 1 of the Constitution provides in part that "full faith and credit shall be given in each State to the public acts, records, and judicial proceedings of every other State," The import of the **full faith and credit clause** is quite clear: The courts of one state must recognize court judgments and other public actions of its sister states. Thus a business firm that obtains a valid judgment against a debtor in one state may enforce that judgment in the courts of any other state in which that debtor's property may be located. The requirement is, however, subject to two important limitations. First, if the court that entered the judgment originally did not have jurisdiction, the courts of other states are not obligated to (and will not) recognize the judgment. Second, if the judgment violates the public policy of the state where enforcement is sought, the courts of that state will not enforce it. For example, if a court in State A awards damages for breach of a loan contract that included a rate of interest that was valid in State A and the creditor then tries to enforce the judgment against the debtor's property in State B, where that interest rate is higher than allowed by State B's law, the courts of State B will refuse to enforce the judgment on public policy grounds.

Our Constitution's full faith and credit clause obviously has no applicability to the enforcement of American state or federal court judgments in other nations or to the enforcement in this country of court judgments from other nations. Similar principles are generally applied, however. Under customary international law, the doctrine of *comity* generally calls for the enforcement of another nation's court judgments, subject to the two exceptions for lack of jurisdiction and public policy. This doctrine and its exceptions

have also been embodied in a number of bilateral and multilateral treaties to which the United States is a party.

Article I, section 10 of the Constitution provides that "no State shall . . . pass any . . . Law impairing the Obligation of Contracts. . . ." The **contract clause,** which applies only to the states and not to the federal government, is intended to prevent states from changing the terms of *existing* contracts by passage of subsequent legislation. When a state passes a statute that might affect contractual obligations, it normally includes a "grandfather clause" specifying that the new law applies only to transactions entered into after the effective date of the law. This not only ensures compliance with the contract clause, but also makes the law fairer. However, even if a state law does have an effect on preexisting contractual rights and obligations, it does not violate the contract clause if the law promotes an important state government interest and interferes with contracts only to an extent that is reasonably necessary to further the state interest.

PROTECTING BASIC RIGHTS

The Constitution contains numerous provisions aimed at protecting individuals and businesses by limiting the powers of the federal and state governments to regulate our affairs. Many of our basic rights are guaranteed in the Bill of Rights—the first 10 amendments to the Constitution. Other protective provisions are found in the body of the original Constitution itself and in subsequent amendments.

Before we look at several of the most important rights-protecting provisions of the Constitution, two preliminary observations are necessary. First, by its express terms, the Bill of Rights applies only to the *federal* government and not to state or local governments. Nothing in the Constitution specifically prohibits the states from infringing freedom of speech, for example. However, the U.S. Supreme Court has used the Fourteenth Amendment's due process clause as a vehicle for applying almost everything in the Bill of Rights to state and local governments. The Fourteenth Amendment, which was passed in 1868 shortly after the Civil War, includes several provisions that expressly limit the powers of the states. As we will see later, one of these provisions—the due process clause—directly guarantees certain important rights. In addition, under the **doctrine of**

incorporation, the Supreme Court has concluded that the concept of due process includes many other basic rights. Thus, the Fourteenth Amendment's due process clause implicitly incorporates almost all the protections in the Bill of Rights and applies them to state and local governments. Among the many guarantees applied to the states in this way are freedom of speech, freedom of the press, freedom of religion, right to an attorney, privilege against self-incrimination in criminal cases, and freedom from unreasonable searches and seizures.[5] Although the doctrine of incorporation has always been very controversial among constitutional scholars, it is now so firmly embedded in our law as to be beyond question.

Second, it must be emphasized that the protective provisions of the Constitution are limitations on *government;* thus, these provisions apply only to governmental actions and not to actions by individuals or business firms. Thus, the Constitution's free speech and assembly provisions do not prevent a private employer from restricting the speech of its employees or a private university from banning a political rally on its campus. However, Constitutional protections apply when a governmental body either compels the private action or substantially participates in it or when governmental power is used to enforce the private action against others. For example, there is a violation of the equal protection clause of the Fourteenth Amendment when a private attorney in a criminal or civil case intentionally excludes potential jurors on the basis of race. The reason for the Constitution's applicability is that jury selection is such an integral part of a governmental process that the government is essentially a co-participant with the private attorney. Another example is found in the rule that a court—an arm of the government—will not enforce a private deed restriction that excludes those of a particular race from purchasing property in a subdivision on the basis of their race; to do so would violate the equal protection clause. However, the mere fact that a particular business or industry is subject to substantial government regulation does not turn the actions of the regulated business firms into governmental actions. For example, public utilities such as telephone

and electric companies are very closely regulated by the states, but their actions are not subject to the Constitution unless the government in a particular situation has actually compelled, substantially participated in, or enforced those actions.

Even though the Constitution does not prohibit private actions, a federal or state statute might. For example, racial discrimination by a private employer or restaurant does not violate the equal protection clause, but it does violate a federal statute—the Civil Rights Act of 1964. We will now turn to a discussion of several important Constitutional guarantees.

Privileges and Immunities

Article IV, section 2 of the Constitution states, in part, that "the citizens of each State shall be entitled to all privileges and immunities of the several states." The basic aim of the **privileges and immunities clause** is to prohibit states from discriminating against residents of other states merely because of their residency. Thus a state cannot prohibit travel by nonresidents within its borders, nor can it deny nonresident plaintiffs access to its court system. The privileges and immunities clause is yet another provision of the Constitution intended to prevent states from erecting barriers around their borders. The fundamental individual right (and also the national interest) that the clause protects from state infringement is that of moving freely among the states without being unreasonably disadvantaged because of the state of residency.

Like other constitutional guarantees, the privileges and immunities clause is not an absolute limitation on governmental power. A state law may treat residents of other states differently if the law protects a legitimate "local" (state) interest and does not discriminate more than is necessary. For example, because state universities are substantially assisted by the taxes that state residents pay, the charging of higher tuition for nonresident students does not violate the privileges and immunities clause. The balancing of a state's local interest against the national interest in individual freedom of travel is a familiar process; the form of the analysis closely resembles the process of resolving claims that state laws unduly burden interstate commerce.

The privileges and immunities clause is one of the few constitutional protections that applies only to individuals and not to corporations. Even though the privileges and immunities clause does not apply,

---

[5]The only two important guarantees in the Bill of Rights that the Supreme Court has held inapplicable to the states are (1) the right to jury trial in *civil* cases and (2) the requirement that a person be indicted by a grand jury before being tried for a criminal offense. The states are free to devise their own rules regarding these two matters; in fact, state constitutional and statutory provisions guarantee these rights in most circumstances.

however, a state's discriminatory treatment of companies incorporated in other states will often have a negative impact on interstate commerce and thus is likely to violate the commerce clause unless it furthers a legitimate state interest and is reasonably limited so as to discriminate no more than necessary.

The following case involves a privileges and immunities clause challenge to a state law in Alaska, in which the Supreme Court balanced the local interest against the individual and national interest, paying careful attention to whether the law was narrowly tailored to fit the state's problem.

HICKLIN V. ORBECK

U.S. Supreme Court, 437 U.S. 518 (1978)

Case

The Alaska legislature passed a statute in 1972 (known as "Alaska Hire") for the stated purpose of reducing unemployment within the state. The key provision of the statute required all employers engaged in specified lines of work to hire qualified Alaska residents in preference to nonresidents. The types of work related to construction of the Trans-Alaska pipeline after discovery of the huge North Slope oil field. To implement the law, persons who had resided in the state for a minimum of one year were furnished "resident cards" as proof of their preferred status.

Hicklin and others, the plaintiffs, were nonresidents who had worked on the Trans-Alaska pipeline for short periods until late 1975, when the law was first enforced. In 1976, when the plaintiffs were refused employment on the pipeline, they brought this action against Orbeck, the state official charged with enforcing Alaska Hire, contending that the law violated the privileges and immunities clause. The Alaska Supreme Court, by a 3-2 vote, upheld the law, and the U.S. Supreme Court granted the plaintiff's request for review.

Brennan, Justice:

. . . The Privileges and Immunities Clause . . . establishes a norm of comity that is to prevail among the States with respect to their treatment of each other's residents. . . . Appellants' appeal to the protection of this Clause is strongly supported by this Court's decisions holding violative of the Clause state discrimination against nonresidents seeking to ply their trade, practice their occupation, or pursue a common calling within the State. For example, [an early case in this Court] . . . recognized that a resident of one State is constitutionally entitled to travel to another State for purposes of employment free from discriminatory restrictions in favor of state residents imposed by the other State.

Again, [in] *Toomer v. Witsell*, 334 U.S. 385 (1948), the leading exposition of the limitations the Clause places on a State's power to bias employment opportunities in favor of its own residents, [this Court] invalidated a South Carolina statute that required nonresidents to pay a fee 100 times greater than that paid by residents for a license to shrimp commercially in the three-mile maritime belt off the coast of that state. The Court reasoned that although the Privileges and Immunities Clause "does not preclude disparity of treatment in the many situations where there are perfectly valid independent reasons for it, it does bar discrimination against citizens of other States where there is no substantial reason for the discrimination beyond the mere fact that they are citizens of other States." A "substantial reason for the discrimination" would not exist, the Court explained, "unless there is something to indicate that noncitizens constitute a peculiar source of the evil at which the statute is aimed." . . .

Even assuming that a State may validly attempt to alleviate its unemployment problem by requiring private employers within the State to discriminate against nonresidents—an assumption made at least dubious [by prior cases]—it is clear under the *Toomer* analysis that Alaska Hire's discrimination against nonresidents cannot withstand scrutiny under the Privileges and Immunities Clause. For although the Statute may not violate the Clause if the State shows [in the words of *Toomer*] "something to indicate that noncitizens constitute a peculiar source of evil," *certainly no showing was made on this record that nonresidents were a peculiar source of the evil [that] Alaska Hire was enacted to remedy, namely, Alaska's uniquely high unemployment.* [Emphasis added.] What evidence the record does contain indicates that the major cause of Alaska's high unemployment was not the influx of nonresidents seeking employment, but rather the fact that a substantial number of Alaska's jobless residents—especially the unemployed Eskimo and Indian residents—were unable to secure employment either because of their lack of education and job training or because of their geographical remoteness from job opportunities. The employment of nonresidents threatened to deny jobs to Alaska residents only to the extent that jobs for which untrained residents were being prepared might be filled by nonresidents before the residents' training was completed.

Moreover, even if the State's showing is accepted as sufficient to indicate

(continues)

HICKLIN V. ORBECK

(continued from previous page)

that nonresidents were "a peculiar source of evil," *Toomer* compels the conclusion that Alaska Hire nevertheless fails to pass constitutional muster, [because] the discrimination the Act works against nonresidents does not bear a substantial relationship to the particular "evil" they are said to present. Alaska Hire simply grants all Alaskans, regardless of their employment status, education, or training, a flat employment preference for all jobs covered by the Act. A highly skilled and educated resident who has never been unemployed is entitled to precisely the same preferential treatment as the unskilled, habitually unemployed Arctic Eskimo enrolled in a job-training program. If Alaska is to attempt to ease its unemployment problem by forcing employers within the State to discriminate against nonresidents—again, a policy which [itself] may present serious constitutional questions—the means by which it does so must be more closely tailored to aid the unemployed the Act is intended to benefit. Even if a statute granting an employment preference to unemployed residents or to residents enrolled in job-training programs might be permissible, Alaska Hire's across-the-board grant of a job preference to all Alaskan residents clearly is not. . . . [For these reasons,] Alaska Hire cannot withstand constitutional scrutiny.

[Judgment reversed.] ⚖

Freedom of Religion

The First Amendment contains two clauses protecting freedom of religion. It provides that "Congress shall make no law (1) respecting an establishment of religion, or (2) prohibiting the free exercise thereof." Although the establishment and free exercise clauses overlap (and sometimes even conflict), they clearly create two separate guarantees. Both guarantees provide that the government's role is to be one of "benevolent neutrality," neither advancing nor inhibiting religion.

Establishment Clause

A large part of the metaphoric "wall" between church and state arises from the **establishment clause,** which prohibits the government from establishing a state religion and, according to the Supreme Court, from financially supporting religion, becoming actively involved in religion, or favoring one religion over another.

The most controversial manifestation of the Supreme Court's view of the establishment clause is probably the "school prayer" case, *Engel v. Vitale,* 370 U.S. 421 (1962). The New York State Board of Regents had written a nondenominational prayer to be recited by students in school on a voluntary basis. The Supreme Court found an establishment clause violation, saying, in part, that "the constitutional prohibition against laws respecting an establishment of a religion must at least mean that in this country it is no part of the business of government to compose official prayers for any group of the American people to recite as a part of a religious program carried on by any government."

An attempt to circumvent *Engel v. Vitale* by institution of a "moment of silence" in the public schools "for meditation or voluntary prayer" was declared unconstitutional in a more recent case, *Wallace v. Jaffree,* 472 U.S. 38 (1985). The legislative history of the law in question made it clear that its primary purpose was to promote religion.

When a state or federal law is challenged as violative of the establishment clause, it will be evaluated by a three-pronged test. First, the court will ask whether the law has a secular (nonreligious) purpose. If there is no such purpose, the law is invalid. Even if the law has a secular purpose, the court will ask, second, whether its *primary* purpose is to advance or inhibit religion. If the answer is in the affirmative, the law is unconstitutional. If the answer is in the negative, the court will ask, third, whether the law fosters excessive government entanglement with religion. Such entanglement might include government evaluation of religious practices, extensive government involvement in church finances and operations, or government attempts to classify what is religious and what is not. Presence of such entanglement obviously indicates an establishment clause violation.

A recent establishment clause case affecting business is *Estate of Thornton v. Caldor, Inc.,* 472 U.S. 703 (1985), which involved a Connecticut statute guaranteeing every employee who "states that a particular day of the week is observed as his Sabbath," the right not to work on his or her chosen day. Because the law gave an absolute preference to the worker's religious practice, no matter how severe the hardship to the employer, the Court held that its primary purpose was to advance religion. Federal law validly requires that employers subject to Title VII, discussed in our later chapter on employment law, make "reasonable accommodations" for the religious practices of employees. But an absolute preference is invalid.

Finally, although the trend across the country is for states to repeal so-called *blue laws*—statutes and ordinances that limit or prohibit the carrying on of specified business activities on Sunday—such laws are generally upheld in the courts on the ground that the primary purpose of such statutes is the furtherance of legitimate social or economic ends, which affect religious beliefs and practices only incidentally.

Free Exercise Clause

The general thrust of the **free exercise clause** is to guarantee to all persons the right of religious belief and the freedom to practice their beliefs without governmental interference. The government may not single out any particular religion for discrimination. To claim the protection of the free exercise clause, a plaintiff must normally prove that he or she is a sincere adherent of an established religion and that a fundamental tenet of that religion is at stake in the case. These requirements weed out spurious, insincere, and trivial claims.

Under the free exercise clause, plaintiffs, frequently belonging to religious minorities, have paved the way for the religious freedoms we all enjoy. For example, in *West Virginia State Board of Education v. Barnette*, 319 U.S. 624 (1943), the Supreme Court held that a board of education requirement that students salute the flag and say the pledge of allegiance was unconstitutional as applied to the plaintiff, a member of the Jehovah's Witnesses. The court said: "If there is any fixed star in our constitutional constellation, it is that no official, high or petty, can prescribe what shall be orthodox in politics, nationalism, religion, or other matters of opinion, or force citizens to confess by word or act their faith therein. If there are any circumstances which permit an exception, they do not now occur to us."

To overcome the very important interest in free exercise of religious beliefs, the government must demonstrate that an unusually important interest is at stake (denominated in various cases "compelling," "of the highest order," or "overriding") and that granting an exemption to the plaintiff will do substantial harm to that interest. The government has succeeded in cases requiring vaccinations for children against their parents' religious objections in furtherance of public health, in cases requiring medical treatment for children over their parents' objections when such treatment was necessary to save the child's life, and in cases banning the handling of poisonous snakes in religious services.

Recently, the Supreme Court reduced the government's burden where incidental effects of government programs interfere with religious practices but do not coerce individuals to act contrary to their religious beliefs. In such cases, the government need not show a "compelling justification" to prevail. Thus, in *Oregon v. Smith*, 494 U.S. 872 (1990), the Supreme Court held that a state's interest in fighting drugs validated its decision to deny unemployment compensation on grounds of "misconduct" to two men who had been fired by a private employer because they ingested peyote, a hallucinogenic drug, for sacramental purposes at a ceremony of their Native American church. The balancing test approach was held inapplicable to an across-the-board criminal prohibition on a particular form of conduct.

Freedom of Speech

No right of Americans receives greater protection than freedom of speech. As with most other constitutional guarantees, the First Amendment's **free speech clause** has been expanded to limit not only the actions of the federal government but also the actions of state and local governments. Unlike citizens in so many other countries, we may freely criticize public officials and the laws of our government.

All methods of expression are within the scope of the free speech clause, including oral and written communications, and those recorded on tape, film, and so on. Moreover, *symbolic expression* is also protected. In other words, expression by nonverbal means such as wearing black arm bands or picketing is protected from government suppression. The giving of money to political candidates, charitable organizations, or various other entities is even treated as a form of protected expression. However, a government limitation of symbolic expression is somewhat more likely to be upheld than a limitation on verbal expression, simply because the conduct that constitutes symbolic expression is somewhat more likely to interfere substantially with some important public interest. If symbolic expression does not substantially interfere with an important public interest, however, it is fully protected.

The right of association is also viewed as a component of free speech. The groups and organizations we join often provide us with one of our most effective means of expressing our beliefs and opinions. Thus, a government limitation on our ability to associate with groups of our choice is a limitation on free speech.

Not only does free speech include the right to express oneself, but it also includes the right to avoid expressing opinions that we do not agree with. For example, in *Pacific Gas & Electric Co. v. Public Utilities Commission of California,* 475 U.S. 1 (1986), the Supreme Court overturned on free speech grounds an order of the California utility regulatory agency that had required an investor-owned utility to include in its billing envelopes a leaflet expressing the views of a consumer group with which the utility disagreed. The Court held that the agency's order unconstitutionally burdened the utility's freedom not to speak, a right that is protected because all speech inherently involves choices of what to say and what to leave unsaid.

Corporate Speech

In addition to protecting the speech of individuals, the First Amendment has also been interpreted to protect the expressions of corporations. This proposition was evident in the above reference to the *Pacific Gas & Electric* case. Corporate speech, like individual speech, has informational value—it contributes to the public debate on important issues. Thus, in *First National Bank of Boston v. Bellotti,* 435 U.S. 765 (1978), the Supreme Court struck down a state statute that prohibited expenditures by business corporations for the purpose of influencing the vote on state referendum proposals, unless a particular proposal "materially affected" the business or property of the corporation. The law was passed to silence the voice of corporations in the public debate over an upcoming referendum concerning a personal income tax. Because the referendum did not deal with a corporate income tax, it did not materially affect the business or property of corporations; thus the statute prohibited corporations from issuing press releases,

publishing advocacy advertisements, or otherwise speaking out on the personal income tax issue. The First National Bank of Boston wished to speak out because it felt that a personal income tax would harm the overall economic climate of the state. In overturning the law, the Supreme Court noted that "the inherent worth of the speech in terms of its capacity for informing the public does not depend upon the identity of its source, whether corporation, association, union, or individual."

Unprotected Speech

Although almost all expression is constitutionally protected, a few categories are not. If a particular type of expression is unprotected, this simply means that the government may limit or prohibit it without violating the First Amendment.

The first category of unprotected speech is *obscenity.* A local, state, or federal law that punishes the dissemination of obscene material is constitutional if the particular material to which the law is applied in a given case meets the Supreme Court's definition of obscenity. In *Miller v. California,* 413 U.S. 15 (1973), the Supreme Court held that, for a book, movie, or other material to be considered obscene, a court must determine that (1) "the average person, applying contemporary community standards" would find that the work, taken as a whole, appeals to the prurient interest; (2) the work depicts or describes, in a patently offensive way, sexual conduct specifically defined by the applicable law; and (3) the work, taken as a whole, lacks serious literary, artistic, political, or scientific value. Under today's community standards in most places, it is very difficult if not impossible to prove that most pornographic material is obscene. When pornography involves children or when children are exposed to such material, however, there is a much higher probability that it will be within the definition of obscenity.

A second category of unprotected speech is *defamation.* Thus it is constitutionally permissible for state tort or criminal laws to be applied to libel or slander—false statements that defame a person's character.

The third category of unprotected speech is a rather amorphous one commonly referred to as *fighting words:* threats, epithets, profanity, false alarms, and the like, which by their nature are likely to lead to violence. Their minimal social value is viewed as being outweighed by the danger to civilized society. This unprotected category of speech is narrowly construed, however; to be outside the scope of constitutional protection, fighting words must contain no significant informational content, must be apparently calculated to lead to violence, and must be made under circumstances in which actual violence is a very real danger.

Unpopular Views

The fact that particular speech is unpopular, or even highly offensive to many people, does not take it out of the zone of constitutional protection. As the Supreme Court said in *Cox v. Louisiana*, 379 U.S. 536 (1965), "Mere expression of unpopular views cannot be held to be a breach of peace." In fact, sometimes the government has an obligation to provide protection for those who express unpopular positions.

Many examples of government attempts to suppress unpopular views have been found unconstitutional. For instance, speech that is critical of the government, even to the point of being very disrespectful or "unpatriotic," is normally protected. In *Texas v. Johnson*, 491 U.S. 397 (1989), the Supreme Court struck down a state law making it a criminal act to "desecrate" the American flag. The Court invalidated the conviction of a communist protestor who had burned the flag at a Republican National Convention, saying: "If there is a bedrock principle underlying the First Amendment, it is that the Government may not prohibit the expression of an idea simply because society finds the idea itself offensive or disagreeable." Indeed, in *Brandenburg v. Ohio*, 395 U.S. 444 (1969), the Supreme Court held that even speech calling for the overthrow of the government is protected by the First Amendment unless it is "directed to inciting or producing *imminent* lawless action and is *likely* to incite or produce such action." This is really just another example of the narrowness of the "fighting words" exception. Among other reasons, providing constitutional protection for the expression of views that are unpopular, distasteful, or offensive to the majority helps to guarantee that the public debate on important issues will be as fully informed and undistorted as possible. The greater number of varied ideas (even bad ones) people are exposed to, the better equipped they will be to recognize worthy ideas.

Scope of Protection

Assuming that speech is protected, a court faced with a First Amendment issue must engage in further analysis to determine the scope of protection to which the expression is entitled under the circumstances. Although powerful, the right of free expression is not absolute and occasionally must yield in limited ways to other public interests.

Commercial Speech. A court must determine whether speech is commercial or noncommercial. **Commercial speech** is intended primarily to propose a commercial transaction. Advertising is the most obvious form of commercial speech. Until the mid-1970s, the general assumption was that commercial expression was not protected. However, the Supreme Court held that it is indeed protected in *Virginia Board of Pharmacy v. Virginia Citizens Consumers Council*, 425 U.S. 748 (1976); in that case, the Court struck down a state law that banned the advertising of prices for prescription drugs. A state law prohibiting advertising by lawyers was invalidated in *Bates v. Arizona State Bar*, 433 U.S. 350 (1977). A city ordinance forbidding the posting of "for sale" signs on real estate was found to violate free speech in *Linmark Associates v. Township of Willingboro*, 431 U.S. 85 (1977), despite the fact that the city had the laudable goal of preventing "white flight" from racially integrated neighborhoods.

According to the Supreme Court, commercial speech is protectable primarily because of its informational value. Prescription drug consumers in the *Virginia Pharmacy* case could not learn, before the advertising ban was struck down, that price variations of up to 600 percent existed among competing pharmacies.

Commercial speech is only protected if it relates to a lawful activity and if it is not misleading. Thus, commercial speech that either relates to an unlawful activity or is misleading could be listed as another category of unprotected speech. Although most commercial speech is protected by the First Amendment, it receives a lower level of protection than noncommercial speech. A restriction on commercial speech will be valid if the government can show that it is necessary to further a significant governmental interest and that the restriction is reasonably related to that interest. The following case is an important one in which the Supreme Court clarified this legal standard for restrictions on commercial speech.

BOARD OF TRUSTEES OF THE STATE UNIVERSITY OF NEW YORK V. FOX

U.S. Supreme Court, 492 U.S. 469 (1989)

Case

The State University of New York (SUNY) adopted a rule (66-156) for its dormitories that banned private commercial enterprises except to provide food, legal beverages, books, vending, linen supply, laundry, and a few other specified services. American Future Systems, Inc. (AFS), sells housewares such as china and crystal to college students by demonstrating and offering products for sale to groups of 10 or more prospective buyers at gatherings assembled and hosted by one of the buyers (for which the host or hostess receives some award). Fox, a student at SUNY's Cortland campus, was hosting one of these "Tupperware-type parties" when campus police asked the AFS representative to leave and arrested her when she refused to do so. Fox and other students sued, claiming that the rule violated the First Amendment. The trial court upheld the rule. The court of appeals reversed, noting that rule 66-156 was not the least restrictive means of advancing the state's interests. The Supreme Court granted certiorari and addressed the commercial speech issue in that portion of the opinion reproduced below.

Scalia, Justice:

. . . We have described our mode of analyzing the lawfulness of restrictions on commercial speech as follows:

At the outset, we must determine whether the expression is protected by the First Amendment. For commercial speech to come within that provision, it at least must concern lawful activity and not be misleading. Next, we ask whether the asserted governmental interest is substantial. If both inquiries yield positive answers, we must determine whether the regulation directly advances the governmental interest asserted, and whether it is not more extensive than is necessary to serve that inter-

est. *Central Hudson Gas & Electric Corp. v. Public Service Comm'n of New York*, 447 U.S. 557, 566 (1980).

The Court of Appeals held, and the parties agree, that the speech here proposes a lawful transaction, is not misleading, and is therefore entitled to First Amendment protection. The Court of Appeals also held, and we agree, that the governmental interests asserted in support of the Resolution are substantial: promoting an educational rather than a commercial atmosphere on SUNY's campuses, promoting safety and security, preventing commercial exploitation of students, and preserving residential tranquility. The Court of Appeals did not decide, however, whether Resolution 66-156 directly advances these interests, and whether the regulation it imposes is more extensive than is necessary for that purpose. As noted earlier, it remanded to the District Court for those determinations. We think that remand was correct, since further factual findings had to be made. It is the terms of the remand, however, that are the major issue here—specifically, those pertaining to the last element of the *Central Hudson* analysis. The Court of Appeals in effect instructed the District Court that it could find the Resolution to be "not more extensive than is necessary" only if it is the "least restrictive measure" that could effectively protect the State's interests.

Our cases have repeatedly stated that government restrictions upon commercial speech may be no more broad or no more expansive than "necessary" to serve its substantial interests. Our jurisprudence has emphasized that "commercial speech [enjoys] a limited measure of protection, commensurate with its subordinate position in the scale of First Amendment values," and is subject to "modes of regulation that might be impermissible in the realm of noncommercial expression." The ample

scope of regulatory authority suggested by such statements would be illusory if it were subject to a least-restrictive-means requirement, which imposes a heavy burden on the State. . . .

None of our cases invalidating the regulation of commercial speech involved a provision that went only marginally beyond what would adequately have served the governmental interest. To the contrary, almost all of the restrictions disallowed under *Central Hudson's* fourth prong have been substantially excessive, disregarding "far less restrictive and more precise means." . . .

On the other hand, our decisions *upholding* the regulation of commercial speech cannot be reconciled with a requirement of least restrictive means. In *Posadas*, for example, where we sustained Puerto Rico's blanket ban on promotional advertising of casino gambling to Puerto Rican residents, we did not first satisfy ourselves that the governmental goal of deterring casino gambling could not adequately have been served (as the appellant contended) "not by suppressing commercial speech that might *encourage* such gambling, but by promulgating additional speech designed to *discourage* it." Rather, we said that it was "up to the legislature to decide" that point, so long as its judgment was reasonable. Similarly, in *Metromedia, Inc. v. San Diego*, 453 U.S., at 513, where we upheld San Diego's complete ban of off-site billboard advertising, we did not inquire whether any less restrictive measure (for example, controlling the size and appearance of the signs) would suffice to meet the City's concerns for traffic safety and esthetics. It was enough to conclude that the ban was "perhaps the only effective approach." . . .

What our decisions require is a "fit between the legislature's ends and the means chosen to accomplish those ends," a fit that is not necessarily

(continues)

BOARD OF TRUSTEES OF THE STATE UNIVERSITY OF NEW YORK v. FOX

(continued from previous page)
perfect, but reasonable; that represents not necessarily the single best disposition but one whose scope is "in proportion to the interest served"; that employs not necessarily the least restrictive means but, as we have put it in the other contexts discussed above, a means narrowly tailored to achieve the desired objective. Within those bounds we leave it to governmental decisionmakers to judge what manner of regulation may best be employed.

We reject the contention that the test we have described is overly permissive. Here we require the government goal to be substantial, and the cost to be carefully calculated. Moreover, since the State bears the burden of justifying its restrictions, it must affirmatively establish the reasonable fit we require. By declining to impose, in addition, a least-restrictive-means requirement, we take account of the difficulty of establishing with precision the point at which restrictions become more extensive than their objective requires, and provide the legislative and executive branches needed leeway in a field (commercial speech) "traditionally subject to governmental regulation." Far from eroding the essential protections of the First Amendment, we think this disposition strengthens them. To require a parity of constitutional protection for commercial and noncommercial speech alike could invite dilution, simply by a leveling process, of the force of the Amendment's guarantee with respect to the latter kind of speech.

[Reversed.]

Noncommercial Speech. If a court determines that particular expression is noncommercial in nature, the degree of constitutional protection is considerably greater than it is for commercial speech. Often the courts use the term *political speech* to refer to noncommercial expression. It should be understood that when the term *political speech* is used, it includes virtually all noncommercial speech—the term is not limited to discussion of political issues.

When noncommercial speech is at issue, a court first must determine whether the restriction merely limits the *time, place, or manner* of expression. (Here, *manner* essentially means *method.*) A governmental body is entitled to place reasonable limits on the time, place, or manner of speech. A time, place, or manner restriction is not based on the content of the expression. For such a restriction to be valid, the government must show that it is necessary to further a significant governmental interest and that the restriction is reasonably related to that interest. Thus, a time, place, or manner restriction on noncommercial speech must meet the same requirements as a restriction on commercial speech. In both cases, the government's burden of justifying the limitation is not extremely difficult. There are countless examples of valid time, place, or manner restrictions. For example, even though I may have a constitutional right to express any view on virtually any subject, a city government has the power to forbid me from expressing my views in the middle of a downtown intersection during rush hour or by means of a sound truck in a residential neighborhood at 3:00 A.M.

Although it often may be obvious that a particular government restriction relates only to the time, place, or manner of expression and not to the content of that expression, sometimes the distinction can be difficult. Suppose, for example, that a statute passed by Congress forbids persons from carrying signs or banners within 500 feet of a foreign embassy in Washington, D.C., if those signs "hold the particular foreign government up to public opprobrium" (that is, scorn or contempt). One might argue that this is merely a time, place, or manner restriction, because it only applies to the area within a 500-foot radius around the embassy. In *Boos v. Barry,* 485 U.S. 312 (1988), however, this statute was treated as a limitation on content and not merely on time, place, or manner. There were two reasons for this conclusion, either of which would have been sufficient: (1) 500 feet was so far away that it would have placed protestors on the other side of the next block, thus completely foreclosing them from their intended audience; and (2) the statute specifically targeted the content of the signs or banners—those expressing disapproval of the foreign government. Thus, if government limits the time, place, or manner of expression in such a way that those wishing to communicate find it either impossible or extremely difficult to reach the intended audience, the restriction will be viewed as one that limits content of expression. The same is true of a restriction that superficially seems to be a mere time, place, or manner restriction, but which, in fact, is tied to the content of the affected expressions.

The greatest degree of constitutional protection is given to *content-based* restrictions on noncommercial speech—restrictions that are based on what is said. When the government attempts to impose a content-based limitation on noncommercial speech, it must bear a very heavy burden of justification. The restriction must be necessary to protect a "compelling" government interest—one that is of extreme importance to society—and the restriction must be "narrowly tailored" to limit expression only to the extent needed to further the government interest. Several examples of compelling government interest are the needs to preserve security and order in prisons, prevent disruptions in public schools, maintain a quiet and reflective environment at the place where election votes are cast, maintain discipline in the armed forces, efficiently and effectively manage the work force at a government agency, protect the national security, and protect the security of a foreign embassy in the United States.

Even if a compelling interest is involved, however, the narrow tailoring requirement can be very difficult for the government to satisfy. For example, in the *Boos v. Barry* case mentioned earlier, the asserted government interest was protecting the security of foreign embassies in Washington, D.C., which is a compelling interest. The statute prohibiting people from negative picketing within 500 feet of embassies was found unconstitutional, however, because the government was unable to demonstrate that the restriction was essential to the security of the embassies. Although prohibiting signs with negative messages around embassies might protect foreign embassy officials from being offended, this is merely a legitimate interest and not a truly compelling one.

Although most content-based restrictions on speech violate the Constitution, one type of content-based limitation is even more likely to be void than others. A content-based restriction that is also *viewpoint discriminatory*—one that favors or disfavors a particular viewpoint—can almost never be justified by the government.

Figure 5.1 summarizes the analytical process employed to resolve questions under the free speech clause.

Equal Protection

The Fourteenth Amendment was passed in 1868, shortly after the Civil War. It states, in part, that "no State shall . . . deny to any person within its jurisdiction the equal protection of the laws." Although no provision of the Constitution explicitly mentions

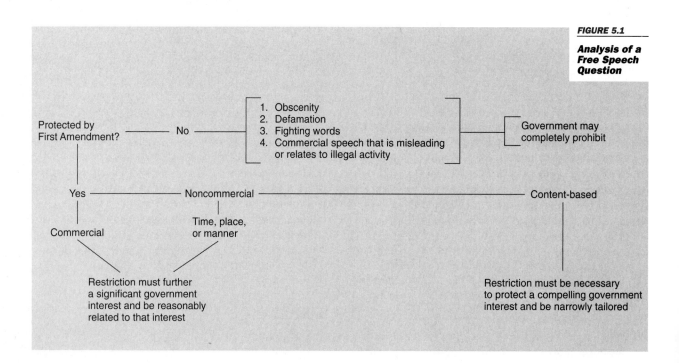

FIGURE 5.1

Analysis of a Free Speech Question

International

As newly independent nations have sought to develop democratic forms of government, it has been relatively common for them to look to the U.S. Constitution as a model. Likewise, emerging democracies often have sought the advice of American constitutional experts when drafting their own new constitutions. For example, former U.S. Supreme Court Justice Thurgood Marshall played a substantial role in drafting a constitution for Kenya in 1960, not long after it became an independent nation.

This is not to say, however, that other nations have simply adopted our Constitution's structure and language. Many countries in such a situation correctly point out, for example, that the real meaning of our Constitution includes 200 years of Supreme Court interpretations. As a consequence, Eastern European nations such as Poland, Hungary, Czechoslovakia, and the Baltic states have embraced many of the fundamental tenets of the U.S. Constitution, such as freedom of speech and the press, freedom of religion, and due process, but they are not satisfied with the broad generalities of the American Constitution. They may agree that the generality and breadth of the U.S. Constitution were appropriate for the late eighteenth century when many of the ideas in that document were novel, but assert that a democratic constitution for the late twentieth and early twenty-first centuries must include more detail than was included in the U.S. Constitution. Many of these nations, while relying heavily on the advice of American constitutional experts, insist on more detail in their modern constitutions than is found in the American Constitution. In setting out basic principles such as free speech, these nations are insisting on the inclusion of exceptions that U.S. courts have created during the 200 years of the U.S. Constitution's existence, such as those permitting government restrictions on the time, place, and method of expressing one's opinions.

The real difficulty, of course, is in the clash of cultures. In Bulgaria, for example, there have been proposals that the new constitution include an exception to the free speech guarantee that prohibits anyone from injuring the reputation of another. This exception goes far beyond the exception in U.S. constitutional interpretation that removes constitutional protection for defamatory statements; such statements in our system are outside the realm of constitutional protection only if they defame a person or business (injure its reputation) and if they are proved to be false, to have been communicated to a third party, and to have caused actual damage. This process of blending and compromising firmly held ideals is, in itself, an integral part of the democratic process that is both inevitable and healthy.

---

equal protection in connection with the *federal* government, the concept has been found to be implicit in the Fifth Amendment's due process clause, which does apply to the federal government. Thus, the guarantee of equal protection acts as a limitation on all levels of government—federal, state, and local.

The fundamental thrust of the **equal protection clause** is to prohibit the government from making arbitrary and unreasonable distinctions among persons. Because virtually every law and regulation involves distinctions and classifications—for example, applying to some industries but not to others, applying to larger companies but not to smaller ones, giving benefits to older people but not to younger ones—legal questions involving the equal protection clause arise frequently. Unfortunately, the Supreme Court's interpretations of the clause have not been as clear or consistent as we would like. The Court has definitely identified two different levels of protection

under the clause and has probably identified a third. For our purposes, we will characterize the equal protection clause as providing three different levels of protection against unreasonable distinctions. We will first examine those aspects of the law under the equal protection clause that are relatively certain and then look briefly at those that are less clear.

Economic and Social Regulation

One area that is quite clear is the application of the equal protection clause to economic and social regulation. The Supreme Court realizes that legislatures must make distinctions in passing such legislation. Only the poor need welfare; the rich do not. Some industries cause pollution; others do not. Some jobs imperil the safety of workers; others do not. Therefore, the Supreme Court uses a lax standard for economic and social legislation when equal protection challenges are raised. This standard is often referred to as the *rational basis test.* The distinction or classification merely has to have a rational basis; in other words, there merely has to be a legitimate government interest (not even a strong one), and the distinction must have some rational relationship with that interest. If a state legislature, for example, has identified a problem and has made a good faith effort to solve it, the test is normally met. Only if the court can conceive of no reasonable set of facts that would justify the distinction and it is clearly a display of arbitrary power and not a matter of judgment will the distinction be invalidated on equal protection grounds.

To decide that the rational basis test applies to economic or social regulation is almost to decide the case. There is such a strong presumption of reasonableness that discrimination in such regulations is almost always upheld. Distinctions need not be drawn with "mathematical nicety," nor must a legislature attack all aspects of a problem at once. Thus, a law requiring operators of "flea markets" who leased space to persons wishing to sell automobiles to have a type of license not required of persons who leased land to regular car dealers constituted permissible discrimination. The state has a legitimate interest in preventing fraud, and it is rational to presume that fraud will be a bigger problem in a flea market than in a stationary car dealership that will probably still be there when a defrauded customer goes back to complain.[6] Similarly, in *Minnesota v. Clover Leaf Creamery Co.,* 449 U.S. 456 (1981), the Supreme Court upheld a state statute that banned the retail sale of milk in nonreturnable, nonrefillable plastic containers but permitted such sale in paperboard containers. The law also did not prohibit the sale of other kinds of products in plastic containers. The state legislature had identified an environmental problem—solid waste disposal—and had made a good faith effort to solve part of the problem. The legislature wanted to encourage the development of environmentally superior containers and had chosen one major industry as a basis for its experiment. Whether the law would work as intended was not the Supreme Court's business; the distinctions in the law did have a rational basis.

Strict Scrutiny

Another relatively clear area of law under the equal protection clause today involves governmental dis-

tinctions based on race or national origin. The highest level of protection applies in such cases. If a law or other government action discriminates against someone because of the person's ethnic group or ancestral origin, the courts apply what they refer to as *strict scrutiny.* The test is essentially the same one that courts apply to content-based restrictions on noncommercial speech. The government must demonstrate that the distinction is necessary to protect a compelling interest and that the distinction is narrowly tailored to discriminate no more than is absolutely needed. A governmental body can almost never meet this test, and a distinction based on race or national origin will almost always be void.[7]

Perhaps the most well-known application of the equal protection clause to a racial classification by the government was the Supreme Court's decision in *Brown v. Board of Education,* 347 U.S. 483 (1954), in which racially segregated public school systems were found to be unconstitutional. A more recent example is *Palmore v. Sidoti,* 466 U.S. 429 (1984), in which the Supreme Court invalidated the action of a state trial judge who took a child away from its mother in a custody fight, because the white mother had married a black man. The legal standard normally applied in child custody cases involves a determination of what is in the best interests of the child; the trial judge had concluded that, in many locales, prevailing societal attitudes against interracial families would make life difficult for the child. However, the Supreme Court said that attempting to shield the child from "the reality of private biases" was not a sufficient justification for a racial distinction.

The courts apply the strict scrutiny test only to *intentional* racial or national origin distinctions by the government. If a distinction or classification is neutral on its face but happens to have a disproportionate impact on a particular ethnic group, strict scrutiny does not apply. In such a case of *de facto* discrimination, the courts apply the rational basis test. Examples include public school districts that follow a "neighborhood school" concept, which may result in particular schools having predominantly white or predominantly black enrollments solely because of housing patterns and not because of any discriminatory act by the

---

[6]*North Dixie Theatre, Inc. v. McCullion,* 613 F. Supp. 1339 (S.D. Ohio 1985).

[7]The courts have also applied the strict scrutiny standard to government distinctions and classifications that interfere with fundamental rights such as free speech, right to privacy, and right to travel interstate. The equal protection clause has no independent significance when applied to such matters, however, because these fundamental rights are protected by other constitutional provisions.

school district. There is no violation of the equal protection clause. (A word of caution is in order, however: If government *employment* practices are challenged for being discriminatory, *de facto* discrimination might be illegal under Title VII of the 1964 Civil Rights Act. Although the equal protection clause of the Constitution would not apply, *de facto* employment discrimination can be illegal under this federal statute whether a government or private employer is involved. Employment discrimination is discussed in Chapter 49.)

Thus far, the only form of racially based distinction that has been upheld is *affirmative action.* Sometimes referred to as "benign" or "reverse" discrimination, affirmative action programs grant limited preferences to ethnic minorities. Affirmative action in the employment setting, by either government or private employers, is governed by Title VII of the 1964 Civil Rights Act, our most important employment discrimination law. Affirmative action occurs in several other contexts, as well; in any nonemployment situation in which an affirmative action program is instituted by a governmental body, the equal protection clause applies. Examples include programs that give limited preferences to minorities in admission to state universities or in the awarding of government contracts for the purchase of goods or services. The purposes of such programs include increasing diversity in state-supported higher education, helping minority-owned businesses become established by enabling them to break into government contract work, and assisting minorities in overcoming the effects of past discrimination in various endeavors.

Although affirmative action has proved to be the only situation in which racial or national origin distinctions have been permitted under the equal protection clause, the government must meet stringent requirements to justify them. For example, in *Richmond v. J. A. Croson Co.*, 488 U.S. 469 (1989), the Supreme Court struck down the minority business enterprise (MBE) set-aside program for awarding city government contracts in Richmond, Virginia. Under this program the City of Richmond required that 30 percent of the dollar volume of all city construction contracts be awarded to businesses that were owned and controlled by blacks, Hispanics, Asians, or Native Alaskans. The percentage could be met by a white-owned general contractor subcontracting work to MBEs. The MBE program was challenged by a white-owned construction company that

lost a small contract to install guard rails on a highway, even though its bid was slightly lower than the successful bid of the MBE. The Supreme Court held that the city did have compelling interests in both remedying the effects of past discrimination and making sure that city tax money was not spent to support an industry that engaged in discriminatory practices (that is, discriminatory subcontracting). However, the Court held that for an MBE program to be valid, the city had to produce evidence demonstrating (1) that discrimination against MBEs in the awarding of city contracts and subcontracts had occurred in the past, (2) a reasonable estimate of the extent of that discrimination, and (3) that it had narrowly tailored the program to take race into account to the least extent possible to serve the city's compelling interest. The city had not fulfilled these requirements. In light of this decision, Richmond let its MBE program expire; thereafter, the amount of MBE participation in city construction contracts dropped to almost zero in Richmond. This result has been repeated in a number of other places. However, many other state and local government agencies are attempting to satisfy the requirements of the *Croson* case.

It should be noted that, at the federal level, Congress has much more latitude to use MBE or other affirmative action programs than do state or local government entities. Such programs enacted by Congress must merely meet a rational basis test. The reason is that in addition to placing a number of limitations on state and local governments, the Fourteenth Amendment also explicitly gave Congress extensive powers to pass legislation carrying out the remedial purposes of that amendment.

Intermediate Scrutiny

We know that the rational basis test applies to classifications in economic regulations and most social legislation, and we also know that the strict scrutiny test applies to government distinctions based on race or national origin. There are a number of other types of distinctions, however, about which the law is not very clear. There appears to be a "middle tier" of protection that applies to distinctions based on important personal characteristics other than race or national origin. Sometimes courts refer to an "intermediate" level of scrutiny. It is fairly clear that this middle tier of protection applies to gender-based distinctions; in such a case, the government must prove that the classification bears a *"substantial* relationship to an *important* government interest."* This test is stricter than the rational basis test but not as stringent as the strict scrutiny test.

When such a test is applied, however, most gender-based distinctions will violate the equal protection clause. For example, in *Arizona v. Norris,* 463 U.S. 1073 (1983), the Supreme Court struck down an Arizona state employees' retirement plan that paid women smaller monthly benefits than men because actuarial tables predicted that the average woman would live longer then the average man. The plan was deemed unfair to the plaintiff, who could not count on living as long as the "average" woman.[8]

Several other kinds of distinctions also apparently fall within this middle tier of protection, including those based on "alienage" (whether a person is a U.S. citizen or merely a legal resident), age, a child's legitimacy or illegitimacy, and a few others involving important personal characteristics. The Supreme Court has not given clear guidance, however. Sometimes it seems to recognize that an intermediate level of scrutiny is being applied; in other cases it claims to be applying only the rational basis test but reaches conclusions indicating that it actually is applying an intermediate level of scrutiny. For example, in *City of Cleburne v. Cleburne Living Center,* 473 U.S. 432 (1985), the plaintiffs wished to establish a closely supervised and highly regulated home for the mentally retarded in Cleburne, Texas. The city required a special use permit for "homes for the lunatic" and denied the plaintiff's request. The Supreme Court specifically stated that it was applying the rational basis test and concluded that there was no rational basis for prohibiting a residential-type home for the mentally retarded within the city. The Court was obviously scrutinizing the city ordinance more closely than it would if it had been an economic regulation. An economic regulation can be practically nonsensical and still pass the rational basis test. Thus, despite the Court's claim that it was merely applying the rational basis test, it was providing some type of middle-tier protection against government distinctions based on mental retardation.

Due Process of Law

Among other clauses in the Fifth Amendment, the due process clause states that "no person shall . . . be deprived of life, liberty, or property without due process of law." The provision applies to actions of the federal government. Among the several provisions of the Fourteenth Amendment, there is also a due process clause that applies to actions of state and local governments. The two clauses are identical, both in their language and in the way they have been interpreted by the courts; thus, there is no reason for distinguishing between the two and people usually refer to the due process clause as a single provision that applies to all levels of government. The courts have interpreted the due process clause as limiting government action in two different ways: the first kind of limitation is referred to as **substantive due process;** the second is called **procedural due process.** Today, procedural due process is much more important than substantive due process.

Substantive Due Process

The substantive component of due process prohibits statutes, regulations, and other kinds of government action that are arbitrary and irrational. Until the late 1930s, the Supreme Court used substantive due process as a basis for invalidating many economic regulations; basically, if the Court disagreed with the law's underlying rationale, it found the law to be arbitrary and irrational. For example, in one leading case, a law limiting the number of hours that bakers could work was found violative of substantive due process because it unreasonably interfered with "the freedom of master and employee to contract in relation to their employment." Since the late 1930s, the Supreme Court has taken a dramatically different view of substantive due process. Under the modern interpretation, the Court refuses to "sit as a super-legislature second-guessing the wisdom of legislation." The standard the Court applies today is essentially the same "rational basis" test that is applied to economic classifications under the equal protection clause. Thus, substantive due process is used only rarely to invalidate economic regulation.

Today, substantive due process still plays a role in several situations, although that role is rather limited:

1. Substantive due process incorporates the standards of the equal protection clause and applies them to the federal government. Thus, the different levels

---

[8]If this same type of sex-discriminatory employee benefit plan is used by a *private* employer, the equal protection clause obviously does not apply. How-

ever, such a benefit plan in private employment will violate the prohibition against sex discrimination in Title VII of the 1964 Civil Rights Act.

of protection that apply under the equal protection clause to classifications by state and local governments are applied to federal government distinctions by means of substantive due process.

2. As mentioned earlier, under the doctrine of incorporation, the protections in the Bill of Rights have been extended to the states by means of the Fourteenth Amendment's due process clause. Substantive due process is the means by which this has been accomplished.

3. Substantive due process protects against extreme instances of statutory vagueness. If a statute is so vague or incomplete that a reasonable person, even after consulting an attorney, would have to engage in sheer guesswork to determine what conduct is permitted or prohibited, the statute violates substantive due process. Sometimes the courts say that a statute must "establish a reasonably ascertainable standard for conduct" to comply with substantive due process. Claims of statutory vagueness are frequently made but are successful only in unusual cases of extreme vagueness.

4. Substantive due process protects against "irrational presumptions." As a matter of practical necessity, the law must make presumptions—presuming the existence of Fact B from proof of Fact A. Presuming one fact because another has been proved is legitimate so long as there is a logical connection between the two. Suppose, for example, that a state law makes it a crime either to steal property or knowingly to take possession of stolen property. Suppose also that, if someone is found in possession of stolen property, the law presumes that the person either stole it or else took possession of it with knowledge that it was stolen. This has been held to be a valid presumption, because the possessor of the property is in a better position than anyone else to explain how he or she acquired it, and he or she is given ample opportunity to explain the circumstances. Thus, he or she is in the best position to explain why the presumption should not be applied in this case. Another example, with an opposite result, involved a federal statute providing that if a kidnapping occurred and nothing was heard from either the kidnapper or the victim for 24 hours after the crime, it was presumed that the kidnapper had crossed state lines. This presumption caused a federal criminal statute to become applicable, thus giving investigative jurisdiction to the Federal Bureau of Investigation. This presumption was found to violate substantive due process, because of the Supreme Court's view that there was no rational connection between a 24-hour period of silence and the act of crossing state lines.

Procedural Due Process

Of much greater importance today is the procedural component of due process. When procedural due process applies, it essentially guarantees that the government will follow fair procedures before taking certain actions against individuals or companies.

Deprivation of Life, Liberty, or Property. The due process clause applies only if particular government action "deprives" a person of "life, liberty, or property." This prerequisite exists whether substantive or procedural due process is at issue; however, most of the problems in determining whether this requirement has been met arise in the procedural due process context. Due process questions almost never involve governmental deprivation of "life," the obvious exception being a criminal prosecution in which the death penalty is a possibility. Thus, the question normally is whether particular government action constitutes a deprivation of "liberty" or "property." These terms are interpreted rather broadly. The term *deprivation of liberty* includes virtually any substantial restriction on the freedom of an individual or company, and the term *deprivation of property* includes virtually any substantial negative effect on any type of property interest. It can be seen from this statement that the term *deprivation* really just means a substantial adverse impact; there does not have to be total destruction of a liberty or property interest to constitute a deprivation. One example of the breadth of the term *property* is that a person can even be viewed as having a property interest in a job with a local, state, or federal government agency. If there is a statutory provision or an agency regulation that gives the employee some type of legally enforceable job security, the person has a property interest in the job and must be given procedural due process before the job can be terminated. The statute or regulation might, for example, provide that the employee can be terminated only for "good cause" or only in other described conditions. Such a guarantee creates a property interest. There are many other examples of situations in which individuals or corporations have legal rights that rise to the level of property interests.

Basic Procedural Requirements. When procedural due process applies to government action, the government must provide the affected party with (1) advance notice of the proposed action, (2) an "opportunity to be heard," that is, a hearing of some type, and (3) an impartial decision maker.[9]

These requirements are very flexible. The type of notice that will be sufficient may vary with the circumstances. The general rule is simply that the timing and content of the notice must be such that the affected party is reasonably apprised of the nature of the proposed action and has an adequate opportunity to prepare a response.

The requirement of a hearing is also very flexible; the fact that procedural due process applies does not mean that there has to be a full-blown court-like hearing. The hearing must be "meaningful under the circumstances" and might range from a very informal face-to-face meeting between the affected party and the decision maker all the way to a very formal trial-type hearing. The kind of hearing required in a particular case depends on how important the affected party's interest is, how important the government's interest is, and what seems to be the best way to optimize those conflicting interests under the circumstances.

The requirement of an impartial decision maker usually just means that a person having the responsibility for making the decision (either alone or as a member of a decision-making group) should not have prejudged the case and should not have a substantial monetary or emotional stake in the outcome of the decision. The mere fact that a decision maker has a particular ideology or has very strong views about the general subject of the decision does not disqualify him or her.

There are several reasons for requiring fair procedures in any decision-making process, including those in government. The most important reason is that fair procedures generally tend to produce better decisions because these procedures improve the chances that all relevant issues will be identified, all important positions will be presented and considered, and relevant information will be adequately screened and tested. Another important reason for

fair procedures is making people feel as if their views count for something, thus increasing their acceptance of decisions even when those decisions go against them. It is much easier to get the compliance and cooperation necessary to carry out decisions when people accept those decisions as being legitimate.

Adjudicative–Legislative Distinction. It is also important to note that the courts have made an important distinction between adjudicative and legislative types of governmental actions. In general, procedural due process applies only to adjudicative types of governmental actions and not legislative ones. The most obvious example of such an action is a court proceeding. Many other kinds of action at all levels of government, however, fall within the definition of adjudicative. Most of the decisions made by government officials, even informal decisions, are of an adjudicative nature. The essential characteristics of an adjudicative process are that (1) it usually seeks to determine a very specific set of facts relating to the prior conduct of an individual or business (or a relatively small number of individuals or businesses); (2) it applies some already established rule or guideline to these facts; and (3) based on the application of the rule to these facts, it produces a decision and imposes legal consequences on an individual or business (or a relatively small group of them).

The most obvious example of a legislative type of action is the enactment of a statute by Congress or a state legislature. Again, however, many other kinds of action at all levels of government are legislative in character. For instance, when a federal agency adopts regulations that will apply in the future to an industry or when a city zoning board adopts a zoning plan to guide future land uses in the city, the action is basically legislative. The essential characteristics of a legislative process are that (1) if it involves fact-finding, those facts are usually of a very general nature; (2) it seeks to develop policies or rules that will apply either to the general population or to a relatively large group of individuals or businesses; and (3) it usually imposes legal consequences only for future conduct and not for prior conduct.

Like most other distinctions, the adjudicative–legislative distinction is sometimes obvious and sometimes not. Some government actions are hybrids. Actually, government decision-making processes run along a continuum from purely adjudicative to purely

[9]As we saw in Chapter 2, in the case of civil lawsuits, procedural due process additionally requires that the case be heard in a state with which the defendant has had significant contacts.

legislative. The more a particular action looks like an adjudicative one, the more likely it is that a court will find that procedural due process applies. Even when a governmental body takes action that is essentially legislative in nature, it may provide notice, hearing, and other procedural safeguards if it so chooses. Thus, Congress has passed legislation requiring federal agencies to provide notice and hearing before certain kinds of agency rule-making activities—this was simply a choice made by Congress despite the fact that the due process clause of the Constitution would not require these procedures. Fair procedures can have great value even if not required by the Constitution.

The basic reasons why the courts have generally applied procedural due process guarantees to adjudicative actions but not to legislative ones are that

(1) fundamental fairness usually demands more procedural safeguards when legal consequences are imposed for past conduct than when rules are developed to guide future conduct; (2) providing advance notice and an opportunity for a hearing becomes extremely difficult and expensive when very large numbers of parties are affected, as is usually the case with legislative actions; and (3) the fact that legislative actions affect a large number of parties usually means that there will be more publicity and more collective economic and political power to guard against arbitrary actions by the government.

The following case illustrates the method courts use to determine whether particular procedures are adequate to fulfill the requirements of procedural due process.

SOUTHERN OHIO COAL CO. v. DONOVAN

U.S. Sixth Circuit Court of Appeals, 774 F.2d 693 (1985)

Case

The Federal Mine Safety and Health Review Commission ("Commission"), a branch of the U.S. Department of Labor, is charged with enforcing the Federal Mine Safety and Health Act ("the Act"). One provision of the Act prohibited a mine operator from discharging a miner for asserting any of his or her safety rights under the law. The Commission implemented this provision of the statute by adopting Rule 44, which specified the detailed procedures to be followed in dealing with a miner's complaint. Under Rule 44, if a miner filed a complaint with the Secretary of Labor alleging that he or she had been discharged as a result of complaining about safety conditions, the Secretary had to commence an investigation within 15 days. If the Secretary decided that the complaint was "not frivolous," the Secretary filed an application with the Commission requesting that the company be ordered to reinstate the miner. The application simply set

forth the Secretary's finding that the complaint was not frivolous, and the application was attached to a copy of the miner's original complaint. The Secretary's application was then examined "on an expedited basis" by an Administrative Law Judge (ALJ), who is a judicial-type official within the agency. The ALJ checked the application and complaint to make sure the documents were in order and, if so, ordered the company immediately to reinstate the miner to the job. The company could then request a hearing before the ALJ, who had to conduct the hearing within 5 days after the request. However, the question to be decided at the hearing was still limited to whether the miner's complaint was "not frivolous." If after the hearing the ALJ agreed with the Secretary that the miner's complaint was not frivolous, the reinstatement order continued. This conclusion by the ALJ could be reviewed by the Commission and ultimately by a federal court of appeals. Still, however, the issue was limited to whether the complaint was frivolous and not whether

the miner actually had been discriminated against for having raised questions about safety. This ultimate question would be determined under separate procedures that would take a substantial period of time; the company was required to keep the miner on the job until final disposition of the claim.

In this case, Southern Ohio Coal Co. (SOCCO) fired a miner for the stated reason of excessive absenteeism. The miner had earlier objected to company officials about unsafe methane levels in SOCCO's mines, and when he was fired he filed a complaint alleging that SOCCO terminated him because of his prior safety objections. Under the procedures described above, the company was ordered to reinstate him. The company challenged the constitutionality of Rule 44 in federal district court. The court held that Rule 44 violated the company's procedural due process rights, and the Secretary of Labor (Donovan) appealed. (It should be noted that the action of Congress in passing the Act, as well

(continues)

SOUTHERN OHIO COAL CO. v. DONOVAN

(continued from previous page)
as the action of the Commission in adopting Rule 44, were legislative actions, and procedural due process did not apply to the methods they used in making these decisions. However, Rule 44 specified procedures for taking adjudicative types of actions; thus, Rule 44's application to particular adjudicative situations was governed by the constitutional guarantee of procedural due process.)

Wellford, Circuit Judge:

Whether the Commission's Rule 44 violates a mine operator's due process rights by failing to provide for a pre-deprivation hearing is at the heart of these controversies. Neither party questions that the mine operators are due some process under the Constitution when a miner claims the opportunity for immediate reinstatement. The Secretary, however, claims that a post-deprivation hearing is sufficient process in light of the (allegedly) overriding governmental interests involved. The mine operators, on the other hand, claim that a post-deprivation hearing is insufficient to protect their Constitutional rights and that a pre-deprivation hearing is mandated, because they could be compelled to make substantial payments before a decision is made initially as to the potential merit of a claim, and because they could be compelled to reinstate a person who is a danger to himself or to others.

Mathews v. Eldridge, 424 U.S. 319 (1976), requires a court to consider three factors to determine whether a particular procedure comports with the requirement of due process:

1. The private interests that will be affected by the official action in question;

2. The risk of an erroneous deprivation of such interests through the procedures involved and the probable value of additional or substitute procedural safeguards; and

3. The government's interest, including the function involved and the fiscal and administrative burdens that the additional or substitute procedural requirement would entail.

The final *Eldridge* factor is met in the instant case. Currently the Secretary is required to give the mine operator a hearing within five days of the temporary reinstatement order. What the mine operators would have this Court require is a pre-deprivation hearing—in other words, the Secretary would have to reverse the order of its procedures and hold a hearing before granting temporary reinstatement. Thus, there would be absolutely no additional fiscal or administrative burdens in granting the operators' desired pre-deprivation hearing.

The first and second factors, however, are not as easily answered as the third. On the first factor, the Secretary correctly notes that "[t]he usual rule has been '[w]here only property rights are involved, mere postponement of the judicial enquiry is not a denial of due process, if the opportunity given for ultimate judicial determination of liability is adequate.'" *Mitchell v. W. T. Grant Co.,* 416 U.S. 600 (1974). Were the employer permitted in all cases to provide merely economic reinstatement rather than normally being required to provide actual physical reinstatement, the Secretary's argument would be more persuasive.

The district court found "compelling" the mine operator's interest in "not being required to employ in a sensitive position a man whom it has discharged."

Prolonged retention of a disruptive or otherwise unsatisfactory employee can adversely affect discipline and morale in the work place, foster disharmony, and ultimately impair the efficiency of an office or agency.

The factor is particularly important

when, as here, the order does not expire by its own terms at any specific time after it issues. Although an operator is given an opportunity to present evidence on its own behalf within five days of the reinstatement, the hearing focuses on whether the miner's complaint was frivolously brought, not whether the complaint is meritorious.

The reliability (or unreliability) of the initial procedures leading to an imposition of temporary reinstatement is perhaps a significant weakness in the administrative scheme under scrutiny. All the Secretary need do to force the mine operator to reinstate the discharged miner is find "minimal supporting evidence" in favor of the complainant. As long as the Secretary finds that the complaint was not "frivolously brought," then the Secretary makes an application for temporary reinstatement. The application itself consists only of the miner's complaint, an affidavit setting forth the Secretary's reasons for his finding that the complaint was not frivolously brought, and proof of service on the operator. The application permits no input from the employer. . . .

. . . [T]he Supreme Court's most recent pronouncement concerning due process requirements, *Cleveland Board of Education v. Loudermill,* 105 S.Ct. 1487 (1985), strongly supports the mine operator's arguments that the Secretary should provide at least some kind of *pre-deprivation* hearing:

Some opportunity for the employee to present his side of these cases is recurringly of obvious value in reaching an accurate decision. Dismissal for cause will often involve factual disputes. Even where the facts are clear, the appropriateness or necessity of the discharge may not be; in such cases, the only meaningful opportunity to invoke the discretion of the decision maker is likely to be before the termination takes effect.

This language is equally applicable to the employer situation in which the issue presented is the issue of forced
(continues)

SOUTHERN OHIO COAL CO. V. DONOVAN

(*continued from previous page*)
reinstatement rather than the other side of the coin, employee termination. We believe this rationale meets the second factor set out in *Mathews v. Eldridge.* While something less "than a full evidentiary hearing is sufficient prior to adverse administrative action," the employers here must be afforded a minimal opportunity to present their side of the dispute before temporary reinstatement is forced upon them. Since the Secretary's Rule 44 fails to insure any reasonable opportunity for at least some minimal pre-deprivation hearing, we hold that it violates the mine operator's due process rights.
[Affirmed.] ⚖

Takings Clause

The final constitutional provision we will examine is the **takings clause** of the Fifth Amendment. It applies explicitly to the federal government and, through the doctrine of incorporation, also applies to state and local governments. The takings clause states that private property shall not "be taken for public use without just compensation." The clause recognizes the ancient principle that a sovereign may take private property for public purposes. This long-recognized governmental power is referred to as the power of **eminent domain.** The takings clause, however, also places limitations on this power. Private property can be taken only for a public purpose, but this requirement is interpreted so broadly that almost any governmental objective will suffice. The most important limitation is that the government must pay "just compensation"—the fair market value—of the property it takes.

The concept of property is very broad under the takings clause. It obviously includes land, as well as the many different types of interests in land such as subsurface mineral rights, easements, and "air rights" (the right to use the air space above land). It also includes any other tangible property, such as a boat or piece of equipment, and intangible property rights such as those that exist in a company's trade secret information.

The government is required to pay the owner when there has been a "taking." It will be remembered that procedural due process applies to any government action that has a significant negative effect on a property interest. To be a taking for which compensation must be paid, however, there must be much more than just a significant negative effect on the property interest. All or most of the property's value and utility must have been appropriated by the government's action. When the government physically appropriates the ownership of property, as when it builds a highway on your land, there obviously is a taking. If you do not agree to sell the land, the government must take legal action to condemn the property and have a court determine its fair value.

Difficult questions can arise, however, when the government does something that has a substantial negative effect on the utility and value of a property interest, without actually appropriating the property. When the government engages in some physical act that greatly diminishes the utility and value of someone's property, courts sometimes view the action as a taking. For example, the government might extend an airport runway so that takeoffs and landings are now very low over an adjoining tract of land. If the government has not bought the adjoining land, either through negotiated purchase or condemnation, the property owner is likely to file suit claiming a *de facto* taking of his or her property. If the court concludes that the government's actions substantially destroyed the owner's ability to make productive use of his or her property, the court usually decides that there has been a taking for which compensation is due. Although the government's action can constitute a taking without totally destroying all possible uses of the property, one of the factors a court will consider in determining whether there has been a sufficiently large destruction of value is whether there are other comparably productive uses for the property.

The issue of whether there has been a taking can also arise when some law or regulation affects the value of property. Most of the time, a regulation that limits the uses an owner can make of his or her property or that otherwise affects its value will not constitute a taking. Courts usually view these regulations as one of the burdens a person or company must bear in return for the many benefits of living in an organized society. The most obvious example is a city zoning law that permits only single-family homes in certain areas, multifamily dwellings in other areas, retail stores elsewhere, and various categories of industry in yet other sections. Despite occasional claims by property owners that they are deprived of the greater financial return they could receive by putting their property to some other use, zoning laws almost never constitute takings. Among other reasons for this conclusion, zoning usually benefits property values on the whole because of the predictability it creates.

The Supreme Court's many cases involving application of the takings clause to regulations have not provided very clear guidance. Unfortunately, the cases in this area are of a rather ad hoc nature. Generally speaking, a regulation that limits use will only constitute a taking in circumstances in which a particular property owner is forced to bear an unusual financial burden that is totally out of proportion with the benefits to be received by either the property owner or the community. For example, in *Nollan v. California Coastal Commission*, 483 U.S. 825 (1987), the Supreme Court held that a state agency had committed a taking when it required a landowner to grant public access across a section of the owner's private beach; the requirement was imposed as a condition before the agency would permit the landowner to demolish an old structure and replace it with a house on the property. The Court found a taking because of a combination of factors: (1) the landowner was singled out for a special burden not imposed on a general community of landowners; (2) the restriction on the owner's ability to demolish and build was not really related to the condition of granting public access; and (3) the granting of access to the public resembled the actual appropriation of an easement by the government (an easement—the right to do something on someone else's land—is a property interest).

SUMMARY

Our Constitution performs many functions. It prevents the undue concentration of power by dividing the authority of the government both vertically and horizontally. Vertically, the federal government is supreme, but is limited to certain enumerated powers set out in the Constitution. All other powers are reserved to the states and their subordinate units of government.

Horizontally, the vast authority of the federal government is separated into the legislative, executive, and judicial branches of government. A system of checks and balances prevents undue influence of any one branch. Although the president of the United States is probably the most powerful person in the world, executive authority to act must be rooted in the Constitution or in congressional acts. If the president acts without authority, or if Congress passes acts inconsistent with the Constitution, the judiciary, pursuant to the doctrine of judicial review, will rein them in. The Constitution, after all, means what the Supreme Court says it means.

The Constitution also protects businesses and individuals from undue government encroachment. We enjoy more freedoms than citizens of any other country, including freedom of religion, freedom of speech, equal protection under the law, and due process of law.

KEY TERMS

Separation of powers
Delegated powers
Reserved powers
State police power
Commerce clause
Federal preemption
Supremacy clause
Full faith and credit clause
Contract clause
Doctrine of incorporation
Privileges and immunities clause
Establishment clause
Free exercise clause
Free speech clause
Commercial speech
Equal protection clause
Substantive due process
Procedural due process
Takings clause
Eminent domain

QUESTIONS AND PROBLEMS

1. Blanco was arrested at his apartment complex for disorderly conduct after he refused numerous requests by neighbors, the apartment manager, and

police to turn down his stereo, which he had positioned in such a manner as to direct the sound of his rock music toward the swimming pool area of the complex. He had turned the stereo's volume up loud enough to cause vibrations in nearby apartments and to force his musical preferences on many neighbors who did not share them. What is the source, if any, of the city's authority to arrest Blanco? (*Blanco v. State,* 761 S.W.2d 38, Tex. App. 1988.)

2. The Heart of Atlanta Motel (P) was a 216-room motel in downtown Atlanta, Georgia. It was not located near a state line, although it was near two interstate highways and two state highways. It did extensive advertising in other states, and 75 percent of its guests were from outside Georgia. P refused to rent rooms to blacks, a practice that Congress outlawed by passage of Title II of the Civil Rights Act of 1964. P sued, claiming that the law was unconstitutional because Congress had no authority to regulate such a motel. Discuss. (*Heart of Atlanta Motel v. United States,* 379 U.S. 241, 1964.)

3. New York passed a law requiring every drug prescription form to have two signature lines, one stating "dispense as written" and one stating "substitution permissible." If the latter line is signed, the doctor must tell the patient that the pharmacist will substitute a (generally cheaper) generic drug for the normal "name brand" drug if the FDA has determined the generic drug to be a bioequivalent substitute. Pharmacists who do not wish to dispense the generic drug challenge the law as unduly burdening interstate commerce. Should this claim prevail? (*Pharmaceutical Society of New York v. Lefkowitz,* 586 F.2d 953, 2d Cir. 1978.)

4. The Montana Fish and Game Commission adopted a regulation in 1976 that set the price of combination hunting licenses at $30 for residents and $225 for nonresidents. (A combination license permitted the taking of one elk, one deer, one black bear, and a specified number of game birds.) This regulation was challenged by nonresident hunters, who contended that it violated the privileges and immunities clause of the U.S. Constitution. The State of Montana contended, among other things, that the interest of Montana residents in the wildlife within its borders was a matter of state protection and that this interest was substantial enough to justify the regulation. Do you think the U.S. Supreme Court agreed with this

defense? Why or why not? (*Baldwin v. Fish and Game Commission of Montana,* 436 U.S. 371, 1978.)

5. Lee, an Amish carpenter and farmer who employed other Amish people in his business, had trouble with the Internal Revenue Service because he did not deduct for or contribute to Social Security. The Internal Revenue Service Code provides a religious exemption for self-employed individuals that Amish can take advantage of. However, there is no such exemption for employment of others. Lee claims that he should not be required to comply with the Code because religious principles prevent him and his employees from claiming Social Security benefits. Discuss the validity of Lee's claim. (*United States v. Lee,* 455 U.S. 252, 1982.)

6. The legislature of Puerto Rico passed a statute that legalized certain forms of casino gambling for the purpose of promoting tourism. The legislature was very concerned, however, that widespread casino gambling by residents of Puerto Rico would have various negative effects on the population. Thus, the legislature prohibited the operators of casinos there from directing their advertising at local residents. Within Puerto Rico and its territorial waters, casino operators were only permitted to advertise gambling on airplanes, cruise ships, or other places where only incoming travelers were likely to be; they also could advertise in the mainland United States and other places outside Puerto Rico. A casino owner wishing to advertise within Puerto Rico challenged the ad restriction on free speech grounds. (The U.S. Constitution applies in Puerto Rico.) Discuss. (*Posadas de Puerto Rico Associates v. Tourism Co. of Puerto Rico,* 478 U.S. 328, 1986.)

7. Rock Against Racism (RAR), furnishing its own sound equipment and technicians, sponsored yearly programs of rock music in a bandshell in New York City's Central Park. Because of complaints about excessive noise from neighbors, the city adopted new guidelines under which it provided the sound equipment and sound technicians for the bandshell. Although the technician generally accommodated any band's requests regarding mixing of sound, the technician controlled the mix and volume. RAR sued, claiming a free speech violation. RAR argued, in part, that it should be allowed to control the sound equipment, subject to an overall volume limit. Discuss. (*Ward v. Rock Against Racism,* 491 U.S. 781, 1989.)

8. For the express purpose of providing a place where teenagers can socialize with each other but not be subjected to the potentially detrimental influence of older teenagers and adults (involving alcohol, drugs, and promiscuous sex), a Dallas ordinance was passed that authorized the licensing of "Class E" dance halls, restricting admission to persons between the ages of 14 and 18 and limiting their hours of operation. Stanglin, whose roller-skating rink and Class E dance hall shared a divided floor space, filed suit contending that the age and hour restrictions violated the minors' equal protection rights. Discuss. (*City of Dallas v. Stanglin*, 490 U.S. 19, 1989.)

9. A motorist was convicted of two traffic offenses in a municipal court in which the city's mayor served as judge, and the convictions were affirmed by the state's supreme court. He appealed this judgment to the U.S. Supreme Court. He contended that he had been denied a trial before "a disinterested and impartial judicial officer as guaranteed by the Due Process clause," in view of the fact that a major part of the village's income was derived from the fines, costs, and fees imposed by the municipal court, and the mayor also served as the city's chief executive with bud-getary responsibility. Do you believe that the appellant's contention is valid? Explain. (*Ward v. Village of Monroeville*, 409 U.S. 57, 1972.)

10. Ewing enrolled a six-year program of study at the University of Michigan that awarded an undergraduate degree and a medical degree on successful completion of the program. To qualify for the final two years of the program, a student must pass an examination known as NBME Part I. Ewing, after an undistinguished academic career, was dismissed from the university when he failed this examination with the lowest score recorded in the history of the program. He sued, seeking readmission to the program and an opportunity to retake the exam on the ground that he had a property interest in the program and that his dismissal was in violation of due process. Evidence showed that academic authorities had given careful consideration to their decision to dismiss Ewing but that all other students in the program who had failed NMBE Part I had been allowed to retake it, some as many as four times. Should Ewing's due process claim prevail? Discuss. (*Regents of the University of Michigan v. Ewing*, 474 U.S. 214, 1986.)

Chapter 6

Rise of the Administrative Agency

The Agency—An Overview

Legislative Delegation of Lawmaking Power

Functions and Powers

Estoppel

Recent Developments

I N THE PRECEDING CHAPTERS we have studied the major processes by which law is made—the formulation of common-law rules by the courts, the enactment of statutes by the legislative bodies, and the interpretation of statutes by the courts. But this examination does not present the total lawmaking picture.

Administrative agencies—the hundreds of boards and commissions existing at all levels of government—also "make law" by their continual promulgation of rules and regulations. The number of administrative agencies has grown so rapidly in the past 40 years that the practical impact of local, state, and federal agencies on the day-to-day activities of individuals and businesses is today probably at least as great as that of legislatures and courts. Every day, boards and commissions across the country engage in such traditional functions as assessing properties for tax purposes, granting licenses and business permits, and regulating rates charged in the transportation and public utility industries—actions that affect millions of Americans. And, more recently, newer agencies such as the Environmental Protection Agency (EPA), Occupational Safety and Health Administration (OSHA), and the National Highway Traffic and Safety Administration (NHTSA) have spawned regulations having a broad impact on the nation's businesses. Justice Jackson was right when he wrote in *FTC v. Ruberoid Co.,* 343 U.S. 470 (1952):

> The rise of administrative bodies probably has been the most significant legal trend of the last century and perhaps more values today are affected by their decisions than by those of all the courts. . . . They also have begun to have important consequences on personal rights. . . . They have become a veritable fourth branch of the Government, which has deranged our three-branch legal theories as much as the concept of a fourth dimension unsettles our three-dimensional thinking.

RISE OF THE ADMINISTRATIVE AGENCY

At the risk of oversimplification, we can say that two major factors are responsible for the dramatic growth of the administrative agency in recent years. First was a change in attitude toward government regulation of business. Until about 1880 the basic attitude of the state and federal governments toward business firms was that of "hands-off"—a philosophy frequently characterized by the *laissez-faire* label. The theory was that trade and commerce could best thrive in an environment free of government controls. By the end of the nineteenth century, however, various monopolistic practices had begun to surface. The passage of the Sherman Act in 1890 reflected the growing idea that a certain amount of government regulation of business was necessary to preserve minimum levels of competition.

A second, and perhaps even more powerful, reason for the emergence of the modern administrative agency is that as our nation grew and became more industrialized, many complex problems sprang up that did not easily lend themselves to traditional types of regulation. Some were posed by technological advances such as the greatly increased generation and distribution of electrical power and the rapid growth of the airline industry. Others resulted from changes in social and economic conditions, particularly the rise of the giant manufacturers and the new methods by which they marketed their products on a national basis. The solution of these problems required expertise and enormous amounts of time for continuous regulation, which the courts and the legislatures simply did not possess. Faced with this situation, the legislative bodies sought new ways to regulate business (and to implement nonbusiness government programs, such as Social Security) that would be more workable.

THE AGENCY—AN OVERVIEW

To understand the basic workings of administrative agencies and the nature of the legal problems we will discuss later, it will be helpful to see how the typical agency is created and how it receives its powers. For this purpose, the Federal Trade Commission provides a good example.

By the turn of the century, it was apparent that some firms in interstate commerce were engaging in practices that, although not violating the Sherman Act, were nonetheless felt to be undesirable.

Although persons who were injured by these practices were sometimes able to obtain relief in the courts, the relief was sporadic, and there was no single body that could maintain surveillance of these practices on a continuing basis.

Accordingly, in 1914 Congress passed the Federal Trade Commission Act, which created the *Federal Trade Commission (FTC)* and authorized it (among other things) to determine what constituted "unfair methods of competition" in interstate commerce. Not only could the commission issue regulations defining and prohibiting such practices, but additionally, it could take action against companies that it believed to be violating such regulations.

Several federal agencies are considered to be part of the executive branch, such as the Small Business Administration (SBA), OSHA, and the Federal Aviation Administration (FAA). Others are structurally independent of the executive branch; once the president's appointment of agency heads and members is confirmed by the Senate, the president has no direct control over the appointee and cannot remove him or her from office. Examples of independent regulatory agencies include the FTC, the Interstate Commerce Commission (ICC), the Securities and Exchange Commission (SEC), the National Labor Relations Board (NLRB), and the Federal Reserve Board (FRB).

LEGISLATIVE DELEGATION OF LAWMAKING POWER

The administrative agency sits somewhat uncomfortably in our tripartite (legislative–executive–judicial) system of government. An agency that is technically part of the executive branch or perhaps an "independent regulatory agency" may exert powers that entail adjudication and rule making as well as traditional executive functions such as investigation and enforcement. A constitutional problem rises because the Constitution in article I, section 1, clearly vests all legislative powers in the Congress and does not provide for delegation of those powers. Therefore, rules and regulations that have been promulgated by agencies and that have the force and effect of law have been challenged as resulting from an unconstitutional delegation of legislative power.

Only in a couple of cases decided during the 1930s, in which the Supreme Court found "delega-

tion running riot," have such challenges succeeded. The courts are well aware of the very practical need for administrative agencies that was described earlier in this chapter. Therefore, they will uphold any agency ruling, regulation, or act that is within standards set forth in an enabling act *if* that act contains "reasonable standards" to guide the agency. What are reasonable standards? Courts have upheld as constitutional delegations of power "to promulgate regulations fixing prices of commodities," to institute rent controls on real property anywhere in the nation under specified circumstances, and even "to issue such orders and regulations as he [the President] deems appropriate to stabilize prices, rents, wages and salaries." Indeed, the doctrine of unconstitutional delegation of legislative power appears moribund at the federal level, although it still has some vitality in litigation involving state agencies.[1]

FUNCTIONS AND POWERS

Ministerial and Discretionary Powers

Before addressing the legal problems that are presented when agencies' rules or orders are appealed to the courts, we will briefly look at the nature of agency activities. The activities of these government boards and commissions vary widely. The functions and powers of some agencies are only **ministerial**—concerned with routinely carrying out duties imposed by law. Boards that issue and renew drivers' licenses fall within this category, as do the many Social Security offices that give information or advice to persons filing for Social Security benefits.

But most agencies also possess broad **discretionary powers**—powers that require the exercise of judgment and discretion in carrying out their duties. Again there is variety in the specific powers of these agencies. Some agencies' discretionary power is largely **investigative** in nature. Two examples are the authority granted to the Internal Revenue Service to inquire into the legality of deductions on taxpayers' returns and the authority of some commissions to make investigations for the purpose of recommending needed statutes to legislatures. Other

---

[1]For example, in *State v. Marana Plantations, Inc.,* 252 P.2d 87 (1953), the power to "regulate sanitary products in the interests of public health" was deemed too vague.

agencies have largely **rule-making powers,** with perhaps some investigative but little **adjudicative power** (enforcement power).

"Full-fledged" federal agencies, such as the FTC and the NLRB, possess all three types of discretionary power—investigative, rule-making, and adjudicative. Thus, typically a board will conduct investigations to determine if conditions warrant the issuance of rules to require (or prohibit) certain kinds of conduct; then it will draw up the regulations and thereafter take action against individuals or firms showing evidence of violating them. In drawing up the rules the board acts quasilegislatively, and in enforcing them it acts quasi-judicially.

Investigative Power
Agencies frequently hold hearings before drafting regulations, and the investigative powers they possess in connection with such hearings are largely determined by the statutes by which they are created. Normally, agencies can order the production of accounts and records relative to the problem being studied and can **subpoena** witnesses and examine them under oath. More disruptive to businesses are the powers most major agencies have to investigate whether statutes they are charged with enforcing and rules they have promulgated are being violated. The two most intrusive forms of investigative power are the subpoena and the physical search and seizure.

Subpoena Power
In the exercise of its adjudicative powers, which are soon to be discussed, agencies may issue subpoenas compelling witnesses to appear and give testimony at an agency hearing.

In any sort of investigation, agencies also may issue *subpoenas duces tecum,* which order the production of books, papers, records, and documents. Agency authority is construed very broadly in this area. According to *United States v. Powell,*[2] an agency must demonstrate that (1) the investigation will be conducted for a legitimate purpose, (2) the inquiry is relevant to the purpose, (3) the information sought is not already possessed by the agency, and (4) the administrative steps required by law have been followed. The agency does not, however, have to prove that there is "probable cause" to believe that a violation of the law has occurred, as is usually required in criminal investigations by the police.

Once the agency has established an apparently valid purpose for the investigation, the burden shifts to the company or individual being investigated to show that the purpose is illegitimate (for example, undertaken for harassment). The following case illustrates the difficulty that the target of a federal agency's investigation may have in attempting to block enforcement of such a subpoena.

[2]379 U.S. 48 (1964).

EEOC v. Peat, Marwick, Mitchell and Co.

U.S. Eighth Circuit Court of Appeals 775, F.2d 928 (1985)

In May 1982, the Equal Employment Opportunity Commission (EEOC) began investigating the retirement practices and policies of Peat, Marwick, Mitchell and Co. (PM) in an effort to determine whether those policies violated the Age Discrimination in Employment Act (ADEA). In accord with its statutory investigative powers, the EEOC subpoenaed from PM documents bearing on the relationship of members to the firm and documents relating to PM's retirement practices and policies.

PM refused to comply with the subpoena, so the EEOC initiated an enforcement proceeding in the district court. The district court ordered enforcement of the subpoena, and PM appealed.

Fagg, Circuit Judge:

PM's primary argument on appeal is that the subpoena should not be enforced because the EEOC's investigation is not for a legitimate purpose authorized by Congress. The ADEA prohibits discrimination by an employer against an employee or prospec-

tive employee on the basis of age. PM contends that its partners are not employees under the ADEA but rather they fall within the definition provided for employers in the Act. Thus, according to PM, the EEOC's investigation of the relationship of PM partners as employers, to the firm and to each other and its investigation of the retirement practices and policies of the partnership is not for a legitimate purpose authorized by Congress.

EEOC maintains that it has subpoenaed the records of PM in an effort to determine whether individuals that PM classifies as "partners" fall within

(continues)

EEOC v. Peat, Marwick, Mitchell and Co.

(continued from previous page)
the definition of "employees" for purposes of the ADEA.

Congress has established the EEOC as the administrative body empowered to investigate violations of the ADEA and has given the EEOC subpoena power in order to carry out its investigations. The authority to investigate violations includes the authority to investigate coverage under the statute. *Donovan v. Shaw,* 668 F.2d 985 (8th Cir. 1982). It can no longer be disputed that "a subpoena enforcement proceeding is not the proper forum in which to litigate the question of coverage under a particular federal statute." *Id.* The initial determination of the coverage question is left to the administrative agency seeking enforcement of the subpoena. Often a coverage question cannot be resolved until the administrative agency has had an opportunity to examine the subpoenaed records.

"The showing of reasonable cause required to support an application for enforcement of a subpoena duces tecum 'is satisfied . . . by the court's determination that the investigation is authorized by Congress, is for a purpose Congress can order, and the documents sought are relevant to the inquiry.'" *Donovan,* 668 F.2d at 989. *See also United States v. Powell,* 379 U.S. 48 (1964). The EEOC's investigation of PM is in an effort to determine whether PM's retirement practices and policies discriminate against individuals classified as employees for purposes of the ADEA. Thus, EEOC's investigation is for a legitimate purpose authorized by Congress. PM has not questioned the relevancy of the documents subpoenaed by the EEOC to a determination of this question.

PM also argues that the district court committed error in enforcing the subpoena because it is abusive, unreasonable, not in good faith, and violative of the constitutional rights of PM and its members. In this regard, PM argues that the EEOC has never made or attempted to make a showing that PM's partners may in fact be employees for purposes of the ADEA, or that it has reason to believe that PM's retirement practices and policies may be violative of the ADEA.

The EEOC is not required to make such a showing. As previously indicated, the EEOC must show that its investigation is for a legitimate purpose authorized by Congress and that the documents subpoenaed are relevant to its inquiry. If this demonstration is made, the EEOC is entitled to the documents subpoenaed unless PM demonstrates that judicial enforcement of the subpoena would amount to an abuse of the court's process. PM has presented no evidence of bad faith or an abuse of the court's process by the EEOC.

[We affirm.] ⚖

Search and Seizure

Many agencies carry out on-site inspections or searches when investigating matters under their jurisdiction. From city health inspectors checking a restaurant's kitchen to OSHA personnel investigating trenches at a construction site to federal mine safety inspectors probing underground coal mines, such investigations are a frequent and, for the investigated company, troublesome occurrence.

These searches have constitutional implications, because the warrant clause of the Fourth Amendment protects commercial buildings as well as private homes. As the Supreme Court pointed out in *Marshall v. Barlow's, Inc.,* 436 U.S. 307 (1978), the searching of businesses by the British immediately preceding the American Revolution was particularly offensive to the colonists and provided part of the rationale for the warrant requirement.

However, we are not accorded as great an expectation of privacy for our businesses as for our homes. For example, several types of businesses, including gun dealers, stone quarries, day care centers, and fishing vessels, have been held to be so "pervasively regulated" that they can have little or no reasonable expectation of privacy. This doctrine appears to be shrinking the protection that businesses have from warrantless searches and seizures, as the following case illustrates.

New York v. Burger

U.S. Supreme Court, 107 S.Ct. 2636 (1987)

Case

Burger owned a junkyard that dismantled cars and sold their parts. Pursuant to a New York statute [Sec. 415-a] authorizing warrantless inspections of such junkyards, police officers entered Burger's junkyard and asked to see his license and records. He replied that he did not have such documents, though they are required by the statute. The officers then announced their intent to search the premises; Burger did not object. The officers found stolen vehicles and parts. Burger was charged in state court with possession of stolen property and unregistered operation of a vehicle dismantler. He moved to suppress the evidence, claiming that the administrative inspection statute was unconstitutional. The trial court denied the motion, but the New York Court of Appeals reversed. The Supreme Court granted the State's application for certiorari.

Blackmun, Justice:

The Court long has recognized that the Fourth Amendment's prohibition on unreasonable searches and seizures is applicable to commercial premises, as well as to private homes. An owner or operator of a business thus has an expectation of privacy in commercial property, which society is prepared to consider to be reasonable. An expectation of privacy in commercial premises, however, is different from and indeed less than a similar expectation in an individual's home. This expectation is particularly attenuated in commercial property employed in "closely regulated" industries.

[A] warrantless inspection, however, even in the context of a pervasively regulated business, will be deemed to be reasonable only so long as three criteria are met. First, there must be a "sub-stantial government interest" that informs the regulatory scheme. Second, the warrantless inspections must be "necessary to further [the] regulatory scheme." *Donovan v. Dewey*, 452 U.S. 594, 600 (1981). Finally, "the statute's inspection program, in terms of the certainty and regularity of its application, [must] provid[e] a constitutionally adequate substitute for a warrant." *Ibid.* In other words, the regulatory statute must perform the two basic functions of a warrant: it must advise the owner of the commercial premises that the search is being made pursuant to the law and has a properly defined scope, and it must limit the discretion of the inspecting officers. To perform this first function, the statute must be "sufficiently comprehensive and defined that the owner of commercial property cannot help but be aware that his property will be subject to periodic inspections undertaken for specific purposes." *Ibid.* In addition, in defining how a statute limits the discretion of the inspectors, we have observed that it must be "carefully limited in time, place and scope." *United States v. Biswell* 406 U.S. 311, 315 (1972).

Searches made pursuant to Sec. 415-a, in our view, clearly fall within this established exception to the warrant requirement for administrative inspections in "closely regulated" businesses. First, the nature of the regulatory statute reveals that the operation of a junkyard, part of which is devoted to vehicle dismantling, is a "closely regulated" business in the State of New York. The provisions regulating the activity of vehicle dismantling are extensive. [The Court then described these regulations in detail.]

The New York regulatory scheme satisfies the three criteria necessary to make reasonable warrantless inspections pursuant to Sec. 415-a5. First, the State has a substantial interest in regulating the vehicle-dismantling and automobile-junkyard industry because motor vehicle theft has increased in the State and because the problem of theft is associated with this industry. In this day, automobile theft has become a significant social problem, placing enormous economic and personal burdens upon the citizens of the United States.

Second, regulation of the vehicle-dismantling industry reasonably serves the State's substantial interest in eradicating automobile theft. It is well established that the theft problem can be addressed effectively by controlling the receiver of, or market in, stolen property.

Moreover, the warrantless administrative inspections pursuant to Sec. 415-a5 "are necessary to further [the] regulatory scheme." *Donovan v. Dewey*, 452 U.S., at 600. We explained in *Biswell*:

> If inspection is to be effective and serve as a credible deterrent, unannounced, even frequent inspections are essential. In this context, the prerequisite of a warrant could easily frustrate inspection; and if the necessary flexibility as to time, scope, and frequency is to be preserved, the protections afforded by a warrant would be negligible.

Third, Sec. 415-a5 provides a "constitutionally adequate substitute for a warrant." The statute informs the owner of a vehicle-dismantling business that inspections will be made on a regular basis. Thus, the vehicle dismantler knows that the inspections to which he is subject do not constitute discretionary acts by a government official but are conducted pursuant to statute. Section 415-a5 also sets forth the scope of the inspection and, accordingly, places the operator on notice as to how to comply with the statute. In addition, it notifies the operator as to who is authorized to conduct an inspection.

Finally, the "time, place, and scope" of the inspection is limited to place appropriate restraints upon the discretion of the inspecting officers. The officers

(continues)

NEW YORK V. BURGER

(continued from previous page)
are allowed to conduct an inspection only "during [the] regular and usual business hours." The inspections can be made only of vehicle-dismantling and related industries. And the permissible scope of these searches is narrowly defined: the inspectors may examine the records, as well as "any vehicle or parts of vehicles which are subject to the record-keeping requirements of this section and which are on the premises."

The Court of Appeals, nevertheless, struck down the statute as violative of the Fourth Amendment because, in its view, the statute had no truly administrative purpose but was "designed simply to give the police an expedient means of enforcing penal sanctions for possession of stolen property." In arriving at this conclusion, the Court of Appeals failed to recognize that a State can address a major social problem *both* by way of an administrative scheme and through penal sanctions. Administrative statutes and penal laws may have the same *ultimate* purpose of remedying the social problem, but they have different subsidiary purposes and prescribe different methods of addressing the problem.

Nor do we think that this administrative scheme is unconstitutional simply because, in the course of enforcing it, an inspecting officer may discover evidence of crimes, besides violations of the scheme itself. The discovery of evidence of crimes in the course of an otherwise proper administrative inspection does not render that search illegal or the administrative scheme suspect.

Finally, we fail to see any constitutional significance in the fact that police officers, rather than "administrative" agents, are permitted to conduct the Sec. 415-a5 inspection. [W]e decline to impose upon the States the burden of requiring the enforcement of their regulatory statutes to be carried out by special agents.

[Reversed.] ⚖

Obviously, warrantless searches may occur in motel lobbies, bars, and other business premises open to the public. The business has no expectation of privacy there. Additionally, the "open field" doctrine allows warrantless searches of areas that are so open to plain view that no reasonable expectation of privacy can exist. For example, the Supreme Court approved a warrantless EPA search carried out by a commercial aerial photographer flying over a 2000-acre chemical plant consisting of numerous covered buildings with outdoor manufacturing equipment and piping conduits.

Although the company had substantial ground-level security, the Court concluded that the plant was more like an open field than it was like "curtilage"— open space in the immediate vicinity of a dwelling, such as a yard. The Court noted that a commercial property owner has to expect less privacy than a homeowner so that, correspondingly, the government's latitude to conduct warrantless searches is greater.[3]

Rule Making
Much of the legislative-type activity of federal agencies is carried out through their rule-making func-tion. Sometimes Congress spells out the procedures for rule-making by a particular agency in that agency's enabling statute. Sometimes the agency is left to follow the Administrative Procedure Act (APA), which the more specific statutes normally follow anyway. The APA provides a comprehensive set of procedural guidelines for a variety of agency activities. In the rule-making area, the APA provides for two basic types—*informal* and *formal*. A third type, called *hybrid rule-making*, has also developed.

Informal Rule Making
Sometimes Congress will authorize informal rule making. To properly promulgate a rule under these procedures, the agency usually publishes a notice of the proposed rule in the *Federal Register*. There follows a comment period, typically of 30 days, in which any interested citizen or company may send written comments to the agency regarding the rule. Such comments might argue that the rule is unnecessary, is unduly burdensome to business, does not go far enough to remedy the problem, goes too far, and the like. The agency is then supposed to digest and react to the comments, perhaps by altering or even scrapping the proposed rule. Normally the rule is modestly altered, and then published in final form in the

---

[3]*Dow Chemical Co. v. U.S.*, 426 U.S. 227 (1986).

Federal Register. At that point, it becomes effective. Ultimately it will be codified in the *Code of Federal Regulations* along with the rules of all other federal administrative agencies.

Formal Rule Making

Formal rule making also involves "notice and comment," but it supplements these with formal hearings at which witnesses testify and are cross-examined by interested parties. Transcripts of the testimony are preserved and become part of the public record. Formal rule making can be very expensive and time-consuming but theoretically leads to especially well-considered results.

Hybrid Rule Making

Hybrid rule making closely resembles formal rule making, except that there is no right to cross-examine the agency's expert witnesses, and, as we shall soon see, a different standard of review is applied by the courts if the rule-making procedure is challenged.

Judicial Review of Rule Making

Naturally some parties are likely to be aggrieved by promulgation of rules that affect them adversely. Few important rules are issued without a subsequent court challenge. Courts will invalidate rules issued pursuant to an unconstitutional delegation of legislative power (as noted above, an extremely rare occurrence) and rules that are unconstitutional (perhaps because they discriminate on the basis of race in violation of equal protection principles).

Courts will also invalidate rules not issued in accordance with applicable procedural standards. For example, if an agency engaged in informal rule making fails to publish a proposed version of the rule in the *Federal Register* so that comments may be received, the rule will likely be invalidated if challenged. The courts will permit minor deviations from APA procedures, but major ones are risky.

Standards of Review. In issuing rules, an agency will have to make several types of decisions. One type of decision will likely turn on a pure **question of law** regarding its powers and the scope of its charge under a law passed by Congress. Courts are experts on the law. Therefore, they have the authority to substitute their interpretations for the meaning of laws passed by Congress for the interpretations made by the agency. Nonetheless, the Supreme Court has

concluded that it makes sense to give deference to the expertise developed by the agency, noting:

> When a court reviews an agency's construction of the statute which it administers, it is confronted with two questions. First, always, is the question whether Congress has spoken to the precise question at issue. If the intent of Congress is clear, that is the end of the matter; for the court, as well as the agency, must give effect to the unambiguously expressed intent of Congress. If, however, the court determines Congress has not directly addressed the precise question at issue, the court does not simply impose its own construction on the statute, as would be necessary in the absence of an administrative interpretation. Rather, if the statute is silent or ambiguous with respect to the specific issue, the question for the court is whether the agency's answer is based on a permissible construction of the statute . . . .
>
> We have long recognized that considerable weight should be accorded to an executive department's construction of a statutory scheme it is entrusted to administer, and the principles of deference to administrative interpretations.[4]

An agency issuing rules must also make decisions as to facts and policy. Two tests predominate review of these types of decisions. The *arbitrary and capricious test* assumes the correctness of an agency's decision, placing the burden on any challenger to prove that the decision was not simply erroneous but so far off the mark as to be arbitrary and capricious. The *substantial evidence test* requires that an agency's decision be based not just on a scintilla of evidence, but on such relevant evidence as a reasonable mind might accept as adequate to support a conclusion.

The arbitrary and capricious test is usually used to judge any policy decision by an agency. Findings of fact made pursuant to formal rule making are judged by the substantial evidence test. Factual determinations made in informal rule making are gauged by the arbitrary and capricious test unless an agency's authorizing act calls for use of the substantial evidence test. Many courts have noted that there is little practical difference in how the two tests are usually applied. Both require court deference to agency decision making, but the following case shows that such deference is not unlimited.

---

[4]*Chevron U.S.A., Inc. v. Natural Resources Defense Council,* 467 U.S. 837 (1984).

MOTOR VEHICLE MANUFACTURERS ASS'N. V. STATE FARM MUTUAL AUTO. INS. CO.

U.S. Supreme Court, 463 U.S.29 (1983)

 Case

To improve highway safety, Congress passed the National Traffic and Motor Vehicle Safety Act of 1966, which directs the Secretary of Transportation or a designated representative to issue motor vehicle safety standards. In 1967, the Secretary's representative, the National Highway Traffic Safety Administration (NHTSA) issued Standard 208, which required installation of seatbelts in all new automobiles. Because usage by consumers was quite low, NHTSA studied passive restraints in the form of automatic seatbelts and airbags, which it estimated could prevent approximately 12,000 deaths and more than 100,000 serious injuries annually. Deadlines for implementation of the passive restraint systems were repeatedly extended until, in 1977, the Secretary promulgated Modified Standard 208, which ordered a phase-in on all new cars to take place between 1982 and 1984. The Secretary assumed that 60 percent of new cars would have airbags and 40 percent would have automobile seatbelts.

However, it soon became apparent that 99 percent of American cars would have detachable seatbelts. In light of this fact and of economic difficulties in the auto industry, the Secretary began in 1981 to reconsider the passive restraint requirement of Modified Standard 208 and ultimately rescinded it.

State Farm Mutual and other insurance companies sued for review of the rescission order. The federal district court and court of appeals held the rescission to be arbitrary and capricious in violation of law. The petitioner Motor Vehicle Manufacturers Association brought the case to the Supreme Court.

White, Justice:

Both the Motor Vehicle Safety Act and the 1974 Amendments concerning occupant crash protection standards indicate that motor vehicle safety standards are to be promulgated under the informal rule-making procedures of §553 of the Administrative Procedure Act. The agency's action in promulgating such standards therefore may be set aside only if found to be "arbitrary, capricious, an abuse of discretion, or otherwise not in accordance with law." We believe that the rescission or modification of an occupant protection standard is subject to the same test.

The Department of Transportation argues that under this standard, a reviewing court may not set aside an agency rule that is rational, based on consideration of the relevant factors and within the scope of the authority delegated to the agency by the statute. We do not disagree with this formulation. The scope of review under the "arbitrary and capricious" standard is narrow and a court is not to substitute its judgment for that of the agency. Nevertheless, the agency must examine the relevant data and articulate a satisfactory explanation for its action including a "rational connection between the facts found and the choice made." *Burlington Truck Lines v. U.S.,* 371 U.S. 156 (1962). In reviewing that explanation, we must "consider whether the decision was based on a consideration of relevant factors and whether there has been a clear error of judgment." *Bowman Transp. Inc. v. Arkansas-Best Freight System, Inc.,* 419 U.S. 281 (1974). Normally, an agency rule would be arbitrary and capricious if the agency has relied on factors which Congress has not intended it to consider, entirely failed to consider an important aspect of the problem, offered an explanation for its decision that runs counter to the evi-

dence before the agency, or is so implausible that it could not be ascribed to a difference in view or the product of agency expertise. The reviewing court should not attempt itself to make up for such deficiencies: "We may not supply a reasoned basis for the agency's action that the agency itself has not given." *SEC v. Chenery Corp.,* 332 U.S. 194 (1947). "We will, however, uphold a decision of less than ideal clarity if the agency's path may reasonably be discerned." *Bowman Transp.*

The ultimate question before us is whether NHTSA's rescission of the passive restraint requirement of Standard 208 was arbitrary and capricious. We conclude, as did the Court of Appeals, that it was. We also conclude, but for somewhat different reasons, that further consideration of the issue by the agency is therefore required. We deal separately with . . . airbags and seatbelts.

The first and most obvious reason for finding rescission arbitrary and capricious is that NHTSA apparently gave no consideration whatever to modifying the Standard to require that airbag technology be utilized. Not one sentence of its rulemaking statement discusses the airbags-only option. [W]hat we said in *Burlington Truck Lines v. United States,* 371 U.S., at 167, is apropos here:

There are no findings and no analysis here to justify the choice made, no indication of the basis on which the [agency] exercised its expert discretion. We are not prepared to and the Administrative Procedures Act will not permit us to accept such . . . practice. . . . Expert discretion is the lifeblood of the administrative process, but "unless we make the requirements for administrative action strict and demanding, expertise, the strength of modern government, can become a monster which rules with no practical limits on its discretion." *New York v. United States,* 342 U.S. 882.

(continues)

MOTOR VEHICLE MANUFACTURERS ASS'N. V. STATE FARM MUTUAL AUTO. INS. CO.

(continued from previous page)

We have frequently reiterated that an agency must cogently explain why it has exercised its discretion in a given manner. [T]he airbag is more than a policy alternative to the passive restraint standard; it is a technological alternative within the ambit of the existing standard. We hold only that given the judgment made in 1977 that airbags are an effective and cost-beneficial life-saving technology, the mandatory passive-restraint rule may not be abandoned without any consideration whatsoever of an airbags-only requirement.

Although the issue is closer, we also find that the agency was too quick to dismiss the safety benefits of automatic seatbelts. NHTSA's critical finding was that, in light of the industry's plans to install readily detachable passive belts, it could not reliably predict "even a 5 percentage point increase as the minimum level of expected usage increase." The Court of Appeals rejected this finding because there is "not one iota"

of evidence that Modified Standard 208 will fail to increase nationwide seatbelt use by at least 13 percentage points, the level of increased usage necessary for the standard to justify its cost.

Recognizing that policymaking in a complex society must account for uncertainty . . . does not imply that it is sufficient for an agency to merely recite the terms "substantial uncertainty" as a justification for its actions. The agency must explain the evidence which is available and must offer a "rational connection between the facts and found and the choice made." *Burlington Truck Lines.* Generally, one aspect of that explanation would be a justification for rescinding the regulation before engaging in a search for further evidence.

The agency is correct to look at the costs as well as the benefits of Standard 208 [but i]n reaching its judgment, NHTSA should bear in mind that Congress intended safety to be the preeminent factor under the Act.

The agency also failed to articulate a basis for not requiring nondetachable belts under Standard 208. By failing to analyze the continuous seatbelt in its own right, the agency has failed to offer the rational connection between facts and judgment required to pass muster under the arbitrary and capricious standard. We agree with the Court of Appeals that NHTSA did not suggest that the emergency release mechanisms used in nondetachable belts are any less effective for emergency egress than the buckle release system used in detachable belts.

"An agency's view of what is in the public interest may change, either with or without a change in circumstances. But an agency changing its course must supply a reasoned analysis. . . ." *Greater Boston Television Corp. v. FCC,* 444 F.2d 841 (CADC).

[Remand to Court of Appeals with directions to remand to NHTSA for further consideration consistent with this opinion.] ⚖

Adjudication

Most major federal agencies also exercise substantial powers of adjudication. That is, they not only issue rules and investigate to uncover violations, they may also charge alleged violators and try them to determine whether a violation has actually occurred.

Because the agency is acting as legislator, police officer, prosecutor, *and* judge and jury, care must be taken to avoid abuse. For that reason, the APA and the courts demand that formal procedural requirements be followed.

Over the years, procedures have evolved such that a person or company brought before an administrative agency for adjudication of a charged violation will usually have the right to notice, the right to counsel, the right to present evidence, and the right

to confront and cross-examine adverse witnesses.

A jury trial is not allowed, but the case is heard by an administrative law judge (ALJ), who is the finder of fact in the first instance. Although the 1000-plus ALJs in the federal system are employees of the agencies whose cases they hear, they cannot be disciplined except for good cause as determined by the federal Merit System Protection Board. Thus, the ALJs exercise substantial autonomy and are seldom puppets of the agency employing them.

Under the APA, all ALJ decisions are reviewable by the employing agency. The agency reviews the record developed in the hearing that was conducted by the ALJ, and reviews the ALJ's fact-findings and legal conclusions. Although the agency usually conducts a limited appellate-type review of the ALJ's

**Box 6.1
The Law
at Work**

As we saw in Chapter 3, various methods of alternative dispute resolution (ADR) are becoming increasingly popular for resolving many kinds of conflicts. In the area of administrative law, one important use of ADR is negotiated *rule making,* sometimes referred to as *regulatory negotiation* or *reg-neg.* Under such a process, the agency proposing to adopt a particular regulation attempts to identify and bring together representatives of various interest groups that might be affected by the regulation. Negotiated rule making is essentially a form of multiparty mediation, with either agency representatives or professional mediators performing the mediation function. The objective is to reach agreement on as many aspects of the regulation as possible, producing rules that accommodate the concerns of affected parties to the greatest extent feasible and reducing the probability of legal challenges to the validity of the rules.

One recent example of an apparently successful use of negotiated rule making involved the U.S. Coast Guard. The 1990 Oil Pollution Act provided that the Coast Guard must adopt regulations requiring operators of oil tankers and barges to develop individual oil spill response plans. Although the Coast Guard could have gone through a typical formal or informal rule-making process, it chose to use a negotiated rule-making process that brought together oil tanker and barge operators, representatives of several environmental groups, and officials from the Coast Guard and other government agencies. Ultimately, the group was able to reach a consensus on a detailed regulation concerning the necessary equipment and personnel to be aboard tankers and barges, the required training for crew members assigned emergency spill response duties, procedures for "lightering" (offloading oil from a tanker to barges or other vessels in the event of a spill or leakage), procedures for coordinating responses with federal officials, and other matters. The agreement reached by the group was then used as the basis for a regulation proposed and issued by the Coast Guard.

findings and conclusions, it does have the power to substitute its own findings and conclusions for those of the ALJ. If the agency does so, however, it still must base its decision on the evidence that appears in the ALJ-hearing record—it cannot disregard this record.

Adjudication is a very influential process. Not only are findings of fact required (for example, did the employer consult the union before deciding to move the plant?), but the ALJ and the agency must also interpret the applicable law (for example, is the employer required to consult the union before deciding to move the plant?). During the Reagan administration, the NLRB largely rewrote American labor policy through the process of adjudication. Although this was done piecemeal through several decisions involving unfair labor practice charges, the change in the law was as complete as if major rule making had been undertaken.

The quasijudicial powers of major federal agencies are so significant that such decisions are normally reviewed directly by the circuit courts of appeal. Other types of decisions—such as the decision to issue a subpoena or to promulgate a new rule—are normally reviewed in the first instance by federal district courts. (Figure 6.1 helps illustrate the adjudicatory process of a federal agency.)

Many different kinds of agency action obviously can have an effect on the liberty or property of individuals and companies. As we saw in the previous chapter, procedural due process requires that many of these actions be preceded by notice and a hearing of some type. These principles were discussed and illustrated at length. The following case involves a procedural due process challenge to an agency action. Because the agency's action was of an adjudicative type—aimed at a particular company based on specific facts—procedural due process applied. The question that remained, however, was whether the agency had provided sufficient procedural protections under the circumstances.

GUN SOUTH, INC. V. BRADY

U.S. Eleventh Circuit Court of Appeals, 877 F.2d 858 (1989)

 Case

Gun South, Inc. (GSI), is a wholesale gun dealer licensed by the Treasury Department's Bureau of Alcohol, Tobacco, and Firearms. In late 1988 and again in early 1989, GSI applied for and was granted permits to import semiautomatic rifles for sporting purposes. On January 23, 1989, GSI ordered 800 AUG-SA semiautomatic rifles and obligated itself to pay $700,000 toward a larger total purchase price. On March 21, 1989, William Bennett, the "Drug Czar," speaking for the secretary of the treasury, announced a temporary 90-day suspension on the importation of five "assault-type" weapons, including those ordered by GSI, so that the bureau could review its conclusion that such rifles are "generally suitable for sporting purposes." Although the bureau assured GSI that the suspension did not apply to weapons purchased under preexisting permits, the Customs Service intercepted GSI's shipment of the aforementioned rifles at the Birmingham Airport.

GSI brought this action to enjoin the government from interfering with the delivery of firearms imported under permits issued before the suspension. The district court issued such an injunction; Brady, Secretary of the Treasury, appealed. The appellate court's discussion of the due process issue follows.

Hatchett, Circuit Judge:

According to GSI, the Government's failure to give it notice of the suspension and an opportunity to respond prior to imposing the suspension deprived GSI of its due process rights. GSI reaches this conclusion by arguing that the Government may not deprive an individual of property without giving such individual an opportunity to be heard. Although GSI correctly argues

the general rule, GSI fails to recognize that the Constitution does not always require such predeprivation procedural protection. *Hodel v. Virginia Surface Mining and Reclamation Assoc.,* 452 U.S. 264, 300 (1981) ("summary administrative action may be justified in emergency situations"). See *Barry v. Barchi,* 443 U.S. 55 (1979) (pending prompt judicial or administrative hearing to determine issue, state's board could properly temporarily suspend horse trainer's license prior to hearing); *Ewing v. Mytinger and Casselberry, Inc.,* 339 U.S. 594 (1950) (allowing seizure of misbranded articles by enforcement agency prior to hearing).

Rather than setting categories of mandatory procedural protections in all cases, the Supreme Court decides the nature and timing of the requisite process in an individual case by accommodating the relevant competing interests.

The Supreme Court's balancing test essentially requires us to weigh three factors: (1) the nature of the private interest; (2) the risk of an erroneous deprivation of such interest; and (3) the government's interest in taking its action, including the burdens that any additional procedural requirement would entail. *Mathews v. Eldridge,* 424 U.S. 319, 335 (1976). Balancing these considerations, we conclude that the Bureau's summary action did not violate GSI's due process rights.

The Bureau imposed the temporary suspension to protect the public by ensuring that nearly three-quarters of a million rifles do not improperly enter the country. The protection of the public's health and safety is a paramount government interest which justifies summary administrative action:

Protection of the health and safety of the public is a paramount governmental interest which justifies summary administrative action. Indeed, deprivation of property to protect the public health and safety is '[o]ne of the oldest examples' of permissible summary action.

Hodel, 452 U.S. at 300 (safety concerns justified summary seizure of vitamin product). The public interest in avoiding the import of possible illegal assault rifles which could contribute significantly to this country's violent crime epidemic is clearly substantial, especially given the large number of rifles approved for importation under the current outstanding permits. The Government could not protect the public interest without imposing the temporary suspension.

On the other side of the balancing equation, we consider the nature of the private interest, including the deprivation's length and finality. GSI has not suffered a permanent loss because the government has not revoked GSI's license or its permits. The Government has merely deprived GSI of the ability to import the AUG-SA rifle for ninety days. The Government has further reassured the court that it will not revoke GSI's permits without giving GSI the right to participate in a hearing.

In addition to being a non-final, temporary deprivation, the ninety-day suspension does not affect a significant portion of GSI's imports. The rifles which GSI seeks to import during this ninety-day period are only a small percent of the number of firearms it plans to import under its permits this year.

Considering the final factor, we do not find that the Government's summary action presents a significant risk of an erroneous deprivation of GSI's right to import the rifles. First, GSI only loses its right to import the rifles for ninety days. Second, as discussed above, the Bureau considered ample evidence before imposing the temporary suspension, and therefore, it minimized the risk that its action would erroneously deprive GSI of its right to import the AUG-SA rifles.

Balancing GSI's temporary nonfinal loss of its right to import one type of rifle against the Government's interest

(continues)

GUN SOUTH, INC. V. BRADY

(*continued from previous page*)
in preventing the unlawful importation of firearms, we conclude that the Government did not err by suspending the importation of the AUG-SA rifle prior to giving GSI an opportunity to respond. The strong public interest in the immediate action outweighs the temporary and limited impact on GSI's alleged property interest. We find support for this decision in other cases which have subordinated more substantial property interests to the Government interest in protecting the public. *See Mackey v. Montrym,* 443 U.S. 1 (1979) (although license to operate motor vehicle is substantial property interest, the substantial nature of such interest is diminished measurably by maximum duration of suspension being ninety days and availability of immediate post-suspension hearing). Furthermore, the availability of a hearing at the end of this temporary suspension provides adequate procedural protection. Thus, the summary imposition of the import suspension does not violate GSI's due process rights.

[Reversed.] ⚖

ESTOPPEL

Often businesses that deal with the government seek advice from government officials, asking such questions as the right way to fill out tax returns, the correct interpretation of a zoning ordinance, or the legality of a securities sale. What all businesspersons must keep in mind is that government officials may from time to time give erroneous advice, but that does not relieve the businesses from culpability.

The legal doctrine of **estoppel** provides in many areas that an entity that takes a particular position that others rely on cannot later change that original position when to do so would injure the party that relied on it. Unfortunately, the general rule is that the

FIGURE 6.1

Administrative Law Process

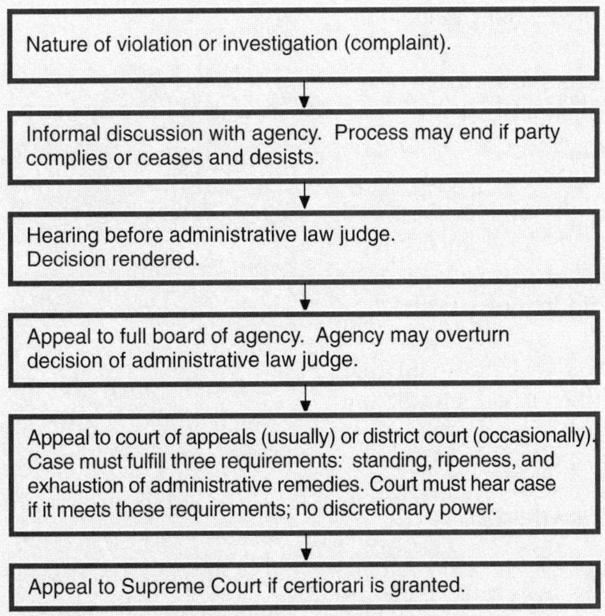

Nature of violation or investigation (complaint).

↓

Informal discussion with agency. Process may end if party complies or ceases and desists.

↓

Hearing before administrative law judge.
Decision rendered.

↓

Appeal to full board of agency. Agency may overturn decision of administrative law judge.

↓

Appeal to court of appeals (usually) or district court (occasionally). Case must fulfill three requirements: standing, ripeness, and exhaustion of administrative remedies. Court must hear case if it meets these requirements; no discretionary power.

↓

Appeal to Supreme Court if certiorari is granted.

doctrine of estoppel does not operate against the government. That is to say, if the government gives erroneous advice, it is not later "estopped to deny" its original position.

The leading case on this subject is *Federal Crop Insurance Corp. v. Merrill*,[5] in which a government official told farmer Merrill that reseeded spring wheat would be covered by federal crop insurance. Unfortunately, the agency's regulations, printed in the *Federal Register*, stated that insurance would not be provided for reseeded crops. Merrill, not knowing of the regulation, relied on the advice. When the crop was destroyed, however, Merrill was unable to recover insurance. The government was not estopped to deny its original position. It was allowed to change its position in a way that the doctrine of estoppel would probably prevent a private insurance company from doing.

The reasoning behind the government exclusion lies, in part, in the notion that federal statutes are contained in the *United States Code* and federal regulations are printed in the *Federal Register* and codified in the *Code of Federal Regulations*, and therefore all citizens are "on notice" of these rules. Still, the exclusion seems unjust to many people, so some exceptions have developed. For example, some courts will invoke estoppel against the government when an official has intentionally misled someone. Others create an exception when the government is acting in a proprietary (business-like) capacity. Today, for example, many courts might decide the 1947 *Merrill* case differently, because in that case the agency was acting more in the role of a private insurance company than as a government agency.

The doctrine's impact when lower levels of government are involved is less clear but cannot be ignored. This lesson was brought home recently when builders given the "go-ahead" by local government officials to build a 31-story building were, after substantial construction, forced to remove everything above the nineteenth floor because the officials had misread a zoning ordinance.[6] The Court said that estoppel is not available "for the purpose of ratifying an administrative error."

RECENT DEVELOPMENTS

The federal administrative process has been closely scrutinized from several angles in recent years. To

make federal agencies more open to public view and more responsive to the needs of constituents and to fiscal and economic concerns, many changes have been made.

Freedom of Information Act

The Freedom of Information Act of 1967 (FOIA), with significant amendments in 1974, is codified as section 552 of the Administrative Procedure Act. Before its enactment it was extremely difficult for a private citizen to obtain and examine government-held documents. The agency from which the information was requested could deny the applicant on the grounds that he or she was not properly and directly concerned or that the requested information should not be disclosed because to do so would not be in the public interest. Under the FOIA, any person may reasonably describe what information is sought, and the burden of proof for withholding information is on the agency. A response is required of the agency within 10 working days after receipt of a request, and denial by the agency may be appealed by means of an expeditable federal district court action. There are, of course, exemptions—nine specific areas to which the disclosure requirements do not apply. That is, if the information concerns certain matters, the agency is not required to comply with the request. The nine exemptions apply to matters that are:

1. Secret in the interest of national defense or foreign policy;

2. Related solely to internal personnel rules and practices of an agency;

3. Exempted from disclosure by statute;

4. Trade secrets and commercial or financial information obtained from a person and privileged or confidential;

5. Interagency or intraagency memoranda or letters;

6. Personnel and medical files, the disclosure of which would constitute an invasion of personal privacy;

7. Certain investigatory records compiled for law enforcement purposes;

8. Related to the regulation or supervision of financial institutions;

9. Geologic and geophysical information and data, including maps concerning wells.

[5]322 U.S. 380 (1947).
[6]*Matter of Parkview Assoc. v. City of New York*, 513 N.Y.S.2d 342, *cert. denied*, 109 S.Ct. 30 (1988).

With regard to the exemptions, Chief Judge Bazelon had this to say in *Soucie v. David,* 448 F.2d 1067 (D.C.Cir. 1971):

The touchstone of any proceedings under the Act must be the clear legislative intent to assure public access to all governmental records whose disclosure would not significantly harm specific governmental interests. The policy of the Act requires that the disclosure requirements be construed broadly, the exemptions narrowly.

Businesses have often complained that confidential information they were required to disclose to the government pursuant to regulatory programs might be vulnerable to disclosure to competitors through the FOIA. In 1987, regulations were issued that require federal agencies to provide early notification to businesses whenever "arguably" confidential business data in government hands are about to be released under the FOIA. Those businesses are given an opportunity to object to the disclosure. Agencies are required to explain in writing if they choose to override such an objection.

Privacy Act
The Federal Privacy Act of 1974 seeks to protect individuals from unnecessary disclosures of facts about them from files held by federal agencies. Although the need of federal agencies for information is recognized through a large series of exceptions and qualifications, the general thrust of the Privacy Act is to prohibit federal agencies from disclosing information from their files about an individual without that individual's written consent. Federal agencies are specifically forbidden from selling or renting an individual's name and address, unless authorized by another law.

Government in the Sunshine Act
A further effort to open up the government is provided by the 1976 Government in the Sunshine Act, codified as section 552b of the Administrative Procedure Act. The purpose of the Act is to assure that "every portion of every meeting of an agency shall be open to public observation." There are, however, exceptions to the open meeting requirement. If the meeting qualifies for one of ten specified exemptions and the agency by majority vote decides to do so, the meeting may be closed to the public. The exemptions of the Act are similar to the nine provided for in the FOIA but are not identical.

Most states have passed some form of open meet-ings laws. There is considerable diversity, but the common purpose is to permit the public to view the decision-making process at all stages.

Regulatory Flexibility Act
We are all presumed to know the law and when final versions of rules are published in the *Federal Register,* legally speaking, we are all put on notice of their existence. Congress realized, however, that as a practical matter many persons, especially small businesses, do not closely follow proposed and final rules printed in the *Federal Register.* Therefore, Congress passed the Regulatory Flexibility Act (RFA) in 1980. Among other provisions, the RFA requires most federal agencies to transmit to the Small Business Administration on a semiannual basis agendas briefly describing areas in which they may propose rules having a substantial impact on small entities (including small businesses, small governmental units, and nonprofit organizations). In this way the small businesses may be on the lookout for potential changes. Also, when any rule is promulgated that will have a significant economic impact on a substantial number of small entities, the agency proposing the rule must give notice not only through the *Federal Register* but also through publications of general notice likely to be obtained by small entities, such as trade journals.

Deregulation
The economic efficiency of many programs of federal regulation is easily questioned. Furthermore, the paperwork burden on many companies attempting to comply with complex federal regulatory schemes can be overwhelming. For these and other reasons, recent administrations have attempted to "deregulate" the economy.

Congress has, at times, assisted the deregulation movement, as evidenced by the Airline Deregulation Act of 1978, the CAB Sunshine Act of 1984, and the Motor Carrier Act of 1980. Various executive orders and agency interpretations have supplemented the effort. During the Reagan administration, for example, there was a noticeably less aggressive enforcement attitude in such agencies as OSHA, the Consumer Products Safety Commission (CPSC), and the EPA.

The advantages and disadvantages of deregulation will be debated for years. Proponents point to the cost savings and the general fare reductions that have occurred in the airline industry through introduction of free competition and elimination of government rate setting. Opponents point to a recent rise in injuries from products and in the work place, the provinces of OSHA and the CPSC, and to alleged increases in various types of pollution caused by EPA inactivity. Neither increases in regulation nor decreases in regulation (as the *Motor Vehicle Manufacturers Ass'n v. State Farm Mutual Auto. Ins. Co.* case shows) come without cost. To a large extent, the positions taken on the deregulation debate are determined by political philosophies and "whose ox is being gored."

SUMMARY

In terms of the influence of administrative agencies on America's economy and society, these agencies truly constitute a "fourth branch of government."

Increased complexity in our economy and society means that our legislatures, state and federal, cannot give personal attention to even a fraction of the problems demanding government attention. Therefore, substantial legislative power is delegated to administrative agencies, sometimes under only the vaguest of guidelines.

Major federal agencies possess both ministerial and discretionary powers. The discretionary powers include those to investigate (as the executive branch does), to make rules (as the legislative branch does), and to adjudicate alleged violations (as the judicial branch does). The courts may review virtually all agency actions.

To be valid, agency rules must be promulgated in accordance with a constitutional delegation of authority, pursuant to proper procedures, in accordance with constitutional strictures—especially those of due process—and must not be arbitrary and capricious.

The power of administrative agencies is very controversial. In recent years the federal government especially has attempted to make administrative procedures more open to public scrutiny and to streamline them so they will be less burdensome for the regulated parties.

KEY TERMS

Administrative agency
Ministerial powers
Discretionary powers
Investigative powers
Rule-making powers
Adjudicative powers
Subpoena
Question of law
Estoppel

QUESTIONS AND PROBLEMS

1. Louisiana passed a statute to regulate commercial marine diving. Among other things, the statute created a Licensing Board, which thereafter promulgated rules and regulations relative to the qualifications of apprentice, journeyman, and master marine divers. One regulation provided that a person could be licensed as a master marine diver only if he or she had "continuously worked for a period of five years under supervision of a master marine diver." Under this regulation, the board refused to license a diver (as a master marine diver) who had had several years' diving experience in the U.S. Navy and who had also had about eight years' commercial diving experience in Louisiana (but not under supervision of a master marine diver). The diver challenged the board's action, contending that the statute was an unconstitutional delegation of legislative authority because it permitted the board to set licensing qualifications without containing any statutory limitations on it, or any standards to which the board should look in setting its qualifications. Do you agree with this contention? Why or why not? (*Banjavich v. Louisiana Licensing Board of Marine Divers,* 111 So.2d 505, 1959.)

2. The U.S. Department of Energy (DOE) issued a subpoena for Phoenix Petroleum Company records during the course of an investigation to determine whether Phoenix had illegally sold crude oil. Phoenix moved to quash (invalidate) the subpoena, claiming DOE was on a "fishing expedition." DOE proved the subpoenaed items were reasonably relevant to the purpose of the investigation but admitted that it could not establish probable cause to believe a violation had taken place. Should the subpoena be quashed by the court? Discuss. (*U.S. v. Phoenix Petroleum Co.,* 571 F.Supp. 16, S.D. Tex. 1982.)

3. Biswell, a pawnshop operator who was federally licensed to deal in sporting weapons, was visited one afternoon by a policeman and a Federal Treasury agent who requested entry into a locked gun storeroom. They had no search warrant but showed

Biswell a section of the Gun Control Act of 1968, which authorized warrantless entry of the premises of gun dealers. Biswell then allowed a search that turned up two sawed-off rifles and led to Biswell's conviction for dealing in firearms without having paid a required special occupational tax. On appeal, Biswell challenged the constitutionality of the warrantless search. Discuss. (*U.S. v. Biswell,* 406 U.S. 311, 1972.)

4. The Federal Trade Commission Act authorizes the Federal Trade Commission (FTC) to determine what kinds of business practices constitute "unfair methods of competition, and deceptive or unfair practices" and to prohibit such practices. Traditionally, when such a practice has been found to exist, the FTC has simply ordered the offending company to stop the practice. In 1975, however, when the FTC ruled that Listerine ads had—for many years—falsely stated that Listerine was "effective in preventing and curing colds and sore throats," the FTC ordered the manufacturer to stop such advertising, and in addition, it ordered the manufacturer to insert in *future* advertising the statement that Listerine would *not* prevent or cure colds and sore throats. The manufacturer then asked the federal courts to rule that the FTC did not have the power, under the Federal Trade Commission Act, to issue such an order (known as *corrective advertising.*) Do you think the manufacturer's argument is a good one? Why or why not? (*Warner-Lambert v. FTC,* 562 F.2d 749, 1977.)

5. A New Jersey statute provided that every taxicab owner who wished to operate in a city within the state had to obtain consent of the "governing body" of the municipality. The statute also provided that the governing body could "make and enforce" ordinances to "license and regulate" all vehicles used as taxis. Under this law a New Jersey city passed an ordinance that set a flat rate taxicab fare of $1.15 for all trips made within the city, regardless of the miles in-

volved. A taxicab owner who wanted to charge $1.50 for some trips attacked this ordinance on the grounds that the statute did *not,* expressly or impliedly, give to cities the power to set taxi fares. (The gist of the attack was that legislatures could not delegate *rate-making* powers to municipalities.) What was the result? Discuss. (*Yellow Cab Corp. v. Clifton City Council,* 308 A.2d 60, 1973.)

6. One section of an Oklahoma law provided that no person shall "knowingly sell" alcoholic beverages to a minor. Certain penalties were provided for, in the event of violations. Another section of the law authorized the Oklahoma Beverage Control Board to promulgate rules and regulations to carry out the act. The board then adopted a rule that, in essence, provided that any liquor license could be revoked if the licensee sold liquor to a minor, even if he or she did *not* know the buyer was a minor. When the license of a liquor retailer, Wray, was revoked by the board as a result of his sale of liquor to a person whom he did not know was a minor, he contended in the Oklahoma courts that the rule of the board was invalid because it conflicted with the quoted statute. Do you agree this argument? Discuss. (*Wray v. Oklahoma Alcoholic Beverage Control Board,* 442 P.2d 309, 1968.)

7. A Social Security Administration field representative erroneously told Hansen that she was not eligible for "mother's insurance benefits." Because of this advice, Hansen did not file a written application, which, by the terms of the law, was a prerequisite to receiving benefits. Nor did the agent follow instructions to advise potential claimants of the written filing requirement and to encourage them to file in a close case. A year or so later, Hansen filed an application and received benefits. She then sued to recover the benefits that she had missed during the period that she had relied on the erroneous advice. Will she succeed? (*Schweiker v. Hansen,* 450 U.S. 785, 1981.)

Chapter 7

Criminal Law and Business

Nature of Criminal Law
Constitutional Protections
General Elements of Criminal Responsibility
General Criminal Defenses
State Crimes Affecting Business
Federal Crimes Affecting Business
Computer Crime
White Collar Crime

B USINESSES ARE THE victims of crime. Businesses commit crimes. This sad reality necessitates a general overview of the role of criminal law in the legal environment of business. Armed robberies, bad checks, employee pilfering, and other criminal acts cost businesses billions of dollars annually. Consumers suffer as well, because these losses are manifested either in the form of higher prices or, worse, failed businesses.

Criminal acts committed by businesses also cause enormous losses to our society. Though crimes committed *by* businesses received little attention in the criminal law until recently, that situation has changed dramatically as we have become aware of such wrongful acts as stifling competition by fixing prices, selling stock based on contrived financial statements, using false advertising to lure customers into buying inferior products, and the like.

The strong interrelationship between criminal law and the vital interests of business is highlighted by frequent references to criminal acts in other chapters of this text. For example, there is discussion of contracts calling for criminal acts in Chapter 14, of criminal securities law violations in Chapter 41, of illegal competitive acts in Chapter 48, and of criminal violation of environmental laws in Chapter 50.

NATURE OF CRIMINAL LAW

A **crime** is a wrong committed against society. Indeed, that wrong is also defined by society, because the criminal law is one of a civilized society's primary tools for conforming the behavior of its citizens to societal norms. Even in a society with as many freedoms as America's, limits must be placed on individual and corporate actions. Today's drug epidemic is a vivid reminder of the damage that certain types of individual activity can inflict on society as a whole. Criminalizing activity is often far from the best way to address the causes of that activity or to solve the problems that arise from it. Nonetheless, criminal law is one of society's most important mechanisms for controlling individual behavior, and that will not change anytime soon.

Civil and Criminal Law Contrasted

Most of this text discusses civil law matters. While there are many similarities between criminal law and civil law, there are also important distinctions. The civil law adjusts rights between or among individuals. The basis of the controversy may be a broken commercial promise, an injury caused by someone's careless driving, or a loss caused by a defective product. The focus is on adjusting the rights of the parties to the transaction. The criminal law, on the other hand, focuses on the individual's relationship to society. In enacting criminal statues, a government is saying that there are certain activities so inherently contrary to the public good that they must be flatly prohibited *in the best interests of society.*

A civil lawsuit is brought by one individual or company (the plaintiff) against another (the defendant). A criminal action, on the other hand, is always brought by an agent of the government (the prosecutor or district attorney) against the alleged wrongdoer. The essence of the civil suit is an injury that the defendant's wrongful act caused to the individual plaintiff. The essence of a criminal prosecution is the injury that the defendant's wrongful act caused society. Of course, there are usually individual victims of criminal acts. The suffering of those victims is not ignored by the criminal law, but greater emphasis is placed on the implications that such conduct has for society at large.

A plaintiff in a civil suit usually requests money damages as compensation for injuries sustained by the defendant's wrongful conduct. In a criminal action, however, even a successful prosecution will not usually produce a dime for the plaintiff. Rather, the remedy sought by the prosecutor typically is punishment for the defendant, such as a fine (which usually goes to the state), imprisonment, or both.

Of course, many types of acts (such as battery) constitute both criminal wrongs and actionable torts. As illustrated in Figure 7.1, the same activity might be the subject of both a civil suit by the victim and a criminal action by the state. A critical difference in such actions lies in the burden of proof. A plaintiff in a civil action must prove the elements of recovery by only "a preponderance of the evidence." Because the

FIGURE 7.1

A Single Act as Both Tort and Crime

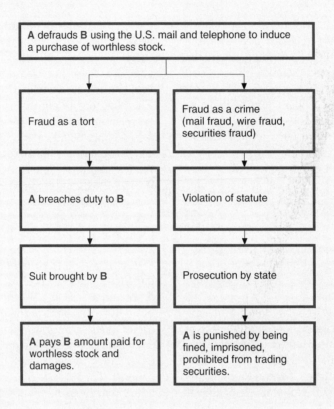

consequences of a criminal conviction are generally considered much more severe, a higher standard of proof must be met by prosecutors. Jurors must be convinced of the defendant's guilt "beyond a reasonable doubt" before the guilty verdict is appropriate. Figure 7.2 outlines major differences between civil and criminal law.

Classification of Crimes

Degree of Seriousness

Except for the most serious crime of treason, crimes are either *felonies* or *misdemeanors,* depending on the severity of the penalty that the statute provides. The definition of **felony** varies from state to state, but it is usually defined as any crime in which the punishment is either death or imprisonment for more than one year in a state penitentiary, as in the cases of murder, robbery, or rape. **Misdemeanors**

are all crimes carrying lesser penalties (such as fines or confinement in county jails)—for example, petit larceny and disorderly conduct. In the federal system, felonies are crimes for which the designated penalty is more than one year in prison; misdemeanors are crimes with lesser designated penalties. Yet another category used in some states is *petty offenses,* covering such infractions as traffic and building code violations.

The distinction between felonies and misdemeanors can be important because of various penalties often imposed on persons convicted of the former, such as loss of the right to vote, to hold public office, or to pursue various careers.

Degree of Moral Turpitude

Crimes such as murder, rape, arson, or robbery are evil in and of themselves. Such acts are called *malum in se,* meaning that they are criminal because they

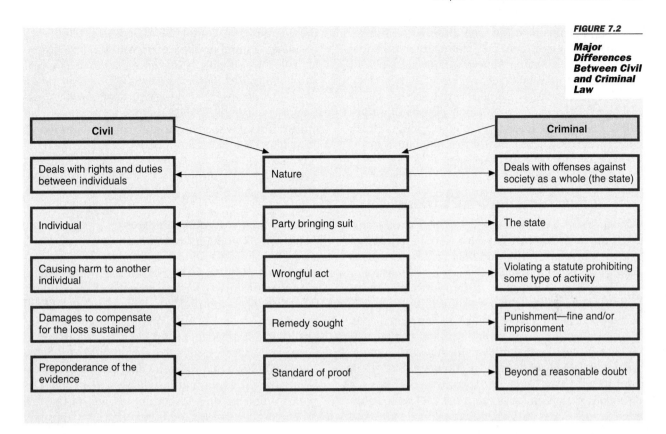

FIGURE 7.2

Major Differences Between Civil and Criminal Law

Civil	Nature	Criminal
Deals with rights and duties between individuals	Nature	Deals with offenses against society as a whole (the state)
Individual	Party bringing suit	The state
Causing harm to another individual	Wrongful act	Violating a statute prohibiting some type of activity
Damages to compensate for the loss sustained	Remedy sought	Punishment—fine and/or imprisonment
Preponderance of the evidence	Standard of proof	Beyond a reasonable doubt

are inherently wicked. Other acts, such as jaywalking or speeding, are *malum prohibitum,* meaning that they are crimes merely because the legislature has said that they are wrongful. Typically, greater punishments attach to crimes that involve moral turpitude.

Jurisdiction

As has already been noted, in America a federal criminal justice system is superimposed over state and local systems. These systems generally address different concerns. Murder is usually a concern only of the state in which it occurred unless, for example, it occurred on federal property, the victim was a federal official, or it occurred as part of an interstate kidnapping. Still, there are several areas of overlap and actions that might well violate both federal and state laws. For example, during the wave of bank robberies during the 1930s Depression, a federal law against bank robberies was passed so that the Federal Bureau of Investigation and federal prosecutors could supplement the efforts of state police and judicial systems.

Purpose of Punishment

Perhaps the most salient feature of the criminal justice system is the punishment that it imposes on wrongdoers. As noted earlier, the punishment is not imposed to compensate the victim. That is the province of the civil tort system. Rather, there are four primary purposes of criminal punishment. First, there is *rehabilitation* or reformation. Although published rates of recidivism (relapse into crime) indicate that this is the most difficult of the punishment goals to attain, it is important that our system at least attempt to reform wrongdoers.

A second, less ambitious, purpose of punishment is simply *restraint* or incapacitation, on the theory that a robber cannot rob and a rapist cannot rape while they are locked up. A third purpose of punishment, and a somewhat controversial one, is that of *retribution.* The concept of retribution predates the Bible's admonition of "an eye for an eye," and society's infliction of retribution on criminals still has strong popular support.

A final purpose of punishment is *deterrence.* The law seeks to persuade the wrongdoer being punished not to err again and, at the same time, to provide an example that might generally deter other potential lawbreakers. The effectiveness of various types of criminal sanctions in deterring crime is not clear. One very controversial subject is the death penalty. Although most evidence makes it clear that a state will not reduce its murder rate by adopting a death penalty, advocates still justify the ultimate punishment on restraint and retribution grounds.

CONSTITUTIONAL PROTECTIONS

Once arrested, a criminal defendant has the considerable power and resources of the government lined up against him or her. The potential for abuse of that power is considerable, and one need not be a student of history to discover blatant examples of such abuses. Because our system operates on the theory that it is better that a guilty man or woman go free than that an innocent man or woman should suffer unjust punishment, we provide manifold protections for criminal defendants. Many of these protections are set forth in the Bill of Rights. Through the controversial process of "incorporation," most of these rights have been applied to the states as well. Additionally, many state constitutions contain parallel protections. The following discussion will help complete the examination of constitutional law begun in Chapter 5.

Fourth Amendment

The Fourth Amendment protects people (and, as we saw in Chapter 6, businesses) against "unreasonable searches and seizures," requiring that search warrants not be issued absent "probable cause." A search warrant will be issued by a judge if the police have produced evidence that would lead a reasonably prudent person to believe there is a substantial likelihood that the defendant is guilty of the offense the police charge. The Fourth Amendment requires that the warrant "particularly describe" the place to be searched and the persons or things to be seized.

A controversial question regards enforcement of this prohibition. What happens to evidence that the police seize without a valid warrant? In *Mapp v. Ohio,* 367 U.S. 643 (1961), the Supreme Court held that "all evidence obtained by searches and seizures in violation of the Constitution is. . . inadmissible in a state court." This holding was very controversial, opponents arguing that "the crook should not go free just because the constable has erred." In recent years

the increasingly conservative Supreme Court has fashioned a number of exceptions to this "exclusionary rule," weakening its impact substantially. For example, in *United States v. Leon,* 468 U.S. 189 (1984), the Court created a "good faith" exception for situations in which the police searched pursuant to an apparently valid search warrant that was later determined to have been improperly issued. The Court reasoned, in part, that the exclusionary rule was meant to deter police abuses rather than to correct errors by judges.

Fifth Amendment

The Fifth Amendment contains a number of provisions that protect criminal defendants from government abuse. For example, individuals cannot be held to answer for major federal criminal charges unless they have been indicted by a **grand jury.** A grand jury typically consists of 23 members of the community who hear evidence presented by the prosecution. If a majority concludes that there is probable cause to believe that the defendant has committed a crime alleged, the grand jury issues a *true bill.* The right to indictment by grand jury is one of the few protections in the Bill of Rights that the Supreme Court has not applied to the states. However, many state constitutions have similar provisions.

The Fifth Amendment also protects defendants from **double jeopardy,** which is being tried twice for the same offense. This means that when a jury finds a defendant "not guilty," the government cannot simply reindict the defendant for the same crime and try again to convict him or her. However, it does not mean that a defendant acquitted of criminal assault and battery could not be sued civilly by his or her alleged victim. Because of the different burden of proof, the same body of evidence that did not convince a criminal jury beyond a reasonable doubt might convince a civil jury applying a preponderance of evidence standard. The fact that a state prosecution will not bar a subsequent federal prosecution and vice versa constitutes another major exception to the double jeopardy prohibition. Thus, theoretically, a defendant who was acquitted of a federal bank robbery charge might be prosecuted by a state claiming that the same alleged robbery violated a state statute.

The Fifth Amendment mandates that no person be deprived of life, liberty, or property without **due process** of law. We know quite a bit about due process from previous chapters. One aspect of due process, for example, is that no one should be convicted of violating a statute that is unduly vague, so that a well-intentional person could not conform his or her conduct to comply with the law. *Kolender v. Lawson*, 461 U.S. 352 (1981), is a good example. In that case, a California criminal statute requiring persons on the street to provide "credible and reliable" identification and to account for their presence when requested to do so by a police officer was held to be unduly vague.

As another example, it would be a due process violation for a prosecutor intentionally to suppress material evidence favorable to the accused. *Brady v. Maryland*, 373 U.S. 83 (1963). But the Supreme Court recently held that the government's accidental destruction of evidence that *might* have supported the defendant's innocence did not violate due process. Nor was due process violated by the government's innocent failure to use the most modern, sophisticated scientific methods of examining evidence. *Arizona v. Youngblood*, 488 U.S. 51 (1988).

The most controversial part of the Fifth Amendment, as interpreted by the Supreme Court, is its protection against self-incrimination. No person "shall be compelled in any criminal case to be a witness against himself." This includes matters of document production as well as of oral testimony. The right is not available to corporations and is individual to the person charged. In a case of interest to all businesspersons, *United States v. Doe*, 465 U.S. 605 (1984), the court held that the sole owner of a corporation could not claim the privilege against self-incrimination to avoid producing records that belong *to the corporation*. Had the business been a sole proprietorship, the owner could have claimed the privilege because the records would have been the owner's, not a separate entity's.

The most famous self-incrimination case is *Miranda v. Arizona*, 384 U.S. 436 (1966), which excluded from evidence any incriminating statements made by a defendant (and evidence to which those statements led police, called "fruit of the poisonous tree") who had not been fully warned of his constitutional right against self-incrimination (and his right to counsel). Thus, the famous "Miranda warning" was born.

As with the exclusionary rule, the current, more conservative members of the Supreme Court have diluted the impact of *Miranda*. For example, in *Duckworth v. Eagan*, 492 U.S. 195 (1989), the police told a criminal suspect that "we have no way of giving you a lawyer, but one will be appointed for you, if you wish, if and when you go to court." Dissenters felt that this statement might have misled the defendant into believing, inaccurately, that he did not have the right to consult an attorney then and there in the stationhouse before being interrogated by the police. But the majority said that "Miranda does not require that attorneys be producible on call . . ." and felt that the statement was not necessarily misleading given that the defendant had already been read the standard Miranda warning, which informs defendants that they have the right to speak to a lawyer before any questions are asked.

Sixth Amendment

The Sixth Amendment contains a litany of constitutional protections for criminal defendants, including the important right to counsel that was mentioned in the previous discussion of the *Miranda* case. Generally speaking, any individual facing potential incarceration has the right to consult an attorney and to have one provided if he or she cannot afford one. The right to counsel is made more meaningful by the defendant's Sixth Amendment rights to be informed of the nature of the accusation, to confront witnesses against him or her, and to call witnesses on his or her own behalf.

There is also the right to a "speedy and public trial." Court backlogs have threatened to make a mockery of the right to a "speedy" trial, but the federal government and most states have now passed "speedy trial" acts that place time limits on the government and give criminal cases priority over civil cases on crowded court dockets.

Importantly, there is also a right to trial by an impartial jury that applies in cases involving "serious" criminal charges. Juries, serving as the "conscience of the community," are a critical safeguard against the heavy hand of the government.

Eighth Amendment

The Eighth Amendment contains important protections for criminal defendants. It states that "excessive bail" shall not be required. Thus, when a judge sets bail before trial, the aim should be not to punish the defendant who is presumed innocent, but simply to guarantee the defendant's appearance at trial. In recent years, Congress has increased the courts' authority to deny bail in situations in which defendants pose special harm to the public.

The Eighth Amendment also bans "excessive fines" and "cruel and unusual punishment." The latter provision has been held not to bar the death penalty, even for juveniles or retarded defendants.

Miscellaneous Protections

Other protections for criminal defendants are scattered throughout the Constitution. For example, there is a ban on *ex post facto* laws—laws that are passed to criminalize conduct *after* the conduct has occurred. Obviously, criminal laws must also be scrutinized to ensure that they do not violate basic freedoms, such as religion and speech. The government could not, for example, make it a crime to be a Baptist. Nor, the court has held, can a state criminalize the burning of the American flag when performed as a form of political expression. *Texas v. Johnson,* 491 U.S. 397 (1989).

GENERAL ELEMENTS OF CRIMINAL RESPONSIBILITY

As a general rule, the prosecutor in a criminal case must do three things to obtain a valid conviction: (1) show that the defendant's actions violated an existing criminal statue, (2) prove beyond a reasonable doubt that the defendant did do the *acts* alleged, and (3) prove that the defendant had the requisite *intent* to violate the law. The first element is important because although many of our crimes have strong common-law roots, today almost all crimes are statutory in nature. The other two elements of act and intent deserve separate consideration.

Guilty Act

A basic element of a criminal conviction is the ***actus reus,*** a Latin term meaning "guilty act." This is a critical part of a criminal conviction because our legal system generally does not punish persons for their thoughts. Evil thoughts alone normally do not injure society and therefore do not justify bringing to bear the full power of the government's criminal justice system. This does not mean that a defendant must always successfully complete a criminal act to be guilty. Generally any act that clearly is a step in the commission of a crime will be sufficient for a conviction for

attempted larceny, murder, and so on, if the intent requirement is also present.

The guilty act must be voluntary and generally must be an act of commission rather than mere omission. However, there are exceptions. Failure to perform a legally imposed duty will constitute a sufficient *actus reus.* An example is failure to fulfill the legally required duty to file an income tax return.

Guilty Mind

Generally, a defendant is not guilty unless his or her guilty act is coupled with a guilty mind, that is, unless the defendant had **mens rea**, an intent to do wrong. A murder conviction, for example, requires the act of killing the victim plus the evil intent to take a life.

Because a person's actual intent can rarely be known with absolute certainty, juries may often presume a criminal intent on the part of the defendant based on the established facts. Thus a jury may presume that an armed prowler apprehended at night entered the house "with the intention of committing a felony," one of the usual statutory elements of the crime of burglary. Intent is often a difficult element to prove beyond a reasonable doubt, but as Justice Oliver Wendell Holmes once stated, "even a dog distinguishes between being stumbled over and being kicked."

Many crimes are called *specific intent* crimes, in that conviction is appropriate only if the defendant had the intent to commit the exact forbidden act charged. For other crimes, *general intent* will suffice, meaning that the defendant had the general intent to commit a wrongful act even though he or she did not intend to bring about the specific result. First degree murder is typically a specific intent crime; to be guilty the defendant must have intended to take a human life. However, if a defendant became very drunk and went on a rampage, killing a man with a gun, he may be found guilty of second degree murder even though he was so drunk he did not know he had a gun. This is an example of general intent.

In the following case, which surprised many observers, the Supreme Court addressed the question of whether a good faith, but objectively unreasonable, belief could negate the intent element.

mens rea
intent to do wrong

CHEEK V. UNITED STATES

U. S. Supreme Court, 498 U.S. 192 (1991)

Petitioner Cheek was charged with multiple counts of willfully failing to file a federal income tax return in violation of section 7203 of the Internal Revenue Code and of willfully attempting to evade his income taxes in violation of section 7201. Cheek admitted that he had not filed the returns but testified that he had not acted willfully because he sincerely believed, based on his indoctrination by a tax protest organization and his own study, that the tax laws were being unconstitutionally enforced and that his actions were lawful. The court of appeals affirmed Cheek's conviction, rejecting his challenge to the trial judge's instructing the jury that an honest but unreasonable belief is not a defense and that Cheek's beliefs that wages are not income and that he was not a taxpayer within the meaning of the code were not objectively reasonable. Cheek appealed.

White, Justice:

The general rule that ignorance of the law or a mistake of law is no defense to criminal prosecution is deeply rooted in the American legal system. Based on the notion that the law is definite and knowable, the common law presumed that every person knew the law.

The proliferation of statutes and regulations has sometimes made it difficult for the average citizen to know and comprehend the extent of the duties and obligations imposed by the tax laws. Congress has accordingly softened the impact of the common-law presumption by making specific intent to violate the law an element of certain federal tax offenses. Thus, the Court almost 60 years ago interpreted the statutory term "willfully" as used in the federal criminal tax statutes as carving out an exception to the traditional rule.

This special treatment of criminal tax offenses is largely due to the complexity of the tax laws.

Willfulness, as construed by our prior decisions in criminal tax cases, requires the Government to prove that the law imposed a duty on the defendant, that the defendant knew of his duty, and that he voluntarily and intentionally violated that duty. We deal first with the case where the issue is whether the defendant knew of the duty purportedly imposed by the provision of the statute or regulation he is accused of violating, a case in which there is no claim that the provision at issue is invalid. In such a case, if the Government proves actual knowledge of the pertinent legal duty, the prosecution, without more, has satisfied the knowledge component of the willfulness requirement. But carrying this burden requires negating a defendant's claim of ignorance of the law or a claim that because of a misunderstanding of the law, he had a good faith belief that he was not violating any of the provisions of the tax laws. This is so because one cannot be aware that the law imposes a duty on him and yet be ignorant of it, misunderstand the law, or believe that the duty does not exist. In the end, the issue is whether, based on all the evidence, the Government has proved that the defendant was aware of the duty at issue, which cannot be true if the jury credits a good-faith misunderstanding and belief submission, whether or not the claimed belief or misunderstanding is objectively reasonable.

It was therefore error to instruct the jury to disregard evidence of Cheek's understanding that, within the meaning of the tax laws, he was not a person required to file a return or to pay income taxes and that wages are not taxable income, as incredible as such misunderstandings of and beliefs about the law might be. Of course, the more unreasonable the asserted beliefs or misunderstandings are, the more likely the jury will consider them to be nothing more than simple disagreement with known legal duties imposed by the tax laws and will find that the Government has carried its burden of proving knowledge.

[Cheek's] claims that some of the provisions of the tax code are unconstitutional are submissions of a different order. They do not arise from innocent mistakes caused by the complexity of the Internal Revenue Code. Rather, they reveal full knowledge of the provisions at issue and a studied conclusion, however wrong, that those provisions are invalid and unenforceable. Thus in this case, Cheek paid his taxes for years, but after attending various seminars and based on his own study, he concluded that the income tax laws could not constitutionally require him to pay a tax.

We do not believe that Congress contemplated that such a taxpayer, without risking criminal prosecution, could ignore the duties imposed upon him by the Internal Revenue Code and refuse to utilize the mechanisms provided by Congress to present his claims of invalidity to the courts and to abide by their decisions. There is no doubt that Cheek, from year to year, was free to pay the tax that the law purported to require, file for a refund and, if denied, present his claims of invalidity, constitutional or otherwise, to the courts. Also, without paying the tax, he could have challenged the claims of tax deficiencies in the Tax Court, with the right to appeal to a higher court if unsuccessful. Cheek took neither course in some years, and when he did was unwilling to accept the outcome. As we see it, he is in no position to claim that his good-faith belief about the validity of the Internal Revenue Code negates willfulness or provides a defense to criminal prosecution.

[T]he judgment of the Court of Appeals is vacated, and the case is remanded for further proceedings consistent with this opinion. ⚖

There are a few crimes for which negligence will suffice and no intent need be proven. Negligent vehicular homicide is an example. There are even some *strict liability* crimes, in which defendants can be found guilty absent intent or even careless behavior. These are typically misdemeanors. Examples include selling liquor to minors, violating traffic rules, and violating pure food and drug laws.

GENERAL CRIMINAL DEFENSES
Defenses Negating Intent

Many defenses raised in a criminal case are aimed at negating the *mens rea* element by showing that the defendant did not intend to commit a crime. Several such defenses exist. We will learn in Chapter 15 that many of these concepts also provide grounds for escaping contractual obligations.

Infancy

The common-law rule was that children younger than seven years were *conclusively* presumed to be incapable of forming criminal intent. Children between seven and fourteen years were accorded the same presumption but in a *rebuttable* form. The presumption could be overcome by proof that the child understood the wrongful nature of his or her act. Many states still follow these basic notions in their criminal statutes. However, virtually all states have created juvenile courts, which treat juveniles as delinquents rather than criminals with the purpose of reforming rather than punishing them. Therefore, infancy as a criminal defense is not as important as it once was, although prosecutors usually have the option of attempting to convince a court to try a juvenile as an adult when a particularly heinous crime has been committed.

Insanity

There are several approaches, none satisfactory, to handling defendants who "plead insanity." Some states use the *M'Naghten* test, which excuses a defendant whose mental defect renders him or her incapable of appreciating the difference between right and wrong. Other excuse defendants who may appreciate the difference between right and wrong but who suffer a mental defect causing an "irresistible impulse" to commit the crime. The District of Co-

lumbia courts developed the *Durham* rule, which simply asks whether the defendant was insane at the time of the crime and, if so, whether the crime was a product of that insanity. Finally, the Model Penal Code provides that a defendant "is not responsible for criminal conduct if at the time of such conduct as a result of a mental disease or defect he lacks substantial capacity either to appreciate the wrongfulness of his conduct or to conform his conduct to the requirements of the law."

Intoxication

If a person *voluntarily* becomes intoxicated (or "high" on drugs), the general rule is that this may negate specific intent but will not negate general intent, as discussed above. Voluntary intoxication is generally no defense to crimes requiring mere negligence or recklessness.

Involuntary intoxication, however, is generally treated as equivalent to insanity. Thus, if a defendant unforeseeably became intoxicated because of an unusual reaction to prescribed medication, courts would be reluctant to hold him or her responsible for crimes he or she might commit under the influence of that medication.

Duress

Occasionally, persons will be forced to commit crimes against their will. When the wrongful threat of others causes a person to commit a crime, *mens rea* is negated. Duress is generally shown when an immediate and inescapable threat of serious bodily injury or death (that is greater than the harm to be caused by the crime) forces a person to commit a crime that he or she does not wish to commit. The threat must come through no fault of the defendant's. If, for example, a defendant voluntarily joins a criminal gang, he or she has no duress defense if the gang leader forces him or her to help in one of the gang's planned crimes.

Mistake

Because ignorance of the law is no excuse, a *mistake of law* is generally no defense to a criminal charge. Thus, a defendant who has intentionally performed a specific act cannot usually defend by saying: "I didn't know that it was illegal," or even "My attorney told me that it was okay." The courts' refusal to hold an attorney's advice to be a valid defense discourages "attorney shopping." However, many courts will find that a mistake of law negates the intent element if (1) the law was not reasonably made known to the public, or (2) the defendant reasonably relied on an erroneous but official statement of the law (such as in a judicial opinion or administrative order).

A defense based on *mistake of fact* is more likely to succeed. Thus, a defendant charged with stealing a blue 12-speed bicycle might successfully defend by showing that he or she owned an identical blue 12-speed bicycle parked at the next rack and mistakenly rode off on the wrong one.

Other Defenses

Entrapment

Police undercover work is often aimed at catching criminals "in the act." If the police not only create an opportunity for a criminal act but also persuade the defendant to commit a crime that he or she would not otherwise have committed, the defendant may have a good **entrapment** defense. The entrapment defense presents difficult factual questions, for the court must draw the line between an unwary innocent and an unwary criminal. The key issue is whether the defendant was *predisposed* to commit the crime. That is, the criminal idea must originate with the defendant, not with the police officer. As the Supreme Court once said, "When the criminal design originates with the [police who] implant in the mind of an innocent person the disposition to commit the alleged offense and induce its commission in order that they may prosecute," entrapment results. *Sorrells v. United States*, 287 U.S. 435 (1932). This standard is applied to the following recent case.

JACOBSON V. UNITED STATES

U.S. Supreme Court, 112 S.Ct. 1535 (1992)

Petitioner Jacobson ordered two "Bare Boys" magazines containing photos of nude preteen and teenage boys at a time when it was legal to do so. Later, the Child Protection Act of 1984 made it illegal to receive through the mails sexually explicit depictions of children. Noticing Jacobson's name on the bookstore mailing list, two government agencies sent mail to him through five fictitious organizations and a bogus pen pal in order to explore his willingness to break the new law. The organizations purported to promote sexual freedom, freedom of choice, and free speech. Jacobson responded to some of the letters. After two and a half years on the government mailing list, Jacobson was solicited to order child pornography. He answered a letter that described concern about child pornography as hysterical nonsense and condemned international censorship, and then received a catalog and ordered a magazine depicting young boys, engaged in sexual activities. Jacobson was arrested; a search of his house found no materials other than those sent by the government.

Jacobson was convicted and his conviction was affirmed, despite his entrapment defense. He then petitioned the Supreme Court for review.

White, Justice:

In their zeal to enforce the law, . . . Government agents may not originate a criminal design, implant in an innocent person's mind the disposition to commit a criminal act, and then induce commission of the crime so that the Government may prosecute. *Sorrells v. United States.*, 287 U.S. 435, 442 (1932). Where the Government has induced an individual to break the law and the defense of entrapment is at issue, as it was in this case, the prosecution must prove beyond reasonable doubt that the defendant was disposed to commit the criminal act prior to first being approached by Government agents.

Thus, an agent deployed to stop the traffic in illegal drugs may offer the opportunity to buy or sell drugs, and, if the offer is accepted, make an arrest on the spot or later. In such a typical case, or in a more elaborate "sting" operation involving Government-sponsored fencing where the defendant is simply provided with the opportunity to commit a crime, the entrapment defense is of little use because the ready commission of the criminal act amply demonstrates the defendant's predisposition. Had the agents in this case simply offered petitioner the opportunity to order child pornography through the mails, and petitioner— who must be presumed to know the law—had promptly availed himself of this criminal opportunity, it is unlikely that his entrapment defense would have warranted a jury instruction.

But that is not what happened here. By the time petitioner finally placed his order, he had already been the target of 26 months of repeated mailings and communications from Government agents and fictitious organizations.
(continues)

entrapment

JACOBSON V. UNITED STATES

(continued from previous page)
Therefore, although he had become predisposed to break the law by May 1987, it is our view that the Government did not prove that this predisposition was independent and not the product of the attention that the Government had directed at petitioner since January 1985.

[The fact that petitioner had previously ordered such magazines does not indicate a predisposition to act illegally because] petitioner was acting within the law at the time he received [those] magazines. . . . When the Government's quest for convictions leads to the apprehension of an otherwise law-abiding citizen who, if left to his own devices, likely would have never run afoul of the law, the courts should intervene.

[Reversed.] ⚖

Self-Defense

Self-defense and defense of others may justify acts of violence that otherwise would be criminal. Although the courts do not require "detached reflection in the presence of an uplifted knife," *Brown v. United States*, 256 U.S. 335 (1921), the general rule permits only that degree of force reasonable under the circumstances. Deadly force can be used if the defendant has a reasonable belief that imminent death or grievous bodily injury will otherwise result. The law does not allow one to shoot an assailant in the back once that assailant is clearly fleeing and poses no further threat. In some cases, retreat might even be required as preferable to deadly force. Nondeadly force can be used in the degree reasonably believed necessary to protect persons or property from criminal acts, although obviously, a lesser degree of force will be viewed as "reasonable" in defense of property.

Immunity

Through the process of *plea bargaining*, defendants often agree to testify against other criminals in return for consideration at time of sentencing and perhaps **immunity** from prosecution of certain potential charges. It is often said that such persons are "turning state's evidence" to help the prosecutor's case.

STATE CRIMES AFFECTING BUSINESS

So many crimes against persons and property are contained in state criminal codes that it would be impossible to list them all. Furthermore, there is such variation from state to state that it is difficult to generalize about criminal law. Nonetheless, this section briefly describes a few of the more common crimes against businesses.

Theft

Many state statutes criminalize the unlawful taking of another's property under a general statute that often terms the crime "theft." Such statutes consolidate a variety of related crimes that developed separately at the common law, such as larceny, burglary, false pretenses, and embezzlement.

Larceny

At common law, **larceny** was the trespassory taking away of the personal property of another with wrongful intent permanently to deprive that person of the use of the property. Larceny is viewed as an injury to the owner's interest in possessing the goods. Shoplifting is a good example. Promising to sell someone your car, taking the money, and then refusing to turn over the car is not larceny, because there is no wrongful taking. The concept of personal property generally does not include trees or personal services but would include computer programs and trade secrets.

There are degrees of larceny. Petit larceny covers theft of smaller amounts (for example, less than $500). Thefts of property worth more would be grand larceny. These statutory distinctions vary in amount from state to state.

Burglary

At common law, **burglary** was the trespassory breaking and entering of the dwelling house of another during the nighttime with intent to commit a felony.

Over time, many of the technical requirements have been dropped. Now, most statutes would find burglary even though the building broken into was not a dwelling house and even though it occurred during the day. Burglary with use of a weapon is called aggravated burglary.

False Pretenses

Obtaining goods by **false pretenses** was defined by the common law as obtaining title to someone else's property by knowingly or recklessly making a false representation of existing material fact that is intended to and does defraud the victim into parting with his or her property. Technically, false pretenses is an injury to title, not mere possession. Title passes to the thief, quite unlike larceny. Examples of such conduct are the filing of false claims with insurance companies, the buying of a VCR with a check the purchaser knows will "bounce," and the taking of buyers' money for goods or services with no intent of delivering such goods or services.

Embezzlement

A wholly statutory offense, **embezzlement** is the fraudulent conversion of the property of another by one who has lawful possession of it. This crime somewhat overlaps with larceny, but the original possession by the wrongdoer is lawful. An example is an attorney who receives funds from a client for payment of a settlement but later decides to spend the money on her- or himself instead.

Some of the key elements of an embezzlement charge are discussed in the following case.

STATE V. JOY

Supreme Court of Vermont, 549 A.2d 1033 (1988)

Defendant Joy was president and sole shareholder of Credit Management Services (CMS), a debt collection agency that collected delinquent accounts for businesses in exchange for 40 percent of the amount collected. CMS was entitled to this percentage regardless of whether the debtor paid CMS or settled with the client directly. When CMS received a payment from a debtor, it would deposit the money with the Barre bank, and within a month an invoice detailing the transaction would be sent to the client. If monies were due the client, a check would accompany the invoice. In addition, CMS maintained an account with a Montpelier bank from which it drew operating expenses.

In early 1981, CMS, suffering financial difficulties, began transferring funds from the Barre account to the Montpelier account to cover its operating expenses. In June 1981, CMS was hired by Stacey Fuel to collect several delinquent accounts. On August 14, CMS received a check from one of Stacey's debtors in the amount of $1,920.25. CMS never forwarded any of this money to Stacey, nor did it inform Stacey that the money had been received. Stacey ended its relationship with CMS in August 1982 and only later learned that CMS had filed for bankruptcy and had listed Stacey as one of its creditors.

Joy was convicted of embezzlement and appealed.

Dooley, Justice:

In his first claim on appeal, defendant suggests that the trial court improperly refused to charge the jury that "[t]he mere fact that C.M.S. Corporation failed or was unable to pay its creditors is not a sufficient showing of intent to justify conviction [of embezzlement]."

Defendant's main objection to the charge is that it failed to state that the jury could consider intent to repay as evidence that the defendant had no fraudulent intent. The elements of embezzlement are detailed in 13 V.S.A. § 2531, which states in pertinent part that:

An officer, agent, bailee for hire, clerk or servant of a banking association or an incorporated company . . . who embezzles or fraudulently converts to his own use, or takes or secretes with intent to embezzle or fraudulently convert to his own use, money or other property which comes into his possession or is under his own care by virtue of such employment, notwithstanding he may have an interest in such property, shall be guilty of embezzlement. . . .

The law is clear that intent to repay is not a defense to embezzlement under a statute like ours. See, e.g., 3 Wharton's Criminal Law § 397, at 405–07 (14th ed. 1980). Further, the proposition that defendant's intent to repay should have been considered by the jury in its determination of whether or not he possessed the necessary *mens rea* is inconsistent with the state of the law. A leading authority on criminal law has observed that "[g]iven a fraudulent appropriation or conversion, an

(continues)

STATE V. JOY

(continued from previous page) embezzlement is committed even if the defendant intends at some subsequent time to return the property or to make restitution to the owner." 3 Wharton's Criminal Law § 397, at 405–06.

The rationale for this rule was stated by the Pennsylvania Supreme Court in *Commonwealth v. Bovaird:*

Where one is charged with embezzlement or fraudulent conversion, the intention to abstract the money and appropriate it to his own use has been fully executed upon its wrongful taking; the ability and intention to indemnify the party from whom it has been withdrawn remains unexecuted, and such intention, even if conscientiously entertained, may become impossible of fulfillment. The crime is consummated when the money is intentionally and wrongfully converted, temporarily or permanently, to the defendant's own use.

Bovaird, 373 Pa. 60, 95 A.2d at 178.

The trial judge properly charged the elements of the offense of embezzlement. Regarding intent, the judge stressed that "there must be a fraudulent intent and the State must prove fraudulent intent beyond a reasonable doubt." And the court properly noted that "the intent to embezzle is a state of mind which can be shown by words or conduct."

Defendant also argues that the trial court erred by not instructing the jury that a mere inability or failure to pay creditors is not sufficient to demonstrate the fraudulent intent necessary for the crime of embezzlement. For the same reasons that intent to repay is not relevant to the existence of fraudulent intent, neither is the ability or inability to repay. Moreover, the charge urged by the defendant misstates the facts of this case and mischaracterizes his relationship with Stacey.

There is no question that "[in] a debtor–creditor relation, the debtor's failure to pay the creditor does not constitute embezzlement." 3 Wharton's Criminal Law § 402, at 417. However, defendant's relationship with Stacey was not that of debtor–creditor, but rather it was one of agent and principal. We are satisfied that the facts and circumstances of this case support defendant's status as an agent of Stacey. The trial court instructed the jury that an agency relationship was critical to the offense charged and that the State was burdened with proving beyond a reasonable doubt that such relationship existed. The court also instructed that "[a] debtor–creditor relationship alone is insufficient to create an agency relationship." The evidence supports a finding of an agency relationship, and the jury so found. Moreover, on appeal, defendant does not argue that he was anything other than an agent of Stacey.

As an agent, rather than a debtor, of Stacey, defendant was obligated to hold and remit to Stacey its percentage of any amounts collected. Given the existence of an agency relationship—as found by the jury—defendant's conversion of the money credited to Stacey's account was precisely the activity prohibited by the embezzlement statute.

[Affirmed.] ⚖

Specialized Statutes

The common-law classifications and general theft statutes have been supplemented by a variety of more specific laws aimed at the same types of conduct. For example, although obtaining money or property by the giving of a bad check would constitute false pretenses or general theft, all states have specific statutes relating to the issuance of bad checks, which impose criminal liability on persons who, with intent to defraud, issue or transfer checks or other negotiable instruments knowing that they will be dishonored. Such knowledge is presumed to exist, under the typical statute, if the drawer had no account with the drawee bank when the check was issued, or if the check was refused payment because of insufficient funds in the drawer's account when it was presented to the bank for payment. Similarly, most states have separate statutes relating to a number of special offenses, such as the setting back of automobile odometers with the intent to defraud and the knowing delivery of "short weights"—the charging of buyers for quantities of goods that are greater than the quantities that were actually delivered.

Robbery

Robbery is stealing from a person or in his or her presence by use of force or threat of force. It is, essentially, a form of larceny but the extra element of force makes it a more serious offense. Removing someone's earring by stealth would be larceny; ripping it from the victim's earlobe would be robbery. Use of a weapon escalates the crime to aggravated robbery.

Forgery

Forgery is the false making or altering of a legally significant instrument (such as a check, credit card, deed, passport, mortgage, or security) with the intent to defraud. Writing an insufficient funds check is not forgery, although it may constitute false pretenses or violate a state bad check law. But changing the true payee's name as written on a check to your own and cashing the check is certainly forgery.

Forgery is a crime with roots deep in the common law, but changing technologies can challenge traditional rules, as the following case illustrates.

PEOPLE V. AVILA

Colorado Court of Appeals, 770 P.2d 1330 (1988)

For fees of between $1500 and $3000, Avila, a lawyer, altered the driver records of two of his clients whose driver's licenses were under revocation for alcohol-related offenses. Avila would instruct his contact in the Motor Vehicle Division (MVD) Office, who had access to the data base where the driving records were maintained on computer disk, to delete the clients' records. The client would later apply for a driver's license, stating that he had no previous driver's license, which the altered computer records would verify. Avila was convicted of two counts of second degree forgery. He appealed.

Van Cise, Judge:

Initially, we note that much of Avila's argument relies on the assertion that forgery cannot be committed on a computer. We reject that contention.

A forgery can be made by any number of artificial means. Indeed, "whether [the forgery] is made with the pen, with a brush[,] . . . with any other instrument, or by any other device whatever; whether it is in characters which stand for words or in characters which stand for ideas . . . is quite immaterial . . ." *Benson v. McMahon,* 127 U.S. 457 (1888).

Avila also contends, in essence, that there was insufficient evidence to sustain his convictions. We disagree.

The elements of second degree forgery pertinent to this case are that (1) the defendant, (2) with intent to defraud, (3) falsely alters, (4) a written instrument, (5) which is or purported to be, or which is calculated to become or to represent if completed, a "written instrument officially issued or created by a public office, public servant, or government agency." Section 18-5-103(1)(c).

Avila contends that there was no written instrument in this case so the forgery conviction cannot stand. We disagree.

Section 18-5-101(9) defines "written instrument" as follows:

"Written instrument" means any paper, document, *or other instrument containing written or printed matter or the equivalent thereof,* used for purposes of reciting, embodying, conveying, or recording information . . . which is capable of being used to the advantage or disadvantage of some person. (Emphasis supplied.)

A fair reading of the statute indicates that a computer disc is included in the definition of a "written instrument."

Next, Avila contends that, since the driving records were deleted, the evidence at trial does not support the finding that he falsely altered a written instrument. He argues that "alter" means to change, while "delete" means to cause to vanish completely. Therefore, he claims he committed no forgery. We are not persuaded.

Section 18-5-101(2) states:

To "falsely alter" a written instrument means to change a written instrument without the authority of anyone entitled to grant such authority, *whether it be* in complete or incomplete form, *by means of erasure,* obliteration, *deletion,* insertion of new matter, transposition of matter, or any other means, so that such instrument in its thus altered form falsely appears or purports to be in all respects an authentic creation of or fully authorized by its ostensible maker. (Emphasis supplied.)

The record shows that the driving records of two of Avila's clients were deleted so that instead of containing their history of driving violations, the computer found no driving records and thus would display the message "no record found."

Under the plain language of the statute, Avila's actions constituted a false alteration within the meaning of § 18-5-101(2).

Next, Avila asserts that there is a distinction between a document falsely made and a genuine document that contains false information. Based on this distinction, he contends that the written instruments were not false but rather were genuine MVD documents which contained false information and, as such, they cannot form the basis for a forgery conviction. We disagree.

In *DeRose v. People,* 64 Colo. 332, 171 P. 359 (1918), the court held that a false statement of fact in an instrument which is genuine is not forgery. It stated:

This writing is what it purports to be—a true and genuine instrument, although it contains false statements. It is not a false paper, and the execution of such a document does not constitute forgery.

(continues)

PEOPLE V. AVILA

(continued from previous page)

In *DeRose*, defendant was a railroad foreman whose job was to draft and submit the time rolls for his men. He was charged with forgery because he credited one of his men with more days than the man had worked. Because the defendant was authorized to draft and submit the time roll, the court found that the document was not "falsely made." It was a genuine railroad time roll prepared by one authorized to do so, but which contained false information.

In *DeRose* the defendant had the authority to perform the general act that led to the production of the document containing the false information.

In contrast, in the instant case, testimony showed that Avila's confederate at the MVD had no authority to delete driver histories. Therefore, under *DeRose*, the documents were forged.

[Affirmed.] ⚖

Arson

At common law, **arson** was the malicious burning of the dwelling house of another. Today, the building burned need not be a dwelling house. And, as all too commonly occurs, people who burn their own house (or other building or personal property) for purposes of defrauding an insurance company are almost certainly violating a state criminal statute prohibiting such fraud.

FEDERAL CRIMES AFFECTING BUSINESS

As with state crimes, there are so many federal criminal statutes that it would be impossible to list them all. Many have been passed in response to perceived crises. In the era of the giant trusts in the late 1800s, Congress passed many antitrust laws, including some carrying criminal penalties (discussed in Chapter 48). As noted earlier, during the Depression Era epidemic of bank robberies, Congress passed a federal bank robbery law. In the wake of the Watergate scandal in the early 1970s, investigation disclosed widespread bribery of foreign officials by U.S. companies, leading to enactment of the Foreign Corrupt Practices Act (discussed in Chapter 41). After the Ivan Boesky case and other insider trading scandals in the late 1980s, Congress increased the criminal penalties for that fraudulent activity (also discussed in Chapter 41). Congress responded to the recent savings and loan scandal by enacting criminal penalties to punish several types of fraudulent activity that required a multibillion dollar taxpayer bailout of savings and loans (see the Financial Institutions Reform, Recovery, and Enforcement Act of 1989). Instead of trying to list all such federal criminal statutes, we will briefly address a few of the more general ones.

Mail and Wire Fraud

Two very general federal statutes punish **mail fraud** (use of the mails to defraud or swindle) and **wire fraud** (similar use of telephone, telegraph, radio, or television). The typical mail or wire fraud case would involve use of the mails or telephones to make false representations to sell products or securities. For example, the mail fraud law has been used to punish fraudulent representations in the use of the mails to advertise such articles as hair-growing products that proved to be worthless, retrofit carburetors that totally failed to improve automobile fuel economy, and false identification cards that the sellers knew were ordered by purchasers for the purpose of deceiving third parties. Similarly, schemes for the operation of "mail-order" schools, where degrees or diplomas are awarded "without requiring evidence of education or experience entitled thereto," and where the operators know such documents are likely to be used by purchasers to misrepresent their qualifications to prospective employers, violate these sections of the law. However, the statutes have been construed to cover a wide variety of factual situations.

For example, in *Carpenter v. United States*, 484 U.S. 19 (1987), a *Wall Street Journal* reporter tipped material nonpublic information (the contents of his columns that were about to be published) to confederates who profitably traded on it. Although the Supreme Court split 4–4 regarding the specific insider trading theory offered by the prosecution, it unanimously affirmed the defendant's conviction for mail and wire fraud. The fraudulent scheme's connection to the mails and wire services used to distribute the newspaper was deemed sufficient to support the conviction.

In the following case the Supreme Court dealt with a difficult mail fraud issue.

SCHMUCK V. UNITED STATES

U.S. Supreme Court, 489 U.S. 705 (1989)

Petitioner Schmuck, a used-car distributor, purchased used cars, rolled back their odometers, and then sold the automobiles to Wisconsin retail dealers for prices artificially inflated because of the low-mileage readings. These unwitting car dealers, relying on the altered odometer figures, then resold the cars to customers, who in turn paid prices reflecting Schmuck's fraud. To complete the resale of each car, the dealer who bought it from Schmuck would submit a title-application form to the Wisconsin Department of Transportation on behalf of the retail customer. The receipt of a Wisconsin title was a legal prerequisite for transferring title and obtaining car tags.

Schmuck was convicted on 12 counts of mail fraud. He appealed, alleging that the mailings that were the crux of the indictment—the submissions of the title-application forms by the auto dealers—were not in furtherance of the fraudulent scheme and, thus, did not satisfy the mailing element of the crime of mail fraud. The circuit court rejected Schmuck's claim but reversed on other grounds. The Supreme Court granted certiorari to resolve both issues. (The following excerpt addresses only the mail fraud issue.)

Blackmun, Justice:

"The federal mail fraud statute does not purport to reach all frauds, but only those limited instances in which the use of the mails is a part of the execution of the fraud, leaving all other cases to be dealt with by appropriate state law." *Kann v. United States*, 323 U.S. 88, 95 (1944). To be part of the execution of the fraud, however, the use of the mails need not be an essential element of the scheme. *Pereira v. United States*, 347 U.S. 1, 8 (1954). It is sufficient for the mailing to be "incident to an essential part of the scheme," *ibid.*, or "a step in [the] plot." *Badders v. United States*, 240 U.S. 391, 394 (1916).

Schmuck argues that mail fraud can be predicated only on a mailing that affirmatively assists the perpetrator in carrying out his fraudulent scheme. The mailing element of the offense, he contends, cannot be satisfied by a mailing, such as those at issue here, that is routine and innocent in and of itself, and that, far from furthering the execution of the fraud, occurs after the fraud has come to fruition, is merely tangentially related to the fraud, and is counterproductive in that it creates a "paper trail" from which the fraud may be discovered. We disagree both with this characterization of the mailings in the present case and with this description of the applicable law.

We begin by considering the scope of Schmuck's fraudulent scheme. Schmuck was charged with devising and executing a scheme to defraud Wisconsin retail automobile customers who based their decisions to purchase certain automobiles at least in part on the low-mileage readings provided by the tampered odometers. This was a fairly large-scale operation. Evidence at trial indicated that Schmuck had employed a man known only as "Fred" to turn back the odometers on about 150 different cars. Schmuck then marketed these cars to a number of dealers, several of whom he dealt with on a consistent basis over a period of about 15 years. Thus, Schmuck's was not a "one-shot" operation in which he sold a single car to an isolated dealer. His was an ongoing fraudulent venture. A rational jury could have concluded that the success of Schmuck's venture depended upon his continued harmonious relations with and good reputation among retail dealers, which in turn required the smooth flow of cars from the dealers to their Wisconsin customers.

Under these circumstances, we believe that a rational jury could have found that the title-registration mailings were part of the execution of the fraudulent scheme, a scheme which did not reach fruition until the retail dealers resold the cars and effected transfers of title. Schmuck's scheme would have come to an abrupt halt if the dealers either had lost faith in
(continues)

SCHMUCK V. UNITED STATES

(continued from previous page)

Schmuck or had not been able to resell the cars obtained from him. These resales and Schmuck's relationships with the retail dealers naturally depended on the successful passage of title among the various parties. Thus, although the registration-form mailings may not have contributed directly to the duping of either the retail dealers or the customers, they were necessary to the passage of title, which in turn was essential to the perpetuation of Schmuck's scheme. As noted earlier, a mailing that is "incident to an essential part of the scheme," *Pereira*, 347 U.S., at 8, satisfies the mailing element of the mail fraud offense. The mailings here fit this description. *See, e.g., United States v. Locklear*, 829 F.2d

1314, 1318–1319 (CA4 1987) (retail customers obtaining title documents through the mail furthers execution of wholesaler's odometer tampering scheme).

Once the full flavor of Schmuck's scheme is appreciated, the critical distinctions between this case and the three cases in which this Court has delimited the reach of the mail fraud statute—*Kann, Parr,* and *Maze*—are readily apparent. In other cases, the Court has found the elements of mail fraud to be satisfied where the mailings have been routine. *See, e.g., Carpenter v. United States*, 484 U.S. 19 (1987) (mailing newspapers).

We also reject Schmuck's contention that mailings that someday may contribute to the uncovering of a

fraudulent scheme cannot supply the mailing element of the mail fraud offense. The relevant question at all times is whether the mailing is part of the execution of the scheme as conceived by the perpetrator at the time, regardless of whether the mailing later, through hindsight, may prove to have been counterproductive and return to haunt the perpetrator of the fraud. The mail fraud statute includes no guarantee that the use of the mails for the purpose of executing a fraudulent scheme will be risk free. Those who use the mails to defraud proceed at their peril.

For these reasons, we agree with the Court of Appeals that the mailings in this case satisfy the mailing element of the mail fraud offenses. ⚖

Travel Act

Section 1952 of Title 18 of the *United States Code* is called the Travel Act. It punishes anyone who travels in interstate or foreign commerce or uses any facility in such commerce to (1) distribute the proceeds of illegal activity, (2) commit any crime of violence or further any unlawful activity, or (3) promote, manage, establish, carry on, or facilitate any unlawful activity. Obviously, this is a very broad act that federalizes all sorts of traditionally state crimes. The "interstate commerce" element can be met by simply mailing a letter or using a telephone, for these are instrumentalities of interstate commerce. The Act has been used, for example, to convict a city electrical inspector who took bribes from private electrical contractors to overlook code violations and to facilitate departmental paperwork even though all the letters mailed by the defendant stayed in one state. The mail is a facility of interstate commerce because it *can* be used to send letters from state to state.

Hobbs Act

The Hobbs Act, 18 U.S.C. sec. 951, punishes anyone who "in any way or degree obstructs, delays, or affects commerce or the movement of any article or

commodity in commerce, by robbery or extortion. . . ." This law punishes extortion (obtaining money or something else of value by use of violence or threat of violence) but not merely accepting bribes. The distinction between the two can be difficult to draw but has been characterized as the difference between "pay me and be assisted" (commercial bribery) and "pay me or be precluded" (extortion).

Because the law punishes those who "in any way" affect commerce, the reach of the federal statute is very broad. In one case, a county sheriff who extorted bribes to protect gamblers and prostitutes was convicted under the Hobbs Act after he solicited payments from an FBI undercover bookie operation. The court held that because the FBI operation bought furniture, paper, food, and natural gas and could have bought more had it not given money to the defendant, interstate commerce was affected. *United States v. Frasch*, 818 F.2d 631 (7th Cir. 1987).

Racketeer Influenced and Corrupt Organizations Act

In 1970 Congress passed the Racketeer Influenced and Corrupt Organizations Act (RICO) to attack organized crime, especially its infiltration into legitimate business. RICO is an unusual criminal statute in that it expressly contains parallel civil provisions. In other words, it provides for both criminal penalties and private civil suits for damages. However, RICO neither included a definition of "organized crime" nor expressly required a link between a defendant's activities and organized crime. Therefore, about nine-tenths of the civil suits and many of the criminal prosecutions brought under RICO have had no connection with professional criminals (as thought of in the common sense) but have, instead, named as defendants accounting firms, banks, law firms, manufacturing corporations, anti-abortion protestors, and a wide variety of others. Because of the importance

of RICO *civil* actions to the area of securities law, RICO is examined in some detail in Chapter 41.

Fortunately, most of the criminal prosecutions brought under RICO have attacked the more traditional manifestations of organized crime. Prosecutors have secured RICO criminal convictions in cases involving marijuana smuggling, kickbacks to judges, extortion of "protection money" by police officers, loansharking, gambling, and the like. However, even in criminal prosecutions the government has occasionally pushed RICO to its limits by prosecuting actions in circumstances it is difficult to believe Congress had in mind when passing RICO. The following case is a more standard RICO criminal action.

UNITED STATES V. LEROY

U.S. Second Circuit Court of Appeals, 687 F.2d 610 (1982)

Defendant LeRoy was vice-president and later business manager of Local 214 of the Laborers International Union. During his terms, LeRoy was placed on the payroll of several contractors hiring Local 214's members. LeRoy did no work but received compensation so the contractors could "keep peace with the laborers." LeRoy also bought gasoline and had his brakes fixed and in so doing had the union pay the bills and then "reimburse" him as though he had paid them. LeRoy appeals his conviction of one count of conspiracy to violate §1962(c) of RICO, in violation of §1962(d).

Moore, Circuit Judge:

Pursuant to §1962(c), it is unlawful "for any person employed by or associated with any enterprise engaged in, or the activities of which affect, interstate or foreign commerce, to conduct or participate, directly or indirectly, in the conduct of such enterprise's affairs through a pattern of racketeering activity. . . ." Unions are expressly included within the term "enterprise."

LeRoy concedes that the Govern-

ment conclusively proved the existence of an enterprise affecting interstate commerce—namely Local 214. He also admits that the Government demonstrated LeRoy's, as well as his co-conspirators', association with the union. LeRoy contends, however, that the Government failed to show that he participated in the conduct of the union's affairs or that his activities constituted a "pattern" of racketeering activity.

Specifically, LeRoy alleges that the Government proved at most illegal conduct committed in furtherance of LeRoy's personal interest, but not in the conduct of the union's business. Accordingly, LeRoy argues, his actions fall beyond the purview of the statute. We find no merit to LeRoy's contention and conclude that his actions took place in the conduct of Local 214's affairs and thus, within the scope of RICO. . . . [W]hile RICO does not specify the degree of interrelationship between the pattern of racketeering and the conduct of the enterprise's affairs, the Act also does not require that predicate acts be in furtherance of the enterprise.

The evidence in this case demonstrates that LeRoy accepted unearned wages while he served as vice-president of Local 214 from various

contractors who testified that they paid him in order to preserve union peace, in violation of the Taft-Hartley Act, and later used his position as business manager to obtain payments from the union treasury for expenses not properly incurred, in violation of the Landrum-Griffin Act. These violations of the Landrum-Griffin and Taft-Hartley Acts were the predicate offenses forming the pattern of racketeering. LeRoy was able to commit these predicate offenses solely by virtue of his positions in Local 214, since the predicate acts were inextricably tied to LeRoy's role as a union official.

We also reject LeRoy's argument that the Government failed to prove that his participation in the union's affairs was "through a pattern of racketeering activity." A "pattern of racketeering activity" is established by proof of the commission of at least two "acts of racketeering" within a ten-year period. Moreover, a violation of either the Landrum-Griffin Act or the Taft-Hartley Act constitutes an act of racketeering. Since the evidence demonstrates that LeRoy violated the provisions of these acts on more than two occasions, the Government clearly proved a pattern of racketeering activity.

[Affirmed.]

COMPUTER CRIME

The explosive growth of the use of computers in the business world in the past few years has brought with it a corresponding increase in computer misuse. The *Avila* forgery case mentioned earlier in this chapter is a good example. Burgeoning computer crime and corresponding government responses justify separate discussion of the area of computer crime. Traditional (precomputer) state and federal laws applicable to such crimes as larceny are not necessarily appropriate for prosecution of cases of computer fraud and computer theft. For example, some cases held that an employee's unauthorized use of his or her employer's computer facilities in private ventures could not support a theft conviction because the employer had not been deprived of any part of value or use of the computer. Other cases have held that use of a computer is not "property" within traditional theft statutes.

Computer crimes fall mainly into three broad categories: unauthorized access, theft of information, and theft of funds. Among schemes that have been subject to prosecution are (1) stealing a competitor's computer program, (2) paying an accomplice to delete adverse information and insert favorable false information into the defendant's credit file, (3) a bank president's having his or her account computer coded so that his or her checks would be removed and held rather than posted so he or she could later remove the actual checks without their being debited, (4) a disgruntled ex-employee's inserting a "virus" into his former employer's computer to destroy its records, and (5) three computer "hackers'" foray into the forbidden recesses of computers that run BellSouth Corporation's phone network.

A recent survey found that 25 percent of businesses responding had recently experienced losses caused by computer crime that averaged between $2 million and $10 million per year. Some estimate that losses caused by computer misuse may be as high as $35 to $40 billion per year (including thefts of funds, losses of computer programs and data, losses of trade secrets, and damage to computer hardware). These estimates may not be reliable, but it is clear that a substantial amount of computer crime is never discovered, and a high percentage of that which is discovered is never reported because (1) companies do not want publicity about the inadequacy of their computer controls and (2) financial institutions such as banks and savings and loans fear that reports of large losses of funds, even when insured, are likely to cause customers to withdraw their deposits.

Whatever the actual loss caused by computer misuse, both Congress and the state legislators have passed statutes to deal specifically with computer crime.

Federal Laws

Although there have been convictions for computer crimes under general federal criminal statutes—such as those dealing with wire fraud, theft, and misappropriation—Congress has recently enacted laws specifically to deal with computer crime. The Access Device and Computer Fraud and Abuse Act of 1984, for example, outlaws (1) obtaining classified information from a computer without authorization and with intent or reason to believe that it is to be used to injure the United States, (2) obtaining from a computer without authorization information that is protected by the Right to Financial Privacy Act or contained in the consumer files of a credit reporting agency, and (3) interfering with the operation of a government computer.

The Comprehensive Crime Control Act of 1984 contained a section on the use of computers in credit card fraud and established penalties for violation. In addition, the Computer Fraud and Abuse Act of 1986 established three federal crimes for computer fraud, destruction, and password trafficking.

State Laws

Almost all states have passed laws dealing with computer crime. Most of the statutes comprehensively address the problem, outlawing (1) computer trespass (unauthorized access), (2) damage to computers or software (for example, use of "viruses"), (3) theft or misappropriation of computer services, and (4) obtaining or disseminating information by computer in an unauthorized manner.

WHITE COLLAR CRIME

The term **white collar crime** generally encompasses nonviolent acts by individuals or corporations to obtain a personal or business advantage in a commercial context. Many of the crimes discussed earlier in this chapter are examples of white collar crime. White collar crime has become an extremely controversial subject in recent years for at least two reasons. First, there is evidence that the economic losses caused by white collar crime are at a staggering level (often estimated at more than $100 billion annually) and growing rapidly. Second, there is a perception, based on substantial fact, that criminal penalties for white collar crimes costing the public millions of dollars are often much less severe than criminal penalties imposed on the average street hood who steals a $75 pair of shoes.

Traditional criminal law did not punish corporations for crimes, reasoning that because a corporation is an artificial entity, it could not form the intent required to supply *mens rea,* and it could not be punished by incarceration. Also, American law was slow to punish corporate officials who committed crimes. One reason is illustrated by the oft-quoted sentiment of a federal judge who said that he would not "penalize a businessman trying to make a living when there are felons out on the street."

In recent years, however, the traditional views have changed rather dramatically. Potential criminal liability must now be a significant concern for both corporations and their officials.

Criminal Liability of Corporations
Today, most criminal statutes include corporations in their definition of "persons" who may violate the statute. The traditional reluctance to impose criminal sanctions on corporations has been overcome by modern reasoning that suggests (1) that the *mens rea* necessary to convict a corporation can be supplied by imputing the intent of the corporation's agents who physically commit the crimes to the corporation (as has long been done in the area of tort law), and (2) that corporations can be punished by fines and by innovative punishments that might, for example, require a corporation that has been caught polluting to fund an environmental education course at a local high school.

The general rule today is that corporations can be held criminally liable for any acts performed by an employee if that employee is acting within the scope of his or her authority for the purpose of benefitting the corporation. The basic idea is that the corporation receives the benefit when the agent acts properly and must bear the responsibility when the agent errs. This is simply an application of the *respondeat superior* doctrine (let the master answer for the wrongs of the agent) that is discussed in more detail in Chap-

ter 32. The corporation can even be held liable when the agent is violating company policy or disobeying a specific order from a superior. Some jurisdictions refuse to hold the corporation criminally liable for crimes committed by lower-level employees, but many states find the corporation responsible no matter how far down the ladder the actual wrongdoer is.

Corporations have been indicted for homicide and a wide variety of lesser offenses, including health and safety violations arising out of toxic waste disposal, failure to remove asbestos from buildings, and construction-site accidents.

On November 1, 1991, federal sentencing guidelines went into effect, significantly increasing the punishments meted out to corporations that violate federal criminal statutes. A sentencing judge now has the prerogative to place a corporation on probation in order to supervise it for a time to ensure that criminal activity is eradicated. Fortunately for corporations, the suggested punishment structure is mitigated substantially if the defendant company has in place an "effective program to prevent and detect violations of law." The purpose of this mitigation factor is to induce corporations to "police their own" by establishing standards of conduct for employees and using various means to enforce those standards.

Criminal Liability of Corporate Officials
The increase in prosecutions of corporations has been matched by an increase in prosecutions of corporate officers as well. Corporate officers will definitely be held liable for criminal acts that they participate in or authorize. In addition, they will be held liable for acts that they aid and abet through any significant assistance or encouragement. Some courts find sufficient encouragement in mere acquiescence of a superior (which a subordinate may read as tacit approval) and even in failure to stop criminal activity that the official knows is occurring. In rare instances involving *strict liability* statutes, corporate officers have been held criminally liable because they failed to control the criminal acts of subordinates (even where they had no knowledge of the acts or had been assured that the acts had stopped). *United States v. Park,* 421 U.S. 658 (1975).

Indicative of the trend toward increased criminal liability are some recent cases in which corporate officials have been tried for *murder* in the deaths of employees exposed to hazardous conditions in the work place. Additionally, federal laws have recently

LEGAL FOCUS

International

As in so many areas of endeavor, criminal activity occurring abroad affects the United States and vice versa. The purchasing in the United States of cocaine that was grown in South America is an obvious example. The interplay of Swiss bank secrecy laws and insider trading in U.S. stocks is another. The international scope of the B.C.C.I. banking scandal that came to light in 1991 is yet another.

Each of these examples highlights the inadequacy of current levels of international cooperation in such matters. But this is not to say that there is no cooperation. American law enforcement agencies do cooperate with similar foreign agencies. The U.S. Securities and Exchange Commission has worked closely with Swiss officials in an attempt to police international insider trading. Many countries have extradition treaties with the United States to facilitate the return of fugitive suspects. Although most attempts at inter-

national cooperation have occurred at a bilateral level, perhaps some day more nations will adopt the model treaties on international criminal cooperation that have been approved by the United Nations Congresses on the Prevention of Crime and the Treatment of Offenders in 1985 and 1990. These include the Model Treaty on Extradition, the Model Treaty on Mutual Assistance in Criminal Matters, and the Model Treaty on the Transfer of Proceedings in Criminal Matters.

---

been enacted or beefed up to encourage criminal actions against individuals who engage in insider trading, environmental pollution, savings and loan fraud, defrauding of the Defense Department, and a host of other activities that have been in the news recently.

SUMMARY

Crime is an unfortunate fact of life for businesses as well as individuals. Some acts of individuals in society are so inimical to the public good that remedy cannot be left to litigation between the victim and the wrongdoer. When that is true, the government initiates criminal actions to protect society at large.

The power of the government is great and potentially subject to abuse. The Bill of Rights contains a host of protections for criminal defendants, including protection from unreasonable searches and seizures, from self-incrimination, from excessive bail, and from cruel and unusual punishment. The Bill of Rights also contains a number of positive rights, including right to counsel, right to grand jury indictment, right to trial by jury, and right to a speedy and public trial.

The basic elements of any criminal conviction are a defendant's guilty act and guilty mind, both of which must be established beyond a reasonable doubt by the prosecutor.

A raft of state laws, such as those criminalizing larceny, embezzlement, forgery, and arson, help to protect business interests. Congress has passed a host of federal criminal acts as well, including the Hobbs Act, the Travel Act, RICO, and the laws outlawing mail and wire fraud. Both federal and state governments have responded to technological innovations by passing new criminal laws dealing specifically with computer crime.

Today, criminal law is not a concern solely for the street criminal. Corporations and those staffing their boardrooms must also abide by society's laws. Criminal prosecutions for white collar crime are definitely increasing in number and severity of penalties meted out.

KEY TERMS

Crime
Felony
Misdemeanor
Grand jury
Double jeopardy
Due process
Actus reus
Mens rea
Entrapment
Immunity
Larceny

Burglary
False pretenses
Embezzlement
Robbery
Forgery
Arson
Mail fraud
Wire fraud
White collar crime

QUESTIONS AND PROBLEMS

1. Minnick was arrested for murder. Federal officials gave him the Miranda warning and suspended interrogation when he requested a lawyer. He consulted with his lawyer two or three times. Then state officials sought to question Minnick, telling him that he would "have to talk" and "could not refuse." Minnick then confessed and was convicted of murder and sentenced to death when his motion to suppress the confession was overruled. Was Minnick denied his right against self-incrimination? Discuss. (*Minnick v. Mississippi,* 111 S.Ct. 486, 1990).

2. To interdict drugs, police in Florida routinely boarded buses at scheduled stops and asked passengers for permission to search their bags. Bostick was such a passenger who was approached without any basis for suspicion, questioned, and informed of his right to refuse a request to search. Bostick gave permission and cocaine was discovered. Bostick was convicted of drug trafficking when his motion to suppress the cocaine was overruled. Were Bostick's Fourth Amendment rights to protection from unreasonable searches and seizures denied? Discuss. (*Florida v. Bostick,* 111 S.Ct. 2382, 1991.)

3. Speckman was an attorney for a partnership that financed a waterslide operation. In 1980, a partner, Schwab, indicated a desire to sell his interest. Speckman told Schwab that he had a buyer and later gave Schwab a check for about $5000. In 1983, Speckman's client, Young, indicated an interest in investment opportunities. Speckman recommended the waterslide operation and Young gave Speckman a check for $7500 to be used to buy Schwab's interest. However, Speckman never altered the partnership records to indicate that Schwab was no longer a partner. Neither Schwab nor Young received any monetary distribution from the partnership. In essence, Speckman bought Schwab's interest, resold it to Young, but then denied Young the benefit of his investment. A jury convicted Speckman of *both* embezzlement and larceny by false pretenses in the obtaining of Young's $7500. Discuss the appropriateness of this verdict. (*State v. Speckman,* 374 S.E.2d 419, N.C.App. 1989.)

4. Using the name "Larry Grimes," Tolliver opened an account at Pioneer Savings & Loan with $50. He applied for a TYME card for use with Pioneer's automated tellers. He later used an automated teller to deposit a $2500 check that had been stolen from Terry McCaughey. He then made several cash withdrawals with his TYME card before the McCaughey check was returned to Pioneer with the notation that the account was closed and the signature unauthorized. Tolliver was convicted of uttering a forged check. Under the statute, the forged writing must be "uttered" or offered as genuine. Tolliver appealed, claiming that it is impossible to offer a writing as genuine to a machine, and therefore the offering or uttering took place when the machines' owners presented the check for payment to the drawee. Is Tolliver's defense valid? (*State v. Tolliver,* 440 N.W.2d 571, Wis.App. 1989.)

5. Matt was a division manager in charge of sales promotion for a tobacco company. One promotion was to give cigarettes to retailers so they could engage in "buy one, get one free" promotions. Matt concocted a scheme that involved removing complimentary tobacco products and exchanging them through sales representatives for salable merchandise. Matt would sell the merchandise and keep the money. To hide the scheme, Matt forced sales representatives to file false reports with respect to the placement of complimentary goods, which he would then mail to the company. Matt was indicted for mail fraud. Should he be convicted? (*United States v. Matt,* 838 F.2d 1356, 5th Cir. 1988.)

6. Mulder was a commissioned salesman for Englehart's wholesale furniture business. He told Bateman, a furniture maker, that he "was in with a couple of new partners" who might have some work for him. Englehart and Mulder met Bateman; Englehart paid Bateman $8750 to build 50 entertainment centers. A few days later, Mulder told Bateman that Englehart had decided to get entertainment centers elsewhere and he would have to give the money back. Bateman, believing Mulder to be Englehart's partner, gave him $6250, retaining $2500 per an agreement with Mulder to stain units Mulder falsely claimed were being

bought elsewhere. Mulder used the $6250 to pay personal debts. When charged with embezzlement, Mulder claimed that, unlike a bank teller, for example, his job was not to handle Englehart's money, and therefore he had not committed embezzlement. Is this a reasonable defense? (*People v. Mulder,* 421 N.W.2d 605, Mich.App. 1988.)

7. Mathews, an administrator for the Small Business Administration, was taped by the FBI as he apparently accepted a bribe. Mathews was indicted for accepting a gratuity in exchange for an official act in violation of federal law. Mathews wished to raise an entrapment defense, but the trial judge refused to allow it unless Mathews first admitted all elements of the offense. In other words, Mathews could not plead in the alternative: "I didn't do it, but if I did I was entrapped." Should a defendant be required to admit the substantive elements of the offense or be barred from raising an entrapment defense? (*United States v. Mathews,* 485 U.S. 58, 1988.)

8. Covino, as Director of Network Services for NYNEX Mobile Communications Co., had substantial influence over selection of and compensation for construction companies working for NYNEX. Great Northeastern was a construction company that did a large proportion of its work for NYNEX. In May 1984, Covino told Brennan, Great Northeastern's president, that one of Brennan's employees had improperly billed $3200 in phone calls to a NYNEX credit card and that it "wouldn't look good" if Covino showed the bill to his superiors. Brennan offered to pay the bill, but Covino said that he would take care of it. Not long thereafter, Covino asked Brennan to build a sun deck on Covino's home, telling him to keep "in mind the phone bill." The project evolved into a $20,000 addition. Covino asked Brennan to take a $15,000 check and then give him back that much in cash so that it would appear Covino had paid for the work. Brennan declined to assist in the coverup but did not charge for the work. Because Brennan was afraid of losing the NYNEX work, he eventually paid over $85,000 in cash to Covino in addition to doing more work on his house. Covino was discovered and indicted for a violation of the Hobbs Act. Discuss the appropriateness of this charge. (*United States v. Covino,* 837 F.2d 65, 2d Cir. 1988.)

9. Covino, from the preceding case, was also charged with a violation of the Travel Act. It was basically alleged that he had phoned Brennan to facilitate the commission of a state crime, specifically, bribery in violation of New York law. Discuss the appropriateness of this charge.

10. Covino was *also* accused of wire fraud. The indictment stated that he had used the wires to "violate his fiduciary duty to NYNEX Communications, by concealing information, to wit, his receipt of money and property . . . , which information was material to the conduct of the business of NYNEX," which was in furtherance of a scheme to defraud NYNEX by depriving it of defendant's "loyal and unbiased services." Discuss the validity of this charge.

Chapter 8

General Tort Law

A Preface

Scope and Complexity of Tort Law

Negligence

Major Intentional Torts

Other Intentional Torts

Special Problems

A PREFACE

Two areas of law, criminal law and contract law, developed at an early time in England. Although both were intended to eliminate, insofar as possible, various kinds of wrongful conduct, each was concerned with markedly different wrongs. The major purposes of criminal law were to define *wrongs against the state*—types of conduct so inherently undesirable that they were flatly prohibited—and to permit the state to punish those who committed such acts by the imposition of fines or imprisonment. The major purposes of contract law, however, were (1) to spell out the nature of the rights and duties springing from *private agreements between individuals* and (2) in the event that one party failed to live up to these duties, to compensate the innocent party for the loss resulting from the other's breach of contract.

When criminal law and contract law were still in their initial stages of development, it became apparent that neither one afforded protection to the large numbers of persons who suffered losses resulting from other kinds of conduct equally unjustifiable from a social standpoint—acts of carelessness, deception, and the like. Faced with this situation, the courts at an early time began to recognize and define other "legal wrongs" besides crimes and breaches of contract—and began to permit persons who were injured thereby to bring civil actions to recover damages against those who committed them. Acts that came to be recognized as wrongs under these rules, which were formulated by judges over the years on a case-by-case basis, acquired the name of **torts** (the French word for *"wrongs"*).

Because tort law applies to such a wide range of activities, any introductory definition of tort must necessarily be framed in general terms—as, for example, "any wrong excluding breaches of contract and crimes," or "any noncontractual civil wrong committed upon the person or property of another." Although such definitions are of little aid in illustrating the specific kinds of torts that are recognized, they do, at least, reflect the historic lines of demarcation between breaches of contract, crimes, and torts.[1]

SCOPE AND COMPLEXITY OF TORT LAW

As our society has become increasingly industrialized and complex, with many relationships existing among individuals that were perhaps unthought of 50 years ago, the legal duties owed by one member of society to others have become considerably more numerous and varied. As a result, tort law encompasses such a wide range of human conduct that the breaches of some duties have little in common with others. For example, some actions are considered tortious (wrongful) only when the actor intended to cause an injury, whereas in other actions—especially those involving negligence—the actor's intentions are immaterial. Similarly, in some tort actions the plaintiff is required to show physical injury to his or her property as a result of the defendant's misconduct, whereas in other actions such a showing is not required. In the latter situations other kinds of legal injury are recognized, such as damage to reputation or mental suffering.

A somewhat clearer picture of the broad sweep of tort law can be gained from the realization that the rules making up this area of law must deal with such diverse matters as the care required of a surgeon in the operating room, the circumstances in which a contracting party has a legal obligation to inform the other party of facts that he or she knows that the other party does not possess, and the determination of the kinds of business information (trade secrets) that are entitled to protection against theft by competitors.

The courts clearly engage in some degree of social engineering as they shape the common law of torts. Common to all successful tort actions are the twin concepts of *interest* and *duty*. Each time a court allows tort recovery, it is saying that the plaintiff has an interest (for example, in bodily integrity, in enjoying the benefits of private property, in a good reputation) sufficiently important for the law to furnish protection and that, correspondingly, in a civilized society the defendant has a duty (for example, not to strike the plaintiff, not to steal the plaintiff's property, not

---

[1]As indicated by these definitions, torts and crimes are essentially two different kinds of wrongs—the first a wrong against the individual and the second a wrong against the state. However, as we will see, in many situations a single wrongful act can constitute both a tort and a crime.

to falsely injure the plaintiff's reputation) that was breached. As society evolves technologically, morally, philosophically, and otherwise, tort law will evolve also. For example, 100 years ago, Americans had very little privacy. However, as increased wealth has allowed us to purchase and enjoy privacy, most of us have come to value privacy very much. In recent years most courts have come to recognize privacy as an interest worth protecting and, as we shall see, have imposed a duty on others not to invade our privacy.

The law of torts is so broad and so pervasive that it cannot be treated in a single chapter. This chapter focuses on the law of negligence and on certain intentional torts. A number of torts of specific concern to business are discussed in Chapter 9. Lawsuits arising out of the sale of defective products are also primarily tort-related; they are discussed in Chapter 22. Although these three chapters are devoted almost solely to tort law, the subject will also make appearances in several other chapters.[2]

This chapter begins with a treatment of negligence law and then studies several important intentional torts.

NEGLIGENCE

Negligence, to oversimplify, is carelessness. The courts long ago decided that our interests in economic well-being and personal safety are sufficiently important to be protected from the careless acts of others. Correspondingly, each of us has a duty as we live our lives and carry on our professions to exercise care not to injure others carelessly. Even though we may not intend to injure, the harm is just as real to the victim who is struck by the careless driver, burned by the carelessly designed product, crippled by the careless surgeon, or ruined financially by embezzlement that an accountant carelessly failed to detect.

The negligence cause of action is the most important method of redress existing today for persons injured accidentally. The newspapers are filled with accounts of negligence actions involving asbestos exposure, Agent Orange, the Exxon *Valdez* oil spill in Alaska, and the like. Whether a plaintiff was injured by a careless driver, a careless product designer, a careless surgeon, or a careless accountant, the same

basic elements must be proved to establish a right of recovery: (1) that the defendant owed the plaintiff a *duty* of due care, (2) that the defendant *breached* that duty of due care, (3) that the defendant's breach *proximately caused* the injury, and (4) that the plaintiff suffered *injury*.

Duty

Few concepts are more fraught with difficulty than that of "duty" in the negligence cause of action. As a general rule, it may be said that we each owe a duty to every person who we can *reasonably foresee* might be injured by our carelessness. If we drive down the street carelessly, pedestrians and other drivers are within the class of foreseeable plaintiffs we might injure. That we do not know the exact names of our prospective victims is unimportant.

To illustrate quickly, in *Burke v. Pan American World Airways, Inc.,*[3] the plaintiff sued the defendants allegedly responsible for a terrible plane collision in the Canary Islands, claiming that she, although in California at the time, felt as though she were being "split in two" and felt an emptiness "like a black hole" at the exact instant of the crash. The plaintiff claimed that in that instant she knew that something terrible had happened to her identical twin sister, who was, in fact, killed in the collision. The plaintiff was prepared to document the phenomenon of "extrasensory empathy" between some pairs of identical twins. Even assuming the plaintiff could establish the point, the court dismissed the suit. When a plane crashes because of an airline's negligence, its passengers are certainly foreseeable plaintiffs, as are any persons on the ground hit by falling wreckage. However, Burke's injuries were too bizarre to be reasonably foreseeable, even if she did sustain them. The defendants owed no legal duty to the plaintiff.

Although foreseeability is a very important consideration in establishing the parameters of a careless actor's duty, it is not the only one. The California courts, which have extended the notion of duty about as far as any jurisdiction, have taken into account such factors as:

the foreseeability of harm to the plaintiff, the degree of certainty that the plaintiff suffered injury, the closeness of the connection between the defendant's conduct and the injury suffered, the moral blame attached to the defendant's

---

[2]For example, Chapter 32 (liability of parties in an agency relationship), and Chapter 51 (consumer transactions and the law).

[3]484 F.Supp. 850 (S.D.N.Y. 1980).

conduct, the policy of preventing future harm, the extent of the burden to the defendant and consequences to the community of imposing a duty to exercise care with resulting liability, and the availability, cost, and prevalence of insurance for the risk involved.[4]

[4]*Rowland v. Christian*, 70 Cal. Rptr. 97 (1968).

Indeed, these are factors the court used in *Soldano v. O'Daniels*, a case discussed in Chapter 1, to impose a duty not to interfere with a Good Samaritan's attempt to aid a victim in distress.

The following case is just one illustration of a court's struggle to meld foreseeability and public policy factors to produce a proper scope of duty.

OTIS ENGINEERING CORP. V. CLARK

Texas Supreme Court, 668 S.W.2d 307 (1983)

Matheson, an employee of defendant Otis Engineering Corporation, had a history of being intoxicated on the job. One night he was particularly intoxicated, and his fellow employees believed he should be removed from the machines. Roy, Matheson's supervisor, suggested that Matheson go home, escorted him to the company parking lot, and asked him if he could make it home. Matheson answered that he could, but 30 minutes later and some three miles away he caused an accident killing the wives of plaintiffs Larry and Clifford Clark.

The Clarks sued Otis in a wrongful death action, but the trial court dismissed the suit, holding that Otis could not be liable because Matheson was not acting within the scope of his employment at the time of the accident. The intermediate court of appeals reversed, and Otis appealed to the Texas Supreme Court.

Kilgarlin, Justice:

The Clarks contend that under the facts in this case Otis sent home, in the middle of his shift, an employee whom it knew to be intoxicated. They aver this was an affirmative act which imposed a duty on Otis to act in a non-negligent manner.

In order to establish tort liability, a plaintiff must initially prove the existence and breach of a duty owed to him by the defendant. As a general rule,

one person is under no duty to control the conduct of another, *Restatement (Second) of Torts* §315 (1965), even if he has the practical ability to exercise such control. Yet, certain relationships do impose, as a matter of law, certain duties upon parties. For instance, the master–servant relationship may give rise to a duty on the part of the master to control the conduct of his servants outside the scope of employment. This duty, however, is a narrow one. Ordinarily, the employer is liable only for the off-duty torts of his employees which are committed on the employer's premises or with the employer's chattels.

Though the decisional law of this State has yet to address the precise issues presented by this case, factors which should be considered in determining whether the law should impose a duty are the risk, foreseeability, and likelihood of injury weighed against the social utility of the actor's conduct, the magnitude of the burden of guarding against the injury and consequences of placing that burden on the employer.

While a person is generally under no legal duty to come to the aid of another in distress, he is under a duty to avoid any affirmative action which might worsen the situation. One who voluntarily enters an affirmative course of action affecting the interests of another is regarded as assuming a duty to act and must do so with reasonable care.

Otis contends that, at worst, its conduct amounted to nonfeasance and under established law it owed no duty

to the Clarks' respective wives. Traditional tort analysis has long drawn a distinction between action and inaction in defining the scope of duty. However, although courts have been slow to recognize liability for nonfeasance, "[d]uring the last century, liability for 'nonfeasance' has been extended still further to a limited group of relations, in which custom, public sentiment and views of social policy have led the courts to find a duty of affirmative action." W. Prosser, *The Law of Torts* at 339. Be that as it may, we do not view this as a case of employer nonfeasance.

What we must decide is if changing social standards and increasing complexities of human relationships in today's society justify imposing a duty upon an employer to act reasonably when he exercises control over his servants. Even though courts have been reluctant to hold an employer liable for the off-duty torts of an employee, "[a]s between an entirely innocent plaintiff and a defendant who admittedly has departed from the social standard of conduct, if only toward one individual, who should bear the loss?" W. Prosser, *supra*, at 257. Dean Prosser additionally observed that "[t]here is nothing sacred about 'duty,' which is nothing more than a word, and a very indefinite one with which we state our conclusion."

During this year, we have taken a step toward changing our concept of duty in premises cases. In *Corbin v. Safeway Stores Inc.*, 648 S.W.2d 292 (Tex. 1983), we held that a store owner has a duty to guard against slips and

(continues)

Ots egi- Ves
duty

OTIS ENGINEERING CORP. v. CLARK

(continued from previous page)
falls if he has actual or constructive knowledge of a dangerous condition and it is foreseeable a fall would occur. Following *Corbin*, why should we be reluctant to impose a duty on Otis? As Dean Prosser has observed, "[c]hanging social conditions lead constantly to the recognition of new duties. No better general statement can be made than that the courts will find a duty where, in general, reasonable men would recognize and agree that it exists."

Therefore, the standard of duty that we now adopt for this and all other cases currently in the judicial process, is: when, because of an employee's incapacity, an employer exercises control over the employee, the employer has a duty to take such action as a reasonably prudent employer under the same or similar circumstances would take to prevent the employee from causing an unreasonable risk of harm to others. The duty of the employer is not an absolute duty to insure safety, but requires only reasonable care.

Therefore, the trier of fact in this case should be left free to decide whether Otis acted as a reasonable and prudent employer considering the following factors: the availability of the nurses' aid station [on the plant premises], a possible phone call to Mrs. Matheson, having another employee drive Matheson home, and the foreseeable consequences of Matheson's driving upon a public street in his stuporous condition.

[Affirm judgment of court of appeals and remand to trial court.] ⚖

Duty of Landowners

A recurring problem in establishing the nature of a duty exists regarding the responsibility of owners or occupiers of land. How much of a duty they owe to visitors to their land has traditionally turned on whether the visitor was a trespasser (one who enters the land with no right to do so), a licensee (one who has a right to come onto the property for self-benefit, such as a door-to-door salesman or a neighbor dropping in uninvited), or an invitee (one invited by the owner or occupier or who enters for the benefit of the owner or occupier, such as a customer at a store). Under this traditional approach (which is still the majority view), trespassers could sue only for intentional torts, licensees could sue also for hidden dangers they should have been warned about, and invitees could sue under the ordinary rules of negligence. Several recent cases have rejected this tripartite approach, not differentiating between plaintiffs and treating all defendants in this context under the general rules of negligence "governed by the test of reasonable care under all the circumstances in the maintenance and operation of their property." *Oulette v. Blanchard*, 364 A.2d 631 (N.H. 1976).

Breach

To be liable for negligence, a defendant must *breach* an existing duty. A breach occurs when the defendant fails to exercise the same care as a "reasonable person under similar circumstances" would have exercised. This hypothetical "reasonable person" or "reasonable man" standard can be fairly strict because of a jury's tendency, confronted with a seriously injured plaintiff, to use 20-20 hindsight:

> [*The reasonable man*] *is one who invariably looks where he is going and is careful to examine the immediate foreground before he executes a leap or bound; who neither star-gazes nor is lost in meditation when approaching trap doors or the margin of a dock; . . . who never mounts a moving omnibus, and does not alight from any car while the train is still in motion . . . and who informs himself of the history and habits of a dog before administering a caress.*[5]

All the Circumstances

Whether or not a defendant's conduct met the "reasonable person" standard of care should be examined in light of all the circumstances of the case. Emergency conditions, for example, may be considered. Normally it would be a clear breach of due care to abandon a moving vehicle, but if a cab driver does so because a robber in the back seat has pulled a gun, a jury might determine that, under all the circumstances, there was no breach of due care to render the cab company liable to a pedestrian who was struck by the driverless cab.[6] An unexpected bee sting might

---

[5]A. P. Herbert, *Uncommon Law: Fardell v. Potts.* Reprinted by permission of Lady Herbert.
[6]*Cordas v. Peerless Transp. Co.*, 27 N.Y.S.2d 198 (N.Y. 1941).

cause a bus driver unavoidably to lose control of a bus, though she was a most careful driver.[7]

The custom of others in the community or of other companies in the industry may also shed light on the proper standard of due care. If the defendant has acted in the same manner as most others in the same situation, it is difficult to conclude that a reasonable person standard was breached. However, custom is not always binding. In one famous case, barges were lost at sea because the tugs towing them had no radio sets to listen to weather reports that would have warned them to take shelter from an approaching storm. That few tug companies used the radio set was not proof that the "reasonable person" standard was met, because "a whole calling may have unduly lagged in the adoption of new and available devices."[8]

Conduct of Others

Traditionally the courts allowed us to assume that other members of society would act carefully and lawfully. In other words, we had no duty to anticipate the negligent or criminal acts of others. However, increasingly courts and juries are concluding that such acts can and must be anticipated in certain circumstances. Thus, operators of a motel located in a high crime area that has itself been the scene of criminal acts in the past may be held to have breached a duty of due care by not providing adequate security for guests who are victimized by crime.[9] Though some courts refuse to impose a duty in such circumstances, providing adequate security is increasingly a concern for motel owners, common carriers, store owners, concert promoters, and even universities.

Negligence *Per Se*

Although the standard of care to which a defendant will be held in a negligence case is usually formulated by the jury's assessment of what a reasonable person would have done, in some cases the conduct is measured in accordance with legislative imposed standards. One example is a "dramshop" act, which many states have passed making it illegal to sell liquor to an intoxicated person. Another is the 55-mile-per-hour speed limit.

Most courts have held that if a defendant violates

such a statute, it is negligence *per se*.[10] That is, if the plaintiff can show that he or she is within the class of persons that the statute was meant to protect and the harm sustained was the type the statute was meant to prevent, the issue of breach of due care is conclusively resolved against the defendant. The jury can be instructed that the defendant had breached the duty of due care. Lack of damages or proximate causation still might prevent recovery.

In one case, a small girl was abducted from the street in front of the building in which she lived, taken across the street to an open, vacant apartment, and assaulted. The girl sued the owners of the apartment building in which the assault occurred for not having locks on the doors, in violation of a city ordinance, and thereby providing a tempting location for the crime. Emphasizing that the ordinance was intended to provide security against crime by requiring all vacant apartments to be secured, the court found negligence *per se* in its violation.[11]

Many courts do not go quite so far, holding only that violation of a statute is one factor the jury can consider among all others in deciding whether the defendant breached the duty of due care.

Proximate Cause

After proving existence and breach of a duty of due care, the plaintiff in a negligence action must demonstrate that the breach proximately caused the plaintiff's alleged injuries. There are many different labels and many different approaches to the proximate cause concept. Fundamentally, **proximate cause** means direct cause—that there is a direct causal connection between the defendant's act of carelessness and the plaintiff's injury—but it is more complicated than that.

"Legal cause," according to many courts, has two requirements. First, *causation in fact* must be shown. Some courts stress that the defendant's carelessness must be an act without which no harm would have occurred. In other words, can we say that "but for" the defendant's act the injuries would not have happened? For example, assume that Jill is driving her car at 40 miles per hour on a street where the speed limit is 30 miles per hour when a small child darts into the street from between two cars and is hit

[7]*Schultz v. Cheney School District*, 371 P.2d 59 (Wash. 1962).
[8]*The T. J. Hooper*, 60 F.2d 737 (2d Cir. 1932).
[9]*Garzilli v. Howard Johnson's Motor Lodges, Inc.*, 419 F.Supp. 1210 (E.D.N.Y. 1976) (the "Connie Francis case").

[10]And, of course, if a plaintiff violates such a statute it is comparative negligence *per se*. This is a concept we shall address directly under the topic of "defenses."
[11]*Nixon v. Mr. Property Management Co.*, 690 S.W.2d 546 (Tex. 1985).

by Jill's car. Assume further that the child was so close to Jill's car when he darted into the street that even had Jill been driving 30 miles per hour, or even 20, she could not have avoided striking the child. In such a case we cannot say that "but for" Jill's speeding the accident would not have happened. Jill's careless speeding was not a proximate cause of the accident, and Jill would not be liable.

Other courts addressing the *causation in fact* element stress that the defendant's carelessness must be a *substantial factor* in bringing about the injury, but not necessarily a "but for" cause, although the two will often overlap.

Factual causation ("but for" or "substantial factor") is insufficient in and of itself, however. Almost every act has consequences that ripple throughout society, and many incidents have several causes. Perhaps "but for" your carelessly running a stop sign, ambulance driver A would never have met nurse B and had child C who at the age of 14 years murdered D. May D's family sue you? Obviously not. For policy reasons, we must limit the liability stemming from our actions in some fashion.

Most courts return to the notion of *foreseeability* in establishing the second element of legal causation. Factual causation ("but for") plus foreseeability will establish proximate or legal causation. Because foreseeability is an important factor in the establishment of both duty and proximate cause, court discussions of the two concepts tend to overlap.

The most famous tort case of all time is perhaps *Palsgraf v. Long Island R.R.*,[12] in which railway employees carelessly pushed a passenger who was trying to board a train. This caused him to drop a package he was carrying which, it turned out, contained fireworks that exploded beneath the wheels of the train. The force of the concussion knocked over a scale at the far end of the train station, injuring Mrs. Palsgraf. Injury to the boarding passenger and his property was a foreseeable result of the negligence of the railroad employees. They owed a duty of care to him, and any injuries to him would have been proximately caused by their actions. However, the court found the injury to Mrs. Palsgraf unforeseeable. The duty owed to the boarding passenger did not protect her.

The *Palsgraf* dissent argued that every person owes to the world a duty to refrain from careless acts and that we should be liable for all injuries flowing

[12]162 N.E. 99 (N.Y. 1928).

directly from our negligence, regardless of foreseeability. The dissenters felt the wrongdoer should be liable for all "proximate consequences," even when they consist of injuries to persons outside the foreseeable radius of danger.

Generally speaking, the "foreseeability" test of *Palsgraf* holds sway in our law today, but the "direct consequences" view of the dissent is frequently applied in various circumstances. For example, if we carelessly injure a person who turns out to be a hemophiliac, who then bleeds to death when most persons would not have, we are still liable for the death. Courts say that we must take our victims as we find them. Although it might not be reasonably foreseeable to us that our victim would be a hemophiliac, the death is a direct result of our carelessness.

Independent Intervening Cause

Especially in terms of foreseeability, the concept of **independent intervening cause** is important. Such a cause is one that emanates from a third party or source to disrupt the causal connection between the defendant's careless act and the plaintiff's injury. Assume that Sue is driving down the street when she comes to an intersection that is blocked by an accident caused by Joe's having run a stop sign. Sue turns her car around and while driving away is hit by a tree that is blown down by a strong wind. Sue can argue that "but for" Joe's carelessness the intersection would not have been blocked and she would have been several miles away from the tree at the time it fell over. But should we hold Joe liable for Sue's injury? No, because the tree's falling is an independent, intervening cause that breaks up the causal chain between Joe's careless driving and Sue's injury. The key, again, is foreseeability. An intervening cause that can reasonably be foreseen by the defendant is usually insufficient to break the causal chain.

There is probably no more complex concept in the law than that of proximate causation, as the following case illustrates. This case is potentially important because it embodies the decision of California's top court to favor "substantial factor" analysis over "but for" analysis, thus making it easier for plaintiffs to recover in cases where a defendant's carelessness may be only one of multiple causes of an injury. Although the controversial decision does not arise in a business context, it has important precedential value for a wide range of cases in which businesses might be defendants (or plaintiffs).

MITCHELL V. GONZALES

California Supreme Court, 819 P.2d 872 (1991)

Case

Damechie Mitchell, 12 years old, standing 4 feet 11 inches tall, and weighing 90 pounds, had a "tag-along, little-brother" relationship with Luis Gonzales, who was 14 years old and weighed 190 pounds. The Gonzales family invited Damechie to go to a lake with them. The parties' testimony conflicted as to whether Mrs. Mitchell told the Gonzales family that Damechie could not swim.

Mrs. Gonzales allowed the children to rent a paddleboat, but told them to stay within 30 feet of the shore in the shallow water. However, Luis began to push the paddleboat carrying Damechie and Luis's sister Yoshi out onto the lake. Damechie told Luis he could not swim, but Luis persisted. Luis said he would save Damechie if the latter fell into the water. Out in the deep water, Luis roughhoused, and the paddleboat tipped over. Damechie fell into the water. Luis and Yoshi did not immediately cry out for help. After a few minutes, Luis told some women nearby, "Lady, my friend's down there." The women then yelled for a lifeguard. Damechie's body was found 120 feet from the shore in 8 feet of water. Luis stated that Damechie had grabbed Luis in an effort to save himself, but that he, Luis, had shaken him off in order to avoid being pulled under. Mr. and Mrs. Gonzales had left supervision of the children to the lifeguards.

Damechie's parents sued the Gonzaleses in negligence. In instructing the jury on the causation element of negligence, the trial court used BAJI No. 3.75, the "but for" causation instruction ("A proximate cause of injury is a cause which, in natural and continuous sequence, produces the injury and without which the injury would not have occurred"), rather

than BAJI 3.76 ("A legal cause of injury is a cause which is a substantial factor in bringing about the injury"), as requested by plaintiffs. The jury found that defendants were negligent, but that their negligence was not a proximate cause of Damechie's death. The court of appeals reversed. The California Supreme Court granted a petition for review.

Lucas, Chief Justice:

In this case we decide whether [jury instruction] BAJI No. 3.75, which contains a "but for" test of cause in fact, should continue to be given in this state, or whether it should be disapproved in favor of BAJI No. 3.76, the so-called legal cause instruction, which employs the "substantial factor" test of cause in fact.

As Dean Prosser observed over 40 years ago, "Proximate cause remains a tangle and a jungle, a palace of mirrors and a maze. . . ." Cases "indicate that 'proximate cause' covers a multitude of sins, that it is a complex term of highly uncertain meaning under which other rules, doctrines and reasons lie buried. . . ." (Prosser, *Proximate Cause in California* (1950) 38 Cal.L.Rev. 369, 375.)

One of the concepts included in the term proximate cause is cause in fact, also referred to as actual cause. Indeed, for purposes of BAJI No. 3.75, "so far as a jury is concerned 'proximate cause' *only* relates to causation in fact." (Commentary to BAJI No. 3.75.) "There are two widely recognized tests for establishing cause in fact. The 'but for' or 'sine qua non' rule, unfortunately labeled 'proximate cause' in BAJI No. 3.75, asks whether the injury would not have occurred but for the defendant's conduct. The other test, labeled 'legal cause' in BAJI No. 3.76, asks whether the defendant's conduct was a substantial factor in bringing about the injury." (*Maupin v. Widling* (1987), 237

Cal.Rptr. 521.)

It has generally been recognized that the "but for" test contained in BAJI No. 3.75 should not be used when two "causes concur to bring about an event and either one of them operating alone could have been sufficient to cause the result. . . . In those few situations, where there are concurrent [independent] causes, our law provides one cannot escape responsibility for his negligence on the ground that identical harm would have occurred without it. The proper rule for such situations is that the defendant's conduct is a cause of the event because it is a material element and a substantial factor in bringing it about." (*Vecchione v. Carlin* (1980) 168 Cal.Rptr. 571).

This case presents the issue of whether BAJI No. 3.75 should be given in *any* negligence action.

Criticism of the term "proximate cause" has been extensive. . . . Prosser and Keeton [did not] hide their dislike for the term: "The word 'proximate' is a legacy of Lord Chancellor Bacon, who in his time committed other sins. The word means nothing more than near or immediate; and when it was first taken up by the courts it had connotations of proximity in time and space which have long since disappeared. It is an unfortunate word, which places an entirely wrong emphasis upon the factor of physical or mechanical closeness." (Prosser & Keeton on Torts, Sec. 42).

It is reasonably likely that when jurors hear the term "proximate cause" they may misunderstand its meaning or improperly limit their discussion of what constitutes a cause in fact. . . . The misunderstanding engendered by the term "proximate cause" has been documented. . . . We believe the . . . authorities properly criticize BAJI No. 3.75 for being conceptually and grammatically deficient. The deficiencies may mislead jurors, causing them, if they can't glean the instruction's meaning despite the grammatical flaws, to focus

(continues)

MITCHELL V. GONZALES

(*continued from previous page*)
improperly on the cause that is spatially or temporally closest to the harm.

In contrast, the "substantial factor" test, incorporated in BAJI No. 3.76 . . . has been comparatively free of criticism and has even received praise. . . . Moreover, the "substantial factor" test subsumes the "but for" test. "If the conduct which is claimed to have caused the injury had nothing at all to do with the injuries, it could not be said that the conduct was a factor, let alone a substantial factor, in the production of the injuries." (*Doupnik v. General Motors Corp.* (1990), 275 Cal.Rptr. 715.)

Not only does the substantial factor instruction assist in the resolution of the problem of independent causes, as noted above, but "[i]t aids in the disposition of two other types of situations which have proved troublesome. One is that where a similar, but not identical result would have followed without the defendant's act; the other where one defendant has made a clearly proved but quite insignificant contribution to the result, as where he throws a lighted match into a forest fire. But in the great majority of cases, *it produces the same legal conclusion as the but-for test.* Except in the classes of cases indicated,

no case has been found where the defendant's act could be called a substantial factor when the event would have occurred without it; nor will cases very often arise where it would not be such a factor when it was so indispensable a cause that without it the result would not have followed." (Prosser & Keeton on Torts, Sec. 41.)

We therefore conclude that BAJI No. 3.75, the so-called proximate cause instruction, should be disapproved and that the court erred when it refused to give BAJI No. 3.76.

[Reversed.]

Injury

As the final element of a negligence cause of action, the plaintiff must prove injury. Negligence recovery is allowed primarily for injury to person or property. Recovery for economic loss not related to personal injury or property damage is generally not allowed, although there are several exceptions for special situations.[13]

Courts traditionally have also been reluctant to allow recovery for emotional distress on grounds that such injuries are too intangible and too easily faked. Over the years, most courts have changed their views as psychiatric testimony regarding the actual existence of emotional distress has become more dependable.

At first, courts allowed recovery for negligently caused emotional distress when the plaintiff also sustained a physical injury in the accident. It was easier to believe that the plaintiff suffered emotional distress if there were accompanying physical injuries. Later courts also awarded recovery to plaintiffs who were not physically injured but were in the "zone of danger." Thus, a pedestrian who was narrowly missed by an automobile that ran down a fellow pedestrian could sue the careless driver for emotional damages.

Because application of the "zone of danger" test sometimes leads to rather arbitrary distinctions, many courts have taken an additional step by allowing "bystander recovery." Thus, according to the leading case,[14] a parent who sees or hears an accident killing the parent's child can recover for emotional distress although not within the zone of danger. Three factors to be weighed in deciding whether to allow recovery are: (1) whether the plaintiff was located near the scene of the accident; (2) whether the emotional shock resulted from a contemporaneous perception of the accident, as opposed to hearing about it later; and (3) whether the plaintiff and the victim were closely related. Many courts have rejected bystander recovery, which obviously entails an extension of the concept of duty. But the modern trend is to recognize that if an actor's carelessness causes an injury that kills or seriously injures someone, the victim's loved ones are almost certain to suffer emotional trauma.

Punitive damages, also known as *exemplary damages,* are not recoverable in mere negligence cases. These are monetary damages, over and above the sums necessary to compensate for the plaintiff's injuries, that are assessed against the defendant to punish for wrongdoing and to deter the defendant and others from engaging in such wrongful conduct.

[13]For example, some courts hold accounting firms liable for injuries caused by negligent auditing when third parties (such as creditors) foreseeably rely on financial documents the firms prepared for their clients. *H. Rosenblum, Inc. v. Adler,* 461 A.2d 138 (N.J. 1983).

[14]*Dillon v. Legg,* 69 Cal. Rptr. 72 (1968).

A defendant in a negligence action is guilty of mere carelessness, so punitive damages are viewed as inappropriate. However, punitive damages are generally available to plaintiffs injured by the intentional torts that we will discuss later in the chapter.

Defenses

Even if the plaintiff establishes all four elements of a negligence cause of action, the defendant may avert or reduce recovery by establishing certain defenses.

Comparative Fault

If the plaintiff is guilty of fault that contributed to the accident, a defense may exist. Under the old system of **contributory negligence,** a plaintiff who was guilty of carelessness that contributed in any material way to the accident was barred from recovery altogether. Even if the jury concluded that the plaintiff was 1 percent at fault and the defendant 99 percent, the plaintiff could recover nothing, no matter how serious the injuries were.

Because of the harshness of the contributory negligence system, most jurisdictions have replaced it with a system of **comparative negligence.** Comparative negligence or comparative fault systems vary widely from jurisdiction to jurisdiction, so it is difficult to generalize. Some states have "pure" comparative negligence systems under which, no matter how great a share of the fault is attributable to the plaintiff, the plaintiff still is entitled to recover the portion of damages caused by the defendant's carelessness. For example, let's assume that in a case arising out of an auto collision between P and D, a jury assesses P's damages at $100,000 and finds P 40 percent at fault and D 60 percent at fault. Rather than being barred from recovery as in a contributory negligence system, P would recover $60,000—that portion of the damages caused by D's fault. Indeed, in a pure system, even if P is found 99 percent at fault and D 1 percent, P would still recover $1,000. That P is many times more at fault than D does not bar recovery for that portion of the loss caused by D's carelessness.

Most jurisdictions have not adopted a pure comparative negligence system. Many allow a plaintiff to recover whatever percentage of damages were caused by the defendant, unless the plaintiff's share of the fault is assessed at 51 percent or higher. If the plaintiff's fault exceeds 50 percent, recovery is barred altogether on the theory that the plaintiff should recover nothing if he or she is more at fault than the defendant. Other states set 49 percent as the cap, not allowing proportionate recovery to a plaintiff found 50 percent or more at fault.

Statute of Limitations

In negligence, as in other causes of action, every state has a **statute of limitations** within which the suit must be filed or forever barred. A typical tort statute of limitations is two years. Thus, a plaintiff injured by a defendant's negligence must file suit within two years of the occurrence. Occasionally a plaintiff may not even know of the injury until more than two years after the occurrence, for example, when carelessly designed drugs with side effects that will not show up for years are sold. Most states have applied tolling devices that provide that in such a case the statute of limitations is tolled; that is, will not begin to run, until the plaintiff knows or should know of the injury. In response to the medical malpractice and products liability "crises," several states have passed statutes of "repose" that bar certain actions after, say, 15 years, whether the injuries sustained were discoverable or not during that period.

No Fault Systems

Negligence has been eliminated as a basis for lawsuits in at least two contexts that should be mentioned here. Every state has a *workers' compensation* system that allows injured employees to recover benefits from their employers when injured on the job. The employee can recover regardless of the presence of employer fault but forfeits the right to sue the employer even if the employer has been careless. Most jurisdictions, however, allow an employee covered by workers' compensation to sue his or her employer in tort if injured by the employer's gross negligence (for example, if the employer has allowed several employees to be injured by the same defective machine without replacing it) or intentional tort. Workers' compensation plays a role in the *Caudle v. Betts* case in the next section and is discussed in more detail in Chapter 49.

Several states have enacted "no fault" automobile statutes. The thrust of these statutes is to reduce litigation by allowing persons who suffer only minor injuries in car accidents to recover only from their own insurance company. Although these laws vary widely from jurisdiction to jurisdiction, in most the plaintiffs' losses must exceed a certain statutory threshold before resort to litigation is allowed.

MAJOR INTENTIONAL TORTS

Assault And Battery

Assault and battery are similar torts that may be treated together. Although modern courts and statutes frequently use the two terms interchangeably, technically a **battery** is a rude, inordinate contact with the person of another. An **assault,** basically, is any act that creates an apprehension of an imminent battery. That we can sue for assault and battery protects our personal dignity from intrusions of the mind (assault) and body (battery). The courts long ago concluded that we have a legitimate interest in being protected from offensive bodily contacts and from fear of them. Indeed, assault and battery also constitute crimes.

Elements

One way to formulate the basic elements of the torts of assault and battery is to require the plaintiff to prove (1) the defendant's affirmative conduct, (2) intent, and (3) the plaintiff's injury.

Affirmative Conduct and Intent. If Sue is carefully driving down the street and is hit by a car that runs a red light, and as a result Sue's car is pushed into a pedestrian, Sue has not committed assault or battery. Although the pedestrian has sustained both apprehension (assuming she saw the accident as it happened) and rude contact, Sue committed no affirmative act that caused the injuries. The driver of the car that ran the red light did commit an affirmative act that was tortious, but that act was negligence, not assault or battery. However, if, while driving down the street, Sue spotted an enemy and deliberately ran down that person in a crosswalk, an assault and battery would have occurred.

The intent required for both assault and battery is the intent either to create an offensive contact to the plaintiff's body or the apprehension of it in the plaintiff. Furthermore, a person is presumed to intend the natural consequences of his or her actions. Thus, if A points an unloaded gun at B and utters threats to use it, an assault occurs if B does not know the gun is unloaded even if A's intent is simply to play a harmless prank. The natural consequences of A's act of pointing the gun is to create an apprehension in B.

Under the *doctrine of transferred intent,* if Sam shoots at Bill, but Bill ducks and the bullet hits Carlos, Carlos has an assault (assuming he saw the incident happening) and battery claim against Sam even if he is Sam's best friend and Sam would not intentionally hurt him for the world. The law transfers the intent Sam had to injure Bill to Carlos.

Injury. If a plaintiff seeks to establish an assault, the injury sustained must be in the nature of an apprehension of imminent bodily contact of an offensive nature. A threat of future contact or a threat by a defendant far away is insufficient. Threats or even attempts at violence that the intended victim does not know about until much later do not create the requisite apprehension, as where D shoots and misses P from so far away that P never realizes the shot was fired. Usually the plaintiff's reactions are judged by what would have caused apprehension in a reasonable person, but if the defendant knows that the plaintiff is an unusually sensitive person and threatens contact that the plaintiff finds offensive although most persons would not, an assault occurs.

If the plaintiff sues for battery, the injury that must be demonstrated is an offensive contact. Being struck with a fist, a knife, or a bullet obviously satisfies the requirement. So does being spat on, poisoned, and having one's clothes ripped or cane knocked away.

The following case illustrates the tort of battery in an employment context, thereby raising also some important workers' compensation issues.

CAUDLE V. BETTS

Supreme Court of Louisiana, 512 So.2d 389 (1987)

Understand Act

Case

Plaintiff Ruben Caudle was a salesman at Betts Lincoln-Mercury, Inc. Shortly before an office Christmas party on December 23, 1983, other employees engaged in horseplay with an electric automobile condenser after discovering that it could be charged by touching one end to a car's spark plug wire and turning the engine over. Once charged, the condenser would deliver a slight electric shock when touched at both ends. Several employees played catch with the charged condenser. Peter Betts, president of the corporation, shocked the back of Caudle's neck with the charged condenser and chased Caudle with it until Caudle escaped by locking himself in an office. After the incident, Caudle suffered headaches and passed out 30 to 40 times in the following months. The condition finally required occipital nerve surgery, leaving a slight numbness on the right side of the plaintiff's head.

Caudle sued Betts individually and Betts Lincoln-Mercury, Inc., for battery, seeking damages for, among other things, pain and suffering, past medical expenses, and loss of earnings. The trial court held that the injury to the plaintiff was not an intentional injury and, therefore, that workers' compensation benefits were the plaintiff's sole remedy. The appellate court affirmed the dismissal of the plaintiff's tort suit, and the plaintiff appealed to the Louisiana Supreme Court.

Dennis, Justice:

The Louisiana Worker's Compensation Act provides for compensation if an employee receives personal injury by accident arising out of and in the course of his employment. As a general rule, the rights and remedies granted to an employee therein are exclusive of all rights and remedies against his employer, any officer or principal of the employer, or any co-employee. However, an exception to this rule provides that nothing therein shall affect the liability of an employer, principal, officer, or co-employee resulting from an "intentional act." . . . [I]n drawing a line between intentional and unintentional acts the legislative aim was to make use of the well established division between intentional torts and negligence.

A harmful or offensive contact with a person, resulting from an act intended to cause the plaintiff to suffer such a contact, is a battery. . . . The intention need not be malicious nor need it be an intention to inflict actual damage. It is sufficient if the actor intends to inflict either a harmful or offensive contact without the other's consent.

The original purpose of the courts in providing the action for battery undoubtedly was to keep the peace by affording a substitute for private retribution. F. Stone, Louisiana Civil Law Treatise, Tort Doctrine, Sec. 125 (1977). The element of personal indignity always has been given considerable weight. Consequently, the defendant is liable not only for contacts that do actual physical harm, but also for those relatively trivial ones which are merely offensive and insulting. W. Prosser and W. Keeton, The Law of Torts, Sec. 9 (5th ed. 1984).

The intent with which tort liability is concerned is not necessarily a hostile intent, or a desire to do any harm. . . . Rather it is an intent to bring about a result that will invade the interests of another in a way that the law forbids. The defendant may be liable although intending nothing more than a good-natured practical joke, or honestly believing that the act would not injure the plaintiff, or even though seeking the plaintiff's own good. [*Id.*]

Bodily harm is generally considered to be any physical impairment of the condition of a person's body, or physical pain or illness. Restatement (Second) of Torts, American Law Institute, Sec. 15 (1965). The defendant's liability for the resulting harm extends, as in most other cases of intentional torts, to consequences which the defendant did not intend, and could not reasonably have foreseen, upon the obvious basis that it is better for unexpected losses to fall upon the intentional wrongdoer than upon the innocent victim. . . .

Applying these precepts to the facts found and affirmed by the lower courts, we conclude that the plaintiff employee proved that a battery had been committed on him by another employee and that he is entitled to recovery for all injuries resulting therefrom including his occipital nerve impairment. It is undisputed that when Mr. Betts shocked the employee, Mr. Caudle, with the condenser, he intended the contact to be offensive and at least slightly painful or harmful. The fact that he did so as a practical joke and did not intend to inflict actual damage does not render him immune from liability. Further, as between the innocent employee victim and the wrongdoer, it is better for unexpected losses to fall upon the intentional wrongdoer. Mr. Caudle is entitled to recover for all consequences of the battery, even those that Mr. Betts did not intend and could not have foreseen.

[Reversed and remanded.] ⚖

Defenses

In addition to the statute of limitations, which typically is two years in such cases, the two primary defenses to assault and battery are **consent** and **self-defense.** A plaintiff who has consented to offensive contacts and the threat of them cannot sue for assault and battery. Thus, a boxer who steps into the ring or the quarterback who steps onto the football field consents to the normal contacts that go with the rules of the game. However, a football player who is forearmed from behind by an opposing player after the play was over, he might have a good battery claim because his consent does not extend to this contact outside the rules of the game any more than it would extend to being shot by an opponent.[15]

Consent cannot be procured by fraud, nor can it be ill-informed. Thus, if M procures F's consent to sexual intercourse by hiding the fact that he has herpes, her consent to intercourse does not constitute consent to the harmful contact with the disease. She may sue for battery.[16] Doctors performing surgery must be very careful to fully inform their patients regarding the contacts that will take place during the surgery to avoid liability for battery. Consent to an appendectomy does not extend to the removal of some of the reproductive organs even though it may be the doctor's best medical judgment that they should be removed.

Self-defense creates a well-recognized privilege to assault and battery. In Chapter 7 we described how the courts restrict one to that degree of force considered reasonable in the circumstances of a crime. The same rule applies in the circumstances of a tort.

Defamation

Long ago the courts decided that we have a legitimate interest in preserving our good reputation in the community. Those who damage our reputation by spreading falsehoods commit the tort of **defamation** and may be liable in damages. Although defamation has historic common-law roots, its development in recent years has been strongly influenced by a series of Supreme Court decisions that have molded the tort in accordance with First Amendment principles.

[15]*Hackbart v. Cincinnati Bengals,* 601 F.2d 516 (10th Cir. 1979).
[16]*Long v. Adams,* 333 S.E.2d 852 (Ga. App. 1985).

Libel versus Slander

Defamation takes two basic forms. **Libel** is written defamation; **slander** is oral. Television and radio broadcasts have generally been categorized as libel. The distinction is important because, traditionally, libel, perhaps because of its more permanent form, was considered more damaging than slander. At common law, a person who proved libel was able to recover damages without any proof of special damages; that is, the very proof that something potentially damaging to the reputation was circulated in public led the court to presume injury. The jury could assess damages without evidence of any specific loss.

Slander, however, required proof of special damages. Generally, a plaintiff had to prove some sort of economic loss stemming from the damage to reputation. Once that was proved, the plaintiff could recover for all sorts of injuries, including humiliation, loss of friendship, and the like. However, in four special categories known as *slander per se,* no special damages needed to be proved. These categories were imputation of serious crime, of loathsome disease, of incompetence in the plaintiff's profession, and of unchastity in women.

However, as we shall see, the Supreme Court's First Amendment decisions have had an impact on this traditional distinction.

Elements

In a defamation case, the plaintiff must generally establish four elements to prevail: (1) that a matter defamatory of the plaintiff, (2) and untrue, (3) was communicated by the defendant, (4) to the plaintiff's injury. Questions of the defendant's fault, as we shall see, also arise.

Matter Defamatory of a Plaintiff. To be defamatory, a statement must be of such a nature as to tend to lower the plaintiff's esteem in the eyes of others. An infinite variety of statements have been held defamatory, but if the defendant falsely tells others that the plaintiff is a thief, a bankrupt, a Nazi, a communist, or a homosexual, it is likely that the plaintiff's esteem in the eyes of others will be lowered. Although most defamation actions are brought by individuals, they can also be brought by corporations and other organizations.

The defamatory statement must be one that the readers or hearers will associate with the plaintiff. Although not mentioned by name, a person who is obviously referred to in a disparaging way in a "novel" that is closely based on reality may have a claim against the author. So may a member of a small group when the defendant defames the entire group (for example, "All the male clerks at this store have AIDS") although the plaintiff is not mentioned by name. When larger groups are referred to (such as "All Republicans are fascists"), the courts hesitate to allow recovery.

Untrue. To be defamatory, a statement not only must tend to lower the plaintiff's esteem in the eyes of others, but also must be untrue. The question may be: Who has the burden of proving truthfulness or falsity? The common law presumed that everyone was a good person; therefore, if the plaintiff proved that a statement tending to defame him or her had been published by the defendant, the burden of proof was on the defendant to prove the truthfulness of the statement. Truth, in other words, was an absolute *defense* to a defamation claim.

A recent Supreme Court case redistributed this burden of proof, at least in some cases, on First Amendment grounds. In *Philadelphia Newspaper, Inc. v. Hepps,*[17] the Court held that if the plaintiff is a public figure (such as a famous actress or athlete), a public official (such as a governor), or a "limited" public figure (a private citizen caught up in a public controversy, such as a businessman whose name appears in a newspaper article about the Mafia), free speech concerns require that the plaintiff be given the burden of proof to demonstrate falsity. The common-law presumption that defamatory speech is false was rejected, at least when the defendant is a member of the media. The implications for a nonmedia defendant or a case involving a private plaintiff not involved in any public controversy are unclear.

Communication. To be defamatory, a statement must be "published" or communicated by the defendant—that is, overheard or read by a third party. If Joe and Kim are standing alone in a field miles from anyone else, Joe can say all the nasty things he wants to Kim without committing defamation. Kim's reputation in the community cannot be hurt if no one else hears the statements. If Kim goes back into town and repeats the statements for others, it is Kim doing the communicating, not Joe.[18]

Injury. As noted earlier, the traditional common-law rule presumed damages in libel and the four special types of slander. If a false statement tending to lower the plaintiff's esteem in the eyes of others appeared in a local newspaper, it was sensible to presume that persons read it and that their impressions of the plaintiff were adversely affected. Injury was presumed, and it made no difference that the defendant did not intend to injure the plaintiff.

The Supreme Court has indicated that this presumption of injury is inconsistent with the First Amendment, at least when the media are reporting about public officials, public figures, or private figures involved in public controversies. In these cases, at least, plaintiffs must introduce some evidence to show that the defamatory publication injured their reputations.

Defenses

Several noteworthy defenses are available in defamation cases.

Statute of Limitations. In most jurisdictions, the statute of limitations for defamation cases is one year, only half the two-year statute of limitations typically found for other types of tort claims.

Absolute Privilege. To encourage certain types of activity, the courts have created an absolute privilege for the potential defendant in several contexts. That is, even if the plaintiff could prove all the elements of defamation just discussed, no liability would attach. The two most important of these are the privileges for judicial and legislative proceedings. To encourage judges to judge, witnesses to testify, lawyers to advocate, and legislators to debate the issues aggressively, all are protected absolutely when involved in their respective activities. Note, however, that the absolute privilege is narrow in scope. An attorney who wrote a book about a case after the trial was over or a legislator making statements not while debating a bill but while campaigning would not be protected.

Qualified Privileges. There are also several qualified privileges when the defendant will be protected if he or she acted in *good faith;* that is, malice must be proved as a prerequisite for recovery. The primary example of this is when the plaintiff is a public figure or public official. Others include, according to some jurisdictions, communications to those who can act in the public interest (for example, complaints to a school board about a teacher) and fair comment on matters of public interest by news commentators.

---

[17]475 U.S. 767 (1986).
[18]This is not to rule out a possible, but probably weak, claim for intentional infliction of emotional distress in this scenario.

Many states have provided a business-related good faith privilege for those who traffic in commercially useful information such as credit reports and employee references. Thus, in many jurisdictions, a job applicant's former employer is protected if he tells the applicant's prospective employer that "We think she stole from us." The plaintiff would have to prove malice to prevail. Note, however, that *Dun & Bradstreet, Inc. v. Greenmoss Builders*, 472 U.S. 749 (1985), makes it clear that this privilege is not constitutionally mandated.

Opinion. Under the First Amendment, there is no such thing as a false idea. We are all entitled to our opinions. Thus, "I think Joe is a jerk" is not actionable. Neither is "I just don't trust Joe; he looks sneaky to me." However, when an editorial writer stated that a plaintiff had lied under oath, the Supreme Court rejected a defense of opinion because the statement was "sufficiently factual to be susceptible of being proved true or false." *Milkovich v. Lorain Journal Co.*, 497 U.S. 1 (1990).

Injurious Falsehood

Closely allied to defamation (and perhaps equally as closely connected to the business torts discussed in Chapter 9) is the tort of **injurious falsehood,** also known as *disparagement, slander of goods,* and *trade libel.* The elements are generally the same as for traditional defamation, but the subject matter relates not to an individual's reputation, but to the plaintiff's title to property or to the quality or conduct of the plaintiff's business. The tort is aimed at protecting economic interests and would allow suit against a defendant who, for example, falsely stated that the plaintiff's business was no longer in existence.

False Imprisonment

The privilege to come and go as we please is important in our society. The courts protect that interest by recognizing the right to sue for the tort of **false imprisonment** when persons are unlawfully confined or restrained without their consent. If the defendant purports to arrest the plaintiff as well, the nearly identical claim of **false arrest** is applicable.

Elements

To prove a false imprisonment claim, the plaintiff must usually prove that the defendant (1) confined or restrained the plaintiff, (2) with intent, (3) without the plaintiff's consent, (4) thereby injuring the plaintiff.

Confinement. False imprisonment can occur when the plaintiff is confined in a room, a building, a car, or even a boat. It can even occur in the wide open spaces if the plaintiff is held in one spot against his or her will by force or threat. If the defendant blocks one exit to a room but another is available to the plaintiff, the confinement requirement is not met.

Intent. If someone accidentally locks another in a room, perhaps negligence is involved, but not false imprisonment. False imprisonment requires a wrongful intent on the defendant's part. As with assault and battery, an intent to injure will suffice, as well as an intent to confine. If the defendant stands outside the plaintiff's house with a gun, issuing threats of bodily injury should the plaintiff emerge, the intent requirement is met. Although the defendant would like nothing better than for the plaintiff to come out of the house, the natural consequence of the defendant's actions is to force the plaintiff to remain in the house.

Without Consent. The same force and threats of force that create an assault may force a person to remain in one place against his or her will. A large man could easily intimidate a small person into staying involuntarily in one place. However, if the plaintiff stays in one place as an accommodation or to clear up an accusation with police, there is no involuntary confinement. If, for example, a store clerk told a customer only "We believe you have stolen from the cash register and we have called the police," and the customer voluntarily stayed in the store to give his or her side of the story, there would be no false imprisonment.

Injury. The injury necessary for a valid false imprisonment claim arises automatically from the confinement, even if it is brief. A restraint of hours or days is not required for the necessary injury to occur. However, because the injury is somewhat mental in nature, it will not occur if the plaintiff is unaware of the confinement. Thus, if the plaintiff sleeps through a confinement, there would be no cognizable injury. But if the plaintiff knows of the confinement, actual and punitive damages are available.

Defenses

In addition to the statute of limitations (typically two years), the defendant's best chance in a false imprisonment case is to prove legal right. Obviously, police officers in possession of probable cause have the right to detain or confine suspects.

Many false imprisonment claims involve shopkeepers. Shoplifting, unfortunately, is a problem of epidemic proportions in the United States. When a shopkeeper detains a suspected shoplifter and presses charges, any number of things can prevent a conviction from being obtained, including prosecutorial or police error, or the failure of a witness to appear. At common law, even a well-founded belief by a shopkeeper that a theft had occurred frequently would not prevent the success of a later false imprisonment claim if, for whatever reason, no criminal conviction was obtained. However, many state legislatures have acted to protect shopkeepers with legislation such as that discussed in the following case. Additionally, some states have updated their protective statutes to reflect usage of modern technology, as the following case illustrates.

ESTES V. JACK ECKERD CORPORATION

Court of Appeals of Georgia, 360 S.E.2d 649 (1987)

As she left Eckerd's store after purchasing some items, the plaintiff Estes activated an anti-shoplifting device's buzzer. Posters warned customers that such devices were in use. Estes was approached by the store manager who told her that he had to look in her shopping bag because the alarm had gone off. His inspection of the bag and the plaintiff's receipt indicated that Estes had paid for all the items, but the sales clerk had not deactivated a special tag on a bottle of shampoo. Estes was soon released. The parties' version of events differed on whether the store manager had treated Estes in a rude and derogatory fashion. The jury apparently believed that he had not, returning a verdict for the defendant on Estes' false imprisonment claim. Estes appealed.

Beasley, Judge:

False imprisonment is "the unlawful detention of the person of another, for any length of time, whereby such person is deprived of his personal liberty." By OCGA 51-7-60, the [legislature] provided a qualified immunity to merchants from tort liability for false arrest or false imprisonment. No recovery is permitted where plaintiff's conduct is such "as to cause a man of reasonable prudence to believe" that the plaintiff was shoplifting or where the manner of detention or arrest and the length of the detention was reasonable under all the circumstances.

Later, OCGA 51-7-61 was added to provide that where a store used an antishoplifting or inventory control device "the automatic activation of the device as a result of a person exiting the establishment or a protected area within the establishment *shall* constitute reasonable cause for the detention of the person so exiting by the owner or operator . . . or employee. . . . Each detention shall be made only in a reasonable manner and only for a reasonable period of time sufficient for any inquiry into the circumstances surrounding the activation of the device." [Emphasis added.] This applies only when a warning notice is conspicuously posted.

In response to Eckerd's position that the statute acts as an absolute bar to Mrs. Estes' recovery, she asserts that immunity is granted only if Eckerd used all reasonable care and due diligence in the use of the device and did not cause harm to her through its negligence.

"False imprisonment is an intentional tort, not a tort of negligence." *Williams v. Smith,* 348 S.E.2d 50 (Ga.App. 1986). . . . The present case is governed by OCGA 51-7-61, not by 51-7-60. . . . A Louisiana court considered a similar Louisiana antishoplifting device statute . . . [and] reasoned that . . . the legislature's clear intention was "to afford to the merchant a right, within statutory limitations, to detain a person when the electronic device has been triggered." The conclusion was that the essential question under such a statute was "not whether 'reasonable cause' exists, but whether the method and extent of plaintiff's detention was reasonable under the circumstances. . . ."

The reasoning of the Louisiana court is persuasive and substantiates our construction of the language of the Georgia statute, which is mandatory, inasmuch as it states that "automatic activation of the device . . . shall constitute reasonable cause. . . ." That is, it makes no difference to "reasonable cause" whether or not negligence on the part of Eckerd's employee in failing to deactivate the special tag on the bottle of shampoo set the device off. What matters is whether the method and time of detention were reasonable within the statutory limitations. Defendant's right to detain is lawful once the device is activated.

Having determined that the defendant's alleged precursor negligence is immaterial when an antishoplifting device has been automatically activated, the only issue under OCGA 51-7-61 is whether the detention was made in a reasonable manner, as she does not contend that it was not for a reasonable period of time, and if proper notice was posted as required. The latter is undisputed as there were at least two warning signs prominently displayed in the

(continues)

ESTES V. JACK ECKERD CORPORATION

(continued from previous page)
store near the entrance and exit.

While the testimony of Estes and Eckerd's manager was conflicting as to what he said when he approached her,

there is no dispute that he searched her bag without any objection on her part, and that the episode lasted only five to ten minutes. Clearly there was no restraint by force or fear here. . . .

We find the evidence sufficient to support the jury's apparent conclusion that Mrs. Estes was not detained unreasonably.

[Affirmed].

Box 8.1 illustrates another remedy given to merchants victimized by shoplifters.

Trespass

We work hard for our money, and when we spend it on property we should have the right to use that property without interference from others. When others infringe on our right to use real property—land and those things attached to it, such as houses—the tort of **trespass** to real property is committed. The tort has a convoluted common-law history that protects property owners from innocent as well as mean-spirited invasions of the right to use real property.

Elements

Generally speaking, to prevail in a trespass case the plaintiff must establish the following elements: (1) af-

firmative conduct by the defendant, (2) with intent to enter onto realty in the possession of another, and (3) resulting in actual entry.

Affirmative Conduct.   If Joe is driving down the street when Alan runs a stop sign with his car, smashes into Joe, and pushes Joe up onto Ed's lawn, no trespass has been committed by Joe. He invaded Ed's real property but not through any affirmative act of his own.

Intent.   Unlike most other intentional torts, the intent element of a trespass cause of action requires the plaintiff to demonstrate only that the defendant intended to enter the place and that the place belonged to the plaintiff. No intent to do harm is required. Thus, if Cindy walks across Ann's land believing that she is walking across her own or across land belonging to her friend Sally who has given her

---

permission to cross it, Cindy commits a trespass actionable by Ann. Cindy's good faith is no defense. However, if Mark has a heart attack and dies instantly while driving down the street, and his car runs onto Ed's lawn, the affirmative conduct element is arguably not met and certainly the intent element is missing. The same may be said of a person who, driving too fast on slick streets, loses control of the car and winds up on someone's lawn. The intent element is missing.

Actual Entry.   Entry is required for completion of the tort, but *usually* no real injury. Damage is presumed from the fact of entry, even if the only injury is trampled blades of grass. A judgment in the form of nominal damages of a dollar or so would still be warranted. According to most courts, the invasion need only be slight, including throwing a rock onto the plaintiff's property, shooting a bullet over it, or tunneling under it. Some courts refuse to recognize injury where the invasion is truly minor, such as where A's tree limb grows so far that it extends over B's property line.

The court must sometimes balance competing interests. For example, in *Bradley v. American Smelting and Refining Co.,* 709 P.2d 782 (Wash. 1985), the defendant operated a copper smelter that emitted particulate matter, including arsenic, cadmium, and other metals. Although undetectable by human senses and not harmful to health, this matter did sometimes settle on the plaintiff's property. The court felt constrained to create an exception to the general rule that any entry constitutes an injury, stating:

> When [airborne] particles or substance accumulates on the land and does not pass away, then a trespass has occurred. While at common law any trespass entitled a landowner to recover nominal and punitive damages for the invasion of his property, such a rule is not appropriate under the circumstances before us. No useful purpose would be served by sanctioning actions in trespass by every landowner within a hundred miles of a manufacturing plant. Manufacturers would be harassed and the litigious few would cause the escalation of costs to the detriment of the many. . . . The plaintiff who cannot show actual and substantial damages should be subject to dismissal.

The trespassory entry is an affront to the use of the property. Therefore, the cause of action is normally recognized as belonging to the possessor of the land. Thus, if T were renting a farm from L, and X trespassed on the farm, T would normally have the right to sue for trespass rather than L.

Defenses

In addition to the typical two-year statute of limitations (which is extended if the trespass is a continuing one, as when the trespasser has erected a small building on the plaintiff's property), the main defenses to a trespass cause of action are *consent* and *legal right.* Thus, a tenant has the landlord's consent, pursuant to a lease, to remain on the landlord's property. However, if the tenant stays beyond the term of the lease and refuses to leave, a trespass is committed because consent has expired.

A legal right might arise from, for example, an *easement,* which is a right to use someone's property for a limited purpose. Thus, if M's land is between N's land and a major highway, N might negotiate an easement from M, paying M a sum of money in exchange for the limited right to travel over M's land going to and from the highway.

OTHER INTENTIONAL TORTS

Invasion Of Privacy

Slowly over the past 75 years or so, the courts have begun to recognize privacy as an interest worthy of legal protection. Today, many jurisdictions have recognized one or more of the following varieties of tort that come under the umbrella of **invasion of privacy.**

Intrusion

Intrusion occurs whenever a defendant intrudes into an area where a plaintiff has a reasonable expectation of privacy. The invasion must be highly offensive to a reasonable person to be actionable. Secretly placing a microphone under the plaintiff's bed to overhear the goings-on would be actionable. So might an employer's secretly searching an employee's locker (where the employee provided his or her own lock and therefore had a justifiable expectation of privacy) without reasonable grounds for doing so.[19]

Disclosure of Embarrassing Private Facts

Where no justification exists, it may be actionable to disclose to the public facts that the plaintiff finds embarrassing or offensive. Because they are "true," the disclosures do not constitute defamation; they may be more akin to blackmail. However, a newsworthiness

---

[19]*K-Mart Corp. Store No. 7441 v. Trotti,* 677 S.W.2d 632 (Tex. App. 1984).

defense exists, at least for the media. In one case, a woman sued for the embarrassment she was caused by a newspaper's disclosing that her husband was killed in a fire in a motel while accompanied by another woman. The court held that fires are newsworthy events, and the newspaper could not be liable for accurately reporting the names of the victims.[20]

False Light
Very similar to the tort of defamation, the action for "false-light" privacy renders liable a defendant who makes statements or does acts that place the plaintiff in a false light in the public eye. Although usually these statements or actions would injure the plaintiff's reputation and also be actionable as defamation, occasionally they might involve false statements that the plaintiff had performed many wonderful deeds. Rather than suing for injury to reputation as in defamation suits, a false-light plaintiff seeks compensation for shame, embarrassment, mental anguish, or humiliation. An attraction of this tort is that it fre-

quently has a two-year statute of limitations, longer than the one-year statutes typical for defamation.

Appropriation of Name or Likeness
A final type of privacy tort protects the economic interests that persons have in the potential exploitation of their names and faces. Thus, if a company uses the name or picture of a famous actress in its advertising campaign without her permission, it has appropriated her name or likeness to her economic detriment. The company should have acquired her consent and paid her for such use. After singer Bette Midler refused to sing for a company's television commercial, it hired one of her back-up singers and asked her to sound as much like Midler as possible. Many listeners thought they were hearing the real Bette Midler, which formed the basis for a successful appropriation suit by Midler.[21]

Several employer–employee disputes have involved claims of invasion of privacy, as the following case illustrates.

[20]*Fry v. Ionia Sentinel Standard*, 300 N.W.2d 687 (Mich. App. 1980).

[21]*Midler v. Ford Motor Co.*, 849 F.2d 460 (9th Cir. 1988).

YOUNG V. JACKSON

Supreme Court of Mississippi, 572 So.2d 378, 1990

Case

The plaintiff, Young, worked at a nuclear power station operated by the defendant, Mississippi Power & Light Co. One day while Young, wearing protective gear, was working in an area highly contaminated by radioactivity, she lost consciousness and was transported to the hospital. Co-worker and defendant Jackson called and visited her at the hospital to inquire about her status. The substance of what happened is disputed. Young claimed that Jackson told her that government safety officials were inquiring about the incident and she needed to tell what happened. Young further claimed that she told Jackson that it was not a safety matter but stemmed from a partial hysterectomy she recently had. The operation was very upset-

ting to Young, who felt like "half a woman now." Young testified that she made Jackson promise to keep the information secret because she had not even told her husband. Jackson, however, testified that Young volunteered the information about her hysterectomy, telling him not to worry about any radiation.

Word spread quickly throughout the plant that Young had collapsed and been taken to the hospital. Rumors spread that Young was a victim of radiation and other employees might be also. In this setting, Jackson told his boss about the hysterectomy and Jackson's boss called employees together and told them there was no reason to worry about radiation because Young had passed out because of the aftereffects of her recent partial hysterectomy.

Later, Young filed this action

against the defendants claiming invasion of privacy. The trial court granted the defendants' motion for summary judgment and Young appealed.

Robertson, Justice:
The positive law of this state affords each person a substantial zone of freedom which, at his election, he may keep private. The zone surrounds person and place and without his consent may not be invaded by other persons. We have made no effort to identify the outer limits of a person's right of privacy and certainly make none here. Suffice it to say that where, as here, the invasion is by private parties, we have recognized a right of action in at least three contexts: (1) the portrayal of Plaintiff in a false light; (2) appropriation of Plaintiff's likeness and unpermitted use; and

(continues)

[handwritten annotations]

YOUNG V. JACKSON

(continued from previous page)
(3) public disclosure of private facts. It is this latter theorum that Betty Young invokes and we accept its more precise statement in Restatement (Second) of Torts Sec. 652D (1977): "One who gives publicity to a matter concerning the private life of another is subject to liability to the other for invasions of his privacy, if the matter publicized is of a kind that (a) would be highly offensive to a reasonable person, and (b) is not of legitimate concern to the public."

No doubt an objective test obtains. A person may not be held liable for public disclosure of facts about another unless he should reasonably have foreseen that the person would be likely offended. It requires little awareness of personal prejudice and human nature to know that, generally speaking, no aspects of life [are] more personal and private than those having to do with one's sexual organs and reproductive system. It may be the fact that many women who have undergone a hysterectomy do not keep that fact secret, but this is not the test. We do not regard it unreasonable that a woman would consider the fact a private matter, nor unforeseeable that she would so consider it.

Without further ado, we hold that the fact that she has undergone a hys-

terectomy is a fact that a woman ordinarily has the right to keep private if she wishes and that public disclosure of that fact by unauthorized persons and without her consent may be actionable.

The [trial court] did not hold Young stated no claim but rather that, in the present state of the record, Defendants' qualified privilege defense prevailed as a matter of law. The defense of qualified privilege has long been accepted in our law of defamation, but we have had no occasion to consider it in an invasion of privacy context. The settings are certainly analogous. We hold that actions for invasion of privacy are subject to the defense of privilege the same as defamation actions. Turning to the contours of the qualified privilege defense as it has evolved in the law of defamation, we can improve little on this Court's early statement:

A communication made in good faith and on a subject-matter in which the person making it has an interest or in reference to which he has a duty, is privileged if made to a person or persons having a corresponding interest or duty, even though it contains matter which without this privilege would be slanderous. There are certain occasions on which a man is entitled to state what he believes to be the truth about another, and in doing so public policy requires that he shall be protected, provided he makes the statement honestly and

not for any indirect or wrong motive. Such occasions are called occasions of qualified privilege, for the reason that the protection is not absolute, but depends entirely upon the honesty of purpose with which the statement is made. Among such statements is one made on a subject-matter in which the person making it, and the person to whom it is made, have a legitimate common interest. The underlying principle is public policy.

Louisiana Oil Corp. v. Renno, 157 So. 705 (Miss. 1934).

Specifically, this Court has recognized that a public policy reason of the sort contemplate[d] exists in the context of the employer/employee relationship.

Today's case arises in such an employer/employee context, and the statements concerning Young's hysterectomy were made against the backdrop of that relationship. The work at [the nuclear power station] was disrupted by rumors concerning Young's accident. Young's co-workers were concerned for her welfare, but for their own as well. Disclosing the true facts of Young's operation could reasonably have been seen likely to allay the fears of her co-workers of excessive levels of radiation in the areas in which they worked.

[Affirmed.] ♻

Intentional Infliction of Mental Distress

As noted earlier, because emotional injuries are difficult to prove and to value, courts have traditionally been reluctant to allow recovery for them. But just as they are now allowed in suitable cases of negligence, they are also allowed when intentionally caused. The turning point may have been cases such as *Wilkinson v. Downtin,*[22] in which, as a practical joke, the defendant called the plaintiff, a woman whose mental state was somewhat suspect anyway, and told her that her

husband had been in a serious accident. This so upset the plaintiff that she had to be hospitalized. Recovery for her emotional distress was allowed.

The requisite elements for proof for the tort of **intentional infliction of mental distress** are generally formulated as follows. First, the defendant must be guilty of extreme and outrageous conduct. Mere insults are usually insufficient, as are profanity and other abuses of a relatively minor nature. Second, the defendant must have intended to cause the plaintiff severe emotional distress. Again, the defendant will be presumed to intend the natural consequences of

[22][1897] 2 Q.B.D. 57.

his or her actions. And a defendant who is aware of a particular plaintiff's susceptibilities to mental distress will be judged accordingly. Finally, the plaintiff must actually suffer such severe distress. Physical consequences are not required, but their presence does assist in establishing proof of severe emotional anguish.

Today, such suits frequently involve attempts by collection agencies to force debtors to pay bills. Thus, in *Turman v. Central Billing, Inc.,* 568 P.2d 1382 (1977), the collection agency was held liable to Turman, who was blind, when it badgered her in trying to collect a small debt assigned to it for collection, even after it knew that she and the creditor had come to a satisfactory settlement. This harassment, which resulted in the plaintiff's hospitalization for anxiety and severe stress, was carried out by repeated phone calls—sometimes twice a day—in which the defendant's agent "shouted" at her, used profanity, told her several times that her husband would lose his job and the house if she did not pay, and called her "scum" and a "deadbeat." (Such egregious acts are also violative of the Federal Debt Collection Practices Act, which we shall study in Chapter 51.)

This tort cannot be used to evade First Amendment restrictions on recovery for defamation. When the Reverend Jerry Falwell sued *Hustler* magazine over an extremely rude parody, showing that it had caused him emotional distress, the Supreme Court held that freedom of expression considerations barred recovery.[23]

Fraud

The essence of the tort of *fraud* is the intentional misleading of one person by another, which results in a loss to the deceived party. Because many kinds of fraudulent conduct occur when the sole purpose of the wrongdoer is to cause the innocent party to enter a contract that the person otherwise would not make, additional consideration of this subject will be undertaken in Chapter 15.

Conversion and Trespass to Personal Property

The tort of **conversion** renders actionable certain invasions of personal property interests, just as trespass protects real property interests. Conversion remedies invasions so serious that they justify forcing the defendant to compensate the plaintiff for the reasonable value of the item involved. An example would be

[23]*Hustler Magazine v. Falwell,* 485 U.S. 46 (1988).

the defendant's theft of the plaintiff's automobile. A tort that generally covers more minor invasions of personal property rights is frequently called trespass to personal property. This tort would remedy, for example, the defendant's minor vandalism of the plaintiff's car.

Nuisance

Like trespass to real property, the tort of **nuisance** protects the enjoyment of such property. Frequently nuisance is used to compensate an intangible disruption of the enjoyment of property, as when the plaintiff is injured by the defendant's invasion through light (erection of tall light poles), noise (rock concerts), vibrations (blasting with dynamite), or smells (pig farming). The courts will consider such factors as the type of neighborhood, the nature of the wrong, its proximity to the plaintiff, its frequency or continuity, and the nature and extent of the injury in deciding whether an actionable nuisance exists.

SPECIAL PROBLEMS

Business Torts

Some torts, such as the theft of trade secrets and the unjustified interference with business contracts, are so peculiarly related to the commercial world that they are called *business torts.* Because of the special issues that these kinds of torts present—and also because of their obvious importance to businesspersons—they are considered at length in Chapter 9.

Employer Liability

Ordinarily, the application of the principles of tort law results in the imposition of liability on the wrongdoer alone. There is one major exception, however, which springs from the principles comprising our master–servant law and our law of agency.

Under these principles, an employer is uniformly held liable for the torts of employees if the employees are acting "within the scope of their employment" at the time of the injury. Thus, if T, a truck driver employed by the D Furniture Company, negligently injures P while delivering a piece of furniture to a customer's home, P has a cause of action against both T and the D Company, as illustrated in Figure 8.1.

Ordinarily, in such a case, P brings just one action against both defendants; if he is successful in proving

FIGURE 8.1

Employer's Liability for Employee's Tort

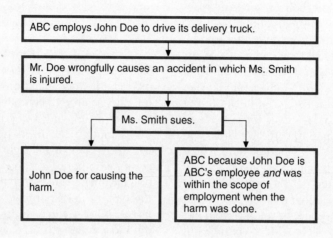

Figure 8.1 Employer's Liability for Employee's Tort

the facts as alleged, he obtains a "joint and several" judgment against T and the D Company. This means that if he is awarded a judgment of $4000, he can enforce the judgment against the assets of either party, or of both, until that sum is recovered. (The "scope of employment" problem is covered further in Chapter 32.)

Joint and Several Liability

When two defendants' actions together contribute to a plaintiff's injury, they are frequently held jointly and severally liable. The "joint" portion of this liability means that each defendant may be held responsible for the entire loss caused to the plaintiff. Thus, theoretically one defendant who is only 10 percent at fault might have to pay also for the 90 percent fault of another defendant, especially if the latter defendant is judgment-proof (lacking assets or insurance to pay). The relatively harsh result that this can have for "deep pocket" defendants is a major cause of criticism of our present tort system. Several states have enacted limits on joint and several liability in certain types of cases.

Statutory Reforms

Increases in the number of tort suits filed, the size of judgments, and consequently, insurance rates have become a major topic of discussion in both the fed-

eral and state legislatures. As this chapter is written both state and federal legislative reforms to limit tort recoveries are being debated and passed across the country. Although the ultimate impact of this wave of legislation cannot yet be gauged, it thus far has concentrated on such matters as medical malpractice and product liability suits, punitive damages, damages for emotional distress, joint and several liability, and statutes of limitation.

SUMMARY

Tort law is, to a great extent, social engineering by the courts. As society evolves, the courts' concept of what interests we have that are worth protecting also evolves. The courts impose duties on us not to injure the protectable interests of others.

The leading remedy for accidental injury in this country is the negligence cause of action. Existence of a duty and proximate causation, both of which turn largely on the notion of foreseeability, are the key elements for a plaintiff's recovery. A plaintiff's own carelessness can lead to a reduction or a bar altogether on recovery.

Among intentional torts, assault and battery protect invasions of our mind and body, defamation protects our good reputation in the community, false imprisonment protects the right to come and go as we please, and trespass protects our right to enjoyment of our real property. To successfully pursue each tort, the plaintiff must prove a variety of specified elements. Each tort involves an intentional act by the defendant. Each has a variety of defenses ranging from self-defense for assault and battery, to absolute and qualified privileges for defamation, to consent and legal right for false imprisonment and trespass.

Intentional torts that are also worth noting include the four varieties of invasion of privacy tort, intentional infliction of emotional distress (which has been often used successfully against aggressive collection agencies), fraud, conversion, and nuisance (which involves lesser invasions of real property than does trespass).

Employers are liable for the torts of their employees committed within the scope of authority. And joint tortfeasors (persons who commit torts) are each potentially liable for the entire judgment awarded to the plaintiff (though the plaintiff cannot have a double recovery). Rapid change in the tort system and escalating monetary awards have led many legislatures to consider strong measures to reform American tort law. We are just now starting to see many of these changes.

KEY TERMS

Torts
Negligence
Proximate cause
Independent intervening cause
Contributory negligence
Comparative negligence
Statute of limitations
Battery
Assault
Consent
Self-defense
Defamation
Libel
Slander
Injurious falsehood
False imprisonment
False arrest
Trespass
Invasion of privacy
Intentional infliction of mental distress
Conversion
Nuisance

QUESTIONS AND PROBLEMS

1. For two years Lee was the patient of Milano, a psychiatrist. Lee was diagnosed as having an adjustment reaction to adolescence. He related many fantasies to Milano about being a hero or an important villain or using a knife to threaten those who frightened him. At a session he showed the knife to Milano. Lee also related certain alleged sexual experiences with Kim, his next-door neighbor. He was emotionally involved, possessive, and had fired a BB gun at a car occupied by Kim and her boyfriend as they drove away on a date. Later, Lee murdered Kim with a knife. Kim's family sued Milano in negligence for not having warned them of the danger from Lee. Should Milano be liable? Discuss. (*McIntosh v. Milano*, 403 A.2d 500, N.J. 1979.)

2. D sent its employee, Wells, into an industrial tank to clean it. The tank contained nitrogen gas and lacked oxygen to breathe. Wells was not wearing protective gear and was overcome by the gas. He became incoherent and delirious. Wells was transported to a nearby hospital where P, a nurse, attended to him. While in a state of delirium, Wells bit off a portion of P's right middle finger. P sued D in negligence. Assuming that P can prove that D's carelessness in safety procedures proximately caused Wells' delirium, should she recover? Discuss. (*Widlowski v. Durkee Foods*, 562 N.E.2d 967, Ill. 1990).

3. Charles and Carolyn needed to repair and clean a well on their property. Charles entered the well and placed a gasoline-powered pump directly above it to remove water. This was a bad idea, because all the carbon monoxide from the engine seeped into the well. When Charles did not respond to Carolyn's calls, she asked her neighbor Bob for help. Bob entered the well to help Charles but was overcome by the fumes himself and died. Bob's family sued Carolyn and Charles's estate for negligence. Should the family recover? Discuss. (*Lowrey v. Horvath*, 689 S.W.2d 625, Mo. 1985.)

4. Two children, Lisa and Deborah, were standing alongside a highway when Lisa was struck by Burd's carelessly driven car. Deborah was barely missed. JoAnne, the girls' mother, saw the whole incident from her front porch. When Lisa, Deborah, and JoAnn sue Burd for the emotional distress caused by his careless driving, who will be allowed to recover? (*Sinn v. Burd*, 404 A.2d 672, Pa. 1979.)

5. Hill took a clock to the defendant's office, and there she found Sapp in charge, sitting behind a four-foot counter that separated him from the public. She handed him the clock. Having had a few drinks and feeling "good and amiable," Sapp said: "If you will come back here and let me love and pet you, I will fix your clock." He then reached forward in an effort to grasp Hill's arm, but she jumped back out of the way, and no physical contact occurred. She later sued for assault. Should she prevail? (*Western Union Telegraph Co. v. Hill,* 150 So. 709, Ala. 1933.)

6. In a review of the plaintiff's restaurant, the defendant newspaper columnist referred to the sauce on the duck as "yellow death on duck" and the poached trout as something that should be renamed "trout à la green plague." The plaintiff sued for defamation, proving that most persons very much liked both dishes. Does the plaintiff have a strong defamation claim? Discuss. (*Mashburn v. Collins,* 355 So.2d 879, La. 1977.)

7. National Bond Company sent two of its employees to repossess Whithorn's car when Whithorn fell behind in his payments. The two repossessors located Whithorn while he was driving his car. They asked him to stop, which he did, but he refused to abandon the car to them. They called a wrecker and ordered the driver to hook Whithorn's car and move it down the street while Whithorn was still in it. Whithorn started the car and tried to escape, but the wrecker lifted the car off the road and progressed 75 to 100 feet before Whithorn managed to stall the wrecker. Whithorn claimed that this incident amounted to a false imprisonment and sued National Bond Company. Does Whithorn have a valid claim? Discuss. (*National Bond Co. v. Whithorn,* 123 S.W.2d 263, Ky. 1939.)

8. The defendant is a crop duster who became confused and flew over the plaintiff's land, spraying poison on the plaintiff's crop. The defendant thought he was spraying the land he had been hired to spray, which was adjacent to the plaintiff's land. The plaintiff sued defendant in trespass. Does the plaintiff have a good claim? Discuss. (*Schronk v. Gilliam,* 380 S.W.2d 743, Tex. Civ. App. 1964.)

9. The defendant credit company called the plaintiff and, to obtain the address of her son for collection purposes, told her that her grandchild had been in a car accident and the defendant needed her son's address. When this turned out to be false, the plaintiff sued for infliction of emotional distress. Does she have a good claim? Discuss. (*Ford Motor Credit Co. v. Sheehan,* 373 So.2d 956, Fla. App. 1979.)

Chapter 9

Business Torts

Interference with Business Relationships
Trademark Infringement
Misuse of Trade Secrets
Patent Infringement
Copyright Infringement
Unfair Competition

CERTAIN KINDS OF business interests and rights have been recognized and protected by common-law rules since very early times. Many of these interests receive supplemental, and sometimes primary, protection from state, and especially federal, statutes. In this chapter we examine some of the most common wrongful invasions of these interests, that is, **business torts,** including (1) interference with existing and prospective contractual and business relationships, (2) trademark infringement, (3) misuse of trade secrets, (4) patent infringement, (5) copyright infringement, and (6) unfair competition.

INTERFERENCE WITH BUSINESS RELATIONSHIPS

Beginning with an 1853 English case in which an opera singer was induced by the defendant theater owner to breach her contract to sing at the plaintiff's theater and appear at the defendant's instead,[1] courts have recognized the general principle that a third party who wrongfully interferes with an existing contract has committed a tort. Most courts have stretched the concept to hold defendants liable for interfering with contracts that do not yet exist but are reasonably certain to be entered into, and with business relationships in general.

A typical case of tortious **interference with business relationships** involved a salesman who followed customers away from his former employer's premises and convinced them to rescind their contracts with that business and to purchase less expensive property from him. Although the customers had the right under federal law to rescind their contracts with the former employer within three days, the salesman was found civilly liable. Although there was arguably no interference with a binding contract, there was interference with prospective advantage flowing from an advantageous business relationship.[2]

Elements of the Tort

In a tortious interference case, the plaintiff must prove (1) the defendant acted intentionally to interfere with a known contract[3] or business relationship (or with one that was reasonably certain to occur), (2) absence of justification or privilege for the defendant's actions, and (3) damage to the plaintiff as a result.

Because defendants are presumed to intend the natural consequences of their actions, the intent element is typically satisfied if the defendant knows the facts that give rise to the plaintiff's contractual rights against another. Wrongful conduct that is intentional and without just cause or excuse gives rise to a finding of implied malice, which is sufficient for liability (as opposed to *actual* malice, which is typically required for an award of punitive damages). Thus, if D Stamp Company knows that X Grocery Store offers P's stamps as an inducement to customers, that such arrangements are typically based on long-term written contracts, and that a store can economically offer only one company's stamps at any one time, D becomes tortiously liable if it proceeds to convince X to begin offering D's stamps.[4]

In one of the most controversial cases in recent legal history, Pennzoil sued Texaco for intentional interference with contract rights when Texaco bought control of Getty Oil after Pennzoil believed it had a contract to acquire Getty. A jury awarded Pennzoil the largest judgment in American legal history— $11.1 billion in compensatory and punitive damages. (That judgment was affirmed on appeal and later settled out of court when Texaco paid $3 billion to Pennzoil.)

Defense of Privilege or Justification

Persons acting with evil motives or improper means to interfere with contracts or business relationships will likely be held liable. For example, as part of a campaign to terrorize Vietnamese-American fishermen competing with native Texas fishermen in Galveston Bay, the Ku Klux Klan told one man who leased his docks to the Vietnamese: "Watch your boats—they're easy to burn" and sent a card to a

---

[1]*Lumley v. Gye,* El & Bl 216.
[2]*Azar v. Lehigh Corp.,* 364 So.2d 860 (Fla. App. 1978).

[3]Most jurisdictions do not even require that the contract be binding. Thus, a defense such as duress or statute of frauds that might protect one of the parties from a breach of contract action will not usually protect a nonparty in a tortious interference suit.
[4]*Top Value Enterprises v. Carlson Marketing,* 703 S.W.2d 806 (Tex. App. 1986).

woman who also leased her docks that said: "You have been paid a 'friendly visit'; do you want the next one to be a 'real one'?" Clearly this outrageous and unjustifiable action constituted tortious interference with the dock leasing contracts.[5]

However, in cases such as the grocery store stamp case mentioned earlier, defendants are likely to argue that their actions constitute examples of good old American free enterprise and should not be the basis of tort liability. Indeed, liability for this tort often turns on a weighing of a plaintiff's interest in having a contract performed or a business expectation fulfilled versus a defendant's interest in competing for that business or in protecting its own economic interests. The law recognizes that no defendant will be liable for tortious interference if its actions are privileged or justified, but these defenses are difficult to delineate precisely.

Justification for a defendant's interference may be found if it is aimed at protecting a third person's legitimate interests, such as when an independent construction inspector hired by a city recommended that the city terminate the plaintiff's construction contract for substandard work,[6] or at protecting the public interest in general.

Furthermore, the defendant can claim justification for interference to protect its own existing contractual or property interests. For example, assume that X gets a new car franchise from D, an auto manufacturer. Later X makes a contract with P, a motorcycle wholesaler, under the terms of which P is permitted to sell motorcycles in a limited area in X's showroom. D subsequently causes X to break the contract with P because of complaints from new car buyers about dirt and noise associated with P's operation. D's interest in the proper conduct of the new car dealership would likely justify its actions, providing a defense to any tortious interference claim P might bring. Thus, P's only recourse would be a breach of contract action against X.

Although the defendant may act to protect *existing* economic interests, it is usually improper to induce a third party to breach an existing contract with the plaintiff solely to gain new customers. In other words, a party's interest in seeing an *existing* contract performed usually outweighs a competitor's right to competition, although many criticize this rule as inconsistent with the principles of free enterprise. However, if a plaintiff's interest has not been reduced to a binding contract but is merely prospective in nature or embodied in a terminable-at-will contract, the *privilege of competition* generally provides a defense so long as the defendant vies for the plaintiff's business with the third party by honest means within the bounds of "fair play."

Even if the means of interference used are proper, such as simply opening up a competing business, the tort will be established if the purpose was improper. In one famous case,[7] the defendant opened up a competing barbershop not to make money, but as part of a malicious scheme to injure the plaintiff by destroying his barbershop's business. "To call such conduct competition is a perversion of terms," the court said in allowing recovery for interference with business conduct.

The shadowy outlines of the competition privilege are discussed in the following case.

[5]*Vietnamese Fishermen's Ass'n v. Knights of the Ku Klux Klan*, 518 F.Supp. 993 (N.D.Tex. 1981).
[6]*Solis v. City of Laredo*, 751 S.W.2d 132 (Tex. App. 1988).

[7]*Tuttle v. Buck*, 119 N.W. 946 (Minn. 1909).

EDWARD VANTINE STUDIOS, INC. V. FRATERNAL COMPOSITE SERVICE

Iowa Court of Appeals, 373 N.W.2d 512 (1985)

Case

The plaintiff, Vantine, and the defendant, Fraternal, are involved in the business of photographing composites of college fraternities and sororities. The plaintiff's booking agent completed signed contracts with several such organizations at Iowa State University for the 1982–1983 school year. In the summers of 1981 and 1982, the defendant's sales manager had visited several Iowa State fraternities and sororities but signed no contracts. In the summer of 1982, he tried again.

Although he was told that the houses had existing contracts with the plaintiff, the sales manager suggested that the legality of the contracts be investigated. He ultimately signed contracts with 12 houses that had initially contracted with the plaintiff. All but one of the contracts contained

(continues)

EDWARD VANTINE STUDIOS, INC. V. FRATERNAL COMPOSITE SERVICE

(handwritten annotations: "was there a tortious interference w/ an existing contract?" "yes, by the insertion of the indemnity clause is wrongful conduct")

(continued from previous page)
an indemnification provision stating that the defendant would pay any legal costs of fees incurred by the organization in breaking the contracts already held with the plaintiff.

The sororities and fraternities expressed dissatisfaction with the plaintiff's previous services. The defendant capitalized on these complaints by offering a lower price and an earlier delivery date. Although the officers who decided to terminate the plaintiff's contract in favor of the defendant's testified that they were not subjected to any undue pressure, they also stated that they would not have terminated the plaintiff's contract except for the insertion of the indemnification clause in the defendant's contract.

The plaintiff sued for tortious interference with existing contracts. The trial court found the defendant liable and awarded the plaintiff $5,016 in actual damages and $10,000 in punitive damages. The defendant appealed.

Hayden, Judge:

There can be little question but that defendant intentionally interfered with plaintiff's contracts. Defendant concedes its awareness of those contracts during the course of its attempts to obtain its own contracts with the twelve houses. Defendant advised the houses to investigate the validity of their contracts with plaintiff and then suggested or at least agreed to insert a clause in its own contracts to indemnify the houses for any legal costs or fees incurred by reason of their breach of their contracts with plaintiff. This is certainly an intentional course of conduct which induced the houses not to perform their contracts with plaintiff.

We also believe and agree with the trial court that defendant's interference was improper to the extent that it agreed to indemnify the houses for any legal costs or fees resulting from their breach of plaintiff's contracts. We concede defendant's point that the business of photographing composites for college fraternities and sororities is very competitive and that the various individual companies in that business will seek to expand their own share of the market, very often at the expense of their competitors. We do not, however, believe that this competitive factor gives defendant free reign [sic] to use whatever inducements it can think of to lure potential customers away from already existing valid and binding contracts. We adopt the trial court's language on this point:

If the contracts had been terminated by reason of better price, better service, or better quality alone. . . . the Court would not have determined that there was a tortious interference with the contracts. It may have caused some claim or cause of action between [plaintiff] and the breaching fraternity or sorority, but it would not have created an actionable tort against Defendant. The Defendant, however, by the insertion, or the encouragement of the insertion, of the indemnity clause has crossed over the line of legitimate competition. It has committed a tort by such activity.

Representatives from five of the fraternities involved testified that they would not have breached their agreements with plaintiff and contracted without the indemnity clause agreed to by defendant. The importance of this clause to defendant is thus obvious. Our acceptance of such a tactic would render the notion of sanctity of contract a nullity and would indicate that a contract could be breached with impunity merely by having the party inducing the breach assume the financial consequences of such breach.

[The court affirmed the judgment for compensatory damages but reversed the award of punitive damages on grounds that the defendant's actions did not rise to the level of legal "malice" required in Iowa for such an award.]

Note: Why did the plaintiff in this case sue its competitor for tortious interference rather than the sororities and fraternities for breach of contract? Two main reasons are obvious. First, the plaintiff wishes to maintain business relations with these organizations and does not wish to alienate them unnecessarily by suing them. Second, punitive damages are virtually never available in a breach of contract action but are often recovered in an intentional tort suit such as this one (although the initial award in this case was not upheld).

Manager's Privilege

When a corporation breaches a contract, the other party will frequently not only sue the corporation for breach of contract but also the corporate officers who made the decision to breach on a tortious interference claim. The corporate officers are usually protected from liability by a doctrine called the "manager's privilege" if their decision to have the corporation breach the contract was based solely or essentially on the best interests of the corporation. Such would be the case when it would be far more advisable for a corporation to pay damages resulting from a breach of contract than to live up to a contract that might be financially disastrous. However, if the officer is acting primarily to further his or her own personal interests, tort liability will be imposed.

TRADEMARK INFRINGEMENT

A **trademark** is any distinctive word, symbol, device, or design adopted for the purpose of identifying the origin of goods being offered for sale. A trademark benefits consumers by acting as a symbol enabling them to identify goods or services that have been satisfactory in the past and to reject those that have been unsatisfactory. A trademark also motivates businesses to maintain or improve the quality of their goods or services over time to reap the benefits of a well-earned public trust in a mark. The tort of infringement, therefore, occurs when a competitor of the owner of the trademark uses a mark so similar to the owned trademark that purchasers of the competitor's goods are misled as to the origin of the goods that they are purchasing. In other words, a deception is accomplished that permits the competitor (typically a manufacturer) to "cash in" on the reputation and goodwill of the trademark owner (who is, typically, another manufacturer).

Although the early trademark rules were exclusively common law in nature, the basis of most of our trademark law today is the Lanham Act—a federal statute passed in 1946.

The act also governs **service marks,** used to identify the origin of services (for example, "Budget," as applied to the car rental business); **trade names** (such as "Amy's Ice Cream"); and **trade dress**—the total image and overall appearance of a product or business, which may include features such as size, shape, color, color combinations, texture, and graphics. Trade dress may include the distinctive packaging of a product, or even, as the Supreme Court held in *Two Pesos, Inc. v. Taco Cabana, Inc.*, 112 S.Ct. 2753 (1992), the distinctive design of a restaurant.

Registration

Under the Lanham Act, as amended in 1988, a person who owns a trademark that is affixed to or applied to his or her goods ("vendible commodities") may register that mark on the Principal Register either by showing that the mark has already been used in commerce or indicating a "bona fide intent" to use the mark at a future date, followed by actual use within three years. Entry on the Principal Register is constructive notice, effective as of the date of filing, of the registrant's exclusive right to use the trademark throughout the entire country. This grant of a nation-wide priority, with few exceptions, gives the registrant a right superior to everyone's except that of a person who used the mark before the filing date, a person who filed an application before that date, and foreign applicants who can claim a priority date under special rules.

The term of the registration is ten years and may be renewed in ten-year increments by registrants who show that they are still genuinely using the mark.

Certain kinds of marks are generally not registrable—the most important of which are those that are merely descriptive or geographic in nature or are persons' surnames. Thus a term that merely describes a general kind of good, which is called a **generic term** (such as aspirin), cannot be registered under any circumstances. And other descriptive terms ("tender" steak), geographical terms ("Nebraska" butter), and surnames ("Henderson" hats) cannot be registered unless they have acquired a *secondary meaning* (a concept discussed later).

In *Zatrains, Inc., v. Oak Grove Smokehouse, Inc.*, 698 F.2d 786 (1983), in which a primary question was whether Zatrains' trademark of FISH FRI batters was so descriptive of batters generally that it could not be protected against the use of the mark FISH FRY batters by the defendant Oak Grove, the court illustrated the applicable principles, as follows:

Courts and commentators have traditionally divided potential trademarks into four categories. A potential trademark may be classified as (1) generic, (2) descriptive, (3) suggestive, or (4) arbitrary or fanciful. These categories, like the tones in a spectrum, tend to blur at the edges and merge together. . . .

A *generic* term is the name of a particular genus or class of which an individual article or service is but a member. A generic term connotes the basic nature of articles or services rather than the more individualized characteristics of a particular product. Generic terms can never attain trademark protection. Furthermore, if at any time a registered trademark becomes generic as to a particular product or service, the mark's registration is subject to cancellation [under the Lanham Act]. Such terms as aspirin and cellophane have been held generic and therefore unprotectable as trademarks.

A *descriptive* term identifies a characteristic or quality of an article or service, such as its color, odor, function, dimensions, or ingredients. Descriptive terms ordinarily are

THE LAW AT WORK

Box 9.1
The Law at Work

The Hard Rock Cafe, founded in 1982, has sold barbecued pork sandwiches under the name "pig sandwich" from Tennessee to New York to Stockholm. However, in 1986, when founder Isaac Tigrett opened up a Hard Rock Cafe in Dallas, he was notified in writing that Texas Pig Stands (TPS) claimed the trademark for the term "pig sandwich." Litigation ensued.

It seems that TPS had sold barbecued pork sandwiches as "pig sandwiches" since the 1920s. At one time, more than 100 TPS restaurants spanned the continent, but by 1986 only 10 were left operating in Texas (and none in Dallas). Still, the jury found for TPS.

On appeal, the Fifth Circuit Court of Appeals, a court that apparently has too much time on its hands, issued a pun-filled ruling that upheld TPS's recovery on the merits. In a section entitled "This Little Piggy Went to See His Lawyer," the court framed the issue as "[w]hether Hard Rock's legal edifice is made of brick, twigs, or straw. . . ."

The court concluded that the terms "pig" and "sandwich" may be generic, but when combined they form a *descriptive mark* that is protectable with a showing of secondary meaning. The court affirmed the jury's finding that TPS had demonstrated secondary meaning, noting that "[s]everal Texas citizens testified to having fond memories of TPS' porcine specialty, supporting TPS' contention that over sixty years of 'pig sandwiches' and 'The Sign of the Pig' had linked the swining and dining. For these reasons, we cannot say that the jury's decision was unfounded."

In its conclusion, entitled "D-D-Dt D-D-Dt That's All, Folks!," the court found that TPS's evidence merited an injunction ordering Hard Rock to cease using the term "pig sandwich," but did not support any award of damages because there was insufficient evidence that TPS had lost any sales or Hard Rock had gained any sales because of the infringement.

Texas Pig Stands v. Hard Rock Cafe International, 951 F.2d 684 (5th Cir. 1992).

---

not protectable as trademarks; they may become valid marks, however, by acquiring a secondary meaning in the minds of the consuming public. . . . [An] example of a descriptive mark would be . . . "Vision Center" in reference to a business offering optical goods and services. . . .

A *suggestive* term suggests, rather than describes, some particular characteristic of the goods or services to which it applies and requires the consumer to exercise the imagination in order to draw a conclusion as to the nature of the goods and services. A suggestive mark is protected without the necessity for proof of secondary meaning. The term "Coppertone" has been held suggestive in regard to sun tanning products.

Arbitrary or *fanciful* terms bear no relationship to the products or services to which they are applied. Like suggestive terms, [these] marks are protectable without proof of secondary meaning. The term "Kodak" is properly classified as a fanciful term for photographic supplies, and "Ivory" is an arbitrary term as applied to soap.[8]

Secondary Meaning

If a trademark appears unregisterable because it is essentially descriptive or geographic or is a surname, the mark may still be registered if the owner can prove that an appreciable number of purchasers within the applicable market do, in fact, associate the mark with the owner (as distinguished from the term's more general meaning). In such a case the mark is said to have acquired a **secondary meaning**—a name that is a misnomer, in view of the fact that such proof indicates the mark has, in fact, a strong meaning.[9] Waltham (watches) and Bavarian (beer) are examples of geographic names registered under the secondary meaning concept, and Safeway (food products) is a descriptive name that achieved registration under the same concept. Another example is given in Box 9.1.

Element of Confusion

In most infringement actions, the plaintiff mark owner has the burden of proving that the defendant's mark is so similar to the plaintiff's that the defendant's use will produce a "likelihood of confusion" in

---

[8]On this aspect of the case, the court held that FISH FRI was essentially descriptive (but, on the basis of other evidence, nonetheless protectable under the secondary meaning concept).

[9]With the exception of generic marks, marks that do not acquire a secondary meaning (or that cannot be registered on the Principal Register for any other reason) can gain some protection by being registered on a Supplemental Register.

buyers' minds as to the true origin of the goods or services. Whether such likelihood exists is a question of fact in any particular case and is determined by such factors as similarity of design of the marks, similarity of product, proof of confusion among actual buyers, and marketing surveys of prospective purchasers showing an appreciable misassociation of the defendant's mark with the plaintiff's product. On the basis of these factors, for example, Rotary De-Rooting was held to be a mark so similar to Roto-Rooter that the owner of Roto-Rooter was successful in recovering damages from the owner of Rotary De-Rooting.[10] But if the products are substantially dis-

similar, even identical marks may not cause confusion. Thus, where a clothing manufacturer had purchased the right to use the mark "Here's Johnny," a court held that the use of that mark by a manufacturer of portable toilets was not likely to cause purchasers of the toilets to associate them with the producer of the suits.[11]

When the trademark at issue is a design on a book, difficult First Amendment questions may arise, as the next case demonstrates.

---

[10]*Roto-Rooter Corp v. O'Neal*, 513 F.2d 44 (5th Cir. 1975).

[11]*Carson v. Here's Johnny Portable Toilets, Inc.*, 698 F.2d 831 (6th Cir. 1983). Although the plaintiff suit manufacturer was unsuccessful in the infringement aspect of the case, the plaintiff, Johnny Carson, was granted an injunction restraining the defendant company from further use of the mark on the invasion of privacy theory.

CLIFFS NOTES, INC. V. BANTAM DOUBLEDAY DELL PUBLISHING GROUP

U.S. Second Circuit Court of Appeals, 886 F.2d 490 (1989)

The plaintiff-appellee publishes "Cliffs Notes," a series of study guides that are condensed versions, with brief analyses, of various short stories, plays, and books. The defendant-appellant Bantam Doubleday Dell Publishing Group, working with the often satirical Spy *magazine, publishes "Spy Notes," a one-time parody both of modern novels (such as Tama Janowitz's* Slaves of New York, *Bret Ellis's* Less Than Zero, *and Jay McInerney's* Bright Lights Big City) *and of Cliffs Notes.* Spy *magazine's editors believed that a study guide would provide an ideal vehicle for a parody of modern novels, because the "flat, straightforward, academic style" of Cliffs Notes would contrast sharply with the "cool, ironic, sophisticated, urbane novels." Spy Notes, like Cliffs Notes, lists on the cover the works it condenses (that is, the three aforementioned novels). It also replicates the distinctive yellow color, black diagonal stripes, and black lettering of Cliffs Notes, a design that is the subject of appellee's registered trademark.*

However, Spy Notes contains

(1) humorous content rather than serious condensation and analysis, (2) the words "A Satire" in bright red lettering five times on the front and four times on the back, (3) colors (red, white, and blue) not used on Cliffs Notes, and (4) wry notations not found on Cliffs Notes (such as "Even Funnier than the Originals"). Spy Notes also is priced substantially higher than Cliffs Notes ($7.95 versus $3.50) and includes "The Spy Novel-O-Matic Fiction-Writing Device," which supposedly can be used by "young, world-weary, urban authors" to create 16,765,056 different plot possibilities.

After Spy Notes had been bound but before it was shipped to bookstores, the appellee sued for trademark infringement under the Lanham Act, claiming that Spy Notes would give consumers the false impression that it was the appellee's product. The trial judge, applying the standards of Polaroid Corp. v. Polarad Elec. Corp., 287 F.2d 492 (2d Cir.), cert. denied, 368 U.S. 820 (1961), *found a "profound likelihood of confusion" and granted the appellee's request for a preliminary injunction barring distribution of Spy Notes. The defendants appealed.*

Feinberg, Circuit Judge:

We start with the proposition that parody is a form of artistic expression, protected by the First Amendment.

At the same time, "[t]rademark protection is not lost simply because the allegedly infringing use is in connection with a work of artistic expression." *Silverman v. CBS Inc.*, 870 F.2d 40, 49 (2d Cir.), cert. denied, 109 S.Ct. 3219 (1989). Books are "sold in the commercial marketplace like other more utilitarian products, making the danger of consumer deception a legitimate concern that warrants some government regulation." *Rogers v. Grimaldi*, 875 F.2d 994, 997 (2d Cir. 1989).

Conflict between these two policies is inevitable in the context of parody, because the keystone of parody is imitation. It is hard to imagine, for example, a successful parody of Time magazine that did not reproduce Time's trademarked red border. A parody must convey two simultaneous—and contradictory—messages: that it is the original, but also that it is *not* the original and is instead a parody. To the extent that it does only the former but not the latter, it is not only a poor parody but also vulnerable under trademark law, since the customer will be confused.

(continues)

CLIFFS NOTES, INC. V. BANTAM DOUBLEDAY DELL PUBLISHING GROUP

(continued from previous page)

Thus, the principal issue before the district court was how to strike the balance between the two competing considerations of allowing artistic expression and preventing consumer confusion.

We believe that the overall balancing approach of *Rogers* and its emphasis on construing the Lanham Act "narrowly" when First Amendment values are involved are both relevant in this case. That is to say, in deciding the reach of the Lanham Act in any case where an expressive work is alleged to infringe a trademark, it is appropriate to weigh the public interest in free expression against the public interest in avoiding consumer confusion. This approach takes into account the ultimate test in trademark law, namely, the likelihood of confusion "as to the source of the goods in question." *Universal City Studios, Inc. v. Nintendo Co.*, 746 F.2d 112, 115 (2d Cir. 1984). At the same time, a balancing approach allows greater latitude for works such as parodies, in which expression, and not commercial exploitation of another's trademark, is the primary intent, and in which there is a need to evoke the original work being parodied.

To apply the *Rogers* approach in this case, we begin by noting the strong public interest in avoiding consumer confusion over Spy Notes. As we put it in *Rogers*, the purchaser of a book, "like the purchaser of a can of peas, has a right not to be misled as to the source of the product." But, taking into account that somewhat more risk of confusion is to be tolerated when a trademark holder seeks to enjoin artistic expression such as a parody, the degree of risk of confusion between Spy Notes and Cliff Notes does not outweigh the well-established public interest in parody. In other words, we do not believe that there is a likelihood that an ordinarily prudent purchaser

would think that Spy Notes is actually a study guide produced by appellee, as opposed to a parody of Cliffs Notes.

First, the district court apparently thought that the parody here had to make an obvious joke out of the cover of the original in order to be regarded as a parody. We do not see why this is so. It is true that some of the covers of the parodies brought to our attention, unlike that of Spy Notes, contain obvious visual gags. But parody may be sophisticated as well as slapstick; a literary work is a parody if, taken as a whole, it pokes fun at its subject. Spy Notes surely does that, and there are sufficient reasons to conclude that most consumers will realize it is a parody. For example, a substantial portion of the potential audience for Spy Notes—i.e., college students or college-educated adults—overlaps with that for Cliffs Notes. Spy magazine, like Cliffs Notes, is widely read on some college campuses, although presumably for different reasons. As a result, the name "Spy" in the title, the notation "A Spy Book" emblazoned on the cover of Spy Notes and the use of a prepack marketing device prominently displaying the "Spy" name should alert the buyer that Spy Notes is a parody of some sort, or, at least, that it is not the same product as Cliffs Notes.

Furthermore, while the cover of Spy Notes certainly conjures up the cover of Cliffs Notes, the two differ in many respects. In addition to the differences listed in the following paragraphs, which indicate that Spy Notes is a parody of Cliffs Notes, the cover of Spy Notes contains red, blue, and white, colors that do not appear on the cover of Cliffs Notes. Also, the Spy Notes cover shows a clay sculpture of New York City rather than a clay sculpture of a bare cliff.

In addition, a Cliffs Notes book is not likely to be bought as an impulse purchase. A prospective reader of Cliffs

Notes probably has a specific book in mind when going to the bookstore for a study guide. And, even if a consumer did go to a store looking for a Cliffs Notes summary of any of the three books condensed in Spy Notes, that purchaser would not find one. Appellee does not produce Cliffs Notes for these novels, and has no plans to do so.

The label "A Satire" is also prominently used five times on the cover (and four on the back) of Spy Notes. Moreover, even for those few readers who might be slightly confused by the cover, the most likely reaction would be to open the book. Both the title page and the copyright notice page indicate that the book is written by the editors of Spy magazine and published by appellant. The copyright notice page states, "Spy Notes is a parody of Cliffs Notes." Furthermore, the reader would encounter the Spy Novel-O-Matic Fiction-Writing Device, which is an immediate tip-off that something non-serious is afoot.

Finally, with few exceptions, most Cliffs Notes are summaries of the traditional "great books," rather than contemporary works or those somewhat outside the mainstream. As indicated above, the Spy editors certainly thought that the three novels were obviously not in the former category and that the purchaser would be aware of the humor of having Cliffs Notes summarize them. Moreover, the books that Spy Notes summarizes are characterized by their spare, stripped-down prose, and uncomplicated plots. The idea of condensing them at all is something of a parody. Thus, the consumer would likely be put on notice from the first that Spy Notes was not Cliffs Notes.

The district court's ruling unjustifiably imposes the drastic remedy of a prepublication injunction upon the cover of a literary parody. Accordingly, for the reasons set forth above, we vacate the injunction against appellant.

Remedies

Where likelihood of confusion is established, the plaintiff's usual remedies under the Lanham Act or common-law principles are the *injunction* and *damages*. The injunction is an order prohibiting the defendant's further use of the mark, and damages is a recovery of money to compensate the plaintiff for the monetary injury (if any) sustained as a result of the infringement.

Because of a tremendous increase in the trafficking of counterfeit designer goods, Congress passed the Trademark Counterfeiting Act of 1984, which provides escalating *criminal* penalties for multiple offenders. For example, a second offender, if an individual, can be fined up to $1 million, imprisoned for up to 15 years, or both.

Antidilution Statutes

Approximately half the states have extended trademark protection beyond situations where a "likelihood of confusion" exists by enacting **antidilution** statutes, which remedy dilution of the distinctive quality of a mark or injury to business reputation even where the parties do not compete and there is no real likelihood that consumers will believe that the plaintiff (trademark owner) is the sponsor of the defendant's products.

Consider the strong TIFFANY trademark, connoting luxury and excellence in products. If someone were to open a bar called TIFFANY, it is unlikely that the public would believe that the owners of the TIFFANY trademark were also responsible for the bar—there would be no likelihood of confusion. However, use of the name TIFFANY on the bar may injure the holder of the TIFFANY trademark in two ways: (1) it lessens the distinctiveness of the mark if it can be used on all manner of products and services (for bars, bicycles, feminine hygiene products, and so on), and (2) it undermines the positive image of the mark if it is no longer restricted to luxury-type products. *Tiffany v. Boston Club,* 231 F.Supp. 836 (D.Mass. 1964). State antidilution laws protect distinctive marks from these types of injuries.

State antidilution laws protect strong and distinctive marks from two types of injuries: (1) a whittling away or dilution of product identification, and (2) injury to business reputation (tarnishment) by the undermining of a positive image. Similar federal dilution legislation has been proposed but not yet passed.

International Trademark Law

The United States is not yet a party to an international trademark treaty affording trademark protection through one international filing. However, the 1988 amendments to the Lanham Act brought U.S. law more in line with international trends and made it more likely that the United States will eventually join the majority of European countries that have already signed the *Madrid Agreement,* which allows for international protection of a proper mark in all member nations through one central filing. The

---

LEGAL FOCUS

International

Legal Focus INTERNATIONAL

Chewing gum carrying American major league baseball team logos sells well in Japan. However, the Japanese patent office barred registration of the Los Angeles base- ball team's name in this connection because the name "Dodgers" to Japanese ears sounded too much like "Rogers," a name already in use by a Japanese food company. However, the Japanese High Court ruled in 1992 that the Dodgers mark can indeed be registered, much to the delight of Japanese baseball fans.

A Suit for Nullification of the Patent Office's Dismissal of the Demand for Retrial of Trademark Application, 71256/1978.

World Intellectual Property Organization (WIPO) is working to implement the new *Madrid Protocol,* which would be a worldwide treaty providing for central filing of trademarks.

Until there are additional advances in international cooperation, U.S. companies seeking to do business abroad must protect their trademarks in foreign countries primarily by complying with those countries' individual trademark laws. Such companies also must deal with "pirates" who register U.S. marks in foreign countries and then demand to be "bought off" when the U.S. company expands its business to those nations.

MISUSE OF TRADE SECRETS

It is an information age, and nothing is more important to most businesses than information. By means of industrial sabotage and the hiring of competitors' employees, companies annually acquire from competitors an estimated $20 billion worth of confidential information. Patent law is often available to protect information, but trade secret law must be considered equally important. Trade secret law can protect a wider range of information at a cheaper cost and do so perpetually, which may be preferable to the 17-year limit to patent protection. "The maintenance of commercial ethics and the encouragement of innovation are the broadly stated policies behind trade secret law."[12]

A **trade secret** is "any formula, pattern, device or compilation of information which is used in one's business, and which gives him an opportunity to obtain an advantage over competitors who do not know or use it."[13] Examples of protectable trade secrets include customer lists, manufacturing processes, chemical formulas, cookie recipes, operating and pricing policies, marketing techniques, raw materials sources, and computer software.

Elements of the Tort

After Manville Corporation spent $9 million over seven years to perfect a new method of insulation, one of its competitors hired six key Manville employees and was able to enter the market in less than two years. Manville later prevailed in a lawsuit against the competitor because simple concepts of fairness sug-

gest that a company that has acquired information or developed processes as a result of its own efforts—information or processes not generally known to others—ought to be protected from the wrongful use of such information or processes by its competitors. The common law and the statutes of almost 20 states that have adopted the Uniform Trade Secrets Act provide such protection.

To successfully bring a misappropriation of trade secrets claim, a plaintiff must prove (1) existence and ownership of a trade secret, (2) the defendant's acquisition of the trade secret by wrongful or improper means, and (3) use or disclosure of the trade secret to the injury of the plaintiff.

In any trade secrets case, two issues are paramount: (1) whether the processes or information the plaintiff is seeking to protect against the defendant's continued use are "secret" in the eyes of the law, and (2) if so, whether the defendant acquired the information by "wrongful means."

Secrecy Requirement

A prototypical trade secret is the formula for Coca-Cola. A Coca-Cola company executive testified by affidavit in *Coca-Cola Bottling Co. v. Coca-Cola Co.,* 227 U.S.P.Q. 18 (D.Del. 1985) that

[t]he written version of the secret formula is kept in a security vault at the Trust Company Bank in Atlanta, and that vault can only be opened by a resolution from the Company's Board of Directors. It is the Company's policy that only two persons in the Company shall know the formula at any one time, and that only those persons may actually oversee the actual preparation of [the product]. The Company refuses to allow the identity of those persons to be disclosed or to allow those persons to fly on the same airplane at the same time.

Coca-Cola knows how to meet the "secrecy" requirement.

Perhaps the extreme measures adopted by Coca-Cola need not be exercised in every case. Nonetheless, to be protected, information must be kept reasonably (not absolutely) secret by its owner. In deciding whether specified information is, in fact, secret, courts generally consider (1) the extent to which the information is known outside the business, (2) the extent to which it is known by employees of the business, (3) the extent of security measures taken by the firm, (4) the value of the information to its owner, (5) the amount of effort or money expended to create

---

[12]*Kewanee Oil Co. v. Bicron Corp.,* 416 U.S. 460 (1973).
[13]*Restatement of Torts* §757, comment b (1939).

the information, and (6) the ease or difficulty with which the information could be properly acquired or duplicated by others. *Restatement (Second) of Torts* §757, comment b. Thus, if a defendant has acquired information that was freely circulated by the plaintiff company among its employees, customers, or suppliers, the secrecy requirement is not met. In contrast, protection will be afforded when a company gives secret information only to a small number of employees on a "need to know" basis, under clear instructions not to disclose it to others. If an employee breaches this trust by passing the information on to a competitor, it remains a trade secret and the competitor's use of it subjects the competitor to tort liability.

Wrongful Acquisition Requirement

Even if information qualifies as a trade secret, its use by a competitor is normally lawful if the competitor has discovered the secret by means that are "not improper." Thus, if X Company discovers a manufacturing process by independent research, or even by means of "reverse engineering"—disassembling a product of Y Company that it has lawfully purchased—the subsequent use of the process by X Company is generally lawful under trade secret rules (which is one reason that patent protection is usually desirable).

Historically, acquisition was considered to be improper only when it was illegal (for example, acquisition by trespass, theft, or wiretapping) or involved breach of a confidential relationship (such as bribery of an employee of the owners). One high-profile example came to light in 1982 when the FBI arrested employees of Hitachi Ltd. on the basis of evidence that it had paid more than $600,000 for stolen data concerning a new IBM computer. More recently, courts have broadened the improper means concept to include methods that "fall below the generally accepted standards of commercial morality, even though not illegal."[14]

The following case illustrates a difficult trade secret question that should be of interest to any would-be inventors.

[14]*E.I. duPont de Nemours & Co., Inc. v. Christopher,* 431 F.2d 1012 (5th Cir. 1970). In this case, duPont recovered damages from a company that had acquired its secret method of producing methanol by means of aerial photographs of a duPont plant under construction. Apparently companies need not use anti-aircraft guns to keep their secrets; only "reasonable" efforts are required.

Smith v. Snap-On Tools Corp.

U.S. Fifth Circuit Court of Appeals, 833 F.2d 578 (1987)

Case

Smith made a rachet by combining parts of two existing tools. Hoping to see his rachet made available for sale, he brought it to the attention of Snap-On Tools, Inc., by showing the rachet to an independent Snap-On dealer and then submitting a tool suggestion form to Snap-On's Wisconsin headquarters. Snap-On began making and selling the rachet without paying anything to Smith. Smith sued, claiming that Snap-On had misappropriated a trade secret. The trial court, applying Wisconsin law, ruled for Smith but did not give him as large a judgment as he desired. Both sides appealed.

Rubin, Circuit Judge:

Wisconsin law prescribes two essential elements in a cause of action for misappropriation of trade secrets: an actual trade secret and a breach of confidence. The essence of the tort of trade secret misappropriation is the inequitable use of the secret. Even when a trade secret exists, a person who learns the secret legitimately, without any duty of confidentiality, is free to use it.

Wisconsin therefore follows trade secret law as set out in Sec. 757 of the Restatement of Torts. Under the Restatement, "[o]ne who discloses or uses another's trade secret, without a privilege to do so, is liable to the other if . . . his disclosure or use constitutes a breach of confidence reposed in him by the other in disclosing the secret

to him." As the comment to this provision states, the proprietor of a trade secret may not unilaterally create a confidential relationship without the knowledge or consent of the party to whom he discloses the secret. No particular form of notice is necessary, however; the question is whether the recipient of the information knew or should have known that the disclosure was made in confidence.

Smith concedes that he never explicitly requested that his disclosure to Snap-On be held in confidence. Nonetheless, he argues, Snap-On knew or should have known that the disclosure was confidential. According to Smith, a "special relationship existed between himself and Snap-On, based on the fact that he, as a relatively unsophisticated individual, submitted his

(continues)

Whether breach of confidentiality

SMITH V. SNAP-ON TOOLS CORP.

(continued from previous page)
invention to Snap-On, a large corporation. Under the circumstances, Smith contends, the manufacturer should have known that he, as the inventor, expected compensation even if he did not request it.

The district court accepted this argument . . . , [but t]his does not reflect Wisconsin law. The Supreme Court of Wisconsin has held [in *RTE Corp. v. Coatings, Inc.*, 267 N.W.2d 226 (1978)] that, when parties are dealing at arm's length, one party's disclosure of an alleged trade secret to another does not automatically create a confidential relationship. Although [*RTE*] involved two corporations, we see no reason to believe that it would have applied a different rule if the inventor had been an individual rather than a corporation.

Under certain circumstances, courts have found liability for misappropriation of trade secrets in cases involving implied confidentiality between an inventor and a manufacturer. When a manufacturer has actively solicited disclosure from an inventor, then made use of the disclosed material, the manufacturer may be liable for use or disclosure of the secret in the absence of any expressed understanding as to confidentiality. In this case, however, Smith disclosed the invention on his initiative, without any prompting from Snap-On. Alternatively, courts have imposed liability when the disclosing inventor did not specifically request confidentiality from the manufacturer, but did make clear that the disclosure was intended as part of a course of negotiations aimed at creating a licensing agreement or entering into a similar business transaction. These cases are also distinguishable because Smith did not indicate that he wanted any pecuniary recompense for his suggestion. . . . When Smith sent Snap-On a tool suggestion report describing the rachet, he did not in any way indicate that he wanted compensation, and indeed wrote on the suggestion form, "I would like to be able to buy a nice new shiney [sic] one from the Snap-On truck." In none of his dealings with Snap-On over the next two years did Smith ever request confidentiality or indicate that he expected or desired any commercial arrangement based on his submission of the rachet suggestion to Snap-On.

In February 1978, more than two years after Smith showed the rachet to Clark, Smith's lawyer sent a letter to the supervisor of Snap-On's Product Management Division in which he asked that Smith receive compensation. Reliance on confidentiality, however, must exist at the time the disclosure is made. An attempt to establish a special relationship long after an initial disclosure comes too late.

Because there was no confidential relationship between Smith and Snap-On, Snap-On violated no obligation to Smith by manufacturing the rachet.

We therefore reverse. ⟁

PATENT INFRINGEMENT

To encourage creation and disclosure of inventions, the Constitution authorizes the federal government to grant **patents** to inventors (*patentees*). In exchange for disclosing the invention, the inventor patentee receives a 17-year (14 years in the case of design patents) exclusive right to make, use, or sell the patented item. The 17-year patent is nonrenewable; after expiration of the period the item goes into the public domain and may be made, used, or sold by anyone.

Subject Matter

Items that may be patented include (1) processes, (2) machines, (3) manufactures (such as products), (4) compositions of matter (for example, new arrangements of elements as in metal alloys), and (5) any improvement on the first four categories. In addition, design patents for ornamental designs have been granted, as have patents on computer software and new varieties of asexually reproducing plants that have been modified by humans and do not naturally occur in nature. In *Diamond v. Chakrabarty*,[15] the Supreme Court even found a new life form (a laboratory-created bacterium for "eating" oil spills) to be patentable.

However, one cannot patent (1) printed matter, (2) naturally occurring substances, (3) methods of doing business, (4) ideas (for example, $E = MC^2$), or (5) scientific principles (such as chemical formulas). This list is nonexclusive, but the idea is that the patentee must create, not find; invent, not merely discover.

A very important question involves whether algorithms used in computer programs may be patented. Although some early Supreme Court cases seemed to

[15]447 U.S. 303 (1980).

discourage such patents because algorithms are akin to "laws of nature," many patents have been granted where the algorithm is *applied* to a practical use. And in *Arrhythmia Research Technology, Inc. v. Corazonix Corp.*, 958 F.2d 1053 (Fed.Cir. 1992), the court held that a "useful process" that incorporates a mathematical algorithm is a proper subject for patent protection.

Patentability

If it fits into a proper subject matter category, an item may be patented if it meets three main tests: utility, novelty, and nonobviousness. An item has *utility* if it produces a direct benefit to humankind. It does not if it is dangerous, immoral, or merely a matter of curiosity. The *novelty* test is met if the item is distinctive from what was present in the prior state of the art. Prior patents, public use or sale, and written descriptions of the item can destroy novelty. *Nonobviousness* is also decided in light of the prior state of the art. If the item could easily have been produced by someone with normal skill in the area or if it is an obvious next step from prior inventions, the nonobviousness test is not met. If a product is immediately a tremendous success or if it fills a long-felt need in the marketplace, there is a presumption of nonobviousness.

In practice, these tests are somewhat vague. For that reason, although the Patent Office grants about 60 percent of the patent applications, when these applications are challenged by alleged infringers, about 60 percent of issued patents are invalidated by the courts.

Patent Procedure

A patent application must be filed in the name of the inventor at the U.S. Patent and Trademark Office in Arlington, Virginia. A person is not entitled to a patent unless the application is filed within one year after the initial public use or sale of the invention. Many inventors have lost all patent rights by failing to file in a timely fashion. The application must include a *specification* (a precise description of the item so that one skilled in the art could make use of it), and *claims* (a description of precisely what makes the item patentable—that is, useful, novel, and nonobvious. The Patent Office will study the application and search for previous patents on the same item. If the application is denied, it may be amended, and frequently substantial negotiation occurs between the applicant and the Patent Office. Decisions can be appealed administratively and, ultimately, to the courts.

Patent procedure is time-consuming and expensive. It is also very complicated, and an inventor would be wise to hire an attorney who specializes in patent law.

Once the application is filed, the patentee can place "Patent Pending" on his or her products for which the patent is sought. This has no legal effect, because the patent is not effective until issued by the Patent Office. However, it puts others on notice of the claim, and if the patent is ultimately granted they can be sued for infringements occurring during the patent pending stage.

Ownership

The patentee can sell his or her title to the patent to a third party. The patentee can also retain the title but grant a license under which a third party can use the patented item in exchange for payment of a royalty to the patentee. Assignments of title must be filed in the Patent Office.

Employees should be aware of the **shop right doctrine.** If an employee is hired for creative or inventive work and invents something on company time while using company resources, the patent belongs to the company. The company will file the application in the employee's name, but the company will own it. Even if the employee was not hired for creative or inventive work, if he or she invents something on company time using company resources, the company will be granted a nonexclusive license to use the patented item without payment of a royalty. Of course, many employers have their employees sign agreements to assign title to all patents generated on company time to the employer.

Infringement

A person infringes a valid patent by using a device that (1) literally meets each of the limitations of the patent's claim, or (2) under the *doctrine of equivalents,* does the "same work in substantially the same way and accomplish[es] substantially the same result" as the patented device, even though the infringing device differs in name, form, or shape.[16]

Defenses

An alleged misuser may raise a number of defenses. First, of course, the misuser may claim that his or her

---

[16]*Autogyro Co. of America v. United States*, 384 F.2d 391 (Ct. Cl. 1967).

device does not meet the doctrine of equivalents. Second, the misuser may challenge the validity of the patent by arguing that it flunks one or more of the tests of novelty, utility, and nonobviousness or that it is not the type of subject matter that may be properly patented. Third, the misuser may claim that the patentee *forfeited* the patent by not filing an application within one year after the invention was in public use, or should have the patent revoked because he or she breached the *duty of candor,* a duty the law imposes to disclose everthing the patentee knows about previous inventions and other facts that might bear on patentability. Finally, the infringer might argue that the patent should be revoked because of *patent*

misuse, which occurs when the patentee abuses the patent, frequently in violation of antitrust laws, to gain more rights than the patent legally confers.

Remedies

A patentee who successfully sues for infringement can obtain an injunction, damages of no less than a reasonable royalty rate (and perhaps trebled in the court's discretion when the plaintiff was damaged to a greater extent than the demonstrated royalty rate), and in exceptional cases, attorneys' fees.

The following case contains a recent Supreme Court discussion of the basic philosophy underlying federal patent policy.

BONITO BOATS, INC. v. THUNDER CRAFT BOATS, INC.

U.S. Supreme Court, 109 S.Ct. 971 (1989)

In September 1976, Bonita Boats, Inc. (petitioner), a Florida corporation, developed a hull design for a fiberglass recreational boat that it marketed under the trade name Bonito Boat Model 5VBR. Designing the hull required substantial effort, including preparation of engineering drawings, creation of a hardwood model, and production of a fiberglass mold from the model. The 5VBR was favorably received by the boating public. Bonito never filed a patent application.

In May 1983, the Florida legislature enacted a statute that makes it "unlawful for any person to use the direct molding process to duplicate for the purpose of sale [or to sell] any manufactured vessel hull or component part of a vessel made by another without the written permission of that other person."

In 1984, Bonito filed this suit alleging that Thunder Craft Boats (respondent) had violated the Florida statute by using the direct molding process to duplicate the Bonito 5VBR fiberglass hull and had sold such duplicates.

The trial court, the Florida Court

of Appeals, and the Florida Supreme Court all concluded that the Florida law was invalid under the supremacy clause of the Constitution in that it impermissibly interfered with the scheme established by the federal patent laws. Bonito brought the matter to the U.S. Supreme Court.

O'Connor, Justice:

From their inception, the federal patent laws have embodied a careful balance between the need to promote innovation and the recognition that imitation and refinement through imitation are both necessary to invention itself and the very lifeblood of a competitive economy. Thomas Jefferson was the first Secretary of State, and the driving force behind early federal patent policy. For Jefferson, a central tenet of the patent system in a free market economy was that "a machine of which we were possessed, might be applied by every man to any use of which it is susceptible." 13 Writings of Thomas Jefferson 335 (Memorial ed. 1904).

Today's patent statute is remarkably similar to the law as known to Jefferson in 1793. Protection is offered to "[w]homever invents or discovers any new and useful process, machine, man-

ufacture, or composition of matter, or any new and useful improvement thereof." 35 U.S.C. § 101. Since 1842, Congress has also made protection available for "any new, original and ornamental design for an article of manufacture." 35 U.S.C. § 171. To qualify for protection, a design must present an aesthetically pleasing appearance that is not dictated by function alone, and must satisfy the other criteria of patentability. The novelty requirement of patentability is presently expressed in 35 U.S.C. §§ 102(a) and (b), which provide:

A person shall be entitled to a patent unless—

(a) the invention was known or used by others in this country, or patented or described in a printed publication in this or a foreign country, before the invention thereof by the applicant for patent, or (b) the invention was patented or described in a printed publication in this or a foreign country or in public use or on sale in this country more than one year prior to the date of application for patent in the United States. . . .

Sections 102(a) and (b) operate in tandem to exclude from consideration for patent protection knowledge which is already available to the public. They express a congressional determination

(continues)

BONITO BOATS, INC. V. THUNDER CRAFT BOATS, INC.

(continued from previous page)

that the creation of a monopoly in such information would not only serve no socially useful purpose, but would in fact injure the public by removing existing knowledge from public use. From the Patent Act of 1790 to the present day, the public sale of an unpatented article has acted as a complete bar to federal protection of the idea embodied in the article thus placed in public commerce.

The federal patent scheme creates a limited opportunity to obtain a property right in an idea. Once an inventor has decided to lift the veil of secrecy from his work, he must choose between the protection of a federal patent, or the dedication of his idea to the public at large.

The applicant whose invention satisfies the requirements of novelty, nonobviousness, and utility, and who is willing to reveal to the public the substance of his discovery and "the best mode . . . of carrying out his invention," 35 U.S.C. § 112, is granted "the right to exclude others from making, using, or selling the invention throughout the United States," for a period of 17 years, 35 U.S.C. § 154. The federal patent system thus embodies a carefully crafted bargain for encouraging the creation and disclosure of new, useful, and nonobvious advances in technology and design in return for the exclusive right to practice the invention for a period of years.

"[The inventor] may keep his invention secret and reap its fruits indefi-

nitely. In consideration of its disclosure and the consequent benefit to the community, the patent is granted. An exclusive enjoyment is guaranteed him for seventeen years, but upon expiration of that period, the knowledge of the invention inures to the people, who are thus enabled without restriction to practice it and profit by its use." *United States v. Dubilier Condenser Corp.,* 289 U.S. 178, 186–187 (1933).

The attractiveness of such a bargain, and its effectiveness in inducing creative effort and disclosure of the results of that effort, depend almost entirely on a backdrop of free competition in the exploitation of unpatented designs and innovations. The novelty and nonobviousness requirements of patentability embody a congressional understanding, implicit in the Patent Clause itself, that free exploitation of ideas will be the rule, to which the protection of a federal patent is the exception. Moreover, the ultimate goal of the patent system is to bring new designs and technologies into the public domain through disclosure. State law protection for techniques and designs whose disclosure has already been induced by market rewards may conflict with the very purpose of the patent laws by decreasing the range of ideas available as the building blocks of further innovation.

Thus our past decisions have made clear that state regulation of intellectual property must yield to the extent that it clashes with the balance struck by Congress in our patent laws.

We believe that the Florida statute at issue in this case so substantially impedes the public use of the otherwise unprotected design and utilitarian ideas embodied in unpatented boat hulls as to run afoul of the teaching of our decisions in [earlier cases].

. . . [T]he Bonito 5VBR fiberglass hull has been freely exposed to the public for a period in excess of six years. For purposes of federal law, it stands in the same stead as an item for which a patent has expired or been denied: it is unpatented and unpatentable. Whether because of a determination of unpatentability or other commercial concerns, petitioner chose to expose its hull design to the public in the marketplace, eschewing the bargain held out by the federal patent system of disclosure in exchange for exclusive use. Yet, the Florida statute allows petitioner to reassert a substantial property right in the idea, thereby constricting the spectrum of useful public knowledge. Moreover, it does so without the careful protections of high standards of innovation and limited monopoly contained in the federal scheme. We think it clear that such protection conflicts with the federal policy "that all ideas in general circulation be dedicated to the common good unless they are protected by a valid patent." *Lear, Inc. v. Adkins,* 395 U.S. 653, 668 (1969).

We therefore agree . . . that the Florida statute is preempted by the Supremacy Clause.

[Affirmed.] ᓚ

International Patent Law

There are several international treaties that protect inventors. For example, the United States and 12 Latin American countries have signed the *Convention for the Protection of Inventions, Patents, Designs and Industrial Methods.* The United States and more than 25 other nations have formed the *International Patent*

Cooperation Union, administered by WIPO, which protects patents in the member countries through one international filing. As with trademarks, however, until additional international cooperation evolves, U.S. companies must be very diligent in order properly to protect their inventions in other nations, especially in those that are not members of these treaties.

Two persons may develop the same idea independently. U.S. law has always granted the patent to the "first to invent." Congress is presently considering changing this to a "first to file" system like that of most countries in the world.

COPYRIGHT INFRINGEMENT

To reward and stimulate intellectual endeavors, federal **copyright** law grants authors protection for the *expression* of their ideas, although not for the ideas themselves. Under the Copyright Act of 1976, all copyrightable works created after January 1, 1978, receive protection for the life of the author plus 50 years after his or her death. If the work is anonymous or a work for hire, the copyright lasts for the shorter of 75 years from its first publication or 100 years from its creation.

During that period, the owner of the copyright has exclusive right to produce the work in any medium, to control derivative works, to distribute copies of the work, to perform the work in public, and to display the work in public.

Subject Matter

Copyrights protect literary works (books, newspapers, magazines), works of a musical, dramatic, graphic, choreographic, or audiovisual nature, and sound recordings. This list is nonexclusive; the law is meant to protect any "original works of authorship." In 1990, Congress (1) gave visual artists such as painters and sculptors the legal right to prevent distorting changes or destruction of their work; (2) explicitly aided architects by extending copyright protection to the constructed design of buildings; and (3) granted copyright owners of computer programs the right to prohibit rental, lending, or leasing of their software, subject to certain exceptions (for example, if the renter is a nonprofit school).

Copyrightability

There are three basic elements of copyrightability. First, the work must be *fixed* in some *tangible medium of expression*. When a book is written, a song is recorded, a picture is painted, or a choreography is filmed, this requirement is met. Until tangibly fixed, a mere idea is unprotected.

Second the work must be *creative* to at least some degree. Creativity, not "sweat-of-the-brow" effort, is the key, as the Supreme Court emphasized in *Feist*

Publications v. Rural Telephone Service Co., 111 S.Ct. 1282 (1991), when it held that a simple compilation of names and addresses in a telephone directory was not copyrightable. The court stressed the fact/expression dichotomy; facts are not copyrightable, although their expression in a compilation might be, but not simply as a reward for hard work. The compilation must show some creativity to be protected. The Court held that a simple alphabetic listing is "devoid of even the slightest creativity."

Third, and most important, the work must be *original*. This does not require novelty, only that the work not be copied from someone else. A person who had never seen the novel *Moby Dick* but wrote a nearly identical book independently could successfully copyright it.

The copyrightability of computer codes is one of the most complicated areas of copyright law. One recent influential case held that programs incorporating the structure of existing software do not necessarily violate copyrights.[17] This case ruled that little other than source codes, the smallest element used in the writing of computer programs, could be copyrightable. On the other hand, another case held that copying of the key elements of a computer program is improper, even if the copy is not an exact one.[18]

Copyright Procedure

Securing a copyright is much easier than securing a patent and has recently become even easier. Copyright law has an important international dimension. Books, songs, movies, and other copyrightable materials quickly travel from continent to continent in today's world. There are two major copyright treaties. Until 1989, the United States belonged only to the Universal Copyright Convention, administered by UNESCO. Effective in 1989, however, the United States also joined the Berne Convention, administered by WIPO.

The process of obtaining a copyright is virtually self-executing. Until 1989, copyright protection for a published work was obtained if each copy of the work contained (1) a copyright notice (such as the word "copyright," the abbreviation "Copr.," or the symbol ©), the date of first publication, and (3) the name of the copyright holder. This relatively simple process

[17]*Computer Associates, Int'l;. v. Altai, Inc.,* 982 F.2d 693 (2d Cir. 1992).
[18]*Lotus Development Corp. v. Borland Int'l,* 799 F.Supp. 203 (D.Mass. 1992).

is now even easier. For works first published after the March 1, 1989, effective date of the Berne Convention, the copyright notice is no longer a requirement. Before March 1989, a person who observed a published work that did not contain a copyright notice could feel assured that the work was in the public domain. For works published after that date, however, this is not necessarily the case.

Copyright registration, although permissive, is still a good idea, because (1) it will protect the author in countries that have not signed the Berne Convention, and (2) it enables plaintiffs to recover statutory damages and an award of attorneys' fees in an infringement action even if actual damages cannot be proven. Registration is accomplished by sending a completed application form with a $20 check to the Register of Copyrights in Washington, D.C., along with one deposit copy of an unpublished work or two copies of a published work.

Infringement

If a plaintiff proves (even by circumstantial evidence) that a defendant had *access* to the plaintiff's work and that the defendant's work bears a *substantial similarity* to the plaintiff's copyrighted work (or a part of it), a claim for infringement is established. The plaintiff need not prove intent; an innocent infringement is actionable. For example, in *Bright Tunes Music Corp. v. Harrisongs Music, Ltd,*[19] the judge did not believe that former Beatle George Harrison intentionally copied an earlier song, "He's So Fine," when he composed "My Sweet Lord." Nonetheless, Harrison had access to the earlier song (which was widely played on popular radio), and his song was

[19]420 F.Supp. 177 (S.D.N.Y. 1977).

substantially similar. Harrison was held to have infringed the owner's copyright.

Fair Use Doctrine

An important, but rather vague, part of copyright law is the *fair use doctrine*. Section 107 of the Copyright Act of 1976 states:

[T]he fair use of a copyrighted work, including such use by reproduction in copies or phono-records or by any other means specified by [§ 106], for purposes such as criticism, comment, newsreporting, teaching (including multiple copies for classroom use), scholarship, or research, is not an infringement of copyright. In determining whether the use made of a work in any particular case is a fair use the factors to be considered shall include—

1. the purpose and character of the use, including whether such use is of a commercial nature or is for nonprofit educational purposes;

2. the nature of the copyrighted work;

3. the amount and substantiality of the portion used in relation to the copyrighted work as a whole; and

4. the effect of the use upon the potential market for or value of the copyrighted work.

Although the applications of this doctrine are controversial, the Copyright Office has issued supplemental guidelines dealing with photocopies: obviously copies used for literary criticism, classroom teaching, and parody fare better than those used for commercial purposes.

The following controversial case illustrates the fair use doctrine.

BASIC BOOKS, INC. v. KINKO'S GRAPHICS CORP.

758 F.Supp. 1522, U.S. District Court, Southern District of New York (1991)

Case

The plaintiffs (major publishing houses) sued the defendant, Kinko's, alleging copyright infringement when Kinko's copied excerpts from books whose rights are held by the plaintiffs without permission and *without payment of required fees and sold the copies for a profit at book stores serving New York University and Columbia University students. Kinko's admits that it copied the excerpts without permission, compiled them into course "packets," and sold them to college students. Twelve in-* *stances of copyright infringement are alleged. To illustrate, six of these instances were contained in "Packet #1: 'Work and Community '," which included 388 pages of copied work taken from 25 books, some in print and some out-of-print.*

Kinko's raised several defenses,
(continues)

BASIC BOOKS, INC. V. KINKO'S GRAPHICS CORP.

(continued from previous page)
including "fair use." After trial, the
district judge entered the following
opinion.

Motley, District Judge:

Coined as an "equitable rule of reason," the fair use doctrine has existed for as long as the copyright law. Justice Story set forth the meaning of fair use to which we adhere today. "In short, we must often . . . look at the nature and objects of the selections made, the quantity and value of the materials used, and the degree in which the use may prejudice the sale, or diminish the profits, or supersede the objects, of the original work." *Folsum v. Marsh,* 9 F.Cas. 342 (C.C.D.Mass. 1841).

This case is distinctive in many respects from those which have come before it. It involves multiple copying. The copying was conducted by a commercial enterprise which claims an educational purpose for the materials. The copying was just that—copying—and did not "transform" the works in suit, that is, interpret them or add any value to the material copied, as would a biographer's or critic's use of a copyrighted quotation or excerpt.

A. The 4 Factors of Fair Use.

1. Purpose and Character of the Use.

Transformative use. The Supreme Court has held that "commercial use of copyrighted material is presumptively an unfair exploitation of the monopoly privilege that belongs to the owner of the copyright." *Sony Corp. v. Universal City Studios,* 464 U.S. 417, 451 (1984). Additionally, the Supreme Court has found that "the distinction between 'productive' and 'unproductive' uses may be helpful in calibrating the balance [of interests.]" *Id.*

It has been argued that the essence of "character and purpose" is the transformative value, that is, productive use of the secondary work compared to the original. "The use . . . must employ the quoted matter in a different manner or for a different purpose from the original. A quotation of copyrighted material that merely republishes the original is unlikely to pass the test." Leval, *Toward a Fair Use Standard,* 103 Harv.L.Rev. 1105, 1111 (1990). Kinko's work cannot be categorized as anything other than a mere repackaging.

Commercial use. The use of the Kinko's packets, in the hands of the students, was no doubt educational. However, the use in the hands of Kinko's employees is commercial. Kinko's claims that its copying was educational and, therefore, qualifies as a fair use. Kinko's fails to persuade us of this distinction. Kinko's has not disputed that it receives a profit component from the revenue it collects for its anthologies. The amount of that profit is unclear; however, we need only find that Kinko's had the intention of making a profit.

While financial gain "will not preclude [the] use from being a fair use," *New York Times Co. v. Roxbury Data Interface,* 434 F.Supp. 217, 221 (D.N.J. 1977), consideration of the commercial use is an important one. "The crux of the profit/nonprofit distinction is not whether the sole motive of the use is monetary gain but whether the user stands to profit from exploitation of the copyrighted material without paying the customary price." *Harper & Row v. Nation Enterprises,* 471 U.S. 539, 562 (1985). This is precisely the concern here and why this factor weighs so heavily in favor of plaintiffs.

2. The Nature of the Copyrighted Work.

Courts generally hold that "the scope of fair use is greater with respect to factual than non-factual works." *New Era Publications v. Carol Publishing Group,* 904 F.2d 152, 157 (2d Cir. 1990). Factual works, such as biographies, reviews, criticism and commentary, are believed to have a greater public value and, therefore, uses of them may be better tolerated by the copyright law. Fictional works, on the other hand, are often based closely on the author's subjective impressions and, therefore, require more protection. These are general rules of thumb. The books infringed in [this] suit were factual in nature. This factor weighs in favor of defendant.

3. The Amount and Substantiality of the Portion Used.

"There are no absolute rules as to how much of a copyrighted work may be copied and still be considered a fair use." *Maxtone-Graham v. Burtchaell,* 803 F.2d 1253 (2d Cir. 1987). This third factor considers not only the percentage of the original used but also the "substantiality" of that portion to the whole of the work; that is, courts must evaluate the qualitative aspects as well as the quantity of material copied.

This court finds and concludes that the portions copied were critical parts of the books copied, since that is the likely reason the college professors used them in their classes. While it may be impossible to determine that the quoted material was "essentially the heart of" the copyrighted material, it may be inferred that they were important parts.

This factor, amount and substantiality of the portions appropriated, weighs against defendant. In this case, the passages copied ranged from 14 to 110 pages, representing from 5.2% to 25.1% of the works. In one case Kinko's copied 110 pages of someone's work and sold it to 132 students. Even for an out-of-print book, this amount is grossly out of line with accepted fair use principles.

In almost every case, defendant copied at least an entire chapter of a plaintiff's book. This is substantial because they are obviously meant to stand alone, that is, as a complete representation of the concept explored in the chapter. This indicates that these excerpts are not material supplemental to the assigned course material but *the* assignment. Therefore, the excerpts, in

(continues)

BASIC BOOKS, INC. V. KINKO'S GRAPHICS CORP.

(continued from previous page) addition to being quantitatively substantial, are qualitatively significant.

4. The Effect of the Use on Potential Markets for or Value of the Copyrighted Work.

The fourth factor, market effect, also fails the defendant. This factor has been held to be "undoubtedly the single most important element of fair use." *Harper & Row,* 471 U.S. at 566. "To negate fair use one need only show that if the challenged use 'should become widespread, it would adversely affect the *potential* market for the copyrighted work'." *Id.* at 568 (quoting *Sony Corp.)*

Kinko's confirms that it has 200 stores nationwide, servicing hundreds of colleges and universities which enroll thousands of students. The potential for widespread copyright infringement by defendant and other commercial copiers is great.

This court has found that plaintiffs derive a significant part of their income from textbook sales and permissions. This court further finds that Kinko's copying unfavorably impacts upon plaintiffs' sales of their books and collections of permission fees. This impact is more powerfully felt by authors and copyright owners of the out-of-print books, for whom permissions fees constitute a significant source of income. This factor weighs heavily against defendant.

Therefore, this court will assess statutory damages in the amount of $50,000 for nine of the 12 infringements, and $20,000 for three of the infringements [because the copying was less] for a total of $510,000 [plus costs and attorney's fees.] ⚖

Remedies

A successful plaintiff in a copyright infringement action usually receives actual damages plus the defendant's profits to the extent they were not calculated into the damage award. If the plaintiffs have registered their copyright, they may elect between actual damages or "statutory damages" in an amount the court finds "just," with the normal range being between $500 and $20,000 for any one work involved in the case, and up to $100,000 if the infringement was willful. In cases where the plaintiff has difficulty proving actual damages, the right to opt for statutory damages can be quite important, as the *Kinko's* case illustrated.

Copyright infringement can also constitute a federal misdemeanor punishable by fines of up to $10,000, one year in jail, or both.

International Copyright Law

We have already noted that international copyright protection is founded on two international treaties. Now that the United States is a party to both the Universal Copyright Convention and the Berne Convention, Americans holding copyrights are entitled to the maximum level of international protection. Unfortunately, the theoretical level of protection is often substantially higher than the actual level of enforcement of the rules in other countries.

UNFAIR COMPETITION

The term **unfair competition** is an imprecise one. In its broadest sense, it covers all tortious business conduct. In its most common usage, however, the term refers only to those business practices that are based on *deception.* In addition to trademark infringement, unfair competition includes any deceptive use by one person of the copyright or patent rights of another. It also embraces many other common-law torts, such as falsely inducing consumers to believe a product is endorsed by another, and "palming off." *Palming off* refers to any word or deed causing purchasers to be misled as to a product's source. It thus includes not only trademark infringement but all other means of source deception as well.

State Deceptive Trade Practices Acts

A consumer who is misled by false advertising or other deceptive practices may have the right to sue under a common-law fraud theory or perhaps a breach of express warranty theory if the advertising involved a product. These theories are discussed in other chapters.[20] However, additional consumer protection legislation, passed at both the state and federal levels, also addresses such activity.

---

[20]Express warranties are discussed in Chapter 22. Fraud is covered in Chapters 8 and 15.

Misleading advertising is often prohibited by state **deceptive trade practices acts.**[21] Other types of unfair competition that are usually prohibited by such statutes are the advertising of goods or services with the intent not to sell them on the advertised terms, representing goods as new when they are used or second-hand, and disparagement—making false statements of fact about competitors' goods or services.

Lanham Act

The federal government has also passed various acts that prohibit unfair competition, such as misleading advertising. In Chapter 51 for example, we will examine the Federal Trade Commission Act's ban on "unfair or deceptive acts or practices." In this chapter, our focus is on section 43(a) of the Lanham Act, which outlaws "any false description or representation." Although this section is frequently used to allow trademark owners to sue competitors for trademark infringement, it has also created a general federal law of unfair competition, which is frequently applied to deceptive advertising. Designed in large part to protect consumers from being misled, the cause of action is given primarily to the competitors of the deceptive advertiser.

---

[21]In states having such statutes, the wrongs are thus statutory torts (rather than common-law torts).

Illicit Acts

Section 43(a) of the Lanham Act has supported suits against companies that (1) used pictures of the plaintiff's product to advertise their own inferior brand; (2) used a confusingly similar color and shape of drug capsule that could mislead consumers into thinking that they were buying the plaintiff's nontrademarked brand; (3) printed "$2.99 as advertised on TV" when only the plaintiff had run such ads; (4) claimed that their pain reliever worked faster than the plaintiff's when it did not; and (5) displayed a rock star's picture on an album creating the impression that the star was a featured performer when, in fact, he or she was not.

As in all advertising, some "puffing" is permitted by the Lanham Act. For example, when a computerized chess game was advertised as "like having Karpov as your opponent," mere puffing was found.[22]

Enforcement

Most courts have not allowed deceived consumers to bring section 43(a) claims. Instead, suit is usually brought by competitors who, while redressing their own injuries, seek to end false advertising that also injures consumers. These competitors have been termed *vicarious avengers* of the consumer interest. A competitor's motive for bringing such a suit is easily seen in the following case.

---

[22]*Data Cash Systems, Inc. v. JS&A Group, Inc.*, 223 U.S.P.Q. 865 (N.D.Ill. 1984).

ALPO PETFOODS, INC. V. RALSTON PURINA CO.

913 F.2d 958, District of Columbia Circuit Court of Appeals (1990)

Two leading dog food producers sued each other for false advertising under section 43(a) of the Lanham Act. ALPO Petfoods sued Ralston Purina for claiming that its Puppy Chow products can lessen the severity of canine hip dysplasia (CHD), a crippling joint condition. Ralston attacked ALPO's claims that ALPO Puppy Food contains "the formula preferred by responding vets two to one over the leading puppy food." After a 61-day bench trial, the district judge decided that both companies had violated section 43(a). He enjoined both from making these or similar claims and awarded ALPO $10.4 million in damages. Only Ralston appealed.

Thomas, Circuit Judge:

[T]o prevail in a false advertising suit under section 43(a), a plaintiff must prove that the defendant's ads were false or misleading, actually or likely deceptive, material in their effects on buying decisions, connected with inter- state commerce, and actually or likely injurious to the plaintiff.

In reviewing the district court's findings on the elements of ALPO's section 43(a) claim, we have no authority to weigh the evidence anew. The district court heard weeks of conflicting expert testimony on the basis for and effectiveness of Ralston's CHD-related advertising. In finding that advertising false, deceptive, material, and injurious, the court cited specific experts' testimony, sometimes crediting that testimony over other evidence.

(continues)

ALPO PETFOODS, INC. V. RALSTON PURINA CO.

(continued from previous page)

Ralston's claims had a weak empirical basis. The hypothesis behind Ralston's CHD-related product change and advertising was the "anion gap theory" of Dr. Richard Kealy, a Ralston nutritionist. This theory holds that the smaller the difference between the chlorine content and the combined sodium and potassium content of a dog's diet, the more snugly the dog's hip joints will tend to fit. [A series of four short-term studies from 1980 to 1984 arguably supported the theory, although none was statistically significant at the 5 percent level. The first long-term study, undertaken in 1985, produced results that] undermined Ralston's CHD-related claims so much that Dr. Kealy ended the study, which he had projected would last for almost three years, after only thirty-three weeks.

We have reviewed the record, and we cannot say that this evidence and other evidence supporting the court's view of Ralston's CHD-related claims were incoherent, facially implausible, or contradicted by extrinsic proof. Accordingly, we affirm the district court's determination that ALPO satisfactorily carried its burdens of proof and persuasion on each element of its false advertising case.

Ralston [also] attacks the monetary remedy [of] $10.4 million in favor of ALPO. [T]he [trial] court actually awarded Ralston's profits [during the time of the false advertising] to ALPO. We doubt the wisdom of an approach to damages that permits courts to award profits for their sheer deterrent effect. Since this case lacks the elements required to support the court's award of Ralston's profits, we vacate the $10.4 million judgment in favor of ALPO. On remand, the court should award ALPO its actual damages, bearing in mind the requirement that any amount awarded have support in the record. In a false advertising case such as this one, actual damages can include: [1] profits lost by the plaintiff on sales actually diverted to the false ad-

vertisers; [2] profits lost by the plaintiff on sales made at prices reduced as a demonstrated result of the false advertising; [3] the cost of any completed advertising that actually and reasonably responds to the defendant's offending ads; and [4] quantifiable harm to the plaintiff's good will, to the extent that completed corrective advertising has not repaired that harm.

[The Lanham Act] also authorizes the court to "enter judgment, according to the circumstances of the case, for any sum above the amount found as actual damages, not exceeding three times the amount." This provision gives the court discretion to enhance damages, as long as the ultimate award qualifies as "compensation and not [as] a penalty." Given this express statutory restriction, if the district court decides to enhance damages, it should explain why the enhanced award is compensatory and not punitive.

[Affirmed as to liability; reversed as to damages and remanded.] ⚖️

Commercial Defamation

Through passage of the Trademark Revision Act of 1988, Congress established a cause of action for commercial defamation, thereby increasing the volume of this type of litigation. The Lanham Act now bans false descriptions or representations about the "nature, characteristics [or] qualities of *any person's* goods, services or commercial activities." (Emphasis added.) Therefore, if Company A runs an ad comparing its products to those of Company B, and in so doing misleadingly describes the characteristics of Company B's products, Company B will be able to recover damages, perhaps including treble damages. For First Amendment reasons, the Act contains express protection for two broad types of activities: (1) political speech, consumer or editorial comment, and satire, and (2) "innocent infringement" (thereby insulating news media that innocently disseminate false advertising).

SUMMARY

Businesses have a strong and legally protectable interest in free and fair competition, and in their intellectual property. The courts will protect against unfair interference not only with existing contractual and business relationships, but also, under proper circumstances, with prospective relationships. The key is frequently whether the defendant is acting with an improper purpose or in an improper manner.

The law protects properly registered trademarks so that producers can enjoy the reputation they have established and consumers are not misled as to the source of the products and services they purchase. To encourage creativity and inventiveness, the law protects intellectual property through patents and copyrights. And it prohibits the theft of trade secrets—the confidential bits of information that can give a business a competitive advantage.

The federal government and the states have also passed laws prohibiting various forms of unfair competition, including many forms of deceptive advertising.

KEY TERMS

Business torts
Interference with business relationships
Justification
Trademark
Service mark
Trade name
Trade dress
Generic term
Secondary meaning
Antidilution
Trade secret
Patent
Shop right doctrine
Copyright
Unfair competition
Deceptive trade practices acts

QUESTIONS AND PROBLEMS

1. The plaintiff, Walner, purchased an ice cream parlor franchise from the defendant, Baskin-Robbins, Inc. The franchise agreement contained language requiring the defendant's approval before the franchise could be sold. Two years later Walner contracted to sell the franchise to Garapet at a substantial profit, but Baskin-Robbins refused to grant permission for the sale. Walner sued for tortious interference with his right to contract with Garapet. Discuss. (*Walner v. Baskin-Robbins Ice Cream Co.*, 514 F.Supp. 1028, N.D.Tex. 1981).

2. A trademark applicant wishes to mark the word "Bundt" in connection with one of its cake pans. Is this term suitable for trademark registration? Discuss. (*In re Northland Aluminum Products, Inc.*, 777 F.2d 1556, Fed. Cir. 1985).

3. Miller Brewing Company purchased the trademark *Lite* and used this name on its labels for beer that was lower in calories than its regular beer. When a competitor, G. Heileman Brewing Company, started marketing a reduced-calorie beer that it labelled as "light beer," Miller brought a trademark infringement action against Heileman. At the trial,

Heileman introduced evidence that the term *light* beer had been used for many years in the beer industry to refer to beers having certain flavors, bodies, or reduced alcoholic contents. On that basis, Heileman contended that *light* was, essentially, a generic term and thus could not be the proper subject of a trademark. The trial court rejected this argument and issued an injunction prohibiting further use of "light" by Heileman. On appeal, do you think the court should accept Heileman's argument? Discuss why or why not. (*Miller Brewing Company v. G. Heileman Brewing Company*, 561 F.2d 75, 1977.)

4. Mead Data Central developed and trademarked LEXIS, a computerized legal research service. Toyota Motor Sales planned to begin selling cars trademarked LEXUS. Discuss Mead Data's possible theories for blocking sale of the cars. (*Mead Data Central, Inc. v. Toyota Motor Sales*, 875 F.2d 1026, 2d Cir. 1989.)

5. The plaintiff bakery filmed one of the defendant bakery's delivery drivers in a grocery store taking the plaintiff's fresh bread out of the plaintiff's wrappers and replacing it with stale loaves. What theory should the plaintiff pursue? Is this a good claim? (*Basque French Bakery v. Toscana Baking Co.*, No. 2937220-0, California Superior Court, Apr. 23, 1984.)

6. In response to complaints by customers of his sons' cycle shop, P developed a device to remedy a stall-out problem occurring when Yamaha racing cycles were run in mud or water. The device closed off the rear air intake, replacing it with an air snorkel located at a higher level under the seat cover. This device was used by P's sons when they raced, and P installed it on the cycles his sons sold. When Yamaha representatives visited the business, P's sons showed them the device. Yamaha soon began using the device on all its cycles. At some point thereafter, P sued Yamaha for trade secret infringement. Will this claim succeed? (*Sheets v. Yamaha*, 657 F.Supp. 319, E.D.La. 1987.)

7. By combining plastic support blocks on pontoons, spaced I-beams, and separate bouyant chambers, Rivet created a machine that could carry heavy loads across stump-filled marshes for extended periods. All three devices had been used before but never in combination. Rivet's machine, which he patented, was significantly more efficient than any previous machine. Later, a former employee began

making a similar machine. In a patent infringement suit, the defendant claimed Rivet's patent was invalid because the invention lacked novelty and nonobviousness. Discuss. (*Kori v. Wilco Marsh Buggies and Draglines, Inc.,* 708 F.2d 151, 5th Cir. 1983.)

8. Johnson Controls, Inc., developed a system of computer programs to control wastewater treatment plants. The "JC-5000S" program is customized for each location and carries a registered copyright. Former employees of Johnson, working for competitor Phoenix Control Systems, Inc., developed a similar program to do similar things. The Phoenix program did not copy the literal elements of Johnson's program (including the source and object code); however, it did copy the structure, sequence, and organization of the JC-5000S. Is such copying sufficient to constitute copyright infringement? (*Johnson Controls v. Phoenix Control Systems, Inc.,* 886 F.2d 1173, 9th Cir. 1989.)

9. Conventional wisdom is that John Dillinger, Public Enemy No. 1, died in a hail of bullets outside Chicago's Biograph Theater on July 22, 1934. Nash wrote two books arguing that Dillinger lived until at least 1979, because the FBI shot the wrong man at the theater. CBS televised an episode of the detective series "Simon and Simon" titled *The Dillinger Print,* which contained a plot featuring Nash's theories. One of the characters (A.J.) even purported to read from a book a description of several physical discrepancies between Dillinger and the corpse described in the 1934 autopsy. Nash cited the same discrepancies in his book. Nash sued CBS for copyright infringement. CBS admitted both access to Nash's books and copying of the books' factual material but argued that copyright law did not protect Nash this far and raised a "fair use" defense. Should Nash prevail? Discuss. (*Nash v. CBS, Inc.,* 899 F.2d 1437, 7th Cir. 1990.)

10. In 1979 U-Haul rented almost all the "self-move" household goods trailers in the United States and 60 percent of the "self-move" trucks. In that year Jartran entered the market and did so well that U-Haul's revenues for 1981 were $49 million less than it had predicted before it knew Jartran would be a competitor. Jartran's success could be traced to a $6 million ad campaign that featured comparison of the one-way rental rates charged by U-Haul and Jartran. Unfortunately, the ads were quite misleading. For example, they compared U-Haul's regular rates to special promotional rates by Jartran without disclosing that these were not the rates Jartran would normally charge. Jartran also published ads showing a Jartran truck and a U-Haul truck with the comparative sizes of the vehicles adjusted to make the U-Haul truck appear smaller and less attractive than it truly was. U-Haul sued Jartran under section 43(a) of the Lanham Act. What was the result? Discuss. (*U-Haul International, Inc. v. Jartran, Inc.,* 793 F.2d 1034, 9th Cir. 1986.)

Chapter 10

Business Ethics, Corporate Social Responsiveness, and the Law

What Is Ethics?
The Relationship between Law and Ethics
Are There Any Moral Standards?
The "Moral Minimum"
Is There a Duty to "Do Good"?
Excusing Conditions
Moral Dilemmas
Moral Reasoning and Decision Making
Are Corporations Moral Agents?
Does Ethics Pay?
Corporate Social Responsiveness

J ILL IS A REGIONAL sales manager for a nation-wide chain of retail consumer electronics stores. She and her assistants at company headquarters design promotional programs for stores in the region, supervise store managers' implementation of company marketing strategies, and conduct sales seminars for salespeople at these stores. Questions continually arise about how far promotional materials and the statements of individual salespeople can go in pushing their products. These questions relate not only to what is legal, but also to what is "appropriate" or "ethical." If particular statements are legal, is there any reason at all to be concerned about them? Are there any other standards? Jill and her associates know that it usually will be illegal to brazenly lie about the quality of a product. But they also know that it is often very difficult for a buyer to prove that a seller made intentionally deceptive statements, so the legal risk is small even in such a case. Jill understands that a company's reputation, and ultimately its sales, may suffer if it becomes known for dealing dishonestly. She also knows, however, that if some forms of subtle deception are practiced with skill, most customers will never know. Although a few customers may discover the deception, the company does not depend on repeat business in most of its product lines.

Even if the legal or financial risks are not great, Jill feels that it is "wrong" to lie to a customer. When she receives a lot of pressure from her superiors to increase sales, however, she begins to ask herself various questions: "Why is it wrong, really?" "Who, after all, defines what is wrong if it isn't illegal?" "We're selling to adults; aren't they supposed to look after themselves?" "Isn't this just the free market at work, and doesn't the market operate impersonally on the assumption that all sellers and buyers pursue their own economic self-interests?" "Isn't it okay to do it if I *feel* okay about it?" "But what if I feel good about it only after some strained rationalizing?" "And . . . let's face it—I don't always feel good about what happens."

When Jill tries to define what is "wrong," she finds it difficult to come up with any standards or any systematic way to develop such standards. Not only that, but she cannot even decide whether there is a rational way to analyze problems of this nature. Assuming, again, that there are no significant legal risks, Jill wonders how much latitude a salesperson should have in extolling the virtues of a product. Must every shortcoming of the item be revealed? Surely not. But why not? May the sales pitch be couched in vague, laudatory terms or must all responses be absolutely factual, precise, and to-the-point? Should the salesperson be concerned about the customer's real need for the product, or is the customer's apparent willingness to purchase the only thing that matters? Should there be any regard for the customer's particular susceptibilities to advertising? What if the advertising campaign that brought the customer into the store was full of "subliminal" messages that subconsciously persuaded him that this product would improve his love life? Jill finally decides that she does not have the time or energy to worry about such things, and that she will just be guided by the opinion of the company's attorneys about the legal risks of particular strategies and statements. Over a period of time, however, she is increasingly bothered by some of the promotional strategies that she initiates or approves. After doing some reading, she realizes that she has been grappling with age-old questions and that there is an entire field of study concerned with questions of this nature. Jill has discovered "business ethics."

WHAT IS ETHICS?

In a formal sense, the term **ethics** refers to the study of **morality** by systematically exploring moral values, moral standards and obligations, moral reasoning, and moral judgments. The terms morality and morals refer to the appropriate treatment of our fellow human beings. Although some people observe a technical distinction between "ethics" and "morals," these terms are often used interchangeably. When someone says, for example, that "Joe did not act ethically in that situation," the word "ethically" means the same thing as "morally." In this chapter, we are not very fussy about the use of these terms. Sometimes we will use them in their technical sense, and sometimes we will not. The context will make the meaning clear.

Is Business Ethics Different?

Should a study of "business ethics" differ from a more general study of the subject? Questions about how we ought to interact with and treat others arise in all aspects of life. Moral issues arise in the realm of the family, social groups, neighborhoods, politics and government, interactions between nations, professional associations, and other relationships, as well as in business. The basic questions, arguments, and problem-solving methods remain the same for all these domains. The factual contexts will vary, of course, depending on the nature of the relationship. In studying "business" ethics, we focus on business relationships and use examples of business problems that raise ethical questions. In other words, business ethics consists of the application of moral principles to people in a business setting.

THE RELATIONSHIP BETWEEN LAW AND ETHICS

One might legitimately ask why a study of business ethics should be included as a unit in a business course about law and the legal system. The material is admittedly somewhat different from the rest of the material in this book, and one could argue that the subject represents a digression from the main focus of the course. There are, however, a number of ways in which ethics and law fit together very naturally. As a result, there are several excellent reasons for dealing with the subject in the context of law. We will first recognize and discuss some of the differences between law and ethics, and then examine the close relationship between the two.

Differences between Legal and Moral Standards

As we will see shortly, legal standards often have their counterparts in the ethical domain, and vice-versa. For example, lying not only may violate a fundamental moral standard but also may constitute fraud under the law of torts and under various criminal statutes. Similarly, breaking a promise not only may be unethical but also may constitute a legally impermissible breach of contract in some circumstances. There are, however, several basic differences between legal and moral standards.

First, legal standards have a different source than moral ones. Whether found in a constitution, statute, judicial decision, or administrative agency regulation, legal standards are defined and applied by governmental processes. It takes governmental power to adopt and enforce laws.

Moral standards, on the other hand, are internal; they are developed within each person. It is true that people develop their moral standards from input they receive from external sources, such as the tenets of their religion and instructions from parents, teachers, friends, and others under whose influence they fall during their formative years. People even pick up information about appropriate and inappropriate moral behavior by observing the conduct and speech of strangers. These moral perceptions are formed, modified, and reinforced over time as we go through the process of having to give rational support and justification for our conduct when it affects others. Despite external influences, people ultimately develop, apply, and modify *their own* moral standards. Legal authority may be complex, even murky, but it is always there. In the personal realm of morality, however, we simply cannot get off the hook by referring to outside authority. Our only human source of authority is our rational thought processes: clear and objective thinking about the dignity, worth, and integrity of people around us and our impact on their lives. Even when one derives his or her basic moral standards from religion, thus referring to a higher authority, conformity with those standards involves an individual choice—an exercise of the will.

Second, the consequences of violating legal and moral standards are different. Violations of the law, if detected, result in concrete sanctions. When lying violates the law against fraud, for example, the guilty person may have to pay damages to the victim in a civil action, and may even be prosecuted in a criminal action and forced to pay a fine to the state or serve a jail term. There are no externally imposed sanctions for violating moral standards, however. Although lying usually is clearly unethical even if it does not meet the legal definition of fraud, the violation of ethical norms by itself is not subject to any definite penalties. It is true that unethical conduct sometimes *can* result in tangible consequences such as lost business because of a damaged reputation. Mostly, however, the consequences are like the standards themselves, internal and difficult to define.

Third, even though legal standards sometimes need to be a bit vague in order to be flexible, they must be more clearly defined than moral standards. The obvious reason is that legal standards are imposed on us by society and we can be punished for violating them; because of this, legal standards must be expressed with enough clarity to give us reasonable notice of society's expectations.

Fourth, moral standards usually require more of us than legal standards. The law tends to seek out the average in human behavior, for at least three reasons: (1) Although people's ideas about what is appropriate behavior vary, the law attempts to prescribe and enforce norms for an entire society. (2) The enforcement of laws requires the use of scarce public resources to support courts, police, and so on. As a result, in order for legal standards to be effective, they must survive a rough cost/benefit analysis. In other words, we should generally allocate society's scarce resources to the enforcement of legal standards only if we feel that the costs of that enforcement are outweighed by the benefits to society of upholding those standards. This is one of the reasons why our legal system often does not do a very good job of providing remedies for small claims. (3) The law must be practical. It may be unethical to break a vaguely expressed promise, for example, but a court can require someone to pay monetary damages for breaking a promise only where the promise describes obligations with reasonable certainty.

Fifth, some laws have little or nothing to do with moral behavior because they exist for other purposes. Some laws, for instance, are adopted solely for the purpose of bringing order to our affairs. There is nothing inherently moral or immoral about driving on one side of the road rather than the other. To prevent chaos, however, a society must decide one way or the other.

The Legal/Ethical Overlap

Despite their differences, law and ethics have much in common. First, as we will see shortly, sound moral reasoning is quite similar in methodology to sound legal reasoning. In other words, the method for rationally identifying and analyzing moral issues is very much like the method for dealing with legal issues.

Second, laws are intended to serve a variety of social purposes including, in some cases, promoting moral conduct. To again use fraud as an example, the laws that prohibit intentional misrepresentations of important facts in business transactions have at least two objectives: promoting adherence to the fundamental moral obligation of honesty in our dealings with others, and improving economic efficiency by improving the quality of information in the market.

Third, regardless of whether a given legal principle has a substantial moral content, evidence of ethical or unethical conduct can have significant effects on the outcome of a dispute. Judges, juries, arbitrators, and other decision makers in legal proceedings cannot help but take note of such behavior. Regardless of their own ethical level, they are likely to recoil when confronted with *your* unethical behavior. Most lawsuits or other dispute resolution procedures involve some close calls on factual and legal questions. When your behavior in the relevant events has been ethically questionable, these close calls are more likely to go against you.

The now-famous dispute between Texaco and Pennzoil, mentioned in Chapter 9, illustrates how the ethical background of a transaction can affect the close decisions that often must be made when legal disputes are being resolved. Pennzoil claimed that it had reached an agreement to merge with Getty Oil Co. Even after the alleged agreement had been reached, Getty secretly shopped around for another merger partner. Within a matter of days, Texaco "pulled the rug out from under" Pennzoil and acquired Getty. Pennzoil sued, claiming that Texaco had committed the tort of intentionally interfering with its contract to buy Getty. As a foundation for its claim, Pennzoil had to show that there had actually been a contract between it and Getty. The facts relevant to this question were quite ambiguous, and the question was a close one. Although the way Texaco and Getty had behaved was not too unusual in the context of mergers and acquisitions, the jury was not favorably impressed by Getty's and Texaco's apparently cavalier attitude toward commitments. Even though the commitments were somewhat vague, and even though many observers thought that the decision was wrong on legal grounds, Pennzoil won a $10.5 billion judgment against Texaco. (Getty and its principals were not defendants because Texaco had agreed to indemnify these parties against any liability that might arise from Texaco's acquisition. The indemnities also did not look good to the jury; even though such clauses are common in merger transactions, the jury was persuaded that Texaco must have known that it and Getty were doing something wrong or it would not have granted the indemnities.)

ARE THERE ANY MORAL STANDARDS?

There are those who believe that it is impossible to identify any concrete rules or standards to serve as a general foundation for evaluating the morality of behavior. The existence and content of particular ethical standards is too personal and individualized to formulate generally applicable rules. Moreover, they argue that what is "ethical" depends a great deal on what is viewed as acceptable behavior in a particular culture and that norms vary greatly from one culture to another. They assert that the formal study and practical application of ethics can consist only of defining and improving the *processes* by which moral issues are identified and analyzed.

Others argue that, although there are no overarching moral "rules" that can be applied to all human behavior, the general standard of **utilitarianism** can serve as a guide for moral behavior. Advanced by noted philosophers such as Jeremy Bentham and John Stuart Mill, utilitarianism is an ethical theory that is committed solely to the purpose of promoting "the greatest good for the greatest number." Utilitarianism essentially permits all conduct that will serve the objective of maximizing the social utility (i.e., the social "benefit" or "good"). As an abstract theory, utilitarianism makes a lot of sense. In actual practice, however, it can be all but impossible to predict, even roughly, which specific actions are likely to provide the greatest benefit to society. Moreover, even deciding how to define "benefit" to society can be an exercise in futility because of the many possible value judgments that may be involved. What one person views as a benefit to society may be quite different from the view of another person. In large part because of these difficulties, other ethicists view utilitarianism as being just one useful component in a rational process of ethical reasoning.

Some well-known philosophers do feel that certain threshold standards of moral behavior can be identified and applied to real problems across various circumstances and cultures. The German philosopher Immanuel Kant wrote that every person's actions should be judged morally by asking the question: "Can this action be justified by reasons that are uniformly applicable to all other persons?" In other words, he suggested as an overarching standard of moral behavior the rule that people cannot make exceptions of themselves; one's behavior is morally defensible only if everyone else could do the same thing without interfering with the optimal functioning of an organized society. This means, among other things, that we should all treat others as we would wish to be treated, a wisdom embodied in the so-called Golden Rule. Each person should be treated as an end in himself, not as a means to an end.

We think there is merit in all of these positions, and that the best approach to questions about ethical behavior includes elements of each. Process is extremely important. It is essential to employ a rational process for analyzing these kinds of questions. (We will present such a process later in this chapter.) We also think, as did Kant, that there are certain fundamental moral standards that are virtually universal. As we discuss these principles, it will become apparent that some elements of utilitarianism are included; we recognize that costs and benefits of alternative courses of action may have to be taken into account when there are extenuating circumstances or conflicting moral obligations.

THE "MORAL MINIMUM"

As we observe human interactions and learn more about human nature, examine and think deeply about the effects that our own actions have on others, and perhaps study the writings of those philosophers who have pondered moral questions over the years, we may begin to discover that certain basic values and standards of conduct are truly necessary for the existence of an advanced civilization. What form do these principles take? Lawrence Kohlberg writes that the morally mature individual bases his actions on "principles chosen because of their logical comprehensiveness, their universality, and their consistency." He then adds: "These ethical principles are not concrete like the Ten Commandments but abstract universal principles dealing with justice, society's welfare, the equality of human rights, respect for the dignity of individual human beings, and with the idea that persons are ends in themselves and must be treated as such."[1]

In our search for generally applicable moral standards, let us assume that we are looking only for those guideposts that are relatively comprehensive, universal, and consistent. We can also assume that the foundation for this search is a view of each human being as unique and as deserving to be treated as we ourselves would wish to be treated. Important questions remain, however: Exactly where do we find these

---

[1]Lawrence Kohlberg, "Moral Stages and Moralization: The Cognitive-Developmental Approach," in Manuel Velasquez, *Business Ethics: Concepts and Cases* (Englewood Cliffs, N.J.: Prentice-Hall, Inc., 1982), 20–23.

standards? If they can be found, can they ever be expressed with enough certainty to provide meaningful guidance for our conduct?

The answer to the first question is that, in order to satisfy the requirements of comprehensiveness, universality, and consistency, we must rely on the rational human thought process as our source. Any other source is likely to produce results that are too variable across cultures, beliefs, circumstances, and even across time.

One approach to the second question is to determine whether there are any standards of behavior that do not need to be defended by a rational person. In other words, from the perspective of a rational mind, are there any general categories of behavior that stand on their own moral foundation, without any need for justification? If so, they could be identified as the **moral minimum**—a set of general standards that constitute the ethical minimum necessary for the functioning of civilization. Stated somewhat differently, violation of these standards is *prima facie* (on its face) wrong. Compliance with such standards requires no defense or justification. To the contrary, a rational person would expect a defense or justification for a *failure to comply* with them. The reason for expecting such a justification is that failure to comply with these standards tends to *destroy the social and economic relationships* that cause a society to function. We suggest the following as components of the moral minimum, fully recognizing that these components sometimes will overlap and that they could be organized and labeled in a variety of ways.

Honesty

A rational person does not have to justify telling the truth. The notion that one should correctly represent the facts is so firmly ingrained in human relations that we expect a justification for not doing so. Without reasonable expectations of honesty, we cannot maintain the personal and business relationships that create order and economic well-being. As we have seen, there are also principles in the *legal* domain that are intended to encourage **honesty,** as with legal prohibitions against fraud. The moral obligation, however, is more encompassing.

Loyalty

In any culture there are certain voluntary relationships in which one party places a higher degree of trust and confidence in the other than one would

place in a stranger. These relationships are not forced upon us; we consent to them either explicitly or implicitly. Examples include an agent or employee's relationship with her principal, the corporate manager's relationship with the company's shareholders, a trustee's relationship with the beneficiary, and each partner's relationship with the others. A moral duty of **loyalty** is based on two facts: First, by virtue of the relationship, we have created in the other person a legitimate expectation that we will further his or her interests. Second, the relationship has placed us in a position where we have the ability to cause serious harm if we do not act in that person's interests. For example, these relationships often give one party some degree of control over information or assets that are valuable to the other person.

When we enter such relationships we take on an affirmative obligation to (1) fully disclose to the other person all material information that is relevant to our dealings; (2) keep confidential any information that the other party reasonably expects us to protect; (3) avoid undisclosed conflicts of interest, (i.e., unless we obtain the other party's consent, stay out of situations that are likely to put pressure on us to act against the other party's best interests); and (4) generally act in the best interests of the other party, even if such action is not entirely in our own best interests. Relationships based on trust and confidence cannot exist without the observance of such behavioral standards, and these kinds of relationships contribute greatly to economic efficiency and social order. The moral duty of loyalty is one of those ethical obligations that has a very close analog in the legal domain. The law identifies certain *fiduciary* relationships, such as agent–principal, in which there are legally enforceable obligations of loyalty. Again, the legal obligation is usually less demanding than the moral one.

Keeping Commitments

Social and commercial relationships among people are quite difficult to maintain without accepting the notion that we should keep the promises we make to each other. For this reason, the rational person is not likely to feel it necessary to defend his actions in **keeping commitments.** Failing to keep them, however, normally requires justification. Sometimes there can be difficult questions about whether a commitment has been made, and if so, about its scope, but once these questions are resolved the rational mind will find little need to justify keeping a promise.

Once again, we can find a narrower legal counterpart to this obligation—when a promise is part of a legally enforceable contract there are sanctions for breaking it.

Doing No Harm

The rational person does not have to defend himself when he refrains from *intentional, reckless, or careless conduct that can cause reasonably foreseeable harm to others.* To the contrary, justification is usually expected for such conduct. Our actions have both expected and unexpected effects on others, and these effects can be positive or negative. Negative effects are those that damage some legitimate interest of another person. It is generally recognized that people have legitimate interests in their physical, economic, and emotional well-being, as well as in their property, privacy, and reputation. There obviously is overlap among these interests but, taken together, they include most of the things that are important to people.

Sometimes our actions have negative consequences for others that we never could have foreseen. When, however, cautious concern for the welfare of others should lead us to anticipate that certain action or inaction may harm the legitimate interests of others, we should do what we can to avoid harm. Narrower legal counterparts for the obligation of **doing no harm** are found throughout the law of torts.

In the following case, the legal issue is whether the defendant committed the tort of fraud. After reading the court's legal analysis and conclusions, carefully consider the following questions: (1) Aside from the legal principles involved, are there any basic moral obligations that are possibly relevant? If so, what are they? (2) Is this a situation in which the extent of any relevant moral obligation is basically the same as the legal obligation? If not the same, is the moral obligation broader or narrower than the legal one? (3) If the moral and legal obligations are somewhat different in scope, can you think of any reasons why this is so?

GRENDELL V. KIEHL

Supreme Court of Arkansas, 723 S.W.2d 830 (1987)

Don Grendell had served as an insurance agent for Loretta and Ferdinand Kiehl since 1971. The Kiehls also relied on Grendell for financial advice. One investment that Grendell promoted to the Kiehls was an oil and gas drilling venture. Grendell told the Kiehls that the investment was "a good thing" and would "make money" for them. On another occasion he "guaranteed that they would make lots of money," and "were going to get 50 barrels a day." No oil was discovered, and the Kiehls lost their investment. They sued Grendell, claiming that he had committed fraud, and they received a judgment against him for $11,329.60. Grendell appealed.

Hays, Justice:

The essential elements of an action for [fraud] are well established: (a) a false,

material representation of fact made by the defendant; (b) scienter—knowledge by the defendant that the representation is false, or an assertion of fact which he does not know to be true; (c) an intention that the plaintiff should act on such representation; (d) justifiable reliance by the plaintiff on the representation; and (e) damage to the plaintiff resulting from such reliance.

. . . The [statement] that the oil investment was a good thing and would make money, even the inference of "50 barrels a day," fails to rise to the level of misrepresentation of fact. Even at its strongest, the proof constitutes expressions of opinion in the nature of "puffing." Admittedly, Mr. and Mrs. Kiehl were relatively inexperienced in business affairs but we cannot conclude they were incapable of recognizing the difference between an opinion that a proposed investment in an oil lease looked promising and was a "good thing," as opposed to a factual assertion that an oil well would become a

producer. Nothing in the testimony suggests the Kiehls were not mindful that while some oil ventures succeed, a good many others, just as inviting at the outset, do not. Indeed, Mrs. Kiehl candidly acknowledged recognizing the risk factor in oil leases and was aware that a "dry hole" was a possibility.

Finding the dividing line between misrepresentation of fact and expression of opinion is often troubling. *Prosser and Keeton on Torts* states that [a claim for fraud] cannot be based on "misstatements of opinion, as distinguished from those of fact. The usual explanation is that an opinion is merely an assertion of one man's belief as to a fact, of which another should not be heard to complain, since opinions are matters about which many many men will be of many minds, and which are often governed by whim and caprice. [Expressions of] judgment and opinion in such a case implies no knowledge."

An opinion may take the form of a statement of quality, of more or less

(continues)

GRENDELL V. KIEHL

(continued from previous page)
indefinite content. One common application of the opinion rule is in the case of loose, general statements made by sellers in commending their wares. No action lies against a dealer who describes the automobile he is selling as a "dandy," a "bear cat," a "good little car," and "a sweet job," or as "the pride of our line" and the "best in the American market," or merely makes use of broad, and vague, commendatory language comparing his goods favorably with others, or praising them as "good," "proper," "sufficient" and the like.

A statement that . . . a real estate investment will insure a handsome profit, that an article is the greatest bargain ever offered, and similar claims are intended and understood to be merely emphatic methods of urging a sale. These things, then, a buyer must disregard in forming a sober judgment as to his conduct in the transaction. If he succumbs to such persistent solicitation, he must take the risk of any loss attributable to a disparity between the exaggerated opinion of the seller and a reasonable or accurate judgment of the value of the article.

The Kiehls point out that their [longstanding] reliance on Don Grendell [in both insurance and financial matters] produced a special relationship of trust and confidence requiring the utmost in good faith and disclosure of all material facts. Even so, there was an absence of proof by the Kiehls that Grendell either knew the assurances made to them were false or made factual representations while lacking knowledge of their truthfulness.

[The court found that Grendell was not guilty of fraud. However, the evidence also showed that he had kept $3,500 of the Kiehl's money that had been deposited with him and not invested, so the court ordered him to pay back that money.] ⚖

IS THERE A DUTY TO "DO GOOD"?

The components of the moral minimum relate only to preventing harm that we may cause, or correcting harm that we have actually caused. What about situations in which harm is being caused through no moral fault on our part? Do we also have a fundamental moral obligation to affirmatively "do good" by trying to prevent or correct harm that we had no part in causing?

Many people, of course, help others without even thinking about the moral implications. They give to charities, volunteer their time, and perform other altruistic acts for many complex reasons. They may do so for religious reasons, because they want to help create a better world for their children, because of the attention it brings them, or just because it makes them feel good. The question we are raising here is whether there is a rationally based moral obligation to do such things and, if so, what are its limits. In other words, is there something resembling the moral minimum for doing good, and can it be defined in any useful way?

Many people do seem to feel a strong sense of obligation to help others. Again, the reasons why they feel this way are varied and complex. It is therefore difficult to isolate the phenomenon's purely rational element. If we study the question solely from the perspective of rational analysis, we will find less general agreement than we did in the case of the moral minimum. At least part of the reasoning process that supports the moral minimum, however, can also be used to argue in favor of a moral obligation to do good. Most rational people would not feel it necessary to defend their actions in doing good. Similarly, they usually would not expect others to defend such actions. On the other hand, does the rational mind expect a justification for *not* doing good? The answer, which is not very helpful, is that some rational minds would and some would not.

If one tries to build an argument that there is a rationally based moral obligation to do good, the argument probably should contain the following elements:

1. In many cases it can be practically impossible to assign a specific moral responsibility for the existence of needs. A family may be desperate because the breadwinner has lost a job from bad health or an economic recession, and they have no family or friends who can help. A Boy Scout troop may need volunteer adult leadership in order to fulfill its goals of teaching, guiding, and nurturing a group of youths. The existence of such needs is really no one's "fault."

Even if we can identify a responsible person or group, it may be totally unrealistic to expect them to take remedial action. The needy family's breadwinner may have lost the job because the company was recklessly or dishonestly managed and went bankrupt. In this case, we can trace moral fault but it is highly unlikely that the blameworthy person or group will correct the harm it has caused. Thus, in an organized society, the rational person should expect there to be unmet needs, and should understand that his efforts to meet these needs will improve the functioning of the society of which he is a member.

2. Although we should use government as one vehicle for meeting people's needs, government cannot serve effectively as our *only* social problem solver. For example, even though government programs can do much good in providing food and shelter for the poor, such programs will usually be inadequate by themselves. Resources will always be too scarce. Government agencies sometimes can be too impersonal, and too remote from the problem, to provide assistance as effectively as individuals or private groups. Moreover, government bureaucracy sometimes can make it a less efficient provider of assistance than individuals and private groups.

3. Helping others is clearly in harmony with the view that we generally should treat others as we would wish to be treated in similar circumstances.

4. In circumstances in which (1) a problem or need is brought to our attention, (2) we are in a good position to help, (3) we have the ability to help, and (4) taking positive action would not require an unreasonable risk or cost, our failure to do something positive is very similar to actually *doing harm by intentional, reckless, or careless conduct.*

If one argues that there is a moral obligation to do good, one must define some limits to the obligation. In item 4, we identified some possible limits which require a bit of further explanation. *First,* we can have no obligation to meet a need that we do not know about. This statement assumes, of course, that we have not consciously tried to avoid knowledge of the situation. If there is such an obligation, it cannot be avoided by intentional ignorance. *Second,* in a given situation we may not be the appropriate persons to take action. There are some cases in which our help is unwanted, or may actually do more harm than good. In addition, there may be some other person, organization or agency that is much better equipped to do the job than we are. This is not an excuse that one should look for, but sometimes good judgment suggests that we are inadequate to be useful. Of course, the fact that we are unable to solve the entire problem does not necessarily mean that we should do nothing at all. One person cannot solve the problem of world hunger, or even hunger in one city, but one person can do *something. Third,* any rational argument that there is a moral duty to do good must incorporate the concept of costs and benefits (or "risks and utility"). A rational person would not expect someone to take positive action that would entail far greater cost or risk to the provider than benefit to the recipient. One cannot be expected to impoverish oneself or one's family in order to give to a worthy cause. (Here, of course, a moral obligation to one's family would be violated at the same time.)

Although we have so far focused on personal situations, the preceding discussion serves as a necessary foundation for our later examination of corporate social responsiveness.

EXCUSING CONDITIONS

There occasionally will be circumstances that may excuse one's violation of a basic moral obligation. The particular conditions surrounding a person's action or inaction may reduce the degree of moral responsibility or even completely remove it. Breaking a promise, for example, is *prima facie* wrong on moral grounds, but it may not always be absolutely wrong. **Excusing conditions** may be present. One must be careful about introducing this concept of excusing conditions into ethical analysis, however, because it so easily can be used improperly as a "cop-out." People are usually quite ready to offer "excuses" for their bad behavior, and they may have to be reminded that "reasons" are not necessarily moral excuses. When we speak of excusing conditions, we assume that they are not the result of carelessness, laziness, or conscious disregard of relevant information.

The kinds of circumstances likely to be viewed by a rational person as excusing conduct that otherwise would be morally blameworthy are those affecting a person's *knowledge* or *freedom of action.* Our status as fully responsible moral beings (or "moral agents") assumes that we act with knowledge of relevant and material information, and that our freedom of action is not substantially impaired by some external force.

Suppose, for instance, that Joe promises to deliver 100 laser printers to Sam by December 1. We are not likely to view Joe as morally blameworthy if he fails to deliver on time because, through no fault of Joe's, one of his main suppliers suddenly cuts him off or his own factory has to shut down for several weeks because of a strike by a labor union. His freedom of action has been impaired. Morally he is still expected, of course, to do everything legally within his power to minimize the harm caused to Sam or to come as close as he can to fulfilling the commitment. His moral responsibility is diminished, however, to the extent that his freedom of action is diminished. In a similar fashion, Joe's moral culpability is reduced to the extent that, when he made the promise, he neither knew nor had reason to know of existing facts that would make it impossible to deliver on time.

As is true of many ethical concepts, the idea of excusing conditions has a roughly similar counterpart in the law. In some situations, evidence showing that a person did not have the knowledge or freedom to have acted differently can prevent liability for breach of contract, negligence, or some other *legal* wrong. Moral excuses and legal excuses are not necessarily equivalent, but the general concepts exist in both domains. Thus, the actions or failures of one of Joe's suppliers might excuse Joe from the *moral* obligation to carry out a promise to deliver printers, but in some circumstances the law may hold that Joe had assumed the risk of such an occurrence and is *legally* responsible. In other situations, extenuating circumstances may provide a legal excuse but not a moral one. In still other cases, both kinds of excuses may exist.

MORAL DILEMMAS

On some occasions fundamental moral obligations may conflict. You know the familiar phrase for such a dilemma: "Caught between a rock and a hard place." Although **moral dilemmas** can arise in a wide variety of situations, *whistleblowing* presents a classic and often agonizing version of such an ethical conflict. The term whistleblowing normally refers to a situation in which an employee objects to or reports to the authorities the illegal or unethical activities of his employer. Because this kind of situation is frequently so rich in ethical questions, we will use the following hypothetical case for two purposes: as an illustration of how moral dilemmas arise and as a basis for our subsequent discussion of moral reasoning.

Suppose that Alexis works in the tax division of a large public accounting firm. One of the firm's major clients is Leviathan Corp. While working on one part of Leviathan's tax return, Alexis discovers that some expense items appear to have been overstated. No single item has been grossly inflated, and the total amount of expense overstatement is significant but not huge. Thus the risk of detection by the Internal Revenue Service probably is relatively small. Also, Alexis cannot tell for sure whether the overstatements are intentional or simply resulted from honest mistakes or incompetence. She speaks with her immediate supervisor about the matter, but the supervisor dismisses the evidence as a "nonproblem." When Alexis presses the issue a little harder, the supervisor says, "Just do your job and don't stick your nose in too far." Should Alexis take up the matter with a higher-level manager, perhaps even with the firm's top management? Suppose that she does so and receives the same kind of response at that level. What then?

Alexis owes a general moral duty of loyalty to her employer, an obligation that requires her to act in the firm's best interests. Moreover, in this case, she owes a duty of loyalty to the client. She also has made commitments, either explicitly or implicitly, to obey her superiors in the firm. Fulfilling these obligations, however, requires actions that are possibly dishonest and that may violate several conflicting moral obligations.

If Alexis refuses to overlook the problem, or if she reports it to the IRS, she stands an excellent chance of losing her job. How likely is it that she will be able to find a comparable job, especially if she cannot get a good reference from her current firm, a possibility that cannot be ignored? Does she have dependents who count on her for support? If so, she probably owes them a moral obligation that could be characterized as one of loyalty, or perhaps doing no harm. Is this duty strong enough to support a decision to keep quiet about something that is possibly dishonest?

Alexis owes a conflicting moral duty of honesty to the government, and to taxpayers who will have to pay more to make up for the underpayments by her firm's clients. It is true that the harm to any other single taxpayer will be extremely small, but the obligation exists nonetheless.

As an accountant, she also has made commitments to other members of her profession to uphold professional standards of honesty and competence. The failures of one member of a professional or trade group taint the reputation of the entire group and thus cause harm to every other member. To overlook the expense overstatements may violate this commitment and, if detected, harm the profession and its members.

Alexis faces a moral dilemma. Is there any way out of it? Of course, there are always ways out, but there may not be a painless way out. In the next section we will examine moral reasoning to see how ethical questions can be analyzed in a rational way. Part of this discussion will focus on moral dilemmas as a part of the overall process of moral reasoning. Clear, rational thinking about moral dilemmas does not necessarily eliminate the conflict or turn a difficult situation into an easy one. On the other hand, fuzzy or irrational thinking can certainly make matters worse. In the next section, we will explore the benefits that structured, rational thinking can bring to ethical problems, including moral dilemmas.

MORAL REASONING AND DECISION MAKING

Ethical issues frequently are emotionally charged. Although it can be quite difficult to think rationally about emotional issues, it is in such situations that clear, organized thinking is most needed. One of the most important lessons one can learn from a study of ethics is that moral questions are capable of being analyzed rationally. The process of analyzing moral questions is essentially the same as rational problem solving or decision making in other situations.

Identifying Issues

The necessary first step in problem solving is to figure out exactly what the problems are. In other words, one must identify the issues. If one is confronted with legal, financial, or marketing issues, for example, they first should be recognized and spelled out as clearly as possible. The same is true of ethical issues. In the hypothetical case involving Alexis, the issue she must cope with immediately is *not* (1) whether it is wrong in general to cheat on one's taxes; (2) whether her superiors are bad people; (3) whether her accounting firm or Leviathan Corp. has developed an organizational structure that is insufficient to establish lines of individual accountability for wrongdoing; or (4) whether she can sue her employer for the tort of wrongful discharge if she is fired for objecting to the expense overstatements or reporting them to the IRS.

Problems have to be defined narrowly enough so that we have the ability both to analyze them adequately *and* exercise some degree of influence over the outcome. The issue that Alexis must confront at the present time is whether her most morally defensible course of action is to keep quiet and go along with her firm's possibly inappropriate behavior or to resist it by "blowing the whistle." Other issues may arise later, but for now this is all she needs to deal with from an ethical perspective.

Identifying the Governing Principles

For every kind of issue there are governing principles or rules that guide or limit our decision. The source of these principles will vary, depending on the nature of the issue. There are legal rules, generally accepted accounting principles, marketing principles, generally accepted courses of medical treatment for particular illnesses, formulas for computing stress in the construction of bridges, and so on. In ethics we have the components of the moral minimum—the foundational moral obligations identified earlier in our discussion.

In some cases the principles will be relatively *specific*, but in others they may be quite *general*. Whether they are specific or general, different principles may be characterized by varying degrees of *certainty* or *acceptance*. In the case of some legal principles, for example, it can be difficult to determine precisely what the rule is. This uncertainty can result from conflicting court decisions, ambiguous statutory language, or other reasons. In addition, some principles are more generally accepted than others, whether the relevant field is law, medicine, accounting, engineering, ethics, or another discipline. These qualifying remarks do not diminish the importance of guiding principles. They represent the collective knowledge gained from experience and rational thought, and should serve as the foundation for rational problem solving.

In ethics, the principles are fairly general. As indicated earlier, however, we think that the *prima facie* duties that constitute the moral minimum are widely accepted across time, culture, and circumstance. Their relative degree of acceptance as societal norms has varied, no doubt, at different times and in different cultures, but in general they have remained intact.

When analyzing ethical issues, it is important to identify the pertinent moral obligations as precisely as possible. What is the *nature* of the obligation? Honesty? Loyalty? Keeping commitments? Doing no harm? After identifying the nature of each moral obligation, we must make sure we understand exactly *who* owes which obligation *to whom.* In Alexis's case we have already done a pretty good job of identifying the obligations that she owes to various parties. If we are doing a complete ethical analysis of the entire situation, we also would find it necessary to identify the moral obligations owed *to* Alexis by her superiors. One can argue persuasively that they are violating their duty of doing no harm by intentionally, recklessly, or negligently engaging in conduct that may cause reasonably foreseeable harm to Alexis. Acting in behalf of the firm, essentially what they have done is ask her to participate in conduct that may be dishonest and possibly even illegal. Even if she does not get into any legal trouble, emotional trauma also can be viewed as "harm" when it is a reasonably foreseeable result of their actions.

Collecting, Verifying, and Drawing Inferences from Information

Issues of any kind always arise in a factual context—they do not exist in a vacuum. In our hypothetical case, the relevant information (i.e., "evidence" or "data") that initially caused Alexis to perceive a problem was the apparent inconsistency between entries in Leviathan's general ledgers used to prepare its tax return and the figures in supporting documentation. When information raises potential ethical, legal, or other issues, we should first do what we can to verify the accuracy, reliability, and completeness of that information. If the issues are sensitive, we obviously must exercise great care in doing this. Caution and good judgment are essential.

We may find that the true facts are very different than we initially suspected, and that there is no problem at all. Of course, we may find that things are much worse than we thought. Frequently we may conclude after an initial inquiry that our information is incomplete and that we need further evidence to understand the situation. Again, in the subsequent search for additional evidence, caution is the watchword. It is usually impossible to acquire information that is so complete and so clearly accurate and reliable as to resolve all doubt. Decisions always have to be made on the basis of information that is less than perfect. When analyzing important issues and preparing to make important decisions, however, it is essential that our information be as complete and accurate as circumstances will allow.

As with any fact-finding process that serves as a foundation for problem solving, in ethical analysis we infer relevant facts from the evidence. In other words, we infer that certain things have happened. In addition to inferring facts, we use the evidence as a basis for making predictions about likely future events. Thus, from the evidence she has at her disposal, Alexis might infer that her firm condones or possibly even assists in tax cheating by clients, although more information is needed to support this inference. Alexis also may have enough information to predict that any further objection to superiors within the firm is likely to be fruitless, and that she may even be penalized in some way for making a fuss.

Applying the Facts to the Principles

The remainder of the ethical problem-solving, or moral reasoning, process involves further application of the guiding principles to the facts that we have inferred from the evidence. In other words, we must determine how the identified moral obligations should apply to these particular facts. This determination should be relatively straightforward, of course, if there are no excusing conditions or moral dilemmas. Such complicating factors are present in many cases, however, and must be incorporated into the analysis.

In our hypothetical scenario, we already have identified the moral dilemmas created by several conflicting duties. The next step is to weigh and balance these obligations against one another. In doing so, we must keep in mind that this is not algebra. Despite being a rational analytical process, it is highly qualitative and involves a degree of subjectivity. The process of balancing conflicting obligations should incorporate at least the following factors.

Excusing Conditions

Are there any excusing conditions that might lessen the strength of one obligation relative to another? Remember that our moral accountability can be diminished or eliminated by genuine lack of knowledge or freedom. In Alexis's case, one can argue that her status as an employee who is acting under orders from her superiors causes her freedom of action to be considerably less than if she were in charge. No doubt this is true; the degree of her moral responsibility surely is not as great as it would be if she had more power over the firm's decisions. Is her freedom of action curtailed so much, however, that she has no moral duty at all? Certainly not—otherwise a person in a subordinate position could be morally answerable for his conduct only if he initiated and controlled the situation. In such a case, of course, either he would be acting outside his authority or else he really would not be acting as a subordinate at all. Completely relieving all subordinates of moral responsibility for their actions within the organization's chain of command has the potential to lower substantially the level of moral behavior within organizations and throughout society. Thus, Alexis should continue to have a moral duty of honesty with respect to her complicity in the firm's possible wrongdoing, although the strength of her obligation may be somewhat less than in other situations where she is not playing a subordinate role.

Conflict Reduction

Are there ways to minimize conflicts? As in this case, a *prima facie* moral duty usually is not eliminated by an excusing condition. Most of the time there either is no such condition or else the condition merely curtails the strength of a duty rather than doing away with it entirely. Thus, any moral dilemma that we previously identified still exists. Before getting to the point of having to make an all-or-nothing choice between conflicting duties, however, we should search for creative solutions that may diminish or remove the conflict.

Alexis might consider requesting reassignment within the firm, perhaps to another geographic location, so as to remove her from any direct role in the questionable activity. Reassignment may not be feasible, and even if it is feasible it may damage her future opportunities in the firm. Moreover, if the attitude of her current superiors is found throughout the organization, she may encounter similar problems in her new position. Assuming that she finds a higher level of ethical standards at her new location, Alexis still *knows* about the possible dishonesty at her previous one. If she remains silent about it, is she guilty of complicity in the questionable behavior even though she is no longer a participant? Many people would say yes. If we take the view that the duty of loyalty to her employer continues to exist, Alexis still owes the same basic duty because she has remained in the same organization. One can see that removing ourselves from direct involvement does not

always eliminate a moral dilemma, although this course of action may reduce the acuteness of the conflict. There remain other options for Alexis, which we will not pursue here.

In other situations, creative ideas for minimizing the degree of conflict between obligations will take other forms. For example, in some cases a person caught in a moral dilemma might be able to work out agreements with one or more of the parties to whom duties are owed so that the duties no longer conflict and all can be fulfilled. If we cannot make agreements that enable us to fulfill all moral duties, it may be possible to work out compromises that permit us to comply fully with one and partially with another. Such opportunities will not always exist, but it is important to give careful consideration to the possibilities.

Prioritizing

When we cannot eliminate a moral dilemma, we must choose between the obligations that we will attempt to satisfy. The choice should be made only after carefully weighing the strength and importance of the conflicting duties. In other words, we must prioritize the obligations. We already may have gone a long way toward weighing and prioritizing our duties as we considered whether excusing conditions were present and sought creative ways to minimize the conflict. We may have found that excusing conditions reduce the significance of one moral duty with respect to another. Similarly, we may have worked out agreements or discovered alternative courses of action that strengthen or weaken different obligations and, consequently, make our choice easier.

If the relative importance of particular obligations, and thus their proper place on our list of priorities, still remains unclear, we should next attempt to evaluate the *harm* that may result from violating the various moral duties. A careful evaluation of harm will take into account both *degree* and *probability*. Other factors being equal, the relative importance of a moral obligation increases proportionately with increases in (1) the degree of harm that is likely to be caused by violating the obligation and (2) the probability (or likelihood) that the harm actually will occur.

In the case of Alexis, for instance, the harm done to taxpayers by this instance of expense overstatement, or even by all similar actions by her employer's clients, is probably pretty small in relative terms. On the other hand, we should also consider cumulative effects. When one tax cheater is reported and gets caught, other cheaters may change their behavior. Thus the harm to taxpayers caused by her firm's conduct, and the harm that may be prevented by her reporting it, could be a lot greater than one might think. With regard to probability, the harm caused by even a single instance of cheating is certain to occur even if it is very small.

The potential harm that Alexis's silence may cause to her profession apparently has a very low probability of occurrence. This harm will occur only if real tax cheating actually happened, she gets into trouble for going along with it, and the profession receives bad publicity as a result. This harm not only has a low probability of occurring, but if limited to this one event, it will also be relatively minor. Again, however, we should consider whether there may be cumulative harmful effects.

If Alexis reports the expense overstatements to the IRS, there is no doubt that short-term harm will be caused to both her employer and Leviathan, especially if the overstatements are found to have been intentional. They will incur penalties, and perhaps substantial legal fees and court costs. These harms appear to be high in both degree and probability. In addition, the accounting firm and Leviathan may suffer long-term harm in the form of damaged company reputations and the various costs associated with an increased level of future oversight by the IRS. This kind of harm probably is somewhat less certain to occur, but if it does occur it could be even more substantial than the short-term damage. At the same time, we must not overlook the possibility that, if Alexis's firm and Leviathan are reported and get into legal trouble now, this event could lead them to clean up their general level of ethical behavior. Arguably, more ethical behavior in the future will reduce their chances of encountering costly legal problems. This leads us to the question of whether ethical behavior produces economic benefit to the ethical company or person. "Does ethics pay?" is an exceedingly difficult and complicated question. We will discuss it later, although we will not even pretend to answer it.

Finally, we need much more information before evaluating the degree or probability of harm that might be caused to others if Alexis loses her job after "blowing the whistle." How likely is it that she will actually lose her job? If she gets fired, how likely is it that she will be able to recover damages from her former employer in a lawsuit claiming the tort of wrongful discharge? Will she have a difficult time finding comparable employment? Do others depend on her for support?

Making a Moral Decision

Ultimately Alexis must make a decision that reflects a choice. Even inaction is a choice. There may be no choice that is totally satisfactory, and there almost certainly will not be one that is completely free of doubt or negative consequences. Whatever course she takes, her choice should be the *conscious* result of a rational process similar to the one we have described.

It is true that quick decisions sometimes have to be made. If so, we may not have the luxury to gather as much information or reflect on our choices as much as we would like. There is almost always *some* time, however, for reflection and rational thinking. When emotionally charged ethical questions arise, we are far more likely to work them out through a rational analytical process if we have already anticipated and carefully thought about general problems of this nature. This is especially true when decisions have to be made under pressure and in relatively short periods of time. If we have not already practiced rational thinking about ethical issues in our actual experiences, we should at least have taken the time to examine our own values and to think about how we would deal with particular moral questions should they arise. Without some preparation, we run a much greater risk of making rash responses under pressure.

It is true that decisions, moral or otherwise, may turn out all right even if not preceded by sound analytical reasoning. Such a result probably represents simple good fortune more than anything else. Conversely, rational thinking does not guarantee optimal results. Although carrying no guarantees, such a process can have the following benefits:

1. It increases our chances of having better and more complete information on which to base a decision.

2. It lowers the risk of completely overlooking an important issue.

3. It improves our chances of making a decision that best balances the various conflicting interests that may be present.

4. If we are later called upon to defend our decision, we will be better prepared to do so. Difficult

decisions that affect others are often challenged, and a decision resulting from the type of process described here is more defensible. We have our facts straighter, and our reasons for making particular choices can be presented more clearly and forcefully because they have been thought through carefully. In addition, we are able to demonstrate a good faith effort to do the right thing. Evidence of good faith is no small matter, and often can make the difference when close judgment calls are at issue.

ARE CORPORATIONS MORAL AGENTS?

There is nearly unanimous agreement that individuals are morally responsible for their actions within business organizations. Managers and employees in corporations, like other individuals in other settings, have moral obligations. These obligations can never be erased by joining anything, be it a club, fraternity, political party, or business organization. We do not,

or at least should not, leave our values at the door when we enter the workplace.

There is less consensus, however, about whether a corporation itself can owe moral obligations independent of the individuals within the organization. A corporation is recognized as a **legal entity** that is capable of owning property, making contracts, being a party to legal proceedings, and so on. It can act, however, only through human beings. Thus, is a corporation a **moral agent** in addition to being a legal entity?

Does It Make Any Difference?

Before examining this question, it is legitimate to ask, "So what?" Does it make any difference? It is no doubt true that in many cases, we can resolve relevant moral questions in business by focusing only on the moral duties of particular individuals within the company. There are situations, however, in which it is impossible to trace decisions or actions to any

---

ETHICS AT WORK

Legal Focus
ETHICS

Secret taping, an activity brimming with ethical and legal questions, has become increasingly common in the work place. Suppose an employee believes that his or her supervisor is "out to get" the employee for reasons that are unjust and possibly illegal. More and more frequently, the response of an employee in such a situation is secretly to tape conversations with the superior. Managers and company lawyers generally view such secret taping as dishonest and disloyal. Even many plaintiffs' lawyers say that the idea of secret taping makes them very uncomfortable. On the other hand, if the supervisor is actually treating the employee in a way that is at least unethical and perhaps illegal, the employee may have no other way to prove

it. It is undoubtedly unethical for an employee to engage in secret taping when the employee has no good reason to believe that the supervisor is acting wrongly. However, if the employee does have good reason to believe that the supervisor is in the process of trying to get rid of the employee for wrongful reasons, such as age, race, or sex discrimination, does the employee have an adequate moral excuse for secret taping? The ethical problem obviously is a difficult one; if there is an "answer" to the question, it depends very much on the particular facts of the case and demands thorough analysis.

From a legal perspective, federal law permits the secret taping of conversations so long as *one* party knows about the taping. Almost one-third of the states have similar legislation. Thus, an employee's secret taping does not violate federal law or the law of

these states. Another group of states, again almost one-third, has laws prohibiting taping unless both parties to the conversation know about it. More than one-third of the states have no relevant legislation. If a fired employee files a lawsuit and has a secret tape that reveals evidence of illegal conduct by the supervisor, the tape certainly will be admissible evidence in the courts of states where such taping is expressly legal. It also is probably admissible in the courts of those states where there is no legislation on the subject of secret taping, and probably in federal courts if the employee is claiming a violation of a federal law such as the 1964 Civil Rights Act prohibition against race or sex discrimination. It is still unclear, however, whether such a tape will be admissible evidence in the courts of a state where the taping is expressly illegal.

given individual. So the question about corporate moral status is not a purely abstract one. Even if we recognize the question as being a real one, does the answer to it have any impact? Suppose that we conclude that corporations themselves do have moral responsibilities. If a particular corporation's actions do not violate the *law*, however, are there any meaningful consequences of a conclusion that it has "acted unethically"?

We think there can be meaningful consequences. The consequences are not nearly as obvious or immediate as they may be when the law is violated, but they are there. The behavior of corporations is a frequent subject of discussion in the media, legislatures, regulatory agencies, classrooms, living rooms, and elsewhere. If there is a general perception in society that corporations are morally accountable for their actions, this perception will have an impact on the public debate over corporate behavior. It can alter the basic structure and direction of the debate, as well as the effect this debate has on people's attitudes about corporations. Feelings that a particular corporation, as an independent moral agent, has acted unethically can affect consumers' buying decisions. Similar feelings about an entire industry, or about corporations in general, can affect the decisions of legislatures and regulatory agencies as to the need for regulation. On the other hand, a company, industry, or the business community in general is much more likely to receive the benefit of the doubt in many different ways when there are no generally negative perceptions about its ethical standards.

The View That Corporations Are Not Moral Agents

The most widely advanced view that corporations cannot have moral obligations is that of philosopher John Ladd, who regards corporations as purely formal organizations analogous to programmable robots or machines.[2] Machines have neither a will nor any freedom of action. Similarly, according to Ladd, a corporation is merely an aggregation of legally binding documents such as a state charter and the corporate bylaws, organizational charts, operating procedures, and customs. The human cogs in this machine are role-players. Moreover, they are replaceable and often virtually interchangeable. Rule-governed activi-

ties and impersonal operating procedures prevent the application, or even the hint, of moral responsibility. Support for Ladd's view may be found, among other places, in Chief Justice John Marshall's description of a corporation in the famous *Dartmouth College* case:

> A corporation is an artificial being, invisible, intangible, and existing only in contemplation of law. Being the mere creature of law, it possesses only those properties which the charter of creation confers upon it, either expressly, or as incidental to its very existence. These are such as are supposed best calculated to effect the object for which it was created.[3]

The fact that corporations are mere "artificial being(s)," or "creature(s) of law," does seem to support the argument that corporations cannot be moral agents with separate moral obligations. The lifeless pieces of paper that bring the corporation into existence and provide governing rules for its operation do not provide it with autonomy or reason. Therefore, we must look elsewhere for support if we are to argue that corporations are moral agents.

The View That Corporations Do Have Moral Responsibilities

We mentioned that violations of moral obligations frequently cannot be traced to a particular individual within a corporation. As a rule, most actions and inactions of relatively large corporations cannot be tallied as the sum of individual actions—the whole is truly greater than the sum of its parts. As a result, individuals tend to escape moral accountability. This fact, in itself, provides considerable support for the argument that corporations should be viewed as separate moral agents.

Organization theory explains this phenomenon in terms of **group dynamics.** Groups often behave very differently than any member would have behaved, because the dynamics of the group transcend individual reason and autonomy. People sometimes just get "caught up in the spirit of things." Examples range all the way from the lynch mob to a corporate board that makes an ethically questionable decision despite the fact that each of its individual members has high personal moral standards. We find the phenomenon not only in groups of co-equal members, but also in chains of command. For example, managers at the top may set policies and give orders but

---

[2]John Ladd, "Morality and the Ideal of Rationality in Formal Organizations," *Monist* 54 (1970): 488–516.

[3]4 Wheat. (17 U.S.) 518 (1819).

deny any responsibility for conduct by their subordinates that they did not intend. Similarly, we often find those at the bottom denying responsibility because they did not make the policy and they themselves intended no harm; they were "just carrying out orders." Several complex factors seem to be responsible for the peculiarities of group dynamics in corporations:

1. Because the action is motivated by corporate purposes rather than personal reasons, participating individuals may not view their conduct as really their own. If they do not associate the action with themselves as human beings, they are not as likely to apply their own personal moral standards to it.

2. A member of a group may feel that there is "safety in numbers." As the number of individual participants in group action increases, each member's feeling of *anonymity* may also increase. Even if a person does recognize and feel somewhat responsible for the moral consequences of his group's proposed action, he nevertheless may go along with a plan because he doubts that he personally will ever be called upon to defend it.

3. Formal lines of authority and accountability within the organization may be fuzzy, thus increasing the chances that no single person really feels responsible. When people do not *feel* responsible, they are less likely to *act* responsibly.

4. Communication among individuals within the decision-making group may be less than perfect, and thus different individuals or subgroups may be acting on the basis of somewhat different facts and assumptions. One individual or subgroup within the organization may not be completely aware of the total picture, leading to the classic situation of the "right hand not knowing what the left hand is doing."

5. Peer pressure can cause a member of a group to be fearful of speaking up when he sees something wrong with the group's proposed action. Many of us do not want to be perceived as "different" or as a "prude." Peer pressure can produce some really strange results. One example is found in the actions preceding the so-called "Watergate cover-up" that ultimately led to President Nixon's resignation in 1974. Later interviews with the participants revealed that, when a group of Nixon's associates was planning to burglarize and plant microphones in Democratic Party headquarters in Washington, D.C.'s Watergate Hotel in the early 1970s, all of the major participants thought it was a dangerous, stupid thing to do. No one voiced this opinion at the time, however; each person thought that the others viewed the break-in as a good idea and no one wanted to risk being tagged as "not a team player." Similar things can happen in business when advertising campaigns, joint ventures, capital restructurings, mergers, new products, research and development programs, personnel policies, and countless other actions are being planned.

On balance, we believe that the arguments in favor of treating corporations as separate moral agents are stronger than those to the contrary. This conclusion is based upon three facts: (1) corporations can act only through the individuals they employ; (2) group dynamics is a reality, and often produces behavior very different than would have occurred had any individual in the group acted alone; and (3) it is frequently impossible to trace ethical failings to an individual in the organization and, consequently, there is no place to attach moral blame if we cannot attach it to the corporation.

DOES ETHICS PAY?

Earlier we alluded to the question of whether ethical behavior by a corporation and the people within it actually produces economic benefit for the company. Ethical behavior ought to be our ideal regardless of the economic consequences. A corporation is, however, created for the primary purpose of operating a business profitably and providing a sufficient return on the shareholders' investment to justify their continuation of that investment. So the question about economic consequences of ethical behavior is a legitimate one.

"Does ethics pay?" is a complex question that is exceptionally difficult to answer. Although there can be no doubt that ethics does pay in some ways some of the time, there is no clear-cut answer that covers all situations. In trying to work toward a general answer, we find a few relevant facts that are based on fairly concrete evidence, but we must rely on intuition and even speculation for many others.

Several possible economic benefits of ethical behavior seem likely to occur, although they are of a long-term nature and are incapable of being measured with any precision. The following are some of these possible economic benefits.

1. It seems almost certain that the maintenance of high ethical standards in a company creates an environment in which very costly violations of the law are less likely to occur.

2. As mentioned earlier, such standards also may reduce the likelihood of new government regulations that are costly to comply with. Although this potential benefit is rather speculative, we do have evidence that *bad* ethical behavior can produce *more* regulation. The Foreign Corrupt Practices Act, for example, was passed by Congress primarily in response to revelations about widespread bribery by American companies in overseas transactions.

3. It also seems reasonable to assume that a high moral tone within a company will have a positive impact on employee morale and productivity. Intuitively, it would seem that, at least for most people, working in a company that observes and requires high ethical standards will be a much more pleasant experience than working in one with low standards. Employees and managers should experience less "cognitive dissonance," a disquieting and disruptive mental state caused by conflicting beliefs. Such a state can be created, for instance, when a manager or employee believes strongly that he should be loyal to the company, obey superiors, and work hard in pursuit of the company's interests, but where prevailing moral attitudes in the company are contrary to his personal moral standards. Since happier employees usually are more productive, the company should be more productive.

4. High ethical standards are likely to generate good will with suppliers and customers. The good reputation that results from ethical behavior does not substitute for quality products, good service, and competitive prices, but it can produce many intangible benefits over time. It makes it possible, for example, to develop long-lasting business relationships based on trust. These kinds of relationships are more economically efficient than those that are based solely on lengthy legal documents, legal threats, and keeping a close watch on the other party.

Balanced against these possible economic benefits is the fact that ethical behavior can sometimes be costly, and when these costs occur they are likely to be direct, immediate, and measurable. For example, it may be quite expensive to install better pollution control equipment than the law requires because of a strong moral commitment to those who drink the water and breathe the air. Competitors may not do the same thing, and their lower costs may enable them to undersell us. Or a company may lose business in the short term because it refuses to pay a bribe or kickback. And, unfortunately, an honest company can lose a business deal to a competitor who misrepresents the facts.

It takes a long-term view to properly assess the economic impact of ethical behavior. Whenever possible, of course, business firms should approach problems with a long-term perspective regardless of whether ethical questions are involved. We believe that the long-term economic benefits of high corporate ethical standards outweigh the more direct short-term economic benefits that low ethical standards sometimes produce. We cannot prove it, however. Studies indicate that very profitable companies *are* more likely to exhibit high standards of ethical behavior than less profitable ones. Although these studies may lend support to the argument that ethics pays, the results could also be interpreted as simply indicating that companies behave more ethically when they can *afford* to do so. Although we can engage in reasonable speculation that ethics pays, we are unable to prove that companies can become more profitable by behaving ethically.

CORPORATE SOCIAL RESPONSIVENESS

If a person accepts the notion that corporations are moral agents and thus owe separate moral obligations, another question arises. Is it appropriate for a corporation to go beyond the moral minimum and correct problems it did not cause? Should a corporation expend corporate resources "doing good" by meeting societal needs? Such actions are sometimes described by the phrase "corporate social responsibility," but "responsiveness" describes the idea better than "responsibility." Going further, if it is *appropriate* for a corporation to do these kinds of things, is there actually an *obligation* to do them?

We first must recognize that questions about **corporate social responsiveness** do not necessarily arise every time a corporation's management considers spending corporate funds for a socially worthwhile cause such as helping a local elementary school offer enrichment programs for gifted students. Voluntarily responding to community needs often can be justified solely on economic grounds. Such actions can provide excellent promotional opportunities for the company and enhance its reputation and goodwill in a variety of ways. Also, improving the local community may improve the company's workforce and even its property values. Essentially, social responsiveness can provide some of the same economic benefits to a corporation that we mentioned earlier in our discussion of whether complying with the moral minimum can produce such benefits. Any attempt to justify socially responsive behavior on economic grounds must focus on long-term rather than short-term benefits, because the kind of benefit derived from such behavior is necessarily indirect and imprecise. Also, we should not put any less value on a corporation's voluntary contribution to society just because management was motivated by the company's self-interest. Indeed, the motives of the managers may have been very complex and indeterminate.

Our main question here, however, is how to deal with the question on moral grounds. Is socially responsive conduct appropriate regardless of whether it pays, and are there any circumstances in which it is morally required?

The Agents of Capital View

One of the most well-known proponents of the view that corporations do not owe a moral duty to be socially responsive is Milton Friedman, a Nobel laureate in economics and an influential spokesman on the role of corporations in society. To begin with, Friedman does not view corporations as moral agents; only managers and employees as individuals have moral status. In addition, he contends that there is no obligation to spend corporate resources correcting problems the company did not cause and, going even further, he asserts that it is not even *appropriate* for the company's managers to do so. They are **agents of capital,** that is, agents of the shareholders who own the corporation and provide its capital. As such, their only duty is to earn as much money as possible for the shareholders, within the limits of the law and customary ethical practices.

Unless specially approved by shareholder resolution, decisions concerning the use of corporate resources to do good necessarily are made by individual managers. According to Friedman, it is completely inappropriate for them to do so. Corporate managers are free to devote their own time and money to whatever pursuits they deem morally or socially appropriate, but when they divert corporate resources to such

projects they breach their duty of loyalty to shareholders. Friedman finds the social responsiveness movement to be a "fundamentally subversive doctrine" that resembles theft—managers are using "someone else's money." The proper function of government is to attend to matters of the common good and social welfare. Corporate managers are not, by training or otherwise, equipped to do that, and even if they were, it would be intolerable in a democracy for unelected, unaccountable "civil servants" to be charged with the responsibility. While government might be slow and unresponsive in addressing current social problems, the insistence that this gap be filled by corporate action is just an acknowledgment of defeat by proponents of corporate social responsiveness who "have failed to persuade a majority of their fellow citizens to be of like mind and [who] are seeking to attain by undemocratic procedures what they cannot attain by democratic procedures."[4]

Another argument along the same lines is that when a social or religious organization or a government agency attempts to meet the needs of society, it usually does so with resources that were placed under the organization's control because of the merits of its social objectives. For example, grants from the American Cancer Society to researchers seeking a cure for cancer are made from funds that were donated to the Society because of the knowledge that the money would be used to fight the disease. Because of scarce resources, there is a "competition among good causes." Although it is unfortunate that all such needs cannot be fully met, this competition provides a method for roughly measuring the relative importance and value to the public of particular social needs. This prioritizing of needs by the marketplace is a very imperfect process that will always leave worthy needs unsatisfied. It does, however, introduce some necessary utilitarianism into the allocation of resources by reducing the chances that too much will go to causes that benefit too few. On the other hand, resources come into a corporation solely because of its business success, unless shareholders invest with the explicit understanding that certain corporate moneys will be spent on identified good causes. Thus, when managers use corporate funds to do good, the needs they meet have not withstood the test of this "market for donated funds."

[4]*New York Times*, Sept. 12, 1962, sect. 6, 122.

The Agents of Society View

There are those who argue that it is both appropriate and morally obligatory for corporations to contribute to the correction of problems they did not cause. They place this duty on the corporation as a moral agent, as well as on managers whose individual and group decisions energize the company. In a speech to the Harvard Business School in 1969, Henry Ford II stated: "The terms of the contract between industry and society are changing. . . . Now we are being asked to serve a wider range of human values and to accept an obligation to members of the public with whom we have no commercial transactions."[5] His words were foreshadowed by those of his grandfather some two generations earlier. "For a long time people believed that the only purpose of industry is to make a profit. They were wrong. Its purpose is to serve the general welfare."[6]

This notion of a "social contract" forms the foundation for many of the arguments that corporate social responsiveness is morally required. Under this view, a corporation is the result of a contract between those forming the corporation and the society that permits its creation. Thus, the corporation has a contract-like obligation to contribute positively to society, and the corporation's managers are not just agents of the shareholders but are also **agents of society.** One noted proponent of this view, philosopher Thomas Donaldson, hypothesized the existence of a society in which individuals always work and produce alone, and never in corporate form. A society such as this, composed of rational persons, would permit the legal creation of corporations only if the benefits to the public are great enough to justify the privileges granted to corporations and to outweigh the potential drawbacks. The privileges include limited liability—only the corporate entity and its assets are liable for corporate debts, not the individual shareholders or managers. This limited liability can come at a cost to other members of society. One potential drawback is that permitting corporations to exist generally leads to much larger aggregations of resources being under the effective control of a smaller number of people. Large resource accumulations in corporations can bring both economic and political power that few, if any, individuals could ever match. Such power can create risks for society.

Supporters of the agents of society view also would use the same basic line of reasoning that one would use to argue that *individuals* have a moral obligation to do good. These arguments were discussed earlier in the chapter. Similarly, for those wishing to build a rational argument in favor of morally required corporate social responsiveness, the same limits that were applied to the individual's obligation to do good would apply to the corporation's duty to be socially responsive.

SUMMARY

In this chapter, we have shown, first, that business, like other human endeavors, is to be evaluated by the same moral standards that are applied throughout our society, and that these moral standards depend on the exercise of free will. Next, we explored the law–ethics relationship, including the differences and similarities between legal and moral standards. Our next step was to question whether there are any fundamental moral standards that are generally accepted across circumstances, cultures, and time. Using the rational human thought process as a foundation, we sought to determine whether there are any basic moral obligations that do not need to be defended by a rational person. From this perspective, we identified four obligations that we referred to as the "moral minimum": honesty, loyalty, keeping commitments, and doing no harm. Our discussion then turned to the question of whether there is anything resembling the moral minimum for "doing good," i.e., is there ever a basic moral obligation to take positive steps to correct harms and meet needs that we had no part in causing? In situations in which some basic moral obligation has possibly been violated, are there any "excusing conditions," and if so, what are their limits? In addition to dealing with this question, we also explored how a rational person should approach "moral dilemmas," i.e., situations in which moral obligations come into conflict.

The chapter then devoted considerable attention to the process of rationally analyzing ethical issues. Two major points made at the outset were that even emotionally charged issues like ethical ones can be analyzed in a rational way, and that this form of reasoning is essentially the same as rational problem solving or decision making in other situations. Next, we looked at the question of whether corporations can be held morally accountable, or whether the

[5]Thomas Donaldson, *Corporations and Morality* (Englewood Cliffs, N.J.: Prentice-Hall, Inc., 1982), 36.
[6]Ibid.

individuals within the firm are the only ones capable of having moral duties. In this regard, we discussed whether the concept makes any real difference, and concluded that it did. We then examined both sides of the issue, and expressed the view that the phenomenon of group dynamics strongly supports an argument that corporations are indeed "moral agents." We explored the difficult and complex question, "Does ethics pay?" without pretending to answer it in any definite way. Finally, we outlined the issues in the "corporate social responsiveness" debate; in other words, is it either appropriate or obligatory for managers to spend corporate funds "doing good"?

KEY TERMS

Ethics
Morality
Utilitarianism
Moral minimum
Honesty
Loyalty
Keeping commitments
Doing no harm
Excusing conditions
Moral dilemmas
Legal entity
Moral agent
Group dynamics
Corporate social responsiveness
Agents of capital
Agents of society

QUESTIONS AND PROBLEMS

1. Robinson and Walters made an oral agreement for Walters to sell five acres of land to Robinson for $138,000. Walters definitely promised to sell and Robinson definitely promised to buy. Robinson wanted the land very badly so that he could build a home for his family in a place that provided them with a lot of space but was still relatively close to the city. Robinson felt that he had gotten a good price. Robinson made a down payment of $6,900. After they made the agreement Robinson prepared a brief written memorandum stating the basic terms of the deal. He signed it and gave a copy to Walters, but Walters never signed. Robinson paid an architect to draw plans for a new home. About this time, however, Walters called Robinson and said he had

changed his mind and no longer wished to sell. Walters wanted to hold on to the land for another couple of years because he thought its value would increase substantially. Robinson was terribly upset, but Walters refused to speak with him any further about the matter. Robinson filed a lawsuit claiming breach of contract. Robinson lost in court, however. In most cases, an agreement for the sale of land is legally enforceable only if it is evidenced by a written document that is signed by the defendant and contains the agreement's essential terms, including an adequate legal description of the land. The memorandum Robinson had prepared was not sufficient for this purpose, because Walters had not signed it and there was not an adequate legal description of the property. Compare the applicable legal rules with any relevant moral standards. Are they different? If so, how are they different, and what are some likely reasons for the difference? Do the reasons make sense?

2. Sally worked as a state government relations specialist for Amalgamated Industries, a large and diversified corporation with operations in many states. She maintained contacts with members of state legislatures and their staffs, as well as with personnel in state regulatory agencies. Her job was to keep top management apprised of proposed legislation and regulations that might affect the company, and to put forth the company's positions on such proposals. The job required her to travel a great deal. Her company reimbursed her for all reasonable business-related travel expenses for which she had receipts. After she had been in the position for a few months, she discovered that many hotels did various things for certain business guests whose jobs would probably bring them to that city on a regular basis. At some hotels, for example, a business guest that the hotel hoped would become a "regular" would be given $20 or $30 cash as a "discount" on the room rate. The written receipt from the hotel, which the guest would submit to his or her employer for reimbursement, did not reflect this discount. What should Sally do if she is offered money in this way? Analyze any ethical questions that are raised by these facts.

3. Frenzoil Corporation is an American oil and gas company engaging in exploration, drilling, production, refining, and wholesale distribution. In addition to doing its own refining and distribution, it also sells crude oil to other refiners, especially smaller ones. One of its tanker ships was carrying a shipment of crude oil to a customer in an African coastal

nation. The three-million-gallon shipment was worth $1.5 million and had to be delivered by March 29 in order to fulfill Frenzoil's commitment to its customer. The customer had to have the oil by this date so that it could meet commitments to its own customers for refined petroleum products. When Frenzoil's captain neared the port at his destination on March 28, he sought permission from the harbor master to dock and unload. The harbor master told the captain that many tankers and other ships were in the harbor and a lot of others were nearby awaiting entry. It would be very difficult for Frenzoil's tanker to dock and unload for at least the next two weeks, the harbor master said, "unless other arrangements were made." He said that one of his assistants would come aboard the tanker and talk to the captain about such arrangements. When the assistant arrived at the tanker, the captain found out that the "arrangements" included substantial bribes to the harbor master and several other officials. If these arrangements were made, the tanker could dock and unload ahead of the many other ships that were waiting. Many of these other ships were operated by companies that were much smaller than Frenzoil, and which could not afford to pay a bribe of this size. The captain radioed his boss at Frenzoil, who took the matter to the company's management and attorneys. They concluded that, even though such bribes might violate federal law— the Foreign Corrupt Practices Act—the chances of the violation being detected were quite small. Some of Frenzoil's managers, however, were still bothered by the ethical implications of paying the bribes. Analyze these implications.

4. Tom Sayles worked as a deck hand on a merchant vessel, the *H.M.S. North Star.* While carrying cargo in the Atlantic Ocean near the north Florida coast, Tom's boss told him to dump the ship's bilge into the sea. The bilge of a ship is the place where foul water containing various wastes collects. At each port there are facilities for pumping out bilges for proper treatment and disposal of the wastes. Tom thought he remembered seeing a U.S. Coast Guard regulation prohibiting bilge-dumping in U.S. territorial waters. Even if the practice does not violate a legal regulation, Tom concluded, it obviously damages the environment. What should Tom do? Analyze the moral issues in this situation.

5. Judith Watson worked for Merritt Flynch & Co., a large New York securities firm with underwriting, brokerage, and investment advising operations throughout the United States and the world. Merritt had branches in many foreign countries. Although serving a stint at one of the foreign offices was not an absolute requirement for advancement, everyone understood that successfully handling a foreign assignment was viewed by top management as very important. Employees who aspired to be on the "fast track" for promotion through the ranks of management almost always had a foreign assignment relatively early in their careers. During her fours years at Merritt, Judith had received two significant promotions. Her work had been universally praised by her superiors, who viewed her as having tremendous potential for advancement into top management.

She was offered a position at the firm's office in Naphtali, an east Asian nation. This was considered a "plum" assignment, successful completion of which could mean a great deal to a person's career. Judith accepted the assignment and began work. She soon found, however, that the business culture in Naphtali was much different than in the United States. Women were generally not well accepted in management positions in that culture. Her immediate superior in the bank's Naphtali office, Dan Moseley, gave Judith much responsibility and always treated her as a co-equal professional, except when they were in the presence of Naphtali clients. In these situations, he referred to her as his "little helper," or his "lovely assistant." Viewed in this way, Merritt's clients felt comfortable dealing with her. On one occasion during discussions with Naphtali clients, Dan treated her as a manager with significant responsibility, and the clients became very uncomfortable, silent, and cold. The deal did not go through, and in all future situations Dan treated and referred to her in ways that made clients comfortable but that infuriated Judith. She discussed the situation with him, and he was very sympathetic and understanding but said he just could not see any other way to handle it. After feeling humiliated a few more times, Judith spoke with Dan's boss, who headed the Naphtali office. He responded in about the same way that Dan had. After continuing in these circumstances for several more months, Judith became irritable and uncooperative, and her performance suffered. The ratings she received on her quarterly performance reviews declined. She really did not know what to do. Analyze the ethical implications of this situation.

PART II

PRINCIPLES OF CONTRACT LAW

ART II IS DEVOTED entirely to the subject of contract law. Here we will be primarily focusing on the basic rules that make up this subject—an approach that is somewhat more traditional than the one taken in Part I. However, to preserve an analytical flavor to our treatment of the subject, the reasons underlying the rules are also given substantial attention.

Chapter 11 presents a brief description of the major classes of contracts recognized by the law. This presentation not only creates an awareness of the diversity of the subject, but also permits an identification of the conceptual principles applicable to all kinds of contracts.

Chapters 12 through 14 are devoted to the heart of contract law—examination of the basic elements that must generally be present in order for an agreement to rise to the level of an enforceable contract. In these chapters, then, we will examine the judicially imposed requirements applicable to the *agreement* (offer and acceptance); *consideration*; and the requirement of a *lawful objective*.

The next chapters deal with somewhat tangential matters, but ones of great significance in those situations where they apply. Thus Chapter 15 explores the circumstances in which the courts may free a person from his or her contractual obligations on the ground of minority, or upon proof of fraud, duress, or mistake of fact. Chapter 16 examines those kinds of contracts that are generally required by law to be in writing, and the rights of third parties are discussed in Chapter 17.

Chapter 18 is largely concerned with two subjects—performance and excuses for nonperformance. The first covers the level of performance that the law requires of a contracting party, whereas the second sets forth the circumstances in which a party may be legally freed of his or her contractual duties even in the absence of fraud, duress, or mistake of fact.

Chapter 19, the concluding chapter of Part II, discusses two important matters: (1) the rules of contractual interpretation that courts use to determine the intent of the parties at the time they entered into the contract, and (2) remedies that are available to parties injured when the promises they have received are not performed.

Throughout Part II, the focus is on the common law of contracts, which governs, for example, contracts dealing with services and land. However, substantial attention will necessarily be given to sales law, which governs contracts dealing with tangible goods. Even though sales law as codified in the Uniform Commercial Code is treated separately in Chapters 20 through 23 of Part III, its interrelationship with the common law of contracts is so complete that neither subject can be treated on its own. ⚖

A Perspective

Nature of a Contract

Classification of Contracts

*Contract Law and Sales Law—
A Special Relationship*

A PERSPECTIVE

In the preceding chapters we took a sweeping look at the aspects of our legal system that are common to all branches of law: the sources of our legal rules, the primary law-making processes, and the manner in which the rules of law are generally implemented by the courts. It is now time to move from the *environmental* approach to more *traditional*, i.e., rule-oriented, areas of the law. The various branches of law that directly control all the legal aspects of business transactions—such as contracts, sales, and corporate dealings—are composed primarily of substantive legal rules.

Contract Law—Special Characteristics

Contract law, which is the subject of Part II, possesses several characteristics that make it the natural starting point for an examination of the other commercial law subjects. First, there is its pervasiveness in the average person's everyday activities. When a person buys a newspaper, leaves a car at a parking lot, or buys a ticket to a football game, a contract of some sort has been entered into. When someone borrows money, or hires someone to paint a house, or insures a car, a contract has again been made. And businesses—whether corner stores or large multinational corporations—must buy or lease office equipment, make agreements with employees, secure heat and light, buy materials from suppliers, and sell their goods and services to customers. All these transactions involve contracts.

Second, the basic principles of contract law are the underpinning of the more specialized business-related subjects, including sales and commercial paper, partnership and corporation law, and other areas.

Third, since the subject of contracts is essentially common-law in nature, the controversies that are presented usually require the courts to examine earlier decisions handed down in cases involving similar fact-patterns. Thus, the doctrine of *stare decisis* is illuminated; and an allied question—whether today's conditions have so changed as to justify a repudiation of earlier decisions—affords an opportunity to analyze more fully the process of judicial reasoning.

NATURE OF A CONTRACT

A contract is a special sort of agreement—one that the law will enforce in some manner in the event that one party does not perform its promise. As will be seen in the next chapter, some agreements are not enforceable because their terms are too indefinite, or they are entered into in jest, or they involve obligations that are essentially social in nature (such as a date to go to a concert). Even seriously intended, definite business agreements, however, are generally not enforceable unless three additional elements are present—what the courts refer to as consideration, capacity, and legality. These concepts will be explored in later chapters also. Indeed, a comprehensive definition of *contract* cannot be attempted until these four elements have been examined in some detail. But for the limited purpose of this chapter, *a contract is an agreement that a court will enforce.*[1]

CLASSIFICATION OF CONTRACTS

Contracts have many facets and, consequently, may be categorized in a variety of ways. Different aspects may be important in different contexts. In one case it may be important that the contract is "bilateral" rather than "unilateral." The outcome of another case may turn on whether the contract is "voidable" rather than "void." An important purpose of this chapter is to introduce the various categories of contracts.

Bilateral and Unilateral Contracts

Most contracts consist of the exchange of mutual promises, the actual performance of which is to occur at some later time. When a manufacturer enters into a contract in May with a supplier, calling for the supplier to deliver 10,000 steel wheels during September at a specified price, each party has promised the other to perform one or more acts at a subsequent time. Such contracts, consisting of "a promise for a promise," are **bilateral contracts.**

---

[1] A more technical definition is the following: "A contract is a promise or set of promises for the breach of which the law gives a remedy, or the performance of which the law in some way recognizes as a duty." *Restatement, Contracts 2d,* §1, The American Law Institute, 1979.

The same terminology applies to offers (proposals) that precede the making of a contract. If the terms of an offer indicate that all the offeror wants at the present time from the offeree is a return promise—rather than the immediate performance of an act—then the proposal can be called a **bilateral offer.**[2] Thus, if a professional football club sends a contract to one of its players in June, offering him $800,000 for the coming season, it is clear that all the club presently wants is the player's promise to render his services at a later time. Such an offer is bilateral; and if the player accepts it by signing and returning the contract, a bilateral contract has been formed.

Some offers, called **unilateral offers,** are phrased in such a way that they can be accepted only by the performance of a particular act. An example of such an offer would be the promise by a TV station to pay $5,000 to the first person who brings to its executive offices any piece of a fallen satellite. This offer can only be accepted by the actual physical production of a portion of the designated satellite, at which time a **unilateral contract** is formed; a mere promise by an offeree that he or she will bring in the item later does not result in the formation of a contract.[3]

True unilateral offers occur rather rarely. And, in cases where there is doubt as to the type of offer made, the courts generally construe them to be bilateral in nature—a view that is usually in keeping with the reasonable expectation of the offeree. One type of unilateral offer, however, *is* made frequently in the real world—the promise by a seller of property to pay a real estate agent a commission when the agent finds a buyer for it. The following case involves such a promise, which comes into being when the seller signs a "listing contract." In the court's decision, attention is focused upon the exact nature of the "act" that such an offer legally requires.

---

[2]The *offeror* is the person making the proposal; the *offeree* is the one to whom it is made.

[3]Under sales law, the distinction between bilateral and unilateral offers is blurred in one limited situation. Section 2-206 of the Uniform Commercial Code is responsible for this result and will be discussed in the next chapter, where the primary focus is on offer/acceptance rules.

Judd Realty, Inc. v. Tedesco

Supreme Court of Rhode Island, 400 A.2d 952 (1979)

Frank Tedesco, defendant, wanted to sell a lot that he owned in Johnston, Rhode Island. On November 18, 1973, he listed the property with Judd Realty, plaintiff, giving it the exclusive right to sell the property for a period of six months—i.e., until the following May 18th. The stated price was $25,000. The "listing contract" signed by Tedesco contained this standard provision: "Should a purchaser be found during the life of this agreement by me, or by you . . . I will pay you a commission of 8 percent of the price received."

About a week before the listing contract expired, plaintiff's president told defendant that she had a buyer for his property. A day or two later she had the prospective purchaser sign the customary "purchase and sale agreement," which was an offer by him to buy the property for $25,000. On May 15, two days before the listing contract expired, plaintiff's president took this offer and a $1,000 check drawn by the prospective purchaser to Tedesco. He told her then that he had decided not to sell. When he subsequently continued in his refusal to accept the offer to purchase, plaintiff brought this action to recover its commission.

The plaintiff claimed that it had produced a "purchaser" within the meaning of that term in the listing contract, even though no sale actually took place. Defendant, in support of the opposite view, contended that the term purchaser was an ambiguous one, in which case the court should follow the rule that the contract be construed against the drafter, the plaintiff. The trial court accepted defendant's contention, and thus ruled that the term "purchaser" meant "someone who actually purchases the property." On this basis it ruled there was no purchaser, and dismissed the complaint. Plaintiff appealed.

The higher court disagreed with the lower court's interpretation, saying that "It is well settled in Rhode Island that a broker has sufficiently performed, and is entitled to compensation under, a brokerage contract when the broker has produced a prospective purchaser who is ready, willing, and able to purchase at the price and terms of the seller." It thus reversed the judgment of the lower court and entered judgment for plaintiff. In that part of its decision

(continues)

JUDD REALTY, INC. v. TEDESCO

(continued from previous page)
appearing below, the higher court emphasized that the contract ultimately formed between plaintiff and defendant was unilateral in nature.

Weisberger, Justice:

. . . Williston distinguishes unilateral and bilateral contracts as follows: "An offer for a unilateral contract generally requires an *act* on the part of the offeree to make a binding contract. This act is consideration for the promise contained in the offer, and [the performance of the act] without more will create a contract. . . . On the other hand, an offer for a bilateral contract requires a *promise* from the of-feree in order that there may be a binding contract." [Emphasis added.] 1 Williston, *Contracts* §65, Third Edition.

Corbin also contrasts unilateral contracts with bilateral contracts in respect to brokerage agreements:

The most commonly recurring case is one in which the owner employs a broker to find a purchaser able and willing to buy, on terms stated in advance by the owner, and in which the owner promises to pay a specified commission for the service. This is an offer by the owner, the [acceptance of which occurs] by the actual rendition of the requested service [by the broker]. Here the only contemplated contract between the owner and the broker is a unilateral contract—a promise to pay a commission for services rendered [i.e., the production of a buyer].

Cases are very numerous in which the owner, after the broker has fully performed the requested service, fails to make conveyance [of the property] to the purchaser, and refuses to pay the commission. Such a refusal is not the revocation of an offer; it is the breach of the fully consummated unilateral contract to pay for services rendered. If the requested service is merely the production of a purchaser able and willing to buy on definitely stated terms, the broker has a right to his commission *even though the owner at once refuses to accept the purchaser's offer.* [Emphasis added.] 1 Corbin, Contracts §50 (1963). . . .

We conclude that the trial justice erred as a matter of law in construing the word "purchaser" in the brokerage agreement to mean "someone who actually purchases the property." . . .

[Judgment reversed.] ⚖

Comment While the *broker* had a cause of action against Tedesco, the *prospective purchaser* in this case does not. As a general rule, a person who lists property for sale has a perfect legal right—insofar as prospective purchasers are concerned—to reject all purchase offers (as long as the rejection is not based on the purchaser's race, color, religion, or national origin).

Express, Implied, and Quasi-Contracts

1. As has been indicated, the essence of a contract is an agreement (an understanding) that has been arrived at in some fashion. If the intentions of the parties are stated fully and in explicit terms, either orally or in writing, they constitute an **express contract.** The typical real estate lease and construction contract are examples of contracts normally falling within this category.

Express contracts are frequently in writing and of considerable length, but this is not necessarily so. If B orally offers to sell his used car to W for $450 cash, and W answers, "I accept," an express contract has been formed. The communications between B and W, while extremely brief, are themselves sufficient to indicate the obligations of each.

2. An **implied contract** is one in which the promises (intentions) of the parties have to be inferred in large part from the facts of their conduct and from the circumstances in which it took place. It is reasonable to infer, for example, that a person who is getting a haircut in a barbershop actually desires the service and is willing to pay for it. If the patron does not pay voluntarily, a court will have no hesitation in saying that by his conduct the patron had made an implied promise to pay a reasonable price, and will hold him liable on this obligation.

The words and conduct test is a good starting point in distinguishing between the two kinds of agreement, but it is also somewhat of an oversimplification. This is primarily so because some agreements are reached through the use of words and conduct both—especially in the case where one person requests a service from another without specifying a price that he or she is willing to pay for it. For example, if T asks J to keep his lawn mowed during the two months that T will be in Europe, and if J performs the requested service, T's request for the service carries with it in the eyes of the law an implied promise that he will pay J the "reasonable value" of his services. Thus the contract that has been formed upon J's completion of the work is an implied contract, even though T requested the service expressly.

3. A **quasi-contract,** in contrast to the express and implied contracts, exists only in those exceptional circumstances where a court feels compelled to impose an obligation upon one person even though he or she had no intention of making a contract at all. The classic illustration is that of a doctor who renders first aid to an unconscious man and later sends a bill for his services. It is perfectly obvious that the patient neither expressly nor impliedly promised to pay for the services when they were rendered; yet to permit him to escape liability entirely on the grounds that a contract was not formed would be to let him get something for nothing—a result the law generally abhors. To solve this dilemma, the courts pretend that a contract was formed and impose a quasi-contractual obligation on the person receiving the service.[4]

A quasi-contractual obligation is imposed only in circumstances where the failure to impose such an obligation would result in one party receiving an "unjust enrichment"—a benefit which, on the grounds of fairness alone, he or she ought to pay for. Suppose, for example, that A plants and cultivates crops on land belonging to B, without B's knowledge. In such a case, B, upon learning the facts, is entitled to bring a *quantum meruit* action to recover from A the reasonable value of the benefit (the profit which A made as a result of the use of the land), for otherwise A would be unjustly enriched.[5]

Three limitations on the quasi-contractual principle should be noted.

1. It cannot be invoked by one who has conferred a benefit unnecessarily or as a result of negligence or other misconduct. Thus, suppose that the X Company contracts to blacktop Y's driveway at 540 Fox Lane for $900, and the company's employees instead mistakenly blacktop the driveway of Y's neighbor, Z, at 546 Fox Lane, in Z's absence. In such a situation Z has no liability to the X Company, since his retention of the blacktop, while a benefit to him, is not an unjust benefit or an unjust retention under the circumstances.

2. Quasi-contracts are contracts in fiction only, since they are not based upon a genuine agreement between the parties. Thus they are not "true" contracts. However, quasi-contractual remedies are often granted in contractual contexts. A combination of contractual rules and quasi-contractual remedies may be employed, for example, to divide losses between the parties where a contract is made and later avoided due to incapacity or fraud (see the discussion of voidable contracts in the next section) or where a contract is made but fails for indefiniteness.

3. A plaintiff generally will not be allowed quasi-contractual recovery from one person if he originally looked to another for compensation. Assume that C sells a house to B, and B hires A to plant shrubs around the house. A does so, but before he is paid, B dies and C generously allows B's widow to rescind the contract. If A sues C on quasi-contractual grounds, claiming that C was unjustly enriched by the planting of the shrubs, recovery will probably be denied because A originally looked to B for compensation and may still proceed against B's estate.

In the first of the following two cases, a state supreme court sets forth the general rules as to the nature and legal effects of implied contracts. The second presents a situation where a recovery of money by the plaintiffs under the quasi-contract principle might be proper.

[4]The technical name for implied contracts is *contracts implied in fact,* and for quasi-contracts *contracts implied in law.* We are using the less formal labels of "implied" and "quasi" for purposes of simplicity.
[5]*Quantum meruit* means, literally, "as much as is deserved."

CARROLL V. LEE

Supreme Court of Arizona, 712 P.2d 923 (1986)

Judy Carroll lived with Paul Lee for fourteen years. Ultimately they settled in Ajo, Arizona, where Paul operated an automobile repair shop. Although Judy used the name Lee during this time, the couple did not marry or ever seriously consider marriage. In 1982 they "went their separate ways."

Prior to the relationship little personal property was owned by either party, and neither owned any real property (i.e., land). During the course of the relationship the couple jointly acquired three parcels of land, several antique or restored automobiles, a mobile home, and various other items of personal property. The real property was titled to the couple in one of three ways. Title was held either (1) as joint tenants with the right of survivorship, (2) as husband and wife, or (3) as husband and wife as joint tenants with the right of survivorship. (The mobile home and some of the automobiles were titled to Paul T. Lee and Judy Lee, with other automobiles titled to Paul T. Lee alone.)

During the time the couple lived together Paul supplied virtually all of the money used to pay their living expenses, while Judy "kept the house" by cleaning, cooking, doing laundry, and working in the yard. After the couple split up Judy filed this partition action claiming a one-half interest in the jointly titled property listed above. (The fact that the properties were titled to both parties did not, in and of itself, convey a one-half interest to Judy. This was because Paul proved that the money used in purchasing them came from the operation of the repair shop, which he owned personally. In such a case, the rule in Arizona—and in most states—is that "where property is paid for by one party and title is

taken in the name of that party and a second party who are not husband and wife, it is presumed that the property was taken for the benefit of the one paying for the property." Thus it was necessary for Judy to prove an agreement existed between them that they be co-owners, in order to rebut this presumption.)

The trial court ruled in favor of Judy, finding that an implied contract existed under which it was agreed that Paul and she would be co-owners of the property. (This finding was based on a 1984 case, Cook v. Cook, *691 P.2d 664, in which the Supreme Court of Arizona upheld an implied contract between an unmarried couple in circumstances similar to those presented by this case.) Paul appealed, and the court of appeals reversed the judgment (for reasons appearing below). Judy petitioned the Supreme Court of Arizona for review.*

Gordon, Vice-Chief Justice:

. . . In *Cook v. Cook, supra,* [this court approved] an agreement between unmarried cohabitants to pool income, acquire assets, and share in the accumulations. We compiled basic concepts of contract law:

The *sine qua non* [essential element] of any contract is the exchange of promises. From this exchange flows the obligation of one party to another. Although it is most apparent that two parties have exchanged promises when their words express a spoken or written statement of promissory intention, mutual promises need not be express in order to create an enforceable contract. *Restatement (Second) of Contracts* §4. Indeed, a promise 'may be inferred wholly or partly from conduct,' *id.,* and 'there is no distinction in the effect of the promise whether it is expressed in writing, or orally, or in acts, or partly in one of these ways and partly in others.' *id.* §19. Thus, two parties may by their course of conduct express their agreement, though no words are ever spoken. From their conduct alone the

trier of fact can determine the existence of an agreement. *Restatement (Second) of Contracts* §4.

The court of appeals [ruled that our decision in *Cook* was not applicable to the instant case because] "no evidence, in words or conduct, suggests mutual promises to contribute funds to a pool. . . ." [In other words, the court of appeals refused to apply the *Cook* rule because in that case both parties were earning income, while in the instant case Paul was the sole income producer. The supreme court disagreed with the court of appeals decision, and continued:]

In Arizona we recognize implied contracts, and there is no difference in legal effect between an express contract and an implied contract. An implied contract is one not created or evidenced by explicit agreement, but inferred by the law as a matter of reason and justice from the acts and conduct of the parties and circumstances surrounding their transaction. Furthermore, in this state monetary consideration is not always required as consideration. . . . Clearly a promise for a promise constitutes adequate consideration. . . .

We believe Judy proved the property requested to be partitioned was acquired through joint common effort and for a common purpose. It is not necessary for her to prove that she produced by her labor a part of the very money used to purchase the property. The parties had an *implied partnership or joint enterprise agreement* at the very least, based on the facts and circumstances presented. [Emphasis added.] Recovery for Judy should be allowed in accordance with these implied expectations. [The court here reviewed testimony by Paul in which he stated that it was his "preference" that Judy stay at home, cook meals, do washing and yardwork, and

(continues)

CARROLL V. LEE

(continued from previous page)
that she did, in fact, perform these services. This testimony ended with the following:]

Q. Did you ever intend that she be an owner with you at that time, at the time that you were acquiring these properties, that she be an owner of those properties at that time?

A. You mean a co-owner?

Q. Yes.

A. *I suppose at the time I had it planned that way.* [Emphasis added by the court.] . . .

[Judy's relevant testimony is as follows:]

Q. All right. What type of an arrangement, if any, did you and Paul discuss about what he expected from your relationship in terms of contribution?

A. We didn't really discuss it. *It just was there.* He went to work. I stayed home and kept the house and, mostly because that's what he wanted me to do. [Emphasis added by the court.]

There was evidence from which the trial court could find the existence of an agreement for property to be acquired and owned jointly, as such was the method in which Paul took title in both the real and personal property. . . . Since Judy was a co-owner of the property under a contract theory, she had the right [under Arizona law] to seek partition and divide the jointly owned assets. . . .

We therefore vacate the opinion of the court of appeals and remand the case to the trial court for a redistribution of property not inconsistent with this opinion.☙

Comment This case has been edited to emphasize the implied contract question. An additional question of equal importance was also presented: whether a finding that an implied contract existed even though the plaintiff's services were entirely of a "homemaking" nature was contrary to public policy, on the ground that enforcement of such a contract might discourage marriage. The court of appeals, by refusing to apply the *Cook* rule, felt that the enforcement of such a contract would have that effect. The higher court, in a part of its decision omitted here, set forth reasons why enforcement of an implied contract in the circumstances presented here was *not* contrary to the public policy of the state.

DESKOVICK ET AL. V. PORZIO

Superior Court of New Jersey, 187 A.2d 610 (1963)

Case

Plaintiffs in this action are brothers, Michael and Peter Deskovick, Jr. Their father, Peter Deskovick, Sr., was hospitalized in 1958 until his death in 1959. During this period Michael paid the hospital and medical bills as they came in, under the impression that the father was financially unable to do so. (This impression was based on statements made by the senior Deskovick in which he indicated an apparently genuine fear that he would not be able to pay the expenses of the hospitalization.) After the father's death it was discovered that, in fact, his estate was adequate to cover all of the payments made by Michael. The

plaintiffs thereupon brought this action against the executor of their father's estate, Porzio, to recover the amounts paid out.

In the trial court, plaintiffs proceeded on the theory that an implied contract existed between them and their father in the foregoing fact-pattern. (No mention of quasi-contractual liability was made.) While the evidence was somewhat conflicting as to whether Michael intended to be repaid out of his father's estate at the time he made the payments, the trial judge ruled as a matter of law that no such intention was present, and, for that reason, no implied contract had been formed. Accordingly, the court directed a verdict for the defendant. On appeal, plaintiffs contended for

the first time that the estate should be liable on the theory of quasi-contract. (As a general rule, the parties cannot raise new issues on appeal. It does not appear why this was permitted in this case.)

Conford, Justice:

. . . If the question whether plaintiffs intended to be repaid at the time they advanced the monies in question were the sole material issue, we would conclude the trial court erred in taking the case out of the jury's hands [because of the conflicting evidence on that point]. However, . . . their intent to be repaid was immaterial in the factual situation presented, for the following reasons.

(continues)

DESKOVICK ET AL. V. PORZIO

(continued from previous page)

It is elementary that the assertion of a contract implied in fact [an "implied contract"] calls for the establishment of a consensual understanding as to compensation or reimbursement inferable from the circumstances under which one furnishes services or property and another accepts such advances. Here an essential for such a mutual understanding was absent *in that the decedent, on behalf of whom these advances were being made, was totally ignorant of the fact.* [Emphasis added.]

[After thus concluding that the proper reason why no implied contract was formed was that the father could not give his implied consent to his sons' actions when he was not aware of them, the appellate court turned to the question of whether recovery might be allowed under the quasi-contract theory, as follows:]

It is elementary that one who pays the debt of another as a volunteer, having no obligation or liability to pay nor any interest menaced by the continued existence of the debt, cannot recover therefor from the beneficiary. Nor can such a volunteer claim the benefit of the law of subrogation. If plaintiffs were mere volunteers, therefore, they would not, within these principles, be entitled to be subrogated to the credi-

tor position of the hospitals and physicians whose bills they paid.

Notwithstanding the foregoing principles, however, we perceive in the evidence adduced at the trial, particularly in the version of the facts reflected in the deposition of Michael, adduced by defendant, a *quasi-contractual* basis of recovery which in our judgment ought to be submitted to a jury at a retrial of the case in the interests of substantial justice.

It is said that a "quasi-contractual obligation is one that is created by the law for reasons of justice, without any expression of assent. . . ." 1 *Corbin on Contracts* (1950), §19, p. 38; 1 *Williston, Contracts* (1957), §3A, p. 13. This concept rests "on the equitable principle that a person shall not be allowed to enrich himself unjustly at the expense of another, and on the principle that whatsoever it is certain that a man ought to do, that the law supposes him to have promised to do." The *Restatement of Restitution* (1937) undertakes to formulate a number of rules growing out of recognized principles of quasi-contract. Id., at p. 5 et seq. Section 26 (p. 116), entitled "Mistake in Making Gifts," reads: "(1) A person is entitled to restitution from another to whom gratuitously and induced thereto by a mistake of fact he has given money if

the mistake (a) was caused by fraud or material misrepresentation. . . ." An innocent misrepresentation by the donee is within the rule. Id., comment, at p. 117. A "mistaken belief in the existence of facts which would create a moral obligation upon the donor to make a gift would ordinarily be a basic error" justifying restitution. Id., at p. 118. . . .

We think the foregoing authorities would apply in favor of sons, who, during their father's mortal illness, believing him without means of meeting medical and hospital bills as a result of what he had previously told them, and wishing to spare him the discomfort of concern over such expenses at such a time, themselves assumed and paid the obligations. The leaving by the father of an estate far more than sufficient to have met the expenditures would, in such circumstances, and absent others affecting the basic equitable situation presented, properly invoke the concept of a *quasi-contractual obligation* of reimbursement of the sons by the estate. [Emphasis added.] Such circumstances would take the payors out of the category of voluntary intermeddlers as to whom the policy of the law is to deny restitution or reimbursement. . . .

Judgment reversed and remanded.⚖

Valid, Voidable, and Void Contracts

A **valid contract** is one in which all of the required elements are present. As a result, it is enforceable against both parties.

In some circumstances, one of the parties to a contract has the legal right to withdraw from it at a later time without liability. Such contracts are referred to as **voidable contracts.** Contracts in which fraud is present fall within this category, because the law permits the one who has been defrauded to set aside the contract. Minors' contracts are another common example of voidable contracts. (Because of their impor-

tance, voidable contracts are considered separately in Chapter 15.)

Courts occasionally designate a third type of contract as being *void*. Such contracts are those which, so far as the law is concerned, never existed at all. Contracts are usually void for either of two reasons: (1) one of the parties is wholly incompetent at the time of contracting (such as a person who has been legally declared insane) or (2) the purpose of the contract is totally illegal (such as an agreement calling for the commission of a crime). The designation **void contract** is admittedly self-contradictory—an improper combination of terms. Nevertheless, this label is used by the courts to distinguish such contracts from those which are merely voidable; and in that sense it is a useful term.

Another type of contract is referred to as being "unenforceable." An **unenforceable contract** was valid at the time it was made but was subsequently rendered unenforceable because of the application of some special rule of law. For example, if a debtor goes through bankruptcy proceedings, the debtor's nonexempt assets are distributed among creditors and the debtor ultimately receives a discharge in bankruptcy. Under bankruptcy law, this discharge prevents a creditor who was not paid in full from bringing legal action to recover the balance of the debt; thus the contract that created the indebtedness was rendered unenforceable by virtue of the discharge. Other examples of unenforceable contracts include those sued upon after the statute of limitations has expired, oral contracts that should have been in writing under the statute of frauds (see Chapter 16), and those calling for performance of personal services by a person who died after the agreement was made.

Negotiated Contracts and Contracts of Adhesion

The terms of many contracts are agreed upon only after a certain amount of bargaining, or "dickering," takes place between the parties. After one party makes an offer to the other, for example, the latter—the offeree—may indicate that he or she will accept only if a specified change is made in the terms of the offer. Or the offeree may respond with a counteroffer, a substantially different proposal from that of the original offer. Contracts that result from these kinds of exchanges are "negotiated contracts."

Contracts of adhesion, by contrast, are formed where one party—usually having greatly superior bargaining power than the other—prepares the terms of a proposed contract and presents it to the other party on a *take-it-or-leave-it basis*. Examples of such "standard form" contracts are apartment leases, hospital admission forms, and sales contracts of new car dealers. While the terms of contracts of adhesion usually favor the parties who have prepared them, such contracts are generally enforceable unless the terms are so shockingly one-sided as to be, in the opinion of the courts, "unconscionable" in nature. (Unconscionable contracts are considered further in Chapter 14.)

HARTLAND COMPUTER LEASING CORP. v. THE INSURANCE MAN, INC.

Missouri Court of Appeals, 770 S.W.2d 525 (1989)

Appellant Hartland (lessor) leases computers. Respondent The Insurance Man, Inc. (lessee), selected computer equipment sold by vendor Multitask. Hartland bought the equipment and in turn leased it to Insurance Man for $229.16 per month for 36 months. Respondents Saulsberry, the sole shareholder of Insurance Man, and Reese guaranteed that they would make the monthly payments if Insurance Man did not. The printed lease stated that the lessor Hartland made no warranties (promises that the computer equipment would perform properly) and that the lessee should look to the vendor for any needed repairs. Lease payments were

due regardless of the condition of the machine. After problems arose with the equipment, respondents stopped making payments. When contacted by Hartland's agent, Hogan, they stated that they did not want the machine and that Hogan should sell it and they would settle the difference.

Hartland sued under the terms of the lease for the payments not made. The trial judge, concluding that the contract was an adhesion contract, disregarded the disclaimers of liability and ruled against Hartland, which appealed.

Gaertner, Judge:

Apparently the trial court concluded that, because he found it to be a con-

tract of adhesion, he was free to disregard appellant's clear and unambiguous express disclaimer of all warranties. This conclusion, under the circumstances of this case, is a misapplication of the law and requires reversal.

In Missouri, an adhesion contract, as opposed to a negotiated contract, has been described as a form contract created and imposed by a stronger party upon a weaker party on a "take this or nothing basis," the terms of which unexpectedly or unconscionably limit the obligations of the drafting party. *Robin v. Blue Cross Hospital Service, Inc.*, 637 S.W.2d 695, 697 (Mo. banc 1982). Some writers view any pre-printed standardized form with filled-in blank spaces to be a contract of adhesion insofar as the pre-printed

(continues)

HARTLAND COMPUTER LEASING CORP. v. THE INSURANCE MAN, INC.

(continued from previous page)
provisions are concerned. Thus, in *Corbin On Contracts*, §559A at 660 (Supp. 1989), it is said "the bulk of contracts signed in this country, if not every major Western nation, are adhesion contracts. . . ." Such form contracts are a natural concomitant of our mass production–mass consumer society. *Id.* Therefore, a rule automatically invalidating adhesion contracts would be completely unworkable. *Corbin, supra* §559A at 660. Accordingly, courts do not view adhesion contracts as inherently sinister and automatically unenforceable. Rather, as with all contracts, the courts seek to enforce the reasonable expectations of the parties garnered not only from the words of a standardized form imposed by its proponent, but from the totality of the circumstances surrounding the transaction. *Robin, supra,* 637 S.W.2d at 697. Only such provisions of the standardized form which fail to comport with such reasonable expectations and which are unexpected and unconscionably unfair are held to be unenforceable. *Corbin, supra,* §559A at 660. Because standardized contracts address the mass of users, the test for "reasonable expectations" is objective, addressed to the average member of

the public who accepts such a contract, not the subjective expectations of an individual adherent.

We look then to all the evidence surrounding this transaction to determine the objectively reasonable expectations of the parties and to the question of unconscionable unfairness imposed upon respondents under the terms of the form contract. We note first that Saulsberry was engaged in the operation of an insurance agency, presumably accustomed to form contracts. The contract at issue is clearly a lease of computer equipment for a term of years. It contains no option to purchase and requires that the equipment be returned to the lessor at the expiration of the term. Indeed, despite Mr. Saulsberry's references at trial to Mr. Hogan as the salesman, Saulsberry's own testimony was that he contacted Multitask, Inc., the vendor, and was referred to "Hartland Computer Leasing about *leasing* a computer system for my business." The lease provides and the evidence shows that, in fact, the equipment Saulsberry selected was purchased by Hartland from Multitask, and delivered to Saulsberry. The lease contains an assignment by Hartland of all warranties by the manufacturer and seller to Saulsberry. At the time of the

first malfunction of the equipment Saulsberry exercised his rights under this assignment and took the equipment to the vendor where it was repaired under the warranty. His refusal to follow the same procedure at the time of the second malfunction, explainable perhaps as exasperation, does not indicate an objectively reasonable expectation that the lessor was obligated under any implied warranty of merchantability or of fitness.

This assignment of warranties did not leave Saulsberry without a remedy, thus militating against any finding of oppressive unconscionability. The retention of full warranty rights against the seller prevents the disclaimer of warranty obligations by the financing lessor from being unconscionable.

Much as we may wish to sympathize with the unrepresented respondents, we cannot escape the fact that it was the equipment, not the terms of the contract, which failed to live up to respondents' expectations. They possessed the right to seek full and complete relief under the express and implied warranties made by the vendor. The fact is they sought relief from the wrong party.

[Reversed.]

Formal and Informal Contracts

Some specialized types of contracts are referred to as **formal contracts.** The term usually is used to refer to sealed contracts—ones that the parties have formalized either by making a physical impression on the paper on which the agreement was written or, in some instances, simply by having the word *seal* or the letters *L.S.* appear at the end of the document.[6]

The great majority of ordinary business contracts are not sealed and are therefore **informal contracts**

(or "simple contracts"). Thus any unsealed contract can be referred to as "simple," even though it may be several pages long and contain complex provisions.

Executory and Executed Contracts

Once a contract is formed, it is an **executory contract** until both parties have fully performed their obligations. When performance has taken place, the contract is said to be an **executed contract.** If one party has fully performed his or her part of the bargain but the other party has not, the contract is executed as to the former and executory as to the latter.

[6]The letters stand for *Locus Sigilli,* meaning "the place for the seal."

RULING MAY HURT LENDER-LIABILITY SUITS

by Wayne Green

Box 11.1
The Law at Work

After years of winning big jury verdicts against banks based on unfair lending conduct, borrowers are finding the pendulum may be swinging the other way. Appeals court judges in lender-liability cases are paying strict attention to the terms of lending contracts, making it harder for plaintiffs to press issues of fairness. And lately, a remarkably tough pro-lender ruling by the federal appeals court in Chicago is hurting their chances even more.

"I think appellate courts are trying to restore some order in this area by giving some deference to contractual provisions," says Daniel R. Fischel, a University of Chicago law professor.

The Chicago case [*Kham & Nate's Shoes v. First Bank of Whiting*, 908 F.2d 1351 (7th Cir. 1990)] . . . upheld the right of lenders to enforce the terms of a loan agreement strictly, even if they know the action will drive a borrower out of business. The case is significant not only for its unyielding support of contractual rights, but also for the intensity of the written opinion, which attacks the idea that fairness should play a major role in lending relationships.

"Parties to a contract are not each others' fiduciaries," the court said in an opinion written by Judge Frank A. Easterbrook. "They are not bound to treat customers with the same consideration reserved for their families."

Lender-liability litigation has exploded in recent years, fueled by disgruntled borrowers ranging from individuals to small and big businesses. Most allege that lenders violated a duty to act in good faith toward borrowers by saying or implying that they would do one thing, then doing something else that hurt the borrowers' business. Several lawsuits shook lenders to their toes in the 1980s, winning big damage awards after a jury or judge found the lender acted in bad faith.

Defense attorneys applaud such . . . rulings [as in the Chicago case] as more "dispassionate" than those coming from emotion-charged trials. Mr. Capello, the plaintiffs' attorney, sees another reason: "Appellate courts generally have very conservative justices—who often come from law firms that represented lenders."

The Chicago court's opinion is hardly dispassionate. There, First Bank of Whiting supplied Kham & Nate's a $300,000 credit line under an agreement where the troubled shoe chain would file for Chapter 11 reorganization and First Bank would be made a priority creditor. After Kham had borrowed $75,000, the bank exercised its contractual right to cancel the credit line on five days notice.

The bankruptcy judge concluded the bank behaved "inequitably" in terminating the credit, and he approved a reorganization plan that weakened the bank's position as creditor.

But Judge Easterbrook was unsympathetic. "Firms that have negotiated contracts are entitled to enforce them to the letter, even to the great discomfort of their trading partners, without being mulcted for lack of 'good faith'," he said.

Acknowledging that literal enforcement of contracts can sometimes bring hardship, Judge Easterbrook said that still doesn't justify some "general duty of 'kindness' in performance, or of judicial oversight into whether a party had 'good cause' to act as it did." A borrower's fate "is legally irrelevant so long as the bank kept its promise," he said.

Source: *Wall Street Journal*, June 30, 1992, p. B7.

CONTRACT LAW AND SALES LAW— A SPECIAL RELATIONSHIP

The subjects of general contract law and sales law deserve separate treatment for at least two reasons:

1. Sales law is applicable only to those contracts calling for the sale of tangible articles of personal property—goods such as automobiles, machine tools, grain, and items of clothing. Contract law, on the other hand, is applicable to virtually all other kinds of agreements—including leases, employment contracts, and real estate sales contracts.

2. Contract law is primarily composed of common-law rules, while sales law is a statutory subject, contained in Article 2 of the Uniform Commercial Code (UCC; see discussion in Chapter 4).

Therefore, Part II of this book, starting with this chapter and proceeding through Chapter 19, will address primarily contract law, and Chapters 20 through 23 of Part III will address sales law.

However, these two subjects cannot be discussed in isolation from each other. Of all the contracts that are entered into, a substantial number *are* sales contracts. Also, the drafters of the UCC Article 2 provisions on sales drew heavily from the common law of contracts, and common-law concepts continue to supplement the more specific UCC provisions. Furthermore, Article 2 of the UCC has been so successful in clarifying and modernizing sales law that judges deciding common-law cases often draw upon Article 2 principles, applying them by analogy. For all these reasons, the discussion of general contract law will refer frequently to Article 2 sales law. In particular, *major UCC modifications of well-established common-law principles will be discussed* in Part II. For example, this chapter has already noted that Section 2–206 blurs the distinction between bilateral and unilateral offers.

SUMMARY

Contracts—agreements that courts will enforce—can be classified in several ways, depending upon the basis used. Sometimes the primary focus is upon the nature of the acceptance which the offeror wants; if the offeror merely wants a return promise from the offeree (and if the offeree makes the requested promise), a bilateral contract is formed. On the other hand, if the offer is phrased in such a way that acceptance can only take place by the performance of a particular act, the performance of that act results in the formation of a unilateral contract. (One significance of this classification is that if the offeror clearly requests performance of an act, a promise by the offeree to perform the act later does not result in the formation of a contract.)

A second basis for classification depends upon the extent to which the parties have manifested their agreement. If the intentions (and obligations) of the parties are set forth clearly in the language used, the agreement is an express contract. By contrast, if the intentions of the parties have to be inferred from their conduct, or where the language used shows an agreement, but requires inferences to be made as to the parties' precise duties, the agreement is an implied contract.

A third basis for classification depends upon the extent to which a contract is enforceable. An agreement that is enforceable by both parties is a valid contract. A contract that one of the parties has a legal right to withdraw from is a voidable contract. And a contract which is so defective that it never existed in the law is a void contract. Other classifications are based upon such factors as the extent to which the terms of the

contract were mutually bargained for, and the extent to which a contract has been performed.

KEY TERMS

Bilateral contract
Bilateral offer
Unilateral offer
Unilateral contract
Express contract
Implied contract
Quasi-contract
Valid contract
Voidable contract
Void contract
Unenforceable contract
Formal contract
Informal contract
Executory contract
Executed contract

QUESTIONS AND PROBLEMS

1. A corporation employed a contractor to build a barn. Later the contractor quit the job, leaving the subcontractor unpaid. A corporation officer then told the subcontractor to finish the job, and promised that the corporation would pay him for his time and materials. Later the subcontractor finished the job, but the corporation refused to pay the amount that the subcontractor demanded. (It was, however, willing to pay a lesser sum.) In the ensuing lawsuit the corporation contended that no contract had ever been entered into here; the subcontractor, on the other hand, argued that the corporation had made a unilateral offer which he, the subcontractor, had accepted by the act of completing the barn. Do you agree with the corporation that no contract of any kind was entered into here? Why or why not? (*Redd v. Woodford County Swine Breeders, Inc.*, 370 N.E.2d 152, 1977.)

2. The law of Ohio required boards of education to furnish transportation to all children who lived more than four miles from the nearest high school. When one board refused to furnish such transportation to one of its eligible students, the student's father drove him to and from school for the school year. When the father then sued the board to recover his driving expenses, the board contended that no contract of any kind ever existed between it and him, and

that it thus had no liability. Do you think an implied contract existed here, under which the board should be liable? If not, could the father recover on the quasi-contract theory? Why or why not? (*Sommers v. Board of Education*, 148 N.E. 682, 1925.)

3. Bio-Zyme (P) sold cattle feed on credit to Preston (D) for a period of 14 months. During this time, D received monthly statements of the amount due. Although sometimes he would be paid up, frequently D was behind in his payments, and P added interest on the unpaid amount to the next month's bill in accordance with a statement on each bill: "Accounts not paid within 30 days will be charged 1% each month." When P finally sued for unpaid amounts, D claimed that he should not have to pay the interest because he had never expressly agreed to pay interest on overdue accounts. Is D correct? Discuss. (*Preston Farm & Ranch Supply v. Bio-Zyme Enterprises*, 625 S.W.2d 295, Tex. 1981.)

4. A county grand jury investigating possible criminal activity in a school for problem children decided that it needed the services of a private investigator. The grand jury was informed that approval of the County Commissioner's Court was needed for such a contract. Upon being asked, the Commissioner's Court authorized the hiring of Stratton at $50/day, not to exceed 20 days. Stratton's services were very helpful, and with the approval of the grand jury foreman, he stayed on the job for 30 days. The Commissioner's Court refused to pay Stratton for the extra 10 days, so he sued in quasi-contract. Will he recover? Discuss. (*Stratton v. County of Liberty*, 582 S.W.2d 252, Tex. Civ. App. 1979.)

5. A schoolteacher owned some land on Lake Michigan. The land was eroding, and the teacher talked to a contractor about having a retaining wall built, but she never told him to go ahead with the job. Nevertheless, the contractor later built the wall without her knowledge. She refused to pay him for the job, whereupon he sued her—on a quasi-contract theory—to recover the reasonable value of the wall. Do you think she should be liable on this theory? What arguments can be made for, and against, recovery by the contractor on this theory? (*Dunnebacke Co. v. Pittman and Gilligan*, 257 N.W. 30, 1934.)

6. Harold Lewis and plaintiff Helen Hall began dating and she eventually moved into his house at his request. They cohabited as "modern unmarrieds without benefit of portfolio" for a year, when Helen decided to move out. Harold begged her to stay and take care of him, promising that if she did so she would be "taken care of." She remained with Harold, taking care of him through his ill health until his death three years later. Several times, Harold asked Helen what she wanted him to leave her; she responded that it was up to him to decide. Perhaps she should have spoken up, for Harold left her nothing in his will. She sued his estate under an implied-in-fact contract theory for $15,840 as compensation for housekeeping and personal services. Should she recover? Discuss. (*Matter of Estate of Lewis*, 423 N.W.2d 600, Mich.App. 1988.)

7. Nye & Nissen Co. (D) bought Olwell's interest in an egg-packing company. Olwell (P) stored an egg-washing machine nearby. Without P's knowledge or permission, D took the egg-washing machine out of storage and used it. When P learned of this three years later, he offered to sell the machine to D for $600; D refused. P then sued in quasi-contract. Will he recover? Discuss. (*Olwell v. Nye & Nissen Co.*, 173 P.2d 652, Wash. 1946.)

8. John Deere Leasing (JDL) leased a tractor to Blubaugh with an option to buy. The lease agreement entitled Blubaugh to exercise an option to purchase at a predetermined price only at the end of the lease period. On the other hand, it gave JDL the right to claim as damages upon default not only the amount due on the lease but also the option-to-purchase price. These provisions were in light-colored fine print on the back of the lease and were nearly illegible because the darker print on the front of the lease showed through to the back. Blubaugh read the front of the lease but not the back, and testified that he assumed this was a typical lease which would not include liability for the purchase price upon default. Will JDL be able to enforce the contract's provisions if Blubaugh defaults? Discuss. (*John Deere Leasing v. Blubaugh*, 636 F.Supp. 1569, D.Kan. 1986.)

Chapter 12

The Agreement

Intention of the Parties

Requirements of the Offer

Termination of the Offer

Preliminary Considerations of the Acceptance

Requirements of the Acceptance

THE FIRST AND FOREMOST element of any contract is an agreement—a reasonably definite understanding between two or more persons. It is for this reason that the liability or obligation resulting from the making of a contract (as distinguished from that imposed by the law of torts or the criminal law) is sometimes described as being "consensual" in nature.

The usual view taken by the law today is that if two or more persons, expressly or by implication, have reached a reasonably clear agreement as to what each party is to do, then that agreement shall be enforceable by the courts (assuming, of course, that the additional elements of consideration and legality are also present).[1] This means that if either party refuses to perform his or her part of the agreement without a lawful excuse, the other party is entitled to recover damages in a breach of contract action. On the other hand, if it is found that a legally sufficient agreement has *not* been formed, neither party has contractual liability to the other.

Because the word *agreement* encompasses a broad spectrum of situations where some kind of understanding has been reached (ranging from the extremely concise to the hopelessly vague), the courts are faced with the problem of deciding just what kinds of agreements are sufficiently definite to warrant judicial relief if they are breached. The best approach to this problem is to break the agreement down into two parts—the offer and the acceptance. The inquiries then become whether either party made an *offer* to the other, and, if so, whether the offer was followed by an *acceptance*. Before considering the legal definitions of these terms, we will briefly mention the rules used by the courts to ascertain the intentions of the parties—with emphasis upon the applicability of these rules to the offer and acceptance.

INTENTION OF THE PARTIES

In cases where the parties disagree as to whether their communications constituted an offer and an acceptance, the court will frequently emphasize the principle that the *intention of the parties* is controlling. If the court finds that their intentions were the same (that there was a "meeting of minds," as it is sometimes phrased), then there is a contract.

One caution about this principle, however, should be noted. When the courts view the parties' communications for the purpose of determining whether their intentions were one and the same, it is the parties' *manifested* (or apparent) intentions that control, rather than their actual intentions.[2] For example, if X writes a letter to Y containing a proposal which meets the legal requirements of an offer, and if Y promptly accepts the offer in a return letter, there is a contract—even if X later claims to have had some mental reservations about the proposal, or says that he really did not intend his letter to be an offer. Thus, when it is said that there must be a *meeting of minds* to have a contract, this usually means that there must only be a legal, or apparent, meeting of minds.

There are two compelling reasons for the frequent use of this objective view:

1. It is virtually impossible for a court to determine what a person's actual intent was at a specific moment.

2. It would be unfair to allow someone to indicate a particular intention to another person and then to come into court and claim that he or she did not mean what was apparently meant.

REQUIREMENTS OF THE OFFER

Inherent in the many definitions of the word **offer** is the idea that it is a proposal made by one person, called the offeror, to another, the offeree, indicating what the offeror will give in return for a specified promise or act on the part of the offeree. That

---

[1]Surprisingly, this has not always been the case. Several centuries ago, the English courts would not enforce agreements (even though the intentions of the parties were quite clear) unless the most rigid formalities had been adhered to—which included not only reducing the agreement to writing but affixing the parties' seals to the document. (See Chapter 13 for a discussion of consideration and Chapter 14 for one of legality.)

[2]A person's manifested or apparent intent is frequently referred to by the courts as "objective" intent, while actual or secret intent is called "subjective" intent. Thus the test used by the courts that is described here is referred to as the "objective test."

is, the offeror must manifest a willingness to enter into a contractual relationship with the other party. Sometimes the manifestation is referred to as a "conditional statement" of what the offeror will do for the offeree. Used in this manner, the term *statement* is broad enough to include both *words* and *conduct* by which the offeror indicates a willingness to contract. Thus, if a person in a drugstore shows a magazine to the cashier and deposits $2.50 (the stated price) on the counter, it is perfectly clear that he or she has made an *offer to purchase* the item without speaking a word. Similarly, when a company delivers an unordered article of merchandise under circumstances which indicate to the recipient that a charge will be made for the article if it is accepted, the company's act constitutes an *offer to sell* the product at the stated price. Of course, the recipient of such unsolicited merchandise does not incur a duty to pay for it unless he or she actually uses it or otherwise indicates acceptance of the sender's offer.[3]

The courts have never tried to specify the exact language or the particular kinds of conduct that must exist in order for one person to make an offer to another, for any attempt to do so would be quite unrealistic in the "real world." What the courts have done, instead, is to formulate several general requirements that must be met in order for a particular communication (or act) to achieve the legal status of an offer. These requirements are (1) a manifestation of an intent to contract; (2) a reasonably definite indication of what the offeror and the offeree are to do; and (3) a communication of the proposal to the intended offeree.

The Intent to Contract

Preliminary Negotiations

Some language is so tentative or exploratory in nature that it should be apparent that an immediate contract is not contemplated. Such communications do not constitute offers; they are designated **preliminary negotiations,** or "dickering." For example, the statement "I'd like to get $4,000 for this car" would normally fall into this category, as would a letter indicating "I will not sell my home for less than $56,000." If the addressee in either of these instances were to reply, "I accept your offer," a contract would not result since no offer was made in either case. Along similar lines, it is usually held that requests for information—called inquiries—do not manifest a genuine intent to contract, and consequently such questions do not constitute offers in most circumstances. Thus, if A writes B, "Would you rent your summer home for the month of June for $900?" and B replies, "Yes, I accept your offer," there is no contract. (The most that can be said in this situation is that B has now made an offer to A, and it will ripen into a contract only if A subsequently accepts it.)

Difficult questions sometimes arise when there are multiple offerees. Suppose that A writes to B: "I hereby offer to sell my farm to you for $120,000." The letter informs B that A is simultaneously making the same offer to several other potential purchasers. B should know that although the language appears to be an offer, this letter is merely preliminary negotiation because A does not intend to be bound to sell the farm to several different persons. On the other hand, if the letter does not disclose that the offer is being made to others, B can make an effective acceptance. (If another offeree, not knowing of the offer to B, also effectively accepts, A faces certain liability in a breach of contract action.)

The decision in the well-known case below helps show how the courts try to draw the lines between preliminary negotiations and offers in several common situations.

---

[3]If the unsolicited goods are sent *by mail,* ordinarily no duty to pay arises even if the recipient uses the goods. Sec. 3009 of Title 39 of the U.S. Code, the Postal Reorganization Act of 1970, provides in part that, except for "merchandise mailed by a charitable organization soliciting contributions," the mailing of any unsolicited merchandise "may be treated as a gift by the recipient, who shall have the right to retain, use, discard, or dispose of it in any manner he sees fit without any obligations whatsoever to the sender."

RICHARDS V. FLOWERS ET AL.

District Court of Appeal, California, 14 Cal. Reptr. 228 (1961)

Mrs. Richards, plaintiff, wrote defendant Flowers on January 15, 1959, as follows: "We would be interested in buying your lot on Gravatt Drive in Oakland, California, if we can deal with you directly and not run through a realtor. If you are interested, please advise us by return mail the cash price you would expect to receive."

On January 19, 1959, Flowers replied: "Thank you for your inquiry regarding my lot on Gravatt Drive. As long as your offer would be in cash I see no reason why we could not deal directly on this matter. . . . Considering what I paid for the lot, and the taxes which I have paid I expect to receive $4,500 for this property. Please let me know what you decide."

On January 25, 1959, Mrs. Richards sent the following telegram to Flowers: "Have agreed to buy your lot on your terms will handle transactions through local title company who will contact you would greatly appreciate your sending us a copy of the contour map you referred to in your letter as we are desirous of building at once. . . ."

On February 5, 1959, Flowers entered into an agreement to sell the property to a third party, Mr. and Mrs. Sutton. Mrs. Richards, after learning of the Sutton transaction, called upon defendant to deliver his deed to her, claiming the above correspondence constituted a contract between him and her. Flowers refused to do so, denying that his letter of January 19 constituted an offer to sell, whereupon Mr. and Mrs. Richards commenced action, asking for specific performance of the alleged contract. (The Suttons intervened in this action to protect their interest by supporting Flowers' contention that

a contract was not formed between him and plaintiffs.)

The trial court ruled that defendant's letter of January 19 did constitute an offer to sell, but it further ruled that plaintiff's telegram of January 25 was not a valid acceptance under a particular section of the California Code known as the "statute of frauds" (the provisions of which are not necessary to our consideration of this case). Accordingly the court entered judgment for the defendant. The Richardses appealed.

Shoemaker, Justice:

. . . Under the factual situation in the instant case, the interpretation of the series of communications between the parties is a matter of law and an appellate court is not bound by the trial court's determination. Respondent Flowers argues that the letter of January 19th merely invited an offer from appellants for the purchase of the property and that under no reasonable interpretation can this letter be construed as an offer. We agree with the respondent. Careful consideration of the letter does not convince us that the language therein used can reasonably be interpreted as a definite offer to sell the property to appellants. As pointed out in *Restatement of the Law, Contracts,* Section 25, comment a: "It is often difficult to draw an exact line between offers and negotiations preliminary thereto. It is common for one who wishes to make a bargain to try to induce the other party to the intended transaction to make the definite offer, he himself suggesting with more or less definiteness the nature of the contract he is willing to enter into. . . ." Under this approach, our letter seems rather clearly to fall within the category of mere preliminary negotiations. Particularly is this true in view of the fact that the letter was written directly in response to appellants' letter inquiring

if they could deal directly with respondent and requesting him to suggest a sum at which he might be willing to sell. From the record, we do not accept the argument that respondent Flowers made a binding offer to sell the property merely because he chose to answer certain inquiries by the appellants. Further, the letter appears to us inconsistent with any intent on his part to make an offer to sell. In response to appellants' question, respondent stated that he would be willing to deal directly with them rather than through a realtor as long as their "offer would be in cash." We take this language to indicate that respondent anticipated a *future offer* from appellants but was making no offer himself. [Emphasis added.]

Appellants refer to the phrase that he would "expect to receive" $4,500 and contend this constitutes an offer to sell to them at this price. However, respondent was only expressing an indication of the lowest price which he was presently willing to consider. Particularly is this true inasmuch as respondent wrote only in response to an inquiry in which this wording was used. We conclude that respondent by his communication confined himself to answering the inquiries raised by appellants, but did not extend himself further and did not make an express offer to sell the property. We have before us a case involving a mere quotation of price and not an offer to sell at that price.

The cause, therefore, comes within the rule announced in such authorities as *Nebraska Seed Co. v. Harsh,* 1915, 152 N.W. 310, wherein the seller had written the buyer, enclosing a sample of millet seed and saying, "I want $2.25 per cwt. for this seed f.o.b. Lowell." The buyer telegraphed his acceptance. The court, in reversing a judgment for plaintiff buyer, stated: "In our opinion the letter of defendant cannot be fairly construed into an offer to sell to the plaintiff. After describing the seed, *(continues)*

RICHARDS V. FLOWERS ET AL.

(*continued from previous page*)
the writer says, 'I want $2.25 per cwt. for this seed f.o.b. Lowell.' He does not say, 'I offer to sell to you.' The language used is general, . . . and is not an offer by which he may be bound, if accepted, by any or all of the persons addressed"; and *Owen v. Tunison*, 1932, 158 A. 926, wherein the buyer had written the seller inquiring whether he would be willing to sell certain store property for $6,000. The seller replied: "Because of improvements which have been added and an expenditure of several thousand dollars it would not be possible for me to sell it unless I was to receive $16,000.00 cash. . . ." The court, in holding that the seller's reply did not constitute an offer, stated: "Defendant's letter . . . may have been written with the intent to open negotiations that might lead to a sale. It was not a proposal to sell." It would thus seem clear that respondent's quotation of the price which he would "expect to receive" cannot be viewed as an offer capable of acceptance. . . .

Since there was never an offer, hence never a contract between respondent Flowers and appellants, the judgment must be affirmed, and it becomes unnecessary to determine whether an appellant's purported acceptance complied with the statute of frauds or whether appellants failed to qualify for specific performance in any other regard.

Judgment affirmed. ♊

Objective versus Subjective Considerations

Up to this point, we have seen that the courts lay great stress on the actual language of a particular communication in determining whether it evidences an intent to contract. Another factor the courts have to consider is the background—the surrounding circumstances in which the communication was made. Examination of the background sometimes makes it quite clear that an intent to contract was not present, even though the language taken by itself meets the requirements of an offer, as where a statement is apparently made in jest, excitement, or anger. In *Higgins v. Lessig*, 49 Ill.App. 459 (1893), for example, a man who learned that his $15 harness had been stolen became so angry that he launched into a tirade in which he stated that he would "give $100 to any man who will find out who the thief is." The court held that this was not an enforceable offer, but merely the "extravagant exclamation of an excited man."

Higgins is consistent with the "objective theory" of contracts mentioned above, because a reasonable person hearing the owner's statement would have realized that once he calmed down he would not seriously wish to pay $100 for the return of a $15 harness. However, under this view parties are not required to read each others' minds. In *Lucy v. Zehmer*, 84 S.E.2d 516 (Va. 1954), for example, a man who claimed that he was only jesting when he offered to sell his farm to his neighbors was held to the bargain because the buyers reasonably believed that he was serious. Although the parties were drinking, they twice reduced their agreement to writing and its terms were reasonable.

This does not mean, however, that parties' intentions are always gauged totally objectively. Suppose, for example, that A promises to pay B $1,000,000 for his ranch. A stranger overhearing the promise might well believe that it was a serious offer because it outwardly appeared to be such. However, if B knows that A is a practical joker and nearly flat broke then B also knows that the statement is not a serious offer. If B attempted to accept the offer, no contract would result because of B's subjective knowledge. A's *apparently* serious offer does not bind him if B knows or should know that A is jesting.

Advertisements

Advertisements are usually considered to be preliminary negotiations, rather than offers to sell. The general rule is that a store advertisement that merely names the company, describes the article to be sold, and gives the price of the article "constitutes nothing more than an invitation to patronize the store." And this is usually true even if the terms "offer" or "special offer" appear in the advertisement.

The historic rationale for this rule is based (1) on the fact that most advertisements are silent on other material matters, such as the available quantity and credit terms, and (2) on the traditional principle that sellers of goods have the right to choose the parties with whom they deal and do not intend to commit themselves to sell to the potentially unlimited numbers of persons who might read advertisements. The rule also applies to catalogs, price quotations, and even articles displayed on a shelf with a price tag.

Thus, when a customer goes to the advertiser's store and tenders the advertised price, a contract is normally *not* formed. Rather, the customer is making an *offer* to purchase, which the store can accept or reject. Exceptions arise when the advertisement is worded so as to limit the number of persons who could reasonably accept the offer. Thus, when the advertisement limits the quantity of goods, e.g., "Three 1990 Mazda Miatas at $20,000 each, on sale Saturday!", most courts hold that at least three buyers can promise to pay the advertised price and thereby create an enforceable contract. Quantity may also be limited by such phrases as "subject to prior sale" or "while they last." A similar exception arises when an advertisement creates a special method of sale (*e.g.*, "1 Black Lapin Stole, Beautiful, Worth $139.50 . . . $1.00, First-Come, First-Served" or "Any person entering our store on Christmas Day wearing a bathing suit can buy an XYZ CD Player for only $220").

An advertised reward for the return of a missing dog would also be an enforceable offer, since realistically only a limited number of people could accept it. Additionally, advertisements promising rewards for information leading to the apprehension of criminals are usually held to constitute offers, even though several people might be in a position to accept; these decisions apparently are based on public policy grounds.

Consumer Protection

The general rule on advertising creates the potential for abuse by unscrupulous merchants who might place advertisements, never intending to live up to their terms. Virtually all states have enacted **consumer protection statutes** which generally impose civil and/or criminal liability upon businesspersons who unfairly refuse to sell goods or services in conformity with the terms of their advertisements. For example, statutes in many states list *deceptive trade practices,* among which is the "advertising of goods or services with the intent not to sell them as advertised." Other states have special "bait and switch" advertising statutes which typically impose liability upon advertisers who lure readers into the store by offering fabulous deals on products, but then either have an insufficient quantity for an expected reason-

able demand or focus all their sales efforts at convincing the shoppers to buy more expensive items that were not advertised.

Auctions

If conducted openly and fairly, auctions are an efficient way of determining a reasonable price in transactions between willing sellers and buyers. The UCC auction provision, Sec. 2-328, is generally consistent with common-law auction rules. In the typical *with reserve* auction, the act of putting a particular item up for auction indicates only a willingness to consider offers to purchase. A bidder's ensuing bid is treated as an offer which may be accepted when the auctioneer (the seller's agent) announces "sold" either verbally or through the fall of the hammer or some other customary means. Because no contract is formed until the hammer falls, the bidders are free to withdraw their bids prior to that event and, more importantly, the seller is free to withdraw the item from sale if no bids are as high as the seller desires.

Auctions are presumed to be with reserve unless they are explicitly represented as being *without reserve*. The act of putting an article up for sale in a without reserve auction is treated as a definite offer. The first bid creates a contract binding on the seller, unless a higher bid is made. The seller can no longer withdraw the item (though, surprisingly, bidders may withdraw their bids until the hammer falls). The highest bidder has a contract for sale that he can enforce.

Reasonable Definiteness

The requirement that the offer be *reasonably definite* is largely a practical one. The terms of an agreement have to be definite enough that a court can determine whether both parties lived up to their promises, in the event that a question of breach of contract arises. If the offer is too indefinite, the court is unable to do this.

As a general rule, then, a communication must cover *all major matters* affecting the proposed transaction in order to constitute an offer. If one or more of these is missing, the communication is merely a preliminary negotiation. Thus if S makes a written proposal to sell his farm Blackacre to B upon specified terms and conditions, "at a mutually agreeable price," and if B promptly sends an acceptance, there is no contract for the reason that S's proposal was not an offer. In a similar case, a company told an injured employee that it would "take care of him" and offer him "light work" when his doctor certified that he was capable of doing such a job. The company later refused to rehire him, and he sued to recover damages, alleging that this was a breach of contract. In ruling against the employee, the court said that since no specific position was mentioned, and there was no discussion of rates of pay or hours of employment, it had no way of determining the amount of the employee's loss. The statement of the company, in other words, was held to be too indefinite to constitute an offer.[4] Similarly, if X writes Y, "I will sell you my car for $1,000, credit terms to be arranged," and Y replies, "I accept," there is no contract. X's statement does not constitute an offer, since there is no way of knowing what credit terms would be acceptable to her

or whether any credit terms will ever be agreed on.

Despite the foregoing, the requirement of "reasonable definiteness" is, as the term itself indicates, relative rather than absolute. Thus it is not necessary that every detail be set forth in a contract, so long as there is agreement on major points. Where there is such agreement, missing terms about routine or mechanical matters may be supplied by the courts to "save" the contract; they may say in regard to such matters that there was *implied agreement*. For example, if X agrees to do certain clean-up work around a construction site for Y for $1,000, neither party can successfully contend that the agreement was too vague simply because no time of performance was specified. In this situation, it is implied that X will have a reasonable time in which to perform.

The case below presents a typical "definiteness" problem in a modern-day setting.

[4]*Laseter v. Pet Dairy Products Company*, 246 F.2d 747 (1957).

Pyeatte v. Pyeatte

Court of Appeals of Arizona, 661 P.2d 196 (1983)

Case

Charles Pyeatte and Margrethe May Pyeatte were married in Tucson, Arizona, in 1972. At the time of the marriage both had received bachelor's degrees. In early 1974 the couple reached an agreement concerning postgraduate education for both of them. The undisputed terms of the agreement were, in Mrs. Pyeatte's words, that she "would put him through three years of law school without his having to work, and when he finished he would put me through my master's degree without my having to work."

Thereafter she supported herself and her husband while he attended law school in Tucson. After his graduation Charles went to work for a law firm in Prescott, Arizona. Because they realized that his salary would not at that time be sufficient to support the marriage and pay for her graduate work simultaneously, she agreed to defer her plans for "a year or two" (during which time she

obtained part-time employment as a teacher).

In April 1978, Charles told Margrethe he no longer wanted to be married, and in June she filed a petition for dissolution of the marriage. During the dissolution proceedings the trial court ruled that the above agreement constituted a reasonably definite and enforceable contract, and found that she had fully performed her part of the contract. The court also found that her husband had not performed his part of the contract, and that she had been damaged as a result of this failure to perform. Thus the court, in addition to granting a decree of dissolution, entered a judgment of $23,000 against Charles on the breach of contract theory (that amount based upon estimates of what her costs of obtaining a master's degree would be). Charles appealed this judgment.

On appeal, the primary questions were (1) whether the trial court was correct in ruling the agreement to be a valid contract, and (2) if not,

whether the award of damages should be, nonetheless, affirmed "as an equitable award of restitution on the basis of unjust enrichment" (on the quasi-contract theory).

Corcoran, Judge:

. . . Although the terms and requirements of an enforceable contract need not be stated in minute detail, it is fundamental that, in order to be binding, an agreement must be definite and certain so that the liability of the parties may be exactly fixed. Terms necessary for the required definiteness frequently include time of performance, place of performance, price or compensation, penalty provisions, and other material requirements of the agreement. . . .

Upon examining the parties' agreement in this instance, *it is readily apparent that a sufficient mutual understanding regarding critical provisions of their agreement did not exist.* [Emphasis added.] For example, no agreement was made regarding the

(continues)

PYEATTE V. PYEATTE

(continued from previous page)
time when appellee [Margrethe] would attend graduate school and appellant [Charles] would be required to assume their full support. Both parties concede that appellee could not have begun her master's program immediately after appellant's graduation because his beginning salary was not sufficient to provide both for her education and the couple's support. Appellee told appellant she was willing to wait a year or two until he "got on his feet" before starting her program. Nothing more definite than that was ever agreed upon. Furthermore, although appellee agreed to support appellant while he attended law school for three years, no corresponding time limitation was placed upon her within which to finish her education. Even if we assume that the agreement contemplated appellee's enrolling as a full-time student, the length of time necessary to complete a master's degree varies considerably depending upon the requirements of the particular program and the number of classes an individual elects to take at one time. Such a loosely worded agreement can hardly be said to have fixed appellant's liability with certainty.

The agreement lacks a number of other essential terms which prevent it from becoming binding. Appellee's place of education is not mentioned at all, yet there are master's programs available throughout the country. . . . Nor was there any agreement concerning the cost of the program to which appellee would be entitled under this agreement. There can be several thousand dollars' difference in tuition, fees, and other expenses between any two master's programs, depending upon resident status, public versus private institutions, and other factors. Appellant testified that at the time of the "contract" neither he nor his wife had any idea as to the specific dollar amounts that would be involved. . . .

We are aware of [the general legal concept that] contracts should be interpreted . . . in such a way as to uphold the contract [whenever possible]. The court's function, however, cannot be that of contract maker. Nor can the court create a contract simply to accomplish a purportedly good purpose. . . .

[After ruling that the trial court's award of damages on the breach of contract theory was erroneous, the court turned to appellee's claim based on quasi-contract as follows:] Appellee's last contention is that the trial court's award should be affirmed as an equitable award of restitution on the basis of unjust enrichment. She argues that appellant's education, which she subsidized and which he obtained through the exhaustion of community assets, constitutes a benefit for which, in equity, he must make restitution.

[The court then ruled that the imposition of a quasi-contractual obligation against one spouse in favor of the other was not contrary to public policy, and continued:] The record shows that the appellee conferred benefits on appellant—financial subsidization of appellant's legal education— with . . . the expectation that she would be compensated therefor by his reciprocal efforts after his graduation and admission to the Bar. Appellant has left the marriage with the only valuable asset acquired during the marriage—his legal education and qualification to practice law. It would be inequitable to allow appellant to retain this benefit without making restitution to appellee. . . .

[The court then reversed the trial court's judgment, and remanded the case to that court for the purpose of determining the amount of recovery that appellee was entitled to, "the amount of the unjust enrichment." In order to determine that amount, the higher court instructed the trial court that "the award to appellee should be limited to the financial contribution by appellee for appellant's living expenses and direct educational expenses," whatever those expenses are found to be.]↺

Comment In a number of states, the ex-spouse's recovery is determined by statute. For example, in *O'Brien v. O'Brien*, 489 N.E.2d 712 (1985), the New York Court of Appeals held that a professional license held by the defendant spouse (the right to practice medicine, in this instance) constituted "marital property" under the state's Domestic Relations Law, the value of which must be considered by a court in making an equitable distribution of the spouses' property. In such states the ex-spouse's recovery does not depend upon proof of an express or implied contract, or upon quasi-contract principles.

Definiteness of the Agreement: Sales Law

Among the most significant modifications of the common law achieved by the UCC is a general relaxation of the degree of definiteness required in the agreement. Several provisions indicate that the drafters of the UCC wanted to make the formation of binding contracts somewhat easier than under common law. They recognized that businesspersons frequently intend to enter into enforceable agreements in situations where it is impracticable to make those agreements as definite as required by common law.

A prime example of this approach is found in Sec. 2-204(3). This section broadly states that a sales contract is enforceable even if one or more terms are left open, so long as (1) the court feels that the parties *intended to make a binding contract* and (2) the agreement and the surrounding circumstances give the court a *reasonably certain basis for granting an appropriate remedy* (such as money damages). Of course, there is a line beyond which the courts will not go. For instance, the larger the number of undecided terms, the less likely it is that a court will find that the parties intended to be legally bound. For this reason, a seller and buyer who wish to make an agreement with one or more terms left for future determination would do well to state specifically whether they intend to be bound in the meantime.

In addition to Sec. 2-204, a number of other sections of the UCC deal with specific omissions or am-biguities often occurring in sales contracts. We will examine the most important of these "gap-fillers" here.

Open Price Provisions

In some circumstances a seller of goods may be primarily concerned with being assured of a market for the goods he or she is producing. Or perhaps a buyer wants a guaranteed supply of certain needed products. In either case, price may be of only secondary importance. Thus buyer and seller might draw up a contract for the sale and purchase of goods at a later date, with the contract providing that the price shall be agreed upon later. Or the contract may say nothing about price at all. (Open price terms may be especially desirable in a market where the going price is subject to daily or weekly fluctuation.)

At common law many courts refused to enforce either type of agreement because of its indefiniteness. Under Sec. 2-305 of the UCC, however, agreements

---

BEWARE THE "CREEPING CONTRACT"

by Kirk Pasich

**Box 12.1
The Law
at Work**

The entertainment industry—in particular, the motion picture and television industries—specializes in "deals": deals to sign a hot new star, deals to sign the new up-and-coming producer and deals to produce motion pictures. Unfortunately, in too many cases, it is never quite clear exactly what the terms of the deal are.

It is almost a daily occurrence that instead of operating pursuant to a detailed comprehensive contract, motion picture and television studios and pro-ducers find themselves dealing with the "creeping contract." The genesis of such contracts is in a deal-making conversation, and their initial terms may be embodied in a "deal memo." Too often, the terms are based on different people's recollections of verbal agreements and on handshake modifications. Ultimately, these deals are resolved by a court or by negotiations among the parties, the outcome of which is determined by the project's success and the desires of the various parties to work together again on the next "sure thing." If the project that is the subject of the creeping contract is successful and all the parties receive the benefits for which they thought they contracted, then disputes might not arise. More likely than not, however, the creeping contract leads to a dispute.

Disputes occur in at least two situations. In the first situation, the parties disagree about the precise terms of the contract and what those terms mean. In the second, the project is never completed—leading to arguments about whether the contract was enforceable or too uncertain to be enforced. In either situation, the creeping contract leaves all parties involved open to substantial financial exposure and the time-consuming and expensive drain of litigation.

Source: *National Law Journal*, March 2, 1992, p. 25.

Comment   In March 1993, a jury awarded a movie producer $8.92 million in damages against actress Kim Basinger based on the producer's evidence that Basinger had, at the last minute, backed out of an oral agreement to star in a movie. The producer maintained that there was a binding oral agreement, though lawyers were still ironing out the details of a written contract. Further evidence showed that Basinger had not signed a written contract in six of her previous 10 movies. She has appealed.

of this nature are now enforceable if the court feels that the parties did intend to be bound by them. (Of course, if the evidence indicates that the agreement was merely tentative and the parties intended to be legally bound only if and when the price was ultimately set, there is no contract until that condition is met. The UCC cannot supply missing contractual intent.)

Whenever a court is called upon to enforce a contract in which the price (for one reason or another) was never actually set, and where it finds that the parties intended to be bound by the open price agreement, the court is faced with the task of providing a price term. Sec. 2-305 establishes a number of principles to guide the court in such a situation.

1. If the parties had expressly left the price *for later agreement* and then failed to agree, the price set by the court should be a "reasonable price at the time for delivery."

2. If the agreement had said *nothing at all about price,* and the price was never settled on, the method of determining it should depend on the circumstances. If the price had failed to be set through no fault of either party, the court should fix a "reasonable price at the time for delivery," as in item 1. But if the failure to set a price was caused by the fault of either party, the party not at fault can either treat the contract as cancelled or fix a "reasonable price" himself or herself. This price is binding and the court will uphold it, so long as it is found to be actually reasonable.

3. If the agreement had provided that the price was to be subsequently fixed *according to a definite standard set or recorded by a third party,* the rules for determining the unresolved price are exactly as they were in item 2. For example, the parties might have agreed that the contract price was to be the market price reported in a certain trade journal on a given date, but no such price was reported in the journal on that date. Or they might have agreed that an impartial third person was to set the price at a future date, but the third party later failed to do so. In either case, the price will be a "reasonable price at the time for delivery." This reasonable price will be set by the court if neither party was at fault; if one party caused the agreed upon method to fail, the other party may set a reasonable price.

4. If the parties had agreed that *one of them was to set the price* at a later time, the deciding party is obligated to set the price in good faith. Although *good faith* is defined differently for merchants and nonmerchants, the most compelling evidence of good or bad faith generally is whether the price fixed was a reasonable market price at that time.[5] If the party responsible for setting the price fails to do so or if he or she fixes a price in bad faith, the other party can either treat the contract as cancelled or set a reasonable price.

Open Time Provisions

The absence of a time provision does not cause a sales contract to be unenforceable. Sec. 2-309 states that, where a contract calls for some type of action by the *seller* (such as shipment or delivery) but does not specify the time for such action, a court may infer a "reasonable time" for performance. Of course, a reasonable time in a given case depends on all the circumstances known to the parties. For instance, suppose that the parties did not set a specific time for delivery but that the seller knew the reason for the buyer's purchase and the use to which the buyer intended to put the goods. A reasonable time for delivery would certainly be soon enough for the buyer to put the goods to their intended use.

Open Delivery Provisions

A sale of goods contract may also be enforceable even if certain delivery terms are to be decided at a later time. (We have already discussed the absence of a *delivery time.*) Another delivery term that might be absent is a provision for the *place of delivery.* Where the parties have not included this provision in their contract, Sec. 2-308 sets forth the following rules to serve as "gap-fillers."

1. The goods should be delivered to the buyer at the *seller's place of business.*

2. If the seller has no place of business, they should be delivered to the buyer at the *seller's residence.*

3. Where the contract refers to specifically identified goods, and both parties knew when making the contract that the goods were located at *some other place,* that place is where delivery should be made.

---

[5] *Good faith* is generally defined in Sec. 1-201(19) of the UCC as "honesty in fact." In the case of a merchant, it is defined in Sec. 2-103(1)(b) as "honesty in fact *and the observance of reasonable commercial standards of fair dealing in the trade.*" (Emphasis added.) Generally, the merchant definition will apply, since open price terms are rare among nonmerchants.

The UCC also attempts to account for other omitted details relating to delivery. For example, if the agreement contemplates shipping the goods but does not mention *shipping arrangements,* the seller has the right under Sec. 2-311 to specify these arrangements. (His or her actions are subject only to the limitation that they be in good faith and within limits set by commercial reasonableness). Another example is the situation where the contract fails to indicate whether the goods are to be delivered *all at once, or in several lots.* In such a case Sec. 2-307 obligates the seller to deliver them all at one time. However, there is one exception to this duty. If both parties, when making the contract, know that the circumstances are such that delivery in a single lot is not practicable, then the seller can deliver in several lots. (This would apply, for instance, to a situation where the quantity involved is so large that both parties realize that a single shipment is not feasible).

Open Payment Provisions

UCC Sec. 2-310 is a "gap-filler" for contracts that are silent as to the time of the buyer's performance—that is, the time of payment. The basic rule is that unless the parties have otherwise agreed, payment is due at the time and place at which the buyer is to receive the goods.[6]

Communication of the Offer

Returning to the subject of contract law (i.e., the common-law principles applicable to the formation of contracts), it is a primary rule that an offer has no effect until it has legally reached the offeree. This requirement of **communication** is based on the obvious proposition that an offeree cannot agree to a proposal before knowing about it. To illustrate: A city council, via a public advertisement, offers to pay $200 to the person or persons who apprehend an escaped criminal. If X captures the fugitive on his farm, only to learn of the offer later, his act does not constitute an acceptance of the offer and he is not entitled to the reward under the principles of contract law. The relatively few cases that involve this kind of fact-pattern generally follow this view.[7]

The principle takes on broader scope—and is more difficult to apply—in situations where there has been clear-cut communication of some terms of the agreement but questionable communication of others. The so-called fine print cases illustrate the problem. For example, statements printed on the back of parking lot tickets frequently provide that "the company shall not be liable for loss of, or injury to, the automobile, regardless of cause," or words of similar import. The usual view is that such provisions have not been legally communicated to the owner of the car and that the owner is not bound by them unless they were actually brought to his or her attention when the contract was made.

One should not conclude, however, that an *actual* communication of terms is required in all cases. If a court feels that the offeror has made a reasonable effort, under the circumstances, to call the terms of the offer to the offeree's attention, then a legal communication has occurred. A subsequent acceptance of the offer would be binding on the offeree in such a case, even though he or she might not have been aware of all its terms.

The case of *Green's Executors v. Smith,* 131 S.E. 846 (1926) is particularly instructive. In that case Smith sent a folder to each of his garage patrons, which indicated on the cover, in large type, that "new storage rates" would be effective at a future date. Inside the folder various rates were set forth, followed by a "note" which provided, in effect, that commencing with the new rates, patrons would also accept all liability for injuries caused by Smith's drivers while taking the cars to and from patrons' homes. Subsequent litigation raised the question whether patrons were bound by the note even if they had not read it. The court held that they were not. Quoting from an earlier decision, the court said: "When an offer contains various terms, some of which do not appear on the face of the offer, the question whether the acceptor is bound by the terms depends on the circumstances. . . . The question arises when a person accepts a railroad or steamboat ticket, bill of lading, warehouse receipt, or other document containing conditions. *He is bound* by all the conditions whether he reads them or not *if he knows that the document contains conditions.* But he is *not bound* by conditions of which he is ignorant . . . *unless he knows that the writing contains terms or unless he ought to know that it contains terms,* by reason of previous dealings, or by reason of the form,

---

[6] As we shall see in Chapter 23, the buyer generally has the *right to inspect* the goods (and reject them if they do not conform to the contractual requirements) before making the payment—unless the contract provides otherwise—as in a collect on delivery (COD) contract.

[7] There are exceptions, however, where recovery has been allowed on non-contract grounds (for example, public policy, inherent fairness, and the like).

size, or character of the document." (Emphasis supplied by the court.) The court continued: "There was nothing on the face of the folder, nor in its form or character, to indicate that it contained [a liability change]. The paper only purported to contain a schedule of rates for services at plaintiff's garage, and defendant had no reason, on account of her previous dealings with plaintiff or otherwise, to know that plaintiff proposed . . . a new contract of such unusual terms."

The case below presents a communication of the offer problem in a much more modern setting.

NEWMAN V. SCHIFF

U.S. 8th Circuit Court of Appeals, 778 F.2d 460 (1985)

Case

Irwin Schiff, defendant, is a self-styled "tax rebel" who has made a career (and substantial profits) out of his tax protest activities. On February 7, 1983, Schiff appeared on CBS News Nightwatch in New York, a program with a viewer participation format. During the program he repeated his long-standing position that "there is nothing in the Internal Revenue Code which I have here, which says anybody is legally required to pay the (federal income) tax." After a number of viewers called in questioning this position, Schiff stated on the air: "If anybody calls this show—I have the Code— and cites any section of this Code that says an individual is required to file a tax return, I will pay them $100,000." A two-minute segment of the program, in which the reward proposal was made, was rebroadcast early the next day on the CBS Morning News.

Newman, plaintiff, is a St. Louis lawyer who saw the rebroadcast (but not the original broadcast). On February 9, a day after viewing the rebroadcast, Newman called the CBS Morning News and cited six sections of the Internal Revenue Code as authority for his position that individuals are legally required to pay federal income taxes. The same day he wrote a letter to CBS Morning News citing the same sections, and stated that the letter represented "performance of the consideration

requested by Mr. Schiff in exchange for his promise to pay $100,000."

Some additional correspondence ensued between CBS, Schiff, and Newman, which culminated in a letter from Schiff to Newman dated April 20, 1983. In that letter Schiff said, in part, "I did make an offer on the February 7, 1983, news." However, he went on to say that Newman had not properly accepted the offer, and was thus not entitled to the money. Newman then brought this action in federal district court to recover damages for breach of contract.

The court entered judgment for Schiff, ruling (1) that Schiff's offer remained open only until the conclusion of the live broadcast; (2) that the rebroadcast did not renew the offer, and (3) that Newman's acceptance was "untimely" (i.e., too late to result in the formation of a contract). Upon reconsideration of the case at Newman's request, the court ruled, in essence, that the offer was renewed when Schiff learned of the rebroadcast "and failed to object to it." The court concluded, however, that Newman's response to the renewed offer still was untimely. (While the court did not give a reason for this conclusion, it was apparently on the theory that Newman's phone call of February 9 was not an acceptance because it was directed to CBS rather than to Schiff, the offeror.) Accordingly, the court affirmed its original judgment that no contract was formed; Newman appealed.

Bright, Senior Circuit Judge:

. . . Newman contends that the district court applied the wrong standard in judging the timeliness of his response to the rebroadcast. We do not [need to decide that issue], however, because we conclude that the district court erred by ruling that Schiff renewed his Nightwatch offer [by failing to disavow] the CBS Morning News rebroadcast. Consequently, we affirm the judgment of the district court on grounds that Newman did not accept Schiff's *initial and only offer* that had been made on the Nightwatch program. [Emphasis added.] . . .

The present case concerns a special type of offer: an offer of a reward [if a particular act is performed]. At least since the time of Lilli Carlill's unfortunate experience with the Carbolic Smoke Ball, courts have enforced public offers to pay rewards [if the offers have been legally communicated to the claimants]. . . . In that case, frequently excerpted and discussed in student law books, the Carbolic Smoke Ball Company advertised that it would pay a "100 £ reward" to anyone who contracted "the increasing epidemic of influenza, colds, or any disease caused by taking cold, after having used the Carbolic Smoke Ball three times daily for two weeks according to the printed directions supplied with each ball." Ms. Carlill, relying upon this promise, purchased and used a Carbolic Smoke Ball. It did not, however, prevent her from catching the flu. The court held that the advertised reward constituted

(continues)

NEWMAN V. SCHIFF

(continued from previous page)
a valid offer which Ms. Carlill had accepted, thereby entitling her to recover. . . .[a]

[The court here ruled that the legal principle relied upon by the trial court to find that the offer was renewed was not applicable to contract law, and thus should not have been invoked by that court. The court continued]: Schiff may have [impliedly] authorized CBS's act of rebroadcasting an excerpt of his Nightwatch interview, yet this did not give the rebroadcast legal effect as a renewed offer. The rebroadcast itself was not an offer, only a news report. Schiff's subsequent conduct and letter do not convert it into an offer.

[a]*Carlill v. Carbolic Smoke Ball Co.*, 1 Q.B. 256(1892).

[After thus distinguishing this case from *Carlill*, the court concluded by saying:]

Schiff's claim that there is nothing in the Internal Revenue Code that requires an individual to file a federal income return demands comment. The kindest thing that can be said about Schiff's promotion of this idea is that he is grossly mistaken, or a mere pretender to knowledge in income taxation. We have nothing but praise for Mr. Newman's efforts which have helped bring this to light. Section 6012 of the Internal Revenue Code . . . provides that individuals having a gross income in excess of a certain amount "shall" file tax returns for the taxable year. Thus section 6012 requires certain individuals to file tax returns. . . . The district court stated that Schiff's

argument is "blatant nonsense," [a ruling that] Schiff did not challenge . . . in his cross-appeal.

We affirm the judgment of the district court for the reasons discussed above.

Although Newman has not "won" his lawsuit in the traditional sense of recovering a reward that he sought, he has accomplished an important goal in the public interest of unmasking the "blatant nonsense" dispensed by Schiff. For that he deserves great commendation by the public. Perhaps now CBS and other communication media who have given Schiff's mistaken views widespread publicity will give John Newman equal time in the public interest.

Affirmed.

TERMINATION OF THE OFFER

Because of the rule that an offer can be accepted at any time before it is legally terminated, it becomes necessary to see what events will cause the offer to die. The rules in this area of the law are rather mechanical in their operation, and we need touch upon them but briefly.

Termination by Act of the Parties

Most offers are terminated by the conduct of the parties themselves by (1) revocation, (2) rejection, or (3) lapse of time.

Revocation

A **revocation** is a withdrawal of the offer by the offeror. Like the offer itself, it is effective only when it has been communicated to the offeree. The mere mailing of a revocation, in other words, ordinarily does not terminate the offer.[8]

The ordinary offer can be revoked at any time—assuming, of course, that it is communicated to the

[8]However, one state—California—provides by statute that a revocation is effective when "dispatched" (when mailed, in this case).

offeree before an acceptance has occurred. This is generally true even if the offeror had promised to keep the offer open a certain length of time. Thus, if X makes an offer to Y, stating that the offer will remain open thirty days, X can revoke it the very next day if he wishes. While this may seem unfair to Y, the reason for this view lies in the fact that Y has not given "consideration" (something of value) in return for X's promise to keep the offer open.

There are two notable exceptions to the general rule that an offer may be revoked at any time prior to its acceptance.

The Option.   In an option (or option contract, as it is frequently called) the offeree—either at the request of the offeror or acting on his or her own initiative—does give the offeror some consideration (usually a sum of money) in return for the offeror's promise to keep the offer open. Once the consideration is accepted by the offeror, the offer cannot be revoked during the specified period of time.

Thus, assume that X says to Y: "I offer to sell my farm to you for $100,000, this offer to remain open for 30 days." Y knows the general rule is that X may revoke this offer at any time before acceptance, yet Y truly wishes to buy the farm and needs time to line up his financing. Y may offer to pay X $50 in exchange for X's promise to keep the offer open for 30 days. If X accepts, an option contract is formed and X must keep the offer open. The amount paid for the option need not be a large sum, and a counteroffer will not terminate the offer.

Sales Law—The Firm Offer.   The general rule and exception noted above apply with equal force to sales transactions. However, the UCC has added a second exception to the general rule by creating another type of irrevocable offer, referred to in Sec. 2-205 as a **firm offer.**

The following requirements must exist for an offer to be irrevocable under this section:

1. It must be an offer to buy or sell goods.

2. It must be made *by* a merchant—though not necessarily *to* a merchant. That is, only the offeror need be a merchant.

3. It must be written and signed by the offeror.

4. It must give assurance that it will be held open.

If all these requirements are met, the offer is irrevocable even if the offeree gives no consideration for the assurance that it will remain open.

The period of time during which the offeror cannot revoke the offer is the time stated in the offer so long as it does not exceed three months. If the offer contains an assurance that it will be held open but mentions no time period, it will be irrevocable for a reasonable time, again not exceeding three months. (The three-month limitation applies only where the offeree is relying on Sec. 2-205 to make the offer irrevocable. If he or she gives *consideration* for the offeror's assurance that the offer will remain open, an *option* exists, and the three-month limitation does not apply.)

Rejection

A **rejection** occurs when the offeree notifies the offeror that he or she does not intend to accept. Like the offer and the revocation, it takes effect only when it has been communicated (in this case, to the offeror). Thus, if an offeree mails a letter of rejection but changes his or her mind and telephones an acceptance before the letter arrives, there is a contract.

One form of rejection is the **counteroffer**—a proposal made by the offeree to the offeror that differs in any material respect from the terms of the original offer. Thus, if the price stated in an offer is $500, and the offeree replies, "I'll pay $400," the original offer is ended forever. A recent case, *Thurmond v. Weiser,* 699 S.W.2d 680 (Tex. 1985), provides a further illustration. There the owner of a small Texas farm offered to sell it for $260,000. The buyer made a counter-offer of $250,000, which was rejected by the seller. Several negotiations ensued, which ended with the buyer sending a written "acceptance" of the $260,000 offer. The owner refused to convey the land, and in subsequent litigation it was held that there was no contract. The court ruled (1) that the original offer to sell for $260,000 was terminated by the buyer's counteroffer of $250,000, and (2) that because the seller did not renew her offer of $260,000 during the negotiations following the counteroffer, there was no outstanding offer capable of being accepted by the buyer.

A response in which the offeree deletes a term from, or adds a term to, the terms of the offer also constitutes a counteroffer. In the preceding case, for example, if the buyer had replied to the original offer, "Accept offer of $260,000; assume highway commission's proposed plan to relocate road on north side will be abandoned," the offer is again terminated.

Lapse of Time

If revocation and rejection were the only recognized means of terminating offers, many offers would remain open forever. To prevent such an unworkable result, a third method of termination is recognized—termination by the *passage of a reasonable length of time.*[9] What is reasonable depends on the circumstances of each case; thus it is virtually impossible to formulate general rules in this area of law.

What we will do instead is list the circumstances or factors that the courts consider in reaching an answer in a given case.

1. A circumstance of particular importance is the language used in the offer. Obviously, if an offeror states, "I must hear from you very soon," the time within which the offeree must accept is somewhat shorter than if such language were not used.

2. Another important circumstance is the means of communication used by the offeror. Sending the

---

[9]A different rule applies to offers in which the offeree is given a *specific* period, such as five days, in which to accept. In such offers, the lapse of the stated period terminates the offer.

offer by telegram normally imports an urgency that the use of the mails does not.[10]

3. Yet another factor of special importance is based upon prevailing market conditions. If the price of a commodity is fluctuating rapidly, for example, a reasonable time might elapse within hours from the time the offer is received.

4. A final factor to be taken into consideration is the method by which the parties have done business in the past.

An offer in some circumstances may thus lapse soon after it has been made, while in other circumstances it may remain open weeks or even months. While there are surprisingly few cases in this area of law, *Ward v. Board of Education*, 173 N.E. 634 (1930) is one of them. In that case Ina Ward received an offer of employment for the following school year on June 18, and she mailed her acceptance on July 5. In subsequent litigation, the higher court stated the applicable rule as follows: "It is a primary rule that a party contracting by mail, as she did, when no time limit is made for the acceptance of the contract, shall have a reasonable time, acting with due diligence, within which to accept." Applying that rule, where Ms. Ward had no explanation for her delay other than the fact that she was hoping to hear from another school board, the court held that the offer had lapsed prior to July 5 and there was, therefore, no contract.

Termination by Operation of Law

The rule that a revocation must be communicated to the offeree in order for it to take effect is based on the grounds of both fairness and logic. In ordinary circumstances, it seems reasonable that the offeree ought to be legally able to accept any offer until he or she has been put on notice that the offer has been terminated.

Certain exceptional events, however, will terminate an offer automatically—without notice to the offeree. These events fall into three categories: (1) death or adjudication of insanity of either party, (2) destruction of the subject matter of the contract, and (3) intervening illegality. The termination of an offer by any of these events is said to occur *by operation of law*.

To illustrate: On September 10, B offers a specific TV set to W for $525. On September 13, B dies. If W mails a letter of acceptance on September 14, there is no contract even if W is unaware of B's death. In the same example the result would be identical if, instead of B's death on September 13, the TV set were destroyed that day through no fault of B's. As another example, X offers to loan $1,000 to Y for one year with interest at the rate of 20 percent. Before the offer is accepted, a state statute takes effect which limits the rate of interest on that particular type of loan to 14 percent. The offer is terminated automatically. Figure 12.1 summarizes these methods of termination.

The various events that automatically terminate *unaccepted offers* generally do not terminate *existing contracts* (except those calling for the rendering of personal services, which we will discuss in Chapter 18). Thus, in the first example, if B's offer of September 10 had been accepted by W *before* B's death on September 13, B's estate would remain bound by the obligation to deliver the TV set.[11]

By the same token, the various terminations by operation of law do not generally apply to options (or option contracts). Thus, if B had promised on September 10 to keep his offer open for ten days, and if W had given B a sum of money in return for this promise, B's death on September 13 would *not* terminate the offer.

PRELIMINARY CONSIDERATIONS OF THE ACCEPTANCE

An offer ripens into a contract if, and only if, it is accepted by the offeree. Remember that a bilateral offer is accepted by the offeree's making the return *promise* that the offeror has requested, while a unilateral offer is accepted only by the actual performance of the requested *act*.

In most situations the offeree's response to the offer is so clearly an acceptance or rejection of it that no misunderstanding between the parties arises. But in a few situations legal difficulties do crop up—as, for example, where the offeree "accepts" the offer but then adds new terms to it or where the offeree's

---

[10]Some courts, for example, adopt the general rule that an offer made via telegram lapses at the close of business hours on the day it is received. (This rule is not applicable, obviously, to offers that by their language expressly or impliedly grant a longer period of time.)

[11]Whether the destruction of the TV on September 13 (instead of B's death) would free B's estate from the duty to deliver another set or would free W from the obligation to pay for the set is controlled by the law of sales, especially sections 2-509 and 2-613 of the Uniform Commercial Code. These sections are discussed in the sales chapters in Part IV.

FIGURE 12.1

Methods of Terminating an Offer

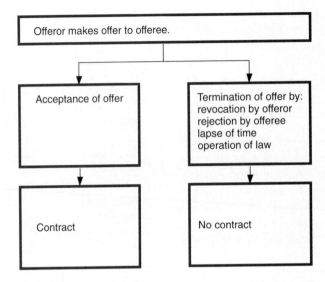

response is vague or indecisive. Another difficulty is the determination of the precise moment at which the acceptance becomes effective—specifically, whether the acceptance has to be actually communicated to the offeror before it becomes legally effective.

In the following discussion, emphasis is given to the acceptance of bilateral offers—those in which the offeror merely wants a return promise on the part of the offeree. Special problems raised by the acceptance of unilateral offers are considered later in the chapter.

REQUIREMENTS OF THE ACCEPTANCE

An acceptance is an expression on the part of the offeree by which he or she indicates a consent to be bound by the terms of the offer. Under general contract law, the acceptance must be a "mirror image" of the offer. Thus if a purported (intended) acceptance varies from the terms of the offer in any way—sometimes called a conditional acceptance—it ordinarily constitutes a counteroffer rather than an acceptance,

as illustrated in Figure 12.2. (While an offeree usually states expressly that he or she is "accepting" the offer, it is not necessary that this particular term be used. Any language showing that the offeree is assenting to the proposal is sufficient.) Regardless of the particular words used by the offeree in his or her response to the offer, the response must meet certain requirements in order to constitute an acceptance. Generally, an acceptance must be (1) unconditional, (2) unequivocal, and (3) legally communicated to the offeror or to the offeror's agent.

Requirement of an Unconditional Acceptance

We have already seen that when an attempted acceptance changes the terms of the offer, it becomes a *counteroffer* and a rejection rather than an acceptance. The same is true when the attempted acceptance adds new terms or conditions to those of the offer.

Thus, if S writes to B: "I hereby offer to sell my farm to you for $50,000," no acceptance would result if B responded: "I accept, if I can pay $2,000 for each of the next 25 years" or "I accept if you promise to

FIGURE 12.2

**Legal Ramifi-
cations of the
Counteroffer**

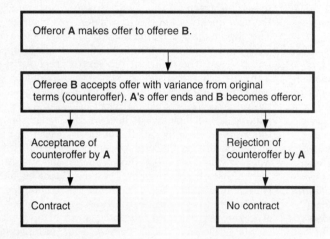

repaint the barn before sale." The general common-law rule is that the acceptance must be a "mirror image" of the offer in order for a contract to result.

The following case presents an intriguing situation in which both parties originally assumed, quite un-

derstandably, that an agreement had clearly been reached—until the sharp-eyed bus driver began to compare the language of the school board's "acceptance" with the language of his offer. At that point, the fun began.

LUCIER V. TOWN OF NORFOLK

Supreme Court of Errors of Connecticut, 122 A. 711 (1923)

Case

Lucier, plaintiff, operated a school bus for the defendant town for the school years of 1915, 1916, 1918, and 1919. In the summer of 1920 plaintiff and defendant began negotiating a contract for the coming year.

After several communications between the parties, plaintiff was asked by the Norfolk Town School Committee to submit a bid covering the transportation of students for the 1920–1921 school year. On August

12, plaintiff submitted his bid, offering to provide transportation at "$175 per week each school week" for that year.

On August 17 the board passed the following resolution: "Voted to award the contract for transporting children to and from Gilbert school and to and from various points in town to Mr. E.A. Lucier for the sum of $35 per day." The next day, a member of the committee, one Stevens, told plaintiff that the board "had voted to award him the contract" and requested plaintiff to have his

buses ready.

On the first day of school, September 7, plaintiff transported the students as agreed. On the evening of September 7 the board presented plaintiff with a formal contract for him to sign, the contract embodying the wording of the August 17 resolution. Plaintiff refused to sign the contract, on the ground that it was not in accordance with his bid for compensation at the rate of $175 per week, but at the rate of $35 per day instead. Thereupon defendant refused to employ plaintiff and

(continues)

LUCIER V. TOWN OF NORFOLK

(continued from previous page)
awarded the transportation contract to a third party.

Plaintiff brought action to recover damages for breach of contract, alleging that a contract was formed on his terms and was breached by defendant. (Specifically, plaintiff's argument was that his bid was accepted on August 18 when Stevens told him that the board "had voted to award him the contract.") Defendant contended that a contract was formed on its terms and that plaintiff was guilty of the breach. The trial court ruled that no contract was formed in this situation (but did award plaintiff $35 dollars, the reasonable value of his services performed on September 7). Plaintiff appealed.

Keeler, Justice:

. . . Summarily stated, the contentions of the plaintiff are: that the negotiations between him and the school board [resulted] in a contract express or implied, and the minds of the negotiating parties met; that Stevens, by reason of his position, had authority to make a contract binding the town; and that [plaintiff's bid, followed by Stevens' actions] resulted in a contract being formed. . . .

[Other] than as to the price to be fixed for the service, there is no dispute between the parties as to the terms submitted in the notice to bidders, and the plaintiff bid with reference to them, his offer conforming to these terms, the price for the service being the only open item in the transaction. The dispute turns upon the question of a rate per week as contrasted with a rate per day. The committee received from the plaintiff a bid of $175 per week; this undoubtedly meant to it the same as $35 per day, a result arrived at by a simple act of division of the larger number by five, the number of school days in the ordinary school week. It would seem that the committee were justified in reaching this conclusion, in that the plaintiff's pay in the contract for the year just past had been at a sum per day, and the notice for bids had called for a bid by the day. . . . When, therefore, the committee received a bid by the week they very naturally in their vote awarding the contract to the plaintiff substituted what they deemed an equivalent sum by the day, to accord with the requirement of the notice. This also was evidently the understanding of Stevens, when he afterward informed the plaintiff that the contract had been awarded to the latter. Subsequent events showed that this construction of his bid was not intended by the plaintiff, and that he intended to insist on the distinction between pay by the day and pay by the week, in that the latter afforded him compensation for work which would not in fact be required, when in any week a school day came upon a holiday.

In the pleadings, each side claimed the equivalence in fact and in effect of the expressions in the bid with those in the vote, each resolving the question of intent favorably to the contention by each, and each consequently claimed a contract which had been broken by the other party. *Both are wrong. It clearly appears from the facts found that the trial judge correctly found that there was no meeting of minds, and hence no contract. The plaintiff had the burden of establishing his construction of the claimed contract and has failed.* [Emphasis added.]

But the plaintiff further insists that he was in effect informed by Stevens that his bid had been accepted by the committee, that the latter was bound by Stevens' statement, and that he [the plaintiff] acted in accordance with the information conveyed to him. Further, that Stevens was the agent of the committee, and had authority to bind it, and that the committee was so bound when Stevens told him that the contract had been awarded to him, which information was in his mind equivalent to a statement that his bid had been accepted in the form tendered. . . . So he says that whatever the committee really intended in the matter, it was bound by Stevens' statement that the contract had been awarded to him on the terms of his bid, even though the vote stated the price of the service at a sum differing therefrom. [The court rejected this contention of plaintiff, ruling that Stevens was simply informing plaintiff of the board's action so that he could get his equipment in readiness, and that Stevens did not intend—nor did he have the authority— to bind the board to anything other than the specific resolution as passed.]

Judgment affirmed.

A Note of Caution

In some situations the offeree's response does constitute an acceptance even though it contains one or more terms that were not set forth in the offer itself. This is true where a reasonable person, standing in the place of the offeree, would justifiably believe that the "new" terms were within the contemplation of, and were agreeable to, the offeror despite the failure to include them in the offer. Following are two illustrations.

1. For several years X has been performing maintenance work upon Y Company's assembly line equipment, and has always granted Y Company 90 days in which to pay for the work. If X writes to Y, offering to perform preventive maintenance on various equipment for $1,000, and Y responds, "We accept on condition that we will have 90 days in which to pay," Y's response very likely constitutes an acceptance. Under the circumstances—the manner in which they had been doing business in the past—Y could assume that it was *implied* that X would grant the usual credit. (Custom in the industry could give rise to a similar implication, if clearly proved by Y.)

2. F offers to sell certain land to D for $55,000 cash. D replies by telegram, "I accept, assuming you will convey good title." This is an acceptance, even though F did not mention the quality of his title, because it is *implied* (under real property law) that a seller of land guarantees good or marketable title unless he or she indicates a contrary intention.

The purpose of the foregoing is simply to warn the student that it is possible for a term or condition to be literally new without necessarily being new in the legal sense. Thus, while the responses of the offerees in the preceding examples appear at first glance to constitute counteroffers, in the eyes of the law they add nothing new and therefore constitute valid acceptances.

New Conditions: Sales Law[12]

Under the UCC's provisions for the sale of goods contracts, an acceptance may be effective (under limited circumstances) even though it contains terms that conflict with, or add to, the terms of the offer. A major reason for rejection of the mirror-image rule by the drafters of the Code lies in the manner in which many sales contracts are entered into. Generally, such contracts are not fully negotiated. For example, commercial buyers often use their own printed forms in ordering goods from manufacturers or wholesalers, and the latter companies frequently use *their* forms in notifying buyers of their acceptance. Naturally, the terms and conditions of the two

forms are rarely identical, because the order forms used by buyers contain buyer-oriented terms, while forms used by sellers to invite, acknowledge, or accept orders contain seller-oriented terms.

In the vast majority of situations, the parties do not pay much attention to the other's forms. The seller provides the goods, the buyer pays for them, and the forms are filed away and forgotten. However, in the occasional situation where problems result and one side or the other wishes to sue for breach of contract, strict adherence to the mirror-image rule would always allow the potential defendant to claim that there was no binding contract because of differences in the forms.

To illustrate: Suppose that on its purchase order form buyer B ordered a quantity of goods at a certain price from seller S, and that seller S sent a purchase acknowledgment form to B indicating that the goods would be shipped. S's form, however, contained a clause stating that interest would be charged on late payments. Later B notified S that he did not want the goods and would not go through with the deal, whereupon S sued B to recover damages for breach of contract. Both parties look at the forms for the first time. In such a case the common law presumes that by responding with the varying term on interest rates, S intended to make a counteroffer, which B has not accepted. Thus no contract was ever formed, with the result that B has no liability to S.

In the modern era where so much commercial activity occurs through "form swapping," the mirror-image rule provides a haven for welshers, such as B in the foregoing example. The drafters of the UCC sought to eliminate such results in situations where the parties truly intended to contract. Section 2-207, which is often called the "Battle of the Forms" provision, addresses this problem. As our analysis will show, Sec. 2-207 reverses the common-law assumption, and presumes instead that an offeree who responds with varying terms intends to contract, unless he clearly indicates that he intends a counteroffer instead. Unfortunately, Sec. 2-207 is one of the most complicated, controversial, and inconsistently applied provisions of the entire Code.

Text of Section 2-207

This section reads, in material part, as follows (emphasis added):

1. A definite and seasonable expression of acceptance or a written confirmation which is sent within a reasonable time *operates as an acceptance* even though it states terms *additional to or different from* those offered or agreed upon unless acceptance is expressly made conditional on assent to the additional or different terms.

2. The additional terms are to be construed as proposals for addition to the contract. *Between merchants, such terms become part of the contract unless:*

a. the offer expressly limits acceptance to the terms of the offer;
b. they materially alter it; or
c. notification of objection to them . . . is given within a reasonable time after notice of them is received.

3. Conduct by both parties which recognizes the existence of a contract is sufficient to establish a contract for sale although the writings of the parties do not otherwise establish a contract. . . . [T]he terms of the particular contract consist of those terms on which the writings of the parties agree [together with terms provided by UCC "gap-filler" rules].

Written Confirmation of Informal Agreement

Section 2-207 provides three routes to contract formation. The first involves *written confirmation of a previous informal agreement.* Often employees of two companies will reach an informal agreement by telephone. They then swap forms which contain terms not discussed. If the parties truly intended to contract, then there is a contract based on the informal understanding. That the terms of the forms do not match will not undo the oral agreement. The terms of the contract consist of those established in the informal agreement, the terms on which the confirmation forms agree, and terms provided by subsection (2) of Sec. 2-207 (which will be discussed in more detail presently).

Exchange of Forms without Prior Agreement

The second route to contract formation arises where there is an *exchange of forms without prior agreement* (though perhaps with prior negotiation). An understanding of this method of contract formation requires careful analysis of subsections (1) and (2) of Sec. 2-207.

Subsection 1—Is There a Contract?

The primary import of this provision is that a seller's response to a buyer's order for goods which clearly indicates that the seller is accepting *constitutes an acceptance* even if it contains terms additional to or different from those found in the offer. Thus Sec. 2-207 clearly rejects the mirror-image rule.

Assume that Buyer B orders 2,000 A-20 widgets from seller S for $9,000, the price appearing in S's catalog. S sends his acknowledgment form as follows: "Accept your sales order #1379; 2,000 A-20 widgets/$9,000"; but on the back of the form is the new term "seller makes no warranties, express or implied, as to goods sold." *A contract now exists,* despite the new term in S's response. In other words, under subsection 1, S's acknowledgment constitutes an acceptance rather than a counteroffer, resulting in a binding contract. If S did not wish to be bound unless the buyer accepted the warranty exclusion, S should have made the matter a subject of negotiation by clearly conditioning the acceptance upon B's approval of the exclusion. If S does not make this condition clear and if it appears that S's response is intended primarily as an acceptance, a contract results.

In situations where the offeree's form agrees with the offeror's as to key terms, such as price, quantity, and date of delivery, differing only as to nonbargained ancillary terms, courts are likely to hold that the offeree's primary purpose was to form a contract. On the other hand, if the offeror's form orders 100,000 pounds of plastic at $2.00 per pound and the offeree's form confirms the order of 100,000 pounds of plastic at $2.25 per pound, the second document is not an acceptance.

Subsection 2—Is the New Term Included in the Agreement?

If subsection 1 analysis leads to the conclusion that a contract has been formed, the remaining question is whether the warranty exclusion has become part of it. If B notices the clause and agrees to it, then it is, of course, included. If B notices the clause and objects to it, then it does *not* become part of the contract. But what about the usual case where B does not notice the clause, or, if he does notice it, simply ignores it? In this situation, a distinction is made between terms that are "different from" those of the offer, and those which are "additional to" those of the offer.

Different Terms. If the term in the acceptance is different from (i.e., conflicts with) a term of the offer, the term does not become a part of the contract. Thus, in the above example, if B's order form had contained a clause setting forth certain warranties that were to be made by the seller (e.g., "seller warrants the widgets to be in conformity with U.S. Department of Defense specification #497 dated 6-15-90"), S's warranty exclusion clause would clearly not be part of the contract.

Additional Terms. As to any term in the acceptance that is an additional term (i.e., regarding a matter not addressed in the offer), Sec. 2-207(2) provides that, *if both parties are merchants,* the term becomes a part of the contract without any further assent on the part of the offeree, unless (a) the offer stated that acceptance is limited to the terms of the offer itself; or (b) the term "materially alters" the contract; or (c) the offeror objects to the new term within a reasonable time after receiving the offeree's acceptance.[13] Thus, in our example involving the

widget purchase, if both B and S were merchants, and if B's order form made no reference to warranties, S's warranty-exclusion clause would automatically become part of the contract, unless barred by a, b, or c.

In this case, most courts would hold that a warranty exclusion clause *does materially alter* an offer and therefore does *not* become part of the contract. The courts decide whether or not there was a material alteration on a case-by-case basis. The thrust of subsection 2(b) is that the offeree is not allowed to slip anything important past the offeror by simply including it in the acceptance form. Rather, the offeree should call the matter to the offeror's attention and make it a subject of negotiation. The case below is typical of those sales controversies in which the courts are called upon to apply the rules of Sec. 2-207.

---

[13]Therefore, in determining whether there is a contract (under subsection 1), it is not necessary that the parties be merchants. But their status as merchants *is* important in determining whether the additional term becomes part of the contract. The reason for this is that the drafters of the UCC felt that additional terms should be included in the contract without express agreement only where the transaction is between two professionals.

ST. CHARLES CABLE TV v. EAGLE COMTRONICS, INC.

U.S. District Court, Southern District of New York, 687 F.Supp. 820 (1988)

Case

St. Charles Cable TV (SCC) and its affiliate Cable Holdings, Inc., construct and operate cable television systems. SCC's representative Behrman had a series of meetings and telephone conversations with representatives of Eagle Comtronics, Inc., which makes addressable descramblers for use in the SCC cable system. On October 12, 1982, Behrman telephoned an order for 4,000 Eagle descramblers. The parties agree that the descramblers were warranted by Eagle for 18 months with an additional 18-month fixed-price replacement option. However, SCC contends that Eagle made various other warranties, which Eagle denies. Eagle sent a sales order acknowledgment to Cable Holdings after Behrman's telephone order. Each acknowledgment stated the

price, the number of descramblers, the 18-month warranty period, and added conspicuously: "Subject to the Terms and Conditions on Reverse Side." Among the terms and conditions listed on the reverse side were provisions that (1) the buyer's remedy under Eagle's warranty is limited to repair or exchange of defective goods and all other warranties are excluded; (2) the buyer is responsible for freight charges and legal costs and interest arising out of any contract dispute; and (3) the buyer must provide notice of defects within 15 days of delivery. Neither Cable Holdings nor SCC ever objected to the terms of the acknowledgment form; but they never signed it nor is there any evidence that their officers were aware of these terms.

Eagle began delivering descramblers in November of 1982. Over the next ten months, numerous problems

arose with the operation of the descramblers. Eagle made numerous repairs and modifications in response to complaints by SCC. Ultimately, SCC and Cable Holdings sued Eagle for breach of warranty, based on a standard implied warranty of merchantability under the UCC rather than on Eagle's limited "replace or repair" warranty. Eagle counterclaimed for the amount due on the purchase price. The following is an excerpt from the judge's ruling following a court trial.

MacMahon, District Judge:

[1. Was there a contract?]

The relevant provision for determining whether a contract has been formed [is] UCC 2-207(1) [which the court then quoted]. Official Comment 1 to the section states that it is intended to apply where "an agreement has been

(continues)

St. Charles Cable TV v. Eagle Comtronics, Inc.

(continued from previous page)
reached either orally or by informal correspondence between the parties and is followed by one or both of the parties sending formal acknowledgments or memoranda embodying the terms so far as agreed upon and adding terms not discussed."

Based on the testimony of Behrman and Eagle's sales manager, Chester Syp ("Syp"), we conclude that an oral agreement was reached by the parties on October 12, 1982. Behrman testified that the extensive negotiations between the parties ended with the determination of the price per unit and his statement that "we have a deal." Syp's testimony was less conclusive, but essentially he agreed that all negotiated terms were settled by telephone calls on October 12.

This conclusion is not changed by Eagle's acknowledgment of sale form. We find that Eagle's acknowledgment form was not "expressly made conditional on assent to the additional terms." First, once the parties have reached an oral agreement, one party cannot unilaterally alter the terms of their agreement by subsequently sending a written form that purports to be conditioned on acceptance of the alterations. Second, the "subject to" language of Eagle's printed form does not satisfy the "expressly made conditional" requirement.

[2. What are the terms of the contract?]

The treatment of the terms and conditions in Eagle's confirmation is governed by UCC 2-207(2) [which the court then quoted]. The parties here are merchants. Behrman did not limit acceptance to particular terms, and no objections to any of Eagle's acknowledgment form terms were made prior to the filing of this action. The terms, therefore, become part of the contract unless they *materially alter* it.

Although the question of when an additional term materially alters an agreement depends on the facts of each case, some guidance is provided by Official Comment 4 [which] suggests that "materially alter" means clauses that would "result in surprise or hardship if incorporated without express awareness by the other party." Generally, disclaimers of warranties or limitations on liability materially alter an agreement. The credible evidence, however, established that the only substantive warranty provision discussed by the parties was Eagle's replace or repair warranty for defects in material and workmanship. Eagle clearly intended that its own warranty apply, as indicated by including it in the acknowledgment form. Moreover, Syp testified credibly that he and Behrman negotiated an extension of *Eagle's* warranty and Behrman did not contradict Syp's statements. There is also consid-

erable indirect evidence that the parties based their agreement on Eagle's warranty term. Cable Holdings had previously received other Eagle equipment with the limited warranty. SCC repeatedly acted in accordance with a replace or repair warranty by returning the descramblers to Eagle and accepting repaired or new descramblers. Excluding additional or different warranties thus would not alter the negotiated oral contract between the parties. Nor can SCC or Cable Holdings claim surprise or hardship from it. Accordingly, we hold that the parties' contract included the limited Eagle warranty and disclaimer.

[The court also held that because interest is typically charged on unpaid bills and freight charges are typically paid by the buyer, no surprise or hardship could be claimed as to those terms in Eagle's form; they became part of the contract. On the other hand, the provisions for attorney's fees and a 15-day notice requirement were neither customary in the industry nor called to SCC's attention; therefore, they would unfairly surprise SCC and did *not* become part of the contract.]

Accordingly, we find that a contract was formed by the parties' oral agreement plus the terms and conditions contained in Eagle's acknowledgment form, except for the notice, [and] legal costs.∿

Agreement Implied from Conduct

To examine Sec. 2-207's third route to contract formation, assume that the parties have no prior informal agreement and even their forms do not produce a contract, perhaps because the offer explicitly limits acceptance to the terms of the offer and the purported acceptance just as clearly adds new terms. In such a case the documents do not appear to produce a contract, yet sellers often ship goods and buyers often pay for them in such instances. Here subsection 3 of 2-207 *implies a contract from the conduct* of

the parties. The terms of the contract consist of those matters that the two forms do agree upon supplemented by the "gap-filler" provisions of the Code.

For example, in one case a buyer and seller exchanged a series of purchase orders, acknowledgments and letters regarding a purchase of aluminum. At no time did the buyer's forms and the seller's forms agree as to a date of delivery. Buyer committed itself to purchase on September 1 and demanded delivery within seven weeks. Seller immediately acknowledged the order, but set a delivery date of nine weeks, later changed to eleven. Buyer stated that this was not acceptable. Seller told buyer either to accept it or obtain the aluminum elsewhere. Nonetheless, seller delivered the aluminum after eleven weeks and buyer accepted and partially paid for the aluminum. Certain defects were found and litigation resulted. The court held that the parties' correspondence did not create a contract. Seller's response materially altered the buyer's offer. In short, the communications indicated that the parties "dickered" over a key term, but never reached agreement. Nonetheless, the *conduct* of the parties (the seller's shipping the goods and the buyer's partially paying for them) did establish formation of a contract under subsection 3 of 2-207. The court then used the UCC "gap-fillers" to establish a reasonable time of delivery in order to determine whether seller had breached.[14]

Unequivocal Assent

Returning to common-law principles, an acceptance is an expression on the part of the offeree by which he or she indicates a consent to be bound by the terms of the offer. Under this definition, the courts require the "expression" be reasonably definite and unequivocal, and be manifested by some overt word or act. These requirements were developed, as a practical matter, to deal with the many situations where—from the language used by the offeree—his or her real intent is not at all clear; that is, the offeree's response is neither a clear-cut acceptance nor a flat rejection of the offer. At best, such responses cause initial delay and uncertainty between the parties as to whether a contract exists; at worst, litigation may ensue, with interpretation left to the courts.

To illustrate: X, in response to an advertisement placed by Y, sends a bid to Y offering to perform the described landscaping work for $23,000. Y replies by telegram: "Offer satisfies all requirements; will give it my prompt attention." Subsequently Y hires another landscaper to do the job, and, when X sues Y to recover damages for breach of contract, Y contends that his response did not constitute an acceptance of the offer. Applying the general rule to this case, Y's reply is too indefinite and tentative to satisfy the "unequivocal" requirement. Thus Y is correct in his contention that a contract was not formed.[15] On the

other hand, each case has to be decided on its own merits, including consideration of the circumstances surrounding the communications. Thus a different result might be reached in the foregoing example if the evidence indicated that X and Y had in the past considered such language to be binding.

Silence

As a general rule, there is no duty on the offeree to reply to an offer. Silence on the part of the offeree, therefore, *does not usually constitute an acceptance.* This is true even when the offer states, "If you do not reply within ten days, I shall conclude that you have accepted," or contains language of similar import. The reasons underlying this view are fairly obvious: (1) the view is consistent with the basic idea that any willingness to contract must be manifested in some fashion, and (2) it substantially prevents an offeree from being forced into a contract against his or her will.

In exceptional circumstances, however, the courts may find that the general rule is unfair to the offeror—that under the facts of the particular case, the offeree owed the offeror a *duty to reject* if he or she did not wish to be bound. In such cases, silence on the part of the offeree does constitute an acceptance.

While it is difficult to generalize about these exceptional situations, two types of case present little controversy.

1. If an *offeree* initially indicates that silence on his or her part can be taken as acceptance, there is no reason why that person should not be bound by the statement. For example: "If you do not hear from me by March 1, you can conclude that we have a contract."

2. If a series of *past dealings* between the parties indicates that the parties consider silence to be an acceptance, it can be assumed by the offeror that this understanding continues until it is expressly changed. For example: a retail jewelry store has, over the years, received periodic shipments of both ordered and unordered jewelry from a large supplier; during this time, the retailer-buyer has always paid for any unordered goods not returned within two weeks. A failure by the retailer to reject a particular shipment, or to give notice of such rejection, within two weeks

---

[14] *Alliance Wall Corp. v. Ampat Midwest Corp.,* 477 N.E.2d 1206 (Ohio App. 1984).

[15] In a case of a similar nature, a school board advertised for bids for the construction of a school building. After fourteen bids were received, the board wired one contractor: "You are low bidder. Come on morning train." The board

and the contractor were subsequently unable to agree to a formal contract, and litigation ensued. The Iowa Supreme Court ruled that the board's telegram did not of itself constitute an acceptance of the contractor's bid, saying that it indicated no more than a willingness on the part of the board to enter into contractual negotiations. (*Cedar Rapids Lumber Co. v. Fisher,* 105 N.W. 595, 1906.)

would very likely operate as an acceptance under the circumstances.

In both the preceding kinds of cases, the courts are likely to say that the offeror "had reason to understand" that silence on the part of the offeree was to be taken as a manifestation of assent, and that the offeree should have been well aware of this fact.

There is another, smaller group of cases in which it has been held that the offeror is justified in believing silence to be a manifestation of assent. These are situations in which a retail buyer gives a salesperson an order (offer) for certain goods, which the salesperson forwards to his or her company. If a reasonable period of time elapses without the company taking action, some courts hold that the buyer can justifiably view such silence as an acceptance of the offer and can hold the company liable for damages if it refuses to deliver the goods. Such courts reason that a company which sends salespeople out to solicit offers owes a duty to buyers to reject their offers within a reasonable time if it does not intend to accept them. (The same rule has sometimes been applied to mailorder houses when they have failed to reject buyers' orders within a reasonable time.)

When Does Acceptance Take Effect?

Reasonable Medium or Mailbox Rule

Offers, revocations, and rejections are effective when received. Acceptances are also effective upon receipt, *but* they may be effective even sooner. That is, under the "mailbox" or **reasonable medium rule,** an acceptance may be effective as soon as it is sent if the medium chosen is reasonable. Although there is variation from jurisdiction to jurisdiction in this area of the law, courts typically deem a chosen medium to be reasonable if (1) it is the same one used by the offeror; (2) it is one customarily used in prior dealings between the parties; (3) it is customarily used within the trade or industry in which the parties are doing business; or (4) it is one which is impliedly authorized by the language of the offer (for example, an acceptance by mail is probably reasonable in response to an offer by telegram if the offer indicated that there was no urgency about reaching an agreement).

If the offeree uses a medium that is not reasonable, the acceptance will be effective only when received. However, if the medium chosen by the offeree is reasonable, the acceptance will be effective *when dispatched* (out of the possession of the offeree). Assume that A mails an offer to B. If B mails an acceptance, there is a contract the minute the acceptance is dispatched even if the post office delays the acceptance or even loses it altogether. (Of course, if the acceptance is lost, the offeree will bear the burden of proving by other evidence that it was, in fact, mailed.) If A calls B to revoke the offer after B has mailed the acceptance, it is too late for the revocation to be effective. The offer, already accepted, has ripened into a binding contract.

Exceptions. There are at least three situations where the reasonable medium rule is generally inapplicable. First, the offeror is the master of his or her offer and may always require that an acceptance be made by a particular medium. If a particular medium (telegraph, for example) is *clearly* specified, then an acceptance sent by any other medium will not result in a contract being formed upon dispatch.

Similarly, the offeror may require that an acceptance be *actually received* in order to be effective. A company that has had difficulty with its mail service might well impose such a requirement, which will override the reasonable medium rule.

Third, if an offeree mails a rejection first, and only later changes his mind and sends an acceptance, the acceptance is not effective until received. Therefore, an offeror who receives the rejection first may assume that it is effective.

Examples

The following examples will illustrate the sequence of events leading to the formation of a contract, given the use of a reasonable medium.

Case 1. June 1— Y receives an offer in the mail from X.
June 2— X mails letter of revocation.
June 3— Y mails acceptance at 5 p.m.
June 4— Y receives the revocation.
June 5— X receives Y's acceptance.

Result. A contract was formed at 5 p.m. on June 3, since use of mail by Y was clearly reasonable. (Since a *revocation* is usually not effective until it is received, the letter that X mailed on June 2 had no effect until June 4, when Y received it. And by that time a contract had already been formed.[16])

---

[16]As noted earlier, in California (and perhaps a few other states) a revocation is effective when mailed—here, on June 2. In such states there would be no contract.

Case 2.   June 1— Y receives an offer in the mail from X.

June 2— Y mails letter of rejection.

June 3— Y changes his mind and at 10 a.m. calls X on the telephone and accepts the offer, telling X to disregard his letter of rejection.

June 4— X receives letter of rejection.

Result.   A contract was formed at 10 a.m. on June 3, when Y gave X actual notice of acceptance. (Since a *rejection* is usually not effective until it is received, Y's letter of rejection had no effect on June 2. The offer was thus open on June 3, when Y accepted it.)

Sales Law Changes

The Uniform Commercial Code generally adopts the reasonable medium rule of the common law, UCC Sec. 2-206(1)(a), providing that an offer may be accepted by "any medium reasonable in the circumstances." However, whereas the common law holds that if an *un*reasonable method of acceptance is utilized, it is not effective until received, UCC Sec. 1-201(38) provides that such an acceptance will be deemed effective as of the time it is sent *if* it is received within the time that a seasonably dispatched acceptance using a reasonable medium would normally arrive.

The following case applies the reasonable medium approach in a common-law context.

CUSHING v. THOMSON

Supreme Court of New Hampshire, 386 A.2d 805 (1978)

Case

An antinuclear protest group, the Clamshell Alliance, sent an application in March of 1978 to the New Hampshire Adjutant General's office, seeking permission to rent the national guard armory in Portsmouth the night of April 29. The alliance hoped to use the armory facilities for a dance it had scheduled on that date.

On March 31 the adjutant general mailed a "contract offer" to the alliance, agreeing to rent the armory upon specified terms. The offer required that a signed acceptance be returned to the adjutant general's office.

Cushing, a member of the alliance, received the offer at the alliance's office on Monday, April 3. That same day he signed it on behalf of the organization, put the acceptance in an envelope, and placed the letter in the office's "outbox."

At 6:30 in the evening of the next day, Tuesday, April 4, Cushing received a phone call from the adjutant general stating that he was withdrawing the offer on orders of Gov-

ernor Meldrim Thomson. Cushing replied that he had already accepted the offer, but the adjutant general repeated the statement that the offer had been withdrawn. (The alliance's acceptance, postmarked April 5, reached the adjutant general's office on April 6.)

When the adjutant general continued in his refusal to give the alliance permission to use the armory, Cushing and other members of the organization brought suit against Governor Thomson and the adjutant general, seeking specific performance of the contract that had allegedly been formed. Defendants contended that there was no contract, claiming that they had revoked the offer prior to plaintiff's "acceptance." Although there was no direct evidence indicating the precise moment at which the outgoing mail was placed in the hands of the U.S. Postal Service, the trial court found that this had presumably occurred prior to the time of the attempted revocation on Tuesday evening. It thus ruled that a contract had been formed, and granted plaintiff a decree of specific performance. Defendants appealed.

Per Curiam:[a]

. . . The [primary] issue presented is whether the trial court erred in determining that a binding contract existed. Neither party challenges the applicable law. [The court quoted the rule from a prior New Hampshire decision as follows:] "To establish a contract of this character, there must be an offer and an acceptance thereof in accordance with its terms. Where the parties to such a contract are at a distance from one another and the offer is sent by mail, the reply accepting the offer may be sent through the same medium, and the contract will be complete when the acceptance is mailed . . . and beyond the acceptor's control." Withdrawal of the offer is ineffectual once the offer has been accepted by posting in the mail.

The defendants argue, however, that there is no evidence to sustain a finding that plaintiff Cushing had accepted the adjutant general's offer before it was withdrawn. Such a finding is necessarily implied in the

[a]"Per curiam" is a phrase used to refer to an opinion of the whole court, as distinguished from an opinion written by any one judge.

(continues)

CUSHING V. THOMSON

(continued from previous page)
court's ruling that there was a binding contract. The implied finding must stand if there is any evidence to support it.

Plaintiffs introduced the sworn affidavit of Mr. Cushing in which he stated that on April 3 he executed the contract and placed it in the outbox for mailing. Moreover, plaintiff's counsel represented to the court that it was custom-ary office practice for outgoing letters to be picked up from the outbox daily and put in the U.S. mail. No [other evidence bearing on this point] was submitted in this informal hearing, and . . . the court's order appears to be [based] in part . . . [on representations made by attorneys for both sides,] a procedure which was not objected to by the parties.

Thus the representation that it was customary office procedure for the let-ters to be sent out the same day that they are placed in the office outbox, supported the implied finding *that the completed contract was mailed before the attempted revocation [occurred].* [Emphasis added.] Because there is evidence to support it, . . . the trial court's finding that there was a binding contract . . . must stand.

Decree affirmed.⚖

Acceptance of Unilateral Offers

Unilateral offers pose two unique problems insofar as offer and acceptance principles are concerned: (1) whether it is necessary for the offeree, having performed the requested act, to notify the offeror of that fact, and (2) whether the offeror has the right to revoke the offer after the offeree has commenced to perform but before the performance is completed.

Is Notice Required?

The general rule is that a unilateral offer is accepted the moment the offeree performs the requested act; giving notice that the act has taken place is usually not required. This rule does not apply, obviously, to offers that expressly request notification. In such offers, a contract is not formed until the requisite notice is given.

Another type of case requiring notice involves those exceptional situations where the act is of such a nature that the offeror "has no adequate means of as-certaining with reasonable promptness and certainty" that the act has taken place.[17] The typical cases in this category are *contracts of guaranty*—those in which one person guarantees a loan made to another. For example: A, in Columbus, asks B, in Miami, to lend $1,000 to C, a Miami resident, A promising to pay the debt if C fails to do so. In this situation, most courts take the view that while a contract is formed between A and B the moment that B makes the loan, A's resulting obligation is discharged (terminated) if B fails to notify him within a reasonable time that the loan has been made.

[17]*Restatement, Contracts 2d,* §54. The American Law Institute, 1979.

When Can Revocation Be Made?

Where the requested act will take a period of time for completion, the traditional rule has been that the offeror can revoke the offer at any time before full performance has taken place, even if the offeree has started to do the job. In such a case a contract is never formed. (However, under the quasi-contract theory, the offeree is ordinarily entitled to recover the reasonable value of his or her performance prior to the revocation. In the event that this partial performance is of no value to the offeror, the offeree will, of course, recover nothing.)

In recent years a growing number of courts have felt that the traditional view is unfair to the offeree in many circumstances, and they have abandoned it in favor of several other approaches. The most widely accepted of the newer views is that where the act is one that of necessity will take a period of time to complete, the *right of revocation is suspended* once the offeree starts to perform and remains suspended until the offeree has had a reasonable time to complete the act. This view is consistent with the traditional view to the extent that no contract is formed until the act has been completed, but it affords an interim protection to the offeree that the traditional view does not. Thus we have yet another illustration of the courts' freedom, within the framework of the common law, to modify those earlier principles whose application has brought about results of questionable merit.

Bilateral/Unilateral Contracts: Sales Law

Many sales contracts are clearly bilateral in nature. For example, a buyer on September 10 sends an order for goods at a specified price for November shipment, and the seller accepts the offer—i.e., promises to ship the goods as ordered—by mailing his or her acknowledgment to the buyer on September 16. Because Sec. 2-206 provides that "an offer to make a contract shall be construed as inviting acceptance in any manner and *by any medium reasonable in the circumstances*," a bilateral contract is formed the moment the acceptance is deposited in the mail on the 16th (assuming the mail was a reasonable medium).

"Prompt Shipment" Offers

Prior to adoption of the UCC, if a buyer ordered goods using such terms as "prompt shipment," "for current shipment," or "ship at once," the offer was usually construed as being an offer for a unilateral contract. Under this common-law view, *actual shipment* was the only way in which the offer could be accepted; a *promise to ship* would not cause a contract to come into existence (a result that sometimes came as a surprise to one or both of the parties). Sec. 2-206(1) of the UCC rejects that view by providing that an offer containing such language shall be construed as inviting acceptance *either* by prompt shipment *or* by a prompt promise to ship. Therefore, an offeree's sending of a return promise to ship forms a bilateral contract in such circumstances (although prompt shipment must follow or the contract will be breached).[18] Sec. 2-206 thus blurs the common-law distinction between bilateral and unilateral offers by permitting the offeree, in this limited instance, a choice as to how his or her acceptance shall be made. The differences between common law and the UCC on this point are illustrated in Figure 12.3.

FIGURE 12.3

Acceptance of a Unilateral Offer under Common-Law and UCC Rules

Common Law

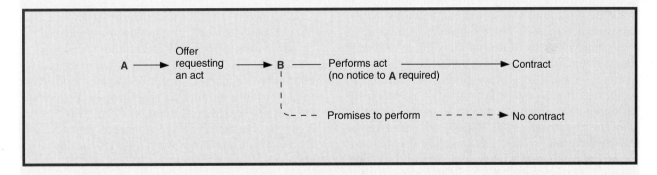

UCC 2-206

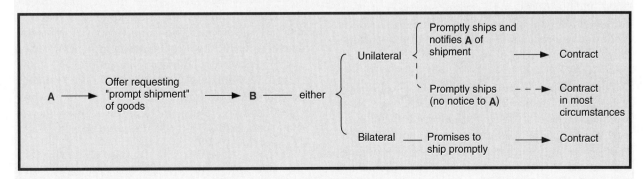

[18]The buyer can still require acceptance of the offer only by the act of shipment itself, but he or she now must explicitly state this in the offer.

SUMMARY

The first element of a contract (excluding quasi-contracts) is an agreement—an offer followed by an acceptance. In order for a communication to constitute an offer, the courts require it to (1) manifest a genuine intent to contract, (2) be reasonably definite, and (3) be legally communicated to the offeree. Communications failing to meet requirement 1 constitute mere "preliminary negotiations." Insofar as requirement 2 is concerned, the common-law rules require that the offer (and thus the ensuing agreement) include all major obligations of the parties. Sales contracts, however, are governed by more liberal rules. Under the UCC, such contracts are enforceable even if they fail to state some of the terms of the agreement. (In such circumstances, the missing terms are supplied by applicable provisions of Article 2 of the UCC.)

Once an offer is made, it remains open until terminated by act of the parties or by operation of law. The most common acts of termination by the parties are revocation and rejection. If a revocation or rejection occurs, any subsequent acceptance is too late and does not result in the formation of a contract. Termination by operation of law—an automatic termination—results where any of the following conditions occur: (1) death or adjudication of insanity of either party, (2) destruction of the subject-matter of the contract, or (3) intervening illegality.

In order for a communication of the offeree to constitute an acceptance, it must show an unequivocal intent to accept and must be in conformity with all of the terms of the offer. If a new term is added, or a term of the offer is deleted, the offeree's communication is a counteroffer (and a rejection of the offer). Under sales law, however (Sec. 2-207 of the UCC), if the offeree's communication is a "definite" acceptance, it constitutes an acceptance even if it contains an additional term. And, in such a case, if both parties are merchants the additional term automatically becomes a part of the contract (with limited exceptions).

When the parties are not dealing face-to-face (or by telephone), the modern rule is that the acceptance of a bilateral offer is effective *when sent* if the offeree uses a reasonable medium of communication. In most situations the U.S. mail is a reasonable medium, and thus, in such cases (under the "mailbox rule") a contract is formed when the acceptance is placed in the mail—even if it is delayed in transmission, or

never reaches the offeror. As to unilateral offers, the traditional rule has been that an acceptance is not effective until the offeree has completed performance of the requested act; thus a revocation before completion is effective. However, an increasing number of courts are taking the view that once the offeree has commenced performance the offeror's right to revoke is suspended until the offeree has had a reasonable time in which to complete the requested performance.

KEY TERMS

Offer
Preliminary negotiations
Consumer protection statutes
Communication (of offer)
Revocation
Firm Offer
Rejection
Counteroffer
Reasonable medium rule

QUESTIONS AND PROBLEMS

1. Capital City Ford advertised that anyone who bought a 1954 model car could turn around and exchange it for a 1955 model at no additional cost. After reading the ad, P bought a 1954 model and then attempted to exchange it for a 1955 model. Capital City refused, pointing out that advertisements generally are not offers that consumers can turn into binding contracts. P sued to enforce an alleged contract. Will P prevail? Discuss. (*Johnson v. Capital City Ford*, 85 So.2d 75, La.App. 1955.)

2. In 1984 evangelist Jerry Falwell was on a TV show with homosexual activist Jerry Sloan. Sloan, who was also a baptist minister, contended that Falwell had said on his "Old-Time Gospel Hour" show that there would be "a celebration in heaven" when mostly gay metropolitan churches around the country were "annihilated." Fallwell responded: "That's an absolute lie, and I'll give you $5,000 if you can produce that tape." Sloan did. Falwell refused to pay. Sloan sued. Will he recover? (*Sloan v. Falwell*, Calif. Superior Court 1986.)

3. Blakeslee, who wished to buy some land owned by the Nelsons, wrote a letter to them asking if they would accept "$49,000 net" for the property. The

Nelsons replied that they would "not sell for less than $56,000," whereupon Blakeslee wired back, "Accept your offer of $56,000 net." Does a contract now exist between the parties? Explain. (*Blakeslee v. Nelson*, 207 N.Y.S. 676, 1925.)

4. Condovest agreed "to use its utmost diligence and good faith" to obtain an FHA or VA loan to finance a condominium project. Upon production of the money, Street was to build the condos, "final plans and specifications to be agreed upon." Initially, Condovest could not secure the loan, so Street declared the agreement "void." A month later, however, Condovest tendered to Street $12,000 as a progress payment; this was the amount to be paid at the time the slab was poured. Condovest promised to make additional progress payments, but Street refused to perform. Condovest sued for breach of contract. Will it prevail? Discuss. (*Condovest Corp. v. John Street Builders*, 662 S.W.2d 138, Tex.App. 1983.)

5. The Jewish War Veterans, Post #58, offered a reward for the arrest and conviction of the killer of one of its members. Glover, not knowing of the offer, gave information to the police regarding the whereabouts of the killer. Glover subsequently learned of the reward and sued to recover it. Will he? Discuss. (*Glover v. Jewish War Veterans*, 68 A.2d 233, D.C. 1949.)

6. The Gator Company, a Florida firm, offered to buy 100 tons of scrap metal from the Sooner Company, located in Norman, Oklahoma, at a specified price. The Sooner Company accepted this offer using one of its own forms, which contained this new term: "It is agreed that any disputes arising out of the performance of this contract will be governed by Oklahoma law." Later the Gator Company wanted to get out of the deal, and contended that the Sooner Company's "acceptance" was legally a counteroffer, and that thus a contract was never formed. Under sales law, Sec. 2-207 of the UCC:

a. Is the Gator Company correct? Why or why not?
b. If a contract were formed, do you think the Sooner Company's new term became a part of that contract? Why or why not?

7. On January 1, 1985, P was injured in a car wreck caused by a person insured by West American Insurance Co. (D). P hired attorney Murnane to negotiate on her behalf. D offered $25,000 in November of 1986. After continued telephonic negotia-

tions, on December 1, 1986, D wrote to Murnane, stating that after further review, its "offer will remain $25,000." This letter did not specify a date on which the offer would terminate. On January 9, 1987, Murnane sent a mailgram to D unconditionally accepting the offer on P's behalf. D refused to pay, pointing out that the statute of limitations on P's right to sue expired on January 1, 1987, eight days before she accepted the offer. P sued to enforce the $25,000 settlement "agreement." Will she prevail? Discuss. (*Vaskie v. West American Insurance Co.*, 556 A.2d 436, 1989.)

8. P delivered eelskins to D four or five times. Each time D accepted delivery, waited a while, and then paid P. This time, D accepted delivery, waited several months, and then simply destroyed the eelskins without paying P. P sued. D claimed that there was no contract because it never expressly accepted any offer. Is this a good defense? Discuss. (*Hobbs v. Massasoit Whip Co.*, 33 N.E. 495, Mass. 1893.)

9. D hired an auctioneer to sell a piece of land for him. Together they prepared an advertisement stating that the land would be sold "without reserve." P started the bidding at $25,000, and it slowly rose to $41,000 (this also being P's bid) when D and his attorney ordered the auction stopped. They announced that they would not sell the land for less than $100,000 and would not allow any more bids to be made. P sued for specific performance, stating his willingness to pay $41,000. D claims that there is no contract. Is D correct? (*Zuhak v. Rose*, 58 N.W.2d 693, Wis. 1953.)

10. Tayloe applied to an insurance company for a fire insurance policy on his home. The company forwarded Tayloe's application to Minor, its agent in Tayloe's area, with a letter telling Minor that he could go ahead and negotiate a policy with Tayloe. Minor then wrote Tayloe, saying that if he desired to effect the insurance coverage for which he had applied, "send me your check for $57 and the business is concluded." Tayloe received this offer on December 20 and deposited his check in the mail on December 21. On December 22, while Tayloe's check was in the mail, his residence burned down. Was an insurance contract between Tayloe and the company in effect at the time of the fire? Explain. (*Tayloe v. The Merchants Fire Insurance Company*, U.S.S.Ct., 9 Howard 390, 1850.)

Chapter 13

Consideration

Historical Note

The Basic Concept of Consideration

Special Situations

A N ELUSIVE THING called **consideration** is the second element ordinarily required in a contract. Generally, if an agreement lacks consideration, neither party can enforce it, even if it is in writing. As a practical matter, consideration is present in most agreements; but since this is not always the case, we need a basic understanding of the *doctrine of consideration* in order to determine when an agreement is legally binding.

HISTORICAL NOTE

Courts have long struggled with the question of what agreements ought to be enforced. No system of law has ever enforced all promises, nor could this feasibly be done. Present-day concepts of consideration have resulted from a mixture of logic and historical accident. At one time, contracts had to be "sealed" in order to be enforced. A **sealed contract** had to have a bit of wax affixed to it, on which the initials or other distinctive marks of each of the parties was imprinted. Today, sealed contracts are virtually unknown, though a few jurisdictions will enforce such a contract even in the absence of consideration. Most jurisdictions, however, will enforce no contract, sealed or unsealed, in the absence of consideration.

The present-day requirements of consideration center in part on the notion that one party to an agreement should not be bound by it if the other party is not similarly bound. A's promise to give a present to B should not be binding on A because B is not bound to do anything. Promises to make gifts are generally unenforceable. Another important aspect of consideration is that it prevents one contracting party from exploiting another, as shall be illustrated later in this chapter in connection with a discussion of the "preexisting obligation" rule.

THE BASIC CONCEPT OF CONSIDERATION

Courts agree substantially about the kinds of promises or acts constituting consideration in most situations. Although several definitions of and tests for consideration have been formulated over the years, most lead to the same conclusion when applied to agreements where the existence of consideration is questioned. Our discussion focuses on a popular approach that emphasizes the "bargain" element of a transaction, which helps distinguish a promise of a mere gift (which may not be enforced) from an enforceable commercial promise to do something that the other party has bargained for.

Assume that Company A promised to deliver 5,000 tires to Company B on July 1 in exchange for Company B's promise to pay $200,000. Assume further that Company B breached the promise; Company A sued for breach of contract; and Company B raised the defense that no consideration existed to support its promise. Many courts would analyze the agreement to determine if three essential elements were present, constituting consideration.[1]

The first determination is whether the promisee (Company A, the party that received the promise that was not performed) suffered a **legal detriment,** defined as (a) doing (or promising to do) something that it was not obligated to do, or (b) refraining from doing (or promising to refrain from doing) something that it had a right to do. Unless Company A had a preexisting legal or contractual obligation to deliver the 5,000 tires, it is clear that Company A did suffer a legal detriment in this transaction. It promised to do something it did not otherwise have to do—to deliver 5,000 tires.

The second element of consideration is that the detriment (A's promise to deliver the 5,000 tires) must induce the promise that was not performed (B's promise to pay $200,000). Unless there is some other explanation for why Company B promised to pay $200,000 to Company A, it is clear that the detriment did induce the promise in this case. This is often called the "bargained for" element—B made its promise while bargaining to induce A to deliver the tires.

The third element of consideration is that the promise (B's promise to pay $200,000) must induce the detriment (A's promise to deliver the 5,000 tires). Again, unless some other reason appears to explain why A promised to deliver the 5,000 tires, it seems

---

[1] *Allegheny College v. National Chautauqua County Bank,* 246 N.Y. 369, 159 N.E. 173 (1927).

clear that it was in order to earn the $200,000 promised by B. All three elements of consideration are present, so the contract is enforceable.

Viewed in this light, consideration at a general level is easy to understand and, obviously, is present in most cases. Companies and individuals promise to deliver goods and services because they want the money that other companies and individuals are willing to pay for those goods and services.

Consider another example. Assume that X promises to install a home air-conditioning unit for Y, and Y promises to pay X $1,100 for the job. Consideration will become important if one of the parties, let us say

X, breaches the promise, is sued by Y, and claims lack of consideration as a defense. A court will quickly find: (1) The promisee (Y) has suffered a legal detriment (promising to do something he did not have to do—pay $1,100). (2) The detriment (Y's promise to pay $1,100) induced the promise (X's promise to install the air-conditioning unit). Obviously X bargained for Y's promise of payment; that is how X makes his living. (3) The promise (X's promise to install the air-conditioning unit) induced the detriment (why else would Y have promised to pay $1,100?). Try to analyze the following cases using the three basic elements of consideration.

HAMER V. SIDWAY

Court of Appeals of New York, 27 N.E. 256 (1891)

Case

William E. Story, Sr., promised to pay his nephew, William E. Story, II, $5,000 if he would refrain from drinking, using tobacco, swearing, and playing cards or billiards for money until he became twenty-one years of age. The nephew refrained from all the specified activities as he was requested to do, and on his twenty-first birthday he wrote his uncle a letter asking him for the money.

The uncle, in reply, assured the nephew, "You shall have the $5,000 as I promised you." The uncle went on, however, to explain that he had worked very hard to accumulate that sum of money and would pay it "when you are capable of taking care of it, and the sooner that time comes the better it will suit me."

Two years later the uncle died, without having made payment. The administrator of the uncle's estate, Sidway, refused to pay the $5,000, and suit was brought to recover that sum. (The plaintiff is Hamer, rather than the nephew, for the reason that at some time before litigation was

begun the nephew had assigned— that is, sold—his rights against the estate to Hamer. Thus Hamer's right to recover is entirely dependent upon whether the nephew had a valid contractual claim against his uncle.)

The trial court ruled that the uncle's promise to pay the $5,000 was not supported by consideration on the part of the nephew (the promisee) and entered judgment for the defendant. The plaintiff appealed.

Parker, Justice:

. . . The defendant contends that the contract was without consideration to support it, and therefore invalid. He asserts that the promisee, by refraining from the use of liquor and tobacco, was not harmed, but benefited; that that which he did was best for him to do, . . . and insists that it follows that, *unless the promisor was benefited,* the contract was without consideration— a contention which, if well founded, would [inject into the law, in many cases, an element so difficult to measure that needless uncertainty would result]. [Emphasis added.] Such a rule could not be tolerated, and is without

foundation in the law. . . .

Pollock, in his work on *Contracts,* page 166, says: "'Consideration' means not so much that one party is profiting as that the other abandons some legal right . . . as an inducement for the promise of the first." Now, applying this rule to the facts before us, the promisee used tobacco, occasionally drank liquor, and he had a legal right to do so. That right he abandoned for a period of years upon the strength of the promise of the [uncle] that for such forbearance he would give him $5,000. We need not speculate on the effort which may have been required to give up the use of those stimulants. *It is sufficient that he restricted his lawful freedom of action within certain prescribed limits upon the faith of his uncle's agreement,* and now, having fully performed the conditions imposed, *it is of no moment whether such performance actually proved a benefit to the promisor, and the court will not inquire into it;* . . . [Emphasis added.] Few cases have been found which may be said to be precisely in point, but such as have been, support the position we have taken. . . .

Judgment reversed. ⚖

Comment Two consideration principles are underscored here, as a result of the higher court's rejection of the defenses raised by the uncle's estate. First, if a promisee incurs a detriment by waiving a legal right, the promisee has given consideration even though he or she may have received an incidental benefit at the same time. (Thus, the nephew gave consideration by giving up certain rights—such as the right to smoke—even though he may have also been physically benefited by this forbearance). Second, consideration exists if the promisee incurs a detriment. It is not a requirement that the promisor must also receive a benefit.

LAMPLEY V. CELEBRITY HOMES, INC.

Colorado Court of Appeals, Division II, 594 P.2d 605 (1979)

Linda Lampley, plaintiff, began work at Celebrity Homes in Denver in May of 1975. On July 29 of that year Celebrity announced the initiation of a profit-sharing plan. Under that plan all employees were to receive bonuses if a certain "profit goal" were reached for the 1975 fiscal year—April 1, 1975, to March 31, 1976. (Linda was working under an at-will agreement—that is, both she and Celebrity could terminate the relationship at any time.)

Plaintiff's employment was terminated in January of 1976. At the end of March 1976, the company announced that the profit goal had been reached, and it made its first distribution of profits in May 1976. When plaintiff was excluded from this distribution, she brought this suit for the share allegedly due her.

In the trial court Celebrity argued that its promise to pay the bonus was a mere "gratuity" on its part, on the ground that there was no considera-tion on the employee's part to sup-port its promise. The trial court re-jected this contention and entered judgment for plaintiff. Celebrity appealed.

Kelly, Judge:

. . . In further support of its claim that the plan is not a binding contract, Celebrity contends that there was no consideration [given by plaintiff]. Ben-efit to the promisor or detriment to the promisee, however slight, can consti-tute consideration. The plan states as its objective:

> "Our goal is . . . to produce added em-ployee benefits gained through a higher qual-ity of operation. Through teamwork in our day to day operation, we can achieve not only higher levels of profits, but also better perfor-mance for our customers, a better quality in design of products, fair treatment of cus-tomers, subcontractors, and suppliers."

This language indicates that the plan was established as an inducement to Celebrity's employees to remain in its employ and to perform more efficient and faithful service. Such result would be of obvious benefit to Celebrity, and thus consideration was present. . . . [The court also impliedly found a detri-ment on the part of the promise, as follows:]

Lampley, who was employed for an indefinite term, was not obligated to re-main until 1976, and it can be inferred from the evidence in the record that she was induced to do so, in part at least, by the profit sharing offer made to her by Celebrity. Thus, this case can be distinguished from [those] which hold that there can be no recovery where the company gets no more service as a result of such a promise than it would if no such promise had been made. The memorandum of the profit sharing plan was an offer to add additional terms to the original employ-ment contract, and Lampley's contin-ued employment with Celebrity [until January 1976] was an acceptance of the offer and the consideration for the contract.

Judgment affirmed. ⚖

Though consideration was found in both these cases and is usually present in commercial transac-tions, obviously it is not always present. Consider the following examples.

- Company A to Company B: "Because you are having such tough times, we will charge you 20 percent less for custodial services than our contract with you calls for." In most jurisdictions (but not all, as we shall see later in the chapter), a court would not hold A to this promise. It is basically a gift, since *B suffered no legal detriment.*

- Company A to Company B: "We have an old metal press that we are no longer using. If you would like to come over some time and pick it up, you may have it." If A renegs on this promise, it will not be deemed enforceable. Even if we assumed that B suffered a detriment in the transaction (making the effort to pick up the press), *that detriment did not induce A's promise.* A was not "bargaining for" that act. Rather, this is basically a promise to make a gift and is unenforceable.

- Wife attacks her husband (D) with an ax, knocking him down. As she is about to decapitate him, P intervenes, catching the ax on its downward flight. P's hand is badly mutilated. D jumps up and promises to pay P $1,000 for saving his life. P has clearly suffered a detriment, and it is exactly what D bargained for. However, the *promise did not induce the detriment.* That is, because D made his promise *after* P acted, we cannot say that his promise caused her to do what she did. Thus, most courts would not enforce this promise. *See Harrington v. Taylor,* 36 S.E.2d 227 (N.C. 1945). (Later in the chapter we shall learn that a minority of courts would enforce the contract to the extent of D's moral obligation.)

Performance of Preexisting Obligations

As a general rule, a promisee does not incur a detriment by performing, or promising to perform, an act that he or she was under a preexisting duty to perform. One can be under a **preexisting obligation** because of the general law of a state or the federal government, or because a prior contract has not yet been carried out.

Obligations Imposed by Law

The following is a simple illustration of an obligation imposed by law. X's store has been burglarized, and X promises a local policeman $75 if he uncovers, and turns over to the authorities, evidence establishing the identity of the culprit. If the policeman furnishes the requested information, he is not entitled to the reward. Under city ordinances and department regulations he already has a duty to do this; therefore it does not constitute a detriment to him.

Contractual Obligations

Greater difficulty is presented in situations where the preexisting obligation exists (or may exist) as the result of a prior contract between the parties. While such situations involve varying fact-patterns, the starting point can be illustrated as follows. D contracts to drill a seventy-foot well for G for $200. After he commences work, D complains that he is going to lose money on the job and may not finish it unless he gets more money. G then says, "All right. Finish up and I'll pay you $100 extra," and D completes the job. G now refuses to pay the additional $100, and D brings suit to hold G to his promise. In this situation most courts would rule that D's act of completing the well was simply the performance of his original obligation—that he incurred no detriment thereby, and cannot enforce G's promise to pay the additional money. Thus, as a general rule, a **modification contract**—a contract that alters the terms of an existing contract—*requires some new consideration in order to be enforceable.* (Consideration would have been present in the above case, for example, had the modification contract required something extra of D—such as drilling the well to a depth of eighty feet.)

The primary rationale for the rule that performance of one's preexisting obligations does not constitute consideration is the prevention of coerced modification contracts. In other words, referring to the original example, the purpose is to prevent D—by threatening to stop work, or by actually stopping it—from enforcing the new promise made by G to pay more, in these circumstances.

Application of the preexisting obligation rule in most instances makes sense and brings about reasonable results. The following case is typical of those in which the rule prevents the enforceability of the modification contract. Following this case, a number of exceptions to the rule (and the reasoning underlying them) will be noted.

QUARTURE V. ALLEGHENY COUNTY ET AL.

Superior Court of Pennsylvania, 14 A.2d 575 (1940)

Case

Quarture, plaintiff, owned land in Pennsylvania. A portion of it was taken when the defendant county relocated and widened a state highway. Plaintiff needed legal help to recover damages from the county, and he employed a lawyer, Sniderman, to represent him in this effort.

A written contract was entered into, under the terms of which Sniderman was to "institute, conduct, superintend or prosecute to final determination, if necessary, a suit or suits, action or claim against the County of Allegheny on account of taking, injuring, and affecting (my, our) property in the relocation, widening, and opening of the State Highway known as Route No. 545." The contract further provided that Sniderman was to receive, as a fee for his services, "10 percent of all that might be recovered."

Sniderman represented plaintiff before the Board of Viewers of Allegheny County, and the board awarded plaintiff $1,650 damages. Plaintiff was dissatisfied with this amount and wished to appeal that award.

Subsequently, a new agreement was entered into between plaintiff and Sniderman. This agreement provided that Sniderman would appeal the case to the court of common pleas and that Quarture would pay him a fee of 33 percent of whatever recovery might be obtained on appeal.

Plaintiff, represented by Sniderman, then brought this action in the court of common pleas, appealing the award of the Board of Viewers, and the court awarded him a judgment of $2,961. At this point Sniderman filed a petition with the court, asking it to distribute to him 33 percent of the judgment—$987.

Quarture objected, contending that his promise to pay the larger percentage was not supported by consideration and that Sniderman was thus bound by his original contract (a fee of 10 percent). The court rejected this contention and awarded Sniderman $987. Plaintiff appealed.

Stadtfeld, Justice:

. . . Our first duty is to construe the original [contract]. What is meant by the terms "final determination?" . . . In the case of *Ex parte Russell,* 20 L.Ed. 632, it was said: "The final determination of a suit is the end of litigation therein. This cannot be said to have arrived as long as an appeal is pending."

The proceedings before the Board of Viewers cannot be considered as a "final determination," as their award is subject to appeal by either the owner of the property or by the municipality. If it were intended to provide for additional compensation in case of appeal from the award of viewers, it would have been a simple matter to have so provided in the contract. We cannot rewrite the contract; we must construe it as the parties have written it. . . .

The general principle is stated in *13 C.J. 351,* as follows: "A promise to do what the promisor is already bound to do cannot be a consideration, for if a person gets nothing in return for his promise but that to which he is already legally entitled, the consideration is unreal." Likewise, at p. 353: "The promise of a person to carry out a subsisting contract with the promisee or the performance of such contractual duty is clearly no consideration, as he is doing no more than he was already obliged to do, and hence has sustained no detriment, nor has the other party to the contract obtained any benefit. Thus a promise to pay additional compensation for the performance by the promisee of a contract which the promisee is already under obligation to the promisor to perform is without consideration."

There are many cases in which this rule of law is laid down or adhered to, but one that clearly sets out the reason for the rule is *Lingenfelder v. Wainwright Brewing Co.,* 15 S.W. 844. In that case, plaintiff, an architect engaged in erecting a brewery for defendant, refused to proceed with his contract upon discovering that a business rival had secured one of the subcontracts. The company, being in great haste for the building, agreed to pay plaintiff additional compensation as an inducement to resume work. It was held that the new promise was void for want of consideration, the court saying:

> It is urged upon us by plaintiff that this was a new contract. New in what? Plaintiff was bound by his contract to design and supervise this building. Under the new promise he was not to do any more or anything different. What benefit was to accrue to defendant? He was to receive the same service from plaintiff under the new [contract] that plaintiff was bound to render under the original contract. What loss, trouble, or inconvenience could result to plaintiff that he had not already assumed? No amount of metaphysical reasoning can change the plain fact that plaintiff took advantage of defendant's necessities, and extorted the promise of 5 percent on the refrigerator plant as the condition of his complying with his contract already entered into. . . . What we hold is that, when a party merely does what he has already obligated himself to do, he cannot demand an additional compensation therefor, and although by taking advantage of the necessities of his adversary he obtains a promise for more, the law will regard it as *nudum pactum,* and will not lend its process to aid in the wrong. . . .

While we do not question the value of the services rendered by Mr. Sniderman, we are nevertheless constrained by reason of our interpretation of the [first] agreement, *to limit the right of recovery to the amount stipulated therein* [*in view of the fact that the carrying on of the appeal was nothing more than what the first agreement required of him*]. [Emphasis added.] It is unfortunate that [that] agreement did not stipulate additional compensation in case of an appeal.

Judgment reversed.

Exceptions to the Preexisting Obligation Rule

Generally, the preexisting obligation rule applies to both coerced promises and uncoerced promises. Thus if a party to a contract later makes a modification contract under which he or she agrees to pay a higher price for property or services to be received under the first contract, such party is not liable on the promise even if it was an entirely voluntary one on his or her part. Because the freeing of the promisor from liability on the second promise, when made voluntarily, is sometimes felt to be unfair to the promisee, the courts (or legislatures) of the various states have fashioned a number of exceptions that cause the voluntary modification contract to be enforceable. The exceptions noted below are often recognized (although the circumstances to which they apply are rather limited ones).

The Unforeseen Difficulties Exception

The **unforeseen difficulties rule** is most easily illustrated by reference to a leading case in which a builder, Schuck, contracted to dig a cellar under a portion of an existing house, to a depth of seven feet, for $1,500. (The contract was made after the parties examined an excavation across the street, where the soil appeared to be normal.) After commencing work, Schuck discovered that the ground below the three-foot level was "swamp-like, black muddy stuff," and that this condition would require the use of piling, which the parties did not contemplate under the contract. Thereupon the home owner, Linz, told Schuck to do whatever was necessary to dig a seven-foot cellar, adding that he would "pay him whatever additional cost" was involved. Schuck completed the job. In ensuing litigation, Linz denied that there was consideration on Schuck's part to support his promise to pay more than the $1,500. The court rejected this contention and permitted Schuck to recover his additional costs.[2]

In reaching this conclusion, the court stated that, in its opinion, *the preexisting obligation rule should not be applied to a situation of this sort*. To support its reasoning the court relied upon these statements from a prior decision:

It is entirely competent [legally possible] for the parties to a contract to modify or waive their rights under it and in-

[2] *Linz v. Schuck*, 67 Atl. 286 (1907). The facts of this case must be distinguished from those presented by the earlier well-drilling example. In that example, the well driller threatened to quit simply because he was losing money, not because of some unknown condition of the soil that required unanticipated efforts.

graft new terms upon it, and in such a case the promise of one party is the consideration for that of the other; but, where the promise to the one is simply a repetition of a subsisting legal promise, there can be no consideration for the promise of the other party, and there is no warrant for inferring that the parties have voluntarily rescinded or modified their contract. But where the party refusing to complete his contract does so by reason of some *unforeseen and substantial difficulties in the performance of the contract, which were not known or anticipated by the parties when the contract was entered into, and which cast upon him an additional burden not contemplated by the parties, and the opposite party promises him extra pay or benefits if he will complete his contract, and he so promises, the promise to pay is supported by a valid consideration.* [Emphasis added.] (*Bryant v. Lord*, 19 Minn. 396, 1872.)

Situations where the rule is applied are admittedly exceptional; the courts of a few jurisdictions do not recognize it at all. And, among courts that do, they have historically taken the view that such circumstances as increased costs, unexpected labor difficulties, or loss of expected sources of materials do not fall within the unforeseen difficulties (or "unanticipated circumstances") rule. However, among such courts today there is a clear trend to recognize such circumstances as being within the rule if (1) the circumstance was truly unanticipated when the contract was made, and (2) the increased compensation is "fair and equitable under the circumstances"—i.e., the extra money promised is no more than a reasonable compensation to the promisee for the additional effort or costs he or she expended in finishing the job. To illustrate: C contracts to build a home for B for $95,000. After work is under way C is unable to get the Pella windows called for in the contract from his local supplier, because of a strike in the Pella plant. C learns, however, he can get the identical Pella windows from a distant supplier at a cost of $500 higher than he originally expected to pay for them. When C tells B this, B tells C to go ahead with the window installation and he will pay C the additional cost. If C completes the job, he is entitled to the extra $500.

The Mutual Rescission Exception

If the parties to the original contract expressly or impliedly rescind (cancel) it before it is fully performed, and enter into a new contract involving the same subject matter, the new contract is enforceable. To illustrate: C contracts to do certain work for B for $1,000. After C starts the job he complains on several occasions that he is going to lose money on the deal. B says that he will consider paying more, and suggests a new contract be made. C, with B's consent, then tears up the contract, and the parties make a new contract under which B agrees to pay C $1,200 for the job. When C finishes the work, he is entitled to the $1,200. The rationale is that the mutual cancellation of the first contract *freed* C of his preexisting duty to do the job, and when C later assumed the same obligation under the new agreement he thus incurred a new detriment sufficient to support B's promise to pay the larger sum. (While this view has been criticized by several authorities, it continues to be followed by most courts today.)

Modification Contracts: Sales Law

The drafters of the UCC made several modifications of the common law aimed at preventing technical rules from impeding enforcement of the parties' factual bargain. As an example, the drafters believed that if the parties to a sales contract subsequently modified it voluntarily, that modification should be enforceable whether or not supported by consideration. Accordingly, UCC Sec. 2-209(1) rejects the general common-law rule by providing that "an agreement modifying a contract [for the sale of goods] needs no consideration to be binding." To illustrate: S and B have agreed that S will sell a certain quantity of goods (such as 10,000 gallons of fuel oil) to B at a certain price. S later finds that he is not going to be able to deliver by the agreed-upon date. He contacts B, *who agrees to an extension of the time for delivery.* B subsequently has a change of heart and demands the goods on the original date. Under the UCC, *B is bound by the agreed-upon modification* even though S gave no additional consideration for the extension of time. (The reasoning behind Sec. 2-209 has prompted several states, including California, New York, and Michigan, to adopt a similar rule for common-law contracts.)

Although the modification agreement need not be supported by new consideration, it must still meet two requirements that the UCC imposes on all contracts falling within its scope. First, the modification must be made in good faith—that is, it must not be a coerced modification. And, second, the contract must not be "unconscionable"—i.e., shockingly one-sided. (The concepts of coercion [duress] and unconscionability are discussed in later chapters.)

To avoid difficulties caused by claims of subsequent modifications, many parties place in their written contracts clauses stating that subsequent modifications not evidenced by a writing shall have no effect. Such NOM ("no oral modification") clauses are expressly made enforceable by Sec. 2-209(2).

Adequacy of Consideration

Whenever the enforceability of a promise is at issue, a finding that the promisee incurred a legally recognized detriment results in the promisor being bound by the contract. This is usually true even if the actual values of the promise and the detriment are unequal—as is reflected in the oft-repeated statement that "the law is not concerned with the **adequacy of consideration.**" To illustrate: X contracts to sell an acreage in Montana to Y for $60,000. Y later discovers that the actual value of the land is under $30,000. Y is liable on his promise to pay $60,000, even though what he received was worth much less. Under the usual test, X incurred a detriment when he promised to convey the land—the surrender of his right to retain the property. The presence of this detriment constituted a consideration sufficient to support Y's promise to pay; and Y's claim of inadequacy is therefore of no relevance. The legal sufficiency of an act or promise, rather than its adequacy, is controlling.[3]

Mutuality of Obligation

The requirement of **mutuality of obligation** dictates that there must be consideration on the part of both parties to the contract. As we have indicated, in the typical bilateral contract each party's promise is supported by the promise of the other, and the requirement is met. If, however, in a particular case there is no mutuality because consideration is lacking on the part of one of the parties, neither party is bound by the agreement. Such an agreement is called an **illusory contract.** For example, A and B enter into a written agreement under the terms of which A promises to employ B as his foreman for one year at a salary of $22,000 and B promises to work in that capacity for the specified time. The last paragraph of the agreement provides that "A reserves the right to cancel this contract at any time." Because A has thus not absolutely bound himself to

---

[3]Adequacy of consideration is, however, inquired into by the courts in exceptional circumstances. They will, for example, refuse to issue a decree of specific performance against a promisor in a contract felt to be "unconscionable"—that is, where the value of the consideration given by the plaintiff-promisee is so grossly inadequate that enforcement of the contract would "shock the conscience and common sense of reasonable people." Additionally, the courts will refuse to enforce promises where the inadequacy of consideration suggests that the promisor has been the victim of fraud (a subject covered in some detail in Chapter 15).

employ B for the year, A has incurred no detriment (no unconditional obligation) by such a promise, with the result that B's promise to work for the year is not binding upon him. Thus, he can quit work at any time without liability to A. In such a case the requirement of mutuality of obligation has not been met, since A is said to have a "free way out" of the contract.

In the next case the right of cancellation was a restricted one. See if you agree with the distinction which the higher court makes between this kind of a clause, on the one hand, and one where the right to cancel is absolute, on the other.

LACLEDE GAS COMPANY V. AMOCO OIL COMPANY

U.S. Eighth Circuit Court of Appeals, 522 F.2d 33 (1975)

 Case

In 1970 a number of mobile home parks were being built by developers in Jefferson County, Missouri. At this time there were no natural gas mains serving these areas, so that persons living in them needed propane gas until the mains would be built.

In order to meet this demand, the Laclede Gas Company (Laclede) entered into a written contract with the American Oil Company (Amoco), under the terms of which Amoco would supply Laclede with propane for its customers living in the parks for a minimum period of one year. The contract contained a clause giving Laclede the right to cancel the agreement after one year upon 30 days written notice to Amoco, but it did not give Amoco any corresponding right to cancel the contract.

For several months Amoco made the required deliveries of propane to Laclede, but thereafter Amoco sent a letter to Laclede saying that it was "terminating" the contract. When Laclede brought this action to recover damages for breach of contract, Amoco contended that it was not bound by the contract because it lacked mutuality (that is, Amoco claimed that its promise to supply the propane was not supported by consideration on the part of Laclede because of the cancellation clause.) The trial court agreed with this contention, and Laclede appealed.

Ross, Judge:

. . . The [trial] court felt that Laclede's right to "arbitrarily cancel the agreement" . . . rendered the contract void "for lack of mutuality." We disagree with this conclusion. . . .

A bilateral contract is not rendered invalid and unenforceable merely because one party has the right to cancellation while the other does not. There is no necessity that for each stipulation in a contract binding the one party there must be a corresponding stipulation binding the other.

The important question in the instant case is whether Laclede's right of cancellation rendered all its other promises in the agreement illusory, so that there was a complete [absence] of consideration. This would be the result had Laclede retained the right of immediate cancellation at any time for any reason.

However, in *1 Williston, Law of Contracts* §104, Professor Williston notes:

Since the courts do not favor arbitrary cancellation clauses, the tendency is to interpret even a slight restriction on the exercise of the right of cancellation as constituting such detriment as will satisfy the requirement of sufficient consideration; for example, where the reservation of right to cancel is for cause, . . . or after a definite period of notice, or upon the occurrence of some extrinsic event. . . .

Professor Corbin agrees, and states simply that when one party has the power to cancel by notice given for some stated period of time, "the contract should never be held to be rendered invalid thereby for lack of mutuality or for lack of consideration." The law of Missouri appears to be in conformity with this general contract rule that a cancellation clause will invalidate a contract only if its exercise is *unrestricted.*

Here Laclede's right to terminate was neither arbitrary nor unrestricted. It was limited by the agreement in at least three ways. First, Laclede could not cancel until one year had passed after the first delivery of propane by Amoco. Second, any cancellation could be effective only on the anniversary date of the first delivery under the agreement. Third, Laclede had to give Amoco 30 days written notice of termination. These restrictions on Laclede's power to cancel clearly bring this case within the rule [and consideration on Laclede's part thus did exist]. . . .

Judgment reversed. ⚖

Requirements Contracts

Buyers and sellers of goods will sometimes enter into contracts where the quantity of the goods being sold—such as gasoline or coal—is not specified; rather, the quantity is to be determined by subsequent events. In some instances, the language of the contract is such that the buyer clearly has a "free way out"; that is, under the terms of the contract the buyer does not absolutely promise to buy any specific amount of goods. For example, S and B enter into a contract under the terms of which B promises to buy from S all the coal that he "might wish" over the next six months at a specified price per ton, with S promising to sell such quantity. Because of the language used, either intentionally or accidentally, B has not bound himself to buy *any* quantity of coal at all; thus the contract is illusory, since B has incurred no detriment. Because mutuality of obligation is lacking, the result is that if B later desires some coal, he is free to buy it from whomever he chooses. Conversely, if B orders coal from S, S has no duty to supply it.

Application of the mutuality of obligation requirement to cases such as the above soon began to cast doubt on the validity of all sales contracts in which buyers did not absolutely commit themselves to purchase some specified minimum quantity of goods. Many contracts, for example, were phrased in such a manner that the quantity of goods the buyer was committed to purchase depended on his or her subsequent needs (whatever they might prove to be) rather than on an obligation to take a fixed number of units at the outset. For example: An ice company contracts to sell to an ice cream manufacturer "all the ice you will need in your business for the next two years" at a specified price per ton.

The courts recognized the practicality of such **requirements contracts** and wanted to enforce them if they could; but the theoretical difficulty was that these contracts did not, by their terms, absolutely bind the buyer to take even a single unit of the product or commodity in question.[4] The courts therefore sought a theory by which many of these contracts could be upheld without demolishing the concept of mutuality.

They accomplished this, in large measure, by adopting the following view. If the parties, by the language of the contract, indicate that the quantity of goods is to be dependent upon the *requirements of the buyer's business,* then the contract is not void for want of mutuality and both parties are bound by it. (The determination of the exact quantity of goods is simply postponed, of necessity, until expiration of the period in question.)[5] Under this theory, while the buyer might not require any of the item or commodity in question, consideration on the part of the buyer exists as follows. In the event that the buyer subsequently requires the product, he or she is obligated to buy it solely from the seller. (That is, the buyer *gives up the right to buy it from others.*) Thus contracts such as the one in the ice case are generally binding on both parties.[6]

Output Contracts

Output contracts are essentially similar to and governed by the same principles as requirements contracts. A seller contracts to sell his or her entire output of a particular article, or of a particular plant, for a specified period of time to the buyer at a designated unit price. The implied promise of the seller (in the event he or she does produce the articles) not to sell them to anyone other than the buyer constitutes a detriment to the seller. And the promise of the buyer to purchase the output, in the event there is any, constitutes a corresponding detriment to the buyer. As a result, such contracts are usually enforceable.[7]

[4]Unlike the ice illustration, for example, it was often highly questionable whether the buyer would require any of the product at all, particularly where the period of time was a short one. (And even in the ice case it was possible that the buyer would go out of business the next day.)

[5]In other words, such contracts are to be distinguished from illusory contracts, in which the quantity is solely dependent upon the buyer's whim or will.

[6]This discussion simply sketches out the basic distinction between illusory and requirements contracts. There are many cases, however, where the courts have difficulty determining whether the contract falls into one category or the other. This is due largely to the fact that the language is frequently vague—terms much less rigid than *require* or *need* are commonly used. As one illustration, the courts by no means agree as to the effect of contracts in which the buyer promises to purchase all goods that he or she "wants" over a specified period. Many feel that this creates a requirements contract; others do not. Thus questions of interpretation arise. And in determining the effect of such terms, an examination of the surrounding circumstances—which differ from case to case—is always relevant. For these reasons, particularly, the results of some cases unquestionably conflict with others (and the student of the law just has to make the best of it).

[7]Sec. 2-306 of the UCC implicitly adopts the general principles stated above in regard to requirements and output contracts. It also tries to limit certain abuses that have occasionally cropped up. For example, a seller under an output contract might take advantage of the buyer by increasing his or her productive capacity far beyond anything the buyer could have anticipated on entering the contract. (A similar hardship can exist in a requirements contract when the buyer's requirements skyrocket far above what was reasonably contemplated by the seller or when the buyer shuts down operations solely for the purpose of escaping liability on the contract.) Sec. 2-306(1) tries to prevent such abuses by providing: "A term which measures the quantity by the output of the seller or the requirements of the buyer means such actual output or requirements as may occur in good faith, except that no quantity unreasonably disproportionate to any stated estimate or in the absence of a stated estimate to any normal or otherwise comparable prior output or requirements may be tendered or demanded."

Settlement of Debts

After a debt becomes due, sometimes the creditor and debtor enter into a *settlement agreement.* This occurs when the creditor, either on his or her own initiative or that of the debtor, promises to release the debtor of all further liability if the debtor pays a specified sum of money. If, after the specified sum is paid, the creditor seeks to recover the balance of the debt on the ground that the agreement lacked consideration on the part of the debtor, the success of the suit usually depends on whether the original debt was "unliquidated" or "liquidated."

Unliquidated Debts

An **unliquidated debt** is one where a genuine dispute exists between the debtor and creditor as to the existence or amount of the indebtedness. *Compromise agreements as to such debts, if executed, are usually binding.* For example: C (creditor) claims that she is owed $150 by D (debtor) for work performed under a contract with D, and D contends that the job was to cost only $100. C then says, "I will settle for $120," and D pays her that sum in cash. If C later sues to recover the balance allegedly owing, *she will be unsuccessful* because her implied promise to release D is supported by D's payment of the $120. (The payment of $120 by D—a sum more than D admitted owing—constitutes consideration because D, by making the payment, thereby gave up the right to have a court rule on his contention that the debt was only $100. Since C's promise to release is thus supported by consideration, D has a good defense to C's suit to recover the balance.) In such a situation, the payment of the $120 by D and the acceptance of that sum by C is said to constitute an "accord and satisfaction"—a binding agreement of a type that will be discussed further in Chapter 18.

Payment by Check   The above rule—preventing a further recovery by the creditor—is also applicable to payments by check if the debtor indicates that the tendered payment is meant to be in full satisfaction of the indebtedness (rather than a partial payment). For example: suppose that in the prior situation, before the parties had reached any agreement on the $120 figure, D simply mailed C a check for $120, bearing the inscription "payment in full." If C endorses the check in the usual manner by signing her name on the back of it, she is—because of D's inscription—impliedly promising to free D of any balance. *This promise is binding on C because D, the*

promisee-debtor, by making the payment again gave up his right to contend in court that the debt was only $100. This common-law rule of "accord and satisfaction" is favored because it promotes out-of-court settlements of disputes. On the other hand, it may be viewed as unfair to creditors.

Suppose that a creditor such as C in the previous example attempts to protect herself by crossing out D's words "in full satisfaction" and adding her own inscription, such as "under protest" or "without prejudice," indicating an intent to collect the remainder of the asserted debt. The general common-law rule has been that this action has no effect—the act of cashing the check implies an acceptance that overrides the words written on the check.[8] *However,* UCC Sec. 1-207 provides that "[a] party who with explicit reservation of rights . . . assents to performance in a manner demanded . . . by the other party does not thereby prejudice the rights reserved." Thus, some courts read Sec. 1-207 to allow C to cash D's check while reserving rights, and then to attempt recovery of the rest of the alleged debt.

Unfortunately, the courts of the various jurisdictions are greatly split as to Sec. 1-207's effect. Some believe that Sec. 1-207 changes the common law only as to the sale of goods. Others hold that it changes the common-law rule in any contract where a check is written. Still others conclude that Sec. 1-207 does not change the common law at all. *Revised* UCC Article 3 (adopted in 27 states as of July 1993) specifies that neither it nor 1-207 alters the common-law rule. As more jurisdictions adopt the RUCC,[9] the split among jurisdictions should be resolved.

Liquidated Debts

In **liquidated debts,** those in which there is *no dispute* as to the amount of the indebtedness, compromise agreements are less frequently binding. For example: A is owed $150 by B. The two parties agree about the amount of the debt and about its due date

---

[8]If the payee of a check does not notice the "in full satisfaction" language, many courts hold that the act of cashing the check cannot support an inference that the creditor assented to the compromise. This is important for companies that may mechanically process thousands of checks a day. Thus, one court held that no inference of accord arose when a creditor's mailroom deposited a conditional check according to internal procedures without the matter coming to the attention of an authorized representative of the creditor. *Slavenburg Corp. v. Kinli Corp.,* 36 U.C.C.Rep. 8 (E.D.Pa. 1983). *Revised* Article 3-311 helps resolve this problem by allowing large corporate payees to notify customers that instruments that are "in full satisfaction" must be sent to a designated office. If the customer does not comply by sending the instrument to the designated office, the claim is not discharged.

[9]See Chapter 24 for more information about Revised UCC Article 3.

of June 1. On June 2, A agrees to accept $120 as payment in full, and B pays that sum in cash. A thereafter brings suit to recover the balance of $30, and B contends that A is bound by the implied promise he made on June 2 to release him.

The common-law view here is that A's promise to release is *not binding, and he can therefore recover the balance of $30.* The reasoning is that the payment of $120 by B did not constitute a detriment to him, since it was less than what he admittedly owed. This rule is followed by the courts of most states even where the promise to release is in writing. (It should be noted, however, that a growing number of states have rejected the latter view by enacting statutes providing that all settlement agreements, *if in writing,* are binding upon the creditor even though consideration is absent. Typical of such statutes is Sec. 1541 of the California Civil Code, which reads as follows: "An obligation is extinguished by a release therefrom given to the debtor by the creditor upon a new consideration, or in writing, with or without new consideration.")

Payment by Check   The common-law view discussed above, permitting further recovery by the creditor in the liquidated debt situation, is also applied by the courts of most states where the compromise payment is made by check rather than in cash. Suppose, for example, that in the above case, where the debt was clearly $150, B sent A a check for $120 with the words "payment in full," and that A cashed it after endorsing it in blank. Even though A did not qualify his endorsement, the common-law view is that the payment of the $120 by B does not constitute the giving of consideration by B, and thus A is not bound by the implied promise to release which he made by cashing the check. Accordingly, A is *permitted to recover the balance,* just as in the case where payment was made in cash.[10] (Once more, a note of caution. In states having the "written release" statute referred to above, the blank endorsement of the check by the creditor is often held to constitute a release "in writing." In such states a recovery by the creditor is thus barred.)

Composition Agreements

A different situation is presented when a debtor makes an agreement with two or more creditors, under the terms of which he or she agrees to pay each creditor who joins in the agreement a stated percentage of that person's claim, with the creditors agreeing in return to accept that percentage as full satisfaction of their claims. Such agreements, called **composition agreements** (or *creditors' composition agreements*), are ordinarily held to be binding on the participating creditors even though each of them receives a sum less than what was originally owed.

To illustrate: X owes Y $1,000 and Z $600. The three parties agree that X will pay each creditor 60 percent of the amount owed and that Y and Z will accept the 60 percent as payment in full. X then pays Y the $600 and Z the $360. If either Y or Z brings suit to recover an additional sum on the theory that his promise to release was not supported by X's payment of the lesser sum, the usual view is that the composition is binding; therefore, the creditor's suit will be dismissed. To reach this result, the courts of many states find consideration to be present in that the promise of each creditor to accept the smaller sum supports the promise of the other creditors to do likewise. Other courts reach the same result by simply ruling that such agreements are binding on the ground of public policy, without trying to find consideration.

SPECIAL SITUATIONS

Up to this point, we have emphasized the usual situations where the courts require consideration to be present in order for promises to be enforced. (Occasional references to minority views were made only for purposes of completeness.) In the remainder of this chapter, we will focus on three exceptional situations where promises can be enforced by the same courts when consideration clearly is not present. The three are promissory estoppel, promises to charitable institutions, and promises made after the statute of limitations has run.

Promissory Estoppel

While it is well established that a promise to make a gift is generally unenforceable by the promisee even where he or she has performed some act in reliance upon the promise, unusual circumstances exist where the application of this view brings about results that are grossly unfair to the promisee. In such circumstances, the courts occasionally will invoke the doctrine of **promissory estoppel** (or "justifiable reliance" theory, as it is often called) to enforce the promise.

---

[10] Since the blank endorser under the general rule applicable to liquidated debts is permitted to recover the balance allegedly due, presumably the "under protest" endorser is similarly protected by the rule.

LEGAL FOCUS

Ethics

Legal Focus
ETHICS

The law's traditional approach to consideration emphasizes the bargain element. As a general rule, the *moral obligation* that results from making a promise is *not* sufficient to cause it to be enforceable. Neither are the motives or feelings of the promisor. Thus, an uncle's promise to pay $500 to his niece "in consideration of the love and affection that I have for you" is not binding. Nor is a promise made "in consideration of your many acts of kindness over the years." These acts (commonly referred to as *acts of past consideration*), which were performed earlier and, presumably, without expectation of payment, have not been bargained

for. Thus, under the traditional approach they do not make a promise enforceable. Should this be the state of the law? Should courts refuse to enforce promises based solely on a moral obligation?

The question becomes more problematic when we address situations such as that arising in *Harrington v. Taylor*, discussed in the text, where a reward promise by a rescue victim to the rescuer made *after* the rescue was held to be unenforceable. This traditional rule is slowly being modified by a trend to allow recovery to the extent of the moral obligation involved, that is, by enforcing a promise that was no more than what the promisor ought to have done. Thus, if a millionaire without close relatives promised a woman who had already rendered household

services to him without compensation for 20 years that upon his death he would leave $25,000 to her, this promise would, in the eyes of some courts, be enforceable against his estate even if the value of her services was much less. *Restatement (Second) of Contracts*, Sec. 86. Also, in *Webb v. McGowin*, 168 So. 196 (Ala. 1935), D's grateful promise to pay P $15 every two weeks for the rest of P's life, made after P permanently injured himself saving D's life, was held enforceable. Does the better rule come from *Harrington v. Taylor or Webb v. McGowin?* How far can the law feasibly go in enforcing promises that our moral sense tells us should be performed, but that fall short of meeting legal requirements applicable to all other promises?

The basic idea underlying this doctrine is that if the promisor makes a promise under circumstances in which he or she should realize that the promisee is almost certainly going to react to the promise in a particular way, and if the promisee does so react, thereby causing a substantial change in his or her position, *the promisor is bound by the promise even though consideration is lacking on the part of the promisee.* To illustrate: Tenant T leases a building from Landlord L from January 1, 1985, to December 31, 1986. In early December 1986, T indicates that he is thinking of remodeling the premises and wants a renewal of the lease for another two years. L replies, "We'll get to work on a new lease soon. I don't know about two years, but you can count on one year for sure." T then spends $500 over the next few weeks in having the first-floor rooms painted, but the parties never execute a new lease. If L seeks to evict T in March 1987 on the ground that his promise to renew was not supported by consideration, he will

probably be unsuccessful—that is, he will be held to his promise regarding the year 1987. In this case, where L should have realized the likelihood of T's conduct in consequence of his promise, L is said to be "estopped by his promise"; that is, he is barred by his promise from contending that the lack of consideration on T's part caused his promise to be unenforceable.

To illustrate further: "A has been employed by B for forty years. B promises to pay A a pension of $200 per month when A retires. A retires and forbears to work elsewhere for several years while B pays the pension. B's promise is binding."[11]

The following case presents a situation where resort to the estoppel doctrine seemed appropriate to the court.

---

[11] *Restatement, Contracts 2d,* The American Law Institute Section 90, 1973. (The text of Section 90 itself appears in the decision in the next case.)

HOFFMAN V. RED OWL STORES, INC.

Supreme Court of Wisconsin, 133 N.W.2d 267 (1965)

Case

In 1960 Hoffman, plaintiff, hoped to establish a Red Owl franchised grocery store in Wautoma, Wisconsin. During that year he and the divisional manager of Red Owl, Lukowitz, had numerous conversations in which general plans for Hoffman's becoming a franchisee were discussed. Early in 1961 Lukowitz advised Hoffman to buy a small grocery in order to gain experience in the grocery business before operating a Red Owl franchise in a larger community.

Acting on this suggestion, Hoffman bought a small grocery in Wautoma. Three months later Red Owl representatives found that the store was operating at a profit, at which time Hoffman told Lukowitz that he could raise $18,000 to invest in a franchise. Lukowitz then advised Hoffman to sell the store, assuring him that the company would find a larger store for him to operate elsewhere—that he would "be operating a Red Owl store in a new location by fall."

Relying on this promise, Hoffman sold the grocery and soon thereafter bought a lot in Chilton, Wisconsin (a site which the company had selected for a new store), making a $1,000 down payment on the lot. Hoffman then rented a home for his family in Chilton and, after being assured by Lukowitz that "everything was all set," made a second $1,000 payment on the lot.

In September 1961 Lukowitz told Hoffman that the only "hitch" in the plan was that he (Hoffman) would have to sell a bakery building he owned in Wautoma and that the proceeds of that sale would have to make up a part of the $18,000 he was to invest, thereby reducing the amount he would have to bor-

row. Hoffman sold the building for $10,000, incurring a loss thereon of $2,000.

About this time, Red Owl prepared a "Proposed Financing for an Agency Store" plan that required Hoffman to invest $24,100 rather than the original $18,000. After Hoffman came up with $24,100, by virtue of several new loans, Red Owl told him that another $2,000 would be necessary.

Hoffman refused to go along with this demand, negotiations were terminated, and the new store was never built. When Hoffman and his wife brought suit to recover damages for breach of contract, Red Owl defended on the ground that its promises were not supported by consideration on Hoffman's part (in view of the facts that no formal financing plan was ever agreed to by Hoffman and no franchise agreement obligations were undertaken by him). Hoffman contended that liability should nonetheless be imposed on the basis of promissory estoppel; the trial court agreed, entering judgment in his favor. Red Owl appealed.

Currie, Chief Justice:

. . . Sec. 90 of Restatement, 1 Contracts, provides: "A promise which the promisor should reasonably expect to induce action or forbearance of a definite and substantial character on the part of the promisee and which does induce such action or forbearance is binding if injustice can be avoided only by enforcement of the promise."

[The Chief Justice then observed that the Wisconsin Supreme Court had never recognized the above rule, but continued:] Many courts of other jurisdictions have seen fit over the years to adopt the principle of promissory estoppel [embodied in Section 90], and

the tendency in that direction continues. . . . The development of the law of promissory estoppel "is an attempt by the courts to keep the remedies abreast of increased moral consciousness of honesty and fair representations in all business dealings." *People's National Bank of Little Rock v. Linebarger Construction Co.*, 240 S.W.2d 12 (1951). . . .

Because we deem the doctrine of promissory estoppel, as stated in Section 90 of Restatement, 1 Contracts, [to be] one which supplies a needed tool which courts may employ in a proper case to prevent injustice, *we endorse and adopt it.* [Emphasis added.]

The record here discloses a number of promises and assurances given to Hoffman by Lukowitz in behalf of Red Owl, [and] upon which plaintiffs relied and acted upon to their detriment.

Foremost were the promises that for the sum of $18,000 Red Owl would establish Hoffman in a store, [and] in November, 1961, [the assurance] to Hoffman that if the $24,100 figure were increased by $2,000, the deal would go through. [In return,] Hoffman was induced to sell his grocery store fixtures and inventory in June, 1961, on the promise that he would be in his new store by fall. In November, plaintiffs sold their bakery building on the urging of defendants and on the assurance that this was the last step necessary to have the deal with Red Owl go through [and on which sale, incidentally, plaintiffs suffered the $2,000 loss earlier referred to].

We determine that there was ample evidence to sustain [the jury's finding that Hoffman relied on the promises of Red Owl], and that his reliance was in the exercise of ordinary care. . . .

[In regard to a contention by Red Owl that its promises were too vague and indefinite to be enforceable in this action, in view of the fact that the size, cost, and design of the proposed store

(continues)

HOFFMAN V. RED OWL STORES, INC.

(continued from previous page)
building were never agreed upon, the court disagreed, saying:] We deem it would be a mistake to regard an action grounded on promissory estoppel as the [precise] equivalent of a breach of contract action. The third requirement [of promissory estoppel,] that the remedy can only be invoked where necessary to avoid injustice, is one that involves a policy decision by the court. Such a policy necessarily embraces an element of discretion.

We conclude that injustice would result here if plaintiffs were not granted some relief because of the failure of defendants to keep their promises which induced plaintiffs to act to their detriment. . . .

Judgment affirmed. ⚖

Applications of Promissory Estoppel

Promissory estoppel is a doctrine of increasing importance and broadening application. We discuss promissory estoppel in this chapter because it is most commonly thought of as a method of enforcing a variety of promises that lack consideration. However, many courts invoke promissory estoppel in a variety of situations where they believe that contractual formalities are unnecessarily blocking attainment of the reasonable intentions and expectations of the parties. Consideration is one such formality; the requirement that some contracts be in writing in order to be enforceable is another. When the writing requirement is discussed in Chapter 16, we will see how promissory estoppel often provides an alternative means of enforcing oral promises that the parties intended to be enforceable, but did not put in writing.

Promissory estoppel doctrine is not completely consistent from jurisdiction to jurisdiction, but typical examples of the wide variety of uses of promissory estoppel include:

- X worries about floods and asks his insurance company whether his current policy protects his house from flood damage, indicating that he will procure a different policy if it does not. The company assures X that his current policy does cover flood damage. After X's house is damaged by a flood, examination of the policy clearly indicates that flood damage is excluded. The insurance company refuses to pay. Many courts would allow X to enforce the company's promise on grounds of promissory estoppel.[12]

- P interviews for a job with D Co., telling D that he has a good job with X Co. but would quit there if D offered him a job. D offers P a job, realizing that he will now resign his job with X. When P reports for work, D tells him that it no longer needs him and points out that his employment was "at-will" anyway (so that D is within its rights to terminate P at any time). Many courts would allow P to recover from D on promissory estoppel grounds.[13]

- Just before L, a general contractor, submits a bid on a construction project, M, a paving subcontractor, calls L and submits an $8,000 bid for the paving work. This is the lowest paving bid, so L reduces his overall bid, submits the bid, and is awarded the contract. Before L can inform M of the bid's success, M calls L to revoke its $8,000 offer, refusing to do the work for less than $15,000. M argues that it revoked its offer before L accepted it and that as of the time of revocation there was nothing to indicate to M that it had a contract it could enforce against L. Many courts would bind M to its promise through the doctrine of promissory estoppel.[14]

Although most courts clearly focus promissory estoppel on the element of a plaintiff's detrimental *reliance*, scholars have recently argued that many courts have actually taken the doctrine beyond this limitation and tend to use promissory estoppel to enforce "any promise made in furtherance of an economic activity."[15]

---

[12] *See Travelers Indemnity Co. v. Holman*, 330 F.2d 142 (5th Cir. 1964).

[13] *See Roberts v. Geosource Drilling Co.*, 757 S.W.2d 48 (Tex.App. 1988).
[14] *See Drennan v. Star Paving Co.*, 333 P.2d 757 (Cal. 1958).
[15] Farber & Matheson. *Beyond Promissory Estoppel: Contract Law and the "Invisible Handshake,"* 52 UNIVERSITY OF CHICAGO LAW REVIEW 903 (1985).

Formal Promises to Charitable Institutions

The law generally looks favorably upon charitable institutions, such as churches, hospitals, and colleges. One result of this policy is that many courts enforce formal promises (e.g., charitable subscriptions) to make gifts to such institutions, even though technically there is no conventional consideration. Among the approaches that courts use to enforce promises to make such gifts are (1) invention of consideration, by finding that each donor's promise is made in consideration of the promises of the other donors (i.e., a donor's promise is supported by the detriment incurred by other donors who made similar promises); (2) promissory estoppel, by finding that donors should foresee that the donee institution will rely on the promised gift, for example, by drawing up plans and beginning construction; and (3) where all else fails, many courts will simply enforce the promise on grounds of public policy.

Promises Made Subsequent to the Running of a Statute of Limitations

All states have **statutes of limitations** limiting the time a creditor has in which to bring suit against the debtor after the debt becomes due.[16] If the specified period of time elapses without the initiation of legal proceedings by the creditor, the statute is said to have "run." While the running of a statute does not extinguish the debt, it does cause the contract to be unenforceable—that is, it prevents the creditor from successfully maintaining an action in court to collect the debt.

New Promise to Pay

To what extent is the situation altered if the debtor, after the statute has run, makes a new promise to pay the debt? One might conclude that such a promise is unenforceable, since there is clearly no consideration given by the creditor in return. This, however, is not the case. *In all states, either by statute or by judicial decision, such a promise, if in writing, is enforceable despite the absence of consideration.*[17] In such a case,

[16]These periods of time vary widely among the states, and there is no typical statute. As a general illustration, however, some states give the creditor three years on an oral contract and six years on a written one.

[17]This rule on the enforceability of promises to pay debts barred by the running of the statute of limitations was, at one time, generally applied to promises to repay debts that were made by debtors after they had gone through *bankruptcy proceedings.* However, under the federal Bankruptcy Reform Act of 1978, effective October 1, 1979, this is no longer true. Thus, today such a promise to repay a debt is not binding unless supported by consideration.

the debt is said to have been "revived," and the creditor now has a new statutory period in which to bring suit. (If the new promise was to pay only a portion of the original indebtedness, such as $200 of a $450 debt, the promise is binding only to the extent of that portion—in this case, $200.)

Part Payment or Acknowledgment

The debt is also revived if a part payment is made by the debtor after the statute has run. If, for example, a five-year statute had run on a $1,000 debt, and the debtor thereafter mailed a check for $50 to the creditor, the creditor now has an additional five years in which to commence legal action for the balance. A mere acknowledgment by the debtor that the debt exists will also revive the obligation to pay.

Imposition of liability in the above instances is based on the theory that the debtor has, by making the part payment or acknowledgment, *impliedly promised* to pay the remaining indebtedness. The debtor can escape the operation of this rule by advising the creditor, when making the payment or acknowledgment, that he or she *is not* making any promise as to payment of the balance.

SUMMARY

As a general rule, a party is not bound by his or her promises unless "consideration" is present. If a defendant in a breach of contract suit claims there was no consideration for the promise he has refused to perform, courts will often ask three questions. First, did the promisee (plaintiff) incur a legal detriment by doing (or promising to do) something that he was not bound to do or by forgoing (or agreeing to forgo) something that he had the right to do? Second, did the promise that has been breached induce the promisee's detriment? Third, did the promisee's detriment induce the defendant's promise? If the answer to all three questions is "yes," as it almost always is in the commercial setting, consideration is present.

Note, however, that under the preexisting duty rule, the promisee generally suffers no detriment by merely promising to do something that he or she is already bound to do, either by statute or by contractual obligation. There are, however, several exceptions to this rule. Most importantly, the UCC allows modifications of contracts to be binding without consideration. (If the contract is for more than $500 either before or after the modification, the modification must be in writing.)

Applying the common-law rules to debt settlement agreements, a distinction is made between unliquidated and liquidated debts. If a debt is unliquidated (i.e., there is a genuine dispute as to the amount of debt), the acceptance by the creditor of the debtor's payment (under circumstances indicating it to be full payment) is binding upon the creditor. In such case, the creditor's express or implied promise to release is supported by consideration on the part of the debtor: the debtor's waiving of his or her right to contest the creditor's claim in court. If the debt is liquidated, however, the payment of a lesser sum than admittedly owing is not consideration, and thus the creditor is not bound by his or her promise to release. (In some states, however, the common-law rules have been modified by statute.)

In limited situations the courts have dispensed with the consideration requirement. The most common of these are situations where (1) the promisee has justifiably relied on the promisor's promise, resulting in the promisor being held liable under the doctrine of promissory estoppel; (2) the promise is made to a charitable institution; or (3) a debtor, after the statute of limitations has run, makes a new promise to pay his or her debt.

KEY TERMS

Consideration
Sealed contract
Legal detriment
Preexisting obligation
Modification contract
Unforeseen difficulties rule
Adequacy of consideration
Mutuality of obligation
Illusory contract
Requirements contract
Output contract
Unliquidated debt
Liquidated debt
Composition agreement
Promissory estoppel
Statute of limitations

QUESTIONS AND PROBLEMS

1. Dr. Browning made a contract with Dr. Johnson, under which he was to sell his practice and equipment to Johnson for a specified price. Before the time for performance, Browning changed his mind and asked Johnson to relieve him of his obligation to sell. Thereafter a new contract was made, under the terms of which Browning promised to pay Johnson $40,000 in return for Johnson's cancellation of the first contract. Later Browning refused to pay the $40,000, contending that this promise of his was not supported by consideration on Johnson's part. Is Browning correct? If not, where is the consideration on Johnson's part? (*Browning v. Johnson,* 422 P.2d 319, 1967.)

2. Hilda and Louis saw a movie, ate at a restaurant, and then had sexual intercourse in the back of Louis's car. Hilda later told Louis that she was pregnant and he was the father. He agreed to pay medical expenses and child support until the child reached the age of 21 if Hilda would promise not to institute bastardy proceedings against him. She agreed. After the child was born, blood tests proved that Louis was not the father, even though it appears that Hilda had believed in good faith that he was. Louis stopped making the child support payments. Hilda sued to enforce his promise. In defense, Louis claimed lack of consideration to support his promise. Is he correct? (*Fiege v. Boehm,* 123 A.2d 316, Md. 1956.)

3. Vinson agreed to do a certain construction job for Leggett, the owner, for $3,950. After work was commenced, Vinson found out that he was going to lose money on the job. Leggett examined Vinson's bills for materials to date and said, "Go ahead and complete the work like we said and I will pay you an additional $1,000." Vinson then completed the job. Is Leggett bound by his promise? Explain. (*Leggett v. Vinson,* 124 So. 427, 1929.)

4. Collins Corporation applied for a loan with the Gwinnett Bank. The bank was willing to loan the money to Collins, but only if its president, Sue, would agree to guarantee the loan in her individual capacity. She did so and the loan was made. When Collins Corp. failed to repay the loan, the bank sued Sue. She raised lack of consideration as a defense, arguing that because the loan went to the corporation, she received no benefit from the transaction. Is this a good defense? (*Collins v. Gwinnett Bank & Trust Co.,* 255 S.E.2d 122, Ga. 1979.)

5. A Pontiac dealer sold a new car to Knoebel under a contract that obligated him to make specified monthly payments. When Knoebel fell behind in his

payments, the dealer repossessed the car, which he had a right to do. On July 26 the dealer told Knoebel that if he would pay off the amount then due ($498.99) by August 10, he—the dealer—would return the car to him at that time. On August 7 Knoebel went to the dealer with the money, but the dealer had sold the car to a third party. When Knoebel sued the dealer for damages for breach of contract (for failure to hold the car for him), the dealer argued that his promise to hold the car was not supported by consideration on Knoebel's part. Is this argument correct? Why or why not? (*Knoebel v. Chief Pontiac, Inc.*, 294 P.2d 625, 1956.)

6. Brian Construction hired Brighenti to perform "All Excavation, Grading, Site Work, Asphalt Pavement, Landscaping, and Concrete Work" and "everything requisite and necessary to finish the entire work properly" at a construction site for $104,326. Before the contract was signed, Brian did test borings in the excavation area, finding nothing unusual. Brighenti relied on these borings in signing the contract, but they turned out to be very misleading. When Brighenti began excavation, he found that an old factory had been located on the site and Brighenti would have to remove concrete foundation walls, slab floors, twisted metals and other debris instead of just dirt. Upon this discovery, Brian agreed to pay Brighenti his costs of removing the material plus 10 percent. Brighenti agreed, but later refused to perform the work. Brian had the work done by someone else, then sued for breach of the second agreement. Brighenti claimed that the second agreement was unenforceable for a lack of consideration under the preexisting obligation rule since he was simply agreeing to perform work that he was already under contract to do. Is this a good defense? (*Brian Construction & Development Co. v. Brighenti*, 405 A.2d 72, Conn. 1978.)

7. Walquist was struck by a car driven by Christensen. The parties were in dispute as to whether or not the accident was Christensen's fault; they were also in disagreement as to the extent of Walquist's injuries. In this setting, they made an agreement: Christensen paid Walquist $500, and Walquist in turn released him from all liability. Later, when it turned out that Walquist's doctor bills alone came to $700, he sued Christensen to recover an additional sum. Christensen used the settlement agreement as a defense, but Walquist contended that Christensen's payment of $500 was not a sufficient consideration to support

his promise to release, in view of the facts that his damages were, in actuality, considerably greater than $500. Is Walquist right? Why or why not?

8. Mrs. Harmon was a long-time employee of the FoxLane Company. Her son's illness had caused her to consider retiring, but she was not sure she was financially able to do so. The president of the company told her, "Marie, I have tried to work something out for you. While I hope you can stay with us for two more years, I want you to know that upon your retirement—whenever it occurs—the company will pay you your present salary as long as you live." Two months later she retired, and the company made several monthly payments. When it then stopped the payments, she sued it for damages. The company contended that its promise was not supported by consideration on her part (i.e., the company did *not* say "Retire now and we will pay.") Was there consideration on Mrs. Harmon's part? If not, is there any principle under which she might recover? Explain.

9. In a dispute arising out of a contract to repair a leaking roof on debtor's building, debtor sent a "full payment" check for $500. The creditor payee endorsed the check below its notation, "Under Protest," and deposited the money into its account. Later, creditor sued debtor for $580 allegedly still due. If creditor can prove that $1,080 was the true amount of the debt, can creditor recover? (*Horn Waterproofing Corp. v. Bushwick Iron and Steel Co.*, 488 N.E.2d 56, N.Y. 1985.)

10. Fretz contracted to construct an office building for Stutts. However, when Stutts could not find financing, the contract was cancelled. A year later Stutts incorporated Aqua-Con, and it received a loan from Southern National Bank to build the building. Stutts again tried to hire Fretz as the builder, but Fretz was worried about being paid. He contacted the Bank, whose officer told him that two million dollars of the loan would not be paid to Stutts but would be held in reserve to insure payment to Fretz. Fretz then agreed to build the building, but when he finished and submitted his final bill of $275,000, he was paid only $50,000 which was all that was left of the loan. Fretz sued the bank for breaching its promise. The bank defended, arguing that its loan was to Aqua-Con and no consideration supported its promise to Fretz. Is this a good defense? (*Fretz Construction Co. v. Southern National Bank*, 626 S.W.2d 478, Tex. 1982.)

Contracts Contrary to Statute

Contracts Contrary to Public Policy

Effect of Illegal Contracts

I N *EVERET V. WILLIAMS,* 9 Law. Quart. Rev. 197 [England], a lawsuit was filed by one partner against another, alleging that they had gone into business together and that the defendant had kept more than his share of partnership profits. The complaint was rather vague regarding the nature of the business, alleging that the parties "proceeded jointly in [dealing for commodities] with good success on Hounslow Heath, where they dealt with a gentleman for a gold watch"; that in Finchley they "dealt with several gentlemen for divers watches, rings, swords, canes, hats, cloaks, horses, bridles, saddles, and other things"; and that a gentleman of Blackheath had items the defendant thought "might be had for little or no money in case they could prevail on the said gentleman to part with the said things." It is told that when it dawned on the court that the partners were highwaymen (the English equivalent of American stagecoach robbers), the solicitors (attorneys) for both parties were jailed and the plaintiff and defendant were both hanged. This possibly apocryphal case vividly makes the point that courts do not generally enforce illegal contracts. Indeed, the third element of an enforceable contract is *legality of purpose*—the attainment of an objective that is not prohibited by state or federal law.

In this chapter we will examine some of the most common kinds of contracts that are ordinarily illegal under state law.[1] Within a given state, a contract is illegal because it is either (1) contrary to that state's statutes (including the regulations of its administrative agencies) or (2) contrary to the public policy of that state, as defined by its courts.

All states have criminal statutes (many of which, as we saw in Chapter 7, are directed towards various kinds of misconduct in the business world). Such statutes not only prohibit certain acts but, additionally, provide for the imposition of fines or imprisonment on persons who violate them. Any contract calling for the commission of a crime is clearly illegal. Many other statutes simply prohibit the performance of specified acts without imposing criminal penalties

for violations. Contracts that call for the performance of these acts are also illegal. (An example of the latter is lending money under an agreement that obligates the borrower to pay interest at a rate in excess of that permitted by statute.)

Still other contracts are illegal simply because they call for the performance of an act that the courts feel has an adverse effect on the general public. (Examples of contracts contrary to public policy are those under which a person promises never to get married or never to engage in a certain profession.)

As a general rule, contracts that are illegal on either statutory or public policy grounds are void. This means that (1) in cases where the contract is entirely executory, neither party is bound by the agreement, and (2) in cases where one of the parties has performed his or her part of the bargain, such party cannot recover the consideration, or the value of the consideration, that has passed to the other party. (Exceptions to this general rule will be discussed later in the chapter.) Furthermore, courts will not allow even quasi-contractual recovery where illegal action is involved. By denying recovery to the parties to an illegal transaction, courts reason that they will deter illegal activity.

CONTRACTS CONTRARY TO STATUTE

Wagering Agreements

All states have statutes relating to **wagering agreements,** or gambling contracts. Under the general language of most of these statutes, making bets and operating games of chance are prohibited. Any obligations arising from these activities are *void* (nonexistent) in the eyes of the law, and thus completely unenforceable by the "winner."

Bets and Lotteries

In most instances wagering agreements are easily recognized. Simple bets on the outcome of athletic events and lotteries such as bingo (when played for money) are the most common of them. On the other hand, merchants holding promotional schemes such

---

[1] Certain federal statutes that have a bearing on the legality of contracts in interstate commerce will be covered in Part VII.

as supermarket drawings sometimes have difficulty determining if they are holding an illegal **lottery,** especially because definitions vary widely from state to state. Courts tend to rule that a scheme that does not require a purchase of goods by the participant is not a lottery because consideration (which most courts view as an essential part of a lottery) is lacking. That is why so many contests state "no purchase necessary." The following case illustrates a common approach to the lottery issue.

PEPSI-COLA BOTTLING CO. OF LUVERNE v. COCA-COLA BOTTLING CO., ANDALUSIA

Supreme Court of Alabama, 534 So.2d 295 (1988)

 Coca-Cola Bottling of Andalusia and Alabama Citizens Action Program sued, claiming that Pepsi-Cola Bottling Company of Luverne had violated a 1982 court order which permanently enjoined Coke and Pepsi "from operation of promotional campaigns whereby consumers of soft drink beverages are participants in 'under the crown' or 'on the tab' games of chance for which a purchase is necessary in all instances except for the right to obtain free crowns, tabs, or chances at some place other than the point of purchase of the beverage." The injunction order found that a 1981 "Pepsi Spirit" campaign in which participants could win cash and "NFL Prizes" (football jerseys and gift certificates) was an illegal lottery that violated the Alabama Constitution. The court found that other than by buying the soft drink, the only way to participate was to request free bottle tops by mail or to visit the Pepsi bottling plant. Only 60 people had done so, and the trial court declared the free participation option to be a sham.

At issue in this case is Pepsi's 1987 "Instant Cash" promotion, in which certain caps were marked $0.25, $1.00, or $100.00, and others were marked with the letters needed to spell "Pepsi Instant Cash" (which could be worth $10,000 to a person with caps containing all the letters).

For this campaign, Pepsi distributed 25,000 cards with a similar opportunity at participating stores, and advertised by means of store displays and radio that no purchase was required. Cards could also be obtained by telephone request and by writing the bottling plant.

The trial court found that Pepsi's "Instant Cash" promotion was a lottery that placed Pepsi in contempt of the 1982 injunction. Pepsi appealed.

Per Curiam:

The three elements of a lottery are (1) a prize, (2) awarded by chance, and (3) for a consideration. Admittedly, the first two elements are present in Pepsi's promotion; however, the element of consideration is absent.

The very question on appeal was recently answered in our response to the Alabama House of Representatives' inquiry as to whether a bill proposing to allow "[a]ny contest for prizes or money as rewards, which is for promotional or advertising purposes, sponsored or conducted by any . . . soft drink bottler in this state . . . not requir[ing] . . . consideration therefor" was constitutional. *Opinion of the Justices No. 277,* 397 So.2d 546 (Ala. 1981). In finding that the proposal did not offend § 65 of the Constitution, this Court relied upon *Clark v. State,* 80 So.2d 308 (1954), stating that "the fact that the business enterprise may be 'expected to gain some benefit by way of increased sales' [does not] constitute [the necessary] consideration." *Opinion of the Justices No. 277,* 397 So.2d at 547.

For the same reason, the "Pepsi Instant Cash" game is not a lottery, because participants were not required to purchase cards in order to play. Any incidental profit or benefit to Pepsi in the sale of the soft drinks containing the "under the crown" chance neither provides the consideration to make the game a lottery nor negates the free participation aspect of the game.

We also find that the promotion did not violate the 1982 injunction. That order prohibited promotional campaigns in which purchases were necessary in all instances; it did not preclude "the right to obtain free crown[s], tabs, or chances at some place other than the point of purchase of the beverage." Less than one month after the promotion began, of the 25,000 free cards distributed, 252 winning free cards had been redeemed. There was also evidence that Pepsi's salesmen were instructed to keep records of the free cards dispersed and to check for the availability of such cards at each store.

The aspect of Pepsi's prior promotions that led to the injunction was the unavailability of free chances. A careful reading of the language of the injunction leads to but one conclusion: that Pepsi complied in good faith with the mandates of the injunction and that Pepsi was within its rights in conducting the "Instant Cash" campaign.

Reversed.

In recent years a growing number of state statutes have been liberalized to permit wagering and lottery activities within narrow limits. For example, so-called "friendly bets"—those defined as not producing substantial sources of income—are frequently exempted from the basic wagering statutes, as are some lotteries operated by religious or charitable organizations. Additionally, several states have sanctioned state-operated lotteries by special statutes.

Insurance Contracts

Many contracts whose performance is dependent upon an element of chance are clearly not wagers. This is particularly true of **risk-shifting contracts** (as distinguished from **risk-creating contracts**). If a person insures his or her home against loss by fire, for example, the contract is perfectly legal even though it is not known at the time the policy is issued whether the insurer will have liability under it. The contract is legal despite this uncertainty because the owner had an "insurable interest" in the home prior to taking out the policy—that is, a financial loss would have resulted if a fire had occurred. Thus an insurance policy is simply a contract by which an existing risk is shifted to an insurance company for a consideration paid by the owner. By contrast, an insurance policy on a building which the insured does not own and in which he or she has no other financial interest is clearly a wager and is unenforceable.

Licensing Statutes

All states have **licensing statutes,** requiring that persons who engage in certain professions, trades, or businesses be licensed. Lawyers, physicians, real estate brokers, contractors, electricians, and vendors of milk and liquor are but a few examples of persons commonly subject to a wide variety of such statutes. In many instances, particularly those involving the professions, passing a comprehensive examination (along with proof of good moral character) is a condition of obtaining a license. In others, only proof of good moral character may be required.

To find out whether an unlicensed person can recover for services rendered under a contract, one must check the particular statute involved. Some licensing statutes expressly provide that recovery by unlicensed persons shall not be allowed (no matter how competent their work).[2] Others, however, are silent on the matter, in which case their underlying purposes must be determined. Most courts take the view in such instances that if the statute is *regulatory*—its purpose being the protection of the general public against unqualified persons—then the contract is illegal and recovery is denied. On the other hand, if the statute is felt to be merely *revenue-raising,* recovery is allowed.

The reasoning behind this distinction, of course, is that allowing recovery of a fee or commission by an unlicensed person in the first category would adversely affect public health and safety, while the enforcement of contracts in the second category does not have this result. Thus an unlicensed milk vendor who has sold and delivered a quantity of milk will ordinarily not be permitted to recover the purchase price from the buyer. Similarly, an unlicensed physician, real estate agent, or attorney will be denied his or her fee. On the other hand, a corporation that has merely failed to obtain a license to do business in a particular city is still permitted to enforce its contracts, because city licensing ordinances applicable to corporations are normally enacted for revenue-raising purposes.

The possibility that a regulatory statute might be passed for the protection of some persons, but not others, is presented in the following case.

---

[2] A provision that contracts made in violation of the statute shall be "void" usually, though not always, has this effect.

BREMMEYER V. PETER KIEWIT SONS COMPANY

Supreme Court of Washington, 585 P.2d 1174 (1978)

Case

The State of Washington awarded Peter Kiewit a prime contract to construct several miles of Interstate 90. The highway right-of-way was overgrown, and needed to have the trees and debris cleared before construction could begin. For this purpose, Peter Kiewit subcontracted the necessary clearing operation to Bremmeyer. Under the subcontract, Bremmeyer agreed to pay Peter Kiewit $35,000 for the right to fall, yard, buck, load and haul to a mill all the merchantable timber within the right-of-way. (Bremmeyer was to keep the proceeds of the sale of the timber as his compensation.)

Bremmeyer paid the $35,000 and began clearing the right-of-way, but before he had finished the job the state terminated Peter Kiewit's prime contract. Peter Kiewit, in turn, cancelled Bremmeyer's subcontract. Peter Kiewit received $1,729,050 from the state for "cancellation costs," but offered to pay Bremmeyer only $38 for cancellation of the contract. Bremmeyer refused the $38 and brought this action to recover the value of the merchantable timber that was still uncut at the time of termination.

In defense, Peter Kiewit's primary argument was that a state statute, RCW 18.27, required contractors to be registered with the state, and that Bremmeyer's failure to register barred his recovery. The trial court, citing a 1973 Washington State case, agreed with this contention and summarily dismissed the action. Bremmeyer appealed.

Stafford, Justice:

. . . We first considered whether the legislature intended RCW 18.27 to bar actions by unregistered subcontractors against prime contractors in *Jeanneret v. Rees*, 511 P.2d 60 (1973). A majority of the court agreed the legislature intended to preclude such actions. [The court then went on to say, however, that it now felt that its decision in that case was based on too literal a reading of the statute, and thus was not necessarily controlling. The court continued:]

Continued reliance upon the literal expression of RCW 18.27 is particularly inappropriate in light of the legislature's amendment to the statute after our divided opinion in *Jeanneret*. . . . A new section now provides:

It is the purpose of this chapter to afford protection *to the public* from unreliable, fraudulent, financially irresponsible, or incompetent contractors. [Emphasis supplied by the court.]

In view of this newly declared statutory purpose and the minimal protections afforded the public by the statute, we are convinced the legislature did not intend to protect prime contractors from actions initiated by unregistered subcontractors. The statutory purpose clearly provides protection *to the public,* i.e., the customers of building contractors. In light of the amendment, and considering the judicial history of RCW 18.27, we do not believe the legislature also intended to protect contractors *from each other*. . . .

Our conclusion that the legislature did not intend to bar actions by unregistered subcontractors against prime contractors is also supported by the practicalities of the contracting trade. Members of the trade are in a more nearly equal bargaining position with respect to *each other*. Not only is information concerning financial responsibility and competence readily attainable within the trade, but each contractor is knowledgeable concerning the financial protections needed for any particular job involved. . . .

Judgment reversed, and case remanded for trial. ↵

Sunday Contracts

Although the trend across the states is to eliminate or minimize the coverage of **Sunday statutes,** several jurisdictions still have some form of law prohibiting certain business transactions on Sunday. Often called "blue laws" (named for the color of paper they were originally printed on), these laws declare void and unenforceable certain contracts entered into on Sunday. Some laws forbid carrying on "all secular labor and business on the Sabbath," thus rendering void virtually all contracts made on a Sunday. Other laws are similar, but riddled with exceptions. Still others merely prohibit the sale of certain kinds of goods on Sunday. Such laws are disappearing, but a merchant moving into a new state should carefully check that jurisdiction's law.

Usury

Partly as a result of religious views going back to early biblical statements, and partly because of the practical hardships resulting from high interest rates charged desperate borrowers, all states have statutes establishing the maximum rate of interest that can be charged on ordinary loans. Charging interest in excess of the permitted rate constitutes **usury.**

The interest ceilings that are imposed by the usury statutes vary from state to state. Traditionally the basic statutes have varied from 6 percent to 12 percent per annum. However, as a result of inflationary pressures in recent years, the basic statutes now generally range from 10 percent to 16 percent per annum.

More important, many kinds of loans are not governed by the basic state statutes. For example, most states put no limit on the rate of interest that can be charged on loans made to corporations. And, under federal regulations, national banks are permitted to charge interest rates that are usually in excess of those permitted by the state usury laws.

Additionally, all states in recent years—again, partly because of inflationary pressures—have adopted special statutes permitting higher rates of interest on other specified kinds of loans. For example, most state laws today provide that interest rates charged by issuers of bank credit cards (such as Visa and MasterCard), and by department stores on

their revolving credit accounts, can be at an annual percentage rate of 18 percent. Similarly, home purchase and construction loans, car loans, and loans by credit unions may generally carry annual interest rates ranging from 18 to 25 percent.[3]

The basic statutes also vary widely insofar as the effect of usury is concerned. Many states permit the usurious lender to recover the principal and interest at the lawful rate, but not the excess interest. In such states the lender suffers no penalty. In others, the lender is permitted to recover the principal only, forfeiting all interest. And in three or four states, the lender forfeits both interest and principal.

It is thus clear that no determination can be made as to the legality or effect of a given loan without inspecting the statutes of the state in which the transaction took place.

---

[3] It should also be noted that most states have adopted special statutes that expressly permit small loan companies, such as "personal loan companies," to charge rates of interest that are considerably higher than those of the general interest statutes. For example, a loan company that qualifies under such statutes may be allowed to charge interest at the rate of 3 percent *per month* on the first $150 of a loan, 2 percent per month on the amount from $151 to $300, and 1 percent on the balance. These statutes usually provide that if interest is charged in excess of the specified rates, the loan is void. In such a case, neither principal nor interest can be recovered.

LEGAL FOCUS

Ethics

In deciding which promises they will enforce or not enforce, courts and legislatures make public policy—engage in "social engineering—just as they do when deciding which types of acts (such as invasion of privacy) will be actionable in tort.

For example, courts have held that contracts in which men pay women to have an abortion are illegal and unenforceable as against public policy. The moral underpinnings of such a ruling are obvious, although to some extent the entire range of arguments underlying our intense national debate over abortion is implicated.

Courts and legislatures have also tended to hold that contracts to pay women to have babies—to be "surrogate mothers"—are unenforceable. So, contracts to terminate fetuses and contracts to give birth to fetuses are both contrary to public policy. Is the law consistent? What moral or practical considerations support such policies?

Along related lines, the federal Transplant Act of 1984 makes it a felony to contract to buy or sell organs such as kidneys or hearts for medical transplants. Many experts believe that this provision is part of the reason for the current shortage of organ donors. For example, in 1991, there were 28,000 prospective kidney recipients, but only 6000 or so available donors, and more than 5000 prospective heart recipients, but only 2000 available donors. What moral or public policy considerations justify the refusal to enforce such contracts? Are those considerations likely to be persuasive to a prospective recipient whose life is on the line?

CONTRACTS CONTRARY TO PUBLIC POLICY
Contracts in Restraint of Trade

Many contracts that unreasonably restrain trade or competition in interstate commerce are in violation of one or more federal statutes, such as the Sherman and Clayton acts.[4] Long before the enactment of these statutes, however, many other contracts in restraint of trade were illegal under the common law of the various states, and this continues to be the case today. Thus a contract that is not subject to the Sherman or Clayton acts may still result in such restraint of trade that courts will set it aside under common-law principles. These principles are briefly summarized here.

Contracts that contain **restrictive covenants**—promises by one party not to engage in a particular occupation or to operate a certain kind of business—compose one group of contracts that are in restraint of trade. However, such promises (sometimes called *covenants not to compete*) are not necessarily illegal.

Generally, covenants not to compete are lawful if two conditions are met. First, the covenant must be of an "ancillary" nature, and second, the restriction (the covenant) must be reasonable under the circumstances.

The Ancillary Requirement

An **ancillary covenant** is one that is a subsidiary or auxiliary part of a larger agreement. A common example of an ancillary covenant is that found in a contract calling for the *sale of a business,* where the contract contains a promise by the seller of the business not to engage in the same type of business within a prescribed geographical area for a certain length of time after the sale. Equally common are covenants in *employment contracts,* under which the employee promises not to compete with the business of his or her employer for a specified period of time after the employment is terminated. (Nonancillary promises, on the other hand, stand alone; they do *not* protect any existing, legally recognized interest such as that in the prior examples. These covenants—such as a promise by a father to pay $10,000 for the son's promise not to engage in medical practice—are generally considered to be an unreasonable restraint of trade in all circumstances, and are thus illegal and unenforceable on public policy grounds.)

Reasonableness—Sale of Business Contracts

When a business is being sold, the interest to be protected relates to the goodwill of the business. A restrictive covenant on the part of the seller, in a particular case, is thus enforceable if its space and time limitations are no broader than are reasonably necessary to afford such protection. For example, a promise by the seller of a retail grocery in Kalispell, Montana, that he will not engage in the retail grocery business "within the City of Kalispell for the period of one year after the sale" is probably reasonable and thus lawful. Similarly, in *Gann v. Morris,* 596 P.2d 43 (1979), a promise by the seller of a silk-screening business in Tucson, Arizona, that he would not operate a competing business within a hundred-mile radius of Tucson for a specified period of time was held to be reasonable in view of the fact that at least one of the business's customers was located that distance away. Thus, in the above instances, if the seller should violate his or her promise, the purchaser of the business is entitled to an injunction against him or her. (On the other hand, if the restraint is found to be excessive—as would be the case if the seller of the grocery in Kalispell was prohibited from engaging in the grocery business "anywhere within the state of Montana" for one year—the restraint is illegal, and thus unenforceable by the buyer.)

Reasonableness—Employment Contracts

Restrictive covenants in employment contracts are reasonable (1) if the restriction is reasonably necessary to protect the employer, and (2) if the restriction is "not unreasonably excessive" as to the employee. Because of this second requirement, **geographical restraints** in employment contracts are more likely to be set aside by the courts than those in contracts where businesses are being sold. In other words, because such restraints may operate with particular harshness upon the employee insofar as his or her ability to make a living is concerned, they are scrutinized with particular care.[5] The following case is illustrative of this approach by the courts.

---

[4]These acts, and other federal statutes of a similar nature, are examined in Part VII.

[5]In contrast to geographical restraints are those covenants under which the employee promises not "to contact or deal with persons who are customers of the employer at the time the employment relationship is terminated" for a stated period of time. Where the time period is found to be reasonable, these kinds of covenants are more likely to be enforced.

BRYCELAND V. NORTHEY

Court of Appeals of Arizona, 772 P.2d 36 (1989)

Case

Bryceland, doing business as Johnny B's Disc Jockey Express, is in the mobile disc jockey business, providing recorded entertainment played by a "deejay" at parties, weddings, dances, and similar functions. He has numerous competitors in the Phoenix area.

Northey and Malvin applied to become deejays for Bryceland in 1985 and 1986, respectively. They received both classroom training and on-the-job help from Bryceland. After completing their training, they signed contracts in which they promised not to compete with Johnny B's for a period of two years within a 50-mile radius of Phoenix and such other areas where they might have performed.

In February 1987, Malvin and Northey both went to work for another mobile disc jockey service owned by Northey's father. Bryceland sued to enforce the covenant not to compete. The trial judge held for Bryceland on this issue, ordering defendants not to compete within a 50-mile radius of Phoenix for two years. Northey and Malvin appealed.

Kleinschmidt, Judge:

Restrictive covenants that tend to prevent an employee from pursuing a similar vocation after termination of employment are disfavored and are strictly construed against the employer. *Amex Distrib. Co. v. Mascari*, 150 Ariz. 510, 514, 724 P.2d 596, 600 (App. 1986). A contrasting rule applies to a covenant given in the sale of a business. As to the latter, courts are more lenient because of the need to see that goodwill is effectively transferred. *Restatement (Second) of Contracts* § 188

comment b (1981). The burden is on the employer to prove the extent of its protectable interest.

Restrictive covenants that are no broader than the employer's legitimately protectable interest will be enforced. An employer may not enforce a post-employment restriction on a former employee simply to eliminate competition *per se*. Comment b to section 188 of the *Restatement* provides in part:

[A post-employment restraint] must usually be justified on the ground that the employer has a legitimate interest in restraining the employee from appropriating valuable trade information and customer relationships to which he has had access in the course of his employment. Arguably the employer does not get the full value of the employment contract if he cannot confidently give the employee access to confidential information needed for [the] most efficient performance of his job. But it is often difficult to distinguish between such information and normal skills of the trade, and preventing use of one may well prevent or inhibit use of the other.

At trial, Bryceland's primary concern was that Malvin and Northey had taken classroom notes, could tell others that they were trained by Bryceland and would use their skills to serve another employer. These will not justify a restraint. A restrictive covenant is not enforceable to prevent a former employee from using the skills and talents he learns on the job in a new job.

The trial court found that there had been no appropriation and disclosure of trade secrets and customer information. Bryceland has not appealed from this finding. Thus, the interest for which Bryceland obtained protection was not its proprietary interest in confidential information.

An employer does have a protectable interest in maintaining customer relationships when an employee leaves. The law will guard this interest by means of a covenant not to compete for

as long as may be necessary to replace the employee and give the replacement a chance to show that he can do the job. Each case hinges on its own particular facts. Malvin and Northey, applying this rule, contend that the restrictive covenant is unreasonable in length. In *Amex,* we said:

In determining whether a restraint extends for a longer period of time than necessary to protect the employer, the court must determine how much time is needed for the risk of injury to be reasonably moderated. When the restraint is for the purpose of protecting customer relationships, its duration is reasonable only if it is no longer than necessary for the employer to put a new man on the job and for the new employee to have a reasonable opportunity to demonstrate his effectiveness to the customers. If a restraint on this ground is justifiable at all, it seems that a period of several months would usually be reasonable. If the selling or servicing relationship is relatively complex, a longer period may be called for.

Amex, 150 Ariz. at 518, 724 P.2d at 604 (quoting Blake, *Employment Agreement Not To Compete,* 73 Harv.L.Rev. 625, 677 (1960)).

The apparent purpose of this principle is to prevent a skilled employee from leaving an employer and, based on his skill acquired from that employment, luring away the employer's clients or business while the employer is vulnerable—that is—before the employer has had a chance to replace the employee with someone qualified to do the job. Here, the evidence showed that it took approximately fourteen weeks for adequate schooling and on-the-job training of new personnel to handle the duties of a deejay, far less than the two-year restriction contained in the agreement. Bryceland did not present evidence, which the trial court accepted as true, of any protectable interest other than the time it would require to replace Malvin and Northey with trained deejays.

(continues)

BRYCELAND V. NORTHEY

(continued from previous page)

We also note, without deciding, that the restriction against employment by any "potential customer or client" of Bryceland may be overly broad. This language goes well beyond protecting Bryceland from Malvin and Northey taking customers away as a result of meeting the customers during the course of their appearances for Johnny B's.

We find that the restrictive covenant is unreasonable in restricting Northey and Malvin's future employment as mobile disc jockeys for a two-year period. Neither the contract itself nor other evidence in the record indicates that this unreasonable portion of the contract was severable.

[Reversed.]

Will the Courts Rewrite the Contract?

The Arizona court in the previous case found that the unreasonably broad time restriction rendered the restrictive covenant completely unenforceable. The modern trend, however, is use of the "blue pencil" rule. Under this approach, courts finding that a contract's restrictions on competition serve an employer's legitimate interests but are unreasonably broad (either in terms of geography or time), will simply rewrite the covenant so that the restrictions are reasonable in scope and then will enforce them to that extent. Thus, a promise not to compete in the entire state of New York for three years might be rewritten to cover only a few counties in New York (where the promisor had worked) for one year.

Exculpatory Clauses

The law of torts imposes certain duties on all persons, one of which is to carry out one's activities in a reasonably careful manner. If a person violates this duty by performing an act carelessly, he or she is guilty of the tort of negligence and is answerable in damages to anyone who was injured thereby.

Businesspersons, and others, often try to avoid this potential liability through the use of **exculpatory clauses** that purport to excuse them from liability resulting from their own negligence. Such clauses are generally—though not always—held to be contrary to public policy, and thus *unenforceable* against the injured party.[6]

The Public Interest Inquiry

The legality of the exculpatory clause depends almost entirely upon the relative strength of the bargaining powers of the contracting parties. Where the party utilizing the clause has *vastly superior bargaining power* over the other, the clause is clearly void. Such disparity is normally found only in those contracts that "substantially affect the public interest"—in other words, in contracts of parties who furnish goods or services that are routinely used by companies and individuals in the carrying on of their everyday business or personal activities. Several examples are listed in this chapter's next major case, *DeVito v. N.Y.U. College of Dentistry*, which addresses the question of whether the medical profession should be allowed to avoid liability for negligence by use of such clauses.

An early landmark case is instructive on the public policy aspects of exculpatory clauses.[7] A brakeman was hired by a railroad only after he promised not to sue the company for any injuries that resulted from the company's negligence. When the company raised the clause as a defense in a negligence suit filed by the brakeman's family after his death in an accident caused by a defective switch, the court stated that parties' contracts are normally enforceable as written. However, parties to contracts are not allowed to make agreements that violate express provisions of the law or injuriously affect public policy. If such clauses as that signed in this case were enforced, the court stated:

[t]he consequence would be that every railroad company, and every owner of a factory, mill, or mine, would make it a condition precedent to the employment of labor,

---

[6] Some exculpatory clauses do *not* attempt to free a party from his or her negligence, but only from liability for injury caused by circumstances ouside his or her control; this kind of clause, not contravening public policy, is ordinarily lawful and binding. One example: a school district's form requiring parental permission for a student's attendance at a field day might provide "The district shall have no liability for injuries arising out of transportation of student to and from said location, other than those directly resulting from negligence of district-employed drivers."

[7] *Little Rock & Fort Smith Ry. Co. v. Eubanks,* 3 S.W. 808 (1886).

MORE FIRMS RESTRICT DEPARTING WORKERS

by Meredith Wadman

**Box 14.1
The Law
at Work**

It was bad enough when Eric Herb lost his job preparing ingredients at Galaxy Cheese Co. last year. But the real shock came last month, when the company threatened to sue him—for landing another job.

Galaxy reminded Mr. Herb and 74 other workers discharged when the company moved from Pennsylvania to Orlando, Fla., that they had signed agreements not to work for competitors for two years after leaving the company. "I didn't understand why they wanted to sue me. . . I was just looking for work," Mr. Herb says.

Managers to minions in businesses ranging from banks to beauty salons are also feeling perplexed and angry over the bite of non-compete agreements. The agreements, designed to prevent workers from decamping with trade secrets or client lists, have become increasingly common, lawyers say, as nervous employers try to cope with ever-stiffening competition.

Companies say they need the agreements now that growing numbers of acquisitions, bankruptcies, mergers and layoffs regularly set loose employees with access to trade secrets and other sensitive information. In some cases, the agreements—which can last for up to five years—ban workers from defecting to local competitors. But others are more universal: Galaxy, for instance, declared the entire continental U.S. off limits.

Courts look carefully at the agreements because they can "keep a person from engaging in his or her livelihood," says Robert Christenson, an Atlanta labor lawyer. And in most states, if judges think the agreements' temporal and geographical limits aren't reasonable, they aren't likely to enforce them.

Companies, however, say they need non-compete clauses because they fear "what [workers] will use against you when in competition with you," says Ronald Green, a New York lawyer who represents companies in employment disputes. The contracts don't aim to restrain fair competition, he maintains, but to prevent unfair competition.

What exactly is unfair becomes less clear when workers are forced out. For instance, BIEC International Inc. of Bethlehem, Pa., owned by Broken Hill Proprietary Co., an Australian steel conglomerate, licenses a steel-protecting alloy called Galvalume. In a management shake-up last year, BIEC slashed by one-third the salaries of three senior executives, including the co-inventor of Galvalume, and fired a fourth. The next month, three of the men decided to start their own steel consulting business—taking mailing lists, supplier and marketing manuals and other confidential documents with them.

BIED sued the four men in U.S. District Court in Easton, Pa. The court ordered the documents returned and issued a preliminary injunction barring the new business from opening its doors until next January. Meanwhile, the court will decide whether the process for making the alloy is a protected trade secret.

The inventor, Angelo R. Borzillo, says the group had a right to the documents because "we wrote the books." What's more, Mr. Borzillo—known as the "godfather of Galvalume"—maintains that he has a right to use the recipe for the alloy he helped invent. He is angry that he might be "blocked from doing something [I] had a very significant part in."

. . . Nearly everyone agrees that non-compete agreements may be reasonable for workers who are privy to valuable technology or inside information. In certain industries, such as biotechnology or pharmaceuticals, "virtually every employment agreement we see" has non-compete clauses, says Mr. Green, the New York lawyer.

But in other industries, the agreements can apply whether employers are protecting high-powered secrets or simply sales routes. For example: Alabama bank executives are blocked from competing in the state for two years; a Kingston, N.Y., pediatrician who quits a certain group practice is barred from practicing within 15 miles of the city for five years; and pest-control workers in Virginia who go to work for a competitor must for two years steer clear of the counties they covered for their former employer.

Critics say the agreements are most controversial when applied to blue-collar workers who, as in the Galaxy case, may simply stir cheese or weigh ingredients. The unequal bargaining power of employers and hourly employees means "the little guy" has "no real power to negotiate anything," says Williams Haushalter, a lawyer for Galaxy competitor Northwood Flavors Co. of Slippery Rock, Pa., where Mr. Herb is now working, . . .

Galaxy, which maintains it is simply trying to survive in a competitive market, concedes its non-compete agreement covers workers who aren't privy to sensitive information. "I don't think any of [the workers] are really in sensitive positions in terms of trade secrets," a spokesman says.

Mr. Herb says he can't recall the specifics of Galaxy's numerous recipes. Now he drives a forklift for Northwood and says he is happy just to have work.

Others are more outspoken. Says Edward Terreri, a Pittsburgh lawyer who has agreed to represent Galaxy employees pro bono if they are sued: "Galaxy's case against these employees looks like Swiss to me. It's full of holes."

Source: *Wall Street Journal*, June 26, 1992, p. B1.

that the laborer should release all right for injuries sustained in the course of the service, whether by the employer's negligence or otherwise. The natural tendency of this would be to relax the employer's carefulness in those matters of which he has the ordering and control, such as the supplying of machinery and materials, and thus increase the perils of occupations which are hazardous even when well managed. And the final outcome would be to fill the country with disabled men and paupers whose support would become a charge upon the counties or upon public charity.

The recent trend has been to enforce exculpatory clauses where they involve only recreational activities, such as where people go rafting, sky-diving, or horseback riding. In such cases the courts are much more likely to give effect to an exculpatory clause than where the consumer is attempting to purchase needed services or to gain housing or employment.

In order to be given effect, even exculpatory clauses that are not declared outright to be against public policy because of the nature of the transaction must be (1) effectively called to the attention of the potential plaintiff, and (2) clearly written. An exculpatory clause buried in the fine print of a lengthy form-contract is unlikely to be given effect because the person against whom it is to operate probably will not notice it. Furthermore, even clauses that are carefully called to the potential plaintiff's attention will operate only to avoid the types of liability that they explicitly and clearly spell out. Any ambiguity in such a clause is construed against its drafter. The *De-Vito* case also addresses this issue.

Finally, keep in mind that exculpatory clauses at best can relieve defendants of liability for simple negligence. Clauses that attempt to avoid liability for acts of intentional wrongdoing or even gross negligence are not enforceable.

DeVito v. N.Y.U. College of Dentistry

Supreme Court, New York County, 544 N.Y.S.2d 109 (1989)

Case

Defendant New York University College of Dentistry ("NYU") operates a dental clinic where, in exchange for reduced fees, patients agree to be treated by students working under faculty supervision. Plaintiff DeVito was treated at the clinic after signing a release which stated: "In consideration of the reduced rates given to me by New York University, I hereby release and agree to save harmless New York University, its doctors, and students, from any and all liability arising out of, or in connection with, any injuries or damages which I may sustain while on its premises, or as a result of any treatment in its infirmaries."

Plaintiff was injured. He sued NYU claiming negligence. Defendant moved for summary judgment based on the release. After noting that the New York courts have not always agreed on the effect of such releases, the trial judge entered the following opinion.

Premenger, Judge:

The threshold consideration is whether the parties have a special relationship which would make enforcement of an exculpatory clause between them against the public interest. This occurs where the party seeking exculpation is in a business or profession which is either publicly regulated or providing an essential service to members of the public. Examples include common carriers and their passengers; public utilities and their customers; employers who impose the clause as a condition of employment and a host of statutorily created prohibited persons, such as landlords, caterers, and those who maintain parking lots, gymnasiums, and other public places.

In these relationships, the consumer's need for the service creates an inequality in bargaining strength which enables the purveyor to insist upon a release, generally on its own prepared form, as a condition to providing the service. As in any adhesion contract a

true and voluntary meeting of the minds on the terms of the agreement is unlikely.

As Williston explains:

Some relationships are such that once entered upon they involve a status requiring of one party greater responsibility than that required of the ordinary person and, therefore, a provision avoiding liability is particularly obnoxious.

Williston, *Contracts* (3rd Ed.1972); § 1751

The courts of this state have not conclusively determined whether it would be against the public interest to allow physicians to insulate themselves from liability for negligence. However, other jurisdictions have held that the physician-patient relationship precludes the enforcement of such exculpatory agreements.

Thus, in *Olson v. Molzen*, 558 S.W.2d 429 (Tenn. 1977) the Supreme Court of Tennessee declared that

the general rule [that] a party may contract
(continues)

DeVito v. N.Y.U. College of Dentistry

(continued from previous page)

against his or her own negligence . . . does not afford a satisfactory solution in a case involving a professional person operating in an area of public interest and pursuing a profession subject to licensure by the State. The rules that govern tradesmen in the marketplace are of little relevancy in dealing with the professional persons who hold themselves out as experts and whose practice is regulated by the state.

Assuming that the status of the parties withstands scrutiny, it next becomes necessary to examine the actual wording of the agreement. One must determine whether its terms are so clear, explicit and unambiguous that it appears certain that the limitation of liability is intended to cover negligent, as well as ordinary, acts of the party seeking to shed responsibility.

In those instances where releases from liability which do not contain the word "negligence" have been construed to include negligent behavior, the words used have referred to the concept of fault in specific and unambiguous terms.

All-encompassing or open-ended phrases such as "any and all claims" or "any and all responsibility or liability of any nature whatsoever" and "all claims and demands whatsoever" are considered insufficient to indicate an intention to waive injury occasioned by fault.

Even if a clause is found to be clear and unambiguous, it must be examined further to determine whether it would be understandable to a layman, which, while not requiring "only monosyllabic language," does compel that the language used be "clear and coherent."

The NYU release cannot survive the close scrutiny mandated by the concepts discussed above. It fails, in all particulars, to meet the established standards. Even if the status of the parties is removed from consideration, the contract cannot be construed to include exemption from negligent acts. There is no reference, either explicitly or implicitly, by "words of similar import" to the concept of negligence or fault. No layman perusing this release would find it immediately understandable that the signatory had contracted to accept not only injuries that might ordinarily and inevitably occur, but also any and all consequences of defendants' carelessness.

Although the law "grudgingly accepts the proposition that men may contract away their liability for negligently caused injuries" (*Van Dyke Prods. v. Eastman Kodak Co.,* 239 N.Y.S.2d 337) it may not do so here. The circumstances of this case and the wording of the release militate against such a result. The parties' status is, at the very least, suspect, the contract is ambiguous, and the language used is far from instantly coherent to a layman.

For all of the foregoing reasons, defendants' motion for summary judgment is denied.

Bailment Contracts

Bailment contracts are similar to leases and employment contracts in that they, too, are so widely used as to substantially affect the public interest. Accordingly, the status of exculpatory clauses in such contracts is essentially the same as those in leases and employment contracts—that is, highly suspect in the eyes of the law.

A *bailment* occurs when the owner of an article of personal property temporarily relinquishes the possession and control of it to another. The person who has parted with the possession is the *bailor,* and the one receiving it is the *bailee.* Typical bailments result from checking a coat at a nightclub, leaving a car at a garage for repairs, and storing goods at a warehouse.

Under general bailment law, a bailee is liable for any damages to, or loss of, the property that is the result of his or her negligence—the failure to use reasonable care under the circumstances. Bailees frequently attempt to escape this liability by the use of an exculpatory clause in the bailment contract. Companies operating parking lots, for example, customarily print on the back of identification tickets something like the following: "The company will endeavor to protect the property of its patrons, but it is agreed that it will not be liable for loss or damage to cars, accessories, or contents, from whatever cause arising."[8]

As suggested earlier, such a clause is *contrary to public policy*—at least to the extent that it purports to free the bailee from liability for loss caused by his or her negligence. The reasoning, of course, is analogous to that applied in the illustration involving the employment contract—specifically, that if such a clause were given effect, all bailees would utilize it,

---

[8]While leaving a car at a parking lot creates a bailor-bailee relationship under ordinary circumstances, this is not always true. Many courts, for example, rule that such a relationship is not created if the patron is permitted to keep the car keys, on the theory that the lot operator in such a case is not given control of the car.

with a consequent lessening of care on their part. As a result, such provisions do not prevent a bailor whose property is damaged while in the bailee's hands from bringing suit. If it is established that the loss was occasioned by negligence on the part of the bailee, the bailor can recover damages.[9]

Unconscionable Contracts

As a general rule, the courts are not concerned with the fairness or unfairness of a particular contract. In other words, where competent parties have struck an agreement it will normally be enforced even if it proves much more advantageous to one party than to the other. However, occasionally the freedom to contract is abused so that the terms of a particular contract are so extremely unfair to one of the parties in light of common mores and business practices that they "shock one's conscience." Courts will not enforce such an **unconscionable contract** against the abused party.

A pre-UCC case vividly illustrating the common-law approach to unconscionability is *Williams v. Walker-Thomas Furniture Co.*, 350 F.2d 445 (D.D.C. 1965). There, a Mrs. Williams purchased some furniture in Washington, D.C., in 1957 on credit under a contract which contained the standard provision that the company would retain title to the goods until all monthly payments were made, and that the company could repossess in event of default. The contract also contained a clause that if Mrs. Williams purchased additional goods on credit, the company had the right to "credit pro-rata" her monthly payments against all such goods. She did, in fact, buy a number of additional items between 1957 and 1962, and the company, as permitted by the pro-rata clause, during that time had applied her payments so that a small balance remained due on all items, even those purchased in 1957 and 1958. In 1962, by which time Mrs. Williams had made payments of over $1,400, she was unable to make additional payments. When the company then sought to repossess all of the goods in her hands, the court refused repossession as to the first items that she had purchased. In part, the court said: "When a party of little bargaining power, and hence little real choice, signs a commercially unreasonable contract with little or no knowledge of its terms, it is hardly likely that his consent, or even an objective manifestation of consent, was ever given to all the terms. In such a case the usual rule that the terms of the agreement are not to be questioned should be abandoned, and the court should consider whether the terms of the contract are so unfair that enforcement should be withheld."

Unconscionability: Sales Law

In most states the common law of unconscionability has been introduced to the sale of goods through UCC Sec. 2-302, which allows a court finding a sales contract or any clause of the contract to be unconscionable to: (1) refuse to enforce the contract, *or* (2) enforce the remainder of the contract without the unconscionable clause, *or* (3) limit the application of any unconscionable clause so as to avoid any unreasonable result.

Most courts require a showing of both procedural and substantive unfairness in order to find a contract unconscionable. *Procedural unconscionability* exists when there is a lack of meaningful choice on the part of one of the parties. Courts must analyze the contract formation process, including such matters as the inability of one of the parties to bargain because of immaturity or old age, lack of sophistication, mental disability, inability to speak English, lack of education or business acumen, and the like; relative bargaining power; whether the party in the strongest economic position simply offered a printed form or boilerplate contract on a take-it-or-leave-it basis to the weaker party (adhesion contracts); whether the terms were explained to the weaker party; whether there were alternative sources for the goods or services; whether high-pressure or deceptive sales tactics were used; and whether important clauses were hidden in the fine print. Contracts entered into in a commercial context are generally presumed not to be unconscionable; businesspersons should be able to protect themselves. Courts are much more likely to find unconscionability in order to aid a consumer than to aid a business, but commercial transactions are not immune from such a finding.

In order to ascertain *substantive unconscionability*, the courts examine the terms of the contract itself to determine whether they are oppressive, perhaps

---

[9]Clauses that place a *limit* on the bailee's liability, in the event of a loss, are viewed more favorably by the courts. Such provisions, if reasonable, are usually not considered to be illegal. Additionally, some bailees are expressly permitted by statute to limit their liability by contract. Under federal law, for example, common carriers in interstate commerce are permitted to do so within limits approved by the Interstate Commerce Commission; thus the limitations commonly found in bills of lading and other transportation contracts are generally enforceable.

because they involve unfair disclaimers of warranty, inflated prices, denial of basic rights and remedies to consumers, penalty clauses, and the like. The courts will decide whether or not a particular contract is unconscionable on a case-by-case basis in light of the overall commercial context in which it was made and

as of the time it was made. Just because a bargain has turned out poorly for one party does not mean that the contract was unconscionable when made. Courts will not use the concept to reallocate the risks taken by the parties when they entered into the contract, as the following case demonstrates.

DOUGHTY V. IDAHO FROZEN FOODS CORP.

Idaho Court of Appeals, 736 P.2d 460 (1987)

In 1983 Doughty contracted to sell a portion of his anticipated potato crop to Idaho Frozen Foods (IFF), a processor of potato products. The parties used a form contract developed through negotiations between IFF and the Potato Growers of Idaho (PGI), an independent bargaining organization which represented 1200 potato growers. Under the contract, Doughty was to receive a base price if the potato crop contained a certain percentage of potatoes weighing ten ounces or more. If the crop contained a higher percentage, the price would be increased; if it contained a lower percentage, the price would be decreased. Size was critical to IFF's processing needs. The contract provided that IFF could refuse any deliveries containing less than 10 percent ten-ounce or larger potatoes.

Unexpected weather conditions resulted in only 8 percent of Doughty's potatoes being ten-ounces or more, so he was entitled to only $2.57 per hundredweight under the IFF contract. After four days of delivery to IFF, Doughty breached the contract, delivering the remainder of his potatoes to the "fresh pack" market where he could receive $4.69 per hundredweight. Pursuant to an agreement with IFF, the proceeds of this sale were placed in a court-controlled bank account.

Doughty then filed this declaratory judgment action, asking the court to declare the contract uncon-

scionable and therefore not binding on him. The trial judge ruled for IFF and Doughty appealed.

Walters, Chief Judge:

Doughty argues that the contract is unconscionable because the terms were disproportionately skewed in favor of IFF. Specifically, Doughty invites a comparison of the built-in step decreases in the contract price based on the percentage of smaller potatoes and the step increases in price for higher percentages of larger potatoes. Doughty contends the contract is unconscionable because the price decreases are steeper than the price increases. Doughty also contends that it was unconscionable for IFF to have the option not to accept the potatoes if they consisted of less than ten percent ten-ounce or larger size potatoes.

In Hershey v. Simpson, 111 Idaho 196, 725 P.2d 196 (Ct. App. 1986), this court recognized that a claim of unconscionability may have procedural and substantive aspects. We stated that procedural unconscionability may arise in the bargaining process leading to an agreement. Procedural unconscionability "is characterized by great disparity in the bargaining positions of the parties, by extreme need of one party to reach some agreement (however unfavorable), or by threats short of duress. These circumstances taint the bargaining process, producing a result that does not reflect free market forces." Regarding substantive unconscionability, we stated that "[o]nly in special circumstances may a court of

equity set aside contracts fairly and freely negotiated." We further noted that such "special circumstances" turn on "whether at the time of making of the contract, and in light of the general commercial background and commercial needs of a particular case, [the contract is] so one-sided as to oppress or unfairly surprise one of the parties."

Doughty's allegations encompass aspects of both procedural and substantive unconscionability. Under either aspect, we do not find the contract to be unconscionable. Although Doughty was not a member of PGI, the group which negotiated the contract with IFF, PGI represented a significant number of growers. Doughty has not shown that he was in any way different from those potato growers who were members of PGI. Moreover, the record clearly establishes that PGI did have substantial bargaining power and negotiating expertise.

Doughty entered into the contract freely and sought the benefits which the collective bargaining power of PGI had obtained. Apparently, Doughty was not dissatisfied with the contract *until* his crop produced small potatoes. There is no indication that Doughty tried or wanted to negotiate different terms under the contract. In fact, the contract would appear to be to the advantage of a farmer such as Doughty—one who through innovation, skill, and aggressiveness sought to produce a crop that would fulfill not only the IFF contract, but also his other processing contract, plus produce potatoes for the "fresh pack" market. Had Doughty's efforts produced the ten-ounce

(continues)

DOUGHTY V. IDAHO FROZEN FOODS CORP.

(continued from previous page)
potatoes he sought, Doughty would have had a very beneficial contract. There was no indication that Doughty was forced by "extreme need" into the contract. Finally, there is no indication from the record of any threats to Doughty that caused him to enter into the IFF contract.

The contract also does not reflect any substantively unconscionable aspects. The prices were based on the size and quality of potatoes that IFF desired and that Doughty hoped he could produce. The pricing variations, as well as the option to refuse potatoes not meeting the contract requirements, do not appear to be unrea-

sonable considering the product the contract was intended to produce—ten-ounce or larger potatoes. The contract was a preharvest contract. Therefore Doughty could attempt to manipulate and manage the crop to produce exactly the size potatoes that would be most financially rewarding. Doughty was thwarted by unexpected weather conditions. Doughty's assertions reflect an attempt to reap the benefits that the contract would have produced if he had grown the kind of potatoes he intended to, yet escape the negative aspects resulting from his inability to produce that type of potato. The contract simply does not appear to be "so one-sided as to op-

press or unfairly surprise one of the parties."

Each party accepted certain risks by signing the preharvest contract. IFF took a chance that market prices might decline, while Doughty took a chance on growing a certain size potato. IFF did have an option to reject potatoes that did not meet IFF's size criteria. However, contracts do not necessarily give identical rights to all parties. That is part of the bargaining process. It does not necessarily make a contract unconscionable. We conclude that the contract was not unconscionable in this case.

[Affirmed.]

Other Illegal Contracts

Many other contracts are generally held to be contrary to public policy. Of these, one broad class deserves comment—contracts that "injure the public service." Promises to pay legislators money in return for their votes and similar promises to judges in return for favorable rulings are clearly injurious to the public and therefore illegal. On the other hand, **lobbying contracts,** under which a person is employed by a third party to influence a legislator's vote or an administrator's decision in the awarding of a contract, are not necessarily illegal. The legality of such contracts largely depends on the propriety of the means used by the lobbyist. If, for example, an engineer simply agrees, for a fee, to present to a lawmaker or administrator factual information tending to show the superiority of one product or material over another, the means are proper and the agreement is not contrary to public policy. A contract, however, that contemplates influencing a government official essentially by reliance on the lobbyist's long personal friendship with that person would be illegal.

In regard to **contingent fee contracts,** under which payment of the fee is conditional upon passage of a particular bill or awarding of a contract, many courts flatly deny the lobbyist recovery of his or her fee under any circumstances—on the ground that

the tendency of such contracts to induce improper activities is, by itself, sufficient to cause them to be contrary to public policy. Other courts, in such cases, permit the lobbyist to recover if he or she can prove proper conduct—that is, conduct free of deception, undue pressure, and the like.

EFFECT OF ILLEGAL CONTRACTS

As noted early in the chapter, illegal contracts are generally void and unenforceable. This means that neither party to such a contract will be assisted by the courts in any way, regardless of the consequences to the parties involved. Thus, if S brings suit to recover the purchase price of a quantity of liquor that he has sold and delivered to B in violation of law, his action will be dismissed. Conversely, if B had paid the purchase price when the contract was made and S subsequently failed to deliver the liquor, any action brought by B to recover the price will also be unavailing.

Courts feel that such a hands-off policy is, in most cases, the best way to discourage the making of illegal contracts. There are exceptional situations, however, in which the courts feel that the results obtained under such a policy are so questionable as to warrant some measure of judicial relief. We will examine three of these situations.

Rights of Protected Parties

Some statutes have as their clear purpose the protection of a certain class of persons. Any contract made in violation of such a statute is enforceable by persons within that class, despite its illegality. For example: a Nebraska insurance company, not licensed to sell insurance in Colorado, issues a fire insurance policy on K's home in Denver. The home is destroyed by fire, and the company refuses to pay on the ground that the contract was illegal. The company is liable on its policy. It would be a ludicrous result if K, a person for whose benefit the licensing statutes were enacted, were to be denied recovery on the ground of illegality.

Parties Not Equally at Fault

In most illegal contracts the parties are equally at fault (or substantially equally at fault). In such instances when an action is brought to enforce the contract, the defendant may successfully assert the defense of *in pari delicto* (literally, "at equal fault").

In some situations, however, the plaintiff may convince the court that he or she was *not* equally at fault with the defendant—i.e., that his or her guilt was substantially less than the defendant's. In such a case the plaintiff's action may be maintained. The exception applies particularly—but not exclusively—where the plaintiff was ignorant of essential facts when the contract was made, through no fault of his or her own. For example: X forges a warehouse receipt, which makes it appear that he is the owner of certain goods stored at a warehouse. X takes the receipt to a trucking company and employs it to pick up the goods at the warehouse and to deliver them to his place of business. The trucking company does so, not knowing that X is not the owner of the goods. The company is entitled to receive its transportation charge from X, even though it was a participant in an illegal transaction.

Severable Contracts

Sometimes a single contract turns out on analysis to be two separate agreements. This can be illustrated by a contract under which a retiring restaurant owner agrees to sell to a former competitor his "ten pinball machines for $50 and one electric broiler for $75." In such a contract, called a **severable contract,** the fact that one of the agreements may be illegal does not prevent the other from being enforced. Thus, if the sale of the pinball machines is prohibited by law, the seller is still under an obliga-tion, enforceable in court, to deliver the broiler. However, most contracts that contain several promises on the part of both parties are not severable. The promises of the two parties usually are so interdependent that the court must rule that they resulted in the creation of a single, indivisible contract. In such cases, if any part of the contract is illegal, the entire agreement is unenforceable.

SUMMARY

A contract may be illegal either because it violates a statute (or administrative regulation), or because it is contrary to public policy. In either event such a contract is generally void and therefore unenforceable. Contracts that are often prohibited by state statute are wagers, those calling for the performance of work by unlicensed persons, contracts entered into (or to be performed) on Sundays, and usurious contracts (those in which a lender charges a rate of interest in excess of that permitted by law). Not all of these contracts, however, are illegal in all states. And even in states where a particular contract is contrary to the letter of a statute, the courts have, in limited circumstances, held the contract to be outside the statute. For example, they usually permit an unlicensed person to recover the contract price of his or her services if the licensing statute was primarily a revenue-raising one (as distinguished from a statute having as its purpose the protection of the health or safety of the citizenry).

The question of whether a particular contract, if enforced, would be injurious to the public at large is determined by the highest court in each state. If the contract is deemed injurious, enforceability is denied on the ground that the contract is contrary to public policy. Contracts that unreasonably restrain trade—being inimical to free and open competition—have long been held to fall within this category. Whether a particular restraint is unreasonable depends upon its purpose, and the scope of its time and space restrictions. Where the restraint is an ancillary part of a contract which itself is lawful, such as a promise by a seller of a business not to compete with the buyer, the restraint is lawful if the protection it affords the buyer is reasonable under the circumstances. Thus a promise by a seller of a single retail establishment not to engage in a similar business anywhere in the state would normally be unreasonably broad, and unenforceable. The test of reasonableness is also applied to restrictive covenants in employment contracts, but such restrictions are subject to closer scrutiny by the courts than are those in sale of business cases.

Exculpatory clauses in contracts that purport to free one party from liability for loss caused by his or her negligence are also viewed with disfavor by the courts, especially where the company utilizing the clause provides a service essential to the business world and, therefore, possesses bargaining power superior to that of the other party.

Unconscionable contracts are a third type of contract held to be contrary to public policy. Such contracts generally possess two characteristics: (1) terms that are shockingly one-sided, and (2) possession of greatly superior bargaining power by the party in whose favor the terms operate.

KEY TERMS

Wagering agreement
Lottery
Risk-shifting contract
Risk-creating contract
Licensing statutes
Sunday statutes
Usury
Restrictive covenant
Ancillary covenant
Geographical restraints
Exculpatory clause
Bailment contract
Unconscionable contract
Lobbying contract
Contingent fee contract
Severable contract

QUESTIONS AND PROBLEMS

1. Wilson was a licensed Hawaii architect who rendered extensive professional services for the owner of a ranch. When he sought his $33,900 fee, the owner refused to pay because Wilson had failed to pay a $15 state "annual registration fee." Does this failure to pay render Wilson's contract illegal, as the ranch owner contends? Explain. (*Wilson v. Kealakekua Ranch, Ltd.*, 551 P.2d 525, 1976.)

2. Bonasera brought an action against Roffe to recover a real estate commission due him for finding a buyer for Roffe's property. Bonasera was not a licensed broker, and Roffe's defense was an Arizona statute providing that only licensed brokers could recover real estate commissions in that state. Bonasera contended that the statute was not applicable to him since he was not in the real estate business, his activity in this instance being but a "single, isolated transaction." Is the statute applicable to Bonasera? Explain. (*Bonasera v. Roffe*, 442 P.2d 165, 1968.)

3. Diadrill, Inc., which makes drill bits for oil well production, sued Gillen, a former employee who had started in the summer of 1980 and was terminated in the spring of 1981. Gillen had signed a covenant not to compete for 12 months within Diadrill's marketing area, which covered several states. When Gillen left Diadrill, he took records, price lists, inventory lists, photos of Diadrill's drill bits, and customer lists. He went to work for a competitor and obtained the business of at least one of Diadrill's former customers for his new boss. Should the court enforce Diadrill's restrictive covenant? (*Gillen v. Diadrill, Inc.*, 624 S.W.2d 259, Tex.Civ.App. 1981.)

4. Lally sold a barbershop located in Rockville, Connecticut, "together with all good will," to Mattis. The bill of sale contained a clause providing that Lally would not engage in the barbering business in any capacity for a period of five years "anywhere in the City of Rockville, or within a radius of one mile" of the shop's location on Market Street in Rockville. (The one-mile alternative was included because the shop was located only a quarter of a mile from the Rockville city limits.) After the sale, Lally operated a restaurant; but when this became unprofitable a year or two later, he opened a one-chair barbershop in his own home, three hundred yards from the shop Mattis had purchased. When Mattis' business fell off thereafter, he brought an action asking the court to enforce the restrictive clause in the contract. Lally contended that the clause in question constituted an unreasonable restraint of trade and was therefore unlawful. Is Lally's contention correct? Explain. (*Mattis v. Lally*, 82 A.2d 155, 1951.)

5. Soble, a lawyer, represented a client in a condemnation suit—a suit in which the client's land was being taken by the state. Soble employed an expert real estate appraiser, Laos, to testify in the suit as to the value of the property. The contract between Soble and Laos provided that Laos was to receive a fee of $1,500 if the court found the value of the property to be $200,000 or less, and $2,500 if the valuation were set at any amount above $200,000.

In subsequent litigation, the question arose as to whether this contingent fee contract was contrary to public policy and thus illegal. On what basis could it be argued that the contract *was* illegal? Discuss. (*Laos v. Soble*, 503 P.2d 978, 1972.)

6. When Bova left her car at a parking lot operated by Constantine, she was given an identification ticket upon which was printed matter, which she did not read, as follows: "This station will endeavor to protect the property of its patrons but it is agreed that it will not be liable for loss or damage of cars, accessories or contents from whatever cause arising." When Bova returned, the car was not in the lot. It had been stolen, and, when found, was in need of repairs totaling $154. In an action brought against Constantine to recover this amount, he contended that the clause on the identification ticket freed him of all liability. Was the clause lawful, and thus a good defense to the suit? Explain. (*Agricultural Insurance Co. v. Constantine*, 58 N.E.2d 658, 1944.)

7. Krazek hired D to take her on a white water rafting trip in West Virginia, signing a "Raft Trip Release and Assumption of Risk," which stated that she was aware of the "substantial risks and dangers" that may occur during white water rafting in remote terrain and that "in consideration of and as part payment for the right to participate," she agreed to assume all risks and to "release, and . . . hold [D] harmless from any and all liability of every kind and nature whatsoever" which might arise out of the trip. During the trip a severe hail storm occurred. D's guide ordered the rafters into the river to protect them from the hail. While in the river, Krazek was swept away by the current and injured. She sued D in negligence. Should the exculpatory clause prevent her from recovering? (*Krazek v. Mountain River Tours, Inc.*, 884 F.2d 163, 4th Cir. 1989.)

8. Plaintiff Michelle Triola Marvin alleged that she and defendant, actor Lee Marvin, orally agreed that they would "live together, hold themselves out to the public as husband and wife, and that she would render services as companion, homemaker,

housekeeper and cook." She claimed further that she gave up her lucrative career as an entertainer in exchange for defendant's promise to "provide for all of plaintiff's financial support and needs for the rest of her life." After six years of living together, the parties split up. Plaintiff sued to enforce the agreement. Defendant moved to dismiss on grounds that the agreement was "immoral" and hence contrary to public policy because it involved a sexual relationship between nonmarital partners. Should a court refuse to enforce the agreement? (*Marvin v. Marvin*, 557 P.2d 106, Cal. 1976.)

9. The Crocker National Bank (D) imposed a charge for processing all checks drawn on accounts without sufficient funds (NSF checks). D requires each depositor to sign a signature card which states that depositors "agree with Crocker National Bank . . . that this account . . . shall be subject to the Bank's present and future rules, regulations, practices, and charges." The card does not identify the amount of the charge for NSF checks and the bank does not furnish the depositor with a copy of the applicable bank rules and regulations. P sued on behalf of himself and all other depositors, claiming that the bank unilaterally and unjustifiably raised the NSF charge at will, eventually charging $6 for each check, though the actual cost incurred was only 30 cents. Is the charge unconscionable, as P claims? (*Perdue v. Crocker National Bank*, 702 P.2d 503, Cal. 1985.)

10. Plaintiffs alleged that D, their stockbroker, gave them a "tip" based on supposedly "inside information." Following the tip, plaintiffs invested, but lost substantial amounts of money when the tipped information turned out to be false. Ps sued D, who raised an "in pari delicto" defense. In essence, D argued that because Ps thought they were receiving secret inside information they knew that they were engaging in illegal "insider trading" violative of the federal securities laws and therefore should be barred from recovering. Is this a good defense? (*Bateman Eichler, Hill Richards, Inc. v. Berner*, 472 U.S. 299, 1985.)

Chapter 15

Voidable Contracts

Capacity
Minors
Mentally Impaired and Intoxicated Persons
Reality of Consent
Fraud
Innocent Misrepresentation
Mistake
Duress
Undue Influence

A

VOIDABLE CONTRACT IS a contract which may be avoided—that is, may be legally set aside—by one of the parties, even though the contract consists of a definite agreement, is supported by consideration, and has a lawful purpose. In this chapter we will examine the most common grounds for the avoidance (disaffirmance) of a contract: *lack of capacity,* and *lack of reality of consent.*

CAPACITY

The term **capacity** means the legal ability—the ability or "competence" in the eyes of the law—to perform a particular act. Within the context of this chapter, the particular act under consideration is the making of a binding contract.

A person's capacity to contract may be limited (or entirely lacking, in some instances) for any of three primary reasons: *minority, mental infirmity,* and *intoxication.* We will consider these subjects in order.[1]

MINORS

Centuries ago, the English courts became aware of the fact that many of the contracts entered into by young persons displayed a shocking lack of judgment; such persons assumed obligations and made purchases that they probably would not have had they possessed greater maturity and experience. The courts, desirous of "protecting the young from the consequences of their own folly," began to wrestle with the question of how this protection could best be brought about.

They initially approached the problem by devising what came to be known as the *harm-benefit test.* Under this view, the courts permitted persons who had entered into contracts while under the age of twenty-one to disaffirm them if they were shown to be harmful to these individuals. This approach was followed for a time in the United States. Its application, however, produced such conflict and uncertainty in the law that a new solution became necessary.

The Common-Law Rule

The U.S. courts finally adopted the sweeping rule that, virtually without exception, *all minors' contracts are voidable at their option.* The right thus given to minors to escape their contractual obligations is no longer dependent upon a showing that the contract is harmful or unwise, or that they have been taken advantage of in some way. To effect a disaffirmance of any contract, all the minor has to do is indicate to the other party his or her intention not to be bound by it. The disaffirmance can be express or implied, and the right to disaffirm continues until the minor reaches the age of majority, plus a "reasonable time thereafter."

Note that a minor's contract is enforceable against the minor *until* an effective disaffirmance occurs. Furthermore, only the minor has the right to disaffirm; the other party to the contract has no corresponding right to disaffirm. If the minor chooses, he or she may enforce the contract against the adult on the other side (assuming that adult's mental competence).

Definition of Minority

In the past twenty years or so virtually every state has lowered the age of majority from the common law's 21 years to 18 years of age for most purposes, including the making of valid contracts.[2] Thus, a **minor** is a person who has not yet attained the age of 18. The agreements of minors of "tender years"—children so young that their minds have not matured sufficiently to understand the meaning of contractual obligations—are void rather than voidable. Because legal actions against this type of minor are virtually nonexistent, the rules considered below are those applicable to the contracts of "older minors"—typically, teenagers.[3]

---

[1] Historically, there have been a number of additional classes of persons who possessed little or no capacity to contract: married women, convicted felons, aliens, American Indians, and unincorporated associations. Today, the legal capacity of some of these classes (e.g., married women, aliens, and felons) has generally been restored by statute or by judicial decision, and cases involving the others do not arise often. Thus we will not discuss these classes of persons in this chapter.

[2] These statutes almost uniformly confer upon 18-year-olds the rights to sue and be sued in their own names, to make wills, to marry without parental consent, and to choose their own domiciles; but generally they do not sanction the right to buy alcoholic beverages until the age of 21 is reached.

[3] There are at least two unusual situations where minors may be treated as adults. First, a few states provide that married persons should be treated as

We will now examine the results of the general rule permitting minors to disaffirm contracts at their option in three basic situations: (1) **ordinary contracts**—that is, contracts under which the goods or services being purchased are not necessities of life; (2) contracts for the purchase of "necessaries," and (3) contracts in which the minor has misrepresented his or her age.

Minors' Liability on Ordinary Contracts

Executory Contracts

Few problems arise where the minor's repudiation occurs before either party has started to perform the obligations under the contract (that is, where the contract is still *executory*). Since the other party is caused little hardship in such a case, all states take the view that the disaffirmance entirely frees the minor of liability. For example, suppose that M, a minor, contracts on July 1 to buy a home stereo system from X for $1,200, the contract providing that the system will be delivered and the purchase price paid on July 15. If M notifies X on July 10 that he will not go through with the deal, the contract is at an end and X has no recourse against M. Similarly, if M contracts to paint Y's house for $400 and later refuses to do the job, the refusal absolves M of liability. If either X or Y were to bring suit against M to recover damages for breach of contract, the suit would be dismissed.

Executed Contracts

Surprising as it may seem, the same rule is also generally applied to executed contracts—those that have been fully performed before the repudiation takes place. Thus, in virtually all states, a minor can purchase a car for cash, drive it until he or she becomes an adult, and still disaffirm the contract (assuming, as is usually the case, that the car is not a necessity of life).[4]

While virtually all courts agree as to the minor's *right to disaffirm* a contract in a situation such as the

above, they do not agree about the *extent of the relief* that should be given to the minor in some circumstances. This can be illustrated by amplifying the facts about the car purchase. Suppose that the purchase price of the car was $2,800 and that the minor brings suit to recover that amount. At the trial, the seller offers evidence establishing that the value of the car at the time the minor offered to return it was $1,500. In such a case the seller can make at least two contentions: (1) that the minor should be charged with the benefit received—that is, the reasonable value of the use of the car prior to disaffirmance or (2) if this contention is rejected, that the minor should at least be charged with the depreciation of the car while it was in the minor's hands.

The Majority View.   The courts of most states reject both contentions, permitting the minor to recover the full price of $2,800. Assuming that the automobile does not constitute a necessity, the majority rule is that the minor's only obligation is *to return the consideration if able to do so.* Under this view, the return of the car—even though it has greatly depreciated in value by reason of use or accident—entitles the minor to recover his or her *entire payment.* Furthermore, if the minor is unable to return the consideration, as would be the case if the car were stolen, the minor is still permitted to recover the $2,800 from the unfortunate seller. And regardless of whether the consideration has depreciated in value or cannot be returned, the minor is not charged with the benefit received from the possession and use of the consideration.

Freedom from liability would also exist if the minor had purchased the car on credit rather than for cash. In that case, if the minor disaffirmed the contract before paying off the balance, and if the seller then brought action to recover that balance, the minor would again be freed of all liability (subject, again, only to the obligation to return the car if he or she is able to do so).[5]

Some Other Views.   The courts of a growing number of states, feeling that the majority view

---

adults for purposes of entering into contracts even if they are not yet 18. Second, several states have procedures where, under court supervision, minors may be treated as adults for purposes of making contracts. Such a procedure allows a child actor, for example, to contract with a movie studio. The studio is protected because the child is unable to disaffirm the contract. The child is protected because the funds he or she is paid under the contract typically go into a trust fund that is administered for the child's benefit.

[4]Standard forms of many car dealers contain a statement that the buyer "hereby certifies that he or she is eighteen years of age, or over." The minor's right to disaffirm this kind of contract is discussed later under the "misrepresentation of age" section.

[5]A procedural note: as the above examples illustrate, minority cases ordinarily arise in one of two ways. In the first (and most common) situation the minor has paid *cash* for the goods or services, and, upon disaffirmance, the minor is the plaintiff seeking return of his or her payment. In the second case, where the minor purchases goods or services *on credit* and then disaffirms, the unpaid seller is the plaintiff, seeking to recover the contract price. Regardless of how the cases arise, the applicable minority rules apply with equal force. (That is, if under the applicable rules the minor in the first case is permitted to recover the full purchase price, he or she in the second case will be entirely freed of the obligation to pay for the goods.)

imposes unreasonable hardship on the other party to the contract, *do* impose liability on the minor under one of two theories. Some states hold the minor liable for the *reasonable value of the benefit* received prior to the disaffirmance, while others reach a similar result by holding the minor liable for the depreciation that has occurred to the goods while in his or her possession. Going back to the original illustration, where the minor had paid cash for the car, the courts of these states would permit the minor to recover the purchase price *minus* the value of the benefit (or depreciation), whatever the jury finds this

to be. Most of these minority jurisdictions would not require a disaffirming minor who had purchased on credit to produce the funds necessary to "make the adult whole" in order to disaffirm. Thus, these minority jurisdictions give less protection to adults who sell to minors on credit than to those who protect themselves by demanding the minors' money "up front."

The case below illustrates the broad protection the majority view affords the minor in a typical fact-pattern. (The rationale underlying this view follows the case.)

HALBMAN V. LEMKE

Supreme Court of Wisconsin, 298 N.W.2d 562 (1980)

James Halbman, a minor, worked at a gas station in Green-field, Wisconsin. During his employment he contracted to buy a 1968 Oldsmobile from Michael Lemke, the station manager, for $1,250. At the time the contract was made Halbman paid Lemke $1,000 cash and took possession of the car. (Title to the vehicle was retained by Lemke.) Under the contract Halbman agreed to pay $25 per week until the balance was paid off.

A little more than a month later, at which time Halbman had paid $1,100 of the price, a connecting rod in the engine broke. He took the car to a garage, where it was repaired at a cost of $637. Halbman did not pay the repair bill. Shortly thereafter Lemke endorsed the car's title over to Halbman, even though the full purchase price had not been paid, in an effort to avoid any liability for the operation and maintenance of the vehicle (including the repair bill). Halbman returned the title to Lemke, with a letter saying he was disaffirming the contract and demanding the return of the $1,100 he had paid. Lemke did not return the money and did not pay the bill. (The car remained in possession of the

repair shop.) Five months later, with the repair bill still unpaid, the garage removed the car's engine and transmission in satisfaction of the debt. The garage then towed the vehicle to the home of Halbman's father. While there it was subjected to vandalism which made the car "unsalvageable."

Halbman then brought this action to recover the $1,100 he had paid, and Lemke counterclaimed for $150, the amount still owing on the contract. The trial court granted judgment for Halbman, ruling that when a minor disaffirms a contract for the purchase of an item, his or her only obligation is to return the property remaining in his hands. The court of appeals affirmed, and Lemke petitioned the Supreme Court of Wisconsin for review.

Callow, Justice:

. . . The sole issue before us is whether a minor, having disaffirmed a contract for the purchase of an item which is not a necessity and having tendered the property back to the vendor, must make restitution to the vendor for damage to the property prior to the disaffirmance. Lemke argues that he should be entitled to recover for the damage to the vehicle up to the time of

disaffirmance, which he claims equals the amount of the repair bill.

Neither party challenges the absolute right of a minor to disaffirm a contract for the purchase of items which are not necessities. That right, variously known as the doctrine of incapacity or the "infancy doctrine," is one of the oldest and most venerable of our common-law traditions. Although the origins of the doctrine are somewhat obscure, it is generally recognized that its purpose is the protection of minors from foolishly squandering their wealth through improvident contracts with crafty adults who would take advantage of them in the marketplace. . . .

As a general rule, a minor who disaffirms a contract is entitled to recover all consideration he has conferred incident to the transaction. In return the minor is expected to restore as much of the consideration as, at the time of disaffirmance, remains in the minor's possession. The minor's right to disaffirm is not contingent upon the return of the property, however, as disaffirmance is permitted even where such return cannot be made. . . .

The law regarding the rights and responsibilities of the parties relative to the consideration exchanged on a disaffirmed contract is characterized by confusion, inconsistency, and a general lack of uniformity as jurisdictions

(continues)

Halbman owes Lemke for the repair bill?

Halbman v. Lemke

(continued from previous page)
attempt to reach a fair application of the infancy doctrine in today's marketplace. [The court then analyzed a number of cases which, Lemke contended, barred recovery by Halbman in this action. The court rejected the rules of those cases, saying:] Because these cases would at some point force the minor to bear the cost of the very improvidence from which the infancy doctrine is supposed to protect him, we cannot follow them.

As we noted in [a prior Wisconsin case], modifications of the rules governing the capacity of infants to contract are best left to the legislature. Until such changes are forthcoming, however, we hold that, absent misrepresentation or tortious damage to the property, a minor who disaffirms a contract for the purchase of an item which is not a necessity may recover his purchase price without liability for use, depreciation, damage, or other diminution in value. . . .

The decision of the court of appeals is affirmed. ⚖

Rationale

There is no question but that the majority rule, as applied to specific situations, frequently results in a severe financial loss to the party who has dealt with the minor. It is also possible that some young people, aware of the rule, enter into contracts with the intention of getting something for nothing. Nevertheless, most courts justify the occasional hardships that result under the majority rule by noting that "the primary purpose of the common-law rule is to afford protection to minors by discouraging others from contracting with them," and this rule no doubt tends to bring about such a result. Thus we have once again a situation where the rights of some individuals, under certain circumstances, must give way to the rights of others because of public policy considerations.

A competent person can, of course, ordinarily escape such hardships by refusing to deal with minors.[6] All persons are presumed to know the law, so that (in theory at least) one who deals with a minor is on notice that it is at his or her peril. A second solution for someone who wishes to make a sale is to refuse to deal with the minor and to contract instead with one of the minor's parents. In such a case the possibility of a disaffirmance is eliminated, since both parties to the contract are competent. A third solution, in situations where the competent party does not know whether the person with whom he or she is dealing is a minor, is to have that person make a statement, preferably in writing, that he or she is over the age of eighteen. (The protection afforded to the competent party by such a representation is considered later in the chapter.)

Ratification

Once a minor reaches the age of majority, he or she has the ability to ratify any contracts made earlier. A **ratification** occurs when the minor indicates to the other party, expressly or impliedly, the intent to be bound by the agreement. Thus, if a minor, after reaching the age of 18, promises that he or she will go through with the contract, an express ratification has taken place and the right of disaffirmance is lost forever. Similarly, if a minor has received an article, such as a typewriter, under a contract and continues to use it for more than a "reasonable time" after reaching the age of 18, an implied ratification has occurred. Another situation in which a ratification can take place involves purchases made under installment contracts. Suppose, for example, that a minor has purchased a motorcycle, agreeing to pay the seller $25 a month until the purchase price has been paid in full. If he continues to make payments for any length of time after reaching the age of 18, it is probable that such payments will be held to constitute a ratification of the contract. (It is obvious, then, that any young person should review all of his or her contracts upon becoming an adult, and refrain from any conduct that would indicate to the other party an intent to be bound by them if he or she wishes to set any of them aside.)

[6]Some persons, such as common carriers, have a legal duty to deal with everyone who requests (and is able to pay for) their services. Disaffirmance against such persons is generally not permitted once the contract has been executed. Thus, a 17-year-old who purchases and uses an airline ticket is not permitted to recover his or her fare.

Minors' Liability on Contracts to Purchase "Necessaries"

When a minor purchases **necessaries** (goods that the law considers necessary to life or health), he or she incurs a greater liability than that imposed (by the majority rule) under contracts calling for the purchase of goods that are not necessities. The rule applicable to contracts calling for the purchase of "necessaries" is that the minor is liable to the other party for the *reasonable value of the goods actually used.* This is the quasi-contractual measure of recovery, because the minor is being held liable not on the contract but, instead, to avoid unjust enrichment. To illustrate: M, 17, buys a topcoat from C, contracting to pay the price of $150 one year later. At the end of that time, when the coat is completely worn out, C brings suit to recover the purchase price. If the court rules that the coat is a necessary, then it must determine what its reasonable value was at the time of the purchase, and M is liable to C in that amount. (In contrast, if the coat is held *not* to constitute a necessary, M is usually freed of all liability—as has been seen earlier.) This imposition of liability occurs only where the goods or services have been used by the minor; contracts calling for the purchase of necessaries can still be set aside as long as they are executory. Thus, if M contracts to purchase a coat from C, which is to be delivered one week later, he can set aside the contract without liability if he notifies C of his disaffirmance before the week is out—and indeed, even later as long as he does not use the coat.

What Constitutes a Necessary?

In answering the question of what constitutes a necessary, it is possible to draw a clear line in most cases. Minimum amounts of food, clothing, and medical services are clearly necessary. So, too, is the rental of a house or apartment by a minor who is married. Many items, on the other hand, are clearly luxuries—such as TV sets, sporting goods, and dancing lessons, under most circumstances.[7] Other items held to be necessaries include legal services, taxes on real property owned by minors, and medical care for a minor's child.

A few states reason that items essential for a minor to earn a living (and therefore to have money to buy necessaries) should also be treated as necessaries. Thus, a minority of states would treat as necessaries such things as a car that a minor uses in his or her work or the services of an employment agency that the minor used to obtain a job.[8]

It should be noted that an item is a necessity only if it is actually needed at the time of purchase. Thus if a minor purchases an item that appears to be a necessity, such as an article of clothing, the minor still has no liability to the seller if he or she can prove that a parent or guardian was "willing and able" to furnish clothing of the type purchased under that particular contract.

Rationale

Why is it that under the majority rule, a minor who buys something frivolous may disaffirm the contract and recover the entire purchase price, whereas a minor who buys something truly needed can disaffirm only where the seller can retain the fair value of what the minor used? These rules seem paradoxical, but the clear rationale is, on the one hand, to discourage merchants from dealing with minors for the frivolous items (by allowing the minors to disaffirm even when it is unfair to the merchant), but on the other hand to induce merchants to sell minors the things they need for survival (by ensuring that the minors will pay at least fair value).

Minors' Liability on Contracts Involving Misrepresentation of Age

We have assumed so far that the minor has not led the other party to believe that he or she is an adult. If such misrepresentation does occur, the minor is guilty of a kind of fraud, and the courts of most jurisdictions will deny the protection that otherwise would be given that person.

Some states have provided by statute that a minor who has misrepresented his or her age is liable on the contract exactly as if he or she were an adult. Most states, however, have left the matter up to the courts, and a spate of rules has resulted. Without attempting to consider all of them, we can make one or two generalizations.

---

[7] In determining whether a doubtful item is a necessary, the courts take into account the "station in life" occupied by the particular minor. Thus a fourth sport coat might be ruled a necessary for a minor who is a member of high society, while it would not be so ruled in regard to others.

[8] *Gastonia Personnel Corp. v. Rogers,* 172 S.E.2d 19 (N.C. 1970).

First, where the minor repudiates the contract while it is entirely executory, most courts permit the disaffirmance just as if there had been no misrepresentation. Although this does not penalize the minor for wrongdoing, it also does not cause particular hardship to the other party in most instances.

Second, where a contract calling for the purchase of a nonnecessary item has been fully or partially executed before the attempted disaffirmance, many courts allow the disaffirmance *only if it will not cause a loss to the other party.*[9] Under this approach, each case is analyzed separately to determine the effect of the disaffirmance. Two illustrations follow.

1. M, a minor, purchases a car from C, a competent party, for $2,500 cash, after telling C that she is 18. A year later, just before becoming 18, M wishes to disaffirm; at this time the market value of the car is $1,400. Despite the misrepresentation, disaffirmance will be permitted. C, however, will be allowed to withhold from the $2,500 the amount of the depreciation, $1,100, which—added to the $1,400 car—will restore him to his original position. M's recovery is thus only $1,400.

2. M purchases a car from C under a contract providing, "Buyer certifies that he or she is 18 years of age or older." The purchase price is $2,500, with $100 paid at the time of purchase and the balance of $2,400 payable in 24 monthly installments. Six months later, when the car is stolen, M notifies C that she wants to be relieved of the balance of the contract. Disaffirmance will probably not be allowed since this would cause a loss to C; thus a suit by C to recover the unpaid balance will be successful.[10]

The contract liability of minors regarding both executory and executed contracts is illustrated in Figure 15.1.

Contracts That Cannot Be Disaffirmed

Not all contracts can be disaffirmed on the ground of minority. For example, disaffirmance of marriage contracts and contracts of enlistment in the armed forces is not permitted on the ground of public policy. For certain other contracts, such as those approved by a court or those made with banks or insurance companies, the same result is generally brought about by statute. For example, a North Carolina statute authorizes banks "in respect to deposit accounts and the rental of safe deposit boxes" to deal with minors as if they were adults. And another North Carolina statute authorizes minors of 15 and over to make life insurance contracts to the same extent as adults. Still other states have held that releases signed by minors to settle litigation are enforceable; otherwise, no suits involving minors could be effectively settled out of court.

Torts and Crimes

The rules permitting minors to disaffirm most contracts do not apply to acts that are tortious or criminal in nature. Generally, minors are fully liable for any torts or crimes they commit (except, of course, minors of "tender years," such as two- or three-year-olds). Thus, if a minor drives a car negligently, anyone injured thereby can recover damages from him or her. Such liability cannot be disaffirmed. Similarly, if a minor operates a motor vehicle while intoxicated, the usual criminal penalties can be imposed (although in the criminal area, the penalties may be tempered under juvenile court procedures).

MENTALLY IMPAIRED AND INTOXICATED PERSONS

Mentally Impaired Persons

Persons with impaired mental capacity are, like minors, given substantial protection by the law insofar as their contractual obligations are concerned. We will briefly examine the general rules applicable to those falling within this broad category which includes mentally retarded, brain damaged, and senile persons, and persons suffering from mental illness. (In the law, the term "insane" is often broadly used to encompass all of the above classes, but sometimes is used more restrictively to refer only to the last class—persons of average intelligence who suffer periods of derangement that often vary widely as to intensity and duration.[11])

Adjudicated Insane

Some mentally impaired persons are formally declared to be incompetent by a court after hearings and

---

[9] In cases of "necessary" contracts, the usual rule normally continues in effect—the minor is liable for the reasonable value of the articles actually used.

[10] This example is based on *Haydocy Pontiac, Inc. v. Lee*, 19 Ohio App.2d 217 (1969). The minor in this case was held to be "estopped" from disaffirming, in view of her misrepresentation; and she continued to be liable for the "fair value of the property."

[11] In any event, the various terms or labels used in the law, such as those we mention here, are often somewhat different from, or less precise than, those used by the medical profession.

FIGURE 15.1

*Contract
Liability of
Minors*

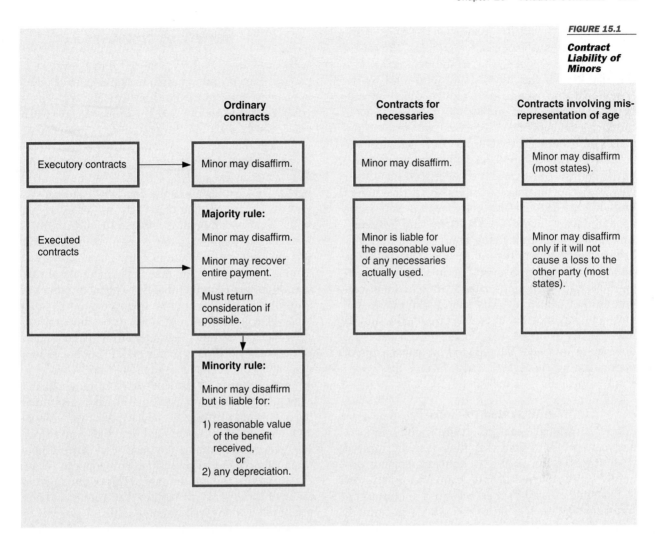

examination by psychologists or psychiatrists. After a person has been **adjudicated insane,** a guardian is appointed. Thereafter, any "contract" made by the insane person rather than by the guardian is absolutely void—that is, creates no liability whatever, even if it is never disaffirmed by the incompetent person or the guardian. (However, if any goods or services furnished under the contracts were *necessities* not being furnished by the guardian, the impaired person would be liable for their fair market value under a quasi-contract theory.)

Insane in Fact

Many mentally impaired persons have never been the subject of incompetency proceedings, but are nonetheless **insane in fact.** If at the time the con-tract was made, the person was so impaired that he or she was *incapable of understanding the nature and effect of the particular agreement,* then the contract is voidable. A court may order rescission of the contract at the request of the impaired party after he or she regains full mental capacity. (Again, if rescission is allowed, liability for the fair market value of any *necessities* furnished under the contract would exist under the quasi-contract principle.)

Hanks v. NcNeill Coal Corporation, 168 P.2d 256 (1946), is typical of those controversies in which the evidence on the "understanding" issue was in sharp conflict. In that case Hanks, a farmer who had never been adjudicated insane, sold coal lands in Colorado to the coal company. At his death his executor sought to rescind the contract on the ground that Hanks was insane in fact—actually insane—at the time of the transaction. In support of this contention, the executor introduced evidence that in the months prior to the sale Hanks was increasingly interested in the "emotional type" of religion; was increasingly abusive to his family members; and manufactured a medicine for horses made of brick dust, burnt shoe leather, and pieces of ground glass. Despite this evidence, the court ruled Hanks to be sane with respect to the sale, on the basis of testimony by lawyers and a banker who had other dealings with him about the time of the sale, who testified that, as to business matters, he appeared to be "in grasp of his affairs" and "rational." In explaining its ruling, the court said: "One may have insane delusions regarding some matters and be insane on some subjects, yet [be] capable of transacting business concerning matters wherein such matters are not concerned, and such insanity does not make one incompetent to contract unless the subject matter of the contract is so connected with an insane delusion as to render the afflicted party incapable of understanding the nature and effect of the agreement, or of acting rationally in the transaction."

Intoxicated Persons

People occasionally seek to escape liability under a contract on the ground that they were intoxicated when it was made. Success in doing so depends primarily on the degree of intoxication found to exist at that time. Disaffirmance is allowed only if a person can establish that he or she was so intoxicated as not to understand the nature of the purported agreement. Thus a question of fact is presented, for a lesser degree of intoxication is not grounds for disaffirmance.

If the required degree of intoxication is found to have existed, the intoxicated person's right to disaffirm, upon regaining sobriety, also substantially parallels that of a minor—again, however, with one basic exception. While we have seen that minors may, as a general rule, disaffirm contracts even though unable to return the consideration that they received, intoxicated persons are required by most courts to return the full consideration as a condition of disaffirmance in all cases (unless they are able to show fraud on the part of the other contracting party). For apparent reasons, contracting parties who are intoxicated receive less protection from the law than do minors or the mentally impaired.

REALITY OF CONSENT

A contract that has been entered into between two persons having full capacity to contract, and which appears to be valid in all other respects, may still be voidable if it turns out that the apparent consent of one or both of the parties was, in fact, not genuine. Contracts that are tainted with *fraud, innocent misrepresentation, mistake, duress,* or *undue influence* can ordinarily be voided (set aside) by the innocent parties. In such instances the courts will allow rescission on the ground that there was "no reality of consent." That is, although it *appears* from the form of the contract alone that the consent of both parties was genuine (or "real"), in fact it was not.

Many areas of law are essentially made up of rules that discourage conduct that is deceitful or otherwise injurious to individuals or to society in general. Some types of conduct are felt to be so detrimental to a stable society that they are flatly prohibited, and punishment for violators is prescribed. From hence have our bodies of criminal law been built up.

In other areas of law rules have come about that attempt to insure at least some degree of care and fairness when private citizens have dealings with one another, and which grant civil remedies against persons who violate them. We have seen, for example, that tortious conduct causes the wrongdoer to answer in damages to the injured party. This continuing filament of thought, to the effect that a person should not be allowed to profit by conduct that is patently offensive, is woven into the law of contracts. It is most apparent in that part of law having to do with fraud and duress and, to a lesser extent, mistake and undue influence.

FRAUD

Leaving aside, for the moment, any attempt to define the term, the essence of **fraud** is deception—the intentional misleading of one person by another. Perhaps the most common type of fraud occurs when one person simply lies to another about a material fact, as a result of which a contract is made. Thus, if S, the owner of a current model car, tells B that he purchased it new six months ago, S knowing that it was in fact "second-hand" when he acquired it, S is guilty of fraud if B, believing this statement to be true, subsequently purchases the car. In this case,

B—after learning the true facts—ordinarily can either rescind the contract and recover the purchase price or keep the car and recover damages from S.

Elements of Fraud

One person can mislead another in so many ways that the courts have been reluctant to fashion a hard and fast definition of fraud; any precise definition almost certainly could be circumvented by persons intent on getting around it. Instead, the courts generally recognize that the various forms of deception they wish to forestall usually contain common elements. When a court is called upon to decide in a given case whether the conduct of one of the parties was fraudulent, its usual approach is to see if the required elements are present. If so, fraud has been established and the victim will be afforded relief.

To be successful in a fraud action, the plaintiff is required to show all of the following:

1. That defendant made a *misrepresentation of a material fact*.

2. That the statement was made with the *intent to deceive* (i.e., defendant knew or should have known the statement was false).

3. That plaintiff *reasonably relied* on the misrepresentation.

4. That plaintiff suffered an *injury* as a result.

Misrepresentation of a Material Fact

Misrepresentation of a material fact (or *misstatement*) is broadly interpreted to include any word or conduct that causes the innocent person to reach an erroneous conclusion of fact. Thus a seller of apples who selects the best ones in a basket and puts them on top of others of inferior quality has, in the eyes of the law, made a "statement" to a prospective buyer that all the apples are of the same quality as those which are visible.

In order for a misstatement to be fraudulent, it must be a **statement of fact**—an actual event, circumstance, or occurrence. Statements about the age of a horse, the number of acres in a tract of land, and the net profit made by a business during a given year are all statements of fact—that is, statements about a fact. And, the misstatement must be material (important). A statement that a 640-acre tract of land holds 642 acres would be false, but probably not materially

so; a statement that it contained 670 acres probably would be materially false. If the innocent person can prove that a particular statement made to him or her was false in a material way, the first element of fraud has been established.

Predictions

Statements as to what will happen in the future are clearly not statements of fact and therefore are not fraudulent even if they turn out to be in error. Thus, if a seller of stock tells a buyer that the stock is "bound to double in value within six months," the buyer is not entitled to relief in the event the increase in value does not come about. The same is true when the seller of a motel states that "it will certainly net $14,000 in the coming year." The reason for the view that such statements do not constitute fraud, of course, is that no one can predict what will happen in the future, and a reasonable person would not put faith in such statements.[12]

Opinion

Statements of opinion, like predictions, are also distinguished from statements of fact. Contracts cannot be set aside on the ground of fraud simply because one of the parties, prior to making the contract, expressed an opinion that later turned out to be incorrect.

Most statements of opinion, in which the declarant is merely expressing personal feelings or judgments on a matter about which reasonable persons might have contrary views, are usually easy to recognize. For example, statements that "this is an excellent neighborhood in which to raise children" or that "this painting will harmonize beautifully with the colors of your living room" involve conclusions with which others might disagree; thus they cannot be the

---

[12] One important type of statement about a present or future event or condition *does* impose a legal obligation on the one making it if it proves to be false: statements that are "warranties"—guarantees as to existing fact or assurances about future performance of a product by the seller. For example: A manufacturer of house paint states on the cans that "this paint, when applied according to the manufacturer's instructions above, will not crack, fade, or peel within two years of its application." If the statement proves to be false, a buyer who has purchased the paint in reliance on the statement can recover damages. The recovery in such a case would be on *breach of warranty* rather than on fraud, except in the rare situation where the buyer can prove that the seller knew the representation to be false when he or she made it. (Most, but not all, warranties are governed by the *law of sales.* Specific questions about the definition and application of express and implied warranties in regard to the sale of goods require reference to Secs. 2-312, 313, 314, 315, and 316 of the UCC, discussed in detail in Chapter 22.)

basis of an action of fraud brought by one who relied upon them.

Other statements, however, are not so easily placed in the "opinion" or "fact" categories. A statement by the seller of a boat that it is "perfectly safe" or a statement by a home owner that "the foundation is sound" are closer to being statements of fact than the previous representations about the neighborhood and the painting. But there are varying degrees of safety and soundness, so these statements too can be held in given situations to constitute only expressions of opinion—particularly if the declarant and the innocent party were on a relatively equal basis insofar as their experience and general knowledge of the subject matter were concerned. (On the other hand, if the declarant is considerably more knowledgeable than the other party, such statements are likely to be viewed as statements of *fact,* and thus fraudulent if false. For example, in the case of *Groening v. Opsata,* 34 N.W.2d 560, 1948, it was held that a false statement by the seller of a summer home located on an eroding cliff on the shore of Lake Michigan that "it isn't too close [to the lake]" and that "there is nothing to fear, everything is all right" constituted fraud, in view of the fact that the seller was a builder of homes in the area.)

Value

Statements about an article's *value* have also caused difficulties. Nevertheless, the courts today adhere to the traditional view (in most circumstances) that the value of an article or piece of property is a matter of opinion rather than fact. Two practical reasons are the basis for this view: (1) an awareness that many types of property are prized by some people but are considered of little value by others, and (2) a recognition of the fact that sellers generally overvalue the things they are attempting to sell, and prospective buyers must accordingly place little or no reliance upon such statements.[13] Consequently, if a seller states that "this apartment building is easily worth $80,000," the buyer normally can not rescind the contract on the ground of fraud, even though he or she relied on the statement and can prove later that the actual market value of the building at the time of sale was nowhere near the stated figure and that the seller knew this at the time.

Again, the general rule is not followed when the declarant's experience and knowledge of the particular subject matter are *markedly superior* to those of the other party—especially if they are so great that the declarant is considered an "expert" in the eyes of the law. (In order to prevent such a person from taking grossly unfair advantage of those who are clearly less knowledgeable, his or her intentional misrepresentations *are* held to be fraudulent.)

The next case presents an allegation of fraud in a modern setting.

---

[13] Statements of gross overvaluation, like others that are grossly extravagant in nature ("this sport coat will wear like iron"), constitute mere "dealers' puffing."

STEINBERG V. CHICAGO MEDICAL SCHOOL

Supreme Court of Illinois, 371 N.E.2d 634 (1977)

The Chicago Medical School, defendant, issued a bulletin for the 1974–1975 school year which stated that applicants would be selected "on the basis of academic achievement, Medical College Admission Test results, personal appraisals by a pre-professional advisory committee or individual instructors, and the personal interview, if requested by the Committee on Admissions."

Steinberg received a bulletin, applied for admission, and paid the required $15 application fee.

After his application was rejected, Steinberg learned that the defendant, in fact, used "nonacademic criteria" in admitting applicants, primarily the ability of the applicant or his family to pledge or make payments of large sums of money to the school. Steinberg then brought this action on behalf of all rejected applicants, claiming that defendant was guilty of fraud in failing to disclose such factors.

A number of issues were raised in the trial court. Two of these were (1) whether a contract was ever formed between the parties, and (2) if so, whether defendant's representations in its bulletin constituted fraud. The trial court ruled against plaintiff on all issues and dismissed the action. An intermediate court of appeals affirmed some rulings of the trial court but reversed others. Plaintiff appealed to the Supreme

(continues)

STEINBERG V. CHICAGO MEDICAL SCHOOL

(continued from previous page)
Court of Illinois. (Only those parts of the highest court's decision applicable to the two selected issues are set forth below).

Dooley, Justice:

. . . An offer [and] an acceptance . . . are basic ingredients of a contract. Steinberg alleges that he and [others] received a brochure describing the criteria that defendant would employ in evaluating applications. He urges that such constituted an invitation for an offer to apply, that the filing of the applications constituted an offer to have their credentials appraised under the terms described by defendant, and that defendant's voluntary reception of the application and fee constituted an acceptance, the final act necessary for the creation of a binding contract.

This situation is similar to that wherein a merchant advertises goods for sale at a fixed price. While the advertisement itself is [usually] not an offer to contract, it constitutes an invitation to deal on the terms described in the advertisement. . . . When the merchant takes the money [there is] an acceptance of the offer to purchase. [The court then agreed with Steinberg's contention that the defendant's receipt of his application and fee constituted an acceptance of his application offer, and that a contract was thus formed. The court next turned to the question of fraud.]

Count III alleges that, with intent to deceive and defraud plaintiffs, defendant stated in its catalogs it would use certain criteria to evaluate applications; that these representations were false in that applicants were selected primarily for monetary considerations; that plaintiffs relied on said representations and were each thereby induced to submit their applications and pay $15, [and that plaintiffs were damaged as a result].

These allegations support a cause of action for fraud. Misrepresentation of an existing material fact coupled with scienter [knowledge], deception, and injury are more than adequate. . . . Plaintiff's allegations of fraud meet the test of common-law fraud.

Not to be ignored is defendant's *modus operandi* as described in *DeMarco v. University of Health Sciences*, 352 N.E.2d 356 (1976):

An analysis of those exhibits shows that in 1970, at least 64 out of 83 entering students had pledges made in their behalves totalling $1,927,900. The pledges varied in amounts from $1400 to $100,000 and averaged $30,123. In 1971, at least 55 out of 83 students had pledges made in their behalves totalling $1,893,000. The pledges varied in amounts from $3000 to $100,000 and averaged $34,418. In 1972, at least 73 out of an entering class of 92 had contributions made in their behalves totalling $3,111,000. The pledges varied in amounts from $20,000 to $100,000 and averaged $42,603. In 1973, at least 78 out of 91 students had contributions made in their behalves totalling $3,749,000. The pledges varied in amounts from $10,000 to $100,000 and averaged $48,064. In addition, there were amounts pledged and partial payments made for students who did not enter or dropped out shortly after entering.

It is immaterial here that the misrepresentation consisted of a statement in the medical school catalog, referring to future conduct, that "student's potential for the study and practice of medicine will be evaluated on the basis of academic achievement, Medical College Admission Test results, personal appraisals by a pre-professional advisory committee or individual instructors, and the personal interview, if requested by the Committee on Admissions." We concede the general rule denies recovery for fraud based on a false representation of intention or future conduct, but there is a recognized exception where the false promise or representation of future conduct is alleged to be the scheme employed to accomplish the fraud. Such is the situation here. . . .

[The higher court, disagreeing with the trial court, thus ruled that Steinberg's allegations, if true, did state a cause of action. It therefore remanded the case to the trial court for determination of the factual issues presented.]

Law

Under the early common-law rule of this country, *statements of law* made by lay persons were clearly held not to constitute statements of fact and thus could not be the basis for actions of fraud. If the seller of a vacant lot that carries a C-1 zoning classification assures the buyer that "this classification permits the erection of duplex rental units," a statement that the seller knows is not true, the buyer who purchases the property in reliance on the statement ordinarily cannot maintain an action for damages. The rule was based on two grounds: (1) the generally reasonable feeling that a statement made by a nonlawyer about a point of law should not be relied upon by the one to whom it is made, and (2) the somewhat more questionable maxim that "everyone is presumed to know the law."

While this is still the rule applied to most cases, it is subject to an increasing number of exceptions. One major exception comprises statements of law made by

LEGAL FOCUS

Ethics

In a recent survey, a surprisingly high percentage of respondents indicated that they believed it was "OK" to lie to an insurance company. What accounts for such responses? Is it OK to steal from a company that is large or a person who is wealthy simply because the victim is large or wealthy? What creates such moral blind spots?

Some courts are beginning to take the profit out of lying to insurance companies. But how far should courts go? In *New York Life v. Johnson*, 923 F.2d 279 (3d Cir. 1991), Johnson falsely indicated that he did not smoke when he filled out a life insurance policy application. Answering truthfully would not have prevented Johnson from obtaining insurance, but would have raised his premiums by 30 to 40 percent. Three years after the $50,000 policy was issued, Johnson died of AIDS, a cause unrelated to his smoking. The insurance company refused to pay on the policy, citing "fraud in the inducement."

The court could have chosen to force the insurance company to pay the entire $50,000 on grounds that the lie was unrelated to the cause of death and the company admitted that it would have issued the policy even had the applicant told the truth. The court could have affirmed the lower court's decision to force the company to pay the face amount reduced by the extra premiums that it did not receive because of the deceit. Or, the court could have simply voided the policy because of the applicant's lie. The court, following recent trends, chose the third alternative. Is this the proper result?

---

persons who—because of their professional or occupational status—can reasonably be expected to know the law relating to their specialty, even though they are not attorneys. Thus intentional misrepresentations of law by persons such as real estate brokers and bank cashiers as to legal matters within their particular specialties are frequently held to be fraudulent.

Silence, Traditionally

The traditional common-law rule was *caveat emptor* ("let the buyer beware"). Under this rule, buyers had the responsibility to look out for themselves in making a purchase. Thus, assume that a seller knew that a car had been involved in an accident that bent the car's frame. If the seller told the buyer: "This car has never been in an accident," a clear misstatement of material fact would have occurred. When the buyer learned the truth, he could rescind due to fraud. But what if the seller did not make such a statement, but simply kept silent about the accident? The traditional rule stated that mere silence (failure to disclose a material fact) *does not constitute fraud*. The reasoning was that in most instances the parties are

dealing at arm's length,[14] possessing roughly the same amount of experience and knowledge relating to the subject matter of the contract. And, in many instances, the facts not disclosed could have been ascertained by the buyer with reasonable inspection or inquiry.

Today, however, *caveat emptor* has been so riddled with exceptions that in many jurisdictions it is difficult to speak of it as being the general rule. Court rulings and state consumer protection statutes have created so many situations where sellers must volunteer adverse information or be charged with fraud that many claim the new general rule is *caveat venditor* ("let the seller beware").

Silence and the Duty to Speak

The courts have found several types of situations where the withholding of information is so manifestly unfair that silence should be held to constitute fraud.

---

[14]Parties are said to deal at "arm's length" when their relationship is such that neither party owes a duty to divulge information to the other party (as distinguished from such exceptional relationships as attorney-client and guardian-ward relationships.)

To prevent unfairness of this degree, the courts say that, in such situations, a "duty to speak" exists. It is difficult to summarize the duty-to-speak categories with precision, because the silence cases involve such a wide variety of fact-patterns, and because the rules of the various states applicable to duty to speak situations are often couched in general terms (to give the courts substantial discretion in their application). Additionally, the law is continuing to evolve in this area, as the courts seek to raise moral standards in the marketplace by applying the rules to situations that were earlier outside their scope.

Despite these factors, several fairly well-defined situations do exist in which the courts generally agree that a duty to speak exists. (In such instances the courts often speak of "intentionally withheld information," of "concealment," and of silence as part of a "plan" to deceive.)

The first of these instances is the sale of property that contains a **latent defect** (or *hidden defect*)—one that a simple or casual inspection by a prospective purchaser ordinarily would not disclose. Common examples are a cracked motor block in an automobile and a termite infestation in a house. A property owner who has knowledge of such conditions is guilty of fraud if he or she does not apprise the prospective purchaser of them—assuming, of course, that the innocent purchaser subsequently enters into a contract to buy the property.

While the latent defect rule, abstractly stated, is highly commendable, the practical protection it affords is less than one might hope for. Frequently it is difficult for the buyer to prove that the defect actually existed at the time of purchase—particularly if a long period of time has elapsed before its discovery. And even if this hurdle is cleared, the buyer has to establish that the seller knew, or should have known, of the defect when the sale occurred. The seller's contention that he or she was honestly unaware of the defective condition is frequently accepted by a jury.[15]

A second duty to speak situation occurs where a **fiduciary relationship** exists—that is, where one of the parties occupies a position of "trust and confidence" relative to the other. (This differs from the ordinary situation, where the parties are dealing "at arm's length.") For example, when a partnership is considering a land purchase, a partner who is part owner of the land under consideration has a duty to divulge his or her interest to the co-partner before the purchase is made. Similarly, a corporate officer who is purchasing stock from a shareholder has a duty to disclose any special facts of which he or she has knowledge, by virtue of that position, which would affect the value of the stock.

The third category comprises situations in which one party has **superior knowledge** about the subject matter of the contract as a result of his or her experience, training, or special relationship with the subject matter. In this type of circumstance the rule has obvious application where the silent party—the one possessing the superior knowledge—is an "expert" in the area, but it often applies to other parties as well. The rule commonly applied is that if one party has superior knowledge, *or* knowledge which is not within the reasonable reach of the other party (and which such party could not discover by the exercise of means open to both parties), there is a duty on the party possessing the knowledge to disclose it. Under this rule, for example, a buyer of Oklahoma land who, by virtue of his employment with an oil company, learns of an oil "strike" on an adjacent ranch would be guilty of fraud if he did not disclose this information to the seller, a rancher. On the other hand, if the buyer was simply another ranch owner in the area, his or her nondisclosure of this information would probably not be fraudulent.

Outside of these situations, most courts take the view that neither party has a duty to volunteer information to the other, even though it might bear materially on the other's decision of whether to contract. Thus the seller of a trash collection business probably has no duty to tell a prospective purchaser of indications that the city is going to institute a collection service of its own—especially if this information is as available to the buyer as it is to the seller.[16]

The following case illustrates, in a rather unusual setting, the courts' struggle to establish fairer rules than a blanket application of *caveat emptor*.

---

[15] Normally the rule on hidden defects does not work in reverse. Thus, if the buyer possesses information about the property that causes its value to be higher than the seller believes it to be, the buyer does not have a duty to divulge this information to the seller (unless the buyer is an expert in the field by reason of training or experience).

[16] *Jappe v. Mandt,* 278 P.2d 940 (1955). Although the buyer's action for damages based upon fraud failed, an action for rescission might have succeeded on the ground of "unilateral mistake"—a subject discussed later in the chapter—*if* the buyer had been able to show that the seller was aware of his ignorance about the proposed city action.

STAMBOVSKY V. ACKLEY

New York Supreme Court, Appellate Division, 572 N.Y.S.2d 672 (1991)

After making a $32,000 down payment on a $650,000 house in Nyack, New York, plaintiff learned that (1) in both Readers' Digest in 1977 and local newspapers in 1982, defendant seller had claimed that she and members of her family had several times over the previous nine years seen poltergeists in the house; and (2) in 1989 the house was included in a five-home walking tour of Nyack and was described in a November 27 newspaper article as "a riverfront Victorian (with ghost)." Plaintiff refused to close on the house and sued both the seller and the seller's real estate agent, seeking both monetary damages and rescission of the contract. The trial court dismissed the suit. Plaintiff appealed.

Rubin, Justice:

While I agree with [the trial court] that the real estate broker, as agent for the seller, is under no duty to disclose to a potential buyer the phantasmal reputation of the premises and that, in his pursuit of a legal remedy for fraudulent misrepresentation against the seller, plaintiff hasn't a ghost of a chance, I am nevertheless moved by the spirit of equity to allow the buyer to seek rescission of the contract of sale and recovery of his down payment. New York law fails to recognize any remedy for damages incurred as a result of the seller's mere silence, applying instead the strict rule of caveat emptor. Therefore, the theoretical basis for relief, even under the extraordinary facts of this case, is elusive if not ephemeral.

"Pity me not but lend thy serious hearing to what I shall unfold" (William Shakespeare, Hamlet, Act I, Scene V [Ghost]).

From the perspective of a person in the position of plaintiff herein, a very practical problem arises with respect to the discovery of a paranormal phenomenon: "Who you gonna' call?" as the title song to the movie "Ghostbusters" asks. Applying the strict rule of caveat emptor to a contract involving a house possessed by poltergeists conjures up visions of a psychic or medium routinely accompanying the structural engineer and Terminex man on an inspection of every home subject to a contract of sale. . . . In the interest of avoiding such untenable consequences, the notion that a haunting is a condition which can and should be ascertained upon reasonable inspection of the premises is a hobgoblin which should be exorcised from the body of legal precedent and laid quietly to rest.

It has been suggested by a leading authority that the ancient rule which holds that mere non-disclosure does not constitute actional misrepresentation "finds proper application in cases where the fact undisclosed is patent, or the plaintiff has equal opportunities for obtaining information which he may be expected to utilize, or the defendant has no reason to think that he is acting under any misapprehension" (Prosser, Law of Torts, at 696 [4th ed. 1971]). However, with respect to transactions in real estate, New York adheres to the doctrine of caveat emptor and imposes no duty upon the vendor to disclose any information concerning the premises unless there is a confidential or fiduciary relationship between the parties or some conduct on the part of the seller which constitutes "active concealment" [such as constructing a dummy ventilation system or covering foundation cracks]. Normally, some affirmative misrepresentation is required to impose upon the seller a duty to communicate undisclosed conditions affecting the premises.

Caveat emptor is not so all-encompassing a doctrine of common law as to render every act of non-disclosure immune from redress, whether legal or equitable. "In regard to the necessity of giving information which has not been asked, the rule differs somewhat at law and in equity, and while the law courts would permit no recovery of damages against a vendor, because of mere concealment of facts under certain circumstances, yet if the vendee refused to complete the contract because of the concealment of a material fact on the part of the other, equity would refuse to compel him so to do, because equity only compels the specific performance of a contract which is fair and open, and in regard to which all material matters known to each have been communicated to the other." (Rothmiller v. Stein, 143 N.Y. 581). Even as a principle of law, long before exceptions were embodied in statute law [for example, the implied warranty provisions of the UCC], the doctrine was held inapplicable to contagion among animals, adulteration of food, and insolvency of a maker of a promissory note and of a tenant substituted for another under a lease. Common law is not moribund. Where fairness and common sense dictate that an exception should be created, the evolution of the law should not be stifled by rigid application of a legal maxim.

Where a condition which has been created by the seller materially impairs the value of the contract and is peculiarly within the knowledge of the seller or unlikely to be discovered by a prudent purchaser exercising due care with respect to the subject matter, non-disclosure constitutes a basis for rescission as a matter of equity. Any other outcome places upon the buyer not merely the obligation to exercise care in his purchase but rather to be omniscient with respect to any fact which may affect the bargain. No practical purpose is served by imposing such a burden upon a purchaser. To the contrary, it encourages predatory business practice and offends the principle that

(continues)

(continued from previous page)
equity will suffer no wrong to be without a remedy.

In the case at bar, defendant seller deliberately fostered the public belief that her home was possessed. Having undertaken to inform the public at large, to whom she has no legal relationship, about the supernatural occurrences on her property, she may be said to owe no less a duty to her contract vendee. It has been remarked

that the occasional modern cases which permit a seller to take unfair advantage of a buyer's ignorance so long as he is not actively misled are "singularly unappetizing" (Prosser, Law of Torts, at 696 [4th ed. 1971]). Where, as here, the seller not only takes unfair advantage of the buyer's ignorance but has created and perpetuated a condition about which he is unlikely even to inquire, enforcement of the contract (in whole or in part) is offensive to the

court's sense of equity. Application of the remedy of rescission, within the bounds of the narrow exception to the doctrine of caveat emptor set forth herein, is entirely appropriate to relieve the unwitting purchaser from the consequences of a most unnatural bargain.

[Reversed. The first cause of action seeking rescission of the contract is reinstated.]

Intent to Deceive

The second element of fraud is *knowledge of falsity* (or, as it is sometimes called, "scienter"). Thus the innocent party must ordinarily prove that the person making the statement knew, or should have known, that it was false at the time it was made. However, the knowledge of falsity requirement is also met if a person makes a statement "with a reckless disregard for the truth," even if the declarant did not actually know it was false. Thus, if the seller of a used car has no idea as to its mileage but nevertheless states that "it has not been driven more than 30,000 miles," the statement constitutes fraud if it is later proven that the true mileage materially exceeded that figure.

Reliance

The victim of a misrepresentation must show that he or she reasonably relied on the misstatement at the time of contracting. Sometimes this is not difficult to establish. The innocent party does not have to prove that the fact in regard to which the misrepresentation was made was the primary factor in inducing him or her to make the contract. It is sufficient that the misrepresentation involved a matter tending to influence the decision.

Reliance does not exist, of course, if the one accused of fraud can prove that the other party actually knew the true facts before making the contract. Also, a charge of fraud will fail if the victim's reliance was not reasonable under the circumstances. While the

old rule of *caveat emptor* is much less significant than formerly, a buyer still cannot blindly accept everything he or she is told. For example, a buyer given an opportunity to view the property is presumed to observe any patent (obvious) defects that might exist. To illustrate—the seller of a used television set tells the buyer it "produces an excellent picture on all channels." If the buyer viewed the set in operation prior to the sale and complained of reception on one channel, that person could hardly contend after the sale that he had reasonably relied on the seller's representation.

Injury

The last element of a successful fraud action is a showing by the innocent party that he or she suffered an injury, usually an economic loss, as a result of the misrepresentation. In most cases proof of injury (or "damage") is the easiest of the fraud elements to prove. For example, in a typical case involving the sale of property, the buyer is able to show that the value of the property he or she received is substantially less than it would have been if the seller's representations had been true.

Remedies for Fraud

Once fraud is established, the defrauded party always has the right to rescind the contract. When such a person chooses the remedy of *rescission,* he or she must ordinarily return the consideration, if any, that was received from the other party. Rescission, then, is designed to restore the parties to their original positions.

In some instances the defrauded party may wish to keep the consideration, for example, a parcel of land, even though it had been misrepresented by the seller. In such a case the buyer may keep the consideration (i.e., "affirm the contract") and bring suit for *damages*—which in the usual situation is, at the minimum, the difference between the actual value of the property the buyer received, and the value it would have had if the representations had been true. (Additionally, because fraud is a tort, the innocent party may be awarded punitive damages as well.)

As a general rule, the defrauded party must elect either to rescind the contract or to recover damages. However, where the fraud involves the making of a sales contract, such an election need not be made. Sec. 2-721 of the UCC provides, in part, that where fraud is established, "Neither rescission nor a claim for rescission of the contract . . . shall bar or be . . . inconsistent with a claim for damages or other remedy." Thus in circumstances where a buyer or seller seeking rescission can show that he or she will suffer a loss notwithstanding the rescission, damages may also be recovered.

INNOCENT MISREPRESENTATION

If all the elements of fraud are present in a particular case, except that the person making the misstatement honestly (and reasonably) believed the statement to be true, that person is guilty of **innocent misrepresentation** rather than fraud. Under the rule of most states, the victim can rescind the contract on that ground, but is usually not given the alternative remedy of damages. Innocent misrepresentation and fraud are contrasted in Figure 15.2.

MISTAKE

Cases are continually arising where one of the parties to a contract attempts to have it set aside by the court on the ground that he or she was mistaken in some respect at the time the contract was made. Often the mistake involves opinion or judgment rather than fact, in which case no relief will be granted. For example, a person contracts to buy land for $30,000 thinking this is its true value. If its actual value proves to be much less, he or she has shown bad judgment

and will not be permitted to rescind the contract. Similarly, if a person purchases stock in the belief that it will greatly increase in value in a short time, he or she obviously cannot have the contract set aside in the event that it does not perform as hoped. If rescission were permitted on grounds such as these, the basic value of all contracts would be destroyed.

However, in certain limited situations a plea of mistake will afford grounds for rescission of a contract, if the mistake was one of *fact*. The general rule is that if both parties were mistaken as to a material fact at the time of contracting, either party can rescind the agreement. On the other hand, if only one of the parties was mistaken, rescission will not be granted unless that person can show that the other party knew, or should have known, of the mistake at the time the contract was made. When both parties are mistaken, the mistake is a **bilateral mistake;** when only one is mistaken, it is a **unilateral mistake.**

Bilateral Mistake

The following examples illustrate the general principle that a contract can be set aside if there is a mutual mistake as to the *existence,* the *identity,* or the *character* of the subject matter of the contract.

1. B purchases S's summer home on April 10. Subsequently, B learns that, unknown to either party, the home was destroyed by fire on April 1. Since both parties entered into the contract under the mistaken assumption that the subject matter of the contract actually existed at that time, B can have the contract set aside.

2. P owns two properties outside Woodsfield, Ohio. G, after viewing both acreages, makes P a written offer to purchase one for $18,000. P accepts the offer. It later develops that G had one property in mind while P, after reading the description contained in G's offer, honestly and reasonably believed that G was referring to the other property. Either party can rescind the agreement, because there was a mutual mistake about the identity of the contract's subject matter.

3. C purchases a gemstone from D for $25. At the time of contracting, both parties believe the stone is a topaz. In fact, it turns out to be an uncut diamond worth $700. Since both parties were mistaken about the true character of the contract's subject matter, D

FIGURE 15.2

Fraud and Innocent Misrepresentation

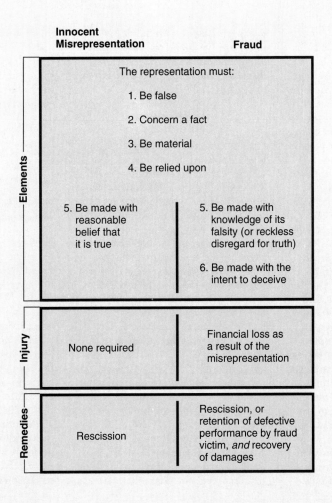

Fraud and Innocent Misrepresentation

can have the contract rescinded, thereby recovering the stone.

The principle is not applicable to situations where both parties realize that they are *in doubt* as to a particular matter, but enter into a contract nonetheless. Thus, in example 3 above, if neither C nor D had any idea what the stone was when they made the contract, D could not rescind the contract when the stone proved to be an uncut diamond (nor could C have rescinded had the stone turned out to be a worthless one). In such an instance both parties had, by contract, "assumed the risk" as to the stone's value.

With these general rules of law in mind let us examine the problem presented by the following case.

(handwritten margin notes): whether custom of coin dealers when buyers when buyer to assume risk of genuineness vs because of mistake

BEACHCOMBER COINS, INC. v. BOSKETT

Superior Court of New Jersey, Appellate Division, 400 A.2d 78 (1979)

Case

Boskett was a part-time dealer in coins in New Jersey. He owned a 1916 dime which bore the letter "D," indicating that it had been minted in Denver. Because of the rarity of such coins, their market value was greatly in excess of their monetary worth.

Beachcomber Coins, plaintiff, was interested in buying the coin, and one of its owners examined the coin to determine its genuineness. After an examination of forty-five minutes he was satisfied that the coin was, in fact, minted in Denver, and he purchased it on behalf of plaintiff for $500. Later plaintiff was advised by the American Numismatic Society that the "D" was a counterfeit. When Boskett, the seller, refused to take back the coin and refund the purchase price, plaintiff brought this action asking rescission of the contract.

The trial judge, sitting without a jury, found that there was a mutual mistake of fact (a mistake as to the coin's genuineness) that would ordinarily justify rescission of the contract. However, he further found that under customary coin dealing procedures a buyer of a coin who

was permitted to examine it before purchase "assumed the risk" that it might be counterfeit. He therefore dismissed the action and plaintiff appealed.

Conford, Judge:

. . . The evidence and trial judge's findings establish this as a classic case [in which rescission should be allowed on the basis of] mutual mistake of fact. As a general rule, "where parties on entering into a transaction that affects their contractual relations are both under a mistake regarding a fact assumed by them as the basis on which they entered into the transaction, it is voidable by either party if enforcement of it would be materially more onerous to him than it would have been had the fact been as the parties believed it to be." *Restatement, Contracts*, §502 (1932). . . .

Moreover, [the *Restatement* provides that] "negligent failure of a party to know or discover the facts as to which both parties are under a mistake does not preclude rescission or reformation on account thereof." The law of New Jersey is in accord. . . .

Defendant's contention that plaintiff assumed the risk that the coin

might be of greater or lesser value is not supported by the evidence. It is [true that] a party to a contract can assume the risk of being mistaken as to the value of the thing sold. The *Restatement* states the rule this way:

Where the parties know that there is doubt in regard to a certain matter and contract on that assumption, the contract is not rendered voidable because one is disappointed in the hope that the facts accord with his wishes. The risk of the existence of the doubtful fact is then assumed as one of the elements of the bargain.

However, for this rule to apply, the parties must be conscious that the pertinent fact may not be true and make their agreement at the risk of that possibility. [That rule is not applicable] in this case, because both parties were certain that the coin was genuine. . . .

[The court then turned to the trial judge's finding that it was customary in the coin dealing business for buyers of coins to assume the risk of genuineness. After examining the testimony on this point at the trial, the court concluded that it was too weak to support the finding of "custom and usage" under New Jersey law. The court thus reversed the judgment, and ordered rescission of the contract.]⚖

Unilateral Mistake

Where only one party to a contract is mistaken about a material fact, rescission is ordinarily not allowed unless the mistake was (or should have been) apparent to the other party. Two examples follow.

1. B purchases a painting from S for $300; B believes it was painted by a well-known artist. B does not, however, disclose this belief to S. In fact, the painting is the work of an amateur and consequently worth no more than $50. Since only B was mistaken as to the identity of the artist, the mistake is unilateral and the contract cannot be rescinded. On the

other hand, B would have been permitted to rescind if S had been aware of B's mistake and had not corrected it.

2. X furnishes three contractors with specifications for a building project and asks them to submit construction bids. C submits a bid for $48,000 and D submits one for $46,500. E's bid, because of an error in addition, is $27,000 rather than the intended $47,000. If X accepts E's bid, E can have the contract set aside if the jury finds (as is likely to be the case) either that X actually knew of the mistake when he accepted the bid or that he should have

been aware of the mistake because of the wide discrepancy in the bids.

Cautions

The "bilateral-unilateral mistake" rule of thumb, while widely followed, by no means settles all cases that arise in the general area of mistake. In the first place, there is some disagreement as to what constitutes a bilateral mistake. Many courts, for example, take the view that such a mistake exists only where the parties have arrived at their erroneous conclusions independently of one another, rather than one party simply relying on information supplied by the other.

Second, a few states have statutes relating to contracts entered into under mistake of fact that sometimes permit rescission where common-law principles would not.

Third, the court will sometimes settle cases purely on "equitable principles"—the basis of overall fairness in particular situations—thereby giving little or no weight to the bilateral-unilateral factor. Many unilateral mistake cases arise in construction contracts when erroneous bids are made. A common approach allows rescission if three factors are present: (1) The mistake was one of mere negligence—for example, the misreading of plans or the erroneous adding of a column of figures due to exhaustion or haste. (2) Rescission would cause no injury to the nonmistaken party other than loss of the erroneous bargain—for example, if the mistake is discovered and called to the attention of the nonmistaken party before the contract is awarded or soon thereafter (i.e., before construction commences while the lowest nonmistaken bid could still be accepted). (3) Holding the mistaken party to his or her bid would be "unconscionable." Thus, a mistaken bidder in a school construction contract was allowed to rescind on the basis of unilateral mistake where the day after the contract was awarded he called the school district's attention to a simple error in addition that had led to a bid of $534,175 rather than the intended $634,175.[17]

Additional Types of Mistake

Occasionally a mistake involves the provisions of the contract itself rather than the contract's subject matter. For example, an offeree might accept an offer that he or she has misread, only to learn later that the offer was in fact substantially different than it

seemed. This is a unilateral mistake, and the offeree is bound by the resulting contract (unless the acceptance itself discloses the mistake to the offeror).

Mutual mistakes as to the value of an article being sold generally are held to constitute mistakes of opinion rather than fact, and rescission is not permitted in such cases. Thus, if B buys a painting from S for $10,000, both parties correctly believing that the artist was Andrew Wyeth, B obviously cannot have the contract set aside simply because he later learns that the painting's true value is only $5,000.

There is somewhat greater uncertainty insofar as mistakes of law are concerned. The courts at one time refused to permit rescission of contracts where a mistake of law existed, either bilateral or unilateral, on the theory that such a mistake was not a mistake of fact. (This idea was consistent with the view that a *misstatement of law* does not constitute a misstatement of fact, under the law of fraud.) Today, however, most courts treat *mistakes of law* and *fact* the same—that is, they will set aside contracts which both parties entered into under a mistake of law as well as those in which the mistake of one party was apparent to the other.

DURESS

Occasionally a person will seek to escape liability under a contract on the ground that he or she was forced to enter into it. Often the courts find that the "force" is insignificant in the eyes of the law, and the complaining party is held to the contract. For example, if a person enters into a contract simply because he or she knows that failure to do so will incur the wrath of some third person, such as his or her employer or spouse, relief will not be granted. If, on the other hand, the degree of compulsion is so great as to totally rob the person of free will, duress exists, and the contract can be rescinded.

One early definition of **duress** that still remains authoritative is the following:

(1) any wrongful act of one person that compels a manifestation of apparent assent by another to a transaction without his volition, or (2) any wrongful threat of one person by words or other conduct that induces another to enter into a transaction under the influence of such fear as precludes him from exercising free will and judgment, if the threat was intended or should reasonably have been expected to operate as an inducement.[18]

---

[17]*Taylor v. Arlington ISD*, 335 S.W.2d 371 (Tex. 1960).

[18]*Restatement, Contracts*, §492. The American Law Institute, 1932.

A necessary element of duress is fear—a genuine and reasonable fear on the part of the victim that he or she will be subjected to an injurious, unlawful act by not acceding to the other party's demands. Thus, if a person signs a contract at gunpoint or after being physically beaten, duress exists, and the victim can escape liability on that ground. Duress also exists when a person makes a contract as a consequence of another person's threat of harm (for instance, kidnapping a child) if the contract is refused.

Generally, the innocent party must show that the act actually committed or threatened was a wrongful one. For instance, a contract entered into between a striking union and an employer cannot be set aside by the latter on the ground of duress if the strike was a lawful one—as, for example, if the strike occurred after an existing "no-strike" contract between union and employer had expired.

The threat of a criminal suit is generally held to constitute duress. For example: X proposes a contract to Y and tells him that if he refuses to sign the agreement, X will turn over evidence to the prosecuting attorney's office tending to prove that Y had embezzled money from his employer six weeks earlier. To prevent this, Y signs the contract. Y can have the contract rescinded on the ground of duress, because a threat to use the criminal machinery of the state for such a purpose is clearly wrongful—regardless of whether or not Y had actually committed the crime in question. Threat of a civil suit, on the other hand, usually does not constitute duress.

While a contract cannot be set aside simply because there is a disparity of bargaining power between the parties, the courts are beginning to accept the idea that *economic duress* (or business compulsion) can be grounds for the rescission of a contract in exceptional situations. The decision in the next case sets forth three requirements that ordinarily must be met in order for a plaintiff to be successful in a suit asking rescission on this ground.

TOTEM MARINE TUG & BARGE v. ALYESKA PIPELINE

Supreme Court of Alaska, 584 P.2d 15 (1978)

Totem Marine Tug and Barge, Inc., entered into a contract with Alyeska Pipeline Services under which Totem was to transport large quantities of pipeline construction materials from Houston, Texas, to Alaska. After Totem began its performance, many problems arose. One major difficulty was the fact that the tonnages to be shipped were six times greater than Alyeska had indicated. Additionally, long delays occurred in getting Totem's vessels through the Panama Canal, which resulted from Alyeska's failure to furnish promised documents to Totem by specified dates. After these and other problems, Alyeska cancelled the contract without cause.

At the time of the wrongful termination, Alyeska owed Totem about $300,000. Officers of Alyeska at first promised that it would pay Totem invoices promptly, but later they told Totem that it would have its money "in six to eight months." (Totem alleged that the delay in payment occurred after Alyeska learned through negotiations with Totem lawyers that Totem's creditors were pressing it for their payments, and that without immediate cash it would go into bankruptcy—allegations that Alyeska did not deny.)

After further negotiations, a settlement agreement was made in 1975, under which Alyeska paid Totem $97,000 in return for surrender of all claims against it. In early 1976 Totem brought this action to rescind the settlement agreement on the ground of economic duress, and to recover the balance allegedly due under the original contract. The trial court ruled as a matter of law that the circumstances under which the settlement occurred did not constitute duress, and dismissed the complaint. Totem appealed.

Burke, Justice:

. . . This court has not yet decided a case involving a claim of economic duress, or what is also called business compulsion. . . . [In recent cases] this concept has been broadened to include myriad forms of economic coercion which force a person to involuntarily enter into a particular transaction. . . .

There are various statements of what constitutes economic duress, but as noted by one commentator, "The history of generalization in the field offers no great encouragement for those who seek to summarize results in any single formula." Dawson, *Economic Duress*, 45 Mich.L.Rev. (1947). . . . [However, many states adopt the view that] duress exists where: (1) one party involuntarily accepted the terms of another, (2) circumstances permitted no other alternative, and (3) such circumstances were the result of coercive acts of the other party. . . .

(continues)

(continued from previous page)

One essential element of economic duress is that the plaintiff show that the other party, by wrongful acts or threats, intentionally caused him to enter into a particular transaction. . . . This requirement may be satisfied where the alleged wrongdoer's conduct is criminal or tortious, but an act or threat may also be wrongful if it is wrongful in the moral sense. . . .

Economic duress does not exist, however, merely because a person has been the victim of a wrongful act; in addition, the victim must have no choice but to agree to the other person's terms or face serious financial hardship. Thus, in order to avoid a contract, a party must also show that he had no reasonable alternative to agreeing to the other party's terms, or as it is often stated, that he had no adequate remedy if the threat were carried out. . . .

Turning to the instant case, we believe that Totem's allegations, if proved, would support a finding that it executed a release of its contract claims against Alyeska under economic duress. Totem has alleged that Alyeska deliberately withheld payment of an acknowledged debt, knowing that Totem had no choice but to accept an inadequate sum in settlement of that debt; that Totem was faced with impending bankruptcy; that Totem was unable to meet its pressing debts other than by accepting the immediate cash payment offered by Alyeska; and that through necessity, Totem thus involuntarily accepted an inadequate settlement offer from Alyeska and executed a release of all claims under the contract. If the release was in fact executed under these circumstances, we think that . . . this would constitute the type of wrongful conduct and lack of alternatives that would render the release voidable by Totem on the ground of economic duress. . . .

Reversed, and case remanded. ⚖

UNDUE INFLUENCE

There are some circumstances in which a person can escape contractual liability by proving that his or her consent was brought about by the **undue influence** of the other party to the contract. While many kinds of influence are perfectly lawful, influence is undue (excessive) where one party so dominates the will of the other that the latter's volition actually is destroyed. A common example occurs where one person, as the result of advanced age and physical deterioration, begins to rely more and more upon a younger, more energetic acquaintance or relative for advice until the point is reached where the older person's willpower and judgment are almost totally controlled by the dominant party. If the older, weaker person can show (1) that he or she was induced to enter into a particular contract by virtue of the dominant party's power and influence, rather than as the result of exercising his or her own volition, and (2) that the dominant party used this power to take advantage of him or her, undue influence is established and he or she is freed of liability on this ground.

The same general rules for undue influence in the making of contracts also apply to the making of wills. Therefore, it may be helpful to read the *Casper v. McDowell* case in Chapter 46, which discusses wills and estate law.

Home Solicitation Statutes

Several states have passed **home solicitation statutes** which protect persons who are subjected to high-pressure sales tactics by salespersons who come to their homes. These statutes supplement the common-law concepts discussed above. The general rule is that a buyer has an automatic three-day period in which to cancel a contract where: (1) the contract is for land, goods or services worth over $25; (2) the sale was initiated by the seller; and (3) the contract was completed at a place other than the seller's place of business (usually the buyer's home). The buyer need not show fraud, undue influence, or mistake. The three-day right to rescind is automatic. The federal government has passed a similar statute which applies to all sales affecting interstate commerce. Home solicitation statutes are discussed in more detail in Chapter 51.

SUMMARY

A voidable contract is an agreement in which one of the parties possesses the legal right to have the contract set aside (i.e., avoided or disaffirmed). The two most common situations in which such a right exists are (1) where there is a lack of capacity, as in minors' contracts, and (2) where reality of consent is lacking, as in contracts tainted with fraud, mistake, or duress.

Minors generally have the right to disaffirm their contracts any time before reaching the age of majority—18 in most states—plus a reasonable time thereafter, even as to contracts that have been fully performed. In such a situation, the minor is required to return the consideration if able to do so. In situations where return of the consideration is not possible, disaffirmance is still generally allowed, in which case the entire loss is borne by the other party to the contract. Additionally, the right to disaffirm is a one-sided one, being possessed only by the minor.

Under the majority rule, where the minor is disaffirming an executed contract calling for the purchase of goods that are not a necessity of life, he or she can recover all of the contract price paid, without being charged with the reasonable value of the use of the goods while in his or her possession. However, where the contract is for the purchase of goods or services that qualify as necessities, the minor in all cases is liable for the reasonable value of the goods actually used, or the services received. And, in any case in which the minor, after reaching the age of majority, expressly or impliedly indicates that he or she will abide by it, the contract has been ratified and the right to disaffirm is lost. The rights of contracting parties who are under a mental disability, or who are intoxicated, generally parallel those of minors.

Even if both parties to a contract are competent, the contract can be set aside if tainted with fraud, innocent misrepresentation, or duress, and—in some circumstances—on the ground of mistake. The elements of fraud are (1) misrepresentation of a fact, (2) made with the intent to deceive (i.e., with knowledge of falsity), (3) reasonable reliance by the other party, and (4) injury to such party. A statement of opinion cannot normally be the basis for a fraud action unless the declarant—the one expressing the opinion—possesses a knowledge of the subject matter of the contract that is markedly superior to that of the other party. And silence does not constitute fraud, except in those limited circumstances in which the courts hold there was a "duty to speak." On the subject of mistake, the basic rule is that a contract can be rescinded only on the ground of mutual mistake of fact, or on the ground of unilateral mistake known to the other party. Duress—when one de-

prives a party of his or her free will to contract by committing (or threatening to commit) a wrongful act—is also a ground for the rescission of a contract.

KEY TERMS

Voidable contract
Capacity
Minor
Ordinary contract
Ratification
Necessaries
Adjudicated insane
Insane in fact
Fraud
Misrepresentation of a material fact
Statement of fact
Statement of opinion
Latent defect
Fiduciary relationship
Superior knowledge
Innocent misrepresentation
Bilateral mistake
Unilateral mistake
Duress
Undue influence
Home solicitation statutes

QUESTIONS AND PROBLEMS

1. McAllister, while a minor, purchased a car under circumstances in which it was clearly not a necessity, and gave the seller his promissory note in payment. The note obligated McAllister to make specified monthly payments beginning with the time of purchase. Just before reaching the age of majority, at which time McAllister had made no payments on the note, he lost possession of the car under circumstances which the trial court found to be "unknown." (It was clear, however, that the car was neither retained by McAllister nor returned to the seller.) Three years after McAllister reached the age of majority, at which time he had still made no payments, the seller sued him on the note, and McAllister then informed the seller that he was disaffirming the purchase and the note. The seller argued that McAllister's attempted disaffirmance was invalid since he waited so long to exercise this right. Is the seller

correct? Explain. (*Warwick Municipal Employees Credit Union v. McAllister*, 293 A.2d 516, 1972.)

2. Ballinger and his wife, while minors, purchased a mobile home. In payment, they gave the seller of the home a promissory note which they signed as co-makers. Before reaching the age of majority they disaffirmed the contract and the note. The seller then brought suit against them to recover the reasonable value of the home, on the ground that it constituted a necessity of life. At the trial, the Ballingers introduced evidence showing that Ballinger's parents were more than willing to furnish them with living accommodations in their own home at the time they made the purchase, and thereafter. What bearing, if any, would this evidence have on the question whether the home constituted a necessity? Explain your reasoning. (*Ballinger v. Craig*, 121 N.E.2d 66, 1953.)

3. Robert Moore opened joint savings accounts in two banks, with the accounts listing a nephew and niece as co-depositors. These accounts, if valid, would result in the money in them passing to the nephew and niece as gifts upon Moore's death. After Moore died, other relatives brought a court action to set aside these joint accounts on the ground that Moore was incompetent to contract at the time that he established them. To support this contention, these relatives produced evidence that over a period of several weeks prior to the opening of the accounts that Moore had often been found wandering on city streets late at night, not knowing where he was; that on one occasion he tried to extinguish the cooking units on his electric stove by pouring water on them; that a neighbor stopped transacting business with him "because he acted so queerly"; and that he was once stopped on a street by a police officer because of "insufficient clothing." Do you think this evidence is sufficient to support the relatives' claim that Moore was incompetent when he made the transactions with the banks? Can you think of other evidence that might contradict this claim? Discuss. (*In re Moore's Estate*, 188 N.E.2d 221, 1962.)

4. Several employees of Empiregas, Inc., plaintiffs, had signed one-year employment contracts with that company over a period of many years. Each time that the employees objected to noncompetition clauses in the contracts they were told by supervisors not to worry about them, just "to sign." At the time of signing their most recent contracts the employees were told by their supervisor that "you know what we have always told you. (These contracts) are not worth a damn; it is just a piece of paper." The employees signed, and after they had fulfilled their contracts they sought employment with a competing firm. Empiregas wrote the competing firm that the employees could not be hired by it because of the noncompetition clauses in their contracts. Empiregas also threatened to sue the firm and employees if it hired them. When the firm decided not to employ them, the employees brought this action against Empiregas alleging that it had "fraudulently induced" them to sign the contracts. Two of Empiregas's defenses were that the statements were not fraudulent because (1) they were merely statements of opinion and (2) they were statements of law rather than fact. Do you agree with either defense? Why or why not? (*Empiregas, Inc. v. Hardy*, 487 So. 2d 244, 1985.)

5. Midwest Supply, a company in the business of preparing income tax returns, advertised "guaranteed accurate tax preparation." Waters, after reading the ad, contacted Midwest and was induced to apply for refunds that he was not legally entitled to. After Waters received the improper refunds, the Internal Revenue Service recovered the payments from him in addition to substantial penalties. Waters then sued Midwest to recover damages on the basis of fraud, alleging that (1) the statement in its ad was false; (2) the employees of Midwest had little or no training in accounting or income tax preparation; and (3) Midwest told its employees not to correct newswriters who described the employees as "specialists and tax experts." On these facts, is Midwest guilty of fraud? Discuss. (*Midwest Supply, Inc. v. Waters*, 510 P.2d 876, 1973.)

6. Whale applied for the position of rabbi with the Jewish Center of Sussex County, New Jersey. The application listed information regarding his education, ordination as a rabbi, and job experience from 1956 to 1977, all of which was true. The Jewish Center employed Whale, but soon thereafter brought action to rescind the contract on the ground of fraud, alleging that Whale failed to disclose the fact that he had earlier been convicted of the crime of using the mails to defraud. Whale defended on the ground that in his résumé accompanying the application he indicated that further information and references would be

furnished on request, but that the center did not avail itself of this opportunity. Is Whale's defense good? Why or why not? (*Jewish Center of Sussex County v. Whale*, 397 A.2d 712, 1978.)

7. In his second or third day in the baseball card business, Irmen was swamped with customers and asked a woman from the shop next door to help him. Twelve-year-old Brian Wrzesinski, owner of 40,000 baseball cards, walked into the store and noticed a 1968 Nolan Ryan rookie card on display in mint condition. The card carried a price sticker of "$1200/." Brian asked the substitute clerk if it was worth $12. She said "yes," and he bought it. However, the sticker was supposed to indicate a price of *twelve hundred dollars* (the card's approximate market value), and when Irmen discovered the sale, he sought return of the baseball card. When Brian refused, Irmen sued to rescind the transaction. How do the rules of mistake apply to this case? (*Irmen v. Wrzesinski*, No. 90 SC 5362, Ill.Cir.Ct. DuPage County [Small Claims Div.], 1990).

8. Black purchased two violins from White for $8,000, the bill of sale describing them as "one Joseph Guarnerius violin and one Stradivarius violin dated 1717." Unknown to either party, neither violin was made by Guarnerius or Stradivarius. Upon discovery of this fact, can Black set aside the purchase and recover payment? Explain.

9. The federal government solicited bids for construction of a Veterans Administration Hospital. Peter Kiewit Sons Co. (D), a general contractor, contacted several subcontractors for purposes of compil-

ing a bid. At the last minute, Heifetz Metal Crafts (P) called D and offered to do the kitchen-equipment part of the job for $99,500, which was $52,000 less than any other subcontractor had estimated. P asked D whether its bid was in accordance with all plans and specifications. P stated that it was and that the bid would remain firm. D then reduced its overall bid by $52,000 and submitted to the government a bid of $17,994,200, and was awarded the contract. After construction was underway, P discovered that it had made a unilateral mistake, believing that kitchen work was to be done in only one of the buildings in the complex, rather than several. P sued to rescind its bid. Should P succeed? (*Heifetz Metal Crafts v. Peter Kiewit Sons Co.*, 264 F.2d 435, 8th Cir. 1959.)

10. IUC, a relatively small construction company, entered into a written contract with New England Telephone & Telegraph (NET) to assemble and install conduits under a river for $149,680. Delays caused by NET forced IUC to perform its work during the winter rather than the summer as originally contemplated. NET repeatedly told IUC that it would pay the extra cost if IUC would complete the work. The changes cost IUC over $800,000. However, it signed a release settling the claim for $575,000 because NET offered the amount on a "take-it-or-leave-it basis" at a time when IUC was in financial distress. Later IUC sought to invoke the theory of duress in order to disaffirm the release so it could sue for more money. Should IUC succeed? (*IUC v. New England Telephone & Telegraph Co.*, 393 N.E.2d 968, Mass.App. 1979.)

The Statute of Frauds
Contracts That Must Be in Writing
Contracts Calling for Sale of Goods
When Is the Writing Sufficient?
The Parol Evidence Rule

M

ANY PEOPLE HAVE the idea that contracts are never enforceable unless they are in writing; thus we hear movie magnate Sam Goldwyn's famous aphorism, "Oral contracts aren't worth the paper they're written on." Insofar as the law is concerned, however, most oral contracts are just as enforceable as written contracts *if their terms can be established in court.*[1] In this chapter we will examine the relatively few kinds of contracts that *are* required by law to be in writing; then we will consider general problems relating to written contracts. (In a situation where the law requires a contract to be in writing, any contract that does not meet that requirement—i.e., one that is entirely oral in nature, or that is written but ambiguous—is an "unenforceable" contract, rather than a "void" or "voidable" one. Thus, as the term indicates, neither party is bound by such a contract—with limited exceptions noted later.)

THE STATUTE OF FRAUDS

In England, prior to the latter part of the seventeenth century, all oral contracts were enforceable as long as their existence and terms could be established. Under this approach, it became apparent that many unscrupulous plaintiffs were obtaining judgments against innocent defendants by the use of *perjured testimony*—false testimony given under oath. To illustrate: P claimed that D had breached a particular oral contract, a contract that D denied making. If P could induce his witnesses (usually by the payment of money) to falsely testify that they heard D agree to the alleged contract, and if D could neither refute such testimony by witnesses of his own nor otherwise prove that P's witnesses were lying, a judgment would ordinarily be granted in favor of P.[2] To eliminate this and other kinds of fraud, Parliament in 1677 passed "An Act for the Prevention of Frauds and Perjuries"—or, as it is commonly called, the **statute of frauds.**

The statute of frauds required certain types of contracts to be in writing in order to be enforceable. Virtually every American state has its own statute of frauds patterned after the original English version, which required the following types of contracts or promises to be in writing (or evidenced by a written memorandum):

1. A contract calling for the sale of land or an interest therein.

2. A contract not to be performed within one year of its making.

3. A promise by one person to pay the debt of another.

4. A promise made in consideration of marriage.

5. A promise by the administrator or executor of an estate to pay a debt of the estate out of his or her own funds.

Modern Rationale

Obviously, a continuing rationale for the statute of frauds is the hope that written agreements will ward off fraud.[3] It also represents a policy judgment that written evidence is more reliable than fading memories. Additionally, the requirement of a writing serves the cautionary function of reminding the parties of the significance of their acts. On the other hand, the statute of frauds also allows some parties to evade obligations that they have willingly undertaken.[4] Indeed, it appears that it is used more often for this purpose than to defeat fraud. This concern has led England, where the statute of frauds originated, to virtually discard it.

Introduction to Exceptions

Criticisms of the statute of frauds have also led courts in America to devise various rules which in certain

---

[1] Many actions based on oral contracts that are otherwise valid are dismissed by the courts because their terms cannot be sufficiently established. For this reason, all contracts of any importance ought to be in writing, even when not required by law.

[2] D's situation was particularly difficult because, at the time we are speaking of, the parties to a civil suit were not permitted to testify in their own behalf; thus the testimony of their witnesses was all-important.

[3] Although we are dealing with something called the statute of frauds, whether or not *fraud* is present has no bearing on the requirement of a writing. The technical concept of fraud is only incidentally connected to the requirement of a writing.

[4] The parties to most oral business contracts do, in fact, perform their obligations in full, even though, because of the statute, they may not be obligated to. The statute is important, then, in those relatively few situations where one of the parties decides to stand on his or her legal rights by refusing to perform under an oral—but otherwise valid—contract.

circumstances will either take oral contracts out of the statute of frauds or grant relief to a party who has performed his or her half of an oral agreement. Thus, even before we address the types of contracts that generally must be in writing to be enforceable, we should mention that each rule has judicially created exceptions. Some courts enforce oral contracts only when there has been an *ancillary promise*—such as where the party against whom the oral promise is to be enforced not only made the promise but also promised to reduce it to writing or promised not to raise the statute of frauds as a defense.

A majority of jurisdictions, however, do not require such an ancillary promise. Rather, where mechanical application of the statute of frauds would cause injustice, these courts will enforce an oral promise to perform upon theories of promissory estoppel (if the promisee foreseeably relied on the oral promise in circumstances where injustice would result if it were not enforced), or part performance (if the promisee has completely or in some instances substantially performed his part of the bargain), or even quasi-contract (to avoid unjust enrichment of the promisor).

These exceptions vary substantially from jurisdiction to jurisdiction and even from category to category among the types of contracts that are supposed to be in writing. It is almost impossible to delineate exactly the scope of these exceptions. However, this chapter will give many examples and notes the strong trend among the courts to use promissory estoppel or related doctrines to enforce oral promises, notwithstanding the statute of frauds, where needed to avoid unfair results. The framers of the Uniform Commercial Code agreed with this trend. As we shall see when we address UCC Sec. 2-201, there are even more exceptions to the sales contract's writing requirement than to the traditional statute of frauds.

CONTRACTS THAT MUST BE IN WRITING
Contracts Calling for the Sale of Land

As a practical matter, the most important contracts required by the statute to be in writing are those calling for the sale of land—real estate. With an exception to be noted later, unwritten agreements of this kind are absolutely unenforceable. Thus, if X orally agrees to sell a farm to Y for a specified price, neither X nor Y can recover damages from the other if one of them refuses to go through with the deal. This is true even in the unlikely event that both parties admit in court that they made the contract.

In most cases it is easy to determine whether a contract does or does not involve the sale of land. Land, or *real property,* essentially consists of the earth's surface, vegetation, buildings, and other structures permanently attached to the soil. Growing crops, being physically attached to the ground, are also generally considered to be real property when sold in conjunction with the land. Thus, if S, by a written agreement, contracts to sell his farm to B for $50,000, B is entitled to receive any crops then growing on it, as well as the land itself—unless the contract provides otherwise. On the other hand, if S contracts merely to sell the crop to B, the crop is considered *personal property* and the contract does not have to be in writing under the statute of frauds. (If, however, the price of the crop were $500 or more, the contract would then be required to be in writing under a special section of the Uniform Commercial Code, which will be discussed later in the chapter.)

Interests in land include real estate mortgages and easements. A real estate **mortgage** is a conveyance of an interest in land by a debtor to a creditor as security for the debt. An **easement** is the right of one person to use or enjoy the land of another in a limited manner. Easements can be created in two general ways—expressly or by implication. If created in an express manner, the granting of the right must be evidenced by a writing—either specific language in a deed or a written contract in place of a deed. An easement created by implication, on the other hand, need not be evidenced by a writing. (One example of such an easement is an "implied easement of necessity." This is created when a landowner sells part of his or her property to another, the land being situated in such a way that the buyer has no access to it except by going across the seller's remaining land.) While real estate *leases* also convey interests in land and thus normally fall within the Statute of Frauds, most states have enacted special statutes providing that oral leases of a year's duration or less are valid.

Effect of Part Performance—Estoppel

As noted earlier, in some circumstances the courts have generally felt that oral contracts ought to be enforceable even though they are not in writing. Accordingly, they have recognized limited exceptions to the rules embodied in the statute of frauds.

One of these exceptions involves oral contracts calling for the sale of land. Such contracts are generally held to be enforceable if the buyer, in reliance upon the oral contract, has (1) paid part of the purchase price, (2) taken possession of the land, and (3) added substantial improvements to it.[5] (In regard to oral *leases* of land of over one year, requirement 1 is, of course, dispensed with.) In these circumstances the courts will permit the buyer to enforce the contract for either of two reasons.

First, the actions of the buyer, in and of themselves, may be felt to be "referable" to the oral contract that the buyer alleges has been formed—that is, the buyer's actions are fairly good evidence that an oral contract has, in fact, been entered into. These

are actions that a person would normally take only if he or she expected to become the owner of the land. The second reason often cited for permitting the buyer to enforce the oral contract is the doctrine of *promissory estoppel* (discussed in Chapter 13). The reasoning here is that where the seller of the land has permitted the buyer to take such actions, it would be manifestly unfair to permit the seller to evict the buyer on the ground that the contract was not in writing. In such a case, the courts are increasingly taking the view that the seller is estopped (i.e., prevented) from using the statute of frauds as a basis for having the oral contract set aside.

The case below presents two common questions: (1) Was a reasonably definite oral contract entered into? and (2) If so, was it saved by the part performance doctrine? (The second case in the chapter presents a situation in which the issue is whether the estoppel doctrine ought to be invoked.)

---

[5] Of course, if both parties have fully performed the contract, the statute is no longer relevant, and neither party can rescind it on the ground that it was originally required to be in writing.

L.U. CATTLE COMPANY V. WILSON

Colorado Court of Appeals, 714 P.2d 1344 (1986)

Case

Prior to September of 1980 the L.U. Cattle Company had been conducting farming operations on some Colorado land it was leasing from the land's owners, the Wilsons. Because the existing lease expired on November 1, 1980, a representative of the company, Kroeger, met with the Wilsons in September for the purpose of entering into a new lease. During the discussion the Wilsons told Kroeger that they wanted the company to plant alfalfa in the future, rather than corn, because this would produce more cash income out of which the company could make its rental payments. Kroeger said that if the acreage was to support alfalfa it had to be fertilized before planting, and, to maximize the efficiency of this plan, it would be necessary to plow and fertilize in the fall of 1980.

After a second meeting, Kroeger felt that as a result of these discus-

sions an oral agreement had been reached for a lease that would be reduced to writing at a later date. Acting on this understanding, Kroeger prepared and mailed a memorandum to the Wilsons on October 4 expressing the terms of the parties' agreement. The last line of the memorandum read: "We will start plowing the last of the week." The Wilsons read and discussed the memorandum, but did not sign it or otherwise respond to it.

During the rest of October and early November the company plowed and fertilized the land, and Wilson was notified of this action. In late January of 1981 the company's owners were concerned that they had no written commitment from the Wilsons. On January 25 Kroeger expressed this concern to Wilson on the phone, who agreed to sign a lease. The next day Kroeger prepared a "Lease Agreement" which he signed on behalf of the company and mailed to the Wilsons. The

Wilsons again did not respond to this document. Nothing further occurred until early March, when Wilson told Kroeger that he would not sign the agreement. Kroeger then removed certain equipment from the land and sent the Wilsons a bill for the cost of the fertilization. Wilson sent a check for the billed amount, but the company did not cash it. The cattle company then filed this suit asking for damages resulting from breach of the oral lease (including lost profits). The Wilsons defended on the ground that the contract was invalid under the statute of frauds.

The trial court found (1) that an oral lease had been entered into, and (2) that the company's actions in fertilizing the land constituted part performance of the agreement which "removed it from the statute of frauds"—i.e., which made the agreement enforceable. Accordingly, the court entered judgment for the company in the amount of $30,862. The

(continues)

(continued from previous page)
Wilsons appealed, disputing both findings of fact.

Sternberg, Judge:

. . . The [first] question here is whether the parties reached an oral contract of lease. The validity of such a contract depends upon proof of a definite agreement as to the extent and bounds of the property leased; . . . a definite and agreed term; and . . . a definite and agreed price of rental, and the time and manner of payment. . . . The memorandum sufficiently indicates the property to be leased, the amount of the rental, and the term [duration] of the lease. [While the memorandum was silent as to the times that rental payments were to be paid,] testimony given by Kroeger, uncontested by lessors [the Wilsons] was sufficient to establish the inference that the parties had contemplated that payment would be made as it had been made under the [prior] lease.[a] Therefore, the trial court

[a] The prior lease was made with one Mason, from whom the Wilsons bought the land.

did not err in concluding that the parties had reached an [oral] lease.

The next question to be resolved concerns the enforceability of the lease. Colorado's statute of frauds provides that contracts for the leasing of lands for periods longer than a year, or notes or memoranda thereof, are void unless in writing and subscribed by the lessor. . . . Where there is part performance of such an oral contract, however, it may be enforceable notwithstanding these requirements.

Here, because lessors did not sign it, the October 4 memorandum was insufficient to remove the lease from the statute of frauds. The trial court, however, made no finding that it did. Rather, it found that the statute was overcome by virtue of lessee's [the company's] actions in plowing the land and in purchasing and applying fertilizer.

This case was presented, argued, and tried on the assumption that the doctrine of part performance is applicable in actions for damages at law. Such performance must be at least substantial part performance. It must

be required by, and fairly referable to, no theory other than that of the alleged agreement. Further, the part performance must be known to the other party . . . at the time of its occurrence.

The evidence in this case established that the parties' agreement obligated lessee to plant alfalfa and that lessors were aware of the necessity for proceeding with field preparation in the fall of 1980. The October 4 memorandum expressly notified lessors of lessee's intent to do so, yet the lessors took no action indicating that they did not want lessee to proceed. Although lessors argue that lessee's action [was referable to the earlier lease made with a prior owner of the land, rather than to the oral lease made by lessors,] there was sufficient evidence in the record from which the trial court could find that it was not. On the facts and circumstances of this case, the trial court did not err in concluding that lessee's actions constituted part performance sufficient to render the lease enforceable despite the statute of frauds. . . .

The judgment is affirmed. ⚖

Contracts Not to Be Performed within One Year

The section of the statute requiring that *agreements not to be performed within one year of the making thereof* be in writing is based on the fact that disputes over the terms of long-term oral contracts are particularly likely to occur; witnesses die, the parties' memories become hazy, and so on. Despite the logic underlying this provision, it has posed numerous problems in practice.

In deciding whether a particular agreement falls within this section, the usual (but not the only) approach taken by the courts is to determine whether it was *reasonably possible,* under its own terms, for the contract in question to have been performed within one year from the time it was made. If so, the contract is outside the statute and need not be in writing.

The fact that performance *actually* may have taken more than one year is immaterial. Consider these examples.

1. A, on June 1, 1990, orally agrees to work for B as a personal secretary at a salary of $3,000 per month "as long as this arrangement is satisfactory to both parties." This is known as an "at-will" employment contract. It gives either party the right to terminate it at any time. It does not have to be in writing to be enforceable, because it can be fully performed *by its own terms* in less than a year. Assume that A worked for B for two years, and in the third year, B refused to pay wages for work A had performed. If A sued, most courts would hold that B could not successfully raise a statute of frauds defense. Even

though performance actually took longer, the contract could have been fully performed in less than one year. (A minority of courts, rejecting the "reasonably possible" test, would hold that if performance longer than one year was *within the contemplation of the parties,* the contract would have to be in writing.)

2. On June 1, 1990, A promises to work for B "as long as you [B] shall live." Most courts, but not all, would hold that this contract also need not be in writing to be enforceable. B might die in less than a year. If he did, the contract would have been fully performed in less than a year. Again, it is irrelevant if B actually did live longer than a year.

3. A promises on June 1, 1990, to work for B "for the next two years." This contract must be in writing to be enforceable, because it is not possible to work for two years in less than one year. True, it is again possible that B might die in less than a year, but the contract will not have been fully performed as written. (Instead, B's death would have *excused* performance under the doctrine of impossibility discussed later in Chapter 18.)

4. A promises on June 1, 1990, to sing a two-hour concert at XYZ University on August 12, 1991. This contract must be in writing to be enforceable. Even though the performance itself will take only two hours, by the contract's terms that performance must occur more than one year after the contract was made.

Exceptions

As with other categories of contracts that usually must be in writing, many courts have enforced oral contracts that would take more than one year from the making to perform where they believed that this was necessary to bring about just results. For instance, in example 1 above, even courts that choose the "contemplation of the parties" approach and conclude that the contract should be in writing would allow A to recover for *work performed* on a part performance basis. The case below is typical of those in which the exceptional result is largely based on the principle of promissory estoppel. This jurisdiction, however, appears to be one of the minority jurisdictions that also requires an ancillary promise (in this case, a promise to put the contract in writing) in order to invoke the exception.

HARMON V. TANNER MOTOR TOURS OF NEVADA, LTD.

Supreme Court of Nevada, 377 P.2d 622 (1963)

This litigation came about as a result of a dispute over which one of two competing common carriers had the exclusive limousine ground transportation franchise for servicing the Las Vegas, Nevada, airport for a period of ten years. The carriers were Tanner Motor Lines, Ltd., plaintiff, and Las Vegas-Tonopah-Reno Stage Lines, Inc. (LTR), one of the defendants.

Five legal issues were involved, one of which had to do with the enforceability of an oral contract entered into between Tanner and the Board of Clark County Commissioners (Board), which was the governing authority of the Las Vegas airport.

(Only that part of the fact-pattern and decision of the case relating to this issue is considered below.)

In late 1959 Tanner submitted a written bid for the limousine service, and that bid was orally *accepted by the board members. Despite this acceptance, the board entered into a written contract in 1960 with the second carrier, LTR, giving it the exclusive transportation rights.*

Tanner then brought this action against Harmon, a representative of the board, and LTR, defendants, asking for specific performance of its 1959 contract. The defendants contended, among other things, that that oral contract was unenforceable under the statute of frauds, because its performance was to take more

than one year. The trial court ruled against the defendants on all points, and entered a decree of specific performance. (That is, the court ruled that Tanner's contract was valid and that he thus did possess the exclusive transportation rights, and it accordingly ordered the board to recognize these rights.) Defendants appealed.

Thompson, Justice:

. . . [The Nevada statute of frauds] provides that every agreement which, by its terms, is not to be performed within one year from the making thereof, shall be void, unless such agreement, or some note or memorandum thereof, expressing the consideration, be in

(continues)

(continued from previous page)
writing and subscribed by the party charged therewith. The Tanner proposal which the board accepted was to provide limousine airport transportation service over a ten year period. It could not be performed within one year and is, therefore, squarely within the mentioned statute. [The court, however, continued:]

Following the acceptance of the Tanner bid, the board [orally] assured Tanner that a formal written agreement would be prepared for signature. *In reliance, Tanner continued to provide limousine service to the air-port, paid $3,600 as the minimum guarantee for the ensuing year, and purchased two new 1960 limousines at the cost of about $9,000.* [Emphasis added].

We acknowledge the general rule that, in the absence of fraud, a promise to reduce an agreement to writing is not, standing alone, a basis for invoking an estoppel against raising the statute of frauds in defense [that is, such a promise alone does not make the moral agreement enforceable]. It is likewise true, as a general rule, that part performance of an agreement within the "one year provision" of the statute of frauds [does not alone make the oral agreement enforceable]. However, where both occur, i.e., a promise to reduce an agreement to writing *and* part performance, an *estoppel* is properly invoked [by the one seeking specific performance], and the main agreement [is enforceable]. We conclude, therefore, that the board cannot rely upon [the statute of frauds] as a defense to this action. . . . The lower court [did not err] in directing the board to execute a formal contract with Tanner and thereafter specifically perform the same. . . .

Affirmed.

Promises to Pay Debts of Another

If A has received a benefit from B, then B's claim that A has made a promise to B is more plausible than if A has received no such benefit. To avoid perjury, the statute of frauds requires that if A has not received such a benefit, A's "promise to answer for the debt, default or miscarriage of another" must be in writing to be enforceable. The classic example is a "guaranty contract" in which A promises B that he will pay C's debt to B *if* C does not. Because A received no benefit in this transaction, the law is suspicious and demands that B provide written evidence of A's promise.

There are three standard elements of a guaranty contract. First, the guarantor promises to pay the debtor's obligation *if* the debtor does not. In other words, guaranty contracts occur in situations of "secondary liability." The creditor is to look primarily to the debtor for repayment, and only if the debtor does not pay is the creditor to look to the guarantor. If, on the other hand, A tells B: "Send C's bills to me," A is the primary debtor to whom B is to look first for payment. A is making the debt his own, not promising to pay the debt of another. Such a promise is not a guaranty and therefore need not be in writing to be enforceable.

Second, a guaranty promise is made for the benefit of the debtor. If the guarantor's "main purpose" in making the promise is to benefit himself, it is not a guaranty contract and need not be in writing to be enforceable. An aunt who, out of pity, promises a landlord that she will pay her niece's rent if the niece does not pay is making a guaranty promise that must be in writing to be enforceable. On the other hand, assume that Guarantor Company has a government contract to build a wind tunnel to test airplanes. Guarantor hires Joe Debtor to do the concrete work. Because Joe does not pay his bills, Creditor Concrete Supply stops delivering concrete, halting construction and endangering Guarantor's contract with the government. If an official of Guarantor called Creditor on the phone and said: "Please keep delivering concrete to Joe Debtor, and we'll pay the bills if he doesn't," the promise would be enforceable though never put in writing because Guarantor's main purpose in making the promise is obviously to benefit itself. Therefore, this is not a guaranty promise and need not be in writing to be enforceable.

Third, a guaranty promise is made to the creditor, not to the debtor. If in the previous example, Guarantor Company had told Joe Debtor: "Keep ordering concrete, and we'll pay the bill if you don't," such a promise is not a guaranty and need not be in writing in order to be enforceable.

Other Promises

Two other relatively insignificant categories of contracts—*promises made in consideration of marriage* and *executors' contracts*—fall within the statute. Thus, if A promises to pay B $5,000 when and if B marries C, A is liable only if his promise is in writing. The same is true in regard to prenuptial agreements, in which parties about to be married to each other expressly spell out their interests in the other's properties. (Indeed, some states have passed statutes requiring that "palimony" contracts—agreements for support or division of property between live-in lovers who are not married—be in writing to be enforceable.) Finally, if the administrator or executor of an estate promises personally to pay a debt of the deceased, the creditor can hold the promisor liable only if the promise is in writing.

In addition, recently many borrowers have sued banks claiming some form of breach of an oral promise to lend, to refinance an existing loan, or to refrain from enforcing remedies contained in a written loan agreement. In one case, for example, a jury awarded $28 million for breach of an alleged oral promise to extend an existing line of credit. In another, a jury awarded $69 million for breach of an alleged oral promise to make a loan. To protect banks and other lending institutions from such liability, many states have recently passed laws barring the enforcement of oral lending agreements without a signed contract.

CONTRACTS CALLING FOR SALE OF GOODS
The UCC Statute of Frauds

Section 2-201 of the code, known as the **UCC statute of frauds,** states that a contract for the sale of goods for a price of $500 or more must be in writing to be enforceable (with exceptions noted subsequently). As is true of other statute of frauds provisions applicable to nongoods transactions, the requirement of Sec. 2-201(1) can be satisfied either (1) by having the contract itself in writing, or (2) by having a subsequent written memorandum of the oral agreement. In either situation, *the writing must be signed by the party against whom enforcement is sought.*

The UCC Confirmation

The language of Sec. 2-201(1) in regard to enforceability parallels that of the basic statute of frauds. That is, if an oral sales contract is followed by a writing signed by only one of the parties, the signer is

bound by the contract but the nonsigner is not. To eliminate this one-sidedness in certain circumstances, subsection 2 of Sec. 2-201 provides another method (in addition to the two set forth above) for satisfying the writing requirement of subsection 1.

Suppose that two parties have orally agreed on a sale of goods. One of the parties then sends a signed letter or other written communication to the other party, saying: "This is to confirm that on June 20 we entered into an agreement for the sale of 175 men's suits on the following terms [the terms being stated in the letter]." If this is the only writing the parties make, the question is whether it can be used to satisfy the requirements of Sec. 2-201(1). If the sender breaches the contract, the letter can be used in a lawsuit by the recipient against the sender because the sender signed it. But if it is the recipient who breaches the contract, can the sender use the letter in his lawsuit to recover damages from the recipient, the nonsigner? In transactions not governed by the UCC, as we have seen, the answer is no. But as to sales of goods, however (as in the above example), the answer sometimes is yes.

Under Sec. 2-201(2), the **UCC confirmation rule,** a confirmation such as the above can be used by the sender against a nonsigning recipient if the following requirements are met:

1. The writing must be "sufficient against the sender." In other words, the *sender* must have *signed* the confirmation, and its contents must meet the relatively lenient sufficiency requirements discussed later in the chapter.

2. Both parties must be *merchants.*

3. The recipient must have had reason to know of the contents of the confirmation *but had not objected to it in writing within ten days after receiving it.*

UCC Exceptions

Section 2-201(3) defines three situations in which an oral contract, if proved, will be enforceable despite the total absence of a writing, even when it involves a sale of goods for a price of $500 or more. The first exception can be used only by a seller; the other two can be used by either a seller or a buyer.

1. If the oral contract is for goods to be specifically manufactured for the particular buyer, it is enforceable against the buyer if two requirements are met:

a. The goods must be of a type not suitable for sale to others in the ordinary course of the seller's business. For example: Suppose that C is an importer of small, foreign-made pickup trucks, and D is a manufacturer of campers that are mounted on pickups. C orally orders from D a number of campers made to fit the pickups imported by C (that is, they will fit no other pickups on the market). If C repudiates the bargain after the campers are made, D will be hard-pressed to sell them elsewhere. He might eventually be able to do so, but considerable effort would probably be required. Thus the goods cannot be sold in the ordinary course of his business.

b. The seller must either have substantially started the manufacture of the goods, or have made commitments for procuring them, before he or she learned of the buyer's repudiation of the agreement.

2. If the defendant "admits in his pleading, testimony or otherwise in court that a contract for sale was made," it will be enforceable even though oral. (The common-law court decisions on this point are conflicting, most courts holding that such an admission does *not* remove the requirement of a writing. Thus the UCC exception represents a significant innovation in this regard.) Observe that not just any admission will suffice; the admission by the defendant must become part of official court records.

3. An oral agreement will be enforced to the extent that payment has been made and accepted or that the goods have been received and accepted. Suppose, for example, that X and Y have made an oral contract for Y to sell X twenty-five television sets at a price of $300 each. Before any of the sets are delivered, X makes a prepayment of $1,800, which Y accepts. Y then refuses to honor the contract. Even if Y were not bound by the contract, X could of course get her money back under the unjust enrichment theory (see Chapter 11). But under the UCC her part payment will make the contract partially enforceable, and she will be able to maintain a suit for breach of a contract obligation to deliver six of the twenty-five television sets. Similarly, if X has made no payment but Y has made a partial shipment which X has accepted, the oral contract is again partially enforceable. That is, if Y delivers and X accepts six

television sets, and X then repudiates the agreement, Y can maintain a suit for breach of a contract obligation to pay $1,800.[6]

The rationale underlying these exceptions is entirely consistent with the purpose of the basic writing requirement of Sec. 2-201(1), which is to forestall the possibility of a party successfully maintaining a fabricated breach of contract suit by the use of perjured testimony. By providing these exceptions, the drafters of the UCC have recognized that, in cases falling within them, it is extremely unlikely that plaintiff's claim will be a complete fabrication. Therefore, because the original purpose for the writing requirement no longer exists in such instances, the oral agreements ought to be binding. Compliance with the statute of frauds under UCC 2-201 is summarized in Figure 16.1.

Modification Contracts

Under Section 2-209 of the UCC, agreements that modify existing sales contracts must be in writing in order to be enforceable in two situations:

1. The modification must be in writing if the original agreement had provided that it could be modified only by a writing.[7]

2. The modification must be in writing if the whole contract, *as modified,* is required to be in writing under the UCC statute of frauds (Sec. 2-201, discussed above).

Other Statutes Requiring a Writing

In addition to the basic statute of frauds and Sections 2-201 and 2-209 of the UCC, all states have additional statutes—usually narrow in scope—that require still other kinds of contracts to be in writing. For example, most states require real estate listing contracts and insurance contracts to be in writing.

---

[6] Prior to enactment of the UCC, part performance of this type made the *entire contract* enforceable. Also, the statutory language in this exception does not address the situation in which the buyer has made a partial prepayment that cannot be allocated to a certain number of individual units of goods. For example, what if buyer makes and seller accepts a $1,000 down payment on a single $6,000 automobile? In the few cases involving this question since enactment of the UCC, most courts have applied the common-law rule and have held the entire contract to be enforceable despite the absence of a sufficient written document.

[7] Section 2-209(2) has an additional provision applicable to those sales contracts entered into between a merchant and a nonmerchant. In such a case, if the contract results from use of the *merchant's form* (with that form containing the requirement that any later modification had to be in writing), that requirement must itself be "separately signed" by the nonmerchant in order to be binding upon him or her.

FIGURE 16.1

Compliance with the Statute of Frauds in Contracts for the Sale of Goods, UCC 2-201

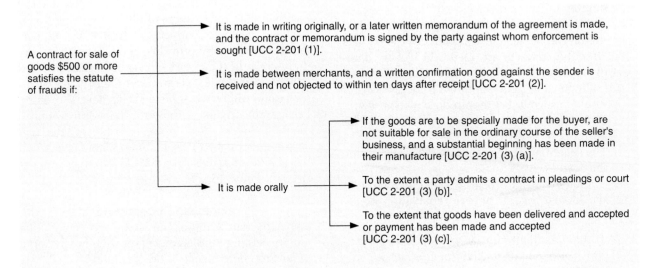

A contract for sale of goods $500 or more satisfies the statute of frauds if:

It is made in writing originally, or a later written memorandum of the agreement is made, and the contract or memorandum is signed by the party against whom enforcement is sought [UCC 2-201 (1)].

It is made between merchants, and a written confirmation good against the sender is received and not objected to within ten days after receipt [UCC 2-201 (2)].

It is made orally

If the goods are to be specially made for the buyer, are not suitable for sale in the ordinary course of the seller's business, and a substantial beginning has been made in their manufacture [UCC 2-201 (3) (a)].

To the extent a party admits a contract in pleadings or court [UCC 2-201 (3) (b)].

To the extent that goods have been delivered and accepted or payment has been made and accepted [UCC 2-201 (3) (c)].

Additionally, Sec. 8-319 of the UCC requires, in general, that contracts calling for the sale of securities (i.e., stocks and bonds) must be in writing, and Sec. 9-203 of the UCC imposes the same requirement upon most "security agreements" governed by Article 9 (i.e., agreements that create security interests in favor of lenders of money or unpaid sellers of goods).

WHEN IS THE WRITING SUFFICIENT?
Contract Law

The original statute of frauds began: "No action shall be brought [upon the following kinds of contracts] unless the agreement upon which such action shall be brought, *or some memorandum or note thereof,* shall be in writing and signed by the party sought to be charged therewith or some other person thereunto by him lawfully authorized." Thus, even if the full contract is not in writing, a "sufficient written memorandum" may satisfy the statute of fraud's requirements. In such situations, the courts *generally require that the writing include at least the following:* (1) names of both parties, (2) the subject matter of the contract, (3) the consideration to be paid, and (4) any other terms

that the court feels are material under the circumstances. Under this fairly strict approach, if any basic term is missing, the contract continues to be unenforceable.

This does not mean, however, that the writing must be in any particular form, or be complete in every detail. And because of the provision that a memorandum or note of the contract may satisfy the statute, it is entirely possible that an oral contract can be validated by the production in court of a confirming telegram, sales slip, check, invoice, or some other writing—assuming, of course, that it contains all the material terms of the agreement.

Additionally, it frequently happens that the contract is evidenced by two or more separate writings, none of which alone is sufficiently complete to satisfy the statute. In such cases the writings may be construed together, thus satisfying the memorandum requirement, if the writings clearly refer to one another (expressly or impliedly), or if they are physically attached to one another.

The requirement that the contract or written memorandum be signed by the party against whom the agreement is to be enforced (or a duly authorized representative) is somewhat loosely applied. It may be satisfied by a signature, by initials, by the letter-head on a sheet of paper, or even by a company's trademark appearing on the paper.

Sales Law

Contracts calling for the sale of goods are often made in the business world under circumstances where, because of the press of time or other factors, the parties put only the barest essentials of the agreement in writing. Recognizing this reality, Sec. 2-201 of the UCC has *greatly relaxed the requirements of the sufficiency of the writing.* For sales of goods, that section provides that the writing (whether the contract itself, or memorandum, or subsequent confirmation) merely has to be "sufficient to indicate that a contract for sale has been made between the parties." The only term that *must be included in the writing is the quantity.* Other terms that are orally agreed upon can be proved in court by oral testimony.[8] Terms that are not agreed upon at all can be supplied by Article 2 itself (as we saw in Chapter 12).

Cases have arisen presenting the question of whether a written "requirements contract" satisfies the quantity requirement of Sec. 2-201. For example, a seller might obligate himself or herself to sell and deliver "all of the 21 oz. plastic your plant can use" over a specified period of time at a specific unit price. In a case in which such language was utilized, *Fortune Furniture Co. v. Mid-South Plastic Co.*, 310 So.2d 725 (1975), the Supreme Court of Mississippi—following the majority rule—held that this type of provision satisfied the requirement that the writing state a quantity.

THE PAROL EVIDENCE RULE

Whenever a contract (or a memorandum thereof) is reduced to writing, the writing ought to contain *all* the material terms of the agreement. This is true not only for contracts that fall within the statute of frauds, but for all other contracts where a writing is utilized as well. One reason for this, as to statute of frauds contracts, is to make sure that the writ-

ing meets the sufficiency requirement under the statute. An equally powerful reason lies in the **parol evidence rule.** This rule provides, in general, that when any contract has been reduced to writing, neither party can introduce "parol" (outside) evidence in court for the purpose of modifying or changing the terms of that contract. More specifically, the rule prohibits a party to a written contract from unilaterally introducing either oral or written statements or agreements made at (or prior to) the time the written contract was made which either conflict with, or add to, the terms of the written contract.

Among the policy reasons for the existence of the parol evidence rule are (1) because a written contract is more reliable than oral testimony, it helps prevent perjury or fraud; (2) it encourages the parties to put their important agreements in writing, thus increasing the reliability of commercial transactions; and (3) it emphasizes a long-standing rule of contract interpretation to the effect that final expressions of intent should prevail over earlier tentative expressions of intent.

As to sales contracts, the UCC's parol evidence rule in Sec. 2-202 is essentially the same as the common-law parol rule, discussed above. However, its wording may increase the chances that extrinsic evidence will be allowed by narrowing the traditional view of what constitutes a *final* expression of the parties' agreement. Obviously, expressions of intent that are only preliminary are not protected by the rule from contradiction by parol sources.

Exceptions

The courts feel that the parol evidence rule brings about clearly undesirable results in some circumstances; accordingly, they have recognized a number of exceptions to it. (In general, these exceptions apply both to cases governed by common-law principles and those governed by sales law.) Following are the most important situations in which a party to a written contract *is* permitted to introduce parol evidence in subsequent legal proceedings:

1. The written contract itself appears to be incomplete. The parol evidence rule applies only to final *and complete* expressions of intent.

2. The written contract is ambiguous, and the parol evidence tends to clear up the ambiguity. Such evidence does not contradict or add to the writing.

---

[8]The oral testimony referred to here is intended to supplement an incomplete writing. If the writing does contain a particular term, oral testimony about anything supposedly agreed upon prior to execution of the writing is not admissible in court for the purpose of contradicting the clear terms of the writing. This is because of the UCC's "parol evidence rule," Sec. 2-202, which will be discussed subsequently.

3. The written contract contains an obvious mistake, such as a typographical or clerical error, and the parol evidence tends to correct the error.

4. The parol evidence shows that the contract was not a valid one, as, for example, that it was induced by fraud or duress on the part of the other party, or was formed under mutual mistake of fact. Alleged fraud is the major exception under which parol evidence is admitted.

5. The evidence shows that the contract was subject to a condition precedent, i.e., that the parties had agreed that a specified event had to occur before the contract would be effective, and that the event had not occurred.

6. The evidence tends to prove that the parties made either an oral or written agreement that modified the written contract *after* the written contract had been entered into. Parties to written contracts often change their minds and later alter the agreements. Admission of such evidence does not contradict the basic reasoning behind the parol evidence rule which is that preliminary contract terms, which may vary substantially as the contract is negotiated, become merged into the final written contract.

A seventh exception, applicable only to sales contracts, allows evidence about the course of prior dealings of the parties or custom of the trade in which the parties are engaged to explain or supplement a writing, even when the evidence appears to contradict its unambiguous terms.

Cumulatively, these exceptions arm the courts with tools to avoid the operation of the parol evidence rule in instances where they believe its application would cause injustice. Thus, a substantial gap may exist between the theory underlying the formal rule on the one hand, and the rule's practical operation on the other.

WRITTEN CONFIRMATION OF DEALS IS UPHELD

by Ellen Joan Pollock and Richard Gibson

**Box 16.1
The Law
at Work**

In a decision likely to affect many financial institutions, New York's highest court ruled [in *Intershoe Inc. v. Bankers Trust Co.*, 569 N.Y.S.2d 333 (1991)] that written confirmation of a deal made over the telephone constitutes the final agreement—even if one side later disputes the terms.

The New York Court of Appeals overturned two lower courts in throwing out a lawsuit filed by Intershoe Inc., a Millersburg, Pa., shoe importer, against Bankers Trust Co. . . . Intershoe and Bankers Trust entered into a foreign currency futures transaction over the phone March 13, 1985, involving Italian *lira*. But the two parties disagreed about the nature of the deal. The confirmation slip, sent by Bankers Trust the day of the transaction, showed that Intershoe had agreed to sell the bank *lira* for $250,000. But Intershoe argued that, in fact, it had agreed over the phone to buy—not sell—the *lira*.

According to the decision, the company's treasurer said he was sure he had not agreed to sell *lira* to the bank, even though he had signed the confirmation slip and returned it to the bank. The treasurer said that Intershoe had sold foreign currency to Bankers Trust in only one of almost 1,000 currency transactions, according to the decision.

The appeals court ruled that under [Sec. 2-202 of] the Uniform Commercial Code, the confirmation slip nonetheless constituted the final expression of the deal and that no contrary evidence based on a prior agreement could be introduced in court. The judges rejected Intershoe's argument that the confirmation slip should have included some indication that the parties intended it to be the final expression of the deal.

"As a practical matter, a confirmation slip or similar writing is usually the only reliable evidence of such transactions, given the unlikely prospect that one who makes scores of similar deals each day will remember the details of any one particular agreement," the court said.

Source: *Wall Street Journal*, April 2, 1991, p. B2.

SUMMARY

Oral contracts are, as a general rule, enforceable if their terms can be proven in court. Under the typical state statute of frauds, however, five classes of contracts must generally be in writing (or be evidenced by a writing) in order to be enforceable. The most important of these are (1) contracts to sell land or an interest in land; (2) contracts not to be performed within one year from the time they were made; and (3) promises to pay debts of another. In all of these cases, however, the courts have recognized exceptions to the rules—thus enforcing the oral contracts—in circumstances where they feel a refusal to enforce would be extremely unfair to one of the parties. In cases where oral contracts have been entered into which clearly fall within the statute, followed by a written confirmation of the contract, the party who has signed the confirmation is bound by the contract, but the other party is not.

Article 2 of the UCC provides a sixth type of contract that must generally be evidenced by a writing: contracts calling for the sale of goods where the price is $500 or more. The UCC statute of frauds substantially removes, as to sales contracts, the one-sidedness that exists under the basic statute where one party has signed a written confirmation but the other party has not. This is achieved by Sec. 2-201(2), which provides that, if both parties are merchants, a written confirmation signed by one party and sent to the other party is binding upon the latter unless he or she objects to its terms within ten days of receiving it. Sec. 2-201(3) also specifies three exceptional situations in which oral contracts of $500 or more are valid even if not evidenced by a writing at all. If a contract falls within the basic statute, the written contract (or memorandum thereof) satisfies the statute only if it contains all the material terms of the agreement. By contrast, to satisfy the UCC requirement, the writing need only indicate that a sales contract has been entered into, and contain the quantity of the goods being sold.

Whenever a contract is in writing, whether or not it is required by law to be in writing, the *parol evidence rule* generally forbids either party from producing outside evidence in a later court action in an effort to change or add to the terms of the contract. The rule achieves this result by prohibiting the introduction of evidence showing that the parties, at or prior to the time of contracting, made oral or written promises in conflict with, or in addition to, the written terms. However, such evidence is allowed in some circumstances, as, for example, where the written contract is incomplete or ambiguous, or where the outside evidence shows that the contract itself was invalid.

KEY TERMS

Statute of frauds
Mortgage
Easement
UCC statute of frauds
UCC confirmation rule
Parol evidence rule

QUESTIONS AND PROBLEMS

1. Dr. Sahlin owned a summer cottage in New York. He told his nurse of many years that if she and her husband—the Strandbergs—would live at the cottage with him on the weekends, and care for him and keep the property in good repair, they would receive the property when he died. The couple rendered the specified services until the time of his death, a period of several years. (Among other things, Mr. Strandberg reconstructed the cottage by shingling it, painting and rewiring it, and putting in new footings and plumbing throughout.) Dr. Sahlin died without a will, and the executor of his estate refused to convey the property to them since there was nothing in writing evidencing the agreement. Do you think the various services the Strandbergs performed caused the contract to be enforceable? Why or why not? (*Strandberg v. Lawrence*, 216 N.Y.S.2d 973, 1961.)

2. Warner wished to build a lumber mill, which would require construction of a railroad switch and spur line from the Texas and Pacific Railroad's main line in Texas. In 1874, he entered into an oral contract with the railroad, under the terms of which he was to supply the ties and grade the ground for the switch, with the railroad promising to construct and maintain the switch and spur line "for Warner's benefit as long as Warner needed it." Warner built the mill, and the railroad built the spur line and switch and maintained service for several years. In 1887, however, the railroad tore up the switch and ties,

leaving Warner without transportation facilities. When Warner sued to recover damages for breach of contract, the railroad contended that the oral agreement "was a contract not to be performed within one year" and within the statute of frauds, and therefore was not enforceable against it. Is the railroad's contention correct? Explain. (*Warner v. Texas and Pacific Ry.*, 164 U.S. 418, 1896.)

3. After reviewing the financial records, Ogle and Melton (Ds) orally agreed to pay Trew (P) $145,000 for his wood-shavings business. Under the agreement, they would pay $1,000 down and then $3,000 per month for 48 months. After two months of operating the business, Ds discovered that it was not as profitable as they had expected and refused to make any further payments. P sued for breach of contract and Ds raised a statute of frauds defense. P showed that Ds had acquired two of his trucks, his stockpile of shavings and storage facilities, and all his existing customers. Additionally, P had made other special arrangements, such as helping Ds obtain insurance. Is the statute of frauds a good defense? (*Trew v. Ogle*, 767 S.W.2d 662, Tenn.App. 1988.)

4. In 1978, Moore, a major depositor in the First National Bank of Clarksville, orally told the bank to open up an account for his sons' trucking company and "I'll cover for them." In 1979, the sons bounced a check which Moore paid off when the bank called it to his attention. In 1980, the sons bounced two more checks simultaneously, totalling almost $500,000. When notified by the bank, Moore said he would cover the checks. However, that night he told his wife, who almost collapsed. The next day Moore told the bank that the deal was off. The bank sued; Moore raised a statute of frauds defense. Is this a good defense? (*First National Bank of Clarksville v. Moore*, 628 S.W.2d 488, Tex.Civ.App. 1982.)

5. Garland Co. sold almost $50,000 worth of materials to Roofco Co., for which Roofco failed to pay. In conversations between Rasor, president and principal shareholder of Roofco, and Garland, Rasor orally guaranteed that he would pay the debt out of personal funds if Roofco did not pay it. When Roofco did not pay, Garland sued to enforce the promise. Rasor raised a statute of frauds defense. Will the defense succeed? (*Garland Co., Inc. v. Roofco Co.*, 809 F.2d 546, 8th Cir. 1987.)

6. Pursuant to an oral contract for the sale of 2000 cattle, seller (P) delivered 222 cattle to buyer (D). Before any further delivery could occur, D breached the contract, claiming that it was unenforceable because it was oral. P sued to enforce the contract. Will P have any success? How much? (*Bagby Land & Cattle Co. v. California Livestock Comm'n Co.*, 439 F.2d 315, 5th Cir. 1971.)

7. After losing his race for the U.S. Senate, Collins did not wish to pay the $29,526.98 he owed for campaign posters that the Williamson Printing Corporation had printed for him and his supporters had spread around the state. So he didn't. Williamson sued for breach of contract. Collins defended by proving that there was no written contract. Is this a good defense? (*Collins v. Williamson Printing Corporation*, 746 S.W.2d 489, Tex.App. 1988.)

8. The owner of a dairy company orally contracted to sell certain land to the Hancock Construction Company, but later refused to go through with the deal. When the construction company brought an action for specific performance (an action seeking the property), the dairy company defended on the ground that the contract was not in writing. The construction company pointed out, however, that after the contract was made it had engineering studies made of the property, and also had made application for a loan of over $292,000 in order to finance the purchase. The construction company then contended that these acts on its part constituted "part performance" of the contract, and thus made the oral contract enforceable. Is this contention correct? Why or why not? (*Hancock Construction Co. v. Kempton & Snedigar Dairy*, 510 P.2d 752, 1973.)

9. In 1982, B&R Co. began buying doors from Lifetime Doors. In early 1983, a sales representative for Lifetime urged B&R to shift all its door purchases to Lifetime, making Lifetime its sole supplier. The sales representative provided literature which invited B&R to join Lifetime's "VIP Club." According to the literature, new purchasers would receive "continuous production availability in full proportion to monthly needs," which would allow them to "order flexible quantities" in shipments of a "desired number." B&R's president secured an oral commitment from Lifetime that Lifetime would supply B&R's requirements of four truckloads of six-panel doors each month in exchange for B&R's promise to purchase

doors exclusively from Lifetime. Three months later, Lifetime began breaching the contract by allowing B&R to obtain the doors it needed only by agreeing to buy certain other types of doors as well. B&R sued for breach of contract. Lifetime raised a statute of frauds defense. Will this defense succeed? Can a "sufficient written memorandum" be found here? (*Barber & Ross Co. v. Lifetime Doors, Inc.,* 810 F.2d 1276, 4th Cir. 1987.)

10. Anderson hired Tri-State Home Improvement Co. to install siding on his home. Anderson claimed that as the contract was being negotiated, Tri-State's president promised that the siding would not rust and guaranteed this for at least 30 years. The written contract, however, did not contain such promises and stated: "The Company prohibits the making of any promises, or representations, unless it is inserted in writing in this agreement before signing." Within two years, extensive rust damage appeared. Anderson sued Tri-State for fraud and deceit. Is evidence as to the oral statements allegedly made by Tri-State's president admissible at trial? (*Anderson v. Tri-State Home Improvement Co.,* 68 N.W.2d 705, Wis. 1955.)

Chapter 17

Third-Party Beneficiaries

Assignments

Delegation of Duties

As a general rule, the rights created by the formation of a contract can be enforced only by the original parties to the agreement. A contract is essentially a private agreement affecting only the contracting parties themselves; both legal and practical difficulties would arise if a stranger to the contract (a **third party**) were permitted to enforce it. Suppose, for example, that X employed B to paint her house and that B subsequently refused to do the job. If Y, one of X's neighbors, were to bring suit against B to recover damages for breach of contract, it would be ludicrous if he were permitted to get a judgment. Since Y was not a party to the contract, he clearly has "no standing to sue," and his suit would be dismissed.

However, in certain exceptional circumstances a third party is permitted to enforce a contract made by others, particularly (1) where it appears, expressly or by necessary implication, that at the time the contract was made the parties to the contract intended that that person receive the benefit of the contract, or (2) where one of the parties, after making the contract, assigned (transferred) his or her rights to a third party. In the former situation the third party is called a *third-party beneficiary,* and in the latter he or she is designated an *assignee* of the contract.

THIRD-PARTY BENEFICIARIES

The law recognizes three kinds of beneficiaries—creditor, donee, and incidental. Generally, creditor and donee beneficiaries (also known as "intended" beneficiaries) can enforce contracts made by others, while incidental beneficiaries cannot.

Creditor Beneficiaries

When a contract is made between two parties for the express benefit of a third person, the latter is said to be a **creditor beneficiary** if he or she had earlier furnished consideration to one of the contracting parties. To illustrate: A owes X $500. A later sells a piano to B, on the understanding that B, in return, is to pay off A's indebtedness to X. Here X is a creditor beneficiary of the contract between A and B, inasmuch as she originally gave consideration to A, which created the debt in her (X's) favor. Once A has delivered the piano, X is entitled to recover the $500 from B—by suit, if necessary.[1]

Assumption of Mortgage

One typical situation involving a creditor beneficiary arises when mortgaged real estate is sold, with the purchaser agreeing to pay off the existing mortgage. For example: S owns a home subject to a $15,000 mortgage held by the Y Bank. S finds a buyer for the home, Z, who is willing to *assume the mortgage.* Thereupon S and Z enter into a contract, under the terms of which S agrees to convey the property to Z, and Z promises to pay S's existing indebtedness to the bank. The Y Bank now has become a creditor beneficiary of the contract between S and Z, since it originally gave consideration to S by making the loan, and it can hold Z liable on his promise to pay the indebtedness. (The assumption of the mortgage by Z does not by itself free S of his liability. Thus the bank can look to either party for payment in case Z defaults—unless it has expressly released S from his obligation.)[2]

Donee Beneficiaries

Where a contract is made for the benefit of a third person who has not given consideration to either contracting party, that person is designated a **donee beneficiary** of the contract. To illustrate: P, an attorney, agrees to perform certain legal services for Q, with the understanding that Q will pay the $200 legal fee to R, P's son-in-law. Here P has made a gift of $200 to R, and R—the donee beneficiary of the contract—can enforce it against Q if Q refuses to pay him voluntarily.

---

[1] If A refused to deliver the piano to B, should B be required to pay X? Obviously, the answer is "no." The promisor (B) can raise the same defenses against an intended beneficiary (X) as he or she can raise against the promisee (A). In this case, the defense is A's failure to perform. Defenses such as lack of consideration, incapacity, fraud, mistake, or statute of frauds would also be effective. If B raises an effective defense to avoid paying X, clearly X could sue A on the original $500 debt.

[2] In most mortgages today, Z, even if willing, would not be allowed to assume the mortgages. "Due on sale clauses" (provisions in the mortgage which make the entire balance owed by S due immediately upon sale of the property) would render the loan "non-assumable."

Life Insurance Contracts

The most common type of contract involving donee beneficiaries is that of the ordinary life insurance policy. If A insures his life with the B Insurance Company, and the policy expressly designates C as the beneficiary of the proceeds of that policy, C—the donee beneficiary—can enforce the contract against the company. The fact that C has not furnished consideration to the company is immaterial; it is sufficient that A, the insured, has done so by making his premium payments.[3]

Incidental Beneficiaries

An **incidental beneficiary** is a person whom the contracting parties did not intend to benefit by making the contract, but who nevertheless will benefit in some way if the contract is performed. Such a beneficiary, unlike a donee beneficiary, has no rights under the contract and thus is not entitled to enforce it. For example, a retail merchant in a college town would benefit from a contract between a construction firm and the university calling for the construction of a four-level parking facility on campus property just across the street from his (or her) store. However, if the builder breaches the contract with the university by refusing to go ahead with the project, the merchant cannot recover damages from the builder.

In determining whether a beneficiary is a donee beneficiary or an incidental beneficiary, the usual test is whether the contract was made primarily for his or her benefit. If so, the beneficiary is a donee beneficiary; if not, he or she is merely an incidental beneficiary. Strong evidence that a beneficiary is intended arises where the contract expressly designates the third party as such or where the promisor's performance is to be rendered directly to the third party.

Consider these illustrations:

1. A hires B Co. to construct a building. Soon after construction begins, A breaches the contract; as a result, B Co. lays off employee X. If X sued A for breach of contract, he would lose. His employment was an incidental benefit of the contract, but clearly A and B Co. did not make the contract for the purpose of benefitting X.

2. A promises to build an office building for B. The plans and specifications call for use of electrical wiring made by L Company. A uses wiring made by M Company instead. L could not sue A for breach of contract because the purpose of this requirement was not to provide business for L.

3. City hires ABC Water Co. to provide water for its citizens' needs at an agreed rate. If ABC charged more than the agreed rate, the citizens would probably be allowed to sue as intended beneficiaries for breach of contract. ABC's performance, after all, was to be directed to the citizens. (However, assume that citizen X's warehouse burns down, in part because ABC did not provide adequate water pressure for the fire fighters. Although the same reasoning would appear to apply, most courts would deny recovery by X against ABC on *public policy* grounds. For fear that allowing recovery in the latter instance would impose crushing financial burdens on entities with government contracts, such as public utilities, most courts would characterize X as a mere incidental beneficiary.[4])

The following is a recent creditor beneficiary case.

---

[3] If A did not pay the premiums that the contract required, obviously B Insurance Co. would not have to pay C the proceeds of the policy, again illustrating that claims of intended beneficiaries against the promisor are subject to the same defenses that could be raised against the promisee.

[4] *H.R. Moch Co. v. Rensselaer Water Co.*, 159 N.E. 896, N.Y. 1928.)

UNITED STATES V. STATE FARM MUTUAL AUTOMOBILE INSURANCE CO.

U.S. Court of Appeals, Fifth Circuit, 936 F.2d 206 (5th Cir. 1991)

Defendant State Farm issued to various armed services members standard boating and automobile accident insurance policies. Twenty-four of these army personnel were injured in accidents that entitled them to recover medical and hospital expenses under the policies. The United States treated these people free of any personal expense at government medical institutions as it is required to do by federal statute 10 U.S.C. Sections 1074, 1076. The government then brought this action seeking reimbursement as a third-party beneficiary to the insurance policies for the value of the medical services provided. The trial court granted summary judgment to the government. State Farm appealed.

(continues)

UNITED STATES V. STATE FARM MUTUAL AUTOMOBILE INSURANCE CO.

(continued from previous page)

Higginbotham, Circuit Judge:

Under Mississippi law, in order for a stranger to a contract to sue to enforce its term, "the contract between the original parties must have been entered into for his benefit, or at least such benefit must be the direct result of the performance within the contemplation of the parties." *Burns v. Washington Savings,* 171 So.2d 322 (Miss.1965). The third party need not be expressly identified in the contract; it is enough that the beneficiary is a member of a class intended to be benefited. At the same time, the right of the third party beneficiary to maintain an action on the contract must "spring" from the terms of the contract itself.

The State Farm policies at issue here contained the following emphasized provisions:

Persons *for Whom* Medical Expenses are Payable.

We will pay medical expenses for bodily injury sustained by:

1. a. The firm person named in the declarations;
   b. his or her spouse; and
   c. her relatives.

Payment of Medical Expenses.

We may pay the injured person or *any person or organization performing the services.*

We have read similar policy language to support third party claims by medical care providers . . . . State Farm urges that it is obligated only for medical expenses actually incurred *by the insured.* No such limitation is imposed by the terms of the policies. State Farm is obligated to pay the costs of reasonable medical services, whether such costs were borne personally by the insured or, as here, directly by the medical care provider. We also cannot accept State Farm's contention that the policies' facility of payment clause—which provides, "We may pay the injured person or any person or organization performing the service"—makes the government an optional payee or incidental beneficiary.

[Affirmed.] ⚖

ASSIGNMENTS

Assignment of Rights

All contracts create certain rights and duties. With exceptions to be noted later, the *rights* a person has acquired under a contract can be transferred, or *assigned,* by that person to a third party.[5] Suppose, for example, that A agrees to add a family room to B's home for $13,500 and that A performs the required work. A thereafter assigns his right to collect the $13,500 to C, in which case A is the **assignor** and C the **assignee.** C can now recover the $13,500 from B, just as A could have done had there been no assignment. The relationship among the parties to an assignment is set forth in Figure 17.1.

Status of the Assignee

Whenever an assignment takes place, the assignee acquires no greater rights than those possessed by the assignor. Putting it another way, the **obligor** (the person with a duty to perform) can assert the same

[5]While a person's *duties* under a contract can also be transferred to a third party in some circumstances, such a transfer is a *delegation* rather than an *assignment.* The delegation of duties is discussed later in the chapter.

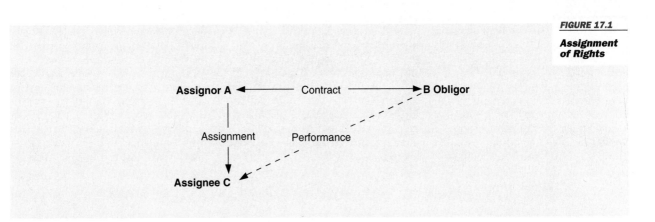

FIGURE 17.1

Assignment of Rights

defenses (if any) against the assignee that he or she had against the assignor.[6]

This can be easily illustrated by referring again to Figure 17.1. If B refuses to pay C and C brings suit against him on the contract, B can escape liability if he can prove that A breached his contract in some material way—by failing to complete the job, for example, or by using materials inferior to those required by the contract. In such a case C's only redress is the right to recover from A any consideration he had given to A in payment for the assignment.

What Rights Can Be Assigned?

Occasionally, when an assignee requests the obligor to perform his or her part of the bargain, the obligor

---

[6]The rule that the assignee of a simple contract acquires no greater rights than those possessed by the assignor does not apply when a particular kind of contract—a *negotiable instrument*—is utilized by the parties. Under the law of commercial paper (which will be discussed in Part III) the purchaser of that special kind of instrument may qualify as a *holder in due course* of such instrument, in which case he or she can enforce the instrument against the obligor in certain situations where the seller of the instrument could not do so. In the above case, for example, if B's obligation were in the form of a negotiable promissory note, and if A negotiated the note to C, a holder in due course, *C is usually entitled to recover the amount of the note from B* even though A breached his contract with B. B's recourse is then to sue A for damages for breach of contract.

refuses to do so on the ground that the assigned right was of such a nature that it could not be legally transferred without his or her consent. Usually, this contention is not accepted by the courts; most contractual rights can be assigned without the obligor's consent. This is especially true where the assigned right was that of *collecting a debt*. The reasoning is that it is ordinarily no more difficult for a debtor (obligor) to pay the assignee than to pay the assignor (the original creditor); hence the obligor has no cause to complain.

Some rights, however, *cannot* be assigned without the obligor's consent. Following are the most common of these situations:

1. The terms of the contract expressly prohibit assignment by one or both parties. (Such clauses are narrowly construed, however, often being interpreted to impose a duty on the assignor not to assign, but not to render invalid an assignment that does occur.)

2. The contract is "personal" in nature; specifically, the right in question involves a substantial *personal relationship* between the original parties to the

---

contract. If X, for example, agrees to be Y's secretary for one year, any assignment by Y of the right to X's services would be invalid unless X consented to it. In fact, many (perhaps most) employment contracts fall within this category.

3. The assignment would materially alter the duties of the obligor. For example: S, of Columbus, Ohio, agrees to sell certain goods to B, also of Columbus, with the contract providing that "S will deliver the goods to the buyer's place of business." If B assigned this contract to the X Company of Cheyenne, Wyoming, S's obligation would be drastically increased and he would not be bound by the assignment unless he consented to it.

Additionally, the assignment of some rights is prohibited by statute. For example, a federal law (31 U.S.C.A. §203) generally prohibits the assignment of claims against the federal government, and some state statutes prohibit the assignment of future wages by wage earners. When the assignment of rights is prohibited by statute, such rights cannot be assigned even with the obligor's consent.

The following case poses a question of assignability in a modern business setting.

SCHUPACH V. MCDONALD'S SYSTEM, INC.

Supreme Court of Nebraska, 264 N.W.2d 827 (1978)

McDonald's, defendant, is the corporation that grants all McDonald's fast food restaurant franchises. In 1959 defendant granted a franchise to a Mr. Copeland, giving him the right to own and operate McDonald's first store in the Omaha-Council Bluffs area. A few days later, in conformity with the negotiations leading up to the granting of the franchise, McDonald's sent a letter to Copeland giving him a "Right of First Refusal"—the right to be given first chance at owning any new stores that might subsequently be established in the area. In the next few years Copeland exercised this right and opened five additional stores in Omaha. In 1964 Copeland sold and assigned all of his franchises to Schupach, plaintiff, with McDonald's consent.

When McDonald's granted a franchise in the Omaha-Council Bluffs area in 1974 to a third party without first offering it to Schupach, he brought this action for damages resulting from establishment of the new franchise, claiming that the assignment of the franchises to him also included the right of first refusal.

A number of issues were raised in this litigation. Defendant contended, among other things, that the right it gave to Copeland was personal in nature, and thus was not transferable without its consent. Plaintiff alleged, on the other hand, that the right was not personal in nature, or, in the alternative, that its transfer was, in fact, agreed to by defendant.

On these issues the trial court ruled that the right was personal in nature. It also ruled, however, after analyzing voluminous correspondence between the parties, that defendant had consented to the transfer. It entered judgment for plaintiff, and defendant appealed. (Only that part of the higher court's opinion relating to these two issues appears below.)

White, Justice:

. . . McDonald's was founded in 1954 by Mr. Ray Kroc. Kroc licensed and later purchased the name of McDonald's [and all other rights relating thereto] from two brothers named McDonald, who were operating a hamburger restaurant in San Bernardino, California. In 1955 Kroc embarked on a plan to create a nationwide standardized system of fast-food restaurants. . . .

At the trial, Kroc testified about the image he sought to create with McDonald's. . . . He wanted to create "an image people would have confidence in. An image of cleanliness. An image where the parents would be glad to have the children come and/or have them work there."

Kroc testified that careful selection of franchisees was to be the key to success for McDonald's and the establishment of this image. . . . People were selected "who had a great deal of pride, and had an aptitude for serving the public, and had dedication."

Fred Turner, the current president of McDonald's, testified [in a similar vein]. . . . He stated that by 1957 it became apparent that McDonald's could only achieve its goal by careful selection of persons who would adhere to the company's high standards. He stated that an individual's managerial skills and abilities were a matter of prime importance in the selection process. . . .

Summarizing, the evidence is overwhelming, [and establishes the conclusion that] the Right of First Refusal was intended to be personal in nature, and was separately a grant independent of the terms of the franchise contract itself. [It also establishes the fact that] the grant depended upon the

(continues)

SCHUPACH V. MCDONALD'S SYSTEM, INC.

(continued from previous page)
personal confidence that McDonald's placed in the grantee, and that to permit the assignability by the grantee without permission of McDonald's would serve to destroy the basic policy of control of the quality and confidence in performance in the event any new franchises were to be granted in the locality. . . .

[The court then reviewed the same correspondence which was examined by the trial court, and ruled that McDonald's had *not* given its permission to the transfer of the right. The judgment for plaintiff was therefore reversed.] ☙

Form of the Assignment

As a general rule, no particular formalities need be observed in order for an assignment to be legally effective. Any words or conduct that indicate an intention on the part of the assignor to transfer his or her contractual rights are normally sufficient. Some assignments, however, are required by statute to be in writing. Thus the assignment of a contract that falls within the statute of frauds must be evidenced by a writing; similarly, under the statutes of most states, the assignment of one's rights to collect wages from an employer must also be in writing.

Absence of Consideration

Once a valid assignment has occurred, the assignee is entitled to enforce the contract against the obligor even if the assignee did not give consideration for the assignment to the assignor. The absence of consideration on the part of the assignee does have one significant effect, however; the assignor in such a case has the right to *rescind the assignment* at any time before the contract has been performed by the obligor, without liability to the assignee. (It is assumed here that the assignment was not meant to be a *gift.* If it were, rescission of the assignment would not, of course, be permitted.)

Notice of Assignment

A valid assignment takes effect the moment it is made, regardless of whether the obligor is aware that the assignment has occurred. However, the assignee should give *immediate notice* to the obligor whenever an assignment is made, in order to protect the rights received under it.

A primary reason for giving notice is that an obligor who does not have notice of an assignment is free to go ahead and render performance to the assignor, thereby discharging his or her contractual duties. Suppose, for example, that X is owed $500 by Y and that X assigns the right to collect the debt to Z. If Y, not knowing of the assignment, pays the debt to X (assignor), Z has lost her right to collect the indebtedness from Y. Any other result would be patently unfair to Y. Z's only redress in such a case is to recover payment from X, who clearly has no right to retain the money. On the other hand, if Y did pay the $500 to X *after* being informed of the assignment, Z could still collect from Y.

Notice of assignment can also be important in a case where successive assignments occur. To illustrate: R owes money to S. S assigns his right to collect the debt to A on June 10, then assigns the same right to B on June 15, B not knowing of the prior assignment. Suppose that the first assignee, A, does not give notice of assignment to R until June 25, while the second assignee, B, gives notice on June 20. In such a situation, a number of courts—though not a majority—would rule that B is entitled to payment of the debt, rather than A; in other words, the assignee who first gives notice prevails. (In states adopting this minority view, A's only redress is to recover the consideration, if any, that he gave to S in exchange for the assignment.) The majority view is that A, the first assignee, collects, even if he did not give notice first.

Sales Contracts

The Uniform Commercial Code's provisions on assignments, primarily Sec. 2-210, are generally similar to the common-law rules discussed above, rendering ineffective only assignments that would (1) materially change the obligor's duties; (2) increase materially the burden or risk imposed on the obligor by contract, or (3) impair materially the obligor's chance of obtaining return performance. The Code is perhaps even more "pro-assignment" than the common law. For example, it contains numerous restrictions on anti-assignment clauses that are not present in the common law.

Most important, perhaps, several types of assignments come within the scope of Article 9's provisions relating to secured transactions. These rules are discussed in some detail in Chapter 29 and will not be repeated here. However, we emphasize that Article 9 does alter several of the common law's rules on assignments where secured transactions occur. For example, it may give priority to a second assignee over a first assignee if the second assignee was the first to file a proper financing statement covering the assignment (UCC 9-312(5)).

DELEGATION OF DUTIES

Our discussion so far has been directed to those cases in which contractual rights alone have been transferred, or assigned—in other words, to those common situations in which it is reasonably clear that the parties understood that the assignor alone would be the party who would perform the contract, as he or she originally contracted to do. In many circumstances, however, a **delegation of duties**—the transfer of one party's contractual duties to another—*is* intended as part of the assignment of rights, and in other circumstances a delegation of duties may occur without an assignment of rights. We will briefly examine these situations.

Delegation in Conjunction with an Assignment
If an assignment occurs in which the assigning party also delegates his or her contractual duties to the assignee, that party is the **delegator** (or assignor-delegator), and the party to whom the duties are transferred is the **delegatee** (or assignee-delegatee). The remaining party—the party to the original contract to whom the performance is owed—is the **obligee.** When a delegation occurs in conjunction with an assignment, the delegatee usually (but not necessarily) expressly or impliedly promises that he or she will perform the delegator's duties under the contract. Assuming such a promise, the relationships are diagrammed in Figure 17.2.[7]

Obligations of the Parties
Where a delegation occurs, and where the delegatee expressly or impliedly promises to perform the delegator's duties, the delegatee assumes the primary responsibility for performance of those duties. The delegator, however, remains secondarily liable for performance of those duties. To illustrate: X contracts to put in a driveway for Y, and X then delegates the duty to Z. If Z fails to do the job, X must either perform the job or be liable to Y, the obligee, for damages for breach of contract. Thus,

[7]This discussion is based upon the assumption of a valid delegation—i.e., one in which the obligee has consented to the delegation, or in which the duty is of such nature that it can be delegated without the obligee's consent. (Non-delegable duties—those that cannot be assigned without the obligee's consent—will be examined later.)

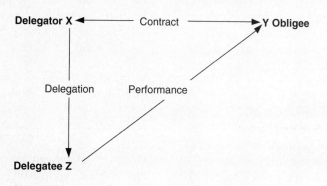

FIGURE 17.2

Delegation of Duties

where the contract is never performed, the obligee has causes of action against both the delegatee and delegator. In other words, a delegation of duties—even when consented to by the obligee—does not in and of itself free the delegator of liability. (Thus, although a delegation is generally defined as a "transfer" of duties, this term is not entirely accurate in view of the retention of secondary liability by the delegator.)

The above discussion has assumed that the delegatee has promised, expressly or by clear implication, to perform the delegator's duties. In some situations, however, it is unclear whether the delegatee has made an implied promise to perform. Going back to the driveway illustration, for example, the assignment document might state that X hereby assigns to Z "all of my rights and obligations under my contract with Y," or it may simply say that X hereby assigns to Z the "entire contract" that he (X) has with Y. In either case, if Z accepts the assignment of rights but neither expressly promises to perform the contract nor commences performance, is he or she liable to Y if the driveway is never built? While there is disagreement on this point, the trend among the courts of most states *is* to find an implied assumption of duties by Z in both cases—with Z thus incurring liability in case he or she fails to perform.

Novation

As noted in the previous section, in the typical delegation, the delegator is secondarily liable on the contract if the delegatee assumes the duty but does not perform. An exception arises where the obligee agrees to substitute the delegatee for the delegator and to look no further to the delegator for performance in exchange for the delegatee's assumption of the duty. Such a consensual substitution of parties is called a **novation.** Mere approval by the obligee of a delegation does not constitute a novation, absent approval of the complete substitution of the delegatee for the delegator. The novation is discussed further in the next chapter.

Delegation in Absence of Assignment—Subcontracts

A delegation of duties may be made without an assignment of the delegator's rights under his or her contract with the obligee. In such cases, where the delegatee by contract promises to perform the delegator's duties, the general rule is that the delegatee's

only obligation is to the delegator. In the "real world" a delegation of duties in the absence of an assignment most often involves a partial delegation of duties. To illustrate: X, a builder, contracts to build a home for Y for $92,000. X then subcontracts the electrical work to the Z Company, an electrical firm. If the Z Company fails to do the work, or does it in an unacceptable manner, it is liable to X but not to Y. (Similarly, it should be noted in passing that if the Z Company *does* perform, it may look only to X, the delegator, for payment. In other words, in the usual situation, the subcontractor is neither an intended beneficiary nor an assignee of the contract between the prime contractor-delegator and the obligee.)

What Duties Are Delegable?

In exceptional circumstances the obligee, upon learning of the delegation, will notify the parties that he or she will not accept performance by the delegatee. The general rule applicable to such a controversy is that any contractual duty may be delegated without the obligee's consent except (1) duties arising out of contracts which expressly prohibit delegation, and (2) contracts in which the obligee has a "substantial interest" in having the obligor-delegator perform personally.

Under the latter rule, contracts calling for the performance of *personal services*—such as those of a teacher, physician, or lawyer—are clearly nondelegable without the obligee's consent (even if the delegatee is as professionally competent as the delegator). Most other contracts call for the performance of duties that are described as essentially *routine* in nature, such as the repair of a building, the sale of goods, or the overhaul of machinery, and these duties are generally held to be delegable. (This result is not as unfair to the objecting obligee as it might appear, because, as we noted earlier, he or she may hold the delegator liable if the delegatee's performance is defective.)

The UCC's rules on delegation are virtually identical to those of the common law.

SUMMARY

While contracts can normally be enforced only by the original contracting parties, some persons—called third parties—can enforce contracts made by others in certain circumstances. The major classes of third parties possessing this ability are beneficiaries and assignees. There are three types of beneficiaries: creditor, donee, and incidental beneficiaries. A creditor beneficiary is a third party to whom one of the contracting parties owes a debt, and who is to receive performance from the other contracting party as a means of extinguishing the debt. A donee beneficiary is a third party who, under the contract, is to receive performance from one of the contracting parties as a gift from the other contracting party. Creditor and donee beneficiaries are permitted to enforce the contracts because in both instances the contracts in question were made primarily for their benefit, i.e., the contracting parties had such beneficiaries in mind as persons who were to receive performance. By contrast, the incidental beneficiary is a person who might have some interest in seeing that the contract be performed, but was *not* a person for whose benefit the contract was made. Accordingly, incidental beneficiaries cannot enforce contracts made by others.

Assignees are persons to whom contractual rights have been assigned after the contract was entered into. As a general rule, one party to a contract may assign his or her rights under the contract without the consent of the other party, the "obligor." (There are, however, limited situations in which the obligor's consent is required.) Once an assignment has occurred, the assignee stands in the same position as the assignor; that is, if the assignor could have enforced the right against the obligor, the assignee has the same power. On the other hand, if the obligor had a valid defense against the assignor (such as breach of contract), the obligor can assert the same defense against the assignee.

In some situations a party to a contract may delegate his duties under the contract to a third party. (In such case, the person transferring his or her duties is the "delegator," the other party to the contract is the "obligee," and the person to whom the duties have been delegated is the "delegatee.") Delegation of duties requires consent of the obligee if the contract was made primarily upon the personal qualities or skill of the delegator, but consent is not required if the performance owed by the delegator to the obligee is "routine in nature." In any event, once a valid delegation occurs the delegator remains secondarily liable to the obligee in the event the delegatee fails to perform the contract (unless the obligee has expressly released the delegator).

KEY TERMS

Third party
Creditor beneficiary
Donee beneficiary
Incidental beneficiary
Assignor
Assignee
Obligor
Delegation of duties
Delegator
Delegatee
Obligee
Novation

QUESTIONS AND PROBLEMS

1. An agency of the State of Washington operated a ferry system providing service between the mainland and offshore islands. The ferry employees were unionized, and they worked under a contract between the union and the state. Just before a Labor Day weekend the union called a strike, which was a breach of its contract. As a result, tourist travel to the islands was substantially cut, and resort owners located on the islands sued the union to recover damages for breach of contract. Should they be able to recover on the theory they were donee beneficiaries? Why or why not? (*Burke and Thomas v. International Organization of Masters,* 585 P.2d 152, 1978.)

2. Rudolph bought a home from Ahlstrom. As a condition of the sale, Ahlstrom agreed to provide Rudolph with a written termite inspection report on the house. He hired ABC Pest Control which, after inspection, furnished Rudolph with a copy of its report which stated that there was no active infestation. Rudolph then bought the house, but less than a year later found a severe and active termite infestation that ABC had overlooked. Rudolph sued ABC for breach of contract. ABC defended by pointing out that it was hired by Ahlstrom and that Rudolph was not a party to the contract. Is this a good defense? (*Rudolph v. ABC Pest Control, Inc.,* 763 S.W.2d 930, Tex. App. 1989.)

3. A labor union entered into a collective bargaining agreement with the Powder Power Tool Corporation, under which the company agreed to pay specified wages to various classes of its employees. When Springer, an employee and union member,

was not paid the full wages to which he was entitled under the agreement, he brought action to recover the additional payments as specified. The company defended on the ground that Springer was not a party to the contract and thus could not maintain the action. Is the company correct? Explain. (*Springer v. Powder Power Tool Co.*, 348 P.2d 1112, 1960.)

4. A (franchisor) agreed to establish B (franchisee) as the holder of a Dairy Queen franchise. The agreement between the two prohibited B from assigning the franchise to a third party without A's permission. Later, B sought to make such an assignment without A's permission. A objected, claiming, in part, that the $90,000 price the third party had agreed to pay was too high and that inflated prices were bad for the business. Also, it appeared that the third party was young and inexperienced in business. The trial court held that the anti-assignment clause violated public policy and refused to give it effect. Did the trial judge rule correctly? (*Hanigan v. Wheeler*, 504 P.2d 972, Ariz.App. 1972.)

5. Abramov, when leaving the employment of a partnership, signed a contract promising not to compete with the partnership for five years. Soon thereafter the partnership incorporated. Abramov later started a business in competition with the corporation, whereupon it brought action for an injunction ordering him to live up to the terms of the contract not to compete. The issue was whether the contract could be assigned by the partnership to the corporation without Abramov's consent. Decide, with reasons. (*Abramov v. Royal Dallas, Inc.*, 536 S.W.2d 388, 1976.)

6. Cullins worked for an insurance agency under an employment contract that prevented him from competing with that agency for a period of three years after leaving its employment. Later, another company, Smith, Bell and Hauck, Inc., purchased the insurance agency. When Cullins quit the agency and formed a new insurance firm, Smith, Bell and Hauck brought an action for an injunction ordering Cullins to live up to his contract not to compete. When Cullins defended on the ground that Smith, Bell and Hauck were not parties to the contract, they contended that an implied assignment of the contract from the insurance agency had taken place and, as assignees, they were entitled to enforce that

contract. Is this a good argument? Discuss. (*Smith, Bell and Hauck, Inc., v. Cullins*, 183 A.2d 528, 1962.)

7. Nexxus Products manufactures hair care products. After some negotiation with Mr. Reicheck, it contracted to have Reicheck's Best Barber & Beauty Supply Co. (Best) become the exclusive distributor of Nexxus hair care products throughout most of Texas. However, two years later, Sally Beauty Company bought all the stock of Best and merged Best into Sally Beauty, acquiring all Best's contracts. Because Sally Beauty was a wholly owned subsidiary of Alberto-Culver Co., one of Nexxus's major competitors in the national hair care products business, Nexxus cancelled the contract. Sally Beauty sued for breach of contract. The trial court held that because the contract was non-assignable, Nexxus had not acted improperly. Did the trial judge rule correctly? (*Sally Beauty Co. v. Nexxus Products Co., Inc.*, 801 F.2d 1001, 7th Cir. 1986.)

8. Coburn, a contractor, was building structures for the City of Boston, and was to be paid according to a certain schedule as jobs were completed. Coburn assigned his right to receive two payments under the contract to P. At the time of the assignment and notice to the City of the assignment, there were no complications. However, thereafter, Coburn defaulted on his contract with the City. The City refused to pay P, who sued. The City sought to raise Coburn's default as a defense against P's suit. Will the City succeed? (*American Bridge Co. v. Boston*, 88 N.E. 1089, Mass. 1909.)

9. Folquet was employed as a school bus driver by the Woodburn Public School District for a contract period of five years at a salary of $125 per school month. The contract required Folquet to furnish and maintain a bus at his own expense, to conduct himself in a proper and moral manner, and to be responsible for the conduct of the pupils while in the bus. Folquet died before the five years elapsed, and his son, an adult, was appointed administrator of his estate. When the son offered to drive the bus for the remainder of the contract, the district refused to let him do so. The son then brought suit to recover damages for breach of contract. The school district contended that the contract was of a personal nature and thus could not be delegated or assigned to any other

driver without its consent. Is the school district's defense valid? Explain. (*Folquet v. Woodburn Public Schools*, 29 P.2d 554, 1934.)

10. A company assigned its accounts receivable to an insurance company and later assigned the same accounts to a bank. The bank gave notice of the assignment to the account debtors before the insurance company did. In subsequent litigation the issue was which of the two assignees was entitled to collect the accounts receivable. (*Boulevard National Bank of Miami v. Air Metals Industries, Inc.*, 176 So.2d 94, 1965.)

a. If the majority rule were applied, who would win?
b. If the minority rule were applied, who would win?

Chapter 18

Discharge of Contracts

Discharge by Operation of Conditions
Discharge by Performance
Discharge by Breach
Discharge by Legal Impossibility
Discharge by Commercial Impracticability
Discharge by Frustration of Purpose
Discharge by Parties' Agreement
Discharge by Operation of Law

SOONER OR LATER all contractual obligations come to an end. When this occurs in a particular case, the contract is said to be *discharged*. What is meant by this is that the *duties* of the contracting parties have been discharged.

There are many ways in which a discharge, or termination, can come about. Most of these result from the conduct of the parties themselves, while others involve events completely outside the control of either party. One leading treatise on contract law recognizes at least twenty separate and distinct ways in which a person's contractual obligations can be discharged.[1] The most important of these are discharge by (1) operation of conditions; (2) performance; (3) breach by the other party; (4) circumstances excusing performance (impossibility, impracticability, and frustration); (5) agreement of the parties; and (6) operation of law.

DISCHARGE BY OPERATION OF CONDITIONS
Conditions, Generally

In many contracts the parties simply exchange mutual promises to perform specified duties, with neither promise being conditioned or qualified in any way. Once such a contract is formed, each party is said to have incurred a "duty of immediate performance"—even though the performance of one or both parties may not be due until some specified time in the future.

In some situations, however, the performance of the contemplated contract is beneficial to one or both of the parties only if a certain event occurs in the future. And in other situations a contract may be mutually beneficial to the parties when entered into, but would be of little benefit if some event should occur before the stated time of performance arrives.

In these situations the parties can achieve substantial protection by the use of conditions in their contract. The term **condition,** in its broadest sense, can be defined as an express or implied provision in a contract which, upon the occurrence or nonoccurrence of a specified event, either creates, suspends, or terminates the rights and duties of the contracting parties. (While this definition refers to a provision or clause in a contract creating the condition, the terms may also be used to refer to the event itself that is designated in such provision.)

The law recognizes three kinds of conditions—*conditions precedent, conditions subsequent,* and *conditions concurrent.* Each type of condition can be further classified as *express* or *implied.* (Our discussion initially will focus on the nature of express conditions, with consideration of implied conditions precedent and implied conditions subsequent being delayed until we reach the subjects of performance and impossibility, respectively.)

Conditions Precedent

A **condition precedent** is a clause in a contract which indicates that the promises made therein are not to be operative until a specified event occurs. For example, X makes this offer to Y: "If the city rezones your property at 540 Fox Lane from C-3 to C-1 within thirty days, I will pay you $18,000 cash for it." Y accepts the offer. While a contract has now been formed, it is clear that the specified event must occur before either party incurs "a duty of immediate performance." The act of rezoning, therefore, is a condition precedent. And, because the condition resulted from the language of the contract, rather than by implication, the rezoning constitutes an *express* condition precedent.[2]

Discharge by Failure (or Nonoccurrence) of a Condition Precedent

Where a contract clearly creates a condition precedent, no "duty of immediate performance" arises until the specified event occurs. In the above case, then, should the rezoning not occur within the specified time, the condition is said to have "failed" and both parties are accordingly discharged of their obligations. In other words, the parties' duties under the contract are terminated.

---

[1]*Restatement, Contracts 2d,* The American Law Institute, 1979.

[2]Conditions precedent can usually be identified by clauses containing the words *if, in the event,* or *when.* Thus the following language creates a condition precedent: "If X is able to obtain a building permit from the city within sixty days" (or "In the event X is able to obtain a building permit . . ."), "it is agreed that Y will construct a swimming pool for her, according to the attached specifications, for $9,000."

Conditions Subsequent

Occasionally both parties to a contract are willing to incur a duty of immediate performance, but want to be freed of their obligations if a particular circumstance arises before the performance date. The parties can achieve this protection by use of an express **condition subsequent**—a clause in a contract providing that upon the happening of a specified event, the contract shall be inoperative (or void).[3] True conditions subsequent are rare, but consider this example: An insurance policy states "If written notice is given to the Company of Mr. A's death within 30 days of its occurrence, the Company will pay $100,000 to the beneficiaries. If the Company refuses to pay, and the beneficiaries do not file suit within one year of the death, any obligation of the Company under this contract shall be discharged."

Discharge by Occurrence of Condition Subsequent

In the above example, the death and the giving of written notice are conditions precedent which give

[3] Thus the essential difference in legal effect between the two basic kinds of conditions is that the occurrence of a condition precedent *imposes* a duty of immediate performance, while the occurrence of a condition subsequent *removes* such a duty.

rise to the Company's duty of immediate performance. However, that duty may be extinguished by the occurrence of a condition subsequent—the failure to file suit within one year. Conditions precedent are contrasted to conditions subsequent in Figure 18.1.

Most conditions subsequent (as is true of conditions generally) are express rather than implied. They can ordinarily be recognized by language providing that the contract is to be void, inoperative, or canceled if a certain event occurs in the future. (The relatively few situations in which implied conditions subsequent exist will be discussed later in the chapter.)

Conditions Concurrent

Conditions concurrent exist when a contract expressly provides (or if one can reasonably infer from its terms) that the performances of the parties are to occur at the same time. A common example is a land sale contract which provides that the seller is to deliver the deed on payment of the purchase price. The duty of each party is thus conditioned on performance by the other. The seller has no duty to deliver the deed until the buyer pays (or tenders) the

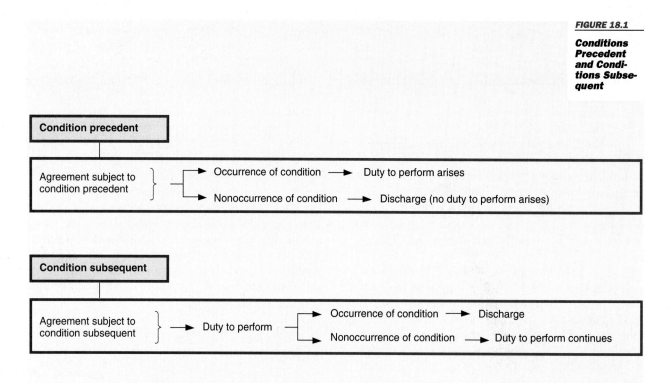

FIGURE 18.1

Conditions Precedent and Conditions Subsequent

purchase price, and the buyer has no duty to pay until the seller delivers (or tenders) the deed.[4]

The legal consequences that result from the use of express conditions precedent and subsequent are clear, once either condition is proven to exist. It is, however, often a more difficult question whether the parties conditioned their obligations at all, and, if so, whether the condition in the particular case fell in the precedent or subsequent category. The following case highlights the impact that such a determination might have on the outcome of a particular controversy.

[4]A tender is an *offer* to perform one's obligation.

RINCONES V. WINDBERG

Court of Appeals of Texas, Austin, 705 S.W.2d 846 (1986)

Rincones and Mena, plaintiffs, entered into a contract with Windberg, defendant, under which they were to "compile, research and edit material for academic and student services for a migrant program handbook." The contract was termed a "Consultant Agreement," and under it each plaintiff was to write specified chapters, for which Windberg would pay each $1,250 per chapter for their respective chapters.

The handbook was ultimately to be used by California authorities, and the parties were aware that the funds to pay plaintiffs would ultimately come from the State of California. The consultant agreement, however, made no mention of Windberg's obligation to pay being contingent upon his receipt of funding by California. Plaintiffs submitted the drafts of their respective chapters to Windberg, but he refused to pay for them because "the publication was not accepted by California," and no funding from that state, therefore, was available for the project.

Plaintiffs then brought this action to recover the monies promised them. The primary question was whether Windberg's receipt of funding from California was a condition precedent to his obligations under the contract, as Windberg contended. The trial court found (1) that the contract was partly written and partly oral; (2) that, under the oral agreement and the circumstances surrounding it, the parties had agreed that the contract was contingent upon California's funding of the project; and (3) that California refused to fund the project. The court concluded that a "condition precedent" existed; that proof of the condition was not barred by the parol evidence rule; that the condition precedent had not been met; that the contract was of no further force and effect, and that Windberg thus had no liability under it.[a] The plaintiffs appealed.

Shannon, Chief Justice:

. . . The meaning of "condition precedent" in Texas jurisprudence is less than clear. For purposes of the parol evidence rule, however, we think that the definition from [a previous case] correctly states that a condition precedent is a condition "which postpones the effective date of the instrument until the happening of a contingency." . . . By way of contrast, a condition subsequent "is a condition referring to a future event, upon the happening of which the obligation no longer becomes binding upon the other party, if he chooses to avail himself of the condition." *Id.* [The court here noted that parol evidence of a condition precedent is admissible to vary or contradict

[a]As was noted in Chapter 16, parol evidence showing a condition precedent is admissible under one of the exceptions to the parol evidence rule.

a written contract, while parol evidence of a condition subsequent is not admissible.]

We now examine the record in an effort to determine whether the evidence supports the court's conclusion that funding from California was a condition precedent to the contract, or whether, to the contrary, the evidence shows an already effective and binding contract subject to a condition subsequent. The admissibility of the parol evidence turns on whether the contract was binding and effective from its inception, or whether it would become binding and effective only upon the occurrence of the contingency.

The evidence shows that all parties devoted substantial amounts of time and money attempting to perform their obligations under the Consultant Agreement. Appellants (plaintiffs) prepared and submitted a first draft of their manuscript, which Hardy [an associate of Windberg] took to California for revisions and recommendations. Thereafter, appellants worked on revisions and submitted a second draft for approval. Hardy, meanwhile, made several trips to California and spent $4,000 of her own money attempting to gain approval and receive funding from the state. All parties initially thought approval and funding for the project was certain, and performed under the contract accordingly. Only after several months had passed did they learn that political changes in California had placed their funding in jeopardy.

(continues)

RINCONES V. WINDBERG

(continued from previous page)

In our opinion the evidence shows that the parties understood that they had a binding and effective contract, and performed accordingly. The evidence is not [consistent] with a determination that the parties had agreed to postpone the effective date of the contract until the condition, funding from California, occurred. . . . [We conclude] that the parol payment condition [is a condition subsequent rather than a condition precedent]. As such, it is inconsistent with the terms of the written contract and is therefore inadmissible under the parol evidence rule. . . .

The judgment is reversed and the case is remanded to the trial court for new trial consistent with this opinion.∞

DISCHARGE BY PERFORMANCE

Most contracts are discharged by performance—by each party completely fulfilling his or her promises. In such cases, obviously, no legal problems exist. Nevertheless, the subject of performance merits special attention for several reasons.

In the first place, many cases arise in which the actual performance of a promisor is, to some extent, defective. Sometimes the performance falls far short of what was promised; other times it deviates from the terms of the contract in only minor respects. As one might expect, the legal consequences of a major breach of contract are more severe and far-reaching than those resulting from a minor breach.

Second, in some cases the courts must determine whether the defective performance constituted a breach of a condition or a mere breach of a promise. A breach of a condition, no matter how slight, usually frees the nondefaulting party, while a breach of a promise generally does not unless it is a material one.

Promises: Degree of Performance Required

Many agreements consist simply of the exchange of mutual promises, with neither party's obligations expressly conditioned in any way. In most of these contracts, however, it is usually apparent from their nature that one of the parties is to perform his or her part of the bargain before the other is obligated to do so. For example: If X contracts to landscape Y's new home for $1,500, it can reasonably be inferred that the work is to be done by X before he can demand payment of Y.[5] Thus, in general, when a promisor seeks to recover the contract price, that person must show that he or she has *fully performed* the promise in some cases or *substantially performed it* in others—depending on the nature of the obligation involved. If it is determined that this performance has met the applicable minimum standard, the promisor is entitled to recover the contract price minus damages (if any) suffered by the promisee. However, if the performance falls short of this minimum, the promisor's obligation has not been discharged, and he or she will recover little or nothing. (The rules determining the extent of recovery in each of these situations will be discussed immediately after the next case in the chapter.)

Total Performance

Some promises are of such a nature that they can be discharged only by complete performance. If a promisor's performance falls short of that called for under such a contract, even though the breach is minor, his or her obligation is not discharged. Suppose, for example, that B contracts in May to buy a car from S for $2,000—the contract providing that the price is to be paid in full by B on June 1, at which time S is to assign the car title to her. If, on June 1, B tenders S a check for $1,950, S has no obligation to transfer the title. A contract under which a seller of land is obligated to convey "merchantable title" falls into the same category; delivery of a deed conveying any interest or title less than that specified will not discharge the seller's obligation.

Substantial Performance

Many obligations are of such a nature that it is unlikely (indeed, not even to be expected, given the frailties of mankind) that a 100 percent performance will actually occur. The typical example involves a construction contract under which a builder agrees

---

[5]In this regard, it is sometimes said that the actual performance of one's promises constitutes an *implied* condition precedent that must be met by that person.

to build a home according to detailed plans and specifications. It is quite possible that the finished building will deviate from the specifications in one or more respects no matter how conscientious and able the builder is. In contracts of this sort, if the promisee-owner seeks to escape liability on the ground of nonperformance of the promisor-builder, it is ordinarily held that the promisor has sufficiently fulfilled the obligation if his or her performance, though imperfect, conformed to the terms of the contract in all major respects. This rule is known as the doctrine of **substantial performance.**

In order for the doctrine to be applicable, two requirements must ordinarily be met:

1. Performance must be "substantial"—that is, the omissions and deviations must be so slight in nature that they do not materially affect the usefulness of the building for the purposes for which it was intended.

2. The omissions or deviations must not have been occasioned by bad faith on the part of the builder. (This is ordinarily interpreted to mean that the omissions or deviations must not have been made knowingly by the builder.)

Using the illustration involving the construction of a house, let us examine three cases where the builder is bringing suit against the owner to recover the last payment of $5,000 called for under the contract and where the owner is refusing to pay on the ground of inadequate performance.

1. The owner proves that the following defects exist: (a) the plaster in all rooms is considerably softer than expected, because the builder used one bag of adamant for each hod of mortar instead of the two bags called for by the contract, and (b) water seepage in the basement is so great as to make the game room

virtually unusable, as a result of the builder's failure to put a required sealant on the exterior of the basement walls. Here the defects are so material, and so affect the enjoyment and value of the home, that the builder has *not substantially performed* his obligations. Thus recovery will be denied, even if the breaches on the part of the builder are shown to be accidental rather than intentional.

2. The owner proves that the following defects exist: (a) the detached garage was given but one coat of paint rather than the two required; (b) the water pipes in the walls were made by the Cohoes Company rather than the Reading Company as was specified (though otherwise the two types of pipe are virtually identical); and (c) the wallboard installed in the attic is ⅛ inch sheeting instead of the ¼ inch that was called for. Here the defects are so slight in nature, even when taken in total, that the builder has substantially performed the contract and can thus probably recover under the doctrine.

3. Same facts as case 2, but, in addition, the owner can show that one or more of the deviations were *intentional;* for example, he produces evidence tending to prove that the builder ordered the installation of the substitute pipe and wallboard knowing that they were not in conformity with the contract. Here the deviations are willful (rather than the result of simple negligence); therefore the builder is guilty of bad faith and the doctrine is not applicable.

Obviously, the requirement that performance be "substantial" is a somewhat elastic one, and necessitates a comparison of the promisor's actual performance with that which the terms of the contract really required of him. The following case is typical of those presenting substantial performance problems.

LANE WILSON COMPANY, INC., v. GREGORY

Court of Appeal of Louisiana, Second Circuit, 322 So.2d 369 (1975)

Case

Lane Wilson Company, plaintiff, contracted to build a swimming pool for Gregory, defendant, at Gregory's KOA Campground outside Monroe, Louisiana, for $12,000. Under the written agreement, the

pool was to be thirty by sixty feet, with a depth varying from three feet to six feet. Later the parties orally modified their contract by agreeing that plaintiff would add a diving board and increase the depth of the pool to accommodate persons using the diving board. It was also orally

agreed that a walkway around the pool would be enlarged and a longer fence built than was originally contemplated. The cost of these modifications raised the contract price to $13,643.

During construction, defendant paid $8,400 on the contract. After the
(continues)

(handwritten: question to substantial performance and done in bad faith)

LANE WILSON COMPANY, INC. v. GREGORY

(continued from previous page)
job was completed, however, he refused to pay the balance due because of various defects in the pool's construction (the most important of which are described in the appellate court's decision following). Plaintiff then brought this action to recover the balance allegedly due. The trial court held that plaintiff had substantially performed the contract, and that plaintiff was thus entitled to the balance of the contract price minus a credit of $300 to remedy one of the defects (the installation of a chlorinator). Defendant appealed.

Burgess, Judge:

. . . Defendant alleged [in his answer] that plaintiff had not constructed the pool according to the terms of the contract. . . . This appeal presents two issues. First, has plaintiff substantially performed the contract, thereby enabling him to recover the balance due on the contract price? Second, if plaintiff has substantially performed, are there any defects in the construction which entitle defendant to damages in an amount sufficient to remedy the faulty performance?

In *Airco Refrigeration Service, Inc., v. Fink,* 134 So.2d 880 (1961), the supreme court considered . . . the meaning of "substantial performance." The court stated:

The principal question presented in this case is whether or not there has been substantial performance so as to permit recovery on the contract. This is a question of fact. Among the factors to be considered are the extent of the defect or non-performance; the degree to which the purpose of the contract is defeated; the ease of correction, and the use or benefit to the defendant of the work performed.

In light of the factors enumerated above, we cannot say the trial court was manifestly erroneous in finding that plaintiff substantially performed the contract. Defendant contracted for a 30 by 60 foot swimming pool deep enough to accommodate persons using a diving board. The defects alleged by defendant are not such that defeat the purpose of the contract or prevent defendant from using the pool. In addition, the defects for which plaintiff may be held accountable are easily remedied.

[The court here examined all of the defects in the job in order to determine whether or not plaintiff had substantially performed the contract. The most important of these defects were described as follows:]

(a) Rather than measuring 30 by 60 feet as called for by the contract, the pool's measurements fluctuate from 59 feet six inches to 59 feet three and one half inches in length, and from 29 feet one-half inch to 29 feet three and one-half inches in width.

(b) The walls of the pool are not vertical, but slope severely to form a bowl-shaped pool.

(c) Plaintiff installed only six water inlets as opposed to twelve water inlets called for by the contract; this deficiency coupled with the poor placement of the inlets results in insufficient water circulation in the pool.

(d) The pool is not ten feet deep as the parties allegedly agreed.

[The court here expressed its opinion as to the materiality of these defects as follows:]

(a) In the instant case we find the deviations in dimensions, which could be discovered only by measuring the pool, *in no way defeat the purpose of the contract.* [Emphasis added.] Plaintiff also testified the method of constructing the pool made it impossible to achieve perfect compliance with the exact measurements called for by the contract. Therefore, under the authority of [earlier cases in this state], we find the slight deviation in measurements did not constitute a breach of the contract.

(b) Defendant made no complaint about the shape of the pool walls until after suit was filed. The defect, if it be one at all, was apparent and defendant is held to have accepted same since he made no objection to the walls until suit was filed.

(c) The number of water inlets was changed at the suggestion of the supplier of the equipment because twelve water inlets would have lowered the water pressure and caused improper circulation in the pool. Defendant agreed to the change in plumbing and cannot now claim that change as a defect.

(d) Defendant failed to prove that the parties agreed to a ten-foot depth for the pool. We find the pool, as constructed, is deep enough to accommodate a diving board and, therefore, there is no defect in regard to the depth of the pool.

[On the basis of this analysis, the court agreed with the trial court that plaintiff had substantially performed the contract. The court then turned to the question of defendant's damages. On this point the court ruled that, in addition to the $300 damages (credit) allowed by the trial court, additional damages should have been allowed to compensate defendant for his removal of incorrect depth markers and the installation of new markers; for his removal of waste cement and cement forms; and to compensate defendant for 200 feet of pipe owned by him that plaintiff used in building the pool. The court summarized these adjustments as follows:]

Totalling the amounts listed above, we find defendant is entitled to $331.02 as damages to correct defects in plaintiff's performance, in addition to the $300 allowed by the trial court for the cost of an additional chlorinator which plaintiff admitted the pool needed.

For the reasons assigned the judgment in favor of plaintiff is amended to reduce the award from $4,943.36 to the sum of $4,612.34, and as amended is affirmed.

Substantial Performance—Amount of Recovery

As noted earlier, if the rule of substantial performance is applicable to a particular case, the promisor-plaintiff is entitled to recover *the contract price minus damages* (that is, the promisor may recover the amount that the promisee agreed to pay under the contract, minus damages—if any—which the promisee sustained as a result of the deviations). Since the damages are typically inconsequential, the promisor usually recovers a high percentage of the contract price. By contrast, where the doctrine is not applicable, the recovery may be little or nothing. The general rules for such situations can be summarized as follows:

1. Where the performance falls short of being substantial and the breach is intentional, the promisor receives nothing. The rationale, of course, is that an intentional wrongdoer should not be rewarded—particularly where the promisee has not received the performance he or she was entitled to. (The rule of nonrecovery also has an affirmative aspect—it strongly "persuades" the promisor to actually finish the job, since he or she will receive nothing otherwise.)

2. In the somewhat rarer case where the performance is not substantial but the breach is unintentional, recovery is allowed on the basis of quasi-contract. For example, if the promisor is permanently injured when only halfway through the job, he or she is entitled to receive the reasonable value of the benefit received by the promisee as a result of the partial performance.

3. If the performance is clearly substantial but the breach is willful, there are conflicting views. Some courts deny any recovery, regardless of other circumstances, embracing the principle that aid should never be given the intentional wrongdoer. Most courts, while endorsing this principle in the abstract, in practice allow the promisor to recover "the reasonable value of the benefit resulting from the performance, minus damages" (as distinguished from the "contract price, minus damages" recovery allowed in situations where the substantial performance requirements are met). Such a recovery is especially common where a failure to allow the promisor anything would result in the promisee being unjustly enriched—a result most likely to occur in cases where the performance is of such a nature that it cannot be returned by the promisee.

Special Problems Relating to Performance
Personal Satisfaction Contracts

Under the ordinary contract, a person who has undertaken the performance of a job impliedly warrants only that he or she will perform in a "workmanlike manner," i.e., the performance will be free of material defect and of a quality ordinarily accepted in that line of work. If the performance meets this standard, he or she is entitled to recover the contract price even if the person for whom the work was done is not satisfied with it.

Some contracts, however, provide that "satisfaction is guaranteed," or contain other language of similar nature. In such cases, it is usually held that such satisfaction is a condition precedent that must be met in order for the promisor to recover under the contract; workmanlike performance alone will not suffice. In determining whether the condition has been met, the courts distinguish between two kinds of contracts: (1) those in which matters of personal taste, esthetics, or comfort are dominant considerations, and (2) those that entail work of mere "mechanical utility."

For contracts in the first category, the condition is fulfilled only if the *promisee is actually satisfied* with the performance that was rendered—no matter how peculiar or unreasonable that person's tastes may be. For example: X, an artist, contracts to paint a portrait of Y for $500 "that will meet with Y's complete satisfaction." When the portrait is completed, Y refuses to pay on the ground that he simply does not like it. If X brings suit to recover the $500, a question of fact is presented: Is Y's claim of dissatisfaction genuine? If the jury so finds, the condition has not been met and X is denied recovery. (Of course, if the jury finds that Y's claim of dissatisfaction is false—that is, he is actually satisfied and is simply using this claim as a ground to escape an otherwise valid contract—then the condition has been met and recovery is allowed.)

For contracts in the second category, where the performance involves work of mere mechanical fitness (or mechanical utility), an objective test is used. For example: M agrees to overhaul the diesel engine in T's tractor-trailer for $200, guaranteeing that T will be "fully satisfied" with the job. In this case, the condition precedent is met if the jury finds that *a reasonable person would have been satisfied* with M's job, even though T himself is dissatisfied.

Performance by an Agreed Time

If a contract does not provide a time by which performance is to be completed, the general rule is that each party has a reasonable time within which to perform his or her obligations. Whether the performance of a promisor in a given case took place within such a time is ordinarily a question for the jury. In practice this rule poses few problems and seems to produce acceptable results.

A more troublesome situation is presented by contracts that *do* contain a stated time of performance. For example: A printer agrees to print up 15,000 letterheads for a customer, with the contract specifying "delivery by April 10." If delivery is not made until April 14, and the customer refuses to accept the goods because of the late performance, the question for the jury is whether the stated time of performance legally constituted a condition precedent. If it did, the condition has obviously not been met and the customer has no obligation to accept the shipment.

The general rule is that such a provision, of and by itself, *does not create a condition precedent.* Under this view, it is sufficient if the performance occurs within a reasonable time after the date specified. Thus, in the preceding illustration, the customer is very likely obligated to accept the letterheads where delivery was only four days late. The customer may recover any damages caused by the delay in accordance with rules of recovery discussed in the next chapter.

Time-of-the-Essence Clauses.   In some situations, however, the parties clearly intend that performance must actually take place by the specified time in order for the promisor to recover from the other party. In such situations, *performance by the agreed-upon time does constitute a condition precedent.* The intention can be manifested in two ways: (1) by the express wording of the agreement itself and (2) by implication (reasonable inference from the nature and subject matter of the contract alone).[6] Two examples may be helpful.

1. P agrees to print up and deliver 15,000 letterheads to Q by April 10, the contract further providing that *time is of the essence.* By this clause, the parties have made the stated time of performance an express condition precedent. Thus, if P fails to deliver the let-

terheads until April 11, Q can refuse to accept the belated performance. P's failure to meet the condition frees Q of her obligations under the contract. Additionally, Q can recover damages from P in a breach of contract suit. (An alternative open to Q is to accept the late performance and "reserve her rights" against P—in which case she is entitled to an allowance against the purchase price to the extent that she has suffered damages as a result of the late performance.)

2. A chamber of commerce purchases fireworks for a Fourth of July celebration it is sponsoring, with the contract providing that "delivery is to be made prior to July 4th." The fireworks arrive too late on July 4th to be used. From the nature of the *subject matter alone* it can be inferred that the stated time is a condition precedent, and the late delivery obviously did not meet that condition. In such a case it is said that time was made a condition "by operation of law" (that is, without regard to other factors).

The courts are reluctant to rule—from the subject matter of the contract or from the nature of the contract alone—that time is of the essence. Limited instances in which such a ruling *may* be made, however (in addition to the rare case typified in example 2), are option contracts—where, for example, a seller of land contracts to keep an offer open ninety days—and contracts in which the value of the subject matter is fluctuating rapidly.

At one time, many courts ruled that time was presumed to be of the essence in sales contracts. Today, however, this is not the general rule. Thus, in most states, a late delivery does not free the buyer unless he or she can clearly prove that delivery by the date contained in the contract *was* material, and that the seller knew or should have been aware of the materiality.

DISCHARGE BY BREACH
Actual Breach

It would be contrary to common sense if a person who had materially breached a contract were nevertheless able to hold the other party liable on it, and the law does not tolerate such a result. As the preceding section on performance indicates, an **actual breach**—failure of the promisor to render performance that meets the minimum required by law (full performance in some cases and substantial

[6]The latter possibility is eliminated in some jurisdictions. A number of states provide by statute that time is never of the essence unless the contract expressly indicates that it is.

performance in others)—ordinarily results in the other party's obligations being discharged. In such cases the promisor's breach operates as "an excuse for nonperformance" insofar as the other's obligation is concerned.

This principle has found its way into the law of sales. Thus, if Seller S on May 1 contracts to deliver a thousand gallons of crude oil to Buyer B on August 15, and on that date S delivers only two hundred gallons with no indication that the balance will be delivered shortly thereafter, B can cancel the entire contract, returning the oil already delivered (see Secs. 2-610 and 2-711 of the UCC).

Anticipatory Breach

If one contracting party indicates to the other, before the time of performance arrives, that he or she is not going to perform his or her part of the bargain, an **anticipatory breach** has occurred; in most cases this has the same effect as an actual breach. For example: In March, X contracts to put in a sewer line for a city, with the contract providing that the work will be commenced by June 1. On April 10, X tells the city that he will not do the job. The city can immediately hire a new contractor to do the work and can institute a suit for damages against X as soon as the damages can be ascertained, without waiting until June to do so. (Such action is not mandatory; the city may ignore the repudiation in the hope that X will have a change of heart and actually commence the work on schedule.)

The doctrine of anticipatory breach does not apply to promises to pay money debts, such as those found in promissory notes and bonds. To illustrate: S borrows $500 from T on February 1, giving T a promissory note in that amount due September 1. If S tells T on August 6 that he will not pay the debt, T must nevertheless wait until September 2 before bringing suit to recover the $500. The UCC has detailed provisions addressing anticipatory breach that are discussed in detail in Chapter 23.

DISCHARGE BY LEGAL IMPOSSIBILITY

Between the time of contracting and the time of performance, some event may occur that will make the performance of the contract—for one party, at least—considerably more difficult or costly than originally expected. When this happens, a promisor may contend that the occurrence legally discharged his or her obligations under the contract—that is, it created a **legal impossibility.**[7] For example: A, an accountant for a large corporation who "moonlights" in his spare time, contracts in May to perform certain auditing services for B during the first three weeks of August, A's regularly scheduled vacation. In June A is transferred to a city five hundred miles away; as a result, he does not perform the promised services. If B were to seek damages for breach of contract, the issue presented would be whether A's transfer discharged his obligations under the contract.

In such a case, the courts resort to a two-step process. The first question to be decided is whether one of the parties had assumed the risk in some manner. For example, in the case above, a court might conclude—from a reading of the entire contract, or from testimony regarding the negotiations leading up to the contract—that B had, in fact, agreed that A need not perform if he were relocated. If so, B had assumed the risk, and A need not perform.

If no assumption of risk is apparent (as is often the case), the court must proceed to the second question: whether it can rule, on the basis of the circumstances under which the contract was made, that the contract necessarily contained an *implied condition subsequent.* In other words, in the case above, A would be excused from performing the contract only if he could convince the court that *he and B agreed by implication* that the contract would be voided if he were transferred before the date of performance.

In most cases of this sort, the promisor's contention that an implied condition subsequent existed is rejected by the courts. The usual view is that such possibilities should have been guarded against by an express condition in the contract. Thus, when a corporation promises to manufacture engines by a certain date under a contract containing no express conditions, the fact that it is unable to do so because of a strike at one of its plants is no legal excuse for its nonperformance of the contract. And when a contractor agrees to construct a building by a certain date, with a monetary penalty imposed for late completion, the law normally does not excuse late performance simply because unexpectedly bad weather delayed the work. Nor will a court normally free a builder from his obligations, in the absence of an express condition, merely because unexpectedly high

---

[7] A related subject, the doctrine of commercial impracticability, will be discussed subsequently.

labor or materials costs will cause him to suffer a loss if he is held to the contract.

Notwithstanding these generalizations, there *are* limited situations in which the defense of legal impossibility is accepted by the courts. We will discuss them briefly.

True Impossibility

Essentially, a contract is rendered impossible of performance only where the supervening event—the event occurring between the making of the contract and the time of performance—was unforeseeable at the time of contracting, and creates an objective impossibility. An objective impossibility results in a situation where, as a result of the unanticipated occurrence, no one can perform the contract—that is, performance is physically impossible. By contrast, an occurrence that makes performance by the promisor, only, impossible (but does not make performance by others impossible) does not discharge the promisor's obligations. For example, the inability of a buyer of a condominium to make a cash payment of $10,000 at the time of closing, as required by the contract, is not excused because his or her business suffered a catastrophic loss just prior to that time. (The difference between the two types of impossibility is often summarized thus: where a promisor is claiming objective impossibility, he is saying "*No one* can perform," while in the subjective impossibility situation he is simply saying "*I* cannot perform.")

Up until recent years, implied conditions subsequent—i.e., conditions resulting in legal (objective) impossibility—have been recognized by the courts in only three situations: (1) in contracts calling for personal services, (2) where the subject matter of the contract is destroyed without the fault of either party, and (3) where the performance of the contract becomes illegal after the contract is formed.[8]

Personal Services

In contracts calling for the rendering of *personal services,* such as the ordinary employment contract, the death or incapacity of the promisor (employee) terminates the agreement. The same is true of contracts that contemplate a *personal relationship* between the promisor and the other party. In such cases the courts will accept the argument that the performer's promise was *subject to the implied condition* that his or her death prior to the time of performance (or illness at the time of performance) rendered the contract null and void.[9]

Destruction of the Subject Matter

The principle is well established that destruction of the subject matter of a contract without the fault of either party, before the time for performance, terminates the contract. Where such a situation occurs, the courts will accept the argument that the destruction *constituted an implied condition subsequent* and will rule, as in the personal service contracts, that a legal impossibility has occurred. For example: If C contracted in January to move D's house in March, the contract would be discharged if the house were destroyed by flood in February. In this regard, it can be said that the destruction of the subject matter of a contract by an act of God creates a legal impossibility. It should be noted, however, that it is the fact of destruction that discharges, rather than the cause (as long as the destruction is not attributable to neglect or misconduct of the parties). To illustrate: X contracts with an investors' syndicate to drive its race car at the next Indianapolis 500, and the night before the race the car is destroyed by a fire set by an arsonist. Both parties are discharged from their obligations, although the arsonist's act is not an act of God.

Beyond cases such as the above, it is often difficult to determine what is meant by the "subject mat-

---

[8]The view is commonly held among lay persons, and sometimes finds its way into court decisions, that promisors are freed of their obligations by any "act of God," or "force majeure"—i.e., a force of nature of such degree that it could not be guarded against or prevented by any degree of care or diligence (such as an earthquake or unprecedented flood). This generalization is true when the subject matter of a contract is destroyed by such an occurrence, but it is not necessarily true in other cases. For example, the destruction of a partially completed building by a tornado may be accepted by a court as grounds for permitting the contractor additional time in which to complete the job, but, as a general rule, it does *not discharge* the contractor from the obligation to rebuild.

[9]Note, however, that many obligations are not personal in nature. For example: If B contracts to sell his land to W for $30,000, and B thereafter dies, the agreement is not terminated. The reason is that B's estate, acting through the executor, is just as capable of delivering a deed to W as was B, had he lived. Nor would the contract be terminated if W rather than B had died. W's estate is just as capable of paying the $30,000 as W would have been, had he lived.

Because of this rule, and because of uncertainty as to application of the act-of-God defense to other contracts, construction contracts (and many others) typically contain *express* conditions subsequent excusing delays in performance, or completely excusing performance, in the event of adverse weather conditions, strikes, and so forth. The following clause, in a maritime shipping contract, is typical. "FORCE MAJEURE: In the event of any strike, fire or other event falling within the term 'Force Majeure' preventing or delaying shipment or delivery of the goods occurring prior to shipment or delivery and preventing or delaying reception of the goods by the buyer, then the contract period of shipment or delivery shall be extended by 30 days on telex request made within seven days of its occurrence. Should shipment or delivery of the goods continue to be prevented beyond 30 days, the unaffected party may cancel the unfulfilled balance of the contract. Should the contract be cancelled and/or performance be prevented during any extension to the shipment or delivery period *neither party shall have any claim against the other.*" [Emphasis added.]

ter" of a contract; the term is often used by the courts to include not only the precise subject matter involved, but any other "thing" or property that performance of the contract necessarily depends on. For example, the X Company in January agrees to manufacture and deliver five hundred widgets to the Y Company in March. In February the X Company's only plant is destroyed by fire, with the result that the widgets cannot be manufactured. In this case the courts will ordinarily rule that the existence of the plant is so necessary to the fulfillment of the contract that its destruction excuses the X Company from its obligations. (Such a ruling would not be made, however, if the X Company operated several plants and if there was no indication in the contract, expressly or impliedly, that the parties intended for the widgets to come from the particular plant that was destroyed.)[10]

[10]Special problems arise in the "destruction" cases involving *sales of goods.* Specific "risk of loss" rules in Article 2 of the UCC govern situations of this sort, and are considered in Chapter 21.

Subsequent Illegality

If, after a contract is made, its performance becomes illegal because of a change in the law (including a promulgation of an administrative agency's regulation), a legal impossibility is created. Thus if B in September contracts to sell fifty pinball machines to G in December, the parties' obligations would be discharged if a state statute prohibiting such a transaction took effect in November.

The case below raises a "destruction of the subject matter" issue in regard to the performance of a construction contract that contained no express conditions subsequent. (However, as noted earlier, the general subject of impossibility should also be considered with a related view, the doctrine of "commercial impracticability," which is discussed immediately after this case.)

[handwritten margin note: who should be responsible for the additional cost after vandalism, meaning there was not total destruction]

LA GASSE POOL CONSTRUCTION CO. v. CITY OF FORT LAUDERDALE

Florida District Court of Appeal, Fourth District, 288 So.2d 273 (1974)

The La Gasse Company, plaintiff, made a contract with the City of Fort Lauderdale under which it was to repair and renovate one of the city's swimming pools for a specified price. One night, when the job was almost completed, vandals damaged the pool so badly that most of the work had to be redone.

When the city refused to pay more than the contract price, plaintiff brought this action to recover compensation for the additional work. The primary contention of plaintiff was that the damage to its work constituted a destruction of the subject matter of the contract, and that it was consequently discharged from any obligation to redo the work. Accordingly, plaintiff argued, when it did do the work over again it was entitled to additional compensation for its services.

The trial court rejected this contention, holding that plaintiff had the responsibility under the original contract to redo the work, and it entered judgment for defendant. Plaintiff appealed.

Downey, Judge:

. . . The question presented for decision is: Where the work done by a contractor, pursuant to a contract for the repair of an existing structure, is damaged during the course of the repair work, but the existing structure is not destroyed, upon whom does the loss fall where neither contractor nor the owner is at fault?

The general rule is that under an indivisible contract to build an entire structure, loss or damage thereto during construction falls upon the contractor, the theory being that the contractor obligated himself to build an entire structure, and absent a delivery thereof he has not performed

his contract. If his work is damaged or destroyed during construction he is still able to perform by rebuilding the damaged or destroyed part; in other words, doing the work over again.

In the case of contracts to repair, renovate, or perform work on existing structures, the general rule is that total destruction of the structure . . . without fault of either the contractor or owner, excuses performance by the contractor and entitles him to recover the value of the work done. The rationale of this rule is that the contract has an implied condition that the structure will remain in existence so the contractor can render performance. Destruction of the structure makes performance impossible, and thereby excuses the contractor's nonperformance.

But where the building or structure to be repaired is *not destroyed,* [and] the contractor's work is damaged so that it must be redone, performance is still possible, and it is the contractor's

(continues)

LA GASSE POOL CONSTRUCTION CO. V. CITY OF FORT LAUDERDALE

(continued from previous page)
responsibility to redo the work so as to complete the undertaking. [Emphasis added.] In other words, absent . . . some other reason for lawful nonperformance, the contractor must perform his contract. Any loss or damage to his work during the process of repairs which can be rectified is his responsibility. The reason for allowing recovery without full performance in the case of total destruction (i.e., impossibility of performance) is absent where the structure remains and simply requires duplicating the work. . . . Accordingly, the judgment for [defendant] is affirmed.♊

DISCHARGE BY COMMERCIAL IMPRACTICABILITY

Under the traditional views just discussed, most contracts did not present situations in which legal impossibility was recognized. Thus most contracting parties were not freed from their obligations even in cases where their performance was clearly made more difficult by events that occurred after the contracts were entered into. Today, however, courts are more likely to free contracting parties than was the case earlier, because of increasing recognition of the **doctrine of commercial impracticability.**

The drafters of the UCC felt that sellers of goods should be excused from their obligations not only where the strict conditions of impossibility existed, but also where performance was literally possible but would necessarily be so radically different from that originally contemplated by the parties that it was impracticable.

Commercial Impracticability under the UCC

Section 2-615 of the UCC reads, in part, as follows: "Delay in delivery or nondelivery in whole or in part by a seller . . . is not a breach of his duty under a contract for sale if performance as agreed has been made impracticable by the occurrence of a contingency the non-occurrence of which was a basic assumption upon which the contract was made."

While a full discussion of the scope and ramifications of the commercial impracticability doctrine cannot be undertaken here, several of its basic characteristics can be noted. These characteristics are best explained in Comment 4 following Sec. 2-615, which reads as follows:

Increased cost alone does not excuse performance unless the rise is due to some unforeseen contingency which alters the essential nature of the performance. Neither is a rise or a collapse in the market in itself a justification, for that is exactly the type of business risk which business contracts made at fixed prices are intended to cover. But a severe shortage of raw materials or of supplies due to a contingency such as war, embargo, local crop failure, unforeseen shutdown of major sources of supply or the like, which either causes a *marked increase in cost* or *altogether prevents the seller* from securing supplies necessary to his performance, is within the contemplation of this section." [Emphasis added.]

Thus this section clearly recognizes certain kinds of contingencies *in addition to* those constituting true impossibilities that may free the seller of his or her obligations under the contract. (In that regard, however, under both Comment 1 to Sec. 2-615 and the case law that has developed with respect to this section, the seller must show that the contingency was not within the contemplation of the parties at the time of contracting.)

A second change brought about by the impracticability doctrine is its recognition that a "marked increase" in cost will free the seller, if caused by an unforeseen contingency. (By contrast, increased cost of performance alone is almost never recognized under the impossibility doctrine as a ground for excusing performance.) However, determination of what constitutes a marked increase in cost is left to the courts to decide on a case-by-case basis, and the courts have interpreted this term quite narrowly. That is, under the decisions, the courts have generally taken the view that the seller must prove that the cost of performance (as a result of the contingency) would at least be double or triple the original cost of

performance. Thus the increased cost provision does not afford sellers relief in as many cases as would at first appear.

After adoption of the UCC, the courts generally recognized commercial impracticability as an excuse for nonperformance in sales contracts only, continuing to require a showing of strict impossibility where other types of contracts were involved. Today, however, *there is a growing tendency among the courts to apply the commercial impracticability yardstick to all kinds of contracts.*

DISCHARGE BY FRUSTRATION OF PURPOSE

Occasionally, after a contract is entered into, some event or condition will occur that clearly does not fall within the impossibility or commercial impracticability doctrines, yet one of the parties will argue that it so *frustrated the purposes of the contract* that its occurrence ought to free him nonetheless. (In other words, such a party is contending that the happening of the event caused the contract to become worthless to him.) To illustrate: D, a car dealer embarking on an ambitious expansion program, makes a contract with C, a contractor, under the terms of which he is to pay C $250,000 for the construction of new showroom facilities. Shortly thereafter, because of an unanticipated national defense emergency, the federal government orders a 90 percent reduction in the production of new automobiles. D contends that this action constitutes grounds for cancelling its construction contract, since he will obviously have few new cars to sell.

Here the courts are on the horns of a dilemma. On the one hand, they understand that the virtual stoppage of new car production substantially eliminates the purpose for which the contract was made—and may even drive D into bankruptcy if he is held to its terms. On the other hand, the adoption of a general rule to the effect that contracts are discharged whenever the _purposes_ of one of the parties cannot be attained as a result of unanticipated future occurrences would cast great uncertainty on the enforceability of almost all contracts.

While it is dangerous to generalize about the kinds of cases in which the doctrine of frustration may be accepted as grounds for avoiding contractual liability, it can safely be said that the courts—while giving the doctrine due consideration in their decisions—actually find it to be *inapplicable* in the great majority of cases. Thus, in the example above, D's contention that he was freed on the ground of frustration of purpose will probably (though not certainly) be rejected.

The following case discusses the entire bundle of doctrines—impossibility, commercial impracticability, and frustration of purpose—tracing their origins and rationale. (Another frustration of purpose case, *Waldinger Corp. v. CRS Group Engineers,* is presented in Chapter 23's discussion of the UCC.)

NORTHERN INDIANA PUBLIC SERVICE CO. v. CARBON COUNTY COAL CO.

U.S. Seventh Circuit Court of Appeals, 799 F.2d 265 (1986)

In 1978 Northern Indiana Public Service Company (NIPSCO), an electric utility in Indiana, contracted to buy 1.5 million tons of coal every year for 20 years, at a price of $24 a ton (subject to various provisions for escalation which by 1985 had driven the price up to $44 a ton) from Carbon County Coal Co., which operated a coal mine in Wyoming. NIPSCO's rates are regulated by the Indiana Public Service Commission which, because of complaints from consumers about higher rates, ordered NIPSCO ("the economy purchase orders") to make a good faith effort to find and purchase electricity from other utilities that could produce it at prices lower than NIPSCO's internal generation. NIPSCO was able to buy substantial amounts of electricity from other utilities at costs below the costs of generating its own electricity using Carbon County's coal. Therefore, NIPSCO stopped accepting coal deliveries from Carbon and brought suit seeking a declaration that it was excused from its obligations under the contract. The trial court ruled against NIPSCO and it appealed.

Posner, Judge:

In the early common law, a contractual undertaking unconditional in terms was not excused merely because something had happened (such as an invasion, the passage of a law, or a natural disaster) that prevented the undertaking. *See Paradine v. Jane,* Aleyn, 26, 82 Eng.Rep. 897 (K.B. 1647). Excuses had to be written into the contract; this is the origin of *force majeure* clauses. Later it came to be recognized that negotiating parties cannot anticipate all the contingencies that may arise in the performance of the contract; a legitimate judicial function in contract cases is to interpolate terms to govern remote contingencies—terms the parties would have agreed on explicitly if they had had the time and foresight to make advance provision for every possible contingency in performance. Later still, it was recognized that physical impossibility was irrelevant, or at least inconclusive; a promisor might want his promise to be unconditional, not because he thought he had superhuman powers but because he could insure against the risk of nonperformance better than the promisee, or obtain a substitute performance more easily than the promisee. Thus the proper question in an "impossibility" case is not whether the promisor could not have performed his undertaking but whether his nonperformance should be excused because the parties, if they had thought about the matter, would have wanted to assign the risk of the contingency that made performance impossible or uneconomical to the promisor or to the promisee; if to the latter, the promisor is excused.

Section 2-615 of the Uniform Commercial Code takes this approach. It provides that "delay in delivery . . . by a seller . . . is not a breach of his duty under a contract for sale if performance as agreed has been made impracticable by the occurrence of a contingency the non-occurrence of which was a basic assumption on which the contract was made. . . ." Performance on schedule need not be impossible, only infeasible—provided that the event which made it infeasible was not a risk that the promisor had assumed. Notice, however, that the only type of promisor referred to is a seller; there is no suggestion that a buyer's performance might be excused by reason of impracticability. The reason is largely semantic. Ordinarily all the buyer has to do in order to perform his side of the bargain is pay, and while one can think of all sorts of reasons why, when the time came to pay, the buyer might not have the money, rarely would the seller have intended to assume the risk that the buyer might, whether through improvidence or bad luck, be unable to pay for the seller's goods or services. To deal with the rare case where the buyer or (more broadly) the paying party might have a good excuse based on some unforeseen change in circumstances, a new rubric was thought necessary, different from "impossibility" (the common law term) or "impracticability" (the Code term), and it received the name "frustration." . . .

The leading case on frustration remains *Krell v. Henry,* [1903] 2 K.B. 740 (C.A.). Krell rented Henry a suite of rooms for watching the coronation of Edward VII, but Edward came down with appendicitis and the

(continues)

Chapter 18 Discharge of Contracts 375

Northern Indiana Public Service Co. v. Carbon County Coal Co.

(continued from previous page)
coronation had to be postponed. Henry refused to pay the balance of the rent and the court held that he was excused from doing so because his purpose in renting had been frustrated by the postponement, a contingency outside the knowledge, or power to influence, of either party. The question was, to which party did the contract (implicitly) allocate the risk? Surely Henry had not intended to insure Krell against the possibility of the coronation's being postponed, since Krell could always relet the room, at the premium rental, for the coronation's new date. So Henry was excused. . . .

Since impossibility and related doctrines are devices for shifting risk in accordance with the parties' presumed intentions, which are to minimize the costs of contract performance, one of which is the disutility created by risk, they have no place when the contract explicitly assigns a particular risk to one party or the other. . . . [A] fixed-price contract is an explicit assignment of the risk of market price increases to the seller and the risk of market price decreases to the buyer, and the assignment of the latter risk to the buyer is even clearer where, as in this case, the contract places a floor under price but allows for escalation. If, as is also the case here, the buyer forecasts the market incorrectly and therefore finds himself locked into a disadvantageous contract, he has only himself to blame and so cannot shift the risk back to the seller by invoking impossibility or related doctrines. . . . It does not matter that it is an act of government that may have made the contract less advantageous to one party. Government these days is a pervasive factor in the economy and among the risks that a fixed-price contract allocates between the parties is that of a price change induced by one of government's manifold interventions in the economy. Since "the very purpose of a fixed-price agreement is to place the risk of increased costs on the promisor (and the risk of decreased costs on the promisee)," the fact that costs decrease steeply (which is in effect what happened here—the cost of generating electricity turned out to be lower than NIPSCO thought when it signed the fixed-price contract with Carbon County) cannot allow the buyer to walk away from the contract. *In re Westinghouse Electric Corp. Uranium Contracts Litigation*, 517 F.Supp. 440, 452 (E.D.Va. 1981).

[Affirmed.]

DISCHARGE BY PARTIES' AGREEMENT

Once a contract has been formed, it is always possible for the parties to make a new agreement that will discharge or modify the obligations of one or both parties under the original contract. The new agreement can take any of several forms, the most common of which are rescission, novation, and accord and satisfaction.

Rescission

A contract can always be canceled by mutual agreement. When this agreement occurs, the contract is *rescinded,* and the obligations of both parties are thereby discharged. An oral rescission agreement is generally valid and binding, even where the original contract was in writing—with one major exception. A rescission agreement must be in writing if it involves a retransfer of real property. (Additionally, under Sec. 2-209(2) of the UCC, modification or rescission of a written *sales contract* must be evidenced by a writing if the original contract so provides.)

Novation

A **novation** occurs when the party entitled to receive performance under a contract agrees to release the party who "owes" the performance and to permit a third party to take that person's place. It is simply a three-sided agreement that results in the substitution of one party for another. For example: X and Y have a contract. Later, they and Z agree that Z will perform X's obligations, with Y expressly releasing X from the original contract. X's obligations are now discharged.

Accord and Satisfaction

After a contract has been formed, the parties may agree that one of them will accept, and the other will render, a performance different from what was originally called for. Such an agreement is an *accord.* Thus, if B owes W $1,800, and they subsequently agree that B will air-condition W's home in satisfaction of the debt, an accord exists. The reaching of an accord does not, of and by itself, terminate the existing obligation. To effect a discharge, a *satisfaction* must take place—the actual performance of the substituted obligation. Thus B's indebtedness is discharged by **accord and satisfaction** only when he completes the air-conditioning job.

DISCHARGE BY OPERATION OF LAW

In addition to the types of discharge already discussed, other events or conditions can bring about a *discharge by operation of law*. The most common of these are bankruptcy proceedings, the running of a statute of limitations, and the fraudulent alteration of a contract.

Bankruptcy Proceedings[11]

Bankruptcy actions today are governed by the federal Bankruptcy Reform Act of 1978. If an individual has been adjudged bankrupt after proper bankruptcy proceedings have taken place, he or she receives a *discharge in bankruptcy* from a court which covers most—but not all—of his or her debts. While the discharge technically does not extinguish the debts that are subject to it, it does so as a practical matter by prohibiting creditors from thereafter bringing court action against the debtor to recover any unpaid balance.

Running of Statutes of Limitations

All states have statutes providing that after a certain amount of time has elapsed, a contract claim is barred. The time limits vary widely from one jurisdiction to another. In some states, for example, claimants are given three years in which to bring suit on oral contracts and five years on written ones; in others, the times vary from two to eight years on oral contracts and from three to fifteen years on written ones.

In any event, if a contract claimant lets the applicable time elapse without initiating legal proceedings, the statute of limitations has run and subsequent court action by that person is barred. The period of time begins the day after the cause of action accrues. Thus, if X promises to pay Y $500 on June 10, 1987, in a state having a three-year statute, the statute begins to run on June 11, with the result that Y has until June 10, 1990, to institute suit. (As in the case of a discharge in bankruptcy, the running of the statute does not extinguish the debt or claim itself; it simply prevents the claimant from subsequently bringing a legal action to recover the indebtedness.)

[11] The subject of bankruptcy is treated in Chapter 30.

Alteration

The law generally strives to discourage dishonest conduct. Consistent with this policy is the rule that the fraudulent, material **alteration** of a written contract by one of the parties discharges the other party as a matter of law. Suppose, for example, that A makes a written contract with B under the terms of which he is to sell 1,000 gallons of paint to B at a specified price per gallon. If B subsequently changes the quantity to 1,200 gallons without A's knowledge, A is excused from delivering any paint at all, if that is his desire. (A also has the right to enforce the contract according to its original terms or as altered—that is, he can tender either 1,000 or 1,200 gallons to B and hold him liable for the quantity chosen.)

SUMMARY

In some situations a contracting party does not want to be obligated by the contract unless and until a certain event occurs. This protection can be achieved by use of an express condition precedent—a clause in the contract providing that performance is to occur only if the specified event occurs. In other circumstances a party might want the contract to be performed unless a certain event occurs within a stated time. In the latter case he or she may achieve protection by use of an express condition subsequent—a clause providing that if the specified event occurs, the contract shall be null and void.

In addition to *express* conditions, in some circumstances the law will recognize that the contract was subject to various *implied* conditions. Most contracts are of such a nature that the parties understood that one party (X) was to perform his part of the bargain (e.g., the painting of Y's house) before the other party (Y) had a duty to pay. In such instances, performance by X constitutes an implied condition to his recovery of the price.

In cases where the promisor's performance falls short of complete performance, he or she may still be able to recover under the doctrine of substantial performance. Under this doctrine, the promisor is entitled to receive the contract price minus damages to the promisee if (1) the defects in his or her performance were slight, and (2) the failure to perform completely was not due to bad faith—i.e., the deviations from 100 percent performance were not intentional.

As seen above, one's contractual obligations may be discharged by the failure of an express condition precedent to occur, the occurrence of an express condition subsequent, or by complete or substantial performance on his or her part. One's contractual obligations are also discharged by breach by the other party, or where a legal impossibility exists. Such an impossibility exists in situations where the courts can rule that, under the circumstances, the contract was subject to an *implied* condition subsequent. Implied conditions are found to exist in only three limited situations: (1) in contracts calling for performance of personal services, and where the promisor dies prior to the time of performance (or is incapacitated at that time); (2) where the subject matter of the contract is destroyed without fault of either party prior to the time of performance; and (3) where performance becomes illegal prior to the time of performance. Because the impossibility view excuses a promisor only in limited circumstances, most courts today are applying the more liberal doctrine of commercial impracticability, instead—a doctrine first recognized under sales law, and one which frees the promisor in more circumstances than does the impossibility view.

KEY TERMS

Condition
Condition precedent
Condition subsequent
Conditions concurrent
Substantial performance
Actual breach
Anticipatory breach
Legal impossibility
Doctrine of commercial impracticability
Novation
Accord and satisfaction
Alteration

QUESTIONS AND PROBLEMS

1. Roper contracted in writing to buy a Wyoming ranch from Lewis for a specified price. At the same time that this contract was made Roper and Lewis also orally agreed, in rather general terms, that Lewis would also sell his 400 head of cattle and some ranch machinery to Roper. Later, when the cattle and ma-chinery deal fell through, Roper brought court action asking for rescission of the ranch contract. Roper's contention was that performance of the cattle and machinery agreement was a *condition precedent* to his obligations under the ranch-purchase contract. Lewis disagreed, pointing out (a) that the written ranch contract did not mention the oral agreement, and (b) that, in fact, the parties never did come to specific terms as to the cattle and machinery prices. Would these factors cause the court to rule that performance of the cattle and machinery contract was *not* a condition precedent? Discuss. (*Lewis v. Roper*, 579 P.2d 434, 1978.)

2. Western Commerce Bank (WCB) was a creditor of the Miller estate, but filed its claim late so that the trustee refused to pay it. WCB sued, claiming that the notice inviting claims published by the estate was defective. On February 10, 1988, the heirs tendered an offer of settlement that provided for the payment of $275,000, subject to the heirs obtaining the necessary financing. WCB accepted. On April 22, when the paperwork for the financing was almost (but not quite) completed, WCB repudiated the settlement agreement. The heirs completed the financing arrangements and asked the court to enforce the settlement. WCB argued that there was no contract because the heirs had not obtained the financing within a reasonable time. Discuss. (*Western Commerce Bank v. Gillespie*, 775 P.2d 737, N.M. 1989.)

3. Cayias owned a pool hall business, which he operated in a leased building. Wishing to sell the business, he listed it with the Associated Investment Company, a broker, under a contract providing that if the company found a buyer at a price agreeable to him, he would pay the company a commission of 10 percent of the purchase price. The company found a buyer willing to pay $3,000, and Cayias and the buyer entered into a contract calling for the sale of the business at that price. The contract provided, however, that if the buyer was not able to obtain a new lease on the building at a monthly rental of $150, "then and in that event the agreement shall become null and void." The purchaser thereafter was apparently not able to get a lease from the owner of the building at this figure, so the sale of the business fell through. The company now sued Cayias, the seller, to recover its commission of $300. Cayias defended on the ground that (a) the quoted clause in the purchase agreement constituted a condition subsequent, and

(b) since the condition (the inability of the buyer to get a lease) occurred with the result that the buyer was released, he (Cayias) was released from his obligation to pay a commission on the "sale." Rule on the correctness of Cayias' contention. (*Associated Investment Co. v. Cayias*, 185 P. 778, 1920.)

4. A contractor who built a country home for Kent for $77,000 sought to recover the unpaid balance of $3,400. Kent refused to make the final payment because the building contract required that all pipe in the home be of "Reading manufacture," and the pipe actually installed was made by a different manufacturer, the Cohoes Company. The contractor proved that the Cohoes pipe met all the specifications of the Reading pipe and that he was not aware of the Reading requirement in the contract when he installed the other pipe. On these facts, does the doctrine of substantial performance apply to the plaintiff, the contractor? Explain. (*Jacobs and Young, Inc. v. Kent*, 129 N.E. 889, 1921.)

5. Waegemann leased commercial space to Montgomery Ward pursuant to an agreement which calculated rent according to the property tax index. During the term of the lease, voters of California passed Proposition 13, which slashed real estate taxes substantially, causing Waegemann to receive only one-third of the current fair market value in rent. In subsequent litigation, Waegeman claimed that the lease should be rescinded on grounds of commercial impracticability or frustration of purposes. Is Waegemann right? (*Waegemann v. Montgomery Ward & Co.*, 713 F.2d 452, 9th Cir. 1983.)

6. A professional football player made a contract with Alabama Football, Inc. (Alabama), which at that time was a member of the World Football League. Under the contract Alabama agreed to pay the player a salary covering the years 1977, 1978, and 1979. Soon after the contract was made, the World Football League folded—ceased to exist. In subsequent litigation, Alabama contended that the failure of the league constituted a *legal impossibility* that freed Alabama of its obligations to the player. Should the court accept this argument? Discuss. (*Alabama Football, Inc. v. Wright*, 452 F.Supp. 182, 1977.)

7. The Republic Creosoting Company contracted to sell and deliver to the City of Minneapolis a quantity of paving blocks, with deliveries to be made in the first six months of 1920. The contract did not contain any clause excusing a late delivery in the event of a strike, a boxcar shortage, or similar events beyond the company's control. Because of a nationwide boxcar shortage, the company was unable to deliver the blocks at the agreed upon time. The city considered this a breach of contract and purchased the blocks from another supplier at a higher price. The city then brought suit against the company to recover damages for breach of contract, and the company defended on the ground that the nationwide boxcar shortage constituted a legal impossibility. Rule on the validity of this defense (a) on the ground of impossibility, and (b) on the ground of commercial impracticability. (*Minneapolis v. Republic Creosoting Co.*, 201 N.W. 414, 1924.)

8. One railroad (the lessor) leased part of its depot facilities in Milwaukee to another railroad (the lessee) under a long-term contract. Thereafter, with several years on the contract remaining, Amtrak was formed by an act of Congress that resulted, among other things, in the lessee's passenger service in the Milwaukee area being very substantially reduced. As a result, the lessee would have very little use for the depot facilities. When the lessor sued the lessee to recover $2 million rental fees for subsequent years, the lessee contended that the formation of Amtrak (and the sharp curtailment of its services) freed it from its remaining obligations under the *frustration of purpose* doctrine. The lessor contested this argument, and offered evidence to show (a) that when the contract was made the lessee was aware that Amtrak might come into existence; (b) that both parties realized that their need for the depot might be substantially cut; and (c) that the lessee, by joining Amtrak—which it was not required by law to do—was itself partly responsible for its cutback of services. Should this evidence convince the court to rule that the frustration of purpose doctrine is *not* applicable? (That is, should this evidence cause the court to rule that the lessee is still bound by the contract?) Why or why not? (*Chicago, M., St.P.&P.R. Co. v. Chicago & N.W.*, 203 N.W.2d 189, 1978.)

Contract Interpretation

Remedies for Breach of Contract

THIS CHAPTER ADDRESSES two of the most practically important areas in all of contract law. Often a contract exists, in that all the basic elements of a binding contract (agreement, consideration, capacity, legality) are present, but its meaning is not clear. It expresses the general rights and obligations of the parties, but what it means *exactly* in relation to the events that have occurred since the contract was formed cannot be agreed upon by the parties to the contract. Indeed, questions regarding the meaning of contracts generate more litigation than any other type of contract question. The first portion of this chapter discusses the basic rules which courts apply when resolving disputes as to the meaning of a contract's terms.

If a plaintiff convinces the court that a contract exists, and that the defendant has breached that contract as interpreted by the court, he has gained nothing unless the law provides him a full and appropriate remedy. The second half of this chapter explores the various avenues of remedy available to a party injured by a breach of contract.

CONTRACT INTERPRETATION

It is told that the defenders of the bastion of Sebasta surrendered to Temures, their besieger, after he promised that "no blood would be shed" should they do so. Temures was good to the letter of his word. But, upon being buried alive, the defenders probably wished they had asked their lawyer to check the fine print. Most modern breach-of-contract lawsuits also involve, often among several issues, a dispute as to the meaning of the contract generally or some of its specific terms. It is a rare situation indeed when both parties to a contract agree as to the meaning of all of its provisions. Such difficulties are perhaps inevitable, a combination of the imprecision of human language, inattention to detail by the drafters of the agreement, and the inability of the parties to foresee events as they will eventually transpire. In Chapter 4, we discussed statutory law and learned that legislators face similar limitations in drafting statutes, giving rise to that "necessary evil"—judicial interpretation.

Similarly courts are often called upon to determine the meaning of contracts and their provisions.

Courts do this through the processes of interpretation and construction. According to some sources, the process of **interpretation** focuses on determining the meaning of words as used in the contract while **construction** deals with the legal effect to be given those words. Generally, however, courts use the terms interchangeably because there is much disagreement as to their technical meaning and as to where one process ends and the other begins. No matter which term is used, the process is complicated.

Intent of the Parties

The primary role of a court asked to interpret a contract is to determine the intent of the parties *at the time the contract was made* and to give effect to that intent. The court's job is not to improve the contract or to rewrite it to address matters that the parties should have considered but did not. As with the process of statutory interpretation, the parties' intent is the centerpiece of the process. The court's own evaluation as to how the contract *should* have been written is irrelevant.

There is disagreement as to the optimum approach to determining contract intent. Most courts speak of an "objective" test that gauges the meaning of a contract's words by how a hypothetical "reasonably intelligent person" would understand them. However, it is not at all rare to see courts strive to determine the common intent of the contracting parties at the time they made the contract.

Contractual interpretation generally raises questions of law to be resolved by the court. However, if a contract's wording is ambiguous, extrinsic evidence may be admitted to determine the parties' intent. Juries often play a role in resolving this question of fact.

While determination of the parties' intent is the overarching goal of contract interpretation, the courts, once they have determined that intent, are constrained by considerations of public policy. In other words, they cannot give effect to a contract where the intent is to produce illegal, unethical, or unconscionable activity.

Plain Meaning Rule

We learned in Chapter 4 that the primary source of legislative intent is the wording of the statute itself. It should not be surprising, then, that in determining the intent of the parties to a contract, courts look first to the language of that contract. The parties' own words are the main evidence of their intentions at the time they made the contract.

Indeed, the words of the contract may be the *only* evidence of the parties' intentions that a court will consider. As in statutory interpretation, there is a well-recognized **plain meaning rule.** If the language of the contract appears clear and unambiguous, the plain meaning rule requires that the courts determine the intent of the parties solely from the face of the instrument. Absent ambiguity, the courts should not resort to extrinsic evidence (such as the actions of the parties, the testimony of the parties, or even the past practices of the parties) in their search for intent. Any attempt to alter the obvious meaning of the words with outside evidence would likely stray from the parties' intent at the time they made the agreement.

A few courts have rejected the plain meaning rule, concluding that it "asserts a semantic perfection which cannot hope to be achieved." *PG&E v. G.W. Thomas Drayage & Rigging Co.,* 442 P.2d 641 (Cal. 1968). Even in plain meaning rule jurisdictions, courts often conclude that the language of the parties, though it appears clear, is not in fact "plain and unambiguous." When that happens, courts resort to extrinsic evidence such as all relevant writings and oral statements, other conduct of the parties manifesting their intent, negotiations, prior course of dealing, and other relevant factors.

The following case examines these divergent approaches to the introduction of extrinsic evidence.

ISBRANDTSEN V. NORTH BRANCH CORPORATION

Supreme Court of Vermont, 556 A.2d 81 (1988)

Case

Plaintiff (grantee) bought from defendant (grantor) a townhouse at a ski resort. Defendant operated recreational facilities, ski trails, parking areas, and assorted outbuildings. There were four townhouses and all adjoined a common area known as the "club" which contained a kitchen, restaurant, and sitting room. Defendant operated and maintained all these areas. Defendant's business depended in part upon rental income derived from lessees of owners of the townhouses who did not use them on a year-round basis. The development was designed so that the temporarily unoccupied townhouses could be rented out to paying guests. This benefitted the owners, who derived a percentage of income from the rentals, and it assured the defendant the income required to continue providing the maintenance services necessary to all occupants.

The deed through which defendant sold the townhouse to plaintiff contained this clause: "The premises hereby conveyed shall be used only for private, single-family residence purposes, except that, under express agreement between Grantor and Grantee, the premises may be rented or used for paying guests in connection with Grantor's operations."

Plaintiff asked the lower court to declare that she could rent her townhouse to paying guests without defendant's knowledge or consent. Defendant claimed that this clause prohibited plaintiff from any such rental except by and with defendant's express consent. The trial judge ruled for the defendant and the plaintiff appealed.

Gibson, Justice:

The question of whether a contract term is ambiguous is a matter of law for the court to decide. A provision in a contract is ambiguous only to the extent that reasonable people could differ as to its interpretation. Here,

plaintiff argues that the deed contains internal inconsistencies which render its terms ambiguous and therefore subject to rules of construction that would warrant judgment in her favor. In particular, plaintiff contends that before the restriction on commercial rental can be given effect, there must first be an agreement between the parties, and that since there is no such agreement, plaintiff is free to do as she wishes.

Before extrinsic evidence may be used to aid in the construction of a written instrument, ambiguity must first be found. In determining whether an ambiguity exists, many courts have adopted the traditional "four corners" test or "plain meaning rule," which states that if a writing appears to be plain and unambiguous on its face, its meaning must be determined from the four corners of the instrument without resort to extrinsic evidence of any nature: "If the term in question does not have a plain meaning it follows that the term is ambiguous." J. Calamari & J. Perillo, The Law of Contracts §3-10, at 166-67 (3d ed. 1987).

(continues)

ISBRANDTSEN V. NORTH BRANCH CORPORATION

(continued from previous page)

A number of courts, recognizing that "plain meaning" cannot exist in a vacuum, have allowed the admission of evidence as to the circumstances surrounding the making of the agreement as well as the object, nature and subject matter of the writing. See, e.g., *Pacific Gas & Elec. Co. v. G.W. Thomas Drayage & Rigging Co.*, 442 P.2d 641 (1968).

We believe it appropriate, when inquiring into the existence of ambiguity, for a court to consider the circumstances surrounding the making of the agreement. Ambiguity will be found where a writing in and of itself supports a different interpretation from that which appears when it is read in light of the surrounding circumstances, and both interpretations are reasonable.

If ambiguity is found on that basis, the court may then rely on subordinate rules of construction in order to interpret the meaning of the disputed terms. If, however, no ambiguity is found, then the language must be given effect in accordance with its plain, ordinary and popular sense.

In making its determination as to ambiguity in the instant case, the trial court properly considered evidence as to the circumstances under which the conveyance was made.

In the late 1960s, plaintiff and her family stayed at North Branch (presumably under a rental agreement as described above) on at least three separate occasions before her husband decided to purchase a townhouse for her. This purchase, which was a gift from Mr. Isbrandtsen to his wife, consisted of one of two new townhouses built in 1969, both of which were joined to the original four buildings. The new townhouses, which had no common "club" areas (having been built after the main buildings), each contained six bedroom units.

At the time defendant conveyed the property to plaintiff, she was asked, like every other owner, to sign a "Business Use Agreement" allowing defendant to rent out the property when she was not in actual occupancy. She declined to do so, advising defendant that she and her family intended to occupy the entire townhouse for their own use. It was uncontested at trial that of the other townhouse owners, all five had executed a "Business Use Agreement."

Plaintiff acknowledges that the restriction to use the property only "for private, single-family residence purposes" limits its use to residential purposes as opposed to business or commercial uses. The clause immediately following that phrase provides one exception to the restriction: the premises may be rented or used for paying guests *under express agreement* between defendant and the owner. The words "under express agreement" were inserted for a purpose and may not be ignored. The law is clear that an agreement must be viewed in its entirety, with an eye toward giving effect to all material parts in order to form a harmonious whole.

While the language of the restrictive clause is somewhat awkward, that in itself does not render it ambiguous. "If a contract, though inartfully worded or clumsily arranged, fairly admits of but one interpretation, it may not be said to be ambiguous or fatally unclear." *Allstate Ins. Co. v. Goldwater*, 163 Mich.App. 646, 648, 415 N.W.2d 2, 4 (1987). Likewise, the fact that a dispute has arisen as to proper interpretation does not automatically render the language ambiguous. Such an approach would merely invite court interference any time a litigant alleged a dispute as to a contractual term.

Viewing the language of the deed in light of the surrounding circumstances, we hold that only one reasonable interpretation exists: that absent an express agreement between plaintiff and defendant, plaintiff is prohibited by the deed from renting her property to paying guests. Likewise, absent such an express agreement, defendant may not rent out plaintiff's property in part or in whole. The restriction serves to protect defendant's interest in maintaining and operating its innkeeping business while serving also to protect plaintiff, who may not want her property rented out indiscriminately to transient individuals.

[Affirmed.]

If courts decide to resort to evidence outside the language of the contract, the best evidence of the parties' intent may be their subsequent conduct in carrying it out. For example, in one case both Jewell and Thomas signed a promissory note. Jewell claimed that he had signed only to assist Thomas in getting the loan and that, therefore, Thomas should repay Jewell for the payments he made to the bank. Thomas claimed that Jewell was the primary obligor on the note. The evidence showed that as soon as the note was signed, Jewell treated the note as his own obligation, taking over complete responsibility for servicing the debt. Thomas never dealt with the bank. Thus, the court concluded, the intent of the parties appeared to be as asserted by Thomas. *Marvin E. Jewell & Co. v. Thomas*, 434 N.W.2d 532 (Neb. 1989).

Rules of Interpretation

As in statutory interpretation, various rules of contract interpretation have developed over the years to assist the courts in determining the parties' intent from the words that they used. Courts should not apply the rules so conservatively as to obstruct the parties' true intentions, nor so liberally as to allow one of the parties to escape his obligations. As noted earlier, the courts are not at liberty to rewrite the contract while purporting to interpret it.

The first task in contract interpretation is to determine to the extent possible the parties' *principal objective* in forming the contract. This principal objective is accorded great weight, and all the contract's terms are construed in order to carry out that objective.

The parties' intentions are generally (though not exclusively) judged in an objective fashion from their expressed intent. Secret intentions are deemed irrelevant. Intentions expressed through either words or actions are given effect unless they conflict with law, morals, or public policy.

Contracts often contain conflicting and inconsistent terms. These will be interpreted, insofar as possible, to achieve the intentions of both parties. If possible, a contract will be construed so as to give effect to all of its provisions. The courts disfavor a construction which requires that a portion of the contract be ignored.

The courts also presume that the parties intended their agreement to be legal, reasonable, and effective. If alternative constructions are both plausible, the one that is preferred is the one least likely to render it illegal, unreasonable, or ineffective. Assume that a contract grants a patent licensee "exclusive use in the U.S.A." of the patented product. If the licensee argues that the right is to be perpetual and the licensor argues that it is to last only the life of the patent, the latter interpretation would be favored because the former would be inconsistent with antitrust laws.

Other aids to interpretation include the following:

1. Words and phrases are given their ordinary meaning, unless the parties indicate otherwise. Although the courts are not slaves to dictionaries, they do frequently consult them. Similarly, technical words are presumed to be used in their commonly accepted technical sense.

2. Specific language controls general language. For example, if a contract provided in one clause that a sole shareholder guaranteed payment for electrical service provided to his company, and another clause provided that the sole shareholder guaranteed electrical service provided to his company at a *specific* address, the court would likely conclude that the sole shareholder was not liable for electrical service provided to the company at other addresses.

3. When a contract is embodied in a printed form, any conflicting provisions added by the parties will prevail. Handwriting will prevail over typewriting. Thus, if a preprinted form contained a provision limiting liability to $1,000, but the figure $2,500 was handwritten into the relevant blank on the form, the latter would set the limit of liability.

4. Ambiguous language is construed against the party who prepares the agreement. This is especially true where the contract is a preprinted adhesion contract where there is little opportunity for negotiation. In *Comprehensive Health Ins. Ass'n v. Dye*, 531 N.E.2d 505 (Ind.App. 1988), for example, an insurance contract prepared by the insurance company contained two different definitions of "preexisting conditions" that would not be covered by the policy. One excluded any sickness that had been diagnosed or treated before the policy was issued; the other excluded any sickness for which a reasonable person would have sought diagnosis or treatment. The court chose to apply the first definition because it was narrower and therefore more favorable to the insured.

5. Where numbers are expressed, words prevail over figures where they are in conflict. For instance, if a typed contract indicated in one place that the purchase price was "four hundred dollars" but in another place indicated that it was "$405," the former would prevail.

6. In every contract, courts will imply a duty of good faith, fair dealing, and cooperation on the part of both parties. The law of the jurisdiction at the place and time the contract is made is also generally read into the contract. Courts will not imply any other terms, unless a contract is silent on a particular point. In such an instance, courts may occasionally imply terms. For example, a contract that is silent as to duration will generally be construed to last for a reasonable time. An obligation to pay money is construed to require that the money be paid in legal tender.

These rules of interpretation, when applied to a specific contract, will not always point in the same direction, as the following case illustrates.

INNES V. WEBB

Texas Court of Civil Appeals, 538 S.W.2d 237 (1976)

Case

Appellee Webb wished to buy a house owned by Huller. Appellant Innes, a real estate broker, prepared an earnest money contract between Webb and Huller. Webb gave Innes a check for $2,000 as earnest money; Innes gave the money to Huller. Huller left town and never completed the contract. Webb seeks return of his $2,000, pointing to a provision in the standard preprinted form that was used for the earnest money contract which provided that if the seller did not comply with the contract for any reason, "Purchaser may demand back the earnest money. . . ." In essence, Webb alleged that Innes held the funds as stakeholder subject to Webb's demand for return of the funds should Huller breach.

Innes emphasized a provision that was typed onto the form which stated: "$2,000 escrow to be turned over to Seller for initial deposit on materials and administrative costs."

The trial court held for Webb in the sum of $2,000 and broker Innes appealed.

Young, Justice:

. . . All of which brings us to the construction of a contract that was prepared by a broker and that contains two apparently inconsistent clauses: one, a printed clause, requiring the return by the broker to the purchaser of the earnest money on purchaser's demand if the seller fails to comply with the contract; and the other, a typewritten clause, requiring the broker to turn over the "$2,000.00 escrow" to the seller "for initial deposit for materials and administrative costs." Appellant urges that we should be guided here by the rule of construction which provides that the written or typewritten part of a contract controls in the event of any conflict thereof with the printed portion of the contract. The rationale for this rule is that the written or typed words are the immediate language of the parties themselves, whereas the language of the printed form is intended for general use only, without reference to the particular aims and objectives of the parties. *Leslie Lowry & Co. v. KTRM, Inc.,* 239 S.W.2d 898, 900 (Tex.Civ.App.—Beaumont 1951, no writ).

On the other hand, appellee contends that our case should be controlled by the rule which requires that an agreement be construed most strictly against the party who drafted it and thus was responsible for the language used.

When we attempt to apply these rules to our case, we find that we apparently have two conflicting rules urged by the parties. The question then arises which rule should prevail here. Our answer to that question is that the rule should be applied which says typed matter controls the printed instead of the rule which says that a contract will be construed against the author. *Universal C.I.T. Credit Corp. v. Daniel,* 150 Tex. 513, 243 S.W.2d 154 (1951); *Leslie Lowry & Co. v. KTRM, Inc.,* supra; 17A C.J.S. Contracts § 324, p.217.

The rule of strict construction against the author has been dealt with in those authorities as follows: In *Daniel,* our Supreme Court held that the rule applies only after ordinary rules of interpretation (such as the typed controls the printed) have been applied. In *KTRM, Inc.,* that Court simply applied the typed controls the printed rule over the authorship rule. In *17A C.J.S.,* the statement is made that the authorship rule is the last one the courts will apply.

For all of those reasons, we hold that the typewritten clause in the contract determines the responsibility of the appellant for his disposition of the "$2,000.00 escrow"; that he delivered that money to the seller under the clause; that, therefore, he did not breach the contract in so delivering the money.

[Reversed.]

Uniform Commercial Code

The UCC in Sec. 2-202 alters common-law practice by permitting more liberal use of extrinsic evidence in determining the parties' intent in sale-of-goods contracts. That is, the UCC backs away from the plain meaning rule, which focuses attention primarily on the language of the parties, by assuming that the parties considered matters such as (1) course of performance, (2) course of dealing, and (3) usage of trade. Thus, in construing a sales contract courts may resort to this extrinsic evidence without finding that the words of the contract are ambiguous.

A **course of performance,** according to UCC 2-208, arises out of "repeated occasions for performance by either party with knowledge of the nature of the performance and opportunity for objection to it by the other." Such performance which is accepted and acquiesced in without objection by the other party is a strong indication of what the parties intended.

A **course of dealing,** according to UCC 1-205, is "a sequence of previous conduct between the parties to a particular transaction which is fairly to be regarded as establishing a common basis of understanding for interpreting their expressions and other conduct." Thus, whereas course of performance arises out of the same contract the court is trying to interpret, course of dealing arises out of earlier transactions between the parties.

Finally, a **usage of trade,** according to UCC 1-205, is "any practice or method of dealing having such regularity of observance in a place, vocation, or trade as to justify an expectation that it will be observed with respect to the transaction in question."

It certainly makes sense to assume that the parties' conduct in performing the contract evidences their intentions and to assume that their intent at the time of making the contract took into account their prior dealings and the customs of their industry. UCC 1-205(4) establishes a priority for interpretation. Express terms of the agreement are the primary source for interpretation. Next in line is course of performance which, where conflicting, controls course of dealing. Course of dealing, in turn, prevails over a conflicting usage of trade. Use of this type of extrinsic evidence is, of course, consistent with the UCC's various "gap-filler" provisions that we studied in Chapter 12.

REMEDIES FOR BREACH OF CONTRACT

Assuming that a valid contract exists and that one of the parties to that contract has breached its obligations (as those obligations were interpreted by the court), the matter of remedies arises.[1] The party who received the promises that were not performed will often look to the judicial system for a remedy (though, as we learned in Chapter 3, remedies may also be provided by alternative means of dispute resolution, such as arbitration). The form, availability, and extent of remedies will play a big part in a party's decision whether to litigate. If the law does not provide a remedy, or provides an inappropriate or inadequate remedy, the wronged party may never sue.

---

[1]We have already touched on the concept of remedies in several chapters. For example, in Chapter 15 we learned that rescission is available as a remedy where contracts were induced by fraud. In Chapter 18, we discussed remedies that are available where parties have only partially, but not completely, performed their contractual obligations.

In our legal system, the freedom to contract entails the freedom to breach one's obligations. Our system of remedies aims not at coercing parties into performing their obligations, but at providing adequate remedies for the other party when breaches do occur. The distinction is subtle, but our free enterprise system's main goal is to encourage people to do business with those who make promises by assuring them that adequate remedies will be available to compensate them should the promisors not perform.

Our discussion is divided into two major sections because of the historical distinction (explored in the introductory chapters) between actions at law and actions in equity. Because the law/equity distinction has largely disappeared, virtually every court can grant remedies that traditionally were available in courts of law (i.e., money damages) *and* those traditionally available in courts of equity (e.g., orders of specific performance and injunction).

As with earlier contract-law chapters, we will note areas where the Uniform Commercial Code alters common-law rules because of the special needs of sale-of-goods transactions. However, these references will be brief, for the matter of Article 2 remedies is explored in detail in Chapter 23.

Money Damages

The primary remedy available for breach of contract is money damages. Because this remedy originated in courts at law, a jury trial is available to plaintiffs seeking such damages. The main goal of an award of damages is to *compensate* the plaintiff for losses caused by the defendant's failure to perform as promised. We will emphasize **compensatory damages** in this discussion, but also explore other types of damages, including nominal damages and liquidated damages.

Compensatory Damages

The amount of money a jury might award depends upon which interest the law is attempting to compensate. There are three such interests that we must address.

1. *Expectation Interest.* The law usually seeks to compensate the plaintiff's *expectation* interest. That is, the law seeks to put the plaintiff in the position in which he expected to be after the defendant performed his promise. In other words, the law attempts to give the plaintiff the "benefit of his bargain."

2. *Reliance Interest.* In situations where it is not feasible or fair to award the plaintiff expectation damages, the law may seek to return the plaintiff to where he was before the contract was entered into. Because this frequently entails reimbursing the plaintiff for funds he spent (or other detriment incurred) in reliance on the defendant's promise, this is called the *reliance* interest.

3. *Restitution Interest.* Finally, a defendant who fails to perform a promise should not be allowed to keep a benefit conferred by a plaintiff who did perform his promise. Therefore, in a breach-of-contract action, the defendant is often ordered to compensate the plaintiff for such a benefit. This is called making restitution, and the law is compensating the plaintiff's *restitution* interest.

Illustration: Assume that D Company hired Ralph to build a storage shed for D for the sum of $10,000. Soon after the contract was made, D repudiated it. If Ralph sued for breach of contract, proving that he could have built the shed for $7,500, he will likely recover $2,500, the profit that he expected to receive from the transaction. This award gives Ralph the benefit of his bargain by placing him in the position he expected to occupy (a $2,500 profit in his pocket) if D performed its promise.

Assume, on the other hand, that sometime after Ralph began building the shed, D breached the contract, telling Ralph not to finish because D would pay nothing. If Ralph could not prove the profit he would have made had the shed been completed, but could show that he had spent $3,400 on labor and materials before the breach, the law would award Ralph that $3,400 to compensate his reliance interest. Ralph spent that amount in reliance on D's promise. (If Ralph could also establish the $2,500 expected profit, he would recover $5,900, because this is the sum required to place him in as good a position as he expected to be in when D performed.)

Assume, on the other hand, that on the day the contract was made, D paid Ralph $2,000 as an advance. Ralph told D the next day that he would not go through with the job, but was keeping the $2,000. If D sued Ralph, it would recover at least $2,000 to compensate its restitution interest.

Expectation Measure. The matter of expectation damages must be explored more thoroughly. Placing a plaintiff in the position he or she expected to be in had the defendant performed as promised is a complicated matter. The general term "expectation damages" can be broken down into at least three subcategories. "Direct" or "general" damages are those losses clearly and directly caused by the defendant's breach. "Consequential" or "special" damages include lost profits and injury to persons or property resulting from the defendant's defective performance. "Incidental" damages include such matters as costs incurred by the plaintiff in arranging for substitute performance.

Assume that D Corporation promised to repair a plastic-molding machine for P Corporation for $15,000 by June 1. D understood that time was of the essence, because P had a big contract to produce plastic cups that called for a June 1 start-up date. On May 20, D informed P that it would not perform its promise. P quickly but thoroughly investigated and found that X Company was willing to make the repairs for $17,000. Working quickly, X completed the repairs on June 15, but P lost $5,000 in profits because the machine was idled for two weeks. Because it cost P $2,000 more to have the machine repaired than it would have had D performed as promised, P can recover $2,000 in *direct damages.* P will also recover $5,000 in *consequential damages* to compensate for the lost profits. Finally, any costs incurred by P in finding X could be recovered as *incidental damages.*

Although this illustration gives a general idea as to calculation of compensatory damages to redress the expectation interest, remember that there are some very important limitations on the plaintiff's recovery:

1. *Causation.* Plaintiff must prove that the defendant's breach was a "substantial factor" in bringing about his or her injury. Assume that Pam proves that she runs a retail clothing store, that Dan promised to deliver winter coats to Pam by September 1, that the coats were not delivered until October 1, and that Pam's revenues for the month of September were down 40 percent from the previous year. Pam appears to have a strong case, but if evidence adduced at trial discloses that the street leading to Pam's store was under construction during the entire month of September so that it was very difficult for customers even to reach Pam's store, and that other stores in the area also sustained lost revenue, a jury might conclude that Dan's delay was not a "substantial factor" in bringing about the plaintiff's loss.

2. *Reasonable Certainty.* Judges and juries should not have to speculate as to the amount of damages the plaintiff sustained that was due to the defendant's breach. Therefore, the plaintiff must establish losses

with "reasonable certainty," a higher standard of proof than is demanded for other issues. This is often a problem in consequential damages, such as lost profits at a sports event.

Assume, for example, that Pete, a candidate for governor in a primary election, contracted to have D Newspaper Co. run one of his ads on the Sunday before election day. The newspaper failed to run the ad, and Pete lost the election. If Pete sued for the salary he would have received as governor, it would be pure speculation to conclude that the missing ad caused Pete to lose the primary election or that Pete would have won the general election had he succeeded in the primary. Therefore, a court probably would deny Pete's claim for these consequential damages.

While the law does not wish to compensate the plaintiff for losses that did not occur, at the same time persons who have breached their promises should not escape liability simply because the plaintiff cannot prove the amount of damages to the penny. For that reason, the law requires reasonable, not absolute, certainty. The UCC reflects the trend in the common law by requiring the plaintiff to prove damages not with mathematical certainty, but with "whatever definiteness and accuracy the facts permit, but no more" (Sec. 1-106, comment 1).

Courts often are less demanding of a plaintiff's proof where the defendant's breach was willful and in situations where precision of proof is inherently impossible (such as in calculation of loss to "goodwill"). Similarly, where a defendant's wrong has caused the difficulty in proof of damages, many courts hold that the defendant "shall not be heard to complain." In short, where the courts are certain that a breach has occurred and that the plaintiff has suffered a loss, they hesitate to deny recovery on grounds that the plaintiff has failed to establish the amount of damages to a reasonable certainty. On the other hand, where the evidence is not clear that a loss even occurred, the reasonable certainty requirement is more likely to bar recovery. An interesting illustration of these general rules follows.

ERICSON V. PLAYGIRL, INC.

California Court of Appeals, 140 Cal.Rptr. 921 (1977)

Case

Plaintiff John Ericson, in an attempt to boost his career as an actor, agreed that defendant Playgirl, Inc., could publish without compensation as the centerfold of its January 1974 issue of Playgirl photographs of Ericson posing naked. No immediate career boost to Ericson resulted. In April 1974, defendant wished to use the pictures again for its annual edition entitled Best of Playgirl, a publication with half the circulation of Playgirl and without the advertising. Ericson agreed to a rerun of his pictures in Best of Playgirl on two conditions: that certain of them be cropped to more modest exposure, and that Ericson's photograph occupy a quarter of the front cover, which would contain photographs of five other persons on its remaining three-quarters. Defendant honored the first of these conditions but, due to an editorial mixup, Ericson's photograph did not appear on the cover of Best of Playgirl. Ericson sued for breach of contract, seeking to recover for the loss of publicity he would have received had his picture appeared on the cover as agreed.

The trial court entered a $12,500 judgment on behalf of Ericson, based in large part on the testimony of an advertising manager for TV Guide who placed the value to an entertainer of an appearance on the cover of a national magazine at $50,000. (¼ cover × $50,000 = $12,500.) Playgirl appealed.

Fleming, Acting Presiding Justice:

Damages must be clearly ascertainable and reasonably certain, both in their nature and origin. (Civ. Code, § 3301.)

Plaintiff's claim of damages for breach of contract was based entirely on the loss of general publicity he would have received by having his photograph appear, alongside those of five others, on the cover of *Best of Playgirl*. Plaintiff proved that advertising is expensive to buy, that publicity has value for an actor. But what he did not prove was that loss of publicity as the result of his non-appearance on the cover of *Best of Playgirl* did in fact damage him in any substantial way or in any specific amount. Plaintiff's claim sharply contrasts with those few breach of contract cases that have found damages for loss of publicity reasonably certain and reasonably calculable, as in refusals to continue an advertising contract. In such cases the court has assessed damages at the market value of the advertising, less the agreed contract price. Plaintiff's claim for damages more closely resembles those which have been held speculative and conjectural, as in the analogous cases of *Jones v. San Bernardino Real Estate*

(continues)

Ericson v. Playgirl, Inc.

(continued from previous page)
Board (1959) 168 Cal.App.2d 661, 665, 336 P.2d 606 where the court declined to award purely conjectural damages for loss of commissions, contacts, business associations, and clientele allegedly occasioned by plaintiff's expulsion from a local realty board; and of *Fisher v. Hampton* (1975) 44 Cal.App.3d 741, 118 Cal.Rptr. 811, where the court rejected an award of damages for defendant's failure to drill a $35,000 oil well when geological reports opined that oil would not be found and no evidence whatever established that plaintiff had been damaged.

An examination of the cases allowing recovery of damages for loss of publicity as a result of breach of contract discloses that in each instance the lost publicity grew out of the loss of the artist's exercise of his profession, i.e., loss of the opportunity to act, to broadcast, to sing, to conduct an orchestra, to entertain; or resulted from the loss of credit to the artist for professional services connected with a particular work, i.e., a script, play, musical composition, design, production, and the like. Publicity in both these categories performs a similar function in that it permits patrons and producers to evaluate the artist's merits in connection with the performance of his art. Damages for the loss of such publicity do not present insuperable difficulties in calculation, for the artist's future earnings can be directly correlated to his box of-

fice appeal or to his known record of successes.

A yawning gulf exists between the cases that involve loss of professional publicity and the instant case in which plaintiff complains of loss of mere general publicity that bears no relation to the practice of his art. His situation is comparable to that of an actor who hopes to obtain wide publicity by cutting the ribbon for the opening of a new resort-hotel complex, by sponsoring a golf or tennis tournament, by presenting the winning trophy at the national horse show, or by acting as master of ceremonies at a televised political dinner. Each of these activities may generate wide publicity that conceivably could bring the artist to the attention of patrons and producers of his art and thus lead to professional employment. Yet none of it bears any relation to the practice of his art. Plaintiff's argument, in essence, is that for an actor all publicity is valuable, and the loss of any publicity as a result of breach of contract is compensable. Carried to this point, we think his claim for damages becomes wholly speculative. It is possible, as plaintiff suggests, that a television programmer might have seen his photograph on the cover of *Best of Playgirl,* might have scheduled plaintiff for a talk show, and that a motion picture producer viewing the talk show might recall plaintiff's past performances, and decide to offer him a role in his next production. But it

is equally plausible to speculate that plaintiff might have been hurt professionally rather than helped by having his picture appear on the cover of *Best of Playgirl,* that a motion picture producer whose attention had been drawn by the cover of the magazine to its contents depicting plaintiff posing naked in Lion Country Safari might dismiss plaintiff from serious consideration for a role in his next production. The speculative and conjectural nature of such possibilities speaks for itself.

Assessment of the value of general publicity unrelated to professional performance takes us on a random walk whose destination is as unpredictable as the lottery and the roulette wheel. When, as at bench, damages to earning capacity and loss of professional publicity in the practice of one's art are not involved, we think recovery of compensable damages for loss of publicity is barred by the Civil Code requirement that damages for breach of contract be clearly foreseeable and clearly ascertainable.

Plaintiff, however, is entitled to recover nominal damages for breach of contract. We evaluate plaintiff's right to nominal damages by analogy to Civil Code section 3344, which provides minimum statutory damages of $300 for knowing commercial use of a person's name or likeness without his consent.

The judgment is modified to reduce the amount of damages to $300, and, as so modified, the judgment is affirmed. ⚖

---

3. *Foreseeability.* Another important limitation on recovery of compensatory damages is that the loss sustained by the plaintiff should have been reasonably foreseeable to the defendant. Assume that Sam's Repair Shop promised to fix Al's car and deliver it to him on June 1. Sam was a day late, delivering the car on June 2. However, on June 1, Al had been bitten by a rabid dog and his injuries had been exacerbated because he had had no car with which to drive himself

to the emergency room. The extra medical injuries (potential consequential damages) could not be compensated because the injury was not reasonably foreseeable to Sam.

The leading case in this area is *Hadley v. Baxendale,* 156 Eng.Rep. 145 (1854), where plaintiff's flour mill suffered a broken gear. Plaintiff hired defendant to transport the gear and its attached drive shaft to the manufacturer for repairs. Plaintiff told defendant that the gear was part of his milling machinery and that defendant should act promptly. Plaintiff did not, however, tell defendant that his entire mill would be shut down until the repairs were made. Defendant breached the contract by performing two days late. Plaintiff sued for the profits lost during this two-day period. The court held that it was not reasonably foreseeable to defendant that plaintiff's entire operation would be shut down for two days; therefore, the lost profits could not be recovered. In so ruling, the English court set forth two important rules. First, it held that a plaintiff can recover direct damages "as may fairly and reasonably be considered . . . arising naturally, i.e., according to the usual course of things" from the breach itself. Second, the court held that plaintiff may recover consequential damages "such as may reasonably be supposed to have been in the contemplation of both parties, at the time they made the contract, as the probable result of it." Thus, the court introduced reasonable foreseeability as an important aspect of recovery for consequential damages.

The following case applies these general rules of foreseeability.

KENFORD COMPANY, INC. v. COUNTY OF ERIE

Court of Appeals of New York, 540 N.Y.S.2d 1 (1989)

 In May of 1968, the County of Erie adopted enabling legislation authorizing it to finance and construct a domed sports stadium in the vicinity of the City of Buffalo. Kenford Co., through its president and sole shareholder, Cottrell, had acquired options on various parcels of land. It offered to sell that land to the county for construction of the stadium; the county rejected the offer. Kenford then offered to donate to the county the land upon which the stadium was to be built, in exchange for which the county was to permit Cottrell and his associate Hofheinz (who together had formed the management company of Dome Stadium Inc. [DSI]) to lease or manage the proposed stadium.

In June 1969, the county adopted a resolution accepting this offer, after which the parties began contract negotiation. During this time, Kenford exercised the options to buy several parcels of land. The contract was signed requiring Kenford to donate 178 acres of land and the county to commence construction within 12 months. The county agreed to negotiate a 40-year lease with DSI under which the county was to receive revenues of not less than $63.75 million

over the 40-year term, comprising (1) all tax revenues received by the county generated by operation of the stadium site; (2) rental payments from DSI; and (3) increased real property taxes resulting from increased assessments received from the "peripheral lands"—those lands near the stadium owned or to be acquired by Kenford.

When the county was unable to raise enough revenue to build the stadium, it adopted a resolution cancelling the contract with Kenford and DSI. DSI and Kenford sued for breach of contract and were awarded summary judgment on the issue of liability. A nine-month trial followed on the matter of damages. Appeals and a retrial followed. The matter then came before New York's highest court for review of a lower court judgment that Kenford was entitled to recover $6.5 million in lost appreciation in the value of its property located on the periphery of the stadium.

Mollen, Judge:

It is well established that in actions for breach of contract, the nonbreaching party may recover general damages which are the natural and probable consequence of the breach. "[I]n order

to impose on the defaulting party a further liability than for damages [which] naturally and directly [flow from the breach], i.e., in the ordinary course of things, arising from a breach of contract, such unusual or extraordinary damages must have been brought within the contemplation of the parties as the probable result of a breach at the time of or prior to contracting" (*Chapman v. Fargo*, 223 N.Y. 32, 36, 119 N.E. 76; *see also, Booth v. Spuyten Duyvil Rolling Mill Co.*, 60 N.Y. 487; *Hadley v. Baxendale*, 9 Exch 341, 156 Eng.Rep. 145; McCormick, Damages § 138, at 562). In determining the reasonable contemplation of the parties, the nature, purpose and particular circumstances of the contract known by the parties should be considered as well as "what liability the defendant fairly may be supposed to have assumed consciously, or to have warranted the plaintiff reasonably to suppose that it assumed, when the contract was made" (*Globe Ref. Co. v. Landa Cotton Oil Co.*, 190 U.S. 540).

In the case before us, it is beyond dispute that at the time the contract was executed, all parties thereto harbored an expectation and anticipation that the proposed domed stadium facility would bring about an economic boom in the County and would result in increased land values and increased

(continues)

KENFORD COMPANY, INC. v. COUNTY OF ERIE

(continued from previous page)
property taxes. We cannot conclude, however, that this hope or expectation of increased property values and taxes necessarily or logically leads to the conclusion that the parties contemplated that the County would assume liability for Kenford's loss of anticipated appreciation in the value of its peripheral lands if the stadium were not built.

Similarly, there is no provision in the contract between Kenford and the County, nor is there any evidence in the record to demonstrate that the parties, at any relevant time, reasonably contemplated or would have contemplated that the County was undertaking a contractual responsibility for the lack of appreciation in the value of Kenford's peripheral lands in the event the stadium was not built. This conclusion is buttressed by the fact that Kenford was under no contractual obligation to the County to acquire or maintain ownership of any land surrounding the 178 acres it was required to donate to the County. Although the County was aware that Kenford had acquired and intended to further acquire peripheral lands, this knowledge, in and of itself, is insufficient, as a matter of law, to impose liability on the

County for the loss of anticipated appreciation in the value of those lands since the County never contemplated at the time of the contract's execution that it assumed legal responsibility for these damages upon a breach of the contract. As this court noted in *Booth v. Spuyten Duyvil Rolling Mill Co.*, 60 N.Y. 487, 494, *supra*) "bare notice of special consequences which might result from a breach of contract, unless under such circumstances as to imply that it formed the basis of the agreement, would not be sufficient [to impose liability for special damages]" (*see also, Czarnikow-Rionda Co. v. Federal Sugar Ref. Co.*, 255 N.Y. 33, 173 N.E. 913, *supra* [the defendant supplier of sugar was not made aware at the time of the contract that the plaintiff purchaser could not acquire sugar on the open market and, therefore, was not liable for the plaintiff's special damages arising out of the breach of contract]; *Baldwin v. United States Tel. Co.*, 45 N.Y. 744, *supra* [the defendant telegraph company was not liable for special damages caused by delay in delivery of message since it was without notice or information indicating that extraordinary care or speed of delivery was necessary].

Thus, the constant refrain which flows throughout the legion of breach of contract cases dating back to the leading case of *Hadley v. Baxendale* provides that damages which may be recovered by a party for breach of contract are restricted to those damages which were reasonably foreseen or contemplated by the parties during their negotiations or at the time the contract was executed. The evident purpose of this well-accepted principle of contract law is to limit the liability for unassumed risks of one entering into a contract and, thus, diminish the risk of business enterprise. In the case before us, although Kenford obviously anticipated and expected that it would reap financial benefits from an anticipated dramatic increase in the value of its peripheral lands upon the completion of the proposed domed stadium facility, these expectations did not ripen or translate into cognizable breach of contract damages since there is no indication whatsoever that the County reasonably contemplated at any relevant time that it was to assume liability for Kenford's unfulfilled land appreciation expectations in the event that the stadium was not built.

[Reversed.]🙐

If the plaintiff establishes causation, reasonable certainty, and foreseeability of loss, recovery often will be calculated according to the following formula:

Damages = Direct Loss + Consequential Loss + Incidental Loss – Cost Avoided – Loss Avoided.

Assume that P had a contract to sell a tract of land to D for $50,000. In order to induce D to make the deal, P also agreed to do $500 worth of grading on the tract and to sell to D a smaller lot for $5,000. The fair market value of the two tracts was $40,000 and $6,000, respectively. D breached his promise and cancelled the deal after P had done half of the grading. P hired a real estate agent who sold the larger tract to X for $40,000, taking an 8 percent commis-

sion. P's direct loss is $10,000 ($50,000 – $40,000), his consequential loss is $250 (the cost of grading), and his incidental loss is $3,200 (the real estate commission). At the same time, P had avoided a cost of $250 (the remainder of the grading) and avoided a loss of $1,000 (for sale of the smaller tract). Therefore, P's recovery would be $10,000 + $250 + $3,200 – $250 – $1,000 = $12,200.

Reliance Measure. If the law cannot compensate the plaintiff's expectation interest, perhaps because the plaintiff cannot establish with reasonable certainty the profit he would make on the transaction, the courts often protect the reliance interest instead. Other situations where the reliance interest is compensated include cases where a contract is frustrated by impossibility of performance or where there has been partial performance of an oral contract that the statute of frauds required to be in writing.

Plaintiffs suing for the reliance interest are allowed to recover such items as expenses incurred in preparing to perform their part of the contract, expenses incurred in actually performing, and losses incurred due to forgone opportunities that they would have pursued absent the contract with the defendant.

Assume that defendant promises to deliver a model stove to plaintiff at a trade fair. Plaintiff plans to demonstrate the stove and take orders from customers. Defendant fails to deliver the stove in time for the fair. If plaintiff could prove with reasonable certainty the profits he would have made from demonstrating the stove, he can recover them under the expectation interest. However, this is likely to be too speculative to establish with reasonable certainty. Therefore, at the very least, the court can compensate plaintiff's reliance interest by making defendant pay the costs, such as rental of the space at the trade fair and of materials to construct a booth, that plaintiff incurred in reliance on defendant's promise.

Restitution Interest. Assume that in the trade fair case, the plaintiff had made an advance payment to the defendant of $400. Because the defendant did not perform, the plaintiff should recover that amount also. The defendant has received a benefit and the law requires the defendant to make restitution to the plaintiff. The key to restitution is "unjust enrichment"—the defendant should forfeit benefits he received from the plaintiff's performance in cases where the defendant did not do as he promised. The concept of restitution pervades the law of both legal and equitable remedies, and we shall return to it later in this chapter.

Mitigation of Damages

There is no reason for the law to compensate the plaintiff for losses arising from the defendant's breach that the plaintiff could reasonably have avoided. Therefore the **mitigation of damages doctrine** requires plaintiffs to take reasonable steps to minimize the accumulation of damages.

Once aware of the other party's breach, a potential plaintiff may not continue his activities so as to increase his damages. For example, assume that Deeco, Inc., hires Peeco, Inc., to build a parking garage. After Peeco has spent $10,000 in commencing performance, Deeco unequivocally tells Peeco that it no longer wants the parking garage built and will not pay for it. If Peeco continues to work on the garage, spending another $8,000, it clearly has failed to mitigate its damages. It may recover the first $10,000, but not the subsequent $8,000, which was clearly avoidable.

A party may even be obliged to take positive steps to minimize damages. For example, assume that Juanita has a five-year contract to work for Acme Corporation as a research chemist. After one year, Acme fires Juanita without cause. Juanita should not sit home for the next four years. If she does, passing up several opportunities to obtain comparable jobs at comparable pay, the law will not compensate her for her lost salary. Instead, the law places on Juanita the obligation to make reasonable efforts to find comparable work. She need not take a job that does not utilize her education, nor need she move across the country in order to find a position. Reasonableness is the key. At the same time, any reasonable expenses Juanita incurs (e.g., hiring an employment agency) in attempting to mitigate her damages are compensable, even if ultimately unsuccessful.

The duty to mitigate is incorporated in Article 2 of the Uniform Commercial Code. We shall see in Chapter 23 that when a buyer of goods breaches a contract, the seller is often obliged to make conscientious efforts to find another buyer for those goods. If the second buyer pays less, the seller may recover from the breaching party not only the difference in purchase price but also the incidental expenses incurred in finding a new buyer.

Although almost every party in every situation has a duty to mitigate, a majority of jurisdictions make an exception for landlords where a lease has been executed. They do not require the landlord to search for a new tenant when the current tenant breaches its lease by moving out and refusing to pay rent. Many jurisdictions, on the other hand, do not recognize this exception.

Consider one other wrinkle. Assume that Acme has contracted to rent a truck from We-Haul Leasing, Inc. Acme breaches, but points out to We-Haul that it can mitigate its damages by leasing the truck to the next customer that comes in needing a truck. However, *if* We-Haul has a different truck that it would have rented to that next customer, then it cannot effectively mitigate its damages. It could have had *two* rentals if Acme had lived up to its part of the lease. Therefore, We-Haul may recover from Acme.

The following case illustrates some important mitigation principles in the employment context.

STEWART V. BOARD OF EDUCATION OF RITENOUR

Missouri Court of Appeals, 630 S.W.2d 130 (1982)

In 1974, plaintiff Stewart was a "permanent teacher" under the Teacher Tenure Act, having taught for 15 years in defendant school district. The Board of Education terminated plaintiff in June 1974. Plaintiff sued. After multiple trials and appeals, the termination was held to be wrongful and damages were assessed. However, the case was heard one more time by the trial court on the issue of mitigation of damages. Despite Stewart's statement that she had made no efforts to secure any type of teaching position during the five years that she was unemployed, the trial judge refused to reduce the damages it had assessed against the Board in the sum of $108,948.01. The Board appealed.

Simon, Judge:

. . . The Board contends that Stewart failed to use reasonable diligence to secure similar employment. In *Wolf v. Missouri State Training School for Boys,* 517 S.W.2d 138, 142-43 (Mo. banc 1974), our Supreme Court stated: "the employer . . . [may] reduce damages recoverable by a wrongfully discharged employee by whatever the employee has earned or by reasonable diligence could have earned during the period of wrongful discharge." *Wolf* involved a wrongfully discharged state corrections officer. Our court, following *Wolf,* held that the doctrine of mitigation applies to wrongfully discharged teachers protected under the Teacher Tenure Act.

A great deal of confusion surrounds the doctrine of mitigation. While it is often stated that the employee has the "duty" to mitigate damages, this characterization is misleading. As Professor Corbin notes, "The law does not penalize . . . [plaintiff's] inaction; it merely does nothing to compensate . . . [plain-

tiff] for the loss that he helped to cause by not avoiding it." 5 Corbin on Contracts § 1039 (1954). Thus, the doctrine of avoidable consequences is the basis for most rules of general damages. Missouri law is in clear agreement with that of the overwhelming majority of jurisdictions to the effect that the Board has the burden of proving that Stewart could have mitigated her damages.

Furthermore, McCormick states, "It is not enough for the employer to prove that the plaintiff made no effort to get other employment, but he must go further and prove that such employment could have been secured." McCormick, Damages 628 (1975 reprint).

In *Ryan v. Superintendent of Schools of Quincy,* 374 Mass. 670, 373 N.E.2d 1178, 1181 (1978), the Massachusetts Supreme Court outlined the defendant's burden:

> A former employer meets its burden of proof of 'mitigation of damages' if the employer proves that (a) one or more discoverable opportunities for comparable employment were available in a location as, or more convenient than, the place of former employment, (b) the improperly discharged employee unreasonably made no attempt to apply for any such job, and (c) it was reasonably likely that the former employee would obtain one of those comparable jobs.

In *Ryan,* defendant school committee wrongfully discharged plaintiff Ryan, a fifty-nine year old art teacher. After winning reinstatement, Ryan sought damages in the form of back pay. As in the case at bar, Ryan did not apply for any teaching positions during the five years of her unemployment. The court stated that "[t]his fact alone . . . is not sufficient to establish that the employee could have mitigated damages."

The court proceeded to examine the facts of the case to determine whether "it was reasonably likely that Ryan could have obtained a compa-

rable job." *Id.* The court noted that the facts indicated that during the period in question the number of art teachers greatly exceeded demand. The court also noted that Ryan would not have been able to get favorable references from her former employer. Finally, the court concluded that Ryan's age would probably have been viewed unfavorably by any prospective employers. On these facts the court held that "the defendants did not sustain their burden of proving that it was 'reasonably likely that the former employee would obtain one of . . . [the] comparable jobs'."

Likewise, we do not believe that the Board met their burden of proof. The evidence introduced at trial reveals that there were teaching jobs available in the St. Louis area during Stewart's period of unemployment for which she was qualified. The Board presented three witnesses who were in charge of hiring teaching personnel in different metropolitan school districts. They testified that in every year from 1974 to 1979, each of their districts hired from zero to 27 teachers in Stewart's subject area. Generally, the number of applicants exceeded the number of vacancies. For example, Dr. Burchard Neel, Associate Superintendent for Personnel for the St. Louis Public Schools, testified that in 1976 when the St. Louis Public Schools hired 27 teachers there were several hundred applicants. The witnesses further testified that from 1974 to 1979 none of their districts had hired a teacher in Stewart's age bracket, with Stewart's qualifications, who had been discharged from another district. None of the evidence indicated that there was a reasonable likelihood that Stewart could have received a teaching position. In fact, the evidence indicated that Stewart's chances of finding a teaching job were slim at best.

Dr. Ellen Harshman, Director of Career Planning and Placement at St.

(continues)

STEWART V. BOARD OF EDUCATION OF RITENOUR

(continued from previous page)
Louis University, testified that a person in Stewart's position would have "very poor" possibilities. Viewing the record in its entirety, we conclude that the Board did not meet its burden of proof. Our holding should not be construed to constitute our approval of a discharged employee's reaping a "reward" as a consequence of her failure to make a reasonable effort to mitigate her damages. Our holding is simply a result of the Board's failure to carry its burden of proof, i.e., of showing there was a reasonable likelihood that Stewart could have obtained one of the available positions. Therefore, we affirm the trial court's decision that Stewart's recovery should not be reduced for her failure to mitigate.⚖

Nominal Damages

Nominal damages are a form of compensatory damages given in a trivial amount (such as six cents or one dollar). It is appropriate to grant nominal damages, for example, where the plaintiff establishes a breach of contract but cannot prove his or her damages with reasonable certainty. *Ericson v. Playgirl, Inc.* is an example (although a special statute established a minimum recovery of $300).

Nominal damages are also appropriate to remedy a technical breach of contract in situations where the plaintiff did not suffer any injury. Assume that P contracts to sell a tract of land to D for $50,000. D breaches, refusing to pay anything, and P sues. Before the suit progresses very far, a new buyer appears and pays P $70,000 for the land. P has not suffered any injury from D's breach. Still, D has breached a promise and the court will, as a matter of principle, allow P to recover nominal damages. In addition to the principle at stake, P is now the prevailing party in the lawsuit, making D responsible for paying court costs (but usually not attorney's fees) in many jurisdictions. (Other jurisdictions do not allow the plaintiff to recover court costs unless a specified minimum amount has been recovered. Such statutes are aimed at discouraging litigation over valid but trivial claims.)

Liquidated Damages

A **liquidated damages** provision is a clause in a contract that stipulates the amount of damages that will be paid in the event of a breach. Such a clause has several purposes. It may avoid a protracted dispute and trial on the issue of damages. This will lower the parties' costs of proof and society's cost of providing a judge and jury. Such a clause may diminish the losses of the defaulting party or, conversely, establish a minimum level of recovery from the nondefaulting party in a case where losses may well be speculative. It allows both parties to better calculate their level of risk in a given transaction.

Courts generally wish to enforce contracts as made by the parties, but they do tend to be leery of liquidated damages clauses, mostly out of a fear that such clauses may be used as a "penalty" to unfairly punish or coerce one of the parties. Typically, courts set forth three criteria for an enforceable liquidated damages clause. First, the injury arising from the breach must be difficult or impossible to estimate accurately. If the amount of damages arising from a breach is easy to determine, a liquidated damages clause does not save trial time and expense and therefore loses much of its justification. Second, the parties must intend for the clause to provide a remedy for the injured party, not a penalty for the defaulting party. This relates back to the notion that part of the freedom of contract is the freedom to breach a contract.

In virtually every case involving the enforceability of a liquidated damages clause, the focus of the court becomes the third criterion—whether the amount established as liquidated damages is a *reasonable estimate* of the actual loss caused by the subsequent breach. The courts will not enforce a clause that sets an amount so far above the true damages sustained that it constitutes a "penalty" imposed on the defendant rather than legitimate compensation for the plaintiff's loss. The reasonableness of the estimate is judged as of the time the contract is entered into, although UCC 2-718(1) allows amounts that are reasonable considering anticipated *or* actual harm.

THE LAW AT WORK

Box 19.1
The Law
at Work

The general rule in contract law is that punitive damages are *not* recoverable in breach-of-contract actions, even if the defendant intentionally refused to perform his or her promise.

However, several jurisdictions do allow recovery of punitive damages when they find that the breach constitutes an independent intentional tort or an independent breach of fiduciary duty. These exceptions have been invoked increasingly in recent years to benefit consumers who have been mistreated by businesses. For example, many jurisdictions recognize that an insurance company's intentional refusal to pay an insured's valid claim may constitute not only a breach of contract, but also an intentional tort often called the *bad faith tort.* Such jurisdictions allow plaintiffs to recover punitive damages in amounts that often dwarf the sum due under the policy.

Although the rationale underlying the bad faith tort seemingly applies to a wide range of situations, most courts have been reluctant to extend their holdings beyond the insurance context. Indeed, courts and academics have struggled with the theory underlying this combination of contract law and tort law, sometimes denominated a *contort.*

Consider two California cases. In the 1984 case *Seaman's Direct Buying Service v. Standard Oil Co.*, 206 Cal.Rptr. 354 (1984), the California Supreme Court expanded the bad faith tort in a lawsuit in which a would-be oil dealer sued an oil company that breached a contract to supply oil. The court stated that the bad faith tort should be available where defendant "in addition to breaching the contract, . . . seeks to shield itself from liability by denying, in bad faith and without probable cause, that the contract exists." However, just four years later in *Foley v. Interactive Data Co.*, 254 Cal.Rptr. 211 (1988), the court refused to apply the bad faith tort to an employee's suit against an employer for wrongful discharge, criticizing the "uncritical incorporation" by some lower California courts "of the insurance model into the employment context, without careful consideration of the fundamental policies underlying the development of tort and contract law in general or of significant differences between the insurer/insured and employer/employee relationship."

If an employer wrongfully fires an employee and then claims in bad faith and without probable cause that no contract exists, should the bad faith tort apply? Most courts would say "no," relegating the plaintiff to simple breach of contract damages. Do you agree with this approach? Do you see principled distinctions between this situation and the insurance scenario?

(Indeed, even under the common law if the estimate turns out to be wildly inaccurate as a gauge of the actual damages, even if it seemed reasonable when the contract was made, the courts are unlikely to enforce it.)

Whether a liquidated damages clause is an unenforceable penalty provision is a matter of law for the judge to decide. The labels used by the parties in the contract do not control. In *U.S. v. Bethlehem Steel Co.*, 205 U.S. 105 (1907), because of a promise for early delivery, the government agreed to buy guns from defendant even though its bid was higher than those of competitors. The contract provided that for each day defendant's delivery was late, a "penalty" of $35 would be imposed. Because this sum represented the average difference in price between defendant's bid and those of the cheaper, but slower, suppliers, it was enforced as a genuine attempt to gauge the government's actual damages.

One form of liquidated damages clause that is almost always enforced is that calling for the breaching party to pay the attorney's fees of the nondefaulting party who is forced to bring a lawsuit.

United Air Lines, Inc. v. Austin Travel Corp.

U.S. Second Circuit Court of Appeals, 867 F.2d 737 (1989)

Case

Plaintiff United Air Lines owns and markets to travel agents the Apollo CRS, a computerized reservation system that provides subscribers access to a vast data bank through which they may make airline reservations, issue tickets, and reserve car rentals and hotel rooms. United is paid a monthly subscription fee and charges airlines a booking fee each time a travel agent uses Apollo to book a flight on another airline. United also markets its ABS, a back-office accounting and management system for travel agents.

Defendant Austin is a travel agency that formerly used a different CRS. However, in 1985 it acquired two small travel agencies (Karson and Fantasy) that subscribed to Apollo. Austin assumed their contracts with United and then executed a five-year Apollo contract to cover its Oceanside and Mitchell Field locations. The contract for Oceanside and Mitchell Field provided for liquidated damages consisting of (1) 80 percent of the remaining monthly fees due under the contract, (2) 80 percent of the variable charges accrued by generation of tickets and itineraries for the month preceding termination, multiplied by the number of months remaining on the contract, and (3) 50 percent of the average monthly booking fee revenues, using the first six months of the contract as a basis for calculation, multiplied by the number of months remaining on the contract. The Fantasy contract contained only the first two elements of liquidated damages.

Austin breached the agreement when one of United's rivals offered to indemnify Austin for any damages incurred for breach if it would terminate the Apollo contracts and buy the rival's system. United brought this breach of contract action. The trial judge held for United, ruling, most importantly, that the liquidated damages clauses were valid and enforceable. Austin appealed.

Miner, Circuit Judge:

It is commonplace for contracting parties to determine in advance the amount of compensation due in case of a breach of contract. 5 *Corbin on Contracts* § 1054, at 319 (1964). A liquidated damages clause generally will be upheld by a court, unless the liquidated amount is a penalty because it is plainly or grossly disproportionate to the probable loss anticipated when the contract was executed. Liquidated damages are not penalties if they bear a "reasonable proportion to the probable loss and the amount of actual loss is incapable or difficult of precise estimation." *Leasing Service Corp. v. Justice,* 673 F.2d 70, 73 (2d Cir.1982).

The liquidated damages fixed in the Apollo contracts were, as the district court found, reasonable at the time the contracts were executed. Most of United's costs when providing Apollo service are either fixed or determined in the early stages of the contractual relationship. The few costs that United would avoid by an early termination of an Apollo contract are estimated to be "less than 20 percent of the amount of revenue from the monthly fixed usage fees and variable charges." The Apollo contracts' liquidated damages clauses provide for recovery by United of only 80% of the fixed and variable charges. Austin is thus provided with better than adequate credit for the costs United is able to avoid by the early removal of the Apollo CRSs from Austin premises.

Austin complains that the 20% discount incorporated by the liquidated damages provisions underestimates the savings realized by United in the event of early contract termination. Austin

points to testimony by a representative of a competing CRS vendor that United's avoidable costs likely equal forty to fifty percent of United's total costs. The testimony of a competitor about United's costs and savings is inherently suspect, and United presented sufficient evidence to justify the 20% figure. The appropriate analysis is not whether a better quantification of damages could have been drafted by the contracting parties, but whether the amount of liquidated damages actually inserted in the contract is reasonable. We note as well, as the district court did, that CRS contracts of United's competitors often call for 100% of rent due on the unexpired term of the contract; United obligated Austin for only 80%. There is no indication that the estimate of probable loss, identified in the contracts as liquidated damages, is either unfair or unreasonable. Indeed, the liquidated damages provisions edge closer toward over-generousness to Austin than they do toward unreasonableness.

Austin further depicts the liquidated damages clauses as imposing penalties because they provide the same amount of damages for each possible breach of the contract, no matter how insignificant. Austin argues that establishing a single liquidated damages amount for any breach indicates that a fair estimation of probable loss for each breach was not conceived when the contract was drafted and executed.

Austin, however, ignores basic tenets of contract law. "A party may terminate a contract only because of substantial nonperformance by the other party so fundamental 'as to defeat the objects of the parties in making the agreement'." *Maywood Sportservice, Inc. v. Maywood Park Trotting Ass'n, Inc.,* 14 Ill.App.3d 141, 302 N.E.2d 79, 84 (1973). Neither United nor Austin can terminate the contracts because of a non-material breach. Thus, liquidated *(continues)*

UNITED AIR LINES, INC. v. AUSTIN TRAVEL CORP.

(continued from previous page)
damages can only be owed to United in the event of a material breach by Austin.

Furthermore, the presumed intent of the parties is that a liquidated damages provision will apply only to material breaches. Additionally, for a non-material breach to allow an ag-grieved party to abrogate the contract, it must be explicitly stated in the agreement of the parties.

We are not persuaded that the liquidated damages outlined in the Apollo contracts were meant to apply to trivial breaches. Article 12 of the Lease Agreement states in unexceptional language that liquidated damages are to be awarded for a failure of "any of the covenants, agreements, terms or conditions." We take this language to refer to material breach. Absent a more explicit demonstration of intent to apply the termination provisions to trivial breaches, the liquidated damages clauses must be enforced.

[Affirmed.]☙

Equitable Remedies

Courts of equity developed in England because the early courts at law could give only one form of remedy—money damages. In other words, they could award a landowner damages caused by a neighbor's trespassing, but could not order the neighbor not to trespass again in the future. Courts of equity developed in large part to provide more flexible forms of remedy in situations where fairness seemed to demand them. Several forms of equitable remedy are available to the party injured by breach of contract. Whereas damages are generally assessed by juries, equitable remedies are within the province of the court and are enforced through the court's authority to hold in contempt persons who violate its orders.

Specific Performance

When a plaintiff asks the court for an order of **specific performance,** he or she is asking the judge to order the defendant to perform the promise that was made. Obviously there may be many instances where specific performance is a remedy that a plaintiff would prefer. If the judge orders specific performance, the plaintiff receives exactly what was bargained for and need not worry about collecting a money judgment or searching for someone to provide substitute performance.

Nonetheless, the courts presume that an award of money damages is the primary remedy in breach-of-contract cases. Specific performance is reserved for the "extraordinary" cases where money damages are inadequate to fully compensate the plaintiff. Specific performance is most frequently ordered when "unique" property is at stake, so that an award of money damages would not fully compensate the plaintiff who could not take the money anywhere to buy the item originally contracted for. Assume, for example, that plaintiff contracted to buy a secret recipe from defendant. If defendant breached its promise to deliver the recipe, an award of damages to plaintiff would not enable plaintiff to obtain the recipe elsewhere, because it remains defendant's trade secret.

Other items often held to be "unique" include rare books and coins, family heirlooms, priceless works of art, items in extremely short supply, patents, copyrights, and shares of closely held corporations which cannot be bought through any market or stockbroker. For historical reasons, courts view every tract of land as unique (even though it may be the same size and have the same characteristics as a tract adjacent to it). Therefore, contracts to sell real property are always enforceable through orders of specific performance. The same may be said of contracts to sell businesses, for these are also presumed to be unique.

Courts will often specifically enforce contracts against *insolvent* defendants, because an award of money damages against a defendant who cannot pay is certainly not adequate compensation. (Conflicts with the priorities given creditors under the bankruptcy laws must be avoided, however.) Specific performance is often granted in cases where the plaintiff's monetary damages are difficult to measure with reasonable certainty; absent specific performance, the plaintiff might be relegated to mere nominal damages.

Limitations. There are several factors that limit the availability of the specific performance remedy.

First and foremost, specific performance is available only within the *discretion* of a court of equity. In attempting to achieve fairness and equity, courts must consider such factors as hardship to the defendant and impact on societal interests.

Additionally, courts consider traditional equitable rules such as the "clean hands" doctrine (no equitable remedy will be granted to a plaintiff who has breached his or her obligations in any material way), the doctrine of unconscionability (the courts will not be a party to enforcing an extremely one-sided bargain), and the doctrine of laches (no remedy for a party who has "slept on his rights" by unduly delaying the bringing of suit). Obviously courts will not order specific performance in contracts that involve illegality, mistake, or fraud.

Specific performance will not be granted in *personal service contracts.* Assume that Sally hires Waldo to paint her portrait because he is the best-known portrait artist in the state and Sally's personal favorite. If Waldo refuses to live up to his obligations the court might allow Sally to recover damages, but would not order specific performance. One reason often given is that it would violate the Thirteenth Amendment's proscription against involuntary servitude to force Waldo to paint against his will. A more plausible policy ground is the *difficulty of supervision* involved. How could a court effectively enforce Waldo's obligation? How could it supervise him to ensure that he did a "good job"? A court can transfer title to land, but it cannot paint for Waldo or sing for a reluctant rock star. For the same reason, courts often refuse to order specific performance in long-term contracts that might require them to undertake years of supervision.

Specific performance and damages are normally thought of as alternative forms of remedies. However, a plaintiff might be able to obtain both in the same case, especially if a court could feasibly order only partial performance by the defendant.

UCC.   If there has been any trend in the common law of specific performance in recent years, it has been to soften the "adequacy" of remedy test, thereby increasing the availability of specific performance. That trend is reflected in UCC 2-716, which authorizes specific performance in sale-of-goods contracts "where the goods are unique *or in other proper circumstances.*" [Emphasis added.] Still, even under the UCC, specific performance remains an "extraordinary" remedy.

Injunction

Assume that Chuck, a football coach, has a five-year contract with the Armadillos, an NFL franchise. In the second year of the contract, Chuck is offered a much more lucrative deal by Big State University and announces that he is accepting it. Obviously the Armadillos will wish to force Chuck to live up to his contract. Just as obviously, no court would order Chuck to specifically perform that contract. In addition to the "involuntary servitude" consideration, there is the difficulty of supervision. How could a court ensure that Chuck hired the right assistants, kept the best players, or called the appropriate plays? However, while a court could not feasibly order Chuck to do what he had promised to do (coach the Armadillos), it could order him *not* to do what he had promised *not* to do (coach Big State U). By signing a full-time contract with the Armadillos, Chuck had implicitly promised not to take any conflicting obligations. Such an order is called an **injunction.**

As with orders of specific performance, injunctive orders are within the court's equitable discretion. Courts will consider factors of fairness, unconscionability, and the plaintiff's "clean hands" in deciding whether to issue such orders. Injunctions are often used in cases involving sports and entertainment, and in normal employment relationships when a party seeks to enforce a covenant not to compete signed by a former employee. We studied the enforceability of these covenants in Chapter 14.

Reformation

Assume that Sharon and Nick reach an oral agreement that Nick's attorney reduces to writing. After the contract is signed, Sharon realizes that because of the attorney's error, the writing does not accurately reflect the oral agreement. Sharon may ask a court for an order of **reformation.** In effect, Sharon is asking the court to rewrite the contract, but only for the limited purpose of enforcing its true terms. The court is not making a new contract, but simply enforcing the parties' agreement as made. Sharon should have read the contract before she signed it, but *if* she can prove that an error has caused a discrepancy between the oral agreement and the written contract, her negligence would not bar reformation in most courts.

The parol evidence rule (see Chapter 16), which prevents introduction of oral testimony to vary the terms of a written contract, would not block Sharon's efforts in this case. It applies only when the writing was intended to be the final and complete statement of the parties' agreement. Most courts conclude that such is not the case where an error in reducing the oral agreement to writing has occurred.

However, the statute of frauds (see Chapter 16, again) does pose serious problems. What if the agreement is the type that the statute of frauds requires to be in writing? Is Sharon asking the court to enforce an oral agreement in contravention of the statute of frauds? Some courts think that this is exactly what she is asking, and will refuse reformation. Other courts reason that they are simply correcting the mistaken written agreement, and will grant reformation.

In relatively rare instances, some courts will reform contracts not to enforce the parties' original agreement, but to modify that original agreement to conform to the law. For example, we learned in Chapter 14 that if a covenant not to compete is drawn too broadly, many courts will rewrite it to cover a smaller geographic area or a shorter time span and will then enforce the modified version.

Rescission

An order of **rescission** is a court order terminating the contractual duties of each party. Usually (but not always) such an order will also allow each party to obtain restitution for any performance rendered to the other party.

Rescission is granted as a remedy in a wide variety of contracts, including those involving voidable agreements (e.g., fraud, mistake, undue influence, innocent misrepresentation, or parties lacking capacity) and those involving illegal activity.

Restitution

An order of **restitution** seeks to place a party in the position he or she was in before the contract was entered into. As noted earlier in this chapter, sometimes such an order will take the form of a damages award telling the defendant to pay the plaintiff the monetary value of the benefit the plaintiff conferred on the defendant. But the notion of restitution is very broad. It can also include an equitable order for the defendant to return specific property that the plaintiff transferred to the defendant pursuant to the agreement that the defendant has breached or the court is rescinding (on grounds of mistake, indefiniteness, lack of capacity, statute of frauds violation, etc.).

Assume, for example, that plaintiff transferred a cow to defendant, both parties believing that the cow was barren but having since discovered that the cow was pregnant at the time of the contract (see mistake cases, Chapter 15). Plaintiff will ask the judge for rescission and for an order of specific restitution, requiring defendant to return the cow. Courts are generally willing to grant restitution in mistake cases (unless defendant has already transferred the cow to an innocent third party). However, had this been a breach case where no mistake was made but the defendant simply failed to pay the purchase price, most courts would refuse to issue an order of rescission, reasoning that money damages would adequately compensate the plaintiff.

Restitution, generally speaking, is used not to enforce promises, but to prevent unjust enrichment by returning the parties to their precontract positions following rescission or breach.

SUMMARY

Judicial interpretation of contracts is, like judicial interpretation of statutes, a necessary evil. The courts' role is to determine the parties' common intent at the time the contract was formed, not to rewrite the contract. Courts will attempt to discover the parties' dominant purpose and construe the terms of the contract to give effect to that purpose.

Many courts apply the plain meaning rule, refusing to consider extrinsic evidence where the parties' intent as spelled out in the language of the contract seems plain and unambiguous. Even these courts will resort to extrinsic evidence of the parties' intentions where the contract is ambiguous. (And other courts will always do so, rejecting the plain meaning rule.) Several rules of interpretation—such as "specific language controls general language," and "unclear language is construed against its drafter"—assist the courts in determining the parties' intent.

The purpose of remedies for breach of contract is not to coerce all promisors into keeping their promises, but to redress injuries to promisees when the promisors fail to perform. Money damages are the main form of remedy for contractual breach. Courts award for damages caused directly by the breach, as well as for consequential and incidental damages under appropriate circumstances. Nominal damages and punitive damages are occasionally available.

The parties often set the amount of damages that should be paid in liquidated damages clauses. Like other contractual provisions, these are usually enforced. However, they are not enforced when they appear to be unreasonable in relation to the true damages sustained, thus constituting a "penalty."

In their discretion, courts may also, in appropriate circumstances (such as where money damages would be inadequate), invoke a raft of equitable remedies such as specific performance, injunction, reformation, rescission, and restitution.

KEY TERMS

Interpretation
Construction
Plain meaning rule
Course of performance
Course of dealing
Usage of trade
Compensatory damages
Mitigation of damages doctrine
Nominal damages
Liquidated damages
Specific performance
Injunction
Reformation
Rescission
Restitution

QUESTIONS AND PROBLEMS

1. Vole owned a parcel of land on which a lessee constructed a hotdog stand pursuant to a 24-year lease. The land was subleased by lessee McGrogan to sublessee Georgacopolous, who owned a restaurant and bar named "Fiddlesticks" next door. McGrogan sent a letter to Vole notifying Vole of his intention to erect a new sign on the leased property. The new sign advertised both the hot dog stand and Fiddlesticks. However, two-thirds of the sign was devoted to Fiddlesticks and indicated that it sold alcoholic beverages. After the sign was erected in this form, Vole objected and sued. Defendants claimed that they had the authority to erect the sign under a lease provision stating that the lessee "shall have the right . . . to make alterations and improvements within said building. . . ." Vole disagreed. Decide. (*Vole, Inc. v. Georgacopoulos*, 538 N.E.2d 205, Ill.App. 1989.)

2. The City of Spokane hired Keltch to construct storm sewers. The contract form, provided by the city, stated that "Sales tax on this Contract . . . will be added to the amount due. . . ." The city's bid form instructed bidders to omit sales taxes from their proposal. The final total read: "Total Bid Price (Not Including Sales Tax) $_____" Keltch claims that these documents indicate that he is entitled to be paid for the sales tax he paid on materials he purchased for installation. The city claims that the provisions simply reflect that the city is exempt from sales tax and that it does not have to reimburse Keltch for sales tax on materials. What rule of interpretation might help resolve this dispute? (*Universal/Land Construction Co. v. City of Spokane*, 745 P.2d 53, Wash.App. 1987.)

3. Tanya Niedbalski was a school teacher in Platte Center for five years. On March 12, 1985, she was offered a "Renewal Agreement" by the School Board. It was an offer to renew her contract and provided that "The failure to return a signed copy of the contract to the . . . Board of Education on or before March 19, 1985 shall constitute a rejection by the Teacher of the offer of employment." The date "March 19, 1985" was typewritten onto the printed form. Another paragraph in the "Renewal Agreement" provided that "Renewal Agreements must be executed by the Teacher and delivered to the . . . Board of Education within 15 calendar days of receipt thereof from the District." Tanya thought about returning the contract on March 19, but forgot to do so. At 11 p.m. she remembered it, but decided that it was too late to call the board members. Therefore, she delivered the contract on March 20. The board told her that she was too late. Was she? Discuss. (*Niedbalski v. Board of Education*, 418 N.W.2d 565, Neb. 1988.)

4. In 1984, defendant Keller hired plaintiff Cencula to build a home for Keller for $161,000. Plaintiff sued in 1985, alleging that he had completed the home, but defendant had failed to pay about $74,000 due under the contract and approximately $4,300 in claimed extras. The complaint sought as consequential damages interest the contractor had paid on a bank loan taken out by him in 1985 for the purpose of paying the subcontractors on the project. The jury found for plaintiff generally, awarding him $20,790 to compensate for the interest paid on the aforementioned loan. Discuss the appropriateness of this award. (*Cencula v. Keller*, 536 N.E.2d 93, Ill.App. 1989.)

5. Blumberg was president and a 50 percent shareholder of Meteor Industries, Inc. While still

with Meteor, he formed a competing corporation, Metalloy Industries. He then resigned from Meteor and during the next three years did business with many of Meteor's customers. Meteor sued, alleging that Blumberg had breached a covenant not to compete, causing a decline in Meteor's profits. The court found that Blumberg had breached the covenant. Regarding damages, the evidence showed that before Blumberg left, 90-98 percent of Meteor's profits came from the sale of brass tubing. Because only Blumberg knew brass tubing, when he left Meteor changed its business "dramatically, completely, and totally" to sale of brass rods. What damages should Meteor recover? (*Meteor Industries, Inc. v. Metalloy Industries, Inc.*, 539 N.Y.S.2d 972, A.D. 1989.)

6. Plaintiff entered a beauty contest and out of 37 contestants was selected as "Miss Legs of Tulsa." The advertisement by the contest's sponsors stated: "And, the first-prize winner receives an all expenses paid Windjammer Cruise to the Caribbean for two." Plaintiff was given two tickets for the cruise, but no expenses for traveling to and from the point of embarkation. Plaintiff sued for breach of contract and fraud, claiming that the sponsors never intended to pay "all expenses." Plaintiff later dropped the breach-of-contract claim. A jury returned a verdict for plaintiff for $6,136 in actual damages and $20,000 in punitive damages. Defendants appealed, claiming that this was essentially a breach-of-contract action where punitive damages should be unavailable. Decide. (*LeFlore v. Reflections of Tulsa, Inc.*, 708 P.2d 1068, Okl. 1985.)

7. Plaintiff Shirley MacLaine Parker contracted to act in defendant Twentieth Century Fox's production of "Bloomer Girl." She was to be paid $750,000. Before production began, defendant wrote to plaintiff, announcing that it would not fulfill its obligations. The letter stated that "to avoid any damage to you," defendant was offering plaintiff a role in "Big Country, Big Man." The compensation offered was identical to that of the original contract, as were 31 of the 34 provisions. However, whereas "Bloomer Girl" was to have been a musical production filmed in California, "Big Country" was to be a dramatic "western type" movie filmed in Australia. Defendant gave plaintiff one week in which to accept the new deal. She did not do so. Rather, she sued for breach of contract. Defendant admitted the breach, but claimed that plaintiff did not mitigate her damages. Discuss. (*Parker v. Twentieth Century Fox Film Corporation*, 474 P.2d 689, Cal. 1970.)

8. Plaintiff H&M Driver Leasing agreed to lease truck drivers as needed to defendant Champion International. The written contract contained Champion's promise that it would not hire any of the drivers furnished by H&M for a period of one year following termination of the agreement. Champion later hired Clifton Sweezy in breach of this promise. H&M sued for breach of contract, invoking a liquidated damages clause under which Champion promised that if it breached the agreement, it would "pay $10,000.00 liquidated damages to H&M, plus any and all actual damages resulting to H&M." Champion admits the breach, but claims that the liquidated damages clause is unenforceable. Discuss. (*H&M Driver Leasing v. Champion International Corp.*, 536 N.E.2d 858, 1989.)

9. After his junior year in college, plaintiff Julius "Dr. J" Erving signed a four-year contract to play professional basketball with defendant Virginia Squires for $500,000 per year. After one year, he signed a contract to play for the Atlanta Hawks for $1,500,000 per year. Plaintiff brought this suit to set aside his contract with the Squires on grounds of fraud. The Squires counterclaimed, seeking arbitration pursuant to a contractual provision and an injunction to bar Erving from playing basketball for any team other than the Squires pending the arbitration. The trial judge granted the injunction and ordered arbitration. Erving appealed. Discuss. (*Erving v. Virginia Squires Basketball Club*, 468 F.2d 1064, 2d Cir. 1972.)

10. Susan Nylen, Elizabeth Lewis, and Julie Reed, students at Indiana University, executed a rental agreement with Park Doral Apartments (PDA) for a term from August 26, 1986 until August 19, 1987, paying a $420 deposit, representing the final month's rent. The lease contained a "savings clause" stating, "Eviction of tenant for breach of lease agreement shall not release tenant from liability for rent payment for the balance of the term of the lease." It also provided that a fee of $2.00 per day, per person, would be assessed for late payments. Julie moved out in December, refusing to pay any further rent. Susan and Elizabeth paid only two-thirds of the total rent due for February and March. PDA sued and the

court preliminarily ordered Susan and Elizabeth to pay full rent or vacate. They vacated. After a trial, the lower court entered judgment in the amounts of $140 per month for February and March, $362 in late fees, $600 in attorney's fees, and $75.24 in conse-quential damages, offset by the $420 security deposit. Defendants appealed. Discuss the validity of the "savings clause" and of the late fee as a liquidated damages provision. (*Nylen v. Park Doral Apartments,* 535 N.E.2d 178, Ind.App. 1989.)

PART III

SALES, COMMERCIAL TRANSACTIONS, AND BANKRUPTCY

PART III BEGINS BY surveying the subjects of sales law and commercial paper. These areas of law govern two of the most important business activities that are carried on in our economic system—sales of personal property (such as television sets and machine tools) and the issuance of negotiable instruments (such as promissory notes and checks). Both of these subjects are governed by the Uniform Commercial Code (UCC); thus, unlike the common-law rules that make up the subject of contracts, the rules we will be considering throughout Part III are entirely statutory in nature.

Chapters 20 through 23 are devoted to *sales law*—the examination and application of the rules of Article 2 of the UCC. The first of these chapters is concerned with defining *goods* and highlighting the essential elements of a sale, so that sales transactions can be distinguished from other transactions in goods (such as bailments) and from contracts calling for the performance of services.

Chapter 21 deals with the rules that determine when title and risk of loss pass from seller to buyer—the latter being of special significance in cases where the goods are damaged or lost before reaching the buyer's hands. Of even more importance in many cases are the areas of warranties and products liability (covered in Chapter 22), which together impose the basic liability that sellers of goods have for injuries caused by defective products. Chapter 23 concludes the subject of sales law by summarizing the rights that a buyer or seller has when the other party breaches a sales contract.

Commercial paper—governed by Article 3 of the UCC—is covered in Chapters 24 through 28. The special characteristics of negotiable instruments and the rules applicable to the negotiation (transfer) of such instruments are summarized in Chapters 24 and 25. The next two chapters deal with the subjects of holders in due course and defenses, and liability of the parties (that is, the liability of makers, drawers, and endorsers of negotiable instruments). Chapter 28 examines the special rules applicable to checks and to the bank–depositor relationship.

Chapter 29 focuses on the rights and responsibilities of the debtor and creditor when items of personal property (inventory, equipment, consumer goods, or intangibles) belonging to the debtor are used as security for the creditor's claim. Chapter 30 concludes Part III by surveying the various methods for dealing with unpaid debts and then focusing on bankruptcy proceedings under federal law. ⚖

Chapter 20

Sales
Introduction to the Law of Sales

Scope of Article 2 of the UCC

*Review of Basic Principles
of Sales Contracts*

Documents of Title

A COLLEGE STUDENT PURCHASES a stereo. A home owner buys several cans of house paint. A manufacturer of tires purchases raw rubber, sulphur, and other materials and ultimately sells tires to automobile owners. A mining company sells coal to an electric utility company. All of the above have at least two things in common. First, they are quite ordinary transactions, occurring countless numbers of times. Second, they involve sales of goods. Thus we can hardly question the relevance of studying the law of sales.

The principles governing sales of goods do not exist in a vacuum. Indeed, Article 2 of the UCC, which provides the legal rules for contracts selling goods, is closely related to the common law which governs other types of contracts. Thus, in Part II's discussion of general contract law (Chapters 11–19), we have already noted pertinent instances where the UCC altered the common law in order to facilitate commercial transactions in goods. (These concepts are briefly recapitulated later in this chapter.) In Chapters 20–23, we will explore in more detail the law governing the sale of goods. In so doing, we will also treat a few closely related matters, for example, the law regarding *leases* of goods and another subject known as *documents of title*.

SCOPE OF ARTICLE 2 OF THE UCC

Article 2 of the UCC deals with the sale of goods.[1] It forms the basis for most of the following discussion of the law of sales.

Sales

A **sale** is defined in Sec. 2-106 of the UCC as "the passing of title from the seller to the buyer for a price." Thus Article 2 does not apply to leases—such as the lease of an automobile—or to other types of bailments—such as the storage of furniture in a warehouse—because only temporary possession of the goods (rather than title) is transferred in these trans-

actions.[2] Neither does Article 2 apply to gifts, because no price is paid. (The section on documents of title later in this chapter briefly discusses bailments, while Chapter 45 contains a more complete treatment of the subject. Gifts are also dealt with in Chapter 45.) A barter transaction (i.e, the trading of goods for other goods or services without the exchange of money) would be within the scope of Article 2.

Goods

In the majority of cases there is no problem ascertaining whether the subject matter should be classified as **goods.** Occasionally, however, the term may present problems. Essentially, two requirements must be met before a particular item of property is classified as a good:

1. It must be *tangible.* In other words, it must have a physical existence. Thus intangible property such as a patent, copyright, trademark, investment security, or contract right would not come within the scope of Article 2.

2. It must be *movable.* This requirement obviously excludes real estate, which is tangible but not movable. (Of course, almost anything, even real estate, is capable of being moved, shovel by shovel, if enough effort is expended. But the word is intended reasonably rather than literally.)

Using these two requirements we can easily envision the wide variety of products that are classified as goods, from airplanes to toothpaste.

Should things that are attached to real estate be considered goods? Because of the movability requirement this question would involve considerable conceptual difficulty were it not for Sec. 2-107 of the UCC, which sets forth the following basic rules:

1. A contract for the sale of *minerals or a structure* (such as a building or its materials) is a contract for the sale of goods if they are to be severed from the land by the *seller.* If, however, they are to be severed

---

[1]Louisiana has adopted parts of the UCC, but not Article 2. Every other state has adopted all of the UCC (excepting the relatively new Article 2A, discussed later in this chapter, and the revised Article 6, discussed in Chapter 21).

[2]Many courts have in the past extended Article 2 sales principles to lease transactions by analogy. In the future, however, *leases* of goods are to be governed by the new Article 2A, discussed later in this chapter.

from the land by the *buyer*, the transaction is a sale of real estate and is governed by the principles of real estate law rather than by the UCC. Two examples may be of some help. First, suppose that S and B agree that S will sell to B a quantity of gravel to be taken from beneath the surface of land owned by S. If their agreement states that S will dig and remove the gravel, the transaction is a sale of goods. If, on the other hand, B is to dig and remove the gravel, the transaction is a sale of real estate. Second, suppose that S and B agree that S will sell to B a storage building (or perhaps the lumber from the building) located on land owned by S. If their agreement indicates that B will remove the building from the land, the transaction is a sale of real estate. If removal is to be by S, it is a sale of goods.

2. A contract for the sale of *growing crops* or *timber* is a contract for the sale of goods, regardless of who is to sever them from the land.

3. A contract for the sale of *anything else attached to real estate* is a sale of goods if it can be severed *without material harm* to the real estate. This rule is, perhaps, not as important as the two rules just discussed, simply because most of the problems regarding things attached to real estate have involved minerals, structures, timber, or growing crops. Situations might exist, however, where this third rule would be pertinent. For example: X and Y agree that X will sell to Y a window air conditioner that is now attached to X's home. (We are assuming it is attached, for otherwise the question would never arise—it would obviously be a sale of goods.) The air conditioner is bolted to a metal shelf supported by braces that are secured to the side of the house by bolts. It is fairly evident that the air conditioner can be removed without material harm to the real estate. Suppose, however, that the subject of the sale is a floor furnace. In this case a gaping hole in the floor would result. This might be a material harm, causing the sale to be treated as a sale of real estate rather than goods.

The rules regarding sales of goods attached to real estate apply to those contracts under which the items are being sold apart from the land. However, if two parties agree that one will sell a tract of land to the other, including a building or some timber located on the land, the sale is treated as a sale of real estate.

The UCC also gives special attention to three other potential problems of classification. It provides that (1) unborn animals are goods; (2) money treated

as a commodity, such as a rare coin, is a good (though money used as a medium of exchange is not); and (3) things that are specially manufactured for the buyer are goods. Although item 3 seems clear-cut, the framers of Article 2 felt that such a sale might be seen as predominantly a sale of services rather than goods and therefore stated it definitely.

Sales of services (such as employment contracts) are obviously not within the scope of Article 2. However, as we saw in item 3, goods and services sometimes are so entwined that classification is no easy task. For example, when a hospital supplies blood to a patient, is the hospital selling a good or supplying a service? When a beautician applies hair dye to a customer's hair in a beauty parlor, is it a contract for goods or services? In such contracts involving both goods and services, most courts attempt to determine whether the *predominant factor, thrust, and purpose* of the transaction as a whole is that of selling a good or supplying a service.[3] This determination often turns on the intent of the buyer, as gauged by several factors, including the relative dollar value involved.

For example, in *De Filippo v. Ford Motor Co.*, 516 F.2d 1313 (3d Cir. 1975), the court held that the sale of a car dealership, which included sales of items that were clearly goods (e.g., cars, parts, and accessories) as well as items that clearly were intangible and therefore not goods (e.g., goodwill, notes receivable, and used car warranties), was predominantly a sale of goods because the contract's terms assigned little dollar value to the intangible items. The court refused to split the contract into two parts, applying the UCC to one portion but not to the other.

And in *Grossman v. Aerial Farm Service, Inc.*, 384 N.W.2d 488 (Minn.App. 1986), the court held that a contract for the aerial spraying of a herbicide on a farm was predominantly a contract for services because the farmers could have applied the herbicide through several methods of ground spraying, but chose a method of application that could only be performed by a contractor equipped to handle their specific request. Thus, the farmers' selection of this type of service gave the contract its predominant character. A comparison of the reasoning in this case to that in the following case illustrates how sticky these issues can be.

---

[3]Although the UCC makes no statement regarding blood transfusions or hair treatments (and the courts are split on the matter), it does specifically provide in Sec. 2–314(1) that food sold in a restaurant is a sale of goods (at least as far as creation of the implied warranty of merchantability is concerned).

MICRO-MANAGERS, INC. V. GREGORY

Court of Appeals of Wisconsin, 434 N.W.2d 97 (1988)

 Case

Stanley Gregory was hired to develop a new programmable controller for a manufacturing firm. Gregory contacted Micro-Managers, Inc. (MMI), which indicated an interest in designing and developing the software required for the controller. After some negotiation, MMI drafted a letter incorporating what it believed to be its working arrangement with Gregory. The letter provided that "all MMI time will be billed by MMI at a rate of $40/hour for software, $50/hour for engineering, and $75/hour for supervision. Direct expenses will be billed as charged MMI."

After MMI delivered the software, Gregory complained that it was unsatisfactory. During litigation that resulted, the question arose as to whether MMI had breached an implied warranty which depended, in turn, upon whether this was a contract for "goods" governed by the UCC. The trial court held for MMI, ruling that Article 2 did not govern the contract and therefore there was no implied warranty to be breached. Gregory appealed.

Dykman, Judge:

It is undisputed that this was a mixed contract, i.e., a contract for both goods and services. The issue is whether the mixed contract was predominantly for goods or for services.

The test for inclusion or exclusion [within the U.C.C.] is not whether [contracts] are mixed, but, granting that they are mixed, whether their predominant factor, their thrust, their purpose, reasonably stated, is the rendition of service, with goods incidentally involved (e.g., contract with artist for painting) or is a transaction of sale, with labor incidentally involved (e.g., installation of a water heater in a bathroom).

Bonebrake v. Cox, 499 F.2d 951, 960 (8th Cir. 1975).

[W]e conclude that *Data Processing v. L.H. Smith Oil Corp.,* 492 N.E.2d 314 (Ind.App.), *aff'd on rehearing,* 493 N.E.2d 1272 (Ind.App. 1986) is on point and more compelling [than cases cited by Gregory]. In that case, as here, the parties contracted for custom computer programming. The trial court had reasoned that the contract was for the development and delivery of a "program," which it concluded was a specially manufactured good covered by U.C.C. warranty provisions. The appellate court phrased the issue as "whether a contract to provide computer programming is a contract for the sale and purchase of goods and thus subject to the provisions of Article 2 of the UCC, or one for the performance of services, and thus subject to common law principles." The court noted that "DPS was *to act* with specific regard to Smith's need. Smith bargained for DPS's skill in developing a system to meet its specific needs." The court concluded that the "mere means by which DPS's skills and knowledge were to be transmitted to Smith's computers was incidental."

In the present case, the contract provided that all MMI charges to Gregory would be on the basis of time, at stated rates, and materials. Under *Bonebrake,* we must determine whether the contract's predominant factor, thrust and purpose is the rendition of a service or the transaction of a sale. We may look to evidence of billing to determine this issue. On January 18, 1983, Terry Coleman, an agent for Gregory, wrote the following in a letter to Sally Peterson, president of MMI: "3. The projected total, excluding bonus, is therefore approximately $59,828, of which $55,968 is labor." In addition, we may look to the language of the contract to determine whether it is more in accord with services instead of sales. The contract speaks in terms of "man-days," "development," "time," "design," etc. These words connote the rendition of services and not a sales transaction.

Based on this evidence, we conclude that this was primarily a service contract. The method by which MMI transmitted that service was merely incidental. Therefore the transaction is not subject to the provisions of the U.C.C.

[Affirmed.] ⚖

Merchants

For the most part, Article 2 applies to all sales contracts, even those in which neither the seller nor the buyer is a merchant. However, a few provisions of Article 2 do require one or both of the parties to be merchants in order for such provisions to be applicable. For this reason, we will now examine the UCC definition of a **merchant.**

Most people who see the word *merchant* probably think of someone engaged in the retail grocery business, the retail clothing business, or similar endeavors. While such people (or corporations) are indeed merchants, the UCC definition includes many others as well.

Sec. 2-104 of the UCC details three different ways in which a person or organization can be considered a merchant.

1. One who "deals in goods of the kind" that are involved under the particular contract in question is a merchant; thus, not only retailers but also wholesalers and probably even manufacturers are merchants. A party is considered a merchant, however, only for the types of goods dealt with regularly in his or her business. That is, a merchant in one type of goods is not a merchant for all purposes. Thus a retail shoe seller is a merchant with respect to transactions involving the purchase or sale of shoes. But if that person buys a new car or sells a secondhand lawn mower, he or she is not a merchant in those transactions.

2. Even if a person does not regularly "deal" in a particular type of goods, he is nevertheless a merchant if he "by his occupation holds himself out as having knowledge or skill peculiar to the practices or goods involved in the transaction." While most persons who fall within this provision are also merchants under the first provision by dealing in the particular goods, there are a few who do not really deal in goods but who are merchants within this second category. For example, if we assume that the word *deal* means "to buy and sell goods," a building contractor does not actually deal in goods. He buys building materials but does not resell them; instead he uses them in the performance of a service—constructing a building. However, he does, by his occupation, hold himself out as having "knowledge or skill peculiar to the practices or goods" involved in certain transactions and thereby is a merchant by definition. Of course, his status is irrelevant in any agreement to construct a building, because that agreement is essentially for services and not within the scope of Article 2. But his status as a merchant can be important with respect to a dispute arising from the sale contract between him and his materials supplier.

3. If a party is not a merchant under either of the first two categories, he or she may nevertheless be treated as one by *employing a merchant* to act in his or her behalf in a particular transaction. The UCC states that one is a merchant if one employs "an agent or broker or other intermediary who by his occupation holds himself out" as having knowledge or skill peculiar to the goods or practices involved in the transaction. Suppose, for example, that Smith, who does not regularly deal in grain, hires a professional grain broker to procure a large quantity of feed for Smith's cattle. In this situation Smith is considered a merchant.

The common thread running through all the above categories of merchants is the possession of or access to a degree of commercial expertise not found in a member of the general public. The UCC occasionally treats merchants differently than nonmerchants. For example, it imposes a higher duty of "good faith" on them. Also, some provisions of the UCC apply only to merchants who are deemed such because they deal in goods, while others apply only to merchants who are deemed such because they hold themselves out as having skill peculiar to the practice. In most provisions, both types of merchants are treated in the same manner.

Courts in different states have taken various views as to whether a farmer or rancher is a "merchant" for UCC purposes. The following case represents a narrow approach that is commonly used in states with a strong agricultural sector, where it often appears that courts are attempting to protect farmers from burdens the UCC imposes on merchants.

Chisolm v. Cleveland

Court of Appeals of Texas, 741 S.W.2d 619 (1987)

Chisolm, a dairyman, bought $9,000 worth of "green chop" (a farm crop used as cattle feed) from Cleveland pursuant to an oral agreement. Cleveland wished to sell by volume; Chisolm wished to buy by weight. After the sale, Cleveland sent Chisolm a written confirmation of the contract, to which Chisolm did not respond within ten days. The terms stated by Cleveland called for price by volume. When the green chop was delivered and payment by volume was requested, Chisolm refused to accept the goods. Cleveland sued for breach of contract. Chisolm raised a statute of frauds defense. The trial court overruled the defense, because Chisolm had not objected within ten days to the written confirmation. This would be an exception to the writing requirement of UCC 2–201

(continues)

CHISOLM V. CLEVELAND

(continued from previous page)
statute of frauds if *both parties were*
"merchants." Chisolm appealed.

Hill, Justice:

Testimony reflected that Chisolm was a dairyman who sought to raise his own dairy feed. He had been a dairyman for thirteen years at the time of the transaction and had purchased feed in 1983 and a little feed in 1984. He acknowledged that if he did not anticipate raising enough feed he would try to purchase enough feed to carry him through. Although Chisolm had raised and bagged green chop, there was no testimony that he had ever bought or sold any.

Chisolm asserts that there is no evidence to support the jury's finding that both Chisolm and Cleveland acted as "between merchants" in the sale of the green chop [for purposes of the exception to the 2–201 statute of frauds]. "Merchant" was defined by the [trial] court as "a person who deals in goods of the kind or otherwise by his occupation holds himself out as having knowledge or skill peculiar to the practices or goods involved in the transaction. . . ." This definition is taken from the longer definition of merchant found in [2–104(a) of the Texas UCC].

The purpose of this definition of "merchant" is to distinguish professionals in a given field from a casual or inexperienced seller or buyer. The evidence here did not show that Chisolm had ever bought and sold green chop, and the evidence showed that he only occasionally bought other types of feed for his cattle, in years when he anticipated that the amount of feed that he had raised would not be sufficient. This evidence establishes that Chisolm is a casual or inexperienced buyer, not that he was a professional buyer or seller of green chop, or any other kind of cattle feed. Since he was only a casual or inexperienced buyer or seller, as opposed to a professional, he was not a merchant as defined by 2-104(a).

Since Chisolm was not a merchant, as defined by 2–104(a), his failure to respond to the written confirmation of the contract within ten days did not remove the contract from the application of the statute of frauds. Thus, Cleveland must establish a written contract with Chisolm before he can enforce it.

Cleveland relies on the opinion of the Texas Supreme Court in *Nelson v. Union Equity Co-op. Exchange*, 548 S.W.2d 352 (Tex. 1977). The facts in *Nelson*, however, are distinguishable from the facts in this case. *Nelson* involved an oral contract for the sale of wheat. The evidence showed that Nelson was a wheat farmer who kept up with the price of wheat by radio every day. He raised his own wheat, brought in one crop a year, and sold it himself. In the five years preceding trial, he sold the wheat to a milling company. His occupation was that of a wheat farmer. As we have previously stated, the evidence in this case shows that Chisolm is a dairy farmer who is only a casual, inexperienced buyer of feed.

[Reversed.]

Leases

Thousands of times a day, Americans rent cars, garden equipment, machines to clean rugs, and numerous other goods. Leasing is also quite common in industry. For example, assume that Company A needs to buy 100 new delivery trucks from Company C, but cannot afford them. Company B ("lessor") agrees to buy the 100 trucks and then to lease them to Company A ("lessee"). In 1986 alone, companies financed $90 billion in equipment such as airplanes, computers, and office equipment through such leases.

Leases of goods present many of the same legal issues that arise in sales of goods. Indeed, some courts have held that Article 2 applies to leases because UCC 2-102 states that it applies to "transactions in goods." Although most courts disagree, many have extended provisions of Article 2 to leases by analogy, reasoning that the rules governing sales could be helpful in resolving lease disputes. This has been unsatisfactory, however, because Article 2 was not designed to address leasing problems.

Therefore, Article 2A, the first new article to be added to the official text of the UCC in more than 35 years, was approved in 1987. Article 2A will probably be slightly revised soon to accommodate changes made by many of the first dozen or so states to adopt it. Thereafter, widespread adoption should quickly follow. Our discussion generally applies to both versions. Article 2A is designed to cover leases of goods in the same manner that Article 2 covers sales. It is intended to apply to virtually every type of lease of tangible personal property.

Article 2A's provisions resemble the common law of bailment for hire (discussed in Chapter 45). This is the most-litigated pre-Article 2A issue related to the difference between a true lease (governed by bailment law) and a lease intended as security for a loan (subject to UCC Article 9). Return, for example, to the hypothetical involving the lease of 100 trucks. If Company A falls behind in its payments, the rights of Company B vis-à-vis Company A's other creditors will depend on whether the agreement is structured as a true lease or as a security interest. This is a matter that we will examine in detail in Chapter 29 which discusses Article 9's rules for secured transactions. For now, it is sufficient to highlight a few of Article 2A's provisions.

Lessee's Remedies

Remedies are usually set forth in the lease contract. The parties to the lease generally have the right to set their own terms and to vary any provision of Article 2A. However, when the lease does not establish remedies, Article 2A provides that in event of default by the lessor, the lessee has the right, among others, to cancel the lease, to recover paid-in rents and security deposits to the extent "just under the circumstances," to obtain substitute goods, and to recover damages.

Lessor's Remedies

If the lessee breaches the lease by wrongfully refusing delivery or failing to make payments when due, the remedies available to the lessor include cancellation of the lease, repossession and disposition, and damages. "Reasonable" liquidated damages clauses will be enforced. Mitigation of damages by re-leasing is not required, but if an item is re-leased, the lessor is not entitled to recover double profits.

Warranties

Finance lessors (those who do not select, manufacture, or supply goods out of inventory, but simply serve as a financial conduit so that the lessee may obtain use of goods—such as Company B in the aforementioned truck example) are automatically exempted from implied warranties. For other lessors, Article 2A's warranty provisions generally track those of Article 2, which will be discussed in detail in Chapter 22. Warranties not affecting third parties may be disclaimed by written and conspicuous provisions.

Consumer Leases

A consumer lease is one that a lessor regularly engaged in the business of leasing or selling makes to an individual lessee who takes primarily for a personal, family, or household purpose, providing total payments do not exceed $25,000. Article 2A contains several provisions to protect consumers in such leases, including one allowing a consumer to recover attorney's fees when a court finds a provision in the lessor's form lease to be "unconscionable."

REVIEW OF BASIC PRINCIPLES OF SALES CONTRACTS

In explaining basic contract law, Chapters 11–19 of Part II focused on the common law of contracts but highlighted changes that Article 2 makes for sales contracts. The first part of this chapter examined the scope of Article 2's coverage. The next three chapters will go into great detail regarding some very important features of Article 2. Before leaving this chapter, however, we will present a quick overview of some basic Article 2 rules on contract formation, enforcement, and interpretation.

Contract Formation

The basic elements needed to form a contract at common law (agreement, consideration, capacity of the parties, legality of purpose) are also essential to formation of a sales contract under Article 2. However, the drafters of the Code meant it to be nontechnical and to operate fairly. For example, the common law says that even if an offeror promises to keep an offer open for a specified period of time, he may revoke the offer at any time before acceptance (unless he has been given consideration to keep it open). As explained in Chapter 12, Sec. 2-205's "firm offer rule" provides a fairer rule, holding merchants to their signed promises to keep offers open for a specified time less than three months' duration even in the absence of consideration.

Even more importantly, the Code's rules on formation of an agreement do not turn on whether there existed a detailed offer and a detailed acceptance, each containing all important elements of the contract. Rather, the drafters of the Code realized that parties often, perhaps pursuant to a quick telephone conversation, intend to form a contract but fail to agree as to a specific term such as price or date of delivery. Therefore, Sec. 2-204 provides that a contract is made if the parties clearly intend one to exist *and* there is a reasonably certain basis for giving an appropriate remedy. Resort may be had to the "gap-fillers" to provide terms the parties omit. For example, 2-305 will provide the price if that term has been omitted, 2-308 fills in the gap if the parties did not determine the place for delivery, 2-309 fills in the time of delivery, and 2-310 fills in the time of payment.

The common law also generally requires that an acceptance be the "mirror image" of the offer on all important terms before a contract exists. The framers of the UCC realized that this requirement was unduly technical, given the modern commercial world's reliance on form contracts that cannot feasibly be fully negotiated for each transaction. Therefore UCC 2-207, the "battle of the forms" provision, states that a contract is formed if the offeree's primary intent is to accept an offer even if the offeree's form does not match the offeror's form in all particulars. That section then gives rules to decide the content of that contract. The essence of 2-207 is that no party is allowed to unfairly surprise the other with contract provisions hidden in fine print.

The area of consideration also illustrates the Code's nontechnical approach. As noted in Chapter 13, Sec. 2-209 states that, unlike at the common law, an agreement modifying a sales contract *needs no consideration to be binding*. Parties are bound to their promises to modify an existing contract, and another technical defense is eliminated. (Somewhat surprisingly, perhaps, the doctrine of promissory estoppel plays almost no role in Article 2.)

Contract Enforcement

No body of commercial law can be free of technical rules, of course. Like the common law, Article 2 carries a statute of frauds requirement that certain contracts for the sale of goods—those of $500 or more—must be in writing in order to be enforceable (Sec. 2-201). However, consistent with its overall approach, the Code makes several exceptions to this technical defense, providing that oral contracts of over $500 are enforceable where (1) the seller has already substantially begun producing specially made goods; (2) payment has been made and accepted or goods have been received and accepted; (3) between merchants there has been a confirmatory memorandum sent and the receiving party did not object to its terms in writing within 10 days; or (4) the party against whom the contract is to be enforced admitted in court proceedings that an oral agreement existed. The Code also has its own parol evidence rule, Sec.

2-202, which again is more generous than the common law, allowing unambiguous final written agreements to be explained or supplemented by course of dealing, usage of trade, or course of performance (see Chapter 16).

The Code also grants the parties the right to shape the contract's terms as they please. For example, they can establish their own remedies with very few limitations. However, in the interests of fairness, the Code does impose some limitations. As explained in Chapter 14, a contractual provision that is unconscionable will not be enforced. A party with superior bargaining power or sophistication will not be allowed to impose unfair terms on an inferior party (UCC 2-302). For example, we will see in Chapter 23 that if a seller with superior bargaining power contractually limits the remedies of the buyer of a defective product so severely that the remedy fails of its essential purpose depriving the buyer of the substantial value of the bargain, the limitation is unenforceable (UCC 2-719(2)).

Contract Interpretation

The Code follows general rules of contract interpretation, but, as noted in Chapter 19, allows more liberal use of extrinsic evidence to determine the parties' intent in sale-of-goods contracts. The Code assumes that the parties considered three important concepts when they formed their agreement. First is *course of performance*, which arises out of "repeated occasions for performance by either party with knowledge of the nature of the performance and opportunity for objection to it by the other." Second is *course of dealing*, "a sequence of previous conduct between the parties to a particular transaction which is fairly regarded as establishing a common basis of understanding for interpreting their expressions and other conduct." Third is *usage of trade*, defined as "any practice or method of dealing having such regularity of observance in a place, vocation or trade as to justify an expectation that it will be observed with respect to the transaction in question." In essence, this means that in determining the meaning of the contract, the courts may consider, in order of importance, the previous course of performance of this particular contract, the past course of dealing between the parties in other contracts they have had, and, finally, the usage of the trade in general as established by contracts and performance of other persons in the industry.

International

Legal Focus

As will be discussed in Chapter 52, the United Nations Convention on Contracts for the International Sale of Goods (CISG) is a multilateral treaty drafted in 1980. The United States adopted the treaty in 1988, and it is only a matter of time before almost all of the world's important trading nations do likewise. In a sale of goods transaction in which the seller and buyer are from different nations, and both nations have adopted the treaty, the CISG is the governing law unless the seller and buyer expressly agree that some other body of law should apply. (The treaty can also apply in some other situations that are too complex to discuss here.) Even if the seller and buyer do not expressly agree to be bound by some other body of law, they can modify any of the CISG's provisions by agreement. The ability of the parties to modify the rules of contract law by their agreement is nothing new, of course; the same is true with regard to almost all of the common law of contracts and the rules of our UCC.

Although much of the CISG resembles Article 2 of our UCC, there are some significant differences. For example, under the UCC a sale of goods contract for $500 or more has to be in writing, but the CISG expressly provides that written documentation is not required so long as other evidence proves the existence and terms of the contract. This difference is more theoretical than real, however, because almost all international sales contracts are actually evidenced by documents that would satisfy the requirements of our UCC.

Another difference between the UCC and the CISG relates to an acceptance containing terms that are additional to or different from the terms of the offer. As you have read, the UCC modifies the common-law "mirror image" rule and consequently makes it easier to form an enforceable sale of goods contract than under common-law rules. The CISG, however, includes a provision that is virtually identical to the common-law mirror image rule: under the CISG, an acceptance containing a term that materially adds to or changes the offer is a counteroffer rather than an acceptance. One other difference relates to the creation of irrevocable offers. The "firm offer" provision of UCC Sec. 2-205 makes it somewhat easier to create an irrevocable offer than do traditional common law contract rules; the CISG makes it even easier than the UCC. Under the CISG, an offer for the sale or purchase of goods is irrevocable if it includes language indicating that it is irrevocable or even if it merely states a time for acceptance. Unlike the UCC, the CISG does not require the offer to be written, and does not include a time limit on an offer's irrevocable status.

Duty of Good Faith

Finally, interpretation and enforcement of contracts for the sale of goods are flavored not only by Article 2's specific policies against surprise, unfairness, and unconscionability, but also by its "good faith" requirements. UCC 1–203 specifically states that "[e]very contract or duty within this Act imposes an obligation of good faith in its performance or enforcement." Section 2-103(1)(b) goes further, defining the "good faith" duty of a merchant to mean acting with "honesty in fact and the observance of reasonable commercial standards of fair dealing in the trade." This again highlights that Article 2 is not a collection of dry rules, but an attempt to establish a framework promoting efficient, but also fair, commercial transactions in goods.

DOCUMENTS OF TITLE

Before concluding this introductory chapter, we need to present some terms that will aid understanding of the subsequent sales chapters. When goods are shipped by a carrier or stored in a warehouse before sale, a *bailment* often occurs. The owner of the goods is the *bailor*; the warehouseman or carrier is the *bailee*. An owner of goods who sends them through a carrier receives a receipt called a **bill of lading,**[4] which contains instructions to the carrier regarding destination and the like, as well as the terms of the shipping agreement. If goods are stored with a

---

[4]Technically, the bill of lading is called an *airbill* when air transportation is used.

bailee/warehouseman before sale, the owner will receive a *warehouse receipt,* which will also contain the terms of the storage agreement. Both instructions are sometimes referred to as *documents of title,* because they provide evidence of title to goods.

Documents of title—such as bills of lading, warehouse receipts, dock warrants, dock receipts, and other orders for delivery of goods which are treated in the regular course of business as adequate evidence that the holder is entitled to receive, hold, and dispose of the goods covered, are governed by Article 7 of the UCC. A **negotiable document of title** is one which by its terms specifies that the goods are to be delivered to "bearer" or to the "order" of a named person. Documents not meeting this requirement are **nonnegotiable documents of title.**[5] A negotiable document of title (e.g., "Deliver to bearer" or "Deliver to order of Dan Owens") entitles whoever is in legal possession of it (as bearer or as Dan Owens's endorsee) to possession of the underlying goods. A nonnegotiable document of title (e.g., "Delivery to Dan Owens"), on the other hand, is not equivalent to ownership of the goods. Regardless of who presents the document, the bailee is under a duty to deliver the goods only to the party who is supposed to receive them under the bailor's instructions. (The difference between a negotiable and a nonnegotiable document is somewhat akin to the difference between a five-dollar bill and a copy of a contract.)

SUMMARY

Sales law—Article 2 of the UCC—applies to sales of goods: items of tangible personal property, such as books, stereos, and structural steel plate. Contracts calling for the sale of land, or the transfer of intangible property (such as the assignment of contractual rights) are not, therefore, governed by Article 2. A sale is a transfer of title to goods from the seller to the buyer for a price. Contracts calling for the sale of growing crops and timber are sales of goods in all cases, but there are special rules for determining the status of sales of minerals, structures, and fixtures. If a sale contract is "mixed," covering goods and nongoods, the rule is that the contract is a sales contract if the bulk of the assets transferred qualify as goods, and is thus governed by Article 2.

As a general rule, sales law applies to sales by both merchants and nonmerchants. However, a few provisions of Article 2 apply only to sales by merchants, and others only to contracts where both parties are merchants. The courts of about half of the states take the view that a farmer is not a merchant, with the result that he or she is not subject to the special rules applicable to merchant sellers. An almost equal number of courts, however, hold the opposite view.

Leases of goods are now covered by Article 2A, which will likely be adopted in most states soon. Although the provisions of 2A are drawn heavily from Article 2's rules for sales, they do make many important modifications for specific problems that arise in the leasing context.

Article 2's rules for the formation, enforcement, and interpretation of contracts for the sale of goods are roughly similar to common-law rules that were discussed in Part II. However, Article 2 does make changes necessary to improve the efficiency of commercial transactions in goods and to eliminate some of the technicalities of the common law.

Sales of goods are frequently made by the transfer of a "document of title" from seller to buyer—e.g., a warehouse receipt or a bill of lading. If the document is "negotiable," the person who is in lawful possession of it is entitled to the goods; that is, such possession is tantamount to ownership of the goods. But if the instrument is nonnegotiable in form, the possessor's rights in the goods are subject to the party who originally delivered them to the warehouse or carrier.

KEY TERMS

Sale
Goods
Merchant
Lease
Bill of lading
Document of title
Negotiable document of title
Nonnegotiable document of title

QUESTIONS AND PROBLEMS

1. Helvey filed suit against Wabash County REMC for breach of a contract to supply electricity to Helvey's furniture factory. During the course of the lawsuit the issue arose as to whether Article 2 of the

[5]A negotiable bill of lading is sometimes called an *order bill* and a nonnegotiable one a *straight bill.*

UCC applied to the dispute. Discuss whether the contract between Helvey and Wabash is covered by Article 2. (*Helvey v. Wabash County REMC*, 278 N.E.2d 608, 1972.)

2. Ernst and Williams agreed to trade an airplane owned by Ernst for an undeveloped residential lot owned by Williams. A dispute arose as to the time, place, and manner of delivering the airplane. Is this dispute governed by the provisions of Article 2? Explain.

3. Hauter agreed to sell 1,500 shares of General Manufacturing Co. common stock to Rogers for $15,000. Later, several terms of the contract became the subject of disagreement between Hauter and Rogers. Hauter filed suit. Does Article 2 govern the transaction? Explain.

4. The City of Twin Falls, Idaho, was in trouble with the EPA for violating federal water pollution standards. It had hired Envirotech to design and construct its sewage treatment plant. Under the contract, Envirotech was to purchase and install equipment which would separate and dispose of sludge produced in the secondary treatment of waste water. Some of the contract documents referred to "construction" and "contractors." On the other hand, one contract provision noted: "Included shall be the percentage of the total selling price for which the supplier is furnishing and installing the particular piece of equipment, to include and cover piping, high pressure pumps and sludge grinders, heat exchangers, reactor boiler, vacuum filters and support equipment, etc., required for the complete installation." When Twin Falls was fined by the EPA, it filed a third party indemnity action against Envirotech under a warranty theory. Did the UCC's warranty provisions apply? Was this a contract for the sale of goods? Discuss. (*U.S. v. City of Twin Falls*, 806 F.2d 862, 9th Cir. 1986.)

5. Contractors Supply (CS) was contacted about a certain type of stucco by Acrylic Stucco Applicators (Acrylic), a subcontractor that had been hired to put stucco on an apartment building being built for Ashley Square. CS secured the stucco from the manufacturer and sold it to Acrylic. Defects began to appear in the stucco soon after it was applied to the building,

and Ashley Square refused to pay. CS sued and Ashley counterclaimed for breach of the implied warranty of merchantability. CS proved that it does not regularly supply the special stucco involved and that Acrylic's order was the first and only time it had been asked to supply the special stucco. Therefore, CS claimed that it was not a "merchant" and that no implied warranty arose. Is CS correct? (*Ashley Square, Inc. v. Contractors Supply of Orlando*, 532 So.2d 710, Fla.App. 1988.)

6. Playboy Clubs International, Inc., operates a number of hotels and nightclubs. Playboy bought fabrics from Loomskill, Inc., which it was going to have made into costumes for its employees by a third party. A dispute arose between Playboy and Loomskill regarding the sale. Relevant to this dispute is a section in Article 2 which applies only if Playboy is considered a merchant. Does this section apply? Discuss. (*Playboy Clubs International, Inc. v. Loomskill*, 13 U.C.C. Rep. Serv. 765, 1974.)

7. Loeb & Co., Inc., marketed raw cotton; Schreiner was a farmer who had grown cotton and other crops for ten years. Although he had sold his own cotton, Schreiner had never sold cotton belonging to anyone else. The parties entered into a contract for Schreiner to sell 150 bales of cotton to Loeb & Co. But when the market price of cotton more than doubled, Schreiner refused to sell. The oral contract was for more than $500, but Loeb & Co. had sent a confirming memorandum to Schreiner that he had never objected to. If Schreiner is a "merchant," he has no statute of frauds defense under 2-201. Is he? (*Loeb & Co., Inc. v. Schreiner*, 320 So.2d 199, Ala. 1975.)

8. Are there any circumstances in which a university might be considered a merchant? Discuss.

9. What part can documents of title play in a sale of goods? Explain.

10. How can one tell whether a document of title is negotiable or nonnegotiable? What is the basic difference between the rights of a person in legal possession of a negotiable document of title and the rights of a person in legal possession of a nonnegotiable document of title?

Chapter 21

Sales

Title, Risk of Loss, and Insurable Interest

Title to Goods

Risk of Loss

Insurable Interest

Sale on Approval and Sale or Return

THE ULTIMATE OBJECTIVE of a sale of goods is to transfer from one party to another the rights and responsibilities that accompany ownership. After negotiation and formation of the sale contract, some amount of time will usually pass before this objective is realized. Time may be needed to produce, procure, or manufacture the goods, or simply to take them from inventory and ship them. And the buyer may not wish to receive the goods until some future date even if the seller is capable of immediate delivery.

Many events can occur during the lapse of time preceding the transfer of ownership. The goods may be destroyed by fire, flood, or other act of God. They may be lost or damaged in transit. The seller or buyer, or both, may attempt to obtain a casualty insurance policy on the goods. A government entity may levy a tax on them. During this lapse of time, then, the question often arises as to which of the contracting parties possesses various rights and is subject to various responsibilities regarding the goods. In this chapter we will examine the rules of Article 2 of the UCC that spell out these rights and responsibilities.

TITLE TO GOODS

Prior to enactment of the UCC, all issues of rights and responsibilities were decided by answering a single question: Who had "title" to the goods at the relevant point in time? This procedure often produced fair and logical results, but sometimes it gave rise to poor ones. Different situations can involve different policy considerations and should therefore not be governed by a single standard. Moreover, the courts were never able to develop an objective method of determining the location of title. For these reasons the UCC has abandoned the concept that title determines all questions of rights and responsibilities, and has adopted the approach of identifying specific problems and establishing rules for their solution that do not depend on who had title to the goods at a given time. *The location of title is thus unimportant in resolving most legal issues arising under the UCC.*

However, in some situations title is still a relevant consideration. A few UCC provisions, for example, do make specific mention of title to the goods. Furthermore, application of various laws other than the UCC can depend on the location of title. (For instance, the issue of title can determine the party upon whom certain tax liabilities rest.) These situations make it desirable to discuss specific UCC rules for locating title and a few special problems relating to title. Later in the chapter we will consider the UCC's treatment of two important and related legal problems—who bears the risk in case of casualty to the goods and who has sufficient interest in the goods to obtain insurance coverage.

Passage of Title

Under Sec. 2-105 of the UCC, goods must be *existing* before any interest in them can pass. Thus **future goods** (such as crops to be grown) can be the subject of a sale contract, but no title to them can pass to the buyer until they actually come into existence.

Other rules relating to passage of title are set forth in UCC 2-401:

1. Goods must be not only existing but also *identified* before title can pass to the buyer. Generally, identification occurs when specific goods are designated as being the subject of the sale contract. Thus, if a seller has an inventory of lumber and agrees to sell a certain described quantity, no title can pass to the buyer until the specific lumber to be sold is marked, segregated, or otherwise identified.

2. Subject to the requirement of identification, title can pass to the buyer in any manner and on any conditions expressly agreed on by the parties.

3. If the parties do not expressly agree as to passage of title, when and where this occurs depends on how the goods are to be delivered. If they are to be shipped to the buyer, title passes to the buyer when the seller "completes his performance with reference to the physical delivery of the goods." In this regard, two situations are possible:

   a. The parties may make a *shipment contract,* authorizing or requiring the seller to ship the goods to the buyer (but not obligating him to see that they actually reach that person). Title passes when the seller delivers the goods to a carrier, such as a trucking company.

b. The parties may make a *destination contract,* obligating the seller to see that the goods are actually delivered to the buyer. Whether the seller personally delivers the goods or ships them through an independent carrier, title passes only when delivery occurs.[1]

4. Sometimes the parties will agree that delivery to the buyer is to be accomplished *without physically moving the goods.* For example, the contract may require the buyer to pick up the goods at the seller's place of business or at a warehouse owned by a third party. When title passes depends on whether a document of title is used.

a. If the seller is required to deliver a document of title (such as a warehouse receipt) to the buyer, title passes *when the document is delivered.* Thus the buyer can have title to the goods even if they are left with the warehouseman for a time.

b. If the seller is not required to furnish a document of title (e.g., where the buyer is to pick up the goods at the seller's premises), passage of title occurs *when the sale contract is made*—if the goods are identified. If the goods are not identified at that time, title passes when identification does occur. These rules are illustrated in Figure 21.1.

Special Problems Regarding Title

Sales by Persons with Imperfect Title

A situation occasionally exists where a party with no title or with imperfect title sells goods to another. To illustrate: Suppose that S sells goods to B. O then appears on the scene and claims to be the true owner or to have some interest in the goods.[2] If O is correct, S will ultimately be responsible for any loss he has caused O or B. Often, however, the real dispute is between O and B over who has the greater right to the goods.

---

[1]"FOB" terms usually determine which type of contract exists. Assume a contract is made between a seller in Dallas and a buyer in Miami. If the stated price is "$2,500 FOB Dallas," or "$2,500 FOB seller's plant," it is a shipment contract. On the other hand, if the price is "$2,500 FOB Miami" or "$2,500 FOB buyer's plant," it is a destination contract. Shipment contracts are more common than destination contracts. "FOB" and other commercial shipping terms are explained further in Chapter 23.

[2]If O is a creditor of S and claims that the goods are the agreed-upon security for the debt, his right to the goods is governed by Article 9 of the UCC, dealing with secured transactions, which is the subject of Chapter 29. At this point we are not dealing with that situation.

In attempting to resolve the conflict between O and B, UCC Sec. 2-403 focuses on the type of title held by S, distinguishing between a void and a voidable title. If S has a void title (which is actually no title at all), he cannot transfer any interest in the goods to B. The most common example of this situation is where S is a thief. If S has stolen goods from O and then sold them to B, O can reclaim the goods from B—even if B had no knowledge of the theft.

The result may be different if S has a **voidable title** at the time he sells to B. Here S actually has title, but O has the power to void S's title for some reason. Common examples are these:

1. S purchases the goods from O through fraud.

2. S purchases the goods from O in a "cash on delivery" transaction and pays with a check that bounces.

3. S is insolvent when he purchases the goods on credit from O. In this case, O's power to void S's title and reclaim the goods generally exists for only ten days after S receives the goods. However, under Sec. 2-702(2), if S has misrepresented his solvency to O in writing within three months before delivery, O's power to void S's title and reclaim the goods is not subject to the ten-day limitation.

4. S purchases the goods from O when O is a minor.

If O asserts his rights in any of the above situations while S still has the goods, no particular problems arise. Suppose, however, that S has already sold them to B. Can O reclaim the goods from B? The answer is yes, unless B is classified as a **bona fide purchaser** (BFP). Section 2-403(1) states that "a person with voidable title has power to transfer *good* title" to a BFP. (Emphasis added.) This represents an important exception to the general rule that a person can transfer no better title than he or she has.

A BFP is defined as a "good faith purchaser for value." Thus two requirements must be met before B can be considered a BFP.

1. B must have acted in "good faith." This essentially means that B purchased without notice of the facts that caused S's title to be voidable. ("Notice" means actual knowledge of such facts, or the possession of information that would have caused a reasonably prudent person to discover such facts.)

FIGURE 21.1

Passage of Title under UCC 2-401

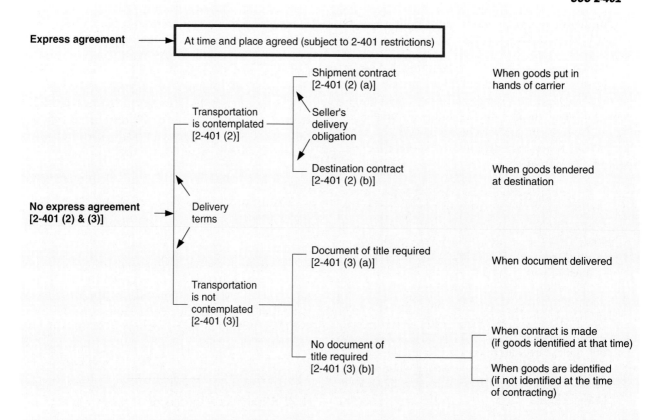

2. B must have given "value" for the goods, that is, "any consideration sufficient to support a simple contract." B meets the value requirement not only by giving S a usual form of consideration—such as payment in cash or by personal check—but also when B receives the goods in satisfaction of a preexisting claim against S. (However, an unreasonably small consideration might be evidence of bad faith on the part of the buyer.)[3]

A buyer cannot simply ignore suspicious circumstances and then claim to have purchased goods without notice that the seller's title was voidable. For example, in *Landshire Food Service, Inc. v. Coghill,* 709 S.W.2d 509 (1986), Bellman bought a Rolls Royce from Coghill with a forged cashier's check.

[3]The requirement of value is easier to satisfy for a BFP than for a holder in due course of a negotiable instrument (see Chapter 26 for details).

Title was transferred to a phony company. Pretending to be Coghill, Bellman then sold the car to Hyken. After the forgery was discovered, a dispute arose as to whether Hyken was a BFP. The court held that he was not, holding that Hyken was put on notice of the irregularities in the title he received because (1) the certificate of title carried evidence of the previous transaction; (2) Bellman gave two contradictory addresses; (3) the asking price was at the low end of fair market value; and (4) Hyken failed to verify the existence and status of a phony company listed as the prior transferee on the title.

Entrustment to a Merchant

One additional situation exists in which a seller can transfer a better title to a buyer than the seller actually has. Under Sec. 2-403(2), if an owner entrusts possession of goods to a merchant who deals in goods of that kind, the merchant has the power to transfer good title to a "buyer in the ordinary course of business." Suppose that Owner O leaves her typewriter to be repaired by M, who is in the business of both repairing and selling typewriters. M then sells O's typewriter to a customer, D. If D purchases the typewriter in an ordinary way from M, and if D has no knowledge that the typewriter actually belongs to O, D has good title. O's only remedy is to sue M for damages; she cannot

reclaim the typewriter from D.[4] The "entrustment" necessary to bring this rule into effect can also occur if a buyer allows a merchant-seller to remain in possession of the goods after the sale. An obvious purpose of the rule is to facilitate the free flow of trade by relieving ordinary customers from the necessity of inquiring into the status of the merchant's title.[5]

The following case illustrates such a situation.

---

[4]D's purchase would not be in the "ordinary course of business," however, if he received the typewriter as security for or in satisfaction of a preexisting debt owed to him by M. D also would not be buying in the ordinary course of

business if the typewriter was part of a bulk purchase of all or a substantial part of M's inventory.

[5]But even though D can acquire greater title in this situation than M had, D's title can be no better than O's.

CANTERRA PETROLEUM, INC. v. WESTERN DRILLING & MINING SUPPLY

North Dakota Supreme Court, 418 N.W.2d 267 (1987)

Mitchell Energy Corporation entrusted oilfield pipe to Port Pipe Terminal, Inc., for storage. Through a paper transaction, two employees of Port Pipe fraudulently transferred apparent ownership of the pipe to Pharoah, Inc., a "dummy" corporation which they created to facilitate the fraudulent sale of merchandise stored at Port Pipe's facilities. In the next few days, Pharoah sold the pipe to Nickel Supply Co., which sold it to Yamin Oil Co., which sold it to NorthStar, which sold it to Western Drilling & Mining Supply, which sold it to Canterra Petroleum, Inc. During these paper transactions, the pipe never left Port Pipe's storage facility until Canterra had it delivered to a trucking company shortly after its purchase. The pipe was stored by the trucking company until law enforcement officers informed Canterra that it was owned by Mitchell. Canterra then surrendered possession to Mitchell and sued Western for breach of warranty of title. Western filed a third-party suit against NorthStar. Canterra received a summary judgment against Western and Western, in turn, received a summary judgment against NorthStar. NorthStar appealed.

Erickstad, Chief Justice:

NorthStar contends that this case falls within the entrustment provision of the Uniform Commercial Code, codified at UCC 2-403:

> 2. Any entrusting of possession of goods to a merchant who deals in goods of that kind gives him power to transfer all rights of the entruster to a buyer in ordinary course of business.

In essence, this statute contains three elements: (1) an entrustment of goods, (2) to a merchant who deals in goods of the kind, (3) followed by a sale to a buyer in the ordinary course of business. If all three elements are present, the rights of the entruster are transferred to the buyer in ordinary course of business. NorthStar argues that Mitchell entrusted the pipe to Port Pipe, a merchant who dealt in pipe, and that through Pharoah the pipe was sold to Nickel, a buyer in the ordinary course of business.

[The court first held that although the trial court had ruled summarily that Port Pipe was merely a storage facility and not a merchant dealing in pipe, there was some evidence indicating that Port Pipe regularly sold pipe. Therefore, summary judgment was inappropriately granted.]

Western also contends that, even if a fact question remains unresolved regarding Port Pipe's merchant status, summary judgment is nevertheless appropriate [because] the entrustment doctrine applies only when the merchant who has been entrusted with the goods sells them in the ordinary course of business. Western contends that the doctrine does not apply where the goods are fraudulently transferred to a dummy corporation by employees of the entrustee and subsequently sold through the dummy corporation to a buyer in the ordinary course of business.

[The rationale of 2-403 has been expressed in] *Sacks v. State*, 360 N.E.2d 21 (Ind.App. 1977):

> Section 2-403 was intended to determine the priorities between two innocent parties: (1) the original owner who parts with his goods through fraudulent conduct of another and (2) an innocent third party who gives value for the goods to the perpetrator of the fraud without knowledge of the fraud. By favoring the innocent third party, the Uniform Commercial Code endeavors to promote the flow of commerce by placing the burden of ascertaining and preventing fraudulent transactions on the one in the best position to prevent them, the original seller.

We believe this policy . . . supports application of the entrustment doctrine

(continues)

CANTERRA PETROLEUM, INC. v. WESTERN DRILLING & MINING SUPPLY

(continued from previous page)
to a situation where employees of the entrustee transfer the entrusted goods to their sham corporation, which in turn sells the goods to a buyer in the ordinary course of business. As between the two innocent parties in this case [Mitchell, which entrusted the pipe to Port Pipe, and Nickel, which bought the pipe in the ordinary course of business from Pharoah], the policy of the Code places the risk of the entrustee's employees fraudulently diverting and selling the goods upon the entruster, Mitchell, which had the opportunity to select its entrustee. Applying the doctrine to this case, Nickel would acquire the title of the entruster, Mitchell, and title would have passed on to the subsequent purchasers of the pipe.

Material issues of fact remain which require resolution upon trial.

[Reversed.] ⚖

Rights of Seller's Creditors against Goods Sold

If a seller for some reason retains possession of the goods after they have been sold, his or her creditors can be misled by this fact. For example, a lender (a "new creditor") may make a loan to the seller, believing that the seller's assets are greater than they really are. Or a person who had a claim against the seller prior to the sale (an "existing creditor"), under the same erroneous belief, might fail to take timely protective measures that he or she would otherwise have taken.

Because of these possibilities, all states have **fraudulent conveyance statutes** which, while not entirely uniform, generally prescribe the circumstances in which the seller's retention of sold goods is fraudulent. When such retention in a particular case is found to be fraudulent, the applicable statute gives certain rights to the creditors insofar as the goods are concerned. The drafters of the UCC, wishing not to interfere with these rights that are created under the local law, achieved this purpose in Sec. 2-402. Section 2-402(2) provides, in essence, that if the seller's retention is "fraudulent under any rule of law of the state where the goods are situated," the seller's creditors *can treat the sale as being void* and the goods as being subject to their claims. Even "unsecured creditors" (those not having a lien on the specific goods) possess this power.[6]

The seller's retention of goods after the sale does not always constitute a fraud on creditors. Indeed, Sec. 2-402(2) states that *it is not fraud* for a seller to retain possession in good faith for a "commercially reasonable time." In other words, the retention must be for a legitimate purpose (such as making adjustments or repairs), and the seller must not keep the goods longer than is reasonably necessary to accomplish this purpose. If the criteria of good faith and a commercially reasonable time are met, the seller's unsecured creditors cannot void the sale.

Retention of possession is not the only way a seller can defraud his or her creditors. Sometimes the sale itself is fraudulent and can be voided by the creditors regardless of who has possession. For instance, a sale made for less than "fair consideration" (thereby depleting the seller's assets) is a fraud on the seller's creditors in either of the following two situations: (1) where the seller is *insolvent* (liabilities exceed assets) at the time of the sale or is made insolvent by the sale, or (2) where the evidence proves that the seller actually intended to hinder, delay, or defraud the creditors. These rules are intended to protect creditors from an attempt by the seller to conceal his or her assets through a sham transaction (usually with a friend or relative).

Bulk Transfers

Suppose that a merchant owing money to creditors sells his or her inventory to a third party. If the merchant uses the proceeds to pay the debts as they fall due, no problems arise. But what if he or she pockets the money and disappears, leaving the creditors unpaid? Can these creditors lay any claim to goods that are now in the buyer's hands? If the buyer has paid a fair consideration, the sale is probably not fraudulent under the rules just discussed.

In such a case, however, if the sale constitutes a "bulk transfer" (or bulk sale, as it is commonly called), the merchant's creditors may be protected by Article 6 of the UCC. The basic rules of that article are as follows:

---

[6]The rights of "secured" creditors will be discussed in Chapter 29.

1. A **bulk transfer** is any transfer (sale) "in bulk and not in the ordinary course of the transferor's business" of a major part of the inventory of an enterprise whose principal business is the sale of merchandise from inventory.

2. Before the bulk transfer takes place, the seller must furnish a list of his or her creditors to the buyer. Then the seller and buyer must prepare a list of the property to be sold. Finally, the buyer must notify the seller's creditors of the bulk sale at least *ten days* before taking possession of or paying for the goods (whichever occurs first). This notice enables creditors to take steps to protect themselves; for example, they can impound the proceeds of the sale if they deem it necessary.

3. If the buyer fails to comply with this advance notice requirement, the sale is ineffective against the seller's existing creditors. (Those who become creditors after the notice is given are not entitled to any notice.) That is, in seeking to obtain satisfaction of their claims, the seller's creditors can treat the goods as still belonging to the seller. For example, a creditor might obtain judgment against the seller and then levy execution on the goods (have them seized) even though they are in the buyer's hands. The creditor must do so, however, within *six months* after the buyer takes possession.

4. Even if a bulk transfer is ineffective because proper notice has not been given, the buyer can transfer good title to a BFP.

The New Article 6.　Article 6 was obviously aimed at protecting creditors from debtors who sold their goods in bulk and then absconded. Since the original promulgation of Article 6, the law and the availability of credit information have both evolved to give substantially more protection to creditors. Today, many believe that Article 6 gives creditors too much protection, impeding normal business transactions. Dissatisfaction with Article 6 led the American Law Institute and National Conference of Commissioners on Uniform State Laws to recommend in 1988 that the states repeal it because it is no longer necessary. Those states believing that they still need a bulk sales statute are urged to replace the current Article 6 with a newer version which would make several changes, including the following:

1. The revised article will apply only when the buyer has notice that the seller will not continue to operate the same or a similar kind of business after the sale.

2. The revised article will not apply to sales in which the value of property otherwise available to creditors is less than $10,000 or greater than $25,000,000.

3. When the seller is indebted to a large number of persons, the buyer need not send individual notices to each, but may give notice by filing.

4. The notice period is increased from 10 days to 45 days and the statute of limitations is increased from six months to one year.

5. A buyer's noncompliance will not render the sale ineffective or adversely affect the buyer's title; rather, the noncomplying buyer will be liable for damages caused by the noncompliance.

6. There is no liability for a buyer who believed in good faith that Article 6 did not apply or who made a good faith attempt to comply with it.

Along with the revised version of Article 6, there also have been many calls for the complete repeal of the Article, leaving the UCC without any sections applying special rules to bulk transfers. Thus, state legislatures are currently faced with three alternatives: retaining the original Article 6, adopting the new Article 6, or repealing Article 6 entirely. As of this writing, 16 states have repealed Article 6 completely, only 4 have adopted the revised version, and the remaining states have not yet taken action. Neither version of Article 6 is included in the text's UCC appendix.

RISK OF LOSS

A warehouse fire damages thousands of dollars' worth of goods. A truck, train, ship, or airplane is involved in an accident that destroys a substantial quantity of goods. In these kinds of situations the question may arise as to who must bear the financial burden of the loss.

The **risk of loss** question is especially provocative when the goods are the subject of a sale contract at the time of damage or destruction. The risk that the goods will suffer some casualty initially rests on the seller, but ultimately it passes to the buyer. The crucial issue is whether the risk had passed from the seller to the buyer at the time of the loss. If it had not yet passed, the financial loss is borne by the seller. (Whether the seller in such a case also remains responsible to fulfill the contract with the buyer is a separate issue, to be discussed in Chapter 23.) If it had already passed, the buyer must bear the loss. This means that the buyer is obligated to pay for the goods if payment had not yet been made, and he or she is not entitled to a refund of any payment already made.

The existence of insurance coverage does not lessen the importance of this question; it simply means that the real issue is whose insurance company must bear the loss. Of course, insurance coverage may be inadequate or totally lacking in a given case. If the goods are damaged, lost, or destroyed while in possession of a bailee such as a carrier or warehouseman, the bailee will often be liable (see Chapter 45 for details). The risk of loss question in such a case is still important, however, because it determines whether the seller or buyer bears the burden of pursuing the bailee for a remedy.

As mentioned earlier in this chapter, risk of loss does not automatically pass with title. In resolving the problem of who bears the risk, the UCC differentiates between two situations: (1) where the contract has not been breached when the loss occurs, and (2) where there has been a breach at the time of the loss.

Risk of Loss Where the Contract Is Not Breached

The rules for placing the risk of loss in the ordinary situation are found in Sec. 2-509, as follows:

1. As was the case with passage of title, the parties can make any agreement regarding the time at which risk of loss passes from seller to buyer.

2. Where there is no agreement as to when the risk passes, the issue is based on *how the goods are to be delivered.* Where the sale contract requires or authorizes the seller to ship the goods by carrier, the timing of the passage of risk depends on the seller's obligation.

    a. If the parties have made a *shipment contract,* in which the seller's obligation is completed upon shipment of the goods, the risk of loss passes to the buyer under Sec. 2-509(1)(a) when the goods are "duly delivered" to the carrier by the seller. In most cases, a due delivery occurs when the seller *puts the goods in the possession of the carrier.* Any loss occurring thereafter falls on the buyer. (The basic shipment section, Sec. 2-504, also requires the seller (1) to make a reasonable

transportation contract with the carrier, including delivery to the buyer of any documents necessary for the buyer to take possession of the goods, and (2) to promptly notify the buyer of the shipment—actions that are, in fact, usually performed by the seller as a matter of routine. However, that section goes on to provide that if the seller fails to perform either of these additional acts, the buyer may reject the shipment only if "material loss ensues"—a clause that most courts interpret as meaning "ensues *as a result of* such failure." Because most cases of loss or damage during shipment are caused by factors unrelated to the seller's nonperformance of either of these duties, the usual result is that the buyer must accept and pay for goods damaged or lost in the carrier's possession even in those cases where the seller fails to perform either of these additional duties.)

    b. If the parties have made a *destination contract,* in which the seller is obligated to see that the goods are actually delivered to the buyer, the risk of loss passes only upon fulfillment of that obligation *by the seller tendering the goods at their destination* under Sec. 2-509(1)(b).

Generally, in 2a and 2b situations, the rules governing risk of loss essentially correspond to those governing passage of title—though differences in wording between the two sections occasionally give rise to a situation where title and risk of loss do not pass at exactly the same time.

3. Sometimes the goods at the time of sale are being held by a **bailee** and are to be delivered *without being moved.* For example, they might be stored in a warehouse, the buyer intending to pick them up there or perhaps to leave them in storage until they are resold to someone else. In such a case, the placing of the risk of loss hinges primarily on whether the bailee has issued a document of title (warehouse receipt) and, if so, what type of document it is. Under Sec. 2-509(2):

    a. If a *negotiable* document of title has been issued for the goods, the risk of loss passes to the buyer when he or she receives the document. Since the holder of a negotiable document generally has an automatic right to receive the goods, it is logical to place the risk of loss on that person.

    b. If a *nonnegotiable* document of title has been issued, the problem is different. A buyer with

FIGURE 21.2

Risk of Loss

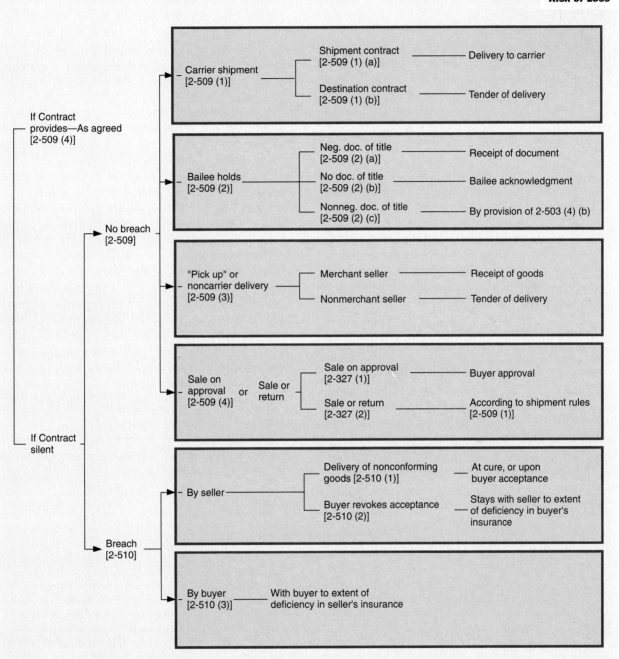

this kind of document is not as well protected as one who has a negotiable document. This person can, for example, lose his or her right to the goods to some third party, such as a creditor of the seller or a purchaser from the bailee.

And the buyer does not actually have a right to the goods until he or she *notifies the bailee of the purchase*. (Indeed, the buyer does not have to accept a nonnegotiable document as performance by the seller; but if the buyer does not object, the seller can satisfy his or her performance requirements with such a document.) Logically, then, the buyer's receipt of a nonnegotiable document does not immediately shift the risk of loss to that person. In fact, the risk does not pass to the buyer until he or she has had a *reasonable amount of time* to present the document to the bailee and demand the goods; and, of course, the risk does not shift if the bailee refuses to honor the document.

c. When the bailee holds goods for which *no document of title* has been issued and the seller wishes to sell the goods without moving them, he or she can do so in either of two ways. First, the seller can give the buyer a writing that directs the bailee to deliver the goods to the buyer. Risk of loss in this instance is determined in the same way as if a nonnegotiable document of title had been issued. Second, the seller can obtain from the bailee an acknowledgment that the buyer is entitled to the goods. In this case, risk of loss passes to the buyer when the bailee acknowledges the buyer's right to possession.

4. Some situations are not covered by any of the foregoing rules. Two common examples are transactions in which the buyer picks up the goods at the seller's premises or in which the seller personally delivers the goods to the buyer (rather than shipping by independent carrier). In such cases, the time at which the risk of loss shifts to the buyer depends on whether the seller is a *merchant*. The rules set forth below are found in Sec. 2-509(3).

If the seller is a merchant, his or her responsibility is somewhat greater than that borne by the nonmerchant; thus the risk of loss does not pass from seller to buyer until the buyer *actually receives the goods*. If the seller is *not* a merchant, the risk of loss passes to the buyer when the seller "tenders" delivery. (The concept of *tender* is discussed in greater detail in Chapter 23, but it essentially means that the seller has placed at the buyer's disposal goods conforming to the contract requirements and has notified the buyer so as to enable that person to take possession.) Suppose, for example, that B purchases a new car from S, a dealer. S is supposed to install an AM-FM radio and speaker system before B takes possession of the car. S does the work and parks the car on his lot, then telephones B and informs her that the car is ready. Before B picks up the car, it is severely damaged by a hailstorm. S must bear the loss. *Since he is a merchant, the risk does not shift to B until the latter actually takes possession.* If S had been an individual selling his personal car, the loss would have been borne by B because risk of loss in that case would have passed to B *at the time of the tender*—the phone call from S prior to the storm.

The preceding points regarding risk of loss are capsulated in Figure 21.2 on page 423.

The following case presents a typical situation in which determination of the time of passage of risk of loss becomes all important.

Schock v. Ronderos

Supreme Court of North Dakota, 394 N.W.2d 697 (1986)

Schock (Buyer) negotiated to buy a mobile home that was owned by the Ronderoses (Sellers) and located on their property. On April 15, 1985, Buyer went to Sellers' home and paid them the agreed purchase price of $3,900. Buyer received a bill of sale and an assurance from Sellers that title would be delivered soon. With Sellers' permission, Buyer prepared the mobile home for re-

moval. Buyer intended to remove the home from Sellers' property on the following Monday, April 22. Sellers had no objection to the mobile home remaining on their premises until that time. They agreed to remove a piano and davenport which were still in the home and to disconnect the electricity and natural gas.

On Friday, April 19, the mobile home was destroyed by high winds as it sat on Sellers' property. Buyer received in the mail a clear certificate

of title on April 23. Buyer later filed this suit for return of the purchase price, arguing that when the home was destroyed, the risk of loss was on the Sellers. The trial judge ruled for Sellers on this claim, and Buyer appealed.

Erickstad, Chief Justice:

The issue of which party in this case must bear the loss of the mobile home is determined by the risk of loss
(continues)

SCHOCK V. RONDEROS

(continued from previous page)
provisions of [UCC 2-509], which provide in relevant part:

3. In any case not within subsection 1 or 2, the risk of loss passes to the buyer on his receipt of the goods if the seller is a merchant; otherwise the risk passes to the buyer on tender of delivery.

It is undisputed that the Sellers are not merchants; therefore, the risk of loss was on them until they made a "tender of delivery" of the mobile home at which time the risk of loss passed to Buyer. The location or status of the title is not a relevant consideration in determining which party must bear the loss of the mobile home.

Pursuant to [UCC 2-503], tender of delivery requires that the seller "put and hold conforming goods at the buyer's disposition. . . ." The trial court determined that there had been payment for and acceptance of the mobile home by Buyer. Within that conclusion is an implicit determination that there was a completed tender of delivery by Sellers.

The Sellers disconnected the electricity and natural gas to the mobile home prior to its destruction, and nothing remained for them to do as a prerequisite to Buyer's taking possession of the home other than the removal of the piano and davenport. Under the circumstances of this case, we believe that their failure to remove those items did not result in an uncompleted tender of delivery. The Sellers testified that following Buyer's payment for the home on April 15, 1985, Buyer could have removed the home from their premises at any time. They further testified that if Buyer had expressed a desire to remove the home prior to Monday, April 22, 1985, they would have removed the piano and davenport immediately so that he could have done so. The Sellers, consistent with a completed tender of delivery, acquiesced in Buyer's decision to prepare, on April 15, 1985, the mobile home for removal. As part of those preparations Buyer removed the skirting, the tie downs, and the [foundation] blocks. He also removed and took with him a set of steps to the mobile home. We believe those actions by Buyer constituted an exercise of possession which is consistent with our conclusion that Sellers had tendered delivery of the mobile home to him on that date. Thus, we hold that on April 15, 1985, the Sellers tendered delivery of the mobile home and the risk of loss passed to Buyer.

[Affirmed.] 🔊

Effect of Breach on Risk of Loss

When one of the parties has breached the contract, that party sometimes is required to shoulder a risk that he or she otherwise would not have to bear. This risk is, of course, in addition to any damages that the party may have to pay. Section 2-510 sets forth three basic rules to cover such situations; rules 1 and 2 apply to breaches by the seller arising out of the delivery of nonconforming goods, while rule 3 applies to breaches by the buyer.

1. When a seller tenders or delivers goods that do not conform to the requirements of the contract, the buyer usually has a right to *reject* the goods. In such a case, the risk of loss does not pass to the buyer until the seller "cures" the defect or the buyer accepts the goods despite their nonconformity.[7] Suppose that S and B have made a shipment contract for the sale of some office furniture. The risk of loss in this situation ordinarily passes to the buyer when the goods are duly delivered to the carrier. However, in this case some of the furniture is improperly upholstered. On receiving and inspecting the furniture, B rejects the shipment. The risk remains with S until he reupholsters the defective pieces of furniture or substitutes good pieces for the bad ones. However, if B had accepted the shipment despite its defects, the risk would have passed to him on acceptance. In other words, if the nonconforming shipment is destroyed or damaged (through no fault of the buyer) prior to cure or acceptance, the loss falls on S.

2. In some situations, a buyer who has accepted goods can *revoke the acceptance.* Suppose, for example, that B does not discover the defect until after he has accepted the shipment. (The circumstances in which B has a right to revoke his acceptance will be discussed in Chapter 23. Here, assume that B does have this right.) If B revokes his acceptance, the risk of

---

[7]The circumstances under which the buyer can reject goods are discussed in Chapter 23. And, in speaking of cure, we are assuming here that the seller has a right to do so—which may or may not be the case. If the seller does not have the right, he or she cannot cure the defect and then force the buyer to take the goods. (The subject of cure is also treated more fully in Chapter 23.)

loss is treated as having remained with S from the beginning. However, the risk borne by S is *only to the extent that B's insurance coverage is deficient.* Suppose, for example, that the value of the goods is $10,000 but that B has insurance coverage of only $5,000. If the goods are destroyed through no fault of either party (for example, by flood or fire), S will bear a loss of $5,000 and B's insurance company will bear the remaining $5,000 loss. If B had had no insurance, S would have borne the entire loss. If B's insurance had covered the entire loss, S would have borne none of it.

3. Situations 1 and 2 involved a breach by the *seller.* What effect does a breach by the *buyer* have on the risk of loss? Stated simply, a breach of the contract by the buyer immediately shifts the risk of loss to him or her. Of course, the risk shifts only if, before B's breach, specific goods had already been identified as the subject of the contract. For example, S might ship conforming goods and B might wrongfully reject them on their arrival. Or, after specific goods had been identified, but before shipment, B might notify S that he will not comply with the contract. In either case, the risk of loss immediately shifts to B even if it would not have passed until later had B not breached the contract. B must bear the risk, however, *only for a reasonable time thereafter* and *only to the extent that S's insurance coverage is deficient.*

In the case that follows, the issues are (a) whether the buyer breached, and (b) if so, how the rules summarized in 3 above would apply.

MULTIPLASTICS, INC. v. ARCH INDUSTRIES, INC.

Supreme Court of Connecticut, 348 A.2d 618 (1974)

The plaintiff, Multiplastics, Inc., brought this action to recover damages from the defendant, Arch Industries, Inc., for the breach of a contract to purchase 40,000 pounds of plastic pellets.

Plaintiff, a manufacturer of plastic resin pellets, agreed with defendant on June 30, 1971, to manufacture and deliver 40,000 pounds of brown polystyrene plastic pellets for nineteen cents a pound. The pellets were specially made for defendant, who agreed to accept delivery at the rate of 1,000 pounds per day after completion of production. Defendant's confirming order contained the notation, "Make and hold for release. Confirmation." Plaintiff produced the order of pellets within two weeks and requested release orders from defendant. Defendant refused to issue the release orders, citing labor difficulties and its vacation schedule. On August 18, 1971, plaintiff sent defendant the following letter:

Against P.O. 0946, we produced 40,000 lbs. of brown high impact styrene, and you have issued no releases. You indicated to us

that you would be using 1,000 lbs. of each per day. We have warehoused these products for more than forty days, as we agreed to do. However, we cannot warehouse these products indefinitely, and request that you send us shipping instructions. We have done everything we agreed to do.

After August 18, 1971, plaintiff made numerous telephone calls to defendant to seek payment and delivery instructions. In response, beginning August 20, 1971, defendant agreed to issue release orders but in fact never did.

On September 22, 1971, plaintiff's plant, containing the pellets manufactured for defendant, was destroyed by fire. Plaintiff's fire insurance did not cover the loss of the pellets, and plaintiff brought action against defendant to recover the contract price.

The trial court concluded that (1) plaintiff had made a valid tender of delivery by its letter of August 18, 1971, and by its subsequent requests for delivery instructions; (2) defendant had repudiated and breached the contract by refusing to accept delivery on August 20, 1971; (3) the period from August 20, 1971, to

September 22, 1971, was not a commercially unreasonable time for plaintiff to treat the risk of loss as resting on defendant under UCC Sec. 2-510(3); and (4) plaintiff was entitled to recover the contract price plus interest. Defendant appealed.

Bogdanski, Justice:

. . . [Section] 2-510, entitled "Effect of breach on risk of loss," reads, in pertinent part, as follows: "(3) Where the buyer as to conforming goods already identified to the contract for sale repudiates or is otherwise in breach before risk of their loss has passed to him, the seller may to the extent of any deficiency in his effective insurance coverage treat the risk of loss as resting on the buyer for a commercially reasonable time." The defendant contends that §2-510 is not applicable because its failure to issue delivery instructions did not constitute either a repudiation or a breach of the agreement. The defendant also argues that even if §2-510 were applicable, the period from August 20, 1971, to September 22, 1971, was not a commercially reasonable period of time within which to treat the

(continues)

MULTIPLASTICS, INC. V. ARCH INDUSTRIES, INC.

(continued from previous page)
risk of loss as resting on the buyer. . . .

The trial court's conclusion that the defendant was in breach is supported by its finding that the defendant agreed to accept delivery of the pellets at the rate of 1,000 pounds per day after completion of production. The defendant argues that since the confirming order instructed the [plaintiff] to "make and hold for release," the contract did not specify an exact delivery date. This argument fails, however, because nothing in the finding suggests that the notation in the confirming order was part of the agreement between the parties. Since, as the trial court found, the plaintiff made a proper tender of delivery, beginning with its letter of August 18, 1971, the plaintiff was entitled to acceptance of the goods and to payment according to the contract. . . .

The remaining question is whether, under §2-510(3), the period of time from August 20, 1971, the date of the breach, to September 22, 1971, the date of the fire, was a "commercially reasonable" period within which to

treat the risk of loss as resting on the buyer. The trial court concluded that it was "not, on the facts in this case, a commercially unreasonable time," which we take to mean that it was a commercially reasonable period. The time limitation in §2-510(3) is designed to enable the seller to obtain the additional requisite insurance coverage. . . . [Under the particular facts of this case,] August 20 to September 22 was a commercially reasonable period within which to place the risk of loss on the defendant. As already stated, the trial court found that the defendant repeatedly agreed to transmit delivery instructions and that the pellets were specially made to fill the defendant's order. Under those circumstances, it was reasonable for the plaintiff to believe that the goods would soon be taken off its hands and so to forego procuring the needed insurance.

We consider it advisable to discuss one additional matter. The trial court concluded that "title" passed to the defendant, and the defendant attacks the conclusion on this appeal. The issue is

immaterial to this case. [Section] 2-401 states: "Each provision of this article with regard to the rights, obligations and remedies of the seller, the buyer, purchasers or other third parties applies irrespective of title to the goods except where the provision refers to such title." As one student of the Uniform Commercial Code has written:

The single most important innovation of Article 2 is its restatement of . . . [the parties'] responsibilities in terms of operative facts rather than legal conclusions; where pre-Code law looked to "title" for the definition of rights and remedies, the Code looks to demonstrable realities such as custody, control and professional expertise. This shift in approach is central to the whole philosophy of Article 2. It means that disputes, as they arise, can focus, as does all of the modern law of contracts, upon actual provable circumstances, rather than upon a metaphysical concept of elastic and endlessly fluid dimensions. Peters, "Remedies for Breach of Contracts Relating to the Sale of Goods Under the Uniform Commercial Code: A Roadmap for Article Two." 73 Yale L.J. 199, 201. . . .

[Affirmed.] ⚖️

INSURABLE INTEREST

Parties often obtain insurance coverage to protect themselves against the possibility that property in which they have an interest might be lost, damaged, or destroyed. An insurance policy is valid only if the party purchasing the protection has an **insurable interest.** Whether a party has this in a given situation is primarily a matter of insurance law rather than sales law. Article 2 of the UCC does, however, contain certain rules regarding insurable interest in goods.

Seller's Insurable Interest

So long as the seller has title to the goods, he or she obviously has an insurable interest. But even if title passes to the buyer, the seller continues to have an insurable interest— and can insure the goods—so long as he or she has a "security interest" (a lien or mortgage to secure payment) in the goods.

Buyer's Insurable Interest

The buyer obtains an insurable interest and can insure the goods as soon as they have been identified as the subject of the sale contract.

Under these rules, seller and buyer can both have an insurable interest in the same goods at the same time. Of course, even if a party has an insurable interest and obtains insurance coverage, that person has no right to recover from the insurance company unless he or she actually sustains a loss.

An application of these rules can be seen in *Bowman v. American Home Assurance Co.,* 213 N.W.2d 446 (Neb. 1973), where Bowman contracted on December 12 to sell his plane to Hemmer. On December 18, before the paperwork was complete or a bill of sale transferred, Bowman loaned the plane to Hemmer so that Hemmer could make a short trip. Hemmer crashed the plane on the 18th. Bowman's

Legal Focus

In sales transactions in which the seller and buyer are based in different nations and both nations have adopted the United Nations Convention on Contracts for the International Sale of Goods (CISG), the CISG provides risk of loss rules unless the parties have agreed otherwise. These rules are quite similar to those of our UCC. Like the UCC, the CISG rules differentiate between situations in which the goods are to be transported and those in which the contract requires the buyer to pick up the goods at the seller's place of business or at some other place. With respect to goods that are to be transported from the seller to the buyer by means of a carrier (or series of carriers), the CISG also differentiates between *shipment* and *destination* contracts in allocating the risk of loss.

Roman law, which formed the basis for the law of many European nations and other countries that did not inherit the common-law traditions of England, specified that the risk of loss passed from seller to buyer at the conclusion of the contract. Some western civil-law countries have retained this rule, and others have changed the rule to place the time of risk transfer at the time of title transfer. Thus, the CISG's adoption of rules closely resembling those of our UCC represents a significant change from the domestic laws of many of the civil-law nations that have adopted the CISG. The CISG rules, much like the UCC, generally transfer the risk of loss at the time the seller has completed its performance obligations under the contract, unless the parties have agreed otherwise.

insurance company refused to pay under a policy that apparently provided coverage until December 23, claiming that Bowman had no insurable interest in the plane at the time of the crash. The court ruled for Bowman, reasoning: (1) under UCC 2-501, a seller has an insurable interest until title passes to the buyer; (2) under UCC 2-401, title passes at the time the seller completes his performance with reference to physical delivery of the goods *or* at any other time explicitly agreed to by the parties; (3) Bowman had only loaned the plane to Hemmer and therefore had not completed physical delivery; and (4) in this case the parties agreed that title would not pass until the paperwork was completed, which had not yet occurred on December 18.

SALE ON APPROVAL AND SALE OR RETURN

Occasionally a seller and buyer agree that the buyer is to have a *right to return the goods to the seller* even though the goods conform to the sale contract. Such transactions possess certain unique characteristics warranting a separate discussion.

A sale of this type is either a **sale on approval** or a **sale or return.** Which of the two forms the transaction takes can always be expressly agreed upon by the parties. If the contract provides for a return of conforming goods but does *not* designate which form is intended, the UCC provides specific rules for classifying the arrangement. Section 2-326 states: "Unless otherwise agreed, if delivered goods may be returned by the buyer even though they conform to the contract, the transaction is (a) a 'sale on approval' if the goods are delivered primarily for *use*, and (b) a 'sale or return' if the goods are delivered primarily for *resale*." (Emphasis added.) This is a common sense test. The purpose of a *sale on approval* is to allow the buyer who will be using the goods an opportunity to try them out before committing himself or herself to pay for them. The purpose of a *sale or return* is to allow the buyer of goods who intends to resell them to others an opportunity to return the unsold items. Copying machines are often sold in a *sale on approval;* textbooks are often sold to bookstores in a *sale or return.*

In either type of transaction the sale contract can specify the period of time within which the buyer must make a decision. If no time is specified, the choice must be made within a *reasonable time.* Failure to decide within this time constitutes acceptance of the goods, and the buyer must pay for them.

In a sale on approval transaction, the buyer can express approval in several ways. For example, as we have already indicated, failure to express disapproval within the required time constitutes approval. Approval can also be given by any statements or actions signifying it. Of course, the buyer can make a *trial use* of the goods without implying approval—though the question sometimes arises as to whether a particular use is really just a trial. While this question must be answered on the basis of the facts of each case, the key is whether the use being made of the goods is consistent with the purpose of a trial.

Consequences of Approval and Return Sales

Under Sec. 2-327, the legal consequences of a sale on approval and a sale or return differ in several significant respects. The most important of these are the following:

1. In a sale on approval, no sale exists until the buyer accepts the goods by giving approval. Up to that time the arrangement is a bailment (the buyer being the bailee), with title and risk of loss *remaining with the seller* until the buyer gives approval.[8] By contrast, in a sale or return a valid sale exists until the buyer returns the goods. Thus title and risk of loss *pass to the buyer* as in any other sale, and remain with him or her until the goods are actually returned to the seller.

2. In a sale on approval, if the goods are returned the seller bears the expense of such return (but if the buyer is a merchant, he or she must follow all reasonable instructions of the seller in making the return). On the other hand, under a sale or return the buyer bears the expense of returning the goods.

3. The rights of creditors also differ with the nature of the transaction. In a sale on approval, the buyer is not the "owner" of the goods in his or her possession prior to approval. Consequently, until an approval occurs, the goods are subject to the claims of the seller's creditors and, with one exception discussed below, not to the claim of the buyer's creditors. By contrast, in a sale or return the buyer *is* the owner of the goods in his or her possession. Therefore, such goods are subject to claims of the buyer's creditors rather than the seller's creditors.

4. We noted earlier that the parties can agree as they wish on whether a particular arrangement permitting the return of conforming goods is a sale on approval or a sale or return. One important exception to this rule places significant constraints on that freedom. Under Sec. 2-326(3), if the buyer maintains a place of business where he or she deals in goods of the kind involved, and if that place of business is conducted under any name other than that of the seller, then the goods in the buyer's possession "are deemed to be on sale or return." *In other words, in such a situation, the goods in the buyer's possession are subject to the claims of his or her creditors.*[9] This is true even though the parties had *agreed* that the arrangement was to be a consignment or a sale on approval, and even though the seller is still the owner of the goods. In order to protect creditors of the buyer, who might be misled by the buyer's possession, this section essentially provides that the agreement of the seller and buyer can simply be ignored. It will still be effective, however, in regard to the rights and obligations existing between the seller and buyer.

In this situation, certain measures are available to the seller to protect his or her ownership rights in the goods. In other words, even though the goods are reachable by the buyer's creditors, a cautious seller can take steps to see that his or her interest prevails. Section 2-326(3) spells out alternatives for the seller, the best of which is compliance with the provisions of Article 9 (secured transactions) with respect to obtaining a "security interest" in the goods and filing public notice of that interest with the appropriate state official. (See Chapter 29 for a detailed discussion of security interests.)

Sale on Consignment

Somewhat akin to a sale on approval and a sale or return is the *sale on consignment*. In such a transaction, a seller (the consignor) delivers goods to another person (the consignee) for the purpose of having the consignee sell them on behalf of the consignor. The consignee is merely an agent of the consignor; both title and risk of loss *remain with the consignor* while the goods are in the consignee's hands. Any unsold goods are, of course, returned to the consignor. The sale on consignment differs from a sale on approval

---

[8]Of course, if the goods are damaged, lost, or destroyed due to the buyer's negligence or intentional wrong, he or she is responsible regardless of where the risk of loss rests.

[9]The exception does not apply if the buyer is an affiliate of the seller doing business under the seller's name. In this case the buyer's creditors should be aware of the seller's interest.

because the consignee does not have possession for the purpose of deciding whether he or she wishes to buy the goods. And it differs from a sale or return because in that transaction the buyer acquires title to the goods for the purpose of reselling them; by contrast, a consignee—being merely an agent of the consignor—does not acquire title to the goods.

SUMMARY

In most circumstances it is immaterial at what moment title to the goods passed from seller to buyer. However, in cases where it is necessary to pinpoint the time of passage, UCC Sec. 2-401 contains rules for making this determination.

There are four situations relevant to the transfer of title which are governed by special code rules, rather than those in Sec. 2-401. Two of these situations are (1) sales by persons having voidable title, and (2) sales by merchants of goods entrusted to them. In these situations an innocent purchaser may receive better title than that possessed by the seller.

Where goods are lost or damaged before receipt by the buyer, it is necessary to determine whether the risk of loss had, or had not, passed from seller to buyer prior to the time of loss or damage. Where neither party has breached the contract, the rules of Sec. 2-509 determine the time of passage of risk. If the parties had made a shipment contract, risk of loss passes when the seller delivers the goods to the carrier. In a destination contract, by contrast, the risk does not pass until the goods have reached their destination and the seller has made a due tender there.

In other situations, where transportation of the goods is not contemplated, the goods at the time of contracting are usually in the possession of a bailee (a warehouse) or in possession of the seller. In the first situation, if the warehouse receipt is negotiable, the risk of loss passes to the buyer when he or she receives the receipt. (If it is nonnegotiable, risk of loss does not pass until the buyer notifies the warehouse of the purchase). In the second situation, where possession is in the seller, the risk of loss does not pass to the buyer until he or she receives the goods *if* the seller is a merchant. If the seller is not a merchant, the risk of loss passes when the seller has tendered delivery (which is usually at some time before the buyer receives the goods).

If one of the parties has breached the contract prior to the time of the loss or damage, special rules set forth in Sec. 2-510 determine the time that risk of loss passes. When one of the parties is attempting to hold his or her insurance company liable for the loss or damage to the goods, such party must show that he or she possessed an insurable interest in the goods at the time of loss or damage. Section 2-501 sets forth the circumstances in which the buyer may have an insurable interest, and those in which the seller may have such an interest.

Sales on approval and sale or return transactions are those in which the buyer has the right to return the goods even though they conform to the terms of the contract. In a sale on approval, title and risk of loss remain with the seller until the buyer expressly or impliedly approves; by contrast, in a sale or return, title and risk of loss pass to the buyer when he or she receives the goods (but reverts to the seller if the buyer returns them).

KEY TERMS

Future goods
Voidable title
Bona fide purchaser
Fraudulent conveyance statutes
Bulk transfer
Risk of loss
Bailee
Insurable interest
Sale on approval
Sale or return

QUESTIONS AND PROBLEMS

1. In 1945, Lieber, then in the United States Army, was among the first soldiers to occupy Munich, Germany. There, he and some companions entered Adolph Hitler's apartment and removed various items of his personal belongings. Lieber brought his share, including Hitler's uniform jacket and cap and some of his decorations and personal jewelry, home to the U.S. after the war. In 1968 the collection was stolen by Lieber's chauffeur, who sold it to a New York dealer in historical Americana. The dealer sold it to the defendant, who purchased it in good faith. Through collectors' circles Lieber soon discovered the whereabouts of his stolen property. Lieber's demand for return of the property was refused, and he filed suit against defendant, seeking the return. Did Lieber or defendant prevail? Explain. (*Lieber v. Mohawk Arms, Inc.*, 64 Misc.2d 206, 1970.)

2. On January 9, 1985, Dartmouth Motor Sales sold a car to Wilcox who not only falsely represented himself to be a licensed car dealer but also paid for the car with a $6300 check that later bounced. The car's title was purportedly transferred by assignment. On January 10, Campbell, a licensed dealer, bought the car from Wilcox for $4300 and title was again transferred by assignment. At 2:00 p.m on January 15, Dartmouth's bookkeeper telephoned Campbell and told him that Dartmouth had a potential claim against the vehicle. Despite this and other communications, Campbell sold the car for $5,500 to Willis later that afternoon. Willis took possession of the car, but a dispute arose as to who was entitled to possession. Can you sort out the various rights of the parties? (*Dartmouth Motor Sales, Inc. v. Wilcox*, 517 A.2d 804, N.H. 1986.)

3. A entrusted goods to B, who was a merchant in the business of selling such goods. B was not authorized to sell A's goods, but he did in fact sell them in his regular manner to C, who thought they belonged to B. C paid for the goods by paying a debt that B owed to X. A filed suit to reclaim the goods from C. Was A successful? Explain.

4. Brown (D) bought five carloads of lumber from Lumber Sales (P). He admitted receiving four carloads but denied receiving the fifth, for which he refused to pay. The fifth carload was delivered to a railroad siding about one-half mile from D's business, as the parties had agreed. One of D's employees was notified of the delivery, but the lumber was not immediately unloaded, partly because the next day was Thanksgiving. The lumber then disappeared. P sued for the price of the fifth carload. Is P entitled to recover? (*Lumber Sales, Inc. v. Brown*, 469 S.W.2d 888, Tenn.App. 1971.)

5. Williams owned a motorboat, which he stored in a hobby shop. He agreed to sell the boat to Sanders. After making the agreement, Williams and Sanders went to the hobby shop, where Williams told the person in charge that Sanders would pick up the boat. Arrangements for the pickup were made between Sanders and the person in charge of the shop. When Sanders later returned to pick up the boat, it was gone. Sanders refused to pay for the boat, and Williams sued Sanders for the purchase price. Did he win his suit? Explain.

6. Lair Co. sold a TV antenna on credit to Crump. The contract provided that Crump could not remove the antenna from his premises while the price remained unpaid. The antenna was delivered and installed by Lair Co. Later it was destroyed by fire, and Crump refused to continue paying for it. When Lair Co. sued for the price, Crump claimed that risk of loss had not yet passed at the time of the fire. His reasoning was that, since the antenna was not shipped by carrier and not held by a bailee, risk would pass from Lair Co. (a merchant) to him only when he actually *received* the antenna. He argued that because of the restrictions placed upon his control of the antenna, Lair Co. technically had retained possession and he had not really received it. Who prevailed? Explain. (*Lair Distrib. Co. v. Crump*, 261 So.2d 904, 1972.)

7. X Company contracted to sell goods to Z Company. Both agreed that Z would pick up the goods at X's premises. The contract called for delivery "FOB purchaser's truck." X notified Z that the goods were ready for Z to pick up. Before Z called for them, however, they were destroyed. X Company sued for the purchase price. Did X win? Explain.

8. Fekkos (D) bought a tractor and various implements from Lykins Oil Co. (P) on April 27, 1985. The next day, while attempting to use the tractor, D discovered several defects, including a dead battery, overheating, missing safety shields, and a missing water pump. On that day D contacted P's employees who believed his objections to be valid and told him they would have the tractor picked up the next day. D stopped payment on the check he had written to P and placed the tractor with a tiller attached in his front yard because his garage was inaccessible and because P's employees would have to jump start the tractor when they picked it up. P did not pick up the tractor on the 30th. On that day, D went to P's store and one of P's employees made the notation "cancelled 4-30-85" on the sale's invoice. The tractor was stolen sometime before 6:00 a.m. on May 1, 1985. The tiller had been removed and was still on the lawn. P later sued D for the purchase price of the tractor. Is D liable? (*Lykins Oil Co. v. Fekkos*, 507 N.E.2d 795, Ohio Ct.Comm.Pleas 1986.)

9. Shook bought electric cable from Graybar Electric Co. Shook was a contractor doing road work, and his place of operation continually changed. Graybar delivered the wrong cable to Shook, who promptly notified Graybar of the error and of the location where Graybar could pick up the cable. Graybar made no effort to take back the cable it had delivered,

and after three months it was stolen. Graybar sued Shook to recover the purchase price for the cable. Did Graybar prevail? Explain. (*Graybar Elec. Co. v. Shook,* 195 S.E.2d 514, 1973.)

10. Scarola purchased goods from Pearsall, not knowing that Pearsall had stolen the goods. Scarola obtained an insurance policy on the goods, which were later destroyed by fire. When Scarola sought to recover their value from the insurance company, the company asserted that Scarola had no insurable interest in the goods. Scarola sued. Did he prevail against the insurance company? Discuss. (*Scarola v. Insurance Co. of North America,* 292 N.E.2d 776, 1972.)

Chapter 22

Sales: Warranties and Products Liability

Warranty

Negligence

Strict Liability

Federal Consumer Legislation

Legislative Limitations on the Products Liability Revolution

I N RECENT YEARS, courts have found themselves plagued with the problem of manufacturer liability, specifically the extent to which a manufacturer should be liable to a consumer who is injured by its product. To address this problem, various rules and legal theories for determining liability have been developed, and these make up the expanding area of law known as *products liability*. Since the 1960s, products liability has become one of the most rapidly changing areas in the history of common law, its bias having undergone a dramatic shift away from the seller to favor, instead, the consumer. The pendulum has taken such a sudden swing that sellers' liability has emerged as one of the most controversial subjects in the business world today.

Under products liability law and sales law, three legal theories may be available to an injured consumer seeking redress: (1) warranty, (2) negligence, and (3) strict liability. The first is a contract theory and is governed by the UCC; the other two are tort theories. The elements of negligence have been discussed in Chapter 8 and are applied here in the context of products liability. The principles of strict liability are taken from section 402A of the American Law Institute's *Restatement (Second) of Torts*. Unlike the UCC, the *Restatement* is not a statute, but a model code of law whose recommendations have been adopted by courts or legislatures in many states. Like the UCC, the strict liability theory applies primarily to transactions involving goods and not to those involving real estate or services.

WARRANTY

A **warranty** is an assurance or guarantee that goods will conform to certain standards. If the standards are not met, the buyer can recover damages from the seller, under a breach of warranty theory.

Such has not always been the case, for although suits involving warranties date as far back as fourteenth century England, a recovery theory was slow in developing. *Caveat emptor* ("let the buyer beware") governed the state of law until recent times—here in America, until the beginning of the twentieth century. The concept of *caveat emptor* allowed the seller to escape liability altogether, in the absence of fraud.

With the growth of business and industry came a clear need to move away from laissez-faire values and to place legal strictures on sales transactions. Chains of distribution were widening the distance between manufacturers and ultimate consumers, and an increasing sophistication in product design made inspection for defects more difficult. As a result, courts came to recognize the existence of three types of warranties, discussed in the following pages: express warranties, implied warranties, and warranties of title.

Express Warranties

Express warranties are those that originate from the words or actions of the seller. To create an express warranty, the seller does not have to use the word *warranty* or *guarantee*, and the buyer does not have to show that the seller intended to make a warranty. Under Sec. 2-313 of the UCC, a seller can create an express warranty in three different ways: (1) by an affirmation of fact or a promise relating to the goods, (2) by a description of the goods, or (3) by providing a sample or model of the goods. Such representations by the seller create contractual obligations to the extent that they become "part of the basis of the bargain."

Affirmation of Fact or Promise

By making an affirmation of fact or a promise relating to the goods, the seller tacitly guarantees that the goods will conform to the specifics he or she sets forth. For example, the seller might claim, "This boat is equipped with a two-year-old, 100-horsepower engine that was overhauled last month." The statement contains several affirmations of fact: (1) the boat is equipped with an engine, (2) the engine is two years old, (3) it generates 100 horsepower, and (4) it was overhauled last month. The seller might further state, "I assure you that this boat will not stall when run in choppy water." The affirmations concern past and present conditions; the promise, by contrast, relates to future events. Both affirmations and promises may create express warranties.

A seller's *commendation* or *expression of opinion* does not constitute an express warranty; neither does a statement that relates only to the *value* of the goods. Thus, the seller could claim that his boat was a "first-class vessel, worth $25,000 at retail" without creating a warranty. The law is not so rigid as to disallow "puffing" of products; it assumes that a consumer can distinguish between sales talk and fact.

But at times the distinction between fact and opinion is not easy to make. Consider, for example, the following statement: "The steering mechanism on this boat has been thoroughly engineered." The claim is rather vague, and as a descriptive phrase, "thoroughly engineered" may not be appreciably different from "first class." Yet the reference to engineering may create an impression of technologic excellence in the mind of an unsophisticated buyer and thus create a wrong impression.

In such cases, the courts tend to consider a number of factors, principally the buyer's frame of reference. If the buyer has limited knowledge of the goods involved, the statement from the seller is apt to be an affirmation of fact. If, however, the buyer is more knowledgeable than the seller, vague statements will be treated as mere expressions of opinion.

These additional generalizations can be made about the creation of express warranties: Statements that are specific and absolute are more readily construed as warranties than indefinite ones. Terms put in writing are more likely to create warranties than those given orally. A warranty is more likely to be found if the statement is objectively *verifiable* (for example, "This machine is one year old."). The nature and seriousness of the defect may also have a bearing on the determination.

Description of Goods

A descriptive word or phrase used in a sale of goods may create an express warranty that the goods will conform to the description. The word *pitted* or *seedless* on a box of prunes or raisins warrants that the fruit will have no seeds. Recognized trade terms may also constitute descriptions. For example, the term *Scotchguard*, used in connection with furniture upholstery, describes fabric that has been treated to make it water- and stain-resistant. Goods described by trade terms are warranted to possess those characteristics generally associated with the terms in the trade or business involved.

Sample or Model

If the seller provides to the buyer a sample or model of the goods to be sold, a warranty arises that the goods will conform to the sample or model. A *sample* is a single item taken from the mass to be sold, whereas a *model* is used to represent the goods. In a sale of wheat, a sample of one bushel might be drawn from the thousand bushels to be sold. But when the item being sold has not yet been manufactured or is too difficult to transport, a model might be used instead.

Although the UCC makes no distinction between express warranties arising out of sales by sample or by model, a sample is more likely to create such a warranty than a model. Because a sample is actually taken from the inventory to be sold, it is usually easier for the buyer to prove that a sample was intended to establish a standard of quality for the sale.

Basis of the Bargain

Under Sec. 2-313, an express warranty is created only if the affirmation or promise, description, model, or sample is "part of the basis of the bargain." Courts have applied this phrase to two types of circumstances. First is the case in which the seller makes a statement about the goods, and circumstances indicate that both parties intended the statement to be a part of the agreement. This would certainly be true if the statement appeared in the sales contract itself and would apply also when it is reasonably clear that the statement played a material part in the buyer's decision to purchase the goods. The second type of case involves statements of fact contained in a brochure, provided to the buyer by the seller. Under pre-Code law, the burden of proof was generally on the buyer to show that he or she had read the statement and relied on it. If reliance could not be shown, the buyer could not recover on the breach of warranty theory. By contrast, under the "basis of the bargain" language, courts *assume* that the statement became a part of the contract unless the seller can show "good reason" for the contrary (Sec. 2-313, comment 8).

A different question arises when, *after* the sale has been made, the buyer requests a promise from the seller that the goods meet certain standards. If given, does this promise become "part of the basis of the bargain"? Before the enactment of the UCC, the answer probably would have been *no;* today it is probably *yes.* Under Sec. 2-209(1), the seller's postsale promise is a modification of the contract and becomes an integral part of the agreement, even without additional consideration from the buyer.

A similar problem occurs sometimes in a sales negotiation, during which the seller makes statements that fail to appear in the written contract. Buyers who attempt to base a claim for breach of warranty on a recollection of oral statements are often thwarted by the *parol evidence rule* of UCC Sec. 2–202. Under this rule, if the court finds that the written form was intended as the final expression of the parties' agreement, any oral statement in contradiction of the written terms will not be admissible as evidence.

The following case illustrates how a company's advertising may expand the scope of an express warranty.

COMMUNITY TELEVISION SERVICES, INC. v. DRESSER INDUSTRIES, INC.

U.S. Court of Appeals, 8th Circuit, 586 F.2d 637 (1978)

In 1965, two television stations in South Dakota created a separate corporation, Community Television Services, Inc. (Community), for the purpose of constructing and operating a 2000-foot tower that would broadcast signals for both stations. Community contracted with Dresser Industries, Inc. (Dresser), who designed, manufactured, and erected the tower for a price of $385,000. The tower was completed in 1969, and Community used it until 1975. During this time, Community regularly inspected and properly maintained the tower. On January 10 and 11, 1975, a severe winter blizzard occurred in the area where the tower was located. During the early morning hours of January 11, as the storm reached its height with wind speeds of up to 80 miles per hour near the top of the tower, the structure collapsed.

Dresser denied responsibility, and Community sued in federal district court for breach of an express warranty. The verdict and judgment in the trial court were in favor of Community, the plaintiff, for damages of $1,274,631.60. Dresser, the defendant, appealed.

Lay, Circuit Judge:

. . . Expert witnesses called by both sides differed in their opinions as to the cause of the collapse. Community's experts testified that they had eliminated metallurgical or mechanical failure or abnormal wind loading as the cause of collapse. They theorized that the cause was high winds setting up a phenomenon known as mechanical resonance. They concluded that because of the resonance, the tower members "were inadequate to support the load that they sustained." On the other hand, Dresser's experts testified that a combination of ice, snow and wind subjected the tower to a total force greater than the ultimate capacity of its structural elements. They theorized that a substantial accumulation of ice on the upper fourth of the tower enlarged the tower members to a greater load than their designed wind loading capacity. Community attempted to refute Dresser's ice theory by calling several witnesses who testified that they did not see any such ice on or near the area where the tower collapsed. In turn, Dresser countered Community's theory through expert testimony that relatively constant winds were necessary for resonance to begin, and the winds were gusty and varied in speed and direction at the time of collapse. Furthermore, Dresser argued that the warranty did not guarantee against mechanical resonance and experts testified that its prevention was beyond the current state of the art.

The specifications incorporated in the sale contract included a specified "Design Wind Load," which set forth the tower's capacity to withstand wind velocity as measured in pounds of pressure per square foot against the flat surface of its members. The specification reads: "The tower shall be designed to resist a uniform wind load per drawing T-5172, sheet S-1, 60 psf on flats." The trial court instructed the jury that this specification constituted an express warranty that the structure would withstand wind exerting pressure of 60 pounds per square foot on the flat surfaces of the tower. Dresser's advertising materials and the testimony of experts at trial revealed that the wind velocity necessary to create 60 pounds of pressure on the flat surfaces of the tower would be approximately 120 miles per hour. The evidence showed that the wind loading specifications referred, at least in engineering parlance, to "a force caused by the wind that is introduced parallel to the ground . . . [which] would be tending to blow the structure over."

Dresser argues that the trial court erred in failing to direct a verdict on the express warranty claim or grant it judgment notwithstanding the verdict, because expert testimony that the tower met the design specification was uncontradicted. Community's own experts stated unequivocally that in their opinion the tower conformed in a mathematical or analytical sense to the 60 pounds per square foot wind loading specification. If the warranty may be restricted to the technical specification set forth in the written contract, we would find Dresser's argument convincing. However, we agree with Community that the warranty was amplified, in advertising materials Dresser gave to Community prior to purchase of the tower, to promise more than mere compliance with technical measurements. In an advertising catalog, Dresser made the following supplementary affirmation:

Wind force creates the most critical loads

(continues)

Community Television Services, Inc. v. Dresser Industries, Inc.

(*continued from previous page*)
to which a tower is normally subjected. When ice forms on tower members thereby increasing the surface area resisting the passage of wind, the load is increased.

Properly designed towers will safely withstand the maximum wind velocities and ice loads to which they are likely to be subjected. Dresser-Ideco can make wind and ice load recommendations to you for your area based on U.S. Weather Bureau data.

In the winter, loaded with ice and hammered repeatedly with gale force winds, these towers absorb some of the roughest punishment that towers take anywhere in the country . . . yet continue to give dependable, uninterrupted service.

Although we agree with Dresser that a seller cannot be held to be the insurer of its product, Dresser nevertheless provided the catalog to Community to induce purchase of its product, and in the absence of clear affirmative proof to the contrary, the above affirmation must be considered part of the "basis of the bargain." Standing alone, the statements provide a warranty that Dresser's tower would be properly designed so as to safely withstand the maximum wind velocities and ice loads to which it would likely be subjected. Dresser did not indicate that this broad affirmation was superseded or cancelled by the technical specification in the contract. When the affirmation is read in tandem with the contract, as part of the "fabric" of the agreement of the parties, it enlarges the warranty created by the technical wind loading specification, giving evidence of its full intent and scope.

We find that the statements in the advertising catalog, which supplement the wind loading specification, could reasonably have been found by the jury to be an affirmation of fact or a promise concerning the actual durability or performance of the tower during the wind and ice storms to which it was likely to be subjected.

Although Dresser's defense was that the tower collapsed by reason of excessive loading due to ice on the tower members, no disclaimer or limitation of the warranty that a properly designed tower would safely withstand the maximum wind and ice loads to which it was likely to be subjected appeared in the advertising materials or the contract. Under the *integrated* warranty given, a purchaser could reasonably assume that the tower, if properly designed for its location, would withstand maximum wind speeds to which it was likely to be subjected, even if ice accumulated on the tower members. While the blizzard was a severe one, the evidence does not support the conclusion that the wind alone, or the combination of wind and ice which Dresser claimed caused the collapse, was not within the range of storm conditions to be reasonably contemplated for the tower's location. Breach of a warranty created by standards describing the specific capacity of goods is proved when the product is shown by direct or circumstantial evidence to have failed to perform reasonably and safely the function for which it was intended by the manufacturer. In view of the affirmation made in the catalog, there was sufficient evidence for the jury to reasonably find that the tower was not as durable as it was warranted to be.

[Affirmed.] ◌

Implied Warranties

An implied warranty is created through the mere act of selling and is imposed on the seller by law. Its purpose is to protect buyers who suffer economic and commercial losses when products fail to serve their needs. Unlike with express warranties, specific representations about a product have not actually been made. The consumer has been guided, instead, by the belief that his or her purchase is suitable for its intended use. In Secs. 2-314 and 2-315, the UCC names two types of implied warranties: the implied warranty of merchantability and the implied warranty of fitness for a particular purpose.

Merchantability

The law injects into the sales contract a warranty that the goods are "merchantable," if the seller is a *merchant with respect to the type of goods being sold.* (When a student sells his or her 1980 VW to a neighbor, no implied warranty of merchantability exists because the student is not a merchant in automobiles.)

Merchantable means essentially that the goods are *fit for the ordinary purpose for which such goods are used.* The warranty of merchantability requires, for example, that shoes have their heels attached well enough that they will not break off under normal use. The warranty does not require, however, that ordinary walking shoes be suitable for mountain climbing. To be merchantable, goods must also serve their ordinary purpose *safely.* A refrigerator that keeps food cold but that gives an electric shock when the handle is touched is not merchantable. This is not to say that the seller becomes an insurer against accident or malfunction; the purchaser is expected to maintain his or her goods against the attrition of use.

The **implied warranty of merchantability** also does not guarantee that goods will be of the highest quality available. They are required to be only of *average or medium grade,* in addition to being adequately packaged and labelled. A growing minority of jurisdictions finds that the implied warranty of merchantability applies to sales of *used* goods; most limit the warranty to sale of new goods.

When applied to food, the implied warranty of merchantability can be related to *wholesomeness.* A tainted pork chop, for instance, is not merchantable. A number of cases decided before enactment of the UCC held that food purchased at a restaurant, hotel, or other such establishment carried no warranty because the sale involved a service rather than a product. The UCC, however, explicitly states that the implied warranty of merchantability extends to food sold at service establishments such as restaurants and hotels, whether the food is consumed on or off the premises.

Many cases alleging a breach of the implied warranty of merchantability have involved objects in food that caused harm to the consumer. Exceptional examples range from a mouse in a bottled soft drink to a screw in a slice of bread. In such cases the courts traditionally have distinguished between "foreign" and "natural" objects. They usually find that if the object is foreign to the mass (such as the mouse or screw mentioned above), the warranty of merchantability has been breached. If, however, the object is natural (such as a bone in a piece of fish), no breach of warranty has occurred.

A growing number of courts have rejected this approach and have based their decisions instead on the "reasonable expectation" of the consumer. The controlling factor in this approach is whether a consumer can reasonably expect the object in question to be in the food. A piece of chicken may be expected to contain a bone but not when in a chicken sandwich; an olive may be expected to contain a pit but not when a hole at the end indicates that it has been pitted. Bones and olive pits will not render food unmerchantable under the "foreign-natural object" test *but may do so under the "reasonable expectation" test.* Thus, the results of a legal suit may vary considerably, depending on which approach is used. A famous case in this area follows.

WEBSTER V. BLUE SHIP TEA ROOM, INC.

Supreme Judicial Court of Massachusetts, 198 N.E.2d 309 (1964)

Plaintiff, Webster, who was born and brought up in New England, ordered a cup of fish chowder while dining at the defendant's "quaint" Boston restaurant. She choked on a fish bone contained in the soup, necessitating two esophagoscopies at the Massachusetts General Hospital. The plaintiff sued for breach of the implied warranty of merchantability. A jury returned a verdict for the plaintiff. The defendant appealed the trial judge's refusal to direct a verdict for the defendant.

Reardon, Justice:

We must decide whether a fish bone lurking in a fish chowder, about the ingredients of which there is no other complaint, constitutes a breach of implied warranty under applicable provisions of the Uniform Commercial Code. As the [trial] judge put it, "Was the fish chowder fit to be eaten and wholesome? Nobody is claiming that the fish itself wasn't wholesome. But the bone of contention here—I don't mean that for a pun—but was this fish bone a foreign substance that made the fish chowder unwholesome or not fit to be eaten?"

The plaintiff has vigorously reminded us of the high standards imposed by this court where the sale of goods is involved.

The defendant asserts that here was a native New Englander eating fish chowder in a "quaint" Boston dining place where she had been before; that "[f]ish chowder, as it is served and enjoyed by New Englanders, is a hearty dish, originally designed to satisfy the appetites of our seamen and fishermen"; that "[t]his court knows well that we are not talking of some insipid broth as is customarily served to convalescents." We are asked to rule in such fashion that no chef is forced "to reduce the pieces of fish in the chowder to miniscule size in an effort to ascertain if they contained any pieces of bone." In so ruling, we are told (in the defendant's brief), "the court will not only uphold its reputation for legal knowledge and acumen, but will, as loyal sons of Massachusetts, save our world-reknowned fish chowder from degenerating into an insipid broth containing the mere essence of its former stature as a culinary masterpiece."

(continues)

WEBSTER V. BLUE SHIP TEA ROOM, INC.

(continued from previous page)

Chowder is an ancient fish dish preexisting even "the appetites of our seamen and fishermen." It was perhaps the common ancestor of the "more refined cream soups, purees, and bisques." Berolzheimer, The American Woman's Cook Book (Publisher's Guild Inc., New York, 1941) p. 176. The all embracing Fannie Farmer states in a portion of her recipe, fish chowder is made with a "fish skinned, but head and tail left on. Cut off head and tail and remove fish from backbone. Cut fish in 2-inches pieces and set aside. Put head, tail, and backbone broken in pieces, in stewpan; add 2 cups cold water and bring slowly to boiling point."

Thus, we consider a dish which for many years, if well made, has been made generally as outlined above. It is not too much to say that a person sitting down in New England to consume a good New England fish chowder embarks on a gustatory adventure which may entail the removal of some fish bones from his bowl as he proceeds. We are not inclined to tamper with age old recipes by any amendment reflecting the plaintiff's view of the effect of the Uniform Commercial Code on them. We are aware of the heavy body of case law involving foreign substances in food, but we sense a strong distinction between them and those relative to unwholesomeness of the food itself, e.g., tainted mackerel, and a fishbone in fish chowder. We consider that the joys of life in New England include the ready availability of fresh fish chowder. We should be prepared to cope with the hazards of fish bones, the occasional presence of which in chowders is, it seems to us, to be anticipated, and which, in the light of a hallowed tradition, do not impair their fitness or merchantability.

Judgment for the defendant. ⚖

Fitness for a Particular Purpose

In Sec. 2-315, the UCC provides: "Where the seller at the time of contracting has reason to know any particular purpose for which the goods are required and that the buyer is relying on the seller's skill or judgment to furnish suitable goods, there is . . . an implied warranty that the goods shall be fit for such purpose" (hence the name **implied warranty of fitness for a particular purpose,** sometimes referred to as *warranty of fitness*). Note that the seller is not required to be a merchant, although merchants are defendants in most cases.

Often the liability incurred by the seller under the implied warranty of fitness is greater than one incurred under the implied warranty of merchantability—a difference that can be best illustrated by a simple example: Suppose a buyer purchases an electric clock and discovers that its hands do not glow in the dark. The packaging carries no reference to visibility of the dial; neither does the instruction card. No breach of the implied warranty of merchantability exists here, for visibility of the dial under all conditions is not within the realm of a clock's "ordinary purpose." Yet, the seller *may* be liable to the buyer for breach of the implied warranty of fitness for a particular purpose if he or she knew that the buyer had a particular reason to need a clock with a lighted dial.[1]

A close examination of facts is required to ascertain whether a warranty of fitness exists, because such a warranty arises only if the following conditions exist:

1. The seller had "reason to know" of the particular purpose for which the goods were purchased. This requirement is obviously met if the seller was *actually informed* of the intended purpose, but such knowledge does not have to be proven. The requirement is also met if the circumstances dictate that the seller, as a reasonable person, *should have known* that the buyer was purchasing the goods for a particular purpose.

2. The seller also had reason to know that the buyer was relying on the seller's skill or judgment to furnish suitable goods. That is, the buyer must have relied on the seller's recommendation and the seller

---

[1]Some confusion exists because courts are split as to whether the "particular purpose" must be something other than the ordinary purpose for which the goods are used for the implied warranty of fitness to arise. Assume that Sally tells the salesman at the ABC Shoe Store that she wants some running shoes for jogging. He selects shoes clearly labelled as running shoes, which turn out to be unsuitable. Some courts would find that there was a breach of the implied warranty of fitness. Others would hold that because running was the ordinary purpose for which the shoes were intended, only an implied warranty of merchantability arose.

must have known or should have known of this dependence. If the buyer shows initiative by presenting brand names or introducing other specifications, recovery will be less likely.

3. Items 1 and 2 above must have existed at the time of contracting. If the seller learns the relevant facts only after the sale contract is made, a warranty does not exist.

These elements are applied in the following unique case.

DEMPSEY v. ROSENTHAL

Civil Court, City of New York, 448 N.Y.S.2d 441 (1983)

Plaintiff bought a poodle, Mr. Dunphy, from defendant for $541.25. Five days later, an inspection by a veterinarian disclosed that Mr. Dunphy had one undescended testicle. The plaintiff returned the dog and demanded a refund. The defendant refused. The plaintiff brought this suit in small claims court, claiming breach of the implied warranties of merchantability and fitness.

Saxe, Judge:

[The judge first found that Mr. Dunphy's condition breached the implied warranty of merchantability because a dog with an undescended testicle would not pass without complaint in the trade. Although fertile, the dog could pass the condition on to future generations. The judge then turned to the matter of implied warranty of fitness.]

The next issue to be resolved here is whether warranty of fitness for a particular purpose has been breached. [The UCC] makes it clear that the warranty of fitness for a particular purpose is narrow, more specific, and more precise

than the warranty of merchantability which involves fitness for the *ordinary* purposes for which such goods are used. The following are the conditions that are not required by the implied warranty of merchantability but that must be present if a plaintiff is to recover on the basis of the implied warranty of fitness for a particular purpose:

1. The seller must have reason to know the buyer's particular purpose.

2. The seller must have reason to know that the buyer is relying on the seller's skill or judgment to furnish appropriate goods.

3. The buyer must, in fact, rely upon the seller's skill or judgment.

Nevertheless, I find that the warranty of fitness for a particular purpose has also been breached. Ms. Dempsey testified that she specified to [defendant's] salesperson that she wanted a dog that was suitable for breeding purposes. Although this is disputed by the defendant, the credible testimony supports Ms. Dempsey's version of the event. Further, it is reasonable for a seller of a pedigree dog to assume that the buyer intends to breed it. But, it is undisputed by the experts here (for both sides) that Mr. Dunphy, with

only one descended testicle, was as capable of siring a litter as a male dog with two viable and descended testicles. This, the defendant contends, compels a finding in its favor. I disagree. While it is true that Mr. Dunphy's fertility level may be unaffected, his stud value, because of this hereditary condition (which is likely to be passed on to future generations) is severely diminished.

The fact that Mr. Dunphy's testicle later descended and assumed the proper position is not relevant. "The parties were entitled to get what they bargained for at the time that they bargained for it. The right of the buyer to rescind must be determined as of the time the election to rescind was exercised. The parties' rights are not to be determined by subsequent events." *White Devon Farm v. Stahl*, 389 N.Y.S.2d 724 (Sup.Ct.N.Y.Co. 1976). *White Devon Farm* involved the "tale of a stud who was a dud." The court there held that the warranty of fitness for a particular purpose was breached despite the fact that the horse's fertility later rose and the stallion sired 27 live foals.

A judgment for the claimant in the amount of $541.25 shall be entered by the clerk.

Warranties in Leases

Article 2A of the UCC contains warranty provisions for *leases* of goods. Except for "finance leases," Article 2A's rules regarding imposition and disclaimer of express and implied warranty liability are generally the same as those of Article 2 that we have just discussed.

Warranties of Title

In most sales of goods, a warranty as to the validity of the seller's title automatically exists. Sec. 2-312 of the UCC imposes two basic types of **warranty of title.** The first is a warranty that *the title conveyed shall be good and its transfer rightful.* This warranty is obviously breached if the seller has stolen the goods from some third party and therefore has no title at all. Other breaches, however, are not so obvious. Suppose that A buys goods from B and then is approached by C who claims to be the rightful owner. Inquiries reveal that there is some basis for C's claim and that the matter can be resolved only through a lawsuit. Will A have to become involved in a lawsuit initiated by C to determine if she bought a good title from B? Or has B breached his warranty of title by conveying a "questionable" title? The answer is that A has the option of returning the goods to B and getting her money back or defending against C's claim. If A takes the latter route and wins the lawsuit, she can recover her legal expenses from B. If A loses the lawsuit, she can recover from B not only her legal expenses, but also the value of the goods lost to C. A breach of the warranty of title exists if C's claim places a "substantial shadow" on the title, even if it ultimately might be proved invalid.

The second type of title warranty is that *the goods shall be delivered free from any security interest or other lien or encumbrance of which the buyer at the time of contracting has no knowledge.* This warranty will be breached, for instance, if B sells mortgaged goods to A without telling A of the mortgage.

Warranties of title accompany a sale of goods unless the seller indicates by specific language that no such assurances are being made or unless the circumstances indicate as much (for example, in a public sale of goods seized by the sheriff to satisfy a debt, rightful transfers of title are generally not guaranteed).

An additional obligation—not, strictly speaking, a warranty of title—is imposed on some sellers by

Sec. 2-312: Unless otherwise agreed, a seller who is a merchant in the type of goods involved is deemed to warrant *that the goods sold do not infringe on the patents, copyrights, or trademarks of a third party.* If a claim of infringement is made by a third party against the buyer, the seller is responsible—unless, of course, the goods were manufactured according to the *buyer's specifications.*

Conflicting and Overlapping Warranties

Two or more warranties sometimes exist in a single sales transaction. For example, a machine might be warranted to perform certain functions and to last for a specified time. In addition to these express warranties, an implied warranty of merchantability or of fitness for a particular purpose, or both, might exist.

When more than one warranty is created in a given transaction, the buyer does not have to choose among them. The warranties are *cumulative,* such that the buyer can take advantage of any or all of them. According to Sec. 2-317, courts should interpret the warranties as being "consistent" whenever such an interpretation is reasonable. In the unusual event that two warranties are in conflict and cannot both be given effect, the court must attempt to determine the intent of the parties as to which warranty should prevail. Several rules offer guidance in determining intention:

1. Exact or technical specifications take precedence over inconsistent samples or models or general language of description.

2. A sample drawn from the goods to be sold takes precedence over inconsistent general language or description.

3. An express warranty, regardless of how it was created, takes precedence over the implied warranty of merchantability if the two are inconsistent. (An express warranty does not take precedence over the implied warranty of fitness for a particular purpose, although it is difficult to imagine a situation in which the two would be inconsistent.)

These rules are not absolute and can be disregarded by the court if they produce an unreasonable result. The following case illustrates a situation in which a seller's express promise conflicted with a claimed implied warranty.

Supreme Court of Nevada, 520 P.2d 234 (1974)

Anderson Halverson Corp., owner of the Stardust Hotel in Las Vegas, Nevada, ordered carpeting to be manufactured by Mohasco and installed in the hotel lobby and casino showroom of the Stardust. After installation the buyer refused to pay, claiming that the carpet "shaded" excessively, giving it a mottled effect and the appearance of being water stained. Mohasco, the plaintiff, sued Anderson Halverson, the defendant, to recover the price of $18,242.50. The trial court held in favor of the defendant, and the plaintiff appealed.

Thompson, Justice:

. . . One Fritz Eden, an interior decorator selected and hired by Stardust, designed a pattern for the carpet to be used in the hotel lobby and casino showroom. A sample run of the chosen pattern was taken to the hotel by Eden, and was approved. Eden then specified the material and grade of carpet which the Stardust also approved. The Stardust then issued a detailed purchase order designating the type and length of yarn, weight per square yard, type of weave, color and pattern. No affirmation of fact or promise was made by any representative of . . . the seller to . . . the buyer. The carpet which was manufactured, delivered and installed was consistent with the sample and precisely conformed to the detailed purchase order. There were no manufacturing defects in the carpet.

Upon installation, however, the carpet did shade and, apparently, to a much greater extent than the Stardust or its representative had anticipated. It is clear from the testimony that "shading" is an inherent characteristic of all pile carpeting. When the tufts of the carpet are bent in different angles, the light reflection causes portions of the carpet to appear in different shades of the same color. The only explanation in the record for the "excessive shading" was that Fritz Eden, the decorator for Stardust, decided not to specify the more expensive "twist yarn." That type yarn causes the tufts to stick straight up (or at least tends to do so) thus aiding in the elimination of excessive shading.

The trial court found that the sale of the carpet was a sale by sample which was made a part of the basis of the bargain and created an express warranty that the carpet delivered for installation would conform to the sample. Moreover, [the trial court found] that the *express* warranty was breached by the seller, thus precluding its claim for relief. [Emphasis added.] . . .

That finding is clearly erroneous. The installed carpet conformed precisely to the description of the goods contained in the purchase order. Moreover, it conformed precisely to the sample which the buyer approved. Whether the sale be deemed a sale by description or by sample, in either event the express warranty of conformity was met. The seller delivered the very carpet which the buyer selected and ordered.

Although there is substantial evidence to support the trial court's finding that the installed carpet shaded excessively, that consequence may not be equated with a breach of an express warranty since the seller delivered and installed the very item which the buyer selected and ordered. Had the buyer, through its interior decorator, selected the more expensive carpet with "twist yarn," perhaps this controversy would not have arisen. The buyer, not the seller, must bear the consequence of that mistake.

[The court then turned to the implied warranty of merchantability question, as follows:] As already noted, the judgment below rests upon an erroneous finding that the seller breached an express warranty that the whole of the carpet would conform to the sample which the buyer had approved. The buyer suggests, however, that the judgment should be sustained in any event since it is otherwise clear that the seller breached the implied warrant[y] of merchantability. . . . We turn to consider this contention.

Unless excluded, or modified, a warranty of merchantability is implied in a contract if the seller is a merchant with respect to the goods in question. We have not, heretofore, had occasion to consider the impact, if any, of the implied warranty of merchantability upon a case where the goods are sold by sample or description and the buyer's specifications are so complete that it is reasonable to conclude that he had relied upon himself and not the seller with regard to the merchantability of the goods. . . .

It is apparent that in a case where the sample or description of the goods may, for some reason, result in an undesirable product, the seller is placed in a dilemma. In Hawkland, A Transactional Guide to the Uniform Commercial Code, Sec. 1.190206, at 65, the following example is given. Suppose a buyer provides his seller with minute specifications of the material, design and method of construction to be utilized in preparation of an order of shoes, and the seller delivers to the buyer shoes which exactly conform to the specifications. If the blueprints are in fact designs of defective shoes, the buyer should not be able to complain that the shoes are defective. For such an order might put the seller in the dilemma of being forced to breach either the express warranty of description or the implied warranty of merchantability.

The matter at hand is similar to the example just given. Although the carpet was not defective, it did shade excessively and was, in the view of the buyer, an undesirable product. Yet, it was the product which the buyer specified and ordered. The manufacturer-

(continues)

MOHASCO INDUSTRIES, INC. v. ANDERSON HALVERSON CORP.

(continued from previous page)
seller was not at liberty to add "twist yarn" and charge a higher price. The buyer relied upon its decorator, Fritz Eden, and the seller performed as directed. . . . [W]e hold that the implied warranty of merchantability is limited

by an express warranty of conformity to a precise description supplied by the buyer, and if the latter warranty is not breached, neither is the former. [Emphasis added.] . . .

The judgment for [the buyer] is reversed, and since there is no dispute

concerning the amount of the plaintiff's claim, the cause is remanded to the district court to enter judgment for the plaintiff against the said defendant for $18,242.50, together with appropriate interest and costs. ◁◁

Disclaimers Excluding and Limiting Warranties

As we have seen, a sales transaction can give rise to three types of warranties: express warranties, implied warranties, and warranties of title. But the creation of these warranties is by no means automatic. The UCC allows a seller to disavow the existence of warranties or to limit the circumstances in which liability will apply by including a **disclaimer** in the sales contract. Theoretically, disclaimers can be justified on the grounds that their use advances freedom of contract, permitting parties to bargain over contract terms and to allocate the risk of loss. Yet in reality, the arrangement tends to be one-sided: consumers usually are in no bargaining position and often do not read disclaimers when making a purchase. For this reason, courts may find a particular disclaimer *unconscionable* under UCC Sec. 2-302.

Disclaimers of Express Warranties

A seller who wishes to avoid liability on an express warranty obviously should not do anything to create a warranty in the first place (a highly impractical measure to take in making sales!). An alternative would be to include a disclaimer in the contract. However, if a warranty has actually become part of the contract, an attempt to disclaim liability will usually not be effective. Sec. 2-316(1) states that a disclaimer will be disregarded if it is inconsistent with the words or conduct that created the express warranty. Suppose that an express warranty has been created by a statement of the seller, by the use of a sample, or by a written description of the goods. Liability could not then be disclaimed by specifying: "These goods are sold without warranties." Such a statement would almost always be inconsistent with the words or conduct that

created the warranty. In short, *it is extremely difficult for a seller to disclaim an express warranty which has become part of the contract.*

Disclaimers of Implied Warranties

Because the existence of an implied warranty depends on circumstances rather than on the precise words used by the seller, such a warranty is relatively easy to disclaim. The UCC permits disclaimers of implied warranties through (1) the use of language specified in Sec. 2-316 of the Code, (2) the buyer's examination of the goods, or (3) custom and usage.

Disclaimer by Language. In the case of the *warranty of merchantability*, the language used by the seller to disclaim liability does not have to be in writing. If written, however, the disclaimer must be "conspicuous" enough to be noticed by any reasonable person involved in the purchase. (A disclaimer printed in larger type or in a different color than the remainder of the document will probably be considered conspicuous.) In addition, the word *merchantability* must be used—unless the seller uses a phrase such as a "with all faults" or "as is," language that serves to disclaim *both* or *either* of the implied warranties.

In the case of the *warranty of fitness for a particular purpose*, the disclaimer must be in writing and must be conspicuous. Yet the statement itself can be a general one, such as, "There are no warranties extending beyond the description on the face hereof."

Disclaimer by Examination. If before making a contract, the buyer fully examines the goods (or a sample or model of them) or deliberately refuses to examine them at all, no implied warranty exists for *reasonably apparent* defects. Yet if the buyer has no opportunity to examine the goods before contracting, the seller becomes liable for such defects.

When defects are hidden, the seller is always liable, unless it can be proved that the buyer had knowledge of the defects before contracting. When deciding whether a defect is "reasonably apparent" or "hidden," a court will take into account the buyer's knowledge or skill. Such a factor obviously has a bearing on what an examination should have revealed to the buyer.

For example, in *Dempsey v. Rosenthal,* Mr. Dunphy's defective condition—the undescended testicle—was not readily observable. A manual manipulation of the scrotal area would have been the only means to verify the condition. The court found that Ms. Dempsey, the buyer, did not know this and should not be charged with knowledge of the fact. The type of examination that would be undertaken by the average buyer of a male puppy would not disclose the defective condition, so recovery was not barred by the inspection provisions of UCC Sec. 2-316.

Disclaimer by Custom or Usage. Implied warranties are sometimes excluded or modified by *trade usage* (industry-wide custom) or by a custom that has been established between the contracting parties. An industry-wide custom will have no effect, however, on a buyer who is not a member of the particular industry and is unaware of the custom.

Limitation on Damages. In contract cases, punitive damages traditionally have not been available to plaintiffs. For this reason, express and implied warranty suits usually involve two types of damages: basis-of-the-bargain damages (the value of the goods warranted less the value received) and consequential damages (personal and property damages proximately caused by the warranty breach, along with any indirect economic loss foreseeable by the defendant).[2] The buyer injured by a breached warranty also has the option to rescind the contract.

The Code allows limitations to be placed by the seller on damages that may be recovered by a breach of warranty. For example, recovery may be limited to *liquidated damages*—that is, a specified amount to be paid in the event of a breach. A limitation may also be placed on the type of remedy available, guaranteeing, for example, only the replacement of the product without charge.

However, such limitations will not be given effect if they are *unconscionable.* For example, UCC Sec. 2-719(3) provides that "[l]imitation of consequential damages for injury to the person in the case of consumer goods is prima facie unconscionable. . . ." Furthermore, comment 1 to Sec. 2-719 provides that "it is of the very essence of a sales contract that at least minimum adequate remedies be available. . . ." Even a clause that appears not to be unconscionable may be ignored if "because of circumstances [it] fails in its purpose or operates to deprive either party of the substantial value of the bargain."

---

[2]In addition to damages, the buyer has an option to rescind the contract when a warranty has been breached.

GREAT DANE TRAILER V. MALVERN PULPWOOD

Supreme Court of Arkansas, 785 S.W.2d 13 (1990)

The plaintiff, Malvern Pulpwood, Inc., bought two drop-deck, 65,000-pound weight-rated pulpwood trailers from the defendant, Great Dane Trailer Sales, Inc. Great Dane issued warranties on the trailers that were limited to the repair or replacement of defective parts, and remedies were limited by the exclusion of consequential and incidental damages. The drop-deck trailers exhibited serious defects, as did their replacements, two straight-decked trailers. Malvern Pulpwood sued for breach of the implied warranties of merchantability and fitness. Great Dane defended on the basis of the "repair or replacement" warranty and disclaimer. Great Dane appealed after a jury verdict in Malvern's favor for $40,000.

Glaze, Justice

Under [UCC] 2-719, parties to an agreement may limit the buyer's remedies to the repair and replacement of nonconforming goods or parts and to make the remedy agreed upon the sole remedy, unless circumstances cause the exclusive or limited remedy to fail of its essential purpose. When there is substantial evidence tending to show that a particular piece of machinery obviously *(continues)*

GREAT DANE TRAILER V. MALVERN PULPWOOD

(continued from previous page)
cannot be repaired or its parts replaced so that it is made free of defects, a jury verdict, which implicitly concludes that a limitation of the remedy to the repair and replacement of nonconforming parts deprived the purchaser of the substantial value of the bargain, should be sustained. Such a limited remedy fails whenever the warrantor, given the opportunity to do so, fails to correct the defect within a reasonable period.

In connection with the sale of two drop-deck trailers sold to Malvern Pulpwood, Great Dane offered the following warranty:

Great Dane Trailers, Inc.'s sole obligation under this warranty shall be limited to the repair or replacement, at its option, of any defective part of said trailer which is the result of defective materials and/or defective workmanship of parts furnished and installed by Great Dane Trailers, Inc. This warranty will expire sixty (60) months from date of delivery to the purchaser, and repairs under this warranty shall be at repair facilities designated by Great Dane Trailers, Inc. Transportation expenses to the repair facility are to be borne by the purchasers. THE EXPRESS WARRANTY HEREIN IS IN LIEU OF ANY AND ALL OTHER WARRANTIES, EXPRESSED OR IMPLIED. NO IMPLIED WARRANTY OF MERCHANTABILITY IS MADE AND THERE ARE NO WARRANTIES WHICH EXTEND BEYOND THE DESCRIPTION ON THE FACE HEREOF.

Although the foregoing five-year warranty was given to repair or replace the 65,000 pound GVWC rated drop-deck trailers, we believe the evidence sufficiently shows the limitation failed of its essential purpose. The drop-deck trailers were described as ten-year trailers with a five-year warranty. Both drop-deck trailers were described as ten-year trailers with a five-year warranty. Both drop-deck trailers "broke" in the same spot within one year from the time Malvern Pulpwood acquired them. Malvern Pulpwood offered testimony that Great Dane's repair job was sloppy and rendered the trailers unsafe. One witness, a welder, stated he did not believe the repairs would fix the trailers; he said that any time steel is welded, the steel would not be as strong as it was before. Great Dane finally replaced the drop-deck trailers with straight-deck trailers. Nevertheless, the replacements, too, broke in the same spot as the drop-deck trailers. [W]e have no doubts that substantial evidence existed to support Malvern Pulpwood's claims that Great Dane failed to correct the trailers' defect within a reasonable period and that the limitation failed of its essential purpose.

[Affirmed.] ᗏ

DEFENSES
Privity Defense
Privity is a legal term for the direct relationship between buyer and seller. **Privity of contract** means relationship of contract: If Manufacturer A sells a yacht to Retailer B who in turn sells it to Consumer C, there is privity of contract between A and B and between B and C, but *not* between A and C. Because a warranty arises from the formation of a contract, privity of contract between the plaintiff and the defendant used to be required for the plaintiff suing for breach of warranty. Warranties did not "run with the goods" to subsequent purchasers and users. Thus, C could sue B but not A.

The privity requirement was not a major hindrance in the early days of our country, when consumers bought most of their goods directly from artisans or local manufacturers. Today, however, when goods travel through chains of distribution, a privity requirement imposes an intolerable burden on consumers. Therefore, it has been greatly relaxed today *and is in the process of being eliminated.* All parties in the chain of distribution (manufacturers, wholesalers, and retailers) are now usually responsible to the last buyer for failure of the goods to live up to the standards of any warranties, especially for personal injuries.

Innocent Bystanders. A final problem with the privity requirement is that defects in goods often injure persons other than the purchaser; yet the privity requirement prevented nonpurchasers (for example, innocent bystanders or persons who borrowed the product from the buyer) from suing anyone in the chain of distribution for breached warranties.

Sec. 2-318 of the UCC has somewhat alleviated this problem by extending warranty protection to (1) members of the buyer's family, (2) members of the buyer's household, and (3) guests in the buyer's home, "if it is reasonable to expect that such person may use, consume or be affected by the goods, and [such person] is injured [physically] by the breach of the warranty." As the language indicates, the extended protection applies only when defective goods have caused a *physical injury to the individual.*

In recent years the drafters of the UCC have proposed alternative versions of Sec. 2-318 to relax the privity requirement further—primarily by granting protection to *any* injured person who could reasonably have been expected to use, consume, or be affected by the goods. Although only 15 or so states have enacted these versions of Sec. 2-318 to date, the trend in most jurisdictions is toward a loosening of the privity requirement in breach of warranty actions.

Plaintiff Misconduct Defenses

When a plaintiff's carelessness contributes to a products-related accident, the defendant can use that carelessness as a defense to warranty claims in most jurisdictions. Because the plaintiff's carelessness defenses to warranty claims are generally the same as such defenses to a strict liability claim, which we are about to discuss, we defer discussion of the matter to the strict liability section.

Statute of Limitations and Notice Requirements

Under UCC Sec. 2-725, an action for breach of contract for sale of goods must be commenced within four years after the cause of action accrues. A traditional tort statute of limitations begins to run only when the right to sue is or should be discovered (and typically lasts two years). The UCC has a similar rule where a warranty *explicitly* extends to future performance of the goods and discovery of the breach must await the time of such performance. In such cases, the statute of limitations does not begin to run until the breach is or should be discovered. However, for all other suits under Article 2, the UCC statute of limitations begins to run when the goods are tendered for delivery. Thus, if the defect is not discovered for four years, the suit may well be time-barred before the defect is discovered. Many potential plaintiffs lose the right to sue by allowing the seller to attempt to effect repairs until after the four-year limit has expired. Furthermore, the Code provides that by agreement the parties may reduce the period of limitation to not less than one year but may not extend it. Thus, the statute of limitations often bars warranty suits.

Some warranty actions are barred by a plaintiff's failure to comply with UCC Sec. 2-607(3), which imposes on the buyer a duty to notify the seller of a breach within a reasonable time after he or she discovers or should discover any breach, or be barred from remedy. The purpose of such a requirement is to minimize litigation by giving the seller a chance to effect repairs or otherwise satisfy the buyer. Courts have generally been reluctant to allow this provision to bar recovery by consumers who suffered personal injuries caused by a breach of warranty. Courts are inclined to construe a "reasonable time" as being a longer period in a personal injury case than in a suit brought for economic loss by a commercial purchaser. The courts are split as to whether a person who bought an item from a retailer must give notice not only to that retailer but also to the manufacturer to be allowed to sue the manufacturer.

NEGLIGENCE

Because the elements of negligence have been discussed at length in Chapter 8, our purpose here is simply to apply them to the area of products liability. Remember that in an action based on negligence, the defendant must have owed a duty to the plaintiff, and this duty must have been breached. Where a sales transaction is involved, the seller's duty to use reasonable care arises from the mere act of placing goods on the market. The economic benefit derived from a sale generates a responsibility to consumers, for the act of selling directly affects the interests of those who have no choice but to rely on the integrity of sellers. Privity of contract is no longer required in the usual negligence suit.

The manufacturer's liability for negligence is often predicated on negligent design or manufacture; in addition, *both* manufacturer and seller may be liable for failure to inspect or failure to adequately warn.

If the seller is a retailer, distributor, or wholesaler, he or she usually has no duty to inspect new goods, barring knowledge of defects. A duty to inspect does exist, however, when the seller is involved in the installation of goods (new or used) or in their preparation for eventual sale. Liability is imposed to the extent that defects are *reasonably apparent*. By the same token, a manufacturer is charged with taking reasonable measures to discover flaws created during the production process.

A *duty to warn* arises when a product's design (or its intended use) subjects the user to hazard or risk of injury. The danger in question need only be reasonably foreseeable—discoverable only within the limits of existing technology. Warnings given must be adequate in their specifics and must extend to all individuals whose harm is reasonably foreseeable. There is no duty to warn of obvious dangers—no duty, for example, to warn about fire on a box of matches.

Negligent manufacture is often cited in cases in which defects are the result of oversight, human or mechanical error, or lack of judgment. For example, production line employees might not be properly trained, or materials selected for construction might not have sufficient strength to resist the stresses of normal use.

In contrast, actions based on charges of *negligent design* hold the manufacturer responsible for more than the exercise of care in production. In addition to warning about risks and hazards inherent in a design, the manufacturer is expected to design a product with optimal safety as the ideal, compromised only when the costs of improving the design exceed the benefits derived therefrom. Under the rule adopted by most states, there is a duty to design products so that accidents are unlikely to occur and so that injuries suffered will be minimal if an accident does occur. To illustrate, say X is driving a car that explodes when struck in the rear by Y, who has negligently maneuvered his truck. X may recover from Y for initial injuries and may possibly recover from the car's manufacturer for additional injuries resulting from the impact if, for example, the gas tank was located vulnerably close to the rear bumper.

Of course, it would be unreasonable to expect cars to be accident-proof in all situations. (If this were the law, some courts have observed, manufacturers would produce nothing but tanks.) In evaluating the adequacy of design standards, courts have considered such factors as the state of existing technology, the expectation of the ordinary consumer, the danger of a product in relation to its social use, and compliance with government safety standards.

To conclude, the negligence theory became viable as an avenue of recovery to injured plaintiffs when the privity requirement was finally abandoned. This theory offers some advantages over the warranty theory; for example, the buyer does not have to prove that a warranty existed, the buyer does not have to notify the seller within a reasonable time after discovering the defect, and disclaimers in the sales contract usually do not allow the seller to escape liability resulting from his or her negligence.

Yet certain disadvantages exist as well. A plaintiff must prove negligent conduct on the part of the manufacturer or seller, and proof of negligence is at times almost impossible to establish. Only in rela-

tively rare cases have courts inferred negligence pursuant to the doctrine of *res ipsa loquitur* ("the thing speaks for itself").[3]

Another impediment to recovery under the negligence theory is that any type of plaintiff misconduct, even simple plaintiff carelessness, will reduce or bar recovery.

In addition, most jurisdictions hold that the UCC provides the only avenue for product liability recovery for mere *economic* loss (generally defined as all losses other than personal injury and tangible damage to property other than the product itself). For example, the majority rule is that if a piece of equipment contains an electrical defect that causes it to be destroyed in a fire resulting in no other loss, warranty provides the buyer's only avenue for recovery. Suit on a negligence theory (and, as we are about to see, a strict liability theory) is precluded in most states.

STRICT LIABILITY

Most courts and legislatures have concluded in recent years that the warranty and negligence theories do not afford consumers as much protection as they ought, in fairness, to have. Many warranty claims are barred, for example, by disclaimers or because of the statute of limitations or failure to give notice of breach within a reasonable time. Many negligence suits fail because the plaintiff is not able to prove specific acts of negligence on the part of the manufacturer.

Recognizing these deficiencies, most jurisdictions have adopted the theory of **strict liability** by which manufacturers and sellers are held liable irrespective of fault. (See Figure 22.1 for a comparison of strict liability with negligence.) Today, strict liability is the most common basis for imposition of product liability for personal injuries.

Justification for the strict liability theory lies in the notion that merchants and manufacturers are better able to bear losses than injured consumers and that, in many cases, losses will be transferred to the buying public in the form of higher prices on products. Thus, society at large assumes the cost of damages suffered by a few—an arrangement that is perhaps more equi-

[3]The doctrine of *res ipsa loquitur* may presume negligence from the fact that the accident did indeed occur. A plaintiff who can show that (1) the defendant controlled the product and (2) the defect would not normally occur absent negligence can benefit from *res ipsa loquitur*'s presumption of negligence. The presumption would be applicable, for example, if a product exploded immediately on being removed from a container that was sealed at the defendant's factory.

FIGURE 22.1

**Differences
between
Negligence
and Strict
Liability**

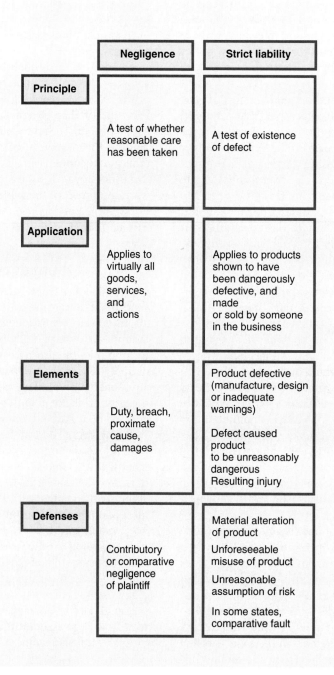

	Negligence	Strict liability
Principle	A test of whether reasonable care has been taken	A test of existence of defect
Application	Applies to virtually all goods, services, and actions	Applies to products shown to have been dangerously defective, and made or sold by someone in the business
Elements	Duty, breach, proximate cause, damages	Product defective (manufacture, design or inadequate warnings) / Defect caused product to be unreasonably dangerous / Resulting injury
Defenses	Contributory or comparative negligence of plaintiff	Material alteration of product / Unforeseeable misuse of product / Unreasonable assumption of risk / In some states, comparative fault

table in that it offers relief for those injured by defective products.

Proponents of strict liability argue, in addition, that eliminating the need to prove negligence in a tort action will make manufacturers and sellers more mindful of accident prevention.

Finally, there is an economic basis for adopting this liability theory: Because negligence is often difficult to prove, litigation becomes excessively costly. From an overall economic standpoint, then, it can make sense to abandon proof of negligence in a products liability action.

Elements of Strict Liability

The elements of strict liability are recorded in section 402 of the American Law Institute's *Restatement (Second) of Torts,* a summary and clarification of American common-law principles. Section 402A reads:

1. One who sells any product in a defective condition unreasonably dangerous to the user or consumer or to his property is subject to liability for physical harm thereby caused to the ultimate user or consumer, or to his property, if

   a. the seller is engaged in the business of selling such a product, and

   b. it is expected to and does reach the user or consumer without substantial change in the condition in which it is sold.

2. The rule stated in Subsection (1) applies although

   a. the seller has exercised all possible care in the preparation and sale of his product, and

   b. the user or consumer has not bought the product from or entered into any contractual relation with the seller.

Two points regarding section 402A merit special emphasis. First, subsection (1)(a) limits application of the strict liability theory to those engaged in the business of selling the products in question. Second, subsection (2) makes it clear that negligence and privity are not issues under the strict liability theory.

Thus in certain respects, strict liability may be viewed as an extension of the implied warranty of merchantability, where the warranty theory was applied to foreign objects in food and drink. (Recall our discussion of the "reasonable expectation" and "foreign-natural object" tests.) Taken further, strict liability is applied in cases involving virtually all kinds of goods. Although there is, in fact, some overlapping here with the warranty theory, actions based on strict liability are nevertheless considered to be actions in tort rather than under warranty.

The crux of a section 402A action is the sale of a *defective product* that is *unreasonably dangerous* to the *user* or *consumer* or to his or her property. Sec-

tion 402A covers only sales of products, not services. A product is defective if it is unreasonably dangerous because of a flaw in the product or a weakness in its design or because adequate warning of risks and hazards related to the design has not been given.

A strict liability action differs from a negligence action in that the plaintiff need not prove the defect resulted from the defendant's failure to use reasonable care. Although in failure-to-warn cases the manufacturer will almost always be found negligent, the same cannot be said of resellers. New products packaged with inadequate warnings may be resold without subjecting intermediaries and retailers to liability under the negligence theory; yet these very resellers could be held liable under section 402A because no fault is required under the strict liability theory.

Defective conditions may result not only from flaws or harmful ingredients within the product but also from foreign objects in its composition and defects in its container. In this regard, a product is not defective "when it is safe for normal handling or consumption." For example, beer consumed only occasionally and in moderate amounts is probably not harmful. If an adult drinks too much beer at a party and then becomes ill, the seller is not liable.

To be safe, a product should be properly packaged and otherwise treated so that it will not deteriorate or be rendered dangerous within a reasonable period of time under normal conditions.

The question of what constitutes an "unreasonably" dangerous product is taken up in section 402A, comments i and k. Presumably, certain products are reasonably dangerous or "unavoidably unsafe"—that is to say, existing technology and scientific knowledge are insufficient to produce a completely safe result. An example often cited is that of the rabies vaccine, which has dangerous side effects but which is the only existing treatment against a deadly disease. Drugs sold under prescription and experimental treatments also fall within this category. Unavoidably unsafe products must be accompanied by instructions and warnings, so that the user can decide whether to undergo the risks involved. If the harmful consequences of using a product generally exceed the benefits and if safer alternatives are available, a product will be considered unreasonably unsafe. In defining what is meant by "unreasonably unsafe," section 402A also considers the expectations of the ordinary consumer, stating: "The articles sold must be dangerous to an extent beyond that which would be contemplated by the ordinary consumer who purchases it, with the ordinary knowledge common to the community as to its characteristics. . . . Good butter is not unreasonably dangerous merely because, if such be the case, it deposits cholesterol in the arteries and leads to heart attacks; but bad butter, contaminated with poisonous fish oil, is unreasonably dangerous."

Another stipulation in section 402A is that products must be in a defective condition when they leave the seller. The burden of proof lies with the plaintiff to show that the product was defective at the time of sale. Subsequent alteration or further processing may operate to relieve the seller of liability.

In addition, the plaintiff's injury must occur as a result of a defect in the product itself, rather than from conditions surrounding its use or consumption. For example, if an Africanized "killer" bee stings a longshoreman unloading crates of tropical fruit, the fruit company is not liable under section 402A because even if there is proof that the bee was a stowaway in the fruit, there is no defect inherent in the fruit itself.

Among the most problematic strict liability cases are those based on a product's allegedly defective warning. The following case is illustrative.

Brune v. Brown Forman Corporation

Texas Court of Appeals, 758 S.W.2d 827 (1988)

 Marie Brinkmeyer, an 18-year-old college freshman, bought a bottle of tequila manufactured by the defendant/appellee, Brown Forman. She drank straight shots of it with some friends until she was escorted to her room. She died that night, allegedly as a direct result of acute alcohol poisoning. Her mother, the plaintiff/appellant Brune, brought this strict liability action on behalf of Brinkmeyer's estate. She alleged that the tequila was an unreasonably dangerous product in that it lacked a warning and/or instructions for its safe use because many teenagers are unaware that the mere ingestion of the drug in excess quantity can cause an overdose resulting in death. The trial court granted summary judgment to Brown Forman. Brune appealed.

Utter, Justice:

The question raised on appeal is: whether the risk of death from acute alcohol poisoning is a matter of common knowledge to the community such that there was no duty on the

manufacturer to warn of the danger as a matter of law.

If a manufacturer knows or should know of potential harm to a user because of the nature of its product, the manufacturer is required to give an adequate warning of such dangers and provide instructions for the safe use of the product. Therefore, in order to prevent the product from being unreasonably dangerous, the seller may be required to give directions or warnings on the container as to its use. This includes the duty to warn against foreseeable misuse.

Appellee submitted no summary judgment proof and argues that there was no duty to warn as a matter of law, because the dangers inherent in its product were within the ordinary knowledge common to the community.

Comment h [to the Restatement (Second) of Torts section 402A] states that:

A product is not in a defective condition when it is safe for normal handling and consumption. If the injury results from . . . abnormal consumption, as where a child eats too much candy and is made ill, the seller is not liable. *Where, however, he has reason to anticipate that danger may result from a particular use, as where a drug is sold which is safe only*

in limited doses, he may be required to give adequate warning of the danger, and a product sold without such warning is in a defective condition.

A close look at comment h, reveals that in a situation where the manufacturer can anticipate a danger from a particular use, such as death resulting from acute alcohol poisoning, he may be required to give adequate warning of that danger. Nowhere does comment h state that there is no duty to warn under any circumstances involved. In fact, appellee may have had reason to anticipate that danger may result from this particular use.

Likewise, comments i and j do not preclude a cause of action based on a duty to warn. In pertinent part, comment i states:

Many products cannot possibly be made entirely safe for all consumption, and any food or drug necessarily involves some risk of harm, if only from overconsumption. *The article sold must be dangerous to an extent beyond that which would be contemplated by the ordinary consumer who purchases it, with the ordinary knowledge common to the community as to its characteristics.* Good whiskey is not unreasonably dangerous merely because it will make some people drunk and is especially dangerous to alcoholics.

(continues)

Rationale

BRUNE V. BROWN FORMAN CORPORATION

(continued from previous page)

Lastly, comment j states in relevant part: Directions or warnings. In order to prevent the product from being [in a defective condition] unreasonably dangerous [to the user or consumer], the seller may be required to give directions or warning, on the container, as to its use. . . . *In the case of poisonous drugs, or those unduly dangerous for other reasons, warnings as to use may be required.*

But a seller is not required to warn with respect to products, or ingredients in them, which are only dangerous, or potentially so, when consumed in excessive quantity, or over a long period of time, *when the danger, or potentiality of danger, is generally known and recognized.* Again the dangers of alcoholic beverages are an example, as are those of foods containing such substances as saturated fats, which may over a period of time have a deleterious effect upon the human heart.

Appellee interprets comment j to mean that the dangers of excessive alcohol consumption are well known to the public. Comment j, however, does not say that the dangers of acute ethyl ingestion resulting in death are necessarily generally known. Rather, it says that when the danger is generally known, no warning is required.

Although there is no question that drinking alcoholic beverages will cause intoxication and possibly even cause illness is a matter of common knowledge, we are not prepared to hold, as a matter of law, that the general public is aware that the consumption of an excessive amount of alcohol can result in death.

Appellant offered evidence which showed that, prior to the time of her death, Brinkmeyer had little exposure to the use of alcohol. Brinkmeyer's mother stated that she had warned Brinkmeyer of the dangers of impaired physical capacity which can result from the consumption of alcohol, but that she had not warned her daughter that alcohol was lethal because she had no knowledge of that fact. In addition, appellant submitted documents showing that the United States Congress has been considering legislation on whether to require warning labels on bottles of alcohol and that the government of Mexico has already instituted such legislation. Appellant further showed that warning labels are presently used in the United States on "Everclear" grain alcohol bottles.

Since we find genuine issues of material fact to exist in this case, we will REVERSE the summary judgment and REMAND for further proceedings.

Limitations and Defenses

As we have already observed, the advantages of the strict liability theory are heavily stacked in favor of the consumer. The focus is no longer on the conduct of the defendant but on the product itself—a far more tangible target. However, the strict liability theory is not an answer to every plaintiff's prayer. Various limitations and defenses operate against him or her, a number of which are effective in some states but not in others.

Limitations

In addition is the requirement that the product undergo no material change in condition after leaving the defendant's hands. One limitation to the strict liability theory is that the plaintiff may find it difficult to prove that a product left the hands of the seller in a defective condition. Where the technology involved in production is complex, witnesses who can testify to defective manufacture may not be available. For this reason, failure-to-warn cases are more common than those alleging errors in the production process.

Although strict liability makes recovery easier in certain respects, the requirement that a defective product be "unreasonably dangerous" precludes recovery in many instances. Damages resulting from the failure of a product to perform its ordinary purpose, for example, would not be covered under section 402A. As a result, some states have eliminated the "unreasonably dangerous" requirement.

In addition, section 402A limits recovery to users and consumers (including family members, guests, and employees of the purchaser; and individuals who prepare a product for consumption, who repair a product, and who passively enjoy the benefit of a product, as in the case of passengers on an airplane). Recovery is not always allowed to injured bystanders or others who are brought into contact with the defective product; courts differ on this point, depending on the state. Most states have extended application of the theory to anyone suffering reasonably foreseeable injury because of the defect (such as the driver of a car struck from behind by another vehicle whose brakes were defectively manufactured).

Finally, damage limitations exist. Plaintiffs can usually recover only for property damages and personal injuries but, as in negligence cases, not for basis-of-the-bargain damages. Recovery for mere economic losses is usually disallowed as inconsistent with the UCC's scheme for warranty recovery. Punitive damages are available in *some* jurisdictions if the defendant evinces utter disregard for the safety of consumers and users of the product. Finally, as we shall discuss in more detail later in the chapter, many states have recently imposed statutory limitations on recoveries in products liability cases in an attempt to stem the "products liability revolution."

Privity Defense

Most states, but not all, follow the section 402A(2)(b) position abolishing the privity requirement. In some states an intermediary is protected from section 402A liability by requirements that the manufacturer be included in the plaintiff's suit whenever possible or that the manufacturer be sued instead of the intermediary.

Sophisticated Purchaser Defense

Some courts recognize a **sophisticated purchaser defense** in strict liability cases based on a defective warning. For example, in one case[4] the defendant sold sand to a foundry firm. The plaintiff, an employee of the buyer, allegedly contracted cancer from long-term inhalation of silica dust contained in the sand. Because the buyer was knowledgeable as to the risks of silica sand, the court granted summary judgment to the defendant seller, allowing it to rely on the knowledgeable intermediate purchaser to supply appropriate warnings. The defense succeeded because most courts treat a duty to warn claim, even under strict liability, according to negligence standards.

Plaintiff Misconduct Defenses

In negligence cases, of course, a plaintiff's carelessness is simply compared with the defendant's in most jurisdictions. The plaintiff's own carelessness can reduce or even bar recovery. In strict liability claims (and, in most jurisdictions, express and implied warranty claims), "plaintiff carelessness" is not treated as a single concept. Rather, several types of plaintiff misconduct are recognized, with differing effects on liability.

One category is *simple plaintiff carelessness*, often described as the failure to detect or guard against a defect in a product. Although some jurisdictions compare such plaintiff carelessness with the defendant's fault under a comparative negligence statute, others conclude that consumers are entitled to as-

sume that products are defect-free. Unwilling to impose an obligation on consumers to assume that products they use might be defective, these latter jurisdictions hold that simple plaintiff carelessness is no defense at all to strict liability (or warranty) claims.

Another category of plaintiff misconduct is **product misuse**, which occurs when a plaintiff uses a product for a purpose for which it was not designed. For example, a consumer might use a pop bottle as a hammer or a lawn mower as a hedge trimmer. In some jurisdictions, unforeseeable product misuse indicates that the product is not defective and constitutes a complete defense to strict liability (and warranty) claims; in other jurisdictions, it is merely evidence of plaintiff misconduct to be compared with the defendant's fault. However, when the plaintiff's misuse is foreseeable to the defendant (for example, that the purchaser of a sports car might exceed the speed limit), many jurisdictions impose on the defendant a duty to warn against the misuse, or perhaps even to install safety devices to guard against the misuse. Therefore, foreseeable misuse typically is no defense.

A final category of plaintiff misconduct is **assumption of risk,** which occurs when a plaintiff, having discovered a defect in the product and fully appreciating its danger, voluntarily uses the product anyway. In one strict liability case,[5] the plaintiff (a professional carpenter) was using the defendant's portable saw when he noticed that the "bumper" for the saw's protective blade guard had fallen off, causing the lower guard to obstruct the front of the blade, preventing it from beginning to cut. Although he had two similar saws on the job site, the plaintiff continued to use the defective one, manually retracting the blade guard before each cut. Six hours later, the plaintiff started the saw and then reached over with his left hand to retract the guard with its lift lever. Unfortunately, he missed the lever and hit the blade, amputating 3/8 inch of his finger. This was held to be an assumption of the risk by the plaintiff. In some jurisdictions, assumption of the risk is a complete bar to recovery; in others, it is evidence of the plaintiff's fault to be compared with that of the defendant under a comparative fault statute.

There is great variation among the states regarding application of these plaintiff misconduct defenses. The following case illustrates one court's thinking regarding a common issue.

[4]*Smith v. Walter C. Best, Inc.,* 927 F.2d 736 (3d Cir. 1990).

[5]*Sargia v. Skil Corp.,* No. 84 Civ. 7107 (S.D.N.Y. 1985).

SMITH V. GOODYEAR TIRE & RUBBER CO.

U.S. District Court, District of Vermont, 600 F.Supp. 1561 (1985)

The plaintiff, Smith, was injured in an automobile accident. He brought this action alleging negligence on the part of the driver, Young, in whose car Smith was riding at the time of the accident, and alleging a strict liability claim against the defendant tire manufacturer, the Goodyear Tire & Rubber Company.

The defendants raised a "seat belt defense," asserting that their liability is reduced or completely erased because Smith was not wearing a seat belt although one was available to him and that wearing it would have reduced, if not eliminated, his injuries. The plaintiff moved to strike this defense. The following is the trial Judge's ruling on the plaintiff's motion.

Coffrin, Chief Judge:

Courts are divided on the issue of whether evidence regarding the non-use of automobile seatbelts should be admissible in comparative negligence cases. Plaintiff relies heavily in his brief on the fact that regulations adopted pursuant to Vermont statutes, although they do require that pleasure cars be equipped with seat belts in their front seats, do not require that the seat belts be used. Plaintiff also points out that Vermont courts have never imposed such a duty.

Plaintiff asserts that courts' reluctance to "find a duty to buckle up" stems from a concern that requiring seat belt use would lead to a flood of litigation in which defendants would argue that, as a matter of law, any plaintiff who fails not only to use his seat belt but also to install an air bag in his car, to adjust his head rest, or, in-

deed, "to drive a Mack Truck" would be more vulnerable to injury and, thus, guilty of contributing to his own injury.

We are unpersuaded by such reasoning. First, admitting such evidence would not create a duty but would merely allow the jury to consider the information on the question of negligence. Second, the test of negligence would continue to be whether the person acted *reasonably under the circumstances presented.* We do not presume to decide whether or not Plaintiff's failure to fasten his seat belt in the instant case was reasonable. We do believe, however, that the arguments on both sides of the issue are such that a reasonable jury could decide either way. As stated by a New York court,

[T]he seat belt affords the automobile occupant an unusual and ordinarily unavailable means by which he or she may minimize his or her damages prior to the accident. [T]he burden of buckling an available seat belt may, under the facts of the particular case, be found by the jury to be less than the likelihood of injury when multiplied by its accompanying severity. *Spier v. Barker*, 323 N.E.2d 164, (Ct.App. 1974).

We hold that the jury should be given the task of making this assessment.

. . . Comment (c) to §402A explains that the justification for this special doctrine of liability is "that the seller, by marketing his product for use and consumption, has undertaken and assumed a special responsibility. . . ." Comment (n) goes on to say that contributory negligence "is not a defense to strict liability when such negligence consists merely in a failure to discover the defect in the product, or to guard against the possibility of its existence." Instead, the Comment states, Plaintiff

will be barred from recovery only if he "discovers the defect and is aware of the danger, and nevertheless proceeds unreasonably to make use of the product."

Even if Goodyear cannot prove the latter, however, we decline to follow the rigid requirements of Comment (n), and hold that Goodyear should be able to introduce evidence of Plaintiff's failure to use his seat belt as a defense to strict liability. Because Vermont follows the doctrine of comparative negligence, it need not be swayed by the "all or nothing" considerations present in the Comment to the Restatement or in contributory negligence jurisdictions. The purpose behind the strict liability doctrine is to hold certain sellers to a higher standard of care due to their assumption of a special responsibility. Our holding does not thwart that purpose, since Plaintiff still would not have to prove negligence on the part of Goodyear. Although we would be reluctant to completely excuse defendants simply because some of a plaintiff's injuries might have resulted from his own actions, it also does not seem fair to allow a negligent plaintiff, who may have contributed to as much as fifty percent of his injuries, to pay for none of them and to recover as much as a plaintiff who had taken all precautions reasonable under the circumstances.

There is a split of authority among other states on this issue. For the reasons stated above, we choose to follow the reasoning of many other comparative fault jurisdictions, and hold that juries may consider evidence of plaintiffs' negligence in assessing damages as to strict liability claims as well as to negligence claims.

Plaintiff's motion is Denied.

LEGAL FOCUS

International

In recent years, the European Economic Community (EEC) adopted a Products Liability Directive imposing strict liability on suppliers of defective products. Although there are several differences, the EEC Directive closely resembles the version of strict liability for defective products applied by almost all states in the United States. The EEC Directive applies only to individual consumers, not to corporate consumers. Although the strict liability doctrine in the United States includes no such absolute limitation, in actual practice almost all strict products liability suits in the United States are brought by individuals because most states apply strict liability only when the defective product has caused bodily injury or damage to some item of property other than the defective item itself.

In some ways the EEC Directive favors the consumer more than U.S. products liability law. For example, the definition of a defective product appears to be broader than in the United States—under the EEC Directive, a product is considered defective when it fails to provide "the safety a person is entitled to expect." In other ways, the EEC Directive is somewhat less protective than U.S. products liability law. For example, the Directive permits member nations to impose an overall ceiling on damages awarded to an injured consumer; however, the ceiling cannot be lower than seventy million ECUs (European Currency Units). This latter provision obviously makes little sense until EEC member nations finally agree on a common currency unit.

The Products Liability Directive must be implemented by legislation in each member nation. Several have been slow to respond, and the EEC has threatened sanctions against those nations. The Directive represents part of a burgeoning movement toward consumer rights in Europe (and in other nations, including Japan) similar to the U.S. movement that began in the early 1960s. Another example of this movement in Europe is an EEC Directive that imposes strict liability on polluters.

In conclusion, the strict liability doctrine favors plaintiffs in that it possesses several advantages: (1) few defenses against liability can be raised by the defendant; (2) disclaimers are ineffectual; (3) privity is not required; and (4) buyers must prove only that goods were *dangerously defective* when they left the seller's hands and that this defect caused the buyer's injury.

However, disadvantages to the plaintiff include (1) applicability of section 402A only against sellers who are merchants, and (2) availability of damages only for physical injuries to person and property and not for economic injuries.

FEDERAL CONSUMER LEGISLATION

Over the years Congress has enacted a number of federal regulatory laws dealing with the safety and quality of goods. For the most part these laws have focused solely on protecting ultimate consumers from physical harm, and until recently, they were enacted piecemeal and were rather narrow in scope. Examples include the Food, Drug and Cosmetic Act (1938), the Flammable Fabrics Act (1953), the Refrigerator Safety Act (1956), the Hazardous Substances Act (1960), and the Poison Prevention Packaging Act (1970).

Consumer Product Safety Act

In 1972 Congress enacted the **Consumer Product Safety Act**—the first law to deal with the safety of consumer products in general—and created a federal agency, the Consumer Product Safety Commission (CPSC), to administer it.[6] This agency possesses broad powers and performs many functions, ranging from safety research and testing to preparing safety rules and standards for more than 10,000 products. It has the power to ban or recall products and to require special labelling in certain circumstances. It can levy civil penalties on those who violate the Act and criminal penalties on those who willfully violate it. Yet de-

---

[6]Some consumer products are not covered by the Consumer Product Safety Act because they come under the aegis of other federal laws. The most important of these are food, drugs, and cosmetics, which are regulated by the Food and Drug Administration under the Food, Drug, and Cosmetic Act. Automobiles are also excluded because of coverage by other legislation.

spite the extensive range of its power, the CPSC has been criticized for not issuing sufficient standards to ensure the integrity of consumer products.

In 1990, Congress raised the civil penalties for Consumer Product Safety Act violations from $2000 to $5000, required manufacturers to report repeated and serious problems with products to the agency, and made other changes to strengthen the CPSC.

Magnuson-Moss Warranty Act

In 1975 Congress passed the **Magnuson-Moss Warranty Act.** Like the federal legislation just discussed, this statute is consumer-oriented. It applies only to purchases by ultimate consumers for personal, family, or household purposes and not to transactions in commercial or industrial settings. The Warranty Act, which is usually enforced by the Federal Trade Commission (FTC), does not regulate the safety or quality of consumer goods. Instead it prevents deceptive warranty practices, makes consumer warranties easier to understand, and provides an effective means of enforcing warranty obligations. The federal Warranty Act is limited to consumer transactions, and it modifies the UCC warranty rules in some respects; in nonconsumer transactions, the UCC rules continue in effect.

The type of warranty to which the Warranty Act applies is much more narrowly defined than is an express warranty under the UCC. Specifically, it is (1), any *written* affirmation of fact made by a supplier to a purchaser relating to the quality or performance of a product and affirming that the product is defect-free or that it will meet a specified level of performance over a period of time; or (2) a written undertaking to "refund, repair, replace, or take other action" if a product fails to meet written specifications. Obviously express warranties that are not in writing, such as those created by verbal description or by sample, will continue to be governed solely by the UCC, even though a consumer transaction is involved.

The Warranty Act does not require anyone to give a warranty on consumer goods. It applies only if the seller *voluntarily chooses* to make an express written warranty (perhaps in an effort to render a product more competitive). When a written warranty is provided for a product costing $10 or more, it must be labelled as either "full" or "limited." When the cost of goods exceeds $15, the warranty must be contained in a single document, must be written in clear language, and must make a number of disclosures, including (1) a description of items covered and those excluded, along with specific service guarantees; (2) instructions on how to proceed in the event of product failure; (3) the identity of those to whom the warranty is extended; and (4) limitations on the warranty period.

Under a full warranty, the warrantor must assume certain minimum duties and obligations.[7] For instance, he or she must agree to *repair or replace* any malfunctioning or defective product within a "reasonable" time and without charge. If the warrantor makes a reasonable number of attempts to remedy the defect and is unable to do so, the consumer can choose to receive a *cash refund* or *replacement* of the product without charge. No *time limitation* can be placed on a full warranty; and consequential damages (such as for personal injury or property damage) can be disclaimed only if the limitation is *conspicuous.*

A written warranty that does not meet the minimum requirements must be designated conspicuously as a *limited warranty.* It may cover, for example, parts but not labor, or it may levy shipping and handling fees. If a time limit (such as 24 months) is all that prevents the warranty from being a full one, it can be designated as a "full 24-month warranty."

Because its purpose is to regulate *written* warranties, the Warranty Act generally does not cover implied warranties of merchantability and fitness for a particular purpose. These are governed by the UCC, and as we have seen, the UCC allows implied warranties to be disclaimed. However, drafters of the Warranty Act saw fit to limit the use of disclaimers where written warranties are involved, because of certain abusive practices prevalent at the time: Sellers were providing limited express warranties in bold print and then disclaiming implied warranties, thus leaving the consumer with few rights while appearing to offer substantial protection.

For this reason, the Magnuson-Moss Act *prohibits a disclaimer of implied warranties* (1) when an express written warranty is given, whether full or limited, or (2) when a service contract is made with the consumer within 90 days after the sale.[8] If the written warranty specifies a *time* limitation, however, implied warranties may be suspended by a disclaimer effective *after* the written warranty expires.

[7]Only the person who actually makes the written warranty—no one else in the chain of distribution—is responsible under the Warranty Act.

[8]Under a service contract the seller agrees to service and repair a product for a set period of time in return for a fixed fee.

The Warranty Act is usually enforced by the FTC, but the Attorney General or an injured consumer can also initiate an action if informal procedures for settling disputes prove ineffective. Sellers are authorized to dictate the informal procedures by which a particular dispute is to be settled. If these procedures follow FTC guidelines, the consumer cannot resort to court action until all established means have been exhausted.

LEGISLATIVE LIMITATIONS ON THE PRODUCTS LIABILITY REVOLUTION

From 1960 until the mid-1980s, the general trend in products liability law was strongly pro-plaintiff. New theories allowed new classes of injured persons to sue defendants that had never before been vulnerable to suit. Injured consumers have been well served, and it is certainly arguable that products liability litigation has been the most influential factor in bringing about improved product designs and safety practices that have saved thousands of lives.

Recent years, however, have seen a countervailing pressure to reform products liability law in order to roll back the "products liability revolution." Damage awards have increased insurance premiums, raised the prices of some products, induced some companies to cease manufacturing certain products, and arguably, caused American business to suffer a competitive disadvantage abroad. The expense of designing eminently safe products, coupled with insurance rates much higher than those in Europe, has added significantly to the costs of production. The apparent "explosion" of products liability has raised a storm of protest among manufacturers and sellers, and at present, almost every state has enacted or is considering tort reform.

Some states have already placed ceilings on damage awards in product liability suits. Others have enacted provisions that prohibit advances in technology from being used, with the benefit of hindsight, against manufacturers. More than one-third of the states have enacted **statutes of repose.** These provide a time period after which the manufacturer is not liable for injuries caused by a product, the statute of limitations notwithstanding. The periods range from 5 to 12 years and begin when a product is sold to an ultimate consumer (one who does not purchase for resale). The purpose of these provisions is to protect manufacturers from liability in situations where

defects do not manifest themselves until many years after the product is sold.

State reform legislation has not been entirely anti-consumer, however. Under a recent California law, companies and managers commit a crime if they fail to notify regulators about known safety defects in their products. Substantial fines and the possibility of prison terms provide enforcement.

Federal Products Liability Legislation

There is substantial variation in the details of products liability law among the 50 state jurisdictions. A manufacturer seeking to market its products on a nationwide basis faces a formidable task in conforming its actions to these varying standards. Although some maintain that optimal products liability law will eventually develop at the state level, the advantages of a comprehensive federal law are obvious.

Several products liability reform measures have been introduced in Congress in recent years, although none has passed. Most bills have sought not only to produce national uniformity but also to limit product liability recoveries through a number of means. At this writing (summer 1993), the leading federal bill (not yet near passage) has the following major provisions: (1) distributors would be liable only for their own negligence and not for simply selling a manufacturer's product; (2) a statute of repose (no suit can be brought involving a product sold more than 25 years earlier) and a narrow statute of limitations (plaintiffs must sue within two years of when they discovered a defect) would be added; (3) punitive damages could be awarded only if a defendant acted with "conscious, flagrant" indifference to public safety; (4) joint and several liability would be restricted to economic damages; (5) workers' compensation recoveries would be subtracted from awards; (6) no suit could be brought by a plaintiff whose injuries resulted primarily from his or her own drug or alcohol use; and (7) nontrial resolution of suits would be encouraged by allowing either party to request alternative dispute resolution and by making possible an award of attorney fees from the opposing party if a settlement offer was rejected and the amount not improved at trial. Although such a bill, if enacted into law, would not satisfy the interests of labor and consumer groups, it would bring uniformity to the area of products liability and afford some relief to manufacturers from the high costs they have come to bear under the strict liability theory.

SUMMARY

A plaintiff injured by a defective product has several possible legal theories to pursue. If the defendant, be it retailer, wholesaler, or manufacturer, made any representations or affirmations of fact regarding the product's performance, an express warranty theory is available if the promises were breached. Although salespersons are allowed to "puff" their product, specific promises made orally or in written "guarantees" or in product advertising may form the basis for an express warranty claim.

Even if the seller makes no representations about a product, the law implies a promise that the good is "merchantable"—of average quality acceptable in the trade of such goods—any time a merchant (one who makes a living selling such goods) sells a consumer a product. Additionally, if that merchant sells a good knowing that the purchaser needs it for a specific purpose and is relying on the seller's expertise to provide a product that can fulfill that purpose, a warranty of fitness for a particular purpose will be implied by the law.

Both implied warranties may be disclaimed, and recovery may be limited, if UCC rules are strictly followed and the disclaimer or limitation is not "unconscionable."

A consumer injured by a defective product can recover against any parties the consumer can prove negligently designed, manufactured, tested, or marketed the product. Careless failure to warn of the unavoidable dangers of a product can also be grounds for suit.

Unlike the negligence theory, which focuses on the conduct of the defendant, the strict liability theory focuses only on the product. If the product is defective and unreasonably dangerous, defendants in the distribution chain (manufacturer-wholesaler-retailer) are liable for injuries caused by the defects, no matter how careful they were.

These remedies are supplemented by several federal statutes designed to protect the consumer, most importantly the Magnuson-Moss Act dealing with express warranties and the Consumer Product Safety Act.

Many believe the law of products liability has become so "pro-consumer" that drastic reforms are needed. Many state legislatures have passed reform legislation which, for example, imposes "statutes of repose" to prevent recovery for injuries caused by old machines and limits on certain types of damage recoveries. As this chapter is written, Congress is considering federal legislation that would dramatically change the law that has evolved during the "consumer revolution" of the past 25 years.

KEY TERMS

Warranty
Express warranty
Implied warranty of merchantability
Implied warranty of fitness for a particular purpose
Warranty of title
Disclaimer
Privity of contract
Res ipsa loquitur
Strict liability
Sophisticated purchaser defense
Product misuse
Assumption of risk
Consumer Product Safety Act
Magnuson-Moss Warranty Act
Statutes of repose

QUESTIONS AND PROBLEMS

1. In August 1980, ITT loaned money to McGinn in return for a security interest in a Caterpillar hydraulic excavator. ITT properly perfected its security interest. In the summer of 1981, ITT learned that McGinn was having financial problems and had discussions with him, the contents of which are disputed. The excavator was sold by McGinn at auction through Vilsmeier in October 1981. Before the auction, Vilsmeier announced that the excavator was being sold free and clear of any liens or security interests. Arnold bought the equipment. In October 1983, however, Arnold surrendered the excavator to ITT on advice of counsel in light of ITT's security interest in the machine. Arnold sued Vilsmeier for breach of warranty of title. The trial judge directed a verdict for Arnold. Vilsmeier claimed that this was improper, for it prevented him from attempting to prove that ITT had waived its security interest in its conversation with McGinn. Did the trial judge err? (*Frank Arnold Contractors, Inc. v. Vilsmeier Auction Co.*, 806 F.2d 462, 3d Cir. 1986.)

2. Walcott & Steele, Inc., sold seed to Carpenter. State law required the package label to give the

percentage of germination. The label on the seed bought by Carpenter carried the required statement, but the seed did not perform at the listed percentage. Carpenter sued for breach of an express warranty, which he claimed was created by the statement regarding percentage of germination. Did Carpenter prevail? Discuss. (*Walcott & Steele, Inc. v. Carpenter*, 436 S.W.2d 820, 1969.)

3. Kassab, a cattle breeder, purchased feed that had been manufactured by Central Soya. The feed was intended for breeding cattle, but Central had accidentally included an ingredient that should be used only for beef cattle. After eating the feed, Kassab's cattle grew and prospered. Kassab was upset, however, when he discovered that the mistakenly included ingredient had caused his entire herd of prize breeding cattle to become sterile. He sued Central for breach of the implied warranty of merchantability. Central claimed that there was no such breach because the feed had made the cattle gain weight exactly as it was supposed to do. Is Central's contention correct? Explain. (*Kassab v. Central Soya*, 246 A. 2d 848, 1968.)

4. Henningsen bought a new automobile from Bloomfield Motors, Inc. Only 10 days after the purchase, when the Chrysler had only 468 miles on the odometer, something under the hood cracked and the car veered 90 degrees into a brick wall. Henningsen's wife was seriously injured. When Henningsen sued Bloomfield and Chrysler on an implied warranty of merchantability theory, they raised as a defense a clause in the purchase contract that provided that the manufacturer's "obligation under this warranty [is] limited to making good at its factory any part or parts thereof which shall, within 90 days after delivery of such vehicle to the original purchaser or before such vehicle has been driven 4,000 miles, whichever event shall first occur, be returned to it with transportation charges prepaid and which its examination shall disclose to its satisfaction to have been thus defective; this warranty being expressly in lieu of all other warranties expressed or implied." Does this disclaimer bar the plaintiff's suit? Discuss. (*Henningsen v. Bloomfield Motors, Inc.*, 161 A.2d 69, N.J. 1960.)

5. Johnson, the plaintiff, raised hogs. He needed ventilating fans for his hog barn. He told the supplier's representative of his needs. When asked, the plaintiff told the representative that there were no unusual humidity or dust problems in the hog barn, but this was not accurate. The plaintiff was advised to purchase certain fans with "open" motors not sealed off from outside air. He bought them, but they malfunctioned because of clogging from humidity and feed dust. Many hogs died; the plaintiff sued the supplier and the manufacturer, among others, for breach of the implied warranty of fitness for a particular purpose. Should the plaintiff prevail? Discuss. (*Johnson v. Lappo Lumber Co.*, 181 N.W.2d 316, Mich. App. 1970.)

6. The defendant manufactures the Rohm .38 caliber revolver, often called a "Saturday Night Special." One of defendant's guns was used in a robbery, causing the death of the clerk at the grocery store being robbed. The gun functioned as it was intended; a bullet was fired with deadly force when the trigger was intentionally pulled. The clerk's family sued the defendant in strictly liability, arguing that the danger of such guns greatly outweighs their utility. The plaintiffs cited evidence that in the United States (1) handgun use results in 22,000 deaths every year; (2) medical care for gunshot victims costs $500 million per year; (3) although handguns constitute only 30 percent of all guns sold, they account for 90 percent of the cases of firearm misuse; (4) a handgun is six times more likely to be used to kill a friend or relative than to repel a burglar; and (5) a person who uses a handgun in self-defense is eight times more likely to be killed than one who quietly acquiesces. How should the judge rule? Discuss. (*Patterson v. Rohm Gesellschaft*, 608 F.Supp. 1206, N.D.Tex. 1985).

7. Daniell felt overburdened and wished to commit suicide. Seeking a place from which she could not escape, she climbed into the trunk of a 1973 Ford LTD and latched it. Later she changed her mind about suicide but could not escape because the trunk contained no internal release mechanism. She was locked in the trunk for nine days and suffered injuries before a passerby heard her cries for help. She sued Ford on the grounds of strict liability, claiming that the truck was defective because it had no internal release mechanism. Is this a good claim? By what standard should the claim be judged? (*Daniell v. Ford Motor Corp.*, 581 F.Supp. 728, D.N.M. 1984.)

8. Laaperi bought a smoke detector from Sears and installed it in his bedroom. The detector was

designed to be powered by AC (electric) current. Six months later a fire broke out in the Laaperi home, killing three of Laaperi's children. The smoke detector did not sound an alarm on the night of the fire, because the fire started in a short circuit in an electric cord. The smoke detector was connected to the circuit, which shorted and cut off. Laaperi sued Sears claiming that it had breached a duty to warn him that the very short circuit that might ignite a fire in his home could, at the same time, incapacitate the smoke detector. Is this a viable theory? Discuss. (*Laaperi v. Sears, Roebuck & Co., Inc.*, 787 F.2d 726, 1st Cir. 1986.)

9. The Hauters, the plaintiffs, purchased a "Golfing Gizmo" for their son from the defendants. The device was designed to provide driving practice for novice golfers. On the package it said, "Completely safe ball will not hit player." But the Hauter's son, while using it as directed, was hit in the head by the ball and severely injured. The plaintiffs sued for breach of express and implied warranties, but the defendants argued that their only obligation was to provide a device that was safe when the ball was hit "properly" and that a drawing on the package depicted a golfer hitting the ball "properly." Is this a good defense? Discuss. (*Hauter v. Zogarts*, 534 P.2d 377, Cal. 1975.)

10. Welch, the plaintiff, bought a new Dodge station wagon from Fitzgerald-Hicks Dodge, Inc. (FHD). During the next six months the car required a large number of repairs—"repairs too numerous to list," in the words of the higher court. Although most repairs were satisfactory, the major continuing problem was a "shimmying" that could be felt when the car was driven. After many unsuccessful attempts by FHD to remedy that problem, the plaintiff left the car with FHD with a letter stating that he was revoking his acceptance. The plaintiff then brought this action against FHD and Chrysler Corporation, the manufacturer, to recover the purchase price. Among the numerous issues at trial was the major question as to whether the shimmy caused the car to be unmerchantable. On that point the plaintiff introduced evidence that the shimmy, while reduced, was still noticeable and bothersome; the defendants, however, contended that, taken as a whole, the car was of such a nature that it would "pass without objection within the automobile industry." The jury found the car to be unmerchantable; on appeal, one of the questions was whether the jury's finding of unmerchantability was supported by the evidence (in view of evidence that all other aspects of the car were, by that time, satisfactory). Do you think the jury's verdict should be upheld? Discuss. (*Welch v. Fitzgerald-Hicks Dodge, Inc.*, 430 A.2d 144, 1981.

Performance of the Sale Contract

Introduction to Remedies

Seller's Remedies

Buyer's Remedies

Lemon Laws

IN THIS FINAL chapter on the law of sales we will discuss two subject areas: (1) performance of the sale contract (the obligations of both seller and buyer that are necessary to fulfill their agreement) and (2) remedies (the various avenues available to a seller or buyer if the other fails to live up to the contract obligations).

PERFORMANCE OF THE SALE CONTRACT

Basically, the seller's obligation is to deliver goods that conform to the contract and to any applicable warranties, and the buyer's obligation is to accept and pay for them. However, *total performance* by the seller may involve a number of other aspects. In addition, several problem areas in the buyer's basic obligations of acceptance and payment require a closer look. The most important thing to remember is that the performance obligations of seller and buyer are ultimately controlled by the agreement of the parties themselves. The primary purposes of the UCC provisions in this area are to help in interpreting the agreement and to establish rules on matters not covered by the agreement.

Seller's Obligations
Tender of Delivery

How does a seller deliver the goods? Must he or she actually put them into the buyer's hands? Has the seller performed the obligation if the buyer has changed his or her mind and refuses to take the goods? The answer to these questions is that the seller fully performs the delivery obligation by "tendering" delivery. According to Sec. 2-503(1), to make a **tender of delivery** the seller must "put and hold conforming goods at the buyer's disposition and give the buyer any notification reasonably necessary to enable him to take delivery." That is, the seller must keep the goods available for the period of time reasonably necessary to enable the buyer to take possession.

Tender must be made at a *reasonable hour.* Suppose, for example, that prices have risen since the making of the contract. The seller cannot perform by tendering delivery at three o'clock in the morning (unless the agreement so provided) in the hope that the buyer will reject the tender.

If the agreement makes no mention of the *place of delivery,* it should be at the seller's place of business or, if the seller has none, at his or her residence. However, if at the time the contract is made the goods are identified and both parties know that they are located at some other location, that place is the place of delivery.

Usually the parties will have agreed on the place of delivery, and most agreements fall within either of two categories:

1. The buyer agrees to pick up the goods at a particular place without the seller having any responsibility for moving them.

2. The seller undertakes responsibility for transporting the goods to the buyer.

The first category may involve an agreement that the buyer will call for the goods at the seller's premises. Or the goods may be in the possession of a bailee (such as a warehouseman), with the buyer being responsible for picking them up. Where the goods are held by a bailee, tender of delivery by the seller is a matter of paperwork. He or she must either deliver to the buyer a *negotiable document of title* (a warehouse receipt) or obtain the *bailee's acknowledgment* that the buyer is entitled to possession (see Chapter 20 for a discussion on documents of title). Delivery by the seller of a nonnegotiable document of title is a proper tender of delivery only if the buyer does not object. Similarly, a mere written direction to the bailee to hand the goods over to the buyer (with no acknowledgment by the bailee of the buyer's rights) is a sufficient tender only if the buyer does not object.

The second category of agreement, in which the seller ships the goods, is further divided into shipment contracts and destination contracts. In a *shipment contract* the seller performs his or her obligations by tendering delivery at the point of shipment. Sec. 2-504 provides that, unless otherwise agreed:

1. The seller must put the goods in the possession of a carrier (such as a trucking or railway company), and the choice of carrier must be reasonable under the circumstances. Further, the seller's contract with the carrier for transporting the goods must also be

reasonable under the circumstances. (For example, a contract with the carrier that understates the value of the goods for insurance purposes is not considered reasonable.)

2. The seller must obtain and promptly deliver in proper form any document (such as a bill of lading) necessary for the buyer to take possession of the goods.

3. The seller must promptly notify the buyer of shipment.

If the seller fails to meet the above requirements, the buyer can reject delivery only if a material loss or delay resulted—unless the parties have agreed differently. For instance, they might agree that failure to give prompt notification is a ground for rejection regardless of the consequences of the failure.

The seller's obligation in a *destination contract* is not fulfilled until delivery is tendered at the destination. Since the seller's required performance extends to the buyer's doorstep, so to speak, special provisions regarding selection of a carrier are not needed for the buyer's protection. The general tender requirements already set forth are sufficient. At the point of destination, the seller must put and hold the goods at the buyer's disposition at a reasonable hour, for a reasonable period of time, and with proper notice. And, of course, the seller must furnish any required documents. Figure 23.1 illustrates the above requirements.

Commercial Shipping Terms

Sales contracts frequently contain terms that have well-established meanings in the commercial world but that are somewhat mysterious to the newcomer. For example, the contract may include phrases such as *FOB Detroit* or *FAS vessel, New York.* These indicate the parties' agreement on particular terms of shipment and are treated as shipping terms even when they appear only in connection with the price ("2.00/lb. FOB seller's plant"). Some of the more common terms are defined below.

FOB ("free on board"). If the named location following the FOB designation is the point of shipment, the agreement is a *shipment contract.* If the vehicle of transportation at the point of shipment is also referred to, the seller must not only put the goods into the possession of a carrier but also bear the expense of loading them on board. An example is

"FOB Car 235Y, Mo. Pac. R.R. Depot, Dallas." If the named location following the FOB designation is the destination, the agreement is a *destination contract.*

FAS ("free alongside" vessel). FAS, frequently found in sale contracts where the goods are to be transported by seagoing vessel, indicates that a *shipment contract* has been made. The seller performs by delivering the goods alongside (on the dock next to) the vessel on which they are to be loaded, but does not bear the expense of loading.

Ex-ship ("from the carrying vessel"). The phrase *ex-ship,* also a maritime term, is actually the reverse of FAS. It denotes a *destination contract* and indicates that the seller's obligation extends to unloading the goods at the port of destination.

CIF ("cost, insurance, and freight") and C & F ("cost and freight"). CIF and C & F are also found almost exclusively in maritime agreements. CIF indicates that the price paid by the buyer includes the cost of the goods, insurance while they are in transit, and all freight charges. C & F means that the price includes the cost of the goods and freight charges but not insurance. Although the terms indicate that the agreement is a *shipment contract,* their inclusion means that the seller assumes obligations in addition to those of an ordinary shipment contract. The C & F term obligates the seller to see that the goods are loaded and to pay the freight charges. The CIF term further obligates the seller to obtain appropriate insurance coverage.

The Perfect Tender Rule

At common law there developed a doctrine known as the **perfect tender rule.** Under this rule, the seller's tender of delivery was required to conform in every detail to the terms of the agreement. In other words, the doctrine of substantial performance (discussed in Chapter 18) did not apply to contracts for the sale of goods. An extreme illustration of the perfect tender rule is found in *Filley v. Pope,* 115 U.S. 213 (1885). The seller agreed to sell pig iron to the buyer, the contract calling for shipment to New Orleans from Glasgow, Scotland. When the time for shipment arrived, no ships were available at Glasgow. The seller's factory in Scotland was halfway between the ports of Glasgow and Leith; and since vessels were available at Leith, he sent the iron to Leith for shipment. The buyer rejected the goods when they arrived. The Supreme Court held that the buyer was entitled to do so, because a contract calling for shipment from

FIGURE 23.1

Seller's Obligations

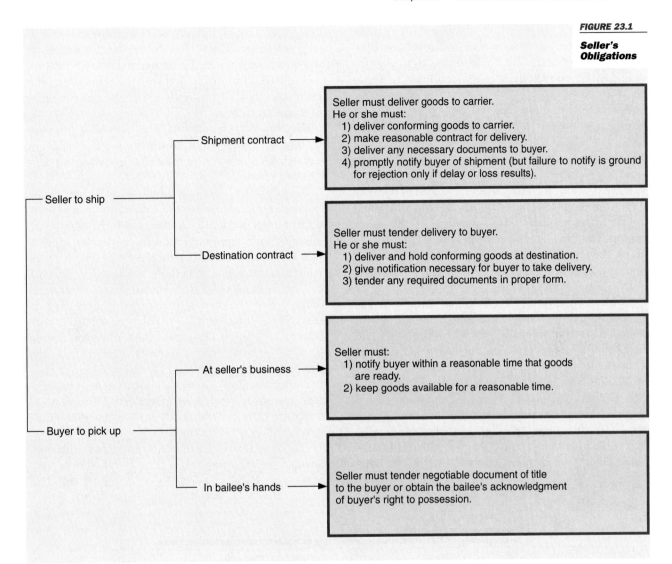

Glasgow is not fulfilled by a shipment from Leith even though no delay results.

UCC Sec. 2-601 essentially restates the perfect tender rule by providing that "if the goods or the tender of delivery fail in *any respect* to conform to the contract," the buyer is not obligated to accept them. (Emphasis added.) Because the perfect tender rule has both limitations and exceptions, it is not absolute.

Limitations of the Perfect Tender Rule

Parties' Agreement. The parties themselves can, of course, limit the perfect tender rule by agreement. For example, they might agree that a delivery of de-

fective goods cannot be rejected if the seller repairs or replaces the defective parts.[1]

Trade Usage, Etc. Because the agreement of the parties to a sale of goods includes that part of their bargain found in usage of trade, course of dealing, and course of performance, sometimes these concepts limit the perfect tender rule. For example, if trade usage in a particular industry recognizes that a contract calling for 100 percent pure industrial plastic is satisfied by 99 percent purity, a buyer has

---

[1]However, insofar as such a clause limits the application of an implied warranty, it must meet all the requirements of the UCC regarding disclaimers of warranty. In a consumer transaction it also must comply with the Magnuson-Moss Warranty Act.

no grounds to object when plastic of 99 percent purity is delivered. This is not an exception to the perfect tender rule; the trade usage simply helps define what constitutes a perfect tender in these circumstances.

Cure. At common law the seller had only one chance to make a perfect tender. Section 2-508 of the UCC gives more latitude to the seller of goods, in an attempt to encourage the parties to mitigate losses by working out their differences. Subsection (1) provides that where the seller makes a tender of delivery that is rejected as nonconforming but the *time for performance has not yet expired,* if the seller promptly notifies the buyer of an intention to "cure," he or she can then make a conforming delivery (or perhaps repair the defective goods) *before* expiration of the time for performance.

Subsection (2) of 2-508 allows cure even *after* the agreed-upon time for performance, where the buyer rejects a nonconforming tender which the seller had *reasonable grounds to believe would be acceptable.* This can occur, for example, (1) where a prior course of dealing between the parties has led the seller to believe that the nonconforming goods would be acceptable because the buyer has accepted such goods before, or (2) where the seller delivers goods that he or she believes to be conforming but which contain a *latent* defect that is only discovered after delivery. As-

sume that a retailer delivered to a customer a television sealed in its factory crate. If, when uncrated in the customer's home, the set had a defective picture, a court would probably find that the retailer had the right to cure after promptly informing the customer of its intent to do so.

Note that the provisions allowing a seller to cure do not preclude a suit by the buyer for damages caused, for example, by the delay in delivering conforming goods.

Good Faith. As noted before, UCC Sec. 1-203 imposes on all parties to the sale of goods a general obligation of good faith. Although this duty applies to all aspects of sales contracts, it has particular application to the perfect tender rule. Assume that a buyer contracts to pay a specified amount for delivery of one million widgets. Soon after the contract is entered into, the market price for widgets drops substantially, so that the buyer wishes to evade its contractual obligation. The good faith provision should prevent the buyer from rejecting the seller's goods on the basis of an insignificant deviation from contractual specifications where the buyer is receiving the true measure of what he bargained for and is attempting to reject the goods for reasons other than the deviation.

The "good faith" limitation is discussed in the following case.

PRINTING CENTER OF TEXAS, INC. v. SUPERMIND PUBLISHING CO.

Court of Appeals of Texas, 669 S.W.2d 779 (1984)

Case

Appellee *Supermind Publishing Co. sued appellant Printing Center of Texas for refund of a deposit made under a written contract to print 5,000 books. Appellee claimed that it rightfully rejected the books upon delivery under UCC 2-601, and that it had the right to cancel the contract and recover its deposit under 2-711. The trial court ruled for appellee, ordering refund of the $2,900 deposit. Appellant appealed.*

Cannon, Justice:

[The key issue is] whether appellee had a right to reject the books under 2-601 which states in part:

if the goods or tender of delivery fail in any respect to conform to the contract, the buyer may (1) reject the whole. . . .

This provision has been called the perfect tender rule because it supposedly allows a buyer to reject whenever the goods are less than perfect. This statement is not quite accurate; under section 2-601 the tender must be perfect only in the sense that the prof-

fered goods must conform to the contract in every respect. Conformity does not mean substantial performance; it means complete performance. The long-standing doctrine of sales law that "there is no room in commercial contracts for the doctrine of substantial performance" is carried forward into section 2-601 of the Code.

Once the contract of the parties has been determined [considering not only the language of the parties but also course of dealing, usage of trade, and course of performance], the evidence must be reviewed to see if the right goods were tendered at the right time *(continues)*

PRINTING CENTER OF TEXAS, INC. v. SUPERMIND PUBLISHING CO.

(continued from previous page)
and place. If the evidence does establish nonconformity in some respect, the buyer is entitled to reject if he rejects in good faith. Section 1-203 provides that "[e]very contract or duty within this Act imposes an obligation of good faith in its performance or enforcement." If the seller alleges that the buyer rejected in bad faith, the seller has the burden of proof on the issue. Evidence of circumstances which indicate that the buyer's motivation in rejecting the goods was to escape the bargain, rather than to avoid acceptance of a tender which in some respect impairs the value of the bar-

gain to him, would support a finding of rejection in bad faith. Thus, evidence of rejection of the goods on account of a minor defect in a falling market would in some instances be sufficient to support a finding that the buyer acted in bad faith when he rejected the goods.

[Turning to the evidence in this case] appellant knew that appellee wanted the books printed for sale to the public. . . . A jury could reasonably conclude that books with crooked and wrinkled pages, off-center cover art, and inadequate perforations are not fit for sale to the public. We find sufficient evidence to support the jury's finding

that the books did not conform to the contract.

Appellant contends that if nonconformities exist, they are minor and that appellee rejected the books in bad faith. Appellant has failed to carry its burden to prove that appellee rejected the books in bad faith. First, we do not agree with the appellant's contention that the alleged nonconformities should be classified as minor. Second, there is no evidence which indicates that appellee's primary motivation in rejection of the books was to escape a bad bargain.

[Affirmed.] ⚖

Exceptions to the Perfect Tender Rule

Buyer Revocation of Acceptance. Assume that a seller delivers nonconforming goods and a buyer, perhaps because of an inadequate inspection, accepts those goods. Only later does the buyer discover the nonconformity. At that point the buyer may well attempt to *revoke his acceptance*, as he is allowed to do under UCC 2-608. However, once the buyer has accepted delivery, the perfect tender rule no longer applies. While a buyer may reject an acceptance for *any* nonconformity, he may revoke an acceptance only by showing that the defect "substantially impaired" the value of the goods. This exception to the perfect tender rule makes sense because the longer buyers have the goods, the higher the likelihood that any defects were caused by them, the greater the benefit buyers may have derived from use of the goods, and the greater the loss to the sellers through depreciation or market fluctuations when the goods are thrown back on them.

Rejection in Installment Contracts. An **installment contract** is defined in Sec. 2-612 as one requiring or authorizing the delivery of goods in separate lots to be separately accepted. Under Sec. 2-612(2), a buyer can reject a particular installment only if the nonconformity *substantially impairs the value of that installment and cannot be cured.* If the

seller gives adequate assurance of cure, the buyer must accept the installment. Under Sec. 2-612(3), the *entire* contract is breached if the nonconformity of the installment substantially impairs the value *of the whole contract.* Again, the "substantial impairment" standard clearly creates an exception to the perfect tender rule. However, in subsection (3) the buyer reinstates the contract if he or she accepts a nonconforming installment without seasonably notifying the seller of cancellation.

Improper Shipping Arrangements. Remember that in a shipping contract the seller must (1) act appropriately in selecting and making a transportation contract with the carrier, (2) provide any documents necessary for the buyer to take possession of the goods, and (3) promptly notify the buyer of the shipment. However, under Sec. 2-504, failure by the seller to fulfill obligations (1) (contract) or (3) (notification) entitles the buyer to reject the delivery only if *material loss or delay* has resulted. (If the UCC had existed at the time of *Filley v. Pope,* the outcome of that case would have been different.) There is no such exception to the perfect tender rule for the obligation to tender documents.

Substitute Means of Delivery. In some cases the parties specifically agree on the type of facilities to be used in loading, shipping, or unloading the goods. If, through no fault of either party, these agreed-upon facilities become unavailable or impracticable, but a *commercially reasonable substitute* is available, the seller and buyer are required to use the substitute.

Effect of Unforeseen Occurrences.

The common-law rules applying to contracts in general also apply to sale of goods contracts unless they have been altered by the UCC. Thus, if the specific subject matter of the sale contract has been destroyed through no fault of either party, or if performance has become illegal because of a change in the law, both parties are excused from their contractual obligations.

Suppose that seller S and buyer B have contracted for the sale of one hundred head of cattle. If the cattle are damaged or destroyed after risk of loss has passed to B (as would be the case in a shipment contract if the carrier is involved in an accident while transporting the cattle), then obviously S has already performed and B will have to pay for the goods. On the other hand, if a flash flood on S's land destroys the cattle *before* risk of loss has passed to B, then the financial loss will have to be borne by S, and B will not have to pay for the cattle.

If the destruction occurs before the risk of loss has passed, a further question remains: Is S excused from performing his part of the bargain? If the contract was for the sale of one hundred head of cattle but not necessarily the specific cattle that were destroyed, the answer is no. Not only has S suffered the loss but he also must still perform the contract by delivering one hundred head of cattle. But if the contract was for the sale of the specific cattle that were subsequently destroyed, S is excused from his obligation and is under no further duty to perform. This common-law rule is restated in UCC Sec. 2-613. (In addition to the basic rule covering cases of *total* destruction, Sec. 2-613 also covers cases where the loss is only *partial*. In such a situation B has a choice. He can treat the contract as canceled, thereby excusing both parties from their obligations. Or he can accept the goods in their damaged condition with an allowance deducted from the contract price.)

Commercial Impracticability.

The UCC also contains a provision, Sec. 2-615, to deal with certain types of unforeseen occurrences that do not result in damage to the specifically identified subject matter of the contract. If, because of unforeseen circumstances, delivery of the goods becomes "commer-

cially impracticable," the parties are excused from their obligations. Of course, an increase in costs or change in the market price alone is not enough to relieve the seller of his or her responsibility; the existence of such risks is one of the main reasons for making binding contracts. But where the difficulty is of an *extraordinary* nature, such as the destruction of a source of supply that had been agreed upon or contemplated by both parties, the seller is excused. In such a case, however, the seller must have taken *all reasonable steps* to assure himself or herself that the source would not fail. The seller also may be excused from delivering if a severe shortage of raw materials due to such events as war, embargo, or local crop failure causes a drastic increase in cost or completely prevents the seller from securing necessary supplies. A seller seeking to be excused because of commercial impracticability, however, must *promptly notify* the buyer of the problem.

Sometimes the commercial impracticability affects only *part* of the seller's capacity to perform. For instance, the unforeseen occurrence might result in a material delay or in a diminution of the quantity of available goods. Where the available quantity is diminished, Sec. 2-615 requires the seller to *allocate deliveries* among customers, including all customers then under contract and, if he or she chooses, regular customers not currently under contract. The seller must give *prompt notification* of either a delay or an allocation and, in the case of an allocation, must make an estimate of the quota available.

Buyer's Choices.

When the buyer is notified of a significant delay or an allocation justified by commercial impracticability, he or she has a choice of cancelling the contract or keeping it in effect. To cancel, the buyer can either notify the seller or merely remain silent. However, if the seller's inability relates only to a particular delivery in an installment contract, the buyer can cancel the contract only if the value of the *whole contract* is substantially impaired. If the buyer has a right to cancel but wishes to keep the contract alive, he or she must give written notice to the seller indicating agreement to the delay or allocation. This notice by the buyer actually amounts to a modification of the contract and must be made within a reasonable time, not exceeding 30 days.

The following case applies the rules of 2-615.[2]

---

[2](Note that the doctrine of commercial impracticability, along with the related common-law concepts of impossibility and frustration of purpose, were discussed in detail in Chapter 18. It may be helpful to reread *Northern Indiana Public Service Co. v. Carbon County Coal Co.* in that chapter.)

WALDINGER CORPORATION V. CRS GROUP ENGINEERS, INC.

U.S. Seventh Circuit Court of Appeals, 775 F.2d 781 (1985)

 A city sanitation district hired Dietz as engineer to prepare specifications for two wastewater treatment facilities required by the EPA. The specifications for required belt-filter presses included both performance capabilities and mechanical components. Waldinger Corporation, a mechanical contractor preparing to bid on the mechanical portions, received a quotation for the belt presses from Ashbrook. Waldinger then bid successfully on the project. Ashbrook, however, was unable to supply the equipment described in the specifications set forth in its contract with Waldinger. Waldinger obtained the equipment from the Ralph B. Carter Company and sued Ashbrook for breach of contract.

In defense, Ashbrook claimed impracticability of performance because of Dietz's intentional or negligent drafting of restrictive specifications. The trial judge found that Dietz had intentionally prepared exclusionary specifications that could be met only by equipment made by Carter, and insisted without justification that Ashbrook comply with them. Thus, he held that Ashbrook was excused from performing its contract with Waldinger because performance was impracticable. Waldinger appealed.

Wood, Circuit Judge:

Assuming the seller has not assumed a greater obligation under the agreement, three conditions must be satisfied before performance is excused [under 2-615]: (1) a contingency has occurred; (2) the contingency has made performance impracticable; and (3) the nonoccurrence of that contingency was a basic assumption upon which the contract was made. The rationale for the defense of commercial impracticability is that the circumstance causing the breach has rendered performance "so vitally different from what was anticipated that the contract cannot be reasonably thought to govern." *Eastern Air Lines, Inc. v. McDonnell Douglas Corp.*, 532 F.2d 957, 991 (5th Cir. 1976). Because the purpose of a contract is to place the reasonable risk of performance upon the promisor, however, it is presumed to have agreed to bear any loss occasioned by an event that was foreseeable at the time of contracting.

The applicability of the defense of commercial impracticability, then, turns largely on foreseeability. The relevant inquiry is whether the risk of the occurrence of the contingency was so unusual or unforeseen and the consequences of the occurrence of the contingency so severe that to require performance is to grant the buyer an advantage he did not bargain for in the contract. If the risk of the occurrence was unforeseeable, the seller cannot be said to have assumed that risk. If the risk of the contingency was foreseeable, that risk is tacitly assigned to the seller. The seller's failure to provide a contractual excuse against the occurrence of a foreseeable contingency may be deemed to be an assumption of an unconditional obligation to perform. Phrased somewhat differently, if a contingency is foreseeable, the section 2-615 defense is unavailable because the party disadvantaged by the fruition of the contingency might have contractually protected itself.

This analysis assumes, of course, that the parties have not restricted the excusing contingencies or eliminated the protection of section 2-615 by imposing upon the seller an absolute contractual duty to deliver. If a particular contingency is contemplated and the risk of its occurrence specifically assigned to the seller, foreseeability is not an issue. The parties will be held to their bargain.

There is, Ashbrook contends, an "irreconcilable conflict" between the language of [the contract] which required it to provide equipment in "strict accordance" with the specifications [which were interpreted by Dietz to be met only by Carter equipment] and the EPA regulations [specifically incorporated in all sub-agreements on EPA projects] prohibiting specifications drawn to only one manufacturer.

Given the EPA regulations prohibiting exclusionary specifications upon which Ashbrook could rightly rely, Ashbrook could not have foreseen the possibility that Dietz would require it to build a Carter machine even if its machine met the performance specifications. The section 2-615 defense is therefore available to Ashbrook if performance was rendered commercially impracticable by Dietz's insistence upon compliance with the exclusionary specifications.

Under the contract documents, Ashbrook was required to guarantee performance. This, the evidence shows, it could not do if required to build its filter press according to Dietz's mechanical specifications [because (1) no Carter machine of this type was in operation, and (2) Dietz had done no independent study to determine if the Carter machine could perform as promised]. We conclude that Ashbrook's inability to supply a filter press that would both satisfy Dietz's mechanical specifications and perform as required is sufficient to establish that performance of its contract with Waldinger was commercially impracticable.

[Affirmed.]

Buyer's Obligations

When the seller has made a sufficient tender of delivery, the burden then falls on the buyer to perform his or her part of the contract.

Providing Facilities

Unless otherwise agreed, the buyer must furnish facilities that are reasonably suited for receipt of the goods.

Right of Inspection

Inspection of the goods by the buyer is a matter depending entirely upon the terms of the agreement. But if the parties have not limited inspection by their agreement, the buyer has a right to inspect the goods before accepting or paying for them—at any reasonable place and time and in any reasonable manner. When the goods are shipped to the buyer, inspection can occur after their arrival. Expenses of inspection must be borne by the buyer but can be recovered from the seller if the goods do not conform and are rejected.

Sometimes the parties' agreement obligates the buyer to make payment before inspecting the goods. For example, when a contract calls for COD ("collect on delivery"), there is no right of inspection before payment unless other terms of the contract expressly grant such a right. Contracts can also require "payment against documents," which means that, unless otherwise agreed, payment is due on receipt of the required documents of title regardless of when the goods themselves actually arrive. CIF and C & F contracts, for example, require payment on receipt of documents unless the parties have agreed to the contrary. Where a contract calls for payment before inspection, payment must be made unless the goods are so obviously nonconforming that inspection is not needed.

When payment is required before inspection, it does not constitute a final acceptance of the goods. Rejection of the goods can still occur if the buyer inspects after the required payment and finds that they are nonconforming.

Acceptance

When conforming goods have been properly tendered, the buyer's basic duty is to accept them, which means simply that the buyer takes the goods as his or her own. This **acceptance** can occur in three different ways:

1. The buyer can expressly indicate acceptance by words. For example, there is an acceptance if the buyer, after having had a reasonable opportunity to inspect, signifies to the seller either that the goods are conforming or that he or she will take them despite their nonconformity.

2. Acceptance also occurs if the buyer has had a reasonable opportunity to inspect the goods and has failed to reject them within a reasonable period of time.

3. The buyer accepts the goods by performing any act inconsistent with the seller's ownership. For example, using, consuming, or reselling the goods usually constitutes an acceptance. However, reasonable use or consumption for the sole purpose of testing is not an acceptance.

Partial Acceptance

If part of the goods are conforming and part are nonconforming, the buyer can make a partial acceptance; he or she cannot, however, accept less than a commercial unit. A *commercial unit* is defined in Sec. 2-105 as a unit of goods recognized in commercial practice as being a "single whole" for purposes of sale, the division of which materially impairs its value. It can be a single article (such as a machine), a set of articles (such as a suite of furniture or an assortment of suits in different sizes), a quantity (such as a bale, gross, or carload), or any other unit treated in use or in the relevant market as a single whole.

Payment

Seller and buyer can agree upon credit arrangements or agree that payment is due when the buyer receives a document of title, regardless of when the goods arrive. But if the parties do not expressly agree on a time for payment, *it is due when the buyer receives the goods.*

While the price is ordinarily payable in money, the parties can agree that some other medium of exchange (such as other commodities) will be used. In addition, the buyer can use any method of making payment that is generally acceptable in the commercial world (such as a check). But the seller can demand payment in *legal tender* (currency) if he or she desires. A seller who makes such a demand must allow the buyer a reasonable amount of time to obtain legal tender. If the buyer pays by check and the check is accepted by the seller, the buyer has performed the obligation of payment unless the check is dishonored (bounced) by the bank.

Some buyers pay with a *letter of credit* (used primarily in foreign commerce). The buyer obtains the letter of credit from his or her own bank, and the bank guarantees to the seller that payment will be made when the proper documents are tendered.

INTRODUCTION TO REMEDIES

Thus far we have focused our discussion on the performance of the sale contract by both parties. But suppose the contract is instead breached by one of the parties. What avenues are open to the other party?

Options in the Event of Anticipatory Repudiation

A breach of contract can occur at any stage in the transaction after the contract is made, even before the time for performance falls due. If, before time for performance, one party clearly communicates to the other the intention not to perform, that party has breached the contract by an **anticipatory repudiation.** In such an event, Sec. 2-610 provides that the "aggrieved party"—the party receiving the repudiation—has two options. First, the party may wait a reasonable length of time before resorting to any remedies, in the hope that the repudiating party will change his or her mind. In the alternative, the aggrieved party may treat the contract as having been breached, and immediately pursue the appropriate remedies. (And, in either case, the aggrieved party may suspend his or her performance.)

Sometimes there is not a clear-cut repudiation but the circumstances are such that one party has reasonable doubts about whether the other is going to perform. In such a case the party who has a reasonable basis for feeling insecure can demand in writing that the other party give *assurance of performance.* Adequate assurance of performance must then be given within a reasonable time (not exceeding thirty days) after receipt of the demand. Failure to give this assurance in response to a justified demand constitutes an anticipatory repudiation.

SELLER'S REMEDIES

The seller's remedies are set forth in Secs. 2-703 to 710 of the UCC. Under these sections, the remedies

that are available to a seller in a particular situation depend on the circumstances existing at the time of the buyer's breach.

Where Buyer Breaches before Receiving the Goods

Following are the remedies for the seller where the buyer has repudiated or otherwise breached the contract before receiving the goods:

1. The seller can cancel the contract.

2. If the goods are in the seller's possession or control but have not yet been identified, he or she can take the steps necessary to identify them (separate them from inventory, tag or label them, and so on). If they are in an unfinished condition, the seller can complete their manufacture if it is reasonable to do so for the purpose of minimizing the loss—or cease manufacture and resell for scrap or salvage value.

3. The seller can *withhold delivery* of goods still in his or her hands, and in some cases even *stop delivery* where the goods have been shipped but have not yet been received by the buyer. Because of the burden to the carrier, seller can stop delivery only if a carload, truckload, planeload, or larger shipment is involved. (The only exception to this quantity requirement is where delivery is stopped because of the buyer's insolvency. In such a case, delivery can be stopped regardless of the quantity of goods involved.) Also, if the carrier has issued a *negotiable bill of lading* (see Chapter 20), the seller can stop delivery only by surrendering the document to the carrier. Thus stoppage in transit cannot occur if the seller has already sent a negotiable bill of lading to the buyer.

4. The seller can *resell* the goods in a commercially reasonable manner at either a private or public (auction) sale. If the resale is *private*, the buyer must be given prior notice of it; if it is *public*, the buyer must be given prior notice unless the goods are perishable or otherwise threaten to rapidly decline in value. A purchaser who buys in good faith at a resale takes the goods free of any rights of the original buyer even if the seller has not conducted the resale in a commercially reasonable manner. When the seller has resold the goods in a proper manner, the damages to which he or she is entitled include the amount by which the contract price exceeds the resale price plus incidental damages such as additional

transportation and handling expenses.[3] Any expenses saved because of the buyer's breach are deducted from the seller's damages.

If the seller *does not resell,* the damages are computed in either of two ways, according to Sec. 2-708. The first measure is the amount by which the contract price exceeds the market price at the time and place for tender (rather than the actual resale price), plus incidental damages, minus expenses saved. If the first measure is inadequate to put the seller in as good a position as buyer's performance would have done, then a second measure is used, which is the profit the seller would have made had the contract been performed, plus incidental damages, minus expenses saved.

5. Under some circumstances the seller can sue to recover the *purchase price* from the buyer, even though the buyer did not receive the goods. This can occur, for example, where (a) the buyer legally accepted the goods while they were still in the seller's possession; (b) the seller shipped conforming goods that were lost or destroyed after risk of loss had passed to the buyer; or (c) the seller made reasonable but unsuccessful efforts to resell the goods at a reasonable price. If the seller receives a court judgment against the buyer for the purchase price, and then, because of changed conditions, is able to resell the goods before the buyer pays the judgment, the pro-

ceeds of the sale must be credited to the buyer. Payment of the judgment entitles the buyer to any of the goods not resold.

Where Buyer Breaches after Receiving the Goods

The seller's remedies where buyer's breach occurs after he or she receives the goods are:

1. If the buyer accepts the goods and does not pay for them, the seller can recover the purchase price plus any incidental damages resulting from the breach.

2. If the buyer wrongfully rejects or revokes acceptance and does not pay, the seller's remedies depend on *whether he or she retakes possession* of the goods. If possession is retaken, the remedies are basically the same as if the buyer had breached *before* receiving the goods. In addition to cancelling the contract, the seller can resell the goods, keep them and recover damages, or recover the purchase price plus incidental damages if resale is impossible. If the seller does not retake possession, the remedies are the same as if the buyer had accepted the goods. In other words, the seller can recover the purchase price plus incidental damages.

The issue raised in the following case, where the buyer breached the contract while the goods were still in the seller's hands, is typical of those which necessitate interpretation of the code sections applicable to sellers' (and buyers') remedies.

LUPROFRESH, INC. V. PABST BREWING COMPANY

Superior Court of Delaware, New Castle County, 505 A.2d 37 (1985)

Luprofresh, Inc., plaintiff, contracted to sell a quantity of hops to Pabst Brewing Company at a specified price. Luprofresh, after processing and storing the hops, notified Pabst that the hops were ready for delivery. Pabst replied with a letter saying it "accepted" the goods, but thereafter breached the contract by refusing to issue shipping orders. Luprofresh then brought this action

to recover the purchase price of the hops from Pabst, defendant.

Defendant, in its pleadings, raised two defenses: (1) a claim that plaintiff's pricing policies (upon which the contract price was based) violated the federal antitrust laws, and (2) the contention that, under Article 2 of the UCC, plaintiff was entitled to recover the purchase price only after making a reasonable effort to resell the goods, and that plaintiff's pleadings did not allege such an effort was made.

The court ruled against defendant on both points. Accordingly, it entered a summary judgment (judgment on the pleadings) for plaintiff in the amount of the contract price. (Only that part of the trial court's decision relating to the UCC issue appears below.)

Taylor, Judge:

. . . [Plaintiff] contends that it is entitled to the full purchase price under

(continues)

LUPROFRESH, INC. V. PABST BREWING COMPANY

(continued from previous page) the contract. Defendant contends that under [Section 2-709 of the UCC] the plaintiff cannot recover the contract price until it proves reasonable effort to resell the goods at a reasonable price, or that such effort would be unavailing.

UCC §2-709 permits the seller to recover the purchase price of goods which have been accepted by the buyer. Plaintiff contends that the hops were accepted by defendant, [pointing to] defendant's letter to plaintiff which states, "we have accepted the following lots (nos. and quantity specified)." A subsequent letter to Luprofresh requests "confirmation of the quantity of hops inventories owned by us and stored on your premises as of December 31, 1984."

UCC §2-606 provides that goods are accepted by the buyer when (1) after reasonable opportunity to inspect the goods, the buyer signifies to the seller that the goods are conforming, or (2) after such opportunity the buyer fails to reject the goods, or (3) the buyer does any act inconsistent with the seller's ownership. The letters from plaintiff referred to above are evidence of identification of specific goods and

acceptance satisfying §2-606. Defendant has presented no [evidence] disputing this.

Defendant contends that any recovery by the seller is subject to the restriction that the seller must have made reasonable effort to resell the goods at a reasonable price. This contention is not supported by the language of §2-709, because it fails to differentiate between the Code provisions applicable to "goods accepted" and "goods identified." §2-709(1)(a) gives an unqualified right to the seller of "goods accepted" to recover the price. §2-709(1)(b) gives a conditional right to the seller to recover the price "if the seller is unable after reasonable effort to resell them at a reasonable price or the circumstances reasonably indicate that such effort will be unavailing." "Goods accepted" are specific goods which have been inspected by the buyer, or at least the buyer must have been afforded reasonable opportunity for such inspection. Hence, all "goods accepted" are "goods identified."

It is noted that subsection (2) [of §2-709] imposes the prerequisite to recovery of the purchase price that the seller "must hold for the buyer any goods which have been identified to

the contract and are still in his control." That section does permit the seller to resell the goods, but since it uses the words "he may resell them at any time prior to collection of the judgment" *it does not mandate resale.* [Emphasis added.]

The status of "goods identified" is achieved by the unilateral action of the seller. The status of "goods accepted" requires that the buyer must have accepted the goods after inspection or waived his right of inspection . . . by inaction, in addition to the seller's action in identifying the goods. The draftsmen of §2-709 contemplated a different standard of recovery for the seller of "goods accepted" from that provided for the seller of "goods identified" [but not accepted]. The apparent objective of §2-709(1)(a) *was to afford a more direct remedy against the buyer who had "accepted" goods than it afforded against the buyer who has not "accepted" goods.* [Emphasis added.]

Based on the foregoing considerations, I find nothing in the portions of the UCC which have been cited which prevents plaintiff from recovering the purchase price. . . .

Judgment for plaintiff. ⚖

BUYER'S REMEDIES

The buyer's remedies are set forth in Secs. 2-711 to 2-718 of the UCC.

Where Seller Fails to Deliver
When the seller breaches the contract by failing to deliver the goods according to the contract, the following remedies are available to the buyer:

1. The buyer can cancel the contract, which relieves him or her of any contractual obligations.

2. The buyer can recover any prepayments made to the seller.

3. The buyer can **cover** (buy the goods elsewhere in a commercially reasonable manner) and receive damages. The damages include (a) the amount by which the cover price exceeds the contract price; (b) any incidental expenses—out-of-pocket costs such as additional transportation and handling expenses; and (c) any consequential losses, such as the buyer's lost profits, that should have been foreseen by the seller as resulting from the breach. Deducted from the buyer's damages, however, are any expenses saved because of the seller's breach. If the buyer does not wish to cover or covers improperly, he or she can receive the amount by which the market price exceeds the contract price, plus any incidental and

consequential damages, minus any expenses saved. The market price is determined as of the time when the buyer learned of the breach and as of the place where delivery should have been tendered.

4. In most cases the buyer will be unable to recover the goods themselves from the seller and will have to be content with money damages. In certain circumstances, however, the buyer can obtain a court decree entitling him or her to possession of the particular goods contracted for. If the goods are *unique* (such as an heirloom) or in other proper circumstances, the buyer can recover them by obtaining a decree of *specific performance* (an order commanding the seller to live up to the agreement). Even if the goods are not unique, the buyer can recover them (a) where they have been specifically identified and (b) where the buyer has made reasonable but unsuccessful efforts to cover or where the circumstances reasonably indicate that such efforts would be fruitless (such as where the goods are in very short supply). The technical name for the buyer's recovery of goods in this type of situation is *replevin.*

Where Seller Delivers Nonconforming Goods

If the seller delivers goods that are defective or in some other way do not conform to the contract, the buyer must notify the seller within a reasonable time after discovering the nonconformity in order to be able to pursue available remedies. The buyer's remedies in this situation are:

1. The buyer can cancel the contract.

2. The buyer can recover any prepayments made to the seller.

3. The buyer can *reject* the delivery. Under the perfect tender rule, the buyer can usually reject if the tender or the goods fail in any respect to conform to the contract. Where the defects are of a type that can be discovered by reasonable inspection, sometimes the buyer can reject only by specifying them in the notice to the seller. This duty to specify defects exists (a) where they can be cured if the seller learns of them promptly or (b) where the specification is requested by one merchant from another merchant.

4. If the buyer has already accepted delivery, however, he or she cannot thereafter reject it. Of course, acceptance is more than just receiving the goods; it means taking them as one's own. However,

in a few circumstances the buyer can *revoke his or her acceptance.*

a. An acceptance can be revoked only if the nonconformity *substantially impairs the value* to the buyer of the delivery or commercial unit in question. For example, a cracked engine block substantially impairs the value of a car, while a malfunctioning clock in the dashboard does not.

b. Where the buyer *knew* of the nonconformity when accepting, he or she can revoke the acceptance only if it was made on the reasonable assumption that the nonconformity would be cured, but it has not been. On the other hand, where the buyer *did not know* of the nonconformity when accepting, he or she can revoke (1) if the acceptance had been made because of the difficulty of discovering the nonconformity at an earlier time or (2) because of the seller's assurances that there were no defects.

c. Revocation of acceptance must occur within a reasonable time after the buyer discovers the basis for it and before any substantial change occurs in the condition of the goods (other than by their own defects).

5. The effect of a rejection or a revocation of acceptance is the same: the goods are not the buyer's and he or she does not have to pay for them. After a justified rejection or revocation the seller usually makes arrangements to take back the goods. The buyer must return the goods on request if the seller refunds any payments made on the price and reimburses the buyer for reasonable expenses incurred in inspecting, receiving, transporting, and caring for them. While in possession of the goods the buyer has certain rights and duties with respect to them:

a. The first duty is to follow all reasonable instructions given by the seller regarding the goods. A seller's instructions are unreasonable if he or she does not guarantee payment of expenses after the buyer has demanded it.

b. If the seller does not pick up the goods or give instructions as to their handling within a reasonable time, the buyer has three alternatives—storing the goods for the seller's account, reshipping them to the seller, or reselling them for the seller's account. (In unusual situations the buyer is actually under a *duty to try to resell the goods* for the seller when reasonable instructions are not given. This duty arises if the buyer is a merchant, the seller has no agent or place of business in the buyer's locality, and the goods are perishable or otherwise threaten to rapidly decline in value.) The buyer has a right to recover reasonable expenses in handling the goods in these situations, just as when following the seller's instructions. One note of caution: a buyer who resells goods without being entitled to do so has legally accepted them.

6. The buyer can cover if he or she wishes, and damages will be computed in the same manner as when the seller breaches by failing to deliver.

7. Finally, the buyer can *accept and keep the goods* despite their nonconformity and still recover all damages caused by the nonconformity. This is frequently the situation in *breach of warranty* cases where the product has already been used or con-

sumed when the defect is discovered. The buyer's damages in such cases are the difference between the actual value of the goods and the value they would have had if they had conformed to the warranty, plus incidental and consequential damages. Consequential damages in a breach of warranty case include bodily injury and property damage caused by the breach and often constitute the largest portion of the buyer's damages. If the goods are not yet paid for, the purchase price is offset against the damages.

Both of the following cases have to do with buyers' remedies. In the first of these, the question is whether the buyer had the right to revoke her acceptance of the goods. The second case illustrates application of the rule that a plaintiff is allowed to recover those damages which are the reasonably direct and foreseeable consequence of the defendant's breach of contract.

ALPERT V. THOMAS

U.S. District Court, District of Vermont, 643 F.Supp. 1406 (1986)

On March 15, 1984, defendant Thomas purchased from plaintiffs Alpert and Wolfman a Russian-Arabian stallion named Raxx. Plaintiffs knew that defendant was buying Raxx for breeding purposes and their agent, Mallory, expressly warranted Raxx's suitability for this purpose and promised to obtain the breeding soundness evaluation that is customary in the industry before sale occurred. Mallory did not procure such an evaluation, though a veterinarian's bill presented to Thomas when Raxx was delivered in May led her to believe that he had. During June and July, and again in September there were several attempts to breed Raxx, but none resulted in a pregnancy. Veterinarians who examined Raxx found that his breeding capability was questionable because of a "low number of morphologically normal, progressively motile sperm."

As late as November 1984, plaintiffs' agents were promising that they would "make things right" for defendant and were still warranting Raxx's breeding abilities. Further examinations in March 1985 again led to the conclusion that Raxx was an unsatisfactory candidate for breeding. On March 26, 1985, defendant sent a letter to plaintiffs revoking the entire contract. At that time, she had paid $94,879.28 of the $175,000 purchase price.

Plaintiffs sued for the balance of the purchase price. Defendant counterclaimed for rescission of the contract or, in the alternative, damages arising from breach of warranty. Following a trial, the judge entered the following opinion.

Billings, District Judge:
[The judge first found that the plaintiffs had made and breached express warranties about Raxx's breeding abili-

ties and that an implied warranty of merchantability arose and was also breached.]

As a result of Raxx's non-conformity to the express and implied warranties that he would be breeding sound, Thomas claims that she revoked her acceptance of Raxx. A buyer's revocation of acceptance of goods must satisfy the provisions of Sec. 2-608. [The judge then quoted the section.]

There are four elements to proper revocation under Sec. 2-608: (1) the goods' non-conformity with the contract substantially impairs the value to the buyer; (2) the buyer's acceptance was (a) forthcoming on the reasonable assumption that the non-conformity would be cured (discovery at the time of acceptance) or (b) reasonably induced by the difficulty of the discovery or by the seller's assurances (no discovery at the time of acceptance); (3) revocation occurred within a reasonable time after the nonconformity was discovered or should have been

(continues)

ALPERT V. THOMAS

(*continued from previous page*)
discovered; and (4) revocation took place before a substantial change occurred in the condition of the goods not caused by their own defects. *White and Summers,* [Uniform Commercial Code] Sec. 8-3, at 303.

As to the first element, Raxx's status as an unsatisfactory prospective breeder rendered him in non-conformity with the purchase and sale agreement's express and implied warranties that he would be merchantable as a breeder. Because Thomas was purchasing Raxx for breeding purposes, this non-conformity substantially impaired his value to her.

The second element of proper revocation under Sec. 2-608 is also satisfied because Thomas was induced to accept Raxx without discovering his non-conformity as a result of Mallory's assurances that [plaintiffs] would perform the breeding soundness evaluation and that Raxx was guaranteed to be breeding sound.

Thomas satisfied the third element of proper revocation in that she formally revoked within a reasonable time after Raxx's non-conformity was discovered or should have been discovered. Among the facts relevant to this finding are: plaintiffs' assurances that they would perform a breeding soundness test rendered the timing of Thomas's discovery of Raxx's infertility reasonable; Thomas promptly notified plaintiffs that Raxx's breedability had become suspect; Thomas or Hultgreen [manager of the farm where Raxx was kept] attempted several times to discuss the problem with plaintiffs and Mallory repeatedly replied that plaintiffs would "make it right"; and [two of the veterinarians who examined Raxx recommended in the Fall of 1984] that Thomas should wait a few months and see if Raxx's problem would correct itself.

As to the final element of revocation, there was no substantial damage in Raxx's condition not caused by his inability to breed.

Judgment shall be entered for defendant on plaintiff's complaint; judgment shall be entered for defendant Thomas on her counterclaim. The attempted sale of Raxx shall be rescinded and declared null and void. Plaintiff will return to Thomas $94,879.29, representing the purchase price already paid for Raxx plus . . . $25,560.00 representing expenses, reasonably incurred in transportation, care, custody and insurance of Raxx from date of delivery to the present. ⚖

CRICKET ALLEY CORPORATION V. DATA TERMINAL SYSTEMS, INC.

Supreme Court of Kansas, 732 P.2d 719 (1987)

Desiring to modernize Cricket Alley's operations as a retail clothing store, its president contacted Data Terminal Systems (DTS) about buying a cash register system compatible with the Wang computer which Cricket Alley already owned. Through advertisements and statements of its employees, DTS seemed to warrant that its cash register system would work with the Wang computer. However, when installed, the system never worked. While DTS tried to remedy the problems, Cricket Alley's old cash registers began to break down. Replacement parts were unavailable. Finally,

DTS's equipment was left in place to perform basic cash register functions, but it never did mesh with the Wang. Cricket Alley sued for breach of warranty.

A jury found that a warranty had been made and breached by DTS. It awarded Cricket Alley consequential and incidental damages in the form of additional labor costs incurred due to the absence of a working cash register system. DTS appealed.

McFarland, Justice:

[The court first quoted both the general damages provision of 2-714 and 2-715's provision for incidental and consequential damages.]

The consequential damages consist of increased labor costs attributable to the failure of the DTS cash registers to communicate with the Wang computer. DTS contends that it did not know the general or particular requirements and needs of plaintiff's business at the time the express warranties were made and, hence, has no liability under 2-715(2)(a) for consequential damages.

Official UCC Comment No. 3 to 2-715 provides, in pertinent part:

. . . the seller is liable for consequential damages in all cases where he had reason to know of the buyer's general or particular requirements at the time of contracting. It is not necessary that there be a conscious acceptance of an insurer's liability on the seller's part, nor is his obligation for consequential damages

(continues)

CRICKET ALLEY CORPORATION V. DATA TERMINAL SYSTEMS, INC.

(continued from previous page)
limited to cases in which he fails to use due effort in good faith.

Particular needs of the buyer must generally be made known to the seller while general needs must rarely be made known to charge the seller with knowledge.

DTS concedes that 2-715(2)(a) is "simply a codification" of the old tests contained in *Hadley v. Baxendale,* 156 Eng.Rep. 145 (1854).

Computerized cash registers are manufactured for use in retail business establishments. . . . The submission of data from the cash registers to the mainline computer on sales, payrolls, inventory, etc., is a common feature of such equipment and the failure of the cash registers to do so would foreseeably create additional labor costs for the afflicted retail merchants. The additional labor costs sought by plaintiff, herein, as consequential damages are not attributable to any unique features of plaintiff's business. We conclude that consequential damages as an element of plaintiff's damages were properly submitted to the jury.

Defendant contends that the damages evidence was speculative and not based upon reasonable certainty. . . . 2-715, Official Comment No. 4, states "the section on liberal administration of remedies rejects any doctrine of certainty which requires almost mathematical precision in the proof of loss. Loss may be determined in any manner which is reasonable under the circumstances."

Evidence submitted to the jury on damages included employee payroll spread sheets that indicated not only dollar expenses but the percentage of time each employee performed manual tasks which would have been unnecessary had the DTS equipment performed satisfactorily the functions needed by plaintiff and warranted by defendant. Testimony was admitted which supported the functions performed and time involved to accomplish them. . . . [W]e conclude the damage award [of $78,781.79] is adequately supported by the evidence.

[Affirmed.] ⚖️

Insolvency

The insolvency of one party may affect the other's remedies. Suppose, for example, that the buyer has prepaid the purchase price and seller becomes insolvent before shipping the goods. If the goods have been identified to the contract, the buyer can compel the seller to turn them over to him or her in certain circumstances. (Sec. 2-502).

If the buyer becomes insolvent during the course of a transaction, under Sec. 2-702 the seller can refuse to deliver except for cash. Also—as noted earlier—if the goods have been shipped and are still in transit, the seller can usually stop delivery unless he or she has already forwarded a negotiable document of title to the buyer.

There are times, however, when the UCC, which is state law, will not prevail. A seller or buyer who becomes insolvent will often go into bankruptcy, a proceeding governed by federal law. Since the federal bankruptcy law prevails over state laws, the remedies granted in the UCC may have little practical significance in cases of insolvency.

Prior Agreement as to Remedies

The parties to a sale contract can provide in their agreement for remedies to be available in the event of breach. Under Sec. 2-718, they can agree on liquidated damages (the measure of damages to be payable in case of breach). Their provision must be reasonable, taking into account the anticipated or actual harm caused by the breach, the difficulties of proof of loss, and the inconvenience of otherwise obtaining an adequate remedy. If the contract sets an unreasonably large amount of liquidated damages, the amount will simply be ignored by the court.

More generally, Sec. 2-719 states that "the agreement may provide for remedies in addition to or in substitution for" those provided in the UCC. For example, the parties might agree that the buyer's only remedy for breach of warranty will be to bring the goods back to the seller for repairs. However, Sec. 2-719 also provides that if the clause limiting remedies "fails of its essential purpose," it will be ignored by a court and the remedies normally available under the UCC will apply. A remedy limitation "fails of its essential purpose" if circumstances cause the limitation to substantially deprive one party of the value of his or her bargain. Thus, in the example above, if the seller does not repair the defective item within a reasonable period of time, the limitation clause will be ineffective and the buyer can resort to whatever remedies the UCC gives him in the circumstances.

International

Legal Focus

The United Nations Convention on Contracts for the International Sale of Goods (CISG) includes provisions specifying the performance obligations of the seller and buyer that are identical in almost every way to those of our UCC. The parties can, of course, modify these obligations by their agreement just as they can under the UCC. There is one major difference between the seller's performance obligations under the CISG and the UCC, however. Under the CISG there is no "perfect tender rule." Under the UCC, when the parties have not agreed otherwise, the general rule is that the buyer has a right to reject the goods within a reasonable time if they do not conform perfectly to the contract and any accompanying remedies.

Under the CISG, however, the buyer has the right to reject the goods only if their nonconformity constitutes a "fundamental breach" of contract by the seller. If the goods' failure to conform to contract specifications or applicable warranties does not constitute a fundamental breach, the buyer must accept the goods; the buyer then has a claim against the seller for any monetary damage caused by the nonconformity.

Article 25 of the CISG defines a fundamental breach, which gives the buyer a right to reject the goods in addition to pursuing any claim for damages caused by nonconformity, in the following way:

A breach of contract committed by one of the parties is fundamental if it results in such detriment to the other party as substantially to deprive him of what he is entitled to expect under the contract, unless the party in breach did not foresee and a reasonable person of the same kind in the same circumstances would not have foreseen such a result.

Although Article 25 of the CISG leaves much room for interpretation, one thing is quite clear: the goods' nonconformity with contract specifications or applicable warranties must be substantial to be a fundamental breach.

Furthermore, a limitation of remedies will be ignored by a court if it is so unfair and represents such a gross abuse of bargaining power that it is deemed *unconscionable*. Section 2-719 provides that, in a sale of *consumer goods*, a clause which limits the availability of damages for *bodily injury* is *presumed* to be unconscionable. Even though a remedy limitation clause is different from a warranty disclaimer (as explained in Chapter 22), such a clause in a consumer transaction must comply with the Magnuson-Moss Warranty Act when applicable.

LEMON LAWS

The purchase of a new car is often part of the American dream. When the new car has repeated and serious problems, however, the dream can turn into a nightmare. Today, purchasers of such disappointing cars often obtain relief under special statutes applicable to motor vehicles known as **lemon laws.** At least 43 states have passed such laws, which represent a legislative judgment that the UCC remedies of rejection, revocation, and breach of warranty do not adequately protect the new car buyer. These laws impose a higher standard of quality and workmanship on the automobile manufacturer than does the UCC. While these laws vary in detail from state to state, in general they provide that (1) if a car under warranty possesses a defect which significantly affects its value or use, and (2) if the dealer is unable to fix the defect in four tries, the owner is entitled to a new car, a "buyback" (an order requiring the manufacturer to refund the purchase price minus a per-mile depreciation charge), recovery of repair costs, or free replacement parts, depending upon the circumstances of the case.

Most lemon laws require that before the buyer is entitled to a buy-back, recovery of repair costs, or some other relief, he or she must go before an "appeal jury" which makes findings of fact relative to the buyer's claim, that is, as to the severity of the defects, and as to the extent of the dealer's correction of the defects. Arbitration is free to the buyer, and usually produces a decision within 40 to 60 days. (Among the major manufacturers, General Motors, American Motors, Honda, Nissan, Volkswagen, and Volvo have designated over 150 Better Business Bureaus to handle their disputes. Ford and Chrysler sponsor their own national mediation programs—Ford's panels are called Consumer Appeals Boards, and Chrysler's are Customer Satisfaction Boards. While mediation boards usually handle only warranty-related disputes, complaints involving out-of-warranty vehicles have sometimes been mediated.)

In general, appeal decisions are binding on the manufacturers but not on the car owners. Thus if a jury orders a buy-back, the manufacturer cannot appeal the decision to the courts, while a jury decision against the buyer is appealable. Although appeal juries have ordered manufacturers either to furnish new cars or make buy-backs in a number of cases, more often they have ordered manufacturers to make refunds of repair costs or to replace defective parts, such as transmissions and engines, with new components. (In a typical year, for example, Better Business Bureaus hear approximately 25,000 cases, but award fewer than 4,000 buy-backs.)

SUMMARY

The basic obligation of the seller is to make a tender of delivery of the goods in conformity with the terms of the contract, and to keep the goods available for a period of time reasonably necessary for the buyer to take possession. If the seller has no responsibility for transporting the goods and they are in the possession of a bailee, the seller must deliver a negotiable document of title to the buyer or obtain the bailee's acknowledgment that the buyer is entitled to possession. If the seller does have responsibility for transporting the goods, under a shipment contract he or she must deliver the goods to a carrier, obtain and deliver any documents necessary for the buyer to take possession of the goods, and notify the buyer of the shipment. Under a destination contract, the seller is required to tender delivery of the goods at their destination.

Although Sec. 2-601 of the UCC adopts the common-law perfect tender rule, this rule is modified by other sections of the UCC. For example, if the seller's performance is deficient, he or she is permitted to "cure" by making a conforming delivery before expiration of the time for performance. (In some situations, cure may even be made after such time.) If, after a sales contract has been entered into, some unanticipated event occurs before the time of performance, the seller may be freed of his or her contractual obligations under the doctrine of commercial impracticability. Under that doctrine a late performance by the seller, or nondelivery in whole or in part, is excused if, because of an unforeseen circumstance, delivery of the goods becomes "commercially impracticable." While the determination of whether a contract has been rendered commercially impracticable is made on a case-by-case basis, in general delivery is impracticable if the unforeseen circumstance makes delivery impossible, or if it so alters the essential nature of the performance that it results in a very marked increase in the cost of performance (with the courts often requiring the seller to show that his or her costs of performance would be doubled or tripled before he or she is freed under this doctrine).

The buyer's basic obligation—to pay for the goods in conformity with the contract—is generally subject to the right of inspection. However, the right of inspection prior to payment is lost if the transaction is a COD one, or contains other terms extinguishing the right. If the buyer breaches the contract before receiving the goods, the *seller's* primary remedies are the right to cancel, to withhold or stop delivery, to resell the goods and recover resulting damages (or, in limited cases, to recover the price). If the buyer breaches after receiving the goods, the seller can recover the price. Also, if the seller reacquires possession, his or her remedies are the same as in the case where the buyer breaches before receiving the goods.

Turning to the *buyer's* remedies, if the seller breaches the contract by failing to deliver, the buyer's primary remedies are the right to cancel, to cover, and to recover damages if the cost of cover exceeds the contract price. If the seller breaches by delivering nonconforming goods, the buyer may cancel, and reject the delivery. And, if the buyer has accepted the goods prior to discovery of the nonconformity, the buyer may revoke his or her acceptance under limited conditions.

KEY TERMS

Tender of delivery
Perfect tender rule
Installment contract
Acceptance
Anticipatory repudiation
Cover
Lemon laws

QUESTIONS AND PROBLEMS

1. Smith purchased a new car. Almost immediately after taking delivery he discovered that the car had a defective transmission, and he promptly took the car back to the dealer. When he told the dealer that he wanted to return the car and cancel the sale, the dealer offered to replace the transmission. Smith refused the dealer's offer of "cure," left the car with the dealer, and made no further payments. The dealer fixed the car, resold it, and sued Smith for damages. Did the dealer prevail? Discuss. (*Zabriskie Chevrolet, Inc. v. Smith*, 240 A.2d 195, 1968.)

2. After Gulf and Sylvan carried on a series of negotiations, they made a contract providing for delivery in three separate lots, to be separately accepted and evidenced by three separate purchase orders sent on the same date. No problems arose in the first two deliveries, but the buyer noticed a minor defect in the third delivery and rejected it, citing the perfect tender rule as his authority. Moreover, he claimed that the seller had breached the entire contract. Is he correct? Explain. (*Gulf Chemical & Metallurgical Corp. v. Sylvan Chemical Corp.*, 12 U.C.C. Rep. Serv. 117, 1973.)

3. A dairy farm contracted with a public school district to supply the latter with half-pints of milk. Between the time of contracting and the time for performance, the price of raw milk rose 23 percent. Other increases in the market price had occurred in the past. The dairy filed suit for a declaratory judgment, asking the court to relieve it from its obligation to deliver the milk under Sec. 2-615. What was the result? Discuss. (*Maple Farms, Inc. v. City School Dist. of the City of Elmira*, 352 N.Y.S.2d 784, 1974.)

4. P advertised his used Triumph automobile for sale in July 1985. D drove the car on two separate occasions and had it inspected by a body shop and a mechanic (who listened to the engine and made a visual inspection). D negotiated the asking price from $2700 down to $2200 and then agreed to buy. The same day that title was signed over and D took possession, he called P and asked for a price adjustment on grounds that the engine was "worn out." P refused. D took the car to a mechanic who said that the car was "run down" and that engine repair work would cost between $1200 and $2000. Three days after the sale, D parked the car in front of P's house with the keys locked inside and placed the certificate of ownership in an envelope in P's mailbox. The car was ultimately towed away by the city. P sued D for $1700 unpaid on the purchase price. Should P recover? (*Herbert v. Harl*, 757 S.W.2d 585, Mo. 1988.)

5. Aubrey's R.V. Center bought a computer system from Tandy to perform certain functions, including most importantly, operating as a point-of-sale recorder of inventory for over 3000 items. Tandy recommended Source Book software, helped Aubrey's procure it, and allegedly stated that it would "stand behind" the software. Because the software never recorded more than 600 items of inventory at once or performed as a point-of-sale recorder, Tandy made several efforts at correction. Unfortunately, they all failed. Almost a year after the system had been purchased, Aubrey's gave up and asked Tandy for rescission of the contract and return of the contract price. Tandy again sought an opportunity to remedy the problems, but soon turned the matter over to its legal department. Does Aubrey's have the right to rescind? (*Aubrey's R.V. Center v. Tandy Corporation*, 731 P.2d 1124, Wash.App. 1987.)

6. In the previous case, evidence showed that Tandy knew that Aubrey's was financing its purchase of the system through a leasing company on a lease-purchase contract. Assuming that Aubrey's *does* have the right to rescind, would Aubrey's also have the right to recover damages in the form of finance charges it incurred in purchasing the system?

7. Great Western Sugar Co. (P) contracted to sell refined beet sugar to Pennant Products (D) in two contracts. The first three-month contract called for purchase of 900,000 lbs. of sugar at $46 per hundred pounds. The second contract covering the next three months was for an additional 500,000 lbs. at $45 per hundred pounds. Both contracts called for periodic shipments to be made in accordance with shipping orders sent by D, and each allowed D to terminate by sending written notice. After receiving and paying for 371,500 lbs. under the first contract, D sent no more shipping orders. Nor did it send a written termination notice. Therefore, P sued for breach of contract. The trial court entered judgment for P. D appealed, arguing (a) that the subject of the contracts was not sufficiently identified for P to recover, and (b) that P had not resold the sugar to mitigate damages and therefore should be barred from recovery. Discuss. (*Great Western Sugar Co. v. Pennant Products, Inc.*, 748 P.2d 1359, Colo.App. 1987.)

8. Under their sale contract seller S was required to deliver goods to buyer B on October 25. On April 30, S called B and demanded more money for the goods. B refused, and S said, "Well, if that's the way you want it." On May 30, B filed suit against S for breach of contract. S contended that B was not entitled to file suit until after the date for performance, October 25. Is S correct? Explain.

9. Plymouth Chemical Co. used propane gas as an essential raw material in producing certain chemicals. It had a long-term supply contract for such gas with Commonwealth Gas Co. A shortage of propane gas occurred, and most suppliers were no longer committing themselves to long-term contracts. Commonwealth breached the contract, and Plymouth sued for specific performance. Commonwealth claimed that Plymouth should be allowed to sue for damages but not for specific performance. Is Commonwealth correct? Explain.

10. After Buyer's breach of contract, Seller resold the goods at a private sale but did not give prior notice of the sale. The resale netted Seller $1000 less than he would have received under the contract with Buyer. Seller sued Buyer for the $1000. Buyer claimed that Seller could not recover the $1000 deficiency because he had not notified Buyer of the sale. Is Buyer correct? Explain.

Development of the Law

Purposes of Commercial Paper

Types of Commercial Paper

Assignee versus Holder in Due Course

Parties to Commercial Paper

T HE TERMS **COMMERCIAL paper** and **negotiable instruments** refer to written promises or orders to pay sums of money, and comprise such instruments as drafts, promissory notes, checks, and certificates of deposit. (The most common of these are notes and checks.) With the advent of "electronic banking" in recent years—such as the widespread use of automated teller machines and experimentation with point-of-sale terminals in retail stores—it has been predicted that someday we will live in an almost checkless society.[1] Because of such developments, the *rate of growth* of check usage has levelled off in recent years. Americans continue to write more than 50 billion checks per year, however, and the checkless society seems far off. Thus the present use of commercial paper in our credit-oriented society is of enormous significance, and will remain so well into the foreseeable future. A knowledge of the basic rules for dealing with this subject therefore continues to be important to the businessperson.

DEVELOPMENT OF THE LAW

Commercial paper has been used for many centuries, probably as early as 1500 B.C according to archaeologists, who tell us that crude promissory notes existed in very early civilizations. By the thirteenth century, merchants in the Middle East were making significant use of both promissory notes and bills of exchange, and by the beginning of the seventeenth century, both kinds of instruments were commonly used in England.

Because the early English courts refused to recognize commercial paper, the merchants created their own methods for enforcing rights arising from the use of these instruments. The rules they developed were enforced by traders at their "fair" or "borough" courts, and together they made up what is known as the *law merchant.*

During the eighteenth and nineteenth centuries these principles were substantially recognized by English and American courts and became part of the common law of both countries. In 1896, the American Bar Association drafted the Uniform Negotiable Instruments Law (NIL), which was soon adopted in all states, codifying our negotiable instruments law.

The Uniform Commercial Code

In 1951, the National Conference of Commissioners on Uniform State Laws and the American Law Institute issued the Uniform Commercial Code (UCC). In all states, Article 3 of the UCC, entitled "Commercial Paper," replaced the old NIL, updating the law to conform to modern practices. The states also adopted Article 4 ("Bank Deposits and Collections"), which must often be consulted regarding problems arising out of the relationship between the drawer of a check and the bank upon which it is written.

Revised Articles 3 and 4

In 1990, major revisions to Article 3 (retitled "Negotiable Instruments") and Article 4 were recommended. As this edition is prepared, almost 30 states have already adopted revised Articles 3 and 4 and it is very likely that the revised versions will soon supplant original Articles 3 and 4 in the large majority of states.[2]

Because (1) the original versions of Articles 3 and 4 remain in effect in many states, and (2) virtually all existing case law is grounded in the earlier versions, our discussion will focus on the pre-1990 Articles 3 and 4. However, major changes wrought by the revised articles will be highlighted. And, whenever a pre-1990 section of Article 3 is cited, we will follow it in brackets with the parallel revised section number, if any. For example, the earlier version of Article 3 defines the term *issue* in UCC Sec. 3-102(1)(a). The revised Article 3 slightly modifies the definition in RUCC 3-105(a). Thus, our discussion would give the definition of *issue* followed by these citations: Sec. 3-102(1)(a) [RUCC 3-105(a)]. Remember, though former and revised versions are likely similar, they probably will not be worded in exactly the same way. As noted, if the revised Article 3 makes a *major* change in the law, that change will be noted separately.

---

[1]More will be said about electronic banking in Chapter 28.

[2]In addition, a new UCC Article 4A, dealing with electronic funds transfers between banks, has been completed and adopted by many states. It will be explored in Chapter 28.

Article 4, to be discussed primarily in Chapter 28, was not as substantially revised in 1990. Major changes will be noted, but we need not give parallel citations as with the more significant changes in Article 3.

PURPOSES OF COMMERCIAL PAPER

During the early part of the Middle Ages, merchants and traders had to carry gold and silver to pay for the goods they purchased at the various international fairs. These precious metals were continually subject to theft or loss through the perils of travel. To minimize dangers of this sort, merchants began to deposit their gold and silver with bankers. When they needed to pay for goods they had purchased, the merchants "drew" on their deposits by giving the seller a written order addressed to the bank, telling it to deliver part of the gold or silver to the seller. These orders, called *bills of exchange*, were *substitutes for money*. Today, checks and the drafts and promissory notes that are payable on demand serve this same purpose.

The second major purpose of commercial paper is to serve as a *credit device*; this came about as a logical extension of its initial use as a money substitute. Soon after bills of exchange became established as substitutes for money, merchants who wished to purchase goods on credit discovered that sellers were sometimes willing to accept bills of exchange that were not payable until a stated time in the future—such as "ninety days after date." If the seller was satisfied as to the commercial reputation of the bill's drawer (the purchaser), the seller would take such an instrument (called a *time bill* or *draft*) and wait until the maturity

date to collect it. In this way, the seller-payee extended credit to the buyer-drawer.

Soon thereafter, ways were devised by which payees could sell these instruments to third parties, usually banks, and receive immediate cash in return. Since the banks would then have to wait for the maturity dates before receiving payment, the payees would have to sell them the paper at a discount—that is, at perhaps 5 to 10 percent less than the face amount. This meant, in effect, that the purchasing banks were charging the sellers interest in advance as compensation for their role in the transaction.

Today, because of the widespread use of time notes and drafts, the credit aspect of commercial paper is as important to the business community as its "substitute for money" aspect.

TYPES OF COMMERCIAL PAPER

There are numerous ways to classify the basic types of commercial paper (negotiable instruments). Of these, the classification specified by Article 3 probably merits top billing.

The UCC Classification

Sec. 3-104 [RUCC 3-104] specifies four types of instruments: drafts, checks, notes, and certificates of deposit.

Drafts

A **draft**, or *bill of exchange*, is an instrument whereby the party creating it (the *drawer*) orders another party (the *drawee*) to pay money to a third party (the

Draft   *A draft is an instrument by which the party creating it, the drawer (Kathi Erley in the example below) orders another party, the drawee (the bank) to pay money to a third party, the payee (Karen Shaw).*

```
$5,000.00                                        January 2        19 XX
         Ninety (90) days after the above date _____ PAY TO THE ORDER OF

                        Karen Shaw

         five thousand and no/100------------------------------------- DOLLARS
                                    WITH EXCHANGE

                   VALUE RECEIVED AND CHARGE TO ACCOUNT OF
         TO   First National Bank of Chicago  ⎫  Kathi Erley
         NO.  02683           Chicago, Illinois ⎭       Kathi Erley

         STOCK FORM 990-8 BANKFORMS, INC.
```

Sales Draft   *A sales draft is a draft or bill of exchange drawn by the seller of goods on the purchaser of those goods and accepted (signed) by the purchaser. The purpose of the transaction is to enable the seller to raise money on the paper before the purchaser's obligation matures under the sales contract.*

```
┌──────────────────────────────────────────────────────────────────────────┐
│         │ Draft                                                            │
│         │ Draft No. 1234                    Date    January 2, 19XX        │
│ ACCEPTED: KMS Imports                                                      │
│ Karen Shaw                                                                 │
│         │ At _____ ***90 Days From Date*** _____          │
│         │ Pay to the Order of _____ ***McNAMARA CORPORATION*** _____       │
│         │ the sum of  Five Thousand and no/100ths ************** Dollars  $5,000.00 │
│         │ Value received and charge to the account of                      │
│         │        ⌠    KMS Imports          The McNamara Corporation       │
│         │  To  ⎨    Hinsdale, Illinois     Joanne McNamara                 │
│         │        ⌡                          Authorized Signature           │
│         │ 1-32-0018 (6/78)                                                 │
└──────────────────────────────────────────────────────────────────────────┘
```

payee). For example, assume that X owes Y $100, and Y owes Z the same amount. Y signs a written order directing X to pay the $100 to Z and gives it to Z. Z presents the instrument to X, who then pays Z. Here, Y is the drawer, X the drawee, and Z the payee.

In order for the draft to work, one of two general conditions must exist. Either (1) the drawee must owe the drawer a debt (in which case the drawer is simply telling the drawee to pay the debt or a portion of it to a third party) or (2) some kind of agreement or relationship must exist between the parties under which the drawee has consented to the drawing of the draft. If neither of these conditions existed, the drawee would not obey the order to pay the amount of the draft to the payee or to any subsequent holder of the instrument.

When a draft is used in connection with a sale of goods, it is called a **sales draft**. A sales draft is a draft drawn by the seller of goods on the purchaser of those goods, which is subsequently accepted (signed) by the purchaser. The purpose of the transaction is to enable the seller to raise money on the paper before the purchaser's obligation matures under the sales contract.

We can illustrate this usage by referring to the specimen sales draft reproduced here. The McNamara Corporation has sold goods to KMS Imports. Because KMS Imports wishes to utilize a negotiable instrument rather than pay cash for the goods immediately, the McNamara Corporation (drawer) draws a draft on KMS Imports for the purchase price of the goods. The instrument orders KMS Imports to pay the stated sum to the order of the McNamara Cor-

poration at a stated time in the future—in this case, 90 days after January 2. (The McNamara Corporation is thus both the drawer and the payee of the instrument.) It is then presented to an officer of KMS Imports—Karen Shaw, in this instance—who accepts it by affixing that company's name to it in the space at the left hand margin. The acceptance, which constitutes a promise by KMS Imports (the drawee-acceptor) to pay the instrument when it become due, is then returned to the McNamara Corporation. It can now negotiate the draft to a third party, usually the McNamara Corporation's bank, and receive cash immediately. Use of the instrument in this manner—by sellers of goods—explains why it is called a *sales* draft. (Other kinds of drafts are also frequently accepted by their drawees; these are discussed in Chapter 27.) Another frequently used draft is the *bank draft*, which is utilized when one bank draws on its funds in another bank.

Checks

A **check** is a particular type of draft. Under Sec. 3-104(2) [RUCC 3-104(f)], it is by definition a "draft drawn on a bank [and] payable on demand." It is thus distinguished from demand drafts drawn on individuals, or on corporations that are not banks. Similarly, it is also distinguished from drafts that are drawn on banks, but that are payable at specific future dates. Checks are by far the most commonly used form of draft. Today, the term *bank* also includes other financial institutions that are legally authorized to receive "demand deposits" and serve as drawees on

Check *A check is the most common type of draft; it is an order (draft or bill of exchange) drawn on a bank and payable on demand.*

KMS IMPORTS		January 2 19 XX	70-681 / 719

PAY TO THE ORDER OF ___Scandinavian Export, Ltd.___ | $ | 5,878.00

___ONLY Five Thousand Eight Hundred Seventy-Eight___ Dollars

BANK OF HINSDALE
Subsidiary of Lake Shore Bancorp
400 E. Ogden Avenue Hinsdale, Illinois 60521

Karen M Shaw

FOR ___Invoice 0899___   BY: _____ DATE: _____

071908814

Source: Courtesy of Bank of Hinsdale, Hinsdale, Illinois.

checks, such as credit unions and savings institutions.

Revised Article 3 specifically indicates that such a draft ("payable on demand and drawn on a bank") "may be a check even if it is described on its face by another term, such as 'money order.'" RUCC 3-104(f).[3] This allows stop-payment orders if a money order is lost or some other problem arises. The status of a money order is unclear under the original Article 3.

One particular form of check is the *cashier's check*, which is drawn by a bank on itself, payable on demand to a payee.[4] Because this check is drawn by the bank ordering itself to pay, the bank must honor the check upon proper presentment. For this reason, in transactions involving the sale of property—where the owner-seller requires some form of guaranteed payment to accompany all offers to purchase—bidders commonly submit cashier's checks along with their bids.

Another type of check specifically defined in the revised Article 3 is a *teller's check*, meaning "a draft drawn by a bank (i) on another bank, or (ii) payable at or through a bank." RUCC 3-104(h). The revised law also defines *certified check* as a check accepted by the bank on which it is drawn. RUCC 3-409(d).

Promissory Note *A promissory note is an instrument by which the maker promises to pay a sum of money to another party (the payee).*

$ ___5,000.00___ , ___2 January___ 19 XX

___Ninety (90) days___ after date ___I___ promise to pay to

the order of ___James J. Walsh___

___Five thousand and no/100___ Dollars

at ___twelve and one-half percent (12.5%) per annum___

Value received.

No. ___083153___ Due ___   *Karen M Shaw*

---

[3]The RUCC thus clarifies that ordinary money orders are to be treated as regular checks rather than as cashier's checks, clarifying a question that had arisen under the earlier Article 3.

[4]A few original Article 3 jurisdictions treat cashier's checks as demand notes

of the bank and the issuing bank as a note maker. Although revised Article 3 labels a cashier's check as a draft, substantively it treats an accepted cashier's check as a demand note.

TAKING THINGS FOR GRANITE

by Joel Schwarz

Box 24.1
The Law
at Work

Joe Mallen of Sequim, Washington, wrote out a 25-pound check to the U.S. District Court in Seattle recently. It didn't bounce.

Mallen was angry after being cited for a leash law violation by the U.S. Fish and Wildlife Service for walking his dog without a leash in a federal refuge for birds. Mallen, who disputed the charge, also hadn't gotten over his irritation with a local bank clerk who had held an out-of-state check made out to Mallen for ten days without cashing it.

To vent his anger at both situations, Mallen spray painted a 25-pound stone from his front yard with three coats of white paint, and with red paint spelled out his account number, the bank's name, the payee, his lease law citation number, and his signature.

The court accepted the stone check and stamped it paid in four places.

Source: *Student Lawyer*, December 1981.

The revised Article 3 also provides that a *traveler's check*, drawn on or payable at or through a bank, may be a negotiable instrument, even if it is conditioned upon presence of a countersignature by a person whose specimen signature appears on the instrument. RUCC 3-104(i).

Notes

A **note** is a promise by one party (the *maker*) to pay a sum of money to another party (the *payee*). Notes differ from drafts in two primary respects. They always contain *promises* to pay money (as distinguished from orders), and they have two parties—maker and payee—rather than three.

Because notes are used in a variety of transactions, they come in many different forms. For example, a note used in a real estate transaction secured by a mortgage on the property being purchased is a *real estate mortgage note*. A note containing a promise to make payments in specified installments, such as payments for a new car, is an *installment note*. And a note secured by personal property is a *collateral note*. While all of these are *promissory notes* in a general sense, that term when used alone usually refers to the simplest kind of notes—those merely containing promises by one person to pay money to another.

Certificate of Deposit   A certificate of deposit *is an instrument by which a bank acknowledges receipt of money and promises to return it at a later date or on demand. Certificates of deposit may be negotiable or nonnegotiable, depending upon their term.*

CERTIFICATE OF DEPOSIT NOT SUBJECT TO CHECK	AUTOMATICALLY RENEWABLE	BANK OF HINSDALE Subsidiary of Lake Shore Bancorp 400 E. Ogden Avenue Hinsdale, Illinois 60521	9010183 January 2 19 XX

Karen M. Shaw _____ HAS DEPOSITED

Five Thousand and no/100 _____ DOLLARS $ **$5,000.00** after date, or at any subsequent

Payable to the Registered Holder hereof in current funds upon the surrender of the Certificate properly endorsed _____ maturity date as herinafter provided.

It is understood and agreed that this Certificate shall be automatically renewed for an additional period of time equal to the original term hereof, dating from the first maturity date, and therafter for similar periods of time equal to the original term, unless the Registered Holder hereof shall present this Certificate for payment at any maturity date, or 7 days thereafter, or unless the bank shall prior to any maturity date, mail written notice to the Registered Holder, at the address appearing on the books of the Bank, of its decision to redeem this Certificate.

Interest at the rate of _____ % per annum shall be paid to the Registered Holder hereof _____ , but the rate of interest be paid in full renewal periods the rate then in effect at this Bank for similarly issued certificates of deposit of like term and amount.

This Certificate and the deposit which it evidences are subject to the Rules and Regulations of any Governmental Agency responsible for supervising this Bank or regulating interest rates and the and Regulations of the Bank in force from time to time. Current FDIC regulation requires a substantial interest penalty if this deposit is withdrawn before maturity date.

ADDRESS One Oak Creek
Buffalo Grove, IL 60089

SOCIAL SEC. NO. 000-00-0000

Kelly L. Burhart

BY: _____ DATE: _____

Source: Courtesy of Bank of Hinsdale, Hinsdale, Illinois.

Certificates of Deposit

A **certificate of deposit** is an acknowledgment by a bank of receipt of money with a return "promise" on the bank's part to repay it at a fixed future date or, in some instances, on demand.

Promises to Pay and Orders to Pay

A second method of classifying commercial paper uses only two categories. All instruments involving the payment of money, regardless of their specialized names within the business community, contain one of two elements—*promises* to pay money or *orders* to pay money. Instruments containing promises to pay can be broadly classified as *notes*, and those containing orders to pay as *drafts*. As already indicated, the certificate of deposit is a special type of note, and the check is a special type of draft.

Demand and Time Instruments

A third method of classifying commercial paper is based solely on the time at which the instrument is payable. Instruments that are payable whenever the holder chooses to present them to the maker (in the case of a note) or to the drawee (in the case of a draft) are called **demand instruments** (or *sight instruments*). Those payable at a specific future date are **time instruments**. Notes, drafts, and certificates of deposit can be either demand or time instruments, whereas checks—by definition—must be payable on demand.

Negotiable and Nonnegotiable Instruments

The term *commercial paper*, used in its broadest sense, embraces both negotiable paper and nonnegotiable paper. *Negotiable instruments* are those whose terms meet the requirements of negotiability appearing in Sec. 3-104 [RUCC 3-104], whereas **nonnegotiable instruments** do not meet such requirements. Thus, whether a particular instrument falls into one category or the other depends entirely on its form and content.

In many instances the negotiable–nonnegotiable classification of commercial paper transcends all others in importance, for two primary reasons:

1. The rules of Article 3 apply (with rare exception) only to instruments that meet the tests of negotiability. (As noted above, *revised* Article 3 is entitled "Negotiable Instruments" rather than "Commercial Paper.") By contrast, nonnegotiable instruments are governed by the ordinary principles of contract law.

In other words, the rights and liabilities of makers, drawers, and indorsers of negotiable instruments are controlled by one body of law, whereas those of parties to nonnegotiable instruments are governed by another.

2. It is possible under the rules of Article 3 for a holder of a negotiable instrument to enjoy the special status of a *holder in due course* (HDC). Such a holder takes the instrument free of many defenses that exist between its original parties. (*Defenses* are matters pled by defendants as a reason in law or fact why the plaintiff should not recover.) The possessor of a nonnegotiable instrument—such as a simple contract—on the other hand, can never qualify as an HDC and always takes subject to these defenses.

Although an examination of the precise rights of the HDC must await the subject of defenses in Chapter 26, the basic distinction between the status of such a holder and that of a mere assignee will be brought to light here.

ASSIGNEE VERSUS HOLDER IN DUE COURSE

As explained in Chapter 17, under contract law the assignee of a simple contract acquires no better rights under the contract than those possessed by the assignor. For example: X contracts to buy a bulldozer from Y for $25,000 under an installment contract. After delivery, Y assigns the contract (the right to collect the price) to a third party, Z. If the machine proves defective, X can successfully assert this fact as a defense against Z, just as X could have asserted it against Y had there been no assignment. This means that the assignee, Z, is not entitled to a judgment against X. The same would be true if X had simply given Y a nonnegotiable note or draft in payment for the bulldozer; Z's rights would be no better than those possessed by Y.

On the other hand, if X had given Y a *negotiable* note, draft, or check in payment for the machine, *and if* Y had then transferred the instrument to Z under circumstances that qualified Z as a holder in due course, then Z would be entitled to recover the full amount of the instrument from X, despite the fact that Y had breached his contract with X by delivering a defective machine.

The above is a simple illustration of one of the basic commercial paper concepts—*that it is possible for a third-party HDC to acquire greater rights under a negotiable instrument than those possessed by the payee-transferor.* This does not mean, however, that the HDC is always legally entitled to payment from the primary party. Sometimes the primary party has available a *real* or *universal defense*, which he or she can successfully assert against any holder, even the HDC. And the holder-in-due course doctrine itself has been sharply limited in recent years, as will be explained in Chapter 26.

PARTIES TO COMMERCIAL PAPER

We have already seen that notes have two original parties—the maker and the payee—whereas drafts and checks have three—the drawer, the drawee, and the payee. But after an instrument is issued, additional parties can become involved. (The liability incurred by each of these parties is spelled out in Chapter 27.)

The Acceptor

Frequently, after a draft is issued, it is presented by the payee (or a subsequent holder) to the drawee (the person to whom the order is addressed) for that person's *acceptance*. Under the UCC some types of drafts require a presentment, whereas for others the presentment is at the option of the holder. In any event, the drawee who "accepts" the draft is called the **acceptor** (or *drawee-acceptor*), and he or she becomes a primary party to the instrument. (An acceptance occurs when the drawee signs his or her name somewhere on the face of the instrument.) In this capacity, the acceptor's liability is roughly akin to that of the maker of a note.

Indorsers

Often the payee of a note or draft transfers it to a third party soon after acquiring it, instead of presenting it to the primary party for repayment. When such a transfer occurs, the payee-transferor almost always "indorses" the instrument by signing his or her name on the back of it before delivering it to the third party; by so doing, the payee becomes an **indorser**. For example, if P, the payee, receives a check from D, P can indorse it to a third party, Z, in payment of a debt that P owes Z (or for any other reason).

Indorsees

The **indorsee** is the person who receives an indorsed instrument; in the example just given, the indorsee is

Z. Z can indorse the instrument to another party, in which case Z also becomes an indorser.

The Bearer

A **bearer** is any person who has physical possession of an instrument that legally qualifies as a *bearer instrument*. For example, if a note is expressly made "payable to bearer" or is simply "payable to cash," whoever possesses it is the bearer.

Another type of bearer instrument comes into existence when an instrument is originally payable to the order of a named person, and the named person indorses it by signing his or her name on the back. An indorsement such as this, called a *blank indorsement*, converts the paper into a bearer instrument; therefore, the subsequent taker of the instrument is also a bearer. The blank indorsement is contrasted with a *special indorsement*, which specifies the person to whom, or to whose order, the instrument is payable. The different kinds of indorsements are discussed in Chapter 25.

Holders

The term *holder* is broader in scope and of greater legal significance than the term *bearer*. Sec. 1-201(20) of the UCC defines a **holder** as a person who possesses a negotiable instrument that is either payable to the bearer or payable to such a person as the payee or indorsee. Thus, the term includes not only persons possessing bearer instruments but also payees and indorsees possessing order instruments. To illustrate: X pays a utility bill by drawing a check "payable to the order of Columbia Gas of Ohio" and mailing it to that company. Although Columbia Gas cannot be called a bearer because the check is not payable to bearer, as payee it clearly qualifies as a holder.

Holder in Due Course

Under Sec. 3-202 [RUCC 3-202], a **holder in due course** is a holder who has given value for the instrument, has acquired it before it was overdue, and has taken it in good faith. As indicated earlier, it is the HDC who is afforded most-favored status under the UCC.[5]

Ordinary Holder

A person who qualifies as a holder but does not meet all the HDC requirements is called an **ordinary**

---

[5]The precise rights of the holder in due course, ordinary holder, and holder through a holder in due course will be examined in Chapter 26.

holder, or sometimes a *mere holder, transferee, or assignee.* Unlike the HDC, an ordinary holder cannot enforce the instrument against the primary party if the latter has a personal defense, such as fraud on the part of the payee. In other words, the ordinary holder takes the instrument subject to all defenses, much like the assignee of a nonnegotiable instrument or contract. However, also like the assignee, the ordinary holder can enforce the instrument against the primary party if the latter has no defense available.

Holder through a Holder in Due Course
If a holder fails to qualify as an HDC, he or she usually can still enjoy the special rights of a holder in due course by showing that any prior holder qualified as an HDC. Such a person is called a *holder through a holder in due course.*

SUMMARY

The terms *commercial paper* and *negotiable instruments* refer to written promises or orders to pay sums of money arising from the use of such instruments as drafts, checks, and promissory notes. These instruments may be either *negotiable* or *nonnegotiable* depending on their terms. The question of negotiability is of primary concern to a purchaser of such an instrument, for if the treatment is negotiable the purchaser may qualify as a holder in due course. In such a case, he or she takes the instrument free of many defenses that might exist between the maker (or drawer) and the payee. Also, if the instrument is nonnegotiable, it is governed by contract law rather than Article 3.

For an instrument to qualify as a negotiable instrument, it must meet the requirements of Sec. 3-104 [RUCC 3-104]. The UCC recognizes four kinds of commercial paper: drafts, checks, notes, and certificates of deposit. Drafts and checks contain orders to pay money. The person to whom the order is addressed is the drawee, the person to whom the order is payable is the payee, and the person issuing the instrument is the drawer. In contrast to drafts, notes contain promises to pay, and have only two parties. The maker is the person making the promise to pay, and the payee is the person to whom the note is payable.

In many instances—usually after the instrument has been issued—two other classes of persons may become parties to it, the acceptor and the indorser.

An acceptance occurs if the holder of a draft presents it to the drawee for his or her signature; by signing, the drawee becomes the acceptor (and is thus primarily liable on the instrument). The indorser, in most instances, is the owner of an instrument who signs his or her name on the back of it before delivering it to a third party, the indorsee.

Other persons recognized under Article 3 are the holder and the bearer. The holder is any person who possesses a negotiable instrument that is payable either to the bearer, to his or her order, or to the indorsee of such an instrument. A holder who meets certain requirements of Article 3 is a holder in due course; one not meeting these requirements is an ordinary holder.

KEY TERMS
Commercial paper
Negotiable instrument
Draft
Sales draft
Check
Note
Certificate of deposit
Demand instrument
Time instrument
Nonnegotiable instrument
Acceptor
Indorser
Indorsee
Bearer
Holder
Holder in due course
Ordinary holder

QUESTIONS AND PROBLEMS
1. On January 18, 1988, Musolino bought a money order from D bank in the sum of $400. She then completed the money order, naming herself as remitter and P, her landlord, as payee. Musolino then presented the money order to Lausch, manager of P's apartment, as the balance due on a security deposit for rental of the apartment. On January 19, Musolino filled out a stop-payment request on the money order. On January 20, Lausch deposited the money order in P's account at D Bank. On January 21, P received notice that his account had been debited $400, the amount of the money order. P sued the

bank, alleging that the stop-payment order was illicit. P argued that although a bank may stop payment on a regular check, a money order is more like a cashier's check upon which payment generally cannot be stopped. Is P correct about the proper characterization of a money order? Discuss. (*Duggan v. State Bank of Antioch*, 540 N.E.2d 1111, Ill.App. 1989.)

2. Norwood was charged with violating California Penal Code Section 475a, which prohibits possession for fraudulent purposes of "a completed check, money order, or traveler's check." Norwood had possessed for fraudulent purposes a completed Los Angeles county "Auditor Controller's General Warrant," reading as follows:

16-66

1220

AUDITOR CONTROLLER'S GENERAL WARRANT COUNTY OF LOS ANGELES
The Treasurer of the County of Los Angeles will pay to the order of:

Apr. 1 1971
Los Angeles, California

[Name and address of payee filled in] $161.00

Approved
Mark H. Bloodgood Auditor-Controller By [facsimile signature] J.S. Rasmussen

Did Norwood violate the statute? Was this warrant a check, money order, or traveler's check? Discuss. (*People v. Norwood*, 103 Cal.Rptr. 7, Cal.App. 1972.)

3. X contracts to paint Y's house for $1200 in June. On June 20, when X is half-way through with the job, Y is called to Europe on a business trip. Before leaving, Y makes out a promissory note for $1200 that is payable July 15, and hands it to X. The next day X sells the note to a local bank for $1000 (he "discounts" the note). In late July, when the bank demands payment from Y, Y refuses to pay the instrument because X never finished the job. If the note in question is *non*negotiable in form, what effect—if any—does this have on Y's liability to the bank? Explain.

4. Tom is owed $1000 by Dick, but in turn owes Harry $400. When Harry presses Tom for payment, Tom gives Harry this letter addressed to Dick: "Out of the $1000 you owe me, please pay $400 of it to Harry as soon as he requests it." Does this letter look like a *draft*, or more like a *note*? Explain.

5. The Scarlet Corporation orders 10 snowmobiles from the Gray Company at a total cost of $12,000. If a *sales draft* were to be used here (instead of a cash payment by the Scarlet Corporation), who would be (a) the drawer, (b) the drawee, and (c) the acceptor?

6. David sells a used car to Emily and takes a promissory note from Emily in payment. When the note comes due, Emily is financially unable to pay it. David then brings suit on the note, and Emily's only defense is that the note is *nonnegotiable* in form. (That is, there was nothing wrong with the car that she received.) If Emily can clearly prove that the note *is nonnegotiable*, is her defense good? Why or why not?

7. B is the maker of a negotiable promissory note, and she issues it to C. C later negotiates it to D. In such a situation, D may qualify as a *holder in due course*, or he may be only an *ordinary holder*. If D was forced to bring suit against B in an effort to obtain payment of the note, under what circumstances might D's success depend entirely on whether he was one type of holder or the other? Explain.

Chapter 25

Commercial Paper
Negotiability and Transfer

Requirements of Negotiability

Transfer

Assignment and Negotiation

Blank, Special, Qualified, and Restrictive Indorsements

Miscellaneous Negotiation Problems

IN MANY SITUATIONS, whether an instrument is negotiable or nonnegotiable is of little importance. Suppose, for example, that P is willing to sell goods to M on credit, taking a promissory ninety-day note signed by M as evidence of the indebtedness. Suppose further that M's financial reputation is good, and that P is perfectly willing to hold the note herself until it matures. In these circumstances P might well be satisfied with a nonnegotiable note, for her chances of being paid on the due date, and her legal rights against M if payment is not made voluntarily, are about as good as those she would possess if the note were negotiable.

In many other circumstances, however, the negotiability or nonnegotiability of an instrument is of vital importance for a number of reasons. First, as noted in Chapter 24, when legal problems arise as to the enforceability of the instrument, the rights and obligations of the parties are resolved under UCC Article 3 if the instrument is negotiable and under ordinary contract law if it is not. And since the holder-in-due-course concept is recognized only under Article 3, any person seeking to enforce the instrument under this concept must (among other things) show at the outset that the instrument meets the tests of negotiability.

In addition, as a practical matter, commercial paper cannot serve its "substitute for money" and "extension of credit" roles unless it is freely transferable (that is, unless prospective purchases of the paper, especially financial institutions, are willing to accept it routinely). And, before such purchasers are willing to accept commercial paper, they not only want to be able to determine that the paper is negotiable in form but, additionally, that the seller/transferor has taken the steps necessary to ensure that the transfer constitutes a "negotiation" of the paper as defined by Article 3.

In this chapter, then, we will discuss (1) the requirements of negotiability and (2) the rules applicable to the transfer of negotiable instruments.

REQUIREMENTS OF NEGOTIABILITY

Today the requirements of negotiability are expressly set forth in Sec. 3-104 [RUCC 3-104] of the UCC.[1] Subsection 1 reads as follows:

Any writing to be a negotiable instrument within this Article must (a) be signed by the maker or drawer; and (b) contain an unconditional promise or order to pay a sum certain in money and [must contain] no other promise, order, obligation, or power given by the maker or drawer except as authorized by this Article; and (c) be payable on demand or at a definite time; and (d) be payable to order or to bearer.

As a result of these requirements, the negotiability of an instrument is entirely dependent on its *form* and *content*. Each of these requirements, together with later sections that help in the interpretation of the negotiability requirements, will now be examined.

The Writing and Signing Requirements
The Writing

Just as there is no such thing as "oral money," an oral promise or order to pay money obviously cannot serve as a substitute for it. Under contract law it is true that an oral promise to pay money can be enforced as long as its existence can be established in court. However, in the commercial world, where large numbers of promises and orders must be transferred daily, the need for such obligations to be evidenced in tangible written form becomes obvious. Under Sec. 1-201(46), this "writing" can be handwritten, printed, or typewritten, or it can consist of "any other intentional [method of] reduction to tangible form."

Normally, of course, the substance on which the writing appears is paper, but the UCC does not require this. Thus we occasionally read in the newspaper about the holder of a "check" written on an egg, a watermelon, or some other unusual object who was able to obtain payment at the drawee bank upon physical presentment of the object. These cases, of course, are rarities; they do, however, bring a welcome degree of humor and ingenuity to the subject of commercial paper (though the bank officials involved might not entirely share this view).[2]

---

[1] As noted in the previous chapter, we are following citations to the original Article 3 with citations to the sections in the revised Article 3 where they have been recodified. This should allow easy cross-referencing. Remember, however, that most of the original sections have been rewritten as well as renumbered, so the language in the two cited sections will be similar but seldom identical. Any major substantive changes made in the RUCC will be noted in the text.

[2] For an amusing look at negotiability in general, see Jennings, *I Want to Know What Bearer Paper Is and I Want to Meet a Holder in Due Course,* 1992 BRIGHAM YOUNG UNIVERSITY LAW REVIEW 385.

The Signing

A negotiable instrument must be signed by the maker in the case of a note or by the drawer in the case of a draft. Ordinarily there is little trouble with this requirement, since such a party almost invariably affixes his or her signature (in longhand) to the instrument at the outset.

In some instances, however, questions do arise. Sec 1-201(39) is designed to alleviate these by stating that the term *signed* means "any symbol executed or adopted by a party with [the] present intention to authenticate a writing." Thus a signing can occur through the use of one's initials, a rubber stamp, or some other type of "signature," such as the mark "X," so long as it is made with the intention of giving assent to the writing's terms.[3]

The Promise or Order Must Be Unconditional

In order for an instrument to be treated as a substitute for money or as a credit extension device, the holder will want assurance that no conditions will be imposed on the instrument's payment. Whether such conditions exist in a given case, thus causing the instrument to be nonnegotiable, depends on the totality of the terms and provisions that make up the instrument. An almost infinite variety of clauses or notations find their way into some instruments and raise legitimate questions as to whether they condition the basic promise or order to pay. We will consider here the most common of these.

Express Conditions

A small percentage of notes and drafts contain clauses that *expressly condition* the primary promise or order to pay. Obviously these clauses destroy negotiability of the instrument at the outset. A note signed by M, maker, which is payable "upon the marriage of my daughter," falls into this category, for it is expressly made payable upon an event that may never occur. Even if the event is very likely to occur (or does, in fact, occur subsequently), the instrument remains nonnegotiable.

Permitted Provisions

A more common situation is one where the basic obligation is itself unconditional but where the in-

strument contains language or clauses that will *possibly* condition the primary obligation—depending, of course, on how the clauses are legally interpreted.

Sec. 3-105 [RUCC 3-106] resolves many of these problems of interpretation. Subsection 1 contains eight express types of clauses or notations that may appear on the face of an instrument that do *not* condition the promise or order to pay. Thus any clause falling within this subsection does not destroy the negotiability of the instrument. For example, subsection 1 permits the maker or drawer to note on the face of the instrument its purpose ("January rent"), or the consideration received in exchange for the instrument ("Payment for 100 bushels wheat"). It also permits the maker or drawer to indicate that the instrument has arisen out of a separate agreement, if such is the case, or is secured by a mortgage on specified property. The UCC recognizes that these kinds of references should have no adverse legal or practical effect on the instrument's negotiability.

Subsections f and g under subsection 1 contain two "fund" provisions. Subsection f permits inclusion on the face of an instrument a clause that merely "indicates a particular account to be debited or any other fund from which *reimbursement* is to be made." Two examples: (1) D draws a check on which he writes the words, "Charge to petty cash"; and (2) the X Corporation, a manufacturer holding several construction contracts with the U.S. Navy, writes on an obligation, "Charge to Navy Contract SX-102." In both instances it is clear that the instruments pledge the general credit of the parties issuing them, and that the extra notations merely refer to funds (or assets) out of which the parties will reimburse themselves after they have paid the instruments. The instruments, therefore, remain negotiable.

Subsection g further provides that two kinds of instruments are negotiable even though they are *payable* out of a specified fund. The more important of these consists of instruments issued by a government, a governmental unit, or a governmental agency. Thus a state-issued bond, payable out of the revenue of that state's turnpike commission, is a negotiable instrument. (In other words, under subsection g the commission's promise to pay is not conditioned upon the existence of a fund at maturity sufficient to permit payment of the full face value of the bonds.) Government obligations are given this special treatment because government funds are

---

[3]Problems relating to forgeries and unauthorized signatures of employers' names by their agents are discussed in Chapter 27.

almost always adequate to honor the obligations, whereas this is less likely to be the case where the maker is an ordinary corporation or individual.[4]

Impermissible Provisions

Subsection 2 of Sec. 3-105 [RUCC 3-106], in contrast to subsection 1, refers to two kinds of clauses or provisions that *do* destroy the negotiability of any note or draft.

"Subject to" Clauses.   Instruments that contain language indicating that the promises or orders to pay are *subject to* some other agreement, such as a mortgage or lease, are nonnegotiable. This results from subsection 2(a), which provides that "A promise or order is not unconditional if the instrument states that it is subject to or governed by any other agreement."

Prior to the adoption of the UCC, some courts took

the view that the negotiability of an instrument that was subject to some other agreement depended on the actual terms of that agreement. This meant that a prospective purchaser had to search out that other agreement in order to know what the status of the instrument was—a most impractical requirement in the commercial world. Subsection 2(a) [RUCC 3-106(a)(ii)] makes such instruments *nonnegotiable as a matter of law*—regardless of what the terms of the other agreement actually are. This subsection underscores the general idea that the negotiability or nonnegotiability of an instrument must be determinable from the face of the instrument alone.

The revised Article 3 refines this requirement by providing that a promise or order is not made conditional, and thereby rendered nonnegotiable, "by a reference to another writing for a statement of rights with respect to collateral, prepayment, or acceleration. . . ." RUCC 3-106(b)(i).

The following case would be decided in the same way under either the original or the revised Article 3.

[4]The second type of instrument that is negotiable, although payable out of a fund, consists of instruments payable out of the "entire assets of a partnership, unincorporated association, trust, or estate by or on behalf of which the instrument is issued."

Carador v. Sana Travel Service, Ltd.

U.S. District Court for the Southern District of New York, 700 F.Supp. 787 (1988)

 Case

Sana Travel Service is a New York corporation, and Paracha is an officer and director of Sana. Paracha drew a check on Sana's account at the National Bank of Pakistan (NBP) for $33,000.00, payable to the order of Jamil Ahmed Kahn (Kahn), Al-Bark Turismo (Al-Bark). Kahn worked for Al-Bark, a travel and tourist service in Brazil. On the memorandum line on the lower left-hand portion of the check, Paracha wrote "Just to hold for the security of future business." Paracha then sent the check to Al-Bark's offices in Brazil.

At the direction of Al-Bark's owner, Kahn indorsed the check in blank and sold it to Carador for cash. Carador then sought to collect on the check by giving it to a firm specializing in foreign currency ex-

change, which then turned it over to a bank in the United States for collection. The U.S. bank sent it to the drawee bank, NBP, in Pakistan. When NBP received the check, it telephoned Sana, and Paracha directed that the check be dishonored. After the check was dishonored, Carador filed suit against Sana and Paracha. (Paracha is also a defendant because he signed the check without indicating on it that he was signing only in a representative capacity for Sana.) Sana and Paracha, the defendants, claimed that the check was rendered nonnegotiable by the notation on its face. If it was not negotiable, they argued, Carador could not be a holder in due course and would be subject to their defense that Al-Bark gave no consideration. Following is the federal district court's opinion on Carador's motion for summary judgment.

Mukasey, Judge:

. . . The parties do not dispute that checks usually are negotiable instruments. However, defendants contend that the notation Paracha wrote on the front of the check destroys its negotiability. Defendants note that a negotiable instrument must be "an unconditional promise or order to pay . . . [containing] no other promise, order, obligation or power . . . except as authorized by this Article." Defendants contend that the notation makes the check a conditional promise to pay because it makes the check subject to, or governed by, another agreement. Alternatively, defendants assert that the notation is so irregular that a reasonably prudent person would be put on notice of the check's restricted purpose, and through reasonable inquiry would discover that the check is not negotiable. In contrast, Carador asserts

(continues)

CARADOR V. SANA TRAVEL SERVICE, LTD.

(continued from previous page)
that the check is negotiable because the notation, on its face, merely indicates that $33,000.00 was conveyed from defendants to Al-Bark as security for performance of a contract.

A check is not a negotiable instrument if the drawer writes on it a promise, order, obligation or power, which, when examined on its face, in any way limits the drafter's unconditional [order] to pay. By contrast, a check which notes that it is a security deposit for future performance of another contract remains negotiable because such a notation does not suggest on its face that the drafter may have reneged on the unconditional promise to honor the instrument. Therefore, the notation on this check does not destroy negotiability because it merely indicates that Al-Bark and Sana have agreed that Sana will give Al-Bark a security deposit to insure future performance of another contract. As a corollary, the check is not so irregular as to put Carador on notice that the check is allegedly not negotiable, or even to require further inquiry into the underlying transaction. Moreover, contrary to defendants' assertion, the notation certainly does not put Carador on notice that the check was never meant to be negotiated.

[The court then found that Carador met all the requirements to be a holder in due course and was not subject to any defense by Sana and Paracha that Al-Bark gave no consideration, even if such defense could be proved. The court also found that Paracha was personally liable on the instrument along with Sana, because Paracha had signed without indicating that he was doing so as a representative of Sana. Thus, the court granted Carador's motion for summary judgment.] ⚖

"Payable Out of Fund" Instruments. The second kind of clause that destroys negotiability, found under subsection 2(b) [no RUCC equivalent] is one that makes the instrument *payable out of a specified fund* (with the narrow exceptions, including instruments issued by government agencies, discussed previously). Because the payment of such instruments is subject to the possibility that there may be no such fund in existence at maturity, the promise or order is viewed by the original Article 3 as conditional in nature. Thus, if in June X promises to pay $5000 to the order of Y on the following December 1 "out of the proceeds of the sale of my Ford Motor stock," the instrument is nonnegotiable when issued to Y, and remains nonnegotiable even if the stock is sold before December 1 for more than $5000.[5]

Note that the revised Article 3 *reverses the specified fund rule,* specifically providing that a promise or order is *not* made conditional simply "because payment is limited to resort to a particular fund or source." RUCC 3-106(b)(ii). Drafters of the revised Article 3 reasoned that there was no strong reason to require that the general credit of the drawer or maker be pledged in order for an instrument to be negotiable. A holder may choose not to accept such a promise or order, but this is insufficient reason to deem it nonnegotiable.

Definite Promise or Order to Pay

Occasionally an instrument refers to the existence of a debt, but its language raises the question of whether the instrument really constitutes a promise or order that the debt be paid. For example, one person may hand to another a written IOU. A statement of this kind, or any other statement that merely acknowledges the existence of a debt, does not constitute a promise to pay, and the instrument thus fails to meet the requirements of negotiability.

FTC Rule 433

As we shall study in Chapter 26, the Federal Trade Commission's rule 433 requires a statement in *consumer* credit notes that a holder or subsequent transferee of a note takes it subject to whatever claims and defenses the consumer can assert against the original payee. The purpose of the rule was mainly to prevent transferees from becoming holders in due course who could collect the note from the consumer regardless of defenses the consumer might have against the

---

[5]The "fund" rules of the original Article 3 can be summarized as follows: (1) An instrument that refers to a fund out of which reimbursement is to be made is negotiable. (2) An instrument that is payable out of a specified fund is nonnegotiable, except for instruments payable out of governmental funds and those payable out of the entire assets of a partnership, unincorporated association, trust, or estate.

original seller (such as that the product was never delivered, or was defective, or was sold under fraudulent pretenses). Under the original Article 3 it is possible to argue that such language renders the note conditional and therefore nonnegotiable. The revised Article 3, however, clearly specifies that such language does *not* render the note conditional or destroy its negotiability. RUCC 3-106(d). However, the effect of rule 433—to prevent subsequent transferees from becoming HDCs—is not altered.

Amount to Be Paid Must Be a Sum Certain in Money

If an instrument is to be a substitute for money and have an equivalent degree of acceptability, the necessity that the amount be a *sum certain* is obvious. This requirement of certainty is met if the holder can determine from the terms of the instrument itself the amount he or she is entitled to receive at maturity.

The original Article 3 recognizes that some instruments contain provisions that at least raise the question of whether they violate this requirement, and Sec. 3-106 [RUCC 3-104(a)] is meant to "save" the negotiability of many of these instruments by providing that:

the sum payable is a sum certain even though it is to be paid (a) with stated interest or by stated installments; or (b) with stated different rates of interest before and after default or a specified date; or (c) with a stated discount or addition if paid before or after the date fixed for payment; or (d) with exchange or less exchange, whether at a fixed rate

or at the current rate; or (e) with costs of collections or an attorney's fee or both upon default.

Subsections a, b, c and e are self-explanatory. Subsection d refers to instruments that are payable in foreign currency. The holder of this kind of instrument may want payment in his or her own country's currency, which requires application of the exchange rate in effect between the two countries. Such instruments, whether payable at fixed exchange rates or at "current rates," are deemed by subsection d to meet the sum certain requirement.

Variable Interest Rate Notes

The original Article 3 was written before variable rate promissory notes (VRNs) became popular. Such notes are now much more widely used, but in most original Article 3 jurisdictions they carry the serious defect of nonnegotiability. Therefore, their holders cannot qualify as HDCs. The revised Article 3 *changes the law by limiting the sum certain requirement to the principal amount.* Under RUCC 3-104(a) and 3-112(b), interest may be "expressed as a fixed or variable rate or rates," and the amount or rate of interest "may require reference to information not contained in the instrument" without destroying negotiability. This is a very important change in the law.

The following case is decided pursuant to the original Article 3, but the result is consonant with the revised Article 3. All necessary facts are included in the court's opinion.

AMBERBOY v. SOCIETE DE BANQUE PRIVEE

Texas Supreme Court, 831 S.W.2d 793 (1992)

Cornyn, Justice:

This case comes to us on a certified question from the United States Court of Appeals for the Fifth Circuit. The question is whether a promissory note requiring interest to be charged at a rate that can be determined only by reference to a bank's published prime rate is a negotiable instrument as defined by the [UCC].

[The court began by quoting UCC Sec. 3-104(a).] The Code does not de-

fine the term "sum certain" [as a requirement of negotiability].

This is not just an ordinary case of statutory construction. Our construction of the provisions of the U.C.C. is grounded in the Code's fundamental purpose, which is to "simplify, clarify and modernize the law governing commercial transactions. . . ." [UCC Sec. 1-102(b)(1)]. Further, the drafters of the U.C.C. expressly contemplated that the courts would advance the basic purpose of the Code by construing the U.C.C.'s provisions "in the light of unforeseen

and new circumstances and practices." [UCC Sec. 1-102, comment 1].

For an instrument to be negotiable . . ., the sum certain to be paid must be capable of computation "from the instrument itself without any reference to any outside source." [UCC Sec. 3-106, comment 1]. However, the Code itself evidences that this is not intended to be a rigid, absolute rule. Section 3-106 lists several instances in which reference to sources outside the instrument are necessary to determine the sum payable under the instrument.

(continues)

AMBERBOY V. SOCIETE DE BANQUE PRIVEE

(continued from previous page)
See, e.g., 3-106(1)(d) (payment in exchange at current rate).

Section 3-106 does not explicitly mention variable rate notes ("VRNs") because when the U.C.C. was developed in the 1950s and adopted in the 1960s, VRNs were virtually unknown. The necessity for VRNs came about as a result of the volatile financial markets of the late 1970s. By the mid-1980s, VRNs accounted for 60% of the total loans made in this country. That dominance in the financial markets has continued into the 90s.

The majority of courts which have addressed the issue before us [pursuant to the original Article 3] have declined to hold that notes which contain variable interest rates are negotiable instruments. . . . A number of states, either in response to court decisions which reject VRNs as negotiable instruments or for reasons that are not readily apparent, have amended 3-106 to provide that the sum certain requirement is not defeated because the rate of interest to be charged is tied to and varies with certain enumerated types of published rates.

We believe the better reasoned view is reflected in the opinions of those courts which have held that VRNs do meet the sum certain requirement and thus are negotiable instruments subject to the terms of article 3 of the UCC. . . . [T]he National Conference of Commissioners on Uniform State law [has proposed], in the interest of uniformity, [revised Article 3] to specifically provide that VRNs are negotiable instruments.

A VRN which contains provision for interest to be paid at a variable rate that is readily ascertainable by reference to a bank's published prime rate is compatible with the Code's objective of commercial certainty. The Code does not require "mathematical certainty" but only "commercial certainty." Commercial certainty serves the purpose of the law of negotiable instruments, which is to make the instrument the functional equivalent of money. If the rate of interest to be paid under the instrument is readily ascertainable by reference to a bank's published prime rate, this purpose is achieved.

We believe that the construction more consistent with the stated purpose of the U.C.C. and modern commercial practices obliges us to answer the Fifth Circuit's certified question affirmatively. ⚖

Payment to Be Made Only in Money

Instruments must be payable only in *money*. Thus, any contract that requires the obligor to perform an act other than, or in addition to, the payment of money is nonnegotiable (with exceptions noted later in this chapter).[6] Three examples of such contracts are: (1) M, in return for a loan, promises to deliver "sixty bushels of U.S. #1 blackeyed peas ninety days after date"; (2) M signs a note that obligates her to pay at maturity $1000 *and* to deliver to the holder at that time sixty bushels of U.S. #1 blackeyed peas; and (3) M signs a note that obligates her to pay $1000 *or* to deliver the peas at maturity.

Money is defined in Sec. 1-201(24) as a "medium of exchange authorized or adopted by a domestic or foreign government as a part of its currency." It thus follows that any instrument payable in the currency of a recognized government is payable in money regardless of where the instrument is to be paid. In that regard, Sec. 3-107(2) [RUCC 3-107] provides that an instrument payable in this country whose amount is stated in a foreign currency (such as 2000 German marks) can be satisfied by the payment of an equivalent number of American dollars at the due date, unless the instrument *expressly* requires payment in marks. In either event the instrument is negotiable. In no case, however, can the instrument be payable in something other than money. To illustrate:

1. An instrument drafted in Mexico City and payable in Dallas expressly calls for payment in ten thousand Mexican pesos. The instrument is payable in money.

2. An instrument payable in U.S. government bonds is not negotiable, since government bonds are not a medium of exchange recognized by the U.S. government.

---

[6]However, contracts that require the *delivery of goods* at a future date often do possess the quality of negotiability. While bills of lading and warehouse receipts fail to qualify as negotiable instruments under Article 3, because they do not contain promises to pay money, they do qualify as negotiable instruments under UCC Article 7.

Payable on Demand or at a Definite Time

Under Sec. 3-108 [RUCC 3-108(a)], to be negotiable an instrument must be either payable on demand or payable at a definite time. This requirement recognizes that the holder of an instrument wants to know with certainty when he or she will be entitled to payment. Any appreciable uncertainty as to time of payment makes the instrument commercially unacceptable and defeats the concept that a negotiable instrument is a substitute for money.

Instruments payable *on demand* (called **demand instruments**) include (1) those that are expressly so payable; (2) those whose terms make the instrument payable "at sight" or "on presentation" by the holder; or (3) those in which no time for payment is stated, as, for example, the following: "I promise to pay to the order of P one hundred dollars. (signed) M."

Instruments that are not payable on demand, called **time instruments,** must be payable at a definite time in order to be negotiable. When issuing this kind of note or draft, the maker or drawer usually wants assurance that there will be no obligation to pay until the specified time period had elapsed. The terms clearly indicate a definite future time for payment, such as "payable one year from date" or "payable July 1, 1994."

Although no problems of negotiability are presented by these kinds of instruments, problems do arise when the note or draft contains additional terms that apparently conflict with the definite time requirement. Sec. 3-109(1) [RUCC 3-108(b)] clears up most of these problem situations, as follows:

(1) An instrument is payable at a definite time if by its terms it is payable (a) on or before a stated date or at a fixed period after a stated date; or (b) at a fixed period after sight; or (c) at a definite time subject to any acceleration; or (d) at a definite time subject to extension at the option of the holder, or to extension to a further definite time at the option of the maker or acceptor or automatically upon or after a specified act or event.

Subsections 1(a) and 1(b)

Subsections a and b of Sec. 3-109(1) [RUCC 3-108(b)] are virtually self-explanatory. An instrument payable on or before a specified date gives the maker, drawer, or acceptor the option of paying before the stated maturity date if he or she wishes. Subsection 1(a) simply points out that such uncertainty does not violate the definite time requirement. Subsection 1(b) refers to a common provision in drafts that the drafts are payable at a specified time (frequently 60 or 90 days) "after sight." That is, the time period does not begin until "sight" (the moment the draft is accepted by the drawee) occurs. Although the time at which the acceptance will occur is unknown when the instrument is first issued, this subsection provides that the instrument nonetheless meets the definite time requirement.

Acceleration Clauses

Instruments due at a fixed future date sometimes have **acceleration clauses** providing that the date of maturity shall be *moved ahead* if a specified event occurs prior to the stated due date. An instrument issued this year with a maturity date two years hence might contain, for example, either of these acceleration clauses: (1) "This instrument shall become immediately due and payable upon the maker's (or acceptor's) bankruptcy"; or (2) for a note payable in monthly installments, "If any installment is not paid when due, the entire instrument is due and payable."

Under Sec. 3-109(1)(c) [RUCC 3-108(b)(ii)], all instruments with acceleration clauses meet the definite time test, even if the events on which the acceleration is based are to some extent within the holder's control. To illustrate, an instrument might provide: "Should the holder deem himself insecure at any time prior to the maturity date, he can demand payment at such time and the entire instrument shall thereupon immediately become due and payable." However, the right of the holder to accelerate an instrument containing a clause such as this is subject to the good faith requirement contained in Sec. 1-208—that the clause "shall be construed to mean that he shall have the power [to accelerate] only if he in good faith believes that the prospect of payment or performance is impaired."

Extension Clauses

Extension clauses are the reverse of acceleration clauses; that is, they appear in notes or drafts having a fixed future maturity date and provide that, under certain circumstances, the date shall be *extended further.* Before enactment of the UCC this kind of clause raised questions about negotiability. Now, Sec. 3-109(1)(d) [RUCC 3-108(b)(iii), (iv)] provides that an instrument is negotiable if by its terms it is payable "at a definite time subject to extension at the option of the holder, or to extension to a further definite time at the option of the maker or acceptor or automatically upon or after a specified event."

Thus, extension clauses that give the *obligor* (maker or acceptor) the right to extend the time of payment meet the definite time test only if they contain a new fixed maturity date. (The same is true for clauses that extend the time of payment automatically on the occurrence of a specified event.) On the other hand, clauses giving the *holder* the right to extend the time of payment need not contain a new fixed maturity date.

This distinction is logical. If the obligor had the right to extend payment without limit, neither the holder nor any potential purchaser could determine with certainty when he or she would have the right to be paid. But when the holder has the option, he or she is free to demand payment at the maturity date or at any time thereafter. (Actually, the holder of any instrument is free to postpone the time of payment even if no extension clause appears.)

We can illustrate the primary effects of this rule as follows:

1. "It is expressly agreed that the holder of this note at the date of maturity can extend the time of payment until the following Thanksgiving or even later if she wishes." *Result:* Negotiability is not destroyed, even though it is not known how long the extension will be, since the option is solely that of the holder.

2. "The maker has the unconditional right to postpone the time of payment of this note beyond its November 1, 1994, maturity date, but for no longer than a reasonable time after such date." *Result:* The definite time requirement is not met and the negotiability of the instrument is thus destroyed, because the right to extend is the maker's and no further time is contained in the extension clause.

Payable upon Happening of Specified Event

An instrument that is payable upon the happening of an event that may never occur (such as "upon the marriage of my daughter") is nonnegotiable for the reason that the promise or order to pay is clearly *conditional* in nature. The instrument remains nonnegotiable even if the event subsequently does occur (although it would, of course, become *payable* at that time).

Sec. 3-109(2) [RUCC has no equivalent provision] goes one step further by providing that "an instru-

ment which by its terms . . . is payable only upon an act or event uncertain as to time of occurrence is not payable at a definite time even though the act or event has occurred." To illustrate: A draft is payable "upon the death of X." Even though X's death is an event that is certain to happen, the draft is nonnegotiable when issued, and remains nonnegotiable after X's death. (As in the prior example, the draft would, however, become *payable* at that time.)

Payable to Order or to Bearer

It is fundamental to the concept of negotiability that the instrument contain language clearly indicating that the maker or drawer intends it to be fully capable of being transferred to some person or persons other than the one to whom it was originally issued. This is why Sec. 3-104(1)(d) [RUCC 3-104(a)(1)] states that the instrument must "be payable to order or to bearer." *Order* and *bearer* are frequently referred to as the "words of negotiability."[7]

Order Instruments

Sec. 3-110 [RUCC 3-109(b)] defines the term **order instrument** and helps interpret Sec. 3-104(1)(d) [RUCC 3-104(a)(1)]; it provides that "an instrument is payable to order when by its terms it is payable to the order or assigns of any person therein specified with reasonable certainty, or to him or his order."[8] Additionally, the instrument can be payable "to the order of (a) the maker or drawer; or (b) the drawee; or (c) a payee who is not maker, drawer, or drawee; or (d) two or more payees together or in the alternative; or (e) an estate, trust or funds. . . . ; or (f) an office or an officer by his title as such. . . .; or (g) a partnership or unincorporated association. . . ."

The requirements of the order instrument are met by such language as "pay to the order of Braden Prentice" and "pay to Melanie Howell or order." However, an instrument "payable to Carolyn Jones" is not an order instrument, and therefore is nonnegotiable.

The revised Article 3 makes an important change in this area. Under the original Article 3, a *check* that

---

[7]We are here concerned with the order-bearer requirement only as it affects *negotiability* of an instrument, but the requirement also affects the manner in which instruments are to be *transferred.* As we will see later in the chapter, a bearer instrument can be "negotiated" to a third party without being indorsed by the transferor, while an indorsement is essential for order instruments.

[8]*Assigns* simply means all third parties to whom the instrument might subsequently be transferred.

did not include the words "to the order of" was non-negotiable. Thus, a drawer could render a check nonnegotiable by simply crossing out the "to the order of" language that is preprinted on most checks. Under RUCC 3-104(c), a check that does not include the words "to the order of" is still negotiable and, thus, there can still be holders in due course. This change in rules applies only to checks, not to notes. One reason for the distinction is that today most checks are processed by machines that do not verify the presence of such wording anyway.

Bearer Instruments

A note or draft that fails to qualify as an order instrument is nonetheless negotiable if it is payable to the *bearer*. Sec. 3-111 [RUCC 3-109(a)] provides that "an instrument is payable to bearer when by its terms it is payable to (a) bearer or the order of bearer; or (b) a specified person or bearer; or (c) 'cash' or the order of 'cash,' or any other indication which does not purport to designate a specific payee."

The following all qualify as **bearer instruments:** "payable to bearer," "payable to the order of bearer," and "payable to X or bearer." However, an instrument that is payable only to a specified person ("payable to X") is not payable to bearer and hence is nonnegotiable.

Terms and Omissions Not Affecting Negotiability

The negotiability of most instruments is settled by reference to the basic sections we have examined. Occasionally, however, instruments present special problems—sometimes because they contain terms not covered by the preceding sections, sometimes because terms are omitted that normally are present, and sometimes because they contain provisions that are in apparent conflict. Secs. 3-112 through 3-118 [RUCC 3-104(a)(3), 3-110(c), (d), 3-311, 3-112, 3-113(a), 3-115, 3-116(a)] are designed to resolve most peripheral problems of this sort. We will discuss the more important of these rules in the context of the original Article 3.

Omissions

Sec. 3-112 [RUCC has no comparable provision][9] provides in part that the negotiability of an instrument is not affected by "the omission of a statement of any consideration, or of the place where the instrument is drawn or payable." This provision rejects the possible view that such omissions cause an instrument to be incomplete and therefore nonnegotiable. Along similar lines, Sec. 3-114 [RUCC has no comparable provision] states that the negotiability of an instrument is not destroyed simply because the date of issue does not appear—unless, of course, the date of maturity is tied to the date of issue, as when an undated note is "payable sixty days after date."

Additional Powers and Promises

We have seen that under Sec. 3-104(1)(b) [RUCC 3-104(a)(3)], any instrument containing a promise or order *in addition to* the "promise or order to pay a sum certain in money" causes the instrument to be nonnegotiable "except as authorized by this Article." Several of these additional promises are expressly authorized by Subsections b and c of Sec. 3-112 [RUCC 3-104(a)(3)(i), (ii)].

Subsection b states that the negotiability of an instrument is not affected by a statement that collateral has been given as security for the obligation. Nor is it affected by a promise on the part of the maker, drawer, or acceptor to *maintain,* to *protect,* or to *give additional collateral* in specified circumstances. To illustrate: The maker of a time note has given the payee a warehouse receipt for 600 bags of beans in the X Warehouse as security. The note further provides that "if a decline in the market value of this collateral should cause the holder of this instrument to deem himself insecure, the maker shall deliver additional collateral upon demand." This note is negotiable.

The reason that these stipulations do not destroy negotiability lies in the fact that they actually *enhance* the value of the basic obligation, rather than limit or condition it. Thus the instruments are more freely acceptable in commerce and even better able to fulfill their role as substitutes for money or as credit instruments than would be the case if the clauses were absent.

The following recent case decided under the original Article 3 applies the four basic elements of negotiability to an instrument that is neither a check, a draft, a certificate of deposit, nor a note.

---

[9]Note that the fact that the RUCC has no comparable provision does not necessarily mean that a rule from the original Article 3 has been changed. It may merely mean, and does in this case, that the revised Article 3 achieves the same result through different means.

NATIONAL BANK OF ALASKA V. UNIVENTURES 1231

Alaska Supreme Court, 824 P.2d 1377 (1992)

Case

The State of Alaska was a tenant in an office building owned by Univentures. On November 24, 1987, the state made a lease payment of $28,143.47 to Univentures with state treasury warrant no. 21045102. LeViege, the managing partner of Univentures, assigned the warrant on behalf of Univentures to Garcia. As a result of a dispute that arose among the partners of Univentures, the state was notified on November 25, 1987, that it should no longer pay LeViege the monthly rent due the partnership. The state was told to refrain from paying rent until a court-appointed receiver was named for Univentures. On November 27, 1987, the state placed a stop-payment order on warrant no. 21045102.

Garcia presented the warrant to the National Bank of Alaska (NBA), the state's clearing bank, on November 30, 1987. NBA paid Garcia $28,143.37 on the warrant but did not debit the state's account because of the stop-payment order. NBA then sued the State of Alaska, LeViege, and Garcia to recover the sum. NBA argued that it was a holder in due course. The trial judge disagreed, holding that the warrant was not a negotiable instrument, disqualifying NBA from HDC status. NBA appealed.

Moore, Justice:

The [trial] court held that NBA was not a holder in due course because the state treasury warrant involved is not a negotiable instrument to which the Uniform Commercial Code applies. As a result, the [trial] court held that NBA took the warrant subject to the state's defense that it had issued a valid stop-payment order.

[UCC 3-104(a)] provides that for a writing to be a negotiable instrument it must:

(1) be signed by the maker or drawer;

(2) contain an unconditional promise or order to pay a sum certain in money and no other promise, order, obligation, or power given by the maker or drawer except as authorized by this chapter;

(3) be payable on demand or at a definite time, and

(4) be payable to order or bearer.

Warrant No. 21045102 satisfies all four elements of the definition of a negotiable instrument. First, the warrant is signed by the maker, Governor Steve Cowper. Second, the warrant contains an unconditional promise or order to pay a sum certain of $28,143.47. A promise or order otherwise unconditional is not made conditional by the fact that the instrument is limited to payment out of a particular fund if the instrument is issued by a government or governmental agency or unit. Third, the warrant is payable at a definite time.

Although the warrant states that it "will be deemed paid unless redeemed within two years after the date of issue," [UCC Sec. 3-109] provides that an instrument is payable at a definite time if by its terms it is payable on or before a stated date. Finally, the warrant clearly indicates that it is payable to the order of Univentures. An "instrument is payable to order if by its terms it is payable to the order or assigns of a person specified in the instrument with reasonable certainty." Because the warrant meets the statutory definition in [UCC Sec. 3-104], we hold that the warrant is a negotiable instrument.

The purposes for which the Uniform Commercial Code was enacted support the conclusion that warrants which satisfy the statutory definition of negotiability must be deemed negotiable. Univentures claims that state warrants should be deemed nonnegotiable because the state must retain its right to assert the defenses of a maker in order to maintain and protect its fiscal policies, practices, and procedures. This argument is directly contrary to the Code's policy of promoting commercial transactions by allowing a party to ascertain the negotiability of an instrument from its face.

[The court then entered judgment for NBA on grounds that, in light of the negotiability of the instrument, NBA qualified as a holder in due course.]

The decision of the [trial] court is REVERSED. ⚖

TRANSFER

Commercial paper is designed primarily for the purpose of circulating freely in the business world. For that reason, we will now look at the various ways such paper can be transferred from one holder to another, and at the basic UCC rules that apply to such transfers.

ASSIGNMENT AND NEGOTIATION

A negotiable instrument has no legal significance of and by itself. In other words, its legal life does not begin until it is issued by the maker or drawer to the first holder.[10] After it has been issued to that person,

---

[10]*Issue* is defined in Sec. 3-102(a)(1) [RUCC 3-105(a)] as "the first delivery of an instrument to a holder."

it can be further transferred by him or her in one of two ways—by *negotiation* or by *assignment*.[11] Although we shall be concerned in this chapter primarily with the legal requirements of a negotiation and the significant rights and duties that flow from it, it is first necessary to distinguish between the two kinds of transfers.

If a payee or other holder of an instrument transfers it to a third party in such a manner that the transfer qualifies as a negotiation under the UCC, the transferee is by definition a holder of the instrument. This makes it possible for the transferee to qualify as a holder in due course (HDC) if he or she meets the other HDC requirements of Article 3. As an HDC, the person can acquire *greater rights* under the instrument than those possessed by the transferor.

Assignment

If the transfer fails to qualify as a negotiation, it is merely an **assignment,** and the transferee is an *assignee* rather than a holder. As such, his or her status is governed by the common-law contract rules discussed in Chapter 17, under which the transferee's rights cannot be greater than those of the transferor. Obviously, then, the purchaser of a negotiable instrument will almost always want to be sure that the transfer qualifies as a negotiation rather than an assignment.

Negotiation

The definition of **negotiation** and the requirements that must be met in order for the transfer of a particular instrument to qualify as a negotiation are found in Sec. 3-202(1) [RUCC 3-201(a)]: "Negotiation is the transfer of an instrument in such form that the transferee becomes a holder. If the instrument is payable to order it is negotiated by delivery with any necessary indorsement; if payable to bearer, it is negotiated by delivery [alone]."[12]

The requirements that must be met, then, in order for a particular transfer to qualify as a negotiation

depend entirely on the form of the instrument at the time of transfer. Before we examine the various kinds of indorsements that can be used, we will illustrate the basic delivery-indorsement requirements.

1. M issues two notes to X, one "payable to bearer" and the other "payable to cash." Because both notes are obviously bearer instruments, X can further negotiate either or both of them to a subsequent purchaser, Y, simply by handing them or mailing them to Y without an indorsement of any kind. (In practice, the purchaser of a bearer instrument normally requests the transferor to indorse it, but the indorsement is not required by the UCC.)

2. Assume the same facts as for example 1, except that the two bearer notes are stolen from X's home by a thief, T. Because *delivery* means a voluntary delivery by the transferor, T's acquisition of the notes in this manner does not constitute a delivery; hence, no negotiation has occurred. However, a further delivery of either note by T to a third party does constitute a negotiation. This points out one of the dangers arising from the use of a bearer instrument. Although a thief (or a finder) does not acquire title to the instrument by virtue of the theft (or finding), he or she can *transfer title* to a subsequent innocent purchaser. In such a case, the original owner, X, has lost all rights to the instrument itself.

3. D draws a check that is "payable to the order of P" and mails it to P. P writes her name on the back of the check (an indorsement) and transfers it to her grocer, G, in payment for groceries. The transfer from P to G constitutes a negotiation of this order instrument, since indorsement and delivery have both occurred. However, if P had delivered the instrument without indorsement, it would not constitute a negotiation. (G's rights in such a case will be discussed near the end of this chapter.)

4. B draws a check that is "payable to the order of C" and mails it to C. T, a thief, steals the check, signs C's name on the back, and delivers it to R, a retailer, in payment for liquor. The transfer from T to R is not a negotiation (nor is it even an assignment) because *a forged indorsement is no indorsement.* Nor would a further transfer by R constitute a negotiation; no one can qualify as a holder under a forged indorsement on an order instrument.

---

[11]By contrast, the transfer of a *non*negotiable instrument *always* constitutes an assignment, no matter how the transfer is effected. This is because the negotiation provisions (and, indeed, all provisions) of Article 3 apply only to *negotiable instruments.*

[12]The issuance of an instrument to the payee technically constitutes a negotiation in view of the fact that the payee (as seen in Chapter 24) is one of the persons who qualifies as a holder under Sec. 1-201(20). However, in actual practice, *negotiation* refers only to transfers that occur after an instrument has been issued.

BLANK, SPECIAL, QUALIFIED, AND RESTRICTIVE INDORSEMENTS

The term *indorsement* is not defined in the original Article 3; RUCC 3-204(a) defines this important term to mean:

a signature, other than that of a signer as maker, drawer, or acceptor, that alone or accompanied by other words is made on an instrument for the purpose of (i) negotiating the instrument, (ii) restricting payment on the instrument, or (iii) incurring indorser's liability on the instrument, but regardless of the intent of the signer, a signature and its accompanying words is an indorsement unless the accompanying words, terms of the instrument, place of the signature, or other circumstances unambiguously indicate that the signature was made for a purpose other than indorsement....

Essentially there are four kinds of indorsements: blank, special, qualified, and restrictive.

Blank Indorsements

Under Sec. 3-204(1) [RUCC 3-205(a)], a **blank indorsement** is one that specifies no particular indorsee; ordinarily it consists only of the name of the payee. If a check is payable "to the order of Mary Glenn," she can indorse it *in blank* by simply writing or stamping her name on the back of the instrument.[13]

A blank indorsement converts an order instrument into a bearer instrument. If Mary Glenn delivers the check to Mark Rhee after indorsing it in blank, Rhee can further negotiate the check by delivery only. A blank indorsement makes the instrument virtually as transferable as cash, and for that reason the instrument should ordinarily be indorsed only at the time it is actually delivered to the transferee.

A person who receives an instrument bearing a blank indorsement can protect himself or herself against the possibility of loss of title through subsequent negotiation by a thief. Sec. 3-204(3) [RUCC 3-205(c)] provides that a "holder may convert a blank indorsement into a special indorsement by writing over the signature of the indorser in blank any contract consistent with the character of the indorse-

ment." Thus, where the instrument was indorsed "Mary Glenn" and delivered to Mark Rhee, he can write above the Glenn signature "pay to the order of Mark Rhee." The instrument is now "indorsed specially" and cannot be negotiated further without Rhee's indorsement. (Special indorsements will be discussed soon.)

Effect of Indorsement

A blank indorsement has three effects (in addition to converting the instrument into a bearer instrument):

1. It transfers title to the instrument to the indorsee on delivery.

2. It extends certain warranties to the indorsee and all subsequent holders.

3. It imposes a legal obligation on the indorser to pay the amount of the instrument to the person holding it at maturity if the maker, acceptor, or drawee does not pay (and if certain other conditions are met). This obligation is sometimes called the *conditional* or *secondary liability* of the blank indorser.[14]

Special Indorsements

Under Sec. 3-204(1) [RUCC 3-205(a)], a **special indorsement** "specifies the person to whom or to whose order it makes the instrument payable." To illustrate: A check is payable to the order of P, and he indorses it, "Pay to the order of X, (signed) P." An instrument indorsed in this manner remains an order instrument, and X's indorsement will be necessary for a further negotiation to occur. An indorsement need not, however, include words of negotiability; an indorsement "Pay to X, (signed) P" has the same legal effect as "Pay to the order of X, (signed) P."

A special indorsement on a bearer instrument converts it into an order instrument. To illustrate: A note is "payable to bearer." The first holder, H, indorses it, "Pay to the order of X, (signed) H" and then delivers it to X. X's indorsement is now necessary for a further negotiation of the instrument. However, if X indorses it in blank, it is now reconverted to a bearer instrument.

The primary effect of a special indorsement, then, is that it requires the indorsement of the special indorsee before it can be negotiated further.

---

[13]Indorsements are ordinarily written on an instrument itself. However, under Sec. 3-202(2) [RUCC 3-204(a)], if there are so many indorsements on the back of an instrument that there is no room for more, subsequent indorsements can be written "on a paper so firmly affixed thereto as to become a part thereof." Such a paper, called an *allonge,* must be firmly pasted or stapled to the instrument; attachment by paper clip alone will not suffice under the original Article 3. RUCC 3-204(a) simply speaks of a paper "affixed to the instrument" with no express reference to the firmness of the attachment.

[14]The warranty and conditional liabilities mentioned here arise from Sec. 3-417(1) [RUCC 3-417] and Sec. 3-414(1) [RUCC 3-415(a), (b)], respectively. Their nature and extent are covered in Chapter 27.

FIGURE 25.1

*Blank,
Special, and
Qualified
Indorsements*

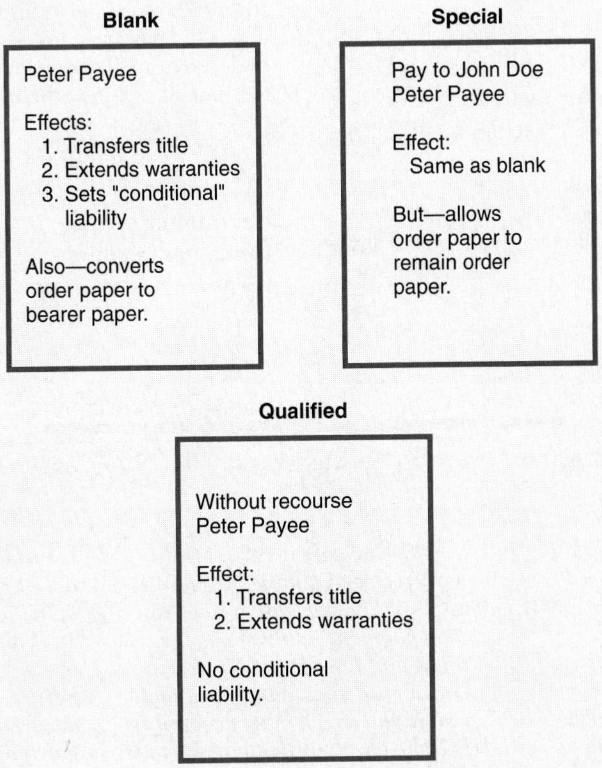

Blank

Peter Payee

Effects:
1. Transfers title
2. Extends warranties
3. Sets "conditional" liability

Also—converts order paper to bearer paper.

Special

Pay to John Doe
Peter Payee

Effect:
   Same as blank

But—allows order paper to remain order paper.

Qualified

Without recourse
Peter Payee

Effect:
1. Transfers title
2. Extends warranties

No conditional liability.

Qualified Indorsements

Blank and special indorsements are "unqualified" indorsements for the reason that indorsers who use them incur *conditional liability* on the instruments negotiated in this manner. Specifically, such indorsers are promising to pay the instruments themselves if the holder is unable to obtain payment from the maker, acceptor, or drawee at maturity. A blank or special indorsement, then, is actually guaranteeing payment of the instrument in addition to transferring title to it.

A **qualified indorsement,** by contrast, is one whose wording indicates that the indorser is not guaranteeing payment of the instrument. The usual qualified indorsement is "without recourse, (signed) X," and the precise effect is illustrated as follows: P receives a check in the mail, drawn on an out-of-town bank and payable to her order. She indorses it "with-out recourse, (signed) P" and negotiates it to H. H deposits the check in his account at a local bank, but a week later the bank returns it to him because the drawer did not have sufficient funds in her account. Because P indorsed the instrument qualifiedly, H cannot recover the amount of the dishonored check from her.

Except for eliminating the conditional liability of the indorser, a qualified indorsement has the same general effect as an unqualified (blank or special) indorsement. "Without recourse" indorsements thus transfer title to the indorsee, permitting further negotiation of the instrument. They also impose a warranty liability on the indorser that is quite similar to the liability of the blank and special indorsers (see Chapter 27 for details).

The effects of blank, special, and qualified indorsements are illustrated in Figure 25.1.

Restrictive Indorsements

It is difficult to make broad generalizations about **restrictive indorsements,** because the original Article 3 recognizes four distinctly separate kinds. Nonetheless, two observations do apply to all of them:

1. Under Sec. 3-206(1) [RUCC 3-206(a)], restrictive indorsements are similar to the other indorsements discussed in this chapter in that they do not (despite their name) restrict the further negotiation of any instrument so indorsed.

2. They differ from the other indorsements by restricting the rights of the indorsee in order to give certain protection to the indorser.

According to Sec. 3-205 [RUCC has no comparable provision]:

An indorsement is restrictive which either (a) is conditional; or (b) purports to prohibit further transfer of the instrument; or (c) includes the words "for collection," "for deposit," "pay any bank," or like terms signifying a purpose of deposit or collection; or (d) otherwise states that it is for the benefit or use of the indorser or of another person.

Before examining the specific kinds of restrictive indorsements, in the following case (decided under the original Article 3) we will see an example of the fundamental differences between a blank indorsement and either a special or restrictive one.

WALCOTT V. MANUFACTURERS HANOVER TRUST

Civil Court of New York City, Kings County, 507 N.Y.S.2d 961 (1986)

Kenneth Walcott filed suit against Manufacturers Hanover Trust (MHT) and Bilko Check Cashing Corp. (Bilko). He claimed that on November 1, 1985, he sent his October 19, 1985 paycheck in the sum of $359.05 together with a Crossland Savings Bank money order in the sum of $251.54 to Midatlantic Mortgage Company in payment of his November 1985 mortgage. According to Walcott, he signed his name on the back of the check and also placed his mortgage number and the Midatlantic mailing sticker on the back with his signature. He asserted that he then put the check and money order in an envelope directed to Midatlantic Mortgage Company and mailed it.

The copy of the check, introduced into evidence, showed Walcott's indorsement and the mortgage number 603052, but no sign of the sticker. The check also showed that it was cashed by Bilko on November 4, 1985 and deposited into the Bilko account at defendant MHT on November 5, 1985.

In mid-November 1985, Mr. Walcott received a notice from Midatlantic that he was late in the November payment of his mortgage. He inquired and found that his paycheck had been cashed at Bilko, who then deposited the check in its account at MHT. The check ultimately cleared through Citibank, the drawee bank, and was charged to the account of the payor, New York Transit Authority (Walcott's employer). The Crossland money order was never cashed; Walcott stopped it on November 22 and replaced it with a new one.

Walcot claimed that someone had stolen the check and cashed it at Bilko. The store manager of Bilko testified that in order for a government check to be cashed, two pieces of identification are required, usually an employee identification card containing an individual's Social Security number and a driver's license. She further testified that the person presenting the check in question must have had such identification since the notations as to the calculation of the check-cashing fees on the front of the check indicate that identification was shown. (The court stated: "This

identification procedure creates doubt as to whether the check was actually stolen.")

Walcott claimed that his placing of the Midatlantic sticker by his signature caused his indorsement to be a special one, and his writing the mortgage number caused it to be a restrictive one. Thus, he claimed, Bilko and MHT improperly treated the check as a bearer instrument. Following is the trial court's decision.

Harkavy, Judge:

. . . The issue presented to this court is whether plaintiff's indorsement of his paycheck was such as to be a special or restrictive indorsement, thus limiting the negotiation of the instrument or did it have the effect of creating a bearer instrument. . . .

Uniform Commercial Code §3-204(1) defines a special indorsement as being one that "specifies the person to whom or to whose order it makes the instrument payable. Any instrument specially indorsed becomes payable to the order of the special indorsee and may be further negotiated only by his indorsement." Examination of the back

(continues)

WALCOTT V. MANUFACTURERS HANOVER TRUST

(continued from previous page)
of the check, a photocopy of which was introduced into evidence, reveals that Mr. Walcott did not specify any particular indorsee. In order for the alleged attached sticker to have served that purpose it must have also complied with UCC 3-202(2): "An indorsement must be written by or on behalf of the holder and on the instrument or on a paper so firmly affixed thereto as to become a part thereof." The back of the check shows no sticker attached at all. Even if it had originally been affixed thereto, as plaintiff claims, it obviously became detached easily, thus failing to meet the indorsement requirements under the UCC to constitute a special indorsement. . . .

As to the numbers written underneath plaintiff's signature, they did not have the effect of restricting plaintiff's indorsement. "An indorsement is restrictive which either (a) is conditional; or (b) purports to prohibit further transfer of the instrument; or (c) includes the words 'for collection,' 'for deposit,' 'pay any bank,' or like terms signifying a purpose of deposit or collection; or (d) otherwise states that it is for the benefit or use of the indorser or of another person." (UCC 3-205). This section of the Uniform Commercial Code is very specific. The series of numbers representing plaintiff's mortgage account was insufficient to restrict negotiation of plaintiff's check.

Plaintiff's indorsement had the effect of converting the check into a bearer instrument. The series of numbers having no restrictive effect, Mr. Walcott indorsed the check in blank, or otherwise stated, he simply signed his name. A blank indorsement under UCC 3-204(2) "specifies no particular indorsee and may consist of a mere signature." Additionally, "[a]n instrument payable to order and indorsed in blank becomes payable to bearer and may be negotiated by delivery alone." Consequently, since plaintiff failed to limit his blank indorsement, the check was properly negotiated by delivery to Bilko and properly cashed by them.

Judgment for the defendants . . . dismissing the complaint. ♐

Conditional Indorsements

As the name indicates, a **conditional indorsement**—recognized under the original Article 3 but not under the revised version—is an order to pay the instrument only if a specified event occurs. As such, the indorsement imposes a condition on the indorsee's right to collect the proceeds of the instrument. This kind of indorsement is not common, but it is useful in certain situations, particularly when combined with a special indorsement. To illustrate: "Pay to the order of Kendyl Dunn upon her delivery to me of one hundred shares of AT&T stock as per our agreement of last November, (signed) Bryan Prentice."

Under the original Article 3, such an indorsement has three basic effects:

1. It does not prohibit further negotiation of the instrument, regardless of whether the condition has or has not occurred.

2. Until the stated condition does occur, however, neither the restrictive indorsee nor any subsequent holder has the right to enforce the instrument.

3. In the event that a holder does receive payment from the maker (or drawee) when the condition has

not yet occurred, both the maker (or drawee) and the holder remain liable to the restrictive indorser for the amount of the instrument.

The RUCC makes another major change here by altering the original Article 3's provision that conditional indorsements are restrictive. Revised Article 3 treats them simply as special indorsements. A person paying or giving value for an instrument so indorsed may ignore the condition. Nor does the condition affect the enforcement right of the indorsee to whom the indorsement was conditional. The revised Article 3 does still recognize the general idea of restrictive (for example, "for deposit only") indorsements.

Special Bank Rules Because of the large volume of commercial paper handled in the bank collection process, certain banks in that process are permitted to disregard any restrictive indorsements (including, of course, conditional indorsements). This result flows from Sec. 3-206(2) [RUCC 3-206(c)(4), (d)], which provides that "an intermediary bank, or a payor bank which is not the depositary bank, is neither given notice nor otherwise affected by a restrictive indorsement of any person excepting the bank's immediate transferor or the person presenting for payment." To illustrate: D, in Worthington, Ohio, draws a check on his Worthington bank and mails it to P, payee, in Bozeman, Montana. P indorses it conditionally and cashes it at his Bozeman bank. The check, now in the bank collection process, is forwarded to a Billings bank, thence to a Chicago bank, and ultimately to the drawee bank in Worthington. Under Sec. 3-206 [RUCC 3-206(c)(4), (d)], the Worthington bank may honor the instrument even if the condition specified in the indorsement has not occurred. Neither that bank nor the Billings and Chicago banks could be held liable to the restrictive indorser in such a situation.[15]

Indorsements Purporting to Prohibit Further Negotiation

Section 3-205(b) [RUCC has no comparable provision] refers to indorsements that intend to prohibit further negotiation, for example, "Pay to the order of X only, (signed) P." Under pre-UCC law such an indorsement terminated negotiability of the instrument, and no subsequent purchaser could qualify as a holder. While this kind of indorsement is rarely used today, the drafters of the UCC reversed the common-law view. Section 3-206(1) [RUCC 3-206(a)] provides expressly that "no restrictive indorsement prevents further transfer or negotiation of the instrument." A "pay to X only" or "pay to the order of X only" indorsement thus has the same legal effect as a special indorsement, and an instrument indorsed in this manner can be further negotiated by X upon proper indorsement and delivery by him or her.

"For Collection" and "For Deposit" Indorsements

Indorsements for collection and for deposit are by far the most commonly used types of restrictive indorsements. Instruments indorsed in either way are almost always put directly into the bank collection process. Under Sec. 3-206(3) [RUCC 3-206(b), (c), (e)], in such situations any depository bank receiving the instrument is responsible for acting consistently with the terms of the indorsement, which ordinarily means that it must credit the restrictive indorser's account.

The protection afforded to the restrictive indorser is best illustrated by a situation where the transferee-

depositary bank fails to live up to its aforementioned duty: D draws and delivers a check payable to P. P indorses the check, "For deposit, (signed) P" and gives the check to her accountant, A, to deposit in P's bank. P's bank gives A cash for the check (or credits A's account), and the cash is not in fact turned over to P (or the funds in A's account are not subsequently made available to P). P can now maintain an *action of conversion* against the bank, and the bank will be liable because it clearly has acted inconsistently with the terms of the restrictive indorsement.

Special Bank Rules As indicated in the discussion of conditional indorsements, drawee and intermediary banks holding restrictively indorsed paper do not have the responsibility that is imposed on depositary banks. Thus, under Sec. 3-206(2) [RUCC 3-206(c)(4), (d)], drawee and intermediary banks in possession of instruments indorsed "for collection" or "for deposit" are neither given notice of nor affected by such indorsements. In other words, these banks cannot be held liable to the restrictive indorser if the restrictive indorsee-depositary bank fails to act consistently with the terms of the indorsements.

A similar type of restrictive indorsement is the *pay any bank or banker indorsement*. This is expressly deemed a restrictive indorsement under Sec. 3-206(3) [RUCC 3-206(b), (c), (e)], and the rules applicable to it are the same as those for the other types of restrictive indorsements discussed in this section.

Trust Indorsements

The fourth type of restrictive indorsement, frequently referred to as a **trust indorsement** or *agency indorsement,* is one that by its terms shows an intent to benefit the indorser or some third party. For example: "Pay to A as agent of P, (signed) P," or "Pay to A in trust for B, (signed) P." In these two situations, two results flow from the indorsements: (1) When the restrictive indorsee, A, receives payment of the instrument, she holds the proceeds in trust for the named beneficiary. (2) Any subsequent purchaser of the instrument takes it free of the restriction, and thus qualifies as an HDC unless he or she has actual knowledge that A's negotiation of the instrument is a breach of A's fiduciary duty.

The following case, decided under the original Article 3, serves notice on bank officers of the unfortunate circumstances that may befall a depositary bank if it fails to pay attention to restrictive indorsements.

---

[15]Here the Bozeman bank is the *depositary bank*—the first bank to which an item is transferred for collection, under Sec. 4-105(a) [RUCC 4-105(2)]. The Billings and Chicago banks are *intermediary banks,* and the Worthington bank is the *payor* (and drawee) bank.

LEHIGH PRESBYTERY V. MERCHANTS BANKCORP.

Superior Court of Pennsylvania, 600 A.2d 593 (1991)

Hunsberger, as secretary/book-keeper for plaintiff/ appellant Lehigh Presbytery, was responsible for opening appellant's mail, affixing a rubber-stamp indorsement to checks received by appellant, and depositing the checks into appellant's account at defendant/appellee bank. Over five years, Hunsberger deposited into her own account 153 of these checks. The bank credited the checks to Hunsberger's account, despite the rubber-stamp restrictive indorsement reading "For Deposit Only To The Credit of Presbytery of Lehigh, Ernest Hutcheson, Treas.," because it relied solely on the account number handwritten on the deposit slips submitted by Hunsberger at the time of deposit. Hunsberger obtained the deposit slips in the lobby of the bank and wrote the proper account title, "Lehigh Presbytery," but inserted her own account number rather than appellant's.

Upon discovering the diversionary scheme, appellant sued the bank. The
bank received a favorable verdict following a trial to the court. The Presbytery appealed.

McEwen, Judge:

[The court first quoted UCC Sec. 3-205, defining restrictive indorsements.] It is undisputed that the indorsement stamped on each check by Ms. Hunsberger is a restrictive indorsement.

Section 3-206 of the U.C.C. addresses the effect of such an indorsement and provides, in pertinent part:

(c) Conditional or specified purpose indorsement.—Except for an intermediary bank, any transferee under an indorsement which is conditional or includes the words "for collection," "for deposit," "pay any bank," or like terms . . . must pay or apply any value given by him for or on the security of the indorsement consistently with the indorsement and to the extent that he does so he becomes a holder for value . . .

Thus, the U.C.C. mandates application of the value of the checks consistently with the indorsement, i.e., for deposit to Lehigh Presbytery's account.

Courts considering the significance of a restrictive indorsement have consistently concluded that the U.C.C. imposes an unwaivable obligation upon the bank to honor the indorsement. The Colorado Supreme Court concluded that "[t]he duty to examine a restrictive indorsement and follow its directions may require a bank to refuse to deposit an item in a particular account if such conduct would be inconsistent with the restrictive indorsement, or to investigate rather than accept an item as a matter of course." *La Junta State Bank v. Travis,* 727 P.2d 48, 54 (Colo.1986). New York State's highest court has held that "[t]he presence of a restriction imposes upon the depository bank an obligation not to accept that item other than in accord with the restriction. By disregarding the restriction, it not only subjects itself to liability for any losses resulting from its actions, but it also passes up what may be the best opportunity to prevent the fraud." *Underpinning & Foundation Constructors, Inc. v. Chase Manhattan,* 386 N.E.2d 1319 (1979).

Judgment reversed.

MISCELLANEOUS NEGOTIATION PROBLEMS

We conclude this chapter with a discussion of several peripheral problems not covered by the general rules of negotiation.

Multiple Payees

Under Sec. 3-116(a) [RUCC 3-110(d)], instruments are sometimes payable to two or more *alternative* persons ("pay to the order of A or B"). Negotiation of such an instrument requires only the indorsement of either of the payees. On the other hand, under Sec. 3-116(b) [RUCC 3-110(d)], if the instrument is payable to the parties *jointly* ("pay to A and B"), then both indorsements are required for a further negotiation of the instrument.

Correction of Names

Sec. 3-203 [RUCC 3-204(d)] provides that "where an instrument is made payable to a person under a misspelled name or [a name] other than his own, he may indorse in that name or his own or both; but signature in both names may be required by a person paying or giving value for the instrument."

Transfer of Unindorsed Order Paper

If an order instrument is transferred without the indorsement of the payee, the transferee is not a holder of the instrument and therefore cannot negotiate it. He or she does, however, have the right (by legal action, if necessary) to require the transferor to indorse the instrument. Upon receiving the indorsement the transferee qualifies as a holder.

There is one exception to the rule that the transferee of an unindorsed order paper cannot negotiate the instrument further. Sec. 4-205 [RUCC 4-205]

permits a depositary bank that received such a check either to supply its customer's indorsement or simply to note on the instrument that it has credited the check to its customer-depositor's account. In either case the bank is a holder and can negotiate the instrument further.

The limits of this exception are tested in the next case.

KELLY v. CENTRAL BANK AND TRUST CO.

Colorado Court of Appeals, 794 P.2d 1037 (1989)

Plaintiffs invested in a Cayman Islands entity, Tradecom, Ltd. Their investments, in the form of cashier's checks, were payable to the order of Tradecom and delivered to Arvey Drown, Tradecom's agent. Drown indorsed the checks and deposited them at defendant Central Bank into a checking account. Most of the $11 million in checks were indorsed in the Tradecom Limited name "for deposit only" and placed in account #072 575 of Equity Trading Corporation, a company owned and managed by Drown that was also purportedly an agent of Tradecom. However, one check for $57,000 was deposited without indorsement and was indorsed by Central Bank's officer as follows:

> For deposit only
> 072 575
> Tradecom by
> Mark E. Thomson
> Commercial Loan officer

Other checks, totalling $519,850, were indorsed as follows:

> For deposit only
> 072 575

Plaintiffs lost most of their money and sued Central Bank on various theories, alleging that neither Drown nor Equity Trading was an agent of Tradecom and that the check in-

dorsements by Drown were unauthorized and ineffective; that over the course of 13 months, the Bank negligently or recklessly permitted Drown improperly to divert the checks, payable to Tradecom, into Equity Trading's checking account; and that Central Bank did not follow reasonable commercial standards. The trial court ordered summary judgment for Central Bank on all claims and plaintiffs appealed.

Tursi, Judge:

[The court first concluded that a power of attorney appointed Drown as Tradecom's agent with authority to indorse and deposit the cashier's checks, and therefore] plaintiffs could not prevail as to the 11 million dollars of checks which contains an indorsement which included the "Tradecom Limited" name. Consequently, with respect to these checks indorsed with Tradecom's name, we conclude that the trial court properly granted summary judgment for Central Bank.

The trial court erred, however, in granting Central Bank summary judgment on the $57,000 check indorsed by Central Bank's commercial loan officer.

In order for Central Bank to have become a holder under this indorsement, and, thus have obtained title, Central Bank would have had to have been authorized to provide Tradecom's indorsement under [UCC Sec. 4-205(1)]. This, however, was impos-

sible since Tradecom was not Central Bank's "customer." Consequently, this indorsement is unauthorized as a matter of law, and summary judgment should not have been ordered for Central Bank on this check.

Plaintiffs also contend that the trial judge erred in granting summary judgment for Central Bank on the remaining $519,850 of cashier's checks lacking any signature and merely indorsed "For deposit only 072 575." We agree.

Under [UCC Sec. 3-419(1)(c)], a check is converted when it is paid on a forged indorsement. In this context, a collecting or depositary bank "pays" a check when it credits its customer's account with the proceeds of a check collected from a drawee bank. If such indorsement occurs on a check with no indorsement or a missing indorsement, it is the legal equivalent of payment on a forged instrument.

The term "indorsement" is generally understood to mean the indorser's writing of his or her signature on the instrument or the affixing of the indorser's name or some designation identifying the indorser on the instrument. A check simply inscribed "For deposit only" to an account other than payee's account and without the payee's signature is not an effective "indorsement."

If the instrument is order paper and the depository bank does not, or cannot, supply the missing indorsement of its customer, the absence of an indorsement can be fatal to negotiation

(continues)

KELLY V. CENTRAL BANK AND TRUST CO.

(continued from previous page)
and transfer of title. One such situation is when the depository bank's customer and the payee are not the same person. In this case, the depository bank is unauthorized to, and cannot, supply the missing indorsement of the payee since the payee is not the bank's "customer" under [UCC Sec. 4-205]. In this situation, the depository bank does not become a holder of the checks and does not obtain good title to them. Payment of such check proceeds to its depositor subjects the depository bank to liability for conversion. [The trial court erred in granting defendant summary judgment on these $576,850 of cashier's checks.

Affirmed in part; reversed in part.]⚖

Forged Indorsements

The original Article 3 provides the general rule that an instrument is converted when it is paid on a forged indorsement. However, a forged indorsement is considered sufficiently effective to impose liability on the drawer, rather than upon the drawee who cashed it, in three main situations that we shall discuss in turn: (1) fictitious payees, (2) impostors, and (3) negligence.

Fictitious Payees

The **fictitious payee** situation most often occurs where a dishonest employee, usually someone in charge of payrolls or payment of bills, draws a company check payable to the order of a nonexistent person or to the order of an actual person who is not entitled to payment. Following are three cases that illustrate the fictitious payee rule. The result and rule will be explained after all three cases are set out.

Case 1. The D company has 50 employees. B, the company's bookkeeper, has authority to issue checks in the corporate name to pay bills and the payroll for the firm's employees. B issues a check to P, who is neither a creditor nor an employee of the company. The check is drawn on the X Bank, where the company has its checking account. After drawing the check, B indorses P's name on the check and cashes it at some other local bank. The X Bank (drawee) receives the check through the collection process and charges the D Company's account.

Case 2. The situation is the same as in Case 1, except that B drafts a check drawn on the X Bank payable to P (an accomplice of B) and puts the check, among others, on T's desk for his signature. T signs the check in the corporate name, believing P to be a creditor of the firm. B takes the check to P after T has signed it; P then indorses it and cashes it at a local bank. The X Bank (drawee) receives the check through the collection process and charges the D Company's account.

Case 3. The situation is the same as for Case 2, except that B, after receiving the signed check payable to the order of P, indorses P's name on the back and transfers it to a third party, H, instead of delivering it to P. H, an innocent purchaser, presents the check to the X Bank for payment but finds that payment has been stopped by the D Company, which had discovered what B had done.

Suppose, in Cases 1 and 2, that the D Company after learning the facts sues the X Bank to recover the amount of the checks on the theory that the indorsements were forgeries. And, in Case 3, suppose that H sues the D Company (drawer) on the check, and the D Company defends on the ground that the indorsement of P was a forgery. Under the original Article 3, the D Company loses all three cases.

In Case 1, where B had the authority to sign checks in the corporate name and did so knowing that P was not entitled to payment, Sec. 3-405(1)(b) [RUCC 404(b)(i)] applies. It provides that "the indorsement by any person in the name of a named payee is effective if a person signing as or on behalf of a maker or drawer intends the payee to have no interest in the instrument." Thus, the signing of P's name by B is an effective indorsement rather than a forgery. Consequently, the bank effectively obeyed the D Company's order to pay, and it was therefore entitled to charge the company's account.

The same is true in Case 2, where B supplied the D Company's treasurer with the checks payable to the order of P, because Sec. 3-405(1)(c) [RUCC 3-405] provides that "the indorsement by any person in

the name of a named payee is effective if an agent or employee of the maker has supplied him with the name of the payee intending the latter to have no such interest." Thus, the X Bank again had the right to charge the company's account with the check—assuming, of course, that the bank had no knowledge of B's misconduct.

In Case 3, for the same reason, the holder of the check, H, can enforce the check against the D Company. (As will be seen in Chapter 28, the fact that the D Company stopped payment on the check does not necessarily insulate it against liability to the holder of the check. A stop-payment order simply prevents the holder from receiving payment on presenting the check to the drawee bank; a subsequent lawsuit by the holder against the drawee will determine the liability or nonliability of the drawer.)

Revised Article 3 makes some changes in this area. First, note that in all of the aforementioned cases, the wrongdoer was an agent of the drawer. Assume the wrongdoer is an agent of the payee. For example, D Company writes a check to X Company. B, an agent of X Company, steals the check and deposits it in an account that B has opened in X Company's name at B's bank. B then uses the funds. The original Article 3 does not apply to this case, meaning that negligence on behalf of X Company would have to be demonstrated before X Company could be held to bear the loss. Revised Article 3 provides, on the other hand, that X Company bears the loss so long as B was an agent of X Company with responsibility for handling the check. [RUCC 3-405(a)(2)(i)].

Most importantly, revised Article 3 imposes a pure *comparative negligence* standard, which may reduce D Company's liability in the aforementioned cases by the amount of any loss caused by negligence on the part of the person paying the instrument or taking it for value or for collection. [RUCC 3-404(d)].[16]

Impostors

An **impostor** is a person who induces a maker or drawer to issue a negotiable instrument in the name of an impersonated payee. Assume that X impersonates Y and is named payee on a check by D who truly believes that X is Y. Because D did not intend X to receive the instrument, X's indorsement is unauthorized when the instrument is transferred to an innocent party. However, under the original Article 3, such an unauthorized indorsement of Y's name can be as effective as if Y herself had signed. Such an impostor's indorsement is effective (not a forgery) insofar as the drawer (D) is concerned. Therefore, if in the aforementioned example X indorsed the instrument by signing Y's name to a good faith holder for value, D would be liable on the instrument and

---

[16]We will learn in Chapter 27 that the revised Article 3 imposes a comparative negligence standard in other areas as well.

would have to seek a remedy from the impostor, X.

Again, the revised Article 3 makes some changes in this area. First, it imposes the comparative negligence standard, which could reduce D's liability if the good faith holder was negligent in accepting the check.

Second, the original Article 3 did not render the drawer liable in the situation where the impostor poses as an *agent of the payee* and the drawer names *the principal* as payee on the check. Assume that X, an impostor, impersonates the president of D Company and is issued a check in the name of "D Company." Under the original Article 3, the drawer is not liable because the drawer took the precaution of making the instrument payable to the principal rather than to the impostor. RUCC 3-404(a) changes this result by providing that a fraud occurs when a wrongdoer impersonates an agent authorized to act for the payee. Therefore, the impostor's rendering of the principal's indorsement would be considered effective so that the drawer is liable for the loss.

Negligence

In many cases involving fictitious payees, the employer's negligence assists the dishonest employee. As we shall learn in Chapter 28 (and discuss in more detail), often the depository bank is in the best position to stop the fraud, but fails to do so. Under the original Article 3, the negligent employer must bear the entire loss *unless* the depository bank acts in bad faith. Under the revised Article 3, however, the comparative negligence principle applies so that part of the loss may be allocated to a depository bank whose carelessness contributes to the loss.

Consider how revised Article 3's comparative negligence provision might have changed the outcome of the following fictitious payee case decided under original Article 3.

SHEARSON LEHMAN BROTHERS, INC. v. WASATCH BANK

U.S. District Court for Utah, 788 F.Supp. 1184 (1992)

Erb worked for plaintiff Shearson Lehman Brothers, Inc. Ashton, Bastian, and Peterson were principals of WordPerfect and its sister corporation, Utah Softcopy. In March 1987, Erb personally accepted on behalf of Shearson a check from Matthews in the amount of $460,150.33 drawn by Utah Softcopy and payable to the order of "ABP [named for each of the WordPerfect principals] Investments." Erb accepted the check for deposit at Shearson, despite the fact that ABP had no account at Shearson at that time. Instead of depositing the check into an authorized WordPerfect account, Erb opened a new account at Shearson in the name of "ABP Investments," forging Bastian's name on the new account documents. He listed as the address of record a post office box unknown to WordPerfect and its principals.

By submitting to the Shearson cashier falsified payment request forms, Erb then induced Shearson to draft checks on the ABP Investments account, payable to ABP Investments. The checks were mailed to the post office box, where Erb received them, indorsed them in the name of ABP Investments, and took them to defendant Wasatch Bank for deposit into his personal account. Fraudulently negotiating 37 checks, Erb procured $504,295.30. Copies of the checks revealed that each was indorsed, in handwriting, in the name of ABP Investments and without Erb's personal indorsement or any other indication of Erb's authority to act on behalf of the payee. No ABP Investments account was maintained at Wasatch, and therefore no signature card or other evidence on the premises of the bank could have been used to verify Erb's authority to deposit checks payable to ABP Investments.

WordPerfect and its principals learned of the misappropriation and settled their claims with Shearson, agreeing to assign to Shearson any rights they might have against Wasatch. Shearson then sued Wasatch, which moved for summary judgment. The following is excerpted from the trial judge's decision on Wasatch's motion.

Anderson, Senior District Judge:

Wasatch acknowledges that, "[a]s a general rule, 'forged indorsements are ineffective to pass title or to authorize a drawee to pay.'" *Western Casualty & Sur. Co. v. Citizens Bank,* 676 F.2d 1344 (10th Cir. 1982) (quoting White & Summers, Handbook of the Law under the Uniform Commercial Code (2d ed. 1980)). Consequently, when a collecting bank makes payment over a forged indorsement, it is generally liable for the amount paid.

Wasatch attempts to avoid such liability, however, by invoking what *(continues)*

SHEARSON LEHMAN BROTHERS, INC. V. WASATCH BANK

(continued from previous page)
is known as the "fictitious payee" defense . . . set forth in 3-405 of the UCC:

(1) An indorsement by any person in the name of a named payee is effective if . . . (c) an agent or employee of the maker or drawer has supplied him [the drawer] with the name of the payee intending the latter to have no such interest.

The official comment to Sec. 3-405 instructs as to its application:

[Section 3-405] extends [the former rule] to include the padded payroll cases, where the drawer's agent or employee prepares the check for signature or otherwise furnishes the signing officer with the name of the payee. The principle followed is that the loss should fall upon the employer as a risk of his business enterprise rather than upon the subsequent holder or drawee. The reasons are that the employer is normally in a better position to prevent such forgeries by reasonable care in the selection . . . of his employees.

According to the Utah high court, when the fictitious payee defense applies, the result is that "the check is deemed to be payable to bearer, and an endorsement of the payee's name on the check is not a forgery." *Braswell Motor Freight Lines, Inc. v. Bank of Salt Lake*, 502 P.2d 560 (Utah 1972).

For the defense to apply, an employee or agent of the drawer must "supply" the name of the payee to the drawer, and the faithless employee must intend that the payee have no interest in the instrument. Although the defense commonly has been referred to as the "fictitious payee" defense, the payee named on the check need not be a fictitious person or entity.

Thus, Wasatch argues that the fictitious payee defense applies to the undisputed facts of the present case. Erb, an employee of the drawer of the check, "supplied" the name of the payee within the meaning of the statute and obviously intended that the named payee have no interest in the checks. He then procured the checks and fraudulently indorsed them for deposit into his account at Wasatch. Wasatch accordingly argues that the effect of Erb's actions was to validate the forged indorsements and to allow good title to pass to Wasatch thereby extinguishing Wasatch's liability for the transaction.

Shearson argues that 3-405 cannot be invoked as a defense unless the party seeking its protection has acted in "good faith." Shearson alleges that Wasatch failed to act with the requisite good faith because (1) Wasatch apparently made no attempt to verify Erb's authority to negotiate the checks

payable to ABP Investments for deposit into his own account; (2) Wasatch personally knew that Erb was employed by the drawer of the check and should have been alerted thereby to the irregularity of the transaction; (3) the large amounts of the checks [up to $60,000 each] were inconsistent with Erb's prior account history; [and] (4) the amounts of the checks exceeded the dollar amount that could be deposited without officer approval according to internal bank policy and such approval was not obtained. . . .

Shearson would have the court conclude that such negligence, assuming it is such, constitutes bad faith and precludes application of [the fictitious payee defense]. . . . The overwhelming majority of jurisdictions considering the question have determined that a collecting bank's simple negligence will not bar a Sec. 3-405 defense to claims resulting from the collecting bank's acceptance of a check over a forged indorsement where the defense is otherwise applicable. . . . [A] bank's failure to follow commercially reasonable banking procedures or to comply with its own policies generally will not constitute a lack of good faith. . . .

[S]ummary judgment is hereby granted in favor of Wasatch. ⚖

SUMMARY

The negotiability or nonnegotiability of an instrument is determined entirely by its form and content. Under Sec. 3-104 [RUCC 3-104], to be negotiable an instrument must (1) be signed by the maker or drawer, (2) contain an unconditional order or promise to pay a sum certain in money, (3) be payable on demand or at a definite time, and (4) be payable to order or to bearer. Subsequent sections of Article 3 clarify these requirements.

The "unconditional" requirement means that the promise or order must be absolute, rather than one payable only in certain circumstances. Two types of provisions generally condition an order or promise, and and thus cause the instrument to be nonnegotiable under the original Article 3: (1) provisions stating that payment is to be out of a specified fund [such a provision does *not* render an instrument nonnegotiable under the revised Article 3], and (2) promises stating that the instrument is "subject to" another agreement.

With respect to the time of payment requirements, an instrument is payable on demand if it so provides, or if it contains no time of payment. An instrument is payable at a definite time if payable at a specified future date, or at such a date with an acceleration clause providing for an earlier maturity date if a certain event occurs. Instruments payable "on or before" a specified date also meet the definite time requirement. An instrument payable "to X" is not negotiable, because it is neither a bearer nor an order instrument.

Turning to the question of transfer, a bearer instrument may be negotiated by delivery only, but an order instrument requires an indorsement in addition to delivery. If a transfer does not meet the negotiation requirements, the transferee is merely an assignee of the transferor's rights, and the transferee cannot achieve the favored holder-in-due course status.

There are four kinds of indorsements: blank, special, qualified, and restrictive. A blank indorsement converts an order instrument into a bearer instrument. Blank and special indorsements have three additional consequences. First, they transfer title to the indorsee when accompanied by delivery of the instrument. Second, such indorsers extend certain warranties, or guarantees, to the indorsee and to all subsequent holders. Third, such indorsers have the legal obligation to pay the instrument at maturity if the maker, acceptor, or drawee dishonors it. A qualified ("without recourse") indorsement has the same consequences as blank and special indorsements except that such an indorser does *not* have the legal obligation to pay the instrument if it is dishonored.

Restrictive indorsements do *not* prohibit further negotiation, but, in general, do restrict the rights of the indorser relative to the proceeds of the instrument upon its payment. A forged indorsement necessary to the negotiation of an order instrument is void. Thus, if a payee's indorsement is forged and the instrument thereafter is transferred, no negotiation has occurred and the transferee is neither a holder of the instrument nor entitled to payment of the instrument. Various exceptions to this general rule arise in cases of fictitious payees and impostors.

KEY TERMS
Demand instrument
Time instrument
Acceleration clause
Extension clause
Order instrument
Bearer instrument
Assignment
Negotiation
Blank indorsement
Special indorsement
Qualified indorsement
Restrictive indorsement
Conditional indorsement
Trust indorsement
Fictitious payee
Impostor

QUESTIONS AND PROBLEMS

1. In response to Aegis Energy System Inc.'s need for capital, purported investor Hagan convinced Carnegie Bank to loan $150,000 to Anderson (falsely represented to be Hagan's wife), secured by a $200,000 note that Aegis had granted to Anderson, and that Anderson then assigned to the bank. When Anderson defaulted, the bank sued Aegis on the note. The note required Anderson to repay the principal sum "with interest thereon from the date hereof at the annual rate of two (2%) percent in excess of the Lender's [Carnegie Bank's] Floating Rate Base, as adjusted from time to time, calculated on the basis of a 360-day year for actual days elapsed. . . ." Is this note negotiable or nonnegotiable? (*Carnegie Bank v. Shalleck,* 606 A.2d 389, N.J.Super. 1992.)

2. In early 1978, Brooks was trying to buy the stock of Otis Smith Ford, Inc. Owner Otis Smith needed a 30-day, $50,000 loan in order to replenish his stock, but United Kentucky Bank would make the loan only if Brooks guaranteed it. While the loan was being processed, bank employees had Brooks sign the second page of a two-page printed form entitled "Unconditional Continuing Guarantee," which stated that Brooks "unconditionally guarantees to the Bank . . . the prompt payment when due of all present and future obligations, liabilities and instruments of any and all kinds constituting or evidencing obligations or liabilities, present or future, of Borrower to Bank. . . ." The blanks were later filled in by bank officers. Smith renewed his note four times, but ultimately went into bankruptcy. The bank sued Brooks on the guaranty. Brooks argued that the guaranty was not enforceable because it was not completely filled out

when he signed it. The court cited UCC Sec. 3-115(1), which provides that an instrument incomplete when signed but later completed in accordance with authority given is enforceable as completed. However, the court believed that Sec. 3-115 applies only when an instrument is negotiable. Was the Brooks guarantee negotiable? Discuss. (*Brooks v. United Kentucky Bank*, 659 S.W.2d 213, Ky.App. 1983.)

3. In September of 1979, the Stewart Company leased a motel to the Downwards under a contract that gave the Downwards the option to buy until May 1, 1980. At the same time Stewart, owner of the company, gave a promissory note to C.J. Realty, the real estate firm handling the deal, which provided that the note would be payable "upon the final closing" between the Stewart Company and the Downwards "on or before May 1, 1980, when [the Downwards] exercise their option to purchase." C.J. Realty sold the note to Calfo, plaintiff. When the note came due, Stewart refused to pay it because the Downwards never exercised their option to buy. Calfo contended that Stewart could not assert the nonsale of property as a defense because the note was a negotiable instrument and that he was an HDC. Was the note negotiable? Discuss. (*Calfo v. D.C. Stewart Co.*, 717 P.2d 697, Utah 1986.)

4. The Sylvias, defendants, signed a promissory note that was payable "within 10 years after date" (that is, date of issue). Ferri demanded payment before the 10 years were up, and the defendants contended that the instrument was not due until the 10 years had elapsed. The trial court ruled that the due date of the instrument was *ambiguous,* and allowed oral testimony as to what the parties' intentions were as to the due date. On the basis of this testimony the court concluded that plaintiff had the right to demand payment at any time after the instrument was issued. Was the trial judge correct? Discuss. (*Ferri v. Sylvia*, 214 A.2d 470, R.I. 1965.)

5. As part of a bankruptcy proceeding, the American Fidelity Fire Insurance Co., plaintiff, issued a certified check for $84,858 payable to the order of "Charles R. Joy, Receiver." Joy indorsed the check restrictively, "For deposit in Quantum Acct. Quantum Bankruptcy," and negotiated it to the Bank of Nova Scotia (BNS), which in return issued certificates of deposit to Joy that were payable to Joy personally. Joy later cashed the certificates and absconded with the money. Plaintiff sued to recover the amount of the check from BNS. Plaintiff's major claim was that BNS's actions were *inconsistent with* the terms of the restrictive indorsement. Will plaintiff prevail? Discuss. (*In re Quantum Development Corporation*, 397 F.Supp. 329, D.V.I. 1975.)

6. The Coles (through a company owned by them) drew a check payable to the order of Wyoming Homes and issued the check to Wyoming Homes in partial payment for a home purchase. The Wyoming Homes salesman, without indorsing the check, deposited it in Wyoming Homes' account in the Gillette Bank, which credited the account. The Gillette Bank put the check into channels of collection and it was duly charged to the Coles' account in the drawee bank, First National Bank of Buffalo. The Coles then discovered that Wyoming Homes was guilty of fraud, and it brought this action against the Gillette Bank (where the check was originally deposited by Wyoming Homes) on the theory that the bank was *merely a transferee* of the check—rather than a holder—since Wyoming Homes did not indorse the check subject to all defenses existing in favor of the Coles, and that the bank is liable in this action. Is the Coles' theory sound? Discuss. (*Cole v. First National Bank of Gillette*, 433 P.2d 837, Wyo. 1967.)

7. Ambassador Financial Services agreed to finance the purchase of seven Mercedes Benz autos. There was a different buyer ("investor") for each car; the buyers intended to lease the cars to Beltax Co. (owned by Walsh) so that it could start a limousine service. Each purchaser signed a promissory note. Ambassador then issued checks made jointly payable to Walsh and each investor to pay for the cars. Each check, drawn on Ambassador's account at defendant Indiana National Bank (INB), was for $16,000. Walsh indorsed his name and that of each of his co-payees and deposited three of the checks into an account in his name "d/b/a Beltax" at First Union Bank. Having failed to notice the forgeries, First Union passed the checks to INB for final payment. INB charged Ambassador's account. Upon discovering the forgeries, Ambassador learned that the cars were never purchased. Ambassador sued INB, claiming that INB was strictly liable for paying the forged check. Is Ambassador correct? Discuss. (*Ambassador Financial Services v. Indiana National Bank*, 605 N.E.2d 746, Ind. 1992.)

Chapter 26

Commercial Paper
Holders in Due Course and Defenses

Holders in Due Course

Defenses

Revised Article 3 Approach to Defenses

*Limitations on Holder in
Due Course Doctrine*

U NDER ORDINARY CONTRACT law, the assignment of a contractual (nonnegotiable) right passes to the assignee the same rights possessed by the assignor—no more and no less. The assignee thus takes the right or claim subject to all defenses that might exist between the original parties to the contract, regardless of whether the assignee knows of them at the time of acquiring the right. As a result, contractual claims are not transferred in large numbers in the business community, for most prospective assignees will purchase a claim only after satisfying themselves that the original obligor on the contract does not have a defense against it. This is usually a time-consuming process and often an impossible one.

The purchasers of negotiable instruments, by contrast, acquire them *free* of many defenses that exist between the original parties to the instrument if such purchasers qualify as **holders in due course** of the instruments. In fact, a major purpose of UCC Article 3 is to facilitate the negotiation of commercial paper by (1) spelling out the requirements that must be met by the purchaser of a negotiable instrument in order for that person to acquire the most favored status of a holder in due course (HDC), and (2) identifying the specific kinds of defenses that are cut off when a purchaser of the instrument attains this status.

In this chapter we will discuss, first, the holder in due course, and, second, the subject of defenses.

HOLDERS IN DUE COURSE
Holder in Due Course Status
It is helpful, at the outset, to understand the typical situation in which an HDC acquires greater rights than those possessed by the transferor. Suppose, for example, that M, a building contractor, has contracted to purchase certain plumbing fixtures from P Company, a plumbing supply firm, for $2250. M makes a negotiable promissory note for that amount, due 60 days later, and gives it to P Company. After receiving the note, P Company negotiates it immediately to the B Bank, receiving, say, $2000 cash in return. When the note comes due, M refuses to pay it because many of the fixtures delivered by P Company are defective. In this situation the B Bank—if it qualifies as an HDC—*is entitled to a judgment*

against M for the full $2250, even though its transferor, P Company, probably would have recovered nothing from M had it held the instrument itself until maturity.

The bank is entitled to a judgment because M's defense—breach of contract on the part of the payee—is one of the defenses cut off by negotiation of the instrument to an HDC. (Such defenses, often called *personal defenses*, will be discussed along with *real defenses* later in the chapter.)

Two further observations about HDCs and other holders should be made.

Status of the Ordinary Holder
In some situations a holder is entitled to payment of the instrument even though he or she is an ordinary holder (one who does *not* qualify as an HDC). In the above illustration, for example, if the plumbing fixtures that were delivered by the P Company to M were not defective in any way—in which case M possesses no defense against the P Company—the B Bank is entitled to recover the full $2250 from M even if it did not meet the HDC requirements of the UCC. Thus, the favored status of the HDC is of significance only in those situations in which the primary party possesses a personal defense against the payee.

Limitations on the Holder in Due Course
Despite the favorable position that the HDC usually occupies, even holders in due course do not *always* prevail against the obligor. In the first place, if the obligor has a *real* defense—such as forgery—he or she may assert this defense against *all* holders, even HDCs. Second, and perhaps more important, *several recently enacted consumer protection statutes and orders of regulatory agencies have cut down the rights of HDCs by permitting obligors to assert personal defenses against them in certain situations.* (These limitations on the HDC doctrine will be discussed later in the chapter.)

Holder in Due Course Requirements
UCC Sec. 3-302 [RUCC 3-302] contains the three basic requirements for HDC status: "A holder in due course is a holder who takes the instrument (a) for

value; and (b) in good faith; and (c) without any notice that it is overdue or has been dishonored or if any defense against or claim to it on the party of any person." The major purpose of these requirements is to define the kind of person who deserves, as a matter of policy, to take the instrument free of certain defenses (such as breach of contract by the payee). Some purchasers of instruments are denied this favored treatment, for example, because they either knew or should have known of an existing defense at the time of purchase.

Before examining each of the requirements, we should remember that a person seeking HDC status must first qualify as a *holder*, defined by Sec. 1-201(20) as "a person who is in possession of . . . an instrument . . . drawn, issued or indorsed to him or to his order or to bearer or in blank." A transferee who acquires an instrument other than by issue or negotiation thus ordinarily fails to qualify as an HDC at the outset, regardless of the other circumstances under which the acquisition took place.

Value

The term **value** is defined in Sec. 3-303 [RUCC 3-303], which states that a holder (usually a purchaser) has given value (1) to the extent that the agreed-upon consideration has been performed (by him or her) or to the extent that he or she acquires a security interest in or a lien on the instrument other than by legal process, or (2) when he or she takes the instrument in payment of, or as security for, an antecedent claim against any person, whether or not the claim is due, or (3) when he or she gives a negotiable instrument in payment for it. The reasoning underlying the value requirement is that if a person receives a note or a check without having given value for it, he or she obviously will suffer no out-of-pocket loss by being unable to recover from the primary party in the event that the latter has a personal defense available.

The following examples illustrate the basic import of the value requirement:

1. P, a payee of an out-of-town check, cashes it at his own bank. The bank, by giving P cash, has obviously given value.

2. P, a retailer, is the payee of a $900 note issued by M. P makes a contract with a third party, H, under which H is to deliver 30 cameras to P in exchange for the note. Before the delivery date P runs into financial difficulties, and H, fearing that the note might be attached by P's creditors, demands that it be negotiated to her immediately. P delivers the note to H, and H later delivers the cameras. H is a holder for value, since she performed the agreed-upon consideration by delivering the cameras. H is entitled to enforce the instrument against the maker, M, at maturity even if M has a personal defense against P.

3. The facts are the same as in 2, above, except that after H received the note, she failed to deliver any of the cameras before learning of M's defense against P. Here H has not given value for the instrument (that is, H's original *promise* to deliver the cameras does not constitute value). This illustration points out the fact that the term *value* in Article 3 is not synonymous with *consideration* under contract law; that is, whereas a promise to perform an act constitutes consideration, it does *not* constitute value.

4. What about a *partial* performance situation? The revised Article 3 clarifies the matter, providing that an HDC "may assert rights as a holder in due course of the instrument only to the fraction of the amount payable under the instrument equal to the value of the partial performance divided by the value of the promised performance." Consider this illustration:

Payee negotiates a $1,000 note to Holder who agrees to pay $900 for it. After paying $500 Holder learns that Payee defrauded Maker in the transaction giving rise to the note. . . . Holder may assert rights as a holder in due course to the extent of $555.55 ($500 divided by $900 = .555 × $1,000 = $555.55).[1]

The following case illustrates the value requirement.

---

[1] RUCC 3-302, comment 6.

FEDERAL LAND BANK V. HARDIN-MAPES COAL CORPORATION

Supreme Court of Kentucky, 817 S.W.2d 225 (1991)

Case

Charles, who performed bookkeeping services for Hardin-Mapes Coal Corp., stole two of its checks and forged the name of the corporation president to both and made Federal Land Bank of Louisville (FLB) the payee. Each check was for the sum of $12,355.29 and was applied as partial payment to a farm loan owed by Charles to FLB. FLB deposited the checks, and the drawee bank mistakenly honored the forged instruments.

Hardin-Mapes filed a lien on the farm property, and when Charles defaulted on the FLB loan. FLB filed suit to foreclose and also named Hardin-Mapes by reason of the lien. FLB claimed the right as an HDC to retain the proceeds of the checks as a credit on the Charles mortgage loan. The trial court ruled for FLB and the court of appeals reversed. FLB appealed.

Reynolds, Justice:

To be a holder in due course is of paramount importance in commercial law and once a party has reached this status, the law provides a mantle of protection wherein most of a maker's legitimate defenses do not get through and he must pay up and settle his quarrel later and with someone else. Necessarily, there are high standards for admission to the rank/status of holder in due course and one of these is that the holder must have given "value." UCC 3-302(1)(a). FLB, upon the receipt of the checks, credited Charles's account, thus taking the instruments in partial payment of the forger's antecedent debt.

The determination that FLB was a holder in due course was error inasmuch as FLB, at the most, extended the forger only partial provisional credit upon the antecedent debt. The security instrument retained by FLB was not released and remained intact.

Value, if any, was provisional. Determinatively, a special situation exists where a payee is a bank that accepts a check from one that is not the maker and that person requests that the bank credit his (the forger's) personal account with the proceeds. The bank is to be held to a higher standard than an individual in a private transaction and notice is deemed to have been given by the terms of the instrument itself. Under these circumstances, the bank is required to hold the proceeds of the instrument subject to the order of the maker and not the presenter (forger) and the bank generally cannot be a holder in due course as against the maker if it has permitted the presenter to otherwise use the proceeds of the check without taking precautions to determine the authority of the presenter. FLB was a holder, not a holder in due course, of the instruments and took the checks subject to all claims against them.

[Affirmed.] ⚖

Good Faith

The requirement that one must take the instrument in good faith in order to qualify as an HDC is contained in Sec. 3-302(b) [RUCC 3-302]. **Good faith** is defined (not too helpfully) in Sec. 1-201(19) as "honesty in fact in the conduct or transaction." The revised Article 3 defines "good faith" in RUCC 3-103(a)(4) to mean "honesty in fact and the observation of reasonable commercial standards of fair dealing." The new definition is meant to emphasize that the law is more concerned with *fairness* than with the care used to perform an act.

In most cases the good faith requirement and the requirement that a holder take an instrument "without notice of a defense" overlap. That is, if a court in a particular case finds the holder to be barred from HDC status because the instrument was acquired under circumstances in which he or she should have known of an existing defense, such holder also often has taken the instrument in bad faith. Conversely, if a court rules that the holder did *not* have reason to know of an existing defense when he or she acquired the instrument, such holder is also usually found to have taken the instrument in good faith. Be that as it may, Article 3 treats the two as separate requirements and so do many defendants when presenting reasons why they believe the plaintiff is not an HDC.

GALATIA COMMUNITY STATE BANK V. KINDY

Supreme Court of Arkansas, 821 S.W.2d 765 (1991)

Case

Kindy agreed to buy four diesel engines from Hicks, who was to deliver them to an address in Canada. Of the $13,000 purchase price, Kindy agreed to wire transfer $6500 and pay the remainder by check. Kindy and Hicks agreed the check would not be cashed until the motors were delivered. In late June 1989, Kindy wired the $6500 and mailed a check postdated July 6, 1989. Kindy placed the number 6500.00 in the box on the right side of the check commonly used for numbers, but a check-writing machine imprinted in the center underlined section of the check, commonly used for stating the amount in words, "°°5550 DOL'S 00 CTS." Kindy placed two different amounts on the check to protect himself from Hicks cashing the checks before the engines were delivered. He testified that he thought if he made the check out with the two different amounts the bank would either call him to find out if it was good, or at least notify him before honoring it.*

Hicks presented the check to the Galatia Bank on July 10, 1989. He received $800 in cash and $4750 in credit to his account from a bank employee who altered the handwritten portion of the check from "$6,550.00" to "$5,550.00," apparently to reconcile the two numbers. Galatia sent the check through the Federal Reserve System for collection, and it was presented to the First National Bank for final payment. Kindy had told First National to call him when the check was presented so he could determine whether Hicks had delivered the en-

gines. First National did so, and Kindy told it not to pay the check because the engines had not been delivered. The check was returned to Galatia. Galatia sent the check through again, but was thwarted by a stop-payment order made by Kindy. Galatia then sued Kindy for $4753.64, the amount it lost as the result of Hicks drawing down the account to which the check had been deposited. The trial court held against Galatia. Galatia appealed.

Newbern, Justice:

If Galatia Bank had made a "fraudulent and material" alteration of the check without Kindy's assent, no doubt Kindy's liability on the instrument would have been discharged [under Sec. 3-407(2)(a) of the original Article 3, in effect at the time of the transaction]. The [revised Article 3 provision adopted in Arkansas in 1991] is slightly different. The Trial Court found specifically that the alteration was not done "fraudulently," and refused to hold Kindy was discharged. That finding was correct. The Court held, rather, that Galatia Bank was not a holder in due course because it did not take the check in "good faith."

"Good faith" is defined at UCC 1-201(9) as "honesty in fact in the conduct or transaction concerned." . . . [T]he good faith requirement is closely related to the requirement of Sec. 3-302(c) that the holder not have "notice that [the instrument] is overdue or has been dishonored or of any defense against or claim to it on the part of any

person."[1] The authors point out that there is a difference between the two requirements, and suggest that the good faith standard should be a subjective one as was intended by the drafters of the [original] Code.

We cannot agree with the Trial Court's conclusion that Galatia Bank was not acting in good faith. There is neither evidence nor legitimate speculation that Galatia Bank or the employee . . . found to have performed the alteration intended harm to any party. . . There was no evidence before the Court to suggest that the change was done other than with "honesty in fact in . . . the transaction concerned."

Because a check imprinting machine's purpose is to protect against alterations, the amount shown on the imprint [$5500] should control [over the handwritten $6550] whether the number is in words or figures.

As Professor Hawkland has written:

A purchaser does not obtain notice of a claim or defense solely because there is a conflict among handwritten, printed and typewritten terms. Although a purchaser might question whether some irregularity has occurred, the premise of section 3-118 seems to be that any conflict is a mere mistake and therefore should be ignored. [W. Hawkland & L. Lawrence, *U.C.C. Series* Sec. 3-118:05 (1984).]

Given these authorities, we conclude that Galatia Bank was a holder in due course with respect to the check and should be allowed to recover against Kindy.

Reversed and remanded. ⚖

[1] J. White and R. Summers, *Uniform Commercial Code* (3rd ed. 1988).

The Taking "Without Notice" Requirement

Section 3-302(1)(c) [RUCC 3-302(a)(2)] provides that, to be an HDC, a holder must take the instrument "without notice that it is overdue or has been dishonored [and without notice] of any defense against it or claim to it on the part of any person." The basic thrust of this section is that a holder should not receive the protection afforded an HDC if he or she acquires an instrument knowing that something is wrong with it.

Under UCC Sec. 1-201(25), a person has notice of a fact when he or she has actual knowledge of it, or from the circumstances "has reason to know" of such fact. Thus, if H acquires an instrument knowing that the payee has breached his or her contract with the maker or drawer, or under circumstances where a prudent person would reasonably suspect such a breach (although H did not have such suspicion), H is not an HDC.

Sec. 3-304 [RUCC 3-304] is an aid to the interpretation of the "without notice" requirement. Because of its length, the application of only a few of its salient provisions are summarized here. (The section can be read in its entirety in Appendix A.)

Notice That Paper Is Overdue or Has Been Dishonored. As we saw in Chapter 24, all negotiable instruments are either *time* or *demand* instruments. Those bearing a fixed future date of maturity, such as "payable July 1, 1995," are time instruments; those stating that they are payable on demand or having no stated maturity date are demand instruments.

A person who purchases a *time instrument* even one day after its stated maturity date takes it with notice that it is overdue. Thus, if a note payable on September 1 is acquired by H on September 2, H does not qualify as an HDC. Sec. 3-304(3) [RUCC 3-302(a)(2)(iii), 3-304(b)(3)] provides in part that "the purchaser has notice that an instrument is overdue if he has reason to know (a) that any part of the principal amount is overdue or that there is an uncured default in payment of another instrument of the same series. . . ." The purchaser has such notice here because the instrument carried its maturity date on its face.

The question as to when *demand* instruments are overdue has caused difficulties because such instruments do not, of course, contain a stated maturity date. The primary rule of Sec. 3-304(3)(c) [RUCC 3-304(a)(1)–(3)] is that a purchaser takes a demand instrument with notice that it is overdue if he or she acquires it more than a "reasonable time after its issue."

What Is a Reasonable Time? The *above section* contains the only provision in the original Article 3 that specifically defines a reasonable time, and applies it only to checks; as to checks drawn and payable in the United States, a reasonable time "is presumed to be 30 days." Thus, if D draws and issues a check on June 1 payable to the order of P, and the check is negotiated to H on July 15, H is not an HDC unless H can provide evidence to overcome the 30-day presumption.

Revised Article 3 *changes* the 30-day presumption to a *90-day absolute rule*. Thus, under no circumstances can someone in an RUCC jurisdiction receive through negotiation a check more than 90 days after its date and become an HDC.

As to other instruments—demand notes and sight drafts—the question of reasonable time is left to the courts by both versions of Article 3. Because these instruments are often held for longer periods of time than are checks, a person may well take such an instrument two or three months (or even longer) after its issue, and still qualify as an HDC. In determining what is a reasonable time in a given case, the courts take into account business and community customs, and other circumstances (for example, interest-bearing notes circulate longer than noninterest-bearing ones, and a reasonable time is generally longer in rural areas than when the parties are residents of larger cities).

Notice of Claim or Defense. Sec. 3-304(1) [RUCC 3-302(a)(1)] reads in part as follows:

The purchaser has notice of a claim or defense if (a) the instrument is so incomplete, bears such visible evidence of forgery or alteration, or is otherwise so irregular as to call into question its validity, terms or ownership or to create an ambiguity as to the party to pay; or (b) the purchaser has notice that the obligation of any party is voidable in whole or in part, or that all parties have been discharged.

The original Article 3 does not make it clear whether the claim or defense has to be related to the irregularity or incompleteness. The RUCC in Sec. 3-302(a)(1) clearly requires an instrument to be complete and regular in order for the holder to qualify as an HDC. This requirement must be met when issue or negotiation occurs and is unrelated to any claim or defense. Thus, under the revised Article 3 a person who accepts an instrument that is "so irregular or incomplete as to call into question its authenticity" (or that bears "apparent evidence of forgery or alteration") cannot be an HDC.

Breach of Fiduciary Duty. Assume that Y, an employee of X Company, converts a check payable to X by paying her bills with it, spending it to benefit herself, or depositing it in her personal account. Under what circumstances the taker of such a check can be an HDC is not totally clear under the original Article 3. RUCC 3-307 seeks to clarify this area by providing that notice to the taker of Y's breach is to be considered notice of the claim of X Company. In the situations mentioned earlier—where an instrument is used to pay a debt known to the taker to be Y's personal debt, *or* for a purpose known to the taker to be Y's personal purpose or placed in Y's personal account, *or* put in an account known to the taker not to be either X's or Y's account—the revised Article 3 *presumes* that the taker has notice of the breach of fiduciary duty, and thus the taker cannot qualify to be an HDC.

If Y makes the instrument payable to herself as an individual rather than as a fiduciary to X, the taker is *not* put on notice of the breach (absent actual knowledge of it).

Related Holder in Due Course Matters
Holder through a Holder in Due Course
If an ordinary holder (who does not independently qualify as an HDC) takes an instrument from someone who is an HDC, or takes an instrument where any prior party qualified as an HDC, he or she is now a "holder with all the rights of an HDC." This results from Sec. 3-201(1) [RUCC 3-203(b)], which provides that "the transfer of an instrument vests in the transferee such rights as the transferor has therein." This section, based on assignment law, is referred to as the *shelter provision* of the code.

One exception to this provision does exist, however. If a purchaser of an instrument negotiates it to a subsequent holder and ultimately repurchases it from either that holder or a later holder, the purchaser's status is determined at the time of first acquiring it. In other words, a holder cannot improve ("launder") his or her position by negotiating the instrument to an HDC and then reacquiring it.

The Payee as a Holder in Due Course
Before adoption of the UCC, some courts took the view that the payee of an instrument was not a

holder, and thus could not qualify as an HDC even if he or she gave value for the instrument, purchased it before it was overdue, and took it without notice of any defense against, or claim to, the instrument. Other courts disagreed. Sec. 3-302(2) [RUCC has no comparable provision] has resolved this conflict by flatly providing that "a payee may be a holder in due course" (assuming, of course, that he or she meets the three basic HDC requirements).

As a practical matter, a payee who has fully performed his or her contract with the maker or drawer of an instrument ordinarily qualifies as an HDC, because in most such instances the payee has given value for the instrument, the maker or drawer possesses no defense, and the payee takes the instrument before it is overdue. In such cases the payee is clearly entitled to payment. On the other hand, if the maker or drawer *does* possess a defense, the payee ordinarily is not an HDC because a defense usually arises out of some default or misconduct on the part of the payee—such as breach of contract, or the perpetration of fraud upon the maker or drawer—or which the payee necessarily has notice. Thus, in an action by the payee in such a case, the maker or drawer may successfully assert the defense.

DEFENSES

Earlier in the chapter we mentioned the two general classes of defenses, using the terms *personal* and *real*. While the original Article 3 refers to these classes as *limited* and *universal*, we will use the older terms, personal and real, because they continue in widespread use today.

Personal defenses, under Article 3, can be asserted only against ordinary holders; generally they cannot be asserted against an HDC or against a holder with all the rights of an HDC. In fact, it is the cutting off of these defenses that gives the HDC status as a favored holder.

Real defenses can be asserted against all holders, including HDCs and holders with all the rights of an HDC.[2]

This is why HDCs are not always entitled to judgments in actions brought against makers, acceptors, or drawers of negotiable instruments.

[2]Throughout this chapter, when we refer to the rights of an HDC, we will assume that whatever is said applies equally to holders with all the rights of an HDC.

Personal Defenses

Sec. 3-306 [RUCC 3-305, 3-306] of the original UCC lists all the **personal defenses** (or *limited defenses*)—those that are ordinarily assertable only against ordinary holders. The major part of that section provides:

Unless he has the rights of a holder in due course, any person takes the instrument subject to (a) all valid claims to it on the part of any person; and (b) all defenses of any party which would be available in an action on a simple contract; and (c) the defenses of want or failure of consideration, nonperformance of any condition precedent, nondelivery, or delivery for a special purpose; and (d) the defense that he or a person through whom he holds the instrument acquired it by theft, or that payment or satisfaction to such holder would be inconsistent with the terms of a restrictive indorsement.

We will now examine the most common kinds of personal defenses under this section.

Breach of Contract

Breach of contract (or *failure of consideration*) is the most common defense falling within the provision of Sec. 3-306(b) [RUCC 3-305(a)(2)]. Many instruments are issued to payees in payment for goods (or services) that the payees are obligated to deliver (or perform) under contracts with the makers or drawers of the instruments. If the contract is breached by the payee, the maker of the note can refuse to pay it, and the drawer of a check can stop payment on it, claiming that the failure of the payee to perform the contract relieves him or her of liability.

Breach of warranty—a form of breach of contract—occurs when a seller of goods makes an express or implied statement or promise about the goods, and the goods do not conform to the statement or promise. For example, under sales law a merchant seller impliedly warrants that the goods are merchantable.[3] If the buyer pays for the goods by giving the seller a negotiable note and later finds that the goods are not merchantable (do not perform in the expected manner), the buyer may assert the defense of breach of warranty against any holder of the note who is not an HDC.

In *United Securities Corp. v. Bruton*,[4] Bruton bought two wigs from a retailer, giving the retailer her promissory note in payment. The retailer payee negotiated the note to United Securities. When United Se-

curities presented the note to Bruton for payment, she refused to pay because the wigs were clearly defective—that is, unmerchantable. In the ensuing lawsuit, Bruton was permitted to assert her defense of breach of warranty against United Securities (which did not qualify as an HDC of the note).

Lack (or *want*) *of consideration*[5] exists in a commercial paper context where a maker or drawer of an instrument issues it to the payee in any case where the payee does not give consideration under ordinary contract law principles. In such situations, want of consideration can be asserted by the maker or drawer against an ordinary holder. To illustrate: D, a distant relative of P, drafts a check and makes a gift of it to P so that P can attend college. P negotiates the check to H. P does not go to college, and D, in disgust, stops payment on the check. If H sues D on the instrument, D can successfully assert the defense of want of consideration—but only if H fails to qualify as an HDC.

Fraud in the Inducement

Two kinds of fraud are recognized in the area of commercial paper: (1) *fraud in the inducement*, which creates a personal defense, and (2) *fraud in the execution* (which we shall soon discuss), which creates a real defense. **Fraud in the inducement** arises where a person who signs a negotiable instrument (knowing it to be such) has been induced to sign by some intentional misrepresentation of the other party. For example, B agrees to buy S's year-old car for $12,000 after being assured by S that the car is a demonstrator that S had purchased just six months earlier from a new car dealer. At the time of purchase, B gives S $2,000 in cash and a promissory note for the balance of $10,000. Soon thereafter, B learns that S had actually bought the car from a private owner who in fact had driven it extensively before selling it to S. S's intentional misrepresentation constitutes fraud in the inducement, and B can assert this defense against S and against any subsequent holder who does not qualify as an HDC.

Illegality

Like the general defense of fraud, some types of *illegality* constitute personal defenses and others constitute real defenses. This is so because although certain transactions are illegal (prohibited) under state statutes or ordinances, the applicable statutes do not

---

[3]See Chapter 22 for further details.
[4]213 A.2d 892 (D.C. 1965).

[5]See Chapter 13 for more details on the doctrine of consideration.

always provide that the prohibited transactions are void. If a statute voids the transaction, the defense is real; if it does not, the defense is merely personal.

To illustrate: A retailer sells goods to D on Sunday in violation of a state statute prohibiting the sale of goods by merchants on that day. However, the statute does not provide that such sales, or the contracts or papers connected with them, are void. The next day the retailer negotiates the check to H, who subsequently learns that D, the buyer-drawer, has stopped payment on it. Here D can assert the defense of illegality against H only if H is an ordinary holder. (Illegality as a real defense is discussed later in the chapter.)

Unauthorized Completion

Although it is ordinarily a bad practice, the maker or drawer of an instrument sometimes signs it while it is incomplete in some respect (for example, leaving blank the amount or the payee's name). He or she usually gives it to a third party—often an employee, but sometimes the payee—with instructions as to how the blank should be filled in (such as, "fill in the amount for no more than $400"). The instrument may then be completed contrary to instructions and

later may be acquired by a subsequent holder. If the latter fails to qualify as an HDC, the maker or drawer usually can assert the defense of **unauthorized completion** and avoid liability. However, under Sec. 3-407(3) [RUCC 3-407(c)], if the subsequent holder does qualify as an HDC (by taking the instrument without knowledge of the wrongful completion and by meeting the other HDC requirements), he or she can enforce the instrument as completed. Thus, where the maximum authorized amount is $400, if the third party completes the instrument to read $1000, a subsequent HDC can recover the full $1000 from the maker or drawer. Therein lies the danger in signing an incomplete instrument.

Nondelivery of an Instrument

Sometimes an instrument finds its way into the hands of a subsequent holder through loss or theft. In such a case the maker or drawer of the instrument has available the defense of *nondelivery*. To illustrate: M is the maker of a bearer instrument that is stolen from her home by X and negotiated to H. If H is merely an ordinary holder, he takes the instrument subject to the defense of nondelivery and therefore cannot enforce it against M.

MATTER OF ESTATE OF BALKUS

Court of Appeals of Wisconsin, 381 N.W.2d 593 (1985)

 James Balkus died on December 4, 1983, leaving no will. A few days after his death his sister, Ann Vesely, examined his personal effects and found, among other things, two promissory notes in the amount of $6,000 each. The notes were payable to her order, and Balkus was the maker of both instruments.

When the administrator of Balkus's estate refused to pay the amount of the notes to Vesely, she filed a claim against Balkus's estate in the amount of $12,000. The circuit court ruled that Vesely was not a holder in due course of the notes, and thus held that the state's defense of nondelivery was assertable against her. Judgment was accordingly entered for the es-

tate, and Vesely appealed.

On appeal, Vesely's primary argument was that the estate did not possess the defense of nondelivery because there had been a "constructive delivery" of the instruments to her—that is, a delivery in the eyes of the law, although not a physical delivery. (If the estate did not possess such defense, Vesely contended that she, as payee, was entitled to payment even if she did not qualify as a holder in due course.)

Nettesheim, Judge:

. . . We now look to the defense of nondelivery asserted by the personal representative [the administrator of the estate]. It is undisputed that Balkus did not physically deliver the notes to

Vesely. She argues, however, that a letter she received from Balkus in August 1974 constituted constructive delivery of the notes. The letter, in pertinent part, stated:

Also you will get & shall say I will bequeath to you all my other junk in my apt. such as tools, radios, TV sets, clothing, clothes and also the money I owe you. I have . . . government bonds made out in your name & the banker told me, nobody could take it away from you. I also have 2 . . . notes made out to you for the amount of money I borrowed from you in 1961 and 1962. That should take care of the interest I was supposed to pay you but I didn't.

The trial court found that Balkus retained dominion and control of the notes, and that he "simply never gave up ownership." These findings are not . . . erroneous.

(continues)

MATTER OF ESTATE OF BALKUS

(continued from previous page)

The general rule is that a promissory note has no effect unless it is delivered. The UCC defines delivery of an instrument as the "voluntary transfer of possession." Sec. 1-201(14). A constructive delivery may be sufficient. [Castro v. Martin, 230 S.E.2d 722, 1976.] A constructive delivery occurs only when the maker indicates an intention to make the instrument an enforceable obligation against him or her by surrendering control over it and intentionally placing it under the power of the payee or a third person.

Balkus never surrendered control nor transferred possession of the note. It is undisputed that the notes were found in Balkus's possessions after his death. The notes were never placed under the control of Vesely or any other party. We therefore reject Vesely's argument that the letter served as constructive delivery of the notes. . . .

Judgment affirmed. ⬧⬧

Prior Payment

When a note or draft is paid by the maker or acceptor, it is routinely surrendered to that person, regardless of whether it is paid at or before maturity. Either way, the instrument normally stops circulating. However, the maker or acceptor may neglect to ask for return of the instrument, or, after its return, it may be stolen. If payment of the instrument occurred before maturity, and if the instrument bears no notation of payment, it is possible that it will get into the hands of an innocent third party. When that holder demands payment at maturity, the maker or acceptor has available the defense of *prior payment* or *payment before maturity* and is therefore not liable if the holder fails to qualify as an HDC. (If the holder is an HDC, the maker or acceptor must pay a second time.)

Incapacity (except Minority)

As seen in Chapter 15, the law recognizes various types and degrees of incapacity. However, unless a maker's or drawer's incapacity is so extreme that under local law the contract or instrument is completely nullified, the defense of *incapacity* is only personal—except in the case of a minor (discussed later in the chapter).

Duress

Similarly, there are varying degrees of duress under the law, most of which are merely personal in nature. Thus, if a person signs an instrument under a vague threat or through fear of economic retaliation, the defense is only personal in nature. (Duress as a real defense is also discussed later in the chapter.)

Real Defenses

Real defenses (or *universal defenses*) are defenses that can be successfully asserted against all holders, including holders in due course. We will now describe the more common types of real defenses, including the offshoots of some of the personal defenses already discussed.

Forgery

A fundamental legal principle of commercial paper, appearing in Sec. 3-401(1) [RUCC 3-401(a)], is that a person cannot be held liable on an instrument unless his or her name appears on it. In the case of **forgery**, the person's name does appear, probably as maker or drawer, but it is signed by another person who has no authority to do so. (An unauthorized signature of indorsement is defined in Sec. 1-201(43) as "one made without actual, implied, or apparent authority and includes a forgery.")

The "pure" forgery case occurs where a person who has no authority, and usually no relationship with the purported drawer or maker, simply commits a criminal act by signing the latter's name to an instrument. For example: A thief steals a book of personalized checks belonging to D. The thief drafts a check and signs D's name as drawer. In this case D has no liability to any holder of the instrument. Sec. 3-401(1) [RUCC 3-403(a)] provides that "any unauthorized signature is *wholly inoperative* as that of the person whose name is signed unless he ratifies it or is precluded from denying it." (Emphasis added.) *Ratification* consists of any conduct on the part of the person whose name has been signed without authority that indicates to third parties that he or she will assume liability on the instrument despite the unauthorized signing. It occurs rarely, and when it does, it is usually in a situation where a principal–agent relationship exists between the purported drawer and the forger.[6]

A situation related to forgery exists when an agent exceeds his or her authority by signing the principal's name on an instrument as drawer or maker. If the principal can show that the agent had no express, implied, or apparent authority to sign, and if the principal does not subsequently ratify the signature, he or she can assert the defense of *unauthorized signing* against any holder, even an HDC.[7]

Fraud in the Execution

Unlike fraud in the inducement, in the case of **fraud in the execution** a person is caused to sign a negotiable instrument under circumstances in which he or she honestly and reasonably believes it to be something other than a negotiable instrument, such as a lease or receipt of some kind.

This commonly occurs when an experienced, high-pressure salesperson talks a home owner who has little education (or perhaps is even illiterate) into signing a promissory note by telling him or her that it is only a request for an estimate or an application of some kind. The salesperson's company then negotiates the instrument to a holder. Here the home owner–maker has a real defense, good against any holder, if certain conditions are met. The maker must show not only that he or she honestly believed the signing was for something other than a negotiable instrument, but also that he or she was not guilty of negligence under the circumstances in failing to realize that the document was a negotiable instrument. The phrase *under the circumstances* takes into account such factors as the signer's age, experience, and schooling. Thus, the maker who is very inexperienced in the business world, or is aged, or has failing eyesight may have a real defense, whereas such a defense would not exist if he or she were a businessperson who hurriedly signed the note after a cursory look (or perhaps without reading it at all) simply because of being in a rush to attend a meeting.

---

[6]Under Sec. 3-404(1) [RUCC 3-403(a)], the primary situation in which a drawer of an instrument may be precluded from asserting the defense of forgery is where he or she is guilty of negligence that contributed to the forgery. This rule, and its alteration in the revised Article 3, will be discussed in Chapter 28.

[7]See Chapter 32 for a treatment of the rules that the courts use in determining whether express, implied, or apparent authority exists.

Article 3's provisions repeatedly address issues of fairness. Matters of efficiency, certainty, and predictability are also always important and often resolve issues that appear to turn on fairness concerns, especially when two innocent parties are at odds.

Consider the case of *Ort v. Fowler*, 2 P. 580 (Kan. 1884). Ort, a farmer, was working alone in his field, about a half mile from his house. A man came by representing himself as the state sale agent for a company selling iron posts and wire fences. He convinced Ort to be the company's local agent. He then had Ort sign two documents that he read to him because Ort did not have his spectacles with him. The man's reading of the documents convinced Ort that both were agency agreements; however, one was a promissory note that the man quickly negotiated to Fowler. When Fowler sued Ort, the court noted, "It is very evident . . . that the defendant has been made the victim of an atrocious swindle. Obviously this stranger, under the pretense of obtaining defendant's signature to two contracts, obtained his signature to this note. . . . Clearly the defendant had no thought of signing a note, and did not suppose he was doing it."

Yet, the court ruled against the victimized farmer *as a matter of law*. Granting that the plaintiff was an "innocent holder for value" (HDC), is this an equitable result? Can we justify enforcing the note that is at the heart of this "atrocious swindle"? On what grounds? Does the UCC provision focusing on whether Ort was guilty of negligence "under the circumstances" provide a fair resolution?

Alteration of a Completed Instrument

As noted earlier, completion of a blank instrument contrary to instructions may create a personal defense. A real defense is created when, after a completed instrument is issued by the maker, one or more of its terms are changed without the maker's knowledge by a holder, and the instrument is thereafter negotiated to a subsequent holder. The issue is thus raised whether the last holder can recover on the instrument—and, if so, to what extent. The answer to these questions depends on two factors: (1) whether the alteration was material and (2) whether the holder qualifies as an HDC.

Sec. 3-407 [RUCC 3-407] essentially defines a material alteration as one that changes the contract of the parties in any respect. A change in the amount of the instrument even by the addition of one cent, or an advance of the date of payment even by one day, is thus material. On the other hand, a correction of the spelling of the payee's name or the addition of the address of the maker would not be material. (If the alteration is not material, all holders are entitled to enforce the instrument as it was originally drawn.)

If the alteration *is* material, the holder's rights depend on whether he or she is an HDC. It is possible to be an HDC when the alteration is so skillfully done that it is not readily apparent to the subsequent purchaser.

Under Sec. 3-407(3) [RUCC 3-407(c)], an HDC can enforce the instrument according to its *original tenor*—that is, as originally drawn. To illustrate: M is the maker of a note payable to the order of P in the amount of $1000. P alters the amount to read $3000 and negotiates the instrument to H, an HDC. At maturity, H is entitled to recover $1000. (Since H cannot recover the balance of $2000 from M, it is said that the defense of material alteration is a defense "to the extent of the alteration.") If, on the other hand, H is not an HDC, he recovers nothing, because a material alteration that is also fraudulent—as is usually the case—is a complete defense against an ordinary holder. (See Figure 26.1.) In the unlikely event that the alteration is not fraudulent, the ordinary holder—like the HDC—is entitled to enforce the instrument according to its original tenor.

Illegality

As we indicated in the section on personal defenses, some kinds of transactions are not only prohibited by statute but are expressly made *void* or *void ab initio* (from the beginning). The defense of *illegality* in these situations is a real defense, assertable against both ordinary holders and HDCs. In a number of states, for example, checks and notes given in payment of gambling debts fall into this category.

The next case presents an interesting application of these principles.

COLUMBUS CHECKCASHIERS V. STILES

Court of Appeals of Ohio, 565 N.E.2d 883 (1990)

In April 1988, appellee Stiles hired Beall to work on his curb. Beall asked appellee to give him $400 "up front" so that he could buy the materials he would need to do the job. Later that day, appellee learned that Beall was not licensed to perform the curb work as required by the Columbus City Code, and placed a stop-payment order on the check. Beall cashed the check at appellant Columbus Checkcashiers' place of business on April 18. When the check was refused payment because of the stop-payment order, appellant sued appellee. The trial court held that appellant was not an HDC and thus was not entitled to recover. Columbus Checkcashiers appealed.

Young, Judge:

[The court first held that the trial court had erred in refusing to find that appellant was an HDC.] [A]lthough appellant was not able to contact the references Beall gave it for check cashing approval, appellant had cashed several checks for Beall, without incident, prior to the time that appellee placed a stop payment order on his $400 check made payable to Beall. Therefore, even though appellant did not pursue every available precaution, its conduct in cashing Stiles' $400 check made payable to Beall constituted good faith, absent evidence of bad faith. There is no evidence in the record to indicate the appellant acted in bad faith. Furthermore, there is no evidence of dishonesty in fact regarding appellant's conduct or the transaction. Thus, the evidence establishes that appellant was a holder in due course, and the trial court's judgment should be modified to reflect this.

(continues)

COLUMBUS CHECKCASHIERS V. STILES

(continued from previous page)

[E]ven though appellant is a holder in due course, appellee can [under original UCC Sec. 3-305(2)(b)] assert the real defense of the illegality of the transaction which rendered Stiles' obligation to Beall a nullity. Columbus City Code 4114.01 provides: "It shall be unlawful for any person to undertake or perform work of any of the licensed contractors . . . as defined in the Columbus Building Code . . . without having first procured the appropriate license . . ."

On April 13, 1988, when Beall entered into the contract with Stiles and accepted Stiles' $400 check, Beall was not licensed nor did he have the proper permit. Yet, he began work on Stiles' property, which was illegal for him to do. He did obtain a permit on April 14, 1988; hoewever, this permit was immediately ruled invalid since Beall was not licensed pursuant to C.C. 4114.01. Furthermore, Beall did not cash the Stiles' check until April 18, 1988, which was a considerable amount of time after the permit was ruled invalid. Beall cashed the Stiles' check with full knowledge that he was not licensed, did not have a permit, and could not complete the work within the city easement without obtaining both. Therefore, the trial court properly found that the contract was void based upon illegality and appellant is not entitled to recover as set forth in [original UCC Sec. 3-305(2)(b)].

Judgment affirmed as modified. ⚖

Incapacity of a Minor or Insane Person

When the maker or drawer of an instrument is a minor, he or she may escape liability on the ground of *incapacity*. Whether this defense is real or personal depends on applicable state law (and as we saw in Chapter 15, state laws differ in their treatment of minors' rights). Still, the defense of *minority* is in most states a real defense. Under this view, if it is asserted by the maker or drawer of an instrument—even against an HDC—the holder recovers nothing. Similarly, if a person signs a note or draft after having been adjudicated insane by a court, his or her defense is also real, the instrument being void *ab initio*.

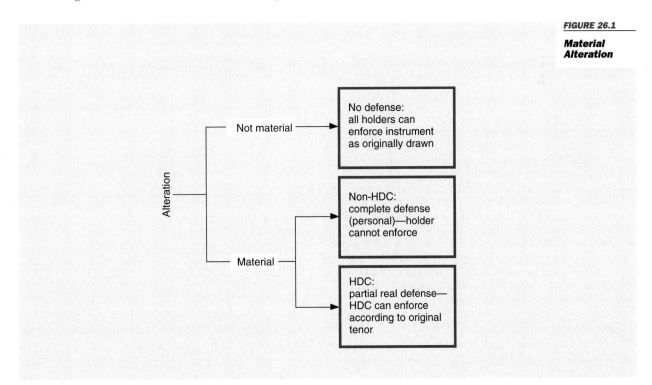

FIGURE 26.1

Material Alteration

Alteration
- Not material → No defense: all holders can enforce instrument as originally drawn
- Material
  - Non-HDC: complete defense (personal)—holder cannot enforce
  - HDC: partial real defense—HDC can enforce according to original tenor

Extreme Duress

Most kinds of duress constitute only personal defenses. *Extreme duress*, however, is another matter; it exists where the force or threat of force is so overwhelming that the victim is entirely deprived of free will. A real defense exists, for example, if a person signs an instrument at gunpoint.

Discharge in Bankruptcy

In some situations the general defense of *discharge* is available to one of the parties to an instrument; yet the instrument can still circulate, and an HDC can still take it free of the defense. One kind of discharge, however, is always a real defense: the *discharge in bankruptcy*. The person who has been discharged under bankruptcy proceedings has no further liability on any outstanding instrument, even if it is held by an HDC.

REVISED ARTICLE 3 APPROACH TO DEFENSES

The revised Article 3 does not make any important changes regarding real and personal defenses, but does attempt to clarify the area by taking a slightly different approach. Subsection a of RUCC 3-305 states that

. . . the right to enforce the obligation of a party to pay an instrument is subject to the following:

(1) a defense of the obligor based on (i) infancy of the obligor to the extent it is a defense to a simple contract, (ii) duress, lack of legal capacity, or illegality of the transaction which, under other law, nullifies the obligation of the obligor, (iii) fraud that induced the obligor to sign the instrument with neither knowledge nor reasonable opportunity to learn of its character or its essential terms, or (iv) discharge of the obligor in insolvency proceedings;

(2) a defense of the obligor stated in another section of this Article or a defense of the obligor that would be available if the person entitled to enforce the instrument were enforcing a right to payment under a simple contract; and

(3) a claim in recoupment of the obligor against the original payee of the instrument if the claim arose from the transaction that gave rise to the instrument; but the claim of the obligor may be asserted against a transferee of the instrument only to reduce the amount owing on the instrument at the time the action is brought.

Subsection b of RUCC 3-305 provides that an *HDC's* right to collect on an instrument is subject to the defenses stated in Subsection 1 above, but not those stated in Subsection 2 or 3.

The revised Article 3 also provides:

A person taking an instrument other than a person having rights of a holder in due course, is subject to a claim of a property or possessory right in the instrument or its proceeds, including a claim to rescind a negotiation and to recover the instrument or its proceeds. A person having rights of a holder in due course takes free of the claim to the instrument.[8]

LIMITATIONS ON HOLDER IN DUE COURSE DOCTRINE

The basic holder in due course concept, which permits an HDC to take an instrument free of all personal defenses, is a necessity if commercial paper is to circulate freely. In certain situations, however, the HDC doctrine has brought about results that have been the subject of increasing scrutiny and dissatisfaction. A typical example is the situation where a person purchases a consumer good, such as a television set, from a retailer and gives the retailer an installment note in payment for it. The retailer then negotiates the instrument to a third party (usually a lending institution), who probably qualifies as an HDC. In such a case, if the television does not work properly (or even if it is never delivered), *the buyer remains fully liable to the HDC*. The buyer's only recourse is to harass the retailer until he or she delivers a workable set or to recover damages for breach of contract—certainly an unsatisfactory solution for the buyer. In recent years, two general kinds of limitations on the HDC doctrine have come into existence in an effort to give the purchaser of consumer goods some relief.

State Statutes

Some state legislatures have enacted statutes that give the consumer a measure of protection in situations such as the one just described. Because of their diversity, these statutes can only be summarized briefly.

A few states have adopted the Uniform Consumer Credit Code (*UCCC* or *U Triple C*, not to be confused with the *UCC*), which prohibits a seller of consumer goods from taking a negotiable instrument—other than a check—as evidence of the buyer's obligation. Some other states have enacted legislation that flatly abolishes the HDC doctrine in

---

[8]RUCC 3-306.

many situations. And a number of states have legislation requiring instruments that evidence consumer indebtedness to bear the words "consumer paper," and providing further that such instruments are non-negotiable.

The Federal Trade Commission Rule

The statutes just mentioned have brought about consumer protection that varies from state to state, and in some states they give less protection than was originally expected. For that reason, the Federal Trade Commission (FTC) promulgated a "Rule to Preserve Buyers' Claims and Defenses in Installment Sales." This rule (rule 433), usually referred to as the **FTC holder in due course rule**, applies in two general situations: (1) where a buyer of consumer goods executes a sales contract that includes giving a promissory note to the seller, and (2) where a seller of consumer goods arranges for a direct loan by a third party—usually a bank or other commercial lending institution—to the customer in order for the sale to be made.

In regard to the first situation, the rule provides in part:

In connection with any sale or lease of goods or services to consumers, in or affecting [interstate] commerce . . . it is an unfair or deceptive trade practice . . . for a seller, directly or indirectly to (a) *Take or receive a consumer credit contract which fails to contain* the following provisions in at least ten point, boldface type:

NOTICE
ANY HOLDER OF THIS CONSUMER CREDIT CONTRACT IS SUBJECT TO ALL CLAIMS AND DEFENSES WHICH THE DEBTOR COULD ASSERT AGAINST THE SELLER OF GOODS OR SERVICES OBTAINED PURSUANT HERETO OR WITH THE PROCEEDS HEREOF. RECOVERY HEREUNDER BY THE DEBTOR SHALL NOT EXCEED AMOUNTS PAID BY THE DEBTOR HEREUNDER.

The failure by a seller who is a "dealer" to include the required notice in each consumer credit contract subjects that person to a possible fine of up to $10,000 and to possible liability in a civil suit brought by the customer to recover damages incurred as a result of such failure.

In regard to the second situation (direct loan by a third party arranged by the merchant who has a relationship with that lender), the rule provides:

In connection with any sale or lease of goods or services to consumers, in or affecting [interstate] commerce . . . it is

an unfair or deceptive trade practice . . . for a seller, directly or indirectly to . . . (b) accept, as full or partial payment for such sale or lease, the proceeds of any purchase money loan . . . unless any consumer credit contract made in connection with such purchase money loan *contains the following provision* in at least ten point, boldface type:

NOTICE
ANY HOLDER OF THIS CONSUMER CREDIT CONTRACT IS SUBJECT TO ALL CLAIMS AND DEFENSES WHICH THE DEBTOR COULD ASSERT AGAINST THE SELLER OF GOODS AND SERVICES OBTAINED WITH THE PROCEEDS HEREOF. RECOVERY HEREUNDER BY THE DEBTOR SHALL NOT EXCEED AMOUNTS PAID BY THE DEBTOR HEREUNDER.

Rule 433 does not, by any means, bring about the death of the HDC doctrine. For example, the rule applies only to *consumer* buyers, not to contracts of commercial buyers, which account for a great deal of commercial paper activity. Also, the rule applies only to consumer purchases on credit; thus purchases in which checks are given in full payment are not subject to it. Finally, the rule permits the assertion of only those personal defenses that the purchaser could assert against the seller of the goods (such as fraud or breach of contract).

SUMMARY

The primary attribute of the holder in due course (HDC) is that such a holder takes the instrument free of personal defenses existing between prior parties. (Ordinary holders, by contrast, take the instrument subject to such defenses.) A holder, to qualify as an HDC, must take the instrument (1) for value, (2) in good faith, and (3) without notice that it is overdue or has been dishonored, or that a defense against or a claim to the instrument exists.

The value requirement reflects the conclusion that a holder who receives an instrument as a gift does not need the protection given to a third party who has given value for it. Similarly, a holder should not be afforded HDC protection if he or she knows or should know of an existing claim to, or defense against, the instrument. This latter requirement essentially overlaps the good faith requirement, because a holder who knows or should know of a claim or defense would often also be a taker in bad faith.

In regard to the overdue requirement, there are three basic rules: (1) A note or draft with a fixed maturity date is overdue the day after such date.

(2) Demand instruments become due a reasonable time after issue, which (except for checks) varies from case to case. (3) Under original Article 3, a reasonable time is presumed to be no more than 30 days after issue; under the revised Article 3, the 30-day presumption is replaced with an absolute 90-day rule.

An HDC, as indicated, takes an instrument free of personal defenses. The most common of these are (1) breach of contract, (2) fraud in the inducement, and (3) unauthorized completion. However, the maker or drawer can assert these defenses against ordinary holders.

Real defenses are those possessed by the maker or drawer that free him or her of liability to HDCs as well as to ordinary holders. Real defenses are less common than personal defenses. The most representative real defenses are forgery, material alteration, and some types of illegality.

To avoid unfairness in situations where a buyer of consumer goods gives a negotiable instrument in payment for them, both state and federal law limit the rights of HDCs who take a consumer's note either through the merchant seller or through a third-party lender arranged by the merchant. Some states have adopted statutes prohibiting sellers of consumer goods from accepting negotiable instruments (except checks) in payment for such goods. Also, the FTC has adopted rule 433, which provides, in general, that any credit contract received by a seller or lessor of consumer goods (or by a party supplying credit for such a sale or lease) must provide that any holder of the contract is subject to all claims and defenses that the buyer or lessee possesses against the seller or lessor.

KEY TERMS
Holder in due course
Value
Good faith
Personal defense
Fraud in the inducement
Unauthorized completion
Real defense
Forgery
Fraud in the execution
FTC holder in due course rule

QUESTIONS AND PROBLEMS

1. Hessler gave a promissory note to a grain company in payment for hogs he purchased from J&J Farms (a company associated with the grain company). The grain company negotiated the check to plaintiff bank. Because Hessler did not get good title to the hogs, he refused to pay the bank when the note matured. Hessler, defendant, contended that the bank was not an HDC, alleging that the bank (1) knew of the defense (defective title to the hogs) and (2) did not take the note in good faith. The trial court found the evidence unclear regarding the bank's knowledge of the defense. On the other hand, evidence showed a close connection between the bank and the grain company in that the president of the grain company was a director of the bank and the bank had been giving financial advice to the grain company on a continuing basis. Is the bank an HDC? Discuss. (*Arcanum National Bank v. Hessler*, 433 N.E.2D 204, Ohio 1982.)

2. The Vanottis purchased a lot in a subdivision from Cochise College Park and gave their promissory note to Cochise in payment for it. After the Vanottis made several monthly payments, Cochise negotiated the note to Salter, plaintiff. The Vanottis refused to pay the balance due, contending that they had several defenses against Cochise, and further contending that Salter was not an HDC. Evidence showed that when Salter acquired the note he knew that the purchase contract that the Vanottis had with Cochise gave them the right to rescind the contract within six months of their purchase and entitled them to a deed to the property after three payments were made and that no deed had been given them. Is Salter an HDC? Discuss. (*Salter v. Vanotti*, 599 P.2d 962, Colo.App. 1979.)

3. Willman was the maker of several notes payable to the order of a designated payee, and he issued them to the payee. Later the payee wanted to borrow money from Wood, and in order to get the loan, the payee had to pledge the notes (deliver them) to Wood as security for the loan. The amount of the loan was substantially less than the total amount of the notes. In subsequent litigation by Wood against Willman, the question arose whether Wood was an HDC to the full extent of the notes or only to the extent of the amount of the loan that Wood had made to the payee. How would you rule on this issue? (*Wood v. Willman*, 423 P.2d 82, Wyo. 1967.)

4. Drexler was attorney and corporate secretary for Eldon's Super Fresh Stores, Inc. (Eldon's), and personal attorney for Prinzing, president and sole

shareholder of Eldon's. Drexler had a trading account in his name with Merrill Lynch; Eldon's did not. Drexler paid for a purchase of Clark Oil stock through his stockbroker at Merrill Lynch with a $4150 check drawn by Eldon's on the Security National Bank. The check, in the exact amount of the purchase price of the shares, was payable to Merrill Lynch and signed by E.C. Prinzing, its president. The check contained no other designation or directive as to its use. Merrill Lynch accepted the check in payment of Drexler's stock purchase, treating Drexler as a remitter. Fifteen months later, Eldon's inquired of Merrill Lynch relative to the stock certificate and asserted a claim to its ownership. In subsequent litigation, Merrill Lynch claimed to be an HDC. Was it? Discuss. (*Eldon's Super Fresh Stores, Inc. v. Merrill Lynch*, 207 N.W.2d 282, Minn. 1973.)

5. A corporation borrowed $25,000 from a bank, with the corporation giving its promissory note to the bank as evidence of the debt. As part of the deal, the bank demanded that four individuals—including Rochman—indorse the instrument as accommodation indorsers who would thereby guarantee payment by the corporation. Rochman told the bank that he would indorse the note only if D'Onofrio would also indorse it, and the bank agreed to this condition. Rochman then indorsed the note, but the bank never got D'Onofrio's indorsement. When the maker of the note (the corporation) later defaulted, the bank sued Rochman on his indorsement. Assuming the bank is not an HDC, can Rochman successfully assert his defense against the bank that his liability was conditioned upon D'Onofrio's indorsement? Discuss. (*Long Island Trust Co. v. International Institute for Packaging Education, Ltd.*, 344 N.E.2d 377, N.Y.App. 1976.)

6. Middle Georgia Livestock Sales (MGLS) drew a check and issued it to a seller of cattle. Thereafter, MGLS learned the cattle it had purchased were stolen, so it issued a stop-payment order to the drawee bank. MGLS (drawer) was sued on the check by Commercial Bank & Trust Co., an HDC. Given that Commercial Bank is an HDC, will it prevail? Discuss. (*Commercial Bank & Trust Co. v. Middle Georgia Livestock Sales*, 182 S.E.2d 533, Ga.App. 1971.)

7. A salesman for a corporation demonstrated a water softening device to the Hutchinsons. Before leaving, the salesman asked them to sign a form so that he could show it to his employer as proof that he had made the demonstration. The Hutchinsons signed, and later learned that they had actually signed a promissory note. The note was subsequently negotiated to a bank, which qualified as an HDC. When the bank sued the Hutchinsons after the note came due, they claimed that they had a real defense in view of the fact that they honestly did not think they were signing a promissory note. The bank sought to overcome that defense by producing evidence that showed the Hutchinsons were intelligent people, and could easily have discovered the true nature of the instrument if they had just read it. If this evidence is true, what effect—if any—does it have on the Hutchinsons' defense? Discuss. (*Reading Trust Co. v. Hutchinson*, Court of Common Pleas of Pennsylvania, 1964.)

8. Thomas bought a car from Monarch Lincoln Mercury, financing the purchase by entering into a retail installment contract assigned to Ford Motor Credit Co. (FMC). Printed on the face of the contract was a notice required by Maryland law identical to that required by FTC rule 433 in consumer credit transactions. The car had been used as a demonstrator model, and though Monarch promised that it was nearly as good as new, it had so many defects that Thomas claimed it was unfit for transportation and constituted a safety hazard. Thomas sued, claiming that the car was worth only a small fraction of the purchase price. FMC claimed that it was an HDC. Is FMC correct? Discuss. (*Thomas v. Ford Motor Credit Co.*, 429 A.2d 277, Md.App. 1981.)

Chapter 27

Commercial Paper
Liability of the Parties

The Signing Requirement

Liability of Primary Parties

*Promissory Liability of
Secondary Parties, Generally*

Promissory Liability of Drawers

Promissory Liability of Indorsers

Warranty Liability of Indorsers

Selected Transferor–Indorser Problems

Discharge of the Parties

Statutes of Limitation

ALL PARTIES TO commercial paper fall into one of two categories. Makers of notes and acceptors of drafts are **primary parties,** and all others are **secondary parties.**

As a general rule, a primary party is absolutely liable on the instrument, while a secondary party is only conditionally liable on it. Before we examine the ramifications of this rule, and its exceptions, it is necessary to see how a person may become a party in the first place.

THE SIGNING REQUIREMENT

Sec. 3-401(1) [RUCC 3-401(a)] provides that "no person is liable on an instrument unless his signature appears thereon." A signature may be made personally, *or by an authorized agent.* The revised Article 3 provides that a person may be liable on an instrument even if his or her signature does not appear thereon so long as an agent or representative signs the instrument and the signature is binding on the represented person.

In clarifying rules implicit in the original Article 3, RUCC 3-401(b) provides that:

A signature may be made (i) manually or by means of a device or machine, and (ii) by the use of any name, including a trade or assumed name, or by a word, mark, or symbol executed or adopted by a person with present intention to authenticate a writing.

Signing by an Agent

When an agent or other representative signs an instrument on behalf of a maker, acceptor, drawer, or indorser, two related problems may arise. The first involves the liability of the principal (represented party) and the second involves the personal liability of the agent or representative. These problems—or potential problems—take on added significance when one realizes that all commercial paper issued by corporations necessarily involves corporate names being signed by agents, because all corporate activity can be carried on *only* through the actions of agents and employees.

Signature by Authorized Agent

Sec. 3-403 [RUCC 3-402] provides that the authority of the agent may be established "as in any other cases of representation"—that is, under the ordinary principles of agency law.[1] Thus, if the treasurer of the X Company has express or implied authority to issue promissory notes in the name of the corporation, the corporation alone would be liable as the maker of a note signed "The X Company, by R. J. Thomas, Treasurer."

Liability of Agent—Improper Signature

Occasionally a signature on an instrument contains the name of both principal and agent, but fails to indicate that the agent signed in a representative capacity. (In the above example, the names of the makers may thus appear as "The X Company" and "R. J. Thomas.") In other cases, the signature does not contain the name of the principal, but does show that the agent signed in a representative capacity ("R. J. Thomas, Treasurer").

Sec. 3-403(2)(b) [RUCC 3-402] of the original Article 3 applies to both of these situations, providing that "except as otherwise established between the immediate parties, the representative (agent) is personally obligated on the instrument." Thus, if the agent is being sued by a third-party holder—someone to whom the instrument has been negotiated—*the agent who fails to indicate agency status is personally liable.* On the other hand, if the agent is being sued by the *payee*, the agent is permitted to introduce evidence showing that he or she actually signed in a representative capacity, and that the payee knew this to be the case. In such a case the agent is not liable. Revised Article 3 emphasizes the distinction between liability to a holder in due course (HDC) who is unaware that the original parties did not intend the agent to be liable and nonliability to the payee who was so aware.

Revised Article 3 makes two important clarifications in this area. First, under the original Article 3 and contrary to basic agency law, agents who failed to disclose their representative capacity fully in signing both their principal's name and their own to an instrument often were held *solely* liable on that instrument. Second, agents were also sometimes held personally liable when signing their principal's preprinted

[1]For a discussion of the different kinds of authority an *agent* might possess, see Chapters 31 and 32.

personalized checks without disclosing their representative capacity in their signature. RUCC 3-402 changes both results. In the first instance, the principal as well as the agent is liable to the third party. In the second instance, the agent is not liable on the principal's check so long as the agent was in fact authorized to sign it. Thus, the result of the following case, representing a popular view under the *original* Article 3, would be just the opposite if decided in an RUCC jurisdiction.

COLONIAL BANKING CO. OF DES MOINES V. DOWIE

Iowa Supreme Court, 330 N.W.2d 279 (1983)

Dowie, president and sole stockholder of Fred Dowie Enterprises, Inc., ordered 325,000 hot dog buns from Colonial Baking Co. in order to stock the concession stands he planned to operate during the Pope's visit to Des Moines in 1979. He gave Colonial a postdated check in the amount of $28,640. The check showed the name of the corporation and its address in the upper left corner. The signature on the check was in the name of "Frederick J. Dowie," and there were no other words of explanation.

Unfortunately, Dowie had badly misjudged consumer demand—he sold only 300 buns. He then stopped payment on the check. Colonial sued both Dowie's corporation and Dowie individually. The trial court refused to grant Colonial's motion for summary judgment against defendants, and the case was tried by a jury. Judgment was entered against both defendants; only Dowie individually appealed. Colonial cross-

appealed, claiming that its summary judgment motion should have been granted.

Schultz, Justice:

[Dowie] argues that he has no personal responsibility on the check because it was imprinted with the corporation's name, even though his signature does not indicate representative capacity. Colonial maintains that a person who signs a corporate check which does not show that he signed in a representative capacity is personally obligated for payment of the check, unless it is otherwise established between the parties that he is not so obligated. . . .

[I]t was necessary for Dowie to have pleaded and provided evidence that there was an agreement, understanding, or course of dealing between the parties that when Dowie signed the check he did so in a representative capacity and was not to be personally liable on the check. [Original UCC Sec. 3-403(2)] assesses liability to a person whose signature is affixed to commercial papers as follows:

An authorized representative who signs his own name to an instrument

a. is personally obligated if the instrument neither names the person represented nor shows that the representative signed in a representative capacity;

b. except as otherwise established between the immediate parties, is personally obligated if the instrument names the person represented but does not show that the representative signed in a representative capacity.

If Dowie wished to avail himself of the exception from liability provided by the phrase "except as otherwise established," it was necessary for him to plead and prove that he fell within the exception. . . . [W]e now hold that this section provides liability against the drawer of a check if there is no evidence that the check was signed in a representative capacity. Other courts have held that the fact that a corporate name is imprinted on the check is not alone sufficient evidence that the drawer who signs his own name to the instrument has otherwise established that he is not personally liable.

[Reversed and remanded for entry of summary judgment against Dowie.] ⚖

Signature by Unauthorized Agent

If an agent executes in the name of a principal an instrument that the agent has absolutely no authority to make, the named principal has no liability on the instrument. Sec. 3-404(1) [RUCC 3-403 (a)] provides, in part, that "[a]ny unauthorized signature is wholly inoperative as that of the person whose name is signed." In effect, therefore, the unauthorized signature is a forgery. There is one exception, however. A principal is

liable if its own negligence contributes substantially to the agent's unauthorized execution of the instrument in the principal's name. Such negligence may take the form, for example, of sloppy supervision and auditing of the agent's instrument-execution activities.[2]

---

[2]Regardless of the principal's liability in such cases, the agent is personally liable on the instrument. The unauthorized signature of the principal operates as the signature of the unauthorized signer as to any person who in good faith pays the instrument or takes it for value.

Revised Article 3 makes some important changes in this area. First, a principal's negligence in supervising an employee does not automatically place all liability on the principal's shoulders. Rather, if the person paying the instrument or taking it for value is *also* careless, comparative negligence applies and the fact-finder may apportion the loss between the third party and the principal. RUCC 3-405(b).

Second, new Article 3 broadens principal liability by holding represented parties liable for the fraudulent indorsements of their employees so long as the employer had given the employee authority to sign, indorse, process, prepare, or otherwise act in a representative capacity *regardless* of whether the principal had negligently contributed to the fraud. Between the innocent, nonnegligent employer and the innocent, nonnegligent third party, the principal loses because it placed the agent in the position to commit the wrong. RUCC 3-405.

Third, revised Article 3 clarifies an area of ambiguity under the original Article 3 by providing in RUCC 3-403(b) that when an organization requires more than one of its agents' signatures on a check, the organization's signature is "unauthorized" if one of the signatures is missing.

LIABILITY OF PRIMARY PARTIES

For the remainder of this chapter we will make two assumptions: (1) that the party whose liability is being examined signed the instrument personally, and (2) that such party does not have an assertable defense against the holder. On this basis we will first examine the liability of *primary parties* (makers of notes and acceptors of drafts).

Liability of the Maker
Contractual Liability

The maker of a note is *primarily liable* on it. That is, the party has the duty to pay the instrument at its maturity date even if the holder does not demand payment at that time. Sec. 3-413 (1) [RUCC 3-412, 3-413(a)] provides that "the maker or acceptor engages [promises] that he will pay the instrument according to its tenor at the time of his engagement or as completed pursuant to Section 3-115 on incomplete instruments."

Furthermore, the maker—unlike the indorser—*is not discharged in any way by the fact that the instrument is presented for payment late;* even if a note is presented for payment many months or even years

after its due date, the maker remains fully liable on it (with some very limited exceptions) until the statute of limitations has run.[3]

Liability on Admissions

By signing a promissory note, the maker *admits* (guarantees) certain facts. Sec. 3-413(3) [RUCC has no comparable provision] provides in part that the maker "admits against all subsequent parties . . . the existence of the payee and his then capacity [capacity at the time of signing the note] to indorse." Thus, if a payee who is a minor negotiates an instrument to a holder and subsequently recovers the instrument by disaffirming his or her indorsement, the holder can recover from the maker any damages incurred as a result of the rescission.

Liability of the Acceptor

As we saw in Chapter 24, time drafts are frequently presented to the drawee prior to maturity for the drawee's *acceptance.* In some instances presentment for acceptance is mandatory, whereas in others it is optional. In any event, when the drawee accepts the instrument, he or she becomes liable on it for the first time.

Once an acceptance occurs, the liability of the drawee-acceptor is virtually identical to that of the maker of a note. Under Sec. 3-413(3) [RUCC has no comparable provision], by accepting, the drawee admits the existence of the payee and that person's then capacity to indorse. More important, under Sec. 3-413(1) [RUCC 3-412, 3-413(a)] the drawer-acceptor promises to pay the instrument at its maturity date. Again, the obligation to pay is not cut off or diminished by a late presentment for payment except under very limited circumstances.[4]

The revised Article 3 makes an important change here. Under the original Article 3, no party to a draft has primary liability until the draft is accepted. Therefore, a drawer of a draft is entitled to notice of dishonor before the drawer is obligated to pay on the draft. RUCC 3–414 imposes *primary* contractual liability on the drawer. Consequently, the drawer in *not* entitled to notice of dishonor as a prerequisite to being obligated to pay.[5]

---

[3]The various Article 3 statutes of limitation are discussed later in the chapter.

[4]The primary rules prescribing the various times at which presentments for acceptance or payment should be made are discussed later in the chapter.

[5]Under the revised Article 3, only an indorser is entitled to notice of dishonor on a draft.

Two further observations regarding acceptances are needed:

1. Until a draft is accepted, the drawee has no liability on the instrument to the payee or to any other holder. As we will see later in this chapter, the drawee usually owes the *drawer* a legal duty to accept the instrument, but does not owe such a duty to any *holder* of the draft. Thus, if a holder presents the draft for acceptance and the drawee refuses to accept, the holder cannot bring action against the drawee (although the holder can bring action against the drawer, who is a secondary party).

2. As a general rule, a refusal by the drawee to accept a draft that is properly presented constitutes a dishonor of the instrument, which triggers the liability of secondary parties on the instrument—the drawer and all indorsers except those indorsing *without recourse* (that is, without guaranteeing payment). The precise elements and ramifications of a dishonor will be examined later in this chapter.

PROMISSORY LIABILITY OF SECONDARY PARTIES, GENERALLY

Under the original Article 3, secondary parties are *drawers* of drafts[6] and checks, and *indorsers* of all instruments. The liability of those parties is often significantly less than that of primary parties.

Primary parties *absolutely promise* to pay the instruments they have signed. Secondary parties promise to pay *only if certain conditions are met:* (1) due presentment, (2) dishonor, and (3) notice of dishonor. Essentially, the secondary party (except for the "without recourse" indorser) is saying, "I will pay this instrument to any holder *if* it is presented to the primary party (or the drawee), and *if* he or she dishonors it (usually by failing to pay), and *if* I am given notice of the dishonor." These conditions, unless waived, must be met in order for the secondary party to be held on his or her **promissory liability**—or *contractual liability,* as it is often called.[7] (These conditions need not be met, however, if a person is seek-

ing to hold the secondary party liable on his or her *warranty* liability, an area we will examine later in this chapter.)

PROMISSORY LIABILITY OF DRAWERS

All drawers, like makers and acceptors, admit the existence of the payee and his or her then capacity to indorse. Of more importance, however, is the drawer's promissory liability.

Under Sec. 3-413(2) [RUCC 3-414(b), (e)], a drawer promises that "upon dishonor of the draft and any necessary notice of dishonor . . . he will pay the amount of the draft to the holder or to any indorser who takes it up." Thus the drawer's contractual liability under original Article 3 is conditioned upon the events of dishonor and the notice of dishonor.

Dishonor of Drafts

Whereas checks and promissory notes require only one kind of presentment, *presentment for payment,* drafts often involve two presentments—*presentment for acceptance* and, later, presentment for payment. Insofar as drafts are concerned, then, a dishonor can occur either by the refusal of the drawee to accept or by the refusal to pay.

Dishonor by Nonacceptance
Under Sec. 3-501(1)(a) [RUCC 3-414(b), 3-502(b) (3)–(4)], presentment for acceptance is required in three situations. This section provides that, unless excused, presentment for acceptance is necessary to charge the drawers and indorsers (1) "where the draft so provides," (2) where it "is payable elsewhere than at the residence or place of business of the drawee," or (3) where its "date of payment depends upon such presentment." This section also provides that "the holder may *at his option* present for acceptance any other draft payable at a stated date"—that is, "time" drafts. Any refusal by the drawee to accept a draft that is properly presented for acceptance, regardless of whether presentment is required or optional, *constitutes a dishonor* that triggers the liability of the drawers and indorsers (assuming that notice of dishonor, if necessary, is also given).

Dishonor by Nonpayment
After an acceptance occurs, as well as in any case where the holder dispenses with an optional presentment for acceptance, a *presentment for payment,* at

---

[6]Remember, as noted in the previous section, the revised Article 3 renders *drawers of drafts* primarily liable.

[7]Some drafts provide that the drawer waives presentment, dishonor, and notice of dishonor. This discussion, however, assumes that no such waiver exists. (Also, under Sec. 3-511 [RUCC 3-504], delay in presentment and notice of dishonor are excused in certain circumstances.)

maturity, is required in order to fix the liability of the drawer (and indorsers, as well). (Until such presentment is made by the holder no dishonor has occurred, and the secondary parties' liability is not fixed.) Once a proper presentment for payment is made, however, a refusal by the drawee to make payment does constitute a dishonor.

Effect of Late Presentment

Sec. 3-503 [RUCC has no comparable provision] brings together the rules that set the time limits within which presentment for acceptance and payment are to be made. Insofar as drafts are concerned, the rules for presentment for payment are as follows:

1. Where a draft is payable at a fixed future date, presentment is due on that date.

2. As to other drafts, presentment must be made within a "reasonable time" after the secondary party became a party; in other words, where the drawer's liability is concerned, within a reasonable time after the draft is issued. Generally, a reasonable time in regard to such a draft under the original Article 3 is determined "by any usage of banking or trade, and the facts of the particular case." However, in the case of an uncertified check it is "presumed" that 30 days after issuance is a reasonable time for presentment insofar as the drawer is concerned (but under the original Article 3 a shorter time applies to indorsers, as will be seen subsequently).

The revised Article 3 makes a big change here, *eliminating presentment as a requirement for liability of secondary parties.* RUCC 3-502. Such presentment has not been a part of normal business practice, typically being waived in the case of promissory notes. (However, notice of dishonor is still required in order to hold secondary parties liable.)

Drawer's Liability Contrasted with Indorser's Liability

Whereas drawers and indorsers are both secondary parties under the original Article 3 (remember that the RUCC eliminates any right of a drawer to notice of dishonor or protest, rendering his or her liability essentially primary), their liabilities differ in one significant respect. While a late presentment automatically frees indorsers of their secondary liability, such a presentment does not free the drawer even under the original Article 3, except in the rare case where a drawee becomes insolvent during the delay in presentment.

Notice of Dishonor

When a dishonor occurs under the original Article 3, notice of dishonor must generally be given to fix the drawer's liability. Sec. 3-508(3) [RUCC 3-503(b)] provides that such notice may either be sent by mail or given orally. This section also provides that where the party giving notice is a bank, notice must be given "before its midnight deadline"—that is, by midnight of the next banking day after dishonor. Where the party giving notice is not a bank, notice must be given by midnight of the third business day following dishonor under the original Article 3. The revised Article 3 changes this rule by granting *non*bank parties thirty days rather than just three. RUCC 3-503(c).

PROMISSORY LIABILITY OF INDORSERS

Unqualified indorsers have two kinds of liability—*secondary liability* (also called *promissory* or *conditional liability*) and *warranty liability.* Qualified (without recourse) indorsers, on the other hand, incur warranty liability only. These two general kinds of liability will be discussed in order.

Conditions: Presentment, Dishonor, and Notice

All unqualified indorsers promise that they will pay the instrument themselves if (1) the instrument is properly presented for acceptance or payment, (2) the instrument is dishonored, and (3) proper notice of dishonor is given them. Thus, under the original Article 3 the conditional liability of the indorser and drawer is the same in this respect: neither party incurs such liability until the specified conditions have occurred.[8] There remains, however, the significant difference, noted earlier, that a *late* presentment frees the indorsers of their conditional liability in all cases, whereas this is not true of drawers.[9]

How Presentments are Made

Under Sec. 3-504(1) [RUCC 3-501(a)], presentment is a demand for acceptance or payment made upon the maker, acceptor, drawee, or other payor by or on

---

[8]Remember that the revised Article 3 changes matters so that drawers of drafts are not entitled to notice of dishonor as a prerequisite to liability. Under RUCC 3-503(a), only indorsers of drafts are entitled to notice of dishonor. Also, revised Article 3 eliminates the presentment requirement to hold secondary parties liable, though they are still entitled to notice of dishonor.

[9]Throughout this section it is assumed that the requirements of dishonor and notice of dishonor, where applicable, are not waived. In some situations, however, the purchaser of an instrument will not take it unless the transferor's indorsement provides that "presentment, dishonor, and notice of dishonor are hereby waived" (by the indorser). In such cases this discussion is inapplicable.

behalf of the holder. It can be made by mail (in which case the time of presentment is the time at which it is received); through a clearing house; at the place specified in the instrument; or, if no place is specified, at the place of business or at the residence of the maker. (In the latter case, if neither the maker "nor anyone authorized to act for him is accessible" at such place, then presentment is excused.) The importance of these rules is that if an attempted presentment is made in any manner other than these authorized ways, a refusal of the maker, acceptor, or drawee at that time does not constitute a dishonor.

Time of Presentment
As indicated, under the original Article 3 a required presentment must be made not only in a proper manner but also at a *proper time* if indorsers are to be held on their secondary (conditional) liability. What is proper depends on the type of presentment (presentment for acceptance or presentment for payment) and the time at which the instrument is payable.

Sec. 3-503(1) [RUCC has no comparable provision] sets forth the rules for determining the times at which *all* presentments must be made. In the interest of brevity, we will concern ourselves only with those parts of this section that apply to presentments for payment.

The two basic rules are provided by Subsections c and e of Sec. 3-503(1) [RUCC has no comparable provision], which provide, in essence, as follows:

1. If an instrument is payable at a specified time (for instance, "November 20, 1995"), presentment must be made *on that date* if secondary parties are to be held liable in the event of a dishonor.

2. As to all other instruments—demand notes, demand drafts, and checks—presentments must be made *within a reasonable time after the secondary party signed the instrument.*

As was indicated earlier, Sec. 3-503(2) [RUCC has no comparable provision] goes on to indicate the factors to be taken into account in determining what is a reasonable time for various instruments, and provides that in regard to uncertified checks drawn and payable in the United States, a reasonable time with respect to the *drawer* is presumed to be thirty days after its date or issue, whichever is later [*changed by the RUCC to an absolute ninety days after its date*]. Additionally, the original Article 3 provides that with respect to the liability of an *indorser* of such a check,

a reasonable time is presumed to be "seven days after his indorsement" [*changed by the RUCC to an absolute period of thirty days after the indorsement*].

Assume that D draws a regular (uncertified) check on his account in the B Bank payable to the order of P on April 6, and he issues it to P on that date. P, by a blank indorsement, negotiates the check to X on April 15, and X, by blank indorsement, negotiates it to H on April 20. On April 26, H presents the check to the drawee, the B Bank, and payment is refused for some reason; H then gives immediate notice of the dishonor to both indorsers, P and X. Under the seven-day rule of Sec. 3-503(2) of the original Article 3 that applies to indorsers of ordinary checks, the last indorser (X) is liable to H, but the prior indorser, P, is not. Since P indorsed on April 15, she could be held liable only if the check were presented to the drawee bank, or at least put into the bank collection process, within seven days—by April 22. In this case presentment on April 26 was late as to P but effective as to X, since the presentment *was* within seven days of X's becoming an indorser. (And if action were brought by H against D, drawer, as well, obviously the presentment *as to him* would be timely, since it would conform to the "within thirty days of issue" rule applicable to drawers.) Obviously, in jurisdictions that have adopted the revised Article 3, both P an X would be liable because the presentment occurred within thirty days of their indorsements. RUCC 3-415(e).

Notice of Dishonor and Protest
When a dishonor occurs, either by a refusal to accept or by nonpayment, any indorser is freed of conditional liability unless he or she is given a *notice of dishonor* within the time specified by Sec. 3-508 [RUCC 3-503]. That section provides in part, as noted earlier, that "any necessary notice must be given by a bank before its midnight deadline,[10] and by any other person before midnight of the third business day after dishonor" [changed to 30 days by the revised Article 3]. The indorser receiving the notice then has the same prescribed time in which to give notice to his or her immediate indorser, if any.

Under Sec. 3–509 [RUCC 3–505(b)], in some situations a *protest* (a formal, notarized notice of

---

[10]The midnight deadline rule requires that if payment cannot be made because of insufficient funds or because a stop payment order has been issued, the drawee bank must give notice to its transferor no later than midnight of the *next business day*. If that transferor is also a bank, it must in turn give notice to *its* transferor by midnight of the day following its receipt of the original notice.

dishonor) can be made. Protest is required only where the dishonored instrument is drawn in or payable in a foreign country. As to other instruments, use of protest in lieu of ordinary notice of dishonor is optional.

When Presentment Is Excused or Delay Permitted
Sec. 3-511(1) [RUCC has no comparable provision] provides: "Delay in presentment, protest or notice of dishonor is excused when the party is without notice that it is due or when the delay is caused by circumstances beyond his control and he exercises reasonable diligence after the cause of the delay ceases to operate." The phrase *without notice that it is due* has particular application to an instrument containing an acceleration clause. It is entirely possible that a holder will take an instrument *after* the time of payment has been accelerated but without knowledge of the acceleration at the time of taking it. The phrase *circumstances beyond his control* excuses delay in presentment or in notice of dishonor when the delay is caused by such things as extreme weather conditions or the emergency closing of businesses in a certain area by act of the governor of the involved state.

Additionally, Sec. 3-511(2) [RUCC 3-504] provides that presentment or notice of dishonor is entirely excused (1) if the party to be charged has waived presentment or notice; (2) if such party has personally dishonored or stopped payment on the instrument; or (3) "if by reasonable diligence the presentment . . . cannot be made, or the notice given."

The fact pattern of the following case is typical of those in which the courts are required to determine whether or not the holders exercised "reasonable diligence" in trying to make presentment. The result would be the same under revised Article 3, RUCC 3-504(a)(i).

GAFFIN V. HEYMANN

Supreme Court of Rhode Island, 428 A.2d 1066 (1981)

In 1967 Gaffin (plaintiff) loaned $10,000 to Michael Heymann so he and a friend could open a travel agency. Later, the business failed and Gaffin told Heymann he wanted the loan repaid.

A series of negotiations between plaintiff, Michael Heymann, and Michael Heymann's father, Paul Heymann (defendant), then ensued: As a result of these discussions, plaintiff finally agreed to accept two promissory notes payable to his order in the amounts of $8000 and $2000 signed by Michael Heymann as maker, on condition that Paul Heymann would also be a party to the $8000 note.

Accordingly, Michael Heymann delivered the notes to plaintiff in March 1968. The $8000 note—the one involved in this litigation—had a maturity date of March 10, 1973. Michael Heymann was the maker of this interest-bearing note, and the instrument bore the signature of Paul Heymann on the back.

Over the next year or two, several payments were missed. For reasons appearing in the decision, plaintiff was unable to locate Michael Heymann in order to collect the payments, and he was also unable to present the note to Michael Heymann for payment on March 10, 1973. Plaintiff then brought this action to recover the amount of the note from defendant.

At the trial, defendant raised two primary issues: (1) whether he was a comaker of the note, as plaintiff contended, or an indorser; and (2) if he was an indorser, whether he was excused from liability because of plaintiff's failure to present the note to the maker at maturity. The trial court ruled that defendant was legally a comaker of the note, in view of plaintiff's refusal to accept the note unless signed by defendant. Accordingly, judgment was entered for plaintiff.

In the appellate court, defendant raised the same issues as those presented in the trial court. As to the first issue, the appellate court accepted defendant's argument that he was an indorser of the instrument, rather than a comaker. This ruling was reached on the basis of Sec. 3-402 of the UCC, which provides that "unless the instrument clearly indicates that a signature is made in some other capacity, it is an indorsement."

The appellate court then turned to the second issue, whether defendant, as indorser, was released of liability by plaintiff's failure to present the note to the maker at maturity. The part of the opinion dealing with this issue appears below.

Kelleher, Justice:

. . . An indorser's liability attaches only after presentment and demand has
(continues)

GAFFIN V. HEYMANN

(continued from previous page) been made on the maker, in this instance, Michael. After the maker has dishonored the note, the indorser is required to pay the instrument according to the tenor at the time he signed it. Unless excused, failure to make presentment to the maker will act to discharge the indorser. [Emphasis added.] Heymann [defendant] argues that since Gaffin [plaintiff] has acknowledged he did not present the note to Michael when due, he has been discharged of his obligation to pay. Gaffin has countered this contention by claiming that presentment was waived by Michael.

[The court here quoted Sec. 3–511, as follows: "Presentment or notice of protest . . . is entirely excused when . . . (c) by reasonable diligence, the presentment or notice of protest cannot be made or the notice given." The court then continued:]

Once Michael delivered the note to Gaffin, he left Massachusetts to live in Rhode Island. After living in Rhode Island for an indeterminate period, he traveled abroad. Heymann told the trial justice that although he had spoken frequently to Michael on the phone since his return to the United States, he was unaware of Michael's address or place of employment. According to his father, Michael, at the time of trial, was residing somewhere in Connecticut.

In ruling that Gaffin had exercised reasonable diligence in attempting to locate Michael, the trial justice noted that Michael had not responded to mail addressed to him at his last-known address, and had not responded to phone messages left at his father's residence. Although these attempts to reach Michael occurred prior to the due date of the note, the trial justice implied that had Gaffin made further efforts after March 10, 1973, they too would have failed. In view of the fact

that Heymann was aware that Gaffin had attempted to contact Michael and that these attempts had been unsuccessful, there would be little to be gained by requiring Gaffin to continue his attempts ad infinitum. This is particularly true when the indorser is in a better position to know the location of the maker than is the payee of the note. Hence, we [agree with the trial court's] finding that Gaffin had indeed exercised due diligence in attempting to locate Michael. [Accordingly, the court said, presentment was excused under Sec. 3-511, and defendant was thus liable as indorser.]

Judgment affirmed in part, reversed in part, and case remanded. [Although both courts held defendant liable for the face amount of the note (on different theories), the case was remanded to the trial court under instructions to recompute the amount of interest due.]∎

WARRANTY LIABILITY OF INDORSERS

An indorser's negotiation of an instrument for value will almost always carry certain warranties (or guarantees) about that instrument. This gives rise to potential **warranty liability,** which is sometimes called the *unconditional liability* of secondary parties, meaning that the liability is *not* conditioned upon proper presentment, dishonor, and notice of dishonor. The revised version of Article 3 makes some important changes in this area, which we shall discuss.

Indorsers without Qualification

Sec. 3-417(2) [RUCC 3-416] provides in part that a person who negotiates an instrument by indorsement and who receives consideration for it makes five warranties to the indorsee and subsequent holders.[11]

(With an exception to be noted later, the same warranties are also made by indorsers who qualify their indorsements.) Under this section the indorser essentially warrants that:

1. He or she has good title to the instrument.

2. All signatures are genuine or authorized.

3. The instrument has not been materially altered.

4. No defense of any party is good against him or her (the indorser).

5. He or she has no knowledge of any insolvency proceeding instituted against the maker, acceptor, or drawer of an unaccepted instrument.

The first four of these warranties are illustrated below. The fifth is rarely encountered.

Under the original Article 3, a breach of *warranty of title* often involves a forged indorsement. For example: D draws and issues an instrument payable to

---

[11]The liability of a person who negotiates an instrument *by delivery* only (without indorsing it) is discussed later in the chapter.

the order of P. The instrument is stolen from P, and the thief forges P's indorsement on the back of it. He then sells the instrument to A, an innocent purchaser, who by blank indorsement negotiates the instrument to B. B presents the instrument for payment, but payment is refused because the maker, acceptor, or drawee has learned that P's indorsement is a forgery. Because of the forged indorsement of P, B has not acquired title to the instrument and cannot hold the maker (or acceptor or drawee, in the case of a draft or check) liable on it. However, B can hold A liable on the warranty of title theory, because A did not have title either, because of the forged indorsement. A is liable on this warranty even if she had no reason to suspect the forgery and (as is true of all other warranties) even if the presentment for payment by B to the primary party was late.

To illustrate the *warranty that all signatures are genuine or authorized,* assume that P received a note of which M was the apparent maker. P later indorsed the note to H, and H recovered nothing from M because M was able to prove that her signature on the note was a forgery. (It may take a lawsuit against M to establish the fact of the forgery, or evidence of the forgery may be so convincing that H forgoes a lawsuit against M.) H can now hold P, the indorser, on his warranty that all signatures on the instrument at the time of the indorsement were genuine. Again, H need not show that P knew of the forgery when he indorsed it; it is the fact of the forgery that is controlling.

The interplay of these first two warranties is examined in the following case decided under the original Article 3.

WHITE V. INDEPENDENCE BANK, N.A.

Court of Appeals of Texas, 794 S.W.2d 895 (1990)

White hired Jansen & Co. to help him collect for a fire loss at his home, assigning 7 percent of the recovery to Jansen. Cambridge Mutual Fire Insurance Co., the insurer, was informed of the arrangement. White settled his claim with Cambridge without informing it that he had earlier fired Jansen & Co. Cambridge submitted the check for the fire loss with two payees—John M. White and Jansen & Co. White asked Jansen & Co. to indorse the draft, but it refused. Therefore, White typed "Jansen & Company" on the back of the check, and signed his name as the indorser. White then presented the draft to Independence Bank ("the collecting bank") for deposit into the account of Alba Corporation (which he owned). White did not tell Cambridge or the collecting bank of his dispute with Jansen & Co. The collecting bank gave Alba immediate conditional credit of the funds.

When the collecting bank presented the check (through a correspondent bank) for payment, the draft was refused for lack of indorsement. Cambridge refused to honor the check until Jansen & Co. indorsed it, and the check was returned to the collecting bank. The bank then charged those funds back to Alba Corporation's account.

White filed suit and lodged a claim against the collecting bank on various theories, including violation of the UCC and of various express and implied warranties. The trial judge ordered the amount of the check ($43,060.80) to be paid 93 percent to White and 7 percent to Jansen. Thereafter, the collecting bank filed a motion for summary judgment on the remainder of White's claims. The motion was granted; White appealed.

O'Connor, Justice:

White claims the collecting bank did not have the right to charge back the funds to the Alba Corporation's account. White admits that any credits to the account were conditional until the collecting bank received cash payment

on drafts. White's theory of liability is that the collecting bank was required to notify him within 24 hours that the draft had been refused. . . . White wants this Court to create a "24 hour rule": If a collecting bank does not notify a customer within 24 hours that the draft the customer presented for collection was refused because the customer forged an endorsement, the customer gets to keep the money.

The collecting bank asserts that White violated [original UCC Secs. 3-116, 3-417, and 4-207]. Section 3-116 defines instruments payable to two or more persons. Section 3-417 discusses presentment warranties [including (2)(b)'s promise that "all signatures are genuine or authorized. . . ."] of the customer.

The collecting bank asserts White breached these warranties because White deposited the draft after he had endorsed Jansen & Company's name without Jansen & Company's approval. The endorsement was not genuine, and White knew this when he presented the draft to the collecting bank.

(continues)

WHITE v. INDEPENDENCE BANK, N.A.

(continued from previous page)
"Good title" means the draft bears no forged endorsements or signatures. When a party presents a draft for acceptance, and knows the draft is forged, the presenting party breaches the warranty of good title. In this case, the facts clearly show that White breached the presentment warranty of good title. He admitted he put Jansen & Company's name on the back of the draft without Jansen & Company's approval.

[Affirmed.]

Remaining Indorser Warranties

We discussed the defense of *material alteration* in Chapter 26, where we saw that a maker or acceptor might escape liability on an instrument by showing that it was materially altered after he or she had made (or accepted) it. The ordinary holder who presents for payment in this situation will probably recover nothing from the maker or acceptor, and an HDC may make only a partial recovery (especially if the alteration involved a raising of the amount of the instrument). However, either holder can hold any *indorser* liable on the breach of warranty theory and thereby recover whatever loss he or she sustained—assuming, of course, that the alteration occurred prior to the indorsement. Thus, ultimate liability will likely fall upon the first solvent indorser who took the instrument following the forgery.

The warranty that *no defense is good against the indorser* refers to any kinds of defenses that do not fall within the first three subsections of Sec. 3-417(2) [RUCC 3-416]—as, for example, the defense of illegality. To illustrate: After a Saturday night poker game, A ends up owing B $175; A gives B a check for that amount in payment. The following Monday, A learns from a lawyer friend that gambling debts are totally unenforceable in his state, so he stops payment on the check. In the meantime, B has indorsed the check to C. In this situation, after being refused payment by the drawee bank, C can hold B (the indorser) liable for breach of the warranty that no defense existed against him.

Revised Article 3 Changes

Revised Article 3 preserves each of the five aforementioned warranties as *transaction warranties* in RUCC 3-416. In a separate section, RUCC 3-417, *presentment warranties* are discussed. Regarding *notes and accepted drafts*, that section eliminates two of the transaction warranties (that the presenter has no knowledge that the signature of the maker or drawer is unauthorized and that there has been no material alteration) from the presentment setting for the obvious reason that the maker or acceptor should know whether the signature is authorized or there has been a material alteration. So, in a presentment of notes or accepted drafts to a maker or an acceptor occurring in a jurisdiction that has adopted the revised Article 3, the only important warranty is that of good title.

Qualified Indorsers

The warranty liability of the person who indorses without recourse is exactly the same as that of the unqualified indorser—with one exception. Whereas the unqualified indorser flatly guarantees that no defense of any party is good against him or her, the qualified indorser warrants only that he or she "has no knowledge of such a defense." Sec. 3-417(3) [RUCC has no comparable provision]. Thus, if a check was given in payment of a totally illegal obligation and subsequently a party indorsed the instrument without recourse, that indorser would not be liable upon dishonor unless it was established that he or she *knew of the defense* at the time of indorsement.

Under the original Article 3, this limitation on warranty liability applies only to defenses falling within Subsection d of 3-417(2) (that "no defense of any party is good against him"). Thus, if the qualified indorser was being sued for breach of the warranty that all signatures were genuine, for example, the qualified indorser would be liable if the drawer's or maker's signature was a forgery, even if he or she did not know of the forgery.

Revised Article 3 Changes

The rule for qualified indorsement just discussed is *changed by revised Article 3*. Under RUCC 3-

416(a)(4), a person making a qualified indorsement in exchange for value warrants that no defense of any party is good against the indorser. Thus, in jurisdictions adopting revised Article 3, this warranty liability applies equally to both unqualified and qualified indorsers.

SELECTED TRANSFEROR–INDORSER PROBLEMS

Liability of Transferor without Indorsement

A person who negotiates a bearer instrument by mere delivery (that is, without indorsing it) has no conditional liability on the instrument. If the primary party is unable to pay the instrument at maturity, the transferor is not liable to the holder.

However, a transferor by mere delivery does have the warranty of an unqualified indorser, with one important exception. While the warranties of indorsers run to all subsequent holders of the instrument, the warranties of the person who transfers without indorsement run only to his or her *immediate transferee.* To illustrate: P receives a bearer note of which M is apparently the maker. P negotiates the note to X by delivery only, and X in turn negotiates it by delivery only to H. If M's signature turns out to be a forgery, H can hold X, her immediate transferor, liable on his warranty that all signatures are genuine, but she cannot hold P, the prior transferor. (Of course, if X has to pay damages to H arising out of the breach of his warranty, X can then hold P because P's warranty did run to him.)

Order of Indorser's Liability

Where two or more indorsements appear on an instrument, it is presumed under Sec. 3-414(2) [RUCC has no comparable provision] that the indorsers are liable in the order in which their signatures appear. For instance, a note is indorsed by X, and the names of Y and Z appear successively below her indorsement. If Z is held liable to the holder (H) following a dishonor, Z can proceed against Y and Y against X. X will then be limited to an attempt to recover the amount of the instrument from the maker.[12]

[12]It is only *presumed* that the indorsers are liable in the order in which their signatures appear; a contrary agreement may exist among the indorsers. In the current example, X will not be liable to Y if she can prove that such an agreement existed between her and Y at the time of her indorsement.

While the holder of a dishonored instrument usually seeks to hold the last indorser liable, the holder is not limited to such a proceeding. For example, in the above case, if, upon dishonor, holder H *gives proper notice* to X, Y, and Z, he can then "skip" Y and Z if he wishes and bring suit directly against X, the first indorser.

Liability of Accommodation Indorsers

Sometimes a person will indorse an instrument merely for the purpose of lending his or her credit to the instrument. Such a person is an **accommodation indorser.** To illustrate: P is the holder of a check of which she is the payee, and she wishes to cash it at a bank where she is unknown. At the bank's suggestion, P asks A, an acquaintance who is a local merchant and depositor at the bank, to indorse the check along with her. A does so, becoming an accommodation indorser. The bank then cashes the check, giving the amount of the instrument to P in cash. (In this case, P is known as the *accommodated party.*)

In general, an accommodation indorser has the same liability to subsequent holders as does any other indorser. The accommodation indorser has both conditional and warranty liability to any subsequent holder (including a holder who knew that he or she was signing merely as an accommodation indorser). Once there is a dishonor of the instrument and proper notice is given to the accommodation indorser, that person is immediately liable to the holder. That is, the holder does not have to bring suit against the primary (accommodated) party in an effort to obtain payment before initiating action against the accommodation indorser.

DISCHARGE OF THE PARTIES

Examination of the rules regarding the liability of secondary parties has already presented several situations in which these parties are discharged, such as failure to make a required presentment or failure to give a notice of dishonor. Now we will briefly describe additional ways in which parties to commercial paper can be discharged.

Discharge by Payment

The vast majority of negotiable instruments are discharged by payment. Under Secs. 3-601(1)(a) and 3-603 [RUCC 3-602(b)(2)], payment in good faith to the holder by a primary party or by the drawee of an unaccepted draft or check usually discharges all parties on the instrument. Payment by any other party, such as an indorser, only discharges the indorser and subsequent parties on the instrument. In such a case, the party making payment can still seek recovery from prior parties on the instrument. If a payment is less than the amount owed, the party making the payment is discharged only to the extent of the payment, as determined by the rules of debt settlement (see

Legal Focus INTERNATIONAL

As noted in Chapter 25, the negotiable instruments discussed in this chapter are of great importance to *international* commercial transactions. Uniformity and predictability in the law, provided by Article 3 on the domestic scene, are just as important internationally. Therefore, on December 9, 1988, the United Nations General Assembly approved for ratification the United Nations Convention on International Bills of Exchange and International Promissory Notes (UNCIBEN), which was produced by the United Nations Commission on International Trade Law (UNCITRAL).

UNCIBEN will apply only if the instrument contains *both* in its heading and in its text the words "International bill of exchange (UNCITRAL Convention)" or "International promissory note (UNCITRAL Convention)," as appropriate. Thus, the parties must "opt in" for the convention to apply. In other words, UNCIBEN's drafters are seeking to create a type of negotiable instrument available only in international business transactions and only on an optional basis.

Note also that UNCIBEN does *not* apply to checks, but does apply to several types of instruments not necessarily viewed as negotiable in all jurisdictions. For example, as noted in Chapter 25, variable interest rate notes (VRNs) are not negotiable in the United States in most jurisdictions following original Article 3. However, they are negotiable in most civil law systems of Europe (and in U.S. jurisdictions adopting the *revised* Article 3). They are deemed negotiable under UNCIBEN. UNCIBEN necessarily contains many compromises between the principles of Article 3 and approaches to similar problems taken in the United Kingdom and in the civil law systems of Europe and elsewhere, although most conflicts were resolved in favor of approaches based on American law.

The ultimate impact of UNCIBEN, of course, depends on how many nations ratify it and then, more importantly, how many persons transacting international business opt in.

Chapter 13).[13] Under Sec. 3-604 [RUCC 3-603], if a party tenders payment, but it is refused, the party is not discharged from liability. However, the holder cannot later recover interest from the time of the tender; nor can he or she recover legal costs or attorneys' fees.

Alteration

Under Sec. 3-407 [RUCC 3-407], alteration of an instrument by a holder discharges any party whose obligation is affected by the alteration, except that an HDC can enforce the instrument according to its original terms.[14] Also, a drawer whose negligence contributes to the alteration may be barred from asserting an alteration defense against a nonnegligent drawee bank.

Cancellation and Renunciation

Sec. 3-605 [RUCC 3-604(a)(i)] reads as follows: "(1) The holder of an instrument may even without consideration discharge any party (a) in any manner apparent on the face of the instrument or the indorsement, as by intentionally cancelling the instrument or the party's signature by destruction or mutilation, or by striking out the party's signature." To illustrate: Marking an instrument "paid" constitutes a cancellation of the instrument itself, as does intentional destruction or mutilation of it. Similarly, striking out a party's indorsement cancels that party's liability (but not the liability of prior parties). Under Sec. 3-605(1)(b) [RUCC 3-604(a)(ii)], *renunciation* occurs when a holder gives up his or her rights against a party to the instrument in a particular way—either by renouncing them in a signed writing given to such party or by surrendering the instrument to that party.

---

[13]Chapter 13 points out that the rules of debt settlement are changed by the revised Article 3 in RUCC 3-311.

[14]Under the original Article 3, an HDC does not give the presentment warranty of material alteration; therefore, if an HDC presents a check that was accepted prior to a material alteration, the acceptor cannot later recover the altered amount from the HDC. RUCC 3-413 (b) *changes* this rule, allowing the acceptor to protect itself by stating an amount on the instrument at the time of acceptance. If the acceptor does so, its obligation is limited to the amount stated. If the acceptor does not do so, its obligation is the amount shown on the instrument when it was negotiated to the HDC.

Discharge of a Prior Party

As a general rule, the intentional cancellation of an instrument discharges all parties to it. Additionally, the discharge of a *particular party* by cancellation or renunciation normally discharges that party and all subsequent parties. These results flow from Sec. 3-606 [RUCC 3-605(b), (c)], which provides, in part, that "[t]he holder discharges any party to the instrument to the extent that without such party's consent the holder . . . without express reservation of rights releases or agrees not to sue any person against whom the party has . . . a right of recourse." To illustrate: A note bears three indorsements: X, Y, and Z, in that order. If the holder, H, gives a valid release to the first indorser, X, both subsequent indorsers, Y and Z, are thereby discharged. It is possible, however, for H in such a situation to release X but expressly to "reserve his rights" against Y and Z. If this occurs, and H later collects the amount of the instrument from either Y or Z, then that party still retains the right of recourse against X, the first indorser. Thus, H's release of X, where he reserves his rights against subsequent indorsers, does not insulate X from liability to the subsequent indorsers.

Discharge by Reacquisition

If a person acquires an instrument that he or she had held at a prior time, all intervening indorsers are discharged as against the reacquiring party and as against subsequent holders who do not qualify as HDCs. To illustrate: P indorses a note to A, and A indorses it to B. If P reacquires the note, indorsers A and B are freed of all liability to P. And if P thereafter recirculates the instrument, A and B will have liability to subsequent holders only if such holders are HDCs.

STATUTES OF LIMITATION

The original version of Article 3 does not contain express statute of limitation provisions. RUCC 3-118 fills this gap by providing time limits for suits on promissory notes payable at a definite time (six years after original or accelerated due date), demand instruments (six years after demand for payment, but no later than ten years after the last payment of principal or interest), drafts (three years after dishonor or ten years after date, whichever comes first), and conversion or warranty theories (three years after the cause of action accrued).

SUMMARY

The primary parties to commercial paper are the makers of notes and acceptors of drafts. Both such parties admit (guarantee) the existence of the payee, and the payee's capacity to indorse. Of much more importance, however, is the promissory liability of makers and acceptors. Assuming they have no defenses against the holder of an instrument, their promises to pay are absolute—that is, their liability is not extinguished by a late presentment for payment. To this there is one limited exception: if an instrument is payable at a designated bank, and if the bank fails between the time presentment should have been made and the time of the late presentment, the maker or acceptor may discharge his or her liability by giving an assignment of his or her rights against the bank in respect to the funds held in the bank for payment.

Secondary parties under the original Article 3 are drawers of drafts and checks, and indorsers of all instruments. (Under the revised Article 3, drawers attain near primary liability; they are not entitled to notice of dishonor.) Such parties, like makers and acceptors, make certain guarantees about the instrument, and also have promissory liability. This promissory liability, however, unlike that of makers and acceptors, is conditional in nature; that is, they promise to pay the holder the amount of the instrument only upon occurrence of three events: (1) a presentment for payment to the maker or drawee-acceptor; (2) a dishonor by such party; and (3) receipt of notice of dishonor. In that regard, however, the promissory liability of the drawer differs markedly from that of an indorser. Whereas it is true that under the original Article 3 the drawer cannot be held liable until the three specified events occur, a late presentment—followed by dishonor and notice of dishonor—does not discharge the drawer from promissory liability (except in the rare case where the drawee fails prior to the time of the late presentment). By contrast, assuming there is no waiver of presentment, dishonor, and notice, a late presentment automatically frees the indorser from promissory liability.

Turning to the subject of warranty liability, the UCC provides that all persons who negotiate an instrument by indorsement (and who receive consideration for the indorsement) make four primary warranties to the indorsee and to all subsequent holders. Under the original Article 3 (note revised Article 3 changes), such an indorser warrants that: (1) he or she has good title to the instrument, (2) all signatures and indorsements on the instrument at the time of indorsement are genuine or authorized, (3) the instrument has not been materially altered, and (4) no defense of any party is good against him or her (the indorser). If there is a breach of any of these guarantees resulting in failure of the indorsee or subsequent holder to obtain payment from the maker or drawee-acceptor, the indorser is liable in damages to such person. The warranty liability of the qualified (without recourse) indorser is the same as that of the unqualified indorser, except that, as to warranty 4, the warranty is that he or she has *no knowledge* of any existing defenses. The warranty liability of an indorser, unlike his or her promissory liability, is not extinguished by a late presentment for payment. The revised Article 3 makes some relatively minor changes in warranty law, especially as regards warranties by qualified indorsers.

The revised Article 3 contains statutes of limitation of the various causes of action that might arise in this area.

KEY TERMS
Primary parties
Secondary parties
Promissory liability
Warranty liability
Accommodation indorser

QUESTIONS AND PROBLEMS

1. On September 23, 1966, Mindy Manufacturing Company issued and distributed payroll checks to its employees payable to their orders and drawn on the Continental Bank and Trust Company. Plaintiffs cashed these checks for a small fee and deposited them in their account at the Provident National Bank, which in turn presented them to Continental, which refused payment because Mindy had insufficient funds. Plaintiffs later sued Apfelbaum, an individual, who signed the aforementioned preprinted payroll checks (with Mindy's name imprinted on them) with his own signature that was "absolute and unqualified" and did not designate his office or capacity. Is Apfelbaum individually liable on these

checks? Discuss. (*Pollin v. Mindy Mfg. Co.*, 236 A.2d 542, Pa.Super. 1967.)

2. Janet Friel became president of New England Office Products Company (the company) in 1981 after the death of her husband who had founded the company. General management of daily operations was handled by her brother-in-law, David Friel, and her role was limited mainly to keeping the checkbook and signing all corporate checks. In 1982 and 1983, the company took out two loans of $10,000 and $30,000 from First Safety Fund National Bank. On both occasions, Janet Friel signed twice: once, directly under the typed name of the company, she wrote "Janet M. Friel, President"; on the line below that signature she wrote, without qualification, "Janet M. Friel." The bank's loan officer said nothing one way or the other about the effect of the signatures. In 1984 the company became insolvent and ceased operations. The bank sued Janet Friel seeking to hold her personally liable on the two notes. Will the bank prevail? Discuss. (*First Safety Fund National Bank v. Friel,* 504 N.E.2d 664, Mass.App. 1987.)

3. Bartus owned all the stock of Rascar, Inc., which opened a checking account with the Bank of Oregon on June 6, 1972. The signature card listed Bartus as one of two required signatures and either George Corning or Kent Corning as the required second signature. During July 1972, the bank paid two checks drawn upon it totalling $3500, each payable to George Corning and signed only by George Corning. Later, the bank paid nine checks payable to George Corning, each bearing the signature of George Corning and the forged signature of Bartus. One issue that arose in subsequent litigation is whether Rascar can recover from the bank because the bank paid on an unauthorized signature. The bank claims that it paid on an authorized signature, because George Corning's valid signature was on all of the checks. Discuss the merits of this issue. (*Rascar, Inc. v. Bank of Oregon*, 275 N.W.2d 108, Wis.App. 1978.)

4. Fourco, defendant, took a promissory note in payment for goods that it sold. It then indorsed the note without recourse and negotiated it to Fair Finance. Fair Finance was not able to recover the full amount of the note from the maker because Fourco, in filling out the note, had computed the interest at a rate higher than that allowed by Ohio law. Fair

Finance then brought an action to recover the balance from Fourco, the indorser. Fourco defended on the ground that a qualified indorser does not guarantee that there are no defenses, but merely guarantees he or she has no knowledge of defenses. The trial court found that Fourco had *no knowledge* of the excess interest and entered judgment for it. Did the trial court rule correctly? Discuss. (*Fair Finance Co. v. Fourco, Inc.*, 237 N.E.2d 406, Ohio App. 1968.)

5. Rzepka, a customer of Society National Bank (SNB), drew two checks totalling $4500 on SNB payable to the ABS Company and delivered them to Mishler, a sales representative of ABS. Mishler forged the payee's indorsements on the two checks, signed his own name, and obtained from SNB in exchange two cashier's checks, payable as before to the ABS Company. He also forged the indorsements on the cashier's checks and deposited them in an account titled "Windows, Inc.," which he maintained at defendant Capital National Bank (Capital). Capital transferred the checks to defendant Union Commerce Bank (Union), which in turn presented them to SNB for payment. SNB paid the checks. After more than a year, Rzepka informed SNB that the indorsements had been forged, whereupon SNB promptly notified Union, the presenting bank, and Capital, the depositary bank, of the forgeries. SNB reimbursed its customer's account and brought suit against Capital and Union. Will SNB prevail? Discuss. (*Society Nat'l Bank v. Capital Nat'l Bank*, 281 N.E.2d 563, Ohio App. 1972.)

6. Plaintiff, a farm machinery dealer, sold machinery on credit to Thomas Sessions to be used on a farm owned and operated by Thomas and his wife Dorothy. In the fall of 1987, Thomas's health was poor; he and Dorothy sold the equipment. To confirm the amounts still owed on the machinery, plaintiff sought and received from Thomas and Dorothy a promissory note in the amount of $42,380.79. Two weeks later, Thomas and Dorothy sold their farm valued at $50,000 to defendant Backus, as trustee for their son Raymond. Thomas died soon thereafter. Plaintiff then sued Dorothy and Backus to collect on the promissory note and to set aside the farm sale as a fraudulent conveyance. The trial court ruled for Dorothy on the note, holding that Thomas rather than Dorothy was liable. The trial judge apparently believed that Dorothy was merely an accommodation party because sales were made solely to Thomas. Was this a proper ruling? Discuss. (*McCarthy v. Sessions*, 572 N.Y.S.2d 749, N.Y.App.Div. 1991.)

7. Marine Midland Bank (MMB) issued as payor a check for $22,036.70, representing the amount payable on an "official check" issued by the bank at the request of plaintiff Biltmore Associates. The check was made payable to the Internal Revenue Service (IRS). Plaintiff mailed the check to its Florida office for forwarding to the IRS. The manager of the Florida office altered, without authority, the name of the payee from "Internal Revenue Service" to "Plantation Island for Internal Revenue Service." The check was indorsed by the Plantation Island Homeowner's Association. A bank in Florida honored the check, and the proceeds were paid into the account of the Plantation Island Homeowner's Association. MMB, in turn, accepted the check and paid the face amount to the Florida bank. Plaintiff then sued MMB, claiming that it had improperly paid the check. Will plaintiff prevail? Discuss. (*Biltmore Associates Ltd. v. Marine Midland Bank*, 578 N.Y.S.2d 798, N.Y.App.Div. 1991.)

8. Plaintiff Ray, eighty years old, was awakened from a nap by a man shaking the screen to her front door. He said he worked for the utility company and needed to check the electrical system of her home because power was off along the block. He pushed his way inside the house and went around placing a device in the electrical outlets. He told Ray that he was not through, but would go get a hamburger while awaiting the arrival of another employee. He told her that she should give him $1.50 for the service charge. She reached for her purse, but he picked up her checkbook and told her that his company required payment by check. He filled in the check for her. She made sure it was in ink so it could not be changed. She signed the check and he left. After waiting a period of time, Ray decided the man was not going to return. She decided to call the bank to stop payment, but her phone line was dead (he had cut it). When she finally talked to the bank two hours later, she learned he had already cashed the check for $1851.50. Because he had written the figures "1.50" far right of the dollar sign, the man was able to add the figures 185. What are Ray's rights against the bank that cashed the check? Discuss. (*Ray v. Farmers State Bank of Hart*, 576 S.W.2d 607, Tex. 1979.)

Chapter 28

Commercial Paper
Checks and the Bank–Depositor Relationship

Checks

The Bank–Depositor Relationship

Selected Bank–Depositor Problems

Increased Federal Control over Checks and the Bank–Depositor Relationship

Electronic Banking

W

HEREAS CHECKS ARE simply one type of commercial paper, they do possess certain characteristics that set them apart from promissory notes and other drafts. Although some of these special aspects have been discussed in prior chapters, others have not. In this chapter we will first summarize the special attributes of checks and then examine the legal relationship between the drawer of a check and the **drawee bank** (the bank on which the check is drawn). As noted earlier, revisions of Articles 3 and 4 have been adopted in several jurisdictions. This chapter will discuss important changes in the law made by these revisions.[1] An important look at the subject of electronic banking and the basic federal law applicable to its various facets—the Electronic Funds Transfer Act—concludes the chapter.

CHECKS

Under Sec. 3-104 [RUCC 3-104], a check is by definition "a draft drawn on a bank payable on demand." (The *demand* requirement thus means that a "post-dated check"—for instance, one issued to the payee on March 10 but dated April 5—is, technically speaking, a draft rather than a check. The primary consequence of postdating is that the drawee bank should not honor the instrument until the specified date arrives, although the RUCC gives banks new protection if they do so, as explained later in the chapter.

Checks generally have a shorter life than other instruments and thus circulate more quickly than ordinary drafts and promissory notes. This is reflected in Sec. 3-503 [RUCC has no comparable provision], which provides that (1) for the drawer of a check, it is presumed that a reasonable time for presentment is to be no more than thirty days after issue, and (2) for an indorser a reasonable time is presumed to be only seven days after indorsement. RUCC 3-415(e) changes the seven-day rule by absolutely (not merely presumptively) discharging indorsers if the check is not presented within thirty days after the indorsement.

The general rule for *drawers* of drafts—that a late presentment excuses them of liability only if they have suffered a loss as a result of the delay—is illustrated as it specifically applies to checks: D draws and issues a check to P on March 1; after several negotiations the check is presented by H, the last holder, to the drawee bank on June 18. Payment is refused at that time (perhaps because D has insufficient funds in her account or because a creditor of D, through legal proceedings, has attached D's funds in the bank). In this case, though presentment has been made more than two months after the thirty-day deadline (March 31), D remains fully liable to H on the instrument *unless* the drawee bank failed after March 31 and before the late presentment on June 18. In that limited situation D can discharge her liability by giving an assignment of funds to H in the amount of the instrument, in the same manner that the maker of a note payable at a bank can (see Chapter 27). RUCC 3-407(f) is similar.

A Check Is Not an Assignment of Funds

As a practical matter, checks are drawn (and received by the payee and subsequent holders) on the assumption that the drawer has funds in his or her account at the drawee bank sufficient to pay the instrument when it is presented. In the great majority of instances this is, in fact, the case. Federal Reserve Board figures indicate that of every thousand checks drawn, only six or seven are dishonored because of insufficient funds.

Despite the likelihood that a given check will actually be honored, under Sec. 3-409(1) [RUCC 3-408] the issuance of a check does not constitute an "assignment of funds" in the drawee bank. Until final payment is made by the drawee bank, the issuance and circulation of the instrument have no effect on the funds in the drawer's account; nor do they discharge the underlying debt in payment for which it was issued.

Thus, whereas a check may be accepted by the payee in payment of a debt owned by the drawer, and whereas the payee may even give the drawer a receipt marked "paid in full," the receipt is conditional upon the check's actually being honored by the drawee

---

[1]One important change is inclusion of a definition of the word *bank* to clarify that the term is no longer limited simply to commercial banks but now includes any "person engaged in the business of banking, including a savings bank, savings and loan association, credit union or trust company." RUCC 4-105(1). As noted earlier, citations to original Article 3 will be immediately followed by citations to the comparable *revised* Article 3 provision. Article 4 was not so thoroughly rewritten.

bank when presented. The same thing is true for bank credits. Thus, where a payee deposits a check in his or her account in a bank (the depositary bank) and receives credit for the deposit, and that bank forwards the check to an intermediary bank which credits the depositary bank's account, the entire process is reversed if the drawee bank dishonors the check. That is, the check is returned to the payee through the same channels, each bank charging its transferor bank with the amount of the instrument. Ultimately the check is returned to the depositary bank, which charges the account of its depositor, the payee, with the amount of the check and returns it to him or her. The payee can then sue the drawer on the check or on the underlying debt itself.

Certification of Checks

In our discussion of drafts we noted that checks (unlike many drafts) are not presented for acceptance. However, they are occasionally presented to the drawee bank for *certification;* if certification is made, the bank's liability is the same as that of the acceptor of a draft.

One of the most common uses of a **certified check** is where a seller of goods, such as a used car dealer, is selling to a buyer with whom he or she has had no business dealings. In such a case the seller will probably want the buyer to have his or her personal check certified before taking it in payment. From a practical standpoint the primary result of certification is that the seller no longer has to worry that the check will be dishonored because of insufficient funds. Frequently, certified checks are required by law from purchasers of real estate at sheriff's sales, and occasionally they are required from persons who are paying fees owed to a state or state agency.

Many banks no longer certify checks, so *teller's checks* (drafts drawn by a bank on another bank, or payable at or through a bank) and *cashier's checks* (drafts with respect to which the drawer and drawee are the same bank or branches of the same bank) are used more often.[2]

[2]These terms are defined in RUCC 3-104.

Mechanics and Effect

In the absence of a special agreement, a bank has no legal duty to certify a check drawn on it; its only duty is to pay the holder in conformity with the terms of the instrument. A bank that accedes to a request for certification does so by stamping the word *certified* on the face of the check, together with the name of the bank and the date, and including the handwritten signature or initials of the officer making the certification. At that time the bank charges the drawer's account with the amount of the check and transfers the funds to its certified check account.

Certification has three basic effects:

1. The certifying bank is now primarily liable on the instrument (it absolutely promises to pay the instrument when it is presented for payment).

2. The certification of a check at the request of a *holder* discharges the drawer and any indorsers who indorsed prior to certification. To illustrate: A check drawn by D is issued to P; P indorses it to H, and H obtains certification from the drawee bank. At this point D (the drawer) and P (the indorser) are released of all liability on the instrument. On the other hand, if the *drawer* requests the certification, he or she remains secondarily liable; that is, in the unlikely event that the certifying bank subsequently cannot or will not honor the check when it is presented for payment, the drawer is liable to the holder.

3. Once a check is certified, the drawer no longer has the right to stop payment on it. This is true no matter who obtained the certification. Under RUCC 3-411, if a bank wrongfully refuses to pay a certified check—or a teller's check or a cashier's check, all of which are to be treated as virtual "cash equivalents"—it is liable for expenses, lost interest, and consequential damage resulting from the refusal to pay. Revised Article 3 rejected cases decided under the original Article 3, which allowed banks to dishonor these three types of checks under certain circumstances.

The following case, decided under the original Article 3, illustrates why banks are increasingly reluctant to certify checks.

QUISTGAARD V. EUROPEAN AMERICAN BANK & TRUST CO.

New York Supreme Court, Appellate Division, 583 N.Y.S.2d 210 (1992)

Plaintiff Quistgaard was payee on a $25,000 check drawn on the account of Video Computer, Inc., and signed by Video's officer, Kiss. Aware of Kiss's reputation for cancelling checks to suppliers, plaintiff visited defendant bank (EAB) on two consecutive days attempting to have the check certified or cashed, only to be told that there were insufficient funds in Video's account. On the next day, EAB did certify the check, marking it with the bank's certification stamp, which read, in large print, "CERTIFIED," and, beneath that, in small print, "Payable only as originally drawn and when properly indorsed." The check was also initialled by a bank officer.

After plaintiff left, an EAB employee called Kiss, who told the bank that he never issued the check; that if plaintiff was in possession of such a check, he must have stolen it and fraudulently completed it; and that the check must not be cashed. When plaintiff returned to the bank, Kiss confronted him and accused him of theft. Plaintiff was arrested and EAB kept the check. Plaintiff then filed this suit to compel payment on the certified check. The Civil Court granted summary judgment dismissing the complaint. The Appellate Term reinstated the complaint. The plaintiff's summary judgment motion was then considered upon further appeal.

Memorandum Decision:

[S]ummary judgment should be granted to plaintiff.

First, we reject EAB's claim that the check was not certified because, under bank policy, the maker should have been contacted before it was certified. Even if EAB were to establish that its policy, before certifying a check, is to contact the maker, it would be irrelevant. Certification must be judged by an objective standard. Thus, once the check was stamped "CERTIFIED" and signed by the bank's agent, the bank may not claim that the check was not really certified because it had not completed its subjectively defined procedures.

EAB also argues that, even if the check was certified, it properly withdrew that certification upon Kiss's stop payment order. We reject this argument. When a bank certifies a check, it accepts it, thereby becoming legally bound to pay it to one rightfully entitled to the funds. UCC 3-413(1). Moreover, since, in this case, the bank certified the check for the holder, it assumed sole liability on the check and the drawer was thereby discharged.

Once a bank has accepted a check by certifying it, it is limited in its right to refuse to honor the check. Thus, under UCC 4-303, a bank must make payment on a certified check regardless of a subsequently received stop payment order. Since, in this case, the stop payment order was received by the bank after the certification became operative, the bank was not entitled to refuse to pay the check on that basis.

[C]ontrary to EAB's assertions, there is some reason to believe that EAB did not actually attempt to withdraw the certification upon receipt of the stop payment order, since, on the day after the stop payment order was received, EAB apparently attempted to pass a "certification debit" on Video's account in order to hold funds to cover the check, only to find that the funds had at that point been withdrawn. Thus, there is a basis to find that EAB's "mistake," and its reason for attempting to withdraw its certification, was in allowing its customer to withdraw the funds after the check was certified.

However, even accepting EAB's assertion that the charges of theft were the basis for withdrawal of the certification, we must reject its argument. EAB has made no allegation that any of the information it relied on in certifying the check, such as the balance in Video's account or the genuineness of Kiss's signature, was incorrect. . . . Since, at the time the check was certified, EAB was not mistaken as to any of the elements which entered into the decision to certify, EAB was not entitled to withdraw the certification on that basis.

Of course, EAB would be fully entitled to defend the within action by reference to certain personal defenses held by the drawer, including theft, or by showing that the certification was obtained from it by fraud. However, EAB has offered no such defense.

[Plaintiff's summary judgment motion is granted.] ⚖

THE BANK–DEPOSITOR RELATIONSHIP

A bank may be liable to a depositor or a depositor liable to a bank solely through Article 3 of the UCC (dealing with commercial paper). However, the bank–depositor relationship is a broad one; thus many of the general rights and duties of the two parties spring from several sources in addition to that article. These sources include the following:

1. A *creditor–debtor relationship* exists between the depositor and the drawee bank, and sometimes

the bank's obligations are essentially those of debtors generally.

2. In some transactions, a *principal–agent relationship* exists between the depositor and the drawee bank, and in these situations the bank has the same obligations as those imposed on all agents—for example, the duty to use reasonable care and the duty not to profit at the principal's expense.

3. In many situations involving controversies between the depositor and the bank, specific sections of Article 4 (dealing with bank deposits and collections) enter the picture.

We begin our discussion by stating the primary duties of a bank. We will then examine some specific situations that commonly cause bank–depositor controversies.

The Bank's Duties
Duty to Honor Orders
The drawee bank is generally obligated to honor checks drawn by the depositor so long as he or she has sufficient funds in the account and has not stopped payment. The bank's failure to honor a check usually makes it liable to the depositor, under ordinary breach of contract principles, for damages resulting from the refusal to pay. (As we will see in more detail later, the bank also is obligated to obey the stop-payment orders of its drawers.)

Assume that an account has insufficient funds to pay a particular check. Can a bank properly honor such a check, thus creating an overdraft in the drawer's account? Original Article 4 does not clearly indicate whether a bank can create an overdraft without customer authorization, although it has been generally understood that a bank may do so and subsequently recover from the drawer the amount of the overdraft. Revised Article 4-401 clearly authorizes a bank to pay an instrument that will create an overdraft if the drawer has authorized the payment and no agreement between the bank and drawer is breached.

Stale Checks. The duty to honor checks is not absolute, however. As noted, a bank obviously does not have to honor checks if there are not sufficient funds in the drawer's account. The bank also does not have to honor **stale checks**. UCC Sec. 4-404 provides that "a bank is under no obligation to a customer having a checking account to pay a check, other than a certified check, which is presented more than six months after its date, but it may charge its

customer's account for a payment made thereafter in good faith." This section suggests that a drawee bank presented with a check beyond the six-month time limit should secure a confirmation from the drawer before honoring it; failure to do so raises at least the possibility that the bank might not be able to show "good faith" in making the payment.

Damages for Wrongful Dishonor. Revised Sec. 4-402(b) clarifies the liability of a bank for wrongful dishonor, providing that "a payor bank is liable to its customer for damages proximately caused by the wrongful dishonor of an item. Liability is limited to actual damages proved and may include damages for an arrest or prosecution of the customer or other consequential damages." The section does not preclude recovery of punitive damages.[3]

Duty to Pay on Only Genuine or Authorized Signatures
As we will see in more detail later in the chapter, a drawee bank that honors a check bearing a forged signature cannot legally charge the purported drawer's account even if the bank did not know of the forgery when it honored the instrument. Thus, if D's signature is forged to a check drawn on the X Bank, and that bank subsequently honors the instrument by paying a holder and charging D's account, D, upon discovery of the forgery, can generally require the bank to recredit her account in the amount of the instrument.

Duty to Use Reasonable Care as Agent
A bank has the duty to use reasonable care in handling commercial paper when acting as an agent for a depositor. This relationship is usually created when a bank's customer deposits in his or her own account a check drawn by a third party (often on some other bank). In such a case, under Sec. 4-201(1), it is presumed that the bank receiving the check is taking it simply as an agent for its depositor rather than purchasing it outright—and this presumption continues even if the bank permits the depositor to make immediate withdrawals against it. As a result of this relationship, the bank owes the depositor (among other things) the duty to use reasonable care in handling and forwarding the instrument through the bank collection process.

---

[3]Original Article 4 provides for similar damages in case of dishonor "by mistake," but does not address situations where the dishonor was for reasons other than mistake.

The Depositor's Duties

The depositor has the general obligation to keep sufficient funds in his or her checking account to permit the bank to honor all checks drawn on the account. In this respect the drawer of a check has a greater potential liability than the drawer of a regular draft. The drawer of a draft is liable only in a civil action to the holder of a draft where it is not paid by the drawee at maturity. The drawer of a check, however, has not only civil liability but also criminal liability for writing a "bad" check (if it is proved that the drawer issued the check with the intent to defraud). Under the statutes of many states there is a presumption of intent to defraud if the drawer does not "make good" to the holder of the check within a specified number of days after the dishonor occurs. Finally, as we will see in more detail later in the chapter, a depositor owes his or her bank the general duty to report forgeries and alterations within a reasonable length of time after he or she knows, or should know, of them.

SELECTED BANK–DEPOSITOR PROBLEMS

Stop-Payment Orders

As we have indicated, it is possible for the drawer of a check[4] to countermand the order contained in it by issuing the drawee bank a **stop-payment order.** The purpose of this, of course, is to prevent the payee or other holder from immediately receiving payment from the bank. Usually the stop-payment order is given only after the drawer discovers some default on the part of the payee (such as fraud or the delivery of defective goods under a sales contract) or after the check has been lost.[5] The order is binding for only a limited time period. Sec. 4-403(2) provides that "an oral order is binding upon the bank only for fourteen calendar days unless confirmed in writing within that period. A written order is effective for only six months unless renewed in writing."

Effect of Stop-Payment Order on Drawer

Assuming that a stop-payment order is given in time to permit the bank to act on it, the immediate effect

is that the holder of the check fails to obtain payment when he or she presents it to the drawee bank. This does not necessarily mean, however, that the drawer is freed of liability on the instrument.

If the payee, after being refused payment, brings suit against the drawer, he or she may be able to prove that the drawer had no legal grounds for stopping payment; that is, the court may determine that the drawer had no valid defense against the payee. In such a case the payee is entitled to recover the amount of the instrument in full. The drawer also might have liability in a situation where he or she does in fact have a personal defense against the payee but where the holder who was refused payment qualifies as an HDC. In a suit against the drawer, such a holder would also be entitled to full payment of the instrument.

Even in these instances, the stop-payment order is of some benefit to the drawer, for it at least assures him or her of the right to present, in a court proceeding, any reason for believing that the holder is not entitled to payment. And, of course, in many such proceedings, the drawer can prove a valid defense and escape all liability to the holder-plaintiff.

Bank's Liability for Disobeying Stop-Payment Order

If the drawee bank honors a check after a valid stop-payment order has been issued against it, the bank is liable to the drawer for any loss he or she suffers by reason of the wrongful payment. However, if the drawer has to bring legal action against the bank in order to have the account recredited in the amount of the check, he or she has the burden of proving the amount of the loss.

Often it is not difficult for the drawer to prove that he or she suffered a loss. Such is the case where the payee obtained payment and the drawer is able to establish clearly that he or she had either a personal or a real defense that could have been asserted against the payee. In this situation, if the stop-payment order had been obeyed by the bank, it is obvious that the payee would never have been able to enforce the instrument against the drawer. The result is that the bank must recredit the drawer's account in the amount of the check.[6] RUCC 4-403(c) expands a bank's liability in this area to include damages for

---

[4]In addition to the drawer of a check, any person authorized to draw on that account and any person claiming an interest in the account of a deceased person can issue stop-payment orders. On the other hand, payees, indorsees, and holders have no right to issue stop-payment orders.

[5]We are speaking throughout this section of *uncertified* checks, rather than certified checks, cashier's checks, or teller's checks. As noted earlier, once a check has been certified, at the request of either the drawer or a holder, no stop-payment order can thereafter be effective. The same is true with accepted drafts.

[6]Written stop-payment orders sometimes contain clauses to the effect that the drawer agrees not to hold the drawee bank liable if it should dishonor the check "through inadvertence or oversight." Such disclaimers are generally invalid. Sec. 4-103(1) provides in part that "no agreement can disclaim a bank's responsibility for its own lack of good faith or failure to exercise ordinary care" in a particular transaction.

FIGURE 28.1

*Bank's
Liability for
Disobeying
Stop Order*

Example 1

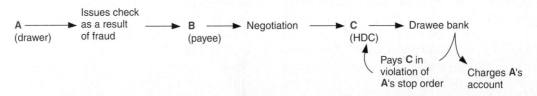

Bank need not recredit **A**'s account. Fraud is a personal defense and not good against HDC; therefore, **A** has suffered no loss.

Example 2

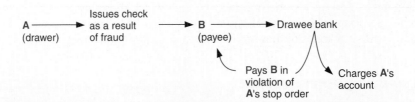

Bank must recredit **A**'s account. **A** has a defense that is good against **B**; therefore **A** has suffered a loss. Bank would be subrogated to **A**'s rights against **B** [UCC Sec. 4-407 (c)].

wrongful dishonor of subsequent items that would not have been dishonored had the stop-payment order been followed.[7]

In some situations, however, the bank may be able to show that the drawer did *not* suffer a loss as a result of its failure to honor the stop-payment order. Such is the case where, in the suit by the drawer against the bank, the drawer did not have a defense of any kind against the payee. In this situation no loss

was incurred by the drawer, because even if the stop-payment order had been obeyed by the bank, the payee would still have been entitled to payment on the check (by legal action against the drawer, if necessary). The payee therefore had the right to the proceeds of the check in any event, and the drawer's suit against the bank will thus fail. The same result will occur (in the suit by the drawer against the bank) if it is determined that although the drawer had a personal defense against the payee, the person who obtained payment was an HDC. These rules are illustrated in Figure 28.1.

The following case applies original Article 3 rules to a stop-payment situation.

[7]A related question is the liability of the bank to the *payee* when the bank wrongfully honors an improper stop-payment order, such as on a certified check. RUCC 3-411(b) allows the payee to collect expenses, loss of interest, and, under some circumstances, consequential damages in order to encourage banks not to honor wrongful stop-payment orders as an accommodation to their customers.

First State Bank of Warren v. Dixon

Court of Appeals of Arkansas, 728 S.W.2d 192 (1987)

 On April 15, 1980, appellee Dixon called appellant First State Bank to stop payment on a check he had written earlier that day. He gave appellant's employee, Hargis, the correct account number, check number, date, and payee of the check but misstated the amount of the check as $1828.73. The correct amount of the check was $1828.15. The bank cashed the check; appellee Dixon sued for recovery of the check amount. A jury held for Dixon and the bank appealed.

Corbin, Chief Judge:

The record reflects appellee testified that when he gave appellant's employee, Frances Hargis, his stop-payment order, he stated it was his only check written to the payee and that it was drawn for $1,800.00 plus dollars. He stated that he was not advised by anyone at the bank that it needed the exact amount of the check in order to stop payment on it. He testified Frances Hargis advised him not to worry about it, that payment on it was stopped. Frances Hargis testified for appellant that appellant's stop-payment requests were computerized, and appellant had to have the exact amount of a check in order to stop payment. She stated that when appellee called her to stop payment on the check, she told him she would need the exact amount. The information she put on the stop-payment order, she testified, was the figure appellee gave her.

[The court then quoted Sec. 4-403 of the original Code.] The Committee Commentary to [this section] is pertinent and provides:

2. The position taken by this section is that stopping payment is a service which depositors expect and are entitled to receive from banks notwithstanding its difficulty, inconvenience and expense. The inevitable occasional losses through failure to stop should be borne by the banks as a cost of the business of banking.

Appellant contends that the necessity of the exact amount of a check for which a stop-payment order is requested is critical because the computerized system it utilized is a key feature of identification in its stop-payment procedure. We believe this argument, if allowed to prevail, would be inconsistent with the intent of the [legislature] . . . [which] clearly contemplated the burden being placed on the bank in the event of loss in such instances as the case at bar.

The issue of whether or not appellee's stop-payment order was received in such manner as to afford appellant a reasonable opportunity to act upon it was submitted to the jury . . . [which] after hearing the conflicting testimony of the parties and the instructions of the court, . . . found for appellee. It is within the province of the jury to believe appellee's theory over appellant's version. . . .

Affirmed. ⚖

Payment on a Postdated Check

Under the original Article 3, a postdated check is deemed a time instrument that is not payable until the indicated date. Thus, a bank that pays such a check acts improperly because the check is not yet "properly payable." This rule imposes a heavy burden on banks, which as a practical matter are unable physically to examine the dates on all checks passing through the system.

RUCC 4-401 puts the burden in jurisdictions adopting the revised Article 4 on the customer who writes a postdated check to give notice to the bank describing the check with "reasonable certainty." Like a stop-payment order, an oral notice is effective for only fourteen days; a written notice is effective for six months. Absent such notice, a bank can without liability pay a postdated check regardless of its date.

Payment on a Forged Indorsement

If a drawee bank honors a depositor's check that bears a *forged indorsement,* the bank must recredit the drawer's account upon his or her discovery and notification of the forgery. To illustrate: D draws a check on the X Bank payable to the order of P. The check is stolen from P by T, and T forges P's indorsement on the back of the instrument. Thereafter, T negotiates the instrument to Y, and Y obtains payment from the X Bank, which has no knowledge of the forgery. The bank then charges D's account and returns the check to D at the end of the month along with D's other cancelled checks. In jurisdictions with the original Article 3, if D soon learns of the forged indorsement and notifies the bank within a reasonable time after this discovery, *the bank must recredit D's account in the amount of the check;* the bank in this case has obviously paid out the money to a person who was not the holder of the instrument.

Usually the bank will recredit the account voluntarily, but if it does not, under Sec. 3-419 [RUCC 3-420] the drawer can bring an action of *conversion* against it to recover the amount of the check. Revised Article 3 makes a minor change here by eliminating the action for conversion; the drawer has an adequate remedy in the form of a suit to have his or her account recredited. RUCC 3-420(a). However, a payee who receives an instrument and whose signature is forged can bring a conversion action against the depositary bank. Such a payee has been injured by the theft.[8]

Bank's Rights against Surrendering Party

Because it is the bank rather than the drawer who initially suffers the loss in the case of a forged instrument, the question arises whether the bank can recover payment from the person who surrendered the check to it for payment (Y in the earlier illustration). The general rule is that the bank can recover, even if the person who surrendered the instrument for payment did not know of the forgery, for breach of the presentment warranty. Sec. 4-207(1)(a) provides that a customer "who obtains payment or acceptance of an item . . . warrants to the payor bank . . . that . . . he has good title to the item." Obviously, a person who surrenders an instrument for payment with a forged indorsement does not have title, so he or she is liable to the drawee bank in the amount of the check on the breach of warranty theory. (After making good to the bank, the person who surrendered the instrument can, of course, proceed against the forger, if that individual can be found.)

The following case is decided under the original Article 3.

---

[8]Payees or indorsees who did not receive delivery of the instrument, on the other hand, may not sue for conversion, RUCC 3-420(a). They have not been injured by the theft and may still recover from the drawer or maker on the underlying obligation.

SEHREMELIS V. FARMERS & MERCHANTS BANK OF LONG BEACH

California Court of Appeals, 7 Cal.Rptr.2d 903 (1992)

Case

George and Athena Sehremelis (plaintiffs) hired Townsend, as construction manager or general contractor, to develop three properties they owned. They obtained three construction loans, one for each project, from Tokai Bank of California (Tokai). The three construction loan agreements provided that the loan funds—together with equity advances by plaintiffs—would be deposited in "loans in process" accounts at Tokai. Under the agreements, plaintiffs were to submit to Tokai applications for payment of construction expenses, documenting the labor and materials in question, upon which Tokai would make payments from plaintiffs' loans in progress accounts, after inspecting the progress of construction. A supplementary document to the third loan, apparently signed by plaintiffs, authorized Townsend or codefendant Friedman to sign payment requests. Plaintiffs claimed that Tokai, without their consent, allowed Townsend and Friedman to insert themselves as authorized signatories on that account.

Between May and September 1988, Townsend and Friedman caused Tokai to issue at least 25 checks in the combined sum of $742,964.27, each payable to Townsend's Western Development Company and another "real or fictitious" subcontractor. The checks were issued on fraudulent invoices. Townsend and Friedman negotiated the checks at Farmers and Merchants Bank (FMB), where Townsend maintained accounts and enjoyed personal relationships with FMB personnel, by forging the copayee-subcontractor's indorsement. Tokai paid the checks and charged them against plaintiffs' loan accounts.

The trial court, inter alia, dismissed plaintiffs' breach of statutory warranty claim against FMB. Plaintiffs appealed. The following excerpt from the appellate court's opinion addresses this issue.

Fukuto, Acting Presiding Judge:

In their primary cause of action against FMB, plaintiffs seek damages for breach of warranties made and extended under Sec. 4-207, [which] provides that a collecting bank—which FMB here was—that obtains payment of a check warrants, "to the payor bank or other payor who in good faith pays or accepts the item that (a) [the collecting bank] has a good title to the item or is authorized to obtain payment or acceptance on behalf of one who has a good title. . . ."

This warranty of "good title" refers to "the validity of the chain of necessary indorsements" (*Sun 'n Sand, Inc.* *(continues)*

SEHREMELIS V. FARMERS & MERCHANTS BANK OF LONG BEACH

(continued from previous page)
v. United California Bank, 21 Cal.3d 671 (1979)), and more specifically to whether "the instrument presented contain[s] all necessary indorsements and are such indorsements genuine or otherwise deemed effective?" *(Id.)* Section 4-207(a) thus imposes a strict liability on the collecting bank, under which the bank, best able to assure the validity of indorsements "since it presumably confronts the indorser," bears ultimate responsibility for forged indorsements.

Plaintiffs' allegation that FMB deposited and collected Tokai checks on which necessary indorsements were "forged, missing or otherwise unauthorized" states facts within the terms of the statutory warranty. The disputed issue is whether plaintiffs, as they allege, "are 'other payors' as defined in Section" 4-207, inasmuch as the warranty in terms extends only to the payor bank (Tokai) "or other payor."

The [California] Supreme Court's decision in *Sun 'n Sand* provides dispositive guidance in resolving this question. In that case an employer sought relief against a collecting-depositary bank at which an unfaithful employee had deposited employer-drawn checks, payable to the bank, which she had altered by raising their amounts. The court first considered "whether Sun 'n Sand, as the drawer of the checks in question, may rely on the warranty provisions" of 4-207. The court answered this question affirmatively, and held "that the drawer of a check whose account is charged is a payor within the meaning of 4-207 and may maintain an action against a collecting bank based on that section's warranties." Analyzing the text and purposes of 4-207, the court observed, "Although the term 'payor' is more commonly used in reference to the drawee than the drawer, it is not defined anywhere in the code and hence should not be regarded as a term of art used in a narrow, technical sense; when a check is negotiated, it is the drawer who ultimately 'pays' when his account is charged in the amount of the check."

The holding and rationale of Sun 'n Sand support treating plaintiffs as payors of the Tokai checks for purposes of 4-207. First, that decision totally refutes FMB's principal argument, that there can be only one payor (in this case Tokai) for purposes of the section. Here, it is alleged plaintiffs were the ones who ultimately paid the checks, when Tokai charged their loans in process accounts after the checks were presented to it.

That plaintiffs were not the drawers of the checks does not require a different conclusion from *Sun 'n Sand* under the facts alleged. Although Tokai was technically both drawer and drawee, in the former capacity it appears to have acted, at least in part, as plaintiffs' agent. Moreover, the checks were paid from accounts containing Tokai's loans to plaintiffs and also plaintiffs' own equity deposits. In sum, plaintiffs' position does not appear so different, legally or practically, from that of the drawer in *Sun 'n Sand* as to require a different application of the statute. [Reversed.] ⚖

Payment on a Forged Drawer's Signature

A somewhat different situation is presented when the drawee bank honors a check on which the *drawer's signature* is a forgery. To illustrate: F, forger, draws a check on the X Bank payable to the order of himself and forging the signature of G, one of the bank's depositors, as the drawer. F indorses the check to H, and H presents the check to the X Bank for payment. The X Bank, not knowing of the forgery, honors the instrument and charges G's account. At the end of the month the forged check is returned to G along with his other cancelled checks.

At this point, assuming that the forgery had occurred without any negligence on the part of G and that G has promptly notified the bank of the forgery, the bank must *recredit G's account in the amount of the check.* This is true because (1) a forged signature is wholly inoperative and (2) a drawee bank is presumed to know the signatures of its depositors. (The latter is based in part on the fact that when a depositor opens a checking account, he or she signs a signature card that is held by the bank and that can be used to determine whether the checks subsequently presented to the bank in the depositor's name are genuine.) The drawee bank is in the best position to prevent the fraud and therefore must typically bear the loss.

Negligent Drawer

The rule that the drawee bank is liable to its depositor in the case of forgery is altered if the bank can show that the drawer was guilty of negligence that substantially contributed to the forgery.

Two primary situations exist in which negligence

on the party of the drawer may be found to exist.

1. If the drawer (usually a corporation in this instance) signs its checks by means of a mechanical check writer, it may be shown that the drawer failed to use reasonable care in preventing unauthorized persons from gaining access to the machine. For example, if the device is left in an area where it is readily accessible to a large number of employees, the drawer may be held negligent. Under the original Article 3, the drawer cannot require the bank to recredit its account; the entire loss falls upon the careless drawer if the bank acted in good faith and consistent with reasonable commercial practices. However, if the bank was careless also, the entire loss shifts back to the bank. In RUCC jurisdictions, a comparative negligence scheme applies and the loss may be split between the careless drawer and a bank that is also careless.

2. It has long been established that a customer owes to the bank the "bank statement duty" of examining his or her cancelled checks within a reasonable time after they have been returned to discover if any of the signatures are forgeries. If the customer fails to do so, under the original Article 4 he or she may be barred from holding the bank liable. This is especially true where a series of forgeries occurs after the initial one that went undetected. We shall examine the rules under original Article 4 and then describe some important changes made by the RUCC.

Sec. 4-406(1) contains the basic provision requiring the drawer to "exercise reasonable care and promptness" in examining checks and statements. Sec. 4-406(2) sets forth specific rules that apply to various "failure to examine" situations. Because these subsections are difficult to understand in the abstract, we will present a hypothetical case along with the appropriate rules:

February 2—D, drawer, receives 30 cancelled checks from the drawee bank that have been charged against her account during the month of January. Her signature has been forged on one check by E, an employee of D's who has access to D's printed check forms.

February 10—E forges another check and cashes it at the drawee bank.

March 2—The February 10 check is returned to D with others honored by the bank during February.

March 3 through March 31—E forges and cashes five more checks; these are also charged to D's account.

April 2—D receives all cancelled checks for the month of March, including the five forged checks.

April 5—D for the first time examines all the checks returned to her in February, March, and April. She discovers the seven forgeries and immediately notifies the bank of them; later she asks the bank to recredit her account for all the forged checks. The bank refuses to do so, contending that it has no liability in view of D's failure to discover the first forgeries promptly.

In this situation, D can probably hold the bank liable for the first two checks but not for the following five. Sec. 4-406(2)(b) of the original Article 4 states in essence that when a forged check is returned to the depositor and that person does not discover it within *14 days from the time of return,* he or she is "precluded from asserting" any *subsequent* forgeries against the bank that are forged "by the same wrongdoer." Thus, since the first forged check was returned to D on February 2, she had until February 16 to give the bank notice in order to protect herself against subsequent forgeries. Since she did not meet this deadline, the liability for the forged checks that were honored after that date is shifted from the bank to D. Because the first two checks had already been paid by the drawee bank before the February 16 deadline, it is probable that the bank could not shift its loss to the drawer, although Sec. 4-406(2)(a) of the original Article 4 keeps this possibility open in exceptional circumstances. However, if the customer shows that the bank was also careless in paying the items, original Article 3 shifts the entire loss back to the bank.

Revised Article 4 makes four important changes in this area. First, because of the increasing use of *check truncation* (the process of check collection that does not physically return checks to the payor from the collecting bank), a bank is required only to provide a statement of account but not to return the actual checks *unless* the customer requests them. Second, the 14-day period for customers to examine their checks is changed to 30 days. Third, as in other areas the comparative negligence concept is adopted. Therefore, a customer who does not act within 30 days is not automatically left to bear all the losses that may be caused, in part, by the bank's honoring of a forged signature. The loss may be apportioned between them. Finally, the bank is held to a duty of "ordinary care," defined in RUCC 3-103(a)(7) as "observance of reasonable commercial standards, prevailing in the area in which the person is located, with respect to the business in which the person is engaged. . . ." With specific regard to this area, the definition goes on to recognize the validity of automated procedures for processing checks, by providing:

In the case of a bank that takes an instrument for processing for collection or payment by automated means, reasonable commercial standards do not require the bank to examine the instrument if the failure to examine does not violate the bank's prescribed procedures and the bank's procedures do not vary unreasonably from general banking usage not disapproved by this Article or Article 4.

If the aforementioned factual scenario occurred in a jurisdiction that had adopted *revised* Articles 3 and 4, how would the result change? The deadline for the customer to inform the bank of the forgeries would change from February 16 (14 days after the checks were returned) to March 4 (30 days after the checks were returned). Therefore, the bank is liable for the January check, the February 10 check, and any checks written on March 3 or 4. Any checks written between March 5 and March 31 would be the responsibility of the drawer. But some responsibility might also be attached to the bank if it is found to have acted without ordinary care [as defined in RUCC 3-103(a)(7)] in honoring the forged signatures.

The following case addresses an important issue under the original Article 3 regarding whether a bank can be found to exercise ordinary care while using mechanical check-processing procedures. The view taken in this case is that adopted by the revised Article 3.

WILDER BINDING CO. v. OAK PARK TRUST & SAVINGS BANK

Illinois Supreme Court, 552 N.E.2d 783 (1990)

Plaintiff Wilder Binding Co. opened a checking account with defendant Oak Park Trust & Savings Bank. The signature card designated plaintiff's president and vice-president as authorized signatories. In December 1983, Daniels was hired as plaintiff's bookkeeper. By June 29, 1984, she had embezzled $25,254.78 from plaintiff by forging plaintiff's vice-president's signature on 42 checks (each drawn for less than $1000) made payable to herself.

The forged checks were cancelled and returned to plaintiff, but under plaintiff's bookkeeping system, Daniels reviewed the monthly statements and cancelled checks. The checks were not discovered until July 15, 1984, when plaintiff's comptroller saw them while examining company records. Plaintiff contacted defendant on July 20 and demanded reimbursement of the embezzled sum. Defendant reimbursed only $5624.78, and plaintiff sued. The trial court entered

summary judgment for plaintiff, so defendant appealed. The intermediate appellate court affirmed, so defendant again appealed.

Moran, Chief Justice:

The [lower courts] reasoned that a bank fails to exercise ordinary care under Sec. 4-406(3) when it uses automated check-sorting equipment and automatically pays checks drawn for less than a designated amount [$1,000 in this case] without manually verifying the signatures of those checks. . . .

Section 4-406 provides banks with an affirmative defense to the general rule that they are liable for paying forged checks. [I]f a bank pays a forged check and later establishes that its customer was negligent in examining bank statements, detecting forgeries and notifying the bank of the forgeries, the customer is precluded from asserting the bank's liability. However, if the customer establishes that his bank failed to exercise ordinary care in paying a forged check, the bank's affirma-

tive defense is inapplicable and, as such, the bank is liable to its customer for the total amount of the forged checks. Therefore, according to plaintiff, even assuming arguendo that it was negligent, defendant is nevertheless liable for the total amount of the forged checks. . . .

[D]efendant argues that its use of automated check-sorting equipment and automatic payment of checks drawn for less than $1,000 without manual verification of the signatures on those checks constitutes the prima facie exercise of ordinary care. Defendant's argument is based on Sec. 4-103(3), which provides in pertinent part:

[I]n the absence of special instructions, *action or nonaction consistent . . . with a general banking usage* not disapproved by this Article, *prima facie constitutes the exercise of ordinary care.*

[D]efendant concludes that its use of automated check-sorting equipment and automatic payment of checks drawn for less than $1,000 without

(continues)

WILDER BINDING CO. V. OAK PARK TRUST & SAVINGS BANK

(continued from previous page) manual verification of the signatures on those checks constitutes the prima facie exercise of ordinary care. Defendant's conclusion is based on [its vice-president's affidavit], which indicates that more than two or three banks in the metropolitan Chicago area also use automated check-sorting equipment and automatically pay checks drawn for less than a designated amount without manually verifying the signatures on those checks.

[W]e believe that a genuine issue of material fact exists regarding whether defendant exercised ordinary care in paying checks. Therefore, it should be left up to the trier of fact to determine whether defendant's use of automated check-sorting equipment and automatic payment of checks drawn for less than $1,000 without manual verification of signatures on those checks is "consistent with general banking usage" and, accordingly, "*prima facie* constitutes the exercise of ordinary care."

[Reversed and remanded for trial on this issue.] ♊

Bank's Rights against Surrendering Party

As seen earlier, if the drawer promptly examines his or her cancelled checks for forgeries and notifies the drawee bank of them, the bank rather than the drawer suffers the loss. The question then arises (as it did in the forged indorsement case) as to whether the bank can recover the amount of the check from the person who surrendered it for payment. The rule here (unlike that involving the forged indorsement) is that if the person did not know of the forged drawer's signature when receiving payment, the bank *cannot* hold him or her liable. Under Sec. 4-207(1)(b), a person who surrenders an instrument for payment guarantees to the drawee bank only that "he has *no knowledge* that the signature of the . . . drawer is unauthorized." (Emphasis added.) Thus, unless the bank can prove such knowledge, its only recourse is an action against the forger (if that person can be identified and located).

Payment on an Altered Check

Although it happens rather rarely, it is possible that the amount of a check will be raised and the instrument will be presented to the drawee bank and paid in its altered form. To illustrate: N draws a check for $75, and P (payee) or a subsequent holder alters the amount—both figures and words—to $175. If the bank charges N's account with the full $175, N can recover from the bank the amount of the alteration— $100. The general rule is that the drawee bank can charge the drawer's account only with the original amount of the check.

The exception to this rule is similar to that involving the forged drawer's signature. If the drawee bank can establish negligence on the part of the drawer that substantially contributed to the alteration, then the drawer is barred under original Article 4 from recovering the difference (but may recover part of his or her loss under a comparative negligence provision of *revised* Article 4). Two common kinds of negligence follow:

1. One kind of negligence occurs where a drawer drafts an instrument so carelessly that it invites alteration. For example, the amount might be written in such a way that there is ample space to insert a digit before (or after) it, or the place where the amount is to appear in words might be left entirely blank.

2: Another kind of negligence occurs where the drawer does not inspect his or her cancelled checks within a reasonable time after they are returned and thus fails to give the bank the notice of alteration that it is entitled to receive. Under Sec. 4-406(1), (2), and (3) of the original Article 4, the drawer in this situation is barred from asserting the fact of alteration against the drawee bank—in the same circumstances and to the same extent as the drawer who negligently failed to detect forged signatures on his or her cancelled checks. Under the revised Article 4, of course, a comparative fault system applies.

Bank's Rights against Surrendering Party

We have seen that where no negligence exists on the part of the drawer, the loss (the amount of the alteration) is borne by the drawee bank. However, as a general rule, the bank is entitled to recover that loss from the person who surrendered the instrument for payment. Sec. 4-207(1)(c) provides that, with limited exceptions, a customer who obtains payment of an item warrants to the payor bank "that the item has not been materially altered." Thus the person who surrenders the check is usually liable on the breach of warranty theory even if he or she did not know of the alteration at the time of obtaining payment.

Breach of Encoding or Retention Warranties

Banks process checks by use of a Magnetic Ink Character Recognition (MICR) system that encodes the checks' face amounts so that they can be "read" by computers. What happens if a $25 check is encoded at a bank for $2500 and the payor bank pays on the basis of the MICR line? Its customer is liable only for the $25 amount for which the check was written. Under *revised* Article 4, an *encoding warranty* has been breached by the encoding bank; the payor bank may recover $2475 from the encoding bank. RUCC 4-209(a).[9]

Revised Article 4 allows banks to use *electronic presentment* (truncation) of instruments. In other words, images of instruments may be presented for payment by electronic means rather than by delivery of the actual instrument. RUCC 4-110. A person who retains an instrument while transmitting its image as presentment for payment under a truncation agreement warrants that the retention and presentment of the item comply with the agreement. RUCC 4-209(b). Persons who take such items in good faith may recover damages from the warranty for losses sustained because of the breach.

INCREASED FEDERAL CONTROL OVER CHECKS AND THE BANK–DEPOSITOR RELATIONSHIP

The Federal Reserve Board (FRB) traditionally has had significant control over the process by which checks move through the banking system. The rules governing the rights and duties among banks and between a depositor and his or her bank, however, have essentially been left to state law as spelled out in the UCC. For a variety of reasons, the degree of federal control is increasing. In this section, we shall describe

certain important federal banking laws that have an impact in this area.

Competitive Equality Banking Act

In the Competitive Equality Banking Act of 1987, Congress gave the FRB broad new authority with respect to the payment system, which includes checks. Specifically, this statute gives the Board responsibility to regulate (1) any aspect of the payment system, including the receipt, payment, collection, or clearing of checks, and (2) any related function of the payment system with respect to checks. This legislation apparently grants the FRB almost unlimited authority to regulate the payment system, notwithstanding existing state laws or private agreements. It remains to be seen how completely this law will *federalize* the use of checks and other payment devices in this country. However, one of the reasons the 1990 revision of Article 4 was less extensive than that of Article 3 is that the FRB has hinted strongly that it may soon exercise its full authority by taking regulatory control of bank collections and deposits.

Expedited Funds Availability Act and Regulation CC

In 1988, Congress passed the Expedited Funds Availability Act (EFAA). In the same year, the FRB adopted **Regulation CC,** which implements the EFAA. (Both the EFAA and Regulation CC will be referred to as Regulation CC.) Regulation CC requires banks to (1) make funds deposited by customers available within specified time periods, (2) provide notices and disclosures describing the bank's funds availability practices, and (3) comply with certain check collection requirements, including the expedited processing and return of checks. The new law applies to U.S. commercial banks, savings banks, thrift institutions, and credit unions (all referred to as "banks"). The EFAA was amended by the Federal Deposit Insurance Corporation Improvement Act of 1991 (the 1991 bank reform act).

Funds Availability

The availability requirements of Regulation CC are based on the type of deposit and the location of the bank in which a check is first deposited (*depositary bank*) relative to the location of the bank by which the check is payable (*paying* or *payor bank*). Under the availability schedules of Regulation CC, banks generally must make deposited funds available on the

---

[9]Original Article 4 does not address this problem.

business day after the day of deposit (referred to as *next-day availability*) for the following deposits: (1) cash; (2) electronic payments, including wire transfers and automated credit transfers such as direct Social Security or payroll deposits; (3) certain government checks and Postal Service money orders; (4) the first $100 of a day's check deposits to an account; (5) certain checks deposited at the bank upon which they were drawn (*on-us items*); and (6) certain cashier's, certified, and teller's checks.[10]

For other types of deposits, primarily deposits of checks beyond $100 in a single day, funds must be made available by the *second* business day after the day of deposit when the paying bank is located in the same check-processing region as the depositary bank (*local checks*). If the paying bank is not located in the same check-processing region as the depositary bank (*nonlocal checks*), funds must be available by the *fifth* business day after the day of deposit.[11] Under Regulation CC, funds must be made available at the *start* of the designated business day. The start of a business day for this purpose is the *later* of (a) 9:00 a.m. local time of the depositary bank, or (b) the time the depositary bank's teller facilities (including automated teller machines, or ATMs) are available for customary account withdrawals.

Exceptions to Availability Requirements

Regulation CC provides several "safeguard exceptions" to the funds availability requirements in order to protect banks from undue risk.

New Accounts. The new accounts exception was created because a substantial portion of bank losses from depositor fraud have traditionally involved new accounts. The exception provides that most of the funds availability requirements do not apply during the first thirty days after a depositor establishes a new account. In the case of ordinary checks deposited to new accounts, the bank is not legally required to make those funds available for withdrawal until thirty days after establishment of the account. Deposits by

cash or electronic transfer to new accounts still must be available on the next day after deposit, however. Also, in the case of government checks and other items that usually must be made available for withdrawal on the next day after deposit, when they are deposited to a new account the bank is required to make them available either five or nine days after deposit, depending on the item.

Large Deposits. Under this exception, only the first $5000 of aggregate deposits to one or more accounts on any banking day must be made available to the depositor pursuant to Regulation CC's funds availability requirements. The bank can extend holds on the amount deposited on any banking day in excess of $5000, but must give the customer written notice. This and several other exceptions permit a bank to delay making funds available to the depositor for a reasonable time beyond the period within which availability is normally required. The law provides that an additional delay of four days beyond the regular hold period is reasonable when an exception applies, and a longer extension may be reasonable in some instances. The large deposits exception is possibly the most important one, because it enables banks to use longer holding periods to avoid really large losses.

Other Exceptions. Several other exceptions also permit banks to hold funds for an additional reasonable time (usually four extra days) beyond the usual availability deadline. There is an exception for a check that has been *returned unpaid and then redeposited* by the customer or the depositary bank.

Another exception applies to an account that has been *repeatedly overdrawn*. An account is defined as repeatedly overdrawn if it had a negative balance (or would have had a negative balance if certain checks or charges had been paid) on at least six banking days during a six-month period. However, if the amount of the negative balance was $5000 or more, negative balances on only two separate days during that period are necessary. If an account meets the definition of repeatedly overdrawn, the exception then applies for six months after the last such overdraft. During operation of the exception, the bank may hold deposited funds for the additional period.

Finally, there are exceptions for certain emergency circumstances and for any check that a bank has reasonable cause to believe is uncollectible.

Originally, the EFAA required banks to give *written notice* each time they invoked any of these

---

[10]Most next-day checks, if not deposited in person at a staffed teller facility, need not be made available for withdrawal until the second business day after deposit.

[11]The EFAA originally allowed banks to treat all deposits made at automated teller machines (ATMs) they did not own or operate (nonproprietary ATMs) as if they were deposits of nonlocal checks, and therefore subject to five-day availability. This treatment was to be permitted until September 1, 1990, at which time banks were to make them available more quickly. However, the 1991 bank reform act made this treatment permanent; therefore, banks may continue to make all check deposits at nonproprietary ATMs available for withdrawal only by the fifth business day after the day of deposit.

exceptions. The 1991 bank reform act changed this rule. In the case of nonconsumer accounts and a few other classes of account, when a bank invokes the large deposit, redeposited check, or repeatedly overdrawn account exceptions, it now need provide only a *one-time* written notice rather than a separate written notice every time it invokes the exception.

The EFAA originally did not allow banks to apply these various exceptions to check deposits for which next-day availability is required (such as certain government checks, cashiers' checks, teller's checks, and on-us checks). The 1991 bank reform act expressly changed this rule so that banks may apply most of the safeguard exceptions to all types of checks.

Disclosure

Regulation CC requires every bank to disclose its funds availability policy to existing and potential customers. These policies must, of course, conform to the minimum availability requirements of Regulation CC. The written disclosure must reflect the policy that the bank actually follows in most cases. Thus, a bank cannot disclose that it will make funds available consistent with the maximum hold periods provided by Regulation CC if it actually makes funds available sooner in most cases. Similarly, a bank that usually makes funds available for withdrawal sooner than required by Regulation CC, but that imposes delays on a case-by-case basis up to the time limit allowed by law, must disclose that it may impose additional delays in some cases and that it will notify the customer if a longer delay will be imposed. A bank also must disclose which exceptions it has determined to apply.

Check Collection and Return Requirements

The EFAA also gives the FRB broad authority to make improvements to the check collection and return system. In another part of Regulation CC, the Board has (1) revised the manner in which banks must handle returned checks and (2) imposed new check indorsement standards.

Under the EFAA, a payor bank that has determined not to pay a check must return the check "expeditiously." The same requirement applies to any other bank handling the checks during the course of return. Although banks can choose either of two different standards for meeting the expeditious return requirement, most have chosen to use the *two-day/four-day standard.* Under this rule a *local check* is returned expeditiously if it is returned so that it will

normally be received by the depositary bank *two business days* after it was presented to the payor bank. For a *nonlocal check,* the requirement is four days.

The new check indorsement standards are aimed at making it easier to identify the name of the depositary bank and promoting the prompt return of checks. The Board's indorsement standards specify the information each indorsement must contain, where on the back of the check it must be placed, and the color of ink that must be used. For example, the space on the back of the check beginning 1.5 inches from the left edge and ending three inches from the right edge is reserved for the indorsement of the depositary bank. Thus, a payee should not put any markings on the back of a check other than in the 1.5-inch space intended for the payee's indorsement. Merchants and other depositors who traditionally have stamped or otherwise marked the back of checks with information intended to identify the drawer or serve other purposes should no longer do so. The regulation permits banks to include provisions in their customer agreements shifting to the customer any loss resulting from customer markings in improper areas on the back of the check. Many banks have done so.

Penalties

A bank that violates the availability, disclosure, or other requirements of Regulation CC may be sued for any actual damages, plus an additional statutory penalty amount. In addition, any person may be able to recover penalties of between $100 and $1000 per violation regardless of whether he or she suffered any actual damages. In class actions, this automatic penalty may be as high as $500,000. A bank's failure to comply with the law's check and return requirements also may result in liability for losses incurred by another bank or its customer. The FRB also may enforce the law's provisions.

ELECTRONIC BANKING

Developments in computer technology have brought about a significant (and growing) phenomenon in recent years—the transfer of funds from one account to another electronically. As **electronic banking** increases in the years ahead, the rules applicable to electronic fund transfers will be of increasing importance insofar as the bank–depositor relationship is concerned. We will here note the most important developments in the area of electronic funds transfers and briefly summarize the basic federal law applicable to these transfers.

Types of Transfers
Automated Teller Machines

It is estimated that roughly half of the adults in the larger cities of the United States today have coded bank cards that enable them to use ATMs. In these cities—and in smaller ones, too—bank customers are becoming increasingly accustomed to using ATMs for such routine tasks as making withdrawals from checking accounts, making deposits in checking accounts, and transferring funds between savings and checking accounts. The use of these "electronic branches" is not only a convenience to bank customers, but also constitutes an effort by banks to rein in their costs by reducing personnel and traditional branches.

Point of Sale Terminals

Point of sale transfers occur when a customer in a retail store pays for a purchase by passing a bank card through a *reading machine* attached to the cash register. When the customer punches his or her personal identification number (PIN) into a keyboard, the cash register electronically charges the customer's account at the bank with the amount of the purchase, and electronically credits the store's account in the same amount. The transaction is verified by a *processing center*, thus enabling the store to give the customer a receipt. Point of sale transactions, if widely accepted, would be a giant step toward our becoming a checkless society. However, customer acceptance of point of sale transactions since their introduction in 1984 has been considerably less than originally expected.

Home Shopping and Banking

Home shopping and banking has sometimes been called the ultimate step in electronic banking. This development, involving a *home information service* consisting of a television set and a personal computer, permits customers to pay bills, make purchases from cooperating retailers, and conduct most of their banking transactions from their own homes. The relevant fund transfers in all of these transactions would, again, be done electronically. For example, in regard to home purchases, the amount of purchase is automatically charged to the buyer's bank account, and automatically credited to the seller's account. Con-

sumer acceptance of home shopping and banking has also been slower than anticipated. Because of such factors as cost and the depersonalizing of retail shopping, their ultimate impact remains to be seen.

Electronic Fund Transfer Act

Electronic banking—even the simple use of ATMs—has carried with it a number of side effects. The stop-payment order, for example, is eliminated (except for preauthorized transfers),[12] and so is **float**—the period between the time a check is issued and the time it is charged to the drawer's account at the drawee bank. More important, because electronic banking radically alters the way in which the bank and its customers have been doing business, it also creates potential new problems for both parties, including the unauthorized transfer of funds, the lack of documents (such as cancelled checks and deposit slips) in the customer's hands in order to prove alleged bank errors, and liabilities of the parties in case the customer's debit card is lost or stolen.

Anticipating these kinds of problems, Congress passed the **Electronic Fund Transfer Act** (EFTA) in 1978. First, the Act defines an *electronic transfer of funds* as "any transfer of funds, other than by check, draft, or similar paper instrument, which is initiated through an electronic terminal, telephone instrument, computer, or magnetic tape so as to order, instruct or authorize a financial institution to debit or credit an account." The Act then requires financial institutions to give disclosure statements to the "consumers" (the institution's customers) that describe the consumers' rights and duties, requires the institutions to keep written documentation of all electronic fund transfers, provides methods of dispute resolution, and spells out the consumers' and institutions' liabilities.

Disclosure Statements

The law requires the institution to provide a **disclosure statement** indicating to the consumer—in "readily understandable language"—such matters as the types of transfers that can be made through its transfer mechanisms; the telephone number and address of the person or office of the institution that

---

[12]A *preauthorized transfer* is a statement in writing by the customer authorizing in advance certain electronic transfers that the institution may automatically make in the future.

should be contacted when the consumer believes an error has been made; the consumer's right to stop payment of a preauthorized fund transfer; and the parties' rights, duties, and liabilities in the case of a breach of duty.

Documentation

The EFTA obligates the institution to keep written documentation of all electronic funds transfers. This documentation must show the amount of the transfer, the number of the account being charged, the date of transfer, the identity of the party receiving the transfer, and the terminal location used in making the transfer. Additionally the institution must send periodic statements to the customer summarizing the transfers made during the prior period.

Dispute Resolution

If a consumer believes that an error has been made by the institution, he or she must give notice of the alleged error to the person or office named in the periodic statement within 60 days of receipt of the institution's statement. The notice can be made either orally or in writing, but it must indicate the account number of the consumer (or information that will enable the institution to determine the number); indicate the consumer's belief that the account contains an error, and the amount of the error; and set forth (where applicable) the "reasons for the consumer's belief" that the error has occurred.

When a notice of error is received by a financial institution, it must "investigate the alleged error, determine whether an error has occurred, and report or mail the results of such investigation and determination within ten business days." If the institution determines that the error did occur, it must correct the error within one business day. If the institution determines that the error did not occur, it must deliver to the consumer an explanation within three business days after the conclusion of its investigation.

As an alternative to these procedures, the institution, upon receipt of a notice of error, may within 10 days *provisionally recredit* the consumer's account with the amount of the alleged error. In such a case, it then has 45 days in which to make its investigation and determination. The Act goes on to provide that the consumer may recover *treble damages* from the institution if it "knowingly and willfully" concluded that the consumer's account was not in error

when such a conclusion could not reasonably have been made, or, in regard to the alternative procedure, if the institution did not recredit the consumer's account within the 10-day period and if the institution (1) did not make a good faith investigation of the alleged error, or (2) did not have a reasonable basis for believing that the account was not in error.

Consumer Liability

The Act requires financial institutions to furnish to consumers wishing to make electronic transfers a *means of access*—usually a personal bank card—by which the consumer can request fund transfers. There are several rules as to the consumer's liability for unauthorized transfers made as a result of loss or theft of the card. The basic rule is that the consumer has the duty to notify the institution when he or she knows of the loss or theft of the card, in which case the consumer's liability is *limited to $50.*

If the consumer fails to give notice to the institution within two business days after learning of the loss or theft, the ceiling on the consumer's liability is raised to $500. And the consumer is liable for the *total amount* of the unauthorized transfers if he or she fails to give notice of such transfers within sixty days of receiving the institution's first periodic statement that reflects the transfers. In extenuating circumstances—for example, where the consumer is away on "extended travel" or is hospitalized—the sixty-day provision is replaced by the duty to give notice "within a reasonable time, under the circumstances."

The Institution's Liability

The Act has a number of provisions imposing *civil liability* on financial institutions for damages the consumer suffers as a result of the institutions' breaches of duty, such as failure to make authorized transfers and failure to make a transfer on the erroneous ground that there were insufficient funds in the consumer's account to permit the transfer.

Generally, an institution's liability for breach of a duty is limited to actual damages incurred by the consumer; however, greater damages are sometimes allowed where bad faith on the part of the institution is shown. (The Act also specifies situations in which class actions can be brought.)

Criminal liability is imposed by the Act on any person (including the consumer as well as the institution) who "knowingly and willfully" gives false information

LEGAL FOCUS

LEGAL FOCUS

Ethics

New technology has many obvious advantages, but it can also create moral problems and ethical dilemmas. Consider poor Mr. Porter. An advertisement stated: "To withdraw funds from your Citibank account at any time all you need do is place your card in our ATM, enter your secret code, and then push a button." Porter did so, but no money was dispensed by the machine. Yet, his checking account was debited $100, as if the money had been dispensed.

Or, perhaps, it's a case of poor Citibank. Maybe Porter really *did* receive and spend the $100, and is just claiming that he didn't. What evidence does he have? What will be the bank's exposure if any customers, with no documentary evidence whatsoever to prove that they did not receive the money, can sue to recover funds that they supposedly did not receive?

The question becomes, in the words of one court, "who (or what) to believe, the person or the machine?" Consider the reasoning of the courts in the following cases similar to that involving Porter. Judd's account was charged with ATM withdrawals that she claimed she did not make and could not have made because she was at work at the time of the withdrawals. The court said that it was not prepared to go so far as to rule that where a credible witness is faced with the adverse "testimony" of a machine, he is as a matter of law faced also with an unmeetable burden of proof. It is too commonplace in our society that when faced with the choice of man or machine we readily accept the "word" of the machine every time. This, despite the tales of computer malfunctions that we hear daily.

On the other hand, in a case where Roscoe claimed to have made a deposit on his employer's behalf in a nighttime depository and to have been fired when the bank denied that it ever received the deposit, the court said:

> Before there can be any cause of action, it must first be alleged and shown to be an established and uncontroverted fact that the bank, after first disclaiming receipt of the deposit and failing to credit it, did in fact receive it. An unexplained loss of a deposit claimed to have been physically placed in a depository is not sufficient, standing alone, to give rise to a cause of action against the bank. . . . To hold otherwise would be sheer folly and permit unrestrained and unlimited suits against banks simply on the bare assertion of an individual that he made a deposit.

Which approach do you prefer? Compare *Porter v. Citibank*, 472 N.Y.S. 2d 582 (N.Y.Civ.Ct. 1984); *Judd v. Citibank*, 435 N.Y.S.2d 210 (N.Y.Civ. Ct. 1980); *Roscoe v. Central Nat'l Bank*, 409 N.Y.S.2d 189 (N.Y.Sup.Ct. 1978).

---

or fails to provide information required by the Act. The liability for these violations is a fine of up to $5000 or imprisonment for not more than one year, or both. Stiffer criminal penalties are provided for other specified wrongs affecting interstate commerce, such as knowingly using forged, fictitious, or lost **debit instruments** (usually personal bank cards); knowingly transporting such instruments in interstate commerce; and knowingly furnishing money, property, or services to another through the use of such instruments.

The following EFTA case involves an interesting scam.

OGNIBENE V. CITIBANK, N.A.

Civil Court of the City of New York, 446 N.Y.S.2d 845 (1981)

Plaintiff Ognibene lost $400 in a scam involving an ATM. Defendant Citibank had for some time been aware of the scam, which worked like this: A customer entered the ATM area. A scam artist was using the customer service telephone located between the two ATM machines and appeared to be telling customer service that one of the machines was malfunctioning. The conversation was only simulated. The scam artist watched the customer press the personal identification code into one of the two machines. Having learned the code, the perpetrator then told the customer that customer service had advised him to ask the customer to insert the Citicard into the allegedly malfunctioning machine to check whether it would work with a card other than the perpetrator's.

(continues)

OGNIBENE V. CITIBANK, N.A.

(continued from previous page)
When a Good Samaritan customer acceded to the request, the other machine was activated. The scam artist then pressed a code into the machine, which the customer did not realize was the customer's own code that had just been observed. After continuing the simulated conversation on the telephone, the perpetrator advised the customer that customer service had asked if the customer would try the Citicard in the allegedly malfunctioning machine once more. A second insertion of the card permitted cash to be released by the machine, and if the customer did as requested, the thief had effectuated a cash withdrawal from the unwary customer's account.

Plaintiff sued Citibank. The following is excerpted from the trial court's opinion.

Thorpe, Judge:

The basic rights, liabilities and responsibilities of the banks which offer electronic money transfer services and the consumers who use them have been established by the Electronic Funds Transfer Act.

The EFT Act places various limits on a consumer's liability for electronic fund transfers from his account if they are "unauthorized." Insofar as is relevant here, a transfer is "unauthorized"

if 1) it is initiated by a person other than the consumer and without actual authority to initiate such transfer, 2) the consumer receives no benefit from it, and 3) the consumer did not furnish such person "with the card, code or other means of access" to his account.

In an action involving a consumer's liability for an electronic fund transfer, such as the one at bar, the burden of going forward to show an "unauthorized" transfer from his account is on the consumer. The EFT Act places upon the bank, however, the burden of proof of any consumer liability for the transfer. To establish full liability on the part of the consumer, the bank must prove that the transfer was authorized. To be entitled to even the limited liability imposed by the statute on the consumer, the bank must prove that certain conditions of consumer liability have been met and that certain [mandated] disclosures have been made.

Plaintiff herein met his burden of going forward. He did not initiate the withdrawals in question, did not authorize the person in the ATM area to make them, and did not benefit from them.

However, defendant's position is, in essence, that although plaintiff was duped, the bank's burden of proof on the issue of authorization has been met by plaintiff's testimony that he permitted his card to be used in the adjoining machine by the other person. The

court does not agree.

The EFT Act requires that the consumer have furnished to a person initiating the transfer the "card, code, or other means of access" to his account to be ineligible for the limitations on liability afforded by the Act when transfers are "unauthorized." The evidence establishes that in order to obtain access to an account via an automated teller machine, both the card and the personal identification code must be used. Thus, by merely giving his card to the person initiating the transfer, a consumer does not furnish the "means of access" to his account. To do so, he would have to furnish the personal identification code as well.

The court finds that plaintiff did not furnish his personal identification code to the person initiating the $400.00 transfer within the meaning of the EFT Act. There is no evidence that he deliberately or even negligently did so. On the contrary, the unauthorized person was able to obtain the code because of defendant's own negligence. Since the bank had knowledge of the scam and its operational details (including the central role of the customer service telephone), it was negligent in failing to provide plaintiff-customer with information sufficient to alert him to the danger when he found himself in the position of a potential victim.

[J]udgment shall be for plaintiff in the sum of $400.00. ⚖

New Article 4A and Commercial Electronic Fund Transfers

The EFTA is a federal *consumer protection law.* As such it does not apply to the more than one trillion dollars transferred electronically from bank to bank ("wholesale") on a daily basis. Articles 3 and 4 of the UCC (original and revised) also do not apply to these huge "commercial" electronic funds transfers. Thus, until recently there had been few settled legal guidelines for these largest of transfers, aside from basic

contract law principles. To fill this void, a new UCC Article 4A was recently enacted. By summer of 1993, it had been adopted in 44 states.

Article 4A defines a *funds transfer* as a "payment order" or series of payment orders by which an "originator" accomplishes payment to the "beneficiary" of the originator's order. Such a transfer can be a very simple transaction in which a corporate originator orders its bank to debit one of its accounts and credit an account of another party at the same bank. Here, the payment order and funds transfer are one and the same. If the originator orders its bank to pay a beneficiary that is a customer of another bank, this payment order will require the originator's bank then to issue at least one other payment order. The additional payment order from the originator's bank may be to the beneficiary's bank directly, probably through a funds transfer system. In other situations, this additional order from the originator's bank may be made to an intermediary bank that will then issue yet another order to the beneficiary's bank.

Essentially, Article 4A creates a set of rules to govern the resolution of legal issues that may arise from commercial electronic funds transfers. Almost all of these rules, like most other UCC principles, can be varied by the agreement of the parties and the operating rules of a funds transfer system. Payment orders, unlike checks, do not establish independent rights and liabilities for the payment of money. Instead, the rights and liabilities of the parties to a payment order arise out of the contract formed when the receiving bank accepts the payment order, perhaps subject to the terms of a prior agreement or the rules of a funds transfer system.

SUMMARY

Checks are governed in some instances by special rules of Article 3 of the UCC, and additionally, the bank–depositor relationship is governed by special rules in both Articles 3 and 4. A check is a draft drawn on a bank payable on demand. The issuance of a check does not, in and of itself, result in an assignment of funds to the payee or to a subsequent holder; this occurs only after the instrument is honored by the drawee bank. A bank has no duty to certify a check, either at the request of the drawer or of a holder. If it does certify, however, the bank becomes primarily liable on the instrument (much like the acceptor of a draft). A certification at the request of a holder of the instrument discharges the drawer from liability, but a certification at the request of the drawer does not have this effect.

There are limited situations where special bank–depositor rules apply, for example, the issuance of stop-payment orders. A drawer may stop payment on a check by giving the drawee bank such an order. An oral order is effective for fourteen days, whereas a written one is effective for six months. If a bank disobeys a stop-payment order by paying the instru-

ment, it is liable to the drawer for any loss resulting from its failure to observe the order. A second example involves payment by a drawee bank of a check drawn by a depositor that—unknown to the bank at the time of payment—bore the forged indorsement of a party whose indorsement was necessary for the negotiation of the instrument. In such a case the bank, having made payment to a person who did not have title, must credit the drawer's account with the amount of the check. The bank—assuming it was not guilty of negligence in failing to know of the forged indorsement—may then recover the amount of the check from the surrendering party (the party to whom it made payment).

A different situation exists when a drawee bank honors an instrument bearing the forged signature of the drawer (its depositor). The bank must again credit the drawer's account, assuming the drawer was negligent in the transaction, but in this situation the bank cannot recover from the surrendering party (unless he or she knew of the forgery when receiving payment).

A drawer may be negligent if a cancelled check bearing the drawer's forged signature is returned by the bank (together with all other cancelled checks for that period), and he or she does not notify the drawee bank of the forgery within 14 days (under the original UCC) or 30 days (under the RUCC) of the time the checks were returned. Under the original Article 4, the drawer cannot require the drawee bank to credit his or her account with the amount of any additional checks (forged by the same person) that the bank honors between the expiration of the 14-day period and the time that the drawer does ultimately give the bank notice of the first forgery. Under revised Article 4, comparative negligence may be used to apportion liability between the careless drawer and a careless bank for all losses occurring after the 30-day period.

Although the rules governing the rights and duties among banks and between a bank and its depositors have historically been found almost exclusively in *state law*, we are beginning to see a great increase in *federal* control over these rules.

Transfers of funds via the use of electronic devices (that is, *electronic banking*) are governed by the federal Electronic Fund Transfer Act, rather than Articles 3 and 4 of the UCC. New Article 4A of the UCC governs commercial electronic funds transfers between banks.

KEY TERMS

Drawee bank
Certified check
Stale check
Stop-payment order
Regulation CC
Electronic banking
Point of sale transfers
Float
Electronic Fund Transfer Act
Disclosure statement
Debit instruments

QUESTIONS AND PROBLEMS

1. Parmet opened an account at Guaranty Federal and later that day used his new account to buy a teller's check by Guaranty Federal for $900,000, payable to "Binion & Co." Guaranty Federal drew the check on its account at Citibank of New York. On the same day, Parmet cashed the check for gambling chips at Binion's Horseshoe Casino in Las Vegas. The next morning, Parmet was at Guaranty Federal when it opened, seeking to stop payment on the teller's check. Guaranty Federal immediately called Citibank to request that payment be stopped. Thus, when Binion's called Citibank, it was told that payment had been stopped. Undaunted, the casino attempted to negotiate the check to its operating company. The Horseshoe Operating Company then sued Guaranty Federal on the check. Will it recover? Discuss. (*Guaranty Federal v. Horseshoe Operating Co.*, 793 S.W.2d 652, Tex. 1990.)

2. Plaintiff stopped payment on a check it drew on defendant bank. The stop-payment order was not renewed, and one year later the check was presented to defendant bank through the bank collection process. The bank honored it and charged plaintiff's account. Plaintiff then sued the bank to recover the amount of the check, claiming wrongful payment by the bank. Should plaintiff prevail? Discuss. (*Granite Equipment Leasing v. Hempstead Bank*, 326 N.Y.S.2d 881, N.Y.Sup.Ct. 1971.)

3. Plaintiff owed money to Westinghouse and drew three checks in a five-month period on its account at First National. Before the checks were delivered, however, an employee of plaintiff forged the indorsement of Westinghouse and presented the

checks to defendant First National Bank & Trust; defendant cashed the checks and gave the proceeds to the employee who used the money for his own purposes. Defendant forwarded the checks to First National and received full compensation charged by First National to plaintiff's account. Plaintiff sued defendant for conversion of the checks. Is conversion a viable theory? Discuss. (*Stone & Webster Eng. Corp. v. First National Bank & Trust Co.*, Mass. 1962.)

4. Accountant Caliendo prepared tax returns for various clients and received from them checks payable to various State of New York taxing entities. Caliendo forged indorsements on these checks, deposited them in his own account with defendant Barclays Bank, and subsequently withdrew the proceeds. Caliendo died shortly after his scheme was uncovered. The state, which never received the checks, sued defendant for conversion. Will the state prevail? Discuss. (*State v. Barclays Bank of New York*, 563 N.E.2d 11, N.Y.Ct.App. 1990.)

5. In early 1985, an employee of defendant Zapata Corporation stole some blank checks from Zapata and wrote a large number of forged checks on Zapata's accounts at plaintiff Rhode Island Hospital Trust National Bank. Plaintiff cashed these checks from March through July 1985. Bank statements reflecting the forged checks were sent to Zapata starting in early April 1985. Zapata did not examine the statements until July; it then found the forgeries and immediately notified plaintiff. Plaintiff then stopped clearing the checks, which already exceeded a total of $100,000. Plaintiff reimbursed Zapata for all checks it cleared before and for 14 days after Zapata received the first statement reflecting forgeries. In ensuing litigation, the question became whether Zapata could recover for the post–April 24 checks on the theory that, even if it was negligent, so was the bank. The bank examined all signatures of checks for more than $1000, examined signatures of checks over $100 if it had reason to suspect a problem, and examined signatures on a randomly chosen 1 percent of all checks between $100 and $1000. Discuss. (*Rhode Island Hospital Trust National Bank v. Zapata Corp.*, 848 F.2d 291, 1st Cir. 1988.)

6. Defendant bank issued a $60,000 cashier's check to Dutt, who attended a real estate auction that day and was the highest bidder on a building. Dutt signed a Real Estate Sale Contract and

indorsed the cashier's check to plaintiff Real Estate Auction (REA). Dutt claims that he then handed the check to an REA agent to allow the agent to photocopy the check and return it to him. Dutt claims that he was not prepared to fully execute the contract and put down earnest money until his attorney examined the contract, but that REA refused to return the check. REA deposited the check on May 31 in a newly opened account at defendant bank. On June 1, the Bank dishonored the cashier's check pursuant to a stop order by Dutt, who claimed that REA obtained the check under false pretenses. After selling the property to another buyer for a higher price, REA sued the bank under the Expedited Funds Availability Act for executing the stop-payment order. Discuss the merits of this suit. (*Real Estate Auctions, Inc. v. National Republic Bank of Chicago,* 1991 U.S. Dist. LEXIS 17625, N.D.Ill. 1991.)

7. Plaintiff Shawmut Bank mistakenly transferred $10,000 from the account of American Optical Corp. to First American Bank & Trust, purportedly for the benefit of Degan, by means of an Electronic Funds Transfer System known as *Fedwire.* The money was credited to an account held jointly by Degan and Merle. Shawmut discovered its error 106 days later, credited the account of its customer American Optical, and asked First American to "reverse" the transfer. When Merle refused to authorize the reversal, First American refused to reverse. Shawmut sued Merle, who was held liable, but the judgment went unsatisfied. So, Shawmut sued First American. Will it prevail on its EFTA claim? Discuss. (*Shawmut Worcester County Bank v. First American Bank,* 731 F.Supp. 57, D.Mass. 1990.)

Chapter 29

Secured Transactions

A VERY LARGE PART of the business that is carried on in this country is done "on credit." While there are many types of transactions in which credit is extended by one person or firm to another, probably the two most common of these arise from sales of goods (in which the buyer promises to pay the purchase price in installments) and loans of money. In these transactions a *debtor-creditor* relationship results, with the buyer (or borrower) being the debtor, and the seller (or lender) being the creditor.

Sometimes a seller or lender is willing to extend credit without receiving any security from the debtor. Such transactions frequently occur at the retail sale level where, for example, a department store will sell a modestly priced article to a buyer who is permitted to charge it to his or her credit card account without executing a security agreement. Unsecured credit may also be extended by wholesalers and manufacturers, and by lenders, especially to debtors who have established a good credit record with the creditor as a result of past dealings.

In all unsecured credit cases, once the creditor delivers the goods or makes the loan to the debtor he or she has lost all rights to the goods or money. This means that if the debtor subsequently defaults, the creditor cannot immediately claim or attach any specific goods or money in the debtor's possession. Instead, he or she is initially limited to bringing an action to recover the amount of the indebtedness. After getting a judgment in such a suit the creditor has the right to have any unencumbered property then in the debtor's possession sold under court order to satisfy the debt.[1] However, it may be that these limited assets will have to be shared with other judgment creditors—or worse still, it may be that the debtor may not own any property at all by the time the judgment is obtained, or that the debtor has even become bankrupt by this time. *Thus an unsecured creditor runs a distinct risk that he or she may recover little or nothing from the debtor.*[2]

[1]Unencumbered property is that which the debtor owns outright—that is, free of any security interest, mortgage, or other lien of a third party.
[2]By contrast, a secured creditor's interest in specific collateral, if "perfected," *is* protected against the claims of judgment creditors. And, if the debtor becomes bankrupt, the security interest survives bankruptcy proceedings—i.e., the collateral cannot be sold by the trustee in bankruptcy for the benefit of unsecured creditors.

SECURED CREDIT TRANSACTIONS

To minimize the above risks, many sellers and lenders routinely require the debtor to enter into a *security agreement* at the time credit is extended—an agreement by which the debtor conveys to the creditor a legally recognized interest in specific personal property owned by the debtor. Once such an interest is created, the creditor has the right to have the specific property sold if the debtor defaults on the payments, and to receive as much of the proceeds of the sale as is necessary to pay off the debt. (If the proceeds are not sufficient to pay the total indebtedness, the creditor then has an *unsecured* claim as to the unpaid balance.)

The dual purpose of a **secured transaction,** then, is to give to the creditor (1) a *specific interest* in the debtor's property that is covered by the security agreement, and (2) a *priority claim* in that property against other creditors who may seek to have the property sold in satisfaction of their claims. This priority, usually obtained by giving notice to all other creditors and third parties who may subsequently become creditors, is called "perfection." (The subject of perfection will be discussed in more detail later in the chapter.)

To illustrate a secured transaction situation: R, an office supply retailer, needs to restock her inventory of electronic word processors, but does not want to pay cash for them. R finds a wholesaler, W, who is able to make immediate delivery of the kind of processor that R wants, and W is willing to sell the goods on credit. R and W therefore sign a security agreement under the terms of which W agrees to sell the word processors to R, with R paying 10 percent down and promising to pay the balance in monthly installments. The agreement describes the goods being sold, and further provides that W is retaining a security interest in them until the total price is paid. At this point a debtor-creditor relationship has been created. W, the secured party, has the inventory collateral of R as security for the debt. W now files a financing statement to give notice to all others of his security interest in the collateral. If R subsequently defaults, W can repossess the remaining inventory to satisfy the debt. Furthermore, assuming that W's filing has given him priority, the collateral will go first to pay off R's debt with W, with only the remaining collateral being available to other creditors.

ARTICLE 9 TERMINOLOGY

Article 9 of the UCC substantially governs secured transactions law.[3] Following are the terms needed for an understanding of the basic concepts of secured transactions law. (These definitions come from Sec. 9-105, except where noted otherwise.)

- *Secured party.* A **secured party** is a lender, seller, or other person in whose favor a security interest exists—including a person to whom accounts or chattel paper have been sold.[4]
- *Debtor.* A **debtor** is a person who owes payment or other performance of the obligation that is secured, regardless of whether he or she owns or has rights in the collateral, and includes the seller of accounts or chattel paper.
- *Security interest.* Under Sec. 1-201(37), a **security interest** is an interest in personal property or fixtures that secures payment or performance of an obligation—that is, the interest granted the secured party.

A recurrent problem has been distinguishing a security interest dressed up as a lease from a true lease. Promulgation of new UCC Article 2A for leasing transactions, which entails a significant amendment to the UCC's definition of "security interest," is aimed at clarifying this distinction. This is important, because Article 2A follows existing law in not requiring lessors to file a financing statement in connection with a true lease in order to protect their interests in leased property. Former case law concentrated

on the intent of the parties in drawing a line between a lease (which does not require a filing to be protected) and a security interest (which usually does require filing for protection). The new amendment to Sec. 1-201(37) provides that for a transaction to be a security interest (and therefore governed by Article 9 rather than a lease governed by Article 2A), the obligation to pay rents must extend for the entire term of the lease and must not be subject to termination by the lessee. If this is the case, then a transaction framed as a lease will be treated as a security interest if it appears that the lessee will enjoy possession and use of the goods *for their entire economic life.* Various criteria are established to assist in this determination. By August 1993, 40 states had adopted Article 2A.

- *Security agreement.* A **security agreement** is a security arrangement between the debtor and the secured party—the agreement that creates the security interest.
- *Collateral.* **Collateral** is the property subject to a security interest, and includes accounts and chattel paper that have been sold.
- *Perfection.* **Perfection** is the taking, by a secured creditor, of those steps which are required under the UCC in order for his or her security interest to be valid as against other creditors.
- *Financing statement.* Under Secs. 9-401 and 9-402, the **financing statement** is the instrument filed to give public notice of the security interest in the collateral.

Following is an illustration of the basic concepts using this terminology. The *secured party* and *debtor* usually enter into a *security agreement* by which the secured party receives a *security interest* in one or more pieces of the debtor's collateral, to be available in the event of the debtor's default. To gain priority over others who may also want a security interest in this same collateral, the secured party files a *financing statement* as notice of his or her claim. The secured interest is now *perfected.* (While the usual security device is expressly labelled "security agreement" to conform to this terminology, older forms creating security interests—the chattel mortgage or conditional sale—are still used occasionally. In such cases these devices, too, are treated today as ordinary security agreements.)

---

[3]Although secured transactions law stems primarily from state laws adopting the UCC, federal law has always exerted an influence through, for example, the Bankruptcy Code. In recent years, the federal government has increasingly superimposed its will in this area. An example, to be discussed later, is the Food Security Act of 1985, which effectively amended Sec. 9-307(1)'s priorities for purchasers of farm products. Another example is *Citicorp Indus. Credit, Inc. v. Brock,* 483 U.S. 27 (1987), in which the Supreme Court held that secured lenders at a foreclosure sale of inventory collateral get in line behind employees who claim that the debtor owed them money because of violations of the minimum wage or overtime provisions of the Fair Labor Standards Act.

[4]An "account" is "any right to payment for goods sold or leased or for services rendered which is not evidenced by an instrument or chattel paper . . ." Sec. 9-106.

"Chattel paper" is a writing which evidences both a monetary obligation and a security interest in specific goods. Sec. 9-105(1)(b).

SCOPE OF ARTICLE 9

Article 9 covers agreements that create security interests in *personal* property. Therefore, security agreements applicable to interests in *real* property, such as those created by the mortgage of a farm or a home, are not governed by this article.[5]

Many times personal property that is subject to a security interest has a tangible existence as **goods.** Typical examples of goods are automobiles, cattle, grain, and television sets. In addition to goods, however, security interests are also commonly created in certain kinds of personal property that have no physical substance. These kinds of property, consisting of rights and interests, are properly termed "intangibles." A third category of personal property is called "indispensable paper." Because this category possesses some characteristics similar to those of goods, it is sometimes called "quasi-intangible." These three categories of property—goods, indispensable paper, and intangibles—may be further classified as indicated below.

Tangible Collateral ("Goods")

Under Sec. 9-109, there are four kinds of goods, classified according to the buyer's primary intent at time of purchase:

- *Consumer goods.* Goods are consumer goods if they are used or bought for use primarily for personal, family, or household purposes.
- *Equipment.* Goods are equipment if they are used or bought for use primarily in business (including farming or a profession).
- *Farm products.* Goods are farm products if they are crops or livestock or supplies used or produced in farming operations, or products of crops or livestock in their unmanufactured state (such as eggs, milk, or sap used in the production of maple syrup), and if they are in the possession of a debtor engaged in raising, fattening, grazing, or other farm operations.
- *Inventory.* Goods are inventory if they are held by the debtor for the purpose of sale or lease to others in the ordinary course of the debtor's business. Also included in the inventory category are goods to be furnished by the debtor to others under service contracts, raw materials, work in process in the hands of a manufacturer, and materials used or consumed in a business. The last category is broad enough to include such items as duplication paper and related supplies of a bank.

A UCC drafters' comment to Sec. 9-109 states that the above classes of goods are "mutually exclusive"; a particular item of property cannot fall into two categories at the same time. However, a particular item of property may fall into different classes at different times. For example, a sofa on the floor of a furniture store is inventory, but is a consumer good when subsequently delivered to a buyer's home or equipment if sold for use in a dentist's office.

In addition to the four classifications of goods noted above, Article 9 also covers security interests in another kind of tangible property, *fixtures.* As we will see in Chapter 43, **fixtures** begin life as items of personal property but are subsequently attached to real estate—land and buildings—in such a manner that they become a part of that real estate.[6] To illustrate: M, a manufacturer, purchases an industrial electric motor on credit from the inventory of W, a wholesaler. The motor is delivered to M's factory, where it is permanently bolted to a concrete bed in the building. (Under special rules discussed later, a security interest in the motor given by M to W at the time of the purchase may continue to exist even though the motor has been converted from personal to real property.)

Indispensable Paper Collateral

Indispensable paper collateral that may be the subject of a security interest can best be described as rights that are created by (in addition to being evidenced by) pieces of paper—written documents such as promissory notes or bills of lading. Under Sec. 9-102, the types of personal property falling within this category include:

- *Documents of Title.* Under UCC Sec. 1-201(15) **documents of title** include bills of lading, dock warrants, dock receipts, warehouse receipts, or any other orders for delivery of goods, and any other documents which in the regular course of

---

[5]Some security interests in personal property fall outside the scope of Article 9. For example, under special statutes an auto mechanic usually obtains a lien on a car while it is in his or her possession, and under Article 2 of the UCC an unpaid seller of goods may have an interest in the goods while they are en route to the buyer. Such security interests are governed by the special statutes that create them. Additionally, security interests in aircraft and maritime vessels are generally governed by specific federal statutes.

[6]This is not true, however, in the case of ordinary building supplies, such as lumber that is used in building a house. In this case the lumber is not a fixture, and any security interest is lost when it becomes a part of the building.

business or financing are treated as adequate evidence that the person in possession is entitled to receive, hold, and dispose of them and the goods they cover. (See Chapter 20 for details.)

- *Instruments.* Under UCC Sec. 9-105(1)(i), the term **instrument** essentially refers to two interests: *negotiable instruments* and *securities.* A negotiable instrument is a promissory note, check, or any other written promise or order to pay money whose terms meet the requirements of negotiability set forth in Sec. 3-104 of the UCC. (See Chapter 25 for details.) Security refers to corporate stocks and bonds.
- *Chattel Paper.* An example of **chattel paper** is a promissory note which not only contains the usual promise to pay a sum of money at a stated future time, but, additionally, contains language that conveys to the holder of the note a security interest. Assume that F, a farmer, purchases a tractor from an implement dealer under a conditional sales contract. The contract (note) that F signs will contain a promise to pay the agreed purchase price in specified monthly installments. This is a negotiable instrument only. If the contract goes on to provide that the dealer-seller shall retain a security interest in the tractor until the note is paid in full, it is chattel paper. The chattel paper may serve as collateral

for a later loan, if the implement dealer (debtor) assigns it to a bank (secured party).

Intangible Collateral

Those types of personal property interests that do not possess the characteristics of goods or indispensable paper collateral are **intangible collateral.** Such interests are either *accounts* or *general intangibles.*

Accounts

Under Sec. 9-106, an **account** is any right to payment for goods sold or leased, or for services rendered, which is not evidenced by an instrument or chattel paper. Generally, the term refers to *accounts receivable.*

General Intangibles

General intangibles is a catch-all category, which is defined under Sec. 9-106 as consisting of any personal property ("including things in action"—rights to collect money or property) *other than* goods, accounts, chattel paper, documents, instruments, and money. Typical examples are literary rights, trademarks, patents, copyrights, and the like.

The case below presents one situation in which a determination of the type of collateral is necessary in order to decide the validity of a secured creditor's claim to the proceeds of that collateral.

In re K. L. Smith Enterprises, Ltd.

U.S. Bankruptcy Court, D. Colorado, 2 B.R. 280 (1980)

K. L. Smith Enterprises operated a large-scale egg production business in Colorado. It housed thousands of laying hens in unique, semi-automated "egg production units" that permitted the efficient collection, sizing, and packaging of large quantities of eggs daily.

In November 1976 the United Bank of Denver loaned $2,400,000 to Smith Enterprises. In connection with the loan, Smith Enterprises executed two security agreements granting the bank security interests in all of its inventory, accounts, contract rights, equipment, and machinery,

and in "the proceeds therefrom"— that is, in the money received by Smith Enterprises from the sale of any of the designated assets.[a]

In November 1979 Smith Enterprises sold $40,000 worth of eggs to Safeway Stores, Inc., its principal customer for many years. That same month it also sold a quantity of eggs to Gonzales, one of its occasional customers, and in December it sold 120,000 hens to the Campbell Soup Company. The sale to Safeway was "on account"—an account receivable was created on Smith Enter-

[a]The subject of "proceeds" will be discussed further under the topic of perfection.

prises' books—and the sale of eggs to Gonzales was a cash transaction. It is not clear whether the sale of the hens to Campbell was on account or for cash.

Shortly thereafter Smith Enterprises went into bankruptcy. In those proceedings the United Bank of Denver claimed that it had a valid security interest in the eggs and chickens, and thus in the proceeds thereof. In response, Smith Enterprises (plaintiff in this action) filed a complaint disputing the bank's claim to the eggs, chickens, and the "cash collateral" in Smith Enterprises' possession at the time of bankruptcy. (In the decision below, Smith

(continues)

IN RE K.L. SMITH ENTERPRISES, LTD.

(continued from previous page)
Enterprises is referred to as "the debtor.")

Keller, Bankruptcy Judge:

This matter came before the court upon the complaint of the Debtor to determine the nature, extent, and validity of a claimed lien by the United Bank of Denver in certain property and certain cash. . . .

The Bank contends that the eggs are inventory within the meaning of its security instruments, and that the chickens may be inventory or may in fact be equipment. It asserts that it, therefore, had a valid security interest in [the] chickens and eggs. Notwithstanding the status of the chickens and eggs, it asserts a security interest in all of the sales to Safeway, which it claims to have been pursuant to contract; the sale to Mr. Gonzales, likewise asserted to have been pursuant to contract; and the sale of the chickens to Campbell Soup Company, which the Bank suggests may have been pursuant to contract as well. The Bank further claims a security interest in the accounts receivable as of the date of the filing of the petition, thus concluding that all of the cash in the Debtor's possession is "cash collateral," to which the Bank's security interest extends.

The Debtor asserts that the chickens and eggs are "farm products" as that term is used in the Colorado version of the Uniform Commercial Code. [§4-9-109.] That section describes farm products as:

crops or livestock or supplies used or produced in farming operations or if they are products of crops or livestock in their unmanufactured states (such as ginned cotton, wool-clip, maple syrup, milk, and eggs), and if they are in the possession of a debtor engaged in raising, fattening, grazing, or other farming operations. If goods are farm products they are neither equipment nor inventory.

It would thus seem that if eggs are products of "livestock," the hens themselves must be "livestock" within the

meaning of that section. There does at least seem to be a biological connection. . . . The Bank has not disavowed this connection but asserts that in the operation such as this, where the sole business is the production of eggs, the eggs lose their characteristic as farm products and instead become inventory in the operation of a business. Great emphasis is placed by the Bank on the fact that there are no residents on the property of the Debtor and that while certain wheat was grown on adjacent land owned by the Debtor, it was not harvested. The Official Comment to UCC §9-109 states:

Products of crops or livestock, even though they remain in the possession of a person engaged in farming operations, lose their status as farm products if they are subjected to a manufacturing process. What is and what is not a manufacturing operation is not determined by this Article. At one end of the scale some processes are so closely connected with farming—such as pasteurizing milk or boiling sap to produce maple syrup or maple sugar—that they would not rank as manufacturing. On the other hand an extensive canning operation would be manufacturing. The line is one for the courts to draw. After farm products have been subjected to a manufacturing operation, they become inventory if held for sale.

[The court then rejected the bank's contention that the debtor's actions of washing, candling, and packaging the eggs constituted a "manufacturing process," in these words:] The pasteurization of milk or the boiling of sap seem to the court to be even more significant treatment of raw product than does the washing, candling, and spraying with oil of eggs. At the very least, they are in the same category, and the internal structure of the egg is not changed. The packaging of eggs in cartons does not seem to this court to be analogous to the "extensive canning operations" characterized by the Official Comment. Nearly all farm products must be packaged in some way for delivery to the farmer's customer. The facts that the packaging is done in the customer's package to eliminate a step in handling or that the operation is

highly mechanized, do not seem to this court to disqualify the operation from the normal farm category. The language of the Code seems reasonably specific in its determination of what are farm products and does not appear to distinguish between the methods of producing the same product. The Bank's refreshing view that only conventional farming techniques which are unmechanized, unsophisticated, and labor intensive can produce farm products is unpersuasive. It is somewhat interesting to note that the loan at the Bank was made through its agricultural loans department.

The cases have uniformly found cattle feeding operations to be "farms" for the purposes of UCC p9-109, although they are not farms in the traditional sense. [The court then conceded that the term "farm" as used in some statutes might be subject to varying interpretations. But the court ruled that such was not the case here, saying:]

The construction of this [particular] statute, however, compels the conclusion that chickens are livestock and eggs are products of livestock. The statutory language is simply too clear [to permit the court to accept the bank's view that only conventional, unmechanized farming techniques can produce farm products]. More importantly, the purposes of the Code could be badly abused [by excessive interpretation]. The Code was designed to provide a simple public explanation of claimed security interests so that the public might know under what conditions they were dealing with a debtor. To strain the statutory construction as sought by the Bank would seriously impair the public notice features which are the hallmark of the Uniform Commercial Code.

[Because of the court's conclusion that the chickens and eggs were farm products rather than inventory, the bank's contention that it had a security interest in the proceeds of the sale of those products necessarily failed. Accordingly, judgment was for Smith Enterprises.] ◊◊

Note

The bank in the previous case should have (1) included "farm products" in its security agreement description, or (2) emphasized terms like "chickens" and "eggs" in its description, rather than mere generic categories like "inventory." Here, the yolk was on the bank.

ATTACHMENT (CREATION) OF A SECURITY INTEREST

Under Sec. 9-203, in order for the businessperson to be sure of having an **attachment,** i.e., an enforceable security interest that attaches to the collateral, three conditions must be met:

1. There must be a *security agreement* entered into which describes the collateral. This agreement must be in writing and signed by the debtor, with one exception: where the collateral is put in the possession of the secured party. Such delivery of possession, called a "pledge," can occur only where the collateral consists of goods (such as jewelry, cattle, or furniture) or quasi-tangibles (such as warehouse receipts or negotiable instruments). Because intangibles are incapable of physical delivery, security agreements creating interests in intangibles must always be in writing.

2. The secured party must give *value* to the debtor. In most instances this consists of a delivery of goods by the secured party to the debtor, or of the advancing of money by the secured party. However, under Sec. 1-201(44) of the UCC a person also gives value for rights in collateral if he or she acquires them (a) as security for a preexisting claim, or (b) in return for a binding commitment to extend credit in the future, or (c) in return for any consideration sufficient to support a simple contract.

3. The debtor must have *rights* (any current or future legally recognized interest) in the collateral. Obviously, if the debtor did not possess any such right, he or she could not convey a right to the secured party.

The following case illustrates the importance of these requirements and also gives a preview of the discussion regarding the priority of competing security interests.

FIRST NATIONAL BANK OF ARIZONA V. CARBAJAL

Arizona Supreme Court, 645 P.2d 778 (1982)

Carbajal owned Baja Vans, which customized vans and sold them wholesale to motor vehicle dealers. In 1976-1977, Baja delivered approximately 12 vans to Arizona Imports, a licensed dealer. About half of these were paid for immediately and half soon thereafter. Until the payments were received, Baja retained the certificates of title and registration slips to the vans. In the summer of 1977, Baja delivered a van to Arizona imports, but was not paid immediately. On June 13, 1977, the Renners bought the van, executing and delivering to Arizona Imports a purchase money security agreement pursuant to which Arizona Imports retained a security interest in the van. On the same day, Arizona

Imports assigned the security agreement to the First National Bank of Arizona, which did not know that the title documents to the vehicle had not been delivered by Baja or that the Renners had returned the van and revoked their acceptance of it. Likewise, Baja did not know that Arizona Imports had sold the van to the Renners.

During this period, Baja had been making repeated demands for payment upon Arizona Imports. Baja learned from an employee of Arizona Imports that its business was "falling apart." Baja took possession of the van and subsequently sold the van in a normal course of business. When First National was not paid by the Renners, it investigated and learned that Baja had reclaimed the van. First National sued Baja for return of

the van or, in the alternative, its fair value. The trial court ruled for First National in the sum of the van's fair value. The Court of Appeals affirmed. Baja appealed.

Cameron, Justice:

[The court first held that because neither party had complied with the filing and registration provisions of Arizona's Motor Vehicle Registration Code, their rights had to be determined exclusively under the UCC.]

Baja maintains that its right to reclamation under Article 2 of the [UCC] is a species of security interest governed by the priority provisions of Article 9. This interest, Baja contends, was perfected when it retook possession of the van after learning that Arizona Imports would not complete the cash sale and is

(continues)

FIRST NATIONAL BANK OF ARIZONA V. CARBAJAL

(continued from previous page)
superior to any unperfected purchase money security interest First National might have had at the time Baja reclaimed the van. We do not agree.

Admittedly, the [UCC] provides that Baja, by retaining title, reserved for itself a security interest in the van. [UCC Secs. 2-401 and 9-113.] Baja's argument that it perfected its security interest by possession alone ignores the provision of the code that before any security interest can be perfected, it must first "attach." Under Article 9, "attach" is a word of art that contemplates the satisfaction of a series of requirements to create an enforceable security interest. [The court then quoted Sec. 9-203.]

The signed writing requirement of [Sec. 9-203] is similar to a statute of frauds and merely requires that for the security interest to attach, it must be reduced to writing and signed by the debtor. Any written agreement, including a bill of sale, will suffice for the interest to attach as long as it has been signed by the debtor and contains a description of the collateral. Baja and Arizona Imports never created such a written security agreement, and Baja was never in possession of the van at a time Arizona Imports held rights in the collateral. Lacking these prerequisites, Baja's interest could never attach and therefore could not have been perfected by possessing the van.

But Baja contends that even if its security interest has not attached or been perfected, First National does not have an enforceable security interest because its debtor, Arizona Imports, did not have sufficient rights to allow First National's interest to attach. [Sec. 9-203(1)(C).] We do not agree. When Baja delivered the van without a written agreement signed by Arizona Imports, Arizona Imports obtained sufficient "rights" and "power" to encumber the van, and therefore First National's security interest attached.

The priority provisions of [UCC Sec. 9-312(5)(b)] dictate that when neither party perfects his interest, priority goes to the first party to attach. Because First National's security interest attached, and Baja's did not, First National is entitled to the proceeds of the van. . . . This may seem unfair to Baja, but it should be remembered that the bank did everything it was required to do in order to have its security interest attach, while Baja failed to insist upon a written agreement signed by Arizona Imports. Baja failed to take advantage of the code provisions for attachment and perfection which would have given it priority over First National.

[Affirmed.] ⚖

PERFECTION OF THE SECURITY INTEREST

Under Sec. 9-201, the security agreement binds the debtor and secured party the moment that it attaches, without the taking of any additional steps by the secured party. In general, however, *the agreement does not protect the creditor against the rights of third parties until the agreement is perfected.* To illustrate: A loans B $500 and takes a security interest in a prize bull belonging to B. A does not perfect the security interest (that is, he neither files a financing statement nor takes possession of the bull). Later a third party, the X Bank, loans B $1000, the bank also taking a security interest in the bull. The X Bank then perfects by duly filing its financing statement. If B thereafter defaults on both loans, under Sec. 9-312 X Bank's perfected security interest will prevail over A's unperfected interest even though A's security interest was created first.[7]

In order for the secured party to obtain *maximum protection against third parties* who may subsequently claim an interest in the collateral—such as the debtor's other secured and unsecured creditors, persons who may have purchased collateral from the debtor, and against a trustee in bankruptcy in case the debtor becomes bankrupt—*the secured party must perfect his or her interest.* Not only does perfection usually give the secured party a protected interest in the collateral, but it also usually gives him or her a protected interest in the *proceeds* of the collateral in case the debtor sells it. Under Sec. 9-306, proceeds is defined as "whatever is received when collateral . . . is sold . . . or otherwise disposed of," and

---

[7]In addition to the priority gained under Sec. 9-312 by a subsequent third party who perfects his or her interest, as in the case of the X Bank above, there are a number of other third parties whose interests in the collateral also supersede those of the unperfected creditor under Sec. 9-301. (Additionally, as will be seen later, the rights of third parties in some situations even take precedence over perfected interests; obviously, the rights of these parties also prevail over unperfected interests.) As a result of these rules, it can be said that an unperfected interest generally affords *no protection against any third party* except a subsequent secured party who also fails to perfect his or her interest.

usually consists of cash and checks which the debtor has received upon sale of the collateral. The right to proceeds is especially important in situations where the collateral cannot be traced, or is in the possession of a third party who, under special UCC provisions noted later, takes the collateral free from the secured party's interest even though perfection has occurred. (The security agreement and financing statement usually expressly provide that the agreement covers proceeds. However, the secured party's right to proceeds exists *even in the absence of such a provision* unless the security agreement—or a subsequent agreement between the secured party and the debtor—provides otherwise. Sec. 9-306(2).)

Methods of Perfection, Generally

The secured party may perfect his or her interest in one of three ways, depending on the type of collateral that is involved. In many situations the secured party has a choice of means of perfection, while in others there is only one method that can be used. Except where the collateral consists of goods which are covered by certificates of title under state law (such as motor vehicles) and fixtures, the three methods of perfection are the following:[8]

1. *Perfection by filing.* As a general rule, perfection requires the creditor to file a financing statement at a designated location specified by the code. (As noted earlier, a financing statement is a document that evidences the secured party's interest and contains a description of the collateral covered by the security agreement.) **Filing** is the most commonly used method of perfection, and is the *only* way that perfection can occur where the collateral consists of intangibles. Because filing is the customary way of achieving perfection, it will be discussed more fully later in this chapter.

2. *Perfection by possession.* Section 9-305 provides, in part, that "a security interest in . . . goods, instruments . . . money, negotiable documents or chattel paper may be perfected by the secured party's taking possession of the collateral." In other words, such a transfer of possession of the collateral to the secured party (a transfer often called a "pledge") can

occur only where the collateral consists of money, goods (such as jewelry), or quasi-tangibles (such as promissory notes or shares of stock).

Two special rules in regard to this kind of perfection of interests in quasi-tangible collateral should be noted. Both of these rules are found in Section 9-304(1).

A. If the collateral consists of negotiable instruments (or of money), possession is the *only* means of perfection; filing will not suffice.

B. If the collateral consists of chattel paper or negotiable documents of title, perfection by filing is permitted. However, Sections 9-308 and 9-309 provide, in general, that security interests in such types of collateral that have been perfected by filing *lose their priority* to good faith purchasers of the collateral. Thus, in order for a party who has a security interest in either chattel paper or negotiable documents of title to receive maximum protection—that is, to insure that the collateral will not be subsequently sold to a good faith purchaser—the secured party *should perfect by taking possession.*

While many kinds of collateral are too bulky for a transfer of possession, and others will not be transferred because the debtor needs to use them in his or her business—as in the case of plant machinery—the pledge, where feasible, does possess two significant advantages over the other kinds of perfection. First, it obviates the need for the security agreement to be in writing (though, in practice, a written agreement is still advisable). And, second, as indicated above, it reduces the possibility that third parties will subsequently acquire or claim interests in the collateral.

3. *Automatic perfection.* Occasionally an interest is perfected by mere attachment—that is, automatically—at the moment that the security interest is created. Such attachment, called **automatic perfection,** is applicable only where the collateral consists of *consumer goods* being purchased by the debtor. It exists in two common situations: (a) where the creditor (usually a retailer) sells the goods on credit and takes a security interest in return, or (b) where the creditor (usually a bank or finance company) loans money to the debtor for the purpose of buying the goods, and takes a security interest in return. To

---

[8]The special rules applicable to motor vehicles and fixtures are discussed subsequently.

illustrate: B buys a washer and dryer on credit from the S Company under a conditional sale agreement (an agreement under which title to the goods is retained by the S Company until the price is paid in full). Under Sec. 9-302(1)(d) the interest of the S Company— called a **purchase money security interest**—is perfected even though it does not file a financing statement, and even though it does not have possession of the goods. Similarly, if B borrows the money to buy the appliances from a finance company, with that company taking a security interest in the goods when purchased, the finance company has a perfected, purchase money security interest in the washer and dryer when B buys them.[9] (The reason for the automatic perfection rule is one of practicality—the fact that secured sales of consumer goods are made in such large numbers by retailers that the filing requirement would place an undue burden upon such sellers.)

While automatic perfection does away with the necessity of filing a financing statement, it should be noted that the security agreement itself *must be in writing;* otherwise there is no attachment to which the perfection can relate.

Perfection: Motor Vehicles and Fixtures
Motor Vehicles
Under Sec. 9-302(3), the usual methods of perfection are not applicable to security interests in collateral which are subject to state certificate of title laws—motor vehicles, boats, and motor homes. Security interests in such goods can be perfected only by compliance with the applicable state statute. In regard to automobiles (and to the other goods in this category), what this means is that—under the law of most states—a security interest can be perfected *only by the notation of such interest on the certificate of title covering the vehicle subject to the interest.* Generally, if such notation is not made, a good faith purchaser of the automobile takes it free of the interest. (In regard to the relatively few states that do not utilize title registration of such vehicles, an examination of the special statutes of such states must be made to determine the priority of conflicting interests.)

Fixtures
As noted above, a fixture is an item or good that becomes so firmly affixed to or so integrally connected to real estate that it is considered part of the real estate. How does the seller of a furnace, for example, obtain a security interest in the furnace that is superior to the interest of the lender who financed the house in which the furnace is to be installed? The rules here are very complicated. Generally, under Sec. 9-313(4)(a), the seller of the furnace who takes a purchase money security interest from the buyer-homeowner has priority over the holder of the mortgage on the real estate *if* the interest is properly filed before the furnace becomes attached to the property or within ten days thereafter. On the other hand, if the furnace is installed when the house is *under construction,* the seller's purchase money security interest will likely be subordinate to a construction mortgage recorded before the installation. The situation is further complicated by substantial variation in state law in this area. See Table 29.1 for clarification of the rules pertaining to perfection.

Filing Requirements, Generally
The Financing Statement
Where perfection is made by the filing of a financing statement, as is usually the case, the requirements of Sec. 9-402 must be met. That section initially provides that "A financing statement is sufficient if it gives the names of the debtor and the secured party, is signed by the debtor, gives an address of the secured party from which information concerning the security interest may be obtained, gives a mailing address of the debtor and contains a statement indicating the types, or describing the items, of collateral." The section goes on to provide that additional information is needed for some types of collateral, so

---

[9]An entirely different situation exists where a purchaser buys consumer goods (such as a washer or dryer) and pays cash for them, and subsequently uses such goods as collateral for a loan. Prior to 1984 these were very common transactions; typically, a person who wanted to borrow money from a lender—usually a small loan company, but sometimes a savings and loan association or a bank— would be asked to check a box in the lender's loan form which gave to the lender a blanket security interest in all of the borrower's household goods. In hearings before the Federal Trade Commission (FTC) in the early 1980s, voluminous testimony was given indicating that the use of such devices ("non-purchase money interests") was attended by a variety of evils. Chief among these were (1) the fact that lenders often used these devices to continually threaten defaulting borrowers with repossession, causing borrowers "mental and psychological" injury; and (2) the fact that in cases where repossession actually occurred, the price of the goods obtained by the lender upon resale was usually so low that the borrower's obligation to the lender was actually reduced very little by the resale. Accordingly, the FTC adopted a rule that, in general, *prohibits lenders in interstate commerce from taking non-purchase money security interests in household goods.* Two observations about the rule: (1) the term "household goods" excludes specified nonnecessities, such as jewelry and works of art; and (2) the rule does not, of course, have application to, or impose limitations upon the use of, *purchase money* security interests in household goods.

TABLE 29.1 PERMISSIBLE TYPES OF PERFECTION FOR VARIOUS KINDS OF COLLATERAL

TYPE OF COLLATERAL	FILING	POSSESSION	AUTOMATIC
Tangible Collateral			
Consumer Goods	X	X	X*
Equipment	X	X	
Farm Products	X	X	
Inventory	X	X	
Fixtures	X		
Indispensable Paper Collateral			
Documents of Title	X**	X	
Instruments	X	X***	
Chattel Paper	X	X	
Intangible Collateral			
Accounts	X		
General Intangibles	X		

*Automatic perfection arises if it is a purchase money security interest. Note also that special rules apply to motor vehicles.
**Temporary 21-day perfection exists without filing.
***Temporary 21-day perfection exists without possession.

that a reading of the full section is necessary to determine the sufficiency of a financing statement in a given situation.

Although many courts are fairly strict in their interpretation of descriptions contained in financing statements, the UCC was intended to create a system of *notice filing* that would eliminate extremely technical readings. The following case is illustrative of the better view.

IN RE FOGARTY

U.S. Bankruptcy Court, Southern District of Florida, 114 B.R. 788 (1990)

Certain mares were owned by Joseph and Virginia Fogarty ("the debtors") and subject to a security interest held by NCNB National Bank of Florida. NCNB became the owner of the mares after it was the successful bidder at the January 5, 1989, foreclosure sale of the mares pursuant to a final judgment foreclosing NCNB's security interest.

NCNB also claimed interest in four thoroughbred foals born to the mares. The claim was based on its security agreement and its properly filed UCC-1 financing statement. The security agreement granted NCNB's predecessor a continuing and unconditional security interest in the mares and any offspring of the mares. The financing statement contained de-

tailed descriptions of the mares including their lineage, birth date, and physical characteristics, but it did not make reference to the offspring or foals of the mares.

In April 1987, NCNB brought a foreclosure action seeking to enforce its security agreement. Prior to the foreclosure sale, the debtors filed a bankruptcy petition under Chapter 11. The foals were conceived in June 1988, two months before the debtor's bankruptcy case; they were born in May 1989, five months after NCNB purchased the mares at foreclosure sale. NCNB had possession of the foals at the time of their birth.

NCNB moved for summary judgment on its claim that it owned the foals. The debtors moved for summary judgment on their claim that NCNB's lien was invalid. The follow-

ing is an excerpt from the bankruptcy court's ruling.

Weaver, Chief Judge:

This court concludes that NCNB must prevail on its claim of ownership of the foals. . . .

To perfect a security interest in collateral such as horses, a financing statement must be filed in the county of the debtor's place of business or the county where the horses are located. A financing statement must be signed by the debtor, contain the name of the debtor and his mailing address, the name and address of the secured party and contain a statement indicating the types, or describing the items, of collateral. The issue here is whether NCNB's financing statements, which contain detailed descriptions of the mares but no

(continues)

In re Fogarty

(continued from previous page)
reference to their offspring, contain a sufficient description of collateral to have perfected NCNB's security interest in the mares *and* the foals as of the commencement of the debtors' bankruptcy case.

Comment 2 to 9-402 of the official text of the Uniform Commercial Code ("UCC") explains that the UCC filing requirements are intended to create a system of "notice filing" to place interested parties on inquiry notice that property of a debtor may be encumbered by a secured creditor:

The notice itself indicates merely that the secured party who has filed may have a security interest in the collateral described. Further inquiry from the parties concerned will be necessary to disclose the complete state of affairs.

"The purpose of the [UCC] filing system is to give notice to creditors and other interested parties that a security interest exists in property of the debtor. Perfect accuracy, however, is not required so long as the financing statement contains sufficient information to 'put any searcher on inquiry.' The emphasis of the Uniform Commercial Code is thus on *commercial realities* rather than on corporate technicalities." *Matter of Glasco, Inc.*, 642 F.2d 793 (5th Cir. 1981)(emphasis added). Thus, the question of whether NCNB's financing statements contain a description of collateral sufficient to place third parties on notice of NCNB's interest in the foals, necessarily involves an examination of the "commercial realities" of the parties' secured transaction within the context of the thoroughbred horse industry.

Based on the evidence presented, this Court finds that the descriptions of collateral contained in NCNB's financing statements were sufficient to place third parties on notice that the foals of the mares were subject to the security interest of NCNB. It is widely acknowledged in the thoroughbred horse industry that the intrinsic value of a thoroughbred mare is based in large part on the mare's ability to produce foals. Furthermore, the link between a thoroughbred mare's value and its ability to produce foals becomes more acute if the mare is older than six years of age when on average, most thoroughbred mares are beyond their prime racing years. In this case, the mares were between seven and fourteen years of age at the commencement of the debtors' bankruptcy case. Accordingly, given the commercial importance of a thoroughbred mare's ability to produce foals, this Court concludes that NCNB's financing statements, containing only a description of the mares, were sufficient to alert third parties to NCNB's interest in the foals thereby perfecting NCNB's security interest in the foals.

[This court finds and concludes that NCNB is entitled to summary judgment as a matter of law.] ⚖️

Place of Filing

In all cases where filing is utilized, the place for doing so depends on the classification of the collateral. In that regard, however, determination of the status of the debtor is not sufficient for a proper classification of the collateral. Rather, the determination in many jurisdictions may depend on how the collateral is used by the debtor. For example, a refrigerator is a *consumer good* if it is sold to a housekeeper, *inventory* if it is in the hands of a merchant selling appliances, *equipment* if it is used by a doctor for storing drugs in his or her office, and *farm equipment* if it is used to store eggs for resale.

Most states have two locations for filing—a *central* one (usually with the secretary of state) and a *local* one (usually with a county clerk). While the states have adopted somewhat varying location rules, most have adopted that version of Sec. 9-401(1) providing, essentially, that where the collateral is *farm equipment, farm products, or consumer goods,* filing is to be at a designated office in the county of the *debtor's residence* (or, if the debtor is not a resident of the state, then at a designated office in the county where the goods are kept). In other words, there is local filing for these kinds of security.

Where the collateral is *timber to be cut, minerals* (including oil and gas), *crops, or fixtures,* local filing is again usually proper—but, in these instances, "in the office where a mortgage on the real estate would be . . . recorded"—in such office in the county *where the land is located.*[10] Filings covering all other kinds of collateral, with minor exception, are to be made centrally—in the office of the secretary of state of the appropriate state. (That state is usually the state of the debtor's residence, or, in the case of a business

[10]Many states require an additional filing (dual filing) in the case of some of these kinds of collateral, especially fixtures.

Box 29.1
The Law at Work

We live in an information and computer age. As we pointed out in Chapter 9, intellectual property rights in trademarks, copyrights, and patents are now as important for some businesses as their bank accounts, buildings, inventory, and other more tangible assets. Indeed, a computer software company's primary assets are its copyrights. A soft drink or athletic shoe company's most valuable asset may well be its trademark.

Lenders, therefore, must familiarize themselves with the basics of intellectual property law and Article 9's requirements for creating security interests in such intellectual property. A lender who thinks solely in terms of buildings and inventory as collateral is missing the boat.

---

firm, a state in which it has a place of business.) Additionally, several states have set up a central filing system for sales of farm product collateral, pursuant to the federal Food Security Act of 1985 (to be discussed presently).

Duration of Filing

Under Sec. 9-403(2), a filed financing statement is effective for five years from the date of filing. After this period, under Sec. 9-403(3), the security interest generally becomes unperfected unless the secured party files a *continuation statement* within six months prior to the expiration date. This continuation, good for five more years, can again be continued using the same procedure. Thus the secured party can continue the perfected interest indefinitely.

Collateral Moved to Another State

There is always the possibility that collateral subject to a perfected security interest will be moved out of the state in which the perfection was made. Such movement may or may not have been contemplated by the parties, and it may or may not be a violation of the terms of the security agreement. In any event, the creditor needs to know what steps must be taken in order to keep his or her interest protected.

General Rule

The perfection of security interests in "multiple state transactions" is governed by Sec. 9-103. In regard to most kinds of collateral ("documents, instruments, and ordinary goods"), Sec. 9-103(1)(d) provides that the perfected creditor has *four months after the collateral has entered another state in which to reperfect*. If reperfection is made within that time, the security interest shall be "deemed to be perfected continuously" under Sec. 9-303(2). Thus if collateral is moved to a new state on March 1, and the creditor refiles there on May 10, his or her interest is generally protected as against any claimants in the state whose claim attached between those dates. On the other hand, if no reperfection is made within the four-month period, the creditor's interest is *unperfected beginning with the time that the collateral entered the state*. In other words, where there is no new perfection within the four-month period, the creditor is not protected by the four-month grace period.

Special Rules—Motor Vehicles

In cases where the collateral consists of accounts, general intangibles, chattel paper, and minerals, special rules apply. (Sec. 9-103[2][3][4] and [5].) Because of the complexity of these rules, the resolution of multistate disputes involving interests in these kinds of collateral can be achieved only by a careful reading of these express provisions and the case law developed under them.

Motor vehicles (and other goods covered by state certificate of title laws) are expressly exempted from the basic filing requirements of Article 9. As to security interests in such collateral as automobiles, then, perfection can be made only pursuant to the applicable state law. The rules here are complicated by the fact that while most states have certificate of title laws, some do not. Additionally, while the laws of most of the states having certificate of title laws provide that a notification of the security interest on the certificate of title is the only means of perfection, the laws of some title states do not so provide. Despite these variations, the rules applicable to two of the most common situations are clear:

1. Where a security interest exists in an automobile (or similar "certificate collateral") in a title state, and where the interest is duly noted on the certificate of title as required by the law of that state, the perfection continues after the automobile is removed to another title state *until it is registered* in the new state—the general four-month rule is inapplicable. Thus the secured party is protected against anyone who purchases the car in the new state prior to the new registration. Additionally, because a new registration normally requires the surrender of the old certificate of title, and the secured party is normally the holder of that certificate, the secured party usually can require that the security interest also be noted on the new certificate of title.

2. Where a security interest exists in an automobile in a non-certificate of title state, and where the interest is perfected by a filing of a financing statement under the basic filing section of Article 9, the security interest is generally protected when the automobile is moved to a new state *for four months* after it is brought into such state.

LIMITATIONS ON PERFECTION

There are limited situations in which certain third parties acquire the collateral *free of* the security interest, even though the interest has been perfected. Following are the primary situations in which these third parties prevail.

Buyers in the Ordinary Course of Business

Section 9-307(1) provides that "a buyer [of goods] in the ordinary course of business . . . takes free of a security interest created by his seller even though the security interest is perfected and even though the buyer knows of its existence." The rationale for this is that the ordinary person who purchases goods from a merchant should not be required to find out if there is an outstanding security interest covering the merchant's inventory. The key words identifying the buyer in this case, a **buyer in the ordinary course of business,** mean that he or she made the purchase in the ordinary course of the debtor's business—that is, that the collateral purchased was of a type which the debtor normally sold (customarily meaning inventory).

To illustrate: M, a merchant in the appliance business, seeks a loan from B Bank, putting up his inventory of refrigerators, stoves, freezers, and other appliances as security for the loan. B Bank perfects its security interest by filing a financing statement centrally with the secretary of state. A week later, C, a consumer, purchases a freezer from M for cash. Since C has purchased in the ordinary course of the seller's business, *he takes the property free of B Bank's security interest.* The ordinary course of business rule does not apply to the rare buyer who not only knows of the existence of the security interest, but also knows that the sale of the goods was a *violation* of the security agreement.

A second limitation on the course of business rule is contained in Sec. 9-307(1), under which ordinary course buyers of farm products (crops or livestock) take subject to a prior perfected security interest covering the products. However, Congress overrode this provision, which had been subject to conflicting court interpretations, in the Food Security Act of 1985. That act gives the same protection to ordinary course buyers of farm products as is accorded buyers of other products. However, the secured party can retain priority by (1) "prenotification," that is, giving *actual* notice to the buyer pursuant to strict guidelines, or (2) filing in a special central filing system for farm products independent of Article 9. Several states have created such a special filing system.

Buyers Not in the Ordinary Course of Business

A second class of buyer who receives protection in some circumstances against a perfected security interest is the buyer who buys consumer goods not in the ordinary course of business, sometimes referred to as "the next-door neighbor buyer." This priority arises under Sec. 9- 307(2), which applies to the situation where consumer goods are sold (usually by a retailer) subject to a purchase money security interest in favor of the seller, in which case—as we saw earlier—perfection is automatic. That section provides, in effect, that if the consumer-buyer (the debtor) resells the goods to a third party not in the ordinary course of business, the third party takes the goods *free of the perfected security interest* if the following conditions are met:

1. The buyer must buy without knowledge of the security interest.

2. He or she must give value for the goods.

3. The purchase must be for the buyer's own personal, family, or household purposes.

4. The purchase must take place before the secured party files a financing statement—a condition that is normally easy to meet, since the secured party in such a case usually does not file at all.

To illustrate: M, a merchant in the appliance business, sells a freezer out of his inventory to C, a consumer, under a conditional sales contract, because C cannot pay the full purchase price. Since this is a purchase money security interest in consumer goods, M makes no filing. C takes the freezer home but decides he does not like it and sells it to his friend, F, who purchases the freezer for his own use without knowledge of M's security interest. If C defaults, M will lose his security interest in the freezer and become a general creditor of C, since F has met the UCC requirements.

Buyers of Chattel Paper, Negotiable Instruments, and Negotiable Documents

Under Article 3 of the UCC, "Commercial Paper," good faith purchasers of negotiable instruments who give value for such instruments generally take the instruments free of claims asserted by prior parties. This same general concept is recognized under Sections 9-308 and 9-309 of the UCC.

Section 9-308 provides, in part, that "a purchaser of chattel paper . . . who gives new value and takes possession of it in the ordinary course of his business *has priority over a security interest in the chattel paper* . . . which is perfected [by filing]." (Emphasis added.) Thus, if a perfected creditor does not take possession of the chattel paper, a person who buys the paper from the debtor in good faith generally takes it free of the perfected interest.

The most common situation (but by no means the only one) to which this section is applicable is the case where a dealer, usually a retailer, sells

goods (for example, furniture) on credit to a consumer, the debtor, with the dealer taking a chattel paper (usually a promissory note coupled with a security interest in favor of the dealer) from the consumer-debtor. The dealer then subsequently assigns the paper to a financial institution, usually a bank, as security for a loan made by the bank to the dealer.[11] In such a case, if the bank perfects by filing only, leaving possession of the paper in the dealer, a person who purchases the paper from the dealer in good faith—that is, without knowledge of the security interest of the bank—and for value takes the chattel paper free of the bank's perfected interest.

Along similar lines, Sec. 9-309 provides, in essence, that a holder in due course of a negotiable instrument, and a holder to whom a negotiable document of title has been duly negotiated, *takes priority over* an earlier security interest in such instrument or document even though the security interest is a perfected one. Further, that section provides that the filing of a security interest in a negotiable instrument or negotiable document (by the original secured party) does not constitute notice of the security interest to such holders.

Other Protected Parties

In addition to buyers of collateral discussed above, there are other third parties whose interests in the collateral (usually arising under other statutes) are excluded from operation of Article 9 by Sec. 9-104. Such interests thus have priority over interests perfected under Article 9. Some of these interests, for example, are those arising under statutes of the United States, landlord liens, and liens "given by statute . . . for services or materials. . . ." To illustrate an interest in the latter category: M, a mechanic, repairs an automobile owned by O that is subject to a security interest in favor of a bank. Under the typical state statute M possesses an *artisan's lien*—the right to retain possession of the car until he or she is paid

---

[11]In the general situation presented here (especially common in the furniture industry), the consumer-debtor is not notified of the assignment to the bank. Thus, in the usual case where the dealer retains possession of the paper *instead of selling it* to a third party, the consumer-debtor continues to make monthly payments to the dealer, and the dealer remits them to the bank. The transaction is referred to as *nonnotification* (or *indirect collection*), as distinguished from the case of *notification* (or *direct collection*), where the consumer-debtor is notified of the assignment and makes payments directly to the bank. In the case of direct notification, common in the automobile industry, possession of the paper is normally transferred to the bank, the secured party.

for the repair work. Generally, under such a lien the mechanic's right to retain possession may be successfully asserted against the bank.

PERFECTION AND THE FLOATING LIEN CONCEPT

Section 9-204 of the UCC permits the security agreement to include a clause providing that the obligation covered by the agreement is also secured by any collateral that may subsequently be acquired by the debtor. Such a provision, called an **after-acquired property clause,** permits the secured creditor to have a **"floating lien"**—a lien on changing or shifting assets of the debtor. This clause is most often used to cover inventories of the debtor, where goods are continuously being sold and restocked by the debtor, but sometimes covers non-inventory assets of the debtor (such as plant machinery).

Section 9-204 also permits the security agreement to contain a **future advances clause** (*dragnet*), which is a clause providing that the debtor's collateral shall also be security for any extensions of credit (advances) which the creditor may make in the future. The following example illustrates the extensive protection that is afforded a secured party who utilizes both the after-acquired property and future advances clauses.

April 2—D borrows money from X (creditor #1) under a security agreement that gives X a security interest in all of the equipment in D's plant. The agreement contains an after-acquired property clause and also a future advances clause. X perfects the same day by filing a financing statement centrally.

June 1—D purchases a new piece of equipment for $50,000, and pays cash for it.

June 15—D decides to replenish his raw material inventory. He does this by getting a loan from Y (creditor #2) for $25,000, putting up his new piece of equipment as security for the loan.

June 16—Y perfects by filing a financing statement centrally.

June 30—D needs additional funds to meet his payroll, and approaches X (creditor #1) for a $20,000 loan for this purpose. X makes the loan.

September 1—D's business is hit by a recession, with the result that D is in default to both X and Y.

In this situation, X's interest in the new piece of equipment has priority over Y's interest, for either of two reasons:

1. If D owes any balance on the original debt incurred April 2, X has a protected security interest in the new equipment by virtue of the after-acquired property clause. Thus, the new equipment can be acquired by X as satisfaction for that debt.[12]

2. If D's indebtedness arises out of the advance made to him by X on June 30, X again has priority even though Y's security interest was perfected prior to that advance. This results from the future advances clause, which causes the June 30 advance *to date back to the April 2 perfection.*

PROCEEDS AND COMMINGLING

The secured party's right to proceeds is extremely important when the debtor sells the collateral to a third party under circumstances in which the secured party loses his or her interest in the collateral. In such a case, any payments (or proceeds) made by the third party to the debtor can be claimed by the secured party in satisfaction of the debt. Under Secs. 9-203 and 306, this right of the secured party is automatic unless the parties agree otherwise, and it is usually continuous in duration until the debt is paid.

In certain business operations, goods under a perfected security interest are commingled with other goods and become part of the product or mass. What then happens to the security interest? Section 9-315(1) provides that the security interest *continues* in the product or mass if the goods lose their identity in processing or manufacturing, or if the financing statement covering the original goods also covers the product into which the goods have been manufactured or processed. Under Sec. 9-315(2), in the same situation, if more than one security interest attaches to the product or mass, they all rank equally according to the cost ratio of their contribution to the total.

The rules relating to after-acquired property, future advances, commingled or processed goods, and proceeds also make it possible for the lien to float on a *shifting stock* of goods. Under Sec. 9-205, the lien

---

[12]The usual priority afforded by an after-acquired property clause may be lost in circumstances where the second creditor's interest is a "purchase money security interest." The special rules applicable to such interests are examined later in the chapter.

can start with raw materials and pass to work in process, to finished inventory, to accounts receivable or chattel paper, and to any cash proceeds under a single perfected security interest.

PRIORITIES AMONG CREDITORS

Earlier, in the section entitled "Limitations on Perfection," we saw that certain *buyers of the collateral* took it free of a perfected security interest. In other words, in a contest between the perfected creditor and a buyer of the collateral, the buyer's interest (in limited circumstances) had priority over that of the creditor.

Here we will examine the rules applicable to even more common controversies—those in which both of the competing parties are *creditors of the debtor* (with both parties' interests arising under Article 9).

Unperfected Security Interests

The basic priority section is Sec. 9-312, and most of the provisions found there deal with priorities between perfected creditors—situations in which both of the claimants to the collateral hold perfected security interests. Before we turn to an examination of these important rules, however, two introductory rules involving priorities relative to *unperfected* interests should be kept in mind.

First, in contests between two secured but unperfected creditors, under Sec. 9-312(5)(b) the creditor's interest that attached first—was created first—takes priority over the other.[13] (It should also be kept in mind, however, that should the debtor go into bankruptcy both unperfected interests are lost, with the unperfected creditors simply sharing in the bankrupt's assets along with his or her unsecured creditors.)

Second, in a contest between an unperfected creditor and a perfected creditor, the perfected creditor's interest, of course, has priority over the unperfected interest—Sec. 9-301(1)(a). And this priority exists even if the unperfected creditor's interest had attached first, and even if the perfected creditor knew of the unperfected interest before he or she perfected.

Perfected Security Interests

Subject to special rules noted later, the basic priority rule applicable to controversies between perfected creditors is that *conflicting security interests rank according to priority in time of filing or perfection, whichever is earlier.* (Sec. 9-312(5)(a).) The following example illustrates the rule.

June 1—Bank A agrees to loan $4000 to D, with the actual advance of the money to be made when subsequently requested by D. D signs a security agreement giving the bank a security interest in his Audemars Piguet watch, valued at $9000. D retains possession of the watch.

June 2—Bank A files its financing statement.

June 5—D borrows $6000 from bank B, signing a security agreement that gives the bank a security interest in the same watch. Bank B, after advancing the money, perfects by filing its financing statement immediately.

June 7—Bank A advances the $4000 to D.

If D defaults on both loans, *bank A's interest has priority over that of bank B*, even though bank B's perfection occurred first.[14] The rationale for the rule, as applied to this situation, is that bank B would have known of bank A's agreement had it checked the appropriate filing system before making its loan.

Two words of caution about the basic rule must be made. First, the "first filing" part of the rule grants priority to such filer over a subsequently perfected interest only in those cases where a security agreement and filing occur at a given time, with the actual advance being made by the filing party at a later date (as in the example above). In the much more common case, where both the first and second creditors immediately advance funds upon the debtor's signing of their respective security agreements, the creditor who *perfects first* prevails. To illustrate: X borrows $1000 from A on June 1, and signs a security agreement on that date giving A a security interest in certain collateral. X then borrows $2000 from B on June 15, giving B a security interest in the same collateral. If B perfects by filing before A does, B's interest has priority over A's.

Second, the basic rule *does not always* give the party who files first or perfects first protection against subsequent creditors who possess purchase money security interests in the collateral (as indicated in the following discussion).

---

[13]This situation does not get into the courts often, because in "real life" when it appears that there is going to be a controversy between two unperfected creditors, one or both of the creditors perfect before litigation begins.

[14]Bank B's perfection occurred on June 5, and bank A's perfection did not occur until June 7. Bank A's filing on June 2 did not constitute a perfection, because its interest had not even attached since it had not yet given value.

SPECIAL RULES APPLICABLE TO PURCHASE MONEY SECURITY INTERESTS

Section 9-312 contains a number of special rules that bring about results different from those obtained under the general rule discussed above. Of these, two that grant special priority to holders of purchase money security interests in limited circumstances merit attention.

Purchase Money Security Interests in Noninventory Collateral

Section 9-312(4) provides that "a purchase money security interest in collateral other than inventory has priority over a conflicting interest in the same collateral . . . if the purchase money security interest is perfected at the time the debtor receives possession of the collateral, or within ten days thereafter." This priority is sometimes referred to as the "super priority" of a purchase money security holder, because his or her interest takes precedence over the person who holds the conflicting interest in the collateral even if that person's interest was perfected prior to the creation of the purchase money interest.

One situation (among several) to which this rule applies is the following: M, a manufacturer, borrows money from bank A, under a written agreement providing that the bank shall have a security interest in the M Company's present and future plant machinery. The bank duly files a financing statement that includes the after-acquired property clause. Thereafter, M buys additional machinery on credit from the XYZ Corporation (a tool and die company) under a security agreement conveying an interest in the additional machinery to the XYZ Corporation. The XYZ Corporation, the purchase money security interest holder, delivers the additional machinery to the M Company and files its financing statement within ten days of delivery. The XYZ Corporation's purchase money security interest in the additional machinery has priority over that of the bank's interest.

Purchase Money Security Interests in Inventories

Purchase money security holders also have "super priority" over existing perfected holders of interests in inventory, but under more limited circumstances. Section 9-312(3)(b) provides, in part, that a perfected purchase money security interest *in inventory* has priority over a conflicting interest in the same inventory if two basic requirements are met: (1) the purchase money security interest must be perfected by the time that the debtor receives the inventory being purchased, and (2) if the holder of the conflicting interest in the inventory has perfected by filing only, the purchase money secured party must give written notification to such holder before the purchase money secured party files his or her financing statement, such notification stating that the purchase money secured party has or expects to acquire a purchase money interest in the debtor's inventory, describing such inventory by item or type. Once this notification is received by the holder of the conflicting interest, it is good for a period of five years.

Again, a note of caution: as to any priority controversies presenting facts that do not clearly fall within the general rule of Sec. 9-312(5) or within the special rules of Sec. 9-312(3)(b) applicable to purchase money security interests, other sections of Sec. 9-312 may apply. (Additionally, the status of perfected security interests in crops is governed by Sec. 9-312(2), a section whose complexity also precludes its treatment in an introductory chapter such as this.)

The next case presents priority issues in a controversy between perfected creditors.

KIMBRELL'S FURNITURE CO., INC. V. FRIEDMAN

Supreme Court of South Carolina, 198 S.E.2d 803 (1973)

This suit deals with two separate purchases made from the plaintiff, Kimbrell's Furniture Company—a new television set by Charlie O'Neal on July 11, 1972, and a tape player by his wife on July 15, *1972. Each purchase was on credit, and in each instance there was executed, as security, a conditional sale contract, designated a **purchase money security agreement.** On the same day of each purchase, O'Neal took the items to defendant, Friedman, a pawnbroker doing busi-* ness as Bonded Loan, and **pledged** *them as security for a loan—the television for a loan of $30 and the tape player for a loan of $25.*

Kimbrell's did not record any financing statement or notice of these security agreements. O'Neal thereafter failed to make his required

(continues)

KIMBRELL'S FURNITURE CO., INC. V. FRIEDMAN

(continued from previous page)
monthly payments to Kimbrell's, whereupon Kimbrell's brought this action to recover possession of the goods.

Bonded Loan, which held possession of the television set and tape player as security for its loan, contended that its lien had priority over Kimbrell's unrecorded security interest. The lower court sustained this contention, and Kimbrell's appealed.

The question to be decided was the following: Is a conditional seller of consumer goods required to file a financing statement in order to perfect his or her security interest as against a pawnbroker who subsequently takes possession of such goods as security for a loan?

Lewis, Justice:

. . . Prior to the adoption of the Uniform Commercial Code (UCC), . . . purchase money security interests, including conditional sales contracts for consumer goods, were required to be recorded in order to perfect such security interests against subsequent creditors, including pawnbrokers.

. . . However, insofar as it applied to the perfection of security interests in consumer goods, this rule has been repealed by the UCC and the provisions of the latter are controlling in the determination of the present question.

Goods are classified or defined for purposes of secured transactions under §10.9-109. Subsection 1 defines "consumer goods" as those "used or bought for use primarily for personal, family or household purposes." The property here involved was a television set and tape player. They are normally used for personal, family or household purposes and the purchasers warranted that such was the intended use. It is undisputed in this case that the collateral involved was consumer goods within the meaning of the foregoing statutory definition.

Kimbrell clearly held a *purchase money security interest* in the consumer goods sold to the O'Neals and, by them, subsequently pledged to Bonded Loan. Section 10.9-107(a).

When filing is required to perfect a security interest, the UCC requires that a document designated as a financing statement (§10.9-402) must be filed. Section 10.9-302. Contrary to the prior provisions of §60-101, supra, the UCC does not require filing in order to perfect a purchase money security interest in consumer goods. Pertinent here, §10.9-302(1)(d) provides:

(1) A financing statement must be filed to perfect all security interests except the following: . . . (d) a purchase money security interest in consumer goods; . . .

Since filing was not necessary, the security interest of Kimbrell attached and was perfected *when the debtors executed the purchase money security agreements and took possession of the property.* Sections 10.9-204, 10.9-303(1). [Emphasis added.] Therefore, Kimbrell's security interest has priority over the security interest of Bonded Loan by virtue of §10.9-312(4), which provides:

(4) A purchase money security interest in collateral other than inventory has priority over a conflicting security interest in the same collateral if the purchase money security interest is perfected at the time the debtor receives possession of the collateral or within ten days thereafter.

This result is consistent with and confirmed by the residual priority rule of 10.9-312(5)(b) providing for priority between conflicting security interests in the same collateral ". . . in the order of perfection unless both are perfected by filing. . . ."

Bonded Loan, however, alleges that its interest takes priority over the security interest of Kimbrell by virtue of §10.9-307(1), which is as follows:

(1) A buyer in ordinary course of business (subsection (9) of Section 10.1-201) other than a person buying farm products from a person engaged in farming operations takes free of a security interest created by his seller even though the security interest is perfected and even though a buyer knows of its existence.

The above section affords Bonded Loan no relief. It was not a buyer in the ordinary course of business so as to take free of the security interest of Kimbrell. A buyer in the ordinary course of business is defined in subsection (9) of p10.1-201 as follows:

"Buyer in ordinary course of business" means a person who in good faith and without knowledge that the sale to him is in violation of the ownership rights or security interest of a third party in the goods buys in ordinary course from a person in the business of selling goods of that kind. . . .

In the Reporter's Comments to §10.9-307(1), supra, Dean Robert W. Foster points out that, under the foregoing definition, a buyer in ordinary course of business "must be 'without knowledge that the sale to him is in violation of the ownership rights or security interest of a third party . . .' *and* the seller must be a 'person in the business of selling goods of that kind. . . .' Thus subsection (1) (of §10.9-307) is limited to the *buyer out of inventory* who may know of the inventory financer's security interest but does not know that the sale to him is unauthorized." [Emphasis added.]

Therefore, Bonded Loan could not have been a buyer in the ordinary course of business when O'Neal pledged the property to it, because O'Neal was not "a person in the business of selling goods of that kind."

The judgment of the lower court is accordingly reversed and the cause remanded for entry of judgment in favor of plaintiff, Kimbrell's Furniture Company, Inc., in accordance with the views herein. ⟂

RIGHTS AND DUTIES PRIOR TO TERMINATION

The security agreement determines most of the rights and duties of the debtor and secured party. However, other rights and duties are imposed by the UCC, some of which are applied in the absence of a security agreement.

Release, Assignment, and Amendment

Under Sec. 9-406, the secured party of record can release all or part of any collateral described in the filed financing statement, thereby ending his or her security interest in the described collateral. Under Sec. 9-405, the secured party can also assign all or part of the security interest to an assignee, who, in order to become the secured party of record, must file either by a disclosure method provided for in the code (such as a notation on the front or back of the financing statement) or by a separate written statement of assignment.

If the debtor and secured party so agree, under Sec. 9-402, the financing statement can be amended (for example, to add new collateral to the security interest). But the filed amendment must be signed by both the debtor and the secured party. This amendment does not extend the time period of the perfection unless collateral is added; in such a case, the perfection for the new collateral applies from the date of filing the amendment.

The debtor's signature is needed for (1) the security agreement, (2) the original financing statement, and (3) amendments to the financing statements. All other documents can be filed with only the signature of the secured party.

Information Requests by Secured Parties

In most states the filing officer must furnish specified information on request to certain parties. For example, under Sec. 9-407(1), the person filing any of the above statements can furnish the filing officer with a duplicate and request that the officer note on such copy the file number, date, and hour of the original filing. The filing officer must send this copy to the person making the request, without charge.

Frequently, prospective secured parties request of the filing officer a certificate giving information on possible perfected financing statements with respect to a named debtor. Under Sec. 9-407(2), if so requested, the filing officer must furnish a copy of any filed financing statement or assignment. Given the priorities of secured interests and the attachment of security interest under the concept of the floating lien, businesspersons ought to request such information before advancing credit to debtors.

Secured Party in Possession of the Collateral

Section 9-207 provides that generally a secured party in possession of the collateral must use reasonable care in the custody and preservation of it and is subject to liability by the debtor for any failure to do so (although he or she does not lose the security interest thereby). The secured party can use or operate the collateral as permitted in the security agreement or to preserve its value. Should the collateral increase in value or profits be derived from it, the secured party can hold these increases as additional security unless they are in the form of money. Any increase in money must be either remitted to the debtor or applied to reduction of the secured obligation.

Under the same section, the secured party must keep the collateral identifiable (except that when the collateral is fungible, it can be commingled with like goods). He or she can repledge the collateral, but this must be done on terms that do not impair the debtor's right to redeem it upon paying the debt.

Again under the same section, unless the security agreement provides to the contrary, the debtor is responsible for all reasonable charges incurred in the custody, preservation, and operation of the collateral possessed by the secured party. These charges include insurance, taxes, storage, and the like.

The following case presents an interesting application of Sec. 9-207's provisions.

CITIBANK, N.A. v. DATA LEASE FINANCIAL CORP.

U.S. Eleventh Circuit Court of Appeals, 828 F.2d 686 (1987)

Case

On April 12, 1973, Citibank loaned $6.2 million to Data Lease. The collateral securing the loan included 870,000 shares (80.2 percent) of the capital stock of Miami National Bank. The pledge agreement expressly provided that, upon any default, Citibank had the absolute and exclusive right to vote the pledged shares. Data Lease defaulted by missing payments due July 12, 1974.

Miami National's financial soundness and competence of management were questioned by bank regulators in early 1975. Beginning in 1976, Citibank exercised its right under the pledge agreement to vote the Miami National stock it held as collateral. Indeed, Citibank elected the entire board. In December 1978, Citibank brought this foreclosure action. On February 29, 1979, the court ordered an emergency judicial sale of the pledged stock, which was purchased by Citibank for $3 million. Data Lease then filed a counterclaim, alleging that Citibank's mismanagement of Miami National had dramatically reduced the value of the collateral, in violation of the UCC, among other provisions. The district court granted summary judgment on this counterclaim to Citibank, and Data Lease appealed.

Vance, Circuit Judge:

Section 9-207 of the Uniform Commercial Code specifies a pledgee's duties with respect to the pledged collateral. Section 679.207(1), Florida Statutes, provides:

> A secured party must use reasonable care in the custody and preservation of collateral in his possession.

This duty applies "when the secured party has possession of the collateral before default, as a pledgee, and also when he has taken possession of the collateral after default." U.C.C. §9-207 comment. A secured party is liable for any loss caused by his failure to meet this standard of care. Fla. Stat. §679.207(3).

The district court held that Citibank had discharged this duty of reasonable care because Citibank "physically preserved" the paper certificates representing Miami National stock. Indeed, the general rule is that,

> a pledgee's duty with regards to the care of the pledged chattel is confined solely to the

physical care of the chattel and a pledgee is not liable for a decline in the value of pledged instruments.

See Tepper v. Chase Manhattan Bank, N.A., 376 So.2d 35, 36 (Fla. Dist.Ct.App. 1979). This rule is based on the common sense notion that a pledgee who has no control over a corporation cannot be held responsible for a dip in the price of stock.

For this reason, the law makes an exception when the pledged stock represents a controlling interest and the pledgee becomes involved in the management of the company. As the pledgee enters this new arena, its duty of reasonable care follows it and attaches to all its activities. In the present case, Data Lease has adduced evidence that Citibank used its power as controlling shareholder to install and maintain incompetent individuals in positions of management at Miami National. Additional evidence suggests that Citibank blithely allowed these individuals to deplete the value of the pledged collateral. We conclude that a jury could find that these actions constituted a breach of Citibank's statutory duty of reasonable care.

[Reversed.]

Debtor's Right to Request Status of Debt

Under Sec. 9-208, the debtor can sign a statement indicating what he or she believes to be the aggregate amount of the unpaid indebtedness as of a specific date (and, under certain circumstances, including a list of collateral covered by the security agreement) with the request that the secured party approve or correct the statement. The secured party, unless he or she has a reasonable excuse, must comply with the request within two weeks of receipt or be liable for any loss caused to the debtor by such failure. Since the debtor could become a nuisance by making numerous and continuous requests to the secured party, he or she is entitled to make such a request without charge only once every six months. For each additional request made during this period, the secured party can require payment of a fee not exceeding $10.

DEFAULT OF THE DEBTOR

In general, under Sec. 9-501, when the debtor is in default, the secured party can reduce his or her claim to judgment, foreclose, or otherwise enforce the security interest by any available judicial procedure. Under Sec. 9-503, unless otherwise agreed, the secured party also has the right to take possession of the collateral on default. This can be done without judicial process only if no breach of the peace occurs. Thus the creditor should not attempt to break into the debtor's home or take the collateral by force. If force is used, the debtor can file criminal charges against the secured party and can bring an action in tort for any damages he or she sustains. Although Section 9-503, the so-called "self-help" section on repossession, has been challenged by debtors in numerous cases on the ground that repossession without judicial process is a violation of the Due Process Clause of the U.S. Constitution, the highest courts of most states have ruled that the section is constitutional.

Duty to Assemble Collateral

Under Sec. 9-503, if the security agreement so provides, the secured party can require the debtor to assemble the collateral upon default and to make it available at a location reasonably convenient to both. If it is impractical to move the collateral or it is too expensive to store, the secured party has the right to render the collateral unusable to the debtor and, following the proper procedure, to dispose of it on the debtor's premises.

Disposal of Collateral

Under Sec. 9-504(1), once the secured party obtains possession, he or she generally has the right to sell, lease, or otherwise dispose of the collateral in its then existing condition or following any commercially reasonable preparation or process. Under 9-507(2), if the secured party sells the collateral, the sale must be handled in a "commercially reasonable manner." Although this is not expressly defined, the code does mention certain actions as being commercially reasonable. Sales made through such actions, or made otherwise and in good faith, are usually held to constitute compliance.

Under Sec. 9-504(3), the collateral can be disposed of at either a public or private sale if done in a commercially reasonable manner. Unless the collateral is perishable, threatens to decline quickly in value, or is of a type customarily sold in a recognized market, the secured party must give the debtor reasonable notice of the time and place of the sale (un-

less the debtor, after default, signed a statement renouncing or modifying this right to notification). No additional notification need be sent in the case of consumer goods, but in other cases notice must also be sent to any other secured creditor from whom the secured party has received written notice of a claim of an interest in the collateral. (Failure of the secured party to give such notice makes him or her liable for any ensuing loss.) The secured party can buy at *any* public sale—and at a private sale if the collateral customarily is sold in a recognized market or is of a type that is the subject of a widely distributed standard price quotation. (Under Sec. 9-501(3)(b), these provisions cannot be waived or varied.)

Under Sec. 9-504(4), when collateral is disposed of by a secured party after default of the debtor, a purchaser for value receives all the debtor's rights in the collateral free from the security interest and subordinate interests and liens. This is true even if the secured party failed to comply with the requirements of disposal under the code or under judicial proceedings, so long as the purchaser bought in good faith, and, at a public sale, had no knowledge of such interests or rights.

Section 9-505 provides that, except where the defaulting debtor has paid 60 percent of an obligation involving consumer goods, the secured party, upon obtaining possession of the goods, can *retain the collateral* in satisfaction of the secured obligation. However, to do so, the secured party must send written notice of such intention to the debtor and (except in the case of consumer goods) to any other secured party from whom written notice of a claim of an interest in the collateral has been received before such notification is sent to the debtor. If no objection is received from such parties within 21 days after notice is sent, the secured party can retain the collateral. But if any timely objection is received, the collateral must be disposed of in compliance with Sec. 9-504.

Section 9-505(1) provides that in the case of consumer goods, where the debtor has paid 60 percent or more of the obligation prior to default, the secured party must *dispose of the collateral* as previously discussed (in Sec. 9-504) within 90 days after taking possession—unless the debtor has signed a statement renouncing all rights in the collateral. Under Sec. 9-507(1), should the secured party fail to do so within this period, the debtor can recover an amount "not less than the credit service charge plus 10 percent of the principal amount of the debt or the time price differential plus 10 percent of the cash price." The secured party may thus suffer a loss by waiting too long to dispose of the collateral in this situation.

Application of Proceeds

The proceeds of the sale are, under Sec. 9-504(1), applied first to the expenses incurred by the secured party in retaking, holding, and selling or leasing the collateral—including reasonable attorney's fees if the security agreement so provides. After these expenses are deducted, the remaining proceeds are applied to the indebtedness of the secured party. If any proceeds are then left, subordinate security interests, if any, are to be satisfied if the subordinate interest holders have made written demand for payment before the proceeds were distributed. (Of course, the secured party can demand that these holders give reasonable proof of their claims.) Thus, even if a businessperson's security interest is second in priority, it is still possible for that person to receive part of the proceeds in satisfaction of the claim by following the UCC procedure.

As a general rule, under Sec. 9-504(2), if any surplus is left after the expenses have been paid and the indebtedness and subordinate security interests have been satisfied, it goes to the debtor. Furthermore, under Sec. 9-501(3)(a), the duty to account to the debtor for this surplus cannot be waived or varied by agreement. Should the proceeds not cover the expenses and the indebtedness to the secured party, under Sec. 9-504(2), the debtor is liable for the deficiency unless otherwise agreed. If the collateral involves the sale of accounts or chattel paper, the rules regarding distribution of surplus and deficiency apply only if they are provided for in the security agreement.

Redemption of Collateral

Section 9-506 provides that the debtor (or any other subordinate secured party) can redeem the collateral at any time before the primary secured party has disposed of (or contracted to dispose of) it, unless he or she has waived the right of redemption in writing after the default. The redemption is accomplished by tendering payment of all obligations secured by the collateral as well as all reasonable costs incurred by the secured party. Under Sec. 9-501(3)(d), a sale of part of the collateral does not remove the right of redemption for any collateral left in the hands of the secured party, and this right can be waived only in the manner indicated here.

TERMINATION

The ultimate goal of the parties is to have the debt paid and the security interest terminated, particularly where it has been perfected by a filing. To accomplish this, when the debt is paid, the secured party files a *termination statement* with the officer with whom the financing statement was filed.

Under Sec. 9-404, if the financing statement covers consumer goods, the secured party must file the termination statement within one month after the secured obligation is no longer outstanding; however, if the debtor demands the statement in writing, it must be filed within ten days after the obligation is no longer outstanding. Thus filing of a termination statement in the case of consumer goods is required even if no demand is made for it by the debtor. In all other cases the secured party must file or furnish the debtor with a termination statement within ten days after written demand is made by the debtor. If the secured party fails to file or furnish the statement to the debtor, he or she is liable to that person for $100 and for any loss caused to the debtor by such failure.

SUMMARY

The purposes of a secured transaction are twofold: (1) to give to a creditor a legally recognized interest in specific property of the debtor, and (2) to give such creditor a priority claim in that property against other creditors who may seek to have the debtor's assets sold in satisfaction of their claims. Secured transactions are governed by Article 9 of the UCC. Under the terminology of that article, the creditor is the secured party, the one owing the debt is the debtor, the interest of the creditor is a security interest, and the property subject to the interest is the collateral.

Secured transactions law applies only to secured interests in personal property. Such property may be classified as tangible collateral (consumer goods, equipment, farm products, and inventory); indispensable paper (documents of title, instruments, and chattel paper); and intangible collateral (accounts and general intangibles such as contractual and patent rights).

A security interest attaches (i.e., is created) by means of a security agreement between the secured party and the debtor. This agreement must be in writing unless the secured party takes possession of the collateral. (Since it is not possible for the creditor to take possession of an intangible, security agreements in intangibles must be in writing). After a security agreement is made, the secured party will ordinarily "perfect" the interest so that it will have maximum protection against claims of other parties to the collateral. (If there is no perfection, the secured party loses his or her interest to a party having a perfected interest in the same collateral; the secured party also loses the interest if the debtor goes into bankruptcy). Perfection is usually achieved by the filing of a financing statement by the creditor (at a designated office specified by the provisions of Article 9). Perfection may be achieved, however, by the secured creditor's taking possession of the collateral, and in some instances involving the sale of consumer goods on credit, perfection is automatic. There are special filing rules as to motor vehicles, fixtures, and to collateral moved to another state.

While a perfected interest is generally valid against all third parties, there are exceptions to this rule. A perfected creditor's interest, for example, is lost if the debtor sells the collateral to a buyer in the ordinary course of the debtor's business. Additionally, such interest is lost to a buyer *not* in the ordinary course of business under certain circumstances, and, where the collateral consists of negotiable instruments left in the debtor's possession, the creditor's interest is lost to a party who purchases them in good faith and for value.

A security agreement may cover a certain type of property (such as machinery or inventory) and such type of property as the debtor may acquire in the future. This protection can be achieved by use of an "after-acquired property" clause in the security agreement. However, this protection might be lost to the unpaid seller of such additional property who himself may have a purchase-money security in that property. A perfected security interest has priority over a nonperfected interest in the same property. Where are two or more perfected interests in the same property, the rule is that the interests rank "according to priority in filing or perfection, whichever is earlier." The rights and duties of the parties prior to termination of the interest generally are spelled out in the security agreement. In the event of a default by the debtor, the creditor's remedies are set forth in Sec. 9-501 of the UCC.

KEY TERMS

Secured transaction
Secured party
Debtor
Security interest
Security agreement
Collateral
Perfection
Financing statement
Goods
Fixtures
Indispensable paper collateral
Documents of title
Instrument
Chattel paper
Intangible collateral
Account
General intangibles
Attachment
Filing
Automatic perfection
Purchase money security interest
Buyer in the ordinary course of business
After-acquired property clause
Floating lien
Future advances clause

QUESTIONS AND PROBLEMS

1. Rike-Kumler, a jeweler, sold a $1,237 diamond ring to Nicolosi which he was going to give to his fiancée. Nicolosi made a down payment and executed a purchase money security agreement to Rike-Kumler for the unpaid balance. Rike-Kumler did not file a financing statement. Nicolosi gave the ring to his fiancée, and later went into bankruptcy. His fiancée called off the engagement and delivered the ring to the trustee in bankruptcy. Rike-Kumler then claimed a protected purchase money security interest in the ring, as against the trustee's claim. At the trial, the trustee in bankruptcy contended that the ring was not a "consumer good," because Nicolosi did not intend to wear it himself. Do you think that the ring was a consumer good? Why or why not? In regard to Rike-Kumler's claim, what difference does it make

whether the ring is or is not a consumer good? Explain. (*In re Nicolosi*, 4 UCC Rptr. 111, 1966.)

2. In order to expand its inventory of car and truck bumpers, Bumper Sales borrowed about $510,000 from Marepcon, a small, asset-based lender whose trade name is Norshipco. In return, Bumper Sales agreed to give Marepcon a security interest in its inventory, accounts receivable, and so on. To perfect its security interest, Marepcon filed three financing statements. The first was filed in the name of "Marepcon." The second two were filed in the name of "Norshipco." Does this inconsistency invalidate the financing statements? Discuss. (*In re Bumper Sales, Inc.*, 907 F.2d 1430, 4th Cir. 1990.)

3. Debtors bought furniture on credit from Factory Outlet Store, giving it a purchase money security interest in the furniture. Factory then assigned the obligation to a creditor. Thereafter, at the request of debtors, who were having trouble making the payments, the creditor refinanced the obligation, reducing the debtor's monthly installment payments from $105.50 to $58.00. The parties cancelled the old note and substituted therefore a new note and security agreement; this note extended the time for repayment and increased the interest rate. The back of the loan application stated that the creditor would retain the purchase money security interest. The creditor took no additional collateral as security and loaned only an additional $9.67 to the debtors. The debtors made one more payment and then declared bankruptcy. The debtors argued in bankruptcy that refinancing automatically extinguishes a purchase money security interest. Should this position be adopted? Discuss. (*In re Billings*, 838 F.2d 405, 10th Cir. 1988.)

4. Citizens National Bank & Trust Co. loaned money to a farmer. The loan was secured by the farmer's growing crops. The bank's security agreement covered crops growing "in and around" sections 22, 27, and 28. Is this description adequate? Discuss. (*In re Burkhart Farm & Livestock*, 938 F.2d 1114, 10th Cir. 1991.)

5. John Oliver Co. borrowed money from John Oliver, Sr. ("Oliver"), who loaned $62,000 to the company pursuant to four promissory notes. Oliver filed four financing statements, signed both by the debtor and the secured party, stating: "This financing statement covers the following types (or items) of prop-

erty: Raw, in process, and finished inventory to cover my interests up to $250,000." There were no separate security agreements. Has Oliver perfected his security interest? Discuss. (*In re John Oliver Co.*, 129 B.R. 1, D.N.H. Bkrtcy. 1991.)

6. Nelson Music Co. (debtor) agreed to guarantee a loan issued by First National Bank (FNB) to Nelson's sister corporation, Wichita Piano and Organ (WPO). One day later, Nelson itself borrowed money from FNB, granting it a security interest in its inventory. The security agreement contained a dragnet clause providing: "The security interest . . . shall secure all obligations of the undersigned to the bank howsoever created. . . ." FNB properly perfected its interest. One year later, Nelson entered into a revolving loan agreement with the Bank of Kansas (BOK), again granting a security interest in its inventory. Nelson paid off the FNB loan, but WPO defaulted. BOK claimed that FNB's security interest in the inventory expired when Nelson paid off its loan. FNB claimed that its guaranty was covered by the dragnet clause and that its security interest therefore still attached to the inventory. Who is right? (*Bank of Kansas v. Nelson Music Co., Inc.*, 949 F.2d 321, 10th Cir. 1991.)

7. A sold a horse to B. B agreed in writing to obtain an insurance policy covering the horse to the extent of the unpaid purchase price, naming A as the beneficiary. However, the buyer named himself as beneficiary and was paid the proceeds of the insurance policy by C, the insurance agent, after the horse died. A sued C, claiming that his written agreement with B had created a security interest in the horse and that C had committed conversion when he paid the insurance proceeds to B. Is A correct? (*Shebester v. Triple Crown Insurers*, 826 P.2d 603, Okla. 1992.)

8. Ziluck applied for a Radio Shack credit card by filling out and executing a Radio Shack RSVP Credit Card Application. He signed on the front above the following language: "I have read the Radio Shack Credit Account and Security Agreement, including the notice provisions in the last paragraph thereof, and it contains no blanks or blank spaces. I agree to the terms of the Agreement and acknowledge receipt of a copy of the Agreement." On the back of the application was the Radio Shack Credit Account and Security Agreement, paragraph 12 of which provided: "SECURITY INTEREST. We retain a

security interest under the Uniform Commercial Code in all merchandise charged to your account." Tandy issued Ziluck a credit card and he used it to buy several items from Radio Shack retail stores. Two years later, Ziluck filed for bankruptcy protection. The bankruptcy court ruled that Tandy's form did not contain a sufficient description of the goods and that Tandy's purchase money security interest therefore failed to attach to the consumer goods bought by Ziluck. Did the bankruptcy court rule correctly? (*In re Ziluck,* 139 B.R. 44, S.D.Fla. 1992.)

9. On September 22, 1981, Bobby Crites bought a new Case tractor from Jensen's Inc., a farm equipment dealer. Crites executed an installment contract and security agreement for the purchase of the tractor. These were assigned to Case, which properly filed a financing statement covering the tractor. The security agreement prohibited Crites from selling or transferring the tractor without Case's consent. In June 1982, Timm bought the tractor from Crites for $35,000 cash. Timm did not know of Case's interest. When Case learned of the sale, it sued Timm for possession of the tractor. Crites soon filed bankruptcy. Is Case entitled to the tractor, or is Timm?

Discuss. (*J.I. Case Credit Corp. v. Crites,* 851 F.2d 309, 10th Cir. 1988.)

10. Plaintiffs owned Golden Manor Corporation, which had borrowed $350,000 from Wainwright Bank and the Small Business Administration (SBA). Golden Manor owned a restaurant that failed and went into receivership. On April 20, 1981, a state court rendered judgment in favor of the SBA, allowing it to foreclose on the property of Golden Manor. The SBA then requested that the county sheriff publish a notice of foreclosure in a local newspaper of general circulation on May 28, June 4, and June 11. Notices were also posted in three public places in the county and at the door of the county courthouse. On July 9, a public sale was held by the county sheriff; Golden Manor's realty was purchased by the SBA as the highest bidder for $235,000. Because earlier appraisals had pegged the value of the reality at $420,000 and $315,000, respectively, plaintiffs sued the SBA, claiming that it had not disposed of the assets in a "commercially reasonable manner." Are plaintiffs correct? Discuss. (*Wainwright Bank v. Railroadmens Federal Savings,* 806 F.2d 146, 7th Cir. 1986.)

Overview of Debtor - Creditor Relations

Bankruptcy Proceedings

Liquidation Proceedings

Business Reorganization

Adjustment of Debts

OVERVIEW OF DEBTOR-CREDITOR RELATIONS

The treatment of debtors has varied greatly over the years. During certain early periods, debtors were forced to become servants of their creditors, were thrown into prison, or even had body parts removed for failure to pay a debt. History finally demonstrated to both creditors and society that very little was accomplished by such methods. In seeking more humane solutions, the general problem has been how to balance the creditor's rights with the debtor's desire for relief from debts.

Numerous devices have been developed through the years for resolving debtor-creditor disputes. In this chapter we will deal primarily with one such procedure—*bankruptcy under federal law.* However, many of the other methods available under state common-law principles, state statutes, and private agreements may actually be preferable to bankruptcy when it is possible to use them. Bankruptcy has traditionally been viewed as an avenue of last resort. Before we turn to a detailed examination of the federal bankruptcy law, we first will survey some of the alternatives.

Alternatives to Bankruptcy

Although time and space do not permit a detailed analysis of each method of debt resolution, the following methods are frequently used when a debtor cannot pay his or her obligation: (1) foreclosure on a real estate mortgage, (2) enforcement of a secured transaction (Article 9 of the UCC), (3) enforcement of an artisan's lien, (4) enforcement of a mechanic's lien, (5) writ of execution on a judgment, (6) garnishment, (7) attachment, (8) receivership, (9) cancelling a fraudulent conveyance, (10) composition of creditors, and (11) assignment for the benefit of creditors.

Foreclosure on a Real Estate Mortgage

When a mortgagor (debtor) defaults under the terms of a mortgage agreement, the mortgagee (creditor) has the right to declare the entire mortgage debt due and enforce his or her rights through a remedy called **foreclosure.** In most states the mortgagee is required to sell the mortgaged real estate (even if it is the person's homestead) under the direction of the court, using the proceeds to pay the foreclosure costs and the balance of the debt. If any proceeds are left over, the surplus goes to the mortgagor. If the proceeds are insufficient to cover the costs of foreclosure and the remaining indebtedness, the mortgagor is liable to the mortgagee for the unpaid balance of the debt. However, before the actual foreclosure sale and for a certain period of time thereafter (set by state statute), the mortgagor can *redeem* the property by full payment of costs, indebtedness, and interest.

Enforcement of a Secured Transaction

As we saw in the last chapter, under Article 9 of the UCC, when a debtor defaults on the security agreement made with a secured party (the creditor), the collateral (personal property) that is the subject of the security agreement can be used to satisfy the debt. The secured party can retain possession of the collateral or take it from the debtor, either by court order or without court action if it can be accomplished peaceably. He or she can then either (1) *keep the collateral* in satisfaction of the debt by giving proper notice to the debtor of such intention (assuming the debtor does not object), or (2) *sell the collateral* through a "commercially reasonable" process. The secured party must always sell the collateral if proper objection is made by the debtor to the party keeping it or if the collateral is classified as "consumer goods" and the debtor has paid 60 percent or more of the debt.

If the collateral is kept by the secured party, the debt is discharged. If the collateral is sold and the proceeds are insufficient to pay the debt and the costs of enforcing the security interest, the secured party is usually entitled to seek a deficiency judgment for the balance. The debtor can redeem the collateral at any time until its sale or disposal.

Enforcement of an Artisan's Lien

The **artisan's lien,** a possessory lien given to creditors who perform services on personal property or take care of goods entrusted to them, was developed at common law. If the debtor does not pay for the services, the creditor is permitted to obtain a judgment and/or to foreclose and sell the property in satisfaction of the debt. Any proceeds remaining from the sale of the property after paying the debt and costs of sale must be returned to the debtor. In order to exercise this lien, the creditor must have retained possession of the property and must not have agreed to provide the services on credit. Many states have passed statutes governing the procedures to be followed in enforcing such a lien. If the creditor operates a warehouse and the claim arises from unpaid storage charges, the procedures which must be followed are set forth in Article 7 of the Uniform Commercial Code.

Enforcement of a Mechanic's Lien

Certain other liens have been made available to creditors by state statutes. One of the most common is the **mechanic's lien**—a lien against real estate for labor, services, or materials used in improving the realty. When the labor or materials are furnished, a debt is incurred. To make the real property itself security for the debt, the creditor must file a notice of lien in a manner provided by statute. To be effective, it usually must be filed within a specified period (usually 60 to 120 days) after the last materials or labor were furnished. If the notice is properly filed and the debt is not paid, the creditor can foreclose and sell the realty in satisfaction of the debt. (This is similar to a foreclosure of a real estate mortgage.)

Writ of Execution on a Judgment

Once a debt becomes overdue, a creditor can file suit for payment in a court of law and, if successful, be awarded a "judgment." If the judgment is not satisfied by the debtor, the creditor has the right to go back to court and obtain a **writ of execution.** The writ, issued by the clerk of the court, directs the sheriff or other officer to levy upon (seize) and sell any of the debtor's *nonexempt property* within the court's jurisdiction. The judgment is paid from the proceeds of the sale, and any balance is returned to the debtor. One limitation on the writ is that it can be levied only on nonexempt property. That is, exempt property, such as the debtor's homestead, cannot be taken to satisfy the judgment.

Garnishment

Another limitation of the writ of execution is that it usually cannot reach debts owed to the judgment debtor by third parties or the debtor's interests in personal property legally possessed by third parties. However, the law does permit the creditor (using the proper court procedure) to require these persons to turn over to the court or sheriff money owed or property belonging to the debtor. This method of satisfying a judgment is called **garnishment;** the third party, called the *garnishee,* is legally bound by the court order. The most common types of "property" garnished are wages and bank accounts. The federal Consumer Credit Protection Act limits garnishment of a debtor's current wages to 25 percent of take-home pay, and prohibits the debtor's employer from discharging him or her because of garnishment for "any one indebtedness." Some state laws place greater restrictions on garnishment of wages.

Attachment

The seizing of a debtor's property under a court order, known as *attachment,* is a statutory remedy and can be exercised only in strict accordance with the provisions of the particular state statutes. It is available to a creditor even *before* a judgment has been rendered, under some statutes. Statutory grounds for attachment prior to judgment are limited, usually including situations where the debtor is unavailable to be served with a summons or where there is a reasonable belief that the debtor may conceal or remove property from the jurisdiction of the court before the creditor can obtain a judgment.

To employ attachment as a remedy, the creditor must file with the court an affidavit attesting to the debtor's default and the legal reasons why attachment is sought. Additionally, the creditor must post a bond sufficient to cover at least the value of the debtor's property, the value of the loss of use of the goods suffered by the debtor (if any), and court costs in case the creditor loses the suit. Most states require the opportunity for some form of hearing before a judge. The court then issues a *writ of attachment,* directing the sheriff or other officer to seize nonexempt property sufficient to satisfy the creditor's claim. If the creditor's suit against the debtor is successful, the property seized can then be sold to satisfy the judgment.

Receivership

Attachment may prove inadequate to protect creditors while they pursue their claims if the debtor's property requires care (such as crops, livestock, etc.). In such cases, on essentially the same grounds as for attachment, the court may appoint a *receiver* to care for and preserve the property pending the outcome of the lawsuit in which one or more creditors are seeking to collect unpaid debts. It is then said that the debtor's property is placed in **receivership.** The object of receivership is to prevent a debtor from "wasting" assets while being pursued by creditors. Receivership may also be the appropriate protective device where the debtor has a going business and where creditors can convince the court that it is being grossly mismanaged.

Cancelling a Fraudulent Conveyance

A debtor may transfer property to a third party by gift or contract under circumstances in which his or her creditors are defrauded. If such fraud can be established, any creditor can have the conveyance (transfer) set aside and the property made subject to his or her claim—even if the property is in the hands of a third party.

The fraud necessary to have a conveyance set aside can be either fraud in fact or fraud implied in law. **Fraud in fact** occurs when a debtor transfers property with the specific intent of defrauding his or her creditors. A creditor will usually encounter difficulty in having a conveyance voided on this ground, simply because of the inherent problems in proving fraudulent intent. The creditor's chances of proving this intent will, however, be somewhat greater if the transfer was to the debtor's spouse or other relative. In addition, it is often the case that the debtor actually had no such fraudulent intent, but the creditor is harmed nevertheless.

To assist the creditor, most states have enacted laws (such as the Uniform Fraudulent Conveyance Act) which create a *presumption* of fraud under certain circumstances. This means that, in some situations, the burden of proof shifts to the debtor. If the debtor fails to prove the absence of fraud, there is **fraud implied in law** and the transfer is voided. Generally speaking, these statutes create a presumption of fraud whenever a debtor transfers property without receiving "fair consideration" in return and the debtor has insufficient assets remaining to satisfy creditors.

Composition of Creditors

Sometimes a debtor or his or her creditors recognize early (before bankruptcy) that the debtor is in financial difficulty. Instead of pursuing remedies under bankruptcy, the debtor and creditors make a *contract* to resolve the debts. The contract—referred to as a **composition of creditors**—calls for the debtor's immediate payment of a sum less than that owed and for the creditor's immediate discharge of the debt. This payment can be made from any of the debtor's assets, including exempt property. Such contracts are held to be binding by the courts. The advantage of an immediate payment and minimum costs makes the composition attractive to creditors. Whether the composition agreement is binding on nonparticipating creditors depends on state law. At common law the agreement was not binding on these creditors.

Assignment for the Benefit of Creditors

Under common-law principles and, in some states, under statute, an **assignment for the benefit of creditors** is available as an alternative to bankruptcy. In such an arrangement, the debtor voluntarily transfers title to some or all assets to a "trustee" or "as-

signee" for the creditors' benefit. By such a transfer, the debtor irrevocably gives up any claim to or control over the property. The trustee or assignee liquidates (sells) the property and makes payment to the creditors on a pro rata basis according to the debt amounts.

Creditors can either accept or reject the partial payment. One accepting such a payment may in effect be releasing the balance of his or her claim. In most states, creditors who do not participate in the assignment cannot reach the assets that have been so assigned. They do, however, have rights to any surplus remaining after participating creditors have been paid, any nonexempt property not assigned, and any nonexempt property acquired after the assignment. Nonparticipating creditors may also be able to force the debtor into bankruptcy.

BANKRUPTCY PROCEEDINGS
History of Bankruptcy Statutes

Bankruptcy as a legal device was initially applied only to commercial business failures. The first Bankruptcy Act in England was adopted in 1542 and applied only to traders or merchants who were unable to pay their debts. It was not until 1861 that bankruptcy was extended to other types of debtors.

The founders of the United States were well acquainted with the problems of debtors. In drafting the U.S. Constitution they stated in Article I, Section 8, clause 4: "The Congress shall have the power . . . to establish . . . uniform laws on the subject of bankruptcies throughout the United States."

Bankruptcy Proceedings Today

Today's bankruptcy law comes primarily from the 1978 Bankruptcy Reform Act, also known as the Bankruptcy Code. The Code has been amended several times since 1978; our discussion will include those changes. Before 1978, federal district courts handled bankruptcy cases, often delegating the responsibility for hearing them to "bankruptcy referees" who were not federal judges but who performed many of the same functions. The 1978 Code established a set of bankruptcy courts, with one such court in each federal district. Bankruptcy judges are complemented by U.S. Trustees who, as we shall see, usually select the trustees who administer the debtors' estates.

Bankruptcy courts hear and decide all of the issues directly involving the bankruptcy proceeding itself, but related nonbankruptcy matters, such as a tort claim by or against the debtor, are decided by the federal district court. An appeal from a bankruptcy court decision is heard by a federal district court or, under certain conditions, by a bankruptcy appellate panel.

As we noted earlier, bankruptcy has traditionally been a solution of last resort. Despite this fact, hundreds of thousands of cases are filed each year under the federal bankruptcy law. The large number of cases is not, however, the only reason for the importance of modern bankruptcy law. Many people have their only direct exposure to our legal system in bankruptcy proceedings. In bankruptcy court debtors and creditors alike find final, if not totally satisfactory, conclusions to disputes that may have seemed endless. In bankruptcy court businesses of all sizes are liquidated or rehabilitated, often affecting the livelihoods of many employees, the security of suppliers and customers, and even the economies of local communities.

The 1978 Code provides for three different kinds of proceedings: (1) liquidation; (2) reorganization; and (3) adjustment of the debts of an individual with regular income. The Family Farmer Bankruptcy Act of 1986 includes an additional kind of proceeding, a separate chapter in the Bankruptcy Code which provides adjustment of debts for family farmers. Our discussion focuses primarily on the liquidation proceeding, often referred to as "straight bankruptcy," because it is the most common type. We will, however, devote some attention to the other three types of proceedings at the end of this chapter. It should also be noted that current bankruptcy law contains a special section dealing with the rehabilitation of bankrupt *municipalities*, which is beyond the scope of our discussion.

LIQUIDATION PROCEEDINGS

Stated very generally, the object of a **liquidation proceeding** under Chapter 7 of the Bankruptcy Act is to sell the debtor's assets, pay off creditors insofar as it is possible to do so, and legally discharge the debtor from further responsibility.

Commencement of the Proceedings

A liquidation proceeding will be either a *voluntary case*, commenced by the debtor, or an *involuntary case*, commenced by creditors.

Voluntary Case

The filing of a **voluntary case** automatically subjects the debtor and its property to the jurisdiction and supervision of the Bankruptcy Court. Any debtor, whether an individual, a partnership, or a corpora-

tion, may file a petition for voluntary bankruptcy, with the following exceptions: (1) banks, (2) savings and loan associations, (3) credit unions, (4) insurance companies, (5) railroads, and (6) governmental bodies. These exempted organizations are covered by special statutes and their liquidation is supervised by particular regulatory agencies.

A debtor does *not* have to be insolvent in order to file a petition for voluntary bankruptcy, but as a practical matter it is usually insolvency that prompts such a petition.[1] In addition, a husband and wife may file a joint case if both consent.

Involuntary Case

The types of organizations which are not permitted to file a voluntary liquidation case also cannot be subjected to an **involuntary case.** In addition to these exemptions, creditors also cannot file an involuntary case against *farmers*,[2] *family farmers*,[3] or *nonprofit corporations*.

If the debtor has twelve or more creditors, at least three must join in filing the case. If there are fewer than twelve creditors, the involuntary case may be filed by one or more of them. Regardless of the number of creditors, those filing the petition must have noncontingent unsecured claims against the debtor totalling in the aggregate at least $5000.

The debtor and its property automatically become subject to the jurisdiction and supervision of the bankruptcy court if the involuntary petition is not challenged. However, if the debtor contests the creditors' petition, they must prove either (1) that the debtor has not been paying debts as they became due or (2) that the debtor's property has been placed in a receivership or an assignment for the benefit of creditors within 120 days before the involuntary petition was filed. If the filing creditors prove either of the above, the debtor and its property are then under the supervision of the court. If no such proof is made, the petition is dismissed.

---

[1] Insolvency is defined in the federal bankruptcy law as the financial condition of a debtor whose debts exceed the fair market value of assets. The definition of insolvency under state law, as set forth in UCC Sec. 1-201(23), is broader. It states that a debtor is insolvent in the above situation *or* when the debtor "fails to pay his debts in the ordinary course of business or cannot pay his debts as they become due."

[2] Farmers other than in the term "family farmers" are defined as persons (which includes individuals, partnerships, or corporations) who received more than 80 percent of their gross income during the preceding taxable year from farming operations owned and operated by them. "Farming operations" includes growing crops, dairy farming, and raising livestock or poultry.

[3] The term "family farmers," important since the 1986 amendment to the Code, is defined later in this chapter.

Automatic Stay

As soon as the petition is filed in either a voluntary or involuntary case, an automatic stay is in operation. The automatic stay puts creditors' claims "on hold" until they are dealt with in the bankruptcy proceeding, and prevents creditors from taking any judicial, administrative, or other action against the debtor. A *secured creditor*, however, may petition the bankruptcy court and receive protection against the loss of its security. The court-ordered protection for secured creditors may take the form of cash payments from the debtor, substitute collateral, or an express grant of relief from the automatic stay permitting foreclosure of the security interest.

The Trustee

After the debtor becomes subject to the bankruptcy proceeding, the U.S. Trustee must appoint an **interim trustee** to take over the debtor's property or business. A U.S. Trustee is appointed in each of 29 regions (consisting of one or more judicial districts) to monitor certain aspects of bankruptcy cases and to appoint and supervise the standing and panel trustees. Within a relatively short time thereafter, a **permanent trustee** will take over. This trustee may be elected by the creditors, but if they do not do so, the interim trustee receives permanent status.

The trustee is an individual or corporation who, under the court's supervision, administers and represents the *debtor's estate*. (Which property is included within the debtor's estate is discussed later.) The basic duties of the trustee are to: (1) investigate the financial affairs of the debtor; (2) collect assets and claims owned by the debtor; (3) temporarily operate the debtor's business if necessary; (4) reduce the debtor's assets to cash; (5) receive and examine the claims of creditors, and challenge in bankruptcy court any claim which the trustee feels to be questionable; (6) oppose the debtor's discharge from its obligations when the trustee feels that there are legal reasons why the debtor should not be discharged; (7) render a detailed accounting to the court of all assets received and the disposition made of them; and (8) make a final report to the court when administration of the debtor's estate is completed. To fulfill these duties as representative of the debtor's estate, the trustee has the power to sue and be sued in that capacity, to use or sell property of the estate, and to employ accountants, attorneys, appraisers, auctioneers, and other professionals with court approval.

If they wish, unsecured creditors may elect a creditors' committee of three to eleven members for the purpose of consulting with the trustee. This committee may make recommendations to the trustee or U.S. Trustee regarding the latter's duties and may submit questions to the court or U.S. Trustee concerning administration of the debtor's estate.

Creditors' Meetings

Within a reasonable time after commencement of the case, the U.S. Trustee must call and preside at a meeting of unsecured creditors. The debtor will have already supplied the court with a list of creditors, so that they may be notified of the meeting. The judge of the bankruptcy court is not permitted to attend a creditors' meeting.

At the first meeting, creditors may elect the trustee. In order for such election to be possible, at least 20 percent of the total amount of unsecured claims which have been filed and allowed must be represented at the meeting. A trustee is elected by receiving the votes of creditors holding a majority, in amount, of unsecured claims represented at the meeting.

The other major item of business at the first creditors' meeting is an *examination of the debtor*. The debtor, under oath, will be questioned by the creditors and the trustee concerning (1) the debtor's assets, and (2) matters relevant to whether the debtor will be entitled to a discharge.

Duties of the Debtor

The bankruptcy law imposes the following duties on the debtor: (1) within a reasonable time after commencement of the proceedings, file with the court a list of creditors, a schedule of assets and liabilities, a schedule of income and expenditures, and a statement of financial affairs; (2) file with the court a statement of intention with respect to the retention or surrender of any property of the estate which secures consumer debt, specifying that such property shall be claimed as exempt, redeemed, or the debt reaffirmed thereon, and perform these intentions within 45 days after filing the notice; (3) cooperate and respond truthfully during the examination conducted at the first creditors' meeting; (4) surrender to the trustee all property to be included in the debtor's estate, as well as all documents, books, and records pertaining to this property; (5) cooperate with the trustee in whatever way necessary to enable the trustee to perform his or her duties; and (6) appear at the hearing conducted by the court concerning whether the debtor should be discharged.

A debtor who fails to fulfill any of these duties may be denied a discharge from liabilities.

The Debtor's Estate
Types of Property

The property owned by the debtor which becomes subject to the bankruptcy proceeding, ultimately to be sold by the trustee, is the **debtor's estate.** This includes all tangible and intangible property interests of any kind, unless specifically exempted. For example, the estate could consist of consumer goods, inventory, equipment, any of the various types of interests in real estate, patent rights, trademarks, copyrights, accounts receivable, and various contract rights.

After-Acquired Property

In addition to property owned at the time the bankruptcy petition (either voluntary or involuntary) was filed, the debtor's estate also includes after-acquired property under some circumstances. Specifically, the estate includes any type of property which the debtor acquires, or becomes entitled to acquire, within 180 days after the petition filing date (1) by inheritance, (2) as a beneficiary of a life insurance policy, or (3) as a result of a divorce decree or a property settlement agreement with the debtor's spouse. And, of course, if a particular item of property is part of the estate, any proceeds, income, production, or offspring from it will also be part of the estate. However, the debtor's earnings from his or her own labor or personal service after the filing date are *not* included in the estate.

Exemptions

A debtor who is an individual (rather than a partnership or corporation) may claim certain **exemptions.** This means that certain types of property are *exempt* and are not included in the debtor's estate. The debtor may keep such property and still receive a discharge from liabilities at the close of the proceedings. Every state has exemption statutes setting forth the types of property which are exempt from seizure under a writ of execution. Before passage of the 1978 Bankruptcy Code, the debtor's exempt property in a federal bankruptcy case was determined solely by the exemption statutes of the state where he or she lived. The 1978 Code, however, included

for the first time a list of federal exemptions which are available to the debtor in bankruptcy regardless of the state of domicile.

Under the 1978 Code the debtor may claim the following exemptions (and *each* spouse may claim them in a joint case): (1) the debtor's interest in a homestead used as a residence, up to a value of $7500; (2) the debtor's interest in a motor vehicle, up to $1200; (3) the debtor's interest, up to $200 *per item*, in household furnishings, appliances, wearing apparel, animals, crops, or musical instruments which are owned primarily for personal, family, or household (nonbusiness) uses, subject to a total of $4000 for all such items; (4) the debtor's interest in jewelry, up to a total of $500, which is owned primarily for personal, family, or household uses; (5) the debtor's interest in any kind of property, up to a limit of $400; (6) any unused portion of the $7500 homestead exemption, subject to a limit of $3750; (7) the debtor's interest in implements, tools, or professional books used in his or her trade, not to exceed $750 in value; (8) any unmatured life insurance policies owned by the debtor (except for credit life policies); (9) professionally prescribed health aids; (10) the debtor's right to receive various government benefits, such as unemployment compensation, social security, and veteran's benefits; (11) the debtor's right to receive various private benefits, such as alimony, child support, and pension payments, to the extent reasonably necessary for support of the debtor or the debtor's dependents; and (12) the right to receive damage awards for bodily injury.

Unfortunately, the 1978 Code has not brought about a great deal of national uniformity in the exemptions given to bankrupt debtors, for two reasons. First, the Code also includes a provision permitting the debtor to choose either the federal exemptions or those of the state where the debtor lives.[4] Because some state exemption laws are more advantageous than the federal exemptions for certain debtors, disparate state exemption laws continue to be important in federal bankruptcy cases. Second, Congress further stated in the 1978 Code that any state legislature can prohibit debtors in that state from using the federal exemptions in a bankruptcy case. The legislatures in a majority of states have done so; in these states, bankrupt debtors must use the state exemptions.

---

[4]The debtor must choose one or the other, as a whole; there cannot be a selection of some exemptions from the federal law and some from a state law.

The debtor also has the power to avoid a lien on his exempt property if such lien is a judicial lien or a non-possessory, nonpurchase-money security interest in personal-use goods, tools of the trade, or health aids. This preserves used, essential personal items for the debtor which were taken as collateral in order to threaten repossession rather than for their resale value.

Even though bankruptcy proceedings are governed by federal law, the ownership interests of a bankrupt debtor in particular items of property ordinarily are determined by *state* law. On the other hand, if a principle of state law conflicts with the overall purposes of the Bankruptcy Code, the state rule will not be applied.

IN RE ATCHISON

U.S. Court of Appeals, Seventh Circuit, 925 F.2d 209 (1991)

Case

On April 16, 1987, less than three months before filing her bankruptcy petition, debtor Anola Atchison executed a disclaimer of inheritance of property given to her under the will of her deceased father. As a result of this disclaimer, the property passed to her children. On July 8, 1987, debtor and her husband filed a joint petition in bankruptcy under Chapter 7. The bankruptcy trustee sued the debtor and her children (defendants), asking the court to rule that the inheritance was part of the bankruptcy estate. The bankruptcy judge ruled for defendants and the trustee appealed. The district court affirmed; the trustee again appealed.

Will, Senior District Judge:

The sole question is whether Anola's disclaimer was a "transfer of an interest of the debtor in property" which the trustee may avoid under Section 548(a). The Bankruptcy Code defines the word

"transfer" to include "every mode . . . of . . . parting with . . . an interest in property," 11 U.S.C. Sec. 101(50), but it does not define what constitutes an interest in property. Absent a federal provision to the contrary, a debtor's interest in property is determined by applicable state law. The parties agree that Illinois law controls.

Under Illinois law, Anola's testamentary gift passed directly to her upon her father's death. She chose to exercise her right to reject the property by executing a disclaimer. Once the disclaimer was executed, the property passed as if Anola had predeceased her father and the disclaimer related back to the date of his death "for all purposes." Ill.Rev.Stat., Ch. 110-1/2, para. 2-7(d). Therefore, the effect of the disclaimer was to prevent Anola from ever acquiring an interest in the property.

The trustee argues that the disclaimer constituted a transfer of an interest in property because when Anola executed the disclaimer she must have had an interest which could be disclaimed. But she did not. The relation back provision of the Illinois disclaimer

statute eliminated any interest Anola held at the time of the disclaimer. Although there is a presumption that a beneficiary accepts a testamentary gift, a valid disclaimer overcomes this presumption and retroactively erases any interest in the beneficiary disclaiming.

A debtor's disclaimer relates back to the death of the testator whether or not it adversely affects the interest of creditors. The relation back doctrine favors the right of beneficiaries to reject a gift over competing interests. This does not unfairly prejudice creditors. Although the doctrine operates to permit a debtor to dodge creditors who might otherwise have access to inherited property, a testamentary gift could not be disclaimed if the debtor had used this property as a basis for acquiring credit. Illinois law protects creditors by limiting the right to disclaim to those beneficiaries who have not acted in a manner inconsistent with a complete renunciation of any rights to the disclaimed property, and there is no allegation that Anola acted in any manner which rendered her disclaimer invalid.

Affirmed.

Voidable Transfers

In a number of circumstances, the trustee has the power to sue and restore to the debtor's estate property or funds which the debtor (or someone acting in the debtor's behalf) had transferred to some third party. These situations, called **voidable transfers**, are as follows:

1. The trustee generally may cancel any transfer of property of the debtor's estate which was made *after* the debtor became subject to the bankruptcy proceeding. The trustee must exercise this power within two years after the transfer was made, or before the bankruptcy case is concluded, whichever occurs first.

2. The trustee may cancel any *fraudulent transfer* made by the debtor within one year prior to the filing of the bankruptcy petition. This power of the trustee applies to both *fraud in fact* and *fraud implied in law,* as discussed earlier in the chapter. It will be remembered that insolvency is an element of fraud implied in law. In determining the fair value of assets for this purpose under the bankruptcy law, exempt property and the property transferred in the particular transaction being challenged are not included.

3. The trustee has the power to cancel a property transfer on any ground that the debtor could have used, such as fraud, mistake, duress, undue influence, incapacity, or failure of consideration.

Voidable Preferences

One of the fundamental objectives of the bankruptcy law is to insure equal treatment of most types of unsecured creditors. The primary reason why we are so concerned with equal treatment of creditors, of course, is that a bankrupt debtor's assets are usually sufficient to pay only a fraction of creditors' total claims. As a result of this concern, the trustee has the power to cancel any transfer by the debtor to a creditor which amounted to a **preference.** A preference is essentially a transfer of property or money, in payment of an existing debt, which causes that creditor to receive more of the debtor's estate than he or she would be entitled to receive in the bankruptcy proceeding had the transfer not occurred.

General Rules for Cancelling Preferences

In the ordinary situation, a preferential transfer to a creditor can be cancelled by the trustee, and the property or funds returned to the debtor's estate, if (1) it occurred within *90 days* prior to the filing of the bankruptcy petition, and (2) the debtor was *insolvent* at the time of the transfer. In this situation, however, insolvency is *presumed.* In other words, if a creditor has received a preferential transfer within the 90-day period prior to the filing of the bankruptcy petition, that creditor must prove that the debtor was *not* insolvent.

Insiders

If the creditor receiving the preference was an **insider,** the trustee's power of cancellation extends to any such transfer made within *one year* before the bankruptcy petition was filed. In general, an insider is an individual or business firm which had a close rela-

tionship with the debtor at the time of the transfer. Examples would include a relative or partner of the debtor, a corporation of which the debtor was a director or officer, or a director or officer of a corporate debtor. In such a case, however, the presumption of insolvency only applies to the 90 days prior to the petition filing. Therefore, if the preference being challenged by the trustee had taken place more than 90 days but less than a year before the petition filing, the trustee must prove that the debtor was insolvent. Figure 30.1 illustrates the rules for cancelling preferences to insiders and other creditors.

Exceptions

In certain circumstances, a payment or transfer to a creditor cannot be cancelled even though it meets the basic requirements of a voidable preference. Three of the most important exceptions are:

1. A transaction which involved a "contemporaneous" (that is, within a very short period of time) exchange between debtor and creditor cannot be cancelled by the trustee. For example, the debtor may have bought goods from the creditor and either paid for them immediately or within a few days. This type of transaction is treated differently than one in which the debtor was paying off a debt which had existed for some time. Such a contemporaneous exchange will be left standing even though it occurred during the 90-day period prior to the filing date.

2. Even though there is no contemporaneous exchange, a payment or transfer to a creditor within the 90-day period will not be cancelled if (1) the particular debt had been incurred by the debtor in the ordinary course of business, (2) the payment was made in the ordinary course of the debtor's business, and (3) the payment was made according to ordinary business terms. An example would be the debtor's payment, during the 90-day period, of the previous month's utility bill.

3. A debtor's repayment during the 90-day period of up to $600 in *consumer debt* is not treated as a voidable preference.

Voidable preferences can occur in an almost infinite variety of circumstances. The following case illustrates one such situation, and also shows one of the many reasons why it is so important for a creditor to obtain and perfect a security interest whenever possible.

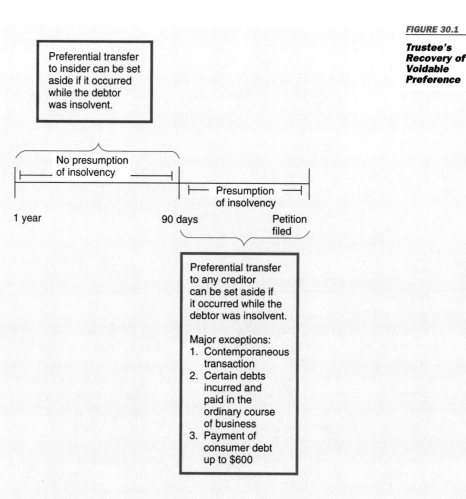

FIGURE 30.1

Trustee's Recovery of Voidable Preference

Preferential transfer to insider can be set aside if it occurred while the debtor was insolvent.

No presumption of insolvency

1 year

Presumption of insolvency

90 days

Petition filed

Preferential transfer to any creditor can be set aside if it occurred while the debtor was insolvent.

Major exceptions:
1. Contemporaneous transaction
2. Certain debts incurred and paid in the ordinary course of business
3. Payment of consumer debt up to $600

In re Fisher

U.S. Bankruptcy Court, S.D. Ohio, 100 Bankr. Rptr. 351 (1989)

Defendant Almiro Fur Fashion Design ("Almiro") was a furrier who supplied furs to Kinston Lee Furriers when it was formerly owned and operated by debtor Julius Fisher under an arrangement giving Fisher the right to return unsold furs. As we saw in Chapter 21 concerning sales of goods, a "sale or return" is a sale transaction in which the buyer has a right to return the items to the seller within an agreed time period. A true sale or return actually transfers title to the buyer until a particular article is returned. In contrast, a "sale on approval" is a transaction in which the buyer has an agreed period of time to decide whether to keep the goods, with no title passing until the expiration of that time or until the buyer affirmatively indicates a desire to keep them. In other words, a sale on approval is a "consignment," the supplier being the "consignor" and the one holding them being the "consignee." A consignee is merely an agent for the purpose of selling the principal's goods, and owns no interest in them. When a right of return exists and the parties have not specified whether it is a sale or return or a sale on approval, the UCC provides that it usually is a "sale or return" if the goods are taken by the buyer for the purpose of resale, and a sale on approval if they are taken by the buyer for the purpose of use.

(continues)

(continued from previous page)

    Under this arrangement with Almiro, Fisher received and held several mink coats ("Minks") having an approximate total wholesale value of $11,155. Almiro did not take a security interest in the Minks. Fisher returned the Minks to Almiro. Less than three months later, Fisher filed a voluntary petition under Chapter 7 of the Bankruptcy Code. The bankruptcy trustee (plaintiff) claimed that Fisher's return of the Minks to Almiro was a voidable preference and filed a complaint against Fisher (defendant) seeking to have the value of the Minks restored to the bankrupt debtor's estate.

Cole, Bankruptcy Judge:

Section 547(b) of the Bankruptcy Code provides as follows:

    (b) Except as provided in subsection (c) of this section, the trustee may avoid any transfer of an interest of the debtor in property—

    (1) to or for the benefit of a creditor;

    (2) for or on account of an antecedent debt owed by the debtor before such transfer was made;

    (3) made while the debtor was insolvent;

    (4) made—

    (A) on or within 90 days before the date of the filing of the petition; . . .

    (5) that enables such creditor to receive more than such creditor would receive if—

    (A) the case were a case under Chapter 7 of this title;

    (B) the transfer had not been made; and

    (C) such creditor received payment of such debt to the extent provided by the provisions of this title.

According to the Trustee, the transfers of the Minks satisfy each and every element of Sec. 547(b) and, therefore, such transfers may be avoided. In response, Almiro submits that it was not a creditor of the Debtor. And, no transfer of property of the Debtor was made, Almiro argues, inasmuch as Debtor had no property interest in the Minks to transfer. This argument is premised upon Almiro's contention that the shipments of the Minks "were not for the purpose of transferring property, but for the sole purpose of consigning the goods to the Debtor for *inspection only.*"

To establish that a transfer constitutes an avoidable preference, the thresholding requirement of a transfer of an interest of the debtor in property must be met. "Transfer" is defined in [the Bankruptcy Code] as "every mode direct or indirect, absolute or conditional, voluntary or involuntary, of disposing of or parting with property or with an interest in property. . . ." In returning the Minks to Almiro, Debtor obviously physically parted with the property in question. The dispute here centers upon whether Debtor possessed a transferable property interest in the Minks. According to Almiro, because the Minks were transferred on a consignment basis, for inspection only, Debtor never obtained a transferrable property interest in the Minks. This argument ignores Ohio law. Debtor's affidavit, as well as Almiro's interrogatory answers, establish that the Minks were shipped to Debtor to be sold on consignment. Because the Minks were delivered to Debtor primarily for resale, and the Debtor could return the Minks to Almiro for credit even if the Minks conformed to the contract, pursuant to Ohio law, this transaction would be classified as a "sale or return." Under [UCC 2-326(b)], goods held on a "sale or return" basis are subject to the claims of the buyer's creditors while in the buyer's possession unless compliance with one of the provisions of [UCC 2-326(c)] is demonstrated. Absent such a showing, then, the Minks were subject to the claims of Debtor's creditors while in his possession and must be deemed to be "property" of the Debtor within the meaning of Sec. 547(b).

Under [UCC 2-326(c)], goods held on "sale or return" are subject to the claims of the buyer's creditors while they are in the buyer's possession, unless the seller of such goods does one of the following:

(1) complies with an applicable state law providing for a consigner's interest to be evidenced by a sign;

(2) establishes that the person conducting the business is generally known by his creditors to be substantially engaged in selling the goods of others; or

(3) complies with the filing requirements of [UCC Article 9].

Almiro's failure to comply with any of the requirements of [2-326(c)] is clear as a matter of fact and law. Ohio has no applicable law providing for a consigner's interest to be evidenced by a sign. And, Almiro does not assert that Debtor was generally known by his creditors to be substantially engaged in the sale of goods of others. Finally, Almiro's failure to file [Article 9] financing statements with respect to the Minks is likewise undisputed. Hence, the relationship between Almiro and the Debtor is not that of consigner-consignee under Ohio law. Rather, the transaction was a "sale or return" and,

. . . the Minks were subject to the claims of Debtor's creditors while in Debtor's possession. It follows, therefore, that under Ohio law Debtor possessed a transferable property interest in the Minks for purpose of Sec. 547(b). Thus, the initial element of an avoidable transfer—transfer of an interest of the Debtor in property—has been established.

According to Almiro, it was not a creditor of the Debtor during the preference period. Hence, Almiro asserts, the Trustee cannot meet the requirement of Sec. 547(b)(1). This contention is without merit. Under [the Bankruptcy Code], a "creditor" is an "entity that has a claim against a debtor that arose at the time of or before the order for relief concerning the debtor." A "claim" is a "right to payment or a right to an equitable remedy." Here, Debtor had the obligation to either return the

(continues)

In re Fisher

(continued from previous page)
Minks or to pay for the merchandise. Put differently, Almiro had a right to payment for the Minks or to an equitable remedy for their return. Accordingly, Almiro was a creditor as defined in [the Code] and the transfers in question were to or for Almiro's benefit.

The transfers of the Minks from Debtor to Almiro were "for or on account of an antecedent debt owed by the Debtor before such transfer[s] . . . [were] made." As noted above, Almiro is a creditor of the Debtor because Debtor had the obligation to either pay for the Minks or return them to Almiro. By the same reckoning, the transfers in question clearly were made on account of claims owned by Debtor to Almiro before such transfers were made.

The third element of a preferential transfer is set forth in Sec. 547(b)(3): the transfer must be made while the Debtor was insolvent. Sec. 547(f) creates the presumption that a debtor is insolvent for the 90 days preceding the petition date. This places the burden of going forward with evidence of the debtor's solvency on the recipient of the alleged preferential transfer. Here, Almiro has offered no evidence, by affidavit or otherwise, to overcome the statutory presumption of insolvency. . . . Hence, the Court finds that Debtor was insolvent at the time of the transfer of the Minks [which admittedly occurred within 90 days preceding the petition date].

The final element which must be shown to establish a preferential transfer is Almiro's receipt of more than it would have received had no transfer taken place and its claim was provided for pursuant to the distributive scheme of the Bankruptcy Code. The affidavit of the Trustee establishes that there will be insufficient assets in the estate for payment of a 100% dividend to general unsecured claimholders. Because the transfer of the Minks permitted Almiro to recover the entire amount of its claim, and because it did not have a perfected security interest in the Minks, Almiro received more by virtue of the transfers than it would have under a Chapter 7 liquidation.

[Therefore] each element of Sec. 547(b) has been established; hence, the transfers of the Minks are subject to avoidance. Judgment is hereby entered in favor of the Trustee and against Defendant in the amount of [$11,155.00]. ⚖

Claims

As a general rule, any legal obligation of the debtor existing pre-petition gives rise to a claim against the debtor's estate in the bankruptcy proceeding. There are, however, several special situations we should mention.

1. If the claim is *contingent* on the happening or nonhappening of some future event or, if its *amount is in dispute,* the bankruptcy court has the power to make an estimate of the claim's value.

2. If the claim against the debtor is for breach of contract, it will include any damages which accrued prior to the filing of the bankruptcy petition, and also those damages attributable to the debtor's failure to perform any future obligations under the contract. Of course, this is no different from an ordinary breach of contract claim when bankruptcy is not involved. However, under the bankruptcy law, if the claim arises out of an *employment contract* or a *real estate lease,* limits are placed on a claim for damages relating to future nonperformance. In the case of an employment contract, such damages are limited to a term of *one year* from the filing date or the date the contract was repudiated, whichever is earlier. In the case of a real estate lease, damages are limited to either *one year* or *15 percent* of the remaining term of the lease, whichever is greater, up to a maximum of *three years.* The starting point for measuring this time is the same as for employment contracts. One reason for these limits is that contracts of these two types are frequently long-term ones, and the farther in the future we try to compute damages, the more speculative they get.

3. A creditor who has received a voidable transfer or preference may not assert a claim of any kind until the wrongfully received property or funds are returned to the debtor's estate.

Subject to the above limitations, any claim filed with the bankruptcy court is allowed unless it is contested by an interested party, such as the trustee, debtor, or another creditor. If challenged, the court will rule on the claim's validity after pertinent evidence is presented at a hearing held for that purpose. In this regard, claims against the debtor's estate will be subject to any defenses that the debtor could have asserted had there been no bankruptcy. The fact that a claim is allowed, of course, does not mean that the particular creditor will be paid in full; it just means that the creditor has the hope of receiving *something*.

Distribution of Debtor's Estate

A secured creditor—one having a security interest or lien in a specific item of property—can proceed directly against that property for satisfaction of his or her claim. This is true even though the debtor is or is about to become subject to a bankruptcy proceeding. In a sense, then, **secured creditors** have priority over all classes of unsecured creditors (usually referred to as **general creditors**). However, if a portion of a secured creditor's claim is not secured, that portion is treated like any other unsecured claim.

When the trustee has gathered all the assets of the debtor's estate and reduced them to cash, these proceeds will be distributed to unsecured creditors. There are certain unsecured claims which are given priority in this distribution. These claims are paid in full *in the order of their priority,* assuming there are sufficient proceeds available. The following seven classes of debts are listed in order of priority. Each class must be fully paid before the next is entitled to anything. If the available funds are insufficient to satisfy all creditors within a class, payment to creditors in that class is made in proportion to the amounts of their claims.

1. First to be paid are all costs and expenses involved in the administration of the bankruptcy proceeding, such as an auctioneer's commission, the trustee's fee, and accountants' and attorneys' fees.

2. If the proceeding is an *involuntary* one, the second priority is any expense incurred in the ordinary course of the debtor's business or financial affairs *after* commencement of the case but *before* appointment of the trustee.

3. Next is any claim for wages, salaries, or commissions, including vacation, severance, and sick leave pay earned by an individual within 90 days before the filing of the petition or the cessation of the debtor's business, whichever occurs first. This priority, however, is limited to $2000 per individual.

4. The fourth priority is any claim for contributions to an employee benefit plan arising from services performed within 180 days before filing or business cessation. Again the limit is $2000 per individual. However, a particular individual cannot re-

ceive more than $2000 under the third and fourth priorities combined.

5. Fifth are claims of grain producers or U.S. fishermen against a debtor who owns or operates a grain or fish storage facility for the produce or its proceeds, limited to $2000 for each such individual.

6. Next are claims of individuals, up to $900 per person, for deposits made on consumer goods or services that were not received.

7. Claims of governmental units for various kinds of taxes, subject to time limits that differ depending on the type of tax, are the last priority.

If all priority claims are paid and funds still remain, general creditors are paid in proportion to the amounts of their claims. Any portion of a priority claim that was beyond the limits of the priority is treated as a general claim. An example would be the amount by which an individual's wage claim exceeded $2000. Figure 30.2 outlines the process of distributing the debtor's estate.

Discharge

After the debtor's estate has been liquidated and distributed to creditors, the bankruptcy court may conduct a hearing to determine whether the debtor should be discharged from liability for remaining obligations.

Grounds for Refusal of Discharge

Under certain circumstances the court will refuse to grant the debtor a **discharge.** These are as follows:

1. Only an *individual* can receive a discharge in a liquidation proceeding. For a corporation to receive a discharge it must go through a reorganization proceeding (discussed later in the chapter), or be dissolved in accordance with state corporation statutes.

2. A debtor will be denied a discharge if he or she had previously received such a discharge within *six years* before the present bankruptcy petition was filed.

3. The debtor will be denied a discharge if he or she has committed any of the following acts: (a) intentionally concealed or transferred assets for the purpose of evading creditors, within one year before the filing of the petition or during the bankruptcy proceedings; (b) concealed, destroyed, falsified, or failed to keep business or financial records unless

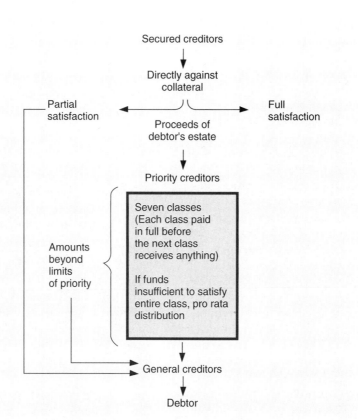

FIGURE 30.2

**Distribution
of Debtor's
Estate**

there was reasonable justification for such action or failure; (c) failed to adequately explain any loss of assets; (d) refused to obey a lawful court order or to answer a material court-approved question in connection with the bankruptcy case; or (e) made any fraudulent statement or claim in connection with the bankruptcy case.

4. If a discharge has been granted, the court may revoke it within one year if it is discovered that the

debtor had not acted honestly in connection with the bankruptcy proceeding.

In the following case, creditors of the bankrupt debtor claimed that the debtor should not be discharged from his obligations because he had demonstrated an actual intent to defraud his creditors. The case demonstrates the importance of looking at a debtor's overall pattern of conduct when determining whether he or she has acted fraudulently.

NORWEST BANK NEBRASKA, N.A. V. TVETEN

U.S. Eighth Circuit Court of Appeals, 848 F.2d 871 (1988)

Tveten was a 59-year-old physician and sole shareholder of Omar A. Tveten, P.A., a professional corporation. He began investing in real estate, initially quite successfully. Joined by other doctors, Tveten

organized ventures that were highly leveraged. Debts were personally guaranteed by Tveten and the other doctors. In mid-1985, Tveten's investments began to sour. Appellees Norwest Bank and Business Development Corporation, and Harold Panuska became creditors of Tveten

as a result of his various investment ventures.

Tveten filed a bankruptcy petition on January 7, 1986. Meanwhile, several creditors already had commenced lawsuits against him. Panuska had obtained a $139,657 judgment against him on October 9,

(continues)

NORWEST BANK NEBRASKA, N.A. V. TVETEN

(continued from previous page)

1985. Norwest Bank and Business Development had commenced an action against him but had not obtained a judgment when Tveten filed for bankruptcy. On the date the petition was filed, Tveten owed his creditors close to $19,000,000.

Before filing for bankruptcy, Tveten consulted a lawyer. As part of his pre-bankruptcy planning, he liquidated almost all of his non-exempt property, converting it into exempt property worth approximately $700,000. This was accomplished through some 17 separate transfers. The non-exempt property he liquidated included land sold to his parents and his brother, respectively, for $70,000 and $75,732 in cash; life insurance policies and annuities with a for-profit company with cash values totaling $96,307.58; his net salary and bonuses of $27,820.91; his KEOGH pension plan and individual retirement fund of $20,487.35; his corporation's profit-sharing plan worth $325,774.51; and a home sold for $50,000. All of the liquidated property was converted into life insurance or annuity contracts with the Lutheran Brotherhood, a fraternal benefit association, which, under Minnesota law, cannot be attached by creditors. Tveten concedes that the purpose of these transfers was to shield his assets from creditors. Minnesota law provides that creditors cannot attach any money or other benefits payable by a fraternal benefit association. Unlike most exemption provisions in other states, the Minnesota exemption has no monetary limit. Indeed, under this exemption, Tveten attempted to place $700,000 worth of his property out of his creditors' reach.

The bankruptcy court held that, even if the exemptions were permissible, Tveten had abused the protections permitted a debtor under the Bankruptcy Code. His awareness of Panuska's judgment against him and of several pending lawsuits, his

rapidly deteriorating business investments, and his exposure to extensive liability well beyond his ability to pay, all led the court to find that Tveten intended to hinder and delay his creditors. Accordingly, the bankruptcy court denied Tveten a discharge. The federal district court affirmed and Tveten appealed.

Timbers, Circuit Judge:

At the outset, it is necessary to distinguish between (1) a debtor's right to exempt certain property from the claims of his creditors and (2) his right to a discharge of his debts. The Code permits a debtor to exempt property either pursuant to the provisions of the Code if not forbidden by state law, or pursuant to the provisions of state law and federal law other than the minimum allowances in the Code. When the debtor claims a state-created exemption, the scope of the claim is determined by state law. It is well established that under the Code the conversion of nonexempt to exempt property for the purpose of placing the property out of the reach of creditors, without more, will not deprive the debtor of the exemption to which he otherwise would be entitled.

The rationale behind this policy is that "[t]he result which would obtain if debtors were not allowed to convert property into allowable exempt property would be extremely harsh, especially in those jurisdictions where the exemption allowance is minimal." This blanket approval of conversion is qualified, however, by denial of discharge if there was extrinsic evidence of the debtor's intent to defraud creditors.

A debtor's right to a discharge, unlike his right to an exemption, is determined by *federal*, not state, law. The Code provides that a debtor may be denied a discharge under Chapter 7 if, among other things, he has transferred property "with intent to hinder, delay, or defraud a creditor" within one year before the date of the filing of the petition.

[T]he standard applied consistently by the courts is the same as that used to

determine whether an exemption is permissible, i.e., absent extrinsic evidence of fraud, mere conversion of non-exempt property to exempt property is not fraudulent as to creditors even if the motivation behind the conversion is to place those assets beyond the reach of creditors.

As the bankruptcy court correctly found here, therefore, the issue in the instant case revolves around whether there was extrinsic evidence to demonstrate that Tveten transferred his property on the eve of bankruptcy with intent to defraud his creditors. The bankruptcy court's finding that there was such intent to defraud may be reversed by us only if clearly erroneous.

In the instant case, the state exemption relied on by Tveten was unlimited, with the potential for unlimited abuse. Indeed, this case presents a situation in which the debtor liquidated almost his entire net worth of $700,000 and converted it to exempt property in seventeen transfers on the eve of bankruptcy while his creditors, to whom he owed close to $19,000,000 would be left to divide the little that remained in his estate. Borrowing the phrase used by another court, Tveten "did not want a *fresh* start, he wanted a *head* start." His attempt to shield property worth approximately $700,000 goes well beyond the purpose for which exemptions are permitted.

The bankruptcy court, as affirmed by the district court, examined Tveten's entire pattern of conduct and found that he had demonstrated fraudulent intent. We agree. While state law governs the legitimacy of Tveten's exemptions, it is federal law that governs his discharge. Permitting Tveten, who earns over $60,000 annually, to convert all of his major non-exempt assets into sheltered property on the eve of bankruptcy with actual intent to defraud his creditors "would constitute a perversion of the purposes of the Bankruptcy Code." Tveten still is entitled to retain, free from creditors' claims, property rightfully exempt under relevant state law.

Affirmed.

Nondischargeable Debts

Even if the debtor is granted a general discharge from obligations, there nevertheless are a few types of claims for which he or she will continue to be liable. These **nondischargeable debts** are as follows:

1. Obligations for payment of taxes are not discharged if (a) the particular tax was entitled to a priority in the distribution of the debtor's estate, but was not paid; or (b) a tax return had been required but was not properly filed; or (c) the debtor had willfully attempted to evade the particular tax.

2. Claims arising out of the debtor's fraud, embezzlement, or larceny are not discharged.

3. The debtor is not excused from liability for a willful and malicious tort.

4. Claims for alimony and child support are not discharged.

5. The debtor is not discharged from a claim that he or she failed to list in the bankruptcy case if this failure caused the creditor not to assert the claim in time for it to be allowed.

6. A fine, penalty, or forfeiture payable to a governmental unit, which is neither compensation for actual pecuniary loss nor a tax penalty, is not discharged.

7. A student loan obligation is not dischargeable, unless (a) it is more than five years old, or (b) the debtor can demonstrate that failure to discharge would cause hardship.

8. Any judgments or awards of damages resulting from the debtor's operation of a motor vehicle while legally intoxicated are not dischargeable.

9. Primarily because of credit card abuse by debtors shortly before filing for bankruptcy, two types of *consumer debts* have been made nondischargeable: (a) debts of more than $500 to a particular creditor for *luxury goods or services*, if incurred within 40 days of the order for relief (i.e., the petition); and (b) cash advances totalling more than $1000 obtained by using a credit card or other open-ended consumer credit arrangement, if incurred within 20 days of the order for relief.

Reaffirmation

Prior to the 1978 Code, a debtor could renew his or her obligation on a debt that had been discharged in bankruptcy simply by expressing a willingness to be bound. This **reaffirmation** required no new consideration by the creditor, but some states did require it to be in writing.

During the course of revising the bankruptcy law, Congress found that many of these reaffirmations were obtained by creditors through the use of coercion or deception. As a result, the new law places significant constraints on the making of a reaffirmation. Specifically, a reaffirmation is not valid unless (1) the bankruptcy court conducted a hearing at which the debtor was fully informed of the consequences of his or her action or the debtor was represented by an attorney who filed an affidavit stating that debtor was fully informed and that the agreement was voluntarily made and does not impose hardship; and (2) the agreement to reaffirm was made *before* the debtor's discharge. In addition, the debtor can rescind the reaffirmation at any time prior to discharge or within 60 days after it is filed with the court.

BUSINESS REORGANIZATION

If it is felt that reorganization and continuance of a business is feasible and is preferable to liquidation, a petition for reorganization may be filed under Chapter 11 of the 1978 Bankruptcy Code. The reorganization procedure is intended for use by *businesses*, but it does not matter whether the owner of the business is an individual, partnership, or corporation. A **reorganization case** can be either voluntary or involuntary, and the requirements for filing an involuntary case are the same as for a liquidation proceeding. In general, the types of debtors exempted from reorganization proceedings are the same as those exempted from liquidation proceedings. The major difference in coverage is that a railroad *can* be a debtor in a reorganization proceeding. The most important aspects of a reorganization case are summarized below.

1. As soon as the petition is filed, an *automatic stay* is in operation just as in a liquidation proceeding. The automatic stay is even more important in a reorganization proceeding, because without such a stay the debtor often would find it impossible to continue operating its business.

2. There may or may not be a trustee in a reorganization case. If a trustee is appointed, he or she will take over and will have basically the same duties and powers as in a liquidation case. Essentially, the court

will appoint a trustee if requested by an interested party (such as a creditor) and if it appears that such an appointment would be in the best interests of all parties involved. Obviously a trustee will be appointed if the court feels there is a possibility of the debtor's business being mismanaged or assets being wasted or concealed. If a trustee is not appointed, the debtor remains in possession and control of the business. In this situation, the debtor is called the **debtor-in-possession,** and has all the powers of a trustee.

3. After commencement of the case, the U.S. Trustee must appoint a committee of unsecured creditors. If necessary, the court or the U.S. Trustee may appoint other creditors' committees to represent the special interests of particular types of creditors. A committee of shareholders may also be appointed to oversee the interests of that group, if the debtor is a corporation.

4. The creditors' and shareholders' committees, and the trustee, if one was appointed, will investigate the business and financial affairs of the debtor. A *reorganization plan* will then be prepared and filed with the bankruptcy court. This plan must divide creditors' claims and shareholders' interests into classes according to their type. For instance, claims of employees, secured creditors, bondholders, real estate mortgage holders, and government units might be segregated into different classes. The plan must indicate how claims within each class are going to be handled and to what extent each class will receive less than full payment, as well as provide adequate means for the plan's execution. Treatment of claims within each class must be equal.

5. The court will "confirm" (approve) the reorganization plan if (a) each class has approved the plan and (b) the court rules that the plan is "fair and equitable" to all classes. A plan is deemed to be accepted by a class of creditors if it received favorable votes from those representing at least two-thirds of the amount of claims and more than half of the number of creditors within that class. Acceptance by a class of shareholders requires an affirmative vote by those representing at least two-thirds of the shares in that class. If the parties are unable to produce an acceptable plan or if the plan subsequently does not work as expected, the court may either dismiss the case or convert it into a liquidation proceeding.

6. After the plan has been confirmed, the debtor is discharged from those claims not provided for in the plan. However, the types of claims that are not discharged in a liquidation case are also not discharged in a reorganization case.

Certain procedural changes were made in 1991 in order to facilitate use of *prepackaged bankruptcies*—reorganization plans negotiated with the debtor's creditors prior to filing as a way to abbreviate the period the debtor company will have to stay in bankruptcy.

Policy Issues in Reorganizations

The attempt by bankruptcy laws to achieve equity among debtors and creditors has always raised questions of ethics and public policy. Indeed, the provisions of the Bankruptcy Code dealing with voidable preferences, refusal of discharge, and nondischargeable debts have ethical and policy questions at their core. The fact that the 1978 Code no longer requires that a debtor be insolvent to file a voluntary case has made these ethical questions even more important: If it is in the best interest of society to provide relief to an insolvent debtor, how far should public policy go in letting a debtor start afresh when that debtor is financially beleaguered but not insolvent?

Since the enactment of the 1978 Code, which increases the flexibility and acceptability of business reorganization cases, ethical and policy questions have arisen with increasing frequency under Chapter 11 of the Code. Again, there is no insolvency requirement, and the ultimate objective of a reorganization is to permit the debtor to continue as a viable entity. Although the reorganization provisions of Chapter 11 pursue worthwhile goals, the process of reorganization does present opportunities for abuse. As we mentioned previously, if a trustee is not appointed in a reorganization proceeding, the debtor becomes a so-called *debtor-in-possession,* with all the powers of a trustee. Although the exercise of such power obviously is under the supervision of the bankruptcy court, creditors, employee unions, and other groups often are understandably concerned about the actions of the debtor-in-possession. Bankruptcy reorganization is today being successfully utilized by major corporations to defer pre-petition debts in order to improve cash flow for post-petition operating costs, to alter obligations under burdensome labor contracts and underfunded pension plans, and to block products liability litigation.

One of the most important powers of the debtor-in-possession, like a trustee, is the power to *cancel executory contracts.* For a time, there was a question whether a debtor-in-possession could cancel a collective bargaining agreement covering its unionized employees. Unions claimed that a debtor-in-possession should not have the power to cancel collective bargaining agreements because an employer could then use a Chapter 11 reorganization as a "union busting" device. The Supreme Court ruled, however, in *NLRB v. Bildisco & Bildisco,* 465 U.S. 513 (1984), that collective bargaining agreements, like other contracts, can be cancelled by the debtor-in-possession when cancellation is in the best interests of a successful reorganization. Shortly thereafter, Congress amended the law so as to place restrictions on this power. Specifically, Congress provided that the debtor-in-possession (i.e., the employer) must first propose reasonable modifications to the existing union contract. If the union rejects these proposed modifications, the Bankruptcy Court then conducts a hearing to determine whether the union has "good cause" for the rejection. A union has good cause for rejecting the proposed modifications if the employer has failed to prove that the contract changes are "fair and equitable" to all parties and necessary for the company's survival. If it is found that the union does have good cause, the burden is then upon the employer to make further proposals. If the court finds that the union did not have good cause for rejecting a particular proposal for modifying the collective bargaining agreement, the employer then has the power to cancel the agreement and set new employment terms unilaterally. An example of the application of these new provisions is found in *Wheeling-Pittsburgh Steel Corp. v. United Steelworkers of America,* 791 F.2d 1074 (3d Cir. 1986), in which the court concluded that the union had good cause for rejection primarily because the employer based its proposals on a "worst case scenario" that required a one-third wage cut for five years and did not include a "snap back" provision that would increase workers' wages and benefits if the company performed better than expected.

One of the most important effects of the filing of a Chapter 11 bankruptcy is the imposition of the automatic stay. This prohibition of collection efforts with regard to pre-petition debts or any other action against the reorganizing debtor raises various ethical and policy questions. Suppose, for example, that a large, profitable company is faced with a great many claims for injuries allegedly arising from products made by the company. A large number of claims have already been filed, and many others are anticipated in the future, making it necessary for the company to set aside extremely large reserves to cover contingent liabilities. Can the company use a Chapter 11 reorganization proceeding to obtain settlements of these claims in an organized, hopefully uniform fashion? This is the question faced by the court in the following case.

In re Johns-Manville Corporation

U.S. Bankruptcy Court, S.D. New York, 36 Bankr. Rptr. 727 (1984)

Johns-Manville Corp. (Manville) was a large, highly successful manufacturing enterprise. It and several other companies were major producers of several products, such as insulation, that contained asbestos. After many people who had been exposed to asbestos for lengthy periods of time developed very serious diseases such as asbestosis and lung cancer, large numbers of lawsuits began to be filed against asbestos producers.

Manville filed a petition for reorganization under Chapter 11 of the Bankruptcy Code, claiming that such filing was made necessary by the "uncontrolled proliferation" of asbestos-related lawsuits. At the time of the court's initial decision in the reorganization case, over 16,000 such suits had been filed against Manville. The company stated that its problems were compounded by the "crushing economic burden to be suffered by it over the next 20-30 years by the filing of an even more staggering number of suits by those who had been exposed but who will not manifest the asbestos-related diseases until some time during this future period." In addition, Manville showed that the insurance industry had generally disavowed coverage for asbestos-related

(continues)

In re Johns-Marville Corporation

(continued from previous page)
claims under products liability insurance policies carried by the company. The question of insurance coverage had been tied up in state court litigation in California for several years.

Several different groups of creditors and asbestos-lawsuit plaintiffs challenged Manville's reorganization petition as inappropriate, and asked that it be dismissed. These groups contended that Manville was a healthy company and was misusing the Bankruptcy Code by attempting to use a reorganization proceeding to resolve products liability claims. The opinion of the Bankruptcy Court follows.

Lifland, Bankruptcy Judge:

Clearly, Manville meets the requirements . . . for debtors under all chapters of the Code in that it is domiciled and has its place of business in the United States. . . . In addition, Manville meets the eligibility requirements applicable to Chapter 11 debtors. . . . Moreover, it should also be noted that neither Section 109 [containing eligibility requirements] nor any other provision relating to voluntary petitions by companies contains any insolvency requirement. . . . This is in striking contrast to the requirement of insolvency . . . with regard to the commencement of involuntary cases. . . .

The filing of a Chapter 11 case creates an estate for the benefit of all creditors and equity holders of the debtor wherein all constituencies may voice their interests and bargain for their best possible treatment. . . .

A principal goal of the Bankruptcy Code is to provide open access to the bankruptcy process. . . . [According to congressional reports,] the rationale behind this "open access" policy is to provide access to bankruptcy relief which is as "open" as "access to the credit economy." Thus, Congress intended that "there should be no legal barriers to voluntary petitions." Another major goal of the Code, that of "rehabilitation of debtors," requires that relief for debtors must be "timely." Congress declared that it is essential to both the open access and rehabilitation goals that

[i]nitiating relief should not be a death knell. The process should encourage resort to it, by debtors and creditors, that cuts short the dissipation of assets and the accumulation of debts. Belated commencement of a case may kill an opportunity for reorganization or arrangement.

Accordingly, the drafters of the Code envisioned that a financially beleaguered debtor with real debt and real creditors should not be required to wait until the economic situation is beyond repair in order to file a reorganization petition. The congressional

purpose in enacting the Code was to encourage resort to the bankruptcy process. This philosophy not only comports with the elimination of an insolvency requirement, but also is a corollary of the key aim of Chapter 11 of the Code, that of avoidance of liquidation. The drafters of the Code announced this goal, declaring that reorganization is more efficient than liquidation because "assets that are used for production in the industry for which they were designed are more valuable than those same assets sold for scrap." Moreover, reorganization also fosters the goals of preservation of jobs in the threatened entity.

In the instant case, not only would liquidation be wasteful and inefficient in destroying the utility of valuable assets of the companies as well as jobs, but, more importantly, liquidation would preclude just compensation of some present asbestos victims and all future asbestos claimants. This unassailable reality represents all the more reason for this Court to adhere to this . . . liquidation avoidance aim of Chapter 11 and deny the motions to dismiss. Manville must not be required to wait until its economic picture has deteriorated beyond salvation to file for reorganization. . . . All of the motions to dismiss the Manville petition are denied in their entirety. ⚖

The Johns-Manville Corporation bankruptcy was described as "one of the most significant Chapter 11 bankruptcy proceedings" by the circuit court that affirmed confirmation of the reorganization plan on appeal. That plan, which resulted from more than four years of negotiations, is described in the opinion that follows.

Kane v. Johns-Manville Corp.

U.S. Second Circuit Court of Appeals, 843 F.2d 636 (1988)

The Bankruptcy Court confirmed Johns-Manville's reorganization plan, and the district court affirmed. Kane, representing 765 "Class-4 creditors"—persons with asbestos-related disease who had filed personal injury suits against Manville prior to Manville's Chapter 11 status—appealed. Kane's primary argument is that the plan does not adequately protect the interests of asbestos victims.

Newman, Circuit Judge:

The cornerstone of the Plan is the Asbestos Health Trust (the "Trust"), a mechanism designed to satisfy the claims of all asbestos health victims, both present and future. The Trust is funded with the proceeds from Manville's settlements with its insurers; certain cash, receivables, and stock of the reorganized Manville Corporation; long term notes; and the right to receive up to 20% of Manville's yearly profits for as long as it takes to satisfy all health claims. According to the terms of the Trust, individuals with as-bestos-related disease must first try to settle their claims by a mandatory exchange of settlement offers with Trust representatives. If a settlement cannot be reached, the claimant may elect mediation, binding arbitration, or traditional tort litigation. The claimant may collect from the Trust the full amount of whatever compensatory damages he is awarded. The only restriction on recovery is that the claimant may not obtain punitive damages.

The purpose of the Trust is to provide a means of satisfying Manville's ongoing personal injury liability while allowing Manville to maximize its value by continuing as an ongoing concern. To fulfill this purpose, the Plan seeks to ensure that health claims can be asserted only against the Trust and that Manville's operating entities will be protected from an onslaught of crippling lawsuits that could jeopardize the entire reorganization effort. To this end, the parties agreed that as a condition precedent to confirmation of the Plan, the Bankruptcy Court would issue an Injunction channeling all asbestos-related personal injury claims to the Trust. The Injunction provides that asbestos claimants may proceed only against the Trust to satisfy their claims and may not sue Manville, its other operating entities, and certain other specified parties, including Manville's insurers. Significantly, the Injunction applies to all health claimants, both present and future, regardless of whether they technically have dischargeable "claims" under the Code.

Manville presented extensive evidence on feasibility at the confirmation hearing, while Kane presented no evidence. The Bankruptcy Judge found that "the Debtor's reasonable and credible projections of future earnings have established that the reorganized corporation is unlikely to face future proceedings under this title." With specific reference to the Trust, the Court found that "[t]he evidence submitted by the Debtor . . . provides a reasonable estimation, based upon known present claimants and reasonable extrapolations from past experience and epidemiological data, of the number and amount of asbestos-related claims that the AH Trust will be required to satisfy. The Debtor has also established that the Trust will, in fact, meet this burden.

[Affirmed.]

Note

Many experts believe that Chapter 11 reorganization bankruptcies are counterproductive. Some studies show that many reorganizations are spectacularly unsuccessful. Although lawyers and accountants are well paid for their work, and managers of the reorganizing companies keep their jobs and run the corporation with a new freedom from old creditors, the corporations tend to end up in liquidation bankruptcy having squandered most of the assets they had when they entered reorganization.

The whole idea behind reorganization bankruptcy is to preserve the going entity in order to protect creditors and shareholders from difficulties caused by short-term credit crunches. However, some studies indicate that creditor losses rise by two-thirds under Chapter 11 when compared with previous law and that shareholder losses are typically almost 100 percent (up from losses of 50 percent or so under prior law). Some experts recommended, therefore, that Chapter 11 be repealed.[5]

The mechanism is costly and cumbersome. For example, in December 1992, the Second Circuit Court

---

[5]See Bradley & Rosenzweig, "Time to Scuttle Chapter 11," *New York Times* (Sunday Forum), March 8, 1992, p. F13.

of Appeals overturned the trial judge's implementation of the Manville asbestos trust fund described in the previous case, and remanded the plan for further consideration by the trial judge. And in mid-1993, Manville asked Congress to enact a legislative cap on its asbestos liability.

ADJUSTMENT OF DEBTS
Of an Individual with Regular Income

Chapter 13 of the 1978 Code, "Adjustment of Debts of an Individual with Regular Income," provides a method by which an individual can pay his or her debts from future income over an extended period of time. It is intended for use by an individual whose primary income is from salary, wages, or commissions (that is, an employee). There is, however, nothing to prevent a self-employed individual, such as the owner of a business, from using this chapter of the bankruptcy law. But the debtor must be an *individual;* partnerships and corporations cannot institute this type of proceeding. Approximately 230,000 of the 830,000 bankruptcies filed in the fiscal year ending March 31, 1991, were Chapter 13s. The most important aspects of an **adjustment case** are summarized below.

1. There is no such thing as an involuntary adjustment case; only the debtor can file the petition. As in the other types of proceedings, an *automatic stay* exists upon filing. To be eligible to file an adjustment case, the debtor must have (a) "regular income," (b) less than $100,000 in noncontingent, undisputed debts which are *unsecured,* and (c) less than $350,000 in noncontingent, undisputed debts which are *secured.*

2. The U.S. Trustee will always appoint a trustee in an adjustment case. The primary function of the trustee in this type of proceeding is to receive and distribute the debtor's income on a periodic basis.

3. The debtor prepares and files an *adjustment plan* with the court. Neither the trustee, creditors, nor anyone else can file the plan. The essential functions of the plan are to designate the portion of the debtor's future income that will be turned over to the trustee for distribution to creditors, to describe how creditors are to be paid, and to indicate the period of time during which payment will be accomplished. If the plan segregates creditors into classes, each creditor within a class must be treated equally. As a gen-

eral rule, the plan cannot extend the period for payment of debts more than three years. It can provide for less than full payment of many types of claims, but must call for full payment of the types of claims which are given priority in a liquidation case.

4. The court will confirm (approve) the plan if (a) the debtor proposed it in *good faith,* and (b) if all secured creditors have accepted it. It is not necessary for unsecured creditors to accept the plan; they are bound by it if the court confirms it, even if it modifies their claims. Furthermore, even if a secured creditor objects to the plan, the court may approve it if special provision is made to insure that the secured creditor is either fully paid or permitted to retain the lien or security interest protecting the claim.

5. At any time before or after confirmation of the plan, the debtor has the privilege of converting the adjustment proceeding to a liquidation case. The bankruptcy court may convert the adjustment proceeding to a liquidation case, or dismiss the case altogether, if the debtor fails to perform according to the plan. On the other hand, if the debtor does perform, he or she will ordinarily be granted a discharge upon completion of the payments provided for in the plan. There is no discharge, however, from the types of claims that cannot be discharged in a liquidation case. A discharge may be revoked within one year if it is discovered that the discharge was obtained through fraud.

Of a Family Farmer with Regular Income

In 1986 in response to the farm economy crisis, Congress enacted Chapter 12, entitled "Adjustment of Debts of a Family Farmer with Regular Annual Income" to provide relief to family farmers who wished to retain and reorganize their farming operations. Most farmers are not eligible for such relief under Chapter 13 because their debts exceed statutory limits. Others are ineligible because they operate as a corporation or partnership. Chapter 11 reorganizations were considered by Congress to be excessively expensive, time-consuming, complicated, and unlikely to result in a confirmed plan for the family farmer.

Chapter 12 was generally modeled after Chapter 13 so that the procedures are basically the same as the Chapter 13 procedures outlined in paragraphs (1) through (5) above. The most striking distinctions found in Chapter 12 are set forth below.

LEGAL FOCUS

International

In the age of large, multinational corporations owning assets and owing obligations in several countries, bankruptcy law has become an exceedingly complex matter. Although the United States has, to some extent, sought to internationalize the process and to cooperate with courts operating in other nations, most nations operate under the "grab" rule. That is, creditors in Country X will be allowed by its courts to grab the debtor's assets in Country X. Outside creditors will be relegated to whatever

crumbs, if any, are left when Country X's creditors are satisfied. Country Y's creditors will grab the debtor's assets located in Country Y, and so on.

Courts of many nations do not even purport to exercise jurisdiction over a debtor's assets located elsewhere. However, if a debtor files in the United States, our Bankruptcy Code claims jurisdiction over the assets of the bankrupt "wherever located" in the world. Many other nations assert similar jurisdiction, but the process breaks down unless there is international respect for these extraterritorial exercises of jurisdiction. Thus far, there has been *less* international cooperation in the area of

bankruptcy than in virtually any other legal area.

Widespread adoption of the proposed Model International Insolvency Cooperation Act (MIICA) would help. Under MIICA, each country's courts would cooperate with foreign bankruptcy proceedings. MIICA would replace the grab rule with a "universalist" rule. In other words, if a company entered bankruptcy proceedings in Country A, courts in Country B would cooperate with courts in Country A, perhaps even to the extent of applying Country A's bankruptcy laws in dealing with creditors and assets located in Country B.

1. The eligibility requirements of Chapter 12 are specifically aimed at the family farmer and exclude large agricultural operators. The debtor must be a **family farmer** defined as an individual engaged in farming whose aggregate debts do not exceed $1,500,000 and not less than 80 percent of whose debts (excluding debt on the principal residence) arise out of farming operations owned and operated by them and who received more than 50 percent of their gross income during the preceding taxable year from such farming operation. Only those partnerships and corporations are included in which more than 50 percent of the outstanding stock or equity is held by one family and its relatives who conduct the farming operation and more than 80 percent of the value of whose assets relate to the farming operation. In addition, the family farmer must have "regular income" defined as income sufficiently regular to enable the debtor to make payments under the Chapter 12 plan.

2. The family farmer's plan need not be filed for 90 days while the Chapter 13 plan must be filed within 15 days of filing the petition. Moreover, a Chapter 13 debtor must commence payments to the trustee within 30 days of filing his or her plan, while Chap-

ter 12 has no provision requiring immediate payments so that a plan may be confirmed even though no payments are provided until the next harvest.

3. Congress has expressly provided that the adequate protection provision which applies in all other bankruptcy cases does not apply in Chapter 12 and has redefined the term more favorably for farmers. In Chapter 12 the customary, reasonable rental value of farmland constitutes adequate protection. Such rental payments should be significantly lower than adequate protection payments in a Chapter 11 case, where costs for lost opportunity to repossess may be included.

4. A Chapter 12 plan may provide for modification of the mortgage on a debtor's principal residence, which is prohibited in Chapter 13. It may also provide for the sale of farmland by parcels or farm equipment by items free and clear of blanket liens as long as the creditor's lien attaches to the proceeds. These modifications of creditors' liens, which would be objectionable in a Chapter 11 or 13 plan, are intended by Congress to permit the family farmer to scale down his operations by selling unnecessary property.

5. Chapter 12 was devised to provide extraordinary relief to eligible farmers during what was perceived by Congress as a temporary crisis and will automatically be repealed on October 1, 1993, unless extended.

SUMMARY

When a debtor encounters difficulty in making repayment to creditors, many alternatives for attempting to resolve the problem exist under state statutory and common-law principles. Although bankruptcy under federal law traditionally has been viewed as a last resort, thousands of federal bankruptcy cases are filed each year. The 1978 Bankruptcy Code, as amended in 1984 and 1986, provides for four basic types of proceedings: liquidation, business reorganization, and adjustment of debts for individuals and for family farmers. Liquidation or reorganization proceedings can be either voluntary or involuntary, and can be instituted by or against either individuals, corporations, or partnerships. An adjustment proceeding can only be filed voluntarily by an individual.

The commencement of any type of proceeding causes an automatic stay of most other proceedings against the debtor. Contrary to prior law, under the 1978 Code a debtor does not have to be insolvent to file a voluntary petition, although insolvency is a requirement for the commencement of an involuntary case by creditors.

In a liquidation proceeding, a trustee is appointed by the bankruptcy court to administer the debtor's estate. The debtor's estate consists of practically all property interests of the debtor except for designated exempt items and is ultimately used to pay the claims of creditors according to a list of priorities contained in the Code. A debtor may select the property exemptions allowed by the law of the state where he or she resides, or the exemptions permitted by the Code; a particular state may, however, require debtors in that state to use only the state exemptions in a bankruptcy proceeding. The powers of the trustee include taking legal action to cancel (1) preferential transfers of property by the debtor to certain creditors and (2) other voidable transfers from the debtor. The trustee may also take legal action to collect claims owed to the debtor.

At the conclusion of a liquidation proceeding, a debtor is normally discharged from the unpaid portion of his or her obligations. Certain types of debts are not dischargeable, however. Moreover, proof of certain facts, such as concealment of assets or other fraudulent conduct by the debtor, may cause the court to deny the debtor a discharge.

A reorganization proceeding is intended to permit a financially overextended business to continue operating and work out a fair plan with creditors for repayment of its debts. A trustee may or may not be appointed in a reorganization proceeding; if one is not appointed, the debtor is called a debtor-in-possession and continues to control the business with all the powers of a trustee. An adjustment case is intended primarily to permit *employees* to work out repayment plans with creditors under court protection and supervision, but it can be used by self-employed individuals. Chapter 12 now provides similar adjustment procedures for family farmers.

KEY TERMS

Foreclosure
Artisan's lien
Mechanic's lien
Writ of execution
Garnishment
Receivership
Fraud in fact
Fraud implied in law
Composition of creditors
Assignment for the benefit of creditors
Liquidation proceeding
Voluntary case
Involuntary case
Interim trustee
Permanent trustee
Debtor's estate
Exemptions
Voidable transfers
Preference
Insider
Secured creditors
General creditors
Discharge
Nondischargeable debts
Reaffirmation
Reorganization case
Debtor-in-possession
Adjustment case
Family farmer

QUESTIONS AND PROBLEMS

1. ZZZ Best Co., Inc. borrowed $7 million from Union Bank. Approximately 18 months later, ZZZZ Best entered Chapter 7 bankruptcy. During the 90 days preceding commencement of the bankruptcy case, ZZZZ Best had made two interest payments totalling $100,000 to Union Bank. The bankruptcy trustee sued to recover those payments as preferential transfers. Union Bank argued that the payments were made in the "ordinary course of business" and therefore were not recoverable. Should the trustee recover? Discuss. (*Union Bank v. Wolas*, 112 S.Ct. 527, 1991.)

2. In 1978, the Dewsnups borrowed $119,000, giving the lenders as security a deed of trust granting a lien in two parcels of farmland. The Dewsnups defaulted in 1979, and the secured creditors issued a notice of default in 1981. The Dewsnups filed for Chapter 11 bankruptcy reorganization before a foreclosure sale could be held. The Chapter 11 proceeding was dismissed because the Dewsnups failed to file a reorganization plan. In 1984, the Dewsnups filed for straight liquidation under Chapter 7. In 1987, the Dewsnups sued to avoid part of the secured creditors' lien, arguing that their $120,000 debt exceeded the fair market value of the collateral (the farmland), and that the bankruptcy court should reduce ("strip down") the creditors' lien to the $39,000 fair market value. Should the bankruptcy court grant the Dewsnups' request? (*Dewsnup v. Timm*, 112 S.Ct. 773, 1992.)

3. James Taylor was the lead singer in a group known as "Kool and the Gang." In 1985 and 1986, the group executed three recording contracts which bound each member of the group to perform thereunder as a solo artist in the event of his departure from the group. In early 1988 Taylor terminated his relationship with Kool and the Gang, and in May 1988 he filed a Chapter 11 bankruptcy petition. He then filed a motion to reject the three personal service contracts under the general power of the trustee to reject or accept executory contracts. The recording companies holding the contracts argued that since earnings for services by a debtor after the commencement of a bankruptcy case are not considered property of the estate, the trustee had no power to accept or reject the contracts in question. Should Taylor be allowed to reject these contracts and be relieved of his obligations to perform thereunder as a part of his "fresh start"? (*Matter of Taylor*, 103 B.R. 511, D.N.J. 1989.)

4. Pennzoil was awarded a judgment against Texaco for more than $11.259 billion. Texaco then filed a Chapter 11 bankruptcy petition. Texaco and Pennzoil, its largest unsecured creditor, filed a Joint Plan of Reorganization which reduced Pennzoil's claim to a cash payment due upon confirmation of $3 billion. This payment was to be in full satisfaction and release of the judgment and all other possible litigation relating to the Getty Oil acquisition out of which the judgment had arisen. The plan also provided for payment of all other creditors in full. Texaco asserted that it was authorized to compromise and settle Pennzoil's claim in this manner under 11 U.S.C. Sec. 1123(b)(3) which provides for "the settlement or adjustment of any claim or interest belonging to the debtor or the estate. . . ." The court disagreed, stating that the Pennzoil claim did not belong to the debtor or the estate. Moreover, Pennzoil obviously was not being treated equally under the plan with all other creditors as required by Sec. 1123(a)(4). Could this plan be confirmed by the court? Discuss. (*In re Texaco, Inc.*, 84 B.R. 893, Bkrtcy. S.D.N.Y. 1988.)

5. Which of the following items of property would *not* be part of a debtor's estate in a bankruptcy case? Explain.

a. A one-half interest in a patent on a machine the debtor had helped invent

b. A fifty-acre tract of ranch land, used by the debtor to pasture cattle

c. An easement which permitted the debtor to drive his pickup and run his cattle over another person's land to get to the public road

d. The debtor's residence in the city

e. One hundred head of cattle

f. A diamond ring, as an inheritance from his father, which the debtor became entitled to receive 30 days after the petition filing date but which he actually received more than seven months later

g. The debtor's salary earned within 180 days after the petition filing date

h. Future payments under a veteran's pension, to which the debtor has a vested right

i. A claim by the debtor against a third party for breach of contract, whose claim could be worth anything from zero to $100,000

6. A Wyoming statute allowed an exemption from bankruptcy proceedings for motor vehicles "used and kept for the purpose of carrying on a trade or business." In his voluntary bankruptcy proceeding, Jerald Johnston claimed an exemption under this law for his 1967 half-ton pickup truck, which he used for transportation to and from his job as a waiter at a restaurant located several miles from his home. The trustee, Gary Barney, objected to the exemption, contending that the pickup did not meet the statute's requirements. Was the pickup exempt? (*Johnston v. Barney*, 842 F.2d 1221, 10th Cir. 1988.)

7. Greenway Plaza Investment Co. (Greenway) owned as its principal asset real property in Austin, Texas, known as the Greenway Plaza Apartments. Beneficial, a creditor with a lien on the apartments, foreclosed on the property. A foreclosure sale was conducted at which Beneficial purchased the apartments for a credit bid against their substantial lien. However, the fair market value of the property at the time of the sale was $2.5 million and the foreclosure price was only roughly 64 percent of that estimated value. Greenway filed a voluntary Chapter 11 bankruptcy petition within one year of the sale. The court found that debtor was insolvent at the time of the sale. A complaint was filed to set aside the foreclosure sale as a fraudulent transfer. What would be the result? (*In re Lindsay*, 98 B.R. 983, Bkrtcy. S.D.Cal. 1989.)

8. In 1986, Joe Henderson, while a manager at Economy Car Leasing (Economy), was discovered to have improperly diverted corporate funds for personal use. Henderson was fired, and on July 30, 1986, entered into an agreement with Economy to make certain restitution payments including $40,000 cash and a non-dischargeable note for $125,000 in exchange for Economy's agreement never to reveal the reasons for his termination. More than 90 days but less than one year later, Henderson filed a Chapter 7 bankruptcy petition. The trustee sought to avoid the payments made to Economy arguing that they constituted voidable preferences. It was stipulated that the debtor was insolvent at the time of the payments and that Economy received more than it would have in a Chapter 7 case. Were the payments voidable as preferences? Explain. (*In re Henderson*, 96 B.R. 820, Bkrtcy. E.D.Tenn. 1989.)

9. Jossee Dias owned and operated a cleaning business known as J.P. Cleaners prior to and after the filing of his Chapter 7 bankruptcy petition. Dias estimated that his annual income for the business was negligible. A creditor objected to discharge on the ground that Dias failed to keep adequate business records without justification. Dias kept no general ledgers of billings, receipts, expenses, or accounts payable. Instead, he kept only the cleaning ticket receipts, bank deposit slips, cancelled checks, and other miscellaneous documents including some cash register tapes from which he argued that a creditor could compile sufficient information to ascertain his financial condition. Dias testified that he did not have time to maintain additional financial records because the operation of his business required all his attention. Should discharge be denied? (*In re Dias*, 95 B.R. 419, Bkrtcy. N.D.Tex. 1988.)

10. Insolvency proceedings involving Polly Peck International plc, a multinational holding company with 200 subsidiaries located worldwide, were the largest in the history of the United Kingdom, involving 2000 nonshareholder creditors with claims of more than $2 billion. Before its insolvency, Polly Peck's shares were traded on the London stock exchange. In late 1990, a court appointed "administrators" (the equivalent of trustees in bankruptcy) for Polly Peck. Under English law, this appointment triggered a stay of all judicial proceedings against Polly Peck without the consent of the administrators or permission of the English court. Thereafter, American citizens filed two lawsuits in the United States against Polly Peck claiming negligence, fraud, and violation of U.S. securities laws. Polly Peck moved to dismiss the U.S. actions in light of the proceedings in the United Kingdom. Should the court dismiss the suits? Discuss. (*Linder Fund, Inc. v. Polly Peck International plc*, 143 Bkrtcy. 807, S.D.N.Y. 1992.)

PART IV

AGENCY AND PARTNERSHIPS

The law of agency deals with the various rights and responsibilities that exist when one person acts in a representative role for another. Because most of the world's work is done by persons acting as representatives of companies or of other individuals, the law of agency is among the most fundamental of subject areas. Moreover, an understanding of the law of agency is essential to the study of business organizations, including partnerships, which are discussed immediately following agency, and corporations, which are discussed in Part V.

The law of employment is also very closely related to the law of agency, because many agents are also employees. Most of our present laws governing employment, however, are statutory in nature, and most of them create legal rights for employees that were not recognized by the common law of agency. For this reason, we are deferring our discussion of employment law to Part VII, Government Regulation of Business.

Chapter 31 focuses on the basic nature of the agency relationship, the methods by which such a relationship is created and terminated, and the duties of the principal and agent to one another. Chapter 32 then examines the duties and liabilities of the principal and agent to third parties.

Following our discussion of agency, we will explore the partnership form of business organization. As you will see, the subject of partnerships ties in very closely with agency, because a business partnership is founded on agency relationships. Chapter 33 looks primarily at the formation of partnerships, Chapter 34 at their daily operation, and Chapter 35 at their termination. Chapter 36 then discusses limited partnerships.⚖⚖

Agency

Nature, Creation, Duties, and Termination

Nature of the Agency Relationship

Creation of the Agency Relationship

Duties of Principal and Agent

Termination of the Agency Relationship

NATURE OF THE AGENCY RELATIONSHIP

In a legal context the term **agency** ordinarily describes a relationship in which two parties—the principal and the agent—agree that one will act as a representative of the other. The **principal** is the person who wishes to accomplish something, and the **agent** is the one employed to act in the principal's behalf to achieve it.

At one time or another, almost everyone has come into contact with the agency relationship. Anyone who has purchased merchandise at a retail store almost certainly has dealt with an agent—the salesclerk. Similarly, anyone who has ever held a job probably has served in some type of representative capacity for the employer.

The usefulness of the agency relationship in the business world is obvious. With few exceptions, no single individual is capable of performing every act required to run a business enterprise. Furthermore, many businesses are organized as corporations, which by definition can act only by employing agents. As a result, most business transactions throughout the world are handled by agents.

The term *agency* is often used loosely to describe many different types of relationships in which one party acts in a representative capacity for another. *Principal* and *agent* are also sometimes used loosely to denote the parties to various types of arrangements. However, throughout our discussion these terms are used narrowly to describe a particular type of relationship. The **principal-agent relationship,** as we use it, means a relationship in which the parties have agreed that the agent is to represent the principal in negotiating and transacting business; that is, the agent is employed to make contracts or enter similar business transactions in behalf of the principal. The term will ordinarily be used in discussions of contractual liability.

Two similar relationships are the **employer-employee relationship** (which is still sometimes referred to by the older term *master-servant relationship*), and the **employer-independent contractor relationship.** The distinction between an employee and an independent contractor is important to many different kinds of legal questions. For example, state workers' compensation laws, federal antidiscrimination statutes, and many other laws regulating employment are applicable only to employees and not to independent contractors. Similarly, federal tax laws requiring the employer to withhold income and social security taxes and to contribute to the worker's social security account are applicable only to employees and not to independent contractors. In the law of agency, the distinction is important when a third party tries to hold the employer legally responsible for a *tort* committed by the employee. As we will see toward the end of the next chapter, an employer often can be held liable for the job-related torts of its employees, but usually cannot be held liable for such torts committed by those working for it as independent contractors.

It also is important to note that the same worker can be both an agent and an employee or both an agent and an independent contractor. Which relationship is relevant depends on the nature of the legal issues in the dispute. When the legal question involves either (1) the rights and duties between the superior and subordinate or (2) the superior's liability to third parties for contracts or other transactions executed by the subordinate, the relevant question usually is whether the subordinate was an agent who acted with authority. On the other hand, if the legal question involves the superior's liability for a tort committed by the subordinate, the relevant question usually is whether the subordinate was an employee who acted within the scope of his or her employment.

Sometimes, however, it is appropriate to use the term agent and to discuss the agent's authority when the legal issue is the superior's tort liability. This happens mainly in two situations: First, it is appropriate to use agent and authority concepts when the superior has directly authorized the agent to engage in the wrongful conduct. In such a case, the superior is liable to the third party for the subordinate's tort regardless of whether the latter is an employee or an independent contractor. Second, courts sometimes use agent and authority concepts when the subordinate's tort was *nonphysical* in nature, such as fraud, defamation, and so on.

Most of our discussion in these two chapters involves the principal-agent relationship; the employer-employee and employer-independent contractor relationships are dealt with in the latter part of the next chapter.

CREATION OF THE AGENCY RELATIONSHIP
Necessary Elements

The agency relationship is *consensual*—that is, based on the agreement of the parties. Many times it is created by a legally enforceable employment contract between the principal and the agent. A legally binding contract is not essential, however. An agency relationship that gives the agent authority to represent the principal and bind him or her by the agent's actions can generally be established by any words or actions that indicate the parties' consent to the arrangement. Consideration is not required.

In fact, no formalities are required for the creation of an agency relationship in most circumstances. For example, it is not usually necessary to spell out the agent's authority in writing; oral authority is ordinarily sufficient. Exceptions do exist, however. The most common one occurs when an agent is granted authority to sell real estate. In a majority of states an agent can make a contract for the sale of real estate that will bind the principal only if the agent's authority is stated in writing.

Even though formalities are usually not required for the creation of an agency, it is certainly wise to express the extent of an agent's authority and any other relevant matters in writing. This precaution often prevents misunderstandings between the principal and agent or between the agent and third parties with whom he or she is dealing. The formal written authorization given by a principal to an agent is frequently referred to as a **power of attorney.** When a formal power of attorney is used, the agent is sometimes referred to as an **attorney-in-fact.** This is simply another term for an agent, and should not be confused with attorney-at-law (a lawyer). Courts generally scrutinize powers of attorney very carefully and interpret their language strictly.

In the following case, an agent learned the hard way about the rule that powers of attorney are interpreted very strictly, and found that good intentions are no substitute for authority.

KING V. BANKERD

Court of Appeals of Maryland, 492 A.2d 608 (1985)

Howard R. Bankerd (Bankerd) and his wife Virginia owned, as "tenants by the entirety," a home in Montgomery County, Maryland. (A "tenancy by the entirety" is one type of joint ownership created by the marriage relationship in some states; see Chapter 41 for details.) They lived there until 1966 when Mrs. Bankerd moved out as a result of marital problems. Bankerd continued to live at the property until July, 1968, when he "left for the west." Mrs. Bankerd then resumed living on the property. For the next twelve years, Bankerd lived at various locations in Nevada, Colorado, and Washington, and made no payments on the mortgage, for taxes, or for the maintenance of the home.

Before Bankerd's departure, he executed a power of attorney to King, an attorney with whom he was acquainted. From 1971 to 1974, Bankerd did not communicate with King in any way. In 1975, however, King sent Bankerd a letter enclosing an updated power of attorney because the Washington Suburban Sanitary Commission was about to put a sewer adjacent to the property, and King believed the new power would be needed. This power of attorney, dated October 30, 1975, was executed by Bankerd and returned to King. It stated:

KNOW ALL MEN BY THESE PRESENTS, that I, Howard R. Bankerd, hereby make, constitute and appoint

ARTHUR V. KING, my attorney for me, and in my name to convey, grant, bargain and/or sell the property designated in the Montgomery County land record as Lot 9 of an unrecorded subdivision as recorded in Liber 3027 at folio 293, situated at 14026 Travilah Road, Rockville, Maryland on such terms as to him may seem best, and in my name, to make, execute, acknowledge and deliver, good and sufficient deeds and conveyances for the same with or without covenants and warranties and generally to do and perform all things necessary pertaining to the future transfer of said property, and generally to do everything whatsoever necessary pertaining to the said property.

After granting this power of attorney, Bankerd had no further communication with King until 1978.

Mrs. Bankerd, who had been living at and maintaining the property
(continues)

KING V. BANKERD

(continued from previous page)
since 1968, requested King in September 1977 to exercise the power of attorney and to transfer Bankerd's interest in the property to her. King was aware that Mrs. Bankerd was nearing retirement and that she was "saddled" with a property she could neither sell nor mortgage because of her husband's legal interest in it. Consequently, King made several attempts to find and communicate with Bankerd, but was unsuccessful.

Mrs. Bankerd informed King that her husband had once attempted to give the property away to a neighbor on the condition that the neighbor assume the mortgage payments. As a result, King asserted that he believed Bankerd "didn't give a damn" about the property, and that given Bankerd's age (approximately sixty-nine years), King believed that Bankerd might even be deceased. King therefore conveyed Bankerd's interest in the property to Mrs. Bankerd by deed in 1978. Mrs. Bankerd paid no consideration for the transfer and King received no compensation for executing the deed. Mrs. Bankerd then sold the property to a third party for $62,500.

In 1981 Bankerd filed suit against King alleging that King had acted negligently and had exceeded his authority as Bankerd's agent. The trial court granted summary judgment to Bankerd against King and awarded $13,555.05 in damages. The intermediate appellate court affirmed, and King appealed to Maryland's highest court.

Cole, Judge:

The single issue presented in this case is whether a power of attorney authorizing the agent to "convey, grant, bargain and/or sell" the principal's property authorizes the agent to make a gratuitous transfer [i.e., a gift] of that property. . . .

Broadly defined, a power of attorney is a written document by which one party, as principal, appoints another as agent (attorney-in-fact) and confers upon the latter the authority to perform certain specified acts or kinds of acts on behalf of the principal. . . . Various rules govern the interpretation of powers of attorney. . . . One well-settled rule is that powers of attorney are strictly construed . . . and are held to grant only those powers which are clearly delineated. . . .

Another accepted rule of construction is to discount or disregard all-embracing expressions found in powers of attorney. Because powers of attorney are ordinarily very carefully drafted and scrutinized, courts give the terms used a technical rather than a popular meaning. In addition, ambiguities in an instrument are resolved against the party who made it or caused it to be made, because that party had the better opportunity to understand and explain his meaning. Finally, general words used in an instrument are restricted by the context in which they are used, and are construed accordingly. . . .

For the reasons below, we conclude that an agent holding a broad power of attorney lacks the power to make a gift of the principal's property, unless that power (1) is expressly conferred, (2) arises as a necessary implication from the conferred powers, or (3) is clearly intended by the parties, as evidenced by the surrounding facts and circumstances.

First, the power to make a gift of the principal's property is a power that is potentially hazardous to the principal's interests. Consequently, this power will not be lightly inferred from broad, all-encompassing grants of power to the agent. Accordingly, "the agent must be circumspect with regard to the powers created—or the lack of them."

Second, the main duty of an agent is loyalty to the interest of his principal. Thus, in exercising granted powers under a power of attorney, the attorney in fact is bound to act for the benefit of his principal and must avoid where possible that which is detrimental unless expressly authorized. It is difficult to imagine how a gift of the principal's real property would be to the benefit of the principal when the power of attorney does not authorize such a gift or the principal does not intend to authorize such a gift. In short, the agent is under a duty to serve his principal with only his principal's purposes in mind. Third, it would be most unusual for an owner of property to grant a power of attorney authorizing the attorney in fact to give his property away. If a person has decided to make a gift of property, he or she usually decides as to who is going to be the donee. . . .

The facts and surrounding circumstances presented in this case do not give rise to any fact or inference that King was authorized to make a gift of Bankerd's real property. In arguing that his conduct was reasonable under the circumstances, King points to his "beliefs" that Bankerd had abandoned the property, that Bankerd did not care about the property, and that Bankerd might be deceased. These arguments completely miss the mark. King's conduct could only be "reasonable" if Bankerd intended for King to give the property away. Although the facts and surrounding circumstances to which King points suggest reasons why he made the gift, they do not support an inference that Bankerd intended to authorize the gift.

Furthermore, the only evidence before the trial court that was relevant to this issue indicated that Bankerd did not intend to authorize King to give the subject property to Bankerd's wife or anyone else. In a letter Bankerd sent to King along with the executed power of attorney, Bankerd wrote that "[y]ou know if I outlive Va., (and I'm ornery enough) you would certainly have a job on that Travilah Road bit *if* you would accept it, that is." Nothing could more clearly belie an assertion that Bankerd

(continues)

KING V. BANKERD

(continued from previous page)
authorized any gift of the property. Bankerd, by virtue of this correspondence, notified King that he clearly anticipated maintaining his interest in the property. Furthermore, King wrote Bankerd assuring him that if the latter executed the new power of attorney he would do nothing detrimental to Bankerd's interests. Certainly, had King believed that he was acquiring the authority to give away Bankerd's property, King would not have made this representation.

In sum, there is no genuine dispute as to any material fact. The trial court did not err in granting Bankerd's motion for summary judgment.

Judgment affirmed. [Note: Instead of suing his agent for damages, Bankerd could have sued to set aside the transfer of his interest to his wife, which, in turn, would have invalidated the transfer by her to the third party.]

Capacity

If an agent, acting in behalf of a principal, makes a properly authorized contract with a third party, the contract is viewed legally as being one between the principal and the third party; that is, it is the *principal's* contract, not the agent's. For this reason the principal's capacity to make contracts may be important in determining the validity of the contract in question. The minority, insanity, or other incapacity of the principal has the same effect on contracts made through an agent as it does on contracts made personally.

LEGAL FOCUS

International

As we have seen, the general rule under state law in the United States is that powers of attorney are interpreted very strictly. The United States is not the only place where this attitude is taken toward powers of attorney. A case decided recently by the Versailles Court of Appeals in France illustrates the same approach. In the case, *Societé Generale v. Erulin*, [1991] ECC 132, Madeline Erulin opened a bank account in her name with Societé Generale. Shortly thereafter, she executed a general power of attorney to her sister-in-law, Francoise Erulin, giving the latter the authority to operate the account as if she were the owner. About three weeks later, Francoise applied to the bank for a "credit card" on the account, signing the application as the owner. Francoise executed a guarantee to the bank for up to 100,000 French Francs (FF). The card operated as a debit card for withdrawing money so long as the account had a positive balance. If the balance became negative, the card served as a credit card that permitted overdrafts.

When the card was issued to Francoise, the account had a significant positive balance. During the next three months, however, Francoise used the card for purchases and withdrawals in huge amounts, resulting in a negative balance of 107,000 FF. During these three months, bank statements were sent to Madeline; she did not examine these statements but forwarded them directly to Francoise. When the negative balance passed 100,000 FF, the bank notified Francoise, not Madeline. The overdraft of 107,000 FF plus interest was not paid, and the bank sued both Madeline and Francoise. Both of the defendants filed counterclaims against the bank.

Ultimately, the Court of Appeals held that the bank acted wrongfully by issuing the credit card to Francoise without notifying Madeline. Although the court spoke in terms of the bank's negligence, its holding clearly was also based on a restrictive view of powers of attorney. The general power of attorney did not specifically give Francoise authority to obtain "extra facilities" such as the credit card; as a consequence, she had no such authority. Although the court admitted that Madeline was somewhat negligent by simply forwarding the bank statements to Francoise without examining them, the court placed the burden of the loss on the bank and Francoise. The bank was held responsible for two-thirds of the loss, and Francoise the other one-third.

On the other hand, the agent's capacity is usually immaterial. The reason is the same—the contract made by the agent for the principal is the principal's contract. A minor, for example, can serve as an agent; his or her lack of contractual capacity ordinarily has no effect on a contract made in behalf of the principal.[1]

DUTIES OF PRINCIPAL AND AGENT

The principal-agent relationship is a **fiduciary relationship**—one of trust. Each party owes the other a duty to act with the utmost good faith. Each should be entirely open with the other, not keeping any information from the other that has any bearing on their arrangement. Other duties, some of which are merely specific applications of the general fiduciary obligation, are discussed below and outlined in Fig. 31.1.

Duties Owed by Principal to Agent

The primary duty owed by the principal to the agent is simply that of complying with the terms of their employment contract, if one exists. Failure of the

---

[1] Of course, the agent's lack of contractual capacity has an effect on his or her own contract of employment with the principal, if one exists. The agent's capacity can also be important if for any reason the third party attempts to hold the agent personally responsible on a contract made with that party.

principal to do so will render him or her liable to the agent for damages; if the breach is material, it will justify the agent in refusing to act for the principal any further. For example: P and A have agreed that A is to be paid a specified percentage of the sales she makes for P. If P refuses or fails to pay A, A can rightfully terminate their arrangement and hold P responsible for damages.

In addition, the principal is under a duty to reimburse the agent for any expenditures reasonably incurred by the agent in furthering the interests of the principal. For example, if P directs A to travel from Chicago to Los Angeles to transact business for P, but does not provide her with any funds for travel expenses, P will be under a duty when A returns to reimburse her for amounts she reasonably expended in making the trip, such as her round-trip air fare.

Similarly, the principal has an obligation to indemnify the agent for liabilities or losses the latter suffers while acting lawfully and within the scope of his or her authority.

Duties Owed by Agent to Principal
Obedience

It is the duty of the agent to obey the clear instructions of the principal, so long as such instructions are legal. If the instructions are ambiguous, the agent cannot disregard them altogether, but he or she can

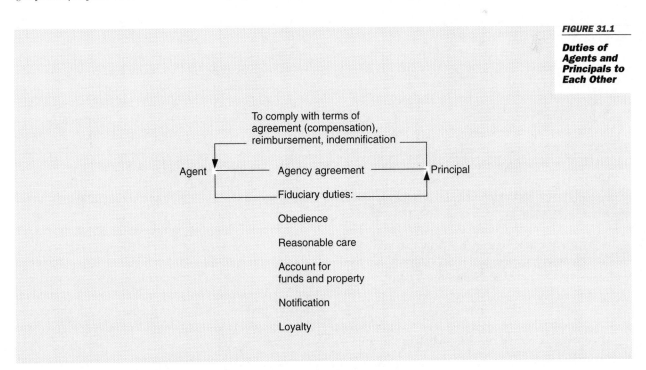

FIGURE 31.1

Duties of Agents and Principals to Each Other

fulfill the duty by acting in good faith and interpreting them in a manner that is reasonable under the circumstances.

Where the instructions are both legal and clear, the agent is justified in departing from them on only rare occasions. One such occasion is when an *emergency* occurs and following the principal's original instructions is not in that person's best interests. The agent should, of course, consult with the principal and obtain new instructions if possible. But if there is no opportunity to consult, the agent is justified in taking reasonable steps to protect the principal, even if it means deviating from priorinstructions. Indeed, the agent may even be under a duty to depart from instructions if following them in the emergency can be considered so unreasonable as to be negligent. (The agent's authority to act in emergencies is discussed more fully in the next chapter.)

Reasonable Care

Unless special provisions in the agreement say otherwise, an agent is normally expected to exercise the degree of care and skill that is reasonable under the circumstances. In other words, the agent has a duty not to be negligent. For example, suppose that B has funds which he wishes to lend to borrowers at current interest rates. He employs C to act in his behalf in locating the borrowers. C lends B's money to T without investigating T's credit rating and without obtaining from T any security for the loan. T turns out to be a notoriously bad credit risk and is actually insolvent at the time of the loan. If B is later unable to collect from T, C will probably be liable to B, because he failed to exercise reasonable care in making the loan.

Under some circumstances, an agent may be under a special duty to exercise more than an ordinary degree of care and skill. For example, if a person undertakes to serve in a capacity that necessarily involves the possession and exercise of a special skill, such as that of a lawyer or stockbroker, he or she is required to exercise the skill ordinarily possessed by competent persons pursuing that particular calling.

In any agency relationship, the principal and agent can by agreement change the agent's duty of care and skill, making it either stricter or more lenient.

Duty to Account

Unless principal and agent agree otherwise, it is the agent's duty to keep and make available to the principal an account of all the money or property received or paid out in behalf of the principal. In this regard, an agent should never mix his or her own money or property with that of the principal. The agent should, for example, set up a separate bank account for the principal's money. If the agent commingles (mixes) his or her own money or property with the principal's in such a way that it cannot be separated or identified, the principal can legally claim all of it.

Duty to Notify

Another important duty of the agent is to notify the principal of all relevant facts—just about any information having a bearing on the interests of the principal—as soon as reasonably possible after learning of them. For example, if A (the agent) discovers that one of P's (the principal's) creditors is about to foreclose a lien on P's property, A should promptly notify P. Or if A learns that one of P's important customers, who owes P a substantial amount of money, has just filed for bankruptcy, A should contact P as soon as possible.

Loyalty

Perhaps the most important duty owed by the agent to the principal is that of loyalty. Violation of this duty can occur in numerous ways. A few of the more significant actions constituting a breach of the duty are discussed below.

Quite obviously, the agent should not *compete* with the principal in the type of business he or she is conducting for the principal, unless the principal expressly gives consent. To illustrate: X, who owns a textile manufacturing business, employs Y to act as his sales agent. Y will be violating his duty of loyalty if, without X's consent, he acquires a personal interest in a textile manufacturing business that competes with X's.

The law presumes that a principal hires an agent to serve the principal's interests and not the personal interests of the agent. Thus the agent should avoid any existing or potential conflict of interest. For example, if B is hired to sell goods for R, he should not sell to himself. Or if he is hired to buy goods for R, he should not buy them from himself. It is difficult, if not impossible, for the agent to completely serve the principal's interests when his or her own personal interests become involved. Of course, such things can be done if the principal is fully informed and gives consent.

In a similar fashion, the agent should not further the interests of any third party in his or her dealings for the principal. The agent also should not work for two parties on opposite sides in a transaction unless both parties agree to it.

If the agent, in working for the principal, acquires knowledge of any *confidential information,* he or she should not disclose this information to outsiders without the principal's consent. To illustrate: G hires H, a lawyer, to represent G in defending a lawsuit filed against G by T. T alleges that his factory was damaged in a fire caused by certain chemicals, purchased by T from G, that were highly flammable and not labeled with an adequate warning. In order to properly defend G, H must learn the secret formulas and processes for producing the chemicals. After learning them, he should not disclose them to anyone without G's consent, either at that time or at any time in the future.

The following case illustrates the strictness of the duty of loyalty owed by an agent to the principal.

GIRARD V. MYERS

Court of Appeals of Washington, 694 P.2d 678 (1985)

Michael Myers was a real estate developer and licensed salesman in the state of Washington. In 1974, he contracted to purchase a 290-acre tract of land known as the Pickering Farm. The purchase contract divided the land into seven parcels, and Myers then obtained groups of investors to purchase each parcel. Myers himself bought one 13.2-acre parcel out of the tract. As a condition of their participation, Myers required these investors to sign a document entitled "Trust and Resale Agreement." This agreement designated Myers as the exclusive sales agent for all of the investors in the event they later desired to resell their parcels, and also gave Myers a "right of first refusal." Under this right of first refusal, if a particular investor or group of investors owning a parcel subsequently desired to resell the land to a third party, they first had to give Myers the opportunity to purchase it at the price offered by the third party, less an 11 percent discount. If Myers chose not to buy the parcel, the investor was obligated to pay Myers an 11 percent commission on the sale to the third party.

In early 1977, two investors, Butler and Kline, decided to sell one-half of their parcel to Girard. Myers indicated that he would refrain from exercising his right of first refusal only if Girard signed a Trust and Resale Agreement identical to that signed by the original investors. This was done and Girard made the purchase, with Myers receiving a sales commission from Butler and Kline.

Myers controlled three limited partnerships that engaged in real estate investment and development. In late 1977 and 1978, these partnerships acquired 51 acres next to the parcel owned by Girard. In 1979 Girard informed Myers that Girard wanted to transfer his land to a partnership that was being formed between Girard and John Sato. Girard also told Myers that Girard considered the Trust and Resale Agreement to be void and that he did not intend to honor it. Girard filed suit asking the court to declare the agreement void and unenforceable. Myers asserted a counterclaim for an 11 percent sales commission on the transfer.

The court ruled that the right of first refusal was unenforceable because it placed no time limit on Myers' exercise of the right and because its terms were too vague, and then held that the sales commission and price discount provisions were void because Myers' ownership and financial interests in the 13.2-acre and 51-acre parcels created an impermissible conflict of interest. Thus the trial court held for Girard and dismissed Myers' counterclaim for the sales commission, and Myers appealed. Only that portion of the appellate court's opinion dealing with the conflict of interest is presented below.

Scholfield, Chief Judge:

The trial court found that the 51 acres acquired by three limited partnerships . . . and the 13.2-acre parcel individually acquired by Myers were "actually or potentially competitive" with the Girard property. . . . Myers argues that his interest in and ownership of property adjacent to the Girard parcel did not violate his fiduciary duties as selling agent "because Girard knew before he purchased the property or signed the agreement that Myers both owned property and intended to remain involved in the coordinated development of the Pickering Farms parcels." He also argues that the Trust and Resale Agreement made the following disclosure:

(8) DISCLOSURE: Agent is in the business of selling and purchasing real property for its own account and as agent for other principals, disclosed and undisclosed. Owner has employed agent for the specific purposes set forth herein and no other relationship of a

(continues)

GIRARD V. MYERS

(continued from previous page)

legal, quasi-legal or of a fiduciary nature exists between the parties.

The record would support a finding Girard knew of Myers' ownership of the 13.2 acres. However, the record is clear that Myers acquired the 51 acres through the three limited partnerships after Girard signed the Trust and Resale Agreement.

Myers does not [challenge] the findings of fact in which the trial court found that the properties Myers owned or had substantial interest in were actually or potentially competitive with the Girard parcel. Thus, a conflict of interest is an established fact in this case. The only issue is whether Myers made a full and timely disclosure to Girard of all material facts regarding the conflict. [As stated by this court in a previous case]:

> We begin with the fundamental rule that a real estate agent has the duty to exercise the utmost good faith and fidelity toward his principal in all matters falling within the scope of his employment. Such agent must exercise reasonable care, skill, and judgment in securing the best bargain possible, and must scrupulously avoid representing interests antagonistic to that of the principal without the explicit and fully informed consent of the principal. Further, the agent must make a full, fair, and timely disclosure to the principal of all facts within the agent's knowledge which are, or may be, material to the transaction and which might affect the principal's rights and interests or influence his actions. Consequently, a dual agency relationship is permissible when both parties have full knowledge of the facts and consent thereto. Before such consent can be held to exist, clear and express disclosure of the dual agency relation and the material circumstances that may influence the consent to the dual agency must be made.

A full and timely disclosure of the facts regarding the 51 acres could not have been made before Girard signed the Trust and Resale Agreement because those properties were not acquired until after the Trust and Resale Agreement was signed. If Myers desired to show that he had made a full disclosure to Girard when the 51 acres were acquired and that he had given Girard the option of either consenting to the conflict of interest or terminating the Trust and Resale Agreement, Myers had the burden of producing evidence on that issue. . . .

The record does not support Myers' argument that all material facts giving rise to the conflict of interest were fully disclosed to Girard. Myers' conflict was unusual in this case because he could profit personally by arranging sales of properties in which he had a personal interest and, at the same time, he could frustrate a sale by Girard to a prospective purchaser interested in both properties, through his claimed right of first refusal and an 11 percent discount. The findings of the trial court on the conflict issue are supported by substantial evidence. We conclude that Myers' claim for a commission should be denied because Myers breached his fiduciary duty as a selling agent.⚖

TERMINATION OF THE AGENCY RELATIONSHIP

Like most private consensual arrangements, the agency relationship usually comes to an end at some point. Termination can occur because of something done by the parties themselves or by operation of law (something beyond their control). Our discussion focuses on the termination of the relationship between the principal and the agent, ignoring for the moment the effects of termination on third parties who might deal with the agent. (The circumstances under which third parties should be notified of the termination and the type of notice required are dealt with in the next chapter.)

Termination by Act of the Parties

Fulfillment of Purpose

Many times an agent is employed to accomplish a particular object, such as the sale of a tract of land belonging to the principal. When this object is accomplished and nothing else remains to be done, the agency relationship terminates.

Lapse of Time

If principal and agent have agreed originally that the arrangement will end at a certain time, the arrival of that time terminates their relationship. If nothing has been said as to the duration of the agency, and if nothing occurs to terminate it, the relationship is deemed to last for a period of time that is reasonable under the circumstances. This generally is a question of whether, after passage of a particular period of time, it is reasonable for the agent to believe that the principal still intends for him or her to act as earlier directed. Of course, if the principal *knows* that the agent is continuing to make efforts to perform, and if the principal does nothing about the situation, the agency relationship may remain alive for a period of time longer than would otherwise be held reasonable.

Occurrence of Specified Event

In a similar fashion, if the principal and agent have originally agreed that the agency, or some particular aspect of it, will continue until a specified event occurs, the occurrence of the event results in termination. For example: P authorizes A to attempt to sell P's farm, Blackacre, for him "only until P returns from New York." When P returns, A's authority to sell Blackacre as P's agent comes to an end. An analogous situation occurs when principal and agent have agreed that the agency, or some aspect of it, will remain in existence only during the continuance of a stated condition. If the condition ceases to exist, the agent's authority terminates. For instance: X directs Y, X's credit manager, to extend $10,000 in credit to T, so long as T's inventory of goods on hand and his accounts receivable amount to $50,000 and his accounts payable do not exceed $25,000. If T's combined inventory and accounts receivable drop below $50,000, the agency terminates insofar as it relates to Y's authority to grant credit to T.

Mutual Agreement

Regardless of what the principal and agent have agreed to originally, they can agree at any time to end their relationship. It makes no difference whether the relationship has been based on a binding employment contract or whether no enforceable employment contract exists; their mutual agreement terminates the agency in either case. It is a basic rule of contract law that the parties can rescind (cancel) the contract by mutual agreement.

Act of One Party

Since the agency relationship is consensual, it can usually be terminated by either the principal or the agent if that person no longer wants to be a party to the arrangement. In most circumstances termination occurs simply by one party indicating to the other that he or she no longer desires to continue the relationship. This is true even if the parties had originally agreed that the agency was to be irrevocable.

If no binding employment contract exists between the two of them, the party terminating the agency normally does not incur any liability to the other by this action. If an enforceable employment contract does exist, one party may be justified in terminating it if the other has violated any of the duties owed under it. Of course, if there are no facts justifying termination, the party taking such action may be responsible to the other for any damages caused by the breach of contract. But the agency relationship is ended nevertheless.

One major exception exists to the ability of either party to terminate the relationship. If the agency is not just a simple one but instead is an **agency coupled with an interest** (that is, the agent has an interest in the subject matter of the agency), the principal cannot terminate the agent's authority without the agent's consent. (Note, however, that an agent is not considered to have an interest in the subject matter simply because he or she expects to make a commission or profit from the activities as agent.) To illustrate: P borrows $5,000 from A. To secure the loan, P grants A a *security interest* (a property interest for the sole purpose of securing a debt) in P's inventory. As part of the agreement, P makes A his agent for the sale of the inventory in case P defaults on the loan. Since A has an interest in the subject matter of the agency (the inventory), the arrangement is an agency coupled with an interest, and P cannot terminate A's authority to sell without A's consent (unless, of course, P repays the loan, in which case A no longer has an interest in the subject matter).

The reason for the exception is that the agent is not really acting for the principal in this situation. By exercising this authority, the agent is acting in his or her own behalf to assert a personal interest.

Termination by Operation of Law

Death or Insanity

The death or insanity of the *agent* immediately terminates an agency relationship. The death or insanity of the *principal* also terminates an agency relationship. In most cases the termination of an agency by the principal's death or insanity occurs immediately, regardless of whether the agent knows what has happened.

Bankruptcy

The insolvency or bankruptcy of the *agent* does not always terminate the agency, but will do so in those circumstances where it impairs the agent's ability to act for the principal. To illustrate: B is authorized by I, an investment house, to act as its agent in advising I's local clients about investments. If B becomes bankrupt, he will no longer be authorized to act for I. The reason is simple; the agent in this situation should realize that the principal probably would not want him to act in its behalf any longer if it knew the facts.

Suppose, however, that the *principal* becomes insolvent or bankrupt, and the agent knows about it. In this case the agent might no longer have authority to act for the principal—but only under circumstances where the agent ought to realize that the principal would no longer want such transactions to be conducted in his or her behalf. For example: P has authorized A to buy an expensive fur coat on credit for P. If P becomes bankrupt, this will probably terminate the agency when A learns of it. A should reasonably infer that under the circumstances P will no longer want him to make such a purchase. However, if A is P's housekeeper and has been authorized to buy groceries for P's household, P's bankruptcy probably will not extinguish that authority. The inference that A should reasonably draw when learning the facts is that P will want her to continue buying necessities such as food until informed otherwise. It is simply a matter of reasonableness.

Change of Law

If a change in the law makes the agency or the performance of the authorized act *illegal*, the agent's authority is ordinarily extinguished when he or she learns of the change. To illustrate: S is a salesperson for T, a toy manufacturer. If a federal agency determines that certain of T's toys are dangerous and bans them, S's authority to sell them to retailers probably will be terminated when she learns of the government ban. That is, upon learning the facts, S should reasonably assume that T will no longer want her to sell the banned items.

Even if the change in the law does not make the agency or the authorized act illegal, termination can still occur if the agent learns of the change and should reasonably expect that the principal will no longer want him or her to act in the manner previously authorized. For instance: A is authorized to purchase fabricated aluminum from a foreign supplier. The federal government imposes a new tariff on imported aluminum that results in substantially higher prices. It is likely that A's authority to buy foreign aluminum will be terminated when he learns of the change.

Loss or Destruction of Subject Matter

The loss or destruction of the subject matter of an agency relationship will terminate the agent's author-

ity. If, for example, X employs Y to sell grain belonging to X that is being stored in a particular storage elevator, the destruction by fire of the elevator and the grain will ordinarily extinguish Y's authority.

Whether the agent's authority terminates automatically or only when he or she learns of the facts depends on the nature and terms of the original agreement between principal and agent. In the instant case, if, instead of a fire, X himself sells the grain to a buyer (which actually amounts to X revoking Y's authority), Y's authority may or may not be automatically terminated. If X has given Y *exclusive authority* to sell, that authority ends only if X notifies Y that he has sold the grain himself. On the other hand, if the authority is not exclusive and Y should realize that X may try to sell the grain himself, Y's authority will terminate when X sells the grain even if Y does not know of the sale.

If the subject matter of the agency (such as the grain) is not lost or destroyed but is merely damaged, Y's authority is terminated if the circumstances are such that Y ought to realize that X would not want the transaction to be carried out.

Miscellaneous Changes of Conditions

The various occurrences we have discussed that terminate an agency by operation of law are by no means an exclusive list. For instance, in some circumstances the outbreak of war, a sudden change in the market value of the subject matter of the agency, or an unexpected loss of some required qualification by the principal or the agent (such as a license) may terminate the agency. Again, if all the circumstances known to the agent are such that he or she, as a reasonable person, ought to realize that the principal would no longer wish him or her to continue in the endeavor, the authority is ended. The agent simply must act in a reasonable fashion until there is an opportunity to consult with the principal.

SUMMARY

The law of agency governs the rights and responsibilities created when one person acts in a representative role for another. When the subordinate transacts business in behalf of the superior, the relationship is usually referred to as that of principal and agent. When the subordinate performs physical tasks for the superior, or when there is any question regarding the superior's tort liability for the actions of the subordinate, the relationship is usually referred to as that of either master and servant or employer and independent contractor. In general, an agency relationship of any type is created by agreement. The agreement may be a legally enforceable employment contract, but it does not have to be. The principal-agent relationship is a fiduciary relationship in which each party owes the other a duty to act in the utmost good faith. The principal owes to the agent the duty to compensate, reimburse for necessary expenses, and comply with any other terms of their agreement. The agent owes to the principal the duty to obey instructions, act with reasonable care, account for the principal's funds or property in the agent's possession, notify the principal of any facts relating to the interests of the principal, and always act with loyalty to the principal's interests. The principal-agent relationship may be terminated by various acts of the parties themselves, or by operation of law.

KEY TERMS

Agency
Principal
Agent
Principal-agent relationship
Employer-employee relationship
Employer-independent
contractor relationship
Power of attorney
Attorney-in-fact
Fiduciary relationship
Agency coupled with an interest

QUESTIONS AND PROBLEMS

1. The Fiscal Court of Adair County, which is a governing body for the county, fills certain county job vacancies in the following way (although the procedure is not in writing):

a. The Lake Cumberland Emergency Medical Systems, Inc. (LCEMSS) interviews job applicants to ensure minimum qualifications;

b. If the position is initially to be funded under the federal Comprehensive Employment and Training Act (CETA), CETA representatives must certify the applicant as "eligible";

c. The Fiscal Court then decides whom to hire.

Carlyne Terbovitz applied for a position which was to be CETA funded. The CETA representatives refused to process Terbovitz's application because she was female. Thus, the Fiscal Court never even reviewed the application. Terbovitz filed suit claiming that the Fiscal Court was guilty of sex discrimination. In the trial, certain officials of LCEMSS testified that the Fiscal Court had told them not to hire a woman for this position. In light of the procedure that was used to screen applicants and make hiring decisions, as well as the statements made by the Fiscal Court to LCEMSS, is the Fiscal Court liable for CETA's discrimination? Discuss. (*Terbovitz v. Fiscal Court of Adair County,* 825 F.2d 111, 6th Cir. 1987.)

2. Lenhardt was the general partner in East Bay Investments, and Petersen was the limited partner. Thus, Lenhardt was the person with authority to manage the business. Lenhardt delegated some of this authority to Petersen by authorizing him to handle all of the financial transactions and sign all documents for East Bay. East Bay sold a piece of land to Barrasso, and there was no question about this transaction because Lenhardt signed the deed. Barrasso borrowed money to make the purchase and gave a mortgage on the property to the lending institution as security. The lender required additional security, however. In order for the sale to go through, East Bay also gave Barrasso's lender a mortgage on some other real estate owned by East Bay. This mortgage was executed and signed only by Petersen in behalf of East Bay. Lenhardt did not know the details of these financial arrangements. Later, Barrasso defaulted on his loan and the lender foreclosed on the mortgages. Lenhardt claimed that the additional mortgage on other East Bay property was void because he had not known of its details, and Petersen was not authorized to execute the mortgage. Is Lenhardt bound by the mortgage that Petersen executed? Discuss. (*Federal Deposit Insurance Corp. v. Barrasso,* 791 F.2d 1529, 11th Cir. 1986.)

3. Whisper Mills is required to bargain with an international union unless the international union authorizes a local union to act as its agent. A local union claims that it has the right to bargain with Whisper Mills even though the international union has not given the local union permission to bind the international union to a collective bargaining contract with

Whisper Mills. Is the local union the international union's agent? (*Whisper Soft Mills v. N.L.R.B.*, 754 F.2d 1381, 9th Cir. 1984.)

4. Treasure Salvors sought to recover the lost treasure of the Spanish ship, the Santa Margarita. Treasure Salvors signed a contract with Captain Jordan, granting him the privilege of working the wrecks, and providing him with pay, specialized supplies, and 5 percent of the recovery of treasures and artifacts. After having great success, Captain Jordan became dissatisfied with the terms of his contract and began to keep his many finds. Does Captain Jordan have any right to more than 5 percent of the treasure? (*Treasure Salvors, Inc. v. Unidentified, Wrecked and Abandoned Sailing Vessel*, 556 F.Supp. 1319, D.Fla. 1983.)

5. Billy Sims hired Argovitz to act as his agent for the purpose of negotiating a contract for Sims as a player in the U.S. Football League (USFL). Unknown to Sims, Argovitz had a very large financial interest in the Houston Gamblers, the USFL's Houston franchise. Argovitz negotiated a very favorable contract for Sims with the Gamblers. Later, Sims found out about Argovitz's interest in the Gamblers, and he wanted out of the contract so that he could play for the Detroit Lions of the National Football League. Is Sims bound by the contract? Discuss. (*Detroit Lions and Sims v. Argovitz*, 580 F.Supp. 542, E.D. Mich. 1984.)

6. St. Croix Homes promised to pay Wilcox management fees for managing St. Croix's housing development. In his seven years as manager, Wilcox did not render full and complete accounts of his service to St. Croix, and the physical and financial condition of the development declined dramatically. Is Wilcox entitled to management fees from St. Croix? (*Wilcox v. St. Croix Labor Union Mutual Homes*, 567 F.Supp. 924, D. Virgin Islands 1983.)

7. Clay was hired by Green to sell Green's boat for not less than $700, out of which Clay was to receive a 10 percent commission. Clay sold the boat for $800

and offered Green $630 in settlement ($700 less 10 percent). Green demanded an additional $90 as the amount due him. Was Green justified in claiming the additional money? Explain.

8. Harkins, a salesman for Watson, was paid a commission on sales made for Watson. Harkins took an order from Boswell for merchandise. Watson accepted the order and shipped the merchandise. In the meantime, Boswell changed his mind and repudiated the transaction, claiming he no longer needed the goods. When they arrived, he refused to accept or pay for them and shipped them back to Watson. Watson claimed that Harkins was not entitled to a commission because the sale had not been completed. Is Watson correct? Explain.

9. Enterprise Federal Savings & Loan Association hired Commonwealth Capital Corp. as its agent for the purpose of acquiring deposits for Enterprise. The parties' contract gave Commonwealth the right to collect commissions from Enterprise, but it did not give Commonwealth any right to the funds it acquired for Enterprise. Can Enterprise unilaterally terminate this agency relationship, and thus terminate Commonwealth's authority, despite the fact that the relationship was created by a legally enforceable contract? Discuss. (*Commonwealth Capital Corp. v. Enterprise Federal Savings & Loan Association*, 630 F.Supp. 1199, E.D. La. 1986.)

10. Wheeler was a sales representative for Burton Enterprises. During his employment—and without telling his employer—Wheeler became a 22 percent owner of a building to be equipped to manufacture and distribute products in direct competition with Burton Enterprises. At the same time, Wheeler lured another of Burton Enterprises' salespersons to join his new company. Wheeler then quit his job with Burton Enterprises and began employment with The Formula One Company. Is Wheeler entitled to commissions earned while employed by Burton Enterprises? (*Burton Enterprises v. Wheeler*, 643 F.Supp. 588, D. Kansas 1986.)

Chapter 32

Agency
Liability of the Parties

Liability of the Principal

Liability of the Agent

Liability of the Third Party

Nonexistent, Partially Disclosed, and Undisclosed Principals

Tort Liability

Criminal Liability

W E HAVE ALREADY discussed the formation and termination of the agency relationship and the duties existing between the parties. Now we will focus our attention on the legal consequences of this relationship, primarily the *contractual liability* of those involved: principal, agent, and third parties. Near the end of the chapter we will deal with a superior's liability for the torts and crimes of his or her subordinates.

LIABILITY OF THE PRINCIPAL

The principal is, of course, liable to the agent if he or she breaches a valid employment contract with the agent or violates any other duty owing to the agent. However, the most important questions in this area relate to the principal's liability to the third parties with whom the agent has dealt. If A, acting in behalf of P, makes a contract with T, what is P's legal responsibility to T? If P does not perform as required in the contract, is P required by law to compensate T for T's losses resulting from P's breach?

The answers to these questions usually depend on the court's decision on another question: Was the agent acting within the scope of his or her *authority* in making this particular contract? We will now examine the approach taken by the courts in arriving at an answer.

The Agent's Authority to Act for the Principal

The fact that you have hired someone to act as your agent does not mean that the person can represent you in any way he or she sees fit. An agent ordinarily can act for the principal in such a way as to make the principal legally responsible only when he or she has **authority** to act that way. The agent's authority can be divided into two basic types: actual and apparent. **Actual authority** is the authority that the agent does, in fact, have. For convenience it can be further divided into *express authority* and *implied authority.* On the other hand, *apparent authority* is something of a contradiction in terms. It describes a concept which, because of unusual circumstances giving rise to an appearance of authority, occasionally holds the principal responsible for certain of the agent's actions that were not really authorized at all.

Express Authority

Express authority is the most obvious and the most common type of authority—that which is directly granted by the principal to the agent. To illustrate: P authorizes A to sell P's farm for at least $25,000. If A sells the farm to T for $30,000, P is bound by the transaction and must honor it. The obvious reason is that A's actions are within the scope of his express authority. Conversely, under most circumstances, P will not be required to honor the transaction if A sells the farm for $20,000.

Implied Authority

As is the case with most business transactions, the principal and agent rarely, if ever, contemplate and provide for every possible event that might occur during the existence of their relationship. The law seeks to allow for this fact through the concept of implied authority. **Implied authority** is primarily a matter of what is *customary.* In other words, where the principal has said nothing about a particular aspect of the agent's authority, whether the agent has such authority normally depends on what type of authority a person in a similar position customarily has. Of course, the principal has the final word as to what authority the agent possesses and can grant more or less authority than such an agent usually has. The concept of implied authority serves only to fill in gaps where the principal has not spoken specifically on the subject but where it is reasonable to assume that the principal would have granted such authority if he or she had thought about it.

Many examples of implied authority can be found. For instance, unless the principal has given indications to the contrary, a traveling salesperson ordinarily has authority to take orders but not to make a binding contract to sell the principal's goods. He or she often will be in possession of samples but there usually is no implied authority to sell them. If, however, the salesperson is one who possesses goods *for immediate sale* (such as a salesclerk in a retail store or a door-to-door sales agent who actually carries the principal's merchandise), he or she ordinarily has authority to sell them and collect payment. But this type of agent still does not have implied authority to grant credit or accept payment from the customer for prior credit purchases. Such authority usually exists only if expressly given by the principal, because it is simply not customary for a salesperson to do these things.

Another common application of the concept of implied authority enables an agent to perform those acts which are merely incidental to the main purpose of the agency. (Some legal writers, in fact, use the term *incidental authority*.) Again, the key is what is customary. The rule regarding such authority is: *Unless the principal has indicated otherwise, his or her agent has implied authority to do those things which are reasonably and customarily necessary to enable that person to accomplish the overall purpose of the agency.*

To illustrate: O, the owner of a retail clothing store, hires M to act as manager of the store and gives M express authority to act in certain ways. For instance, M probably will be expressly authorized to purchase inventory and make sales. In addition, M will have implied authority to handle matters that are incidental to the main purpose of the agency. Thus, if the plumbing in the store begins to leak, M can hire a plumber, and O is bound to pay for the services. Similarly, unless instructed otherwise, M can hire an electrician to repair a short in the wiring or a janitorial service to clean the floors. He can also hire a salesclerk or other necessary assistants.

Of course, if the transaction is out of the ordinary or involves a substantial expenditure, the agent should first consult with the principal, because the agent's implied authority may not extend to such matters. Thus, if the electrician hired by M to repair a shorted wire informs him that the wiring in the building is badly worn and does not comply with city building code requirements, M should not act on his own to contract for the rewiring at a substantial cost. Instead he should consult with O before taking further action.

Interesting questions regarding an agent's authority are sometimes raised by the occurrence of an *emergency*. Although it is often said that the scope of an agent's implied authority is "expanded" in emergency situations, this is only sometimes true. If an emergency occurs and there is no opportunity to consult with the principal, the agent has implied authority to take steps that are reasonable and prudent under the circumstances—including actions that may be contrary to prior instructions by the principal.

To illustrate: A has been ordered by P to purchase badly needed raw materials from country X and to ship them through country Y, which has the nearest port facility where the goods can be loaded on vessels. A makes the purchase but then learns from a usually reliable source that a revolution is imminent in country Y and will probably break out while the goods are en route. Fearing that transportation may be impaired or that the goods may be seized by the revolutionaries, A attempts to contact P but is unable to do so. Since he knows that P needs the goods quickly, A arranges for shipment to another port through country Z. Shipment over the other route will be slightly more expensive and time-consuming but also presumably safe, and P will still receive the goods in time to meet his needs.

In this case, A was impliedly authorized to act as he did—even if no revolution actually occurred. What is important is that two elements were present: (1) A, the agent, was *unable to consult with his principal;* and (2) he acted *reasonably,* in light of all the knowledge available to him, to protect the interests of his principal.

Apparent Authority

Thus far we have dealt with situations where the agent has actual authority, either express or implied. Now we will examine the peculiar concept of **apparent authority** (sometimes called **ostensible authority**). As we mentioned earlier, speaking of apparent authority as a specific type of authority is something of a contradiction, because the phrase describes a situation where the agent actually has no authority. If the agent acts outside the scope of his or her actual (express or implied) authority, the principal is normally not responsible on the unauthorized transaction. However, if the principal, *by his or her own conduct,* has led reasonable third parties to believe that the agent actually has such authority, the principal may be responsible. In discussing implied authority, we were concerned with what appeared reasonable to the *agent*. But for apparent authority, our concern is with the viewpoint of reasonable *third parties*. Obviously, some situations can fall within the scope of either implied or apparent authority. In such cases we usually speak in terms of implied authority; apparent authority is used as a basis for holding the principal responsible only where no express or implied authority is present.

The importance of apparent authority can be illustrated by two examples:

1. S, a salesman for R, has in his possession R's goods (not just samples). It is customary for an agent in S's position who is handling this type of goods to have authority to actually sell and collect payment for them. While making his rounds, S calls the home office. R tells him that he is afraid some of the items S has are defective and instructs him not to sell the goods in his possession but merely to take orders for a period of time. Contrary to instructions, S sells the goods. R is bound by the transactions and will be responsible to T, the buyer, if the goods actually are defective. It appears that R has acted in a reasonable fashion under the circumstances. However, by allowing S to have possession of the goods, he has led T to believe that S is authorized to sell—because it is *customary*. T has no way of knowing that S's actual authority has been expressly limited to something less than what is customary. The basis of R's liability is *not* S's implied authority, because S *knew* that he had no authority and was acting contrary to express instructions. Instead, the basis for R's liability is apparent authority—arising out of the fact that T has been misled by the *appearance of authority*.

2. When the agency is terminated, the agent's *actual authority* is also terminated. But this does not automatically dispose of the problem of *apparent authority*. It is sometimes necessary to notify third parties of the termination in order to keep the principal from being liable under the concept of apparent authority. As a general rule, where termination has occurred *as a matter of law* (see Chapter 31 for details), all authority ceases automatically and the principal is not responsible for the agent's further actions regardless of whether the third party has been notified.[1] Most problems involving termination and apparent authority arise when the agency has been ended *by act of the parties* (such as the principal firing the agent). Where termination is by act of the parties, the principal may still be bound by the agent's actions (because of apparent authority) unless and until the third party is notified of the termination. The principal must notify third parties with

whom the agent has dealt in the past by letter, telegram, telephone, or some other method of *direct communication* if their identities are reasonably easy to ascertain. Regarding all other third parties, the principal can protect himself simply by giving *public notice*. An advertisement in a local newspaper is the most common form of such notice, but other methods may be sufficient if they are reasonable under the circumstances.

Ratification of Unauthorized Transactions

If an agent's action is not within the scope of his or her actual (express or implied) authority, and if the facts are such that no apparent authority is present, the principal generally is not liable to the third party for that action. Even in the absence of actual or apparent authority, however, the principal may become responsible if he or she *ratifies* (or *affirms*) the agent's unauthorized actions. An unauthorized act ratified by the principal is treated by the courts in the same manner as if it had been actually authorized from the beginning. The two forms of **ratification**—express and implied—are discussed below.

Express Ratification

If, upon learning of the agent's unauthorized dealings, the principal decides to honor the transaction, he or she can simply inform the agent, the third party, or someone else of that intention. In this situation an **express ratification** has obviously occurred.

Implied Ratification

Even if the principal has not expressly communicated the intent to ratify, the person can nevertheless be deemed to have done so if his or her words or conduct reasonably indicate that intent. *Inaction* and *silence* may even amount to ratification if, under the circumstances, a reasonable person would have voiced an objection to what the agent had done. The following five examples will help clarify the concept of **implied ratification.** For each example, no actual authority exists, and there are no facts present to indicate apparent authority.

Example 1. A, who is a driver of a truck owned by P, enters into an unauthorized agreement with T, under which A is to haul T's goods on P's truck. Sometime later, while A is en route, T becomes concerned about the delay and calls P. Upon learning of the transaction, P does not repudiate it but instead

---

[1] However, a few courts have held that where the agency is terminated by the principal's *death,* his or her estate can continue to be liable for the agent's actions, under the doctrine of apparent authority, until the third party learns of the death.

assures T that "A is a good driver and the goods will be properly cared for." P has ratified the agreement.

Example 2.   Same facts as Example 1. This time, however, T does not call P. The goods arrive safely at their destination, and T sends a check for the shipping charges to P. This is when P first learns of the transaction. If P cashes or deposits the check and uses the money, he will be deemed to have ratified the agreement. Even if he simply retains the check for an appreciable period of time and says nothing, he will probably be held to have ratified.

Example 3.   A makes an unauthorized contract to sell P's goods to T. Upon learning of the contract, P says nothing to A or T but assigns the right to receive payment for the goods to X. P has ratified the agreement.

Example 4.   Same facts as Example 3. This time, however, P does not assign the right to receive payment. Instead he ships the goods to T. P has ratified the agreement.

Example 5.   Same facts as Example 4, but the goods are shipped to T without P's knowledge. P then learns of the transaction, and when T does not make payment by the due date, P files suit against T to collect the purchase price. P has ratified the transaction. (P would not have ratified if he had filed suit to rescind the sale and get his goods back.)

Requirements for Ratification

Certain requirements must be present for ratification to occur. Following are the most important of them:

1. The courts generally hold that a principal can ratify only if the agent, in dealing with the third party, has indicated that he or she is acting *for a principal* and not in his or her own behalf.

2. At the time of ratification, the principal must have *known* or *had reason to know* of the essential facts about the transaction. What this means is that the principal must have had either actual knowledge of the relevant facts or sufficient knowledge so that it would have been easy to find out what the essential facts were. The requirement of knowledge is usually important when the third party tries to hold the principal liable by claiming that some words or actions of the principal had amounted to ratification.

3. Ratification must occur within a *reasonable time* after the principal learned of the transaction. What constitutes a reasonable time will, of course, depend on the facts of the particular case. However, a court will automatically rule that a reasonable time period has already expired, and thus that there can be no ratification, if there has been a fundamental change in the facts that had formed the basis of the transaction. An example would be damage to or destruction of the subject matter of the transaction. Similarly, the principal will not be permitted to ratify if the third party has already indicated a desire to withdraw from the transaction. The third party has the right to withdraw prior to ratification and, when he or she does so, any later attempt by the principal to ratify will be treated as being too late.

4. If the principal ratifies, he or she must ratify the *entire transaction* rather than ratifying that part which is to his or her advantage and repudiating that which is to his or her disadvantage. For example, a principal ratifying a contract for the sale of goods to a third party is obligated on any warranties that accompany the goods.

5. The transaction obviously must be *legal,* and the principal must have the *capacity* required to be a party to the transaction.

6. If any *formalities* (such as a writing) would have been required for an original authorization, the same formalities must be met in ratifying the transaction. Of course, if formalities are required, the ratification will have to be express—it cannot be implied. Since most authorizations do not require any special formalities, this usually poses no problem.

The following two cases both deal with the question of apparent authority. The second case also involves the issue of ratification.

INDUSTRIAL MOLDED PLASTIC PRODUCTS, INC. V. J. GROSS & SON, INC.

Superior Court of Pennsylvania, 398 A.2d 695 (1979)

Case

Industrial Molded Plastic Products (Industrial) is in the business of manufacturing custom injection molded plastics by specification for various manufacturers. Industrial also manufactures various "fill-in" items during slack periods, such as electronic parts, industrial components, mirror clips, and plastic clothing clips. J. Gross & Sons (Gross) is a wholesaler to the retail clothing industry, selling mostly sewing thread, but also other items such as zippers, snaps, and clips.

Sometime in the fall of 1970, Stanley Waxman (Gross's president and sole stockholder) and his son Peter (a twenty-two-year-old salesman for Gross) appeared at the offices of Industrial's president, Judson T. Ulansey. They suggested to him that they might be able to market Industrial's plastic clothing clips in the retail clothing industry, in which they had an established sales force. At this initial meeting, there was no discussion of Peter Waxman's authority or lack thereof in the company. After this meeting, Stanley authorized Peter to purchase a "trial" amount of clips (not further specified) to test the market, but neither this authorization nor its limitation was communicated to Ulansey. All subsequent negotiations were between Ulansey and Peter Waxman only. Deceiving both his father and Ulansey, Peter held himself out as vice-president of Gross, and on December 10, 1970, signed an agreement obligating Gross to purchase from Industrial five million plastic clothing clips during the calendar year of 1971, at a price of $7.50 per thousand units, delivery at Industrial's plant in Blooming Glen, Pennsylvania. Before the execution of this agreement, Ulansey telephoned Stanley Waxman, who told Ulansey that Peter could act on behalf of

Gross. There was no discussion of the specific terms of the agreement, such as the quantity purchased.

Industrial immediately began production of the five million clips during "fill-in" time. As they were manufactured, they were warehoused in Industrial's plant as specified in the contract. In February 1971, Peter Waxman picked up and paid for 772,000 clips. Stanley Waxman, who had to sign Gross's check for payment, thought that this was the "trial amount" he had authorized Peter to buy. These were the only clips which Gross ever took into its possession. On numerous occasions during the year Ulansey urged Peter to pick up more of the clips, which were taking up more and more storage space at Industrial's plant as they were being manufactured. Peter told Ulansey that he was having difficulty selling the clips and that Gross had no warehousing capacity for the inventory that was being accumulated. At no time, however, did Peter repudiate the contract or request Industrial to halt production. By the end of 1971, production was completed and Industrial was warehousing 4,228,000 clips at its plant.

On January 19, 1972, Industrial sent Gross an invoice for the remaining clips of $31,506.45. However, Gross did not honor the invoice or pick up any more of the clips. Ulansey wrote to Stanley Waxman on February 7, 1972, requesting him to pick up the clips. Receiving no response, Ulansey wrote to Stanley Waxman again on February 23, 1972, threatening legal action if shipping instructions were not received by March 1, 1972. Finally, on March 30, 1972, Peter Waxman responded with a letter to Ulansey, which stated that Gross's failure to move the clips was due to a substantial decline in the clothing industry in 1971 and competition with new

lower-cost methods of hanging and shipping clothes. The letter asked for Industrial's patience and predicted that it would take at least the rest of the year to market the clips successfully. At this point, Industrial sued. Stanley Waxman learned of the five-million clip contract for the first time when informed by his lawyer of the impending lawsuit. At this time, Peter began an extended (four years) leave of absence from Gross.

The trial court ruled in favor of Industrial, the plaintiff, but awarded damages of only $2,400. Both parties appealed, plaintiff claiming that it should be entitled to the entire contract price of over $31,000, and defendant claiming that it should not be liable at all.

Hoffman, Judge:

. . . Gross contends that it was not bound by the agreement to purchase the clips because Peter Waxman had no authority to sign the contract for Gross. However, Peter was an agent of Gross and did have express authority to purchase for Gross, as its president instructed him to purchase a "trial amount" of clips. A principal's limitation of his agent's authority in amount only, not communicated to the third party with whom the agent deals, does not so limit the principal's liability. Although the agent violates his instructions or exceeds the limits set to his authority, he will yet bind his principal to such third persons, if his acts are within the scope of the authority which the principal has caused or permitted him to possess. Such limitations will be binding [only] upon third persons *who know of them.*

An admitted agent is presumed to be acting within the scope of his authority where the act is legal and the third party has no notice of the agent's limitation. The third person must use reasonable diligence to ascertain the

(continues)

INDUSTRIAL MOLDED PLASTIC PRODUCTS, INC. V. J. GROSS & SON, INC.

(continued from previous page)
authority of the agent, but he is also entitled to rely upon the apparent authority of the agent when this is a reasonable interpretation of the manifestations of the principal.

Here, the limitation on Peter's authority was not communicated to Industrial. As Stanley Waxman brought Peter into the initial meeting soliciting business from Industrial, Ulansey could reasonably presume his authority to act

for Gross in consummating the deal. Gross complains that Ulansey was not diligent in ascertaining Peter's authority, but in fact Ulansey telephoned Stanley Waxman precisely for the purpose of verifying Peter's authority. As Stanley said that Peter was authorized to act on behalf of Gross, the principal thus completed clothing the agent in apparent authority to bind the corporate entity on the agreement. If anybody was lacking in diligence, it was

Stanley Waxman in not inquiring as to the amount of the contract Peter proposed to sign. Thus, we affirm the conclusion of the court below that Gross was bound by the agreement to purchase the clips.

[The court then held that the trial court had incorrectly computed damages, and that Industrial was entitled to the total contract price of $31,506.45 plus interest from the invoice date.]⚖

CITY ELECTRIC V. DEAN EVANS CHRYSLER-PLYMOUTH

Supreme Court of Utah, 672 P.2d 89 (1983)

Case

Dave Sturgill was a salesman for Dean Evans Chrysler-Plymouth, a retail automobile dealership. Dean Evans was president of the firm, and Mike Evans was assistant secretary. Mike Evans was also a partner with Johnny Rider in another business, Johnny Rider's Backstage Restaurant. On one occasion, Mike Evans and Johnny Rider were discussing the remodeling of their restaurant. Sturgill happened to be present during the discussion, and volunteered to contact City Electric, an electric materials supplier that Sturgill had previously worked for. Sturgill said that he might be able to get them a good price on the electrical materials they would need for the remodeling project. Sturgill called Don Hatch, a salesman for City Electric, and told Hatch that Sturgill was trying to do a favor for his boss (Mike Evans). Sturgill asked if City Electric would give Mike Evans a fair price, and if the restaurant could establish an*

account. Shortly after this conversation, and before City Electric had time to set up an account for the restaurant, Mike Evans told Sturgill that the materials should be purchased on the auto dealership's account with City Electric.

The next day, Sturgill again called Hatch and placed an order for materials, stating that the materials were to be charged to the account of Dean Evans Chrysler-Plymouth. Sturgill said that he was acting pursuant to Mike Evans's directions, but there was never any representation that the auto dealership owned or was affiliated with the restaurant. Hatch checked his firm's computer printouts of open accounts and found that the auto dealership did have such an account with City Electric. Hatch put this and several later orders on the account, and the materials were delivered to the restaurant. Several invoices were sent to the auto dealership, and two of them dated October 8 and 9, 1978, were paid in December, 1978. There was no evidence indicating who paid these two

invoices in behalf of the auto dealership. Apparently, either Mike Evans or Sturgill paid the two invoices with company funds before the dealership's president, Dean Evans, discovered what had happened. Thereafter, the dealership refused to make any further payments, leaving an unpaid balance of $2,332.70. City Electric, plaintiff, filed suit against Dean Evans Chrysler-Plymouth, defendant, for this unpaid balance. The trial court held that both Mike Evans and Dave Sturgill had apparent authority to charge the orders to the dealership's account, and ruled in favor of plaintiff. Defendant appealed.

Howe, Justice:

It is well settled law that the apparent or ostensible authority of an agent can be inferred only from the acts and conduct of the principal. Where corporate liability is sought for acts of its agent under apparent authority, liability is premised upon the corporation's knowledge of and acquiescence in the
(continues)

Apparent authority

CITY ELECTRIC V. DEAN EVANS CHRYSLER-PLYMOUTH

(continued from previous page)
conduct of its agent which has led third parties to rely upon the agent's actions. Nor is the authority of the agent "apparent" merely because it looks so to the person with whom he deals. It is the principal who must cause third parties to believe that the agent is clothed with apparent authority. (See *Forsyth v. Pendleton,* 617 P.2d 358 (Utah 1980), where the referral by seller to her attorney of a letter written to her by buyers constituted an act sufficient to clothe the attorney with apparent authority to act for seller.) It follows that one who deals exclusively with an agent has the responsibility to ascertain that agent's authority despite the agent's representations. Moreover, it has been held that apparent authority vanishes when the third party has actual knowledge of the real scope of the agent's authority. . . .

Under the applicable standard of review this Court will accord the findings of the trial court a presumption of validity and correctness so long as there is support for them in the evidence. That support is singularly absent in this case. . . . Sturgill's apparent authority was never established. His request for electrical materials for the remodeling of the restaurant fell wide of the mark of his scope of employment. . . . His own statement could not establish any authority in him.

Plaintiff's credit manager testified that all purchases made between October and December of 1978 were made out to Johnny Rider of the Backstage Restaurant and that none of the receipts was signed by anyone on behalf of the defendant. None of the materials was delivered to the defendant and most of them were picked up by workers involved with the remodeling. Hatch testified that Sturgill told him he was trying to do his boss (Mike Evans) a favor by getting him good prices. Hatch never talked to Mike, who he knew was a son of Dean Evans, and who he assumed had a management position with defendant. His only contact was with Sturgill, who he assumed had no management position with the defendant. Sturgill made no representation to Hatch that defendant owned the Backstage Restaurant and the only authority Hatch relied upon was Sturgill's telling him that Mike told Sturgill to call and arrange for the materials. When questioned whether he took credit information from Sturgill from which he could determine whether to extend credit, Hatch answered "No. I looked on our computer printout for addresses and open accounts, and Dean Evans Chrysler-Plymouth had an account with us." Hatch did not claim that plaintiff had an agreement with the defendant relating to the materials. Hatch's dealings were exclusively with Sturgill and on a matter unrelated to the business of the defendant. Whatever apparent authority Sturgill might have otherwise had vanished for that reason alone. Unless otherwise agreed, general expressions used in authorizing an agent are limited in application to acts done in connection with the act or business to which the authority primarily relates.

Plaintiff's argument that the contract was ratified by payments made of the October 8 and October 9 invoices fares no better. Plaintiff's exhibit offers no clue as to who paid them. A penciled notation "Paid in Dec 1978" does not rise to the level of ratification by defendant as required by law. Ratification is premised upon the knowledge of all material facts and upon an express or implied intention on the part of the principal to ratify. There is not a shred of evidence in the record that defendant paid the two mentioned invoices, nor is the court's statement that "everybody knew that Mike was connected" sufficient to impute knowledge of Sturgill's actions to the defendant, let alone an intent to subsequently ratify those actions.

The plaintiff failed to establish its case and it was error for the trial court to find in its favor. The judgment is reversed.🔯

Importance of the Agent's Knowledge

In deciding the question of a principal's liability to a third party, sometimes a key issue is whether the principal has received notice of a particular fact. For example, P is obligated under a contract to make payment to T. T assigns her right to receive this payment to X, an assignee. Assuming that T's right is assignable, P is bound to honor the assignment and pay X instead of T only if he has received notice of the assignment. But what if P's agent, A, receives this notice rather than P himself? If A promptly relays the information to P, there is usually no problem. What happens, though, if A fails to do so and P, not knowing of the assignment, pays T instead of X? Is P liable to X because P's agent had received notice?

Ordinarily, in any case where notice to the principal is important, *notice to the agent is treated as notice to the principal if the agent's receipt of the notice is within the scope of his or her actual or apparent authority.* In other words, in such cases the law will treat the principal as if he or she had received notice even if the agent did not transmit it. Obviously, however, this does not apply where the third party who notifies the agent knows that the agent is acting adversely to the interests of the principal (as where the third party and the agent are conspiring to defraud the principal).

LIABILITY OF THE AGENT

When the agent is acting for the principal, the agent ordinarily incurs no personal responsibility if he or she acts in a proper fashion. However, circumstances do exist where the agent can become liable.

Breach of Duty

If the agent violates any of the duties owed to the principal, he or she naturally is liable for the damages caused by the breach. Where the duty which has been violated is that of loyalty, the penalties may be even more severe. A disloyal agent is not only responsible to the principal for any resulting loss sustained by the latter but also usually forfeits his or her right to be compensated for services rendered. Furthermore, the agent must turn over to the principal any profits made from his or her disloyal activity.

Exceeding Authority

The agent who exceeds his or her actual authority is personally responsible unless the principal ratifies the unauthorized actions. Whether this responsibility is to the principal or to the third party depends on the circumstances. If the agent exceeds his or her actual authority, but the principal is liable to a third party on the ground of apparent authority, the agent's liability is to the *principal*. On the other hand, if the agent exceeds his or her actual authority and the facts are such that the principal is not liable to a third party under apparent authority, then the agent's liability is to the *third party*.

Assuming Liability

If the agent personally assumes liability for a particular transaction, then he or she obviously is responsible. For instance: A is attempting to purchase goods for P on credit. T, the seller, is wary of P's credit rating and refuses to grant credit unless A also becomes obligated. A signs the agreement as P's agent and in his own individual capacity. A is in effect a *co-principal* and therefore personally liable to T if P defaults.

Nondisclosure of Principal

If the agent, in dealing with a third party, fails to disclose that he or she is *acting for a principal* or fails to disclose the *principal's identity,* the agent is personally responsible to the third party. Additionally, the agent will sometimes be liable if he or she acts for a nonexistent principal or for one not having legal capacity. (These subjects are dealt with specifically later in the chapter.)

Commission of a Tort

If the agent commits a *tort*, he or she is personally responsible to the injured party for the resulting harm. This is true regardless of whether the agent was working for the principal at the time. (Sometimes the principal also is responsible. This problem is discussed later in the chapter.)

LIABILITY OF THE THIRD PARTY

Relatively little need be said about the liability of the third party. Since that party is acting in his or her own behalf, he or she is personally responsible to the other party to the transaction. This ordinarily means that:

1. If the third party fails to live up to his or her part of the bargain, that person will be liable to the principal.

2. The third party owes no responsibility to the agent unless the agent has personally become a party to the transaction.

3. The third party is liable for his or her torts to any party injured as a result.

NONEXISTENT, PARTIALLY DISCLOSED, AND UNDISCLOSED PRINCIPALS

In discussing the principal-agent relationship we have thus far assumed that the principal exists when the agent executes the transaction in question and that both the existence and the identity of the principal are disclosed to the third party. This is usually, but not always, the case. The special problems that arise in connection with *nonexistent, partially disclosed*, and *undisclosed principals* are discussed below.

Nonexistent Principals

If an agent purports to act for a principal who does not exist at the time, the agent is usually liable to the third party. Of course, since there is no principal, the agent is not really an agent at all; he or she merely *claims* to be one.

While this situation does not occur frequently, it is by no means rare. A common instance of the **nonexistent principal** is that of a person attempting to act for an organization that is not legally recognized as a separate entity. (A *legal entity* is an organization—such as a corporation—that is recognized by the law as having the rights and duties of a person, although it is not flesh and blood. It can, for example, make contracts, sue, and be sued in its own name.) Thus a member of an unincorporated association, such as a church, club, fraternity, or the like, may attempt to contract in behalf of the association. Since the "principal" is not legally recognized as one, the members who make the agreement are personally responsible. It is for this reason that many churches and other such organizations form corporations.

The contracts of *corporate promoters* (those who play a part in the initial organization of a corporation) have posed similar problems. Quite often, these people make various types of agreements before the proposed corporation is formed. They may, for example, enter contracts for the purpose of raising capital, purchasing a building site, or procuring the services of an attorney, an accountant, or other professionals. The liabilities of the promoter, of the corporation once it is formed, and of the third party are discussed in Chapter 36.

A similar situation occurs when a principal has existed but is now dead or lacks contractual capacity when the agent contracts with the third party. As we mentioned in Chapter 18, such an occurrence often terminates the agency, and the principal (or that person's estate) is not bound. If the agency is not terminated, the principal's status affects his or her own liability in the same way as if the principal had personally dealt with the third party.

Whether the *agent* is personally liable depends on the circumstances. If the principal is *dead* or has been *declared insane by a court* at the time of the transaction, the agent invariably is held personally liable to the third party. On the other hand, if, at the time the transaction is made, the principal is either a *minor* or *insane* (but not officially declared insane by a court), the agent is personally responsible to the third party in only two situations:

1. The agent is liable if he or she has made representations to the effect that the principal has contractual capacity. This is true even if the agent is honestly mistaken.

2. The agent who has made no such representations is still liable to the third party if he or she *knew or had reason to know* of the principal's lack of capacity *and* the third party's ignorance of the facts.

Partially Disclosed Principals

As we indicated earlier, an agent usually is responsible to the third party if the agent discloses the fact that he or she is acting for a principal but does not *identify* that person. If the agent acts with authority, the principal is also responsible and may be held liable when the third party learns his or her identity.[2] Since the third party knows that the agent is acting for someone else, the third party is, in turn, liable to the principal. In sum, the liability of the principal and the third party is the same as in the case of a completely disclosed principal. The only difference is that in the case of a **partially disclosed principal,** *the agent is also liable,* unless the agent and the third party agree otherwise.

Undisclosed Principals

Individuals and business organizations sometimes prefer not to have their connection with a transaction be known. If an agent acts in behalf of a principal but does not disclose to the third party the fact that he or she is representing another, it is said that the agent acts for an **undisclosed principal.** In other words, the third party, not knowing that a principal-agent relationship exists, thinks that the agent is dealing solely for himself.

In a case such as this, the agent is personally liable to the third party. If and when the principal makes himself known, that person is also liable to the third party if the agent acted within the scope of his authority. In such an event, the third party must *elect* whether to hold the agent or the principal responsible.[3]

---

[2]There is conflict among the courts on whether the third party must make a choice (or *election*) between the agent and the principal in such a case or whether he or she can hold both of them responsible.

[3]Different jurisdictions apply different rules as to what constitutes an *election.* Demanding payment from the agent or the principal or even filing suit against one of them usually *is not* considered the third party's "point of no return." Obtaining satisfaction of the claim obviously *is* an election. However, courts differ on whether *obtaining a court judgment* (which has not yet been collected) constitutes an election. Of course, if the third party obtains a judgment against the agent before knowing the principal's identity, there is no binding election and the third party can still pursue the principal.

Thus far we have focused on the liability of the undisclosed principal and the agent. But what about the liability of the *third party?* Since the *agent* is a party to the contract, he or she can enforce the agreement against the third party. Once revealed, the *principal* ordinarily can also enforce the agreement. In three situations, however, the third party can refuse to perform for the undisclosed principal and can continue to treat the agent as the sole party to whom he or she is obligated.

1. If the third party has already performed for the agent before the principal is revealed, the third party is not required to render a second performance.

2. If, prior to the transaction, the third party has indicated that he or she will not deal with the one who is the undisclosed principal, the third party is not required to perform for that principal. Similarly, the third party is not responsible to the undisclosed principal if the former has indicated beforehand or in the agreement that he or she will not deal with *anyone* other than the agent.

3. In all other situations the undisclosed principal is treated in much the same way as an *assignee* from the agent (see Chapter 16 for a discussion of assignees). He or she can demand performance from the third party only if the contract is of a type that can be assigned. Thus, if the contract calls for personal service by the agent or if the agent's personal credit standing, judgment, or skill played an important part in the third party's decision to deal with that individual, the third party cannot be forced to accept the undisclosed principal as a substitute.

TORT LIABILITY

Until now, our discussions of legal responsibility have focused almost exclusively on the parties' contractual liability. Now we will turn to their *tort liability.*

Circumstances in which the Superior Is Liable for the Subordinate's Torts

Obviously, if either the superior, the subordinate, or the third party personally commits a tort, that person is liable to the one injured by the wrongful act. If the *subordinate* commits a tort, the additional question often arises whether his or her *superior* is also liable to the injured third party. This is often important because ordinarily the superior is insured or otherwise more financially capable of paying damages.

If the superior personally is at fault, that person obviously is liable because he or she has committed a tort. This can be seen in the following situations:

1. If the superior *directs* the subordinate to commit the tort (or even if the superior *intends* that the tort be committed), he or she is responsible.

2. If the superior carelessly allows the subordinate to operate potentially dangerous equipment (such as an automobile or truck), even though he or she knows or should know that the subordinate is unqualified or incapable of handling it safely, the superior is responsible for any resulting harm. The phrase *negligent entrustment* is often used to describe this situation.

3. Similarly, the superior is held liable if he or she is negligent in *failing to properly supervise a subordinate.*

Most often, however, the superior has not directed or intended the commission of a tort and has no reason to suppose that he or she is creating a dangerous situation. Therefore, the third party usually seeks to impose **vicarious liability** (liability imposed not because of one's own wrong but solely because of the wrong of one's subordinate) on the superior. The imposition of liability on the superior for a tort committed by a subordinate is based on the doctrine of **respondeat superior** ("let the master answer").

The theoretical justification for holding the superior responsible is that he or she can treat the loss—or the premiums for liability insurance—as a cost of doing business. The cost is thus reflected in the price of his or her product, and the loss is ultimately spread over that segment of the population benefiting from that product.

When the superior is required to pay damages to a third party because of the tort of a subordinate, the superior usually has a legal right to recoup the loss from that subordinate. As a practical matter, this is an illusory right in many cases, because the subordinate frequently is unable to pay.

Of course, the superior is not always responsible for the torts of subordinates. In this regard, two issues must ordinarily be dealt with:

1. Was the relationship that of employer-employee (i.e., master-servant) or employer–independent contractor?

2. If an employer-employee relationship existed, was the employee acting within the scope of his or her employment at the time of committing the alleged tort?

Employer–Employee or Employer–Independent Contractor

Legal Significance of the Distinction

The imposition of vicarious liability often depends on the nature of the relationship involved. If it is found to be that of employer-employee, the employer is liable for a tort committed by the employee if it was committed in the scope of the employee's employment for the employer.

On the other hand, if the relationship is found to be that of employer and independent contractor, the employer generally is not liable for a tort committed by the independent contractor. Those few instances in which the employer *is liable* for a tort are as follows.

1. If the task for which the independent contractor was hired is *inherently dangerous,* the employer will be responsible for harm to third parties caused by the dangerous character of the work. The employer's responsibility in such a case is based on the tort concept of *strict liability.* That is, the responsibility exists solely because of the nature of the activity, regardless of whether any negligence or other fault brought about the damage. Activities deemed to be inherently dangerous include blasting, using deadly chemicals, or working on buildings in populated areas where people must pass below the activity.

2. If the employer owes a *nondelegable duty,* he or she cannot escape ultimate responsibility for performing that duty by obtaining an independent contractor to perform it. Thus, if the independent contractor is negligent or commits some other tort in the performance of such a task, the employer is liable to the injured third party. Nondelegable duties are those duties owed to the public which courts feel to be of such importance that responsibility cannot be delegated. Examples are (a) a duty imposed by statute, such as the statutory duty of a railroad to keep highway crossings in a safe condition; (b) the duty of a city to keep its streets in a safe condition; (c) the duty of a landlord who has assumed responsibility for making repairs to the premises to see that those repairs are done safely; and (d) the duty

of a business proprietor whose premises are open to the public to keep the premises in a reasonably safe condition.

3. As is usually the case regardless of the exact nature of the relationship between the superior and subordinate, an employer is liable for the independent contractor's tort if the employer specifically directed, authorized, or intended the wrongful conduct.

Making the Distinction

The determination of whether a particular subordinate is an employee or an independent contractor depends essentially on the issue of *control.* If the employer has hired the subordinate merely to achieve a result and has left decisions regarding the method and manner of achieving that result up to the subordinate, the latter is an independent contractor. On the other hand, if the superior actually controls or has the right to control the method and manner of achieving the result, then the subordinate is an employee. Thus a construction contractor hired to erect a building is usually an independent contractor, while a secretary hired to type and take dictation is usually an employee.

However, the delineation is not always easy, and sometimes it produces problems of extreme conceptual difficulty. The most important question, of course, is whether the employer *controls or has the right to control the method and manner of doing the work.* Where the matter of control is not so obvious as to make the determination readily apparent, other factors can be taken into account. Some facts which would increase the likelihood of a subordinate being viewed as an independent contractor are: (1) the subordinate has his own independent business or profession; (2) the subordinate uses his own tools, equipment, or workplace to perform the task; (3) the subordinate is paid by the job, not by the hour, week, or month; (4) the subordinate has irregular hours; and (5) the subordinate is performing a task that is not part of the employer's regular business. None of these facts automatically makes a subordinate an independent contractor; each is simply a factor to be weighed along with all the other evidence.

The following case illustrates the importance of the employer's right of control when there is a question about the subordinate's status as an employee or an independent contractor.

Branco Wood Products, Inc. v. C.C. Huxford Trust

Court of Civil Appeals of Alabama, 521 So. 2d 73 (1988)

The defendant, Branco Wood Products, is a corporation engaged in the business of supplying wood to large purchasers, such as Container Corporation of America (CCA), the purchaser in this case. Branco has a number of individuals who act as its wood producers, i.e., individuals who cut and deliver the timber which Branco then supplies to its purchasers.

CCA buys wood from Branco by means of a "ticket system." The way this system works is that the wood producer cuts and delivers to CCA the amount of wood indicated on the ticket. CCA then pays Branco for the wood delivered, and Branco pays the wood producer. On the occasion that led to this dispute, CCA gave tickets to Branco which entitled the bearer to deliver a certain amount of wood to CCA. Branco gave the CCA tickets to Edward Bell, one of its producers, who began cutting timber on property located adjacent to land owned by the C.C. Huxford Trust, the plaintiff in this case. Mistakenly, Bell crossed the boundary line between the two tracts and cut timber on the Trust's property. When the Trust learned that Bell was cutting timber on its property, it immediately informed Branco's president who told Bell to stop cutting the timber.

The Trust sued Branco, claiming that it was liable for the damages caused by Bell's trespass because Bell was Branco's employee and was acting in the scope of his employment. Branco claimed that it was not responsible because Bell was an independent contractor. The trial court ruled in favor of the Trust, and Branco appealed.

Holmes, Judge:

. . . Under the doctrine of respondeat superior, [an employer] may be liable for the acts of his [employee] that are done in the interest of and in the prosecution of the [employer's] business if the [employee] is acting within the scope of his employment.

The test for determining if one is an agent or employee, as opposed to an independent contractor, is whether the alleged employer has reserved the right of control over the means and agencies by which the work is done, not the actual exercise of such control. Moreover, the control reserved by the employer must be over the manner in which—or the means by which—the employee's work is done, as well as the result accomplished. In other words, the employer must have the right to control, "not only what shall be done, but how it shall be done."

Because working relationships take a wide variety of forms, each case must depend upon its own facts, and all features of the relationship must be considered together. Thus, whether an [employer-employee] relationship exists is determined by the facts of the case, not by how the parties characterize their relationship.

Applying these rules to the case now before us, we can only conclude that the evidence does not support the trial court's conclusion that Bell was acting as the defendant's agent or employee when he cut timber on the plaintiff's land. In other words, the evidence does not show that the defendant had a reserved right of control over the means, or the manner, by which Bell performed his job of producing the quantity of timber called for by the CCA tickets that could make the defendant liable under the theory of respondeat superior.

The testimony of George I. Edwards, the defendant's president, was that the defendant did not direct or supervise Bell or its other wood producers in their work. Edwards testified that he did not tell Bell how to cut down trees, load his truck, or haul the wood; that he did not offer Bell any advice on cutting and removal techniques; that the defendant did not supply Bell with any equipment, trucks, or gas to use in his wood producing; that Bell was not on the "payroll per se" of the defendant; and that he did not tell Bell when he was supposed to go to work or when he was to quit work or how long he was to work each day.

Moreover, in this particular instance, the defendant did not direct Bell as to where he was to cut timber to fill the amount called for by the CCA tickets. Rather, the testimony indicated that Bell made arrangements independently with the property owner to cut timber on her land.

We do note that the testimony was to the effect that Edwards does go out periodically to the sites where the defendant's wood producers are cutting to check on their work. In addition, Bell testified that "whenever [Edwards] told me something I was cutting for him or something like that and he told me, that is what I did."

We do not think that any of the testimony, even that last recited, shows that the defendant retained the right to control the manner in which Bell performed his job of producing wood to fill the amount called for by the CCA tickets given to him by the defendant.

The control necessary for the existence of an employer-employee relationship is not established merely because the employer retains the right to supervise or inspect the work of an independent contractor to determine if he is performing in conformity with the contract. . . .

We must reverse [because the trial] court's conclusion that the defendant is liable for the trespass of Bell is not supported by the evidence when the applicable law is applied. This case is reversed and remanded to the trial court for entry of a judgment [consistent with this opinion].

[handwritten margin note: Myt Workers Comp -]

Scope of Employment

If the subordinate is deemed to be an employee, the employer is liable to third parties for those torts committed by the employee in the *scope of his or her employment*. There exists no simple definition of the **scope of employment** (sometimes called *course of employment*) concept. Obviously, an employee is acting within the scope of employment while performing work that he or she has been *expressly directed to do by the employer*. To illustrate: X has directed Y to drive X's truck from New York to Albany via a certain route. While on that route, Y drives negligently and injures T. X is liable to T.

In the absence of a specific directive given by the employer, an act usually is in the scope of employment if it is *reasonably incidental to an activity that has been expressly directed*. Thus, in the above example, if Y had stopped to buy gasoline and had negligently struck a parked car belonging to T, X would have been liable to T.

Deviations

The employer sometimes can be held liable even though the employee has deviated from the authorized activity. The employer's liability in such cases depends on the *degree* and *foreseeability* of the deviation. If the deviation is great, the employer usually is not responsible. Suppose that Y, in driving X's truck from New York to Albany, decides to go a hundred miles off his authorized route to visit an old friend. On the way there, Y negligently collides with T. In this situation, X is not liable.

But what if Y has been to see his friend and was returning to his authorized route when the collision occurred? Three different viewpoints have been taken by various courts. Where there has been more than a slight deviation from the scope of employment, as in this case, some courts have held that the reentry into the scope of employment occurs only when the employee has *actually returned to the authorized route or activity*. Others have held that there is reentry the moment that the employee, with an intent to serve the employer's business, *begins to turn back toward the point of deviation*. However, a majority of courts have held that reentry occurs when the employee, with an intent to serve the employer's business, *has turned back toward and come reasonably close to the point of deviation*.

If the deviation from the authorized route or activity is only slight, many courts have held that the employee is still within the scope of employment if the type of deviation was *reasonably foreseeable* by the master. For example: While driving from New York to Albany, Y stops at a roadside establishment to get something to eat or buy a pack of cigarettes. While pulling off the road, he negligently strikes a parked car. In this situation X is liable. Although buying something to eat or smoke may not be necessary to drive a truck from New York to Albany (as is the purchase of gasoline) and although Y was not really serving his employer, the deviation was only slight and was of the type that any employer should reasonably expect.

Many examples of the scope of employment issue—such as the next two cases—involve auto accidents (though certainly the issue is not limited to them). These two cases illustrate some typical problems in this area.

LAZAR v. THERMAL EQUIPMENT CORP.

Court of Appeals of California, 195 Cal. Rptr. 890 (1983)

Richard Lanno was employed as a project engineer for Thermal Equipment Co., which was a manufacturer of heating equipment and pressure vessels for the aerospace industry. In connection with his job, Lanno was sometimes required to proceed from his home *directly to a job site in the mornings. In addition, he was constantly on call as a trouble-shooter, and, consequently, Thermal's customers occasionally called him at his home after hours and on weekends. In order to answer these calls, Lanno needed the company truck, in which he sometimes carried tools; if the truck was not at his home, he would stop at* *Thermal to pick up needed tools on the way to answer the call. To facilitate these duties, Thermal allowed Lanno to take the company truck home with him on a daily basis. Thermal provided Lanno with gasoline for the truck, and allowed him to use it for personal purposes.*

On one occasion, Lanno finished work and left Thermal's business

(continues)

LAZAR V. THERMAL EQUIPMENT CORP.

(continued from previous page)
premises. Driving the company
truck, he headed in a direction away
from both the workplace and his
home; Lanno testified that he planned
to stop at a store, purchase some-
thing, and then go home. Before
reaching the store, Lanno was in-
volved in an accident with Lazar,
who suffered bodily injury and dam-
age to his car. Lazar filed suit against
Thermal, claiming that Lanno had
driven the truck negligently and that
Lanno was within the scope of his
employment at the time of the acci-
dent. The jury found that Lanno was
not acting within the scope of his em-
ployment at the time of the accident,
but the trial court granted Lazar's
motion for judgment notwithstanding
the verdict, holding that Lanno was
within the scope of employment as a
matter of law. The jury had found
Lazar's damages to be $81,000, and
the trial court rendered judgment for
Lazar against Thermal in this
amount. Thermal appealed.

Schauer, Presiding Judge:

Under the doctrine of respondeat superior, an employer is responsible for
the torts of his employee if these torts
are committed within the scope of employment. The "going and coming"
rule acts to limit an employer's liability
under respondeat superior. This rule
deems an employee's actions to be outside the scope of employment when
these actions occur while the employee
is going to or returning from work. The
"going and coming" rule, in turn, has
been limited in recent years. Under
the modern rule, if the employee's
trip to or from work "involves an incidental benefit to the employer, not
common to commute trips made by ordinary members of the work force," the
"going and coming" rule will not apply.
Thus in *Hinman v. Westinghouse Electric Co.*, 2 Cal.3d 956 (1970), it was
held that the "going and coming" rule
did not apply where the employer had

made the commute part of the workday by compensating the employee
for his travel time. Similarly, in *Hunt-
singer v. Glass Containers Corp.*, 22
Cal. App.3d 803 (1972), an employee
was required to drive to and from work
in order to have his vehicle available
for company business. The court held
that these circumstances, if confirmed
by a jury, would support a finding that
the employee's commute conferred an
incidental benefit on the employer;
a jury could therefore find that the
commute fell within the scope of employment.

In the [present] case, the trial court
was presented with uncontroverted
evidence that Thermal derived a special benefit from Lanno's commute.
This commute was made in the company vehicle, and an object of the commute was to transport the vehicle to
Lanno's home where it would be ready
for business use in case Lanno received
emergency after-hours calls for repair
from the employer's customers. In
traveling to and from work, Lanno was
thus acting in the scope of his employment, conferring a tangible benefit on
his employer; the "going and coming"
rule is thus inapplicable.

A further issue, however, is presented in this case. . . . Lanno decided
that, before going home, he would stop
at a shop and buy a certain, now forgotten, item. To further complicate the
question, this shop and item were located in the opposite direction from
Lanno's home. . . .

Categorization of an employee's action as within or outside the scope of
employment . . . begins with a question
of foreseeability. . . . Foreseeability as a
test for respondeat superior merely
means that in the context of the particular enterprise an employee's conduct
is not so unusual or startling that it
would seem unfair to include the loss
resulting from it among other costs of
the employer's business.

One traditional means of defining
this foreseeability is seen in the distinction between minor "deviations" and

substantial "departures" from the employer's business. The former are
deemed foreseeable and remain within
the scope of employment; the latter are
unforeseeable and take the employee
outside the scope of his employment.

Witkin [an authority on the law of
agency] describes the traditional distinction as follows: "The question is
often one of fact, and the rule now established is that only a substantial deviation or departure takes the employee
outside the scope of his employment.
If the main purpose of his activity is
still the employer's business, it does
not cease to be within the scope of the
employment by reason of incidental
personal acts, slight delays, or deflec-
tions from the most direct route. . . ."

In the [present] case, we are asked
to decide whether Lanno's personal
errand was a foreseeable deviation
from the scope of his employment, or
whether evidence or inferences therefrom have been presented which
would lead a jury to believe that this
errand was an unforeseeable, substantial departure from his duties. . . .

The evidence presented to the trial
court was not controverted. Lanno testified that on the day of the accident he
left work and headed away from his
home, planning to buy an item and
then return directly home. The evidence thus clearly showed that Lanno
planned a minor errand to be carried
out, broadly speaking, on the way
home. Lanno further testified that this
type of errand occurred with his employer's permission. No evidence was
presented, nor could any inference be
drawn from the evidence, showing that
Lanno had any other object in mind
that day than a brief stop at a store before going home.

The evidence, then, leads ineluc-
tably to the conclusion that Lanno's errand was a minor deviation from his
employer's business. While the specific
act was one "strictly personal" to
Lanno, it was "necessary to his convenience" under the standard [set forth
in] *Alma W. v. Oakland Unified School*
(continues)

LAZAR V. THERMAL EQUIPMENT CORP.

(continued from previous page)
Dist., 123 Cal. App.3d 133. While this standard was suggested for deviations "at work," we think it is applicable to deviations made on the way home, in the employer's vehicle, when the trip home benefits the employer. Here, it would have been unreasonable and inconvenient for Lanno to drive his truck home, stop there, then return to purchase the needed item, passing work on the way. The decision to stop to buy the item on the way home was one reasonably necessary to Lanno's comfort and convenience. For this reason the detour must be considered a minor deviation.

The detour was foreseeable for much the same reason. While a decision to stop at a party, or a bar, or to begin a vacation, might not have been foreseeable, we can think of no conduct more predictable than an employee's stopping at a store to purchase a few items on the way home. Where, as here, the trip home is made for the benefit of the employer, in the employer's vehicle, accidents occurring during such minor and foreseeable deviations become part of the "inevitable toll of a lawful enterprise." . . .

Finally, we note that Thermal makes much of the fact that Lanno was headed in the direction opposite his home at the time of the accident. . . . An employer's liability, however, should not turn simply on a point of the compass; the fact that the store Lanno decided to visit was to the north of his workplace, rather than to the south, is not the controlling factor in this case. Instead, the modern rationale for respondeat superior requires that liability be hinged on the foreseeability and substantiality of the employee's departure from his employer's business. Where, as here, the deviation is insubstantial and foreseeable, the doctrine of respondeat superior will apply.

The judgment is affirmed.⚖

Comment If the deviation had been substantial and unforeseeable, such as a two-hour stop at a bar, Lanno would have been outside the scope of his employment during the deviation. However, because the "coming and going" rule did not apply to this case, Lanno would have *reentered* the scope of employment upon getting back into the truck and resuming the trip toward home.

DINKINS V. FARLEY

New York Supreme Court, Monroe County, 434 N.Y.S.2d 325 (1980)

As part of its personnel policy, Xerox Corporation maintained a National Tuition Aid Program that provided financial assistance to employees taking advanced college courses. An employee's application to participate in the program had to be approved by the employee's immediate supervisor. The company provided tuition assistance only for those courses directly related to a present job or to a future job to which an employee might reasonably aspire at Xerox. Upon approval of the employee's application, Xerox advanced 100 percent of the tuition and lab fees and then deducted 35 percent of that amount from the employee's paychecks in installments. Thereafter, the employee was required to verify enrollment by submitting itemized receipts from the college, and later to verify successful completion of a course by submitting a grade report to Xerox within 30 days after the end of the semester. If a grade report for a course was not submitted to Xerox within 50 days after semester's end, the company initiated steps to collect the other 65 percent of course expenses from the employee. However, if the employee ultimately received an advanced degree as a result of his participation in the tuition aid program, Xerox would refund the 35 percent that had been paid by the employee. A course taken under the program was expected to be scheduled outside of working hours if possible; if this was not possible, the employee could have limited time off during the workday to attend classes, subject to approval by the employee's supervisor. Such time off had to be made up at another time decided by the supervisor. Xerox spent about $1,000,000 annually on the program, and at the time of this case over 6,000 of Xerox's employees had participated.

Victor Farley, an employee of Xerox, had a bachelor's degree in engineering and wished to take a linear systems course that would better prepare him for pursuing a master's degree in that field. His application for the tuition aid program was approved by Xerox and he enrolled in

(continues)

(continued from previous page)
the course at the Rochester Institute of Technology. He usually got out of work at 4:20 or 4:30 p.m., and frequently was a few minutes late for the class, which began at 4:20. One afternoon as Victor was driving to class, he was involved in an automobile accident at an intersection on campus. The other driver, Diane Dinkins, sued both Victor and Xerox, claiming that Victor was guilty of negligence and that Xerox was also liable because Victor was acting within the scope of his employment at the time of the accident. Before trial, Xerox filed a motion for summary judgment on the ground that, as a matter of law, Victor was not acting within the scope of his employment when the accident occurred. Below is the opinion of the trial court on this issue.

Boehm, Justice:

Although Xerox subsidizes the outside education of an employee who successfully completes course work for a degree, this alone should not be controlling in creating a "scope of employment" status, at least while the course is still in progress, because failure to complete the course would make the employee responsible to pay the entire tuition. Thus, if tuition payments alone were the criterion by which scope of employment was determined, one would not know whether or not an employee was within the scope of his employment during the course year until his work had been graded at the end of the school year. Until that time an employee's status would be a contingent one, ripening only after the grades were issued. If, in the meantime, the employee had an accident driving to or from class, Xerox would not know whether it could be held responsible as his employer until the employee had passed or flunked.

Further, the purpose of Victor Farley in working toward a master's degree was predominantly personal. Although it may also serve a purpose of Xerox to have its employees better trained or more satisfied on the job by being promoted from within the organization, this purpose is subservient to the personal motive of Victor to better his own employment and economic status by obtaining a master's degree, a degree which would remain his and continue to benefit him even if he should no longer work for Xerox. . . .

No doubt there is a good business and policy reason for Xerox to subsidize the education of its employees within certain areas of value to Xerox, but it cannot be said that such a purpose is necessary or vital to its operation except insofar as ambitious, well-trained or satisfied employees are vital to any organization in the same way as healthy employees are. . . .

Further, it is undisputed that Xerox does not direct the number of times an employee must attend class nor whether he must attend at all. Hypothetically, if an employee were able to successfully complete a course by home study and never attend class, Xerox would still be obligated for 100 percent of the tuition. It is not going to and from class which determines whether an employee is reimbursed; it is whether he successfully completes his educational course.

If Xerox could be held liable in this case under respondeat superior, other circumstances come to mind which would also appear to impose liability upon it. For example, if Victor Farley carelessly handled volatile materials in a chemistry class and another student were injured or property were destroyed, Xerox could be held responsible. If Xerox is responsible for what an employee does on his way to class, why would it not be equally responsible for what an employee does in class? Or, if educational sabbaticals funded by scholarship grants under the same aid program were encouraged by Xerox, it could be responsible for injuries caused by one of its employees during such a sabbatical driving to or from class at a university hundreds of miles away from the plant. Or, if Xerox encouraged its employees to take paid leaves of absence to participate in worthwhile community organizations or projects, it could be responsible for injuries caused by an employee while so participating.

Other areas of liability come to mind. If Xerox encouraged noontime physical activity by its employees, such as jogging, would it be responsible for an injury caused to a pedestrian by one of its jogging employees in the area around Xerox Square? . . .

In none of these examples would an employee be acting in the scope of his employment as that term has been historically understood. Scope of employment "refers to those acts which are so closely connected with what the servant is employed to do, and so fairly and reasonably incidental to it, that they may be regarded as methods, even though quite improper ones, of carrying out the objectives of the employment." (Prosser, Law of Torts [4th ed], pp. 460-461.)

The Restatement of Agency sets forth the requirements as follows: *(1) Conduct of a servant is within the scope of employment if, but only if: (a) it is of the kind he is employed to perform; (b) it occurs substantially within the authorized time and space limits; (c) it is actuated . . . by a purpose to serve the master. . . .*

(2) Conduct of a servant is not within the scope of employment if it is different in kind from that authorized, far beyond the authorized time or space limits, or too little actuated by a purpose to serve the master.

Victor's activity at the time of the accident in driving to a course whose successful completion was of primary and direct benefit to him cannot be said to be in the scope of his employment. Taking the course was not "closely connected" with what he had been employed to do nor was it "fairly and reasonably incidental" to

(continues)

DINKINS V. FARLEY

(continued from previous page)
the carrying out of the objectives of his employment. It was "too little actuated by a purpose to serve the master"; his own purpose was clearly the prevailing one. Nor was Xerox exercising control over him, directly or indirectly, at the time. He was driving a car not owned by Xerox; he selected his own mode of transportation; he chose the course which he was attending, but he could have gone or not gone as he saw fit and if he failed to attend class after enrolling the jeopardy he suffered was not his job but only the tuition Xerox had advanced on his behalf. It is difficult to see how Xerox was in control or could have been in control of Victor when the accident happened.

The case of *Makoske v. Lombardy,* 47 A.D.2d 284, is not to the contrary for there the employees were required to attend the training session at Saratoga. They were obliged to go. They did not have the same option which Victor had. . . .

The motion of defendant Xerox Corporation is granted. [Thus, Xerox would not be liable even if Victor was found to have been guilty of negligence. The question of Victor's liability for negligence would be decided at trial, because genuine fact issues existed with regard to this question.]⟟

Intentional Torts

Thus far we have assumed the tort to be that of *negligence* (simple carelessness). Most cases in fact are concerned with the employee's negligence. However, an employee's *intentional tort,* such as assault and battery, libel, slander, fraud, trespass, or the like, can also subject the employer to liability. The test is the same. The employer is liable if the employee was acting within the scope of his or her employment at the time. It should be emphasized, though, that an employer is *less likely* to be responsible if the employee's tort was *intentional* rather than merely negligent. The reason is that when an employee intentionally commits a wrongful act, he or she is more likely to be motivated by personal reasons rather than by a desire to serve the employer. Those cases where the employer *has* been held liable for his or her employee's intentional torts usually fall within one of four broad categories.

1. *Where the tort occurs in a job in which force is a natural incident.* An example is a bouncer in a saloon, who is naturally expected to use force occasionally. But if *excessive* force is used, the employer is liable.

2. *Where the employee is actually attempting to promote the employer's business but does it in a wrongful manner.* For example, two competing tow truck drivers are attempting to beat each other to the scene of an accident to get the business for their respective employers. One intentionally runs the other off the road. The employer of the one committing the tort is liable.

3. *Where the tort results from friction naturally brought about by the employer's business.* For instance, the employee, who works for a building contractor, argues with an employee of a subcontractor about the method for laying a floor. They become angry, and the building contractor's employee strikes the other party. The building contractor, as employer, is probably liable.

4. *Where the tort was directly authorized or clearly intended by the employer.* This situation usually, but not always, involves a nonphysical tort such as fraud or defamation. As mentioned at the beginning of this discussion of the employer's tort liability, an employer who authorizes or intends the subordinate's wrongful act is usually held liable regardless of the kind of tort or the type of relationship between superior and subordinate.

Concluding Note on Tort Liability

Two additional problems regarding an employer's tort liability need to be discussed:

1. A minor is not necessarily the employee of his or her parents. Thus, in the absence of a special statute, the parent is not liable for the torts of a minor child unless the child was acting as an employee in the scope of employment for the parent. The parent can, of course, be held liable for his or her own wrongful act in negligently supervising the child.

LEGAL FOCUS

International

Legal Focus
INTERNATIONAL

The legal concept that an employer can be held liable for the wrongful acts of an employee committed within the scope of employment is not just an American rule. It has been applied for centuries in various legal systems, including those derived from the English common law, the Roman civil law, and others. Today, it operates to impose both tort liability and criminal responsibilities on employers throughout the world. In fact, it is used to impose criminal liability on employers in many nations to a greater extent than in the United States.

One recent example is found in *Anklagemyndigheden [Public Prosecutor] v. Hansen & Son,* decided in 1990 by the European Court of Justice (the judicial organ of the European Economic Community (EEC)). In that case, an EEC regulation required truck drivers to drive no more than eight hours consecutively and to have a rest period of at least eleven hours between eight-hour driving stints. Hansen & Son was a trucking company based in Denmark. One of its drivers was found to have violated the EEC rest-period regulation while hauling cargo in the Netherlands. The regulation provided for criminal penalties; both the driver and his employer were prosecuted, convicted, and ordered to pay fines in Denmark. The European Court of Justice ultimately upheld both convictions. The employer's conviction was upheld because the driver was acting within the scope of his employment at the time of the violation. The court held that it was irrelevant that the employer, Hansen & Son, had taken all reasonable steps to ensure that its drivers complied with the regulation and was not blameworthy in any other way. The company's liability was based purely on the concept of respondeat superior.

Also, several states have passed statutes making parents liable within set limits for intentional property damage caused by a minor child.

2. Although the subject of bailments is beyond the scope of this discussion, it should be mentioned that a bailee is not necessarily the employee of the bailor. A *bailment* occurs when the owner of an item of property (the bailor) turns over temporary custody (not ownership) of the item to the bailee for any reason. The bailor ordinarily is *not* liable to third parties for torts committed by the bailee while using the bailor's property. The bailor *is* liable, however, if he or she was negligent in entrusting the item to one whom he or she knew not to be qualified or capable of handling it safely. Otherwise, the bailor generally is liable only if the bailee was acting as the bailor's *employee* in the scope of employment at the time of the tort. Two exceptions exist with regard to *bailments of automobiles:*

a. A few states follow the *family purpose doctrine.* Under that judge-made doctrine, a member of the family is treated as the employee of the head of the household when driving the family car, regardless of whether such a relationship actually existed.

b. A few states have passed *owner-consent statutes,* which hold the owner of an automobile liable to a third party injured by the negligence of anyone who is driving it with the consent of the owner. This liability exists regardless of any employer-employee relationship and regardless of whether the owner was personally negligent.

CRIMINAL LIABILITY

As a general rule, a superior cannot be *criminally* prosecuted for a subordinate's wrongful act unless the superior expressly authorized it. Thus, if Y, a subordinate, while acting within the scope of her employment, injures T, and T dies, Y's superior can be held liable in a civil suit for damages but cannot be subjected to criminal liability. Any criminal responsibility rests on the shoulders of the subordinate. The rule exists because crimes ordinarily require intent, and the superior in this situation has no criminal intent.

Exceptions to the rule usually fall within one of two categories:

1. The statute making the particular act a crime may specifically provide for placing criminal responsibility

on the superior. For example, the federal antitrust laws provide for criminal penalties to be levied against corporations, which can commit crimes only through their human agents.

2. A superior can sometimes be criminally prosecuted under statutes that do not require intent for a violation. A specific example is the offense of selling adulterated food under the federal Food, Drug, and Cosmetic Act. Other examples can be found in some state laws regulating liquor sales and the accuracy of weights of goods sold on that basis.

SUMMARY

The contractual liability of the principal to third parties for transactions made by the agent is dependent on the agent's authority. If the agent acted within the scope of his or her authority when executing the transaction, the resulting contract is the principal's contract and the principal is bound by it. An agent's authority may be express—that which is directly granted by the principal to the agent. It may also be implied—that which is customary for an agent in such a position, or which is reasonably incidental to the agent's express authority. Even if the agent has no express or implied authority, it is possible for the principal to be liable for the agent's actions on the grounds of apparent authority. Apparent authority exists when the principal, by his or her conduct, has misled a reasonably acting third party to believe that the agent had authority. In addition, it is possible for a principal to become liable to the third party by subsequently ratifying the agent's unauthorized transaction. When a principal's liability to a third party depends on whether the principal had notice or knowledge of particular facts, notice to the agent is treated as notice to the principal if receipt of such information was within the scope of the agent's actual or apparent authority.

The agent usually does not incur personal liability when acting in behalf of the principal. The agent can become liable, however, by breaching a duty to the principal, exceeding his or her authority, personally assuming liability, not fully disclosing to the third party that the agent is acting for a particular principal, or committing a tort against a third party.

When a subordinate commits a tort harming a third party, the subordinate clearly is legally responsible to the third party. The superior also can be liable to the third party if it is found that the subordinate was an employee rather than an independent contractor, and if the subordinate was acting within the scope of his or her employment when the tort was committed. A subordinate is an employee if the superior had the right to exercise detailed control over the method and manner by which the subordinate was to accomplish the task. A subordinate is an independent contractor if he or she was hired to accomplish a particular result, and the details of how to do it were within the subordinate's discretion.

KEY TERMS

Authority
Actual authority
Express authority
Implied authority
Apparent authority (or ostensible authority)
Ratification
Express ratification
Implied ratification
Nonexistent principal
Partially disclosed principal
Undisclosed principal
Vicarious liability
Respondeat superior
Scope of employment

QUESTIONS AND PROBLEMS

1. Capital Dredge & Dock Corp. hired an attorney, Alteri, to represent the corporation. Capital Dredge held Alteri out to the City of Detroit as having authority to represent Capital Dredge in personal injury claims and "certain related claims against the City." However, Capital Dredge representatives specifically instructed Alteri not to compromise any of Capital Dredge's claims against the City of Detroit for extra work and delay. Alteri signed a document releasing all of Capital Dredge's claims against the City. Is the release valid? (*Capital Dredge & Dock Corp. v. City of Detroit*, 800 F.2d 525, 6th Cir. 1986.)

2. Consolidated Foods Corp. authorized Newman only to draft an agreement for David Chase to buy the Fuller Brush Company, a division of Consolidated Foods. The agreement was expressly to be subject to the approval of Consolidated Foods' board of directors. Upon drafting such an agreement, New-

man sent a telegram to Chase stating that the board of directors had ratified the agreement to sell the Fuller Brush Company, even though the board had done no such thing. Is Consolidated bound by the terms of the agreement? (*Chase v. Consolidated Foods Corp.*, 744 F.2d 566, 7th Cir. 1984.) No

3. Jerry Beck represented himself as acting on behalf of two partnerships investing in real estate in order to obtain investment money from the Stolmeiers. The partnerships had not authorized Beck to be their agent, but they used the money solicited from the Stolmeiers to renovate partnership properties. The Stolmeiers became dissatisfied with their investment. When the members of the partnerships learned of this fact, they made no effort to repudiate Beck's authority to solicit funds on their behalf. Are the partnerships bound by Beck's guarantee to the Stolmeiers that they would receive a return on their investment? (*Stolmeier v. Beck*, 441 N.W.2d 889, Neb. 1989.) Ratified by accepting the $

4. Rodriguez was a salesman at a retail carpet outlet owned by Carpet World, Inc. He usually was the only employee in the store, and the company's sales manager only made occasional visits to the store. Although he had no hiring authority, Rodriguez hired Amy Schoonover on a salary and commission basis. Amy worked for two months, earning salary and commissions of $714, but was never paid. Rodriguez disappeared, and Amy sued Carpet World for her unpaid compensation. Is Carpet World liable? Discuss. (*Schoonover v. Carpet World, Inc.*, 588 P.2d 729, 1978.) Appar. auth.

5. Bruton lent a D-8 Caterpillar rent-free to David Eckvall, who wanted to clear some land owned by Eckvall. It was agreed that Eckvall would provide an operator and pay for fuel and routine maintenance. Nothing was said about major repairs. While Eckvall was using the Cat, it broke down. Without contacting Bruton, he took it to Automatic Welding & Supply (AWS), where extensive repairs were made at a cost of $2,340. When the repairs were almost completed, Bruton happened to come into the AWS shop on other business and saw his Cat. He spoke to an AWS mechanic and learned of the scope of the repairs, but nothing was said about cost. After the repairs were completed, the Cat was returned to Eckvall's property, where he used it for some time thereafter. AWS billed Bruton for the repairs. Bruton denied liability,

and AWS sued. Is Bruton responsible for the $2,340? Discuss. (*Bruton v. Automatic Welding & Supply*, 513 P.2d 1122, 1973.)

6. Chipman, an employee at Barrickman's service station, was towing a disabled car for Barrickman. Estell, Chipman's girlfriend, was a passenger in the tow truck. She was just along for the ride, without Barrickman's knowledge. The tow truck was involved in an accident and Estell, who was injured, sued Chipman and Barrickman. The trial court dismissed the suit against Barrickman, because he had an official "no rider" rule, even though he didn't always enforce it. Estell appealed. How should the appellate court rule? Discuss. (*Estell v. Barrickman*, 571 S.W.2d 650, 1978.) Estell won. look @ foreseeability & scope of employment

7. Chambers was in the business of moving mobile homes. On previous occasions, Chambers had hired Ross and Bridges to help move mobile homes. Chambers had provided Ross with a truck that had on it magnetic signs bearing the name "Chambers Mobile Home Movers," but asked Ross to remove the signs after Ross damaged two mobile homes. Benny Tate hired Ross and Bridges to move Tate's mobile home based upon Ross's assurances that he was experienced and had insurance. When Tate met Ross and Bridges on the appointed day, both Ross and Bridges were wearing shirts with the name "Chambers Home Movers." The truck did not have the signs on it on that day, but it did on the second day. Tate overheard Ross tell a North Carolina Department of Transportation official that Chambers Home Movers was Ross's business. Tate's mobile home was damaged during the move. Ross told Tate that he worked for Chambers. Is Chambers responsible for the damaged mobile home? (*Tate v. Chambers*, 379 S.E.2d 681, N.C. App. 1989.) No agency chambers not liable

8. Jimmy and Bonnie Gilkeson, husband and wife, jointly owned a farm. Dennis Holliday and a number of his friends gathered on the Gilkeson's property for the purpose of playing their radio and drinking beer. The Gilkesons heard the music. Mr. Gilkeson investigated the activity, and told Holiday and his friends that they were trespassing. In the altercation that followed, Mr. Gilkeson negligently shot Holiday. Holiday sued both Mr. and Mrs. Gilkeson for damages. Is Mrs. Gilkeson liable, based on the argument that she consented to her husband's role in investigating the activity, and that he was

no auth
no ratification
→ Bruton doesn't have to pay

therefore representing her? Discuss. (*Holliday v. Gilkeson,* 363 S.E.2d 133, W.Va. 1987.)

9. Annie Brown was employed by Burlington Industries, Inc. For nearly two years, Ernest Whitmore, a manager at Burlington, made sexually suggestive remarks and gestures towards Brown. During this period of time, Brown complained on numerous occasions to her immediate supervisor and department head about the sexual harassment. (Burlington's open-door policy, as contained in its employee handbook, instructed employees to bring any complaints initially to their supervisor or department head.) Whitmore's sexual harassment of Brown continued despite Brown's complaints to her supervisor and department head. Is Burlington liable for Whit-

more's intentional infliction of emotional distress upon Brown? (*Brown v. Burlington Industries, Inc.,* 378 S.E.2d 232, N.C. App. 1989.)

10. Supervisors at Church's Fried Chicken are authorized to engage in limited forms of disciplinary action. A particular supervisor attempted to reprimand one of the employees under his supervision for what he regarded as an instance of unsatisfactory job performance. The supervisor made several disparaging remarks about the employee's personal life, and then grabbed the employee by her collar, threw her to the ground, and kicked her in the back. Is Church's liable for this supervisor's actions? (*Hester v. Church's Fried Chicken,* 499 N.E.2d 923, Ohio App. 1986.)

Chapter 33

Partnerships
Nature, Formation, and Property

The Nature of Partnerships

Formation of a Partnership

Partnership Property

THE NATURE OF PARTNERSHIPS
Governing Law

Court-developed common law provided the governing rules for partnerships until 1914, when the Uniform Partnership Act (UPA) was promulgated. The UPA codified most of the common-law rules and significantly altered some of them. It has been adopted by 49 states (the exception being Louisiana), giving us a relatively uniform body of national partnership law.[1]

Naturally, 80 years of service has revealed some cracks and flaws in the UPA. As this edition is being prepared, work on a Revised Uniform Partnership Act (RUPA) has just been completed. *If* the RUPA is adopted by several states, it will significantly change many of the rules discussed in the next three chapters. Because only two states (Wyoming and Montana) have adopted RUPA as of this writing, however, we defer any thorough discussion of the RUPA to following editions. However, in footnotes we will make reference to some of the major changes that adoption of RUPA would bring.

Defining a Partnership

Section 6 of the UPA defines a *partnership* as "an association of two or more persons to carry on as co-owners a business for profit." This definition can be broken into elements as follows.

Association

The term *association* indicates that a partnership is a voluntary arrangement formed by agreement.

Person

Under the UPA the term *person* includes not only individuals but also corporations, other partnerships, and other types of associations. With regard to minors and insane persons, the same basic rules apply to partnership agreements as to other types of contracts. Thus a minor can treat the partnership agreement with the other partners as voidable. The minor usually can also repudiate personal liabilities to creditors beyond the amount of his or her investment in the business. But this investment *is* subject to the claims of partnership creditors, although it is the maximum liability that the minor ordinarily can incur.

Co-owners

The partners are defined as co-owners of the business, which distinguishes them from those who are merely agents, servants, or other subordinates. Courts often say that true partners share in three communities of interest: capital, management, and profits. Typically, partners will contribute money, property, or services to the enterprise's capital, have a voice in management, and enjoy a right to share in the profits.

To Carry on a Business

The term *business* has been defined in Section 2 of the UPA as including "every trade, occupation, or profession."

For Profit

An association cannot be a partnership unless the purpose of forming it is to make profits directly through its business activities. Associations for other purposes (including religious, patriotic, or public improvement purposes, or furtherance of the *separate* economic interests of members) are not partnerships, even if they engage in business transactions. Thus the local chapter of a fraternal lodge cannot be a partnership, and the rights and duties of partners cannot attach to its members. For example, individual members are not personally liable for debts incurred for the lodge by its officers unless an agency relationship has been expressly created.

The Entity Theory versus the Aggregate Theory

Drafters of the UPA could not agree as to whether a partnership should be treated (1) like a corporation, as an *entity*, separate and apart from its owners, or (2) as it traditionally had been at common law as a mere *aggregation* of its partners. They eventually reached a compromise so that a partnership today is treated as an entity for some purposes and as a mere

---

[1]The UPA, which appears in its entirety in Appendix B, and other "uniform" laws were created by the American Law Institute and the National Conference of Commissioners on Uniform State Laws. Since these groups possessed no legislative powers, the rules they promulgate have no effect until formally adopted by state legislatures.

aggregation for others. In a sense, the UPA has retained the **aggregate theory** by defining a partnership as "an association of two or more persons. . . ." The pass-through taxation feature of partnerships is also consistent with an aggregation theory.

On the other hand, the UPA uses the **entity theory** for selected purposes. For example, the UPA recognizes the concept of *partnership property* and allows a partnership to own and convey property in the partnership name. In addition, it places liability for acts of the partners in conducting partnership business primarily on the partnership itself and the partnership property, and only secondarily on individual partners and their individual property. Also, under various UPA provisions every partner is an agent *of the partnership*, capital contributions are made *to the partnership*, books are kept *for the partnership*, and every partner is accountable as a fiduciary *to the partnership*. The UPA even defines the term *person* to include partnerships.

The general trend is to treat partnerships as entities for more and more purposes, a practice that is consistent with common expectations in the commercial world.[2] However, in difficult cases courts often apply whichever theory allows them to reach an equitable result consistent with policy and pragmatic considerations. For example, in *Lawler v. Dallas Statler Hilton,*[3] the plaintiff, a maid supervisor, was injured on the job and received a workers' compensation award. The exclusive nature of such an award barred her from suing her employer, a joint venture,[4] so she sued the hotel's manager for negligence. That manager, however, was also a venturer (partner) in the joint venture. The court believed that the policy considerations underlying the exclusive recovery rule were so important that the joint venture should be treated as an aggregation so that benefits flowing from it should be viewed as flowing from its members as well, thereby barring civil damages recovery not only against the joint venture but also against its members.

Contrast *Lawler* with *Kuehl v. Means,*[5] wherein several minors formed a partnership that contracted with the plaintiff. When the plaintiff sued on the contract, the minors attempted to disaffirm it. Had the court used the aggregate theory, it would have held that the partnership was a mere collection of its partners and if all of them had the right to disaffirm, so would the partnership. However, apparently believing that such disaffirmance would be unfair, the court held that the plaintiff's contract was with the partnership *entity,* which could not disaffirm on grounds of minority.

FORMATION OF A PARTNERSHIP
The Partnership Agreement

As previously mentioned, the partnership is formed by agreement, either express or implied. It is not created by statute, as is a corporation. Few, if any, statutory requirements must be met in order to *form* a partnership. While the UPA governs many aspects of the *operation* of a partnership, it is intended primarily to fill in the gaps of the partnership agreement. Many UPA rules are applicable only if the partners do not agree otherwise.

The agreement obviously must have a *legal object,* but a partnership can be formed even if one or more of the other elements of a valid contract is absent. A valid contract usually does exist as a practical matter, but it is not required. A partnership can be created without a written document, although any part of the agreement falling within the statute of frauds does require a writing for enforceability.

Despite the fact that a written partnership agreement is usually not required, it is highly desirable. Formation of a business is a substantial undertaking and should not be left to the oral declarations of the parties—for several reasons:

1. There are many inherent problems in proving the exact terms of an oral agreement.

2. Numerous problems (such as those relating to taxation) can be satisfactorily resolved only by a carefully drafted written instrument.

3. If the parties go through the process of drafting a formal document with the aid of an attorney, they are much more likely to foresee many problems they otherwise would not have thought about. For example, matters such as procedures for expulsion of a partner or for settlement of disputes between partners are easily overlooked because they seem so remote when the partnership is first formed.

---

[2]The RUPA substantially increases the tilt toward the entity theory. For example, it defines a partnership as "an *entity* resulting from the association of two or more persons to carry on as co-owners a business for profit." RUPA Sec. 201(a).

[3]793 S.W.2d 27 (Tex.App. 1990).

[4]A *joint venture* is simply a partnership formed for a single undertaking with no expectation of continuity. In almost all instances, joint ventures are governed by the UPA, which provides identical results to cases involving partnerships.

[5]218 N.W. 907 (Iowa 1928).

Desirable Elements of a Partnership Agreement

The formal partnership agreement, often referred to as the **articles of partnership,** should clearly reflect the intent of the partners as to the rights and obligations they wish to assume in the business. What is contained in these articles will depend on the nature of the business and the desires of the partners, but ordinarily the written instrument should include such items as the following:

1. Name of the firm. The partnership is not required to have a firm name, but it is usually a good idea to have one. The name can be that of one or more of the partners, or it can be fictitious. (But it cannot be deceptively similar to that of another business for the purpose of attracting its customers.) If the name is fictitious, it usually must be registered. Most states have **assumed name statutes** (sometimes called **fictitious name statutes**) that require any firm, including a partnership, to register with a state official the fictitious name under which the firm is doing business. The purpose of such statutes is to enable creditors of the firm to learn the identities of those responsible.

2. Nature and location of the business.

3. Date of commencement and duration of the partnership.

4. Amount of contributions in money or property each partner is to make (in other words, the amount of their investments in the business).

5. Time within which the contribution of each partner is to be made.

6. Salaries and drawing accounts of each partner, if such are desired.

7. Division of work and duties of each partner, including rights in management.

8. Admission requirements for new partners.

9. Each partner's proportionate share of net profits while the business is continuing to operate and upon dissolution.

10. Any proposed restrictions on the power of individual members to bind the firm.

11. Clear delineation of partnership assets as distinguished from individual partners' assets.

12. Bookkeeping and accounting methods to be used and location of and access to books.

13. Procedures for withdrawal or exclusion of a partner.

14. Indication of whether withdrawal or exclusion causes dissolution, and if not, rules for continuing the business after such an event.

15. Method for determining the value of a withdrawing or excluded partner's interest.

16. Requirements and procedures for notice to partners and partnership creditors in case of dissolution.

17. Which partner or partners will be in charge of winding up the business upon dissolution.

18. Procedures for settling disputes between partners, such as submitting them to arbitration.

Determining the Existence of a Partnership

When the parties have clearly expressed their intentions in a written instrument, there is ordinarily no difficulty in determining whether a partnership exists. But when the parties have not been explicit in declaring their intentions, problems frequently arise. The most fundamental, of course, is whether a partnership has even been _created._ This issue arises with surprising frequency, because of its importance in regard to the rights and obligations of the "partners" and third parties as well. For example, a creditor may seek to hold several persons liable for the transactions of one of them on the ground that they are partners. Or one party might claim that he and another are partners and that the other party has violated a resulting fiduciary duty by having a conflicting business interest.

When the existence of a partnership is disputed by an interested party, such existence becomes a question of fact to be decided on the basis of all the circumstances. Typically, no single factor is controlling, and the court's ultimate decision commonly is based on several considerations. *Intent* of the parties is important, but not the labels that they use. If persons associated in business call themselves *partners,* that label is indicative, but not necessarily controlling. Similarly, the fact that persons believe and perhaps even explicitly state that they are *not* partners is irrelevant if the actual substance of the relationship they intend to create is what the law calls a *partnership.*

Substance controls over form. The most important substantive factors in determining the parties' intent are (1) sharing of profits and losses, (2) joint control of the business, and (3) joint ownership and control of capital or property.

Sharing of Profits and Losses

If there has been no sharing of profits or agreement to share them, a court is very likely to find that no partnership exists. On the other hand, the sharing of *net profits* (as opposed to mere *gross revenues*) usually gives rise to a rebuttable presumption that a partnership exists. That the presumption is *rebuttable* means that it may be overcome by the weight of contrary evidence, but it remains a potent aid to the party seeking to establish the existence of a partnership who has the burden of proof in such matters.

There are certain situations, however, where the sharing of profits does *not* give rise to a rebuttable presumption of partnership existence. These are situations where logical alternative explanations for the sharing of profits are present. Following are several situations that fall in this category.

First, no presumption of partnership exists where the profits are received by a creditor in payment of a debt. For example, O, the owner of a business in financial difficulty, owes a debt to X. In settlement of this debt, X agrees to accept a certain percentage of O's profits for a period of time. No inference of partnership is created by the sharing of profits, and no partnership exists between O and X (unless, perhaps, X takes title to a portion of the business property and takes an active role in managing the business).

Second, no presumption of partnership arises where profits are received as wages by an employee. Employers often key salary bonuses to profits in order to encourage employees to work harder. This is an obvious and common explanation for the sharing of profits that indicates nothing more than an employment relationship, so long as X withholds federal taxes from employees' salaries, exercises control over the employees, and does not allow them any management powers or co-ownership of business property.

Third, where the profits are received as consideration for the sale of property no presumption of partnership exists. When an item of property having uncertain value is sold to someone who expects to use it in carrying on a business, it is sometimes agreed that the price payable to the seller will include a share of the profits made from use of the property.

Two common examples are *goodwill* and *trademarks*. The seller often retains no ownership of the property or control over its use; nor is he or she usually expected to share any losses incurred by the buyer. In many instances this is simply the best way of computing the value of a particular property right. No partnership presumption is created by such an arrangement.

Other situations where sharing of profits does not give rise to a presumption of partnership are where the profits are received as rent by a landlord, as an annuity by a spouse or representative of a deceased partner, or as interest on a loan by a creditor.

Absence of an agreement to share losses does not necessarily weigh heavily against the existence of a partnership. Often partners will agree to share profits, but they may not even consider that they might suffer a loss, or they may believe it will bring bad luck to even think about the possibility. Hence, they will have no agreement as to losses even though they clearly intended to be partners. On the other hand, if there *is* an agreement to share losses, an extremely strong presumption of partnership arises. As noted previously, there are many nonpartnership explanations for why persons would agree to share profits, but there are few nonpartnership reasons that would explain an agreement to share losses.

Joint Control and Management

Although sharing of profits is a cardinal element of the partnership, another factor often felt to be important by the courts is whether the parties have *joint control* over the operation of the business. For instance, where sharing of profits by itself is not sufficient to indicate existence of a partnership, the addition of the factor of joint control might well cause a court to hold that a partnership has been created. *Exercise of management powers* is obviously very strong evidence of control. But the fact that management powers have been expressly delegated to one or more of the partners does not mean that those who do not manage are not true partners if the other facts indicate that they are. In a sense, agreeing to relinquish control is itself an exercise of the right of control.

Joint Ownership of Property

Another factor that frequently finds its way into court opinions is *joint ownership of assets*. Of the three basic tests for existence of a partnership, this is the least important, although it certainly is taken into account by the court, along with all the other evidence. The UPA takes the position that co-ownership of property does not, of itself, establish a partnership. An inference of partnership is also not necessarily created by the fact that the co-owners share any profits made by the use of the property. This seems at first to be inconsistent with our earlier discussion of the presumption of partnership that is usually engendered by profit sharing. But there is no real inconsistency. In the case of co-owners of property, the sharing of profits made from the property is a basic part of co-ownership. In most cases the owner of property wishes to receive whatever income it generates; thus it is reasonable to assume that co-owners will want to share the income from their jointly owned property. A partnership should not be presumed simply because the owners act in a way totally consistent with simple co-ownership.

On the other hand, if the property and its use are only part of a larger enterprise, and the parties share profits from the whole enterprise, an inference of partnership is justified. For instance, co-ownership of a commercial building and sharing of its rental income by A and B does not necessarily make them partners. If, however, they use part of the building as premises for the operation of a going business of some type, sharing not only the rental income from the remainder of the building but also the profits and management of the business, they are quite likely to be considered partners.

The following case illustrates the type of evidence considered by courts in determining whether a partnership exists.

BASS V. BASS

Supreme Court of Tennessee, 814 S.W.2d 38 (1991)

When Linda Bass (plaintiff) and William Bass (the deceased) first started living together in 1975, she was employed full-time and he was drawing unemployment compensation. They "just joined [their incomes] together and paid bills and bought food and things." A year later William leased a restaurant, and plaintiff worked there 17 hours a day while William worked in a beer store nearby. Eventually they each worked 12-hour shifts at the restaurant in order to keep it open 24 hours a day. Linda was not compensated for her efforts at the restaurant, though she worked there from 1976 to 1981, when it burned.

Linda and William were married in 1980, but divorced that same year. Immediately after the divorce they resumed living together and Linda began working in a video game business William had begun. Linda assisted William in daily servicing of the machines, helped to decide where

new machines would be located, and kept most of the business records. Although she was not listed as a partner or co-owner of the businesses, she wrote and signed most of the checks for the operation of the 18 locations, worked on the machines, and collected money from them. She was not paid a salary or wages for her efforts. All property and checking accounts were in the name of William Bass. The video game businesses prospered so that William was able to buy a convenience store and used car business.

When William died intestate in 1986, a dispute arose between Linda and William's brother. The trial court held that Linda was William's partner and therefore equitable owner of one-half of the assets of his estate. The court of appeals reversed. Linda appealed.

Drowota, Justice:

In Tennessee, a partnership is defined as an association of two or more persons to carry on as co-owners a business for profit, and the receipt of a share of the profits of that business is prima facie evidence that a partnership exists. In determining whether one is a partner, no one fact or circumstance may be pointed to as a conclusive test, but each case must be decided upon consideration of all relevant facts, actions, and conduct of the parties. If the parties' business brings them within the scope of a joint business undertaking for mutual profit—that is to say if they place their money, assets, labor, or skill in commerce with the understanding that profits will be shared between them—the result is a partnership whether or not the parties understood that it would be so.

Moreover, the existence of a partnership depends upon the intention of the parties, and the controlling intention in this regard is that ascertainable from the actions of the parties. Although a contract of partnership, either express or implied, is essential to the creation of partnership status, it is not essential that the parties actually intend to become partners. The existence of a partnership is not a question

(continues)

BASS V. BASS

(continued from previous page)
of the parties' undisclosed intention or even the terminology they use to describe their relationship, nor is it necessary that the parties have an understanding of the legal effects of their acts. It is the intent to do the things which constitute a partnership that determines whether individuals are partners, regardless if it is their purpose to create or avoid the relationship. Stated another way, the existence of a partnership may be implied from the circumstances where it appears that the individuals involved have entered into a business relationship for profit, combining their property, labor, skill, experience, or money.

. . . [Some earlier cases indicate that] an individual should not be denied the opportunity to establish the existence of a *business* partnership into which they, like any other competent individual, may enter into, whether or not cohabitation exists.

There is no question that the plaintiff and William Bass carried on as co-owners a business for profit. The parties pooled their money to purchase "food and things," to pay bills and,

most importantly, to lease the restaurant. This was done, initially at least, while the plaintiff was working full time and the deceased was unemployed. The implication is that the plaintiff made a significant financial contribution, particularly when the couple began the first business, the restaurant. Moreover, the proceeds from the restaurant business were used to birth the video machine venture, and the profits from this undertaking were used to buy the convenience store. When asked about who kept up with the financial aspect of the businesses, Linda Bass stated that "mostly, we took care of it together." The uncontroverted evidence before the trial court was that all income from the businesses was pooled and that the plaintiff received whatever was necessary from those funds to maintain her standard of living. Similarly, plaintiff, by virtue of her reliance on the pooled funds, necessarily incurred business obligations whenever expenditures were made from those funds. Linda Bass shared in the profits of these businesses, in that she had all of the advantages and obligations of running the businesses.

Aside from making a financial contribution and sharing profits, the plaintiff invested considerable time and labor into operating both the restaurant and the video machine businesses. . . . Additionally, the plaintiff kept the financial records of the businesses, writing the vast majority of the checks, taking care of the daily bookkeeping work, as well as most of the banking business.

It is of little or no consequence that the plaintiff and the deceased did not formally regard themselves as "partners." As we have pointed out previously, the existence of a partnership may be implied from the circumstances where it appears that the individuals involved have entered into a business relationship for profit, commingling their property, labor, skill, experience, or money. This is precisely what the parties involved in this case did. It was through the joint efforts of William Bass and Linda Bass that the business prospered. That prosperity was due in equal part to the effort of Linda Bass.

The judgment of the Court of Appeals is reversed, and that of the trial court is reinstated.⚖

Note

Courts traditionally have been somewhat reluctant to find partnerships in the domestic setting, often finding labors such as Linda Bass's to be simply those of a "helpful spouse." Indeed, the court of appeals in this case held that although William treated Linda "shabbily," she had no remedy. Perhaps the Tennessee Supreme Court's decision in *Bass* signals a new trend.

Partnership By Estoppel

Even when no partnership exists, partnership-like liability may be imposed on a *partnership by estoppel* theory under Sec. 16 of the UPA, if these elements are present: (a) words or conduct by or attributable

to the party to be charged amounting to a representation of partnership, (b) detrimental action taken by the plaintiff in reliance upon the representation, and (c) reasonableness of the representation.

Thus, if C knowingly allows A and B to represent to D that C is their partner, and, reasonably believing this representation to be true, D loans money to A and B based on C's good financial standing, C will be held liable on a partnership by estoppel theory even if she is not, in fact, a partner of A and B.

Another common application of this doctrine arose in *Colo-Tex Leasing, Inc. v. Neitzert,*[6] where D and his brother, as partners, signed on May 28, 1983,

[6]746 P.2d 972 (Colo.App. 1987).

a lease agreement for refrigeration equipment to be used in a retail liquor store managed by D's brother. P approved the lease on June 9, and relying on the lease and the partners' financial statements, advanced funds to a refrigerator manufacturer for custom fabrication of the equipment. D saw the equipment being installed at the grand opening of the store in July 1983, but in later litigation claimed that by that time he had sold his partnership interest to his sister. Because D had never informed P of his withdrawal as partner, he was still liable on the lease based on a partnership by estoppel theory.

The partnership by estoppel doctrine seldom applies in tort cases because tort plaintiffs typically cannot satisfy the reliance element. Also note that a plaintiff may rely on representations made to her personally, but not on representations made to others that she has not heard *unless* the defendant has held himself out as a partner in a *public* manner. One court described a *public holding out* (which may be relied on by the whole world), as distinguished from a *private holding out* (which may be relied on only by those who heard it), in these terms:

The holding out to the public generally must appear so public and so long continued as to justify an inference, as matter of fact, that one dealing with the partnership knew of it and relied on it, without direct testimony to that effect.[7]

PARTNERSHIP PROPERTY

A partnership commonly requires various types of property for the operation of its business, including, for example, real estate, equipment, inventory, or intangibles such as cash or securities. Under the UPA, a partnership is recognized as an entity insofar as property ownership is concerned and can own either real estate or other types of property. The UPA uses the phrase **tenants in partnership** to describe the status of individual partners with respect to the partnership property. (The rights that individual partners have regarding partnership property will be discussed in the next chapter.)

Although today a partnership can (and quite often does) own such property itself, it is not essential that it own any property at all. The partners themselves may wish to *individually* own the property needed for the operation of the business.

[7] *Baich v. Campbell*, 791 P.2d 1080 (Ariz.App. 1990).

For a number of reasons it is sometimes important to determine whether an item of property belongs to the partnership or to an individual partner. Among them:

1. In most states, creditors of the partnership must resort to partnership property for satisfaction of their claims before they can take property of individual partners.

2. The right of a partner to use partnership property is usually limited to purposes of furthering the partnership business.

3. The question of ownership can also be important with regard to taxation, distribution of assets upon dissolution of the partnership, and other matters.

Factors in Determining Ownership
Agreement
The ownership of property is determined by *agreement* of the partners. Sound business practices dictate that the partners should explicitly agree on the matter and keep accurate records of their dealings with property. Unfortunately, partners often fail to indicate clearly their intentions as to whether ownership of particular items of property rests with the partnership or with one or more individual partners. In such cases, the courts consider all pertinent facts in an attempt to discover the partners' *intent*. Where it appears that the matter of property ownership never occurred to the partners, so that they actually had no definite intention, the court determines which of the possible alternatives—partnership or individual ownership—more closely accords with their general intentions and objectives for the business as a whole and which is fairer both to partners and to third parties.

Legal Title
In the absence of a clear agreement as to ownership, the strongest evidence of property ownership is the name in which the property is held, often referred to as the **legal title.** If an item of property is held in the name of the partnership, courts will hold it to be partnership property in almost every case. This principle most often plays a part where *real estate* is involved, because a deed has been executed in the name of some party and usually has been "recorded" (made part of official county records). Such formal

evidence of ownership is frequently not available for property other than real estate, but if it is available, it will play the same important role. For example, this principle applies to motor vehicles, for which there is usually a state-issued certificate of title.

Problems regarding ownership seldom arise if title to the property in question is held in the partnership name. Those that do arise usually occur in either of two situations: (1) where the property is of a type for which there is no deed, certificate, or other formal evidence of ownership; or (2) where title is held in the name of one or more individual partners, but there is a claim that it is actually partnership property. In the first instance, evidence must be presented to establish just where ownership actually rests. In the second, evidence must be introduced to overcome the presumption of individual ownership and prove that the property actually belongs to the partnership. No single factor is controlling; the court's determination ordinarily is based on the cumulative weight of several factors.

Specific Factors

Property *purchased with partnership funds* is presumed to be partnership property. This presumption is rebuttable, but typically it is very difficult to overcome.

Evidence indicating that the property has been used in the business of the partnership also weighs in favor of the conclusion that it is partnership property. This factor, however, is not conclusive because courts realize that it is not uncommon for an individual partner to allow his or her property to be used in the partnership business without intending to surrender ownership of it.

If property is carried in the partnership books as an asset of the firm, this strongly indicates that it is partnership property. The inference is even stronger if an unpaid balance on the property's purchase price is carried in the records as a partnership liability.

Among other factors[8] that a court may consider in determining whether specific property belongs to the partnership or an individual partner are the following:

1. If property had been purchased with funds of an individual partner, the fact that partnership funds were later used to improve, repair, or maintain the property *tends* to show that it now belongs to the partnership. (But additional evidence usually is required, because most courts have been unwilling to infer that the property is owned by the partnership *solely* on the basis that partnership funds were later used to maintain it.)

2. The fact that *taxes* on the property have been paid by the partnership can be important.

3. The receipt by the partnership of *income* generated by the property is evidence that the partnership is the owner.

4. Any other conduct of those involved is considered if it tends to indicate their intent regarding property ownership.

The following case illustrates the strong presumption that property acquired with partnership funds or labor is partnership property, as well as some of the problems that may sometimes result from having partnership property in the name of one of the partners instead of the partnership.

[8]RUPA Sec. 203 adds detail to the UPA's guidelines for determining whether property is owned by individual partners or by the partnership. Most of the guidelines are consistent with current case law.

ECKERT V. ECKERT

Supreme Court of North Dakota, 425 N.W. 2d 914 (1988)

Case

Ben Eckert was Donovan Eckert's uncle. In 1959 the two formed a farming and ranching partnership called the "E-7 Ranch." No formal partnership agreement was ever executed. Donovan died in 1982, and Gaila Eckert, the representative of Donovan's estate, filed suit seeking dissolution and liquidation of the partnership.

Ben and Gaila agreed on the division of all partnership property except for cooperative patronage credits with the Minot Farmers Union Elevator, Minot Farmers Union Oil, and Harvest States Cooperative. Gaila asserted that these patronage credits are partnership property which should be equally split. Ben asserted that these credits were titled in his name individually and are not partnership property.

A portion of the cooperatives' profits each year are allocated to each member-patron and the cooperative is required to pay out at least 20 percent of this amount in cash to the member-patron. The remaining 80 percent is retained by the cooperative but shows on its books as a patronage credit to the member-patron. Although this portion is not distributed to the member-patron at the time it is earned, it must be reported as income by the member-patron. These unpaid distributions typically are retained by the cooperative until the member-patron reaches a certain age or the cooperative's board of directors votes to "retire" the credits for a specified past year.

In this case, patronage credits were earned on business generated by the partnership. The 20 percent annual cash distributions were paid to Ben Eckert, who placed them in the partnership account and included them as income to the partnership on the partnership tax return. The partnership return then allocated one-half of this income to Ben and one-half to Donovan. The 80 percent patronage credits were also included as partnership income each year, and again one-half of this income was allocated to each partner.

Upon reaching age 65 in 1978, Ben began receiving distributions of the retained patronage credits from Farmers Union Oil. Between 1978 and 1983, Ben received $28,612.28 of those credits. Ben kept all of these funds. None of the retained patronage credits earned on partnership business with Farmers Union Elevator and Harvest States had been distributed at the time of trial.

The trial court placed the burden on Gaila to prove that the patronage credits earned through partnership business were partnership property. In large part because the credits were held in Ben's name, the trial court concluded that Gaila had failed to meet her burden of proof and dismissed her claim. Gaila appealed.

Gierke, Justice:

The trial court relied heavily upon the fact that the patronage credits were held in Ben's name, but that fact is not conclusive of the issue of ownership. Property which is titled in the name of an individual partner may nevertheless be partnership property. The determination whether property held in the name of an individual partner belongs to the partnership is a question of fact. The relevant inquiry is whether the partners intended that the property in question be partnership property or individual property.

Section 45-05-07, N.D.C.C. [U.P.A. @ 8], provides:

1. All property originally brought into the partnership stock or subsequently acquired by purchase or otherwise, on account of the partnership, is partnership property.

2. Unless the contrary intention appears, property acquired with partnership funds is partnership property.

. . . The above-quoted provisions of the Uniform Act have consistently been construed to create a presumption that property acquired with partnership funds is partnership property. . . . The presumption extends beyond purchases with partnership funds to any acquisition of property derived from partnership labor, materials, or other assets.

In this state, a presumption shifts the burden of proof to the party against whom it is directed. A review of the record in this case establishes that the presumption should have been applied and the burden of proof shifted to Ben. Ben does not dispute that the vast majority of the patronage credits were derived from partnership business with the cooperatives. Inasmuch as these credits were property acquired or derived through partnership funds, assets, labor, or materials, they are presumed to be partnership property. . . . The burden then shifts to Ben to establish that there was an intention between the partners that the patronage credits earned through partnership business were to be Ben's individual property.

The judgment of the district court is reversed and the matter is remanded for a new trial in accordance with this opinion.

**Box 33.1
The Law
at Work**

In recent years accounting firms, and to a lesser degree law firms, have taken a beating from liability judgments. In 1991, law and accounting firms paid nearly $1 billion in liability judgments. In 1992 alone, Ernst & Young agreed to pay $400 million to settle federal charges that it inadequately audited several failed savings and loans, and KPMG Peat Marwick paid $67.9 million in England for an allegedly faulty audit. By some estimates, more than $30 billion in lawsuits are still pending against major accounting firms.

Given these staggering figures, many law and accounting firms are reducing partners' compensation, laying off partners, and, in extreme cases, even going out of business. The dream of many professionals—to be a partner in a major law or accounting firm—now may seem to be more of a nightmare, given the potential liability that attaches to partner status. An accounting firm partner in New York may be forced to dip into personal assets to help pay a judgment against the firm arising out of malpractice committed by a partner in Seattle whom the New York partner has never met.

In light of this situation, many law and accounting firms are abandoning the traditional partnership and are seeking alternative ways of organizing themselves to avoid this open-ended liability exposure. For example, some regional accounting firms are reorganizing from partnerships into separate professional corporations—one corporation for each state in which the firm does business. Under state professional corporation or professional association statutes, partners remain individually liable for their own malpractice, but their liability for the negligent acts of their former partners (now co-shareholders) is limited to the amount of money they have invested in the partnership.

Texas, Louisiana, and Delaware have authorized *limited liability partnerships*, which achieve the same effect. In Texas, for example, if a lawyer, doctor, accountant, or similar professional files a proper statement with the secretary of state indicating that the firm is reorganizing into a limited liability partnership and that it maintains a certain level of liability insurance to cover typical malpractice cases, that professional will be individually liable only for his or her own malpractice. Malpractice committed by other partners must be compensated out of the liability policy and firm assets only.

Such reforms are controversial because protection for the professionals may come at the expense of compensation for clients and others injured by malpractice. The struggle continues to be an effort to protect the economic viability of professional firms on the one hand, while adequately compensating malpractice victims and encouraging careful performance of professional obligations on the other. There is, as yet, no sign that the partnership form of organization for law and accounting firms will disappear, but many firms have already sought out alternatives.

SUMMARY

A partnership is defined as "an association of two or more persons to carry on as co-owners a business for profit." In some respects, a partnership is treated as a separate legal entity. For example, it is legally capable of owning property and making contracts, and partnership property is primarily liable for partnership debts. In other respects, however, the law treats a partnership as an aggregation of individuals rather than an entity. For example, individual partners are personally responsible for partnership debts after partnership assets are exhausted.

The partnership is created by agreement. Although this agreement does not have to be a formal written one, it ought to be. Partners should devote great care to the creation of a formal written partnership agreement, a document often called the articles of partnership.

Courts may examine a variety of factors to determine whether a partnership exists when there is no formal partnership agreement. The sharing of profits is an important indicator of partnership status, but there are several situations in which profit sharing does not mean that the parties intended to be partners. Showing that the parties each exercised control and management over the business is another important way of establishing the existence of a partnership. Joint ownership of property is a relevant factor, but it is not weighed as heavily in determining whether a partnership exists.

A partnership is legally capable of owning property, although it is not necessary that a partnership own property in order to operate its business. A partnership can use property that is owned by individual partners. It can be important to determine whether a particular item of property is owned by the partnership or by one or more individual partners, for several reasons. For example, partnership creditors must look first to partnership property for satisfaction of their claims, and an individual partner's right to use partnership property is restricted. The articles of partnership should specify which property is to be owned by the partnership. When a question of property ownership is not resolved by the articles of partnership, courts consider such things as the name in which legal title is held, whether the property was purchased with partnership funds, the way the property is used, and its treatment in the partnership records.

KEY TERMS

Aggregate theory
Entity theory
Articles of partnership
Assumed name statute (or fictitious name statute)
Tenants in partnership
Legal title

QUESTIONS AND PROBLEMS

1. The U.S. government filed suit against the "Bonanno Organized Crime Family of La Cosa Nostra," claiming that the family's activities violated the Racketeer Influenced and Corrupt Organizations Act (RICO). The government sought both monetary damages and forfeiture of property that allegedly had been used to carry out illegal purposes. In order to maintain the suit against the family as an organization, however, the government had to prove that the family was a legal "person," or entity. The government's argument was that the family operated as a partnership or a joint venture. The defendants filed a motion to dismiss the government's complaint, and the issue for the court at this point was whether the allegations in the complaint, if ulti-

mately proved, would establish that the Bonanno family was a partnership.

The allegations in the government's complaint stated that the Bonanno family operates through groups known as "crews." Each crew has as its leader a person known as a "Capo," who is the captain or boss of a crew. A "Capo" of a crew is supervised by, reports to, and, where necessary, is supported by the head of the Bonanno Family, who is known as the "Boss." The Boss has a second-in-command, known as the "Underboss." The Bonanno Family also has a counselor or advisor, known as a "Consigliere," who advises about intra-Family disputes. The Bonanno Family rules dictate that a crew member cannot participate in illegal activities without the prior approval of the crew member's Capo. Likewise, a Capo can only undertake an illegal activity after the Boss or the Underboss has approved the activity. There is no indication that family members agree to share losses. Is the Bonanno family a partnership? Discuss. (*United States v. The Bonanno Organized Crime Family of La Cosa Nostra,* 879 F.2d 20, 2d Cir. 1989.)

2. Dr. Citrin had the following oral agreement with Dr. Mehta: Dr. Mehta would perform medical services in Dr. Citrin's office while Dr. Citrin was away on vacation. Thirty percent of all fees collected from Medicare, Medicaid, and insurance companies were to be paid to Dr. Citrin, with such amounts characterized as rent and administrative services. Fees received directly from patients, however, were to be kept entirely by Dr. Mehta. In addition, while covering Dr. Citrin's office, Dr. Mehta had authority to use Dr. Citrin's prescription pads, and full use of equipment and staff. Does this relationship rise to the level of partnership? Discuss. (*Impastato v. De Girolamo,* 459 N.Y.S.2d 512, N.Y. Sup. Ct. 1983.)

3. Tandy Corporation hired Larson under a Special Manager Incentive Agreement (SMIA) pursuant to which Larson agreed to manage a Radio Shack store for compensation equal to one-half of the adjusted gross profit of the store as computed by a specified formula. Larson also agreed to make a "security deposit" of $20,000 that would cover any loss sustained by Tandy by reason of Larson's failure to manage the store or protect its assets with reasonable care. The agreement was automatically renewable annually until either party gave notice of termination.

Nine years later, Tandy terminated the agreement because, in Larson's view, it wanted to replace SMIA managers with salaried company managers so as to increase Tandy's share of the profits generated by the stores. Larson sued, claiming that he was a partner with Tandy and therefore Tandy could not simply dismiss him with no offer of compensation for the value of the enterprise as a going concern. Was there a partnership? Discuss. (*Larson v. Tandy Corp.*, 371 S.E.2d 663, Ga.App. 1988.)

4. Lowell and Eldon Indvik had a joint ownership interest in farmland bought from their parents. They had no written partnership agreement and did not file partnership tax returns. Lowell testified that they had no intent to become partners, but farmed under the name "Indvik Brothers" as a convenience. They did agree to share profits and losses equally. In borrowing money from a bank, each signed a document entitled "Authority of Partnership to Open Deposit Account and to Procure Loans," a document that described "Indvik Brothers" as the trade name to be used by the partnership of Eldon and Lowell Indvik. Subsequent loan documents were executed using "Indvik Brothers" as the name of the artificial entity borrowing money. Additionally, an agricultural security agreement executed by the brothers identified the document as a partnership financial statement. Were they partners or, as Lowell testified, "just brothers farming together"? Discuss. (*In re Indvik*, 118 B.R. 993, N.D.Iowa Brktcy. 1990.)

5. Could the brothers in the previous case be held liable as partners on a partnership by estoppel theory? Discuss.

6. Zinke, sole general partner and significant investor in a limited partnership, misappropriated partnership funds by writing checks to himself on partnership money market accounts. After failing to recover the funds, the limited partners and their insurers had Zinke charged with embezzlement. The judge dismissed the indictment, holding that a person cannot steal from himself. In so ruling, did the judge apply the entity or the aggregate theory of partnerships? Discuss. (*People v. Zinke*, 76 N.Y.2d 8, 1990.)

7. Rider opened a dairy farm enterprise with his father. Both worked on the farm. Each received half of the income from the business, including the sale of cattle. Each claimed only half the business's income on his individual income tax return. Farm equipment used by the enterprise was depreciated on a partnership basis and funds generated by the enterprise were used to buy equipment and feed. When Rider's father died, Rider claimed that all the cattle on the farm and most of the equipment were owned by him personally. Other heirs claimed that the cattle and equipment were partnership property. Discuss. (*In re Estate of Rider*, 409 A.2d 397, Pa. 1979.)

8. Frank owned two parcels of property—a store and a rental house. At the store, he ran a sole proprietorship known as Mountain Armory in a building he had constructed using borrowed funds secured by a mortgage on both properties. In 1975, Frank entered into a partnership with his son "to engage in the purchase, sale, and maintenance of firearms, ammunition, and other sporting goods." As a Christmas present in 1978, Frank raised his son's partnership interest to 49 percent. A dispute occurred in 1986, and Frank told his son that he never wanted to see him again. The son sued for dissolution of the partnership, claiming that the house was part of the partnership property. The son cited evidence that the rental house was listed as an asset on partnership tax returns, that rental income was listed on the returns as partnership income, and that his duties included maintenance of the store and the house. Frank cited evidence that both buildings were listed in his name, that the rental house was not used by the business, that his son's wife was paid separately by Frank for managing the rental house, that his son really did little work at the rental house, and that Frank's will listed the house as a personal asset to be devised but did not mention the store. Was the rental house partnership property? Discuss. (*Standring v. Standring*, 794 P.2d 1089, Colo.App. 1990.)

Chapter 34

Partnerships
Operating the Business

Partners' Rights

Partners' Duties

*Partnership Contractual Liability
to Third Parties*

Partnership Tort Liability to Third Parties

Satisfaction of Creditors' Claims

PARTNERS' RIGHTS

The UPA governs matters of partners' rights and duties; however, the rights and duties of the partners as to one another (but not, naturally, as to third parties) may be altered by agreement of the partners. A partnership that is properly planned and implemented with a written partnership agreement can be conformed to fit the partners' desires. We begin this chapter by examining the basic rights of partners.

Right to Choose Associates

Embodying the concept *delectus personae*—that a person should enjoy freedom of association—UPA Sec. 18(g) provides that "[n]o person can become a member of a partnership without the consent of all partners." Given the fiduciary nature of the partnership relationship and the open-ended liability of partners, it certainly makes sense that persons should not have partners foisted on them against their will. By agreement, of course, partners may waive this right to freedom of association by authorizing the addition of new partners by majority vote, for example.

In an important recent case, a court held that one exception to the *delectus personae* right existed where a major national accounting firm refused to admit a woman as a partner in circumstances indicating gender bias. The court held that the Civil Rights Act's policies against discrimination on the basis of race, gender, and religion outweighed the freedom of association (See Box 34.1).[1]

Management Rights

One of the basic rights of a partner is to participate in the management of the enterprise. Unless the partnership agreement provides otherwise, all partners have equal rights in the conduct and management of the partnership business. This is true regardless of the amount of their capital contributions or services to the business.

Many partnership agreements expressly provide that a particular partner will be the "managing partner," exercising control over the daily operations of the business. Such agreements can also be implied

from the conduct of the partners. For example: Ajax Co. is a partnership composed of partners A, B, C, D, and E. Over a substantial period of time, C, D, and E have left the management of the business to A and B, who possess recognized ability and experience as managers. If C, D, and E suddenly complain about a management decision made by A and B, the court probably will find that there was an implied agreement to give management powers completely to A and B and that they were therefore justified in acting without first consulting C, D, and E.

Unless it has been expressly or impliedly agreed otherwise, differences among the partners regarding management are usually settled by a *majority vote*. A few matters, however, such as admission of a new partner or amendment of the articles of partnership, require the consent of *all* the partners unless they have previously agreed that a less-than-unanimous vote will suffice.

Individual Rights in Partnership Property

Although a partner does not actually *own,* as an individual, any part of the partnership property (the partnership is the owner), he or she does have *rights* in specific partnership assets. However, the interests of the partnership as a business entity are of greater importance than the rights of any of the individual partners. Let us assume that a partnership owns a piece of equipment and that this ownership is undisputed. If one of the partners wishes to make use of the property or otherwise control it, he or she is subject to a number of limitations.

Limitations by Agreement

The first limitation is that of the *partnership agreement*. If the agreement among the partners stipulates the rights each is to have with respect to partnership property, then the individual who wants to use or control the property is bound by the agreement. For example, the agreement might provide that one of the other partners has the exclusive right to possess or deal with the property.

Equal Right to Possession

Where there has been no agreement regarding partnership property, certain limitations are imposed by

---

[1] *Hopkins v. Price Waterhouse,* 737 F.Supp. 1202 (D.D.C. 1990), *aff'd,* 920 F.2d 967 (D.C.Cir. 1990).

BUSINESSES FEAR CASE MAY BRING COURTS INTO PARTNERSHIP MATTERS

by Eric J. Wallach

**Box 34.1
The Law
at Work**

The celebrated *Hopkins v. Price Waterhouse* case produced another momentous decision recently when the U.S. District Court for the District of Columbia ruled that Price Waterhouse had discriminated against Anne Hopkins because of her sex in denying her partnership status and ordered the accounting firm to reinstate her, as a partner, effective July 1, 1990. The holding by Judge Gerhard Gesell sent shock waves through the professional and business communities. It is one of the first court-mandated reinstatement decisions that goes beyond mere continuation of employment or even enforced promotion of an employee.

Judge Gesell's ruling potentially opens the door for judicial intervention in the up-to-now highly subjective and largely unregulated field of partnership and senior executive decisions. What remains to be seen is whether this ruling augurs a new era of increased regulation of employment decisions, or whether it is an aberration—the product of the combination of an insensitive employer, a sympathetic plaintiff, and an activist judge.

Ms. Hopkins had been working as a senior manager at Price Waterhouse's Washington, D.C., office for approximately five years when she first came up for partnership consideration in 1982. She was the only female among 88 candidates for partnership that year. Exceptional in her job-related accomplishments, she was described by colleagues as "an outstanding professional" and as "extremely competent, intelligent." In addition, Ms. Hopkins had distinguished herself from other candidates for partnership by her remarkable success in producing new business for her firm.

Yet Anne Hopkins was not elected a partner at Price Waterhouse. Certain partners evaluating her claimed that she was difficult to get along with and especially short-tempered with the staff. These otherwise facially valid criticisms took on another tone, however, when the commenting partners also characterized Ms. Hopkins as too "macho" and needing a course in charm school. A key partner in Ms. Hopkins' office at Price Waterhouse advised her to "walk more femininely, talk more femininely, wear make-up, have her hair styled, and wear jewelry."

. . . [After finding Price Waterhouse liable for gender discrimination in vio-

lation of Title VII, Judge Gesell turned to consideration of a remedy.] He portrayed [Price Waterhouse] as an entity that, although nominally functioning as a partnership, was more accurately described as a "national concern [that] lacks the intimacy and interdependence of smaller partnerships." The court emphasized the size (approximately 900 partners in 90 offices) and structure (no ceiling placed on the number of partners) of the firm in depicting Price Waterhouse not as a tight-knit partnership whose delicate balance of cooperation and collegiality would be upset by the imposition of an unwanted partner, but instead as an immense, impersonal outpost of corporate America.

. . . Even by its own terms, the reinstatement decision in *Hopkins v. Price Waterhouse* does not change the traditional disinclination of courts to interfere with the financial or commercial affairs or the governance of businesses and professional firms. Instead, it appears to reflect the simple determination that, given the extreme circumstances of this particular case, a large concern such as Price Waterhouse could tolerate without undue difficulty or disharmony the addition of Ms. Hopkins to the partnership.

Source: *National Law Journal*, September 24, 1990, p. 18.

---

law on individual partners. Under the UPA, each partner has an *equal right to possess partnership property for partnership purposes*. Without the consent of all the other partners, an individual is not entitled to exclusive possession or control of partnership assets. Furthermore, the equal right of possession enjoyed by each partner is limited to purposes that further the partnership business, unless the other partners consent to a use for some different purpose.

Nontransferability

A partner's right to possess and control partnership property for partnership purposes *cannot be transferred by that person to a third party outside the partnership*. The reason is simple. In this situation the third party would be exercising a right that for all practical purposes would make him or her a new partner, and a new partner can be brought into the partnership only by the agreement of all the partners. For similar reasons, this right cannot be reached by a partner's personal creditors. Additionally, it does not pass to the executor or administrator of a partner's estate when he or she dies; instead it passes to the surviving partner or partners. A partner's rights with respect to specific partnership property should not be confused with his or her interest in the partnership. The **interest in the partnership** is each partner's share of the profits and surplus, and it is subject to different rules than the right to use partnership property. (This concept is more fully developed later in the chapter.)

The next case discusses and illustrates the principle that a partner does not actually own specific items of partnership property. It also foreshadows our later discussion of the satisfaction of claims made by creditors of the partnership as well as of individual partners.

In re GROFF

U.S. Tenth Circuit Court of Appeals, 898 F.2d 1475 (1990)

To secure a debt of Lee and Gwen Groff, Citizens Bank took a security interest in specified cattle the Groffs owned and all cattle "after acquired." Unbeknownst to the bank, Lee Groff was about to enter a cattle-feeding joint venture with Ed Pickering. On several subsequent occasions, Groff and Pickering bought cattle from Agri-Tech Services with Morgan County Feeders, Inc. providing purchase money financing.

When Lee and Gwen filed a bankruptcy petition, a question arose regarding creditors' rights to the Groff-Pickering cattle. Citizens Bank argued that the cattle came within the after-acquired property clause of their security agreement with the Groffs. The bankruptcy court ruled that the Groff's estate did not contain the Groff-Pickering cattle, but did contain Lee's interest in the Groff-Pickering venture. The district court affirmed and Citizens Bank appealed.

Logan, Circuit Judge:

[The court first held that like a general partnership, a joint venture is governed by the UPA.]

The UPA provides that the partnership owns property as an entity, separate and distinct from the partners. Sec. 8. The right of the partners in specific partnership property is as co-owners, holding as tenants in partnership. Sec. 25(1). But "[a] partner's right in specific partnership property is not assignable except in connection with the assignment of rights of all the partners in the same property," Sec. 25(2)(b), and "[a] partner's right in specific partnership property is not subject to attachment or execution, except on a claim against the partnership." Sec. 25(2)(c). Individual partners can only assign their residual interests in the entire partnership. This is also the only partnership interest that the partners' individual creditors can reach; only partnership creditors can attach partnership property. Secs. 26-28. On dissolution of the partnership, partner-ship creditors have priority in the distribution of partnership property. If an individual partner becomes insolvent, that partner's individual creditors have priority over partnership creditors with regard to his separate property. Secs. 38(1), 40(h)-(i). So the UPA treats the partnership and its assets and liabilities as a separate entity, distinct from the assets and liabilities of its owners. This scheme is necessary to prevent disruption of, and facilitate credit for, the partnership business. It is equally necessary in the context of joint ventures.

In this case, because the Groffs purported to act solely on their own behalf in granting a lien on their cattle to Citizens Bank, they could transfer no interest in the Groff-Pickering cattle. The Groff-Pickering cattle could not enter the Groffs' bankruptcy estate; only the Groffs' residual interest in the Groff-Pickering joint venture [the right to share in profits and in surplus assets, if any, upon dissolution] became property of the estate.

Affirmed. ⚖

Profits, Losses, and Other Compensation

As previously mentioned, a partner's *interest in the partnership* is his or her share in the profits of the business as well as a share of what the excess would be at a given time if all the partnership's debts were paid and all the accounts were tallied up and settled. The proportion of partnership profits to be received by each partner is ordinarily determined by an express provision in the articles of partnership. This proportion can be determined on the basis of each partner's contribution of capital, property, or services or by any other method the partners wish to use. If the agreement makes no provision for distributing profits, they will be divided *equally.* The rule requiring equal division in the absence of contrary agreement applies without regard to the amount of capital, property, or service contributed by each partner.

The agreement may also provide for the sharing of losses, although it is often silent on the matter, since few people enter a business expecting to lose money. If the agreement says nothing about losses, they are shared *in the same proportion as profits.* Thus, if nothing is agreed as to either profits or losses, both are shared equally.

The articles of partnership may provide for salaries or other compensation to be paid an individual partner or partners for services rendered in behalf of the partnership. If, however, the agreement does not so provide, a partner is *not entitled to any compensation for such services.* The law presumes in such cases that the parties' intent was that a share of the profits be each partner's only compensation. There are two minor exceptions to this rule.[2] First, if a partnership's dissolution is caused by the death of a partner, a surviving partner who winds up the affairs of the partnership is entitled to reasonable compensation for these services. Second, if a partner performs "extraordinary" services beyond the typical scope of the partnership, perhaps by moving the partnership into successful new lines of business while a co-partner is taking a leave of absence, reasonable compensation is due.[3]

Unless otherwise agreed, a partner is *not entitled to interest on his or her contribution of capital* to the partnership (the partner's investment). But if the partners originally agreed upon a date for repayment to individual partners of their capital contributions, a partner has a right to receive interest on his or her contribution from that date if it remains unpaid. As we saw in the previous chapter, a partner's payment of money to the partnership is presumed to be a capital contribution rather than a *loan.* However, if a payment is clearly a loan, then the partner is entitled to receive interest computed from the date of the loan.

If an individual partner, acting reasonably in the ordinary and proper conduct of partnership business,

makes a payment or incurs personal liability to a third party, the partner is entitled to be *reimbursed* or *indemnified* by the partnership. For example, suppose that the partnership has contracted to sell goods to a buyer. The buyer breaches the contract and refuses to accept the goods. While attempting to find another buyer, it is necessary for the partner handling the transaction to store the goods or to ship them elsewhere. If that partner personally pays such expenses, he or she is entitled to be reimbursed by the partnership.

Right to an Account

Under certain circumstances a partner can institute a legal proceeding called an **account** (or an **accounting**). In such a suit, all records of the partnership must formally be produced and all balances computed under court supervision. Since each partner ordinarily has free access to the books, this kind of lawsuit usually is filed only when the partnership has been dissolved.

There are circumstances, however, in which a partner may demand a formal account from his or her copartners without seeking the dissolution of the partnership. Then, if the copartners refuse or if the partner making the demand is dissatisfied with the accounting, he or she may institute legal action. Under Sec. 22 of the UPA, a partner has the right to a formal account as to partnership affairs under any of the following circumstances:

1. He or she has been *wrongfully excluded* by the other partners from the partnership business or from possession of partnership property.

2. The right to a formal account has been provided for in an *agreement* between the partners.

3. One of the other partners has, without consent, derived a *personal benefit* from a transaction related to partnership business.

4. Other circumstances render it "just and reasonable" (for example, if he or she has been traveling for a long period of time on partnership business and the other partners are in possession of the company's records).

Right to Inspect

In order to allow partners to protect their own interests, the UPA accords them a broad, but not unlimited, power to inspect partnership records. Naturally,

---

[2] The general rule is illustrated in *Birnbaum v. Birnbaum,* a major case discussed later in this chapter.

[3] *Altman v. Altman,* 653 F.2d 755 (3d Cir. 1981).

no partner is allowed to inspect for a fraudulent purpose or to gain unfair advantage over other partners. In almost all other circumstances, however, the partner's right to inspect will be protected, even after dissolution of the partnership during the winding up period.

PARTNERS' DUTIES
Duty of Obedience

Naturally, partners' rights entail corresponding obligations. For example, partners are obliged to abide by the partnership agreement and to comply with properly made partnership decisions. If the partners vote on a matter of ordinary business, they must abide by the majority's decision. For example, assume that A, B, and C are equal partners. If A and B vote to strip C of the authority to hire and fire employees, C should abide by that vote. C will be liable for any damages caused the partnership by failure to comply.

Duty to Render Services

There is no UPA provision requiring each partner to work 40 hours per week for the partnership business. Nonetheless, there is a general expectation that partners will provide services to the firm in order to assist it in the enterprise it undertakes. The guideline is the expectations of the parties. It may be the partners' expectation that A will be the "money" partner, providing the capital for the business without any notion of participating actively in its operation, and that B, because of her expertise in the area, will be the partner responsible for overseeing day-to-day operations. In such a case, B's failure actively to render services would likely be a breach of the duty to render services; A's similar failure would not.

A partner who fails to live up to reasonable expectations regarding the rendering of services may have his or her partnership interest charged with either (1) the cost of hiring a replacement or (2) financial losses caused the partnership by the breach.

Duty of Care

In providing services, partners owe a basic duty of care to the partnership. If partners injure the partnership by their careless performance of partnership duties, some jurisdictions allow the other partners to recover damages. These courts generally set "gross negligence" as the standard of liability, evidencing

a reluctance to encourage such suits. Other jurisdictions simply refuse to allow such suits. One recent statement of the unsettled law in this area is that:

Generally, a [partner] is not liable to his [copartners] for damages caused by his mistakes of judgment. He may be liable for negligence, however, if it causes injury to the *person or property* of the other [partners] or if the [partnership agreement] calls for him to exercise a particular or extraordinary degree of diligence and skill.[4]

Fiduciary Duty

The most important duty of any partner is the fiduciary duty of highest trust and confidence owed to the partnership and the other partners. The scope of the duty was outlined by the Supreme Court many years ago:

[It is] well settled that one partner cannot, directly or indirectly, use partnership assets for his own benefit; that he cannot, in conducting the business of a partnership, take any profit clandestinely for himself; that he cannot carry on the business of the partnership for his private advantage; that he cannot carry on another business in competition or rivalry with that of the firm, thereby depriving it of the benefit of his time, skill, and fidelity without being accountable to his copartners for any profit that may accrue to him therefrom; that he cannot be permitted to secure for himself that which it is his duty to obtain, if at all, for the firm of which he is a member; nor can he avail himself of knowledge or information which may be properly regarded as the property of the partnership, in the sense that it is available or useful to the firm for any purpose within the scope of the partnership business.[5]

Justice Cardozo issued the most famous description of the tenor of the fiduciary duty:

[Partners] owe to one another, while the enterprise continues, the duty of the finest loyalty. Many forms of conduct permissible in a workaday world for those acting at arm's length, are forbidden to those bound by fiduciary ties. A [partner] is held to something stricter than the morals of the marketplace. Not honesty alone, but the punctilio of an honor the most sensitive, is then the standard of behavior. As to this there has developed a tradition that is unbending and inveterate.[6]

[4] *Duffy v. Piazza Const., Inc.,* 815 p.2d 267 (Wash.App. 1991), *citing Ferguson v. Williams,* 670 S.W.2d 327 (Tex.App. 1984) ("negligence in the management of the affairs of a general partnership or joint venture does not create any right of action against that partner by other members of the partnership").
[5] *Latta v.Kilbourn,* 150 U.S. 524 (1893).
[6] *Meinhard v. Salmon,* 164 N.E. 545 (N.Y. 1928).

The most common breaches of fiduciary duty occur when partners place themselves in a conflict of interest with the partnership or seize a partnership business opportunity for themselves. A partner may engage in his or her own enterprises outside the partnership so long as the articles of partnership do not prohibit such activity and so long as the outside involvement does not cause the partner to neglect partnership affairs. But a partner cannot *compete* with the partnership. For example, a partner in a grocery store business obviously cannot legally run a competing store in the neighborhood.

The following case is a typical conflict of interest scenario.

BIRNBAUM V. BIRNBAUM

New York Court of Appeals, 539 N.E.2d 574 (1989)

Saul Birnbaum was a 50 percent owner of a partnership that owned and operated a shopping center. His niece and nephew, Jay and Ilene, each owned 25 percent. The partnership agreement named Saul and Jay as managing partners, but because of a conflict with Saul, Jay never took an active role in management. Jay and Ilene brought this suit after they discovered that Saul had hired Victoria Tree, who later became his wife, to help develop the property and charged her compensation amounting to hundreds of thousands of dollars to the partnership, without the consent of Jay and Ilene.

The trial court held that Victoria's compensation could not be charged to the partnership and that Saul was not entitled to compensation for his services in developing the property. The Appellate Division reversed the ruling as to Victoria's compensation and then certified an appeal to the New York Court of Appeals.

Wachtler, Chief Judge:

Partners, and particularly managing partners, owe a fiduciary duty to the other partners. Consequently, [Saul] owed a fiduciary duty to Jay and Ilene to protect their interests in the Cherry Hill shopping center.

Saul's financial transactions with Victoria violated his fiduciary duty to Jay and Ilene in two fundamental aspects. First, as a general proposition, absent an agreement to the contrary, partners, joint venturers, and tenants in common look solely to the appreciation of their interest in the endeavor for their financial rewards, and are not entitled to separate compensation for services rendered. Saul does not dispute the lower court's determination that no agreement exists entitling him to compensation for the services he rendered, and thus, personally, he cannot be compensated for the services he provided. Moreover, the trial court's finding, left undisturbed by the Appellate Division, was that the services that are attributed to Victoria are precisely those that Saul was obligated and expected to perform free of individual compensation. Under the facts of this case, Saul acted inconsistently with his obligation to protect the interests of Jay and Ilene, when he charged the property for services that he personally was obligated to perform without direct compensation.

Second, it is elemental that a fiduciary owes a duty of undivided and undiluted loyalty to those whose interests the fiduciary is to protect. This is a sensitive and "inflexible" rule of fidelity, barring not only blatant self-dealing, but also requiring avoidance of situations in which a fiduciary's personal interest possibly conflicts with the interest of those owed a fiduciary duty. Included within this rule's broad scope is every situation in which a fiduciary, who is bound to single-mindedly pursue the interests of those to whom a duty of loyalty is owed, deals with a person "in such close relation [to the fiduciary] that possible advantage to such other person might consciously or unconsciously" influence the fiduciary's judgment. *Albright v. Jefferson County Nat'l Bank,* 53 N.E.2d 753 (N.Y.). In this case, Saul's financial relationship with his wife conflicted with his duty to Jay and Ilene and therefore violated the precept of undiluted trust at the core of his responsibilities as a fiduciary.

Consequently, Saul's departure from his basic obligation to Jay and Ilene cannot be countenanced by this court in the absence of both full disclosure and the assent of Jay and Ilene. The trial court determined that there was neither disclosure nor assent. Thus, we conclude that the trial court properly held that Victoria's compensation could not be charged to the property.

This is not to say, nor would we suggest that a person occupying a position of trust is barred from hiring employees. We only reaffirm here the most basic principle that a court will not countenance the behavior of a fiduciary who, without full disclosure and consent, enters into a financial arrangement placing his spouse's interests at odds with the interests of those to whom he owes a duty of undivided loyalty.

[The trial court's order is reinstated.]

Nor may a partner acquire a *business opportunity* that fairly belongs to the partnership in that it is within the scope of the partnership's current business or a natural expansion thereof. Assume that A and B are in the business of locating and investing in promising oil and gas properties. If A discovers an interesting and potentially profitable property near where the partnership has invested before, A may pursue it as her own personal opportunity only after (1) she has fully disclosed the opportunity to the partnership and (2) either (a) the partnership decides not to pursue the opportunity or (b) the partnership is for some largely irremediable reason unable to pursue the opportunity.

Duty of Accounting

Each partner's right to an accounting (discussed earlier) entails a concomitant duty on the part of each partner to account to the partnership by keeping records of all transactions with the partnership or on its behalf and giving those records to the designated partnership recordkeeper.

The duty to keep records lies with the managing partner or any other partner who agrees to undertake the task. That partner must keep complete and accurate accounts and can be held liable for the failure to do so.

PARTNERSHIP CONTRACTUAL LIABILITY TO THIRD PARTIES

General Application of Agency Rules

In partnership transactions with third parties, the law of agency governs the liabilities of the partnership, the partners, and the third party. UPA Sec. 9(1) provides that each "partner is an agent of the partnership for purposes of its business." Technically, the partnership is the principal and each partner an agent with respect to partnership affairs. Most courts state that each partner is also an agent for the other partners (who are principals), as well as for the partnership entity. Of course, this is often the practical result anyway, since the other partners can be held personally liable if partnership assets are insufficient to satisfy the partnership liability.

Consistent with agency principles, the partnership is liable to third parties for contracts negotiated by a partner who acts within (1) actual (express or implied) authority or (2) apparent authority. Partnership liability can also exist if the partnership, acting through the other partners, ratifies an unauthorized transaction of a partner.

Express Authority

The first type of actual authority, that which is expressly stated, can arise from written partnership agreements, formal votes at partnership meetings, or even an informal meeting of the partners over a meal. If in this manner the partners explicitly agree that partner Jones will have the authority to buy all cars and trucks needed in the partnership business, Jones's act of buying those cars and trucks will bind the partnership.

Implied Authority

Implied authority, which is also a type of actual authority, is inferred by the courts from the statements or actions of the partners. Perhaps the partners mentioned in the prior paragraph never expressly agreed that Jones should buy cars and trucks for the partnership. However, if they place Jones in a position where such purchases are necessary or incidental to carrying out his assigned tasks in the usual way, courts will infer that Jones has the authority to act. Also, as noted in the chapters on agency law, partners will have implied authority to act in good faith in emergency situations where they do not have the opportunity to consult with copartners.

Apparent Authority

Perhaps the partnership operates a restaurant and names Jones the managing partner. Managers of restaurants typically have the authority to hire and fire waiters and waitresses, but the partners are concerned that Jones lacks experience in this area and expressly agree that he should not hire and fire without the approval of all other partners. By their express act, the partners have eliminated any actual authority of Jones to hire and fire. No implied authority may arise in the face of this express agreement. However, a third party who did not know of the limitation on Jones's authority would reasonably assume that he could hire and fire as most restaurant managers may. Thus, if Jones hired Smith as a waiter, the partnership would be bound on the contract *unless* Smith had notice of the limitation.

Scope of Authority

In attempting to fix partnership contractual liability, a key is often to determine the scope of a particular partner's authority. All express statements are extremely helpful, of course. Where actual authority has not been expressed, or if expressed, is unknown to third parties, the courts inquire: What matters are within the *scope of authority* of a partner carrying out business in the *usual way?*

Generally speaking, courts assume that partners have the authority to borrow money needed to stock the shelves of a retail store, to buy property and equipment needed by the enterprise, to make deliveries of products sold and receive payment therefor, to endorse partnership checks and notes, to hire and fire employees, and to sue to enforce partnership claims. The underlying assumption is that a partner has the inherent power of a "general management agent" of the partnership.

In determining the scope of a partner's authority in difficult cases, courts tend to generalize by looking to (1) past practices of this particular partnership and (2) normal practices of similar partnerships in the area. For example, in *Smith v. Dixon,*[7] a contract to sell a tract of farmland to the plaintiff for $200,000 was negotiated by W. R. Smith, the "predominant" partner. The remaining partners later claimed that Smith's actual authority was to sell the land for no less than $225,000. The court enforced the contract after finding that in several earlier situations Smith had bought and sold land on the partnership's behalf. In selling to the plaintiff, Smith was merely acting within the apparent scope of his authority as judged by past practices of the partnership.

One example of a case illustrating customary practices of similar partnerships in the locality as a source

[7]386 S.W.2d 244 (Ark. 1965).

of authority is *Womack v. First National Bank of Augustine.*[8] Lane and Charles McClanahan were partners in a pig farming operation. Lane, a doctor, simply invested money. Charles operated the farm. Early on, both partners signed promissory notes borrowing money from the plaintiff bank on a revolving basis. As with many farms and retail operations, the partners would borrow money, buy pigs, raise and sell the pigs, use the proceeds to pay off their loans, and then borrow more money to start the process again. After a time, only Charles signed the notes. When Lane died, his estate claimed that it was not liable on the later notes. The court, however, held that the notes bound the partnership not only because the borrowing was consistent with its past practices, but also because the borrowing was consistent with the manner in which other such farms conducted business in the area:

> Where the partnership business contemplated periodical or continuous or frequent purchasing, not as incidental to an occupation, but for the purpose of selling again the thing purchased, it is usual and customary to purchase on credit and to execute paper evidencing the existence of the partnership debt.[9]

The following case addresses a question that often arises: When is the act of selling land within the scope of authority for carrying out the partnership business in the usual way?

[8]613 S.W.2d 548 (Tex.Civ.App. 1981).
[9]By noting the difference between an occupational partnership (such as a firm of accountants or lawyers) and a partnership that makes its money selling goods (such as a retail store or farm), the court was ruling consistently with a distinction courts have traditionally made between **nontrading partnerships** (where the power to borrow will be narrowly interpreted) and **trading partnerships** (where the power to borrow will be interpreted broadly).

OWENS V. PALOS VERDES MONACO

Court of Appeal of California, 191 Cal. Rptr. 381 (1983)

Seymour Owens, Albert Fink, and Manny Borinstein were in the business of acquiring, holding, and developing real estate on the Palos Verdes peninsula in California. They bought 250 acres, divided it into four tracts, and formed four separate partnerships to own and develop the tracts. Borinstein died, and the surviving partners agreed that Borinstein's widow, Pearl, would become a partner, but would hold the interests in the four partnerships in trust for her daughter Joan. Several years later, Kajima International, Inc., became interested in buying one of these tracts of land. The tract in question, 57 acres, was held by a partnership called Monaco Land Holders (MLH).

A representative of Kajima contacted a real estate brokerage

(continues)

OWENS V. PALOS VERDES MONACO

(continued from previous page) firm in the Palos Verdes area. The brokerage firm contacted Owens, one of the three partners in MLH and the other partnerships. Owens told the broker to show the 57-acre tract to the Kajima representative, to "pursue the sale," and "keep him [Owens] informed." After Kajima's representative had seen the land and conferred with his superiors, Kajima made a written offer to buy. This offer was delivered by the broker to both Owens and Fink. They rejected the offer and Owens told the broker that "Al Fink will be handling this from now on; just keep me apprised of what's going on." A second offer was made and was again delivered to both Owens and Fink. Fink met with Owens and they decided to reject this offer, as well. At this time, and later, Pearl Borinstein was kept informed about the negotiations and indicated that she would go along with any proposal that met with Owens' approval.

Over the next several months, the broker tried to put together a deal that would be agreeable to both sides. Three different meetings were held to negotiate the sale. Present at all three meetings were the broker and several representatives of Kajima, including a vice-president and another high-ranking officer. At the first two meetings, MLH was represented by Fink and Joan Borinstein (Pearl's daughter). Owens was informed about each of the meetings in advance, but each time he indicated that if Fink was going to be present, there was no need for him (Owens) to be there. At the third meeting, when the sale was finally concluded and the

written contract was signed, only Fink was present in behalf of MLH, although Owens, Pearl, and Joan had all been notified of the meeting. Thus, Fink was the only partner signing the contract for the partnership. At this meeting, a question was raised about the fact that only one partner was signing, and Fink assured the buyers that he had authority to act for the partnership.

About two weeks after this third meeting, Owens indicated that he was unhappy with the terms of the sale contract and did not want the sale to go forward. The buyer insisted on completing the sale, and Owens filed suit against both the partnership and Kajima. In the suit, Owens sought a declaratory judgment that the contract was invalid and an injunction prohibiting the partnership from transferring title to the 57-acre tract to Kajima. Kajima filed a counterclaim against the partnership, Owens, and the other partners, seeking a decree of specific performance that would require the contract to be carried out by transferring title to Kajima. (Because initially there was some confusion as to whether the 57-acre tract was owned by MLH or by one of the other partnerships, Palos Verdes Monaco, both partnerships were named as parties to the lawsuit. Consequently, the name of Palos Verdes Monaco appears in the title of the case. After the suit was filed, it was determined that MLH owned this particular tract.) The trial court ruled that the contract was valid because Fink had authority to sign in behalf of the partnership, denied Owens' request for an injunction, and granted Kajima's request for

specific performance of the contract. Owens, the partnership, and the other partners appealed.

Feinerman, Presiding Justice:

The seminal issue in this appeal is whether Fink's signature alone was sufficient to bind MLH to the terms of the April 1 agreement. The resolution of that question depends upon the conclusion we reach regarding Fink's authority to act for the partnership. . . .

In our view of the matter, the provisions of [the Uniform Partnership Act, §9] are dispositive of the issue of Fink's authority to bind the partnership. . . .

Section 9 provides in pertinent part as follows:

(1) Every partner is an agent of the partnership for the purpose of its business, and the act of every partner, including the execution in the partnership name of any instrument, for apparently carrying on in the usual way the business of the partnership of which he is a member binds the partnership, *unless the partner so acting has in fact no authority to act for the partnership in the particular matter, and the person with whom he is dealing has knowledge of the fact that he has no such authority.* [Emphasis added by the court.]

(2) *An act of a partner which is not apparently for carrying on the business of the partnership in the usual way does not bind the partnership unless authorized by the other partners. . . .*

The Supreme Court in analyzing section 9 in *Ellis v. Mihelis* (1963) 384 P.2d 7, stated: "These provisions distinguish between acts of a partner which bind the partnership because of his status as a partner without any express authority being required and acts binding on the partnership only after express authorization by all partners. Under the express terms of subdivision (1) of the section all acts of a partner which are apparently within the usual course of the particular business bind the partnership. The effect of the provision is that the status of a partner, *(continues)*

Owens v. Palos Verdes Monaco

(continued from previous page)
without more, serves as a complete authority with respect to such acts, obviating the necessity of any express authority, either oral or written, from the other members of the firm. It necessarily follows that insofar as a partner limits his conduct to matters apparently within the partnership business, he can bind the other partners without obtaining their written consent. Subdivision (2), however, provides that there must be express authority for acts of a partner which do not appear to be in the usual course of the business. . . ."

In the case before us, Fink's signature alone was sufficient to bind the partnership if the sale of the subject property was an act "for apparently carrying on in the usual way the business of the partnership." The apparent scope of the partnership business depends primarily on the conduct of the partnership and its partners and what they cause third persons to believe about the authority of the partners. . . .

The trial court found that "[t]he sale of the land to Kajima was apparently in the ordinary course of the selling partnership's business. . . . Fink was the only partner who ever attended meetings with representatives of Ka-

jima regarding this transaction up to and including April 1, 1977. Fink conducted the negotiations on behalf of the sellers. In the context of the negotiations for the sale of the land, Fink's role as sale negotiator for the sellers, and Owens' statements [to the broker] that Fink would handle the deal on behalf of the sellers, statements which were reported to Kajima, [reasonably led] Kajima to believe that Fink had authority to sell the land."

The conduct of the partnership and its partners in this case was sufficient to sustain the findings that the partnership was in the business of selling property and that Fink, a partner, was authorized to act for the partnership.

[The partners also] argue that sale of the subject property cannot be considered to be within the apparent scope of the partnership business because sale of said property would make it impossible to carry on the partnership business. Section 9, subdivision (3) specifies certain acts which are not within the scope of the usual course of business. It provides: "Unless authorized by the other partners or unless they have abandoned the business, one or more but less than all the partners have no authority to:. . . (c) Do any

other act which would make it impossible to carry on the ordinary business of a partnership." . . .

A number of reported decisions, including *Petrikis v. Hanges* (1952) 245 P.2d 39, hold that the sale of a partnership's only asset is beyond the scope of usual partnership business and thus cannot be effected by a single partner. In *Petrikis*, the seller of real property, Mr. Petrikis, sold the partnership's only asset, a cocktail lounge, without written authority from his partners. The Court of Appeal held that Petrikis had not bound the partnership because he had acted beyond the scope of usual business in selling the partnership's only asset. *Petrikis* is distinguishable from the present case in that. . . . Petrikis' partnership was in the business of running a bar, not the business of holding a bar in anticipation of its eventual sale. In the present case, MLH had a singular purpose. It existed solely to hold and sell a piece of real property. The business of MLH was selling its land. Thus, the sale was in the ordinary course of MLH's business. . . .

[The judgment of the trial court that the contract was valid and ordering its enforcement is affirmed.]⚖

Matters Typically Outside the Scope of Partnership Authority

Acts Requiring Unanimity

As noted in *Owens*, UPA Sec. 9(3) provides that certain acts by a single partner are completely unauthorized. In other words, a partner cannot bind the partnership by these acts regardless of the nature of the business or what is customary. Furthermore, even a *majority* of the partners do not have the power to bind the partnership by these acts; there must be *unanimous* agreement.

The acts requiring unanimous action are (1) assigning partnership property for the benefit of creditors; (2) disposing of the goodwill of the business, as

for example, by selling the right to use its trade name; (3) confessing a judgment;[10] (4) submitting a partnership claim or liability to arbitration;[11] and, most importantly, (5) doing "any other act which would make it impossible to carry on the ordinary business of a partnership."

Furthermore, there are several types of actions for which implied authority usually does not exist. The

[10] A *confession of judgment* is an agreement of a debtor allowing the creditor to obtain a court judgment for a specified sum against the debtor without the necessity of legal proceedings.

[11] The UPA was written in 1914 when there was a general hostility to arbitration that, fortunately, no longer exists. The RUPA, if adopted, would eliminate the unanimity requirement of Sec. 9(3), leaving things to be decided according to general rules of agency.

UPA does not require unanimity for such actions, but a single partner acting alone typically would not have authority to do these acts, *unless* the partners had expressly or impliedly agreed to grant such authority. Among these actions are (1) assuming or guaranteeing in the name of the partnership a third party's debt; (2) converting partnership assets to the personal benefit of a partner; or (3) engaging in a gratuitous undertaking, such as giving property away. Third parties dealing with a partner who is attempting to do these acts should realize that no binding authority exists.

Ratification

Remember, even if a partner's act is outside the scope of both actual and apparent authority, the partnership may still be bound by it if the partnership knowingly and voluntarily *ratifies* the act. The ratification may be *express,* perhaps pursuant to a formal partnership vote. The ratification may also be *implied from the circumstances,* such as the partnership's voluntarily accepting the benefits of the contract or suing to enforce the contract. Either evidences a partnership determination to be bound by the agreement.

PARTNERSHIP TORT LIABILITY TO THIRD PARTIES

Partnership vicarious tort liability for the actions of its agents (and other employees, for that matter) is also governed by general rules of agency. Sec. 13 of the UPA provides that where "by any wrongful act or omission of any partner acting within the ordinary course of the business of the partnership or with the authority of his co-partners, loss or injury is caused to any person," the partnership is liable to the same extent as the wrongdoing partner.

As with contractual liability, the key question often boils down to whether the partner was acting "within the scope of authority" or in the "ordinary course of business" of the partnership. Cases of negligence may be difficult, but they are typically less troublesome than cases involving intentional torts. When a doctor in a medical partnership commits malpractice in operating on a patient, the partnership will be liable for that negligence. When a partner carelessly causes an auto accident while delivering partnership goods to a customer, the partnership will almost certainly be vicariously liable also.

Intentional torts are more difficult, because it is less likely that commission of such a tort is within the partner's scope of authority. For example, if a partner in a retail business simply loses his temper with a customer and commits assault and battery, the partnership will probably not be held liable to the customer. Courts often hold that acts of arson, false imprisonment, and defamation do not aid the partnership and therefore are not within the scope of authority.

However, if the partner's act is intended to advance the partnership's interests, even in a wrongful manner, the partnership will likely be held liable. For example, if a partner strikes a customer while attempting to collect a debt owed to the partnership or lies to a prospective customer in a fraudulent attempt to sell the partnership's goods, the partnership will probably be held liable.

The following case addresses the partnership's vicarious liability for partners' intentional torts and also discusses a partnership's direct tort liability for its own failings.

KELSEY-SEYBOLD CLINIC V. MACLAY

Supreme Court of Texas, 466 S.W.2d 716 (1971)

Plaintiff John Maclay filed suit against Dr. Brewer and the Kelsey-Seybold Clinic, a medical partnership, for the tort of alienation of affection. Plaintiff alleged that Dr. Brewer, while treating plaintiff's wife, showered her with attention and gifts in order to alienate her affections for plaintiff; that various acts of undue familiarity occurred between Mrs. Maclay and Dr. Brewer on and off partnership property; that these acts occurred in the course and scope of Brewer's employment as a partner at the Clinic; that the Clinic, through Dr. Kelsey, a senior partner, knew of Brewer's actions; and that the partnership approved of, ratified, and consented to Brewer's conduct.

The Clinic moved for summary judgment on grounds that it could not legally be held responsible for

(continues)

KELSEY-SEYBOLD CLINIC V. MACLAY

(continued from previous page)
Dr. Brewer's actions. The trial court agreed. The intermediate appellate court reversed and remanded the case for trial. The Clinic appealed.

Walker, Justice:

The bases of liability alleged in the petition are (1) that Dr. Brewer's wrongful conduct was in the course and scope of the partnership business and was approved, consented to, ratified, and condoned by the Clinic, and (2) that the Clinic, after notice of the alleged relationship between Dr. Brewer and Mrs. Maclay, failed to take any action. Plaintiff is thus relying upon the vicarious or partnership liability of the Clinic for the acts of one of the partners and also its liability for breach of a duty owing by the Clinic when it learned of Dr. Brewer's relationship with Mrs. Maclay.

On the question of vicarious liability, plaintiff argues that the affidavit of the members of the Clinic's executive committee will not support a summary judgment since it comes from interested parties and contains mere conclusions. No attempt will be made to consider this contention, because the judgment of the Court of Civil Appeals must be affirmed for other reasons that will be discussed below. We are unwilling to believe that plaintiff seriously expects to prove in a conventional trial that the acts alleged to have been committed by Dr. Brewer were in the course and scope of the partnership business or were either authorized or ratified by the Clinic. Rather than concern ourselves about possible deficiencies in the affidavit filed by the Clinic, we assume for the purpose of this opinion that Dr. Brewer was not acting in the ordinary course of the Clinic's business and that his conduct was neither authorized nor ratified by the partnership. This will enable us to reach questions that may well arise at the trial of the case.

The Court of Civil Appeals reasoned that the summary judgment was improper because the Clinic had not conclusively negated consent on its part to the alleged wrongful conduct of Dr. Brewer. . . . Where a partner proposes to do, in the name or for the benefit of the partnership, some act that is not in the ordinary course of the business, consent by the other partners may constitute his authority to do the act for the partnership. We also recognize that even a willful or malicious act outside the ordinary scope of the partnership business may be so related to the business that tacit consent of the other partners could fairly be regarded as a grant of authority. In this instance, however, Dr. Brewer was acting solely for his personal gratification. His conduct could not benefit the Clinic in any way, and no one would have supposed that he was acting for the partnership. It is our opinion that in these circumstance the "consent" that might be inferred from the silence or inaction of the Clinic after learning of his conduct does not render the Clinic vicariously liable for the damage claimed by the plaintiff.

On the basis of the present record and the facts we are assuming in this case, the liability of the Clinic must rest, if at all, upon some theory akin to [negligent supervision]. The Clinic was under a duty, of course, to exercise ordinary care to protect its patients from harm resulting from tortious conduct of persons upon the premises. A negligent breach of that duty could subject the Clinic to liability without regard to whether the tortious conduct immediately causing the harm was that of an agent or servant or was in the ordinary scope of the partnership business. For example, it might become liable, as a result of its own negligence, for damage done by a vicious employee while acting beyond the scope of his authority.

We are also of the opinion that the Clinic owed a duty to the families of its patients to exercise ordinary care to prevent a tortious interference with family relations. It was not required to maintain constant surveillance over personnel on duty or to inquire into and regulate the personal conduct of partners and employees while engaged in their private affairs. But if and when the partnership received information from which it knew or should have known that there might be a need to take action, it was under a duty to use reasonable means at its disposal to prevent any partner or employee from improperly using his position with the Clinic to work a tortious invasion of legally protected family interests. This duty relates only to conduct of a partner or employee on the premises of the Clinic or while purportedly acting as a representative of the Clinic elsewhere. Failure to exercise ordinary care in discharging that duty would subject the Clinic to liability for damages proximately caused by its negligence.

The rather meager information in the present record . . . does not affirmatively and clearly [show] that the Clinic could or should have done nothing.

The judgment of the Court of Civil Appeals is affirmed.

Criminal Liability

Many intentional torts also constitute crimes (as do many nontortious acts). Courts are reluctant to impose criminal liability on a partnership or on the other partners for the act of one of them. Such liability is, of course, placed on any partner who participated in, directed, or expressly authorized the act of the other. However, the partnership as an entity (and other partners who did *not* participate in, direct, or expressly authorize the wrongful act) will be criminally liable for the crime of the partner only if (1) it was committed in the ordinary course of the partnership business *and* (2) proof of criminal intent is *not* required for conviction. Examples include illegal liquor sales, mislabelling of goods, and unsafe transporting of explosives.

SATISFACTION OF CREDITORS' CLAIMS
Partnership Creditors

One of the cardinal characteristics of the partnership form of business is that the individual partners are *personally liable* for the obligations of the partnership. Under Sec. 15 of the UPA, all partners are *jointly* liable for partnership contractual obligations, but *jointly and severally* liable for partnership tort liabilities.

At common law, a plaintiff suing jointly liable defendants had to sue *all* the joint obligors. A release of any one defendant through settlement had the effect of releasing all other defendants. On the other hand, in situations of joint and several liability, the plaintiff could choose individual defendants. For example, a plaintiff could sue one of four partners, rather than all. And, if a settlement or judgment against one did not satisfy the entire obligation, the plaintiff could proceed to sue one or more of the other partners.

Several states have altered these rules by statute, and some states have amended their UPAs to provide for joint and several liability in *both* contract and tort cases.[12] However, it is important to remember that if liability is joint, almost all courts require a plaintiff to pursue the partnership as an entity first and *exhaust* its assets before pursuing the individual assets of any partner. However, where the liability is joint and sev-

eral, most courts hold that partnership assets need *not* be exhausted before plaintiff pursues the individual assets of the partners.[13]

Individual Creditors

Assume that C of the ABC partnership has "credit card fever" and runs up a bill at a local department store that he cannot hope to pay anytime soon. The department store sues C and obtains a judgment, only to learn that C's only nonexempt asset is an interest in the ABC partnership. How can the store proceed in order to recover its judgment? We learned earlier the difference between C's interest in the partnership (the right to a share of profits and of assets upon dissolution) and C's interest in specific partnership property (to use it for partnership purposes only). C may not assign specific partnership property to the store and the store cannot attach it.

Therefore, the store's only recourse is to obtain a **charging order** against the partner's *interest in the partnership.* A charging order issued by a court will order that partner's share of the profits to be paid to his or her creditor until the debt is fully discharged. If the debt has not been completely paid when the partnership is dissolved, the charging order will require payment to the creditor of that partner's share in the surplus, if any remains when all partnership affairs are settled.

The charging order protects the other partners and the going concern value of the enterprise. A and B continue the partnership as always, except that when they write a check for C's share of the profits they send it to the store instead of to C. C remains a partner. The store does not become a partner. It has no voice in management and no right to inspect partnership books. The charging order may be satisfactory to the store if the stream of profits is sufficient to pay off the debt in a relatively short period of time.

But what if the store's judgment is very large and the amount of profits generated by the partnership is very small? For example, assume that the debt is $100,000, that C's share of the profits is only $2000 annually, and that the partnership's assets are $300,000. At this rate, it will take 50 years for the store's judgment to be satisfied. The store would love

---

[12]The RUPA also provides for joint and several liability for both contract and tort claims.

[13]The RUPA would require exhaustion of partnership assets in virtually every case before a partnership creditor could proceed against the individual assets of a partner.

to liquidate the partnership so that it could get C's share of the $300,000 of partnership assets.

However, the store can move past a charging order only with court permission. Courts will grant permission only in a situation like that described—when it would take an inordinately long time to pay off the creditor's debt. In such circumstances, the court *may* order foreclosure of C's interest in the partnership. Usually, an auction is held and the creditor purchases C's interest at auction.

The following case involves such a foreclosure.

HELLMAN V. ANDERSON

Court of Appeal of California, 284 Cal.Rptr. 830 (1991)

 Anderson and Tallstrom were partners in Rancho Murieta Investors (RMI). Anderson, as an individual, owed almost $500,000 to numerous judgment creditors (known collectively as "Hellman"). Hellman obtained a charging order against Anderson's 80 percent interest in RMI. No profits were paid by RMI to Hellman, and Anderson testified that RMI had not generated profits and was not expected to do so in the near future. Hellman then applied to the court for an order that Anderson's interest in RMI be sold at auction. The trial judge held that the interest could not be sold without Tallstrom's consent and denied the request. Hellman appealed.

Sims, Associate Justice:

In this case, we hold that a judgment debtor's interest in a partnership (meaning the right to share in the profits and surplus) may be foreclosed upon and sold, even though other partners do not consent to the sale, provided the foreclosure does not unduly interfere with the partnership business.

[In *Crocker Nat. Bank v. Perroton,* 255 Cal.Rptr. 794 (1989)], the court said:

A creditor with a judgment against a partner but not against the partnership ordinarily cannot execute directly on partnership assets or on the partner's interest in the partnership. . . . It was to prevent [the] "hold up" of the partnership business and the consequent injustice done the other partners resulting from execution against partnership property [that the UPA provisions were adopted].

Therefore, a judgment creditor must seek a charging order to reach the debtor partner's interest in the partnership. Through a charging order, the court may charge the debtor's interest in the partnership with payment of the unsatisfied judgment, plus interest.

Courts from other jurisdictions have agreed that the charging order provision of the UPA authorizes sale of a charged partner's interest [but not partnership property which may not be sold].

[The nondebtor partner's consent to sale of the debtor partner's interest is not required for the following reasons.] First, the statutes do not say that nondebtor partner consent is required for foreclosure on a charging order.

A second consideration is the policy underlying the UPA of avoiding undue interference with partnership business. However, we do not think that foreclosure of a partner's interest will always unduly interfere with the business of the partnership. This is because the statutory scheme itself limits the interest subject to foreclosure and sale. As we have mentioned, a partner's "interest in the partnership" is a personal property right separate and distinct from the partner's (1) rights in specific partnership property and (2) right to participate in management. The "interest in the partnership" means only the partner's share of profits and surplus. Foreclosure entails no execution upon partnership assets, and the interest acquired by foreclosure does not include the right to participate in management.

We conclude that since the interest acquired by the purchaser of a partnership interest is limited by operation of law to the partner's share of profits and surpluses, with no acquisition of interest in partnership property or no management participation, the foreclosure and sale of the partnership interest will not always unduly interfere with the partnership business to the extent of requiring consent of the nondebtor partners. In some cases, foreclosure might cause a partner with essential managerial skills to abandon the partnership. In other cases, foreclosure would appear to have no appreciable effect on the conduct of partnership business. Thus, the effect of foreclosure on the partnership should be evaluated on a case-by-case basis by the trial court in connection with its equitable power to order a foreclosure.

[The case was remanded so that the trial court could make such a determination in this case.]⚖

Note

The creditor purchasing a partnership interest still does not become a partner. Indeed, it has not advanced its position except to gain some leverage in negotiating with the nondebtor partners, *unless* the partnership is at will or the partnership is for a term that has passed or for a purpose that has been accomplished, in which case the creditor apparently gains the right to dissolve the partnership with court assistance.[14] In such a situation, the creditor will finally be able to lay its hands on the value of partnership assets.

SUMMARY

One of the basic rights of a partner is to participate in the management of the business. It is possible, however, for partners to alter their management rights by agreement. If there is no agreement otherwise, most management decisions in a partnership are made by majority vote of the partners. A few unusual matters require consent of all the partners unless they had previously agreed to let such decisions be made by less-than-unanimous vote.

Unless the articles of partnership provide otherwise, an individual partner's right in partnership property is limited to the equal right (with other partners) to possess such property for partnership purposes. This right is not transferable. When the agreement does not provide otherwise, all partners share equally in profits and losses, regardless of the relative amounts of capital they contributed. A partner normally is entitled to compensation other than a share of profits, unless the partnership agreement states otherwise.

Partners owe fiduciary duties to each other and must act with reasonable care and with the utmost good faith. Each partner has a right to have complete access to partnership records. Under certain circumstances, a partner has the right to an account, which is a court-supervised audit of all partnership records.

The partnership's relations with third parties are governed by the basic rules of the law of agency. Each partner is an agent of the partnership for the purposes of its business, and the partnership is bound by a partner's actions when they have the apparent purpose of operating the partnership's business in the usual manner.

[14] UPA Sec. 32(2).

KEY TERMS

Interest in the partnership
Account (or accounting)
Nontrading partnership
Trading partnership
Charging order

QUESTIONS AND PROBLEMS

1. Under the Nassau Queens Medical Group's partnership agreement, a partner could be terminated by a majority vote if the partner had reached the age of 70. Dr. Levy was expelled from the partnership on the ground that he was over 70 years old. Other partners over the age of 70, however, were not terminated. There was no evidence that the partnership acted out of a desire to gain a business or property advantage for the remaining partners. Was Dr. Levy's termination allowable under the partnership agreement? Discuss. (*Levy v. Nassau Queens Medical Group,* 102 A.2d 845, N.Y.App.Div. 1984.)

2. Five sisters sued their father to establish the existence of a partnership among them for management and disposition of the community of assets of the father and his first wife (mother of the plaintiffs) in an oil drilling company that the father had operated for 15 years. The trial court found that a partnership did exist. In rendering judgment, the trial court debited $54,751.05 from the father's capital account to compensate for "unauthorized drawings" of funds for his own use. The father appealed, claiming that the draws were to compensate him for acting as the sole manager of the partnership over the years. Should the father's appeal succeed? (*Conrad v. Johnson,* 465 S.W.2d 819, Tex.Civ.App. 1971.)

3. Alexander and Sims were partners in a retail business. An operation revealed that Sims had cancer and would not live long. Before this information was given to Sims, Alexander went to the hospital and presented Sims with an agreement providing "that in the event of the decease of either of the partners, all of the partnership assets shall immediately become the sole and exclusive property of the surviving partner." Both partners signed the agreement. Only later did Sims learn of the seriousness of her illness; she then signed a will leaving all of her property to her parents. Who should receive Sims's interest in the

partnership? Discuss. (*Alexander v. Sims,* 249 S.W.2d 832, Ark. 1952.)

4. Oswald and Leckey, certified public accountants, executed a partnership agreement to conduct an accounting practice. After forming the partnership, each partner continued to bill the clients that he personally served. The relationship between Oswald and Leckey was not harmonious, and the partnership was dissolved about two years later. Oswald filed suit for an accounting to determine each partner's share of a partnership bank account. In the lawsuit, Oswald claimed that Leckey had improperly "written down" several accounts while they were partners, and that Leckey should have to repay the partnership for the amount of the write-downs. (An account is "written down" when the amount actually billed is less than the amount due as shown on the books.) The evidence showed that part of Leckey's motive in writing down the accounts was to keep these clients as his own. Did Leckey violate his fiduciary duty of loyalty to Oswald? Discuss. (*Oswald v. Leckey,* 572 P.2d 1316 (Or. 1977.)

5. Voeller, managing partner of a partnership operating a drive-in movie theater business, sold a parcel of partnership land to Hodge. Sale of the land would not have impaired operation of the business, but the other partners objected to the sale. Hodge sued to enforce the contract. Is it binding on the partnership? Discuss. (*Hodge v. Garrett,* 614 P.2d 420, Idaho 1980.)

6. Pius and Albinus Scherr began a general partnership to construct and invest in buildings. They opened a checking account at the First National Bank; the signature card indicated that money could be withdrawn and notes signed by either partner. Later the Scherrs drafted a partnership agreement that withdrew the authority to borrow money from the partners acting singly, requiring both partners to sign for any loan. The agreement was placed in the bank's file. The bank made several loans to the partners, with both signing the notes, including a $100,000 loan on October 26, 1983. The next day Pius alone signed a $65,000 short-term note giving as the purpose final construction on a restaurant being built by the partners. The $65,000 note was not repaid; litigation ensued. Is the partnership bound on the note? Discuss. (*First Nat'l Bank & Trust v. Scherr,* 467 N.W.2d 427, N.D. 1991.)

7. Attorney Grandeau stole money from his clients. The state had a Clients' Security Fund, funded by contributions from lawyers, which repaid 373 clients $589,829 for their losses and then took an assignment from the injured clients in order to sue Grandeau, his law partnership, and his partner *Dahowski* for reimbursement. *Dahowski* claims that he is not liable for Grandeau's misappropriation of client funds. Assume that *Dahowski* did not know of or participate in Grandeau's illicit activities. Is *Dahowski* liable? Discuss. (*Clients' Security Fund v. Grandeau,* 526 N.E.2d 270, N.Y. 1988.)

8. The Davis Packing Co. was awarded a judgment against R. A. Myles individually. To enforce the judgment, Davis had the sheriff levy upon 10 cows owned by R. A. Myles & Co., a partnership of which Myles was a member. The cows were sold and the money was applied toward the judgment. The partnership sued, claiming the cattle were wrongfully converted. Discuss. (*R. A. Myles & Co. v. A. D. Davis Packing Co.,* 81 So. 863, Ala. 1919.)

Chapter 35

Partnerships
Termination

Dissolution

Winding Up Partnership Affairs

COMPLETE TERMINATION OF the partnership as a business organization is composed of two elements: *dissolution* and *winding up*. Dissolution does not of itself bring the partnership business to a close; it is, rather, the "beginning of the end." Essentially, the word **dissolution** designates that point in time when the object of the partners changes from continuing the organization in its present form to discontinuing it.[1] The partnership is not terminated at that time, but its object has become termination.

The second element of termination, commonly referred to as **winding up,** involves the actual process of settling partnership affairs after dissolution. After both dissolution and winding up have occurred, the partnership as an organization will have terminated.

DISSOLUTION
Causes of Dissolution

The events that cause dissolution can be divided into four categories: (1) act of one or more partners not in violation of their agreement, (2) act of one or more partners in violation of their agreement, (3) operation of law, and (4) court decree.

Act of One or More Partners Not in Violation of Their Agreement

As we have seen in the discussion of partnership formation and operation, the partnership is created by agreement. Thus, when the question becomes one of dissolution, the partnership agreement (articles of partnership) should be the first place to look for guidance.

The partnership agreement may provide, for example, that the partnership will exist for only a specified period of time. Upon expiration of this period, the partnership dissolves in accordance with the original agreement, unless all the partners agree to amend the articles of partnership and extend the prescribed duration.[2] The partnership agreement similarly could provide for automatic dissolution of the partnership upon the occurrence of some particular event. When this event takes place, the partnership dissolves unless the partners unanimously amend the agreement.

Where the partnership agreement makes no provision for a definite duration and places no other limitations on a partner's right to withdraw, a **partnership at will** exists. This means that any partner can withdraw at any time without violating the agreement and, therefore, without incurring contractual liability to the other partners. Such a withdrawal automatically dissolves the partnership unless the partnership agreement provides that withdrawal will not result in dissolution.[3]

Similarly, the partnership agreement may allow for exclusion of a partner by the other partners. Such a provision might permit exclusion of a partner only for specified reasons, or it might even permit exclusion without cause by vote of a specified number of the other partners. In any event, the partners relying on the exclusion clause are not in violation of the agreement if they act in accordance with its terms. Moreover, an exclusion clause in the partnership agreement usually is interpreted by a court as an agreement among the partners that dissolution will not occur when a partner is excluded according to the clause.

Since a partnership is created by agreement, it can be dissolved by agreement. Regardless of the terms of the original partnership agreement, a partnership can be dissolved at any time without violating that agreement if all the partners consent to dissolution. A unanimous dissolution agreement overrides the original articles of partnership. A dissolution agreement that is not unanimous, however, constitutes a violation of the original partnership agreement by

---

[1] Later in the chapter we will discuss the situation where certain of the partners wish to continue the *business,* even though the partnership as an organization is dissolved. It might be continued as a new partnership or in some other organizational form. In such a case, the termination of the partnership consists primarily of bookkeeping entries and purchase of the interests of noncontinuing partners.

[2] Continuance of the business by the partners after expiration of the agreed term constitutes an implied partnership agreement even in the absence of an express amendment of the articles of partnership. The partnership will then be one "at will," which means that the individual partners are legally free to withdraw at any time thereafter. So long as they actually continue, however, the partnership exists and the terms of the implied partnership agreement are those of the original agreement, insofar as they are applicable.

[3] RUPA reorganizes the causes of dissolution, but generally resembles the UPA except that it provides that a partnership does not automatically dissolve simply because partners are added or subtracted.

those causing dissolution unless their action is in accordance with a provision in the original agreement expressly permitting dissolution by a less-than-unanimous vote.[4]

[4] However, if a partner has assigned his or her interest in the partnership to a third party, or if a partner's personal creditor has subjected the partner's

The following case more fully explains the overriding nature of the partnership agreement in resolving questions relating to dissolution.

interest in the partnership to a "charging order," the consent of that partner is not required for dissolution.

OSBORNE V. WORKMAN

Supreme Court of Arkansas, 621 S.W.2d 478 (1981)

Case

In 1966 Merrill Osborne, a physician, joined with five other physicians in a partnership to operate a medical clinic. Their written partnership agreement specified no definite term, but only that it would continue "until said partnership is dissolved mutually or by law." The agreement also provided that if a doctor withdrew from the partnership he was to be paid his percentage share of the clinic's asset value at the time of withdrawal, excluding accounts receivable. When the partnership was formed, the clinic's accounts receivable were $105,000 and were treated as a partnership asset. The accounts gradually increased, and by 1979 totalled $513,000. Estimates of actual collectability of these accounts in 1979 varied from $100,000 to $400,000. Between 1966 and 1979 a number of new physicians were admitted to the partnership, and a total of seven withdrew. In six of the seven withdrawals, the withdrawing physicians received nothing from accounts receivable; one had received a portion of the accounts by unanimous vote of the remaining partners in 1968.

In 1978 Osborne announced his intention to withdraw from the partnership, and by 1979 he had relocated to a private medical practice. The remaining partners offered to pay him his percentage share of the partnership's present asset value,

excluding accounts receivable, but Osborne insisted on receiving a share of those accounts. When the remaining partners refused, he filed suit seeking dissolution of the partnership and a winding up that would include liquidation of its assets. The trial court held for the partnership and remaining partners, and Osborne, appellant, appealed to the Supreme Court of Arkansas.

Hays, Associate Justice:

Appellant contends that dissolution should have been ordered under [§31 of the UPA], entitled "Causes of Dissolution," which provides some nine instances of dissolution by operation of law, including the express will of any partner where no definite term is specified in the agreement. The agreement here did not provide for a specific term; hence it is urged that any partner could dissolve the partnership at will. But the argument fails in two respects: It ignores the precondition clearly stated in §31, that the section applies "without violation of the agreement between the parties"; and it fails to consider what was intended by the partnership agreement itself. Moreover, §29 defines dissolution:

The dissolution of a partnership is the change in the relation of the partners caused by any partner ceasing to be associated in the carrying on as distinguished from the winding up of the business; provided that this change in the relation of the partners shall not effect a dissolution of the partnership *in contraven-*

tion or violation of the agreement between the partners. [Emphasis added by the court.]

Self-limiting language appears throughout the UPA which renders it "subject to any agreement to the contrary." Even the section for the settling of accounts after dissolution and winding up, which provides the method of distribution among the partners, is "subject to any agreement to the contrary." The clear intent of the UPA [is] to defer to any existing partnership agreement. . . .

Turning to the agreement itself, we note that in construing the agreement we are governed by what the parties intended. Appellant contends that the wording "until said partnership is dissolved mutually or by law" triggers that provision in UPA Section 31 giving any partner the right to dissolve at will. Certainly any partner can withdraw at will and to the extent that withdrawal is a dissolution he is correct. But appellant seeks . . . the termination of the partnership by liquidation, and we cannot agree these partners intended such a result. We think the clear intent was that [actual] termination would occur only by mutual agreement and not by the unilateral act of a single partner. Appellant's contention cannot be reconciled with the words "mutually dissolved," [because according to his argument] the dissolution could be achieved by a single partner—the reverse of mutual. It is undisputed that seven doctors withdrew over the years and [with only one unanimously voted
(continues)

OSBORNE V. WORKMAN

(continued from previous page)
exception] the partnership retained all of the accounts receivable and in determining what the parties intended, reference is made to what they did. It is inconceivable that six doctors would form a partnership, enter into an elaborate agreement intended to promote longevity, set up a common practice, pool their equipment, records and resources, [but to have] intended that any one of them could end it at any time by demanding dissolution and liquidation. . . .

Persons with professional qualifications commonly associate in business partnerships. The practice of continuing the operation of the partnership business, even though there are some changes in partnership personnel, is also common. The reasons for an agreement that a medical partnership should continue without disruption of the services rendered are self-evident. If the partnership agreement provides for continuation, sets forth a method of paying the withdrawing partner his agreed share, and does not jeopardize

the rights of creditors, the agreement is enforceable. . . .

In conclusion, where competent parties knowingly enter into an agreement suited to their purposes, keep that agreement in effect over many years to their mutual benefit, it is not for the courts to nullify such agreement. . . .

The decree is affirmed. [Dr. Osborne is bound by the express terms of the partnership agreement, cannot force liquidation, and it not entitled to a share of the accounts receivable.]⚖

Act of One or More Partners in Violation of Their Agreement

Regardless of the terms of the partnership agreement, one or more partners can withdraw from the partnership at any time. However, a distinction must be drawn between the ever-present *power* to withdraw and the *right* to withdraw. Although the power to withdraw from a partnership always exists, any partner whose withdrawal violates the partnership agreement is liable to the nonwithdrawing partners for damages caused by the withdrawal. Such withdrawal causes a dissolution of the partnership unless the partnership agreement provided that dissolution would not result in these circumstances. Although withdrawal can cause dissolution without any formal court action, one or more of the withdrawing or nonwithdrawing partners often will seek a court decree of dissolution if there is any disagreement about whether the withdrawal actually violated the partnership agreement or about the amount of damages.

By Operation of Law

The partnership automatically dissolves if an event occurs that makes it illegal to carry on the business. The *business itself* may become illegal, as where a partnership for the purpose of selling liquor loses its liquor license. Or it may become illegal for *these particular partners* to carry on the business together, as where an individual partner in a medical practice has his or her license revoked.

Unless otherwise agreed, dissolution also occurs automatically on the *death* of a partner or on the *bankruptcy* of either a partner[5] or the partnership itself. The articles of partnership may, of course, provide that the death or bankruptcy of an individual partner will not cause a dissolution.

By Court Decree

Section 32 of the UPA specifically enumerates several situations in which dissolution of a partnership can be accomplished by seeking and obtaining a formal court decree. They can be divided into two broad categories: (1) situations in which a *partner* can obtain a decree of dissolution and (2) situations in which a *third party* can obtain such a decree.

Decree Obtained by a Partner. When a partner has become *insane*, either that person or another partner can obtain a court decree dissolving the partnership. In such a case dissolution does not occur automatically (as it does in the case of death or bankruptcy). A formal court decree is required in the instance of insanity because a person's mental competency is inherently subject to doubt and dispute, whereas death and bankruptcy are more certain events. The decree can be sought (1) when a partner

---

[5] Some courts hold that a partner's bankruptcy under the reorganization provisions of Chapter 11 of the Bankruptcy Code does not dissolve the partnership. These courts reason that at the time the UPA was drafted in 1914, only Chapter 7 liquidation bankruptcy existed and that the differences between the two types of bankruptcy justify different treatment. See, for example, *In re Hawkins*, 113 B.R. 315 (Bkrtcy.N.D.Tex. 1990).

has already been declared insane by a court in a sanity hearing or (2) when such a formal adjudication has not yet occurred. In the latter case, the court asked to dissolve the partnership will itself determine whether the partner is insane. The court will not dissolve the partnership in either case, however, unless it appears probable that the insanity will continue for a substantial part of the partnership's duration.

Dissolution also can be obtained by court decree if a partner becomes in any other way *incapable of performing his or her part of the partnership agreement.* This provision is usually applied to disabilities other than insanity (such as prolonged illness, a paralytic stroke, or a serious accident) when it appears that the disability will continue for a substantial period of time and will materially obstruct or negatively affect the objectives of the partnership. The court decree in this case can be sought by either the partner suffering the disability or any other partner.

A partner can obtain a decree of dissolution when one of the other partners has been guilty of *serious misconduct.* Breach of the partnership agreement is, of course, one example of such misconduct. Even if the partnership agreement has not been breached, under the UPA a decree of dissolution can be obtained if another partner has been "guilty of such conduct as tends to affect prejudicially the carrying on of the business" or if the other partner "so conducts himself in matters relating to the partnership business that it is not reasonably practicable to carry on the business in partnership with him." Examples of such conduct are fraud in dealing with partnership property or funds, substantial overdraft of a drawing account by a partner who has been temporarily left in charge of the business, and serious neglect of partnership affairs.

Where misconduct has occurred, the guilty partner cannot obtain dissolution by court decree; this right belongs solely to one or more of the other partners. Furthermore, if the other partner or partners so desire, they can simply withdraw and cause dissolution. A court decree is not essential, and the guilty partner cannot sue them for damages even if their withdrawal is contrary to the partnership agreement. Although formal court action is not essential in cases of misconduct, it is often desirable where any doubt exists as to whether the misconduct is serious enough to warrant dissolution or where disagreement exists regarding damages or the value of partners' interests.

Finally, any partner can obtain a decree of dissolution when it becomes evident that the business is *unprofitable* and will probably not be profitable in the future.

Decree Obtained by a Third Party. Two types of third parties are considered to have a sufficient interest in partnership affairs to obtain a decree of dissolution in certain circumstances: (1) an *assignee* of a partner's interest in the partnership and (2) a partner's *personal creditor* who has subjected that partner's interest to a charging order. Either of these third parties, however, can obtain a decree of dissolution in only two situations: (1) after expiration of the period of time or accomplishment of the purpose specified in the articles of partnership, in cases where the articles include such a provision, or (2) at any time, if the partnership is a partnership "at will" when the third party acquires his or her interest.

In the next case, a partner sought dissolution by court decree on the basis of a claim that one of the other partners had breached the partnership agreement. The question also arose whether the partner who violated the agreement forfeited all of his rights as a partner, or whether he was just liable for whatever monetary damage his breach caused to the other partners.

STASZAK V. ROMANIK

U.S. Sixth Circuit Court of Appeals, 690 F.2d 578 (1982)

Joseph Staszak and his cousin, Walter Romanik, formed a partnership in 1959 under the name North Star Tree Company for the purpose of growing and selling Christmas trees. Walter lived in Michigan, and Joseph in Maryland; both owned land in Michigan where the trees were to be grown. They made an oral agreement that Walter's 20 acres and Joseph's 80 acres both would be used in the business: Walter would supply labor and manage the operation, Joseph would supply the working capital, and profits and losses would be shared equally. In 1968 Walter and Joseph agreed that Walter should begin receiving a salary for his management services. Between 1959 and 1969 the partnership purchased and leased substantial additional land, so that by 1969 trees were being grown on 1,573 acres. Also by 1969, 94 full-time and part-time employees worked for the partnership.

In early 1969 Walter and Joseph purchased another Christmas tree business in Michigan, Sno Kist Tree Corporation, using as a down payment $134,000 that Joseph had personally borrowed and contributed to the partnership. The purchase included the Sno Kist trademark, a long-term lease on Sno Kist's land and equipment, and assignments of leases held by Sno Kist on several other tracts of land used for growing and harvesting trees. All of these leases included tree harvesting rights. Walter and Joseph agreed at the same time to admit Joseph's son Richard Staszak as an equal partner in the larger enterprise. Essentially, a new partnership was formed at this time, and the purchase of Sno Kist Tree Company was made in the names of all three partners. Thereafter, North Star and Sno Kist were operated as a single business, and in

1970 the three partners executed a written partnership agreement that formally adopted the Sno Kist name for the entire operation, and provided that the capital contributions of the partners were to be their interests in partnership real estate and other assets. The written agreement also stated that profits were to be shared equally, but that these profits were to be distributed in such a way as to eventually equalize the partners' capital contributions.

During the first year's harvest after formation of the three-way partnership, Richard Staszak went from Maryland to Michigan and stayed throughout the harvest season, overseeing the work on a portion of the operation. Richard spent part of each succeeding year, during the harvesting season, in Michigan. Beginning in 1972, Walter began complaining that Richard was not doing what was required by their agreement, because they had an unwritten understanding that Richard was to move to Michigan and work full time in the business. By 1975 relations between Walter and the Staszaks had completely deteriorated, and Joseph and Richard tried to buy out Walter's interest in the partnership. Walter refused to sell and filed suit claiming that the partnership should be dissolved because of Richard's breach of the partnership agreement. The trial court concluded that, even though the partnership agreement did not so state, there was an implied agreement that Richard Staszak would move to Michigan and work full time in the business, and that Richard had breached this agreement. Because the agreement had required Richard initially to contribute only services, and no capital, to the partnership, the trial court found that there was a complete failure of consideration on Richard's part. Consequently, the trial court held that Richard had never become a

partner and had to return to the partnership over $80,000 in profit distributions he had received since 1969. Joseph and Richard appealed.

Lively, Circuit Judge:

The [trial court] found that Richard Staszak was a partner at the inception of the Sno Kist partnership. This finding was correct. . . .

Since the UPA is intended to be comprehensive, whenever its provisions cover a situation involving a partnership those provisions should be applied. Only when presented with a case not provided for in the Act should a court be governed by general rules of law and equity. The Act provides [that] when dissolution is caused by the wrongful act of a partner, that partner is entitled to his share of partnership [surplus] subject to the right of partners who have not breached the agreement to recover from him any damages caused by his breach.

Instead of applying the foregoing provisions of the UPA the trial court determined that Richard Staszak should, in effect, be removed retroactively as a partner, should be denied all equity in partnership assets and should be required to refund to the partnership all profits previously distributed to him. . . .

It is clear that at least part of the consideration for formation of the Sno Kist partnership was the agreement of each partner to contribute his interest in real and personal property transferred to the partnership as capital and to permit distributions of profit in such a manner as to equalize the capital contribution of each. . . .

The partnership agreement described the capital of the partnership as the real estate described in Schedule A and the personal property described in Schedule B. . . . Both schedules were attached. . . . The [next] paragraph of the agreement provided that the contribution of each partner consisted of

(continues)

STASZAK V. ROMANIK

(continued from previous page)
his interest in the property described in Schedules A and B and any other property or money "conveyed" to the partnership. Richard Staszak had a one-third interest in the assets purchased from the . . . Sno Kist Tree Corporation which became the property of the Sno Kist partnership. Yet the trial court found that Richard's only contribution was to consist of personal services to the partnership. Further, Richard Staszak's share of the profits of the partnership between 1970 and 1977 was substantially in excess of the approximately $80,000 which he withdrew. Paragraph XIV of the agreement provided that the undistributed profits of the partners were to be applied to equalize their capital contributors. The finding that Richard Staszak made no contribution to the capital of the partnership was clearly erroneous. Thus, even though Richard Staszak failed to perform services as promised, there was not a total failure of consideration.

Richard Staszak has not appealed from the finding that there was an implied agreement that he would move to Michigan and work full time for the partnership or from the conclusion that his breach of this agreement was sufficient to require dissolution of the partnership. He contends, however, that the proper remedy for this breach is that provided in [the Uniform Partnership Act]. We agree. . . .

In this case the trial court found that a partnership was formed. It is clear that Richard Staszak made some contribution to capital—his share of the assets purchased by the three partners in equal shares from the . . . Sno Kist Tree Corporation. The partners were equally liable for payment of the balance of the purchase price above the down payment of $100,000. Richard Staszak made further contributions of capital by withdrawing less than his total share of partnership prof-

its. Finally, he performed services for the corporation each year until 1976. His breach of partnership duties consisted only of his failure to move to Michigan and work full time for the partnership. The other partners are entitled to recover any damages which this breach caused the partnership. But forfeiture of Richard's interest was not a permitted sanction for the breach.

The judgment of the district court is reversed insofar as it holds that Richard Staszak was not entitled to a partner's share in the assets of the partnership and insofar as it directs Richard Staszak to repay to the partnership the amounts which he has previously withdrawn as distributions of partnership profits. Upon remand the district court will determine the amount of damages, if any, sustained by the partnership as the result of Richard Staszak's breach and award such damages equally to the other partners. ⚖

Effect of Dissolution on Partners' Authority

Despite the fact that dissolution does not sound the instantaneous death knell of the partnership, it is frequently important to ascertain the precise moment when it occurs. The reason is simple. When dissolution takes place, certain significant changes occur in the nature of the partners' relationships with one another and with outsiders. Of paramount significance is the effect dissolution has on the *authority of partners to bind the partnership*. In most cases, of course, a partner acting without authority must personally shoulder the burden of any liability resulting from such action.

Upon dissolution, the authority of individual partners to act in behalf of the partnership usually ceases, *except for acts necessary to complete unfinished transactions or those appropriate for winding up partnership affairs*. For example, suppose that a partnership, before dissolution, had made a contract to sell goods. After dissolution, a partner would have authority to arrange for shipping those goods in accordance with the existing contract. However, he or she would not have authority to make new contracts without the consent of the other partners, unless these contracts were in furtherance of liquidating the business. Thus the partner probably would be authorized to make contracts for the sale of existing inventory. Similarly, he or she usually would be able to do such things as hire an accountant to take inventory and perform an audit, pay partnership debts and receive payment of obligations owing to the partnership, and make reasonable compromise agreements with debtors and creditors. Obviously a partner's authority to borrow money would be severely restricted after dissolution. Borrowing in order to pay existing obligations would probably be authorized in many situations, but borrowing for any other reason probably would not.

If, instead of liquidating the business, some of the partners intend to continue it as a new partnership or other type of organization, these limitations on authority may cause short-term difficulties. During the changeover period, certain transactions not within the scope of this limited authority may be necessary to keep the business going. In such a case, the consent of *all* partners must be obtained to authorize this kind of transaction.

In the absence of a contrary agreement among the partners, the type of authority still existing after dissolution can be exercised by *any* of the partners. If they choose, however, they can agree that such authority rests only with a certain partner. The person delegated this type of responsibility is sometimes referred to as the **liquidating partner** (or **winding-up partner**). Then, if third parties are so notified, they can hold the partnership liable only if they deal with the designated partner.

Special Situations

Regarding the effect of dissolution, three exceptional situations must be mentioned.

Partner's Knowledge. Under some circumstances it is important to determine whether the partner transacting business for the partnership after dissolution has *knowledge* of certain facts. If dissolution is caused either by the *act* of any partner (whether in violation of the partnership agreement or not), the *death* of any partner, or the *bankruptcy* of any partner, the partnership will be bound by any transaction made by a partner who *did not know* the facts that caused dissolution.[6] This liability exists even if the transaction was not merely a completion of unfinished business and was not otherwise appropriate for winding up partnership affairs. (Of course, the transaction must be of a type that would have been binding upon the partnership if dissolution had *not* occurred.)

Notice to Third Parties. In some situations the *absence of notice to third parties* may result in partnership liability for unauthorized transactions entered into after dissolution. If the transaction is of a type that would have bound the partnership if dissolution had *not* taken place, the firm will be liable for it *after* dissolution if the third party being dealt with has not been properly notified of the dissolution. If, before dissolution, the third party has extended credit to the partnership, a transaction with this person after dissolution will bind the partnership unless he or she is proven to have had knowledge of the dissolution. The best way to prevent such a pos-

sibility is to directly notify all the partnership's creditors that dissolution has occurred. Since their names and addresses will almost certainly be in the partnership records, no undue inconvenience will result. If the third party had not extended credit to the partnership in the past but did know of its existence prior to dissolution, *the partnership is not liable for transactions with that party* made after dissolution if he or she either knows of the dissolution or if the fact of dissolution has been advertised in a newspaper of general circulation in those places where the partnership has regularly done business.[7] These rules regarding notice to third parties are simply an application of the principle of *apparent authority*.

The Bankrupt Partner. Under the UPA, the partnership is not bound in any circumstances where the postdissolution transaction is made by a partner who is personally *bankrupt*. In such a case it does not matter whether the third party knows of the partner's bankruptcy or of the resulting dissolution; the UPA's view is that one should know the status of the person with whom one is dealing.

Effect of Dissolution on Existing Liabilities

A cardinal rule of partnership law is that dissolution in and of itself does not alter the existing liabilities of the partnership or of individual partners. In some circumstances the event causing dissolution may also cause a discharge from certain liabilities, but it is not the dissolution itself that causes the discharge. Contracts in force at the time of the event that causes dissolution may or may not be discharged, depending upon the rules of contract law. For instance, the death of a partner might terminate an existing partnership contract if the contract had called for some type of personal service by the deceased partner. And bankruptcy of the partnership will not only result in dissolution but also will discharge partnership liabilities that are in excess of the combined assets of the partnership and all the partners. Whether existing liabilities in other situations will be discharged depends entirely on the circumstances.

WINDING UP PARTNERSHIP AFFAIRS

Winding up is the second and final step after dissolution in the termination of a partnership.

---

[6] Section 3 of the UPA makes a distinction between *knowledge* and *notice*. This distinction makes no difference in the majority of cases and its technicality is of too refined a nature for our discussion.

[7] Before enactment of the UPA, some courts had recognized other methods of publicizing the dissolution, but the UPA speaks only of advertisement by newspaper.

The Right to Wind Up

The question of which partners have the right to wind up partnership affairs can be determined by agreement of the partners.[8] In the absence of an agreement, all partners have an equal right to settle partnership affairs, with two notable exceptions. A partner who has *wrongfully caused dissolution* and a partner who is *personally bankrupt* do not have the right to exercise any control over the winding up process.

Distribution of Assets

When dissolution has occurred and the business is to be terminated, the winding up process entails such activities as liquidating partnership property (turning it into cash), collecting outstanding accounts, paying outstanding debts, and any other actions required to bring partnership affairs to a close.

After all partnership assets have been liquidated, they are distributed to those having claims against the partnership. The order in which they are distributed is of little importance if the partnership has been profitable and all claims can be paid in full. Where partnership assets are insufficient to completely satisfy all claims, however, the issue obviously becomes quite significant.

As previously noted, when partnership assets are insufficient to pay partnership debts, assets of individual partners can be used insofar as necessary. Before this can happen, however, any claims of that partner's individual creditors must be satisfied.

Claims against the partnership are paid in the following order:

1. First to be paid are claims of outside creditors of the partnership.

2. Next are claims of individual partners for repayment of loans they have made to the partnership. Interest is ordinarily payable unless it had been agreed that the loan would be interest-free.

3. Claims of individual partners for return of contributions they have made to the partnership's working capital are third in line. Interest is not payable on contributions to capital unless the partners had agreed otherwise.[9]

4. If any partnership assets remain after satisfying the other claims, these are distributed as profits to the partners in the proportion in which profits were to be shared.

To illustrate: Jones and Smith are partners in the retail clothing business. The partnership has not been profitable and is dissolved. The financial position of the partnership after all assets have been reduced to cash is summarized as follows (assuming no interest payable on partners' loans or capital contributions):

ASSETS		LIABILITIES AND PARTNER'S EQUITY		
Cash ...	$200,000	*Liabilities*		
	$200,000	Accounts payable	$225,000	
		Loans from partners		
		Jones	25,000	
		Smith	10,000	$260,000
		Partners' equity		
		Jones (contribution to capital)	$ 50,000	
		Smith (contribution to capital)	50,000	100,000
				$360,000

As we can see, the operations of the partnership have resulted in an overall loss of $160,000. Assuming that losses are to be divided equally, Jones and Smith will each have to personally bear an $80,000 loss. The following summary indicates the personal financial positions of Jones and Smith:

	Jones	*Smith*
Assets...	$150,000	$200,000
Liabilities.......................................	−75,000	−250,000
	$75,000	($50,000)

Here we see that Smith is insolvent. Since his individual assets must first be used to pay his individual debts, he is financially unable to pay partnership obligations. As a result, Jones must use his personal assets to pay the remaining partnership debts to partnership creditors. This obligation amounts to $25,000, since partnership accounts payable were $225,000 and partnership assets were $200,000. The

---

[8] If the partners disagree as to who shall wind up, a court may appoint a qualified disinterested third party as a *receiver* to handle the winding up process.

[9] RUPA generally preserves the UPA order of distribution, paying outsiders first and partners as creditors second. However, the UPA's final two categories (capital and profits) are combined and worded "to partners in accordance with their rights to distributions." In theory, contributions to capital and shares in profits and losses work together to determine the partners' rights to distributions.

losses actually borne by each partner are summarized as follows:

	Jones	Smith
Loans to partnership (unrepaid)	$ 25,000	$10,000
Contributions to partnership capital (unreturned)	50,000	50,000
Use of individual's assets to pay partnership creditors	25,000	—
	$100,000	$60,000

Since each partner should have borne a loss of $80,000, Jones now has a claim against Smith for $20,000. Whether this claim will be collectible, as a practical matter, is a problem Jones must face.

Continuing the Business

The business of a partnership is not always terminated after dissolution, even though the partnership as an organization comes to an end. Where the operations of the partnership have been profitable and customer goodwill has been built up, the business will be more valuable as a going concern than it will if it is liquidated. Thus some of the partners may wish to continue the business—and they can do so unless continuation would be illegal for some reason. If they decide to continue, the winding up process will consist primarily of bookkeeping entries and the purchase by continuing partners of the interests of withdrawing partners. Customers may never know there has been any change, unless some change is made in the firm name. And creditors of the dissolved partnership will continue to be creditors of the reorganized partnership.[10]

According to Agreement

If the articles of partnership provide for continuing the business after dissolution, these provisions dictate the procedures to be followed. For instance, the articles of partnership might specify procedures for continuing the business after the withdrawal, expul-

sion, or death of a partner, including methods for valuing that partner's interest and settling accounts between the continuing and noncontinuing partners. It also is possible for the partners to make a binding agreement concerning the continuation of the business at the time of dissolution.

Without Agreement

When there is no agreement for continuing the business, either in the articles of partnership or in a separate agreement made at the time of dissolution, the procedures for continuation are guided by the UPA. In this regard, the UPA makes a distinction between two situations: (1) where dissolution has occurred *without* a wrongful act by any partner, and (2) where it *has been caused* by such a wrongful act.

Where Dissolution Occurred without a Wrongful Act. The most common situations of no wrongful act are dissolution caused by death of a partner or by the withdrawal of a partner in a situation where he or she had the right to do so. In such a case, the continuing partners must immediately settle with the withdrawing partner or the estate of the deceased partner (the term *withdrawing partner* hereafter will also include the estate of a deceased partner) if the latter so desires. If settlement is made *immediately,* it consists only of a payment to the withdrawing partner of an amount equal to the value of that partner's interest in the partnership at the time of dissolution. This, of course, will be his or her share of any existing surplus of partnership asset value (including goodwill) over partnership liabilities. If settlement is *postponed,* the withdrawing partner receives not only the value of his or her interest in the partnership (computed as of the moment of dissolution) but also an additional amount to compensate for the delay. The additional amount is computed in one of two ways, depending on the choice of the withdrawing partner—either as *interest* on the amount due since dissolution or as an amount equal to that partner's proportionate share of partnership *profits* earned since dissolution.

This choice granted to the withdrawing partner is intended to encourage the remaining partners to settle accounts promptly. Otherwise, the withdrawing partner may share in profits if the partnership does well, or choose interest payments if the partnership flounders. In other words, the withdrawing partner has no downside risk, as the following case illustrates.

[10]The situation may be different if the business is reorganized and continued in some form other than a partnership, such as a corporation. In such a case, all those who were partners in the dissolved partnership will be liable for debts incurred by the partnership before dissolution, unless the creditors release them. This is true for those persons continuing the business (who may now be officers, directors, and/or stockholders in the new corporation) and for those who have left it. The corporation itself is a separate legal entity not liable for these old debts unless it assumes them. This frequently occurs, however, because the new corporation ordinarily is controlled by at least some of the former partners, and it will often assume the old debts in return for a release by creditors of the former partners.

KING V. EVANS

Texas Court of Appeals, 791 S.W.2d 531 (1990)

In 1969, King and Evans agreed to form a farming partnership. King contributed a 725-acre tract of land to the partnership; this contribution was reimbursed from partnership income by 1981. Evans left the partnership as of July 31, 1981; the value of Evans's share of the partnership interest at the date of dissolution was $203,198. King continued to operate the farm until 1988 without settling with Evans, so Evans and his wife brought this action.

A jury found in favor of the noncontinuing partner (Evans) in the sum of $203,198 (the value of his partnership interest at the time of dissolution in 1981) plus interest in the amount of $192,155. King appealed.

Biery, Judge:

If [after dissolution] the business is not wound up but instead continued, with or without agreement, the noncontinuing partner may elect between one of two alternatives. First, he may force a liquidation, taking his part of the proceeds and this sharing in profits and losses after dissolution. Alternatively, he may permit the business to continue (or accept the fact that it has) and claim as a creditor the value of his interest at dissolution. If the noncontinuing partner selects the latter alternative, he has an additional election to receive either interest or profits from the date of dissolution. [Sec. 42.]

The jury determined from the evidence that the value of Mr. Evans' partnership interest at the date of dissolution was $203,198.00. Therefore, [Evans was] entitled to that sum.

Section 42 is intended to give the noncontinuing partner the benefit of asset appreciation at dissolution, and leave him unaffected by later post-dissolution losses. Crane & Bromberg, *Partnership* 496–97 (1968). According to the California Supreme Court, the statute was obviously intended to put the risk of operating the business after dissolution on the continuing partner. *Casida v. Roberts*, 337 P.2d 829 (1959). This is the reason that the value of an outgoing partner's interest must be computed as of the date of dissolution rather than the later time of settlement. Conversely, neither would an outgoing partner receive the benefit of post-dissolution appreciation, should such occur.

Another California appellate court recently reiterated the principle that the UPA Sec. 42's "date of dissolution" valuation purposely places future risk on the continuing partner, regardless of who is thus favored at a future settlement. The California court reasoned that a withdrawing partner has no downside risk, given the fact that his interest was fixed as of the date of dissolution, and thus the withdrawing partner should not be entitled to share in the upside potential which involved risk on the part of the remaining partners.

The risk of continuation of the farming business after dissolution, including the risks of land depreciation in a falling real estate market, have been placed by statute on King as a continuing partner. We recognize that the real estate depression of the 1980s has created an inequitable situation for Mr. King, but we are bound by the provisions of Sec. 42. . . .

[King also appeals the recovery by Evans of $192,155 in prejudgment interest on one-half of the land's 1981 value.] The dissolution of the King-Evans partnership occurred in 1981, but Mr. King continued the business until 1988. Under these circumstances, Mr. Evans, the non-continuing partner, has two options. The recovery of his share in the value of the partnership, including the value of land, is one of the two valid alternatives. Because appellees selected that particular method of recovery, they are also entitled to an additional election of either interest or profits as of the date of dissolution. Appellees validly recovered interest as of the date of dissolution.

[Affirmed.]

Where Dissolution Was Caused by a Partner's Wrongful Act. In the second situation, where dissolution has been caused by a partner's wrongful act, somewhat different rules are applied. The wrongfully withdrawing partner is still entitled to receive the value of his or her interest in the partnership, but the value of partnership *goodwill* is not included in computing this value. Further, the damages caused by the wrongful dissolution are deducted from the total amount. If settlement is not made immediately, the rules for compensating the withdrawing partner for the delay are the same as in the first situation.

Notice to Third Parties

Notice of dissolution to third parties is as important when the business is continued as when it is terminated. Those continuing the business must take it upon themselves to provide proper notification (as explained earlier). If they do not, they may be bound by certain later acts of a former partner who has left the business. Also, if those continuing the business reorganize it as a *corporation* rather than as another partnership, they will need to notify their business creditors of the change in status. If this is not done, and new obligations to these creditors are incurred (the creditors still thinking they are dealing with a partnership), the former partners might find themselves personally liable for the new obligations as if they were still partners. If proper notice is given, of course, they will be able to claim the limited liability that is enjoyed by those who are officers, directors, or stockholders in a corporation.

As we observed earlier, it is always best to deal thoroughly with the question of dissolution, continuation of the business, valuation of partners' interests, and similar matters in the original partnership agreement. In the case that follows, the partners had done

so in a comprehensive fashion. Later, several of the partners pulled out of the partnership and tried to get around some of the terms of the partnership agreement relating to dissolution.

If the original partnership agreement does not deal with dissolution and its many implications, or if the partners wish to modify the original agreement's dissolution provisions, they can make a separate agreement at the time of dissolution.[11] This can be a risky proposition, however, because at such a time the partners are less likely to be in an agreeable frame of mind than they were when the partnership was formed. But if an agreement can be reached at this later time, it can resolve the various issues arising from dissolution.

---

[11] Because the adding and subtracting of partners does not automatically dissolve a partnership under RUPA, the drafting of buy-sell agreements becomes especially important and is given special attention under that Act.

CURTIN V. GLAZIER

Supreme Court of New York, Appellate Division, 464 N.Y.S.2d 899 (1983)

Case

In 1968 Louis Glazier and Joseph Jackler formed a partnership, Glazier, Jackler & Company, for the practice of accounting. In 1972 Robert Nelkin was admitted as a partner with a 10 percent interest in the partnership. At that time, Articles of Partnership (the basic partnership agreement) and a Partnership Continuation Agreement were executed by the three partners. Thereafter, these agreements were executed in basically the same form each time a new partner was admitted. Paragraph 15 of the Articles of Partnership provided for removal of a partner without cause by the affirmative vote of partners representing a majority interest. In the event of such removal, the Articles also provided for the purchase by remaining partners of the removed partner's interest in accordance with the terms of the Partnership Continuation Agreement. The Partnership Continuation Agreement contained "Buy-Sell"

provisions specifying the remaining partners' right to buy the removed partner's interest at a price to be computed according to a stated formula. The formula attempted to value the partnership's total value as a going concern, with the removed partner receiving his or her pro rata share of that value. Under the agreed formula in the buy-sell provisions, this value was to be based on the net service receipts of the prior calendar year adjusted to account for future income from accounts receivable and work in progress, as well as for future expenses and accounts payable.

In the event of a dissolution of the partnership and actual termination of the business, the buy-sell provisions of the Continuation Agreement obviously would not apply. Instead, the dissolution provisions of the Articles would apply, which provided for payment to each partner of his or her share of the partnership's surplus. The going concern value of the partnership

could not be taken into account in such a case, and a partner's share necessarily would be less than if the going concern value were included. Basically, these two methods of computing the values of partners' interests dealt with fundamentally different situations. However, the Articles also contemplated that the partners might remove one of the group and then attempt to circumvent the buy-sell provisions by dissolving the partnership and forming a new partnership to assume the business. In other words, the remaining partners might try to disguise a removal and continuation as a dissolution and liquidation, thus depriving the removed partner of his part of the going concern value computed under the buy-sell provisions. To prevent such a result, paragraph 10 of the Articles stated:

The parties hereto are further in accord in their desire that under no circumstances are the obligations of the remaining partners who continue the business of this partnership to be circumvented by said

(continues)

CURTIN V. GLAZIER

(continued from previous page) remaining partners upon legal dissolution of the partnership caused by the termination of any partner by the formation of a "different" partnership, which would nevertheless take over the business of the present partnership without satisfying its obligations.

The same idea was also expressed in paragraph 16, in which the partners had agreed that, in the case of a removal, if the remaining partners chose not to continue the partnership they should not attempt to accomplish a continuation in an indirect manner without giving the removed partner the benefit of the buy-sell provisions.

In May 1982 all of the partners except Thomas Curtin signed a written agreement to dissolve the partnership and distribute their shares of partnership surplus in accordance with the dissolution provisions of the original Articles of Partnership. The buy-sell provisions of the original Continuation Agreement were not used. These partners, minus Curtin, then split into two groups and formed two new partnerships. One of the new partnerships continued to do business at the offices previously used by Glazier, Jackler & Co., and served the same clients. Curtin, plaintiff, filed suit against the other partners, defendants, claiming that there had actually been a continuation of the business, and the buy-sell provisions of the Continuation Agreement should be enforced. The trial court granted summary judgment in favor of Curtin, and the other partners appealed.

Denman, Judge:

Plaintiff contends that defendants' action in dissolving the partnership and forming two different partnerships from which he has been excluded is precisely the situation which the parties sought to avoid by incorporating paragraphs 10 and 16 in the articles. He argues that defendants "constructively removed" him from the partnership and that he is entitled to be compensated for the value of his interest based on the formula governing involuntary removal in the Buy-Sell Provisions. The applicability of that formula is of substantial financial consequence to plaintiff: the value of his interest under the Buy-Sell Provisions is $100,638.78 as opposed to only $26,057.65 under the dissolution agreement.

Defendants [argued] that there was a true dissolution of Glazier, Jackler & Company, CPAs, occasioned by unresolved differences of opinion between defendants Glazier and Jackler; that the partnership was in the process of complete liquidation; and that under the dissolution provision of the articles of partnership, plaintiff was entitled only to the value of his respective share of partnership assets. . . .

Defendants claim that [disputed] issues of fact exist with respect to whether there was a true dissolution of the partnership or whether there has been a continuation of the partnership by the remaining partners, albeit in a different form. [The trial court] treated the issue as one of contract interpretation and construed paragraphs 10 and 16 of the articles of partnership as precluding defendants from continuing to practice accounting under the arrangement described without purchasing plaintiff's interest for the amount determined under the Buy-Sell Provisions. We agree that the issue turns on interpretation of the partnership agreements and that it was properly determined as a matter of law.

It has long been settled that partnership rights and obligations may be fixed by agreement. Where, as here, there is a writing intended to be a complete expression of the parties' intention, the language of the agreement controls. It is not open to speculation and cannot be rewritten. Intention plainly expressed in clear, unambiguous terms raises no question of fact and summary judgment is appropriate. . . . Additionally, the facts upon which [the trial court] relied were undisputed. The dissolution agreement provided for defendants to purchase all of the outstanding accounts receivable and permitted them to purchase assets of the partnership including its computer, Xerox machine and word processor. Defendants did not controvert the fact that the "new" partnership formed by defendants Jackler, Nelkin, Liberman and Ewanyk would continue to maintain its office at the location previously occupied by Glazier, Jackler & Company. Although defendants dispute the fact that partnership debts have been canceled with respect to some of the defendants by offsetting their obligations against their interests in the new partnership, one is hard-pressed to find another explanation as to why defendants Gerber, Jackler, Liberman and Ewanyk, [whose shares of existing partnership debts were] $44,000, $56,000, $56,000 and $97,000, respectively, would agree to dissolution under which their respective distributive shares are estimated to be $21,520, $17,520, $17,520 and $7,720. In any event, the worksheet attached to plaintiff's affidavit . . . clearly provides for cancellation of partnership debts, which is an indirect method of offsetting those obligations against defendants' interests in the newly formed partnerships. Once plaintiff alleged the offsetting of these partnership debts, it was incumbent upon defendant to come forward with [evidence to rebut] that allegation. Inasmuch as defendants failed to do so, interpreting the partnership agreement in light of the undisputed facts and uncontroverted allegations before it, [the trial court] properly found a constructive removal as a matter of law and granted summary judgment. We also agree that an accounting is unnecessary as the figures used to calculate the value of plaintiff's interest under the Buy-Sell Provisions were undisputed.

[The judgment is affirmed. Plaintiff is entitled to receive an interest under the buy-sell provisions that takes into account the going concern value of the business.]

LEGAL FOCUS

International

A *joint venture* is a type of partnership; specifically, the term *partnership* implies a long-term relationship, whereas *joint venture* implies a one-shot, project-oriented venture. The forming of partnerships or joint ventures between American companies has become an increasingly common phenomenon in recent years. Perhaps more importantly, American companies have used joint ventures with foreign companies in order to pierce foreign markets. Indeed, since 1985 the formation of joint ventures between American companies and international co-venturers has increased at an annual rate of almost 30 percent.

Several factors account for this increased use. For example, some host countries restrict direct foreign investment in order to maintain local control and avoid exploitation by foreign powers. A joint venture with a foreign firm often will enable an American firm to evade such restrictions. Also, such a joint venture allows the American firm to make use of the host country firm's existing work force, operations, and marketing structures, as well as its understanding of the local business environment.

Differences in law, linguistics, and culture make the proper formation and operation of such ventures difficult. Increasingly, however, enterprises are concluding that the potential benefits justify the undertaking.

SUMMARY

Termination of a partnership involves dissolution and winding up. Dissolution is the point when the object of the partners changes from continuing the organization in its present form to discontinuing it. Winding up is the actual process of settling partnership affairs after dissolution. The partnership agreement may specify the events that will or will not cause dissolution. In the absence of agreement to the contrary, withdrawal of a partner causes dissolution. Whether such withdrawal also amounts to a breach of the partnership agreement depends on the terms of that agreement.

Dissolution occurs by operation of law in the case of the death of a partner or the bankruptcy of either the partnership or an individual partner. Dissolution can be obtained by court decree when a partner becomes insane or otherwise incapable of performing his or her part of the partnership agreement. Dissolution by court decree also can be obtained when the partnership is unprofitable, or when a partner is found guilty of serious misconduct. Dissolution substantially restricts the authority of a partner to act as an agent for the partnership, but dissolution in and of itself has no effect on existing partnership liabilities.

In the winding up process, claims against the partnership by outside creditors are paid first, followed by repayment of loans from partners and repayment of partners' capital contributions; any remainder is distributed to partners as profits. When the business itself is continued after dissolution, winding up does not involve an asset liquidation but consists primarily of bookkeeping changes and payment to a withdrawing or excluded partner or to the estate of a deceased partner.

KEY TERMS

Dissolution
Winding up
Partnership at will
Liquidating partner (or winding-up partner)

QUESTIONS AND PROBLEMS

1. Plaintiffs Richard and Barbara Logan entered into a partnership agreement with defendant Donald

Logan, Richard's brother. Plaintiffs contributed more than their share of the capital in exchange for Donald's agreeing to locate, purchase, and manage apartment buildings on behalf of the partnership. Plaintiffs hired a financial advisor, Shymko, to represent their interests in the partnership. The partnership prospered under defendant's supervision, but friction between Shymko and defendant led plaintiffs to seek a court-ordered dissolution. Should such a dissolution be granted? Under what circumstances? Discuss. (*Logan v. Logan*, 675 P.2d 1242, Wash.App. 1984.)

2. Owen and Cohen agreed to open and operate a bowling alley as equal partners for a 10-year term. The enterprise was profitable at first, but Cohen soon refused to do any work around the alley, telling Owen that he "had not worked yet in 47 years and did not intend to start now." Cohen told Owen that Owen could do the manual labor while Cohen managed and "wore the dignity." Cohen did his best to humiliate Owen in front of employees and told a friend that "Owen won't be around long." Cohen also wished to put a gambling parlor on the second floor of the building, which Owen opposed. These disagreements caused sufficient problems that the business began to lose money and fell behind on its loan payments. Owen sued for a court-ordered dissolution. Cohen opposed, arguing that a few minor disagreements were not grounds for this drastic remedy. Is Cohen correct? Discuss. (*Owen v. Cohen*, 119 P.2d 713, Cal. 1941.)

3. Father and son engaged in a partnership leasing mini-warehouses. They agreed in writing that (1) 75 percent of the profits would go to the father, and 25 percent to the son; (2) they would share equal management rights; (3) both would devote all their time to the business, working without a salary; (4) the business would continue upon the death or retirement of either; and (5) either partner could retire at the end of any fiscal year and the remaining partner would have the right to purchase the retiring partner's interest or to liquidate. After a year, troubles developed. The son refused to sign notes to borrow money and moved away. The father continued the business, taking out loans and suffering losses, with no help from the son. Later, the son gave notice of retirement, but could not reach an agreement with the father on the purchase of his interest. Should a court order dissolution? Has the son forfeited all interest in

the partnership? Discuss. (*Dobson v. Dobson*, 549 S.W.2d 177, Tex.Civ.App. 1980.)

4. Lyman Stoddard, Sr., his wife Alda, and their son Lyman, Jr. ("Junior") operated a newspaper in partnership. Alda died in 1963; Lyman, Sr. died on February 3, 1964. Junior continued to operate the newspaper. Lyman, Sr.'s executor, his son John, attempted to persuade Junior to wind up the business and to sell the newspaper, but Junior resisted. In 1965, John sued for a liquidation and accounting, and the case was settled on September 6, 1966, with Junior agreeing to be responsible for all debts arising after February 13, 1964. The business was in a weak condition and was soon discontinued. Plaintiff accountants had rendered services to the newspaper for years. They sued the estate of Lyman, Sr. and Alda for bills incurred after their deaths, arguing that these were proper winding up expenses chargeable to the partnership. Is this a viable claim? Discuss. (*King v. Stoddard*, 194 Cal.Rptr. 903, Cal.App. 1972.)

5. Defendants George and Alice Long formed a partnership called Long's Auto Sound. In June 1978, Jensen Sound Laboratories (Jensen) loaned money to the partnership, which incorporated in January 1979, acquiring the partnership's business. For the next two years, Jensen did business with the Longs, always being paid by a check drawn on the corporation, Long's Sound Systems, Inc. Eventually, the business fell behind on payments, and Jensen sued the Longs individually, claiming that it had no knowledge that they had incorporated other than the checks. Should the Longs be personally liable? Discuss. (*Jensen Sound Laboratories v. Long*, 447 N.E. 2d 464, Ill.App. 1983.)

6. Handler and Cauble were equal partners in a retail furniture and appliance store until Cauble's death on May 18, 1971. Handler continued to operate the store successfully, making profits of $40,163.42, but not settling up with Cauble's estate, which finally sued. What is the estate entitled to recover from Handler? Discuss. (*Cauble v. Handler*, 503 S.W.2d 362, Tex.Civ.App. 1973.)

7. Vassallo and Sexauer were equal partners in an enterprise that purchased the stock of a corporation with $10,000 contributed by Vassallo. The remainder of the purchase price of the stock was paid out of profits. Neither partner contributed any other capital. When the partnership was wound up and the

stock sold, it brought $21,474. The trial judge found that the $10,000 capital contribution had been repaid to Vassallo out of these proceeds shortly after sale of the stock. He then held Vassallo's 50 percent share of the $21,474 to be $10,737 and subtracted the $10,000 already paid. He rendered final judgment for Vassallo in the sum of $737. Did the trial judge rule correctly? Discuss. (*Vassallo v. Sexauer,* 177 N.W.2d 470, Mich.App. 1970.)

8. A partnership was created by Atkins, Benson, and Collier, who agreed to share profits equally.

Nothing was agreed as to the sharing of losses. The partners decided to dissolve the partnership after one year of operation, at which time the partnership's books revealed the following: Atkins had loaned the partnership $10,000 and had made a capital contribution of $20,000; Benson had made a $10,000 capital contribution; Collier had made no capital contribution; and the partnership had assets of $80,000 and owed outside creditors $55,000. How should the assets be distributed to the creditors and partners? Discuss.

Chapter 36

Limited Partnerships

*The Nature and History of Limited
Partnerships*

Forming the Limited Partnership

Control

Protecting Limited Partners

*Assignment of an Interest in a
Limited Partnership*

*Dissolution and Winding Up of the
Limited Partnership*

THE NATURE AND HISTORY OF LIMITED PARTNERSHIPS
The Nature of the Limited Partnership

The amount of capital required in a business often is greater than an individual is able to obtain or willing to risk. Meeting these capital requirements is one of the most important reasons for the formation of partnerships. In an ordinary partnership, however, each partner is personally liable for the partnership's obligations. The prospect of unlimited personal liability in the case of a partnership may create a major obstacle to capital raising efforts because many potential investors will be unwilling to accept such a risk.

As we will see in subsequent chapters, the creation of a corporation may provide the necessary means for meeting a firm's capital requirements. In many situations, however, the *limited partnership* is an attractive alternative for this purpose. A limited partnership is a partnership formed by two or more persons *and having at least one general partner and at least one limited partner.* The **general partners** essentially run the business as they would an ordinary partnership. The **limited partners,** on the other hand, are merely investors. Limited partners have little voice in the basic operation of the business, and their liability usually is limited to the amount of their investment in the enterprise.

The limited partnership is a blend of the characteristics of general partnerships and corporations. Like a general partnership, a limited partnership (1) has at least one general partner with general liability, and (2) has "pass through" taxation in that the profits of the enterprise are passed through the partnership and taxed to the individual partners. Like a corporation, a limited partnership (1) is a creature of statute, (2) carries limited liability for its limited partners akin to that enjoyed by corporate shareholders, and (3) features centralized management by the general partner (or partners).

Uses

The combination of limited liability for investors and partnership taxation makes the limited partnership an attractive vehicle for many types of investments, especially those in enterprises that are likely to show losses in their early stages or that show tax losses despite positive cash flows because of deductions such as those for depreciation. These losses are passed on to the partners, who can use them to offset other income. The dreaded "double taxation" of corporations is avoided.[1] Although tax reforms enacted in 1986 reduced the explosive popularity of limited partnership "tax shelters" in such areas as oil and gas development and real estate, limited partnerships have served as a vehicle for investment in thousands of types of businesses, including motion pictures, cattle feedlots, and amusement parks.

Governing Law

The need for uniformity and consistency in the way limited partnerships were treated in the various states led to the drafting of the Uniform Limited Partnership Act (ULPA) in 1916. The ULPA eventually was adopted in 49 states. Because of various shortcomings in the ULPA, the National Conference of Commissioners on Uniform State Laws drafted a Revised Uniform Partnership Act in 1976 (1976 RULPA) and substantially revised it in 1985 (1985 RULPA). Although the strong trend is toward adoption of the 1985 RULPA, the laws of many states are still based, in whole or in part, upon the ULPA or the 1976 RULPA (or both). Furthermore, most existing case law has naturally been decided under the ULPA. Therefore, all three versions of the law will be discussed. Nonetheless, our primary focus will be on the most modern version of limited partnership law—the 1985 RULPA.[2]

FORMING THE LIMITED PARTNERSHIP
Name

The ULPA's only requirement relating to the name of the partnership is that the name generally should

---

[1] Unlike partnerships, which pay no income tax, corporations pay income tax on their corporate earnings. After-tax earnings are then often distributed to shareholders in the form of dividends upon which the shareholders must also pay income tax.

[2] Remember that when an issue is not covered by a state's version of the ULPA or the RULPA, courts refer to the UPA and then to the common law for supplemental guidance.

not contain the surname of a limited partner. The drafters feared that creditors might be misled by the name "Rockefeller and Prentice," believing that they could always tap the rich Rockefeller's personal assets when, in fact, Rockefeller was a limited partner and Prentice, a pauper, the only general partner. The ULPA punishes violation by forfeiture of the limited partner's limited liability status.

Both versions of the RULPA continue this prohibition, but allow use of the corporate name of a corporate general partner or of a name the business had used before admission of that limited partner. Importantly, they also divest of limited liability only those limited partners who "knowingly permit" their names to be used. Even then, such limited partners are liable only to creditors who extend credit to the limited partnership lacking knowledge that the limited partner is not a general partner. As a practical matter, this "reliance" requirement provides substantial shelter to limited partners.

Both versions of the RULPA also provide that the limited partnership name (1) shall contain the words "limited partnership" without abbreviation, (2) may not contain words or phrases misleading as to the partnership's purpose, and (3) may not be the same as or deceptively similar to that of existing limited partnerships or corporations.

Filing Requirements

Forming a limited partnership, like forming a corporation, requires compliance with statutory requirements. The ULPA requires the filing of a **certificate of limited partnership** in either the secretary of state's office or the county clerk's office. The certificate must set forth numerous specified items, including the name of the limited partnership, the general character of its business, the names and addresses of its general and limited partners, the cash contributions made by each and obligations to make future contributions, the right to distributions, and the time or circumstances when the partnership is to be dissolved.

The 1985 version of the RULPA significantly increases the privacy available to limited partners by reducing the amount of information that the certificate must contain. Under the 1985 RULPA, the certificate need contain only the name of the partnership, the name and address of its agent for service of process, the names and business addresses of its general partners, and the latest date upon which the limited partnership is to dissolve. Other items may be disclosed, but need not be.

Consequences of Defective Formation

The ULPA provides that a limited partnership is formed if there is "substantial compliance in good faith" with filing requirements. Both versions of the RULPA contain the "substantial compliance" language, but omit the "good faith" requirement. But what is "substantial compliance"? And what happens if substantial compliance is not achieved? Under the ULPA, some courts took the view that limited partnerships are creatures of statute that must comply with statutory provisions for their existence. If substantial compliance was not achieved, limited partners would forfeit their limited liability status.

Most ULPA courts, however, took the view that the primary purpose of the filing requirement is to give notice to creditors that they are dealing with a limited partnership. Therefore, limited partners would be generally liable only to creditors who were affirmatively misled by the failure to comply substantially with statutory requirements. A third party who did not rely on a misleading filing could not later gain a windfall by discovering a filing defect and suing limited partners who, the third party knew, had claimed limited liability status all along. Both versions of the RULPA adopt this reliance requirement, thereby substantially protecting limited partners. The following case illustrates the majority approach.

FABRY PARTNERSHIP V. CHRISTENSEN

Supreme Court of Nevada, 794 P.2d 719 (1990)

Case

Plaintiff/appellant Fabry Partnership sold the Silver Queen Motel to the Silver Queen Limited Partnership ("Limited Partnership") for $3.185 million on April 24, 1980. Only $500,000 was paid in cash; the balance was secured by a note and deed of trust. On April 1, 1980, four general partners had signed the limited partnership certificate. During April, May, and June 1980, the defendants invested money in the Limited Partnership, signing the signature page of the certificate as limited partners. However, the certificate was not filed with the County Recorder as required by Nevada law until December 29, 1980.

By November 1982, the Limited Partnership fell behind in payments. Fabry foreclosed on the motel, but its sale did not bring enough to satisfy the note. So, Fabry sued defendants for the deficiency, claiming that they were individually liable. The trial court granted summary judgment to defendants, ruling that their liability was limited to the amount they had invested in the limited partnership. Fabry appealed.

Per Curiam:

Fabry contends that the limited partners failed to comply with the statutory requirements for the creation of a limited partnership . . . because no certificate was filed with the Nye County Recorder at the time of the transaction between Fabry and the Limited Partnership. Fabry further argued that the filing of the certificate of limited partnership in December of 1980 cannot relate back to the April transaction. We disagree.

[First, the Nevada version of the ULPA requires only "substantial compliance" with the filing requirements. Second, the Nevada ULPA "provides for a liberal construction of the Act." Finally, the Nevada ULPA] does not specify a time limit for recordation of the required certificate.

Based upon the aforementioned statutes, we are persuaded that the trial court properly entered summary judgment dismissing the limited partners from the action below. There was substantial compliance with the Act by the limited partners and the certificate was filed within a "reasonable time." *See Stowe v. Merrilees,* 44 P.2d 368 (Cal. 1935) (what is reasonable time must be determined by the circumstances of the particular case).

Furthermore, in the instant case, Fabry knew from the outset that the sale of the Silver Queen Motel involved a limited partnership. This knowledge is supported by the note and deed of trust which clearly identified the Silver Queen Limited Partnership as the purchaser of the motel. Additionally, the business relationship between the parties continued without protest for nearly two years after the filing of the certificate and before default was declared. Fabry cannot now circumvent the Limited Partnership in an attempt to impose individual liability on the limited partners.

Affirmed.

False Statements

A limited partner may also forfeit limited liability status by signing a limited partnership certificate containing a statement known to be false. The ULPA provides that anyone who relies on such false statements and thereby suffers a loss is entitled to hold the limited partner individually liable. For example, in *Walraven v. Ramsey,*[3] a limited partner who signed a certificate knowing that certain land he had contributed to the partnership was not worth nearly as much as represented was held personally liable to a subsequent creditor.

Both RULPAs are similar, clearly imposing a reliance requirement on plaintiffs. They allow recovery from any limited partner who knew, and any general partner who knew or should have known, that the statement was false at the time it was signed. The RULPAs also impose liability on general partners who learn of a changed fact that makes the certificate inaccurate but fail to cancel or amend it. Remember that under either version of the RULPA, any liability for false statements extends only to those "who suffer loss by *reliance* on the [false] statement." Also, under the 1985 RULPA, limited partners need not sign the limited partnership certificate or its amendments, thus reducing the risk of limited partner liability for false statements contained therein.

[3] 55 N.W.2d 853 (Mich. 1953).

Renunciation

Persons who *erroneously* believe that they are limited partners can avoid being treated as general partners under Sec. 11 of the ULPA, "provided that on ascertaining the mistake [they] promptly renounce [their] interest in the profits of the business, or other compensation." Both versions of the RULPA are similar, providing that persons who erroneously and in good faith believe that they are limited partners will not have general liability if, upon learning of the mistake, they file a missing certificate or amend an erroneous one or "withdraw from future equity participation in the enterprise" by filing a certificate of withdrawal in the secretary of state's office.

There is a clear reliance requirement here. Sec. 304 of the 1985 RULPA provides that a person erroneously believing that he or she is a limited partner

is liable as a general partner to any third party who transacts business with the enterprise (i) before the person withdraws and an appropriate certificate is filed to show withdrawal, or (ii) before an appropriate certificate is filed to show that he is not a general partner, but in either case *only if the third party actually believed in good faith* that the person was a general partner at the time of the transaction. (Emphasis added.)

The following ULPA case illustrates a proper renunciation.

VOUDOURIS V. WALTER E. HELLER & CO.

Court of Civil Appeals of Texas, 560 S.W.2d 202 (1977)

Nick Voudouris needed credit to start a carpet business. He induced a relative, Johnny Voudouris, to co-sign a promissory note as his capital contribution to the business. A limited partnership agreement was drawn up naming Johnny as a limited partner with a 20 percent interest. However, Nick never filed the limited partnership certificate as required by the Texas ULPA. As soon as Johnny discovered that Nick was not paying the business's bills and had not filed the limited partnership certificate, he secured a list of creditors from Nick and wrote to all of them indicating that he had sold his interest to Nick and was no longer liable on any past or future indebtedness of the business. Johnny did repay the original promissory note that he had co-signed.

When plaintiff Heller's invoices went unpaid, it sued Nick and Johnny Voudouris d/b/a/ Carpet Gallery of Austin, Ltd. Plaintiff claimed that Johnny was generally liable because of Nick's failure to form the limited partnership properly. The *trial court ruled for plaintiff and Johnny appealed.*

Coleman, Chief Justice:

The limited partnership agreement evidences the fact that Johnny Voudouris agreed to become a limited partner . . . . There is no other evidence to contradict these recitations. While the limited partnership agreement never became effective according to its terms because it was never filed with the Secretary of State, it does illuminate the intent of the parties. Whether a particular association is in fact a partnership depends largely on the intention or understanding of the parties involved.

An indication of the interpretation to be given [to Sec. 11 of the ULPA] is found in *United States v. Coson*, 286 F.2d 453 (9th Cir. 1961). The court quoted from *Giles v. Vette*, 263 U.S. 553, where the Supreme Court said:

Section 11 is broad and highly remedial. The existence of a partnership—limited or general—is not essential in order that it shall apply. The language is comprehensive, and covers all cases where one has contributed to the capital of a business conducted by a partnership or person erroneously believing that he is a limited partner. It ought to be con-

strued liberally, and with appropriate regard for the legislative purpose to relieve from the strictness of the earliest statutes and decisions.

In a footnote, the court said:

Of course an intent to become a general partner may be inferred from conduct. In this case no such conduct was shown. Coulson had nothing to do with management of Moulin Rouge, or with its organization. The only conduct shown on his part was consistent solely with his belief that he was dealing with a limited partnership. The ancient rule that failure to comply with statutory provisions renders the association a general partnership, vanished with the enactment of the Uniform Limited Partnership Act. As stated in the Commissioners' note on the act: "Third: The limited partner not being in any sense a principal of the business, failure to comply with the requirements of the act in respect to the certificate, while it may result in the nonformation of an association, does not make him a partner or liable as such. The exact nature of his liability in such cases is set forth in Section 11."

The 9th Circuit went on to hold that it was not important whether the renunciation operated to relieve Coson from liability *ab initio* or whether it operated to compel a finding that Coson was not a general partner at any time, first, because he never had the
(continues)

VOUDOURIS V. WALTER E. HELLER & CO.

(continued from previous page)
necessary intent to join a partnership in that capacity and, second, because his renunciation under Section 11 was fully effective.

Here we find that the limited partnership failed to become effective because it was not filed with the Secretary of State. [However, t]here is testimony from the defendant that immediately upon learning that the partnership agreement had not been filed he renounced the partnership. This testimony is supported by documentary evidence. . . . [Johnny's] testimony that he intended to enter a limited partnership, took no part in the management of the enterprise, and gave up his interest therein soon after his discovery that the partnership agreement had never been filed with the Secretary of State was clear and positive. [Section 11 of the ULPA] prevents the imposition of liability on Johnny Voudouris for the debts of Carpet Gallery of Austin, Ltd.

Reversed.☙

CONTROL

As noted earlier, a theme underlying limited partnership law is that the limited partners renounce the right to control their investment in exchange for limited liability. Therefore, theoretically, they are not to take an active role in *control* of the partnership business. Sec. 7 of the ULPA, for example, provides that "[a] limited partner shall not be liable as a general partner unless, in addition to the exercise of his rights as a limited partner, he takes control of the business." But what activities constitute taking "control"?

Under the ULPA, courts concluded that limited partners exerted the forbidden control when they exercised "decision-making authority that may not be checked or nullified by the general partner."[4] On the other hand, limited partners were not deemed to be taking part in control when they merely served as subordinate employees of the enterprise, participated in the choice of key employees where their decisions were often vetoed by the general partner, or rendered advice to the general partners.

Both versions of the RULPA, especially the 1985 version, go even further to allow limited partners to take an active role in the business of the partnership without forfeiting their limited liability. Sec. 303(b) of the 1985 RULPA provides the following *nonexclusive* list:

A limited partner does not participate in the control of the business . . . solely by doing one or more of the following:

(1) being a contractor for or an agent or employee of the limited partnership or of a general partner or being an officer, director, or shareholder of a general partner that is a corporation;

(2) consulting with and advising a general partner with respect to the business of the limited partnership;

(3) acting as surety for the limited partnership or guaranteeing or assuming one or more specific obligations of the limited partnership;

(4) taking any action required or permitted by law to bring or pursue a derivative action in the right of the limited partnership;

(5) requesting or attending a meeting of the partners;

(6) voting on one or more of the following matters:

(i) the dissolution and winding up of the limited partnership;

(ii) the sale, exchange, lease, mortgage, pledge, or other transfer of all or substantially all of the assets of the limited partnership;

(iii) the incurrence of indebtedness by the limited partnership other than in the ordinary course of business;

(iv) a change in the nature of the business;

(v) the admission or removal of a general partner;

(vi) the admission or removal of a limited partner;

(vii) a transaction involving an actual or potential conflict of interest between a general partner or the limited partners;

(viii) an amendment to the partnership agreement or certificate of limited partnership; or

(ix) matters related to the business of the limited partnership not otherwise enumerated in this subsection (b), which the partnership agreement states in writing may be subject to the approval or disapproval of limited partners;

(7) winding up the limited partnership pursuant to Section 803; or

(8) exercising any right or power permitted to limited partners under this Act and not specifically enumerated in this subsection.

[4]*Gast v. Petsinger*, 323 A.2d 371 (Pa.Super. 1971).

Even if the limited partner's activities do exceed this liberal list of permitted activities so as to constitute an exercise of control, the 1985 RULPA imposes a reliance requirement on any plaintiff seeking to impose general liability. Sec. 303(a) provides that "if the limited partner participates in control of the business, he or she is liable only to persons who transact business with the limited partnership reasonably believing, *based upon the limited partner's conduct,* that the limited partner is a general partner." (Emphasis added.) The 1976 version of RULPA imposed such a reliance requirement *unless* the level of participation by the limited partner was "substantially the same" as that of a general partner.

The following case applies these principles.

MOUNT VERNON SAVINGS & LOAN V. PARTRIDGE ASSOCIATES

U.S. District Court for the District of Maryland, 679 F.Supp. 522 (1987)

Case

MIW Investors sold an apartment project named Partridge Courts to Dreyfuss in 1971 for $4.8 million. During the next ten years Dreyfuss paid very little on the loan, and the note he had signed became an unproductive asset in MIW's portfolio. MIW then made an agreement to repurchase Partridge Courts by assuming the outstanding balance of the $4.8 million note plus certain other consideration. MIW planned to convert Partridge Courts into a condominium complex, and formed a limited partnership, Partridge Associates (Partridge), for that purpose. MIW was one of two limited partners and owned a 50 percent interest in Partridge. Friendship Services, Inc., a subsidiary of Friendship Savings & Loan Association, was the other limited partner and owned a 48 percent interest. American Housing, Inc., was the general partner and owned a 2 percent interest. MIW assigned its rights under the Dreyfuss repurchase agreement to Partridge. MIW also loaned $6 million to Partridge, $4.8 million of which was used by Partridge to buy the original 1971 Dreyfuss note from MIW.

The participants in Partridge put together a number of other complex financial arrangements. In one of these, representatives of Friendship (the other limited partner) and American Housing (the general partner) obtained for Partridge a $2.6 million loan from Mount Vernon Savings. The loan was on terms that were not very favorable to Mount Vernon, apparently because Mount Vernon's president, Russell, needed Friendship's help in an unrelated deal in which Mount Vernon had committed itself to a loan that was above its lending authority under federal regulations.

Several months later Partridge more or less fell apart. Mount Vernon never received any payments on its loan to the limited partnership. Later, Mount Vernon became insolvent and was taken over by the Federal Savings & Loan Insurance Corporation (FSLIC). In behalf of Mount Vernon, FSLIC sued Partridge Associates, American Housing (the general partner), and MIW. FSLIC's claim against MIW was based on the theory that, because MIW had been the driving force behind the organization of Partridge and had played an active role in helping it put together various financial arrangements, MIW should have the same unlimited liability for Partridge's obligations as a general partner. All parties filed motions for summary judgment. The federal district court held that there were disputed issues of fact regarding FSLIC's claims against Partridge and American Housing, so that a trial was necessary for these claims. The court's discussion of FSLIC's claim against MIW follows.

Motz, Judge:

. . . FSLIC contends that MIW has unlimited liability for Partridge Associates' obligations because MIW took part in the control of the business of the partnership. Theoretically, a threshold question is presented whether this case is governed by the "old" Uniform Limited Partnership Act, which was in effect in Maryland when Partridge Associates was formed and which governed Partridge Associates at the time of the occurrence of the events giving rise to this action, or under the "new" Revised Uniform Limited Partnership Act, which became applicable to partnerships formed under the old Act on July 1, 1985. However, this Court believes that insofar as the statutory provisions here involved are concerned, the new Act merely clarifies what was [implicit] in the old. Therefore, this threshold question need not be resolved.

Section 7 of the old Act provided as follows: "A limited partner shall not become liable as a general partner unless, in addition to the exercise of his rights and powers as a limited partner, he takes part in the control of the business." Some courts held that, under this section, a limited partner could not be held liable as a general partner unless he had led the plaintiff to believe that he was a general partner. These cases drew support from an official comment to Section 1 of the old Act that "no public policy requires a person who contributes to the capital of a

(continues)

MOUNT VERNON SAVINGS & LOAN v. PARTRIDGE ASSOCIATES

(*continued from previous page*)

business . . . to become bound for the obligations of the business; provided creditors have no reason to believe that the times their credits were extended that such person was so bound." [A few other courts] held, however, that reliance by the plaintiff was not an element of control under the old Act.

Although undoubtedly in conflict with one another, these two dichotomous lines of authority can be explained by recognizing that the different courts had different focuses. Those which required reliance as an element of control were concentrating upon the external relationship between the plaintiff and the limited partner, and were concerned with the equities arising from that relationship. The [courts looking only at control, and not reliance appear] to have been concerned about the broader public policy of requiring those who choose to accept the benefits of the limited partnership form to preserve the integrity of the partnership's internal relationships. This distinction is made explicit in the new Act. Under Section 303(a) a limited partner who disregards the limited partnership form to such an extent that he becomes substantially the same as a general partner has unlimited liability regardless of a plaintiff's knowledge of his role. At the same time, a limited partner may have unlimited liability for exercising less than a general partner's power if the fact that he acted as more than a limited partner was actually known to the plaintiff.

Against this background it is too facile simply to say that "control" is a question of fact which must be resolved by the fact finder. Such an approach begs the question of what "control" means. Rather, analysis must first proceed by asking whether Mount Vernon had actual knowledge that MIW was acting as something more than a limited partner. FSLIC has presented no evidence to prove that fact. There is no indication whatsoever that Russell was led into the Partridge transaction by knowledge of MIW's participation in the partnership, and Donald Eversoll, the then chairman of the Board of Mount Vernon, has testified that he did not learn of the Partridge transaction until November, 1982, long after Mount Vernon had entered the Memorandum of Understanding and turned over the mortgages. Furthermore, the documents promoting the Partridge venture to which FSLIC points as mentioning MIW's participation clearly identify MIW as a limited partner.

Therefore, it must then be asked, as phrased in the new Act, whether MIW's "participation in the control of . . . [Partridge Associates] . . . was substantially the same as the exercise of the powers of a general partner." As to this question, FSLIC properly maintains that the record is clear that MIW originated the basic concept of Partridge Associates in order to breathe life into a dormant loan. Further, the affidavit of Michael J. Ferraguto, Jr., the president of an American Housing subsidiary which did construction for the Partridge project, does establish that MIW's president attended and participated in periodic operational meetings concerning the progress of the project. However, the law does not confine the role of a limited partner to that of a passive investor, as in a conventional syndication.

To the contrary, as is expressly recognized in the new Act, and as was implicit in the old, a limited partner may be actively involved in the day-to-day operation of the partnership's affairs, provided that he does not have ultimate decision-making responsibility. Thus, the question is not whether MIW provided advice and counsel to Partridge Associates (which, undoubtedly, it did in light of its long association with the Partridge project) but whether it exercised at least an equal voice in making partnership decisions so as, in effect, to be a general partner. On that issue FSLIC has presented no evidence, and summary judgment against it is therefore proper.∽

Note   Had the 1985 version of RULPA been applied in *Mt. Vernon*, once it was decided that Mt. Vernon did not rely on MIW's status as a general partner, whether or not MIW exercised "substantially the same" control as a general partner would have been irrelevant.

Corporate General Partners

Under either the ULPA or RULPA, most jurisdictions allow corporations to be general partners of limited partnerships, or even the sole general partner.[5] This allows a limited partner an opportunity to enjoy limited liability status, yet control the partnership, by forming and controlling a corporate general partner. However, corporate formalities must be observed. In *Gonzalez v. Chalpin*,[6] a limited partner who was the sole shareholder and director of the only general partner was held personally liable for

---

[5]*Western Camps, Inc. v. Riverway Enterprises*, 138 Cal.Rptr. 918 (Cal.App. 1977).

[6]564 N.Y.S.2d 702 (Ct.App. 1990).

partnership obligations because he appeared to be acting on behalf of himself and not in a representative capacity. For example, he signed checks in his own name without indicating in any way that he was acting as an officer or director of a corporation.

Being a General Partner and a Limited Partner at the Same Time

It is possible for a person to be both a general partner and a limited partner at the same time. Such a person is liable to outsiders as a general partner. His or her additional status as a limited partner is important only with respect to the dealings among the partners themselves. Thus, that portion of the person's investment designated as a limited partner contribution is treated as such for assignment, distribution, or other purposes.

PROTECTING LIMITED PARTNERS

Limited partners are essentially *investors*. Generally speaking, they have no right to control the business or to use partnership property or to conduct business on behalf of the partnership. Especially in larger enterprises, limited partners are essentially at the mercy of general partners, *except* for protections provided by statutes and courts.

For example, as noted in the previous section, limited partners may, especially under the RULPA, have substantial input into the operation of the limited partnership without being deemed to participate in control. However, this input must be authorized by the partnership agreement; the ULPA and the RULPA themselves do not confer such rights. Furthermore, in larger limited partnerships, this activity is likely to be limited to voting on various issues.

Limited partners are entitled to inspect and copy partnership records and to receive full disclosure of any information affecting the partnership. Whereas Sec. 10 of the ULPA grants limited partners the same rights as general partners to inspect and copy partnership books, to have those books kept at the principal place of business, to demand full and true information from the general partner at all times, and to demand a formal accounting whenever "circumstances render it just and reasonable," both versions of the RULPA provide even broader inspection rights. Sec. 105 of the 1976 RULPA, for example, specifies in great detail certain records that must be kept at the partnership office and held available for

inspection and copying by partners during ordinary business hours. Because the 1985 RULPA reduces substantially the amount of information that must be contained in the certificate of limited partnership filed with the secretary of state, it necessarily expands the categories of information that must be maintained and left available for inspection under Sec. 105.

Under the ULPA, many courts held that limited partners could file derivative actions on behalf of the limited partnership when the general partners refused to act. Both versions of the RULPA specifically provide that limited partners have the right to sue derivatively.

Perhaps the most important protection granted limited partners is the fiduciary duty imposed on general partners. This fiduciary duty is, if anything, heightened in the limited partnership context because of the vulnerability of limited partners who have no right to participate actively in the control of the partnership. A general partner owes limited partners "the duty of exercising good faith, honesty, and fairness in his dealings with them and the funds of the partnership," and this duty may not be diluted by the partnership agreement.[7]

ASSIGNMENT OF AN INTEREST IN A LIMITED PARTNERSHIP

The rules regarding assignment of a partner's interests in a limited partnership are basically the same as for an ordinary partnership. The interests of both general and limited partners can be assigned, totally or partially, to third parties. An assignment by either a general or limited partner does not terminate the limited partnership.

Such an assignment also does not cause the assignee to become a partner—the assignee merely becomes entitled to receive the assigning partner's share of profits or other asset distributions.

The assignee of a *general partner's* interest can be admitted as a new general partner only by written consent of all the general and limited partners (other than the assigning partner), followed by formal amendment of the certificate. The assignee of a *limited partner's* interest can be admitted as a new limited partner by written consent of all general and limited partners (other than the assigning partner), *or* by a provision in the certificate permitting the

[7]*Labovitz v. Dolan*, 545 N.E.2d 304 (Ill.App. 1989).

PITFALLS FOR PARTNERSHIP INVESTORS MAY LURK IN THAT SEEMINGLY INSIGNIFICANT FINE PRINT

by Ann Monroe

Box 36.1
*The Law
at Work*

Like many investors, Tulsa, Okla., businessman Paul Shindell paid little attention to the fine print when he bought into a horse-breeding limited partnership two years ago.

One of the provisions he overlooked gave investors only 15 days to respond to any changes proposed by Kinderhill Corp., the general partner. Thus, last fall when Kinderhill proposed a reorganization that Mr. Shindell and a number of other investors didn't like, they found themselves struggling against the clock.

Ultimately, Kinderhill agreed to resubmit its proposals with some changes—but only after some investors took the matter to court. Next time, Mr. Shindell vows, "I will read every word, and we'll look every word up in a legal dictionary."

Investors who skip over seemingly insignificant provisions in a limited-partnership agreement can find that they come back and bite. It's "a bit like a pre-nuptial agreement," says Philip Oppenheimer of Oppenheimer & Bigelow, which buys partnership interests from investors. As long as the deal works, it doesn't matter—but if things go bad, it's crucial.

A common provision gives the general partners the right of first refusal when limited partners want to sell their interests. That may sound innocuous, but it can discourage outside buyers, effectively preventing investors from selling to anyone but the general partner.

Because the general partner has the right to equal any bid, outsiders know they can buy the limited partner's interest only by overpaying. Some firms that buy partnership interests on the secondary market won't look at one with that provision.

Another flag is the "overcall provision," which allows the general partner to ask investors to put up more cash. While the fresh contribution generally isn't mandatory, other, accompanying provisions typically reduce the equity of investors who don't contribute. . . .

Fine print can also turn what looks like investor protection into exactly the opposite. Lee L. Errickson, a senior vice president at Robert A. Stanger & Co., a Shrewsbury, N.J., consulting firm, notes that general partners often own interests that don't start paying until the limited partners get a certain amount of cash. But in some cases, he says, the fine print allows the partnership to borrow, if necessary, to keep the general partner's yield on the same level as that of limited partners.

Some other provisions to watch:

The "754 election." Investors want a partnership that's easy to sell. Lawyers, consultants, and others who specialize in partnerships say that a provision allowing a 754 election helps. That's because such an election increases the tax basis of the interest being sold, preventing a buyer from being taxed because of write-offs claimed by the original owner.

Voting. As Mr. Shindell and other investors in the Kinderhill horse-breeding partnership discovered, stopping a general partner's proposals can be difficult. But it can be even harder. Under the Kinderhill voting limitations, it takes a 51% "no" vote of the limited partners to block the general partner; many partnerships require a negative vote by 66%, 75%, or even 90% of the limited partners.

Service limits. Many general partners provide lots of services to the partnerships. But if they aren't strictly limited, says Mr. Oppenheimer, "when you get done all kinds of hands are potentially in the limiteds' pockets."

Limits on business dealings. Strict limits should be placed on the general partner's dealings—sales, leases, loans, and so forth—with the partnership. One agreement Mr. Errickson cites allows the general partner to contribute property to the partnership at higher than its appraised value.

. . . Once investors are in a partnership, [Stan Ross, co-managing partner of Kenneth Leventhal & Co.] advises that they "keep in contact with the general partner—make up reasons to call, if you have to." After all, he warns, "no matter how good the contract is, if he's going to be flaky, you'll suffer."

Source: *Wall Street Journal*, February 13, 1987, p. 23.

assigning limited partner to designate an assignee as a new limited partner. In either case, the certificate must be amended formally to reflect admission of the new limited partner.

The provisions of the RULPA relating to assignments are substantially the same as those of the ULPA. There are two differences, however: (1) under the RULPA, the partnership agreement may specifically make the interests of general or limited partners *nonassignable;* and (2) the RULPA states that a general or limited partner ceases to be a partner upon assignment of *all* of his or her interest, unless the partnership agreement provides for a different result.

DISSOLUTION AND WINDING UP OF THE LIMITED PARTNERSHIP
Dissolution

A limited partnership dissolves at the time or under the circumstances specified in the certificate. It also can be dissolved at any time by written agreement of all the general and limited partners, followed by formal cancellation of the certificate.

Under both the ULPA and the RULPA, the death, insanity, or withdrawal of a *general partner* causes dissolution of the limited partnership *unless* continuation of the business is provided for (1) in the certificate or (2) by written consent of all remaining general and limited partners. To continue the business as a limited partnership in any event, there must remain at least one general partner and one limited partner. To meet this requirement, new partners may be admitted.

Under the ULPA, a general partner's bankruptcy or involvement in some other insolvency proceeding is not treated as an automatic withdrawal from the limited partnership. The RULPA does, however, treat such an event as a withdrawal unless the certificate or unanimous written agreement of the partners provides otherwise.

The death, insanity, withdrawal, or bankruptcy of a *limited partner* does not cause dissolution of the limited partnership. (This statement assumes, of course, that at least one limited partner remains.) When a limited partner dies, the executor or administrator of the person's estate exercises control over the interest

in the limited partnership. In the case of insanity, such control is exercised by the limited partner's guardian. The interest of a bankrupt limited partner is controlled by the trustee in bankruptcy.

Winding Up

As is true of an ordinary partnership, a limited partnership continues to exist after dissolution for so long as necessary to wind up its affairs. Control of the winding up process is in the hands of the general partners. Their authority to act in behalf of the partnership is restricted to those activities necessary to bring the business to an end. Limited partners may supervise the process, however, if no general partners remain. Moreover, any general or limited partner, as well as the representative or assignee of any general or limited partner, may obtain court supervision of the winding up process.

After winding up, the assets of the limited partnership are liquidated and distributed. Under both the ULPA and RULPA, the claims of creditors must be satisfied first. The claims of *outside* creditors obviously are included in this priority group. The ULPA also includes the claims of limited partners who are creditors, but the claims of general partners who have lent money to the business are given a lower priority. The RULPA includes in the top priority the claims of both general and limited partners who are creditors of the partnership.

The certificate may specify the order in which the partners receive a return of their capital contributions and an allocation of any surplus. If not so specified, Section 23 of the ULPA or Section 804 of the RULPA governs the distribution. The most important difference between the asset distribution rules of the two statutes is that the ULPA gives priority to limited partners while the RULPA treats general and limited partners essentially the same.

A well-conceived and well-drafted agreement is as important to the participants in a limited partnership as it is in the case of a regular partnership. When beginning such a venture, the parties must realize that things may go wrong, and provide for such contingencies in the agreement. The most difficult distribution problems arise when the limited partnership loses money.

RETZKE V. LARSON

Court of Appeals of Arizona, 803 P.2d 439 (1990)

Howard (general partner) and Larson (limited partner) formed a limited partnership (Great Salt River) that owned and operated a mobile home park. Larson contributed $5250 to the partnership and later loaned it $18,350. Plaintiff Retzke sued the limited partnership and Howard for $63,734, claiming that he had loaned money to Howard for use by the partnership and had not been repaid. Soon after suit was filed, the mobile home park property was sold and Larson received $20,000 from the proceeds of the sale.

Great Salt River did not answer the complaint and Retzke received a default judgment of $78,126.54. Retzke then initiated garnishment proceedings against Larson, claiming that Larson was indebted to him for assets of the limited partnership. The trial court found that Retzke might be able to sue Larson, the limited partnership, or both for wrongful distribution under the Arizona version of the 1976 RULPA, but concluded he would have to file a separate suit to do so. Retzke appealed.

Gerber, Judge:

[The judge first held that Retzke could pursue his claim for garnishment in this suit. The judge then turned to the merits of Retzke's claim.]

Larson contends that he was entitled to receive the $20,000.00 from the sale of the mobile home park because it was repayment of the principal and interest on the loans he made to the partnership. Retzke argues that it was wrong for Larson to receive this money when the partnership was without other funds to pay Retzke's claim.

Under [Sec. 107 of the 1975 RULPA], a partner lending money to the limited partnership has the same rights and obligations with respect to the money loaned as do other creditors who are not partners, unless the partnership agreement or other applicable law provides to the contrary.

An example of "other applicable law" referred to in [Sec. 107] is found in [Sec. 607 of the 1975 RULPA], which provides:

A partner may not receive a distribution from a limited partnership to the extent that, after giving effect to the distribution, all liabilities of the limited partnership, other than liabilities to partners on account of their partnership interests, exceed the fair value of the partnership assets.

This provision parallels Sec. 44-1008 of the Uniform Fraudulent Conveyance Act which provides:

Every conveyance of partnership property and every partnership obligation incurred when the partnership is or will be thereby rendered insolvent, is fraudulent as to partnership creditors, if the conveyance is made or obligation is incurred:

1. To a partner, whether with or without a promise by him to pay partnership debts, or

2. To a person not a partner without fair consideration to the partnership as distinguished from consideration to the individual partners.

Under either of these provisions, a partner is not entitled to repayment of a loan if that repayment renders the partnership insolvent. A partner who is also a creditor is not entitled to preferential treatment. The rules governing limited partnerships clearly state otherwise. [Sec. 804 of the 1976 RULPA] provides that upon the winding up of a limited partnership, assets shall be first distributed in satisfaction of liabilities of the limited partnership to all creditors including partners who are creditors.

The burden of proof in the trial court is on [Retzke] to show a garnishable debt. Here, [Retzke] met his burden because [Larson's] own pleadings in the trial court admitted that [he] received $20,000.00 as the proceeds of the sale of the partnership's real property. Garnishee Larson has not denied that the limited partnership had no other assets beyond the mobile home park. When the park was sold and the sale proceeds were distributed to the partners, Retzke's claim for money loaned to the partnership was already in existence, although not yet reduced to judgment. The distribution of the sale proceeds rendered the partnership insolvent and therefore violated [Sec. 607 of the 1976 RULPA] as well as [the Uniform Fraudulent Conveyance Act].

The matter is remanded to the trial court for determining Retzke's pro rata share of the $20,000.00 in assets of the limited partnership wrongfully distributed to Larson.⚖

SUMMARY

A limited partnership is a partnership consisting of one or more general partners and one or more limited partners. The general partners have the same au-

thority and liability as partners in an ordinary partnership. Limited partners, on the other hand, are merely investors who have little voice in the basic operation of the business and whose liability is limited to their investment in the partnership. Today, the law of limited partnerships is found primarily in the Revised Uniform Limited Partnership Act (RULPA) and in the original Uniform Limited Partnership Act (ULPA).

Because limited liability can be created only by statute, creation of a limited partnership involves compliance with statutory requirements in addition to a partnership agreement. The most important statutory requirement is the filing of a certificate of limited partnership. The capital requirements of a limited partnership are met in basically the same way as in an ordinary partnership, by contributions from partners. Although the general partners normally have the power to manage the partnership, they must have the written consent of all general and limited partners, or express authorization in the certificate, to perform certain actions that fundamentally affect the business. Limited partners may lose their limited liability if they participate in the control of the business. Some courts have found the limited partner liable if such control has been exercised, regardless of whether the particular creditor has relied on the limited partner's actions. Most courts, however, have found the limited partner liable only if the evidence indicates that the limited partner's conduct probably caused the creditor to view the limited partner as a general partner. The RULPA specifies certain "safe harbors" in which particular types of conduct by a limited partner definitely will not cause a limited partner to be personally liable for partnership debts.

A limited partnership is dissolved by the death, insanity, or withdrawal of a general partner unless continuation is provided for by the certificate or written consent of all general and limited partners. The winding up of a limited partnership is very similar to that of an ordinary partnership. Outside creditors have first priority in the distribution of partnership assets. Remaining partnership assets are distributed as specified in the certificate of limited partnership; if the certificate does not so specify, the ULPA gives limited partners priority over general partners but the RULPA treats general and limited partners essentially the same.

KEY TERMS
General partner
Limited partner
Certificate of limited partnership

QUESTIONS AND PROBLEMS

1. An agreement for the creation of a limited partnership was signed in November. It named Dimentia Corporation and its president, Wilson, as general partners. Franklin and several others were named as limited partners. In December the limited partnership, acting through Wilson and Dimentia Corp., contracted to buy land from Rigg. The next April the limited partnership defaulted on the contractual obligation. It was not until shortly after this default that a certificate was filed to bring the limited partnership legally into existence. The limited partners then formally renounced (disclaimed) their interests in the limited partnership. Rigg sued and obtained a judgment against Dimentia Corp. and Wilson. Almost two years later, after discovering that the certificate had been filed late, Rigg also sued Franklin and the other limited partners to hold them personally liable. Should the limited partners be personally liable in this situation? Discuss. (*Franklin v. Rigg*, 237 S.E.2d 526, Ga. Ct. App. 1977.)

2. McRea owned an automobile dealership, and Rowlett operated an automobile repair business. The manufacturer for whom McRea was a dealer insisted that McRea have a repair shop as part of the dealership. As a result, McRea and Rowlett agreed to form a limited partnership with McRea as sole general partner and Rowlett as sole limited partner. Rowlett moved his equipment to the dealership premises, and also contributed cash to the limited partnership's capital. Rowlett served as foreman of the repair shop, while McRea continued to run the dealership as a whole. Although Rowlett supervised the repair shop, he was under the ultimate direction and control of McRea. McRea had to approve all extensions of credit in the repair shop, except in the case of customers personally known by Rowlett. If a credit customer known and approved by Rowlett did not pay, however, Rowlett had to make up the loss. The partnership's bank account was under the complete control of McRea, and he was the only person authorized to draw checks on the account. Some time later, the business ran into financial difficulties. Silvola, a creditor of the dealership, was unable to collect his claim from McRea or the partnership. Consequently, Silvola sued Rowlett on the debt, claiming that Rowlett's activities had made him liable as a general partner. Should Rowlett be

held liable? Discuss. (*Silvola v. Rowlett*, 272 P.2d 287, Colo. Sup. Ct. 1954.)

3. Diversified Properties was a limited partnership engaged in buying, selling, and managing real estate. The limited partnership consisted of Weil as the sole general partner and a group of limited partners. About a year after its formation the business ran into severe cash flow problems and was on the verge of collapse. The limited partners had several meetings and hired two new employees to take over management of the business from Weil. During this time all of the limited partners also were personally involved in negotiations with creditors concerning the refinancing of Diversified's obligations. Weil was still formally the sole general partner, and creditors still recognized him as such. However, he no longer received a salary or occupied the partnership office, and exercised little authority. He subsequently went to work for another real estate firm. Weil then filed a lawsuit in which he sought a declaratory judgment that the limited partners had become liable as general partners because of their activities. Is Weil's contention correct? Discuss. (*Weil v. Diversified Properties*, 319 F.Supp. 778, D.D.C. 1970.)

4. Hacienda Farms, Limited, was organized as a limited partnership to engage in vegetable farming, with de Escamilla as the general partner and Russell and Andrews as limited partners. Most of Hacienda's vegetable crops were marketed through a separate produce company controlled by Andrews. Decisions as to which crops to plant were always made jointly by the three partners. Sometimes de Escamilla disagreed with Russell and Andrews on planting decisions; when this happened, de Escamilla was overruled by the limited partners. Checks could be drawn on the partnership account only with the signatures of at least two partners. Most of the checks were actually signed by Russell and Andrews, although a few were signed by de Escamilla and one of the limited partners. The firm went bankrupt, and Holzman, the trustee in bankruptcy, filed suit for the purpose of determining whether Russell and Andrews had become personally liable for partnership debts. Were the limited partners liable as general partners? Discuss. (*Holzman v. de Escamilla*, 195 P.2d 833, Cal. Dist. Ct. App. 1948.)

5. Professional football player Alzado induced champion boxer Muhammed Ali into fighting an exhibition match with him. Ali conditioned his agree-

ment upon Alzado putting up a $250,000 letter of credit guaranteeing compensation. Alzado formed Combat Promotions, Inc. (CPI) to promote the bout, but had difficulty raising the $250,000. As a publicity move, Blinder-Robinson (B-R), a stock brokerage firm, agreed to put up the money. CPI and B-R formed a limited partnership, Combat Associates, with CPI as the general partner and B-R as the limited partner. The match was a financial disaster for all but Ali. In subsequent litigation, Alzado claimed that B-R was liable as a general partner because it had taken an active role in promotion of the bout. Evidence showed that B-R made no investment, accounting, or other financial decisions for the limited partnership. However, B-R used its Denver office as a ticket outlet, gave two parties to promote the match, and provided a meeting room for many of Combat Associates' meetings. B-R's owner personally appeared on a television talk show and gave television interviews to promote the match. Did B-R engage in control so as to forfeit its limited liability? (*Alzado v. Blinder-Robinson*, 752 P.2d 544, Colo. 1988.)

6. GPI, a corporation, was the only general partner in USACafes Ltd. (Cafes), a limited partnership. Sam and Charles owned 100 percent of GPI and 47 percent of Cafes as limited partners. Sam and Charles were also directors of GPI, and in that capacity proposed and pushed through a sale of Cafe's assets to Mesta. Plaintiffs, other limited partners in Cafes, sued Sam and Charles, claiming that Mesta bought at a bargain price because it made side payments, forgave loans, and otherwise benefitted GPI's directors. Plaintiffs claimed that the GPI directors, including Sam and Charles, breached a fiduciary duty owed to them. Defendants claimed that they owed a fiduciary duty only to GPI and not to Cafes or its limited partners. Is this claim accurate? (*In re USACafes Limited Partnership Litigation*, 600 A.2d 43, Del.Ch. 1991.)

7. For many years the general partners of Mt. Hood Meadows Ltd., a limited partnership, voted to distribute only 50 percent of the limited partners' taxable profits and to retain the rest in order to reinvest it in the business. Limited partners sued to compel the general partners to distribute to them all the profits allocated to them under the provisions of the partnership agreement. The agreement gave broad discretion to the general partners in making allocation decisions, but plaintiffs claimed that by retaining earnings in this fashion, the general partners

effectively required them to make additional capital contributions against their will. Is this a valid claim? (*Brooke v. Mt. Hood Meadows, Oreg., Ltd.*, 725 P.2d 925, Or.App. 1986.)

8. Plaintiffs invested as limited partners in a limited partnership sponsored by Dolan, the general partner. In 1985 and 1986, the partnership reported earnings of over $34 million and $18 million, respectively. The limited partners were required to report their pro rata share of income on their personal income tax returns for those years. Although the partnership had the cash available to fund these obligations, Dolan chose to make only a nominal distribution of cash to the limited partners. For example, in 1985, each partner had to report taxable income of $415,331 per unit, whereas Dolan distributed only $12,000 per unit. Accordingly, in both years plaintiffs had to dig deeply into their personal funds to pay their tax obligations. In late November of 1986, a company controlled by Dolan offered to buy out the limited partners' interests for approximately two-thirds of their book value. More than 90 percent of the plaintiffs accepted the offer, but they immediately sued Dolan for breach of fiduciary duty. Will plaintiffs win? (*Labovitz v. Dolan*, 545 N.E.2d 304, Ill.App. 1989.)

PART V

CORPORATIONS AND SECURITIES REGULATION

AFTER OUR DISCUSSION OF the principal–agent relationship in Part IV, we studied two closely related forms of business organization, the partnership and the limited partnership. We dealt with those kinds of organizations at that point because agency relationships serve as their basic building blocks. We now turn our attention to the form of organization that is the most important in terms of its overall contribution to business activity in this country—the corporation. Chapter 37 examines the nature and formation of corporations, and Chapter 38 discusses the role of corporate shareholders. Chapter 39 looks at the roles and responsibilities of corporate managers, and Chapter 40 deals with mergers and other major structural changes in corporations. Chapter 41 surveys the law of Securities Regulation, a subject that could logically be studied in Part VII along with other topics in Government Regulation of Business, but that is examined at this juncture because it places important limitations on the fundamental capital-raising activities of corporations. Although the federal and state laws that regulate securities can also apply to individuals and to organizations other than corporations, the heaviest impact is on corporations. Finally, Chapter 42 deals with the legal responsibilities of the certified public accountant (CPA). This subject is discussed here because most of a CPA's legal responsibilities arise from his or her relationship with corporations. ⚖

Chapter 37

Corporations
Nature and Formation

The Nature and History of Corporations

Preincorporation Activities

The Incorporation Process

The Corporation as a Legal Entity

Financing the Corporation

THE NATURE AND HISTORY OF CORPORATIONS
The Nature of the Corporation

Suppose for a moment that you have been given the authority to create a new organizational form for conducting a business enterprise. You probably would want to create an artificial being with a legally recognized identity of its own, so that it could make contracts, own property, sue and be sued, and do all the other things necessary for running a business. This artificial being, having existence only on paper but nevertheless recognized by law as a "person," could have perpetual existence. It would be completely unfettered by the limitations of a flesh-and-blood existence. There would be no worries about death and its effect upon the continuing vitality of the business. True, it would have to act through human agents, but these agents could be replaced with no effect on the artificial being.

You probably would want the ownership of this new organizational form to rest in the hands of investors who would have no management responsibilities. In this way, an investor's interest in the business could be sold to another investor with no effect on the operation of the enterprise. And management would be centralized, thus improving the efficiency of the business.

Investors could be attracted by making their ownership interests freely transferable and by shielding them from liability for business debts. The possibilities for raising capital would be practically endless. New shares in the ownership of the business could be issued as needed for capital requirements, and if the business had been successful, investors would buy them.

But despite the worthiness of your creation, it possesses one flaw: it is not new. It has already been conceived of and put into practice. *It is called a corporation.*

Sources of American Corporation Law

During the first few decades after the Revolutionary War, corporations in the United States were formed only by special acts of state legislatures. Fear of large accumulations of capital led legislatures to limit the formation of corporations. In the 1800s, however, states gradually enacted "general incorporation" laws under which persons could form corporations by following specified procedures and without special legislative permission.

All states have corporate codes, and the law of corporations is generally the same from state to state. However, this body of law is not as uniform nationally as, say, partnership law. The Model Business Corporation Act (MBCA), drafted by the American Bar Association in 1969, has provided a basic guideline for the modern corporation statutes of many states. More recently, the Revised Model Business Corporation Act (RMBCA) has had substantial influence as well. Because the RMBCA represents the most modern comprehensive statement of corporation law, its provisions will be the focus of our descriptions of corporation law.

Despite our focus on the RMBCA, note that the state of Delaware enacted an extremely flexible corporation statute at the end of the nineteenth century, when most state laws were quite inflexible. Because Delaware law permitted corporate management more alternatives in structuring and operating the enterprise, and also because Delaware courts developed a relatively well-settled body of judicial precedent at an early time, many companies incorporated in Delaware even though their principal places of business were elsewhere. Delaware has maintained its preeminent position; today more than half of the "Fortune 500" companies are incorporated in Delaware, and several states have modeled their corporate codes after Delaware's. Therefore, in areas where Delaware law has special influence—including mergers and acquisitions, derivative litigation, and the liability of officers and directors for poor business judgments—Delaware law will receive our special attention.

Classification of Corporations
Domestic and Foreign Corporations

A corporation that has been incorporated in a particular state is referred to as a **domestic corporation** in that particular state. One that has been incorporated in some other state or in another nation is called a **foreign corporation.**

Private and Government Corporations

A corporation formed by private parties is a **private corporation.** Almost all corporations, including those formed for business and nonprofit purposes, fall within this category. The **government corporation,** on the other hand, is one formed by the state or federal government. Incorporated cities and towns are examples of government corporations at the state level; the Tennessee Valley Authority and the United States Postal Service are examples at the federal level. (Government corporations are sometimes referred to as *public* corporations, but it is best to avoid this term because it tends to be confused with the *publicly held* corporation, discussed below.)

Business and Nonprofit Corporations

Private corporations are either of the business or the nonprofit variety. A **business corporation** is simply one that is formed to engage in a business activity for profit. A **nonprofit corporation** (sometimes called a *not-for-profit* corporation) is one formed for social, charitable, religious, or other nonprofit purposes.

Publicly Held and Close Corporations

A **publicly held corporation** is one whose shares of stock are offered for sale to the public. (Sometimes such a corporation is called a *public* corporation, a term that should be avoided because of potential confusion with the government corporation.) A **close corporation** is one whose shares of stock are not offered for sale to the public, but instead are owned by either a single shareholder or a small, closely knit group of shareholders. The shareholders themselves are usually active in managing the business of a close corporation. (The close corporation is sometimes referred to by a variety of other names, such as a *closed, closely held, one-person,* or *family corporation.*)

Professional Corporations

Until the early 1960s, state corporation laws usually did not allow persons to form corporations for the purpose of engaging in the practice of a profession such as medicine or law. Since that time, however, most states have enacted statutes permitting one or a group of professionals to form a **professional corporation.** Probably the most important result of these statutes is that physicians, attorneys, and members of other professions can now receive several federal tax advantages (such as tax-deductible insurance or pension plans) as "employees" of the corporation that they could not receive as sole proprietors or as members of a partnership.

Subchapter S Corporations

Corporations are entities generally taxed under Subchapter C of the Internal Revenue Code. Because the corporation and its shareholders have separate identities, the distribution of the corporation's post-tax income to shareholders as "dividends" is again taxed, this time as personal income to the individuals receiving it. Thus, *double taxation* can result from the separate identities of the corporation and its owners. On the other hand, certain small corporations may elect to be taxed as partnerships in some circumstances in order to avoid this double taxation. The *Subchapter S corporation* pays no taxes; its income is passed through to its shareholders who pay personal income tax on it.

Subchapter S of the Internal Revenue Code allows such a choice to be made by corporations meeting several requirements, including: (1) 35 or fewer shareholders; (2) unanimous shareholder agreement to the election, (3) a single class of shares, and (4) no nonresident alien shareholders.

Limited Liability Companies

A new development that should be mentioned, even though it is an *un*incorporated association, is the *limited liability company* (LLC). In an attempt to foster a favorable business climate, several states have authorized the formation of LLCs (and several more states are presently considering doing so). An LLC is like a Subchapter S corporation in that it offers both the limited liability of a corporation and, if formed properly, the "pass through" taxation of a partnership. However, the states authorizing LLCs loosen the standards for qualification. For example, they typically impose no limitation as to the number of shareholders, do not ban nonresident alien ownership, and allow multiple classes of shares (See Box 37.1).

PREINCORPORATION ACTIVITIES
Promoters' Activities

For various reasons the word *promoter* sometimes elicits unfavorable reactions from people. The negative connotations of the word are generally unwarranted, though, because promoters usually serve a legitimate and socially useful function. In essence, a **promoter** is the motivating force behind the creation

PARTNERSHIP, CORPORATION AREN'T ONLY WAYS TO START OUT

by Jeffrey Tannenbaum

Box 37.1
The Law
at Work

Robert H. Kane's start-up enterprise is a mouthful: Octagon Communications Limited Liability Co.

The name doesn't exactly have a ring to it. It's rather awkward on stationery and business cards. It even fails to convey the company's intended business: investments in rural cellular-telephone companies.

But loud and clear, the name conveys something else: a new form of ownership that Mr. Kane and his seven partners expect will serve them well. Their enterprise—to be based in Denver—is neither a traditional partnership nor a traditional corporation. Rather, under Colorado law, it is a "limited liability company," or LLC.

Mr. Kane and his partners are expecting to enjoy the best of both worlds: the tax advantages of a partnership and the legal safeguards of a corporation. Yet they face none of the drawbacks associated with forming a so-called subchapter-S corporation,

which also is taxed much like a partnership. For example, S corporations can't have corporate shareholders, but LLCs can. "If some corporation ever wants to offer me jillions of dollars for my interest, I'll be able to sell it," Mr. Kane says.

Not yet worth jillions, Octagon doesn't even have an office. But it is in the forefront of a movement toward the LLC as a form of ownership for small U.S. businesses and joint ventures. "Interest in the LLC concept is growing remarkably fast," says John R. Maxfield, a Denver lawyer who helped write the LLC law there.

Fast, anyway, by the slow-paced standards of lawmaking. In 1977, Wyoming became the first state to authorize LLCs, but it took until 1988 for the Internal Revenue Service to confirm that the new Wyoming entities would be treated as partnerships for federal tax purposes.

One appeal of LLCs is that, as with partnerships, any income flows through untaxed to the individual owners. Such owners don't avoid personal taxes, but they do avoid corporate

taxes. Regular corporations face higher maximum taxes in the first place. And if the corporations pay dividends, owners are taxed again.

Of course, S corporations avoid double taxation—but they don't enjoy all the advantages of partnerships when it comes to juggling income and deductions. For example, the 20%-owner of an S corporation normally must pay taxes on 20% of any income. By contrast, partnership members are free to divvy up any income and tax liability as they see fit. Thus, equal partners might change the allocations of profit or loss year to year to fit their individual tax needs. LLCs offer the same freedom.

With LLCs, as with regular corporations, only the company's assets, and not the owners' personal assets, are at risk in business-related lawsuits. In partnerships, so-called limited partners enjoy such protection, but general partners don't. And limited partners face restrictions on how active they can be in the business. LLCs are designed to protect all partners while imposing no limits on their activity.

Source: *Wall Street Journal*, May 14, 1991, p. B2.

of the corporation. He or she recognizes the business opportunity, analyzes it to determine its economic feasibility, and brings together the necessary resources and personnel.

In planning for the proposed corporation, the promoter often finds it necessary to employ the services of attorneys, accountants, architects, or other professionals. He or she may also have to borrow money or contract for the purchase of real estate, equipment, patent rights, or other property. And in some circumstances the promoter may find it desirable prior to incorporation to contract with persons to serve as officers and employees upon formation of the corporation. Several legal questions can arise in connection with such transactions. For example: Is the promoter

personally liable on these contracts? Is the corporation liable once it is formed? What if the corporation is never actually formed? The approach taken by the courts is summarized as follows.

Where Corporation Is Formed and Contract Adopted

If the proposed corporation *is* later formed, it can adopt the promoter's contract and become a party to it. The corporation is not bound unless it adopts the transaction. Assuming that the corporation is formed and does adopt the contract, the question remains whether the promoter is still liable on the contract. If the promoter made the contract in his or her own name, with no reference to the proposed corporation, the promoter obviously continues to be liable unless released by the third party. On the other hand, if the promoter made the contract in the name of, or with reference to, the proposed corporation, there is a split of opinion among the various states: courts in several states have held that the promoter is automatically discharged from responsibility under the contract when the corporation adopts it, but in a majority of states courts have ruled that the promoter continues to be liable unless released by the third party.

Where Corporation Is Not Formed or Contract Not Adopted

If the proposed corporation is not ever formed, or if it is formed but does not adopt the contract, the promoter usually is personally liable on the contract. Under basic principles of contract law, however, the promoter is not liable if (1) the contract expressly provided that the promoter would be discharged from responsibility if the corporation was not formed or did not adopt the contract; (2) the third party later releases the promoter from liability; or (3) the court concludes that the promoter and the third party had originally intended only an informal agreement and that neither of them had intended to be bound unless the corporation ultimately was formed and became a party to the agreement.

Many times two or more promoters are involved. Prior to the actual creation of the corporation these promoters are viewed by the law as being engaged in a *joint venture.* As a result, they maintain the same kind of fiduciary relationship that exists among partners. In their dealings with one another they must exercise the highest standards of honesty and openness.

Once the corporation is formed, the promoters also owe the same type of fiduciary responsibility to the corporation itself and to all interested parties. Complete disclosure must be made, for example, to the board of directors and to all investors (shareholders). Promoters are not allowed to make secret profits on the promotional scheme.

In the two cases that follow, the courts deal with two difficult questions arising from the activities of corporate promoters. The first case illustrates that promoters are generally presumed to be liable on the contracts they sign on behalf of the corporation-to-be, especially if the corporation never comes into existence. Only clear evidence of an agreement to the contrary will absolve the promoter of liability. The second case addresses the question of when a corporation that does come into existence will be liable for contracts signed on its behalf by promoters before it came into existence.

COOPERS & LYBRAND V. FOX

Court of Appeals of Colorado, 758 P.2d 683 (1988)

On November 8, 1981, defendant Fox met with a representative of plaintiff Coopers & Lybrand (Coopers), to request a tax opinion and other accounting services. Fox informed Coopers that he was acting on behalf of a corporation he was in the process of forming, G. Fox & Partners, Inc. Coopers accepted the engagement knowing that the corporation was not yet in existence. G. Fox and Partners, Inc. was incorporated on December 4, 1981. Coopers finished its work in mid-December and billed "Mr. Garry R. [sic] Fox, Fox and Partners, Inc." in the amount of $10,827. When neither the corporation nor Fox individually paid the bill, Coopers sued Fox for breach

of contract.

The trial court held that Fox was not individually liable, presumably because Coopers had failed to prove the existence of any agreement on his part regarding payment. Coopers appealed.

Kelly, Chief Judge:

Coopers asserts that the trial court erred in finding that Fox was under no obligation to pay Coopers' fee in the absence of an agreement that he would be personally liable. We agree.

As a general rule, promoters are personally liable for the contracts they make, though made on behalf of a corporation to be formed. The well-recognized exception to the general rule of promoter liability is that if the

contracting party knows the corporation is not in existence but nevertheless agrees to look solely to the corporation and not to the promoter for payment, then the promoter incurs no personal liability. In the absence of an express agreement, the existence of an agreement to release the promoter from liability may be shown by circumstances making it reasonably certain that the parties intended to and did enter into the agreement.

Here, the trial court found there was *no* agreement, either express or implied, regarding Fox's liability. Thus, in the absence of an agreement releasing him from liability, Fox is liable.

Coopers also contends that the trial court erred in ruling, in effect, that Coopers had the burden of proving any agreement regarding Fox's personal

(continues)

COOPERS & LYBRAND V. FOX

(*continued from previous page*)
liability for payment of the fee. We agree.

Release of the promoter depends on the intent of the parties. As the proponent of an alleged agreement to release the promoter from liability, the promoter has the burden of proving the release agreement.

Fox seeks to bring himself within the exception to the general rule of promoter liability. However, as the proponent of the exception, he must bear the burden of proving the existence of the alleged agreement releasing him from liability. The trial court found that there was no agreement regarding Fox's liability. Thus, Fox failed to sustain his burden of proof, and the trial court erred in granting judgment in his favor. ⚖

STOLMEIER V. BECK

Supreme Court of Nebraska, 441 N.W.2d 888 (1989)

In early 1983, Beck phoned his sister-in-law and her husband, the Stolmeiers (plaintiffs), representing that he had recently begun a business investing in real estate. Beck asserted that he was the day-to-day manager of properties owned by a group of investors who bought delapidated properties and fixed them up. Beck assured the Stolmeiers that if they agreed to invest, their investment would double every six months. Plaintiffs invested $20,000 through checks payable to Beck that were deposited in an Omaha bank and applied to real estate either owned or controlled by defendant individuals, partnerships, and corporations, including Group V Management and Development, Inc. All defendants knew that plaintiff's money had been invested through Beck and was being used to finance the enterprise.

When none of the Stolmeiers' funds were returned, they sued Beck as the promoter and the corporations and partnerships he formed that used plaintiffs' money. The trial court found that, among others, Group V Management and Development was liable to plaintiffs, and that defendant appealed.

White, Justice:

In the absence of a subsequent adoption by the corporation, a contract made by a promoter is not binding on the corporation. However, a contract made by a promoter for a corporation may be adopted by the corporation after it comes into existence. This adoption may be by express corporate action, or it may be established by implication from the conduct of the corporation. Particularly pertinent to this action, where the corporation voluntarily accepts the benefits accruing to it from the engagement of its promoters, after full knowledge and having the opportunity to decline the same, it is to be regarded as adopting the contract.

In the present case, Group V Management and Development, through its officers, knew that Beck had obtained money from the Stolmeiers for use by the corporation in its business of renovating older buildings for investment purposes. The Stolmeiers adduced evidence that the money invested by them was placed in an account at First Westside Bank in Omaha and then was used by the corporation in operating its business. Through these actions, the corporation adopted the burdens and benefits of the contract made by Beck on behalf of the corporation, and is now properly held resonsible for the breach of the agreement made by Beck on behalf of the corporation.

[Affirmed.] ⚖

THE INCORPORATION PROCESS

The word **incorporation** refers to the procedural mechanics of forming a corporation. Although the details of these procedures differ from state to state, substantial similarity exists with respect to their basic outline.

Articles of Incorporation

The first step in the formative process is preparation of **articles of incorporation,** a legal document that should be prepared by an attorney and that must be signed by the **incorporators.** The incorporators are those individuals who *technically* apply to the state for incorporation. They must be adults, but they need not have any interest in the business enterprise itself. Often they are the persons actually forming the corporation, but they can be completely disinterested parties (such as secretaries in the office of the attorney who is preparing the articles).

The following is a summary of those matters which generally should be included in the articles of incorporation.

1. *The name of the corporation:* This name cannot be the same as, or deceptively similar to, that of any other corporation legally doing business within the state.

2. *The duration of the corporation:* In most states this can be perpetual. And in the few states that do place limitations on the number of years a corporation can exist, it is usually only a formality to renew the corporation's existence on expiration of the stated time period.

3. *The purpose or purposes for which the corporation is organized:* While most states allow the formation of a business corporation for any lawful purpose, a few still prohibit corporations from practicing medicine, law, or other professions. Also, many states do not allow banks, loan companies, insurance companies, public utilities, or railroads to be formed under the general incorporation statutes. These types of businesses are often required to incorporate under other, specialized statutes.

4. *The financial structure of the corporation:* Detailed information must usually be included about the methods by which the corporation will raise capital needed for its operations.

5. *Provisions for regulating the internal affairs of the corporation:* Examples of such provisions are the location of shareholders' meetings, quorum and voting requirements at shareholders' and board of directors' meetings, removal of directors, and filling director vacancies.

6. *The address of the corporation's registered office and the name of its registered agent at this address:* The registered office is simply the corporation's official office in the state, and the registered agent is its official representative. The purpose of requiring a corporation to have a registered office and registered agent is to insure that there will be an easily identifiable place and person for the receipt by the corporation of summonses, subpoenas, and other legal documents.

7. *Information relating to the first board of directors of the corporation:* The board of directors is the group of individuals who manage the affairs of the corporation. The number of directors constituting the initial board must be indicated in the articles. Additionally, the articles usually must include the names and addresses of those individuals who will serve as directors until the first annual shareholders' meeting or until another board of directors is otherwise selected.

8. *The name and address of each incorporator.*

Certificate of Incorporation

The articles of incorporation must be filed with the designated state official (usually the secretary of state). If they are in conformance with all legal requirements and if all required fees are paid, the state official will issue a **certificate of incorporation** (sometimes called a **charter**). This certificate represents the permission given by the state to conduct business in the corporate form. The corporation traditionally comes into existence when the certificate of incorporation is issued. After issuance, the certificate and an attached copy of the articles of incorporation are returned to the incorporators.

Initial Organization

Under the laws of most states, the incorporators must hold an *organizational meeting* after issuance of the charter. In states where the first board of directors is not named in the articles of incorporation, the incorporators elect the directors at this meeting. In all states, authorization will usually be given to the board of directors to issue shares of stock. Perhaps the most important purpose of the meeting, however, is to adopt bylaws.

Bylaws are the rules or "private laws" that regulate and govern the actions and affairs of the corporation. Although they ordinarily are *not* filed with a state official, the bylaws must not conflict in any way with the provisions of the articles of incorporation. The relationship between the articles and the bylaws is analogous to the relationship between the constitution and the statutes of a state. A corporation's bylaws sometimes amount to only a brief statement of rules for internal management of the corporation. Often, however, the bylaws are extremely detailed, sometimes even including a restatement of applicable statutes as well as provisions from the articles of incorporation. As an example of the type of details frequently included in the bylaws, many provisions relate to the specifics of conducting directors' and shareholders' meetings.

The board of directors also holds an organizational meeting, at which time it transacts whatever business is necessary to launch the operations of the enterprise. In some states the incorporators do *not* hold an organizational meeting, and in these states the board of directors adopts bylaws and performs the other tasks described earlier as functions of the incorpora-

tors. In the states in which incorporators *do* meet, the directors at their initial meeting usually approve all actions taken by the incorporators. In addition, the agenda of the first directors' meeting includes such matters as approval of the corporate seal, election of corporate officers, adoption of preincorporation agreements made by the promoters, selection of a bank for depositing corporate funds, and other pertinent items of business. Figure 37.1 outlines the steps in forming the corporation.

FIGURE 37.1

Basic Steps in Forming a Corporation

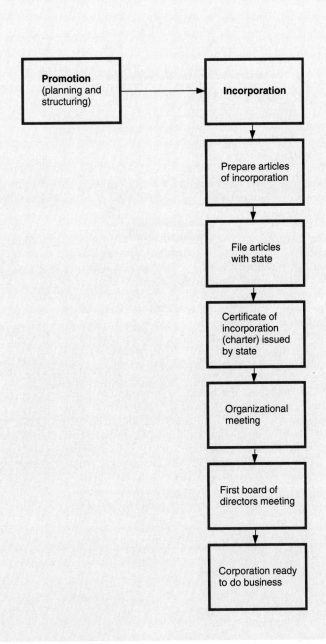

THE CORPORATION AS A LEGAL ENTITY
Consequences of Entity Status

Once formed, the corporation is a legal entity—an artificial being or person. It can own property, make contracts, sue and be sued in court, and generally perform all legal functions that an individual can perform.

The individuals who own the corporation (the shareholders) and those who manage it (the officers and directors) generally are not personally liable for its debts. Conversely, the corporation usually is not liable for the personal debts of those who own and manage it. The corporation even enjoys some of the same constitutional rights as individuals,[1] but not all.

The legal identity of the corporation is thus distinct from the identities of its owners and managers. The following famous case starkly illustrates the firmly established notion that a corporation is an entity separate and distinct from its owners.

---

[1]For example, corporations enjoy freedom of speech, the right to due process and equal protection under the laws, the right not to be tried twice for the same offense (*double jeopardy*), and the right to be secure from unreasonable searches and seizures. On the other hand, corporations do not enjoy freedom of religion or the privilege against self-incrimination.

PEOPLE'S PLEASURE PARK CO. V. ROHLEDER

Supreme Court of Virginia, 61 S.E. 794 (1908)

Case

Appellee Rohleder and appellant Butts bought lots from owners who had platted 125 acres with the intention of establishing a "settlement of white persons." The purchase contracts contained a "restrictive covenent" providing that "[t]he title to this land is never to vest in a person or persons of African descent." (Fortunately, such racially discriminatory covenants have long since been declared unconstitutional, but they were enforceable in 1908.)

Butts later sold his land to Fulton, who on the same day conveyed it to appellant People's Pleasure Park Company, Inc. All owners of this corporation were "colored persons," and the land was bought for the express purpose of converting it into a "park or place of amusement for colored persons."

Appellee sued to annul the conveyance as inconsistent with the restrictive covenant. Appellants appealed from a lower court ruling that in order to have the sale sustained, they must pay appellee the market value of the three lots she purchased.

Cardwell, Justice:

[Plaintiff's complaint] fails to allege facts showing a violation of the restriction, and should have been dismissed. Such a conveyance, by no rule of construction, vests the title to the property conveyed in "a person or persons of African descent." Although a copy of the charter of the [corporation] is filed as an exhibit with the [complaint] and made a part thereof, and which sets out that the object for which the corporation is formed is "to establish and develop a pleasure park for the amusement of colored people," a contemplated sale of the property to "a person or persons of African descent" is not even alleged, but only a contemplated use of the property as a place of amusement for colored persons, which the restriction relied on neither expressly nor by implication, prohibits.

"A corporation is an artificial person like the state. It is a distinct existence—an existence separate from that of its stockholders and directors"—1 Cook on Corp. (4th ed.).

Prof. Rudolph Sohm, in his *Institutes of Roman Law,* pp. 104–106, says:

In Roman law the property of the corporation is the sole property of the collective whole; and the debts of a corporation are the sole debts of the collective whole. . . . It represents a kind of ideal private person, an independent subject capable of holding property, totally distinct from all previous existing persons, including its own members. It possesses, as such, rights and liabilities of its own. It leads its own life, as it were, quite unaffected by any change of members. It stands apart as a separate subject or proprietary capacity, and, in contemplation of law, as a stranger to its own members. The collective whole, as such, can hold property. Its property, therefore, is, as far as its members are concerned, another's property, its debts another's debts.

Reversed.

Piercing the Corporate Veil

As noted previously, the general rule is that a corporation possesses an identity separate from its owners, who enjoy limited liability. For example, suppose that Beta Corporation becomes insolvent and goes into bankruptcy. Under most circumstances, the shareholders of Beta are not personally liable to Beta's creditors for its debts. These shareholders, whether they are individuals or other corporations, will lose their investments in Beta because their stock will be worthless, but Beta's creditors normally can reach only Beta's corporate assets to satisfy their claims.

In unusual situations, however, courts may ignore the separate status of the corporation and its owners. This disregard of the corporate entity in order to impose liability for a corporation's obligations on its shareholders is often referred to as **piercing the corporate veil.** Naturally, the difficult matter is determining under what circumstances the corporate veil should be pierced. When the corporation does not have sufficient assets to pay its liabilities, should the loss remain on the third-party creditors or be shifted to the corporation's shareholders? This is essentially a loss-allocation question. On the one hand, we wish to encourage persons to do business by allowing them to enjoy limited liability. On the other hand, we do not wish to allow the corporate entity to be used "to defeat public convenience, to justify wrong, protect fraud, or defend crime."[2]

[2]*U.S. v. Milwaukee Refrig. Transit Co.,* 142 F.2d 247 (C.C.E.D. Wis. 1905).

The case law in this area is inconsistent, but generally the courts attempt to do what is "fair" under the circumstances, without subverting the basic policies underlying creation of the corporate entity. Courts will never pierce the corporate veil of a large, publicly held corporation such as Chrysler or IBM, but small, closely held corporations are fair game for piercing, especially if their owners (1) fail to follow corporate formalities such as holding shareholders' and directors' meetings, (2) commingle personal and corporate funds, (3) begin the business with assets that are insufficient in light of the risks faced, (4) bleed assets out of the corporation for personal use, or (5) use the corporation as a mere shell or conduit to operate a single venture or some particular aspect of their individual businesses. Many of these factors go to the same point: the corporation should have an existence and purpose separate from that of its owners and should not merely be their "alter ego."

In a breach of contract case, the biggest issue will probably be whether the defendant shareholders defrauded the plaintiff. Absent fraud, courts are reluctant to pierce the corporate veil in contract cases because third parties generally have every opportunity to protect themselves by refusing to do business with inadequately capitalized corporations. In tort cases, where plaintiffs typically do not have an opportunity to choose their tortfeasors, inadequate capitalization of the corporation is perhaps the most important factor in determining whether to pierce.

The following case discusses some of the more important principles in this area.

CASTLEBERRY V. BRANSCUM

Supreme Court of Texas, 721 S.W.2d 270 (1987)

Plaintiff Castleberry and defendants Branscum and Byboth were equal shareholders in Texan Transfer, Inc. (TTI). TTI delivered new furniture for Freed's Furniture Co. Branscum also operated Elite Moving as a sole proprietorship; this company moved household goods, sometimes using TTI's trucks and employees. A dis- *pute arose when Castleberry learned of Elite Moving's existence, and the three men agreed that TTI would buy Castleberry's stock for $42,000. One thousand dollars was to be paid right away and the rest in later installments. Branscum and Byboth were not personally obligated to pay. TTI soon had financial trouble and never paid more than the original $1000. TTI's assets were sold to pay corporate liabilities, and thereafter* *Branscum and Byboth formed Custom Carriers, Inc., which obtained the contract to deliver for Freed's Furniture Co. that had been held by TTI. Castleberry sued TTI and Branscum and Byboth personally. The trial court pierced the corporate veil in accordance with a jury finding, imposing liability on Branscum and Byboth personally. The appellate court reversed. Castleberry appealed.*

(continues)

CASTLEBERRY V. BRANSCUM

(continued from previous page)

Spears, Justice:

The corporate form normally insulates shareholders, officers, and directors from liability for corporate obligations; but when these individuals abuse the corporate privilege, courts will disregard the corporate fiction and hold them individually liable.

We disregard the corporate fiction, even though corporate formalities have been observed and corporate and individual property have been kept separately, when the corporate form has been used as part of a basically unfair device to achieve an inequitable result. Specifically, we disregard the corporate fiction:

(1) when the fiction is used as a means of perpetuating fraud;

(2) where a corporation is organized and operated as a mere tool or business conduit of another corporation;

(3) where the corporate fiction is resorted to as a means of evading an existing legal obligation;

(4) where the corporate fiction is employed to achieve or perpetrate monopoly;

(5) where the corporate fiction is used to circumvent a statute; and

(6) where the corporate fiction is relied upon as a protection of crime or to justify wrong.

The basis used here to disregard the corporate fiction, a sham to perpetrate a fraud, . . . is sometimes confused with intentional fraud; however, "[n]either fraud nor an intent to defraud need be shown as a prerequisite to disregarding the corporate entity; it is sufficient if recognizing the separate corporate existence would bring about an inequitable result." *Fletcher,* Cyclopedia Corporations Sec. 41.30 at 30 (Supp. 1985).

Because disregarding the corporate fiction is an equitable doctrine, Texas takes a flexible fact-specific approach focusing on equity. [In this case, Castleberry testified that after he found out about Brascum's formation of Elite Moving, Branscum stated that he would see to it that Castleberry never got anything out of Texan Transfer.] Castleberry testified that after the buy-out, Elite Moving began to take over more and more of Texan Transfer's business. Texan Transfer supposedly loaned Elite Moving its trucks, but Branscum admitted that the companies had no written rental agreement and that no mileage records were kept to show how much Elite Moving owed Texan Transfer. Branscum also conceded that Texan Transfer could do Elite Moving's work.

For the eighteen months prior to the buy-out agreement, Texas Transfer had a net income of $65,479. After the agreement in 1981 Texan Transfer's annual net income fell to $2,814 and in 1982 it lost more than $16,000. In contrast, the newly formed Elite Moving declared an income in 1982 of $195,765.

Sometimes after Castleberry filed suit in April 1982, Branscum told Sue Campbell, then his wife, that Castleberry "would never get a dime, that he would file bankruptcy before Castleberry got any money out of the company . . ." At trial, Byboth conceded that Custom Carriers was formed because of this lawsuit.

We hold that this is some evidence of a sham to perpetrate a fraud. A jury could find that Byboth and Branscum manipulated a closely-held corporation, Texan Transfer, and formed competing businesses to ensure that Castleberry did not get paid. Castleberry had little choice but to sell his shares back to the corporation.

In determining if there is an abuse of corporate privilege, courts must look through the form of complex transactions to the substance. The variety of shams is infinite, but many fit this case's pattern: a closely held corporation owes unwanted obligations; it siphons off corporate revenues, sells off much of the corporate assets, or does other acts to hinder the on-going business and its ability to pay off its debts; a new business then starts up that is basically a continuation of the old business with many of the same shareholders, officers and directors.

[The court of appeals' judgment is reversed; the trial court judgment is affirmed.] ⚖

FINANCING THE CORPORATION

After incorporation, the corporation must obtain the funds necessary to launch and initially operate the business. When the business has been in operation for a substantial period of time, a wider range of financing alternatives are available, including retained earnings, short-term borrowing, and accounts receivable financing. At the beginning, however, fewer alternatives exist.

The principal method of initially financing a corporation is by the issuance of **securities,** which are sold to investors. The board of directors usually authorizes their issuance during its initial organizational meeting. The most common types are equity securities and debt securities.

Equity securities are usually referred to as **shares of capital stock,** or simply as *shares.* Each share represents an interest in the ownership of the corporation. Therefore, the investors who purchase them (the **shareholders** or **stockholders**) are the owners of the corporation. (More is said about the various types of shares in Chapter 38.)

Debt securities are usually referred to as **bonds.** Corporate bonds do not represent ownership interests in the corporation, but are loans to the corporation from the investors who purchase them. The relationship between the investor who purchases bonds and the corporation which issues them is that of creditor and debtor.

Consideration for Securities

Shares may generally be issued (sold by the corporation for the first time) only in exchange for proper consideration as gauged by both quantity and quality tests.

In terms of quantity, in most states shares must be issued for no less than the sale price established by the board of directors and for no less than their *par value* (an arbitrary face amount established by the board).[3] The RMBCA eliminates the concept of par

[3]Virtually every state now allows issuance of *low par* stock (with par value established at a dollar or perhaps even less) and *no par* stock in order to avoid any question that shares were issued for consideration below par value.

value and provides simply that shares be issued for at least the sale price established by the board. Shares issued for less than the required amounts are *watered stock.* Under either the traditional majority approach or the RMBCA, a shareholder who pays inadequate consideration is usually liable to pay the full amount to the corporation or its creditors. Directors may also be held liable for allowing shares to be issued for inadequate consideration.

In terms of quality, the traditional majority approach provides that shares may be issued only for money *paid,* property *received,* or labor *performed.* In other words, shares may not be issued in exchange for mere promises to pay money, convey property, or perform services. The RMBCA alters this approach, authorizing shares to be issued "for consideration consisting of any tangible or intangible property or benefit to the corporation, including cash, promissory notes, services performed, contracts for services to be performed, or other securities of the corporation." The RMBCA relies on the good faith of the board of directors to ensure that corporate shares are not simply given away.

The following case applies the traditional approach to reach a result that would be easily embraced under the RMBCA.

LYNCH V. ASSET PROTECTION ASSOCIATES, INC.

Supreme Court of Alabama, 505 So.2d 344 (1987)

Case

Lynch owned and operated a sole proprietorship, Asset Protection Associates, which provided guard and security services to businesses on a contract basis. His business had operated for six months and contracted with several businesses when Lynch joined with Heflin and Kelly to incorporate the business. The corporation (Asset) was formed with $50,000 of authorized capital and 50,000 shares of $1 par value common stock authorized to be issued. Lynch paid for 3000 shares and Kelly and Heflin each paid for 2000. In addition, according to Lynch and

Heflin, Lynch was issued another 25,000 shares in exchange for the transfer of the business and contracts of his sole proprietorship. Kelly testified that it was his understanding that Lynch would pay $25,000 for the shares.

Current shareholders of Asset brought suit to "invalidate" Lynch's 25,000 shares as improperly issued for illicit consideration. The trial court declared the shares null and void. Lynch appealed.

Houston, Justice:

[The Alabama Constitution] provides, in pertinent part, that "No corporation

shall issue stock or bonds except for money, labor done, or property actually received; and all fictitious increase of stock or indebtedness shall be void. . . ."

Further, Tit. 10, Sec. 21(36), 1940 Code . . . , provided:

The consideration for the issuance of shares *may be paid,* in whole or in part, in money, *in other property,* tangible or intangible, or in labor or services actually performed for the corporation. When payment of the consideration for which shares are to be issued shall have been received by the corporation, such shares shall be deemed to be fully paid and nonassessable.

Neither promissory notes nor future services shall constitute payment or part payment, for shares of a corporation.

(continues)

LYNCH V. ASSET PROTECTION ASSOCIATES, INC.

(continued from previous page)

In the absence of fraud in the transaction, the judgment of the board of directors or the stockholders, as the case may be, as to the value of consideration received for shares shall be conclusive. (Emphasis added.)

The trial court . . . ruled that the requirements [set forth above] "cannot be satisfied by the transfer of an executory contract which requires the performance of services in futuro." We disagree and for the following reasons hold that the contracts transferred by Lynch, in exchange for the issuance of the disputed stock, were "valuable contract rights," and, as such, could constitute valid consideration for the payment of stock.

Pursuant to Sec. 21(36), a corporation could issue paid-up shares of stock in exchange for property, tangible or intangible. This principle, that stock may be paid for in property, comprehends various kinds of property, including "valuable contract rights." *Sterling Varnish Co. v. Sonom Co.*, 133 So.2d 624 (Miss. 1961). The term "property" is not used in its broad sense, which includes anything susceptible of ownership, but is limited to that which may readily be applied to the debts of the corporation. . . .

We are of the opinion that the contracts which Lynch transferred, in exchange for the issuance of the disputed stock, were "valuable contract rights," and as such could have constituted consideration for the payment of shares of stock. Heflin testified:

As of the moment we incorporated, from the time we changed the—the operation changed from Mr. Lynch as a sole proprietor to the time Asset Protection Associates [Inc.] was established, there were ongoing contracts, guards in place, uniforms on them, salaries being paid, contracts being negotiated, payments being received for services provided which in that amount of time shifted from James Lynch, proprietor, to Asset Protection.

As referred to in Heflin's testimony, the right to continue Lynch's ongoing negotiations for additional security contracts, as well as his labor expended in establishing, organizing, and staffing his ongoing security business, accrued to the benefit of Asset at the date of its incorporation.

Furthermore, in response to a question concerning the three incorporators' valuation of the contracts, Heflin testified that "we talked in terms of maybe $100,000–$200,000 of value plus the intangibles such as goodwill and the ongoing effort that [Lynch] was making." Clearly, the general service contracts, as transferred by Lynch, were not mere promises to perform future personal services, but, instead, were valuable contract rights, from which income was expected to and did occur without regard to the rendition of future services by Lynch. We are of the opinion that a corporation may treat as payment for stock any property which it is authorized to own and which is necessary to its business, provided that the property is taken in good faith and at a fair valuation. Therefore, we hold that the business and contracts of Lynch's proprietorship could satisfy the applicable constitutional and statutory requirements as previously set out in this opinion.

[Reversed and remanded for a factual determination regarding whether the 25,000 shares were issued in exchange for the contracts (which would be legal), as testified by Heflin or Lynch, or were issued in exchange for Lynch's promise to pay $25,000, as testified by Kelly.] ◇◇

Registration of Securities

When a corporation issues securities to meet either its initial capital requirements or its later financial needs, it usually must comply with the securities laws of those states in which they are offered for sale.[4] The laws of some states simply prohibit fraud in the sale of securities. In many states, however, the issue of securities must be *registered* with the state agency empowered to administer the law. To register, the corporation must supply extremely detailed financial and other information about itself. Some state agencies have broad discretionary powers to pass judgment on the merits of a particular issue of securities— even to forbid such issuance—and penalties for failing to register with them can be quite severe.

Many issues of securities, such as those sold in interstate commerce or through the mails, must also be registered under the **Securities Act of 1933,** a federal law. Here again, detailed financial and other information must be supplied. This information must be given both to the appropriate federal agency—the **Securities and Exchange Commission (SEC)**— and to the persons to whom the securities are offered for sale. The SEC does not pass judgment on the merits of a particular issue of securities but attempts only to insure full and complete disclosure of relevant information. The underlying rationale is that the

---

[4]These state laws are often referred to as *blue-sky laws,* because they are largely antifraud statutes intended to prevent the sale of worthless securities ("pieces of the blue sky").

light of publicity will serve to deter misconduct in the sale of securities. Under the Securities Act of 1933, failing to register or willfully making false statements in the registration is punishable by a fine of up to $10,000 and/or imprisonment of up to five years. Civil actions for damages can also be brought by injured private parties.

The purpose of both state and federal securities laws is protection of the investing public. Although compliance with these laws is costly and time-consuming, failure to comply can be even more costly. What is more, the protection afforded by these laws benefits not only the investors but also the corporations themselves by encouraging investment in corporate enterprises.

Securities laws are discussed in depth in Chapter 41, "Securities Regulation."

SUMMARY

The concept of the corporation is of ancient origin, dating to the twenty-first century B.C. in Babylonian law. The famous overseas trading companies of the sixteenth and seventeenth centuries became the models for modern corporations. American corporation law today is found primarily in state statutes and the judicial interpretations of those statutes, although federal securities regulation law also plays an important role.

The most important characteristic of the corporation is its status as a legal entity with an identity separate from that of its owners and managers. In most situations the separateness of the corporate identity is recognized, but in unusual circumstances courts will disregard the corporate entity, or "pierce the corporate veil," in order to prevent the separateness of the corporation from being used as a mere tool to perpetrate fraud.

The promoter serves as the motivating force for the identification of a business opportunity, the marshalling of resources to exploit the opportunity, and the formation of the corporation as an operating format. The corporation, once formed, is liable for the promoter's preincorporation contracts only if the corporation adopts them. The promoter usually is liable on such contracts even if the corporation is later formed and adopts them. When two or more promoters act together, they are viewed prior to formation of the corporation as participants in a joint venture, and owe fiduciary duties to each other. A promoter also owes fiduciary duties to the corporation and its shareholders when the corporation is formed.

The actual procedure of forming a corporation is referred to as *incorporation,* and must strictly follow the statutory requirements of the state in which it is registered. The most important means for obtaining a corporation's necessary financing is the issuance of securities. The two most important types of securities are equity securities and debt securities. Equity securities are commonly called shares of capital stock. The purchasers of these securities, shareholders, are the owners of the corporation. Debt securities are commonly called bonds. The purchasers of these securities are creditors rather than owners of the corporation. New issues of securities usually must be registered with federal and state government agencies.

KEY TERMS

Domestic corporation
Foreign corporation
Private corporation
Government corporation
Business corporation
Nonprofit corporation
Publicly held corporation
Close corporation
Professional corporation
Promoter
Incorporation
Articles of incorporation
Incorporators
Certificate of incorporation (charter)
Bylaws
Piercing the corporate veil
Securities
Equity securities
Shares of capital stock
Shareholders (stockholders)
Debt securities
Bonds
Securities Act of 1933
Securities and Exchange Commission (SEC)

QUESTIONS AND PROBLEMS

1. Goodman contracted to perform renovation of apartments for their owner DDS, with the work to be completed by October 15, 1979. While the renovation contract was being negotiated, Goodman told

the managing partner of DDS that he was going to form a corporation to limit his liability. Goodman signed the contract as "Building Design & Development, Inc. (In Formation), John A. Goodman, President." DDS wrote out its first progress payment check to "Building Design & Dev., Inc.—John Goodman." Goodman struck out his name and endorsed it as president of the company, instructing DDS to make out all future checks to the corporation, which DDS did. Goodman did not actually form the corporation until November 1979. The work was late and of poor quality, and litigation began. The contract contained an arbitration clause, and the question arose whether Goodman was personally bound by the contract. Was he? (*Goodman v. Darden, Doman & Stafford Associates,* 670 P.2d 648, Wash. 1983.)

2. The Craigs needed $100,000 to start a retail business. Lacking credit, they formed a corporation and sought investors. They asked four friends to invest $12,000 each, with the understanding that the Craigs would borrow $52,000 to buy their shares, completing the $100,000 capitalization. Instead, the Craigs, with the knowledge of the First National Bank, invested only $3000 of their own money and had the corporation borrow the remaining $49,000. Not knowing about this corporate debt, three of the investors were later induced to sign guaranties covering notes of the corporation. When the business went broke, the bank sought to enforce the guaranties as covering the $49,000 loan. Should the bank prevail? (*First National Bank of Council Bluffs v. One Craig Place, Ltd.,* 303 N.W.2d 688, Iowa 1981.)

3. Progress Tailoring Co. advertised that it manufactured garments, although these garments actually were manufactured by its wholly owned subsidiary. The Federal Trade Commission instituted proceedings in which it sought to stop such advertising on the ground that it was deceptive. Did the FTC prevail? Discuss. (*Progress Tailoring Co. v. FTC,* 153 F.2d 103, 1946.)

4. A federal statute prohibited railroads from giving rebates to those using the railroad for shipping goods. X Corp. shipped substantial quantities of goods by rail. The officers and principal shareholders of X Corp. formed a separate corporation for the purpose of obtaining what were, in actuality, rebates. Did X Corp. violate the antirebate law by receiving rebates through the separate corporation? Explain.

5. Defendant financed a corporation to be operated primarily by his son. He advanced the $1000 statutory minimum capital, and received 98 of the 100 authorized shares. He later transferred most of his shares to his son. He took no role in control of the corporation, but loaned it money from time to time. Plaintiff sued defendant on a corporate contract, seeking to pierce the corporate veil in order to hold defendant personally liable for a debt the corporation could not pay. Should the corporate veil be pierced? (*Texas Industries, Inc. v. Dupuy & Dupuy Development, Inc.,* 227 So.2d 265, La.App. 1969.)

6. Plaintiffs' daughter drowned in a swimming pool operated by Seminole Hot Springs Corporation. When a $10,000 judgment against the corporation went unsatisfied, plaintiffs sought to hold defendant Cavaney, who was one of three incorporators and shareholders, and who also was the corporation's attorney, personally liable. Plaintiffs sought to pierce the corporate veil, in part, because the corporation had been started with virtually no assets. Cavaney argued that he could not be held personally liable because he had become a shareholder and incorporator simply as an "accommodation" to his clients, the other two owners of Seminole. Should the corporate veil be pierced to allow recovery from Cavaney? (*Minton v. Cavaney,* 364 P.2d 473, Cal. 1961.)

7. Thomas was president of Jon-T Chemicals, Inc. ("Chemicals"), which incorporated Jon-T Farms ("Farms") as a wholly owned subsidiary engaged in farming and land-leasing. Farms had $10,000 in capital. It shared officers, directors, offices, accountants, and more with Chemicals. Chemicals made ongoing, informal advances whenever Farms needed money; eventually the advances totaled $7.1 million. Thomas (acting through a partnership) and Farms were criminally convicted of submitting more than $2 million worth of fraudulent applications for agricultural subsidies. Because of the insolvency of Thomas and Farms, the government sued to recover from Chemicals the amount paid. Should the corporate veil of Farms be pierced to allow the government to reach Chemicals's assets? (*U.S. v. Jon-T Chemicals, Inc.,* 768 F.2d 686, 5th Cir. 1985.)

8. Terry and Carl Prickett formed Data General, Inc. to handle data processing needs of banks, feedlots, and other general businesses. As the only directors, they issued 45,000 shares of no par stock to

Terry and 5000 to Carl. When the corporation became bankrupt, its creditors challenged the issuance of these shares. Terry and Carl pointed out that they had done a lot of research and traveling to put together computers, software, and techniques that they had transferred to the corporation as consideration for the shares. Are the creditors right in claiming that this consideration was too "unsubstantial and shadowy" in nature to be valid? (*Prickett v. Allen*, 475 S.W.2d 308, Tex.Civ.App. 1971.)

Chapter 38

Corporations
The Shareholders' Role

Shareholder Voting Rights

Other Basic Shareholder Rights

Shareholder Liabilities

Shareholders in the Close Corporation

Management of Close Corporations

ONE TRADITIONAL WAY to view the corporate management structure is the *inverted pyramid.* At the top of the pyramid are the shareholders, owners of the enterprise. As owners, they are theoretically the ultimate source of authority for corporate operations. Just below the shareholders are the directors, elected by the shareholders to make the broad policy decisions regarding the corporation's direction. At the bottom are the officers, chosen by the directors and invested with the authority to run the day-to-day operations of the business. Figure 38.1 reflects such a view.

This traditional view has much validity. However, if we are speaking of large, publicly held corporations, it may exaggerate the influence of both shareholders and directors. In such corporations, many believe that the officers not only make the day-to-day decisions regarding the corporation's operations, but also control the agenda at directors' meetings and have substantial influence regarding who will be directors. And if we are speaking of small, closely held corporations, the traditional model may not account for the fact that in such companies the owners of the corporation typically serve as both officers and directors, making it somewhat artificial to distinguish among the three layers.

In this chapter we will describe in detail the role of shareholders in the corporate structure, focusing on their voice in management as well as their more general rights and liabilities. We will note in particular the special rights accorded shareholders by the *close corporation statutes* enacted in several jurisdictions. In the next chapter, we will turn our attention to a similar examination of the role of officers and directors.

SHAREHOLDER VOTING RIGHTS

Shareholder Voting Procedure

The power to control the details of daily corporate operation resides with the board of directors, which often delegates much of the responsibility to officers and other employees. In most situations, the remedy for shareholder dissatisfaction with the manner in which corporate affairs are being handled is to elect a new board of directors. The most important shareholder functions are (1) election and removal of directors, (2) amendment of articles and bylaws, and (3) approval of certain extraordinary corporate matters.

Election and Removal of Directors

Although the initial board of directors is either named in the articles of incorporation or selected by the incorporators, its term ordinarily extends only until the first meeting of shareholders. The selection of directors then becomes a shareholder function.

Except for death or resignation, a director usually serves until the expiration of his or her term of office, and frequently is reelected to one or more subsequent terms. However, shareholders have always had the inherent power to remove directors at any time *for cause* (fraud, misconduct, neglect of duties, and so on)—subject, of course, to court review. On the other hand, the traditional common-law rule was that a director could not be removed *without cause* during his or her term unless the shareholders had expressly reserved that right at the time of election. Today, however, this rule has been changed by statute in a majority of states to permit shareholders to remove directors at any time *with or without cause.* Removal of a director in either case is accomplished by majority vote. However, if "cumulative voting" was used to elect the director, removing him or her may be somewhat more difficult. The concept of cumulative voting and its effects will be discussed shortly.

Amendment of Articles and Bylaws

Shareholders have the power to amend the articles of incorporation. Of course, since the corporation's articles must be filed with the secretary of state, any later amendments must also be filed.

In different states the bylaws are initially adopted by either the incorporators, the directors, or the shareholders. But regardless of which body possesses the power of original adoption, the shareholders are empowered to amend or even repeal them subsequently.

In many jurisdictions the directors have the power to amend or repeal the bylaws, but this power is really subordinate in nature. In other words, even when the directors are given such authority by statute, by the articles, or by the bylaws themselves, the ultimate power rests with the shareholders. Because they possess an inherent power with respect to

FIGURE 38.1

Relationship of Shareholders, Directors, and Officers in a Corporation

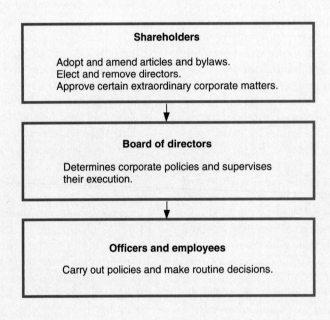

bylaws, they can override the directors' actions even if such actions were authorized.

Approval of Extraordinary Corporate Matters

Although the authority to conduct most corporate affairs is held by the directors, certain matters are of such an unusual nature as to require shareholder approval. This approval is ordinarily given in the form of a "resolution" voted on at a shareholders' meeting. Extraordinary matters requiring shareholder approval include (1) sale or lease of corporate assets not in the regular course of the corporation's business, and (2) merger, consolidation, or dissolution of the corporation.

Exercise of Shareholder Voting

Shareholders as such are not agents of the corporation and therefore cannot bind the corporation by acting *individually;* their powers must be exercised *collectively.* The most common vehicle for the exercise of shareholder functions is the *shareholders' meeting.* In recent years, however, most states have amended their corporation laws to allow shareholders to take action by *written consent.* This consent must ordinarily be signed by all shareholders entitled to vote on the matter.[1] But the shareholders' meeting still remains the most common forum for shareholder action.

Types of Meetings

Shareholders' meetings are either *annual* or *special.* Corporations are usually required by state law to hold annual meetings; the most important item of business at these meetings is usually the election of some or all of the directors. Between annual meetings, special meetings may be called to transact business that cannot or should not wait until the next annual meeting.

Time and Place of Meetings

The time of annual meetings and the place for annual and special meetings may be set forth in the articles,

---

[1]A few states allow shareholder action by a less-than-unanimous written consent.

but they are more commonly found in the bylaws. Most annual meetings are held in the spring. Older statutes often required shareholders' meetings to be held in the state of incorporation, but this generally is no longer a requirement.

Notice of Meetings

State laws usually require written notice of any shareholders' meeting to be sent to each shareholder a reasonable time prior to the meeting, although shareholders can waive this requirement by signing a waiver before or after the meeting. In some instances a shareholder's *conduct* may constitute a waiver of notice. For example, where a shareholder receives no formal notice but knows of the meeting and attends without protesting the lack of notice, he or she waives the requirement of notice.

The notice generally must state the place, day, and hour of the meeting; and in the case of a special meeting, the notice must state the purpose or purposes for which the meeting is being called. The business transacted at a special meeting must be limited to the purposes set forth in the notice.

Quorum

Before action can validly be taken at a shareholders' meeting, a **quorum** must be present. Quorum requirements are expressed in terms of either a specific portion of outstanding shares or a specific portion of shares entitled to vote. These requirements are usually set forth in the articles or the bylaws within limits defined by state statute. The RMBCA provides that, if the articles are silent on the matter, a majority of outstanding shares entitled to be voted on the matter constitutes a quorum. The RMBCA allows the articles to raise or lower the quorum requirement, but many jurisdictions do not allow it to be lower than one-third of all outstanding shares.

Voting

Action at a shareholders' meeting is taken by voting. The number of votes a shareholder has is determined by the number of shares he or she owns. A majority of votes present and entitled to vote will constitute effective action unless a statute or the articles of incorporation require a higher percentage. Assume 10,000 shares outstanding and articles silent on a quorum. In most states 5001 would be a quorum. Assume further that only 5001 votes appear at the meeting. In most states if 2450 voted for, 2150 voted

against, and 401 abstained, the measure would fail, because a majority of the shares voting (2501) did not approve the action. However, states following the RMBCA reach a contrary result by disregarding abstentions in matters other than the election of directors, providing that approval occurs if the votes cast in favor of an action exceed those cast against.

State laws frequently require that a corporation keep a record of all its shareholders, listing their names and addresses as well as the number and type of shares held by each. Usually corporations are also required to prepare a *voting list* (a list of shareholders who can vote and the number of votes each is entitled to) prior to each shareholders' meeting. The record of shareholders and the voting list must be kept at a designated place (such as the principal corporate office) and must be available for inspection by shareholders.

Impartial individuals referred to as *tellers* (or sometimes as *judges* or *inspectors*) are usually present to supervise elections at the shareholders' meetings. Although tellers are not generally required by law, many state statutes do require them if a shareholder so requests or if they are called for in the bylaws.

Cumulative Voting

Practically every state provides for **cumulative voting** by shareholders. A few states *require* it, but most merely *permit* it if the articles of incorporation provide for it and a shareholder gives written notice before the meeting that he or she intends to exercise the right to vote cumulatively.

In normal (*straight*) voting, a majority faction can elect *all* directors and thereby dominate the corporation. Assume that Sue owns 51 out of 100 outstanding shares in X Corporation, and that Al owns the other 49. With 51 percent of the votes, Sue can elect 100 percent of the directors in straight voting; each of her candidates will be among the three highest vote recipients. To allow proportional representation, cumulative voting grants each share the number of votes corresponding to the number of directors to be elected. Furthermore, those votes may be cumulated—grouped for just one or a few candidates. Thus, if five directorships are up for election, Al will have a total of 245 votes (49 shares multiplied by five directorships). If Al casts 123 votes for one of his candidates and 122 for the other, they will both be elected to the board. There is no way that Sue can spread her 255 votes (51 times 5) around so that Al's three candidates will not be among the top five recipients.

A simple formula determines how many shares must be controlled to elect a given number of directors:

$$\# \text{ needed to elect } X \ \# \text{ of directors} = \frac{\# \text{ of shares voting} \times X}{\# \text{ to be elected } + \ 1} + 1$$

(or fraction needed to produce next highest whole)

OTHER BASIC SHAREHOLDER RIGHTS

Right to Inspection and Information

Absent access to reasonable information about the corporation, shareholders may not be able to preserve or exercise any of their other rights effectively, including the right to vote.

Common Law

The common law provides every shareholder with the basic right of *access to corporate records*. This includes not only the right to inspect and copy corporate records personally, but also the right to employ accountants, attorneys, or other assistants as may reasonably be required to obtain the necessary information.

Compliance with a shareholder's inspection request can be costly and time-consuming for a corporation. Because of the potential for abuse by shareholders seeking simply to harass the corporation, the common law places the burden on the shareholder to demonstrate that he or she seeks to inspect relevant records at a proper time and place for a *proper purpose.*

Statutory Inspection Rights

The corporate codes of most states supplement (rather than replace) the common law inspection rights. Many provide, for example, that any shareholder who owns more than 5 percent of the corporation's stock *or* who has held any number of shares for more than six months shall have the right to examine corporate records for a *proper purpose.* Many others follow the RMBCA in granting these rights to *all* shareholders. As noted previously, at common law the shareholder has the burden to prove a proper purpose; most of these statutes shift to the corporation the burden to prove that a qualified shareholder has an *improper purpose* before inspection will be denied.

The concept of a proper purpose is discussed in the following recent case.

TATKO v. TATKO BROTHERS SLATE CO., INC.

Supreme Court of New York, Appellate Division, 569 N.Y.S.2d 783 (1991)

Petitioner Tatko sought to sell his shares in respondent, a family-owned corporation. A 1948 shareholders' agreement required Tatko to sell his shares to the corporation for "book value" as shown on respondent's annual balance sheet prepared by its regular accountants. Petitioner had been furnished with respondent's latest financial report, which contained a balance sheet listing assets, liabilities, stockholder equity, and portions of the minutes from a 1973 stockholders' meeting. Respondent expressed a willingness to buy petitioner's shares for $35,789.40, but refused to make

available other records sought by petitioner.

Petitioner brought this suit seeking a court order allowing inspection of respondent's records. The trial court ruled for petitioner, and respondent corporation sought this review.

Yesawich, Justice:

A shareholder has a common-law right to inspect corporate books and records where the request is made in good faith and for a proper purpose. At issue here is whether petitioner's avowed purpose in bringing this proceeding, namely, to help him determine the true value of his stock, is proper; cor-

porate mismanagement or malfeasance is not charged. Respondent speculates that petitioner's demand to inspect its records is driven by bad faith. Improper purposes are those which are inimical to the corporation, for example, to discover business secrets to aid a competitor of the corporation, to secure prospects for personal business, to find technical defects in corporate transactions to institute "strike suits", and to locate information to pursue one's own social or political goals (Henn and Alexander, Corporations Sec. 199, at 358 [3d ed.]).

In contrast, proper purposes are those reasonably related to the shareholder's interest in the corporation. They include, among others, efforts to

(continues)

TATKO V. TATKO BROTHERS SLATE CO., INC.

(continued from previous page)
ascertain the financial condition of the corporation, to learn the propriety of dividend distribution, to calculate the value of stock, to investigate management's conduct, and to obtain information in aid of legitimate litigation (Henn and Alexander). Petitioner's decision to sell his stock to respondent presents a valid reason for inspecting financial records relating to the value of his individual holdings. Although such information may serve no useful purpose to a shareholder who has agreed in advance to be bound by an accountant's report as to the stock's value, that is not the factual posture of this case.

As noted, the 1948 agreement between the parties provided that book value is to be determined by resort to the annual balance sheet prepared by respondent's regular accountants. Here the accountants, in their letter transmitting respondent's balance sheet and comparative statement of income and retained earnings to it, did so with the caveat that these documents had been compiled from "information that [was] the representation of management," and a further warning that they had neither audited nor reviewed the financial statements and, indeed, expressed no opinion on them. At a minimum, book value requires not only that the entries be complete and correct, but that accepted accounting principles not be entirely disregarded. As for respondent's apprehension, that if the inspection sought is permitted to take place petitioner may divulge to competitors confidential information regarding corporate activities to respondent's detriment, that can be appeased by holding petitioner and his representatives to his counsel's averment that they will consent to an order prohibiting them from disclosing to respondent's competitors "anything they learn of concerning the business." Given the foregoing circumstances, petitioner should be accorded an opportunity to determine the accuracy of the values of those items fixed by management and reflected in respondent's financial statement which bear on book value.

[Affirmed.] ⚖

Courts often struggle with requests for inspection that seem to be aimed at advancing a shareholder's moral or political agenda. Unaccompanied by any legitimate *economic* motivation grounded in one's status as a shareholder, such requests are generally viewed as invalid. However, if a proper economic purpose accompanies a political, moral, or religious motivation, most courts will allow inspection. And some courts seemingly will allow inspection solely on grounds of such a good faith social motivation.[2]

Right to Dividends

A person who purchases corporate shares is making an investment from which he or she obviously intends to receive a profit. Depending on the nature of the business and the type of shares purchased, the shareholder may expect such profit to arise either from increases in the market value of the shares, or from dividends, or perhaps from both.

Dividends are simply payments made by the corporation to its shareholders, representing income or profit on their investment. The payment is usually in the form of money, but it can consist of some type of property, such as the securities of another company that the corporation has been holding as an asset.

Sometimes the corporation pays a **stock dividend,** which is the issuance to shareholders of additional shares of the corporation's own stock. Such a distribution is *technically not a dividend*, because it does not represent a transfer of any property from the corporation to its shareholders. Instead, each shareholder simply becomes the owner of a larger number of shares, and the ownership proportions do not change. Although shareholders may not benefit immediately from a stock dividend, because the value of the preexisting shares is diluted, they usually do benefit in the long run because of the tendency of such shares to increase later in value.

The laws of the various states differ substantially with respect to the circumstances in which dividends can legally be paid. Generally, however, the following limitations are imposed:

1. In many states dividends ordinarily can be paid only from particular sources. For example, some

[2] *Food and Allied Service Trades Dept. v. Wal-Mart Stores, Inc.,* 1992 Del. Ch. LEXIS 108 (Del. Ch. 1992).

states allow dividends to be paid only from "current net earnings." This means that the source of funds for the payment must be the net profits of the corporation for the current year or the year just ended. Many states, however, permit dividends to be paid from any existing "surplus." In effect, this means that the payment must not be made out of the original capital investment of the corporation. Other states allow payments from other sources, such as "revaluation" surplus—the appreciation in value of property held by the corporation.

2. Dividends ordinarily cannot be paid if the corporation is insolvent or if the payment itself will cause the corporation to become insolvent. Depending on the particular state statute involved, *insolvency* is defined either as (1) the inability of the corporation to pay its debts as they come due *(equity insolvency)*, or (2) the possession of insufficient assets to meet all outstanding liabilities *(bankruptcy insolvency)*. The modern trend, exemplified in the RMBCA, is to eliminate any restrictions on the payment of dividends, except the insolvency tests. Under the RMBCA, a dividend payment is proper, regardless of the account from which it is paid, so long as it does not render the corporation insolvent under either the equity or the bankruptcy approach to measuring insolvency.

Other Distributions

Dividend rules are meant to strike a fair balance between the interests of corporate shareholders on the one hand and those of corporate creditors on the other. Obviously, corporate creditors are potentially injured when funds are paid out of the corporate treasury and into the pockets of shareholders whether those transfers are via dividend payments or via some other form, such as the repurchase of shares by the corporation. Although many states have different restrictions on the payment of dividends from those on similar transactions, the RMBCA recognizes the economic equivalency of these types of transactions and places the same limitations (no equity or bankruptcy insolvency) on both of them.

Right to Preferences

The rights enjoyed by individual shareholders sometimes depend on the class of shares they own. In a given situation, a corporation might issue only one class of stock or it might issue several, depending on the needs of the business.

Corporate stock is generally classified either as *common* or *preferred.* **Common stock,** the most basic and frequently issued type, enjoys no special privileges or preferences. The overwhelming majority of small corporations issue only one class of stock. **Preferred stock,** on the other hand, guarantees to its owners some type of special privilege or "preference" over the owners of common stock.[3]

For example, most preferred shares carry a *dividend preference.* This does not mean that their owners are guaranteed the right to receive dividends. What it does mean is that *if a dividend is declared,* owners of preferred stock are ahead of common stockholders in line. For example: Zeta Corp. has issued common stock and one class of "$3 preferred." In any given year, the owners of the common stock cannot be paid a dividend until the owners of the preferred stock have received a dividend of $3 per share.

Some preferred shares carry a *liquidation preference,* which means a preference as to the distribution of corporate assets in the event that the corporation is dissolved. Although the preference puts preferred shareholders ahead of common shareholders in the line for distributions of corporate assets, they are still behind corporate creditors.

Preemptive Rights

Suppose Jupiter Corporation has a capitalization of $100,000 and 1000 outstanding shares. X owns 100 shares of this stock. The corporation is in need of additional capital funds, so the shareholders vote to amend the articles in order to authorize the issuance of another 1000 shares. If X is not given an opportunity to purchase shares of the new issue of stock, her proportionate interest in the right to control the corporation and her right to share in dividends will be halved. Worse yet, if the shares are issued for an amount less than the pre-issuance per share value of X's shares, then the value of X's share of net assets upon dissolution will be substantially diluted.

To avoid this adverse impact on X, the courts traditionally have recognized a concept known as the **preemptive right.** When a corporation issues new stock, the preemptive right gives each shareholder an opportunity to purchase the number of new shares that will maintain his or her proportionate interest in the corporation. A shareholder possessing a preemptive

[3]Because it is possible to create classes of "common" stock that have economic preferences or classes of "preferred" shares that can be economically subordinate to common shares in some regards, the RMBCA eliminates use of the term *preferred* shares and speaks only of *classes* of shares.

right must be given notice and a reasonable amount of time to exercise the right by purchasing the new shares. Anyone who fails to exercise this right within a particular time may be held to have waived the right with respect to that particular issue of stock.

Most states provide that the preemptive right will be available to shareholders *unless* excluded by the articles of incorporation. Virtually all publicly held corporations exclude preemptive rights, which are burdensome to the corporation and not very important because few shareholders of a company such as IBM or General Motors will have a large enough stock ownership percentage to be injured by the issuance of new shares. However, for closely held corporations with only a few shareholders, preemptive rights can be very important. Nonetheless, the RMBCA reverses the default position. States adopting its approach presume that *no* preemptive right exists unless expressly provided for in the articles.

Virtually all states provide that the preemptive right will not exist in certain situations, including when shares are issued as compensation to employees (allowing corporations to compensate employees with shares) and when shares are sold otherwise than for money (allowing corporations to issue shares in order to pay for real estate they wish to buy or as part of a merger without having shareholders disrupt the deal by exercising preemptive rights). Also, preferred shares carry no preemptive rights, and common shares carry no preemptive rights as to offerings of preferred shares. Many states provide that when *treasury shares* (shares once issued and later reacquired by the corporation and now held in the corporation's name) are issued, no preemptive right exists.

Share Transferability

Shares of corporate stock are property that may ordinarily be sold or otherwise transferred as the owner wishes. Free transferability of ownership interests is often viewed as a major advantage of the corporate form, and it certainly is if the shares are of a public corporation. However, if a closely held corporation is involved, there may be a practical limitation to transferability—no one other than current owners of the corporation may be interested in buying the shares. There may also be *legal* limitations on transferability.

Share Transfer Restrictions

In some circumstances (usually involving close corporations), it may be desirable for the corporation to restrict the shareholder's right to transfer his or her shares. Assume that A, B, and C are the only shareholders of Prestige Corporation. As with most small corporations, all are actively involved in running the business. A and B will not want to wake up one morning and find that C has transferred his interest to D, a complete stranger with whom they will then have to share the management of the business. A slightly larger corporation might worry that a large shareholder would sell her shares to several buyers, perhaps causing the corporation to exceed the 35-shareholder limit for Subchapter S status or similar numerical limitations under various state laws. To avoid these types of problems, A, B, and C may impose **share transfer restrictions** (STRs), limiting the free transferability of the shares.

Among the basic types of STRs are the following:

1. *Simple Prohibitions.* For example, owners of a medical corporation might impose a restriction forbidding the sale of shares to nonphysicians in jurisdictions where such ownership is prohibited.

2. *Consent Restrictions.* For example, an STR might prohibit any shareholder from selling shares without the consent of the board of directors or all other shareholders. This could prevent sale of shares to a third party whom the current owners do not like or trust.

3. *First Options.* An STR might prohibit a shareholder from selling shares without first offering them to the other shareholders or the corporation at an established price or, perhaps, at the price the third party is willing to pay.

4. *Buy-Sell Agreements.* An STR might require the corporation to buy at an agreed price or pursuant to an established formula the shares of any shareholder who dies. This would prevent the continuing owners of the corporation from being saddled with new and perhaps unwanted "partners" (the deceased owner's heirs) and helps to provide financial security for the heirs.

In order to be legal, STRs must generally be *conspicuously* noted on the face of the stock certificates (for example, in bold print or red ink), and must be *reasonable* under the circumstances. The more restrictive the STR, the stronger the justification needed to establish its reasonableness. Many courts are slightly hostile to STRs; most construe them narrowly. Therefore, an STR must be clearly written in order to have the desired effect.

Shareholder Derivative Suits

Shareholders have the right to bring and defend lawsuits in the corporation's name. Suits brought on the corporation's behalf are called **shareholder derivative suits** because the right to sue derives primarily from an injury done to the corporation, not an injury done to the shareholder personally.[4] Derivative suits are controversial because, on the one hand, they provide discipline for wrongdoing officers and directors, but on the other hand, they have often been abused by shareholders seeking to harass corporate management into an out-of-court settlement of an essentially frivolous claim.

A shareholder seeking to bring a derivative suit must overcome several difficult procedural hurdles. Because the discretion to sue, along with most other matters, is within the purview of the board of directors, the shareholder seeking to bring a derivative action must either (1) make a written demand upon the board of directors that it bring suit on behalf of the corporation, or (2) be prepared to establish the *futility of demand* so as to excuse the requirement, perhaps by providing plausible evidence that a majority of the directors on the board were guilty of wrongdoing or otherwise were acting in the board's own self-interest. If the shareholder does make a demand and it is accepted, obviously the corporation will control the lawsuit thereafter. If the shareholder makes a demand and it is rejected, the shareholder may then file the derivative suit.

In either a *demand excused* (futility) case or a *demand rejected* case, courts may review to determine whether action to terminate a suit would be in the best interests of the corporation. In both cases, the **business judgment rule** grants to the board's decision substantial protection from judicial review. The contours of the business judgment rule will be analyzed in more detail in the next chapter.

SHAREHOLDER LIABILITIES

Having discussed the basic rights of shareholders, it makes sense to address their basic liabilities.

Liability on Stock Subscriptions

A **stock subscription** is an offer by a prospective investor (a *subscriber*) to buy shares of stock in a corporation. The ordinary rules of contract law apply to such offers, with some minor modifications. Although formal stock subscriptions are not used as often as they once were to launch a corporation, an accepted stock subscription is a contract, and the subscriber is liable for damages to the corporation if he or she breaches that contract by refusing to pay the agreed price.

Liability for Watered Stock

As noted in the previous chapter, shareholders who buy newly issued shares directly from the corporation are liable for any "water" in their shares. In other words, if a shareholder pays less than the par value or less than the sale price fixed by the board, he or she will be liable for the difference to the corporation or under proper circumstances, to its creditors.

Liability for Illegal Dividends

The general rule is that shareholders are liable for the return of improperly paid dividends in two situations. First, if the dividend is paid while the corporation is *insolvent* or if payment renders it insolvent, shareholders are *always* liable for its return. Second, if the dividend is illegal for any other reason, a shareholder usually is required to account for its return only if he or she *knew* of the illegality when receiving payment. Examples of such illegal dividends are those paid from an unauthorized source and those paid in breach of legitimate preferences owed to other shareholders.[5]

SHAREHOLDERS IN THE CLOSE CORPORATION

Introduction

As noted in the introduction to this chapter, the inverse pyramid model of corporate governance does not fully describe the typical closely held corporation in the United States. In such a corporation, the legal theory may be that the shareholders elect the directors who, in turn, choose the officers who will run the daily affairs of the business. In reality, the same persons are typically the owners *and* the directors *and* the officers. They probably operate more like a partnership than like a publicly held corporation, such as General Motors or IBM. Such a setting creates special problems for shareholders.

---

[4]If the shareholder is only injured incidentally as a result of an injury to the corporation, a derivative suit should be brought. However, if a shareholder is injured as an individual in a manner not shared commonly with other shareholders, an individual suit should be brought.

[5]As we shall see in the next chapter, directors who authorize illegal dividends are also generally liable to the corporation and creditors.

Shareholder Control Devices

Absent special provisions, a majority shareholder can easily dominate a corporation under a general state corporate code. Assume that a three-owner corporation is formed, with Alice owning 55 percent of the shares, Beth owning 25 percent, and Cyd owning 20 percent. If things start amicably, Alice, Beth, and Cyd will probably elect one another to the board and then select one another to be officers. Then they will hire one another as corporate employees. However, if a disagreement arises, Beth and Cyd will quickly learn how tenuous their position is. Under most states' laws, Alice can call a shareholders' meeting, remove without cause Beth and Cyd as directors, and then fire them as officers and employees. If we change the above facts to make Alice, Beth, and Cyd equal one-third owners of shares, the same danger lingers if any shareholder falls out of grace with the other two. Any two of the shareholders could band together and freeze out a third.

By consulting attorneys, shareholders can devise special control devices to protect minorities from abuse and to accomplish many other worthwhile goals. The following are among the leading devices used to allocate control and management powers in a closely held corporation.

Classification of Stock

A corporation's shares may be divided into two or more classes of stock. For example, in a corporation formed by A and B, the articles could specify that Class A shares would be issued to A and Class B shares issued to B. Furthermore, the articles could specify that the board of directors would be composed of three directors elected by Class A shares and three directors elected by Class B shares. In this way, equal voice in the management of the corporation can be preserved.

Supermajority Provisions

Assume that Gina is planning to become an equal one-third owner of Y Corporation stock with Sue and Kim. Gina may be more risk-averse than her co-owners; she may well insist that the articles impose a requirement that any corporate borrowing exceeding $10,000 be approved not by the normal majority vote of directors, but by a supermajority of 75 percent. Such a requirement would effectively grant Gina a veto over borrowing transactions that she views as too risky.

Proxies

Assume that Jay and Kay are minority shareholders in a small corporation, each owning 26 percent of the shares. They may wish to control the corporation, but can do so only by coordinating their voting. Perhaps Jay and Kay have difficulty agreeing on specific matters. They may decide to grant a **proxy** to a third party, Ray, to vote their shares in a block. A proxy is simply a signed, written document authorizing a person present at the annual shareholders' meeting to vote the shares of a shareholder. In this way, Ray can elect a majority of directors (and, in the absence of cumulative voting, all the directors) to represent the interests of Jay and Kay.[6]

Shareholder Agreement

Agreements in which a group of shareholders decide prior to a meeting to cast their votes in certain ways are sometimes employed to concentrate voting power. For example, Jay and Kay may agree in advance to vote for each other to be directors. These agreements are usually valid and enforceable if they are in writing, deposited with the corporate secretary, and noted on all stock certificates. Some states also impose time limitations on the existence of such agreements, typically providing that they can run no longer than 10 years.

The following case involves such a shareholder agreement.

---

[6]The use of proxies in corporate board elections of major public corporations is discussed in detail in Chapters 39 (state regulation) and 41 (federal regulation).

SANDERS V. MCMULLEN

U.S. Fifth Circuit Court of Appeals, 868 F.2d 1465 (1989)

Case

The Houston Sports Association (HSA) is a Texas corporation that owns and operates the Astrodome and the Houston Astros Baseball Club. In 1979, McMullen formed the Houston Astros Limited Partnership (HALP) to purchase the capital stock of HSA from its creditors. McMullen was a general partner of HALP and personally owned 25 percent of the partnership. His family owned an additional 8 percent. Sanders, as one of 25 other investors, owned a 2 percent interest in HALP. After the 1980 baseball season, investors sought to oust McMullen as a general partner of HALP, and the organization was dissolved. HSA, however, was recapitalized and the partners of HALP received HSA stock. The result was that McMullen controlled 34 percent of the stock and became chairman of the board. Sanders still owned 2 percent.*

In 1984, minority shareholders tried to enter a voting agreement with 51 percent of the stockholders to remove McMullen from management of HSA. Sanders's 2 percent interest was included in the 51 percent, but he decided to withdraw from the agreement, leaving the shareholders with only 49 percent. Sanders claims he agreed to withdraw because of promises made by McMullen. McMullen was able to retain control of HSA, and even purchased more shares when the organization was restructured. McMullen then controlled 63 percent of the shares and Sanders increased his shares to 13 percent with a $4 million stock purchase.

Sanders contended that McMullen promised him the following items in exchange for withdrawing from the voting trust: (1) He would participate in all management decisions involving the baseball team; (2) he would have access to all operational infor-

mation; (3) the baseball manager and staff would be advised of his status; (4) he would participate in league meetings, World Series, and All Star Game activities; (5) he would have access to all baseball facilities; (6) his shares would be included in the control block for any sale; and (7) McMullen would vote his shares to keep Sanders on the board of directors.

Sanders contends that he purchased the additional stock and withdrew from the voting agreement that would have ousted McMullen in reliance on these promises. A continuing shareholder's agreement and a collateral agreement were both signed by the parties. The agreements reflected Sanders's additional investment of $4 million. The promises were not contained in the documents or mentioned on the stock certificates. In November 1986, Sanders was not reelected to the board of directors of HSA and McMullen sent him a letter stating that he was not entitled to any special privileges as a shareholder. Sanders sued McMullen for breaching the agreement and for fraudulent misrepresentation. He sought a decree of specific performance requiring McMullen to honor his agreement, or an order requiring McMullen to purchase Sanders's stock at the fair market price.

The trial court granted McMullen's motion for summary judgment, finding that there was no genuine issue of material fact, and Sanders appealed.

Gee, Judge:

. . . The trial court determined that any agreement between McMullen and Sanders was a "voting agreement" that fell under the Texas Business Corporation Act, article 2.30(B). . . . This statute requires . . . three things: (1) a writing; (2) a deposit of a counterpart

[i.e., a copy or duplicate original of the written agreement] at the corporation's main office; (3) reference to the agreement on the [stock] certificates. . . .

Since the promises were not in writing, the court granted summary judgment on the issue. The trial court treated all of the issues as constituting a voting agreement, although not all of them related to voting. In fact, of the seven alleged promises, only the one that required McMullen to vote his shares so as to keep Sanders on the board is without question controlled by article 2.30(B). The trial court's summary judgment on alleged promises not relating to the voting of shares is therefore reversed and remanded. . . .

[Sanders] also argues that Texas courts do not require literal adherence to the voting agreement statute, and cites *R.H. Sanders Corp. v. Haves*, 541 S.W.2d 262 (Tex. Civ. App. 1976) in support of that argument. The argument, however, is overbroad. The [court in that case upheld] a voting agreement that failed to comply with all of the technical requirements of the statute, but only because the purpose of the statute was not frustrated. Although no copy was filed with the corporation, and the stock certificates failed to refer to the agreement, all shareholders had knowledge of the agreement. The notice requirement of the statute was therefore satisfied. The [court in that case] wisely looked to the purpose of the statute, one to give notice to shareholders and potential buyers of the stock. The court continued to state that, "since the parties here are all of the shareholders and had knowledge of the agreement, and since no outside buyers were involved, no compelling policy reason exists here for requiring technical compliance with these notice provisions."

[The holding in that case] cannot apply to this case. While Texas courts may not require literal conformity with the statute they do at least require that

(continues)

SANDERS V. MCMULLEN

(continued from previous page)
the purpose of the statute not be undermined. In this case, other shareholders existed who were totally unaware of the agreement. The notice element of the statute is therefore unsatisfied. The alleged promise to vote so as to keep [Sanders] on the board was clearly a voting agreement not in compliance with statutory requirements. The trial court properly awarded summary judgment on that issue and we affirm. . . .

[However,] the order of the trial court fails completely to address [Sanders's] fraud complaint. The elements for a prima facie case of fraudulent misrepresentation are: (1) a material misrepresentation; (2) the representation was false; (3) the speaker knew it was false when made; (4) the speaker intended reliance; (5) the other party did rely on it; and (6) the party in reliance was injured.

From the materials presented by [Sanders], there was evidence for each of these elements. Whether [he] will prevail at trial is a matter of contention, but at least for the purpose of summary judgment, the court must consider the evidence in the light most favorable to the non-movant [i.e., Sanders].

Perhaps the trial court considered the tort claim moot since the contract claim failed. This, however, would not eliminate the tort claim. . . . The gist of the fraud in cases involving promises made with no intention to perform is not breach of the promise, but the fraudulent intent of the promisor, the false representation of an existing intention to perform where such intent is in fact nonexistent, and the deception of the promisee by such false promise. . . . [There is enough evidence to create a genuine issue of disputed fact on each of these elements of fraud, so the trial court should not have granted McMullen's motion for summary judgment on Sanders's fraud claim.]

Summary judgment for [McMullen] on the alleged promise of McMullen to vote so as to keep Sanders on the Board is affirmed. . . . The trial court's grant of summary judgment [for McMullen] on the fraud claim relating to the other promises is reversed, and the case is remanded for a trial on these issues. ⛬

Note than in *McMullen*, the essence of the agreement was: "I will vote for you if you will vote for me." In other words, both were agreeing as to what they would do in their capacity as *shareholders*. It is a different thing, however, to agree as to what you will do once you are elected to be a director (for example, "I will vote to hire you as an employee" or "I will vote to pay large dividends"). Decisions taken as a director are subject to the fiduciary duty that directors owe to shareholders. Many courts hold that a shareholder agreement is invalid if it substantially restricts the discretion of a director in making decisions about what is in the best interests of the corporation. This is a formalistic view based on the traditional distinction between the roles of shareholders on the one hand and directors on the other hand. As we shall soon see, this distinction may not be valid in the closely held corporation.

Voting Trusts

A similar method of concentrating voting power is the **voting trust.** This is formed by an agreement in which the *record ownership* of shares is transferred to trustees whose sole function is to vote the shares.

Voting trust certificates are given by the trustees to the original shareholders, entitling them to all rights of share ownership other than voting rights. As a general rule, voting trusts must meet the same legal requirements as shareholder voting agreements.

MANAGEMENT OF CLOSE CORPORATIONS

Most corporate codes are written with the largest companies in mind. As noted earlier, the divisions among the roles of shareholder, director, and officer are artificial in a close corporation, where the same persons often occupy all three roles. For example, in *Galler v. Galler,* [7] a corporation was owned by two married couples. The four owners entered into a shareholders' agreement that, among other things, provided that they would vote for one another as directors *and* vote to pay certain amounts as dividends. As noted previously, the second portion of this agreement purports to bind the Gallers in their role *as directors*, impinging on the authority of directors traditionally granted under state corporate codes.

[7]203 N.E.2d 577 (Ill. 1964).

RE-DEFINING CLOSE CORPORATIONS

by Ivery D. Foreman

Box 38.1
The Law at Work

The ineffectiveness of traditional corporate law principles in protecting minority shareholders in closely-held, or "close," corporations has resulted in increased judicial and legislative intervention to prohibit attempts by majority shareholders to squeeze out minority shareholders.

Increasingly, courts and legislatures are recognizing that the inherent relationship among shareholders of a close corporation unmistakably resembles a partnership, and, consequently, they are applying partnership principles to settle shareholder disputes.

. . .Because of the unusual and intimate relationship between shareholders and the actual operations of the close corporation, many courts have recognized that control of this entity is peculiarly susceptible to misuse or abuse by majority shareholders, including failure to declare dividends, unfair distribution of business profits to majority shareholders in the form of salaries or bonuses, and discharge of minority shareholders as corporate employees.

To avoid such misuse or abuse, courts have held shareholders of a close corporation to owe each other the same heightened fiduciary duty that exists between partners, a duty of utmost good faith and loyalty. . . .

Many states have adopted laws to codify the partnership features that apply to close corporations. . . . Other states have adopted statutes that specifically permit the use of close corporations to take advantage of the limited liability, tax benefits and perpetual existence features of a corporation while permitting the parties to set forth the terms of their business relationship in an agreement similar to those describing partnerships. . . .

The treatment of close corporations as "incorporated partnerships" has resulted in other developments. For example, while majority shareholders frequently assume that their actions are justifiable if they have a legitimate business purpose, since they have the right to control the corporation, their heightened partner-like fiduciary duty in close corporations actually limits their rights to control.

In addition, some courts have determined that majority shareholders should not be permitted to exercise powers arbitrarily or without regard to the legitimate expectations of minority shareholders.

Accordingly, the principle of good faith and fair dealing among shareholders of a close corporation may override traditional corporate principles of majority control. Principles of fiduciary duty are even being applied to close corporations in the absence of any formal agreement among shareholders.

. . . It is important that a close corporation agreement be used to clarify the relationship of shareholders. The use of outside or disinterested directors also may serve to avoid disputes between majority and minority shareholders and the manipulative use of corporate control by majority shareholders to unfairly deprive minority shareholders of the advantages and opportunities to which they are entitled.

Source: *ABA Journal*, March 1992, p. 76.

However, the *Galler* court ignored the traditional view and upheld the agreement as a practical necessity in the close corporation context, after spelling out the obvious differences between close and publicly held corporations:

It should be emphasized that we deal here with a so-called close corporation. For our purposes, a close corporation is one in which the stock is held in a few hands, or in a few families; and wherein it is not at all, or only rarely, dealt in by buying and selling. Moreover, it should be recognized that shareholder agreements similar to that in question here are often, as a practical consideration, quite necessary for the protection of those financially interested in the close corporation. While the shareholder of a public issue corporation may readily sell his shares on the open market should management fail to use, in his opinion, sound business judgment, his counterpart of the close corporation often has a large total of his entire capital invested in the business and has no ready market for his shares should he desire to sell. He feels, understandably, that he is more than a mere investor and that his voice should be heard concerning all corporate activity. Without a shareholder agreement, specifically enforceable by the courts, insuring him a modicum of control, a large minority shareholder might find himself at the mercy of an oppressive or unknowledgeable majority. Moreover, as in the case at bar, the shareholders of a close corporation are often also the directors and officers thereof. With substantial shareholder interests abiding in each member of the board of directors, it is often quite impossible to secure, as in the large public issue corporation, independent board judgment free from personal motivations concerning corporate policy. For these and other reasons too voluminous to enumerate here, often the only sound basis for protection is afforded by a lengthy, detailed shareholder agreement securing the rights and obligations of all concerned.

Thus, increasingly courts and legislatures have realized that the closely held corporation functions more like a partnership than like a large corporation. This realization has several ramifications, including (1) the imposition of a partner-like fiduciary duty upon shareholders in closely held corporations, and (2) the enactment of "close corporation statutes" to supplement traditional state corporate codes (See Box 38.1).

Fiduciary Duty

As courts have increasingly recognized the similarity between a small, closely held business and a partnership, they have increasingly imposed fiduciary duties upon shareholders to treat each other fairly that would not exist in an IBM or General Motors. The following case describes this duty and helps set its outer limits.

GOODE V. RYAN

Supreme Judicial Court of Massachusetts, 489 N.E.2d 1001 (1986)

Alice Marr owned 800 shares out of a total of 11,340 outstanding shares of the common stock of Gloucester Ice & Cold Storage Co. Gloucester engaged in the manufacture and sale of ice to fishing industry customers. Until 1980, Gloucester also operated a separate fish cold storage business. When Alice Marr died, the administrator of her estate, Thomas Goode, demanded that Gloucester purchase Marr's 800 shares. The demand was refused, and Goode filed suit against the officers, directors, and a controlling shareholder of Gloucester, seeking an order of the court requiring the corporation to purchase the 800 shares. The trial court granted the defendants' motion for summary judgment, and plaintiff appealed.

Hennessey, Chief Justice:

Gloucester is a close corporation. . . . The number of shareholders is small, no ready market exists for the Gloucester stock, and majority shareholder participation in the management of the corporation is substantial. The parties agree that no provisions restricting the transfer of stock or requiring the corporation or remaining shareholders to redeem its stock on the death of a shareholder appear in the corporation's articles of organization or by-laws, or in any agreement among the shareholders.

In *Donahue v. Rodd Electrotype Co.*, 367 Mass. 578 (1975), we [held] that shareholders in a close corporation owe one another substantially the same fiduciary duty of utmost good faith and loyalty in operation of the enterprise that partners owe one another. Applying that rule, we held in *Donahue* that a controlling shareholder selling a close corporation its own shares must cause the corporation to offer to purchase shares ratably from all other shareholders. Subsequently [in another case], we applied the rule to provide relief to a minority shareholder in a close corporation whose employment and income from the corporation were terminated without cause by the majority shareholders. The plaintiff in the instant case asks us to apply the fiduciary principles established in those cases to hold that, on the death of a minority shareholder, majority shareholders are obligated to purchase, or to cause the corporation to purchase, the shares owned by the minority shareholder.

As we stated in the *Donahue* case, one identifying characteristic of a close corporation is the absence of a ready market for corporate stock. A shareholder wishing to convert an investment in a close corporation to cash for personal financial reasons or because of unhappiness with the management of the enterprise will have only a limited number of opportunities for disposing of the asset. Similarly, the executor or administrator of the estate of a deceased shareholder in a close corporation will be confronted with an illiquid asset that may have a high value in the estate, but have little, if any, dividend value for the beneficiaries. In both situations, the only prospective purchasers for the stock may be the remaining shareholders in the corporation or the corporation itself.

Investors in other types of firms have easier mechanisms available for disposing of their interests. A shareholder in a large, public-issue corporation can sell the stock on the financial markets at no price disadvantage relative to other sellers of that stock. A member of a partnership can convert the investment to cash by exercising the right to dissolve the partnership.

The shareholder who owns less than a majority interest in a close corporation does not have any of these options. In the absence of an agreement among shareholders or between the corporation and the shareholder, or a provision in the corporation's articles of organization or by-laws, neither the corporation nor a majority of shareholders is under any obligation to purchase the shares of minority shareholders when

(continues)

GOODE V. RYAN

(continued from previous page)
minority shareholders wish to dispose of their interest in the corporation.

The minority shareholder in a close corporation is susceptible to oppression by the majority or controlling shareholders. In the instant case, there is no evidence of any oppressive conduct on the part of defendants directed at excluding the shares Goode represented from participation in the affairs of the corporation. In fact, the deceased shareholder, Alice Marr, never held corporate office, or served on the board of directors, or received any salary from Gloucester, and there is no indication that she or her estate was aggrieved by the absence of involvement in corporate management. The majority shareholders made no effort to curtail, or interfere with, any benefits to which Marr or her estate was entitled as a minority shareholder in Gloucester. The majority shareholders simply refused to purchase the Marr estate stock. This refusal violated no agreement or corporate governance provision and did not violate any fiduciary obligation they owed to the plaintiff. Nor are any facts present to permit us to conclude that the majority used assets of the corporation to enrich themselves at the expense of minority shareholders.

While the plaintiff's predicament in not being able to dispose of the Gloucester stock to facilitate prompt settlement of the Marr estate is unfortunate, the situation was not caused by the defendants but is merely one of the risks of ownership of stock in a close corporation. It is not the proper function of this court to reallocate the risks inherent in the ownership of corporate stock in the absence of corporate or majority shareholder misconduct. . . .

Judgment affirmed. ⚖

Close Corporation Statutes

Recognizing the need for special treatment of closely held corporations, 20 or so states have made special provision for them either by enacting separate supplements to their corporate codes or by sprinkling provisions throughout existing codes. The RMBCA also has a Close Corporation Supplement based on four principles:

(1) the need for a flexible, useful statutory framework; (2) the desirability of having adequate basic protection against oppression of minority shareholders; (3) the desirability of codifying some of the customary practices used by experienced practitioners to achieve the objectives and expectations of investors in close corporations; and (4) the necessity of integrating the special close corporation statutory provisions in the supplement with all other statutory provisions governing business operations.

Generally speaking, close corporations whose shareholders "opt in" (choose to be governed by the statute) may be operated formally like large corporations, informally like partnerships, or anywhere between these polar extremes. For example, many states provide that the shareholders may choose to be governed by the traditional board of directors, *or* by a majority vote of all shareholders, *or* by a committee of shareholders, *or* by a nonshareholder manager, *or* in any other manner they choose. They may enter into shareholder agreements that govern virtually every aspect of internal corporate life. They may not prejudice third-party creditors, but as among themselves the shareholders may make of the corporation what they will.

SUMMARY

The traditional view is that the corporate management structure is in an inverted pyramid with the shareholders electing directors and voting on major changes, the directors setting broad policy and selecting the officers, and the officers running the day-to-day affairs of the business. However, that model is only a rough guideline and has certain limitations in describing the actual operation of both large public corporations and small, closely held corporations.

Shareholders usually elect directors and take other actions by voting at an annual shareholders' meeting. Voting power corresponds to the number of shares owned; shareholders may, however, be allowed to vote cumulatively in proper circumstances. Other shareholder rights include the right to receive properly paid dividends, the right to inspect corporate records for a valid purpose, and the right to transfer shares.

Potential abuses in the close corporation context have led to creation of numerous devices aimed at averting oppression of minority shareholders and other purposes, including the shareholder agreement, the voting trust, and the proxy.

Additionally, realizing that closely held corporation are very much like partnerships, many states have imposed a fiduciary duty upon shareholders in such corporations to treat one another fairly, and several other states have adopted specific statutes designed to give ultimate management flexibility to small corporations.

KEY TERMS

Quorum
Cumulative voting
Dividends
Stock dividends
Common stock
Preferred stock
Preemptive right
Share transfer restrictions
Shareholder derivative suit
Business judgment rule
Stock subscription
Proxy
Voting trust

QUESTIONS AND PROBLEMS

1. There are 1000 outstanding shares of X Corporation stock that will be voted at next month's election of five directors. Sharon, a dissident shareholder, seeks to form a faction that can elect at least two directors to the board by asserting its right to vote cumulatively. What is the minimum number of shares that the faction must control in order to be able to elect two directors?

2. Bostic was hired by Wrights Beauty College, Inc. in 1978 as the director of one of its schools. In 1984, Bostic and his wife acquired stock in the corporation and joined the Wagoners (Martin, Vicky, and Don) as its only shareholders. In 1990, Bostic was discharged from his position. Thereafter he sought to inspect several corporate records, including loan documents, agreements to purchase other beauty colleges, profit and balance sheets, and financial statements. The corporation denied inspection, and Bostic sued alleging three purposes for his inspection: (1) to fulfill his obligations as a member of the board of directors, (2) to determine whether he bears any individual liability for loans for which he had signed both individually and as an officer, and (3) to evaluate the financial worth of his holdings. Are these "proper purposes" that should entitle Bostic to inspect the records? (*Wrights Beauty College, Inc. v. Bostic,* 576 N.E.2d 626, Ind.App. 1991.)

3. Browning owned 320 shares out of 1000 outstanding of C.C. Plywood Corp. After suffering losses in its first two years, C.C. became profitable. The other shareholders sought to force Browning out of the company by authorizing 500,000 shares of new stock to be issued at $1 each, knowing that Browning had no money to exercise his preemptive rights to 151,696 shares. Browning's holdings were reduced from 32 percent to less than 1 percent. Browning sued, but defendants argued that Browning had voluntarily waived his preemptive rights. Should the court act to protect Browning? (*Browning v. C.C. Plywood Corp.,* 434 P.2d 339, Or. 1967.)

4. Paul owned 43 percent of the shares of F-L Property, Inc. Its articles provided that no shareholder could "sell, assign, transfer, pledge, hypothecate or in any other manner dispose of" F-L shares without first offering in writing to sell the shares to F-L and its shareholders and receiving their consent to the sale. Paul's wife Marilyn sued him for divorce, and the divorce judge ordered Paul to transfer half of his F-L shares to Marilyn as part of the divorce settlement. The other shareholders voted not to consent to the transfer. Who now owns Paul's shares? (*Castonguay v. Castonguay,* 306 N.W.2d 143, Minn. 1981.)

5. Crosby owned 26 percent of Seascape Corporation. He sued the four controlling shareholders, officers, and directors of Seascape, claiming that they paid themselves unreasonable salaries; caused Seascape to pay their personal expenses; used Seascape's property for personal enterprise; caused Seascape to buy life insurance for their benefit; and took improper, low-interest loans from Seascape. Defendants moved to dismiss on grounds that this was a derivative suit, yet Crosby had neither made demand upon the board nor showed that demand should be excused as futile. Is this a derivative action or a direct action by an injured shareholder? (*Crosby v. Beam,* 548 N.E.2d 217, Ohio 1989.)

6. Eaton formed a corporation to acquire his business. The California Commissioner of Corporations

authorized the corporation to sell not more than 4500 shares of $10 par value stock to defendant and others, and required that 1022 shares be held in escrow until certain conditions were met. These shares were never released from escrow. Plaintiff recovered a $21,000 judgment against the corporation that went unsatisfied. Plaintiff then sought to recover from Eaton personally the difference between the par value of the 4500 shares he allegedly received and the value of the consideration he gave for it, a sum of $35,000. Plaintiff showed that the 1022 shares supposedly held in escrow were treated as though they belonged to plaintiff. Should plaintiff be able to recover the deficiency paid for this allegedly "watered" stock? (*Bing Crosby Minute Maid Corp. v. Eaton*, 297 P.2d 5, Cal. 1956.)

7. On February 1, 1983, Cox, Powell, and Thomas, equal one-third owners of the shares of two corporations, entered into an STR to protect "their best interests." Pursuant to the agreement, all shares owned by a shareholder at the time of his or her death were to be acquired by the corporation through life insurance policies established to fund the transaction. The agreement provided that "[e]ach price shall be reviewed at least annually no later than the annual meeting of shareholders" and that "[t]he purchase price shall remain in full force and effect until so changed." No annual meeting was held in February 1984. Cox died in an accidental fire in March 1984. The price at which the corporation was bound to buy Cox's shares, as established in the agreement, was $374,976, though they were worth perhaps twice that much. The administrator of Cox's estate refused to tender the shares because of the price-value differential and the failure to review the repurchase price in 1984. Is the STR enforceable under these circumstances? (*Concord Auto Auction, Inc. v. Rustin*, 627 F.Supp. 1526, D.Mass. 1986.)

8. Robert and Virginia Gaylord (Ps) owned 50 percent of the stock of Imperial Travel, Inc. Hagshenas (D) owned the other 50 percent. These three, and D's wife, were the officers, directors, and key employees of Imperial. Unfortunately, they became involved in a bitter dispute, and D sued seeking dissolution of the corporation. The trial court entered certain orders designed to keep the business operating pending a full trial. Soon thereafter, D and his wife resigned as officers and directors of Imperial and then opened a competing travel agency, luring away some of Imperial's employees and customers. Ps asked the judge for an injunction ordering D not to compete with Imperial. D argued that since he was no longer an officer or director of Imperial and had never signed a covenant not to compete, he was free to compete with Imperial. Is D correct? (*Hagshenas v. Gaylord*, 557 N.E.2d 316, Ill.App. 1990.)

Chapter 39

Corporations
Corporate Managers

Board of Directors: Choice and Functions
Exercise of Board Functions
Officers: Selection and Functions
Powers of Officers
Rights of Corporate Managers
Liabilities of Corporate Managers
Contract, Tort, and Criminal
Liabilities of Managers

As NOTED IN THE previous chapter, the *board of directors* is in many ways a corporation's center of power. Elected by the shareholders, the board theoretically sets broad corporate policy and selects and supervises the *officers* who manage the daily operations of the business. In this chapter, we will explore the role of these managers in the operation of the corporation. We will also examine in detail their rights and responsibilities.

BOARD OF DIRECTORS: CHOICE AND FUNCTIONS

Number and Qualifications

The number of directors is usually established in either the articles or the bylaws of a corporation. Although many states formerly required that there be at least three directors, today most permit a corporation to have as few as one.

Most states have eliminated minimum age requirements and state residency requirements for directors. Also, most states no longer require a director also to be a shareholder, unless the articles or bylaws so provide. In actual practice, most directors *are* shareholders; however, in large corporations there is a growing trend toward use of *outside directors* who are not corporate officers and typically have minimal share holdings. These outside directors theoretically serve as "watchdogs" to avoid abuses by the *inside directors* (directors who are also officers).

Election and Term

The initial board ordinarily serves until the first annual shareholders' meeting, when new directors are elected by majority vote of the shareholders. The term of office for corporate directors is one year unless the board is *classified*. A **classified board** is divided into classes, with only one class elected each year, the result being that the directors serve "staggered" terms.

Directors may be removed by shareholders *for cause* and, in most states, *without cause*. The power to remove a director for cause can also be given, in the articles or bylaws, to the board of directors itself.

Management Functions

Even though the corporation generally is bound by the actions of the board, the directors are not agents of the corporation or of the shareholders who elect them. There are two reasons for this. First, their powers are conferred by the *state* rather than by the shareholders. And second, they do not have *individual* power to bind the corporation, as agents do; instead, they can only act *as a body.*[1] Directors thus occupy a position unique in our legal system. They are ultimately responsible not to the shareholders who elected them, but to the best interests of the corporation as perceived by the directors. Indeed, directors may properly ignore the wishes of a majority of shareholders (although they may risk being removed).

With the exception of certain extraordinary matters requiring shareholder vote (such as mergers and amendments of articles) described in the previous chapter, the board of directors is empowered to manage all affairs of the corporation.[2] It not only determines the corporate policies but also supervises their execution. The management powers of the board of directors usually include the following:

1. Setting of basic corporation policy in such areas as product lines, services, prices, wages, and labor-management relations.

2. Decisions relating to financing the corporation, such as the issuance of authorized shares or bonds.

3. Determination of whether (and how large) a dividend is to be paid to shareholders at a particular time.

4. Selection, supervision, and removal of corporate officers and other managerial employees.

5. Decisions relating to compensation of managerial employees, pension plans, and similar matters.

---

[1]However, if one director signs a contract on the corporation's behalf and all other directors knowingly acquiesce, it will bind the corporation. Courts disagree as to whether acquiescence by a mere majority of directors will bind the company.

[2]Our discussion in this chapter assumes that the corporate shareholders have not elected to operate the corporation pursuant to a close corporation statute, which, as noted in Chapter 38, would allow them to dispense with directors and officers altogether.

EXERCISE OF BOARD FUNCTIONS

Most state statutes allow boards (and shareholders, as pointed out in Chapter 38) to act by unanimous written consent. The traditional and most common method for board action, however, is the board of directors' meeting.

Time and Place of Board Meetings

There are two types of board meetings: *regular* and *special*. The time and place of regular meetings is ordinarily established by the bylaws, by a standing resolution of the board, or simply by custom. Unless expressly required, notice of such meetings does not have to be given to directors. If the need arises, special meetings can be called between regular meetings. Prior notice of special meetings is required in most cases.

Quorum and Voting

Before action can validly be taken at a board of directors' meeting, a quorum must be present. Most states allow the articles or bylaws to establish the level of attendance for a quorum, although some states provide that it cannot be lower than, say, one-third of the membership.

Board action is taken by voting; each director has only one vote, and effective action usually requires only a *majority* vote of those present.[3] However, the articles or bylaws may have a greater-than-majority requirement for certain actions.

Later in this chapter, we will discuss the fiduciary duties of directors. Although a director's conflict of interest can cause the director to be liable for resulting harm to the corporation, such a conflict also can affect the fundamental power of the board to take action, as the next case demonstrates.

[3]The RMBCA and most states allow directors to participate in a meeting via conference call.

WEISS MEDICAL COMPLEX, LTD. V. KIM

Appellate Court of Illinois, 408 N.E.2d 959 (1980)

Weiss Medical Complex, Ltd., a professional corporation, operated a medical clinic in Harvey, Illinois. Sun Kim and Chusak Ladpli, licensed physicians, entered into employment contracts with the corporation in 1972 and 1973, respectively. The contracts were for a term of one year, to be automatically renewed unless either party gave written notice of termination at least 90 days prior to the end of the year. Each contract contained a restrictive covenant in which the employee agreed not to practice medicine within a ten-mile radius of the corporation for a period of one year after termination of the employment.

In early 1977 the board of directors voted to cancel the restrictive covenants in physicians' contracts. At this time the corporation's bylaws provided for thirteen directors, but only seven directors had been elected. All seven directors attended the board meeting at which this action was taken. The minutes of this meeting were subsequently reviewed by the corporation's attorney, who indicated that the board's action was questionable because four of the directors had restrictive covenants in their own contracts, thus creating a possible conflict of interest. The attorney advised that the board should attempt to get shareholder approval of the action. At the shareholders' meeting that was held subsequently, the board's action was not ratified, mainly because the majority shareholder, Dr. Weiss, opposed the action.

In 1979 Dr. Kim and Dr. Ladpli terminated their employment with the corporation and opened their own medical practices within a ten-mile radius of the Weiss facility. At

the insistence of Dr. Weiss, the corporation filed suit seeking an injunction enforcing the restrictive covenants in its former employees' contracts. The trial court held that the board's action had been valid, and dismissed the suit. The corporation appealed.

McNamara, Justice:

Plaintiff urges that it was legal error to allow four personally interested directors having restrictive covenants in their employment contracts to be counted toward the quorum and majority vote of plaintiff's board of directors.

A quorum is composed of a majority of the number of directors fixed by the corporation's bylaws. The act of a majority of the directors at a meeting at which a quorum is present is the act of the board of directors. At the times of the resolution in issue, plaintiff's bylaws

(continues)

WEISS MEDICAL COMPLEX, LTD. v. KIM

(continued from previous page) provided for 13 directors; thus seven directors constituted a quorum.

Duties imposed upon a director of the corporation as a fiduciary require him to manage the corporation with undivided and unqualified loyalty, and prohibit him from profiting personally at corporate expense or permitting his private interests to clash with those of his corporation. In Illinois, a director who has a personal interest in a subject under consideration is disqualified to vote on the matter and may not be counted for the purpose of making a quorum. The only exception is that a director, irrespective of any personal interest, may vote to establish reasonable compensation to all directors for service to the corporation. Whether a director is personally interested in a matter is a question of fact. Where there is no quorum because of the disqualification of directors, a contract executed pursuant to a resolution of the board is voidable and may be rendered valid by shareholder ratification.

Four of the seven directors who voted affirmatively to delete the restrictive covenant from all existing contracts had a restrictive covenant in their own employment contracts with plaintiff. The trial court did not make a determination whether these four directors had a personal interest in the matter under consideration by the board, although it did note that they benefited from the action.

We believe that the evidence conclusively demonstrated that these four directors had a personal interest in the matter under consideration by the board. They were among the intended beneficiaries of the board's resolution. Removal of the restrictive covenant would enable a director to leave the clinic and yet continue to render services to patients previously treated at the clinic. This access to plaintiff's patients would provide clientele and a source of income to physicians leaving the clinic. Consequently, a director who was restrained from such ongoing patient contact by the restrictive covenant in issue stood to benefit from a favorable outcome on the vote to delete the provision from all existing contracts. . . . We conclude, therefore, that the directors with restrictive covenants in their contracts were clearly disqualified to vote this benefit of removal to themselves.

In view of the personal interest of four board members, when the matter of restrictive covenants was considered, there were only three directors whose lack of personal interest entitled them to be counted towards a quorum. Consequently, no affirmative action on restrictive covenants was taken by a qualified majority of the board of directors.

Under such circumstances, the board's action was voidable. Although the action could have been ratified by the shareholders, the shareholders expressed objections at a meeting on June 6, 1977, and ratification was not achieved. . . .

In view of the personal interest of four directors, there was no quorum present at the board meeting on February 3, 1977. And since shareholder ratification was refused, the resolution to remove restrictive covenants from all existing employment contracts was not binding on the corporation. Consequently, the trial court erred in finding that the board's action cancelled the restrictive covenant in [the] employment contracts. . . .

For the reasons stated, the order of the circuit court of Cook County . . . denying plaintiff's motion for a preliminary injunction . . . is reversed, and the cause is remanded for further proceedings not inconsistent with this opinion. ∽

Delegation of Board Powers to Officers and Employees

The board can, and quite often does, delegate its authority to manage the corporation to officers and other employees. Not only is authority usually given to carry out board decisions, but managerial personnel also are generally given authority to make management decisions. The delegation of decision-making authority is usually a practical necessity, because daily business activities require too many decisions for each one to be made by the board. The powers delegated by the board, however, must relate only to ordinary corporate affairs (not to matters of an unusual nature), and must not be so broad as to give an officer or employee complete managerial discretion.

Thus, even though certain management functions are often delegated to officers and other employees, the ultimate power to manage still rests with the board. For example, RMBCA 8.01 provides that "[a]ll corporate powers shall be exercised by *or under the authority of,* and the business and affairs of the corporation managed *under the direction of,* its board of directors. . . ." (Emphasis added.)

Most states *do* allow the board to delegate certain decisions to committees composed of only some of the board members. Most public corporations now have (1) an executive committee to act on matters requiring attention between formal board meetings, (2) an audit committee to review the independent auditor's report on auditing and accounting matters, (3) a nomination committee to ensure directors' input into the nomination of new directors, (4) a compensation committee to set the compensation of directors and officers, and perhaps (5) a special litigation committee to determine whether derivative litigation should be dismissed (more on this later).

However, typical of most state statutes, RMBCA 8.25 provides that certain actions must be undertaken by the entire board and may not be delegated to committees, including (1) authorizing dividends, (2) initiating any extraordinary action (such as a merger) requiring shareholder approval, (3) filling vacancies on the board, (4) amending the articles or bylaws, and (5) authorizing the issuance or repurchase of shares.

OFFICERS: SELECTION AND FUNCTIONS
Number and Titles
Most commonly, the corporate officers are the president, one or more vice-presidents, the secretary, and the treasurer. Most state laws say little or nothing about the responsibilities of these various officers. Some corporations also have other officers, such as chief executive officer, chairman of the board, general manager, comptroller (or controller), and general counsel. The RMBCA illustrates the modern trend by providing simply that a corporation shall have the officers listed in its bylaws or appointed by its board. It requires neither any certain number of officers nor that they bear any specific title. In many states, and under the RMBCA, one person may hold *all* corporate offices, though many states still require that the offices of president and secretary, at least, be held by different persons.

Appointment, Tenure, and Removal
Most commonly, officers are selected by the board of directors, although in some states they may be chosen by the shareholders directly. They typically serve at the pleasure of the board and are removable without cause at any time.[4]

---
[4]If an officer is hired pursuant to a long-term contract, he or she may be removed by the board at any time but may have a breach of contract action against the corporation.

POWERS OF OFFICERS
Because agency law governs, the corporation is bound by the *contracts* formed by its officers when they act within (1) actual authority, express or implied; (2) apparent authority; or (3) no authority but the action is later *ratified* by the corporation. This section explores in more detail the powers of officers to bind the corporation contractually.[5]

Express Authority
Express authority is authority that is put into words—written or oral. Officers' express authority usually derives from (1) state corporate codes, (2) the articles of incorporation, (3) bylaws, and (4) board of directors resolutions. Most state statutes are incomplete in this regard; bylaws typically are the most fruitful source of expressions of officer authority. If the bylaws are stingy in granting authority, officers will often have to seek board resolutions to authorize contemplated actions.

Implied Authority
Another type of actual authority, *implied authority*, is authority that is not spelled out in words, but is derived by "reading between the lines" of the statutes, articles, bylaws, and board resolutions. It is often based on customary practice of other corporations in the area or on the past practices of this specific corporation. Some courts hold that certain officers have inherent power simply by virtue of the office they hold. Other courts infer the existence of all authority needed to carry out the tasks assigned to the officer by the bylaws or board of directors.

President
Some courts hold that the president has no more inherent power than any other officer, although some expand the president's powers when he or she is also acting as a "general manager." Most courts hold that the president has inherent authority to bind the corporation in *ordinary business transactions*, but not extraordinary transactions (which require board approval). The following are usually deemed to be extraordinary transactions that would require express authorization: (1) entering new lines of business, (2) making significant capital investments, (3) promising to pay large bonuses to employees, (4) selling or

---
[5]Traditional agency rules also govern *tort* questions; when officers or other corporate employees commit torts while acting within the scope of their authority, the corporation will generally be liable to pay damages for any injury caused.

mortgaging corporate real estate, (5) borrowing large sums of money, and (6) signing managerial employees to long-term contracts.

A third view representing the modern trend is that the office of president should be deemed inherently to carry broad powers to act on the corporation's behalf in almost any manner that could be authorized by the board of directors. This view is consistent with the reasonable expectations of most persons operating in the business world.

The majority view is applied in the following case.

ULLMAN-BRIGGS, INC. v. SALTON, INC.

U.S. District Court for the Southern District of New York, 754 F.Supp. 1003 (1991)

Dick Ullman and Charles Briggs owned plaintiff Ullman-Briggs, Inc., a manufacturer's representative that solicited orders from any merchants to whom its clients were willing to sell their products. These included department stores, specialty stores, distributors, and discounters. One of the plaintiff's clients was Salton, Inc. (defendant), whose president, Finesman, was a friend of Ullman's. Indeed, Ullman had introduced Finesman to the inventor of "Wet Tunes," a battery-operated shower radio that was Salton's most successful item in its line of electronic products.

On August, 5 1985, defendant Salton and plaintiff entered into a written contract providing that plaintiff would be Salton's exclusive representative in the Northeast for two years. Finesman, as president of Salton, signed the contract on its behalf. Soon thereafter, Sevko, Inc. bought Salton, fired Finesman, and immediately terminated its contract with plaintiff. In subsequent negotiations between plaintiff's principals and Sevko's officers, Sevko offered to allow plaintiff to be Salton's exclusive representative for two years as to just one store—J.C. Penney. Plaintiff rejected the offer and brought this action for breach of contract. Salton argued that it was outside the scope of Finesman's authority to sign the two-year contract. The following is excerpted from the trial court's order following trial.

Sprizzo, District Judge:

"[T]here was in fact a contract between Ullman-Briggs and Salton which was breached by defendant's termination of plaintiff. The Court finds that Alvin Finesman, as president of [Salton] at the time of the contract, had actual authority to enter into that contract. The corporate by-laws clearly gave Finesman broad authority to enter into contracts on behalf of the company. Moreover, it is well-settled that the president of a corporation has the [inherent] authority to enter into any necessary contract in the ordinary course of the company's business.

Defendant's argument that this contract was so unusual or extraordinary that Finesman exceeded his authority in entering into it is unpersuasive and must be rejected. This case is not analogous to cases, such as those relied upon by defendant, where the company's president sells the only asset the corporation owned or enters into an employment contract which provides for unusually large compensation in the form of the company's stock.

Moreover, there was evidence, which the Court finds credible, that a two-year written representation contract was not so unusual in the electronic appliance industry that Finesman clearly lacked authority to make it. This conclusion is supported by evidence that Salton subsequently offered Ullman-Briggs a two year contract with respect to sales to J.C. Penney.

[Judgment entered for plaintiff.]

Other Officers

Many large corporations have hundreds of vice-presidents, such as senior vice-presidents, junior vice-presidents, executive vice-presidents, and vice-presidents in charge of public relations. Most courts hold that vice-presidents have no authority by virtue of their office to deal with third parties; rather, their inherent powers are primarily internal—mainly to step into the president's shoes in an emergency. However, modern courts are beginning to hold more frequently that vice-presidents have broader authority, at least the authority to bind the corporation as to matters within their area of responsibility.

Most courts hold that secretaries and treasurers have no power by virtue of their office to bind the corporation as to contracts with third parties. Only internal and ministerial powers inhere in these offices. For example, the secretary has authority to give notice of meetings, to keep certain corporate records, and to certify copies of board resolutions and other corporate documents. Treasurers generally have the authority to collect and disburse corporate funds, but only as authorized by the board or other officers.

Apparent Authority
As we know from the discussion of agency law in Chapter 32, even in the absence of express or implied authority, *apparent authority* may still exist to bind the corporation. For example, in the *Ullman-Briggs* case, the court, after finding that actual authority existed to bind Salton to the two-year contract, went on to hold, as an alternative basis for its judgment, that apparent authority existed:

> Furthermore, even assuming [for purposes of argument] that Finesman did not have the actual authority to enter into the contract, plaintiff was certainly entitled to rely upon his apparent authority to execute the contract on behalf of Salton. Where a principal engages in words or conduct that give rise to the appearance that an agent has the authority to enter into a transaction, then the principal will be bound if a third party reasonably relies upon that appearance of authority. Here, Salton held Finesman out to the industry as its president and allowed him to enter into contracts on its behalf. Accordingly, he was clothed with a broad apparent authority and Ullman-Briggs's reliance upon that apparent authority was reasonable, especially since, as noted above, the contract was not so unusual that plaintiff should reasonably have known that he had no authority to make it.

Naturally there can be no apparent authority to do an act that the board of directors could not legally authorize.

Ratification
Even if an officer has neither actual (express or implied) nor apparent authority to enter into a contract, the corporation is still bound if it *ratifies* the contract expressly (such as by board resolution) or impliedly (for example, by knowingly and voluntarily accepting the benefits of the agreement).

RIGHTS OF CORPORATE MANAGERS
In the following discussion, the rights of directors will be dealt with separately from the rights of officers and other managerial employees. The reason for

this is that some of the rights possessed by directors are unique to their position.

Directors
Recognition and Participation
A director who has been properly elected possesses several rights of a very basic nature—for instance, the right to be recognized as a director by his or her associates, the right to receive notice of board meetings, and the right to attend and participate in them. A duly elected director who is excluded from recognition or participation by his or her associates can obtain a court order enforcing these rights.

Inspection
The right of directors to inspect all corporate records is somewhat similar to the inspection right possessed by shareholders. However, the reasons for allowing inspection by directors are even stronger than those for allowing shareholder inspection. Directors *must* have complete access to corporate records in order to fully discharge their decision-making responsibilities. It obviously would be unfair to hold them responsible for paying an illegal dividend, for example, if corporate financial records had not been completely at their disposal.

Because of this compelling need for access to corporate books, most states hold that a director's right of inspection is *absolute and unqualified* (that is, not subject to the various limitations that are often placed on a shareholder's inspection right). Of course, a director's abuse of this right can provide a basis for his or her removal from the board. And a director is liable for any damage to the corporation resulting from abuse of the right (such as its use for an improper purpose). But in the majority of states where the director's inspection right is absolute, *neither the other directors, the officers, nor the shareholders can restrict his or her examination of corporate records.*[6]

Compensation
The traditional rule was that directors were not entitled to compensation for their services to the corporation. This rule was predicated on the assumption that directors were usually shareholders and would receive their compensation in the form of dividends.

---

[6]The courts in a *few* states, however, have held that a director's inspection right can be denied where his or her motive is obviously hostile or otherwise improper.

It also took into account the fact that some directors also served as corporate officers and received compensation for their services in those positions.

The basis for this rule is not applicable to many modern corporations, however. It is not uncommon today for individuals having little or no stock ownership to serve as directors. Furthermore, a great many directors serve only as directors and do not hold other positions with the corporation.

For these reasons, there is a growing trend in modern corporations toward compensation of directors as such. The traditional rule provides no real obstacle to this trend, because it simply holds that directors have no inherent *right* to be compensated. They can in fact be paid if there is a valid authorization for such payment in the articles or bylaws. Indeed, the statutes of some states today go even further, providing, for example, that the board of directors can fix the compensation of its own members unless the articles or bylaws state otherwise. Directors are, of course, responsible for any abuse of this power.

Indemnification

The performance of their management responsibilities sometimes causes directors to become involved in legal proceedings. For example, the directors may be sued by a shareholder who claims that they acted negligently in managing the corporation. Or they may be charged by the government in a civil or criminal suit with a violation of the antitrust laws.

The costs of such lawsuits to the individual director, in terms of both expenses and potential liability for damages or fines, may be quite substantial. Under the common-law rule a director had no right to be indemnified (reimbursed) by the corporation for expenses or other losses. Today, however, the statutes of most states do permit, or even require, indemnification of corporate directors in some circumstances. The rationale for indemnity is that it (1) encourages innocent managers to defend themselves, (2) induces qualified people to agree to serve as directors, and (3) deters frivolous suits by shareholders and others.

Representative of the modern trend, RMBCA 8.51 authorizes a corporation to indemnify directors if (1) they conducted themselves in good faith, (2) they reasonably believed their conduct was in the corporation's best interests, and (3) in the case of criminal proceedings, they had no reasonable cause to believe that their conduct was unlawful. This *permissive*

indemnification covers judgments, penalties, fines, settlements, and expenses actually incurred in suits brought by third parties. However, if the suit was brought by or on behalf of the corporation, indemnification extends only to expenses and shall not be paid at all if the director is held liable to the corporation. It makes no sense for the corporation to receive a judgment against a director and then have to pay the money out again to reimburse the director.

RMBCA 8.52 states that unless the articles of incorporation provide otherwise, directors *shall* be indemnified for reasonable expenses if they have been wholly successful in their defense of any suit brought because they are or were directors. So, directors who prevail entirely are entitled to *mandatory indemnification*.[7]

Officers and Other Managerial Employees

Corporate officers and other individuals who have managerial responsibilities are simply *employees* of the corporation.[8] It naturally follows, therefore, that the rights they have with respect to compensation and other matters are determined by their employment contracts.

Since their positions involve them in corporate decision making, officers and other managerial employees are subject to many of the same risks of litigation as are directors. Thus the rules regarding indemnification are the same for directors, officers, and managerial employees. That is, everything we have said about indemnification of directors applies with equal force to all others occupying management positions.

LIABILITIES OF CORPORATE MANAGERS

Those who manage the corporate enterprise owe to the corporation and its shareholders a number of basic duties that can be classified under the headings of *obedience, due care,* and *loyalty.* A corporate manager incurs personal liability for the failure to fulfill any of these duties. In addition to these fundamental duties, certain special liabilities are imposed by federal securities laws. Unlike the previous sec-

---

[7]RMBCA 8.54 also provides for court-ordered indemnification if the court determines that the director is entitled to mandatory indemnification under 8.52 *or* that "the director is fairly and reasonably entitled to indemnification in view of all the relevant circumstances."

[8]The word *employee* is used in a nontechnical sense. Managers and supervisors are not considered "employees" under some other specialized laws, such as those governing labor-management relations. But such laws are not our concern here.

LEGAL FOCUS

Ethics

Legal Focus
ETHICS

Assume that Company A wishes to buy all the shares of Company B. The deal will produce a nice profit for Company B shareholders, but Company B's directors know that Company A's first step upon acquiring control will be to close several plants in Ohio currently owned by Company B. Thousands of Company B's employees will lose their jobs.

Large corporations face a difficult question: For whose benefit do they exist? The traditional view, explicated in the classic case *Dodge v. Ford Motor Co.*, 170 N.W. 668 (Mich. 1919), is that "[a] business corporation is organized and carried on primarily for the profit *of the stockholders.*" (Emphasis added.)

In recent years, some ethicists have argued that because the large

corporation has become a major institution—comparable at some level to government, school, and church—it should be operated with a broader perspective. In other words, corporate officers and directors should take into account the concerns of other "stakeholders" whose interests are directly affected by the operation of the corporation. For example, employees, customers, and suppliers obviously have a large stake in numerous corporate decisions. Communities in which corporate plants and offices are located have similar interests.

A decision that might benefit shareholders—for example, to sell all Company B shares at a profit to Company A—may adversely affect the employees who are laid off in Ohio, the customers in Ohio who lose their local supplier, and the communities in Ohio who count on the corporation's tax

payments and charitable contributions.

Some argue that it is unethical to make corporate decisions based *solely* on a policy of maximizing profits without concern for the adverse ramifications such decisions may have on the lives of nonshareholders. They argue that it is myopic to mandate that all business judgment decisions be made with the express goal of maximizing short-term share prices. Others argue just as vehemently that the shareholders do, after all, own the corporation and its assets, and therefore their interests must be paramount. To permit or require consideration of the interests of other stakeholders (as many recent state statutes do in the takeover context) is an arguable appropriation of the property of the shareholders, converting their for-profit investment into an involuntary charitable enterprise.

What do you think?

---

tion on the *rights* of corporate managers, our discussion of *liabilities* makes no distinction between directors and other types of managers. The duties and liabilities of all who manage the corporation are essentially the same.

Obedience

Corporate managers have a duty to see that the corporation obeys the laws and confines its operations to those activities that are within the limits of its corporate powers. If they knowingly or carelessly involve the corporation in either an illegal or unauthorized act, they are personally liable for any resulting damage to the corporation.[9]

Due Care and the Business Judgment Rule

The duty of due care is sometimes referred to as the duty of "diligence." It is, in effect, a duty "not to be

[9]Of course, any manager who participates in the commission of an illegal act also may be personally subject to fines or other penalties imposed by the particular law.

negligent." In applying this standard, courts normally require a director, officer, or other manager to exercise the kind of care that an ordinarily prudent person would exercise in a similar position and under similar circumstances.

Although held to a standard of reasonable care, a manager is not liable for honest mistakes of judgment. Under normal circumstances, courts are extremely reluctant to interfere with the business decisions of a corporation's managers, and will not second-guess the wisdom of those decisions. Courts feel that if bad decisions are made, the proper remedy is for shareholders to exercise their voting power to bring in new management, and not to subject business decisions to judicial review. Under this so-called **business judgment rule,** a court will not hold a manager liable for the consequences of a decision, even if harm resulted to the corporation, so long as the manager made a reasonably informed decision and apparently acted in a good faith belief at the time that the decision was in the best interests of the corporation. The term "business judgment rule" is simply another way of referring to the manager's basic duty of due care.

Examples of those relatively unusual situations in which a manager might be liable despite the business judgment rule would include (1) the failure to review corporate records or to carefully consider other relevant evidence before making an important decision; (2) the failure to seek expert advice (such as that of an attorney, accountant, or engineer) about a technical matter that clearly called for input from such an expert; and (3) the complete reliance on someone else's opinion without making a reasonable inquiry, where the person giving the opinion clearly had a selfish interest in the matter, or where the opinion itself obviously was erroneous or baseless (such as relying totally on the opinion of another director who had a personal interest in the matter, or relying on the advice of an attorney that bid rigging or bribery was perfectly legitimate).

Although the business judgment rule, or duty of due care, is applied to all aspects of the manager's decision-making role, in recent years courts have been called upon with increasing frequency to apply the standard to managers' actions when the corporation is the target of an attempted takeover by another company. For this reason, in the discussion of mergers in the next chapter, a separate section deals with the responsibilities of corporate managers when responding to a takeover attempt.

In a non-takeover context, the next two cases each involve claims that corporate directors violated the duty of due care in their management of the business.

Shlensky v. Wrigley

Appellate Court of Illinois, 237 N.E.2d 776 (1968)

 Shlensky, the plaintiff, was a majority shareholder in Chicago National League Ball Club, Inc. The corporation owned and operated the major league professional baseball team known as the Chicago Cubs. The individual defendants were directors of the Cubs. Defendant Philip K. Wrigley was also president of the corporation and owner of approximately 80 percent of the corporation's shares.

Shlensky filed suit in behalf of the corporation (a derivative suit), claiming that it had been damaged by the failure of the directors to have lights installed in Wrigley Field, the Cubs' home park. No trial was held, however, because the trial court dismissed his complaint on the ground that it did not set forth a claim that the law would recognize even if his version of the facts were correct. Shlensky appealed.

Sullivan, Justice:

. . . Plaintiff alleges that since night baseball was first played in 1935 nineteen of the twenty major league teams have scheduled night games. In 1966, out of a total of 1620 games in the major leagues, 932 were played at night. Plaintiff alleges that every member of the major leagues, other than the Cubs, scheduled substantially all of its home games in 1966 at night, exclusive of opening days, Saturdays, Sundays, holidays and days prohibited by league rules. Allegedly this has been done for the specific purpose of maximizing attendance and thereby maximizing revenue and income.

The Cubs, in the years 1961–65, sustained operating losses from its direct baseball operations. Plaintiff attributes these losses to inadequate attendance at Cubs' home games. He concludes that if the directors continue to refuse to install lights at Wrigley Field and schedule night baseball games, the Cubs will continue to sustain comparable losses and its financial condition will continue to deteriorate.

Plaintiff alleges that, except for the year 1963, attendance at Cubs' home games has been substantially below that at their road games, many of which were played at night.

Plaintiff compares attendance at Cubs' games with that of the Chicago White Sox, an American League club, whose weekday games were generally played at night. The weekend attendance figures for the two teams was similar; however, the White Sox weeknight games drew many more patrons than did the Cubs' weekday games. . . .

Plaintiff further alleges that defendant Wrigley has refused to install lights, not because of interest in the welfare of the corporation but because of his personal opinions "that baseball is a 'daytime sport' and that the installation of lights and night baseball games will have a deteriorating effect upon the surrounding neighborhood." It is alleged

(continues)

SILENSKY V. WRIGLEY

(continued from previous page)
that he has admitted that he is not interested in whether the Cubs would benefit financially from such action because of his concern for the neighborhood, and that he would be willing for the team to play night games if a new stadium were built in Chicago. . . .

Plaintiff . . . argues that the directors are acting for reasons unrelated to the financial interest and welfare of the Cubs. However, we are not satisfied that the motives assigned to Philip K. Wrigley, and through him to the other directors, are contrary to the best interests of the corporation and the stockholders. For example, it appears to us that the effect on the surrounding neighborhood might well be considered by a director who was considering patrons who would or would not attend the games if the park were in a poor neighborhood. Furthermore, the long run interest of the corporation in its property value at Wrigley Field might demand all efforts to keep the neighborhood from deteriorating. By these thoughts we do not mean to say that we have decided that the decision of the directors was a correct one. That is beyond our jurisdiction and ability. We are merely saying that the decision is one [for the] directors [to make]. . . .

Finally, we do not agree with plaintiff's contention that failure to follow the example of the other major league clubs in scheduling night games constituted negligence. Plaintiff made no allegation that these teams' night schedules were profitable or that the pur-pose for which night baseball had been undertaken was fulfilled. Furthermore, it cannot be said that directors, even those of corporations that are losing money, must follow the lead of the other corporations in the field. Directors are elected for their business capabilities and judgment and the courts cannot require them to forego their judgment because of the decisions of directors of other companies. Courts may not decide these questions in the absence of a clear showing of dereliction of duty on the part of the specific directors and mere failure to "follow the crowd" is not such a dereliction.

For the foregoing reasons the order of dismissal entered by the trial court is affirmed. ⚖

FRANCIS V. UNITED JERSEY BANK

Superior Court of New Jersey, 392 A.2d 1233 (1978)

Pritchard & Baird Intermediaries Corp. ("Pritchard & Baird") was engaged in the business of being a "reinsurance broker." (If an insurance company has a very large individual risk or a number of similar risks on which it has given coverage, it often protects itself from too heavy a loss by shifting the risk to another large insurer or group of insurers. It does this by "reinsuring," that is, by purchasing insurance on all or part of the underlying risk from one or more other insurers. A reinsurance broker brings the parties together in a reinsurance arrangement.) Charles Pritchard, Sr., the founder of the company, was for many years its principal shareholder and controlling force. In 1970 he took his sons, Charles, Jr. and William, into the business. Because of the father's advancing age, the two sons played an increasingly dominant role in the affairs of the corporation. After the father's death in 1973, the sons took complete control.

Pritchard & Baird had been a successful company under the control of Charles, Sr., even though he engaged in various questionable business practices. He commingled the funds of different clients, commingled the company's funds with his own per-sonal funds, and kept incredibly poor records. However, his clients were always taken care of and his creditors were always paid. After his sons took over, they continued his sloppy business practices but did not continue taking care of clients and paying creditors. In essence, they "looted" the company of millions of dollars and by the end of 1975 had plunged it into bankruptcy.

Francis was appointed as trustee in bankruptcy for Pritchard & Baird. In this capacity he sought to recover for Pritchard & Baird's creditors several million dollars which had been wrongfully taken from the company. He brought suit against two

(continues)

FRANCIS V. UNITED JERSEY BANK

(continued from previous page)
defendants: (1) the father's estate, of which United Jersey Bank was administrator; and (2) the estate of Lillian Pritchard. Lillian Pritchard was the wife of Charles Sr., and had served as a director of the corporation from its creation until its bankruptcy. She died after the bankruptcy proceedings began. Apparently because of the size of Lillian Pritchard's personal estate, the primary question in the case was whether she had acted negligently in her role as a director by not discovering and stopping the illegal actions of her sons. If so, her estate would be liable for that negligence. The trial court's opinion follows. (Note: There was no mention of the whereabouts of the two sons.)

Stanton, Judge:

. . . Directors are responsible for the general management of the affairs of a corporation. They have particular responsibility with respect to distributions of assets to shareholders and with respect to loans to officers and directors. It is true that in this case the directors were never asked to take explicit and formal action with respect to any of the unlawful payments made to members of the Pritchard family. I am satisfied that, in terms of her actual knowledge, Mrs. Pritchard did not know what her sons were doing to the corporation and she did not know that it was unlawful. She did not intend to cheat anyone or to defraud creditors of the corporation. However, if Mrs. Pritchard had paid the slightest attention to her duties as a director, and if she had paid the slightest attention to the affairs of the corporation, she would have known what was happening.

Financial statements were prepared for Pritchard & Baird every year. They were simple statements, typically no longer than three or four pages. The annual financial statements accurately and clearly reflected the payments to

members of the Pritchard family, and they clearly reflected the desperate financial condition of the corporation. For example, a brief glance at the statement for the fiscal year ending on January 31, 1970 would have revealed that Charles, Jr. had withdrawn from the corporation $230,932 to which he was not entitled, and William had improperly withdrawn $207,329. A brief glance at the statement for the year ending January 31, 1973 would have shown Charles, Jr. owing the corporation $1,899,288 and William owing it $1,752,318. The same statement showed a working capital deficit of $3,506,460. The statement for the fiscal year ending January 31, 1975, a simple four-page document, showed Charles, Jr. owing the corporation $4,373,928, William owing $5,417,388, and a working capital deficit of $10,176,419. All statements reflected the fact that the corporation had virtually no assets and that liabilities vastly exceeded assets. In short, anyone who took a brief glance at the annual statements at any time after January 31, 1970 and who had the slightest knowledge of the corporation's business activities would know that Charles, Jr. and William were, in simple and blunt terms, stealing money which should have been paid to the corporation's customers.

. . . [T]he inherent nature of a corporate director's job necessarily implies that he must have a basic idea of the corporation's activities. He should know what business the corporation is in, and he should have some broad idea of the scope and range of the corporation's affairs. In terms of our case, Mrs. Pritchard should have known that Pritchard & Baird was in the reinsurance business as a broker and that it annually handled millions of dollars belonging to, or owing to various clients. Charged with that knowledge, it seems to me that a director in Mrs. Pritchard's position had, at the bare minimum, an obligation to ask for and read the annual financial statements of the corporation. She would then have

the obligation to react appropriately to what a reading of the statements revealed.

It has been urged in this case that Mrs. Pritchard should not be held responsible for what happened while she was director of Pritchard & Baird because she was a simple housewife who served as a director as an accommodation to her husband and sons. Let me start by saying that I reject the sexism which is unintended but which is implicit in such an argument. There is no reason why the average housewife could not adequately discharge the functions of a director of a corporation such as Pritchard & Baird, despite a lack of business career experience, if she gave some reasonable attention to what she was supposed to be doing. The problem is not that Mrs. Pritchard was a simple housewife. The problem is that she was a person who took a job which necessarily entailed certain responsibilities and she then failed to make any effort whatever to discharge those responsibilities. The ultimate insult to the fundamental dignity and equality of women would be to treat a grown woman as though she were a child not responsible for her acts and omissions.

It has been argued that allowance should be made for the fact that during the last years in question Mrs. Pritchard was old, was grief-stricken at the loss of her husband, sometimes consumed too much alcohol and was psychologically overborne by her sons. I was not impressed by the testimony supporting that argument. There is no proof whatever that Mrs. Pritchard ever ceased to be fully competent. There is no proof that she ever made any effort as a director to question or stop the unlawful activities of Charles, Jr. and William. The actions of the sons were so blatantly wrongful that it is hard to see how they could have resisted any moderately firm objection to what they were doing. The fact is that Mrs. Pritchard never knew what they were doing because she never made

(continues)

FRANCIS V. UNITED JERSEY BANK

(continued from previous page)
the slightest effort to discharge any of her responsibilities as a director of Pritchard & Baird.

Defense counsel have argued that Mrs. Pritchard should not be held liable because she was a mere "figurehead director." . . . In legal contemplation there is no such thing as a "figurehead" director. This has been clearly recognized for many years so far as banking corporations are concerned. 3A *Fletcher, Cyclopedia of the Law of Private Corporations, §1090,* has this to say:

It frequently happens that persons become directors of banking houses for the purpose of capitalizing the position in the community where the bank does business, without any intention of watching or participating in the conduct of its affairs. It is a dangerous practice for the director, since such figureheads and rubber stamps are universally held liable on the ground that they have not discharged their duty nor exercised the required amount of diligence exacted of them.

There is no reason why the rule stated by *Fletcher* should be limited to banks. Certainly, there is no reason why the rule should not be extended to a corporation such as Pritchard & Baird which routinely handled millions of dollars belonging to, or owing to, other persons. . . .

I hold that Mrs. Pritchard was negligent in performing her duties as a director of Pritchard & Baird. Had she performed her duties with due care, she would readily have discovered the wrongdoing of Charles, Jr. and William shortly after the close of the fiscal year ending on January 31, 1970, and she could easily have taken effective steps to stop the wrongdoing. Her negligence caused customers and creditors of Pritchard & Baird to suffer losses amounting to $10,355,736.91. There will be a judgment against her estate in that amount. ⚖

Protecting the Director

The outcome in *Francis* notwithstanding, the duty of care typically has not been applied in a burdensome manner, in part because the RMBCA and other state statutes accord to officers and directors, especially outside directors, a *right to rely* on information, reports, opinions, financial statements, and financial data prepared or provided by officers, employees, attorneys, accountants, or committees of directors that are reasonably believed to be reliable. In other words, a director need not hire a private investigator or a separate auditing firm to double check every corporate record provided; he or she may assume that they are accurate. On the other hand, as one court noted, if a director "has recklessly reposed confidence in an obviously untrustworthy employee, has refused or neglected cavalierly to perform his duty as a director, or has ignored either willfully or through inattention obvious danger signs of employee wrongdoing, the law will cast the burden of liability on him."[10]

Furthermore, remember that a shareholder derivative suit seeking to impose liability on a director for breach of a duty of due care must overcome not only the business judgment rule defense, but also the many procedural hurdles discussed in the last chapter, such as the demand requirement. Even if a shareholder managed to demonstrate that demand is properly excused, for example, his or her suit may still be derailed by a **special litigation committee** (SLC). How does an SLC work? Assume that a shareholder files a derivative suit against several board members alleging that they have defrauded the company. The board may appoint an SLC, composed of "independent" (nondefendant) directors or nondirectors, charging the SLC with determining whether allowing the suit to be prosecuted is in the best interests of the corporation.

Perhaps not surprisingly, most SLCs conclude that continuation of the lawsuit is not in the corporation's best interests. Although some jurisdictions accord little weight to SLCs, many view their decisions as *binding* so long as they are truly independent and appear to have conducted a careful investigation. Courts in other jurisdictions, including Delaware, reserve the right substantively to review the SLC's conclusions before dismissing the lawsuit. All in all, the SLC is yet another difficult hurdle for a derivative suit plaintiff to surmount in attempting to impose liability on careless or crooked directors.

[10]*Graham v. Allis-Chalmers Mfg. Corp.,* 188 A.2d 125 (Del.Ch. 1963).

Finally, in the next chapter, in the takeover context, we shall discuss *Smith v. Van Gorkom*,[11] a landmark Delaware case in which major liability was imposed on directors for carelessly and inattentively approving the sale of a corporation for an amount arguably much less than its true worth. Although *Van Gorkom* is one of very few cases ever imposing such liability, it scared corporations and potential directors so much that they ran to state legislatures for protection. In the late 1980s, most states passed laws authorizing shareholders to eliminate director and officer liability for breaches of due care. For example, RMBCA 2.02(b)(4) authorizes articles of incorporation to contain

a provision eliminating or limiting the liability of a director to the corporation or its shareholders for money damages for any action taken, or any failure to take any action, as a director, except liability for (A) the amount of a financial benefit received by a director to which he is not entitled; (B) an intentional infliction of harm on the corporation or the shareholders; (C) a violation of [provisions regarding unlawful dividends and other distributions]; or (D) an intentional violation of a criminal law.

Loyalty

Directors, officers, and other corporate managers are deemed to be *fiduciaries* of the corporation they serve. Their relationship to the corporation and its shareholders is one of trust. They must act in good faith and with the highest regard for the corporation's interests as opposed to their personal interests. Several problems that commonly arise in the context of the duty of loyalty are discussed below.

Use of Corporate Funds

Obviously, a director or other party who occupies a fiduciary position with respect to the corporation must not use corporate funds for his or her own purposes.

Confidential Information

A director or other manager sometimes possesses confidential information that is valuable to the corporation, such as secret formulas, product designs, marketing strategies, or customer lists. The manager is not allowed to appropriate such information for his or her own use.

[11]488 A.2d 858 (Del. 1985).

Contracts with the Corporation

A corporate manager who enters into a contract with the corporation should realize that it is not an "arm's-length" transaction. That is, the manager must make a full disclosure of all material information he or she possesses regarding the transaction. Furthermore, if the contract is at all unfair to the corporation, it is *voidable* at the corporation's option.

For obvious reasons, courts have not looked kindly upon contracts in which a *director* has a personal interest. (The contract might be with the director personally or with another company in which he or she has a financial stake.) If a contract of this nature was authorized at a board meeting where the presence of the interested director was necessary for a quorum or where this director's vote was required for a majority, many states hold the contract to be voidable at the corporation's option *regardless of its fairness*.

Corporate Opportunity

The **corporate opportunity doctrine** prohibits corporate managers from personally taking advantage of business opportunities that, in all fairness, should belong to the corporation. An obvious violation of this doctrine occurs when a manager has been authorized to purchase land or other property for the corporation but instead purchases it for himself.

Application of the corporate opportunity doctrine is sometimes not so clear-cut, however. A much more difficult problem is presented, for instance, when a director or other manager is confronted with a business opportunity arising from an *outside source* rather than from direct corporate authorization. For example: C is a director of Ace Air Freight, a corporation engaged in the business of transporting freight by air. C learns that M, a third party, has a used airplane in excellent condition that he is offering for sale at a low price. Can C purchase the airplane for himself? If the plane is of a type suitable for the corporation's freight business, the answer probably is no. He is obligated to inform the corporation of the opportunity.

This example illustrates the so-called "line of business" test employed by most courts in resolving such problems. Under this approach, a corporate manager cannot take personal advantage of a business opportunity that is *closely associated with the corporation's line of business*. Furthermore, the rule includes opportunities not only in the area of current corporate business but also in areas where the corporation might naturally expand.

Of course, if the corporation is actually offered the opportunity and *rejects* it, an individual manager can then exploit it. Some courts also have held that if the corporation is financially *unable* to take a business opportunity, a manager can lawfully take personal advantage of it without first disclosing it to the corporation. Other courts, however, have held that the manager always must first disclose the opportunity

and give the corporation a reasonable time to decide whether it is able and willing to exploit the opportunity before the manager can personally seize it.

The following case illustrates the type of double-dealing that the corporate opportunity doctrine is designed to prevent. In addition, the case involves the question whether a corporation's financial inability to take a business opportunity excuses a manager's failure to disclose the opportunity to the corporation.

KLINICKI v. LUNDGREN

Supreme Court of Oregon, 695 P.2d 906 (1985)

Case

In January 1977 Klinicki conceived the idea of engaging in the air transportation business in Berlin, West Germany. He discussed the idea with his friend Lundgren. At that time, both men were furloughed Pan American Airlines pilots stationed in West Germany. They decided to enter the air transportation business, planning to begin operations with an air taxi service and later to expand into other service, such as regularly scheduled or charter flights. In April 1977 they incorporated Berlinair, Inc., as an Oregon corporation. Lundgren was the corporation's president and a director; Klinicki was vice-president and a director. Each owned 33 percent of the corporation's stock. Lelco, Inc., a corporation owned by Lundgren and members of his family, also owned 33 percent, and the corporation's attorney owned the remaining 1 percent. Berlinair obtained the necessary government licenses, purchased an aircraft, and in November 1977 began passenger service.

As president, Lundgren was primarily responsible for developing and promoting Berlinair's transportation business. Klinicki was in charge of operations and maintenance. In November 1977 Klinicki and Lundgren, as

representatives of Berlinair, met with representatives of the Berliner Flug Ring (BFR), a consortium of Berlin travel agents that contracts for charter flights to take German tourists to various vacation resorts. The BFR contract was considered a lucrative business opportunity by those familiar with the air transportation business, and Klinicki and Lundgren had contemplated pursuing the contract when they formed Berlinair. After the initial meeting, all subsequent contacts with BFR were made by Lundgren or other Berlinair employees acting under his direction.

During the early stages of negotiations, Lundgren believed that Berlinair could not obtain the contract because BFR was then satisfied with its existing carrier. In early June 1978, however, Lundgren learned that there was a good chance that the BFR contract might be available. He informed a BFR representative that he would make a proposal on behalf of a new company. On July 7, 1978, he incorporated Air Berlin Charter Co. (ABC) and was its sole owner. On August 20, 1978, ABC presented BFR with a contract proposal, and after a series of discussions it was awarded the contract on September 1, 1978. Lundgren effectively concealed from Klinicki his negotiations with BFR and his diversion of the BFR contract.

Klinicki, as a minority stockholder in Berlinair, filed suit against ABC and Lundgren for usurping a corporate opportunity of Berlinair. The trial court ruled in Klinicki's favor and imposed a constructive trust on ABC, which required ABC's profits to be turned over to Berlinair. The court of appeals affirmed, and Lundgren and ABC appealed.

Jones, Justice:

ABC . . . contend[s] that the concealment and diversion of the BFR contract was not a usurpation of a corporate opportunity, because Berlinair did not have the financial ability to undertake that contract. ABC argues that proof of financial ability is a necessary part of a corporate opportunity case. . . .

There is no dispute that the corporate opportunity doctrine precludes corporate fiduciaries from diverting to themselves business opportunities in which the corporation has an expectancy, property interest or right, or which in fairness should otherwise belong to the corporation. The doctrine follows from a corporate fiduciary's duty of undivided loyalty to the corporation. . . . If there is presented to [a director or officer] a business opportunity which is within the scope of the [corporation's] activities and of present or potential advantage to it, the law will

(continues)

KLINICKI V. LUNDGREN

(continued from previous page)
not permit him to seize the opportunity for himself; if he does so, the corporation may elect to claim all of the benefits of the transaction. . . .

We first address the issue . . . of the relevance of a corporation's financial ability to undertake a business opportunity. . . . This is an issue of first impression in Oregon. . . .

A rigid rule was applied in *Irving Trust Co. v. Deutsch,* 73 F.2d 121 (2nd Cir. 1934). In that case a syndicate made up of directors of Acoustic Products Co. purchased for themselves . . . the rights to manufacture under certain radio patents which were essential to Acoustic. They justified this on the ground that Acoustic was not financially able to purchase the patents on which the defendants later made very substantial profits. The courts refused to inquire whether the conclusion of financial inability was justified. Referring to the facts which raised a question whether Acoustic actually did lack the funds or credit necessary to make the acquisition, the court said:

Nevertheless, [the facts in the case concerning whether Acoustic lacked funds to carry out the contract] tend to show the wisdom of a rigid rule forbidding directors of a solvent corporation to take over for their own profit a corporate contract on the plea of the corporation's financial inability to perform. If

the directors are uncertain whether the corporation can make the necessary outlays, they need not embark upon the venture; if they do, they may not substitute themselves for the corporation any place along the line and divert possible benefits into their own pockets.

On the other end of the legal spectrum from *Irving Trust Co. v. Deutsch* [is a] Minnesota case, *Miller v. Miller,* 222 N.W.2d 71 (1974). . . . In *Miller,* the Minnesota Supreme Court . . . found that [the corporation's] financial ability [to pursue the business opportunity] is a prerequisite to establishing a corporate opportunity. . . . Defendant, relying on *Miller,* contends [that the plaintiff must prove that the corporation was financially able to obtain the BFR contract]. We reject this argument. . . .

Where a director or [officer] wishes to take personal advantage of a "corporate opportunity," the director or [officer] must . . . promptly offer the opportunity and disclose all material facts known regarding the opportunity to the disinterested directors or, if there is no disinterested director, to the disinterested shareholders. . . . The director or [officer] may take advantage of the corporate opportunity only after full disclosure and only if the opportunity is rejected by a majority of the disinterested directors or, if there are no disinterested directors, by a ma-

jority of the disinterested shareholders. If, after full disclosure, the disinterested directors or shareholders unreasonably fail to reject the offer, the interested director or [officer] may proceed to take the opportunity if he can prove the taking was otherwise "fair" to the corporation. Full disclosure to the appropriate corporate body is, however, an absolute condition precedent to the validity of any forthcoming rejection as well as to the availability to the director or [officer] of the defense of fairness. . . .

The BFR contract was a "corporate opportunity" of Berlinair. . . . Lundgren did not offer Berlinair the BFR contract . . . and did not attempt to obtain the consent of Berlinair to his taking of the BFR corporate opportunity. . . . Berlinair never rejected the opportunity presented by the BFR contract . . . [and did not subsequently ratify] the appropriation of the BFR contract. . . .

Because of the above, the defendant may not now contend that Berlinair did not have the financial ability to successfully pursue the BFR contract.

The Court of Appeals is affirmed. [ABC holds the BFR contract in trust for Berlinair, and all profits from the contract must be paid to Berlinair.] ⚖️

Controlling Shareholders
In some situations, **controlling shareholders** are placed under fiduciary duties similar to those owed by directors, officers, and other managers. If a single shareholder, or a group of shareholders acting in concert, owns a sufficient number of shares to control the direction of corporate affairs, the possibility exists that they will try to exercise this control so as to further their own personal interests at the expense of the corporation and the other shareholders. Corporate control must not be abused, however, and the

controlling shareholders are required to act in the best interests of the corporation as a whole and with complete fairness to minority shareholders.

Miscellaneous Statutory Duties
In addition to the duties of care and loyalty, directors and officers face numerous specific duties imposed by statutes, both state and federal. For example, most states (and RMBCA 8.33) impose liability on directors who vote for or assent to illegal corporate distributions, such as a payment of dividends that renders

the corporation insolvent. Similar provisions in many jurisdictions impose on directors liability for such actions as issuance of shares without receiving proper consideration, preferential transfers to shareholders during corporate liquidation, and beginning business without a statutorily required minimum of capital.

There are also various statutes, state and federal, that subject officers and directors to liability for OSHA violations, antitrust violations, overtime due workers under the federal Fair Labor Standards Act, failure to withhold federal income tax payments, Employee Retirement Income Security Act violations, and unpaid employee wages.

Areas of potential liability also arise under various federal securities laws, including the **Securities Act of 1933** and the **Securities Exchange Act of 1934.** Directors are often sued under these laws for such acts as (1) issuing shares pursuant to misleading prospectuses, (2) issuing shares without registering them with the SEC, (3) soliciting proxies by making misleading statements to shareholders, and (4) insider trading. All of these matters are discussed in detail in Chapter 41.

CONTRACT, TORT, AND CRIMINAL LIABILITIES OF MANAGERS
Contract Liabilities

When officers (or other employees) contract on behalf of a corporation, they generally do not intend to be individually liable on the contract. Rather, they believe they are acting only as agents for the company. However, agency rules dictate that an officer may be *personally* liable on a contract if he or she (1) exceeds actual authority, (2) signs the contract without indicating his or her representative capacity, (3) signs a personal guarantee to support the corporate obligation, or (4) appears to be the contracting party while acting on behalf of an undisclosed corporate principal.

Tort Liabilities

Any director, officer, or employee of a corporation who commits or directs the commission of a tort that injures third parties will be liable for that tort, even if acting with the purpose of helping the corporation. Naturally, if the act is within the scope of the employee's authority, the corporation will be vicariously liable as well.

Criminal Liabilities

As state and federal prosecutors have cracked down on white collar crime in recent years, corporate managers have increasingly become the targets of criminal charges. The criminal liability of corporations and of their managers was discussed in detail in Chapter 7 and will not be repeated here.

SUMMARY

The board of directors sets basic corporate policy and makes important business decisions; often it delegates to officers and other corporate employees the authority to make daily operational decisions. Directors take formal action only as a body; such action is usually taken at meetings, although many states permit board action by written consent or conference call in some situations. Each director has one vote, regardless of whether he or she owns shares in the corporation and regardless of the number of shares owned. Directors usually have regularly scheduled meetings, but special meetings may also be called upon the giving of adequate notice of the time, place, and purpose of the meeting.

A corporate director is given a number of rights necessary to the effective performance of his or her functions, including the right to be recognized as a director by associates, the right to receive notice of board meetings, and the right to attend and participate in those meetings. A director also has the right of inspection. Although there is no inherent right to compensation, the law normally permits corporations to compensate directors, and the trend is clearly toward the granting of substantial compensation. A director also has no inherent right to be indemnified for liabilities incurred while acting on corporate matters, but today the law usually does permit such indemnification. The rights of other managers, such as officers, are normally determined by their employment contracts with the corporation.

Directors, officers, and other corporate managers owe to the corporation and its shareholders the duties of obedience, due care, and loyalty. The business judgment rule is used by courts when interpreting and applying the duty of due care. Corporate managers may be held liable under federal securities laws in several situations, including those in which they either fail to file required registration statements or file statements that are misleading, buy or sell the company's securities on the basis of material inside information, make short-swing profits on the company's securities, and fail to reveal in a clear and truthful manner all relevant material information in a proxy solicitation.

KEY TERMS

Classified board
Business judgment rule
Special litigation committee
Corporate opportunity doctrine
Controlling shareholder
Securities Act of 1933
Securities Exchange Act of 1934

QUESTIONS AND PROBLEMS

1. Charlestown Company was dissolved, and its shareholders elected a committee to work with the board of directors in winding up the business. The laws of New Hampshire, where the case arose, provided that "the business of every such corporation shall be managed by the directors thereof, subject to the bylaws and votes of the corporation, and under their direction by such officers and agents as shall be duly appointed by the directors or by the corporation." The board ignored the committee. A shareholder sued, challenging the board's failure to recognize the committee. Did the board act properly? Discuss. (*Charlestown Boot and Shoe Co. v. Dunsmore*, 60 N.H. 85, 1880.)

2. SCLD Company was incorporated in October 1960 by Florence. It had nine directors, including Kring, who was issued 30,000 shares of stock in exchange for some cash and a promissory note. The corporation never made money and ceased operation in about a year. In August 1961, three directors—Kring, Florence, and Mathis—met and agreed that Kring would return his shares in exchange for cancellation of his note. Plaintiff sued on behalf of creditors to enforce the note as an unpaid subscription. Was the August 1961 meeting effective to cancel the note? Discuss. (*Doyle v. Chladek*, 401 P.2d 18, Or. 1965.)

3. The president of Hessler, Inc., made a contract with an employee, Farrell, in which retirement benefits were promised to Farrell. For many years, the president had been allowed to manage the corpora-

tion more or less independently of the board; he also owned approximately 80 percent of the corporation's stock. If any board members opposed him, the president removed them. When Farrell retired, the corporation refused to pay the benefits and Farrell sued. The corporation claimed that the agreement made with Farrell by the president was invalid because it had not been approved by the board of directors. Is the corporation correct? Discuss. (*Hessler, Inc. v. Farrell*, 226 A.2d 708, Del. 1967.)

4. Plaintiff was given a long-term contract to manage an incorporated restaurant business. The contract was signed by plaintiff and by Rapp, president and sole shareholder of the corporation. The contract was never approved at a formal meeting of the board of directors, and later the corporation argued that the contract was not binding on it. Is the corporation correct? Discuss. (*Rapp v. Felsenthal*, 628 S.W.2d 258, Tex.Civ.App. 1982.)

5. Tastee Freez Industries was a holding company owning four subsidiaries, including Drive-In. Tastee Freez sought to borrow money from Boulevard Bank, but the bank would not loan money without a guarantee from Drive-In. Maranz, president of Drive-In, signed the guarantee. Because a guarantee of another corporation's debt is usually considered an "extraordinary" act, the bank asked to see a copy of the directors' resolution authorizing Maranz's signing. Maranz produced a resolution with the corporate seal duly affixed by Drive-In's secretary, Dick. It turned out that Maranz and Dick had forged the resolution; Drive-In's board had never authorized the action. Is the guarantee binding on Drive-In? Discuss. (*In re Drive-In Development Corp.*, 371 F.2d 215, 7th Cir. 1966.)

6. In 1976, American Express (AE) found itself holding 2 million shares of DLJ stock worth $26 million less than when purchased four years before. AE's board decided to issue the shares as a special "in kind" dividend to its shareholders. Two shareholders sued the directors, alleging a breach of its duty of due care. They contended that if AE were to sell the shares on the market rather than distribute them to shareholders, it would sustain a capital loss of $26 million that could be offset against taxable capital gains on other investments, thus saving the corporation about $8 million in income tax. The board had considered this plan but rejected it because of the

adverse effect that a $26 million loss on its balance sheet might have on the market price of AE stock. Plaintiffs did not claim fraud or self-dealing by the board, but strongly argued that defendants made a very imprudent decision. Should plaintiffs' claim prevail? Discuss. (*Kamin v. American Express,* 383 N.Y.S.2d 807, 1976.)

7. Marvin and Anderson were directors of IVAC. Marvin instigated a loan to ISS, Inc., without disclosing that he was a shareholder and director of ISS. Anderson knew of Marvin's interest, but did not tell the other directors. After IVAC went into bankruptcy, Marvin and Anderson were sued for having breached their fiduciary duty to IVAC in approving loans to ISS that were not repaid. Discuss their liability. (*In re Illinois Valley Acceptance Corp.,* 531 F.Supp. 737, C.D.Ill. 1982.)

8. Bio-Lab, Inc. was formed for the purpose of establishing a plasmapheresis business that involved separating red blood cells from the plasma of paid donors, returning the red blood cells to the donor's circulatory system, and selling the plasma to biological manufacturing companies. Its first office was opened in Montgomery, Alabama, but it was envisioned that the business would expand to other cities. Dissension arose among Bio-Lab's three owners, Morad (42 percent), Thomson (28 percent), and Coupounas (30 percent). Morad and Thomson removed Coupounas from the board and soon founded Med-Lab, Inc., which began operating a plasmapheresis business in Tuscaloosa, Alabama. Both corporations were profitable; both sold 95 percent of their products to the same three purchasers. Coupounas sued, alleging that Morad and Thomson had appropriated a business opportunity properly belonging to Bio-Lab. Is Coupounas right? Discuss. (*Morad v. Coupounas,* 361 So.2d 6, Ala. 1978.)

Chapter 40

Corporations
Merger, Consolidation, and Termination

Mergers and Consolidations

Termination

I N THE PRECEDING chapters we examined the nature and formation of the corporation, its basic operation, and the rights and liabilities of its individual participants. This final chapter focuses on more unusual aspects of corporate operation. Initially, we discuss changes in the fundamental structure of the corporation brought about by mergers and consolidations. Then we deal with the various circumstances in which the corporate existence can be terminated.

MERGERS AND CONSOLIDATIONS

The terms *merger* and *consolidation* are often used interchangeably to describe any situation in which two or more independent businesses are combined under a single ownership. Technically, however, there is a difference in meaning between the two terms. A **merger** is the absorption of one existing corporation by another; the absorbing corporation continues to exist while the one being absorbed ceases to exist. A **consolidation,** on the other hand, is a union resulting in the creation of an entirely new corporation and the termination of the existing ones. Symbolically, a merger can be illustrated by the equation A + B = A, while a consolidation is represented by A + B = C.

The distinction between mergers and consolidations has very little practical significance. Whether a particular combination is a merger or consolidation, the rights and liabilities of the corporations and their shareholders and creditors are the same. For this reason, the RMBCA has eliminated use of the term *consolidation,* and the popular term *merger* is often used by courts (and in the following discussion) to describe both combinations.

Reasons for Merging

The reasons for merging two corporations vary greatly, depending on the particular circumstances. The most common reasons are discussed below.

General Advantages of Size

In many cases the motive for a merger is the acquisition of some or all of the benefits that result from an increase in size. An ability to buy and produce in larger amounts, for example, may bring about greater efficiency and lower overhead costs.

Because the combination possesses greater resources than its constituent companies had possessed separately, it may be able to obtain capital more easily and to engage in more extensive advertising and research. Furthermore, the larger organization sometimes finds it easier to attract the best managers, technical advisers, and other personnel.

These advantages of size are usually legitimate. Occasionally, however, the motives of corporate managers in pursuing mergers may be less valid. Sometimes growth is sought merely for its own sake, without any resulting increase in efficiency. For instance, a merger might produce a much more impressive set of financial statements for the acquiring company, not through any improvement in its performance but simply because of the "larger numbers" brought about by the acquisition. And, of course, the personal rewards of the corporate managers may increase accordingly.

Eliminating Competition

Some mergers are motivated by the desire to lessen the rigors of competition. The most obvious example, of course, is the acquisition of a direct competitor for the purpose of suppressing competition between the two.[1] Mergers brought about solely for this purpose are less common than in the past, however, because of the enforcement of the antitrust laws.

Acquisition of Know-how

A large corporation might acquire a much smaller one in the same or a related line of business for the purpose of obtaining patents or other technological know-how owned by the smaller company. In addition, some of that company's employees might possess useful capabilities.

Guaranteed Supplies or Outlets

A company might seek to assure itself of an adequate supply of an essential item by acquiring a producer of that item. Conversely, a guaranteed outlet might be the motivating factor behind the acquisition of a company that purchases a product supplied by the acquiring firm.[2]

---

[1]A merger between two competitors is called a *horizontal merger.*
[2]A merger between firms in a supplier-customer relationship is called a *vertical merger.*

Diversification

One corporation sometimes wishes to acquire another in a totally unrelated line of business solely for the purpose of diversifying. Doing business in several diversified lines removes some of the economic risks that exist when a corporation commits all its resources to a single industry.[3]

Defensive Mergers

Occasionally a corporation actually seeks to be acquired by another. For example, suppose that X Corporation is attempting to acquire Y Corporation. However, the managers and shareholders of Y Corporation are opposed to the takeover because of differing business philosophies. Y Corporation thus arranges a merger with Z Corporation to avoid the takeover attempt by X. Such a merger is often called a **defensive merger.**

Another merger that might be classified as defensive is illustrated as follows. Jones, the founder of General Steel Corp. and its primary manager throughout its existence, now wishes to retire. Jones is afraid that "his" company will not be managed properly in his absence, so he arranges for General Steel to be acquired by a larger company whose management capabilities he trusts.[4]

Tax Savings

Although tax considerations are beyond the scope of this discussion, the lessening of federal income tax liability sometimes is an important reason for undertaking a particular merger. For example, a company facing a huge tax liability might acquire another company with large tax credits or loss carry-overs. Obviously, however, there should be good reasons for a merger other than just tax benefits, or the combination may later turn out to be problematic.

Unused Capital

Sometimes a merger may simply be an investment outlet for unused capital. For example, a corporation may have accumulated profits that it does not choose to pay out as dividends. The acquisition of another corporation may be an attractive investment opportunity for these funds.

---

[3]A merger between firms in unrelated lines of business is called a *conglomerate merger.*
[4]In this case Jones is probably a controlling shareholder in General Steel Corp. and thus has the power to carry out his wish.

Procedures

The procedure for a merger or consolidation is governed by statute. Every state has a statute that authorizes the combination of two or more *domestic* corporations. In almost every state, the statutory procedures also allow the combination of a domestic and a *foreign* (out-of-state) corporation. The procedures vary somewhat from state to state, but they can be outlined generally as follows:

1. The board of directors of each corporation must adopt a resolution approving the merger or consolidation. This resolution should set forth:

   a. The names of the combining corporations and the name of the corporation that will result from the combination.
   b. The terms and conditions of the proposed combination.
   c. The method and basis to be used in converting the securities of each corporation into securities of the resulting corporation.
   d. In the case of a merger, any changes caused thereby in the articles of incorporation of the surviving corporation. In the case of a consolidation, the resolutions of the respective boards should include the entire articles of incorporation for the resulting new corporation.

2. The plan must then be approved by the shareholders of each corporation, at either an annual or a special meeting. The vote required for approval varies among the states from a simple majority to four-fifths of the outstanding shares; a *two-thirds* vote is a common requirement.

3. After shareholder approval, the plan for the combination must be submitted to the appropriate state official (usually the secretary of state) in a document referred to as the **articles of merger or consolidation.**

4. If all documents are in the proper form, the state official issues a **certificate of merger or consolidation** to the surviving or new corporation.

Merger with a Subsidiary

In a majority of states, the procedures have been greatly simplified for the merger of a subsidiary corporation into its parent. These streamlined procedures allow such a merger to be consummated *without shareholder approval.*

If the parent owns *all* the subsidiary's shares, the only requirements are that (1) the parent's board of directors adopt a resolution setting forth the plan for the merger, (2) articles of merger be filed, and (3) a certificate of merger be issued. If some of the subsidiary's shares are owned by others, there is an additional requirement that these minority shareholders be given prior notice of the merger. These simplified procedures for "short form" mergers can be used, however, only if the parent owns a *very large portion* of the subsidiary's shares (90 or 95 percent in most states).

Effects of Merger or Consolidation

The effects of a merger or consolidation can be summarized as follows:

1. The corporations who are parties to the merger become a single corporation.

2. All of the corporate parties to the merger, other than the surviving or new corporation, cease to exist.

3. The surviving or new corporation possesses all the rights, privileges, and powers of the combining corporations.

4. The surviving or new corporation acquires all the property of the combining corporations without the necessity of a deed or other formal transfer.

5. The surviving or new corporation is liable for all the debts and obligations of the combining corporations.

6. In the case of a merger, the articles of incorporation of the surviving corporation are deemed to be amended to the extent, if any, that changes in these articles are stated in the articles of merger. In the case of a consolidation, the articles of consolidation serve as the articles of incorporation for the new corporation.

Figure 40.1 illustrates the steps in a typical merger or consolidation.

The Appraisal Right

At common law a merger, consolidation, or other combination required the *unanimous* approval of the shareholders of each corporation. In an effort to lessen the severity of this restriction on corporate actions, all the states changed their laws to provide for approval by less than a unanimous vote.

In exchange for elimination of their "veto" power over structural changes such as mergers and consoli-

dations, as well as radical amendments to the articles of incorporation, sales of substantially all corporate assets, and other changes that dramatically alter the nature of the shareholders' original investment, shareholders who opposed such changes were granted the **appraisal right**—the right to sell their shares back to the corporation for cash. Thus, if Corporation A's shareholders approve its merger with Corporation B, giving up their A shares in exchange for a certain number of shares of B, those shareholders of A who opposed the merger and refused to vote for the deal may seek the "fair value" of their A shares in cash rather than accept their allotment of B shares pursuant to terms of the merger.[5]

Dissenting shareholders must strictly follow the required procedures, or the appraisal right will be forfeited. The most important requirement is that dissenting shareholders refuse to vote for the merger (or other transaction) and demand payment within the designated time period, often within 10 days after approval of the transaction.

Fair Value

If the corporation and the shareholders cannot agree on the *fair value* of the shares, litigation often ensues. In calculating fair value, many courts apply the "Delaware block" method of valuing shares, which evaluates them from three perspectives: asset value, market value, and earnings value. These factors are then weighted and factored together.

Asset value is often determined by subtracting total liabilities from total assets and dividing by the number of outstanding shares. *Market value* is determined by looking at the price quoted on an exchange or over-the-counter by a stock broker, if any. If no reliable market exists, evidence may be garnered by examining recent sales.

There are typically two steps to calculating *earnings value*. First, earnings per share is calculated by dividing average earnings during the previous five years by the total number of outstanding shares. Second, that figure is then "capitalized" by use of a price/earnings multiplier derived by comparisons of the price/earnings ratio of competing corporations.

[5]In 20 or so states, including Delaware, no appraisal right is accorded to shareholders of large, publicly held corporations. This *market exception* assumes that if shareholders are upset with the course such corporations are charting, they may protect themselves adequately by simply selling their shares on the efficient open market, a market that likely does not exist for the shares of a close corporation.

FIGURE 40.1

***Steps in
Merger or
Consolidation***

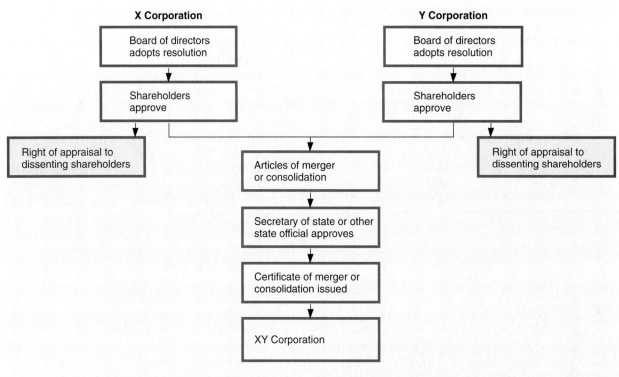

To illustrate, in *Gibbons v. Schenley Industries*,[6] the court's calculations were as follows:

	VALUE FACTORS	WEIGHT	ASSIGNED VALUE
Market Value	$29.00	55%	$15.75
Earnings Value	$39.79	45%	$17.91
Asset Value	$49.83	0%	$ 0.00
			Fair Value = $33.86

[6]339 A.2d 460 (Del. Ch. 1975).

Asset value was given no weight because the court believed that it had little predictive value in determining future income in this particular case. Schenley's assets consisted largely of an overvalued inventory containing many unpopular brands, and most of its distilleries were no longer operating.

The Delaware block method has been criticized on several grounds, including giving insufficient weight to *future* earnings potential. The following case modified the Delaware block in the jurisdiction of its birth.

WEINBERGER V. UOP, INC.

Delaware Supreme Court, 457 A.2d 701 (1983)

Signal Companies, Inc. owned 50.5 percent of the common stock of UOP Inc. when it decided to acquire all the rest in a "cash out" merger. A merger was proposed at $21 per share and recommended by the boards of both companies (although the UOP board was not informed that a study by two officers of Signal—Arledge and Chitiea—who sat on UOP's board indicated that $24 per share would still be a good price for Signal).

Given the majority requirement for approval of such mergers in Delaware and the fact that Signal owned more than a majority of UOP's shares, the transaction was easily approved. Plaintiff, a dissident shareholder who had met all procedural requirements, sued to enforce his appraisal rights. The following portion of the court's opinion deals only with the valuation of plaintiff's shares.

Moore, Justice:

Turning to the matter of price, plaintiff also challenges its fairness. His evidence was that on the date the merger was approved the stock was worth at least $26 per share. In support, he offered the testimony of a chartered investment analyst who used two basic approaches to valuation: a comparative analysis of the premium paid over market in ten other tender offer-merger combinations and a discounted cash flow analysis.

[The Chancellor (trial judge)] rejected plaintiff's method of proof and accepted . . . the so-called "Delaware block" or weighted average method . . . wherein the elements of value, that is,

assets, market price, earnings, etc., were assigned a particular weight and the resulting amounts added to determine the value per share. This procedure has been in use for decades. However, to the extent it excludes other generally accepted techniques used in the financial community and the courts, it is now clearly outmoded. It is time we recognized this in appraisal and other stock valuation proceedings and bring our law current on the subject.

While the Chancellor rejected plaintiff's discounted cash flow method of valuing UOP's stock, as not corresponding with "either logic or the existing law," it is significant that this was essentially the focus, that is, earnings potential, of Messrs. Arledge and Chitiea in their evaluation of the merger. Accordingly, the standard "Delaware block" or weighted average method of valuation, formerly employed in appraisal and other stock valuation cases, shall no longer exclusively control such proceedings. We believe that a more liberal approach must include proof of value by any techniques or methods which are generally considered acceptable in the financial community and otherwise admissible in court. . . . This will obviate the very structured and mechanistic procedure that has heretofore governed such matters.

Fair price obviously requires consideration of all relevant factors involving the value of a company. This has long been the law of Delaware as stated in *Tri-Continental Corp.*, 74 A.2d at 72:

> The basic concept of value under the appraisal statute is that the stockholder is entitled to be paid for that which has been taken from him, viz., his proportionate interest in a going concern. By value of the stockholder's proportionate interest in the corporate enter-

prise is meant the true or intrinsic value of his stock which has been taken by the merger. In determining what figure represents this true or intrinsic value, the appraiser and the courts must take into consideration all factors and elements which reasonably might enter into the fixing of value. Thus, market value, asset value, dividends, earnings prospects, the nature of the enterprise and any other facts which would throw any light on *future* prospects of the merged corporation are not only pertinent to an inquiry as to the value of the dissenting stockholders' interest, but *must* be considered by the agency fixing the value (emphasis added).

This is not only in accord with the realities of present-day affairs, but it is thoroughly consonant with the purpose and intent of our statutory law [which] mandates the determination of "fair" value based upon "all relevant factors." Only the speculative elements of value that may arise from the "accomplishment or expectation" of the merger are excluded. We take this to be a very narrow exception to the appraisal process, designed to eliminate use of pro forma data and projections of a speculative variety relating to the completion of a merger. But elements of future value, including the nature of the enterprise, which are known as susceptible of proof as of the date of the merger and not the product of speculation, may be considered.

. . . While we do not suggest a monetary result one way or another, we do think the plaintiff's evidence should be part of the factual mix and weighed as such. Until the $21 price is measured on remand by the valuation standards mandated by Delaware law, there can be no finding at the present stage of these proceedings that the price is fair.

[Reversed and remanded.] ⬠

Note

Weinberger also stands for the proposition that the appraisal remedy is not the *sole* remedy of dissenting shareholders in transactions that involve fraud, misrepresentation, self-dealing, deliberate waste of corporate assets, or gross and palpable overreaching. . . ." In such situations, an "entire fairness" test is applied to the transaction and remedies beyond appraisal may appropriately be granted.

Asset and Stock Acquisitions

Thus far our discussion has been largely limited to "statutory" mergers and consolidations, in which all of the requisite formalities have been carried out. However, corporations can achieve the same practical results by less formal means, particularly through *asset acquisition* and *stock acquisition.* In legal circles these transactions are sometimes called *de facto* **mergers,** as contrasted with "statutory" mergers and consolidations. In everyday usage they are more frequently referred to simply as "mergers," or "takeovers."

Asset Acquisitions

Suppose that X Co. wishes to acquire all or most of the assets of Y Co. It may purchase these assets with cash or with a combination of cash and promissory notes. Or it may make the purchase by issuing shares of its stock to Y in return for Y's assets.

Although the practical effect of such an asset acquisition is to merge one company into the other, the *acquiring company* usually does not have to obtain shareholder approval. Ordinarily, the only situation in which the approval of the acquiring company's shareholders must be obtained is when the assets are to be bought with shares and there are not enough authorized but unissued shares to make the purchase. In such a case the shareholders will have to amend the articles of incorporation to authorize the issuance of additional shares.

The rules are substantially different, however, with respect to the *acquired company.* The sale of all or most of its assets puts its shareholders into a position very different from the one they previously occupied. Therefore, they must approve the sale. Indeed, in the past, the common-law rule required unanimous approval. This strict requirement was relaxed, however, along with the relaxation of the approval requirement for formal mergers and acquisitions. Today, the general rule is that the shareholders of the acquired company must approve the sale by the same vote required for a merger or consolidation. And the dissenting shareholders of the acquired company possess an appraisal right just as in a formal merger or consolidation.

After the sale, the corporation that has sold its assets may simply choose to dissolve. It may, however, decide to start its operations anew (either in the same or some other line of business). A third alternative is for the corporation to continue in existence as a **holding company** (or **investment company**). In the latter case, its sole (or at least primary) function will be to own and receive income from securities, such as those it may have received as the purchase price for its assets.

Stock Acquisitions

A frequently employed method for achieving a combination between two corporations is the purchase by one corporation of the shares of another. This generally is accomplished by action of the acquiring company's board of directors, without any need for approval by its shareholders. Unless the purchase is being made merely for investment purposes, the aim of the purchaser obviously is to obtain a sufficient number of shares so that it *controls* the company whose shares are acquired. Control usually requires ownership of over 50 percent of a corporation's voting shares. Although the present discussion assumes acquisition by one *corporation* of a controlling stock interest in another corporation, the same principles apply to such an acquisition by an *individual.*

Open Market Purchases. Although it is theoretically possible for the acquiring company to negotiate individually with the target company's shareholders for the purchase of their shares, this usually is not done. If the target company's shares are publicly traded, the large number of shareholders involved makes individual negotiation practically impossible; if the target company is a close corporation, transfer of the shares is usually restricted by a shareholder agreement that can be changed only by the shareholders as a group. Instead of individual negotiation, if the target company's shares are publicly traded the acquiring company can purchase the shares on the open market. Even if a sufficient number of shares can be obtained on the market, however, this method of acquiring control may be too slow if the target company's board opposes the change of control. Although the formal approval of the target company's board of directors is not a legal requirement for acquisition of the company's shares, the board is in a position to make acquisition of a controlling interest much more difficult. As we will see in a separate section on directors' responsibilities in a takeover situation, the target company's board often will take various steps either to persuade its shareholders not to sell their shares or to make the acquisition less attractive to the acquiring company. The slowness of open market purchases for the purpose of acquiring control gives the target company's board ample time to devise various strategies to defeat the attempted takeover.

Tender Offers. Because fast action is often necessary, it has become common for the acquiring company to make a **tender offer** for the target company's shares. A tender offer is a publicly advertised offer to the target company's shareholders to buy at a specified price those shares that are "tendered" (i.e., made available) to the acquiring company. The main advantage of a tender offer is speed—the acquiring company is more likely to obtain enough shares for control before the target company's board can erect effective barriers to the acquisition.

The price specified in a tender offer usually is substantially above the prevailing market price for the shares, because only by offering such a "premium" can the offeror assure swift acceptance of its offer. Although this price often is in cash, it may consist of a stated number of the acquiring company's shares per share of the target company, or a combination of cash and a stated number of the acquiring company's shares. The specified price can even take the form of bonds or other property owned by the acquiring company, or a combination of such property with cash.

If the acquiring company's objective is to obtain control over the target company, the acquiring company may not want to purchase any shares unless it is assured of gaining control. Thus, the tender offer may provide that it will be valid only if accepted by the holders of a stated number of shares. On the other hand, the acquiring company may not want to buy any more shares than are necessary to achieve control. Thus, the tender offer may expressly limit the number of shares to be purchased and may provide that if more than this number are tendered, they will be purchased on a proportionate basis from all tendering shareholders.

The **Williams Act,** passed by Congress in 1968, amended the Securities Exchange Act of 1934 to regu-late tender offers. One of the primary aspects of this law is the requirement that the individual or corporation making a tender offer supply a wide variety of detailed information to the target company's shareholders so that those shareholders can make a completely informed decision whether to tender their shares. (The Williams Act is discussed in more detail in Chapter 41, Securities Regulation.)

Proxy Contests. Sometimes a relatively small stock acquisition can provide a launching pad for a proxy contest that ultimately leads to a merger. In a publicly held corporation acquiring proxies from a large number of shareholders is the most common method of concentrating voting power to gain or keep control. Existing managers usually maintain control by acquiring proxies giving them the power to vote for themselves, or others they choose as directors. Occasionally one or more shareholders desiring a change in control may challenge existing management by attempting to persuade other shareholders to give their proxies to the challengers instead of current management.

An individual or company wishing to accomplish a merger sometimes will use a strategy that involves an initial stock acquisition followed by a proxy contest and then a formal merger. Suppose, for example, that X Corp. wishes to acquire and merge with Y Corp. X Corp. might acquire a significant (but much less than controlling) interest in Y Corp. by purchasing some of Y's shares in the open market. As a shareholder of Y Corp., X Corp. then launches a proxy contest prior to Y's next annual shareholders' meeting. In its communications with Y's other shareholders, X Corp. must reveal its true intentions. If X Corp.'s contest with Y Corp.'s management for proxies is successful, X Corp. will be able to elect its own candidates to Y Corp.'s board of directors. These directors will then vote to merge with X Corp. and again solicit proxies from Y's shareholders for formal approval of the merger. (Federal regulation of proxy contests is discussed in more detail in Chapter 41.)

Management Responsibilities in a Takeover Attempt

In modern times, many of the court cases applying corporation law principles arise in the takeover context, and much of this litigation focuses on the response of the target company's board to a tender offer. When one corporation attempts to acquire a controlling stock interest in another corporation, the target company's board of directors occupies a central role, for two reasons. First, the board's recommendation to accept or reject a tender offer often will strongly influence the decision of the target company's shareholders. Second, as mentioned previously, the board has the ability to erect a number of obstacles to the takeover.

Sometimes the target company's board will view a tender offer favorably and will recommend to the shareholders that they sell their shares. It must be realized, however, that a formal merger probably would have been negotiated and presented to the target company's shareholders if that company's board had been favorably disposed toward the takeover. Consequently, in most situations the target company's board will resist the takeover attempt. A tender offer that is resisted by the target company's board is referred to as a "hostile" or "unfriendly" tender offer.

When responding to a tender offer, directors owe to the corporation and its shareholders the same fundamental duties of obedience, due care, and loyalty as they owe in other circumstances. Fulfilling these duties becomes especially demanding in the takeover setting, however, because the future ownership, control, and direction of the company are suddenly at stake, and tender offers do not permit a great deal of time for study and reflection.

The Duty of Loyalty in the Takeover Setting

Directors are fiduciaries of the corporation and its shareholders, and the duty of loyalty requires that directors act in the best interests of the shareholders. Inside directors, who also hold office or own significant numbers of shares, must be especially vigilant to fulfill the duty of loyalty because the takeover attempt presents them with an inherent conflict. Their position as directors requires them always to serve the interests of shareholders as a group, and often a takeover by another company is clearly in the best interests of those shareholders, who typically are being offered a large premium over the market price of their shares. On the other hand, inside directors face the probable loss of their management jobs if the takeover is successful. A court will conclude that directors have violated the duty of loyalty if it finds that they acted primarily for the purpose of maintaining their positions and control, or if they did not properly disclose relevant facts to shareholders. Directors must fully assess the tender offer and make a good faith decision whether the shareholders will receive the greatest benefit by accepting or rejecting it. If the directors make any recommendation to shareholders concerning a tender offer or other takeover attempt, they must fully disclose all material information relevant to that recommendation.

The Williams Act contains detailed disclosure provisions that govern the roles of all parties to a tender offer, including the tender offeror and target management. Those requirements are generally consistent with the "duty of candor" that most states impose upon management in other types of transactions, including mergers, as the following case illustrates.

Shell Petroleum, Inc. v. Smith

Delaware Supreme Court, 606 A.2d 112 (Del. 1992)

Royal Dutch Petroleum Co., through SPNV Holdings, Inc. ("Holdings"), owned 94.6 percent of the outstanding shares of Shell Oil Co. Holdings initiated a short-form merger offering Shell's minority shareholders $58 per share, but specifying that shareholders who before July 1, 1985, waived their right to seek an appraisal would receive an extra $2 per share. Holdings distributed several documents to the minority shareholders, including one called "Certain Information About Shell" (CIAS).

The CIAS contained a table of discounted future net cash flows (DCF) for Shell's oil and gas reserves. Because of a computer programming error, the DCF failed to account for the cash flows from approximately 295 million barrels of proved oil and gas reserves, resulting in an understatement of DCF of approximately $1 billion, or at least $3 per share.

After the merger was approved, some of Shell's minority shareholders sued, alleging that the error constituted a breach of Holdings's state law duty of candor. The trial court
(continues)

(continued from previous page)
found for plaintiffs, awarding them
$2 per share. Holdings appealed.

Moore, Justice:

Holdings' duty with respect to disclosure is clear. As the majority shareholder, Holdings bears the burden of showing complete disclosure of all material facts relevant to a minority shareholder's decision whether to accept the short-form merger consideration or seek an appraisal. Thus, the question is one of materiality. A fact is considered material if there is a "substantial likelihood that the disclosure of the omitted fact would have been viewed by the reasonable investor as having significantly altered the 'total mix' of information available." *Rosenblatt v. Getty Oil Co.*, 493 A.2d 929 (Del. 1985).

Holdings argues that the [trial] court's decision was incorrect because: 1) the error was insignificant when viewed in context; 2) the error was not significant enough to affect a shareholder's decision whether to seek an appraisal; and 3) the error was not material because the DCF was only an estimate.

Holdings contends that the billion dollar error was insignificant because it resulted in only a 5.5% understatement in the total discounted cash flows reported. However, the significance of the error is clearly demonstrated by the fact that a Shell executive vice president stated in the *Wall Street Journal* that a 220 million barrel discovery in the Gulf of Mexico was considered a major find. Thus, it is difficult to accept Holdings' argument that the failure to report cash flows from 295 million barrels was insignificant. . . .

Holdings also argues that a $3 per share error was not significant enough to make a reasonable stockholder change his decision and seek an appraisal. However, the question is not whether the information would have changed the stockholder's decision to accept the merger consideration, but whether "the fact in question would have been relevant to him." *Barkan v. Amsted Industries, Inc.*, 567 A.2d 1279 (Del. 1989). "[T]he real worth of an oil company is centered in its reserves." *Rosenblatt*, at 941. We cannot agree that a billion dollar understatement of the value of Shell's reserves would have been anything but highly relevant and material to a reasonable stockholder.

Finally, Holdings contends that the DCF is only an estimate of future cash flows and, therefore, it would be unreasonable for a shareholder to conclude that Shell's oil and gas reserves were worth the amount presented in the DCF. In fact, according to Holdings, a reasonable shareholder should anticipate a certain margin of error simply due to the uncertainties inherent in the estimate process.

Although the DCF presents an estimate of future cash flows, a shareholder could reasonably conclude that the DCF was accurately prepared based on all available information. Moreover, a reasonable shareholder could conclude that the 1985 DCF was prepared in a manner consistent with the 1984 DCF. Thus, a comparison of the 1984 and 1985 DCFs should present an accurate indication of whether the value of Shell's reserves was increasing or decreasing. Such was not the case. A comparison of the 1984 and 1985 DCFs inevitably leads to the erroneous conclusion, as stated in the CIAS, that the value of Shell's reserves had declined. Most importantly, the misleading statement that the value of the reserves had declined was not based upon the inherent inaccuracies of the estimate process, but upon an error made by Shell. The fact that the error was included in a schedule which contained estimates does not diminish its materiality.

[Affirmed.]

Due Care and the Business Judgment Rule in the Takeover Setting

Courts apply the business judgment rule (discussed in Chapter 39) when determining whether directors have fulfilled their duty of due care in responding to a takeover attempt or similar transaction. Directors are expected to give the matter the type of concentrated attention warranted by its great importance, but courts do take into account the fact that tender offers frequently do not give the target company's board a substantial amount of time for study. Essentially, the business judgment rule requires directors to make a decision that is as fully informed as the circumstances permit.

The following case illustrates the duty of directors to inform themselves fully before making the momentous decision to sell a corporation.

SMITH v. VAN GORKOM

Supreme Court of Delaware, 488 A.2d 858 (1985)

 Case

Trans Union was a widely diversified company, with its most substantial earnings coming from its railcar leasing business. Federal tax laws gave Trans Union a tremendous amount of investment tax credits (ITCs) to offset against income, but accelerated depreciation deductions were decreasing its taxable income to such an extent that it was unable to use all of its ITCs. By not using its ITCs, Trans Union was losing millions of dollars in tax benefits. Van Gorkom had been an officer of Trans Union for 24 years, its Chief Executive Officer for 17 years, and Chairman of the Board for two years. He was nearing retirement, and personally owned 75,000 shares of Trans Union stock. Trans Union's board consisted of five outside and five inside directors. In late August, 1980, the board, strongly led by Van Gorkom, concluded that it should seek a merger with a company having large amounts of taxable income so that the ITCs could be used. The type of merger they wished to pursue was a "leveraged buyout," in which the acquirer would borrow the funds necessary to purchase Trans Union's stock and then use the cash flow from Trans Union's operations to service the debt. Van Gorkom and two other Trans Union officers and directors, Romans and Chelberg, performed calculations indicating that such a leveraged buyout would be "easy" at $50 per share and "very difficult" at $60 per share. No independent financial advisors were consulted, and no study was done to determine what actually would be a fair price for Trans Union's shares. The only studies were aimed at determining what price would make a leveraged buyout feasible.

Van Gorkom then arranged meetings on September 13 and 15 with

Jay Pritzker, a social acquaintance and well-known takeover specialist. At the first meeting, Van Gorkom proposed that Pritzker accomplish a leveraged buyout of Trans Union at $55 per share, and at the second meeting Pritzker indicated a definite interest in the proposal. Two other Van Gorkom–Pritzker meetings were held on the 16th and 17th, which were also attended by two other Trans Union officers (Chelberg and Peterson) and a paid consultant. At a final private meeting between Van Gorkom and Pritzker on September 18, Pritzker stated definitely that a corporation completely owned by Pritzker would offer to buy all of Trans Union's stock for $55 per share, that Trans Union's board would have only three days to act on the proposal, and that Trans Union would have to arrange the financing needed by Pritzker to make the acquisition.

Pritzker then had his attorney draft a formal merger agreement. In the meantime, Van Gorkom arranged for Trans Union's banks to finance Pritzker's purchase. On Friday, September 19, Van Gorkom called a special meeting of the Trans Union board for the next day. The directors were not given an agenda or told of the purpose of the meeting. At the meeting on September 20, which lasted two hours, presentations were made only by Van Gorkom and his personal attorney. Romans, one of the inside directors who had earlier performed the calculations concerning an appropriate price per share, told the board that his calculations did not deal with the question of a fair price but only with the question of a price that would make a leveraged buyout feasible. Copies of the formal merger agreement did not arrive until the end of the meeting, and were not examined by the directors. The board then voted to approve the

merger and submit it to shareholders. That night at a social event hosted by Van Gorkom for the opening of the Chicago Lyric Opera, Van Gorkom and Pritzker signed the formal merger agreement. Neither Van Gorkom nor any other Trans Union board member read the agreement before it was executed.

The proposed merger between Trans Union and Pritzker's company was submitted to Trans Union's shareholders, and they voted to approve it. They were not informed about the basis for the $55 per share figure, however. Several shareholders then discovered how the transaction came about, and filed a class action in behalf of all Trans Union shareholders. The plaintiffs claimed that Trans Union's directors violated their duty of due care to the shareholders. The trial court ruled in favor of Trans Union's directors, and the shareholders appealed.

Horsey, Justice:

Under the business judgment rule there is no protection for directors who have made "an unintelligent or unadvised judgment." A director's duty to inform himself in preparation for a decision derives from the fiduciary capacity in which he serves the corporation and its stockholders. . . . Representation of the financial interests of others imposes on a director an affirmative duty to protect those interests and to proceed with a critical eye in assessing information of the type and under the circumstances present here. . . .

The standard of care applicable to a director's duty of care has been recently restated by this Court. In *Aronson v. Lewis*, we stated:

While the Delaware cases use a variety of terms to describe the applicable standard of care, our analysis satisfies us that under the business judgment rule director liability is predicated upon concepts of gross negligence.

(continues)

SMITH V. VAN GORKOM

(continued from previous page)
We again confirm that view. We think the concept of gross negligence is the proper standard for determining whether a business judgment reached by a board of directors was an informed one. . . .

On the record before us, we must conclude that the Board of Directors did not reach an informed business judgment on September 20, 1980 in voting to "sell" the Company for $55 per share pursuant to the Pritzker merger proposal. Our reasons, in summary, are as follows:

The directors (1) did not adequately inform themselves as to Van Gorkom's role in forcing the "sale" of the Company and in establishing the per share purchase price; (2) were uninformed as to the intrinsic value of the Company; and (3) given these circumstances, at a minimum, were grossly negligent in approving the "sale" of the Company upon two hours' consideration, without prior notice, and without the exigency of a crisis or emergency. . . .

Without any documents before them concerning the proposed transaction, the members of the Board were required to rely entirely upon Van Gorkom's 20-minute oral presentation of the proposal. No written summary of the terms of the merger was presented; the directors were given no documentation to support the adequacy of $55 price per share for sale of the company; and the Board had before it nothing more than Van Gorkom's statement of his understanding of the substance of an agreement which he admittedly had never read, nor which any member of the Board had ever seen.

Considering all of the surrounding circumstances—hastily calling the meeting without any prior notice of its subject matter, the proposed sale of the Company without any prior consideration of the issue or necessity therefor, the urgent time contraints imposed by Pritzker, and the total absence of any documentation whatsoever—the directors were duty bound to make reasonable inquiry of Van Gorkom and Romans, and if they had done so, the inadequacy of that upon which they now claim to have relied would have been apparent.

[The judgment of the trial court for the directors is reversed, and the case is remanded to the trial court for a determination of the fair value of Trans Union's stock and calculation of damages to the shareholders.] ⚖

Evaluating Defensive Tactics

As pointed out in *Shlensky v. Wrigley* in Chapter 39, the *business judgment rule*—the courts' determination to defer to the business expertise of the board of directors—provides broad protection for the good faith judgments of directors, at least when they have done their homework. For a long time, the business judgment rule provided a virtually impregnable barrier protecting the directors of a target company in erecting defenses to a hostile takeover. Those directors have in some cases used their discretion to spend corporate cash and borrow large sums of money in order to make the target corporation less attractive and to prevent an offeror from using the target's own assets to help pay off debts incurred in the takeover. In other cases, directors have moved the corporation to states with laws that tend to make tender offers more difficult to consummate successfully. They have acquired competitors of the offeror in an attempt to create an antitrust impediment to the takeover. They have launched "Pac-Man" counter tender offers for control of the offeror. They have sold the corporation's "crown jewel" (the subsidiary or division that attracted the offer in the first place). They have granted "lock-up options" (opportunities to purchase part of the company at bargain prices) to "white knights" (friendly third-party bidders) to assure their ability to complete a **defensive merger** in order to defeat a hostile bid. They have issued "poison pills" (shares of stock that carry, for example, the right, effective in the event of a change of control, to buy the corporation's shares for 50 cents on the dollar, thereby dramatically diluting the position of the offeror). They have launched "self tender" offers, using the target's own funds and credit to repurchase shares from disgruntled shareholders in order to keep them out of the hands of a hostile bidder. They have even threatened "corporate suicide" (liquidation and dissolution).

Legal challenges to these defensive tactics have taken two major forms. One, based on *federal* law, has been generally ineffective, as will be explained in Chapter 41. The second basis for attack is the argument, based on *state* corporation law, that target managers are breaching their fiduciary duties to shareholders by using defensive tactics to save their jobs at the expense of the shareholders' opportunity to sell their shares at a profit to the tender offeror. For many years, such challenges were uniformly unsuccessful as the courts repeatedly held that defensive actions taken by target managements were protected by the business judgment rule.

In recent years, however, it has dawned on the courts that the target directors are in a conflict-of-interest situation in evaluating a tender offer that may cost them their jobs but promises big profits to target shareholders. The following case is one of the first to recognize that, in light of this conflict of interest, the business judgment rule should not be blindly applied to protect director decisions in this context.

NORLIN CORP. v. ROONEY, PACE INC.

U.S. Second Circuit Court of Appeals, 744 F.2d 255 (1984)

Norlin Corp. is a company whose shares are listed on the New York Stock Exchange. It is incorporated in Panama, but with its principal place of business in New York. Piezo Electric Products, Inc., on two trading days, January 6 and 12, 1984, in conjunction with the investment banking firm of Rooney, Pace Inc., purchased 32 percent of Norlin's common stock in a series of separate market transactions. Fearful of an imminent takeover, on January 20 Norlin transferred 28,295 shares of common stock to Andean Enterprises, Inc., a wholly owned subsidiary, incorporated in Panama, purportedly in consideration for Andean's cancellation of a Norlin promissory note of $965,454. On January 25, Norlin's board approved a transfer of 800,000 authorized but unissued shares of preferred stock to Andean in exchange for a $20 million promissory note. Also on January 25, Norlin created an ESOP and appointed three board members as trustees. The board immediately transferred 185,000 common shares to the ESOP in exchange for a promissory note of $6,824,945. In its filings of required disclosures with the SEC, Norlin admitted that its board was the beneficial owner of, and had voting control over, all transferred shares. As a result of these transactions, the Norlin board controlled 49 percent of the corporation's outstanding stock. Norlin's

chairman, Stevens, and president, Simpkins, wrote the company's shareholders indicating that they were taking all necessary steps to oppose the Rooney, Pace-Piezo offer. The letter offered no justification for the transactions other than to defeat the potential takeover.

Norlin's attorneys warned Norlin directors that their actions might cause the New York Stock Exchange to delist Norlin stock, and on March 15, the NYSE suspended trading in Norlin stock and indicated an intent to delist because issuance of stock to Andean and the ESOP resulted in a change of control of the company, which, under NYSE rules, requires shareholder approval.

Norlin filed suit in federal district court seeking a preliminary injunction against Piezo that would prohibit it from acquiring any more Norlin shares and require it to sell those it had already acquired. Norlin's suit was based on a claim that Piezo had violated federal securities laws in making the acquisitions, but the district court found that Piezo's acquisitions had been completely lawful and denied Norlin's request. Norlin did not appeal this ruling. Piezo filed a counterclaim against Norlin in district court, alleging that Norlin had acted illegally in issuing the stock to the ESOP and the subsidiary. The district court ruled for Piezo on its counterclaim and issued a preliminary injunction barring Norlin from voting any of the transferred shares. Norlin appealed.

Kaufman, Judge:

Piezo asserts, and the district court appropriately found, that the illegality of voting the stock transferred to Andean and the ESOP had been demonstrated with sufficient certainty to warrant injunctive relief. As we will explain, the right of a wholly owned subsidiary to vote shares of a parent company's stock is controlled by statute. The propriety of an issuance of stock to an ESOP in the context of a contest for corporate control has not been legislatively resolved, and so must be assessed in relation to fiduciary principles governing the conduct of officers and directors. Thus, we must analyze the two issues separately.

[Regarding the transfers of stock to Andean, the court first addressed the "conflict of laws" issue by attempting to decide whether Panamanian or New York law should apply. Ultimately, it made no difference because "the relevant rules of law in New York and Panama are identical on this point: A wholly owned subsidiary may not vote shares of its parent's stock," because this is essentially the same as the parent corporation voting its own shares, with its board deciding how to vote them. The court then turned to the validity of the transfers to the ESOP.]

We now turn to the district court's conclusion that appellee had demonstrated probable illegality stemming from the voting of Norlin shares held by the ESOP. This is a somewhat more difficult problem, for we have little statutory authority to guide us. . . . We must look instead to those fiduciary

(continues)

NORLIN CORP. v. ROONEY, PACE INC.

(continued from previous page)
principles of state common law that constrained the actions of corporate officers and directors.

A board member's obligation to a corporation and its shareholders has two prongs, generally characterized as the duty of care and the duty of loyalty. The duty of care refers to the responsibility of a corporate fiduciary to exercise, in the performance of his tasks, the care that a reasonably prudent person in a similar position would use under similar circumstances. In evaluating a manager's compliance with the duty of care, New York courts adhere to the business judgment rule, which "bars judicial inquiry into actions of corporate directors taken in good faith and in the exercise of honest judgment in the lawful and legitimate furtherance of corporate purposes."

The second restriction traditionally imposed, the duty of loyalty, derives from the prohibition against self-dealing that inheres in the fiduciary relationship. Once a showing is made that directors have a self-interest in a particular corporate transaction, the burden shifts to them to demonstrate that the transaction is fair and serves the best interests of the corporation and its shareholders.

In applying these principles in the context of battles for corporate control, we begin with the business judgment rule, which affords directors wide latitude in devising strategies to resist unfriendly advances. However, the business judgment rule governs only where the directors are not shown to have a self-interest in the transaction at issue. Once self-dealing or bad faith is demonstrated, the duty of loyalty supersedes the duty of care, and the burden shifts to the directors to "prove that the transaction was fair and reasonable to the corporation."

In this case, the evidence was more than adequate to constitute a prima facie showing of self-interest on the board's part. All the stock transferred to Andean and the ESOP was to be voted by the directors; indeed, members of the board were appointed trustees of the ESOP. The precipitous timing of the share issuances, and the fact that the ESOP was created the very same day that stock was issued to it, give rise to a strong inference that the purpose of the transaction was not to benefit the employees but rather to solidify management's control of the company. This is buttressed by the fact that the board offered its shareholders no rationale for the transfers other than its determination to oppose, at all costs, the threat to the company that Piezo's acquisitions ostensibly represented. Where, as here, directors amass voting control of close to a majority of a corporation's shares in their own hands by complex, convoluted, and deliberate maneuvers, it strains credulity to suggest that the retention of control over corporate affairs played no part in their plans.

We reject the view, propounded by Norlin, that once it concludes that an actual or anticipated takeover attempt is not in the best interests of the company, a board of directors may take any action necessary to forestall acquisitive moves. The business judgment rule does indeed require the board to analyze carefully any perceived threat to the corporation and to act appropriately when it decides that the interests of the company and its shareholders might be jeopardized. As we have explained, however, the duty of loyalty requires the board to demonstrate that any actions it does take are fair and reasonable. We conclude that Norlin has failed to make that showing.

ESOPs, like other employee benefit plans, may serve a number of legitimate corporate purposes, and their creation is generally upheld in the courts when they do so. By establishing an ESOP, corporate managers may seek to improve employee morale and loyalty, to raise capital for the corporation, or to supplement employee compensation or retirement benefits. When an ESOP is set up in the context of a contest for control, however, it devolves upon the board to show that the plan was in fact created to benefit the employees, and not simply to further the aim of managerial entrenchment. In applying that distinction, courts have looked to factors such as the timing of the ESOP's establishment, the financial impact on the company, the identity of the trustees, and the voting control of the ESOP shares.

In this case, an examination of each of these factors indicates that the ESOP was created solely as a tool of management self-perpetuation. It was created a mere five days after the district court refused to enjoin further stock purchases by Piezo, and at a time when Norlin's officers were clearly casting about for strategies to deter a challenge to their control. No real consideration was received from the ESOP for the shares. The three trustees appointed to oversee the ESOP were all members of Norlin's board, and voting control of all the ESOP shares was retained by the directors. We therefore conclude that the record supports the finding that the transfer of stock to the ESOP was part of a management entrenchment effort. . . .

We thus find that Piezo has succeeded in demonstrating the likelihood of success on the merits, with regard to the share issuances to both Andean and the ESOP. We move on to the other requirement for the issuance of a preliminary injunction: a showing of irreparable harm. . . .

[The court then found that the potential delisting by the NYSE constituted irreparable harm. The court then stated:] Because Piezo has succeeded in demonstrating probable illegality in the issuance of shares to Andean and the ESOP, as well as irreparable harm therefrom, we agree that the voting of those shares should, pending further proceedings, be enjoined. Accordingly, the order of the district court is affirmed.

Legal Focus

When takeovers of American companies are proposed by *foreign* firms, additional legal considerations may come into play. Naturally, the United States generally welcomes infusions of foreign capital. Around $300 billion of direct foreign investment occurred in the 1980s alone, leading to a situation where foreign companies control about 5 percent of the American economy and 15 percent of manufacturing assets in the United States.

But assume, for example, that a company from China or Germany seeks to buy control of an American company that makes critical components for several U.S. military defense systems. Congress has passed special legislation requiring the federal government to give special scrutiny to acquisitions with national security ramifications.

Under the law, called the "Exon-Florio Amendment," the President is given authority to block any takeover that might threaten national security. The President has delegated that authority to a government panel called the *Committee on Foreign Investment in the United States* (CFIUS), which reviews prospective foreign takeovers to determine whether there is "credible evidence" that the transaction "could threaten to impair the national security."

At this writing, very few proposed transactions have been barred on national security grounds, but the level of scrutiny is increasing and a new law functionally puts the burden on acquiring companies to prove that they are *not* a threat to U.S. national security; previously, the burden had been more on opponents to prove that the acquirers *were* such a threat. In the fall of 1992, a French-owned company, Thomson-CSF, withdrew its bid to buy the missiles business of U.S.-owned LTV Corp. in light of difficulties raised during the CFIUS review process.

Following *Norlin*, Delaware (the leading jurisdiction in such matters) has developed several important rules to govern target director discretion in hostile tender offers. Three cases are among the most important decided in Delaware.

First, in *Unocal Corp. v. Mesa Petroleum Co.*, 493 A.2d 946 (Del. 1985), the Delaware Supreme Court held that a target management's defensive tactics must be *reasonable in relation* to the threat posed. If a hostile bidder's tender offer is coercive or clearly inadequate, target management will be given substantial leeway to use some of the aforementioned defensive tactics (such as poison pills or white knights) to defeat it. However, if the bid is not coercive and is at a fair price that target shareholders can take or leave at their own discretion, target management "does not have unbridled discretion to defeat any perceived threat by any draconian means available."

Second, once target managers have decided that the corporation is for sale—for example, they respond to a hostile bid by bringing in a white knight to make a competing bid, or they make their own bid through a management-sponsored leveraged buyout (an attempt by target management to buy out the public investors by using huge amounts of credit secured by the corporation's own assets)—they become "auctioneers" with a responsibility to obtain the highest possible price for the shareholders. *Revlon, Inc. v. MacAndrews & Forbes Holdings, Inc.*, 506 A.2d 173 (Del. 1986) holds that use of lockup options to sell crown jewels to a white knight may unduly favor that white knight, thereby impermissibly stifling a bidding contest. Absent a fair auction, the target shareholders might not receive the highest possible price for their shares.

Third, in *Paramount Communications, Inc. v. Time, Inc.*, 571 A.2d 1140 (Del. 1990), the Delaware Supreme Court's interpretation of these rules gave additional leeway to a target board by holding that directors "are not obliged to abandon a deliberately conceived corporate plan for a short-term shareholder profit [in the form of a tender offer] unless there is clearly no basis to sustain the corporate strategy." *Time* approved a target board's use of a poison pill to "just say no" to a hostile bid that would have disrupted the target's long-term strategic plan to merge with another corporation. The court appeared to give credence to *Time*'s assertion that it was also protecting its "corporate culture" from a hostile invasion.

TERMINATION

As we saw earlier, a primary characteristic of the corporation is that it can have a perpetual existence. (While a few states do place time limits on the duration of the certificate of incorporation, this is of no real consequence because renewal is usually only a formality.) This is not to say, however, that a corporation *must* exist forever. A number of different circumstances can bring about an end to its existence.

In discussing the termination of a corporation, a distinction must be made between liquidation and dissolution. **Liquidation** is the conversion of the corporation's assets to cash and the distribution of these funds to creditors and shareholders. **Dissolution** is the actual termination of the corporation's existence as an artificial person—its "legal death." A liquidation can occur without an actual dissolution, as where the corporation sells its assets to another company. The shareholders might then choose to dissolve the corporation, but it would not be required. On the other hand, dissolution sometimes takes place before liquidation. The remainder of our discussion is devoted primarily to the various circumstances that bring about dissolution, with a final mention of the process of winding up corporate affairs after dissolution.

Voluntary Dissolution

A corporation can voluntarily terminate its own existence. Dissolution can be accomplished by the incorporators in some unusual circumstances, but the shareholders are ordinarily the only ones with such power. The board of directors does *not* have the power to dissolve the corporation.

By Incorporators

If the corporation has never gotten off the ground, it can be voluntarily dissolved by the incorporators. This can occur where the corporation has not done any business and no shares have been issued. In such a situation, the incorporators dissolve the corporation by filing "articles of dissolution" with the appropriate state official, who then issues a "certificate of dissolution."

By Shareholders

If the shareholders wish to discontinue the corporation's existence for any reason, they can do so. The most common reason for voluntary dissolution is that the enterprise has proved unprofitable.

The procedures for voluntary dissolution vary somewhat from state to state, but their general outline is basically the same. The process is usually initiated by resolution of the board of directors. A meeting of the shareholders is then called, at which time the matter is voted on. The vote required for approval varies among the states in the same manner as for mergers and consolidations, from a simple majority to four-fifths, with a *two-thirds* vote being a common requirement. After shareholder approval, articles of dissolution are filed and the certificate of dissolution is issued.

Dissenting shareholders can challenge the dissolution in court. However, a court will issue an injunction prohibiting dissolution only if these shareholders are able to prove that the controlling shareholders dissolved the corporation in *bad faith*, with the intent of defrauding the minority.

Involuntary Dissolution

In some circumstances, a court action can be instituted for the purpose of dissolving the corporation. A legal proceeding of this nature can be brought by a shareholder or by the state. Dissolution ordered by a court in such a proceeding is often referred to as an "involuntary" dissolution.

By Shareholders

The laws of the various states generally provide that one or more shareholders can file a lawsuit requesting that the court dissolve the corporation. Those situations in which a shareholder can obtain dissolution by court order are listed below.

Oppression of Minority Shareholders. In most states, oppression of minority shareholders by those in control is a ground for judicial dissolution. Oppressive conduct generally includes any act by which controlling shareholders seek to take unfair advantage of the minority. One example is the purchase of corporate assets by controlling shareholders, who then lease them back to the corporation for exorbitant rental fees.

Deadlock. Most states authorize dissolution by the court if it is proved that the corporation is unable to function because of a management deadlock. This is not a common occurrence and ordinarily could only happen in a closely held corporation. In order for there to be an unbreakable management deadlock, of course, there would have to be equal ownership interests by two separate factions and a board of directors with an even number of members split into equal, opposing groups.

Mismanagement. Courts are generally reluctant to interfere with decisions made by corporate managers. However, a court may order dissolution of the corporation if it is being so grossly mismanaged that its assets are actually being wasted.

The following case illustrates the difficulty a shareholder may encounter in seeking to have the corporation involuntarily dissolved because of alleged mismanagement.

GRUENBERG v. GOLDMINE PLANTATION, INC.

Court of Appeal of Louisiana, 360 So.2d 884 (1978)

Goldmine Corp's. principal asset was a 900-acre tract of land fronting on the Mississippi River in Louisiana. Acquired in 1941 for $65,000, the property was appraised at $3,000 per acre in 1975, giving it a value at that time of $2,700,000. Since its acquisition the land had been used solely for growing sugar cane, a business which in recent years had not been very profitable. However, since 1966 various industrial interests had expressed a desire to buy the land, the latest proposed price being $3,600 per acre.

Without even investigating the merits of these offers, Goldmine's directors voted to reject them. The directors apparently were motivated by a feeling that the land would probably continue to increase in value, but they made no effort to obtain information that would enable them to intelligently weigh the proposals and determine the best interests of the shareholders.

Ten of Goldmine's shareholders, who collectively owned 40 percent of its stock, filed suit seeking to have the corporation dissolved by court order. They were opposed by four shareholders who collectively owned the remaining 60 percent. These four also served as the company's directors. Louisiana law provided several grounds for involuntary dissolution, the following two of which were asserted by plaintiffs as applying to Goldmine's situation: (1) "The objects of the corporation have wholly failed,

or are entirely abandoned, or their accomplishment is impracticable"; or (2) "It is beneficial to the interests of the shareholders that the corporation should be liquidated and dissolved."

The trial court dismissed the suit, and plaintiffs appealed.

Stoulig, Judge:

. . . Meanwhile, back at the farm, the sugar cane crop was yielding dismal dividends which, over the past 10 years, averaged a net profit of less than one-half of 1 percent and the only reason the operation did not result in a loss for most of these years was that no charge for the use of the land was included in the operating expenses. . . .

From the minority standpoint, approximately $1,080,000 of their collective funds are tied up in a farming operation that has no future and from which they realize sparse returns. Aware of the tax consequences of liquidating, they nonetheless reason that 50 percent plus of something they can use is better than 100 percent of a paper asset beyond their reach.

In the light of this situation, we consider whether plaintiffs have sustained the proof to support their demands for involuntary dissolution. . . . First we hold the evidence does not support our concluding the objects of incorporation have "wholly failed" or "been abandoned" or that "their accomplishment is impracticable." Sugar cane has been grown continuously on this property since 1941. . . . Although the future of sugar cane farming on plantations the size of Goldmine is at best speculative

and the record leaves no doubt that the highest and best use of this land at present is for industrial purposes, we cannot conclude that the accomplishment of sugar farming is impracticable.

Low profits per se do not render the accomplishment of the objects of the corporation impracticable. . . . To us "impracticability" connotes an element of obsolescence as well as a low return operation. Therefore relief is not available [on this ground].

We next consider whether the record supports the view that dissolution would be more beneficial to the shareholders. It can be urged validly in this case that the low returns of the past have been more than offset by the appreciation of the corporate assets. With the completion of the river bridge at Luling within the next few years, the land value, according to [an expert appraiser], should increase tremendously. Thus the proof required [for this ground] is lacking.

. . . We appreciate the frustrations of the minority who are locked into a financial situation in which they have a substantial interest but no control. They suggest the shareholders be equated to partners and be permitted to disengage from the corporation as they could were Goldmine operated as a partnership. Our substantive law provides for involuntary dissolution but offers no remedy for the minority shareholder with substantial holdings who is out of control and trapped in a closed corporation. We will not arrogate the legislative function to provide relief. . . .

Affirmed.

By the State

Because a corporation derives its right to exist from the state where it is incorporated, it seems natural that the state should also be able to take away that right. This power can be exercised, however, only in certain circumstances. The primary grounds for state-initiated dissolution are a corporation's consistently exceeding or abusing the powers conferred on it by law, a corporation's never having commenced business or becoming dormant after abandoning its business, and a corporation's failure to comply with administrative requirements such as (1) failure to file required reports with the secretary of state, (2) failure to pay franchise fees or other state taxes, and (3) failure to appoint or maintain a registered agent. Many states acknowledge the relative insignificance of such administrative omissions by providing for easy reinstatement upon compliance and payment of any penalties owed.

By Creditors

The RMBCA provides for court-ordered dissolution of a corporation upon application of a corporate creditor if it is shown that (1) the creditor's claim has been reduced to an unsatisfied judgment and the corporation is insolvent, or (2) the corporation has admitted in writing that the creditor's claim is due and that the corporation is insolvent.

Winding Up

Where Dissolution Is Voluntary

When voluntary dissolution occurs, the corporation's directors become *trustees* who hold corporate assets for the benefit of creditors and shareholders. They usually are allowed to wind up corporate affairs without court supervision. The directors in this situation have four duties:

1. They must not undertake any new business. Their authority is limited to the fulfillment of existing corporate obligations.

2. They must make a reasonable attempt to collect debts owed to the corporation.

3. After liquidation of corporate assets, they must pay creditors insofar as these assets are sufficient to do so.

4. When the claims of corporate creditors have been satisfied, they must distribute any remaining funds to shareholders. This distribution is required to be in the proportion of shareholders' respective interests and in accordance with any special rights enjoyed by preferred shareholders.

The directors can be held personally responsible for the breach of any of these winding-up duties. However, if they are unwilling to serve as trustees in liquidating the corporation, a *receiver* will be appointed and supervised by a court for the purpose of winding up corporate affairs. The court can also take such action if a creditor or shareholder shows cause why the directors should not be allowed to perform this function.

Where Dissolution Is Involuntary

In any case where dissolution is involuntary, the liquidation of corporate assets and other winding-up activities are always performed by a court-appointed receiver.

Post-Dissolution Liability of Shareholders

Occasionally, corporations dissolve and distribute remaining assets to shareholders *without* settling all known debts. Also, unknown obligations may later arise. Should the corporate creditors be allowed to reach the assets distributed to former shareholders? Most jurisdictions provide some procedures to grant protection to creditors in this situation. At the same time, interests of the shareholders of the dissolving corporation must also be considered.

Although the RMBCA contains new procedures for dealing with this problem,[7] most jurisdictions follow, at least roughly, the 1969 MBCA's provision that the dissolution of a corpoation "shall not take away or impair any remedy available to or against such corporation, its directors, officers, or shareholders, for any right or claim existing, or any liability incurred, prior to such dissolution if action or other proceeding thereon is commenced *within two years* after the date of dissolution." Assume, for example, that a corporation dissolves shortly after one of its delivery truck drivers causes a serious accident. If the injured party sues within two years of the dissolution, the shareholders who receive corporate assets in the dissolution may be liable pro rata to repay those assets to satisfy the injured plaintiff's claim.

SUMMARY

Although there are technical differences between a merger and a consolidation, there really are no

[7]RMBCA Secs. 1406, 1407.

practical differences, and the two terms are often used interchangeably to describe a combination of independent corporations under common ownership. The term merger is usually used to describe both types of combinations, as well as a number of other variations.

The reasons for a merger between two corporations are many and varied. A merger begins with approval by the board of each company, and then must also be approved by a vote of each company's shareholders, usually by a majority. A dissenting shareholder, one who voted against an approved merger, usually has the right of appraisal. This right permits the shareholder to have his or her shares appraised and bought by the corporation at their fair value.

In addition to formal mergers and consolidations, corporations may be combined under common ownership by other means, such as asset or stock acquisitions. These variations often are also referred to as mergers in everyday usage. Stock acquisitions may be accomplished in different ways, including open market purchases and tender offers. When the target company's board resists an attempted takeover by stock acquisition, the acquiring company is likely to use a tender offer because it is faster and allows the target company's board less time to raise obstacles to the takeover. In responding to a takeover attempt, however, the target company's board must continue to fulfill its basic duties of obedience, due care, and loyalty. In the takeover setting, these duties require the board to act in good faith, make decisions that are as completely informed as possible under the circumstances, and seek the best interests of their company's shareholders.

A corporation can be dissolved in several different ways: there may be a voluntary dissolution by vote of a majority of the shareholders, or there may be an involuntary dissolution for prescribed reasons in a court action instituted by a shareholder or by the state.

KEY TERMS

Merger
Consolidation
Defensive merger
Articles of merger or consolidation
Certificate of merger or consolidation
Appraisal right
De facto merger
Holding company (or investment company)

Tender offer
Williams Act
Liquidation
Dissolution

QUESTIONS AND PROBLEMS

1. In valuing the dissenters' shares of Kirby Lumber Corporation via the "Delaware block," a court concluded that the earnings value was $120 per share and the asset value $456 per share. There had been so little trading in the corporation's stock that the court could not reconstruct a market value. The court therefore assigned 60 percent weight to the earnings value and 40 percent weight to the asset value. What is the "fair value" of the dissenters' shares? (*Bell v. Kirby Lumber Corp.*, 395 A.2d 730, Del.Ch. 1976.)

2. The Opatut family owned 75 percent of the stock of Colonial Foods Corp., and totally controlled it. The Opatuts often transacted business with Colonial, and minority Colonial shareholders ultimately brought a derivative action claiming that the Opatuts had profited unfairly in several business dealings with Colonial. To end the derivative suit, the Opatuts initiated a merger with a subsidiary they owned in order to buy out the minority shareholders. Once the merger was completed, the plaintiffs were no longer shareholders and therefore had no standing to bring the derivative suit. However, they brought suit challenging the motives behind the merger and the $3 per share price that the Opatuts had selected unilaterally. Is the appraisal right plaintiffs' only remedy? (*Merritt v. Colonial Foods, Inc.*, 505 A.2d 797, Del.Ch. 1986.)

3. Moran, a director of Household International, was considering a takeover of Household by another company he controlled. He contemplated a "front-end-loaded, two-tiered bid," a two-step takeover featuring a tender offer to gain majority control and a freeze-out merger to buy the rest of the shares, with a higher price paid in the tender offer than in the merger. In the face of its vulnerability, the Household board issued a poison pill. Among other features, the pill had a provision that, if activated by a merger or consolidation, allowed Household shareholders to buy $200 of the common stock of the tender offeror for $100. Moran challenged the validity of the pill. Is

this a valid defensive arrangement? (*Moran v. Household International,* 500 A.2d 1346, Del. 1985.)

4. After a court enjoined a management-sponsored corporate restructuring aimed at defeating a hostile bid by the Bass Group, Macmillan, Inc.'s board chose to put the company up for auction. The two main bidders were KKR and MCC. KKR's bid featured participation by management of Macmillan, and management rather shamelessly favored KKR in all its negotiations, repeatedly giving it extra information and additional chances to raise its bid, when these things were denied MCC. Should MCC's challenge to the auction succeed? (*Mills Acquisition Co. v. Macmillan, Inc.,* 559 A.2d 1261, Del. 1989.)

5. VAC, the world's largest maker of cutting tools and quality hand tools, was dominated by the Thomas family. Throughout its history, VAC had pursued long-term profit maximization, often investing large amounts in capital at the expense of short-term profit. It had been quite successful. Newell Company also had been a successful company, primarily by acquiring other companies. Some 90 percent of Newell's sales and profits were generated by past acquisitions, often achieved through two-tier offers. Newell slowly accumulated 11 percent of VAC's stock and then made a tender offer for 10 percent more. The VAC board, dominated by outside directors, authorized a repurchase of shares that would increase the holdings of the Thomas family to more than 50 percent, effectively blocking any takeover. Discuss the validity of this defensive maneuver. (*Newell Co. v. Vermont American Corp.,* 725 F.Supp. 351, N.D.Ill. 1989.)

6. Grand Met made an all-cash bid for all shares that might be tendered of Pillsbury. Pillsbury's board rejected the bid, refused to cancel its poison pill, and adopted a plan that allegedly provided greater value to its shareholders. The plan involved (1) a spin-off of its Burger King subsidiary, (2) sale of its Steak & Ale restaurants, and (3) sale of the rest of its food business. The Grand Met bid was $63 per share. Pillsbury's alternative, if optimistic assumptions turned out to be accurate, would be worth $68 per share within five years. Grant Met sued for an order enjoining operation of the poison pill and enjoining the Burger King spin-off. Should the court issue such an order? (*Grand Metropolitan Public Ltd. v. Pillsbury Co.,* 558 A.2d 1049, Del.Ch. 1988.)

7. Two factions of shareholders of Barlum Hotel, Inc. were at each other's throats. A third party's offer to buy the hotel for a million dollars was rejected by the Kowal faction, much to the regret of the Keywell faction. A shareholders' meeting degenerated into fisticuffs. Thereafter, the leaders of the two factions refused to speak to each other, except through third parties. No meeting of shareholders or directors with a quorum was held for more than four years. The corporation profited in three of the years, but lost money in the fourth. No dividends had been paid for six years. The hotel was run-down and poorly managed. The Keywell group asked a court for an order of involuntary dissolution. Should the court grant the request? (*Levant v. Kowal,* 86 N.W.2d 336, Mich, 1957.)

8. Van County Insurance Agency, Inc. (Van) was voluntarily dissolved on September 24, 1982. Its assets were distributed to Thompson, Turner, and Jones, its sole shareholders. On September 21, 1983, plaintiff creditor filed a lawsuit against the aforementioned shareholders for $4700 owed it by Van. The suit had originally been filed against Van on August 6, 1981. Are the Van shareholders liable even though the corporation has been voluntarily dissolved? (*Thompson v. A.G. Nash & Co., Inc.,* 704 S.W.2d 822, Tex.App. 1985.)

Introduction to Securities Regulation

1933 Act: Regulating the
Issuance of Securities

1934 Act: Regulating the
Trading of Securities

State Regulation

International Implications

THE GREAT STOCK market crash of 1929 was one of the most dramatic turning points in American economic history. That event not only ushered in the Great Depression but also heralded the creation of modern securities regulation. Securities regulation is one of the most complicated areas of the law; attorneys who practice in the securities field are among the most specialized and well paid of all lawyers. Although this vast, everchanging subject may be intimidating to the novice, few persons in business can afford to remain ignorant of its effects on the way business is done in this country.

Many aspects of securities regulation are highly visible. Most Americans are familiar with the hustle and bustle of the New York Stock Exchange. More than 45 million Americans own stock, many in major corporations such as General Motors and IBM. Through securities regulation, the federal government, and to a lesser degree the states, regulate trading on the stock exchanges, protect the interests of shareholders, and attempt to ensure that the collapse of 1929 is never repeated.

In this chapter, some of the more important aspects of the law of securities regulation are surveyed.

INTRODUCTION TO SECURITIES REGULATION

A security such as a stock or a bond has no intrinsic value—its value lies in the ownership interest that it represents. The value of that ownership interest may be difficult to discover and easy to misrepresent. Securities may be produced in nearly limitless supply at virtually no cost by anyone with access to a printing press. For all these reasons, fraud, manipulation, and deceit have been frequent companions of the security. Government regulation of securities dates back to at least 1285, when King Edward I of England attempted to gain some control over the capital markets by licensing brokers located in London.

Securities regulation in the United States was almost nonexistent until 1911, when Kansas enacted securities laws. Other states soon followed suit, but without federal laws, companies could evade regulation by operating across state lines.

The 1920s were an especially active time for the issuance and trading of securities. The securities business was then characterized by price manipulation, deceitful practices, selling on excessive credit, and the abuse of secret information by corporate insiders. Of the $50 billion of new securities offered for sale in the United States in the 1920s, about one-half were worthless. The public and the national economy were devastated when stock market prices fell 89 percent between 1929 and 1933, a situation that finally produced federal action.

Federal Legislation

The first federal securities law was the *Securities Act of 1933* (the 1933 Act), which regulated the initial issuance of securities by companies. Fraudulent and deceptive practices were outlawed, and registration was required before a new security could be offered or sold, unless that security was entitled to an exemption from registration.

A year later, Congress passed the *Securities Exchange Act of 1934* (the 1934 Act), which extended federal regulation to trading in securities already issued and outstanding, required registration of securities brokers and dealers, and created the Securities and Exchange Commission (SEC), the federal agency that enforces the federal securities laws through its extensive powers.

In 1935, Congress passed the *Public Utility Holding Company Act* in response to manipulative and monopolistic practices in the public utilities industry. The SEC in its early years was largely concerned with correcting abuses in the financing and operating of large public utilities. Because the commission has been very successful in this area, separate enforcement of the Public Utility Holding Company Act is no longer a major SEC priority.

The next securities law passed by Congress was the *Trust Indenture Act of 1939,* which helped protect persons investing in bonds, debentures, notes, and other debt securities by imposing qualification requirements on trustees of such instruments. A year later, the *Investment Company Act of 1940* imposed additional requirements on companies engaged primarily in the business of investing, reinvesting, and trading securities. For example, that act prohibits anyone found guilty of securities fraud from being associated with investment companies and bans transactions between such companies and their officers without prior SEC approval. The *Investment Advisers Act of 1940* required persons or firms who engaged in the business of advising others about investments for compensation to register with the SEC, as brokers and dealers are required to register under the 1934 Act.

The *Securities Investor Protection Act of 1970* amended the 1934 Act in response to a rash of failures in the late 1960s in the broker-dealer business. The act creates the Securities Investor Protection Corporation (SIPC), which manages a fund to protect investors from the failure of broker-dealers in the same manner as the Federal Deposit Insurance Corporation protects the customers of banks.

Although not a securities act in a strict sense, the *Racketeer Influenced and Corrupt Organizations Act of 1970* (RICO) affects the securities business. The basics of RICO were explained in Chapter 7. Because one of RICO's "predicate acts" is securities fraud, many lawsuits complaining primarily of securities law violations have been parlayed into RICO claims by aggressive prosecutors and inventive civil plaintiffs.

Of these acts, the 1933 Act and the 1934 Act remain the most important.

What Is A Security?

Securities are commonly thought of as the stock issued by corporations. The shares of common and preferred stock issued by corporations constitute a major type of security. These are *equity securities,* which evidence an ownership interest in the corpora-

tion. Holders of equity securities are normally entitled to vote on important corporate matters and to receive dividends as their share of the corporate profits. The other major type of security is the *debt security,* such as the bond, note, or debenture. Holders of debt securities are creditors rather than owners. They have no voice in corporate affairs but are entitled to receive regular interest payments according to the terms of the bond or note.

Because the inventive human mind has devised an inordinate variety of investment interests, securities regulation goes beyond items that are clearly labelled *stocks* or *bonds.* Sec. 2(1) of the 1933 Act broadly defines *security* to include

> any note, stock, treasury stock, bond, debenture, evidence of indebtedness, certificate of interest or participation in any profit-sharing agreement, . . . investment contract, voting-trust certificate, fractional undivided interest in oil, gas or other mineral rights, or, in general, any interest or instrument commonly known as a 'security.'. . .

This broad definition has, of necessity, been liberally construed by the courts. Interests in limited partnerships, condominiums, farm animals with accompanying agreements for their care, franchises, whiskey warehouse receipts, and many other varied items have been deemed to be securities.

The inclusion of the term *investment contract* in the 1933 Act's definition of security has produced much litigation. Some very interesting investment opportunities have been held to constitute investment contracts, as the following case illustrates.

Smith v. Gross

U.S. Ninth Circuit Court of Appeals, 604 F.2d 292 (1979)

Case

Gross used a promotional newsletter to solicit buyer-investors to raise earthworms to help him reach his quota of selling earthworms to fishermen. Buyers were promised that the seller's instructions would enable them to have a profitable worm farm, that the time required was similar to that of a

garden, that the worms doubled in quantity every 60 days, and that Gross would buy back all bait-size worms produced by buyers at $2.25 per pound.

The Smiths invested but later sued claiming that contrary to Gross's representations, the worms multiplied at a maximum of eight rather than 64 times per year and that the promised profits could be achieved

only if the multiplication rate were as fast as represented and if Gross repurchased the Smiths' production at $2.25 per pound, which was much higher than the true market value. Gross could pay that amount only by selling the worms to new worm farmers at inflated prices.

The Smiths claimed that Gross made false representations, which violated the federal securities laws.

(continues)

SMITH V. GROSS

(continued from previous page)
The federal district court dismissed the action for want of subject matter jurisdiction after concluding that no "security" was involved in the case. The Smiths appealed.

Per Curiam:

. . . The Smiths contend that the transactions between the parties involved an investment contract type of security. In *SEC v. W. J. Howey Co.*, 328 U.S. 293, 301 (1946), the Supreme Court set out the conditions for an investment contract: "[t]he test is whether the scheme involves [1] an investment of money [2] in a common enterprise [3] with profits to come solely from the efforts of others." This court in *SEC v. Glenn W. Turner Enterprises, Inc.*, 474 F.2d 476, 482 (9th Cir.), *cert. denied*, 414 U.S. 821 (1973), held that, despite the Supreme Court's use of the word "solely," the third element of the *Howey* test is "whether the efforts made by those other than the investor are the undeniably significant ones, those essential managerial efforts which affect the failure or success of the enterprise." The *Turner* court defined a common enterprise as "one in which the fortunes of the investor are interwoven with and dependent upon the efforts and success of those seeking the investment or of third parties."

We find this case virtually identical with *Miller v. Central Chinchilla Group, Inc.*, 494 F.2d 414 (8th Cir. 1974). In *Miller* the defendants entered into contracts under which they sold chinchillas to the plaintiffs with the promise to repurchase the offspring. The plaintiffs were told that it was simple to breed chinchillas according to the defendants' instructions and that the venture would be highly profitable. The plaintiffs alleged that the chinchillas were difficult to raise and had a high mortality rate, and that the defendants could return the promised profits only if they repurchased the offspring and sold them to other prospective chinchilla raisers at an inflated price.

The *Miller* court focused on two features in holding there was an investment contract: (1) the defendants persuaded the plaintiffs to invest by representing that the efforts required of them would be very minimal; and (2) that if the plaintiffs diligently exerted themselves, they still would not gain the promised profits because those profits could be achieved only if the defendants secured additional investors at the inflated prices. Both of these features are present in the instant case. We find *Miller* to be persuasive and consistent with *Turner*. . . .

There was a common enterprise as required by *Turner*. The Smiths alleged that, although they were free under the terms of the contract to sell their production anywhere they wished, they could have received the promised profits only if the defendants repurchased above the market price, and that the defendants could have repurchased above the market price only if the defendants secured additional investors at inflated prices. Thus, the fortune of the Smiths was interwoven with and dependent upon the efforts and success of the defendants.

We also find that here, as in *Miller* the third element of an investment contract set forth in *Turner*—that the efforts of those other than the investor are the undeniably significant ones—was present here. The *Miller* court noted that the plaintiffs there had been assured by the sellers that the effort needed to raise chinchillas was minimal. The significant effort necessary for success in the endeavor was that of the seller in procuring new investors who would purchase the chinchillas at inflated prices. Here, the Smiths alleged that they were promised that the effort necessary to raise worms was minimal and they alleged that they could not receive the promised income unless the defendants purchased their harvest.

We find the analysis in *Miller* persuasive and hold that the Smiths alleged facts that, if true, were sufficient to establish an investment contract. . . .

The judgment of the district court is reversed.

1933 ACT: REGULATING THE ISSUANCE OF SECURITIES

A major portion of federal securities regulation concerns the issuance of securities by companies. Congressional investigations after the 1929 stock market crash disclosed that enthusiasm for investment opportunities in the 1920s was often so great that large offerings of stock would be gobbled up by an investing public that knew virtually nothing about the selling company.

The goal of the 1933 Act is to protect the investing public. The 1933 Act is a disclosure statute frequently called the "Truth in Securities" law. The Act requires full disclosure by companies wishing to issue and sell stock to the public. By requiring such companies to file a registration statement with the SEC and to use an offering called a **prospectus** when attempting to sell securities, the law attempts to enable the investor to make an informed decision. The SEC, which is charged with enforcement of the law, does not attempt to pass on the value of the securities offered nor to advise investors to purchase or not purchase the securities of particular companies.

The 1933 Act also protects investors by prohibiting fraud and deceit in the distribution of shares, even those that the law does not require to be registered.

Registration Process
Elements of the Process

Securities are distributed much like any product. The corporation selling securities to raise capital, the *issuer,* is analogous to the manufacturer of goods. *Underwriters* act as wholesalers, *dealers* act as retailers, and the *investor* is a consumer. By regulating the activities of the issuer, underwriter, and dealer, the 1933 Act seeks to ensure that the investor has access to adequate information before purchasing a particular security.

The keystones to the disclosure process are the registration statement and the prospectus, the contents of which are discussed presently. Sec. 5(a) of the 1933 Act makes it unlawful to sell or deliver any security without first filing with the SEC a registration statement that has become effective. Sec. 5(b)(1) makes it unlawful to sell a security by means of a prospectus that does not meet statutory standards. Sec. 5(b)(2) makes it unlawful to sell securities that are not accompanied or preceded by a prospectus. Finally, Sec. 5(c) makes it illegal even to *offer* to sell or buy securities before a registration statement is filed.

SEC Approval

The registration statement filed with the SEC is not automatically effective. Rather, the staff of the SEC may review the statement for omissions and inaccuracies. Some reviews may be more thorough than others. Because of budgetary cutbacks and staff reductions, the SEC in recent years has had to give cursory reviews to many registration statements, reserving the full review process primarily for statements filed by new issuers selling to the public for the first time. Indeed, today most registration statements are not reviewed at all.

Sec. 8(a) of the 1933 Act provides that if the SEC is silent, the registration statement automatically becomes effective on the twentieth day after its filing. The registration process may be analyzed in terms of its three major time periods. The first stage of the process is the period before the registration statement is filed (the *prefiling period*). The second stage lasts from the filing of the statement until it becomes effective (the *waiting period*). The final stage is, of course, after the statement becomes effective (the *post-effective period*).

Prefiling Period. To prevent circumvention of the provisions of Sec. 5, an issuer is strictly limited during the prefiling period. The issuer may not sell or even offer to sell a security before the registration statement is filed. The term *offer* is broadly construed and encompasses not only formal sales campaigns, but any type of activity meant to "precondition" the market. A simple speech by a corporate executive or a press release about how well the company is doing may be improper if it "just happens" to be soon followed by the filing of a registration statement.

The only activities permitted during the prefiling period, other than normal advertising and communications with shareholders by an issuer, are preliminary negotiations between the issuer and underwriters. This is necessary because a large distribution of securities may require that an entire syndicate of underwriters be assembled.

Waiting Period. The purpose of the waiting period is to slow the distribution process so that the dealers and the public have time to familiarize themselves with the information disclosed in the registration process. Although no sales may be consummated during this period, certain types of offers are allowed, and underwriters may now make arrangements with dealers for their assistance in distribution.

In addition to oral offers, certain types of written offers are permissible during the waiting period. For example, an issuer may place in *The Wall Street Journal* a short announcement known as a *tombstone ad* because it is usually surrounded by a black border. Under SEC rule 134, the announcement may contain only a few limited items, such as (1) the kind of security, (2) the amount, (3) by whom purchase orders will be executed, and (4) the location at which a prospectus may be obtained. The announcement must state that no offer to purchase can actually be accepted during the waiting period and that an indication of interest is not binding on a prospective investor.

Offers may also be made by use of a preliminary prospectus, which contains information from the registration statement then under review. These are called *red herring prospectuses,* because SEC rule 430 requires that a special legend be printed in red ink on each one labelling it a preliminary prospectus, stating that a registration statement has been filed but is not yet effective, that no final sale can be made during the waiting period, and that it does not constitute an offer to sell.

Post-Effective Period. Once the registration statement becomes effective, sales of securities may be completed. However, the law still imposes requirements aimed at encouraging dissemination of information. With some exceptions, the issuer, underwriter, and dealer must provide a copy of the final prospectus with every written offer, supplemental sales literature, written confirmation of sale, or delivery of securities. The prospectus must be used as long as the distribution is taking place; if this period extends beyond nine months, Sec. 10(a)(3) requires that the prospectus be updated to reflect more recent information on the status of the issuer. In addition, the issuer must update the prospectus whenever important new developments occur; otherwise the information can become stale and misleading, resulting in liability for fraud under Sec. 17(a) of the 1933 Act.

Shelf Registration

Originally, an insurer was required to file a new registration statement every time it sought to initiate a new distribution of stock. However, rule 415 now establishes a system known as **shelf registration.** Under this system a company is allowed to file one registration statement announcing its long-term plans for sales of securities. Then, whenever the company thinks market conditions and its own financial needs require the sale of securities, it can issue the additional securities without going through the registration process described above to achieve SEC approval because it already has a registration statement and a prospectus "on the shelf." If periodically updated, the registration statement will remain continuously effective. Rule 415 enhances the ability of corporations to raise capital on short notice, but its use has been restricted primarily to the larger, more reliable corporations.

Disclosure Requirements

The information disclosure requirements of the 1933 Act and the 1934 Act were for a long time separate, often overlapping and sometimes conflicting. In recent years, the SEC has made an effort to coordinate the requirements for information disclosure con-

tained in the two acts. The filing requirements of the 1934 Act must be mentioned here because they now bear significantly on the disclosure requirements of the 1933 Act regarding the registration statement and prospectus.

Registration and Reporting

Sec. 12 of the 1934 Act requires all companies whose securities are traded on the national stock exchanges (such as the New York Stock Exchange) and any other companies with more than $5 million in assets and more than 500 shareholders to register their securities with the SEC. These companies are referred to as registered or reporting companies. There are about 10,000 such companies. The required registration statement must contain extensive information about such areas as the organization, financial structure, and nature of the business; the structure of present classes of stock; the directors and officers and their remuneration; important contracts; balance sheets; and profit-and-loss statements for the three preceding fiscal years.

Sec. 13 requires that the registration statement be continually updated with annual reports (called *10-Ks*) and quarterly reports (*10-Qs*). In addition, if important facts change between quarterly reports, the company should amend the registration statement by use of an 8-K report.

Integration of Registration Requirements

Despite all the information made public under the 1934 Act, even reporting companies traditionally had to go through the expensive registration process under the 1933 Act, which required disclosure of information already made public in the 1934 Act reports. Because of complaints about duplication and needless expense, the SEC changed the rules in 1982 to make disclosure requirements uniform under the 1933 and 1934 Acts and to use the periodic reports of the 1934 Act to satisfy many of the disclosure requirements of the 1933 Act registration statements by a process of incorporation by reference. The core of this procedure is a three-tiered registration structure that creates three distinct categories of registration statement, depending on the issuer's financial size and reporting history. The largest, most dependable companies can file very basic prospectuses that incorporate by reference all the information contained in previously filed 1934 Act reports. Medium-sized companies with less reliable reporting histories are allowed some incorporation by reference, and the remaining companies must file complete registration statements with no incorporation by reference.

Sec. 10 of the 1933 Act, as supplemented by various rules issued by the SEC, controls the content of the prospectus. The most important information in the registration statement regarding the financial structure, organization, operations, and officers and directors of the issuer must be summarized in the prospectus (unless incorporation by reference is allowed under the new system).

Materiality

Exactly which details must be included in the registration statement and prospectus is a matter governed not only by statutes and rules but also by the concept of **materiality.** The most important element in the disclosure provisions of both the 1933 and 1934 Acts is that all matters that are important or material to an investor's decision should be disclosed.

Materiality is an elusive concept, but the Supreme Court has described information as material "if there is a substantial likelihood that a reasonable shareholder would consider it important" in making an investment decision.[1] This is usually limited to matters having a significant bearing on the economic and financial performance of the company.

Examples of material facts include an erratic pattern of earnings, an intention to enter into a new line of business, adverse competitive conditions, litigation with the government that might lead to imposition of a financially damaging fine, and a substantial disparity between the price at which the shares are being offered to the public and the cost of the shares owned by officers, directors, and promoters. The following case illustrates one application of the concept of materiality in the context of the 1933 Act disclosure requirements.

---

[1]*TSC Industries, Inc. v. Northway, Inc.,* 426 U.S. 438, 449 (1976).

In re Doman Helicopters, Inc.

Securities and Exchange Commission, 41 S.E.C. 431 (1963)

Case

Doman Helicopters, Inc., was formed in 1945 but never was able to do business on a profitable basis. Except for one experimental model sold in 1950, two prototypes delivered to the Army in 1956 and 1957 (both subsequently repurchased by Doman), and one helicopter on loan to its Italian licensee, by 1962 Doman had never manufactured or sold any helicopters. Instead, it had continually flirted with bankruptcy. By September 30, 1961, its accumulated losses totalled more than $5.7 million. On January 31, 1962, Doman's current liabilities were $292,446, whereas its assets were only $13,178.

On April 19, 1962, Doman filed a Form S-1 registration statement proposing to offer publicly 681,971 shares, some to current shareholders, some to creditors, and some to the public. The contemplated price was

$1.50 per share. Doman's future plans were predicated on development of a proposed helicopter, the D-10B.

The SEC commenced a proceeding under Sec. 8(d) of the 1933 Act to determine whether a stop order should issue suspending the effectiveness of Doman's registration statement. The focus of the investigation was on deficiencies in the prospectus.

The Commission:

. . . 1. Status and Prospectus of the Model D-10B. The prospectus describes the D-10B as though it were an existing and operational helicopter possessing superiority in specified respects [economy of operation, range, payload per dollar invested] over other helicopters offered on the market. . . . There is no adequate factual foundation for the[se] statements, and they were false and misleading.

The D-10B has never been flown or

tested or even assembled in prototype form, crucial facts which are nowhere disclosed in the registration statement.

2. The Doman Hingeless Rotor System. The prospectus makes the following claims for the so-called "Doman Hingeless Rotor System": "In comparison with other devices, this system provides greater inherent stability in forward flight, less vibration in any flight attitude or maneuver, long life for the rotor and blade assembly, relatively low initial and maintenance costs and exceptional permissible range of the center of gravity of the fuselage and its cargo.". . .

These representations present in their totality a misleading picture of uniqueness and substantiated superiority of the Doman rotor system. That system has been used only on a few converted or prototype models. No production model using the Doman rotor system has ever been subjected to normal day to day usage by a user or customer. In

(continues)

IN RE DOMAN HELICOPTERS, INC.

(continued from previous page)
such circumstances the unqualified claims as to superior durability and lower maintenance costs were not warranted, and it was deceptive to describe the system as "fully developed and proven.". . .

3. Efforts to Secure Defense Contracts. The prospectus makes only a passing reference to the fact that registrant unsuccessfully attempted to secure a military market for its helicopters. It does not disclose the nature of those attempts or of the action of the Department of Defense with respect to them. Registrant had from 1951 to 1962 made strenuous and persistent efforts to interest that Department in its proposals and devices. The Department made a number of tests with the two prototype helicopters that it purchased from the registrant and made an extensive study of the Doman rotor system. It found "no significant advantages in the Doman rotor system over other types," and those findings were reaffirmed upon successive reviews following objections raised by registrant. . . . Irrespective of the correctness of the Department's conclu-

sions, they constitute a determination by the technical staff and responsible authorities of the largest single purchaser of helicopters that for their purposes registrant's rotor system had no special merit. Such determination was a significant adverse factor, and the failure to disclose it rendered the prospectus misleading.

4. Application of Proceeds. The prospectus stated that the proceeds of the offering would be used to develop the D-10B, but failed to state the order of priority in which the proceeds would be applied as required by Instruction 2 to Item 3 of Form S-1. The prospectus did not adequately disclose that except to the extent that the creditors to whom part of the offering is to be made elected to take stock in exchange for their debt claims, $292,466 of the proceeds from the public offering would first have to be applied to the liquidation of registrant's outstanding indebtedness, thereby reducing and perhaps exhausting the funds that the prospectus stated would be allocated to the D-10B. It also failed to disclose that approximately $13,000 of the estimated proceeds would have to be used

to pay the accrued salaries of certain officers and directors, and that a large portion of the proceeds would have to be used to meet current expenses, which were being incurred at the rate of $11,000 per month, and would be used for that purpose even if the proceeds of the offering were insufficient to permit registrant to go forward with its D-10B program.

5. Dilution Aspects of Offering. The prospectus fails to disclose the dilution aspects of the offering. As of January 31, 1962, registrant's shares had a book value of minus 30 cents per share. If all the shares that the registrant proposes to offer to its existing stockholders and to its creditors were in fact sold at the proposed offering prices, that book value would increase to 55 cents per share. Purchasers paying $1.50 per share would therefore suffer an immediate dilution of 95 cents per share, the benefit of which will inure entirely to the present stockholders. It was pertinent to an informed appraisal by the persons to whom the securities being offered may be sold that this dilution be described in the prospectus. . . .

A stop order will issue. ⚖

Exemptions

In certain situations where there is less need for regulation, Secs. 3 and 4 of the 1933 Act provide exemptions from Sec. 5's registration requirements (although not from the antifraud provisions of the 1933 and 1934 Acts).

Perhaps the most important exemption is that for "transactions by any person other than an issuer, underwriter, or dealer" provided by Sec. 4(1). This simply means that once the issue is sold to the investing public, the public may trade, and the dealers may handle most transactions, without any worry about registration or prospectus delivery requirements. Thus, the 1933 Act does not generally apply to so-called secondary trading, which is regulated by the 1934 Act.

Sec. 3(a) exempts from registration the securities of governments (state and federal), charitable organizations, banks, savings and loans, and common carriers, which are regulated under other federal laws.

Small Issues

There are also exemptions for small issues and small issuers. Sec. 4(2) exempts "transactions by an issuer not involving any public offering," an exemption used primarily in connection with (1) bank loans, (2) privately negotiated sales of securities to large institutional investors (private placements), and (3) the promotion of business ventures by a few closely related persons. Sec. 3(b) authorizes the SEC to exempt securities if it finds that registration "is not necessary in the public interest and for the protection of investors by reason of the small amount involved [a $5 million ceiling] or the limited character of the public offering." Pursuant to a 1992 amendment, small companies may now solicit indications of interest from investors before proceeding to raise up to $5 million annually (with minimal SEC filings) under regulation A.

Regulation D.   The SEC's regulation D fleshes out the 3(b) exemption in rules 504 and 505 and the 4(2) exemption in rule 506. Rule 504 exempts from registration any offering in a 12-month period totalling less than $1 million (reduced by amounts sold in reliance on other exemptions). This exemption is aimed at smaller businesses and is not available to 1934 Act reporting companies.

Rule 505 allows a company, including reporting companies, to sell up to $5 million in securities (reduced by amounts sold in reliance on other exemptions) in any 12-month period without registering, provided the sales are to no more than 35 unaccredited investors. **Accredited investors** are persons and institutions—such as pension funds, banks, corporate insiders, and millionaires—who because of their very nature are unlikely to need government protection in making investment decisions. The number of sales to accredited investors is not limited, although no general advertising or soliciting is allowed.

Rule 506 allows all companies to sell an unlimited amount of securities in an issuance where sales are limited to 35 unaccredited investors, if the issuer makes a determination that all purchasers are "sophisticated" and therefore capable of protecting themselves without the assistance of a registration statement and prospectus. Accredited investors are assumed to be sophisticated, and an unsophisticated purchaser may act through a sophisticated purchaser representative. As with rule 505, no general advertising or soliciting is allowed, which is why these are often called "private placement" offerings. Typically, an issuer, rather than offering shares to the open market, will place them through private direct negotiations with an institutional investor, such as an insurance company.

Local Offerings

A final important exemption is Sec. 3(a)(11)'s exemption for intrastate offerings, which applies where a selling company doing business in a state offers and sells securities only to residents of the same state and intends to use the proceeds there. An issuer, accord-

ing to rule 147, is doing business within a state if (1) it derives 80 percent or more of its revenue from operations within the state, (2) at least 80 percent of its assets are located within the state, (3) at least 80 percent of the net proceeds of the issuance will be used within the state, and (4) the issuer's principal office is located there. Offer of the shares for sale to a single nonresident will void the exemption. Federal regulation is deemed unnecessary because of the availability of state regulation and the close proximity of purchaser to seller.

Institutional Investors

Buyers of private placement securities under rule 506 have traditionally been hindered in attempts to resell them. To encourage trading in the private placement markets by large institutional investors, in 1990 the SEC adopted rule 144A, which exempts a sale of securities so long as (1) they are not of the same class as those listed on an exchange or quoted on the National Association of Securities Dealers Automated Quotation (NASDAQ) system, (2) the buyer is a qualified institutional buyer (QIB), and (3) the seller and prospective purchaser may request basic financial information from an issuer. A QIB must in the aggregate own and invest at least $100 million, ensuring that QIBs are large institutions that can take care of themselves. Rule 144A functionally allows large investors to trade among themselves without worrying about registration and disclosure requirements.

Enforcement and Civil Liabilities
Government Action

The SEC has numerous powers to enforce compliance with the provisions of the 1933 Act. For example, if the SEC believes that a registration statement is incomplete or inaccurate, Sec. 8(b) authorizes issuance of a "refusal order," which prevents the statement from becoming effective until SEC objections are satisfied. If inaccuracies are discovered after the effective date, the SEC may issue a *stop order* pursuant to Sec. 8(d), as was done in the *Doman Helicopters* case, to suspend the effectiveness of the statement. Sec. 8(e) authorizes the SEC to conduct an "examination" to investigate fully whether a stop order should issue.

More generally, Sec. 19(b) gives the SEC power of subpoena to aid investigations of any potential violation of the 1933 Act. Sec. 20(b) allows the SEC to go into federal district court to seek an injunction whenever it appears that any person is violating the 1933 Act.

The 1933 Act even contains criminal provisions. Sec. 24 provides that any person who willfully violates any provision of the act or any SEC rule or any person who willfully makes an untrue statement or omits a material fact in a registration statement is subject to a fine of not more than $10,000, imprisonment of not more than five years, or both.

Private Suit

The 1933 Act provides remedies for violation of its provisions in the form of lawsuits that may be brought by injured investors.

Sec. 11. An investor who is injured after buying securities with reliance on a rosy picture falsely painted in a prospectus will probably not be satisfied with the SEC's injunction remedy or even criminal prosecution. The investor will desire to recoup losses through a civil action for damages, and the 1933 Act has express provision for such lawsuits. Sec. 11 states that if "any part of the registration statement, when such part became effective, contained an untrue statement of a material fact or omitted to state a material fact required to be stated therein or necessary to make the statements therein not misleading, any person acquiring such security" may file a civil action. Potential defendants in such an action include every person who signed the registration statement (which includes the issuer, its principal executive officers, chief financial officer, principal accounting officers, and most of the board of directors), every person who was a director or identified as about to become a director, every accountant, every appraiser or other expert who is named as having helped prepare it, and every underwriter.

The Sec. 11 cause of action is loosely patterned after a common-law fraud action but is modified to greatly ease a plaintiff's burdens in seeking recovery. For example, the common-law fraud elements of privity of contract and reliance are not necessary in a Sec. 11 claim so long as the plaintiff can trace the purchased shares back to the defective offering and show they were not previously issued shares of the same company being publicly traded at the same time.

If the plaintiff proves the registration statement contained misstatements or omissions of material facts, the law presumes that these caused the plaintiff's damages, and the burden of proof shifts to the defendants to prove that other factors were the true cause of the plaintiff's losses.

Furthermore, Sec. 11 does not require proof of fraudulent intent. Proof of misstatement or omission shifts the burden of proof to the defendants to establish that they were guilty of neither fraudulent intent nor negligence in preparing the registration statement. Individual defendants must establish that they used "due diligence" in preparing the registration statement. The amount of diligence that is due from a defendant depends on his or her position as an *insider* (with full access to key information) or an *outsider*, and a defendant is generally allowed to rely on "expertised" portions of the statement—those portions prepared by experts such as independent auditors. The due diligence defense is not available to the issuing company, which is strictly liable for inaccuracies in the registration statement.

Sec. 12. Complementing Sec. 11 are Sec. 12(1), which allows an investor to recover when offers or sales are made in violation of Sec. 5 (that is, without the filing of a registration statement, by use of a defective prospectus, or where securities are delivered without an accompanying prospectus), and Sec. 12(2), which allows recovery by investors injured by misrepresentations made outside a prospectus (such as in an oral sales pitch or in literature accompanying an unregistered offering). The elements of recovery and defenses in Sec. 12 suits are roughly the same as under Sec. 11, although the range of potential defendants is limited to "sellers" of securities—those who actually pass title or those who "solicit" transactions, such as brokers and dealers.

1934 ACT: REGULATING THE TRADING OF SECURITIES

Although the 1933 Act regulates primarily the initial issuance of securities, the 1934 Act regulates the trading of those securities. An array of complex problems comes within the purview of the 1934 Act. The general registration and reporting requirements of the 1934 Act have already been discussed. Attention is now turned to several other major concerns of the act.

Insider Trading

Knowledge of the inner workings of a corporation can be very valuable in making investment decisions. For example, if a corporate vice-president learned that his company's scientists had just been granted an important patent that will open up a new sales field, he would have a distinct and arguably unfair trading advantage over the general investing public. Insider trading was a widespread phenomenon in the 1920s, yet the common law provided little protection from such abusive practices.

Sec. 16(b)

One response to the insider trading problem is Sec. 16 of the 1934 Act, which applies to three categories of persons: officers, directors, and owners of more than 10 percent of the shares of any one class of stock of a 1934 reporting company. Thus, the provision applies only to persons reasonably assumed to have influence in and therefore access to inside information of large, publicly traded companies. Subsection (a) of Sec. 16 requires that these three categories of insider file three types of reports with the SEC. The two most important are an initial report revealing the holdings when a director or officer takes office or when a stockholder first obtains a 10 percent holding, and an

additional report each month thereafter in which a change in holdings occurs. Because many insiders had been lax in filing such reports, in 1991 the SEC added a requirement that in their proxy statements sent to shareholders, issuers list any insiders who did not comply with Sec. 16(a).

Subsection b of Sec. 16 provides that any profits realized (or losses avoided) by such an insider in connection with a purchase and sale (or sale and purchase) within a six-month period is an illegal "short-swing" profit. Any such profit may be recovered on the issuer's behalf. The striking thing about Sec. 16(b) is the near absolute nature of the liability it imposes. Thus, assume that Sherry, a director of ABC Company, buys ABC shares on January 1. If she sells any ABC shares (not necessarily the same ones she bought on January 1) within six months thereafter at a higher price than she purchased, she is liable to forfeit her profit *even if* she did not use any inside information. A classic Sec. 16(b) case follows.

SMOLOWE V. DELENDO CORPORATION

U.S. Court of Appeals, Second Circuit, 136 F.2d 231 (1943)

Litigation over a tax claim disrupted Delendo Corp.'s negotiations for sale of its assets to Schenley Distillers. Four years later, negotiations were reopened and the sale was completed on April 30, 1940. In the six months before the sale, defendants Seskis and Kaplan—both officers, directors, and major shareholders of Delendo—bought Delendo shares, which they then sold at substantial profits in the Schenley deal. Plaintiff shareholders of Delendo sued to recover those profits for the benefit of the corporation, apparently claiming that Seskis and Kaplan had inside information that the tax problem with the government was being negotiated away, thus clearing the way for the profitable sale of assets.

The defendants claimed they did not use inside information in making their purchases, thus raising the issue

of whether such use is a necessary element of recovery in a Sec. 16(b) claim. The trial court ruled for the plaintiffs; the defendants appealed.

Clark, Circuit Judge:

The primary purpose of the Securities Exchange Act . . . was to insure a fair and honest market, that is, one which would reflect an evaluation of securities in the light of all available and pertinent data. Furthermore, the Congressional hearings indicate that Sec. 16(b), specifically, was designed to protect the "outsider" stockholders against at least short-swing speculation by insiders with advance information. It is apparent too, from the language of Sec. 16(b) itself, as well as from the Congressional hearings, that the only remedy which its framers deemed effective for this reform was the imposition of a liability based upon an objective measure of proof. This is

graphically stated in the testimony of Mr. Corcoran, chief spokesman for the drafters and proponents of the Act, in Hearings before the Committee on Banking and Currency: "You hold the director, irrespective of any intention or expectation to sell the security within six months after, because it will be absolutely impossible to prove the existence of such intention or expectation, and you have to have this crude rule of thumb, because you cannot undertake the burden of having to prove that the director intended, at the time he bought, to get out on a short swing."

A subjective standard of proof, requiring a showing of an actual unfair use of inside information, would render senseless the provisions of the legislation limiting the liability period to six months, making an intention to profit during the period immaterial, and exempting transactions wherein there is a bona fide acquisition of stock in connection with a previously contracted

(continues)

SMOLOWE V. DELENDO CORPORATION

(continued from previous page)
debt. . . . And its total effect would be to render the statute little more of an incentive to insiders to refrain from profiteering at the expense of the outside stockholders than are the common law rules of liability; it would impose a more stringent statute of limitations upon the party aggrieved at the same time that it allowed the wrongdoer to share in the spoils of recovery. Had Congress intended that only profits from an actual misuse of inside information should be recoverable, it would have been simple enough to say so.

The present case would seem to be of the type which the statute was designed to include. Here it is conceded that the defendants did not make unfair use of information they possessed as officers at the time of the transactions. When these began they had no offer from Schenley. But they knew they were pressing the tax suit; and they, of course, knew of the corporate offer to settle it which reestablished the offer to purchase and led to the favorable sale. It is naive to suppose that their knowledge of their own plans as officers did not give them most valuable inside knowledge as to what would probably happen to the stock in which they were dealing. It is difficult to find this use "unfair" in the sense of illegal; it is certainly an advantage and a temptation within the general scope of the legislature's intended prohibition.

Affirmed. ⚖

Sec. 10(b)

Another provision of the 1934 Act that regulates insider trading, as well as many other facets of securities trading, is Sec. 10(b). This provision makes it unlawful to "use or employ, in connection with the purchase or sale of any security, . . . any manipulative or deceptive device or contrivance in contravention of such rules and regulations as the Commission may prescribe. . . ."

Pursuant to Sec. 10(b), the SEC has issued the most famous of all its rules, rule 10b-5, quoted in full:

It shall be unlawful for any person, directly or indirectly, by the use of any means or instrumentality of interstate commerce, or of the mails, or of any facility of any national securities exchange,

(1) to employ any device, scheme or artifice to defraud,

(2) to make any untrue statement of a material fact or to omit to state a material fact necessary in order to make the statements made, in the light of the circumstances under which they were made, not misleading, or

(3) to engage in any act, practice, or course of business which operates or would operate as a fraud or deceit upon any person, in connection with the purchase or sale of any security.

General Provisions. One important category of rule 10b-5 cases involves insider trading. Although a Sec. 10(b) case is more difficult to prove, its coverage is broader than Sec. 16(b)'s. The broad purpose of Sec. 10(b) and rule 10b-5 is to protect the investing public by preventing fraud and equalizing access to material information. Sec. 10(b) applies to any purchase or sale by any person of any security—there are no exceptions. Thus, small, close corporations (the shares of which are not offered to the public for sale but are typically held by just a few, perhaps members of a single family) are covered as well as the largest public corporations. Transactions covered include those occurring on the stock exchanges, in over-the-counter sales through stockbrokers, or even in privately negotiated sales. Any person connected with the transaction is regulated, not only insiders as in Sec. 16(b).

Unlike Sec. 16(b), Sec. 10(b) requires proof of actual use of inside information to establish a violation. There is no automatic presumption. Furthermore, the information must be material, and it must be nonpublic.

Enforcement. A willful violation of any provision of the 1934 Act, including those banning insider trading, subjects the violator to the criminal provisions of Sec. 32, which carry penalties of imprisonment up to 10 years, and/or a fine of up to $1 million for individuals. Corporations can be fined up to $2.5 million.

The SEC refers criminal cases to the Department of Justice for prosecution. But the SEC itself can take steps against inside traders. It can hold disciplinary proceedings if a regulated broker, dealer, or underwriter is involved. It can go to federal district court to obtain an injunction to halt illegal practices and perhaps an order rescinding the fraudulent sale. In 1988, the SEC was authorized to seek civil fines against securities firms that "knowingly and recklessly" fail properly to supervise their employees who engage in insider trading. Additionally, the SEC is authorized in civil insider trading cases to seek relief in the form of disgorgement of illicit profits and assessment of a civil penalty of up to three times the profit gained or loss avoided. Pursuant to these provisions, infamous arbitrageur Ivan Boesky consented to disgorge insider trading profits of $50 million and to pay a civil fine of $100 million.

In 1990, the SEC was further authorized to issue its own "cease and desist" orders to persons engaged in illicit activity and to seek *civil* fines in court ranging up to $100,000 for each violation by individuals and $500,000 for each violation by organizations. Although the insider trading scandals of the 1980s largely prompted this new legislation, these new SEC powers apply to many violations of federal securities law.

In addition to government civil and criminal actions, a private civil lawsuit for damages may be brought by victims of fraud, such as insider trading, against the perpetrators. Although the 1934 Act does not explicitly provide for such a right of action, the courts have implied one since 1946.[2] Private lawsuits brought under Sec. 10(b) and rule 10b-5 in the 1960s and 1970s dramatically altered the law of securities regulation in the United States.

Potential Defendants.   The key to insider trading liability is the *disclose or abstain rule,* which requires that certain persons either disclose material nonpublic information that they possess or abstain from trading in the relevant company's stock until that information becomes public. The disclose or abstain rule promotes fairness in securities trading by equalizing *access* to important information affecting the value of securities. Equal information is not the goal, only equal access. Although the goal cannot be perfectly achieved, small investors will likely be more willing to enter the market if they know the SEC is actively promoting equal access.

Four major categories of persons owe a duty to disclose or abstain. The first category consists of *corporate insiders,* a term defined more broadly than in the Sec. 16 provisions to include any corporate employee with access to material inside information, not just officers and directors.

A second major category of potential insider trading defendants are *temporary insiders.* These are persons who receive confidential corporate information for a corporate purpose and with the expectation that it will be kept confidential but then use it in insider trading. Classic examples are attorneys, accountants, and investment bankers hired temporarily by a corporation. For example, if an attorney is hired to help Corporation A merge with Corporation B and the attorney realizes that this will be a very favorable arrangement for Corporation A, she may be tempted to trade in its stock. That would be illegal so long as the information is nonpublic.

A third category of potential insider trading defendant consists of *misappropriators*—noninsiders who steal confidential inside information. The "disclose or abstain" obligation must rest on a *duty* to someone. Insiders, their tippees, and temporary insiders all owe a duty to the corporation in whose shares they trade. It can be a little more elusive to determine the duty owed by a misappropriator. The misappropriation theory was used by the lower courts to criminally convict a *Wall Street Journal* reporter who secretly leaked information about articles the newspaper was about to publish to confederates who traded profitably on the information. In *Carpenter v. United States,* 484 U.S. 19 (1987), the Supreme Court addressed the misappropriation theory and split 4–4 in a vote on its validity, although the Court affirmed the conviction on the basis of the federal wire fraud statute.

The fourth category includes any tippee of any of the first three categories. Unless tippees are covered, a corporate president could tip his or her spouse and then enjoy the fruits of the spouse's trading. The Supreme Court has held that a tippee cannot be liable for insider trading unless he or she knows that the tipper breached a duty in passing along the information.[3] Such a breach occurs if the information is passed for personal benefit (whether monetary or otherwise) rather than for a corporate purpose.

The "misappropriation" category of insider trading is the most controversial and is illustrated in the following case.

---

[2]*Kardon v. National Gypsum Co.,* 69 F.Supp. 512 (E.D.Pa. 1946).

[3]*Dirks v. SEC,* 436 U.S. 646 (1983).

SEC v. CHERIF

U.S. Court of Appeals, Seventh Circuit, 933 F.2d 403 (1991)

Defendant Cherif worked for the First National Bank of Chicago until he was terminated in late 1987. He had a magnetic identification card that allowed him to enter the bank after normal business hours. He was supposed to surrender the card on termination. Instead, Cherif persuaded a bank secretary with whom he was romantically involved to type a fake memorandum that led to this card being reactivated. During the year after his termination, Cherif used this card 30 times to enter the bank on nights and weekends. He went to the Special Finance Department of the bank, which assisted in tender offers, corporate restructurings, and leveraged buyouts. He discovered confidential information about upcoming deals that had not been publicly announced. He then would buy stock in the companies involved in the proposed deals, selling his shares after the price rose following public announcement. Cherif profited more than $200,000.

The SEC brought this civil enforcement action against Cherif claiming, inter alia, that he had violated section 10(b) and rule 10b-5. The trial court held that Cherif had committed such violations. Cherif appealed.

Cummings, Circuit Judge:

The "classical" theory [of insider trading] brings corporation insiders and tippees of those insiders within the ambit of Rule 10b-5. Under the classical theory, a person violates the rule when he or she buys or sells securities on the basis of material, non-public information and at the same time is an insider of the corporation whose securities are traded, or a tippee who knows or should know of the insider's breach. The theory is that an insider owes a fiduciary duty to the corporation's shareholders not to trade on inside information for his personal benefit. A tippee of an insider owes a fiduciary duty which is derivative of the duty owned by the insider.

The misappropriation theory extends the reach of Rule 10b-5 to outsiders who would not ordinarily be deemed fiduciaries of the corporate entities in whose stock they trade. The misappropriation theory focuses not on the insider's fiduciary duty to the issuing company or its shareholders but on whether the insider breached a fiduciary duty to any lawful possessor of material non-public information.

[I]n *SEC v. Materia*, 745 F.2d 197 (2d Cir. 1984), the employee of a financial printer was held liable under Rule 10b-5 for trading upon information the printing company had acquired in confidence from its clients. The Second Circuit found that Materia had perpetrated a fraud upon this employer by misappropriating information entrusted to the printing company. ("By purloining and trading on confidences entrusted to [the printer], it cannot be gainsaid that Materia undermined his employer's integrity.")

There is a common sense notion of fraud behind the misappropriation theory. As the court [in *SEC v. Clark*, 915 F.2d 439 (9th Cir. 1990)] put it: "[B]y becoming part of a fiduciary or similar relationship, an individual is implicitly stating that she will not divulge or use to her own advantage information entrusted to her in the utmost confidence. She deceives the other party by playing the role of the trustworthy employee or agent; she defrauds it by actually using the stolen information to its detriment."

The only possible barrier to application of the misappropriation theory to Cherif's case is, as Cherif points out, the fact that his employment with First Chicago ended before he stole and traded upon inside information. Cherif argues that no fiduciary duty existed between him and his employer at any time after December 1987, when he began to obtain information about upcoming transactions from the Specialized Finance Department.

As an initial matter, Cherif misconstrues the nature of his duty to First Chicago. He argues that the terms of the bank's "integrity policy" [which explicitly identified its "internal policies" as confidential information which "should not be utilized for personal gain"] only prevented him from using information specifically about future transactions obtained while he was on the job. He also believes that the use of such inside information was restricted only to the term of his employment.

Notwithstanding the contractual agreement, Cherif was bound by a broader common law duty. The common law duty obligates an employee to protect any confidential information entrusted to him by his employer during his employment. In addition, an employee is obligated to continue to protect such information after his termination.

Cherif betrayed a trust in a way that a mere thief does not. He used property and information belonging to First Chicago, and made available to him only through his fiduciary relationship, against the bank's own interests. His actions were fraudulent in the common understanding of the word because they deprived some person of something by "trick, deceit, chicane or overreaching." *McNally v. United States*, 483 U.S. 350 (1987). Cherif may have eroded client confidence in First Chicago, by suggesting the company's susceptibility to treachery from within. We have little difficulty concluding that his course of conduct was fraudulent within the meaning of Rule 10b-5.

Affirmed.

[*Note*: Cherif was also *criminally* convicted of mail and wire fraud in connection with these transactions. *United States v. Cherif*, 943 F.2d 692 (7th Cir. 1991).]

False or Inadequate Corporate Disclosures

A second major category of Sec. 10(b) cases relates to disclosures of information about corporations. Already noted are the registration and reporting requirements of the 1934 Act. The registration forms—the 10-Ks, 10-Qs, and 8-Ks—are all designed to promote full disclosure of information important to the investing public. When a corporation or some person fraudulently misstates or fails to disclose material information, a Sec. 10(b) violation may occur.[4]

An investor who is injured because he or she bought or sold shares on the basis of inaccurate or incomplete corporate information may bring a private cause of action under the antifraud provisions of Sec. 10(b). The requirements of a valid claim in such a lawsuit are patterned after those of common-law fraud: (1) a misrepresentation of material fact, (2) made by defendant with knowledge of the falsity, (3) an intent to induce the plaintiff to rely, (4) actual reliance by the plaintiff, (5) privity of contract between the plaintiff and the defendant, and (6) damage sustained. Modification of some of these common-law elements has been a source of controversy in this type of Sec. 10(b) case.

Privity

Privity of contract has been largely eliminated as a requirement of a Sec. 10(b) cause of action in the corporate disclosure setting. An injured shareholder is normally allowed to sue those persons responsible for false statements whether or not the stockholder purchased shares from or sold shares to the defendants.

Intent

Actual intent to defraud arising from knowledge of the falsity of a statement is a traditional element of common-law fraud. To advance the remedial purposes of the 1934 Act, many lower courts formerly interpreted Sec. 10(b) virtually to eliminate the requirement of intent by holding defendants liable although they were guilty of nothing more than simple negligence.

The Supreme Court overruled these cases, however, in *Ernst & Ernst v. Hochfelder*, 425 U.S. 185 (1976). There the Court held that the defendant ac-

counting firm was not liable for a Sec. 10(b) violation "in the absence of any allegation of **scienter**—intent to deceive, manipulate, or defraud."

The question has subsequently arisen as to whether a defendant should be liable if guilty of "recklessness," which means being highly negligent or so careless as to exhibit a complete disregard for possible damage to others. Most lower courts have concluded that reckless conduct is sufficient for imposition of liability, although the Supreme Court has not spoken on the issue.

Reliance

In a common-law fraud case, the plaintiff must normally prove that the defendant's fraudulent statement was relied on in making the sale or purchase. To advance the broadly remedial purposes of the 1934 Act, some adjustments have been made to the traditional reliance requirement.

A misleading corporate disclosure can occur either when a material fact is concealed or when it is misrepresented. Because it is impractical to require an investor to prove reliance on a fact that was concealed from him or her, the Supreme Court has eliminated the reliance requirement in concealment cases. In *Affiliated Ute Citizens v. United States*, 406 U.S. 128 (1972), the plaintiffs, mixed-blood Ute Indians, sold shares in the Ute Development Corporation through the defendants, bank officials. The defendants failed to disclose to the plaintiffs their own interest in the transactions or the fact that shares were trading at higher prices among whites. The Court held:

Under the circumstances of this case, involving primarily a failure to disclose, positive proof of reliance is not a prerequisite to recovery. All that is necessary is that the facts withheld be material in the sense that a reasonable investor might have considered them important in the making of this decision. This obligation to disclose and this withholding of a material fact establish the requisite element of causation in fact.

In cases of active misrepresentation, proof of reliance is practicable; nonetheless, there have been some important modifications of the reliance requirements even in misrepresentation cases, partly because of the impersonal nature of transactions that occur through the stock exchanges. The leading case follows.

[4]False or misleading statements in documents filed with the SEC may also lead to liability under Sec. 18(a) of the 1934 Act.

BASIC, INC. V. LEVINSON

U.S. Supreme Court, 485 U.S. 224 (1988)

Case

In 1965, Combustion Engineering, Inc. expressed an interest in acquiring Basic, Inc. That interest was reawakened by regulatory developments in late 1976. Beginning in September 1976, Combustion representatives had meetings and phone calls with Basic officers and directors about a possible merger. During 1977 and 1978, Basic made three public statements denying that it was engaged in merger negotiations. On December 18, 1978, Basic was asked by the New York Stock Exchange to suspend trading in its shares. It issued a press release stating that it had been "approached" about a merger. On December 19, Basic's board accepted Combustion's offer, and this was publicly announced on December 20.*

Former Basic shareholders (respondents), who sold their stock after Basic's first denial that it was engaged in merger talks (October 21, 1977) and before the suspension of trading, sued Basic and its directors (petitioners). The respondents claim that petitioners' misleading statements caused them to miss the opportunity to sell at the higher merger price, in violation of Sec. 10(b) of the 1934 Securities Act.

The district court (1) granted class action status to the respondents, adopting a presumption that they had relied on petitioners' public statements, thereby satisfying the "common question of fact or law" requirement of the Federal Rules of Civil Procedure; and (2) granted summary judgment to petitioners on the merits, holding that petitioners had no obligation to disclose the ongoing merger negotiations.

The circuit court affirmed on the class action issue, adopting the district court's "fraud on the market" theory, but reversed on the merits,

finding that a duty to disclose the merger talks might have existed. Petitioners appealed.

Blackmun, Justice:

[The Supreme Court first rejected the circuit court's resolution of the merits of the case. Unlike the circuit court, which held that almost any misleading statement about merger negotiations could be material, the Supreme Court held that materiality must depend on a balancing of (1) the indicated probability that the merger will occur, and (2) the anticipated magnitude of the merger in light of the totality of the company's activities. It then catalogued various factors, such as board resolutions and instructions to investment bankers (which might show probability that the merger would occur) and the size of the corporations involved and of the premium over market price being discussed (which might show magnitude of the event), for lower courts to consider in applying its subjective, fact-specific approach.]

We turn to the question of reliance and the fraud-on-the-market theory. Succinctly put:

The fraud-on-the-market theory is based on the hypothesis that, in an open and developed securities market, the price of a company's stock is determined by the available material information regarding the company and its business. . . . Misleading statements will therefore defraud purchasers of stock even if the purchasers do not directly rely on the misstatements. . . . The causal connection between the defendants' fraud and the plaintiffs' purchase of stock in such a case is no less significant than in a case of direct reliance on misrepresentations. *Peil v. Speiser,* 806 F.2d 1154, 11600–1161 (CA3 1986).

We agree that reliance is an element of a rule 10b-5 cause of action. See *Ernst & Ernst v. Hochfelder,* 425 U.S. [185], at 206 [(1976)]. Reliance provides the requisite causal connection between a defendant's misrepresenta-

tion and a plaintiff's injury. . . . There is, however, more than one way to demonstrate the causal connection. . . .

The modern securities markets, literally involving millions of shares changing hands daily, differ from the face-to-face transactions contemplated by early fraud cases [that required a showing of privity], and our understanding of Rule 10b-5's reliance requirement must encompass these differences.

In face-to-face transactions, the inquiry into an investor's reliance upon information is into the subjective pricing of that information by that investor. With the presence of a market, the market is interposed between the seller and buyer and, ideally, transmits information to the investor in the processed form of a market price. Thus the market is performing a substantial part of the valuation process performed by the investor in a face-to-face transaction. The market is acting as the unpaid agent of the investor, informing him that given all the information available to it, the value of the stock is worth the market price. *In re LTV Securities Litigation,* 88 F.R.D. 134, 143 (N.D. Tex. 1980).

. . . Requiring a plaintiff to show a speculative state of facts, *i.e.,* how he would have acted if omitted material information had been disclosed, . . . or if the misrepresentation had not been made . . . would place an unnecessarily unrealistic evidentiary burden on the Rule 10b-5 plaintiff who has traded on an impersonal market.

The presumption of reliance employed in this case is consistent with, and, by facilitating Rule 10b-5 litigation, supports the congressional policy embodied in the 1934 Act. In drafting that Act, Congress expressly relied on the premise that securities markets are affected by information, and enacted legislation to facilitate an investor's reliance on the integrity of those markets. . . .

The presumption is also supported by common sense and probability. Recent empirical studies have tended to

(continues)

(continued from previous page)
confirm Congress' premise that the market price of shares traded on well-developed markets reflect all publicly available information, and, hence, any material misrepresentation. It has been noted that "it is hard to imagine that there ever is a buyer or seller who does not rely on market integrity. Who would knowingly roll the dice in a crooked crap game?" *Schlanger v. Four Phase Systems, Inc.*, 555 F.Supp. 535, 538 (SDNY 1982). . . .

Any showing that severs the link between the alleged misrepresentation and either the price received (or paid) by the plaintiff, or his decision to trade at a fair market price, will be sufficient to rebut the presumption of reliance.

[Court of Appeals' judgment is vacated and remanded.] ⚖

Although the outer limit of permissible rule 10b-5 actions is not completely settled, the Supreme Court has attempted to confine the actions to situations involving deceit and manipulation. Simple corporate mismanagement or breaches of fiduciary duty by corporate officials, not involving deceit, are not actionable under rule 10b-5.[5]

Proxy Regulation

Although most corporate decisions are made by the officers and directors, shareholders do occasionally vote on matters of importance. At the annual shareholders' meeting required by state incorporation laws, the shareholders elect directors to the board of directors. Their approval may also be required for certain extraordinary matters, such as amendments to corporate bylaws or articles of incorporation, mergers, or sales of major assets.

Valid shareholder approval requires at least a majority vote (and sometimes two-thirds or three-fourths approval) of a quorum of shares eligible to vote. However, in a large corporation with thousands of shareholders, it is very unusual for more than a small percentage of shareholders to appear at the annual meeting. To obtain a quorum, corporate management is usually required to solicit *proxies* from the shareholders. A **proxy** is an authorization to vote shares owned by someone else. At a typical corporation's annual meeting, incumbent management will solicit and receive proxies from a sufficient number of shareholders to vote itself into control for another year.

Sec. 14(a) of the 1934 Act prohibits solicitation of proxies for any shares registered under the Act in contravention of rules promulgated by the SEC. The rules that the SEC has issued have three broad goals: full disclosure, fraud prevention, and increased shareholder participation.

Full Disclosure

State laws have not always required corporate management to be responsive to the informational needs and desires of shareholders. The SEC, knowing that most major corporations solicit proxies at least annually, requires in rule 14a-3 that no soliciting occur unless each person solicited is furnished with a written proxy statement containing the information specified in Schedule 14A.

Schedule 14A contains more than 20 items, some of which are applicable only if specified matters, such as merger approval, are involved. In the typical solicitation by management relating to election of directors, the proxy statement must be accompanied by an annual report to contain, *inter alia*, comparative financial statements for the last two fiscal years, a summary of operations, a brief description of the business done by the issuer and its subsidiaries, and identification of the issuer's directors and executive officers and their principal occupations. This information must be clearly presented. Indeed, unfavorable publicity given to the extremely high pay of many American executives, whose companies were performing less well than foreign competitors whose executives were paid much less, led to a 1992 SEC reform that requires proxy materials to spell out for shareholders the specifics of executive compensation via charts rather than often unreadable legalistic text.

Proxy Contests

Normally, incumbent management will face no organized opposition in the election of directors at the

---

[5]*Santa Fe Industries v. Green*, 430 U.S. 462 (1977).

annual meeting. But if the corporation is floundering financially, perhaps a group of "insurgent" shareholders will attempt to elect its own slate of candidates to the board of directors. Or perhaps the insurgents have lined up a merger with or tendered their shares to another corporation, which intends to fire incumbent management, and incumbent management has negotiated a proposed defensive merger with yet another company, which would be willing to retain the incumbents in their present positions. In these and other situations, proxy contests arise over the control of the corporation. Incumbent managements and insurgent shareholders vie for sufficient proxies to prevail in the shareholders' vote. Federal regulations specify the procedure for such contests and punish any fraud that may occur.

Changes promulgated in 1992 made it easier for dissident shareholders to communicate with each other. Previously, any time 10 or more shareholders communicated, they were required to file a Schedule 14B with the SEC disclosing such matters as employment history, stock holdings, and past criminal violations. The 1992 changes make it much easier for dissident shareholders to cooperate in formulating plans to reform a poorly performing company.

Antifraud.   Proxy contests sometimes become quite heated. To prevent fraud, rule 14a-9 prohibits the use of false or misleading statements to solicit proxies. The term *solicitation* is broadly defined to cover both statements seeking proxies and communications urging shareholders to refuse to give proxies. Thus, if incumbent management falsely states or omits to state a material fact in urging shareholders not to grant proxies to an insurgent group, a violation of rule 14a-9 and Sec. 14(a) occurs. A private cause of action is available to remedy such a violation.

Tender Offers

A final important area of federal securities law regulates a method of taking control of a corporation, called a **tender offer.** In a typical tender offer, one corporation (the *offeror*) will publicly offer to purchase a controlling interest (more than 50 percent of the shares) in another corporation (the *target*). The target's shareholders are invited to tender their shares to the offeror in return for cash or the offeror's equity or debt securities (or a combination) in an amount usually well above the prior market price of the target's stock.

Because of the easy availability of credit and lack of government regulation, the tender offer gained widespread usage in the 1960s. One variety, termed the *Saturday Night Special,* featured a "take-it-or-leave-it" offer to the target's shareholders with a very short time for them to make up their minds. Afraid of losing an opportunity to sell shares at above the market price, shareholders frequently would tender their shares without time to learn anything about the offeror or to evaluate the possibility of a higher offer from a different source.

Federal Legislation

Comprehensive federal regulation of tender offers began with the passage of the Williams Act of 1968. That Act amended Secs. 13 and 14 of the 1934 Act with the basic purpose of increasing both the amount of information flowing to target shareholders and the time available to use that information.

Filing Requirements.   Sec. 13(d) of the 1934 Act requires that any person or group acquiring more than 5 percent of the shares of any corporation must file a Schedule 13D within 10 days with the SEC. That schedule requires disclosure of the background of the person or group, their source of funds, their purpose, the number of shares owned, relevant contracts or other arrangements with the target, and any plans for change of the target's affairs.

Procedural Rules.   Sec. 14(d) and rule 14d-2 provide that a tender offer is commended on the date of public announcement of the offer. On that date, rule 14d-3 requires the offeror to file with the SEC a Schedule 14D-1, which requires informational disclosures similar to those of Schedule 13D.

The target's management may support a tender offer; perhaps the management even negotiated it. But tender offers frequently are "hostile," and the offeror intends to replace the target's management with its own people. Even if the target's management opposes the offer, Sec. 14(d) and rule 14d-5 require the target's management to mail the tender offer to the target's shareholders or promptly to provide the offeror with a shareholder list so it can do the mailing itself.

Target management must file with the SEC a Schedule 14D-9. This document (1) discloses whether the officers and directors intend to hold their shares or to tender, (2) describes any contractual arrangement management may have with the offeror (for instance, the offeror sometimes can obtain management's support through monetary incentives), and (3) discloses any concrete negotiations with a "white knight"—a company willing to make a competing tender offer that is more advantageous to incumbent management.

Substantive Rules. Substantively, Sec. 14(d) and rule 14e-1 provide that a tender offer must be held open for a minimum of 20 business days, so the target's shareholders will have an opportunity to evaluate the offer fully. No more Saturday Night Specials will occur. If more shares are tendered than the offeror wishes to purchase, the offeror must purchase from each shareholder on a pro rata basis. This requirement promotes equal treatment of shareholders.

What if an offeror initiates the tender offer at $40 per share, seeking to purchase 51 percent of the target's shares, but only 25 percent are tendered? The offeror may choose to extend the offering period and amend the offer to $50 per share. This higher price must be given to all tendering shareholders, including those who were willing to sell at the lower price.

The final important provision of the Williams Act is Sec. 14(e), the prohibition of fraud or manipulation in either supporting or opposing a tender offer.

Remedies. Violations of Secs. 13(d), 14(d), and 14(e) may be remedied by civil actions for injunctive relief. Injured shareholders who, relying on fraudulent statements, either tendered when they would not have done so had they known the truth, or failed to tender when they would have had they not been defrauded, also can sue for damages under Sec. 14(e).

Defensive Tactics

A recent controversy has focused on the latitude that should be accorded target management in opposing hostile tender offers. Normally, courts hesitate to review the business judgments of any corporation's management, but the recent use by target managers of such tactics as "poison pills," sale of "crown jewels," recruiting of "white knights," and other devices explained in Chapter 40 has brought two major types of legal challenges. First is a state law challenge based on a claim that target managers using these devices are breaching their fiduciary duty to target shareholders. Our discussion in Chapter 40 summarized the key holdings in this area, demonstrating that there is substantial state court review of such actions.

The second basis for attacking defensive tactics is the argument that they are "manipulative" in violation of Sec. 14(e) of the Williams Act. The Supreme Court rejected this argument in the following case—thus relegating any significant court review to state jurisdiction.

SCHREIBER V. BURLINGTON

U.S. Supreme Court, 472 U.S. 1 (1985)

On December 21, 1982, Burlington Northern, Inc. made a hostile tender offer for 25 million shares of El Paso Gas Co. at $24 per share. Although El Paso's management initially opposed the offer, its shareholders fully subscribed it. Burlington did not accept the tendered shares, however. Instead, after negotiations with El Paso's management, Burlington rescinded the December tender offer, purchased 4 million shares from El Paso, substituted a new tender offer for only 21 million shares at $24 each, and recognized certain contractual arrangements between El Paso

and its management that guaranteed the managers substantial compensation upon a change of control ("golden parachutes"). More than 40 million shares were tendered in response to the second tender offer.

Rescission of the first offer diminished payment to those shareholders who had tendered during the first offer. Not only were fewer shares purchased, but the shareholders who retendered were subjected to substantial proration. Petitioner Schreiber sued on behalf of similarly situated shareholders, alleging that Burlington, El Paso, and members of El Paso's board had violated § 14(e). She claimed that withdrawal of the first tender offer coupled with substi-

tution of the second was a "manipulative" distortion of the market for El Paso stock.

The trial court dismissed the suit for failure to state a claim. The U.S. Court of Appeals for the Third Circuit affirmed. Schreiber petitioned to the Supreme Court.

Burger, Chief Justice:

We are asked in this case to interpret § 14(e) of the Securities Exchange Act. The starting point is the language of the statute. Section 14(e) provides:

It shall be unlawful for any person to make any untrue statement of a material fact or omit to state any material fact necessary in order to

(continues)

SCHREIBER V. BURLINGTON

(continued from previous page)

make the statements made, in the light of the circumstances under which they are made, not misleading, or to engage in any fraudulent, deceptive or manipulative acts or practices, in connection with any tender offer or request or invitation for tenders, or any solicitation of security holders in opposition to or in favor of any such offer, request, or invitation. The Commission shall, for the purposes of this subsection, by rules and regulations define, and prescribe means reasonably designed to prevent, such acts and practices as are fraudulent, deceptive, or manipulative.

Petitioner reads the phrase "fraudulent, deceptive or manipulative acts or practices" to include acts which, although fully disclosed, "artificially" affect the price of the takeover target's stock. Petitioner's interpretation relies on the belief that § 14(e) is directed at purposes broader than providing full and true information to investors.

Petitioner's reading of the term "manipulative" conflicts with the normal meaning of the term. We have held in the context of an alleged violation of § 10(b) of the Securities Exchange Act:

Use of the word "manipulative" is especially significant. It is and was virtually a term of art when used in connection with the securities markets. It connotes intentional or willful conduct designed to deceive or defraud investors by controlling or artificially affecting the price of securities. *Ernst & Ernst v. Hochfelder, 425 U.S. 185, 199 (1976)*

The meaning the Court has given the term "manipulative" is consistent with the use of the term at common law, and with its traditional dictionary definition.

Our conclusion that "manipulative" acts under § 14(e) require misrepresentation or nondisclosure is buttressed by the purpose and legislative history of the provision. "The purpose of the Williams Act is to insure that public shareholders who are confronted by a cash tender offer for their stock will not be required to respond without adequate information." *Rondeau v. Mosinee Paper Corp., 422 U.S. 49, 58 (1975).*

The expressed legislative intent was to preserve a neutral setting in which the contenders could fully present their arguments. The Senate sponsor [said]:

We have taken extreme care to avoid tipping the scales either in favor of management or in favor of the person making the takeover bids. S. 510 is designed solely to require full and fair disclosure for the benefit of investors. The bill will at the same time provide the offeror and management equal opportunity to present their case.

Congress' consistent emphasis on disclosure persuades us that it intended takeover contests to be addressed to shareholders. In pursuit of this goal, Congress, consistent with the core mechanism of the Securities Exchange Act, created sweeping disclosure requirements and narrow substantive safeguards. The same Congress that placed such emphasis on shareholder choice would not at the same time have required judges to oversee tender offers for substantive fairness. It is even less likely that a Congress implementing that intention would express it only through the use of a single word placed in the middle of a provision otherwise devoted to disclosure.

We hold that the term "manipulative" as used in § 14(e) requires misrepresentation or nondisclosure. Without misrepresentation or nondisclosure, §14(e) has not been violated.

Applying the definition to this case, we hold that the actions of respondents were not manipulative. The amended complaint fails to allege that the cancellation of the first tender offer was accompanied by any misrepresentation, nondisclosure or deception. The District Court correctly found, "All activity of the defendants that could have conceivably affected the price of El Paso shares was done openly."

Petitioner also alleges that El Paso management and Burlington entered into certain undisclosed and deceptive agreements during the making of the second tender offer. The substance of the allegations is that, in return for certain undisclosed benefits, El Paso managers agreed to support the second tender offer. But both courts noted that petitioner's complaint seeks redress only for injuries related to the cancellation of the first tender offer. Since the deceptive and misleading acts alleged by the petitioner all occurred with reference to the making of the second tender offer—when the injuries suffered by petitioner had already been sustained—these acts bear no possible causal relationship to petitioner's alleged injuries.

Affirmed. ◊

STATE REGULATION

Because every state has its own system of securities regulation, corporations must always be cognizant of these rules also. The Commissioners on Uniform State Laws have produced the Uniform Securities Act, which has been used as a pattern for many states' laws. Still, because many large states have not followed this act and many have amended it to varying degrees, there is a lack of uniformity that complicates

LEGAL FOCUS

Ethics

If ethical standards were sufficiently high and widely practiced, there would be little need for much of the securities regulation currently performed by the federal and state governments. Indeed, there is a school of thought that most areas of securities law should be deregulated and investors should be left to look out for themselves in terms of gathering information about companies in which they might wish to invest. There is substantial evidence, however, that vigorous securities regulation is needed now and will continue to be a necessary fixture.

At one level, scam artists continually victimize unsophisticated (and sometimes sophisticated) investors with whatever is the latest "get rich quick" scheme. In the mid- to late 1980s, the SEC investigated such scams as (1) a company claiming to have developed a fuel-processing device that could turn low-grade coal, rubber, and household garbage into crude oil (the company demonstrated the machine without disclosing that hidden inside its works was a 23-gallon tank that promoters filled with oil before each demonstration); (2) a company that falsely claimed to have developed a "self-chilled" soda can; and (3) a company that may have raised $300 million by claiming to have a secret process for turning sand from Costa Rica's black sand beaches into gold.

In the early 1990s, the bigger problem appeared to be false financial data disclosed to investors and the SEC. Even sophisticated investors demanding detailed financial information cannot protect themselves if companies provide false information. In the year preceding September 1992, for example, some 20 public companies whose shares were widely traded on national stock exchanges admitted to serious lapses in past financial statements. Some of the cases were particularly egregious. Phar-Mor, a drugstore chain, took a $350 million charge and filed for bankruptcy protection after it was disclosed that the company had for several years inflated earnings by overstating payments from large vendors and that several million dollars had been "borrowed" by a company founder. Cascade International, a retail chain, collapsed and its founder and chairman disappeared after it became clear that the company's financial statements were wildly inaccurate. The company claimed to be selling cosmetics in counters at 255 stores when the real number was one-tenth that amount. MiniScribe Corporation was sued for millions after it was disclosed that senior management had fooled company directors, auditors, and creditors by inflating sales and inventory and even shipping bricks to distributors and recording them as disk-drive sales.

Such schemes reinforce the necessity of a regulatory presence in the securities field. But they also raise serious questions about ethical practices in American business. Such frauds often require (1) active wrongdoing by the director participants and, equally troubling, (2) passive acquiescence by peripheral participants such as lawyers and accountants. What does this say about the state of ethics in American business?

the marketing of securities. Perhaps the Revised Uniform Securities Act, promulgated in late 1985, will lead to more uniformity. It will likely change some of the present state practices described below.

Registration

Most states have laws that, like the 1933 Securities Act, regulate the original distribution of securities. A corporation that intends to market its shares nationwide must comply with not only the 1933 Act but also approximately 40 separate state registration laws. There are three basic systems of state registration. Some states use *registration by notification,* which requires the filing of certain material and then a waiting period before the securities may be sold, similar to the procedure under the 1933 Act.

Registration by qualification is used by some states. This process goes beyond the simple disclosure philosophy of the 1933 Act and actually involves merit review of the securities by state officials. Typically, states using merit review refuse to allow sales of securities that do not meet a "fair, just, and equitable" standard. The standard may not be met, for example, if the organizers and promoters of the corporation intend to sell to the public at per share prices much greater than they themselves paid.

The third type is *registration by coordination,* which results in automatic state approval whenever a security's registration has become effective under the 1933 Act at the federal level.

Some states allow registration by more than one method.

Exemptions

State registration laws contain exemptions, as does the 1933 Act. There is an ongoing effort to coordinate state and federal exemption to produce uniformity. A uniform system of exemptions would greatly simplify matters for a corporation planning a widespread distribution of securities, but the chances of achieving complete uniformity appear slim.

Other Provisions

Many state securities laws also contain antifraud provisions similar to those in the 1933 and 1934 federal laws. In states without such laws, the courts have extended the common law of fraud to prohibit deceitful securities practices.

Some states also have qualification and registration provisions governing the activities of securities brokers and dealers, which are usually similar to federal registration provisions in the 1934 Act.

Many states also regulate tender offers in a manner that burdens offerors and therefore discourages such transactions. The Supreme Court held one such state act to be constitutional in *CTS Corp. v. Dynamics Corp.*, 481 U.S. 69 (1987).

INTERNATIONAL IMPLICATIONS

Each year, Americans buy tens of billions of dollars worth of foreign securities, and foreign investors purchase tens of billions of dollars of U.S. securities. Many American investors watch the London and Tokyo stock markets almost as closely as they monitor the New York Stock Exchange. Because our economy increasingly intersects with those of other nations, international concerns affect virtually every sphere of U.S. securities law.

Registration Exemptions

Earlier we listed the important domestic exemptions to the registration requirements of the 1933 Act. To encourage foreign issuers to raise equity in American markets, in 1990 the SEC added a foreign exemption—regulation S. Generally speaking, regulation S provides that Sec. 5's registration requirement does not apply to sales or resales of securities if two requirements are met. First, the sale must be an *offshore transaction,* defined as one in which no offer is made to a person in the United States, *and* either (1) at the time the buy order is originated the buyer is outside the United States or (2) the transaction is executed through the facilities of a designated offshore securities market. Second, there can be no "directed selling efforts" in the United States. Issuers must take additional precautions to assure that the shares, once purchased outside the United States, are not quickly resold in the United States as a means of circumventing the registration requirements.

Antifraud

Regulation S provides an exemption only from registration, not from antifraud rules. Therefore, Sec. 10(b) and rule 10b-5 continue to apply whenever (1) fraudulent conduct occurs in the United States (even if the impact is on American or foreign investors in other countries), or (2) fraudulent conduct occurs abroad, having significant effects in the United States. To illustrate the *conduct test:* Foreign investors who bought the issuer's shares abroad were allowed to sue an American accounting firm for a fraud involving allegedly fraudulent certified financial statements that occurred primarily in Ireland, because, in large part, the audit was directed primarily by the firm's American office where engagement partner responsibility lay (even though the field work was performed mostly in Ireland).[6] To illustrate the *effects test:* American investors were allowed to sue in the United States the directors of a Canadian corporation who allegedly authorized the sale of the company's stock in Canada at an unfairly low price, thus affecting the value of the company's shares that were traded on the American Stock Exchange.[7]

Insider Trading

As noted in Chapter 7, many of the insider trading schemes occurring in the United States in the 1980s were aided by the bank secrecy laws of Switzerland and other countries. In recent years, with pressure from the United States, many of these nations have become more cooperative in divulging information,

---

[6]*Dept. of Economic Development v. Arthur Andersen & Co.*, 683 F.Supp. 1463 (S.D.N.Y. 1988).

[7]*Schoenbaum v. Firstbrook*, 405 F.2d 200 (2d Cir. 1969).

thereby allowing the SEC to prosecute more successfully foreign citizens who are inside traders as well as U.S. citizens who attempt to cover their tracks with use of foreign bank accounts.

Tender Offers

As foreign investors from Japan, Europe, and elsewhere have bought American companies through tender offers, some Americans have become uneasy with the implications of these purchases. Therefore, Congress passed the Exon-Florio Amendment to a 1988 trade bill. Exon-Florio authorizes the President or the President's delegates to prevent or even reverse such a takeover if it threatens national security. (See the Legal Focus International box in Chapter 40.)

SUMMARY

Securities law is enmeshed in federal and state regulation. Securities, whether debt or equity, must upon initial issuance be registered with the SEC, unless an exemption is available. The goal of registration is to force disclosure of material facts regarding the issuing company so that potential investors can make an informed decision.

The registration process is burdensome and expensive. Companies are severely limited in terms of the publicity in which they can engage before and immediately after registration. To reduce the paperwork burden, the SEC has done its best in recent years to integrate the requirements of the 1933 Act, which govern the one-time registration of shares about to be issued, with those of the 1934 Act, which govern the continuous disclosures larger corporations must make.

If errors of omission or misrepresentation appear in a registration statement, a battery of government and private actions are available to punish the wrongdoers.

The 1934 Act governs a number of important areas of trading in securities. Insider trading is an unfair practice of particular concern to the SEC these days. Both Sec. 16(b), which provides a form of strict liability for trading by officers, directors, and 10 percent owners, and Sec. 10(b) which ranges more broadly but requires proof of actual use of material, nonpublic information, are available to punish such trading.

Sec. 10(b) is also available to remedy false or inadequate corporate disclosures in press releases, SEC filings, annual reports, and the like. Private litigation under Sec. 10(b) for damages has reshaped securities law in the United States.

Two methods of gaining control of a corporation, proxy fights and tender offers, involve particularly high stakes. The opportunities for profit and abuse of shareholder interests are great. Both processes are subject to a web of federal regulation designed to protect shareholder interests. In the proxy realm, the key is full disclosure. In tender offers, it is disclosure plus fair treatment of all shareholders.

Though federal regulation tends to dominate the scene, no securities attorney may safely ignore the securities rules that most states have enacted to cover issuance of shares, fraud, tender offers, and other related matters.

KEY TERMS

Securities
Prospectus
Shelf registration
Materiality
Accredited investor
Scienter
Proxy
Tender offer

QUESTIONS AND PROBLEMS

1. Co-op City was a massive, government-subsidized housing complex, operated as a nonprofit corporation. To acquire an apartment, eligible prospective tenants had to buy 18 shares of Co-op stock for each room at $25 per share. The purchase was in effect a recoverable deposit. The shares could not be transferred to a nontenant, did not carry votes as to management of the co-op, and had to be offered to the co-op for sale at the initial selling price whenever the tenant moved out. When rental rates went up, some tenants sued claiming inadequate disclosure under the federal securities law. Discuss whether these "shares of stock," as they were labelled, constituted securities under federal law. (*United Housing Foundation, Inc. v. Forman,* 421 U.S. 837, 1975.)

2. Wherehouse Entertainment, Inc., offered convertible subordinated debentures, stressing that purchasers would have the right to redeem the bonds in

the event of certain triggering events that might endanger the value of the debentures, *unless* the transaction was approved by a "majority of the Independent Directors." Eighteen months later, Wherehouse entered into a merger, which triggered the right to tender. Plaintiff purchasers attempted to redeem the bonds but were rejected on grounds that the board had nullified the right to tender by approving the merger. The plaintiffs sued under Secs. 11 and 12(2) of the 1933 Act and Sec. 10(b) of the 1934 Act, alleging that the right to redeem, presented as a valuable feature in the offering materials, was in fact illusory. The defendant claimed that every individual statement that it had made in selling the debentures was literally true. The plaintiffs argued that even if that were the case, the defendant gave the misleading overall impression that exercise of the right to redeem would be the norm and waiver by directors would be the exception. Can statements that are literally true still be materially misleading in cumulative effect? Discuss. (*McMahan & Co. v. Wherehouse Entertainment, Inc.*, 900 F.2d 576, 2d Cir. 1990.)

3. After the terrible industrial accident in Bhopal, India, caused by a leak of methyl isocyanate (MIC) at a Union Carbide plant, Union Carbide shareholders sued the corporation under Sec. 10(b), claiming that Union Carbide had made material omissions in several of its annual reports, quarterly reports, and similar documents. Basically, the plaintiffs claimed that Union Carbide failed to describe the manufacture, storage, risks, and personnel requirements attendant to MIC and that Union Carbide failed to disclose the financial implications of a possible MIC accident. Should this information have been disclosed? Discuss. (*In re Union Carbide Class Action Securities Litigation*, 648 F.Supp. 1322, S.D.N.Y. 1986.)

4. Lee bought the stock of Pal's Finer foods but became unhappy with the purchase and filed suit under Sec. 12(2) of the 1933 Act against Pal's former owners, their lawyer, and their accountant, Diodate. Diodate filed a motion for summary judgment, claiming that he was merely the seller's accountant and not a "seller" himself within the meaning of the statute. Lee submitted an affidavit swearing that Diodate participated in the stock sale and recommended that Lee buy the stock. Should the court grant Diodate's motion? Discuss. (*Lee v. Spicola*, FED.SEC.L.REP. (CCH) 94,120, M.D. Fla. 1988.)

5. Claiming the intrastate exemption of Sec. 3(a)(11) of the 1933 Act, McDonald Investment Company did not register its offering of shares with the SEC. McDonald is a Minnesota corporation with its only offices in that state. It sold shares only to Minnesota residents. However, the funds were raised to lend to real estate developers in Arizona. Discuss the availability of the exemption. (*SEC v. McDonald Investment Co.*, 343 F.Supp. 343, D. Minn. 1972.)

6. Moore, a psychiatrist, was treating the wife of an officer of Posi-Seal. Another company was planning to acquire Posi-Seal. At a treatment session with the wife that the Posi-Seal officer attended to facilitate the treatment process, Moore learned of the planned acquisition. Before public announcement of the acquisition, Moore bought 9000 shares of Posi-Seal stock. He sold them after the acquisition at a profit of $26,933.74. Discuss whether Moore has violated Sec. 10(b)'s ban on insider trading. (*SEC v. Morgan F. Moore*, No. N-86-88-PCD, D.Conn. 1986.)

7. Lund was CEO of Verit Industries. Horowitz was on Verit's board and was CEO of P&F Company. Lund and Horowitz were friends. P&F began negotiating a particular deal, and Horowitz called Lund to ask him if Verit would be interested in providing capital and being an investor in the acquisition. Lund said that Verit would not be interested. However, he soon bought 10,000 shares of P&F stock in his own name at $1.25 per share—his only purchase of P&F stock in 10 years. Soon the P&F deal was completed and announced to the public. Lund sold his shares for a $12,500 profit. The SEC charged that Lund that violated rule 10b-5 insider trading prohibition. Did he? (*SEC v. Lund*, 570 F.Supp. 1397, C.D. Cal. 1983.)

8. A registered broker-dealer's sales force repeatedly made false and misleading statements in an effort to sell Lawn-A-Mat common stock. After several complaints were ignored, the SEC sought an injunction to halt the illicit practices. One respondent was the sales supervisor, who was informed of the misdeeds but did not take affirmative steps to prevent a recurrence of the deceit. One issue that arose was whether the SEC would have to prove scienter to obtain an injunction against practices that allegedly violated rule 10b-5. Discuss. (*Aaron v. SEC*, 446 U.S. 680, 1980.)

9. Hamm bought 1000 shares of Playboy stock at $17 per share in September 1979. On April 13, 1981, Playboy announced that it was in danger of losing the operating licenses for its three London gambling casinos, which provided a substantial portion of Playboy's operating revenue. The market price of Playboy stock dropped after these disclosures, and Hamm sued under Sec. 10(b), claiming that Playboy had known as early as 1979 that its licenses were in danger but had not revealed this in its quarterly and annual reports. Playboy defended by pointing out that Hamm had not read those reports anyway. Is this a good defense? Discuss. (*HSL, Inc. v. Daniels*, FED.SEC.L.REP. (CCH) 99,577, N.D. Ill. 1983.)

Common-Law Liability to Clients
Common-Law Liability to Third Parties
Management Advisory Services
Tax Practice
Accountants and the
Federal Securities Laws
Criminal Liability of Accountants
Accountants' Privilege and Confidentiality

M ODERN ECONOMIES ARE critically dependent on accurate, reliable financial information, which provides the basis by which investors and businesspersons value assets and enterprises. As accumulations of capital grow larger and economic transactions become more complex, the importance of this information grows ever greater.

Accountants provide much of this financial information. An accountant who audits a corporation's books is relied on not just by the corporation but also by investors, creditors, government agencies, and others to provide an accurate financial picture. Because the role of the accountant is so critical to our economy and the potential damage if the accountant errs is so great, all states regulate use of the title *certified public accountant* (*CPA*). All states require examinations for qualification, and many require additional experience and continuing education for CPAs. An extensive code of ethics promulgated by the American Institute of Certified Public Accountants (AICPA) sets out rules of conduct.

Despite a generally good record, the accounting profession occasionally stubs its collective toe. Being a potential "deep pocket," accounting firms are often an inviting target in lawsuits where more active wrongdoers have fled the scene or become insolvent. For that reason, the financial consequences of errors by accountants can be devastating. Indeed, the accounting profession now faces a truly critical situation. Between 1980 and 1988, major accounting firms paid out $300 million in audit-related litigation. At the time, it was believed that the situation could hardly worsen. It has.

In 1992, a jury assessed a $200 million punitive damages judgment against Coopers & Lybrand (which apparently was later settled out of court by a payment of around $50 million). Ernst & Young paid $63 million to settle a negligence suit, and KPMG Peat Marwick paid $67.9 million in England for an allegedly faulty audit. More than 4000 lawsuits claiming damages of over $30 *billion* are currently pending against accounting firms. Many of these are suits by the FDIC seeking to recover losses sustained in the savings and loan debacle of the late 1980s. These are *staggering* numbers that threaten the very existence of some large firms. Indeed, in 1990, Laventhol &

Horwath, facing $2 billion in lawsuits, went out of business.

Such judgments have many consequences. Liability insurance premiums are 10 times what they were in 1985 for much less coverage. Many smaller CPA firms are shying away from auditing work, where most of the liability judgments have arisen. Bigger accounting firms are refusing to do audit work for small companies that cannot also give the accountants substantial amounts of tax and consulting work. The AICPA is attempting to raise its members' standard of conduct, while at the same time lobbying both federal and state legislatures for helpful changes in the law. The formerly coveted "partnership" promotions in big accounting firms are now sometimes turned down by persons who do not wish to shoulder the liability that goes along with it. Many accounting partnerships are restructuring into corporations or limited liability companies in hopes of limiting liability.

It is obviously important to be familiar with the legal obligations of accountants. This chapter surveys the many potential sources of an accountant's legal liability. Of the three major accounting functions—auditing, tax practice, and management advisory services—auditing is emphasized because it generates the most accounting revenue and gives rise to most of the lawsuits filed against accountants.

COMMON-LAW LIABILITY TO CLIENTS
Contractual Liability

An accountant hired to audit a company's books is an independent contractor who must perform the auditing responsibilities properly and with due care. Though not a guarantor of the accuracy of the client's financial records, the auditor must act diligently, independently, and honestly. The auditor's responsibilities are established by the contract with the client.

An audit is an independent critique of a business entity's financial statements in order to determine their accuracy and reliability. The audit consists of three phases: (1) collection of data, (2) analysis of data, and (3) report of data and conclusions in an appropriate form. The goal of the audit is an opinion by the auditor regarding the quality of the client's financial statements.

An auditor who is unable to form a valid opinion as to the accuracy of the company's records—perhaps because the company has allowed only a limited review, or the underlying financial records are incomplete, or the accuracy is dependent upon an event that has not yet transpired, such as the closing of a pending sale— uses a **disclaimer.** A disclaimer informs the reader that the auditor has had to qualify the opinion and is therefore not vouching that the company's financial statements fairly present the stated information. In one case an auditor was able to avoid legal liability by clearly noting that the auditors did not confirm the accounts receivable or review their collectability and that the balance sheet had not been adjusted for uncollectable receivables.[1] However, if the disclaimer is not sufficiently clear and definite to qualify a general impression of accuracy in the financial statements, the auditor may still be liable. Furthermore, an accountant who knows that statements compiled by the company are inaccurate cannot pass them along with a disclaimer and thereby avoid liability. A disclaimer does not relieve an accountant from the duty to refrain from knowingly being a party to fraud.[2]

The defensibility of the auditor's opinion is frequently the subject of litigation. Any number of auditing errors can produce an inaccurate opinion and constitute a breach of the auditing contract. The auditor may be inadequately trained or supervised or not sufficiently familiar with the client's business. Lapses in examination, such as the failure to verify inventory, or to discover that accounts receivable are uncollectable, may occur. Poor judgment in analyzing the data or a misleading manner of reporting conclusions are other errors. Such mistakes constitute a breach of the auditing contract and may result in liability on a breach of contract claim.

Negligence Liability

The same auditing mistakes that constitute a breach of contract will normally also constitute a breach of the auditor's duty of due care and therefore provide a basis for a tort claim of negligence. An auditor who fails to observe professional standards is liable just like a doctor or lawyer who commits malpractice.

Standard of Care in Auditing

The duty of an auditor is to exercise the special care and skill that the typical professional auditor would exercise in the same circumstances. At trial, expert testimony will help establish that standard of care.

Where does the standard of care come from? The auditor may be guided by **Generally Accepted Auditing Standards (GAAS),** which establish the objectives to be obtained by an audit and set the quality of performance in terms of skill, independence, and care. **Generally Accepted Accounting Principles (GAAP)** address the theoretical aspects of how various transactions should be carried on the books. GAAS and GAAP are derived from such sources as (1) pronouncements of the AICPA, (2) pronouncements of the Financial Accounting Standards Board (FASB), (3) Securities and Exchange Commission accounting rules and releases, (4) rules of state boards of accounting and societies of CPAs, and (5) Internal Revenue Service rules of practice. These standards can be raised in a specific instance if more is promised by the auditor in a particular engagement contract.

A violation of GAAP or GAAS will be considered *prima facie* evidence of negligence by the auditor. On the other hand, compliance with GAAP and GAAS does not ensure an auditor of nonliability. Even if proper procedures and standards are used, poor judgment in analyzing the data collected can lead to liability. Furthermore, some courts demand more of auditors than mere mechanical application of GAAP and GAAS. For example, in *United States v. Simon,*[3] defendant auditors were convicted of conspiring to commit criminal fraud by knowingly certifying a false and misleading financial statement, despite their calling eight expert independent accountants who testified that defendants had complied with GAAP and GAAS. The court held such expert testimony to be "persuasive" but not "conclusive" and left to the jury the ultimate decision as to whether the financial statements as a whole did not fairly present the client's financial position. In most recent cases, however, courts have held that auditors fulfill their duty of due care by complying with GAAP and GAAS in good faith.[4]

Standard of Care in Nonauditing Situations

Sometimes accountants are hired to do less exacting work than a full audit. Traditionally, if the accountant did an unaudited financial statement or bookkeeping, he or she could avoid liability by marking each page

---

[1]*Stephens Industries, Inc. v. Haskins & Sells,* 438 F.2d 357 (10th Cir. 1971).
[2]*Ashland Oil, Inc. v. Arnett,* 875 F.2d 1271 (7th Cir. 1989).

[3]425 F.2d 796 (2d Cir. 1969), *cert. denied,* 397 U.S. 1006 (1970).
[4]*SEC v. Arthur Young & Co.,* 590 F.2d 785 (9th Cir. 1979).

as unaudited and accompanying all documents with a disclaimer to clearly indicate the auditor expressed no opinion on accuracy.

However, cases decided in the 1970s held accountants civilly and even criminally liable for their "unauditor" activities. The courts clearly expected the auditors to take a more active role in detecting fraud and misstatements than did the accounting profession in these situations.

Because there was a lack of guidance as to what was expected of an accountant doing "unauditor" work, the AICPA issued Statements on Standards for Accounting and Review Services No. 1 (SSARS No. 1), which provides the heretofore missing standards. SSARS No. 1 divides nonaudit work into **compilation** (assembly and preparation of financial statements from records of the client) and **review** (limited review of financial statements prepared by the client), and provides specific guidelines as to what is expected of the accountant in both activities. Although some courts have recently hinted that they will accept the notion that accountants should be held to a less stringent standard when performing nonaudit work,[5] others have found accountants liable for negligence even though SSARS No. 1 was followed.[6]

Fraud Detection

Auditors have often taken the position that it is not their job to detect fraud, but only to ensure that their clients prepare financial statements in accordance with GAAP and GAAS. They say that they are "watchdogs, not bloodhounds." Courts sometimes demand a higher standard than auditors desire, one stating: "general accounting standards . . . require the auditor to use his professional skill to follow up any signs of fraud that he discovers in the audit. . . . Auditors are not detectives hired to ferret out fraud, but if they chance on signs of fraud they may not avert their eyes—they must investigate."[7]

Numerous instances of "audit failure" (where firms took bankruptcy soon after their auditors had given them unqualified audit opinions attesting to the reliability of their financial reports) in the 1970s and 1980s led to pressure to increase the auditor's role as financial detective. In 1990, the Auditing Standards Board's SAS No. 53, dealing with an auditor's responsibility to detect fraud, became effective. Basically, SAS No. 53 states that an auditor should not only exercise due care in planning, performing, and evaluating the results of audit procedures, but also bring to bear the proper degree of "professional skepticism" to achieve reasonable assurance that material errors or irregularities will be discovered. (Under earlier standards, auditors were allowed to assume that management was honest, absent information to the contrary.)

Professional skepticism means assuming neither dishonest management nor unquestioned honesty. Auditors should certainly be alert to mistakes in gathering or processing accounting data, incorrect accounting estimates due to oversight or misrepresentation, and mistakes in application of accounting principles. It is important that auditors assess the integrity of management by considering circumstances that may indicate a tendency on management's part to distort financial statements, such as frequent disputes about aggressive application of accounting rules or evasive responses to audit inquiries. Accounting firms must keep a client's audit committee informed as to any significant irregularities discovered.

Still, auditors are not required to be lawyers or criminal investigators. SAS No. 53 recognizes that auditors cannot *guarantee* the accuracy of their reports. On the other hand, as this edition is being prepared, Congress is debating a bill that would place a greater burden on independent auditors to design procedures to detect illegal acts and to inform top corporate management, and in some cases the SEC, of any illegalities that are detected. Sponsors of the bill aim to make accountants the "first line of defense against cooked books and fraud" in publicly traded corporations. Opponents believe that such a law turning accountants into "whistleblowers" would greatly widen the already significant liability exposure of auditors in this area.

Independence

The following guidelines serve to preserve the auditor's independence.

1. Accountants must not have any direct or material indirect financial interest in the client.

2. Auditors should not loan money to or accept loans from the client.

3. Auditors should not be officers or directors of the client.

---

[5]*William Iselin & Co., Inc. v. Landau*, 513 N.Y.S.2d 3 (1987).
[6]*Robert Wooler Co. v. Fidelity Bank*, 479 A.2d 1027 (Pa.Super. 1984).
[7]*Cenco, Inc. v. Seidman & Seidman*, 686 F.2d 449 (7th Cir. 1982).

4. Auditors should not work for a contingent fee.

5. Auditors should not allow clients to indemnify them for their professional liability exposure.

If independence is lacking, any issued reports should indicate it in an accompanying disclosure.

Obvious problems arise when accountants who are auditing a client receive large, unsecured loans from that client, a practice that the AICPA only recently explicitly barred after SEC allegations that Arthur Young partners had borrowed over $20 million from their client RepublicBank, a failed Texas bank holding company. Furthermore, the simple fact that the client pays the auditor's fee may make it difficult for the auditor to remain independent. In 1984, for example, approximately 450 public corporations changed auditors. Though most switches were supposedly motivated by an opportunity for lower fees, 20 percent of the changes followed issuance of a qualified opinion. This development has led both Congress and the SEC to scrutinize possible "opinion shopping"—a corporation's scouting about until it can find an accounting firm willing to support a favorable accounting treatment. As the SEC has stated: "If the manner in which the issuer changes its auditors restricts the independence of the new auditors or calls into question their objectivity, such conduct erodes the public's belief in the integrity of both the financial markets and the independent audit function."[8]

[8]*In re Broadview Financial Corp.*, Securities Exchange Act Release No. 21949.

The SEC has adopted rules mandating prompt disclosure by large public companies of changes in auditors under circumstances indicating possible "opinion shopping." The disclosure must include the grounds of disagreement with the former auditor and any discussions the company had with the new auditor before the switch.

Defenses
Lack of Reliance

Plaintiffs cannot recover on account of an auditor's careless mistake if they knew the true facts and therefore did not rely on the erroneous opinion of the auditor.

Contributory Negligence

Contributory negligence by the client has been asserted successfully as a defense by careless auditors, but the courts disagree as to the scope of the defense. If the client's contributory negligence consists of disregarding the auditor's recommendations or of activity which prevented the auditor from effectively performing his or her duties, most courts would either bar recovery or reduce it.

If, on the other hand, the auditor's negligence lies in failure to detect fraud by the client's employees, the courts are split. Some hold that careless supervision by client management contributing to the success of the fraud constitutes contributory negligence. Other courts hold that careless supervision is not the type of conduct which should block or reduce recovery.

The following case illustrates one school of thought.

HALLA NURSERY, INC. V. BAUMANN-FURRIE & CO.

Minnesota Supreme Court, 454 N.W.2d 905 (1990)

From 1983 to 1985, defendants Baumann-Furrie & Co. and Allen Furrie provided accounting services to plaintiff, Halla Nursery, a retail nursery. During this time, Halla's bookkeeper embezzled $135,000 from the company. In 1986, Halla brought this malpractice action against defendants, alleging negligent

performance of accounting services in failing to detect the embezzlement. Defendants denied liability and raised an affirmative defense of Halla's contributory negligence for, among other things, failing to put in place internal financial controls to protect the company from embezzlement.

The jury found Halla 80 percent at fault and Baumann-Furrie 20 percent at fault, and assessed damages of

$309,761. The trial court ordered judgment of no recovery, but then granted a new trial because it had erred in failing to instruct the jury on the effect of its answers to the comparative fault questions, as required by Minnesota law. (In other words, the jury was not instructed that a finding that plaintiff was 80 percent at fault would bar any recovery by it.) Baumann-Furrie appealed the

(continues)

Halla Nursery, Inc. v. Baumann-Furrie & Co.

(continued from previous page)
order for a new trial. The court of
appeals affirmed the order of a new
trial and ruled that at the new trial
contributory negligence could be
raised as a defense only if that negli-
gence directly interfered with Bau-
mann-Furrie's ability to perform the
contract in accordance with GAAP.
Baumann-Furrie appealed.

Wahl, Justice:

The case was tried as a negligence action. The trial court . . . allowed the
jury to determine under Minnesota's
comparative fault statute whether
Halla was negligent in the day-to-day
management and operation of its business, and whether that negligence was
a direct cause of its damages, then to
compare Halla's negligence with that
of Baumann-Furrie. The court of appeals reversed, adopting instead the
rule of *Lincoln-Grain, Inc. v. Coopers
& Lybrand*, 345 N.W.2d 300 (Neb.
1984), which held that the contributory
negligence of a client in an accountant
malpractice case is a defense only
where it had contributed to the accountant's failure to perform the contract and report the truth.

The *Lincoln Grain* rule had its genesis in *National Surety Corp. v. Lybrand*, 9 N.Y.S.2d 554 (1939). . . . In
National Surety, during an audit, the
accountants failed to discover that a
cashier was embezzling funds from a
stockbroker. The court rejected the accountant's defense that the client had
been contributorily negligent in running its business such that it was impossible to determine that the cashier was
embezzling funds. The court stated:

We are not prepared to admit that accountants are immune from the consequences of
their negligence because those who employ
them have conducted their own business negligently. Accountants, as we know, are commonly employed for the very purpose of

detecting defalcations which the employer's
negligence has made possible. Accordingly, we
see no reason to hold that the accountant is
not liable to his employer in such cases. Negligence of the employer is a defense only when
it has contributed to the accountant's failure to
perform his contract and report the truth.

Halla argues the *Lincoln Grain*
rule, based on *National Surety*, is more
fair, that without it accountants are
rendered immune from the consequences of their own negligence
simply because those who employ
them may have conducted their own
businesses negligently. The *National
Surety-Lincoln Grain* rule has been
adopted in some other jurisdictions
[including New York, Illinois, Pennsylvania, and Texas], and has been considered by commentators to be the better
rule on policy grounds.

Baumann-Furrie, on the other
hand, argues that the contributory negligence exception adopted by the court
of appeals is inappropriate in the context of our broad, expansive doctrine of
comparative fault. They argue further
that the exception was adopted initially
to mitigate the harsh consequence of
the common law rule of negligence
[which totally barred a plaintiff's recovery for even the slightest contributory
negligence], an exception not necessary in a comparative fault state like
Minnesota. Finally, they argue that the
rule imposes a heavy evidentiary burden on the accountant: applying *Lincoln Grain* to a malpractice case would
require that the defendant-accountant
must prove not only that the plaintiff's
negligence caused or contributed to
the plaintiff's loss, but also that the
plaintiff's negligence caused defendant's negligence.

Baumann-Furrie correctly points
out that earlier interpretations of comparative fault by this court would seem
to mandate that the same liberal construction apply to malpractice actions
against accountants. We have on nu-

merous occasions indicated our broad
view of comparative fault. Furthermore, we have applied principles of
comparative fault to [legal and medical]
malpractice actions. We recognize, however, that professional malpractice actions pose peculiar problems and that
the comparison of fault between a
layperson and a professional should be
approached with caution. Accountants,
like other professionals, are held to a
standard of care which requires that
they "exercise the average ability and
skill of those engaged in that profession." *Vernon J. Rockler & Co. v. Glick-
man, Isenberg, Lurie & Co.*, 273
N.W.2d 647 (Minn. 1978). Failure to
exercise ordinary care in conducting accounting activities may expose an accountant to allegations of negligence.
By the same token, the persons who
hire accountants, usually businesspersons, should also be required to
conduct their business activities in a
reasonable and prudent manner.

Because we have broadly construed
the comparative fault act and applied it
to other professional malpractice actions, we reverse the court of appeals
and hold that the trial court did not err
in applying the principles of comparative fault in this action by a client
against an accountant for negligent failure to discover embezzlement in the
client's business. The application of the
broad definition of fault as set forth in
the comparative fault statute can be
particularly appropriate in such actions. This is not to say that there
would never be a case where a limiting exception might be necessary, for
example, where the scope of employment is such that discovery of defalcations is clearly encompassed. This is
not such a case.

[The trial court did err in not informing the jury of the effects of its
findings regarding comparative fault.]

The judgment of the court of appeals is reversed. ⚖

COMMON-LAW LIABILITY TO THIRD PARTIES

In recent years auditors have increasingly found themselves subject to suit by nonclient plaintiffs. As the defense of lack of privity has slowly eroded in many other areas of the law, so it has diminished as a shield for auditors. Increasing reliance by client creditors, investors, and others on the work of the auditors has led to their increasing liability.

Fraud

An auditor is guilty of fraud whenever he or she intentionally assists a client in deceiving others with false financial statements. If an auditor makes a false statement which he or she does not know is false but does not have reasonable grounds to believe is true, the act is deemed constructive fraud or gross negligence and the result is the same—liability to injured parties. Many years ago, a court said:

A representation certified as true to the knowledge of the accountants when knowledge there is none, reckless misstatement, or an opinion based on grounds so flimsy as to lead to the conclusion that there was no genuine belief in its truth, are all sufficient upon which to base liability. A refusal to see the obvious, a failure to investigate the doubtful, if sufficiently gross, may furnish evidence leading to an inference of fraud so as to impose liability for losses suffered by those who rely on the balance sheet. In other words, heedlessness and reckless disregard of consequence may take the place of deliberate intention.[9]

An auditor's liability to third parties in fraud cases was firmly established many years ago in *Ultramares Corp. v. Touche* wherein the defendants certified a firm's accounts knowing that banks and other lenders were relying on the audit. The certified balance sheet showed a net worth of a million dollars when, in reality, the company's capital had been wiped out. Justice Cardozo held that "To creditors and investors to whom the [auditor's] employer exhibited the certificate, the defendants owed a . . . duty to make it without fraud, since there was notice in the circumstances of its making that the employer did not intend to keep it to himself." Regarding fraud, constructive fraud, recklessness, or gross negligence, Justice Cardozo's statement remains the rule today.[10]

Negligence

In the *Ultramares* opinion, Justice Cardozo drew a sharp distinction between fraudulent conduct and negligent conduct, holding that the auditor would not be liable to third parties for the latter:

If liability for negligence exists, a thoughtless slip or blunder, the failure to detect a theft or forgery beneath the cover of deceptive entries, may expose accountants to a liability in an indeterminate amount for an indeterminate time to an indeterminate class. The hazards of a business conducted on these terms are so extreme as to enkindle doubt whether a flaw may not exist in the implication of a duty that exposes to these consequences.

The *Ultramares* privity approach (adopted in about 10 jurisdictions) now constitutes only one of three primary approaches to the scope of auditor liability for negligence, and it was slightly modified in *Credit Alliance Corp. v. Arthur Andersen & Co.*,[11] which extended liability to third parties relying on inaccurate financial reports only where (1) the accountant was aware that the financial reports were to be used for a particular purpose, (2) in furtherance of this purpose, a known party intended to rely on the reports, and (3) some conduct on the part of the accountants *linking* them to that party evinced the accountants' understanding of that party's reliance. Later cases indicated that *Credit Alliance* represents only a slight loosening of the privity standard.[12]

Approximately 18 jurisdictions have rejected the privity standard in favor of Sec. 552 of the Restatement (Second) of Torts, which permits recovery only "by the person or one of a limited group of persons for whose benefit and guidance [an accountant] intends to supply the information or knows that the recipient intends to supply it." Thus, the Restatement approach expands the accountant's liability beyond the contracting party, but only slightly. As a supplier of information, an accountant is liable for negligence to a third party only if the accountant intends to supply time information for the benefit of the third party (or parties) in a specific transaction or type of transaction identified to the accountant.

A few other jurisdictions have adopted the third major approach to this problem—the *reasonable foreseeability standard*. These courts hold that an

[9]*State St. Trust Co. v. Ernst*, 15 N.E.2d 416 (N.Y. 1938).
[10]*Ultramares Corp. v. Touche*, 174 N.E. 441 (N.Y. 1931).
[11]493 N.Y.S.2d 435 (1985).
[12]See *Security Pacific Business Credit, Inc. v. Peat Marwick Main & Co.*, 79 N.Y.2d 695 (1992).

accountant owes a duty of care to all parties who are reasonably foreseeable users of the accountant's audit. This is the most liberal approach; it applies general negligence principles without recognizing any special need to protect accountants.

Cases involving hundreds of millions of dollars may turn on which of these three views a particular jurisdiction adopts. The following recent case is expected to be very influential.

BILY V. ARTHUR YOUNG & CO.

Supreme Court of California, 834 P.2d 745 (1992)

Osborne Computer Corporation grew quickly during 1980–1982. In 1981, it hired defendant Arthur Young to audit its financial statements. To raise capital essential to its continued growth, Osborne planned to make an initial public offering of its stock.

There were significant weaknesses in Osborne's internal accounting procedures. As a result, the November 1982 financial statements were far too optimistic. Osborne took bankruptcy in 1983 and its shares and warrants became basically worthless. Plaintiffs, persons who invested in Osborne stock and warrants or loaned money to Osborne, sued Arthur Young on claims of negligence and negligent misrepresentation. A jury found in favor of plaintiffs; Arthur Young appealed. The court of appeals affirmed, following an earlier California case applying the "foreseeability" test described previously. Arthur Young appealed again.

Lucas, Justice:

We granted review to consider whether and to what extent an accountant's duty of care in the preparation of an independent audit of a client's financial statements extends to persons other than the client. [The court then summarized the *Ultramares* privity approach, the Restatement approach, and the liberal foreseeability approach.]

[W]e decline to permit all merely foreseeable third party users of audit reports to sue the auditor on a theory of professional negligence. Our holding is premised on three central concerns. . . .

1. Liability Out of Proportion to Fault.

An auditor is a watchdog, not a bloodhound. . . . As a matter of commercial reality, audits are performed in a client-controlled environment. The client typically prepares its own financial statements; it has direct control over and assumes primary responsibility for their content. . . .

Client control also predominates in the dissemination of the audit report. Once the report reaches the client, the extent of its distribution and the communications that accompany it are within the exclusive province of client's management. Thus, regardless of the efforts of the auditor, the client retains effective primary control of the financial reporting process.

Moreover, the audit report is not a simple statement of verifiable fact that, like the weight of [a] load of beans . . . can be easily checked against uniform standards of indisputable accuracy. Rather, an audit report is a professional opinion based on numerous and complex factors. . . . [T]he report is based on the auditor's interpretation and application of hundreds of professional standards, many of which are broadly phrased and readily subject to different constructions. Although ultimately expressed in shorthand form, the report is the final product of a complex process involving discretion and judgment on the part of the auditor at every stage. Using different initial assumptions and approaches, different sampling techniques, and the wisdom of 20-20 hindsight, few CPA audits would be immune from criticism.

. . . Although hindsight suggests [that plaintiffs] misjudged a number of major factors (including, at a minimum, the product, the market, the competition, and the company's manufacturing capacity), plaintiffs' litigation-focused attention is now exclusively on the auditor and its report. Plaintiffs would have us believe that, had the Arthur Young report disclosed deficiencies in accounting controls and the $3 million loss (on income of over $68 million), they would have ignored all the other positive factors that triggered their interest (such as the company's rapid growth in sales, its dynamic management, and the intense interest of underwriters in a public offering) and flatly withheld all their funds.

. . . [J]udicial endorsement of third party negligence suits against auditors limited only by the concept of foreseeability raises the spectre of multibillion-dollar professional liability that is distinctly out of proportion to: (1) the fault of the auditor (which is necessarily secondary and may be based on complex differences of professional opinion); and (2) the connection between the auditor's conduct and the third party's injury (which will often be attenuated by unrelated business factors that underlie investment and credit decisions). . . . [S]uch disproportionate liability cannot fairly be justified on moral, ethical, or economic grounds.

(continues)

BILY V. ARTHUR YOUNG & CO.

(continued from previous page)

2. The Prospect of Private Ordering.
. . . [T]he third party in an audit negligence case . . . can "privately order" the risk of inaccurate financial reporting by contractual arrangements with the client. For example, a third party might expand its own resources to verify the client's financial statements or selected portions of them that were particularly material to its transaction with the client. Or it might commission its own audit or investigation. . . .

As a matter of economic and social policy, third parties should be encouraged to rely on their own prudence, diligence, and contracting power, as well as other informational tools. This kind of self-reliance promotes sound investment and credit practices and discourages the careless use of monetary resources. If, instead, third parties are simply permitted to recover from the auditor for mistakes in the client's financial statements, the auditor becomes, in effect, an insurer of not only the financial statements, but of bad loans and investments in general.

3. The Effect on Auditors of Negligence Liability to Third Persons.
Courts and commentators advocating auditor negligence liability to third parties also predict that such liability might deter auditor mistakes, promote more careful audits, and result in a more efficient spreading of the risk of inaccurate financial statements. . . . We are not directed to any empirical data supporting these prognostications.

In view of the inherent dependence of the auditor on the client and the labor-intensive nature of auditing, we doubt whether audits can be done in ways that would yield significantly greater accuracy without disadvantages. Auditors may rationally respond to increased liability by simply reducing audit services in fledgling industries where the business failure rate is high, reasoning that they will inevitably be singled out and sued when their client goes into bankruptcy regardless of the care or detail of their audits. . . . Consistent with this reasoning, the economic result of unlimited negligence liability could just as easily be an increase in the cost and decrease in the availability of audits and audit reports with no compensating improvement in overall audit quality. . . .

[W]e hold that an auditor's liability for general negligence in the conduct of an audit of its client financial statements is confined to the client, i.e., the person who contracts for or engages the audit services. Other persons may not recover on a pure negligence theory.

There is, however, a further narrow class of persons who, although not clients, may reasonably come to receive and rely on an audit report and whose existence constitutes a risk of audit reporting that may fairly be imposed on the auditor. Such persons are specifically intended beneficiaries of the audit report who are known to the auditor and for whose benefit it renders the audit report. While such persons may not recover on a negligence theory, we hold they may . . . recover on a theory of negligent misrepresentation.

[Reversed.] ⚖

Note

Most courts do not distinguish between the torts of negligence and negligent misrepresentation. By adopting the privity approach to a negligence theory and the Restatement approach to the negligent misrepresentation theory, the California Supreme Court effectively adopted the middle-ground, Restatement approach to auditor third-party negligence liability.

MANAGEMENT ADVISORY SERVICES

A second basic function of accountants is to perform consulting or management advisory services (MAS). More and more accountants are expanding into management consulting, giving general advice on such matters as mergers and acquisitions, modernizing manufacturing plants, personnel training, office management, and choosing types of computers, methods of inventory control, and tax shelters. Some major accounting firms have earned more than a billion dollars a year in consulting fees.

Because the AICPA has promulgated few concrete standards to govern MAS and there have been few litigated cases, the accountant venturing into MAS has little guidance. Many predict litigation in this area will increase, especially because accountants are starting to give advice as to matters outside their traditional competence.

Potential liability in this area is high. In a case involving the band Creedence Clearwater Revival, a jury rendered an $8.6 million verdict against an accounting firm which placed $5 million of the band's money in a Bahamian bank which the firm should have known was in financial trouble.[13]

---

[13]*Clifford v. Kanter*, #778142 (San Francisco Superior Court, 1983).

In the past the SEC discouraged accounting firms from expanding into MAS. For example, the SEC has banned direct business relationships between accountants and the companies they audit, reasoning that an accounting firm's auditors would have difficulty being objective about decisions the firm's consultants had played a part in making. However, in 1990 the SEC ruled that accounting firms could spin off separate entities to do consulting work for their audit clients. For its part, the AICPA has stated that CPAs performing consulting work for audit clients must not assume the role of employee or manager in audit client operations or exercise authority on behalf of audit clients (such as by consummating transactions or holding custody of assets).

TAX PRACTICE

The tax practice in which many accountants engage is an increasingly big business. Heavy government regulation of the area exposes the accountant to a variety of legal constraints.

For example, the Tax Reform Act of 1976 requires a preparer of tax returns to furnish a complete copy of each return to the taxpayer at the time or before the taxpayer signs the return, and to retain copies of the returns for three years or retain lists of client names and taxpayer identification numbers for IRS inspection. All returns prepared by CPAs must be signed by them even if no fee is charged (however, they should be signed only if the accountant is satisfied that all relevant information has been provided and all questions answered).

The Internal Revenue Code penalizes accountants who prepare returns yet do not (1) furnish copies to the taxpayer; (2) retain copies of returns or lists of names and taxpayer identification numbers; or (3) correct incorrectly prepared returns. The law also imposes civil liability on accountants who aid and abet taxpayers in substantial underpayment of taxes, and criminal liability for aiding, abetting, or counseling the preparation of false tax returns. Penalties for violation are not insubstantial. For example, in a recent case the IRS assessed penalties of $10,000 for each of eight quarterly corporate employment tax forms (Form 941) and $1000 for each of 19 W-2 forms for corporate employees that had been prepared by an independent accountant. The $99,000 fine was imposed under Sec. 6071 of the Internal Revenue Code, which punishes any person who assists in preparing or presenting a tax return or supporting document while knowing (or believing) that the material will be used to understate tax liability. In preparing returns, the accountant had not included cash payments made to the corporation's employees.[14]

An accountant who carelessly advises a client on tax matters, miscalculates a client's tax liability, forgets to file a client's return on time, or loses a client's papers can be held liable for negligence. Liability can extend to fees and penalties incurred by the client in correcting the mistake, occasional punitive damages, and even loss on prospective transactions. In one case, for example, defendant accountants advised plaintiff she could sell certain stock at a loss to reduce her income tax liability by offsetting an earlier gain in selling North American Company stock. Unfortunately, defendants had erroneously calculated the North American sale which really resulted in a loss. Because there was no reason to sell the additional stock at a loss, plaintiff was entitled to recover the difference between the sale price and the cost of replacement after she learned of the mistake.[15]

The IRS has substantial powers to obtain the papers of an accountant in investigating the tax liability of the accountant's client. Failure to comply with IRS subpoenas can lead to a contempt citation.

ACCOUNTANTS AND THE FEDERAL SECURITIES LAWS

In the wake of the great stock market crash of 1929, Congress passed several laws to regulate the sale of securities in this country. These acts protect the investing public by requiring companies to fully disclose information about themselves, by punishing fraudulent activity, and by promoting fair dealing.

The impact of these laws upon the accounting profession has been profound. Both Congress and the Securities Exchange Commission rely on auditors to play a major role in producing accurate financial information. Recently the SEC noted:

During the past several years, public and Congressional attention has been focused to an unprecedented degree on the accounting profession and on its role in promoting public confidence in the integrity of financial reporting. The Federal securities laws, since their enactment in the

[14]*Mullikin v. U.S.*, 952 F.2d 920 (6th Cir. 1991).
[15]*Rassieur v. Charles*, 188 S.W.2d 817 (Mo. 1945).

aftermath of the economic crisis of the early 1930's, have authorized the Commission to require that independent accountants audit the financial statements of publicly-held corporations. Thus, those laws have placed upon the accountant unique and important responsibilities in facilitating the proper functioning of this nation's capital formation processes and, more broadly, of our economic system as a whole.[16]

Recognizing the importance of reliable accounting and auditing to the effectiveness of the securities law, Congress gave the SEC substantial powers to make and enforce rules for accounting. Although the SEC has let the accounting profession lead the way, it has retained final authority and issues several types of rules and pronouncements governing the accounting practices of companies and the proper form for information in financial statements which must be filed with the SEC. Any accountant who audits for a public company is vitally concerned with the rules that the SEC promulgates, and with those of the Financial Accounting Standards Board (FASB), which the SEC recognizes as the private sector's primary standard-setting entity. Although the SEC's express authority to regulate accounting practices extends only to those public companies which must file statements with it on a regular basis, its influence on the actions of the FASB and AICPA ultimately affects the work of all independent auditors no matter how small the client company.

So important is the quality of auditing of public companies that the AICPA voted in 1990 to require *peer reviews* for accounting firms auditing such large companies. Under this system, implemented under pressure from the SEC, a firm's audit procedures are scrutinized by outside accountants from other firms to ensure that proper standards are followed. Peer review will be expensive, but should raise the quality of audits.

SEC Rule 2(e) provides for discipline of those who "practice" before the commission. An accountant who prepares any statement, opinion, or other paper filed with the SEC with the preparer's consent is deemed to be "practicing" before the commission. Under Rule 2(e), the SEC can punish those who are unqualified, unethical, or in violation of its rules, or who have lost their state license or been convicted of various crimes. Intentional wrongdoing by the accountant is not a prerequisite for Rule 2(e) punishment.

Though the audit failure rate among public corporations is less than 1 percent, SEC enforcement actions against accountants directly and against public corporations for their accounting activities have greatly increased in recent years. In 1983 and 1984 there were 23 SEC enforcement actions brought against accounting firms. Fifteen of these led to suspensions of one or more accountants. The suspensions ranged from thirty days to over five years. Typically, a suspended accountant may reapply for the right to practice before the SEC after taking additional coursework and joining the AICPA's SEC Practice Section (a peer review group).

Any accountant who undertakes to audit for a public corporation must also face the possibility of substantial liability in *civil lawsuits* filed under various provisions of the securities laws.[17]

Securities Act of 1933

The Securities Act of 1933 regulates the initial sale of new stock by corporations to the public. It is frequently called the "truth in securities" law because its major goal is full disclosure to the investing public. If the financial statements required by the Securities Act of 1933 are inaccurate and investors are injured, lawsuits frequently follow. Accountants are often defendants in such lawsuits because of their role in preparing and auditing these statements.

Section 11

Section 11 of the Securities Act of 1933 expressly provides that if any part of a registration statement when it became effective contained an untrue statement of a material fact (or omitted a fact necessary to insure that the statements made were not misleading), any person who acquired such a security may sue for injuries sustained. Section 11 then expressly lists as among potential defendants the issuing company, directors, the underwriter who sold the stock, and "every accountant" who helped prepare any part of the registration statement or any financial statement used in it.

---

[16]Report of the Securities and Exchange Commission on the Accounting Profession and the Commission's Oversight Role (1978). The Supreme Court's statements in *United States v. Arthur Young & Co.*, the last major case in this chapter, clearly indicate that the Supreme Court also believes in the public responsibilities of the accounting profession.

[17]A lengthier discussion of the substance of the U.S. securities laws is contained in Chapter 41. Here we only highlight those provisions most directly pertaining to accountants.

A plaintiff making a Section 11 claim need prove only that a false statement was made in the registration statement and that a loss was sustained. Section 11 plaintiffs need not prove that they relied on the false statements or that the false statements caused their loss; these are presumed. Significantly, plaintiffs need not prove that defendants acted fraudulently, nor do they have the burden of proving mere negligence. Negligence, which is a sufficient basis for liability, is presumed from the fact of the misleading statement.

An issuing company has virtually no defense under Section 11 if there has been a false statement and a loss. Individual defendants, such as accountants, can defend by proving (1) the false statements had no causal connection to plaintiff's loss; (2) plaintiff knew of the falsity of the statement at the time of the stock purchase; or (3) the defendant acted with "due diligence." The harsh negligence standard of Section 11 is made even more stringent by placing the burden of proof on defendants to prove they were not negligent, but subsection (b)(3)(B) provides that accountants may carry that burden by showing that both at the time of registration and at the time the statement became effective (after SEC review and approval) they "had after reasonable investigation, reasonable grounds to believe and did believe . . . that the statements were true and that there was no omission to state a material fact required to be stated therein or necessary to make the statements therein not misleading."

In a leading Section 11 case, *Escott v. Barchris Construction Corp.*, a company (Barchris) which constructed bowling alleys became insolvent soon after selling stock to the public pursuant to a registration statement. Among the many defendants in a Section 11 suit by investors was Peat, Marwick, the company's auditor. The registration statement contained reference to Peat, Marwick's 1960 audit of the company, which had several defects. The court noted that the accountant whom Peat, Marwick assigned to the task (Berardi) had little experience, was unfamiliar with the bowling industry, asked questions but did nothing to verify the answers, did not discover Barchris was listing sales that had not occurred, did not discover Barchris was holding up checks in substantial amounts because there was no money to pay them, and did not learn about some major problems Barchris was having with delinquent notes. In summary, the court held:

Accountants should not be held to a standard higher than that recognized in their profession. I do not do so here. Berardi's review did not come up to that standard. He did not take some of the steps which Peat, Marwick's written program prescribed. He did not spend an adequate amount of time on a task of this magnitude. Most important of all, he was too easily satisfied with glib answers to his inquiries.

. . . [T]here were enough danger signals in the materials which he did examine to require some further investigation on his part. Generally accepted accounting principles required such further investigation under these circumstances. It is not always sufficient merely to ask questions. . . . I conclude that Peat, Marwick has not established its due diligence defense.[18]

Section 12(2)

In the past accountants were often sued under Section 12(2) of the Securities Act of 1933, which provides that any person who offers or sells a security by means of false statements, whether or not made in a prospectus, shall be liable to the purchaser for damages sustained. Only the "seller" was liable, but courts took a very broad view of the definition of "seller." Because the Supreme Court recently limited the definition of "seller" to those who actually pass title or those who "solicit" transactions (such as brokers or dealers), accountants who stick to traditional accounting functions should no longer be held liable under Section 12(2).[19]

Securities Exchange Act of 1934

The Securities Exchange Act of 1934 complements the Securities Act of 1933 by regulating the trading of securities after their initial issuance. The 1934 Act regulates such diverse matters as proxy solicitation, tender offers to purchase shares of other companies, and the activities of brokers and dealers who sell stock at the "retail" level. It contains numerous antifraud provisions and allows the SEC to keep tabs on major public companies by requiring them to file a registration statement with the Commission and to update that statement with annual reports, quarterly reports, and interim reports whenever material changes occur in the company's financial situation. The work of accountants in preparing and auditing the financial statements that go into the registration documents and supplemental reports is critical to the success of the Securities Exchange Act of 1934. If the accountant errs, liability may ensue.

[18]*Escott v. Barchris Construction Corp.*, 283 F.Supp. 643 (S.D.N.Y. 1968).
[19]*Pinter v. Dahl*, 486 U.S. 622 (1988).

Section 10(b)

Perhaps the most litigated of all securities provisions are Section 10(b) of the 1934 Act and Rule 10b-5 which supplements it. The elements of a Section 10(b) violation are a manipulative or deceptive practice in connection with a purchase or sale of stock which results in a loss to plaintiff. Additionally, in most instances plaintiff must prove reliance on the deceptive statements or acts. Unlike in Section 11 of the Securities Act of 1933, the plaintiff carries the burden of proof under Section 10(b).

For many years it was unclear whether a defendant under Section 10(b) could be liable if guilty only of negligence in making a deceptive statement, or if plaintiff would have to prove fraudulent *intent* on defendant's part. The Supreme Court clarified the matter in the following case, which involved an accountant defendant.

ERNST & ERNST V. HOCHFELDER

U.S. Supreme Court, 425 U.S. 185 (1976)

Defendant-petitioner Ernst & Ernst is an accounting firm which from 1946 through 1967 periodically audited the books of First Securities Company of Chicago, a small brokerage firm. Plaintiffs-respondents, including Hochfelder, were induced by Nay, president of First Securities, to invest in "escrow" accounts which he said would yield a high return. In fact, there were no such accounts; Nay immediately converted these funds to his personal use. The accounts were not carried on First Securities' books, and were not discovered until after Nay committed suicide in 1968, leaving behind a note that described the escrow accounts as "spurious" and First Securities as bankrupt. Plaintiffs sued Ernst & Ernst under Section 10(b) and Rule 10b-5. Plaintiffs did not claim Ernst & Ernst knew of Nay's scheme or intentionally committed any wrong. Rather, plaintiffs claimed defendant's audits were negligently performed in that they failed to detect Nay's "mail rule"—that he was the only person in the office who could open mail. Had Ernst & Ernst discovered this unusual practice, it would have had to have been reported in the audit reports, leading to discovery of the fraud.

The trial court dismissed the action, and on appeal the Seventh Circuit held that negligence could be a proper basis for Section 10(b) liability. Ernst & Ernst petitioned for Supreme Court review.

Powell, Justice:

. . . We granted certiorari to resolve the question whether a private cause of action for damages will lie under §10(b) and Rule 10b-5 in the absence of any allegation of "scienter"—intent to deceive, manipulate, or defraud. We conclude that it will not and therefore we reverse. . . . In addressing this question, we turn first to the language of §10(b), for "[t]he starting point in every case involving construction of a statute is the language itself." *Blue Chip Stamps* [*v. Manor Drug Stores,* 421 U.S. 723, 756 (1975)].

Section 10(b) makes unlawful the use or employment of "any manipulative or deceptive device or contrivance" in contravention of Commission rules. The words "manipulative or deceptive" used in conjunction with "device or contrivance" strongly suggest that §10(b) was intended to proscribe knowing or intentional misconduct.

In its *amicus curiae* ["friend of the court"] brief, however, the Commission contends that nothing in the language "manipulative or deceptive device or contrivance" limits its operation to knowing or intentional practices. In support of its view, the Commission cites the overall congressional purpose in the 1933 and 1934 Acts to protect investors against false and deceptive practices that might injure them. The Commission then reasons that since the "effect" upon investors of given conduct is the same regardless of whether the conduct is negligent or intentional, Congress must have intended to bar all such practices and not just those done knowingly or intentionally. The logic of this effect-oriented approach would impose liability for wholly faultless conduct where such conduct results in harm to investors, a result the Commission would be unlikely to support. But apart from where its logic might lead, the Commission would add a gloss to the operative language of the statute quite different from its commonly accepted meaning. The argument simply ignores the use of the words "manipulative," "device," and "contrivance"—terms that make unmistakable a congressional intent to proscribe a type of conduct quite different from negligence. Use of the word "manipulative" is especially significant. It is and was virtually a term of art when used in connection with securities markets. It connotes intentional or willful conduct designed to deceive or defraud investors by controlling or artificially affecting the price of securities.

In addition to relying upon the Commission's argument with respect to the operative language of the statute, respondents contend that since we are dealing with "remedial legislation," it must be construed "'not technically and restrictively, but flexibly to effectuate its remedial purposes.'"

(continues)

ERNST & ERNST V. HOCHFELDER

(*continued from previous page*)
Affiliated Ute Citizens v. United States,
405 U.S. 128, 151 (1972). They argue
that the "remedial purposes" of the
Acts demand a construction of §10(b)
that embraces negligence as a standard
of liability. But in seeking to accomplish its broad remedial goals, Congress did not adopt uniformly a
negligence standard even as to express
civil remedies. In some circumstances
and with respect to certain classes of
defendants, Congress did create express liability predicated upon a failure
to exercise reasonable care. E.g., 1933
Act §11(b)(3)(B) (liability of "experts,"
such as accountants, for misleading
statements in portions of registration
statements for which they are responsible). But in other situations good
faith is an absolute defense. 1934 Act
§18 (misleading statements in any document filed pursuant to the 1934 Act).
And in still other circumstances, Congress created express liability regardless of the defendant's fault, 1933
Act §11(a) (issuer liability for misleading statements in the registration
statement).

It is thus evident that Congress
fashioned standards of fault in the express civil remedies in the 1933 and
1934 Acts on a particularized basis. As-
certainment of congressional intent
with respect to the standard of liability
created by a particular section of the
Acts must rest primarily on the language of that section. Where, as here,
we deal with a judicially implied liability, the statutory language is no less important. In view of the language of
§10(b), which so clearly connotes intentional misconduct, and mindful that
the language of a statute controls when
sufficiently clear in its context, further
inquiry may be unnecessary. We turn
now, nevertheless, to the legislative
history of the 1934 Act to ascertain
whether there is support for the meaning attributed to §10(b) by the Commission and respondents. . . .

Neither the intended scope of
§10(b) nor the reasons for the changes
in its operative language are revealed
explicitly in the legislative history of
the 1934 Act, which deals primarily
with other aspects of the legislation.
There is no indication, however, that
§10(b) was intended to proscribe conduct not involving scienter. The extensive hearings that preceded passage of
the 1934 Act touched only briefly on
§10, and most of the discussion was devoted to the enumerated devices that
the Commission is empowered to proscribe under §10(a). The most relevant
exposition of the provision that was to
become §10(b) was by Thomas G. Corcoran, a spokesman for the drafters.
Corcoran indicated:

Subsection (c) [§10(b)] says, 'Thou shalt
not devise any other cunning devices'. . . . Of
course subsection (c) is a catch-all clause to
prevent manipulative devices. I do not think
there is any objection to that kind of clause.
The Commission should have the authority to
deal with new manipulative devices.

This brief explanation of §10(b) by a
spokesman for its drafters is significant.
The section was described rightly as a
"catchall" clause to enable the Commission "to deal with new manipulative [or cunning] devices." It is difficult
to believe that any lawyer, legislative
draftsman, or legislator would use
these words if the intent was to create
liability for merely negligent acts or
omissions. . . .

When a statute speaks so specifically in terms of manipulation and deception, and of implementing devices
and contrivances—the commonly understood terminology of intentional
wrongdoing—and when its history reflects no more expansive intent, we are
quite unwilling to extend the scope of
the statute to negligent conduct.
[Reversed.] ⚖

Comment Although the Supreme Court has not spoken on the issue, a majority of lower courts have held that "recklessness" by a defendant is sufficient to satisfy the scienter requirement of Section 10(b), though mere negligence is not.

Section 14

Section 14 of the 1934 Act sets forth a comprehensive scheme governing solicitation of proxies. The
SEC requires management to include an annual
statement when it mails proxy solicitations to shareholders. The annual statement contains much useful
information about the company, including financial
statements which accountants helped compile and
audit. If a group of shareholders (called insurgents)
would like to oust incumbent management and gain
control of the board of directors, a proxy fight may
result in which insurgents and incumbents vie for
shareholders' proxies to vote at the annual meeting.
Proxy fights may also revolve around policy decisions
which must be made by shareholders, such as
whether to approve a merger. These elections frequently turn on the financial performance of the
company, so the accuracy of the accountants' work is
of vital importance.

Rule 14a-9, promulgated by the SEC, outlaws
proxy solicitation by use of false statements or misleading omissions.

Individual causes of action are permitted under Section 14, and, although the courts are in disagreement, accountants have been held liable for both primary violations of Section 14 and for aiding and abetting violations by others. In one influential but controversial case, *Adams v. Standard Knitting Mills, Inc.*, Standard shareholders such as Adams were solicited to cast their proxies in favor of a merger with Chadbourn, Inc. The proxy statement was accompanied by Chadbourn's financial statements which had been prepared by its accountants, Peat, Marwick. Although Standard shareholders were convinced to approve the merger and exchange their Standard shares for Chadbourn shares of equal value and supposedly higher dividends, when Chadbourn's sales declined the following year it was unable to pay the promised dividends because of certain restrictions in its loan agreements with banks. These restrictions were not disclosed in the proxy statement, and the court held Peat, Marwick was negligent, but not guilty of scienter, in omitting them.[20]

Although it recognized other courts had held corporations liable for mere negligence under Section 14, the *Adams* court declined to do so, stating "we are influenced by the fact that the accountant here, unlike the corporate issuer, does not directly benefit from the proxy vote and is not in privity with the stockholder. Unlike the corporate issuer, the preparation of financial statements to be appended to proxies and other reports is the daily fare of accountants, and the accountant's potential liability for mistakes would be enormous under a negligence standard."

Adams not withstanding, the courts remain divided with the trend being toward application of a negligence standard. Accountants guilty of scienter or recklessness are not only liable civilly, but also could face criminal liability.

Foreign Corrupt Practices Act of 1977

In the wake of Watergate and other political scandals of the 1970s, hundreds of American corporations were found to have been paying bribes to foreign political officials to obtain or keep business in foreign countries. Congress responded by passing the Foreign Corrupt Practices Act of 1977 (FCPA), which has broad implications for accountants.

The first part of the FCPA bans bribes to foreign officials by U.S. companies attempting to obtain or retain business in foreign countries. These rules

[20]623 F.2d 422 (6th Cir. 1980), *cert. denied*, 449 U.S. 1067 (1980).

were discussed in Chapter 41 and will not be repeated here.

The second part of the FCPA more directly involves accountants. Because bribes had been concealed by doctoring corporate records, Congress decided all public companies must (1) keep detailed records which "accurately and fairly" reflect the company's financial activities, and (2) devise a system of internal accounting controls sufficient to provide "reasonable assurance" that all transactions are authorized and accounted for. Though designed primarily to aid detection of foreign bribes, these accounting provisions are not limited to that function.

The FCPA has strengthened financial accounting of public corporations. The requirement of record-keeping and internal accounting controls are more stringent than the previous financial materiality standard that accountants had used.

Rule 13b2-1 prohibits any person from falsifying any book, record, or account subject to the FCPA. Rule 13b2-2 prohibits officers and directors of companies from making false statements to accountants. Penalties for violation of FCPA provisions are substantial and may include jail terms.

Because the accounting provisions of the FCPA are somewhat vague as to when records "accurately and fairly" reflect a company's financial picture or when an internal accounting control system allows "reasonable assurance" of accuracy, Congress in 1988 amended the FCPA to ensure that penalties will not be imposed for insignificant or technical infractions or inadvertent conduct. Additional guidance as to an auditor's evaluation of a company's internal accounting controls derives from the Accounting Standards Board's SAS No. 55, effective in 1990, which enlarges the auditor's traditional obligation to evaluate a client's internal control system by requiring him or her to focus not merely on the client's accounting controls but on its entire control structure, including the "control environment" (attitude of the board and management) and the control policies and procedures set up by management to ensure that the firm's specific objectives will be attained.

RICO

The Racketeering Influenced and Corrupt Organizations Act (RICO) was passed in an attempt to blunt organized crime's infiltration into legitimate business. Perhaps unfortunately, Congress drafted the law in such broad terms that it has led to a plethora of suits against businesses having no connection to real mobsters. The elements of RICO civil liability are (1) the conduct, (2) of an enterprise, (3) through a pattern, (4) of racketeering activity. Because "racketeering activity" is defined to include several "garden varieties" of fraud (such as mail fraud and securities fraud), virtually all traditional securities cases can now include a RICO count.

The incentive to include a RICO count is simple— RICO provides for recovery of treble damages and attorneys' fees. Furthermore, RICO can provide a powerful bargaining chip—no mild-mannered accountant wants the neighbors reading in the morning paper that the accountant has been named in a "racketeering" lawsuit. Along with the nation's most respected corporations, banks, and insurance companies, virtually every major accounting firm has been sued in one or more RICO suits.

Because many people believe RICO has gotten out of hand, as this chapter is written, the AICPA has joined many other groups in lobbying Congress to amend RICO to end the flood of lawsuits against "legitimate" businesses.[21]

CRIMINAL LIABILITY OF ACCOUNTANTS

Accountants face a number of criminal provisions which constrain their activities. Some accountants have gone to jail for violating these provisions.

Federal Securities Acts

The two most important criminal provisions for accountants are those of the Securities Act of 1933 and the Securities Exchange Act of 1934. Section 24 of the 1933 Act makes it a crime to willfully violate any section or rule of the Act or to willfully make a false statement in any registration statement. Section 32 of the 1934 Act similarly makes it a crime to willfully violate any section or rule of the 1934 Act or to willfully make a false statement in any document filed with the SEC. Because the accounting provisions of the FCPA amended the 1934 Act, willful violation of these provisions is also a crime.

Section 24 of the 1933 Act carries a potential penalty of up to five years in jail and/or a $10,000 fine. Individual accountants intentionally violating provisions of the 1934 Act face up to 10 years in jail, a fine of up to $1 million, or both. Criminal punishment for FCPA violations is separately provided.

Because these provisions require violations be "willful" before they constitute crimes, scienter is an element of a criminal violation. Courts have held that negligence or mistake is insufficient for liability, but recklessness may be sufficient. For example, in *U.S. v. Natelli*, defendant auditors helped a company cover up the fact that previously reported sales had not really occurred by hiding a discrepancy in a footnote.[22] The appellate court approved the trial judge's instruction that "good faith, an honest belief in the truth of the data set forth in the footnote and entries in the proxy statement would constitute a complete defense here." On the other hand, the court quoted a holding that "Congress equally could not have intended that men holding themselves out as members of these ancient professions [law and accounting] should be able to escape criminal liability on a plea of ignorance when they shut their eyes to what was plainly to be seen or have represented a knowledge they knew they did not possess."

Other Criminal Provisions

The most important additional criminal provision for accountants is the federal mail fraud statute, discussed in Chapter 7, which outlaws use of the federal mails to carry out fraudulent schemes. The penalty for violation is a fine up to $1,000, imprisonment of not more than five years, or both. Scienter is required for violation. In *U.S. v. Glick*, Chisolm, a con man with some flair, induced people to pay him nonrefundable front end fees to obtain loans for them. He represented himself as a man of great wealth who would guarantee the loans. Chisolm would show his victims financial statements prepared by his accountant, Glick. Glick knew the financial statements contained blatant violations of GAAP and that no lending institution would furnish a loan to Chisolm based on them. Glick also knew of Chisolm's use of the statements. Although Glick professed his good faith belief that Chisolm really did possess substantial wealth, the appellate court affirmed his conviction under the mail fraud law, holding he could not deliberately close his eyes to what was obvious to him.[23]

Accountants must also be wary of the federal false filing statement statute, which attaches criminal penalties to the filing of knowingly false statements with any federal agency, including the SEC.

---

[21]For more detail on RICO, consult Chapter 7.

[22]*U.S. v. Natelli*, 527 F.2d 311 (2d Cir. 1975), *cert. denied*, 425 U.S. 934 (1976).
[23]710 F.2d 639 (10th Cir. 1983).

Furthermore, most state securities statutes, called "blue sky" laws, contain criminal provisions comparable to those of the 1933 and 1934 Acts.

As noted earlier, intentionally filing false income tax returns on behalf of a taxpayer-client is also a crime.

Finally, accountants must be aware of federal statutes which outlaw **conspiracy** (agreement) to violate, or aiding and abetting (taking action) violations of other federal laws, such as securities statutes. Again, these provisions require intentional wrongdoing. For example, the required elements of aiding and abetting a securities violation are "that [defendant-auditor] knew of the [securities law] violations and of its role in the scheme, and, with this knowledge, substantially assisted in the violation."[24] Such actions are more likely to lead to civil liability, but may also provide the basis for criminal violations.

ACCOUNTANTS' PRIVILEGE AND CONFIDENTIALITY

Just as lawyers and doctors receive confidential, sensitive information from their clients and patients, so

do accountants frequently receive extremely sensitive financial information from their clients. Indeed, AICPA ethics standards provide that accountants should not disclose confidential client information unless (1) the client consents; (2) it is necessary to avoid violation of GAAP or GAAS; (3) disclosure is in response to an enforceable subpoena; or (4) disclosure is necessitated by an inquiry made by the ethics division or trial board of the AICPA or a state CPA regulatory body.

To the chagrin of most accountants, the common law does not recognize an accountant-client privilege similar to that afforded to lawyers, doctors, or members of the clergy. A part of the rationale for this is that much of what the accountant does is aimed at preparing forms and documents which will be disclosed publicly anyway.

The Federal Rules of Evidence do not provide for an accountant-client privilege, and traditionally there has been none at the federal level. Recently the Supreme Court confirmed the traditional federal approach by reversing a lower court decision which had created a limited confidential accountant-client privilege for tax accrual papers. The next case is a summary of that proceeding. (Note the opinion's emphasis on the *public* nature of an accountant's responsibilities.)

[24]*Seiffer v. Topsy's Int'l, Inc.*, 487 F.Supp. 653 (D.Kan. 1980).

UNITED STATES V. ARTHUR YOUNG & CO.

U.S. Supreme Court, 465 U.S. 805 (1984)

Respondent Arthur Young was the independent auditor of respondent Amerada Hess Corp., and therefore responsible for reviewing the corporation's financial statements as required by the federal securities laws. In so doing it verified Amerada's statement of contingent tax liabilities, preparing tax accrual workpapers relating to the evaluation of the corporation's reserves for such liabilities. In an IRS criminal investigation of Amerada's tax returns, the auditor's workpapers were summoned under §7602 of the IRS Code. Amerada instructed Arthur Young not to comply with the summons, so the IRS commenced an enforcement action in federal district court.

The district court ordered enforcement of the summons. On appeal, the Court of Appeals, while concluding that the papers were relevant to the IRS investigation, created a work-product immunity for independent auditors' work for public corporations. It found that the IRS had not made a sufficient showing to overcome the immunity and refused to enforce the summons. The government appealed.

Burger, Chief Justice:

. . . Based upon its evaluation of the competing policies of the federal tax and securities laws, the Court of Appeals found it necessary to create a so-called privilege for the independent auditor's workpapers.

Congress has endowed the IRS with expansive information-gathering authority; §7602 is the centerpiece of that congressional design. . . . [C]ourts should be chary in recognizing exceptions to the broad summons authority of the IRS or in fashioning new privileges that would curtail disclosure under §7602.

The Court of Appeals nevertheless concluded that "substantial countervailing policies" required the fashioning of a work-product immunity for an independent auditor's tax accrual workpapers. To the extent that the Court of Appeals, in its concern for the "chilling effect" of the disclosure of tax accrual workpapers, sought to facilitate communication between independent auditors and their clients, its remedy more closely resembles a testimonial accountant-client privilege than a work-product immunity for accountants' workpapers. But as this Court stated in Couch v. United States, 409 U.S. 322 (1973), "no confidential accountant-client privilege exists under federal law, and no state-created privilege has been recognized in federal cases."

Nor do we find persuasive the argument that a work-product immunity for accountants' tax accrual workpapers is a fitting analogue to the attorney work-product doctrine established in Hickman v. Taylor, 329 U.S. 495 (1947). The Hickman work-product doctrine was founded upon the private attorney's role as the client's confidential adviser and advocate, a loyal representative whose duty it is to present the client's case in the most favorable possible light. An independent certified public accountant performs a different role. By certifying the public reports that collectively depict a corporation's financial status, the independent auditor assumes a *public* responsibility transcending any employment relationship with the client. The independent public accountant performing this special function owes ultimate allegiance to the corporation's creditors and stockholders, as well as to the investing public. This "public watchdog" function demands that the accountant maintain total independence from the client at all times and requires complete fidelity to the public trust. To insulate from disclosure a certified public accountant's interpretations of the client's financial statements would be to ignore the significance of the accountant's role as a disinterested analyst charged with public obligations.

We cannot accept the view that the integrity of the securities markets will suffer absent some protection for accountants' tax accrual workpapers. The Court of Appeals apparently feared that, were the IRS to have access to tax accrual workpapers, a corporation might be tempted to withhold from its auditor certain information relevant and material to a proper evaluation of its financial statements. But the independent certified public accountant cannot be content with the corporation's representations that its tax accrual reserves are adequate; the auditor is ethically and professionally obligated to ascertain for himself as far as possible whether the corporation's contingent tax liabilities have been accurately stated. Responsible corporate management would not risk a qualified evaluation of a corporate taxpayer's financial posture to afford cover for questionable positions reflected in a prior tax return. Thus, the independent auditor's obligation to serve the public interest assures that the integrity of the securities markets will be preserved without the need for a work-product immunity for accountants' tax accrual workpapers.

[Reversed.] ⚖

At the state level, only about 15 jurisdictions still recognize an accountant-client privilege. The scope of the privilege varies from state to state, with most having exceptions for criminal actions, bankruptcy proceedings, and the like.

The privilege, where it exists, belongs to the client, not to the accountant. The client waives the privilege by relying on the accountant's audits or opinions in litigation. Obviously clients cannot rely on the auditor's opinion and then prevent the opposing litigant from examining the procedures that the accountant used to reach the opinion.

SUMMARY

Plaintiffs are reaching into the "deep pocket" of accountants with growing frequency. On a variety of fronts, litigation, the size of judgments, and liability insurance rates are all increasing.

Accountants can be held liable to their clients for both breach of contract and negligence when they fail to carefully and reasonably perform their agreed-upon services. At the same time, they must maintain independence from their clients, or the auditing function will be thwarted. If the client is also negligent, the courts are divided on how that fact should influence the liability of a negligent accountant.

There is also a trend to hold accountants liable to foreseeable third parties, such as creditors or investors, who rely on prepared financial statements for business decisions.

Accountants do extensive tax work and are expanding into management advisory services. There is likely to be an increase in litigation against them in these areas.

Numerous provisions in both the 1933 and 1934 securities acts give rise to potential liability for accountants. The standard of care imposed on the auditor varies from section to section; thus, each rule must be analyzed independently. In recent years the Foreign Corrupt Practices Act, and especially RICO, have expanded accountants' liability extensively.

In addition to being subject to civil penalties, accountants may have criminal penalties imposed on them if they are found to have intentionally violated any of a number of federal rules.

Unlike attorneys, at the federal level at least accountants have been denied an accountant-client privilege.

KEY TERMS

Disclaimer
Generally Accepted Auditing Standards (GAAS)
Generally Accepted Accounting Principles (GAAP)
Compilation
Review
Conspiracy

QUESTIONS AND PROBLEMS

1. The Professional Rodeo Cowboys Association (PRCA) hired the accounting firm of Wilch, Smith & Brock (WSB) to verify the prize money winnings of professional rodeo cowboys so that it could crown the World's Champion All-Around Cowboy on the basis of who had won the most prize money in sanctioned rodeos during the season. WSB determined that Camarillo was the top money winner, so he was crowned champion. Unfortunately, WSB had made two errors in its calculations; Ferguson was actually entitled to be champion. This led to a dispute which was settled by PRCA declaring the cowboys co-champions and awarding prizes and money to Ferguson equal to what had been awarded Camarillo. PRCA then sued the accountants, WSB. Are the accountants liable? Discuss. (*Professional Rodeo Cowboys Assoc. v. Wilch, Smith & Brock*, 589 P.2d 510, Colo. App. 1978.)

2. Shortly before a large corporation declared bankruptcy, three checks totaling $315,000 were drawn on the corporation's account and paid to the corporation's sole shareholder and to a corporate officer, to the detriment of corporate creditors. Birnie, who worked for Wilkes & Co., which had long been the corporation's outside auditor, helped conceal the transfers. Birnie then told the bankruptcy trustee that the corporate records were not complete, so the trustee hired Wilkes to compile complete records. Wilkes did so, and included false entries intended to conceal the fraudulent transfers. Later the fraud was discovered, and the trustee sued Wilkes for breach of contract. Wilkes argued the fraud occurred before the trustee had hired him. Is this a good defense? Discuss. (*In re F.W. Koenecke & Sons, Inc.*, 605 F.2d 310, 7th Cir. 1979.)

3. Timm, Schmidt & Co. (Timm) audited the financial statements of CFA, Inc., from 1973 to 1976.

In November 1975, CFA obtained a $300,000 loan from Citizens State Bank (Citizens), which relied on the financial statements prepared by Timm. In early 1977, Timm discovered material errors totaling over $400,000 in the 1974 and 1975 statements of CFA. When Citizens learned of these errors, it called CFA's loan due, and CFA went into receivership. Citizens lost $150,000 on its loans and sued Timm for negligence. All Timm employees swore they did not know the financial statements would be used by CFA to obtain loans, but the senior partner stated "as a certified public accountant, I know that audited statements are used for many purposes and that it is common for them to be supplied to lenders and creditors, and other persons." Timm claimed its contract was with CFA and it had no liability to Citizens. Is Timm correct? Discuss. (*Citizens State Bank v. Timm, Schmidt & Co.*, 335 N.W.2d 361, Wis. 1983.)

4. Alexander Grant & Co. (AGC) was engaged by GHP Corp. to prepare an unaudited financial statement based on information provided by GHP. GHP submitted copies of the statement to Spherex, Inc., to obtain credit. Later Spherex sustained losses in its dealings with GHP, it appearing that the information in the unaudited statements was inaccurate. Spherex sued AGC, which argued that it should not be liable in negligence to a third party with whom it had no contract, especially on an *unaudited* statement. Does it matter that the statement was unaudited? Discuss. (*Spherex, Inc. v. Alexander Grant & Co.*, 451 A.2d 1308, N.H. 1982.)

5. Reid, a fashion designer, turned $1.4 million over to her accountant, Silver, who in effect became her business manager. Over the course of his employment, Silver paid himself $90,000 for services rendered and $72,500 for accounting fees, frequently made interest-free loans to himself from Reid's funds, and was reluctant to make full and fair disclosure to Reid about the details of his activities. Reid sued for an accounting. Will Reid prevail? Discuss. (*Reid v. Silver*, 354 F.2d 600, 7th Cir. 1965.)

6. Beck Industries' trustee in bankruptcy sued Beck's auditors, Ernst & Ernst, alleging the auditors were guilty of negligence and breach of contract in failing to detect that Beck's earnings and overall financial condition had been much worse than publicly reported. The trustee alleged that the false statements caused Beck's board of directors to embark on

an ill-advised acquisition program which led to ruin. Two of Beck's directors, including its president, knew of the overstatements; the other directors did not. Ernst & Ernst raised a contributory negligence defense. Is this defense valid? Discuss. (*Shapiro v. Glekel*, 380 F.Supp. 1053, S.D.N.Y. 1974.)

7. Early in 1964, PMM acted as independent auditor for Yale Express System. Later PMM was hired to do some "special studies" of Yale's past and current income and expenses. While engaged in these studies sometime in 1964, PMM discovered that the earlier financial statements it had audited were substantially misleading. PMM did not disclose this fact to the stock exchanges on which Yale stock was traded until May 1965. Investors who had traded in Yale stock during the interim sued PMM for common-law fraud and for a Section 10(b) violation. PMM claimed it had no duty to disclose the information since the original error was not its fault. Is PMM liable under Section 10(b)? Discuss. (*Fischer v. Kletz*, 266 F.Supp. 180, S.D.N.Y. 1967.)

8. Peat Marwick prepared a tax return for plaintiff. Plaintiff signed the return without reviewing it. The return contained errors caused by Peat Marwick's negligence. Because of the errors, the IRS imposed penalties on the taxpayer, who sued Peat Marwick for indemnity (reimbursement of the penalty amount). Should plaintiff recover? Discuss. (*Bick v. Peat Marwick and Main*, 799 P.2d 94, Kan.App. 1990.)

9. Al had Aberrant Fund, Inc. (AF), which he controlled, purchase substantial amounts of Dilly Modest Systems (DMS) shares. These purchases kept the market price of DMS stock high, allowing Al to sell his personal DMS stock holdings at a big profit. AF later sold at a big loss because, *inter alia,* DMS's registration statement had stated that DMS had over $12 million in back orders when in reality it had much less, and had not disclosed that the primary back order customer was in financial trouble, could not pay its debts, and was controlled by DMS. AF sued Etan & Etan (E&E), accountants who helped prepare the registration statement. E&E showed that although it knew of the overstatement of back orders, GAAP did not require that the back orders be audited or that the overreporting be noted in the audit. Does compliance with GAAP insulate E&E from liability? Discuss. (*Admiralty Fund v. Hugh Johnson & Co.*, 677 F.2d 1301, 9th Cir. 1982.)

10. D accounting firm, which has been P's financial adviser for seven years, convinced P to invest in a truck leasing scheme that D arranged and managed through a corporation that its individual accountant/members owned. D's principals altered some investment documents, signed documents on P's behalf without a power of attorney, and made several misrepresentations to P about the progress of the venture. P sued D under Sec. 12(2) of the 1933 Securities Act. Can D be liable as a "seller"? Discuss. (*En Yun Hsu v. Leaseway Transportation Corp.*, FEDERAL SECURITIES LAW REPORTS, Para. 92,043, N.D.Cal. 1985.)

PART VI

PROPERTY: OWNERSHIP, CONTROL, AND PROTECTION

All of the world's material wealth consists of *property* of one type or another. The acquisition of property has been and continues to be one of the primary goals of a major portion of the world's population. What is more, a substantial percentage of all civil lawsuits ever commenced have arisen out of disputes over some sort of property. For these reasons, the rules of law governing the ownership of property are among the most fundamental in our legal system.

In a society without a system of laws, "ownership" of property would consist merely of physical possession plus the strength and wits to keep it. In an organized society, however, with rights and duties determined by law, the concept of ownership is considerably more sophisticated, in terms of both its complexity and the orderliness of its protection. In the modern sense, then, ownership comprises a group of rights (such as possession, use, enjoyment, and transfer) that are *protected and guaranteed by governmental authority*.

All property is divided into two basic categories: real property and personal property. Essentially, *real property* (often called *real estate* or *realty*) is land and most things affixed to it. *Personal property*, on the other hand, consists of every item of tangible or intangible property not included within the definition of real property. Items of tangible personal property are usually called *goods*.

In Part VI we explore various legal aspects of owning, controlling, and protecting real and personal property. Chapter 43 surveys the law of real property. In Chapter 44 we examine the landlord-tenant relationship, which is created when real property is leased. Chapter 45 surveys the law of personal property and then discusses the bailment relationship, which is created when the owner of an item of personal property transfers posssession, but not title, to another. In Chapter 46, we deal with (1) the disposition of both real and personal property upon the death of the owner and (2) the transfer of real and personal property through the establishment of a trust. Finally, Chapter 47 discusses insurance—one of the most important means of protecting the value of all types of property. The chapter also examines other kinds of insurance, such as life insurance.⚖

Chapter 43

Real Property

The Nature of Real Property

Interests in Real Property

Concurrent Ownership

Sales of Real Property

Adverse Possession

Regulation of Real Property Ownership, Use, and Sale

IN THIS CHAPTER we survey the principles of law relating to the ownership and control of real property. After exploring the fundamental nature of real property, we examine the various types of ownership interests and the process of transferring these interests.

THE NATURE OF REAL PROPERTY

The most important element of real property is, of course, the land itself. Things affixed to the land take the form of either vegetation or fixtures.

Land

The definition of *land* includes not only the surface of the earth but also everything above and beneath it. Thus the ownership of a tract of land theoretically includes both the air space above it and the soil from its surface to the center of the earth.

Air Rights

A landowner's rights with respect to the air space above the surface are called **air rights.** In recent years, air rights have become an important part of land ownership in some areas. In densely populated metropolitan areas, for instance, air space is often quite valuable from a commercial standpoint. Thus the owner of an office building might sell a portion of its air space to a party who wishes to build and operate a restaurant or group of apartments atop the building. And railroad companies with tracks running through downtown areas, where building space is at a premium, sometimes sell the space above their tracks for office building construction.

For practical reasons, modern courts have held that a landowner's air rights are not violated by airplanes flying at reasonable heights. If, however, a flight is low enough to actually interfere with the owner's use of the land (such as when the plane is taking off or landing), there is a violation of these air rights.

Subsurface Rights

The most practical result of the rule extending a landowner's property rights to the center of the earth is that he or she owns the *minerals* beneath the surface. When the land is sold, the buyer acquires any existing minerals, such as coal, even if they are not expressly mentioned. These minerals in the ground can also be owned *separately.* Thus a landowner might sell only the minerals or sell the rest of the land and expressly retain the minerals.

In some states (such as Texas and Pennsylvania) oil and natural gas are treated like other minerals with respect to ownership. That is, they can be owned while they are still in the ground.[1] The courts in a few states (such as California) take a contrary view, holding that oil and gas are not owned by anyone until pumped out of the ground. Of course, regardless of the type of mineral or the particular jurisdiction, an owner who *first removes* the minerals and *then sells* them is making a sale of personal property (i.e., goods), not real property.

Vegetation

Both natural vegetation, such as trees, and cultivated vegetation, such as corn, wheat, or other growing crops, are considered to be real property. Thus, in a land-sale transaction, the vegetation passes to the buyer along with the land unless expressly excluded from the sale.

When growing vegetation is sold by itself, and not with the land, the general rule today is that the transaction is a sale of personal property (goods). This rule holds true almost universally for growing crops.[2] The same rule is followed for growing timber in a majority of states, but several states treat a sale of growing timber as a sale of real property.

Fixtures

A **fixture** is an item that was originally personal property but that has been attached to the land (or to another fixture) in a relatively permanent fashion. Fixtures are viewed by the law as *real property.* Thus title to them passes to the buyer of real property unless the seller expressly excludes them from the transaction. In other words, even if the documents employed in the transaction describe only the land and are silent with respect to fixtures, title to them

---

[1] Ownership of oil, gas, or other minerals while still in the ground is referred to as *ownership in place.*
[2] See UCC Sec. 2-107.

nevertheless passes to the buyer. Items that are not fixtures, however, do not pass along with a sale of land unless they are expressly included in the terms of the transaction.

To illustrate: Jones contracts to sell his farm to Williams, and the contract describes only the boundaries of the land. Located on the farm are a house and a barn. These buildings are fixtures and will pass to Williams as part of the real property, as will the fence around the land. Inside the house, Jones's clothing and furniture are not fixtures, but the built-in cabinets and plumbing are. The hay stored in the barn is not a fixture, but the built-in feeding troughs are.

As is true of minerals, when a landowner removes a fixture from the soil or from the building to which it was attached and then sells the item *by itself,* it is considered a sale of *personal property* rather than real property. In fact, if a landowner removes a fixture with the intention that removal will be permanent, the item reverts back to its original status as personal property regardless of whether it is sold.

Determining Whether an Item Is a Fixture

Although the decision on whether a particular article is a fixture is often obvious (as in the case of a house), many items are difficult to classify. In general, a court will hold that an item is a fixture if there was *an intent that it become a permanent part of the real property.*

When the owner or occupier of land has not clearly expressed his or her intent, it must be determined from all the circumstances of the case. Following are three factors that are often considered in determining whether an item was intended to be a fixture.

Attachment.   An item is usually classified as a fixture if it is attached to a building in such a manner that it cannot be removed without damage to the building. Examples include shingles on the roof, built-in cabinets or appliances, a floor furnace, or a floor covering that is cemented in place.

Specialized Use.   An item is usually considered a fixture if it was specially made or altered for installation in a particular building. Examples include specially fitted window screens, drapes custom-made for an odd-sized window, and a neon sign created for particular business premises.

Custom.   Sometimes local custom dictates whether an item is a fixture. For example, in some parts of the country it is customary for houses to be sold with refrigerators. Where this custom exists a landowner's intent when installing the refrigerator is probably that it be a permanent addition. Thus it is a fixture. (The same principle applies, of course, to any other "customary" item.)

The following case illustrates the analytical approach employed by courts when determining whether an item was intended to be a fixture.

JOHNSON V. HICKS

Court of Appeals of Oregon,626 P.2d 938 (1981)

Case

Margaret and Hoy Johnson owned a tract of land in Klamath County, Oregon. Neil and Maxine Hicks (Hoy Johnson's sister) lived on an adjoining tract. In 1964, Hoy Johnson and Neil Hicks installed an irrigation system to serve both pieces of land. They shared both the labor and costs of installation. After installation, they also shared equally the maintenance and electricity costs for the system. The irrigation system contained approximately 700 feet of two-inch pipe that crossed the Johnson land and ran along the edge of

the Hicks land. In addition, the system included 1,500 feet of aluminum pipe used to irrigate the pasture on the Johnson land, and a pump, motor, and pump house not located on the Johnson or Hicks land. About three-fourths of the system was underground. Later, in this lawsuit, Hoy Johnson testified that his purpose in installing the system was to irrigate the pastureland, on which he raised cattle and horses. He also testified that the installation was to be permanent and that when he sold the pastureland he "let the sprinkler system go with it." Neil Hicks wanted the system primarily to irrigate his yard.

In April 1967, when Margaret and Hoy Johnson were experiencing marital problems, Hoy Johnson and Neil Hicks entered into an agreement declaring the irrigation system to be their joint property and "upon the death or incapacity of either of the parties hereto the property shall be in the ownership and control of the surviving party." Hicks later testified in this lawsuit that their intent in drawing up the agreement was as follows:

Well, at the time we made it up Hoy was the one—I told Hoy we were going to have trouble because—if something happened to him and she was involved in it. You know,

(continues)

JOHNSON V. HICKS

(continued from previous page)
we can't get along with her to begin with and he said that he can see our point and that we'll go to a lawyer and have him write this paper up, you know, in case something happened to him or to myself and there wouldn't be no women involved into it.

In 1969 Margaret and Hoy Johnson were divorced. The divorce decree awarded to Margaret the family home and the one-third of an acre on which it was located, her personal property, and all furniture and fixtures in the home. Hoy was awarded two other parcels of land and all other personal property. The irrigation system was not mentioned in the decree. From 1969 until April 1979 a portion of the irrigation pipe remained on Margaret's land, and she continued to use the water from the system for watering her yard and trees. During this time she neither offered nor was asked to contribute to the expense of operating the system; Hoy Johnson and Neil Hicks continued to split all costs for the system. Margaret did, however, pay an annual assessment to the Klamath Basin Improvement District for the right to use the irrigation water.

In 1979 Neil suggested to Hoy that they "cut her off," but Hoy refused because the amount of water Margaret used was very small and he had no objection to it. On April 1, 1979, however, Neil moved 140 feet of irrigation pipe from Margaret's land and placed it on his land and on adjoining land owned by a brother of Hoy's. Margaret, plaintiff, filed suit against Neil Hicks, defendant, alleging that the irrigation system was a fixture and that the part of the system on her property passed to her in the divorce decree as part of the real estate. She sought an injunction requiring Neil to restore the pipe to its original position on her land and prohibiting him from further interference with it. Margaret also sought damages caused by the loss of water, and Neil asserted a counterclaim for

the expenses of maintaining and operating the system. The trial court held that the part of the system on Margaret's property was not a fixture, and dismissed all claims. Margaret appealed.

Roberts, Judge:

In deciding whether an article used in connection with real property should be considered as a fixture and a part of the land . . . the usual tests are: (1) real or constructive annexation of the article to the realty; (2) appropriation or adaptation to the use or purposes of the realty with which it is connected; (3) the intention to make the annexation permanent.

The intention of making the article permanently accessory to the real property is to be inferred from the nature of the article, the relation of the party making or maintaining the annexation, the policy of the law in relation thereto, the structure and mode of annexation, and the purpose and use for which it is made. . . . It is the trend of judicial opinion to regard all of those things as fixtures which have been attached, whether physically or constructively to the realty with a view to the purposes for which the real property is held or employed, however slight or temporary the connection between the articles and the land. The important element to be considered is the intention of the party making the annexation. . . . The controlling intention is that which the law deduces from all of the circumstances of the installation of the article upon the land. [Many courts] have emphasized intent at the time of the attachment of the item to the real property as the controlling factor.

In this case we have the intent of both defendant Neil Hicks and plaintiff's former husband to consider, as well as their April 1, 1967, agreement, which purports to formalize their intent. A written agreement that a chattel [i.e., an item of personal property] already annexed to the soil shall [revert

to its original status as personal property], however, is binding only upon the parties to the agreement and those having notice. Plaintiff had no knowledge of the 1967 agreement. We therefore have to determine the intent of plaintiff's former husband and Neil Hicks with respect to the permanency of the pipe at the time of its installation in 1964. . . .

It is apparent that [Hoy Johnson and Neil Hicks] installed the irrigation system on the farm with a view to enhancing the production of the [land]. Irrigation in a semiarid region, like parts of Klamath County, is the very life of the land. It is beyond comprehension that the system was installed for any temporary purpose. . . . We infer Mr. Hicks' intent to be that the system they installed would be used to provide water for the two properties for so long as the Johnsons remained in possession of their parcel. We think it obvious that if Hoy Johnson had remained in possession of the entire three-acre parcel, he would have viewed the irrigation system as a permanent accessory, increasing the value and use of the property. That the parcel of land was later, in effect, subdivided, makes no difference as to his intention at the time of installation or in the status of the pipe at the present time. Further, Mr. Johnson said he had always been content to let plaintiff use the water and had resisted attempts to remove her supply.

It is important to note that we are not here determining water rights of any kind, but only plaintiff's right to continued possession of the irrigation pipe which had been on her property for 15 years and for 10 years in her exclusive possession. We find the pipe installed on plaintiff's property was a fixture and that defendants' removal of the pipe and subsequent possession wrongfully interfered with her rights. The trial court's order denying the mandatory injunction is therefore reversed. The injunction should be issued on remand.

(continues)

JOHNSON V. HICKS

(continued from previous page)

We remand to the trial court on the issue of damages. The only evidence in the record is that by the time of trial plaintiff had suffered some $870 in damages to trees, shrubs and lawn on her property due to lack of water after the removal of the irrigation pipe.

There is also evidence, however, that there was city water available to her but that she had this hookup removed. We therefore remand to the trial court to ascertain the actual damage to plaintiff's property, and whether she could have mitigated these damages. We express no opinion on defendant Hicks'

right to recover for contribution to the repair and maintenance of the system, since, because of the disposition of the case, no evidence was taken on this issue.

Reversed and remanded for further proceedings consistent with this opinion.⚖

INTERESTS IN REAL PROPERTY

Ownership of real property is not an "all or nothing" proposition. The total group of legal rights constituting complete ownership can be divided among several individuals. The particular set of rights owned in a given situation is referred to as an *estate* or an *interest* in real property. The common law developed a complex system of classifying and defining these various interests, a system which is described here in simplified form. Much of the terminology used to classify real property interests is of ancient origin. At the outset, the law distinguishes those interests that include the right of possession from those that do not. The so-called **possessory interests** are further subdivided into **freehold estates** and **nonfreehold estates.** The following discussion examines these types of possessory interests, and then outlines the different **nonpossessory interests.** It concludes by describing another classification, the so-called future interests in real property.

Freehold Estates

A freehold estate is one that can legally exist for an indefinite period of time.

Fee Simple

When a person has complete ownership of real property, his or her interest is described as a **fee simple estate.**[3] This is the most important type of freehold estate. In everyday usage, when someone is spoken

of as the "owner" or as "having title," it generally means that the individual owns a fee simple interest. The characteristics of a fee simple interest are: (1) ownership is of unlimited duration and (2) so long as the owner abides by the law and does not interfere with the rights of adjoining landowners, the owner is free to do whatever he or she chooses with the property.

If O, the owner of a fee simple interest in real property, conveys (transfers) the property to B, it is presumed that the entire fee simple is being conveyed. B will acquire a lesser interest only if the terms of the conveyance clearly so indicate. Thus a conveyance of the property "from O to B," with nothing said about the type of interest being conveyed, is deemed to transfer the entire fee simple interest to B.

Fee Simple Defeasible

Some interests in real property are classified as fee simple interests despite the fact that ownership is not absolute. Suppose, for example, that O conveys a fee simple interest to B, subject to the limitation that B's interest will cease upon the occurrence of a specified event. B's interest in this case is called a **fee simple defeasible.** It is a fee simple in every respect except that it is subject to the possibility of termination.

One of the most common limitations of this type relates to the *use* that is to be made of the land. For instance, the terms of the conveyance from O to B may state that B's ownership will continue only if the land is used for recreational purposes. The person entitled to the property if and when B's interest terminates is said to own a *future interest.* Future interests are discussed later in the chapter.

---

[3]Various other phrases are also employed. It is sometimes said that the person is the *fee owner* or that he or she owns the land *in fee, in fee simple,* or *in fee simple absolute.*

Life Estate

A **life estate** is an interest in real property, the duration of which is measured by the life of some designated person. For example, O, the fee simple owner, might convey the property to B "for B's lifetime." During his lifetime B would own a life estate. Similarly, if O's conveyance to B was "for the life of X," B would still own a life estate. (The latter is a much less common situation.) The person entitled to ownership after termination of a life estate owns a future interest.

Owning a life estate is not the equivalent of owning a fee simple for one's lifetime. It is true that the owner of the life estate (called the "life tenant") has the right to *normal use* of the property. For example, the life tenant can use it as a residence, farm it, conduct a business on it, allow another to use it in return for the payment of rent, or make any other reasonable use of it. However, the life tenant cannot do anything that will permanently damage the property and thus harm the owner of the future interest.

As an example of the limitations on a life tenant's use of the property, the right to cut timber on the land is somewhat restricted. The timber can be cut if it is required for fuel, fencing, or agricultural operations. But it cannot be cut for the purpose of *sale* unless (1) the life estate was conveyed to the life tenant specifically for that purpose, or (2) selling timber is the only profitable use that can be made of the land, or (3) the land was used for that purpose at the time the person became a life tenant, or (4) the owner of the future interest expressly permits the cutting.

Similarly, a life tenant can take oil and gas from existing wells and other minerals from existing mines if subsurface rights were not expressly excluded from the life estate. But this party cannot drill *new* wells or open *new* mines without authorization either in the document creating the life estate or at a later time from the owner of the future interest.

Although a life tenant is responsible to the owner of the future interest for any permanent damage he or she personally causes to the land, there is no such responsibility for damage caused by accidents, by third parties, or otherwise without the life tenant's fault.

A life tenant is also under a duty to pay taxes on the property. If this duty is neglected and the land is taken by the taxing authority, the life tenant is liable to the owner of the future interest.

Nonfreehold Estates

The nonfreehold estates, sometimes called **leasehold estates,** are created by a *lease* of real property in which the owner grants to another the temporary right to possess the property in return for the payment of rent.[4] In such a case, the owner is called the *lessor,* or *landlord,* and the occupier is called the *lessee,* or *tenant.*[5] Several different types of nonfreehold, or leasehold, estates may be created, depending on the terms of the lease agreement. The next chapter discusses the landlord-tenant relationship in detail.

Nonpossessory Interests
Easements

Essentially, an **easement** is the right to make some limited use of another's real property without taking possession of it. Stated another way, it is the right to do a specific thing on another's land. Sometimes an easement is referred to informally as a *right-of-way.* Examples of easements include the right to run a driveway or road across another's land, to run a power or telephone line above it, or to run a pipeline under it.

Types of Easements. Easements are either *appurtenant* or *in gross.* An **easement appurtenant** is one created specifically for use in connection with another tract of land. For example: A and B own adjoining tracts. A grants to B an easement to cross A's land to get to and from a highway. Here the easement on A's land is appurtenant, because it was created for use in connection with B's land. In this situation, A's land is called the **servient estate** and B's the **dominant estate.**

An **easement in gross,** on the other hand, is one *not* used in connection with another tract of land. For example, a telephone company has an easement in gross when it acquires the right to run poles and wires across A's land.

Whenever a tract of land subject to either type of easement is sold, the purchaser must continue to recognize the easement if he or she knew or should have known of its existence at the time of purchase. Even without such knowledge, the purchaser's ownership is subject to the easement if a document creating the interest was *recorded* (filed with the appropriate county official) prior to the purchase.

[4] Although the granting of a *right to drill* for oil and gas is often called a *lease* in popular usage, it is not truly a lease because it does not convey a possessory interest in real property.
[5] The "owner" in this situation might be the owner of a fee simple, of a fee simple defeasible, of a life estate, or even of a leasehold.

An easement appurtenant is said to "run with the land." This means that if the land being benefited by the easement (the dominant estate) is sold, the easement goes along with it. However, the owner of an easement appurtenant cannot sell or otherwise transfer it *by itself,* apart from the dominant estate. On the other hand, the owner of an easement in gross today is generally allowed to transfer it to another party.

Creation of Easements.   An easement can be created in several ways. Creation of an **easement by express grant or reservation** is the most common method. An express grant occurs when a landowner expresses an intent to convey an easement to another party. An express reservation occurs when a landowner sells the land itself but expressly reserves, or keeps, an easement on the land being sold. Because an easement is an interest in real property, the expression of an intent to grant or reserve such an interest must be made in a written document containing a legally sufficient description of both the land and the scope of the easement. The document also must contain the names of the parties, the duration of the interest, and the signature of at least the party making the grant or reservation. The document could be either a *deed,* discussed later in the chapter, or a *will,* discussed in Chapter 46.

An **easement by implication** also can be created where surrounding circumstances reasonably indicate that the parties probably intended to create such an interest. An easement exists by implication only if the following facts are proved:

1. An easement will be implied only when land is subdivided into two or more segments. This would occur, for example, when A, who owns twenty acres of land, sells ten acres out of the tract to B.

2. Prior to the subdivision, the owner of the entire tract must have been making a particular use of the property, and continuance of this use after the subdivision would require recognition of an easement. Thus, suppose that prior to A's sale of ten acres to B, A had constructed and used a ditch to improve the drainage of one part of the property. The ditch went through the portion that A kept, but it benefited the part sold to B by improving the drainage of that portion.

3. The use that A was making of the property before the subdivision must have been apparent; in other words, it must have been observable to anyone conducting a reasonable inspection of the property.

4. Continuation of the use must be reasonably necessary to B's use of his ten acres. In this case, because the drainage improvement benefited the land purchased by B, the ditch across A's ten acres probably would be viewed as reasonably necessary.

In the circumstances just described, B would have an easement across A's land giving B the right to continue using the ditch to drain water from B's land.

An **easement by necessity** also can be created in some circumstances. In contrast with an easement by implication, neither a subdivision of land nor a particular prior use is a prerequisite for the existence of an easement by necessity. However, the easement must be an absolute necessity, not just a reasonably necessary use. For example, a person leasing space in an office building has an easement by necessity that permits use of the stairs, elevators, hallways, and other common areas. Another example could be found in a situation similar to the one in which A sold a portion of his land to B. If B's ten acres had been at the back of the original tract, with no means of access to a public road other than by crossing A's ten acres, B would have an easement by necessity to cross A's land when going to and from B's land.

An **easement by prescription** (or **prescriptive easement**) may be created when someone actually does something on another's land for a period of time. Creation of an easement by prescription is similar to the acquisition of title by adverse possession, which is discussed later in the chapter. Such an easement is created if one party has actually exercised an easement (such as a driveway) on someone else's land continuously for a period of time specified by state statute, the use was made without the express consent of the landowner, and the use was an apparent one. The required period of time for creation of a prescriptive easement in a particular state is usually the same as for acquisition of title by adverse possession.

Profits

A **profit,** technically called a *profit à prendre,* is the right to go upon land and take something from it. Examples include the right to mine minerals, drill for oil, or take wild game or fish. A *right to take* minerals, which is a profit, must be distinguished from an actual *sale* of the fee simple interest in the minerals in the ground. The form the transaction takes depends on the intent of the parties, as evidenced primarily by the language used. Of course, in those states where oil and gas are not deemed capable of being owned while in the ground, any transaction in which the buyer is to drill for oil and gas is a profit.

The legal principles applicable to the creation, classification, transfer, and enforceability of profits are exactly the same as in the case of easements.

Licenses

In essence, a **license** is simply the landowner's permission for someone else to come upon his or her land. It does not create an interest in real property, because the landowner can revoke it at any time. But even though the grantee of the license does not have a legally enforceable *right* to go upon the land, the license (prior to its revocation) does keep the grantee from being considered a trespasser. Two examples of situations where licenses exist are:

1. The purchaser of a ticket to a movie or other amusement or sporting event has a license to enter the premises.

2. Sometimes a license is created when there is an ineffective attempt to create an easement or profit. For example, since these are required to be in writing, an oral easement or profit is merely a license.

Mortgages and Liens

A person who borrows money frequently has to grant the lender an interest in some item of property to secure payment of the debt. When the property to be used as security is real property, the landowner grants the lender an interest by executing a **mortgage.** The landowner-debtor is called the *mortgagor,* and the lender is called the *mortgagee.* In most states, the interest created by the mortgage is a **lien.**[6] If the mortgagor defaults on the obligation, the mortgagee has a right to *foreclose* the mortgage. This means that the real property can be seized and sold, usually at a public sale (auction), and the proceeds used to pay off the debt. The most common situation in which a mortgage is executed occurs when a buyer of real property borrows a portion of the purchase price and

signs a mortgage giving the lender an interest in the property being purchased. Because a mortgage conveys an interest in real property, it must be expressed in a written document that is sufficient to satisfy the statute of frauds.

In some situations, real property may be subjected to a creditor's interest without the landowner's consent. Such an interest is referred to very generally as an **involuntary lien,** to contrast it with the voluntary lien created by a mortgage. Statutes or constitutional provisions in most states provide for the involuntary creation of a **mechanic's lien** to secure payment for work done on or materials added to real property. For example, the contractor who builds a house on the land or adds a new room to an existing house usually has a mechanic's lien on the real estate that can be foreclosed if payment is not made. Many states require that, before any work is done or materials provided, the person claiming the lien give the landowner written notice that a mechanic's lien will be asserted. In addition, most states require that a written document in which the mechanic's lien is claimed be filed with the county clerk, recorder of deeds, or other designated county official.

Other types of involuntary liens also exist. When a plaintiff in a civil lawsuit receives a judgment for money damages against the defendant, and the defendant does not pay, in some states the plaintiff may create a **judgment lien** against the defendant's real property by filing a copy of the judgment with the appropriate county official.

It is important to note that, in the case of mechanic's liens, judgment liens, and other involuntary liens, the act of filing the written document with a public official actually *creates* the lien. As we will discuss later in the chapter, deeds, mortgages, and other documents creating *voluntary* interests in real property can be recorded to give greater protection to the person holding the interest, but the act of recording does not create the interest in such situations.

Future Interests

A final category of real property interest is the **future interest,** which consists of the residue remaining when the owner of a fee simple estate transfers less than a fee simple to someone else. Despite its name, a future interest does have a present existence and can be transferred, mortgaged, and so on. It is the actual use and enjoyment of the interest that is unavailable until a future time.

---

[6] In several states, however, a mortgage actually transfers *legal title* to the property to the mortgagee. In such a state, the mortgage normally provides that the mortgagee does not have the right of possession unless the mortgagor defaults on the underlying obligation; but the mortgagor does not actually own the property until the debt is paid and the mortgage released.

The subject of future interests is quite complex, with its own system of classification. Very generally, there are two basic types of future interest: the reversion and the remainder. A **reversion** exists when the owner of a fee simple transfers a lesser interest and retains the residue. For example, suppose that O, the owner of a fee simple estate, conveys a fee simple defeasible or life estate to B. If no provision is made for ownership of the future interest, it is owned by O and is called a reversion. O can separately transfer the reversion to someone else, or let it pass to his or her heirs. Upon expiration of B's interest, the reversion becomes a present fee simple estate. On the other hand, a **remainder** exists when the owner of a fee simple transfers a lesser interest and expressly provides that ownership will pass to a third party upon expiration of the lesser interest. Suppose that when O conveys the fee simple defeasible or life estate to B, O expressly provides that ownership will pass to C upon expiration of B's interest. In this case, C's future interest is called a remainder. C can separately transfer the future interest or let it pass to his or her heirs. When B's interest terminates, the remainder becomes a fee simple estate.

CONCURRENT OWNERSHIP

Any interest in real property that can be owned by one person can also be owned jointly by two or more persons. We will examine some of the more important types of concurrent ownership.

Tenancy in Common and Joint Tenancy
Characteristics
The most frequently encountered types of concurrent ownership are the **tenancy in common** and the **joint tenancy.** In a tenancy in common, the co-owners are called *tenants in common* or *cotenants.* In a joint tenancy they are called *joint tenants.*

The most important distinction between these two types of concurrent ownership has to do with disposition of a co-owner's interest when he or she dies. The interest of a tenant in common passes to that person's heirs according to his or her will, or according to state statute if there was no will. The heirs and the surviving co-owner(s) then become tenants in common. The joint tenancy, on the other hand, is characterized by a *right of survivorship*, which means that the interest of a deceased joint tenant passes to the surviving joint tenant(s).

Creation
A tenancy in common can be created in several ways. For example, if O conveys a fee simple estate "to A and B," the real property will be owned by A and B as tenants in common. Similarly, if O dies and his land passes to his heirs, A and B, the property will be owned by A and B as tenants in common. Or if O conveys a fractional interest (such as one-half or one-third) to A, the property will be owned by O and A as tenants in common.

A joint tenancy is more difficult to create and, consequently, is not as frequently used or as important as a tenancy in common. In most states, concurrent ownership of real property is presumed to be a tenancy in common, and will be a joint tenancy only if explicitly created. Even the use of the terms "joint tenancy" or "joint tenants" is not a clear enough expression to create a joint tenancy in most states, because people often use such terms in a nontechnical sense to refer to a tenancy in common. Thus, if O wishes to create a joint tenancy between A and B, in most states O would have to refer expressly to the *right of survivorship* in addition to using the terms joint tenancy or joint tenants. Moreover, a joint tenancy traditionally could be created only if the joint tenants received their interests at the same time and in the same document, and only if their fractional interests were *equal*. In recent years, statutes in a few states have removed the requirement that a joint tenancy must be created at the same time by a single document. These requirements have never existed for the creation of a tenancy in common.

Partition
In either a tenancy in common or a joint tenancy, none of the co-owners owns any segregated portion of the land. Instead, each owns an undivided fractional interest in the entire tract of land. The tenants in common or joint tenants can agree in writing to *partition* the land; but if they do so, their relationship as co-owners ends, and each becomes the owner of a specifically designated section of the property. If one or more of the co-owners wants to partition the land but the parties are unable to reach unanimous agreement on the division, any one of them can initiate a lawsuit to have the land partitioned. In their decisions, courts commonly express a preference for a partition *in kind,* which is a physical division of the property into sections of equal value. As a practical matter, however, it is extremely difficult for a court to

accomplish a physical division that gives each former co-owner a section of clearly equal value. Consequently, most court-ordered partitions ultimately involve a sale of the property and an equal division of the proceeds.

Condominiums and Cooperatives

Although the **condominium** form of ownership was used in some European cities before and during the Middle Ages, only in recent years has it become popular in this country. Most buildings subject to condominium ownership today are physically similar to apartments, and may contain only a few units or as many as several hundred. Ordinarily, a person owns a fee simple estate in the living space of a particular unit, but not in the land on which the unit rests. The fee simple interest in the living space may be owned solely by an individual, or it may be subject to any of the various forms of concurrent ownership such as a tenancy in common. In addition, a tenancy in common among the owners of the living space units exists with respect to other areas such as common roofs and walls, parking lots, and recreation areas.

Although a building subject to **cooperative** ownership may also physically resemble an apartment building, this form of ownership is quite different than a condominium. A *cooperative corporation* is formed under special state statutory provisions, and the corporation owns the building. Each occupier of a living unit owns a share of stock in the corporation and leases the unit from the corporation. Because the corporate entity itself owns the real property, a cooperative is not technically a form of concurrent ownership.

Marital Property

Tenancy by the Entireties

Under the English Common law, a conveyance of real property to husband and wife created a **tenancy by the entireties.** A tenancy by the entireties is essentially the same as a joint tenancy with right of survivorship, the surviving spouse taking complete ownership on the death of the other. Unlike a joint tenancy, a tenancy by the entireties cannot be severed by one party. A tenancy by the entireties also cannot be transferred by one spouse without the consent of the other, and the creditors of one spouse cannot reach the property without consent of the other.

The tenancy by the entireties has been abolished in several states and modified in others during recent years. Today, the tenancy by the entireties exists in about 20 states. In those states abolishing this form of ownership, a conveyance of real property to husband and wife will create either a joint tenancy or tenancy in common, depending on the language of conveyance.

Traditionally, the husband had the exclusive right to control and possession of property held in a tenancy by the entireties. Today, in those states still recognizing the tenancy by the entireties, statutory changes have given the spouses equal rights of control and possession.

Community Property

Another system of marital property ownership in this country is referred to as **community property.** The origin of the community property system can be traced directly to Spanish marital property law, which had borrowed the concept from medieval Germanic tribes in Europe. Nine American states presently employ the community property system. In five of these—Arizona, California, Louisiana, New Mexico, and Texas—the community property system was simply a continuation of Spanish law that had been in effect before statehood. Idaho, Nevada, and Washington voluntarily adopted the system early in their settlement, and Wisconsin adopted it in 1986.

The community property system recognizes two types of property: community property and separate property. Each spouse owns an undivided one-half interest in all community property, an interest which passes to his or her heirs upon death. Each has complete ownership of his or her separate property.

Because the community property system is based on the concept that the marital relationship itself is an entity, and that this entity benefits materially from the time and effort of both spouses, most property acquired by the husband or wife during marriage is community property. This includes the salary, wages, or other income earned by either spouse, income earned from community property, and property bought with the proceeds or income from community property. Money or property is the separate property of one of the spouses only if it was acquired by that person before marriage, or acquired after marriage by gift or inheritance. The income generated by one spouse's separate property is his or her separate property in a majority of the community property states. In any situation in which there is a question whether an item of property is community or separate, there is a strong legal presumption that it is community. The various community property states have their own specific rules for determining which spouse has management rights over particular types of community property.

Other Marital Property Rights

Various other property rights are created by marriage. The English common law gave the wife a right called **dower,** consisting of a life estate in one-third of her husband's real property after his death. The husband had a right called **curtesy,** consisting of a life estate in all of his wife's real property after her death. Almost all states have abolished or greatly altered these common-law rights in recent years. Most states, however, do provide a surviving spouse with some type of interest after the death of the other spouse to insure that the survivor will at least be able to continue living in their shared residence (i.e., the **homestead**).

SALES OF REAL PROPERTY

Next to leases, sales are the most commonly occurring real estate transactions. Whether such sales involve a residential house and lot, a farm, or other real property, they are the most monetarily significant transactions many people ever experience.

Most real estate sales involve the transfer of a fee simple interest in the surface, minerals, or both. Transfer of other types of interests may be accomplished in much the same way, but the procedures are often modified to fit the particular circumstances. Leasehold interests are usually created simply by the signing of a lease contract. Throughout the following discussion we will assume that the transaction is of the most common type—the sale of a fee simple interest.

Brokers

When a landowner wishes to sell property, the first step usually is to contact and employ a real estate broker (or "agent"). Although this is not required (the landowner can, of course, sell the land without help), it is usually desirable unless the owner already has a buyer lined up.

The function of the broker is to find a buyer. This is usually the extent of the broker's authority; he or she ordinarily is not given authority to actually sell or even to make a contract to sell. In return for finding a

buyer the broker is entitled to be compensated by receiving an agreed-upon *commission,* which is usually a percentage of the selling price.

A formal employment contract setting out the terms of the arrangement should be made with the broker. Indeed, in many states a broker has no legally enforceable right to a commission unless the agreement to pay it is in writing.

The arrangement with the broker can be of several types, including an open listing, exclusive agency, or exclusive right to sell. In an **open listing,** the broker is entitled to a commission only if he or she is the *first one* to procure a buyer who is "ready, willing, and able" to buy at the stated selling price. The owner is free to sell the land personally or through another broker without incurring liability to the employed broker. Open listings are not extremely common today.

A second type, the **exclusive agency,** arises when the owner gives assurance that no other broker will be hired during the term of the agreement. If the owner does employ another broker who procures a buyer, the sale is valid but the original broker is still entitled to the agreed commission. However, the owner is entitled to sell the land *personally,* without the aid of the employed broker or any other broker. If the owner makes the sale without assistance, the employed broker is not entitled to a commission.

The type of arrangement most advantageous to the broker is an **exclusive right to sell,** in which the employed broker is entitled to the agreed commission if the property is sold during the agreement's duration by anyone, whether done with the aid of the employed broker or some other broker or by the owner acting alone.

Multiple Listing Services

In many localities today, real estate brokers have formed multiple listing services. A **multiple listing service (MLS)** is an arrangement whereby brokers in the area pool their listings, each member having access to the pool. A participating broker ordinarily obtains either an exclusive agency or exclusive right to sell agreement from the landowner, and then places that listing in the local MLS. If another broker who also is a member of the MLS finds a buyer for the property, the commission is split between the listing and selling brokers under the terms of the MLS membership agreement signed by each participating broker.

LEGAL FOCUS

Ethics

Legal Focus

Today the law in most states requires a real estate broker to reveal to a prospective buyer any information about the condition of the property that would materially affect its value. In some states, the broker (and the seller as the broker's principal) is liable to a buyer for failing to disclose such information only if it is proved that the broker actually knew about the condition at the time of sale; in other states, however, the broker is liable to the buyer even without actual knowledge if a reasonable investigation by the broker would have uncovered the information.

This duty normally applies to physical defects in the real estate, such as a cracked foundation or a leaky roof. Recently, however, questions have arisen as to whether a broker should also be required to disclose to the buyer whether the seller or a prior occupant had AIDS. Despite compelling scientific evidence that it is impossible for a person to contact AIDS by occupying a house that previously had been occupied by an AIDS victim, many buyers would shy away from buying such a house. Such a buyer might be acting on the basis of misinformation, hysteria, or the fear that the home's resale value would be diminished. The Federal Fair Housing Act prohibits discrimination against handicapped buyers or renters of residential real estate, and AIDS clearly qualifies as a handicap. This law, and a number of similar state statutes, do not provide such protection for *seller*, however. Thus, these laws neither prohibit nor require the broker's disclosure that the prior occupant had AIDS. The small number of state court decisions on the question, based primarily on the common-law duty of disclosure in real estate transactions, have produced no discernible trend.

Because of the virtual absence of applicable legal standards, the primary question for a broker caught in such a situation is an ethical one. The broker normally represents the seller. As the seller's agent, the broker owes the seller several moral duties in addition to those legal duties created by the law of agency. Perhaps the most important moral obligation owed by the broker to the seller is that of loyalty—the duty always to act in the seller's best interests unless the law requires otherwise. On the other hand, one might argue that the broker also owes to the buyer a moral duty to refrain from acting in a way that would cause reasonably foreseeable harm to the buyer. Such harm to the buyer might take the form of psychological trauma if the facts are later discovered, or more tangibly, reduced resale value of the property if the buyer later wishes to sell and the facts become known.

If the broker knows, or reasonably should know, that the seller or another previous occupant had AIDS, and does not tell the buyer, does the broker violate a moral duty to the buyer? Although a nonfrivolous argument may be made that such a moral duty does exist, this duty would conflict with the broker's duty to the seller, creating a moral dilemma. Most students of ethics would view the broker's duty of loyalty to the seller as weighing more heavily in an ethical analysis than the duty to the buyer. Thus, the broker probably acts most ethically by not disclosing, again assuming that the law in a particular state does not require disclosure. (It should be noted, however, that several states are currently considering legislation that would specifically determine whether such a disclosure by the broker is required, permitted, or prohibited.) The moral dilemma becomes far more difficult to resolve, however, if the broker knows that the prior occupant had AIDS, and the prospective buyer specifically asks the broker about the fact. Here, the broker cannot fulfill the duty to the seller without telling an out-and-out lie to the buyer. In such a case, the law probably resolves the broker's dilemma, because lying in response to a specific question will normally be illegal fraud.

The Contract

When a buyer is found, a contract for sale will ordinarily be made. When making an offer to buy, or when entering the contract itself, the buyer often makes a deposit referred to as **earnest money.** The real estate sale contract sometimes is called an *earnest money contract,* and normally provides that the buyer will forfeit the earnest money if he or she breaches the contract.

To be enforceable, a contract for the sale of land has to be in writing in almost all circumstances. Although the contract usually is evidenced by a detailed formal document signed by both seller and buyer, the requirement of written documentation can be satisfied by informal instruments such as letters or telegrams. The writing, whether formal or not, must contain *all the essential terms* of the agreement and must be signed by the party against whom enforcement is sought.[7] If any of the essential terms are missing, the writing is considered insufficient; oral testimony will not be allowed to fill in the gaps, and the contract is unenforceable.

Specifically, the terms that must be included in the written contract for sale are (1) the *names* of the seller and buyer and an indication of their intent to be bound, (2) a *description* of the property sufficient to identify it, and (3) the *price*.

More is said about the required description in the discussion of deeds later in this chapter. (Incidentally, if the seller does ultimately convey title by giving a deed, it is immaterial whether there was an enforceable contract. The contract simply prevents one party from reneging prior to transfer of title.)

Title Examination, Insurance, and Survey

One of the main reasons for initially making a sale contract rather than immediately transferring ownership is to give the buyer an opportunity to investigate the seller's title (often called a **title examination**). This essentially involves an examination of all officially recorded documents concerning the property. The examination is usually made by an attorney employed either by the purchaser, by the lending institution from which the purchase price is being borrowed, or by a title insurance company.

The attorney may personally search the public records and on the basis of this investigation issue a "certificate of title" giving his or her opinion as to the validity of the seller's title. Or the attorney may examine an **abstract,** which is a compilation of the official records relating to a particular parcel of land. Privately owned *abstract companies* or *abstracters* produce such abstracts and keep them current.

The sale contract often requires the seller to provide evidence of a good title. The certificate of title is used as such evidence in some parts of the country, while in other areas the abstract and the attorney's opinion based thereon provide the required evidence. It is also becoming more frequent for the contract to require the seller to provide the buyer with "title insurance." This may be used as the sole evidence of title, or it may be required in addition to other evidence. Title insurance, which is purchased from a company engaged in the business of selling such insurance (often called a *title company*), simply provides that the issuing company will compensate the buyer for any loss if the title ultimately proves defective. Of course, the title company will issue such a policy only if its own attorneys feel, after making a title examination, that the title is good.

Unless a survey has been made very recently, the seller is often required under the contract to have a new survey made. A licensed surveyor will be employed to make sure that the described boundaries are correct and that no buildings or other encroachments lie on the boundary line.

Financing and Closing the Sale

Many times the buyer does not have sufficient funds available to pay the agreed price. In such cases, after the contract is made but before the transfer of title, the buyer must obtain the necessary financing. Savings and loan associations are one of the most frequently used sources of such funds, especially for the purchase of residential property. As we mentioned earlier, the buyer (mortgagor) normally executes a mortgage to the lender (mortgagee) as security for the loan.

Sometimes the seller provides the financing by permitting the buyer to pay the purchase price in installments. In such a case, the seller may immediately transfer title to the buyer and take a mortgage to secure payment, or the seller and buyer may agree that title will not be transferred to the buyer until the purchase price is completely paid. The latter type of ar-rangement is often called a **contract for deed.**

The actual transfer of ownership usually takes place at the **closing** (or **settlement**)—the meeting attended by the seller and buyer as well as other interested parties such as their attorneys, the broker, and a representative of the mortgagee. At the meeting the seller signs and delivers to the buyer a *deed* that transfers the ownership; and the buyer pays the purchase price. (As a practical matter, however, the representative of the mortgagee may actually pay the seller.) It is also common for the mortgage to be executed at the closing and for other incidental financial matters to be settled (such as apportionment of property taxes and insurance that the seller may have prepaid).

---

[7]The signature can be that of the party's authorized agent. However, in most states, a contract for the sale of real estate signed by an agent is enforceable only if the agent's authorization is also in writing. (The same rule is true for the signing of a deed, discussed later in this chapter.)

Sometimes a closing occurs in a different manner, by the use of an "escrow agent." The **escrow agent** is a disinterested third party to whom the seller has delivered the deed and to whom the buyer has made payment. It is fairly common for an institution such as a title insurance company to serve as escrow agent. This party's instructions generally are to close the deal by delivering the deed to the buyer and the payment to the seller on receipt of the required evidence of good title.

The Deed

Types of Deeds

As we stated earlier, title to real property is conveyed by means of a written deed. Several types of deeds exist, each involving particular legal consequences.

General Warranty Deed. From the buyer's point of view, the **general warranty deed** is by far the most desirable kind to obtain, because it carries certain warranties, or covenants, that the title is good. These warranties may be expressed in the deed, but even if not expressed they are *implied* if the document is actually a general warranty deed. Whether a particular deed is one of general warranty depends on the language used in it. The wording necessary to create such a deed varies from state to state. In Illinois and Michigan, for example, the verb phrase *convey and warrant* makes it a general warranty deed. The warranties, which overlap somewhat, usually consist of the following: (1) **Covenant of seisin.** The seller (called *grantor* in the deed) guarantees that he or she has good title to the land conveyed. (2) **Covenant against encumbrances.** The grantor guarantees that there are no encumbrances on the land except as stated in the deed. (An *encumbrance* includes any type of lien or easement held by a third party.) The existence of such an encumbrance causes a breach of this warranty by the grantor, even if the grantee (the buyer) knows about it when receiving the deed, unless the deed states that the title is "subject to" the particular encumbrance. (3) **Covenant for quiet enjoyment.** The grantor guarantees that the grantee (or those to whom the grantee later conveys the property) will not be evicted or disturbed by a person having a better title or a lien.

Special Warranty Deed. In a **special warranty deed,** there is a warranty only that the title has not been diminished in any way by a personal act of the grantor. For example, suppose the grantor had previously executed a mortgage on the land that the deed does not mention. If the grantee later has to pay off the mortgage or if it is foreclosed and the grantee loses the property, the grantor will be liable to the grantee for damages. On the other hand, if the grantor has not personally encumbered the title but an outstanding title or interest in the land is later asserted by some third person, the grantor incurs no liability. This situation might arise, for instance, if the land is encumbered by a valid lien created by someone who owned the land prior to the grantor. The special warranty deed is a sufficient performance of the seller's obligations under the sale contract unless that contract specifically required a general warranty deed.

Quitclaim Deed. In a **quitclaim deed,** the grantor does not really purport to convey any title at all to the grantee. The deed says, in essence, "If I have any present interest in this land, I hereby convey it to you." This deed is not a sufficient performance of the grantor's obligations under the sale contract unless the contract so provides. Quitclaim deeds are often used as a form of *release.* For example: A owns the land, but X arguably has some type of interest in it, and A negotiates with X for a release of X's claim. One way of accomplishing the release is for A to obtain a quitclaim deed from X. Quitclaim deeds are also frequently employed by government entities (such as cities and counties) when they sell land.

Deed of Bargain and Sale. The **deed of bargain and sale** purports to convey title but does not contain any warranties. Even though differing in form, this deed conveys the same type of title as a quitclaim deed. It also is not a sufficient performance of the grantor's obligations under the sale contract unless the contract so provides.

Requirements of a Valid Deed

Because a deed accomplishes a present transfer of a property interest, *consideration* is not required. The owner can give away the property if he or she wishes. Of course, a *sale contract* must be supported by consideration, as must any other executory contract. A promise to make a gift of land or of anything else is generally not enforceable; but a completed gift by delivery of a deed is perfectly valid, assuming that there is no intent to defraud the grantor's creditors. Even though there is no requirement that a grantee give consideration for a deed or that consideration be stated in the deed, it is customary for the deed to contain a *recital of consideration*—a statement of what consideration is being given by the grantee. It is also customary for the recital to state merely a nominal consideration (such as $10) rather than the price actually paid.

There are several requirements that a deed must meet in order to transfer a real property interest. Although these requirements vary slightly among the states, they may be summarized as follows.

Grantor and Grantee.   The deed must name a grantor and grantee. The grantor must have legal capacity. If the grantor is married, it is generally desirable to have the grantor's spouse named as a grantor as well, for several reasons. In most states, if the property is occupied by husband and wife as their residence, or homestead, both must join in a conveyance of the property even if only one of them owns it. And as previously mentioned, the laws of many states give one spouse certain types of rights with respect to the property of the other regardless of whether the property is their homestead, and these rights are extinguished only if the grantor's spouse joins in the deed.

Words of Conveyance.   The deed must contain words of conveyance—words indicating a present intent to transfer ownership to the grantee, such as "I, Ruth Smith, do hereby grant, sell, and convey. . . ."

Description.   The deed must contain an adequate description of the land being conveyed.

Signature.   The deed must be signed by the grantor. For the reasons already discussed, it is also usually desirable to obtain the signature of a married grantor's spouse.

Delivery.   The deed must be delivered to the grantee.

Methods of Describing Land

As previously mentioned, a valid deed must contain an adequate description of the property being conveyed. Although this description should be (and usually is) stated in the deed, it is permissible for the deed to refer to a sufficient description contained in another document.

Land can be adequately described in several ways, but regardless of the method employed the property must be identified in such a way that there can be no mistake about exactly which parcel of land is being conveyed. There is a general tendency for the courts to require a greater degree of precision in a deed than in a sale contract. For example, in the case of

residential property, a sale contract usually is enforceable if the description is merely a street name and number in a particular city and state. In many states, however, such a description is not sufficient for a deed to be a valid conveyance of title to the property.

Government Survey.   In those states west of the Mississippi River (except Texas) and in Alabama, Mississippi, Florida, Illinois, Indiana, Ohio, and Michigan, land can be described by reference to the **United States Government Survey.** This survey was adopted by Congress in 1785 for the purpose of describing government-owned land that was to be transferred to states, railroads, and settlers. It uses meridians and parallels to divide the surveyed areas into quadrangles that are approximately 24 miles on each side. Each quadrangle is further divided into 16 tracts called **townships** that are approximately 6 miles on each side.

Metes and Bounds.   In those states not using the U.S. Government Survey (the eastern states and Texas), it is common for land to be described by **metes and bounds.** *Metes* means measures of length; *bounds* refers to the boundaries of the property. A metes and bounds description essentially just delineates the exterior lines of the land being conveyed. It may make use of a *monument* (a natural or artificial landmark such as a river or street) to constitute a boundary or to mark a corner of the tract. A metes and bounds description begins at a well-identified point and runs stated distances at stated angles, tracing the boundary until it returns to the starting point.

Plat.   The two methods just discussed, reference to the government survey and metes and bounds, are normally used to describe land in rural and semirural areas that have not been formally subdivided and platted. Most land in urban areas has been surveyed by private developers and subdivided into numbered blocks and lots on a **plat** (map) that is recorded (filed) with a designated county official. In almost all parts of the country, it is common to describe urban land by reference to the lot and block number in the recorded plat.

In the following case, we will see how problems can arise from "homemade" deeds. The case also illustrates that a court will, where it is possible to do so, attempt to make sense out of an imprecisely drafted deed.

BAKER V. ZINGELMAN

Superior Court of Pennsylvania, 393 A.2d 908 (1978)

Margaret and Carl DeBow owned a tract of land known as the Lakeland Allotment. There was a plat subdividing the land into lots, but no actual subdivision had occurred. The property was mostly farmland, and the DeBows lived in the farm house and operated an antique shop in the barn behind the house. There also were several other sheds and garages on their property. In 1968 they built and moved into a new home west of the land in question. They then asked Marie Baker (Margaret's sister) and her husband George to leave their home in Cleveland, Ohio, move to the farmhouse on the Lakeland Allotment, and operate the antique shop. They agreed to do so, and Margaret prepared a deed conveying the property to the Bakers.

Before preparing the deed, Margaret had "walked off" (measured) the land to be transferred, and asked the Bakers if they thought it was sufficient footage to include the buildings located on the land. Margaret stated that if the land she measured off was not sufficient to include the buildings, "we can clear it up later." The deed prepared by Margaret began "at a point where the east line of the proposed Michigan Avenue intersects the south line of West Erie Street" and then followed the directional and distance description matching a lot on the Lakeland Allotment plat. Michigan Avenue was an unopened street, and Margaret admitted that she did not know exactly where it began when she prepared the deed.

The Bakers moved into the farmhouse and reopened and operated the antique shop in 1971. During the same year Carl DeBow died. In 1973 Margaret married Zingelman, her present husband. It appears that this remarriage contributed in some way to the problems that later arose. Sometime in 1973 George Baker became upset with Margaret because she parked her truck in the garage which the Bakers claim is located on their property. There was a falling out between the families about this time. Margaret informed the Bakers that part of the barn, the garage, and sheds located on the land extended onto her adjacent land. By early 1975, Margaret's attorney informed the Bakers that the part of the barn which projected onto Margaret's property would be forcibly removed unless the Bakers chose to purchase for $10,000 the strip of property which would clear up the location problem of the buildings. The Bakers, plaintiffs, then sued to enjoin Margaret from parking her truck in the garage and from cutting off part of the barn.

At the trial, the testimony of two surveyors disclosed that all of one shed and garage and a portion of another shed and 13 feet of the barn extended onto Margaret's property. The lower court, however, enjoined Margaret from any further trespass and ordered her to convey to the Bakers the strip of land which would then place the buildings on the Baker property, in order to effectuate the original intent of the parties in their conveyance of 1971. Margaret, the defendant, appealed.

Cercone, Judge:

... Defendant's argument stems from the legal principles and cases stating that when the language of a deed is clear and unambiguous, the intent of the parties must be gleaned solely from the instrument. Where a portion of a building is not included in the description of the deed and it is not clear from the deed that the parties meant for the entire building to pass, only that portion of the building passes that is covered in the description. In the case before us, defendant argues that the description in the deed was clear, ... [and] that since there was no mention of any of the buildings in the deed, the judge should not have allowed parol evidence concerning the alleged inducement by Margaret for her sister to move to Pennsylvania.

Although this is a correct statement of the law, we must remember the lower court sat in equity. It is a general proposition of equity that when a person grants a thing, he intends to grant also that without which the thing cannot be enjoyed. We must assume the parties intended a reasonable result. The description in the deed before us was not prepared by a professional, but by defendant, who admitted she did not know exactly where Michigan Avenue began at the time of the deed preparation. There very easily could have been a mistake or ambiguity in the deed concerning the description, regardless of the omission of the word "building." Where such an ambiguity exists, the surrounding circumstances may be considered to determine the intent of the parties, and the subsequent acts of the parties are important to manifest their intentions. The actions of the parties subsequent to the deed were that the Bakers moved into the farmhouse and operated the antique shop in the barn. They obviously relied on the deed as having conveyed to them their interest in the property and in the buildings. It was only after the sisters' "falling out" that the boundary dispute arose. The proposed sale of the strip of land which would clear the building at a price of $10,000 seems extremely unreasonable in light of the fact that the deed of 1971 conveyed the majority of the land without any consideration passing.

(continues)

BAKER V. ZINGELMAN

(continued from previous page)

Even if the language of the deed can be construed as being precise and clear on its face, the cases do make exceptions where encroachments are minor and where it would be illogical and unreasonable for the grantor to have conveyed only part of buildings. Here, plaintiffs were living in the house and operating the antique shop in the barn unhindered until the argument occurred. It is extremely unlikely that 13 feet of the barn, one garage, and part of two other sheds were deliberately excluded from the conveyance.

Taking all these facts into consideration, we must agree with the lower court that the defendant intended to convey sufficient footage to cover the house, barn, and related buildings to her sister and her husband at the time of the original deed in 1971.

[Judgment for plaintiffs, the Bakers, is affirmed.]◇◇

Acknowledgment

An **acknowledgment** is a formal declaration before a designated public official, such as a notary public, by a person who has signed a document, that he or she executed the document as a voluntary act. The public official places his or her signature and seal after the declaration and the declarant's signature. The resulting instrument, referred to as a *certificate of acknowledgment,* is attached to the document to which it relates.

In most states an acknowledgment is not required for a deed to be valid, but it is required as a prerequisite to "recording."

Recording

Recording is the act of filing the deed with a public official, referred to in different states as the "recorder of deeds," "register of deeds," or any of several other titles. The official copies the deed into the record books, indexes it, and returns the original to the person who filed it.

As between the grantor and grantee, an otherwise valid deed is perfectly good even if it is not recorded. The purpose of recording procedures, which exist in every state, is to give notice to the world at large that the transfer of title has taken place. Frequently referred to as "constructive notice," this means that third parties are treated as having notice regardless of whether they actually do.

State recording statutes generally provide that an unrecorded deed, though valid between grantor and grantee, is void with respect to any subsequent bona fide purchaser. A **bona fide purchaser (BFP)** is a good faith purchaser for value. For example, suppose that O sells a tract of land to B, and B does not record her deed. O then sells the same land to C by executing another deed. If C pays for the land rather than receiving it as a gift, he is giving *value.* If C does not know of the earlier conveyance to B when he purchases, he is acting in *good faith.* Thus C qualifies as a BFP and has good title. In this situation B has no title. But if B has recorded her deed prior to C's purchase, B would have title even if C later gave value and acted in good faith. The reasoning is that C could have discovered B's interest if he had checked the records.

Although there is some conflict on the point, the courts in a majority of states hold that C qualifies as a BFP even if he does not record his own deed. (Of course, if he does not do so, he runs the risk of having the same thing happen to him that happened to B. If there was a "C," there could later be a "D.")

Regarding the status of C as a BFP, another point must be made. If B, the first grantee from O, is actually *in possession of the land* when C acquires his interest, this possession serves as notice to C. Thus, even if B did not record and C did not have actual knowledge of B's interest, C nevertheless is not a BFP.

Recording statutes apply not only to the sale of a fee simple interest but also to the conveyance of any other type of interest in land. For example, if O executes a mortgage to B, giving her a lien on the property, B should record her mortgage. If she does not, she risks losing her interest to a subsequent BFP.

Furthermore, the word *purchaser* actually means a grantee of any type of interest in the land, even such interests as liens or easements. Suppose, for instance, that O sells to B, who does not record her deed. O later borrows money from C and executes a mortgage purporting to give C a lien on the land. By making the loan to O, C is giving value. If C receives the mortgage without knowledge of the earlier conveyance to B, he is acting in good faith and is treated as a BFP. Thus C's mortgage is valid, and B's ownership is subject to it. If B had been a mortgagee herself instead of an actual grantee of the title, the same rules would apply to the conflict between B and C, the two mortgagees.

ADVERSE POSSESSION

Under some circumstances, a party can acquire ownership of land by taking possession of it and staying in possession for a certain number of years. The required time period is established by statute and varies from state to state, ranging from five years in California to thirty years in Louisiana.

Ownership acquired in this manner is frequently referred to as **title by adverse possession** or **title by limitation**.[8] Since it is not acquired by deed, there is nothing to record. Thus the recording statutes do not apply, and title by adverse possession, once acquired, cannot be lost to a subsequent BFP. Of course, even though such title is not *acquired* by deed, it can be *conveyed* by deed to someone else. Such a deed would be subject to all the rules applicable to deeds in general, including the recording statutes.

Requirements for Title by Adverse Possession

Not all types of possession will ripen into ownership. The possession must be "adverse," which means, in effect, that it must be actual, hostile, open and notorious, and continuous.[9]

Actual Possession

The requirement that possession be *actual* simply means that the possessor must have exercised some type of *physical control* over the land that indicates a claim of ownership. The person need not actually live on the property, although this certainly constitutes

actual possession. What is required is that the possessor act toward the land as an average owner probably would act, taking into account the nature of the land. For example, if it is farmland, the farming of it constitutes actual possession. Erecting buildings or other improvements may also be sufficient.

Construction of a fence or building that extends over the true boundary line and onto the land of an adjoining property owner generally constitutes actual possession of that part of the land encompassed by the fence or located under the building. Thus, if the other requirements of adverse possession are met, the party erecting the fence or building will become the owner of the area in question after the prescribed period of time.

Hostile Possession

The requirement that the possession be *hostile* does not mean that it must be accompanied by ill feelings. What it means is that possession must be *nonconsensual;* it is not adverse if it occurs with the consent of the true owner. Thus a tenant's possession of the landlord's property under a lease agreement is not hostile unless the tenant clearly communicated to the landlord that the tenant was claiming ownership.

Similarly, if two parties are co-owners of a tract of land, each of them has a right to possession. Therefore, possession by one co-owner is not hostile as to the other unless the possessor notifies the other that he or she is claiming sole ownership.

Open and Notorious Possession

The possession must be *open and notorious* rather than secretive. In other words, it must be a type of possession that will be easily noticeable by the true owner if a reasonable inspection is made.

Continuous Possession

In order for adverse possession to ultimately ripen into ownership, it must be *reasonably continuous* for the required period of time. The possessor does not have to be in possession every single day of the period. For instance, he or she could leave temporarily with an intent to return, and the law would treat the possession as not having been interrupted.

In answering the question of whether possession has been continuous, a court will take into account the nature of the land and the type of use being made of it. Thus farming the land only during the growing season each year constitutes continuous possession.

---

[8] The latter phrase is explained by the fact that the prescribed time periods are, in essence, statutes of limitations setting forth the maximum length of time an owner has to sue someone who is wrongfully in possession of the owner's land.

[9] Some courts have also said that the possession must be "exclusive" and "under claim of right." These requirements will not be discussed because they overlap with the four listed here and really add nothing to what is required for adverse possession to exist.

Also, the uninterrupted possession by two or more successive possessors can sometimes be added together, or "tacked," to satisfy the statutory time requirement. For "tacking" to be permitted, there must have been *privity* between the successive possessors. This simply means that the possessions by different persons must not have been independent of each other; rather, there must have been a transaction between them which purported to transfer the property. To illustrate: In State X the required period for adverse possession is ten years. O is the true owner. B meets all the requirements for adverse possession except that he stays on the land only six years. B then purports to sell or otherwise transfer the land to C. If C stays in possession for four more years, continuing to meet all the requirements for obtaining title by adverse possession, C becomes the owner of the land.

The following case illustrates the applicability of the adverse possession doctrine to a common problem—a boundary dispute between "unneighborly" neighbors.

KLINE V. KRAMER

Court of Appeals of Indiana, 386 N.E.2d 982 (1979)

 The Klines and the Kramers were adjoining landowners who both claimed ownership of a strip of land 1 to 4 feet wide and 309 feet long. The disputed strip formed the northern boundary of the Kramer property and the southern boundary of the Kline property. Both claimed ownership through previous owners. The Klines, who acquired their property in 1972, based their claim to the strip on the legal description contained in their deed. The Kramers, who purchased their property in 1968, claimed the strip on the theory of adverse possession. The position of the Kramers was that the ten-year period of possession necessary to establish adverse possession had been satisfied by the previous owners of the Kramer property, Harry and Hazel Britt.

The Kramers, plaintiffs, filed suit against the Klines, defendants, seeking to establish ownership of the boundary strip. The trial court granted the plaintiffs' motion for summary judgment, ruling that they had title by adverse possession, and the defendants appealed.

Staton, Judge:

. . . Harry Britt testified at the hearing on Kramer's motion for summary judgment that when he purchased the present-day Kramer property in 1947, a fence existed along the northern boundary of the land. Britt maintained the fence during his period of ownership. Photographs of the fence-line were introduced into evidence at the hearing in which Britt identified old fence posts he had set in maintaining the existing fence and familiar trees which had grown in the fence-line during his tenure on the land. While Britt testified that he never contemplated that he was claiming land that belonged to his neighbor, the fence in fact described a line which ran roughly one to four feet north of and parallel to the legally-described northern boundary of his property.

Britt testified that he felt that he owned the property up to the fence line and that he used it to plant crops and pasture cattle. It was his belief that he had bought "what was inside the fence." Similarly, Britt stated that when he sold the land to the Kramers in 1968 he intended to convey to them all the land enclosed by the fence.

F. Richard Kramer testified that he believed that he had purchased the property up to the fence that ran along the northern edge of his acreage. In 1972, Kramer inadvertently allowed his tractor to roll through the fence, tearing out a middle portion of it. Kramer repaired the break in the fence by stretching new fencing between the remaining old fence and fence posts to the east and west of the break. The new portion of the fence was set in the exact location of the old fence, according to Kramer, who noted that the new section followed a trail which cattle had worn along the old section.

Kramer concluded his testimony by stating that he had made improvements which encroached on the disputed stretch of land, that he had no knowledge of the true boundary line until Kline had conducted a survey of the land, and that he had paid taxes on his property according to the tax receipts sent to him by the County Treasurer.

. . . The trial court's entry of summary judgment was predicated on its conclusion that the Kramers had acquired title to the property through adverse possession. The ten year possessory period necessary to acquire title on that basis is a statute of limitations which runs against the titleholder. If the titleholder fails to oust the intruder within the ten year period, title to the property vests in the intruder, assuming all other elements of adverse possession are satisfied.

. . . The Klines contend that summary judgment was improper because the undisputed evidence reveals the absence of the elements necessary to acquire title by adverse possession. Specifically, the Klines maintain that

(continues)

KLINE V. KRAMER

(continued from previous page)
the Kramers' predecessors-in-interest, the Britts, whose possessory period provides the foundation for the Kramers' claim, lacked the necessary adverseness, hostility, and intention to claim title to the strip. This argument is premised largely on the testimony of both Harry and Hazel Britt that they never intended to lay claim to any land that belonged to their neighbor to the north. Accordingly, the Klines argue, the Britts held the land by mistake and lacked the adverse intent or hostility which is requisite to establishing a claim of adverse possession.

We note that in the law of adverse possession, "adverse" is synonymous with "hostile." So long as an occupant of another's land does not disavow his or her right to possession of the property nor acknowledge that the posses-

sion is subservient to the title held by the true owner, the possession is adverse or hostile.

. . . While it is true that the Britts did not intend to claim the land of their neighbors, the record clearly reveals that they intended to claim all the land within the parameters of the fence which ran along the northern boundary of their property. They did not recognize that their ownership was subservient to their neighbor's title, nor did they acknowledge that they had no legal right to possession of the property. In all respects they acted as the sole owner of the property, maintaining the fence and using the land in a manner consistent with its normal purposes. This evidence clearly establishes that the Britts intended to claim title to the disputed strip of land. The only mistake involved in the Britts' posses-

sion was their belief that they were merely acting in a manner consistent with their ownership rights, a fact which does not negate the conclusion that their possession was adverse.

This uncontroverted evidence also establishes the Britts' "intent to claim title" to the contiguous strip of land, as the Klines have characterized the element of adverse possession. This element is more aptly defined as "a claim of ownership." The element is satisfied by entering upon and occupying the land with the intent to hold the land as one's own. The trial court was thus justified in finding that the Britts' possession was both hostile and under a claim of ownership. . . .

[Affirmed. The Kramers, plaintiffs, own the boundary strip because of adverse possession.]⚖

REGULATION OF REAL PROPERTY OWNERSHIP, USE, AND SALE

Eminent Domain

The power of the government to take private property for public purposes (such as a highway) is referred to as the power of **eminent domain.** The federal government derives the power of eminent domain from the Fifth Amendment to the U.S. Constitution. Individual states draw the power from their own constitutions. In addition, states have delegated the power of eminent domain by statute to local governments (such as counties, cities, and school districts) and to railroads and public utilities.

The power can be exercised without the owner's consent, but the government must pay *just compensation* (i.e., the fair value of the property) to the owner. In many cases, a governmental body seeking to acquire property for a public purpose will negotiate a purchase from the owner. If the owner does not consent, or if there is disagreement as to the fair value of the property, the government exercises the

power of eminent domain by instituting a court action called **condemnation.** In a condemnation proceeding the court will set a fair value for the property based on the evidence of that value.

In some situations, a property owner may claim that an activity by a governmental body has so deprived the owner of the use of the property that a "taking" of the property has actually occurred. The property owner can institute a legal action known as **inverse condemnation,** in which a court will determine whether there has been a taking of the property and, if so, the fair value to be paid the owner. The mere fact that a governmental activity has diminished the use or value of property does not establish that there has been a "taking"; the evidence must demonstrate that the owner has been effectively deprived of any reasonable use of the land. For example, the taking off and landing of airplanes at a city-owned airport could constitute a taking of an adjoining property owner's land if the land was so close to the airport that the planes flew over it at extremely low altitude.

Land Use Control
Restrictive Covenants

A deed may contain significant restrictions on the use of the property. For example, it might provide that only a single-family dwelling can be built on the land. Such **restrictive covenants** are usually valid and can be enforced by surrounding landowners. It also is common for a real estate developer to place restrictive covenants on all the residential lots in a subdivision and to specify those restrictions in the recorded plat. Such restrictions, such as those relating to the type and appearance of structures that can be built on the lots, are intended to preserve property values and can also be enforced by surrounding landowners in the subdivision.

Zoning

Pursuant to their constitutional police power, all states have passed legislation giving cities the power to enact zoning ordinances. In some states, similar powers have been given to counties. A **zoning ordinance** is essentially a law specifying the permissible uses of land in designated areas. Such an ordinance might specify zones for single-family dwellings, several categories of multiple-family dwellings, office buildings, various classifications of commercial structures, industrial facilities, and so on. Moreover, a zoning ordinance may impose even more detailed restrictions on use, such as minimum distances of structures from streets, lot sizes, and minimum parking accommodations for commercial buildings. The purposes of zoning laws are to permit the orderly planning of growth, protect against deterioration of surrounding property values by obnoxious uses, maintain the residential character of neighborhoods, and further other public purposes such as the prevention of overcrowding.

To prevent zoning from constituting a "taking" of property, zoning ordinances usually permit the continuance of a preexisting use even though it does not conform to the zoning restrictions for that area. In addition, a landowner may obtain a **variance**—permission from the city to make a use of the property that does not conform to the zoning ordinance—if he or she proves the following: (1) The zoning ordinance makes it impossible for the owner to receive a reasonable return on his or her investment in the land. (2) The negative effect of the zoning ordinance is unique to this owner's property; it is not an effect that is common to other landowners in the zone.

(3) Granting the variance will not substantially alter the basic character of the surrounding neighborhood.

The Implied Warranty of Habitability

In recent years courts in a majority of states have recognized an **implied warranty of habitability** in the sale of new residential housing. The warranty exists separately from, and in addition to, any express warranties made by the seller. The warranty of habitability does not apply to minor defects, but only to major defects that substantially interfere with the buyer's use of the property as a residence. Examples of defects that probably would be a breach of the warranty include a defective foundation, leaking roof, malfunctioning heating or cooling system, and unsafe electrical wiring. Breach of the warranty entitles the buyer to receive damages from the seller based on the cost of repairing defects that are reasonably correctable, or the amount by which the home's market value has been reduced in the case of noncorrectable defects.

The implied warranty of habitability generally has been applied only to sales by a builder or other seller who is in the housing business. Real estate brokers and agents normally have not been held responsible under this warranty. Although some courts have extended the builder's liability under the implied warranty of habitability to the subsequent sale of used homes, a majority of courts have restricted it to the first sale of new homes. In recent years most states also have imposed an implied warranty of habitability on the landlord who leases residential property; a detailed discussion of the warranty in that setting is included in the next chapter.

SUMMARY

Real property includes (1) land, consisting of the surface, air rights, and subsurface rights, and (2) things affixed to the land, consisting of vegetation and fixtures. A fixture is an item that formerly was personal property and that has been attached to the land with an intent that it become a permanent part of the land.

The complete ownership of land can be divided in a number of ways. The particular set of rights owned in a given situation is an estate, or interest, in real property. These interests can be classified as freehold, nonfreehold, nonpossessory, and future. Any interest in real property that can be owned by one individual can also be owned concurrently by two or more individuals. There are several forms of co-ownership of real property.

Sales of real property commonly involve a transfer of complete ownership—the fee simple estate—but similar procedures may be employed to transfer lesser interests. In the typical sale of real property, the owner obtains the services of a broker, a buyer is found, a sale contract is executed, the buyer procures the necessary financing, various steps are taken to insure that the seller has a good title, and the closing or settlement occurs. The seller transfers title by executing and delivering a written deed. Although there are several types of deed, the general warranty deed is the best from the buyer's perspective. The deed must meet several requirements in order to transfer ownership effectively. Deeds should be acknowledged and recorded for the buyer's protection.

Title to real property can also be acquired by adverse possession, in which the taking of land must be actual, hostile, open and notorious, and the taking party must have continuous possession for a period of time specified by state statute. The ownership, use, and sale of real property is subject to several types of regulation, including the government's power of eminent domain, restrictive covenants, zoning ordinances, and the implied warranty of habitability.

KEY TERMS
Air rights
Fixture
Possessory interests
Freehold estates
Nonfreehold estates
Nonpossessory interests
Fee simple estate
Fee simple defeasible
Life estate
Leasehold estates
Easement
Easement appurtenant
Servient estate
Dominant estate
Easement in gross
Easement by express grant or reservation
Easement by implication
Easement by necessity
Easement by prescription
(or prescriptive easement)
Profit

License
Mortgage
Lien
Involuntary lien
Mechanic's lien
Judgment lien
Future interest
Reversion
Remainder
Tenancy in common
Joint tenancy
Condominium
Cooperative
Tenancy by the entireties
Community property
Dower
Curtesy
Homestead
Open listing
Exclusive agency
Exclusive right to sell
Multiple listing service (MLS)
Earnest money
Title examination
Abstract
Contract for deed
Closing (or settlement)
Escrow agent
General warranty deed
Covenant of seisin
Covenant against encumbrances
Covenant for quiet enjoyment
Special warranty deed
Quitclaim deed
Deed of bargain and sale
United States Government Survey
Townships
Metes and bounds
Plat
Acknowledgment
Recording
Bona fide purchaser (BFP)
Title by adverse possession (or title by limitation)
Eminent domain
Condemnation
Inverse condemnation
Restrictive covenants
Zoning ordinance
Variance
Implied warranty of habitability

QUESTIONS AND PROBLEMS

1. Talley and Warren were adjoining landowners. Talley drilled a producing oil well on his land close to the boundary line between his and Warren's property. Warren sued Talley for trespass. Although the entire well was on Talley's property, Warren proved that the well was drawing oil not only from beneath Talley's land but also from beneath Warren's. Will Warren prevail? Discuss.

2. In the above situation, suppose that Talley had drilled a "slant well," which began on his land but ended beneath Warren's land because it had been drilled at an angle. What will be the result if Warren sues for trespass in this case? Discuss.

3. Jenkins sold a 10-acre tract of land to Watkins. In the past, Jenkins had engaged in the business of raising rabbits, and at the time of the sale a number of rabbit hutches were still on the land. They were not attached to the soil but merely rested upon it. Each hutch had a wire-covered wooden frame and a tin roof; each measured approximately 4 feet by 4 feet by 4 feet. These hutches were never mentioned in the transaction. When Jenkins moved from the premises after the sale, he claimed that the rabbit hutches were still his and that he was entitled to take them. Watkins disagreed. Who is correct? Discuss.

4. Discuss whether wall-to-wall carpeting should be considered a fixture.

5. What are some probable reasons for the rule that the owner of a fee simple interest is presumed to be selling the entire interest unless the terms of the conveyance clearly indicate transference of a lesser interest? Explain.

6. Kempin was the owner of a life estate in a 60-acre parcel of land. A valuable stand of growing timber was situated on the property, and substantial deposits of lignite were located beneath it. Kempin began cutting the timber, both for firewood and for the purpose of sale. He also undertook to mine the lignite, some of which he intended to use for fuel and some of which he intended to sell. Moskovitz, who was to become the fee simple owner on Kempin's death, sued Kempin to enjoin him from all of the above activities. Who will prevail? Explain.

7. Explain the difference between easements, profits, and licenses.

8. In connection with the employment of a real estate broker, what is the difference between an open listing, an exclusive agency, and an exclusive right to sell?

9. Poindexter sold his farm to Samuelson, who did not record his deed. Several weeks later, before Samuelson had taken possession of the land, Poindexter sold the same property to Rosser, who made a large down payment and knew nothing of the earlier sale to Samuelson. Does Samuelson or Rosser have title to the land? Explain. Would it matter whether Rosser recorded his deed? Explain. Would it make any difference if Samuelson had already taken possession of the land when Rosser bought it? Explain.

10. Arnold and Ross were adjoining landowners. The opening of a cave was located on Arnold's land, but the cave ran beneath Ross's land. Ross did not know of the cave's existence. For a continuous period of 25 years, Arnold used the entire cave for various purposes, including storage. On a number of occasions, doing business as the Marengo Cave Co., he also guided visitors through the cave for a fee. Ross finally learned of the cave and of the use Arnold had been making of it. He demanded that Arnold cease his use of the part of the cave beneath Ross's land. Arnold refused, claiming that he had acquired title to the cave by adverse possession. The pertinent state statute provided for acquisition of such title after 20 years. Ross filed suit to establish ownership of the cave. Who owned the portion of the cave located beneath Ross's land? Discuss. (*Marengo Cave Co. v. Ross*, 10 N.E.2d 917, 1937.)

R bona fide purchaser

Chapter 44

Landlord and Tenant

THE NATURE OF THE LANDLORD–TENANT RELATIONSHIP

The landlord-tenant relationship is created when the owner of real estate transfers temporary possession of the property to another person in return for the payment of rent.[1] The agreement providing for this transfer of possession and payment of rent is a **lease,** or *rental agreement.* The owner is referred to as the *landlord,* or *lessor,* and the one taking possession is the *tenant,* or *lessee.*

The identifying characteristic of a lease is the tenant's temporary acquisition of *exclusive possession* and *control* of the premises or the particular portion of it which he or she occupies. The tenant is distinguished from a *purchaser* because no title passes. On the other hand, the tenant is distinguished from a mere *licensee* who receives the temporary right to park a car in a space, occupy a seat in a theater, or make some other nonexclusive, revocable use of the premises. The tenant also is different from a *lodger* who occupies a room in a hotel but does not have legal control over the occupied area.

The law governing the landlord-tenant relationship consisted almost solely of common-law principles until recent times. Today many states have specific statutes concerning the rights and duties of landlords and tenants. A Uniform Residential Landlord and Tenant Act was proposed in 1972 by the National Conference of Commissioners on Uniform State Laws and, with some variations, has been adopted in one-third of the states. Common-law principles still control, however, in many situations not covered by specific statutes. This area of law is thus a mixture of statutory provisions and case precedents.

Landlord-tenant law developed in a basically agrarian economy when the focal point of the lease was the land itself. As a result, the transaction was viewed primarily as one for the transfer of an interest in real estate, and the principles of real estate law governed most aspects of the arrangement. In the great majority of leases today, however, the focal point of the transaction is the house, apartment, office, or other structure on the land. Consequently, the law has gradually changed so as to view the arrangement primarily as a contract, with the rules of contract law governing more and more aspects of the relationship. The movement in recent years toward greater legal protection for the consumer also has had a substantial impact on landlord-tenant law.

CREATION AND TERMINATION OF THE LANDLORD–TENANT RELATIONSHIP

The Lease

The Importance of the Lease

The landlord-tenant relationship is created by agreement. Therefore, the lease and its particular terms determine the rights and duties of the parties. Most of the relevant legal principles serve only to specify rights and duties when the lease is silent on a disputed matter. There are a few legal principles, however, which do take precedence over a conflicting lease term.

Because the specific terms of the lease are of such great importance, it is critical that the parties draft their agreement carefully to clearly reflect their intent and to provide for various contingencies that might arise. It is also important for one party to closely examine any lease form proposed by the other. There is no standard form that must be used. Some groups, such as landlord associations, have developed their own standard form, but there is no law requiring it to be followed or preventing it from being changed.

Form of the Lease

A lease may be oral unless a state statute requires it to be written. Most states have statutes requiring a written document for any lease extending beyond a stated time period. In some states, leases for a term greater than one year must be written; in other states the period is three years.

Whether oral or written, a valid lease agreement must (1) indicate an intent to create the landlord-tenant relationship; (2) identify the parties, each of whom must have contractual capacity; (3) clearly identify the premises; and (4) state the amount of the rent and when it is to be paid.

Covenants and Conditions

A lease provision in which the landlord or the tenant promises to do something or not to do something is

---

[1] The "owner" might own a fee simple interest, life estate, or other type of possessory interest. See Chapter 43 for details.

either a **covenant** or a **condition.** The difference lies in the consequences resulting from the breach of a promise. If one party fails to perform a *covenant,* the other party's recourse normally is to file suit for money damages. The innocent party is not relieved from his or her obligations, and the breaching party does not forfeit his or her rights under the lease.

On the other hand, the failure to perform a *condition* does cause a forfeiture of the lease and relieves the innocent party from further obligations. Because of the drastic nature of forfeiture, most lease provisions traditionally have been viewed as covenants unless the lease expressly provides for forfeiture as a consequence of breach.

For example, suppose that the tenant fails to make a rent payment within the agreed time. If the lease does not expressly provide for forfeiture of the lease as a result of nonpayment, the landlord's only remedy under the common-law rule is to sue for the unpaid rent. However, if the lease had expressly made rent payment a condition by providing for forfeiture in the event of nonpayment, the landlord could declare the lease terminated and evict the tenant. Today it is common for many lease clauses to provide for forfeiture as the penalty for breach of the clause. This is especially true of clauses spelling out tenants' duties in standard form leases prepared by landlords.

In recent years, statutes have been enacted in most states which make forfeiture the penalty for a tenant's failure to pay rent, even without an express lease clause to that effect.

Types of Tenancies

The interest acquired by a tenant is called a **tenancy,** or **leasehold.** Several types of tenancies exist.

Tenancy for Years

The most common tenancy is one that is technically called a **tenancy for years.** The name of this tenancy is rather misleading because it actually is created whenever a lease provides for a specific duration, such as thirty days, six months, one year, or fifty years. Such a tenancy terminates automatically when the term expires.

Periodic Tenancy

A **periodic tenancy** exists when the parties have not agreed on a specific duration, but have agreed that rent is to be paid at particular intervals (such as monthly or yearly). In such a case, the tenancy exists from period to period and can be terminated by one party giving notice to the other. The parties may expressly agree on the form and timing of the notice. If the lease is silent on the question, the common-law rule required that such notice be given at least one full rental period prior to termination. An exception was made for leases having rental periods of one year or more—in such cases six months' notice was required. Most states now have statutes which modify the common-law rule. Many of these statutes shorten the notice requirement to thirty days for periodic tenancies having rental periods longer than one month.

Tenancy at Will

A **tenancy at will** is a landlord-tenant relationship which may be terminated at any time by either party without advance notice. It exists when the parties have not agreed on either an express duration or a particular interval for rental payment. A tenancy at will is an uncommon occurrence.

Tenancy at Sufferance

When a valid tenancy is terminated, but the tenant continues to occupy the premises after he or she no longer has the right to do so, a **tenancy at sufferance** is created. The landlord can choose to make another lease or force the tenant to leave. The phrase tenancy at sufferance merely distinguishes the tenant from a complete trespasser who never had permission to be on the premises in the first place.

Termination for Reasons Other than Expiration of the Lease

We already have seen some of the ways in which tenancies can terminate: expiration of the term in a tenancy for years, advance notice in a periodic tenancy, and breach of a condition in the lease.

Although leases usually are *not* terminated by the death or disability of either party, there are several other ways in which leases may come to an end.[2] The parties may, for example, terminate the lease by mutual agreement. This is sometimes called **surrender and acceptance**—the tenant surrenders the lease, and the landlord accepts the surrender.

---

[2] In the event of death, the rights and duties under the lease are part of the estate of the deceased under the control of the executor or administrator. In the event of insanity, the insane person's guardian exercises the rights and duties existing under the lease.

If the primary subject matter of a lease is a structure, such as a house or apartment, most courts hold that destruction of the structure through no fault of either party (such as fire or flood) will terminate the lease. As with other contracts, leases can also be terminated because of fraud, mistake, duress, undue influence, or minority.

Sale of the Leased Property

The landlord continues to own an interest in the premises during the term of the lease. This interest is called a **reversion** and consists of the landlord's future right to possession after termination of the lease.

A landlord may sell the leased property during the term of the lease, but such a sale does not terminate the lease. In actuality, the landlord merely sells what he has—the reversion. The purchaser buys the property subject to the rights of the tenant.

There are a few limited exceptions to this principle. In some ways a modern-day lease is still considered to be a transfer of an interest in real estate, rather than a mere contract, and to be subject to some of the rules of real estate law. For example, real estate *recording statutes* (discussed in Chapter 43) generally do apply to leases. Therefore, a purchaser from the landlord does not have to honor the preexisting lease if (1) the lease had not been recorded prior to the sale, *and* (2) the tenant was not in possession of the premises at the time of the sale. Either the recording or the tenant's possession will put the purchaser on notice of the tenant's rights, and the purchaser must honor the lease.

POSSESSION OF THE PREMISES

Landlord's Obligation to Turn Over Possession

One of the most important obligations of the landlord is to give the tenant possession. However, the laws of the various states are in conflict as to the extent of this obligation. One group of states follows the so-called "English rule," which requires the landlord to give the tenant actual physical possession. Under this rule, for example, if a holdover tenant from a previous lease is still in possession when the new tenant becomes entitled to possession, the landlord breaches the obligation to the new tenant.

Another group of states follows the "American rule," which requires only that the landlord transfer the *legal right to possession* to the tenant. Under this rule, the presence of a holdover tenant who has no legal right to be there is really the new tenant's problem, not the landlord's. The new tenant must take the necessary steps to remove the holdover.

Covenant of Quiet Enjoyment

During the term of the lease, the landlord owes to the tenant an obligation not to interfere with the tenant's lawful possession and use of the premises. This obligation, the **covenant of quiet enjoyment,** is expressly stated in most leases, but in most states is implied by law even if not stated in the lease. The covenant may be breached by the conduct of the landlord, someone acting under the landlord's authority, or someone having better title to the premises than the landlord has. It ordinarily may not be breached by other third parties—for example, in a majority of states the independent conduct of another tenant does not make the landlord liable for breach of this obligation. Therefore, if tenant X interferes with tenant Y's lawful possession and use, Y's remedy is against X and not against the landlord.

The most common actions of the landlord that breach this covenant are *eviction* and *constructive eviction.*

Eviction

An **eviction** occurs if the landlord padlocks the premises, changes the door lock and refuses to give the tenant a new key, or in some other way physically bars the tenant from entering the premises. A tenant who has a legal right to possession has a choice. He or she may (1) sue for damages or (2) treat the eviction as a breach of *condition* and be relieved from further obligations under the lease.

Constructive Eviction

Even without physically barring the tenant from entry, the landlord's action or inaction may cause the property to be unsuitable for the purpose for which it was leased. An example would be the failure to provide heat in the winter as promised in the lease. In such a case, the tenant may remain on the premises and sue for damages. If the tenant remains, he or she usually continues to be liable for rent. The tenant may, however, choose to abandon the property and treat the landlord's conduct as a **constructive eviction.** The tenant then is under no further obligation to pay rent.

USE OF THE PREMISES BY THE TENANT
Restrictions on Use

The uses that can be made of the property by the tenant usually are specified by agreement. In fact, clauses detailing permissible and impermissible uses are among the most common and important parts of leases. Such provisions frequently concern matters such as number of occupants, whether pets are permitted, and so forth.

In the absence of a lease provision prohibiting a particular use, the tenant is entitled to make any use of the premises that is (1) legal and (2) reasonably in line with the basic purpose for which the property was leased.

Damaging the Landlord's Reversionary Interest

The tenant has no right to use the property in such a way as to cause permanent damage to it. The duty of a tenant not to damage the landlord's reversionary interest is sometimes referred to as the duty not to commit **waste.** For example, a tenant cannot take timber or minerals from the land unless the right to do so was (1) expressly permitted by the lease or by later agreement or (2) clearly implied from surrounding circumstances. The right may be implied, for instance, when the primary value of the leased property is its timber or minerals, so that the parties probably would not have executed the lease if these materials had not been there.[3]

A tenant can be held liable for either intentionally or negligently damaging the leased property. When determining whether a tenant was negligent, the courts apply general principles of tort law. Many cases of this type involve claims by landlords that fire damage was caused by the tenant's negligence. For the landlord to prevail in such a case, there must be evidence that the tenant failed to act with reasonable care, such as by smoking in bed or leaving the premises to go shopping while food was left cooking on the kitchen range. Many cases also involve assertions by the tenant that the provisions of the lease excused him or her from liability for negligent damage to the leased premises. The language of the lease itself is the starting point for resolving most disputes arising from the landlord-tenant relationship, including this type of dispute. In the following case, the question for the court is whether the provisions of the lease should be interpreted so as to excuse the tenant from liability for fire damage caused by the tenant's negligence.

---

[3] A point that was made in Chapter 43 must be reiterated. What is ordinarily called an oil and gas "lease" is not really a lease at all. It is either the sale of a fee simple interest in the minerals in the ground or it is the sale of a right to take the minerals from the ground (a so-called "profit").

ACQUISTO V. JOE R. HAHN ENTERPRISES, INC.

Supreme Court of New Mexico, 619 P.2d 1237 (1980)

The defendant, Acquisto, leased a building from the plaintiff, Hahn Enterprises. During the term of the lease a fire broke out in the building, and the landlord sued Acquisto for damages caused by the fire. The landlord claimed that Acquisto had negligently caused the fire. Based upon a jury verdict, the trial court found that Acquisto had been guilty of negligence, and that there was no provision in the lease excusing Acquisto from responsibility for his negligence. The court of appeals reversed, holding that the lease did excuse Acquisto from such liability, and the landlord appealed to the New Mexico Supreme Court.

Sosa, Chief Justice:

The relevant provisions of the lease pertinent to the disposition of this case are as follows:

IV. USE OF PREMISES. Lessee . . . hereby agrees and covenants with Lessor . . . not to use . . . said premises in any manner . . . so as to tend to increase the existing rate of fire insurance for the said demised premises.

V. CONDITION OF PREMISES AND REPAIRS. Lessee . . . hereby agrees . . . that . . . at the expiration of the term of this Lease, or any renewal or extension thereof, Lessee will yield up peaceably the said premises to Lessor in as good order and condition as when the same were entered upon by Lessee, *loss by fire or inevitable accident, damage by the elements, and reasonable use and wear excepted.* . . . [Emphasis added by court.]

XII. TAXES, OTHER ASSESSMENTS, AND INSURANCE. . . . Fire and extended coverage insurance upon all buildings . . . upon the said premises shall be provided for as follows: [blank]   and fire and extended coverage insurance upon all of the contents . . .

(continues)

ACQUISTO V. JOE R. HAHN ENTERPRISES, INC.

(continued from previous page)
situated upon the said premises shall be provided for as follows: [blank]   ....

XV. DESTRUCTION. Lessee . . . agrees and covenants with Lessor that if at any time during the term of this Lease . . . the said demised premises shall be totally or partially destroyed by fire, earthquake, or other calamity, then Lessor shall have the option to rebuild or repair the same. . . .

The tenant contends that the lease provisions operate to relieve him of liability for all fires, including those he negligently causes. Whether express language must be used to exculpate [i.e., excuse] a party to the lease is a question of first impression in New Mexico. The courts in other jurisdictions are divided on the issue. One line of cases hold that no specific exculpatory language is required and that the intent to relieve one of the parties from liability for negligence must be determined from the lease as a whole. These cases hold that the parties' intent must be determined from the lease as a whole, in light of the subject matter, surrounding circumstances and the natural meaning of the language used. In all of these cases, the court found that the parties had intended that the landlord provide fire insurance for the benefit of both parties; this finding, coupled with the clause excepting loss by fire or other casualty, was sufficient to show an intent not to hold the tenant liable for his negligence. This is the line of cases upon which the Court of Appeals based its opinion. The second line of cases, rejected by the Court of Appeals, hold that the lease must state explicitly that the tenant is released from liability for a fire resulting from his own negligence. We hold that leases are to be construed as a whole to determine the parties' intent. In the absence of an agreement between the parties specifying which of them will carry fire insurance for the benefit of both parties, or an express clause in the lease relieving a party from his negligence, each party must bear the risk of loss for his own negligence.

A lease is subject to the basic rules of contract construction. It must be read as a whole to effectuate the intent of the parties. We will not look beyond the four corners of the document unless the lease is ambiguous. The Court of Appeals found that the lease was patently ambiguous because Paragraph XII, which would have provided which party would carry fire insurance, was left blank. We disagree that this constitutes an ambiguity; rather it is a clear indication that the parties failed to agree which of them would provide the insurance. This conclusion is supported by the fact that the other blanks in the same paragraph providing for the payment of taxes were completed. We conclude that the parties were aware of the blanks relative to fire insurance and chose not to fill them in. Since we hold that the lease is complete, plain and unambiguous, parol evidence may not be introduced to vary the terms of the agreement. The trial court properly excluded extrinsic evidence of the parties' intent with respect to fire insurance.

The tenant contends that the use of "fire" in Paragraph V of the lease operates to exculpate him from his negligence because it refers to all fires, including those caused by his negligence. We disagree. The word "fire" must be construed in the context of the other words in the clause, which provide that the tenant is to surrender the premises to the landlord in the same condition they were in at the beginning of the lease term, "loss by fire or inevitable accident, damage by the elements . . . excepted." The plain meaning of this language is that only fire caused by unavoidable consequences or acts of God were to be exempt, but not fire caused by negligence. The use of such phrases as "inevitable accident" and "damage by the elements" support this construction. These are all non-negligent occurrences and we must construe "fire" to fall within the same type of occurrence.

The arguments that Paragraph IV, which prohibits the tenant from doing anything which would increase the insurance rates, or Paragraph XV, which gives the landlord the option of rebuilding the premises when loss by "fire, earthquake or other calamity" occurs, indicate an intent by the parties that the landlord provide fire insurance thereby relieving tenant from liability, are rejected. First, the type of "fire" referred to in Paragraph XV is that which can be classified as purely accidental and non-negligent. This is clear from the use of "other calamity" in the same clause, indicating a use of "fire" in the context of a calamity rather than in the context of negligence. Secondly, Paragraph IV is a clause found in many leases without regard to which party is responsible for providing insurance. It does not follow from the language therein that the landlord agreed to provide insurance. This is especially so when read in conjunction with Paragraph XII which is specifically designed to establish which party will carry the insurance. Since Paragraph XII is blank, the only logical conclusion to be drawn is that the parties did not agree that either of them would carry insurance.

Having decided that the lease is not ambiguous, that the landlord did not agree to provide fire insurance, and that the use of "fire" does not include negligently caused fire, it follows that the responsibility for loss of the premises due to negligence must be borne by the negligent party. This is merely a restatement of the common law rule of tort liability. While the law allows one to exculpate himself by contract, it will do so only if the exculpation is set forth with such clarity that the intent to negate the usual consequences of tortious conduct is made plain. In this case, where the parties failed to agree that one, or both, of them would carry fire insurance, and where there is no specific exculpatory language relieving the tenant from liability for negligence,

(continues)

ACQUISTO V. JOE R. HAHN ENTERPRISES, INC.

(continued from previous page)
each party will be responsible for damages caused by his negligence. This is more equitable than requiring the innocent landlord to pay for a fire he did not cause.

For the foregoing reasons we reverse the decision of the Court of Appeals and affirm the decision of the trial court. [Thus, although the court held that an express exculpatory clause was not required to excuse the

tenant from liability for negligent damage to the premises, in this case the lease as a whole did not indicate that the parties intended to excuse the tenant.]

Altering the Premises

Suppose that a tenant in an apartment or house wants to add some built-in bookshelves or paint the interior walls. Or suppose that a business tenant wishes to build an additional storage area for inventory. Does the tenant have a right to alter the property?

Many leases expressly forbid the tenant from making alterations to the premises without specific consent of the landlord. Even if the lease contains no such clause, however, the tenant generally has no right to make alterations without consent.

In many states the law imposes an absolute requirement that the tenant return the premises to the landlord at the end of the lease in exactly the same condition they were in at the beginning, except for normal wear and tear. If the tenant has made any changes without the landlord's consent, the tenant is liable for the cost of putting the property back into the condition it was in at the beginning of the lease.

In a growing number of states, however, the tenant is not liable for the cost of "undoing" such alterations if (1) the alteration was consistent with and necessary for the tenant's reasonable use of the premises, and (2) the alteration did not diminish the value of the property.

Fixtures

We saw in Chapter 43 that an item of personal property becomes a *fixture* when it is affixed to real property. Even if not actually attached, the item is a fixture if circumstances indicate that it was intended to be part of the real estate.

If a tenant affixes an item to the leased property, the same basic rules are applied to determine whether the item is a fixture as are applied in other

situations. Thus, a tenant who installs built-in bookshelves, new cabinets, or other such items probably has added fixtures to the property and cannot remove them when the lease expires.

However, many courts traditionally have drawn a distinction between fixtures added by a residential tenant and those added by a tenant who conducts a business on the leased property. Fixtures added by a business tenant are called **trade fixtures.** Courts generally have held that a business tenant probably did not intend for a trade fixture to become part of the real estate. Thus if an item such as a gasoline pump or neon sign can be removed without substantial damage to the real estate, the business tenant usually can remove it at the end of the lease.

This distinction between residential and business tenants has been frequently criticized as illogical.

THE DUTY TO MAINTAIN THE PREMISES

The traditional common-law view was that the landlord was not responsible for the condition of the premises at the beginning of the lease or for making repairs during the lease. The tenant leased the premises "as is," and was responsible for making later repairs so that the premises were substantially in the same condition at the end of the lease as at the beginning.

The tenant's duty to repair has always been subject to certain important limits. The duty does not apply to major structural components such as the foundation and framework, but only to relatively minor items like windows, venetian blinds, and so forth. However, whether classified as major or minor, the tenant is responsible for making emergency repairs to protect the premises from the elements and thus prevent further damage. This responsibility is part of the tenant's overall duty not to commit waste by negligently or intentionally damaging the property.

The general rule that a landlord has no duty to maintain the premises still exists *in theory.* However, over the years the courts have recognized many exceptions to the rule. Today the exceptions are practically as broad as the general rule. We will examine the most important situations in which the landlord does have a duty to make repairs.

Express Covenant

As with most other matters, the obligation to make repairs may be dealt with in a specific lease clause. If the landlord expressly promises to keep the premises in good repair, he or she is legally responsible for complying with the promise.[4] The extent of the obligation is determined by the language used.

A lease may sometimes place certain repair duties on the tenant. In such a situation, the language of the clause again determines the scope of the obligation.

Common Areas

When a landlord leases several units of a multi-unit property to different tenants, the landlord is responsible for maintaining common areas in a reasonably safe condition. The most common example of a multi-unit property is an apartment complex. Common areas include swimming pools, stairs, halls, and similar places over which the landlord retains control. The duty of repair extends to defects that the landlord actually knows about and to those that he or she reasonably *should* know about. Thus, the landlord is obligated to make reasonable, periodic inspections of common areas.

Like any other individual or company, a landlord is responsible for the actions of its agents and employees when they are acting within the scope of their authority or employment. Thus, when an apartment manager is notified of an unsafe condition in a common area, the landlord is treated legally as knowing about the condition. Similarly, the manager or other agent's failure to inspect common areas is treated as the landlord's failure.

Building Codes

Many state statutes and city ordinances specify certain standards for both the construction and maintenance of buildings. In the case of leased premises, the landlord, as owner, is ordinarily responsible for compliance with these codes. Provisions dealing with electrical wiring, heating, and other structural concerns usually apply to both commercial and residential structures. Some codes, however, impose a greater duty on the landlord in leases of residential property by requiring that the owner keep the premises in overall good repair. A few state legislatures have even adopted separate "housing codes" dealing especially with residential property.

Implied Warranty of Habitability

Perhaps the most important development in landlord-tenant law in recent years has been the recognition of an **implied warranty of habitability** in leases of residential property.[5] Most courts that have considered the question recently have adopted the warranty. A few have based their decisions on particular language in state housing codes placing certain duties of repair on residential landlords. Most of them, however, have recognized the warranty as a matter of public policy regardless of the existence or wording of a housing code. In addition, several states have adopted the implied warranty of habitability by express legislative enactment.

The warranty of habitability requires landlords to maintain residential property, such as a house, apartment, or duplex, in a "habitable" or livable condition. Although this warranty is most commonly applied to physical defects in the property, it has also been applied to the provision of essential services such as garbage collection. The obligation of the landlord exists at the time the property is leased and throughout the term of the lease. Defects in the premises constitute a breach of the warranty only when the landlord knows or should know about them and has had a reasonable time to make repairs.

A dwelling can be habitable even though it has minor defects. Therefore, the warranty of habitability only applies to major deficiencies. Of course, in some cases a whole host of minor problems existing at the

---

[4]When such a promise is separately made *after* the lease has been agreed to, the new promise must be supported by new consideration.

[5]Judicial recognition of the implied warranty of habitability has also been a major development in the law relating to the *sale of new homes,* as was mentioned in the previous chapter.

same time may render a dwelling unlivable even though each defect alone is not major.

Some defects, such as a large hole in the ceiling or the lack of heat in a cold climate, obviously cause a dwelling to be unhabitable. Others, such as an occasional drip from the kitchen faucet, just as obviously do not cause the premises to be unhabitable. In many cases, however, the question is much closer. The courts in such situations must determine whether the particular defect involves an item which is truly essential or merely an amenity. One court observed:

> [I]n a modern society one cannot be expected to live in a multi-storied apartment building without heat, hot water, garbage disposal, or elevator service. Failure to supply such things is a breach of the implied covenant of habitability. Malfunction of venetian blinds, water leaks, wall cracks, lack of painting, at least of the magnitude presented here, go to what may be called "amenities." Living with lack of painting, water leaks and defective venetian blinds may be unpleasant, aesthetically unsatisfying, but does not come within the category of unhabitability.[6]

When determining whether defects are substantial enough to violate the warranty of habitability, the courts consider a variety of factors, including the following: (1) the impact of the defect on basic life functions—sleeping, eating, relaxing, and so on; (2) the actual or possible effect of the defect on the safety and health of tenants; (3) the length of time the defect has existed; (4) the age of the building—the newer the building, the higher are the tenant's reasonable expectations regarding its condition; and (5) whether the defect violates a building or housing code.

The next case discusses the public policy considerations underlying the implied warranty of habitability, and illustrates the standards used by courts in applying the warranty.

[6]*Academy Spires, Inc. v. Brown,* 111 N. J. 477, 268 A.2d 556, 559 (1970).

PARK WEST MANAGEMENT CORP. v. MITCHELL

Court of Appeals of New York, 391 N.E.2d 1288 (1979)

Case

Park West owned an apartment complex consisting of seven highrise buildings on the Upper West Side of Manhattan in New York City. Because of a strike by Employees' Union Local 32-B, the landlord's entire maintenance and janitorial staff did not report to work for a 17-day period. All of the incinerators were wired shut, thus requiring the tenants to dispose of garbage at the curbs in paper bags. Because employees of the New York Sanitation Department refused to cross the striking employees' picket lines, uncollected trash piled up to the height of the first floor windows. The garbage and the stench it produced led the Health Department to declare a health emergency at the complex.

Also during this period, regular exterminating service was not performed, which, together with the ac-
cumulated trash, created conditions in which rats, roaches, and vermin flourished. Routine maintenance and other service was not performed, and common areas were not cleaned.

A group of tenants withheld their rent payments during the period, and the landlord sued for the rent. About 400 tenants ultimately joined in the legal proceeding. The tenants defended against the landlord's suit by claiming a breach of the implied warranty of habitability. The trial court and intermediate appellate courts ruled that the warranty had been breached, and granted a 10 percent reduction in the tenants' June rent bill. The landlord appealed to the highest court in New York.

Cooke, Chief Judge:

Under the traditional common-law principles governing the landlord-tenant relationship, a lease was regarded as a
conveyance of an estate for a specified term and thus as a transfer of real property. Consequently, the duty the law imposed upon the lessor was satisfied when the legal right of possession was delivered to the lessee. The lessor impliedly warranted only the continued quiet enjoyment of the premises by the lessee. This covenant of quiet enjoyment was the only obligation imposed upon the landlord which was interdependent with the lessee's covenant to pay rent. As long as the undisturbed right to possession of the premises remained in the tenant, regardless of the condition of the premises, the duty to pay rent remained unaffected.

Because the common law of leasehold interests developed in rural, agrarian England, the right to possession of the land itself was considered the essential part of the bargain; structures upon the land were deemed incidental. . . .

(continues)

PARK WEST MANAGEMENT CORP. V. MITCHELL

(continued from previous page)

As society slowly moved away from an agrarian economy, the needs and expectations of tenants underwent a marked change. No longer was the right of bare possession the vital part of the parties' bargain. The urban tenant seeks shelter and the services necessarily appurtenant thereto—heat, light, water, sanitation and maintenance. . . .

A number of factors mandated departure from the antiquated common-law rules governing the modern landlord-tenant relationship. The modern-day tenant, unlike his medieval counterpart, is primarily interested in shelter and shelter-related services. He is usually not competent to perform maintenance chores, even assuming ability to gain access to the necessary equipment and to areas within the exclusive control of the landlord. . . .

The transformation of the nature of the housing market occasioned by rapid urbanization and population growth was further impetus for the change. Well-documented shortages of low- and middle-income housing in many of our urban centers has placed landlords in a vastly superior bargaining position, leaving tenants virtually powerless to compel the performance of essential services. . . . While it is true that many municipalities have enacted housing codes setting minimum safety and sanitation standards, historically those codes could be enforced only by municipal authorities.

In short, until development of the warranty of habitability in residential leases, the contemporary tenant possessed few private remedies and little real power, under either the common law or modern housing codes, to compel his landlord to make necessary repairs or provide essential services. . . . A residential lease is now effectively deemed a sale of shelter and services by the landlord who impliedly warrants: first, that the premises are fit for human habitation; second, that the condition of the premises is in accord with the uses reasonably intended by the parties; and,

third, that the tenants are not subjected to any conditions endangering or detrimental to their life, health or safety. . . . The obligation of the tenant to pay rent is dependent upon the landlord's satisfactory maintenance of the premises in habitable condition.

Naturally, it is [an] impossibility to attempt to document every instance in which the warranty of habitability could be breached. Each case must, of course, turn on its own peculiar facts. However, the standards of habitability set forth in local housing codes will often be of help in resolution of this question. . . . However, a simple finding that conditions on the leased premises are in violation of an applicable housing code does not necessarily constitute automatic breach of the warranty. In some instances, it may be that the code violation is *de minimis* or has no impact upon habitability. . . .

But, while certainly a factor in the measurement of the landlord's obligation, violation of a housing code or sanitary regulation is not the exclusive determinant of whether there has been a breach. Housing codes do not provide a complete delineation of the landlord's obligation, but rather serve as a starting point in that determination by establishing minimal standards that all housing must meet. In some localities, comprehensive housing, building or sanitation codes may not have been enacted; in others, their provisions may not address the particular condition claimed to render the premises uninhabitable. Threats to the health and safety of the tenant—not merely violations of the codes—de-termine the reach of the warranty of habitability. . . .

To be sure, absent an express agreement to the contrary, a landlord is not required to ensure that the premises are in perfect or even aesthetically pleasing condition; he does warrant, however, that there are no conditions that materially affect the health and safety of tenants. For example, no one will dispute that health and safety are adversely affected by insect or rodent infestation,

insufficient heat and plumbing facilities, significantly dangerous electrical outlets or wiring, inadequate sanitation facilities or similar services which constitute the essence of the modern dwelling unit. If, in the eyes of a reasonable person, defects in the dwelling deprive the tenant of those essential functions which a residence is expected to provide, a breach of the implied warranty of habitability has occurred.

Under the facts presented here, respondents [tenants] have proven that petitioner [landlord] breached its implied warranty of habitability. As a result of the strike, essential services bearing directly on the health and safety of the tenants were curtailed, if not eliminated. Not only were there numerous violations of housing and sanitation codes, but conditions of the premises were serious enough to necessitate the declaration of a health emergency. In light of these factors, it ill behooves petitioner to maintain that the tenants suffered only a trifling inconvenience. . . .

Problematical in these cases is the method of ascertaining damages occasioned by the landlord's breach. That damages are not susceptible to precise determination does not insulate the landlord from liability. Inasmuch as the duty of the tenant to pay rent is coextensive with the landlord's duty to maintain the premises in habitable condition, the proper measure of damages for breach of the warranty is the difference between the fair market value of the premises if they had been as warranted, as measured by the rent reserved under the lease, and the value of the premises during the period of the breach. . . . In ascertaining damages, the finder of fact must weigh the severity of the violation and duration of the conditions giving rise to the breach as well as the effectiveness of steps taken by the landlord to abate those conditions. . . . The record here amply supports the 10% reduction in rent ordered by Civil Court.

[Affirmed.]

Tenant's Remedies for Landlord's Failure to Maintain the Premises

The instances in which a landlord has the duty to maintain the premises have been increasing in recent times. Along with the expansion of the landlord's obligation to maintain the premises, there has also been a general expansion of the tenant's remedies for breach of the obligation. The remedies available to the tenant will depend on the circumstances and on the law of the particular state.

Suit for Damages

Any time the landlord breaches a duty to repair, the tenant may sue for the damages caused by the landlord's failure. Damages in the case of relatively minor defects are based on the cost of repairing them. For major defects, damages usually are calculated as the difference between the rental value of the premises in unrepaired and repaired conditions. Because of the time and expense of pursuing a damage suit, it is a feasible remedy only for major defects. Even in the case of major defects, a damage lawsuit usually makes economic sense only if (1) the lease is a long-term one or (2) the tenant uses the premises for business purposes so that the attorney fees and other expenses of pursuing the claim can be treated as a business expense for tax purposes.

Repair and Deduct

In the past several years many states have enacted so-called **repair and deduct** statutes. This type of legislation permits the tenant to make repairs and then deduct the cost of such repairs from the rent. Courts in several states have recognized the right to repair and deduct even without a specific statute. The right of tenants to use this remedy is subject to several important limitations: (1) the defect must have been one that the landlord was legally obligated to repair; (2) the landlord must have been notified of the defect and failed to repair it within a prescribed period of time; (3) the amount that can be deducted by the tenant usually is limited—in some states the limitation is expressed as a specific maximum amount, such as $200; in other states it is based on a set formula, such as one month's rent; and (4) in several states, the tenant's right to repair and deduct applies only to defects that relate to essential services such as water and electricity.

The repair and deduct remedy has been applied most commonly to situations in which a landlord breached the implied warranty of habitability.

Rent Withholding

By statute or court decision, many states in recent years have authorized a reduction in the tenant's rent until the landlord makes required repairs. The amount of the reduction is computed in various ways, but generally must be proportionate to the diminishment of rental value caused by the defect. When the **rent withholding** right is created by statute, the statute usually requires the tenant to deposit the amount withheld with a court or other designated agency until the dispute is resolved.

Regardless of whether the right to reduce and withhold rent has been created by statute or judicial decision in a particular state, a tenant exercising the right always runs the risk of withholding too much. If a court ultimately determines that a tenant has withheld more than the law permits, the tenant is liable to the landlord for the amount that was impermissibly withheld.

Like the repair and deduct remedy, the rent withholding remedy also has usually been connected with the implied warranty of habitability. The *Park West* case provides an illustration of this remedy.

Lease Cancellation

The landlord's breach of a duty to repair ordinarily does not give the tenant a right to cancel the lease. However, when the defects are so major that the implied warranty of habitability is breached, most courts permit the tenant to cancel the lease, abandon the premises, and be relieved of any further rent payment obligation. When the tenant chooses this alternative, the implied warranty of habitability is essentially the same as the older principle of constructive eviction.

INJURIES ON THE PREMISES

Suppose that a defect in the leased premises causes injury to the tenant, a member of the tenant's family, or someone else who is lawfully on the premises. Who is legally responsible for the damages caused by these injuries? Liability commonly depends upon whether the landlord or tenant has control over the particular area where the injury occurred. In a few situations, however, the existence of a duty to repair may create such liability regardless of control.

Liability of the Tenant

The tenant has a general duty to maintain in a reasonably safe condition that part of the leased premises which is under his or her control. Thus, if a visitor on residential property or a customer on business property is injured by an unsafe condition, the tenant usually is responsible. Clearly, however, the tenant's responsibility does not extend to injuries occurring in those common areas controlled by the landlord.

The tenant's duty to maintain the premises in a safe condition exists even in situations where the landlord has a duty to make repairs. Consequently, in some situations both landlord and tenant may be legally responsible for injuries to a third party. Making both of them responsible increases the likelihood that the premises will be kept in a safe condition. Such a policy takes into account the fact that outsiders are less familiar with the property and less likely to be aware of potentially dangerous conditions than the landlord or tenant.

Liability of the Landlord

The landlord's liability for injuries may be based on control, on an affirmative duty to make repairs, or on both factors.

Public Purpose

Ordinarily, the circumstances in which a landlord is liable for injuries are the same whether the injured person is a tenant or anyone else lawfully on the premises. There is, however, one major exception to this principle. When premises are leased for a purpose that involves admission of the public, such as a retail store, the landlord owes a continuing duty to the public to maintain the premises in a safe condition. This duty makes the landlord liable for injuries to members of the public even when there would have been no basis for landlord liability if the *tenant* had been the injured party.

When premises are leased for a public purpose, and a member of the public is injured by a defect in the property, the tenant also is responsible. The injured party could thus take action against both landlord and tenant.

Common Areas

The landlord is liable for injuries caused by defects in common areas over which the landlord has control. This liability to tenants or others lawfully on the premises is coextensive with the landlord's general duty to make repairs in common areas.

The following case presents a situation in which the landlord was held liable for injuries caused by defects in an outside porch.

CRUZ V. DREZEK

Supreme Court of Connecticut, 397 A.2d 1335 (1978)

 Case

The Cruz family rented a third-floor apartment in a three-family house in New Britain, Connecticut, from the owners, Edward and Jeanette Drezek. Outside the third-floor apartment was a porch. The evidence did not indicate whether other tenants also had access to the porch. Regardless of whether it was a true "common" area, the evidence did clearly show that the landlord retained control over this exterior porch.

Fourteen-year-old Hector Cruz was helping his family move in. A small mattress was being raised by

ropes from the ground to the third-floor porch. Hector was on the porch pulling the mattress up. As he leaned on the railing surrounding the porch, it gave way and he fell to the ground. The Cruzes sued the Drezeks for damages resulting from Hector's injuries. Based on a jury verdict, the trial court awarded judgment in favor of Hector for $20,000 and Hector's parents for $1,952.40 to cover the medical bills they had paid. The Drezeks, defendants, appealed on the grounds that there was not enough evidence of negligence on their part to even create a jury question, and that the trial court should have ruled in their favor as a matter of law.

Healey, Justice:

. . . The defendants were under the duty to use reasonable care to keep those portions of the premises, and specifically the third-floor porch, together with its railings, over which they had control, in a reasonably safe condition. . . . There could be no breach of the duty resting upon the defendants unless they knew of the defective condition or were chargeable with notice of it because, had they exercised a reasonable inspection of their premises, they would have discovered it; and it was the defendants' duty to make a reasonable inspection of premises in their control to discover possible defects therein.

(continues)

CRUZ V. DREZEK

(continued from previous page)
Turning to the question of the specific defective condition, the evidence, while contradictory, furnished a reasonable basis for the jury's conclusion that the plaintiffs had proven that there did exist at the time of this accident a specific defective condition pertaining to the front porch railing, that the specific defective condition in fact caused Hector's fall and that that specific condition had existed for a sufficient length of time so as to have afforded the defendants an opportunity on a reasonable inspection to discover and remedy it. . . .

The following evidence was also before the jury: Detective Walsh of the New Britain Police Department, who had been a policeman for twenty-three years and a detective for sixteen years, arrived at the scene of this accident within two or three minutes after receiving a radio call. He learned that two men had fallen from the third-floor porch and had been injured. He testified, with respect to the railing, that the railing, where it pulled away, looked "rotted"; that there were nails sticking out and that the wood "looked rotted; it looked old"; that "the railing had carried away from its anchor, from the nails which anchored it to the side of the building, of the posts"; that when he found the railing, the nails were still

in it and that he recalled that some nails were left in the posts upstairs and some stayed with the railing which fell below; and that, with respect to both the railing and posts, the exterior wood was "badly weathered," and that "the paint was chipped away, and where the paint was chipped away the wood was gray from weathering." Mrs. Ehritz, a witness called by the defendants, had lived two houses away for about fifteen years. She testified that the "railing was old and the nails were rusty." . . .

The defendants had purchased this house about ten weeks or two months before this accident. While admitting the house needed a paint job, Edward Drezek claimed it did not need new porches. He applied, however, in November, 1970, for a building permit to repair and enclose three front porches on this house. Before buying this property Edward Drezek personally inspected it. With reference to the third-floor porch, he visually inspected it and specifically checked that porch's railings and banisters, all of which he claimed were fine.

Frank Costanzo is a foreman for a moving company for which he has worked for fifty years and he has spent at least forty years working on the trucks, helping people to move. He has had "plenty of occasions" to move mattresses and, in the course of his work,

ropes have been used many times to pull up mattresses. According to him, this was a customary and common way of handling them because they are otherwise too hard to handle. . . .

This was a third-floor porch, and the greater the likelihood of danger, the greater the amount of care required in making an inspection of the premises to meet the standard of due care. The controlling question in deciding whether the defendants had constructive notice of the defective condition is whether the condition existed for such a length of time that the defendants should, in the exercise of reasonable care, have discovered it in time to remedy it. Given the evidence before the jury, they could reasonably have found that this specific defective condition existed for a reasonable length of time within which the defendants should have learned of it, especially because of Edward Drezek's having been on that porch approximately two months before, just before he bought this property, at which time he looked at the railings, and that a reasonable length of time had passed for remedying the condition of which he should have known. . . .

A permissible and reasonable view of the evidence by the jury permitted them to find for the plaintiffs.

[Affirmed.]

Latent Defects

A **latent defect** is one that is hidden to such an extent that the tenant is not likely to discover it during a normal initial inspection. If such a defect exists at the time a lease is made, and the landlord either knows or reasonably should know about it, the landlord has a duty to disclose the defect to the tenant. Failure to disclose makes the landlord liable for injuries subsequently caused by the defect. It is important to note that the landlord fulfills his or her duty by disclosing the existence of the defect—the landlord is not re-

quired to actually fix it unless there is some other legal basis for imposing a duty of repair.

The landlord's nondisclosure of hidden defects may bring about other consequences as well, such as giving the tenant a legal basis for cancelling the lease.

Negligent Repairs

Regardless of whether the landlord has a duty to make repairs, if he or she makes them and does so in a *negligent* manner, the landlord is liable for any injuries caused by the negligent repairs.

Express Agreement, Statutory Duty, and Implied Warranty

In the previous section we saw that, in modern times, the landlord has increasingly been placed under a duty to make repairs. This duty may exist because the landlord has agreed in an express lease provision to make repairs, or the duty may be imposed by a building or housing code or the implied warranty of habitability. In these situations, the landlord may have the duty to make repairs even with respect to those parts of the premises under the tenant's control.

Suppose that Thompson has leased an apartment from Leonard. Assume that, because of an express lease clause, an applicable code provision, or an implied warranty, Leonard has a duty to repair and maintain the apartment. Leonard then breaches this duty by failing to make certain repairs. If either Thompson or someone else lawfully on the premises is injured because of the defect, is Leonard liable for the injury?

The court decisions in the various states are somewhat evenly split on this issue. Some of them focus on the repair duty itself and conclude that liability for injuries is a logical component of the duty. Others focus on the factor of control and conclude that the landlord's liability for injuries should not extend to areas over which the landlord has very little daily control, even when the landlord has a duty to repair those areas.

Of course, when the injured person is an outsider who does not live on the leased premises, the tenant generally is liable for the injuries even though the landlord may also be liable.

Exculpatory and Indemnification Clauses

Leases often contain **exculpatory clauses,** which state that the landlord is not liable for injuries on the premises. Such a clause cannot excuse the landlord from liability to outsiders who are not parties to the lease. However, it is also common for an **indemnification clause** to accompany the exculpatory clause. The indemnification clause states that the tenant must indemnify, or reimburse, the landlord for damages the landlord has to pay to outsiders.

The courts have reached different conclusions on the question of whether exculpatory and indemnification clauses are effective to shield the landlord. Some of these different results are based upon the language of the particular clause or the existence of a specific statute in the particular state. However, many of the decisions are simply in conflict with one another.

As a general proposition, courts are much more likely to throw out such clauses in residential leases than in commercial ones. Moreover, regardless of the type of lease, there is a gradual trend in the courts toward invalidating these clauses.

It should be emphasized that here we are speaking of exculpatory clauses that seek to excuse the *landlord* from liability. If the lease contains a clause purporting to excuse the *tenant* from liability, such a clause is normally valid. The question whether a lease expresses an intent to excuse the tenant was dealt with earlier in the chapter.

LANDLORD'S RESPONSIBILITY TO PROTECT TENANTS FROM CRIMES

The landlord does not have an absolute duty to protect tenants from the criminal acts of outsiders. As part of the general expansion of the landlord's duties in recent years, however, several courts have found landlords responsible for providing such protection in certain circumstances. The situations in which the landlord has been found liable for crimes committed against tenants usually involve evidence that (1) the area around the leased premises has a high crime rate, (2) the landlord knew or should have known of the danger caused by criminal activity in the area, and (3) the landlord did not take precautions that were reasonably necessary to protect tenants under the circumstances.

When these facts are proved, the landlord is held responsible for criminal conduct occurring both in common areas and in the leased premises itself. The landlord's responsibility can take several forms. First, he or she may be held liable to a tenant for damages caused by the crime. Courts have based this liability on either the tort of negligence or the implied warranty of habitability. Second, a landlord's inadequate precautions in the face of known criminal activity could constitute a breach of the implied warranty of habitability or the covenant for quiet enjoyment even if the particular tenant making the claim has not actually been injured by a crime. In this situation, the tenant would be entitled to the normal remedies for breach of those obligations, including rent reduction, cancellation of the lease, and so on. The following case provides an illustration of the latter type of situation.

HIGHVIEW ASSOCIATES V. KOFERL

District Court of Suffolk County, 477 N.Y.S.2d 585 (1984)

Case

Jeanne Koferl, a single woman with an eight-year-old son, was a tenant in a large garden apartment complex owned by Highview in Selden, New York. Burglaries and robberies had become fairly common in the complex, and the landlord had done nothing to improve security. On one occasion, Koferl discovered a "peeping tom" looking through her window on the first floor, and she notified the apartment manager of the incident. Somewhat later, toward the end of January 1983, two unknown men attempted to burglarize Koferl's apartment at 3:00 a.m. She was awakened when one of the burglars started to rip the screen from the sliding glass door. She was able to ward off the criminals, and in terror she then grabbed her son and fled to her mother's home, never to return to the apartment. The lease did not expire until May 26, and the landlord was not able to rerent the apartment to another tenant until April 1.

The landlord sued Koferl, claiming that she breached the lease by moving out and paying no further rent. The landlord sought damages of $588, consisting of unpaid rent, painting and repairs, expenses involved in finding another tenant, and attorney fees, minus Koferl's $930 security deposit that the landlord had kept. Koferl defended by asserting that the landlord had breached the implied warranty of habitability and the covenant for quiet enjoyment by failing to provide adequate protection against criminals, thus relieving her of any responsibility under the lease. She did not seek damages or the return of her security deposit.

Colaneri, Judge:

The issue posed by the defendant is . . .: Should the landlord of a large gar-

den apartment complex in a rural or suburban community furnish protection to its tenants . . . against the depredations of burglars, thieves and other criminals?

This court is mindful of the cases of *Brownstein v. Edison,* 425 N.Y.S.2d 773 and *Sherman v. Concourse Realty Corp.,* 365 N.Y.S.2d 239. The fact situations in these cases differ from the facts in the instant case in that the landlords in both cases had provided special locks and buzzer systems on the front doors to prevent criminal types from intruding into high-rise apartment buildings in New York City.

In both cases the landlord had raised the rent to include the cost of the special locks and protective systems. In both cases the locks and protective devices were broken and inoperable. The tenant in the *Brownstein* case was murdered in the apartment lobby, and the tenant in the *Sherman* case was severely assaulted—again in the apartment lobby.

The courts in both cases held that the landlord had assumed the duty to provide some degree of protection to the tenants by providing these protective devices, and the landlords in both cases were to render an essential service affecting habitability. Thus, when the locks and devices became inoperable, the landlords breached the implied warranty of habitability.

In [*Park West Management Corp. v. Mitchell,*] Chief Judge Cooke discussed the transition of landlord-tenant law from the common-law concept of a tenant's estate in land to the modern day theory that a lease is not an estate in land, but is a contract between the owner of real property and the occupier of real property. It was held in that case that the landlord "is not a guarantor of every amenity customarily rendered in the landlord-tenant relationship," and that the warranty of habitability was not [created]

for the purpose of rendering landlords absolute insurers of services which do not affect habitability. The [New York statute adopting this warranty] was designed to give rise to an implied promise on the part of the landlord that both the leased premises and areas within the landlord's control are fit for human occupation at the inception of the tenancy, and the premises will remain so throughout the lease term.

In the present case, there was no initial obligation on the part of the landlord to supply security devices for the protection of the tenants. After a number of years, however, this apartment complex has become the object of burglars and thieves, so that break-ins and thefts have become frequent. Mr. David Orenstein, the manager of the plaintiff's complex, testified that there were approximately 5 to 10 burglaries each year in the entire complex. Mr. Orenstein, however, was quite evasive and vague about the actual number of burglaries.

If this court accepts the figure of (only) 10 burglaries per year as the number of burglaries committed in the subject premises, this amounts to one burglary in every 36.6 apartments. Thus, if we use this one statistic, and, if we extend this ratio over a period of years, almost 10% of the tenants in the plaintiff's garden apartment complex will be victims of burglaries, thefts and worse over a three-year period.

Relying upon the reasoning of Chief Judge Cooke [in the *Park West* case], this court shall extend the concept of the implied warranty of habitability and make it applicable to the present case. This court finds that living conditions in the plaintiff's garden apartment complex had become dangerous and that the landlord had become obligated to take steps to protect its tenants by whatever means available to it.

(continues)

HIGHVIEW ASSOCIATES V. KOFERL

(continued from previous page)

Despite many notices to the plaintiff of thefts and burglaries committed in the plaintiff's garden apartment complex, the landlord had not (and has not) taken any steps to protect its tenants. The plaintiff has thus breached the implied warranty of habitability, as well as the [covenant] of use and quiet enjoyment.

The defendant acted reasonably and properly when she fled the premises, since it became apparent to her that it was not safe to live in the apartment any longer.

Accordingly, judgment is rendered for the defendant dismissing the plaintiff's complaint, with costs awarded to the defendant. ↵↵

RENT AND OTHER FINANCIAL OBLIGATIONS OF THE TENANT

Rent

Rent is the compensation paid to the landlord for the tenant's possession and use of the leased premises. Leases almost always contain provisions expressly setting the rent. If this is omitted, the law of most states obligates the tenant to pay the reasonable rental value of the property. The right to receive rent can be *assigned,* or transferred, to a third party.

The time, method, and place for rent payment usually are specified in the lease. Most leases expressly require advance payment at the *beginning* of each rental period. If the parties do not agree on the time for payment, however, the general rule is that rent is due at the *end* of each rental period.

When the lease expressly requires payment of rent on or before a stated date, payment by this date usually is an absolute requirement. The tenant breaches his or her obligation by late payment. In a few states, however, statutes have been passed which provide a short "grace period" beyond the due date, such as five days. Until expiration of this grace period, the landlord may not terminate the lease for nonpayment. Also, if the landlord has customarily accepted late rental payments, he or she may have *waived* the right to prompt payment. In such a case, the landlord must continue to accept similarly late payments unless he or she expressly announces that late payments will not be accepted in the future.

Rent normally is not considered "paid" until actually received by the landlord or the landlord's agent. However, most courts do not permit lease termination because of relatively short, unexpected delays in mail delivery.

Rent is payable in money unless the parties agree on some other form of consideration. Payment by check is sufficient unless the landlord expressly requires cash.

The lease usually specifies the place for payment. If it does not, the leased property itself is the place where the rent is payable. In such a case, before the landlord can legally terminate the lease for nonpayment he or she must come onto the leased premises and demand the rent.

Security Deposits

A **security deposit** of cash or property by the tenant is required only if the lease provides for it. Most leases do provide for security deposits. The purpose of a security deposit is to provide the landlord with a quick and sure remedy when the tenant damages the property, fails to pay rent, or breaks the lease.

Some landlords attempt to keep security deposits regardless of whether there is any justification for doing so. Legally, the landlord is entitled to keep only so much of the deposit as is necessary to compensate him or her for damages that actually can be proved. Today, many states have statutes specifically regulating the landlord's handling of the security deposit when a lease is terminated.

Typically, these statutes require that the landlord return the tenant's security deposit within a certain period of time, such as 30 days, and prohibit any deduction from the deposit that is not explained on an accompanying itemized list of damages and repairs.

Other Payments

Unless the lease provides otherwise, the landlord is obligated to pay taxes on the leased property and the tenant is required to pay utility bills.

THE LANDLORD'S REMEDIES

Detainer

A lease legally may be terminated for several reasons, as we saw earlier in the chapter. For instance, expiration of the agreed duration terminates the lease. Also, in most states today, the landlord may terminate the lease for nonpayment of rent.

If the tenant wrongfully remains in possession after termination, the landlord may file a court action to have the tenant removed. This action, usually called **unlawful detainer, forcible entry and detainer,** or some similar name, is given special expedited treatment by the court and decided very quickly. If the landlord proves a right to possession, the sheriff or other officer removes the tenant from the property.[7]

Landlord's Lien

At common law, the landlord had the right to seize, and hold or sell, the tenant's personal property for nonpayment of rent. The **landlord's lien** extended only to items actually located on the leased premises. Today in most states this remedy is regulated by statute. In some states the landlord must file a court action to exercise his or her lien. In these states, items of the tenant's property located on the leased premises are seized by a sheriff or other officer. Other states permit the landlord to seize the tenant's belongings, but a court proceeding normally is required before they can be sold.

Many leases, particularly residential ones, expressly grant the landlord a lien on the tenant's belongings located on the leased premises. The extent of the lien and method of enforcement are governed primarily by the language of the lease.

Damages

When the tenant fails to pay rent or harms the property, the landlord is entitled to receive money damages to compensate for the loss. If the security deposit is inadequate to pay these damages, the landlord may file suit to collect the remainder.

Duty to Mitigate Damages

Suppose that T, the tenant, and L, the landlord, have agreed to the lease of a house for eighteen months at a monthly rental of $500. After six months T stops paying rent, and two months later she leaves (either voluntarily or involuntarily). T certainly is liable to L for $1,000—two months' unpaid rent. But is T also responsible for the $5,000 rent for the remaining ten months of the lease?

Traditionally, L could recover the $5,000 and was not obligated to *mitigate,* or lessen, his damages by seeking another tenant. He could simply leave the premises vacant. If L actually does find another tenant, the damages L can recover from T are reduced by the rent L receives from the substitute tenant during the remainder of the original lease term.

In a substantial minority of states, L is under a duty to mitigate his damages by making reasonable efforts to find a new tenant. Suppose that L finds a new tenant six months after T leaves (that is, with four months remaining in the original lease term). Obviously, L still could recover the $1,000 unpaid rent from T. But what about L's claim for $3,000 rent for the six months during which the house was vacant? In one of those states requiring L to mitigate his damages, the court will determine whether L had made a reasonable effort to find a new tenant after T left. If the court concludes that such an effort was made, and that the period of vacancy was not due to any lack of diligence on L's part, L can recover $3,000 in addition to the $1,000. On the other hand, if the court concludes that L did not make a reasonable effort and probably could have found a new tenant in *three months* had such an effort been made, L's recovery from T will be limited to $1,000 plus $1,500.

The requirement that L mitigate damages is being adopted by more and more courts and legislatures as they have an opportunity to consider the question, and probably will become the majority rule in the next few years.

ASSIGNMENTS AND SUBLEASES

A tenant sometimes may want to transfer his or her rights and obligations under the lease to a third party. Such a transfer is either an assignment or a sublease.

Distinction between Assignment and Sublease

An **assignment** of the lease occurs when the tenant transfers the entire remaining portion of the lease to a third party. A **sublease** occurs when the tenant transfers the lease for only part of its remaining

---

[7]An older type of remedy, *ejectment,* still exists in many states. It is a much slower procedure for evicting tenants and has not often been used by landlords since statutes have created the quicker detainer procedure.

LEGAL FOCUS

International

When comparing the law of various nations, it is often interesting to find that similar results have been achieved through quite different lines of reasoning. One example in the area of landlord-tenant law is the doctrine of *retaliatory eviction*. This doctrine, which is recognized by statute or judicial decision in well over one-half of the states in the United States, generally provides that a landlord (especially a residential one) cannot lawfully evict a tenant in retaliation for certain actions by the tenant. Such actions by the tenant include complaining to the landlord or to local housing authorities about defects in the premises, or exercising the right to make repairs and deduct the reasonable cost of those repairs from the rent. In a jurisdiction recognizing the doctrine of retaliatory eviction, the landlord commits a separate illegal act by evicting the tenant in retaliation for the tenant's actions, even if the eviction is not a breach of a lease contract. The theoretical basis for the doctrine of retaliatory eviction in the United States is that a person should not be punished for exercising a legal right.

In the civil law as found in European countries, and indeed, in most developed countries throughout the world that do not trace their legal heritage to the English common law, the doctrine of retaliatory eviction has been recognized for a longer period of time than in the United States. Although application of the doctrine in these countries generally produces the same results as in those U.S. states recognizing the doctrine, the original theoretical foundation for it was quite different. The civil law underpinning for the retaliatory eviction rule is the "abuse of rights" doctrine, which essentially states that a person with a legal right (such as the landlord) should not abuse it by exercising it unfairly. Thus, the U.S. common-law version of retaliatory eviction is based on tenants' rights, whereas the civil law version in much of the rest of the world is based on the exercise of landlords' rights. It is also worth noting that the abuse of rights doctrine is generally not recognized in U.S. common law in other legal subject areas where it could have potential applicability.

---

duration. Suppose, for example, that two years remain on what was originally a three-year lease. If the tenant transfers the lease to another party for the remaining two years, the transfer is an assignment. If the tenant executes a transfer for less than two years, such as twelve or eighteen months, the transfer is a sublease.

When an assignment occurs, the third party (assignee) essentially takes the place of the original tenant. The landlord-tenant relationship, with all of its rights and responsibilities, then exists between the landlord and the assignee. The landlord and assignee each have the right to legally enforce the lease obligations of the other. However, the original tenant is not excused from his or her obligations unless expressly released by the landlord. Thus, if the assignee fails to pay rent, the landlord can proceed against the assignee, the original tenant, or both. If the original tenant has to pay, he or she is entitled to recoup the loss from the assignee.

In the case of a sublease, no legal relationship is created between the landlord and the third party (sublessee). Neither the landlord nor the sublessee has legally enforceable obligations to or rights against the other. The landlord-tenant relationship, with all its rights and duties, continues to exist between the landlord and the original tenant. Another landlord-tenant relationship is created between the original tenant and the sublessee.

The Tenant's Right to Transfer

As a general rule, a tenant has the right to execute an assignment or sublease unless (1) the lease places express limitations on the right, or (2) a specific state statute modifies the right in some way. Today, most leases expressly prohibit assignments or subleases unless the landlord consents. Moreover, several states have statutes which regulate the execution of assignments and subleases. In some states, the transfer must be in writing to have any effect, and in some states recording statutes must be complied with to protect the interest of the assignee or sublessee.

SUMMARY

The landlord-tenant relationship is created by an agreement commonly called a lease, which provides for the transfer of exclusive possession and control of real property in return for the payment of rent. The interest acquired by the tenant, or lessee, is called a tenancy, or leasehold, and takes different forms depending on the terms of the lease. The landlord, or lessor, is the owner of the reversionary fee simple interest, and owes the tenant the duty to allow possession and not to interfere with the lawful possession and use of the premises. The tenant, on the other hand, has a duty not to intentionally or negligently damage the premises, and usually has no right to add fixtures or otherwise alter the premises without the landlord's consent.

Although the traditional rule that a landlord has no duty to maintain the premises still exists theoretically, in modern times it has become subject to a great many important exceptions, including the duty to keep common areas in a reasonably safe condition and to observe the maintenance obligations imposed by building codes and the implied warranty of habitability. Both the tenant and the landlord can be held liable in some circumstances for injuries occurring on the premises. The tenant's liability is based on the duty to maintain in a reasonably safe condition that part of the premises under his or her control. The landlord can be held liable for injuries on premises that were leased for a purpose involving admission of the public and for those occurring in common areas, as well as for injuries resulting from latent defects or negligent repairs. In some states the landlord is liable for injuries caused by breach of an express lease provision, statutory duty, or implied warranty.

There is a modern trend for landlords to be held responsible for taking reasonable precautions to protect tenants from criminal activities. The landlord has a basic right to receive rent from the tenant, and may require the tenant to post a security deposit to cover possible damage to the property. The landlord has several remedies for the tenant's breach of the lease agreement, including detainer, exercise of the landlord's lien, and a suit for damages. As a general rule, a tenant has the right to transfer the right to possession by assignment or sublease unless such right is restricted by the lease or by statutory provision.

KEY TERMS

Lease
Covenant
Condition
Tenancy (or leasehold)
Tenancy for years
Periodic tenancy
Tenancy at will
Tenancy at sufferance
Surrender and acceptance
Reversion
Covenant of quiet enjoyment
Eviction
Constructive eviction
Waste
Trade fixtures
Implied warranty of habitability
Repair and deduct
Rent withholding
Latent defect
Exculpatory clause
Indemnification clause
Rent
Security deposit
Unlawful detainer (or forcible entry and detainer)
Landlord's lien
Assignment
Sublease

QUESTIONS AND PROBLEMS

1. Kolea rented a building from Greenfield for the purpose of storing automobiles. Approximately one year later, while the lease was still in effect, the building was destroyed by fire. The lease agreement was silent as to the effect of such an occurrence on the rental obligation. Thereafter, Kolea refused to continue paying rent, claiming that the destruction of the building excused him from any further obligation to pay rent. Greenfield sued for the unpaid rent under the remaining portion of the lease. Will Greenfield be successful? Discuss. (*Albert M. Greenfield & Co. v. Kolea,* 380 A.2d 758, Pa. 1977.)

2. Kilbourne rented an apartment from Forester for one year, beginning in June 1966. A provision in the lease stated that it was "renewable at the end of the year period." Kilbourne renewed the lease for an additional year in June 1967. Toward the end of the second year Kilbourne gave notice to Forester that she wished to renew the lease for a third one-year term. Forester refused to execute another lease, Kilbourne refused to leave, and Forester filed suit

to have Kilbourne removed from the apartment. Who will prevail? Discuss. (*Kilbourne v. Forester*, 464 S.W.2d 770, Mo. Ct. App. 1971.)

3. Applegate and Turnquist leased an apartment from Inland for a one-year term. Before signing the lease agreement, Applegate inspected the apartment with the building manager. The apartment was very dirty and a couple of dead roaches could be seen. The manager said "it would be fixed" before Applegate moved in. At the time the lease was being signed, Applegate asked the manager if the apartment had any problem with roaches, because she didn't want to move in if it did. The manager replied that she hadn't heard anything about roaches. The next day, Applegate and Turnquist moved into the apartment and immediately saw roaches everywhere. They attempted for two days to exterminate the roaches, but were unsuccessful. The two tenants then moved out and refused to pay rent. Inland kept the security deposit. Applegate filed suit in which she sought to recover the security deposit, claiming that Inland had committed a constructive eviction. Inland asserted a counterclaim for damages, claiming that Applegate breached the lease agreement. Discuss whether a constructive eviction had occurred. (*Applegate v. Inland Real Estate Corporation*, 441 N.E.2d 379, Ill. App. Ct. 1982.)

4. The Norwoods rented a second-floor apartment from Lazarus. There were seven other apartments on the second floor, and a common hallway served all eight units. Children of various tenants, including the Norwoods' two-year-old daughter, regularly played in the hallway. Lazarus periodically inspected the building and saw the children playing. The paint on the walls and baseboards of the hallway was cracked and flaking. Flakes of paint were on the hall floor. On several occasions the Norwoods saw their daughter put paint flakes in her mouth. Each time they spanked her and told her to stop. Later she became ill and was diagnosed as having chronic lead poisoning. The paint in the hallway was tested by the Lead Poison Control Unit of the City of St. Louis, and was found to contain high levels of lead in violation of a city ordinance. The Norwoods sued Lazarus for damages, claiming that he was negligent in permitting an unsafe condition to exist. Are the Norwoods correct? Discuss. (*Norwood v. Lazarus*, 634 S.W.2d 584, Mo. Ct. App. 1982.)

5. Winslar rented an apartment from Bartlett. The police came to the apartment to arrest Winslar.

When they knocked on the door, Winslar shot through the door with a gun, wounding one of the police officers. The police then threw tear gas canisters into the apartment and subsequently arrested Winslar. The tear gas caused substantial damage to the apartment, and Bartlett filed suit against Winslar. Should Winslar be held responsible to Bartlett for the damages to the apartment? Why or why not? (*Winslar v. Bartlett*, 573 S.W.2d 608, Tex. Ct. Civ. App. 1978.)

6. Williams worked for a company which conducted its business in offices leased from Koplin. To get to and from work, it was necessary for Williams to use an outside stairway. One day when Williams was leaving the building after work, she slipped on snow and ice which had accumulated on the stairs. She was injured in the resulting fall, and filed suit against Koplin, the owner of the building, and Hinsdale, who managed the building for Koplin. Should Williams win? Discuss. (*Williams v. Alfred N. Koplin & Co.*, 448 N.E.2d 1042, Ill. App. Ct. 1983.)

7. Crowell leased an apartment from the City of Dallas Housing Authority, a city government agency serving the purpose of providing safe and sanitary dwellings to persons of low income. In the standard lease agreement provided by the Housing Authority, a clause stipulated that the Authority would not be liable for any damages caused by the condition of the premises. A heater in Crowell's apartment was defective and caused the apartment to fill with carbon monoxide, killing Crowell. Crowell's son, in behalf of his father's estate, sued for damages resulting from medical expenses and his father's pain and suffering. The Housing Authority defended on the grounds that it was excused from liability by the clause in the lease. Is the Housing Authority's defense a good one? Discuss. (*Crowell v. Housing Authority of the City of Dallas*, 495 S.W.2d 887, Tex. 1973.)

8. In anticipation of his upcoming marriage, Kridel leased an apartment from Sommer for a two-year period. Shortly before the wedding, however, Kridel's fiancée broke the engagement. Kridel notified Sommer that he was breaking the lease. Sommer made no effort to rent the apartment to anyone else. In fact, another person wanted to rent it shortly thereafter, but Sommer refused, stating that the apartment was already leased to Kridel. Sommer finally put the apartment up for rent fifteen months later and immediately leased it to another tenant. Sommer sued Kridel for the unpaid rent during the time the

apartment was vacant. Was Kridel responsible for the rent during this period? (*Sommer v. Kridel,* 378 A.2d 767, N. J. 1977.)

9. Trentacost was a 61-year-old widow who had rented an apartment from Brussel for more than ten years. The apartment was located in a building containing a total of eight units located over street-level stores. Access was provided by front and rear entrances. A padlock secured the back entrance, but there was no lock on the front entrance. One afternoon Trentacost was returning to her apartment from a shopping trip. After she had entered the building from the front and reached the top of a flight of stairs leading to her apartment, an assailant grabbed her ankles from behind and dragged her down the stairs. Her purse was stolen and she suffered severe injuries. She later filed suit against Brussel, claiming that he was negligent in not providing a lock or other adequate security for the front entrance. The evidence showed that during the past three years, police had investigated from 75 to 100 crimes in the neighborhood, mostly burglaries and street muggings. Two months before the attack, Trentacost herself had reported to Brussel an attempt by someone to break into the building's cellar. At other times she had notified him of the presence of unauthorized persons in the hallways. She claimed that Brussel had promised to put a lock on the front door, but he denied ever discussing the subject. Should the court hold Brussel liable for Trentacost's damages? Discuss. (*Trentacost v. Brussel,* 412 A.2d 436, N. J. 1980.)

Chapter 45

Personal Property and Bailments

Ownership of Personal Property
Gifts of Personal Property
Other Methods of Acquiring Ownership
Bailments of Personal Property
Special Bailments

OWNERSHIP OF PERSONAL PROPERTY

As we saw in the introduction to Part VI, all property is classified as either real or personal property. In some ways, the legal framework for personal property ownership is similar to that for real property. For example, personal property can be subject to many of the same categories of concurrent ownership as real property, including tenancy in common and joint tenancy, as well as marital co-ownership categories such as tenancy by the entireties and community property. The rules for creating and regulating these types of co-ownership are essentially the same for personal property as for real property.

In addition, a creditor can acquire a voluntary security interest in an item of personal property that is similar to the interest created by a real property mortgage. The debtor retains title to the property, but the creditor with such a security interest owns an interest that serves as security until the debt is paid. The creation, protection, and enforcement of security interests in personal property are governed by Article 9 of the Uniform Commercial Code, and are discussed separately in Chapter 29, "Secured Transactions."

In many ways, however, ownership of personal property is legally quite different than ownership of real property. Ownership of personal property is usually a simpler matter than ownership of real property, primarily because the law does not formally recognize the numerous types of interests that it does for real property. Ordinarily, a person either is the owner of an item of personal property or is not. There sometimes can be a difficult question regarding *who* is the owner of an item of personal property, but once that question is resolved, ownership usually is an all-or-nothing proposition. One example of this fact is found in the use of leases. As we saw in the previous chapter, a lease of real property actually creates another type of ownership interest. A lease of personal property, however, merely creates a *bailment;* the lessee has temporary possession but no ownership interest in the item of personal property.

This chapter deals with several basic topics concerning the ownership, possession, and use of personal property. It first discusses gifts of personal property, and then examines several other methods by which ownership of personal property can change. The chapter then provides a detailed discussion of bailments, an important form of personal property transaction in which possession but not ownership is transferred. It should be pointed out that several other topics related to personal property are sufficiently specialized and complex that they are dealt with in separate chapters. The subject of *sales of goods,* for instance, is thoroughly explored in Chapters 20 through 23. As already mentioned, the topic of secured transactions is covered in Chapter 29. In addition, transfers of both real and personal property by *will* are discussed in Chapter 46.

GIFTS OF PERSONAL PROPERTY

A gift occurs when an owner of property (the **donor**) voluntarily transfers ownership of the property to another (the **donee**) without receiving any consideration in return. In order for the donor to accomplish a transfer of ownership by gift, two fundamental requirements must be met: (1) the donor must have a *present intent* to transfer ownership and (2) the donor must *deliver possession* to the donee.[1]

Present Intent to Transfer Ownership

The language and conduct of the donor, considered in the light of all the surrounding circumstances, must indicate a present intent to transfer ownership. Thus, a promise or expression of intent to transfer ownership in the future is not sufficient. A promise to make a gift is not the same thing as an actual gift. By its very nature, such a promise is not made in return for consideration, as required by contract law. Accordingly, it usually confers no rights on the promisee and cannot be enforced.

It also is critical that the expression of present intent relate to *ownership*. If the evidence indicates that the current owner merely intends to transfer present custody or the right to use the property, there is no gift.

---

[1] There is also a requirement that the donee accept the gift, but acceptance is presumed unless the donee expressly rejects the gift. This issue arises only on rare occasions.

Delivery of Possession

The donor also must actually carry out the expression of intent by delivering possession of the property to the donee. Once there has been an expression of present intent to transfer ownership coupled with actual delivery, the absence of consideration from the donee becomes irrelevant. Title to the property has passed. Many of the disputes involving gifts of personal property have centered on the question of whether there was delivery of possession to the donee. The most common problems relating to the question of delivery are outlined below.

Retention of Control

If the donor attempts to retain a degree of control over the property, there usually is not a legally effective gift. As one court stated, there must be "a complete stripping of the donor of dominion or control over the thing given."[2] To illustrate: X indicates he wants to give a diamond ring to Y. If X then places the ring in a safe-deposit box to which both X and Y have access, there is not a sufficient delivery. Another example is found in the case of *Lee v. Lee*, 5 F.2d 767 (1925): The widow of a grandson of General Robert E. Lee prepared a written document stating that she was giving to her two sons a trunk containing several items which had belonged to the general. She deposited the trunk with a storage company, with instructions to the company obligating it to deliver the trunk to either her or her sons. In holding that there had not been an adequate delivery, the court said, "[T]here was not that quality of completeness present in the transaction which distinguishes a mere intention to give from the completed act, and where this element is lacking the gift fails."

Delivery to an Agent

If delivery of the property is made to the donor's *own agent,* with instructions to deliver to the donee, there is not a completed gift until the donee actually receives the item. The reason, again, is that the donor does not part with sufficient control until the donee takes possession. If the donor delivers possession to the *donee's agent,* however, a valid gift has been made.

Property Already in Possession of the Donee

If the donee already possesses the property when the donor indicates an intent to presently make a gift, the

---

[2]*Allen v. Hendrick,* 206 Pac. 733 (1922).

gift is immediately effective. There is no need to make a formal delivery in this situation.

Constructive Delivery

In most cases, delivery of actual physical possession is required. In two types of circumstances, however, a **constructive delivery** (or **symbolic delivery**) will suffice.

Impracticality. If it is *impractical or inconvenient* to deliver actual physical possession because the item is too large or because it is located at too great a distance from the parties, constructive delivery is allowed. In such cases it ordinarily takes the form of a delivery of something that gives the donee *control* over the property. For example, if the item being given is a car, delivery of the car's key to the donee is sufficient. Similarly, delivery to the donee of a key to a building, room, or container in which an item is located constitutes a valid delivery if physical delivery of the property itself is impractical or inconvenient.

Intangibles. Constructive delivery is permissible for a gift of *intangible* personal property, for the obvious reason that there is nothing physical to deliver. Some types of intangible property rights are evidenced by written documents that by either law or business custom are accepted as representing the intangible right itself. Examples are bonds, promissory notes, corporate stock certificates, insurance policies, and savings account books. For these types of property rights, delivery of the written instrument evidencing the right is treated as delivery of the right itself. If the property right is an ordinary contract right not represented by any commercially recognized document, most courts allow constructive delivery of it by delivery of a writing setting forth the *present intent* to assign the right to the donee.

Grounds for Invalidating Gifts

Of course, a gift will not be valid if the donor's action was induced by fraud, duress, mistake, or undue influence. In addition, the courts always examine very carefully any gift occurring between persons in a "fiduciary" relationship. Thus, if X owes a higher degree of trust to Y because of a fiduciary relationship, and X receives a gift from Y, the law places the burden upon X to prove that all was fair. The following case illustrates this important principle.

GORDON V. BIALYSTOKER CENTER & BIKUR CHOLIM, INC.

Court of Appeals of New York, 385 N.E.2d 285 (1978)

 *Ida Gorodetsky,
who was 85 years
old at the time, suf-
fered a stroke and
was admitted to*
**Brookland-Cumberland Hospital in
August 1972. Her closest relatives,
two brothers and a niece, had not
seen her for several years, and she
had lived alone since 1962. From
the time of her stroke until her death
four months later, Ida remained partially paralyzed, confused, and sometimes semicomatose.**

*At the suggestion of one of Ida's
acquaintances, the Bialystoker nursing home sent one of its social workers to visit the elderly lady in the
hospital in October 1972. After learning that Ida had funds of her own,
the director of the nursing home sent
the social worker back to visit Ida on
November 3 for the purpose of having her sign a withdrawal slip. A
request had already been made for
her admittance to the home, and the
purpose of the withdrawal slip was
to obtain funds for her care at the
home. Using her withdrawal slip, the
home obtained a $15,000 check from
Ida's account payable to the home
"for the benefit of Ida Gorodetsky."*

*On November 13 Ida was moved
to the infirmary of the nursing home.
That same day, within an hour and a
half of admission, she was visited by
a group consisting of the home's executive director, its fund raiser, one of
its social workers, and a notary public. She was presented with a collection of instruments on each of which
she placed her mark. These instruments included an application for admission to the home, an admission
agreement, a withdrawal slip for the
$12,864.46 remaining in her bank ac-
count, an assignment of that amount
to the home, and a letter making a
donation to the home of any part of
the $27,864.46 remain-ing after pay-
ing expenses for her lifetime care.*

*Ida died on December 5 while still
a resident of the nursing home. Her
brother, Sam Gordon, administrator
of her estate, filed suit against the
nursing home to recover these funds,
less the amount necessary to pay her
expenses. The trial court ruled for
the defendant nursing home on the
ground that a valid gift had been
made. The intermediate level appellate court reversed, ruling in favor of
plaintiff administrator, and defendant
appealed to New York's highest court.*

Jones, Justice:

. . . It is indisputable that on November 13, 1972, when the gift on which
defendant predicates its claim to the
funds in dispute was made, there existed between the donor and donee a
fiduciary relationship arising from the
nursing home's assumption of complete control, care and responsibility of
and for its resident. As the executive
director of that institution testified at
some length, the residents of the nursing home are dependent on the home
"to take care in effect of their very
livelihood, their existence;" they "rely
upon the people in the home to take
care of them . . . ; they have no means
of taking care of themselves;" and ask
and receive help from the staff of
the home. According to the witness,
"every one of the residents' particular
needs . . . is administered to them by
the help, the nurses or the doctors" of
the home and in many instances—as
was the case with the decedent—"they
have no other source of getting that
kind of help and don't get any help
other than from the institution." The
acceptance of such responsibility with
respect to the aged and infirm who, for
substantial consideration availed themselves of the custodial care offered by
the institution, resulted in the creation
of a fiduciary relationship and the applicability of the law of constructive
fraud. Under that doctrine, where a

fiduciary relationship exists between
parties, transactions between them
are scrutinized with extreme vigilance,
and clear evidence is required that the
transaction was understood, and that
there was no fraud, mistake, or undue
influence. Where those relations exist
there must be clear proof of the integrity and fairness of the transaction,
or any instrument thus obtained will be
set aside, or held as invalid between
the parties. As was said long ago, in ar-
ticulating the concept of constructive
fraud: "It may be stated as universally
true that fraud vitiates all contracts,
but as a general thing it is not presumed but must be proved by the party
seeking to relieve himself from an
obligation on that ground. Whenever,
however, the relations between the
contracting parties appear to be of
such a character as to render it certain
that they do not deal on terms of equality but that either on the one side from
superior knowledge of the matter derived from a fiduciary relation, or from
an overmastering influence, or on the
other from weakness, dependence, or
trust justifiably reposed, unfair advantage in a transaction is rendered probable, there the burden is shifted, the
transaction is presumed void, and it is
incumbent upon the stronger party to
show affirmatively that no deception
was practiced, no undue influence was
used, and that all was fair, open, voluntary and well understood. This doctrine
is well settled." (*Cowee v. Cornell*, 75
N.Y. 91, 99–100). So here, the defendant, rather than plaintiff, bore the
burden of proof on the issue whether
Ida's gift of funds was freely, voluntarily and understandingly made. *Examination of the record demonstrates that
that burden had not been met.* [Em-
phasis added.]

. . . The home was aware of the
patient's mental and physical infirmi-
ties and weakness. Nothing to that
point had remotely suggested that the
patient might be disposed to make a
(continues)

GORDON V. BIALYSTOKER CENTER & BIKUR CHOLIM, INC.

(*continued from previous page*)
gift to the home, or indeed that she even knew of its existence. The parties were brought together only in contemplation of the patient's transfer to the home; the transaction between them had no other meaning. That the patient was inescapably reposing confidence in the home from the moment of their first encounter was implicit in the circumstances.

We reject out of hand defendant's contention that, as a charitable organization, it should not be made subject to the same evidentiary burden that would be imposed on a profitmaking institution. However worthy may be the objectives to which its funds are dedicated, no justification exists for relieving it of the obligation, when circumstances suggest a substantial risk of overreaching, of affirmatively demonstrating that assets it has acquired have come to it from a willing and informed donor, untainted by impermissible initiative on the part of the donee.

. . . [T]he testimony offered, in conjunction with the other evidence in the case, was insufficient as a matter of law to sustain the burden of proof resting on the nursing home.

[The judgment of the intermediate level appellant court is affirmed; defendant nursing home must return to Ida's estate all funds beyond what was necessary to pay her expenses.]⚖

Special Treatment of Joint Bank Accounts

It is rather common for a bank account to be in the names of two persons, such as husband and wife. The phrase *joint account* is often used in a nontechnical sense to describe any bank account in the names of two people. These accounts are either a tenancy in common or a joint tenancy with survivorship rights, depending on the terms of the agreement with the bank.

In connection with the law of gifts, the requirement that the donor part with all control over the property is frequently an issue in cases involving a bank account jointly owned by the donor and the donee. For example, suppose that X deposits money belonging to him in a bank account that is in the name of X and Y. Both X and Y have the right to withdraw funds from the account. Obviously there is a completed gift from X to Y of all money actually taken from the account by Y. But because of the retention of control by X, money that is not withdrawn from the account by Y is not considered a gift.

Suppose, however, that the agreement between X and the bank provides that on the death of X or Y, the funds remaining in the account will go to the *survivor* (that is, a "joint tenancy" is created). If X dies first, the question will arise whether a valid gift of the remaining funds has been made by X to Y. A few courts have held that in such a situation there is not a sufficient relinquishment of control by X to create a gift. However, they also have usually held that Y is nevertheless entitled to the money as a *third party*

beneficiary of an enforceable contract between X and the bank. On the other hand, a majority of courts have simply relaxed the delivery requirement in this type of case and have held that there is a valid gift to Y despite the retention of some control by X.

Of course, as is true of any other gift, X must have *intended* to make a gift to Y. In the case of a joint tenancy bank account (one with a right of survivorship), there is a *presumption* of intent on the part of X to make a gift to Y, and this presumption can be rebutted only by evidence clearly showing that X did *not* intend to make a gift. For instance, the evidence might show that the joint account was established solely to give Y access to X's funds so as to enable Y to help X handle his financial affairs.

Gifts *Inter Vivos* and *Causa Mortis*

Gifts are classified as either *inter vivos* or *causa mortis*. A **gift *inter vivos*** is simply an ordinary gift between two living persons. A **gift *causa mortis*** is also between living persons, but it is made by the donor in contemplation of his or her death from some existing affliction or impending peril.

Although a gift *causa mortis* resembles a *will,* because both involve gifts in contemplation of death, it is important to emphasize their differences. As we will see in Chapter 46, a will must meet several formal statutory requirements such as written documentation and the signed attestation of a specified number of witnesses. A gift *causa mortis*, on the other hand, must meet the same requirements as a regular gift, intent and delivery. Execution of a formal will is the only way to make a gift conditional on the donor's death without an immediate transfer of possession.

Two special rules apply to the gift *causa mortis*, distinguishing it slightly from a regular gift: (1) The gift is revoked automatically if the donee dies before the donor, with the result that ownership reverts back to the donor. (2) The gift is also revoked automatically if the donor does not die from the current illness or peril.

OTHER METHODS OF ACQUIRING OWNERSHIP

Ownership of Wild Game

As a general rule, the law views wild animals, fish, and birds as being *unowned* property. The first person who takes possession with an intent to become an owner usually acquires legal ownership. The technical name for such acquisition is **occupation.** The one taking possession does not become the owner, however, if that person is a *trespasser* or is acting in violation of state or federal game and fish laws. A trespasser is one who is on land without the express or implied consent of the owner or tenant who has legal control of the land. Wild game taken by a trespasser belongs to the owner or the tenant of the land. In addition, no title is acquired to wild game taken in violation of state or federal laws.

Abandoned, Lost, and Mislaid Property

The common law made a distinction between abandoned, lost, and mislaid property. An item was deemed to be **abandoned property** if found under circumstances indicating either that it was left by someone who did not want it anymore, or was left so long ago that the former owner almost certainly was no longer living. The nature of the property, its location, and other relevant factors can be taken into account in determining whether the property should be classified as abandoned. The common law characterized an item as **lost property** if it was discovered under circumstances indicating that it was *not* placed there voluntarily by the owner (such as a purse, billfold, or ring found on a street or sidewalk or on the floor of a hotel or theater lobby). **Mislaid property,** on the other hand, was property discovered under circumstances indicating that it was placed there voluntarily by the owner and then forgotten (such as a suitcase under the seat of an airplane or bus or a purse on a table in a restaurant).

The common law treated abandoned property in the same manner as wild game, the first person taking possession becoming the owner. If the acquirer was a trespasser on the land where the game was taken, however, the landowner or tenant became the owner. The finding of lost or mislaid property, on the other hand, did not change ownership of the item. Either the finder or the landowner (or tenant, if leased) acquired only a right to possession that was superior to the rights of everyone but the true owner. The finder or landowner taking possession was required to take reasonable steps to preserve the property and locate its owner. If the owner appeared to claim the property, he or she was obligated to pay the reasonable costs of storing and preserving it, but was not legally required to pay a reward. All of this assumes, of course, that the identity of the true owner was unknown; if known, the finder or landowner voluntarily taking possession had an absolute duty to deliver the property to its owner and was guilty of a crime for not doing so.

The distinction between lost and mislaid property was used to determine who was entitled to possession in the situation where the item was found by someone who did not own or control the premises. The owner or tenant of the land was entitled to possession if the item was characterized as mislaid property, because of the possibility that the true owner might remember where it was left and return to reclaim it. In the case of lost property, however, the finder was entitled to possession unless he or she was a trespasser, in which case the landowner or tenant had the possessory right.

Finding Statutes

In modern times, almost all jurisdictions have enacted legislation regulating the possession and ownership of found property. These laws are referred to as **finding statutes** (or **estray statutes**), and vary substantially from state to state. Several of these statutes, as interpreted by the courts, have retained the common-law distinctions between abandoned, lost, and mislaid property. Some of them apply only to lost property, not to mislaid or abandoned property. However, the courts in some of these states have applied a strong presumption that found property is lost and therefore subject to the statute. In other states, the finding statutes have completely preempted the common-law rules and apply to any found property regardless of its characterization as abandoned, mislaid, or lost.

State finding statutes typically require that the finder of an item of personal property turn it over to a designated governmental authority within a certain period of time, such as ten days. Some statutes designate a local authority for receipt and custody of the item, such as the city police, county sheriff, or county clerk. Others designate a state authority such as the state police. Depending on the provisions of the statute, either the finder or the custodial authority must then take specified steps to locate the true owner, such as by publishing newspaper notices a certain number of times during a particular time period. If the prior owner does not appear and establish ownership within a stated period of time, such as one year, most statutes provide that the finder acquires ownership (not just possession) of the property. A finder who does not comply with the finding statute in a particular state does not acquire ownership or a right to possession, and usually is guilty of a crime. Finding statutes normally place obligations and give rights to the *finder,* regardless of who owns or controls the land where the property is found. Some of these statutes, however, have been interpreted as incorporating the common-law rule that a finder who is a willful trespasser acquires no rights in found property; in such a case, the owner or tenant of the land where the item was found acquires the rights granted by the statute.

Escheat Statutes

All states also have enacted **escheat statutes,** which normally provide that intangible property such as money, corporate stock, or bonds is presumed abandoned if it has remained in the possession of a custodian, such as a bank or securities dealer, for a specified time period without any deposits, withdrawals, or other contact by the owner. The time period provided by these statutes is usually lengthy, seven years being a common term. After passage of this time period, a state governmental authority ordinarily is required to publish notices identifying the property; if the property still remains unclaimed for a shorter period, such as six months, the state becomes the owner. Escheat statutes generally apply also to unclaimed stolen property recovered by police, and to the unclaimed property of a person who dies without heirs or a will. Some escheat statutes include other abandoned property as well.

The following case illustrates the application of a finding statute to a hunter's unexpected discovery.

WILLSMORE V. TOWNSHIP OF OCEOLA

Michigan Court of Appeals, 308 N.W.2d 796 (1981)

 While hunting on unposted (i.e., there were no signs prohibiting entry) and unoccupied land, Duane Willsmore's attention was drawn to a place on the ground where branches were arranged in a crisscross pattern. When he kicked aside the branches and some loose dirt, he found a watertight suitcase in a freshly dug hole. Inside the suitcase he found $383,400, which he immediately turned over to the state police. The police noted that some of the money had teller bands around it, indicating that it recently had been in a bank, but they were not able to trace the money to any particular source. The police placed the money in an interest-bearing account, and shortly thereafter Willsmore complied with the Michigan Lost Goods Act by notifying the clerk of the township where the money was found and properly publicizing the find. The statute provided that, one year after the required public notice, a finder who had complied with the law became owner of one-half of the property and the township in which it was found became owner of the other half.

After expiration of the one year, Willsmore filed suit against the township to determine ownership. The state of Michigan also asserted ownership of the money as abandoned property under the Code of Escheats—the Michigan escheat statute. The land on which the money was found was the subject of a sale contract at the time of the finding, although the landowner rightfully cancelled the transaction before the trial of this case because the buyer had breached the contract. The landowner expressly refused to assert any claim to the money. However, the person who had been the buyer under the contract, Powell, alleged that he was the true owner of the money and asserted a claim in the lawsuit. At the trial, Powell offered his deposition into evidence, but it was not admitted because he was available to testify and he had refused to answer any questions on cross-examination at the taking of the deposition. Powell refused to testify

(continues)

WILLSMORE V. TOWNSHIP OF OCEOLA

(continued from previous page)
at the trial, asserting his constitutional right to remain silent on the grounds that his statements might tend to incriminate him. The trial court granted a directed verdict awarding Willsmore and the township one half of the money each according to the Lost Goods Act. Powell and the state of Michigan appealed.

Corsiglia, Judge:

The Lost Goods Act of Michigan . . . provides that the finder shall give notice to potential owners, post notice in two places within the township of the find, publish notice in a newspaper if the goods are of a value of $10 or more and give notice in writing to the township clerk. The statute requires that these things be done within very short time periods. Willsmore did not comply with the strict language of the statute. This lapse is understandable in light of the advice he received from the police. After the State Police took custody of the suitcase, they told the finder and his wife to keep silent about the money, informed them that their lives might be in danger, suggested that leaving town for a time might be a good idea and even transported them in a state vehicle at speeds reaching up to 100 m.p.h. accompanied by officers armed with rifles. There is no indication on the record that the delay in complying with the provisions of the Lost Goods Act was a willful refusal to comply, or that it caused it to be more difficult for the true owner of the money to be located. Indeed, Willsmore's initial action upon finding the property was to notify a governmental authority, not attempt to keep it himself. It is understandable that after receiving instructions from the State Police to keep quiet, Willsmore did not act within the time limits set in the statute. [We hold] that Willsmore substantially complied with the notice provisions of the Lost Goods Act. . . .

[Regarding Powell's claim of ownership,] it is required that a party claiming as true owner prove his ownership. When faced with questions about how he obtained the money and hid it, Powell had the right to assert his constitutional privilege to remain silent. However, the court not only had the right, but also the duty, to conclude from such silence that Powell did not carry his burden of proof. . . . Powell's claim as true owner fails as a matter of law. . . . Because of his continued assertion of the right to remain silent at his deposition, relevant cross-examination was impossible. Powell, by choice, did not testify at the trial. Other evidence bearing on his alleged ownership of the money was not admissible because of its nature as hearsay. . . .

The brief period of time that the money was buried also effectively eliminates the Code of Escheats from application to this case. . . . The state carries the burden of establishing its right to escheatable property. The Attorney General has the power to intervene to claim property as escheatable upon one of three grounds:

(1) Death of an owner intestate (without a will) with no known heirs;
(2) Owner's disappearance or absence from last known place of residence for a continuous period of seven years leaving no known heirs; or
(3) Owner's abandonment of the property.

It is the third basis of standing which might appear to apply in this case. However, the Code of Escheats establishes a clear, narrow definition of "abandonment" which could not apply to the money based on undisputed facts before the trial court. Under the Code of Escheats, "abandoned property" is defined as "property against which a full period of dormancy has run." A "period of dormancy" is defined to mean a full and continuous period of seven years during which an owner has ceased, failed, or neglected to exercise dominion or control over his property or to assert a

right of ownership or possession. . . .

Clearly, money in the ground for only a few months does not fall within the plain language of the Code of Escheats. Nor does it fall within the policy and historical derivation of the Code. The Law of Escheats developed out of the need for a sovereign to take title when tenure failed because of the absence of heirs. The statute has always been strictly construed, and the burden is on the state to prove that the property is escheatable. Initially, the Code of Escheats involved only real property. It was later expanded to cover personal property in certain narrow instances. In general, it covers personal property in situations where the property has been left with holders who would not be considered "finders" in the usual sense. For example, it is commonly applied to banks and similar institutions. It is generally not applied to individual holders of funds. . . . The Code of Escheats is not applicable to the present case. . . .

This Court finds that the Lost Goods Act is applicable to this property. It could be argued that applying the Lost Goods Act to a suitcase buried on another's land will encourage inappropriate behavior on the part of people in order that they might become "finders" under the provisions of the act. However, upon reflection, this argument is of limited merit. In the type of case where such a "find" would be inappropriate, the publicity given under the provisions of the Lost Goods Act would bring forward the true owner of the property, very possibly the property owner upon whose land it was found. Notice provisions would require notice to this potential true owner. In addition, in a different factual context, the remedy of trespass would be appropriate to discourage such "finds." The facts of this case do not support a trespass argument against the finder. The testimony indicated that the land was unposted and unoccupied, and that it had been hunted upon for many years by claimant Willsmore without objection.

(continues)

WILLSMORE V. TOWNSHIP OF OCEOLA

(continued from previous page)

The Lost Goods Act encourages the goals which this Court considers important in such cases. It provides certainty of title to property by eventually vesting clear title after a set period of time. It encourages honesty in finders by providing penalties for not turning in property in accord with its provisions and providing incentives for compliance. The act provides notice to potential true owners and publication to seek them out. It provides for registration of the find in a central location where an owner could locate the goods with ease. The Lost Goods Act provides for appraisal of the goods. There is a reasonable time limit before title to goods is cut off from the former owner or holder. The public obtains a portion of the benefit of a find through receipt of one half of the value by the township. The finder receives an award for his honesty by receiving one half of the value of the property plus costs. . . .

Parties to this suit urge this Court to draw a distinction between categories of found property [which] are derived from the common law. . . . "Lost property," as used in the [Lost Goods Act], is a broad generic category. . . . The statute is in effect a "finder's statute."

The provisions of the act are an eminently reasonable solution to a troublesome problem. Obviously there is a potential for a true owner to turn up in a year and a day to discover that his title has been cut off. However, a line must be drawn to establish clear title to goods at some point. . . .

The trial court correctly . . . [granted] motions for a directed verdict in favor of the finder, Duane Willsmore, and the Township of Oceola.

Affirmed.⚖

Accession

An **accession** is a change in or an addition to an item of personal property. If the change or addition occurs with the owner's knowledge or consent, there is no effect on ownership of the item of property, and the question of compensation to the one making the addition or change depends entirely on the express or implied contract between the parties.

If the change or addition occurs without the owner's knowledge or consent, however, it is possible for ownership to be affected. The person causing the change or addition might have acted with knowledge that the action was wrongful (in bad faith), or with the honestly mistaken belief that he or she owned the item or otherwise had the right to make the change or addition (in good faith). Good faith accessions frequently occur when someone buys an item such as a boat or automobile, makes substantial changes or additions, and then finds out that the title to the purchased item was void because the seller had stolen it. The rules regarding accessions are outlined below.

Change in Personal Property by Labor

If a change in an item of personal property is brought about entirely or almost entirely by a nonowner's *labor,* ownership passes to the person performing the labor only if (1) the *identity* of the property has been changed, or (2) the value of the property is *many times greater* than it was prior to the change. An example of a change in identity is shown in the situation where A makes B's grapes into wine without B's consent. An example of a sufficiently great increase in value is found in the case where A takes a piece of stone belonging to B and carves a statue from it without B's consent. There is a definite tendency on the part of courts to deal more harshly with someone who caused the accession while knowing that it was wrong. A greater magnitude of change is often required to pass title to such a party than to someone who acted in good faith.

Addition of Other Property

When one person permanently attaches something to another's personal property without the latter's consent, ownership of the resulting product goes to the owner of the "principal" item. For example, if A puts a new engine in a car owned by B, the car and the new engine belong to B. On the other hand, if A puts an engine owned by B in A's car, the car and engine are owned by A.

Compensation to Owner

In either of these situations, where an item is changed by a nonowner's labor or where other property has been added to the item, the party who caused the accession (the improver) is responsible for any loss to the other party. Thus, if the circumstances are such that the improver acquired title to the item as a result of the accession, that person must compensate the original owner. If the improver acted in good faith, he or she is required to pay the original owner only for the value of the property in its original condition. But if the improver acted in bad faith, he or she is required to pay to the original owner the value of the property in its improved state.

Where the accession itself does not cause title to pass to the improver, but the original owner simply chooses not to reclaim the property, the situation is treated the same as if the accession *had* caused title to pass. Where the accession does not cause title to pass to the improver, and the original owner *reclaims* the improved property, the improver usually is not entitled to any compensation at all, regardless of whether he or she acted in good faith.

Confusion of Goods

A **confusion of goods** occurs where there has been an intermingling of the goods of different persons. It usually occurs in connection with **fungible goods** (i.e., each unit is identical), such as the same grade of grain, oil, or chemicals. It can, however, occur with nonfungible goods, such as cattle or quantities of packaged merchandise.

If the goods of A and B have been confused (1) by agreement between A and B, (2) by an honest mistake or accident, or (3) by the act of some third party, a tenancy in common is created. Here, A and B each owns an undivided interest in the mass according to the particular proportions they contributed to it.

Suppose, however, that A caused the confusion by deliberately wrongful or negligent conduct. In this case, if the goods of A and B are fungible, A can get his portion back if he proves with reasonable certainty how much that portion is. On the other hand, if the goods are not fungible, A must prove which specific items are his or else he gets nothing.

After there has been a confusion, the quantity of goods might be diminished by fire, theft, or other cause so that not enough is left to give each owner a complete share. If one owner caused the confusion by deliberately wrongful or negligent conduct, that person must bear the entire burden of the decrease. If the confusion came about by agreement, by accident or honest mistake, or by an act of a third party, the burden of the decrease is borne proportionately by both owners.

BAILMENTS OF PERSONAL PROPERTY

The term *bailment* initially evokes a feeling of puzzlement in most people. Once it is described, however, it is immediately recognized as a simple and commonplace occurrence in everyday life. The taking of a dress to a dry cleaner, the lending of a car to a friend, and the delivering of goods to a railroad for shipment are all actions that result in the creation of bailments. A **bailment** can be defined as the delivery of possession of personal property from one person to another under an agreement by which the latter is obligated to return the property to the former or to deliver it to a third party. The person transferring possession is the **bailor,** and the one receiving it is the **bailee.**

The rules governing most ordinary bailment relationships are common-law in nature. Certain kinds of bailments, however, are subject to statutory enactments. As we will see later in this chapter, Article 7 of the Uniform Commercial Code governs many aspects of the bailment relationships created when one ships goods by common carrier or stores goods with a warehouseman. Also discussed later is the fact that special state statutes regulate some of the obligations of "innkeepers" (i.e., hotel owners) toward the property of guests. As discussed earlier in Chapter 20 (Introduction to the Law of Sales), a new Article 2A of the Uniform Commercial Code has recently been drafted and submitted to state legislatures for adoption. Article 2A covers *leases* of personal property, which are a form of bailment that occurs when one pays rent to the owner of an item such as a car, equipment, home appliance, etc., for the right to use the item for a designated time. Article 2A leaves most of the traditional common-law rules intact for this kind of bailment. One important step taken by Article 2A is that it applies the same basic warranty obligations to lessors in lease transactions that Article 2 applies to sellers in sales transactions. Although many courts had already adopted the sales warranty provisions for personal property leases, Article 2A attempts to do so formally and uniformly.

Elements of a Bailment

By definition, the creation of a bailment requires that (1) one party must deliver possession (but not title) to the other, (2) the property delivered must be classified as personal property, and (3) the parties must agree that the recipient of the property will later return it, deliver it to a third party, or otherwise dispose of it in some specified manner.

Delivery of Possession

The requirement that possession of the property be delivered normally means that (1) the property must be transferred to the bailee, (2) the bailee must acquire control over the item, and (3) the bailee must knowingly accept the property.

Although actual physical possession of the bailed property is almost always transferred to the bailee, it is possible for a bailment to be created by delivery of something that gives the bailee effective control over the item, such as the keys or certificate of title to a boat or car.[3]

In addition to a transfer of the property, the circumstances must indicate that the recipient acquired control over it. For example, when a customer hangs his or her coat on a coatrack at a restaurant, and can get it back without notifying the restaurant's management or employees, there is no bailment of the coat because the restaurant did not acquire control over it. Similarly, if a waiter or other restaurant employee takes the coat and hangs it on a rack that is freely accessible to the customer, who may retrieve it without notice or assistance, there still is no bailment. On the other hand, if the coat is left with a coatroom attendant or other restaurant employee, who puts it in a place that is not accessible to the customer without assistance, a bailment has been created because the restaurant has control over the coat.

For the same reason, leaving a car at a parking lot or parking garage is generally held to constitute a bailment only if the car owner is required to leave the keys with an attendant. Otherwise, the parking lot company does not have sufficient control over the car. In a situation in which the car owner is permitted to lock the car and keep the keys, the transaction usually is not a bailment, but is merely a *license*—a contractual permission to use the parking space. The owner of the parking lot is a *licensor* and the car owner is a *licensee.*

Although the bailor normally is the owner of the bailed property, this is not always the case. What is required is that the bailor have a "superior right of possession" with regard to the bailee. Thus, if Joe lends his lawn mower to Robert for the summer and

---

[3]This is another example of the concept of *constructive delivery,* which was discussed earlier in the chapter with regard to gifts of personal property.

Robert takes it to a repair shop in September before returning it to Joe, a bailment exists between Robert and the repair shop while the mower is being repaired.

As we have seen, a physical delivery of property by one person to another does not create a bailment unless the recipient knowingly accepts the property. For example, suppose that Joan has several packages of merchandise in the trunk of her car when she leaves it at a parking lot under circumstances in which a bailment exists as to the car. There is no bailment of the packages unless Joan notifies the parking lot attendant of their presence.

Personal Property

As we previously observed, all property is either *real* or *personal.* By definition, bailments involve only transfers of personal property. Although owners of real property frequently transfer possession of it to others for limited periods of time, such transactions are not bailments.

Most bailments involve items of tangible personal property, such as automobiles or jewelry. It is possible, however, for intangible personal property to be the subject of a bailment. This occurs, for example, when a stock certificate representing ownership of corporate stock is delivered by a debtor to a creditor as security for the debt.

The Agreement to Return

A bailment necessarily involves an agreement that the property ultimately is to be returned by the bailee to the bailor or delivered to a designated third party. The bailment contract can be either express or implied, and in most cases is not legally required to be in writing. Obviously, however, it is advisable to have the bailment contract in writing if the value of the bailed property is substantial and particularly if a commercial bailor or bailee is involved. Most commercial bailors, such as car rental agencies, and commercial bailees, such as a company that is in the business of storing the property of others, customarily use detailed written contracts.

As a general rule, the bailee is required to return or deliver the *identical* goods at the end of the bailment. Thus, if a Buick dealer delivers a car to Joyce under a contract providing that in return she will deliver her used motor home to the dealer within a month, the transaction is a sale rather than a bailment. The arrangement also would be a sale if the

contract gives Joyce the option of returning the car or delivering the motor home in a month.

The rule requiring delivery of the identical property is subject to two well-established exceptions, which are outlined below.

Fungible Goods.   If the subject matter of the transaction is *fungible goods,* each unit of which is interchangeable, with the contract obligating the recipient merely to later redeliver the same quantity of goods of the same description to the owner or to a third party, the transaction is still a bailment. This rule is especially important in grain storage situations, with the result that grain elevators taking in grain for storage are bailees even though the grain they later return to their customers or deliver to third parties is not the same grain they originally received.

Options to Purchase.   The second exception arises in a situation where the one receiving possession of the property has a specified period of time within which to decide whether to purchase or return it. This type of transaction, sometimes called a *bailment with the option to purchase,* is a bailment despite the fact that the bailee has the choice of turning it into a sale by giving the bailor the agreed price rather than the property itself. Bailments of this type can take several forms, e.g., a *lease with the option to purchase.* Another example is the *sale on approval,* which was discussed in Chapter 21 concerning sale transactions.

Constructive Bailments

There are a few cases in which the courts treat transactions as if they are bailments even though one of the ordinarily required elements is missing. One example of such a **constructive bailment** is found in the use of a bank safe-deposit box. When a customer places property in a safe-deposit box, the bank does not acquire *exclusive* control because access to the box requires both the customer's and the bank's key. In addition, the bank usually does not have actual knowledge of the contents of the box. Despite these differences from a traditional bailment, a majority of courts treat the arrangement as a bailment and hold the bank to the responsibilities of a bailee. In a few states, however, legislation has been passed declaring the use of a safe-deposit box to be only a rental of the space—that is, a *license* rather than a bailment.

The courts also usually treat a finder of personal property as a bailee even though the owner did not deliver the item to the finder. The bailment continues until the finder surrenders possession to a governmental authority or becomes the owner of the property by complying with a state finding statute.

Types of Bailments

Bailments can be broadly classified as *ordinary bailments* and *special bailments.* As the name implies, ordinary bailments comprise the vast majority of bailment transactions. Special bailments are discussed briefly at the end of the chapter. Ordinary bailments may be further subdivided into (1) bailments for the sole benefit of the bailee, (2) bailments for the sole benefit of the bailor, and (3) mutual benefit bailments.

Sole Benefit of the Bailee

A bailment for the sole benefit of the bailee exists when the owner of an item permits another to use it without compensation or any other benefit. Examples include the loan of a car to a friend or a lawn mower to a neighbor.

Sole Benefit of the Bailor

A bailment for the sole benefit of the bailor exists when a person stores or takes care of someone else's property as a favor, without receiving any compensation or other benefit. Such a bailment would arise, for example, where Ruth permits George to store his furniture in her garage while he is away for the summer, with no benefit at all to Ruth.

Mutual Benefit Bailments

Because people ordinarily do not enter into bailments unless they receive some sort of gain from the transaction, mutual benefit bailments are by far the most common kind. Most mutual bailments involve a bailor or bailee who receives direct compensation, as in the case of an equipment rental firm or a company that is in the business of storing the property of others.

It is possible, however, for the benefit to be an indirect one. Suppose, for example, that an employer prohibits its employees from keeping their coats or other personal belongings in the immediate working area, and maintains a separate coatroom or other area where such items are left under the control of an attendant. Even though no direct compensation is paid, there is a mutual benefit bailment. The employees benefit by having a secure place to keep their property during working hours. The employer, on the other hand, benefits in several ways, including having an uncluttered working area with fewer distractions for employees, and with less potential for problems arising from theft among employees.

The example of the restaurant's provision of a coatroom where it takes control of customers' coats and hats, presented earlier in the discussion of bailments, also illustrates a mutual benefit bailment involving indirect compensation.

Rights of the Bailee

The bailee's rights in a bailment transaction depend almost entirely on the express or implied terms of the parties' contract. These rights normally involve *possession, use,* and *compensation.*

If the contract provides that the bailee is to have possession for a specified period of time and if the bailor is receiving consideration in return, the bailee ordinarily has the right to retain possession for the entire time. And if the bailor wrongfully retakes possession before the agreed time has expired, the bailee is entitled to damages for breach of contract. The bailee also can enforce this possessory right against a third party who wrongly interferes with it. Thus, if the bailed property is stolen, destroyed, or damaged by a third party, the bailee has the right to initiate legal action to recover the property or receive money damages from the third party.

Whether the bailee has the right to use the bailed property depends on the express terms of the contract or, if there are no such terms, on the general purposes of the bailment. If the contract is for *storage,* for example, the bailee usually has no right to use the property while it is in his or her possession. On the other hand, if the bailee is *renting* the property, he or she obviously has the right to use it in a normal manner.

Except for bailments in which the bailee is renting property for the purpose of using it, or in situations where there is a clear understanding that he or she is not to receive any payment, the bailee normally has the right to some form of compensation for the safekeeping of the property. In the case of a bailee who is in the business of storing the property of others, the compensation is almost always spelled out in the contract. Where the amount of the compensation is not expressly agreed upon, the bailee is entitled to the reasonable value of his or her services. If the purpose of the bailment is to have the bailee perform a service, such as automobile repairs, the amount of the compensation again depends on the express or implied terms of the contract.

Duties of the Bailee

A bailee has the fundamental duties of using and returning the bailed property in accordance with the bailment contract and exercising due care (or reasonable care) in handling the property.

Use and Return

If the bailee uses it in a way that is beyond the consent granted in the agreement, such use constitutes a breach of contract and the bailee is liable for any damages resulting from the unauthorized use regardless of whether he or she committed negligence or any other tort. For instance, Vance, a resident of Sacramento, California, borrows a pickup truck from his neighbor, Perez, to move some furniture from Stockton to Sacramento. After Vance reaches Stockton and loads the furniture, he decides to go on to Modesto, about 25 miles farther, to visit his brother. If the truck is damaged in an accident while Vance is in Modesto, he is fully liable to Perez for the damage even if the accident was not his fault in any respect.

A bailee who intentionally does not return the bailed property at the end of the bailment commits both a breach of contract and the tort of conversion, and is liable to the bailor for the value of the property.

Due Care and the Presumption of Negligence

When the bailed property is damaged, lost, stolen, or destroyed because the bailee has failed to exercise due care in handling the item, he or she is guilty of the torts of negligence and conversion and is responsible to the bailor for the amount of the damage or loss.

A variety of circumstances are taken into account to determine whether the bailee exercised due care, including the value of the bailed property, the susceptibility of this particular type of bailed property to damage or theft, and the amount of experience the bailee has had in dealing with similar types of property in the past. Thus, a bailee is expected to exercise greater care in handling a $2,000 diamond ring than a $100 chair. A bailee also would be expected to exercise more care in handling extremely flammable chemicals or a thoroughbred horse than a truckload of bricks.

Until recent years, most courts applied different degrees of care to the different categories of bail-

ment. The bailee was required to exercise great care in a bailment for the sole benefit of the bailee, and only slight care in a bailment for the sole benefit of the bailor. In a mutual benefit bailment the bailee was required to exercise reasonable care, which was defined as the amount of care a reasonable person would exercise in protecting his or her own property. Although the courts in some states still make this rigid distinction, many of them have abandoned it as a strict basis for determining the bailee's required degree of care. These courts apply the general standard of reasonable care to all types of bailments, and simply treat the amount of benefit the bailee was receiving from the bailment as another one of the factors relevant to the question of whether he or she exercised such care.

Courts often emphasize that the bailee is ordinarily not an absolute insurer of the safety of the property, however, and is not liable unless the damage or loss results from his or her intentional or negligent act. Although true, this statement is somewhat misleading. The reason is that when a bailee fails to return the property in its former condition, there is a **presumption of negligence.** In other words, when the bailor proves that the property was not returned at all, or was returned in a damaged condition, the burden then shifts to the bailee to explain exactly what happened and to demonstrate how the loss occurred without his or her fault. Sometimes the courts use different terminology to refer to this presumption and say that the bailor's proof of damage or loss establishes a *prima facie* case of negligence. However it is stated, the rule makes it very difficult for a bailee to avoid liability once it is established that a bailment existed and the property was damaged or not returned.

The presumption of negligence greatly increases the importance of determining whether a bailment actually existed. A person who causes damage to or loss of another's property by failing to exercise due care is ordinarily liable for that damage or loss regardless of whether a bailment or any other particular relationship existed between the parties. In most situations, however, the property owner must prove specific acts on the part of the defendant that constituted negligence. In some cases, as where the item was stolen or destroyed by fire while on the defendant's premises, it can be almost impossible for the plaintiff to produce any specific evidence of what happened. Therefore, the question of whether a bailment existed frequently determines the outcome of such a case.

Exculpatory Clauses

Bailees frequently attempt to contractually excuse themselves from liability for harm to the bailed property. It is common, for example, for parking lots, automotive repair shops, or dry cleaners to post signs or give tickets or documents to bailors containing statements such as "The owner assumes all risk for damage to or loss of the property, and the proprietor is not responsible for such damage or loss resulting from fire, theft, flood, or negligence." Statements of this nature are referred to as **exculpatory clauses.**

In most situations exculpatory clauses are not effective to free the bailee from liability, for two reasons. First, as discussed in Chapter 11 regarding the formation of contracts, courts normally hold that such provisions are *not legally communicated* to the bailor unless specifically called to the bailor's atten-

tion. Second, even if the exculpatory clause is legally communicated and thus becomes part of the bailment contract, courts usually conclude that the clause *violates public policy* and is unenforceable on the grounds of illegality. This conclusion is almost always reached when the bailee is in the business of handling the property of others and the terms of the bailment contract are presented by the bailee to the bailor on a nonnegotiated "take it or leave it" basis. (In other words, the agreement is a *contract of adhesion,* a concept that was discussed at several points in the chapters on contracts.)

The following two cases illustrate the approach taken by courts to determine whether a bailment exists, and emphasize the critical importance of that question in situations where no one really knows exactly what happened to the bailed property. In addition, the second case provides an example of the courts' usual attitude toward exculpatory clauses in bailment contracts.

Pinto v. Bridgeport Mack Trucks, Inc.

Superior Court of Connecticut, Appellate Session, 458 A.2d 696 (1983)

Alfred Pinto had worked as a diesel mechanic for Bridgeport Mack Trucks for nine years. As was the custom in the industry, the employer supplied all the larger tools and employees furnished their own hand tools. It also was customary for employees to leave their tools in the work area of the employer's premises after finishing a day's work. Pinto was hired with the understanding that he would provide his own hand tools, and he maintained a two-piece tool chest in the employer's work area. The top section of the chest loaded with his tools weighed approximately 500 pounds. There were about 25 other tool boxes scattered around the work area. This work area consisted of a 39,000 square foot space in the rear of the employer's build-

ing; a showroom area was in the front.

As often was the case, on the occasion in question the employer's volume of work required the services of two shifts of mechanics. The first shift worked from 8:00 a.m. to 4:30 p.m., and the second shift from 3:00 p.m. to 11:30 p.m. The employer was open for business until 11:00 p.m., but at the end of the first shift a chain link fence surrounding the sides and rear of the building was locked, leaving a front door leading into the showroom area as the only means of access to the work area. After finishing his work on the first shift, Pinto locked his tools in his box and left it beside the truck he was repairing. The second shift reported for work as usual and, as was their custom, the employees on the second shift took a meal break between 7:00 and 7:30 p.m. Some of the employees

left the building during their break, while others ate in a lunchroom at the rear of the work area. During this half hour, McDonald, the foreman of the second shift, went back and forth between the lunchroom and work area answering the telephone and attending to other business matters. He was out of the work area a total of ten minutes during the entire break.

Upon returning from the break, an employee noticed that a battery charger was missing. The next morning Pinto discovered that the top section of his tool chest was also missing. The foreman had locked the building after the second shift the previous evening, and an investigation disclosed no signs of forced entry during the night. The employer refused to pay for Pinto's tools, so he filed suit against the employer seeking damages for their value. At the trial, evidence was presented showing that
(continues)

PINTO V. BRIDGEPORT MACK TRUCKS, INC.

(continued from previous page)
during the preceding year there had been discussions among employees and managers about storing the employees' tools to avoid their damaging or being damaged by the large trucks moving about the area. The employer's managers offered to provide a separate area where tool boxes could be wheeled and stored, and to obtain chains to secure them, but this action was never taken. The evidence also showed that, prior to the loss of the battery charger and Pinto's tools, there had been no thefts from the employer's building in nine years.

The trial court found that there was not a bailment of Pinto's tools, but held the employer liable because there was independent evidence of the employer's negligence. The employer appealed.

Covello, Judge:

A bailment is a consensual relation and it includes, in its broadest sense, any delivery of personal property in trust for a lawful purpose. Assumption of control is the determinative factor. A bailee is one who receives personal property from another in trust for a specific purpose, with a contract, express or implied, that the trust shall be faithfully executed and the property returned or duly accounted for when the special purpose is accomplished.

Here there was no delivery of the plaintiff's tools to the defendant nor receipt of them in a sense that could serve as a basis for concluding that the defendant had assumed control over them. Delivery connotes a handing over or surrender of possession to another. Locking the tools in a box and leaving the box wherever one chooses in the work area of the employer's premises, pursuant to a trade custom, is not consistent with a handing over or surrender of possession of either the tools or the box to the employer within the meaning of a bailment.

A conclusion that there was no bailment is not necessarily dispositive of the ultimate issue, as the existence of a bailment does nothing more than create a presumption of negligence. The failure of a bailee to return goods delivered to him raises a presumption that their nonproduction is due to his negligence. This presumption prevails unless and until the bailee proves the actual circumstances involved in the damaging of the property. If those circumstances are proved, then the burden is upon the bailor to satisfy the court that the bailee's conduct in the matter constituted negligence. If negligence may be independently demonstrated, the absence of the benefit of a presumption is not necessarily fatal to the plaintiff's cause of action.

In this connection, the trial court concluded that "[b]y not following up on the offer to set aside a caged or protected area or in supplying chains and insisting that the tool boxes be made secure each night, the defendant could be easily aware of the harm that was eventually suffered." The court further concluded that "[t]he employer controlled the work area and also set general policies to be followed by the employees. That control and management imposed an affirmative duty upon the employer that it failed to meet. If the adequate protection of the caged or locked area had been provided and a general policy of seeing that the employees used the protection had been enforced by the employer, then the duty would have been met."

[We disagree with the trial court's conclusion.] Negligence is a breach of duty. That duty is to exercise due care. The ultimate test of the existence of a duty to use care is found in the foreseeability that harm may result if it is not exercised. By that is not meant that one charged with negligence must be found actually to have foreseen the . . . particular injury which resulted . . . but the test is, would the ordinary person in the defendant's position, knowing what he knew or should have known, anticipate that harm of the general nature of that suffered was likely to result?

On the facts, the defendant could not be charged with that reasonable anticipation of harm which would be the basis of liability in negligence. Reasonable care does not require that one must guard against eventualities which, at best, are too remote to be reasonably foreseeable. The defendant did not know, nor did its employees have any knowledge of facts which would charge it with knowledge that thieves might steal an employee's 500 pound tool chest. There was no evidence of prior thefts. On the contrary, there was evidence that there had been no thefts in the preceding nine years. A chain link fence surrounding the sides and rear of this commercial building was secured by the day shift. The sole night access to the 39,000 square foot building was through a single door leading into the showroom. The tool chests, meanwhile, were in a maintenance area in the rear of the building. Employees were in and out of this area constantly. The totality of the facts and the circumstances militating against such a thing occurring remove the theft from the realm of what was reasonably foreseeable. . . .

There is error. The judgment is set aside and the case is remanded with direction to render judgment for the defendant. ⚖

EMPLOYERS INSURANCE OF WAUSAU V. CHEMICAL BANK

Civil Court of New York, 459 N.Y.S.2d 238 (1983)

Case

Suncrest Pharmacal Corp. claimed that Chemical Bank failed to credit one of Suncrest's deposits, resulting in a loss of over $11,000. Suncrest received $3,000 from its insurer, Employers Insurance of Wausau, and both Suncrest and the insurance company then filed suit against the bank to recover damages for the loss.

At the trial, Weintraub, president of Suncrest, testified that on a Friday evening about 7:00 p.m. he placed a paper bag containing two of the bank's cloth deposit bags in a night depository. Before leaving, he checked to see that the paper bag did in fact go down the chute. One of the deposit bags contained 850 one dollar bills, and the other contained cash and checks totalling $19,191.52. The deposit slip for both bags was in the one that contained $850. The following Monday the bank notified Weintraub that it had received only the bag containing the deposit slip and $850. Suncrest was able to have payment stopped on all of the checks in the missing bag on which it was the payee, but was unable to do so on any of the checks payable to others and endorsed over to Suncrest, because there was no record of the names of the makers of those checks. The lost cash and checks totalled $11,084.50.

An officer of the bank described the procedure used by the bank in opening the night deposit vault, and Suncrest conceded that it was unable to prove any specific acts of negligence relating to the bank's procedure in handling night deposits. Suncrest asserted, however, that the deposit had created a bailment, and that the bank had the burden of explaining exactly what happened to the lost bag. The bank claimed that there was no bailment, and that its

liability was limited by the written deposit agreement between it and Suncrest, which provided that permission to use the night depository was a "privilege" and "gratuitous," and that "the exercise of that privilege [was] at the sole risk" of Suncrest. The following is the opinion of the trial court.

Lehner, Judge:

Until a deposit bag is opened and the contents credited to the depositor's account, the relationship between the bank and its night depository customer is that of bailor and bailee and only ordinary care is required of the bank in operating the facility. . . . [Authors' note: After the deposit is credited, a debtor-creditor relationship is created between the bank and its customer, and the bank is absolutely liable for the amount of the deposit.]

However, plaintiff must first establish that a bailment was in fact created by a proper deposit. For the trier of fact to determine whether a bailment was created many factors should be taken into account, such as the depositor's prior deposit history, method of depositing, his over-all character, and corroboration. Suncrest has been a long-time customer of the bank, a frequent user of its night depository service, and has never registered any complaints about the facility until now. Its method of depositing was as precautionary and circumspect as possible. Mr. Weintraub's testimony was, in part, corroborated by the foreman of Suncrest, who accompanied him to the bank and saw him place a paper bag in the night depository, but was unable to testify with respect to its contents.

Observing Mr. Weintraub from the witness stand leads the court to find him a rather credible witness. The bank acknowledged that many customers will place the bank's cloth de-

posit bag in a paper bag for security purposes in order to conceal possession. The bank officer testified that after the cloth bags are removed from the vault each morning, any paper bags used are thrown on the floor and discarded. The bank's supposition that Mr. Weintraub may not have checked to see that the deposit went down the chute is not a viable contention if the court believes (which it does) that both cloth bags were contained in the one paper bag, [because] the bank did receive one of the cloth bags. Finally, the fact that so many checks that had to be stopped were contained in the missing bag tends to lessen any concern that the claim is fraudulent.

In light of the above, the court finds that the aforesaid second bag containing cash and checks totaling $19,191.52 was in fact properly placed in the night depository vault in the paper bag with the other bag containing $850. When the paper bag entered the chute, a bailment was created. Although in the typical bailment there is personal delivery from the bailor to the bailee, here the bailment occurred upon delivery into a device under the exclusive care and control of the bank.

The finding of the creation of a bailment brings the court to the question of where the loss shall lie when neither plaintiffs nor defendant alleged any wrongdoing by the other. It is difficult to impose a burden upon either party to demonstrate fault, as the bank is never aware of a night deposit until the next morning when the vault is opened, and the depositor is never present when the vault is opened.

The general rule is that when a bailee is unable to advance an adequate explanation for the failure to return property subject to a bailment, it is liable for the loss, but that if the bailee provides a sufficient explanation for the loss so as to raise an issue of fact, the bailor must then prove negligence. . . .

(continues)

EMPLOYERS INSURANCE OF WAUSAU v. CHEMICAL BANK

(continued from previous page)

In *Gramore Stores v. Bankers Trust Co.*, 402 N.Y.S.2d 326, the court held that a bank "may not contract away its liability for negligence" and struck an affirmative defense based on an exculpatory provision similar to that executed herein. . . .

Chemical Bank is not claiming exemption from liability for negligence, but rather is arguing that unless negligence or a conversion is established, the contract prohibits a recovery. In its brief it states: "The bank has merely defined its liability to protect itself against fraudulent claims." . . . It is hard to see where the contract provision would apply unless defendant is seeking to distinguish between negligence established by conduct as opposed to a presumption thereof that might ensue from application of the rules of bailment. If this is defendant's argument, the court cannot accept it. First, the court agrees with the holding in *Gramore Stores* that public policy [does not look favorably on an attempt by] a public institution such as a bank [to contract] away its liability for negligence. Second, [in any kind of transaction an attempt to contract away one's liability for negligence is not effective] unless it is absolutely clear that this was the understanding. Such an interpretation could not be garnered from an examination of the agreement herein. . . .

In *Vilner v. Crocker National Bank*, 152 Cal. Rptr. 850, a similar set of facts to those herein was presented with the bank arguing that proof that it exercised ordinary care met its conceded burden of explaining the failure to return the depositor's bag. The court disagreed, stating: "A simple showing of the exercise of ordinary care is not a sufficient explanation. Something has gone terribly awry. There is no evidence that explains it but, as Thoreau reminds us, 'Some circumstantial evidence is very strong, as when you find a trout in the milk.' A general showing of prudence and caution will not do absent an explanation of the cause of the disappearance." . . .

The court is acutely aware of the possibility of opening the floodgates to numerous fraudulent claims. But each and every claimant must first overcome the not insignificant threshold of demonstrating that a deposit was in fact made. Thereafter, the burden shifts to the bank to offer an explanation of how the loss occurred. Needless to say, requiring a bank to prove that it was not negligent in handling a particular deposit it claims it did not receive is rather difficult. But in the present case, with a court finding that the deposit was made, the court can only presume that the loss thereafter occurred as a result of the negligence of or conver-

sion by the bank's employees. Possibly the second cloth bag was left in the paper bag that was thrown away, was dropped or even stolen. In any event, the exculpatory provision, which defendant concedes would not preclude a recovery for negligence or conversion, cannot therefore prohibit the imposition of liability.

Between the bank, that can offer no evidence with respect to how the deposit was made, and the depositor, who is in a similar position with respect to the opening of the bags, the loss should fall on the bank if it cannot explain what happened to the bag. . . . The excuse that the deposit was not received can consequently be analogized to the position of the warehouse in *I.C.C. Metals v. Municipal Warehouse Co.*, 50 N.Y.2d 657, which when it was unable to return stored goods merely offered the supposition that they were stolen. The Court of Appeals held that such explanation was insufficient to shift the burden back to the bailor to establish the bailee's fault and therefore allowed a recovery based on conversion to stand.

The defendant having failed to offer any explanation as to how the loss occurred is liable to the plaintiff Suncrest in the sum of $8,084.50, with interest from the date of the loss, and to plaintiff Employers Insurance Company of Wausau for $3,000, with interest from the date it paid Suncrest.🔌

Rights of the Bailor

Essentially, the rights of the bailor arise from the duties of the bailee. Thus, the bailor's most important rights are to have the bailed property returned at the end of the bailment period, to have the bailee use due care in protecting the property, and to have the bailee use the property (if use is contemplated at all) in conformity with the express or implied terms of the bailment contract. Additionally, if the bailor is having work performed on the property by the bailee, the bailor is entitled to have it done in a workmanlike fashion. If the purpose of the bailment is use of the property by the bailee, the bailor has the right to compensation under the express or implied terms of the contract.

Duties of the Bailor

Liability for Defects in the Bailed Property
Obviously, the bailor has duties corresponding to the rights of the bailee discussed previously. In addition,

the bailor has certain basic duties with respect to the condition of the bailed property.

Negligence. The bailor must not knowingly deliver property containing a hidden defect that is likely to cause injury. In either a mutual benefit bailment or one for the sole benefit of the bailee, the bailor is legally required to notify the bailee of any dangerous defect about which the bailor has *actual knowledge.* In a mutual benefit bailment, the bailor's duty regarding the condition of the bailed property is somewhat greater, and he or she can be held responsible for injury caused by hidden defects about which the bailor *either knew or should have known.*[4] Thus, in a mutual benefit bailment, the bailor's duty includes reasonably inspecting the property and maintaining it in a safe condition before delivery to a bailee.

In either of these situations, a violation of the bailor's duty constitutes negligence, and the bailor is liable for resulting harm to the bailee and to others coming into contact with the defective property in a reasonably foreseeable manner. For example, a bailor's liability for delivering a defective automobile to the bailee would include injuries to the bailee and his or her immediate family, as well as to innocent third parties such as the driver of another automobile involved in an accident because of the defect.

Warranty and Strict Liability. In addition to imposing liability for the bailor's negligence, most courts in recent years have placed additional liability on commercial bailors. In the case of bailors who are in the business of renting property, such as automobiles, construction equipment, and so on, a majority of courts have held the bailor responsible for dangerous defects in the bailed property on basis of the *implied warranty* and *strict products liability* theories. These courts have drawn an analogy from the liability imposed on merchants in *sales* transactions. The importance of this development, as we saw in Chapter 22, "Warranties and Products Liability," is that the supplier of a defective item can be held liable without any proof that the supplier knew or should have known of the defect. Moreover, the supplier's defenses are much more limited under the warranty and strict liability theories.

As mentioned earlier, new Article 2A of the Uniform Commercial Code formally adopts the same

basic warranty obligations for lessors of personal property as exist under Article 2 for sellers of personal property.

Bailor's Disclaimers

We saw previously that commercial *bailees* frequently attempt to limit their liability contractually. It also is very common for commercial *bailors* to make similar attempts. This type of provision, whether it is called an exculpatory clause, disclaimer, or liability limitation, is given essentially the same treatment by the courts as bailees' exculpatory clauses. In fact, in the majority of states that have drawn an analogy between the bailor who is in the business of renting personal property and the merchant who is in the business of selling goods, a disclaimer by the bailor is given even harsher treatment by the courts. Such a provision violates public policy and thus is not allowed to shield a commercial bailor from liability for negligence, breach of warranty, or strict liability when a defect in the bailed property causes personal injury or property damage to either the bailee or someone else whose contact with the item was reasonably foreseeable.

SPECIAL BAILMENTS

Special bailments are those involving common carriers, warehouse companies, and innkeepers (or hotelkeepers). Although bailments involving these types of bailees have most of the characteristics of ordinary bailments and are subject to most of the same rules, they are singled out because of certain unique aspects.

Common Carriers

A **common carrier** is a company that is licensed by the state or federal government to provide transportation services to the general public. Most airlines, trucking companies, and railroad companies are common carriers. A company doing business as a common carrier must make its services available to the public on a nondiscriminatory basis. A common carrier can be contrasted with a **contract carrier,** which does not hold itself out as providing transportation services to the public and is not licensed to do so. A contract carrier provides service under contract only to a few selected customers.

Suppose that a furniture manufacturer in Pittsburgh, Pennsylvania, delivers a large quantity of furniture to a railroad company for shipment to a

[4]Questions concerning the condition of the bailed property almost never arise in a bailment for the sole benefit of the bailor, because the bailee does not *use* the property. If the bailed property was defective and harmed the bailee in such a case, however, the bailor's duty presumably would be the same as in a mutual benefit bailment.

wholesale furniture distributor in St. Louis, Missouri. When the manufacturer, called the *shipper,* turns over possession of the furniture to the railroad company, called the *carrier,* a type of mutual benefit bailment has been created.

Bailments of this type are different from ordinary bailments in several important respects.

Obligation to Transport

Unlike most bailees, the carrier has a contractual obligation to transport the bailed property.

Bills of Lading

Also unlike other bailees, the carrier issues a **bill of lading** to the shipper. The bill of lading, the rules for which are set forth in Article 7 of the Uniform Commercial Code, serves as both a *contract of bailment* and a *document of title.* In other words, it sets forth the terms of the agreement between shipper and carrier and also serves as evidence of title to the goods.

As was discussed in Chapter 20 dealing with sales of goods, a bill of lading or other document of title can be either *negotiable* or *nonnegotiable.* A bill of lading ordering the carrier to "deliver to X" is a nonnegotiable document of title. The carrier's obligation in such a case is to deliver the goods only to X, and the nonnegotiable document does not confer the right to receive the goods to anyone else who might come into possession of the document.

On the other hand, a bill of lading ordering the carrier to "deliver to the order of X," or to "deliver to bearer," is a negotiable document of title. Lawful possession of a negotiable document is tantamount to ownership of the goods, and the carrier is obligated to deliver them to anyone having such possession. In the case of a bill of lading ordering the carrier to "deliver to the order of X," the carrier is required to surrender the goods to Y if X has endorsed and delivered the document to Y and Y presents it to the carrier. In the case of a bill of lading ordering the carrier to "deliver to bearer," the carrier is required to surrender the goods to anyone to whom the document has been delivered, even without the presence of an endorsement.

Bills of lading, especially negotiable ones, are often used to facilitate sales transactions by providing the seller (shipper) a document that can be sent to the buyer and then used by the buyer to take possession of the goods when they reach their destination. This document may be sent directly from the seller to the buyer, or it may be sent through banking channels with the seller's and buyer's banks acting as agents for delivery of the document and receipt of payment.

Strict Liability

Contrary to ordinary bailments, the carrier is absolutely liable to the shipper for damage to or loss of the goods. In other words, the carrier's liability is not based upon negligence or other fault.[5] There are, however, several narrow categories of circumstances in which the carrier is not liable. If the goods are damaged, stolen, lost, or destroyed during shipment, the carrier has the burden of proving that the situation falls within one of these categories. The categories are as follows.

Act of God. The carrier is not liable if it can show that the loss was caused by an unexpected force of nature that was of such magnitude that damage to the goods could not have been prevented. The term Act of God is interpreted very strictly; evidence that the goods were damaged or destroyed by a flood, for example, will not suffice to excuse the carrier unless the flood was of such an unprecedented nature that no reasonable precautions could have forestalled the loss.

Act of a Public Enemy. This term is also interpreted very narrowly, and is usually applied only to a situation in which the goods were damaged, destroyed, or seized by a foreign nation at war with the United States.

Act of a Public Authority. The term public authority is much broader, and applies to actions by various local, state, or federal government officials. Examples would include the seizure of an illegal drug shipment by law enforcement officers, or the seizure of goods by a sheriff acting under a *writ of execution.* A writ of execution is a court order requiring an officer to seize property and sell it for the purpose of paying off a judgment against the owner.

Act of the Shipper. The carrier is not responsible if the shipper's own actions are shown to have caused the loss. For example, the carrier is not liable for the death of the shipper's chickens if proved to have been caused by the shipper's improperly ventilated crates.

---

[5] Frequently, one carrier will transport the goods for only part of the total trip, and other carriers will provide transportation for other portions of the journey. In such a situation, involving *connecting carriers,* the last carrier to have the goods is presumed to have received them in good condition, and is liable to the shipper for damage to the goods. If this carrier claims that the goods were damaged while in the hands of an earlier carrier, it must initiate legal action against the other carrier to recoup its loss.

The Inherent Nature of the Goods. The carrier is not liable if the loss is caused by an inherent characteristic of the goods themselves that the carrier had no control over. This category also is construed very strictly. For example, it would not be sufficient for the carrier to show that a shipment of fruit spoiled and that fruit is prone to spoilage. To escape liability, the carrier would have to prove that the fruit spoiled for a very specific reason, such as the fact that it was overripe at the time of shipment, and that the carrier could not have prevented the spoilage.

Liability Limitations

Despite the fact that carriers are liable for harm to the bailed property even without being at fault, they are permitted to limit their liability contractually to a greater extent than ordinary bailees. Under federal and state regulations, common carriers may obtain the shipper's agreement to place a dollar limit on the carrier's liability, and the limitation is valid if the shipper was given a choice of paying a higher transportation fee for a higher dollar limitation.

Warehouse Companies

A **warehouse company** is in the business of storing other people's property for compensation. A *public* warehouse company is obligated to serve the general public without discrimination. Most of the principles applicable to warehouse companies are exactly the same as those for ordinary bailees. In fact, some of the illustrations presented in the discussion of ordinary bailments involved warehouses.

The most important characteristic that warehouse operators have in common with other bailees is the nature of the bailee's liability. A warehouse company is not absolutely liable like a common carrier, but is liable for damage to or loss of the bailed property only in those circumstances in which an ordinary bailee is liable, namely, where the damage or loss is caused by the bailee's negligence, conversion, or breach of contract. Warehouse companies, however, are also subject to the same presumption of negligence as ordinary bailees.

Thus, for most purposes a warehouse company is an ordinary bailee. It is often singled out as a special bailee, however, for three reasons: (1) Like a common carrier, and unlike other bailees, a warehouse operator may obtain the bailor's agreement to limit the warehouse's liability, and the limitation is valid if the bailor was given a choice of a higher dollar limitation in return for a higher fee. (2) Also like a common

carrier, a warehouse company issues documents of title for the goods it receives. The document of title issued by a warehouse company is called a **warehouse receipt,** and is governed by the same rules as bills of lading under Article 7 of the UCC. (3) A warehouse company is subject to more extensive regulation by the state than most other bailees. For example, warehouses are usually subject to special building standards and fire prevention measures.

Innkeepers

The taking of articles of personal property to a hotel or motel room by a guest does not create a bailment, for two reasons. First, the **innkeeper** (i.e., the hotel owner) normally does not have knowledge of the specific items that are brought into the room. Second, because the guest is free to remove the items from the room without notice to the innkeeper, the latter does not have exclusive possession of the items.

Despite the absence of a true bailment relationship, under common-law principles the innkeeper had exactly the same absolute liability as a common carrier for damage to or loss of guest's personal property. In modern times, however, all states have passed statutes diminishing the innkeeper's liability. The typical statute requires innkeepers to maintain a safe or other appropriate facility for the safekeeping of its guests' valuables. If a guest deposits property with the innkeeper, a bailment is created. Under most statutes, if the property then is damaged or lost, the innkeeper has the same absolute liability as a common carrier. Some statutes, however, place dollar limits on the innkeeper's liability.

With regard to property that is *not* turned over to the innkeeper for safekeeping, the statutes vary. Many provide that the innkeeper's common-law liability is reduced to that of an ordinary bailee. Other statutes do not remove the innkeeper's absolute responsibility, but place a dollar limit such as $50 on that liability.

SUMMARY

Although the legal framework for personal property ownership bears a number of similarities to that for real property, there are also many differences. Primary among the differences is that ownership of personal property usually is an all-or-nothing proposition, and is not subdivided into the wide variety of interests that characterize real property ownership. Ownership of personal property can be acquired in a sale transaction or by will, subjects that are dealt with elsewhere in this book. Personal property ownership can be transferred by gift, which requires expression of a present intent to transfer ownership and delivery of possession. Other methods by which title to an article of personal property can be affected are occupation, finding, accession, and confusion.

A bailment of personal property arises when one party transfers temporary possession (but not title) to another under an agreement in which the recipient is required to return the property later or to deliver it to a designated third person. Bailments can be ordinary or special. Ordinary bailments can be further subdivided into those for the sole benefit of the bailee, sole benefit of the bailor, and mutual benefit of the parties. The most important duties of the bailee in an ordinary bailment are to use and return the property only in accordance with the bailment contract, and to exercise due care in protecting the property. When bailed property is not returned or is returned in a damaged condition, there is a presumption of negligence.

The most important duties of the bailor are to conform to the terms of the contract regarding the bailee's use and possession of the property, and not to deliver bailed property having a known dangerous defect. This duty is somewhat greater in a mutual benefit bailment than in one for the sole benefit of the bailee. In addition to this liability for negligence, in recent years liability under warranty and strict products liability theories has been imposed on commercial bailors.

Special bailments are those involving common carriers, warehouse companies, and innkeepers. A common carrier is absolutely liable for damage to or loss of the goods unless the carrier can prove that the damage or loss was caused by one of five narrowly interpreted events. A warehouse company has the liability of an ordinary bailee, but is different in that it issues warehouse receipts and is subject to greater regulation. An innkeeper, though not technically a bailee of the property its guests keep in their rooms, had the same absolute liability as a common carrier under common-law rules. All states have passed statutes modifying this liability in certain ways.

KEY TERMS
Donor
Donee
Constructive delivery (or symbolic delivery)
Gift inter vivos
Gift causa mortis
Occupation
Abandoned property
Lost property
Mislaid property
Finding statute (or estray statute)
Escheat statute
Accession
Confusion of goods
Fungible goods
Bailment
Bailor
Bailee
Constructive bailment
Presumption of negligence
Exculpatory clause
Special bailments
Common carrier
Contract carrier
Bill of lading
Warehouse company
Warehouse receipt
Innkeeper

QUESTIONS AND PROBLEMS

1. Closter was despondent and had decided to commit suicide. Before doing so, he inserted into an envelope a promissory note that he owned. On the note he wrote that he was giving it to Schutz. Closter then shot and killed himself. Schutz, who occupied another room in the same boardinghouse, heard the shot, rushed to his friend's room and found his body there. Schutz saw the envelope lying on the desk where Closter had placed it. Thinking that it might be a suicide note, Schutz opened it and found the promissory note containing Closter's expression of donative-intent. Schutz pocketed the envelope and note. The existence of the note later came to light, and Liebe, the administrator of Closter's estate, filed suit to collect on the note from Battman, who had originally executed it. Schutz claimed that *he* was the owner of the note and was entitled to collect on it from Battman. Who won? Discuss. (*Liebe v. Battman,* 54 Pac. 179, 1898.)

2. Walters suffered a heart attack. Fearful of impending death, he gave his diamond ring to his

sister while he was still in the hospital. Walters' condition improved, and he was discharged from the hospital two months later. He asked his sister to return the ring, but she refused. Not wanting to cause a family quarrel, he said nothing more. Five years later he died from heart disease. Does the ring belong to his sister? Explain. Would it make any difference if he had never asked for the return of the ring? Discuss.

3. Hillebrant indicated to Brewer that he was making a gift to Brewer of a herd of cattle. Hillebrant then obtained Brewer's branding iron and branded the cattle with Brewer's registered brand. Before the cattle were delivered to Brewer, however, Hillebrant changed his mind. Brewer sued, claiming that a completed gift of the cattle had been made. Was Brewer correct? Discuss. (*Hillebrant v. Brewer*, 6 Tex. 45, 1851.)

4. Harkness was elderly and bedridden. So that his close friend Kuntz could pay his bills for him a joint account was established with money belonging to Harkness. The account was a joint tenancy with right of survivorship. It was used for its intended purpose until Harkness died two years later (that is, Kuntz never used the funds for any purpose other than to pay bills for Harkness). When Harkness died, Kuntz claimed the money remaining in the account, asserting that it was his as a gift. Harkness' heirs disagreed. What is the result? Explain.

5. X and Y consented to the mixing of their wheat in a grain storage elevator owned by Z. What is the status of the ownership of the wheat? Explain. Would the answer be different if Z had caused the confusion accidently? Explain. Would the answer be different if X had intentionally caused the confusion with knowledge that he had no right to do so? Explain.

6. Hanson agreed to loan $1,000 to Kristofferson only after Kristofferson agreed to *pledge* a ring valued at $3,000 with Hanson. A pledge involves transfer of possession of personal property to a creditor as security for the debt. Soon after the loan was made, the ring was stolen while in Hanson's possession. In subsequent litigation between the parties, Hanson contended that he was not a bailee in this situation because his obligation to return the ring was not absolute—he would not have to return it if Kristofferson defaulted on his loan. Is Hanson's contention correct? Why or why not?

7. X left her expensive leather handbag in a medical clinic waiting room when she was called into her doctor's office for her appointment. When she returned to the waiting room 45 minutes later, the handbag was gone. She later brought suit against the clinic to recover its value. At the trial the clinic receptionist and X's doctor testified that they did not see the handbag at any time during the day of her appointment. Assuming the receptionist and the doctor were telling the truth, would this testimony necessarily rule out a bailment relationship? Explain. If the receptionist had testified that she had noticed X placing the handbag in a corner of a couch before entering the doctor's office, would this fact clearly establish a bailment? Discuss.

8. Scarlet, a Ford dealer, delivered a new Taurus automobile to his neighbor, Gray, for ten days; the understanding between the two men was that at the end of that period Gray would have the option of (a) giving his 1913 Ford Model T to Scarlet in payment for the Taurus, or (b) paying Scarlet $15,000 in cash for the Taurus. During the ten-day period while Gray is in possession of the Taurus, is he a bailee of the car? Discuss. Would your answer be any different if the agreement had simply given Gray, at the end of the ten-day period, the option of either returning the Taurus or paying $15,000 cash for it? Explain.

9. X leaves his car at the Y Company's parking lot and returns an hour later to find that it has been badly damaged while in the Y Company's possession. In this situation, X's right to recover damages from the parking lot company might be seriously jeopardized if the legal relationship between X and the Y Company was merely that of licensee and licensor rather than bailor and bailee. Explain why this is so.

10. David Crystal, Inc., delivered goods to a trucking company for transportation. While in the trucking company's possession, the goods were lost when the truck carrying them was hijacked in New York City. In a legal action by David Crystal against the trucking firm, a common carrier, the trucking firm defended on the ground that truck hijackers are "public enemies," and that it thus was not liable for the loss. Is this contention correct? Why or why not? (*David Crystal, Inc. v. Ehrlich-Newmark Truck Co.*, 314 N.Y.S.2d 559, 1970.)

Wills

Intestacy—Statutes of Descent and Distribution

Administration of the Estate

Trusts

Estate Planning

Although few people amass large fortunes in their lifetimes, most will not die penniless. Many people are surprised at the actual value of what they may have considered to be modest holdings. Real estate acquired early in life may appreciate dramatically; life insurance, both individual and group, may be owned in substantial amounts, and investment in the stock market through mutual funds is commonplace. One's personal property, slowly acquired over a period of years, may constitute a sizable asset. Some knowledge of wills, trusts, and other estate planning devices is essential to make informed decisions about one's personal situation.

The case of Pablo Picasso is a good example of what can happen when a person with a substantial estate fails to provide for its orderly disposition. When the famous artist died in 1973 he left a tremendous fortune—millions of dollars in assets. To whom did he leave it? As a matter of fact, Picasso died **intestate;** that is, at the time of his death he had not prepared a document—a will—to provide specific and detailed instructions about what to do with his property. A properly planned, drafted, and executed will might have eliminated most of the bitter controversy that arose among those close to him over the disposition of his wealth.

Picasso apparently felt that making a will was an act in contemplation of death and therefore an unpleasant subject to be avoided. He resisted all efforts by those who anticipated protracted legal proceedings to persuade him to make a will to provide for an orderly disposition of his property. When any person of considerable means refuses to provide for his or her estate's distribution on death, controversy is almost as certain as death itself.

WILLS

A will transforms a person's wishes about the disposition of his or her property into a valid, legal instrument. This section covers formal, written wills in detail and mentions other types briefly. Following are some commonly used terms with which the student may be unfamiliar. A man who makes a will is a **testator,** a woman is a **testatrix.** A person who dies is a **decedent.** A decedent leaving a valid will is said to die *testate.* It is customary for a testator to designate a personal representative to carry out the provisions of the will. This person is an **executor** if male and an **executrix** if female. If there is no will or the will does not designate a personal representative, the court will appoint an **administrator** (or *administratrix*) to handle the decedent's estate. With regard to the testator's property, disposition of real estate is properly called a **devise,** money passing under a will is a **legacy,** and other property is disposed of by **bequest.**[1] (Today, lawyers use these terms interchangeably.)

Testamentary Capacity

A will is valid only if the testator had **testamentary capacity** at the time of its making. In most states the testator must have attained a specific minimum age, usually 18. In all states the testator must possess the mental capacity to dispose of the property intelligently. Testamentary capacity is not identical to capacity to contract. In general, testators have the capacity to make wills if they have attained the statutory age, if they know what property they own, and if they reasonably understand how and to whom they want to leave their property. The following case illustrates this principle.

[1] The Uniform Probate Code, which has been largely adopted in about 15 states and partially in some others, uses the term "devise" to refer to any sort of testamentary gift whether of land, money, or personal property.

HOLLADAY V. HOLLADAY

Court of Appeals of Kentucky, 172 S.W.2d 36 (1943)

This action was a will contest involving the will of Lewis Holladay. A college graduate, Holladay made his home on his mother's farm with her and a sister until his mother's death in 1929. He remained on the farm until he died in 1940 at age 66. He was survived by a brother, Joe, and three sisters. Joe was the sole beneficiary under Lewis's will. When he submitted the will for probate, the sisters opposed the proceeding on a number of grounds. The primary basis for the contest was the allegation by the sisters, the contestants, that Lewis did not possess sufficient mental capacity to execute a will.

Upon a verdict rendered in the Clark Circuit Court a judgment was entered adjudging that a paper executed by Lewis Holladay was his last will and testament. This appeal is prosecuted from that judgment.

Sims, Justice:

. . . Lewis Holladay had a college education and made his home on his mother's farm with her and a maiden sister, Miss Denia, until his mother's death in 1929. His mother was quite old and her death greatly upset him. The testimony for contestants is that Lewis was far from normal mentally years before his mother died, but was much more unstable afterwards. It was testified he shot and killed his pet dog without reason in 1917 or 1918. During electrical storms he would take his seat under a tree, saying it was safer there than in the house. He was afflicted with stomach ulcers and could not sleep at nights and would roam over the premises and farm, and on occasion would stand like a statue in the county road even at midnight, requiring travelers to drive around him. At times he would go to the barn during the night and throw down hay for his stock when it was not in the barn but was out on pasture. He would bathe at night in a pond which was little more than a hog wallow, saying it gave him relief. It was testified that if the least thing went wrong, such as some meat falling down or the spilling of some lard from a bucket, he became so upset that it was necessary to put him to bed to quiet him. Pages could be consumed in reciting the testimony relative to his queer, weird and unnatural actions. There were many suicides and much insanity on both sides of his family, and it appears in the evidence that he threatened to destroy himself.

Opposing such testimony, twenty-six of his neighbors, friends, business acquaintances and associates testified he was perfectly sane and normal; that he was a good farmer and a successful business man. These twenty-six witnesses made up a cross section of the community and included people from all walks of life: doctors, bankers, veterinarians, livestock buyers, farmers and shop keepers, practically all of whom had business or social contacts with him. Upon the written request of his sisters, he and his brother, Joe, were named administrators of his mother's $23,000 estate, which testator wound up practically without assistance from Joe. In 1930, the year he wrote his will, Lewis contracted with his sisters that he would bid $137.50 per acre for his mother's farm of 146 acres if it were sold at public auction; and he carried out his contract and purchased the farm. He raised and sold registered sheep; was the moving spirit in some important and successful litigation in 1929 involving damages to farm lands in the community when a water dam broke. From 1929 to 1933 he served twice on the petit jury and twice on the grand jury; and in the interim between 1927 and 1940 he wrote more than 2,000 checks aggregating $29,000.

. . . The court did not err in refusing to give contestants' proffered instruction on the alleged insane delusions Lewis had against his sisters. His feelings toward them were unkind and even bitter, but they were based upon facts and not delusions. His sisters had objected to the fee allowed him as administrator of his mother's estate, although it was slightly less than the statutory limit of 5 percent. They had insinuated that when he and Joe, the morning after the death of their brother Felix, went through the deceased's personal effects they were looking for his will with the sinister motive of destroying it if they found one in favor of the sisters. Miss Denia had intimated that Lewis had sensual plans in bringing in a housekeeper after his mother's death. Then after Lewis had agreed to bid $137.50 per acre on his mother's farm, his three sisters attempted to raise the price. This combination of incidents had turned Lewis against his sisters, but it cannot be said his feelings were insane delusions, which are ideas or beliefs springing spontaneously from a diseased or perverted mind without reason or foundation in fact. A belief which is based upon reason and evidence, be it ever so slight, cannot be an insane delusion. . . .

The judgment is affirmed.

Undue Influence

Even if a testator or testatrix has the legal capacity to make a will, that will should not be admitted to probate if it is the product of fraud, duress, or, more typically, undue influence. Many courts use a four-factor test to determine the existence of undue influence. That test is applied in the following case.

CASPER V. MCDOWELL

Wisconsin Supreme Court, 205 N.W.2d 753 (1973)

Case

On April 2, 1970, 78-year-old Joseph Casper died. His will, drafted ten months before his death by a local attorney, provided for payment of debts and funeral expenses, bequeathed $1,500 to each of Casper's two sons (Alger and Richard), and left the residue and remainder of the estate to Wilma Jean McDowell, who had lived with Casper as housekeeper and friend from October 1964 to his death. Nothing was left to Joseph's brother, John. The will specified Wilma Jean's father or her brother as executor.

After the will was submitted for admission to probate, objections were filed by Alger and Richard. Later they also challenged, on undue influence grounds, transactions in which Joseph had named Wilma Jean a joint tenant on a bank account and two deposit certificates. A jury found no undue influence in the transactions, and the trial court admitted the will to probate. Alger and Richard appealed.

Wilkie, Justice:

This court has often reiterated the elements necessary to establish undue influence. In Will of Freitag [101 N.W.2d 108 (Wis. 1960)] they were capsulized as follows:

. . . Susceptibility, opportunity to influence, disposition to influence, and coveted result; stated more completely: 1. A person who is susceptible of being unduly influenced by the person charged with exercising undue influence; 2. the opportunity of the person charged to exercise such influence on the susceptible person to procure the improper favor;

3. a disposition on the part of the party charged, to influence unduly such susceptible person for the purpose of procuring an improper favor either for himself or another; 4. a result caused by, or the effect of such undue influence.

Joseph Casper's first marriage ended in divorce in the early 1930s. After the divorce the sons [Alger and Richard] lived with their mother but continued to see their father. Both sons eventually moved to California in the 1950s. Joseph Casper remarried but . . . his second wife died in 1958. In October 1964, the testator placed an advertisement in the Kenosha newspaper for a housekeeper. Wilma Jean McDowell, then twenty-two years old, answered the ad . . . and continuously resided in the testator's home until his death in 1970. Although Jean McDowell testified that she had not had sexual relations with the testator, several witnesses testified the two were intimate. There was very little contact [between testator and his sons] after 1965. The testator's brother, John, testified that after 1965 he did not see his brother very often.

A. *Susceptibility.* As evidence of Joseph Casper's susceptibility to undue influence, appellants cite his deteriorating physical condition, his dissociation from family members, former friends and associates, and his inordinate attraction to this young girl. Testimony from various witnesses regarding Casper's odd conduct included his failure to recognize a grandchild and an old friend; his cutting off the top of several of his trees and one of his neighbor's trees; the severe cutting of his hand by placing it in his lawnmower. Appellants also cite as conclu-

sive proof of susceptibility a boast made by Jean McDowell to a neighbor that she could get anything she wanted from Casper.

The prevailing evidence, however, is that Joseph Casper was a strong willed and independent person. A neighbor, Frank Novelen, stated: "Well, he had a mind of his own. . . . Yeah, I'd say if he wanted to do something, he'd do it." Casper's stockbroker, Harry Myers, testified he had talked with Casper a couple of days before his death. According to Myers the two men had a conversation for fifteen minutes concerning the stock market. Myers stated the only difference he perceived in Casper was that his hair was a "shade grayer than the time I'd seen him before."

His personal physician testified that, in his opinion, Casper was "orientated" during the fourteen years they were acquainted. We conclude from this evidence that Casper, during the last half dozen years of his life, did not lose his characteristic independence. He was not susceptible to undue influence as claimed by appellants. While his health declined with age, his mental condition did not deteriorate severely.

B. *Disposition.* The disposition to influence is shown by "a willingness to do something wrong or unfair, and grasping or overreaching characteristics." [Estate of Brehmer, 164 N.W.2d 318 (Wis. 1969).] Not every act of kindness may be considered as indicating a disposition to influence a testator. In Estate of McGonigal [174 N.W.2d 205 (Wis. 1970)] we noted "There is nothing wrong with aiding and comforting a failing testator; indeed, such activity should be encouraged."

(continues)

CASPER V. McDOWELL

(continued from previous page)
While Jean McDowell's aid and comfort to Joseph Casper may have exceeded that which is normally expected of a nurse or housekeeper, this fact, standing alone, does not require the inference of a disposition to unduly influence.

While Casper's diminished contacts with his friends and family may give rise to the suspicion that Jean McDowell was "poisoning" the testator's mind, such inference or suspicion is not necessarily true. Casper's friend, John Schanock, stated that he felt Casper's interests simply turned to love. Quite natural is Casper's diminished need to depend upon friends and family after Jean McDowell's arrival. The two, despite several spats, were quite close.

[Also] on June 2, 1964, [testator] designated Linda Corn as beneficiary of [a savings] account. This indicates that Casper, although maintaining contact with friends and family, did not regard them as potential recipients of his bounty even before he and Jean McDowell met.

C. *Coveted result.* At first blush, the will and [property] transfers in the instant case appear unnatural. Indeed, as stated in Estate of Culver [126 N.W.2d 536 (Wis. 1964)], they raise a "red flag of warning." It does not automatically follow, however, that Joseph Casper's giving the majority of his wealth to nonkin is unnatural. The naturalness of a will depends upon the circumstances of each case.

Here, the testator's closest kin, his two sons, lived in California and had

for many years. It appears that Casper's closest friend was Jean McDowell.

Although there is a claim that Casper deviated from socially acceptable behavior for a man of his age in hiring Jean McDowell, fifty years his junior, as a resident housekeeper and in considering her as his closest friend through his last years, this does not necessarily lead to but one inference that his giving the majority of his estate to her was an unnatural testamentary result obtained by undue influence.

D. *Opportunity.* The only element of the four essential to a finding of undue influence that is present here is the "opportunity" to influence the testator.

[Affirmed.]

The Formal Will
The term *formal* indicates that the will has been prepared and executed in compliance with the state's law of wills ("probate code"). Although the right to make a will generally exists independent of statute, the procedures for drafting, executing, and witnessing the formal written document are governed by statute. Such statutory requirements, although basically similar, vary from state to state. Therefore the drafter must be thoroughly acquainted with the law of the state in which the testator's will is to be effective and must be sure to comply with its provisions. Noncompliance usually means that the will is declared invalid. If this happens, the decedent's property passes in accordance with the state's law of descent and distribution. (Such statutes and their application are discussed later in another section.)

General Requirements
A will must be written; it must be signed by the testator or testatrix or at his or her direction. In most states, the signing must be witnessed by two competent persons who themselves must sign as witnesses in the presence of each other and of the testator or testatrix.[2] Most states require an **attestation clause,** a paragraph beneath the testator's signature to the effect that the will was *published*—that is, declared by the testator to be the last will and testament, and signed in the presence of the witnesses, who themselves signed as attesting witnesses. These are the formalities required by statute, and they must be strictly observed. The witnesses do not need to read or know the contents of the will. The testator or testatrix simply announces to them that the document is the will and that he or she is going to sign it. The function of the attestation clause is to serve as a self-proving affidavit to relieve the witnesses of the burden of testifying when the will is submitted for admission to probate after the death of the testator or testatrix.

Specific Provisions
The main function of a will is to provide for the disposal of property. However, it can appoint an executor and cancel all previous wills if it so states. It

[2] A few states require three witnesses

can also provide for an alternative disposition of property in the event the primary beneficiary predeceases the testator. If the testator or testatrix is married, the surviving spouse is usually appointed as the executor or executrix; if unmarried, a close relative or friend may be designated.

A will can also cover the disposition of property in the event that husband and wife die nearly simultaneously. It is essential for the will to state that it revokes any and all prior wills. The existence of two or more wills can create insurmountable problems. Sometimes none are admitted to probate (the court proceedings whereby a will is proved and the estate of the decedent is disposed of), in which event the state's statutory provisions for the division of an estate are followed.

The will can also name a guardian for minor children. If both husband and wife die, the guardian they have appointed in their wills can be confirmed by the court if he or she is qualified and willing to serve in that capacity. This will obviate the necessity for a court-appointed guardian and a possible controversy between the two competing, though well-meaning, sides of the family.

Modification

While it is possible in some states to change one's will by erasure, by striking out portions, or by interlineation, such procedures are risky undertakings at best. The proper method is to modify by means of a **codicil.** This is an addition to the will and must be executed with the same formalities as the original document. Consequently, if extensive modification is necessary, the testator would be well-advised to consider making a new will.

Revocation

A will becomes effective only at the death of the testator. The testator can revoke or amend the will at any time until death. Revocation can be accomplished in several ways, but usually must be done in strict compliance with statute by means evincing a clear intent to revoke. Executing a new will with a clause expressly revoking all prior wills and codicils is a customary method of revoking a will. The necessity for strict statutory compliance is illustrated in the following case.

IN RE ESTATE OF HAUGK

Wisconsin Supreme Court, 280 N.W.2d 684 (1979)

On January 6, 1965, Marie Haugk executed a will naming the Lutheran Children's Friend Society and the Easter Seal Society of Milwaukee County ("appellants") as residual beneficiaries. On September 2, 1976, Marie's husband, Horst Haugk, burned the 1965 will in the family basement, while Marie, who was suffering from a heart condition and was thus unable to descend the stairs into the basement, stayed upstairs in the kitchen. Soon thereafter, Marie spoke to her attorney about execution of a new will which would have eliminated appellants as beneficiaries, purportedly because she had wearied of their repeated requests for funds. However, Marie died before the new will could be executed.

Haugk filed a petition with the probate court claiming his wife died intestate, leaving him as sole beneficiary of her $130,000 estate. Appellants then petitioned the court for admission of the 1965 will. The trial court found that the 1965 will was properly revoked and ruled for Haugk. Appellants challenge this ruling on appeal.

Coffey, Justice:

The common law requirements for revocation of a will by physical act have been codified in sec. 853.11(1)(b), Stats., which recites:

853.11 Revocation (1) subsequent writing or physical act. A will is revoked in whole or in part by:

. . .

(b) Burning, tearing, canceling or obliterating the will or part, with the intent to revoke, by the testator or by some person in the testator's presence and by his direction.

Thus the revocation statute clearly delineates that, in order for the revocation of Marie's will to be effective, Haugk had to burn the will: (1) in Marie's presence, and (2) at her direction.

The record discloses that Marie was in the kitchen of her apartment while Haugk was in the basement burning the will in the incinerator. He explained that Marie's heart condition prevented her from going to the basement because of the strain of climbing the stairs. Contrary to the strict wording of sec. 853.11(1)(b), Stats., the trial court found that Marie, being in near proximity in the same house, 13 steps away, was in Haugk's "constructive

(continues)

IN RE ESTATE OF HAUGK

(*continued from previous page*)
presence" at the time the will was destroyed.

In *Estate of Murphy*, 259 N.W. 430 (1935), this court discussed the necessity of the testator's presence during the destruction of a will.

> Inasmuch as revocation involves intention, the inference arises that the physical act must be performed by the testatory himself or under his sanction and direction. . . . Both presence and direction of the testator being usually essential where the act is performed by another, a will is not legally revoked though destroyed by the testator's own order, if burned or torn where he did not or could not see or take cognizance of the deed done, as statutes commonly require the revocation by physical act to be by testator himself or in his presence and in such states cancellation by a third party out of the presence of testator is of no effect.

In the present case, a valid revocation could have been achieved if Haugk had torn up and destroyed the will in Marie's presence; thus she would not have had to endanger her health by climbing the basement stairs. It makes even more sense and eliminates all suggestion of fraud if the testator personally revoked the will, defacing each page of the document and placing her initials thereon.

The requirement that a will must be destroyed in the "testator's presence" must be strictly construed. This strict construction is necessary so as to prevent the inadvertent or more importantly the fraudulent destruction of a will contrary to the testator's intentions. Each element must be established by adequate evidence as this court will not adopt a position that will promote either intestacy or the fraudulent destruction of an individual's last will and testament.

[Reversed.]

Revocation can also be caused by operation of law. Marriage, divorce, or the birth of a child subsequent to making a will may affect its validity by revoking it completely or partially. State laws on wills are not uniform—the birth of a child may revoke a will completely in one state but only partially in another. Marriage and divorce also affect wills differently from state to state.

Limitations

There are a few limitations on a person's right to dispose of property through a will. For example, if a married person's will leaves no provision for inheritance by the spouse, many states allow the spouse to claim a share of the estate, typically one-third, under what is called a "forced share," "widow's share," or "elective share." If the spouse is left less than the statutory "forced share," the spouse has the right to renounce the actual devise and take the larger "forced share." In addition, many states provide the spouse a "homestead right" to a specific amount of land (for example, 1 acre in town or 160 acres in the country).

In community property states, each spouse owns one-half of the community property. In most of these states, the surviving spouse receives title to half the community property and the deceased spouse's share passes by will, if one exists, or by intestacy if no will exists. In no event can either spouse dispose of more than one-half the community property by will.

Holographic Wills

Almost half the states allow testators to execute their own wills without formal attestation. These **holographic wills** must be entirely in the testator's own handwriting, including the signature. These wills differ from formal wills in that no attestation clause or witnesses are required. However, most states allowing holographic wills require that the testator's handwriting and signature be proved by two witnesses familiar with them during probate of the will. Competent witnesses would include persons who had received correspondence from the testator. A holographic will is purely statutory—that is, it must be made in accordance with the appropriate state's law and is subject to prescribed conditions and limitations. The principal requirement is that it be entirely in the testator's own handwriting. In *Estate of Thorn*, a testator in a holographic will used a rubber stamp to insert "Cragthorn" in the phrase "my country place Cragthorn." The will was held to be invalid since it was not entirely in the testator's handwriting.[3] In some jurisdictions the holographic will must be dated in the testator's handwriting. The requirements of

---

[3] 183 Cal. 512, 192 P. 19 (1920).

testamentary capacity and intent are the same as those for formal wills, but a holographic will is otherwise informal and may even take the form of a letter if it conveys testamentary intent (the mental determination or intention of the testator that the document constitute the person's will).

Nuncupative Wills

About half the states permit **nuncupative wills,** or *oral wills.* In general, statutes impose strict limitations on the disposal of property through a nuncupative will. Most states require that it be made during the testator's "last sickness"; that it be written down within a short period; that it be proved by two witnesses who were present at its making; and that the value of the estate bequeathed not exceed a certain amount, usually quite small. Some states also require that the decedent have been a soldier in the field or a sailor at sea in actual contemplation or fear of death.[4] Nuncupative wills, where recognized, usually effect distribution of personal property only, not real property.

Nuncupative wills are difficult to establish, and the restrictions placed on them are intended to discourage their use. There is always the possibility of mistake or fraud and, except on rare occasions, a testator can easily plan sufficiently ahead to use the more traditional and acceptable type of will.

INTESTACY—STATUTES OF DESCENT AND DISTRIBUTION

State laws govern the disposition of a decedent's estate when the decedent has died without a will— intestate. Such laws are called statutes of descent and distribution. They provide for disposition of the decedent's property, both real and personal, in accordance with a prescribed statutory scheme. Real property descends; personal property is distributed. Consequently, the law of the state where the decedent's real estate is located will determine the heirs, by class, to whom it will descend. The decedent's personal property will be distributed in accordance with the law of the state in which he or she is domiciled. In addition to prescribing the persons who will inherit a decedent's property, statutes of descent and distribution also prescribe the order and proportions in which they will take. The effect of this is that intes-

[4]These are commonly known as soldiers' and sailors' wills.

tate decedents permit the state to select their heirs by default.

The Surviving Spouse

Without exception, statutes of descent and distribution specify the portion of a decedent's estate that will be taken by his or her lawful, surviving spouse. Variation in this area is significant from state to state. Formerly, under common law, the surviving spouse was entitled only to a life estate (ownership for life) or *dower* (to the widow) or *curtesy* (to the widower) in the real property owned by the decedent. Personal property was divided among the surviving spouse and any children of the marriage. Today, the law of dower and curtesy has been either abolished or altered significantly by statute in all jurisdictions. Typically, if a husband or wife dies intestate, the statutes provide that the surviving spouse takes one-half or one-third of the estate if there are children or grandchildren. If there are no children or grandchildren, in most jurisdictions the surviving spouse takes the entire estate. However, the states vary considerably in their treatment of this matter. In one jurisdiction, for example, children of the decedent take the real estate, to the exclusion of a surviving spouse, with the spouse taking one-third of the personal property. If there are no children or descendants of children the spouse takes the entire estate. In another, if there are children or representatives of deceased children, the surviving wife takes a child's share but not less than one-fifth of the estate.

In general, if there are children the surviving spouse must share the estate with them. The number of children or grandchildren will determine the share which is to pass to the surviving spouse. If there are no children or grandchildren, or none have survived the decedent, the surviving spouse takes everything.

As noted earlier, in a community property state, one-half of the community property is owned by the surviving spouse. The remaining half is subject to intestacy rules if no will exists.

Descendants of the Decedent

There is little disparity in the statutes that govern the shares of an intestate's children or other lineal descendants (those in a direct line from the decedent— children and grandchildren). It is generally the case that, subject to the statutory share of a surviving spouse, children of the decedent share and share alike, with the children of a deceased child taking that child's share. This latter provision is known as a **per stirpes** distribution. For example, assume that a decedent dies after his spouse, leaving two children, a son and a daughter, who have two and three children of their own, respectively. If both son and daughter survive the decedent, each will take half the estate. However, if the son predeceases the decedent, his two children will take his share, each of them taking one-fourth of the estate with the daughter taking the other half. (If the decedent's spouse were still alive, the fractions described here would still apply, but only to that portion of the estate remaining after the spouse took her share.)

If the descendants are all of one class, that is, children or grandchildren, they will take **per capita,** each getting an equal share. Thus, if the intestate had a son and daughter who predeceased him, but those children left behind five living grandchildren, each grandchild would take one-fifth of what is left after the surviving spouse's share has been provided for. Figure 46.1 illustrates these differences.

Adopted children are generally treated the same as natural children; illegitimate children generally inherit only from their mother unless their father's paternity has been either acknowledged or established through legal proceedings.

The Surviving Ascendants

There is general agreement that children of the decedent and subsequent generations of lineal

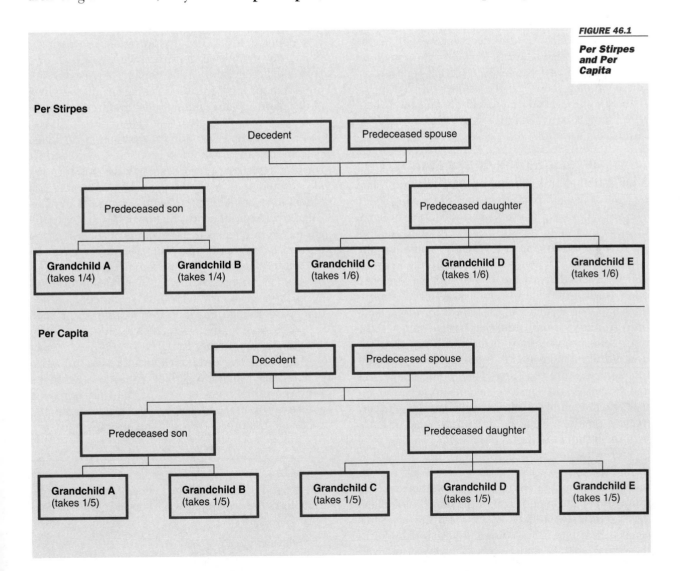

FIGURE 46.1

Per Stirpes and Per Capita

descendants will take to the exclusion of other blood relatives such as parents or brothers and sisters. With regard to the ascendants of the intestate (parents and grandparents), there is much less uniformity in state law. In most states, where decedents leave no descendants, their parents will take the estate, with brothers and sisters (known as collaterals) taking if the parents are not living. In other jurisdictions, brothers and sisters share with the parents. Nephews and nieces may take the share of a predeceased parent if other brothers and sisters of the decedent are still living. If not, the nephews and nieces, as sole survivors, share and share alike in a *per capita* distribution. In any event, a distribution to ascendants and collaterals is made only if there are no surviving descendants or spouse.

Other than the surviving spouse, relatives by marriage have no claim on the decedent's estate. If the intestate has died leaving no heirs or next-of-kin whatsoever—no spouse, children, grandchildren, ascendants, or collaterals—the estate will pass to the state by a process known as **escheat.** This rarely happens, but it is provided for by law.

ADMINISTRATION OF THE ESTATE

Administration of decedents' estates is accomplished by a proceeding in **probate** if they die leaving a will. The word derives from the Latin *probatio,* proof. In the law of wills it means the proof or establishment of a document as the valid last will and testament of the deceased. In most states, the court having jurisdiction is called the probate court, and the principal question to be decided by judicial determination is the validity or invalidity of the will. Once the will has been admitted to probate—that is, determined to be valid—the probate court insures efficient distribution of the estate. Funeral expenses, debts to creditors and taxes are paid first. Then homestead rights and forced shares must be taken into account. Finally, the remaining assets are distributed impartially to heirs, devisees, legatees, and others, in accordance with the testator's wishes.

The *personal representative* of the decedent (called the executor if appointed by will and the administrator if appointed by the court) administers the estate under the supervision of the court—to collect decedent's assets, to pay or settle any lawful claims against the estate, and to distribute the remainder to those who will take under the will. If there is no will,

the state's law of descent and distribution will determine how the estate is to be distributed.

Probate and the administration of decedents' estates are strictly regulated by statute and can be complex procedures when the estate is substantial and the interest in property of the deceased is not clear. Many parties may be affected by the administration process, so attention to detail and compliance with the state's probate law or code are essential. A personal representative who has effectively handled the estate and wound up its affairs may petition the court and be discharged from any further responsibilities.

Avoiding Administration

Quite frequently, the formal administration of decedents' estates can be wholly or partially avoided. In fact, it is safe to say that fewer than half the deaths in this country result in administration proceedings. Obviously, if the decedent died with no assets or a very small estate, there is no need for an involved administration. Most jurisdictions permit the handling of decedents' affairs without official administration in such cases.

There are, however, still other situations in which probate or formal administration can be avoided, at least for a portion of the decedent's assets. For example, if some or all of the property was co-owned with others as a "joint tenancy" with a right of survivorship, it passes to the surviving owners and not to the estate.[5] Joint tenancy bank accounts or securities or a residence owned as a joint tenancy or as a tenancy by the entirety all pass to the surviving owner. This method of owning property is sometimes referred to as the "poor man's will." It should be noted, however, that even though the decedent's interest in such property bypasses the estate, it can still be subject to an estate or inheritance tax.

If the decedent owned one or more life insurance policies, they will not be subject to administration if a beneficiary has been named. If one has not been named or if the one named has predeceased the decedent, the proceeds pass to the estate.

TRUSTS

The trust is a versatile legal concept that is typically used to conserve family wealth from generation to

---

[5]See Chapter 45 for a discussion of concurrent ownership and the right of survivorship.

Box 46.1
The Law at Work

Several years ago, Jamaican reggae singer and songwriter Bob Marley became a star with such songs to his credit as "I Shot the Sheriff," "War," "Jammin'," and others. Many of his songs were made even more popular when recorded by others such as Eric Clapton. When he died at age 36 from brain cancer, Marley had an international network of music publishing and recording companies and was personally worth over $30 million. After his death, his estate continued to earn millions of dollars annually from royalties on his music. Marley died without leaving a will, despite the advice he had received many times that he should have one. Marley was of the Rastafarian religion; many people believed that his religious beliefs caused

him to spurn the making of a will. His mother stated that "[h]is" mind wasn't on those material t'ings because he know no man never bring nuttin' into this world. Naked they come and naked shall they go." Others claim that Marley simply got too busy and forgot to have a will prepared.

Under Jamaican law, which applied to the disposition of his estate because this was his domicile, the lack of a will meant that his wife Rita was entitled to only 10 percent of his assets. The other 90 percent was to be divided among his eleven children, of whom Rita was the mother of four. Rita thought, perhaps correctly, that Marley would have left her far more than 10 percent if he had made his wishes known by executing a will. Several years after his death, the court-appointed administrator of Marley's estate charged Rita and her accountant and lawyer with fraud and other legal violations. The basis for the

administrator's claims was the assertion that Rita and her advisors had forged Marley's signature to a number of documents that were backdated to a time before his death; these documents purported to transfer controlling ownership of several companies to Rita, thus removing them from the assets of his estate. Several years of litigation have now taken place, with no end in sight. A will does not guarantee that there will be no disputes after a person's death, but it certainly improves the odds either that there will not be any significant disputes or that any such issues will be resolved more quickly. In this case, knowing Marley's true wishes probably would have had a substantial impact on the actions of various interested parties, especially in light of the fact that he very likely would have provided more for Rita if he had made a will.

generation, to provide for the support and education of children, and to minimize the tax burden on substantial estates. Trust law recognizes two types of property ownership, legal and equitable. One person can hold legal title to property while another can have the equitable title.

To establish a trust, the party intending to create a trust, called a **settlor** or *trustor,* transfers legal ownership of property to a *trustee* for the benefit of a third party, the **beneficiary.** The trustee is the legal owner of the property, called the *res* or *corpus,* but it is owned in trust to be used and managed solely for the benefit of others, who own the equitable title. A trust established and effective during the life of the settlor is known as an *inter vivos* or "living" **trust.** If it is created by the settlor's will, to be effective on that person's death, it is a **testamentary trust.** Trusts are also classified as *express, implied, private,* or *charitable,* depending on the purpose they serve and how they are created.

The Express Private Trust

An express private trust is created when a settlor, with clear intent to do so, and observing certain formalities, sets up a fiduciary relationship involving a trustee, the beneficiaries, and management of the trust *res* for a lawful purpose. There is little uniformity in the statutes that govern trusts and their creation. It is a general requirement, however, that trusts be established by a writing or, if oral, subsequently proved by a writing. The writing need not be formal so long as it clearly identifies the trust property and the beneficiary and states the purpose for which the trust is created. The intent of the settlor to create a trust must be clear from the circumstances and the action taken. No particular language is required, but the settlor's instructions should be direct and unambiguous. If the purpose of the trust is to put children through college, this should be stated clearly. Language that "requests," or "hopes," or "desires" that the trustee do certain things is considered to be precatory in nature (a mere request and not an order or command) and may not be binding on the trustee. Further, words or phrases that fall short of appointing a trustee or imposing positive responsibilities should be avoided. For example, when a husband left his estate to his wife, stating in the will that it was his "request" that upon her death his wife "shall give my interest to each of my brothers," the language was viewed as purely **precatory.** The brothers had no legal right to object when the wife gave the land to her nephew instead.[6]

The Trust Property

The subject matter of a trust may be any property of value. Money, interests in real estate, securities, and insurance are commonly used. However, settlors must own the property at the time they create the trust. They cannot transfer in trust property they expect to acquire and own at a later date. When the property is transferred to the trustee it becomes his or hers to manage for the benefit of the beneficiaries and in accordance with the terms of the trust. If the essential elements of a valid trust are missing or if the trust fails, the property will revert to the settlor, if living, or to that person's estate, if deceased.

The Trustee

A **trustee** is, of course, essential; a trust without one cannot be effective. However, the courts will not let an otherwise valid trust fail for want of a trustee. If the named trustee dies or declines to serve or is removed for cause, the court will appoint a replacement. The court will also appoint a trustee when the settlor fails to name one in the trust. No special qualifications are necessary. Since trustees take title to property and manage it, they must be capable of owning property. Minors and incompetents can own property, but they are under a disability in regard to contractual capacity. Consequently, since their contracts are voidable, they cannot function as trustees. Settlors can appoint themselves trustees and, in fact, designate themselves as beneficiaries. The settlor cannot, however, be the sole trustee and the sole beneficiary of a single trust. This relationship would merge both legal and equitable titles to the trust property in the trustee, and he or she would hold it free of any trust.

If a corporation (an artificial person) is not prohibited by its charter from doing so, it can act as a

[6]*Comford v. Cantrell,* 151 S.W.2d 1076 (Tenn. 1941).

trustee. Trust companies and banks, for example, frequently serve as trustees for both large and small trusts. They typically charge fees amounting to 1 percent of the value of the *res* per year.

Beneficiaries

The express private trust is ordinarily created for the benefit of identified, or identifiable, beneficiaries. A father can establish a trust for the care and education of his minor children—and can name them in the trust instrument. However, a settlor can also simply specify as the beneficiaries a class of persons, such as "my minor children" or "my brothers and sisters." In either case, the persons who are to benefit are readily identifiable. Trusts have also been held to be valid when established for domestic animals, household pets, and even inanimate objects. Such trusts present problems, since nonhuman and inanimate beneficiaries are incapable of holding title to property. Additionally, there will be no beneficiary with the capacity to enforce the provisions of the trust against the trustee. This is not to say that a charitable trust for animals in general or a trust for humane purposes will fail. (The charitable trust is discussed in a following section.)

The beneficiary does not have to agree to accept the benefits of the trust. It is presumed that beneficiaries accept the trust unless they make a specific rejection. Their interest in the trust can, in general, be reached by creditors, and they can sell or otherwise dispose of their interests. However, beneficiaries can transfer only the interests they hold—the equitable title. If a beneficiary holds more than a life estate, and the trust does not make other provisions, this interest can be disposed of in a will or can pass to the beneficiary's estate after death.

Managing the Trust

The administration of a trust is highly regulated by statute. Trustees must know the law of their jurisdictions. In general, they must make every effort to carry out the purpose of the trust. They must act with care and prudence and use their best judgment, and at all times they must exercise an extraordinary degree of loyalty to the beneficiary—the degree of loyalty required of those in a fiduciary position.

In carrying out the purposes of a trust, the trustees ordinarily have broad powers that are usually described in the trust instrument. In addition, they may have implied powers that are necessary to carry out their express duties. For example, trustees can have express authority to invest the trust property and pay the beneficiary the income from such investments. They can also have the implied power to incur reasonable expenses in administering the trust.

Insofar as it is possible trustees should exercise the care and skill of a "prudent person" in managing the trust. A reasonable goal for a trustee is to exercise the diligence necessary to preserve the corpus and realize a reasonable return on income from "prudent" investments at the same time. State laws often specify the types of investments a trustee can make. In Georgia, for example, trust law authorizes investment in bonds or securities issued by the state and by the U.S. government and certain of its agencies and in certain banks or trust companies insured by the Federal Deposit Insurance Corporation. With certain exceptions, any other investment of trust funds must be under an order of the superior court or at the risk of the trustee. If the trust instrument gives the trustee wide discretion to invest in "other" securities, many jurisdictions allow this. Statutes often indicate that prudent persons should diversify their investments. However, the trustee can still be held accountable for a failure to exercise proper care. In other words, the law discourages bad investments.

The relationship between the trustee and the beneficiary is fiduciary in nature. Consequently, in managing trusts, trustees must act solely for the benefit of the beneficiaries. For example, trustees cannot borrow any portion of the trust funds or sell their own property to the trust. Neither can they purchase trust property for themselves. Even though the trustee's personal dealings with the trust may prove to be advantageous to the beneficiary, the duty of loyalty is breached and the trustee can be charged with such breach. If there are multiple trustees, an innocent trustee may well be held liable for not preventing a co-trustee's breach of fiduciary duty.

The duties of a trustee are highlighted in the following case.

WITMER V. BLAIR

Missouri Court of Appeals, 588 S.W.2d 222 (1979)

Case

At his death in 1960, Henry Nussbaum's will created a trust for the education of his grandchildren. Defendant Jane Ann Blair, Nussbaum's niece, was named trustee. Nussbaum's daughter, Dorothy Janice Witmer (defendant's cousin) was given a reversionary interest in the residue of the trust should none of the grandchildren survive to inherit the estate. Marguerite Janice Witmer (Dorothy's daughter) became the only beneficiary of the trust.

Defendant Blair received the trust estate in 1961. It consisted of $1,905 in checking and savings accounts, $5,700 in certificates of deposit, and a house valued at $6,000. The house was sold in 1962, netting $4,467 to the trust estate, which amount was deposited in a trust checking account. For the next several years, the trustee kept funds in checking and savings

accounts and in certificates of deposit. As of December 31, 1975, the trust assets consisted of $2,741 checking account, $5,474 savings, and $8,200 certificates of deposit.

Marguerite was 23 years old at the time of trial. She had not attended college, but various sums of money had been expended from the trust for her benefit, including a typewriter, clothes, glasses, modeling school tuition and expenses, and a tonsillectomy, all totalling some $1,250. The trust also spent $350 for dentures for Dorothy.

Marguerite and Dorothy brought this suit against Blair for breach of trust for failure to properly invest the funds of the trust. The trial judge removed the trustee and surcharged her account for $309 in unexplained expenditures, but refused to assess actual or punitive damages for breach of trust. Plaintiffs appealed.

Welborn, Special Judge:

The trust was handled by appellant rather informally. She kept no books for the trust. The expenditures were in most cases advanced by her from her personal account and she reimbursed herself from the trust income. In 1965, the bank erroneously credited the trust account with $560 which should have gone to the trustee's personal account. The mistake was not corrected and that amount remained in the trust account. The trustee received no compensation for her services. Asked at the trial whether she had ever been a trustee before, she responded negatively, adding "And never again." She explained the large checking account balances in the trust account by the fact that college for Janice "was talked about all the way through high school. . . . [I]n my opinion, it was the sensible way to keep the money where I could get it to her without any

(continues)

WITMER V. BLAIR

(continued from previous page)
problems at all in case she needed it quickly."

An accountant testified that had $800 been kept in the checking and savings accounts (the $800 was based upon the maximum disbursement in any year) and the balance of the trust placed in one-year certificates of deposit, $9,138 more interest would have been earned as of September 30, 1976.

A concise summary of the law applicable to the situation appears in 76 Am. Jur.2d *Trusts* §379 (1975):

It is a general power and duty of a trustee, implied if not expressed, at least in the case of an ordinary trust, to keep trust funds properly invested. Having uninvested funds in his hands, it is his duty to make investments of them, where at least they are not soon to be applied to the purposes and objects or turned over to the beneficiaries of the trust. Generally, he cannot permit trust funds to lie dormant or on deposit for a prolonged period, but he may keep on hand a fund sufficient to meet expenses, including contingent expenses, and he need not invest a sum too small to be prudently invested. A trustee ordinarily may not say in excuse of a failure to invest that he kept the funds on hand to pay the beneficiaries on demand.

The trustee is under a duty to the beneficiary to use reasonable care and skill to make the trust property productive. Restatement (Second) of Trusts §181 (1959).

A breach of trust is a violation by the trustee of any duty which as trustee he owes to the beneficiary. Restatement (Second) of Trusts §201 (1959).

Comment b to this section states:

Mistake of law as to existence of duties and powers. A trustee commits a breach of trust not only where he violates a duty in bad faith, or intentionally although in good faith, or negligently, but also where he violates a duty because of a mistake as to the extent of his duties and powers. This is true not only where his mistake is in regard to a rule of law, whether a statutory or common-law rule, but also where he interprets the trust instrument as authorizing him to do acts which the court determines he is not authorized by the instrument to do. In such a case, he is not protected from liability merely because he acts in good faith, nor is he protected merely because he relies upon the advice of counsel.

Under the above rules, there has been a breach of trust by the trustee in this case and her good faith is not a defense to appellants' claim. In 1962, appellant Marguerite was some nine years of age. Obviously there was no prospect of the beneficiary's attending college for a number of years. However, when Marguerite became of college age [around 1971] and was considering a college education, the respondent should not be faulted for keeping readily available a sum of money which would permit the use of the trust fund for such purpose.

Reversed, and remanded with directions [to enter judgment for plaintiffs for $2,840].

The Spendthrift Trust

Settlors may be concerned that beneficiaries may be incapable of managing their own affairs either because of inexperience and immaturity or simply because they are "spendthrifts." Settlors can therefore determine that beneficiaries will not sell, mortgage, or otherwise transfer their rights to receive principal and income and that the beneficiaries' creditors will not reach the income or principal while it is in the hands of the trustee. Such a provision no longer applies after the income or principal has been paid over to the beneficiary. Further, some modern statutes limit the **spendthrift trust.** They either limit the income that is protected from creditors or they permit creditors to reach amounts in excess of what the beneficiary is considered to need.

Trust Termination

In most states, settlors can revoke a trust at any time if they have reserved that power. However, most trusts are terminated when the stated period has elapsed or when the trust purpose has been served. In a trust for the care of minor children, it logically ends when the beneficiaries have reached their majority. In a trust for the college education of the beneficiary, it will terminate when that goal has been attained. In any event, upon termination of a trust, any balance of funds remaining reverts to the settlor or is disposed of in accordance with the instructions contained in the trust.

Charitable Trusts

The purpose of a charitable trust is the general benefit of humanity. Its beneficiaries can be education, science, religion, hospitals, homes for the aged or handicapped, and a host of other charitable or public entities. Charitable trusts are much like private trusts. Furthermore, the courts of most jurisdictions will find another suitable purpose for a charitable trust when the settlor's stated purpose is impossible or difficult to achieve. The courts do so under the doctrine of *cy pres,* meaning so near or as near. The doctrine is used to prevent a charitable trust from failing for want of a beneficiary. To illustrate: a testator establishes a testamentary trust for the support and maintenance of orphans in a specified orphanage. If the specified orphanage ceased to exist before the testator's death, the court could use the *cy pres* doctrine, find that the trustor's intent was to benefit orphans generally, and apply the trust to some other orphanage in the area. The *cy pres* doctrine applies only where there is definite charitable intent, never to private trusts.

Implied Trusts

An implied trust, constructive or resulting, is created by law. While the distinction is not always clear, a **constructive trust** is usually imposed upon property by the courts to correct or rectify fraud or to prevent one party from being unjustly enriched at the expense of another. In reality, it is a fiction or remedy to which a court of equity will resort to prevent injustice. Suppose that A and B have agreed to purchase a tract of land jointly with the deed to list both of them as grantees. If, despite the agreement, A secretly buys the land alone, and the deed fails to list B as grantee, the court will impose a constructive trust on the property to the extent of the half interest B should have. This procedure assumes that B is ready and willing to pay half the purchase price. In another case, directors of corporations who take advantage of their positions to make secret profits from corporate opportunities will be constructive trustees for the corporations to the extent of the profits they make. Constructive trusts commonly arise out of the breach of a fiduciary relationship where no trust intent is present or required.

The **resulting trust** arises out of, or is created by, the conduct of the parties. It is imposed in order to carry out the apparent intentions of the parties at the time they entered into the transaction that gave rise to the trust. The most frequent use of the resulting trust occurs when one party purchases property but records the title in the name of another. For example, A wants to purchase a tract of real estate but does not want it subjected to the hazards of his business ventures. He therefore buys the land but has the deed made out in the name of a friend, B. There is no problem if B conveys the real estate to A on demand in accordance with their understanding of the nature of the transaction. However, if B refuses to convey the land, the courts can impose a resulting trust on B for A's benefit. Some difficulty can arise if, in the situation above, A has title taken in the name of his wife or a close relative, because it could be valid to presume that A intended the land as a gift. And if A had purchased in the name of another to defraud his creditors, it is likely that the courts would refuse to impose the resulting trust, being reluctant to afford relief to a wrongdoer.

ESTATE PLANNING

"*Estate Planning* is applying the law of property, trusts, wills, future interests, insurance, and taxation to the ordering of one's affairs, keeping in mind the possibility of retirement and the certainty of death."[7] Wills and trusts are the most commonly used estate planning devices. This final section briefly explores other aspects of the estate planning process, touching first on the philosophy that has previously guided or misguided many in the disposition of their property—a disposition that usually occurs after death, with dire results for the surviving heirs. The general public equates estate planning with death; lifetime planning is more important than death planning. The aim is not merely to dispose of one's estate at death but to organize resources during life in order to provide for the present and future well-being of one's family.

The major consideration in preserving estate integrity today is the impact taxes may have if little thought is given to methods for reducing estate shrinkage. In fact, it is quite likely for the decedent's survivors to find on settling the estate that the principal heir is the government. It is, of course, unlawful to evade taxes, but there is nothing illegal about doing everything possible to avoid paying unnecessary taxes. Various planning devices can keep unwanted heirs, in the form of estate and inheritance taxes, and the expense of probate and administration to a minimum.

Gifts

One of the keys to cutting estate taxes is to give away some assets before death. The gifts shift income to children or perhaps retired parents who may be in

[7]R. J. Lynn, *An Introduction to Estate Planning* (St. Paul, Minn.: West Publishing, 1975), 1.

lower tax brackets. Giving, as an estate planning device, may be hard to accept for the donor who has spent a lifetime slowly accumulating an estate. Nevertheless, it is something to consider, keeping in mind one's personal situation. Amateur philanthropy, however, can be dangerous. Property given outright to a poor manager can be wasted away; a gift with too many strings attached can be something less than useful to the donee. Gift taxes must also be considered. Under current tax law, each parent may transfer $10,000 each year to any recipient, including children, without any gift tax liability.

Life Insurance

Life insurance, in its various forms, can serve many purposes in estate planning. Ownership can be so arranged that the proceeds will not become part of the insured's estate to be taxed. It is a good means of providing liquid funds so that forced sales of other property to pay estate charges or debts can be avoided. In general, life insurance is not subject to probate and administration expenses and is a good way to make *inter vivos* (during lifetime) gifts to children, to grandchildren, or, if the donor is so inclined, to charity. Many kinds of policies are available—term, whole life, and endowment, for example—and there may be a place for one or more types in an estate plan. For the average wage earner life insurance is the major, perhaps the only, means of providing security for the family. Indeed, it may be all that is necessary, other than a valid will. With regard to business ventures, the members of a partnership often enter into buy and sell agreements with a view to continuing the partnership after the death of a partner. The partnership agreement sometimes provides that the estates of deceased partners will sell their interests to surviving partners and that the partners will buy such interests. Insurance is frequently used by the partnership to fund the agreement.

The Marital Deduction

For federal estate tax purposes the **marital deduction** is a useful device in estate planning involving substantial assets. It reflects the social concept that property accumulated during marriage should be treated as community property, disregarding the fact that differing amounts could have been contributed by the husband and wife. The marital deduction was designed to more nearly equate tax treatment between residents of states that have community property laws and those of states which do not. No matter what amount a decedent spouse passes to a surviving spouse, that amount will not be taxed in the decedent spouse's estate. This allows the surviving spouse to continue to have the use of up to all of the "community" assets for the rest of his or her life. The amount passing to the surviving spouse is included in his or her estate and will be taxed at the surviving spouse's death. The amount passing to the surviving spouse under the marital deduction must be determined through careful planning to maximize tax savings and meet the objectives of a particular family. Competent legal counsel and financial advice should be sought early in the estate planning process.

SUMMARY

The inevitability of death makes proper estate planning a very wise idea. A basic method of distributing property upon death is through an instrument known as a will. A testator must have testamentary capacity, that is, the mental ability to understand the property owned and the persons to whom he or she would like to give it, and not be under the undue influence of any particular person. A formal will must meet several statutory requirements, including being signed in the presence of witnesses. Modifications and even revocations must similarly follow a proper statutory pattern; for example, a will burned at the direction of a testatrix may not be effectively revoked if the destruction does not take place in her presence.

Many states allow handwritten wills, and even oral wills may be effective in limited circumstances. Should no valid will exist, a decedent's possessions will pass to relatives under state laws of descent and distribution, which impose a standardized division of the property.

Use of a trust is another method of estate planning. The settlor of a trust places property in the control of a trustee who administers the property for the advantage of beneficiaries. There are several types of trusts, and tax laws have traditionally had a significant impact on their numbers and use. The trustee owes a fiduciary duty to the beneficiaries, and may be liable in damages for wrongful or negligent administration of the assets.

Intelligent estate planning frequently uses gifts and life insurance in addition to wills and, where appropriate, trusts.

KEY TERMS

Intestate
Testator
Testatrix
Decedent
Executor
Executrix
Administrator
Devise
Legacy
Bequest
Testamentary capacity
Attestation clause
Codicil
Holographic will
Nuncupative will
Per stirpes
Per capita
Escheat
Probate
Settlor
Beneficiary
Res
Inter vivos trust
Testamentary trust
Precatory
Trustee
Spendthrift trust
Cy pres
Constructive trust
Resulting trust
Marital deduction

QUESTIONS AND PROBLEMS

1. Decedent, Matilda Manchester, prepared the following document, wholly in her own handwriting:

I, Matilda Manchester, leave and bequeath all my estate and effects, after payment of legal, funeral and certain foreign shipment expenses (as directed) to the following legatees, viz.

Then followed a statement of devises and bequests to divers persons. It ended as follows:

Whereunto I hereby set my hand this fourteenth day of January, 1914.

Decedent did not sign the document, her name appearing only in the opening clause as shown above. The paper was folded and sealed in an envelope

which was endorsed by the decedent: "My Will, Ida Matilda Manchester." Should the document be admitted to probate as a valid holographic will? (*Estate of Manchester,* 163 P. 358, Cal. 1917.)

2. A father purchased 100 shares of stock for each of his two children, using money he had withdrawn from their savings accounts. The shares of stock were issued to the mother and registered in her name. When the mother died, a question arose as to ownership of the stock. What are the children's rights in this matter? (*Markert v. Bosley,* 207 N.E.2d 414, 1965.)

3. A state's law required that all formal wills must be "subscribed at the end thereof by the testator" and that attesting witnesses must "sign the instrument as a witness, at the end of the will." The will in question consisted of three pages. The first page was a printed form entitled "Last Will and Testament." Typed on the form were two testamentary provisions and the appointment of executors. On the same form, in the spaces provided, appeared the signature of the testatrix and an attestation clause signed by three witnesses. There were two additional typewritten pages containing testamentary clauses, each of the two pages being signed at the bottom by only the testatrix. The attesting witnesses had not signed the additional pages, their signatures appearing only on the first, "form" page. Does the document qualify as a will? (*Estate of Howell,* 324 P.2d 578, Cal. 1958.)

4. A testator wanted to revoke his will by having his wife burn it. In his presence she burned an envelope which she fraudulently represented to him to contain his will. (*Brazil v. Silva,* 185 P. 174, 1919.)

   a. If she was the sole legatee under his will, is she likely to take his estate?
   b. If the testator had two children, are they, in effect, disinherited?

5. A widow died intestate. There had been four children; but one, who had two children, predeceased his mother. How will the estate be divided among the widow's descendants?

6. Edward Muder died on March 15, 1984, leaving behind an unwitnessed "will form" that, in addition to the preprinted words, contained the following handwritten statement: "My wife Retha F. Muder, our home and property in Shumway, Navajo County, car-pick up, travel trailer, and all other earthly possessions belonging to me, livestock, cattle, sheep, etc.

Tools, savings accounts, checking accounts, retirement benefits, etc." Retha submitted the will to probate as either a proper formal will, or as a valid holographic will. Should the will be admitted to probate? (*Matter of Estate of Muder,* 751 P.2d 986, Ariz. App. 1987.)

7. The will of Lauren M. Townsend, after a statement of several specific bequests, provided: ". . . that the remainder be made into a fund, the interest of which shall be used to help defray the expense of educating some girl or boy in music or art. I appoint Paul Gill to have charge of selecting the recipient of this last bequest." Is the quoted language sufficiently specific to create a charitable trust? (*Estate of Huebner,* 15 P.2d 758, Cal. 1932.)

8. Reed died on March 2, 1982, leaving behind a tape recording in a sealed envelope on which was handwritten "Robert Reed To be played in the event of my death only! (signed) Robert G. Reed." Buckley sought to have the tape recording admitted to probate as a holographic will. Should the tape be admitted? (*Matter of Estate of Reed,* 672 P.2d 829, Wyo. 1983.)

9. McGurrin signed his will when no one else was present. An intermediary then took the will to other persons who added their signatures to the document.

The testator's only contact with these persons was by telephone after all signatures had been affixed. He thanked them for "witnessing" his will. Should this will be accepted in probate? (*Matter of Estate of McGurrin,* 743 P.2d 994, Idaho App. 1987.)

10. In 1960, Leonard Garver executed a will which created a trust. The trust instrument named the Baker Boyer National Bank (Bank) as trustee and included certain farmland. After Leonard's wife and son had enjoyed a life estate in the farmland, it was to be held in trust until Leonard's grandsons, Russell and Gregory (beneficiaries) reached the age of 25. After Leonard and his wife died, his son Richard, as executor of the estates, sold some of the land and invested the $194,000 proceeds in tax-free municipal bonds. For the next nine years the bank, as trustee, continued to invest the funds in tax-free municipal bonds at the recommendation of Richard's attorney and his broker. After a dispute between the bank as trustee and Russell and Gregory as beneficiaries, the portfolio of bonds was liquidated at a loss of $63,750. Russell and Gregory sued the bank for breach of its duty as trustee, claiming that the bank should have diversified the investment portfolio. Discuss the merits of this claim. (*Baker Boyer National Bank v. Garver,* 719 P.2d 583, Wash. App. 1986.)

Chapter 47

Insurance Law

Nature and Functions of Insurance

Types of Insurance

NATURE AND FUNCTIONS OF INSURANCE

Almost every type of endeavor or venture, individual or business, involves risk or uncertainty concerning financial loss. Insurance is a means of transferring or shifting risk from the individual or business to a group whose members agree to share losses on some equitable basis. Suppose that a manufacturer produces and markets a line of products the use of which poses considerable risk, such as bicycles, swings and slides, and power lawnmowers. An injury or death caused by such products may result in a lawsuit and a substantial damages award to the injured user or, if the product has caused death, to his or her surviving family. Such awards may be in the millions of dollars, causing extreme economic hardship to an individual manufacturer. The design, manufacture, and marketing of a potentially dangerous product may pose a risk too great for a single business to assume.

Manufacturers can collectively share products liability losses by transferring the risk to a professional risk bearer, the insurer, through the purchase of an insurance contract. The group of manufacturers share the cost of losses as they occur so that no one of them will be forced to bear the entire cost of a substantial judgment awarded as the result of a products liability lawsuit.

The exact cost of insurance is established statistically based upon the loss costs and expenses of insurers writing the coverage involved. The premium paid by the insured is an expense of doing business.

This chapter examines briefly the general types of insurance, placing major emphasis on the coverages that are relevant for business: *life, health, property,* and *liability.* In addition, the concept of risk management is presented.

The Insurance Contract

An insurance contract is often called a *policy.* The person or company purchasing insurance coverage is called the *insured,* or the *policyholder.* The company issuing the insurance policy is called the *insurer,* or the *insurance company.* To be an enforceable agreement, a contract of insurance must contain the essential elements of contract: *offer and acceptance, consideration, legal purpose, competent parties,* and *legal form.*

Offer and Acceptance

The offer is customarily made by the prospective insured when he or she makes an application for the desired coverage. The acceptance occurs when the agent or broker issues a **binder** (a temporary contract) or when the policy itself is issued by the insurance company. A binder can be either written or oral and is used to bind the company immediately prior to the receipt of the application and issuance of the policy.

Consideration

The considerations exchanged in an insurance transaction are the payment of the **premium** by the insured or other responsible party (such as the parents of an insured minor), and the promise of the insurer to pay if the covered contingency occurs.

Legal Purpose

A contract made for an illegal purpose, or containing an illegal provision, is usually void and cannot be enforced by either party. This general principle is equally applicable to contracts of insurance. If the insurance company violates state law by failing to include a required provision that was intended to protect policyholders, however, the policyholder can still enforce the contract under a well-established exception to the illegality doctrine. The most important application of the requirement of a legal purpose is the *insurable interest* rule, which is discussed separately in the following section.

Insurable Interest

A fundamental requirement of a legally valid insurance contract is that an insured must have an **insurable interest** in the subject matter of the insurance, that is, a benefit to be derived from the continued existence of the person or property insured. Without the existence of an insurable interest, the policyholder is simply wagering on the occurrence of death, in the case of life insurance, or property damage, in the case of property insurance. Because gambling contracts are void, an insurance policy issued to an insured not having an insurable interest is unenforceable. In addition to furthering the general prohibition against gambling agreements, the requirement of insurable interest also helps protect against murder or property destruction for the purpose of collecting insurance proceeds. The rationale for the insurable interest requirement in the life insurance context was expressed as follows by the court in *New England Mutual Life Insurance Co. v. Null*, 605 F.2d 421 (1979):

> It is contrary to sound public policy to permit one, having no interest in the continuance of the life of another, to speculate upon that other's life—and it should be added that to permit the same might tend to incite the crime of murder—and the rule is enforced, and the defense permitted, not in the interest of the defendant insurer, but solely for the sake of the law, and in the interest of a sound public policy.

The absence of an insurable interest causes the contract to be void, and no benefits are payable under the policy. In such a case the insured is entitled to a refund of premiums paid, however. Other legal consequences can also result from the issuance of a policy to someone without an insurable interest. For instance, if an insurance company issues a life insurance policy to someone who does not have an insurable interest, and the insured then murders the subject of the life insurance, the insurance company can be held liable for negligence to the estate of the murder victim. Similarly, if an insurance company issues a policy covering property to someone not having an insurable interest, and the insured then intentionally destroys the property, the insurance company can be held liable for negligence to the owner of the property.

Insurable Interest Distinguished from Other Concepts. It is important to distinguish the insurable interest requirement from other related concepts. For example, life insurance policies normally contain a provision expressly excluding liability if the person whose life is insured commits suicide. This provision applies even if the person taking out the policy had an insurable interest. Also, courts do not permit a beneficiary named in a life insurance policy to recover under the policy if the beneficiary murders the person whose life is insured. Again, this rule applies even if the person taking out the insurance had an insurable interest in the life being insured, and the policy itself is valid. In such a case, since the policy is valid, the proceeds are payable either to a secondary beneficiary specified in the policy or to the estate of the deceased if there is no secondary beneficiary. Similarly, a person who intentionally damages or destroys property is not permitted to collect under an insurance policy covering the property, even if the insured had an insurable interest.

Insurable Interest in Life. A person obviously may obtain a policy of insurance on his or her own life. If one person takes out life insurance on someone else's life, however, it is required that the policyholder have an insurable interest in the life of the person who is the subject of the insurance. In the case of life insurance, the insurable interest must exist at the time the policy is issued, but does not have to exist at the time of death. Thus, if a wife takes out life insurance on her husband, there is an insurable interest at the time the policy is issued; the policy remains valid even after divorce unless a specific provision calls for termination upon divorce.

As a general rule, an insurable interest exists when the policyholder and the person whose life is being insured have a relationship such that the policyholder will benefit from the continuance of the person's life or suffer financial loss from the person's death. State laws usually specify the types of relationships that create insurable interests, and these laws vary somewhat. In all states, husband and wife have an insurable interest in each other's life. In some states, other relationships within the immediate family, such as parent-child or brother-sister, also create an insurable interest. The relationship between a nephew or niece and an aunt or uncle usually does not create an insurable interest. Except for husband and wife, relationships through marriage do not create insurable interests. For example, a person does not have an insurable interest in the life of his or her mother-in-law.

An employer has an insurable interest in the life of a *key employee*, that is, an employee whose death would cause substantial hardship to the employer. An employee with significant managerial or supervisory responsibilities, or especially valuable knowledge or skills would, for example, be a key employee. In addition, an unsecured creditor usually has an insurable interest in the life of the debtor up to the amount of the indebtedness. The following case presents an illustration and discussion of the insurable interest requirement in life insurance.

New York Life Insurance Co. v. Baum

U.S. Fifth Circuit Court of Appeals, 700 F.2d 928 (1983)

Case

Baum and Cook made preliminary plans for the formation of a media advertising business in Louisiana. It was agreed that Baum would provide capital and Cook would furnish the experience necessary to launch the venture. Their understanding was that a corporation would be formed to carry on the business. Over the next several months, Baum lent Cook $16,500 for getting the business started. Shortly after Baum and Cook had made their agreement, however, Cook made a separate agreement with Cutler to form a partnership in Texas under the name of Media Sales. The Cook-Cutler partnership, also engaged in the media advertising business, was unknown to Baum.

After Baum had lent money to Cook, Baum decided to obtain "key man" life insurance coverage on Cook to protect Baum's investment, and a policy was purchased from New York Life Insurance Company. At first, Baum listed himself as the beneficiary; upon the insistence of the insurance company, however, the named beneficiary was changed to Media Sales & Marketing, Inc., the planned name of the corporation Baum and Cook were to form. The name of the prospective corporation was used because Baum was an agent of New York Life, and the insurance company would not permit one of its agents to be named as a beneficiary except in a policy issued on the life of one of the agent's family members. A few days after Baum obtained this policy, Cook and Cutler incorporated their business in Texas as Media Sales Corporation, and totally excluded Baum. Baum paid premiums on the life insurance policy until Cook died one year later. After Cook's death, Baum filed suit in federal district court asserting a claim to

the life insurance proceeds because his money had provided the primary capital for the business and he was actually the intended beneficiary. Media Sales Corporation also asserted a claim because it claimed to be the same corporation as the one that was expressly named as beneficiary. (Presumably, Cutler was behind the assertion of a claim by Media Sales.)

The trial court held that neither Baum nor Media Sales Corporation had an insurable interest in Cook's life, and that the policy was completely void. Both parties appealed to the U.S. Court of Appeals.

Thornberry, Circuit Judge:

[The court initially concluded that New York law applied to the case because the life insurance contract was formed in New York and most of its performance was to take place in that state.] Section 146 [of the New York Insurance Law] defines an insurable interest in the case of persons not related by blood or by law as follows:

[I]n the case of other persons, a lawful and substantial economic interest in having the life, health or bodily safety of the person insured continue, as distinguished from an interest which would arise only by, or would be enhanced in value by, the death, disablement or injury, as the case may be, of the person insured.

[In one New York case, the court said:] "It may be generally stated that the reasoning behind legislation requiring an insurable interest . . . is in furtherance of the public policy against wagering or gambling on human lives. This policy has been adopted in most jurisdictions to prevent speculation in human life, since the incentive to shorten the life of the insured would be increased." While discussing the subject of insurable interest between creditors and their debtors another New

York court held as follows: "It is now well settled that the bank had an insurable interest in the life of [the deceased debtor] at the time it made the loan to him and under such circumstances the bank had the right to enter into any agreement with the insurance company so that it would receive a sum of money as indemnity in case its interest in the subject matter should suffer diminution of value by reason of certain specified causes or contingencies. The bank with such an insurable interest in the borrower clearly had the right to secure itself against the death of the borrower." . . .

Applying these principles to our case, we hold that . . . Baum had an insurable interest in the life of Cook, his debtor, as a matter of law. A creditor-debtor relationship existed between Baum and Cook at the time the policy was executed and Baum loaned the majority of the funds to Cook after the policy went into effect. The facts fail to show that the policy was taken as a wager. As creditor, Baum had a reasonable ground to expect some benefit or advantage from the continuation of Cook's life, namely, repayment of the loan. Furthermore, there are compelling arguments against allowing the insurer to escape its obligation.

It is surely not a sound policy to permit insurers to contract to insure the lives of persons, receive premiums therefor as long as the . . . beneficiary . . . will continue to pay, and then, when the time comes for the insurers to pay what they agreed to pay, allow them to escape their contract on the ground of want of insurable interest in the life insured, unless it clearly appears that such contracts are pernicious and dangerous to society.

Regarding Media Texas, the situation is less clear. While it is true that, as a general rule, a corporation has an insurable interest in the life of its key employees, the district court found that "the record clearly demonstrates
(continues)

NEW YORK LIFE INSURANCE CO. V. BAUM

(continued from previous page)
that Media Sales (Texas) was nothing more than a nonfunctioning corporate shell." Indeed, no stock was apparently ever issued by Media Texas. The district court also found that "the creation of a Texas corporation was never contemplated by the parties, as evidenced by the representations made by Baum

in the application for the life insurance policy." . . .

For the reasons stated above, the judgment of the district court is reversed. [Baum did have an insurable interest in the life of Cook. In a rehearing of this case, the court of appeals ordered that the case be remanded to the district court for resolution of several

remaining factual issues, including the question whether it was possible under the facts for Media Sales Corp. also to have an insurable interest. The appeals court's directions to the lower court made it highly likely that Baum would ultimately receive all of the insurance proceeds.] ⚖

Insurable Interest in Property. The underlying rationale for the requirement of an insurable interest in property is essentially the same as the requirement of an insurable interest in life: one should be permitted to obtain insurance coverage on property only if that person would suffer a financial loss as a result of damage to or destruction of the property. While an insurable interest in life must be present when the policy is issued, the rule is different for property. An insurable interest in property must exist at the time the loss occurs, and is not required to have existed when the policy was issued. An owner of property obviously has an insurable interest in it, but

others also may have such an interest. Thus, the mortgagee has an insurable interest in the mortgaged real estate, and a secured creditor has an insurable interest in the specific item of personal property (such as an automobile) that serves as collateral to secure the debt. In cases in which a nonowner has an insurable interest in property, the owner continues to have such an interest as well. Both parties may obtain insurance coverage on the value of their respective interests in the property.

The next case provides a further example of one of the many types of situations in which a person may have an insurable interest in property.

MOTORISTS MUTUAL INSURANCE CO. V. RICHMOND

Court of Appeals of Kentucky, 676 S.W.2d 478 (1984)

 Case

After thirteen years of marriage and two children, Linda Richmond and Eddie Durham were divorced in 1977. The divorce decree called for their house to be sold within six months, but no sale ever took place. Instead, the couple attempted to reconcile their differences until March 1981 when Richmond and the two children moved out. During this four-year period between the divorce and Richmond's departure, the couple made extensive im-

provements in the house, including interior remodeling and the addition of exterior walkways and a porch. Each of them contributed equally to the labor and expense of the improvements. In February 1980, while they were still living together, Richmond executed a deed transferring her interest in the house and lot to Durham. In March 1980, Durham executed a second mortgage on the property to secure a loan of almost $5,000. In June 1981, three months after Richmond moved out, Durham died of chronic heart disease.

Richmond immediately moved back into the house with her two children and made it their residence. She assumed liability on the second mortgage and made the payments. In January 1982 Richmond took out a fire insurance policy on the home and its contents from Motorists Mutual Insurance Co. When making application for the insurance policy, Richmond was asked by the insurance company's agent whether there was a lien on the property. She replied that there was, and stated that the lien was in her name.

(continues)

MOTORISTS MUTUAL INSURANCE CO. V. RICHMOND

(continued from previous page)
Although this statement was technically in error because the mortgage was still in Durham's name, Richmond's reply was based on a good faith belief that her assumption of liability on the mortgage meant that the lien was in her name. Nothing was said about legal title to the property, but the agent checked a box on the application form indicating that Richmond was the sole owner of the property. In actuality, her two children owned legal title as the only heirs of Durham, who died without a will.

In October 1982 the property was totally destroyed by fire. In response to Richmond's claim under the policy, the insurance company paid her $11,740 for the value of the contents, but refused to pay anything for the value of the house on the grounds that she had no insurable interest in the real estate. Richmond, her two children, and her mortgagee, Farmers National Bank (which was entitled to a portion of the insurance proceeds to satisfy the mortgage), sued the insurance company to recover the policy amount for the house. The trial court held that she had an insurable interest, and awarded her and the mortgagee a judgment of $29,000. The insurance company appealed.

Clayton, Judge:

Seeking to avoid payment under the contract, Motorists would now cast Richmond as nothing more than a trespassing squatter who "surreptitiously" returned to the residence and thereafter fraudulently represented her true lack of ownership interest. . . . We cannot accept these characterizations.

Linda Richmond, both before and after the death of her late former husband, made substantial monetary contribution to the maintenance and improvement of the destroyed residence. As natural guardian for her minor children, and later as administratrix of the Durham estate, she was obligated to provide for the care and custody of their offspring, including the duty to protect their home, of which the children became sole owners in fee simple by statute of descent upon the death of their father. Thus, when Richmond returned to the property following Durham's death she was not a surreptitious trespasser. Her offspring and she as their guardian were fully entitled to use and dominion over the premises. While not possessed of title, Richmond certainly possessed an insurable interest in the residence; first, by her status as natural guardian for the protection of her minor children's interest; and second, by her extensive investment in the residence. . . . In general, it is well-settled law that a person has an insurable interest in the subject matter insured where he has such a relation or connection with, or concern in, such subject matter that he will derive pecuniary benefit or advantage from its preservation, or will suffer pecuniary loss or damage from its destruction, termination, or injury by the happening of the event insured against.

Nor does the present record contain any suggestion of fraud or unwitting assumption of risk by Motorists. Richmond made no claim of ownership to the residence. Her only direct action with regard to the [application] was to place her signature upon it. Motorists' own agent was responsible for completing the remainder of the document including the portion indicating Richmond's ownership. Had he so cho-

sen, he could have easily verified his assumptions concerning Richmond's ownership simply by calling Farmers State Bank. It is a well settled principle of law in this state that an insurer as principal is bound by the acts of his agent within the scope of his apparent authority. . . .

Motorists is further obligated to make payment by the definition provisions of its policy. Under that policy "insured" is defined as:

You and the following representatives of your household:
a. your relatives; b. any other person under the age of 21 who is in the care of any person named above.

At the time of issuance of the policy, Linda's children, Melody and James, were each, by statute of descent, fee simple owners of an indivisible one-half interest in the residence. As minors under the age of 15, neither child was legally capable of contracting for insurance in his or her own behalf. Therefore, absent Linda's efforts in securing insurance, neither Melody nor James could have directly protected his or her ownership interest in the home. By defining the terms of its policy so as to include the ownership interest of the children, Motorists undertook exactly the risk it bargained for. . . . The contract speaks for itself.

[After] having determined that both Richmond and her children possessed an insurable interest in the residence throughout the life of the policy, [the court then concluded that the mortgagee also had such an interest because it would benefit by the continuing existence of the home as security for its loan.]

The judgment [against the insurance company] is affirmed. ⚖

Competent Parties

As is the case with other contracts, the parties to an insurance contract must have contractual capacity. Certain persons (minors and mental incompetents, for example) lack capacity or are under a disability. Minors, defined by statute in most states as anyone under the age of eighteen, may disaffirm a contract. In the absence of a statute regulating insurance for minors, a minor could purchase insurance, pay premiums until nearly eighteen, and then disaffirm and demand the refund of premiums paid. However, most states have conferred capacity on minors to contract for annuities, endowments, life insurance, accident and health insurance, and other forms of insurance in which the minor has an insurable interest. The minor may cancel the policy, as may an adult, but he or she may not demand return of the premiums paid. The age at which a minor may contract for insurance varies from state to state.

Legal Form

The form and content of insurance contracts are highly regulated by state law. Certain standard provisions relating to the specific type of insurance must be included in the policy and are spelled out in detail by statute in most states. Consequently, the proper form of insurance contracts is prescribed by law.

An agreement as complex as an insurance policy obviously should be in writing. Some states require that all insurance contracts be in writing, but several states merely prohibit oral agreements for certain types of insurance. Even in those states that do not prohibit all oral insurance contracts, it is exceedingly rare for an insurance agreement to be oral because of its inherently complex nature.

Other Aspects of the Insurance Contract

Unilateral in Nature

Most commercial contracts are *bilateral:* each of the parties makes a legally enforceable promise and each is therefore obligated to perform as promised. An insurance contract, however, is *unilateral.* Only one party, the insurer, makes an enforceable promise. After the insurance is in effect, the insured having paid the first premium, he or she is under no obligation to pay further premiums or to comply with other policy provisions. Payment must be made to continue the coverage, but only the insurer is legally required to perform.

Contract of Adhesion

Even though state laws prescribe the form and provisions of insurance contracts, the insurer prepares the contract, and it can be accepted or rejected by the other party, the insured. There is little negotiation as to terms; if the insured wishes to accept the contract it must be taken "as is" (this type of contract is called a **contract of adhesion**). Because the insurer prepares the contract, questions of construction or interpretation are construed most strictly against the insurer. Ambiguity in the wording of the contract is interpreted by the courts in favor of the insured.

Aleatory in Nature

The ultimate discharge of the parties to an insurance contract is governed by chance. The profit and loss involved usually depend upon an uncertain event or contingency; the values exchanged by the contracting parties will quite likely be unequal. For example, a motorist may pay automobile insurance premiums for years and never have reason to make a claim against the insurance company. In this case, the insured pays a substantial sum and the insurer pays nothing to that particular insured.

TYPES OF INSURANCE
Life Insurance

A contract of life insurance typically provides that the insurer will pay a specified sum of money—the face amount of the policy—upon the death of the insured if the premiums have been paid in accordance with the terms of the contract. There are basically three types of life insurance policies, *whole life, term insurance,* and *endowment insurance.*

Whole Life

The key characteristic of **whole life insurance** is that it provides protection for the whole of life (or to age 100, the end of the mortality table on which premiums are based). There are two primary types of whole life coverage: ordinary life and limited payment whole life. Under *ordinary life* contracts, premiums are payable for the entire lifetime of the insured or until he or she reaches age 100. Under *limited payment whole life* policies (examples are twenty payment, thirty payment, or paid-up at age sixty-five), premiums are payable until death or until the end of the predetermined premium paying period, whichever occurs first. Under both ordinary and limited payment whole life policies, payment of the specified sum of money is made upon the death of the insured to a named beneficiary or to the estate of the deceased. Payment to a named beneficiary may be a lump sum or periodic payments, as elected by the insured or the beneficiary. After the policy has been in effect for a specified number of years, the insured can discontinue paying premiums and receive a paid-up policy to the extent that his or her premiums have purchased such coverage.

During the life of the policy the insured has a right to borrow from the insurer an amount approximately equal to the cash surrender value of the policy. Should the insured die with all or part of such a loan unpaid the unpaid loan or balance would be deducted from the proceeds paid to the beneficiary.

Term Insurance

Term insurance is written for a specified period of time. It is relatively inexpensive but provides protection for death occurring only during the period of the policy. Term insurance can be written for any number of years. The insured may, in most cases, renew the policy for additional terms at increased premiums as age increases, and may have the option to convert the policy to some form of permanent insurance without a medical examination.

Because it is temporary protection, term insurance does not build cash values, nor may the insured borrow on the policy. Because of its low cost for younger ages, it is useful for those who cannot afford the higher cost of whole life. This might be the case for a young person with a family who wants to provide protection but is not yet in a position to purchase insurance as part of his or her estate plan.

Endowment Insurance

Endowment insurance provides that the insurer will pay the policy face amount to the insured when he or she reaches the end of the policy period (such as at age 65) or, should the insured die before the end of the period, to a designated beneficiary. Since maturity of the policy is ordinarily prior to the death of the insured, the cost of the endowment policy is substantially higher than that of whole life or term insurance.

Universal Life

Universal life insurance is a new form that combines some features of both whole life and term life.

Payments are often called "contributions." One portion of each payment is a charge for term life coverage, and another portion is for the insurance company's overhead and profit. The remaining part of each payment goes into an account that earns interest at a variable rate that is set periodically by the company. The amount in this account is similar to the cash surrender value of whole life insurance.

State Regulation of Life Insurance

The states exercise extensive regulatory control over the insurance industry within their jurisdictions. State insurance laws require that certain provisions be included in each policy delivered or issued within the state. Examples of typical required provisions include:

1. *Grace period:* Beginning with the second premium, a period of not less than 30 days within which the payment of any premium may be made without the policy lapsing.

2. *Incontestability:* After a policy has been in force for a period of two years from its date of issue, the policy shall become incontestable during the lifetime of the insured.

3. *Misstatement of age:* Where the age of the insured has been misstated, the benefit accruing under the policy shall be that which the premium would have purchased at the correct age.

Health Insurance

Many types of health insurance are available both to individuals and to employees as a group under a company-sponsored health plan. Health insurance can be divided into two basic types, *income replacement* and *medical expense* insurance.

Income Replacement

Income replacement policies provide for the payment of a stated periodic sum in the event the insured becomes disabled through sickness or injury and is unable to work. Eligibility for benefits is usually based on the fact that the insured is so sick or severely injured that he or she is unable to pursue the usual line of work.

The benefit period purchased under income replacement policies can be either short-term or long-term. A period longer than two years is considered long-term; the majority of policies are short-term.

Medical Expense

Medical expense insurance pays the cost of medical care required as a result of injury or sickness. Included are payments for physicians, hospital, nursing, and medicines and medical supplies. The insured is reimbursed for medical expenses within certain limits; the payments may be made either to the facility providing the medical service or to the insured.

The Health Maintenance Organization. A **health maintenance organization (HMO)** is a formal organization of physicians who provide medical care to their subscriber patients on an as-needed basis. HMOs provide benefits that are in many respects broader than those offered by other plans. For example, the typical HMO stresses prevention of sickness by offering preventive medical care. The Health Maintenance Organization Act of 1973 requires employers of more than 25 employees to offer enrollment in an HMO as an option to existing health care plans.

An HMO subscriber pays a fixed fee in exchange for all the medical care that may be required. In addition to the fee, the subscriber may pay a nominal fee, $1 or $2, for each visit to the facility, but the charge is the same regardless of the nature of the service or treatment rendered by the physician.

Social Insurance

While the normal expectation is that individuals and families should be able to care for themselves, economic security is beyond the reach of part of society. The concept of **social insurance** involves the notion that a certain segment of society is unable to fully care for itself and is thus subject to the risk of existing without an adequate standard of living. Social insurance, as defined by the Committee on Social Insurance of the Commission on Insurance Terminology of the American Risk and Insurance Association, is a device for pooling risks by transfer to a governmental service organization.

Various governmental programs have been enacted into law to assure each member of society at least a minimum standard of living. These include far-reaching social insurance programs.

Old-Age, Survivors', Disability, and Health Insurance

Known as Social Security, old-age, survivors', disability, and health insurance is an extremely comprehensive social insurance program that affects almost every individual in the country. As enacted in 1935 and extensively amended over the years, it provides a measure of security for eligible workers and their families against the risks associated with old age and the loss of ability to provide for themselves (although the benefits were never intended to provide full financial support). Its chief features are *old-age benefits, survivors' benefits, disability benefits,* and *medicare benefits.* Many claims may be controversial with regard to eligibility. An administrative hearing is frequently required to resolve a disputed claim for benefits. To illustrate the scope of the problem, there are approximately 1,100 administrative law judges assigned to federal agencies to conduct administrative hearings. Of that number, about 700 are assigned to the Social Security Administration alone.

Unemployment Compensation

Unemployment compensation is intended for workers who have been laid off and are unable to find other work through no fault of their own. Individual states operate the system, with each state levying a tax on employers to finance benefits. Each state has its own rules for determining eligibility. Benefit amounts are usually based on a fraction of average wages during a recent period, subject to minimum and maximum amounts, and are paid for a prescribed period. (When the general level of unemployment reaches a certain level, benefits may be paid for an additional period, usually 13 weeks. One-half of the benefits paid during this extended period are financed by the federal government.)

State Workers' Compensation Laws

As discussed in Chapter 49, Employment Law, the basic thrust of **workers' compensation** legislation is to provide medical care expense, income replacement, and rehabilitation benefits to employees suffering from work-related injury or occupational disease. The costs of these benefits, or the premiums for insurance to pay them, are borne by the employer and reflected in the cost of producing the employer's product or service. Although most employment is covered by workers' compensation, many states exclude farm laborers, domestic servants, and casual employees because their work is often of a sporadic or multi-employer nature. Workers' compensation is a no-fault system. If the agency (or the court) decides that the injury was job-related, compensation is awarded regardless of whether the employer, employee, or anyone else was at fault in causing the injury.

Property Insurance

Property insurance protects against financial loss because of damage to or destruction of the covered property. It is available in many forms and can be written to protect against a variety of perils. The basic kinds of coverage and a few of the important principles that apply are examined here.

Standard Fire Policy

Fire is the most common type of peril to which buildings and other structures are susceptible. Consequently, insurance coverage to protect against the risk of fire loss is the oldest, and still the most important, form of property insurance. A standard fire insurance policy was adopted by the state of New York in 1943 and has served as a model for standard fire policies in most states. Even though the standard fire policies in most states still retain the basic provisions of the New York Standard Fire Policy, much of the language has been changed by many states in recent years in an effort to make policies more easily understood by policyholders.

Homeowner's Policy

The **homeowner's policy** is a package agreement covering (1) damage to the dwelling, (2) damage to or loss of the policyholder's personal property located either on or off the premises, and (3) legal liability of the homeowner for injury to others. Each type of coverage is subject to dollar limitations specified in the policy. Because of its broad coverage, the homeowner's policy has become very popular in modern times.

The typical homeowner's policy covers damage to the home, its contents, and many other items of personal property caused by fire, lightning, wind, hail, vandalism, and other specified perils. Coverage against theft of items of personal property is also frequently included. The coverage for personal property normally excludes motor vehicles, farm equipment, and airplanes, as well as boats while they are in the water. Such items are the subject of separate insurance policies. In addition, coverage is often excluded or limited for several other types of personal property, such as money, securities, and jewelry unless additional coverage is obtained in return for a higher premium.

One of the most attractive features of the typical homeowner's policy is its provision of coverage on a **replacement cost basis.** In other words, subject to the policy's dollar limits, and sometimes subject to other restrictions, the insurance company pays the amount required to repair or replace the structure without deduction for depreciation or obsolescence.

Interpretation of Fire Coverage

Most property insurance policies cover fire losses only from so-called *hostile* fires, and do not cover losses from *friendly* fires. If a fire is characterized as hostile, covered losses include those from fire and smoke as well as from water or other efforts to save the property. A hostile fire is one that begins in a place that was not intended or escapes from its originally intended place; a friendly fire is one that is confined to the place where it should be. The lighted burner of a gas cooking stove is a friendly fire, as is the fire in a fireplace or a backyard incinerator, because these fires are confined to their intended places. Consequently, damage caused by smoke from the fireplace or incinerator is normally not covered by insurance. Similarly, the loss is not covered when someone accidently throws a ring or other valuable property into the incinerator. On the other hand, a fire started by an electrical short in the attic is a hostile fire, as is a fire started when furniture or clothing catches fire from a fireplace or heater. In addition, if the flame from a cooking stove flares up because of spilled or overheated grease and spreads to the kitchen window curtains, the fire has become a hostile one within the meaning of fire insurance coverage.

Coinsurance Requirement

Today, most property insurance policies include a **coinsurance clause.** The basic purpose of such a clause is to encourage policyholders to insure their property for an amount that is at least close to its full value. If a policyholder does not insure the property for an amount that is sufficiently close to its full replacement cost, the policyholder must bear a proportionate part of any loss from fire or other covered peril. The coinsurance requirement applies only to partial losses. Coinsurance clauses do not apply to cases of total destruction.

In most policies, the coinsurance clause requires that the amount of the coverage be at least 80 percent of the property's replacement cost. If the coverage amount is less than 80 percent, the insurance company pays a fraction of the replacement cost, the fraction derived by dividing the policy amount by the

**Box 47.1
The Law
at Work**

The use of arbitration, mediation, and other forms of alternative dispute resolution (ADR) has increased dramatically in the insurance industry as in other businesses. A number of large insurance companies have recently gone a step further, however, in the compelling circumstances presented by mass disasters. After Hurricane Andrew devastated southern Florida and Louisiana, followed shortly by similar devastation in Hawaii by Hurricane Iniki, 10 major insurance companies entered into an agreement with the Center for Public

Resources regarding the handling of billions of dollars in claims. The Center is a nonprofit organization devoted to alternative dispute resolution; it promotes alternatives to litigation in a number of ways, including educational efforts, encouraging large companies to make commitments to try ADR, and offering dispute resolution services.

In this particular instance, the Center secured commitments from these insurance companies to attempt arbitration, mediation, and other ADR techniques to resolve all the claims arising from these mass disasters. Obviously, the policyholders could not be forced into using ADR, but when insurance companies make an all-out effort to avoid litigation of claims and to

inform claimants of the many advantages of ADR, most policyholders are likely to try some form of binding or nonbinding ADR. The insurance companies in this case conditioned their commitment in only one way; it was agreed that they would not hesitate to contest claims in court, and would not attempt ADR, in any case in which they were convinced that the claims were fraudulent or made in bad faith. Although alternatives to litigation hold much promise for handling many kinds of claims more quickly and less expensively without unduly sacrificing fairness, claims arising from mass disasters represent one of the most fruitful uses of ADR.

amount that would have satisfied the coinsurance clause. Suppose, for example, that Otto owns a home with a current replacement cost of $100,000. To satisfy the usual coinsurance clause, he must obtain and pay for insurance in an amount of at least $80,000. If he insures the home for $80,000 or more and it is damaged by fire or other covered peril, he will receive the replacement cost for the damage. Thus, if it will cost $15,000 to repair the damage, he will receive the full $15,000 (minus, of course, any deductible the parties have agreed upon and specified in the policy). If he insures the home for only $60,000, however, the insurance company will pay only $12,000 (again, minus any agreed deductible). This amount is calculated as follows: Otto's policy amount ($60,000) divided by the amount of coverage that would have been necessary to satisfy the coinsurance clause ($80,000) is 3/4. The $15,000 replacement cost multiplied by this fraction equals $12,000.

In times of inflation, it is particularly important for the policyholder to review the amount of coverage periodically and increase it as necessary to continue meeting the coinsurance requirement. Today, many insurance companies offer an *inflation guard endorse-*

ment, an optional provision in homeowner's policies that periodically increases the coverage automatically by predetermined amounts.

Pro Rata Coverage

An owner who obtains two or more policies from different insurance companies covering the same property could potentially profit by receiving more than the replacement cost. Today, most property insurance policies (as well as other types of insurance, such as health insurance) contain a **pro rata clause,** which specifies that each insurance company is responsible only for a proportionate share of the loss. Thus, if Ruth obtains two homeowner's policies on her house, one from X insurance company for $100,000 and the other from Y insurance company for $50,000, the pro-rata clauses in the policies would result in X being responsible for 2/3 and Y for 1/3 of any covered loss.

Liability Insurance

Liability insurance provides protection against the risk of a legal action for damages that may be brought against the policyholder. Liability insurance may be written to meet a variety of needs.

Each year individuals and businesses are exposed to legal liability resulting in the payment of millions of dollars to compensate plaintiffs for injury to their persons or property. A homeowner may fail to remove ice from a sidewalk, and a caller falls and is injured. A bottle of cooking oil has been broken on the floor of a supermarket, and a patron is injured. A manufacturer produces and markets a consumer product that proves to be dangerously defective, and a user is injured. Lawsuits by injured parties against the property owner or manufacturer are being filed with increasing frequency as our society has become more consumer-protection oriented. And the judgments awarded by juries, both of actual damages, to compensate the plaintiff, and punitive damages, to punish the defendant, are sometimes staggering. The possibility that accidents will occur on residential or commercial premises presents another form of risk that can be transferred to an insurer. General liability exposure can be classified as *personal liability, business liability,* and *professional liability.*

Personal Liability—Coverage by the Homeowner's Policy

Personal liability coverage is an integral part of the homeowner's policy. In essence, it protects the policyholder against the financial risk of injuries or property damage to others. This coverage usually applies to damage caused to others by the unsafe condition of the policyholder's premises, or by the negligence of the policyholder. As in other types of insurance, the coverage limits are specified in the policy. A typical homeowner's policy might limit personal liability coverage, for example, to $100,000, with higher limits available upon payment of a higher premium.

Liability coverage in the homeowner's policy normally applies only to personal activities, not to business or professional activities. In addition, liability resulting from the operation of a motor vehicle or airplane usually is not covered. The risks associated with these excluded activities are the subject of separate insurance policies.

The basic thrust of liability coverage is to insure against the policyholder's *negligence* or carelessness. Consequently, most liability insurance provisions do not cover damage claims against the policyholder resulting from his or her *intentionally wrongful acts.* As is true of most other issues, the question whether someone has been harmed by the policyholder's negligence, or by his or her intentional conduct, is not always easy to resolve. In the following case, these principles are applied to a situation in which harm certainly was intended, but the policyholder made a mistake in his choice of a target.

PETERS V. TROUSCLAIR

District Court of Appeal of Florida, 431 So.2d 296 (1983)

 James Trousclair was a riverboat pilot whose occupation required extended absences from his wife and home. During one of those absences, Peters, Mrs. Trousclair's cousin, had been residing at Trousclair's home for several days. The record reflects that although Trousclair had extended the invitation, he had only met Peters on two prior occasions, was not familiar with him, and was unaware that Peters had begun residing in the home. In the meantime, one Humphreys, not at Trousclair's invitation, was also re- siding at the home, having become amorously involved with Mrs. Trousclair. On the occasion that led to this lawsuit, Trousclair returned home without forewarning to find his wife and the two men lounging in the living room in the early morning hours. In a fit of jealous rage, Trousclair burst into the room, grabbed Peters, whom he did not recognize, and repeatedly stabbed him, causing serious injury. He then pursued Humphreys.

Upon venting the remainder of his frustration on Humphreys, Trousclair suddenly realized that Peters was his wife's cousin and promptly took him to a hospital. Peters initiated a civil lawsuit alleging that Trousclair had committed the tort of either assault and battery or negligence, in the alternative. Trousclair held a homeowner's insurance policy with American Liberty Insurance Company that included personal liability coverage. His request that the company defend him was denied. Judgment was rendered for Peters against Trousclair for compensatory and punitive damages totalling $105,606.55. Peters then sought to have the court hold the insurance company responsible for this amount under the personal liability provision

(continues)

PETERS V. TROUSCLAIR

(continued from previous page)
of Trousclair's policy. The trial court found no coverage because the insurance policy expressly excluded liability for intentional harm, and Peters appealed.

Wigginton, Judge:

[The insurance company claimed, and the trial court concluded, that] Trousclair's act was intentional and excluded from the policy, the exclusion reading:

1. Coverage E—Personal Liability and Coverage F—Medical Payments to Others do not apply to bodily injury or property damage:
   a. which is expected or intended by the insured. . . .

The record supports the trial court's finding. It reveals that although Trousclair was unaware at the time of the stabbing of the identity of Peters as being his wife's cousin, knowledge which might have otherwise stayed his hand, the act was nonetheless intentionally, specifically directed toward the person of Peters. This feature serves to distinguish the instant case from *Grange Mutual Casualty Co. v. Thomas,* 301 So.2d 158 (Fla. Dist. Ct. App. 1974), which [held that liability coverage applied to a case involving] the shooting of a nonparticipant observer of a family quarrel who was the unfortunate recipient of an errant bullet intended for another. Compare also *Phoenix Insurance Co. v. Helton,* 298 So.2d 177 (Fla. Dist. Ct. App. 1974), and *Cloud v. Shelby Mutual Insurance Co.,* So.2d 217 (Fla. Dist. Ct. App. 1971), in which it was ruled that coverage was not excluded as a matter of law where there was an "intentional act" but not an "intentionally caused" injury. However, as pointed out in *Hartford Fire Insurance Co. v. Spreen,* 343 So.2d 649 (Fla. Dist. Ct. App. 1977): "Running through all of these cases is an act of negligence by the insured, sometimes gross or even culpable negligence. But never has coverage been found under such policies where the insured's act was deliberately designed to cause harm to the injured party."

Here, it is evident from Trousclair's own statements in the record that Peters was the immediate and intended object of his wrath. There is no doubt that Trousclair's act was "deliberately designed to cause harm" to Peters at the moment he committed the act. . . .

[The judgment of the trial court is affirmed. The insurance company is not liable.] ⚖

Business Liability Coverage

Businesses that need broad, all-risk coverage against the perils of doing business may obtain what is known as the comprehensive general liability form of insurance. This form covers a variety of risks and, with appropriate endorsements, can be tailored to fit specific business needs. The broad form comprehensive general liability endorsement adds coverage for a wide range of liability exposures that are otherwise excluded from the basic coverage. Included are such items as blanket contractual liability, personal injury and advertising injury, premises medical payments, host liquor liability (this covers the selling or serving of liquor at social events), and other coverages that a business may need but has overlooked.

There are special policies to cover storekeepers, the owners and operators of small shops, and so-called dram shop (bar or saloon) owners or operators. In some states owners of dram shops may be liable for injury or damage caused by their patrons to third parties. For example, a saloon keeper who permits a patron to overimbibe may be guilty of negligence and therefore liable for the injury or damage caused by the patron who, while driving, is involved in an auto accident.

Products Liability Coverage. Manufacturers of consumer and other products face special risks. In the Federal District Courts, there were over 10,000 products liability cases commenced between July 1, 1984, and June 30, 1985. This number, of course, does not include the many products liability suits filed in *state* courts. Products liability and the risks faced by the manufacturer whose product may injure a user are discussed in the risk management section of this chapter.

Professional Malpractice Liability Coverage

The term malpractice is often used to refer to negligence by a professional. The proliferation of lawsuits alleging malpractice against physicians and hospitals in recent years has generated a heavy demand for medical **malpractice insurance.** Moreover, the number and size of damage awards and settlements against insurance companies providing malpractice coverage have increased dramatically. As a result, premium rates for such insurance have skyrocketed.

While malpractice insurance is generally thought of as needed only by physicians and hospitals, others who render specialized services to the public also find themselves increasingly liable for malpractice. Attorneys, engineers, pharmacists, and architects, for example, have experienced greater exposure to damage claims and much higher liability insurance premiums in the last few years. Similarly, the demand and the premiums for liability insurance covering the activities of corporate managers have grown. Today, so-called "D & O" (directors and officers) insurance is frequently demanded by executives as part of their compensation packages, although it is becoming extremely expensive and much more difficult to obtain.

Automobile Insurance

Ownership of an automobile poses risks that are too great for most individuals to assume on their own. Consequently, the automobile owner must transfer the risk to a professional risk bearer by purchasing automobile insurance of the various kinds and in the amounts of coverage that fit his or her needs. These needs may be dictated by statute.

Types of Coverage

The typical automobile insurance policy includes several types of coverage which are discussed below.

Liability Coverage. The liability coverage in the automobile policy protects the insured, the insured's family members, and certain others against loss that may arise as a result of legal liability when the insured's auto is involved in an accident and causes personal injury or property damage. The policy is written subject to limits and is expressed in terms such as $25/$50/$5. In this example, coverage is provided for up to $50,000 for all persons injured in a single accident, with a limit of $25,000 for any one individual; the $5 figure indicates that up to $5,000 will be paid for property damage resulting from a single accident. Larger amounts can be purchased and, as the limits are increased, the cost is proportionately greater.

Most states have enacted **financial responsibility laws** that, in effect, require a driver to have at least a specified amount of coverage or risk the imposition of some form of state sanction. State requirements vary, ranging from $5/$10/$1 to $25/$50/$10 (numbers expressed in thousands). And more than half the states have "compulsory" insurance laws requiring some form of state-approved security.

Under the automobile insurance policy the insurer is obligated to pay for injuries "arising out of the ownership, maintenance, or use" of the insured vehicle. In litigation involving the insurer's obligation to pay, the issue is frequently "use," that is, was there a causal relationship or connection between the injury and the use of the vehicle? Obviously, if the vehicle is being driven for some legitimate purpose it is being "used" and resulting injuries would be covered. But suppose that a plaintiff slips and falls while pushing an insured auto, with a dead battery, on an icy driveway. Did the injury from the fall arise out of the use of the vehicle? The court in *Union Mutual Fires Ins. Co. v. King,* 300 A.2d 335 (N.H. 1973), said yes and the insurer paid. The following case also confronts the "use" question.

McNeill v. Maryland Insurance Guaranty Association

Court of Special Appeals of Maryland, 427 A.2d 1056 (1981)

When Charlie McNeill could not start his car, he asked his friend, Evelyn Watkins, to bring her car to where McNeill's was located so that he could use her car's battery to "jump start" his own. Watkins got a third person, Edwin Hill, to drive her car and keep it running during the operation. McNeill correctly attached the jumper cables to the battery posts of both cars while the engine of the Watkins car was running, and removed one or more of the caps from his battery to check its fluid level. (These caps were removable for the addition of water to the battery; at the time of these events, car batteries were not of the sealed, maintenance-free variety.) While Hill was operating Watkins' car, Hill lit a match, presumably to light a cigarette, and tossed it out the window. The match evidently landed close to the battery, and the flame caused McNeill's battery to explode. McNeill, who was standing beside and leaning over his battery, was seriously injured.

(continues)

McNeill v. Maryland Insurance Guaranty Association

(continued from previous page)

Watkins had an insurance policy covering her car, and it included provisions making the insurance company liable for any bodily injury or property damage to others that Watkins would be responsible for. These provisions expressly applied, however, only to such injuries or damages "arising out of the ownership, maintenance, or use" of Watkins' car. McNeill filed suit against the insurance company that had issued the policy on Watkins' car. Attorneys for both parties stipulated that the accident was caused by the negligence of Hill, acting as Watkins' agent, and that McNeill was not contributorily negligent. The trial court ruled that McNeill's injuries did not arise out of the ownership, maintenance, or use of Watkins' car, and held that the insurance company was not liable. McNeill appealed.

Liss, Judge:

The Watkins vehicle was covered by the . . . policy which provided in pertinent part:

Coverage A—Bodily Injury Liability . . . To pay on behalf of the insured all sums which the insured shall become legally obligated to pay as damages because of:

A. bodily injury . . . arising out of the ownership, maintenance or use of the owned automobile. . . .

The standard adopted by the Court of Appeals [i.e., Maryland's highest court] in the interpretation of provisions of an insurance policy where the disputed provision is susceptible to more than one construction is that the provision must be "literally construed in order to promote . . . recovery for innocent victims of motor vehicle accidents." "Ownership, maintenance or use clauses" do not limit recovery solely to injuries that are caused by direct physical contact with the insured vehicle; nor is it necessary that the damages be directly sustained or in-

flicted by the operation of the motor vehicle. . . .

[The insurance company] relies heavily upon *Plaxco v. United States Fidelity & Guaranty Co.*, 166 S.E.2d 799 (S.C. 1969). . . . The issue in *Plaxco* was whether the use by an insured of his automobile battery to crank the engines of his airplane by connecting the batteries with jumper cables constituted a use of an automobile within the meaning of the automobile liability insurance policy providing coverage arising out of the ownership, maintenance or use of any automobile. In *Plaxco*, the plaintiff drove his automobile to the airport for the purpose of making a trip in his airplane. The plane battery was either dead or too weak to start the engine so he drove his automobile to the left wing and connected the batteries of the plane to the auto by use of a jumper cable. When this was done he entered the plane, started the engine and engaged the brakes and alighted to disconnect the jumper cables, leaving the airplane engine running. After the plaintiff disconnected one of the cables from the automobile battery, and while attempting to disconnect the other, the airplane brakes failed to hold and struck another aircraft. The court held that the accident did not result from the use of plaintiff's automobile, when it stated:

The accident in question did not result from the use of plaintiff's automobile. The only connection between the automobile and the airplane was the use of the automobile battery to start the airplane engine. This purpose had been completed when the airplane moved forward, after the brakes failed to hold. We find nothing in the facts or circumstances to show a causal connection between the use of the automobile battery as a source of power to start the airplane engine and the subsequent forward movement of the airplane. . . . The facts show that the accident resulted from the use of the airplane and not the insured automobile.

We conclude that the facts in *Plaxco* are distinguishable from the present case. The use of the Watkins vehicle

was clearly a use which was or should have been contemplated and anticipated by the insurance carrier and the owner of the vehicle. It is not unusual that an insured might on occasion be required to use his vehicle to charge the battery of another vehicle. At the time the explosion took place, the Watkins vehicle was still being used in an activity permitted by her policy. . . . The Watkins vehicle was still attached by the jumper cables to McNeill's vehicle at the time Watkins' driver negligently threw the match. McNeill's activity in unscrewing the battery caps was entirely consistent with an effort to determine whether the battery had sufficient fluid and charge to permit McNeill's car to operate without being attached to the jumper cables. The lighting of the cigarette by Watkins' driver was not an intervening or independent cause, as was the failure of the airplane brakes in *Plaxco*.

Our conclusion, under a policy such as is here before us, is that where a dangerous situation causing injury is one which arose out of or had its source in, the use or operation of the automobile, the chain of responsibility must be deemed to [continue] until broken by the intervention of some event which has no direct or substantial relation to the use or operation. . . . [In other words,] the event which breaks the chain, and which, therefore, would exclude liability under the automobile policy, must be an event which bears no direct or substantial relation to the use or operation; and until an event of the latter nature transpires the liability under the policy exists. . . .

Under the facts in this case we conclude that there was a causal relationship between the use of the Watkins vehicle to start McNeill's automobile and . . . the explosion. . . . We find that at the time [the negligently caused explosion] occurred, the Watkins vehicle was being "used" as contemplated by the Watkins liability insurance policy.

Judgment reversed. [Watkins' insurance company is liable.]

Medical Payments Coverage. The medical payments coverage provides that the insurer will pay reasonable expenses for necessary medical and funeral services rendered because of bodily injury or death caused by an accident and suffered by a person covered by the policy. Included would be any occupant of the insured's automobile. There are limitations on the medical payments, usually ranging from $500 to $5,000 per person per accident.

Uninsured Motorist Coverage. Another part of the automobile policy covers the driver and passengers in the event of bodily injury caused by a hit-and-run driver or by a negligent driver who is financially irresponsible (unable to pay). Under the coverage the insurer will pay up to a specified amount to compensate for the insured's being unable to collect from the negligent driver. Uninsured motorist coverage usually has the same limits as the bodily injury limits of the liability coverage.

Additionally, if an insured purchases increased uninsured motorist coverage he or she may also purchase *underinsured* motorist coverage. This endorsement to the policy covers the situation in which the other driver, at fault, has some insurance but the limits of his or her policy are less than those of the insured's uninsured motorist coverage.

Physical Damage—Collision and Comprehensive Coverage. Physical damage coverage protects the insured against the loss of or damage to his or her automobile. There are two basic forms, *collision* and *comprehensive* (other than collision). As the term implies, collision coverage protects the insured against the perils of upset of the covered automobile or its impact with some object. Many perils are not covered by the collision insurance. These include damage or loss caused by thrown or falling objects, explosion, windstorm, earthquake, hail, flood, vandalism, and glass breakage. For example, suppose that the insured's car is severely pitted by large hailstones or dented by a tree limb blown down in a storm. There has been impact, but the collision insurance would not cover the damage.

To protect against the perils not covered by collision insurance the insured can purchase comprehensive coverage. The items noted above as being excluded would thus be covered.

Both types of physical damage coverage are less costly if there is a deductible provision. That is, the insured agrees to pay for any damages that do not exceed the amount of the deductible, perhaps $100 or $200. If the insured with $200 deductible collision coverage suffers collision damage of $500, the insurer would pay $300 and the balance, $200, would be paid by the insured.

Duties after an Accident or Loss

An insured involved in an auto accident is under a contractual agreement to promptly notify his or her insurer of all the details of the accident together with the names and addresses of any injured persons and any witnesses. The policy further provides for the insured to cooperate fully with the insurance company in its conduct of an investigation, settlement, or defense of a claim or suit. In its handling of a claim or lawsuit, the insurer will settle, or defend the insured, as it deems appropriate and will pay all defense costs. However, the insurer's duty to settle or defend ends when the limits of its liability have been reached.

Subrogation

Subrogation may be defined as the substitution of one person in another's place, allowing the party substituted the same rights and claims as the party being substituted. The subrogation clause in the automobile policy provides:

A. If we make a payment under this policy and the person to or for whom payment was made has a right to recover damages from another we shall be subrogated to that right. That person shall do:
1. Whatever is necessary to enable us to exercise our rights; and
2. Nothing after loss to prejudice them.

To illustrate, suppose that the insured's car is totally demolished in an accident, the other driver being at fault. The insurance company would pay the insured in accordance with the terms of the policy. However, the insured has the right to proceed against the negligent driver but, having been paid by his or her own insurance company, relinquishes that right to the company. The insurer may now proceed against the negligent driver to recover the amount it had paid the insured. In other words, the insurer is subrogated to the rights of the insured.

Cancellation of the Automobile Policy

By state law, after the insured has had the policy for a specified number of days, from 30 to 90 depending upon the state, it may be terminated by the insurer only for certain reasons. Typical of these reasons are:

1. Nonpayment of required premiums.

2. Material misrepresentations by the insured in the policy application.

3. Making of a fraudulent claim by the insured.

4. Suspension or revocation of the insured's driver's license.

5. The insured's addiction to drugs.

6. The insured or other customary operator has been convicted or forfeited bail during the 36 months preceding cancellation for any felony, criminal negligence while operating a motor vehicle, driving under the influence, leaving the scene of an accident, theft of a motor vehicle, or making false statements in an application for a driver's license.

No-Fault Insurance

Under traditional tort law a party who drives negligently and causes personal injury or property damage may be held liable and forced to pay damages. Traditionally, it must be determined which insured is at fault with his or her insurer then paying the damages. Under certain states' *no-fault* systems the determination of fault is unnecessary; each insured collects for injuries and damages from his or her own insurer. Both negligent and nonnegligent parties are covered.

A strict **no-fault insurance** system would do away with tort actions for bodily injuries caused by automobile accidents. There would be no recovery for damages other than bodily injury, and recovery for "pain and suffering" would not be allowed. However, in most of the 23 states having no-fault laws, modification of the pure no-fault concept permits tort suits subject to specific restrictions and limitations on the right to sue. There is considerable variation from state to state, with no state having a pure no-fault law.

Since the first no-fault insurance law, enacted by Massachusetts in 1970, considerable dissatisfaction with the concept has been expressed by those with a vested interest in automobile insurance. American trial lawyers and certain segments of the insurance industry have voiced objections on grounds ranging from unconstitutionality to claims that under no-fault the allocation of the costs of accidents will be unfair and incentives for careful driving will be reduced.

On the other hand, proponents of the system argue that the long-run effect will be to cut costs and reduce premiums for motorists. Whether or not this will happen remains to be seen. The many factors to be taken into account in determining costs in those states having no-fault systems have made it difficult to ascertain how much is being saved if indeed lower premiums are being realized.

Proposals for Federal No-Fault Legislation. Because there is little or no uniformity among the states in their approach to no-fault laws, many proponents of the concept feel that federal regulation is a necessity. Several no-fault proposals have been introduced in Congress but none have been received with much enthusiasm. They have been opposed by a large segment of the insurance industry, the American Bar Association, and the American Trial Lawyers Association. Consequently, passage of a federal no-fault bill, at least for the immediate future, seems a remote possibility. A more likely solution may be federal legislation that prescribes standards for the states to follow in developing their own no-fault laws. There has been some movement in this direction.

SUMMARY

An insurance contract, or policy, must possess the same essential elements as other contracts. The person purchasing the insurance makes an offer by submitting the application; the offer is accepted either by the agent's issuance of a binder or the insurance company's issuance of the policy itself. One of the most important elements in the case of insurance is that the insured, or policyholder, must possess an insurable interest in the subject matter of the policy. Insurance issued to one without an insurable interest amounts to an illegal gambling contract, and is void. The policyholder also must be of sufficient age, and most insurance contracts are required by state law to be in writing.

Insurance contracts are usually contracts of adhesion and are therefore construed in the insured's favor when an ambiguity arises. They also are unilateral and aleatory in nature.

The major types of insurance are life, health, social, property, liability, and automobile. Several subcategories exist within each type, and many aspects of the different types are overlapping. Homeowner's insurance, for example, includes both property and liability coverage. Automobile insurance is a specialized type of property and liability insurance. The typical property insurance policy includes a coinsurance clause that encourages the owner to insure his or her property for at least close to its full value by requiring the owner to bear a proportionate part of any loss if coverage is not maintained for a specified percentage of the property's replacement cost. Most types of liability insurance cover the policyholder's liability only for negligence, and not for intentionally wrongful acts.

KEY TERMS
Binder
Premium
Insurable interest
Contract of adhesion
Whole life insurance
Term insurance
Endowment insurance
Universal life insurance
Health maintenance organization (HMO)
Social insurance
Unemployment compensation
Workers' compensation
Homeowner's policy
Replacement cost basis
Coinsurance clause
Pro rata clause
Liability insurance
Malpractice insurance
Financial responsibility laws
No-fault insurance

QUESTIONS AND PROBLEMS

1. Kludt and his family live on a farm that is entirely owned by his wife. The deed to the farm names only his wife as the owner. However Kludt operates the farm and applies any profit he makes to improvements and the support of himself and his family. He has insured the property naming himself as the insured. When the farm was damaged by fire the insurance company refused to pay Kludt's claim, alleging that the policy was void because Kludt has no insurable interest in the property. Is the insurer correct? (*Kludt v. German Mutual Fire Ins. Co.*, 140 N.W. 321, Wis. 1913.)

2. John Smith and Jane Doe have been close to each other since childhood and made plans to marry in June 1984. With this in mind, and to take advantage of the lower premiums for younger persons, in February 1984 Jane purchased a policy of life insurance on John naming herself as beneficiary. Should John die after they are married will Jane be paid the proceeds of the policy?

3. The X, Y, Z partnership has been in business for twenty years and has been profitable. It is estimated that each partner's interest in the firm amounts to approximately $120,000. Partner X died suddenly, and his surviving spouse wants to be paid her deceased husband's share of partnership assets as soon as the amount has been determined. What problems might this pose for the surviving partners if they want to continue the business? How could these problems have been avoided?

4. Plaintiff was the insured under an accidental death and dismemberment policy that provided full coverage for, among other things, the "total and irrecoverable loss of entire sight of an eye." After a cataract operation on his right eye the plaintiff was fitted with a contact lens that permitted him very limited vision in the eye. However, he could not tolerate the contact lens and without it the eye was practically sightless with no medical assurance that it would ever be any better. When the insurer denied coverage plaintiff filed an action against it claiming the total and irrecoverable loss of entire sight of an eye. A major issue in the case was the meaning of the phrase "irrecoverable loss of sight." In deciding this case what rule of construction will the court apply? (*Roy v. Allstate Ins. Co.*, 383 A.2d 637, Conn. 1978.)

5. A bakery oven was badly damaged in the amount of $2160 when its thermostatic control failed and caused it to overheat to 650° and become red hot on the outside. This charred the wooden floor, which was damaged to the extent of $800. On what grounds might the insurer attempt to deny coverage? Will it be successful? (*L.L. Freeberg Pie Co. v. St. Paul Mut. Ins. Co.*, 100 N.W.2d 753, Minn. 1960.)

6. A home has a market value of $80,000. To replace the home in the event of total destruction would cost $120,000. The owner has a homeowner's policy with $90,000 of coverage. If a fire damages the house in the amount of $20,000, at replacement cost, how much will the insurer pay?

7. A woman operates a beauty salon in a building she owns that in 1980 was valued at $85,000. She has a policy of fire insurance for $85,000 with a 90

percent coinsurance clause. In 1982 a hair dryer overheated and resulted in a fire that caused $25,000 in damages. After the fire it was determined that the building, in its pre-fire state, was worth $130,000. How much will the owner collect from her insurer?

8. The phrase "arising out of the . . . use" of the insured automobile frequently raises questions as to the kinds of things that constitute "use" so that the in-jured insured, or others, are covered by the insured's policy. A truckdriver, while fueling the truck for a trip, is injured when the fuel tank explodes. The driver was not in the truck at the time of the explosion. Did this accident result from "use" of the truck so that there was coverage? (*Red Ball Motor Freight, Inc. v. Employers Mut. Liab. Ins. Co.*, 189 F.2d 374, 1951.)

PART VII

GOVERNMENT REGULATION OF BUSINESS

ODAY, FOR BETTER OR for worse, the major business activities that are carried on in this country are subject to a substantial amount of federal and state regulation. This fact of life was mentioned in Chapter 6 (Lawmaking by Administrative Agencies), because much of the regulation is, in fact, carried on by government boards and commissions.

In that chapter, however, our primary mission was to see how administrative agencies—whether regulatory or not—actually "make law." We did not attempt to cover the entire subject of government regulation itself. In these final chapters we will make several excursions into this highly complex area of law. It is important to note, also, that several state and federal regulatory laws have been examined elsewhere in the text. For example, in Chapter 22, Warranties and Products Liability, the Magnusson-Moss and Consumer Product Safety Acts are discussed along with other aspects of products liability law. In Chapter 41, we examined the federal and state laws that regulate the issuance and trading of stocks, bonds, and other securities.

The subject of government regulation of business is so broad, far-reaching, and varied that a balanced treatment of it, in any degree of depth, would require a work of several volumes. Obviously, that is not our purpose here.

Instead, our goals will be more modest. In Chapter 48, we provide an overview of the federal antitrust laws, which are aimed at promoting competition in American markets. Then, in Chapter 49, we focus on a variety of federal and state laws that regulate the employment relationship. Chapter 50 discusses several important federal and state regulatory laws that seek to protect our physical environment. Chapter 51 surveys federal and state regulatory provisions aimed at protecting the consumer. Finally, Chapter 52 discusses some of the regulations imposed by the United States and other nations on international business transactions.⚖

Chapter 48

Antitrust Law

Introduction

Monopolization

Mergers

Horizontal Restraints of Trade

Vertical Restraints of Trade

INTRODUCTION
The Objectives of Antitrust Law

An economy such as that of the United States, which depends primarily on the operation of market forces, cannot function properly without competition. Although the word "competition" is subject to various shades of meaning, it most often refers to a condition of economic rivalry among firms. That is, firms should be engaged in a contest for customers, the outcome of that contest depending on each firm's ability to satisfy customer wants.

The primary purpose of antitrust law is to promote competition. In the various types of markets, competition can take somewhat different forms. In the case of many kinds of products, for example, price is a very important factor in customers' buying decisions (that is, "price elasticity" is high), and much of the competitive rivalry among sellers may focus on price. On the other hand, in some markets price may not be quite as important to most customers as good service, availability of many product options, convenience, or other factors. In such markets, competition among sellers is likely to emphasize these nonprice attributes to a greater extent. Not only does the form of competition vary somewhat among markets, but the intensity of competition also is less in some markets than in others. The job of antitrust law is to encourage competition in its various forms and to preserve it to the extent feasible in a given market.

Most economists feel that a competitive, market-based economy produces a number of beneficial results such as efficient allocation of scarce resources, lower prices, higher quality, greater innovation, and economic freedom. In the view of some authorities, there is another reason for having a strong antitrust policy in the United States—more competition in an economic sense may diminish the amount of power that large firms have over the political process and over the lives of large numbers of people.

Has antitrust law achieved its goals? This question cannot be answered with certainty because it is practically impossible to measure the effects of antitrust law on the American economy. There are many markets (so-called **oligopolies**) in which most of the sales are made by a few large companies. Many of these firms are very efficient; some are not. Many do not abuse their power; some do. In some of these markets, competition appears to be quite vigorous, but in others it is rather stagnant. Moreover, in many of these markets concentration of power in a few firms is an inevitable result of extremely large capital requirements and economies of scale. On the other hand, the *degree* of economic concentration is clearly not always inevitable.

Thus, it is not surprising to find substantial disagreement among authorities concerning the wisdom and effect of antitrust law. Some say the law has not been enforced aggressively enough, while others say that it has been applied too aggressively to the wrong things. Many points of criticism and support have been raised over the years. Only two conclusions are relatively certain: (1) although the interpretation of some of the antitrust rules will vary over time, the fundamental principles are probably going to remain with us; and (2) antitrust law will always be controversial. With that, we will examine the law itself.

The Federal Antitrust Statutes

The first, and still the most important, of the federal antitrust laws is the Sherman Act, passed by Congress in 1890. Section 1 of this Act prohibits "contracts, combinations, and conspiracies in restraint of trade." The focus of Section 1 is collusion among firms that are supposed to be acting independently when making basic business decisions. Section 2 prohibits "monopolization, attempts to monopolize, and conspiracies to monopolize." The prohibition of monopolization, which is the most important part of Section 2, focuses on single-firm domination of a market.

In 1914, Congress enacted the Clayton Act with two main purposes in mind: (1) to make the prohibitions against certain anticompetitive practices more specific, and (2) to make it easier to challenge certain practices, such as mergers, when the evidence shows only probable future anticompetitive effects and not actual present effects. Section 2 of the Act prohibits price discrimination; Section 3 prohibits some tying and exclusive dealing agreements; and Section 7 forbids anticompetitive mergers. In any of these cases, the law is violated only if the evidence demonstrates an actual or highly probable anticompetitive effect of a substantial nature. Section 8 of the Clayton Act prohibits *interlocking directorates* between certain large corporations that are in direct competition with each other. An interlocking directorate occurs when the same individual serves on the boards of directors of two corporations.

Also in 1914, Congress passed the Federal Trade Commission Act (FTC Act). In addition to creating the Federal Trade Commission (FTC) as an enforcement agency, the Act also prohibited "unfair methods of competition" in Section 5. Any conduct that violates one of the other antitrust laws, plus a few other types of conduct, constitutes an unfair method of competition. In 1938, Congress added another phrase to Section 5 prohibiting "unfair or deceptive acts or practices." Thus the first part of the statute deals with antitrust matters, and the second part deals with various forms of consumer deception such as false advertising.

In 1936 Congress passed the Robinson-Patman Act, which amended Section 2 of the Clayton Act in an effort to make the law against price discrimination more effective.

Even though antitrust law is based on statutory enactments, most of the language in those statutes is so broad that court interpretations account for most of the lawmaking process. Also, our attention in this chapter is focused only on *federal* antitrust law. Most states have their own antitrust laws, which usually apply to the same basic practices that are forbidden by federal law.

Coverage and Exemptions

Coverage

Like many other federal statutes that are based on the Commerce Clause of the U.S. Constitution, the federal antitrust laws apply to business activities that either directly involve or substantially affect interstate commerce. Business activities occurring in foreign commerce, such as imports and exports, are also covered by U.S. antitrust law if there is a substantial effect on an American market.

Exemptions

The actions of the federal government are exempt from the antitrust laws, as are most actions of state governments so long as they are acting pursuant to legitimate and clearly expressed state regulatory interests. In this regard, actions of cities and other local governments are treated as state action if the local government is essentially just carrying out some aspect of state regulatory policy. Actions by foreign governments also are not within the scope of the antitrust laws.

If particular activities of a firm are subject to special regulation by a federal agency, such as the Securities Exchange Commission or the Commodity Futures Trading Commission, any possible anticompetitive consequences of those activities will usually not be scrutinized under the antitrust laws if the responsible agency has approved the activities after carefully considering the impact on competition.

In addition, the formation and ordinary activities (collective bargaining and strikes, for instance) of labor unions are exempt. Similarly, the actions of firms are exempt to the extent that they form a legitimate part of the union-company collective bargaining agreement and do not affect parties outside the union-company relationship. Finally, the joint activities of two kinds of selling cooperatives are exempt from the antitrust laws: (1) those formed by agricultural or livestock producers, and (2) export groups, so long as the limitation on export competition among members of the group does not adversely affect a domestic U.S. market.

Enforcement

Enforcement of the federal antitrust laws can take one or more of several different forms. The Antitrust Division of the U.S. Department of Justice, which operates under the attorney general as part of the executive branch, can institute civil lawsuits and criminal prosecutions in federal district court. In a civil suit, if the Justice Department proves a violation of the Sherman, Clayton, or Robinson-Patman Acts, the remedy it normally obtains from the court is an injunction. The injunction will order the cessation of particular illegal actions, and may even require substantial modification of a firm's everyday business practices so as to lessen the likelihood of future violations. Many times the terms of an injunction are the result of an agreed settlement between the Justice Department and the defendant. In such cases, the injunction issue by the court after approving the terms of the settlement is called a *consent decree*. A firm or individual violating the terms of an injunction will be held in contempt of court.

If the case falls under the Sherman Act and involves a flagrant violation, such as blatant price fixing among competitors, the Justice Department may file a criminal prosecution in federal court. Upon conviction (which is a felony), the maximum penalty in a criminal case is a $1 million fine for corporations, and a $100,000 fine and three years' imprisonment for individuals.

The FTC also has authority to enforce the Clayton, Robinson-Patman, and FTC Acts. Even though it technically has no power to enforce the Sherman Act, any conduct that would violate the Sherman Act will also constitute an "unfair method of competition" under Section 5 of the FTC Act. FTC enforcement, which is civil in nature, consists of a hearing before an administrative law judge of the agency, with subsequent review by the five-member FTC. If a violation is found, the FTC will issue a "cease and desist order," which is essentially the same as an injunction. Violation of an FTC order is punishable by a penalty of up to $10,000 for each day of noncompliance.

A private party can file a civil lawsuit in federal court claiming a violation of the Sherman, Clayton, or Robinson-Patman Acts. The plaintiff sometimes can obtain an injunction in such a suit, but the remedy normally sought is *treble damages*. This means that if the plaintiff proves it was damaged by the defendant's violation, the law automatically multiplies the plaintiff's money damages by three.

In the following pages, we look first at that portion of the law concerned primarily with industry structure, namely the law of *monopolization* and *mergers*. We then turn to the antitrust laws that focus on particular kinds of conduct in our discussion of *horizontal restraints of trade, vertical restraints of trade*, and *price discrimination*.

MONOPOLIZATION

In trying to formulate a working definition of **monopoly** under Section 2 of the Sherman Act, as a practical matter the courts could not simply adopt the classical economic model of monopoly: one seller, very high entry barriers to the market, and no close substitutes for the product. Instead, they defined a monopoly in more pragmatic terms as "a firm having such an overwhelming degree of market power that it is able to control prices or exclude competition."

The center of this definition is *market power*. Essentially, market power is the ability of a firm to behave differently than it could behave in a perfectly competitive market. Stated differently, market power is the ability to exercise some degree of control over the price of its product, that is, to raise its price without losing most of its customers. In virtually every market, there will be firms with *some* control over the price they charge, although the degree of control varies greatly from case to case.

The concept of market power is critical to any examination of competition under the antitrust laws, because competition usually cannot be harmed unless one firm, or a group of firms acting together, possesses some degree of market power. With respect to other issues in antitrust law, degrees of market power that are less than monopolistic can be very important. However, in deciding whether there is a monopoly under Section 2 of the Sherman Act, courts look for an *overwhelming* degree of market power. This exists when one firm dominates a market to such an extent that it does not have to worry much about the response of competitors.

Measuring Market Power

Traditionally, the enforcement agencies and courts have looked primarily at the *structure* of a market when trying to draw inferences about degrees of market power. The most important structural factor is usually the firm's **market share.** In other words, what percentage share of the relevant market does the firm have? The courts have not developed hard and fast rules as to what market share definitely does or does not demonstrate overwhelming market power. However, the cases indicate that a market share of less than 50 percent will never be enough, and a share of 75 percent will frequently (but not always) be enough. Although other indicators of market power are always important, they become critical when the share is below or above this range.

Other structural factors include the following:

1. The *relative size of other firms* in the market can be important. If M has, say, 60 percent of the market, M generally will have less market power if there are at least one or two other very large firms with perhaps 20 or 30 percent shares than if the remainder of the market is occupied by a large number of very small firms. The reason is that if the other firms are themselves quite large, even though smaller than M, they are more likely to have economies of scale and costs similar to M. Thus, although oligopoly may not be the most desirable market structure, it is usually much better than monopoly.

2. The *size and power of customers* is also relevant, because the existence of large, powerful buyers

can put a damper on the market power of a potentially monopolistic seller.

3. The market's **entry barriers** are quite important. Entry barriers are conditions that make entry into the market by a new competitor significantly more costly and risky. If a market has low entry barriers, and a powerful firm in the market earns very high returns by using its power to charge high prices, the high returns will attract new competition to the market that will diminish the dominant firm's power. High entry barriers, on the other hand, provide substantial insulation for the powerful firm so that it can fully exploit its market power. Examples of entry barriers include excess production capacity in the market, higher costs of capital for potential competitors than for the dominant firm, strong customer preferences for brands produced by the dominant firm, important technology or know-how that is protected by patents or by trade secret law, complex distribution channels, and so forth. Entry barriers are not necessarily good or bad; they are just conditions that may be relevant. It also should be noted that some entry barriers are inevitable, whereas some can be intentionally erected by a dominant firm. Although the importance of entry barriers has long been recognized, in recent years some authorities have come to view them as even more important to the question of market power than the internal composition of the market.

4. In addition to market share and other structural factors, the *dynamics* of the market can also be relevant to the question of how much power a firm has. For instance, if the market is characterized by rapidly developing technology, or if total market demand is expanding rapidly, it will be much harder for a firm to hold on to its dominant position for very long.

Defining the Relevant Market
Before seeking to determine whether a firm has overwhelming power, it is necessary to define the relevant market. Essentially, the process of market definition involves an attempt to identify a category of business transactions that accurately reflects the operation of competitive forces. A market can be thought of as the context within which competitive forces can be measured with reasonable accuracy. Any market must be defined in terms of two elements: (1) a particular product or service, or some grouping of products or services, and (2) a geographic area.

Product Market
Suppose that M Company is charged with monopolizing the market for the sale of zippers in the United States. Most of M's zippers are sold to clothing manufacturers, but some are sold to fabric stores and other retail outlets for resale to consumers. M produces 90 percent of the zippers sold in the United States. If "zippers" is the proper market definition, M's market share almost certainly demonstrates overwhelming market power. M argues, however, that zippers actually face stiff competition from buttons, snaps, hooks, and Velcro, and that the 90 percent figure does not accurately portray M's power. If buttons, snaps, hooks, and Velcro are included in the market definition, let us suppose that M's share of this larger "clothing fastener" market will be only 23 percent, a figure that certainly does not indicate overwhelming power.

The approach that most courts have taken to such a problem is to look first at the **cross elasticity of demand** among the products in question. The term describes the concept of interchangeability. If there is a substantial degree of cross elasticity of demand between two or more products, they usually will be treated as occupying the same product market. In other words, if the evidence indicates that a substantial portion of customers view two products as being reasonable substitutes for one another, a court is likely to treat the products as being part of a single market.

The evidence in such a case, like so many others, will usually not be very "neat." It probably will show that zippers are preferred by most customers for particular uses, and that these customers are willing to pay significantly more for zippers than other fasteners for these uses. Buttons are probably preferred for certain other uses, snaps for others, and Velcro for still others. For some uses, two or more types of fasteners may be viewed as basically equivalent, and customers may choose solely on the basis of price. Courts necessarily must employ some fairly rough approximations in such cases. Thus, if the evidence convinces a court that a substantial body of customers views two or more products as reasonably interchangeable for a substantial number of important uses, they probably will be included in a single product market. It is also possible, of course, that the evidence will justify a conclusion that fasteners for one particular use constitute a separate market, and that one or more other markets exist for other uses. This conclusion is likely only if the use is quite distinctive from other uses and the volume of business for this use is very substantial.

Another factor that sometimes is relevant to the process of product market definition is **cross elasticity of supply.** This refers to the relative ease or difficulty with which producers of related products may respond to increases in demand. Suppose, for example, that many customers view buttons and zippers as basically interchangeable for certain important uses. Thus, there may be a high degree of cross elasticity of *demand.* However, all button manufacturers are operating at close to their production capacity, and the building of additional button-making facilities is very costly and time-consuming. Therefore, if M raises the price of zippers substantially and many customers would consider switching to buttons, button manufacturers cannot absorb the additional demand. These zipper customers will have to keep buying zippers at a higher cost. Button makers will not build additional capacity unless they think that zipper prices will remain high for the foreseeable future, so they could count on the additional demand for buttons for a long enough time to justify the investment in new button-making capacity. Thus, even though *demand* cross elasticity may be relatively high, there is low *supply* cross elasticity, and courts will probably treat zippers and buttons as two separate markets. It is also true that high cross elasticity of supply can support a conclusion that two products should be in the same market even though there is currently a low degree of demand cross elasticity. Suppose, for example, that most customers view zippers and Velcro as not being interchangeable for a particular use. However, if a price increase for zippers causes many customers to look for a substitute, and if Velcro manufacturers could modify their product easily and inexpensively so that it would be a reasonable zipper substitute for this particular use, zippers and Velcro may be treated as one market.

Geographic Market

Depending on the situation, the relevant geographic market can be local, regional, national, or international. It represents the area within which buyers can reasonably be expected to seek alternative sources of supply. Retail geographic markets tend to be smaller than wholesale markets, which tend to be smaller than manufacturing markets, although there are many exceptions to this generalization. The factor that usually determines the size of a geographic market is the relative cost of searching for and shipping products from more distant geographic locations. When we speak of relative cost, we mean relative to the cost of the product itself. Buyers obviously will spend more time and money searching for better deals and shipping from more distant places when the desired purchase is 100 million computer chips than when it is a loaf of bread.

Intent to Monopolize

If a firm has overwhelming market power and thus is a monopolist, is there automatically a violation of Section 2 of the Sherman Act? Or must something else be proved? The answer is that the evidence must also demonstrate that the dominant firm had an intent to monopolize, that is, that it willfully acquired or maintained its monopoly power. This obviously means that there can be legal monopolies. For example, a monopoly is legal if it exists solely because of lawful patents or trade secrets, or because economies of scale are so large that the market will support only one profitable firm.

As in other areas of law, intent is inferred from conduct. In the case of monopolization, courts usually will infer an intent to monopolize only if the dominant firm has engaged in *predatory* conduct, that is, conduct which is aimed at inflicting economic harm on one or more other firms for reasons that are not related to greater efficiency or better performance. There are two very general categories of predatory behavior: predatory pricing and nonprice predation.

Predatory pricing is usually found where the dominant firm has persistently sold at prices below its average variable cost. Such pricing is viewed as predatory because it cannot be justified by a legitimate profit motive; while these prices are being charged, it is a money-losing proposition for the dominant firm. Instead, predatory pricing can only pay off for the dominant firm if it permits that firm to maintain its monopoly position so that it can later recover its losses by charging very high prices and earning monopoly profits. Predatory pricing can be used to drive another firm out of the market, although this is so costly for the dominant firm and has such uncertain long-term payoffs for that firm that it may not happen very often. Strategic predatory pricing can also be used on a periodic basic to discourage other firms from entering the market, or to send a clear signal to smaller firms in the market that they had better not engage in aggressive price competition. Predatory pricing for these purposes is probably more common than for the purpose of actually driving a competitor out.

Nonprice predation is probably more common than any kind of predatory pricing because it does not cost the dominant firm as much. Most forms of nonprice predation are aimed at increasing the costs of competitors or increasing entry barriers for potential competitors. A few examples are (1) tying up customers with long-term contracts that are not justified by cost savings, so that it is much more difficult for existing and potential competitors to engage in a fair

contest for those customers; (2) taking away key employees from a smaller competitor; (3) falsely disparaging the products of smaller competitors; (4) forcing smaller firms into completely unjustified lawsuits and administrative proceedings because the costs of such proceedings hurt the smaller firms more than the dominant firm; and (5) various forms of sabotage. Some kinds of nonprice predation may violate other laws as well, but many kinds do not.

The following case illustrates a form of nonprice predation that the U.S. Supreme Court found sufficient to fulfill the intent requirement of Section 2.

Aspen Skiing Co. v. Aspen Highlands Skiing Corp.

U.S. Supreme Court, 105 S.Ct. 2847 (1985)

The plaintiff, Aspen Highlands Skiing Corp. (Highlands), and the defendant, Aspen Skiing Co. (Ski Co.), were involved in the business of operating downhill skiing facilities in the Aspen, Colorado, area. There are four major mountain facilities in the area, and most customers prefer a ticket that permits them to use all four facilities. Because of this customer preference, the companies operating the facilities at the four mountains had for several years cooperated in offering an "all-Aspen" ticket that would permit customers to use any of the four facilities. Although the four facilities were originally developed by separate firms, over a period of years Ski Co. acquired ownership of three of these facilities. The fourth was owned and operated by Highlands. After several years of cooperating to the extent necessary to offer an all-Aspen ticket because of strong customer demand for such a ticket, Ski Co. stopped the practice and began offering only a ticket that permitted access to its three facilities. Highlands suffered substantial economic damage as a result, because there was not a great demand for a ticket to just its one

mountain. The skiing school operated by Highlands, which was generally recognized as the best in the area, also lost a great deal of business because of the termination of the all-Aspen ticket program.

Highlands sued Ski Co., alleging illegal monopolization in violation of Section 2 of the Sherman Act. Based upon a jury verdict, the trial court found that Aspen Ski Co. had a monopoly in the market for downhill skiing facilities in the Aspen area, and that its refusal to deal with Highlands demonstrated the requisite intent to monopolize. Highlands was awarded a judgment of $7.5 million (after trebling). The court of appeals affirmed. The only issue presented to the Supreme Court was whether the evidence was sufficient for an inference of intent to monopolize.

Stevens, Justice:

Ski Co. contends that even a firm with monopoly power has no duty to engage in joint marketing with a competitor, that a violation of §2 cannot be established without evidence of substantial exclusionary conduct, and that none of its activities can be characterized as exclusionary. . . . Ski Co. is surely correct in [stating] that even a firm with mo-

nopoly power has no general duty to engage in a joint marketing program with a competitor. . . . [In general, a firm is free to choose those with whom it wishes to deal, and this proposition also applies in most situations to a monopolist. In the case of a monopolist, however, this freedom is qualified somewhat, because a monopolist's refusal to deal may constitute evidence of unlawful exclusionary intent when it apparently was not motivated by efficiency concerns or other legitimate business justifications.]

In the actual case that we must decide, the monopolist did not merely reject a novel offer to participate in a cooperative venture that had been proposed by a competitor. Rather, the monopolist elected to make an important change in a pattern of distribution that had originated in a competitive market and had persisted for several years. The all-Aspen, 6-day ticket with revenues allocated on the basis of usage was first developed when three independent companies operated three different ski mountains in the Aspen area. It continued to provide a desirable option for skiers when the market was enlarged to include four mountains, and when the character of the market was changed by Ski Co.'s acquisition of monopoly power. Moreover, since the

(continues)

ASPEN SKIING CO. V. ASPEN HIGHLANDS SKIING CORP.

(*continued from previous page*)
record discloses that interchangeable tickets are used in other multimountain areas which apparently are competitive, it seems appropriate to infer that such tickets satisfy consumer demand in free competitive markets. . . .

Perhaps most significantly, however, Ski Co. did not persuade the jury that its conduct was justified by any normal business purpose. Ski Co. was apparently willing to forgo daily ticket sales. . . . [The evidence supports the jury's conclusion] that Ski Co. elected to forgo these short-run benefits because it was more interested in reducing competition in the Aspen market over the long run by harming its smaller competitor. . . . That conclu-

sion is strongly supported by Ski Co.'s failure to offer any efficiency justification whatever for its pattern of conduct. . . . Ski Co. claimed that usage could not be properly monitored. The evidence, however, established that Ski Co. itself monitored the use of the 3-area passes based on a count taken by lift operators, and distributed the revenues among its own mountains on that basis. Ski Co. contended that coupons were administratively cumbersome, and that the survey takers had been disruptive and their work inaccurate. Coupons, however, were no more burdensome than the credit cards accepted at Ski Co. ticket windows. Moreover, in other markets Ski Co. itself participated in interchange-

able lift tickets using coupons. As for the survey, its own manager testified that the problems were much overemphasized by Ski Co. officials, and were mostly resolved as they arose. Ski Co.'s explanation for its rejection of Highlands' offer to hire—at Highlands' own expense—a reputable national accounting firm to audit usage of the 4-area tickets at Highlands' mountain, was that there was no way to "control" the audit. . . .

Thus the evidence supports an inference that Ski Co. was not motivated by efficiency concerns and that it was willing to sacrifice short-run benefits and customer good will in exchange for a perceived long-run impact on its smaller rival. . . . Affirmed. ⚖

Comment Although the all-Aspen 4-mountain ticket program had been a legitimate joint venture because it resulted in a product for which there was strong demand and which could not have been offered by a single firm, the participants in such an arrangement would have to maintain independent control of their own pricing and be careful not to let the joint venture limit competition any more than necessary to achieve its legitimate goals. If the participants cooperated in pricing more than necessary to make the joint venture work, they could be guilty of violating the prohibition in Section 1 of the Sherman Act against "contracts, combinations, or conspiracies in restraint of trade."

MERGERS

Basic Principles

A **merger** between two companies clearly is a "combination" that could be scrutinized under Section 1 of the Sherman Act, which prohibits "contracts, combinations, and conspiracies in restraint of trade." In the early years after Congress passed the Sherman Act, however, the Supreme Court interpreted Section 1 in such a narrow way, at least as applied to mergers, that a merger could be illegal only if it occurred between two direct competitors with very large market shares. Because Congress intended antitrust law to reach some other mergers as well, in 1914 it enacted Section 7 of the Clayton Act. The statute was amended substantially by the Cellar-Kefauver Act of 1950, further demonstrating an intent to prevent mergers when the evidence indicates either actual harm to

competition or a substantial probability of such harm in the future. Another amendment in 1976 requires the participants in most mergers of any significant size to give both the Justice Department and the FTC advance notice of a merger so that these agencies can assess its possible effects before it occurs.

Section 7 prohibits one company from acquiring the stock or assets of another company if the acquisition is likely to diminish competition in a substantial way. Total or partial acquisitions are covered. Obviously, however, a stock acquisition cannot raise any concerns about harming competition unless the acquiring company obtains a large enough stake in the acquired company either to control it or at least to have substantial influence over its board of directors. Similarly, an acquisition of assets cannot harm competition unless the assets are very important to competition in the particular market, such as major manufacturing facilities, airline routes, critical patented technology, and so on.

So long as there is an acquisition of assets or shares of stock, the exact form of the transaction does not matter. It may be a "friendly" merger or consolidation negotiated between the boards of the two firms and then approved by shareholders, a "hostile" stock acquisition by means of a public tender offer, a series of stock purchases either on the open market or through negotiations with individual shareholders, or any other form.

In attempting to assess a merger's actual or probable effects on competition, a court will first define the relevant market or markets. This is done in exactly the same way as in a monopoly case. As we will see in our discussion of the different types of mergers, the question of market power is also very important in merger cases. It is important to note, however, that a merger does not have to result in market power that is even close to being monopolistic in order to be ruled illegal. Although substantial market power is necessary for substantial anticompetitive effects, that power does not have to be overwhelming for such effects to occur.

Another important point about the law in this area is that periodic political changes in Washington affect the enforcement and interpretation of Section 7 to a greater extent than the other antitrust laws. Although such changes affect antitrust law in general, private lawsuits are much less important as an enforcement tool in the case of mergers than in other areas of antitrust. Most challenges to mergers are made by either the Justice Department or the FTC, rather than by private plaintiffs. Thus, when the current political climate is relatively conservative and probusiness, the enforcement attitude toward mergers is likely to be quite lenient. On the other hand, when an administration is in power that distrusts large concentrations of economic power and does not really believe that most mergers contribute to economic efficiency, more mergers are usually challenged under Section 7. In recent times, the attitude toward mergers was rather strict between the mid-1950s and early 1970s. It was somewhat less strict during the remainder of the 1970s, and was quite lenient during the 1980s.

Types of Mergers

Mergers traditionally have been classified as horizontal, vertical, or conglomerate. A *horizontal merger* occurs if the two firms are competitors, and a *vertical*

merger occurs if one of the firms sells something that the other firm buys. Any other is a *conglomerate merger.* Although these classifications are useful to describe very broadly some relevant differences in the various factual settings in which mergers occur, the same basic test applies to all mergers: does the merger substantially diminish competition, or is it quite likely to do so in the future? Moreover, a merger may sometimes fit more than one category. For instance, in *Brown Shoe Co. v. United States,* 370 U.S. 294 (1962), the challenged merger had both horizontal and vertical aspects because each of the merging firms, Brown Shoe Co. and Kinney Shoe Co., was both a manufacturer *and* a retailer of shoes.

Horizontal Mergers

A merger between competitors poses the greatest danger to competition because the market has one less competitor. In assessing the impact of a **horizontal merger,** the courts usually emphasize the same general kinds of evidence that are important in measuring market power in a monopoly case.

Market Share. The *combined market share* of the merging firms is often the first thing the courts look at. During earlier periods when the attitude toward mergers was very strict, a number of them were challenged and ruled illegal when the combined market shares were under 10 percent and other evidence indicated a definite trend toward concentration of economic power in the relevant market. Today, however, a horizontal merger is not likely to get much attention under Section 7 unless the combined market share exceeds 30 percent.

Market Concentration. The *overall concentration of the market* is also important. In general, the more concentrated the market is at the time of the merger, the more likely it is that a questionable merger will be held illegal. Suppose, for example, that a merger occurs between two firms having market shares of 20 percent and 15 percent, and the remainder of the market consists of three other firms with shares of 25 percent, 20 percent, and 20 percent. This merger would be somewhat more likely to violate Section 7 than it would if the remainder of the market consisted of, say, six other firms with shares of approximately 11 percent each.

Acquisition by Leading Firm. In addition, if a single firm already dominates a market rather completely and there are no other firms that can come close to its resources and scale economies, *any* acquisition of a competitor by the *dominant firm* runs a great risk of being held illegal.

Entry Barriers. If the market is characterized by high entry barriers, a borderline merger is much more likely to be ruled illegal, and vice versa. Indeed, as we mentioned in the discussion of monopoly, an increasing number of authorities have begun to view a market's entry barriers as being at least as important to the market power question as the market's internal composition. One practical difficulty with this view, however, is that entry barriers usually are much more difficult to measure with any kind of precision than the market's internal structure.

Increased Risk of Collusion. Another relevant factor could be the existence of evidence indicating that collusion among competitors had been a problem in this market in the past, and that by further reducing the number of competitors this merger could make collusion even easier in the future. In general, the lower the number of competitors, the easier it is for them to put together and maintain a price-fixing conspiracy or other collusive anticompetitive arrangement.

Other Factors. Other factors can also be important to the evaluation of horizontal mergers. For example, a firm with 15 or 20 percent of a market ordinarily could acquire a firm with a 2 or 3 percent share without much fear of legal challenge. Suppose, however, that the smaller firm had recently developed patented technology of major significance to future competition in the market, or that it had traditionally been a very efficient "maverick" and frequently had led the way in vigorous price competition. In such a case, the acquisition would run a significantly higher risk of being challenged successfully under Section 7.

Vertical Mergers

Although a **vertical merger** is much less likely to harm competition than a horizontal one, it is possible for such a merger to diminish competition. Essentially, a vertical merger creates **vertical integration,** which occurs when one firm operates at more than one level of the distribution chain for a product. (Obviously, a firm can also become vertically integrated, without a merger, by creating new facilities to operate at another level.) Suppose that S Company is an important producer of a key component or ingredient used by B Company in manufacturing an end product, and that S acquires B.

S would be using the merger to vertically integrate "downstream." If B had acquired S, B would be vertically integrating "upstream."

The Debate. There has been a long-standing debate about the merits of vertical integration. Some experts have viewed vertical integration as being primarily a vehicle for greater efficiency. Others have viewed it as being primarily a tool for locking up markets and supply sources, raising entry barriers, and making collusion easier. Still others have viewed vertical integration as something of a "mixed bag" of economic effects that is exceptionally difficult to sort out. Currently, the prevailing attitude among a majority of economists and enforcement officials toward vertical integration is basically a favorable one. Not everyone shares that view, however, and the pendulum of expert opinion could swing in the other direction at some point in the future.

Efficiency Argument. Undoubtedly, vertical integration can create efficiencies, primarily by saving transaction costs. If the vertically integrated firm ("S-B") is managed properly, it usually should be able to transfer goods and services from one level to another more cheaply than if it were two separate firms operating at the two levels. Being part of one company ideally should permit better coordination and planning. Having an assured source of supply for B and an assured market for S should permit better inventory control. This, in turn, should produce lower carrying costs by avoiding excess inventory and lower delay-related costs by reducing instances of shortage. Vertical integration also can reduce the various kinds of selling costs between S and B, such as those associated with promotion, sales personnel, and contract drafting and monitoring. Opponents of vertical integration reply that, even if these efficiencies are created, the cost savings are not going to be passed along to consumers unless competition in the downstream market is vigorous. They also argue that many of the same efficiencies can be achieved through relatively long-term contracts without creating the same degree of risk for competition.

Entry Barriers. Some observers argue that vertical integration can increase entry barriers and thus insulate firms in the market from new competition. The reason, they say, is that a firm thinking about entering a market in which the major competitors are vertically integrated will have to come into the market at two levels simultaneously, which is more costly and difficult. Those favoring vertical integration, however, reply that new entry into such a market is more difficult simply because the vertically integrated firms in the market are more efficient, and that it is more difficult to compete against efficient firms with low costs.

Making Collusion Easier. Some critics of vertical integration also claim that it can make collusion easier for the vertically integrated firms, especially those at the "upstream" level (in our example, S's level). This can happen, they claim, because removing the layer of independent buyers from the downstream level does away with an important set of "watchdogs" on the upstream firms. Those with a favorable view of vertical integration often admit that this is a possibility, but point out that it is likely to happen only if there are very few firms at both levels and if most of these large firms are already vertically integrated. Besides, they say, antitrust enforcers can just watch out for the collusion and take action if they find it.

Current Law. Because of today's generally favorable attitude toward vertical integration, a vertical merger will usually be legal. A successful challenge to such a merger is likely only if most of the firms in the market are already vertically integrated, this vertically combined market is a highly concentrated oligopoly, and both S and B have large market shares. It is mainly the fear of collusion being made easier in this kind of situation that creates the risk of a successful legal challenge.

Conglomerate Mergers

Mergers without horizontal or vertical characteristics are usually called **conglomerate mergers.** Although several grounds for striking down conglomerate mergers have been employed in the past, such a merger creates very little legal risk today. About the only situation where such a risk exists now is in the following circumstances: (1) X enters the widget market in the western U.S. by acquiring Y, a major producer of widgets in that area. (2) That market was already a highly concentrated oligopoly. (3) For a substantial period of time before the merger, X had a special incentive to enter the market and the resources to do it. Other potential new entrants did not have similar incentives. This special incentive may have existed because the widget market was an unusually attractive extension of X's product line, or perhaps because X already sold widgets elsewhere and this was an ideal geographic expansion. In either case, X could get into the market and compete more easily and cheaply than other new firms because of

the product or geographic relationship. (4) The western widget market had high entry barriers that discouraged other firms from entering, but that were not so high as to discourage X because of its large resources and special incentive. (5) Prior to the merger, the major firms in the western widget market knew that X was a probable future entrant.

In this situation, the presence of X "on the edge" of the western widget market prior to the merger was probably having a beneficial effect by causing widget makers in the market to keep their prices lower than they would have otherwise, in the hope of discouraging X from actually entering. When X enters, this beneficial "edge effect" is removed. If X had entered by building new facilities, or by acquiring a very small firm in the market and expanding it into a major competitor, X's entry would have positive effects that would offset the removal of its former "edge effect." But when X enters by acquiring a firm that is already a major player, there is nothing positive to counteract the negative, and the merger may be illegal.

Failing Company Defense

Even if a merger is one that normally would violate Section 7 of the Clayton Act, proof of the *failing company defense* prevents a violation. This defense exists if one of the merging firms probably will not be able to meet its financial obligations in the near future; (2) it appears unlikely that the failing firm will be able to reorganize successfully under Chapter 11 of the Bankruptcy Code and emerge as a viable company; and (3) the failing firm has made a good faith, but unsuccessful, effort to obtain a merger offer from another firm that would pose less danger to competition than does the merger being challenged.

Merger Guidelines

The Justice Department's Antitrust Division first issued Merger Guidelines in 1968. The guidelines, which are also followed by the FTC, were completely rewritten in 1982, and again revised slightly in 1984. These guidelines are not binding law but do provide business with a valuable planning tool by specifying the circumstances in which the two agencies can ordinarily be expected to challenge a merger.

One of the key innovations of the current guidelines is the use of the Herfindahl-Hirschman Index (HHI) for measuring the relative level of economic concentration in a market. This index involves squaring the market share of each firm in the market and then adding the squares. Thus, a market with 10 firms of equal size would have an HHI of 1,000. The guidelines consider a market with an HHI under 1,000 to be unconcentrated, between 1,000 and 1,800 to be moderately concentrated, and over 1,800 to be concentrated. The greater the level of concentration in the relevant market, the more likely it is that a merger will be challenged and that it will be ruled illegal.

The following Supreme Court decision is from a case involving a horizontal merger between two relatively large competitors. It is an important decision because, among other things, it illustrates how evidence of surrounding economic circumstances may convince a court that such a merger is legal.

UNITED STATES V. GENERAL DYNAMICS CORP.

U.S. Supreme Court, 415 U.S. 486 (1974)

Material Service Corp. owned Freeman Coal Mining Co. In 1954 Material Service began purchasing the stock of United Electric Coal Co., and by 1959 had acquired effective control of United. General Dynamics Corp. then acquired Material Service Corp. Subsequently, the government sued General Dynamics, claiming that the merger of Freeman and United violated Section 7 of the Clayton Act.

Freeman and United together accounted for about 23 percent of total coal production in the state of Illinois. If the geographic market was defined more broadly as the Eastern Interior Coal Province, one of the country's four major coal distribution areas, the combined share would have been about 12 percent. The district court found that the merger did not violate Section 7, and the government appealed to the Supreme Court. The Supreme Court pointed out that such market share figures likely would lead to a ruling of illegality except for the existence of other important factors. These other economic factors caused the court to approve the merger regardless of the market shares.

Stewart, Justice:

. . . Much of the District Court's opinion was devoted to a description of the changes that have affected the coal industry since World War II. . . . To a growing extent since 1954, the electric utility industry has become the mainstay of coal consumption. While electric utilities consumed only 15.76% of the coal produced nationally in 1947, their share of total consumption increased every year thereafter, and in 1968 amounted to more than 59% of all the coal consumed throughout the Nation.

To an increasing degree, nearly all coal sold to utilities is transferred under long-term requirements contracts, under which coal producers promise to meet utilities' coal consumption requirements for a fixed period of time, and at predetermined prices. . . .

Because of these fundamental changes in the structure of the market for coal, the District Court was justified in viewing the statistics relied on by the Government as insufficient to sustain its case. Evidence of past production does not, as a matter of logic, necessarily give a proper picture of a company's future ability to compete. In most situations, of course, the unstated assumption is that a company that has maintained a certain share of a market in the recent past will be in a position to do so in the immediate future. . . .

In the coal market, however, statistical evidence of coal *production* was of considerably less significance. The bulk of the coal produced is delivered under long-term requirements contracts, and such sales thus do not represent the exercise of competitive power but rather the obligation to fulfill previously negotiated contracts at a previously fixed price. The focus of competition in a given time-frame is not on the disposition of coal already produced but on the procurement of new long-tem supply contracts. In this situation, a company's past ability to produce is of limited significance, since it is in a position to offer for sale neither its past production nor the bulk of the coal it is presently capable of producing, which is typically already committed under a long-term supply contract. A more significant indicator of a company's power effectively to compete with other companies lies in the state of a company's uncommitted reserves of recoverable coal. . . .

The testimony and exhibits in the District Court revealed that United Electric's coal reserve prospects were "unpromising." United's relative position of strength in reserves was considerably weaker than its past and current ability to produce. While United ranked fifth among Illinois coal producers in terms of annual production, it was 10th in reserve holdings, and controlled less than 1% of the reserves held by coal producers in Illinois, Indiana, and western Kentucky. Many of the reserves held by United had already been depleted, at the time of trial, forcing the closing of some of United's midwest mines. Even more significantly, the District Court found that of the 52,033,304 tons of currently mineable reserves in Illinois, Indiana, and Kentucky controlled by United, only four million tons had not already been committed under long-term contracts. United was found to be facing

(continues)

UNITED STATES V. GENERAL DYNAMICS CORP.

(*continued from previous page*)
the future with relatively depleted resources at its disposal, and with the vast majority of those resources already committed under contracts allowing no further adjustment in price. In addition, the District Court found that "United Electric has neither the possibility of acquiring more [reserves] nor the ability to develop deep coal reserves," and thus was not in a position to increase its reserves to replace those already depleted or committed.

Viewed in terms of present and future reserve prospects—and thus in terms of probable future ability to compete—rather than in terms of past production, the District Court held that United Electric was a far less significant factor in the coal market than the Government contended or the production statistics seemed to indicate. While the company had been and remained a "highly profitable" and efficient producer of relatively large amounts of coal, its current and future power to compete for subsequent long-term contracts was severely limited by its scarce uncommitted resources. Irrespective of the company's size when viewed as a producer, its weakness as a competitor was properly analyzed by the District Court and fully substantiated that court's conclusion that [the merger] would not "substantially . . . lessen competition. . . ."

Affirmed. ⟁

HORIZONTAL RESTRAINTS OF TRADE

In examining the law pertaining to monopolies and mergers, we were concerned primarily with market structure and only secondarily with specific instances of conduct. We now turn our attention to particular types of business behavior. Market structure continues to be relevant here, but its role is a secondary one.

Our first inquiry into the behavioral side of antitrust is **horizontal restraints of trade**—arrangements between two or more competitors that suppress or limit competition. The applicable statute is Section 1 of the Sherman Act which, as stated earlier, prohibits "contracts, combinations, or conspiracies in restraint of trade."

The Requirement of Collusion

Section 1 of the Sherman Act can be applied only if there was **collusion** between two or more independent entities. Many different terms are used to describe the concept: joint action, concerted action, agreement, combination, conspiracy, and others. As is true of all things that must be proved in the law, the collusion requirement is sometimes obvious and sometimes not. An example of a case in which the requirement obviously was present is *National Society of Professional Engineers v. United States*, 435 U.S. 679 (1978), in which the Court held illegal an ethical rule of the society that prohibited competitive bidding by its 69,000 members. The collusion requirement was so obviously satisfied that it was not even an issue. In such a case, even if the association has been incorporated and thus is a single independent entity, its rules and other actions are in reality the collective actions of its members who explicitly or implicitly granted their approval.

If collusion is not obvious, courts normally have to rely on circumstantial evidence to decide the question. Evidence of any *communications* among the parties can be very important, but such evidence may or may not be strong enough to permit the fact finder to conclude that collusion has taken place. If there is no such evidence, or if it is not sufficient to prove collusion, there must at least be evidence demonstrating that the parties had an *opportunity to conspire*. To establish a circumstantial case of collusion, it usually is also necessary to prove *uniformity of action* among the defendants. Thus, a court is quite unlikely to find that collusion occurred unless the defendants acted in a very similar fashion in pricing, refusing to deal with another party such as a customer or supplier, or other important matter.

It is not enough, however, merely to prove that the firms did about the same thing, because there can be many legitimate reasons for such an occurrence. This is especially true in a market with a relatively small number of firms. In an oligopoly, for example, it sometimes is inevitable that several companies will make similar pricing moves within a relatively short time span, primarily because they all know what the others are doing and the actions of each one are quite important. In other situations, there also may be reasonable explanations for uniformity; for instance, the same external factor such as a supply shortage may have affected all firms simultaneously. If there is substantial uniformity, however, without any legitimate explanation, the situation is suspicious and the firms' parallel conduct is fairly strong evidence of collusion. Also, the greater the *degree* of uniformity, the more strongly this evidence points toward collusion.

The Rule of Reason

Assuming that collusion has been proved, the defendants' action violates Section 1 only if it "restrains trade." What this means is that their conduct must have suppressed or limited competition. Relatively early in the history of the Sherman Act, in *Standard Oil Co. v. United States,* 221 U.S. 1 (1911), the Supreme Court held that Section 1 does not forbid *all* arrangements that limit competition. If the statute had been interpreted in a literal, all-inclusive fashion, it could have produced strange and inefficient results such as prohibiting the formation of partnerships, corporations, and other business organizations because they involve the combination of individuals who might otherwise be competitors. Instead, the Court adopted the so-called **rule of reason,** under which arrangements are illegal only if they "unreasonably" restrict competition.

The next question, of course, is how do the courts decide whether a particular arrangement is reasonable or unreasonable? In essence, the rule of reason involves an examination of the *purpose* and the *effect* of the conduct being challenged.

Purpose

The firms will always claim that their purpose was legitimate—i.e., not anticompetitive. They may insist, for example, that their motive was to promote ethical conduct in their industry, prevent fraudulent practices by their suppliers or customers, encourage product standardization or safety, or any one of many other lawful purposes. The court will examine all pertinent evidence before deciding whether the defendants are to be believed, or whether their predominant motive was to restrict competition. If the court concludes that their primary motive was to limit competition, the arrangement is illegal if there is a likelihood of even a small restriction on competition. If, on the other hand, the court decides that their primary motive was a legitimate one, the court

will find a violation of Section 1 only if the evidence indicates that competition will be diminished in a substantial way. There is actually something of a rough sliding scale. The greater the apparent bad effect on competition, the less weight the court will give to any legitimate motive.

Effect on Competition

Perhaps the most important factor in the analysis of an arrangement's effect on competition is the collective *market power* of the group. Market power is evaluated in the same way here as in the more structurally oriented situations of monopoly and merger. A group's aggregate market power does not have to be huge for an arrangement to violate the rule of reason, but if the group's purpose was apparently all right, its power must be substantial enough to convince a court that serious anticompetitive effects are likely to result.

Another factor that often plays a part in the court's analysis is the existence of a *less restrictive alternative.* Thus, if the evidence establishes that the firms could have achieved their claimed objectives by using some other arrangement that would have posed less danger to competition, a court is somewhat more likely to find a violation of Section 1. The existence of a less restrictive alternative does not automatically cause their arrangement to be illegal, but it does tip the scales a bit in that direction, for two reasons. First, it demonstrates that the firms caused a greater negative effect on competition than they really had to. Second, such evidence may even cause a court to view their alleged motive with more suspicion.

If evidence of market power and other relevant factors indicates that a substantial negative effect on competition is possible, the legality of the arrangement sometimes can be saved by clear evidence that it also will have *offsetting procompetitive effects.* These are just positives to offset the negatives, and usually involve some aspect of the arrangement that will improve the efficiency of the market. The court will engage in a rough balancing of these effects against the anticompetitive ones and decide which seem to predominate. Examples of procompetitive effects include creating a new kind of market that otherwise would not exist, stimulating competition by bringing more transactions into the market, improving the quality or quantity of information available to buyers and sellers, and so on.

The following landmark Supreme Court case illustrates most of these aspects of rule-of-reason analysis.

You will be able to see the Court examining (1) motives; (2) market power (although it does not use this term); (3) the fact that the scope of the arrangement seemed to be limited so that it was not any more restrictive than it had to be; and (4) what the judges viewed as offsetting procompetitive effects brought about by taking quite a few transactions from a few large dealers and bringing them into the organized market where information was more accurate and up-to-date and trading more open and competitive.

CHICAGO BOARD OF TRADE V. UNITED STATES

U.S. Supreme Court, 246 U.S. 231 (1918)

 In the late 1800s and early 1900s Chicago was the leading grain market in the world, and the Board of Trade was the commercial center through which most of the trading in grain was done. Its 1,600 members included brokers, commission merchants, dealers, millers, manufacturers of corn products, and grain elevator owners. Grain transactions usually took one of three forms: (1) spot sales—sales of grain already in Chicago in railroad cars or elevators ready for immediate delivery; (2) future sales—agreements for delivery of grain at a later time; (3) sales "to arrive"—agreements for delivery of grain which was already in transit to Chicago or which was to be shipped almost immediately from other parts of the Midwest.

On each business day, sessions of the Board of Trade were held at which all bids and sales were publicly made. Spot sales and future sales were made during the regular session between 9:30 a.m. and 1:15 p.m. Special sessions, referred to as the "Call," were held immediately after the close of the regular session. During the Call, which usually lasted about 30 minutes, members of the Board of Trade engaged only in "to arrive" transactions. These transactions usually involved purchases from farmers or small dealers in one of the Midwestern states. Participation in the Call session was limited to members, but they could trade on behalf of nonmembers if they wished. Members also could make any of the

three types of transaction privately with each other at any place, either during or after board sessions. Members could engage privately in any type of transaction at any time with nonmembers, but not on the board's premises.

With respect to "to arrive" transactions, a particular market price would be established by the public trading during the short Call session. Until 1906, however, members were not bound by that price during the remainder of the day. In that year the Board of Trade adopted what was known as the "Call rule." The rule, which applied only to "to arrive" transactions, required members to use the market price established at the public Call session when they bought grain in private transactions between the end of that session and 9:30 the next morning.

The government filed suit in federal district court, claiming that the Call rule violated Section 1 of the Sherman Act. The board contended that the purpose and effect of the rule was to bring more of the "to arrive" transactions into the public market at the Call session. By bringing more of these transactions into the public market, the board felt that four or five large grain warehouse owners in Chicago would no longer have such a controlling grip over "to arrive" transactions. The district court, however, ruled that evidence relating to the history and purpose of the rule was irrelevant and issued an injunction against the operation of the rule. The Board of Trade then appealed to the U.S. Supreme Court.

Brandeis, Justice:

. . . Every agreement concerning trade, every regulation of trade, restrains. To bind, to restrain, is of their very essence. The true test of legality is whether the restraint imposed is such as merely regulates and perhaps thereby promotes competition or whether it is such as may suppress or even destroy competition. To determine that question the court must ordinarily consider the facts peculiar to the business to which the restraint is applied; its condition before and after the restraint was imposed; the nature of the restraint and its effect, actual or probable. The history of the restraint, the evil believed to exist, the reason for adopting the particular remedy, the purpose or end sought to be attained, are all relevant facts. This is not because a good intention will save an otherwise objectionable regulation or the reverse; but because knowledge of intent may help the court to interpret facts and to predict consequences. The District Court erred, therefore, in striking from the [Board's] answer allegations concerning evidence on that subject. But the evidence admitted makes it clear that the rule was a reasonable regulation of business consistent with the provisions of the AntiTrust Law.

First: The nature of the rule: The restriction was upon the period of price-making. It required members to desist from further price-making after the close of the Call until 9:30 a.m. the next business day: but there was no restriction upon the sending out of bids after close of the Call. Thus it required members who desired to buy grain "to
(continues)

CHICAGO BOARD OF TRADE v. UNITED STATES

(continued from previous page)
arrive" to make up their minds before the close of the Call how much they were willing to pay during the interval before the next session of the Board. The rule made it to their interest to attend the Call; and if they did not fill their wants by purchases there, to make the final bid high enough to enable them to purchase from country dealers.

Second: The scope of the rule: It is restricted in operation to grain "to arrive." It applies only to a small part of the grain shipped from day to day to Chicago, and to an even smaller part of the day's sales: members were left free to purchase grain already in Chicago from anyone at any price throughout the day. It applies only during a small part of the business day; members were left free to purchase during the sessions of the Board grain "to arrive," at any price, from members anywhere and from nonmembers anywhere except on the premises of the Board. It applied only to grain shipped to Chicago: members were left free to purchase at any price throughout the day from either members or nonmembers, grain "to arrive" at any other market. Country dealers and farmers had available in practically every part of the territory called tributary to Chicago some other market for grain "to arrive."

Thus Missouri, Kansas, Nebraska, and parts of Illinois are also tributary to St. Louis; Nebraska and Iowa, to Omaha; Minnesota, Iowa, South and North Dakota, to Minneapolis or Duluth; Wisconsin and parts of Iowa and of Illinois, to Milwaukee; Ohio, Indiana and parts of Illinois, to Cincinnati; Indiana and parts of Illinois, to Louisville.

Third: The effects of the rule: As it applies to only a small part of the grain shipped to Chicago and to that only during a part of the business day and does not apply at all to grain shipped to other markets, the rule had no appreciable effect on general market prices; nor did it materially affect the total volume of grain coming to Chicago. But within the narrow limits of its operation the rule helped to improve market conditions thus:

(a) It created a public market for grain "to arrive." Before its adoption, bids were made privately. Men had to buy and sell without adequate knowledge of actual market conditions. This was advantageous to all concerned, but particularly so to country dealers and farmers.

(b) It brought into the regular market hours of the Board sessions more of the trading in grain "to arrive."

(c) It brought buyers and sellers into more direct relations; because on the Call they gathered together for a free and open interchange of bids and offers.

(d) It distributed the business in grain "to arrive" among a far larger number of Chicago receivers and commission merchants than had been the case there before.

(e) It increased the number of country dealers engaging in this branch of the business; supplied them more regularly with bids from Chicago; and also increased the number of bids received by them from competing markets.

(f) It eliminated risks necessarily incident to a private market, and thus enabled country dealers to do business on a smaller margin. In that way the rule made it possible for them to pay more to farmers without raising the price to consumers.

(g) It enabled country dealers to sell some grain "to arrive" which they would otherwise have been obliged either to ship to Chicago commission merchants or to sell for "future delivery."

(h) It enabled those grain merchants of Chicago who sell to millers and exporters to trade on a smaller margin and, by paying more for grain or selling it for less, to make the Chicago market more attractive for both shippers and buyers of grain. . . .

The decree of the District Court is reversed with directions to dismiss the [government's complaint]. ⚖

The Per Se Rule

Also relatively early in the history of the Sherman Act, the Supreme Court recognized that certain types of practices are obviously anticompetitive and do not really have any redeeming social virtues. In such a case, the **per se rule** applies. This means that, once the particular type of activity is identified as one that falls within a per se category, it is automatically illegal and the inquiry ends. Of the various horizontal restraints of trade, price fixing, market division, and boycotts are per se illegal. It is very important to understand, however, that the per se rule has its greatest impact in situations where the challenged activity can be easily labeled as price fixing, market division, or a boycott. If there is a close question whether the arrangement should be characterized in this way, the court must analyze its purpose and effect in order to decide how to label it. This analysis is basically the same as in a rule-of-reason case.

Price Fixing

Price fixing among competitors is per se illegal. This activity occurs when two or more competitors agree explicitly to charge a specific price, or to set a price floor, but many other arrangements can also constitute price fixing because they substantially interfere with the price-setting function of the market. Some examples include agreements or understandings among competitors to (1) not submit competitive bids; (2) rotate the privilege of being low bidder on contracts; (3) artificially manipulate supply or demand in a way that affects price substantially; (4) not advertise prices; (5) not grant certain discounts; (6) maintain uniformity on a particular term that constitutes a component of price, such as shipping or credit charges; (7) keep prices within a particular range; and even (8) maintain a *ceiling* on prices.

Many other joint arrangements may have an arguable effect on the market's pricing mechanism. If the court is convinced that the parties' main purpose is to suppress price competition, it will probably call the arrangement price fixing and find it illegal. As mentioned earlier, however, if there is significant doubt about the question, a court will probably engage in a rule-of-reason type analysis, regardless of whether it uses that phrase.

Market Division

Market division among competitors is also per se illegal, assuming that such division is found to be the primary objective of a particular arrangement. The same rule can be applied to market division agreements involving *potential* competitors making decisions about entering new markets. Market division arrangements can take at least three forms: (1) in a *territorial* market division, the firms agree to refrain from competing with each other in designated geographic areas; (2) in a *customer allocation* arrangement, the firms assign particular customers or classes of customers to each seller and agree not to solicit customers of another seller; (3) in a *product line* division, the firms agree to limit their activities to particular types of products or services so as to avoid competing with each other.

Boycotts

A firm ordinarily has freedom to choose those with whom it will transact business. However, when two or more parties agree not to deal with some other party, antitrust problems arise. When the agreeing parties are competitors and their primary purpose apparently is to curtail competition, the resulting **boycott** is per se illegal. Two or more firms will violate Section 1, for example, if they agree to quit selling to a customer be-

cause the latter is trying to integrate upstream and become their competitor. Likewise, a group of firms would be engaged in an illegal boycott if they agreed to stop selling to certain customers unless those customers quit buying from a competitor of those in the agreeing group. A similar violation would occur if the group agreed not to buy from a supplier unless that supplier refrained from selling to a competitor or potential competitor of the group. Boycotts are sometimes used to drive a firm out of a market, keep it from entering in the first place, or discipline a firm by "showing it who's boss" and thus convincing it to stop competing so aggressively.

Although labelling problems occur with respect to all of the per se categories, they seem to be especially troublesome in the case of boycotts. The reason is that there are many group activities that have legitimate reasons for existing, but that also may have the tendency to *exclude* other firms. Suppose for example, that many of the automotive repair businesses in Missouri, Kansas, and Oklahoma form an organization called the Midwest Auto Repair Association (MARA). The stated purposes of the group are to promote the auto repair business in various ways and encourage high ethical standards in the industry. Like any organization, MARA establishes rules for membership that might require such things as full-time participation in the auto repair business, a fee to cover the organization's costs, fewer than a specified number of verified customer complaints during a given period of time, and so on. Jones does not meet one of the requirements and is either denied membership initially or is forced out later. He claims that he has been the victim of a boycott.

There are many other examples. Similar problems can arise if a group of firms in the same industry tries to establish uniform product standards for the purpose of either safety or reducing customer confusion and dissatisfaction. One firm's product does not meet the standard and thus does not receive the approval of the group. The firm claims a boycott.

Yet another example arises where a group of firms pool their resources to develop a facility such as a research lab. This can be legitimate where the great cost, risk, and uncertainty of constructing a major facility or engaging in a particular undertaking is too much for a single firm. (This last example describes a "joint venture," which will be discussed shortly.) A competitor is not permitted to join the venture and claims a boycott.

When confronted with such claims, courts first look at the group's apparent *purpose*. If the primary purpose was to exclude others and achieve some restriction on competition, it will be per se illegal as a boycott. If the main purpose appears to have been a legitimate one, the court engages in a rule-of-reason type of analysis. The court will try to determine just how important it is for a firm to participate. (This is just another kind of inquiry into a group's collective market power.) If exclusion really does *not* harm a firm's ability to compete in the relevant market, the arrangement is legal. On the other hand, if participation *is* very important to a firm's ability to compete, the rules or restrictions that have the result of excluding others must be *reasonable*. To be reasonable, they must (1) have a logical relationship to the group's legitimate objectives, and (2) not exclude others any more than is necessary to accomplish those objectives.

Trade Associations

A trade association is a loosely knit organization of firms with mutual interests. Its membership usually includes firms within the same industry, but sometimes also includes suppliers or customers of these firms, and perhaps others with an interest in the field, such as consultants. The mere existence of a trade association presents no antitrust problems—most industries have some type of trade association. Moreover, the activities of these associations usually are legitimate and socially useful. Associations in some industries have been instrumental, for example, in setting product safety standards, maintaining ethical norms, providing arbitration or other procedures for resolving disputes between members, forming group self-insurance pools, and so on.

The problem with trade associations is that they can present very tempting opportunities for illegal group activities such as price fixing, market divisions, boycotts, or other arrangements that stifle competition. Members must be vigilant to ensure that the association's activities do not harm competition, and have all proposals reviewed by attorneys with antitrust expertise. If a firm believes that action about to be taken by the group is legally questionable, the firm should voice its dissent and not participate.

Joint Ventures

Although the term **joint venture** has no precise meaning, it has been likened to a partnership for a limited purpose. The joint research lab used earlier as an illustration is a type of joint venture. When two or more firms collaborate for some reason, their joint undertaking may or may not be a joint venture. The basic characteristics of a legitimate joint venture are (1) a partial pooling of resources by two or more firms, (2) a limited degree of integration of some aspect of the firms' operations, and (3) an intent to accomplish a defined business objective that could not be accomplished as efficiently (or at all) by a single firm. Situations in which joint ventures are commonly accepted as legitimate include those in which extremely large economies of scale, very high risks, or unusually extended long-term payoffs are involved, or where the nature of the product is such that it cannot be produced or marketed efficiently without collaboration between two or more firms.

Joint ventures usually do not violate the antitrust laws, but they can do so on occasion. Section 1 of the Sherman Act is the primarily applicable statute, and joint ventures are normally judged under the rule of reason. If formation of the joint venture involves an asset or stock acquisition, Section 7 of the Clayton Act also can be applied, although the legal standards for joint ventures are basically the same under both statutes.

The risk of illegality obviously is greater when actual or potential competitors are involved. In addition, certain kinds of activities are more likely to limit competition than those involving other kinds of activities. A joint venture might involve matters ranging along a continuum from basic research to applied research, product development, production, promotion and other marketing activities, selling, and finally, distribution. The risk of harm to competition, and thus the degree of scrutiny under the antitrust laws, increases as the activity moves along the continuum away from research. Joint ventures involving activities farther along the continuum, such as production, can be valid, but their justification must be stronger.

Assuming that the basic objectives of the joint venture are legitimate, three basic types of antitrust questions can still be raised. First, the formation of a joint venture occasionally may create dangers to competition that probably will not be outweighed by increased efficiency or other positive effects. This may happen if the venture is just *too big*—that is, if it is larger than really necessary to accomplish its legitimate objectives. Second, even if the venture is not too large, it may include some *ancillary restriction* that limits competition among the participants more than necessary.

Even universities are subject to antitrust laws. Recently, the U.S. Department of Justice filed a civil suit charging a group of Ivy League schools and the Massachusetts Institute of Technology (M.I.T.) with price fixing. The basis for the charge was that these schools had operated what they called an "overlap group" for many years. Universities in the group had met periodically to discuss and reach consensus on the levels of financial aid to be given to eligible students who had applied to more than one of the schools, thus limiting competition among these schools for those students.

The U.S. Justice Department had additional evidence that the Ivy League schools, and sometimes M.I.T., also met separately outside the formal meetings of the overlap group to discuss planned tuition increases and faculty salaries, thus diminishing competition further in two separate markets.

All of the Ivy League universities charged with price fixing settled the case by agreeing to a federal court injunction prohibiting any such collusion in the future. M.I.T. did not join in the settlement, instead choosing to fight the charges in court. A federal district court found that M.I.T. was guilty of price fixing in violation of Sec. 1 of the Sherman Act and issued an injunction prohibiting this activity. The agreed

settlement by the Ivy League schools could not be used against them as evidence of guilt in any subsequent private suits by students or former students; the court's finding of a violation by M.I.T. could be used for this purpose, however.

After the government filed the suit, Congress passed a statute permitting universities to discuss and agree to general guidelines for financial aid, but prohibiting them from discussing individual students. Thus, something like the overlap group could continue operating for very limited purposes. In addition to not being permitted to discuss financial aid for any identified student, this or any other group of universities obviously may not agree explicitly or implicitly on tuition or faculty salaries.

For example, participants might agree to exchange certain kinds of information which, if misused, could make it fairly easy to engage in horizontal price fixing. This restriction would require a very strong justification. Third, the joint venture may harm outsiders who are excluded from participation. This situation is analyzed as described earlier in the discussion of various group activities that tend to exclude others.

VERTICAL RESTRAINTS OF TRADE

When firms operating at different levels of the distribution chain enter some arrangement that may harm competition, we call it a **vertical restraint of trade.**

Resale Price Maintenance
Nature and Effects

Resale price maintenance (RPM), which is also called vertical price fixing, occurs when a seller and buyer agree on the price at which the buyer will resell to its own customers. RPM usually is a method by which a manufacturer or other supplier limits price competition among its dealers or distributors in the

market for resale of the product. Competition among such dealers for sales of the manufacturer's product is called **intrabrand competition,** in contrast with the **interbrand competition** that occurs between different manufacturers' brands.

RPM has always been controversial. Many economists and legal scholars believe that RPM and other forms of restriction on intrabrand competition are usually employed to increase efficiency. They claim that these limits on intrabrand competition can be used by a manufacturer to make sure that its dealers invest in the facilities, trained personnel, and promotional activities necessary to stimulate sales and properly serve customers. If one dealer makes such an investment and thereby stimulates demand for the manufacturer's product, but another dealer does not, the latter has lower costs and can underprice the former. The first dealer will then be discouraged and will stop making such investments. Because of some dealers' **free riding,** the argument goes, many (or most) of the manufacturer's dealers will not do those things necessary to compete vigorously with other brands. If the manufacturer uses RPM to put a floor below its dealers' resale prices, however, some argue that this will solve the problem by reducing dealers' incentives to take a free ride on the investment of other dealers. The incentive is gone because they cannot use their lower costs to underprice and take customers from another dealer. Those arguing that the law should treat RPM very leniently also claim that, because any potential harm to competition is only intrabrand, customers are protected so long as competition among different brands remains active.

Other experts have serious doubts about the "free rider" justification for RPM. They argue that free rider problems are really not that common, and that many cases of resale price maintenance have involved products like toothpaste or blue jeans, for which there is not much need for the kinds of costly facilities or services that are susceptible to free riding. They also claim that, even if free rider problems are common, other means are available for solving them that do not cause similar harm to price competition. Such means include contractual commitments from dealers to provide the necessary facilities, personnel, promotion, and services. Opponents of RPM claim that the true reason for the practice often may be the manufacturer's desire to keep dealers' prices up and relieve them from intrabrand competition so that they do not pressure the manufacturer to lower its prices to them. They also sometimes argue that RPM can be used as a device to carry out a horizontal price-fixing conspiracy among dealers.

Legal Standards
The statute applicable to RPM is Section 1 of the Sherman Act. From the early days of the Sherman Act, RPM was viewed as per se illegal. In 1937, Congress passed legislation that delegated to state legislatures the power to determine the status of RPM in their particular states. Most states passed so-called Fair Trade laws that permitted RPM on branded merchandise within their borders if meaningful competition existed among different brands of the same product. Congress strengthened the power of the states to permit this practice in 1945. Gradually, however, the notion of permitting RPM fell out of favor. Many states repealed their Fair Trade laws, and many state supreme courts held that the statutes violated provisions in their state constitutions. Most of the remaining Fair Trade statutes fell into disuse, either because ambiguous interpretations created uncertainty, or simply because it was difficult for an

interstate seller to use RPM legally when it was illegal in so many places. In 1975, Congress repealed the federal law that permitted states to enact Fair Trade laws. Thus, RPM became per se illegal everywhere in the nation once again.

Although resale price maintenance is per se illegal, there continues to be a vigorous debate about whether it should be. Until the early 1980s, the U.S. Justice Department aggressively prosecuted cases of RPM and the federal courts generally took a very harsh view of the practice. (Until 1975, the Justice Department and courts dealt with RPM only if it occurred in a state where it was illegal.) Since the early 1980s, the law against RPM has not been enforced as aggressively, and the courts have begun to interpret the law so as to make it somewhat more difficult for either the Justice Department or private parties to prove RPM. These attitudes and interpretations could easily change again in the future, as they have several times in the past.

Proving a Vertical Agreement
Most of the difficult issues in RPM cases have involved the question of whether there actually has been an "agreement" to set resale prices. "Suggested" resale prices at the retail level are quite common. They do not constitute RPM unless there is evidence that there really has been an agreement (either voluntary or coerced) that gives the manufacturer or other supplier effective control over the dealer's resale prices. This point also illustrates the fact that there can be an illegal RPM "agreement" even if one party has coerced the other into participating; Section 1 of the Sherman Act does not require that the agreement be completely voluntary.

One of the most difficult issues in this area involves the extent to which a seller lawfully may use a *refusal to deal* in an attempt to control buyers' resale prices. In *United States v. Colgate & Co.*, 250 U.S. 300 (1919), the Supreme Court stated that a "unilateral refusal to deal" cannot violate Section 1 of the Sherman Act even if controlling resale prices is the seller's ultimate goal. In other words, so long as a seller acts entirely on its own ("unilaterally") it can refuse to sell to anyone it chooses, regardless of the motive. The problem, of course, is distinguishing between unilateral action by the seller and action that is part of an RPM arrangement between the seller and others. Suppose that M, a manufacturer, either initially refuses to sell to R, a retailer, or later terminates an existing supplier-customer relationship with R. (When RPM is claimed, the second situation is the most common.) To create a genuine fact issue for the jury, R must present evidence indicating that (1) there was an agreement to fix resale prices at R's level, and (2) M refused to deal with R because R would not go along with the arrangement. The agreement to limit price competition at R's level could be between M and wholesalers who act as intermediaries between M and R, between M and other retailers who compete with R, or even between M and R if the evidence shows that R previously had been part of an RPM arrangement with M and then tried to get out of it.

Vertical Nonprice Restrictions

Nature and Effects

Vertical restrictions may relate to matters other than price. The **vertical nonprice restrictions (VNRs)** that can cause some concern under Section 1 of the Sherman Act generally are those involving some type of market division. VNRs take many forms, depending on several factors. These factors include the relative bargaining power of the manufacturer and its dealers or distributors, and the nature of the product and the markets in which it sells.

One type of VNR is the *territorial exclusive*, in which M, the manufacturer, guarantees its dealers that they will have the exclusive right to market M's product in their respective geographic areas. In order to honor this arrangement with each dealer, M obviously must keep all dealers from reselling outside their own areas. Because this restriction places a contractual limitation on M's freedom, M will not use exclusive territories in its distribution system unless it has relatively less bargaining power than its dealers. More often, M will use *territorial and customer restrictions*, without any promise of exclusive territories. Such an arrangement requires dealers or distributors to resell only within their respective territories or only to particular customers, but does not guarantee them exclusive rights to sell in those areas or to those customers. A similar provision that restricts dealers somewhat less is the *area of primary responsibility*, which does not absolutely prohibit a dealer from reselling outside its designated territory but requires only that the territory be thoroughly served before sales can be made outside the area. Another fairly common provision is the *location requirement*, which requires a dealer to sell only from a specified location. In most cases, a location requirement has the same effect as a territorial restriction.

Like RPM, all forms of VNRs have the common characteristic of limiting *intrabrand* competition. Also like RPM, there is a long-standing debate about the competitive benefits and dangers of VNRs. Today, and commonly during the past, the prevailing attitude toward these restrictions has been more favorable than the attitude toward RPM. Generally, the feeling has been that VNRs are more likely than RPM (1) to be based on legitimate motives and (2) to help *intrabrand* competition more than they hurt *intrabrand* competition. A significant number of authorities think, however, that the law should not treat VNRs and RPM any differently because they are usually employed for the same purposes, have basically the same effects, and can be difficult to distinguish in practice.

Legal Standards

The legal status of VNRs has varied over the years. Until 1967, they were analyzed under the rule of reason. In that year, a decision of the U.S. Supreme Court caused some kinds of nonprice restriction on dealers to be per se illegal. This decision was overruled by the Court in 1977, and since then the rule of reason has been applied to all forms of VNRs.

In the case of VNRs, the question of motive is usually not as important as it can be when the rule of reason is applied to horizontal restrictions. Courts generally accept as legitimate M's objective of using a VNR to limit intrabrand competition, so long as there apparently is some business justification for the limitation. Under the rule of reason, M's market share will be the most important factor. If it is below approximately 10 percent, the restriction usually will be legal without further inquiry. If the share is at or above this level, courts normally will look at other factors. Other factors that could increase the chances of illegality in a close case include (1) evidence that *interbrand* competition in this particular market is not very strong, and that *intrabrand* competition is especially important; (2) evidence that most other manufacturers in this market also use such restrictions to limit intrabrand competition among their dealers; and (3) evidence that M selected a form of VNR that limits intrabrand competition much more than is really necessary under the circumstances.

The following case is the one in which the U.S. Supreme Court switched from the per se rule back to the rule of reason for judging VNRs. The Court's discussion outlines and adopts some of the arguments made by those who feel that VNRs usually produce more economic benefits than harms.

CONTINENTAL T.V., INC. V. G.T.E. SYLVANIA, INC.

U.S. Supreme Court, 433 U.S. 36 (1977)

 Case

Sylvania manufactured and sold television sets through its Home Entertainment Products Division. Prior to 1962, like most other television manufacturers, Sylvania sold televisions to independent or company-owned wholesale distributors who then resold them to a large and diverse group of retailers. Prompted by a decline in its market share to a relatively insignificant 1 to 2 percent of national television sales, Sylvania conducted an intensive reassessment of its marketing strategy and in 1962 adopted the franchise plan challenged here. Sylvania phased out its wholesale distributors and began to sell its televisions directly to a smaller and more select group of franchised retailers. The main purpose of the change was to decrease the number of competing Sylvania retailers in the hope of attracting the more aggressive and competent retailers, which Sylvania felt was necessary to improve its market position.

Thus, Sylvania limited the number of franchises granted for any given area and required each retail dealer to sell Sylvania products only from the location or locations specified in the franchise agreement. These retailers were not prohibited from selling the products of competing manufacturers. A franchise did not constitute an exclusive territory, and Sylvania retained sole discretion to increase the number of retailers in an area in light of the success or failure of existing retailers in developing their market. The revised marketing strategy apparently was successful, and by 1965 Sylvania's share of national television sales increased to 5 percent, making it the eighth largest manufacturer of televisions.

In 1965 Sylvania proposed to franchise an additional retailer in San Francisco. This proposal upset

Continental T.V., an existing Sylvania dealer in the city. Continental then proposed to open a new store in Sacramento. Sylvania denied Continental's request because it felt that Sacramento presently was being adequately served. Continental then began selling Sylvania televisions in Sacramento in defiance of Sylvania, and the manufacturer stopped selling to Continental.

Continental filed a treble damage suit against Sylvania, claiming that the restrictions on dealer location violated Section 1 of the Sherman Act. In federal district court Continental received a jury verdict against Sylvania for approximately $600,000 and a judgment for $1.8 million. In ruling for Continental, the district court applied the Supreme Court's 1967 decision in United States v. Arnold, Schwinn & Co., *which had held vertical nonprice restrictions to be per se illegal. When Sylvania appealed to the court of appeals, that court reversed and ordered a retrial because it thought that the* Schwinn *case was inapplicable to the present situation. Continental then appealed to the U.S. Supreme Court. The Supreme Court felt that the* Schwinn *case was indeed applicable to the facts of the present case, but wished to decide whether* Schwinn *should still be the law. Thus, the issue for the Supreme Court was whether to follow its earlier decision in the* Schwinn *case and apply the per se rule, or to overrule that case and apply the rule of reason to vertical nonprice restrictions.*

Powell, Justice:

. . . Since its announcement, *Schwinn* has been the subject of continuing controversy and confusion, both in the scholarly journals and in the federal courts. The great weight of scholarly opinion has been critical of the decision, and a number of the federal

courts confronted with analogous vertical restrictions have sought to limit its reach. In our view, the experience of the past 10 years should be brought to bear on this subject of considerable commercial importance. . . .

Per se rules of illegality are appropriate only when they relate to conduct that is manifestly anti-competitive. As the Court explained in *Northern Pac. R. Co. v. United States*, 356 U.S. 1, 5, 78 S.Ct. 514, 518, 2 L.Ed.2d 545 (1958), "there are certain agreements or practices which because of their pernicious effect on competition and lack of any redeeming virtue are conclusively presumed to be unreasonable and therefore illegal without elaborate inquiry as to the precise harm they have caused or the business excuse for their use."

In essence, the issue before us is whether *Schwinn's per se* rule can be justified under the demanding standards of *Northern Pac. R. Co.* . . .

The market impact of vertical restrictions is complex because of their potential for a simultaneous reduction of intrabrand competition and stimulation of interbrand competition. . . .

Vertical restrictions reduce intrabrand competition by limiting the number of sellers of a particular product competing for the business of a given group of buyers. Location restrictions have this effect because of practical constraints on the effective marketing area of retail outlets. Although intrabrand competition may be reduced, the ability of retailers to exploit the resulting market may be limited both by the ability of consumers to travel to other franchised locations and, perhaps more importantly, to purchase the competing products of other manufacturers. . . .

Vertical restrictions promote interbrand competition by allowing the manufacturer to achieve certain efficiencies in the distribution of his products. These "redeeming virtues" are implicit in every decision sustaining

(*continues*)

Continental T.V., Inc. v. G.T.E. Sylvania, Inc.

(*continued from previous page*)
vertical restrictions under the rule of reason. Economists have identified a number of ways in which manufacturers can use such restrictions to compete more effectively against other manufacturers. For example, new manufacturers and manufacturers entering new markets can use the restrictions in order to induce competent and aggressive retailers to make the kind of investment of capital and labor that is often required in the distribution of products unknown to the consumer. Established manufacturers can use them to induce retailers to engage in promotional activities or to provide service and repair facilities necessary to the efficient marketing of their products. Service and repair are vital for many products, such as automobiles and major household appliances. The availability and quality of such services affect a manufacturer's good will and the competitiveness of his product. Because of market imperfections such as the so-called "free rider" effect, these services might not be provided by retailers in a purely competitive situation, despite the fact that each retailer's benefit would be greater if all provided the services than if none did. . . .

Certainly, there has been no showing in this case, either generally or with respect to Sylvania's agreements, that vertical restrictions have or are likely to have a "pernicious effect on competition" or that they "lack . . . any redeeming virtue." Accordingly, we conclude that the *per se* rule stated in *Schwinn* must be overruled. In so holding we do not foreclose the possibility that particular applications of vertical restrictions might justify *per se* prohibition under *Northern Pac. R. Co.* But we do make clear that departure from the rule of reason standard must be based upon demonstrable economic effect. . . .

In sum, we conclude that the appropriate decision is to return to the rule of reason that governed vertical restrictions prior to *Schwinn*. When anti-competitive effects are shown to result from particular vertical restrictions they can be adequately policed under the rule of reason, the standard traditionally applied for the majority of anti-competitive practices challenged under § 1 of the Act. Accordingly, the decision of the Court of Appeals is affirmed. ⚖

Comment On retrial, the district court found that Sylvania's vertical restrictions were valid under the rule of reason. This holding was based primarily on (1) Sylvania's legitimate business justification, (2) Sylvania's small market share, and (3) the court's feeling that Sylvania had chosen the "least restrictive alternative"—in other words, that the location clause was less restrictive of competition than other methods Sylvania might have used to accomplish its objectives.

Tying Agreements
Nature and Effects

When one party agrees to supply (sell, lease, etc.) a product or service only on the condition that the customer also take another product or service, a **tying agreement** has been made. The desired item is the *tying* product, and the item the customer is required to take is the *tied* product. Tying agreements are scrutinized under both Section 1 of the Sherman Act and Section 3 of the Clayton Act. Section 3 of the Clayton Act applies only to the tying of two tangible commodities. Section 1 of the Sherman Act applies to all tying arrangements, including those in which either or both products is not a tangible commodity (such as a service, an intangible property right, or land). Today tying agreements are analyzed the same way under the two statutes, so Section 3 of the Clayton Act is largely redundant.

An early landmark case provides a clear example of tying. In *IBM v. United States*, 298 U.S. 131 (1936), IBM was found guilty of illegal tying by requiring all customers leasing its tabulating machines to also purchase their tabulating cards from IBM.

The main concern about tying is that a supplier may use power in one market (the market for the *tying* product) to distort competition in another market (the market for the *tied* product). Such distortion can occur, it is argued, because the supplier's sales of the tied product are not based on the independent competitive merits of that product.

Several different motivations may lead a supplier to use tying arrangements. In some cases, the supplier may be trying to use the power it has in the tying market to expand its power in the tied market. Such a practice is sometimes referred to as *leveraging*. There is quite a bit of debate among experts as to the extent to which power actually can be leveraged from one market to another.

A supplier also might use tying in an attempt to *protect its goodwill*. This could be the motive, for example, where the supplier sells or leases product X, and where product Y must be used in conjunction with X. The supplier may be concerned that some customers might use inferior versions of Y that will cause X to perform poorly, and thus hurt the reputation of X. In such a case, the supplier might require buyers to buy the supplier's own version of Y along with X. The general feeling under the antitrust laws, however, has been that the supplier should accomplish its objective by requiring the customer to use any version of Y that meets specifications set by the supplier, unless the use of specifications is very difficult.

Another possible motive for tying is to *discriminate among customers* according to the intensity with which they use the supplier's product. Suppose that M manufactures a machine used by food processing companies to inject salt into foods during processing. If M feels that customers who use the machine more may be willing to pay more for it, M may try to charge them based on intensity of use so as to maximize its total revenues. Direct metering may be very difficult. Sometimes, however, intensity of use is directly proportional to the amount of a second product the customer uses in connection with M's product. In the case of the salt-dispensing machine, intensity of use can be measured by the amount of salt used by the customer. Thus, M may try to measure intensity by requiring customers of its machines also to buy its salt. Through the salt sales, M's total revenue will be greater in transactions with high-intensity users.

Legal Standards

Tying can occur only if two separate products are involved. Often this is obvious, but sometimes it is not, as for example in the case of various options on new automobiles. Generally, a transaction will be viewed as including two separate products if the evidence demonstrates that there really are two separate markets in which the different items are commonly demanded. However, even if there are two separate markets, courts usually will treat a transaction as involving only one product if packaging two items is significantly more efficient than selling them separately.

If there are two separate products, tying is illegal only if the supplier has *substantial power in the market for the tying product*. The reason for this requirement is the generally accepted proposition that tying

cannot cause any substantial harm in the *tied* market unless the supplier has quite a bit of power in the *tying* market. Market power is measured in the same way here as in other cases. Today, a supplier probably has to have at least a 30 percent share of the tying market to be viewed as having substantial power in that market. Other factors, such as entry barriers, are also very important. According to the courts, there is a second requirement for tying to be illegal, namely, that the supplier's tying arrangements must generate a substantial amount of business in the *tied* market. This requirement is so easy to establish, however, that it is practically always present.

Exclusive Dealing
Nature and Effects

The most common form of **exclusive dealing** agreement is one in which the customer makes a commitment that it will purchase a particular product or service only from the supplier (and, implicitly or explicitly, *not* from the supplier's competitors). Many times these arrangements are called "requirements contracts" because the parties often speak in terms of the buyer's commitment to purchase its "requirements" of a product from the seller. The primary concern caused by this type of arrangement is that there may be fewer and less frequent opportunities for the seller's competitors to compete for those customers who are parties to the exclusive dealing. Widespread use of such agreements in a market may also increase entry barriers for potential competitors.

Another kind of exclusive dealing that occurs less often is one in which the seller agrees to sell only to a particular buyer (and, thus, not sell to the buyer's competitors). This is sometimes called an "output" contract, because the seller obligates itself to sell all of its output of a product to the buyer. Output contracts usually raise no competitive concerns, but occasionally might unreasonably prevent the buyer's competitors from acquiring products needed to compete.

Legal Standards

Today, exclusive dealing is likely to be illegal under Section 1 of the Sherman Act or Section 3 of the Clayton Act only if a dominant share—probably more than 30 percent—of the relevant market is locked away from competitors. Thus, the practice creates a real legal risk only when a leading or dominant firm in a market makes widespread use of it.

Price Discrimination

Although the original version of Section 2 of the Clayton Act contained a prohibition of **price discrimination,** it proved ineffective because of certain major loopholes. In 1936 Congress enacted the Robinson-Patman Act in an effort to make the law against price discrimination more effective. Congress's main purpose in passing this law was to protect small businesses from having to pay higher prices than larger companies.

Basic Elements

The interstate commerce requirement in the Robinson-Patman Act is more difficult to prove than in any other of the antitrust laws. It is not enough that the seller or buyer is an interstate company or that the transaction affects interstate commerce—at least one of the relevant sales must actually cross state lines. Only a few states have laws prohibiting intrastate price discrimination within their borders. It should also be noted that many nations, including the United States, have *antidumping laws* that prohibit a foreign producer from selling goods in the country at a lower price than in that producer's home country.

Assuming that the interstate commerce requirement is met, the following must be proved to establish a violation of the Robinson-Patman Act. (1) The seller must have charged *different prices* to two or more different customers. (2) The transaction must have involved *tangible commodities,* not services, land, or intangibles. (3) The transactions must have been *sales,* rather than consignments, leases, or some other form of transaction. (4) The goods sold in the transactions being compared must have been *of like grade and quality,* which means that the products sold to different customers at different prices must have been essentially the same. Trivial differences are ignored. (5) The evidence must demonstrate a likelihood of *substantial harm to competition.* Generally speaking, isolated or sporadic instances of price discrimination will not violate the Act because it usually will be impossible to prove competitive injury. Such injury often can be proved only where the discrimination was recurring and systematic. To prove injury to one of the seller's competitors, it is usually necessary to show that the discriminatorily lower prices to favored customers were *predatory* (below cost). To prove injury to one of the favored customer's competitors, it is usually necessary to show that the disfavored buyer actually lost substantial business to the favored buyer because of the discrimination.

Defenses

When the basic elements of a Robinson-Patman Act violation are proved, the seller is guilty unless it can prove one of three available defenses. The first is *cost justification.* There is no violation if the seller's different prices are simply a reflection of differences in the costs of "manufacture, sale, or delivery." Thus the seller wins if it proves that the higher prices to one buyer or group of buyers are directly attributable to the higher costs of providing the goods to that buyer or group. The second defense is *meeting competition.* A seller does not violate the Act if a lower price to one buyer "was made in good faith to meet an equally low price of a competitor." Suppose S generally charges $10 for a product, but learns that its competitor is offering the product to a certain customer for $9. S can legally meet the $9 price to that customer even while keeping its price to other buyers at $10. Another version of the meeting competition defense permits a seller to charge different prices in different geographic markets in order to meet different prevailing market prices in those different areas. The third defense is *changing conditions.* The seller is permitted to change prices in response to changing conditions that affect the marketability of the goods, such as imminent deterioration of perishable commodities or obsolescence of seasonal goods.

SUMMARY

The primary objective of antitrust law is to promote competition in markets. The various antitrust laws generally apply to activities occurring in or affecting interstate commerce. The laws are subject to a few limited exemptions, and are enforced by the U.S. Justice Department, Federal Trade Commission, and private parties. Section 2 of the Sherman Act prohibits monopolization, which occurs when one firm dominates a market so completely that it really does not have to worry about the responses of competitors. In addition to proving that a firm has overwhelming market power, it also must be shown that the monopolist willfully acquired or maintained its power by predatory conduct. Mergers—acquisitions of stock or assets—are prohibited by Section 7 of the Clayton Act if the evidence indicates that they are likely to diminish competition in a substantial way. Mergers are usually classified as horizontal (between competitors), vertical (where one of the merging firms buys something that the other sells), and conglomerate. Horizontal mergers pose the greatest risk to competition and thus are more likely to violate Section 7.

Horizontal restraints of trade—arrangements between competitors that restrict competition—are covered by Section 1 of the Sherman Act, which prohibits "contracts, combinations, or conspiracies in restraint of trade." Horizontal price fixing, market divisions, and boycotts are per se illegal, which means that these arrangements are automatically illegal once they are identified. Other arrangements between competitors are judged under the rule of reason, and are illegal only if they are likely to cause substantial restrictions on competition.

Vertical restraints of trade occur between firms at different levels of the distribution chain. Resale price maintenance involves arrangements by which a seller and buyer agree on the price at which the buyer will resell the products to its own customers. Despite substantial controversy, the practice is per se illegal under Section 1 of the Sherman Act. Vertical nonprice restrictions, on the other hand, are judged under Section 1's rule of reason. These restrictions normally relate to the area within which or the customers to whom the buyer can resell.

A tying arrangement occurs where the supplier provides a product only on the condition that the customer take another product. Tying agreements violate Section 1 of the Sherman Act or Section 3 of the Clayton Act when the supplier has substantial power in the market for the tying product. An exclusive dealing agreement occurs where the buyer agrees to buy all of its requirements of a product from the seller (and not from the seller's competitors), or where the seller agrees to sell all of its output to the buyer (and not to the buyer's competitors). The requirements type of exclusive dealing is much more common. Exclusive dealing violates Section 1 of the Sherman Act or Section 3 of the Clayton Act only if the arrangements lock up a substantial portion of the relevant market, probably at least 30 percent today.

Price discrimination violates the Robinson-Patman Act when the seller sells the same tangible product to two or more different purchasers at different prices, state lines are crossed, and competitive injury

results. There are three defenses to a Robinson-Patman Act violation.

KEY TERMS

Oligopoly
Monopoly
Market share
Entry barriers
Cross elasticity of demand
Cross elasticity of supply
Predatory pricing
Nonprice predation
Merger
Horizontal merger
Vertical merger
Vertical integration
Conglomerate merger
Horizontal restraint of trade
Collusion
Rule of reason
Per se rule
Price fixing
Market division
Boycott
Joint venture
Vertical restraint of trade
Resale price maintenance (RPM)
Intrabrand competition
Interbrand competition
Free riding
Vertical nonprice restriction (VNR)
Tying agreement
Exclusive dealing
Price discrimination

QUESTIONS AND PROBLEMS

1. Alcoa was charged with monopolizing the U.S. market for aluminum ingot. Aluminum ingot is sold in blocks or bars to fabricators, who use it to make aluminum sheets, conduit, wiring, and other end products. Alcoa produced 90 percent of the "virgin" aluminum ingot sold in the United States. Some of its ingot production, however, was actually fabricated by Alcoa into end products before being sold. Another factor in the market was "secondary" ingot, or aluminum ingot made from recycled aluminum. Secondary ingot was acceptable for many of the same

uses as virgin ingot, but not for all of them. If the product market was defined to include all of Alcoa's virgin ingot production, including that part which Alcoa itself fabricated before selling, but not to include secondary ingot, Alcoa's market share would be about 90 percent. If the market definition also included secondary ingot, Alcoa's share would be 64 percent. If the market definition included secondary ingot, but did not include that part of Alcoa's ingot which it fabricated before selling, Alcoa's share would be 33 percent. Discuss how the product market should be defined. (*United States v. Aluminum Co. of America*, 148 F.2d 416, 2d Cir. 1945.)

2. Suppose that in a particular three-state region there are only two granite quarries from which granite suitable for cemetery monuments can be obtained. This type of granite is not available anywhere else in this region, and transportation costs are too high for granite to be shipped in from outside the region. Ace owns one quarry and Beta owns the other. Ace produces 60 percent of the region's total granite production from its quarry, and Beta produces the other 40 percent. Ace does not fabricate any of its granite but sells it in large blocks to firms who make cemetery monuments. Beta is also a cemetery monument maker and uses all of its granite production to manufacture monuments. It sells none to other monument manufacturers. Ace is charged by the Justice Department with monopolizing the sale of granite in this three-state region. Discuss how the product and geographic market should be defined and whether Ace is likely to be found in violation of Section 2 of the Sherman Act.

3. Martex Co. produces a special type of scalpel used by surgeons. The scalpel effectively cauterizes the incision as the surgeon operates, thus eliminating much of the bleeding problem in surgery. Although Martex was not able to obtain a patent on the scalpel when it was developed several years ago, there still is only one other manufacturer of this type of scalpel. Of the total sales of the cauterizing scalpel, Martex accounts for 85 percent. The scalpel is used by most surgeons for major surgical procedures, and Martex sales represent 70 percent of the total sales of all types of scalpels. Whenever Martex sells these scalpels to surgeons or hospitals, it does so under a contract requiring the buyer to return the scalpel to Martex when it is worn out. Martex uses the worn-out scalpels in its research lab for experimentation, with the objective of improving the product.

Discuss whether Martex may have violated Section 2 of the Sherman Act.

4. The nation's second largest can producer acquired the nation's third largest producer of glass containers. Cans and bottles did not compete for all end uses, but for some uses they did compete. For example, there was clear rivalry between cans and bottles for the business of soft drink and beer producers. Both industries were relatively concentrated: the top two can manufacturers had 70 percent of can sales; the top three bottle manufacturers had 55 percent of bottle sales. If cans and bottles were viewed as a single market, the two firms would have, respectively, 22 percent and 3 percent of that market. Discuss whether this merger would violate Section 7 of the Clayton Act. (*United States v. Continental Can Co.*, 378 U.S. 441, 1964.)

5. General Motors, Ford, and Chrysler, in that order, were the largest automobile producers in America. Together they accounted for 90 percent of domestic production. The domestic spark plug market was dominated by Champion (40 percent), AC (30 percent—wholly owned by General Motors), and Autolite (15 percent). The remainder of the spark plug market was accounted for by very small producers.

The independent spark plug makers (primarily Champion and Autolite) sold spark plugs to the automakers (primarily Ford and Chrysler) at cost or below. These original equipment (OE) plugs were sold so cheaply because auto mechanics almost always replace worn out plugs with the same brand that had been original equipment (called the OE tie). Thus, it was essential to get into the OE market in order to get into the market for replacement plugs—the aftermarket. Large profits were made in this aftermarket.

Ford, whose purchases of OE plugs from the independent spark plug makers amounted to 10 percent of all the spark plugs produced domestically, wanted to gain entry into the profitable spark plug aftermarket. It did so by purchasing Autolite's only spark plug factory, as well as its trademark and distribution facilities. Discuss whether this merger might violate Section 7 of the Clayton Act. (*Ford Motor Co. v. United States*, 405 U.S. 562, 1972.)

6. Theatre Enterprises, Inc., owned and operated the Crest Theatre in a suburban shopping center

located about six miles from downtown Baltimore. At that time, the downtown area was still the most important shopping district. As a result, a downtown movie theatre generally had about 10 times the drawing power of a suburban theatre like the Crest. Before and after the opening of the Crest, Theatre Enterprises sought to obtain first-run films from several major film distributors. It approached each distributor individually, and was turned down on every occasion. As a result, the Crest was able to show first-run films only after the downtown theatres had shown them. Other than these delayed first-runs, Crest was left with "subsequent runs" (films that had been re-released). Theatre Enterprises sued the distributors, claiming that they had violated Section 1 of the Sherman Act by engaging in a group refusal to deal. There was no direct evidence of agreement among the distributors. Discuss whether and under what circumstances Theatre Enterprises could prevail. (*Theatre Enterprises, Inc. v. Paramount Film Distributing Corp.*, 346 U.S. 537, 1954.)

7.   During a period of time in which demand for refined sugar was falling because of increasing consumer preferences for artificial sweeteners, several sugar refiners began offering price discounts to some of their larger customers in an effort to stimulate sales and decrease inventories. These discounts were generally in the form of secret rebates. Before long, most other sugar refiners and their customers learned about these rebates. Claiming that these discriminatory rebates were "demoralizing the industry at a time when market conditions were already bad" and that customers were "losing faith in the integrity of the sugar industry," these other refiners urged those granting rebates to stop the practice. The rebating refiners argued, however, that their practices were completely legitimate because "everybody knows it's cheaper to sell to large customers." The nonrebating refiners then put pressure on sugar cane and sugar beet growers and within a short time the rebating refiners were unable to buy cane and beets for making sugar. Within a month the rebating refiners all stopped the practice of favoring certain customers. The Justice Department filed suit in federal district court, claiming that the "nonrebating" sugar refiners and the growers had violated Section 1 of the Sherman Act. Discuss whether Section 1 has been violated.

8.   Many retail department stores provide delivery service for large items purchased by their customers.

In the New York City area, the presidents of three stores were talking privately about delivery problems at a Chamber of Commerce luncheon. One of them mentioned that the costs involved in maintaining delivery trucks, forklifts, and other equipment and employees were becoming too great to justify the service. The other two agreed, but all of them were concerned about the business they might lose if they discontinued delivery service. They decided to contact other department stores in the metropolitan area to find out what their feelings were. After a series of discussions among the presidents of 18 of the 20 largest department stores in the area, they came up with the following alternative proposals:

a. They could all simultaneously stop providing delivery service.
b. They could jointly select and deal with an existing independent delivery service. The group would investigate existing services, invite them to submit bids, and ultimately select one and jointly contract with it.

Upon hearing of these proposals, the U.S. Department of Justice initiated an investigation. The department was interested in whether any of these proposals might violate Section 1 of the Sherman Act. Discuss the legality of proposals a and b.

9.   Chemco is a manufacturer of various agricultural chemicals such as herbicides and insecticides. Most of these products were sold to wholesale distributors who then resold either to retail dealers or directly to farmers. During a 20-day period in late 1980, Chemco received individual complaints from five of its distributors in the Pacific Coast region of the country. These distributors complained that a sixth distributor, Ace, had been significantly undercutting their prices and hurting their sales. Chemco made no promises to them, but a month later it announced to all of its distributors across the nation that it was implementing a new policy. Chemco's new policy was that, in the future, it would sell only to those distributors who would indicate in advance their intent to abide by Chemco's schedule of suggested resale prices. Most distributors responded affirmatively to Chemco's new policy. Those few who did not respond affirmatively were discontinued as Chemco distributors. One of those who did not respond affirmatively and who was discontinued was

Ace. Discuss whether Chemco and its distributors may have violated Section 1 of the Sherman Act.

10. Sarco, Inc., a manufacturer of various types of electronic equipment and devices used for industrial and medical purposes, sold its products to franchised dealers who then resold to their customers. Many of the products were complicated and relatively expensive. As a result, dealers needed to be carefully selected and trained so that they would be knowledgeable about the products and could offer essential consultation and demonstration services to potential customers. In addition, it was necessary that dealers be able to expertly perform repairs on the products. Sarco, which accounted for between 10 and 18 percent of national sales in its various product lines, granted each dealer an exclusive territory and required each to sell only in that territory. Sarco's distribution system was challenged under Section 1 of the Sherman Act. Discuss whether the system is likely to be legal or illegal under Section 1 of the Sherman Act.

Chapter 49

Employment Law

Labor Relations Law

Employment Discrimination Law

Protection of Safety and Welfare

Employer's Right to Discharge Employees

Protection of Employee Privacy

The law of employment relations has undergone a fundamental transformation within recent years and change continues even today. For much of our nation's history, the legal relationship between employer and employee was governed by general traditional principles of common law, which in practice typically tilted in the direction of the employer's authority. For example, employers lawfully could discharge their workers for any (or no) reason, including the individual employee's race, union membership, or job-related injury.

The growth of unions was the working person's first response to this legal regime, which seemingly favored employers to an inordinate degree. Unionization was frustrated at first by a series of judicial decisions, but once Congress provided statutory protection in the 1930s, the new labor organizations were able to thrive and provided considerable benefits to member workers.

Notwithstanding the advantages provided the majority of employees, unions had some serious shortcomings, especially when it came to protecting small groups of employees and dealing with noneconomic issues. In the 1960s Congress once again intervened to expand the protection of workers in areas where unions had contributed little. A number of antidiscrimination laws were enacted, the most significant being the Civil Rights Act of 1964. The Occupational Safety and Health Act of 1968 established a new agency and granted it considerable power to guard against workplace hazards. Legislation expanded worker rights in other areas as well. Perhaps prodded by this congressional activity, the courts also began to reexamine old precedents and initiate new common-law protections for employees. This chapter explores these developments in the law of employment relations and the complications the changes create for employers.

LABOR RELATIONS LAW

In the early nineteenth century, attempts to unionize were stymied by the doctrine that they represented unlawful criminal conspiracies at common law. This theory gradually fell into disfavor and by the end of the century unions began to achieve some success, especially with the advent of industrialization and a rise in perceived employer abuse of power. Even in the early twentieth century, however, the courts continued to frustrate union development by enjoining critical functions of such organizations, such as striking and picketing. This was an era of much labor strife and periodic outbreaks of violence associated with labor/management disputes.

Recognizing the existence of a serious national problem, Congress passed several laws in an attempt to resolve labor/management difficulties, including the Railway Labor Act and the Norris-La Guardia Act, which prohibited, among other provisions, the use of injunctions against many union activities. Although these statutes eased the situation somewhat, it soon became clear that more extensive legislation was necessary. In 1935 Congress created a comprehensive framework for labor relations law by passing the National Labor Relations Act (NLRA). While this act has been amended, the basic rules established by the original NLRA survive today as the foundation of current law.

The NLRA unambiguously recognized an employee's right to organize by forming unions and authorized these labor organizations to bargain collectively with employers. Certain practices were declared to be **unfair labor practices,** and these were prohibited. Unfair labor practices were defined to include employer domination of unions, interference with employee organizing, discrimination against union members, and refusal to bargain collectively.

In order to enforce these requirements, the NLRA established a new agency, the National Labor Relations Board (NLRB). The NLRB consists of the General Counsel and the Board itself. The General Counsel investigates charges of unfair labor practices and, if they are found meritworthy, initiates an action against the responsible party. These actions are heard by an administrative law judge and may be appealed to the entire Board. If the Board finds a violation, it can seek enforcement of a number of sanctions, including cease-and-desist orders and back pay awards. Board decisions may be appealed to the U.S. Courts of Appeals.

Coverage

The NLRA applies generally to all employers involved in or affecting interstate commerce. As discussed in Chapter 5 (Constitutional Law), this language is quite broad in scope. The act is limited to protection of employees, however, and does not cover independent contractors, a distinction explained in Chapter 19. In addition, some categories of employees are specifically excluded from the act's coverage. Government employees, as well as workers for railways and airlines (protected under a different statute) are outside the NLRA's coverage. Significantly, managerial and supervisory employees are not covered by the act, as they are considered to be part of "management" rather than "labor."

Right to Organize

Central to the NLRA is its guarantee of a right to form unions. Once a group of employees determines that it desires to form an organization for collective bargaining, the group seeks out other workers for support. Once 30 percent of the eligible employees in an appropriate job category sign authorization cards, the employee group may petition for an election to certify a union as the employees' bargaining representative. Conduct of such elections is carefully scrutinized by the NLRB to ensure "laboratory conditions" of fairness. Employers opposing unionization must take special care in their actions and statements lest they be found to have committed an unfair labor practice, in which case the union may be automatically certified by the Board, regardless of the election's outcome. The following case illustrates the care that an employer must take to avoid disturbing the laboratory conditions required for a unionization election.

NLRB v. Exchange Parts Co.

U.S. Supreme Court, 375 U.S. 405 (1964)

Case

Exchange Parts Co. is in the automobile parts rebuilding business. On November 9, 1959, the International Brotherhood of Boilermakers, Iron Shipbuilders, Blacksmiths, Forgers and Helpers informed the company that a majority of workers favored unionization and on February 19 the Board granted an election petition.

On February 25, the company held a dinner for employees, at which a vice-president announced that a previously granted extra vacation day could be either a floating holiday or could be taken on the individual employee's birthday. The workers chose the latter. The vice-president also mentioned the upcoming election as an opportunity for employees to "determine whether they wished to hand over their right to speak and act for themselves."

On March 4, the company sent its employees a letter that spoke of the "Empty Promises of the Union" and "the fact that it is the Company that puts things in your envelope. . . ." *After mentioning a number of benefits, the letter stated:* "The Union can't put any of those things in your envelope—only the Company can do that." *The letter also went on to state that* "it didn't take a Union to get any of those things and . . . it won't take a Union to get additional improvements in the future." *Past company benefits were summarized and new benefits were announced, including the new birthday holiday, a new system for computing overtime that had the effect of increasing wages, and a new vacation schedule that enabled employees to take more time off per year.*

The election was held on March 18, and the union lost. The union promptly filed a charge with the Board, which held that the company actions had the intent to induce employees to vote against the union, thereby disrupting laboratory condi- tions and amounting to an unfair labor practice. The Board sought enforcement of its ruling in the Court of Appeals, which held against the Board. The Board then appealed this decision to the Supreme Court.

Harlan, Justice:

. . . [The NLRA] makes it an unfair labor practice for an employer "to interfere with, restrain, or coerce employees in the exercise of [their rights to form labor unions]." . . . We think the Court of Appeals was mistaken in concluding that the conferral of employee benefits while a representation election is pending, for the purpose of inducing employees to vote against the union does not "interfere with" the protected right to organize. . . .

In *Medo Photo Supply Corp. v. N.L.R.B.*, 321 U.S. 678, 686, this Court said: "The action of employees with respect to the choice of their bargaining agents may be induced by favors bestowed by the employer as well as by

(continues)

NLRB v. Exchange Parts Co.

his threats or domination." . . . The danger inherent in well-timed increases in employee benefits is the suggestion of a fist inside the velvet glove. Employees are not likely to miss the inference that the source of benefits now conferred is also the source from which future benefits must flow and which may dry up if it is not obliged. . . .

We cannot agree with the Court of Appeals that enforcement of the Board's order will have the "ironic" result of "discouraging benefits for labor." The beneficence of an employer is likely to be ephemeral if prompted by a threat of unionization which is subsequently removed. Insulating the right of collective organization from calculated good will of this sort deprives employees of little that has lasting value.

Reversed. [The Board's order shall be enforced.] ♫

In addition to benefits, employers must be careful not to say anything that may be interpreted as a "threat." An employer's statement that a plant shutdown was possible because the union would make company survival impossible was held to be unlawful.

Collective Bargaining

Collective bargaining is the term for negotiations between an employer and the union representative. Once a union has been certified as an official bargaining representative of a category of employees, the NLRA imposes a duty to bargain in good faith on both employer and union. Mandatory subjects of bargaining include wages and most working conditions. The good faith provision requires the parties to make a sincere effort to reach agreement. Approaches such as "take it or leave it" proposals may support an inference of bad faith and hence an unfair labor practice finding. An employer also must be willing to furnish certain information to the union and cannot delay unduly in doing so.

Strikes

The most powerful device possessed by unions under the NLRA is the right to strike. This right is available when collective bargaining has reached an impasse. For a strike to be legal it must be supported by a majority of members and cannot be a "wildcat" strike by a disgruntled minority. The NLRA also restricts strikes to those against the primary employer and prohibits strikes against third parties in an attempt to coerce that third party to pressure the primary employer. Even primary strikes are unlawful if they are violent or designed to compel "featherbedding" (the hiring of unnecessary employees) or other illegal contract terms.

The NLRA imposes other conditions on the conduct of strikes. For example, if workers are on strike against one employer at a multi-employer location (such as a construction site), the employees may not picket the entire site, as this applies unlawful secondary pressure against the other employers. Workers may picket a portion of the site that is used largely by their primary employer. If a strike is legal, the employer may be restricted in dealing with his striking employees. If the workers are engaged in an authorized strike protesting the employer's unfair labor practices, the strikers are automatically entitled to reinstatement after the strike is resolved. In the more traditional economic wage strike, the employer need not necessarily rehire strikers but never can discriminate against strikers, who have a right to seek reemployment on terms equal to those offered other prospective employees.

Nonunion Employees

Although the NLRA was designed primarily to protect unionization, it extends certain rights to nonunion workers as well. Where nonunion employees engage in concerted activity, such as a walkout in response to perceived unsafe working conditions, they are protected much like strikers on behalf of a union. In general, however, employers have a relatively free hand in dealing with nonunion workers. This situation gives rise to one potentially serious pitfall, however. If an employer sets up "employee committees" or other groups to address grievances in the absence of a union, the committee's independence from management must be carefully ensured. Otherwise, the employer may be found to have created a company-dominated labor organization, which is an unfair labor practice under the NLRA.

The above discussion represents an exceedingly brief review of labor relations law. There is a huge body of precedent under the NLRA elaborating on the above principles. Many of the legal rules in this field have become quite picayune. Consequently, employers must take special care in any controversy involving an organization of employees.

EMPLOYMENT DISCRIMINATION LAW

For much of America's history, employers had the legal right to discriminate among employees on any basis other than union membership. Recently, however, antidiscrimination laws have been enacted that affect all phases of the employment process and that prohibit discrimination based on race, color, religion, sex, age, national origin, or perceived handicap. Worker use of these laws has grown to the point where they may exceed the NLRA as a source of litigation and potential employer liability.

Title VII
Coverage
The Civil Rights Act of 1964 is a comprehensive federal enactment prohibiting discrimination in various settings, including housing, public accommodations, and education. Title VII of the Act deals specifically with discrimination in employment. Title VII prohibits discrimination against individuals because of their *race, color, religion, sex, or national origin.* Although Title VII was one of the earliest laws prohibiting employment discrimination, it remains the most significant.

The provisions of Title VII apply to employers, employment agencies, and labor unions. An employer is subject to Title VII if it (1) has 15 or more employees *and* (2) is engaged in business that affects interstate or foreign commerce. State and local governments are also within the definition of employer, and their employment practices are covered by Title VII. In most instances, the federal government's employment practices are also covered.

Scope of Protection
Title VII's prohibition against discrimination on the basis of race or color is very broad. It obviously protects blacks, but it also protects many other classes from unequal treatment, including Hispanics, American Indians, and Asian-Americans. Even whites are protected against racial discrimination.

The prohibition against national origin discrimination is violated if an employer discriminates on the basis of a person's country of origin. It is not illegal, however, for an employer to require employees to be U.S. citizens. (However, a *government* employer must have a very good reason for requiring its employees to be U.S. citizens, or the requirement will violate the equal protection clause of the U.S. Constitution.) Title VII also protects individuals against discrimination based on the race, color, or national origin of their family members or friends.

Title VII's prohibition against sex discrimination, which forbids unequal treatment based on *gender,* is aimed primarily at discrimination against females, but it also protects males against gender-based discrimination. The law makes it illegal to use sex as a factor in employment decisions, and also to engage in sexual harassment. Title VII protects women from discrimination because of pregnancy or childbirth, as well. It does not apply to discrimination based on sexual practices, preferences, or lifestyles, so long as the employer treats employees of both sexes equally.

Although religious organizations can lawfully hire employees based on their religious beliefs, other employers cannot make distinctions for religious reasons. The term religion not only includes well-recognized religious faiths, but also unorthodox ones. For Title VII purposes, the courts use the same broad definition of religion that they use in freedom-of-religion cases under the first amendment to the Constitution: "a sincere and meaningful belief occupying in the life of its possessor a place parallel to that filled by the God of those admittedly qualified."

In addition to forbidding discrimination based on religion, the law also requires an employer to make "reasonable accommodation" for employees' religious beliefs and practices. Employers do not have to go to great lengths or incur significant expense in order to make reasonable accommodation, however. For example, in *TWA v. Hardison*, 432 U.S. 63 (1977), Hardison worked in a department of TWA that had to operate 7 days a week, 24 hours a day. He became an adherent of a religious denomination that observed a Saturday sabbath, and tried to get Saturdays off. The collective bargaining agreement between TWA and the labor union included a seniority system that controlled many aspects of employment, including priorities in getting particular days off. Hardison did not have enough seniority to get Saturdays off most of the time. TWA tried unsuccessfully to find other employees who would voluntarily switch days with him so that he would not have to work Saturdays. Hardison requested that TWA use supervisors to fill in for him, hire additional personnel, or require other employees to switch with him regardless of seniority. TWA declined, Hardison refused to work on Saturday, and the employer fired him. When Hardison claimed a Title VII violation, the Supreme Court ruled that TWA had acted properly. The company fulfilled its obligation to make reasonable accommodation by reducing weekend shifts to minimum crews and trying to find volunteers to trade shifts.

Procedures and Remedies

Title VII establishes special procedures for enforcing its dictates. An individual who believes him- or herself to be the victim of unlawful discrimination cannot simply take an employer to court. Rather, the Civil Rights Act created the Equal Employment Opportunity Commission (EEOC) to receive complaints of violations. The EEOC investigates these complaints and, when they are adequately supported by facts, the Commission attempts conciliation measures between the employer and employees. If conciliation efforts fail, the EEOC may file suit in federal district court. Individuals may sue to enforce Title VII only after EEOC and the particular state equal employment opportunity agency has had the opportunity to take action.

Once a court finds that Title VII has been violated, the court is empowered to grant an injunction prohibiting future violations and correcting past actions. Retroactive back pay or seniority may be ordered for employees who have suffered from unlawful discrimination. In addition, a court may compel an offending company to implement an "affirmative action" program to recruit and retain minority employees.

What Constitutes Discrimination Under Title VII?

Illegal discrimination can be proved in either of two ways. First, the plaintiff may show that the defendant had engaged in *intentional* discrimination—sometimes referred to as "disparate treatment." Second, the plaintiff may show that some employment practice or policy of the defendant has had a discrimina-

tory *effect*, or impact—sometimes referred to as "disparate impact." The following discussion explains the use of these terms.

Intentional Discrimination

In general, any employment decision or practice which treats individuals unequally *because of* race, color, religion, sex, or national origin violates Title VII. Illegal discrimination might occur, for example, in connection with firing, refusing to hire, refusing to train or promote, granting unequal compensation or fringe benefits, or practicing any type of segregation or classification of employees or applicants that tends to deprive them of employment opportunities.

A violation of Title VII may be proved by showing that an employer *intended* to discriminate for a prohibited reason. There obviously would be a violation, for instance, if an employer maintained an express policy of "whites only" for admission of employees to a management training program.

Prima Facie *Case*. Express discrimination such as this became much less common after employers became fully aware of Title VII and its requirements. Intentional discrimination still occurs, but that intent usually is not expressed so openly as before. Recognizing this fact, the courts have ruled that an inference of discriminatory intent may be drawn in certain circumstances. When the EEOC or an individual plaintiff proves facts which make it logical to conclude that intentional discrimination probably has occurred, the courts hold that a ***prima facie* case** of discrimination exists.

Suppose, for example, that an individual job applicant is rejected and has reason to believe that the employer's refusal to hire was motivated by unlawful discrimination. Even though there was no explicit discriminatory motive on the employer's part, a *prima facie* violation of Title VII can be established by showing that (1) the applicant is within a protected class (racial or ethnic minority or female); (2) the applicant applied for a job for which the employer was seeking applicants; (3) the applicant was qualified to perform the job; (4) the applicant was not hired for the job; and (5) the employer either filled the position with a nonminority person or continued trying to fill it. If the claim of discrimination is based on a discharge rather than a refusal to hire, a *prima facie* case can be established by showing that (1) the plaintiff is within a protected class; (2) the plaintiff was performing the job satisfactorily; (3) the plaintiff was discharged; and

(4) the plaintiff's work was then assigned to someone who was not within a protected class. In other employment decisions, the requirements of a *prima facie* case would similarly have to be modified to fit the circumstances. (It should be noted that when courts speak of "protected class," they are referring to the usual situation in which a female or nonwhite person is the plaintiff; it is possible, however, for a male or white to be the plaintiff.)

Employer's Rebuttal. When the plaintiff in such a case introduces evidence sufficient to create a *prima facie* case, the burden then shifts to the employer to bring forth evidence of a *legitimate, nondiscriminatory reason* for plaintiff's rejection. To overcome plaintiff's *prima facie* case, the employer can introduce evidence relating to matters such as the applicant's past experience and work record, letters of recommendation, or the superior qualifications of the person actually hired. An example is found in *Peters v. Jefferson Chemical Co.*, 516 F.2d 447 (5th Cir. 1975), in which the employer successfully rebutted the female plaintiff's *prima facie* case by showing that she had not been hired as a laboratory chemist because she had not done laboratory work for several years. The court did not require the employer to prove that her skills were actually inadequate, but accepted the employer's assumption that laboratory skills diminish from nonuse over a substantial period of time. In another case, *Boyd v. Madison County Mutual Insurance Co.*, 653 F.2d 1173 (7th Cir. 1981), a male employee established a *prima facie* case of sex discrimination against the employer by showing that the employer had a policy of awarding attendance bonuses only to clerical employees, all of whom were women. The employer was able to rebut the *prima facie* case successfully by demonstrating that there had been a serious absenteeism problem with clerical staff and that the bonus policy was aimed at correcting that problem.

In a case based on an allegedly discriminatory discharge, the employer might overcome the plaintiff's *prima facie* case by showing evidence of the plaintiff's poor performance, absenteeism, insubordination, and so on.

The types of reasons that are sufficient to rebut a plaintiff's *prima facie* case may vary from one kind of job to another. For instance, some jobs require skills that are quite subjective and extremely difficult to measure. Many executive and professional jobs are of such a nature, requiring traits such as creativity, initiative, ability to delegate and supervise, communicative skills, and a facility for persuasion. With regard to jobs that are inherently subjective, an employer usually will be permitted to use subjective justifications for the action taken. Thus, an attorney could be rejected because of "poor reputation," so long as the employer actually had some evidence of this fact. On the other hand, a court ordinarily will not accept an employer's purely subjective evaluation of an individual when the job in question requires little skill or responsibility or when it requires skills that can be objectively measured.

Pretext. If the plaintiff establishes a *prima facie* Title VII violation and the employer fails to come forth with acceptable evidence of a legitimate, nondiscriminatory reason, the plaintiff wins. If the employer does produce such evidence, the plaintiff will lose unless he or she can then convince the court that the employer's asserted reason was really just a "pretext"—that is, a cover-up for intentional discrimination. Plaintiff might be able to show, for example, that the employer's "legitimate reason" was applied discriminatorily. In *Corley v. Jackson Police Dept.*, 566 F.2d 994 (5th Cir. 1978), the employer proved that the plaintiffs, black police officers, had been fired for accepting bribes. Although this clearly was a legitimate reason for firing them, the plaintiffs proved that white officers who also had been accused of the same conduct by an informant were not investigated as thoroughly and were not fired. The court held that the employer's reason was a pretext for racial discrimination and that Title VII had been violated.

Discriminatory Impact

We have seen that a violation of Title VII can be proved by showing that the employer intended to discriminate. This proof is accomplished either by presenting direct evidence of discriminatory motive or by establishing a *prima facie* case from which discriminatory intent can be inferred.

Another way to prove that an employer has violated Title VII is to show that a particular employment rule or practice, although apparently neutral on its face, actually has an unequal impact on a protected group. Examples include height and weight requirements having the effect of excluding a disproportionate number of females, or a standardized test or educational requirement having the effect of excluding a disproportionate number of persons from a particular ethnic group. In such a case, the plaintiff is not required to show that the defendant had an intent to discriminate.

Prima Facie Case. The individual plaintiff, or the EEOC acting in the individual's behalf, must initially prove that the employment practice in question has an adverse impact on the protected group of which the individual is a member. This can be accomplished by the use of several different types of evidence. It could be shown, for example, that the employment practice has caused the employer to hire 40 percent of the whites who had applied, but only 20 percent of black applicants. Or, in another situation, discriminatory impact might be proved by showing that some action of the employer had the effect of eliminating 75 percent of all women from possible consideration, even though women comprise approximately one-half of the total population. Another method for proving discriminatory impact is to do a statistical comparison of the composition of the employer's work force with the composition of the relevant labor pool. For example, if the plaintiff alleges that a job criterion or selection method has a discriminatory impact on blacks, the plaintiff might attempt to show that the percentage of blacks working for the employer is much smaller than the percentage of qualified blacks in the available labor market. When a statisitcal disparity is used to prove discriminatory impact, the plaintiff must produce evidence linking the particular practice being challenged to the statistical imbalance in the employer's work force. If several employment practices are being challenged on the grounds that they have an aggregate discriminatory impact, the plaintiff will be permitted to lump them together if it is not feasible to single out a specific practice and show its impact alone.

It is important to realize, however, that the method used to prove discriminatory impact must be tailored to fit the particular employment practice being challenged and the particular group allegedly being affected. Thus, a court usually would not accept a comparison of the employer's minority hiring rate with general population statistics where the job in question required special qualifications. For example, if the job required a degree in mechanical engineering, the employer's experience in filling that job would need to be compared with the available population of mechanical engineers. The geographic area in which the statistical comparison should be made will also differ from one case to another. Suppose, for instance, that a plaintiff is trying to establish discriminatory impact in the case of an employer in San Francisco. If the job in question involves unskilled or semiskilled labor, general population statistics for the San Francisco-Oakland Bay area would probably be appropriate for comparison. However, if the job requires such special training and qualifications that the employer normally would have to recruit over a wider geographic area, the appropriate base for statistical comparison would be the population of qualified individuals in that larger area, such as the United States.

Employer's Rebuttal As we have seen, an employer may rebute a *prima facie* case of discriminatory intent merely by producing some plausible evidence of a nondiscriminatory reason for the employer's action. When the plaintiff has established a *prima facie* case by proving discriminatory *impact,* however, the employer's task of rebuttal is somewhat more difficult. In an impact case, the employer has to *prove* (not just introduce some plausible evidence) "business necessity." To meet this burden, the employer must prove that (1) the challenged employment practice was necessary to achieve an important business objective, and (2) the practice actually achieves this objective.

GRANT V. BETHLEHEM STEEL CORP.

U.S. Court of Appeals, Second Circuit, 635 F.2d 1007 (1980)

Bethlehem Steel Corporation's Fabricating Steel Construction Division was engaged in the construction of steel framework for skyscrapers, bridges, and other structures. The employees on these construction projects, who were called ironworkers, worked together in groups of three to six. Each group worked under the leadership of a foreman. No special education or training was required for the job of ironworker. To be a foreman, an ironworker needed safety consciousness, leadership qualities, and productiveness.

Before enactment of Title VIII, there had been a long history of racial discrimination in the hiring of ironworkers in the New York City area. Several factors, including title VII, a shortage of ironworkers, and

(continues)

GRANT V. BETHLEHEM STEEL CORP.

(continued from previous page)
community pressure, led to the admission of blacks into the ironworker trade by the 1960s. Black and other minority ironworkers did not, however, advance to become foremen. On ten representative projects in the 1970s, Bethlehem employed blacks in 10 percent of its 1018 ironworker jobs but hired only one black for 126 foreman jobs.

The method used for selection of foremen on Behtlehem's steel projects was rather haphazard. On each steel construction project Bethlehem employed a project superintendent, who chose the foreman for the project. The superintendents, all of whom were white, were given uncontrolled discretion to hire whom they pleased. These superintendents hired by word of mouth on the basis of wholly subjective criteria. No foreman's jobs were posted, and no list of eligible foreman was kept. Instead, on hearing informally of an upcoming Bethlehem project (the superintendent would learn this fact as much as eight months to a year in advance), the superintendent would communicate with persons in the trade whom he knew or who were recommended to him by others and line them up as prospective foremen for the project. Others interested in the job of foreman would rarely have the chance to apply for the job on any given project, because only persons solicited by the superintendent would know of the project in advance. By the time the project became known generally and notice of it was posted in the union hiring hall, there would usually no longer be any foreman openings available.

Three individuals, Grant, Ellis, and Martinez, attempted on several occasions to obtain foreman jobs with Bethlehem but were unsuccessful. Grant and Ellis were black, and Martinez was a dark-skinned Puerto Rican. All were in their forties and fifties and had many years of wide-ranging experience in ironwork, spot-less work records, and excellent reputations. In addition, Ellis had worked as a foreman for two other companies, Martinez had been a foreman on one previous project for Bethlehem, and Grant had been supervisor on several projects for other companies outside the United States.

Their repeated efforts to become foremen for Bethlehem were frustrated primarily by two Bethlehem superintendents, Deaver and Driggers. Both had been Bethlehem superintendents in New York for many years and had never hired a black or Puerto Rican foreman. They both hired foremen by word of mouth from among friends and those recommended by other foremen, union officials, or superintnedents. Neither of them ever kept any list of ironworkers qualified to become foremen. They defended their subjective hiring practices by pointing to the dangers of ironwork and asserting that no objective method of evaluation would have let them effectively determine an individual's competence to handle the heavy responsibility of the position.

Grant, Ellis, and Martinez, plaintiffs, brought a class action suit in federal district court against Bethlehem, Deaver, and Driggers, contending that the hiring practices in question were discriminatory both in treatment (intent) and impact. The district court ruled that the defendants had not violated Title VII, and the plaintiffs appealed.

Mansfield, Circuit Judge:

. . . [Plaintiffs] assert that friendship and nepotism rather than assessment of ability formed the basis for the superintendents' selections, and that since blacks tended to be excluded from the all-white superintendents' friendship, they were also unlawfully excluded from jobs as foremen. In support of these allegations, [plaintiffs] point out that the supervisors often went to considerable length to solicit people whom they knew for foreman positions, sometimes calling them on the phone or personally going to ask them to work. One superintendent, Driggers, hired his two sons as foremen, notwithstanding that they had less ironwork experience than the three named plaintiffs and had not served as foremen before. On another occasion, Superintendent Deaver hired a foreman whom he knew had a drinking problem. One member of the gang which this man supervised suffered a fatal accident because he was not following safety regulations. Similarly, Deaver rehired a foreman who had lost a gang member on his last project when a column for which he was responsible fell; the same foreman lost a derrick on the new project, and left work with a nervous breakdown. [Plaintiffs] urge that concern for workers' safety could not have been the primary motive behind these hirings. . . .

[W]e find insufficient the district court's grounds for holding that plaintiffs failed to make out a prima facie case of discriminatory treatment. . . .

The Supreme Court's holding in *Furnco Construction Co. v. Waters*, 438 U.S. 567 (1978), does not dictate a different result. There the Court held that employers had a responsibility only to offer blacks the same employment opportunities as whites, not to solicit blacks or otherwise devise hiring methods that would maximize black employment. Here blacks were not offered the same employment opportunities as whites. The district court stated that "if Bethlehem had taken affirmative steps to find qualified blacks, one or more additional black foremen would have been appointed," but concluded that Bethlehem's failure to take such steps could not be illegal, given the logic of *Furnco*. Contrary to the district court's conclusion, we believe that the failure to solicit qualified blacks as foremen constitutes a form of unacceptable discrimination in this case, since whites were here being solicited at the same time, even though the whites made no applications for the foreman's jobs for which they were hired. . . .

(continues)

GRANT V. BETHLEHEM STEEL CORP.

(continued from previous page)

[Plaintiffs] made out a strong prima facie case of discriminatory treatment under Title VII. . . .

Nor can we accept the district court's conclusion that [plaintiffs] failed to make out a prima facie case of discriminatory impact under Title VII. The undisputed statistics point strongly toward discrimination. After a "long history of discrimination against blacks in the hiring of ironworkers" Bethlehem during the 1970–75 period employed 1018 ironworkers, of whom 102 were black or Puerto Rican. During the same period it appointed 126 whites as foremen and only 1 black. . . .

Prior foreman experience is a factor properly considered in weighting the defense of business necessity. But without an inquiry into the nature and extent of the experience insofar as it may indicate superior competence on the part of the ironworkers, it cannot be categorized as [absolutely necessary] for appointment as foremen. An incompetent foreman should not be repeatedly hired over a qualified ironworker without foreman experience merely because the former had the good fortune to have been hired once as a foreman. Here, [plaintiffs] produced creditable evidence that the superintendents selected some foremen on the basis of friendship without knowledge of or inquiry into their prior safety history. Some of these foremen, as noted above, possessed bad safety records that would have excluded them from rehiring in a strictly merit-based hiring system. No business necessity dictated that these men be rehired without superintendents assuming any responsibility to consider qualified blacks for the job.

The record, moreover, shows that fully 50% of the foremen hired on the 10 sample projects had worked for Bethlehem less than a year before being made foremen. Each of the named plaintiffs, who were qualified to be foremen, had longer Bethlehem tenure. Many of these other foremen did not have the extensive experience gained by [plaintiffs] as ironworkers and foremen in outstanding companies other than Bethlehem. [Plaintiffs] adduced evidence that Bethlehem supervisors hired their sons, friends, and persons whom they trusted, often despite these men's relatively slight experience as Bethlehem ironworkers, even though persons with Bethlehem foreman experience (including [plaintiff] Martinez) were available for the job. . . .

[On the question of discriminatory impact, defendants also argue] that it was incorrect to view the entire Bethlehem ironworker force as the pool of qualified candidates for foreman positions. The presence of 10% blacks in the ironworkers' labor force, the argument goes, does not suggest that 10% participation in the foreman ranks should follow. Before 1972 there were few minority workers in the union, and most blacks who belonged to the union in 1975 had been members a relatively short time. Those blacks who belonged to the workforce during the early 1970s took up a comparatively larger segment of the apprentice and trainee pools. The legacy of admitted past discrimination gave blacks less average experience per man than whites. The ratio of qualified blacks to qualified whites in the workforce, [defendants] concluded, was therefore substantially smaller than the overall percentage of blacks in the workforce.

This background, though partially true, does not justify the assumption that there were *no* appreciable blacks in the workforce with the ability to be good foremen. Though the union had few black members in the early 1970s, many black "permit" workers were working on iron work projects during that period, and some even earlier. Some black workers, including the three named plaintiffs, had more experience at Bethlehem and elsewhere than at least several of the whites hired as foremen. Moreover, as all parties have recognized, experience is only one of several factors to be considered when selecting foremen. It defies common sense to suggest that only one black was sufficiently experienced and competent to merit selection as a foreman during this period when 126 foreman jobs were filled. It would not have created any substantial difficulty for supervisors to maintain a pool of "eligibles" to be notified of foreman openings, from whom they would choose the foreman for new projects. Such a pool would undoubtedly have contained some qualified blacks. . . .

For all of these reasons we hold that [plaintiffs] have made out a prima facie case of not only discriminatory treatment but discriminatory impact as well. We remand the case to permit [defendants] to introduce additional evidence that their discriminatory conduct may have been justified by business necessity, and for any rebuttal testimony by the plaintiffs. As the evidence thus far introduced is insufficient to meet the burden on the defendants, if no additional defensive evidence is offered the sole remaining issue would be backpay damages.

[Reversed and remanded.]

Bona Fide Occupational Qualification

Once discrimination has been proved, the employer has few defenses. One such defense in Title VII provides that it is not illegal to discriminate on the basis of religion, sex, or national origin in situations where religion, sex, or national origin is a **bona fide occupational qualification (BFOQ).** Race or color cannot be a BFOQ. Congress intended the BFOQ defense to be a very limited exception that would apply only to rare situations. The EEOC and the courts have followed this intent by recognizing the exception very infrequently.

Most of the situations in which BFOQ has been an issue have involved sex discrimination. Stereotypes or traditional assumptions about which jobs are appropriate for males or females do not establish the BFOQ exception. A basic principle of Title VII is that the individual should decide whether the job is appropriate, assuming that person is qualified to perform it. Thus, males cannot automatically be barred from jobs such as airline flight attendant or secretary,

and females cannot be barred from mining, construction, or other jobs requiring lifting, night work, and so forth. Even the fact that the employer's customers strongly prefer employees to be of one sex or the other does not create the BFOQ exception.

In a few circumstances, however, gender is an essential element of the job. For example, the BFOQ defense has been permitted where one sex or the other is necessary for authenticity, as in the case of models or actors. In addition, being a woman has been held to be a BFOQ for employment as a salesperson in the ladies' undergarments department of a department store, and as a nurse in the labor and delivery section of an obstetrical hospital. Being a man has been held to be a BFOQ for employment as a security guard, where the job involved searching male employees, and also as an attendant in a men's restroom.

The following case applies the BFOQ defense to a difficult problem faced by both employers and employees—exposure of women workers to substances that create risks of harm to fetuses.

United Automobile, Aerospace, & Agricultural Workers Union v. Johnson Controls, Inc.

U.S. Supreme Court, 111 S.Ct. 1196 (1991)

Case

Johnson Controls, Inc., manufactures batteries. In the manufacturing process, the element lead is a primary ingredient. Occupational exposure to lead entails health risks, including the risk of harm to any fetus carried by a female employee. Lead exposure to men also carries some risk for their unborn children, but not to the same extent as in the case of exposure to women. Before the Civil Rights Act of 1964 became law, Johnson Controls did not employ any woman in a battery-manufacturing job. In 1977 it adopted a policy of fully informing its female employees of the fetal risks associated with exposure to lead, permitting them to make a voluntary decision about whether they wished to work in a job that would expose them to lead. In 1982, the company changed its policy to one of exclusion. Under this policy, women were ab-

solutely excluded from jobs involving significant lead exposure unless they presented medical documentation of sterility.

Several employees and the union filed a class action in federal district court, alleging that the company's fetal protection policy constituted sex discrimination in violation of Title VII. Among the individual plaintiffs were Mary Craig, who had chosen to be sterilized in order to avoid losing her job; Elsie Nason, a 50-year-old divorcee who had suffered a loss in compensation when she was transferred out of a job where she was exposed to lead; and Donald Penney, a male employee who had been denied a request for a leave of absence for the purpose of lowering his lead level because he intended to become a father. The district court treated the fetal protection policy as a neutral employment practice having a discriminatory impact on women. The court concluded that the plaintiffs

had established a prima facie case of discriminatory impact, but that the company had established business necessity, and the plaintiffs had failed to demonstrate reasonable alternatives that would not have such a discriminatory impact. It granted summary judgment for the company. The U.S. Court of Appeals affirmed. The plaintiffs appealed to the U.S. Supreme Court. In their appeal, they claimed that the fetal protection policy was not a gender-neutral practice, but was explicitly discriminatory on the basis of sex. Because it was explicit gender discrimination, they contended that the defendant could prevail only by proving the BFOQ defense, which is much more difficult than showing business necessity in an impact case.

Blackmun, Justice:

The bias in Johnson Controls' policy is obvious. Fertile men, but not fertile
(continues)

United Automobile, Aerospace, & Agricultural Workers Union v. Johnson Controls, Inc.

(continued from previous page)
women, are given a choice as to whether they wish to risk their reproductive health for a particular job. The policy excludes women with childbearing capacity from lead-exposed jobs and so creates a facial [that is, explicit] classification based on gender. . . .

[Johnson Controls] does not seek to protect the unconceived children of all its employees. Despite evidence in the record about the debilitating effect of lead exposure on the male reproduction system, Johnson Controls is concerned only with the harms that may befall the unborn offspring of its female employees. . . . Johnson Controls' fetal-protection policy is [explicit] sex discrimination forbidden under Title VII unless respondent can establish that sex is a "bona fide occupational qualification."

Under section 703(e)(1) of Title VII, an employer may discriminate on the basis of "religion, sex, or national origin in those certain instances where religion, sex, or national origin is a bona fide occupational qualification reasonably necessary to the normal operation of that particular business or enterprise." . . . The BFOQ defense is written narrowly, and this Court has read it narrowly. We have read the BFOQ language of section 4(f) of the Age Discrimination in Employment Act of 1967 (ADEA), which tracks the BFOQ provision in Title VII, just as narrowly. . . . The wording of the BFOQ defense contains several terms of restriction that indicate that the exception reaches only special situations. The statute thus limits the situations in which discrimination is permissible to "certain instances" where sex discrimination is "reasonably necessary" to the "normal operation" of the "particular" business. Each one of these terms—certain, normal, particular—prevents the use of general subjective standards and favors an objective, verifiable requirement. But the most telling term is "occupational" this indicates that these objective, verifiable

requirements must concern job-related skills and aptitudes. . . .

Johnson Controls argues that its fetal-protection policy falls within the so-called safety exception to the BFOQ. Our cases have stressed that discrimination on the basis of sex because of safety concerns is allowed only in narrow circumstances. In *Dothard v. Rawlinson*, this Court indicated that danger to a woman herself does not justify discrimination. We there allowed the employer to hire only male guards in contact areas of maximum-security male penitentiaries only because more was at stake than the "individual woman's decision to weigh and accept the risks of employment." We found sex to be a BFOQ inasmuch as the employment of a female guard would create real risks of safety to others if violence broke out because the guard was a woman. Sex discrimination was tolerated because sex was related to the guard's ability to do the job—maintaining prison security. We also required in *Dethard* a high correlation between sex and ability to perform job functions and refused to allow employers to use sex as a proxy for strength although it might be a fairly accurate one. Similarly, some courts have approved airlines' layoffs of pregnant flight attendants at different points during the first five months of pregnancy on the ground that the employer's policy was necessary to ensure the safety of passengers. In two of these cases, the courts pointedly indicated that fetal, as opposed to passenger, safety was best left to the mother.

We considered safety to third parties in *Western Airlines, Inc. v. Criswell*, 472 U.S. 400 (1985), in the context of the ADEA. We focused upon "the nature of the flight engineer's tasks," and the "actual capabilities of persons over age 60" in relation to those tasks. Our safety concerns were not independent of the individual's ability to perform the assigned tasks, but rather involved the possiblity that, because of age-connected debility, a flight engineer

might not properly assist the pilot, and might thereby cause a safety emergency. Furthermore, although we considered the safety of third parties in *Dothard* and *Criswell*, those third parties were indispensable to the particular business at issue. In *Dothard*, the third parties were the inmates; in *Criswell*, the third parties were the passengers on the plane. We stressed that in order to qualify as a BFOQ, a job qualification must relate to the "essence," or to the "central mission of the employer's business.". . .

Third-party safety considerations properly entered into the BFOQ analysis in *Dothard* and *Criswell* because they went to the core of the employee's job performance. Moreover, that performance involved the central purpose of the enterprise. The essence of a correctional counselor's job is to maintain prison security; the central mission of the airline's business was the safe transportation of its passengers. . . . The unconceived fetuses of Johnson Controls' female employees, however, are neither customers nor third parties whose safety is essential to the business of battery manufacturing. No one can disregard the possibility of injury to future children; the BFOQ, however, is not so broad that it transforms this deep social concern into an essential aspect of batterymaking.

Our case law, therefore, makes clear that the safety exception is limited to instances in which sex or pregnancy actually interferes with the employee's ability to perform the job. . . . Women as capable of doing their jobs as their male counterparts may not be forced to choose between having a child and having a job. . . .

Pregnant women who are able to work must be permitted to work on the same conditions as other employees. . . . [E]mployers may not require a pregnant woman to stop working at any time during her pregnancy unless she is unable to do her work. Employment late in pregnancy often imposes risks on the unborn child, but Congress
(continues)

UNITED AUTOMOBILE, AEROSPACE, & AGRICULTURAL WORKERS UNION V. JOHNSON CONTROLS, INC.

(continued from previous page)
indicated that the employer may take into account only the woman's ability to get her job done. . . . Congress made clear that the decision to become pregnant or to work while being either pregnant or capable of becoming pregnant was reserved for each individual woman to make for herself. . . .

We have no difficulty concluding that Johnson Controls cannot establish a BFOQ. Fertile women, as far as appears in the record, participate in the manufacture of batteries as efficiently as anyone else. Johnson Controls' professed moral and ethical concerns about the welfare of the next generation do not suffice to establish a BFOQ of female sterility. Decisions about the welfare of future children must be left to the parents who conceive, bear, support, and raise them rather than to the employers who hire those parents. . . .

A world about tort liability and the increased cost of fertile women in the workplace is perhaps necessary. One of the [concurring] judges in this case expressed concern about an employer's tort liability and concluded that liability for a potential injury to a fetus is a social cost that Title VII does not require a company to ignore. . . . More than 40 States currently recognize a right to recover for a prenatal injury based either on negligence or on wrongful death. According to Johnson Controls, however, the company complies with the lead [exposure] standard developed by OSHA and warns its female employees about the damaging effects of lead. . . . Without negligence, it would be difficult for a court to find liability on the part of the employer [in a case alleging injury to a fetus]. If . . . Title VII bans sex-specific fetal-protection policies, the employer fully informs the woman of the risk, and the employer has not acted negligently, the basis for holding an employer liable [under general tort principles] seems remote at best.

[Without ruling on the question because it was not presented, the Supreme Court then noted that Title VII's prohibition of gender-specific fetal protection policies might preclude a tort claim for injury to a fetus on the constitutional theory of federal presumption.] . . . We, of course, are not presented with, nor do we decide, a case in which costs would be so prohibitive as to threaten the survival of the employer's business. We merely reiterate our prior holdings that [an] incremental cost of hiring women cannot justify discriminating against them. . . .

It is no more appropriate for the courts than it is for individual employers to decide whether a woman's reproductive role is more important to herself and her family than her economic role. Congress has left this choice to the woman as hers to make. The judgment of the Court of Appeals is reversed and the case is remanded.

Seniority Systems

Seniority refers to the length of time an employee has worked for a company, or perhaps the time worked within a particular department or other division of the company. Many companies, especially those having collective bargaining agreements with unions, have seniority systems. These systems provide that many kinds of employment rights and privileges are to be determined on the basis of seniority. For example, the right to bid for another job or another shift within the company, or the right to be protected from lay-off, may be determined by seniority. Although far from perfect, seniority systems are generally recognized as one of the few truly objective means for making many kinds of employment decisions. Such systems, however, can sometimes have a discriminatory impact on women and minorities, because these employees on the average are likely to have less seniority than white males. Because of their positive aspects, seniority systems are partially exempted from Title VII. A "bona fide" (good faith) seniority system does not violate Title VII just because it has a discriminatory impact; the system is illegal only if it is intentionally used to discriminate.

Other Issues under Title VII
Sexual Harassment

Harassment or intimidation of an employee violates Title VII when it is based on that person's sex just as it does when based on race, color, religion, or national origin. **Sexual harassment** may take the same form that other illegal harassment normally takes, namely, slurs, taunts, epithets, or other abuses that create a hostile, intimidating, or offensive working environment. In some situations, however, sexual harassment may be quite different from harassment for racial or other reasons. Sexual harassment may take the form of unwelcome requests for sexual favors. Indeed, it probably takes the form of unwelcome requests more often than slurs, taunts, and so on.

The courts and EEOC have recognized two general kinds of situations in which such unwelcome requests constitute illegal sexual harassment. These two varieties, which may sometimes overlap, are referred to as *"quid pro quo"* and "hostile environment" sexual harassment.

Quid Pro Quo Harassment.   The term **quid pro quo** means "something for something," and refers to the situation in which continued employment, a favorable review, promotion, or some other tangible job benefit is explicitly or implicitly conditioned upon an employee's positive response to a requested sexual favor. To prove this kind of illegal sexual harassment, the following facts must be established:

1. The employer, or someone for whose actions the employer is responsible, requested sexual favors from an employee, and the request was *unwelcome*.

2. The request was a term or condition of employment, or was reasonably seen by the employee as such a term or condition. This means that the request either (a) was actually part of the employment and would have an effect on the employee's status or opportunity, or (b) the employee reasonably interpreted the request as being part of the employment and having such an effect.

Hostile Environment Harassment.   This form of sexual harassment can occur where there are requests for sexual favors, but the evidence does not prove that the requests were tied to tangible job benefits. To prove **hostile environment** sexual harassment, the following facts must be established:

1. Like the *quid pro quo* variety, the employer, or someone for whose actions the employer is responsible, requested sexual favors from an employee, and the request or requests must have been *unwelcome*.

2. The request or requests must have been of such a nature as to create an intimidating, hostile, or offensive working environment. Although it is conceivable that a single unwelcome request could seriously infect the working environment, in most cases it will be difficult to prove that the hostile environment form of sexual harassment has occurred unless the unwelcome requests and accompanying conduct were repeated over a period of time.

Affirmative Action

The primary strategy in the legal battle against employment discrimination has been simply to prohibit discriminatory practices and to strike them down when they are discovered. Another important weapon, however, has been **affirmative action**— actually giving preferences to minorities and women in the hiring process. In many cases, affirmative action programs include goals and timetables for increasing the percentage of minorities and women in the employer's work force. The basic purpose of affirmative action is to rectify previous discrimination.

Affirmative action has been used by some courts as a remedy in specific cases of discrimination. In other words, after concluding that an employer had practiced discrimination, some courts have both ordered the cessation of the practice and required the employer to implement an affirmative action program. In addition, some employers, either on their own or in connection with union collective bargaining agreements, have instituted voluntary affirmative action programs.

Since their inception, affirmative action programs have raised difficult legal questions. By granting preferences to minorities and women, these programs discriminate in some degree against white males. White males are protected against race and sex discrimination by Title VII; does so-called reverse discrimination, brought about by affirmative action programs, violate Title VII or other discrimination laws?

In *United Steelworkers of America v. Weber*, 443 U.S. 193 (1979), the Supreme Court ruled that *voluntary* affirmative action programs are permissible under Title VII in certain circumstances. In several other cases, lower courts have upheld *mandatory* affirmative action programs in similar circumstances. As a limited exception to the basic prohibition against discrimination, reverse discrimination brought about by affirmative action programs is legal under the following conditions.

1. There must be a formal, systematic program— the employer cannot discriminate against nonminorities on an isolated, ad hoc basis.

2. Any such program must be temporary—it must operate only until its reasonable minority hiring goals are reached.

3. The program cannot completely bar the hiring or promotion of nonminority workers.

4. The program cannot result in the actual firing of nonminority workers.

5. The program cannot force the employer to hire or promote unqualified workers.

6. If the program is court-ordered, it must be based on evidence that there actually had been discrimination by the employer in the past. If the program is voluntary, it can be based either on evidence of past discrimination or merely on evidence that

there has been a substantial underutilization of minorities or women by the employer.

7. In general, an affirmative action plan cannot override preexisting employee rights that have been established by a valid seniority system. The following case illustrates this additional limitation on the operation of an affirmative action program.

FIREFIGHTERS LOCAL UNION NO. 1784 V. STOTTS

U.S. Supreme Court, 467 U.S. 561 (1984)

In 1977, Carl Stotts brought a Title VII action alleging that the Memphis Fire Department was engaged in unlawful racial discrimination. In 1980, the case was settled by consent decree between the parties. To increase black participation in the department, the consent decree established the goal of 50 percent black hiring and 20 percent black promotions for a designated time. In 1981, budget constraints in Memphis necessitated the layoff of numerous firefighters. Under the "last hired, first fired" protection of the Fire Department's seniority system, the laid off workers were predominantly blacks hired under the terms of the consent decree.

Mr. Stotts went back to court seeking an injunction that would prevent layoffs from obstructing the goal of the consent decree to increase the number of black firefighters. The union intervened to oppose this request and protect the terms of their seniority system. The district court

held for Stotts and entered an injunction that effectively required the department to fire white firefighters with seniority protection rather than the more recently hired black firefighters. This injunction was upheld on appeal, and the union appealed to the U.S. Supreme Court.

White, Justice:

Section 703(h) of Title VII provides that it is not an unlawful employment practice to apply different terms, conditions, or privileges of employment pursuant to a bona fide seniority system, provided that such differences are not the result of an intention to discriminate because of race. It is clear that the city had a seniority system, that its proposed layoff plan conformed to that system, and that in making the settlement the city had not agreed to award competitive seniority to any minority member whom the city later proposed to lay off. The District Court held that the city could not follow its seniority system in making its proposed layoffs because its proposal was dis-

criminatory in effect. Section 703(h) permits the routine application of a seniority system absent proof of an intention to discriminate. Here, the layoff proposal was not adopted with the purpose or intent to discriminate on the basis of race.

[The injunction to enforce the consent decree] overstates the authority of the trial court to disregard a seniority system in fashioning a remedy after an employer has followed a pattern or practice having a discriminatory effect on black applicants or employees. If individual members of a plaintiff class demonstrate that they have been actual victims of the discriminatory practice, they may be given their rightful place on the seniority roster. However, mere membership in the disadvantaged class is insufficient to warrant a seniority award; each individual must prove that the discriminatory practice had an impact on him. Here, there was no finding that any of the blacks protected from layoff had been a victim of discrimination and no award of competitive seniority to any of them. [Reversed.]

Comparable Worth

As we will see shortly, a separate federal statute, the Equal Pay Act of 1963, prohibits sex-based discrimination in rates of pay. This law applies only when a male and a female are doing jobs that are substantially the same. Therefore, the Equal Pay Act does

not apply to a situation in which a male and a female receive different pay for jobs that are different, even if the evidence indicates that the two jobs are of equal economic value to the employer. Although the doctrine of **comparable worth** does not provide a basis for a claim under the Equal Pay Act, the fact that men and women receive different pay for jobs that are of comparable worth to the employer might be relevant in a Title VII case in some circumstances. Suppose, for example, that a female employee claims that her employer violated Title VII by intentionally placing males and females in different categories of job because of their sex, or by setting different rates of pay for different jobs because one category of job was held primarily by men and the other primarily by women. In such a situation, evidence that the two categories of job were of comparable economic value to the employer would be a relevant factor to be considered by a court when it decides whether an inference of discriminatory intent is warranted.

Although evidence of different pay for jobs of comparable worth may in some circumstances be relevant to a possible inference of discriminatory intent, the courts thus far have held that evidence of comparable worth, by itself, does not establish a violation of Title VII. In other words, the fact that an employer has different pay rates for two different jobs of comparable worth, one type of job being held primarily by males and the other primarily by females, does not establish a violation of Title VII. Other evidence of gender-based discrimination would have to be present.

It is quite common for employers to base pay rates for different jobs on prevailing market rates for such jobs in the area. If such dependence on the market creates a situation in which women and men are paid differently for jobs of comparable worth, has the employer violated Title VII? In the leading case on this question, *American Federation of State, County, and Municipal Employees v. State of Washington*, 770 F.2d 1401 (9th Cir. 1985), the court of appeals concluded that an employer does not violate Title VII merely by basing pay scales on prevailing market rates even if the result is a differential between men and women. After this case and some others, the doctrine of comparable worth probably is of limited value in challenging a compensation system under Title VII. It should be noted, however, that several state legislatures have adopted comparable worth systems for state government employees. Because government jobs usually are classified in a systematic fashion, with substantial uniformity within a classification, the concept of comparable worth may have its greatest utility in government employment.

Equal Pay Act

The first antidiscrimination in employment act, predating even Title VII, is the Equal Pay Act. This statute prohibits an employer from paying an employee of one sex less than an employee of the opposite sex, when the two are performing jobs that require "equal skill, effort, and responsibility" and "under similar working conditions." Proof that the pay differential is due to the workers' varying merit or pursuant to a legitimate seniority system are available defenses under the Act. The Equal Pay Act is limited to sex discrimination in the form of wages and overlaps considerably with Title VII. There are slight differences in employers covered by the two Acts, however, and the Equal Pay Act may be a worker's only recourse for wage discrimination in some companies with fewer than 15 employees.

Age Discrimination in Employment Act

Title VII expanded the scope of employment discrimination protection in 1967, when it passed the Age Discrimination in Employment Act (ADEA). The coverage of this Act is quite similar to Title VII, except that it applies only to situations where there is a minimum of 20 employees. The ADEA prohibits discrimination based on age against anyone over age 40. Prohibited discrimination may take the form of disparate individual treatment, when an individual is penalized for being part of the protected age range, or disparate impact, when an employer's general policy needlessly discriminates against those aged 40 and over. Only the age of the victim of discrimination is relevant. Thus, an employer automatically favoring a 45-year-old over a 60-year-old, or vice versa, has violated the ADEA just as surely as if the employer had favored a 25-year-old.

The ADEA provides several statutory defenses for employers. An employee may always be discharged or otherwise penalized for good cause other than age. A bona fide occupational qualification defense also exists and closely resembles that under Title VII. Bona fide seniority systems or employee benefit plans are also exempted from ADEA violation. Courts have interpreted these defenses somewhat more expansively, in the employer's favor, than in most cases decided under Title VII.

Discrimination against Persons with Disabilities

In the Rehabilitation Act of 1973, Congress prohibited discrimination in employment against handicapped persons. That law, however, applied only to the employment practices of federal government agencies, businesses having contracts with the federal government, and organizations or programs receiving federal funding (such as universities receiving federal research funds). The Rehabilitation Act continues to apply to these three groups of employers.

In 1990, Congress passed the Americans with Disabilities Act (ADA), which provides comprehensive protection against discrimination to persons with disabilities. The ADA includes provisions dealing not only with discrimination in employment, but also with problems of discrimination and access in public transportation, public accommodations (such as restaurants and office buildings), and communications. Title I of the ADA, dealing with employment, is the only part relevant to our discussion in this chapter. The employment portions of the ADA cover the same employers as Title VII of the 1964 Civil Rights Act; in addition, the new law adopts most of the procedures and methods of proving discrimination from Title VII.

The ADA borrows most of its basic concepts and definitions, however, from the Rehabilitation Act. Instead of speaking of "handicapped persons," as did the Rehabilitation Act, the ADA speaks of "persons with disabilities." It uses the same basic definition for such persons as was used for handicapped persons under the Rehabilitation Act. Under the ADA, a person has a disability if he or she has a "physical or mental impairment that substantially affects one or more of the major life activities" of that person. Major life activities include functions such as caring for one's self, performing manual tasks, walking, seeing, hearing, speaking, breathing, learning, and participating in social relationships and activities. The law does not attempt to include an exhaustive list of disabilities. However, conditions that obviously would constitute disabilities include orthopedic, visual, speech, and hearing impairments; cerebral palsy; muscular dystrophy; multiple sclerosis; HIV infection; cancer; diseases of the heart or other major organs; diabetes; seizure disorders (formerly called epilepsy); mental retardation; emotional illness; serious learning disabilities; drug addiction; and alcoholism. Although alcoholism and drug addiction constitute disabilities, the ADA expressly provides that a *current user* of alcohol or illegal drugs is not protected by the law.

Finally, the ADA also contains a list of conditions referred to as "behavioral" that are expressly excluded from the definition of disability, including homosexuality, bisexuality, gender identity disorders, exhibitionism, voyeurism, compulsive gambling, kleptomania, pyromania, and several others.

In addition to prohibiting discrimination in employment against a person actually having a "physical or mental impairment substantially affecting a major life activity," the ADA also prohibits discrimination against a person who either *has a record* of such an impairment or *is regarded as having* such an impairment. That part of the law dealing with having a record of an impairment is intended to protect those victimized by mistaken records (which are often difficult to correct) or by the stigma of a past affliction that no longer constitutes an impairment. Although that part of the law dealing with one who is "regarded" as having an impairment will sometimes overlap with the "record of" provision, its main purpose is to protect those who are victimized by stereotypes. In other words, there are some conditions that may cause no impairment at all, or at least no impairment for a certain kind of job, but because of stereotypes those with the condition are treated as if they are impaired.

Even if a person is protected by the ADA, an employer is under no obligation to hire unless the person is qualified to do the job. If the person can do the job without any special accommodation, the employer should not even bring up the subject of changing the job, changing the working environment, or similar subjects. However, if an individual is not qualified as the job now exists, but would be qualified if the employer makes a "reasonable accommodation" for the person's impairment, then the person is viewed by the law as being qualified. The question of reasonable accommodation should not be dealt with, however, unless the disabled person brings it up or unless the need to make some adjustment in the job becomes obvious after the individual has been performing it for a time. An adjustment of the work environment or schedules may be reasonable, or perhaps rearranging a job into different parts if such a change does not significantly affect efficiency. To meet the burden of making a reasonable accommodation for a person's disability, however, the employer is not required to incur an "undue hardship."

The ADA responds to a real social problem, and has the potential to tap a large pool of previously unused talent for our work force. Many people believe, however, that it reaches too far, includes too many physical or mental conditions, and has too many vague terms and concepts that will result in years of litigation. Some argue that the government (that is, taxpayers) should bear more of the burden for helping the truly disabled move into the mainstream of

American economic and social life, and that the ADA places too much of the burden on private businesses. Some also argue that mandatory use of arbitration or other alternative dispute resolution techniques should have been included in the law to avoid the huge amount of litigation that is expected.

PROTECTION OF SAFETY AND WELFARE

Although unions undoubtedly have improved the safety and welfare of individual employees, they have failed to provide full protection, at least in the judgment of Congress and the states. Numerous laws have been passed to protect workers from on-the-job injuries and the financial consequences of such injuries. Congress also has legislated to preserve the financial welfare of workers, especially in the context of pension and other employee benefit plans.

Workers' Compensation

In the 19th century, workers were frequently injured on the job and often without legal recourse to compensate them for their injuries. In response, state legislatures passed workers' compensation statutes. All fifty states have such laws and while they vary somewhat, the laws all share certain common features. Workers' compensation is paid without regard to employer negligence and workers receive a predetermined amount, based on the injury suffered. Benefits payable include medical costs, income replacement, death benefits, and rehabilitation costs. Levels of compensation are typically lower than a worker might receive in a lawsuit, but the statutory system avoids much of the attorney and other costs of litigation, while eliminating most employer defenses to payment of the lesser sum.

The main restriction on recovery under workers' compensation statutes is the requirement that the injury must have arisen "out of and in the course of employment." Although the majority of injuries are clearly job-related, a large number of cases lie on the disputed borderline of work. For example, an employee whose job requires travel will ordinarily be able to receive benefits for injuries incurred in the course of such travel. By contrast, a mere commuter will not be compensated if injured on the way to work.

Employees typically are also covered while engaging in activities reasonably incidental to job duties. Thus, an employee on a lunch break who slips and falls in the employer's cafeteria would be covered.

State laws also cover diseases arising out of employment, but proof of the source of disease is much more complicated to obtain than is proof of work injuries, and such cases are more often disputed.

Occupational Safety and Health Act

In 1970, Congress passed the Occupational Safety and Health Act to help prevent workplace disease and injuries. The Act created the Occupational Safety and Health Administration (OSHA), part of the U.S. Department of Labor, to administer its provisions. This statute applies to virtually every United States employer.

Central to OSHA's powers is its standard-setting authority. The agency promulgates regulations compelling employers to make their workplaces safer in a variety of ways. Most of the early standards were intended to prevent job injuries, and OSHA suffered considerable ridicule because of the highly detailed nature of its rules. For example, the agency devoted considerable effort to regulating the number of toilets to be available and the allowable design of such facilities. As the agency has gained experience, its standards have allowed more flexibility for employers, and the regulatory focus has shifted toward prevention of occupational diseases.

Unlike some agencies that have been largely co-opted by the industries they regulate, OSHA has maintained standards that are often quite strict. These rules have given rise to litigation that has helped define the extent of the agency's powers. In an attempt to prevent a cancer associated with the inhalation of benzene, a petroleum byproduct, OSHA promulgated a stringent standard without attempting to specify the magnitude of the harm created by existing levels. The agency believed that it was simply fulfilling its mandate to create the healthiest workplace feasible, but the Supreme Court overturned the regulation in *Industrial Union Department v. American Petroleum Institute,* 448 U.S. 607 (1980). The Court held that OSHA could regulate only "significant risks" and generally should quantitatively measure a risk before promulgating rules. Shortly after this decision, industry challenged an OSHA regulation limiting exposure to cotton dust, which causes several lung diseases. Industry contended that OSHA had to base regulation on a cost/benefit analysis, but the Supreme Court upheld the agency's regulation in *American Textile Manufacturers Inst. v. Donovan,* 452 U.S. 490 (1981). This decision held that OSHA possessed authority to require any health protection "feasible" for industry and was not required to weigh the costs of a rule against its benefits before acting.

While OSHA has broad standard-setting authority, the task of establishing rules against all workplace hazards is beyond the capabilities of any agency. In recognition of this limit, Congress created a "general duty clause" in the Safety Act. This provision requires all employers to provide a place of employment free from recognized hazards of death or serious harm, regardless of whether a federal standard applies to the particular situation. As an example of the application of this clause, one employer was found in violation for permitting untrained employees to attempt electrical repairs on a wet floor without any protective equipment.

Beyond standards development, OSHA is also responsible for enforcing the Act, and considerable controversy has circulated around these enforcement powers. The agency's compliance officers make unannounced inspections. While search warrants are required for the inspections, they are liberally granted. When violations are found, OSHA may issue citations to an employer that include penalties of up to $1000 per violation. An employer may contest these penalties before a separate, independent organization known as the Occupational Safety and Health Review Commission.

Fair Labor Standards Act

The Fair Labor Standards Act (FLSA) was among the federal government's first employment law statutes. Passed in response to the Great Depression, the FLSA regulates the hours that employees may be required to work and the wages they must be paid. As was the case in the statutes discussed above, the coverage of the FLSA is extremely broad. An employer involved in any way in interstate commerce falls under the Act's purview. An exception is made for managerial employees, as well as those employed in the professions, such as lawyers and accountants.

Among the most controversial provisions of FLSA immediately after its passage was the Act's prohibition of certain forms of child labor. Employees under 18 years of age are excluded from occupations designated as hazardous, such as mining, logging, and excavation work. Hours are strictly regulated for employees who are less than 16 years old.

The FLSA is also the source of the federal minimum wage requirements. This wage level is currently set at $4.25 per hour for each of the first 40 hours worked in a week. Any work in excess of 40 hours per week must be paid at a "time-and-a-half" rate, 50 percent greater than the employee's normal wage. If employees are not paid on an hourly basis, the FLSA requires at least as much compensation as a per hour minimum wage rate would require for the hours they actually worked. Employers must maintain complete employment and payroll records for review by the Department of Labor. Substantial penalties are imposed for violations. With the exception of the above provisions, the Act imposes no other requirements on the employment relationship, such as mandatory vacations or rest periods.

EMPLOYER'S RIGHT TO DISCHARGE EMPLOYEES

An employer must have considerable freedom to discipline or fire employees in order to manage its work force effectively and efficiently. If an employer is unable to discharge disgruntled or shirking workers, we all pay. On the other hand, many feel that employees deserve protection from unjustified dismissals. (Incidentally, when we speak of an employee being fired or discharged, we are referring not only to actual firing but also to "constructive discharges," where the employer creates such an intolerable situation for the employee that he or she is forced to quit.)

An employee who has a legally enforceable employment contract obviously has whatever job security the contract specifies. Most employees, however, do not have such a contract. An employee who is covered by a labor-management collective bargaining agreement usually enjoys considerable protection from improper discharge. Most such contracts provide that employees can be fired or otherwise disciplined only for "good cause." Approximately 30 percent of the American work force is covered by collective bargaining agreements. Public employees, i.e., those who work for a federal, state, or local government agency, also enjoy significant job security under federal and state "civil service" laws. In general, after a designated probationary period, these employees can be fired only for good cause and only after specified procedures have been followed. Public employees account for about 17 percent of the American work force.

Employment at Will

All other employees (over half of the work force) are covered by the so-called **employment-at-will** doctrine. This traditional common-law rule provides that, in the absence of a contract, either the employer or employee can terminate the relationship at any time, for any reason or no reason. In recent years, however, many people have come to view this rule as overly harsh toward employees and, consequently, a number of exceptions have been created.

Statutory Exceptions

A few federal and state statutes provide protection for employees in specific situations. For example, federal employment laws like Title VII, FLSA, and OSHA include provisions making it illegal for an employer to punish an employee for filing a complaint or cooperating with an investigation or proceeding under the particular law. In some states, employees are protected from being penalized for filing a workers' compensation claim or taking time off to serve on a jury. Also, several states now have statutes giving an employee a right to sue an employer for damages if the employer fired the employee for "whistle-blowing." Whistle-blowing occurs when a worker objects to or reports the employer's suspected illegal activities. Even if the employee turned out to be wrong, and the employer was not actually doing anything illegal, these statutes apply so long as the employee was sincere and had a solid factual basis for believing that illegal practices were occurring.

The Public Policy Exception

Although a number of statutes such as these have been enacted during recent times, the most important developments in the area have been judicial ones. On their own, the courts in a majority of states have carved out several important exceptions to employment at will. The most notable of these exceptions can be grouped together under the idea of "public policy." In other words, these courts have ruled that an employee should be able to recover damages for the tort of "wrongful discharge" (or "retaliatory discharge") when the employer's conduct is contrary to a clearly established public policy. Defining public policy is not always an easy task, however. Most courts are fully aware that a vague, expansive public policy concept will provide very little guidance to employers or employees. Without reasonable guidance, employers will find it very difficult to maintain an effective personnel management system because of the fear that every discharge might lead to an expensive lawsuit.

As a result, most courts have concluded that the public policy claimed to have been violated by the employer must be clearly stated in a federal or state statute, constitutional provision, or widely recognized and accepted judicial decision. In those states permitting an employee to assert a claim for wrongful discharge based on public policy, a fired employee is likely to have a good claim in the following situations:

1. The employer may not discharge a worker for refusing to commit an act that is *illegal* under a statute, constitutional provision, or prior judicial decision. For example, courts have found employers liable for firing employees who refused to participate in an illegal price-fixing scheme, commit perjury, mislabel food products, falsify a pollution control test, sign a false defamatory statement about a co-employee, perform a medical procedure for which the nurse-employee was not licensed, or pump a ship's bilges into the water.

2. Generally, an employee has a good wrongful discharge claim if he or she has been fired for *exercising a statutory right.* For example, an employer has been held liable for damages to an employee who was fired for exercising the right to sign a union authorization card. Similarly, employers have been held liable for discharging employees because they filed workers' compensation claims or served on juries, even if there was no specific antiretaliation statute in that state covering the situation.

3. An employer often will be held liable to an employee who was fired for *whistleblowing*—objecting to or disclosing the employer's violations of the law. The employee normally has a valid claim if he or she (a) acted in good faith and (b) had reasonable cause to believe that the employer was violating the law, even if later investigation reveals that the employer actually did not act illegally. On the question of whether an employee must first give company management an opportunity to correct the problem before complaining to the authorities, the courts are split. A majority of them, however, recognize the wrongful discharge claim regardless of where the employee first lodged an objection.

Courts usually have stressed that an employee is not protected from discharge just because he or she acted out of strong, and even admirable, convictions if a purely private matter is involved that does not affect the public interest. For example, one court concluded that there was no wrongful discharge claim where the employee was fired for refusing to follow a particular research program. As a matter of personal conscience, the employee felt that the research was not proper, but there was nothing illegal, immoral, or hazardous about it. Two Illinois cases also provide an illustrative contrast. In one, the court found that no violation of public policy had occurred when a company's chief financial officer was fired for a continuing disagreement with the company's president about accounting methods. There was no plausible claim that the president's methods were deceptive or violated securities or tax laws or generally accepted accounting principles. In the other case, the court held that the employee did have a claim for wrongful discharge where he had been fired for complaining about the company's use of accounting methods that substantially overstated income and assets in a way that very likely would violate tax laws and the disclosure provisions of federal securities laws.

The following case illustrates an unfortunate situation that led one state supreme court to consider and adopt the public policy exception to employment at will.

WAGENSELLER V. SCOTTSDALE MEMORIAL HOSPITAL

Arizona Supreme Court, 710 P.2d 1025 (1985)

Case

Catherine Wagenseller worked as an emergency room nurse for the Scottsdale Memorial Hospital. She had originally been recruited personally by the emergency department's manager, Kay Smith, and for four years maintained a superior work record and enjoyed excellent professional and personal relationships with Smith and others in the department. She was an "at-will" employee, with no contractual or other job guarantees.

Wagenseller, Smith, and several others from the emergency department, as well as a number of employees from other area hospitals, went on an eight-day camping and rafting trip down the Colorado River. While on the trip, Wagenseller became very uncomfortable because of the behavior of Smith and a few others. This behavior included heavy drinking, group nude bathing and other public nudity, and a lot of unnecessary closeness while rafting. In addition, Smith and others staged a parody of the song "Moon River," which ended with members of the group "mooning" the audience. Wagenseller declined to participate in any of these activities. Smith and others also per-formed the "Moon River" skit twice at the hospital after the group's return from the river, but Wagenseller declined to participate there as well.

After the trip, relations between Wagenseller and Smith deteriorated. Smith began harassing Wagenseller, using abusive language and embarrassing her in the presence of other staff. These problems continued, and Wagenseller was fired about five months after the camping trip. Wagenseller appealed her dismissal to the hospital's administrative and personnel department, but the dismissal was upheld. She then filed suit for damages against Smith, the hospital, and several of its personnel administrators. In the suit, she alleged that her termination violated public policy and therefore constituted the tort of wrongful discharge. Although Wagenseller's claims had been substantiated by the pretrial statements of several others, the trial court refused to recognize any exception to the employment-at-will doctrine and granted the defendants' motions for summary judgment. The appeals court reversed part of the judgment, but still did not grant Wagenseller the relief she sought, so she appealed to the Arizona Supreme Court.

Feldman, Justice:

. . . Under the traditional employment-at-will doctrine, an employee without an employment contract for a definite term can be fired for cause, without cause, or for "bad" cause. . . . In recent years there has been apparent dissatisfaction with the absolutist formulation of the common law at-will rule. . . . The trend has been to modify the at-will rule by creating exceptions to its operation. . . . The most widely accepted approach is the "public policy" exception, which permits recovery upon a finding that the employer's conduct undermined some important public policy. . . . A majority of the states have now either recognized a cause of action based on the public policy exception or have indicated their willingness to consider it, given appropriate facts. The key to an employee's claim in all of these cases is the proper definition of a public policy that has been violated by the employer's actions.

Before deciding whether to adopt the public policy exception, we first consider what kind of discharge would violate the rule. The majority of courts required, as a threshold showing, a "clear mandate" of public policy. The leading case recognizing a public policy exception to the at-will doctrine is

(continues)

WAGENSELLER V. SCOTTSDALE MEMORIAL HOSPITAL

(continued from previous page)
Palmateer v. International Harvester Co., 421 N.E.2d 876, 878 (Ill. 1981), which holds that an employee stated a cause of action for wrongful discharge when he claimed he was fired for supplying information to police investigating alleged criminal violations by a co-employee. Addressing the issue of what constitutes "clearly mandated public policy," the court stated:

> There is no precise definition of the term. In general, it can be said that public policy concerns what is right and just and what affects the citizens of the State collectively. It is to be found in the State's constitution and statutes and, when they are silent, in its judicial decisions. Although there is no precise line of demarcation dividing matters that are the subject of public policies from matters purely personal, a survey of cases in other States involving retaliatory discharges shows that a matter must strike at the heart of a citizen's social rights, duties, and responsibilities before the tort will be allowed.

. . . It is difficult to justify this court's further adherence to a rule which permits an employer to fire someone for a cause that is morally wrong. . . . Certainly, a court would be hard-pressed to find a rationale to hold that an employer could with impunity fire an employee who refused to commit perjury. . . . We therefore adopt the public policy exception to the at-will termination rule. We hold that an employer may fire for good cause or for no cause. He may not fire for bad cause—that which violates public policy. . . .

. . . In the case before us, Wagenseller refused to participate in activities which arguably would have violated our indecent exposure statute. This statute provides that a person commits indecent exposure by exposing certain described parts of the body when someone else is present and when the defendant is "reckless about whether such other person, as a reasonable person, would be offended or alarmed by the act." . . . While this statute may not embody a policy which "strikes at the heart of a citizen's social rights, duties, and responsibilities" as clearly and forcefully as some other statutes, such as a statute prohibiting perjury, we believe that it was enacted to preserve and protect the commonly recognized right of public privacy and decency. The law does, therefore, recognize bodily privacy as a "citizen's social right." . . . We are compelled to conclude that termination of employment for refusal to participate in the public exposure of one's buttocks is a termination contrary to the policy of this state. . . .

[The trial court's action granting summary judgment against Wagenseller was in error. The decision is reversed and remanded to the trial court for a trial where Wagenseller will have a full opportunity to prove her allegations.] ⚖

PROTECTION OF EMPLOYEE PRIVACY

Lie Detector Testing

Employers have extremely important interests in learning certain kinds of background information about people who are applying for jobs. Incompetent, dishonest, or violent employees can cause untold harm to an employer. A company may need to know about a job applicant's past work record, criminal record, and general character when legitimately attempting to protect itself against lawsuits and against a damaged reputation, as well as to protect its customers and its other employees from physical harm. Employers also have a valid interest in obtaining information from existing employees when theft or other wrongdoing has occurred at the workplace.

During the past several decades, more and more employers used the lie detector (polygraph) examination in an effort to get accurate information from employees and job applicants. Because of mounting evidence that these examinations are not very reliable, and that thousands of employees and applicants were being harmed each year by erroneous results, Congress passed the Employee Polygraph Protection Act of 1988. This law prohibits most uses of the polygraph by private employers, subject only to a few limited exceptions. The most important exception permits a private employer to require an employee to take a lie detector test as part of an ongoing investigation of theft, sabotage, or other property loss, if this employee had custody of the property and if there is other independent evidence creating a reasonable suspicion that this employee was involved in the incident. The law also does not prohibit federal, state, or local government agencies from requiring their employees and job applicants to take lie detector tests, mainly because the Constitution applies to government employers. The constitutional right of privacy protects against many unreasonable uses of the polygraph by government employers, but clearly does not protect employees to the extent that the federal polygraph statute does.

Employee Drug Testing

Employees who are impaired by drugs or alcohol endanger the public and their fellow workers, and cost their employers millions of dollars annually as a result of accidents, absenteeism, higher health insurance claims, low productivity, and poor workmanship. Employers have legitimate interests in minimizing these costs; maintaining a safe, secure, and productive workplace; and protecting themselves against liability to those injured by the actions of impaired employees. Both co-workers and members of the public have a legitimate claim to protection against the unsafe conduct or defective products resulting from employees' drug or alcohol use.

Employees subjected to drug testing, on the other hand, have important interests in preventing harm to their reputations and economic security resulting from inaccurate test results and avoiding unwarranted intrusions into their personal lives. Drug tests are not always accurate, and the analysis of urine, blood, or hair specimens often reveals a lot of private information about the subject that has nothing to do with the use of illicit drugs. It is certainly true that alcohol use causes the same kinds of workplace problems as drug use, but alcohol-impaired employees often can be identified more easily without the risk of erroneous test results or the disclosure of irrelevant private information that may be revealed in drug testing. Most of the difficult legal issues, therefore, have involved employers testing for controlled substances other than alcohol.

Most employers take some kind of action against an employee who refuses a test or who tests positive for illicit drugs. This action can range from required enrollment in a rehabilitation program to immediate discharge. Similarly, job applicants who refuse testing or test positive are virtually assured of not getting the job. As a result, legal action by employees challenging drug-testing programs is becoming increasingly common. The legal system has not yet had sufficient time, however, to develop a coherent, uniform set of principles to balance the various interests that are involved. Although the law pertaining to employee drug testing is still in a formative stage, it is possible to make some generalizations.

If the employer is a federal, state, or local government agency, the Constitution provides a measure of protection for the legitimate privacy interests of employees. The Constitution also applies if the government requires a private employer to do drug testing.

The most obviously applicable constitutional provision is the Fourth Amendment prohibition of *unreasonable searches and seizures.* The taking of a urine, blood, or hair specimen is a "search and seizure." Generally, people and their belongings can be searched only if there is "probable cause" to believe that they possess evidence of a violation of the law. Recently, in *National Treasury Employees Union v. Von Raab*, 109 S.Ct. 1384 (1989) (involving testing by a government agency), and *Skinner v. Railway Labor Executives Ass'n*, 109 S.Ct. 1402 (1989) (involving government-required testing by private employers), the U.S. Supreme Court held that drug testing sometimes is constitutionally permissible even without any evidence that a particular employee is a drug user. The Court said that, in the case of employees whose work creates significant safety, health, or security risks, testing may be done on a random or mass basis so long as the testing program is conducted in a reasonable manner overall. To be reasonable, the program must include ample safeguards to ensure accuracy and privacy.

The Constitution does not apply to drug testing by private employers unless the testing is required by the government. Tort law does apply, however, if an employer conducts a test or uses the results in such a way that a tort is committed. If the employer intentionally reveals private information from the test to others who have no legitimate interest in receiving it, the employer may be liable to the employee for the tort of invasion of privacy. If the test produces a false positive result, and the employer reveals it to others without a legitimate interest in knowing it, the employer may be liable for defamation. In some cases, carelessness in the administration of the test or use of the results may cause the employer to be liable for the tort of negligence.

A few states have passed statutes specifically regulating the design and implementation of drug testing programs by private employers. The objective of these statutes is to increase the likelihood that results will be accurate and that employee privacy will be protected to the fullest extent possible.

In the case of unionized workers, the implementation of a drug testing program is a so-called "mandatory subject of collective bargaining." This means that the employer cannot make such a decision on its own, but must submit the question to the process of collective bargaining with the union. If the company and the union cannot agree, either or both may use

THE LAW AT WORK

Box 49.1
The Law
at Work

Employment law is another area where alternative dispute resolution has become increasingly common. Mediation and arbitration have been used for many decades in the resolution of workplace disputes when a labor union is involved. Almost all collective bargaining agreements include procedures for resolving disputes, with legally binding arbitration often being the capstone of the procedure. The most common situation in which arbitration is used in this context occurs when an employee is disciplined or terminated, and contends that the punishment was not for "good cause" as specified in the collective bargaining agreement. If the matter cannot be resolved informally between union and company representatives, arbitration is typically used as a final resolution method.

Until recently, arbitration was not used frequently to resolve employment disputes outside the labor union context. Today, however, it is becoming much more common for employers and employees to enter into individual employment contracts containing predispute arbitration clauses even when no union is involved. The trend was already developing rapidly, but accelerated when the U.S. Supreme Court held that an arbitrator's decision in such a case is legally binding even when the employee asserts a claim based on some federal statute, such as the laws against various forms of employment discrimination. Thus, if an employee who has signed an employment contract containing a clause calling for legally binding arbitration of any future disputes arising from the employment relationship is later fired and wishes to sue the employer, the dispute must be submitted to arbitration even if the employee claims a violation of some right created by statute. The decision of the arbitrator is final, and the employee cannot file a lawsuit alleging such a right.

In many situations in which companies traditionally would not have entered into a binding employment contract at all (that is, where there would be only an "at will" relationship, with no enforceable contract rights on either side), more and more companies are using employment contracts containing arbitration clauses when hiring employees. There is no evidence that arbitrators are more likely than judges or juries to find in favor of companies in such disputes, but when the employee does win, the damage awards tend to fall within a narrower range. Thus, in addition to the typical savings of time and expense associated with arbitration, employees and their attorneys are less likely to operate with a "lottery" mentality, hoping for an extremely large jury verdict. (In another area where arbitration has become much more commonly used, disputes between securities brokers and their customers, empirical studies have shown that arbitrators are at least as likely as judges or juries to rule in favor of the customer; moreover, the average damage awards by arbitrators in these securities cases are slightly higher than those in federal court, but the amounts of those awards do not vary as wildly in arbitration as in court. Although this situation is different, it is sufficiently similar for us to infer that employees submitting various claims to arbitration probably will do as well, on the average, as they would have done in court, although the damage awards are likely to fall within a narrower range overall.)

economic weapons such as lockouts or strikes to put pressure on the other side.

SUMMARY

The law of employment relationships has undergone a series of fundamental changes in recent decades. For much of our nation's history, employment was governed by traditional common-law rules of contracts, with little government involvement. Today's employer, however, must be cognizant of numerous government requirements in the areas of health and safety, discrimination, wages, employee benefits, and labor organization.

The first inroads in the common law came in the National Labor Relations Act. This legislation facilitated unionization of the workplace by protecting organizing campaigns, compelling collective bargaining between management and lawfully recognized employee representatives, prohibiting discrimination against union members, and guaranteeing the right to strike, among other provisions. A long list of employer activities may be considered unfair labor practices, for which the employer may be penalized. This labor law also provides some benefits to employers in terms of prohibiting certain types of actions by union and nonunion employees.

The most significant recent labor laws are those against employment discrimination. Under Title VII of the Civil Rights Act, employers are prohibited from intentionally discriminating against employees because of their race, sex, color, religion, or national origin. Moreover, even seemingly neutral employment practices may be found illegal if they have the effect of discriminating against one or more of the protected classes. This statute has given rise to the controversial social issue of affirmative action, in which protected classes are granted special benefits, often at the expense of other workers. While some forms of affirmative action are legal, courts have placed limits on many programs. Other related legislation proscribes discrimination because of age or handicap and compels equal pay for equal work.

Another significant area of employment law regulation deals with worker safety and welfare. The Occupational Safety and Health Act enables the federal government to set standards for workplace safety. When accidents do occur, state workers' compensation statutes ensure that employees are compensated for their injuries. The Fair Labor Standards Act regulates pay levels for workers.

Yet another employment law issue involves standards for firing workers. Recent statutes and court decisions are placing important limits upon an employer's discretion in discharging employees. Such a decision may be unlawful if it violates public policy principles.

Finally, a number of legal developments in recent years have focused on the privacy rights of employees. An important federal law now restricts employers' use of the lie detector, and provisions of constitutional and tort law are being applied to workplace drug testing.

KEY TERMS

Unfair labor practice
Collective bargaining
Prima facie case
Bona fide occupational qualification (BFOQ)
Sexual harassment
Quid pro quo
Hostile environment
Affirmative action
Comparable worth
Employment at will

QUESTIONS AND PROBLEMS

1. Republic Aviation Corp. operated a large military aircraft manufacturing plant that was not unionized. Republic had a rule against soliciting union membership within the plant. A worker ignored the rule and passed out application cards on his own time during lunch periods. Republic fired the worker for violating company rules, and the worker filed a complaint with the NLRB. Has the company committed an unfair labor practice? (*Republic Aviation Corp. v. NLRB*, 324 U.S. 793, 1945.)

2. A building stone supplier and its union were involved in a labor dispute and a strike was called. The company's customers at construction sites rented independent trucking companies to deliver the company's stones during the strike and deducted the rental cost from their payments to the supplier. The stone supplier's union picketed the construction site customers and the rental trucking companies. Has the union committed an unfair labor practice? (*Laborers Local 859 v. NLRB (Thomas S. Byrne, Inc.)*, 446 F.2d 1319, D.C. Cir. 1971.)

3. As a protest against the Russian invasion of Afghanistan, members of the International Longshoremen's Association refused to handle cargoes arriving from or departing to the Soviet Union. An American company that imports Russian wood products for sale in the United States complained to the NLRB that the union action was illegal. Has the union committed an unfair labor practice? (*Int'l Longshoremen's Assn. v. Allied Int'l Inc.*, 102 S.Ct. 1656, 1982.)

4. The Los Angeles Dept. of Water & Power provided retirement and death benefits for its employees. Because, statistically speaking, the women employees would outlive the male employees by a number of years, the total retirement benefits paid out would be greater. Consequently, the Department required female employees to pay more toward the retirement fund. A female employee claimed that this was unlawful sex discrimination and sued. Should she win? (*L.A. Dept. of Water & Power v. Manhart*, 435 U.S. 702, 1978.)

5. A male airline pilot decided that he would be more comfortable as a woman and underwent a sex change operation. The pilot's employment record as a man was very good. After the operation, however, the airline fired the pilot, expressing a variety of medical and psychological concerns for safety. The pilot claimed that she was discriminated against as a transsexual in a way "based on sex" and that her firing therefore constituted illegal discrimination. Should she win?

6. Employee X has been exposed to the AIDS virus. After admitting this fact on a questionnaire, he was fired by the employer. Assume that the employer receives federal funds. Can the employee successfully sue for unlawful discrimination under the Rehabilitation Act?

7. A railroad had an absolute policy of refusing consideration for employment to any person convicted of a crime other than a minor traffic offense. Green, a prospective employee, had been convicted for refusing military induction in 1967. Statistics showed that in urban areas between 37 and 78 percent of all blacks would be excluded by this policy, while 11 to 17 percent of whites would be so excluded. Green, refused employment as a consequence of the policy, sued the railroad under Title VII of the Civil Rights Act. Should Green win? (*Green v. Missouri Pacific Railroad Co.*, 523 F.2d 1290, 8th Cir. 1975.)

8. McKeever worked as an attorney of New Jersey Bell Telephone Co. While driving home from work one day he was killed in an auto accident. His family claimed for workers' compensation death benefits, noting that at-home work was a regular part of McKeever's job, that the employer encouraged and benefited from this at-home work, and that he had work in his briefcase in the car at the time he was killed. Is this a valid workers' compensation claim? (*McKeever v. New Jersey Bell Telephone Co.*, Workmen's Comp. Law Rep. (CCH) Sec. 2566, N.J. Super. Ct. App. Div. 1981.)

9. An employee of Sanders Roofing Co. fell from the flat roof where he was working. Because there was no catch platform around the roof the Labor Department issued a citation to Sanders for violating the "general duty" clause of OSHA. Sanders argued in defense that OSHA had a specific standard requiring catch platforms around sloped roofs but not flat ones. Should Sanders be found guilty of violating OSHA? (*R.L. Sanders Roofing Co. v. OSHRC*, 620 F.2d 97, 5th Cir. 1980.)

10. Cleary worked for American Airlines for 20 years as a payroll clerk and an airport operations agent. American fired Cleary for being absent from his work area and threatening another employee, but provided him no hearing to answer these charges. Cleary alleged that the real reason for his firing was his union activities and sued American Airlines for unlawful discharge, claiming that the company violated an implied covenant of good faith. Should Cleary prevail? (*Cleary v. American Airlines, Inc.*, 168 Cal. Rptr. 722, 2nd Ct. App. 1980.)

Chapter 50

Environmental Protection Law

Common Law and Pollution
National Environmental Policy Act
Water Pollution Control
Air Pollution Control
Solid Waste and Its Disposal
Regulation of Toxic Substances
Noise Pollution
Indoor Pollution
Endangered Species
The Environment, Industry, and Society

ONCERN FOR THE environment is growing both domestically and internationally. As Americans have gradually become more aware of the adverse impact that human consumption of resources and human technology can have on the land, sea, and air, their support for more comprehensive governmental regulation of environmental matters has grown. Well-known incidents such as the accident at the Three Mile Island nuclear facility; the contamination by dioxins of Times Beach, Missouri; the indiscriminate dumping of hazardous wastes in Love Canal, New York; and the Alaskan oil spill caused by the Exxon *Valdez* have intensified public concern. Problems such as acid rain, depletion of the ozone layer, and the "greenhouse effect" are creating similar concerns on an international scale.

In recent years these concerns have led to a strengthening of state and local regulation of pollution, to the creation of a mammoth array of federal pollution regulations, and to some initial efforts at international cooperation in pollution control. For businesses, these rules and regulations are decidedly a mixed blessing. On the one hand, the owners, officers, and employees of businesses are individuals who need a clean, safe environment as much as anyone else. On the other hand, many of these laws impose additional burdens on what many consider to be an already overregulated economy.

The thousands of rules and regulations issued by the Environmental Protection Agency (EPA), for example, have become a part of the legal environment of business with which industry must become familiar. Many small firms have gone out of business because they could not meet various antipollution requirements imposed by the EPA. Others, both large and small, have found that compliance has become an extremely costly budget item. As we shall see in this chapter, two obvious manifestations of the heightened level of environmental regulation lie in (1) the increasing use of *criminal* sanctions against environmental offenders (134 criminal indictments for violations of federal environmental laws were brought in fiscal 1990 alone) and (2) regulations that require persons who did not actually pollute to pay for the cleanup of pollution caused by others (for example, landowners may be liable for millions of dollars to clean up pollution caused entirely by previous owners of the land).

Nothing could be more important than the saving of our planet's environment. However, the many governmental regulations outlined in this chapter place a tremendous burden on industry, much of which is passed on to the consuming public. During the coming years there will be continuing debate as to the proper balancing of environmental versus economic interests both domestically and internationally. However, there is no doubt that environmental regulation will continue to be a consideration of enormous importance in most domestic and multinational businesses. Modern managers must view the environment and its legal regulation as a challenge, as an opportunity, and as a factor that must be continuously considered as decisions are made. New rules and regulations will create costs that must be managed. They will terminate some lines of business but open up others.

In this chapter we examine several of the known causes of pollution and the major remedial measures designed to prevent further deterioration of the environment. We also briefly address the matter of *indoor* air pollution. And we will explore the fledgling international efforts to preserve the global environment by multinational cooperation. Initially, however, we will look at common-law remedies that have long been available at the state level to remedy certain types of pollution.

COMMON LAW AND POLLUTION

Common-law remedies founded on the law of torts are totally inadequate to provide a comprehensive method of regulating air, land, and water pollution in the United States. However, as a remedial or loss-shifting device, common-law torts may be useful to individual plaintiffs who may have suffered some environmental harm. A farmer's water supply may be contaminated by industrial discharge of pollutants into a stream. Homeowners near a sanitary landfill may be exposed to noxious fumes from the constant trash fires used by the landfill to dispose of burnable refuse. Or homeowners may suffer property damage when caustic fumes from a chemical plant blanket their property, killing vegetation and causing house-paint to peel and crack. In each case the individual plaintiff may seek injunctions to prohibit further damage from the pollutants and, in appropriate cases, recover money damages. The common-law tort remedies available include nuisance, negligence, trespass, and strict liability.

Nuisance

When property is used in such a manner that it inflicts harm on others, there may be a cause of action in tort for **nuisance** against the owner. If the harm is widespread, affecting the common rights of a substantial segment of a community, it is considered a *public* nuisance. Because fishing rights belong to the public, a discharge of pollutants into a navigable stream that killed fish would be a public nuisance. If an individual's right to quiet enjoyment of his or her land is disturbed by unreasonable and unwarranted use of property by another property owner, a *private* nuisance has occurred. Most public nuisances are abated through action by public officials charged with controlling the facility that is causing the harm. An action to abate a private nuisance is usually brought by the party affected against the party whose conduct gives rise to the nuisance.

In the case of either public or private nuisances, courts are often called on to balance the interests of plaintiffs and defendants. No court would eagerly close an offending industrial plant that employs an entire community. Similarly, residents near a large airport may be expected to endure some inconvenience caused by noise and vibration. A homeowner who buys near an existing airport or industrial facility may not find the courts sympathetic when a complaint is registered, but this is not invariably the case. To balance the interests of the community properly, courts often cannot simply rule in favor of the party who arrived first.

For example, in *Spur Industries, Inc. v. Del E. Webb Development Co.*,[1] a major developer bought 20,000 acres of farm land near Phoenix to develop Sun City, a retirement village. Nearby were cattle feedlots, later purchased and expanded by Spur Industries. As the developer completed houses and Spur expanded, only 500 feet separated the two operations. Prevailing winds blew flies and odors from the cattle pens over the homesites, thus making it difficult to sell the sites most affected. The developer filed a

nuisance suit against Spur, asking that Spur be enjoined from operating its cattle feedlots in the vicinity of the housing development. In an attempt to balance the parties' competing interests reasonably, the court permanently enjoined Spur from operating the feedlots but further held that Spur should be awarded damages, a reasonable amount of the cost of moving or shutting down, because the developer had brought people to the nuisance, thus causing Spur damage.

Negligence, Trespass, and Strict Liability

The tort of **negligence** involves the breach by the defendant of a duty owed to the plaintiff to use reasonable care to avoid injury to the plaintiff's person or property. If the operator of a plant negligently maintained its equipment so that harmful pollutants were discharged into a waterway, neighbors injured by the pollution would probably have a valid negligence claim against the careless plant operator.[2]

An intentional entering onto another's land without permission is a **trespass.** So too, causing particles to be borne onto another's land may be a trespass if the owner of the source of the particles has reason to believe that the activity would cause damaging deposits. For example, a physical and obvious trespass occurs when cement dust from a plant is deposited, layer on layer, on the property of nearby residents. Of course, if the particles deposited are undetectable by human senses and not harmful to health, although undeniably real, a court, in balancing the interests of society, will likely dismiss any trespass action.[3]

In certain cases in which the threat or damage is caused by abnormally or inherently dangerous activities, the theory of **strict liability** may be used to recover damages or to halt the activity. The spraying of crops with toxic chemicals and the storage of explosive or other hazardous materials are examples of activities that may result in a defendant being held strictly liable. In such cases, a defendant's reasonable care is no defense. The inherent danger of the activity and resulting damages are sufficient to justify the plaintiff's recovery.

Although much attention is focused on the federal regulations that we are about to discuss, the role of these state common-law causes of action must not be overlooked. Even in situations addressed by federal laws, they provide a tremendously important

[2]The concept of negligence was fully discussed in Chapter 8.
[3]See *Bradley v. American Smelting and Refining Co.*, 709 P.2d 782 (Wash. 1985), in Chapter 8.

[1]494 P.2d 700 (Ariz. 1972).

supplement. For example, litigation over the costs of cleaning up hazardous waste sites is usually based on the federal "Superfund" statute to be discussed later. However, the New Jersey Supreme Court, for example, has ruled that a company that pollutes a property can be held strictly liable for cleanup and other costs, giving an important remedy to the purchasers of such sites.[4]

These common-law theories are of ancient origin but have been adapted to the environmental context in "toxic tort" litigation in recent years. In addressing the *enhanced risk doctrine* and the *medical monitoring doctrine*, the following case illustrates the modern evolution of the doctrine of negligence made necessary by the peculiar problems caused by exposure to environmental hazards.

[4]*T&E Indus. v. Safety Light Corp.*, 587 A.2d 1249 (N.J. 1991).

IN RE PAOLI RAILROAD YARD PCB LITIGATION

U.S. Court of Appeals, Third Circuit, 916 F.2d 829 (1990)

The plaintiffs are 38 persons who have either worked in or lived adjacent to the Paoli railyard, an electric railcar maintenance facility in Philadelphia. Their primary claim is that they have contracted a variety of illnesses as the result of exposure to polychlorinated biphenyls (PCBs). PCBs are toxic substances that, as the result of decades of PCB use in the Paoli railcar transformers, can be found in extremely high concentration at the railyard and in the surrounding air and soil. Defendants include Monsanto (maker of PCBs), General Electric (maker of transformers), Amtrak (owner of the site since 1976), and Conrail (operator of the site).

The district court excluded much of the plaintiffs' proffered testimony and thereafter granted summary judgment to the defendants. The trial court also rejected as a matter of law the plaintiffs' claim based on the medical monitoring doctrine. The plaintiffs appealed.

Becker, Circuit Judge:

[The court held that the trial judge had improperly excluded plaintiffs' expert testimony and therefore concluded that summary judgment had been inappropriately granted. In the following excerpt, the court addressed the plaintiffs' medical monitoring theory.]

We turn . . . to the viability of certain plaintiffs' "medical monitoring" claims, by which plaintiffs sought to recover the costs of periodic medical examinations that they contend are medically necessary to protect against the exacerbation of latent diseases brought about by exposure to PCBs. [Pennsylvania state courts have not] decided whether a demonstrated need for medical monitoring creates a valid cause of action. Therefore, sitting in diversity, we must predict whether the Pennsylvania Supreme Court would recognize a claim for medical monitoring under the substantive law of Pennsylvania and, if so, what its elements are.

Medical monitoring is one of a growing number of non-traditional torts that have developed in the common law to compensate plaintiffs who have been exposed to various toxic substances. Often, the diseases or injuries caused by this exposure are latent. This latency leads to problems when the claims are analyzed under traditional common law tort doctrine because, traditionally, injury needed to be manifest before it could be compensable.

Nonetheless, in an effort to accommodate a society with an increasing awareness of the danger and potential injury caused by the widespread use of toxic substances, courts have begun to recognize claims like medical monitoring, which can allow plaintiffs some relief even absent present manifestations of physical injury. More specifically, in the toxic tort context, courts have al-

lowed plaintiffs to recover for emotional distress suffered because of the fear of contracting a toxic exposure disease, the increased risk of future harm, and the reasonable costs of medical monitoring or surveillance. . . .

It is easy to confuse the distinctions between these various non-traditional torts. However, the torts just mentioned involve fundamentally different kinds of injury and compensation. Thus, an action for medical monitoring seeks to recover only the quantifiable costs of periodic medical examinations necessary to detect the onset of physical harm, whereas an enhanced risk claim seeks compensation for the anticipated harm itself, proportionately reduced to reflect the chance that it will not occur. We think that this distinction is particularly important because . . . in *Martin v. Johns-Manville Corp.*, 494 A.2d 1088 (Pa. 1985), the [Pennsylvania Supreme Court] made clear that a plaintiff in an enhanced risk suit must prove that future consequences of an injury are reasonably probable, not just possible.

Martin does not lead us to believe that Pennsylvania would not recognize a claim for medical monitoring, however. First, the injury that the court was worried about finding with reasonable probability in *Martin* is different from the injury involved here. The injury in an enhanced risk claim is the anticipated harm itself. The injury in a medical monitoring claim is the cost of the medical care that will, one hopes,

(continues)

In re Paoli Railroad Yard PCB Litigation

(continued from previous page)
detect that injury. The former is inherently speculative because courts are forced to anticipate the probability of future injury. The latter is much less speculative because the issue for the jury is the less conjectural question of whether the plaintiff needs medical surveillance. Second, the Pennsylvania Supreme Court's concerns about the degree of certainty required can easily be accommodated by requiring that a jury be able reasonably to determine that medical monitoring is probably, not just possibly, necessary.

[We predict] that the Supreme Court of Pennsylvania would recognize a cause of action for medical monitoring established by proving that:

1. Plaintiff was significantly exposed to a proven hazardous substance through the negligent actions of the defendant.

2. As a proximate result of exposure, plaintiff suffers a significantly increased risk of contracting a serious latent disease.

3. That increased risk makes periodic diagnostic medical examinations reasonably necessary.

4. Monitoring and testing procedures exist which make the early detection and treatment of the disease possible and beneficial.

. . . The policy reasons for recognizing this tort are obvious. Medical monitoring claims acknowledge that, in a toxic age, significant harm can be done

to an individual by a tortfeasor, notwithstanding latent manifestation of that harm. Moreover, as we have explained, recognizing this tort does not require courts to speculate about the probability of future injury. It merely requires courts to ascertain the probability that the far less costly remedy of medical supervision is appropriate. Allowing plaintiffs to recover the cost of this care deters irresponsible discharge of toxic chemicals by defendants and encourages plaintiffs to detect and treat their injuries as soon as possible. These are conventional goals of the tort system as it has long existed in Pennsylvania. [Reversed.] ⚖

Note: This court guessed wrong. Pennsylvania's highest court rejected medical monitoring in a case decided just before this book went to press. Nonetheless, the approach taken in *Paoli* is popular elsewhere.

Regulation by State Legislatures

In addition to the common-law role played by the courts, all state governments (and many subordinate governmental units) have passed laws dealing with the quality of the environment. These laws deal with all types of pollution—water, air, solid waste, noise, and others. Often state laws are patterned after federal laws. For example, several states have "mini-Superfunds" for hazardous waste site cleanup patterned after the federal Superfund law discussed later in this chapter. One popular type of state statute is the "bottle bill," designed to regulate the dumping of cans and bottles. Additionally, many federal laws presently provide a substantial state role in the establishing and enforcing of pollution standards.

NATIONAL ENVIRONMENTAL POLICY ACT

Although all states and many localities have significant environmental rules and regulations, federal regulations clearly dominate the regulatory landscape. Recognizing that a national environmental policy was needed, Congress enacted the National Environmental Policy Act (NEPA) in 1969 to "en-

courage productive and enjoyable harmony between man and his environment and biosphere and stimulate the health and welfare of man; to enrich the understanding of the ecological systems and natural resources important to the Nation; and to establish a Council on Environmental Quality." NEPA is a major step toward making each generation responsible to succeeding ones for the quality of the environment.

Environmental Impact Statements

NEPA requires that an **environmental impact statement** (EIS) be prepared by the appropriate agency whenever proposed major federal action will *significantly* affect the quality of the human environment. This requirement affects private enterprise as well because an EIS will be required if federal funds have been committed to a particular private venture. For example, a contractor building a federal highway or a naval base may have to help provide a detailed statement describing the environmental impact of the proposed action, unavoidable adverse effects, acceptable alternatives to the proposed project, and any irreversible and irretrievable commitments of resources involved.

Preparation of an EIS can be a costly and time-consuming task, even though regulations now limit the length to 150 pages (except in unusual circumstances.) NEPA requires that the statement be clear, to the point, and in simple English. It also requires that all key points and conclusions be set forth in a summary of no more than 15 pages. No matter how well prepared, an EIS is merely a prediction as to future environmental consequences of a proposed federal action. The proposed agency action, evaluated in light of the EIS, can be successfully challenged in court only if it can be shown to be "arbitrary and capricious."

Litigation over EISs often substantially delays and increases the costs of federal projects. Although very few federal projects have ever been halted by court actions based on NEPA, it is likely that many environmentally unsound projects have been abandoned or never begun because of EIS requirements. The EIS requirement remains controversial because it is impossible to quantify whether the environmental benefits of this process outweigh the additional time and expense incurred.

Environmental Protection Agency

In 1970 the EPA was created, consolidating into one agency the power to regulate various aspects of the environment that previously had been scattered across several federal agencies and departments. The EPA establishes and enforces environmental protection standards, conducts research on pollution, provides assistance to state and local antipollution programs through grants and technical advice, and generally assists the Council on Environmental Quality (CEQ). The CEQ was established to facilitate implementation of NEPA by issuing guidelines for the preparation of impact statements and generally to assist and advise the President on environmental matters. In its guidelines, CEQ has required that EISs be prepared as early in the decision-making process as possible and that other agencies and the public be given a chance to comment and criticize before any final decision is made to go ahead with major federal action.

Consolidation of diverse functions under the EPA has provided a center of control for the continuing war on pollution. How it works can be illustrated by studying the major areas of concern.

WATER POLLUTION CONTROL

As in other areas of environmental concern, federal regulation of water pollution is based on a series of measures passed over the years. For example, the Rivers and Harbors Act of 1890 prohibited the dumping of refuse into all navigable waters, and the 1899 Rivers and Harbors Appropriations Act made it unlawful for ships and manufacturing establishments to discharge refuse into any navigable waterway of the United States or into any tributary of a navigable waterway. Efforts to clean up the nation's waterways began in earnest with passage of the Federal Water Pollution Control Act in 1948, which has been repeatedly amended over the years.

Clean Water Act

The Clean Water Act (passed in 1971 and subsequently amended) is the major federal law governing water pollution. It provided a comprehensive plan to eliminate water pollution, setting standards and guidelines on an industry-by-industry basis for controlling water pollution from industrial sources. The types of discharges with which the law is concerned are as varied as the industries to be controlled. Thermal pollution from heat-generating plants and particulates and toxic wastes from manufacturing activities are subject to regulation and continual monitoring to assure that prescribed standards are being met. In general, industry is expected to control and eliminate its discharge of pollutants as soon as possible through the "best available technology (BAT) economically achievable."

The law placed primary responsibility on the states but provided for federal aid to local governments and small businesses to help them in their efforts to comply with the law's requirements. It also provided a licensing and permit system, at both state and federal levels, for discharging into waterways and a more workable enforcement program.

Citizen Suits

The Clean Water Act also allows citizens or organizations whose interests are affected by water pollution to sue violators of standards established under the law. Similar provisions are contained in several other environmental laws. The following case addresses a major issue raised by these "citizen suit" provisions. The factual summary sheds additional light on the working mechanism of the Clean Water Act.

GWALTNEY OF SMITHFIELD V. CHESAPEAKE BAY FOUNDATION, INC.

U.S. Supreme Court, 484 U.S. 49 (1987)

Case

The Clean Water Act was enacted in 1972 "to restore and maintain the chemical, physical, and biological integrity of the Nation's water." The Act establishes the National Pollutant Discharge Elimination System (NPDES), under which the EPA, or a state that has its own program conforming to federal standards, may issue permits authorizing the discharge of pollutants in accordance with specified conditions. If the holder of such permit violates its conditions, he or she is subject not only to federal and state action, but also to civil suits by private citizens, which are authorized against any person "alleged to be in violation of" the conditions of a federal or state NPDES permit. Sec. 505(a)(1).

Between 1981 and 1984, petitioner Gwaltney violated the conditions of its permits by discharging pollutants. These violations are chronicled in the Discharge Monitoring Reports (DMRs) that the permit (and the Act) require the petitioner to maintain. Although the petitioner was improving its equipment to minimize problems, in February 1984 Chesapeake Bay Foundation and Natural Resources Defense Council ("respondents"), two nonprofit organizations, sent notice to Gwaltney, the EPA, and Virginia regulators indicating their intention to commence a citizen suit under the Act. The suit requested declaratory and injunctive relief, imposition of civil penalties, and attorneys' fees and costs.

*Gwaltney's new equipment solved its problems; the permit was not violated after May 15, 1984. Respondents filed their suit in June 1984, alleging that Gwaltney "has violated [and] will continue to violate" its NPDES permit. Gwaltney moved to dismiss on grounds that the court lacked subject matter jurisdiction be-*cause a citizen's complaint brought under Sec. 505(a) must allege a violation occurring at the time the complaint is filed. The trial court denied that motion. Gwaltney appealed, and the Fourth Circuit Court of Appeals affirmed. Gwaltney appealed to the Supreme Court.

Marshall, Justice:

The most natural reading of "to be in violation" is a requirement that citizen-plaintiffs allege a state of either continuous or intermittent violation—that is, a reasonable likelihood that a past polluter will continue to pollute in the future. Congress could have phrased its requirement in language that looked only to the past (" to have violated"), but it did not choose this readily available option.

Our reading of the "to be in violation" language of Sec. 505(a) is bolstered by the language and structure of the rest of the citizen suit provisions in Sec. 505 of the Act. These provisions together make plain that the interest of the citizen suit is primarily forward-looking.

One of the most striking indicia of the prospective orientation of the citizen suit is the pervasive use of the present tense throughout Sec. 505.

Any other conclusion would render incomprehensible Sec. 505's notice provision, which requires citizens to give 60 days notice of their intent to sue to the alleged violator as well as to the Administrator and the State. If the Administrator or the State commences enforcement action within that 60 day period, the citizen suit is barred, presumably because governmental action has rendered it unnecessary. It follows logically that the purpose of notice to the alleged violator is to give it an opportunity to bring itself into complete compliance with the Act and thus likewise render unnecessary a citizen suit.

Adopting respondents' interpreta-tion of Sec. 505's jurisdictional grant would create a second and even more disturbing anomaly. The bar on citizen suits when governmental enforcement action is underway suggests that the citizen suit is meant to supplement rather than to supplant governmental action. The legislative history of the Act reinforces this view of the role of the citizen suit. The Senate Report noted that "[t]he Committee intends the great volume of enforcement actions [to] be brought by the State," and that citizen suits are proper only "if the Federal, State, and local agencies fail to exercise their enforcement responsibility." Respondents' interpretation of the scope of the citizen suit would change the nature of the citizens' role from interstitial to potentially intrusive. We cannot agree that Congress intended such a result.

The legislative history of the Act provides additional support for our reading of Sec. 505. Members of Congress frequently characterized the citizen suit provisions as "abatement" provisions or as injunctive measures. Moreover, both the Senate and House Reports explicitly connected Sec. 505 to the citizen suit provisions authorized by the Clean Air Act, which are wholly injunctive in nature.

Our conclusion that Sec. 505 does not permit citizen suits for wholly past violations does not necessarily dispose of the lawsuit. Section 505 confers jurisdiction over citizens suits when the citizen-plaintiffs make a good-faith allegation of continuous or intermittent violation. The statute does not require that a defendant "be in violation" of the Act at the commencement of suit; rather, the statute requires that a defendant be "*alleged* to be in violation."

Because the court below declined to decide whether respondents' complaint contained a good-faith allegation of ongoing violation by the petitioner, . . . we remand the case for consideration of this question. ⚖

Note

Between 1984 and 1988, some 806 notices of intent to sue under the Clean Water Act were filed, primarily by such groups as the National Resources Defense Fund, the Sierra Club Legal Defense Fund, and the Friends of the Earth. Only a tiny percentage of such suits are preempted by governmental enforcement action, and most lead to negotiations and court-approved settlements and consent decrees. Such citizen suits have become quite controversial. Supporters believe that they are a beneficial supplement to actions brought by overworked agencies such as the EPA and its state counterparts. Critics believe that the suits have become so numerous (and arguably driven by provisions allowing for recovery of attorneys' fees) that they do not bring about cost-effective results and subvert consistency and fairness in national enforcement. The Supreme Court's decision to deny the right to sue to environmental groups in *Lujan v. Defenders of Wildlife*, 112 S.Ct. 2130 (1992), a citizens' suit brought under the Endangered Species Act, reflects a hostility to such suits that may foreshadow future imposition of restrictive procedural requirements.

Water Quality Act of 1987

In the Water Quality Act of 1987, Congress amended the Clean Water Act by emphasizing a state-federal program to control *non-point source* pollution. Whereas *point sources* such as municipal or industrial discharge pipes account for much water pollution, Congress determined that non-point source pollution such as oil and grease runoff from city streets, pesticide runoff from farmland, and runoff from mining areas must be addressed. The states were charged with developing programs to improve water quality by combatting this pollution, which is so difficult to track.

The 1987 Act also clamped down on toxic water pollution and empowered the EPA to assess administrative penalties for water pollution. The penalties were placed on a sliding scale. For more serious offenses (considering the nature, circumstances, extent, and gravity of the violation, and the violator's ability to pay, history of violations, degree of culpability, and savings resulting from the violation), the EPA must provide relatively formal hearings but can assess larger penalties. Smaller penalties are assessed for minor violations after less formal procedures.

Responding to concerns about abuses of citizen suits, the 1987 Act also gave the EPA more supervision of settlement agreements in such cases, and a greater ability to preclude such suits administratively.

Oil Spills

All too frequently, vessels from small coastal barges to huge supertankers accidentally discharge their cargos into the sea near the coast. The ecologic effect on fish, shellfish, and waterfowl and on the public and private shorelines and beaches may be immense. Consequently, the Clean Water Act imposes severe sanctions on those responsible for such pollution. The owner or operator of a grounded oil-carrying vessel can be liable for up to $250,000 of the cost of cleaning up its spilled oil; if the oil spill is the result of willful negligence or misconduct, the owner or operator of the vessel can be held liable to the U.S. government for the full cost of cleaning up the shore. Operators of onshore and offshore facilities are also held liable for spillage and pollution, under ordinary conditions, to the extent of $50 million and, where willful negligence and misconduct are involved, to the full extent of the cost of cleanup and removal, including the restoration or replacement of natural resources damaged or destroyed by the discharge of oil or hazardous substances.

After the Exxon *Valdez* oil spill in Alaska, Exxon was charged with a variety of criminal offenses and sued by all manner of private and governmental officials. A wide variety of laws and regulations dealing with water pollution and wildlife were allegedly violated. Exxon settled state and federal litigation by agreeing to pay $900 million over 11 years (in civil penalties), plus $100 million for restoration of the injured area to be split between the United States and Alaska and $25 million in criminal fines. The settlement did not affect about $59 billion in private civil suits then pending against Exxon.

Additional Regulations

Of related concern are the Marine Protection, Research, and Sanctuaries Act, which regulates the discharge and introduction of pollutants into coastal waterways and marine areas, and the Safe Drinking Water Act of 1974, which gave the states primary responsibility for enforcing national standards for drinking water. Under the act, the EPA has set maximum drinking water contaminant levels of certain chemicals, pesticides, and microbiologic pollutants.

AIR POLLUTION CONTROL

Clean Air Act

The Clean Air Act of 1970 empowered the EPA to set standards to attain certain primary ambient (outside) air quality standards designed by Congress to protect public health. Because achieving the standards is costly, the EPA's role is to balance the economic, technologic, and social factors that must be considered in attaining the clean air goals that have been set.

Several programs formed the essential elements of the Clean Air Act. Foremost was the setting of primary (health) and secondary (welfare) ambient air quality standards. Because the Clean Air Act's approach involved a federal-state partnership, another program required the states to draft state implementation plans (SIPs) for achieving ambient air quality standards. When approved by the EPA, such plans permitted the states to enforce air quality standards within their borders. Operators of air pollution sources could be required to monitor, sample, and keep appropriate records, all of which were subject to on-premises inspection by the EPA. When a proper SIP was not prepared, the burden fell to the EPA to adopt a Federal Implementation Plan (FIP).

To reduce emissions in accordance with prescribed schedules, the act also set new source performance standards (NSPSs)—emission standards for various categories of large industrial facilities. Major polluters must use the best acceptable control devices, those with proven capabilities to reduce emissions. To ease the burden on industry, the EPA adopted the **bubble concept,** under which a large plant with multiple emission points (stacks) does not have to meet standards for each one. The plant instead is under a "bubble" with a single allowable emission level. Plant management can manage each point source within the bubble to meet the sum total of emission limits by the most economical means.

Finally, the act addressed automobile pollution by developing emission standards and fuel additive regulations. Use of unleaded gasoline and catalytic converters has resulted in substantial progress. However, industry continues to complain that the standards are too burdensome, and environmentalists still claim that the rules are too lax and are ineffectually enforced.

1990 Amendments

Although measurable progress was made in many areas pursuant to the 1970 Clean Air Act, it is undeniable that serious air pollution problems remain. Therefore, in 1990, Congress enacted significant amendments to the act. With predicted costs for implementation between $20 billion and $100 billion annually, the 1990 amendments emphasized four critical areas.

First, the amendments addressed ozone, carbon monoxide, and particulate matter—where there had been significant failures to attain established standards. For example, the amendments established five categories for ozone nonattainment, ranging from marginal to extreme, with attainment deadlines stretching from 1993 to 2010, and increasingly stringent control requirements tied to the degree of nonattainment.

A second key area is air toxics. A list of 189 hazardous substances or groups of substances was added to a previous list of eight air pollutants. The EPA is to target categories of major sources of such pollutants. For each source, the EPA is required to establish emission control standards based on maximum achievable control technology (MACT).

The third major area is **acid rain.** With a phased-in timetable, the amendments require a reduction in emissions of sulfur dioxide by electric utility steam generating units by 10 million tons from 1980 levels. After full implementation, the national cap for such emissions will be 8.9 million tons annually, with the EPA issuing freely transferable "allowances" within that total to existing generating units. Holders who do not use their allowances may sell them or carry them forward for future use.

Fourth, in addressing automobile pollution, the law set emission standards that might add as much as $500 to the cost of a new car. Among other provisions, the 1990 amendments prohibited the sale of leaded gasoline for highway use after December 31, 1995, and prohibited the manufacture of an engine that requires leaded gasoline after 1992.

The amendments mean increased expenses and record-keeping for giant corporations and many small businesses as well. As many as 50,000 points of pollution may be required to obtain permits under the amendments. Those who fail to comply face the stiffest penalties yet. For example, previously violations were generally misdemeanors, but now they are felonies with criminal penalties that may run up to $1 million per violation. Additionally, the EPA Administrator may assess civil administrative penalties up to $25,000 a day per violation, and the role of litigation by citizens and private organizations in the enforcement process has been expanded. For example, as we saw earlier, in *Gwaltney of Smithfield Ltd. v. Chesapeake Bay Foundation*,[5] the Supreme Court held that citizens could sue only for ongoing violations of the Clean Water Act, a holding applied to the Clean Air Act as well. The 1990 amendments specifically permit citizens to file complaints over *past* violations that have been repeated.

Another form of citizen input comes in the permit process. All large pollution sources (except vehicles) must obtain permits from state pollution authorities specifying that their emissions do not violate Clean

[5]484 U.S. 49 (1987).

Air Act limits. Those permits are subject to EPA review, and if the EPA does not object to a permit, citizens may petition the agency to do so and may comment on permits and request public hearings during the approval process. Some 34,000 facilities will be covered by the permit program.

Proponents stress that the long-term benefits to the environment and public health may well outweigh the burdens that the act places on industry and on consumers who purchase products.

In the area of air pollution, as well as most others, major environmental programs have been established in a sequential fashion. That is, instead of having a master comprehensive plan, major initiatives have been amended and then amended again to address new problems or old problems that have proved to be intractable. The difficulties of such an approach are illustrated in the following recent case.

Coalition for Clean Air v. Southern California Edison Co.

U.S. Court of Appeals, Ninth Circuit, 971 F.2d 219 (1992)

Case

Before the Clean Air Act was amended in 1990, California's state implementation plan (SIP) for the South Coast Air Basin was rejected, and the EPA acquired the obligation to prepare a federal implementation plan (FIP). The appellants brought this suit to force the EPA to prepare an FIP. EPA recognized its obligation to do so, and a settlement agreement was entered into that, as later amended, granted the EPA until February 28, 1991, to produce such a plan. However, when the 1990 amendments to the Clean Air Act were passed, the district court vacated the settlement agreement and dismissed appellants' action on grounds that California should have the chance to promulgate an SIP under the new standards before the EPA completed its FIP. Appellants appealed.

Norris, Circuit Judge:

California's South Coast Air Basin has the dirtiest air in the United States. Twenty-two years have passed since Congress first enacted legislation requiring implementation plans to attain national air quality standards, and yet today the South Coast still lacks implementation plans for ozone and carbon monoxide. In 1989, EPA entered into a settlement agreement with appellants requiring it to perform its statutory duty and promulgate federal implementation plans for the South Coast on an expeditious schedule. EPA now argues that, when Congress passed the Clean Air Act Amendments of 1990, it relieved EPA of this obligation and returned the implementation plan process to square one. We disagree and reverse.

EPA's statutory obligation to promulgate FIPs is contained in Sec. 110(c)(1) of the Clean Air Act, as amended in 1990:

The Administrator shall promulgate a Federal implementation plan at any time within two years after the Administrator—

(A) finds that a State has failed to make a required submission or finds that the plan or plan revision submitted by the State does not satisfy the minimum criteria established under . . . this title, or

(B) disapproves a State implementation plan submission in whole or in part, unless the State corrects the deficiency, and the Administrator approves the plan or plan revision, before the Administrator promulgates such Federal implementation plan.

Appellants contend that under subsection (B), EPA is obligated to promulgate ozone and CO FIPs for South Coast based on its disapproval in January 1988 of California's proposed SIPs. EPA, on the other hand, contends that [this section] was intended to operate prospectively only, so that EPA's obligation to promulgate a FIP for the South Coast will be triggered only if California fails to submit a SIP that meets the requirements of the Clean

(continues)

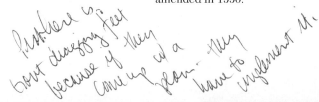

COALITION FOR CLEAN AIR V. SOUTHERN CALIFORNIA EDISON CO.

(continued from previous page)
Air Act by the deadlines set forth in the 1990 Amendments.

We begin with the language of the provision: "The Administrator shall promulgate a Federal implementation plan at any time within 2 years after the Administrator . . . disapproves a State implementation plan submission in whole or in part." This language is not, by its terms, limited to EPA's disapproval of "newly submitted" SIPs or SIPs "submitted under the 1990 Amendments." Instead it refers to disapproval of state implementation plans generally, either in whole or in part. EPA must promulgate a FIP within two years of such disapproval, unless the state submits and EPA approves revisions to the SIP that correct the deficiency. Since EPA disapproved the South Coast SIPs in January 1988, the statute on its face requires EPA to promulgate FIPs for the South Coast by January 1990.

EPA also argues that requiring it to promulgate FIPs for the South Coast at this time would be inconsistent with the 1990 Amendments as a whole because those Amendments impose new deadlines and change certain requirements of the Clean Air Act. The district court found this argument persuasive. It reasoned that if the Act were interpreted to continue EPA's existing obligation to promulgate FIPs for the South Coast, "there would be the anomaly that the SIP prepared by the State under the former criteria and rejected is to be replaced by a FIP prepared under new criteria that the State has never had an opportunity to address."

. . . Running throughout EPA's argument is the notion that federal involvement necessarily preempts state planning to control air pollution. However, this is a misleading conception. The Clean Air Act creates "a federal-state partnership for the control of

air pollution," *Abramowitz v. EPA*, 832 F.2d 1071 (9th Cir. 1987), which continues after EPA's obligation to promulgate a FIP has been triggered. [T]he state may propose and EPA may approve revisions to a proposed SIP that meet the requirements of the act at any time prior to the actual promulgation of a FIP. Even after a FIP is promulgated, the states remain responsible for submitting revisions to the FIP if EPA changes the air quality standards, or if Congress changes the provisions of the Act. Thus, we fail to see how enforcing the plain terms of Sec. 110(c)(1)(B) will create an unintended anomaly.

REVERSED. The case is REMANDED for reinstatement of the agreement. On remand the district court is instructed to establish an expeditious schedule for promulgation of final ozone and CO FIPs for the South Coast consistent with this opinion. ♫

SOLID WASTE AND ITS DISPOSAL

The disposal of millions of tons of solid waste produced annually in this country presents a problem of staggering proportions. Periodic garbage pickups at residences or small businesses or weekly trips to the county or municipal sanitary landfill solve the problem for most people. However, less than 10 percent of solid waste is classified as residential, commercial, or institutional. The greater portion is classified as agricultural or mineral. Agriculture alone contributes more than 50 percent. Undisposed of, the waste creates enormous health and pollution problems; inadequate disposal methods often create greater hazards. If burned, solid waste pollutes the air. If dumped into waterways, lakes, or streams, the Clean Water Act is violated. Consequently, federal statutes have been enacted to combat the problem.

Solid Waste Disposal Act/Resource Conservation Recovery Act

The primary goal of the Solid Waste Disposal Act of 1965 and the 1976 amendment known as the Resource Conservation and Recovery Act (RCRA) is more efficient management of waste and its disposal through financial and technical assistance to state and local agencies in the development and implementation of new methods of waste disposal. RCRA defined **hazardous waste** as a solid waste, or combination of solid wastes, that because of its quantity, concentration, physical, chemical, or infectious characteristics may

(A) cause, or significantly contribute to an increase in mortality or an increase in serious irreversible, or incapacitating reversible, illness; or

(B) pose a substantial present or potential hazard to human health or the environment when improperly treated, stored, transported, or disposed of, or otherwise managed.

RCRA also established an Office of Solid Waste within the EPA to regulate the generation and transportation of solid waste (both toxic and nontoxic), as well as its disposal, thus providing "cradle-to-grave" regulation. Although RCRA focuses primarily on the regulation and granting of permits for ongoing hazardous waste activities, it does have a corrective action program for site cleanup. The EPA is authorized to sue to force the cleanup of existing waste disposal sites presenting imminent hazards to the public health.

These acts generally treat toxic wastes more harshly than nontoxic wastes. But where is the line drawn? The Hazardous and Solid Waste Amendments (to RCRA) of 1984 required the EPA to expand the list of constituents characterized as toxic. In 1990, the EPA issued its rules, adding 25 organic chemicals to a preexisting list of eight metals and six pesticides regulated for toxicity. Nearly 20,000 small (and large) businesses generating solid waste containing these substances must now comply with rules regarding hazardous waste, and a substantial number of landfills must now be treated as hazardous waste facilities, greatly expanding the costs of required disposal and cleanup. The 1984 amendments also created a comprehensive program for regulating underground storage tanks, such as gasoline tanks at service stations.

Comprehensive Environmental Response, Compensation, and Liability Act of 1980 (CERCLA/Superfund)

Although RCRA provides cradle-to-grave regulation of active hazardous waste sites, in the wake of the Love Canal incident referred to earlier, Congress passed the **Comprehensive Environmental Response, Compensation, and Liability Act of 1980 (CERCLA),** better known as the **Superfund** legislation, to clean up abandoned or inactive sites. CERCLA initially established a $1.6 billion Hazardous Substance Response Trust Fund to cover the cost of "timely government responses to releases of hazardous substances into the environment."

Addressing a much broader range of hazardous substances than RCRA, CERCLA holds the polluter, rather than society, responsible for the costs of cleaning up designated hazardous waste sites, instruct-

ing the EPA to list the nation's worst toxic waste sites, identify responsible parties, and sue them for cleanup costs, if necessary. The following **potentially responsible parties** (PRPs) were initially enumerated: (1) present owners and operators of facilities; (2) any person who, at the time of disposal, owned or operated such a facility; (3) generators of hazardous substances who arrange for disposal or treatment at another's facility; or (4) transporters of hazardous substances. These parties are strictly liable for cost of removal and remediation, response costs incurred by others, and damages to natural resources owned or controlled by any government. Due care and compliance with existing laws are no defense. Once determined to be responsible, a PRP may have to bear the entire cost of cleanup because liability is joint and several. In other words, if the government proves that owner A, prior owner B, and transporter C are all PRPs, and B and C are insolvent, A may have to pay for the entire cleanup. Furthermore, CERCLA is retroactive, covering both disposal acts committed and response costs incurred before the law was passed. Thus, potential CERCLA liability can be staggering.

The act also allows a category of exceptions, including owners of property incident to a security interest (*security interest exception*) and owners of land contaminated by the acts or omissions of third parties who are not contractually related to the owner (*third-party defense*).[6] The third-party defense is unavailable if the polluter is an employee or agent of the responsible party or one in a direct or indirect contractual relationship with that party.

Under the original version of CERCLA, completely innocent current owners of hazardous dumps faced liability for cleanup. In 1986, Congress passed the Superfund Amendments and Reauthorization Act (SARA), which provided an *innocent landowner defense* for those who could not only establish the third-party defense but also show (1) they had no reason to know of the contamination of the property when they purchased it and (2) they had made all appropriate inquiry into the previous ownership and uses of the property consistent with good commercial and customary practice. SARA also replaced the original CERCLA trust fund with the $8.5 billion Hazardous Substance Superfund (Superfund) financed by

---

[6]CERCLA also allows a PRP to avoid liability when pollution is caused by an act of God or of war.

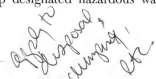

general revenue appropriations, certain environmental taxes, and monies recovered under CERCLA on behalf of the Superfund, and CERCLA-authorized penalties and punitive damages. SARA authorized civil penalties of up to $25,000 per day for willful failure to comply with EPA regulations.

Although in the earlier years, the costs of Superfund fell primarily on large corporations, in recent years, those corporations have spread the pain by suing small businesses and even municipalities for contributions specifically authorized by CERCLA. For example, two large corporations, who had settled an EPA action by agreeing to pay for a $9 million cleanup of a landfill, sued a tiny pizzeria (among several other small businesses), surmising that it might have included cleanser, insecticide cans, or other items containing traces of toxins in its garbage sent to the landfill. Small companies often settle such cases out of court because the cost of defending would be so high.[7]

The financial threat that CERCLA poses to industries that generate toxic wastes and companies that dispose of them is obvious. Additionally, CERCLA

poses substantial hidden liabilities for a wide range of entities, including the pizzeria mentioned above; real estate buyers, lessees, and landlords; purchasers of corporations with unknown environmental liabilities; and indirect owners and operators such as lenders or parent corporations. For example, a lender might under certain circumstances be liable to clean up a borrower's waste site at an expense far in excess of the amount of the loan. Furthermore, several courts have held that despite traditional notions of limited liability for corporations, parent corporations may be liable for pollution caused by subsidiaries over which the parents exert substantial influence,[8] and that when two corporations merge the acquiring corporation may well be responsible for pollution caused long before by the acquired corporation.[9]

For a long time, the government automatically assumed that any company linked to a hazardous waste site was potentially liable for *all* damages. The government then left it to the parties to decide who was responsible for what portion of the loss. The following is the first significant case to reject that view.

[7]Tomsho, *Big Corporations Hit by Superfund Cases Find Way to Share Bill,* Wall Street Journal, April 2, 1991, p. A1.

[8]For example, *United States v. Kayser-Roth Corp.,* 910 F.2d 24 (1st Cir. 1990).

[9]For example, *Anspec Co. v. Johnson Controls, Inc.,* 922 F.2d 1240 (6th Cir.. 1991).

UNITED STATES V. ALCAN ALUMINUM CORP.

U.S. Court of Appeals, Third Circuit, 964 F.2d 252 (1992)

A "borehole" on the premises of Hi-Way Auto Service emptied into a complex of five square miles of underground mines and related tunnels that, in turn, emptied through the Butler Tunnel into the Susquehanna River. In the 1970s, the Mahler Companies collected liquid wastes from numerous plants and deposited 2 million gallons of such waste into the borehole. Among Mahler's customers was defendant Alcan Aluminum Co., which used an emulsion in its process of hot-rolling aluminum ingots. Because Alcan treated the emulsion before Mahler picked it up, its levels of CERCLA

hazardous substances such as copper, chromium, cadmium, lead, and zinc were far below toxic levels and, indeed, below naturally occuring background levels. Mahler deposited about 35,000 gallons of Alcan's emulsion into the hole in 1978 and 1979. In September 1985, approximately 100,000 gallons of water contaminated with hazardous substances were released from the site into the Susquehanna; the discharge was composed of wastes deposited there in the late 1970s.

The United States sued 20 defendants, including Alcan, for the recovery of costs it incurred in cleaning up the river. All other defendants settled with the government. The trial court

granted the government's motion for summary judgment in the sum of $473,790.18—the difference between the full response costs the government had incurred and the amount it had recovered from the settling defendants. Alcan appealed.

Greenberg, Circuit Judge:

In response to widespread concern over the improper disposal of hazardous wastes, Congress enacted CERCLA, a complex piece of legislation designed to force polluters to pay for costs associated with remedying their pollution. . . . [O]f great significance in this case, CERCLA imposes strict liability on responsible parties.

(continues)

joint ≃ several liability

UNITED STATES V. ALCAN ALUMINUM CORP.

(continued from previous page)

Alcan argues that it should not be held liable for response costs incurred by the Government in cleaning the Susquehanna River because the level of hazardous substances in its emulsion was below that which naturally occurs and thus could not have contributed to the environmental injury. . . . [C]ourts that have addressed this issue have almost uniformly held that CERCLA liability does not depend on the existence of a threshold quantity of a hazardous substance. . . . If Congress had intended to impose a threshold requirement, it could easily have so indicated. We should not rewrite the statute simply because the definition of one of its terms ["hazardous substances"] is broad in scope.

Alcan maintains that, if we decline to construe the determination of "hazardous substance" to encompass a concentration threshold, we must at least require the Government to prove that *Alcan's emulsion* caused or contributed to the release or the Government's incurrence of response costs. . . . [V]irtually every court that has considered this question has held that a CERCLA plaintiff need not establish a direct causal connection between the defendant's hazardous substances and the release or the plaintiff's incurrence of response costs. . . . [T]he Government must simply prove that the defendant's hazardous substances were deposited at the site from which there was a release and that the *release*

caused the incurrence of response costs. . . .

The foregoing conclusions that (1) there is no quantitative threshold in the definition of hazardous substances and (2) the plaintiff need not establish a causal connection between a given defendant's waste and the release or the incurrence of response costs would initially appear to lead to unfair imposition of liability. As Alcan asserts, this definition of "hazardous substances" effectively renders everything in the universe hazardous, including, for example, federally approved drinking water. When this definition is read in conjunction with the rule that specific causation is not required, CERCLA seemingly would impose liability on every generator of hazardous waste, although that generator could not, on its own, have caused any environmental harm.

While Alcan's assertion is of considerable strength, the Government's rebuttal is equally forceful. It notes that individual defendants must be held responsible for environmental injury brought about by the actions of multiple defendants, even if no single defendant itself could have produced the harm, for otherwise "each defendant in a multi-defendant case could avoid liability by relying on the low concentrations of hazardous substances in its waste, while the plaintiff is left with the substantial clean-up costs associated with the defendants' accumulated wastes. . . ."

We find some merit in the arguments advanced by both the Government and Alcan. Accordingly, in our view, the common law principles of joint and several liability provide the only means to achieve the proper balance between Alcan's and the Government's conflicting interests and to infuse fairness into the statutory scheme without distorting its plain meaning or disregarding congressional intent.

Under the Restatement [of Torts, Sec. 433A], where a joint tortfeasor seeks to apportion the full amount of a plaintiff's damages according to that tortfeasor's own contribution to the harm, it is the tortfeasor's burden to establish that the damages are capable of such apportionment. . . . [W]e will remand this case for the [trial] court to determine whether there is a reasonable basis for limiting Alcan's liability based on its personal contribution to the harm to the Susquehanna River. . . . Alcan's burden in attempting to prove the divisibility of harm to the Susquehanna River is substantial, and the analysis will be factually complex as it will require an assessment of the relative toxicity, migratory potential and synergistic capacity of the hazardous waste at issue. But Alcan should be permitted this opportunity to limit or avoid liability. If Alcan succeeds in this endeavor, it should only be liable for that portion of the harm fairly attributable to it.

[Reversed.] ♐

Before *Alcan*, the government typically recovered the entire sum of its costs and left it to PRPs such as Alcan to sue the other PRPs for contribution. Thus, the *Alcan* holding, if adopted by other courts, substantially increases the government's burden in such cases.

CERCLA is controversial not only because of its potential for extremely high and potentially un-

fair liability for PRPs. Its administration has also been attacked. As of mid-1992, only 84 of 1245 designated sites had been cleaned up, at an average cost approaching $50 million per site. Additionally, substantial amounts of money expended by CERCLA defendants and their insurance companies had gone to litigation expenses, rather than cleanup efforts.

REGULATION OF TOXIC SUBSTANCES

In addition to the identifiable pollutants that are controlled at the source by the EPA, a more serious threat may be posed by the thousands of chemicals and compounds that are manufactured for commercial and generally beneficial use. These include herbicides, pesticides, and fertilizers, some of which may be highly toxic as single elements or may become toxic when combined with other elements. It is now apparent that toxic substances, initially applied to serve some useful purpose, are working their way into the environment, often with potentially dangerous results to humans exposed to those substances. An infamous example occurred at Times Beach, Missouri, where deadly dioxins deposited years before may have caused severe health problems for local residents.

Toxic Substances Control Act

In 1976 Congress enacted the Toxic Substances Control Act (TSCA) to create a review and control mechanism for the process of bringing chemical substances into the marketplace. The EPA is required to develop a comprehensive inventory of existing chemicals by calling on manufacturers to report the amount of each chemical substance they produce. TSCA imposes testing requirements on manufacturers and requires notice to the EPA when a new substance is being considered for development and production. The main purpose of the act is to prohibit the introduction of substances that would present an uncontrollable risk. Additionally, TSCA provides for testing, warnings, and instructions leading to the safe use of toxic chemicals with minimal effects on humans and the environment. Enforcement procedures permit the EPA to issue an order to prohibit the manufacture of high-risk substances. Pursuant to TSCA, the EPA has developed specific standards for PCBs, asbestos, chlorofluorocarbons, dioxins, and other substances.

Unlike some other environmental laws (the Clean Air Act, for example), TSCA orders the EPA to consider the economic and social impact of its decisions as well as the environmental effects. Therefore, more than some environmental regulations, TSCA seeks to avoid unnecessary burdens on the economy.

Pesticide Regulation

Obviously pests such as insects and mice cause significant crop damage and health problems. For that rea-son, chemicals that can kill or inhibit the reproduction of such pests are quite valuable for the health and economic welfare of Americans. Unfortunately, the widespread and long-term use of such substances can itself endanger the environment, injuring wildlife and human health. For that reason, Congress passed the Federal Environmental Pesticide Control Act in 1972, amending an earlier 1947 law, the Federal Insecticide, Fungicide, and Rodenticide Act (FIFRA). These acts together require that pesticides be registered with the EPA before they can be sold. Applicants for registration must provide comprehensive safety testing information to the EPA, which will approve the application only if the pesticide is properly labelled, lives up to its claims, and does not cause "unreasonable adverse effects on the environment." Such substances, when applied to crops that provide food for animals or people, may be used only within established limits. It is under this legislation that the EPA substantially banned the well-known insecticide DDT.

NOISE POLLUTION

The Noise Control Act of 1972, the first major federal assault on excessive noise emanating from sources to which the public is exposed on a continual basis, empowers the EPA to establish noise emission standards for specific products in cooperation with agencies otherwise concerned with them and to limit noise emissions from those products that can be categorized as noise producers. The act specifically targets transportation vehicles and equipment, machinery, appliances, and other commercial products. The act subjects federal facilities to state and local noise standards and expressly reserves the right to control environmental noise in the state through licensing and regulation or restriction of excessively noisy products.

The thrust of the Noise Control Act is to reduce environmental noise in an effort to prevent what are recognized as long-range effects (hearing problems) on public health and welfare. Violations of the prohibitions of the act are punishable by fines, imprisonment, or both.

Many states and localities have their own noise pollution rules and regulations.

INDOOR POLLUTION

Until recently, indoor pollution was given relatively little attention by environmentalists, businesses, and

LEGAL FOCUS

International

Legal Focus
INTERNATIONAL

The various forms of pollution do not respect national borders. Therefore, pollution has a critical international dimension that cannot be overlooked. International law and international organization now play an increasingly important role in solving important environmental problems. Unfortunately, as in nonenvironmental areas, their weaknesses prevent truly effective action. Nonetheless, important strides have been made.

International Organizations

Naturally, a look at international organizations must begin with the United Nations. Unfortunately, the United Nations has no executive environmental agency. Its strongest arm is UNEP (United National Environment Programme), which has helped formulate international treaties on pollution but has a limited budget and therefore can neither fund major projects nor comprehensively enforce international law.

The International Court of Justice plays at least a minor role in enforcing customary international law on transnational pollution. For example, in the *Corfu Channel Case (Greece v. Italy*, 1949 I.C.J. 18), that body ruled that countries have an obligation not to allow their territory to be used for acts (including polluting acts) contrary to the rights of other states. An International Joint Commission established a similar "good neighbor" principle in a pollution dispute between the United States and Canada in the *Trail Smelter Arbitration* (United States v. Canada, 3 R. Int'l. Arb. Awards 1907 (1949)), which involved claims by citizens of the state of Washington against smelters located in the British Columbia province, ruling that "under the principles of international law, . . . no state has the right to use or permit the use of its territory in such a manner as to cause in-

jury by fumes in or to the territory of another or the properties or persons therein, when the case is of serious consequence and the injury is established by clear and convincing evidence."

International Conventions

The international community has in recent years attacked various aspects of the pollution problem through conventions and conferences. For example, as a starting point, Principle 21 of the Stockholm Conference (1972) provides that

> States have, in accordance with the Charter of the United Nations and the principles of international law, the sovereign right to exploit their own resources pursuant to their own environmental policies, and the responsibility to ensure that activities within their own jurisdiction or control do not cause damage to the environment of other States or of areas beyond the limits of national jurisdiction.

Pursuant to that principle, several important conventions have been formulated. To attack the problem of "garbage imperialism" (the exporting of waste by developed countries for disposal in underdeveloped countries), the Basel Convention (1989) sought to prohibit transboundary movement of hazardous wastes absent written consent by all countries involved. Another requirement is that the receiving country have an environmentally sound way to dispose of the waste.

Water pollution in the form of oil spills by tankers has been addressed several times, including through the Protocol of 1984 to Amend the International Convention on Civil Liability for Oil Pollution Damage and the Protocol of 1984 to Amend the International Fund for Compensation for Oil Pollution Damage. The goal of these conventions was to create international standards of liability and an internationally enforced insurance scheme.

The endangering of species has been addressed in the 1973 Convention on

International Trade in Endangered Species and Wild Fauna and Flora and the 1979 Convention on Conservation of Migratory Species of Wild Animals. These conventions address such matters as the illicit international trade in ivory, exotic birds, and rhinoceros horns.

The matter of ozone depletion is of primary importance in the international legal community because of the potential for worldwide adverse effects. Recently the Montreal Protocol called for industrialized nations to completely phase out the use of ozone-depleting chlorofluorocarbons (CFCs) by the year 2000. It also provided a $100 million "financial mechanism" trust fund to enable developing countries to reduce their reliance on CFCs and to fund the attempt to find nonpolluting substitutes.

The June 1992 U.N. Conference on the Environment and Development ("Earth Summit") in Brazil led to several potential advances in international cooperation, including two treaties—the U.N. Framework Convention on Climate Change and the Convention on Biological Diversity. These two treaties will be binding upon all countries that ratify them; 153 nations signed the Biological Diversity treaty (only the United States refused).

Limitations

Unfortunately, although most of these conventions look good on paper and all are important symbolic steps, most suffer in varying degrees from limitations that are common to all international legal measures. Most of the conventions were signed by substantially more nations than ultimately ratified them. Most do not apply to nations that did not ratify. Most lack methods of enforcement and suffer from vagueness in terminology. Still, international cooperation is essential to saving the planet, and every effective step in the right direction should be appreciated and supported.

regulators. Recently, however, many experts have concluded that indoor air is many times more hazardous than outdoor air. Because Americans spend a very high percentage of their time indoors, a serious problem is presented by such indoor pollutants.

Among the most serious indoor pollutants are radon gas (a colorless, odorless gas that often percolates from the soil into homes and other buildings), asbestos (natural fibers often used as insulation and for other construction purposes), and formaldehyde (a chemical also often found in insulation and other construction materials). The tendency of these substances and others to cause cancer or other diseases is widely accepted.[10]

Despite the dangers presented by these and other substances, as of this writing there is no comprehensive federal policy on indoor air quality. Nor have the states taken any uniform action. For example, the federal government's efforts at regulating radon have not yet moved past the research and study phase. Hit-and-miss attempts have led to substantial amounts being spent to clean up asbestos, especially in schools, and to the demise of the formaldehyde insulation industry. Nonetheless, the regulatory efforts have been incomplete. Therefore, the substantial dangers posed by indoor air pollution will undoubtedly lead to additional state and federal regulation in the near future.

Litigation in the area of indoor pollution is also in its infancy, but increased activity will likely be seen in coming years. In *Pinkerton v. Georgia Pacific Corp.*[11] for example, $16.2 million was recovered to compensate for sensitivity reactions in the plaintiffs to indoor formaldehyde exposure caused by the defendant's negligence.

ENDANGERED SPECIES

The 1973 Endangered Species Act (ESA) has been called the world's most stringent environmental law because of its unstinting protection of plant and animal species endangered or threatened with extinction. Aside from the moral principles underlying preservation of endangered species, there is the simple utilitarian consideration that an extinct species can no longer provide food, medicine, and other benefits to mankind.

[10]See F. Cross, *Legal Responses to Indoor Air Pollution* (Quorum Books 1990).
[11]No. CV 186-4651CC (Mo. Cir. Ct. 1990).

On the other hand, a tiny fish (the snail darter) interrupted the construction of a $100 million dam project, a bird (the northern spotted owl) arguably has endangered thousands of jobs in the lumber industry in the Northwest, and millions of acres of land have been subject to land use restrictions under the ESA.

This clash of values inevitably created controversy. That controversy is currently before Congress as it begins considering the task, ongoing at this writing, of reauthorizing the ESA, which expired in October 1992.

THE ENVIRONMENT, INDUSTRY, AND SOCIETY

At least two things should be clear from this chapter. First, businesses are faced with a myriad of environmental rules and regulations, some extremely costly and difficult to implement. To cover them fully would require a discussion hundreds of pages long. We have scarcely touched on the thousands of state and local antipollution ordinances and have not mentioned several matters of intense federal concern, such as the controversies over preserving national parks and drilling for oil and gas offshore. Nor have we mentioned some very important federal laws, including the Hazardous Materials Transportation Act (promoting safe movement of "hazardous materials" through our nation's transportation system), the Emergency Planning and Community Right-to-Know Act (aimed at forcing communities to prepare for a Bhopal-type spill of hazardous chemicals in the United States), or the Occupational Safety and Health Administration's numerous rules to protect workers from chemical injury, including the Worker Right-to-Know Rule (under which chemical manufacturers and employers using hazardous chemicals must communicate their hazards to affected employees).

Second, it should be obvious that striking a balance among competing interests—protection of the environment, economic health of business, long-term health of citizens—is exceedingly difficult. For that reason, the national debate on our priorities in this area and the best way to meet them will continue long into the future.

SUMMARY

Few matters are more important than the future of our environment. The enormous number of state and federal environmental regulations with which businesses must contend are testimony to this fact.

Common law torts such as nuisance, negligence, and strict liability for damage caused by inherently dangerous activity (such as handling hazardous materials) have long afforded grounds for recovery. Now they are supplemented by a wide range of state legislative requirements.

The most important actor in environmental regulation is the EPA. It is in charge of enforcing a wide range of federal environmental laws, including the Clean Water Act, the Clean Air Act, the Resource Conservation and Recovery Act, the Endangered Species Act, and perhaps most frightening of all in terms of potential liability, the Comprehensive Environmental Response, Compensation, and Liability Act (CERCLA or "Superfund"). Many of these acts feature "citizen suits" as a supplemental means of enforcement.

Because pollution does not respect international boundaries, it is especially critical that nations cooperate in attacking environmental problems. Many important steps have been taken, but much remains to be done.

KEY TERMS

Nuisance
Negligence
Trespass
Strict liability
Environmental impact statement
Bubble concept
Acid rain
Hazardous waste

Comprehensive Environmental Response, Compensation, and Liability Act of 1980 (CERCLA/Superfund)
Potentially responsible parties

QUESTIONS AND PROBLEMS

1. Defendant Atlantic Cement operated a large cement plant near Albany, New York. Neighboring landowners brought an equitable action seeking damages and an injunction. Their complaint alleged that they had suffered, and would continue to suffer, property damage caused by dirt, smoke, and vibration from the cement plant. The trial court found that the cement plant was a nuisance and awarded tempo-

rary damages but refused to issue an injunction. The record disclosed that Atlantic Cement had more than $45 million invested in the plant and provided employment for some 300 employees. In awarding temporary damages to landowners, the trial court further granted the right to bring later suits for future damages. Is this a reasonable resolution of this suit? Discuss. (*Boomer v. Atlantic Cement Co.,* 257 N.E.2d 870, N.Y. App. 1970.)

2. In 1974 the Secretary of Defense announced the closing of an Army Depot near Lexington, Kentucky. The closing would eliminate 18 military and 2630 civilian jobs in the area. The Army prepared an environmental assessment that concluded that a formal EIS would not be needed because the closing would cause no significant impact on the human environment. A nongovernmental research institution concluded that the area would suffer only minimal short-term unemployment after the closing. In litigation that followed, the question arose whether the impact on employment would constitute "a major Federal action significantly affecting the quality of the human environment," necessitating the filing of an EIS. What did Congress intend when it passed NEPA? Discuss. (*Breckinridge v. Rumsfeld,* 537 F.2d 864, 6th Cir. 1976.)

3. T&E bought property once owned by U.S.R. Corporation, which had processed radium there. In 1981, the EPA placed the property on its CERCLA National Priorities List. T&E closed the facility and sued all the successor corporations of U.S.R., alleging, among others, a state-law claim of strict liability for an abnormally dangerous activity. The defendants claimed that strict liability could be imposed only if defendants knew *at the time of performance* that their activity was in fact abnormally dangerous. Are they right? Discuss. (*T&E Industries v. Safety Light Corp.,* 587 A.2d 1249, N.J. Sup. Ct. 1991.)

4. In facts similar to the previous case, Anspec Company bought land from Ultraspherics, later selling the land to a third party and leasing it back from him. After Anspec had bought the property, Ultraspherics merged into Hoover Group, which was designated as the corporation to survive the merger. Hoover assumed all assets and liabilities of Ultraspherics. Johnson Controls is the sole shareholder of Hoover Group and of Ultraspherics' parent corporation, Hoover Universal. Before Anspec bought the

property, Ultraspherics had disposed of hazardous waste on the site. The Michigan Department of Natural Resources notified Anspec of the contamination, and Anspec spent substantial amounts in response. Anspec sought reimbursement of these costs under CERCLA. Johnson Controls, Hoover Universal, and Hoover Group all moved to dismiss on grounds that they had not owned, occupied, or stored chemicals on the property. Is this a good defense? Discuss. (*Anspec Co., Inc. v. Johnson Controls, Inc.*, 922 F.2d 1240, 6th Cir. 1991.)

5. The plaintiff, Anthony, leased office space from the defendant, Commonwealth Enterprises, but a fire in the building caused exposure and release of asbestos material into the offices. The air was polluted, and asbestos dust contamination on the plaintiff's property made its use, movement, or removal hazardous. When the defendant refused to decontaminate the asbestos, the plaintiff hired consultants for the job. The plaintiff then sued the defendant under CERCLA for reimbursement of the costs incurred. Should the plaintiff recover? Discuss. (*Anthony v. Blech*, 760 F.Supp. 832, C.D. Cal. 1991.)

6. Sec. 7(a)(2) of the Endangered Species Act divides responsibilities regarding the protection of endangered species between the Secretaries of Interior and Commerce. They issued a regulation limiting the section's geographic scope to the United States and the high seas, exempting actions taken in foreign nations. Plaintiffs, wildlife conservation and other environmental organizations, sued for a declaratory judgment that the regulation erred as to the section's geographic scope. The Secretary of the Interior moved for dismissal on grounds that plaintiffs lacked "standing" to file the suit. Obviously an endangered species cannot sue on its own behalf. Under what circumstances should an environmental group be allowed to bring a suit such as this? Discuss. (*Lujan v. Defenders of Wildlife*, 112 S.Ct 2130, 1992.)

7. When OSHA set standards for cotton dust permissible in the air in plants preparing and manufacturing cotton, it set the level according to what would be economically feasible for the industry. The cotton industry challenged the standards on grounds that

the costs imposed were excessive in relation to the health benefits gained. Does the failure to undertake a cost-benefit analysis render the standards invalid? Discuss. (*American Textile Manufacturers Inititute v. Donovan*, 452 U.S. 490, 1981.)

8. Union Electric Company, an electrical utility company servicing St. Louis and much of Missouri, was informed that sulfur dioxide emissions from its coal-fired generating plants violated the Missouri plant sulfur dioxide restrictions. Union claimed that it had encountered economic and technologic difficulties that made compliance with the emission limitations impossible. For example, it claimed that low-sulfur coal had become too scarce and expensive; that the installation of sulfur dioxide removal equipment would cost more than $500 million; and that to operate and maintain such equipment would cost more than $120 million a year. Should the EPA grant Union a variance if to do so would permit the company to operate? Discuss. (*Union Electric Co. v. EPA*, 427 U.S. 246, 1975.)

9. An employee of Standard Oil of Kentucky accidentally left open a shut-off valve, causing a large quantity of aviation gasoline to flow into the St. Johns River in Florida. The Rivers and Harbors Act of 1899 provides, in part, that "[i]t shall not be lawful to throw, discharge, or deposit . . . any refuse matter of any kind or description whatever other than that flowing from streets and sewers and passing therefrom in a liquid state, into any navigable water of the United States." Should commercially valuable gasoline be considered refuse for purposes of the Act, thus making Standard Oil guilty of a violation? Discuss. (*United States v. Standard Oil Co.*, 384 U.S. 224, 1966.)

10. The EPA limited the rights of Quivera Mining Co. and Homestake Mining Co. to discharge pollutants into Arroyo del Puerto and San Mateo Creek. Because these were nearly dry "gullies," the companies challenged the EPA's order, pointing out that the Clean Water Act authorizes the EPA to regulate discharges only into "navigable waters." Was the EPA within its jurisdiction? Discuss. (*Quivera Mining Co. v. EPA*, 765 F.2d 126, 10th Cir. 1985.)

Chapter 51

Consumer Transactions and the Law

Deceptive Trade Practices

Federal Trade Commission Act

Consumer Credit Protection Act

Uniform Consumer Credit Code

Real Estate Settlement Procedures Act

Additional Consumer Protection Measures

DURING RECENT YEARS the creditor–debtor relationship has undergone a significant shift in emphasis from protection of the creditor to protection of the debtor in the **consumer transaction,** in which a consumer borrows to purchase a product or purchases on credit. Consumer protection law is designed to protect the buyer-debtor from such things as **usury** (lending money at interest rates higher than the law allows), excessive **garnishments,** and hidden costs in credit transactions. This is not to say that the creditor, or seller, is completely at the mercy of the buyer, or debtor. However, the rights of the seller-creditor are defined by numerous laws on the subject. Therefore, a knowledge of the basic provisions of consumer protection statutes is essential to the businessperson wanting to operate a commercially successful venture and, at the same time, conduct consumer transactions within the law.

The law of consumer transactions is primarily statutory. Consumers derive their rights and incur their obligations from the many state and federal statutes available for their benefit. Some laws protect consumers from false advertising and other deceptive practices. A number of statutes protect consumers in the financial dealings associated with borrowing or buying. Others afford protection in the purchasing process and set guidelines for the degree of performance and satisfaction it is reasonable to expect from a purchase. Finally, some statutes and a large body of case law relate to product safety. They provide a measure of protection against unsafe products and allow recovery for damages or injury caused by such products. Table 51.1 is a guide to some of the more important statutes. This information is important to all business students so that they may know their rights as consumers and their obligations as businesspersons.

DECEPTIVE TRADE PRACTICES

A consumer who is misled by false advertising or other deceptive practices may have the right to sue under a common-law fraud theory or perhaps a breach of express warranty theory if the advertising involved a product. These theories have been discussed in earlier chapters.[1] However, two federal

statutes help protect consumers from such deceptive practices without involving the consumers as plaintiffs. These are Sec. 5 of the Federal Trade Commission (FTC) Act and Sec. 43(a) of the Lanham Act.

FEDERAL TRADE COMMISSION ACT

Sec. 5(a)(1) of the FTC Act declares invalid (1) unfair methods of competition and (2) unfair or deceptive acts or practices. Both must at least "affect" interstate commerce for federal jurisdiction to exist. Unfair methods of competition substantially duplicate the antitrust violations that were covered earlier.[2] Our major concern in this chapter relates to the prohibition against "unfair or deceptive acts or practices."

Illicit Acts

Deceptive advertising is the main target of FTC concern in the realm of "unfair or deceptive acts or practices." With assistance from the courts, the FTC has prohibited and often punished (1) deceptive price advertising (for example, advertising a sale as 20 percent off a "suggested retail price" when in fact the goods are hardly ever sold at that price); (2) affirmative product claims that cannot be substantiated (such as claiming without evidence that a mouthwash helps fight the common cold); (3) deceptive advertising demonstrations (such as claiming that a shaving cream moisturizes so well that sandpaper can easily be shaved, yet demonstrating this by passing a razor through loose sand scattered on plexiglass); (4) product endorsements by celebrities who do not really use the product; (5) failure to indicate the origin of foreign goods; (6) use of "no cholesterol" on food labels that, although literally true, still mislead consumers into thinking that the products are also low in fat; (7) production of "infomercials"—half-hour television commercials designed to look like consumer programs rather than paid advertisements;

---

[1]Fraud was covered in Chapter 15, products liability warranty claims were

discussed in Chapter 22, along with the Mangnuson-Moss Act and the Consumer Products Safety Act, which also protect consumers from dangerous products. Indeed, in Chapter 6 the *Sun and Sands Imports* case illustrated the CPSC in action to protect consumers from potentially dangerous products. Trademark law also naturally protects consumers. It was discussed in Chapter 9 along with regulation of deceptive advertising under the Lanham Act. Obviously, the law is a web of regulations with lots of overlap.

[2]Antitrust law is discussed in Chapter 48.

TABLE 51.1 CURRENT CONSUMER PROTECTION STATUTES

POPULAR NAME	PURPOSE	REFERENCES
Child Protection and Toy Safety	Requires special labeling and child proof devices	15 U.S.C.A. §§1261 *et seq.*
Cigarette Labeling and Advertising	Surgeon general's warning of possible health hazard	15 U.S.C.A. §§1331 *et seq.*
Consumer Credit Protection	Comprehensive protection, all phases of credit transactions	15 U.S.C.A. §§1601 *et seq.*
Consumer Leasing Act	Improves disclosure of true costs in leasing transactions	15 U.S.C.A. §§1667
Consumer Product Safety	Protects consumer against defective or dangerous products	15 U.S.C.A. §§2051 *et seq.*
Equal Credit Opportunity	Prohibits discrimination in extending credit	15 U.S.C.A. §1691
Fair Credit and Charge Card Disclosure	Allows consumers to comparison shop for credit	15 U.S.C.A. §1610
Fair Credit Reporting	Protects consumer's credit reputation	15 U.S.C.A. §1681
Fair Debt Collection Practices	Prohibits abuses by debt collectors	15 U.S.C.A. §1692
Fair Packaging and Labeling	Requires accurate name, weight, quantity	15 U.S.C.A. §§1451 *et seq.*
Federal Trade Commission	Prohibits unfair or deceptive trade practices	15 U.S.C.A. §45
Flammable Fabrics	Eliminates or controls manufacture and marketing of dangerous fabrics	15 U.S.C.A. §§1191 *et seq.*
Food, Drug, and Cosmetic	Prohibits marketing of impure, adulterated products	21 U.S.C.A. §§301 *et seq.*
Fur Products Labeling	Prohibits misbranding of fur products	15 U.S.C.A. §69
Home Equity Loan Consumer Protection Act	Protects consumers who use homes as collateral	15 U.S.C.A. §1637a
Interstate Land Sales Act	Protects against land sale abuses	15 U.S.C.A. §1701
Lanham Act	Prohibits deceptive acts or practices in product sales	15 U.S.C.A. §43(a)
Magnuson-Moss Warranty	Governs content of warranties	15 U.S.C.A. §§2301 *et seq.*
National Traffic and Motor Vehicle Safety	Promotes traffic and auto safety	15 U.S.C.A. §§1381 *et seq.*
Real Estate Settlement Procedures	Requires disclosure of home buying costs	HUD Reg. X
Truth in Lending	Requires complete disclosure of credit terms	15 U.S.C.A. §§1601 *et seq.*
Uniform Commercial Code	Law of sales—unconscionable contracts	§2-302
Uniform Consumer Credit Code	Similar to federal Truth in Lending	9 states have adopted[a]

[a]Colorado, Idaho, Indiana, Iowa, Kansas, Maine, Oklahoma, South Carolina, Utah, Wisconsin and Wyoming have adopted substantial parts of some version of the Uniform Consumer Credit Code (UCCC).

and (8) product claims that tend to deceive, such as giving the name "Fresh Choice" to an orange juice made from concentrate.

The FTC's reach under Sec. 5 extends beyond deceptive advertising to other deceptive practices, including (1) "bait and switch" tactics (for example, advertising a low-quality good at a low price to induce consumers to come to the store and then pressuring them to buy a higher-priced model); (2) deceptive debt collection practices (such as sending letters to delinquent creditors that promised that a suit would be filed if no payments were made when, in fact, a determination to sue had not been made); and (3) unfair door-to-door selling—the FTC has promulgated a rule allowing consumers three days to rescind purchases made in their homes from door-to-door salesmen.[3]

[3]A similar provision under the Uniform Consumer Credit Code is discussed later in this chapter.

Enforcement

The FTC issues various rules, regulations, and guidelines regarding deceptive or unfair acts and practices. If the FTC discovers a potential violation, it can institute proceedings by filing a formal administrative complaint against the offender. The charge is normally heard before an FTC administrative law judge (ALJ), whose decision is reviewed by the FTC. The FTC's decisions may be reviewed by the courts.

Normally the FTC issues a "cease and desist" order to recalcitrant violators, ordering them to stop the deceptive acts or practices. Violation of such an order can precipitate fines of up to $10,000 per day. If the FTC has a strong case, an offender may agree to a "consent" order in which the FTC promises no further prosecution if the offender agrees to "go and sin no more."

In addition to obtaining injunctive orders from courts to support its cease and desist orders, the FTC is empowered to seek redress for consumers, perhaps in the form of refunds or cancellation of unfair contracts.

In advertising cases, the FTC has occasionally ordered *corrective advertising* by a company that has long deceived the public. In such a case, the company must spend its own money to inform the public that its prior claims were untrue. *Multiproduct orders* are more frequently issued. Such an order, which is typically used against a company that has

flagrantly engaged in falsely advertising for a few of its products, is aimed at *all* the company's products. The rationale for such an order is that a company that has engaged flagrantly in the false advertising of some of its products is likely to do the same with other products.

Although the FTC Act is aimed primarily at false advertising, it has been applied to other types of behavior, as the following case illustrates.

ORKIN EXTERMINATING CO., INC. v. FTC

U.S. Eleventh Circuit Court of Appeals, 849 F.2d 1354 (1988)

In a series of promotions between 1968 and 1975, the defendant, Orkin, made guarantees of lifetime termite control in exchange for timely payment of an annual fee that would not be raised unless the homeowner structurally modified the covered house. In 1978, Orkin decided that it could no longer afford to live up to this guarantee, so it substantially raised the annual fee on 207,000 contracts, pleading "inflation" as an excuse. Many customers complained, leading Orkin to roll back increases on 21,500 contracts. Those who did not complain or who did not have the documentation that Orkin required did not receive a roll-back, however. Pursuant to its Sec. 5 authority to block behavior constituting "unfair or deceptive" acts, the FTC ordered Orkin to rescind the price increases as to all the contracts. Orkin sought review of this order.

Clark, Circuit Judge:

Section 5 declares that "unfair or deceptive acts or practices in or affecting commerce" are unlawful, 15 U.S.C. § 45(a)(1); it also empowers the Commission to prevent certain entities from engaging in behavior that constitutes "unfair or deceptive acts or practices." 15 U.S.C. § 45(a)(2).

Orkin contends that a "mere breach of contract," which does not involve

some sort of deceptive or fraudulent behavior, is outside the ambit of section 5. In support of this proposition, Orkin cites cases that have interpreted state statutes similar to the FTCA, commonly referred to as "little" section 5 laws, to require "something more" than a simple breach of contract before a given course of conduct can be found "unfair or deceptive."

In 1980, the Commission promulgated a policy statement containing an abstract definition of "unfairness" which focuses upon unjustified customer injury. Under the standard enunciated in this policy statement,

[t]o justify a finding of unfairness the injury must satisfy three tests. It must be substantial; it must not be outweighed by any countervailing benefits to consumers or competition that the practice produces; and it must be an injury that consumers themselves could not reasonably have avoided.

The first prong of the unfairness standard requires a finding of substantial injury to consumers. In finding that Orkin's conduct has caused the requisite harm, the Commission said,

The harm resulting from Orkin's conduct consists of increased costs for services previously bargained for and includes the intangible loss of the certainty of the fixed price term in the contract.

108 F.T.C. at 362. The Commission's finding of "substantial" injury is supported by the undisputed fact that Orkin's breach of its pre-1975 con-

tracts generated, during a four-year period, more than $7,000,000 in revenues from renewal fees to which the Company was not entitled. As the Commission noted, although the actual injury to individual customers may be small on an annual basis, this does not mean that such injury is not "substantial."

As for the second prong of the unfairness standard, the Commission noted that "conduct can create a mixture of both beneficial and adverse consequences." But because "[t]he increase in the fee was not accompanied by an increase in the level of service provided or an enhancement of its quality," the Commission concluded that no consumer benefit had resulted from Orkin's conduct. The Commission also rejected various arguments that an order requiring Orkin to roll back its fee increases "would have adverse effects on its entire customer base and on many of its competitors." On appeal, Orkin has not challenged the Commission's conclusions regarding consumer benefits and benefits to competition.

With regard to the third prong of the unfairness standard, the Commission concluded that consumers could not have reasonably avoided the harm caused by Orkin's conduct. The Commission's focus on a consumer's ability to reasonably avoid injury "stems from the Commission's general reliance on free and informed consumer choice as the best regulator of the market." As the Commission

(continues)

ORKIN EXTERMINATING CO., INC. V. FTC

(continued from previous page)
explained, "Consumers may act to avoid injury before it occurs if they have reason to anticipate the impending harm and the means to avoid it, or they may seek to mitigate the damage afterward if they are aware of potential avenues toward that end." 108 F.T.C. at 366.

The Commission determined that "neither anticipatory avoidance nor subsequent mitigation was reasonably possible for Orkin's pre-1975 customers." *Id.* at 366. Anticipatory avoidance through consumer choice was impossible because these contracts give no indication that the company would raise the renewal fees as a result of inflation, or for any other reason.

As for mitigation of consumer injury, the Commission concluded that the company's "accommodation program" could not constitute an avenue for avoiding injury because relief from Orkin's conduct was available only to those customers who complained about the increases in the renewal fees.

There remains, however, the question whether this case represents a significant departure from prior Commission precedent. We note what has been written in a recent law review article:

Some of the oldest "unfairness" decisions involve sellers' refusals to live up to the terms of their contract. The Commission has often challenged sellers for traditional breaches of contract: failure to fill orders, delivery of inferior merchandise, refusal to return goods taken for repair, or refusal to return promised deposits. Recent trade regulation rules have focused on similar issues. These actions have attracted little controversy. Breach of contract has long been condemned as a matter of law economics, and public policy.

Craswell, 1981 Wis.L.Rev. at 128–29.

An adoption of Orkin's position would mean that the Commission could never proscribe widespread breaches of retail consumer contracts unless there was evidence of deception or fraud. The statutory scheme at issue here "necessarily gives the Commission an influential role in interpreting section 5 and in applying it to facts of particular cases arising out of *unprecedented situations.*" *F.T.C. v. Colgate-Palmolive Co.*, 380 U.S. 374, 385 (1965).

This case may be "unprecedented" to the extent it concerns non-deceptive contract breaches. But given the extraordinary level of consumer injury which Orkin has caused and the fact that deceptiveness is often not a component of the unfairness inquiry, we think the limitation of the Commission's section 5 authority urged by Orkin would be inconsistent with the broad mandate conferred upon the Commission by Congress. Thus, because the Commission's decision fully and clearly comports with the standard set forth in its Policy Statement, we conclude that the Commission acted within section 5 authority.

Orkin's final argument is that the Commission erred in declining to consider evidence that it relied, in good faith, upon advice of counsel when it decided to increase its annual renewal fees. Orkin's reliance upon counsel—a fact we assume—is irrelevant to an action brought pursuant to section 5. The unfairness standard, focusing as it does upon consumer injury, does not take into account the mental state of the party accused of a section 5 violation. "The purpose of the Federal Trade Commission Act is to protect the public, not punish the wrong doer. . . ." *Regina Corp. v. F.T.C.*, 322 F.2d 765, 768 (3d Cir. 1963).

[The FTC's injunction order is upheld.] ᗌᗍ

Lanham Act

The Lanham Act is another important federal act that outlaws "any false description or representation" in connection with any person's goods, services, or commercial activities. The pertinent provisions of Sec. 43(a) of the Lanham Act have been discussed in Chapter 9 and will not be repeated here.

CONSUMER CREDIT PROTECTION ACT

It is a fairly easy matter for the average householder to obtain and use any number of credit cards. The cash purchase of major appliances and automobiles is now a rare occurrence. The proliferation of credit has required legislation to define the rights and obligations of those who deal in it.

Congress enacted the Consumer Credit Protection Act (CCPA) in 1968 in response to unscrupulous and predatory practices on the part of creditors extending credit in consumer transactions. Congress was concerned with consumer credit disclosure methods, credit advertising, garnishment methods, questionable procedures used by some credit reporting agencies, and certain debt collection practices (a problem recognized in a 1977 amendment to the Act).

Truth in Lending

Before the **truth-in-lending** portion of the CCPA was passed in 1969, it was very difficult for consumers to understand what they were being charged for borrowing money or buying on time. Some lenders or sellers on credit would quote a "discount," others would refer to an "add on," and still others to various fees plus "simple interest." Some would quote monthly rates, whereas others quoted annual rates. The purpose of the Truth in Lending Act (TILA) is not to limit interest rates but to mandate disclosure of the true cost of credit so consumers borrowing money or buying on time can comparison shop.

Coverage

TILA, as amended, applies to credit transactions involving personal, family, or household purposes. Loans for commercial or agricultural purposes are not covered. And because Congress assumed that borrowers of large sums can protect themselves, TILA only applies to consumer loans not exceeding $25,000. Unlike many other consumer protection statutes, however, TILA also applies to credit secured by real property or a dwelling, such as a mortgage loan. There is no ceiling amount for this type of transaction; TILA applies even if the amount involved exceeds $25,000.

Only natural persons are protected by TILA's provisions. Debtors such as corporations or other organizations are not protected. All creditors who in the ordinary course of business lend money or sell on credit must comply with TILA provisions. TILA would not, however, apply to one consumer's loan to another.

Disclosure

TILA is primarily a disclosure act. It is clarified by regulation Z, a set of rules promulgated by the Federal Reserve Board. TILA's two key disclosure requirements relate to the **annualized percentage rate (APR),** which is the yearly cost of credit calculated on a uniform basis, and the *finance charge,* which is any additional amount the consumer pays as a result of buying on credit instead of paying cash. Examples of a finance charge would include application and processing charges such as a loan origination fee charged by mortgage lenders, investigation or credit reporting fees, and premiums for required credit insurance.

All disclosures must be written, clear, and conspicuous. The APR and finance charge must be more conspicuous than the other required disclosures.

Specific disclosure requirements are keyed to the type of transaction. On the one hand is an *open-end* (revolving) transaction, such as a gasoline credit card or VISA and MasterCard. On the other hand are all transactions other than open-end, usually character-

ized as closed-end (installment) sales or loans with a fixed number of payments. If repeated transactions are reasonably expected by the creditor, the open-end requirements apply.

In an open-end transaction, there are two types of required disclosure: an initial disclosure and periodic supplementary disclosures. The initial disclosure, which should be made before the first transaction, is general in nature, covering important terms of the credit plan rather than specific transactions. Required initial disclosures include (1) a statement of when finance charges begin to accrue, including any "free-ride" period; (2) the APR; (3) in a variable rate plan, conditions under which the interest rate may increase; (4) an explanation of the method used to determine the balance on which the finance charge may be computed and of how the amount of finance charge will be determined; (5) conditions under which the creditor may acquire a security interest in the debtor's property; and (6) a statement of the debtor's billing rights.

Creditors in open-end transactions must also make periodic disclosures at the end of each billing cycle. These disclosures are geared to the specific transactions that have occurred, and include such things as (1) the account balance at the beginning of the cycle; (2) identification of each transaction with descriptions of date, amount, and creditor; (3) the periodic rates that may be used to compute the finance charge and corresponding APR; (4) amounts of other charges; (5) account balance as of the closing date of the cycle; (6) any free-ride period; and (7) an address to be used for notice of billing errors. These disclosures are contained in the monthly statements credit card holders receive.

Disclosures in a closed-end transaction are somewhat different. They must be made before consummation of the transaction in question. An important concept is the *federal box.* The written disclosures should, by use of lines, a separate sheet of paper, boldface type, or the like, call attention to the required TILA disclosures. If the creditor puts too much information in the federal box, thus detracting from attention given the required federal disclosures, a TILA violation occurs just the same as if insufficient information is disclosed.

Among the required disclosures in a closed-end transaction are (1) the creditor's identity; (2) the amount financed and how it is computed; (3) the finance charge and APR (and circumstances under which it may be increased); (4) number, amounts, and timing of payments; (5) total dollar value of all payments; and (6) effect of prepayment.

Substantive Provisions

Although TILA is primarily a disclosure statute, it does shape some credit practices through substantive provisions. For example, it provides a three-day right of rescission for consumers who use their residence to secure credit in a nonpurchase money transaction. The rule does not apply to the first mortgage, issued when a house is purchased. But assume a home-owner contracts to buy a new air conditioner on credit. If the credit purchase is secured by the re-tailer's receiving a second mortgage on the residence, the right of rescission would apply. Absent an emergency, the seller should not deliver goods or perform services during that three-day period.

TILA also contains certain rules regarding how credit may be advertised. Again, the purpose is to create uniform, clear statements that will allow for comparison shopping. Furthermore, TILA contains numerous provisions regarding use of credit cards, even when no finance charge exists. One such provision is the $50 maximum ceiling for credit card holder liability, which is discussed later in this chapter.

Enforcement

Various federal agencies, most importantly the FTC, enforce the civil provisions of TILA, and the Department of Justice can bring criminal charges for TILA violations. The maximum criminal penalty is one year in jail, a $5,000 fine, or both for *each* violation.

Consumers are accorded a private right of action under TILA and may recover their actual damages *plus* two times the finance charge (not to be less than $100 or more than $1000) and attorneys' fees. Suit should be brought within one year of a disclosure violation. The statute of limitations in a case involving a house being used as collateral is three years from the date of violation. TILA also contains a limited good-faith defense, which is applied in the following case.

HENDLEY V. CAMERON-BROWN CO.

U.S. Eleventh Circuit Court of Appeals, 840 F.2d 831 (1988)

On April 1, 1984, the Hendleys and the Blacks (appellants) obtained discounted variable rate mort-gage loans from Cameron-Brown Co. (appellee) to finance the purchase of their homes. The loans featured an annual adjustment of the interest rate. The annual interest rate was based on an "index plus margin" formula that was deter-mined by adding to the margin, then at 2.79 percent, the current index (subject to a 2 percent annual cap and an overall cap of 5.75 percent for the lifetime of the loan). Appellants claim they were told that the interest rate would adjust annually in the same direction as the index.

At the end of the first year, ap-pellee informed appellants that the interest rate for the second year would increase from 9.875 percent to 11.875 percent. Appellee claims that this increase was based on the "index plus margin" formula checked by the 2 percent cap. Objecting to this increase, appellants filed this suit claiming that appellee had violated TILA's disclosure requirements. Be-cause the index actually declined in the second year from 10.53 percent to 9.61 percent, appellants main-tained that the increase was inconsis-tent with the disclosure statement's language that the interest rate would be adjusted annually in the same di-rection as the index. Appellants ar-gued that appellee failed to disclose the initial index and that the initial interest rate was discounted (lower than it would have been if it had been calculated by using the "index plus margin" formula).

The trial court granted summary judgment to appellee, finding that it had "technically complied" with TILA and that any deficiencies were protected by its "good-faith" effort

at complying with relatively new rules. Appellants appealed.

Vance, Circuit Judge:

Congress enacted the Truth In Lend-ing Act to ensure meaningful disclo-sures in consumer credit transactions. The Federal Reserve Board ("Board") promulgated Regulation Z to execute the purposes of the Truth In Lending Act. The Board established the disclo-sure requirements for variable rate loans in 12 C.F.R. § 226.18(f). This provision provides:

If the annual percentage rate may increase after consummation, the following disclosures [are required]:

(1) The circumstances under which the rate may increase.

(2) Any limitations on the increase.

(3) The effect of an increase.

(4) An example of the payment terms that would result from an increase.

(continues)

HENDLEY V. CAMERON-BROWN CO.

(continued from previous page)

We hold that appellee did not comply with the first requirement by fully disclosing the "circumstances under which the rate may increase." The disclosure statement provided that "the interest rate may increase during the term of this transaction if the index increases." This, however, was not the only circumstance which could cause an increase in the interest rate. As the district court stated, "The problem is that the statement fails to note that the initial interest rate is discounted, creating the possibility of an increase even when the index does not rise." Due to the initial discounted interest rate, the annual interest rate could increase if the index remained constant, or even if the index declined. Absent this information, the disclosure failed to meet regulatory standards.

Appellee argues that at the time these transactions occurred the Board had recently amended its official staff interpretation of regulation § 226.18(f) to explain its application to discounted variable rate loans. The amended interpretation required the disclosure to "reflect a composite annual percentage rate based on the initial rate for as long as it is charged and, for the remainder of the term, the rate that would have been applied using the index or formula at the time of consummation." Appellee maintains that this amended interpretation was only optionally effective on April 1, 1984, and that due to the "dramatic change in the disclosure requirements" appellee was not required to go beyond the requirements of the existing interpretation. Regardless of the effective date of the amended interpretation, however, the regulation's requirements did not change and we believe that appellee failed to comply with the clear disclosure requirements of the regulations.

Appellee also argues that even if the disclosure were improper, it is insulated from liability under 15 U.S.C. § 1640(f) because it acted in good faith in accordance with the Board's official interpretation of regulation § 226.18(f). Section 1640(f) provides:

No provision of this section, section 1607(b), section 1607(c), section 1607(e), or section 1611 of this title imposing any liability shall apply to any act done or omitted in good faith in conformity with any rule, regulation, or interpretation thereof by the Board or in conformity with any interpretation or approval by an official or employee of the Federal Reserve System duly authorized by the Board to issue such interpretations or approvals under such procedures as the Board may prescribe therefor, notwithstanding that after such act or omission has occurred, such rule, regulations, interpretation, or approval is amended, rescinded, or determined by judicial or other authority to be invalid for any reason.

Section 1640(f) "does not protect a creditor who *fails* to conform with a regulation or interpretation through an honest, good faith mistake." *Cox v. First Nat'l Bank of Cincinnati*, 751 F.2d 815, 825 (6th Cir. 1985). So a creditor's honest and reasonable but mistaken interpretation is not protected. Appellee's belief that the regulation did not require further disclosure based on its mistaken interpretation of the regulation and reliance on an inapplicable interpretation does not protect it from liability. As a matter of law, the section 1640(f) good faith defense is not available.

[Reversed.] ⚖

Home Equity Loan Consumer Protection Act

Consumers occasionally use their homes as security when applying for open-end credit. The consequences for the homeowner who defaults on such a loan are obviously quite significant. Therefore, in an amendment to TILA, Congress passed the Home Equity Loan Consumer Protection Act of 1988 (HELCPA). Basically, this Act requires lenders to provide an application-stage disclosure statement in addition to a consumer education pamphlet whenever a consumer puts up his or her "principal dwelling" (defined, unusually, to include second or vacation homes) as security for open-end credit. In addition to a broad range of disclosure requirements, HELCPA also contains several substantive provisions, including (1) restrictions on the creditor's ability to change unilaterally the plan's terms; (2) limitations on grounds for terminating the loan and requiring immediate repayment of the balance ("acceleration"); and (3) requirements that an external, publicly available index or formula be used if the home equity plan allows for rate changes.

Restrictions on Garnishment

Garnishment can be defined as the legal proceedings of a judgment creditor to require a third person owing money to the debtor or holding property belonging to the debtor to turn over to the court or sheriff the property or money for the satisfaction of the judgment. Congressional hearings leading to the enactment of the CCPA revealed that the unrestricted garnishment of wages encouraged predatory extension of credit, that employers were often quick to discharge an employee whose wages were garnished, and that the laws of the states on the subject were so different they effectively destroyed the uniformity of the bankruptcy laws and defeated their purpose. Consequently, the CCPA section on garnishment set limits on the extent to which the wages of an individual could be garnished. In general, wages cannot be garnished in any work week in excess of 25 percent of the individual's disposable (after-tax) earnings or the amount by which the disposable earnings for that work week exceed 30 times the federal minimum hourly wage, whichever is less. Such restrictions do not apply in the case of a court order for the support of any person (wife or child, for example); any order of a court of bankruptcy under Chapter 13, Adjustment of Debts of an Individual with Regular Income, of the Federal Bankruptcy Act; or any debt due for state or federal taxes.

Of particular interest to students is that in the 1991 Federal Unemployment Benefits Bill, Congress authorized a 10 percent garnishment of wages of persons who are more than 180 days behind in repayment of student loans.

Fair Credit Reporting Act

The section of the CCPA known as the *Fair Credit Reporting Act* is directed at consumer reporting agencies. It is an effort by Congress to ensure that the elaborate mechanism developed for investigating and evaluating the credit worthiness, credit standing, credit capacity, character, and general reputation of consumers is fair with respect to the confidentiality, accuracy, relevance, and proper use of the reported information. Too often in the past, the consumer was denied credit because of misleading or inaccurate information supplied to a prospective creditor by a consumer reporting agency.[4] The effect could be devastating, particularly as it affected the consumer's credit standing and general reputation in the business community.

The information on individual consumers is derived from many sources, including creditors and

court and other official records, and, in many cases, from facts consumers supply themselves. Information accumulated in a **consumer report** and disseminated to users can and often does include such items as judgments, liens, bankruptcies, arrest records, and employment history. In addition, the Fair Credit Reporting Act covers the **investigative reports** made by credit reporting agencies. Often used by prospective employers or by insurance companies, investigative reports are more personal in nature than consumer reports and can contain information on the subject's personal habits, marital status (past and present), education, political affiliation, and so on.

With regard to both consumer reports and investigative reports, the law requires that, on request and proper identification, consumers are entitled to know the nature and substance of all information about them (except medical information) in the agency's file, the sources of the information, and the identity of those who have received the report from the credit reporting agency. Those entitled to receive consumer reports include businesses that may want to extend credit to the consumer, prospective employers or insurers, and government licensing agencies that may be concerned with the financial responsibility of the consumer. Access to the information can also be gained by court order. In addition, an investigative report cannot be prepared on an individual consumer unless that person is first notified and given the right to request information on the nature and scope of the pending investigation.

An important provision of the Act requires that all information in consumer reports be current and that consumer reporting agencies maintain reasonable procedures designed to avoid violations of certain other provisions. This is an obvious effort to reduce the incidence of carelessly prepared reports having inaccurate information. (See Box 51.1)

Finally, civil penalties for a *negligent* violation of the Act include the actual damages to the consumer and, in a successful action, court costs and reasonable attorneys' fees. In case of *willful* noncompliance, punitive damages may also be awarded to the successful plaintiff-consumer. Administrative enforcement of the Act is a function of the FTC because violations are considered unfair or deceptive acts or practices.

---

[4]This is not an agency of the government. Such agencies are persons or businesses that regularly assemble credit information and provide it to others for a fee.

COMEAUX V. BROWN & WILLIAMSON TOBACCO CO.

U.S. Court of Appeals, Ninth Circuit, 915 F.2d 1264 (1990)

Case

The defendant, B&W, offered the plaintiff, Comeaux, a job. Comeaux accepted, gave notice to his then-current employer, and moved to Fremont, California, where the job was. While Comeaux made these arrangements, B&W ran a credit check on Comeaux without telling him that it was going to do so or that the results could affect his employment. The credit report from Trans Union Credit Information Co. revealed that Comeaux had a poor credit history. B&W then told Comeaux that it would not hire him. Comeaux sued B&W, inter alia, for breach of contract. In February 1988, soon after the lawsuit was filed, B&W ran a second credit check on Comeaux, not because it was considering hiring him but to prepare for the litigation. When Comeaux learned of this, he amended his complaint to add a claim for violation of the FCRA.*

The trial judge granted B&W summary judgment on all claims. Comeaux appealed. [The following portion of the court's opinion addresses only the FCRA claim.]

Sneed, Circuit Judge:

The FCRA provides for civil and criminal penalties for those who do not comply with the Act. Sections 1681n and 1681o, respectively, make consumer reporting agencies and users liable for willful or negligent noncompliance with "any requirement" imposed under the Act. Section 1681q provides a criminal penalty for "knowingly and willfully obtain[ing] information on a consumer from a consumer reporting agency under false pretenses." Noncompliance with 1681q thereby forms a basis for civil liability under 1681n.

B&W told Trans Union that it wanted the February 1988 credit report on Comeaux "for employment purposes." The record before us establishes that this statement was false, even though B&W claimed at one stage in the litigation that it was true. Thus, B&W requested the report under false pretenses, thereby violating section 1681q and providing Comeaux with a cause of action under section 1681n or 1681o.

B&W argues, however, that its receipt and use of the February 1988 credit report is not governed by the FCRA, which only regulates "consumer reports." It claims that the report was not a consumer report because it sought the report for a *non-consumer* purpose. The term "consumer report" is defined in section 1681a(d). [Its] plain language reveals that a credit report will be construed as a "consumer report" under the FCRA if the credit bureau providing the information *expects* the user to use the report for a purpose permissible under the FCRA, without regard to the ultimate purpose to which the report is *actually* put. B&W's construction of the statute [which the district court adopted] would render meaningless the FCRA's goal of allowing the release of credit reports for certain purposes only.

If a consumer reporting agency provides a report based on a reasonable expectation that the report will be put to a use permissible under the FCRA, then that report is a "consumer report" under the FCRA and the ultimate use to which the report is actually put is irrelevant to the question of whether the FCRA governs the report's use and the user's conduct.

[The district court's summary judgment order on the FCRA claim is REVERSED.]

Credit Cards

The widespread use of credit cards, issued by all manner of companies, created much legal controversy when a card fell into the wrong hands through loss or theft. Many companies provided their credit cards indiscriminately to any person who might want one and to many who had not requested them. It became a major problem to determine who was to assume the liability for unauthorized credit card purchases: the person to whom the card was issued, the unauthorized user, the merchant who made the sale, or the credit card issuer. Congress addressed the problem in CCPA provisions that prohibit the issuance of credit cards except in response to a request or application and that place limits on the liability of a cardholder for its unauthorized use. In general, if a cardholder loses a credit card and it is used by someone without authority to do so, the cardholder is liable if (1) the liability does not exceed $50; (2) the card is an accepted card; (3) the issuer has given notice to the cardholder as to the potential liability; (4) the issuer has provided the cardholder with a self-addressed, prestamped notification to be mailed by the cardholder in the event of loss or theft; (5) the unauthorized use occurs before

GETTING THE KINKS OUT OF YOUR CREDIT REPORT

by Michele Galen

Box 51.1
The Law at Work

When Senator Richard Bryan (D-Nev.) and his wife went to buy a house in Las Vegas last year, a routine credit check turned up a few surprises. His report listed credit cards that just "weren't ours," he says. It also showed several lawsuits that had been filed against the state of Nevada, naming Bryan because he was then governor. Bryan again found errors when he refinanced the house in January. The most glaring was a tax lien that didn't exist. "I was frankly shocked to see some of that stuff in there," he says.

Both times, Bryan got the errors deleted by writing to the credit bureaus. But, the senator says, "I'm not unmindful that John Q. Public would have more problems." Bryan is pushing a bill amending the Fair Credit Reporting Act of 1970 to help consumers fix false credit reports. The provisions include a 30-day deadline for the bureaus to resolve disputes. The bill follows a wave of criticism and lawsuits over practices by the Big Three: Equifax, Trans Union, and TRW.

The furor is also encouraging the credit agencies to take steps on their own. They have made it easier and cheaper to get credit reports, but it can still be tough to delete errors. Says Edmund Mierzwinski, consumer advocate for the U.S. Public Interest Research Group: "The short answer to how to fix your credit report is be vigilant and persistent."

Start by knowing what information is collected. Credit reports contain data supplied by banks and other institutions about loans, credit cards, and bill payments. They also include job information and data culled from public records, including legal judgments. Most negative data remain on file for seven years, but bankruptcies can stay for 10 years. Creditors and others use the reports for making such decisions as granting a mortgage or renting an apartment.

Consumers can minimize errors by completing credit applications carefully, always using the same name. For example, if you use a middle initial, be sure to include it. Don't wait until you've been denied credit or shut out of a job before checking for accuracy. The Big Three enter 2 billion pieces of data into credit records monthly, so the odds of errors slipping in are high.

Consumer advocates suggest getting copies of your credit report once a year from each bureau because they collect different data. Also review your reports six months in advance of a major purchase such as a house or before seeking a job that requires a security clearance or background check.

The credit bureaus will send you the reports upon request, but they differ in how much they charge. If you're denied credit, the bureaus must provide a free copy if you request it within 30 days after being turned down. Industry practice expands that period to 60 days.

For consumers who are just curious, TRW now provides one free report annually. Equifax charges $8, except in a few states where the caps are lower. The company requires that you send your request in writing. Trans Union has some 300 offices that will supply the reports for an average of $15.

When making your request, ask the bureau to include a pamphlet explaining your legal rights. You can also get the information from the Federal Trade Commission, Bureau of Consumer Protection, Division of Credit Practices, Room S-4429, 6th St. and Pennsylvania Ave., NW, Washington, D.C. 20580 (202 326-3758).

The most common mistakes include credit data that belong to someone else and outstanding credit-card balances that you actually paid. If you find an error, follow the dispute resolution process set forth in the credit report. Fill out the form and return it, along with any documentation that supports your side. Send copies to the original creditor, as well as to any collection agencies.

Source: *Business Week*, May 25, 1992, p. 132.

---

the cardholder has notified the issuer that an unauthorized use of the card has occurred; and (6) the card issuer has provided a method whereby the user of the card can be identified by the merchant, either by photograph or signature, as the authorized user.

The provisions just mentioned are for the protection of a lawful cardholder. Unauthorized use of a credit card can result in severe penalties. If the unauthorized transaction involves goods or services, or both, having a retail value of $5000 or more, the penalty can be a fine of up to $10,000 or imprisonment for up to five years, or both.

AMERICAN EXPRESS TRAVEL RELATED SERVICES CO. v. WEB, INC.

Supreme Court of Georgia, 405 S.E.2d 652 (1991)

WEB, Inc. opened a corporate credit account with American Express in New York. Under the agreement, credit cards were issued to William E. Becker, the "individual applicant," and to his wife, his daughter, and Madelyn Lazich, the "additional applicants," who were authorized to charge to the corporate account. Under the agreement, WEB and Becker were responsible for all charges made to the account, whereas the additional applicants were liable only for their own charges.

Lazich, a real estate broker who had a personal relationship with Becker, was hired by Becker to open an Atlanta office of WEB. When the relationship soured, she went on a spending spree, charging over $27,000 on the American Express card alone. Lazich used the card itself on some of the charges, but on others, after WEB retrieved her card, used only the account number.

WEB filed this suit seeking a declaratory judgment that it was not responsible for Lazich's personal charges. American Express counterclaimed for the amount due. The trial court ruled for American Express. The intermediate appellate court reversed. American Express appealed.

Hunt, Justice:

The Truth-in-Lending Act sets out the terms to be used in applying its principles. 15 U.S.C.A. Sec. 1602(m) provides:

> The term "cardholder" means any person to whom a credit card is issued or any person who has agreed with the card issuer to pay obligations arising from the issuance of a credit card to another person[;]

while subsection (o) defines "unauthorized use":

> The term "unauthorized use" . . . means a use of a credit card by a person *other than the cardholder* who does not have actual, implied, or apparent authority for such use and from which the cardholder receives no benefit. [Emphasis supplied.]

15 U.S.C.A. Sec. 1643, sets out the conditions for limiting the liability of a cardholder for the "unauthorized use" of a credit card:

> A cardholder shall be liable [up to $50] for the unauthorized use of a credit card if . . . (E) the unauthorized use occurs before the card issuer has been notified that an unauthorized use of the credit card has occurred or may occur *as the result of loss, theft, or otherwise;* . . . [Emphasis supplied.]

Thus, under section 1643, a cardholder is protected from liability only from "unauthorized use" and is not protected from misuse by an authorized user. WEB argues, however, that when it gave notice to American Express, Lazich became an "unauthorized user" subject to the limitations of section 1643.

In setting out the limits of the liability of credit cardholders in sections 1643, Congress did not provide for mitigation of cardholders' liability where notice of miuse is given to the issuer. We must conclude that Congress intended no such limitation and notice of misuse does not convert the cardholder into an "unauthorized" user. Lazich, herself a cardholder, was, beyond doubt, an authorized user as to all the carges she made . . . . Lazich's charges were not "unauthorized" within the meaning of [TILA].

Reversed.

Fair Credit and Charge Card Disclosure Act

Concerned over high interest rates charged credit card borrowers, Congress considered enacting a ceiling on such charges, but ultimately decided that competition was the best regulation. Therefore, to enable consumers to comparison shop, Congress enacted the Fair Credit and Charge Card Disclosure Act (FCCCDA) of 1988 (an amendment to TILA), which requires disclosure of certain key items of information at the solicitation and application stages for credit and charge card accounts.

The amount of disclosure required varies with the type of solicitation. Direct mail applications and solicitations must disclose more information, for example, than solicitations made by telephone or through ads contained in magazines. A complete catalog of the required disclosures would be too lengthy to repeat here. However, among the key disclosures that must be made in connection with a direct mail solicitation for a *credit card* are (1) each periodic rate of finance charge expressed as an annual percentage rate; (2) if the plan includes a variable rate of interest, the fact that the rate may vary, how the rate is determined, and the APR in effect within 30 days before the time of the mailing; (3) any annual or other periodic fee imposed for issuance of the credit card; (4) any transaction fee imposed in connection with purchase transactions; and (5) any minimum or fixed finance charge that could be imposed during a billing cycle. These and other "core disclosures" must be placed in a prominent location either on or with the application or solicitation.

Less onerous disclosures are required for applications or solicitations for a "charge card," defined as "a card, plate, or other single credit device that may be used from time to time to obtain credit which is *not* subject to a finance charge." The Act also requires disclosure of any fees charged to renew a credit or charge card account. Atypically, it preempts rather than supplements state laws in the area.

Fair Debt Collection Practices Act

The Fair Debt Collection Practices Act was designed to eliminate abusive debt collection practices by debt collectors and to protect individual debtors against debt collection abuses. The following excerpt from *Duty v. General Finance Co.*, 273 S.W.2d 64 (Tex. 1954), illustrates some of the tactics used by an overzealous debt collector. It is important to note that each and every tactic employed by the General Finance Company debt collector is now prohibited by the Fair Debt Collection Practices Act.

The harassment alleged may be summarized as follows: Daily telephone calls to both Mr. & Mrs. Duty which extended to great length; threatening to blacklist them with the Merchants' Retail Credit Association; accusing them of being deadbeats; talking to them in a harsh, insinuating, loud voice; stating to their neighbors and employers that they were deadbeats; asking Mrs. Duty what she was doing with her money; accusing her of spending money in other ways than in payments on the loan transaction; threatening to cause both plaintiffs to lose their jobs unless they made the payments demanded; calling each of the plaintiffs at the respective places of their employment several times daily; threatening to garnish their wages; berating plaintiffs to their fellow employees; requesting their employers to require them to pay; calling on them at their work; flooding them with a barrage of demand letters, duncards, special delivery letters, and telegrams both at their homes and their places of work; sending them cards bearing this opening statement. "Dear Customer: We made you a loan because we thought that you were honest"; sending telegrams and special delivery letters to them at approximately midnight, causing them to be awakened from their sleep; calling a neighbor in the disguise of a sick brother of one of the plaintiffs, and on another occasion as a stepson; calling Mr. Duty's mother at her place of employment in Wichita Falls long distance, collect; leaving red cards in their door, with insulting notes on the back and thinly-veiled threats; calling Mr. Duty's brother long distance, collect, in Albuquerque, New Mexico, at his residence at a

cost to him in excess of $11, and haranguing him about the alleged balance owed by plaintiffs.

The debt collector's communications with others and with the debtor in an effort to locate the debtor are governed by a provision of the Act. The debt collector is prohibited from making false representations or misleading the debtor about the nature of the collection process. The collector cannot solicit or take from any person a check postdated by more than five days without notice of the intent to deposit the check. On occasion, debt collectors have encouraged the debtor to write a postdated check for the amount of the debt knowing that the debtor had insufficient funds to cover the check. A threat to deposit the postdated check was often enough to compel the debtor to seek the funds necessary to pay the collector and thereby avoid criminal prosecution for issuing a bad check. The Act further provides that written notice of the amount of the debt and the name of the creditor be sent to the customer together with a statement that, unless the consumer disputes the validity of the debt within 30 days, the debt collector can assume it is a valid obligation. If the consumer owes multiple debts and makes a single payment, the debt collector cannot apply the payment to any debt that is disputed by the consumer.[5]

The Fair Debt Collection Practices Act protects the consumer-debtor and places significant burdens on the debt collector. Compliance with the Act is enforced by the Federal Trade Commission, because violations are considered to be unfair or deceptive trade practices. A debt collector who fails to comply with the provisions of the Act may incur civil liability to the extent of actual damages sustained by the plaintiff, additional punitive damages not to exceed $1000, and court costs and reasonable attorneys' fees.

Fair Credit Billing

Before the Fair Credit Billing Act, the burden of resolving a billing dispute rested mainly on the customer-debtor. This is no longer true. The Fair Credit Billing Act requires that creditors maintain procedures whereby consumers can complain about billing errors and obtain satisfaction within a specified period, not later than two billing cycles or 90 days. The consumer must give the creditor notice of the billing

---

[5]This provision may be contrary to a commonly accepted principle of contract law: Where a debtor owes multiple debts and fails to specify to which debt the payment is to be applied, the creditor can make the choice.

error with a statement explaining the reasons for questioning the item or items felt to be in error. The creditor must then either make appropriate corrections in the consumer's account or conduct an investigation into the matter. If, after the investigation, the creditor feels that the statement is accurate, it must so notify the debtor and explain why it believes the original statement of account to be correct. The Act also requires that payments be credited promptly and that any overpayment be refunded (on request by the debtor) or credited to the debtor's account.

Equal Credit Opportunity

The Equal Credit Opportunity Act (ECOA), as amended, quite simply prohibits discrimination based on race, color, religion, national origin, sex, marital status, or age in connection with extensions of credit. The applicant must, however, have contractual capacity; minors, for example, cannot insist on credit under the Act. The enactment is the result of complaints by married persons that credit frequently was denied unless both parties to the marriage obligated themselves. Each party can now separately and voluntarily apply for and obtain credit accounts, and state laws prohibiting separate credit no longer apply. The Act also directs the Board of Governors of the Federal Reserve System to establish a Consumer Advisory Council to provide advice and consultation on consumer credit and other matters. The following case offers an interesting application of the ECOA.

UNITED STATES V. AMERICAN FUTURE SYSTEMS, INC.

U.S. Third Circuit Court of Appeals, 743 F.2d 169 (1984)

Case

American Future Systems (AFS) sold china, cookware, crystal, and tableware, 95 percent of the time on credit. AFS marketed its wares through three separate programs. Its summer programs targeted as preferred customers single white women between the ages of 18 and 21 years who lived at home. AFS hoped parents would co-sign the order but would extend credit and automatically ship goods to the buyer even without a co-signature. Nonpreferred customers, almost always young black women, were extended credit only after a satisfactory credit check. If the buyer did not pass the check, goods would not be shipped. AFS sales employees were urged to sell only in areas believed to be all or predominantly white and worked under commission arrangements that encouraged sales to whites.

AFS's winter program had two aspects. Its preferred sales targets were single white women in their final three years of college. They were given immediate credit and the ordered goods were shipped to them immediately, regardless of age, credit

histories, or any other normal indicia of creditworthiness. Nonpreferred customers for the winter program included all minorities, men, married persons, and freshmen in college. AFS would not ship goods to these customers until they had made three successive monthly payments. Although these customers were led to believe they were being treated the same as other AFS customers, AFS had made a marketing judgment to prefer white women.

The Department of Justice sued AFS, its president, and an affiliated company, claiming violation of the ECOA. AFS defended, claiming that minority customers are, as a group, less creditworthy than their white counterparts. AFS could produce no reliable evidence to support this position, so the trial court found both the winter and summer programs to violate the ECOA. AFS appealed as to the winter program only.

Higginbotham, Circuit Judge:

The Equal Credit Opportunity Act proscribes discrimination in the extension of credit. Section 1691(a) of the ECOA states that

[i]t shall be unlawful for any creditor to discriminate against any applicant, with respect to any aspect of a credit transaction—(1) on the basis or race, color, religion, national origin, sex or marital status, or age (provided the applicant has the capacity to contract).

The ECOA does provide, however, for special purpose credit programs responsible to special social needs of a class of persons. Section 1691(c)(3) carves out this exception:

It is not a violation of this section for a creditor to refuse to extend credit offered pursuant to . . . any special purpose credit program offered by a profit-making organization to meet special social needs which meets standards prescribed in regulations by the [Federal Reserve] Board.

The district court made a finding which shows that the class of persons between the ages of 18 and 21 are in special need of credit assistance. [The court then found that AFS's program met the three conditions for this exception in that (1) there was a "special social need" for credit for this age group, (2) the program was in writing, and (3) the preferred class "probably would not receive such credit or probably would receive it on less favorable terms" absent the program.]

(continues)

UNITED STATES V. AMERICAN FUTURE SYSTEMS, INC.

(continued from previous page)

Notwithstanding a credit program having satisfied these three requirements, a program once established cannot discriminate on prohibited bases such as race, sex or marital status.

Congressman Annunzio, who recommended key amendments which broadened the types of discrimination prohibited by the ECOA, elaborated on the purpose of the ECOA:

The essential concept of nondiscrimination in the extension of credits is that each individual has a right when he applies for credit to be evaluated as an individual: to be evaluated on his individual creditworthiness, rather than based on some generalization or stereotype about people who are similar to him in race, color, national origin, religion, age, sex, or marital status. Bias is not creditworthiness. Impression is not creditworthiness. An individual's ability and willingness to repay an extension of credit is creditworthiness.

Thus the specific issue before us is whether the ECOA permits [preferred treatment to single white women] where the district court expressly found that each person in the group of individuals between the ages of 18 and 21 shares the same credit disability. . . .

There is a particular irony in AFS's approach where it singles out white women as a "disadvantaged" group and gives them a special advantage that it unhesitatingly denies to black and other minority women.

Despite all of the disadvantages that women have had, historically and at present, the significant disadvantages suffered by white women have been far less than those disadvantages black women, Native American women (Indians), Hispanic and other minority American women have had to endure for centuries. Yet, the paradox of AFS's plan is that it perpetuates the past disparities between white and minority women and rather than helping all women it aids only white women and slams the door of equal credit opportunity in the faces of minority women.

We do not believe that it was the intention of Congress to accentuate the disparities among disadvantaged groups by helping those women who have been the *least* deprived while denying equal opportunity to those women who have been the most deprived.

[Affirmed.] ⚖

Supplementing the ECOA is the Women's Business Ownership Act of 1988, aimed at eliminating discrimination in the extension of credit to businesses owned and controlled by women.

UNIFORM CONSUMER CREDIT CODE

Federal legislation does not necessarily preclude similar state legislation. For example, Sec. 1610 of the Consumer Credit Protection Act generally preempts only state laws that are *less* protective of debtors. State laws that are *more* protective probably are not precluded.[6] This principle—that state laws are enforceable even though they may regulate an area already covered by federal statutes—is illustrated by the Uniform Consumer Credit Code (UCCC).

The UCCC has been promulgated by the National Conference of Commissioners on Uniform State Laws in two versions—one in 1968 and one in 1974.

Eleven states have adopted substantial parts of one form or another of the UCCC. Many other states have similar provisions. However, there is great variation from state to state, even among the UCCC adopters. Therefore, our discussion of the UCCC's features must be somewhat general.

The UCCC is much like the Federal Consumer Credit Protection Act. It covers consumer credit sales, loans, garnishment, and insurance provided in relation to a consumer credit sale. Its truth-in-lending provisions require full disclosure to the consumer of all aspects of the credit transaction and further require that charges to the consumer be computed and disclosed as an annual percentage rate. The code does not prescribe any specific rates for credit service charges, but it sets maximums based on unpaid balances—36 percent per year on $300 or less in non-open-end accounts, 21 percent per year for balances of $300 to $1000, and 15 percent for unpaid balances in excess of $1000. Because the law permits higher charges for smaller transactions, it forbids creditors from breaking large transactions down into smaller ones to take advantage of higher credit charges.

---

[6]For example, state laws that prohibit garnishments or provide for more limited garnishments than are allowed under the federal statute are effective and enforceable despite the federal regulations on the same subject.

Home Solicitation Sales

The UCCC covers door-to-door solicitation in some detail, because this is a troublesome area for consumers. Consumers tend to be more vulnerable to high-pressure selling tactics in their homes; after signing an agreement to purchase, they often regret the decision. The UCCC therefore permits the rescission of a credit sale solicited and finalized in the customer's home if the customer gives written notice to the seller within 72 hours after signing the agreement to purchase.[7] The cancellation notice is effective when deposited in a mailbox and can take any form so long as it clearly expresses the buyer's intention to void the home solicitation sale. Sellers are required to provide a statement informing buyers of their right to cancel, including the mailing address for the written cancellation notice.

[7]Many of the states that have not adopted the UCCC do have statutes governing door-to-door solicitation, and many municipalities have ordinances regulating solicitors, peddlers, and transient merchants. The latter regulations are known as Green River ordinances. See *Green River v. Fuller Brush Co.*, 65 F.2d 112 (1933).

COLE V. LOVETT

U.S. District Court, Southern District of Mississippi, 672 F.Supp 947 (1987)

Case

On Tuesday, November 9, 1982, at approximately 6:00 p.m., the plaintiffs, Norman and Judy Cole, were visited by two representatives of Capitol Roofing, Tony Stepp and Ken Smith. That same evening the plaintiffs signed a contract for the installation of vinyl siding on their home. At that time, Stepp provided several documents for the Coles to sign but did not allow them to read them, representing that they were work papers, credit applications, and insurance papers. The Coles received only a single carbon copy of the work order contract and a copy of a disclosure statement. Shortly after Stepp and Smith left, the plaintiffs changed their minds and decided to obtain more estimates. The next morning Judy called Stepp and informed him of this decision, but Stepp replied that the papers had already been processed, the workers would be out at the end of the week, and there was nothing he could do.

When she returned home from work that day, Judy discovered Capitol's workers installing siding. She did not tell them to leave, because she thought she had no choice. As soon as the work was completed, Capitol Roofing assigned the contract to defendant UCM. Problems resulted with the siding but repeated calls to Capitol brought no satisfaction. After having made 11 monthly payments to UCM on the $4900 bill, the plaintiffs consulted a lawyer who, by letter of December 19, 1984, informed both Capitol and UCM that the Coles desired to exercise their right of rescission under both the Truth in Lending Act (TILA) and the Mississippi Home Sales Solicitation Act (MHSSA). On receiving no response, the plaintiffs sued J.L. Lovett d/b/a Capitol Roofing to rescind. UCM counterclaimed for the remaining sum due on the contract. After hearing the evidence, the trial judge rendered the following opinion.

Lee, District, Judge:

[The judge first found that the plaintiffs were entitled to rescind the contract for TILA violations. For example, Capitol had failed to disclose the security interest it was acquiring in the plaintiffs' home, a violation of 12 C.F.R. Sec. 226.23(a)(1) (which grants a right to rescind in any "credit transaction in which a security interest is or will be retained or acquired in the consumer's principal dwelling") and failed to furnish plaintiffs with adequate notice of their right to rescind as required by 12 C.F.R. Sec. 226.23(a) and (b). The judge found that the violations were not mere clerical errors; therefore, the plaintiffs were entitled to cancellation of the finance charges on the transaction and to have the security interest in their home voided.]

In addition to their TILA claims, plaintiffs have alleged violations of the MHSSA. Like TILA, the MHSSA imposes notice and disclosure requirements upon a seller in a transaction which is a "home solicitation sale." A home solicitation sale is defined as "a consumer credit sale of goods or services in which the seller engages in a personal solicitation of the sale at a residence of the buyer and the buyer's agreement or offer to purchase is then given to the seller. . . ." Miss. Code Ann. Sec. 75-66-1. This section excludes from coverage sales which are initiated by the buyer.

In the present case, there was substantial disagreement between the parties as to the manner in which the initial contact between Capitol Roofing and the Coles occurred. Stepp testified that in November 1982 Capitol Roofing had installed siding on the home of Wanda Collins, a neighbor of the Coles. He claimed that while the crew was working at the Collins home, Judy Cole approached a member of the installation crew and, as a result of a conversation between them, the applicator told Ken Smith to see if the Coles wanted siding. According to Stepp's

(continues)

(continued from previous page)
version, the sales call was at the insistence of Judy Cole. The Coles' testimony that their first contact with anyone from Capitol Roofing occurred when Smith and Stepp came to their home on November 9 was corroborated by Wanda Collins, who explained that she had suggested to Stepp that Judy Cole might be interested in purchasing siding . . . and Stepp promised Wanda Collins a $100 commission on any referrals by her which resulted in sales. The court finds the sales call . . . was not at the Coles' request. Consequently, this transaction constituted a "home solicitation sale" within the meaning of MHSSA.

MHSSA provides the buyer a right to cancel a home solicitation sale until midnight of the third business day following the day on which the buyer signs an agreement or offer to purchase. With limited exceptions, none of which are applicable here, the seller is required to obtain the buyer's signature on a statement, executed simultaneously with the agreement to purchase, which must conspicuously inform the buyer of his rights under the Act. Until the seller has complied with the notice provisions of the Act, the buyer may cancel the home solicitation sale by notifying the seller "in any manner and by any means of his intention to cancel." . . . As the court has concluded that the transaction constituted a home solicitation sale, and as Capitol Roofing never informed the Coles of their right to cancel under the Mississippi Act, the Coles properly and timely exercised their right to cancel by letter from their attorney to defendants dated December 19, 1984.

The obligations of the parties to a home solicitation sale upon cancellation are set forth [in the Act] which requires the seller, within ten days of cancellation of a home solicitation sale to tender to the buyer "any payments made by the buyer and any note or other evidence of indebtedness." If the seller complies with this obligation, he is allowed to retain a cancellation fee of five percent of the case price, not to exceed any cash down payment. Until the seller complies, "the buyer may retain possession of the goods delivered to him by the seller or has a lien on the goods in his possession or control for any recovery to which he is entitled." Section 75-66-9 provides in pertinent part that:

(1) . . . within a reasonable time after a home solicitation sale has been cancelled or an offer to purchase revoked, the buyer upon demand must tender to the seller any goods delivered by the seller pursuant to the sale. . . . If the seller fails to demand possession of goods within a reasonable time after cancellation or revocation, the goods become the property of the buyer, without obligation to pay for them. For the purposes of this section forty (40) days is presumed to be a reasonable time. . . .

(3) If the seller has performed any services pursuant to a home solicitation sale prior to its cancellation, the seller is entitled to no compensation except the cancellation fee provided in this chapter.

. . . Hence, as a result of defendants' noncompliance with the requirements of MHSSA, they are required to cancel the deed of trust and to return to plaintiffs payments made in the amount of $1703.57. The Coles are also entitled to cancellation of the underlying contract. Finally, as a result of Capitol Roofing's failure to demand possession of the siding within a reasonable time after cancellation, the siding became the property of the Coles and they are relieved of any further obligation to pay for it.

As one court has observed,

If this result appears to deal harshly with merchants who have fully performed under their contracts, it seems clear to this court that the message which the legislature has attempted to convey by the [law] is "Caveat Vendor." Merchants, put on notice by the statute, can easily and inexpensively protect themselves, . . . by including a right to cancel provision and an accompanying notice of cancellation as a matter of course in all contracts signed outside their trade premises.

Weatherall Aluminum Products Company v. Scott, 139 Cal. Rptr. 329, 331 (1977).

[It is so ordered.]

Debtor Default

Generally, if a consumer defaults on payments, creditors can repossess the property the consumer has purchased and sell it to satisfy the unpaid debt. If the sale earns too little to discharge the debt, the creditor can normally sue the debtor and obtain a deficiency judgment. However, the 1968 UCCC distinguishes between debts incurred in the purchase of goods for $1000 or less and debts exceeding $1000. If the goods purchased were worth $1000 or less, the credi-tor must *either* repossess the goods *or* sue the debtor for the unpaid balance. If the creditor chooses to repossess, the debtor is not personally liable for the unpaid balance. Only if the original sale exceeded $1000 can the creditor repossess *and* seek a deficiency judgment if repossession fails to cover the unpaid balance.

With regard to garnishment, the UCCC prevents any prejudgment attachment of the debtor's unpaid earnings and limits the garnishment to 25 percent of net income or to that portion of the income in excess of 40 times the federal minimum hourly wage. The UCCC also prohibits an employer from discharging an employee whose wages are garnished to pay a judgment arising from a consumer credit sale, lease, or loan.

Although the UCCC has been adopted by nine states, the law as adopted can vary considerably from state to state. It is generally true of the so-called uniform laws that a state can make significant changes so the law reflects local attitudes or conforms to local policy in the particular matter covered.

REAL ESTATE SETTLEMENT PROCEDURES ACT

The purchase of a residence is the largest single transaction most consumers ever make. It can be a traumatic experience for the novice who finds that, in addition to the down payment, substantial sums of money will be required on settlement, or closing day. Items to be paid for may include attorney's fees; title insurance; various inspections, surveys, and appraisals; agent's or broker's services; taxes and insurance; and many other miscellaneous items. Congress found that because of the variation in the kinds of items included in the settlement costs and the amount charged for each, significant reforms were needed in the real estate settlement process. The purpose of the Real Estate Settlement Procedures Act (RESPA), enacted in 1974 and subsequently amended, is to ensure that buyers of residential property are given timely information on the nature and costs of the settlement process and that they are protected against obvious abuses. The Act requires that effective advance disclosure be made to home buyers and sellers. It prohibits kickbacks or referral fees and, in general, affords considerable protection by letting the home buyer know what it is going to cost to buy a given home.

RESPA applies to all federally related mortgage loans and is administered and enforced by the Secretary of Housing and Urban Development.[8] The Secretary has issued comprehensive regulations, known as regulation X, to prescribe procedures for curbing questionable practices in real estate transactions. Various forms have been devised and are in use, and

---

[8]Most, if not all, mortgage loans on residential property are federally related. The deposits or accounts of the lending institution may be insured by an agency of the federal government or the lender may be regulated by a federal agency.

a special information booklet has been developed for the lender to distribute to the borrower at the time a loan application is made. The lender is also required to provide the borrower with "good-faith estimates" of the dollar amount or range of each settlement service charge that the borrower is likely to incur. Generally speaking, RESPA places the burden on the lender to provide the borrower good advance information about the costs of purchasing a home—the basic cost and the substantial sums needed on settlement day.

ADDITIONAL CONSUMER PROTECTION MEASURES

Federal legislation primarily ensures fair treatment for consumers seeking credit, borrowing money, or contemplating the purchase of a residence or automobile. For the most part, the statutes studied in this chapter have been remedial in nature. Their purpose is to correct what Congress has determined to be persistent abuses. Many other statutes, however, are designed to protect the consumer's safety and well-being. These laws concern general health and welfare and alert the consumer to the possibility of harm from the use or misuse of certain products.

Packaging and Labeling

The Public Health Cigarette Smoking Act of 1969, popularly known as the Cigarette Labeling and Advertising Act, establishes a comprehensive federal program to deal with labelling and advertising the ill effects of smoking on health. The Act completely bans advertising of cigarettes and little cigars on any medium of electronic communication subject to the jurisdiction of the Federal Communications Commission. It also requires that every cigarette package, every cigarette advertisement, and every billboard carrying such an advertisement carry one of four warning labels. These labels warn consumers about the various adverse health effects of smoking.

In *Cipollone v. Liggett Group*, 112 S.Ct. 2608 (1992), the Supreme Court held that compliance with federal labelling laws preempts state law products liability claims by smokers or their families against cigarette makers based on a failure-to-warn theory. However, the Court held that claims are not preempted if based on breach of express warranty, fraudulent misrepresentation by way of false statements and concealment of material facts in advertising, or conspiracy to misrepresent or conceal material facts concerning health hazards by cigarette companies.

The Wholesome Poultry Products Act and the Wholesome Meat Act are also examples of protective statutes. Each establishes procedures to ensure that only wholesome products are distributed to consumers and that they are properly labeled and packaged.

The Nutrition Labeling and Education Act of 1990 (NLEA) required that particular nutrition information—regarding amounts of cholesterol, sodium, sugar, and protein, for example—be included in most food labeling. It also authorized the Food and Drug Administration to regulate the labelling of claims that can be made for foods regarding the characteristics (for example, "low salt," "reduced fat") and disease prevention or other health benefits (such as "fiber prevents cancer"). These rules were issued in December 1992, requiring compliance by 1994. The new uniform labels for hundreds of thousands of consumer products will cost industry around $2 billion to implement, but Congress hopes that improved nutrition arising from better informational disclosure about such matters as fat, cholesterol, fiber, and sodium content will produce many billions of dollars of savings through reduced health costs.

The Federal Food, Drug, and Cosmetic Act establishes extensive controls over various products and regulates their development, premarket testing, labelling, and packaging.

In the Fair Packaging and Labeling Act, Congress has stated that informed consumers are essential to the fair and efficient functioning of a free-market economy and that packages and labels should enable consumers to obtain accurate information about the quantity of the contents and should facilitate value comparisons. The Act therefore establishes comprehensive requirements for the identification of commodities and provides that net quantities must be conspicuously displayed in a uniform location on the principal panel of the product. The main purpose of the Act, set forth in some detail, is the prevention of unfair or deceptive packaging and labelling and general misbranding of consumer commodities.

An important amendment, the Poison Prevention Packaging Act of 1970, resulted in the mandatory development and use of childproof devices on household substances that could harm young children if mishandled or ingested. Other statutes for children are the Flammable Fabrics Act and the Child Protection and Toy Safety Act. The Consumer Product Safety Commission is responsible for administering many of the statutes relating to product safety.

SUMMARY

Many state and federal consumer protection laws now create an atmosphere in which many believe *caveat venditor* ("let the seller beware") has replaced the traditional *caveat emptor*.

Consumers are protected from deceptive practices, including deceptive advertising, by Sec. 5 of the Federal Trade Commission Act and Sec. 43(a) of the Lanham Act. These laws authorize the FTC, as well as competitors of the misleading advertiser, to bring suit to correct deceptive ads.

The Consumer Credit Protection Act creates an arsenal of weapons that protect the borrower or purchaser on credit. The Truth in Lending Act mandates extensive disclosures whenever a consumer borrows money or buys on credit. The purpose is to ensure that the consumer knows the true cost of the borrowing and can comparison shop. The Fair Credit Reporting Act protects consumers from the serious damage that misleading credit reports can have on consumers' economic status. The Fair Debt Collection Practices Act protects debtors from abusive collection practices by professional collection agencies. Also, in this nonexclusive listing of protective statutes, the Equal Credit Opportunity Act promotes equality in the extension of credit by outlawing discrimination on the basis of sex, age, race, and other grounds.

The Uniform Consumer Credit Code, which has been adopted by nine states and copied in many others, also contains credit disclosure requirements and home solicitation provisions protecting vulnerable consumers from unfair practices by door-to-door salesmen.

Packaging and labeling laws and the Real Estate Settlement Procedures Act are just two of an extensive battery of proconsumer statutes that every businessperson must understand and comply with.

KEY TERMS

Consumer transaction
Usury
Garnishment

Truth in lending
Annual percentage rate (APR)
Consumer report
Investigative report

QUESTIONS AND PROBLEMS

1. Removatron International makes and sells an epilator machine designed to remove unwanted hair permanently without the side effects associated with electrolysis. The machine uses a pair of tweezers to remove the hair; while the tweezers grasp the hair but before it is removed, the machine emits radio frequency energy that travels down the tweezers and along the hair. Removatron advertises in beauty industry trade magazines. Removatron's ads state that hair removal can be "permanent" and that unwanted hair will no longer be a problem, that the machine has been "clinically tested and endorsed," and that it is approved by the Federal Communications Commission (FCC). When the FTC challenged these ads, evidence showed that the machines cost $4000 and treatment costs $35 per hour. During the sales process, purchasers are informed that the machine will not work for everyone and that permanent removal will be obtained only after several treatments. The FCC does not approve the product but only approved the machine to emit radio waves at a particular frequency. No controlled scientific studies have been performed to test the effectiveness and safety of the machine. Should the FTC be allowed to block Removatron's ads in their current form? How should a cease and desist order be structured? (*Removatron International Corp. v. FTC*, 884 F.2d 1489, 1st Cir. 1989.)

2. Litton Industries advertised that a survey of "independent microwave oven service technicians" indicated that 76 percent of the surveyed population "recommend Litton." Evidence showed that in conducting its survey, Litton used only its own service agency lists, although it had lists of its competitors; Litton knew at least 100 agencies were excluded from the survey; Litton surveyed only one technician at each agency; Litton knew its list contained some dealers who sold Litton microwaves and therefore had reason to favor them and certainly were not "independent"; and Litton knew many of those surveyed had insufficient experience with other brands to respond accurately. In a Sec. 5 action, the FTC entered a multiproducts order, prohibiting Litton from misusing survey information with all its products, not just microwaves. Should the court uphold this order? (*Litton Industries, Inc. v. FTC*, 676 F.2d 364, 9th Cir. 1982.)

3. An ambulance company charges its customers an additional $5 when they do not pay by cash or check at the time services are rendered. Does this arrangement constitute a "finance charge" that must be disclosed under the Truth in Lending Act? Discuss. (*Hahn v. Hank's Ambulance Service, Inc.*, 787 F.2d 543, 11th Cir. 1986.)

4. Maurice had an American Express card. Later, his wife Virginia was granted a supplementary card. When Maurice died, Virginia's card was cancelled under American Express's general policy of automatically terminating supplemental cards on the death of the basic cardholder. The cancellation had nothing to do with Virginia's creditworthiness or ability to pay. Virginia did reapply for a card and was granted it. Still, she sued American Express for violation of the ECOA. Discuss. (*Miller v. American Express Co.*, 688 F.2d 1235, 9th Cir. 1982.)

5. The odometer of a motorcycle purchased by the plaintiff indicated that it had been driven 875 miles. The actual mileage was 14,000. Plaintiff sought damages claiming that the defendant failed to disclose the actual mileage or that the true mileage was unknown; that the defendant altered the odometer intending to defraud; or that the defendant repaired the odometer, failed to adjust it to zero, and failed to so notify the purchaser of the repair. Such allegations, if proven would constitute violations of the Motor Vehicle Information and Cost Savings Act. Defendant moved to dismiss, claiming that the Act did not apply to motorcycles and, if it did, was unconstitutionally vague. The Act provided that notice of any alteration in mileage must be attached to the left door frame of the vehicle. Motorcycles, claimed the defendant, do not have door frames. Is this a good defense? Discuss. (*Grambo v. Loomis Cycle Sales, Inc.*, 404 F.Supp. 1073, N.D. Ind. 1975.)

6. In October, 1974, Sheehan purchased a Ford automobile that was financed by Ford Credit on a retail installment contract. Later Sheehan moved to various locations and became delinquent on his account. When Ford Credit was unable to locate Sheehan it assigned the delinquent account to a central

recovery office for collection or repossession. A short time later Sheehan's mother, who resided in Rhode Island, received a phone call from a woman who identified herself as an employee of the Mercy Hospital in San Francisco. (The call actually emanated from Ford Credit's office in Dearborn, Michigan.) She advised Sheehan's mother that one or both of Sheehan's children had been involved in a serious automobile accident and that she, the caller, was attempting to locate Sheehan. The mother supplied the caller with Sheehan's home and business addresses and phone numbers. The following day Sheehan's car was repossessed and subsequent inquiry revealed that the phone call was a ruse and that Sheehan's children had not been injured. Are consumers protected against such practices? (*Ford Motor Credit Company v. Frances C. Sheehan*, 373 So.2d 956, Fla. 1979.)

7. A consumer who tried to obtain information from a credit reporting agency on the nature and substance of items in his file was denied such information and was forced to return to the credit reporting agency's office several times. The consumer was finally given some of the information held by the agency, but several items were withheld. Discuss this situation with regard to the Fair Credit Reporting Act. (*Millstone v. O'Hanlon Reports, Inc.*, 383 F.Supp. 269, 1974.)

8. Betty Jones had a VISA and Master Charge account with the defendant bank. On her request, the bank issued cards on those accounts to her husband also. On November 11, 1977, Jones informed the bank by two separate letters that she would no longer honor charges made by her husband on the two accounts, whereupon the bank immediately revoked both accounts and requested the return of the cards. Despite numerous notices and requests for surrender of the cards, both Jones and her husband retained the cards and continued to make charges

against the accounts. Not until March 9, 1978, did Jones relinquish her credit cards. Is Jones responsible for the balance owing on the account, which includes sums charged by her husband after November 11, 1977? Discuss. (*Walker Bank & Trust Co. v. Jones*, 672 P.2d 73, Utah 1983.)

9. The plaintiff was responsible for one-half of her daughter's medical bills; her ex-husband (Julius) was responsible for the rest. When Julius did not pay two bills—one of $100 for their daughter and one of $35 for Julius's next wife—the defendant credit bureau sent a notice to the plaintiff. A second notice stated in capital letters: "48 Hour Notice, Notice Is Hereby Given That This Item Has Already Been Referred for Collection Action, We Will at Any Time after 48 Hours Take Action as Necessary and Appropriate to Secure Payment in Full, Pay This Amount Now if Action Is to Be Averted." The plaintiff never paid any amount, including the $50 that she conceded owing, because she did not get a breakdown on the $135 bill. The defendant admits that it was mistaken regarding the $35 amount, for which the plaintiff was not responsible. Defendant's president admits that it never sues for amounts less than $150 but limits its collection actions to letters and telephone calls. The plaintiff sued, claiming violation of the FDCPA. Is this a valid claim? Discuss. (*Pipiles v. Credit Bureau of Lockport*, 886 F.2d, 22, 2d Cir. 1989.)

10. D liked P's work when he remodeled D's bedroom, so D called P when he wanted his kitchen remodeled. After some discussion, a contract prepared by P was signed in D's home. It did not provide that D could cancel within three days; D was not provided with a form "notice of cancellation." D was unhappy with P's work on the kitchen and refused to pay. P sued. D counterclaimed, arguing that P breached the state's home solicitation act. May D rescind the contract? Discuss. (*Langston v. Brewer*, 649 S.W.2d 827, Tex. App. 1983.)

Chapter 52

The Legal Environment of International Business

Introduction
International Sales Contracts
Resolving International Trade Disputes
National Regulation of the
Import/Export Process
Organizing for International Trade
Other Ways of Doing Business
Regulating the Transnational Corporation

INTRODUCTION

As early as 1816 in *The Schooner Exchange v. Mc-Fadden*,[1] Chief Justice Marshall wrote: "The world [is] composed of distinct sovereignties . . . whose mutual benefit is promoted by intercourse with each other, and by an exchange of those good offices which humanity dictates and its wants require." As long as nations have existed, there has been commercial activity among them. That activity is generally very beneficial to all the parties involved, and in our modern world the amount of international commercial activity is exploding.

For example, worldwide exports of goods exceed $2 trillion annually. The United States alone exports more than $200 billion in goods per year. (Unfortunately for our trade balance, we import a substantially greater amount annually than that.) Many of the largest U.S. corporations derive more than half their profits from sales outside the country. On the flip side of the coin, more than 70 percent of U.S. manufacturers face direct foreign competition for sales in the United States.

Direct U.S. investment[2] in foreign countries exceeds $475 billion. In turn, foreigners have directly invested about $300 billion in the United States. This accounts for the fact that more than 3 million Americans are employed by companies directly owned by foreign investors. Furthermore, half of all products made in the U.S. have foreign components and half of all imports and exports are between companies and their foreign parents of affiliates. Increasingly, U.S. companies are forming joint ventures with foreign companies to do business overseas. Conversely, many foreign companies are entering U.S. markets through similar means.

This is only one aspect of the situation, because foreign entities also own more than a trillion dollars of U.S. securities.[3] Two hundred thousand traders watching computer screens around the world help make up international financial markets that send a stream of capital 50 times the value of international trade flowing across the international borders.

All in all, an already small world is growing smaller. Every day, investors in the United States watch the Tokyo stock market, for its fluctuations will affect the U.S. stock markets. The collapse of the Soviet Union and the tearing down of the Berlin Wall are cause for celebration in the United States not only because they portend democracy but also because of the commercial opportunities opening for U.S. businesses in Eastern Europe. Just as dramatically, the events of Tiananmen Square in China in 1989 quickly put a damper on the interests of foreign investors.

Just as each company or investor hoping to do business abroad must be concerned with the events occurring in other countries, so must they be concerned with *legal* aspects of international transactions. The laws of the countries in which they intend to do business, as well as *international law*, must be considered in each and every transaction.

Legal problems are pervasive and inescapable. Can a U.S. company selling its goods in South Korea expect protection from trademark infringement by local companies?[4] Must a Japanese company operating its plant on American soil comply with U.S. laws when making its employment decisions?[5] Does a European company wishing to purchase an American company face any barriers that a potential U.S. purchaser would not face?[6] An endless variety of legal questions shape international commerce.

This chapter provides an introduction to the basic aspects of international legal rules as they bear most directly on persons and business organizations engaged in commercial transactions across national borders. It does not pursue in any detail many related and very important fields such as public international

---

[1]Cranch 116 (1812).

[2]*Direct investment* means that the investor not only invests money but also takes an active role in the foreign enterprise.

[3]The purchasing of securities of a foreign business (but not actively taking part in its operation) is often called *portfolio investment*.

[4]Under American pressure, South Korea has strengthened its trademark laws, but these laws are often underenforced.

[5]Generally, Japanese companies must follow U.S. antidiscrimination law, but they are allowed to prefer Japanese nationals for top management positions. U.S. courts have not been completely consistent in interpreting laws in this area. The Supreme Court did rule that U.S. antidiscrimination laws embodied in Title VII do not apply extraterritorially to regulate the employment practices of U.S. firms that employ American citizens abroad, *EEOC v. Arab American Oil Co.*, 111 S. Ct. 1227 (1991), but Congress quickly passed legislation to reverse this result.

[6]In 1988, the Omnibus Trade and Competitiveness Act authorized the president to block purchases of U.S. firms by foreign buyers when the takeover would threaten national security.

law, which regulates legal and political relationships among sovereign states.

Classifying International Trade

Today we classify within the term *international trade* any movement of goods, services, or capital across national boundaries. In its normal use, the term includes three major components:

1. *Export* of goods, services, or commodities from one country to another.

2. *Import* of goods, services, or commodities into one country from another.

3. Of increasing importance since the end of the Second World War, *foreign direct investment,* such as the acquisition of interests in capital facilities in one country by investors from another.

Each of these components of international trade is distinct from the other; each raises particular legal and business issues; and each has been met with a distinct legal response intended to facilitate, harmonize, and regulate this aspect of global commercial and economic relations. With the growth in complexity of modern trade, the competition among nations as expressed in trade policy, and the shrinking presence of centrally planned economies in socialist bloc and Third World countries, the three main facets of international trade noted above have come to demonstrate, to varying degrees, three different sources of regulations:

1. Procedures developed by the *international trading community,* intended to ease trading relations and foster the resolution of disputes.

2. Regulations developed by *national governments* designed to protect national trading interests and to make them more competitive in international markets.

3. Laws and standards for international trade relations established by *international governmental organizations* such as the United Nations and the Organization for Economic Cooperation and Development, intended to harmonize trading community and national principles; to eliminate trade abuses; and to develop a greater participation in world trade, especially on the part of those nations that form the Third World.

This chapter looks at some of the major features of each of these components of the international trade framework.

INTERNATIONAL SALES CONTRACTS

Although foreign direct investment and foreign portfolio investment have become increasingly important factors in world commerce in recent years, the transfer of goods across national frontiers remains extremely important. This type of transaction—an export from the seller's perspective and an import from the buyer's point of view—is fundamentally a contract of sale, much like its domestic cousin in its essential features. However, special factors such as the great distances involved, accompanying insurance considerations, and differences in legal systems present special problems. An overriding factor in the formation of the international sales contract is that the parties do not, in the normal situation, know each other well; this ignorance can lead to uneasiness over the creditworthiness of the buyer and the dependability of the seller, and anxiety about the enforcement of the obligations of the parties if there should be a breach of contract.

In response to these and other concerns, international private sector traders have over time devised a series of specialized but fairly standard techniques and legal devices that take the form of a series of "side" contracts that supplement the basic sales contract.

Financing the Transaction:
The Letter of Credit

Because of the presumed lack of knowledge on the part of the seller as to the creditworthiness of the buyer, the export trade has developed a reliance on the **letter of credit** financing device.[7] Basically, the letter of credit is an irrevocable assurance by the bank of the importer/buyer that funds for the payment of goods sold by the exporter/seller are available beyond the control of the buyer and that these can be obtained by the seller on provision of documentary proof that the goods have been shipped and that other contractual obligations of the seller have been fulfilled and are thus beyond the arbitrary control of the seller.

---

[7]Standardization in the use and implications of the letter of credit device has been advanced by the publication of *Uniform Customs and Practice for Documentary Credits,* Publication No. 400 (Paris: The International Chamber of Commerce, 1984).

The documents that the seller must produce to be paid can include (1) inland and ocean **bills of lading** to establish receipt of the goods by the shipper and to serve as "documents of title" for the merchandise; (2) commercial invoices and packing lists to attest to the contents of bulk and packaged materials; (3) an **export license** and shipper's export declaration to show compliance with any applicable export controls; and (4) any **import licenses,** consular invoices, or **certificates of origin** necessary to comply with the import laws of the receiving country.

Because the buyer's bank is typically a foreign bank, the seller may have no more confidence in it that in the buyer itself. It is not unusual, then, for the seller to involve its own bank in the transactions to transmit the funds or to confirm or guarantee the performance of the buyer's bank that is issuing the letter of credit. In these circumstances, the seller's bank may undertake only to accept the transfer of funds from the buyer's bank and to credit these to the account of the seller (an *advising bank*); it may go further, however, and contract to guarantee this payment to the seller (a *standby* or *confirming bank*). In either event, an additional layer of contractual obligation will appear, this time between the seller and its bank and, further, between the seller's bank and the buyer's bank.

The letter of credit is essentially a means to make the seller comfortable that the goods will be paid for and to assure the buyer that the purchase money will not be released to the seller until proper, conforming goods are suitably shipped. Strict compliance with the letter of credit is generally required, as the following case illustrates.

BOARD OF TRADE OF SAN FRANCISCO v. SWISS CREDIT BANK

U.S. Ninth Circuit Court of Appeals, 728 F.2d 1241 (1984)

Swiss Credit Bank (SCB) refused to honor a letter of credit issued in favor of the plaintiff's assignor (Antex Industries) for the sale of 92,000 microchips to Electronic Arrays for use in electronic computers. When the letter was presented to the bank it was accompanied by an air waybill showing that the goods had been air-freighted to their destination. The letter of credit stipulated that a "full set clean on board bills or lading," evidencing ocean shipments of the microchips, was to have been presented. The trial court refused to order SCB to honor the letter of credit, and Antex appealed.

Boochever, Circuit Judge:

. . . SCB dishonored the letter of credit because of Antex's failure to comply with its terms. [It is conceded] for the purposes of this appeal that the letter of credit required marine shipment and that Antex's air shipment was nonconforming. [It is maintained], however, that the dishonor was improper, because the manner of shipment was not material.

This court's earlier decision in the case precludes [the] argument that Antex's noncompliance with the terms of the letter of credit was not a material defect. . . . As we noted in the prior decision, strict compliance with the letter's terms was required:

The bank notes that strict compliance with the terms of the letter of credit is required. . . .In this case the shipment was by air, not ocean; and if the Bank's interpretation of the letter of credit is correct, the refusal to pay was not wrongful.

Even if we were not bound by prior decision, we would reach the same result. The issuer of a letter of credit should not be placed in the position of having to determine whether an unauthorized method of shipment is material. In this instance, whether air shipment would have been considered hazardous by the parties or apt to cause damage to sensitive electronic equipment is not the type of evaluation that should be required in a transaction where promptness and certainty are of the essence. Absent a waiver, an issuer may insist on strict compliance with the terms of a letter of credit. In fact, the parties here agreed to be bound by the Uniform Customs and Practice or Documentary Credits (1974 Revision) International Chamber of Commerce (Brochure No. 290), which requires strict compliance with all terms of the letter of credit.

We conclude that SCB was justified in dishonoring the letter of credit because of Antex's failure to comply with its terms. The district court's judgment is affirmed. ⚖

FIGURE 52.1

Financing Techniques of Typical International Sales Transaction

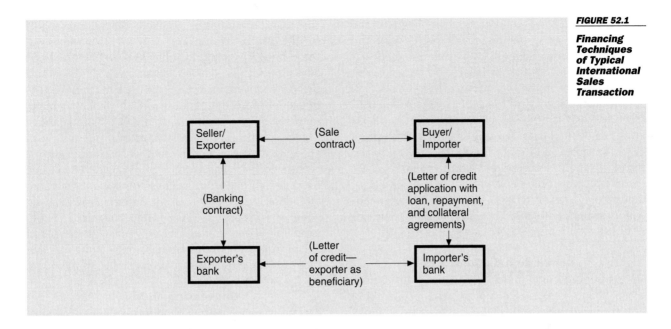

The complexity of these multilayered arrangements is greatly reduced by the frequency with which they are used and their corresponding familiarity in the international trading community. It may help to chart the usual financing techniques of a typical international sales transaction in goods (see Figure 52.1).

Trade Terms

Financing is, of course, only a means to an end, and a myriad of other factors—almost all of them bearing directly on the ultimate price paid for the goods—will be resolved in the terms of the international sales contract. The parties may wish to provide for a fixed rate of currency exchange or to specify the currency of payment for the contract; they may elect to identify the "official" language of the sales contract or to provide that two or more languages each represent the agreed terms of the transaction; they may choose the applicable law and identify the court that will have jurisdiction in the event of a subsequent disagreement; or they may decide to refer any contract disputes to binding or nonbinding arbitration. Clauses such as these, although very important, may or may not appear in the final contract, depending on a host of subtle factors, including the current economic and political climate, the degree of mutual trust and familiarity between the parties, and the extent to which they share common linguistic, cultural, business, or legal tradition. For instance, an American exporter will have, in most cases, fewer questions about the conditions of commerce with a long-time Canadian business associate than, for instance, with a first-time trading partner in Sri Lanka or Liechtenstein.

Various commonly accepted **trade terms,** addressing matters of universal concern such as factors of distance, language barriers, and general unfamiliarity between the parties, have evolved over time within the international trading community.[8] These terms are often used to allocate responsibility between the parties. For example, *CIF* stands for "cost, insurance, and freight," meaning that the seller's quoted price is inclusive of the cost of goods, shipping charges, and marine insurance policy providing at least minimum coverage. This implies that the seller will bear the risk of loss during transit from the factory to the port of shipment; thereafter the risk shifts to the buyer who pays for the marine insurance policy that is usually arranged by the seller.

---

[8]Attempts have been made to further standardize these trade terms by the publication of uniform trade term definitions. This work was undertaken in the Revised American Foreign Trade Definitions (RAFTD) of 1941 and subsequently by the International Chamber of Commerce (ICC) in the 1953 publication of "International Commercial Terms" (Incoterms), which has been periodically revised since that time. The Uniform Commercial Code also sets forth definitions of some of these terms, and these are, in states that have adopted the UCC, binding as law although subject to express modification by agreement of the parties. The 1980 U.N. Convention on the International Sale of Goods will displace inconsistent UCC provisions in circumstances where the Convention applies.

The term *FAS* (Fee Alongside) implies that the risk of loss will pass from the seller/exporter when the goods are delivered alongside a vessel, usually designated by the buyer. Risk of damage in the onloading operation rests on the buyer. *FOB* (Free On Board) contemplates delivery of the goods by the seller, usually on a designated vessel where shipment has been arranged by the buyer; risk of loss passes at the ship's rail. *CAF* (Cost and Freight) is similar to CIF but the buyer arranges for insurance during carriage. *Ex* terms (exfactory) can be used to designate a place of delivery from seller to buyer that is other than the location of the carrier—for instance, at the factory, or perhaps at the ultimate destination of the goods.

Convention on Contracts

In an attempt to add uniformity and certainty to the terms of international sales of goods contracts, several countries have ratified the 1980 United Nations Convention on Contracts for the International Sale of Goods (CISG). The CISG became part of American law on January 1, 1988, and has been ratified by more than 30 nations, including Germany, Canada, China, Finland, France, Italy, and Mexico. It is predicted that most of America's major trading partners will soon ratify the CISG.

Assume that Country A and Country B have both ratified the CISG. If a purchaser with a place of business in A makes a contract to buy goods from a company with a place of business in B, the CISG's provisions will automatically govern the contract unless the parties opt out of its coverage. The CISG does not apply to consumer sales and has no provisions governing the validity of contracts, ownership claims of third parties, or liability claims for death or personal injury. However, it does have provisions governing most other issues that could arise in a contractual setting. The parties may provide their own variations, but the CISG augments contractual terms and provides the rules for situations the parties did not contemplate or address in their agreement.

The CISG could be loosely termed an international Uniform Commercial Code. It addresses most of the same subjects as Article 2 of the UCC, such as definiteness and revocability of offers, timeliness of acceptances, risk of loss, excuse from performance, and remedies. However, the CISG differs from the UCC in several respects. For example, Article 11 of the Convention largely abolishes the statute of frauds requirement of a written contract. Article 16 states

that an offer cannot be revoked if it was reasonable for the offeree to rely on it as being irrevocable and the offeree has acted in reliance thereon. Article 35 alters the UCC's "perfect tender" rule. A seller must deliver goods fit for ordinary use of the buyer's particular purpose that is known to the seller. A buyer may reject goods only if there is a "fundamental breach." Article 50 addresses buyer's remedies, providing that a buyer may require a seller to perform in accordance with the promise or fix an additional time for the seller to perform. This latter option is not contained in the UCC but is derived from German law. A complete discussion of the CISG's provisions is beyond the scope of this chapter, but a single set of rules should greatly assist businesspersons in planning and executing international sales transactions.

Convention on Notes

The CISG's attempt to add uniformity to international sales law may soon be supplemented by the U.N. Convention on International Bills of Exchange and International Promissory Notes. Approved by the U.N. General Assembly on December 9, 1988, and now open for ratification, the Convention creates a new type of international negotiable instrument and represents an attempt to provide the same uniformity for international commercial paper transactions that Article 3 of the UCC provides from interstate transactions. This convention (known as UNCIBEN) was introduced in Part III of this book.

In various stages of development are several other international conventions regarding subjects addressed by the UCC, including (1) the UNCITRAL Model Law on International Credit Transfers, (heavily influenced by UCC Article 4A on Electric Funds Transfers) (2) the UNIDROIT Convention on International Financial Leasing and the UNIDROIT Convention on International Factoring (addressing subjects governed by Article 9 of the UCC), and (3) a revision of the Uniform Customs and Practices for Documentary Credits and drafting (in process) of uniform rules on stand-by letters of credit and bank guarantees (see UCC Article 5).

RESOLVING INTERNATIONAL TRADE DISPUTES

No contract—including one for an international business transaction—can be so tightly drawn that it is totally impervious to later disagreement; similarly, unforeseen changes in circumstances may make performance of the contract impossible or, perhaps, more difficult or expensive than originally contemplated by the parties. An international trader should, therefore, have a clear understanding of the means available to resolve such disputes if they should arise.

Judicial litigation is rarely the best means to resolve any business dispute: The costs associated with it (attorneys' fees, court costs, and general expenses) will often offset any profit expected from the transaction. These factors are compounded in transnational litigation.

Difficulties often arise in identifying a court with proper jurisdiction over the subject matter of the action or the parties to the transaction. In many types of litigation the question will arise as to which state has the authority to assert its law over the transaction and the parties.

Domestic Court Jurisdiction

In business litigation, and in other types of litigation touching the international sphere, the rules of jurisdiction are evolving but are as yet unclear. The as yet unadopted American Law Institute *Restatement of the Foreign Relations Law of the United States (Revised)* may be a good indicator of the direction in which the law is heading. Rather than use the traditional categories of subject matter jurisdiction and personal jurisdiction, the proposed revision to this Restatement establishes three categories: (1) *jurisdiction to prescribe,* that is, the authority of a state to make its law applicable to persons or activities; (2) *jurisdiction to adjudicate,* that is, the authority of a state to subject particular persons or things to its judicial process; and (3) *jurisdiction to enforce,* that is, the authority to use the resources of government to induce or compel compliance with its law.

Attempts by the United States to impose its legal regulations on activities occurring abroad has caused substantial resentment in foes and allies alike in recent years. The revised Restatement's Sec. 402 would recognize a nation's *jurisdiction to prescribe* with respect to

(1) (a) conduct, a substantial part of which takes place within its territory; (b) the status of persons, or interests in things, present within its territory; (c) conduct outside its territory which has or is intended to have substantial effect within its territory;

(2) the activities, status, interests or relations of its nationals outside as well as within its territory; or

(3) certain conduct outside its territory by persons not its nationals which is directed against the security of the state [example: terrorism] or a limited class of other state interests.

Thus, links of territoriality and nationality are ordinarily necessary to the power to prescribe law, although they are not sufficient in all cases. Furthermore, these criteria are expressly limited by Sec. 403, which states that even when they are present, jurisdiction to prescribe should not be exercised when it would be "unreasonable" as determined by an evaluation of all relevant factors, including (1) the extent to which the activity takes place in the regulating state and has a substantial, direct, and foreseeable effect there; (2) the connections, such as nationality, residence, or economic activity, between the regulating state and the persons responsible for the activity to be regulated or between the state and those whom the law is designed to protect; (3) the character of the activity to be regulated, the extent to which other states regulate it, and its general acceptability; (4) the existence of justified expectations that might be injured; (5) the importance of the regulation to the international political, legal, or economic system; (6) the extent to which such regulation is consistent with the traditions of the international system; (7) the extent to which another state may have an interest in regulating the activity; and (8) the likelihood of conflict with regulation by other states. A state should defer to another state whose interest in regulating the same conduct is clearly greater.

The *Timberlane* case, which soon follows, illustrates a court's independent formulation of a "reasonableness" approach.

Reasonableness also is the hallmark of the revised Restatement's approach to *jurisdiction to adjudicate.* According to proposed Sec. 421, personal jurisdiction is to be exercised only if reasonable. Such exercise will generally be deemed reasonable if an individual defendant is present (other than transitorily) in the territory of the state; *or* is a domiciliary, resident, or national of the state; *or* regularly carries on business there; *or* has consented to the exercise of jurisdiction. Additionally, exercise of jurisdiction to adjudicate will be reasonable if the person has carried on activity in the state that created the liability in question or has carried on outside the state an activity having substantial, direct, or foreseeable effect within the state that created the liability in question.

Finally, under Sec. 431 of the proposed revised Restatement, *jurisdiction to enforce* will be present only where a state had the power to prescribe, in accordance with Secs. 402 and 403, and the power to adjudicate as to the particular defendant. Enforcement measures must be proportional to the gravity of the violation and may be used against persons located outside the territory of the enforcing state only if such persons are given fair notice and an opportunity to be heard.

TIMBERLANE LUMBER CO. v. BANK OF AMERICA

U.S. Ninth Circuit Court of Appeals, 549 F.2d 597 (1976)

Timberlane Lumber Company, an American corporation with subsidiary corporations in Honduras, brought a Sherman Act antitrust suit against the Bank of America and several Honduran citizens alleging that the defendants had conspired to shut down the plaintiff's milling operations in Honduras so that the bank (and its Honduran affiliates and customers) could monopolize Honduran lumber exports to the United States. Timberlane filed suit in a federal court in California, arguing that the illegal activities of the defendants in Honduras had effects in the United States sufficient to vest the American court with personal jurisdiction over the foreign defendants. The district court dismissed the action for lack of jurisdiction, and the plaintiff appealed.

Choy, Circuit Judge:

. . . There is no doubt that American antitrust laws extend over some conduct in other nations. . .

That American law covers some conduct beyond this nation's borders does not mean that it embraces all, however. Extraterritorial application is understandably a matter of concern for the other countries involved. Those nations have sometimes resented and protested, as excessive intrusions into their own spheres, broad assertions of authority by American courts. . . . Our courts have recognized this concern and have, at times, responded to it, even if not always enough to satisfy all the foreign critics. . . . In any event, it is evident that at some point the interests of the United States are too weak and the foreign harmony incentive for restraint too strong to justify an extraterritorial assertion of jurisdiction.

What that point is or how it is determined is not defined by international law. . . .

Even among American courts and commentators, however, there is no consensus on how far the jurisdiction should extend. The district court here concluded that a "direct and substantial effect" on United States foreign commerce was a prerequisite, without stating whether other factors were relevant or considered. . . .

Few cases have discussed the nature of the effect required for jurisdiction, perhaps because most of the litigated cases have involved relatively obvious offenses and rather significant and apparent effects on competition within the United States. . . . It is probably in part because the standard has not often been put to a real test that it seems so poorly defined. . . .

Implicit in [the] observation . . . in several of the cases and commentaries employing the "effects" test, is the suggestion that factors other than simply the effect on the United States are weighed, and rightly so. As former Attorney General (then Professor) Katzenbach observed, the effect on American commerce is not, by itself, sufficient information on which to base a decision that the United States is the nation primarily interested in the activity causing the effect. "[A]nything that affects the external trade and commerce of the United States also affects the trade and commerce of other nations, and may have far greater consequences for others than for the United States." Katzenbach, *Conflicts on an Unruly Horse,* 65 Yale L.J. 1087, 1150 (1956).

The effects test by itself is incomplete because it fails to consider other nations' interests. Nor does it expressly take into account the full nature of the relationship between the actors and this country. Whether the alleged offender is an American citizen, for instance, may make a big difference; applying American laws to American citizens raises fewer problems than application to foreigners. . . .

American courts have, in fact, often displayed a regard for comity and the prerogatives of other nations and considered their interests as well as other parts of the factual circumstances, even when professing to apply an effects test. To some degree, the requirement for a "substantial" effect may silently incorporate these additional considerations, with "substantial" as a flexible standard that varies with other factors. . . .

[T]he antitrust laws require in the first instance that there be effect—actual or intended—on American foreign commerce before the federal courts may legitimately exercise subject matter jurisdiction under those statutes. . . . [Also], there is the additional question which is unique to the international setting of whether the interests of, and links to, the United States—including the magnitude of the effect on American foreign commerce—are sufficiently strong, vis-à-vis those of other nations,

(continues)

TIMBERLAND LUMBER CO. V. BANK OF AMERICA

(continued from previous page)
to justify an assertion of extraterritorial authority.

It is this final issue which is both obscured by undue reliance on the "substantiality" test and complicated to resolve. An effect on United States commerce, although necessary to the exercise of jurisdiction under the antitrust laws, is alone not a sufficient basis on which to determine whether American authority *should* be asserted in a given case as a matter of international comity and fairness. In some cases, the application of the direct and substantial test in the international context might open the door too widely by sanctioning jurisdiction over an action when these considerations would indicate dismissal. At other times, it may fail in the other direction, dismissing a case for which comity and fairness do not require forbearance, thus closing the jurisdictional door too tightly—for the Sherman Act does reach some restraints which do not have both a direct and substantial effect on the foreign commerce of the United States. A more comprehensive inquiry is necessary. . . .

What we prefer is an evaluation and balancing of the relevant consideration in each case—in the words of King-man Brewster, a "jurisdictional rule of reason." . . .

The elements to be weighed include the degree of conflict with foreign law or policy, the nationality or allegiance of the parties and the locations or principal places of business of corporations, the extent to which enforcement by either state can be expected to achieve compliance, the relative significance of effects on the United States as compared with those elsewhere, the extent to which there is explicit purpose to harm or affect American commerce, the foreseeability of such effect, and the relative importance to the violations charged of conduct within the United States as compared with conduct abroad. A court evaluating these factors should identify the potential degree of conflict if American authority is asserted. A difference in law or policy is one likely sore spot, though one which may not always be present. Nationality is another; though foreign governments may have some concern for the treatment of American citizens and business residing there, they primarily care about their own nationals. Having assessed the conflict, the court should then determine whether in the face of it the contracts and interests of the United States are sufficient to support the exercise of extraterritorial jurisdiction.

The comity question is . . . complicated. [Author's note: Generally speaking, "comity" is respect for another nation's sovereignty.] From Timberlane's complaint it is evident that there are grounds for concern as to at least a few of the defendants, for some are identified as foreign citizens. . . . Moreover, it is clear that most of the activity took place in Honduras, though the conspiracy may have been directed from San Francisco, and that the most direct economic effect was probably in Honduras. However, there has been no indication of any conflict with the law or policy of the Honduran government, nor any comprehensive analysis of the relative connections and interests of Honduras and the United States. Under these circumstances, the dismissal by the district court cannot be sustained on jurisdictional grounds.

We, therefore, vacate the dismissal and remand the Timberlane action. [In other words, it is not obvious that Honduran sovereignty will be offended by permitting this case to proceed, so this by itself is not reason enough to dismiss the case. The case is remanded to the district court for full consideration of the various factors discussed.] ⚖

Foreign Sovereign Immunities Act

Even in circumstances in which the court should be willing to assert its jurisdiction over the defendant under the effects or reasonableness tests, it may be barred from doing so because of a personal immunity of the defendant. This bar is most often encountered when the defendant is a foreign state or state agency, a circumstance more frequently present today when many nations—especially those with centrally planned economies—are engaging directly in trading activities. The Foreign Sovereign Immunities Act (FSIA), passed by Congress in 1976, modifies the absolute sovereign immunity that the common law had recognized but continues to limit a plaintiff's ability to recover a judgment from a foreign state or state agency.

Under the FSIA, U.S. courts have jurisdiction over foreign sovereigns primarily in cases arising out of the latters' *commercial activities*, as illustrated in the following case.

REPUBLIC OF ARGENTINA V. WELTOVER, INC.

U.S. Supreme Court, 112 S.Ct. 2160 (1992)

 Case

In order to stabilize petitioner Argentina's currency, that country issued bonds, called Bonods, which provided for repayment in U.S. dollars through transfer on the market in one of several locations, including New York City. Because it lacked sufficient foreign exchange to retire the Bonods when they began to mature, Argentina unilaterally extended the time for payment, offering bondholders substitute instruments as a means of rescheduling the debts. Respondent bondholders, two Panamanian corporations and a Swiss bank, rejected the rescheduling and insisted on payment in New York. Argentina refused, so respondents brought this breach-of-contract suit in New York.

Argentina moved to dismiss for lack of subject matter jurisdiction. The trial court denied the motion and was affirmed on appeal on grounds that the FSIA provided jurisdiction. Argentina then appealed to the Supreme Court.

Scalia, Justice:

The Foreign Sovereign Immunities Act of 1976 establishes a comprehensive framework for determining whether a court in this country, state or federal, may exercise jurisdiction over a foreign state. Under the Act, a "foreign state *shall* be immune from the jurisdiction of the courts of the United States and of the States" unless one of several statutorily defined exceptions applies. The FSIA thus provides the "sole basis" for obtaining jurisdiction over a foreign sovereign in the United States. See *Argentine Republic v. Amerada Hess Shipping Corp.*, 488 U.S. 428 (1989). The most significant of the FSIA's exceptions—and the one at issue in this case—is the "commercial" exception of Sec. 1605 (a) (2), which provides that a foreign state

is not immune from suit in any case in which the action is based upon a commercial activity carried on in the United States by the foreign state; or upon an act performed in the United States in connection with a commercial activity of the foreign state elsewhere; or upon an act outside the territory of the United States in connection with a commercial activity of the foreign state elsewhere and that act causes a direct effect in the United States.

Respondents relied only on the third clause [so] our analysis is limited to considering whether this lawsuit is (1) "based . . . upon an act outside the territory of the United States"; (2) that was taken "in connection with a commercial activity" of Argentina outside this country; and (3) that "cause[d] a direct effect on the United States. . . . The fact that the cause of action is in compliance with the first of the three requirements—that it is "based upon an act outside the territory of the United States" (presumably Argentina's unilateral extension)—is uncontested.

[Turning to the second element, the] FSIA defines "commercial activity" to mean:

[E]ither a regular course of commercial conduct or a particular commercial transaction or act. The commercial character of an activity shall be determined by reference to the nature of the course of conduct or particular transaction or act, rather than by reference to its purpose.

[W]e conclude that when a foreign government acts, not as a regulator of a market, but in the manner of a private player within it, the foreign sovereign's actions are "commercial" within the meaning of the FSIA. Moreover, because the Act provides that the commercial character of an act is to be determined by reference to its "nature" rather than its "purpose," the question is not whether the foreign government is acting with a profit motive or instead with the aim of fulfilling uniquely sovereign objectives. Rather, the issue is whether the particular actions that the foreign state performs (whatever the

motive behind them) are the *type* of actions by which a private party engages in "trade and traffic or commerce," Black's Law Dictionary 270 (6th ed. 1990). Thus, a foreign government's issuance of regulations limiting foreign currency exchange is a sovereign activity, because such authoritative control of commerce cannot be exercised by a private party; whereas a contract to buy army boots or even bullets is a "commercial" activity, because private companies can similarly use sales contracts to acquire goods.

The commercial character of the Bonods is confirmed by the fact that they are in almost all respects garden-variety debt instruments: they may be held by private parties; they are negotiable and may be traded on the international markets (except in Argentina); and they promise a future stream of cash income.

The remaining question is whether Argentina's unilateral rescheduling of the Bonods had a "direct effect" in the United States. . . . [W]e reject [any] suggestion that Sec. 1605 (a)(2) contains any unexpressed requirement of "substantiality" or "foreseeability." As the Court of Appeals recognized, an effect is "direct" if it follows "as an immediate consequence of the defendant's . . . activity."

We . . . have little difficulty concluding that Argentina's unilateral rescheduling of the maturity dates on the Bonods had a "direct effect" in the United States. Respondents had designated their accounts in New York as the place of payment, and Argentina made some interest payments into those accounts before announcing that it was rescheduling the payments. Because New York was thus the place of performance for Argentina's ultimate contractual obligations, the rescheduling of those obligations necessarily had a "direct effect" in the United States: Money that was supposed to have been delivered to a New York bank for deposit was not forthcoming.

AFFIRMED.

Act of State Doctrine

Closely related in effect to the doctrine of sovereign immunity is the **act of state doctrine.** This doctrine is based on the concept that it is beyond the sensible exercise of judicial powers for a court in this country to sit in judgment on the actions of another sovereign nation taken in its own territory. Any redress of grievances caused by such actions should be obtained by the United States government dealing directly with the other sovereign. Thus, in *Banco Nacional de Cuba v. Sabbatino,* 376 U.S. 398 (1964), a case challenging Cuba's expropriation of a Cuban corporation that was largely owned by U.S. residents, the Supreme Court held:

[T]he Judicial Branch will not examine the validity of a taking of property within its own territory by a foreign sovereign government, extant and recognized by this country at the time of the suit, in the absence of treaty or other unambiguous agreement regarding controlling legal principles, even if the complaint alleges that the taking violates customary international law.

Also related to sovereign immunity is the doctrine of **sovereign compulsion,** under which American courts will refuse to hold a defendant liable for actions that it was compelled to take under the law of a recognized foreign sovereign.

The following case illustrates some of the difficult questions that can arise in application of the act of state doctrine.

W. S. KIRKPATRICK & CO. V. ENVIRONMENTAL TECTONICS CORPORATION

U.S. Supreme Court, 110 S.Ct. 701 (1990)

Petitioner W. S. Kirkpatrick & Co. pleaded guilty to a violation of the Foreign Corrupt Practices Act for having paid a bribe to a Nigerian official to obtain a contract with the Republic of Nigeria. Respondent Environmental Tectonics Corporation, an unsuccessful bidder on the contract, then brought this suit claiming that petitioner had violated the Racketeer Influenced and Corrupt Organizations Act (RICO) among others. Despite having received a letter from the Department of State indicating its view that this case posed no "unique embarrassment" to execution of American foreign policy, the trial court granted summary judgment to the petitioner on grounds that the act of state doctrine barred the claim. The court of appeals reversed, concluding that no embarrassment of the executive in its conduct of foreign affairs was evident. Petitioner appealed.

Scalia, Justice:

This Court's description of the jurisprudential foundation for the act of state doctrine has undergone some evolution over the years. We once viewed the doctrine as an expression of international law, resting upon "the highest considerations of international comity and expediency," *Oetjen v. Central Leather Co.,* 246 U.S. 297, 303–304 (1918). We have more recently described it, however, as a consequence of domestic separation of powers, reflecting "the strong sense of the Judicial Branch that its engagement in the task of passing on the validity of foreign acts of state may hinder" the conduct of foreign affairs. *Banco Nacional de Cuba v. Sabbatino,* 376 U.S. 398, 423 (1964). Some Justices have suggested possible exceptions to application of the doctrine where one or both of the foregoing policies would seemingly not be served: an exception, for example, for acts of state that consist of commercial transactions, since neither modern international comity nor the current position of our Executive Branch accorded sovereign immunity to such acts . . . or an exception for cases in which the Executive Branch has represented that it has no objection to denying validity to the foreign sovereign act, since then the courts would

be impeding no foreign policy goals.

The parties have argued about the applicability of these possible exceptions, and, more generally, about whether the purposes of the act of state doctrine would be furthered by its application in this case. We find it unneccessary, however, to pursue those inquiries, since the factual predicate for application of the act of state doctrine does not exist. Nothing in the present suit requires the court to declare invalid, and thus ineffective as "a rule of decision for the courts of this *country," Ricaud v. American Metal Co.,* 246 U.S. 304, 310 (1918), the official act of a foreign sovereign.

In every case in which we have held the act of state doctrine applicable, the relief sought or the defense interposed would have required a court in the United States to declare invalid the official act of a foreign sovereign performed within its own territory. . . . In the present case, by contrast, neither the claim nor any asserted defense requires a determination that Nigeria's contract with Kirkpatrick International was, or was not, effective.

The short of the matter is this: Courts in the United States have the power, and ordinarily the obligation, to

(continues)

W. S. Kirkpatrick & Co. v. Environmental Tectonics Corporation

(continued from previous page)
decide cases and controversies properly presented to them. The act of state doctrine does not establish an exception for cases and controversies that may embarrass foreign governments, but merely requires that, in the process of deciding, the acts of foreign sovereigns taken within their own jurisdiction shall be deemed valid. That doctrine has no application to the present case because the validity of no foreign sovereign act is at issue.

[Affirmed.] ⚖

International Litigation: Other Concerns

In the domestic setting, it can be quite troublesome to obtain service of summons over a proper defendant; obtain evidence to support the claim through oral depositions, written interrogatories, and document production; and ultimately enforce the judgment against a recalcitrant defendant. In the international context, such tasks can be overwhelming. To reduce these barriers to the civil prosecution of a valid claim, several international agreements have been reached that are intended generally to increase international cooperation in these respects.

The Hague Convention on Service Abroad of Judicial and Extrajudicial Documents in Civil or Commercial Matters provides that each signatory state will maintain a Central Authority to process judicial documents, such as complaints, and expedite their transmission. The Hague Convention on the Taking of Evidence Abroad in Civil or Commercial Matters of 1970 seeks to reduce the barriers raised by national laws to obtaining evidence for use in court and to streamline the discovery process in international litigation. The Convention creates Central Authorities in each signatory nation through which discovery requests (*Letters of Request*) are channeled; it permits consuls to conduct some discovery procedures regarding their own nationals; and, finally, it allows the use of court-appointed commissioners for discovery purposes in limited circumstances. The United States is a signatory of both Conventions.

What happens if an American company, for example, receives a judgment against a foreign defendant in a foreign country's court and wishes to enforce that judgment against the defendant's property located in the United States? Will U.S. courts recognize such foreign judgments? Enforcement of foreign judgments is a matter of state law, which varies somewhat from jurisdiction to jurisdiction. Guidance is pro-vided by the Restatement (Third) of the Foreign Relations Law of the United States, which provides that final money judgments of the courts of a foreign state will generally be enforced in the United States. However, a U.S. court is prohibited from enforcing a judgment that (1) was rendered by a judicial system that does not provide impartial tribunals or due process of law or (2) was rendered by a court lacking personal jurisdiction over the defendant under its own law or international law. Furthermore an American court has discretion to refrain from enforcing a foreign judgment on several grounds, including that the rendering court did not have subject matter jurisdiction, that the defendant did not receive notice of the proceedings in time to defend, that the judgment was obtained by fraud, or that the judgment is based on a cause of action repugnant to American public policy.

Arbitration

In view of the special difficulties encountered in international court litigation, it is not surprising that the international business community has actively sought alternative methods of commercial dispute resolution. Quite popular is **arbitration,** a process whereby parties to a transaction agree (either within the terms of their basic agreement or subsequently) to submit any future (or existing) disputes to an impartial third party (or panel) for nonjudicial resolution. The decision of the arbitrator—termed an *award*—may, depending on the agreement of the parties, be binding or nonbinding.

Binding arbitration within the international trading context has a long and colorful history and today is the preferred alternative to litigation in international commercial circles. The advantages of arbitration are many, including: (1) it is less expensive and more speedy than court procedures; (2) it is more private than litigation; and (3) the parties may choose knowledgeable experts (rather that generalist judges and untrained juries) to decide the matter based on commercial realities.

Arbitration is not, however, without its disadvantages. Arbitral panels generally do not have the power to compel the attendance of witnesses or the production of other information relevant to the case. The informality of the procedure can lead to an undesired degree of "looseness" in the process; and, because arbitrators are generally not bound by the strict letter of the law, final outcomes may be difficult to forecast.

Several organizations have sought to facilitate this means of dispute resolution by providing standard arbitral rules and procedures. Chief among these organizations are the International Chamber of Commerce (headquartered in Paris), the U.N. Commission on International Trade Law (UNCITRAL), the American Arbitration Association, the International Centre for Settlement of Investment Disputes (ICSID—created by the 1965 Convention on the Settlement of Investment Disputes Between States and Nationals of Other States), the Inter-American

Commercial Arbitration Commission, and the London Court of Arbitration.

So well accepted is the use of arbitration in international commercial disputes that most nations readily enforce such awards. In the United States, such enforcement is a matter of federal law. As with foreign court judgments, guidance is provided by the Restatement (Third) of Foreign Relations, which provides that awards pursuant to valid written arbitral agreements will generally be enforced, although a court may deny recognition on such grounds as: (1) the agreement to arbitrate was not valid under applicable law; (2) the losing party was not given an opportunity to present its case; (3) the award deals with matters outside the terms of the agreement to arbitrate; or (4) recognition of the award would be contrary to public policy. The Restatement's rules are based on the U.N. Convention on the Recognition and Enforcement of Foreign Arbitral Awards (known as the *New York Convention*). Almost 80 nations are parties to this Convention, reflecting the widespread acceptance of arbitration in the international sphere. The following case is illustrative.

MITSUBISHI MOTORS CORP. V. SOLER CHRYSLER-PLYMOUTH, INC.

U.S. Supreme Court, 473 U.S. 614 (1985)

Petitioner Mitsubishi, a Japanese corporation that manufactures automobiles, is the product of a joint venture between Chrysler International, S.A. (CISA), a Swiss corporation, and another Japanese corporation, aimed at distributing automobiles manufactured by the petitioner through Chrysler dealers outside the continental United States. Respondent Soler, a Puerto Rican corporation, entered into distribution and sales agreements with CISA. These agreements contained a clause providing for arbitration by the Japan Commercial Arbitration Association of all disputes arising out of certain articles of the agreement or for the breach thereof. Disagreements did arise, and petitioner filed suit in federal district

court in Puerto Rico under the federal Arbitration Act and the Convention on the Recognition and Enforcement of Foreign Arbitral Awards, seeking an order to compel arbitration of the dispute in accordance with the arbitration clause. Respondent filed a counterclaim alleging antitrust violations by petitioner and CISA. The district court ordered arbitration of almost all issues. On appeal, the circuit court affirmed, except as to the antitrust issues, which it held to be inappropriate for arbitration.

Blackmun, Justice:

By agreeing to arbitrate a statutory claim, a party does not forgo the substantive rights afforded by the statute; it only submits to their resolution in an arbitral, rather than a judicial, forum. It

trades the procedures and opportunity for review of the courtroom for the simplicity, informality, and expedition of arbitration. We must assume that if Congress intended the substantive protection against waiver of the right to a judicial forum, that intention will be deducible from text or legislative history. . . . Having made the bargain to arbitrate, the party should be held to it unless Congress itself has evinced an intention to preclude a waiver of judicial remedies for the statutory rights at issue. . . .

We now turn to consider whether Soler's antitrust claims are nonarbitrable even though it agreed to arbitrate them. In holding that they are not, the Court of Appeals followed the decision of the Second Circuit in *American Safety Equipment Corp. v. J. P. McGuire & Co.*, 391 F.2d 821 (1968) [finding] that "the pervasive
(continues)

MITSUBISHI MOTORS CORP. V. SOLER CHRYSLER-PLYMOUTH, INC.

(continued from previous page)
public interest in enforcement of the antitrust laws, and the nature of the claims that arise in such cases, combine to make . . . antitrust claims . . . inappropriate for arbitration." We find it unnecessary to assess the legitimacy of the *American Safety* doctrine as applied to agreements to arbitrate arising from domestic transactions. As in *Scherk v. Alberto-Culver Co.,* 417 U.S. 506 (1974), we conclude that concerns of international comity, respect for the capacities of foreign and transnational tribunals, and sensitivity to the need of the international commercial system for predictability in the resolution of disputes require that we enforce the parties' agreement, even assuming that a contrary result would be forthcoming in a domestic context.

Even before *Scherk,* this Court had recognized the utility of forum-selection clauses in international transactions. In *The Bremen v. Zapata Off-Shore Co.,* 407 U.S. 1 (1972), an American oil company, seeking to evade a contractual choice of an English forum and, by implication, English law, filed a suit in admiralty in a United States District Court against the German corporation which had contracted to tow its rig to a location in the Adriatic Sea. Notwithstanding the possibility that the English court would enforce provisions in the towage contract exculpating the German party which an American court would refuse to enforce, this Court gave effect to the choice-of-forum clause. It observed:

The expansion of American business and industry will hardly be encouraged if, notwithstanding solemn contracts, we insist on a parochial concept that all disputes must be re-

solved under our laws and in our courts. . . . We cannot have trade and commerce in world markets and international waters exclusively on our terms, governed by our laws, and resolved in our courts.

. . . In *Scherk,* . . . this Court [enforced] the arbitration agreement even while assuming for purposes of the decision that the controversy would be nonarbitrable had it arisen out of a domestic transaction. Again, the Court emphasized:

A contractual provision specifying in advance the forum in which disputes shall be litigated and the law to be applied is . . . an almost indispensable precondition to achievement of the orderliness and predictability essential to any international business transaction.

A parochial refusal by the courts of one country to enforce an international arbitration agreement would not only frustrate these purposes, but would invite unseemly and mutually destructive jockeying by the parties to secure tactical litigation advantages. . . . [It would] damage the fabric of international commerce and trade, and imperil the willingness and ability of businessmen to enter into international commercial agreements.

. . . There is no reason to assume at the outset of the dispute that international arbitration will not provide an adequate mechanism. To be sure, the international arbitral tribunal owes no prior allegiance to the legal norms of particular states; hence, it has no direct obligation to vindicate their statutory dictates. The tribunal, however, is bound to effectuate the intentions of the parties. Where the parties have agreed that the arbitral body is to decide a defined set of claims which includes, as in these cases, those arising from the application of American antitrust law, the tribal therefore should

be bound to decide that dispute in accord with the national law giving rise to the claim. And as long as the prospective litigant effectively may vindicate its statutory cause of action in the arbitral forum, the statute will continue to serve both its remedial and deterrent function. . . .

As international trade has expanded in recent decades, so too has the use of international arbitration to resolve disputes arising in the course of that trade. The controversies that international arbitral institutions are called upon to resolve have increased in diversity as well as in complexity. Yet the potential of these tribunals for efficient disposition of legal disagreements arising from commercial relations has not yet been tested. If they are to take a central place in the international legal order, national courts will need to "shake off the old judicial hostility to arbitration," *Kulukundis Shipping Co. v. Amtorg Trading Corp.,* 126 F2d. 978 (CA2 1942), and also their customary and understandable unwillingness to cede jurisdiction of a claim arising under the domestic law to a foreign or transnational tribunal. To this extent, at least, it will be necessary for national courts to subordinate domestic notions of arbitrability to the international policy favoring commercial arbitration.

Accordingly, we "require this representative of the American business community to honor its bargain," . . . by holding this agreement to arbitrate "enforce[able]" in accord with the explicit provisions of the Arbitration Act." *Scherk,* 417 U.S., at 520.

The judgment of the Court of Appeals is affirmed in part and reversed in part. ☙

NATIONAL REGULATION OF THE IMPORT/EXPORT PROCESS

The impact of export trade transcends, of course, the private interests of the parties to the international

sales contract. Concerns at the national level touch on defense and security matters (especially in the export of high technology with military applications) and the depletion of national stocks of critical materials. Moreover, the volumes and direction of flow of export sales are inextricably bound up in the general economic posture of a nation and thus bear directly on its overall pattern of foreign relations. Not surprisingly, almost all nations have responded to these factors by adopting broad regulatory schemes to control exports. The implementation of these programs will directly affect the international trader and the methods used in that trade.

In the United States, the power to regulate international trade is vested in the Congress under the provisions of the commerce clause of the federal Constitution. Congress has used this power repeatedly since the early days of the Republic and the trail of congressional legislation dealing with import and export matters continues into the present day. The Export Administration Act of 1979 is perhaps the most important piece of federal legislation affecting American export traders today.

Export Administration Act

The Export Administration Act is a comprehensive scheme to regulate exports from the United States and, together with the regulations adopted pursuant to it, extends its controls in some instances to the re-export of certain American goods to third countries. The Act grants discretionary authority to the Office of Export Administration (OEA) of the Department of Commerce to impose export controls for three basic reasons: (1) national security (to prevent "dual use" products that might have military applications from reaching our enemies), (2) foreign policy (for example, to prevent goods from reaching countries that practice terrorism or apartheid), and (3) short supply of goods in the United States.

In general terms, the act provides for three broad types of required export licenses:

1. A general license authorizing exports—this type of license covers the vast bulk of American exports and is normally issued by the OEA without a formal application by the exporter. (There is also a qualified general license authorizing multiple imports.)

2. A validated license relating to a specific export.

3. A distribution license permitting export of unlimited quantities of certain commodities under an international marketing program without additional approval from the OEA.

The Export Administration Regulations (found in the *Code of Federal Regulations*) round out, define,

and implement the provisions of the 1979 Act. They contain a Commodity Control List, which will assist the exporter in identifying circumstances when a general license will not suffice. In most instances, this decision is a function of what commodity is going to what country. Some few nations (Iraq and Cuba, among others) are virtually closed to American exports. These regulations also contain provisions relating to the export of technical data (as opposed to commodities, which are treated as a separate and distinct category for licensing purposes). The general license *GTDR* controls the export of technical data in terms of both destination and the degree of "public accessibility" to the information; a more liberal license, the general license *GTDA* allows technical data exports to virtually any destination if the data meet the regulations' standard of public availability. A 1985 amendment to the Export Administration Act also provides for a comprehensive operations license to govern exports from American corporations to off-shore affiliates and subsidiaries. This type of license will have frequent use within transnational corporate systems.

Although the Export Administration Act is a major source of export regulation in the United States, it is by no means the only one.[9] Export control provisions are also found in the Nuclear Non-Proliferation Act (1978) and the Atomic Energy Act (1954), which govern the nuclear materials. The Arms Export Control Act, the Trading with the Enemy Act, and the International Emergency Economic Power Act also contain important export restrictions.

In addition, the United States is a member of the Coordinating Committee for Multilateral Export Controls (COCOM) along with Japan and most NATO members. This is an international group that cooperates in the control of exports of strategic goods to sensitive destinations. COCOM has no authority to enforce its own policies but relies on regulations of its member states. During the 1980s, the United States was much more sensitive to export of technology than were other COCOM members. The culmination in 1992 of the European Economic Community (EEC) (to be discussed soon) and the disintegration of the Soviet Union are combining to pressure the United States to reduce its attempts to impose its technology export controls extraterritorially. However, in the

---

[9]Note, too, the impact of other federal legislation on the conduct of international business. For instance, the Foreign Corrupt Practices Act controls bribery and other undesirable acts abroad.

aftermath of Operation Desert Storm and the information it brought regarding Iraq's ability to obtain western weapons technology, this area is receiving new attention.

Export Incentives

U.S. export policy and legislation is not, however, totally negative. Important legislation has long been on the books to encourage increased export trade by manufacturers and suppliers in this country.

As early as 1918, Congress adopted the Webb-Pomerene Act to promote American export trade by granting limited exemptions to exporters from the application of U.S. antitrust laws, principally the Sherman and Clayton acts. Congress acted in the belief that American traders could better compete in foreign markets if they were permitted to form associations capturing the benefits of economies of scale and greater efficiency; such associations, however, involved a danger of criminal or civil liability under American antitrust laws. The Webb-Pomerene Act, therefore, relieved export associations of this risk but conditioned the exemption in important respects. Principally, such an association is prohibited by the act from entering into any agreement that "artificially or intentionally" depresses commodity prices within the United States or that "substantially lessens competition within the United States, or otherwise restrains trade therein." Further, the benefits of the act (obtained by registration of the association with the Federal Trade Commission) are limited to associations formed for the export of commodities; transactions for services or technology are not protected. As a result of these limitations and lingering anxiety about possible antitrust liability, comparatively few Webb-Pomerene associations are registered with the FTC.

Export Trading Company Act

The failure of the 1918 legislation to promote greater American export trade, coupled with increasing U.S. trade deficits in the mid- and late 1970s,[10] created a sense of urgency in Congress to devise new and more effective means to encourage increased exports from this country, especially by small- and medium-sized

companies historically underrepresented in international trade transactions. The legislative response was the Export Trading Company Act of 1982.

At the heart of this Act is the provision that

no criminal or civil action may be brought under the antitrust laws [of the United States] against a person to whom a certificate of review is issued [by the Secretary of Commerce] which is based on conduct which is specified in, and complies with the terms of, a certificate . . . which . . . was in effect when the conduct occurred.

This exemption is available to individual persons residing in the United States, partnerships or corporations created under state or federal law, and significantly for antitrust purposes, "any association or combination, by contract or other arrangement" between or among any of these.

The Act's scope is comprehensive. It extends its antitrust protection to activities related to the export of goods and merchandise and (going beyond the reach of the Webb-Pomerene Act) to services. This latter category is defined to include services that are the subject of the transaction (as in transborder management agreements) and includes accounting, architectural, data processing, business, communications, consulting, and legal services. Also eligible for exemption from possible antitrust liabilities are "export trade services," that is, international market research, product research and design, transportation, warehousing, insurance, and the like.

The Export Trading Company Act also contains important provisions that modify statutory impediments that separate the banking community from participation in international trade. Title II of the Act (termed the *Bank Export Services Act*) permits banks to invest in export trading companies up to the statutory limit of 5 percent of their consolidated capital and surplus; further, they are also allowed to own such companies outright. These provisions are intended to marshal substantial capital to promote international trade. The absence of such funding has hobbled export trade in the past because many small- and medium-sized banks were reluctant to finance "speculative foreign ventures" over which they had little or no control.

Regulating Imports

Compared with the elaborate nature of export controls and incentives, the regulation of imports into the United States is relatively straightforward. The

---

[10]The United States never experienced a trade deficit—an excess of imports over exports—until 1971. Between 1971 and 1976, however, the American trade deficit rose to $5 billion, largely because of massive oil imports that amounted to $77 billion in 1981 alone. The deficit exploded, reaching $170 billion in 1986. (U.S. Bureau of the Census, *Highlights of U.S. Export and Import Trade*, FT1990, Feb. 1987.)

application of these import control laws can, however, be quite complex.

Under the import–export clause of the federal Constitution, the power to levy import customs and duties rests exclusively with the federal government. Using federal power in this regard, the government has established a comprehensive system of tariff schedules that apply to goods entering the United States—the Tariff Schedules of the United States (TSUS). The TSUS will be applied by federal customs officials first to classify the entering goods and then to determine the applicable tariff rate to the goods so classified. The federal government sets the actual rate, but does so subject to bilateral or multilateral restraints that it has assumed. For example, a treaty with another nation may stipulate the tariff level or, more generally, the applicable tariff may have been negotiated within the framework of a multinational commitment, for example, the General Agreement on Tariffs and Trade (GATT). In either event, the tariff generally must be paid before the goods are admitted into this country.

An important exception to this principle is the use of a foreign trade zone (FTZ). Established by federal law, these zones are fenced-off, policed warehouses and industrial parks usually located near American ports of entry. Goods entering the port from abroad may be taken into the FTZ and stored there without paying any applicable tariff and with a minimum of formality and procedure. As long as the goods are warehoused within the FTZ, no duty is payable and the goods may be further processed, assembled, or finished. Only when the merchandise leaves the confines of the FTZ will the duty be imposed, frequently at a reduced rate. The FTZ has shown itself to be an effective device for encouraging additional international trade in the United States.

Whereas import licenses are generally not required for imports into the United States, certain goods may be denied entry altogether. Bans on importation may be applied against undesirable imports such as narcotics, pornographic material, or printed materials advocating the violent overthrow of the United States. Import bans may be applied to prevent entry of automobiles that do not meet vehicle safety regulations or against other products not meeting standards established to protect public health and safety. Products violating the patent, trademark, and copyright laws of the United States may also be excluded. Moreover, certain goods may be subjected to

tariff increases to offset foreign government subsidies that unfairly reduce their U.S. market price or to counteract a foreign producer's deliberate attempt to destabilize or destroy the product's domestic production in the United States. These *countervailing* and *antidumping* measures are considered again in this chapter with regard to the GATT.

Trade and Tariff Act

One method of increasing the access of U.S. companies to foreign markets is retaliation against countries that treat U.S. companies unfairly. A series of acts over the years have authorized and encouraged the President to take such retaliatory action. In recent years Congress has been specifically concerned with the difficulty U.S. companies have had gaining access to markets in Asia, especially Japan. At various times Congress has authorized, and even mandated, the President to respond to unfair trade practices by use of higher tariffs, import quotas, or withdrawal from existing trade agreements with offending parties. Prying open new markets for U.S. companies without unduly antagonizing existing trading partners requires the striking of a delicate balance.

Protection from Unfair Competition

Various provisions of federal law protect U.S. companies from unfair practices by foreign competitors selling in this country. The primary protective provision is Sec. 337 of the Tariff Act of 1930, which protects "domestic industries" from "substantial injury" stemming from "unfair methods of competition and unfair acts in the importation of articles into the United States, or in their sale. . . ." Sec. 337 has been invoked most often in cases of alleged patent infringement, but it also protects U.S. businesses from copyright and trademark infringement, false advertising, trade secret misappropriation, palming off (misleading consumers into thinking they are buying another company's goods), and even "dumping."

Sec. 337 is activated by a domestic company's complaint to the U.S. International Trade Commission, an independent federal regulatory commission. The commission follows the Administrative Procedure Act in investigating the complaint and determining whether there has been a violation. The President has 60 days to review the commission's decision. Remedies can include cease and desist orders, temporary exclusion orders, and even permanent exclusion orders.

Because American businesses were losing as much as $40 billion annually from foreign infringement of U.S. patents and other intellectual property rights, in 1988 Congress directed the President to identify countries that do not protect copyrights and patents and to initiate expedited unfair trade investigations in egregious cases unless to do so would harm national economic interests.

ORGANIZING FOR INTERNATIONAL TRADE

The massive devastation of the Second World War had among its many casualties the international trade infrastructure, which had been growing slowly but perceptibly since the middle of the nineteenth century. One of the major tasks of reconstruction following 1945 was the recreation of a framework for international trade. Negotiations focusing on trade, money, and finance led to establishment of the current international economic institutions, including the GATT, the International Monetary Fund, and the International Bank for Reconstruction and Development. More recently, regional trade agreements have become a prominent means of facilitating international trade.

The GATT

The United Nations Conference on Trade and Employment met in Havana in late 1947 and was attended by more than 50 countries. Although the conference was unsuccessful in creating a proposed International Trade Organization, it led almost two dozen countries to conclude the GATT (General Agreement on Tariffs and Trade), the essential purpose of which was to achieve a significant reduction of the general level of national tariffs and, further, to provide an institutional framework within which future tariff conflicts could be resolved. The GATT has, since its creation, shown itself to be of enduring significance in international economic and trade relations. According to its supporters, the GATT trading system has achieved unprecedented trade expansion and world prosperity. (Its detractors note that GATT provisions are often breached by participating countries.)

The GATT achieves its overall objective of liberalized international trade by addressing a series of key issues regarding important restrictions. It requires that each signatory state extend "most favored nation" tariff rates to goods from other signatory nations and, further, obligates participating nations to afford "national treatment" to the imported goods from other signatory countries. Article III of the agreement provides:

The products of the territory of any contracting party imported into the territory of any other contracting party shall be accorded treatment no less favorable than that accorded to like products of national origin in respect of all laws, regulations and requirements affecting their internal sale, offering for sale, purchase, transportation, distribution or use.

The GATT prohibits discrimination by participating states through quantitative trade restrictions by providing that import quotas, if adopted at all by a state, shall be applied equally to all nations that are parties to the agreement. An even more ambitious objective of the GATT is the elimination of all prohibitions or restrictions (other than duties, taxes, or other charges) on imports and exports among the member nations.

In large measure, the GATT implements its goals of free trade through a series of published tariff schedules that are developed through an intricate negotiation process within the framework of the organization and that, once published, are binding on each of the participating states. In recognition of inevitable trade anomalies and to secure the willing participation and cooperation of member states in its tariff reduction program, the GATT provides special circumstances when unilateral exceptions to the schedules of tariffs may be made. The most well known of these relate to antidumping duties and countervailing subsidies.

If the products of one country are "dumped" into another at prices below their fair market value in the exporting country in an effort to disrupt or destroy the domestic production of those goods in the receiving nation, the GATT contemplates that the government of the receiving country may impose an "antidumping duty" in an effort to equalize the domestic price in those goods with the prevailing fair market price in the exporting country. Similarly, when the production of certain goods in the exporting state is heavily subsidized by the government of that nation (leading to a reduced export price for that product), the GATT permits the receiving state to impose a "countervailing duty" to bring the market price up to a competitive level.

In its formative years, the GATT concentrated almost exclusively on measures to reduce tariff barriers to increase international trade. More recently, it has turned its attention to the reduction of nontariff barriers, such as unreasonably restrictive local standards and inaccessible national distribution systems, to further increase the volume of trade among nations.

During the rounds of negotiation, nations bargain to advance their positions. The United States, for example, seeks to induce Europe and Japan to lower subsidies for their farmers who compete with American agriculture and to induce Third World nations to refrain from pirating U.S. trademarks, copyrights, and patents. Many nations seek to induce Japan to open its economy to foreign sellers and urge the United States to reduce its protection for textiles. For their part, underdeveloped nations seek freer access to advanced technology and to markets for their agricultural products.

The IMF and the IBRD

The International Monetary Fund (IMF), like the GATT, is intended to coordinate the activities of governments regarding international trade functions and does not primarily address the individual international trader. Growing out of discussions held at Bretton Woods, New Hampshire, late in the Second World War, the IMF was designed to speed international financial and economic reconstruction by providing an institutional structure within which intergovernmental loans would be used to stabilize currency exchange rates and, through a system of credits (termed *Special Drawing Rights* or *SDRs*), to enable member countries to borrow from the fund or from each other as a means of stabilizing their national currencies with the international monetary system.

Affiliated with the International Monetary Fund is the International Bank for Reconstruction and Development (IBRD), which was founded to "assist in the reconstruction and development of territories of members by facilitating the investment of capital for productive purposes" and to "promote private foreign investment by means of guarantees or participations in loans and other investments made by private investors." The IBRD, located in Washington, D.C., is permitted under its charter to guarantee, participate in, or make loans to member states and to any business, industrial, or agricultural enterprise in the territories of a member state. The availability through IMF and IBRD of massive amounts of financial credit was particularly significant in Western Europe during the immediate postwar years and has

had, in addition, a very significant role in the industrial development of Asia and Africa in the past several decades.

Regional Trade Agreements

The multilateral approach to trade negotiation embodied in GATT is complemented by various regional trading arrangements. Latin American countries, Pacific Rim countries, and various other regional groupings have acted in concerted fashion to enhance trade and investment among their members. Two such regional agreements are of particular importance to American businesses.

United States–Canada Free Trade Act

The United States and Canada have the world's largest trading partnership. Trade between the two countries rose from $74 billion in 1980 to more than $150 billion by 1988. To further enhance this already productive relationship, the two countries entered into the Free Trade Act (FTA), which took effect on January 1, 1989, and, over a 10-year period, is intended to phase out virtually all remaining tariffs.

The FTA will not result in the complete integration that exists among American states or Canadian provinces. However, it will curtail trade barriers and ensure that any still existing serve legitimate purposes, such as protection of health, environment, or national security. Approximately 80 percent of all goods were already crossing the border between the two countries duty-free. The FTA will reduce tariffs on most other items and will significantly relax foreign investment restrictions (especially those existing in Canada) to facilitate direct investment between businesses of the two nations. The FTA also aims to facilitate fair competition, to establish effective dispute-resolution procedures, and to lay the foundation for further bilateral and multilateral trade cooperation.

United States–Mexico Free Trade

As this edition is written, the United States, Canada, and Mexico have signed the North American Free Trade Agreement (NAFTA), designed to create among the three countries the same type of free-trade relationship that the FTA created between the United States and Canada. These efforts are aimed at creating a unified continental market in North America similar to that in Europe discussed in the next section. NAFTA is aimed at securing the rights and privileges of transnational corporations in North America and granting, in general, national treatment and most-favored-nation treatment to NAFTA investors. If adopted by Congress, NAFTA will cause many short-term dislocations for the American economy, but presents exciting long-term prospects.

European Economic Community

By the Treaty of Rome in 1958, six European countries (Belgium, France, Italy, Luxembourg, The Netherlands, and West Germany) formed the European Economic Community (EEC). Eventually joined by six other nations (Denmark, Ireland, the United Kingdom, Greece, Portugal, and Spain), the EEC seeks economic integration and the creation of a single internal European market.[11] The Single European Act of 1987 set December 31, 1992, as target date for completion of implementing legislation.

EEC members are motivated not only by the hope of gaining an economic advantage by combining their markets, but also by a desire to bind Western Europe more tightly in a political and social sense. A basic principle of the EEC is creation of a Community Law, which will preempt national law wherever national law might conflict. The EEC is not likely to create a "United States of Europe." After all, there are still twelve separate governments and nine different languages. However, by harmonizing economic regulations in the various states and breaking down trade barriers, the EEC will probably become a very strong economic entity with which all trading competitors, including U.S. businesses, will have to reckon.

As of this writing, the EEC has already transferred to Community institutions the power to set tariff policies and abolish customs duties among member states, harmonized the system for designation and codification of goods, empowered the Community to counteract anticompetitive practices and to defend itself politically, and issued 300 very precise directives concerning industrial products, metrology, textiles, electricity, labelling, advertising, sale of hazardous materials, and the like—all aimed at expediting trade among Community members. However, Denmark's summer 1992 rejection of certain EEC accords (the "Maastricht treaty") derailed at least

temporarily the fast-track to the goals of a single European currency by 1999 and common foreign and defense policy soon thereafter. The single trade market still took effect in December 1992.

OTHER WAYS OF DOING BUSINESS

Thus far, we have spoken of international trade mainly in terms of direct sales from a seller in one country to a buyer in another. However, there are many other forms of international transactions. Take the case of an American corporation wishing to export its goods. Rather than send its own employees to the foreign markets to drum up business at the retail or wholesale level, it might hire an **agent** in that foreign country to act on its behalf. Such agents would typically have authority to contract on behalf of the American sellers. Complications would likely arise from the differences between agency law and customs in the United States and those of the foreign country.

Or the American company might choose to do business through a **licensee** in the foreign country. That licensee would pay a fee to the American company for the right to sell the company's goods. Such licensees, of course, will want exclusive rights to sell the American company's products, if possible. Legal problems here may result from antitrust laws of the United States and the foreign country. An increasingly popular form of such licensing arrangement is the franchising of trademarks, trade names, and copyrights. Many American service industries, such as fast food chains and convenience store chains, are expanding to foreign markets through use of this device.

Or an American seller may wish to have a foreign subsidiary corporation formed in the foreign nations in which it seeks to do business. This process is complicated by the many restrictions that most countries, especially in the underdeveloped world, place on such corporations. Such restrictions may take the form of **currency controls,** which make it difficult to take profits out of the country. Or the host country may require a certain percentage of host country ownership of the American company's subsidiary or require that the company enter into a joint venture with the host government or a local company.

India, for example has endeavored to "Indianize" foreign companies operating there. In the wake of the terrible 1984 Bhopal, India, gas leak that killed 2700 and injured perhaps 200,000, the Union Car-

---

[11]Greenland joined the EEC but later withdrew. Turkey has asked to become a member, and it is expected that Austria will also apply for membership.

bide Corporation has *claimed* that its subsidiary—Union Carbide India Ltd.—was so "Indianized" that Union Carbide could not have shut the plant down out of safety concerns had it wanted to. All 9000 employees of the company were Indian, and quasi-governmental Indian financial institutions owned 25 percent of its stock. Union Carbide itself retained only 50.9 percent of the subsidiary's stock. In many lesser developed countries, foreign corporations are limited to 49 percent ownership; local entities must retain control.

The following case illustrates legal issues that may arise with the use of one of these methods of doing business abroad—the franchise.

DAYAN V. MCDONALD'S CORPORATION

Appellate Court of Illinois, 466 N.E.2d 958 (1984)

Case

In 1971, Dayan and McDonald's Corp. signed a master license agreement (MLA), granting Dayan a 30-year franchise right to use the McDonald's patents, trademarks, and trade names in Paris. The agreement bound Dayan to meet McDonald's Quality, Service, and Cleanliness (QSC) standards, because his departure from them would impede the successful operation of McDonald's restaurants in other parts of the world. If Dayan defaulted, McDonald's had the right to terminate the agreement. McDonald's issued operating licenses to Dayan for 14 restaurants. However, McDonald's was never satisfied with Dayan's compliance with QSC standards. In 1976, McDonald's told Dayan that his substandard operation could no longer be tolerated and that he would have six months to bring his restaurants into compliance with the QSC standards. When Dayan failed to do so, McDonald's sued in Paris to terminate the MLA. Dayan then brought this action in Illinois to enjoin the termination.

The trial judge, after 65 days of testimony, refused to issue the injunction, ruling that McDonald's properly terminated the MLA because of Dayan's breach of its QSC provisions. Dayan appealed.

Buckley, Presiding Justice:

[Several] cases reflect judicial concern over longstanding abuses in franchise relationships, particularly contract provisions giving the franchisor broad unilateral powers of termination at will. Taken collectively, they stand for the proposition that the implied convenant of good faith restricts franchisor discretion in terminating a franchise agreement to those cases where good cause exists.

After finding good cause for termination existed, the trial court found that McDonald's sole motive for termination was Dayan's failure to maintain QSC standards.

Our review of the evidence admits of no doubt; the trial court properly resolved this issue in favor of McDonald's. To characterize the condition of Dayan's restaurants as being in substantial noncompliance with McDonald's QSC standards is to engage in profound understatement. Throughout the trial the various witnesses struggled to find the appropriate words to describe the ineffably unsanitary conditions observed in these restaurants, as did the trial court in its memorandum opinion. Terms describing the uncleanliness—such as "indescribable," "extremely defective sanitary conditions," "filthy, grimy, cruddy," "deplorable," "significantly unsanitary," "contaminated," "insanitary," "very dirty," "very, very dirty," "disgusting," "abundance of filth," "pig pens"—tell only part of the story. The accuracy of these epithets is supported by voluminous, detailed testimonial evidence which consumed many weeks of trial and thousands of pages of transcript and is also corroborated by over 1,000 photographs admitted in evidence at trial. The conditions of filth were so widespread and reported by so many persons that any attempt to catalog them all would only unduly lengthen this opinion.

[Dayan's complaint that McDonald's did not provide a trained, French-speaking operations man] rings false. As the trial court correctly realized:

"It does not take a McDonald's trained French speaking operational man to know that grease dripping from the vents must be stopped and not merely collected in a cup hung from the ceiling, that dogs are not permitted to defecate where food is stored, that insecticide is not blended with chicken breading, that past-dated products should be discarded, that a potato peeler should be somewhat cleaner than a tire-vulcanizer and that shortening should not look like crankcase oil."

[Affirmed.] ⚖️

The Foreign Corrupt Practices Act (FCPA) of 1977 bars American companies from paying bribes to get business from foreign governments. More specifically, the FCPA bans these companies (and their officers and agents) from offering money or "anything of value" to foreign officials, foreign political candidates, or foreign political parties if the purpose is to induce that entity to assist the American company in obtaining or retaining business. (In addition to antibribery provisions, the FCPA also has accounting provisions designed to prevent large corporations from maintaining "off-the-book accounts" or "slush funds" from which such payments might be made without alerting auditors or senior corporate officials.)

Penalties for violation of the FCPA are severe. An American company may be fined up to $2 million for criminal violations of the FCPA. Individual agents of these companies may be fined up to $100,000, imprisoned for up to five years, or both. Lesser civil penalties may be imposed in actions brought by the Securities and Exchange Commission.

The antibribery provisions carry exceptions permitting (1) "grease" payments made to officials in order to obtain routine government actions, such as the issuing of permits or licenses, the processing of government papers such as visas, the providing of police protection or mail delivery, and the providing of telephone, electrical power, or water service; (2) any payments lawful under the written laws and regulations of the recipient's home country; and (3) bona fide expenses, such as for travel and lodging, directly related to promoting or demonstrating a product.

Despite these exceptions, American companies are convinced that the FCPA places them at a disadvantage in competing for global business against other nations not so punctilious about their business practices. There is some statistical evidence to support this view, although U.S. exports have increased greatly since the FCPA's passage.

Opponents of the FCPA also argue that the United States should not export its values regarding proper business practices. These persons argue that it is improper for the United States to attempt to impose its ethical standards on foreign nations. What do you think? Are we doing Third World nations any favors by "playing their game"? Are we developing nations well served by business practices based heavily on bribery and corruption? Are our companies ethically justified in paying bribes because foreign competitors may do so?

REGULATING THE TRANSNATIONAL CORPORATION

The rise of huge and powerful **transnational corporations** (TNCs) is one of the defining elements of the post–World War II global economic environment. TNCs such as IBM, Exxon, and Toyota can have tremendous impact on the economy, culture, and environment of developing host countries. In the early 1970s, a series of economic, political, and legal factors focused international attention on the role and impact of these TNCs in global economic relationships.

TNCs are naturally interested in gaining free entry to foreign economies and protecting the investments they make there. For their part, developing countries are concerned with avoiding repetition of the consequences of earlier colonialism. They wish to have their local laws and autonomy respected and to protect their resources, culture, environment, and workers. They wish to be fairly treated and assisted to develop and not merely exploited.

For the past two decades efforts at balancing these competing interests have been ongoing in a number of spheres. Several bilateral treaties have been signed between developed and developing nations, wherein the former promised certain concessions to obtain the latters' protection of TNC investments. Some regional pacts have also have been signed.

Perhaps most importantly, the United Nations has played a major role. Completion of the U.N. Code of Conduct on Transnational Corporations may finally be at hand. The code specifies that treatment of TNCs by host countries should be fair and equitable. Specific standards on matters of nationalization and compensation, national regulation, transfer of payments, and settlements of disputes are all set forth.

Additional guiding principles include an International Code of Marketing of Breast-Milk Substitutes (under the jurisdiction of the World Health Organization), Guidelines of Consumer Protection (adopted by the U.N. General Assembly), and Criteria for Sustainable Development (aimed at discouraging overexploitation by TNCs).

SUMMARY

International commercial relations is a growing field. Each year an increasing volume of diverse goods is traded among an expanding number of nations. Both direct and indirect investment in foreign economies are also expanding. Such commercial relations are governed by a network of rules arising from multiple sources, including the domestic rules of the trading partners; the rules established by the international trading community; and the rules promulgated by regional organizations, such as the European Economic Community, and by international organizations, such as the United Nations and its various organs.

The international trading community has developed various uniform trade terms, financing devices (such as the letter of credit), and even trade rules such as those embodied in the Convention on Contracts for the International Sale of Goods in order to facilitate international trade. The Convention on Notes will probably be the next development.

When disputes over international agreements arise, the difficulties of domestic litigation are multiplied many times. U.S. courts must juggle such doctrines as the act of state doctrine and the doctrine of sovereign compulsion, as well as examine domestic legislation such as the Foreign Sovereign Immunities Act in order to determine which cases they can and cannot hear. These difficulties make arbitration a natural answer and, indeed, many international disputes are settled through arbitration.

Every nation is concerned with its export and import process. Like other nations, the United States has passed legislation to encourage the overall level of exports, while at the same time controlling the items that are exported in the interest of national security. Imports are also regulated to protect U.S. industry from unfair competition.

The international trade scene features not only bilateral trade agreements between nations, but also the multinational approach of the GATT, and regional trade agreements such as that embodied in the European Economic Community.

Investment by developed nations in lesser developed nations can stimulate the latters' economies. At the same time, if not properly handled, that investment can lead to charges of exploitation. Both international organizations and the lesser developed nations themselves have worked on investment codes designed to facilitate beneficial investment, while limiting the adverse side effects that sometimes arise.

KEY TERMS

International law
Letter of credit
Bill of lading
Export license
Import license
Certificate of origin
Trade terms
Act of state doctrine
Sovereign compulsion
Comity
Agent
Licensee
Currency controls
Transnational corporation

QUESTIONS AND PROBLEMS

1. Schlunk, an American whose parents were killed in an accident, filed suit in the United States against a German company, Volkswagen AG (VWAG), and its wholly owned U.S. subsidiary, Volkswagen of America (VWOA). Schlunk did not attempt to serve VWAG in West Germany. Instead, he argued that service on VWOA in the United States constituted adequate service on VWAG. VWAG took the view that it could be served only in its West German headquarters pursuant to the provisions of the Hague Convention on the Service of Process. Which view seems to be the better one? (*Volkswagenwerk Aktiengesellschaft v. Schlunk*, 108 S. Ct. 2104, 1988.)

2. Defendants are two corporations owned by the Republic of France. They design, manufacture, and market aircraft, including the "Rallye." The plaintiffs were injured when a Rallye crashed in Iowa; they filed a breach of warranty suit in federal court in Iowa. The plaintiffs made various discovery requests under the Federal Rules of Civil Procedure. The defendants complied with initial requests but later took

the position that because they were French corporations, "and the discovery sought can only be found in a foreign state, namely France," the Hague Convention on the Taking of Evidence Abroad in Civil or Commercial Matters provided the exclusive means of pretrial discovery. Should this be the case? (*Societe Nationale Industrielle Aerospacetiale v. U.S. District Court*, 482 U.S. 522, 1987.)

3. In *Board of Trade of San Francisco v. Swiss Credit Bank*, the court held that the shipper's use of aircraft to transport goods did not strictly comply with the provision of the letter of credit stipulating ocean shipment. Does the manner of shipment make any difference if, in fact, they arrive on time and undamaged? What if the commercial invoices presented to the bank by the seller do not use the same unit of measurement for the goods as used in the letter of credit? The court in *Atari, Inc. v. Harris Trust and Savings Bank*, 599 F. Supp. 592 (N.D. Ill. 1984) said that this was not a basis on which to dishonor the letter of credit. How strict, then, is the doctrine of strict compliance?

4. It is normally important to an exporter that the letter of credit issued in payment for the goods be "irrevocable" so that the buyer/importer cannot cancel the letter after the seller has shipped under the contract. Must the term *irrevocable* be used in the letter of credit to make it so? Will words having the same significance make the letter "irrevocable?" If the letter of credit states that it "shall remain in force for a period of six (6) months," is it an irrevocable letter of credit for that period of time? *Conco, Inc. v. Norwest Bank Mason City*, 767 F.2d 470 (8th Cir. 1985) held that such language made the letter of credit an irrevocable one.

5. Lamb grows tobacco in Kentucky. He sells to Phillip Morris and B.A.T. (defendants) and in so doing competes with foreign tobacco growers. Lamb filed an antitrust action against the defendants, claiming that their subsidiaries in Venezuela agreed to make periodic contributions to the favorite charity of the Venezuelan president's wife, in exchange for price controls on Venezuelan tobacco, elimination of controls on retail cigarette prices in Venezuela, and other concessions. The trial court dismissed the antitrust claim, holding that the act of state doctrine blocked their prosecution. Was the trial court correct? Discuss. (*Lamb v. Phillip Morris, Inc.*, 915 F.2d 1024, 6th Cir. 1990.)

6. In deciding a dispute over the ownership of a trademark originally owned by a company formed in pre-World War II Germany, a New York federal court had to decide whether to give effect to a judgment rendered by a court in post-World War II East Germany. The judge determined that the defendant had not received advanced notice of the opinion rendered by the Supreme Court of East Germany, that defendant had not participated in the proceedings, that East German courts did not have before them much of the essential proof needed to decide the case, and that the East German court's opinion lacked a "reasoned objective approach" and was "thoroughly saturated with a combination of communist propaganda, diatribes against the 'capitalist oriented' decision of the West German courts, and the absence of judicial restraint." Should the East German court's decision be given effect? Discuss. (*Carl Zeiss Stiftung v. VEB Carl Zeiss Jena*, 433 F.2d 686, 2d Cir. 1970.)

7. Geosource, Inc., of Houston, Texas, owned Sensor, a Netherlands business organization. Sensor made a contract, governed by the law of The Netherlands, to deliver 2400 strings of geophones to C.E.P. by September 1982, with the ultimate destination identified as the U.S.S.R. In June 1982, pursuant to the Export Administration Act of 1979, President Reagan prohibited the shipment to the U.S.S.R of equipment manufactured in foreign countries under license from U.S. firms. The purpose of the embargo was to sanction the imposition of martial law in Poland. Sensor notified C.E.P. that as a subsidiary of a U.S. company, it was bound to follow this ban and could therefore not fulfill this contract. C.E.P. sued in District Court at The Hague, Netherlands. To what extent should the court be bound to follow U.S. political policies? (*Compagnie Europeenne Des Petroles v. Sensor Nederland*, 22 ILM 66, District Court at The Hague, 1983.)

8. The possibility of damage is not the only risk that passes to the buyer at ship's rail in a C.I.F. contract. In *Badhwar v. Colorado Fuel & Iron Corp.*, 138 F. Supp. 595 (S.D.N.Y. 1955), goods shipped under a C.I.F. contract from California to Bombay were delayed en route almost six months because of a labor strike on the West Coast, causing damage to the Indian buyer. Neither buyer nor seller was responsible for the delay or the consequent loss to the buyer. The court nonetheless held that the risk of this

loss had passed to the buyer when the goods cleared ship's rail in California. Does fault play no role in allocating the risk of loss? What if a seller is responsible for delay or damage after the goods are unloaded? Will this make any difference in a C.I.F. contract?

9. Nelson was hired in the United States to be a monitoring systems engineer for a hospital in Saudi Arabia. During the course of his duties, Nelson claims that he was detained and tortured by agents of the Saudi government in Saudi Arabia in retaliation for reporting safety violations at the hospital. Nelson sued Saudi Arabia, the hospital where he worked, and Royspec, a corporation owned and controlled by the Saudi government, claiming subject matter jurisdiction under the FSIA. The trial court dismissed for lack of such jurisdiction. Did the trial court err? Discuss. (*Nelson v. Saudi Arabia,* 923 F.2d 1528, 11th Cir. 1991.)

10. Chuidian, a Philippine citizen, has various business interests in California. In 1985, a Philippine government agency (Guarantee Corporation) sued Chuidian, who counterclaimed. The suit was settled out of court with the Philippine National Bank (Bank), a state-owned bank, issuing an irrevocable letter of credit to Chuidian on behalf of the Guarantee Corporation. Soon thereafter, the Philippine government of President Ferdinand Marcos was overthrown and replaced by a government led by Corazon Aquino. The new regime formed a Presidential Commission on Good Government for the purpose of recovering "ill-gotten wealth" accumulated by Marcos and his associates. Daza was appointed a member of the commission. Because the commission suspected that Marcos and Chuidian had entered into a fraudulent settlement of the aforementioned litigation to pay off Chuidian for not revealing certain facts about Marcos's involvement in Chuidian's business enterprises, Daza instructed the Bank not to make payment on the letter of credit issued to Chuidian. Chuidian filed suit against the Bank and added Daza as a defendant. The trial court granted Daza's motion to dismiss on grounds of sovereign immunity. Did the trial court err? Discuss. (*Chuidian v. Philippine Nat'l Bank,* 912 F.2d 1095, 9th Cir. 1990.)

Appendix A

The Uniform Commercial Code
(Selected Sections)

ARTICLE 1/GENERAL PROVISIONS
Part 1/Short Title, Construction, Application and Subject Matter of the Act
§ 1–101
Short Title

This Act shall be known and may be cited as Uniform Commercial Code.

§ 1–102
Purposes; Rules of Construction; Variation by Agreement

(1) This Act shall be liberally construed and applied to promote its underlying purposes and policies.

(2) Underlying purposes and policies of this Act are
(a) to simplify, clarify and modernize the law governing commercial transactions;
(b) to permit the continued expansion of commercial practices through custom, usage and agreement of the parties;
(c) to make uniform the law among the various jurisdictions.

(3) The effect of provisions of this Act may be varied by agreement, except as otherwise provided in this Act and except that the obligations of good faith, diligence, reasonableness and care prescribed by this Act may not be disclaimed by agreement but the parties may by agreement determine the standards by which the performance of such obligations is to be measured if such standards are not manifestly unreasonable.

(4) The presence in certain provisions of this Act of the words "unless otherwise agreed" or words of similar import does not imply that the effect of other provisions may not be varied by agreement under subsection (3).

(5) In this Act unless the context otherwise requires
(a) words in the singular number include the plural, and in the plural include the singular;
(b) words of the masculine gender include the feminine and the neuter, and when the sense so indicates words of the neuter gender may refer to any gender.

§ 1–103
Supplementary General Principles of Law Applicable

Unless displaced by the particular provisions of this Act, the principles of law and equity, including the law merchant and the law relative to capacity to contract, principal and agent, estoppel, fraud, misrepresentation, duress, coercion, mistake, bankruptcy, or other validating or invalidating cause shall supplement its provisions.

. . . .

§ 1–106
Remedies to Be Liberally Administered

(1) The remedies provided by this Act shall be liberally administered to the end that the aggrieved party may be put in as good a position as if the other party had fully performed but neither consequential or special nor penal damages may be had except as specifically provided in this Act or by other rule of law.

(2) Any right or obligation declared by this Act is enforceable by action unless the provision declaring it specifies a different and limited effect.

§ 1–107
Waiver or Renunciation of Claim or Right after Breach

Any claim or right arising out of an alleged breach can be discharged in whole or in part without consideration by a written waiver or renunciation signed and delivered by the aggrieved party.

. . . .

Part 2/General Definitions and Principles of Interpretation
§ 1–201
General Definitions

Subject to additional definitions contained in the subsequent Articles of this Act which are applicable to specific Articles or Parts thereof, and unless the context otherwise requires, in this Act:

(1) "Action" in the sense of a judicial proceeding includes recoupment, counterclaim, set-off, suit in equity and any other proceedings in which rights are determined.

(2) "Aggrieved party" means a party entitled to resort to a remedy.

(3) "Agreement" means the bargain of the parties in fact as found in their language or by implication from other circumstances including course of dealing or usage of trade or course of performance as provided in this Act (Sections 1–205 and 2–208). Whether an agreement has legal consequences is determined by the provisions of this Act, if applicable; otherwise by the law of contracts (Section 1–103). (Compare "Contract".)

(4) "Bank" means any person engaged in the business of banking.

(5) "Bearer" means the person in possession of an instrument, document of title, or certified security payable to bearer or indorsed in blank.

(6) "Bill of lading" means a document evidencing the receipt of goods for shipment issued by a person engaged in the business of transporting or forwarding goods, and includes an airbill. "Airbill" means a document serving for air transportation as a bill of lading does for marine or rail transportation, and includes an air consignment note or air waybill.

(7) "Branch" includes a separately incorporated foreign branch of a bank.

(8) "Burden of establishing" a fact means the burden of persuading the triers of fact that the existence of the fact is more probable than its non-existence.

(9) "Buyer in ordinary course of business" means a person who in good faith and without knowledge that the sale to him is in violation of the ownership rights or security interest of a third party in the goods buys in ordinary course from a person in the business of selling goods of that kind but does not include a pawnbroker. All persons who sell minerals or the like (including oil and gas) at wellhead or minehead shall be deemed to be persons in the business of selling goods of that kind. "Buying" may be for cash or by exchange of other property or on secured or unsecured credit and includes receiving goods or documents of title under a pre-existing contract for sale but does not include a transfer in bulk or as security for or in total or partial satisfaction of a money debt.

(10) "Conspicuous": A term or clause is conspicuous when it is so written that a reasonable person against whom it is to operate ought to have noticed it. A printed heading in capitals (as: NON-NEGOTIABLE BILL OF LADING) is conspicuous. Language in the body of a form is "conspicuous" if it is in larger or other contrasting type or color. But in a telegram any stated term is "conspicuous". Whether a term or clause is "conspicuous" or not is for decision by the court.

(11) "Contract" means the total legal obligation which results from the parties' agreement as affected by this Act and any other applicable rules of law. (Compare "Agreement".)

(12) "Creditor" includes a general creditor, a secured creditor, a lien creditor and any representative of creditors, including an assignee for the benefit of creditors, a trustee in bankruptcy, a receiver in equity and an executor or administrator of an insolvent debtor's or assignor's estate.

(13) "Defendant" includes a person in the position of defendant in a cross-action or counterclaim.

(14) "Delivery" with respect to instruments, documents of title, chattel paper or securities means voluntary transfer of possession.

(15) "Document of title" includes bill of lading, dock warrant, dock receipt, warehouse receipt or order for the delivery of goods, and also any other document which in the regular course of business or financing is treated as adequately evidencing that the person in possession of it is entitled to receive, hold and dispose of the document and the goods it covers. To be a document of title a document must purport to be issued by or addressed to a bailee and purport to cover goods in the bailee's possession which are either identified or are fungible portions of an identified mass.

(16) "Fault" means wrongful act, omission or breach.

(17) "Fungible" with respect to goods or securities means goods or securities of which any unit is, by nature or usage of trade, the equivalent of any other like unit. Goods which are not fungible shall be deemed fungible for the purposes of this Act to the extent that under a particular agreement or document unlike units are treated as equivalents.

(18) "Genuine" means free of forgery or counterfeiting.

(19) "Good faith" means honesty in fact in the conduct or transaction concerned.

(20) "Holder" means a person who is in possession of a document of title or an instrument or a certificated investment security drawn, issued or indorsed to him or to his order or to bearer or in blank.

(21) To "honor" is to pay or to accept and pay, or where a credit so engages to purchase or discount a draft complying with the terms of the credit.

(22) "Insolvency proceedings" includes any assignment for the benefit of creditors or other proceedings intended to liquidate or rehabilitate the estate of the person involved.

(23) A person is "insolvent" who either has ceased to pay his debts in the ordinary course of business or cannot pay his debts as they become due or is insolvent within the meaning of the federal bankruptcy law.

(24) "Money" means a medium of exchange authorized or adopted by a domestic or foreign government as a part of its currency.

(25) A person has "notice" of a fact when
    (a) he has actual knowledge of it; or
    (b) he has received a notice or notification of it; or
    (c) from all the facts and circumstances known to him at the time in question he has reason to know that it exists.

A person "knows" or has "knowledge" of a fact when he has actual knowledge of it. "Discover" or "learn" or a word or phrase of similar import refers to knowledge rather than to reason to know. The time and circumstances under which a notice or notification may cease to be effective are not determined by this Act.

(26) A person "notifies" or "gives" a notice or notification to another by taking such steps as may be reasonably required to inform the other in ordinary course whether or not such other actually comes to know of it. A person "receives" a notice or notification when
    (a) it comes to his attention; or
    (b) it is duly delivered at the place of business through which the contract was made or at any other place held out by him as the place for receipt of such communications.

(27) Notice, knowledge or a notice or notification received by an organization is effective for a particular transaction from the time when it is brought to the attention of the individual conducting that transaction, and in any event from the time when it would have been brought to his attention if the organization had exercised due diligence. An organization exercises due diligence if it maintains reasonable routines for communicating significant information to the person conducting the transaction and there is reasonable compliance with the routines. Due diligence does not require an individual acting for the organization to communicate information unless such communication is part of his regular duties or unless he has reason to know of the transaction and that the transaction would be materially affected by the information.

(28) "Organization" includes a corporation, government or governmental subdivision or agency, business trust, estate, trust, partnership or association, two or more persons having a joint or common interest, or any other legal or commercial entity.

(29) "Party," as distinct from "third party", means a person who has engaged in a transaction or made an agreement within this Act.

(30) "Person" includes an individual or an organization (see Section 1–102).

(31) "Presumption" or "presumed" means that the trier of fact must find the existence of the fact presumed unless and until evidence is introduced which would support a finding of its nonexistence.

(32) "Purchase" includes taking by sale, discount, negotiation, mortgage, pledge, lien, issue or re-issue, gift or any other voluntary transaction creating an interest in property.

(33) "Purchaser" means a person who takes by purchase.

(34) "Remedy" means any remedial right to which an aggrieved party is entitled with or without resort to a tribunal.

(35) "Representative" includes an agent, an officer of a corporation or association, and a trustee, executor or administrator of an estate, or any other person empowered to act for another.

(36) "Rights" includes remedies.

(37) "Security interest" means an interest in personal property or fixtures which secures payment or performance of an obligation. The retention or reservation of title by a seller of goods notwithstanding shipment or delivery to the buyer (Section 2–401) is limited in effect to a reservation of a "security interest". The term also includes any interest of a buyer of accounts or chattel paper which is subject to Article 9. The special property interest of a buyer of goods on identification of those goods to a contract for sale under Section 2–401 is not a "security interest", but a buyer may also acquire a "security interest" by complying with Article 9. Unless a consignment is intended as security, reservation of title thereunder is not a "security interest", but a consignment is in any event subject to the provisions on consignment sales (Section 2–326).

Whether a transaction creates a lease or security interest is determined by the facts of each case; however, a transaction creates a security interest if the consideration the lessee is to pay the lessor for the right to possession and use of the goods is an obligation for the term of the lease not subject to termination by the lessee, and

   (a) the original term of the lease is equal to or greater than the remaining economic life of the goods,

   (b) the lessee is bound to renew the lease for the remaining economic life of the goods or is bound to become the owner of the goods,

   (c) the lessee has an option to renew the lease for the remaining economic life of the goods for no additional con-

sideration or nominal additional consideration upon compliance with the lease agreement, or

   (d) the lessee has an option to become the owner of the goods for no additional consideration or nominal additional consideration upon compliance with the lease agreement.

A transaction does not create a security interest merely because it provides that

   (a) the present value of the consideration the lessee is obligated to pay the lessor for the right to possession and use of the goods is substantially equal to or is greater than the fair market value of the goods at the time the lease is entered into,

   (b) the lessee assumes risk of loss of the goods, or agrees to pay taxes, insurance, filing, recording, or registration fees, or service or maintenance costs with respect to the goods,

   (c) the lessee has an option to renew the lease or to become the owner of the goods,

   (d) the lessee has an option to renew the lease for a fixed rent that is equal to or greater than the reasonably predictable fair market rent for the use of the goods for the term of the renewal at the time the option is to be performed, or

   (e) the lessee has an option to become the owner of the goods for a fixed price that is equal to or greater than the reasonably predictable fair market value of the goods at the time the option is to be performed.

For purposes of this subsection (37):

   (x) Additional consideration is not nominal if (i) when the option to renew the lease is granted to the lessee the rent is stated to be the fair market rent for the use of the goods for the term of the renewal determined at the time the option is to be performed, or (ii) when the option to become the owner of the goods is granted to the lessee the price is stated to be the fair market value of the goods determined at the time the option is to be performed. Additional consideration is nominal if it is less than the lessee's reasonably predictable cost of performing under the lease agreement if the option is not exercised;

   (y) "Reasonably predictable" and "remaining economic life of the goods" are to be determined with reference to the facts and circumstances at the time the transaction is entered into; and

   (z) "Present value" means the amount as of a date certain of one or more sums payable in the future, discounted to the date certain. The discount is determined by the interest rate specified by the parties if the rate is not manifestly unreasonable at the time the transaction is entered into; otherwise, the discount is determined by a commercially reasonable rate that takes into account the facts and circumstances of each case at the time the transaction was entered into.

(38) "Send" in connection with any writing or notice means to deposit in the mail or deliver for transmission by any other usual means of communication with postage or cost of transmission provided for and properly addressed and in the case of an instrument to an address specified thereon or otherwise agreed, or if there be none to any address reasonable under the circumstances. The receipt of any writing or notice within the time at which it would have arrived if properly sent has the effect of a proper sending.

(39) "Signed" includes any symbol executed or adopted by a party with present intention to authenticate a writing.

(40) "Surety" includes guarantor.

(41) "Telegram" includes a message transmitted by radio, teletype, cable, any mechanical method of transmission, or the like.

(42) "Term" means that portion of an agreement which relates to a particular matter.

(43) "Unauthorized" signature or indorsement means one made without actual, implied or apparent authority and includes a forgery.

(44) "Value". Except as otherwise provided with respect to negotiable instruments and bank collections (Sections 3–303, 4–208 and 4–209) a person gives "value" for rights if he acquires them

   (a)   in return for a binding commitment to extend credit or for the extension of immediately available credit whether or not drawn upon and whether or not a chargeback is provided for in the event of difficulties in collection; or

   (b)   as security for or in total or partial satisfaction of a pre-existing claim; or

   (c)   by accepting delivery pursuant to a pre-existing contract for purchase; or

   (d)   generally, in return for any consideration sufficient to support a simple contract.

(45) "Warehouse receipt" means a receipt issued by a person engaged in the business of storing goods for hire.

(46) "Written" or "writing" includes printing, typewriting or any other intentional reduction to tangible form.

Amended in 1962, 1972 and 1977.

§ 1–202
Prima Facie Evidence by Third Party Documents

A document in due form purporting to be a bill of lading, policy or certificate of insurance, official weigher's or inspector's certificate, consular invoice, or any other document authorized or required by the contract to be issued by a third party shall be prima facie evidence of its own authenticity and genuineness and of the facts stated in the document by the third party.

§ 1–203
Obligation of Good Faith

Every contract or duty within this Act imposes an obligation of good faith in its performance or enforcement.

§ 1–204
Time; Reasonable Time; "Seasonably"

(1)   Whenever this Act requires any action to be taken within a reasonable time, any time which is not manifestly unreasonable may be fixed by agreement.

(2)   What is a reasonable time for taking any action depends on the nature, purpose and circumstances of such action.

(3)   An action is taken "seasonably" when it is taken at or within the time agreed or if no time is agreed at or within a reasonable time.

§ 1–205
Course of Dealing and Usage of Trade

(1)   A course of dealing is a sequence of previous conduct between the parties to a particular transaction which is fairly to be regarded as establishing a common basis of understanding for interpreting their expressions and other conduct.

(2)   A usage of trade is any practice or method of dealing having such regularity of observance in a place, vocation or trade as to justify an expectation that it will be observed with respect to the transaction in question. The existence and scope of such a usage are to be proved as facts. If it is established that such a usage is embodied in a written trade code or similar writing the interpretation of the writing is for the court.

(3)   A course of dealing between parties and any usage of trade in the vocation or trade in which they are engaged or of which they are or should be aware give particular meaning to and supplement or qualify terms of an agreement.

(4)   The express terms of an agreement and an applicable course of dealing or usage of trade shall be construed wherever reasonable as consistent with each other; but when such construction is unreasonable express terms control both course of dealing and usage of trade and course of dealing controls usage trade.

(5)   An applicable usage of trade in the place where any part of performance is to occur shall be used in interpreting the agreement as to that part of the performance.

(6)   Evidence of a relevant usage of trade offered by one party is not admissible unless and until he has given the other party such notice as the court finds sufficient to prevent unfair surprise to the latter.

§ 1–206
Statute of Frauds for Kinds of Personal Property
Not Otherwise Covered

(1)   Except in the cases described in subsection (2) of this section a contract for the sale of personal property is not enforceable by way of action or defense beyond five thousand dollars in amount or value of remedy unless there is some writing which indicates that a contract for sale has been made between the parties at a defined or stated price, reasonably identifies the subject matter, and is signed by the party against whom enforcement is sought or by his authorized agent.

(2)   Subsection (1) of this section does not apply to contracts for the sale of goods (Section 2–201) nor of securities (Section 8–319) nor to security agreements (Section 9–203).

§ 1–207
Performance or Acceptance under Reservation of Rights

A party who with explicit reservation of rights performs or promises performance or assents to performance in the manner demanded or offered by the other party does not thereby prejudice the rights reserved. Such words as "without prejudice", "under protest" or the like are sufficient.

§ 1–208
Option to Accelerate at Will

A term providing that one party or his successor in interest may accelerate payment or performance or require collateral or additional collateral "at will" or "when he deems himself insecure" or in words of similar import shall be construed to mean that he shall have power to do so only if he in good faith believes that the prospect of payment or performance is impaired. The burden of establishing lack of good faith is on the party against whom the power has been exercised.

§ 1–209
Subordinated Obligations

An obligation may be issued as subordinated to payment of another obligation of the person obligated, or a creditor may subordinate his right to payment of an obligation by agreement with either the person obligated or another creditor of the person obligated. Such a subordination does not create a security interest as against either the common debtor or a subordinated creditor. This section shall be construed as declaring the law as it existed prior to the enactment of this section and not as modifying it. Added 1966.

Note: *This new section is proposed as an optional provision to make it clear that a subordination agreement does not create a security interest unless so intended.*

ARTICLE 2/SALES
Part 1/Short Title, General Construction and Subject Matter
§ 2–101
Short Title

This Article shall be known and may be cited as Uniform Commercial Code—Sales.

§ 2–102
Scope; Certain Security and Other Transactions Excluded from This Article

Unless the context otherwise requires, this Article applies to transactions in goods; it does not apply to any transaction which although in the form of an unconditional contract to sell or present sale is intended to operate only as a security transaction nor does this Article impair or repeal any statute regulating sales to consumers, farmers or other specified classes of buyers.

§ 2–103
Definitions and Index of Definitions

(1) In this Article unless the context otherwise requires
  (a) "Buyer" means a person who buys or contracts to buy goods.
  (b) "Good faith" in the case of a merchant means honesty in fact and the observance of reasonable commercial standards of fair dealing in the trade.
  (c) "Receipt" of goods means taking physical possession of them.
  (d) "Seller" means a person who sells or contracts to sell goods.

(2) Other definitions applying to this Article or to specified Parts thereof, and the sections in which they appear are:

> "Acceptance". Section 2–606.
> "Banker's credit". Section 2–325.
> "Between merchants". Section 2–104.
> "Cancellation". Section 2–106(4).
> "Commercial unit". Section 2–105.
> "Confirmed credit". Section 2–325.
> "Conforming to contract". Section 2–106.
> "Contract for sale". Section 2–106.
> "Cover". Section 2–712.
> "Entrusting". Section 2–403.
> "Financing agency". Section 2–104.
> "Future goods". Section 2–105.
> "Goods". Section 2–105.
> "Identification". Section 2–501.
> "Installment contract". Section 2–612.
> "Letter of Credit". Section 2–325.
> "Lot". Section 2–105.
> "Merchant". Section 2–104.
> "Overseas". Section 2–323.
> "Person in position of seller". Section 2–707.
> "Present sale". Section 2–106.
> "Sale". Section 2–106.
> "Sale on approval". Section 2–326.
> "Sale or return". Section 2–326.
> "Termination". Section 2–106.

(3) The following definitions in other Articles apply to this Article:

> "Check". Section 3–104.
> "Consignee". Section 7–102.
> "Consignor". Section 7–102.
> "Consumer goods". Section 9–109.
> "Dishonor". Section 3–507.
> "Draft". Section 3–104.

(4) In addition Article 1 contains general definitions and principles of construction and interpretation applicable throughout this Article.

§ 2–104
Definitions: "Merchant"; "Between Merchants"; "Financing Agency"

(1) "Merchant" means a person who deals in goods of the kind or otherwise by his occupation holds himself out as having knowledge or skill peculiar to the practices or goods involved in the transaction or to whom such knowledge or skill may be attributed by his employment of an agent or broker or other intermediary who by his occupation holds himself out as having such knowledge or skill.

(2) "Financing agency" means a bank, finance company or other person who in the ordinary course of business makes advances against goods or documents of title or who by arrangement with either the seller or the buyer intervenes in ordinary course to make or collect payment due or claimed under the contract for sale, as by purchasing or paying the seller's draft or making advances against it or by merely taking it for collection whether or not documents of title accompany the draft. "Financing agency" includes also a bank or other person who similarly intervenes

between persons who are in the position of seller and buyer in respect to the goods (Section 2–707).

(3) "Between merchants" means in any transaction with respect to which both parties are chargeable with the knowledge or skill of merchants.

§ 2–105
Definitions: Transferability; "Goods"; "Future" Goods; "Lot"; "Commercial Unit"

(1) "Goods" means all things (including specially manufactured goods) which are movable at the time of identification to the contract for sale other than the money in which the price is to be paid, investment securities (Article 8) and things in action. "Goods" also includes the unborn young of animals and growing crops and other identified things attached to realty as described in the section on goods to be severed from realty (Section 2–107).

(2) Goods must be both existing and identified before any interest in them can pass. Goods which are not both existing and identified are "future" goods. A purported present sale of future goods or of any interest therein operates as a contract to sell.

(3) There may be a sale of a part interest in existing identified goods.

(4) An undivided share in an identified bulk of fungible goods is sufficiently identified to be sold although the quantity of the bulk is not determined. Any agreed proportion of such a bulk or any quantity thereof agreed upon by number, weight or other measure may to the extent of the seller's interest in the bulk be sold to the buyer who then becomes an owner in common.

(5) "Lot" means a parcel or a single article which is the subject matter of a separate sale or delivery, whether or not it is sufficient to perform the contract.

(6) "Commercial unit" means such a unit of goods as by commercial usage is a single whole for purposes of sale and division of which materially impairs its character or value on the market or in use. A commercial unit may be a single article (as a machine) or a set of articles (as a suite of furniture or an assortment of sizes) or a quantity (as a bale, gross, or carload) or any other unit treated in use or in the relevant market as a single whole.

§ 2–106
Definitions: "Contract"; "Agreement"; "Contract for Sale"; "Sale"; "Present Sale"; "Conforming" to Contract; "Termination"; "Cancellation"

(1) In this Article unless the context otherwise requires "contract" and "agreement" are limited to those relating to the present or future sale of goods. "Contract for sale" includes both a present sale of goods and a contract to sell goods at a future time. A "sale" consists in the passing of title from the seller to the buyer for a price (Section 2–401). A "present sale" means a sale which is accomplished by the making of the contract.

(2) Goods or conduct including any part of a performance are "conforming" or conform to the contract when they are in accordance with the obligations under the contract.

(3) "Termination" occurs when either party pursuant to a power created by agreement or law puts an end to the contract otherwise

than for its breach. On "termination" all obligations which are still executory on both sides are discharged but any right based on prior breach or performance survives.

(4) "Cancellation" occurs when either party puts an end to the contract for breach by the other and its effect is the same as that of "termination" except that the cancelling party also retains any remedy for breach of the whole contract or any unperformed balance.

§ 2–107
Goods to Be Severed from Realty: Recording

(1) A contract for the sale of minerals or the like (including oil and gas) or a structure or its materials to be removed from realty is a contract for the sale of goods within this Article if they are to be severed by the seller but until severance a purported present sale thereof which is not effective as a transfer of an interest in land is effective only as a contract to sell.

(2) A contract for the sale apart from the land of growing crops or other things attached to realty and capable of severance without material harm thereto but not described in subsection (1) or of timber to be cut is a contract for the sale of goods within this Article whether the subject matter is to be severed by the buyer or by the seller even though it forms part of the realty at the time of contracting, and the parties can by identification effect a present sale before severance.

(3) The provisions of this section are subject to any third party rights provided by the law relating to realty records, and the contract for sale may be executed and recorded as a document transferring an interest in land and shall then constitute notice to third parties of the buyer's rights under the contract for sale.

Part 2/Form, Formation and Readjustment of Contract
§ 2–201
Formal Requirements; Statute of Frauds

(1) Except as otherwise provided in this section a contract for the sale of goods for the price of $500 or more is not enforceable by way of action or defense unless there is some writing sufficient to indicate that a contract for sale has been made between the parties and signed by the party against whom enforcement is sought or by his authorized agent or broker. A writing is not insufficient because it omits or incorrectly states a term agreed upon but the contract is not enforceable under this paragraph beyond the quantity of goods shown in such writing.

(2) Between merchants if within a reasonable time a writing in confirmation of the contract and sufficient against the sender is received and the party receiving it has reason to know its contents, it satisfies the requirements of subsection (1) against such party unless written notice of objection to its contents is given within ten days after it is received.

(3) A contract which does not satisfy the requirements of subsection (1) but which is valid in other respects is enforceable

    (a) if the goods are to be specially manufactured for the buyer and are not suitable for sale to others in the ordinary course of the seller's business and the seller, before notice of repudiation is received and under circumstances which reasonably indicate that the goods are for the buyer, has made either a substantial beginning of their manufacture or commitments for their procurement; or

(b) if the party against whom enforcement is sought admits in his pleading, testimony or otherwise in court that a contract for sale was made, but the contract is not enforceable under this provision beyond the quantity of goods admitted; or

(c) with respect to goods for which payment has been made and accepted or which have been received and accepted (Section 2–606).

§ 2–202
Final Written Expression: Parol or Extrinsic Evidence

Terms with respect to which the confirmatory memoranda of the parties agree or which are otherwise set forth in a writing intended by the parties as a final expression of their agreement with respect to such terms as are included therein may not be contradicted by evidence of any prior agreement or of a contemporaneous oral agreement but may be explained or supplemented

(a) by course of dealing or usage of trade (Section 1–205) or by course of performance (Section 2–208); and

(b) by evidence of consistent additional terms unless the court finds the writing to have been intended also as a complete and exclusive statement of the terms of the agreement.

§ 2–203
Seals Inoperative

The affixing of a seal to a writing evidencing a contract for sale or an offer to buy or sell goods does not constitute the writing a sealed instrument and the law with respect to sealed instruments does not apply to such a contract or offer.

§ 2–204
Formation in General

(1) A contract for sale of goods may be made in any manner sufficient to show agreement, including conduct by both parties which recognizes the existence of such a contract.

(2) An agreement sufficient to constitute a contract for sale may be found even though the moment of its making is undetermined.

(3) Even though one or more terms are left open a contract for sale does not fail for indefiniteness if the parties have intended to make a contract and there is a reasonably certain basis for giving an appropriate remedy.

§ 2–205
Firm Offers

An offer by a merchant to buy or sell goods in a signed writing which by its terms gives assurance that it will be held open is not revocable, for lack of consideration, during the time stated or if no time is stated for a reasonable time, but in no event may such period of irrevocability exceed three months; but any such term of assurance on a form supplied by the offeree must be separately signed by the offeror.

§ 2–206
Offer and Acceptance Formation of Contract

(1) Unless otherwise unambiguously indicated by the language or circumstances

(a) an offer to make a contract shall be construed as inviting acceptance in any manner and by any medium reasonable in the circumstances;

(b) an order or other offer to buy goods for prompt or current shipment shall be construed as inviting acceptance either by a prompt promise to ship or by the prompt or current shipment of conforming or nonconforming goods, but such a shipment of nonconforming goods does not constitute an acceptance if the seller seasonably notifies the buyer that the shipment is offered only as an accommodation to the buyer.

(2) Where the beginning of a requested performance is a reasonable mode of acceptance an offeror who is not notified of acceptance within a reasonable time may treat the offer as having lapsed before acceptance.

§ 2–207
Additional Terms in Acceptance or Confirmation

(1) A definite and seasonable expression of acceptance or a written confirmation which is sent within a reasonable time operates as an acceptance even though it states terms additional to or different from those offered or agreed upon, unless acceptance is expressly made conditional on assent to the additional or different terms.

(2) The additional terms are to be construed as proposals for addition to the contract. Between merchants such terms become part of the contract unless:

(a) the offer expressly limits acceptance to the terms of the offer;

(b) they materially alter it; or

(c) notification of objection to them has already been given or is given within a reasonable time after notice of them is received.

(3) Conduct by both parties which recognizes the existence of a contract is sufficient to establish a contract for sale although the writings of the parties do not otherwise establish a contract. In such case the terms of the particular contract consist of those terms on which the writings of the parties agree, together with any supplementary terms incorporated under any other provisions of this Act.

§ 2–208
Course of Performance or Practical Construction

(1) Where the contract for sale involves repeated occasions for performance by either party with knowledge of the nature of the performance and opportunity for objection to it by the other, any course of performance accepted or acquiesced in without objection shall be relevant to determine the meaning of the agreement.

(2) The express terms of the agreement and any such course of performance, as well as any course of dealing and usage of trade, shall be construed whenever reasonable as consistent with each other; but when such construction is unreasonable, express terms shall control course of performance and course of performance shall control both course of dealing and usage of trade (Section 1–205).

(3) Subject to the provisions of the next section on modification and waiver, such course of performance shall be relevant to show a waiver or modification of any term inconsistent with such course of performance.

§ 2–209
Modification, Rescission and Waiver

(1) An agreement modifying a contract within this Article needs no consideration to be binding.

(2) A signed agreement which excludes modification or rescission except by a signed writing cannot be otherwise modified or rescinded, but except as between merchants such a requirement on a form supplied by the merchant must be separately signed by the other party.

(3) The requirements of the statute of frauds section of this Article (Section 2–201) must be satisfied if the contract as modified is within its provisions.

(4) Although an attempt at modification or rescission does not satisfy the requirements of subsection (2) or (3) it can operate as a waiver.

(5) A party who has made a waiver affecting an executory portion of the contract may retract the waiver by reasonable notification received by the other party that strict performance will be required of any term waived, unless the retraction would be unjust in view of a material change of position in reliance on the waiver.

§ 2–210
Delegation of Performance; Assignment of Rights

(1) A party may perform his duty through a delegate unless otherwise agreed or unless the other party has a substantial interest in having his original promisor perform or control the acts required by the contract. No delegation of performance relieves the party delegating of any duty to perform or any liability for breach.

(2) Unless otherwise agreed all rights of either seller or buyer can be assigned except where the assignment would materially change the duty of the other party, or increase materially the burden or risk imposed on him by his contract, or impair materially his chance of obtaining return performance. A right to damages for breach of the whole contract or a right arising out of the assignor's due performance of his entire obligation can be assigned despite agreement otherwise.

(3) Unless the circumstances indicate the contrary a prohibition of assignment of "the contract" is to be construed as barring only the delegation to the assignee of the assignor's performance.

(4) An assignment of "the contract" or of "all my rights under the contract" or an assignment in similar general terms is an assignment of rights and unless the language or the circumstances (as in an assignment for security) indicate the contrary, it is a delegation of performance of the duties of the assignor and its acceptance by the assignee constitutes a promise by him to perform those duties. This promise is enforceable by either the assignor or the other party to the original contract.

(5) The other party may treat any assignment which delegates performance as creating reasonable grounds for insecurity and may without prejudice to his rights against the assignor demand assurances from the assignee (Section 2–609).

Part 3/General Obligation and Construction of Contract
§ 2–301
General Obligations of Parties

The obligation of the seller is to transfer and deliver and that of the buyer is to accept and pay in accordance with the contract.

§ 2–302
Unconscionable Contract or Clause

(1) If the court as a matter of law finds the contract or any clause of the contract to have been unconscionable at the time it was made the court may refuse to enforce the contract, or it may enforce the remainder of the contract without the unconscionable clause, or it may so limit the application of any unconscionable clause as to avoid any unconscionable result.

(2) When it is claimed or appears to the court that the contract or any clause thereof may be unconscionable the parties shall be afforded a reasonable opportunity to present evidence as to its commercial setting, purpose and effect to aid the court in making the determination.

§ 2–303
Allocations or Division of Risks

Where this Article allocates a risk or a burden as between the parties "unless otherwise agreed", the agreement may not only shift the allocation but may also divide the risk or burden.

§ 2–304
Price Payable in Money, Goods, Realty, or Otherwise

(1) The price can be made payable in money or otherwise. If it is payable in whole or in part in goods each party is a seller of the goods which he is to transfer.

(2) Even though all or part of the price is payable in an interest in realty the transfer of the goods and the seller's obligations with reference to them are subject to this Article, but not the transfer of the interest in realty or the transferor's obligations in connection therewith.

§ 2–305
Open Price Term

(1) The parties if they so intend can conclude a contract for sale even though the price is not settled. In such a case the price is a reasonable price at the time for delivery if
    (a) nothing is said as to price; or
    (b) the price is left to be agreed by the parties and they fail to agree; or
    (c) the price is to be fixed in terms of some agreed market or other standard as set or recorded by a third person or agency and it is not so set or recorded.

(2) A price to be fixed by the seller or by the buyer means a price for him to fix in good faith.

(3) When a price left to be fixed otherwise than by agreement of the parties fails to be fixed through fault of one party the other may at his option treat the contract as cancelled or himself fix a reasonable price.

(4) Where, however, the parties intend not to be bound unless the price be fixed or agreed and it is not fixed or agreed there is no contract. In such a case the buyer must return any goods already received or if unable so to do must pay their reasonable value at the time of delivery and the seller must return any portion of the price paid on account.

§ 2–306
Output, Requirements and Exclusive Dealings

(1) A term which measures the quantity by the output of the seller or the requirements of the buyer means such actual output or requirements as may occur in good faith, except that no quantity unreasonably disproportionate to any stated estimate or in the absence of a stated estimate to any normal or otherwise comparable prior output or requirements may be tendered or demanded.

(2) A lawful agreement by either the seller or the buyer for exclusive dealing in the kind of goods concerned imposes unless otherwise agreed an obligation by the seller to use best efforts to supply the goods and by the buyer to use best efforts to promote their sale.

§ 2–307
Delivery in Single Lot or Several Lots

Unless otherwise agreed all goods called for by a contract for sale must be tendered in a single delivery and payment is due only on such tender but where the circumstances give either party the right to make or demand delivery in lots the price if it can be apportioned may be demanded for each lot.

§ 2–308
Absence of Specified Place for Delivery

Unless otherwise agreed
    (a) the place for delivery of goods is the seller's place of business or if he has none his residence; but
    (b) in a contract for sale of identified goods which to the knowledge of the parties at the time of contracting are in some other place, that place is the place for their delivery; and
    (c) documents of title may be delivered through customary banking channels.

§ 2–309
Absence of Specific Time Provisions; Notice of Termination

(1) The time for shipment or delivery or any other action under a contract if not provided in this Article or agreed upon shall be a reasonable time.

(2) Where the contract provides for successive performances but is indefinite in duration it is valid for a reasonable time but unless otherwise agreed may be terminated at any time by either party.

(3) Termination of a contract by one party except on the happening of an agreed event requires that reasonable notification be received by the other party and an agreement dispensing with notification is invalid if its operation would be unconscionable.

§ 2–310
Open Time for Payment or Running of Credit; Authority to Ship under Reservation

Unless otherwise agreed
    (a) payment is due at the time and place at which the buyer is to receive the goods even though the place of shipment is the place of delivery; and
    (b) if the seller is authorized to send the goods he may ship them under reservation, and may tender the documents of title, but the buyer may inspect the goods after their arrival before payment is due unless such inspection is inconsistent with the terms of the contract (Section 2–513); and
    (c) if delivery is authorized and made by way of documents of title otherwise than by subsection (b) then payment is due at the time and place at which the buyer is to receive the documents regardless of where the goods are to be received; and
    (d) where the seller is required or authorized to ship the goods on credit the credit period runs from the time of shipment but post-dating the invoice or delaying its dispatch will correspondingly delay the starting of the credit period.

§ 2–311
Options and Cooperation Respecting Performance

(1) An agreement for sale which is otherwise sufficiently definite (subsection (3) of Section 2–204) to be a contract is not made invalid by the fact that it leaves particulars of performance to be specified by one of the parties. Any such specification must be made in good faith and within limits set by commercial reasonableness.

(2) Unless otherwise agreed specifications relating to assortment of the goods are at the buyer's option and except as otherwise provided in subsections (1)(c) and (3) of Section 2–319 specifications or arrangements relating to shipment are at the seller's option.

(3) Where such specification would materially affect the other party's performance but is not seasonably made or where one party's cooperation is necessary to the agreed performance of the other but is not seasonably forthcoming, the other party in addition to all other remedies
    (a) is excused for any resulting delay in his own performance; and
    (b) may also either proceed to perform in any reasonable manner or after the time for a material part of his own performance treat the failure to specify or to cooperate as a breach by failure to deliver or accept the goods.

§ 2–312
Warranty of Title and against Infringement; Buyer's Obligation against Infringement

(1) Subject to subsection (2) there is in a contract for sale a warranty by the seller that

(a) the title conveyed shall be good, and its transfer rightful; and

(b) the goods shall be delivered free from any security interest or other lien or encumbrance of which the buyer at the time of contracting has no knowledge.

(2) A warranty under subsection (1) will be excluded or modified only by specific language or by circumstances which give the buyer reason to know that the person selling does not claim title in himself or that he is purporting to sell only such right or title as he or a third person may have.

(3) Unless otherwise agreed a seller who is a merchant regularly dealing in goods of the kind warrants that the goods shall be delivered free of the rightful claim of any third person by way of infringement or the like but a buyer who furnishes specifications to the seller must hold the seller harmless against any such claim which arises out of compliance with the specifications.

§ 2–313
Express Warranties by Affirmation, Promise, Description, Sample

(1) Express warranties by the seller are created as follows:

(a) Any affirmation of fact or promise made by the seller to the buyer which relates to the goods and becomes part of the basis of the bargain creates an express warranty that the goods shall conform to the affirmation or promise.

(b) Any description of the goods which is made part of the basis of the bargain creates an express warranty that the goods shall conform to the description.

(c) Any sample or model which is made part of the basis of the bargain creates an express warranty that the whole of the goods shall conform to the sample or model.

(2) It is not necessary to the creation of an express warranty that the seller use formal words such as "warrant" or "guarantee" or that he have a specific intention to make a warranty, but an affirmation merely of the value of the goods or a statement purporting to be merely the seller's opinion or commendation of the goods does not create a warranty.

§ 2–314
Implied Warranty: Merchantability; Usage of Trade

(1) Unless excluded or modified (Section 2–316), a warranty that the goods shall be merchantable is implied in a contract for their sale if the seller is a merchant with respect to goods of that kind. Under this section the serving for value of food or drink to be consumed either on the premises or elsewhere is a sale.

(2) Goods to be merchantable must be at least such as

(a) pass without objection in the trade under the contract description; and

(b) in the case of fungible goods, are of fair average quality within the description; and

(c) are fit for the ordinary purposes for which such goods are used; and

(d) run, within the variations permitted by the agreement, of even kind, quality and quantity within each unit and among all units involved; and

(e) are adequately contained, packaged, and labeled as the agreement may require; and

(f) conform to the promises or affirmations of fact made on the container or label if any.

(3) Unless excluded or modified (Section 2–316) other implied warranties may arise from course of dealing or usage of trade.

§ 2–315
Implied Warranty: Fitness for Particular Purpose

Where the seller at the time of contracting has reason to know any particular purpose for which the goods are required and that the buyer is relying on the seller's skill or judgment to select or furnish suitable goods, there is unless excluded or modified under the next section an implied warranty that the goods shall be fit for such purpose.

§ 2–316
Exclusion or Modification of Warranties

(1) Words or conduct relevant to the creation of an express warranty and words or conduct tending to negate or limit warranty shall be construed wherever reasonable as consistent with each other; but subject to the provisions of this Article on parol or extrinsic evidence (Section 2–202) negation or limitation is inoperative to the extent that such construction is unreasonable.

(2) Subject to subsection (3), to exclude or modify the implied warranty of merchantability or any part of it the language must mention merchantability and in case of a writing must be conspicuous, and to exclude or modify any implied warranty of fitness the exclusion must be by a writing and conspicuous. Language to exclude all implied warranties of fitness is sufficient if it states, for example, that "There are no warranties which extend beyond the description on the face hereof."

(3) Notwithstanding subsection (2)

(a) unless the circumstances indicate otherwise, all implied warranties are excluded by expressions like "as is", "with all faults" or other language which in common understanding calls the buyer's attention to the exclusion of warranties and makes plain that there is no implied warranty; and

(b) when the buyer before entering into the contract has examined the goods or the sample or model as fully as he desired or has refused to examine the goods there is no implied warranty with regard to defects which an examination ought in the circumstances to have revealed to him; and

(c) an implied warranty can also be excluded or modified by course of dealing or course of performance or usage of trade.

(4) Remedies for breach of warranty can be limited in accordance with the provisions of this Article on liquidation or limitation of damages and on contractual modification of remedy (Sections 2–718 and 2–719).

§ 2–317
Cumulation and Conflict of Warranties Express or Implied

Warranties whether express or implied shall be construed as consistent with each other and as cumulative, but if such construction is unreasonable the intention of the parties shall determine which warranty is dominant. In ascertaining that intention the following rules apply:

(a) Exact or technical specifications displace an inconsistent sample or model or general language of description.

(b) A sample from an existing bulk displaces inconsistent general language of description.

(c) Express warranties displace inconsistent implied warranties other than an implied warranty of fitness for a particular purpose.

§ 2–318
Third Party Beneficiaries of Warranties Express or Implied

Note: *If this Act is introduced in the Congress of the United States this section should be omitted. (States to select one alternative.)*

Alternative A

A seller's warranty whether express or implied extends to any natural person who is in the family or household of his buyer or who is a guest in his home if it is reasonable to expect that such person may use, consume or be affected by the goods and who is injured in person by breach of the warranty. A seller may not exclude or limit the operation of this section.

Alternative B

A seller's warranty whether express or implied extends to any natural person who may reasonably be expected to use, consume or be affected by the goods and who is injured in person by breach of the warranty. A seller may not exclude or limit the operation of this section.

Alternative C

A seller's warranty whether express or implied extends to any person who may reasonably be expected to use, consume or be affected by the goods and who is injured by breach of the warranty. A seller may not exclude or limit the operation of this section with respect to injury to the person of an individual to whom the warranty extends. As amended 1966.

§ 2–319
F.O.B. and F.A.S. Terms

(1) Unless otherwise agreed the term F.O.B. (which means "free on board") at a named place, even though used only in connection with the stated price, is a delivery term under which

(a) when the term is F.O.B. the place of shipment, the seller must at that place ship the goods in the manner provided in this Article (Section 2–504) and bear the expense and risk of putting them into the possession of the carrier; or

(b) when the term is F.O.B. the place of destination, the seller must at his own expense and risk transport the goods to that place and there tender delivery of them in the manner provided in this Article (Section 2–503);

(c) when under either (a) or (b) the term is also F.O.B. vessel, car or other vehicle, the seller must in addition at his own expense and risk load the goods on board. If the term is F.O.B. vessel the buyer must name the vessel and in an appropriate case the seller must comply with the provisions of this Article on the form of bill of lading (Section 2–323).

(2) Unless otherwise agreed the term F.A.S. vessel (which means "free alongside") at a named port, even though used only in connection with the stated price, is a delivery term under which the seller must

(a) at his own expense and risk deliver the goods alongside the vessel in the manner usual in that port or on a dock designated and provided by the buyer; and

(b) obtain and tender a receipt for the goods in exchange for which the carrier is under a duty to issue a bill of lading.

(3) Unless otherwise agreed in any case falling within subsection (1)(a) or (c) or subsection (2) the buyer must seasonably give any needed instructions for making delivery, including when the term is F.A.S. or F.O.B. the loading berth of the vessel and in an appropriate case its name and sailing date. The seller may treat the failure of needed instructions as a failure of cooperation under this Article (Section 2–311). He may also at his option move the goods in any reasonable manner preparatory to delivery or shipment.

(4) Under the term F.O.B. vessel or F.A.S. unless otherwise agreed the buyer must make payment against tender of the required documents and the seller may not tender nor the buyer demand delivery of the goods in substitution for the documents.

§ 2–320
C.I.F. and C. & F. Terms

(1) The term C.I.F. means that the price includes in a lump sum the cost of the goods and the insurance and freight to the named destination. The term C. & F. or C.F. means that the price so includes cost and freight to the named destination.

(2) Unless otherwise agreed and even though used only in connection with the stated price and destination, the term C.I.F. destination or its equivalent requires the seller at his own expense and risk to

(a) put the goods into the possession of a carrier at the port for shipment and obtain a negotiable bill or bills of lading covering the entire transportation to the named destination; and

(b) load the goods and obtain a receipt from the carrier (which may be contained in the bill of lading) showing that the freight has been paid or provided for; and

(c) obtain a policy or certificate of insurance, including any war risk insurance, of a kind and on terms then current at the port of shipment in the usual amount, in the currency of the contract, shown to cover the same goods covered by the bill of lading and providing for payment of loss to the order of the buyer or for the account of whom it may concern; but the seller may add to the price the amount of the premium for any such war risk insurance; and

(d) prepare an invoice of the goods and procure any other documents required to effect shipment or to comply with the contract; and

(e) forward and tender with commercial promptness all the documents in due form and with any indorsement necessary to perfect the buyer's rights.

(3) Unless otherwise agreed the term C. & F. or its equivalent has the same effect and imposes upon the seller the same obligations and risks as a C.I.F. term except the obligation as to insurance.

(4) Under the term C.I.F. or C. & F. unless otherwise agreed the buyer must make payment against tender of the required documents and the seller may not tender nor the buyer demand delivery of the goods in substitution for the documents.

§ 2–321
C.I.F. or C. & F.: "Net Landed Weights"; "Payment on Arrival"; Warranty of Condition on Arrival

Under a contract containing a term C.I.F. or C. & F.

(1) Where the price is based on or is to be adjusted according to "net landed weights", "delivered weights", "out turn" quantity or quality or the like, unless otherwise agreed the seller must reasonably estimate the price. The payment due on tender of the documents called for by the contract is the amount so estimated, but after final adjustment of the price a settlement must be made with commercial promptness.

(2) An agreement described in subsection (1) or any warranty of quality or condition of the goods on arrival places upon the seller the risk of ordinary deterioration, shrinkage and the like in transportation but has no effect on the place or time of identification to the contract for sale or delivery or on the passing of the risk of loss.

(3) Unless otherwise agreed where the contract provides for payment on or after arrival of the goods the seller must before payment allow such preliminary inspection as is feasible; but if the goods are lost delivery of the documents and payment are due when the goods should have arrived.

§ 2–322
Delivery "Ex-Ship"

(1) Unless otherwise agreed a term for delivery of goods "ex-ship" (which means from the carrying vessel) or in equivalent language is not restricted to a particular ship and requires delivery from a ship which has reached a place at the named port of destination where goods of the kind are usually discharged.

(2) Under such a term unless otherwise agreed
    (a) the seller must discharge all liens arising out of the carriage and furnish the buyer with a direction which puts the carrier under a duty to deliver the goods; and
    (b) the risk of loss does not pass to the buyer until the goods leave the ship's tackle or are otherwise properly unloaded.

§ 2–323
Form of Bill of Lading Required in Overseas Shipment; "Overseas"

(1) Where the contract contemplates overseas shipment and contains a term C.I.F. or C. & F. or F.O.B. vessel, the seller unless otherwise agreed must obtain a negotiable bill of lading stating that the goods have been loaded on board or, in the case of a term C.I.F. or C. & F., received for shipment.

(2) Where in a case within subsection (1) a bill of lading has been issued in a set of parts, unless otherwise agreed if the documents are not to be sent from abroad the buyer may demand tender of the full set; otherwise only one part of the bill of lading need be tendered. Even if the agreement expressly requires a full set
    (a) due tender of a single part is acceptable within the provisions of this Article on cure of improper delivery (subsection (1) of Section 2–508); and
    (b) even though the full set is demanded, if the documents are sent from abroad the person tendering an incomplete set may nevertheless require payment upon furnishing an indemnity which the buyer in good faith deems adequate.

(3) A shipment by water or by air or a contract contemplating such shipment is "overseas" insofar as by usage of trade or agreement it is subject to the commercial, financing or shipping practices characteristic of international deep water commerce.

§ 2–324
"No Arrival, No Sale" Term

Under a term "no arrival, no sale" or terms of like meaning, unless otherwise agreed,
    (a) the seller must properly ship conforming goods and if they arrive by any means he must tender them on arrival but he assumes no obligation that the goods will arrive unless he has caused the non-arrival; and
    (b) where without fault of the seller the goods are in part lost or have so deteriorated as no longer to conform to the contract or arrive after the contract time, the buyer may proceed as if there had been casualty to identified goods (Section 2–613).

§ 2–325
"Letter of Credit" Term; "Confirmed Credit"

(1) Failure of the buyer seasonably to furnish an agreed letter of credit is a breach of the contract for sale.

(2) The delivery to seller of a proper letter of credit suspends the buyer's obligation to pay. If the letter of credit is dishonored, the seller may on seasonable notification to the buyer require payment directly from him.

(3) Unless otherwise agreed the term "letter of credit" or "banker's credit" in a contract for sale means an irrevocable credit issued by a financing agency of good repute and, where the shipment is overseas, of good international repute. The term "confirmed credit" means that the credit must also carry the direct obligation of such an agency which does business in the seller's financial market.

§ 2–326
Sale on Approval and Sale or Return; Consignment Sales and Rights of Creditors

(1) Unless otherwise agreed, if delivered goods may be returned by the buyer even though they conform to the contract, the transaction is
    (a) a "sale on approval" if the goods are delivered primarily for use, and
    (b) a "sale or return" if the goods are delivered primarily for resale.

(2) Except as provided in subsection (3), goods held on approval are not subject to the claims of the buyer's creditors until acceptance; goods held on sale or return are subject to such claims while in the buyer's possession.

(3) Where goods are delivered to a person for sale and such person maintains a place of business at which he deals in goods of the kind involved, under a name other than the name of the person making delivery, then with respect to claims of creditors of the person conducting the business the goods are deemed to be on sale or return. The provisions of this subsection are applicable even though an agreement purports to reserve title to the person making delivery until payment or resale or uses such words as "on consignment" or "on memorandum". However, this subsection is not applicable if the person making delivery

(a)   complies with an applicable law providing for a consignor's interest or the like to be evidenced by a sign, or

(b)   establishes that the person conducting the business is generally known by his creditors to be substantially engaged in selling the goods of others, or

(c)   complies with the filing provisions of the Article on Secured Transactions (Article 9).

(4) Any "or return" term of a contract for sale is to be treated as a separate contract for sale within the statute of frauds section of this Article (Section 2–201) and as contradicting the sale aspect of the contract within the provisions of this Article on parol or extrinsic evidence (Section 2–202).

§ 2–327
Special Incidents of Sale on Approval and Sale or Return

(1) Under a sale on approval unless otherwise agreed

(a)   although the goods are identified to the contract the risk of loss and the title do not pass to the buyer until acceptance; and

(b)   use of the goods consistent with the purpose of trial is not acceptance but failure seasonably to notify the seller of election to return the goods is acceptance, and if the goods conform to the contract acceptance of any part is acceptance of the whole; and

(c)   after due notification of election to return, the return is at the seller's risk and expense but a merchant buyer must follow any reasonable instructions.

(2) Under a sale or return unless otherwise agreed

(a)   the option to return extends to the whole or any commercial unit of the goods while in substantially their original condition, but must be exercised seasonably; and

(b)   the return is at the buyer's risk and expense.

§ 2–328
Sale by Auction

(1) In a sale by auction if goods are put up in lots each lot is the subject of a separate sale.

(2) A sale by auction is complete when the auctioneer so announces by the fall of the hammer or in other customary manner. Where a bid is made while the hammer is falling in acceptance of a prior bid the auctioneer may in his discretion reopen the bidding or declare the goods sold under the bid on which the hammer was falling.

(3) Such a sale is with reserve unless the goods are in explicit terms put up without reserve. In an auction with reserve the auctioneer may withdraw the goods at any time until he announces completion of the sale. In an auction without reserve, after the auctioneer calls for bids on an article or lot, that article or lot cannot be withdrawn unless no bid is made within a reasonable time. In either case a bidder may retract his bid until the auctioneer's announcement of completion of the sale, but a bidder's retraction does not revive any previous bid.

(4) If the auctioneer knowingly receives a bid on the seller's behalf or the seller makes or procures such a bid, and notice has not been given that liberty for such bidding is reserved, the buyer may at his option avoid the sale or take the goods at the price of the last good faith bid prior to the completion of the sale. This subsection shall not apply to any bid at a forced sale.

Part 4/Title, Creditors and Good Faith Purchasers
§ 2–401
Passing of Title; Reservation for Security; Limited Application of This Section

Each provision of this Article with regard to the rights, obligations and remedies of the seller, the buyer, purchasers or other third parties applies irrespective of title to the goods except where the provision refers to such title. Insofar as situations are not covered by the other provisions of this Article and matters concerning title become material the following rules apply:

(1) Title to goods cannot pass under a contract for sale prior to their identification to the contract (Section 2–501), and unless otherwise explicitly agreed the buyer acquires by their identification a special property as limited by this Act. Any retention or reservation by the seller of the title (property) in goods shipped or delivered to the buyer is limited in effect to a reservation of a security interest. Subject to these provisions and to the provisions of the Article on Secured Transactions (Article 9), title to goods passes from the seller to the buyer in any manner and on any conditions explicitly agreed on by the parties.

(2) Unless otherwise explicitly agreed title passes to the buyer at the time and place at which the seller completes his performance with reference to the physical delivery of the goods, despite any reservation of a security interest and even though a document of title is to be delivered at a different time or place; and in particular and despite any reservation of a security interest by the bill of lading

(a)   if the contract requires or authorizes the seller to send the goods to the buyer but does not require him to deliver them at destination, title passes to the buyer at the time and place of shipment; but

(b)   if the contract requires delivery at destination, title passes on tender there.

(3) Unless otherwise explicitly agreed where delivery is to be made without moving the goods,

(a)   if the seller is to deliver a document of title, title passes at the time when and the place where he delivers such documents; or

(b)   if the goods are at the time of contracting already identified and no documents are to be delivered, title passes at the time and place of contracting.

(4) A rejection or other refusal by the buyer to receive or retain the goods, whether or not justified, or a justified revocation of acceptance revests title to the goods in the seller. Such revesting occurs by operation of law and is not a "sale".

§ 2–402
Rights of Seller's Creditors against Sold Goods

(1) Except as provided in subsections (2) and (3), rights of unsecured creditors of the seller with respect to goods which have been identified to a contract for sale are subject to the buyer's rights to recover the goods under this Article (Sections 2–502 and 2–716).

(2) A creditor of the seller may treat a sale or an identification of goods to a contract for sale as void if as against him a retention of possession by the seller is fraudulent under any rule of law of the state where the goods are situated, except that retention of possession in good faith and current course of trade by a merchant-seller for a commercially reasonable time after a sale or identification is not fraudulent.

(3) Nothing in this Article shall be deemed to impair the rights of creditors of the seller
    (a) under the provisions of the Article on Secured Transactions (Article 9); or
    (b) where identification to the contract or delivery is made not in current course of trade but in satisfaction of or as security for a pre-existing claim for money, security or the like and is made under circumstances which under any rule of law of the state where the goods are situated would apart from this Article constitute the transaction a fraudulent transfer or voidable preference.

§ 2–403
Power to Transfer; Good Faith Purchase of Goods; "Entrusting"

(1) A purchaser of goods acquires all title which his transferor had or had power to transfer except that a purchaser of a limited interest acquires rights only to the extent of the interest purchased. A person with voidable title has power to transfer a good title to a good faith purchaser for value. When goods have been delivered under a transaction of purchase the purchaser has such power even though
    (a) the transferor was deceived as to the identity of the purchaser, or
    (b) the delivery was in exchange for a check which is later dishonored, or
    (c) it was agreed that the transaction was to be a "cash sale", or
    (d) the delivery was procured through fraud punishable as larcenous under the criminal law.

(2) Any entrusting of possession of goods to a merchant who deals in goods of that kind gives him power to transfer all rights of the entruster to a buyer in ordinary course of business.

(3) "Entrusting" includes any delivery and any acquiescence in retention of possession regardless of any condition expressed between the parties to the delivery or acquiescence and regardless of whether the procurement of the entrusting or the possessor's disposition of the goods have been such as to be larcenous under the criminal law.

(4) The rights of other purchasers of goods and of lien creditors are governed by the Articles on Secured Transactions (Article 9), Bulk Transfers (Article 6) and Documents of Title (Article 7).

Part 5/Performance
§ 2–501
Insurable Interest in Goods; Manner of Identification of Goods

(1) The buyer obtains a special property and an insurable interest in goods by identification of existing goods as goods to which the contract refers even though the goods so identified are nonconforming and he has an option to return or reject them. Such identification can be made at any time and in any manner explicitly agreed to by the parties. In the absence of explicit agreement identification occurs
    (a) when the contract is made if it is for the sale of goods already existing and identified;
    (b) if the contract is for the sale of future goods other than those described in paragraph (c), when goods are shipped, marked or otherwise designated by the seller as goods to which the contract refers;
    (c) when the crops are planted or otherwise become growing crops or the young are conceived if the contract is for the sale of unborn young to be born within twelve months after contracting or for the sale of crops to be harvested within twelve months or the next normal harvest season after contracting whichever is longer.

(2) The seller retains an insurable interest in goods so long as title to or any security interest in the goods remains in him and where the identification is by the seller alone he may until default or insolvency or notification to the buyer that the identification is final substitute other goods for those identified.

(3) Nothing in this section impairs any insurable interest recognized under any other statute or rule of law.

§ 2–502
Buyer's Right to Goods on Seller's Insolvency

(1) Subject to subsection (2) and even though the goods have not been shipped a buyer who has paid a part or all of the price of goods in which he has a special property under the provisions of the immediately preceding section may on making and keeping good a tender of any unpaid portion of their price recover them from the seller if the seller becomes insolvent within ten days after receipt of the first installment on their price.

(2) If the identification creating his special property has been made by the buyer he acquires the right to recover the goods only if they conform to the contract for sale.

§ 2–503
Manner of Seller's Tender of Delivery

(1) Tender of delivery requires that the seller put and hold conforming goods at the buyer's disposition and give the buyer any notification reasonably necessary to enable him to take delivery. The manner, time and place for tender are determined by the agreement and this Article, and in particular
    (a) tender must be at a reasonable hour, and if it is of goods they must be kept available for the period reasonably necessary to enable the buyer to take possession; but

(b) unless otherwise agreed the buyer must furnish facilities reasonably suited to the receipt of the goods.

(2) Where the case is within the next section respecting shipment tender requires that the seller comply with its provisions.

(3) Where the seller is required to deliver at a particular destination tender requires that he comply with subsection (1) and also in any appropriate case tender documents as described in subsections (4) and (5) of this section.

(4) Where goods are in the possession of a bailee and are to be delivered without being moved

    (a) tender requires that the seller either tender a negotiable document of title covering such goods or procure acknowledgment by the bailee of the buyer's right to possession of the goods; but

    (b) tender to the buyer of a non-negotiable document of title or of a written direction to the bailee to deliver is sufficient tender unless the buyer seasonably objects, and receipt by the bailee of notification of the buyer's rights fixes those rights as against the bailee and all third persons; but risk of loss of the goods and of any failure by the bailee to honor the non-negotiable document of title or to obey the direction remains on the seller until the buyer has had a reasonable time to present the document or direction, and a refusal by the bailee to honor the document or to obey the direction defeats the tender.

(5) Where the contract requires the seller to deliver documents

    (a) he must tender all such documents in correct form, except as provided in this Article with respect to bills of lading in a set (subsection (2) of Section 2–323); and

    (b) tender through customary banking channels is sufficient and dishonor of a draft accompanying the documents constitutes non-acceptance or rejection.

§ 2–504
Shipment by Seller

Where the seller is required or authorized to send the goods to the buyer and the contract does not require him to deliver them at a particular destination, then unless otherwise agreed he must

    (a) put the goods in the possession of such a carrier and make such a contract for their transportation as may be reasonable having regard to the nature of the goods and other circumstances of the case; and

    (b) obtain and promptly deliver or tender in due form any document necessary to enable the buyer to obtain possession of the goods or otherwise required by the agreement or by usage of trade; and

    (c) promptly notify the buyer of the shipment.

Failure to notify the buyer under paragraph (c) or to make a proper contract under paragraph (a) is a ground for rejection only if material delay or loss ensues.

§ 2–505
Seller's Shipment under Reservation

(1) Where the seller has identified goods to the contract by or before shipment:

    (a) his procurement of a negotiable bill of lading to his own order or otherwise reserves in him a security interest in the goods. His procurement of the bill to the order of a financing agency or of the buyer indicates in addition only the seller's expectation of transferring that interest to the person named.

    (b) a non-negotiable bill of lading to himself or his nominee reserves possession of the goods as security but except in a case of conditional delivery (subsection (2) of Section 2–507) a non-negotiable bill of lading naming the buyer as consignee reserves no security interest even though the seller retains possession of the bill of lading.

(2) When shipment by the seller with reservation of a security interest is in violation of the contract for sale it constitutes an improper contract for transportation within the preceding section but impairs neither the rights given to the buyer by shipment and identification of the goods to the contract nor the seller's powers as a holder of a negotiable document.

§ 2–506
Rights of Financing Agency

(1) A financing agency by paying or purchasing for value a draft which relates to a shipment of goods acquires to the extent of the payment or purchase and in addition to its own rights under the draft and any document of title securing it any rights of the shipper in the goods including the right to stop delivery and the shipper's right to have the draft honored by the buyer.

(2) The right to reimbursement of a financing agency which has in good faith honored or purchased the draft under commitment to or authority from the buyer is not impaired by subsequent discovery of defects with reference to any relevant document which was apparently regular on its face.

§ 2–507
Effect of Seller's Tender; Delivery on Condition

(1) Tender of delivery is a condition to the buyer's duty to accept the goods and, unless otherwise agreed, to his duty to pay for them. Tender entitles the seller to acceptance of the goods and to payment according to the contract.

(2) Where payment is due and demanded on the delivery to the buyer of goods or documents of title, his right as against the seller to retain or dispose of them is conditional upon his making the payment due.

§ 2–508
Cure by Seller of Improper Tender
or Delivery; Replacement

(1) Where any tender or delivery by the seller is rejected because non-conforming and the time for performance has not yet expired, the seller may seasonably notify the buyer of his intention to cure and may then within the contract time make a conforming delivery.

(2) Where the buyer rejects a non-conforming tender which the seller had reasonable grounds to believe would be acceptable with or without money allowance the seller may if he seasonably notifies the buyer have a further reasonable time to substitute a conforming tender.

§ 2–509
Risk of Loss in the Absence of Breach

(1) Where the contract requires or authorizes the seller to ship the goods by carrier

    (a) if it does not require him to deliver them at a particular destination, the risk of loss passes to the buyer when the goods are duly delivered to the carrier even though the shipment is under reservation (Section 2–505); but

    (b) if it does require him to deliver them at a particular destination and the goods are there duly tendered while in the possession of the carrier, the risk of loss passes to the buyer when the goods are there duly so tendered as to enable the buyer to take delivery.

(2) Where the goods are held by a bailee to be delivered without being moved, the risk of loss passes to the buyer

    (a) on his receipt of a negotiable document of title covering the goods; or

    (b) on acknowledgment by the bailee of the buyer's right to possession of the goods; or

    (c) after his receipt of a non-negotiable document of title or other written direction to deliver, as provided in subsection (4)(b) of Section 2–503.

(3) In any case not within subsection (1) or (2), the risk of loss passes to the buyer on his receipt of the goods if the seller is a merchant; otherwise the risk passes to the buyer on tender of delivery.

(4) The provisions of this section are subject to contrary agreement of the parties and to the provisions of this Article on sale on approval (Section 2–327) and on effect of breach on risk of loss (Section 2–510).

§ 2–510
Effect of Breach on Risk of Loss

(1) Where a tender or delivery of goods so fails to conform to the contract as to give a right of rejection the risk of their loss remains on the seller until cure or acceptance.

(2) Where the buyer rightfully revokes acceptance he may to the extent of any deficiency in his effective insurance coverage treat the risk of loss as having rested on the seller from the beginning.

(3) Where the buyer as to conforming goods already identified to the contract for sale repudiates or is otherwise in breach before risk of their loss has passed to him, the seller may to the extent of any deficiency in his effective insurance coverage treat the risk of loss as resting on the buyer for a commercially reasonable time.

§ 2–511
Tender of Payment by Buyer; Payment by Check

(1) Unless otherwise agreed tender of payment is a condition to the seller's duty to tender and complete any delivery.

(2) Tender of payment is sufficient when made by any means or in any manner current in the ordinary course of business unless the seller demands payment in legal tender and gives any extension of time reasonably necessary to procure it.

(3) Subject to the provisions of this Act on the effect of an instrument on an obligation (Section 3–802), payment by check is conditional and is defeated as between the parties by dishonor of the check on due presentment.

§ 2–512
Payment by Buyer before Inspection

(1) Where the contract requires payment before inspection non-conformity of the goods does not excuse the buyer from so making payment unless

    (a) the non-conformity appears without inspection; or

    (b) despite tender of the required documents the circumstances would justify injunction against honor under the provisions of this Act (Section 5–114).

(2) Payment pursuant to subsection (1) does not constitute an acceptance of goods or impair the buyer's right to inspect or any of his remedies.

§ 2–513
Buyer's Right to Inspection of Goods

(1) Unless otherwise agreed and subject to subsection (3), where goods are tendered or delivered or identified to the contract for sale, the buyer has a right before payment or acceptance to inspect them at any reasonable place and time and in any reasonable manner. When the seller is required or authorized to send the goods to the buyer, the inspection may be after their arrival.

(2) Expenses of inspection must be borne by the buyer but may be recovered from the seller if the goods do not conform and are rejected.

(3) Unless otherwise agreed and subject to the provisions of this Article on C.I.F. contracts (subsection (3) of Section 2–321), the buyer is not entitled to inspect the goods before payment of the price when the contract provides

    (a) for delivery "C.O.D." or on other like terms; or

    (b) for payment against documents of title, except where such payment is due only after the goods are to become available for inspection.

(4) A place or method of inspection fixed by the parties is presumed to be exclusive but unless otherwise expressly agreed it does not postpone identification or shift the place for delivery or for passing the risk of loss. If compliance becomes impossible, inspection shall be as provided in this section unless the place or method fixed was clearly intended as an indispensable condition failure of which voids the contract.

§ 2–514
When Documents Deliverable on Acceptance; When on Payment

Unless otherwise agreed documents against which a draft is drawn are to be delivered to the drawee on acceptance of the draft if it is payable more than three days after presentment; otherwise, only on payment.

§ 2–515
Preserving Evidence of Goods in Dispute

In furtherance of the adjustment of any claim or dispute

    (a) either party on reasonable notification to the other and for the purpose of ascertaining the facts and preserving evidence has the right to inspect, test and sample the goods including such of them as may be in the possession or control of the other; and

(b) the parties may agree to a third party inspection or survey to determine the conformity or condition of the goods and may agree that the findings shall be binding upon them in any subsequent litigation or adjustment.

Part 6/Breach, Repudiation and Excuse
§ 2–601
Buyer's Rights on Improper Delivery

Subject to the provisions of this Article on breach in installment contracts (Section 2–612) and unless otherwise agreed under the sections on contractual limitations of remedy (Sections 2–718 and 2–719), if the goods or the tender of delivery fail in any respect to conform to the contract, the buyer may

(a) reject the whole; or

(b) accept the whole; or

(c) accept any commercial unit or units and reject the rest.

§ 2–602
Manner and Effect of Rightful Rejection

(1) Rejection of goods must be within a reasonable time after their delivery or tender. It is ineffective unless the buyer seasonably notifies the seller.

(2) Subject to the provisions of the two following sections on rejected goods (Sections 2–603 and 2–604),

(a) after rejection any exercise of ownership by the buyer with respect to any commercial unit is wrongful as against the seller; and

(b) if the buyer has before rejection taken physical possession of goods in which he does not have a security interest under the provisions of this Article (subsection (3) of Section 2–711), he is under a duty after rejection to hold them with reasonable care at the seller's disposition for a time sufficient to permit the seller to remove them; but

(c) the buyer has no further obligations with regard to goods rightfully rejected.

(3) The seller's rights with respect to goods wrongfully rejected are governed by the provisions of this Article on seller's remedies in general (Section 2–703).

§ 2–603
Merchant Buyer's Duties as to Rightfully Rejected Goods

(1) Subject to any security interest in the buyer (subsection (3) of Section 2–711), when the seller has no agent or place of business at the market of rejection a merchant buyer is under a duty after rejection of goods in his possession or control to follow any reasonable instructions received from the seller with respect to the goods and in the absence of such instructions to make reasonable efforts to sell them for the seller's account if they are perishable or threaten to decline in value speedily. Instructions are not reasonable if on demand indemnity for expenses is not forthcoming.

(2) When the buyer sells goods under subsection (1), he is entitled to reimbursement from the seller or out of the proceeds for reasonable expenses of caring for and selling them, and if the expenses include no selling commission then to such commission as is usual in the trade or if there is none to a reasonable sum not exceeding ten per cent on the gross proceeds.

(3) In complying with this section the buyer is held only to good faith and good faith conduct hereunder is neither acceptance nor conversion nor the basis of an action for damages.

§ 2–604
Buyer's Options as to Salvage of Rightfully Rejected Goods

Subject to the provisions of the immediately preceding section on perishables if the seller gives no instructions within a reasonable time after notification of rejection the buyer may store the rejected goods for the seller's account or reship them to him or resell them for the seller's account with reimbursement as provided in the preceding section. Such action is not acceptance or conversion.

§ 2–605
Waiver of Buyer's Objections by Failure to Particularize

(1) The buyer's failure to state in connection with rejection a particular defect which is ascertainable by reasonable inspection precludes him from relying on the unstated defect to justify rejection or to establish breach

(a) where the seller could have cured it if stated seasonably; or

(b) between merchants when the seller has after rejection made a request in writing for a full and final written statement of all defects on which the buyer proposes to rely.

(2) Payment against documents made without reservation of rights precludes recovery of the payment for defects apparent on the face of the documents.

§ 2–606
What Constitutes Acceptance of Goods

(1) Acceptance of goods occurs when the buyer

(a) after a reasonable opportunity to inspect the goods signifies to the seller that the goods are conforming or that he will take or retain them in spite of their non-conformity; or

(b) fails to make an effective rejection (subsection (1) of Section 2–602), but such acceptance does not occur until the buyer has had a reasonable opportunity to inspect them; or

(c) does any act inconsistent with the seller's ownership; but if such act is wrongful as against the seller it is an acceptance only if ratified by him.

(2) Acceptance of a part of any commercial unit is acceptance of that entire unit.

§ 2–607
Effect of Acceptance; Notice of Breach; Burden of Establishing Breach after Acceptance; Notice of Claim or Litigation to Person Answerable Over

(1) The buyer must pay at the contract rate for any goods accepted.

(2) Acceptance of goods by the buyer precludes rejection of the goods accepted and if made with knowledge of a non-conformity cannot be revoked because of it unless the acceptance was on the reasonable assumption that the non-conformity would be seasonably cured but acceptance does not of itself impair any other remedy provided by this Article for non-conformity.

(3) Where a tender has been accepted

(a) the buyer must within a reasonable time after he discovers or should have discovered any breach notify the seller of breach or be barred from any remedy; and

(b) if the claim is one for infringement or the like (subsection (3) of Section 2–312) and the buyer is sued as a result of such a breach he must so notify the seller within a reasonable time after he receives notice of the litigation or be barred from any remedy over for liability established by the litigation.

(4) The burden is on the buyer to establish any breach with respect to the goods accepted.

(5) Where the buyer is sued for breach of a warranty or other obligation for which the seller is answerable over

(a) he may give his seller written notice of the litigation. If the notice states that the seller may come in and defend and that if the seller does not do so he will be bound in any action against him by his buyer by any determination of fact common to the two litigations, then unless the seller after seasonable receipt of the notice does come in and defend he is so bound.

(b) if the claim is one for infringement or the like (subsection (3) of Section 2–312) the original seller may demand in writing that his buyer turn over to him control of the litigation including settlement or else be barred from any remedy over and if he also agrees to bear all expense and to satisfy any adverse judgment, then unless the buyer after seasonable receipt of the demand does turn over control the buyer is so barred.

(6) The provisions of subsections (3), (4) and (5) apply to any obligation of a buyer to hold the seller harmless against infringement or the like (subsection (3) of Section 2–312).

§ 2–608
Revocation of Acceptance in Whole or in Part

(1) The buyer may revoke his acceptance of a lot or commercial unit whose non-conformity substantially impairs its value to him if he has accepted it

(a) on the reasonable assumption that its non-conformity would be cured and it has not been seasonably cured; or

(b) without discovery of such non-conformity if his acceptance was reasonably induced either by the difficulty of discovery before acceptance or by the seller's assurances.

(2) Revocation of acceptance must occur within a reasonable time after the buyer discovers or should have discovered the ground for it and before any substantial change in condition of the goods which is not caused by their own defects. It is not effective until the buyer notifies the seller of it.

(3) A buyer who so revokes has the same rights and duties with regard to the goods involved as if he had rejected them.

§ 2–609
Right to Adequate Assurance of Performance

(1) A contract for sale imposes an obligation on each party that the other's expectation of receiving due performance will not be impaired. When reasonable grounds for insecurity arise with respect to the performance of either party the other may in writing demand adequate assurance of due performance and until he receives such assurance may if commercially reasonable suspend any performance for which he has not already received the agreed return.

(2) Between merchants the reasonableness of grounds for insecurity and the adequacy of any assurance offered shall be determined according to commercial standards.

(3) Acceptance of any improper delivery or payment does not prejudice the aggrieved party's right to demand adequate assurance of future performance.

(4) After receipt of a justified demand failure to provide within a reasonable time not exceeding thirty days such assurance of due performance as is adequate under the circumstances of the particular case is a repudiation of the contract.

§ 2–610
Anticipatory Repudiation

When either party repudiates the contract with respect to a performance not yet due the loss of which will substantially impair the value of the contract to the other, the aggrieved party may

(a) for a commercially reasonable time await performance by the repudiating party; or

(b) resort to any remedy for breach (Section 2–703 or Section 2–711), even though he has notified the repudiating party that he would await the latter's performance and has urged retraction; and

(c) in either case suspend his own performance or proceed in accordance with the provisions of this Article on the seller's right to identify goods to the contract notwithstanding breach or to salvage unfinished goods (Section 2–704).

§ 2–611
Retraction of Anticipatory Repudiation

(1) Until the repudiating party's next performance is due he can retract his repudiation unless the aggrieved party has since the repudiation cancelled or materially changed his position or otherwise indicated that he considers the repudiation final.

(2) Retraction may be by any method which clearly indicates to the aggrieved party that the repudiating party intends to perform, but must include any assurance justifiably demanded under the provisions of this Article (Section 2–609).

(3) Retraction reinstates the repudiating party's rights under the contract with due excuse and allowance to the aggrieved party for any delay occasioned by the repudiation.

§ 2–612
"Installment Contract"; Breach

(1) An "installment contract" is one which requires or authorizes the delivery of goods in separate lots to be separately accepted, even though the contract contains a clause "each delivery is a separate contract" or its equivalent.

(2) The buyer may reject any installment which is non-conforming if the non-conformity substantially impairs the value of that installment and cannot be cured or if the non-conformity is a defect in the required documents; but if the non-conformity does not fall within subsection (3) and the seller gives adequate assurance of its cure the buyer must accept that installment.

(3) Whenever non-conformity or default with respect to one or more installments substantially impairs the value of the whole contract there is a breach of the whole. But the aggrieved party reinstates the contract if he accepts a non-conforming installment without seasonably notifying of cancellation or if he brings an action with respect only to past installments or demands performance as to future installments.

§ 2–613
Casualty to Identified Goods

Where the contract requires for its performance goods identified when the contract is made, and the goods suffer casualty without fault of either party before the risk of loss passes to the buyer, or in a proper case under a "no arrival, no sale" term (Section 2–324) then

    (a) if the loss is total the contract is voided; and

    (b) if the loss is partial or the goods have so deteriorated as no longer to conform to the contract the buyer may nevertheless demand inspection and at his option either treat the contract as voided or accept the goods with due allowance from the contract price for the deterioration or the deficiency in quantity but without further right against the seller.

§ 2–614
Substituted Performance

(1) Where without fault of either party the agreed berthing, loading, or unloading facilities fail or an agreed type of carrier becomes unavailable or the agreed manner of delivery otherwise becomes commercially impracticable but a commercially reasonable substitute is available, such substitute performance must be tendered and accepted.

(2) If the agreed means or manner of payment fails because of domestic or foreign governmental regulation, the seller may withhold or stop delivery unless the buyer provides a means or manner of payment which is commercially a substantial equivalent. If delivery has already been taken, payment by the means or in the manner provided by the regulation discharges the buyer's obligation unless the regulation is discriminatory, oppressive or predatory.

§ 2–615
Excuse by Failure of Presupposed Conditions

Except so far as a seller may have assumed a greater obligation and subject to the preceding section on substituted performance:

    (a) Delay in delivery or non-delivery in whole or in part by a seller who complies with paragraphs (b) and (c) is not a breach of his duty under a contract for sale if performance as agreed has been made impracticable by the occurrence of a contingency the non-occurrence of which was a basic assumption on which the contract was made or by compliance in good faith with any applicable foreign or domestic governmental regulation or order whether or not it later proves to be invalid.

    (b) Where the causes mentioned in paragraph (a) affect only a part of the seller's capacity to perform, he must allo-

cate production and deliveries among his customers but may at his option include regular customers not then under contract as well as his own requirements for further manufacture. He may so allocate in any manner which is fair and reasonable.

    (c) The seller must notify the buyer seasonably that there will be delay or non-delivery and, when allocation is required under paragraph (b), of the estimated quota thus made available for the buyer.

§ 2–616
Procedure on Notice Claiming Excuse

(1) Where the buyer receives notification of a material or indefinite delay or an allocation justified under the preceding section he may by written notification to the seller as to any delivery concerned, and where the prospective deficiency substantially impairs the value of the whole contract under the provisions of this Article relating to breach of installment contracts (Section 2–612), then also as to the whole,

    (a) terminate and thereby discharge any unexecuted portion of the contract; or

    (b) modify the contract by agreeing to take his available quota in substitution.

(2) If after receipt of such notification from the seller the buyer fails so to modify the contract within a reasonable time not exceeding thirty days the contract lapses with respect to any deliveries affected.

(3) The provisions of this section may not be negated by agreement except in so far as the seller has assumed a greater obligation under the preceding section.

Part 7/Remedies
§ 2–701
Remedies for Breach of Collateral Contracts Not Impaired

Remedies for breach of any obligation or promise collateral or ancillary to a contract for sale are not impaired by the provisions of this Article.

§ 2–702
Seller's Remedies on Discovery of Buyer's Insolvency

(1) Where the seller discovers the buyer to be insolvent he may refuse delivery except for cash including payment for all goods theretofore delivered under the contract, and stop delivery under this Article (Section 2–705).

(2) Where the seller discovers that the buyer has received goods on credit while insolvent he may reclaim the goods upon demand made within ten days after the receipt, but if misrepresentation of solvency has been made to the particular seller in writing within three months before delivery the ten day limitation does not apply. Except as provided in this subsection the seller may not base a right to reclaim goods on the buyer's fraudulent or innocent misrepresentation of solvency or of intent to pay.

(3) The seller's right to reclaim under subsection (2) is subject to the rights of a buyer in ordinary course or other good faith purchaser under this Article (Section 2–403). Successful reclamation of goods excludes all other remedies with respect to them.

§ 2–703
Seller's Remedies in General

Where the buyer wrongfully rejects or revokes acceptance of goods or fails to make a payment due on or before delivery or repudiates with respect to a part or the whole, then with respect to any goods directly affected and, if the breach is of the whole contract (Section 2–612), then also with respect to the whole undelivered balance, the aggrieved seller may

(a) withhold delivery of such goods;

(b) stop delivery by any bailee as hereafter provided (Section 2–705);

(c) proceed under the next section respecting goods still unidentified to the contract;

(d) resell and recover damages as hereafter provided (Section 2–706);

(e) recover damages for non-acceptance (Section 2–708) or in a proper case the price (Section 2–709);

(f) cancel.

§ 2–704
Seller's Right to Identify Goods to the Contract Notwithstanding Breach or to Salvage Unfinished Goods

(1) An aggrieved seller under the preceding section may

(a) identify to the contract conforming goods not already identified if at the time he learned of the breach they are in his possession or control;

(b) treat as the subject of resale goods which have demonstrably been intended for the particular contract even though those goods are unfinished.

(2) Where the goods are unfinished an aggrieved seller may in the exercise of reasonable commercial judgment for the purposes of avoiding loss and of effective realization either complete the manufacture and wholly identify the goods to the contract or cease manufacture and resell for scrap or salvage value or proceed in any other reasonable manner.

§ 2–705
Seller's Stoppage of Delivery in Transit or Otherwise

(1) The seller may stop delivery of goods in the possession of a carrier or other bailee when he discovers the buyer to be insolvent (Section 2–702) and may stop delivery of carload, truckload, planeload or larger shipments of express or freight when the buyer repudiates or fails to make a payment due before delivery or if for any other reason the seller has a right to withhold or reclaim the goods.

(2) As against such buyer the seller may stop delivery until

(a) receipt of the goods by the buyer; or

(b) acknowledgment to the buyer by any bailee of the goods except a carrier that the bailee holds the goods for the buyer; or

(c) such acknowledgment to the buyer by a carrier by reshipment or as warehouseman; or

(d) negotiation to the buyer of any negotiable document of title covering the goods.

(3) (a) To stop delivery the seller must so notify as to enable the bailee by reasonable diligence to prevent delivery of the goods.

(b) After such notification the bailee must hold and deliver the goods according to the directions of the seller but the seller is liable to the bailee for any ensuing charges or damages.

(c) If a negotiable document of title has been issued for goods the bailee is not obliged to obey a notification to stop until surrender of the document.

(d) A carrier who has issued a non-negotiable bill of lading is not obliged to obey a notification to stop received from a person other than the consignor.

§ 2–706
Seller's Resale Including Contract for Resale

(1) Under the conditions stated in Section 2–703 on seller's remedies, the seller may resell the goods concerned or the undelivered balance thereof. Where the resale is made in good faith and in a commercially reasonable manner the seller may recover the difference between the resale price and the contract price together with any incidental damages allowed under the provisions of this Article (Section 2–710), but less expenses saved in consequence of the buyer's breach.

(2) Except as otherwise provided in subsection (3) or unless otherwise agreed resale may be at public or private sale including sale by way of one or more contracts to sell or of identification to an existing contract of the seller. Sale may be as a unit or in parcels and at any time and place and on any terms but every aspect of the sale including the method, manner, time, place and terms must be commercially reasonable. The resale must be reasonably identified as referring to the broken contract, but it is not necessary that the goods be in existence or that any or all of them have been identified to the contract before the breach.

(3) Where the resale is at private sale the seller must give the buyer reasonable notification of his intention to resell.

(4) Where the resale is at public sale

(a) only identified goods can be sold except where there is a recognized market for a public sale of futures in goods of the kind; and

(b) it must be made at a usual place or market for public sale if one is reasonably available and except in the case of goods which are perishable or threaten to decline in value speedily the seller must give the buyer reasonable notice of the time and place of the resale; and

(c) if the goods are not to be within the view of those attending the sale the notification of sale must state the place where the goods are located and provide for their reasonable inspection by prospective bidders; and

(d) the seller may buy.

(5) A purchaser who buys in good faith at a resale takes the goods free of any rights of the original buyer even though the seller fails to comply with one or more of the requirements of this section.

(6) The seller is not accountable to the buyer for any profit made on any resale. A person in the position of a seller (Section 2–707) or a buyer who has rightfully rejected or justifiably revoked acceptance must account for any excess over the amount of his security interest, as hereinafter defined (subsection (3) of Section 2–711).

§ 2–707
"Person in the Position of a Seller"

(1) A "person in the position of a seller" includes as against a principal an agent who has paid or become responsible for the price of goods on behalf of his principal or anyone who otherwise holds a security interest or other right in goods similar to that of a seller.

(2) A person in the position of a seller may as provided in this Article withhold or stop delivery (Section 2–705) and resell (Section 2–706) and recover incidental damages (Section 2–710).

§ 2–708
Seller's Damages for Non-Acceptance or Repudiation

(1) Subject to subsection (2) and to the provisions of this Article with respect to proof of market price (Section 2–723), the measure of damages for non-acceptance or repudiation by the buyer is the difference between the market price at the time and place for tender and the unpaid contract price together with any incidental damages provided in this Article (Section 2–710), but less expenses saved in consequence of the buyer's breach.

(2) If the measure of damages provided in subsection (1) is inadequate to put the seller in as good a position as performance would have done then the measure of damages is the profit (including reasonable overhead) which the seller would have made from full performance by the buyer, together with any incidental damages provided in this Article (Section 2–710), due allowance for costs reasonably incurred and due credit for payments or proceeds of resale.

§ 2–709
Action for the Price

(1) When the buyer fails to pay the price as it becomes due the seller may recover, together with any incidental damages under the next section, the price
> **(a)** of goods accepted or of conforming goods lost or damaged within a commercially reasonable time after risk of their loss has passed to the buyer; and
> **(b)** of goods identified to the contract if the seller is unable after reasonable effort to resell them at a reasonable price or the circumstances reasonably indicate that such effort will be unavailing.

(2) Where the seller sues for the price he must hold for the buyer any goods which have been identified to the contract and are still in his control except that if resale becomes possible he may resell them at any time prior to the collection of the judgment. The net proceeds of any such resale must be credited to the buyer and payment of the judgment entitles him to any goods not resold.

(3) After the buyer has wrongfully rejected or revoked acceptance of the goods or has failed to make a payment due or has repudiated (Section 2–610), a seller who is held not entitled to the price under this section shall nevertheless be awarded damages for non-acceptance under the preceding section.

§ 2–710
Seller's Incidental Damages

Incidental damages to an aggrieved seller include any commercially reasonable charges, expenses or commissions incurred in stopping delivery, in the transportation, care and custody of goods after the buyer's breach, in connection with return or resale of the goods or otherwise resulting from the breach.

§ 2–711
Buyer's Remedies in General; Buyer's Security Interest in Rejected Goods

(1) Where the seller fails to make delivery or repudiates or the buyer rightfully rejects or justifiably revokes acceptance then with respect to any goods involved, and with respect to the whole if the breach goes to the whole contract (Section 2–612), the buyer may cancel and whether or not he has done so may in addition to recovering so much of the price as has been paid
> **(a)** "cover" and have damages under the next section as to all the goods affected whether or not they have been identified to the contract; or
> **(b)** recover damages for non-delivery as provided in this Article (Section 2–713).

(2) Where the seller fails to deliver or repudiates the buyer may also
> **(a)** if the goods have been identified recover them as provided in this Article (Section 2–502); or
> **(b)** in a proper case obtain specific performance or replevy the goods as provided in this Article (Section 2–716).

(3) On rightful rejection or justifiable revocation of acceptance a buyer has a security interest in goods in his possession or control for any payments made on their price and any expenses reasonably incurred in their inspection, receipt, transportation, care and custody and may hold such goods and resell them in like manner as an aggrieved seller (Section 2–706).

§ 2–712
"Cover"; Buyer's Procurement of Substitute Goods

(1) After a breach within the preceding section the buyer may "cover" by making in good faith and without unreasonable delay any reasonable purchase of or contract to purchase goods in substitution for those due from the seller.

(2) The buyer may recover from the seller as damages the difference between the cost of cover and the contract price together with any incidental or consequential damages as hereinafter defined (Section 2–715), but less expenses saved in consequence of the seller's breach.

(3) Failure of the buyer to effect cover within this section does not bar him from any other remedy.

§ 2–713
Buyer's Damages for Non-Delivery or Repudiation

(1) Subject to the provisions of this Article with respect to proof of market price (Section 2–723), the measure of damages for non-delivery or repudiation by the seller is the difference between the market price at the time when the buyer learned of the breach and the contract price together with any incidental and consequential damages provided in this Article (Section 2–715), but less expenses saved in consequence of the seller's breach.

(2) Market price is to be determined as of the place for tender or, in cases of rejection after arrival or revocation of acceptance, as of the place of arrival.

§ 2–714
Buyer's Damages for Breach in Regard to Accepted Goods

(1) Where the buyer has accepted goods and given notification (subsection (3) of Section 2–607) he may recover as damages for any non-conformity of tender the loss resulting in the ordinary course of events from the seller's breach as determined in any manner which is reasonable.

(2) The measure of damages for breach of warranty is the difference at the time and place of acceptance between the value of the goods accepted and the value they would have had if they had been as warranted, unless special circumstances show proximate damages of a different amount.

(3) In a proper case any incidental and consequential damages under the next section may also be recovered.

§ 2–715
Buyer's Incidental and Consequential Damages

(1) Incidental damages resulting from the seller's breach include expenses reasonably incurred in inspection, receipt, transportation and care and custody of goods rightfully rejected, any commercially reasonable charges, expenses or commissions in connection with effecting cover and any other reasonable expense incident to the delay or other breach.

(2) Consequential damages resulting from the seller's breach include
　　(a) any loss resulting from general or particular requirements and needs of which the seller at the time of contracting had reason to know and which could not reasonably be prevented by cover or otherwise; and
　　(b) injury to person or property proximately resulting from any breach of warranty.

§ 2–716
Buyer's Right to Specific Performance or Replevin

(1) Specific performance may be decreed where the goods are unique or in other proper circumstances.

(2) The decree for specific performance may include such terms and conditions as to payment of the price, damages, or other relief as the court may deem just.

(3) The buyer has a right of replevin for goods identified to the contract if after reasonable effort he is unable to effect cover for such goods or the circumstances reasonably indicate that such effort will be unavailing or if the goods have been shipped under reservation and satisfaction of the security interest in them has been made or tendered.

§ 2–717
Deduction of Damages from the Price

The buyer on notifying the seller of his intention to do so may deduct all or any part of the damages resulting from any breach of the contract from any part of the price still due under the same contract.

§ 2–718
Liquidation or Limitation of Damages; Deposits

(1) Damages for breach by either party may be liquidated in the agreement but only at an amount which is reasonable in the light of the anticipated or actual harm caused by the breach, the difficulties of proof of loss, and the inconvenience or nonfeasibility of otherwise obtaining an adequate remedy. A term fixing unreasonably large liquidated damages is void as a penalty.

(2) Where the seller justifiably withholds delivery of goods because of the buyer's breach, the buyer is entitled to restitution of any amount by which the sum of his payments exceeds
　　(a) the amount to which the seller is entitled by virtue of terms liquidating the seller's damages in accordance with subsection (1), or
　　(b) in the absence of such terms, 20 percent of the value of the total performance for which the buyer is obligated under the contract or $500, whichever is smaller.

(3) The buyer's right to restitution under subsection (2) is subject to offset to the extent that the seller establishes
　　(a) a right to recover damages under the provisions of this Article other than subsection (1), and
　　(b) the amount or value of any benefits received by the buyer directly or indirectly by reason of the contract.

(4) Where a seller has received payment in goods their reasonable value or the proceeds of their resale shall be treated as payments for the purposes of subsection (2); but if the seller has notice of the buyer's breach before reselling goods received in part performance, his resale is subject to the conditions laid down in this Article on resale by an aggrieved seller (Section 2–706).

§ 2–719
Contractual Modification or Limitation of Remedy

(1) Subject to the provisions of subsections (2) and (3) of this section and of the preceding section on liquidation and limitation of damages,
　　(a) the agreement may provide for remedies in addition to or in substitution for those provided in this Article and may limit or alter the measure of damages recoverable under this Article, as by limiting the buyer's remedies to return of the goods and repayment of the price or to repair and replacement of non-conforming goods or parts; and
　　(b) resort to a remedy as provided is optional unless the remedy is expressly agreed to be exclusive, in which case it is the sole remedy.

(2) Where circumstances cause an exclusive or limited remedy to fail of its essential purpose, remedy may be had as provided in this Act.

(3) Consequential damages may be limited or excluded unless the limitation or exclusion is unconscionable. Limitation of consequential damages for injury to the person in the case of consumer goods is prima facie unconscionable but limitation of damages where the loss is commercial is not.

§ 2–720
Effect of "Cancellation" or "Rescission" on Claims for Antecedent Breach

Unless the contrary intention clearly appears, expressions of "cancellation" or "rescission" of the contract or the like shall not be construed as a renunciation or discharge of any claim in damages for an antecedent breach.

§ 2–721
Remedies for Fraud

Remedies for material misrepresentation or fraud include all remedies available under this Article for non-fraudulent breach. Neither rescission or a claim for rescission of the contract for sale nor rejection or return of the goods shall bar or be deemed inconsistent with a claim for damages or other remedy.

§ 2–722
Who Can Sue Third Parties for Injury to Goods

Where a third party so deals with goods which have been identified to a contract for sale as to cause actionable injury to a party to that contract

(a) a right of action against the third party is in either party to the contract for sale who has title to or a security interest or a special property or an insurable interest in the goods; and if the goods have been destroyed or converted a right of action is also in the party who either bore the risk of loss under the contract for sale or has since the injury assumed that risk as against the other;

(b) if at the time of the injury the party plaintiff did not bear the risk of loss as against the other party to the contract for sale and there is no arrangement between them for disposition of the recovery, his suit or settlement is, subject to his own interest, as a fiduciary for the other party to the contract;

(c) either party may with the consent of the other sue for the benefit of whom it may concern.

§ 2–723
Proof of Market Price: Time and Place

(1) If an action based on anticipatory repudiation comes to trial before the time for performance with respect to some or all of the goods, any damages based on market price (Section 2–708 or Section 2–713) shall be determined according to the price of such goods prevailing at the time when the aggrieved party learned of the repudiation.

(2) If evidence of a price prevailing at the times or places described in this Article is not readily available the price prevailing within any reasonable time before or after the time described or at any other place which in commercial judgment or under usage of trade would serve as a reasonable substitute for the one described may be used, making any proper allowance for the cost of transporting the goods to or from such other place.

(3) Evidence of a relevant price prevailing at a time or place other than the one described in this Article offered by one party is not admissible unless and until he has given the other party such notice as the court finds sufficient to prevent unfair surprise.

§ 2–724
Admissibility of Market Quotations

Whenever the prevailing price or value of any goods regularly bought and sold in any established commodity market is in issue, reports in official publications or trade journals or in newspapers or periodicals of general circulation published as the reports of such market shall be admissible in evidence. The circumstances of the preparation of such a report may be shown to affect its weight but not its admissibility.

§ 2–725
Statute of Limitations in Contracts for Sale

(1) An action for breach of any contract for sale must be commenced within four years after the cause of action has accrued. By the original agreement the parties may reduce the period of limitation to not less than one year but may not extend it.

(2) A cause of action accrues when the breach occurs, regardless of the aggrieved party's lack of knowledge of the breach. A breach of warranty occurs when tender of delivery is made, except that where a warranty explicitly extends to future performance of the goods and discovery of the breach must await the time of such performance the cause of action accrues when the breach is or should have been discovered.

(3) Where an action commenced within the time limited by subsection (1) is so terminated as to leave available a remedy by another action for the same breach such other action may be commenced after the expiration of the time limited and within six months after the termination of the first action unless the termination resulted from voluntary discontinuance or from dismissal for failure or neglect to prosecute.

(4) This section does not alter the law on tolling of the statute of limitations nor does it apply to causes of action which have accrued before this Act becomes effective.

ARTICLE 2A/LEASES
Part 1/General Provisions
§ 2A–101
Short Title

This Article shall be known and may be cited as the Uniform Commercial Code—Leases.

§ 2A–102
Scope

This Article applies to any transaction, regardless of form, that creates a lease.

§ 2A–103
Definitions and Index of Definitions

(1) In this Article unless the context otherwise requires:
(a) "Buyer in ordinary course of business" means a person who in good faith and without knowledge that the sale to him [or her] is in violation of the ownership rights or security interest or leasehold interest of a third party in the goods buys in ordinary course from a person in the business of selling

goods of that kind but does not include a pawnbroker. "Buying" may be for cash or by exchange of other property or on secured or unsecured credit and includes receiving goods or documents of title under a pre-existing contract for sale but does not include a transfer in bulk or as security for or in total or partial satisfaction of a money debt.

(b) "Cancellation" occurs when either party puts an end to the lease contract for default by the other party.

(c) "Commercial unit" means such a unit of goods as by commercial usage is a single whole for purposes of lease and division of which materially impairs its character or value on the market or in use. A commercial unit may be a single article, as a machine, or a set of articles, as a suite of furniture or a line of machinery, or a quantity, as a gross or carload, or any other unit treated in use or in the relevant market as a single whole.

(d) "Conforming" goods or performance under a lease contract means goods or performance that are in accordance with the obligations under the lease contract.

(e) "Consumer lease" means a lease that a lessor regularly engaged in the business of leasing or selling makes to a lessee, except an organization, who takes under the lease primarily for a personal, family, or household purpose, if the total payments to be made under the lease contract, excluding payments for options to renew or buy, do not exceed $25,000.

(f) "Fault" means wrongful act, omission, breach, or default.

(g) "Finance lease" means a lease in which (i) the lessor does not select, manufacture or supply the goods, (ii) the lessor acquires the goods or the right to possession and use of the goods in connection with the lease, and (iii) either the lessee receives a copy of the contract evidencing the lessor's purchase of the goods on or before signing the lease contract, or the lessee's approval of the contract evidencing the lessor's purchase of the goods is a condition to effectiveness of the lease contract.

(h) "Goods" means all things that are movable at the time of identification to the lease contract, or are fixtures (Section 2A–309), but the term does not include money, documents, instruments, accounts, chattel paper, general intangibles, or minerals or the like, including oil and gas, before extraction. The term also includes the unborn young of animals.

(i) "Installment lease contract" means a lease contract that authorizes or requires the delivery of goods in separate lots to be separately accepted, even though the lease contract contains a clause "each delivery is a separate lease" or its equivalent.

(j) "Lease" means a transfer of the right to possession and use of goods for a term in return for consideration, but a sale, including a sale on approval or a sale or return, or retention or creation of a security interest is not a lease. Unless the context clearly indicates otherwise, the term includes a sublease.

(k) "Lease agreement" means the bargain, with respect to the lease, of the lessor and the lessee in fact as found in their language or by implication from other circumstances including course of dealing or usage of trade or course of performance as provided in this Article. Unless the context clearly indicates otherwise, the term includes a sublease agreement.

(l) "Lease contract" means the total legal obligation that results from the lease agreement as affected by this Article and any other applicable rules of law. Unless the context clearly indicates otherwise, the term includes a sublease contract.

(m) "Leasehold interest" means the interest of the lessor or the lessee under a lease contract.

(n) "Lessee" means a person who acquires the right to possession and use of goods under a lease. Unless the context clearly indicates otherwise, the term includes a sublessee.

(o) "Lessee in ordinary course of business" means a person who in good faith and without knowledge that the lease to him [or her] is in violation of the ownership rights or security interest or leasehold interest of a third party in the goods, leases in ordinary course from a person in the business of selling or leasing goods of that kind but does not include a pawnbroker. "Leasing" may be for cash or by exchange of other property or on secured or unsecured credit and includes receiving goods or documents of title under a pre-existing lease contract but does not include a transfer in bulk or as security for or in total or partial satisfaction of a money debt.

(p) "Lessor" means a person who transfers the right to possession and use of goods under a lease. Unless the context clearly indicates otherwise, the term includes a sublessor.

(q) "Lessor's residual interest" means the lessor's interest in the goods after expiration, termination, or cancellation of the lease contract.

(r) "Lien" means a charge against or interest in goods to secure payment of a debt or performance of an obligation, but the term does not include a security interest.

(s) "Lot" means a parcel or a single article that is the subject matter of a separate lease or delivery, whether or not it is sufficient to perform the lease contract.

(t) "Merchant lessee" means a lessee that is a merchant with respect to goods of the kind subject to the lease.

(u) "Present value" means the amount as of a date certain of one or more sums payable in the future, discounted to the date certain. The discount is determined by the interest rate specified by the parties if the rate was not manifestly unreasonable at the time the transaction was entered into; otherwise, the discount is determined by a commercially reasonable rate that takes into account the facts and circumstances of each case at the time the transaction was entered into.

(v) "Purchase" includes taking by sale, lease, mortgage, security interest, pledge, gift, or any other voluntary transaction creating an interest in goods.

(w) "Sublease" means a lease of goods the right to possession and use of which was acquired by the lessor as a lessee under an existing lease.

(x) "Supplier" means a person from whom a lessor buys or leases goods to be leased under a finance lease.

(y) "Supply contract" means a contract under which a lessor buys or leases goods to be leased.

(z) "Termination" occurs when either party pursuant to a power created by agreement or law puts an end to the lease contract otherwise than for default.

(2) Other definitions applying to this Article and the sections in which they appear are:

"Accessions". Section 2A–310(1).
"Construction mortgage". Section 2A–309(1)(d).
"Encumbrance". Section 2A–309(1)(e).
"Fixtures". Section 2A–309(1)(a).
"Fixture filing". Section 2A–309(1)(b).
"Purchase money lease". Section 2A–309(1)(c).

(3) The following definitions in other Articles apply to this Article:
"Accounts". Section 9–106.
"Between merchants". Section 2–104(3).
"Buyer". Section 2–103(1)(a).
"Chattel paper". Section 9–105(1)(b).
"Consumer goods". Section 9–109(1).
"Documents". Section 9–105(1)(f).
"Entrusting". Section 2–403(3).
"General intangibles". Section 9–106.
"Good faith". Section 2–103(1)(b).
"Instruments". Section 9–105(1)(i).
"Merchant". Section 2–104(1).
"Mortgage". Section 9–105(1)(j).
"Pursuant to commitment". Section 9–105(1)(k).
"Receipt". Section 2–103(1)(c).
"Sale". Section 2–106(1).
"Sale on Approval". Section 2–326.
"Sale or Return". Section 2–326.
"Seller". Section 2–103(1)(d).

(4) In addition Article 1 contains general definitions and principles of construction and interpretation applicable throughout this Article.

§ 2A–104
Leases Subject to Other Statutes

(1) A lease, although subject to this Article, is also subject to any applicable:
(a) statute of the United States;
(b) certificate of title statute of this State: (list any certificate of title statutes covering automobiles, trailers, mobile homes, boats, farm tractors, and the like);
(c) certificate of title statute of another jurisdiction (Section 2A–105); or
(d) consumer protection statute of this State.

(2) In case of conflict between the provisions of this Article, other than Sections 2A–105, 2A–304(3) and 2A–305(3), and any statute referred to in subsection (1), the provisions of that statute control.

(3) Failure to comply with any applicable statute has only the effect specified therein.

§ 2A–105
Territorial Application of Article to
Goods Covered by Certificate of Title

Subject to the provisions of Sections 2A–304(3) and 2A–305(3), with respect to goods covered by a certificate of title issued under a statute of this State or of another jurisdiction, compliance and the effect of compliance or noncompliance with a certificate of title statute are governed by the law (including the conflict of laws rules) of the jurisdiction issuing the certificate

until the earlier of (a) surrender of the certificate, or (b) four months after the goods are removed from that jurisdiction and thereafter until a new certificate of title is issued by another jurisdiction.

§ 2A–106
Limitation on Power of Parties to Consumer Lease to Choose
Applicable Law and Judicial Forum

(1) If the law chosen by the parties to a consumer lease is that of a jurisdiction other than a jurisdiction in which the lessee resides at the time the lease agreement becomes enforceable or within 30 days thereafter or in which the goods are to be used, the choice is not enforceable.

(2) If the judicial forum chosen by the parties to a consumer lease is a forum that would not otherwise have jurisdiction over the lessee, the choice is not enforceable.

§ 2A–107
Waiver or Renunciation of Claim or Right after Default

Any claim or right arising out of an alleged default or breach of warranty may be discharged in whole or in part without consideration by a written waiver or renunciation signed and delivered by the aggrieved party.

§ 2A–108
Unconscionability

(1) If the court as a matter of law finds a lease contract or any clause of a lease contract to have been unconscionable at the time it was made the court may refuse to enforce the lease contract, or it may enforce the remainder of the lease contract without the unconscionable clause, or it may so limit the application of any unconscionable clause as to avoid any unconscionable result.

(2) With respect to a consumer lease, if the court as a matter of law finds that a lease contract or any clause of a lease contract has been induced by unconscionable conduct or that unconscionable conduct has occurred in the collection of a claim arising from a lease contract, the court may grant appropriate relief.

(3) Before making a finding of unconscionability under subsection (1) or (2), the court, on its own motion or that of a party, shall afford the parties a reasonable opportunity to present evidence as to the setting, purpose, and effect of the lease contract or clause thereof, or of the conduct.

(4) In an action in which the lessee claims unconscionability with respect to a consumer lease:
(a) If the court finds unconscionability under subsection (1) or (2), the court shall award reasonable attorney's fees to the lessee.
(b) If the court does not find unconscionability and the lessee claiming unconscionability has brought or maintained an action he [or she] knew to be groundless, the court shall award reasonable attorney's fees to the party against whom the claim is made.
(c) In determining attorney's fees, the amount of the recovery on behalf of the claimant under subsections (1) and (2) is not controlling.

§ 2A–109
Option to Accelerate at Will

(1) A term providing that one party or his [or her] successor in interest may accelerate payment or performance or require collateral or additional collateral "at will" or "when he [or she] deems himself [or herself] insecure" or in words of similar import must be construed to mean that he [or she] has power to do so only if he [or she] in good faith believes that the prospect of payment or performance is impaired.

(2) With respect to a consumer lease, the burden of establishing good faith under subsection (1) is on the party who exercised the power; otherwise the burden of establishing lack of good faith is on the party against whom the power has been exercised.

Part 2/Formation and Construction of Lease Contract

§ 2A–201
Statute of Frauds

(1) A lease contract is not enforceable by way of action or defense unless:
> **(a)** the total payments to be made under the lease contract, excluding payments for options to renew or buy, are less than $1,000; or
> **(b)** there is a writing, signed by the party against whom enforcement is sought or by that party's authorized agent, sufficient to indicate that a lease contract has been made between the parties and to describe the goods leased and the lease term.

(2) Any description of leased goods or of the lease term is sufficient and satisfies subsection (1)(b), whether or not it is specific, if it reasonably identifies what is described.

(3) A writing is not insufficient because it omits or incorrectly states a term agreed upon, but the lease contract is not enforceable under subsection (1)(b) beyond the lease term and the quantity of goods shown in this writing.

(4) A lease contract that does not satisfy the requirements of subsection (1), but which is valid in other respects, is enforceable:
> **(a)** if the goods are to be specially manufactured or obtained for the lessee and are not suitable for lease or sale to others in the ordinary course of the lessor's business, and the lessor, before notice of repudiation is received and under circumstances that reasonably indicate that the goods are for the lessee, has made either a substantial beginning of their manufacture or commitments for their procurement;
> **(b)** if the party against whom enforcement is sought admits in that party's pleading, testimony or otherwise in court that a lease contract was made, but the lease contract is not enforceable under this provision beyond the quantity of goods admitted; or
> **(c)** with respect to goods that have been received and accepted by the lessee.
> **(5)** The lease term under a lease contract referred to in subsection (4) is:
> **(a)** if there is a writing signed by the party against whom enforcement is sought or by that party's authorized agent specifying the lease term, the term so specified;

> **(b)** if the party against whom enforcement is sought admits in that party's pleading, testimony, or otherwise in court a lease term, the term so admitted; or
> **(c)** a reasonable lease term.

§ 2A–202
Final Written Expression: Parol or Extrinsic Evidence

Terms with respect to which the confirmatory memoranda of the parties agree or which are otherwise set forth in a writing intended by the parties as a final expression of their agreement with respect to such terms as are included therein may not be contradicted by evidence of any prior agreement or of a contemporaneous oral agreement but may be explained or supplemented:
> **(a)** by course of dealing or usage of trade or by course of performance; and
> **(b)** by evidence of consistent additional terms unless the court finds the writing to have been intended also as a complete and exclusive statement of the terms of the agreement.

§ 2A–203
Seals Inoperative

The affixing of a seal to a writing evidencing a lease contract or an offer to enter into a lease contract does not render the writing a sealed instrument and the law with respect to sealed instruments does not apply to the lease contract or offer.

§ 2A–204
Formation in General

(1) A lease contract may be made in any manner sufficient to show agreement, including conduct by both parties which recognizes the existence of a lease contract.

(2) An agreement sufficient to constitute a lease contract may be found although the moment of its making is undetermined.

(3) Although one or more terms are left open, a lease contract does not fail for indefiniteness if the parties have intended to make a lease contract and there is a reasonably certain basis for giving an appropriate remedy.

§ 2A–205
Firm Offers

An offer by a merchant to lease goods to or from another person in a signed writing that by its terms gives assurance it will be held open is not revocable, for lack of consideration, during the time stated or, if no time is stated, for a reasonable time, but in no event may the period of irrevocability exceed 3 months. Any such term of assurance on a form supplied by the offeree must be separately signed by the offeror.

§ 2A–206
Offer and Acceptance in Formation of Lease Contract

(1) Unless otherwise unambiguously indicated by the language or circumstances, an offer to make a lease contract must be construed as inviting acceptance in any manner and by any medium reasonable in the circumstances.

(2) If the beginning of a requested performance is a reasonable mode of acceptance, an offeror who is not notified of acceptance within a reasonable time may treat the offer as having lapsed before acceptance.

§ 2A–207
Course of Performance or Practical Construction

(1) If a lease contract involves repeated occasions for performance by either party with knowledge of the nature of the performance and opportunity for objection to it by the other, any course of performance accepted or acquiesced in without objection is relevant to determine the meaning of the lease agreement.

(2) The express terms of a lease agreement and any course of performance, as well as any course of dealing and usage of trade, must be construed whenever reasonable as consistent with each other; but if that construction is unreasonable, express terms control course of performance, course of performance controls both course of dealing and usage of trade, and course of dealing controls usage of trade.

(3) Subject to the provisions of Section 2A–208 on modification and waiver, course of performance is relevant to show a waiver or modification of any term inconsistent with the course of performance.

§ 2A–208
Modification, Rescission and Waiver

(1) An agreement modifying a lease contract needs no consideration to be binding.

(2) A signed lease agreement that excludes modification or rescission except by a signed writing may not be otherwise modified or rescinded, but, except as between merchants, such a requirement on a form supplied by a merchant must be separately signed by the other party.

(3) Although an attempt at modification or rescission does not satisfy the requirements of subsection (2), it may operate as a waiver.

(4) A party who has made a waiver affecting an executory portion of a lease contract may retract the waiver by reasonable notification received by the other party that strict performance will be required of any term waived, unless the retraction would be unjust in view of a material change of position in reliance on the waiver.

§ 2A–209
Lessee under Finance Lease as Beneficiary of Supply Contract

(1) The benefit of the supplier's promises to the lessor under the supply contract and of all warranties, whether express or implied, under the supply contract, extends to the lessee to the extent of the lessee's leasehold interest under a finance lease related to the supply contract, but subject to the terms of the supply contract and all of the supplier's defenses or claims arising therefrom.

(2) The extension of the benefit of the supplier's promises to the lessee does not: (a) modify the rights and obligations of the parties to the supply contract, whether arising therefrom or otherwise, or (b) impose any duty or liability under the supply contract on the lessee.

(3) Any modification or rescission of the supply contract by the supplier and the lessor is effective against the lessee unless, prior to the modification or rescission, the supplier has received notice that the lessee has entered into a finance lease related to the supply contract. If the supply contract is modified or rescinded after the lessee enters the finance lease, the lessee has a cause of action against the lessor, and against the supplier if the supplier has notice of the lessee's entering the finance lease when the supply contract is modified or rescinded. The lessee's recovery from such action shall put the lessee in as good a position as if the modification or rescission had not occurred.

§ 2A–210
Express Warranties

(1) Express warranties by the lessor are created as follows:
  (a) Any affirmation of fact or promise made by the lessor to the lessee which relates to the goods and becomes part of the basis of the bargain creates an express warranty that the goods will conform to the affirmation or promise.
  (b) Any description of the goods which is made part of the basis of the bargain creates an express warranty that the goods will conform to the description.
  (c) Any sample or model that is made part of the basis of the bargain creates an express warranty that the whole of the goods will conform to the sample or model.

(2) It is not necessary to the creation of an express warranty that the lessor use formal words, such as "warrant" or "guarantee", or that the lessor have a specific intention to make a warranty, but an affirmation merely of the value of the goods or a statement purporting to be merely the lessor's opinion or commendation of the goods does not create a warranty.

§ 2A–211
Warranties against Interference and against Infringement; Lessee's Obligation against Infringement

(1) There is in a lease contract a warranty that for the lease term no person holds a claim to or interest in the goods that arose from an act or omission of the lessor, other than a claim by way of infringement or the like, which will interfere with the lessee's enjoyment of its leasehold interest.

(2) Except in a finance lease there is in a lease contract by a lessor who is a merchant regularly dealing in goods of the kind a warranty that the goods are delivered free of the rightful claim of any person by way of infringement or the like.

(3) A lessee who furnishes specifications to a lessor or a supplier shall hold the lessor and the supplier harmless against any claim by way of infringement or the like that arises out of compliance with the specifications.

§ 2A–212
Implied Warranty of Merchantability

(1) Except in a finance lease, a warranty that the goods will be merchantable is implied in a lease contract if the lessor is a merchant with respect to goods of that kind.

(2) Goods to be merchantable must be at least such as

(a) pass without objection in the trade under the description in the lease agreement;

(b) in the case of fungible goods, are of fair average quality within the description;

(c) are fit for the ordinary purposes for which goods of that type are used;

(d) run, within the variation permitted by the lease agreement, of even kind, quality, and quantity within each unit and among all units involved;

(e) are adequately contained, packaged, and labeled as the lease agreement may require; and

(f) conform to any promises or affirmations of fact made on the container or label.

(3) Other implied warranties may arise from course of dealing or usage of trade.

§ 2A–213
Implied Warranty of Fitness for Particular Purpose

Except in a finance of lease, if the lessor at the time the lease contract is made has reason to know of any particular purpose for which the goods are required and that the lessee is relying on the lessor's skill or judgment to select or furnish suitable goods, there is in the lease contract an implied warranty that the goods will be fit for that purpose.

§ 2A–214
Exclusion or Modification of Warranties

(1) Words or conduct relevant to the creation of an express warranty and words or conduct tending to negate or limit a warranty must be construed wherever reasonable as consistent with each other; but, subject to the provisions of Section 2A–202 on parol or extrinsic evidence, negation or limitation is inoperative to the extent that the construction is unreasonable.

(2) Subject to subsection (3), to exclude or modify the implied warranty of merchantability or any part of it the language must mention "merchantability", be by a writing, and be conspicuous. Subject to subsection (3), to exclude or modify any implied warranty of fitness the exclusion must be by a writing and be conspicuous. Language to exclude all implied warranties of fitness is sufficient if it is conspicuous and states, for example, "There is no warranty that the goods will be fit for a particular purpose".

(3) Notwithstanding subsection (2), but subject to subsection (4),

(a) unless the circumstances indicate otherwise, all implied warranties are excluded by expressions like "as is" or "with all faults" or by other language that in common understanding calls the lessee's attention to the exclusion of warranties and makes plain that there is no implied warranty, and is conspicuous;

(b) if the lessee before entering into the lease contract has examined the goods or the sample or model as fully as desired or has refused to examine the goods, there is no implied warranty with regard to defects that an examination ought in the circumstances to have revealed; and

(c) an implied warranty may also be excluded or modified by course of dealing, course of performance, or usage of trade.

(4) To exclude or modify a warranty against interference or against infringement (Section 2A–211) or any part of it, the language must be specific, be by a writing, and be conspicuous, unless the circumstances, including course of performance, course of dealing, or usage of trade, give the lessee reason to know that the goods are being leased subject to a claim or interest of any person.

§ 2A–215
Cumulation and Conflict of Warranties Express or Implied

Warranties, whether express or implied, must be construed as consistent with each other and as cumulative, but if that construction is unreasonable, the intention of the parties determines which warranty is dominant. In ascertaining that intention the following rules apply:

(a) Exact or technical specifications displace an inconsistent sample or model or general language of description.

(b) A sample from an existing bulk displaces inconsistent general language of description.

(c) Express warranties displace inconsistent implied warranties other than an implied warranty of fitness for a particular purpose.

§ 2A–216
Third-Party Beneficiaries of Express and Implied Warranties

Alternative A

A warranty to or for the benefit of a lessee under this Article, whether express or implied, extends to any natural person who is in the family or household of the lessee or who is a guest in the lessee's home if it is reasonable to expect that such person may use, consume, or be affected by the goods and who is injured in person by breach of the warranty. This section does not displace principles of law and equity that extend a warranty to or for the benefit of a lessee to other persons. The operation of this section may not be excluded, modified, or limited, but an exclusion, modification, or limitation of the warranty, including any with respect to rights and remedies, effective against the lessee is also effective against any beneficiary designated under this section.

Alternative B

A warranty to or for the benefit of a lessee under this Article, whether express or implied, extends to any natural person who may reasonably be expected to use, consume, or be affected by the goods and who is injured in person by breach of the warranty. This section does not displace principles of law and equity that extend a warranty to or for the benefit of a lessee to other persons. The operation of this section may not be excluded, modified, or limited, but an exclusion, modification, or limitation of the warranty, including any with respect to rights and remedies, effective against the lessee is also effective against the beneficiary designated under this section.

Alternative C

A warranty to or for the benefit of a lessee under this Article, whether express or implied, extends to any person who may reasonably be expected to use, consume, or be affected by the goods and who is injured by breach of the warranty. The operation of this section may not be excluded, modified, or limited with respect to injury to the person of an individual to whom the warranty extends, but an exclusion, modification, or limitation of the warranty, including any with respect to rights and remedies, effective against the lessee is also effective against the beneficiary designated under this section.

§ 2A–217
Identification

Identification of goods to which a lease contract refers may be made at any time and in any manner explicitly agreed to by the parties. In the absence of explicit agreement, identification occurs:

(a)   when the lease contract is made if the lease contract is for a lease of goods that are existing and identified;

(b)   when the goods are shipped, marked, or otherwise designated by the lessor as goods to which the lease contract refers, if the lease contract is for a lease of goods that are not existing and identified; or

(c)   when the young are conceived, if the lease contract is for a lease of unborn young of animals.

§ 2A–218
Insurance and Proceeds

(1)   A lessee obtains an insurable interest when existing goods are identified to the lease contract even though the goods identified are nonconforming and the lessee has an option to reject them.

(2)   If a lessee has an insurable interest only by reason of the lessor's identification of the goods, the lessor, until default or insolvency or notification to the lessee that identification is final, may substitute other goods for those identified.

(3)   Notwithstanding a lessee's insurable interest under subsections (1) and (2), the lessor retains an insurable interest until an option to buy has been exercised by the lessee and risk of loss has passed to the lessee.

(4)   Nothing in this section impairs any insurable interest recognized under any other statute or rule of law.

(5)   The parties by agreement may determine that one or more parties have an obligation to obtain and pay for insurance covering the goods and by agreement may determine the beneficiary of the proceeds of the insurance.

§ 2A–219
Risk of Loss

(1)   Except in the case of a finance lease, risk of loss is retained by the lessor and does not pass to the lessee. In the case of a finance lease, risk of loss passes to the lessee.

(2)   Subject to the provisions of this Article on the effect of default on risk of loss (Section 2A–220), if risk of loss is to pass to the lessee and the time of passage is not stated, the following rules apply:

(a)   If the lease contract requires or authorizes the goods to be shipped by carrier.

(i) and it does not require delivery at a particular destination, the risk of loss passes to the lessee when the goods are duly delivered to the carrier; but

(ii) if it does require delivery at a particular destination and the goods are there duly tendered while in the possession of the carrier, the risk of loss passes to the lessee when the goods are there duly so tendered as to enable the lessee to take delivery.

(b)   If the goods are held by a bailee to be delivered without being moved, the risk of loss passes to the lessee on acknowledgment by the bailee of the lessee's right to possession of the goods.

(c)   In any case not within subsection (a) or (b), the risk of loss passes to the lessee on the lessee's receipt of the goods if the lessor, or, in the case of a finance lease, the supplier, is a merchant; otherwise the risk passes to the lessee on tender of delivery.

§ 2A–220
Effect of Default on Risk of Loss

(1)   Where risk of loss is to pass to the lessee and the time of passage is not stated:

(a)   If a tender or delivery of goods so fails to conform to the lease contract as to give a right of rejection, the risk of their loss remains with the lessor, or, in the case of a finance lease, the supplier, until cure or acceptance.

(b)   If the lessee rightfully revokes acceptance, he [or she], to the extent of any deficiency in his [or her] effective insurance coverage, may treat the risk of loss as having remained with the lessor from the beginning.

(2)   Whether or not risk of loss is to pass to the lessee, if the lessee as to conforming goods already identified to a lease contract repudiates or is otherwise in default under the lease contract, the lessor, or, in the case of a finance lease, the supplier, to the extent of any deficiency in his [or her] effective insurance coverage may treat the risk of loss as resting on the lessee for a commercially reasonable time.

§ 2A–221
Casualty to Identified Goods

If a lease contract requires goods identified when the lease contract is made, and the goods suffer casualty without fault of the lessee, the lessor or the supplier before delivery, or the goods suffer casualty before risk of loss passes to the lessee pursuant to the lease agreement or Section 2A–219, then:

(a)   if the loss is total, the lease contract is avoided; and

(b)   if the loss is partial or the goods have so deteriorated as to no longer conform to the lease contract, the lessee may nevertheless demand inspection and at his [or her] option either treat the lease contract as avoided or, except in a finance lease that is not a consumer lease, accept the goods with due allowance from the rent payable for the balance of the lease term for the deterioration or the deficiency in quantity but without further right against the lessor.

Part 3/Effect Of Lease Contract
§ 2A–301
Enforceability of Lease Contract

Except as otherwise provided in this Article, a lease contract is effective and enforceable according to its terms between the parties, against purchasers of the goods and against creditors of the parties.

§ 2A–302
Title to and Possession of Goods

Except as otherwise provided in this Article, each provision of this Article applies whether the lessor or a third party has title to the goods, and whether the lessor, the lessee, or a third party has possession of the goods, notwithstanding any statute or rule of law that possession or the absence of possession is fraudulent.

§ 2A–303
Alienability of Party's Interest under Lease Contract or of Lessor's Residual Interest in Goods; Delegation of Performance; Assignment of Rights

(1) Any interest of a party under a lease contract and the lessor's residual interest in the goods may be transferred unless

    (a) the transfer is voluntary and the lease contract prohibits the transfer; or

    (b) the transfer materially changes the duty of or materially increases the burden or risk imposed on the other party to the lease contract, and within a reasonable time after notice of the transfer the other party demands that the transferee comply with subsection (2) and the transferee fails to comply.

(2) Within a reasonable time after demand pursuant to subsection (1)(b), the transferee shall:

    (a) cure or provide adequate assurance that he [or she] will promptly cure any default other than one arising from the transfer;

    (b) compensate or provide adequate assurance that he [or she] will promptly compensate the other party to the lease contract and any other person holding an interest in the lease contract, except the party whose interest is being transferred, for any loss to that party resulting from the transfer;

    (c) provide adequate assurance of future due performance under the lease contract; and

    (d) assume the lease contract.

(3) Demand pursuant to subsection (1)(b) is without prejudice to the other party's rights against the transferee and the party whose interest is transferred.

(4) An assignment of "the lease" or of "all my rights under the lease" or an assignment in similar general terms is a transfer of rights, and unless the language or the circumstances, as in an assignment for security, indicate the contrary, the assignment is a delegation of duties by the assignor to the assignee and acceptance by the assignee constitutes a promise by him [or her] to perform those duties. This promise is enforceable by either the assignor or the other party to the lease contract.

(5) Unless otherwise agreed by the lessor and the lessee, no delegation of performance relieves the assignor as against the other party of any duty to perform or any liability for default.

(6) A right to damages for default with respect to the whole lease contract or a right arising out of the assignor's due performance of his [or her] entire obligation can be assigned despite agreement otherwise.

(7) To prohibit the transfer of an interest of a party under a lease contract, the language of prohibition must be specific, by a writing, and conspicuous.

§ 2A–304
Subsequent Lease of Goods by Lessor

(1) Subject to the provisions of Section 2A–303, a subsequent lessee from a lessor of goods under an existing lease contract obtains, to the extent of the leasehold interest transferred, the leasehold interest in the goods that the lessor had or had power to transfer, and except as provided in subsection (2) and Section 2A–527(4), takes subject to the existing lease contract. A lessor with voidable title has power to transfer a good leasehold interest to a good faith subsequent lessee for value, but only to the extent set forth in the preceding sentence. When goods have been delivered under a transaction of purchase the lessor has that power even though:

    (a) the lessor's transferor was deceived as to the identity of the lessor;

    (b) the delivery was in exchange for a check which is later dishonored;

    (c) it was agreed that the transaction was to be a "cash sale"; or

    (d) the delivery was procured through fraud punishable as larcenous under the criminal law.

(2) A subsequent lessee in the ordinary course of business from a lessor who is a merchant dealing in goods of that kind to whom the goods were entrusted by the existing lessee before the interest of the subsequent lessee became enforceable against the lessor obtains, to the extent of the leasehold interest transferred, all of the lessor's and the existing lessee's rights to the goods, and takes free of the existing lease contract.

(3) A subsequent lessee from the lessor of goods that are subject to an existing lease contract and are covered by a certificate of title issued under a statute of this State or of another jurisdiction takes no greater rights than those provided both by this section and by the certificate of title statute.

§ 2A–305
Sale or Sublease of Goods by Lessee

(1) Subject to the provisions of Section 2A–303, a buyer or sublessee from the lessee of goods under an existing lease contract obtains, to the extent of the interest transferred, the leasehold interest in the goods that the lessee had or had power to transfer, and except as provided in subsection (2) and Section 2A–511(4), takes subject to the existing lease contract. A lessee with a voidable leasehold interest has power to transfer a good leasehold interest to a good faith buyer for value or a good faith sublessee for value, but only to the extent set forth in the preceding sentence. When goods have been delivered under a transaction of lease the lessee has that power even though:

    (a) the lessor was deceived as to the identify of the lessee;

    (b) the delivery was in exchange for a check which is later dishonored; or

    (c) the delivery was procured through fraud punishable as larcenous under the criminal law.

(2) A buyer in the ordinary course of business or a sublessee in the ordinary course of business from a lessee who is a merchant dealing in goods of that kind to whom the goods were entrusted by the lessor obtains, to the extent of the interest transferred, all of the lessor's and lessee's rights to the goods, and takes free of the existing lease contract.

(3) A buyer or sublessee from the lessee of goods that are subject to an existing lease contract and are covered by a certificate of title issued under a statute of this State or of another jurisdiction takes no greater rights than those provided both by this section and by the certificate of title statute.

§ 2A–306
Priority of Certain Liens Arising by Operation of Law

If a person in the ordinary course of his [or her] business furnishes services or materials with respect to goods subject to a lease contract, a lien upon those goods in the possession of that person given by statute or rule of law for those materials or services takes priority over any interest of the lessor or lessee under the lease contract or this Article unless the lien is created by statute and the statute provides otherwise or unless the lien is created by rule of law and the rule of law provides otherwise.

§ 2A–307.
Priority of Liens Arising by Attachment or Levy on, Security Interests in, and Other Claims to Goods

(1) Except as otherwise provided in Section 2A–306, a creditor of a lessee takes subject to the lease contract.

(2) Except as otherwise provided in subsections (3) and (4) of this section and in Sections 2A–306 and 2A–308, a creditor of a lessor takes subject to the lease contract:
    (a) unless the creditor holds a lien that attached to the goods before the lease contract became enforceable, or
    (b) unless the creditor holds a security interest in the goods that under the Article on Secured Transactions (Article 9) would have priority over any other security interest in the goods perfected by a filing covering the goods and made at the time the lease contract became enforceable, whether or not any other security interest existed.

(3) A lessee in the ordinary course of business takes the leasehold interest free of a security interest in the goods created by the lessor even though the security interest is perfected and the lessee knows of its existence.

(4) A lessee other than a lessee in the ordinary course of business takes the leasehold interest free of a security interest to the extent that it secures future advances made after the secured party acquires knowledge of the lease or more than 45 days after the lease contract becomes enforceable, whichever first occurs, unless the future advances are made pursuant to a commitment entered into without knowledge of the lease and before the expiration of the 45-day period.

§ 2A–308
Special Rights of Creditors

(1) A creditor of a lessor in possession of goods subject to a lease contract may treat the lease contract as void if as against the creditor retention of possession by the lessor is fraudulent under any statute or rule of law, but retention of possession in good faith and

current course of trade by the lessor for a commercially reasonable time after the lease contract becomes enforceable is not fraudulent.

(2) Nothing in this Article impairs the rights of creditors of a lessor if the lease contract (a) becomes enforceable, not in current course of trade but in satisfaction of or as security for a pre-existing claim for money, security, or the like, and (b) is made under circumstances which under any statute or rule of law apart from this Article would constitute the transaction a fraudulent transfer or voidable preference.

(3) A creditor of a seller may treat a sale or an identification of goods to a contract for sale as void if as against the creditor retention of possession by the seller is fraudulent under any statute or rule of law, but retention of possession of the goods pursuant to a lease contract entered into by the seller as lessee and the buyer as lessor in connection with the sale or identification of the goods is not fraudulent if the buyer bought for value and in good faith.

§ 2A–309
Lessor's and Lessee's Rights When Goods Become Fixtures

(1) In this section:
    (a) goods are "fixtures" when they become so related to particular real estate that an interest in them arises under real estate law;
    (b) a "fixture filing" is the filing, in the office where a mortgage on the real estate would be recorded or registered, of a financing statement concerning goods that are or are to become fixtures and conforming to the requirements of subsection (5) of Section 9–402;
    (c) a lease is a "purchase money lease" unless the lessee has possession or use of the goods or the right to possession or use of the goods before the lease agreement is enforceable;
    (d) a mortgage is a "construction mortgage" to the extent it secures an obligation incurred for the construction of an improvement on land including the acquisition cost of the land, if the recorded writing so indicates; and
    (e) "encumbrance" includes real estate mortgages and other liens on real estate and all other rights in real estate that are not ownership interests.

(2) Under this Article a lease may be of goods that are fixtures or may continue in goods that become fixtures, but no lease exists under this Article of ordinary building materials incorporated into an improvement on land.

(3) This Article does not prevent creation of a lease of fixtures pursuant to real estate law.

(4) The perfected interest of a lessor of fixtures has priority over a conflicting interest of an encumbrancer or owner of the real estate if:
    (a) the lease is a purchase money lease, the conflicting interest of the encumbrancer or owner arises before the goods become fixtures, the interest of the lessor is perfected by a fixture filing before the goods become fixtures or within ten days thereafter, and the lessee has an interest of record in the real estate or is in possession of the real estate; or
    (b) the interest of the lessor is perfected by a fixture filing before the interest of the encumbrancer or owner is of

record, the lessor's interest has priority over any conflicting interest of a predecessor in title of the encumbrancer or owner, and the lessee has an interest of record in the real estate or is in possession of the real estate.

(5) The interest of a lessor of fixtures, whether or not perfected, has priority over the conflicting interest of an encumbrancer or owner of the real estate if:

(a) the fixtures are readily removable factory or office machines, readily removable equipment that is not primarily used or leased for use in the operation of the real estate, or readily removable replacements of domestic appliances that are goods subject to a consumer lease, and before the goods become fixtures the lease contract is enforceable; or

(b) the conflicting interest is a lien on the real estate obtained by legal or equitable proceedings after the lease contract is enforceable; or

(c) the encumbrancer or owner has consented in writing to the lease or has disclaimed an interest in the goods as fixtures; or

(d) the lessee has a right to remove the goods as against the encumbrancer or owner. If the lessee's right to remove terminates, the priority of the interest of the lessor continues for a reasonable time.

(6) Notwithstanding paragraph (a) of subsection (4) but otherwise subject to subsections (4) and (5), the interest of a lessor of fixtures is subordinate to the conflicting interest of an encumbrancer of the real estate under a construction mortgage recorded before the goods become fixtures if the goods become fixtures before the completion of the construction. To the extent given to refinance a construction mortgage, the conflicting interest of an encumbrancer of the real estate under a mortgage has this priority to the same extent as the encumbrancer of the real estate under the construction mortgage.

(7) In cases not within the preceding subsections, priority between the interest of a lessor of fixtures and the conflicting interest of an encumbrancer or owner of the real estate who is not the lessee is determined by the priority rules governing conflicting interests in real estate.

(8) If the interest of a lessor has priority over all conflicting interests of all owners and encumbrancers of the real estate, the lessor or the lessee may

(a) on default, expiration, termination, or cancellation of the lease agreement by the other party but subject to the provisions of the lease agreement and this Article, or

(b) if necessary to enforce his [or her] other rights and remedies under this Article, remove the goods from the real estate, free and clear of all conflicting interests of all owners and encumbrancers of the real estate, but he [or she] must reimburse any encumbrancer or owner of the real estate who is not the lessee and who has not otherwise agreed for the cost of repair of any physical injury, but not for any diminution in value of the real estate caused by the absence of the goods removed or by any necessity for replacing them. A person entitled to reimbursement may refuse permission to remove until the party seeking removal gives adequate security for the performance of this obligation.

(9) Even though the lease agreement does not create a security interest, the interest of a lessor of fixtures is perfected by filing a financing statement as a fixture filing for leased goods that are or are to become fixtures in accordance with the relevant provisions of the Article on Secured Transactions (Article 9).

§ 2A–310
Lessor's and Lessee's Rights When Goods Become Accessions

(1) Goods are "accessions" when they are installed in or affixed to other goods.

(2) The interest of a lessor or a lessee under a lease contract entered into before the goods became accessions is superior to all interests in the whole except as stated in subsection (4).

(3) The interest of a lessor or a lessee under a lease contract entered into at the time or after the goods became accessions is superior to all subsequently acquired interests in the whole except as stated in subsection (4) but is subordinate to interests in the whole existing at the time the lease contract was made unless the holders of such interests in the whole have in writing consented to the lease or disclaimed an interest in the goods as part of the whole.

(4) The interest of a lessor or a lessee under a lease contract described in subsection (2) or (3) is subordinate to the interest of

(a) a buyer in the ordinary course of business or a lessee in the ordinary course of business of any interest in the whole acquired after the goods became accessions; or

(b) a creditor with a security interest in the whole perfected before the lease contract was made to the extent that the creditor makes subsequent advances without knowledge of the lease contract.

(5) When under subsections (2) or (3) and (4) a lessor or a lessee of accessions holds an interest that is superior to all interests in the whole, the lessor or the lessee may

(a) on default, expiration, termination, or cancellation of the lease contract by the other party but subject to the provisions of the lease contract and this Article, or

(b) if necessary to enforce his [or her] other rights and remedies under this Article, remove the goods from the whole, free and clear of all interests in the whole, but he [or she] must reimburse any holder of an interest in the whole who is not the lessee and who has not otherwise agreed for the cost of repair of any physical injury but not for any diminution in value of the whole caused by the absence of the goods removed or by any necessity for replacing them. A person entitled to reimbursement may refuse permission to remove until the party seeking removal gives adequate security for the performance of this obligation.

Part 4/Performance of Lease Contract: Repudiated, Substituted and Excused
§ 2A–401
Insecurity: Adequate Assurance of Performance

(1) A lease contract imposes an obligation on each party that the other's expectation of receiving due performance will not be impaired.

(2) If reasonable grounds for insecurity arise with respect to the performance of either party, the insecure party may demand in writing adequate assurance of due performance. Until the insecure party receives that assurance, if commercially reasonable the insecure party may suspend any performance for which he [or she] has not already received the agreed return.

(3) A repudiation of the lease contract occurs if assurance of due performance adequate under the circumstances of the particular case is not provided to the insecure party within a reasonable time, not to exceed 30 days after receipt of a demand by the other party.

(4) Between merchants, the reasonableness of grounds for insecurity and the adequacy of any assurance offered must be determined according to commercial standards.

(5) Acceptance of any nonconforming delivery or payment does not prejudice the aggrieved party's right to demand adequate assurance of future performance.

§ 2A–402
Anticipatory Repudiation

If either party repudiates a lease contract with respect to a performance not yet due under the lease contract, the loss of which performance will substantially impair the value of the lease contract to the other, the aggrieved party may:

(a) for a commercially reasonable time, await retraction of repudiation and peformance by the repudiating party;

(b) make demand pursuant to Section 2A–401 and await assurance of future performance adequate under the circumstances of the particular case; or

(c) resort to any right or remedy upon default under the lease contract or this Article, even though the aggrieved party has notified the repudiating party that the aggrieved party would await the repudiating party's performance and assurance and has urged retraction. In addition, whether or not the aggrieved party is pursuing one of the foregoing remedies, the aggrieved party may suspend performance or, if the aggrieved party is the lessor, proceed in accordance with the provisions of this Article on the lessor's right to identify goods to the lease contract notwithstanding default or to salvage unfinished goods (Section 2A–524).

§ 2A–403
Retraction of Anticipatory Repudiation

(1) Until the repudiating party's next performance is due, the repudiating party can retract the repudiation unless, since the repudiation, the aggrieved party has cancelled the lease contract or materially changed the aggrieved party's position or otherwise indicated that the aggrieved party considers the repudiation final.

(2) Retraction may be by any method that clearly indicates to the aggrieved party that the repudiating party intends to perform under the lease contract and includes any assurance demanded under Section 2A–401.

(3) Retraction reinstates a repudiating party's rights under a lease contract with due excuse and allowance to the aggrieved party for any delay occasioned by the repudiation.

§ 2A–404
Substituted Performance

(1) If without fault of the lessee, the lessor and the supplier, the agreed berthing, loading, or unloading facilities fail or the agreed type of carrier becomes unavailable or the agreed manner of delivery otherwise becomes commercially impracticable, but a commercially reasonable substitute is available, the substitute performance must be tendered and accepted.

(2) If the agreed means or manner of payment fails because of domestic or foreign governmental regulation:

(a) the lessor may withhold or stop delivery or cause the supplier to withhold or stop delivery unless the lessee provides a means or manner of payment that is commercially a substantial equivalent; and

(b) if delivery has already been taken, payment by the means or in the manner provided by the regulation discharges the lessee's obligation unless the regulation is discriminatory, oppressive, or predatory.

§ 2A–405
Excused Performance

Subject to Section 2A–404 on substituted performance, the following rules apply:

(a) Delay in delivery or nondelivery in whole or in part by a lessor or a supplier who complies with paragraphs (b) and (c) is not a default under the lease contract if performance as agreed has been made impracticable by the occurrence of a contingency the nonoccurrence of which was a basic assumption on which the lease contract was made or by compliance in good faith with any applicable foreign or domestic governmental regulation or order, whether or not the regulation or order later proves to be invalid.

(b) If the causes mentioned in paragraph (a) affect only part of the lessor's or the supplier's capacity to perform, he [or she] shall allocate production and deliveries among his [or her] customers but at his [or her] option may include regular customers not then under contract for sale or lease as well as his [or her] own requirements for further manufacture. He [or she] may so allocate in any manner that is fair and reasonable.

(c) The lessor seasonably shall notify the lessee and in the case of a finance lease the supplier seasonably shall notify the lessor and the lessee, if known, that there will be delay or nondelivery and, if allocation is required under paragraph (b), of the estimated quota thus made available for the lessee.

§ 2A–406
Procedure on Excused Performance

(1) If the lessee receives notification of a material or indefinite delay or an allocation justified under Section 2A–405, the lessee may by written notification to the lessor as to any goods involved, and with respect to all of the goods if under an installment lease contract the value of the whole lease contract is substantially impaired (Section 2A–510):

(a) terminate the lease contract (Section 2A–505(2)); or

(b) except in a finance lease that is not a consumer lease, modify the lease contract by accepting the available quota in substitution, with due allowance from the rent payable for the balance of the lease term for the deficiency but without further right against the lessor.

(2) If, after receipt of a notification from the lessor under Section 2A–405, the lessee fails so to modify the lease agreement within a reasonable time not exceeding 30 days, the lease contract lapses with respect to any deliveries affected.

§ 2A–407
Irrevocable Promises: Finance Leases

(1) In the case of a finance lease that is not a consumer lease the lessee's promises under the lease contract become irrevocable and independent upon the lessee's acceptance of the goods.

(2) A promise that has become irrevocable and independent under subsection (1):
    (a) is effective and enforceable between the parties or against third parties including assignees of the parties, and
    (b) is not subject to cancellation, termination, modification, repudiation, excuse, or substitution without the consent of the party to whom the promise runs.

Part 5/Default
A. In General
§ 2A–501
Default: Procedure

(1) Whether the lessor or the lessee is in default under a lease contract is determined by the lease agreement and this Article.

(2) If the lessor or the lessee is in default under the lease contract, the party seeking enforcement has rights and remedies as provided in this Article and, except as limited by this Article, as provided in the lease agreement.

(3) If the lessor or the lessee is in default under the lease contract, the party seeking enforcement may reduce the party's claim to judgment, or otherwise enforce the lease contract by self-help or any available judicial procedure or nonjudicial procedure, including administrative proceeding, arbitration, or the like, in accordance with this Article.

(4) Except as otherwise provided in this Article or the lease agreement, the rights and remedies referred to in subsections (2) and (3) are cumulative.

(5) If the lease agreement covers both real property and goods, the party seeking enforcement may proceed under this Part as to the goods, or under other applicable law as to both the real property and the goods in accordance with his [or her] rights and remedies in respect of the real property, in which case this Part does not apply.

§ 2A–502
Notice after Default

Except as otherwise provided in this Article or the lease agreement, the lessor or lessee in default under the lease contract is not entitled to notice of default or notice of enforcement from the other party to the lease agreement.

§ 2A–503
Modification or Impairment of Rights and Remedies

(1) Except as otherwise provided in this Article, the lease agreement may include rights and remedies for default in addition to or in substitution for those provided in this Article and may limit or alter the measure of damages recoverable under this Article.

(2) Resort to a remedy provided under this Article or in the lease agreement is optional unless the remedy is expressly agreed to be exclusive. If circumstances cause an exclusive or limited remedy to fail of its essential purpose, or provision for an exclusive remedy is unconscionable, remedy may be had as provided in this Article.

(3) Consequential damages may be liquidated under Section 2A–504, or may otherwise be limited, altered, or excluded unless the limitation, alteration, or exclusion is unconscionable. Limitation of consequential damages for injury to the person in the case of consumer goods is prima facie unconscionable but limitation of damages where the loss is commercial is not.

(4) Rights and remedies on default by the lessor or the lessee with respect to any obligation or promise collateral or ancillary to the lease contract are not impaired by this Article.

§ 2A–504
Liquidation of Damages

(1) Damages payable by either party for default, or any other act or omission, including indemnity for loss or diminution of anticipated tax benefits or loss or damage to lessor's residual interest, may be liquidated in the lease agreement but only at an amount or by a formula that is reasonable in light of the then anticipated harm caused by the default or other act or omission.

(2) If the lease agreement provides for liquidation of damages, and such provision does not comply with subsection (1), or such provision is an exclusive or limited remedy that circumstances cause to fail of its essential purpose, remedy may be had as provided in this Article.

(3) If the lessor justifiably withholds or stops delivery of goods because of the lessee's default or insolvency (Section 2A–525 or 2A–526), the lessee is entitled to restitution of any amount by which the sum of his [or her] payments exceeds:
    (a) the amount to which the lessor is entitled by virtue of terms liquidating the lessor's damages in accordance with subsection (1); or
    (b) in the absence of those terms, 20 percent of the then present value of the total rent the lessee was obligated to pay for the balance of the lease term, or, in the case of a consumer lease, the lesser of such amount or $500.

(4) A lessee's right to restitution under subsection (3) is subject to offset to the extent the lessor establishes:
    (a) a right to recover damages under the provisions of this Article other than subsection (1); and
    (b) the amount or value of any benefits received by the lessee directly or indirectly by reason of the lease contract.

§ 2A–505
Cancellation and Termination and Effect of Cancellation, Termination, Rescission, or Fraud on Rights and Remedies

(1) On cancellation of the lease contract, all obligations that are still executory on both sides are discharged, but any right based on prior default or performance survives, and the cancelling party also retains any remedy for default of the whole lease contract or any unperformed balance.

(2) On termination of the lease contract, all obligations that are still executory on both sides are discharged but any right based on prior default or performance survives.

(3) Unless the contrary intention clearly appears, expressions of "cancellation", "rescission", or the like of the lease contract may not be construed as a renunciation or discharge of any claim in damages for an antecedent default.

(4) Rights and remedies for material misrepresentation or fraud include all rights and remedies available under this Article for default.

(5) Neither rescission nor a claim for rescission of the lease contract nor rejection or return of the goods may bar or be deemed inconsistent with a claim for damages or other right or remedy.

§ 2A–506
Statute of Limitations

(1) An action for default under a lease contract, including breach of warranty or indemnity, must be commenced within 4 years after the cause of action accrued. By the original lease contract the parties may reduce the period of limitation to not less than one year.

(2) A cause of action for default accrues when the act or omission on which the default or breach of warranty is based is or should have been discovered by the aggrieved party, or when the default occurs, whichever is later. A cause of action for indemnity accrues when the act or omission on which the claim for indemnity is based is or should have been discovered by the indemnified party, whichever is later.

(3) If an action commenced within the time limited by subsection (1) is so terminated as to leave available a remedy by another action for the same default or breach of warranty or indemnity, the other action may be commenced after the expiration of the time limited within 6 months after the termination of the first action unless the termination resulted from voluntary discontinuance or from dismissal for failure or neglect to prosecute.

(4) This section does not alter the law on tolling of the statute of limitations nor does it apply to causes of action that have accrued before this Article becomes effective.

§ 2A–507
Proof of Market Rent: Time and Place

(1) Damages based on market rent (Section 2A–519 or 2A–528) are determined according to the rent for the use of the goods concerned for a lease term identical to the remaining lease term of the original lease agreement and prevailing at the time of the default.

(2) If evidence of rent for the use of the goods concerned for a lease term identical to the remaining lease term of the original lease agreement and prevailing at the times or places described in this Article is not readily available, the rent prevailing within any reasonable time before or after the time described or at any other place or for a different lease term which in commercial judgment or under usage of trade would serve as a reasonable substitute for the one described may be used, making any proper allowance for the difference, including the cost of transporting the goods to or from the other place.

(3) Evidence of a relevant rent prevailing at a time or place or for a lease term other than the one described in this Article offered by one party is not admissible unless and until he [or she] has given the other party notice the court finds sufficient to prevent unfair surprise.

(4) If the prevailing rent or value of any goods regularly leased in any established market is in issue, reports in official publications or trade journals or in newspapers or periodicals of general circulation published as the reports of that market are admissible in evidence. The circumstances of the preparation of the report may be shown to affect its weight but not its admissibility.

B. Default by Lessor
§ 2A–508
Lessee's Remedies

(1) If a lessor fails to deliver the goods in conformity to the lease contract (Section 2A–509) or repudiates the lease contract (Section 2A–402), or a lessee rightfully rejects the goods (Section 2A–509) or justifiably revokes acceptance of the goods (Section 2A–517), then with respect to any goods involved, and with respect to all of the goods if under an installment lease contract the value of the whole lease contract is substantially impaired (Section 2A–510), the lessor is in default under the lease contract and the lessee may:
   (a) cancel the lease contract (Section 2A–505(1));
   (b) recover so much of the rent and security as has been paid, but in the case of an installment lease contract the recovery is that which is just under the circumstances;
   (c) cover and recover damages as to all goods affected whether or not they have been identified to the lease contract (Sections 2A–518 and 2A–520), or recover damages for nondelivery (Sections 2A–519 and 2A–520).

(2) If a lessor fails to deliver the goods in conformity to the lease contract or repudiates the lease contract, the lessee may also:
   (a) if the goods have been identified, recover them (Section 2A–522); or
   (b) in a proper case, obtain specific performance or replevy the goods (Section 2A–521).

(3) If a lessor is otherwise in default under a lease contract, the lessee may exercise the rights and remedies provided in the lease contract and this Article.

(4) If a lessor has breached a warranty, whether express or implied, the lessee may recover damages (Section 2A–519(4)).

(5) On rightful rejection or justifiable revocation of acceptance, a lessee has a security interest in goods in the lessee's possession or control for any rent and security that has been paid and any expenses reasonably incurred in their inspection, receipt, transportation, and care and custody and may hold those goods and dispose of them in good faith and in a commercially reasonable manner, subject to the provisions of Section 2A–527(5).

(6) Subject to the provisions of Section 2A–407, a lessee, on notifying the lessor of the lessee's intention to do so, may deduct all or any part of the damages resulting from any default under the lease contract from any part of the rent still due under the same lease contract.

§ 2A–509
Lessee's Rights on Improper Delivery; Rightful Rejection

(1) Subject to the provisions of Section 2A–510 on default in installment lease contracts, if the goods or the tender or delivery fail in any respect to conform to the lease contract, the lessee may reject or accept the goods or accept any commercial unit or units and reject the rest of the goods.

(2) Rejection of goods is ineffective unless it is within a reasonable time after tender or delivery of the goods and the lessee seasonably notifies the lessor.

§ 2A–510
Installment Lease Contracts: Rejection and Default

(1) Under an installment lease contract a lessee may reject any delivery that is nonconforming if the nonconformity substantially impairs the value of that delivery and cannot be cured or the nonconformity is a defect in the required documents; but if the nonconformity does not fall within subsection (2) and the lessor or the supplier gives adequate assurance of its cure, the lessee must accept that delivery.

(2) Whenever nonconformity or default with respect to one or more deliveries substantially impairs the value of the installment lease contract as a whole there is a default with respect to the whole. But, the aggrieved party reinstates the installment lease contract as a whole if the aggrieved party accepts a nonconforming delivery without seasonably notifying of cancellation or brings an action with respect only to past deliveries or demands performance as to future deliveries.

§ 2A–511
Merchant Lessee's Duties as to Rightfully Rejected Goods

(1) Subject to any security interest of a lessee (Section 2A–508(5)), if a lessor or a supplier has no agent or place of business at the market of rejection, a merchant lessee, after rejection of goods in his [or her] possession or control, shall follow any reasonable instructions received from the lessor or the supplier with respect to the goods. In the absence of those instructions, a merchant lessee shall make reasonable efforts to sell, lease, or otherwise dispose of the goods for the lessor's account if they threaten to decline in value speedily. Instructions are not reasonable if on demand indemnity for expenses is not forthcoming.

(2) If a merchant lessee (subsection (1)) or any other lessee (Section 2A–512) disposes of goods, he [or she] is entitled to reimbursement either from the lessor or the supplier or out of the proceeds for reasonable expenses of caring for and disposing of the goods and, if the expenses include no disposition commission, to such commission as is usual in the trade, or if there is none, to a reasonable sum not exceeding 10 percent of the gross proceeds.

(3) In complying with this section or Section 2A–512, the lessee is held only to good faith. Good faith conduct hereunder is neither acceptance or conversion nor the basis of an action for damages.

(4) A purchaser who purchases in good faith from a lessee pursuant to this section or Section 2A–512 takes the goods free of any rights of the lessor and the supplier even though the lessee fails to comply with one or more of the requirements of this Article.

§ 2A–512
Lessee's Duties as to Rightfully Rejected Goods

(1) Except as otherwise provided with respect to goods that threaten to decline in value speedily (Section 2A–511) and subject to any security interest of a lessee (Section 2A–508(5)):

(a) the lessee, after rejection of goods in the lessee's possession, shall hold them with reasonable care at the lessor's or the supplier's disposition for a reasonable time after the lessee's seasonable notification of rejection;

(b) if the lessor or the supplier gives no instructions within a reasonable time after notification of rejection, the lessee may store the rejected goods for the lessor's or the supplier's account or ship them to the lessor or the supplier or dispose of them for the lessor's or the supplier's account with reimbursement in the manner provided in Section 2A–511; but

(c) the lessee has no further obligations with regard to goods rightfully rejected.

(2) Action by the lessee pursuant to subsection (1) is not acceptance or conversion.

§ 2A–513
Cure by Lessor of Improper Tender or Delivery; Replacement

(1) If any tender or delivery by the lessor or the supplier is rejected because nonconforming and the time for performance has not yet expired, the lessor or the supplier may seasonably notify the lessee of the lessor's or the supplier's intention to cure and may then make a conforming delivery within the time provided in the lease contract.

(2) If the lessee rejects a nonconforming tender that the lessor or the supplier had reasonable grounds to believe would be acceptable with or without money allowance, the lessor or the supplier may have a further reasonable time to substitute a conforming tender if he [or she] seasonably notifies the lessee.

§ 2A–514
Waiver of Lessee's Objections

(1) In rejecting goods, a lessee's failure to state a particular defect that is ascertainable by reasonable inspection precludes the lessee from relying on the defect to justify rejection or to establish default:

(a) if, stated seasonably, the lessor or the supplier could have cured it (Section 2A–513); or

(b) between merchants if the lessor or the supplier after rejection has made a request in writing for a full and final written statement of all defects on which the lessee proposes to rely.

(2) A lessee's failure to reserve rights when paying rent or other consideration against documents precludes recovery of the payment for defects apparent on the face of the documents.

§ 2A–515
Acceptance of Goods

(1) Acceptance of goods occurs after the lessee has had a reasonable opportunity to inspect the goods and

(a) the lessee signifies or acts with respect to the goods in a manner that signifies to the lessor or the supplier that the goods are conforming or that the lessee will take or retain them in spite of their nonconformity; or

(b) the lessee fails to make an effective rejection of the goods (Section 2A–509(2)).

(2) Acceptance of a part of any commercial unit is acceptance of that entire unit.

§ 2A–516
Effect of Acceptance of Goods; Notice of Default; Burden of Establishing Default after Acceptance; Notice of Claim or Litigation to Person Answerable Over

(1) A lessee must pay rent for any goods accepted in accordance with the lease contract, with due allowance for goods rightfully rejected or not delivered.

(2) A lessee's acceptance of goods precludes rejection of the goods accepted. In the case of a finance lease, if made with knowledge of a nonconformity, acceptance cannot be revoked because of it. In any other case, if made with knowledge of a nonconformity, acceptance cannot be revoked because of it unless the acceptance was on the reasonable assumption that the nonconformity would be seasonably cured. Acceptance does not of itself impair any other remedy provided by this Article or the lease agreement for nonconformity.

(3) If a tender has been accepted:

(a) within a reasonable time after the lessee discovers or should have discovered any default, the lessee shall notify the lessor and the supplier, or be barred from any remedy;

(b) except in the case of a consumer lease, within a reasonable time after the lessee receives notice of litigation for infringement or the like (Section 2A–211) the lessee shall notify the lessor or be barred from any remedy over for liability established by the litigation; and

(c) the burden is on the lessee to establish any default.

(4) If a lessee is sued for breach of a warranty or other obligation for which a lessor or a supplier is answerable over:

(a) The lessee may give the lessor or the supplier written notice of the litigation. If the notice states that the lessor or the supplier may come in and defend and that if the lessor or the supplier does not do so he [or she] will be bound in any action against him [or her] by the lessee by any determination of fact common to the two litigations, then unless the lessor or the supplier after seasonable receipt of the notice does come in and defend he [or she] is so bound.

(b) The lessor or the supplier may demand in writing that the lessee turn over control of the litigation including settlement if the claim is one for infringement or the like (Section 2A–211) or else be barred from any remedy over. If the demand states that the lessor or the supplier agrees to bear all expense and to satisfy any adverse judgment, then unless the lessee after seasonable receipt of the demand does turn over control the lessee is so barred.

(5) The provisions of subsections (3) and (4) apply to any obligation of a lessee to hold the lessor or the supplier harmless against infringement or the like (Section 2A–211).

§ 2A–517
Revocation of Acceptance of Goods

(1) A lessee may revoke acceptance of a lot or commercial unit whose nonconformity substantially impairs its value to the lessee if he [or she] has accepted it:

(a) except in the case of a finance lease, on the reasonable assumption that its nonconformity would be cured and it has not been seasonably cured; or

(b) without discovery of the nonconformity if the lessee's acceptance was reasonably induced either by the lessor's assurances or, except in the case of a finance lease, by the difficulty of discovery before acceptance.

(2) Revocation of acceptance must occur within a reasonable time after the lessee discovers or should have discovered the ground for it and before any substantial change in condition of the goods which is not caused by the nonconformity. Revocation is not effective until the lessee notifies the lessor.

(3) A lessee who so revokes has the same rights and duties with regard to the goods involved as if the lessee had rejected them.

§ 2A–518
Cover; Substitute Goods

(1) After default by a lessor under the lease contract (Section 2A–508(1)), the lessee may cover by making in good faith and without unreasonable delay any purchase or lease of or contract to purchase or lease goods in substitution for those due from the lessor.

(2) Except as otherwise provided with respect to damages liquidated in the lease agreement (Section 2A–504) or determined by agreement of the parties (Section 1–102(3)), if a lessee's cover is by lease agreement substantially similar to the original lease agreement and the lease agreement is made in good faith and in a commercially reasonable manner, the lessee may recover from the lessor as damages (a) the present value, as of the date of default, of the difference between the total rent for the lease term of the new lease agreement and the total rent for the remaining lease term of the original lease agreement and (b) any incidental or consequential damages less expenses saved in consequence of the lessor's default.

(3) If a lessee's cover does not qualify for treatment under subsection (2), the lessee may recover from the lessor as if the lessee had elected not to cover and Section 2A–519 governs.

§ 2A–519
Lessee's Damages for Non-Delivery, Repudiation, Default and Breach of Warranty in Regard to Accepted Goods

(1) If a lessee elects not to cover or a lessee elects to cover and the cover does not qualify for treatment under Section 2A–518(2), the measure of damages for non-delivery or repudiation by the lessor or for rejection or revocation of acceptance by the lessee is the present value as of the date of the default of the difference between the then market rent and the original rent, computed for the remaining lease term of the original lease agreement together with incidental and consequential damages, less expenses saved in consequence of the lessor's default.

(2) Market rent is to be determined as of the place for tender or, in cases of rejection after arrival or revocation of acceptance, as of the place of arrival.

(3) If the lessee has accepted goods and given notification (Section 2A–516(3)), the measure of damages for non-conforming tender or delivery by a lessor is the loss resulting in the ordinary course of events from the lessor's default as determined in any manner that is reasonable together with incidental and consequential damages, less expenses saved in consequence of the lessor's default.

(4) The measure of damages for breach of warranty is the present value at the time and place of acceptance of the difference between the value of the use of the goods accepted and the value if they had been as warranted for the lease term, unless special circumstances show proximate damages of a different amount, together with incidental and consequential damages, less expenses saved in consequence of the lessor's default or breach of warranty.

§ 2A–520
Lessee's Incidental and Consequential Damages

(1) Incidental damages resulting from a lessor's default include expenses reasonably incurred in inspection, receipt, transportation, and care and custody of goods rightfully rejected or goods the acceptance of which is justifiably revoked, any commercially reasonable charges, expenses or commissions in connection with effecting cover, and any other reasonable expense incident to the default.

(2) Consequential damages resulting from a lessor's default include:
  (a) any loss resulting from general or particular requirements and needs of which the lessor at the time of contracting had reason to know and which could not reasonably be prevented by cover or otherwise; and
  (b) injury to person or property proximately resulting from any breach of warranty.

§ 2A–521
Lessee's Right to Specific Performance or Replevin

(1) Specific performance may be decreed if the goods are unique or in other proper circumstances.

(2) A decree for specific performance may include any terms and conditions as to payment of the rent, damages, or other relief that the court deems just.

(3) A lessee has a right of replevin, detinue, sequestration, claim and delivery, or the like for goods identified to the lease contract if after reasonable effort the lessee is unable to effect cover for those goods or the circumstances reasonably indicate that the effort will be unavailing.

§ 2A–522
Lessee's Right to Goods on Lessor's Insolvency

(1) Subject to subsection (2) and even though the goods have not been shipped, a lessee who has paid a part or all of the rent and security for goods identified to a lease contract (Section 2A–217) on making and keeping good a tender of any unpaid portion of the rent and security due under the lease contract may recover the goods identified from the lessor if the lessor becomes insolvent within 10 days after receipt of the first installment of rent and security.

(2) A lessee acquires the right to recover goods identified to a lease contract only if they conform to the lease contract.

C. Default by Lessee
§ 2A–523
Lessor's Remedies

(1) If a lessee wrongfully rejects or revokes acceptance of goods or fails to make a payment when due or repudiates with respect to a part or the whole, then, with respect to any goods involved, and with respect to all of the goods if under an installment lease contract the value of the whole lease contract is substantially impaired (Section 2A–510), the lessee is in default under the lease contract and the lessor may:
  (a) cancel the lease contract (Section 2A–505(1));
  (b) proceed respecting goods not identified to the lease contract (Section 2A–524);
  (c) withhold delivery of the goods and take possession of goods previously delivered (Section 2A–525);
  (d) stop delivery of the goods by any bailee (Section 2A–526);
  (e) dispose of the goods and recover damages (Section 2A–527), or retain the goods and recover damages (Section 2A–528), or in a proper case recover rent (Section 2A–529).

(2) If a lessee is otherwise in default under a lease contract, the lessor may exercise the rights and remedies provided in the lease contract and this Article.

§ 2A–524
Lessor's Right to Identify Goods to Lease Contract

(1) A lessor aggrieved under Section 2A–523(1) may:
  (a) identify to the lease contract conforming goods not already identified if at the time the lessor learned of the default they were in the lessor's or the supplier's possession or control; and
  (b) dispose of goods (Section 2A–527(1)) that demonstrably have been intended for the particular lease contract even though those goods are unfinished.

(2) If the goods are unfinished, in the exercise of reasonable commercial judgment for the purposes of avoiding loss and of effective realization, an aggrieved lessor or the supplier may either complete manufacture and wholly identify the goods to the lease contract or cease manufacture and lease, sell, or otherwise dispose of the goods for scrap or salvage value or proceed in any other reasonable manner.

§ 2A–525
Lessor's Right to Possession of Goods

(1) If a lessor discovers the lessee to be insolvent, the lessor may refuse to deliver the goods.

(2) The lessor has on default by the lessee under the lease contract the right to take possession of the goods. If the lease contract so provides, the lessor may require the lessee to assemble the goods and make them available to the lessor at a place to be designated by the lessor which is reasonably convenient to both parties. Without removal, the lessor may render unusable any goods employed in trade or business, and may dispose of goods on the lessee's premises (Section 2A–527).

(3) The lessor may proceed under subsection (2) without judicial process if that can be done without breach of the peace or the lessor may proceed by action.

§ 2A–526
Lessor's Stoppage of Delivery in Transit or Otherwise

(1) A lessor may stop delivery of goods in the possession of a carrier or other bailee if the lessor discovers the lessee to be insolvent and may stop delivery of carload, truckload, planeload, or larger shipments of express or freight if the lessee repudiates or fails to make a payment due before delivery, whether for rent, security or otherwise under the lease contract, or for any other reason the lessor has a right to withhold or take possession of the goods.

(2) In pursuing its remedies under subsection (1) the lessor may stop delivery until
    (a) receipt of the goods by the lessee;
    (b) acknowledgment to the lessee by any bailee of the goods, except a carrier, that the bailee holds the goods for the lessee; or
    (c) such an acknowledgment to the lessee by a carrier via reshipment or as warehouseman.

(3) **(a)** To stop delivery, a lessor shall so notify as to enable the bailee by reasonable diligence to prevent delivery of the goods.
    (b) After notification, the bailee shall hold and deliver the goods according to the directions of the lessor, but the lessor is liable to the bailee for any ensuing charges or damages.
    (c) A carrier who has issued a nonnegotiable bill of lading is not obliged to obey a notification to stop received from a person other than the consignor.

§ 2A–527
Lessor's Rights to Dispose of Goods

(1) After a default by a lessee under the lease contract (Section 2A–523(1)) or after the lessor refuses to deliver or take possession of goods (Section 2A–525 or 2A–526), the lessor may dispose of the goods concerned or the undelivered balance thereof in good faith and without unreasonable delay by lease, sale or otherwise.

(2) If the disposition is by lease contract substantially similar to the original lease contract and the lease contract is made in good faith and in a commercially reasonable manner, the lessor may recover from the lessee as damages (a) accrued and unpaid rent as of the date of default, (b) the present value as of the date of default of the difference between the total rent for the remaining lease term of the original lease contract and the total rent for the lease term of the new lease contract, and (c) any incidental damages allowed under Section 2A–530, less expenses saved in consequence of the lessee's default.

(3) If the lessor's disposition is by lease contract that for any reason does not qualify for treatment under subsection (2), or is by sale or otherwise, the lessor may recover from the lessee as if the lessor had elected not to dispose of the goods and Section 2A–528 governs.

(4) A subsequent buyer or lessee who buys or leases from the lessor in good faith for value as a result of a disposition under this section takes the goods free of the original lease contract and any rights of the original lessee even though the lessor fails to comply with one or more of the requirements of this Article.

(5) The lessor is not accountable to the lessee for any profit made on any disposition. A lessee who has rightfully rejected or justifiably revoked acceptance shall account to the lessor for any excess over the amount of the lessee's security interest (Section 2A–508(5)).

§ 2A–528
Lessor's Damages for Non-Acceptance or Repudiation

(1) Except as otherwise provided with respect to damages liquidated in the lease agreement (Section 2A–504) or determined by agreement of the parties (Section 1–102(3)), if a lessor elects to retain the goods or a lessor elects to dispose of the goods and disposition is by lease agreement that for any reason does not qualify for treatment under Section 2A–527(2), or is by sale or otherwise, the lessor may recover from the lessee as damages for non-acceptance or repudiation by the lessee (a) accrued and unpaid rent as of the date of default, (b) the present value as of the date of default of the difference between the total rent for the remaining lease term of the original lease agreement and the market rent at the time and place for tender computed for the same lease term, and (c) any incidental damages allowed under Section 2A–530, less expenses saved in consequence of the lessee's default.

(2) If the measure of damages provided in subsection (1) is inadequate to put a lessor in as good a position as performance would have, the measure of damages is the profit, including reasonable overhead, the lessor would have made from full performance by the lessee, together with any incidental damages allowed under Section 2A–530, due allowance for costs reasonably incurred and due credit for payments or proceeds of disposition.

§ 2A–529
Lessor's Action for the Rent

(1) After default by the lessee under the lease contract (Section 2A–523(1)), if the lessor complies with subsection (2), the lessor may recover from the lessee as damages:
    (a) for goods accepted by the lessee and for conforming goods lost or damaged within a commercially reasonable time after risk of loss passes to the lessee (Section 2A–219), (i) accrued and unpaid rent as of the date of default, (ii) the present value as of the date of default of the rent for the remaining lease term of the lease agreement, and (iii) any incidental damages allowed under Section 2A–530, less expenses saved in consequence of the lessee's default; and
    (b) for goods identified to the lease contract if the lessor is unable after reasonable effort to dispose of them at a reasonable price or the circumstances reasonably indicate that effort will be unavailing, (i) accrued and unpaid rent as of the date of default, (ii) the present value as of the date of default of the rent for the remaining lease term of the lease agreement, and (iii) any incidental damages allowed under Section 2A–530, less expenses saved in consequence of the lessee's default.

(2) Except as provided in subsection (3), the lessor shall hold for the lessee for the remaining lease term of the lease agreement any goods that have been identified to the lease contract and are in the lessor's control.

(3) The lessor may dispose of the goods at any time before collection of the judgment for damages obtained pursuant to subsection (1) and the lessor may proceed against the lessee for damages pursuant to Section 2A–527 or Section 2A–528.

(4) Payment of the judgment for damages obtained pursuant to subsection (1) entitles the lessee to use and possession of the goods not then disposed of for the remaining lease term of the lease agreement.

(5) After a lessee has wrongfully rejected or revoked acceptance of goods, has failed to pay rent then due, or has repudiated (Section 2A–402), a lessor who is held not entitled to rent under this section must nevertheless be awarded damages for non-acceptance under Sections 2A–527 and 2A–528.

§ 2A–530
Lessor's Incidental Damages

Incidental damages to an aggrieved lessor include any commercially reasonable charges, expenses, or commissions incurred in stopping delivery, in the transportation, care and custody of goods after the lessee's default, in connection with return or disposition of the goods, or otherwise resulting from the default.

§ 2A–531
Standing to Sue Third Parties for Injury to Goods

(1) If a third party so deals with goods that have been identified to a lease contract as to cause actionable injury to a party to the lease contract (a) the lessor has a right of action against the third party, and (b) the lessee also has a right of action against the third party if the lessee:
    (i) has a security interest in the goods;
    (ii) has an insurable interest in the goods; or
    (iii) bears the risk of loss under the lease contract or has since the injury assumed that risk as against the lessor and the goods have been converted or destroyed.

(2) If at the time of the injury the party plaintiff did not bear the risk of loss as against the other party to the lease contract and there is no arrangement between them for disposition of the recovery, his [or her] suit or settlement, subject to his [or her] own interest, is as a fiduciary for the other party to the lease contract.

(3) Either party with the consent of the other may sue for the benefit of whom it may concern.

ARTICLE 3/COMMERCIAL PAPER*
Part 1/Short Title, Form and Interpretation
§ 3–101
Short Title

This Article shall be known and may be cited as Uniform Commercial Code–Commercial Paper.

*Authors' Note: Revised Articles 3 and 4 are included after the original version of these articles.

§ 3–102
Definitions and Index of Definitions

(1) In this Article unless the context otherwise requires
    (a) "Issue" means the first delivery of an instrument to a holder or a remitter.
    (b) An "order" is a direction to pay and must be more than an authorization or request. It must identify the person to pay with reasonable certainty. It may be addressed to one or more such persons jointly or in the alternative but not in succession.
    (c) A "promise" is an undertaking to pay and must be more than an acknowledgment of an obligation.
    (d) "Secondary party" means a drawer or endorser.
    (e) "Instrument" means a negotiable instrument.

(2) Other definitions applying to this Article and the sections in which they appear are:

"Acceptance". Section 3–410.
"Accommodation party". Section 3–415.
"Alteration". Section 3–407.
"Certificate of deposit". Section 3–104.
"Certification". Section 3–411.
"Check". Section 3–104.
"Definite time". Section 3–109.
"Dishonor". Section 3–507.
"Draft". Section 3–104.
"Holder in due course". Section 3–302.
"Negotiation". Section 3–202.
"Note". Section 3–104.
"Notice of dishonor". Section 3–508.
"On demand". Section 3–108.
"Presentment". Section 3–504.
"Protest". Section 3–509.
"Restrictive Indorsement". Section 3–205.
"Signature". Section 3–401.

(3) The following definitions in other Articles apply to this Article:

"Account". Section 4–104.
"Banking Day". Section 4–104.
"Clearing House". Section 4–104.
"Collecting Bank". Section 4–105.
"Customer". Section 4–104.
"Depositary Bank". Section 4–105.
"Documentary Draft". Section 4–104.
"Intermediary Bank". Section 4–105.
"Item". Section 4–104.
"Midnight deadline". Section 4–104.
"Payor Bank". Section 4–105.

(4) In addition Article 1 contains general definitions and principles of construction and interpretation applicable throughout this Article.

§ 3–103
Limitations on Scope of Article

(1) This Article does not apply to money, documents of title or investment securities.

(2) The provisions of this Article are subject to the provisions of the Article on Bank Deposits and Collections (Article 4) and Secured Transactions (Article 9).

§ 3–104
Form of Negotiable Instruments; "Draft"; "Check"; "Certificate of Deposit"; "Note"

(1) Any writing to be a negotiable instrument within this Article must

(a)   be signed by the maker or drawer; and

(b)   contain an unconditional promise or order to pay a sum certain in money and no other promise, order, obligation or power given by the maker or drawer except as authorized by this Article; and

(c)   be payable on demand or at a definite time; and

(d)   be payable to order or to bearer.

(2) A writing which complies with the requirements of this section is

(a)   a "draft" ("bill of exchange") if it is an order;

(b)   a "check" if it is a draft drawn on a bank and payable on demand;

(c)   a "certificate of deposit" if it is an acknowledgment by a bank of receipt of money with an engagement to repay it;

(d)   a "note" if it is a promise other than a certificate of deposit.

(3) As used in other Articles of this Act, and as the context may require, the terms "draft", "check", "certificate of deposit" and "note" may refer to instruments which are not negotiable within this Article as well as to instruments which are so negotiable.

§ 3–105
When Promise or Order Unconditional

(1) A promise or order otherwise unconditional is not made conditional by the fact that the instrument

(a)   is subject to implied or constructive conditions; or

(b)   states its consideration, whether performed or promised, or the transaction which gave rise to the instrument, or that the promise or order is made or the instrument matures in accordance with or "as per" such transaction; or

(c)   refers to or states that it arises out of a separate agreement or refers to a separate agreement for rights as to prepayment or acceleration; or

(d)   states that it is drawn under a letter of credit; or

(e)   states that it is secured, whether by mortgage, reservation of title or otherwise; or

(f)   indicates a particular account to be debited or any other fund or source from which reimbursement is expected; or

(g)   is limited to payment out of a particular fund or the proceeds of a particular source, if the instrument is issued by a government or governmental agency or unit; or

(h)   is limited to payment out of the entire assets of a partnership, unincorporated association, trust or estate by or on behalf of which the instrument is issued.

(2) A promise or order is not unconditional if the instrument

(a)   states that it is subject to or governed by any other agreement; or

(b)   states that it is to be paid only out of a particular fund or source except as provided in this section.

§ 3–106
Sum Certain

(1) The sum payable is a sum certain even though it is to be paid

(a)   with stated interest or by stated installments; or

(b)   with stated different rates of interest before and after default or a specified date; or

(c)   with a stated discount or addition if paid before or after the date fixed for payment; or

(d)   with exchange or less exchange, whether at a fixed rate or at the current rate; or

(e)   with costs of collection or an attorney's fee or both upon default.

(2) Nothing in this section shall validate any term which is otherwise illegal.

§ 3–107
Money

(1) An instrument is payable in money if the medium of exchange in which it is payable is money at the time the instrument is made. An instrument payable in "currency" or "current funds" is payable in money.

(2) A promise or order to pay a sum stated in a foreign currency is for a sum certain in money and, unless a different medium of payment is specified in the instrument, may be satisfied by payment of that number of dollars which the stated foreign currency will purchase at the buying sight rate for that currency on the day on which the instrument is payable or, if payable on demand, on the day of demand. If such an instrument specifies a foreign currency as the medium of payment the instrument is payable in that currency.

§ 3–108
Payable on Demand

Instruments payable on demand include those payable at sight or on presentation and those in which no time for payment is stated.

§ 3–109
Definite Time

(1) An instrument is payable at a definite time if by its terms it is payable

(a)   on or before a stated date or at a fixed period after a stated date; or

(b)   at a fixed period after sight; or

(c)   at a definite time subject to any acceleration; or

(d)   at a definite time subject to extension at the option of the holder, or to extension to a further definite time at the option of the maker or acceptor or automatically upon or after a specified act or event.

(2) An instrument which by its terms is otherwise payable only upon an act or event uncertain as to time of occurrence is not payable at a definite time even though the act or event has occurred.

§ 3–110
Payable to Order

(1) An instrument is payable to order when by its terms it is payable to the order or assigns of any person therein specified with reasonable certainty, or to him or his order, or when it is conspicuously designated on its face as "exchange" or the like and names a payee. It may be payable to the order of
(**a**) the maker or drawer; or
(**b**) the drawee; or
(**c**) a payee who is not maker, drawer or drawee; or
(**d**) two or more payees together or in the alternative; or
(**e**) an estate, trust or fund, in which case it is payable to the order of the representative of such estate, trust or fund or his successors; or
(**f**) an office, or an officer by his title as such in which case it is payable to the principal but the incumbent of the office or his successors may act as if he or they were the holder; or
(**g**) a partnership or unincorporated association, in which case it is payable to the partnership or association and may be indorsed or transferred by any person thereto authorized.

(2) An instrument not payable to order is not made so payable by such words as "payable upon return of this instrument properly indorsed."

(3) An instrument made payable both to order and to bearer is payable to order unless the bearer words are handwritten or typewritten.

§ 3–111
Payable to Bearer

An instrument is payable to bearer when by its terms it is payable to
(**a**) bearer or the order of bearer; or
(**b**) a specified person or bearer; or
(**c**) "cash" or the order of "cash", or any other indication which does not purport to designate a specific payee.

§ 3–112
Terms and Omissions Not Affecting Negotiability

(1) The negotiability of an instrument is not affected by
(**a**) the omission of a statement of any consideration or of the place where the instrument is drawn or payable; or
(**b**) a statement that collateral has been given to secure obligations either on the instrument or otherwise of an obligor on the instrument or that in case of default on those obligations the holder may realize on or dispose of the collateral; or
(**c**) a promise or power to maintain or protect collateral or to give additional collateral; or
(**d**) a term authorizing a confession of judgment on the instrument if it is not paid when due; or
(**e**) a term purporting to waive the benefit of any law intended for the advantage or protection of any obligor; or
(**f**) a term in a draft providing that the payee by indorsing or cashing it acknowledges full satisfaction of an obligation of the drawer; or
(**g**) a statement in a draft drawn in a set of parts (Section 3–801) to the effect that the order is effective only if no other part has been honored.

(2) Nothing in this section shall validate any term which is otherwise illegal.

§ 3–113
Seal

An instrument otherwise negotiable is within this Article even though it is under a seal.

§ 3–114
Date, Antedating, Postdating

(1) The negotiability of an instrument is not affected by the fact that it is undated, antedated or postdated.

(2) Where an instrument is antedated or postdated the time when it is payable is determined by the stated date if the instrument is payable on demand or at a fixed period after date.

(3) Where the instrument or any signature thereon is dated, the date is presumed to be correct.

§ 3–115
Incomplete Instruments

(1) When a paper whose contents at the time of signing show that it is intended to become an instrument is signed while still incomplete in any necessary respect it cannot be enforced until completed, but when it is completed in accordance with authority given it is effective as completed.

(2) If the completion is unauthorized the rules as to material alteration apply (Section 3–407), even though the paper was not delivered by the maker or drawer; but the burden of establishing that any completion is unauthorized is on the party so asserting.

§ 3–116
Instruments Payable to Two or More Persons

An instrument payable to the order of two or more persons
(**a**) if in the alternative is payable to any one of them and may be negotiated, discharged or enforced by any of them who has possession of it;
(**b**) if not in the alternative is payable to all of them and may be negotiated, discharged or enforced only by all of them.

§ 3–117
Instruments Payable with Words of Description

An instrument made payable to a named person with the addition of words describing him
(**a**) as agent or officer of a specified person is payable to his principal but the agent or officer may act as if he were the holder;
(**b**) as any other fiduciary for a specified person or purpose is payable to the payee and may be negotiated, discharged or enforced by him;
(**c**) in any other manner is payable to the payee unconditionally and the additional words are without effect on subsequent parties.

§ 3-118
Ambiguous Terms and Rules of Construction

The following rules apply to every instrument:

(a)   Where there is doubt whether the instrument is a draft or a note the holder may treat it as either. A draft drawn on the drawer is effective as a note.

(b)   Handwritten terms control typewritten and printed terms, and typewritten control printed.

(c)   Words control figures except that if the words are ambiguous figures control.

(d)   Unless otherwise specified a provision for interest means interest at the judgment rate at the place of payment from the date of the instrument, or if it is undated from the date of issue.

(e)   Unless the instrument otherwise specifies two or more persons who sign as maker, acceptor or drawer or indorser and as a part of the same transaction are jointly and severally liable even though the instrument contains such words as "I promise to pay".

(f)   Unless otherwise specified consent to extension authorizes a single extension for not longer than the original period. A consent to extension, expressed in the instrument, is binding on secondary parties and accommodation makers. A holder may not exercise his option to extend an instrument over the objection of a maker or acceptor or other party who in accordance with Section 3-604 tenders full payment when the instrument is due.

§ 3-119
Other Writings Affecting Instrument

(1)   As between the obligor and his immediate obligee or any transferee the terms of an instrument may be modified or affected by any other written agreement executed as a part of the same transaction, except that a holder in due course is not affected by any limitation of his rights arising out of the separate written agreement if he had no notice of the limitation when he took the instrument.

(2)   A separate agreement does not affect the negotiability of an instrument.

§ 3-120
Instruments "Payable Through" Bank

An instrument which states that it is "payable through" a bank or the like designates that bank as a collecting bank to make presentment but does not of itself authorize the bank to pay the instrument.

§ 3-121
Instruments Payable at Bank

Note: *If this Act is introduced in the Congress of the United States this section should be omitted.*
   (States to select either alternative)

Alternative A

A note or acceptance which states that it is payable at a bank is the equivalent of a draft drawn on the bank payable when it falls due

out of any funds of the maker or acceptor in current account or otherwise available for such payment.

Alternative B

A note or acceptance which states that it is payable at a bank is not of itself an order or authorization to the bank to pay it.

§ 3-122
Accrual of Cause of Action

(1)   A cause of action against a maker or an acceptor accrues
   (a)   in the case of a time instrument on the day after maturity;
   (b)   in the case of a demand instrument upon its date or, if no date is stated, on the date of issue.

(2)   A cause of action against the obligor of a demand or time certificate of deposit accrues upon demand, but demand on a time certificate may not be made until on or after the date of maturity.

(3)   A cause of action against a drawer of a draft or an indorser of any instrument accrues upon demand following dishonor of the instrument. Notice of dishonor is a demand.

(4)   Unless an instrument provides otherwise, interest runs at the rate provided by law for a judgment
   (a)   in the case of a maker, acceptor or other primary obligor of a demand instrument, from the date of demand;
   (b)   in all other cases from the date of accrual of the cause of action.

Part 2/Transfer and Negotiation
§ 3-201
Transfer: Right to Indorsement

(1)   Transfer of an instrument vests in the transferee such rights as the transferor has therein, except that a transferee who has himself been a party to any fraud or illegality affecting the instrument or who as a prior holder had notice of a defense or claim against it cannot improve his position by taking from a later holder in due course.

(2)   A transfer of a security interest in an instrument vests the foregoing rights in the transferee to the extent of the interest transferred.

(3)   Unless otherwise agreed any transfer for value of an instrument not then payable to bearer gives the transferee the specifically enforceable right to have the unqualified indorsement of the transferor. Negotiation takes effect only when the indorsement is made and until that time there is no presumption that the transferee is the owner.

§ 3-202
Negotiation

(1)   Negotiation is the transfer of an instrument in such form that the transferee becomes a holder. If the instrument is payable to order it is negotiated by delivery with any necessary indorsement; if payable to bearer it is negotiated by delivery.

(2) An indorsement must be written by or on behalf of the holder and on the instrument or on a paper so firmly affixed thereto as to become a part thereof.

(3) An indorsement is effective for negotiation only when it conveys the entire instrument or any unpaid residue. If it purports to be of less it operates only as a partial assignment.

(4) Words of assignment, condition, waiver, guaranty, limitation or disclaimer of liability and the like accompanying an indorsement do not affect its character as an indorsement.

§ 3–203
Wrong or Misspelled Name

Where an instrument is made payable to a person under a misspelled name or one other than his own he may indorse in that name or his own or both; but signature in both names may be required by a person paying or giving value for the instrument.

§ 3–204
Special Indorsement; Blank Indorsement

(1) A special indorsement specifies the person to whom or to whose order it makes the instrument payable. Any instrument specially indorsed becomes payable to the order of the special indorsee and may be further negotiated only by his indorsement.

(2) An indorsement in blank specifies no particular indorsee and may consist of a mere signature. An instrument payable to order and indorsed in blank becomes payable to bearer and may be negotiated by delivery alone until specially indorsed.

(3) The holder may convert a blank indorsement into a special indorsement by writing over the signature of the indorser in blank any contract consistent with the character of the indorsement.

§ 3–205
Restrictive Indorsements

An indorsement is restrictive which either
  (a) is conditional; or
  (b) purports to prohibit further transfer of the instrument; or
  (c) includes the words "for collection", "for deposit", "pay any bank", or like terms signifying a purpose of deposit or collection; or
  (d) otherwise states that it is for the benefit or use of the indorser or of another person.

§ 3–206
Effect of Restrictive Indorsement

(1) No restrictive indorsement prevents further transfer or negotiation of the instrument.

(2) An intermediary bank, or a payor bank which is not the depositary bank, is neither given notice nor otherwise affected by a restrictive indorsement of any person except the bank's immediate transferor or the person presenting for payment.

(3) Except for an intermediary bank, any transferee under an indorsement which is conditional or includes the words "for collection", "for deposit", "pay any bank", or like terms (subparagraphs (a) and (c) of Section 3–205) must pay or apply any value given by him for or on the security of the instrument consistently with the indorsement and to the extent that he does so he becomes a holder for value. In addition such transferee is a holder in due course if he otherwise complies with the requirements of Section 3–302 on what constitutes a holder in due course.

(4) The first taker under an indorsement for the benefit of the indorser or another person (subparagraph (d) of Section 3–205) must pay or apply any value given by him for or on the security of the instrument consistently with the indorsement and to the extent that he does so he becomes a holder for value. In addition such taker is a holder in due course if he otherwise complies with the requirements of Section 3–302 on what constitutes a holder in due course. A later holder for value is neither given notice nor otherwise affected by such restrictive indorsement unless he has knowledge that a fiduciary or other person has negotiated the instrument in any transaction for his own benefit or otherwise in breach of duty (subsection (2) of Section 3–304).

§ 3–207
Negotiation Effective Although It May Be Rescinded

(1) Negotiation is effective to transfer the instrument although the negotiation is
  (a) made by an infant, a corporation exceeding its powers, or any other person without capacity; or
  (b) obtained by fraud, duress or mistake of any kind; or
  (c) part of an illegal transaction; or
  (d) made in breach of duty.

(2) Except as against a subsequent holder in due course such negotiation is in an appropriate case subject to rescission, the declaration of a constructive trust or any other remedy permitted by law.

§ 3–208
Reacquisition

Where an instrument is returned to or reacquired by a prior party he may cancel any indorsement which is not necessary to his title and reissue or further negotiate the instrument, but any intervening party is discharged as against the reacquiring party and subsequent holders not in due course and if his indorsement has been cancelled is discharged as against subsequent holders in due course as well.

Part 3/Rights of a Holder
§ 3–301
Rights of a Holder

The holder of an instrument whether or not he is the owner may transfer or negotiate it and, except as otherwise provided in Section 3–603 on payment or satisfaction, discharge it or enforce payment in his own name.

§ 3–302
Holder in Due Course

(1) A holder in due course is a holder who takes the instrument
  (a) for value; and
  (b) in good faith; and
  (c) without notice that it is overdue or has been dishonored or of any defense against or claim to it on the part of any person.

(2)   A payee may be a holder in due course.

(3)   A holder does not become a holder in due course of an instrument:
   (a)   by purchase of it at judicial sale or by taking it under legal process; or
   (b)   by acquiring it in taking over an estate; or
   (c)   by purchasing it as part of a bulk transaction not in regular course of business of the transferor.

(4)   A purchase of a limited interest can be a holder in due course only to the extent of the interest purchased.

§ 3–303
Taking for Value

A holder takes the instrument for value
   (a)   to the extent that the agreed consideration has been performed or that he acquires a security interest in or a lien on the instrument otherwise than by legal process; or
   (b)   when he takes the instrument in payment of or as security for an antecedent claim against any person whether or not the claim is due; or
   (c)   when he gives a negotiable instrument for it or makes an irrevocable commitment to a third person.

§ 3–304
Notice to Purchaser

(1)   The purchaser has notice of a claim or defense if
   (a)   the instrument is so incomplete, bears such visible evidence of forgery or alteration, or is otherwise so irregular as to call into question its validity, terms or ownership or to create an ambiguity as to the party to pay; or
   (b)   the purchaser has notice that the obligation of any party is voidable in whole or in part, or that all parties have been discharged.

(2)   The purchaser has notice of a claim against the instrument when he has knowledge that a fiduciary has negotiated the instrument in payment of or as security for his own debt or in any transaction for his own benefit or otherwise in breach of duty.

(3)   The purchaser has notice that an instrument is overdue if he has reason to know
   (a)   that any part of the principal amount is overdue or that there is an uncured default in payment of another instrument of the same series; or
   (b)   that acceleration of the instrument has been made; or
   (c)   that he is taking a demand instrument after demand has been made or more than a reasonable length of time after its issue. A reasonable time for a check drawn and payable within the states and territories of the United States and the District of Columbia is presumed to be 30 days.

(4)   Knowledge of the following facts does not of itself give the purchaser notice of a defense or claim
   (a)   that the instrument is antedated or postdated;
   (b)   that it was issued or negotiated in return for an executory promise or accompanied by a separate agreement, unless the purchaser has notice that a defense or claim has arisen from the terms thereof;
   (c)   that any party has signed for accommodation;

   (d)   that an incomplete instrument has been completed, unless the purchaser has notice of any improper completion;
   (e)   that any person negotiating the instrument is or was a fiduciary;
   (f)   that there has been default in payment of interest on the instrument or in payment of any other instrument, except one of the same series.

(5)   The filing or recording of a document does not of itself constitute notice within the provisions of this Article to a person who would otherwise be a holder in due course.

(6)   To be effective notice must be received at such time and in such manner as to give a reasonable opportunity to act on it.

§ 3–305
Rights of a Holder in Due Course

To the extent that a holder is a holder in due course he takes the instrument free from

(1)   all claims to it on the part of any person; and

(2)   all defenses of any party to the instrument with whom the holder has not dealt except
   (a)   infancy, to the extent that it is a defense to a simple contract; and
   (b)   such other incapacity, or duress, or illegality of the transaction, as renders the obligation of the party a nullity; and
   (c)   such misrepresentation as has induced the party to sign the instrument with neither knowledge nor reasonable opportunity to obtain knowledge of its character or its essential terms; and
   (d)   discharge in insolvency proceedings; and
   (e)   any other discharge of which the holder has notice when he takes the instrument.

§ 3–306
Rights of One Not Holder in Due Course

Unless he has the rights of a holder in due course any person takes the instrument subject to
   (a)   all valid claims to it on the part of any person; and
   (b)   all defenses of any party which would be available in an action on a simple contract; and
   (c)   the defenses of want or failure of consideration, nonperformance of any condition precedent, non-delivery, or delivery for a special purpose (Section 3–408); and
   (d)   the defense that he or a person through whom he holds the instrument acquired it by theft, or that payment or satisfaction to such holder would be inconsistent with the terms of a restrictive indorsement. The claim of any third person to the instrument is not otherwise available as a defense to any party liable thereon unless the third person himself defends the action for such party.

§ 3–307
Burden of Establishing Signatures, Defenses and Due Course

(1)   Unless specifically denied in the pleadings each signature on an instrument is admitted. When the effectiveness of a signature is put in issue

(a) the burden of establishing it is on the party claiming under the signature; but

(b) the signature is presumed to be genuine or authorized except where the action is to enforce the obligation of a purported signer who has died or become incompetent before proof is required.

(2) When signatures are admitted or established, production of the instrument entitles a holder to recover on it unless the defendant establishes a defense.

(3) After it is shown that a defense exists a person claiming the rights of a holder in due course has the burden of establishing that he or some person under whom he claims is in all respects a holder in due course.

Part 4/Liability of Parties
§ 3–401
Signature

(1) No person is liable on an instrument unless his signature appears thereon.

(2) A signature is made by use of any name, including any trade or assumed name, upon an instrument, or by any word or mark used in lieu of a written signature.

§ 3–402
Signature in Ambiguous Capacity

Unless the instrument clearly indicates that a signature is made in some other capacity it is an indorsement.

§ 3–403
Signature by Authorized Representative

(1) A signature may be made by an agent or other representative, and his authority to make it may be established as in other cases of representation. No particular form of appointment is necessary to establish such authority.

(2) An authorized representative who signs his own name to an instrument

(a) is personally obligated if the instrument neither names the person represented nor shows that the representative signed in a representative capacity;

(b) except as otherwise established between the immediate parties, is personally obligated if the instrument names the person represented but does not show that the representative signed in a representative capacity, or if the instrument does not name the person represented but does show that the representative signed in a representative capacity.

(3) Except as otherwise established the name of an organization preceded or followed by the name and office of an authorized individual is a signature made in a representative capacity.

§ 3–404
Unauthorized Signatures

(1) Any unauthorized signature is wholly inoperative as that of the person whose name is signed unless he ratifies it or is precluded from denying it; but it operates as the signature of the

unauthorized signer in favor of any person who in good faith pays the instrument or takes it for value.

(2) Any unauthorized signature may be ratified for all purposes of this Article. Such ratification does not of itself affect any rights of the person ratifying against the actual signer.

§ 3–405
Impostors; Signature in Name of Payee

(1) An indorsement by any person in the name of a named payee is effective if

(a) an impostor by use of the mails or otherwise has induced the maker or drawer to issue the instrument to him or his confederate in the name of the payee; or

(b) a person signing as or on behalf of a maker or drawer intends the payee to have no interest in the instrument; or

(c) an agent or employee of the maker or drawer has supplied him with the name of the payee intending the latter to have no such interest.

(2) Nothing in this section shall affect the criminal or civil liability of the person so indorsing.

§ 3–406
Negligence Contributing to Alteration or
Unauthorized Signature

Any person who by his negligence substantially contributes to a material alteration of the instrument or to the making of an unauthorized signature is precluded from asserting the alteration or lack of authority against a holder in due course or against a drawee or other payor who pays the instrument in good faith and in accordance with the reasonable commercial standards of the drawee's or payor's business.

§ 3–407
Alteration

(1) Any alteration of an instrument is material which changes the contract of any party thereto in any respect, including any such change in

(a) the number or relations of the parties; or

(b) an incomplete instrument, by completing it otherwise than as authorized; or

(c) the writing as signed, by adding to it or by removing any part of it.

(2) As against any person other than a subsequent holder in due course

(a) alteration by the holder which is both fraudulent and material discharges any party whose contract is thereby changed unless that party assents or is precluded from asserting the defense;

(b) no other alteration discharges any party and the instrument may be enforced according to its original tenor, or as to incomplete instruments according to the authority given.

(3) A subsequent holder in due course may in all cases enforce the instrument according to its original tenor, and when an incomplete instrument has been completed, he may enforce it as completed.

§ 3–408
Consideration

Want or failure of consideration is a defense as against any person not having the rights of a holder in due course (Section 3–305), except that no consideration is necessary for an instrument or obligation thereon given in payment of or as security for an antecedent obligation of any kind. Nothing in this section shall be taken to displace any statute outside this Act under which a promise is enforceable notwithstanding lack or failure of consideration. Partial failure of consideration is a defense pro tanto whether or not the failure is in an ascertained or liquidated amount.

§ 3–409
Draft Not an Assignment

(1)   A check or other draft does not of itself operate as an assignment of any funds in the hands of the drawee available for its payment, and the drawee is not liable on the instrument until he accepts it.

(2)   Nothing in this section shall affect any liability in contract, tort, or otherwise arising from any letter of credit or other obligation or representation which is not an acceptance.

§ 3–410
Definition and Operation of Acceptance

(1)   Acceptance is the drawee's signed engagement to honor the draft as presented. It must be written on the draft, and may consist of his signature alone. It becomes operative when completed by delivery or notification.

(2)   A draft may be accepted although it has not been signed by the drawer or is otherwise incomplete or is overdue or has been dishonored.

(3)   Where the draft is payable at a fixed period after sight and the acceptor fails to date his acceptance the holder may complete it by supplying a date in good faith.

§ 3–411
Certification of a Check

(1)   Certification of a check is acceptance. Where a holder procures certification the drawer and all prior indorsers are discharged.

(2)   Unless otherwise agreed a bank has no obligation to certify a check.

(3)   A bank may certify a check before returning it for lack of proper indorsement. If it does so the drawer is discharged.

§ 3–412
Acceptance Varying Draft

(1)   Where the drawee's proffered acceptance in any manner varies the draft as presented the holder may refuse the acceptance and treat the draft as dishonored in which case the drawee is entitled to have his acceptance cancelled.

(2)   The terms of the draft are not varied by an acceptance to pay at any particular bank or place in the United States, unless the acceptance states that the draft is to be paid only at such bank or place.

(3)   Where the holder assents to an acceptance varying the terms of the draft each drawer and indorser who does not affirmatively assent is discharged.

§ 3–413
Contract of Maker, Drawer and Acceptor

(1)   The maker or acceptor engages that he will pay the instrument according to its tenor at the time of his engagement or as completed pursuant to Section 3–115 on incomplete instruments.

(2)   The drawer engages that upon dishonor of the draft and any necessary notice of dishonor or protest he will pay the amount of the draft to the holder or to any indorser who takes it up. The drawer may disclaim this liability by drawing without recourse.

(3)   By making, drawing or accepting the party admits as against all subsequent parties including the drawee the existence of the payee and his then capacity to indorse.

§ 3–414
Contract of Indorser; Order of Liability

(1)   Unless the indorsement otherwise specifies (as by such words as "without recourse") every indorser engages that upon dishonor and any necessary notice of dishonor and protest he will pay the instrument according to its tenor at the time of his indorsement to the holder or to any subsequent indorser who takes it up, even though the indorser who takes it up was not obligated to do so.

(2)   Unless they otherwise agree indorsers are liable to one another in the order in which they indorse, which is presumed to be the order in which their signatures appear on the instrument.

§ 3–415
Contract of Accommodation Party

(1)   An accommodation party is one who signs the instrument in any capacity for the purpose of lending his name to another party to it.

(2)   When the instrument has been taken for value before it is due the accommodation party is liable in the capacity in which he has signed even though the taker knows of the accommodation.

(3)   As against a holder in due course and without notice of the accommodation oral proof of the accommodation is not admissible to give the accommodation party the benefit of discharges dependent on his character as such. In other cases the accommodation character may be shown by oral proof.

(4)   An indorsement which shows that it is not in the chain of title is notice of its accommodation character.

(5)   An accommodation party is not liable to the party accommodated, and if he pays the instrument has a right of recourse on the instrument against such party.

§ 3–416
Contract of Guarantor

(1)   "Payment guaranteed" or equivalent words added to a signature mean that the signer engages that if the instrument is not paid when due he will pay it according to its tenor without resort by the holder to any other party.

(2) "Collection guaranteed" or equivalent words added to a signature mean that the signer engages that if the instrument is not paid when due he will pay it according to its tenor, but only after the holder has reduced his claim against the maker or acceptor to judgment and execution has been returned unsatisfied, or after the maker or acceptor has become insolvent or it is otherwise apparent that it is useless to proceed against him.

(3) Words of guaranty which do not otherwise specify guarantee payment.

(4) No words of guaranty added to the signature of a sole maker or acceptor affect his liability on the instrument. Such words added to the signature of one or two or more makers or acceptors create a presumption that the signature is for the accommodation of the others.

(5) When words of guaranty are used presentment, notice of dishonor and protest are not necessary to charge the user.

(6) Any guaranty written on the instrument is enforceable notwithstanding any statute of frauds.

§ 3–417
Warranties on Presentment and Transfer

(1) Any person who obtains payment or acceptance and any prior transferor warrants to a person who in good faith pays or accepts that

   (a) he has a good title to the instrument or is authorized to obtain payment or acceptance on behalf of one who has a good title; and

   (b) he has no knowledge that the signature of the maker or drawer is unauthorized, except that this warranty is not given by a holder in due course acting in good faith

      (i) to a maker with respect to the maker's own signature; or

      (ii) to a drawer with respect to the drawer's own signature, whether or not the drawer is also the drawee; or

      (iii) to an acceptor of a draft if the holder in due course took the draft after the acceptance or obtained the acceptance without knowledge that the drawer's signature was unauthorized; and

   (c) the instrument has not been materially altered, except that this warranty is not given by a holder in due course acting in good faith

      (i) to the maker of a note; or

      (ii) to the drawer of a draft whether or not the drawer is also the drawee; or

      (iii) to the acceptor of a draft with respect to an alteration made prior to the acceptance if the holder in due course took the draft after the acceptance, even though the acceptance provided "payable as originally drawn" or equivalent terms; or

      (iv) to the acceptor of a draft with respect to an alteration made after the acceptance.

(2) Any person who transfers an instrument and receives consideration warrants to his transferee and if the transfer is by indorsement to any subsequent holder who takes the instrument in good faith that

   (a) he has a good title to the instrument or is authorized to obtain payment or acceptance on behalf of one who has a good title and the transfer is otherwise rightful; and

   (b) all signatures are genuine or authorized; and

   (c) the instrument has not been materially altered; and

   (d) no defense of any party is good against him; and

   (e) he has no knowledge of any insolvency proceeding instituted with respect to the maker or acceptor or the drawer of an unaccepted instrument.

(3) By transferring "without recourse" the transferor limits the obligation stated in subsection (2)(d) to a warranty that he has no knowledge of such a defense.

(4) A selling agent or broker who does not disclose the fact that he is acting only as such gives the warranties provided in this section, but if he makes such disclosure warrants only his good faith and authority.

§ 3–418
Finality of Payment or Acceptance

Except for recovery of bank payments as provided in the Article on Bank Deposits and Collections (Article 4) and except for liability for breach of warranty on presentment under the preceding section, payment or acceptance of any instrument is final in favor of a holder in due course, or a person who has in good faith changed his position in reliance on the payment.

§ 3–419
Conversion of Instrument; Innocent Representative

(1) An instrument is converted when

   (a) a drawee to whom it is delivered for acceptance refuses to return it on demand; or

   (b) any person to whom it is delivered for payment refuses on demand either to pay or to return it; or

   (c) it is paid on a forged indorsement.

(2) In an action against a drawee under subsection (1) the measure of the drawee's liability is the face amount of the instrument. In any other action under subsection (1) the measure of liability is presumed to be the face amount of the instrument.

(3) Subject to the provisions of this Act concerning restrictive indorsements a representative, including a depositary or collecting bank, who has in good faith and in accordance with the reasonable commercial standards applicable to the business of such representative dealt with an instrument or its proceeds on behalf of one who was not the true owner is not liable in conversion or otherwise to the true owner beyond the amount of any proceeds remaining in his hands.

(4) An intermediary bank or payor bank which is not a depositary bank is not liable in conversion solely by reason of the fact that proceeds of an item indorsed restrictively (Sections 3–205 and 3–206) are not paid or applied consistently with the restrictive indorsement of an indorser other than its immediate transferor.

Part 5/Presentment, Notice of Dishonor and Protest
§ 3–501
When Presentment, Notice of Dishonor, and Protest Necessary or Permissible

(1) Unless excused (Section 3–511) presentment is necessary to charge secondary parties as follows:

(a) presentment for acceptance is necessary to charge the drawer and indorsers of a draft where the draft so provides, or is payable elsewhere than at the residence or place of business of the drawee, or its date of payment depends upon such presentment. The holder may at his option present for acceptance any other draft payable at a stated date;

(b) presentment for payment is necessary to charge any indorser;

(c) in the case of any drawer, the acceptor of a draft payable at a bank or the maker of a note payable at a bank, presentment for payment is necessary, but failure to make presentment discharges such drawer, acceptor or maker only as stated in Section 3–502(1)(b).

(2) Unless excused (Section 3–511)

(a) notice of any dishonor is necessary to charge any indorser;

(b) in the case of any drawer, the acceptor of a draft payable at a bank or the maker of a note payable at a bank, notice of any dishonor is necessary, but failure to give such notice discharges such drawer, acceptor or maker only as stated in Section 3–502(1)(b).

(3) Unless excused (Section 3–511) protest of any dishonor is necessary to charge the drawer and indorsers of any draft which on its face appears to be drawn or payable outside of the states, territories, dependencies and possessions of the United States, the District of Columbia and the Commonwealth of Puerto Rico. The holder may at his option make protest of any dishonor of any other instrument and in the case of a foreign draft may on insolvency of the acceptor before maturity make protest for better security.

(4) Notwithstanding any provision of this section, neither presentment nor notice of dishonor nor protest is necessary to charge an indorser who has indorsed an instrument after maturity.

§ 3–502
Unexcused Delay; Discharge

(1) Where without excuse any necessary presentment or notice of dishonor is delayed beyond the time when it is due

(a) any indorser is discharged; and

(b) any drawer or the acceptor of a draft payable at a bank or the maker of a note payable at a bank who because the drawee or payor bank becomes insolvent during the delay is deprived of funds maintained with the drawee or payor bank to cover the instrument may discharge his liability by written assignment to the holder of his rights against the drawee or payor bank in respect of such funds, but such drawer, acceptor or maker is not otherwise discharged.

(2) Where without excuse a necessary protest is delayed beyond the time when it is due any drawer or indorser is discharged.

§ 3–503
Time of Presentment

(1) Unless a different time is expressed in the instrument the time for any presentment is determined as follows:

(a) where an instrument is payable at or a fixed period after a stated date any presentment for acceptance must be made on or before the date it is payable;

(b) where an instrument is payable after sight it must either be presented for acceptance or negotiated within a reasonable time after date or issue whichever is later;

(c) where an instrument shows the date on which it is payable presentment for payment is due on that date;

(d) where an instrument is accelerated presentment for payment is due within a reasonable time after the acceleration;

(e) with respect to the liability of any secondary party presentment for acceptance or payment of any other instrument is due within a reasonable time after such party becomes liable thereon.

(2) A reasonable time for presentment is determined by the nature of the instrument, any usage of banking or trade and the facts of the particular case. In the case of an uncertified check which is drawn and payable within the United States and which is not a draft drawn by a bank the following are presumed to be reasonable periods within which to present for payment or to initiate bank collection:

(a) with respect to the liability of the drawer, thirty days after date or issue whichever is later; and

(b) with respect to the liability of an indorser, seven days after his indorsement.

(3) Where any presentment is due on a day which is not a full business day for either the person making presentment or the party to pay or accept, presentment is due on the next following day which is a full business day for both parties.

(4) Presentment to be sufficient must be made at a reasonable hour, and if at a bank during its banking day.

§ 3–504
How Presentment Is Made

(1) Presentment is a demand for acceptance or payment made upon the maker, acceptor, drawee or other payor by or on behalf of the holder.

(2) Presentment may be made

(a) by mail, in which event the time of presentment is determined by the time of receipt of the mail; or

(b) through a clearing house; or

(c) at the place of acceptance or payment specified in the instrument or if there be none at the place of business or residence of the party to accept or pay. If neither the party to accept or pay nor anyone authorized to act for him is present or accessible at such place presentment is excused.

(3) It may be made

(a) to any one of two or more makers, acceptors, drawees or other payors; or

(b) to any person who has authority to make or refuse the acceptance or payment.

(4) A draft accepted or a note made payable at a bank in the United States must be presented at such bank.

(5) In the cases described in Section 4–210 presentment may be made in the manner and with the result stated in that section.

§ 3–505
Rights of Party to Whom Presentment Is Made

(1) The party to whom presentment is made may without dishonor require

(a) exhibition of the instrument; and

(b) reasonable identification of the person making presentment and evidence of his authority to make it if made for another; and

(c) that the instrument be produced for acceptance or payment at a place specified in it, or if there be none at any place reasonable in the circumstances; and

(d) a signed receipt on the instrument for any partial or full payment and its surrender upon full payment.

(2) Failure to comply with any such requirement invalidates the presentment but the person presenting has a reasonable time in which to comply and the time for acceptance or payment runs from the time of compliance.

§ 3–506
Time Allowed for Acceptance or Payment

(1) Acceptance may be deferred without dishonor until the close of the next business day following presentment. The holder may also in a good faith effort to obtain acceptance and without either dishonor of the instrument or discharge of secondary parties allow postponement of acceptance for an additional business day.

(2) Except as a longer time is allowed in the case of documentary drafts drawn under a letter of credit, and unless an earlier time is agreed to by the party to pay, payment of an instrument may be deferred without dishonor pending reasonable examination to determine whether it is properly payable, but payment must be made in any event before the close of business on the day of presentment.

§ 3–507
Dishonor; Holder's Right of Recourse;
Term Allowing Re-Presentment

(1) An instrument is dishonored when

(a) a necessary or optional presentment is duly made and due acceptance or payment is refused or cannot be obtained within the prescribed time or in case of bank collections the instrument is seasonably returned by the midnight deadline (Section 4–301); or

(b) presentment is excused and the instrument is not duly accepted or paid.

(2) Subject to any necessary notice of dishonor and protest, the holder has upon dishonor an immediate right of recourse against the drawers and indorsers.

(3) Return of an instrument for lack of proper indorsement is not dishonor.

(4) A term in a draft or an indorsement thereof allowing a stated time for re-presentment in the event of any dishonor of the draft by nonacceptance if a time draft or by nonpayment if a sight draft gives the holder as against any secondary party bound by the term an option to waive the dishonor without affecting the liability of the secondary party and he may present again up to the end of the stated time.

§ 3–508
Notice of Dishonor

(1) Notice of dishonor may be given to any person who may be liable on the instrument by or on behalf of the holder or any party who has himself received notice, or any other party who can be compelled to pay the instrument. In addition an agent or bank in whose hands the instrument is dishonored may give notice to his principal or customer or to another agent or bank from which the instrument was received.

(2) Any necessary notice must be given by a bank before its midnight deadline and by any other person before midnight of the third business day after dishonor or receipt of notice of dishonor.

(3) Notice may be given in any reasonable manner. It may be oral or written and in any terms which identify the instrument and state that it has been dishonored. A misdescription which does not mislead the party notified does not vitiate the notice. Sending the instrument bearing a stamp, ticket or writing stating that acceptance or payment has been refused or sending a notice of debit with respect to the instrument is sufficient.

(4) Written notice is given when sent although it is not received.

(5) Notice to one partner is notice to each although the firm has been dissolved.

(6) When any party is in insolvency proceedings instituted after the issue of the instrument notice may be given either to the party or to the representative of his estate.

(7) When any party is dead or incompetent notice may be sent to his last known address or given to his personal representative.

(8) Notice operates for the benefit of all parties who have rights on the instrument against the party notified.

§ 3–509
Protest; Noting for Protest

(1) A protest is a certificate of dishonor made under the hand and seal of a United States consul or vice consul or a notary public or other person authorized to certify dishonor by the law of the place where dishonor occurs. It may be made upon information satisfactory to such person.

(2) The protest must identify the instrument and certify either that due presentment has been made or the reason why it is excused and that the instrument has been dishonored by non-acceptance or nonpayment.

(3) The protest may also certify that notice of dishonor has been given to all parties or to specified parties.

(4) Subject to subsection (5) any necessary protest is due by the time that notice of dishonor is due.

(5) If, before protest is due, an instrument has been noted for protest by the officer to make protest, the protest may be made at any time thereafter as of the date of the noting.

§ 3–510
Evidence of Dishonor and Notice of Dishonor
The following are admissible as evidence and create a presumption of dishonor and of any notice of dishonor therein shown:

(a) a document regular in form as provided in the preceding section which purports to be a protest;

(b) the purported stamp or writing of the drawee, payor bank or presenting bank on the instrument or accompanying it stating that acceptance or payment has been refused for reasons consistent with dishonor;

(c) any book or record of the drawee, payor bank, or any collecting bank kept in the usual course of business which shows dishonor, even though there is no evidence of who made the entry.

§ 3–511
Waived or Excused Presentment, Protest or Notice of Dishonor or Delay Therein

(1) Delay in presentment, protest or notice of dishonor is excused when the party is without notice that it is due or when the delay is caused by circumstances beyond his control and he exercises reasonable diligence after the cause of the delay ceases to operate.

(2) Presentment or notice or protest as the case may be is entirely excused when

(a) the party to be charged has waived it expressly or by implication either before or after it is due; or

(b) such party has himself dishonored the instrument or has countermanded payment or otherwise has no reason to expect or right to require that the instrument be accepted or paid; or

(c) by reasonable diligence the presentment or protest cannot be made or the notice given.

(3) Presentment is also entirely excused when

(a) the maker, acceptor or drawee of any instrument except a documentary draft is dead or in insolvency proceedings instituted after the issue of the instrument; or

(b) acceptance or payment is refused but not for want of proper presentment.

(4) Where a draft has been dishonored by nonacceptance a later presentment for payment and any notice of dishonor and protest for nonpayment are excused unless in the meantime the instrument has been accepted.

(5) A waiver of protest is also a waiver of presentment and of notice of dishonor even though protest is not required.

(6) Where a waiver of presentment or notice or protest is embodied in the instrument itself it is binding upon all parties; but where it is written above the signature of an indorser it binds him only.

Part 6/Discharge
§ 3–601
Discharge of Parties

(1) The extent of the discharge of any party from liability on an instrument is governed by the sections on

(a) payment or satisfaction (Section 3–603); or

(b) tender of payment (Section 3–604); or

(c) cancellation or renunciation (Section 3–605); or

(d) impairment of right of recourse or of collateral (Section 3–606); or

(e) reacquisition of the instrument by a prior party (Section 3–208); or

(f) fraudulent and material alteration (Section 3–407); or

(g) certification of a check (Section 3–411); or

(h) acceptance varying a draft (Section 3–412); or

(i) unexcused delay in presentment or notice of dishonor or protest (Section 3–502).

(2) Any party is also discharged from his liability on an instrument to another party by any other act or agreement with such party which would discharge his simple contract for the payment of money.

(3) The liability of all parties is discharged when any party who has himself no right of action or recourse on the instrument

(a) reacquires the instrument in his own right; or

(b) is discharged under any provision of this Article, except as otherwise provided with respect to discharge for impairment of recourse or of collateral (Section 3–606).

§ 3–602
Effect of Discharge against Holder in Due Course

No discharge of any party provided by this Article is effective against a subsequent holder in due course unless he has notice thereof when he takes the instrument.

§ 3–603
Payment or Satisfaction

(1) The liability of any party is discharged to the extent of his payment or satisfaction to the holder even though it is made with knowledge of a claim of another person to the instrument unless prior to such payment or satisfaction the person making the claim either supplies indemnity deemed adequate by the party seeking the discharge or enjoins payment or satisfaction by order of a court of competent jurisdiction in an action in which the adverse claimant and the holder are parties. This subsection does not, however, result in the discharge of the liability

(a) of a party who in bad faith pays or satisfies a holder who acquired the instrument by theft or who (unless having the rights of a holder in due course) holds through one who so acquired it; or

(b) of a party (other than an intermediary bank or a payor bank which is not a depositary bank) who pays or satisfies the holder of an instrument which has been restrictively indorsed in a manner not consistent with the terms of such restrictive indorsement.

(2) Payment or satisfaction may be made with the consent of the holder by any person including a stranger to the instrument.

Surrender of the instrument to such a person gives him the rights of a transferee (Section 3–201).

§ 3–604
Tender of Payment

(1) Any party making tender of full payment to a holder when or after it is due is discharged to the extent of all subsequent liability for interest, costs and attorney's fees.

(2) The holder's refusal of such tender wholly discharges any party who has a right of recourse against the party making the tender.

(3) Where the maker or acceptor of an instrument payable otherwise than on demand is able and ready to pay at every place of payment specified in the instrument when it is due, it is equivalent to tender.

§ 3–605
Cancellation and Renunciation

(1) The holder of an instrument may even without consideration discharge any party
    (a) in any manner apparent on the face of the instrument or the indorsement, as by intentionally cancelling the instrument or the party's signature by destruction or mutilation, or by striking out the party's signature; or
    (b) by renouncing his rights by a writing signed and delivered or by surrender of the instrument to the party to be discharged.

(2) Neither cancellation nor renunciation without surrender of the instrument affects the title thereto.

§ 3–606
Impairment of Recourse or of Collateral

(1) The holder discharges any party to the instrument to the extent that without such party's consent the holder
    (a) without express reservation of rights releases or agrees not to sue any person against whom the party has to the knowledge of the holder a right of recourse or agrees to suspend the right to enforce against such person the instrument or collateral or otherwise discharges such person, except that failure or delay in effecting any required presentment, protest or notice of dishonor with respect to any such person does not discharge any party as to whom presentment, protest or notice of dishonor is effective or unnecessary; or
    (b) unjustifiably impairs any collateral for the instrument given by or on behalf of the party or any person against whom he has a right of recourse.

(2) By express reservation of rights against a party with a right of recourse the holder preserves
    (a) all his rights against such party as of the time when the instrument was originally due; and
    (b) the right of the party to pay the instrument as of that time; and
    (c) all rights of such party to recourse against others.

Part 7/Advice of International Sight Draft
§ 3–701
Letter of Advice of International Sight Draft

(1) A "letter of advice" is a drawer's communication to the drawee that a described draft has been drawn.

(2) Unless otherwise agreed when a bank receives from another bank a letter of advice of an international sight draft the drawee bank may immediately debit the drawer's account and stop the running of interest pro tanto. Such a debit and any resulting credit to any account covering outstanding drafts leaves in the drawer full power to stop payment or otherwise dispose of the amount and creates no trust or interest in favor of the holder.

(3) Unless otherwise agreed and except where a draft is drawn under a credit issued by the drawee, the drawee of an international sight draft owes the drawer no duty to pay an unadvised draft but if it does so and the draft is genuine, may appropriately debit the drawer's account.

Part 8/Miscellaneous
§ 3–801
Drafts in a Set

(1) Where a draft is drawn in a set of parts, each of which is numbered and expressed to be an order only if no other part has been honored, the whole of the parts constitutes one draft but a taker of any part may become a holder in due course of the draft.

(2) Any person who negotiates, indorses or accepts a single part of a draft drawn in a set thereby becomes liable to any holder in due course of that part as if it were the whole set, but as between different holders in due course to whom different parts have been negotiated the holder whose title first accrues has all rights to the draft and its proceeds.

(3) As against the drawee the first presented part of a draft drawn in a set is the part entitled to payment, or if a time draft to acceptance and payment. Acceptance of any subsequently presented part renders the drawee liable thereon under subsection (2). With respect both to a holder and to the drawer payment of a subsequently presented part of a draft payable at sight has the same effect as payment of a check notwithstanding an effective stop order (Section 4–407).

(4) Except as otherwise provided in this section, where any part of a draft in a set is discharged by payment or otherwise the whole draft is discharged.

§ 3–802
Effect of Instrument on Obligation for Which It Is Given

(1) Unless otherwise agreed where an instrument is taken for an underlying obligation
    (a) the obligation is pro tanto discharged if a bank is drawer, maker or acceptor of the instrument and there is no recourse on the instrument against the underlying obligor; and
    (b) in any other case the obligation is suspended pro tanto until the instrument is due or if it is payable on demand until its presentment. If the instrument is dishonored action may be maintained on either the instrument or the obligation;

discharge of the underlying obligor on the instrument also discharges him on the obligation.

(2) The taking in good faith of a check which is not post-dated does not of itself so extend the time on the original obligation as to discharge a surety.

§ 3–803
Notice to Third Party

Where a defendant is sued for breach of an obligation for which a third person is answerable over under this Article he may give the third person written notice of the litigation, and the person notified may then give similar notice to any other person who is answerable over to him under this Article. If the notice states that the person notified may come in and defend and that if the person notified does not do so he will in any action against him by the person giving the notice be bound by any determination of fact common to the two litigations, then unless after seasonable receipt of the notice the person notified does come in and defend he is so bound.

§ 3–804
Lost, Destroyed or Stolen Instruments

The owner of an instrument which is lost, whether by destruction, theft or otherwise, may maintain an action in his own name and recover from any party liable thereon upon due proof of his ownership, the facts which prevent his production of the instrument and its terms. The court may require security indemnifying the defendant against loss by reason of further claims on the instrument.

§ 3–805
Instruments Not Payable to Order or to Bearer

This Article applies to any instrument whose terms do not preclude transfer and which is otherwise negotiable within this Article but which is not payable to order or to bearer, except that there can be no holder in due course of such an instrument.

ARTICLE 4/BANK DEPOSITS AND COLLECTIONS*
Part 1/General Provisions and Definitions
§ 4–101
Short Title

This Article shall be known and may be cited as Uniform Commercial Code–Bank Deposits and Collections.

§ 4–102
Applicability

(1) To the extent that items within this Article are also within the scope of Articles 3 and 8, they are subject to the provisions of those Articles. In the event of conflict the provisions of this Article govern those of Article 3 but the provisions of Article 8 govern those of this Article.

(2) The liability of a bank for action or non-action with respect to any item handled by it for purposes of presentment, payment

*Authors' Note: Revised Articles 3 and 4 are included after the original versions of these articles.

or collection is governed by the law of the place where the bank is located. In the case of action or non-action by or at a branch or separate office of a bank, its liability is governed by the law of the place where the branch or separate office is located.

§ 4–103
Variation by Agreement; Measure of Damages; Certain Action Constituting Ordinary Care

(1) The effect of the provisions of this Article may be varied by agreement except that no agreement can disclaim a bank's responsibility for its own lack of good faith or failure to exercise ordinary care or can limit the measure of damages for such lack or failure; but the parties may by agreement determine the standards by which such responsibility is to be measured if such standards are not manifestly unreasonable.

(2) Federal Reserve regulations and operating letters, clearing house rules, and the like, have the effect of agreements under subsection (1), whether or not specifically assented to by all parties interested in items handled.

(3) Action or non-action approved by this Article or pursuant to Federal Reserve regulations or operating letters constitutes the exercise of ordinary care and, in the absence of special instructions, action or non-action consistent with clearing house rules and the like or with a general banking usage not disapproved by this Article, prima facie constitutes the exercise of ordinary care.

(4) The specification or approval of certain procedures by this Article does not constitute disapproval of other procedures which may be reasonable under the circumstances.

(5) The measure of damages for failure to exercise ordinary care in handling an item is the amount of the item reduced by an amount which could not have been realized by the use of ordinary care, and where there is bad faith it includes other damages, if any, suffered by the party as a proximate consequence.

§ 4–104
Definitions and Index of Definitions

(1) In this Article unless the context otherwise requires
  (a) "Account" means any account with a bank and includes a checking, time, interest or savings account;
  (b) "Afternoon" means the period of a day between noon and midnight;
  (c) "Banking day" means that part of any day on which a bank is open to the public for carrying on substantially all of its banking functions;
  (d) "Clearing house" means any association of banks or other payors regularly clearing items;
  (e) "Customer" means any person having an account with a bank or for whom a bank has agreed to collect items and includes a bank carrying an account with another bank;
  (f) "Documentary draft" means any negotiable or non-negotiable draft with accompanying documents, securities or other papers to be delivered against honor of the draft;
  (g) "Item" means any instrument for the payment of money even though it is not negotiable but does not include money;
  (h) "Midnight deadline" with respect to a bank is midnight on its next banking day following the banking day on which it

receives the relevant item or notice or from which the time for taking action commences to run, whichever is later;

(i) "Properly payable" includes the availability of funds for payment at the time of decision to pay or dishonor;

(j) "Settle" means to pay in cash, by clearing house settlement, in a charge or credit or by remittance, or otherwise as instructed. A settlement may be either provisional or final;

(k) "Suspends payments" with respect to a bank means that it has been closed by order of the supervisory authorities, that a public officer has been appointed to take it over or that it ceases or refuses to make payments in the ordinary course of business.

(2) Other definitions applying to this Article and the sections in which they appear are:

"Collecting bank". Section 4–105.
"Depositary bank". Section 4–105.
"Intermediary bank". Section 4–105.
"Payor bank". Section 4–105.
"Presenting bank". Section 4–105.
"Remitting bank". Section 4–105.

(3) The following definitions in other Articles apply to this Article:

"Acceptance". Section 3–410.
"Certificate of deposit". Section 3–104.
"Certification". Section 3–411.
"Check". Section 3–104.
"Draft". Section 3–104.
"Holder in due course". Section 3–302.
"Notice of dishonor". Section 3–508.
"Presentment". Section 3–504.
"Protest". Section 3–509.
"Secondary party". Section 3–102.

(4) In addition Article 1 contains general definitions and principles of construction and interpretation applicable throughout this Article.

§ 4–105
"Depositary Bank"; "Intermediary Bank"; "Collecting Bank"; "Payor Bank"; "Presenting Bank"; "Remitting Bank"

In this Article unless the context otherwise requires:

(a) "Depositary bank" means the first bank to which an item is transferred for collection even though it is also the payor bank;

(b) "Payor bank" means a bank by which an item is payable as drawn or accepted;

(c) "Intermediary bank" means any bank to which an item is transferred in course of collection except the depositary or payor bank;

(d) "Collecting bank" means any bank handling the item for collection except the payor bank;

(e) "Presenting bank" means any bank presenting an item except a payor bank;

(f) "Remitting bank" means any payor or intermediary bank remitting for an item.

§ 4–106
Separate Office of a Bank

A branch or separate office of a bank [maintaining its own deposit ledgers] is a separate bank for the purpose of computing the time within which and determining the place at or to which action may be taken or notices or orders shall be given under this Article and under Article 3.

Note: *The brackets are to make it optional with the several states whether to require a branch to maintain its own deposit ledgers in order to be considered to be a separate bank for certain purposes under Article 4. In some states "maintaining its own deposit ledgers" is a satisfactory test. In others branch banking practices are such that this test would not be suitable.*

§ 4–107
Time of Receipt of Items

(1) For the purpose of allowing time to process items, prove balances and make the necessary entries on its books to determine its position for the day, a bank may fix an afternoon hour of 2:00 PM or later as a cut-off hour for the handling of money and items and the making of entries on its books.

(2) Any item or deposit of money received on any day after a cut-off hour so fixed or after the close of the banking day may be treated as being received at the opening of the next banking day.

§ 4–108
Delays

(1) Unless otherwise instructed, a collecting bank in a good faith effort to secure payment may, in the case of specific items and with or without the approval of any person involved, waive, modify or extend time limits imposed or permitted by this Act for a period not in excess of an additional banking day without discharge of secondary parties and without liability to its transferor or any prior party.

(2) Delay by a collecting bank or payor bank beyond time limits prescribed or permitted by this Act or by instructions is excused if caused by interruption of communication facilities, suspension of payments by another bank, war, emergency conditions or other circumstances beyond the control of the bank provided it exercises such diligence as the circumstances require.

§ 4–109
Process of Posting

The "process of posting" means the usual procedure followed by a payor bank in determining to pay an item and in recording the payment including one or more of the following or other steps as determined by the bank:

(a) verification of any signature;

(b) ascertaining that sufficient funds are available;

(c) affixing a "paid" or other stamp;

(d) entering a charge or entry to a customer's account;

(e) correcting or reversing an entry or erroneous action with respect to the item.

Part 2/Collection of Items:
Depository and Collecting Banks
§ 4–201
Presumption and Duration of Agency Status of Collecting Banks and Provisional Status of Credits; Applicability of Article; Item Indorsed "Pay Any Bank"

(1) Unless a contrary intent clearly appears and prior to the time that a settlement given by a collecting bank for an item is or becomes final (subsection (3) of Section 4–211 and Sections 4–212 and 4–213) the bank is an agent or sub-agent of the owner of the item and any settlement given for the item is provisional. This provision applies regardless of the form of indorsement or lack of indorsement and even though credit given for the item is subject to immediate withdrawal as of right or is in fact withdrawn; but the continuance of ownership of an item by its owner and any rights of the owner to proceeds of the item are subject to rights of a collecting bank such as those resulting from outstanding advances on the item and valid rights of setoff. When an item is handled by banks for purposes of presentment, payment and collection, the relevant provisions of this Article apply even though action of parties clearly establishes that a particular bank has purchased the item and is the owner of it.

(2) After an item has been indorsed with the words "pay any bank" or the like, only a bank may acquire the rights of a holder
  (a) until the item has been returned to the customer initiating collection; or
  (b) until the item has been specially indorsed by a bank to a person who is not a bank.

§ 4–202
Responsibility for Collection; When Action Seasonable

(1) A collecting bank must use ordinary care in
  (a) presenting an item or sending it for presentment; and
  (b) sending notice of dishonor or non-payment or returning an item other than a documentary draft to the bank's transferor [or directly to the depositary bank under subsection (2) of Section 4–212] (*see note to Section 4–212*) after learning that the item has not been paid or accepted, as the case may be; and
  (c) settling for an item when the bank receives final settlement; and
  (d) making or providing for any necessary protest; and
  (e) notifying its transferor of any loss or delay in transit within a reasonable time after discovery thereof.

(2) A collecting bank taking proper action before its midnight deadline following receipt of an item, notice or payment acts seasonably; taking proper action within a reasonably longer time may be seasonable but the bank has the burden of so establishing.

(3) Subject to subsection (1)(a), a bank is not liable for the insolvency, neglect, misconduct, mistake or default of another bank or person or for loss or destruction of an item in transit or in the possession of others.

§ 4–203
Effect of Instructions

Subject to the provisions of Article 3 concerning conversion of instruments (Section 3–419) and the provisions of both Article 3 and this Article concerning restrictive indorsements only a collecting bank's transferor can give instructions which affect the bank or constitute notice to it and a collecting bank is not liable to prior parties for any action taken pursuant to such instructions or in accordance with any agreement with its transferor.

§ 4–204
Methods of Sending and Presenting; Sending Direct to Payor Bank

(1) A collecting bank must send items by reasonably prompt method taking into consideration any relevant instructions, the nature of the item, the number of such items on hand, and the cost of collection involved and the method generally used by it or others to present such items.

(2) A collecting bank may send
  (a) any item direct to the payor bank;
  (b) any item to any non-bank payor if authorized by its transferor; and
  (c) any item other than documentary drafts to any non-bank payor, if authorized by Federal Reserve regulation or operating letter, clearing house rule or the like.

(3) Presentment may be made by a presenting bank at a place where the payor bank has requested that presentment be made.

§ 4–205
Supplying Missing Indorsement; No Notice from Prior Indorsement

(1) A depositary bank which has taken an item for collection may supply any indorsement of the customer which is necessary to title unless the item contains the words "payee's indorsement required" or the like. In the absence of such a requirement a statement placed on the item by the depositary bank to the effect that the item was deposited by a customer or credited to his account is effective as the customer's indorsement.

(2) An intermediary bank, or payor bank which is not a depositary bank, is neither given notice nor otherwise affected by a restrictive indorsement of any person except the bank's immediate transferor.

§ 4–206
Transfer between Banks

Any agreed method which identifies the transferor bank is sufficient for the item's further transfer to another bank.

§ 4–207
Warranties of Customer and Collecting Bank on Transfer or Presentment of Items; Time for Claims

(1) Each customer or collecting bank who obtains payment or acceptance of an item and each prior customer and collecting bank warrants to the payor bank or other payor who in good faith pays or accepts the item that
  (a) he has a good title to the item or is authorized to obtain payment or acceptance on behalf of one who has a good title; and
  (b) he has no knowledge that the signature of the maker or drawer is unauthorized, except that this warranty is not given

by any customer or collecting bank that is a holder in due course and acts in good faith

  (i) to a maker with respect to the maker's own signature; or

  (ii) to a drawer with respect to the drawer's own signature, whether or not the drawer is also the drawee; or

  (iii) to an acceptor of an item if the holder in due course took the item after the acceptance or obtained the acceptance without knowledge that the drawer's signature was unauthorized; and

(c) the item has not been materially altered, except that this warranty is not given by any customer or collecting bank that is a holder in due course and acts in good faith

  (i) to the maker of a note; or

  (ii) to the drawer of a draft whether or not the drawer is also the drawee; or

  (iii) to the acceptor of an item with respect to an alteration made prior to the acceptance if the holder in due course took the item after the acceptance, even though the acceptance provided "payable as originally drawn" or equivalent terms; or

  (iv) to the acceptor of an item with respect to an alteration made after the acceptance.

(2) Each customer and collecting bank who transfers an item and receives a settlement or other consideration for it warrants to his transferee and to any subsequent collecting bank who takes the item in good faith that

(a) he has a good title to the item or is authorized to obtain payment or acceptance on behalf of one who has a good title and the transfer is otherwise rightful; and

(b) all signatures are genuine or authorized; and

(c) the item has not been materially altered; and

(d) no defense of any party is good against him; and

(e) he has no knowledge of any insolvency proceeding instituted with respect to the maker or acceptor or the drawer of an unaccepted item.

In addition each customer and collecting bank so transferring an item and receiving a settlement or other consideration engages that upon dishonor and any necessary notice of dishonor and protest he will take up the item.

(3) The warranties and the engagement to honor set forth in the two preceding subsections arise notwithstanding the absence of indorsement or words of guaranty or warranty in the transfer or presentment and a collecting bank remains liable for their breach despite remittance to its transferor. Damages for breach of such warranties or engagement to honor shall not exceed the consideration received by the customer or collecting bank responsible plus finance charges and expenses related to the item, if any.

(4) Unless a claim for breach of warranty under this section is made within a reasonable time after the person claiming learns of the breach, the person liable is discharged to the extent of any loss caused by the delay in making claim.

§ 4–208
Security Interest of Collecting Bank in Items, Accompanying Documents and Proceeds

(1) A bank has a security interest in an item and any accompanying documents or the proceeds of either

(a) in case of an item deposited in an account to the extent to which credit given for the item has been withdrawn or applied;

(b) in case of an item for which it has given credit available for withdrawal as of right, to the extent of the credit given whether or not the credit is drawn upon and whether or not there is a right of charge-back; or

(c) if it makes an advance on or against the item.

(2) When credit which has been given for several items received at one time or pursuant to a single agreement is withdrawn or applied in part the security interest remains upon all the items, any accompanying documents or the proceeds of either. For the purpose of this section, credits first given are first withdrawn.

(3) Receipt by a collecting bank of a final settlement for an item is a realization on its security interest in the item, accompanying documents and proceeds. To the extent and so long as the bank does not receive final settlement for the item or give up possession of the item or accompanying documents for purposes other than collection, the security interest continues and is subject to the provisions of Article 9 except that

(a) no security agreement is necessary to make the security interest enforceable (subsection (1)(b) of Section 9–203); and

(b) no filing is required to perfect the security interest; and

(c) the security interest has priority over conflicting perfected security interests in the item, accompanying documents or proceeds.

§ 4–209
When Bank Gives Value for Purposes of Holder in Due Course

For purposes of determining its status as a holder in due course, the bank has given value to the extent that it has a security interest in an item provided that the bank otherwise complies with the requirements of Section 3–302 on what constitutes a holder in due course.

§ 4–210
Presentment by Notice of Item Not Payable by, through or at a Bank; Liability of Secondary Parties

(1) Unless otherwise instructed, a collecting bank may present an item not payable by, through or at a bank by sending to the party to accept or pay a written notice that the bank holds the item for acceptance or payment. The notice must be sent in time to be received on or before the day when presentment is due and the bank must meet any requirement of the party to accept or pay under Section 3–505 by the close of the bank's next banking day after it knows of the requirement.

(2) Where presentment is made by notice and neither honor nor request for compliance with a requirement under Section 3–505 is received by the close of business on the day after maturity or in the case of demand items by the close of business on the third banking day after notice was sent, the presenting bank may treat the item as dishonored and charge any secondary party by sending him notice of the facts.

§ 4–211
Media of Remittance; Provisional and Final Settlement in Remittance Cases

(1) A collecting bank may take in settlement of an item
(a) a check of the remitting bank or of another bank on any bank except the remitting bank; or
(b) a cashier's check or similar primary obligation of a remitting bank which is a member of or clears through a member of the same clearing house or group as the collecting bank; or
(c) appropriate authority to charge an account of the remitting bank or of another bank with the collecting bank; or
(d) if the item is drawn upon or payable by a person other than a bank, a cashier's check, certified check or other bank check or obligation.

(2) If before its midnight deadline the collecting bank properly dishonors a remittance check or authorization to charge on itself or presents or forwards for collection a remittance instrument of or on another bank which is of a kind approved by subsection (1) or has not been authorized by it, the collecting bank is not liable to prior parties in the event of the dishonor of such check, instrument or authorization.

(3) A settlement for an item by means of a remittance instrument or authorization to charge is or becomes a final settlement as to both the person making and the person receiving the settlement
(a) if the remittance instrument or authorization to charge is of a kind approved by subsection (1) or has not been authorized by the person receiving the settlement and in either case the person receiving the settlement acts seasonably before its midnight deadline in presenting, forwarding for collection or paying the instrument or authorization,–at the time the remittance instrument or authorization is finally paid by the payor by which it is payable;
(b) if the person receiving the settlement has authorized remittance by a non-bank check or obligation or by a cashier's check or similar primary obligation of or a check upon the payor or other remitting bank which is not of a kind approved by subsection (1)(b),–at the time of the receipt of such remittance check or obligation; or
(c) if in a case not covered by sub-paragraphs (a) or (b) the person receiving the settlement fails to seasonably present, forward for collection, pay or return a remittance instrument or authorization to it to charge before its midnight deadline,–at such midnight deadline.

§ 4–212
Right of Charge-Back or Refund

(1) If a collecting bank has made provisional settlement with its customer for an item and itself fails by reason of dishonor, suspension of payments by a bank or otherwise to receive a settlement for the item which is or becomes final, the bank may revoke the settlement given by it, charge back the amount of any credit given for the item to its customer's account or obtain refund from its customer whether or not it is able to return the items if by its midnight deadline or within a longer reasonable time after it learns the facts it returns the item or sends notification of the facts. These rights to revoke, charge-back and obtain refund ter-

minate if and when a settlement for the item received by the bank is or becomes final (subsection (3) of Section 4–211 and subsections (2) and (3) of Section 4–213).

[(2) Within the time and manner prescribed by this section and Section 4–301, an intermediary or payor bank, as the case may be, may return an unpaid item directly to the depositary bank and may send for collection a draft on the depositary bank and obtain reimbursement. In such case, if the depositary bank has received provisional settlement for the item, it must reimburse the bank drawing the draft and any provisional credits for the item between banks shall become and remain final.]

Note: *Direct returns are recognized as an innovation that is not yet established bank practice, and therefore, Paragraph 2 has been bracketed. Some lawyers have doubts whether it should be included in legislation or left to development by agreement.*

(3) A depositary bank which is also the payor may chargeback the amount of an item to its customer's account or obtain refund in accordance with the section governing return of an item received by a payor bank for credit on its books (Section 4–301).

(4) The right to charge-back is not affected by
(a) prior use of the credit given for the item; or
(b) failure by any bank to exercise ordinary care with respect to the item but any bank so failing remains liable.

(5) A failure to charge-back or claim refund does not affect other rights of the bank against the customer or any other party.

(6) If credit is given in dollars as the equivalent of the value of an item payable in a foreign currency the dollar amount of any charge-back or refund shall be calculated on the basis of the buying sight rate for the foreign currency prevailing on the day when the person entitled to the charge-back or refund learns that it will not receive payment in ordinary course.

§ 4–213
Final Payment of Item by Payor Bank; When Provisional Debits and Credits Become Final; When Certain Credits Become Available for Withdrawal

(1) An item is finally paid by a payor bank when the bank has done any of the following, whichever happens first:
(a) paid the item in cash; or
(b) settled for the item without reserving a right to revoke the settlement and without having such right under statute, clearing house rule or agreement; or
(c) completed the process of posting the item to the indicated account of the drawer, maker or other person to be charged therewith; or
(d) made a provisional settlement for the item and failed to revoke the settlement in the time and manner permitted by statute, clearing house rule or agreement.

Upon a final payment under subparagraphs (b), (c) or (d) the payor bank shall be accountable for the amount of the item.

(2) If provisional settlement for an item between the presenting and payor banks is made through a clearing house or by debits or credits in an account between them, then to the extent that provisional debits or credits for the item are entered in accounts between the presenting and payor banks or between the presenting and successive prior collecting banks seriatim, they become final upon final payment of the item by the payor bank.

(3) If a collecting bank receives a settlement for an item which is or becomes final (subsection (3) of Section 4–211, subsection (2) of Section 4–213) the bank is accountable to its customer for the amount of the item and any provisional credit given for the item in an account with its customer becomes final.

(4) Subject to any right of the bank to apply the credit to an obligation of the customer, credit given by a bank for an item in an account with its customer becomes available for withdrawal as of right

    (a) in any case where the bank has received a provisional settlement for the item,–when such settlement becomes final and the bank has had a reasonable time to learn that the settlement is final;

    (b) in any case where the bank is both a depositary bank and a payor bank and the item is finally paid,–at the opening of the bank's second banking day following receipt of the item.

(5) A deposit of money in a bank is final when made but, subject to any right of the bank to apply the deposit to an obligation of the customer, the deposit becomes available for withdrawal as of right at the opening of the bank's next banking day following receipt of the deposit.

§ 4–214
Insolvency and Preference

(1) Any item in or coming into the possession of a payor or collecting bank which suspends payment and which item is not finally paid shall be returned by the receiver, trustee or agent in charge of the closed bank to the presenting bank or the closed bank's customer.

(2) If a payor bank finally pays an item and suspends payments without making a settlement for the item with its customer or the presenting bank which settlement is or becomes final, the owner of the item has a preferred claim against the payor bank.

(3) If a payor bank gives or a collecting bank gives or receives a provisional settlement for an item and thereafter suspends payments, the suspension does not prevent or interfere with the settlement becoming final if such finality occurs automatically upon the lapse of certain time or the happening of certain events (subsection (3) of Section 4–211, subsections (1) (d), (2) and (3) of Section 4–213).

(4) If a collecting bank receives from subsequent parties settlement for an item which settlement is or becomes final and suspends payments without making a settlement for the item with its customer which is or becomes final, the owner of the item has a preferred claim against such collecting bank.

Part 3/Collection of Items: Payor Banks
§ 4–301
Deferred Posting; Recovery of Payment by
Return of Items; Time of Dishonor

(1) Where an authorized settlement for a demand item (other than a documentary draft) received by a payor bank otherwise than for immediate payment over the counter has been made be-

fore midnight of the banking day of receipt the payor bank may revoke the settlement and recover any payment if before it has made final payment (subsection (1) of Section 4–213) and before its midnight deadline it

    (a) returns the item; or

    (b) sends written notice of dishonor or nonpayment if the item is held for protest or is otherwise unavailable for return.

(2) If a demand item is received by a payor bank for credit on its books it may return such item or send notice of dishonor and may revoke any credit given or recover the amount thereof withdrawn by its customer, if it acts within the time limit and in the manner specified in the preceding subsection.

(3) Unless previous notice of dishonor has been sent an item is dishonored at the time when for purposes of dishonor it is returned or notice sent in accordance with this section.

(4) An item is returned:

    (a) as to an item received through a clearing house, when it is delivered to the presenting or last collecting bank or to the clearing house or is sent or delivered in accordance with its rules; or

    (b) in all other cases, when it is sent or delivered to the bank's customer or transferor or pursuant to his instructions.

§ 4–302
Payor Bank's Responsibility for Late Return of Item

In the absence of a valid defense such as breach of a presentment warranty (subsection (1) of Section 4–207), settlement effected or the like, if an item is presented on and received by a payor bank the bank is accountable for the amount of

    (a) a demand item other than a documentary draft whether properly payable or not if the bank, in any case where it is not also the depositary bank, retains the item beyond midnight of the banking day of receipt without settling for it or, regardless of whether it is also the depositary bank, does not pay or return the item or send notice of dishonor until after its midnight deadline; or

    (b) any other properly payable item unless within the time allowed for acceptance or payment of that item the bank either accepts or pays the item or returns it and accompanying documents.

§ 4–303
When Items Subject to Notice, Stop-Order, Legal Process or
Setoff; Order in Which Items May Be Charged or Certified

(1) Any knowledge, notice or stop-order received by, legal process served upon or setoff exercised by a payor bank, whether or not effective under other rules of law to terminate, suspend or modify the bank's right or duty to pay an item or to charge its customer's account for the item, comes too late to so terminate, suspend or modify such right or duty if the knowledge, notice, stop-order or legal process is received or served and a reasonable time for the bank to act thereon expires or the setoff is exercised after the bank has done any of the following:

    (a) accepted or certified the item;

    (b) paid the item in cash;

    (c) settled for the item without reserving a right to revoke the settlement and without having such right under statute, clearing house rule or agreement;

(d) completed the process of posting the item to the indicated account of the drawer, maker or other person to be charged therewith or otherwise has evidenced by examination of such indicated account and by action its decision to pay the item; or

(e) become accountable for the amount of the item under subsection (1)(d) of Section 4–213 and Section 4–302 dealing with the payor bank's responsibility for late return of items.

(2) Subject to the provisions of subsection (1) items may be accepted, paid, certified or charged to the indicated account of its customer in any order convenient to the bank.

Part 4/Relationship between Payor Bank and Its Customer
§ 4–401
When Bank May Charge Customer's Account

(1) As against its customer, a bank may charge against his account any item which is otherwise properly payable from that account even though the charge creates an overdraft.

(2) A bank which in good faith makes payment to a holder may charge the indicated account of its customer according to

(a) the original tenor of his altered item; or

(b) the tenor of his completed item, even though the bank knows the item has been completed unless the bank has notice that the completion was improper.

§ 4–402
Bank's Liability to Customer for Wrongful Dishonor

A payor bank is liable to its customer for damages proximately caused by the wrongful dishonor of an item. When the dishonor occurs through mistake liability is limited to actual damages proved. If so proximately caused and proved damages may include damages for an arrest or prosecution of the customer or other consequential damages. Whether any consequential damages are proximately caused by the wrongful dishonor is a question of fact to be determined in each case.·

§ 4–403
Customer's Right to Stop Payment; Burden of Proof of Loss

(1) A customer may by order to his bank stop payment of any item payable for his account but the order must be received at such time and in such manner as to afford the bank a reasonable opportunity to act on it prior to any action by the bank with respect to the item described in Section 4–303.

(2) An oral order is binding upon the bank only for fourteen calendar days unless confirmed in writing within that period. A written order is effective for only six months unless renewed in writing.

(3) The burden of establishing the fact and amount of loss resulting from the payment of an item contrary to a binding stop payment order is on the customer.

§ 4–404
Bank Not Obligated to Pay Check
More Than Six Months Old

A bank is under no obligation to a customer having a checking account to pay a check, other than a certified check, which is presented more than six months after its date, but it may charge its customer's account for a payment made thereafter in good faith.

§ 4–405
Death or Incompetence of Customer

(1) A payor or collecting bank's authority to accept, pay or collect an item or to account for proceeds of its collection if otherwise effective is not rendered ineffective by incompetence of a customer of either bank existing at the time the item is issued or its collection is undertaken if the bank does not know of an adjudication of incompetence. Neither death nor incompetence of a customer revokes such authority to accept, pay, collect or account until the bank knows of the fact of death or of an adjudication of incompetence and has reasonable opportunity to act on it.

(2) Even with knowledge a bank may for ten days after the date of death pay or certify checks drawn on or prior to that date unless ordered to stop payment by a person claiming an interest in the account.

§ 4–406
Customer's Duty to Discover and Report
Unauthorized Signature or Alteration

(1) When a bank sends to its customer a statement of account accompanied by items paid in good faith in support of the debit entries or holds the statement and items pursuant to a request or instructions of its customer or otherwise in a reasonable manner makes the statement and items available to the customer, the customer must exercise reasonable care and promptness to examine the statement and items to discover his unauthorized signature or any alteration on an item and must notify the bank promptly after discovery thereof.

(2) If the bank establishes that the customer failed with respect to an item to comply with the duties imposed on the customer by subsection (1) the customer is precluded from asserting against the bank

(a) his unauthorized signature or any alteration on the item if the bank also establishes that it suffered a loss by reason of such failure; and

(b) an unauthorized signature or alteration by the same wrongdoer on any other item paid in good faith by the bank after the first item and statement was available to the customer for a reasonable period not exceeding fourteen calendar days and before the bank receives notification from the customer of any such unauthorized signature or alteration.

(3) The preclusion under subsection (2) does not apply if the customer establishes lack of ordinary care on the part of the bank in paying the item(s).

(4) Without regard to care or lack of care of either the customer or the bank a customer who does not within one year from the time the statement and items are made available to the customer (subsection (1)) discover and report his unauthorized signature or any alteration on the face or back of the item or does not within three years from that time discover and report any unauthorized indorsement is precluded from asserting against the bank such unauthorized signature or indorsement or such alteration.

(5) If under this section a payor bank has a valid defense against a claim of a customer upon or resulting from payment of an item and waives or fails upon request to assert the defense the bank may not assert against any collecting bank or other prior party presenting or transferring the item a claim based upon the unauthorized signature or alteration giving rise to the customer's claim.

§ 4–407
Payor Bank's Right to Subrogation on Improper Payment

If a payor bank has paid an item over the stop payment order of the drawer or maker or otherwise under circumstances giving a basis for objection by the drawer or maker, to prevent unjust enrichment and only to the extent necessary to prevent loss to the bank by reason of its payment of the item, the payor bank shall be subrogated to the rights

(a) of any holder in due course on the item against the drawer or maker; and

(b) of the payee or any other holder of the item against the drawer or maker either on the item or under the transaction out of which the item arose; and

(c) of the drawer or maker against the payee or any other holder of the item with respect to the transaction out of which the item arose.

Part 5/Collection of Documentary Drafts

§ 4–501
Handling of Documentary Drafts; Duty to Send for Presentment and to Notify Customer of Dishonor

A bank which takes a documentary draft for collection must present or send the draft and accompanying documents for presentment and upon learning that the draft has not been paid or accepted in due course must seasonably notify its customer of such fact even though it may have discounted or bought the draft or extended credit available for withdrawal as of right.

§ 4–502
Presentment of "On Arrival" Drafts

When a draft or the relevant instructions require presentment "on arrival", "when goods arrive" or the like, the collecting bank need not present until in its judgment a reasonable time for arrival of the goods has expired. Refusal to pay or accept because the goods have not arrived is not dishonor; the bank must notify its transferor of such refusal but need not present the draft again until it is instructed to do so or learns of the arrival of the goods.

§ 4–503
Responsibility of Presenting Bank for Documents and Goods; Report of Reasons for Dishonor; Referee in Case of Need

Unless otherwise instructed and except as provided in Article 5 a bank presenting a documentary draft

(a) must deliver the documents to the drawee on acceptance of the draft if it is payable more than three days after presentment; otherwise, only on payment; and

(b) upon dishonor, either in the case of presentment for acceptance or presentment for payment, may seek and follow instructions from any referee in case of need designated in the draft or if the presenting bank does not choose to utilize his services it must use diligence and good faith to ascertain the reason for dishonor, must notify its transferor of the dishonor and of the results of its effort to ascertain the reasons therefor and must request instructions.

But the presenting bank is under no obligation with respect to goods represented by the documents except to follow any reasonable instructions seasonably received; it has a right to reimbursement for any expense incurred in following instructions and to prepayment of or indemnity for such expenses.

§ 4–504
Privilege of Presenting Bank to Deal with Goods; Security Interest for Expenses

(1) A presenting bank which, following the dishonor of a documentary draft, has seasonably requested instructions but does not receive them within a reasonable time may store, sell, or otherwise deal with the goods in any reasonable manner.

(2) For its reasonable expenses incurred by action under subsection (1) the presenting bank has a lien upon the goods or their proceeds, which may be foreclosed in the same manner as an unpaid seller's lien.

Note: *Revised Articles 3 and 4. As this text went to press, 19 states had adopted Revised Articles 3 and 4 as substitutes for the original versions. Many more states are expected to enact Revised Articles 3 and 4 during the next few years.*

REVISED ARTICLE 3/NEGOTIABLE INSTRUMENTS
Part 1/Short Title, Form, and Interpretation

§3–101
Short Title

This Article may be cited as Uniform Commercial Code–Negotiable Instruments.

§ 3–102
Subject Matter

(a) This article applies to negotiable instruments. It does not apply to money, to payment orders governed by Article 4A, or to securities governed by Article 8.

(b) If there is conflict between this Article and Article 4 or 9, Articles 4 and 9 govern.

(c) Regulations of the Board of Governors of the Federal Reserve System and operating circulars of the Federal Reserve Banks supersede any inconsistent provision of this Article to the extent of the inconsistency.

§ 3–103
Definitions

(a) In this Article:
(1) "Acceptor" means a drawee who has accepted a draft.
(2) "Drawee" means a person ordered in a draft to make payment.
(3) "Drawer" means a person who signs or is identified in a draft as a person ordering payment.

(4) "Good faith" means honesty in fact and the observance of reasonable commercial standards of fair dealing.

(5) "Maker" means a person who signs or is identified in a note as a person undertaking to pay.

(6) "Order" means a written instruction to pay money signed by the person giving the instruction. The instruction may be addressed to any person, including the person giving the instruction, or to one or more persons jointly or in the alternative but not in succession. An authorization to pay is not an order unless the person authorized to pay is also instructed to pay.

(7) "Ordinary care" in the case of a person engaged in business means observance of reasonable commercial standards, prevailing in the area in which the person is located, with respect to the business in which the person is engaged. In the case of a bank that takes an instrument for processing for collection or payment by automated means, reasonable commercial standards do not require the bank to examine the instrument if the failure to examine does not violate the bank's prescribed procedures and the bank's procedures do not vary unreasonably from general banking usage not disapproved by this Article or Article 4.

(8) "Party" means a party to an instrument.

(9) "Promise" means a written undertaking to pay money signed by the person undertaking to pay. An acknowledgment of an obligation by the obligor is not a promise unless the obligor also undertakes to pay the obligation.

(10) "Prove" with respect to a fact means to meet the burden of establishing the fact (Section 1–201(8)).

(11) "Remitter" means a person who purchases an instrument from its issuer if the instrument is payable to an identified person other than the purchaser.

(b)   Other definitions applying to this Article and the sections in which they appear are:

"Accommodated party". Section 3–419
"Accommodation party". Section 3–419
"Alteration". Section 3–407
"Anomalous indorsement". Section 3–205
"Blank indorsement". Section 3–205
"Cashier's check". Section 3–104
"Certificate of deposit". Section 3–104
"Certified check". Section 3–409
"Check". Section 3–104
"Consideration". Section 3–303
"Draft". Section 3–104
"Holder in due course". Section 3–302
"Incomplete instrument". Section 3–115
"Indorsement". Section 3–204
"Indorser". Section 3–204
"Instrument". Section 3–104
"Issue". Section 3–105
"Issuer". Section 3–105
"Negotiable instrument". Section 3–104
"Negotiation". Section 3–201
"Note". Section 3–104
"Payable at a definite time". Section 3–108
"Payable on demand". Section 3–108
"Payable to bearer". Section 3–109
"Payable to order". Section 3–109

"Payment". Section 3–602
"Person entitled to enforce". Section 3–301
"Presentment". Section 3–501
"Reacquisition". Section 3–207
"Special indorsement". Section 3–205
"Teller's check". Section 3–104
"Transfer of instrument". Section 3–203
"Traveler's check". Section 3–104
"Value". Section 3–303

(c)   The following definitions in other Articles apply to this Article:

"Bank". Section 4–105
"Banking day". Section 4–104
"Clearing house". Section 4–104
"Collecting bank". Section 4–105
"Depositary bank". Section 4–105
"Documentary draft". Section 4–104
"Intermediary bank". Section 4–105
"Item". Section 4–104
"Payor bank". Section 4–105
"Suspends payments". Section 4–104

(d)   In addition, Article 1 contains general definitions and principles of construction and interpretation applicable throughout this Article.

§ 3–104
Negotiable Instrument

(a)   Except as provided in subsections (c) and (d), "negotiable instrument" means an unconditional promise or order to pay a fixed amount of money, with or without interest or other charges described in the promise or order, if it:

(1)   is payable to bearer or to order at the time it is issued or first comes into possession of a holder;

(2)   is payable on demand or at a definite time; and

(3)   does not state any other undertaking or instruction by the person promising or ordering payment to do any act in addition to the payment of money, but the promise or order may contain (i) an undertaking or power to give, maintain, or protect collateral to secure payment, (ii) an authorization or power to the holder to confess judgment or realize on or dispose of collateral, or (iii) a waiver of the benefit of any law intended for the advantage or protection of an obligor.

(b)   "Instrument" means a negotiable instrument.

(c)   An order that meets all of the requirements of subsection (a), except paragraph (1), and otherwise falls within the definition of "check" in subsection (f) is a negotiable instrument and a check.

(d)   A promise or order other than a check is not an instrument if, at the time it is issued or first comes into possession of a holder, it contains a conspicuous statement, however expressed, to the effect that the promise or order is not negotiable or is not an instrument governed by this Article.

(e)   An instrument is a "note" if it is a promise and is a "draft" if it is an order. If an instrument falls within the definition of both "note" and "draft," a person entitled to enforce the instrument may treat it as either.

(f)   "Check" means (i) a draft, other than a documentary draft, payable on demand and drawn on a bank or (ii) a cashier's check or teller's check. An instrument may be a check even though it is described on its face by another term, such as "money order".

(g) "Cashier's check" means a draft with respect to which the drawer and drawee are the same bank or branches of the same bank.

(h) "Teller's check" means a draft drawn by a bank (i) on another bank, or (ii) payable at or through a bank.

(i) "Traveler's check" means an instrument that (i) is payable on demand, (ii) is drawn on or payable at or through a bank, (iii) is designated by the term "traveler's check" or by a substantially similar term, and (iv) requires, as a condition to payment, a countersignature by a person whose specimen signature appears on the instrument.

(j) "Certificate of deposit" means an instrument containing an acknowledgment by a bank that a sum of money has been received by the bank and a promise by the bank to repay the sum of money. A certificate of deposit is a note of the bank.

§ 3–105
Issue of Instrument

(a) "Issue" means the first delivery of an instrument by the maker or drawer, whether to a holder or nonholder, for the purpose of giving rights on the instrument to any person.

(b) An unissued instrument, or an unissued incomplete instrument that is completed, is binding on the maker or drawer, but nonissuance is a defense. An instrument that is conditionally issued or is issued for a special purpose is binding on the maker or drawer, but failure of the condition or special purpose to be fulfilled is a defense.

(c) "Issuer" applies to issued and unissued instruments and means a maker or drawer of an instrument.

§ 3–106
Unconditional Promise or Order

(a) Except as provided in this section, for the purposes of Section 3–104(a), a promise or order is unconditional unless it states (i) an express condition to payment, (ii) that the promise or order is subject to or governed by another writing, or (iii) that rights or obligations with respect to the promise or order are stated in another writing. A reference to another writing does not of itself make the promise or order conditional.

(b) A promise or order is not made conditional (i) by a reference to another writing for a statement of rights with respect to collateral, prepayment, or acceleration, or (ii) because payment is limited to resort to a particular fund or source.

(c) If a promise or order requires, as a condition to payment, a countersignature by a person whose specimen signature appears on the promise or order, the condition does not make the promise or order conditional for the purposes of Section 3–104(a). If the person whose specimen signature appears on an instrument fails to countersign the instrument, the failure to countersign is a defense to the obligation of the issuer, but the failure does not prevent a transferee of the instrument from becoming a holder of the instrument.

(d) If a promise or order at the time it is issued or first comes into possession of a holder contains a statement, required by applicable statutory or administrative law, to the effect that the rights of a holder or transferee are subject to claims or defenses that the issuer could assert against the original payee, the promise or order is not thereby made conditional for the purposes of Section 3–104(a); but if the promise or order is an instrument, there cannot be a holder in due course of the instrument.

§ 3–107
Instrument Payable in Foreign Money

Unless the instrument otherwise provides, an instrument that states the amount payable in foreign money may be paid in the foreign money or in an equivalent amount in dollars calculated by using the current bank-offered spot rate at the place of payment for the purchase of dollars on the day on which the instrument is paid.

§ 3–108
Payable on Demand or at Definite Time

(a) A promise or order is "payable on demand" if it (i) states that it is payable on demand or at sight, or otherwise indicates that it is payable at the will of the holder, or (ii) does not state any time of payment.

(b) A promise or order is "payable at a definite time" if it is payable on elapse of a definite period of time after sight or acceptance or at a fixed date or dates or at a time or times readily ascertainable at the time the promise or order is issued, subject to rights of (i) prepayment, (ii) acceleration, (iii) extension at the option of the holder, or (iv) extension to a further definite time at the option of the maker or acceptor or automatically upon or after a specified act or event.

(c) If an instrument, payable at a fixed date, is also payable upon demand made before the fixed date, the instrument is payable on demand until the fixed date and, if demand for payment is not made before that date, becomes payable at a definite time on the fixed date.

§ 3–109
Payable to Bearer or to Order

(a) A promise or order is payable to bearer it if:
    (1) states that it is payable to bearer or to the order of bearer or otherwise indicates that the person in possession of the promise or order is entitled to payment;
    (2) does not state a payee; or
    (3) states that it is payable to or to the order of cash or otherwise indicates that it is not payable to an identified person.

(b) A promise or order that is not payable to bearer is payable to order if it is payable (i) to the order of an identified person or (ii) to an identified person or order. A promise or order that is payable to order is payable to the identified person.

(c) An instrument payable to bearer may become payable to an identified person if it is specially indorsed pursuant to Section 3–205(a). An instrument payable to an identified person may become payable to bearer if it is indorsed in blank pursuant to Section 3–205(b).

§ 3–110
Identification of Person to Whom Instrument Is Payable

(a)   The person to whom an instrument is initially payable is determined by the intent of the person, whether or not authorized, signing as, or in the name or behalf of, the issuer of the instrument. The instrument is payable to the person intended by the signer even if that person is identified in the instrument by a name or other identification that is not that of the intended person. If more than one person signs in the name or behalf of the issuer of an instrument and all the signers do not intend the same person as payee, the instrument is payable to any person intended by one or more of the signers.

(b)   If the signature of the issuer of an instrument is made by automated means, such as a check-writing machine, the payee of the instrument is determined by the intent of the person who supplied the name or identification of the payee, whether or not authorized to do so.

(c)   A person to whom an instrument is payable may be identified in any way, including by name, identifying number, office, or account number. For the purpose of determining the holder of an instrument, the following rules apply:

   (1)   If an instrument is payable to an account and the account is identified only by number, the instrument is payable to the person to whom the account is payable. If an instrument is payable to an account identified by number and by the name of a person, the instrument is payable to the named person, whether or not that person is the owner of the account identified by number.

   (2)   If an instrument is payable to:

      (i)   a trust, an estate, or a person described as trustee or representative of a trust or estate, the instrument is payable to the trustee, the representative, or a successor of either, whether or not the beneficiary or estate is also named;

      (ii)   a person described as agent or similar representative of a named or identified person, the instrument is payable to the represented person, the representative, or a successor of the representative;

      (iii)   a fund or organization that is not a legal entity, the instrument is payable to a representative of the members of the fund or organization; or

      (iv)   an office or to a person described as holding an office, the instrument is payable to the named person, the incumbent of the office, or a successor to the incumbent.

(d)   If an instrument is payable to two or more persons alternatively, it is payable to any of them and may be negotiated, discharged, or enforced by any or all of them in possession of the instrument. If an instrument is payable to two or more persons not alternatively, it is payable to all of them and may be negotiated, discharged, or enforced only by all of them. If an instrument payable to two or more persons is ambiguous as to whether it is payable to the persons alternatively, the instrument is payable to the persons alternatively.

§ 3–111
Place of Payment

Except as otherwise provided for items in Article 4, an instrument is payable at the place of payment stated in the instrument. If no place of payment is stated, an instrument is payable at the address of the drawee or maker stated in the instrument. If no address is stated, the place of payment is the place of business of the drawee or maker. If a drawee or maker has more than one place of business, the place of payment is any place of business of the drawee or maker chosen by the person entitled to enforce the instrument. If the drawee or maker has no place of business, the place of payment is the residence of the drawee or maker.

§ 3–112
Interest

(a)   Unless otherwise provided in the instrument, (i) an instrument is not payable with interest, and (ii) interest on an interest-bearing instrument is payable from the date of the instrument.

(b)   Interest may be stated in an instrument as a fixed or variable amount of money or it may be expressed as a fixed or variable rate or rates. The amount or rate of interest may be stated or described in the instrument in any manner and may require reference to information not contained in the instrument. If an instrument provides for interest, but the amount of interest payable cannot be ascertained from the description, interest is payable at the judgment rate in effect at the place of payment of the instrument and at the time interest first accrues.

§ 3–113
Date of Instrument

(a)   An instrument may be antedated or postdated. The date stated determines the time of payment if the instrument is payable at a fixed period after date. Except as provided in Section 4–401(c), an instrument payable on demand is not payable before the date of the instrument.

(b)   If an instrument is undated, its date is the date of its issue or, in the case of an unissued instrument, the date it first comes into possession of a holder.

§ 3–114
Contradictory Terms of Instrument

If an instrument contains contradictory terms, typewritten terms prevail over printed terms, handwritten terms prevail over both, and words prevail over numbers.

§ 3–115
Incomplete Instrument

(a)   "Incomplete instrument" means a signed writing, whether or not issued by the signer, the contents of which show at the time of signing that it is incomplete but that the signer intended it to be completed by the addition of words or numbers.

(b)   Subject to subsection (c), if an incomplete instrument is an instrument under Section 3–104, it may be enforced according to its terms if it is not completed, or according to its terms as augmented by completion. If an incomplete instrument is not an instrument under Section 3–104, but, after completion, the requirements of Section 3–104 are met, the instrument may be enforced according to its terms as augmented by completion.

(c) If words or numbers are added to an incomplete instrument without authority of the signer, there is an alteration of the incomplete instrument under Section 3–407.

(d) The burden of establishing that words or numbers were added to an incomplete instrument without authority of the signer is on the person asserting the lack of authority.

§ 3–116
Joint and Several Liability; Contribution

(a) Except as otherwise provided in the instrument, two or more persons who have the same liability on an instrument as makers, drawers, acceptors, indorsers who indorse as joint payees, or anomalous indorsers are jointly and severally liable in the capacity in which they sign.

(b) Except as provided in Section 3–419(e) or by agreement of the affected parties, a party having joint and several liability who pays the instrument is entitled to received from any party having the same joint and several liability contribution in accordance with applicable law.

(c) Discharge of one party having joint and several liability by a person entitled to enforce the instrument does not affect the right under subsection (b) of a party having the same joint and several liability to receive contribution from the party discharged.

§ 3–117
Other Agreements Affecting Instrument

Subject to applicable law regarding exclusion of proof of contemporaneous or previous agreements, the obligation of a party to an instrument to pay the instrument may be modified, supplemented, or nullified by a separate agreement of the obligor and a person entitled to enforce the instrument, if the instrument is issued or the obligation is incurred in reliance on the agreement or as part of the same transaction giving rise to the agreement. To the extent an obligation is modified, supplemented, or nullified by an agreement under this section, the agreement is a defense to the obligation.

§ 3–118
Statute of Limitations

(a) Except as provided in subsection (e), an action to enforce the obligation of a party to pay a note payable at a definite time must be commenced within six years after the due date or dates stated in the note or, if a due date is accelerated, within six years after the accelerated due date.

(b) Except as provided in subsection (d) or (e), if demand for payment is made to the maker of a note payable on demand, an action to enforce the obligation of a party to pay the note must be commenced within six years after the demand. If no demand for payment is made to the maker, an action to enforce the note is barred if neither principal nor interest on the note has been paid for a continuous period of 10 years.

(c) Except as provided in subsection (d), an action to enforce the obligation of a party to an unaccepted draft to pay the draft must be commenced within three years after dishonor of the draft or 10 years after the date of the draft, whichever period expires first.

(d) An action to enforce the obligation of the acceptor of a certified check or the issuer of a teller's check, cashier's check, or traveler's check must be commenced within three years after demand for payment is made to the acceptor or issuer, as the case may be.

(e) An action to enforce the obligation of a party to a certificate of deposit to pay the instrument must be commenced within six years after demand for payment is made to the maker, but if the instrument states a due date and the maker is not required to pay before that date, the six-year period begins when a demand for payment is in effect and the due date has passed.

(f) An action to enforce the obligation of a party to pay an accepted draft, other than a certified check, must be commenced (i) within six years after the due date or dates stated in the draft or acceptance if the obligation of the acceptor is payable at a definite time, or (ii) within six years after the date of the acceptance if the obligation of the acceptor is payable on demand.

(g) Unless governed by other law regarding claims for indemnity or contribution, an action (i) for conversion of an instrument, for money had and received, or like action based on conversion, (ii) for breach of warranty, or (iii) to enforce an obligation, duty, or right arising under this Article and not governed by this section must be commenced within three years after the [cause of action] accrues.

Notice of Right to Defend Action

In an action for breach of an obligation for which a third person is answerable over pursuant to this Article or Article 4, the defendant may give the third person written notice of the litigation, and the person notified may then give similar notice to any other person who is answerable over. If the notice states (i) that the person notified may come in and defend and (ii) that failure to do so will bind the person notified in an action later brought by the person giving the notice as to any determination of fact common to the two litigations, the person notified is so bound unless after seasonable receipt of the notice the person notified does come in and defend.

Part 2/Negotiation, Transfer, and Indorsement
§ 3–201
Negotiation

(a) "Negotiation" means a transfer of possession, whether voluntary or involuntary, of an instrument by a person other than the issuer to a person who thereby becomes its holder.

(b) Except for negotiation by a remitter, if an instrument is payable to an identified person, negotiation requires transfer of possession of the instrument and its indorsement by the holder. If an instrument is payable to bearer, it may be negotiated by transfer of possession alone.

§ 3–202
Negotiation Subject to Rescission

(a) Negotiation is effective even if obtained (i) from an infant, a corporation exceeding its powers, or a person without capacity, (ii) by fraud, duress, or mistake, or (iii) in breach of duty or as part of an illegal transaction.

(b)   To the extent permitted by other law, negotiation may be rescinded or may be subject to other remedies, but those remedies may not be asserted against a subsequent holder in due course or a person paying the instrument in good faith and without knowledge of facts that are a basis for rescission or other remedy.

§ 3–203
Transfer of Instrument; Rights Acquired by Transfer

(a)   An instrument is transferred when it is delivered by a person other than its issuer for the purpose of giving to the person receiving delivery the right to enforce the instrument.

(b)   Transfer of an instrument, whether or not the transfer is a negotiation, vests in the transferee any right of the transferor to enforce the instrument, including any right as a holder in due course, but the transferee cannot acquire rights of a holder in due course by a transfer, directly or indirectly, from a holder in due course if the transferee engaged in fraud or illegality affecting the instrument.

(c)   Unless otherwise agreed, if an instrument is transferred for value and the transferee does not become a holder because of lack of indorsement by the transferor, the transferee has a specifically enforceable right to the unqualified indorsement of the transferor, but negotiation of the instrument does not occur until the indorsement is made.

(d)   If a transferor purports to transfer less than the entire instrument, negotiation of the instrument does not occur. The transferee obtains no rights under this Article and has only the rights of a partial assignee.

§ 3–204
Indorsement

(a)   "Indorsement" means a signature, other than that of a signer as maker, drawer, or acceptor, that alone or accompanied by other words is made on an instrument for the purpose of (i) negotiating the instrument, (ii) restricting payment of the instrument, or (iii) incurring indorser's liability on the instrument, but regardless of the intent of the signer, a signature and its accompanying words is an indorsement unless the accompanying words, terms of the instrument, place of the signature, or other circumstances unambiguously indicate that the signature was made for a purpose other than indorsement. For the purpose of determining whether a signature is made on an instrument, a paper affixed to the instrument is a part of the instrument.

(b)   "Indorser" means a person who makes an indorsement.

(c)   For the purpose of determining whether the transferee of an instrument is a holder, an indorsement that transfers a security interest in the instrument is effective as an unqualified indorsement of the instrument.

(d)   If an instrument is payable to a holder under a name that is not the name of the holder, indorsement may be made by the holder in the name stated in the instrument or in the holder's name or both, but signature in both names may be required by a person paying or taking the instrument for value or collection.

§ 3–205
Special Indorsement; Blank Indorsement; Anomalous Indorsement

(a)   If an indorsement is made by the holder of an instrument, whether payable to an identified person or payable to bearer, and the indorsement identifies a person to whom it makes the instrument payable, it is a "special indorsement." When specially indorsed, an instrument becomes payable to the identified person and may be negotiated only by the indorsement of that person. The principles stated in Section 3–110 apply to special indorsements.

(b)   If an indorsement is made by the holder of an instrument and it is not a special indorsement, it is a "blank indorsement." When indorsed in blank, an instrument becomes payable to bearer and may be negotiated by transfer of possession alone until specially indorsed.

(c) The holder may convert a blank indorsement that consists only of a signature into a special indorsement by writing, above the signature of the indorser, words identifying the person to whom the instrument is made payable.

(d)   "Anomalous indorsement" means an indorsement made by a person who is not the holder of the instrument. An anomalous indorsement does not affect the manner in which the instrument may be negotiated.

§ 3–206
Restrictive Indorsement

(a)   An indorsement limiting payment to a particular person or otherwise prohibiting further transfer or negotiation of the instrument is not effective to prevent further transfer or negotiation of the instrument.

(b)   An indorsement stating a condition to the right of the indorsee to receive payment does not affect the right of the indorsee to enforce the instrument. A person paying the instrument or taking it for value or collection may disregard the condition, and the rights and liabilities of that person are not affected by whether the condition has

been fulfilled.

(c)   If an instrument bears an indorsement (i) described in Section 4–201(b), or (ii) in blank or to a particular bank using the words "for deposit," "for collection," or other words indicating a purpose of having the instrument collected by a bank for the indorser or for a particular account, the following rules apply:

(1)   A person, other than a bank, who purchases the instrument when so indorsed converts the instrument unless the amount paid for the instrument is received by the indorser or applied consistently with the indorsement.

(2)   A depositary bank that purchases the instrument or takes it for collection when so indorsed converts the instrument unless the amount paid by the bank with respect to the instrument is received by the indorser or applied consistently with the indorsement.

(3)   A payor bank that is also the depositary bank or that takes the instrument for immediate payment over the counter from a person other than a collecting bank converts the instrument unless the proceeds of the instrument are received by the indorser or applied consistently with the indorsement.

(4) Except as otherwise provided in paragraph (3), a payor bank or intermediary bank may disregard the indorsement and is not liable if the proceeds of the instrument are not received by the indorser or applied consistently with the indorsement.

(d) Except for an indorsement covered by subsection (c), if an instrument bears an indorsement using words to the effect that payment is to be made to the indorsee as agent, trustee, or other fiduciary for the benefit of the indorser or another person, the following rules apply:

> **(1)** Unless there is notice of breach of fiduciary duty as provided in Section 3–307, a person who purchases the instrument from the indorsee or takes the instrument from the indorsee for collection or payment may pay the proceeds of payment or the value given for the instrument to the indorsee without regard to whether the indorsee violates a fiduciary duty to the indorser.
>
> **(2)** A subsequent transferee of the instrument or person who pays the instrument is neither given notice nor otherwise affected by the restriction in the indorsement unless the transferee or payor knows that the fiduciary dealt with the instrument or its proceeds in breach of fiduciary duty.

(e) The presence on an instrument of an indorsement to which this section applies does not prevent a purchaser of the instrument from becoming a holder in due course of the instrument unless the purchaser is a converter under subsection (c) or has notice or knowledge of breach of fiduciary duty as stated in subsection (d).

(f) In an action to enforce the obligation of a party to pay the instrument, the obligor has a defense if payment would violate an indorsement to which this section applies and the payment is not permitted by this section.

§ 3–207
Reacquisition

Reacquisition of an instrument occurs if it is transferred to a former holder, by negotiation or otherwise. A former holder who reacquires the instrument may cancel indorsements made after the reacquirer first became a holder of the instrument. If the cancellation causes the instrument to be payable to the reacquirer or to bearer, the reacquirer may negotiate the instrument. An indorser whose indorsement is canceled is discharged, and the discharge is effective against any subsequent holder.

Part>Part 3/Enforcement of Instruments

§ 3–301
Person Entitled to Enforce Instrument

"Person entitled to enforce" an instrument means (i) the holder of the instrument, (ii) a nonholder in possession of the instrument who has the rights of a holder, or (iii) a person not in possession of the instrument who is entitled to enforce the instrument pursuant to Section 3–309 or 3–418(d). A person may be a person entitled to enforce the instrument even though the person is not the owner of the instrument or is in wrongful possession of the instrument.

§3–302
Holder in Due Course

(a) Subject to subsection (c) and Section 3–106(d), "holder in due course" means the holder of an instrument if:

> **(1)** the instrument when issued or negotiated to the holder does not bear such apparent evidence of forgery or alteration or is not otherwise so irregular or incomplete as to call into question its authenticity; and
>
> **(2)** the holder took the instrument (i) for value, (ii) in good faith, (iii) without notice that the instrument is overdue or has been dishonored or that there is an uncured default with respect to payment of another instrument issued as part of the same series, (iv) without notice that the instrument contains an unauthorized signature or has been altered, (v) without notice of any claim to the instrument described in Section 3–306, and (vi) without notice that any party has a defense or claim in recoupment described in Section 3–305(a).

(b) Notice of discharge of a party, other than discharge in an insolvency proceeding, is not notice of a defense under subsection (a), but discharge is effective against a person who became a holder in due course with notice of the discharge. Public filing or recording of a document does not feel of itself constitute notice of a defense, claim in recoupment, or claim to the instrument.

(c) Except to the extent a transferor or predecessor in interest has rights as a holder in due course, a person does not acquire rights of a holder in due course of an instrument taken (i) by legal process or by purchase in an execution, bankruptcy, or creditor's sale or similar proceeding, (ii) by purchase as part of a bulk transaction not in ordinary course of business of the transferor, or (iii) as the successor in interest to an estate or other organization.

(d) If, under Section 3–303(a)(1), the promise of performance that is the consideration for an instrument has been partially performed, the holder may assert rights as a holder in due course of the instrument only to the fraction of the amount payable under the instrument equal to the value of the partial performance divided by the value of the promised performance.

(e) If (i) the person entitled to enforce an instrument has only a security interest in the instrument and (ii) the person obliged to pay the instrument has a defense, claim in recoupment, or claim to the instrument that may be asserted against the person who granted the security interest, the person entitled to enforce the instrument may assert rights as a holder in due course only to an amount payable under the instrument which, at a time of enforcement of the instrument, does not exceed the amount of the unpaid obligation secured.

(f) To be effective, notice must be received at a time and in a manner that gives a reasonable opportunity to act on it.

(g) This section is subject to any law limiting status as a holder in due course in particular classes of transactions.

§ 3–303
Value and Consideration

(a) An instrument is issued or transferred for value if:

> **(1)** the instrument is issued or transferred for a promise of performance, to the extent the promise has been performed;

(2) the transferee acquires a security interest or other lien in the instrument other than a lien obtained by judicial proceeding;

(3) the instrument is issued or transferred as payment of, or as security for, an antecedent claim against any person, whether or not the claim is due;

(4) the instrument is issued or transferred in exchange for a negotiable instrument; or

(5) the instrument is issued or transferred in exchange for the incurring of an irrevocable obligation to a third party by the person taking the instrument.

(b) "Consideration" means any consideration sufficient to support a simple contract. The drawer or maker of an instrument has a defense if the instrument is issued without consideration. If an instrument is issued for a promise of performance, the issuer has a defense to the extent performance of the promise is due and the promise has not been performed. If an instrument is issued for value as stated in subsection (a), the instrument is also issued for consideration.

§ 3–304
Overdue Instrument

(a) An instrument payable on demand becomes overdue at the earliest of the following times:

(1) on the day after the day demand for payment is duly made;

(2) if the instrument is a check, 90 days after its date; or

(3) if the instrument is not a check, when the instrument has been outstanding for a period of time after its date which is unreasonably long under the circumstances of the particular case in light of the nature of the instrument and usage of the trade.

(b) With respect to an instrument payable at a definite time the following rules apply:

(1) If the principal is payable in installments and a due date has not been accelerated, the instrument becomes overdue upon default under the instrument for nonpayment of an installment, and the instrument remains overdue until the default is cured.

(2) If the principal is not payable in installments and the due date has not been accelerated, the instrument becomes overdue on the day after the due date.

(3) If a due date with respect to principal has been accelerated, the instrument becomes overdue on the day after the accelerated due date.

(c) Unless the due date of principal has been accelerated, an instrument does not become overdue if there is default in payment of interest but no default in payment of principal.

§ 3–305
Defenses and Claims in Recoupment

(a) Except as stated in subsection (b), the right to enforce the obligation of a party to pay an instrument is subject to the following:

(1) a defense of the obligor based on (i) infancy of the obligor to the extent it is a defense to a simple contract, (ii) duress, lack of legal capacity, or illegality of the transaction which, under other law, nullifies the obligation of the obligor, (iii) fraud that induced the obligor to sign the instru-

ment with neither knowledge nor reasonable opportunity to learn of its character or its essential terms, or (iv) discharge of the obligor in insolvency proceedings;

(2) a defense of the obligor stated in another section of this Article or a defense of the obligor that would be available if the person entitled to enforce the instrument were enforcing a right to payment under a simple contract; and

(3) a claim in recoupment of the obligor against the original payee of the instrument if the claim arose from the transaction that gave rise to the instrument; but the claim of the obligor may be asserted against a transferee of the instrument only to reduce the amount owing on the instrument at the time the action is brought.

(b) The right of a holder in due course to enforce the obligation of a party to pay the instrument is subject to defenses of the obligor stated in subsection (a)(1), but is not subject to defenses of the obligor stated in subsection (a)(2) or claims in recoupment stated in subsection (a)(3) against a person other than the holder.

(c) Except as stated in subsection (d), in an action to enforce the obligation of a party to pay the instrument, the obligor may not assert against the person entitled to enforce the instrument a defense, claim in recoupment, or claim to the instrument (Section 3–306) of another person, but the other person's claim to the instrument may be asserted by the obligor if the other person is joined in the action and personally asserts the claim against the person entitled to enforce the instrument. An obligor is not obliged to pay the instrument if the person seeking enforcement of the instrument does not have rights of a holder in due course and the obligor proves that the instrument is a lost or stolen instrument.

(d) In an action to enforce the obligation of an accommodation party to pay an instrument, the accommodation party may assert against the person entitled to enforce the intrument any defense or claim in recoupment under subsection (a) that the accommodated party could assert against the person entitled to enforce the instrument, except the defenses of discharge in insolvency proceedings, infancy, and lack of legal capacity.

§ 3–306
Claims to an Instrument

A person taking an instrument, other than a person having rights of a holder in due course, is subject to a claim of a property or possessory right in the intrument or its proceeds, including a claim to rescind a negotiation and to recover the instrument or its proceeds. A person having rights of a holder in due course takes free of the claim to the instrument.

§ 3–307
Notice of Breach of Fiduciary Duty

(a) In this section:

(1) "Fiduciary" means an agent, trustee, partner, corporate officer or director, or other representative owing a fiduciary duty with respect to an instrument.

(2) "Represented person" means the principal, beneficiary, partnership, corporation, or other person to whom the duty stated in paragraph (1) is owed.

(b) If (i) an instrument is taken from a fiduciary for payment or collection or for value, (ii) the taker has knowledge of the fiduciary status of the fiduciary, and (iii) the represented person makes a claim to the instrument or its proceeds on the basis that the transaction of the fiduciary is a breach of fiduciary duty, the following rules apply:

(1) Notice of breach of fiduciary duty by the fiduciary is notice of the claim of the represented person.

(2) In the case of an instrument payable to the represented person or the fiduciary as such, the taker has notice of the breach of fiduciary duty if the instrument is (i) taken in payment of or as security for a debt known by the taker to be the personal debt of the fiduciary, (ii) taken in a transaction known by the taker to be for the personal benefit of the fiduciary, or (iii) deposited to an account other than an account of the fiduciary, as such, or an account of the represented person.

(3) If an instrument is issued by the represented person or the fiduciary as such, and made payable to the fiduciary personally, the taker does not have notice of the breach of fiduciary duty unless the taker knows of the breach of fiduciary duty.

(4) If an instrument is issued by the represented person or the fiduciary as such, to the taker as payee, the taker has notice of the breach of fiduciary duty if the instrument is (i) taken in payment of or as security for a debt known by the taker to be the personal debt of the fiduciary, (ii) taken in a transaction known by the taker to be for the personal benefit of the fiduciary, or (iii) deposited to an account other than an account of the fiduciary, as such, or an account of the represented person.

§ 3–308
Proof of Signatures and Status as Holder in Due Course

(a) In an action with respect to an instrument, the authenticity of, and authority to make, each signature on the instrument is admitted unless specifically denied in the pleadings. If the validity of a signature is denied in the pleadings, the burden of establishing validity is on the person claiming validity, but the signature is presumed to be authentic and authorized unless the action is to enforce the liability of the purported signer and the signer is dead or incompetent at the time of trial of the issue of validity of the signature. If an action to enforce the instrument is brought against a person as the undisclosed principal of a person who signed the instrument as a party to the instrument, the plaintiff has the burden of establishing that the defendant is liable on the instrument as a represented person under Section 3–402(a).

(b) If the validity of signatures is admitted or proved and there is compliance with subsection (a), a plaintiff producing the instrument is entitled to payment if the plaintiff proves entitlement to enforce the instrument under Section 3–301, unless the defendant proves a defense or claim in recoupment. If a defense or claim in recoupment is proved, the right to payment of the plaintiff is subject to the defense or claim, except to the extent the plaintiff proves that the plaintiff has rights of a holder in due course which are not subject to the defense or claim.

§ 3–309
Enforcement of Lost, Destroyed, or Stolen Instrument

(a) A person not in possession of an instrument is entitled to enforce the instrument if (i) the person was in possession of the instrument and entitled to enforce it when loss of possession

occurred, (ii) the loss of possession was not the result of a transfer by the person or a lawful seizure, and (iii) the person cannot reasonably obtain possession of the instrument because the instrument was destroyed, its whereabouts cannot be determined, or it is in the wrongful possession of an unknown person or a person that cannot be found or is not amenable to service of process.

(b) A person seeking enforcement of an instrument under subsection (a) must prove the terms of the instrument and the person's right to enforce the instrument. If that proof is made, Section 3–308 applies to the case as if the person seeking enforcement had produced the instrument. The court may not enter judgment in favor of the person seeking enforcement unless it finds that the person required to pay the instrument is adequately protected against loss that might occur by reason of a claim by another person to enforce the instrument. Adequate protection may be provided by any reasonable means.

§3–310
Effect of Instrument on Obligation for Which Taken

(a) Unless otherwise agreed, if a certified check, cashier's check, or teller's check is taken for an obligation, the obligation is discharged to the same extent discharge would result if an amount of money equal to the amount of the instrument were taken in payment of the obligation. Discharge of the obligation does not affect any liability that the obligor may have as an indorser of the instrument.

(b) Unless otherwise agreed and except as provided in subsection (a), if a note or an uncertified check is taken for an obligation, the obligation is suspended to the same extent the obligation would be discharged if an amount of money equal to the amount of the instrument were taken, and the following rules apply:

(1) In the case of an uncertified check, suspension of the obligation continues until dishonor of the check or until it is paid or certified. Payment or certification of the check results in discharge of the obligation to the extent of the amount of the check.

(2) In the case of a note, suspension of the obligation continues until dishonor of the note or until it is paid. Payment of the note results in discharge of the obligation to the extent of the payment.

(3) Except as provided in paragraph (4), if the check or note is dishonored and the obligee of the obligation for which the instrument was taken is the person entitled to enforce the instrument, the obligee may enforce either the instrument or the obligation. In the case of an instrument of a third person which is negotiated to the obligee by the obligor, discharge of the obligor on the instrument also discharges the obligation.

(4) If the person entitled to enforce the instrument taken for an obligation is a person other than the obligee, the obligee may not enforce the obligation to the extent the obligation is suspended. If the obligee is the person entitled to enforce the instrument but no longer has possession of it because it was lost, stolen, or destroyed, the obligation may not be enforced to the extent of the amount payable on the instrument, and to that extent the obligee's rights against the obligor are limited to enforcement of the instrument.

(c) If an instrument other than one described in subsection (a) or (b) is taken for an obligation, the effect is (i) that stated in subsection (a) if the instrument is one on which a bank is liable as maker or acceptor, or (ii) that stated in subsection (b) in any other case.

§ 3–311
Accord and Satisfaction by Use of Instrument

(a) If a person against whom a claim is asserted proves that (i) that person in good faith tendered an instrument to the claimant as full satisfaction of the claim, (ii) the amount of the claim was unliquidated or subject to a bona fide dispute, and (iii) the claimant obtained payment of the instrument, the following subsections apply.

(b) Unless subsection (c) applies, the claim is discharged if the person against whom the claim is asserted proves that the instrument or an accompanying written communication contained a conspicuous statement to the effect that the instrument was tendered as full satisfaction of the claim.

(c) Subject to subsection (d), a claim is not discharged under subsection (b) if either of the following applies:
(1) The claimant, if an organization, proves that (i) within a reasonable time before the tender, the claimant sent a conspicuous statement to the person against whom the claim is asserted that communications concerning disputed debts, including an instrument tendered as full satisfaction of a debt, are to be sent to a designated person, office, or place, and (ii) the instrument or accompanying communication was not received by that designated person, office, or place.
(2) The claimant, whether or not an organization, proves that within 90 days after payment of the instrument, the claimant tendered repayment of the amount of the instrument to the person against whom the claim is asserted. This paragraph does not apply if the claimant is an organization that sent a statement complying with paragraph (1)(i).

(d) A claim is discharged if the person against whom the claim is asserted proves that within a reasonable time before collection of the instrument was initiated, the claimant, or an agent of the claimant having direct responsibility with respect to the disputed obligation, knew that the instrument was tendered in full satisfaction of the claim.

§ 3–312
Lost, Destroyed, or Stolen Cashier's Check, Teller's Check, or Certified Check

(a) In this section:
(1) "Check" means a cashier's check, teller's check, or certified check.
(2) "Claimant" means a person who claims the right to receive the amount of a cashier's check, teller's check, or certified check that was lost, destroyed, or stolen.
(3) "Declaration of loss" means a written statement, made under penalty of perjury, to the effect that (i) the declarer lost possession of a check, (ii) the declarer is the drawer or payee of the check, in the case of a certified check, or the remitter or payee of the check, in the case of a cashier's check or teller's check, (iii) the loss of possession was not the result of a transfer by the declarer or a lawful seizure, and (iv) the declarer cannot reasonably obtain possession of the check because the check was destroyed, its whereabouts cannot be determined, or it is in the wrongful possession of an un-

known person or a person that cannot be found or is not amenable to service of process.
(4) "Obligated bank" means the issuer of a cashier's check or teller's check or the acceptor of a certified check.

(b) A claimant may assert a claim to the amount of a check by a communication to the obligated bank describing the check with reasonable certainty and requesting payment of the amount of the check, if (i) the claimant is the drawer or payee of a certified check or the remitter or payee of a cashier's check or teller's check, (ii) the communication contains or is accompanied by a declaration of loss of the claimant with respect to the check, (iii) the communication is received at a time and in a manner affording the bank a reasonable time to act on it before the check is paid, and (iv) the claimant provides reasonable identification if requested by the obligated bank. Delivery of a declaration of loss is a warranty of the truth of the statements made in the declaration. If a claim is asserted in compliance with this subsection, the following rules apply:
(1) The claim becomes enforceable at the later of (i) the time the claim is asserted, or (ii) the 90th day following the date of the check, in the case of a cashier's check or teller's check, or the 90th day following the date of the acceptance, in the case of a certified check.
(2) Until the claim becomes enforceable, it has no legal effect and the obligated bank may pay the check or, in the case of a teller's check, may permit the drawee to pay the check. Payment to a person entitled to enforce the check discharges all liability of the obligated bank with respect to the check.
(3) If the claim becomes enforceable before the check is presented for payment, the obligated bank is not obliged to pay the check.
(4) When the claim becomes enforceable, the obligated bank becomes obliged to pay the amount of the check to the claimant if payment of the check has not been made to a person entitled to enforce the check. Subject to Section 4–302(a)(1), payment to the claimant discharges all liability of the obligated bank with respect to the check.

(c) If the obligated bank pays the amount of a check to a claimant under subsection (b)(4) and the check is presented for payment by a person having rights of a holder in due course, the claimant is obliged to (i) refund the payment to the obligated bank if the check is paid, or (ii) pay the amount of the check to the person having rights of a holder in due course if the check is dishonored.

(d) If a claimant has the right to assert a claim under subsection (b) and is also a person entitled to enforce a cashier's check, teller's check, or certified check which is lost, destroyed, or stolen, the claimant may assert rights with respect to the check either under this section or Section 3–309.

Part 4/Liability of Parties
§ 3–401
Signature

(a) A person is not liable on an instrument unless (i) the person signed the instrument, or (ii) the person is represented by an agent or representative who signed the instrument and the signature is binding on the represented person under Section 3–402.

(b) A signature may be made (i) manually or by means of a device or machine, and (ii) by the use of any name, including a trade or assumed name, or by a word, mark, or symbol executed or adopted by a person with present intention to authenticate a writing.

§ 3–402
Signature by Representative

(a)   If a person acting, or purporting to act, as a representative signs an instrument by signing either the name of the represented person or the name of the signer, the represented person is bound by the signature to the same extent the represented person would be bound if the signature were on a simple contract. If the represented person is bound, the signature of the representative is the "authorized signature of the represented person" and the represented person is liable on the instrument, whether or not identified in the instrument.

(b)   If a representative signs the name of the representative to an instrument and the signature is an authorized signature of the represented person, the following rules apply:

(1)   If the form of the signature shows unambiguously that the signature is made on behalf of the represented person who is identified in the instrument, the representative is not liable on the instrument.

(2)   Subject to subsection (c), if (i) the form of the signature does not show unambiguously that the signature is made in a representative capacity or (ii) the represented person is not identified in the instrument, the representative is liable on the instrument to a holder in due course that took the instrument without notice that the representative was not intended to be liable on the instrument. With respect to any other person, the representative is liable on the instrument unless the representative proves that the original parties did not intend the representative to be liable on the instrument.

(c)   If a representative signs the name of the representative as drawer of a check without indication of the representative status and the check is payable from an account of the represented person who is identified on the check, the signer is not liable on the check if the signature is an authorized signature of the represented person.

§ 3–403
Unauthorized Signature

(a)   Unless otherwise provided in this Article or Article 4, an unauthorized signature is ineffective except as the signature of the unauthorized signer in favor of a person who in good faith pays the instrument or takes it for value. An unauthorized signature may be ratified for all purposes of this Article.

(b)   If the signature of more than one person is required to constitute the authorized signature of an organization, the signature of the organization is unauthorized if one of the required signatures is lacking.

(c)   The civil or criminal liability of a person who makes an unauthorized signature is not affected by any provision of this Article which makes the unauthorized signature effective for the purposes of this Article.

§ 3–404
Impostors; Fictitious Payees

(a)   If an impostor, by use of the mails or otherwise, induces the issuer of an instrument to issue the instrument to the impostor, or to a person acting in concert with the impostor, by impersonating the payee of the instrument or a person authorized to act for the payee, an indorsement of the instrument by any person in the name of the payee is effective as the indorsement of the payee in favor of a person who, in good faith, pays the instrument or takes it for value or for collection.

(b)   If (i) a person whose intent determines to whom an instrument is payable (Section 3–110(a) or (b)) does not intend the person identified as payee to have any interest in the instrument, or (ii) the person identified as payee of an instrument is a fictitious person, the following rules apply until the instrument is negotiated by special indorsement:

(1)   Any person in possession of the instrument is its holder.

(2)   An indorsement by any person in the name of the payee stated in the instrument is effective as the indorsement of the payee in favor of a person who, in good faith, pays the instrument or takes it for value or for collection.

(c)   Under subsection (a) or (b), an indorsement is made in the name of a payee if (i) it is made in a name substantially similar to that of the payee or (ii) the instrument, whether or not indorsed, is deposited in a depositary bank to an account in a name substantially similar to that of the payee.

(d)   With respect to an instrument to which subsection (a) or (b) applies, if a person paying the instrument or taking it for value or for collection fails to exercise ordinary care in paying or taking the instrument and that failure substantially contributes to loss resulting from payment of the instrument, the person bearing the loss may recover from the person failing to exercise ordinary care to the extent the failure to exercise ordinary care contributed to the loss.

§ 3–405
Employer's Responsibility for Fraudulent Indorsement by Employee

(a)   In this section:

(1)   "Employee" includes an independent contractor and employee of an independent contractor retained by the employer.

(2)   "Fraudulent indorsement" means (i) in the case of an instrument payable to the employer, a forged indorsement purporting to be that of the employer, or (ii) in the case of an instrument with respect to which the employer is the issuer, a forged indorsement purporting to be that of the person identified as payee.

(3)   "Responsibility" with respect to instruments means authority (i) to sign or indorse instruments on behalf of the employer, (ii) to process instruments received by the employer for bookkeeping purposes, for deposit to an account, or for other disposition, (iii) to prepare or process instruments for issue in the name of the employer, (iv) to supply information determining the names or addresses of payees of instruments to be issued in the name of the employer, (v) to control the disposition of instruments to be issued in the name of the employer, or (vi) to act otherwise with respect to instruments in a responsible capacity. "Responsibility" does not include authority that merely allows an employee to have access to instruments or blank or incomplete instrument forms that are being stored or transported or are part of incoming or outgoing mail, or similar access.

(b) For the purpose of determining the rights and liabilities of a person who, in good faith, pays an instrument or takes it for value or for collection, if an employer entrusted an employee with responsibility with respect to the instrument and the employee or a person acting in concert with the employee makes a fraudulent indorsement of the instrument, the indorsement is effective as the indorsement of the person to whom the instrument is payable if it is made in the name of that person. If the person paying the instrument or taking it for value or for collection fails to exercise ordinary care in paying or taking the instrument and that failure substantially contributes to loss resulting from the fraud, the person bearing the loss may recover from the person failing to exercise ordinary care to the extent the failure to exercise ordinary care contributed to the loss.

(c) Under subsection (b), an indorsement is made in the name of the person to whom an instrument is payable if (i) it is made in a name substantially similar to the name of that person or (ii) the instrument, whether or not indorsed, is deposited in a depositary bank to an account in a name substantially similar to the name of that person.

§ 3–406
Negligence Contributing to Forged Signature or Alteration of Instrument

(a) A person whose failure to exercise ordinary care substantially contributes to an alteration of an instrument or to the making of a forged signature on an instrument is precluded from asserting the alteration or the forgery against a person who, in good faith, pays the instrument or takes it for value or for collection.

(b) Under subsection (a), if the person asserting the preclusion fails to exercise ordinary care in paying or taking the instrument and that failure substantially contributes to loss, the loss is allocated between the person precluded and the person asserting the preclusion according to the extent to which the failure of each to exercise ordinary care contributed to the loss.

(c) Under subsection (a), the burden of proving failure to exercise ordinary care is on the person asserting the preclusion. Under subsection (b), the burden of proving failure to exercise ordinary care is on the person precluded.

§ 3–407
Alteration

(a) "Alteration" means (i) an unauthorized change in an instrument that purports to modify in any respect the obligation of a party, or (ii) an unauthorized addition of words or numbers or other change to an incomplete instrument relating to the obligation of a party.

(b) Except as provided in subsection (c), an alteration fraudulently made discharges a party whose obligation is affected by the alteration unless that party assents or is precluded from asserting the alteration. No other alteration discharges a party, and the instrument may be enforced according to its original terms.

(c) A payor bank or drawee paying a fraudulently altered instrument or a person taking it for value, in good faith and without notice of the alteration, may enforce rights with respect to the instrument (i) according to its original terms, or (ii) in the case of an incomplete instrument altered by unauthorized completion, according to its terms as completed.

§ 3–408
Drawee Not Liable on Unaccepted Draft

A check or other draft does not of itself operate as an assignment of funds in the hands of the drawee available for its payment, and the drawee is not liable on the instrument until the drawee accepts it.

§ 3–409
Acceptance of Draft; Certified Check

(a) "Acceptance" means the drawee's signed agreement to pay a draft as presented. It must be written on the draft and may consist of the drawee's signature alone. Acceptance may be made at any time and becomes effective when notification pursuant to instructions is given or the accepted draft is delivered for the purpose of giving rights on the acceptance to any person.

(b) A draft may be accepted although it has not been signed by the drawer, is otherwise incomplete, is overdue, or has been dishonored.

(c) If a draft is payable at a fixed period after sight and the acceptor fails to date the acceptance, the holder may complete the acceptance by supplying a date in good faith.

(d) "Certified check" means a check accepted by the bank on which it is drawn. Acceptance may be made as stated in subsection (a) or by writing on the check which indicates that the check is certified. The drawee of a check has no obligation to certify the check, and refusal to certify is not dishonor of the check.

§ 3–410
Acceptance Varying Draft

(a) If the terms of a drawee's acceptance vary from the terms of the draft as presented, the holder may refuse the acceptance and treat the draft as dishonored. In that case, the drawee may cancel the acceptance.

(b) The terms of a draft are not varied by an acceptance to pay at a particular bank or place in the United States, unless the acceptance states that the draft is to be paid only at that bank or place.

(c) If the holder assents to an acceptance varying the terms of a draft, the obligation of each drawer and indorser that does not expressly assent to the acceptance is discharged.

§ 3–411
Refusal to Pay Cashier's Checks, Teller's Checks, and Certified Checks

(a) In this section, "obligated bank" means the acceptor of a certified check or the issuer of a cashier's check or teller's check bought from the issuer.

(b) If the obligated bank wrongfully (i) refuses to pay a cashier's check or certified check, (ii) stops payment of a teller's check, or (iii) refuses to pay a dishonored teller's check, the person asserting the right to enforce the check is entitled to compensation for expenses and loss of interest resulting from the nonpayment and may recover consequential damages if the obligated bank refuses to pay after notice of particular circumstances giving rise to the damages.

(c) Expenses or consequential damages under subsection (b) are not recoverable if the refusal of the obligated bank to pay occurs because (i) the bank suspends payments, (ii) the obligated bank asserts a claim or defense of the bank that it has reasonable grounds to believe is available against the person entitled to enforce the instrument, (iii) the obligated bank has a reasonable doubt whether the person demanding payment is the person entitled to enforce the instrument, or (iv) payment is prohibited by law.

§ 3–412
Obligation of Issuer of Note or Cashier's Check

The issuer of a note or cashier's check or other draft drawn on the drawer is obliged to pay the instrument (i) according to its terms at the time it was issued or, if not issued, at the time it first came into possession of a holder, or (ii) if the issuer signed an incomplete instrument, according to its terms when completed, to the extent stated in Sections 3–115 and 3–407. The obligation is owed to a person entitled to enforce the instrument or to an indorser who paid the instrument under Section 3–415.

§ 3–413
Obligation of Acceptor

(a) The acceptor of a draft is obliged to pay the draft (i) according to its terms at the time it was accepted, even though the acceptance states that the draft is payable "as originally drawn" or equivalent terms, (ii) if the acceptance varies the terms of the draft, according to the terms of the draft as varied, or (iii) if the acceptance is of a draft that is an incomplete instrument, according to its terms when completed, to the extent stated in Sections 3–115 and 3–407. The obligation is owed to a person entitled to enforce the draft or to the drawer or an indorser who paid the draft under Section 3–414 or 3–415.

(b) If the certification of a check or other acceptance of a draft states the amount certified or accepted, the obligation of the acceptor is that amount. If (i) the certification or acceptance does not state an amount, (ii) the amount of the instrument is subsequently raised, and (iii) the instrument is then negotiated to a holder in due course, the obligation of the acceptor is the amount of the instrument at the time it was taken by the holder in due course.

§ 3–414
Obligation of Drawer

(a) This section does not apply to cashier's checks or other drafts drawn on the drawer.

(b) If an unaccepted draft is dishonored, the drawer is obliged to pay the draft (i) according to its terms at the time it was issued or, if not issued, at the time it first came into possession of a holder, or (ii) if the drawer signed an incomplete instrument, according to its terms when completed, to the extent stated in Sections 3–115 and 3–407. The obligation is owed to a person entitled to enforce the draft or to an indorser who paid the draft under Section 3–415.

(c) If a draft is accepted by a bank, the drawer is discharged, regardless of when or by whom acceptance was obtained.

(d) If a draft is accepted and the acceptor is not a bank, the obligation of the drawer to pay the draft if the draft is dishonored by the acceptor is the same as the obligation of an indorser under Section 3–415(a) and (c).

(e) If a draft states that it is drawn "without recourse" or otherwise disclaims liability of the drawer to pay the draft, the drawer is not liable under subsection (b) to pay the draft if the draft is not a

check. A disclaimer of the liability stated in subsection (b) is not effective if the draft is a check.

(f) If (i) a check is not presented for payment or given to a depositary bank for collection within 30 days after its date, (ii) the drawee suspends payments after expiration of the 30-day period without paying the check, and (iii) because of the suspension of payments, the drawer is deprived of funds maintained with the drawee to cover payments of the check, the drawer to the extent deprived of funds may discharge its obligations to pay the check by assigning to the person entitled to enforce the check the rights of the drawer against the drawee with respect to the funds.

§ 3–415
Obligation of Indorser

(a) Subject to subsections (b), (c), and (d) and to Section 3–419(d), if an instrument is dishonored, an indorser is obliged to pay the amount due on the instrument, (i) according to the terms of the instrument at the time it was endorsed, or (ii) if the indorser indorsed an incomplete instrument, according to its terms when completed, to the extent stated in Section 3–115 and 3–407. The obligation of the indorser is owed to a person entitled to enforce the instrument or to a subsequent indorser who paid the instrument under this section.

(b) If an indorsement states that it is made "without recourse" or otherwise disclaims liability of the indorser, the indorser is not liable under subsection (a) to pay the instrument.

(c) If notice of dishonor of an instrument is required by Section 3–503 and notice of dishonor complying with that section is not given to an indorser, the liability of the indorser under subsection (a) is discharged.

(d) If a draft is accepted by a bank after an indorsement is made, the liability of the indorser under subsection (a) is discharged.

(e) If an indorser of a check is liable under subsection (a) and the check is not presented for payment, or given to a depositary bank for collection, within 30 days after the day the indorsement was made, the liability of the indorser under subsection (a) is discharged.

§ 3–416
Transfer Warranties

(a) A person who transfers an instrument for consideration warrants to the transferee and, if the transfer is by indorsement, to any subsequent transferee that:

   (1) the warrantor is a person entitled to enforce the instrument;
   (2) all signatures on the instrument are authentic and authorized;
   (3) the instrument has not been altered;
   (4) the instrument is not subject to a defense or claim in recoupment of any party which can be asserted against the warrantor; and
   (5) the warrantor has no knowledge of any insolvency proceeding commenced with respect to the maker or acceptor or, in the case of an unaccepted draft, the drawer.

(b) A person to whom the warranties under subsection (a) are made and who took the instrument in good faith may recover from the warrantor as damages for breach of warranty an amount equal to the loss suffered as a result of the breach, but not more than the amount of the instrument plus expenses and loss of interest incurred as a result of the breach.

(c) The warranties stated in subsection (a) cannot be disclaimed with respect to checks. Unless notice of a claim for breach of warranty is given to the warrantor within 30 days after the claimant has reason to know of the breach and the identity of the warrantor, the liability of the warrantor under subsection (b) is discharged to the extent of any loss caused by the delay in giving notice of the claim.

(d) A [cause of action] for breach of warranty under this section accrues when the claimant has reason to know of the breach.

§ 3–417
Presentment Warranties

(a) If an unaccepted draft is presented to the drawee for payment or acceptance and the drawee pays or accepts the draft, (i) the person obtaining payment or acceptance, at the time of presentment, and (ii) a previous transferor of the draft, at the time of transfer, warrant to the drawee making payment or accepting the draft in good faith that:

    (1) the warrantor is, or was, at the time the warrantor transferred the draft, a person entitled to enforce the draft or authorized to obtain payment or acceptance of the draft on behalf of a person entitled to enforce the draft;

    (2) the draft has not been altered; and

    (3) the warrantor has no knowledge that the signature of the drawer of the draft is unauthorized.

(b) A drawee making payment may recover from any warrantor damages for breach of warranty equal to the amount paid by the drawee less the amount the drawee received or is entitled to receive from the drawer because of the payment. In addition, the drawee is entitled to compensation for expenses and loss of interest resulting from the breach. The right of the drawee to recover damages under this subsection is not affected by any failure of the drawee to exercise ordinary care in making payment. If the drawee accepts the draft, breach of warranty is a defense to the obligation of the acceptor. If the acceptor makes payment with respect to the draft, the acceptor is entitled to recover from any warrantor for breach of warranty the amounts stated in this subsection.

(c) If a drawee asserts a claim for breach of warranty under subsection (a) based on an unauthorized indorsement of the draft or an alteration of the draft, the warrantor may defend by proving that the indorsement is effective under Section 3–404 or 3–405 or the drawer is precluded under Section 3–406 or 4–406 from asserting against the drawee the unauthorized indorsement or alteration.

(d) If (i) a dishonored draft is presented for payment to the drawer or an indorser or (ii) any other instrument is presented for payment to a party obliged to pay the instrument, and (iii) payment is received, the following rules apply:

    (1) The person obtaining payment and a prior transferor of the instrument warrant to the person making payment in good faith that the warrantor is, or was, at the time the warrantor transferred the instrument, a person entitled to enforce the instrument or authorized to obtain payment on behalf of a person entitled to enforce the instrument.

    (2) The person making payment may recover from any warrantor for breach of warranty an amount equal to the

amount paid plus expenses and loss of interest resulting from the breach.

(e) The warranties stated in subsections (a) and (d) cannot be disclaimed with respect to checks. Unless notice of a claim for breach of warranty is given to the warrantor within 30 days after the claimant has reason to know of the breach and the identity of the warrantor, the liability of the warrantor under subsection (b) or (d) is discharged to the extent of any loss caused by the delay in giving notice of the claim.

(f) A [cause of action] for breach of warranty under this section accrues when the claimant has reason to know of the breach.

§ 3–418
Payment or Acceptance by Mistake

(a) Except as provided in subsection (c), if the drawee of a draft pays or accepts the draft and the drawee acted on the mistaken belief that (i) payment of the draft has not been stopped pursuant to Section 4–403 or (ii) the signature of the drawer of the draft was authorized, the drawee may recover the amount of the draft from the person to whom or for whose benefit payment was made or, in the case of acceptance, may revoke the acceptance. Rights of the drawee under this subsection are not affected by failure of the drawee to exercise ordinary care in paying or accepting the draft.

(b) Except as provided in subsection (c), if an instrument has been paid or accepted by mistake and the case is not covered by subsection (a), the person paying or accepting may, to the extent permitted by the law governing mistake and restitution, (i) recover the payment from the person to whom or for whose benefit payment was made or (ii) in the case of acceptance, may revoke the acceptance.

(c) The remedies provided by subsection (a) or (b) may not be asserted against a person who took the instrument in good faith and for value or who in good faith changed position in reliance on the payment or acceptance. This subsection does not limit remedies provided by Section 3–417 or 4–407.

(d) Notwithstanding Section 4–215, if an instrument is paid or accepted by mistake and the payor or acceptor recovers payment or revokes acceptance under subsection (a) or (b), the instrument is deemed not to have been paid or accepted and is treated as dishonored, and the person from whom payment is recovered has rights as a person entitled to enforce the dishonored instrument.

§ 3–419
Instruments Signed for Accommodation

(a) If an instrument is issued for value given for the benefit of a party to the instrument ("accommodated party") and another party to the instrument ("accommodation party") signs the instrument for the purpose of incurring liability on the instrument without being a direct beneficiary for the value given for the instrument, the instrument is signed by the accommodation party "for accommodation."

(b) An accommodation party may sign the instrument as maker, drawer, acceptor, or indorser and, subject to subsection (d), is obliged to pay the instrument in the capacity in which the accommodation party signs. The obligation of an accommodation party may be enforced notwithstanding any statute of frauds and whether or not the accommodation party receives consideration for the accommodation.

(c) A person signing an instrument is presumed to be an accommodation party and there is notice that the instrument is signed for accommodation if the signature is an anomalous indorsement or is accompanied by words indicating that the signer is acting as surety or guarantor with respect to the obligation of another party to the instrument. Except as provided in Section 3–605, the obligation of an accommodation party to pay the instrument is not affected by the fact that the person enforcing the obligation had notice when the instrument was taken by that person that the accommodation party signed the instrument for accommodation.

(d) If the signature of a party to an instrument is accompanied by words indicating unambiguously that the party is guaranteeing collection rather than payment of the obligation of another party to the instrument, the signer is obliged to pay the amount due on the instrument to a person entitled to enforce the instrument only if (i) execution of judgment against the other party has been returned unsatisfied, (ii) the other party is insolvent or in an insolvency proceeding, (iii) the other party cannot be served with process, or (iv) it is otherwise apparent that payment cannot be obtained from the other party.

(e) An accommodation party who pays the instrument is entitled to reimbursement from the accommodated party and is entitled to enforce the instrument against the accommodated party. An accommodated party who pays the instrument has no right of recourse against, and is entitled to contribution from, an accommodation party.

§ 3–420
Conversion of Instrument

(a) The law applicable to conversion of personal property applies to instruments. An instrument is also converted if it is taken by transfer, other than a negotiation, from a person not entitled to enforce the instrument or a bank makes or obtains payment with respect to the instrument for a person not entitled to enforce the instrument or receive payment. An action for conversion of an instrument may not be brought by (i) the issuer or acceptor of the instrument or (ii) a payee or indorsee who did not receive delivery of the instrument either directly or through delivery to an agent or a co-payee.

(b) In an action under subsection (a), the measure of liability is presumed to be the amount payable on the instrument, but recovery may not exceed the amount of the plaintiff's interest in the instrument.

(c) A representative, other than a depositary bank, who has in good faith dealt with an instrument or its proceeds on behalf of one who was not the person entitled to enforce the instrument is not liable in conversion to that person beyond the amount of any proceeds that it has not paid out.

Part 5/Dishonor

§ 3–501
Presentment

(a) "Presentment" means a demand made by or on behalf of a person entitled to enforce an instrument (i) to pay the instrument made to the drawee or a party obliged to pay the instrument or, in the case of a note or accepted draft payable at a bank, to the bank, or (ii) to accept a draft made to the drawee.

(b) The following rules are subject to Article 4, agreement of the parties, and clearing-house rules and the like:

(1) Presentment may be made at the place of payment of the instrument and must be made at the place of payment if the instrument is payable at a bank in the United States; may be made by any commercially reasonable means, including an oral, written, or electronic communication; is effective when the demand for payment or acceptance is received by the person to whom presentment is made; and is effective if made to any one of two or more makers, acceptors, drawees, or other payors.

(2) Upon demand of the person to whom presentment is made, the person making presentment must (i) exhibit the instrument, (ii) give reasonable identification and, if presentment is made on behalf of another person, reasonable evidence of authority to do so, and (. . .) sign a receipt on the instrument for any payment made or surrender the instrument if full payment is made.

(3) Without dishonoring the instrument, the party to whom presentment is made may (i) return the instrument for lack of a necessary indorsement, or (ii) refuse payment or acceptance for failure of the presentment to comply with the terms of the instrument, an agreement of the parties, or other applicable law or rule.

(4) The party to whom presentment is made may treat presentment as occurring on the next business day after the day of presentment if the party to whom presentment is made has established a cut-off hour not earlier than 2 PM for the receipt and processing of instruments presented for payment or acceptance and presentment is made after the cut-off hour.

§ 3–502
Dishonor

(a) Dishonor of a note is governed by the following rules:

(1) If the note is payable on demand, the note is dishonored if presentment is duly made to the maker and the note is not paid on the day of presentment.

(2) If the note is not payable on demand and is payable at or through a bank or the terms of the note require presentment, the note is dishonored if presentment is duly made and the note is not paid on the day it becomes payable or the day of presentment, whichever is later.

(3) If the note is not payable on demand and paragraph (2) does not apply, the note is dishonored if it is not paid on the day it becomes payable.

(b) Dishonor of an unaccepted draft other than a documentary draft is governed by the following rules:

(1) If a check is duly presented for payment to the payor bank otherwise than for immediate payment over the counter, the check is dishonored if the payor bank makes timely return of the check or sends timely notice of dishonor or nonpayment under Section 4–301 or 4–302, or becomes accountable for the amount of the check under Section 4–302.

(2) If a draft is payable on demand and paragraph (1) does not apply, the draft is dishonored if presentment for payment is duly made to the drawee and the draft is not paid on the day of presentment.

(3) If a draft is payable on a date stated in the draft, the draft is dishonored if (i) presentment for payment is duly made to the drawee and payment is not made on the day the draft becomes payable or the day of presentment, whichever is later, or (ii) presentment for acceptance is duly made before the day the draft becomes payable and the draft is not accepted on the day of presentment.

(4) If a draft is payable on elapse of a period of time after sight or acceptance, the draft is dishonored if presentment for acceptance is duly made and the draft is not accepted on the day of presentment.

(c) Dishonor of an unaccepted documentary draft occurs according to the rules stated in subsection (b)(2), (3), and (4), except that payment or acceptance may be delayed without dishonor until no later than the close of the third business day of the drawee following the day on which payment or acceptance is required by those paragraphs.

(d) Dishonor of an accepted draft is governed by the following rules:

(1) If the draft is payable on demand, the draft is dishonored if presentment for payment is duly made to the acceptor and the draft is not paid on the day of presentment.

(2) If the draft is not payable on demand, the draft is dishonored if presentment for payment is duly made to the acceptor and payment is not made on the day it becomes payable or the day of presentment, whichever is later.

(e) In any case in which presentment is otherwise required for dishonor under this section and presentment is excused under Section 3–504, dishonor occurs without presentment if the instrument is not duly accepted or paid.

(f) If a draft is dishonored because timely acceptance of the draft was not made and the person entitled to demand acceptance consents to a late acceptance, from the time of acceptance the draft is treated as never having been dishonored.

§ 3–503
Notice of Dishonor

(a): The obligation of an indorser stated in Section 3–415(a) and the obligation of a drawer stated in Section 3–414(d) may not be enforced unless (i) the indorser or drawer is given notice of dishonor of the instrument complying with this section or (ii) notice of dishonor is excused under Section 3–504(b).

(b) Notice of dishonor may be given by any person; may be given by any commercially reasonable means, including an oral, written, or electronic communication; and is sufficient if it reasonably identifies the instrument and indicates that the instrument has been dishonored or has not been paid or accepted. Return of an instrument given to a bank for collection is sufficient notice of dishonor.

(c) Subject to Section 3–504(c), with respect to an instrument taken for collection by a collecting bank, notice of dishonor must be given (i) by the bank before midnight of the next banking day following the banking day on which the bank receives notice of dishonor of the instrument, or (ii) by any other person within 30 days following the day on which the person receives notice of dishonor. With respect to any other instrument, notice of dishonor must be given within 30 days following the day on which dishonor occurs.

§ 3–504
Excused Presentment and Notice of Dishonor

(a) Presentment for payment or acceptance of an instrument is excused if (i) the person entitled to present the instrument cannot with reasonable diligence make presentment, (ii) the maker or acceptor has repudiated an obligation to pay the instrument or is dead or in insolvency proceedings, (iii) by the terms of the instrument presentment is not necessary to enforce the obligation of indorsers or the drawer, (iv) the drawer or indorser whose obligation is being enforced has waived presentment or otherwise has no reason to expect or right to require that the instrument be paid or accepted, or (v) the drawer instructed the drawee not to pay or accept the draft or the drawee was not obligated to the drawer to pay the draft.

(b) Notice of dishonor is excused if (i) by the terms of the instrument notice of dishonor is not necessary to enforce the obligation of a party to pay the instrument, or (ii) the party whose obligation is being enforced waived notice of dishonor. A waiver of presentment is also a waiver of notice of dishonor.

(c) Delay in giving notice of dishonor is excused if the delay was caused by circumstances beyond the control of the person giving the notice and the person giving the notice exercised reasonable diligence after the cause of the delay ceased to operate.

§ 3–505
Evidence of Dishonor

(a) The following are admissible as evidence and create a presumption of dishonor and of any notice of dishonor stated:

(1) a document regular in form as provided in subsection (b) which purports to be a protest;

(2) a purported stamp or writing of the drawee, payor bank, or presenting bank on or accompanying the instrument stating that acceptance or payment has been refused unless reasons for the refusal are stated and the reasons are not consistent with dishonor;

(3) a book or record of the drawee, payor bank, or collecting bank, kept in the usual course of business which shows dishonor, even if there is no evidence of who made the entry.

(b) A protest is a certificate of dishonor made by a United States consul or vice consul, or a notary public or other person authorized to administer oaths by the law of the place where dishonor occurs. It may be made upon information satisfactory to that person. The protest must identify the instrument and certify either that presentment has been made or, if not made, the reason why it was not made, and that the instrument has been dishonored by nonacceptance or nonpayment. The protest may also certify that notice of dishonor has been given to some or all parties.

Part 6/Discharge and Payment
§ 3–601
Discharge and Effect of Discharge

(a) The obligation of a party to pay the instrument is discharged as stated in this Article or by an act or agreement with the party which would discharge an obligation to pay money under a simple contract.

(b) Discharge of the obligation of a party is not effective against a person acquiring rights of a holder in due course of the instrument without notice of the discharge.

§ 3-602
Payment

(a) Subject to subsection (b), an instrument is paid to the extent payment is made (i) by or on behalf of a party obliged to pay the instrument, and (ii) to a person entitled to enforce the instrument. To the extent of the payment, the obligation of the party obliged to pay the instrument is discharged even though payment is made with knowledge of a claim to the instrument under Section 3–306 by another person.

(b) The obligation of a party to pay the instrument is not discharged under subsection (a) if:

(1) a claim to the instrument under Section 3–306 is enforceable against the party receiving payment and (i) payment is made with knowledge by the payor that payment is prohibited by injunction or similar process of a court of competent jurisdiction, or (ii) in the case of an instrument other than a cashier's check, teller's check, or certified check, the party making payment accepted, from the person having a claim to the instrument, indemnity against loss resulting from refusal to pay the person entitled to enforce the instrument; or

(2) the person making payment knows that the instrument is a stolen instrument and pays a person it knows is in wrongful possession of the instrument.

§ 3-603
Tender of Payment

(a) If tender of payment of an obligation to pay an instrument is made to a person entitled to enforce the instrument, the effect of tender is governed by principles of law applicable to tender of payment under a simple contract.

(b) If tender of payment of an obligation to pay an instrument is made to a person entitled to enforce the instrument and the tender is refused, there is discharge, to the extent of the amount of the tender, of the obligation of an indorser or accommodation party having a right of recourse with respect to the obligation to which the tender relates.

(c) If tender of payment of an amount due on an instrument is made to a person entitled to enforce the instrument, the obligation of the obligor to pay interest after the due date on the amount tendered is discharged. If presentment is required with respect to an instrument and the obligor is able and ready to pay on the due date at every place of payment stated in the instrument, the obligor is deemed to have made tender of payment on the due date to the person entitled to enforce the instrument.

§ 3-604
Discharge by Cancellation or Renunciation

(a) A person entitled to enforce an instrument, with or without consideration, may discharge the obligation of a party to pay the instrument (i) by an intentional voluntary act, such as surrender of the instrument to the party, destruction, mutilation, or cancellation of the instrument, cancellation or striking out of the party's signature, or the addition of words to the instrument indicating discharge, or (ii) by agreeing not to sue or otherwise renouncing rights against the party by a signed writing.

(b) Cancellation or striking out of an indorsement pursuant to subsection (a) does not affect the status and rights of a party derived from the indorsement.

§ 3-605
Discharge of Indorsers and Accommodation Parties

(a) In this section, the term "indorser" includes a drawer having the obligation described in Section 3–414(d).

(b) Discharge, under Section 3–604, of the obligation of a party to pay an instrument does not discharge the obligation of an indorser or accommodation party having a right of recourse against the discharged party.

(c) If a person entitled to enforce an instrument agrees, with or without consideration, to an extension of the due date of the obligation of a party to pay the instrument, the extension discharges an indorser or accommodation party having a right of recourse against the party whose obligation is extended to the extent the indorser or accommodation party proves that the extension caused loss to the indorser or accommodation party with respect to the right of recourse.

(d) If a person entitled to enforce an instrument agrees, with or without consideration, to a material modification of the obligation of a party other than an extension of the due date, the modification discharges the obligation of an indorser or accommodation party having a right of recourse against the person whose obligation is modified to the extent the modification causes loss to the indorser or accommodation party with respect to the right of recourse. The loss suffered by the indorser or accommodation party as a result of the modification is equal to the amount of the right of recourse unless the person enforcing the instrument proves that no loss was caused by the modification or that the loss caused by the modification was an amount less than the amount of the right of recourse.

(e) If the obligation of a party to pay an instrument is secured by an interest in collateral and a person entitled to enforce the instrument impairs the value of the interest in collateral, the obligation of an indorser or accommodation party having a right of recourse against the obligor is discharged to the extent of the impairment. The value of an interest in collateral is impaired to the extent (i) the value of the interest is reduced to an amount less than the amount of the right of recourse of the party asserting discharge, or (ii) the reduction in value of the interest causes an increase in the amount by which the amount of the right of recourse exceeds the value of the interest. The burden of proving impairment is on the party asserting discharge.

(f) If the obligation of a party is secured by an interest in collateral not provided by an accommodation party and a person entitled to enforce the instrument impairs the value of the interest in collateral, the obligation of any party who is jointly and severally liable with respect to the secured obligation is discharged to the extent the impairment causes the party asserting discharge to pay more than that party would have been obliged to pay, taking into account rights of contribution, if impairment had not occurred. If the party asserting discharge is an accommodation party not entitled to discharge under subsection (e), the party is deemed to have a right to contribution based on joint and several liability rather than a right to reimbursement. The burden of proving impairment is on the party asserting discharge.

(g) Under subsection (e) or (f), impairing value of an interest in collateral includes (i) failure to obtain or maintain perfection or recordation of the interest in collateral, (ii) release of collateral without substitution of collateral of equal value, (iii) failure to perform a duty to preserve the value of collateral owed, under Article 9 or other law, to a debtor or surety or other person secondarily liable, or (iv) failure to comply with applicable law in disposing of collateral.

(h) An accommodation party is not discharged under subsection (c), (d), or (e) unless the person entitled to enforce the instrument knows of the accommodation or has notice under Section 3–419(c) that the instrument was signed for accommodation.

(i) A party is not discharged under this section if (i) the party asserting discharge consents to the event or conduct that is the basis of the discharge, or (ii) the instrument or a separate agreement of the party provides for waiver of discharge under this section either specifically or by general language indicating that parties waive defenses based on suretyship or impairment of collateral.

REVISED ARTICLE 4/BANK DEPOSITS AND COLLECTIONS
Part 1/General Provisions and Definitions

§ 4–101
Short Title

This Article may be cited as Uniform Commercial Code–Bank Deposits and Collections.

§ 4–102
Applicability

(a) To the extent that items within this Article are also within Articles 3 and 8, they are subject to those Articles. If there is conflict, this Article governs Article 3, but Article 8 governs this Article.

(b) The liability of a bank for action or non-action with respect to an item handled by it for purposes of presentment, payment, or collection is governed by the law of the place where the bank is located. In the case of action or non-action by or at a branch or separate office of a bank, its liability is governed by the law of the place where the branch or separate office is located.

§ 4–103.
Variation by Agreement; Measure of Damages; Action Constituting Ordinary Care

(a) The effect of the provisions of this Article may be varied by agreement, but the parties to the agreement cannot disclaim a bank's responsibility for its lack of good faith or failure to exercise ordinary care or limit the measure of damages for the lack or failure. However, the parties may determine by agreement the standards by which the bank's responsibility is to be measured if those standards are not manifestly unreasonable.

(b) Federal Reserve regulations and operating circulars, clearing-house rules, and the like have the effect of agreements under subsection (a), whether or not specifically assented to by all parties interested in items handled.

(c) Action or non-action approved by this Article or pursuant to Federal Reserve regulations or operating circulars is the exercise of ordinary care and, in the absence of special instructions, action or non-action consistent with clearing-house rules and the like or

with a general banking usage not disapproved by this Article, is prima facie the exercise of ordinary care.

(d) The specification or approval of certain procedures by this Article is not disapproval of other procedures that may be reasonable under the circumstances.

(e) The measure of damages for failure to exercise ordinary care in handling an item is the amount of the item reduced by an amount that could not have been realized by the exercise of ordinary care. If there is also bad faith it includes any other damages the party suffered as a proximate consequence.

§ 4–104
Definitions and Index of Definitions

(a) In this Article, unless the context otherwise requires:
(1) "Account" means any deposit or credit account with a bank, including a demand, time, savings, passbook, share draft, or like account, other than an account evidenced by a certificate of deposit.
(2) "Afternoon" means the period of a day between noon and midnight.
(3) "Banking day" means the part of a day on which a bank is open to the public for carrying on substantially all of its banking functions.
(4) "Clearing house" means an association of banks or other payors regularly clearing items.
(5) "Customer" means a person having an account with a bank or for whom a bank has agreed to collect items, including a bank that maintains an account at another bank.
(6) "Documentary draft" means a draft to be presented for acceptance or payment if specified documents, certificated securities (Section 8–102) or instructions for uncertificated securities (Section 8–308), or other certificates, statements, or the like are to be received by the drawee or other payor before acceptance or payment of the draft.
(7) "Draft" means a draft as defined in Section 3–104 or an item, other than an instrument, that is an order.
(8) "Drawee" means a person ordered in a draft to make payment.
(9) "Item" means an instrument or a promise or order to pay money handled by a bank for collection or payment. The term does not include a payment order governed by Article 4A or a credit or debit card slip.
(10) "Midnight deadline" with respect to a bank is midnight on its next banking day following the banking day on which it receives the relevant item or notice or from which the time for taking action commences to run, whichever is later.
(11) "Settle" means to pay in cash, by clearing-house settlement, in a charge or credit or by remittance, or otherwise as agreed. A settlement may be either provisional or final.
(12) "Suspends payments" with respect to a bank means that it has been closed by order of the supervisory authorities, that a public officer has been appointed to take it over, or that it ceases or refuses to make payments in the ordinary course of business.

(b) Other definitions applying to this Article and the sections in which they appear are:

"Agreement for electronic presentment". Section 4–110
"Bank". Section 4–105
"Collecting bank". Section 4–105

"Depositary bank". Section 4–105
"Intermediary bank". Section 4–105
"Payor bank". Section 4–105
"Presenting bank". Section 4–105
"Presentment notice". Section 4–110

(c) The following definitions in other Articles apply to this Article:

"Acceptance". Section 3–409.
"Alteration". Section 3–407
"Cashier's check". Section 3–104
"Certificate of deposit". Section 3–104
"Certified check". Section 3–409
"Check". Section 3–104
"Good faith". Section 3–103
"Holder in due course". Section 3–302
"Instrument". Section 3–104
"Notice of dishonor". Section 3–503
"Order". Section 3–103
"Ordinary care". Section 3–103
"Person entitled to enforce". Section 3–301
"Presentment". Section 3–501
"Promise". Section 3–103
"Prove". Section 3–103
"Teller's check". Section 3–104
"Unauthorized signature". Section 3–403

(d) In addition, Article 1 contains general definitions and principles of construction and interpretation applicable throughout this Article.

§ 4–105
"Bank"; "Depositary Bank"; "Payor Bank"; "Intermediary Bank"; "Collecting Bank"; "Presenting Bank"

In this Article:

(1) "Bank" means a person engaged in the business of banking, including a savings bank, savings and loan association, credit union, or trust company.
(2) "Depositary bank" means the first bank to take an item even though it is also the payor bank, unless the item is presented for immediate payment over the counter.
(3) "Payor bank" means a bank that is the drawee of a draft.
(4) "Intermediary bank" means a bank to which an item is transferred in course of collection except the depositary or payor bank.
(5) "Collecting bank" means a bank handling an item for collection except the payor bank.
(6) "Presenting bank" means a bank presenting an item except a payor bank.

§ 4–106
Payable through or Payable at Bank: Collecting Bank

(a) If an item states that it is "payable through" a bank identified in the item, (i) the item designates the bank as a collecting bank and does not by itself authorize the bank to pay the item, and (ii) the item may be presented for payment only by or through the bank.

Alternative A

(b) If an item states that it is "payable at" a bank identified in the item, the item is equivalent to a draft drawn on the bank.

Alternative B

(b) If an item states that it is "payable at" a bank identified in the item, (i) the item designates the bank as a collecting bank and does not by itself authorize the bank to pay the item, and (ii) the item may be presented for payment only by or through the bank.

(c) If a draft names a nonbank drawee and it is unclear whether a bank named in the draft is a co-drawee or a collecting bank, the bank is a collecting bank.

§ 4–107
Separate Office of Bank

A branch or separate office of a bank is a separate bank for the purpose of computing the time within which and determining the place at or to which action may be taken or notices or orders shall be given under this Article and under Article 3.

§ 4–108
Time of Receipt of Items

(a) For the purpose of allowing time to process items, prove balances, and make the necessary entries on its books to determine its position for the day, a bank may fix an afternoon hour of 2 PM or later as a cutoff hour for the handling of money and items and the making of entries on its books.

(b) An item or deposit of money received on any day after a cutoff hour so fixed or after the close of the banking day may be treated as being received at the opening of the next banking day.

§ 4–109
Delays

(a) Unless otherwise instructed, a collecting bank in a good faith effort to secure payment of a specific item drawn on a payor other than a bank, and with or without the approval of any person involved, may waive, modify, or extend time limits imposed or permitted by this [Act] for a period not exceeding two additional banking days without discharge of drawers or indorsers or liability to its transferor or a prior party.

(b) Delay by a collecting bank or payor bank beyond time limits prescribed or permitted by this [Act] or by instructions is excused if (i) the delay is caused by interruption of communication or computer facilities, suspension of payments by another bank, war, emergency conditions, failure of equipment, or other circumstances beyond the control of the bank, and (ii) the bank exercises such diligence as the circumstances require.

§ 4–110
Electronic Presentment

(a) "Agreement for electronic presentment" means an agreement, clearing-house rule, or Federal Reserve regulation or operating circular, providing that presentment of an item may be made by transmission of an image of an item or information describing the item ("presentment notice") rather than delivery of the item itself. The agreement may provide for procedures governing retention, presentment, payment, dishonor, and other matters concerning items subject to the agreement.

(b) Presentment of an item pursuant to an agreement for presentment is made when the presentment notice is received.

(c) If presentment is made by presentment notice, a reference to "item" or "check" in this Article means the presentment notice unless the context otherwise indicates.

§ 4–111
Statute of Limitations

An action to enforce an obligation, duty, or right arising under this Article must be commenced within three years after the [cause of action] accrues.

Part 2/Collection Items: Depository and Collecting Banks

§ 4–201
Status of Collecting Bank as Agent and Provisional Status of Credits; Applicability of Article; Item Indorsed "Pay Any Bank"

(a) Unless a contrary intent clearly appears and before the time that a settlement given by a collecting bank for an item is or becomes final, the bank, with respect to an item, is an agent or subagent of the owner of the item and any settlement given for the item is provisional. This provision applies regardless of the form of indorsement or lack of indorsement and even though credit given for the item is subject to immediate withdrawal as of right or is in fact withdrawn; but the continuance of ownership of an item by its owner and any rights of the owner to proceeds of the item are subject to rights of a collecting bank, such as those resulting from outstanding advances on the item and rights of recoupment or setoff. If an item is handled by banks for purposes of presentment, payment, collection, or return, the relevant provisions of this Article apply even though action of the parties clearly establishes that a particular bank has purchased the item and is the owner of it.

(b) After an item has been indorsed with the words "pay any bank" or the like, only a bank may acquire the rights of a holder until the item has been:
(1) returned to the customer initiating collection; or
(2) specially indorsed by a bank to a person who is not a bank.

§ 4–202
Responsibility for Collection or Return; When Action Timely

(a) A collecting bank must exercise ordinary care in:
(1) presenting an item or sending it for presentment;
(2) sending notice of dishonor or nonpayment or returning an item other than a documentary draft to the bank's transferor after learning that the item has not been paid or accepted, as the case may be;
(3) settling for an item when the bank receives final settlement; and
(4) notifying its transferor of any loss or delay in transit within a reasonable time after discovery thereof.

(b) A collecting bank exercises ordinary care under subsection (a) by taking proper action before its midnight deadline following receipt of an item, notice, or settlement. Taking proper action within a reasonably longer time may constitute the exercise of ordinary care, but the bank has the burden of establishing timeliness.

(c) Subject to subsection (a)(1), a bank is not liable for the insolvency, neglect, misconduct, mistake, or default of another bank or person or for loss or destruction of an item in the possession of others or in transit.

§ 4–203
Effect of Instructions

Subject to Article 3 concerning conversion of instruments (Section 3–420) and restrictive indorsements (Section 3–206), only a collecting bank's transferor can give instructions that affect the bank or constitute notice to it, and a collecting bank is not liable to prior parties for any action taken pursuant to the instructions or in accordance with any agreement with its transferor.

§ 4–204
Methods of Sending and Presenting; Sending Directly to Payor Bank

(a) A collecting bank shall send items by a reasonably prompt method, taking into consideration relevant instructions, the nature of the item, the number of those items on hand, the cost of collection involved, and the method generally used by it or others to present those items.

(b) A collecting bank may send:
(1) an item directly to the payor bank;
(2) an item to a nonbank payor if authorized by its transferor; and
(3) an item other than documentary drafts to a nonbank payor, if authorized by Federal Reserve regulation or operating circular, clearing-house rule, or the like.

(c) Presentment may be made by a presenting bank at a place where the payor bank or other payor has requested that presentment be made.

§ 4–205
Depository Bank Holder of Unindorsed Item

If a customer delivers an item to a depositary bank for collection:

(1) the depositary bank becomes a holder of the item at the time it receives the item for collection if the customer at the time of delivery was a holder of the item, whether or not the customer indorses the item, and, if the bank satisfies the other requirements of Section 3–302, it is a holder in due course; and

(2) the depositary bank warrants to collecting banks, the payor bank or other payor, and the drawer that the amount of the item was paid to the customer or deposited to the customer's account.

§ 4–206
Transfer between Banks

Any agreed method that identifies the transferor bank is sufficient for the item's further transfer to another bank.

§ 4–207
Transfer Warranties

(a) A customer or collecting bank that transfers an item and receives a settlement or other consideration warrants to the transferee and to any subsequent collecting bank that:
(1) the warrantor is a person entitled to enforce the item;
(2) all signatures on the item are authentic and authorized;
(3) the item has not been altered;

(4) the item is not subject to a defense or claim in recoupment (Section 3–305(a)) of any party that can be asserted against the warrantor; and

(5) the warrantor has no knowledge of any insolvency proceeding commenced with respect to the maker or acceptor or, in the case of an unaccepted draft, the drawer.

(b) If an item is dishonored, a customer or collecting bank transferring the item and receiving settlement or other consideration is obliged to pay the amount due on the item (i) according to the terms of the item at the time it was transferred, or (ii) if the transfer was of an incomplete item, according to its terms when completed as stated in Sections 3–115 and 3–407. The obligation of a transferor is owed to the transferee and to any subsequent collecting bank that takes the item in good faith. A transferor cannot disclaim its obligation under this subsection by an indorsement stating that it is made "without recourse" or otherwise disclaiming liability.

(c) A person to whom the warranties under subsection (a) are made and who took the item in good faith may recover from the warrantor as damages for breach of warranty an amount equal to the loss suffered as a result of the breach, but not more than the amount of the item plus expenses and loss of interest incurred as a result of the breach.

(d) The warranties stated in subsection (a) cannot be disclaimed with respect to checks. Unless notice of a claim for breach of warranty is given to the warrantor within 30 days after the claimant has reason to know of the breach and the identity of the warrantor, the warrantor is discharged to the extent of any loss caused by the delay in giving notice of the claim.

(e) A cause of action for breach of warranty under this section accrues when the claimant has reason to know of the breach.

§ 4–208
Presentment Warranties

(a) If an unaccepted draft is presented to the drawee for payment or acceptance and the drawee pays or accepts the draft, (i) the person obtaining payment or acceptance, at the time of presentment, and (ii) a previous transferor of the draft, at the time of transfer, warrant to the drawee that pays or accepts the draft in good faith that:

(1) the warrantor is, or was, at the time the warrantor transferred the draft, a person entitled to enforce the draft or authorized to obtain payment or acceptance of the draft on behalf of a person entitled to enforce the draft;

(2) the draft has not been altered; and

(3) the warrantor has no knowledge that the signature of the purported drawer of the draft is unauthorized.

(b) A drawee making payment may recover from a warrantor damages for breach of warranty equal to the amount paid by the drawee less the amount the drawee received or is entitled to receive from the drawer because of the payment. In addition, the drawee is entitled to compensation for expenses and loss of interest resulting from the breach. The right of the drawee to recover damages under this subsection is not affected by any failure of the drawee to exercise ordinary care in making payment. If the drawee accepts the draft (i) breach of warranty is a defense to the obligation of the acceptor, and (ii) if the acceptor makes payment with respect to the draft, the acceptor is entitled to recover from a warrantor for breach of warranty the amounts stated in this subsection.

(c) If a drawee asserts a claim for breach of warranty under subsection (a) based on an unauthorized indorsement of the draft or an alteration of the draft, the warrantor may defend by proving that the indorsement is effective under Section 3–404 or 3–405 or the drawer is precluded under Section 3–406 or 4–406 from asserting the drawee the unauthorized indorsement or alteration.

(d) If (i) a dishonored draft is presented for payment to the drawer or an indorser or (ii) any other item is presented for payment to a party obliged to pay the item, and the item is paid, the person obtaining payment and a prior transferor of the item warrant to the person making payment in good faith that the warrantor is, or was, at the time the warrantor transferred the item, a person entitled to enforce the item or authorized to obtain payment on behalf of a person entitled to enforce the item. The person making payment may recover from any warrantor for breach of warranty an amount equal to the amount paid plus expenses and loss of interest resulting from the breach.

(e) The warranties stated in subsections (a) and (d) cannot be disclaimed with respect to checks. Unless notice of a claim for breach of warranty is given to the warrantor within 30 days after the claimant has reason to know of the breach and the identity of the warrantor, the warrantor is discharged to the extent of any loss caused by the delay in giving notice of the claim.

(f) A cause of action for breach of warranty under this section accrues when the claimant has reason to know of the breach.

§ 4–209
Encoding and Retention Warranties

(a) A person who encodes information on or with respect to an item after issue warrants to any subsequent collecting bank and to the payor bank or other payor that the information is correctly encoded. If the customer of a depositary bank encodes, that bank also makes the warranty.

(b) A person who undertakes to retain an item pursuant to an agreement for electronic presentment warrants to any subsequent collecting bank and to the payor bank or other payor that retention and presentment of the item comply with the agreement. If a customer of a depositary bank undertakes to retain an item, that bank also makes this warranty.

(c) A person to whom warranties are made under this section and who took the item in good faith may recover from the warrantor as damages for breach of warranty an amount equal to the loss suffered as a result of the breach, plus expenses and loss of interest incurred as a result of the breach.

§ 4–210
Security Interest of Collecting Bank in Items,
Accompanying Documents and Proceeds

(a) A collecting bank has a security interest in an item and any accompanying documents or the proceeds of either:

(1) in case of an item deposited in an account, to the extent to which credit given for the item has been withdrawn or applied;

(2) in case of an item for which it has given credit available for withdrawal as of right, to the extent of the credit given, whether or not the credit is drawn upon or there is a right of charge-back; or

(3) if it makes an advance on or against the item.

(b) If credit given for several items received at one time or pursuant to a single agreement is withdrawn or applied in part, the security interest remains upon all the items, any accompanying documents or the proceeds of either. For the purpose of this section, credits first given are first withdrawn.

(c) Receipt by a collecting bank of a final settlement for an item is a realization on its security interest in the item, accompanying documents, and proceeds. So long as the bank does not receive final settlement for the item or give up possession of the item or accompanying documents for purposes other than collection, the security interest continues to that extent and is subject to Article 9, but:

    (1) no security agreement is necessary to make the security interest enforceable (Section 9–203(1)(a));

    (2) no filing is required to perfect the security interest; and

    (3) the security interest has priority over conflicting perfected security interests in the item, accompanying documents, or proceeds.

§ 4–211
When Bank Gives Value for Purposes of Holder in Due Course

For purposes of determining its status as a holder in due course, a bank has given value to the extent it has a security interest in an item, if the bank otherwise complies with the requirements of Section 3–302 on what constitutes a holder in due course.

§ 4–212
Presentment by Notice of Item Not Payable by, through, or at Bank; Liability of Drawer or Indorser

(a) Unless otherwise instructed, a collecting bank may present an item not payable by, through, or at a bank by sending to the party to accept or pay a written notice that the bank holds the item for acceptance or payment. The notice must be sent in time to be received on or before the day when presentment is due and the bank must meet any requirement of the party to accept or pay under Section 3–501 by the close of the bank's next banking day after it knows of the requirement.

(b) If presentment is made by notice and payment, acceptance, or request for compliance with a requirement under Section 3–501 is not received by the close of business on the day after maturity or, in the case of demand items, by the close of business on the third banking day after notice was sent, the presenting bank may treat the item as dishonored and charge any drawer or indorser by sending it notice of the facts.

§ 4–213
Medium and Time of Settlement by Bank

(a) With respect to settlement by a bank, the medium and time of settlement may be prescribed by Federal Reserve regulations or circulars, clearing-house rules, and the like, or agreement. In the absence of such prescription:

    (1) the medium of settlement is cash or credit to an account in a Federal Reserve bank of or specified by the person to receive settlement; and

    (2) the time of settlement, is:

        (i) with respect to tender of settlement by cash, a cashier's check, or teller's check, when the cash or check is sent or delivered;

        (ii) with respect to tender of settlement by credit in an account in a Federal Reserve Bank, when the credit is made;

        (iii) with respect to tender of settlement by a credit or debit to an account in a bank, when the credit or debit is made or, in the case of tender of settlement by authority to charge an account, when the authority is sent or delivered; or

        (iv) with respect to tender of settlement by a funds transfer, when payment is made pursuant to Section 4A–406(a) to the person receiving settlement.

(b) If the tender of settlement is not by a medium authorized by subsection (a) or the time of settlement is not fixed by subsection (a), no settlement occurs until the tender of settlement is accepted by the person receiving settlement.

(c) If settlement for an item is made by cashier's check or teller's check and the person receiving settlement, before its midnight deadline:

    (1) presents or forwards the check for collection, settlement is final when the check is finally paid; or

    (2) fails to present or forward the check for collection, settlement is final at the midnight deadline of the person receiving settlement.

(d) If settlement for an item is made by giving authority to charge the account of the bank giving settlement in the bank receiving settlement, settlement is final when the charge is made by the bank receiving settlement if there are funds available in the account for the amount of the item.

§ 4–214
Right of Charge-Back or Refund; Liability of Collecting Bank; Return of Item

(a) If a collecting bank has made provisional settlement with its customer for an item and fails by reason of dishonor, suspension of payments by a bank, or otherwise to receive settlement for the item which is or becomes final, the bank may revoke the settlement given by it, charge back the amount of any credit given for the item to its customer's account, or obtain refund from its customer, whether or not it is able to return the item, if by its midnight deadline or within a longer reasonable time after it learns the facts it returns the item or sends notification of the facts. If the return or notice is delayed beyond the bank's midnight deadline or a longer reasonable time after it learns the facts, the bank may revoke the settlement, charge back the credit, or obtain refund from its customer, but it is liable for any loss resulting from the delay. These rights to revoke, charge back, and obtain refund terminate if and when a settlement for the item received by the bank is or becomes final.

(b) A collecting bank returns an item when it is sent or delivered to the bank's customer or transferor or pursuant to its instructions.

(c) A depositary bank that is also the payor may charge back the amount of an item to its customer's account or obtain refund in accordance with the section governing return of an item received by a payor bank for credit on its books (Section 4–301).

(**d**) The right to charge back is not affected by:
(**1**) previous use of a credit given for the item; or
(**2**) failure by any bank to exercise ordinary care with respect to the item, but a bank so failing remains liable.

(**e**) A failure to charge back or claim refund does not affect other rights of the bank against the customer or any other party.

(**f**) If credit is given in dollars as the equivalent of the value of an item payable in foreign money, the dollar amount of any charge-back or refund must be calculated on the basis of the bank-offered spot rate for the foreign money prevailing on the day when the person entitled to the charge-back or refund learns that it will not receive payment in ordinary course.

§ 4–215
Final Payment of Item by Payor Bank; When Provisional Debits and Credits Become Final; When Certain Credits Become Available for Withdrawal

(**a**) An item is finally paid by a payor bank when the bank has first done any of the following:
(**1**) paid the item in cash;
(**2**) settled for the item without having a right to revoke the settlement under statute, clearing-house rule, or agreement; or
(**3**) made a provisional settlement for the item and failed to revoke the settlement in the time and manner permitted by statute, clearing-house rule, or agreement.

(**b**) If provisional settlement for an item does not become final, the item is not finally paid.

(**c**) If provisional settlement for an item between the presenting and payor banks is made through a clearing house or by debits or credits in an account between them, then to the extent that provisional debits or credits for the item are entered in accounts between the presenting and payor banks or between the presenting and successive prior collecting banks seriatim, they become final upon final payment of the item by the payor bank.

(**d**) If a collecting bank receives a settlement for an item which is or becomes final, the bank is accountable to its customer for the amount of the item and any provisional credit given for the item in an account with its customer becomes final.

(**e**) Subject to (i) applicable law stating a time for availability of funds and (ii) any right of the bank to apply the credit to an obligation of the customer, credit given by a bank for an item in a customer's account becomes available for withdrawal as of right:
(**1**) if the bank has received a provisional settlement for the item, when the settlement becomes final and the bank has had a reasonable time to receive return of the item and the item has not been received within that time;
(**2**) if the bank is both the depositary bank and the payor bank, and the item is finally paid, at the opening of the bank's second banking day following receipt of the item.

(**f**) Subject to applicable law stating a time for availability of funds and any right of a bank to apply a deposit to an obligation of the depositor, a deposit of money becomes available for withdrawal as of right at the opening of the bank's next banking day after receipt of the deposit.

§ 4–216
Insolvency and Preference

(**a**) If an item is in or comes into the possession of a payor or collecting bank that suspends payment and the item has not been finally paid, the item must be returned by the receiver, trustee, or agent in charge of the closed bank to the presenting bank or the closed bank's customer.

(**b**) If a payor bank finally pays an item and suspends payments without making a settlement for the item with its customer or the presenting bank which settlement is or becomes final, the owner of the item has a preferred claim against the payor bank.

(**c**) If a payor bank gives or a collecting bank gives or receives a provisional settlement for an item and thereafter suspends payments, the suspension does not prevent or interfere with the settlement's becoming final if the finality occurs automatically upon the lapse of certain time or the happening of certain events.

(**d**) If a collecting bank receives from subsequent parties settlement for an item, which settlement is or becomes final and the bank suspends payments without making a settlement for the item with its customer which settlement is or becomes final, the owner of the item has a preferred claim against the collecting bank.

Part 3/Collection of Items: Payor Banks
§ 4–301
Deferred Posting; Recovery of Payment by Return of Items; Time of Dishonor; Return of Items by Payor Bank

(**a**) If a payor bank settles for a demand item other than a documentary draft presented otherwise than for immediate payment over the counter before midnight of the banking day of receipt, the payor bank may revoke the settlement and recover the settlement if, before it has made final payment and before its midnight deadline, it
(**1**) returns the item; or
(**2**) sends written notice of dishonor or nonpayment if the item is unavailable for return.

(**b**) If a demand item is received by a payor bank for credit on its books, it may return the item or send notice of dishonor and may revoke any credit given or recover the amount thereof withdrawn by its customer, if it acts within the time limit and in the manner specified in subsection (a).

(**c**) Unless previous notice of dishonor has been sent, an item is dishonored at the time when for purposes of dishonor it is returned or notice sent in accordance with this section.

(**d**) An item is returned:
(**1**) as to an item presented through a clearing house, when it is delivered to the presenting or last collecting bank or to the clearing house or is sent or delivered in accordance with clearing-house rules; or
(**2**) in all other cases, when it is sent or delivered to the bank's customer or transferor or pursuant to instructions.

§ 4–302
Payor Bank's Responsibility for Late Return of Item

(**a**) If an item is presented to and received by a payor bank, the bank is accountable for the amount of:

(1) a demand item, other than a documentary draft, whether properly payable or not, if the bank, in any case in which it is not also the depositary bank, retains the item beyond midnight of the banking day of receipt without settling for it or, whether or not it is also the depositary bank, does not pay or return the item or send notice of dishonor until after its midnight deadline; or

(2) any other properly payable item unless, within the time allowed for acceptance or payment of that item, the bank either accepts or pays the item or returns it and accompanying documents.

(b) The liability of a payor bank to pay an item pursuant to subsection (a) is subject to defenses based on breach of a presentment warranty (Section 4–208) or proof that the person seeking enforcement of the liability presented or transferred the item for the purpose of defrauding the payor bank.

§ 4–303
When Items Subject to Notice, Stop-Payment Order, Legal Process, or Setoff; Order in Which Items May Be Charged or Certified

(a) Any knowledge, notice, or stop-payment order received by, legal process served upon, or setoff exercised by a payor bank comes too late to terminate, suspend, or modify the bank's right or duty to pay an item or to charge its customer's account for the item if the knowledge, notice, stop-payment order, or legal process is received or served and a reasonable time for the bank to act thereon expires or the setoff is exercised after the earliest of the following:

(1) the bank accepts or certifies the item;

(2) the bank pays the item in cash;

(3) the bank settles for the item without having a right to revoke the settlement under statute, clearing-house rule, or agreement;

(4) the bank becomes accountable for the amount of the item under Section 4–302 dealing with the payor bank's responsibility for late return of items; or

(5) with respect to checks, a cutoff hour no earlier than one hour after the opening of the next banking day after the banking day on which the bank received the check and no later than the close of that next banking day or, if no cutoff hour is fixed, the close of the next banking day after the banking day on which the bank received the check.

(b) Subject to subsection (a), items may be accepted, paid, certified, or charged to the indicated account of its customer in any order.

Part 4/Relationship between Payor Bank and Its Customer
§ 4–401
When Bank May Charge Customer's Account

(a) A bank may charge against the account of a customer an item that is properly payable from the account even though the charge creates an overdraft. An item is properly payable if it is authorized by the customer and is in accordance with any agreement between the customer and bank.

(b) A customer is not liable for the amount of an overdraft if the customer neither signed the item nor benefited from the proceeds of the item.

(c) A bank may charge against the account of a customer a check that is otherwise properly payable from the account, even though payment was made before the date of the check, unless the customer has given notice to the bank of the postdating describing the check with reasonable certainty. The notice is effective for the period stated in Section 4–403(b) for stop-payment orders, and must be received at such time and in such manner as to afford the bank a reasonable opportunity to act on it before the bank takes any action with respect to the check described in Section 4–303. If a bank charges against the account of a customer a check before the date stated in the notice of postdating, the bank is liable for damages for the loss resulting from its act. The loss may include damages for dishonor of subsequent items under Section 4–402.

(d) A bank that in good faith makes payment to a holder may charge the indicated account of its customer according to:

(1) the original terms of the altered item; or

(2) the terms of the completed item, even though the bank knows the item has been completed unless the bank has notice that the completion was improper.

§ 4–402
Bank's Liability to Customer for Wrongful Dishonor; Time of Determining Insufficiency of Account

(a) Except as otherwise provided in this Article, a payor bank wrongfully dishonors an item if it dishonors an item that is properly payable, but a bank may dishonor an item that would create an overdraft unless it has agreed to pay the overdraft.

(b) A payor bank is liable to its customer for damages proximately caused by the wrongful dishonor of an item. Liability is limited to actual damages proved and may include damages for an arrest or prosecution of the customer or other consequential damages. Whether any consequential damages are proximately caused by the wrongful dishonor is a question of fact to be determined in each case.

(c) A payor bank's determination of the customer's account balance on which a decision to dishonor for insufficiency of available funds is based may be made at any time between the time between the time the item is received by the payor bank and the time that the payor bank returns the item or gives notice in lieu of return, and no more than one determination need be made. If, at the election of the payor bank, a subsequent balance determination is made for the purpose of reevaluating the bank's decision to dishonor the item, the account balance at that time is determinative of whether a dishonor for insufficiency of available funds is wrongful.

§ 4–403
Customer's Right to Stop Payment; Burden of Proof of Loss

(a) A customer or any person authorized to draw on the account if there is more than one person may stop payment of any item drawn on the customer's account or close the account by an order to the bank describing the item or account with reasonable certainty received at a time and in a manner that affords the bank a reasonable opportunity to act on it before any action by the bank with respect to the item described in Section 4–303. If the signature of more than one person is required to draw on an account, any of these persons may stop payment or close the account.

(b) A stop-payment order is effective for six months, but it lapses after 14 calendar days if the original order was oral and was not confirmed in writing within that period. A stop-payment order may be renewed for additional six-month periods by a writing given to the bank within a period during which the stop-payment order is effective.

(c) The burden of establishing the fact and amount of loss resulting from the payment of an item contrary to a stop-payment order or order to close an account is on the customer. The loss from payment of an item contrary to a stop-payment order may include damages for dishonor of subsequent items under Section 4–402.

§ 4–404
Bank Not Obliged to Pay Check More Than Six Months Old

A bank is under no obligation to a customer having a checking account to pay a check, other than a certified check, which is presented more than six months after its date, but it may charge its customer's account for a payment made thereafter in good faith.

§4–405
Death or Incompetence of Customer

(a) A payor or collecting bank's authority to accept, pay, or collect an item or to account for proceeds of its collection, if otherwise effective, is not rendered ineffective by incompetence of a customer of either bank existing at the time the item is issued or its collection is undertaken if the bank does not know of an adjudication of incompetence. Neither death nor incompetence of a customer revokes the authority to accept, pay, collect, or account until the bank knows of the fact of death or of an adjudication of incompetence and has reasonable opportunity to act on it.

(b) Even with knowledge, a bank may for 10 days after the date of death pay or certify checks drawn on or before that date unless ordered to stop payment by a person claiming an interest in the account.

§ 4–406
Customer's Duty to Discover and Report Unauthorized Signature or Alteration

(a) A bank that sends or makes available to a customer a statement of account showing payment of items for the account shall either return or make available to the customer the items paid or provide information in the statement of account sufficient to allow the customer reasonable to identify the items paid. The statement of account provides sufficient information if the item is described by item number, amount, and date of payment.

(b) If the items are not returned to the customer, the person retaining the items shall either retain the items or, if the items are destroyed, maintain the capacity to furnish legible copies of the items until the expiration of seven years after receipt of the items. A customer may request an item from the bank that paid the item, and that bank must provide in a reasonable time either the item or, if the item has been destroyed or is not otherwise obtainable, a legible copy of the item.

(c) If a bank sends or makes available a statement of account or items pursuant to subsection (a), the customer must exercise rea-

sonable promptness in examining the statement or the items to determine whether any payment was not authorized because of an alteration of an item or because a purported signature by or on behalf of the customer was not authorized. If, based on the statement or items provided, the customer should reasonably have discovered the unauthorized payment, the customer must promptly notify the bank of the relevant facts.

(d) If the bank proves that the customer failed, with respect to an item, to comply with the duties imposed on the customer by subsection (c), the customer is precluded from asserting against the bank:

    (1) the customer's unauthorized signature or any alteration on the item, if the bank also proves that it suffered a loss by reason of the failure; and

    (2) the customer's unauthorized signature or alteration by the same wrongdoer on any other item paid in goof faith by the bank if the payment was made before the bank received notice from the customer of the unauthorized signature or alteration and after the customer had been afforded a reasonable period of time, not exceeding 30 days, in which to examine the item or statement of account and notify the bank.

(e) If subsection (d) applies and the customer proves that the bank failed to exercise ordinary care in paying the item and that the failure substantially contributed to loss, the loss is allocated between the customer precluded and the bank asserting the preclusion according to the extent to which the failure of the customer to comply with subsection (c) and the failure of the bank to exercise ordinary care contributed to the loss. If the customer proves that the bank did not pay the item in good faith, the preclusion under subsection (d) does not apply.

(f) Without regard to care or lack of either the customer or the bank, a customer who does not within one year after the statement or items are made available to the customer (subsection (a)) discover and report the customer's unauthorized signature on or any alteration on the item is precluded from asserting against the bank the unauthorized signature or alteration. If there is a preclusion under this subsection, the payor bank may not recover for breach or warranty under Section 4–208 with respect to the unauthorized signature or alteration to which the preclusion applies.

§ 4–407
Payor Bank's Right to Subrogation on Improper Payment

If a payor bank has paid an item over the order of the drawer or maker to stop payment, or after an account has been closed, or otherwise under circumstances giving a basis for objection by the drawer or maker, to prevent unjust enrichment and only to the extent necessary to prevent loss to the bank by reason of its payment of the item, the payor bank is subrogated to the rights

    (1) of any holder in due course on the item against the drawer or maker;

    (2) of the payee or any other holder of the item against the drawer or maker either on the item or under the transaction out of which the item arose; and

    (3) of the drawer or maker against the payee or any other holder of the item with respect to the transaction out of which the item arose.

Part 5/Collection of Documentary Drafts

§ 4–501
Handling of Documentary Drafts; Duty to Send for Presentment and to Notify Customer of Dishonor

A bank that takes a documentary draft for collection shall present or send the draft and accompanying documents for presentment and, upon learning that the draft has not been paid or accepted in due course, shall seasonably notify its customer of the fact even though it may have discounted or bought the draft or extended credit available for withdrawal as of right.

§ 4–502
Presentment of "On Arrival" Drafts

If a draft or the relevant instructions require presentment "on arrival", "when goods arrive" or the like, the collecting bank need not present until in its judgment a reasonable time for arrival of the goods has expired. Refusal to pay or accept because the goods have not arrived is not dishonor: the bank must notify its transferor of the refusal but need not present the draft again until it is instructed to do so or learns of the arrival of the goods.

§ 4–503
Responsibility of Presenting Bank for Documents and Goods; Report of Reasons for Dishonor; Referee in Case of Need

Unless otherwise instructed and except as provided in Article 5, a bank presenting a documentary draft:

(1) must deliver the documents to the drawee on acceptance of the draft if it is payable more than three days after presentment; otherwise, only on payment; and

(2) upon dishonor, either in the case of presentment for acceptance or presentment for payment, may seek and follow instructions from any referee in case of need designated in the draft or, if the presenting bank does not choose to utilize the referee's services, it must use diligence and good faith to ascertain the reason for dishonor, must notify its transferor of the dishonor and of the results of its effort to ascertain the reasons therefor, and must request instructions.

However the presenting bank is under no obligation with respect to goods represented by the documents except to follow any reasonable instructions seasonably received; it has a right to reimbursement for any expense incurred in following instructions and to prepayment of or indemnity for those expenses.

§ 4–504
Privilege of Presenting Bank to Deal with Goods; Security Interest for Expenses

(a) A presenting bank that, following the dishonor of a documentary draft, has seasonably requested instructions but does not receive them within a reasonable time may store, sell, or otherwise deal with the goods in any reasonable manner.

(b) For its reasonable expenses incurred by action under subsection (a) the presenting bank has a lien upon the goods or their proceeds, which may be foreclosed in the same manner as an unpaid seller's lien.

ARTICLE 5/LETTERS OF CREDIT [OMITTED]
. . . .

ARTICLE 6/BULK TRANSFERS [OMITTED]
. . . .

ARTICLE 7/WAREHOUSE RECEIPTS, BILLS OF LADING AND OTHER DOCUMENTS OF TITLE [OMITTED]
. . . .

ARTICLE 8/INVESTMENT SECURITIES [OMITTED]
. . . .

ARTICLE 9/SECURED TRANSACTIONS; SALES OF ACCOUNTS AND CHATTEL PAPER

Note: *The adoption of this Article should be accompanied by the repeal of existing statutes dealing with conditional sales, trust receipts, factor's liens where the factor is given a non-possessory lien, chattel mortgages, crop mortgages, mortgages on railroad equipment, assignment of accounts and generally statutes regulating security interests in personal property.*

Where the state has a retail installment selling act or small loan act, that legislation should be carefully examined to determine what changes in those acts are needed to conform them to this Article. This Article primarily sets out rules defining rights of a secured party against persons dealing with the debtor; it does not prescribe regulations and controls which may be necessary to curb abuses arising in the small loan business or in the financing of consumer purchases on credit. Accordingly there is no intention to repeal existing regulatory acts in those fields by enactment or re-enactment of Article 9. See Section 9–203(4) and the Note thereto.

Part 1/Short Title, Applicability and Definitions
§ 9–101
Short Title

This Article shall be known and may be cited as Uniform Commercial Code–Secured Transactions.

§ 9–102
Policy and Subject Matter of Article

(1) Except as otherwise provided in Section 9–104 on excluded transactions, this Article applies

(a) to any transaction (regardless of its form) which is intended to create a security interest in personal property or fixtures including goods, documents, instruments, general intangibles, chattel paper or accounts; and also

(b) to any sale of accounts or chattel paper.

(2) This Article applies to security interests created by contract including pledge, assignment, chattel mortgage, chattel trust, trust deed, factor's lien, equipment trust, conditional sale, trust receipt, other lien or title retention contract and lease or consignment intended as security. This Article does not apply to statutory liens except as provided in Section 9–310.

(3) The application of this Article to a security interest in a secured obligation is not affected by the fact that the obligation is itself secured by a transaction or interest to which this Article does not apply. Amended in 1972.

§ 9–103
Perfection of Security Interest in Multiple State Transactions

(1) Documents, instruments and ordinary goods.

(a) This subsection applies to documents and instruments and to goods other than those covered by a certificate of title described in subsection (2), mobile goods described in subsection (3), and minerals described in subsection (5).

(b) Except as otherwise provided in this subsection, perfection and the effect of perfection or non-perfection of a security interest in collateral are governed by the law of the jurisdiction where the collateral is when the last event occurs on which is based the assertion that the security interest is perfected or unperfected.

(c) If the parties to a transaction creating a purchase money security interest in goods in one jurisdiction understand at the time that the security interest attaches that the goods will be kept in another jurisdiction, then the law of the other jurisdiction governs the perfection and the effect of perfection or non-perfection of the security interest from the time it attaches until thirty days after the debtor receives possession of the goods and thereafter if the goods are taken to the other jurisdiction before the end of the thirty-day period.

(d) When collateral is brought into and kept in this state while subject to a security interest perfected under the law of the jurisdiction from which the collateral was removed, the security interest remains perfected, but if action is required by Part 3 of this Article to perfect the security interest,

(i) if the action is not taken before the expiration of the period of perfection in the other jurisdiction or the end of four months after the collateral is brought into this state, whichever period first expires, the security interest becomes unperfected at the end of that period and is thereafter deemed to have been unperfected as against a person who became a purchaser after removal;

(ii) if the action is taken before the expiration of the period specified in subparagraph (i), the security interest continues perfected thereafter;

(iii) for the purpose of priority over a buyer of consumer goods (subsection (2) of Section 9–307), the period of the effectiveness of a filing in the jurisdiction from which the collateral is removed is governed by the rules with respect to perfection in subparagraphs (i) and (ii).

(2) Certificate of title.

(a) This subsection applies to goods covered by a certificate of title issued under a statute of this state or of another jurisdiction under the law of which indication of a security interest on the certificate is required as a condition of perfection.

(b) Except as otherwise provided in this subsection, perfection and the effect of perfection or non-perfection of the security interest are governed by the law (including the conflict of laws rules) of the jurisdiction issuing the certificate until four months after the goods are removed from that jurisdiction and thereafter until the goods are registered in another jurisdiction, but in any event not beyond surrender of the certificate. After the expiration of that period, the goods are not covered by the certificate of title within the meaning of this section.

(c) Except with respect to the rights of a buyer described in the next paragraph, a security interest, perfected in another jurisdiction otherwise than by notation on a certificate of title, in goods brought into this state and thereafter covered by a certificate of title issued by this state is subject to the rules stated in paragraph (d) of subsection (1).

(d) If goods are brought into this state while a security interest therein is perfected in any manner under the law of the jurisdiction from which the goods are removed and a certificate of title is issued by this state and the certificate does not show that the goods are subject to the security interest or that they may be subject to security interests not shown on the certificate, the security interest is subordinate to the rights of a buyer of the goods who is not in the business of selling goods of that kind to the extent that he gives value and receives delivery of the goods after issuance of the certificate and without knowledge of the security interest.

(3) Accounts, general intangibles and mobile goods.

(a) This subsection applies to accounts (other than an account described in subsection (5) on minerals) and general intangibles (other than uncertificated securities) and to goods which are mobile and which are of a type normally used in more than one jurisdiction, such as motor vehicles, trailers, rolling stock, airplanes, shipping containers, road building and construction machinery and commercial harvesting machinery and the like, if the goods are equipment or are inventory leased or held for lease by the debtor to others, and are not covered by a certificate of title described in subsection (2).

(b) The law (including the conflict of laws rules) of the jurisdiction in which the debtor is located governs the perfection and the effect of perfection or non-perfection of the security interest.

(c) If, however, the debtor is located in a jurisdiction which is not a part of the United States, and which does not provide for perfection of the security interest by filing or recording in that jurisdiction, the law of the jurisdiction in the United States in which the debtor has its major executive office in the United States governs the perfection and the effect of perfection or non-perfection of the security interest through filing. In the alternative, if the debtor is located in a jurisdiction which is not a part of the United States or Canada and the collateral is accounts or general intangibles for money due or to become due, the security interest may be perfected by notification to the account debtor. As used in this paragraph, "United States" includes its territories and possessions and the Commonwealth of Puerto Rico.

(d) A debtor shall be deemed located at his place of business if he has one, at his chief executive office if he has more than one place of business, otherwise at his residence. If, however, the debtor is a foreign air carrier under the Federal Aviation Act of 1958, as amended, it shall be deemed located at the designated office of the agent upon whom service of process may be made on behalf of the foreign air carrier.

(e) A security interest perfected under the law of the jurisdiction of the location of the debtor is perfected until the expiration of four months after a change of the debtor's location to another jurisdiction, or until perfection would have ceased by the law of the first jurisdiction, whichever period first expires. Unless perfected in the new jurisdiction before the end of that period, it becomes unperfected thereafter and is deemed to have been unperfected as against a person who became a purchaser after the change.

(4) Chattel paper.

The rules stated for goods in subsection (1) apply to a possessory security interest in chattel paper. The rules stated for accounts in subsection (3) apply to a non-possessory security interest in chattel paper, but the security interest may not be perfected by notification to the account debtor.

(5) Minerals.

Perfection and the effect of perfection or non-perfection of a security interest which is created by a debtor who has an interest in minerals or the like (including oil and gas) before extraction and which attaches thereto as extracted, or which attaches to an account resulting from the sale thereof at the wellhead or minehead are governed by the law (including the conflict of laws rules) of the jurisdiction wherein the wellhead or minehead is located.

(6) Uncertificated securities.

The law (including the conflict of laws rules) of the jurisdiction of organization of the issuer governs the perfection and the effect of perfection or non-perfection of a security interest in uncertificated securities.

Amended in 1972 and 1977.

§ 9–104
Transactions Excluded from Article

This Article does not apply

(a) to a security interest subject to any statute of the United States, to the extent that such statute governs the rights of parties to and third parties affected by transactions in particular types of property; or

(b) to a landlord's lien; or

(c) to a lien given by statute or other rule of law for services or materials except as provided in Section 9–310 on priority of such liens; or

(d) to a transfer of a claim for wages, salary or other compensation of an employee; or

(e) to a transfer by a government or governmental subdivision or agency; or

(f) to a sale of accounts or chattel paper as part of a sale of the business out of which they arose, or an assignment of accounts or chattel paper which is for the purpose of collection only, or a transfer of a right to payment under a contract to an assignee who is also to do the performance under the contract or a transfer of a single account to an assignee in whole or partial satisfaction of a preexisting indebtedness; or

(g) to a transfer of an interest in or claim in or under any policy of insurance, except as provided with respect to proceeds (Section 9–306) and priorities in proceeds (Section 9–312); or

(h) to a right represented by a judgment (other than a judgment taken on a right to payment which was collateral); or

(i) to any right of set-off; or

(j) except to the extent that provision is made for fixtures in Section 9–313, to the creation or transfer of an interest in or lien on real estate, including a lease or rents thereunder; or

(k) to a transfer in whole or in part of any claim arising out of tort; or

(l) to a transfer of an interest in any deposit account (subsection (1) of Section 9–105) except as provided with respect to proceeds (Section 9–306) and priorities in proceeds (Section 9–312).

Amended in 1972.

§ 9–105
Definitions and Index of Definitions

(1) In this Article unless the context otherwise requires:

(a) "Account debtor" means the person who is obligated on an account, chattel paper or general intangible.

(b) "Chattel paper" means a writing or writings which evidence both a monetary obligation and a security interest in or a lease of specific goods, but a charter or other contract involving the use or hire of a vessel is not chattel paper. When a transaction is evidenced both by such a security agreement or a lease and by an instrument or a series of instruments, the group of writings taken together constitutes chattel paper.

(c) "Collateral" means the property subject to a security interest, and includes accounts and chattel paper which have been sold.

(d) "Debtor" means the person who owes payment or other performance of the obligation secured, whether or not he owns or has rights in the collateral, and includes the seller of accounts or chattel paper. Where the debtor and the owner of the collateral are not the same person, the term "debtor" means the owner of the collateral in any provision of the Article dealing with the obligation, and may include both where the context so requires.

(e) "Deposit account" means a demand, time, savings, passbook or like account maintained with a bank, savings and loan association, credit union or like organization, other than an account evidenced by a certificate of deposit.

(f) "Document" means document of title as defined in the general definitions of Article 1 (Section 1–201), and a receipt of the kind described in subsection (2) of Section 7–201.

(g) "Encumbrance" includes real estate mortgages and other liens on real estate and all other rights in real estate that are not ownership interests.

(h) "Goods" includes all things which are movable at the time the security interest attaches or which are fixtures (Section 9–313), but does not include money, documents, instruments, accounts, chattel paper, general intangibles, or minerals or the like (including oil and gas) before extraction. "Goods" also includes standing timber which is to be cut and removed under a conveyance or contract for sale, the unborn young of animals, and growing crops.

(i) "Instrument" means a negotiable instrument (defined in Section 3–104), or a security (defined in Section 8–102) or any other writing which evidences a right to the payment of money and is not itself a security agreement or lease and is of a type which is in ordinary course of business transferred by delivery with any necessary indorsement or assignment.

(j) "Mortgage" means a consensual interest created by a real estate mortgage, a trust deed on real estate, or the like.

(k) An advance is made "pursuant to commitment" if the secured party has bound himslf to make it, whether or not a subsequent event of default or other event not within his control has relieved or may relieve him from his obligation.

(l) "Security agreement" means an agreement which creates or provides for a security interest.

(m) "Secured party" means a lender, seller or other person in whose favor there is a security interest, including a person to whom accounts or chattel paper have been sold. When the holders of obligations issued under an indenture of trust, equipment trust agreement or the like are represented by a trustee or other person, the representative is the secured party.

(n) "Transmitting utility" means any person primarily engaged in the railroad, street railway or trolley bus business, the electric or electronics communications transmission business, the transmission of goods by pipeline, or the transmission or the production and transmission of electricity, steam, gas or water, or the provision of sewer service.

(2) Other definitions applying to this Article and the sections in which they appear are:

"Account". Section 9–106.
"Attach". Section 9–203.
"Construction mortgage". Section 9–313(1).
"Consumer goods". Section 9–109(1).
"Equipment". Section 9–109(2).
"Farm products". Section 9–109(3).
"Fixture". Section 9–313(1).
"Fixture filing". Section 9–313(1).
"General intangibles". Section 9–106.
"Inventory". Section 9–109(4).
"Lien creditor". Section 9–301(3).
"Proceeds". Section 9–306(1).
"Purchase money security interest". Section 9–107.
"United States". Section 9–103.

(3) The following defintions in other Articles apply to this Article:

"Check". Section 3–104.
"Contract for sale". Section 2–106.
"Holder in due course". Section 3–302.
"Note". Section 3–104.
"Sale". Section 2–106.

(4) In addition Article 1 contains general definitions and principles of construction and interpretation applicable throughout this Article.

Amended in 1966, 1972, and 1977.

§ 9–106
Definitions: "Account"; "General Intangibles"

"Account" means any right to payment for goods sold or leased or for services rendered which is not evidenced by an instrument or chattel paper, whether or not it has been earned by performance.

"General intangibles" means any personal property (including things in action) other than goods, accounts, chattel paper, documents, instruments, and money. All rights to payment earned or unearned under a charter or other contract involving the use or hire of a vessel and all rights incident to the charter or contract are accounts.

Amended in 1966, 1972.

§ 9–107
Definitions: "Purchase Money Security Interest"

A security interest is a "purchase money security interest" to the extent that it is

(a) taken or retained by the seller of the collateral to secure all or part of its price; or

(b) taken by a person who by making advances or incurring an obligation gives value to enable the debtor to acquire rights in or the use of collateral if such value is in fact so used.

§ 9–108
When After-Acquired Collateral Not Security for Antecedent Debt

Where a secured party makes an advance, incurs an obligation, releases a perfected security interest, or otherwise gives new value which is to be secured in whole or in part by after-acquired property his security interest in the after-acquired collateral shall be deemed to be taken for new value and not as security for an antecedent debt if the debtor acquires his rights in such collateral either in the ordinary course of his business or under a contract of purchase made pursuant to the security agreement within a reasonable time after new value is given.

§ 9–109
Classification of Goods; "Consumer Goods"; "Equipment"; "Farm Products"; "Inventory"

Goods are

(1) "consumer goods" if they are used or bought for use primarily for personal, family or household purposes;

(2) "equipment" if they are used or bought for use primarily in business (including farming or a profession) or by a debtor who is a non-profit organization or a governmental subdivision or agency or if the goods are not included in the definitions of inventory, farm products or consumer goods;

(3) "farm products" if they are crops or livestock or supplies used or produced in farming operations or if they are products of crops or livestock in their unmanufactured states (such as ginned cotton, woolclip, maple syrup, milk and eggs), and if they are in the possession of a debtor engaged in raising, fattening, grazing or other farming operations. If goods are farm products they are neither equipment nor inventory;

(4) "inventory" if they are held by a person who holds them for sale or lease or to be furnished under contracts of service or if he has so furnished them, or if they are raw materials, work in process or materials used or consumed in a business. Inventory of a person is not to be classified as his equipment.

§ 9–110
Sufficiency of Description

For the purposes of this Article any description of personal property or real estate is sufficient whether or not it is specific if it reasonably identifies what is described.

§ 9–111
Applicability of Bulk Transfer Laws

The creation of a security interest is not a bulk transfer under Article 6 (see Section 6–103).

§ 9–112
Where Collateral Is Not Owned by Debtor

Unless otherwise agreed, when a secured party knows that collateral is owned by a person who is not the debtor, the owner of the collateral is entitled to receive from the secured party any surplus under Section 9–502(2) or under Section 9–504(1), and is not liable for the debt or for any deficiency after resale, and he has the same right as the debtor

(a) to receive statements under Section 9–208;

(b) to receive notice of and to object to a secured party's proposal to retain the collateral in satisfaction of the indebtedness under Section 9–505;

(c) to redeem the collateral under Section 9–506;

(d) to obtain injunctive or other relief under Section 9–507(1); and

(e) to recover losses caused to him under Section 9–208(2).

§ 9–113
Security Interests Arising Under Article on Sales

A security interest arising solely under the Article on Sales (Article 2) is subject to the provisions of this Article except that to the extent that and so long as the debtor does not have or does not lawfully obtain possession of the goods

(a) no security agreement is necessary to make the security interest enforceable; and

(b) no filing is required to perfect the security interest; and

(c) the rights of the secured party on default by the debtor are governed by the Article on Sales (Article 2).

§ 9–114
Consignment

(1) A person who delivers goods under a consignment which is not a security interest and who would be required to file under this Article by paragraph (3)(c) of Section 2–326 has priority over a secured party who is or becomes a creditor of the consignee and who would have a perfected security interest in the goods if they were the property of the consignee, and also has priority with respect to identifiable cash proceeds received on or before delivery of the goods to a buyer, if

(a) the consignor complies with the filing provision of the Article on Sales with respect to consignments (paragraph (3)(c) of Section 2–326) before the consignee receives possession of the goods; and

(b) the consignor gives notification in writing to the holder of the security interest if the holder has filed a financing statement covering the same types of goods before the date of the filing made by the consignor; and

(c) the holder of the security interest receives the notification within five years before the consignee receives possession of the goods; and

(d) the notification states that the consignor expects to deliver goods on consignment to the consignee, describing the goods by item or type.

(2) In the case of a consignment which is not a security interest and in which the requirements of the preceding subsection have not been met, a person who delivers goods to another is subordinate to a person who would have a perfected security interest in the goods if they were the property of the debtor.

Added in 1972.

Part 2/Validity of Security Agreement and Rights of Parties Thereto
§ 9–201
General Validity of Security Agreement

Except as otherwise provided by this Act a security agreement is effective according to its terms between the parties, against purchasers of the collateral and against creditors. Nothing in this Article validates any charge or practice illegal under any statute or regulation thereunder governing usury, small loans, retail installment sales, or the like, or extends the application of any such statute or regulation to any transaction not otherwise subject thereto.

§ 9–202
Title to Collateral Immaterial

Each provision of this Article with regard to rights, obligations and remedies applies whether title to collateral is in the secured party or in the debtor.

§ 9–203
Attachment and Enforceability of Security Interest; Proceeds; Formal Requisites

(1) Subject to the provisions of Section 4–208 on the security interest of a collecting bank, Section 8–321 on security interests in securities and Section 9–113 on a security interest arising under the Article on Sales, a security interest is not enforceable against the debtor or third parties with respect to the collateral and does not attach unless:

(a) the collateral is in the possession of the secured party pursuant to agreement, or the debtor has signed a security agreement which contains a description of the collateral and in addition, when the security interest covers crops growing or to be grown or timber to be cut, a description of the land concerned;

(b) value has been given; and

(c) the debtor has rights in the collateral.

(2) A security interest attaches when it becomes enforceable against the debtor with respect to the collateral. Attachment occurs as soon as all of the events specified in subsection (1) have taken place unless explicit agreement postpones the time of attaching.

(3) Unless otherwise agreed a security agreement gives the secured party the rights to proceeds provided by Section 9–306.

(4) A transaction, although subject to this Article, is also subject to . . . . °, and in the case of conflict between the provisions of this Article and any such statute, the provisions of such statute control. Failure to comply with any applicable statute has only the effect which is specified therein.

Amended in 1972 and 1977.

Note: *At ° in subsection (4) insert reference to any local statute regulating small loans, retail installment sales and the like.*

The foregoing subsection (4) is designed to make it clear that certain transactions, although subject to this Article, must also comply with other applicable legislation.

This Article is designed to regulate all the "security" aspects of transactions within its scope. There is, however, much regulatory legislation, particularly in the consumer field, which supplements this Article and should not be repealed by its enactment. Examples are small loan acts, retail installment selling acts and the like. Such acts may provide for licensing and rate regulation and may prescribe particular forms of contract. Such provisions should remain in force despite the enactment of this Article. On the other hand if a retail installment selling act contains provisions on filing, rights on default, etc., such provisions should be repealed as inconsistent with this Article except that inconsistent provisions as to deficiencies, penalties, etc., in the Uniform Consumer Credit Code and other recent related legislation should remain because those statutes were drafted after the substantial enactment of the Article and with the intention of modifying certain provisions of this Article as to consumer credit.

§ 9–204
After-Acquired Property; Future Advances

(1) Except as provided in subsection (2), a security agreement may provide that any or all obligations covered by the security agreement are to be secured by after-acquired collateral.

(2) No security interest attaches under an after-acquired property clause to consumer goods other than accessions (Section 9–314) when given as additional security unless the debtor acquires rights in them within ten days after the secured party gives value.

(3) Obligations covered by a security agreement may include future advances or other value whether or not the advances or value are given pursuant to commitment (subsection (1) of Section 9–105).

Amended in 1972.

§ 9–205
Use or Disposition of Collateral without Accounting Permissible

A security interest is not invalid or fraudulent against creditors by reason of liberty in the debtor to use, commingle or dispose of all or part of the collateral (including returned or repossessed goods) or to collect or compromise accounts or chattel paper, or to accept the return of goods or make repossessions, or to use, commingle or dispose of proceeds, or by reason of the failure of the

secured party to require the debtor to account for proceeds or replace collateral. This section does not relax the requirements of possession where perfection of a security interest depends upon possession of the collateral by the secured party or by a bailee.

Amended in 1972.

§ 9–206
Agreement Not to Assert Defenses against Assignee; Modification of Sales Warranties Where Security Agreement Exists

(1) Subject to any statute or decision which establishes a different rule for buyers or lessees of consumer goods, an agreement by a buyer or lessee that he will not assert against an assignee any claim or defense which he may have against the seller or lessor is enforceable by an assignee who takes his assignment for value, in good faith and without notice of a claim or defense, except as to defenses of a type which may be asserted against a holder in due course of a negotiable instrument under the Article on Commercial Paper (Article 3). A buyer who as part of one transaction signs both a negotiable instrument and a security agreement makes such an agreement.

(2) When a seller retains a purchase money security interest in goods the Article on Sales (Article 2) governs the sale and any disclaimer, limitation or modification of the seller's warranties.

Amended in 1962.

§ 9–207
Rights and Duties When Collateral Is in Secured Party's Possession

(1) A secured party must use reasonable care in the custody and preservation of collateral in his possession. In the case of an instrument or chattel paper reasonable care includes taking necessary steps to preserve rights against prior parties unless otherwise agreed.

(2) Unless otherwise agreed, when collateral is in the secured party's possession
    (a) reasonable expenses (including the cost of any insurance and payment of taxes or other charges) incurred in the custody, preservation, use or operation of the collateral are chargeable to the debtor and are secured by the collateral;
    (b) the risk of accidental loss or damage is on the debtor to the extent of any deficiency in any effective insurance coverage;
    (c) the secured party may hold as additional security any increase or profits (except money) received from the collateral, but money so received, unless remitted to the debtor, shall be applied in reduction of the secured obligation;
    (d) the secured party must keep the collateral identifiable but fungible collateral may be commingled;
    (e) the secured party may repledge the collateral upon terms which do not impair the debtor's right to redeem it.

(3) A secured party is liable for any loss caused by his failure to meet any obligation imposed by the preceding subsections but does not lose his security interest.

(4) A secured party may use or operate the collateral for the purpose of preserving the collateral or its value or pursuant to the order of a court of appropriate jurisdiction or, except in the case of consumer goods, in the manner and to the extent provided in the security agreement.

§ 9–208
Request for Statement of Account or List of Collateral

(1) A debtor may sign a statement indicating what he believes to be the aggregate amount of unpaid indebtedness as of a specified date and may send it to the secured party with a request that the statement be approved or corrected and returned to the debtor. When the security agreement or any other record kept by the secured party identifies the collateral a debtor may similarly request the secured party to approve or correct a list of the collateral.

(2) The secured party must comply with such a request within two weeks after receipt by sending a written correction or approval. If the secured party claims a security interest in all of a particular type of collateral owned by the debtor he may indicate that fact in his reply and need not approve or correct an itemized list of such collateral. If the secured party without reasonable excuse fails to comply he is liable for any loss caused to the debtor thereby; and if the debtor has properly included in his request a good faith statement of the obligation or a list of the collateral or both the secured party may claim a security interest only as shown in the statement against persons misled by his failure to comply. If he no longer has an interest in the obligation or collateral at the time the request is received he must disclose the name and address of any successor in interest known to him and he is liable for any loss caused to the debtor as a result of failure to disclose. A successor in interest is not subject to this section until a request is received by him.

(3) A debtor is entitled to such a statement once every six months without charge. The secured party may require payment of a charge not exceeding $10 for each additional statement furnished.

Part 3/Rights of Third Parties; Perfected and Unperfected Security Interests; Rules of Priority
§ 9–301
Persons Who Take Priority over Unperfected Security Interests; Rights of "Lien Creditor"

(1) Except as otherwise provided in subsection (2), an unperfected security interest is subordinate to the rights of
   (a) persons entitled to priority under Section 9–312;
   (b) a person who becomes a lien creditor before the security interest is perfected;
   (c) in the case of goods, instruments, documents, and chattel paper, a person who is not a secured party and who is a transferee in bulk or other buyer not in ordinary course of business or is a buyer of farm products in ordinary course of business, to the extent that he gives value and receives delivery of the collateral without knowledge of the security interest and before it is perfected;
   (d) in the case of accounts and general intangibles, a person who is not a secured party and who is a transferee to the extent that he gives value without knowledge of the security interest and before it is perfected.

(2) If the secured party files with respect to a purchase money security interest before or within ten days after the debtor re-

ceives possession of the collateral, he takes priority over the rights of a transferee in bulk or of a lien creditor which arise between the time the security interest attaches and the time of filing.

(3) A "lien creditor" means a creditor who has acquired a lien on the property involved by attachment, levy or the like and includes an assignee for benefit of creditors from the time of assignment, and a trustee in bankruptcy from the date of the filing of the petition or a receiver in equity from the time of appointment.

(4) A person who becomes a lien creditor while a security interest is perfected takes subject to the security interest only to the extent that it secures advances made before he becomes a lien credit or within 45 days thereafter or made without knowledge of the lien or pursuant to a commitment entered into without knowledge of the lien.

Amended in 1972.

§ 9–302
When Filing Is Required to Perfect Security Interest; Security Interests to Which Filing Provisions of this Article Do Not Apply

(1) A financing statement must be filed to perfect all security interests except the following:
   (a) a security interest in collateral in possession of the secured party under Section 9–305;
   (b) a security interest temporarily perfected in instruments or documents without delivery under Section 9–304 or in proceeds for a 10 day period under Section 9–306;
   (c) a security interest created by an assignment of a beneficial interest in a trust or a decedent's estate;
   (d) a purchase money security interest in consumer goods; but filing is required for a motor vehicle required to be registered; and fixture filing is required for priority over conflicting interests in fixtures to the extent provided in Section 9–313;
   (e) an assignment of accounts which does not alone or in conjunction with other assignments to the same assignee transfer a significant part of the outstanding accounts of the assignor;
   (f) a security interest of a collecting bank (Section 4–208) or in securities (Section 8–321) or arising under the Article on Sales (see Section 9–113) or covered in subsection (3) of this section;
   (g) an assignment for the benefit of all the creditors of the transferor, and subsequent transfers by the assignee thereunder.

(2) If a secured party assigns a perfected security interest, no filing under this Article is required in order to continue the perfected status of the security interest against creditors of and transferees from the original debtor.

(3) The filing of a financing statement otherwise required by this Article is not necessary or effective to perfect a security interest in property subject to
   (a) a statute or treaty of the United States which provides for a national or international registration or a national or international certificate of title or which specifies a place of filing different from that specified in this Article for filing of the security interest; or

(b) the following statutes of this state; [list any certificate of title statute covering automobiles, trailers, mobile homes, boats, farm tractors, or the like, and any central filing statute]; but during any period in which collateral is inventory held for sale by a person who is in the business of selling goods of that kind, the filing provisions of this Article (Part 4) apply to a security interest in that collateral created by him as debtor; or

(c) a certificate of title statute of another jurisdiction under the law of which indication of a security interest on the certificate is required as a condition of perfection (subsection (2) of Section 9–103).

(4) Compliance with a statute or treaty described in subsection (3) is equivalent to the filing of a financing statement under this Article, and a security interest in property subject to the statute or treaty can be perfected only by compliance therewith except as provided in Section 9–103 on multiple state transactions. Duration and renewal of perfection of a security interest perfected by compliance with the statute or treaty are governed by the provisions of the statute or treaty; in other respects the security interest is subject to this Article.

Amended in 1972 and 1977.

§ 9–303
When Security Interest Is Perfected; Continuity of Perfection

(1) A security interest is perfected when it has attached and when all of the applicable steps required for perfection have been taken. Such steps are specified in Sections 9–302, 9–304, 9–305 and 9–306. If such steps are taken before the security interest attaches, it is perfected at the time when it attaches.

(2) If a security interest is originally perfected in any way permitted under this Article and is subsequently perfected in some other way under this Article, without an intermediate period when it was unperfected, the security interest shall be deemed to be perfected continuously for the purposes of this Article.

§ 9–304
Perfection of Security Interest in Instruments, Documents, and Goods Covered by Documents; Perfection by Permissive Filing; Temporary Perfection without Filing or Transfer of Possession

(1) A security interest in chattel paper or negotiable documents may be perfected by filing. A security interest in money or instruments (other than certificated securities or instruments which constitute part of chattel paper) can be perfected only by the secured party's taking possession, except as provided in subsections (4) and (5) of this section and subsections (2) and (3) of Section 9–306 on proceeds.

(2) During the period that goods are in the possession of the issuer of a negotiable document therefor, a security interest in the goods is perfected by perfecting a security interest in the document, and any security interest in the goods otherwise perfected during such period is subject thereto.

(3) A security interest in goods in the possession of a bailee other than one who has issued a negotiable document therefor is perfected by issuance of a document in the name of the secured party or by the bailee's receipt of notification of the secured party's interest or by filing as to the goods.

(4) A security interest in instruments (other than certificated securities) or negotiable documents is perfected without filing or the taking of possession for a period of 21 days from the time it attaches to the extent that it arises for new value given under a written security agreement.

(5) A security interest remains perfected for a period of 21 days without filing where a secured party having a perfected security interest in an instrument (other than a certificated security), a negotiable document or goods in possession of a bailee other than one who has issued a negotiable document therefor

(a) makes available to the debtor the goods or documents representing the goods for the purpose of ultimate sale or exchange or for the purpose of loading, unloading, storing, shipping, transshipping, manufacturing, processing or otherwise dealing with them in a manner preliminary to their sale or exchange, but priority between conflicting security interests in the goods is subject to subsection (3) of Section 9–312; or

(b) delivers the instrument to the debtor for the purpose of ultimate sale or exchange or of presentation, collection, renewal or registration of transfer.

(6) After the 21 day period in subsections (4) and (5) perfection depends upon compliance with applicable provisions of this Article.

Amended in 1972 and 1977.

§ 9–305
When Possession by Secured Party Perfects Security Interest without Filing

A security interest in letters of credit and advices of credit (subsection (2)(a) of Section 5–116), goods, instruments (other than certificated securities), money, negotiable documents or chattel paper may be perfected by the secured party's taking possession of the collateral. If such collateral other than goods covered by a negotiable document is held by a bailee, the secured party is deemed to have possession from the time the bailee receives notification of the secured party's interest. A security interest is perfected by possession from the time possession is taken without a relation back and continues only so long as possession is retained, unless otherwise specified in this Article. The security interest may be otherwise perfected as provided in this Article before or after the period of possession by the secured party.

Amended in 1972.

§ 9–306
"Proceeds"; Secured Party's Rights on Disposition of Collateral

(1) "Proceeds" includes whatever is received upon the sale, exchange, collection or other disposition of collateral or proceeds. Insurance payable by reason of loss or damage to the collateral is proceeds, except to the extent that it is payable to a person other than a party to the security agreement. Money, checks, deposit accounts, and the like are "cash proceeds". All other proceeds are "non-cash proceeds".

(2) Except where this Article otherwise provides, a security interest continues in collateral notwithstanding sale, exchange or other disposition thereof unless the disposition was authorized by the secured party in the security agreement or otherwise, and also continues in any identifiable proceeds including collections received by the debtor.

(3) The security interest in proceeds is a continuously perfected security interest if the interest in the original collateral was perfected but it ceases to be a perfected security interest and becomes unperfected ten days after receipt of the proceeds by the debtor unless

    (a) a filed financing statement covers the original collateral and the proceeds are collateral in which a security interest may be perfected by filing in the office or offices where the financing statement has been filed and, if the proceeds are acquired with cash proceeds, the description of collateral in the financing statement indicates the types of property constituting the proceeds; or

    (b) a filed financing statement covers the original collateral and the proceeds are identifiable cash proceeds; or

    (c) the security interest in the proceeds is perfected before the expiration of the ten day period.

Except as provided in this section, a security interest in proceeds can be perfected only by the methods or under the circumstances permitted in this Article for original collateral of the same type.

(4) In the event of insolvency proceedings instituted by or against a debtor, a secured party with a perfected security interest in proceeds has a perfected security interest only in the following proceeds:

    (a) in identifiable non-cash proceeds and in separate deposit accounts containing only proceeds;

    (b) in identifiable cash proceeds in the form of money which is neither commingled with other money nor deposited in a deposit account prior to the insolvency proceedings;

    (c) in identifiable cash proceeds in the form of checks and the like which are not deposited in a deposit account prior to the insolvency proceedings; and

    (d) in all cash and deposit accounts of the debtor in which proceeds have been commingled with other funds, but the perfected security interest under this paragraph (d) is

    (i) subject to any right to set-off; and

    (ii) limited to an amount not greater than the amount of any cash proceeds received by the debtor within ten days before the institution of the insolvency proceedings less the sum of (I) the payments to the secured party on account of cash proceeds received by the debtor during such period and (II) the cash proceeds received by the debtor during such period to which the secured party is entitled under paragraphs (a) through (c) of this subsection (4).

(5) If a sale of goods results in an account or chattel paper which is transferred by the seller to a secured party, and if the goods are returned to or are repossessed by the seller or the secured party, the following rules determine priorities:

    (a) If the goods were collateral at the time of sale, for an indebtedness of the seller which is still unpaid, the original security interest attaches again to the goods and continues as a perfected security interest if it was perfected at the time when the goods were sold. If the security interest was originally perfected by a filing which is still effective, nothing fur-

ther is required to continue the perfected status; in any other case, the secured party must take possession of the returned or repossessed goods or must file.

    (b) An unpaid transferee of the chattel paper has a security interest in the goods against the transferor. Such security interest is prior to a security interest asserted under paragraph (a) to the extent that the transferee of the chattel paper was entitled to priority under Section 9–308.

    (c) An unpaid transferee of the account has a security interest in the goods against the transferor. Such security interest is subordinate to a security interest asserted under paragraph (a).

    (d) A security interest of an unpaid transferee asserted under paragraph (b) or (c) must be perfected for protection against creditors of the transferor and purchasers of the returned or repossessed goods.

Amended in 1972.

§ 9–307
Protection of Buyers of Goods

(1) A buyer in ordinary course of business (subsection (9) of Section 1–201) other than a person buying farm products from a person engaged in farming operations takes free of a security interest created by his seller even though the security interest is perfected and even though the buyer knows of its existence.

(2) In the case of consumer goods, a buyer takes free of a security interest even though perfected if he buys without knowledge of the security interest, for value and for his own personal, family or household purposes unless prior to the purchase the secured party has filed a financing statement covering such goods.

(3) A buyer other than a buyer in ordinary course of business (subsection (1) of this section) takes free of a security interest to the extent that it secures future advances made after the secured party acquires knowledge of the purchase, or more than 45 days after the purchase, whichever first occurs, unless made pursuant to a commitment entered into without knowledge of the purchase and before the expiration of the 45 day period.

Amended in 1972.

§ 9–308
Purchase of Chattel Paper and Instruments

A purchaser of chattel paper or an instrument who gives new value and takes possession of it in the ordinary course of his business has priority over a security interest in the chattel paper or instrument

    (a) which is perfected under Section 9–304 (permissive filing and temporary perfection) or under Section 9–306 (perfection as to proceeds) if he acts without knowledge that the specific paper or instrument is subject to a security interest; or

    (b) which is claimed merely as proceeds of inventory subject to a security interest (Section 9–306) even though he knows that the specific paper or instrument is subject to the security interest.

Amended in 1972.

§ 9–309
Protection of Purchasers of Instruments, Documents and Securities

Nothing in this Article limits the rights of a holder in due course of a negotiable instrument (Section 3–302) or a holder to whom a negotiable document of title has been duly negotiated (Section 7–501) or a bona fide purchaser of a security (Section 8–302) and the holders or purchasers take priority over an earlier security interest even though perfected. Filing under this Article does not constitute notice of the security interest to such holders or purchasers.

Amended in 1977.

§ 9–310
Priority of Certain Liens Arising by Operation of Law

When a person in the ordinary course of his business furnishes services or materials with respect to goods subject to a security interest, a lien upon goods in the possession of such person given by statute or rule of law for such materials or services takes priority over a perfected security interest unless the lien is statutory and the statute expressly provides otherwise.

§ 9–311
Alienability of Debtor's Rights: Judicial Process

The debtor's rights in collateral may be voluntarily or involuntarily transferred (by way of sale, creation of a security interest, attachment, levy, garnishment or other judicial process) notwithstanding a provision in the security agreement prohibiting any transfer or making the transfer constitute a default.

§ 9–312
Priorities among Conflicting Security Interests in the Same Collateral

(1) The rules of priority stated in other sections of this Part and in the following sections shall govern when applicable: Section 4–208 with respect to the security interests of collecting banks in items being collected, accompanying documents and proceeds; Section 9–103 on security interests related to other jurisdictions; Section 9–114 on consignments.

(2) A perfected security interest in crops for new value given to enable the debtor to produce the crops during the production season and given not more than three months before the crops become growing crops by planting or otherwise takes priority over an earlier perfected security interest to the extent that such earlier interest secures obligations due more than six months before the crops become growing crops by planting or otherwise, even though the person giving new value had knowledge of the earlier security interest.

(3) A perfected purchase money security interest in inventory has priority over a conflicting security interest in the same inventory and also has priority in identifiable cash proceeds received on or before the delivery of the inventory to a buyer if

    (a) the purchase money security interest is perfected at the time the debtor receives possession of the inventory; and

    (b) the purchase money secured party gives notification in writing to the holder of the conflicting security interest if the holder had filed a financing statement covering the same

types of inventory (i) before the date of the filing made by the purchase money secured party, or (ii) before the beginning of the 21 day period where the purchase money security interest is temporarily perfected without filing or possession (subsection (5) of Section 9–304); and

    (c) the holder of the conflicting security interest receives the notification within five years before the debtor receives possession of the inventory; and

    (d) the notification states that the person giving the notice has or expects to acquire a purchase money security interest in inventory of the debtor, describing such inventory by item or type.

(4) A purchase money security interest in collateral other than inventory has priority over a conflicting security interest in the same collateral or its proceeds if the purchase money security interest is perfected at the time the debtor receives possession of the collateral or within ten days thereafter.

(5) In all cases not governed by other rules stated in this section (including cases of purchase money security interests which do not qualify for the special priorities set forth in subsections (3) and (4) of this section), priority between conflicting security interests in the same collateral shall be determined according to the following rules:

    (a) Conflicting security interests rank according to priority in time of filing or perfection. Priority dates from the time a filing is first made covering the collateral or the time the security interest is first perfected, whichever is earlier, provided that there is no period thereafter when there is neither filing nor perfection.

    (b) So long as conflicting security interests are unperfected, the first to attach has priority.

(6) For the purposes of subsection (5) a date of filing or perfection as to collateral is also a date of filing or perfection as to proceeds.

(7) If future advances are made while a security interest is perfected by filing, the taking of possession, or under Section 8–321 on securities, the security interest has the same priority for the purposes of subsection (5) with respect to the future advances as it does with respect to the first advance. If a commitment is made before or while the security interest is so perfected, the security interest has the same priority with respect to advances made pursuant thereto. In other cases a perfected security interest has priority from the date the advance is made.

Amended in 1972 and 1977.

§ 9–313
Priority of Security Interests in Fixtures

(1) In this section and in the provisions of Part 4 of this Article referring to fixture filing, unless the context otherwise requires

    (a) goods are "fixtures" when they become so related to particular real estate that an interest in them arises under real estate law

    (b) a "fixture filing" is the filing in the office where a mortgage on the real estate would be filed or recorded of a financing statement covering goods which are or are to become fixtures and conforming to the requirements of subsection (5) of Section 9–402

(c) a mortgage is a "construction mortgage" to the extent that it secures an obligation incurred for the construction of an improvement on land including the acquisition cost of the land, if the recorded writing so indicates.

(2) A security interest under this Article may be created in goods which are fixtures or may continue in goods which become fixtures, but no security interest exists under this Article in ordinary building materials incorporated into an improvement on land.

(3) This Article does not prevent creation of an encumbrance upon fixtures pursuant to real estate law.

(4) A perfected security interest in fixtures has priority over the conflicting interest of an encumbrancer or owner of the real estate where

    (a) the security interest is a purchase money security interest, the interest of the encumbrancer or owner arises before the goods become fixtures, the security interest is perfected by a fixture filing before the goods become fixtures or within ten days thereafter, and the debtor has an interest of record in the real estate or is in possession of the real estate; or

    (b) the security interest is perfected by a fixture filing before the interest of the encumbrancer or owner is of record, the security interest has priority over any conflicting interest of a predecessor in title of the encumbrancer or owner, and the debtor has an interest of record in the real estate or is in possession of the real estate; or

    (c) the fixtures are readily removable factory or office machines or readily removable replacements of domestic appliances which are consumer goods, and before the goods become fixtures the security interest is perfected by any method permitted by this Article; or

    (d) the conflicting interest is a lien on the real estate obtained by legal or equitable proceedings after the security interest was perfected by any method permitted by this Article.

(5) A security interest in fixtures, whether or not perfected, has priority over the conflicting interest of an encumbrancer or owner of the real estate where

    (a) the encumbrancer or owner has consented in writing to the security interest or has disclaimed an interest in the goods as fixtures; or

    (b) the debtor has a right to remove the goods as against the encumbrancer or owner. If the debtor's right terminates, the priority of the security interest continues for a reasonable time.

(6) Notwithstanding paragraph (a) of subsection (4) but otherwise subject to subsections (4) and (5), a security interest in fixtures is subordinate to a construction mortgage recorded before the goods become fixtures if the goods become fixtures before the completion of the construction. To the extent that it is given to refinance a construction mortgage, a mortgage has this priority to the same extent as the construction mortgage.

(7) In cases not within the preceding subsections, a security interest in fixtures is subordinate to the conflicting interest of an encumbrancer or owner of the related real estate who is not the debtor.

(8) When the secured party has priority over all owners and encumbrancers of the real estate, he may, on default, subject to the provisions of Part 5, remove his collateral from the real estate but he must reimburse any encumbrancer or owner of the real estate who is not the debtor and who has not otherwise agreed for the cost of repair of any physical injury, but not for any diminution in value of the real estate caused by the absence of the goods removed or by any necessity of replacing them. A person entitled to reimbursement may refuse permission to remove until the secured party gives adequate security for the performance of this obligation.

Amended in 1972.

§ 9–314
Accessions

(1) A security interest in goods which attaches before they are installed in or affixed to other goods takes priority as to the goods installed or affixed (called in this section "accessions") over the claims of all persons to the whole except as stated in subsection (3) and subject to Section 9–315(1).

(2) A security interest which attaches to goods after they become part of a whole is valid against all persons subsequently acquiring interests in the whole except as stated in subsection (3) but is invalid against any person with an interest in the whole at the time the security interest attaches to the goods who has not in writing consented to the security interest or disclaimed an interest in the goods as part of the whole.

(3) The security interests described in subsections (1) and (2) do not take priority over

    (a) a subsequent purchaser for value of any interest in the whole; or

    (b) a creditor with a lien on the whole subsequently obtained by judicial proceedings; or

    (c) a creditor with a prior perfected security interest in the whole to the extent that he makes subsequent advances.

If the subsequent purchase is made, the lien by judicial proceedings obtained or the subsequent advance under the prior perfected security interest is made or contracted for without knowledge of the security interest and before it is perfected. A purchaser of the whole at a foreclosure sale other than the holder of a perfected security interest purchasing at his own foreclosure sale is a subsequent purchaser within this section.

(4) When under subsections (1) or (2) and (3) a secured party has an interest in accessions which has priority over the claims of all persons who have interests in the whole, he may on default subject to the provisions of Part 5 remove his collateral from the whole but he must reimburse any encumbrancer or owner of the whole who is not the debtor and who has not otherwise agreed for the cost of repair of any physical injury but not for any diminution in value of the whole caused by the absence of the goods removed or by any necessity for replacing them. A person entitled to reimbursement may refuse permission to remove until the secured party gives adequate security for the performance of this obligation.

§ 9–315
Priority When Goods Are Commingled or Processed

(1) If a security interest in goods was perfected and subsequently the goods or a part thereof have become part of a product or mass, the security interest continues in the product or mass if

    (a) the goods are so manufactured, processed, assembled or commingled that their identity is lost in the product or mass; or

    (b) a financing statement covering the original goods also covers the product into which the goods have been manufactured, processed or assembled.

In a case to which paragraph (b) applies, no separate security interest in that part of the original goods which has been manufactured, processed or assembled into the product may be claimed under Section 9–314.

(2) When under subsection (1) more than one security interest attaches to the product or mass, they rank equally according to the ratio that the cost of the goods to which each interest originally attached bears to the cost of the total product or mass.

§ 9–316
Priority Subject to Subordination

Nothing in this Article prevents subordination by agreement by any person entitled to priority.

§ 9–317
Secured Party Not Obligated on Contract of Debtor

The mere existence of a security interest or authority given to the debtor to dispose of or use collateral does not impose contract or tort liability upon the secured party for the debtor's acts or omissions.

§ 9–318
Defenses against Assignee; Modification of Contract after Notification of Assignment; Term Prohibiting Assignment Ineffective; Identification and Proof of Assignment

(1) Unless an account debtor has made an enforceable agreement not to assert defenses or claims arising out of a sale as provided in Section 9–206 the rights of an assignee are subject to

    (a) all the terms of the contract between the account debtor and assignor and any defense or claim arising therefrom; and

    (b) any other defense or claim of the account debtor against the assignor which accrues before the account debtor receives notification of the assignment.

(2) So far as the right to payment or a part thereof under an assigned contract has not been fully earned by performance, and notwithstanding notification of the assignment, any modification of or substitution for the contract made in good faith and in accordance with reasonable commercial standards is effective against an assignee unless the account debtor has otherwise agreed but the assignee acquires corresponding rights under the modified or substituted contract. The assignment may provide that such modification or substitution is a breach by the assignor.

(3) The account debtor is authorized to pay the assignor until the account debtor receives notification that the amount due or to become due has been assigned and that payment is to be made to the assignee. A notification which does not reasonably identify the rights assigned is ineffective. If requested by the account debtor, the assignee must seasonably furnish reasonable proof that the assignment has been made and unless he does so the account debtor may pay the assignor.

(4) A term in any contract between an account debtor and an assignor is ineffective if it prohibits assignment of an account or prohibits creation of a security interest in a general intangible for money due or to become due or requires the account debtor's consent to such assignment or security interest.

Amended in 1972.

Part 4/Filing
§ 9–401
Place of Filing; Erroneous Filing; Removal of Collateral

First Alternative Subsection (1)

(1) The proper place to file in order to perfect a security interest is as follows:

    (a) when the collateral is timber to be cut or is minerals or the like (including oil and gas) or accounts subject to subsection (5) of Section 9–103, or when the financing statement is filed as a fixture filing (Section 9–313) and the collateral is goods which are or are to become fixtures, then in the office where a mortgage on the real estate would be filed or recorded;

    (b) in all other cases, in the office of the [Secretary of State].

Second Alternative Subsection (1)

(1) The proper place to file in order to perfect a security interest is as follows:

    (a) when the collateral is equipment used in farming operations, or farm products, or accounts or general intangibles arising from or relating to the sale of farm products by a farmer, or consumer goods, then in the office of the . . . . in the county of the debtor's residence or if the debtor is not a resident of this state then in the office of the . . . . in the county where the goods are kept, and in addition when the collateral is crops growing or to be grown in the office of the . . . . in the county where the land is located;

    (b) when the collateral is timber to be cut or is minerals or the like (including oil and gas) or accounts subject to subsection (5) of Section 9–103, or when the financing statement is filed as a fixture filing (Section 9–313) and the collateral is goods which are or are to become fixtures, then in the office where a mortgage on the real estate would be filed or recorded;

    (c) in all other cases, in the office of the [Secretary of State].

Third Alternative Subsection (1)

(1) The proper place to file in order to perfect a security interest is as follows:

    (a) when the collateral is equipment used in farming operations, or farm products, or accounts or general intangibles arising from or relating to the sale of farm products by a farmer, or consumer goods, then in the office of the . . . . in the county of the debtor's residence or if the debtor is not a resident of this state then in the office of the . . . . in the county where the goods are kept, and in addition when the collateral is crops growing or to be grown in the office of the . . . . in the county where the land is located;

(b)   when the collateral is timber to be cut or is minerals or the like (including oil and gas) or accounts subject to subsection (5) of Section 9–103, or when the financing statement is filed as a fixture filing (Section 9–313) and the collateral is goods which are or are to become fixtures, then in the office where a mortgage on the real estate would be filed or recorded;

(c)   in all other cases, in the office of the [Secretary of State] and in addition, if the debtor has a place of business in only one county of this state, also in the office of . . . . of such county, or, if the debtor has no place of business in this state, but resides in the state, also in the office of . . . . of the county in which he resides.

Note: *One of the three alternatives should be selected as subsection (1).*

(2)   A filing which is made in good faith in an improper place or not in all of the places required by this section is nevertheless effective with regard to any collateral as to which the filing complied with the requirements of this Article and is also effective with regard to collateral covered by the financing statement against any person who has knowledge of the contents of such financing statement.

(3)   A filing which is made in the proper place in this state continues effective even though the debtor's residence or place of business or the location of the collateral or its use, whichever controlled the original filing, is thereafter changed.

Alternative Subsection (3)

[**(3)**   A filing which is made in the proper county continues effective for four months after a change to another county of the debtor's residence or place of business or the location of the collateral, whichever controlled the original filing. It becomes ineffective thereafter unless a copy of the financing statement signed by the secured party is filed in the new county within said period. The security interest may also be perfected in the new county after the expiration of the four-month period; in such case perfection dates from the time of perfection in the new county. A change in the use of the collateral does not impair the effectiveness of the original filing.]

(4)   The rules stated in Section 9–103 determine whether filing is necessary in this state.

(5)   Notwithstanding the preceding subsections, and subject to subsection (3) of Section 9–302, the proper place to file in order to perfect a security interest in collateral, including fixtures, of a transmitting utility is the office of the [Secretary of State]. This filing constitutes a fixture filing (Section 9–313) as to the collateral described therein which is or is to become fixtures.

(6)   For the purposes of this section, the residence of an organization is its place of business if it has one or its chief executive office if it has more than one place of business.

Amended in 1962 and 1972.

Note: *Subsection (6) should be used only if the state chooses the Second or Third Alternative Subsection (1).*

§ 9–402
Formal Requisites of Financing Statement; Amendments; Mortgage as Financing Statement

(1)   A financing statement is sufficient if it gives the names of the debtor and the secured party, is signed by the debtor, gives an address of the secured party from which information concerning the security interest may be obtained, gives a mailing address of the debtor and contains a statement indicating the types, or describing the items, of collateral. A financing statement may be filed before a security agreement is made or a security interest otherwise attaches. When the financing statement covers crops growing or to be grown, the statement must also contain a description of the real estate concerned. When the financing statement covers timber to be cut or covers minerals or the like (including oil and gas) or accounts subject to subsection (5) of Section 9–103, or when the financing statement is filed as a fixture filing (Section 9–313) and the collateral is goods which are or are to become fixtures, the statement must also comply with subsection (5). A copy of the security agreement is sufficient as a financing statement if it contains the above information and is signed by the debtor. A carbon, photographic or other reproduction of a security agreement or a financing statement is sufficient as a financing statement if the security agreement so provides or if the original has been filed in this state.

(2)   A financing statement which otherwise complies with subsection (1) is sufficient when it is signed by the secured party instead of the debtor if it is filed to perfect a security interest in

(a)   collateral already subject to a security interest in another jurisdiction when it is brought into this state, or when the debtor's location is changed to this state. Such a financing statement must state that the collateral was brought into this state or that the debtor's location was changed to this state under such circumstances; or

(b)   proceeds under Section 9–306 if the security interest in the original collateral was perfected. Such a financing statement must describe the original collateral; or

(c)   collateral as to which the filing has lapsed; or

(d)   collateral acquired after a change of name, identity or corporate structure of the debtor (subsection (7)).

(3)   A form substantially as follows is sufficient to comply with subsection (1):

Name of debtor (or assignor)

Address . . . .

Name of secured party (or assignee) . . . .

Address . . . .

1. This financing statement covers the following types (or items) of property:

(Describe) . . . .

2. (If collateral is crops) The above described crops are growing or are to be grown on:

(Describe Real Estate) . . . .

3. (If applicable) The above goods are to become fixtures on°

°Where appropriate substitute either "The above timber is standing on . . . ." or "The above minerals or the like (including oil and gas) or accounts will be financed at the wellhead or minehead of the well or mine located on . . . ."

(Describe Real Estate) ....
and this financing statement is to be filed [for record] in the real estate records. (If the debtor does not have an interest of record) The name of a record owner is
4. (If products of collateral are claimed) Products of the collateral are also covered.

(use whichever signature is applicable)

....
Signature of Debtor (or Assignor)
....
Signature of Secured Party (or Assignee)
....

(4) A financing statement may be amended by filing a writing signed by both the debtor and the secured party. An amendment does not extend the period of effectiveness of a financing statement. If any amendment adds collateral, it is effective as to the added collateral only from the filing date of the amendment. In this Article, unless the context otherwise requires, the term "financing statement" means the original financing statement and any amendments.

(5) A financing statement covering timber to be cut or covering minerals or the like (including oil and gas) or accounts subject to subsection (5) of Section 9–103, or a financing statement filed as a future filing (Section 9–313) where the debtor is not a transmitting utility, must show that it covers this type of collateral, must recite that it is to be filed [for record] in the real estate records, and the financing statement must contain a description of the real estate [sufficient if it were contained in a mortgage of the real estate to give constructive notice of the mortgage under the law of this state]. If the debtor does not have an interest of record in the real estate, the financing statement must show the name of a record owner.

(6) A mortgage is effective as a financing statement filed as a fixture filing from the date of its recording if
   (a) the goods are described in the mortgage by item or type; and
   (b) the goods are or are to become fixtures related to the real estate described in the mortgage; and
   (c) the mortgage complies with the requirements for a financing statement in this section other than a recital that it is to be filed in the real estate records; and
   (d) the mortgage is duly recorded.
No fee with reference to the financing statement is required other than the regular recording and satisfaction fees with respect to the mortgage.

(7) A financing statement sufficiently shows the name of the debtor if it gives the individual, partnership or corporate name of the debtor, whether or not it adds other trade names or names of partners. Where the debtor so changes his name or in the case of an organization its name, identity or corporate structure that a filed financing statement becomes seriously misleading, the filing is not effective to perfect a security interest in collateral acquired by the debtor more than four months after the change, unless a new appropriate financing statement is filed before the expiration of that time. A filed financing statement remains effective with respect to collateral transferred by the debtor even though the secured party knows of or consents to the transfer.

(8) A financing statement substantially complying with the requirements of this section is effective even though it contains minor errors which are not seriously misleading.

Amended in 1972.

Note: *Language in brackets is optional.*

Note: *Where the state has any special recording system for real estate other than the usual grantor-grantee index (as, for instance, a tract system or a title registration or Torrens system) local adaptations of subsection (5) and Section 9–403(7) may be necessary. See Mass.Gen.Laws Chapter 106, Section 9–409.*

§ 9–403
What Constitutes Filing; Duration of Filing; Effect of Lapsed Filing; Duties of Filing Officer

(1) Presentation for filing of a financing statement and tender of the filing fee or acceptance of the statement by the filing officer constitutes filing under this Article.

(2) Except as provided in subsection (6) a filed financing statement is effective for a period of five years from the date of filing. The effectiveness of a filed financing statement lapses on the expiration of the five year period unless a continuation statement is filed prior to the lapse. If a security interest perfected by filing exists at the time insolvency proceedings are commenced by or against the debtor, the security interest remains perfected until termination of the insolvency proceedings and thereafter for a period of sixty days or until expiration of the five year period, whichever occurs later. Upon lapse the security interest becomes unperfected, unless it is perfected without filing. If the security interest becomes unperfected upon lapse, it is deemed to have been unperfected as against a person who became a purchaser or lien creditor before lapse.

(3) A continuation statement may be filed by the secured party within six months prior to the expiration of the five year period specified in subsection (2). Any such continuation statement must be signed by the secured party, identify the original statement by file number and state that the original statement is still effective. A continuation statement signed by a person other than the secured party of record must be accompanied by a separate written statement of assignment signed by the secured party of record and complying with subsection (2) of Section 9–405, including payment of the required fee. Upon timely filing of the continuation statement, the effectiveness of the original statement is continued for five years after the last date to which the filing was effective whereupon it lapses in the same manner as provided in subsection (2) unless another continuation statement is filed prior to such lapse. Succeeding continuation statements may be filed in the same manner to continue the effectiveness of the original statement. Unless a statute on disposition of public records provides otherwise, the filing officer may remove a lapsed statement from the files and destroy it immediately if he has retained a microfilm or other photographic record, or in other cases after one year after the lapse. The filing officer shall so arrange matters by physical annexation of financing statements to continuation statements or other related filings, or by other means, that if he physically destroys the financing statements of a period more than five years past, those which have been continued by a continuation statement or which are still effective under subsection (6) shall be retained.

(4) Except as provided in subsection (7) a filing officer shall mark each statement with a file number and with the date and hour of filing and shall hold the statement or a microfilm or other photographic copy thereof for public inspection. In addition the filing officer shall index the statement according to the name of the debtor and shall note in the index the file number and the address of the debtor given in the statement.

(5) The uniform fee for filing and indexing and for stamping a copy furnished by the secured party to show the date and place of filing for an original financing statement or for a continuation statement shall be $ . . . . if the statement is in the standard form prescribed by the [Secretary of State] and otherwise shall be $ . . . . , plus in each case, if the financing statement is subject to subsection (5) of Section 9–402, $ . . . . The uniform fee for each name more than one required to be indexed shall be $ . . . . The secured party may at his option show a trade name for any person and an extra uniform indexing fee of $ . . . . shall be paid with respect thereto.

(6) If the debtor is a transmitting utility (subsection (5) of Section 9–401) and a filed financing statement so states, it is effective until a termination statement is filed. A real estate mortgage which is effective as a fixture filing under subsection (6) of Section 9–402 remains effective as a fixture filing until the mortgage is released or satisfied of record or its effectiveness otherwise terminates as to the real estate.

(7) When a financing statement covers timber to be cut or covers minerals or the like (including oil and gas) or accounts subject to subsection (5) of Section 9–103, or is filed as a fixture filing, [it shall be filed for record and] the filing officer shall index it under the names of the debtor and any owner of record shown on the financing statement in the same fashion as if they were the mortgagors in a mortgage of the real estate described, and, to the extent that the law of this state provides for indexing of mortgages under the name of the mortgagee, under the name of the secured party as if he were the mortgagee thereunder, or where indexing is by description in the same fashion as if the financing statement were a mortgage of the real estate described.

Amended in 1972.

Note: *In states in which writings will not appear in the real estate records and indices unless actually recorded the bracketed language in subsection (7) should be used.*

§ 9–404
Termination Statement

(1) If a financing statement covering consumer goods is filed on or after . . . . , then within one month or within ten days following written demand by the debtor after there is no outstanding secured obligation and no commitment to make advances, incur obligations or otherwise give value, the secured party must file with each filing officer with whom the financing statement was filed, a termination statement to the effect that he no longer claims a security interest under the financing statement, which shall be identified by file number. In other cases whenever

there is no outstanding secured obligation and no commitment to make advances, incur obligations or otherwise give value, the secured party must on written demand by the debtor send the debtor, for each filing officer with whom the financing statement was filed, a termination statement to the effect that he no longer claims a security interest under the financing statement, which shall be identified by file number. A termination statement signed by a person other than the secured party of record must be accompanied by a separate written statement of assignment signed by the secured party of record complying with subsection (2) of Section 9–405, including payment of the required fee. If the affected secured party fails to file such a termination statement as required by this subsection, or to send such a termination statement within ten days after proper demand therefor, he shall be liable to the debtor for one hundred dollars, and in addition for any loss caused to the debtor by such failure.

(2) On presentation to the filing officer of such a termination statement he must note it in the index. If he has received the termination statement in duplicate, he shall return one copy of the termination statement to the secured party stamped to show the time of receipt thereof. If the filing officer has a microfilm or other photographic record of the financing statement, and of any related continuation statement, statement of assignment and statement of release, he may remove the originals from the files at any time after receipt of the termination statement, or if he has no such record, he may remove them from the files at any time after one year after receipt of the termination statement.

(3) If the termination statement is in the standard form prescribed by the [Secretary of State], the uniform fee for filing and indexing the termination statement shall be $ . . . . , and otherwise shall be $ . . . . , plus in each case an additional fee of $ . . . . for each name more than one against which the termination statement is required to be indexed.

Amended in 1972.

Note: *The date to be inserted should be the effective date of the revised Article 9.*

§ 9–405
Assignment of Security Interest;
Duties of Filing Officer; Fees

(1) A financing statement may disclose an assignment of a security interest in the collateral described in the financing statement by indication in the financing statement of the name and address of the assignee or by an assignment itself or a copy thereof on the face or back of the statement. On presentation to the filing officer of such a financing statement the filing officer shall mark the same as provided in Section 9–403(4). The uniform fee for filing, indexing and furnishing filing data for a financing statement so indicating an assignment shall be $ . . . . if the statement is in the standard form prescribed by the [Secretary of State] and otherwise shall be $ . . . . , plus in each case an additional fee of $ . . . . for each name more than one against which the financing statement is required to be indexed.

(2) A secured party may assign of record all or part of his rights under a financing statement by the filing in the place where the original financing statement was filed of a separate written statement of assignment signed by the secured party of record and setting forth the name of the secured party of record and the debtor, the file number and the date of filing of the financing statement and the name and address of the assignee and containing a description of the collateral assigned. A copy of the assignment is sufficient as a separate statement if it complies with the preceding sentence. On presentation to the filing officer of such a separate statement, the filing officer shall mark such separate statement with the date and hour of the filing. He shall note the assignment on the index of the financing statement, or in the case of a fixture filing, or a filing covering timber to be cut, or covering minerals or the like (including oil and gas) or accounts subject to subsection (5) of Section 9–103, he shall index the assignment under the name of the assignor as grantor and, to the extent that the law of this state provides for indexing the assignment of a mortgage under the name of the assignee, he shall index the assignment of the financing statement under the name of the assignee. The uniform fee for filing, indexing and furnishing filing data about such a separate statement of assignment shall be $ . . . . if the statement is in the standard form prescribed by the [Secretary of State] and otherwise shall be $ . . . . , plus in each case an additional fee of $ . . . . for each name more than one against which the statement of assignment is required to be indexed. Notwithstanding the provisions of this subsection, an assignment of record of a security interest in a fixture contained in a mortgage effective as a fixture filing (subsection (6) of Section 9–402) may be made only by an assignment of the mortgage in the manner provided by the law of this state other than this Act.

(3) After the disclosure or filing of an assignment under this section, the assignee is the secured party of record.

Amended in 1972.

§ 9–406
Release of Collateral; Duties of Filing Officer; Fees

A secured party of record may by his signed statement release all or a part of any collateral described in a filed financing statement. The statement of release is sufficient if it contains a description of the collateral being released, the name and address of the debtor, the name and address of the secured party, and the file number of the financing statement. A statement of release signed by a person other than the secured party of record must be accompanied by a separate written statement of assignment signed by the secured party of record and complying with subsection (2) of Section 9–405, including payment of the required fee. Upon presentation of such a statement of release to the filing officer he shall mark the statement with the hour and date of filing and shall note the same upon the margin of the index of the filing of the financing statement. The uniform fee for filing and noting such a statement of release shall be $ . . . . if the statement is in the standard form prescribed by the [Secretary of State] and otherwise shall be $ . . . . , plus in each case an additional fee of $ . . . . for each name more than one against which the statement of release is required to be indexed.

Amended in 1972.

§ 9–407
Information from Filing Officer

[**(1)** If the person filing any financing statement, termination statement, statement of assignment, or statement of release, furnishes the filing officer a copy thereof, the filing officer shall upon request note upon the copy the file number and date and hour of the filing of the original and deliver or send the copy to such person.]

[**(2)** Upon request of any person, the filing officer shall issue his certificate showing whether there is on file on the date and hour stated therein, any presently effective financing statement naming a particular debtor and any statement of assignment thereof and if there is, giving the date and hour of filing of each such statement and the names and addresses of each secured party therein. The uniform fee for such a certificate shall be $ . . . . if the request for the certificate is in the standard form prescribed by the [Secretary of State] and otherwise shall be $ . . . . Upon request the filing officer shall furnish a copy of any filed financing statement or statement of assignment for a uniform fee of $ . . . . per page.]

Amended in 1972.

Note: *This section is proposed as an optional provision to require filing officers to furnish certificates. Local law and practices should be consulted with regard to the advisability of adoption.*

§ 9–408
Financing Statements Covering Consigned or Leased Goods

A consignor or lessor of goods may file a financing statement using the terms "consignor," "consignee," "lessor," "lessee" or the like instead of the terms specified in Section 9–402. The provisions of this Part shall apply as appropriate to such a financing statement but its filing shall not of itself be a factor in determining whether or not the consignment or lease is intended as security (Section 1–201(37)). However, if it is determined for other reasons that the consignment or lease is so intended, a security interest of the consignor or lessor which attaches to the consigned or leased goods is perfected by such filing.

Added in 1972.

Part 5/Default
§ 9–501
Default; Procedure When Security Agreement Covers Both Real and Personal Property

(1) When a debtor is in default under a security agreement, a secured party has the rights and remedies provided in this Part and except as limited by subsection (3) those provided in the security agreement. He may reduce his claim to judgment, foreclose or otherwise enforce the security interest by any available judicial procedure. If the collateral is documents the secured party may proceed either as to the documents or as to the goods covered thereby. A secured party in possession has the rights, remedies and duties provided in Section 9–207. The rights and remedies referred to in this subsection are cumulative.

(2) After default, the debtor has the rights and remedies provided in this Part, those provided in the security agreement and those provided in Section 9–207.

(3) To the extent that they give rights to the debtor and impose duties on the secured party, the rules stated in the subsections referred to below may not be waived or varied except as provided with respect to compulsory disposition of collateral (subsection (3) of Section 9–504 and Section 9–505) and with respect to redemption of collateral (Section 9–506) but the parties may by agreement determine the standards by which the fulfillment of these rights and duties is to be measured if such standards are not manifestly unreasonable:

(a) subsection (2) of Section 9–502 and subsection (2) of Section 9–504 insofar as they require accounting for surplus proceeds of collateral;

(b) subsection (3) of Section 9–504 with subsection (1) of Section 9–505 which deal with disposition of collateral;

(c) subsection (2) of Section 9–505 which deals with acceptance of collateral as discharge of obligation;

(d) Section 9–506 which deals with redemption of collateral; and

(e) subsection (1) of Section 9–507 which deals with the secured party's liability for failure to comply with this Part.

(4) If the security agreement covers both real and personal property, the secured party may proceed under this Part as to the personal property or he may proceed as to both the real and the personal property in accordance with his rights and remedies in respect of the real property in which case the provisions of this Part do not apply.

(5) When a secured party has reduced his claim to judgment the lien of any levy which may be made upon his collateral by virtue of any execution based upon the judgment shall relate back to the date of the perfection of the security interest in such collateral. A judicial sale, pursuant to such execution, is a foreclosure of the security interest by judicial procedure within the meaning of this section, and the secured party may purchase at the sale and thereafter hold the collateral free of any other requirements of this Article.

Amended in 1972.

§ 9–502
Collection Rights of Secured Party

(1) When so agreed and in any event on default the secured party is entitled to notify an account debtor or the obligor on an instrument to make payment to him whether or not the assignor was theretofore making collections on the collateral, and also to take control of any proceeds to which he is entitled under Section 9–306.

(2) A secured party who by agreement is entitled to charge back uncollected collateral or otherwise to full or limited recourse against the debtor and who undertakes to collect from the account debtors or obligors must proceed in a commercially reasonable manner and may deduct his reasonable expenses of realization from the collections. If the security agreement secures an indebtedness, the secured party must account to the debtor for any surplus, and, unless otherwise agreed, the debtor is liable for any deficiency. But, if the underlying transaction was a sale of accounts or chattel paper, the debtor is entitled to any surplus or is liable for any deficiency only if the security agreement so provides.

Amended in 1972.

§ 9–503
Secured Party's Right to Take Possession after Default

Unless otherwise agreed a secured party has on default the right to take possession of the collateral. In taking possession a secured party may proceed without judicial process if this can be done without breach of the peace or may proceed by action. If the security agreement so provides the secured party may require the debtor to assemble the collateral and make it available to the secured party at a place to be designated by the secured party which is reasonably convenient to both parties. Without removal a secured party may render equipment unusable, and may dispose of collateral on the debtor's premises under Section 9–504.

§ 9–504
Secured Party's Right to Dispose of Collateral after Default; Effect of Disposition

(1) A secured party after default may sell, lease or otherwise dispose of any or all of the collateral in its then condition or following any commercially reasonable preparation or processing. Any sale of goods is subject to the Article on Sales (Article 2). The proceeds of disposition shall be applied in the order following to

(a) the reasonable expenses of retaking, holding, preparing for sale or lease, selling, leasing and the like and, to the extent provided for in the agreement and not prohibited by law, the reasonable attorneys' fees and legal expenses incurred by the secured party;

(b) the satisfaction of indebtedness secured by the security interest under which the disposition is made;

(c) the satisfaction of indebtedness secured by any subordinate security interest in the collateral if written notification of demand therefor is received before distribution of the proceeds is completed. If requested by the secured party, the holder of a subordinate security interest must seasonably furnish reasonable proof of his interest, and unless he does so, the secured party need not comply with his demand.

(2) If the security interest secures an indebtedness, the secured party must account to the debtor for any surplus, and, unless otherwise agreed, the debtor is liable for any deficiency. But if the underlying transaction was a sale of accounts or chattel paper, the debtor is entitled to any surplus or is liable for any deficiency only if the security agreement so provides.

(3) Disposition of the collateral may be by public or private proceedings and may be made by way of one or more contracts. Sale or other disposition may be as a unit or in parcels and at any time and place and on any terms but every aspect of the disposition including the method, manner, time, place and terms must be commercially reasonable. Unless collateral is perishable or threatens to decline speedily in value or is of a type customarily sold on a recognized market, reasonable notification of the time and place of any public sale or reasonable notification of the time after which any private sale or other intended disposition is to be made shall be sent by the secured party to the debtor, if he has not signed after default a statement renouncing or modifying his right to notification of sale. In the case of consumer goods no other notification need be sent. In other cases notification shall be sent to any other secured party from whom the secured party has received (before sending his notification to the debtor or before the debtor's renunciation of his rights) written notice of a claim of an interest in the collateral. The secured party may buy at any public sale and if the collateral is of a type customarily sold in a recognized market or is of a type which is the subject of widely distributed standard price quotations he may buy at private sale.

(4) When collateral is disposed of by a secured party after default, the disposition transfers to a purchaser for value all of the debtor's rights therein, discharges the security interest under which it is made and any security interest or lien subordinate thereto. The purchaser takes free of all such rights and interests even though the secured party fails to comply with the requirements of this Part or of any judicial proceedings

   (a) in the case of a public sale, if the purchaser has no knowledge of any defects in the sale and if he does not buy in collusion with the secured party, other bidders or the person conducting the sale; or

   (b) in any other case, if the purchaser acts in good faith.

(5) A person who is liable to a secured party under a guaranty, indorsement, repurchase agreement or the like and who receives a transfer of collateral from the secured party or is subrogated to his rights has thereafter the rights and duties of the secured party. Such a transfer of collateral is not a sale or disposition of the collateral under this Article.

Amended in 1972.

§ 9–505
Compulsory Disposition of Collateral; Acceptance of the Collateral as Discharge of Obligation

(1) If the debtor has paid sixty per cent of the cash price in the case of a purchase money security interest in consumer goods or sixty per cent of the loan in the case of another security interest in consumer goods, and has not signed after default a statement renouncing or modifying his rights under this Part a secured party who has taken possession of collateral must dispose of it under Section 9–504 and if he fails to do so within ninety days after he takes possession the debtor at his option may recover in conversion or under Section 9–507(1) on secured party's liability.

(2) In any other case involving consumer goods or any other collateral a secured party in possession may, after default, propose to retain the collateral in satisfaction of the obligation. Written notice of such proposal shall be sent to the debtor if he has not signed after default a statement renouncing or modifying his rights under this subsection. In the case of consumer goods no other notice need be given. In other cases notice shall be sent to any other secured party from whom the secured party has received (before sending his notice to the debtor or before the debtor's renunciation of his rights) written notice of a claim of an interest in the collateral. If the secured party receives objection in writing from a person entitled to receive notification within twenty-one days after the notice was sent, the secured party must dispose of the collateral under Section 9–504. In the absence of such written objection the secured party may retain the collateral in satisfaction of the debtor's obligation.

Amended in 1972.

§ 9–506
Debtor's Right to Redeem Collateral

At any time before the secured party has disposed of collateral or entered into a contract for its disposition under Section 9–504 or before the obligation has been discharged under Section 9–505(2) the debtor or any other secured party may unless otherwise agreed in writing after default redeem the collateral by tendering fulfillment of all obligations secured by the collateral as well as the expenses reasonably incurred by the secured party in retaking, holding and preparing the collateral for disposition, in arranging for the sale, and to the extent provided in the agreement and not prohibited by law, his reasonable attorneys' fees and legal expenses.

§ 9–507
Secured Party's Liability for Failure to Comply with This Part

(1) If it is established that the secured party is not proceeding in accordance with the provisions of this Part disposition may be ordered or restrained on appropriate terms and conditions. If the disposition has occurred the debtor or any person entitled to notification or whose security interest has been made known to the secured party prior to the disposition has a right to recover from the secured party any loss caused by a failure to comply with the provisions of this Part. If the collateral is consumer goods, the debtor has a right to recover in any event an amount not less than the credit service charge plus ten per cent of the principal amount of the debt or the time price differential plus 10 percent of the cash price.

(2) The fact that a better price could have been obtained by a sale at a different time or in a different method from that selected by the secured party is not of itself sufficient to establish that the sale was not made in a commercially reasonable manner. If the secured party either sells the collateral in the usual manner in any recognized market therefor or if he sells at the price current in such market at the time of his sale or if he has otherwise sold in conformity with reasonable commercial practices among dealers in the type of property sold he has sold in a commercially reasonable manner. The principles stated in the two preceding sentences with respect to sales also apply as may be appropriate to other types of disposition. A disposition which has been approved in any judicial proceeding or by any bona fide creditors' committee or representative of creditors shall conclusively be deemed to be commercially reasonable, but this sentence does not indicate that any such approval must be obtained in any case nor does it indicate that any disposition not so approved is not commercially reasonable.

ARTICLE 10/EFFECTIVE DATE AND REPEALER [OMITTED]
. . . .

Appendix B

The Uniform Partnership Act

Part I/Preliminary Provisions
§ 1
Name of Act

This act may be cited as Uniform Partnership Act.

§ 2
Definition of Terms

In this act, "Court" includes every court and judge having jurisdiction in the case.

"Business" includes every trade, occupation, or profession.

"Person" includes individuals, partnerships, corporations, and other associations.

"Bankrupt" includes bankrupt under the Federal Bankruptcy Act or insolvent under any state insolvent act.

"Conveyance" includes every assignment, lease, mortgage, or encumbrance.

"Real property" includes land and any interest or estate in land.

§ 3
Interpretation of Knowledge and Notice

(1) A person has "knowledge" of a fact within the meaning of this act not only when he has actual knowledge thereof, but also when he has knowledge of such other facts as in the circumstances shows bad faith.

(2) A person has "notice" of a fact within the meaning of this act when the person who claims the benefit of the notice:

    (a) States the fact to such person, or

    (b) Delivers through the mail, or by other means of communication, a written statement of the fact to such person or to a proper person at his place of business or residence.

§ 4
Rules of Construction

(1) The rule that statutes in derogation of the common law are to be strictly construed shall have no application to this act.

(2) The law of estoppel shall apply under this act.

(3) The law of agency shall apply under this act.

(4) This act shall be so interpreted and construed as to effect its general purpose to make uniform the law of those states which enact it.

(5) This act shall not be construed so as to impair the obligations of any contract existing when the act goes into effect, nor to affect any action or proceedings begun or right accrued before this act takes effect.

§ 5
Rules for Cases Not Provided for in This Act

In any case not provided for in this act the rules of law and equity, including the law merchant, shall govern.

Part II/Nature of Partnership
§ 6
Partnership Defined

(1) A partnership is an association of two or more persons to carry on as co-owners a business for profit.

(2) But any association formed under any other statute of this state, or any statute adopted by authority, other than the authority of this state, is not a partnership under this act, unless such association would have been a partnership in this state prior to the adoption of this act; but this act shall apply to limited partnerships except in so far as the statutes relating to such partnerships are inconsistent herewith.

§ 7
Rules for Determining the Existence of a Partnership

In determining whether a partnership exists, these rules shall apply:

(1) Except as provided by section 16 persons who are not partners as to each other are not partners as to third persons.

(2) Joint tenancy, tenancy in common, tenancy by the entireties, joint property, common property, or part ownership does not of itself establish a partnership, whether such co-owners do or do not share any profits made by the use of the property.

(3) The sharing of gross returns does not of itself establish a partnership, whether or not the persons sharing them have a joint or common right or interest in any property from which the returns are derived.

(4) The receipt by a person of a share of the profits of a business is prima facie evidence that he is a partner in the business, but no such inference shall be drawn if such profits were received in payment:

    (a) As a debt by installments or otherwise,

    (b) As wages of an employee or rent to a landlord,

    (c) As an annuity to a widow or representative of a deceased partner,

    (d) As interest on a loan, though the amount of payment vary with the profits of the business,

    (e) As the consideration for the sale of a good-will of a business or other property by installments or otherwise.

§ 8
Partnership Property

(1)   All property originally brought into the partnership stock or subsequently acquired by purchase or otherwise, on account of the partnership, is partnership property.

(2)   Unless the contrary intention appears, property acquired with partnership funds is partnership property.

(3)   Any estate in real property may be acquired in the partnership name. Title so acquired can be conveyed only in the partnership name.

(4)   A conveyance to a partnership in the partnership name, though without words of inheritance, passes the entire estate of the grantor unless a contrary intent appears.

Part III/Relations of Partners to Persons Dealing with the Partnership
§ 9
Partner Agent of Partnership as to Partnership Business

(1)   Every partner is an agent of the partnership for the purpose of its business, and the act of every partner, including the execution in the partnership name of any instrument, for apparently carrying on in the usual way the business of the partnership of which he is a member binds the partnership, unless the partner so acting has in fact no authority to act for the partnership in the particular matter, and the person with whom he is dealing has knowledge of the fact that he has no such authority.

(2)   An act of a partner which is not apparently for the carrying on of the business of the partnership in the usual way does not bind the partnership unless authorized by the other partners.

(3)   Unless authorized by the other partners or unless they have abandoned the business, one or more but less than all the partners have no authority to:

    (a)   Assign the partnership property in trust for creditors or on the assignee's promise to pay the debts of the partnership,

    (b)   Dispose of the goodwill of the business,

    (c)   Do any other act which would make it impossible to carry on the ordinary business of a partnership,

    (d)   Confess a judgment,

    (e)   Submit a partnership claim or liability to arbitration or reference.

(4)   No act of a partner in contravention of a restriction on authority shall bind the partnership to persons having knowledge of the restriction.

§ 10
Conveyance of Real Property of the Partnership

(1)   Where title to real property is in the partnership name, any partner may convey title to such property by a conveyance executed in the partnership name; but the partnership may recover such property unless the partner's act binds the partnership under the provisions of paragraph (1) of section 9, or unless such property has been conveyed by the grantee or a person claiming through such grantee to a holder for value without knowledge that the partner, in making the conveyance, has exceeded his authority.

(2)   Where title to real property is in the name of the partnership, a conveyance executed by a partner, in his own name, passes the equitable interest of the partnership, provided the act is one within the authority of the partner under the provisions of paragraph (1) of section 9.

(3)   Where title to real property is in the name of one or more but not all the partners, and the record does not disclose the right of the partnership, the partners in whose name the title stands may convey title to such property, but the partnership may recover such property if the partners' act does not bind the partnership under the provisions of paragraph (1) of section 9, unless the purchaser or his assignee, is a holder for value, without knowledge.

(4)   Where the title to real property is in the name of one or more or all the partners, or in a third person in trust for the partnership, a conveyance executed by a partner in the partnership name, or in his own name, passes the equitable interest of the partnership, provided the act is one within the authority of the partner under the provisions of paragraph (1) of section 9.

(5)   Where the title to real property is in the names of all the partners a conveyance executed by all the partners passes all their rights in such property.

§ 11
Partnership Bound by Admission of Partner

An admission or representation made by any partner concerning partnership affairs within the scope of his authority as conferred by this act is evidence against the partnership.

§ 12
Partnership Charged with Knowledge of or Notice to Partner

Notice to any partner of any matter relating to partnership affairs, and the knowledge of the partner acting in the particular matter, acquired while a partner or then present to his mind, and the knowledge of any other partner who reasonably could and should have communicated it to the acting partner, operate as notice to or knowledge of the partnership, except in the case of a fraud on the partnership committed by or with the consent of that partner.

§ 13
Partnership Bound by Partner's Wrongful Act

Where, by any wrongful act or omission of any partner acting in the ordinary course of the business of the partnership or with the authority of his co-partners, loss or injury is caused to any person, not being a partner in the partnership, or any penalty is incurred, the partnership is liable therefor to the same extent as the partner so acting or omitting to act.

§ 14
Partnership Bound by Partner's Breach of Trust

The partnership is bound to make good the loss:

    (a)   Where one partner acting within the scope of his apparent authority receives money or property of a third person and misapplies it; and

    (b)   Where the partnership in the course of its business receives money or property of a third person and the money or property so received is misapplied by any partner while it is in the custody of the partnership.

§ 15
Nature of Partner's Liability

All partners are liable

(a)   Jointly and severally for everything chargeable to the partnership under sections 13 and 14.

(b)   Jointly for all other debts and obligations of the partnership; but any partner may enter into a separate obligation to perform a partnership contract.

§ 16
Partner by Estoppel

(1)   When a person, by words spoken or written or by conduct, represents himself, or consents to another representing him to any one, as a partner in an existing partnership or with one or more persons not actual partners, he is liable to any such person to whom such representation has been made, who has, on the faith of such representation, given credit to the actual or apparent partnership, and if he has made such representation or consented to its being made in a public manner he is liable to such person, whether the representation has or has not been made or communicated to such person so giving credit by or with the knowledge of the apparent partner making the representation or consenting to its being made.

(a)   When a partnership liability results, he is liable as though he were an actual member of the partnership.

(b)   When no partnership liability results, he is liable jointly with the other persons, if any, so consenting to the contract or representation as to incur liability, otherwise separately.

(2)   When a person has been thus represented to be a partner in an existing partnership, or with one or more persons not actual partners, he is an agent of the persons consenting to such representation to bind them to the same extent and in the same manner as though he were a partner in fact, with respect to persons who rely upon the representation. Where all the members of the existing partnership consent to the representation, a partnership act or obligation results; but in all other cases it is the joint act or obligation of the person acting and the persons consenting to the representation.

§ 17
Liability of Incoming Partner

A person admitted as a partner into an existing partnership is liable for all the obligations of the partnership arising before his admission as though he had been a partner when such obligations were incurred, except that this liability shall be satisfied only out of partnership property.

Part IV/Relations of Partners to One Another
§ 18
Rules Determining Rights and Duties of Partners

The rights and duties of the partners in relation to the partnership shall be determined, subject to any agreement between them, by the following rules:

(a)   Each partner shall be repaid his contributions, whether by way of capital or advances to the partnership property and share equally in the profits and surplus remaining after all liabilities, including those to partners, are satisfied; and must contribute towards the losses, whether of capital or otherwise, sustained by the partnership according to his share in the profits.

(b)   The partnership must indemnify every partner in respect of payments made and personal liabilities reasonably incurred by him in the ordinary and proper conduct of its business, or for the preservation of its business or property.

(c)   A partner, who in aid of the partnership makes any payment or advance beyond the amount of capital which he agreed to contribute, shall be paid interest from the date of the payment or advance.

(d)   A partner shall receive interest on the capital contributed by him only from the date when repayment should be made.

(e)   All partners have equal rights in the management and conduct of the partnership business.

(f)   No partner is entitled to remuneration for acting in the partnership business, except that a surviving partner is entitled to reasonable compensation for his services in winding up the partnership affairs.

(g)   No person can become a member of a partnership without the consent of all the partners.

(h)   Any difference arising as to ordinary matters connected with the partnership business may be decided by a majority of the partners; but no act in contravention of any agreement between the partners may be done rightfully without the consent of all the partners.

§ 19
Partnership Books

The partnership books shall be kept, subject to any agreement between the partners, at the principal place of business of the partnership, and every partner shall at all times have access to and may inspect and copy any of them.

§ 20
Duty of Partners to Render Information

Partners shall render on demand true and full information of all things affecting the partnership to any partner or the legal representative of any deceased partner or partner under legal disability.

§ 21
Partner Accountable as a Fiduciary

(1)   Every partner must account to the partnership for any benefit, and hold as trustee for it any profits derived by him without the consent of the other partners from any transaction connected with the formation, conduct, or liquidation of the partnership or from any use by him of its property.

(2)   This section applies also to the representatives of a deceased partner engaged in the liquidation of the affairs of the partnership as the personal representatives of the last surviving partner.

§ 22
Right to an Account

Any partner shall have the right to a formal account as to partnership affairs:

(a) If he is wrongfully excluded from the partnership business or possession of its property by his co-partners,

(b) If the right exists under the terms of any agreement,

(c) As provided by section 21,

(d) Whenever other circumstances render it just and reasonable.

§ 23
Continuation of Partnership beyond Fixed Term

(1) When a partnership for a fixed term or particular undertaking is continued after the termination of such term or particular undertaking without any express agreement, the rights and duties of the partners remain the same as they were at such termination, so far as is consistent with a partnership at will.

(2) A continuation of the business by the partners or such of them as habitually acted therein during the term, without any settlement or liquidation of the partnership affairs, is prima facie evidence of a continuation of the partnership.

Part V/Property Rights of a Partner
§ 24
Extent of Property Rights of a Partner

The property rights of a partner are (1) his rights in specific partnership property, (2) his interest in the partnership, and (3) his right to participate in the management.

§ 25
Nature of a Partner's Right in Specific Partnership Property

(1) A partner is co-owner with his partners of specific partnership property holding as a tenant in partnership.

(2) The incidents of this tenancy are such that:

(a) A partner, subject to the provisions of this act and to any agreement between the partners, has an equal right with his partners to possess specific partnership property for partnership purposes; but he has no right to possess such property for any other purpose without the consent of his partners.

(b) A partner's right in specific partnership property is not assignable except in connection with the assignment of rights of all the partners in the same property.

(c) A partner's right in specific partnership property is not subject to attachment or execution, except on a claim against the partnership. When partnership property is attached for a partnership debt the partners, or any of them, or the representatives of a deceased partner, cannot claim any right under the homestead or exemption laws.

(d) On the death of a partner his right in specific partnership property vests in the surviving partner or partners, except where the deceased was the last surviving partner, when his right in such property vests in his legal representative. Such surviving partner or partners, or the legal representative of the last surviving partner, has no right to possess the partnership property for any but a partnership purpose.

(e) A partner's right in specific partnership property is not subject to dower, curtesy, or allowances to widows, heirs, or next of kin.

§ 26
Nature of Partner's Interest in the Partnership

A partner's interest in the partnership is his share of the profits and surplus, and the same is personal property.

§ 27
Assignment of Partner's Interest

(1) A conveyance by a partner of his interest in the partnership does not of itself dissolve the partnership, nor, as against the other partners in the absence of agreement, entitle the assignee, during the continuance of the partnership, to interfere in the management or administration of the partnership business or affairs, or to require any information or account of partnership transactions, or to inspect the partnership books; but it merely entitles the assignee to receive in accordance with his contract the profits to which the assigning partner would otherwise be entitled.

(2) In case of a dissolution of the partnership, the assignee is entitled to receive his assignor's interest and may require an account from the date only of the last account agreed to by all the partners.

§ 28
Partner's Interest Subject to Charging Order

(1) On due application to a competent court by any judgment creditor of a partner, the court which entered the judgment, order, or decree, or any other court, may charge the interest of the debtor partner with payment of the unsatisfied amount of such judgment debt with interest thereon; and may then or later appoint a receiver of his share of the profits, and of any other money due or to fall due to him in respect of the partnership, and make all other orders, directions, accounts and inquiries which the debtor partner might have made, or which the circumstances of the case may require.

(2) The interest charged may be redeemed at any time before foreclosure, or in case of a sale being directed by the court may be purchased without thereby causing a dissolution:

(a) With separate property, by any one or more of the partners, or

(b) With partnership property, by any one or more of the partners with the consent of all the partners whose interests are not so charged or sold.

(3) Nothing in this act shall be held to deprive a partner of his right, if any, under the exemption laws, as regards his interest in the partnership.

Part VI/Dissolution and Winding Up
§ 29
Dissolution Defined

The dissolution of a partnership is the change in the relation of the partners caused by any partner ceasing to be associated in the carrying on as distinguished from the winding up of the business.

§ 30
Partnership not Terminated by Dissolution

On dissolution the partnership is not terminated, but continues until the winding up of partnership affairs is completed.

§ 31
Causes of Dissolution

Dissolution is caused:

(1) Without violation of the agreement between the partners,
(a) By the termination of the definite term or particular undertaking specified in the agreement,
(b) By the express will of any partner when no definite term or particular undertaking is specified,
(c) By the express will of all the partners who have not assigned their interests or suffered them to be charged for their separate debts, either before or after the termination of any specified term or particular undertaking,
(d) By the expulsion of any partner from the business bona fide in accordance with such a power conferred by the agreement between the partners;

(2) In contravention of the agreement between the partners, where the circumstances do not permit a dissolution under any other provision of this section, by the express will of any partner at any time;

(3) By any event which makes it unlawful for the business of the partnership to be carried on or for the members to carry it on in partnership;

(4) By the death of any partner;

(5) By the bankruptcy of any partner or the partnership;

(6) By decree of court under section 32.

§ 32
Dissolution by Decree of Court

(1) On application by or for a partner the court shall decree a dissolution whenever:
(a) A partner has been declared a lunatic in any judicial proceeding or is shown to be of unsound mind,
(b) A partner becomes in any other way incapable of performing his part of the partnership contract,
(c) A partner has been guilty of such conduct as tends to affect prejudicially the carrying on of the business,
(d) A partner wilfully or persistently commits a breach of the partnership agreement, or otherwise so conducts himself in matters relating to the partnership business that it is not reasonably practicable to carry on the business in partnership with him,
(e) The business of the partnership can only be carried on at a loss,
(f) Other circumstances render a dissolution equitable.

(2) On the application of the purchaser of a partner's interest under sections 28 or 29:
(a) After the termination of the specified term or particular undertaking,
(b) At any time if the partnership was a partnership at will when the interest was assigned or when the charging order was issued.

§ 33
General Effect of Dissolution on Authority of Partner

Except so far as may be necessary to wind up partnership affairs or to complete transactions begun but not then finished, dissolution terminates all authority of any partner to act for the partnership,

(1) With respect to the partners,
(a) When the dissolution is not by the act, bankruptcy or death of a partner; or
(b) When the dissolution is by such act, bankruptcy or death of a partner, in cases where section 34 so requires.

(2) With respect to persons not partners, as declared in section 35.

§ 34
Right of Partner to Contribution from Co-partners after Dissolution

Where the dissolution is caused by the act, death or bankruptcy of a partner, each partner is liable to his co-partners for his share of any liability created by any partner acting for the partnership as if the partnership had not been dissolved unless
(a) The dissolution being by act of any partner, the partner acting for the partnership had knowledge of the dissolution, or
(b) The dissolution being by the death or bankruptcy of a partner, the partner acting for the partnership had knowledge or notice of the death or bankruptcy.

§ 35
Power of Partner to Bind Partnership to Third Persons after Dissolution

(1) After dissolution a partner can bind the partnership except as provided in Paragraph (3)
(a) By any act appropriate for winding up partnership affairs or completing transactions unfinished at dissolution;
(b) By any transaction which would bind the partnership if dissolution had not taken place, provided the other party to the transaction
(I) Had extended credit to the partnership prior to dissolution and had no knowledge or notice of the dissolution; or
(II) Though he had not so extended credit, had nevertheless known of the partnership prior to dissolution, and, having no knowledge or notice of dissolution, the fact of dissolution had not been advertised in a newspaper of general circulation in the place (or in each place if more than one) at which the partnership business was regularly carried on.

(2) The liability of a partner under Paragraph (1b) shall be satisfied out of partnership assets alone when such partner had been prior to dissolution
(a) Unknown as a partner to the person with whom the contract is made; and
(b) So far unknown and inactive in partnership affairs that the business reputation of the partnership could not be said to have been in any degree due to his connection with it.

(3) The partnership is in no case bound by any act of a partner after dissolution

(a) Where the partnership is dissolved because it is unlawful to carry on the business, unless the act is appropriate for winding up partnership affairs; or

(b) Where the partner has become bankrupt; or

(c) Where the partner has no authority to wind up partnership affairs; except by a transaction with one who

(I) Had extended credit to the partnership prior to dissolution and had no knowledge or notice of his want of authority; or

(II) Had not extended credit to the partnership prior to dissolution, and, having no knowledge or notice of his want of authority, the fact of his want of authority has not been advertised in the manner provided for advertising the fact of dissolution in Paragraph (1bII).

(4) Nothing in this section shall affect the liability under Section 16 of any person who after dissolution represents himself or consents to another representing him as a partner in a partnership engaged in carrying on business.

§ 36
Effect of Dissolution on Partner's Existing Liability

(1) The dissolution of the partnership does not of itself discharge the existing liability of any partner.

(2) A partner is discharged from any existing liability upon dissolution of the partnership by an agreement to that effect between himself, the partnership creditor and the person or partnership continuing the business; and such agreement may be inferred from the course of dealing between the creditor having knowledge of the dissolution and the person or partnership continuing the business.

(3) Where a person agrees to assume the existing obligations of a dissolved partnership, the partners whose obligations have been assumed shall be discharged from any liability to any creditor of the partnership who, knowing of the agreement, consents to a material alteration in the nature or time of payment of such obligations.

(4) The individual property of a deceased partner shall be liable for all obligations of the partnership incurred while he was a partner but subject to the prior payment of his separate debts.

§ 37
Right to Wind Up

Unless otherwise agreed the partners who have not wrongfully dissolved the partnership or the legal representative of the last surviving partner, not bankrupt, has the right to wind up the partnership affairs; provided, however, that any partner, his legal representative or his assignee, upon cause shown, may obtain winding up by the court.

§ 38
Rights of Partners to Application of Partnership Property

(1) When dissolution is caused in any way, except in contravention of the partnership agreement, each partner, as against his copartners and all persons claiming through them in respect of their interests in the partnership, unless otherwise agreed, may have

the partnership property applied to discharge its liabilities, and the surplus applied to pay in cash the net amount owing to the respective partners. But if dissolution is caused by expulsion of a partner, bona fide under the partnership agreement and if the expelled partner is discharged from all partnership liabilities, either by payment or agreement under section 36(2), he shall receive in cash only the net amount due him from the partnership.

(2) When dissolution is caused in contravention of the partnership agreement the rights of the partners shall be as follows:

(a) Each partner who has not caused dissolution wrongfully shall have,

(I) All the rights specified in paragraph (1) of this section, and

(II) The right, as against each partner who has caused the dissolution wrongfully, to damages for breach of the agreement.

(b) The partners who have not caused the dissolution wrongfully, if they all desire to continue the business in the same name, either by themselves or jointly with others, may do so, during the agreed term for the partnership and for that purpose may possess the partnership property, provided they secure the payment by bond approved by the court, or pay to any partner who has caused the dissolution wrongfully, the value of his interest in the partnership at the dissolution, less any damages recoverable under clause (2aII) of this section, and in like manner indemnify him against all present or future partnership liabilities.

(c) A partner who has caused the dissolution wrongfully shall have:

(I) If the business is not continued under the provisions of paragraph (2b) all the rights of a partner under paragraph (1), subject to clause (2aII), of this section,

(II) If the business is continued under paragraph (2b) of this section the right as against his co-partners and all claiming through them in respect of their interests in the partnership, to have the value of his interest in the partnership, less any damages caused to his co-partners by the dissolution, ascertained and paid to him in cash, or the payment secured by bond approved by the court, and to be released from all existing liabilities of the partnership; but in ascertaining the value of the partner's interest the value of the goodwill of the business shall not be considered.

§ 39
Rights Where Partnership Is Dissolved for Fraud or Misrepresentation

Where a partnership contract is rescinded on the ground of the fraud or misrepresentation of one of the parties thereto, the party entitled to rescind is, without prejudice to any other right, entitled,

(a) To a lien on, or a right of retention of, the surplus of the partnership property after satisfying the partnership liabilities to third persons for any sum of money paid by him for the purchase of an interest in the partnership and for any capital or advances contributed by him; and

(b) To stand, after all liabilities to third persons have been satisfied, in the place of the creditors of the partnership for any payments made by him in respect of the partnership liabilities; and

(c)   To be indemnified by the person guilty of the fraud or making the representation against all debts and liabilities of the partnership.

§ 40
Rules for Distribution

In settling accounts between the partners after dissolution, the following rules shall be observed, subject to any agreement to the contrary:

(a)   The assets of the partnership are:
    (I)   The partnership property,
    (II) The contributions of the partners necessary for the payment of all the liabilities specified in clause (b) of this paragraph.
(b)   The liabilities of the partnership shall rank in order of payment, as follows:
    (I)   Those owing to creditors other than partners,
    (II) Those owing to partners other than for capital and profits,
    (III) Those owing to partners in respect of capital,
    (IV) Those owing to partners in respect of profits.
(c)   The assets shall be applied in order of their declaration in clause (a) of this paragraph to the satisfaction of the liabilities.
(d)   The partners shall contribute, as provided by section 18 (a) the amount necessary to satisfy the liabilities; but if any, but not all, of the partners are insolvent, or, not being subject to process, refuse to contribute, the other partners shall contribute their share of the liabilities, and, in the relative proportions in which they share the profits, the additional amount necessary to pay the liabilities.
(e)   An assignee for the benefit of creditors or any person appointed by the court shall have the right to enforce the contributions specified in clause (d) of this paragraph.
(f)   Any partner or his legal representative shall have the right to enforce the contributions specified in clause (d) of this paragraph, to the extent of the amount which he has paid in excess of his share of the liability.
(g)   The individual property of a deceased partner shall be liable for the contributions specified in clause (d) of this paragraph.
(h)   When partnership property and the individual properties of the partners are in possession of a court for distribution, partnership creditors shall have priority on partnership property and separate creditors on individual property, saving the rights of lien or secured creditors as heretofore.
(i)   Where a partner has become bankrupt or his estate is insolvent the claims against his separate property shall rank in the following order:
    (I)   Those owing to separate creditors,
    (II) Those owing to partnership creditors,
    (III) Those owing to partners by way of contribution.

§ 41
Liability of Persons Continuing the Business in Certain Cases

(1)   When any new partner is admitted into an existing partnership, or when any partner retires and assigns (or the representative of the deceased partner assigns) his rights in partnership property to two or more of the partners, or to one or more of the partners and one or more third persons, if the business is continued without liquidation of the partnership affairs, creditors of the first or dissolved partnership are also creditors of the partnership so continuing the business.

(2)   When all but one partner retire and assign (or the representative of a deceased partner assigns) their rights in partnership property to the remaining partner, who continues the business without liquidation of partnership affairs, either alone or with others, creditors of the dissolved partnership are also creditors of the person or partnership so continuing the business.

(3)   When any partner retires or dies and the business of the dissolved partnership is continued as set forth in paragraphs (1) and (2) of this section, with the consent of the retired partners or the representative of the deceased partner, but without any assignment of his right in partnership property, rights of creditors of the dissolved partnership and of the creditors of the person or partnership continuing the business shall be as if such assignment had been made.

(4)   When all the partners or their representatives assign their rights in partnership property to one or more third persons who promise to pay the debts and who continue the business of the dissolved partnership, creditors of the dissolved partnership are also creditors of the person or partnership continuing the business.

(5)   When any partner wrongfully causes a dissolution and the remaining partners continue the business under the provisions of section 38(2b), either alone or with others, and without liquidation of the partnership affairs, creditors of the dissolved partnership are also creditors of the person or partnership continuing the business.

(6)   When a partner is expelled and the remaining partners continue the business either alone or with others, without liquidation of the partnership affairs, creditors of the dissolved partnership are also creditors of the person or partnership continuing the business.

(7)   The liability of a third person becoming a partner in the partnership continuing the business, under this section, to the creditors of the dissolved partnership shall be satisfied out of partnership property only.

(8)   When the business of a partnership after dissolution is continued under any conditions set forth in this section the creditors of the dissolved partnership, as against the separate creditors of the retiring or deceased partner or the representative of the deceased partner, have a prior right to any claim of the retired partner or the representative of the deceased partner against the person or partnership continuing the business, on account of the retired or deceased partner's interest in the dissolved partnership or on account of any consideration promised for such interest or for his right in partnership property.

(9)   Nothing in this section shall be held to modify any right of creditors to set aside any assignment on the ground of fraud.

(10) The use by the person or partnership continuing the business of the partnership name, or the name of a deceased partner as part thereof, shall not of itself make the individual property of the deceased partner liable for any debts contracted by such person or partnership.

§ 42
Rights of Retiring or Estate of Deceased Partner When the Business Is Continued

When any partner retires or dies, and the business is continued under any of the conditions set forth in section 41(1, 2, 3, 5, 6), or section 38(2b) without any settlement of accounts as between him or his estate and the person or partnership continuing the business, unless otherwise agreed, he or his legal representative as against such persons or partnership may have the value of his interest at the date of dissolution ascertained, and shall receive as an ordinary creditor an amount equal to the value of his interest in the dissolved partnership with interest, or, at his option or at the option of his legal representative, in lieu of interest, the profits attributable to the use of his right in the property of the dissolved partnership; provided that the creditors of the dissolved partnership as against the separate creditors, or the representative of the retired or deceased partner, shall have priority on any claim arising under this section, as provided by section 41(8) of this act.

§ 43
Accrual of Actions

The right to an account of his interest shall accrue to any partner, or his legal representative, as against the winding up partners or the surviving partners or the person or partnership continuing the business, at the date of dissolution, in the absence of any agreement to the contrary.

Part VII/Miscellaneous Provisions
§ 44
When Act Takes Effect

This act shall take effect on the . . . . day of . . . . one thousand ninehundred and . . . .

§ 45
Legislation Repealed

All acts or parts of acts inconsistent with this act are hereby repealed.

Appendix C

Revised Uniform Limited Partnership Act (1976) with the 1985 Amendments

ARTICLE 1/GENERAL PROVISIONS
§ 101
Definitions

As used in this Act, unless the context otherwise requires:

(1) "Certificate of limited partnership" means the certificate referred to in Section 201, and the certificate as amended or restated.

(2) "Contribution" means any cash, property, services rendered, or a promissory note or other binding obligation to contribute cash or property or to perform services, which a partner contributes to a limited partnership in his capacity as a partner.

(3) "Event of withdrawal of a general partner" means an event that causes a person to cease to be a general partner as provided in Section 402.

(4) "Foreign limited partnership" means a partnership formed under the laws of any state other than this State and having as partners one or more general partners and one or more limited partners.

(5) "General partner" means a person who has been admitted to a limited partnership as a general partner in accordance with the partnership agreement and named in the certificate of limited partnership as a general partner.

(6) "Limited partner" means a person who has been admitted to a limited partnership as a limited partner in accordance with the partnership agreement.

(7) "Limited partnership" and "domestic limited partnership" means a partnership formed by 2 or more persons under the laws of this State and having one or more general partners and one or more limited partners.

(8) "Partner" means a limited or general partner.

(9) "Partnership agreement" means any valid agreement, written or oral, of the partners as to the affairs of a limited partnership and the conduct of its business.

(10) "Partnership interest" means a partner's share of the profits and losses of a limited partnership and the right to receive distributions of partnership assets.

(11) "Person" means a natural person, partnership, limited partnership (domestic or foreign) trust, estate, association, or corporation.

(12) "State" means a state, territory, or possession of the United States, the District of Columbia, or the Commonwealth of Puerto Rico.

§ 102
Name

The name of each limited partnership as set forth in its certificate of limited partnership:

(1) shall contain without abbreviation the words "limited partnership";

(2) may not contain the name of a limited partner unless (i) it is also the name of a general partner or the corporate name of a corporate general partner, or (ii) the business of the limited partnership had been carried on under that name before the admission of that limited partner.

(3) may not be the same as, or deceptively similar to, the name of any corporation or limited partnership organized under the laws of this State or licensed or registered as a foreign corporation or limited partnership in this State; and

(4) may not contain the following words [here insert prohibited words].

§ 103
Reservation of Name

(a) The exclusive right to the use of a name may be reserved by:

(1) any person intending to organize a limited partnership under this Act and to adopt that name;

(2) any domestic limited partnership or any foreign limited partnership registered in this State which, in either case, intends to adopt that name;

(3) any foreign limited partnership intending to register in this State and adopt that name; and

(4) any person intending to organize a foreign limited partnership and intending to have it register in this State and adopt that name.

(b) The reservation shall be made by filing with the Secretary of State an application, executed by the applicant, to reserve a specified name. If the Secretary of State finds that the name is available for use by a domestic or foreign limited partnership, he shall reserve the name for the exclusive use of the applicant for a period of 120 days. Once having so reserved a name, the same applicant may not again reserve the same name until more than 60 days after the expiration of the last 120-day period for which that applicant reserved that name. The right to the exclusive use of a reserved name may be transferred to any other person by filing in the office of the Secretary of State a notice of the transfer, executed by the applicant for whom the name was reserved and specifying the name and address of the transferee.

§ 104
Specified Office and Agent

Each limited partnership shall continuously maintain in this State;

(1) an office, which may but need not be a place of its business in this State, at which shall be kept the records required by Section 105 to be maintained; and

(2) an agent for service of process on the limited partnership, which agent must be an individual resident of this State, a domestic corporation, or a foreign corporation authorized to do business in this State.

§ 105
Records to Be Kept

(a) Each limited partnership shall keep at the office referred to in Section 104(1) the following:

(1) a current list of the full name and last known business address of each partner, separately identifying the general partners (in alphabetical order) and the limited partners (in alphabetical order);

(2) a copy of the certificate of limited partnership and all certificates of amendment thereto, together with executed copies of any powers of attorney pursuant to which any certificate has been executed;

(3) copies of the limited partnership's federal, state and local income tax returns and reports, if any, for the 3 most recent years;

(4) copies of any then effective written partnership agreements and of any financial statements of the limited partnership for the 3 most recent years; and

(5) unless contained in a written partnership agreement, a writing setting out:

(i) the amount of cash and a description and statement of the agreed value of the other property or services contributed by each partner and which each partner has agreed to contribute;

(ii) the times at which or events on the happening of which any additional contributions agreed to be made by each partner are to be made;

(iii) any right of a partner to receive, or of a general partner to make, distributions to a partner which include a return of all or any part of the partner's contribution; and

(iv) any events upon the happening of which the limited partnership is to be dissolved and its affairs wound up.

(b) Records kept under this section are subject to inspection and copying at the reasonable request and at the expense of any partner during ordinary business hours.

§ 106
Nature of Business

A limited partnership may carry on any business that a partnership without limited partners may carry on except [here designate prohibited activities.]

§ 107
Business Transactions of Partner with the Partnership

Except as provided in the partnership agreement, a partner may lend money to and transact other business with the limited partnership and, subject to other applicable law, has the same rights and obligations with respect thereto as a person who is not a partner.

ARTICLE 2/FORMATION: CERTIFICATE OF LIMITED PARTNERSHIP
§ 201
Certificate of Limited Partnership

(a) In order to form a limited partnership, a certificate of limited partnership must be executed and filed in the office of the Secretary of State. The certificate shall set forth:

(1) the name of the limited partnership;

(2) the address of the office and the name and address of the agent for service of process required to be maintained by Section 104;

(3) the name and the business address of each general partner;

(4) the latest date upon which the limited partnership is to dissolve; and

(5) any other matters the general partners determine to include therein.

(b) A limited partnership is formed at the time of the filing of the certificate of limited partnership in the office of the Secretary of State or at any later time specified in the certificate of limited partnership if, in either case, there has been substantial compliance with the requirements of this section.

§ 202
Amendment to Certificate

(a) A certificate of limited partnership is amended by filing a certificate of amendment thereto in the office of the Secretary of State. The certificate shall set forth:

(1) the name of the limited partnership;

(2) the date of filing the certificate; and

(3) the amendment to the certificate.

(b) Within 30 days after the happening of any of the following events an amendment to a certificate of limited partnership reflecting the occurrence of the event or events shall be filed:

(1) the admission of a new general partner;

(2) the withdrawal of a general partner; or

(3) the continuation of the business under Section 801 after an event of withdrawal of a general partner.

(c) A general partner who becomes aware that any statement in a certificate of limited partnership was false when made or that any arrangements or other facts described have changed, making the certificate inaccurate in any respect, shall promptly amend the certificate.

(d) A certificate of limited partnership may be amended at any time for any other proper purpose the general partners determine.

(e) No person has any liability because an amendment to a certificate of limited partnership has not been filed to reflect the occurrence of any event referred to in subsection (b) of this section if the amendment is filed within the 30-day period specified in subsection (b).

(f) A restated certificate of limited partnership may be executed and filed in the same manner as a certificate of amendment.

§ 203
Cancellation of Certificate

A certificate of limited partnership shall be cancelled upon the dissolution and the commencement of winding up of the partnership or at any other time there are no limited partners. A certificate of cancellation shall be filed in the office of the Secretary of State and set forth:

(1)   the name of the limited partnership;

(2)   the date of filing of its certificate of limited partnership

(3)   the reason for filing the certificate of cancellation;

(4)   the effective date (which shall be a date certain) of cancellation if it is not to be effective upon the filing of the certificate; and

(5)   any other information the general partners filing the certificate determine.

§ 204
Execution of Certificates

(a)   Each certificate required by this Article to be filed in the office of the Secretary of State shall be executed in the following manner:

(1)   an original certificate of limited partnership must be signed by all general partners;

(2)   a certificate of amendment must be signed by at least one general partner and by each other general partner designated in the certificate as a new general partner;

(3)   a certificate of cancellation must be signed by all general partners.

(b)   Any person may sign a certificate by an attorney-in-fact, but a power of attorney to sign a certificate relating to the admission of a partner must specifically describe the admission.

(c)   The execution of a certificate by a general partner constitutes an affirmation under the penalties of perjury that the facts stated therein are true.

§ 205
Execution by Judicial Act

If a person required by Section 204 to execute any certificate fails or refuses to do so, any other person who is adversely affected by the failure or refusal may petition the [designate the appropriate court] to direct the execution of the certificate. If the court finds that it is proper for the certificate to be executed and that any person so designated has failed or refused to execute the certificate, it shall order the Secretary of State to record an appropriate certificate.

§ 206
Filing in Office of Secretary of State

(a)   Two signed copies of the certificate of limited partnership and of any certificates of amendment or cancellation (or of any judicial decree of amendment or cancellation) shall be delivered to the Secretary of State. A person who executes a certificate as an agent or fiduciary need not exhibit evidence of his authority as a prerequisite to filing. Unless the Secretary of State finds that any certificate does not conform to law, upon receipt of all filing fees required by law he shall:

(1)   endorse on each duplicate original the word "Filed" and the day, month, and year of the filing thereof;

(2)   file one duplicate original in his office; and

(3)   return the other duplicate original to the person who filed it or his representative.

(b)   Upon the filing of a certificate of amendment (or judicial decree of amendment) in the office of the Secretary of State, the certificate of limited partnership shall be amended as set forth therein, and upon the effective date of a certificate of cancellation (or a judicial decree thereof), the certificate of limited partnership is cancelled.

§ 207
Liability for False Statement in Certificate

If any certificate of limited partnership or certificate of amendment or cancellation contains a false statement, one who suffers loss by reliance on the statement may recover damages for the loss from:

(1)   any person who executes the certificate, or causes another to execute it on his behalf, and knew, and any general partner who knew or should have known, the statement to be false at the time the certificate was executed; and

(2)   any general partner who thereafter knows or should have known that any arrangement or other fact described in the certificate has changed, making the statement inaccurate in any respect within a sufficient time before the statement was relied upon reasonably to have enabled that general partner to cancel or amend the certificate, or to file a petition for its cancellation or amendment under Section 205.

§ 208
Scope of Notice

The fact that a certificate of limited partnership is on file in the office of the Secretary of State is notice that the partnership is a limited partnership and the persons designated therein as general partners are general partners, but it is not notice of any other fact.

§ 209
Delivery of Certificates to Limited Partners

Upon the return by the Secretary of State pursuant to Section 206 of a certificate marked "Filed", the general partners shall promptly deliver or mail a copy of the certificate of limited partnership and each certificate of amendment or cancellation to each limited partner unless the partnership agreement provides otherwise.

ARTICLE 3/LIMITED PARTNERS
§ 301
Admission of Limited Partners

(a)   A person becomes a limited partner on the later of:

(1)   the date the original certificate of limited partnership is filed; or

(2)   the date stated in the records of the limited partnership as the date that person becomes a limited partner.

(b)   After the filing of a limited partnership's original certificate of limited partnership, a person may be admitted as an additional limited partner:

(1) in the case of a person acquiring a partnership interest directly from the limited partnership, upon compliance with the partnership agreement or, if the partnership agreement does not so provide, upon the written consent of all partners; and

(2) in the case of an assignee of a partnership interest of a partner who has the power, as provided in Section 704, to grant the assignee the right to become a limited partner, upon the exercise of that power and compliance with any conditions limiting the grant or exercise of the power.

§ 302
Voting

Subject to Section 303, the partnership agreement may grant to all or a specified group of the limited partners the right to vote (on a per capita or other basis) upon any matter.

§ 303
Liability to Third Parties

(a) Except as provided in subsection (d), a limited partner is not liable for the obligations of a limited partnership unless he is also a general partner or, in addition to the exercise of his rights and powers as a limited partner, he participates in the control of the business. However, if the limited partner participates in the control of the business, he is liable only to persons who transact business with the limited partnership reasonably believing, based upon the limited partner's conduct, that the limited partner is a general partner.

(b) A limited partner does not participate in the control of the business within the meaning of subsection (a) solely by doing one or more of the following:

(1) being a contractor for or an agent or employee of the limited partnership or of a general partner or being an officer, director, or shareholder of a general partner that is a corporation;

(2) consulting with and advising a general partner with respect to the business of the limited partnership;

(3) acting as surety for the limited partnership or guaranteeing or assuming one or more specific obligations of the limited partnership;

(4) taking any action required or permitted by law to bring or pursue a derivative action in the right of the limited partnership;

(5) requesting or attending a meeting of partners;

(6) proposing, approving, or disapproving, by voting or otherwise, one or more of the following matters:

(i) the dissolution and winding up of the limited partnership;

(ii) the sale, exchange, lease, mortgage, pledge, or other transfer of all or substantially all of the assets of the limited partnership;

(iii) the incurrence of indebtedness by the limited partnership other than in the ordinary course of its business;

(iv) a change in the nature of the business;

(v) the admission or removal of a general partner;

(vi) the admission or removal of a limited partner;

(vii) a transaction involving an actual or potential conflict of interest between a general partner and the limited partnership or the limited partners;

(viii) an amendment to the partnership agreement or certificate of limited partnership; or

(ix) matters related to the business of the limited partnership not otherwise enumerated in this subsection (b), which the partnership agreement states in writing may be subject to the approval or disapproval of limited partners;

(7) winding up the limited partnership pursuant to Section 803; or

(8) exercising any right or power permitted to limited partners under this Act and not specifically enumerated in this subsection (b).

(c) The enumeration in subsection (b) does not mean that the possession or exercise of any other powers by a limited partner constitutes participation by him in the business of the limited partnership.

(d) A limited partner who knowingly permits his name to be used in the name of the limited partnership, except under circumstances permitted by Section 102(2), is liable to creditors who extend credit to the limited partnership without actual knowledge that the limited partner is not a general partner.

§ 304
Person Erroneously Believing Himself [or Herself] Limited Partner

(a) Except as provided in subsection (b), a person who makes a contribution to a business enterprise and erroneously but in good faith believes that he has become a limited partner in the enterprise is not a general partner in the enterprise and is not bound by its obligations by reason of making the contribution, receiving distributions from the enterprise, or exercising any rights of a limited partner, if, on ascertaining the mistake, he:

(1) causes an appropriate certificate of limited partnership or a certificate of amendment to be executed and filed; or

(2) withdraws from future equity participation in the enterprise by executing and filing in the office of the Secretary of State a certificate declaring withdrawal under this section.

(b) A person who makes a contribution of the kind described in subsection (a) is liable as a general partner to any third party who transacts business with the enterprise (i) before the person withdraws and an appropriate certificate is filed to show withdrawal, or (ii) before an appropriate certificate is filed to show that he is not a general partner, but in either case only if the third party actually believed in good faith that the person was a general partner at the time of the transaction.

§ 305
Information

Each limited partner has the right to:

(1) inspect and copy any of the partnership records required to be maintained by Section 105; and

(2) obtain from the general partners from time to time upon reasonable demand (i) true and full information regarding the state of the business and financial condition of the limited partnership, (ii) promptly after becoming available, a copy of the limited partnership's federal, state and local income tax returns for each year, and (iii) other information regarding the affairs of the limited partnership as is just and reasonable.

ARTICLE 4/GENERAL PARTNERS
§ 401
Admission of Additional General Partners

After the filing of a limited partnership's original certificate of limited partnership, additional general partners may be admitted as provided in writing in the partnership agreement or, if the partnership agreement does not provide in writing for the admission of additional general partners, with the written consent of all partners.

§ 402
Events of Withdrawal

Except as approved by the specific written consent of all partners at the time, a person ceases to be a general partner of a limited partnership upon the happening of any of the following events:

(1)   the general partner withdraws from the limited partnership as provided in Section 602;

(2)   the general partner ceases to be a member of the limited partnership as provided in Section 702;

(3)   the general partner is removed as a general partner in accordance with the partnership agreement;

(4)   unless otherwise provided in writing in the partnership agreement, the general partner: (i) makes an assignment for the benefit of creditors; (ii) files a voluntary petition in bankruptcy; (iii) is adjudicated a bankrupt or insolvent; (iv) files a petition or answer seeking for himself any reorganization, arrangement, composition, readjustment, liquidation, dissolution or similar relief under any statute, law, or regulation; (v) files an answer or other pleading admitting or failing to contest the material allegations of a petition filed against him in any proceeding of this nature; or (vi) seeks, consents to, or acquiesces in the appointment of a trustee, receiver, or liquidator of the general partner or of all or any substantial part of his properties;

(5)   unless othewise provided in writing in the partnership agreement, [120] days after the commencement of any proceeding against the general partner seeking reorganization, arrangement, composition, readjustment, liquidation, dissolution or similar relief under any statute, law, or regulation, the proceeding has not been dismissed, or if within [90] days after the appointment without his consent or acquiescence of a trustee, receiver, or liquidator of the general partner or of all or any substantial part of his properties, the appointment is not vacated or stayed or within [90] days after the expiration of any such stay, the appointment is not vacated;

(6)   in the case of a general partner who is a natural person,
(i) his death; or
(ii) the entry of an order by a court of competent jurisdiction adjudicating him incompetent to manage his person or his estate;

(7)   in the case of a general partner who is acting as a general partner by virtue of being a trustee of a trust, the termination of the trust (but not merely the substitution of a new trustee);

(8)   in the case of a general partner that is a separate partnership, the dissolution and commencement of winding up of the separate partnership;

(9)   in the case of a general partner that is a corporation, the filing of a certificate of dissolution, or its equivalent, for the corporation or the revocation of its charter; or

(10)   in the case of an estate, the distribution by the fiduciary of the estate's entire interest in the partnership.

§ 403
General Powers and Liabilities

(a)   Except as provided in this Act or in the partnership agreement, a general partner of a limited partnership has the rights and powers and is subject to the restrictions of a partner in a partnership without limited partners.

(b)   Except as provided in this Act, a general partner of a limited partnership has the liabilities of a partner in a partnership without limited partners to persons other than the partnership and the other partners. Except as provided in this Act or in the partnership agreement, a general partner of a limited partnership has the liabilities of a partner in a partnership without limited partners to the partnership and to the other partners.

§ 404
Contributions by General Partner

A general partner of a limited partnership may make contributions to the partnership and share in the profits and losses of, and in distributions from, the limited partnership as a general partner. A general partner also may make contributions to and share in profits, losses, and distributions as a limited partner. A person who is both a general partner and a limited partner has the rights and powers, and is subject to the restrictions and liabilities, of a general partner and, except as provided in the partnership agreement, also has the powers, and is subject to the restrictions, of a limited partner to the extent of his participation in the partnership as a limited partner.

§ 405
Voting

The partnership agreement may grant to all or certain identified general partners the right to vote (on a per capita or any other basis), separately or with all or any class of the limited partners, on any matter.

ARTICLE 5/FINANCE
§ 501
Form of Contribution

The contribution of a partner may be in cash, property, or services rendered, or a promissory note or other obligation to contribute cash or property or to perform services.

§ 502
Liability for Contribution

(a)   A promise by a limited partner to contribute to the limited partnership is not enforceable unless set out in a writing signed by the limited partner.

(b)   Except as provided in the partnership agreement, a partner is obligated to the limited partnership to perform any enforceable promise to contribute cash or property or to perform services, even if he is unable to perform because of death, disability or any other reason. If a partner does not make the required contribution of property or services, he is obligated at the option of the limited partnership to contribute cash equal to that portion of the value, as stated in the partnership records required to be kept pursuant to Section 105, of the stated contribution which has not been made.

(c)   Unless otherwise provided in the partnership agreement, the obligation of a partner to make a contribution or return money or other property paid or distributed in violation of this Act may be compromised only by consent of all partners. Notwithstanding the compromise, a creditor of a limited partnership who extends credit or otherwise acts in reliance on that obligation after the partner signs a writing which reflects the obligation and before the amendment or cancellation thereof to reflect the compromise may enforce the original obligation.

§ 503
Sharing of Profits and Losses

The profits and losses of a limited partnership shall be allocated among the partners, and among classes of partners, in the manner provided in writing in the partnership agreement. If the partnership agreement does not so provide in writing, profits and losses shall be allocated on the basis of the value, as stated in the partnership records required to be kept pursuant to Section 105, of the contributions made by each partner to the extent they have been received by the partnership and have not been returned.

§ 504
Sharing of Distributions

Distributions of cash or other assets of a limited partnership shall be allocated among the partners and among classes of partners in the manner provided in writing in the partnership agreement. If the partnership agreement does not so provide in writing, distributions shall be made on the basis of the value, as stated in partnership records required to be kept pursuant to Section 105, of the contributions made by each partner to the extent they have been received by the partnership and have not been returned.

ARTICLE 6/DISTRIBUTIONS AND WITHDRAWAL
§ 601
Interim Distribution

Except as provided in this Article, a partner is entitled to receive distributions from a limited partnership before his withdrawal from the limited partnership and before the dissolution and winding up thereof to the extent and at the times or upon the happening of the events specified in the partnership agreement.

§ 602
Withdrawal of General Partner

A general partner may withdraw from a limited partnership at any time by giving written notice to the other partners, but if the withdrawal violates the partnership agreement, the limited partnership may recover from the withdrawing general partner damages

for breach of the partnership agreement and offset the damages against the amount otherwise distributable to him.

§ 603
Withdrawal of Limited Partner

A limited partner may withdraw from a limited partnership at the time or upon the happening of events specified in writing in the partnership agreement. If the agreement does not specify the time or the events upon the happening of which a limited partner may withdraw or a definite time for the dissolution and winding up of the limited partnership, a limited partner may withdraw upon not less than 6 months' prior written notice to each general partner at his address on the books of the limited partnership at its office in this State.

§ 604
Distribution Upon Withdrawal

Except as provided in this Article, upon withdrawal any withdrawing partner is entitled to receive any distribution to which he is entitled under the partnership agreement and, if not otherwise provided in the agreement, he is entitled to receive, within a reasonable time after withdrawal, the fair value of his interest in the limited partnership as of the date of withdrawal based upon his right to share in distributions from the limited partnership.

§ 605
Distribution in Kind

Except as provided in writing in the partnership agreement, a partner, regardless of the nature of his contribution, has no right to demand and receive any distribution from a limited partnership in any form other than cash. Except as provided in writing in the partnership agreement, a partner may not be compelled to accept a distribution of any asset in kind from a limited partnership to the extent that the percentage of the asset distributed to him exceeds a percentage of that asset which is equal to the percentage in which he shares in distributions from the limited partnership.

§ 606
Right to Distribution

At the time a partner becomes entitled to receive a distribution, he has the status of, and is entitled to all remedies available to, a creditor of the limited partnership with respect to the distribution.

§ 607
Limitations on Distribution

A partner may not receive a distribution from a limited partnership to the extent that, after giving effect to the distribution, all liabilities of the limited partnership, other than liabilities to partners on account of their partnership interests, exceed the fair value of the partnership assets.

§ 608
Liability Upon Return of Contribution

(a)   If a partner has received the return of any part of his contribution without violation of the partnership agreement or this

Act, he is liable to the limited partnership for a period of one year thereafter for the amount of the returned contribution, but only to the extent necessary to discharge the limited partnership's liabilities to creditors who extended credit to the limited partnership during the period the contribution was held by the partnership.

(b)   If a partner has received the return of any part of his contribution in violation of the partnership agreement or this Act, he is liable to the limited partnership for a period of 6 years thereafter for the amount of the contribution wrongfully returned.

(c)   A partner receives a return of his contribution to the extent that a distribution to him reduces his share of the fair value of the net assets of the limited partnership below the value, as set forth in the partnership records required to be kept pursuant to Section 105, of his contribution which has not been distributed to him.

ARTICLE 7/ASSIGNMENT OF PARTNERSHIP INTERESTS
§ 701
Nature of Partnership Interest

A partnership interest is personal property.

§ 702
Assignment of Partnership Interest

Except as provided in the partnership agreement, a partnership interest is assignable in whole or in part. An assignment of a partnership interest does not dissolve a limited partnership or entitle the assignee to become or to exercise any rights of a partner. An assignment entitles the assignee to receive, to the extent assigned, only the distribution to which the assignor would be entitled. Except as provided in the partnership agreement, a partner ceases to be a partner upon assignment of all his partnership interest.

§ 703
Rights of Creditor

On application to a court of competent jurisdiction by any judgment creditor of a partner, the court may charge the partnership interest of the partner with payment of the unsatisfied amount of the judgment with interest. To the extent so charged, the judgment creditor has only the rights of an assignee of the partnership interest. This Act does not deprive any partners of the benefit of any exemption laws applicable to his partnership interest.

§ 704
Right of Assignee to Become Limited Partner

(a)   An assignee of a partnership interest, including an assignee of a general partner, may become a limited partner if and to the extent that (i) the assignor gives the assignee that right in accordance with authority described in the partnership agreement, or (ii) all other partners consent.

(b)   An assignee who has become a limited partner has, to the extent assigned, the rights and powers, and is subject to the restrictions and liabilities, of a limited partner under the partnership agreement and this Act. An assignee who becomes a limited partner also is liable for the obligations of his assignor to make and return contributions as provided in Articles 5 and 6. However, the assignee is not obligated for liabilities unknown to the assignee at the time he became a limited partner.

(c)   If an assignee of a partnership interest becomes a limited partner, the assignor is not released from his liability to the limited partnership under Sections 207 and 502.

§ 705
Power of Estate of Deceased or Incompetent Partner

If a partner who is an individual dies or a court of competent jurisdiction adjudges him to be incompetent to manage his person or his property, the partner's executor, administrator, guardian, conservator, or other legal representative may exercise all of the partner's rights for the purpose of settling his estate or administering his property, including any power the partner had to give an assignee the right to become a limited partner. If a partner is a corporation, trust, or other entity and is dissolved or terminated, the powers of that partner may be exercised by its legal representative or successor.

ARTICLE 8/DISSOLUTION
§ 801
Nonjudicial Dissolution

A limited partnership is dissolved and its affairs shall be wound up upon the happening of the first to occur of the following:
   (1) at the time specified in the certificate of limited partnership;
   (2) upon the happening of events specified in writing in the partnership agreement;
   (3) written consent of all partners;
   (4) an event of withdrawal of a general partner unless at the time there is at least one other general partner and the written provisions of the partnership agreement permit the business of the limited partnership to be carried on by the remaining general partner and that partner does so, but the limited partnership is not dissolved and is not required to be wound up by reason of any event of withdrawal if, within 90 days after the withdrawal, all partners agree in writing to continue the business of the limited partnership and to the appointment of one or more additional general partners if necessary or desired; or
   (5) entry of a decree of judicial dissolution under Section 802.

§ 802
Judicial Dissolution

On application by or for a partner the [designate the appropriate court] court may decree dissolution of a limited partnership whenever it is not reasonably practicable to carry on the business in conformity with the partnership agreement.

§ 803
Winding Up

Except as provided in the partnership agreement, the general partners who have not wrongfully dissolved a limited partnership or, if none, the limited partners, may wind up the limited partnership's affairs; but the [designate the appropriate court] court may wind up the limited partnership's affairs upon application of any partner, his legal representative, or assignee.

§ 804
Distribution of Assets

Upon the winding up of a limited partnership, the assets shall be distributed as follows:

(1)   to creditors, including partners who are creditors, to the extent otherwise permitted by law, in satisfaction of liabilities of the limited partnership other than liabilities for distributions to partners under Section 601 or 604;

(2)   except as provided in the partnership agreement, to partners and former partners in satisfaction of liabilities for distributions under Section 601 and 604; and

(3)   except as provided in the partnership agreement, to partners first for the return of their contributions and secondly respecting their partnership interests, in the proportions in which the partners share in distributions.

ARTICLE 9/FOREIGN LIMITED PARTNERSHIPS
§ 901
Law Governing

Subject to the Constitution of this State, (i) the laws of the state under which a foreign limited partnership is organized govern its organization and internal affairs and the liability of its limited partners, and (ii) a foreign limited partnership may not be denied registration by reason of any difference between those laws and the laws of this State.

§ 902
Registration

Before transacting business in this State, a foreign limited partnership shall register with the Secretary of State. In order to register, a foreign limited partnership shall submit to the Secretary of State, in duplicate, an application for registration as a foreign limited partnership, signed and sworn to by a general partner and setting forth:

(1)   the name of the foreign limited partnership and, if different, the name under which it proposes to register and transact business in this State;

(2)   the State and date of its formation;

(3)   the name and address of any agent for service of process on the foreign limited partnership whom the foreign limited partnership elects to appoint; the agent must be an individual resident of this State, a domestic corporation, or a foreign corporation having a place of business in, and authorized to do business in, this State;

(4)   a statement that the Secretary of State is appointed the agent of the foreign limited partnership for service of process if no agent has been appointed under paragraph (3) or, if appointed, the agent's authority has been revoked or if the agent cannot be found or served with the exercise of reasonable diligence;

(5)   the address of the office required to be maintained in the state of its organization by the laws of that state or, if not so required, of the principal office of the foreign limited partnership;

(6)   the name and business address of each general partner; and

(7)   the address of the office at which is kept a list of the names and addresses of the limited partners and their capital contributions, together with an undertaking by the foreign limited partnership to keep those records until the foreign limited partnership's registration in this State is cancelled or withdrawn.

§ 903
Issuance of Registration

(a)   If the Secretary of State finds that an application for registration conforms to law and all requisite fees have been paid, he shall:

(1)   endorse on the application the word "Filed," and the month, day, and year of the filing thereof;

(2)   file in his office a duplicate original of the application; and

(3)   issue a certificate of registration to transact business in this State.

(b)   The certificate of registration, together with a duplicate original of the application, shall be returned to the person who filed the application or his representative.

§ 904
Name

A foreign limited partnership may register with the Secretary of State under any name, whether or not it is the name under which it is registered in its state of organization, that includes without abbreviation the words "limited partnership" and that could be registered by a domestic limited partnership.

§ 905
Changes and Amendments

If any statement in the application for registration of a foreign limited partnership was false when made or any arrangements or other facts described have changed, making the application inaccurate in any respect, the foreign limited partnership shall promptly file in the office of the Secretary of State a certificate, signed and sworn to by a general partner, correcting such statement.

§ 906
Cancellation of Registration

A foreign limited partnership may cancel its registration by filing with the Secretary of State a certificate of cancellation signed and sworn to by a general partner. A cancellation does not terminate the authority of the Secretary of State to accept service of process on the foreign limited partnership with respect to [claims for relief] [causes of action] arising out of the transactions of business in this State.

§ 907
Transaction of Business Without Registration

(a)   A foreign limited partnership transacting business in this State may not maintain any action, suit, or proceeding in any court of this State until it has registered in this State.

(b) The failure of a foreign limited partnership to register in this State does not impair the validity of any contract or act of the foreign limited partnership or prevent the foreign limited partnership from defending any action, suit, or proceeding in any court of this State.

(c) A limited partner of a foreign limited partnership is not liable as a general partner of the foreign limited partnership solely by reason of having transacted business in this State without registration.

(d) A foreign limited partnership, by transacting business in this State without registration, appoints the Secretary of State as its agent for service of process with respect to [claims for relief] [causes of action] arising out of the transaction of business in this State.

§ 908
Action by [Appropriate Official]

The [designate the appropriate official] may bring an action to restrain a foreign limited partnership from transacting business in this State in violation of this Article.

ARTICLE 10/DERIVATIVE ACTIONS
§ 1001
Right of Action

A limited partner may bring an action in the right of a limited partnership to recover a judgment in its favor if general partners with authority to do so have refused to bring the action or if an effort to cause those general partners to bring the action is not likely to succeed.

§ 1002
Proper Plaintiff

In a derivative action, the plaintiff must be a partner at the time of bringing the action and (i) must have been a partner at the time of the transaction of which he complains or (ii) his status as a partner must have devolved upon him by operation of law or pursuant to the terms of the partnership agreement from a person who was a partner at the time of the transaction.

§ 1003
Pleading

In a derivative action, the complaint shall set forth with particularity the effort of the plaintiff to secure initiation of the action by a general partner or the reasons for not making the effort.

§ 1004
Expenses

If a derivative action is successful, in whole or in part, or if anything is received by the plaintiff as a result of a judgment, compromise, or settlement of an action or claim, the court may award the plaintiff reasonable expenses, including reasonable attorney's fees, and shall direct him to remit to the limited partnership the remainder of those proceeds received by him.

ARTICLE 11/MISCELLANEOUS [OMITTED]

Appendix D

Revised Model Business Corporation Act (1984)

CHAPTER 1/GENERAL PROVISIONS
Subchapter A/Short Title and Reservation of Power
§ 1.01
Short Title

This Act shall be known and may be cited as the "[name of state] Business Corporation Act."

§ 1.02
Reservation of Power to Amend or Repeal

The [name of state legislature] has power to amend or repeal all or part of this Act at any time and all domestic and foreign corporations subject to this Act are governed by the amendment or repeal.

Subchapter B/Filing Documents
§ 1.20
Filing Requirements

(a) A document must satisfy the requirements of this section, and of any other section that adds to or varies these requirements, to be entitled to filing by the secretary of state.

(b) This Act must require or permit filing the document in the office of the secretary of state.

(c) The document must contain the information required by this Act. It may contain other information as well.

(d) The document must be typewritten or printed.

(e) The document must be in the English language. A corporate name need not be in English if written in English letters or Arabic or Roman numerals, and the certificate of existence required of foreign corporations need not be in English if accompanied by a reasonably authenticated English translation.

(f) The document must be executed:
  (1) by the chairman of the board of directors of a domestic or foreign corporation, by its president, or by another of its officers;
  (2) if directors have not been selected or the corporation has not been formed, by an incorporator; or
  (3) if the corporation is in the hands of a receiver, trustee, or other court-appointed fiduciary, by that fiduciary.

(g) The person executing the document shall sign it and state beneath or opposite his signature his name and the capacity in which he signs. The document may but need not contain: (1) the corporate seal, (2) an attestation by the secretary or an assistant secretary, (3) an acknowledgement, verification, or proof.

(h) If the secretary of state has prescribed a mandatory form for the document under section 1.21, the document must be in or on the prescribed form.

(i) The document must be delivered to the office of the secretary of state for filing and must be accompanied by one exact or conformed copy (except as provided in sections 5.03 and 15.09), the correct filing fee, and any franchise tax, license fee, or penalty required by this Act or other law.

§ 1.21
Forms

(a) The secretary of state may prescribe and furnish on request forms for: (1) an application for a certificate of existence, (2) a foreign corporation's application for a certificate of authority to transact business in this state, (3) a foreign corporation's application for a certificate of withdrawal, and (4) the annual report. If the secretary of state so requires, use of these forms is mandatory.

(b) The secretary of state may prescribe and furnish on request forms for other documents required or permitted to be filed by this Act but their use is not mandatory.

§ 1.22
Filing, Service and Copying Fees

(a) The secretary of state shall collect the following fees when the documents described in this subsection are delivered to him for filing:

Document	Fee
(1) Articles of incorporation	$_____ .
(2) Application for use of indistinguishable name	$_____ .
(3) Application for reserved name	$_____ .
(4) Notice of transfer of reserved name	$_____ .
(5) Application for registered name	$_____ .
(6) Application for renewal of registered name	$_____ .
(7) Corporation's statement of change of registered agent or registered office or both	$_____ .
(8) Agent's statement of change of registered office for each affected corporation	$_____ .
not to exceed a total of	$_____ .
(9) Agent's statement of resignation	No fee.
(10) Amendment of articles of incorporation	$_____ .
(11) Restatement of articles of incorporation with amendment of articles	$_____ .

(12) Articles of merger or share exchange $_____ .
(13) Articles of dissolution $_____ .
(14) Articles of revocation of dissolution $_____ .
(15) Certificate of administrative dissolution   No fee.
(16) Application for reinstatement following administrative dissolution $_____ .
(17) Certificate of reinstatement   No fee.
(18) Certificate of judicial dissolution   No fee.
(19) Application for certificate of authority $_____ .
(20) Application for amended certificate of authority $_____ .
(21) Application for certificate of withdrawal $_____ .
(22) Certificate of revocation of authority to transact business   No fee.
(23) Annual report $_____ .
(24) Articles of correction $_____ .
(25) Application for certificate of existence or authorization $_____ .
(26) Any other document required or permitted to be filed by this Act. $_____ .

(b)   The secretary of state shall collect a fee of $_____ each time process is served on him under this Act. The party to a proceeding causing service of process is entitled to recover this fee as costs if he prevails in the proceeding.

(c)   The secretary of state shall collect the following fees for copying and certifying the copy of any filed document relating to a domestic or foreign corporation:

(1) $_____ a page for copying; and

(2) $_____ for the certificate.

§ 1.23
Effective Time and Date of Document

(a)   Except as provided in subsection (b) and section 1.24(c), a document accepted for filing is effective:

(1)   at the time of filing on the date it is filed, as evidenced by the secretary of state's date and time endorsement on the original document; or

(2)   at the time specified in the document as its effective time on the date it is filed.

(b)   A document may specify a delayed effective time and date, and if it does so the document becomes effective at the time and date specified. If a delayed effective date but no time is specified, the document is effective at the close of business on that date. A delayed effective date for a document may not be later than the 90th day after the date it is filed.

§ 1.24
Correcting Filed Document

(a)   A domestic or foreign corporation may correct a document filed by the secretary of state if the document (1) contains an incorrect statement or (2) was defectively executed, attested, sealed, verified, or acknowledged.

(b)   A document is corrected:

(1)   by preparing articles of correction that (i) describe the document (including its filing date) or attach a copy of it to the articles, (ii) specify the incorrect statement and the rea-

son it is incorrect or the manner in which the execution was defective, and (iii) correct the incorrect statement or defective execution; and

(2)   by delivering the articles to the secretary of state for filing.

(c)   Articles of correction are effective on the effective date of the document they correct except as to persons relying on the uncorrected document and adversely affected by the correction. As to those persons, articles of correction are effective when filed.

§ 1.25
Filing Duty of Secretary of State

(a)   If a document delivered to the office of the secretary of state for filing satisfies the requirements of section 1.20, the secretary of state shall file it.

(b)   The secretary of state files a document by stamping or otherwise endorsing "Filed," together with his name and official title and the date and time of receipt, on both the original and the document copy and on the receipt for the filing fee. After filing a document, except as provided in sections 5.03 and 15.10, the secretary of state shall deliver the document copy, with the filing fee receipt (or acknowledgement of receipt if no fee is required) attached, to the domestic or foreign corporation or its representative.

(c)   If the secretary of state refuses to file a document, he shall return it to the domestic or foreign corporation or its representative within five days after the document was delivered, together with a brief, written explanation of the reason for his refusal.

(d)   The secretary of state's duty to file documents under this section is ministerial. His filing or refusing to file a document does not:

(1)   affect the validity or invalidity of the document in whole or part;

(2)   relate to the correctness or incorrectness of information contained in the document;

(3)   create a presumption that the document is valid or invalid or that information contained in the document is correct or incorrect.

§ 1.26
Appeal from Secretary of State's Refusal to File Document

(a)   If the secretary of state refuses to file a document delivered to his office for filing, the domestic or foreign corporation may appeal the refusal to the [name or describe] court [of the county where the corporation's principal office (or, if none in this state, its registered office) is or will be located] [of $_____ county]. The appeal is commenced by petitioning the court to compel filing the document and by attaching to the petition the document and the secretary of state's explanation of his refusal to file.

(b)   The court may summarily order the secretary of state to file the document or take other action the court considers appropriate.

(c)   The court's final decision may be appealed as in other civil proceedings.

§ 1.27
Evidentiary Effect of Copy of Filed Document

A certificate attached to a copy of the document filed by the secretary of state, bearing his signature (which may be in facsimile) and the seal of this state, is conclusive evidence that the original document is on file with the secretary of state.

§ 1.28
Certificate of Existence

(a) Anyone may apply to the secretary of state to furnish a certificate of existence for a domestic corporation or a certificate of authorization for a foreign corporation.

(b) A certificate of existence or authorization sets forth:
(1) the domestic corporation's corporate name or the foreign corporation's corporate name used in this state;
(2) that (i) the domestic corporation is duly incorporated under the law of this state, the date of its incorporation, and the period of its duration if less than perpetual; or (ii) that the foreign corporation is authorized to transact business in this state;
(3) that all fees, taxes, and penalties owed to this state have been paid, if (i) payment is reflected in the records of the secretary of state and (ii) nonpayment affects the existence or authorization of the domestic or foreign corporation;
(4) that its most recent annual report required by section 16.22 has been delivered to the secretary of state;
(5) that articles of dissolution have not been filed; and
(6) other facts of record in the office of the secretary of state that may be requested by the applicant.

(c) Subject to any qualification stated in the certificate, a certificate of existence or authorization issued by the secretary of state may be relied upon as conclusive evidence that the domestic or foreign corporation is in existence or is authorized to transact business in this state.

§ 1.29
Penalty for Signing False Document

(a) A person commits an offense if he signs a document he knows is false in any material respect with intent that the document be delivered to the secretary of state for filing.

(b) An offense under this section is a [_____] misdemeanor [punishable by a fine of not to exceed $_____].

Subchapter C/Secretary of State
§ 1.30
Powers

The secretary of state has the power reasonably necessary to perform the duties required of him by this Act.

Subchapter D/Definitions
§ 1.40
Act Definitions

In this Act:
(1) "Articles of incorporation" include amended and restated articles of incorporation and articles of merger.

(2) "Authorized shares" means the shares of all classes a domestic or foreign corporation is authorized to issue.
(3) "Conspicuous" means so written that a reasonable person against whom the writing is to operate should have noticed it. For example, printing in italics or boldface or contrasting color, or typing in capitals or underlined, is conspicuous.
(4) "Corporation" or "domestic corporation" means a corporation for profit, which is not a foreign corporation, incorporated under or subject to the provisions of this Act.
(5) "Deliver" includes mail.
(6) "Distribution" means a direct or indirect transfer of money or other property (except its own shares) or incurrence of indebtedness by a corporation to or for the benefit of its shareholders in respect of any of its shares. A distribution may be in the form of a declaration or payment of a dividend; a purchase, redemption, or other acquisition of shares; a distribution of indebtedness; or otherwise.
(7) "Effective date of notice" is defined in section 1.41.
(8) "Employee" includes an officer but not a director. A director may accept duties that make him also an employee.
(9) "Entity" includes corporation and foreign corporation; not-for-profit corporation; profit and not-for-profit unincorporated association; business trust, estate, partnership, trust, and two or more persons having a joint or common economic interest; and state, United States, and foreign government.
(10) "Foreign corporation" means a corporation for profit incorporated under a law other than the law of this state.
(11) "Governmental subdivision" includes authority, county, district, and municipality.
(12) "Includes" denotes a partial definition.
(13) "Individual" includes the estate of an incompetent or deceased individual.
(14) "Means" denotes an exhaustive definition.
(15) "Notice" is defined in section 1.41.
(16) "Person" includes individual and entity.
(17) "Principal office" means the office (in or out of this state) so designated in the annual report where the principal executive offices of a domestic or foreign corporation are located.
(18) "Proceeding" includes civil suit and criminal, administrative, and investigatory action.
(19) "Record date" means the date established under chapter 6 or 7 on which a corporation determines the identity of its shareholders and their shareholdings for purposes of this Act. The determinations shall be made as of the close of business on the record date unless another time for doing so is specified when the record date is fixed.
(20) "Secretary" means the corporate officer to whom the board of directors has delegated responsibility under section 8.40(c) for custody of the minutes of the meetings of the board of directors and of the shareholders and for authenticating records of the corporation.
(21) "Shares" mean the unit into which the proprietary interests in a corporation are divided.
(22) "Shareholder" means the person in whose name shares are registered in the records of a corporation or the beneficial owner of shares to the extent of the rights granted by a nominee certificate on file with a corporation.

(23) "State," when referring to a part of the United States, includes a state and commonwealth (and their agencies and governmental subdivisions) and a territory, and insular possession (and their agencies and governmental subdivisions) of the United States.

(24) "Subscriber" means a person who subscribes for shares in a corporation, whether before or after incorporation.

(25) "United States" includes district, authority, bureau, commission, department, and any other agency of the United States.

(26) "Voting group" means all shares of one or more classes or series that under the articles of incorporation or this Act are entitled to vote and be counted together collectively on a matter at a meeting of shareholders. All shares entitled by the articles of incorporation or this Act to vote generally on the matter are for that purpose a single voting group.

§ 1.41
Notice

(a) Notice under this Act shall be in writing unless oral notice is reasonable under the circumstances.

(b) Notice may be communicated in person; by telephone, telegraph, teletype, or other form of wire or wireless communication; or by mail or private carrier. If these forms of personal notice are impracticable, notice may be communicated by a newspaper of general circulation in the area where published; or by radio, television, or other form of public broadcast communication.

(c) Written notice by a domestic or foreign corporation to its shareholder, if in a comprehensible form, is effective when mailed, if mailed postpaid and correctly addressed to the shareholder's address shown in the corporation's current record of shareholders.

(d) Written notice to a domestic or foreign corporation (authorized to transact business in this state) may be addressed to its registered agent at its registered office or to the corporation or its secretary at its principal office shown in its most recent annual report or, in the case of a foreign corporation that has not yet delivered an annual report, in its application for a certificate of authority.

(e) Except as provided in subsections (c) and (d), written notice, if in a comprehensible form, is effective at the earliest of the following:

   (1) when received;

   (2) five days after its deposit in the United States Mail, as evidenced by the postmark, if mailed postpaid and correctly addressed;

   (3) on the date shown on the return receipt, if sent by registered or certified mail, return receipt requested, and the receipt is signed by or on behalf of the addressee.

(f) Oral notice is effective when communicated if communicated in a comprehensible manner.

(g) If this Act prescribes notice requirements for particular circumstances, those requirements govern. If articles of incorporation or bylaws prescribe notice requirements, not inconsistent with this section or other provisions of this Act, those requirements govern.

§ 1.42
Number of Shareholders

(a) For purposes of this Act, the following identified as a shareholder in a corporation's current record of shareholders constitutes one shareholder:

   (1) three or fewer co-owners;

   (2) a corporation, partnership, trust, estate, or other entity;

   (3) the trustees, guardians, custodians, or other fiduciaries of a single trust, estate, or account.

(b) For purposes of this Act, shareholdings registered in substantially similar names constitute one shareholder if it is reasonable to believe that the names represent the same person.

CHAPTER 2/INCORPORATION
§ 2.01
Incorporators

One or more persons may act as the incorporator or incorporators of a corporation by delivering articles of incorporation to the secretary of state for filing.

§ 2.02
Articles of Incorporation

(a) The articles of incorporation must set forth:

   (1) a corporate name for the corporation that satisfies the requirements of section 4.01;

   (2) the number of shares the corporation is authorized to issue;

   (3) the street address of the corporation's initial registered office and the name of its initial registered agent at that office; and

   (4) the name and address of each incorporator.

(b) The articles of incorporation may set forth:

   (1) the names and addresses of the individuals who are to serve as the initial directors;

   (2) provisions not inconsistent with law regarding:

      (i) the purpose or purposes for which the corporation is organized;

      (ii) managing the business and regulating the affairs of the corporation;

      (iii) defining, limiting, and regulating the powers of the corporation, its board of directors, and shareholders;

      (iv) a par value for authorized shares or classes of shares;

      (v) the imposition of personal liability on shareholders for the debts of the corporation to a specified extent and upon specified conditions; and

   (3) any provision that under this Act is required or permitted to be set forth in the bylaws.

(c) The articles of incorporation need not set forth any of the corporate powers enumerated in this Act.

§ 2.03
Incorporation

(a) Unless a delayed effective date is specified, the corporate existence begins when the articles of incorporation are filed.

(b) The secretary of state's filing of the articles of incorporation is conclusive proof that the incorporators satisfied all conditions precedent to incorporation except in a proceeding by the state to cancel or revoke the incorporation or involuntarily dissolve the corporation.

§ 2.04
Liability for Preincorporation Transactions

All persons purporting to act as or on behalf of a corporation, knowing there was no incorporation under this Act, are jointly and severally liable for all liabilities created while so acting.

§ 2.05
Organization of Corporation

(a) After incorporation:

(1) if initial directors are named in the articles of incorporation, the initial directors shall hold an organizational meeting, at the call of a majority of the directors, to complete the organization of the corporation by appointing officers, adopting bylaws, and carrying on any other business brought before the meeting;

(2) if initial directors are not named in the articles, the incorporator or incorporators shall hold an organizational meeting at the call of a majority of the incorporators:

(i) to elect directors and complete the organization of the corporation; or

(ii) to elect a board of directors who shall complete the organization of the corporation.

(b) Action required or permitted by this Act to be taken by incorporators at an organizational meeting may be taken without a meeting if the action taken is evidenced by one or more written consents describing the action taken and signed by each incorporator.

(c) An organizational meeting may be held in or out of this state.

§ 2.06
Bylaws

(a) The incorporators or board of directors of a corporation shall adopt initial bylaws for the corporation.

(b) The bylaws of a corporation may contain any provision for managing the business and regulating the affairs of the corporation that is not inconsistent with law or the articles of incorporation.

§ 2.07
Emergency Bylaws

(a) Unless the articles of incorporation provide otherwise, the board of directors of a corporation may adopt bylaws to be effective only in an emergency defined in subsection (d). The emergency bylaws, which are subject to amendment or repeal by the shareholders, may make all provisions necessary for managing the corporation during the emergency, including:

(1) procedures for calling a meeting of the board of directors;

(2) quorum requirements for the meeting; and

(3) designation of additional or substitute directors.

(b) All provisions of the regular bylaws consistent with the emergency bylaws remain effective during the emergency. The emergency bylaws are not effective after the emergency ends.

(c) Corporate action taken in good faith in accordance with the emergency bylaws:

(1) binds the corporation; and

(2) may not be used to impose liability on a corporate director, officer, employee, or agent.

(d) An emergency exists for purposes of this section if a quorum of the corporation's directors cannot readily be assembled because of some catastrophic event.

CHAPTER 3/PURPOSES AND POWERS
§ 3.01
Purposes

(a) Every corporation incorporated under this Act has the purpose of engaging in any lawful business unless a more limited purpose is set forth in the articles of incorporation.

(b) A corporation engaging in a business that is subject to regulation under another statute of this state may incorporate under this Act only if permitted by, and subject to all limitations of, the other statute.

§ 3.02
General Powers

Unless its articles of incorporation provide otherwise, every corporation has perpetual duration and succession in its corporate name and has the same powers as an individual to do all things necessary or convenient to carry out its business and affairs, including without limitation power:

(1) to sue and be sued, complain and defend in its corporate name;

(2) to have a corporate seal, which may be altered at will, and to use it, or a facsimile of it, by impressing or affixing it or in any other manner reproducing it;

(3) to make and amend bylaws, not inconsistent with its articles of incorporation or with the laws of this state, for managing the business and regulating the affairs of the corporation;

(4) to purchase, receive, lease, or otherwise acquire, and own, hold, improve, use, and otherwise deal with, real or personal property, or any legal or equitable interest in property, wherever located;

(5) to sell, convey, mortgage, pledge, lease, exchange, and otherwise dispose of all or any part of its property;

(6) to purchase, receive, subscribe for, or otherwise acquire; own, hold, vote, use, sell, mortgage, lend, pledge, or otherwise dispose of; and deal in and with shares or other interests in, or obligations of, any other entity;

(7) to make contracts and guarantees, incur liabilities, borrow money, issue its notes, bonds, and other obligations, (which may be convertible into or include the option to purchase other securities of the corporation), and secure any of its obligations by mortgage or pledge of any of its property, franchises, or income;

(8) to lend money, invest and reinvest its funds, and receive and hold real and personal property as security for repayment;

(9) to be a promoter, partner, member, associate, or manager of any partnership, joint venture, trust, or other entity;

(10) to conduct its business, locate offices, and exercise the powers granted by this Act within or without this state;

(11) to elect directors and appoint officers, employees, and agents of the corporation, define their duties, fix their compensation, and lend them money and credit;

(12) to pay pensions and establish pension plans, pension trusts, profit sharing plans, share bonus plans, share option plans, and benefit or incentive plans for any or all of its current or former directors, officers, employees, and agents;

(13) to make donations for the public welfare or for charitable, scientific, or educational purposes;

(14) to transact any lawful business that will aid governmental policy;

(15) to make payments or donations, or do any other act, not inconsistent with law, that furthers the business and affairs of the corporation.

§ 3.03
Emergency Powers

(a) In anticipation of or during an emergency defined in subsection (d), the board of directors of a corporation may:

(1) modify lines of succession to accommodate the incapacity of any director, officer, employee, or agent; and

(2) relocate the principal office, designate alternative principal offices or regional offices, or authorize the officers to do so.

(b) During an emergency defined in subsection (d), unless emergency bylaws provide otherwise:

(1) notice of a meeting of the board of directors need be given only to those directors whom it is practicable to reach and may be given in any practicable manner, including by publication and radio; and

(2) one or more officers of the corporation present at a meeting of the board of directors may be deemed to be directors for the meeting, in order of rank and within the same rank in order of seniority, as necessary to achieve a quorum.

(c) Corporate action taken in good faith during an emergency under this section to further the ordinary business affairs of the corporation:

(1) binds the corporation; and

(2) may not be used to impose liability on a corporate director, officer, employee, or agent.

(d) An emergency exists for purposes of this section if a quorum of the corporation's directors cannot readily be assembled because of some catastrophic event.

§ 3.04
Ultra Vires

(a) Except as provided in subsection (b), the validity of corporate action may not be challenged on the ground that the corporation lacks or lacked power to act.

(b) A corporation's power to act may be challenged:

(1) in a proceeding by a shareholder against the corporation to enjoin the act;

(2) in a proceeding by the corporation, directly, derivatively, or through a receiver, trustee, or other legal representative, against an incumbent or former director, officer, employee, or agent of the corporation; or

(3) in a proceeding by the Attorney General under section 14.30.

(c) In a shareholder's proceeding under subsection (b)(1) to enjoin an unauthorized corporate act, the court may enjoin or set aside the act, if equitable and if all affected persons are parties to the proceeding, and may award damages for loss (other than anticipated profits) suffered by the corporation or another party because of enjoining the unauthorized act.

CHAPTER 4/NAME
§ 4.01
Corporate Name

(a) A corporate name:

(1) must contain the word "corporation," "incorporated," "company," or "limited," or the abbreviation "corp.," "inc.," "co.," or "ltd.", or words or abbreviations of like import in another language; and

(2) may not contain language stating or implying that the corporation is organized for a purpose other than that permitted by section 3.01 and its articles of incorporation.

(b) Except as authorized by subsections (c) and (d), a corporate name must be distinguishable upon the records of the secretary of state from:

(1) the corporate name of a corporation incorporated or authorized to transact business in this state;

(2) a corporate name reserved or registered under section 4.02 or 4.03;

(3) the fictitious name adopted by a foreign corporation authorized to transact business in this state because its real name is unavailable; and

(4) the corporate name of a not-for-profit corporation incorporated or authorized to transact business in this state.

(c) A corporation may apply to the secretary of state for authorization to use a name that is not distinguishable upon his records from one or more of the names described in subsection (b). The secretary of state shall authorize use of the name applied for if:

(1) the other corporation consents to the use in writing and submits an undertaking in form satisfactory to the secretary of state to change its name to a name that is distinguishable upon the records of the secretary of state from the name of the applying corporation; or

(2) the applicant delivers to the secretary of state a certified copy of the final judgment of a court of competent jurisdiction establishing the applicant's right to use the name applied for in this state.

(d) A corporation may use the name (including the fictitious name) of another domestic or foreign corporation that is used in this state if the other corporation is incorporated or authorized to transact business in this state and the proposed user corporation:

(1) has merged with the other corporation;

(2) has been formed by reorganization of the other corporation; or

(3) has acquired all or substantially all of the assets, including the corporate name, of the other corporation.

(e) This Act does not control the use of fictitious names.

§ 4.02
Reserved Name

(a) A person may reserve the exclusive use of a corporate name, including a fictitious name for a foreign corporation whose corporate name is not available, by delivering an application to the secretary of state for filing. The application must set forth the name and address of the applicant and the name proposed to be reserved. If the secretary of state finds that the corporate name applied for is available, he shall reserve the name for the applicant's exclusive use for a nonrenewable 120-day period.

(b) The owner of a reserved corporate name may transfer the reservation to another person by delivering to the secretary of state a signed notice of the transfer that states the name and address of the transferee.

§ 4.03
Registered Name

(a) A foreign corporation may register its corporate name, or its corporate name with any addition required by section 15.06, if the name is distinguishable upon the records of the secretary of state from the corporate names that are not available under section 4.01(b)(3).

(b) A foreign corporation registers its corporate name, or its corporate name with any addition required by section 15.06, by delivering to the secretary of state for filing an application:

    (1) setting forth its corporate name, or its corporate name with any addition required by section 15.06, the state or country and date of its incorporation, and a brief description of the nature of the business in which it is engaged; and

    (2) accompanied by a certificate of existence (or a document of similar import) from the state or country of incorporation.

(c) The name is registered for the applicant's exclusive use upon the effective date of the application.

(d) A foreign corporation whose registration is effective may renew it for successive years by delivering to the secretary of state for filing a renewal application, which complies with the requirements of subsection (b), between October 1 and December 31 of the preceding year. The renewal application renews the registration for the following calendar year.

(e) A foreign corporation whose registration is effective may thereafter qualify as a foreign corporation under that name or consent in writing to the use of that name by a corporation thereafter incorporated under this Act or by another foreign corporation thereafter authorized to transact business in this state. The registration terminates when the domestic corporation is incorporated or the foreign corporation qualifies or consents to the qualification of another foreign corporation under the registered name.

CHAPTER 5/OFFICE AND AGENT
§ 5.01
Registered Office and Registered Agent

Each corporation must continuously maintain in this state:
    (1) a registered office that may be the same as any of its places of business; and

    (2) a registered agent, who may be:
        (i) an individual who resides in this state and whose business office is identical with the registered office;
        (ii) a domestic corporation or not-for-profit domestic corporation whose business office is identical with the registered office; or
        (iii) a foreign corporation or not-for-profit foreign corporation authorized to transact business in this state whose business office is identical with the registered office.

§ 5.02
Change of Registered Office or Registered Agent

(a) A corporation may change its registered office or registered agent by delivering to the secretary of state for filing a statement of change that sets forth:
    (1) the name of the corporation,
    (2) the street address of its current registered office;
    (3) if the current registered office is to be changed, the street address of the new registered office;
    (4) the name of its current registered agent;
    (5) if the current registered agent is to be changed, the name of the new registered agent and the new agent's written consent (either on the statement or attached to it) to the appointment; and
    (6) that after the change or changes are made, the street addresses of its registered office and the business office of its registered agent will be identical.

(b) If a registered agent changes the street address of his business office, he may change the street address of the registered office of any corporation for which he is the registered agent by notifying the corporation in writing of the change and signing (either manually or in facsimile) and delivering to the secretary of state for filing a statement that complies with the requirements of subsection (a) and recites that the corporation has been notified of the change.

§ 5.03
Resignation of Registered Agent

(a) A registered agent may resign his agency appointment by signing and delivering to the secretary of state for filing the signed original and two exact or conformed copies of a statement of resignation. The statement may include a statement that the registered office is also discontinued.

(b) After filing the statement the secretary of state shall mail one copy to the registered office (if not discontinued) and the other copy to the corporation at its principal office.

(c) The agency appointment is terminated, and the registered office discontinued if so provided, on the 31st day after the date on which the statement was filed.

§ 5.04
Service on Corporation

(a) A corporation's registered agent is the corporation's agent for service of process, notice, or demand required or permitted by law to be served on the corporation.

(b) If a corporation has no registered agent, or the agent cannot with reasonable diligence be served, the corporation may be served by registered or certified mail, return receipt requested, addressed to the secretary of the corporation at its principal office. Service is perfected under this subsection at the earliest of:

    (1) the date the corporation receives the mail;

    (2) the date shown on the return receipt, if signed on behalf of the corporation; or

    (3) five days after its deposit in the United States Mail, if mailed postpaid and correctly addressed.

(e) This section does not prescribe the only means, or necessarily the required means, of serving a corporation.

CHAPTER 6/SHARES AND DISTRIBUTIONS
Subchapter A/Shares
§ 6.01
Authorized Shares

(a) The articles of incorporation must prescribe the classes of shares and the number of shares of each class that the corporation is authorized to issue. If more than one class of shares is authorized, the articles of incorporation must prescribe a distinguishing designation for each class, and prior to the issuance of shares of a class the preferences, limitations, and relative rights of that class must be described in the articles of incorporation. All shares of a class must have preferences, limitations, and relative rights identical with those of other shares of the same class except to the extent otherwise permitted by section 6.02.

(b) The articles of incorporation must authorize (1) one or more classes of shares that together have unlimited voting rights, and (2) one or more classes of shares (which may be the same class or classes as those with voting rights) that together are entitled to receive the net assets of the corporation upon dissolution.

(c) The articles of incorporation may authorize one or more classes of shares that:

    (1) have special, conditional, or limited voting rights, or no right to vote, except to the extent prohibited by this Act;

    (2) are redeemable or convertible as specified in the articles of incorporation (i) at the option of the corporation, the shareholder, or another person or upon the occurrence of a designated event; (ii) for cash, indebtedness, securities, or other property; (iii) in a designated amount or in an amount determined in accordance with a designated formula or by reference to extrinsic data or events;

    (3) entitle the holders to distributions calculated in any manner, including dividends that may be cumulative, noncumulative, or partially cumulative;

    (4) have preference over any other class of shares with respect to distributions, including dividends and distributions upon the dissolution of the corporation.

(d) The description of the designations, preferences, limitations, and relative rights of share classes in subsection (c) is not exhaustive.

§ 6.02
Terms of Class or Series Determined by Board of Directors

(a) If the articles of incorporation so provide, the board of directors may determine, in whole or in part, the preferences, limitations, and relative rights (within the limits set forth in section 6.01) of (1) any class of shares before the issuance of any shares of that class or (2) one or more series within a class before the issuance of any shares of that series.

(b) Each series of a class must be given a distinguishing designation.

(c) All shares of a series must have preferences, limitations, and relative rights identical with those of other shares of the same series and, except to the extent otherwise provided in the description of the series, of those of other series of the same class.

(d) Before issuing any shares of a class or series created under this section, the corporation must deliver to the secretary of state for filing articles of amendment, which are effective without shareholder action, that set forth:

    (1) the name of the corporation;

    (2) the text of the amendment determining the terms of the class or series of shares;

    (3) the date it was adopted; and

    (4) a statement that the amendment was duly adopted by the board of directors.

§ 6.03
Issued and Outstanding Shares

(a) A corporation may issue the number of shares of each class or series authorized by the articles of incorporation. Shares that are issued are outstanding shares until they are reacquired, redeemed, converted, or cancelled.

(b) The reacquisition, redemption, or conversion of outstanding shares is subject to the limitations of subsection (c) of this section and to section 6.40.

(c) At all times that shares of the corporation are outstanding, one or more shares that together have unlimited voting rights and one or more shares that together are entitled to receive the net assets of the corporation upon dissolution must be outstanding.

§ 6.04
Fractional Shares

(a) A corporation may:

    (1) issue fractions of a share or pay in money the value of fractions of a share;

    (2) arrange for disposition of fractional shares by the shareholders;

    (3) issue scrip in registered or bearer form entitling the holder to receive a full share upon surrendering enough scrip to equal a full share.

(b) Each certificate representing scrip must be conspicuously labeled "scrip" and must contain the information required by section 6.25(b).

(c) The holder of a fractional share is entitled to exercise the rights of a shareholder, including the right to vote, to receive dividends, and to participate in the assets of the corporation upon liquidation. The holder of scrip is not entitled to any of these rights unless the scrip provides for them.

(d) The board of directors may authorize the issuance of scrip subject to any condition considered desirable, including:

(1) that the scrip will become void if not exchanged for full shares before a specified date; and

(2) that the shares for which the scrip is exchangeable may be sold and the proceeds paid to the scripholders.

Subchapter B/Issuance of Shares
§ 6.20
Subscription for Shares Before Incorporation

(a) A subscription for shares entered into before incorporation is irrevocable for six months unless the subscription agreement provides a longer or shorter period or all the subscribers agree to revocation.

(b) The board of directors may determine the payment terms of subscriptions for shares that were entered into before incorporation, unless the subscription agreement specifies them. A call for payment by the board of directors must be uniform so far as practicable as to all shares of the same class or series, unless the subscription agreement specifies otherwise.

(c) Shares issued pursuant to subscriptions entered into before incorporation are fully paid and nonassessable when the corporation receives the consideration specified in the subscription agreement.

(d) If a subscriber defaults in payment of money or property under a subscription agreement entered into before incorporation, the corporation may collect the amount owed as any other debt. Alternatively, unless the subscription agreement provides otherwise, the corporation may rescind the agreement and may sell the shares if the debt remains unpaid more than 20 days after the corporation sends written demand for payment to the subscriber.

(e) A subscription agreement entered into after incorporation is a contract between the subscriber and the corporation subject to section 6.21.

§ 6.21
Issuance of Shares

(a) The powers granted in this section to the board of directors may be reserved to the shareholders by the articles of incorporation.

(b) The board of directors may authorize shares to be issued for consideration consisting of any tangible or intangible property or benefit to the corporation, including cash, promissory notes, services performed, contracts for services to be performed, or other securities of the corporation.

(c) Before the corporation issues shares, the board of directors must determine that the consideration received or to be received for shares to be issued is adequate. That determination by the board of directors is conclusive insofar as the adequacy of consideration for the issuance of shares relates to whether the shares are validly issued, fully paid, and nonassessable.

(d) When the corporation receives the consideration for which the board of directors authorized the issuance of shares, the shares issued therefor are fully paid and nonassessable.

(e) The corporation may place in escrow shares issued for a contract for future services or benefits or a promissory note, or make other arrangements to restrict the transfer of the shares, and may

credit distributions in respect of the shares against their purchase price, until the services are performed, the note is paid, or the benefits received. If the services are not performed, the note is not paid, or the benefits are not received, the shares escrowed or restricted and the distributions credited may be cancelled in whole or part.

§ 6.22
Liability of Shareholders

(a) A purchaser from a corporation of its own shares is not liable to the corporation or its creditors with respect to the shares except to pay the consideration for which the shares were authorized to be issued (section 6.21) or specified in the subscription agreement (section 6.20).

(b) Unless otherwise provided in the articles of incorporation, a shareholder of a corporation is not personally liable for the acts or debts of the corporation except that he may become personally liable by reason of his own acts or conduct.

§ 6.23
Share Dividends

(a) Unless the articles of incorporation provide otherwise, shares may be issued pro rata and without consideration to the corporation's shareholders or to the shareholders of one or more classes or series. An issuance of shares under this subsection is a share dividend.

(b) Shares of one class or series may not be issued as a share dividend in respect of shares of another class or series unless (1) the articles of incorporation so authorize, (2) a majority of the votes entitled to be cast by the class or series to be issued approve the issue, or (3) there are no outstanding shares of the class or series to be issued.

(c) If the board of directors does not fix the record date for determining shareholders entitled to a share dividend, it is the date the board of directors authorizes the share dividend.

§ 6.24
Share Options

A corporation may issue rights, options, or warrants for the purchase of shares of the corporation. The board of directors shall determine the terms upon which the rights, options, or warrants are issued, their form and content, and the consideration for which the shares are to be issued.

§ 6.25
Form and Content of Certificates

(a) Shares may but need not be represented by certificates. Unless this Act or another statute expressly provides otherwise, the rights and obligations of shareholders are identical whether or not their shares are represented by certificates.

(b) At a minimum each share certificate must state on its face:
(1) the name of the issuing corporation and that it is organized under the law of this state;
(2) the name of the person to whom issued; and
(3) the number and class of shares and the designation of the series, if any, the certificate represents.

(c) If the issuing corporation is authorized to issue different classes of shares or different series within a class, the designations, relative rights, preferences, and limitations applicable to each class and the variations in rights, preferences, and limitations determined for each series (and the authority of the board of directors to determine variations for future series) must be summarized on the front or back of each certificate. Alternatively, each certificate may state conspicuously on its front or back that the corporation will furnish the shareholder this information on request in writing and without charge.

(d) Each share certificate (1) must be signed (either manually or in facsimile) by two officers designated in the bylaws or by the board of directors and (2) may bear the corporate seal or its facsimile.

(e) If the person who signed (either manually or in facsimile) a share certificate no longer holds office when the certificate is issued, the certificate is nevertheless valid.

§ 6.26
Shares Without Certificates

(a) Unless the articles of incorporation or bylaws provide otherwise, the board of directors of a corporation may authorize the issue of some or all of the shares of any or all of its classes or series without certificates. The authorization does not affect shares already represented by certificates until they are surrendered to the corporation.

(b) Within a reasonable time after the issue or transfer of shares without certificates, the corporation shall send the shareholder a written statement of the information required on certificates by section 6.25(b) and (c), and, if applicable, section 6.27.

§ 6.27
Restriction on Transfer of Shares and Other Securities

(a) The articles of incorporation, bylaws, an agreement among shareholders, or an agreement between shareholders and the corporation may impose restrictions on the transfer or registration of transfer of shares of the corporation. A restriction does not affect shares issued before the restriction was adopted unless the holders of the shares are parties to the restriction agreement or voted in favor of the restriction.

(b) A restriction on the transfer or registration of transfer of shares is valid and enforceable against the holder or a transferee of the holder if the restriction is authorized by this section and its existence is noted conspicuously on the front or back of the certificate or is contained in the information statement required by section 6.26(b). Unless so noted, a restriction is not enforceable against a person without knowledge of the restriction.

(c) A restriction on the transfer or registration of transfer of shares is authorized:

(1) to maintain the corporation's status when it is dependent on the number or identity of its shareholders;
(2) to preserve exemptions under federal or state securities law;
(3) for any other reasonable purpose.

(d) A restriction on the transfer or registration of transfer of shares may:

(1) obligate the shareholder first to offer the corporation or other persons (separately, consecutively, or simultaneously) an opportunity to acquire the restricted shares;
(2) obligate the corporation or other persons (separately, consecutively, or simultaneously) to acquire the restricted shares;
(3) require the corporation, the holders of any class of its shares, or another person to approve the transfer of the restricted shares, if the requirement is not manifestly unreasonable;
(4) prohibit the transfer of the restricted shares to designated persons or classes of persons, if the prohibition is not manifestly unreasonable.

(e) For purposes of this section, "shares" includes a security convertible into or carrying a right to subscribe for or acquire shares.

§ 6.28
Expense of Issue

A corporation may pay the expenses of selling or underwriting its shares, and of organizing or reorganizing the corporation, from the consideration received for shares.

Subchapter C/Subsequent Acquisition of Shares by Shareholders and Corporation
§ 6.30
Shareholders' Preemptive Rights

(a) The shareholders of a corporation do not have a preemptive right to acquire the corporation's unissued shares except to the extent the articles of incorporation so provide.

(b) A statement included in the articles of incorporation that "the corporation elects to have preemptive rights" (or words of similar import) means that the following principles apply except to the extent the articles of incorporation expressly provide otherwise:

(1) The shareholders of the corporation have a preemptive right, granted on uniform terms and conditions prescribed by the board of directors to provide a fair and reasonable opportunity to exercise the right, to acquire proportional amounts of the corporation's unissued shares upon the decision of the board of directors to issue them.
(2) A shareholder may waive his preemptive right. A waiver evidenced by a writing is irrevocable even though it is not supported by consideration.
(3) There is no preemptive right with respect to:
　(i) shares issued as compensation to directors, officers, agents, or employees of the corporation, its subsidiaries or affiliates;
　(ii) shares issued to satisfy conversion or option rights created to provide compensation to directors, officers, agents, or employees of the corporation, its subsidiaries or affiliates;
　(iii) shares authorized in articles of incorporation that are issued within six months from the effective date of incorporation;
　(iv) shares sold otherwise than for money.
(4) Holders of shares of any class without general voting rights but with preferential rights to distributions or assets have no preemptive rights with respect to shares of any class.

(5) Holders of shares of any class with general voting rights but without preferential rights to distributions or assets have no preemptive rights with respect to shares of any class with preferential rights to distributions or assets unless the shares with preferential rights are convertible into or carry a right to subscribe for or acquire shares without preferential rights.

(6) Shares subject to preemptive rights that are not acquired by shareholders may be issued to any person for a period of one year after being offered to shareholders at a consideration set by the board of directors that is not lower than the consideration set for the exercise of preemptive rights. An offer at a lower consideration or after the expiration of one year is subject to the shareholders' preemptive rights.

(c) For purposes of this section, "shares" includes a security convertible into or carrying a right to subscribe for or acquire shares.

§ 6.31
Corporation's Acquisition of Its Own Shares

(a) A corporation may acquire its own shares and shares so acquired constitute authorized but unissued shares.

(b) If the articles of incorporation prohibit the reissue of acquired shares, the number of authorized shares is reduced by the number of shares acquired, effective upon amendment of the articles of incorporation.

(c) Articles of amendment may be adopted by the board of directors without shareholder action, shall be delivered to the secretary of state for filing, and shall set forth:
(1) the name of the corporation;
(2) the reduction in the number of authorized shares, itemized by class and series; and
(3) the total number of authorized shares, itemized by class and series, remaining after reduction of the shares.

Subchapter D/Distributions
§ 6.40
Distributions to Shareholders

(a) A board of directors may authorize and the corporation may make distributions to its shareholders subject to restriction by the articles of incorporation and the limitation in subsection (c).

(b) If the board of directors does not fix the record date for determining shareholders entitled to a distribution (other than one involving a purchase, redemption, or other acquisition of the corporation's shares), it is the date the board of directors authorizes the distribution.

(c) No distribution may be made if, after giving it effect:
(1) the corporation would not be able to pay its debts as they become due in the usual course of business; or
(2) the corporation's total assets would be less than the sum of its total liabilities plus (unless the articles of incorporation permit otherwise) the amount that would be needed, if the corporation were to be dissolved at the time of the distribution, to satisfy the preferential rights upon dissolution of shareholders whose preferential rights are superior to those receiving the distribution.

(d) The board of directors may base a determination that a distribution is not prohibited under subsection (c) either on financial statements prepared on the basis of accounting practices and principles that are reasonable in the circumstances or on a fair valuation or other method that is reasonable in the circumstances.

(e) Except as provided in subsection (g), the effect of a distribution under subsection (c) is measured:
(1) in the case of distribution by purchase, redemption, or other acquisition of the corporation's shares, as of the earlier of (i) the date money or other property is transferred or debt incurred by the corporation or (ii) the date the shareholder ceases to be a shareholder with respect to the acquired shares;
(2) in the case of any other distribution of indebtedness, as of the date the indebtedness is distributed; and
(3) in all other cases, as of (i) the date the distribution is authorized if the payment occurs within 120 days after the date of authorization or (ii) the date the payment is made if it occurs more than 120 days after the date of authorization.

(f) A corporation's indebtedness to a shareholder incurred by reason of a distribution made in accordance with this section is at parity with the corporation's indebtedness to its general, unsecured creditors except to the extent subordinated by agreement.

(g) Indebtedness of a corporation, including indebtedness issued as a distribution, is not considered a liability for purposes of determinations under subsection (c) if its terms provide that payment of principal and interest are made only if and to the extent that payment of a distribution to shareholders could then be made under this section. If the indebtedness is issued as a distribution, each payment of principal or interest is treated as a distribution, the effect of which is measured on the date the payment is actually made.

CHAPTER 7/SHAREHOLDERS
Subchapter A/Meetings
§ 7.01
Annual Meeting

(a) A corporation shall hold annually at a time stated in or fixed in accordance with the bylaws a meeting of shareholders.

(b) Annual shareholders' meetings may be held in or out of this state at the place stated in or fixed in accordance with the bylaws. If no place is stated in or fixed in accordance with the bylaws, annual meetings shall be held at the corporation's principal office.

(c) The failure to hold an annual meeting at the time stated in or fixed in accordance with a corporation's bylaws does not affect the validity of any corporate action.

§ 7.02
Special Meeting

(a) A corporation shall hold a special meeting of shareholders:
(1) on call of its board of directors or the person or persons authorized to do so by the articles of incorporation or bylaws; or
(2) if the holders of at least 10 percent of all the votes entitled to be cast on any issue proposed to be considered at the proposed special meeting sign, date, and deliver to the corporation's secretary one or more written demands for the meeting describing the purpose or purposes for which it is to be held.

(b) If not otherwise fixed under sections 7.03 or 7.07, the record date for determining shareholders entitled to demand a special meeting is the date the first shareholder signs the demand.

(c) Special shareholders' meetings may be held in or out of this state at the place stated in or fixed in accordance with the bylaws. If no place is stated or fixed in accordance with the bylaws, special meetings shall be held at the corporation's principal office.

(d) Only business within the purpose or purposes described in the meeting notice required by section 7.05(c) may be conducted at a special shareholders' meeting.

§ 7.03
Court-Ordered Meeting

(a) The [name or describe] court of the county where a corporation's principal office (or, if none in this state, its registered office) is located may summarily order a meeting to be held:

(1) on application of any shareholder of the corporation entitled to participate in an annual meeting if an annual meeting was not held within the earlier of 6 months after the end of the corporation's fiscal year or 15 months after its last annual meeting; or

(2) on application of a shareholder who signed a demand for a special meeting valid under section 7.02 if:

(i) notice of the special meeting was not given within 30 days after the date the demand was delivered to the corporation's secretary; or

(ii) the special meeting was not held in accordance with the notice.

(b) The court may fix the time and place of the meeting, determine the shares entitled to participate in the meeting, specify a record date for determining shareholders entitled to notice of and to vote at the meeting, prescribe the form and content of the meeting notice, fix the quorum required for specific matters to be considered at the meeting (or direct that the votes represented at the meeting constitute a quorum for action on those matters), and enter other orders necessary to accomplish the purpose or purposes of the meeting.

§ 7.04
Action Without Meeting

(a) Action required or permitted by this Act to be taken at a shareholders' meeting may be taken without a meeting if the action is taken by all the shareholders entitled to vote on the action. The action must be evidenced by one or more written consents describing the action taken, signed by all the shareholders entitled to vote on the action, and delivered to the corporation for inclusion in the minutes or filing with the corporate records.

(b) If not otherwise determined under sections 7.03 or 7.07, the record date for determining shareholders entitled to take action without a meeting is the date the first shareholder signs the consent under subsection (a).

(c) A consent signed under this section has the effect of a meeting vote and may be described as such in any document.

(d) If this Act requires that notice of proposed action be given to nonvoting shareholders and the action is to be taken by unanimous consent of the voting shareholders, the corporation must give its nonvoting shareholders written notice of the proposed action at least 10 days before the action is taken. The notice must contain or be accompanied by the same material that, under this Act, would have been required to be sent to nonvoting shareholders in a notice of meeting at which the proposed action would have been submitted to the shareholders for action.

§ 7.05
Notice of Meeting

(a) A corporation shall notify shareholders of the date, time, and place of each annual and special shareholders' meeting no fewer than 10 nor more than 60 days before the meeting date. Unless this Act or the articles of incorporation require otherwise, the corporation is required to give notice only to shareholders entitled to vote at the meeting.

(b) Unless this Act or the articles of incorporation require otherwise, notice of an annual meeting need not include a description of the purpose or purposes for which the meeting is called.

(c) Notice of a special meeting must include a description of the purpose or purposes for which the meeting is called.

(d) If not otherwise fixed under section 7.03 or 7.07, the record date for determining shareholders entitled to notice of and to vote at an annual or special shareholders' meeting is the day before the first notice is delivered to shareholders.

(e) Unless the bylaws require otherwise, if an annual or special shareholders' meeting is adjourned to a different date, time, or place, notice need not be given of the new date, time, or place if the new date, time, or place is announced at the meeting before adjournment. If a new record date for the adjourned meeting is or must be fixed under section 7.07, however, notice of the adjourned meeting must be given under this section to persons who are shareholders as of the new record date.

§ 7.06
Waiver of Notice

(a) A shareholder may waive any notice required by this Act, the articles of incorporation, or bylaws before or after the date and time stated in the notice. The waiver must be in writing, be signed by the shareholder entitled to the notice, and be delivered to the corporation for inclusion in the minutes or filing with the corporate records.

(b) A shareholder's attendance at a meeting:

(1) waives objection to lack of notice or defective notice of the meeting, unless the shareholder at the beginning of the meeting objects to holding the meeting or transacting business at the meeting;

(2) waives objection to consideration of a particular matter at the meeting that is not within the purpose or purposes described in the meeting notice, unless the shareholder objects to considering the matter when it is presented.

§ 7.07
Record Date

(a) The bylaws may fix or provide the manner of fixing the record date for one or more voting groups in order to determine the shareholders entitled to notice of a shareholders' meeting, to demand a special meeting, to vote, or to take any other action. If the bylaws do not fix or provide for fixing a record date, the board of directors of the corporation may fix a future date as the record date.

(b) A record date fixed under this section may not be more than 70 days before the meeting or action requiring a determination of shareholders.

(c) A determination of shareholders entitled to notice of or to vote at a shareholders' meeting is effective for any adjournment of the meeting unless the board of directors fixes a new record date, which it must do if the meeting is adjourned to a date more than 120 days after the date fixed for the original meeting.

(d) If a court orders a meeting adjourned to a date more than 120 days after the date fixed for the original meeting, it may provide that the original record date continues in effect or it may fix a new record date.

Subchapter B/Voting
§ 7.20
Shareholders' List for Meeting

(a) After fixing a record date for a meeting, a corporation shall prepare an alphabetical list of the names of all its shareholders who are entitled to notice of a shareholders' meeting. The list must be arranged by voting group (and within each voting group by class or series of shares) and show the address of and number of shares held by each shareholder.

(b) The shareholders' list must be available for inspection by any shareholder, beginning two business days after notice of the meeting is given for which the list was prepared and continuing through the meeting, at the corporation's principal office or at a place identified in the meeting notice in the city where the meeting will be held. A shareholder, his agent, or attorney is entitled on written demand to inspect and, subject to the requirements of section 16.02(c), to copy the list, during regular business hours and at his expense, during the period it is available for inspection.

(c) The corporation shall make the shareholders' list available at the meeting, and any shareholder, his agent, or attorney is entitled to inspect the list at any time during the meeting or any adjournment.

(d) If the corporation refuses to allow a shareholder, his agent, or attorney to inspect the shareholders' list before or at the meeting (or copy the list as permitted by subsection (b)), the [name or describe] court of the county where a corporation's principal office (or, if none in this state, its registered office) is located, on application of the shareholder, may summarily order the inspection or copying at the corporation's expense and may postpone the meeting for which the list was prepared until the inspection or copying is complete.

(e) Refusal or failure to prepare or make available the shareholders' list does not affect the validity of action taken at the meeting.

§ 7.21
Voting Entitlement of Shares

(a) Except as provided in subsections (b) and (c) or unless the articles of incorporation provide otherwise, each outstanding share, regardless of class, is entitled to one vote on each matter voted on at a shareholders' meeting. Only shares are entitled to vote.

(b) Absent special circumstances, the shares of a corporation are not entitled to vote if they are owned, directly or indirectly, by a second corporation, domestic or foreign, and the first corporation owns, directly or indirectly, a majority of the shares entitled to vote for directors of the second corporation.

(c) Subsection (b) does not limit the power of a corporation to vote any shares, including its own shares, held by it in a fiduciary capacity.

(d) Redeemable shares are not entitled to vote after notice of redemption is mailed to the holders and a sum sufficient to redeem the shares has been deposited with a bank, trust company, or other financial institution under an irrevocable obligation to pay the holders the redemption price on surrender of the shares.

§ 7.22
Proxies

(a) A shareholder may vote his shares in person or by proxy.

(b) A shareholder may appoint a proxy to vote or otherwise act for him by signing an appointment form, either personally or by his attorney-in-fact.

(c) An appointment of a proxy is effective when received by the secretary or other officer or agent authorized to tabulate votes. An appointment is valid for 11 months unless a longer period is expressly provided in the appointment form.

(d) An appointment of a proxy is revocable by the shareholder unless the appointment form conspicuously states that it is irrevocable and the appointment is coupled with an interest. Appointments coupled with an interest include the appointment of:

(1) a pledgee;
(2) a person who purchased or agreed to purchase the shares;
(3) a creditor of the corporation who extended it credit under terms requiring the appointment;
(4) an employee of the corporation whose employment contract requires the appointment; or
(5) a party to a voting agreement created under section 7.31.

(e) The death or incapacity of the shareholder appointing a proxy does not affect the right of the corporation to accept the proxy's authority unless notice of the death or incapacity is received by the secretary or other officer or agent authorized to tabulate votes before the proxy exercises his authority under the appointment.

(f) An appointment made irrevocable under subsection (d) is revoked when the interest with which it is coupled is extinguished.

(g) A transferee for value of shares subject to an irrevocable appointment may revoke the appointment if he did not know of its existence when he acquired the shares and the existence of the irrevocable appointment was not noted conspicuously on the certificate representing the shares or on the information statement for shares without certificates.

(h) Subject to section 7.24 and to any express limitation on the proxy's authority appearing on the face of the appointment form, a corporation is entitled to accept the proxy's vote or other action as that of the shareholder making the appointment.

§ 7.23
Shares Held by Nominees

(a)   A corporation may establish a procedure by which the beneficial owner of shares that are registered in the name of a nominee is recognized by the corporation as the shareholder. The extent of this recognition may be determined in the procedure.

(b)   The procedure may set forth:
(**1**)   the types of nominees to which it applies;
(**2**)   the rights or privileges that the corporation recognizes in a beneficial owner;
(**3**)   the manner in which the procedure is selected by the nominee;
(**4**)   the information that must be provided when the procedure is selected;
(**5**)   the period for which selection of the procedure is effective; and
(**6**)   other aspects of the rights and duties created.

§ 7.24
Corporation's Acceptance of Votes

(a)   If the name signed on a vote, consent, waiver, or proxy appointment corresponds to the name of a shareholder, the corporation if acting in good faith is entitled to accept the vote, consent, waiver, or proxy appointment and give it effect as the act of the shareholder.

(b)   If the name signed on a vote, consent, waiver, or proxy appointment does not correspond to the name of its shareholder, the corporation if acting in good faith is nevertheless entitled to accept the vote, consent, waiver, or proxy appointment and give it effect as the act of the shareholder if:
(**1**)   the shareholder is an entity and the name signed purports to be that of an officer or agent of the entity;
(**2**)   the name signed purports to be that of an administrator, executor, guardian, or conservator representing the shareholder and, if the corporation requests, evidence of fiduciary status acceptable to the corporation has been presented with respect to the vote, consent, waiver, or proxy appointment;
(**3**)   the name signed purports to be that of a receiver or trustee in bankruptcy of the shareholder and, if the corporation requests, evidence of this status acceptable to the corporation has been presented with respect to the vote, consent, waiver, or proxy appointment;
(**4**)   the name signed purports to be that of a pledgee, beneficial owner, or attorney-in-fact of the shareholder and, if the corporation requests, evidence acceptable to the corporation of the signatory's authority to sign for the shareholder has been presented with respect to the vote, consent, waiver, or proxy appointment;
(**5**)   two or more persons are the shareholder as cotenants or fiduciaries and the name signed purports to be the name of at least one of the coowners and the person signing appears to be acting on behalf of all the coowners.

(c)   The corporation is entitled to reject a vote, consent, waiver, or proxy appointment if the secretary or other officer or agent authorized to tabulate votes, acting in good faith, has reasonable basis for doubt about the validity of the signature on it or about the signatory's authority to sign for the shareholder.

(d)   The corporation and its officer or agent who accepts or rejects a vote, consent, waiver, or proxy appointment in good faith and in accordance with the standards of this section are not liable in damages to the shareholder for the consequences of the acceptance or rejection.

(e)   Corporate action based on the acceptance or rejection of a vote, consent, waiver, or proxy appointment under this section is valid unless a court of competent jurisdiction determines otherwise.

§ 7.25
Quorum and Voting Requirements for Voting Groups

(a)   Shares entitled to vote as a separate voting group may take action on a matter at a meeting only if a quorum of those shares exists with respect to that matter. Unless the articles of incorporation or this Act provide otherwise, a majority of the votes entitled to be cast on the matter by the voting group constitutes a quorum of that voting group for action on that matter.

(b)   Once a share is represented for any purpose at a meeting, it is deemed present for quorum purposes for the remainder of the meeting and for any adjournment of that meeting unless a new record date is or must be set for that adjourned meeting.

(c)   If a quorum exists, action on a matter (other than the election of directors) by a voting group is approved if the votes cast within the voting group favoring the action exceed the votes cast opposing the action, unless the articles of incorporation or this Act require a greater number of affirmative votes.

(d)   An amendment of articles of incorporation adding, changing, or deleting a quorum or voting requirement for a voting group greater than specified in subsection (b) or (c) is governed by section 7.27.

(e)   The election of directors is governed by section 7.28.

§ 7.26
Action by Single and Multiple Voting Groups

(a)   If the articles of incorporation or this Act provide for voting by a single voting group on a matter, action on that matter is taken when voted upon by that voting group as provided in section 7.25.

(b)   If the articles of incorporation or this Act provide for voting by two or more voting groups on a matter, action on that matter is taken only when voted upon by each of those voting groups counted separately as provided in section 7.25. Action may be taken by one voting group on a matter even though no action is taken by another voting group entitled to vote on the matter.

§ 7.27
Greater Quorum or Voting Requirements

(a)   The articles of incorporation may provide for a greater quorum or voting requirement for shareholders (or voting groups of shareholders) than is provided for by this Act.

(b)   An amendment to the articles of incorporation that adds, changes, or deletes a greater quorum or voting requirement must meet the same quorum requirement and be adopted by the same vote and voting groups required to take action under the quorum and voting requirements then in effect or proposed to be adopted, whichever is greater.

§ 7.28
Voting for Directors; Cumulative Voting

(a) Unless otherwise provided in the articles of incorporation, directors are elected by a plurality of the votes cast by the shares entitled to vote in the election at a meeting at which a quorum is present.

(b) Shareholders do not have a right to cumulate their votes for directors unless the articles of incorporation so provide.

(c) A statement included in the articles of incorporation that "[all] [a designated voting group of] shareholders are entitled to cumulate their votes for directors" (or words of similar import) means that the shareholders designated are entitled to multiply the number of votes they are entitled to cast by the number of directors for whom they are entitled to vote and cast the product for a single candidate or distribute the product among two or more candidates.

(d) Shares otherwise entitled to vote cumulatively may not be voted cumulatively at a particular meeting unless:

> **(1)** the meeting notice or proxy statement accompanying the notice states conspicuously that cumulative voting is authorized; or
> **(2)** a shareholder who has the right to cumulate his votes gives notice to the corporation not less than 48 hours before the time set for the meeting of his intent to cumulate his votes during the meeting, and if one shareholder gives this notice all other shareholders in the same voting group participating in the election are entitled to cumulate their votes without giving further notice.

Subchapter C/Voting Trusts and Agreements
§ 7.30
Voting Trusts

(a) One or more shareholders may create a voting trust, conferring on a trustee the right to vote or otherwise act for them, by signing an agreement setting out the provisions of the trust (which may include anything consistent with its purpose) and transferring their shares to the trustee. When a voting trust agreement is signed, the trustee shall prepare a list of the names and addresses of all owners of beneficial interests in the trust, together with the number and class of shares each transferred to the trust, and deliver copies of the list and agreement to the corporation's principal office.

(b) A voting trust becomes effective on the date the first shares subject to the trust are registered in the trustee's name. A voting trust is valid for not more than 10 years after its effective date unless extended under subsection (c).

(c) All or some of the parties to a voting trust may extend it for additional terms of not more than 10 years each by signing an extension agreement and obtaining the voting trustee's written consent to the extension. An extension is valid for 10 years from the date the first shareholder signs the extension agreement. The voting trustee must deliver copies of the extension agreement and list

of beneficial owners to the corporation's principal office. An extension agreement binds only those parties signing it.

§ 7.31
Voting Agreements

(a) Two or more shareholders may provide for the manner in which they will vote their shares by signing an agreement for that purpose. A voting agreement created under this section is not subject to the provisions of section 7.30.

(b) A voting agreement created under this section is specifically enforceable.

Subchapter D/Derivative Proceedings
§ 7.40
Subchapter Definitions

In this subchapter:

> **(1)** "Derivative proceeding" means a civil suit in the right of a domestic corporation or, to the extent provided in section 7.47, in the right of a foreign corporation.
> **(2)** "Shareholder" includes a beneficial owner whose shares are held in a voting trust or held by a nominee on the beneficial owner's behalf.

§ 7.41
Standing

A shareholder may not commence or maintain a derivative proceeding unless the shareholder:

> **(1)** was a shareholder of the corporation at the time of the act or omission complained of or became a shareholder through transfer by operation of law from one who was a shareholder at that time; and
> **(2)** fairly and adequately represents the interests of the corporation in enforcing the right of the corporation.

§ 7.42
Demand

No shareholder may commence a derivative proceeding until:

> **(1)** a written demand has been made upon the corporation to take suitable action; and
> **(2)** 90 days have expired from the date the demand was made unless the shareholder has earlier been notified that the demand has been rejected by the corporation or unless irreparable injury to the corporation would result by waiting for the expiration of the 90 day period.

§ 7.43
Stay of Proceedings

If the corporation commences an inquiry into the allegations made in the demand or complaint, the court may stay any derivative proceeding for such period as the court deems appropriate.

§ 7.44
Dismissal

(a) A derivative proceeding shall be dismissed by the court on motion by the corporation if one of the groups specified in subsections (b) or (f) has determined in good faith after conducting a reasonable inquiry upon which its conclusions are based that the maintenance of the derivative proceeding is not in the best interests of the corporation.

(b) Unless a panel is appointed pursuant to subsection (f), the determination in subsection (a) shall be made by:

(1)   a majority vote of independent directors present at a meeting of the board of directors if the independent directors constitute a quorum; or

(2)   a majority vote of a committee consisting of two or more independent directors appointed by majority vote of independent directors present at a meeting of the board of directors, whether or not such independent directors constituted a quorum.

(c) None of the following shall by itself cause a director to be considered not independent for purposes of this section:

(1)   the nomination or election of the director by persons who are defendants in the derivative proceeding or against whom action is demanded;

(2)   the naming of the director as a defendant in the derivative proceeding or as a person against whom action is demanded; or

(3)   the approval by the director of the act being challenged in the derivative proceeding or demand if the act resulted in no personal benefit to the director.

(d) If a derivative proceeding is commenced after a determination has been made rejecting a demand by a shareholder, the complaint shall allege with particularity facts establishing either (1) that a majority of the board of directors did not consist of independent directors at the time the determination was made or (2) that the requirements of subsection (a) have not been met.

(e) If a majority of the board of directors does not consist of independent directors at the time the determination is made, the corporation shall have the burden of proving that the requirements of subsection (a) have been met. If a majority of the board of directors consists of independent directors at the time the determination is made, the plaintiff shall have the burden of proving that the requirements of subsection (a) have not been met.

(f) The court may appoint a panel of one or more independent persons upon motion by the corporation to make a determination whether the maintenance of the derivative proceeding is in the best interests of the corporation. In such case, the plaintiff shall have the burden of proving that the requirements of subsection (a) have not been met.

§ 7.45
Discontinuance or Settlement

A derivative proceeding may not be discontinued or settled without the court's approval. If the court determines that a proposed discontinuance or settlement will substantially affect the interests of the corporation's shareholders or a class of shareholders, the court shall direct that notice be given to the shareholders affected.

§ 7.46
Payment of Expenses

On termination of the derivative proceeding the court may:

(1)   order the corporation to pay the plaintiff's reasonable expenses (including counsel fees) incurred in the proceeding

if it finds that the proceeding has resulted in a substantial benefit to the corporation;

(2)   order the plaintiff to pay any defendant's reasonable expenses (including counsel fees) incurred in defending the proceeding if it finds that the proceeding was commenced or maintained without reasonable cause or for an improper purpose; or

(3)   order a party to pay an opposing party's reasonable expenses (including counsel fees) incurred because of the filing of a pleading, motion or other paper, if it finds that the pleading, motion or other paper was not well grounded in fact, after reasonable inquiry, or warranted by existing law or a good faith argument for the extension, modification or reversal of existing law and was interposed for an improper purpose, such as to harass or to cause unnecessary delay or needless increase in the cost of litigation.

§ 7.47
Applicability to Foreign Corporations

In any derivative proceeding in the right of a foreign corporation, the matters covered by this subchapter shall be governed by the laws of the jurisdiction of incorporation of the foreign corporation except for sections 7.43, 7.45 and 7.46.

CHAPTER 8/DIRECTORS AND OFFICERS
Subchapter A/Board of Directors
§ 8.01
Requirement for and Duties of Board of Directors

(a) Except as provided in subsection (c), each corporation must have a board of directors.

(b) All corporate powers shall be exercised by or under the authority of, and the business and affairs of the corporation managed under the direction of, its board of directors, subject to any limitation set forth in the articles of incorporation.

(c) A corporation having 50 or fewer shareholders may dispense with or limit the authority of a board of directors by describing in its articles of incorporation who will perform some or all of the duties of a board of directors.

§ 8.02
Qualifications of Directors

The articles of incorporation or bylaws may prescribe qualifications for directors. A director need not be a resident of this state or a shareholder of the corporation unless the articles of incorporation or bylaws so prescribe.

§ 8.03
Number and Election of Directors

(a) A board of directors must consist of one or more individuals, with the number specified in or fixed in accordance with the articles of incorporation or bylaws.

(b) If a board of directors has power to fix or change the number of directors, the board may increase or decrease by 30 percent or less the number of directors last approved by the shareholders, but only the shareholders may increase or decrease by more than 30 percent the number of directors last approved by the shareholders.

(c)   The articles of incorporation or bylaws may establish a variable range for the size of the board of directors by fixing a minimum and maximum number of directors. If a variable range is established, the number of directors may be fixed or changed from time to time, within the minimum and maximum, by the shareholders or the board of directors. After shares are issued, only the shareholders may change the range for the size of the board or change from a fixed to a variable-range size board or vice versa.

(d)   Directors are elected at the first annual shareholders' meeting and at each annual meeting thereafter unless their terms are staggered under section 8.06.

§ 8.04
Election of Directors by Certain Classes of Shareholders

If the articles of incorporation authorize dividing the shares into classes, the articles may also authorize the election of all or a specified number of directors by the holders of one or more authorized classes of shares. Each class (or classes) of shares entitled to elect one or more directors is a separate voting group for purposes of the election of directors.

§ 8.05
Terms of Directors Generally

(a)   The terms of the initial directors of a corporation expire at the first shareholders' meeting at which directors are elected.

(b)   The terms of all other directors expire at the next annual shareholders' meeting following their election unless their terms are staggered under section 8.06.

(c)   A decrease in the number of directors does not shorten an incumbent director's term.

(d)   The term of a director elected to fill a vacancy expires at the next shareholders' meeting at which directors are elected.

(e)   Despite the expiration of a director's term, he continues to serve until his successor is elected and qualifies or until there is a decrease in the number of directors.

§ 8.06
Staggered Terms for Directors

If there are nine or more directors, the articles of incorporation may provide for staggering their terms by dividing the total number of directors into two or three groups, with each group containing one-half or one-third of the total, as near as may be. In that event, the terms of directors in the first group expire at the first annual shareholders' meeting after their election, the terms of the second group expire at the second annual shareholders' meeting after their election, and the terms of the third group, if any, expire at the third annual shareholders' meeting after their election. At each annual shareholders' meeting held thereafter, directors shall be chosen for a term of two years or three years, as the case may be, to succeed those whose terms expire.

§ 8.07
Resignation of Directors

(a)   A director may resign at any time by delivering written notice to the board of directors, its chairman, or to the corporation.

(b)   A resignation is effective when the notice is delivered unless the notice specifies a later effective date.

§ 8.08
Removal of Directors by Shareholders

(a)   The shareholders may remove one or more directors with or without cause unless the articles of incorporation provide that directors may be removed only for cause.

(b)   If a director is elected by a voting group of shareholders, only the shareholders of that voting group may participate in the vote to remove him.

(c)   If cumulative voting is authorized, a director may not be removed if the number of votes sufficient to elect him under cumulative voting is voted against his removal. If cumulative voting is not authorized, a director may be removed only if the number of votes cast to remove him exceeds the number of votes cast not to remove him.

(d)   A director may be removed by the shareholders only at a meeting called for the purpose of removing him and the meeting notice must state that the purpose, or one of the purposes, of the meeting is removal of the director.

§ 8.09
Removal of Directors by Judicial Proceeding

(a)   The [name or describe] court of the county where a corporation's principal office (or, if none in this state, its registered office) is located may remove a director of the corporation from office in a proceeding commenced either by the corporation or by its shareholders holding at least 10 percent of the outstanding shares of any class if the court finds that (1) the director engaged in fraudulent or dishonest conduct, or gross abuse of authority or discretion, with respect to the corporation and (2) removal is in the best interest of the corporation.

(b)   The court that removes a director may bar the director from reelection for a period prescribed by the court.

(c)   If shareholders commence a proceeding under subsection (a), they shall make the corporation a party defendant.

§ 8.10
Vacancy on Board

(a)   Unless the articles of incorporation provide otherwise, if a vacancy occurs on a board of directors, including a vacancy resulting from an increase in the number of directors:
    (1)   the shareholders may fill the vacancy;
    (2)   the board of directors may fill the vacancy; or
    (3)   if the directors remaining in office constitute fewer than a quorum of the board, they may fill the vacancy by the affirmative vote of a majority of all the directors remaining in office.

(b)   If the vacant office was held by a director elected by a voting group of shareholders, only the holders of shares of that voting group are entitled to vote to fill the vacancy if it is filled by the shareholders.

(c)   A vacancy that will occur at a specific later date (by reason of a resignation effective at a later date under section 8.07(b) or otherwise) may be filled before the vacancy occurs but the new director may not take office until the vacancy occurs.

§ 8.11
Compensation of Directors

Unless the articles of incorporation or bylaws provide otherwise, the board of directors may fix the compensation of directors.

Subchapter B/Meetings and Action of the Board
§ 8.20
Meetings

(a)   The board of directors may hold regular or special meetings in or out of this state.

(b)   Unless the articles of incorporation or bylaws provide otherwise, the board of directors may permit any or all directors to participate in a regular or special meeting by, or conduct the meeting through the use of, any means of communication by which all directors participating may simultaneously hear each other during the meeting. A director participating in a meeting by this means is deemed to be present in person at the meeting.

§ 8.21
Action Without Meeting

(a)   Unless the articles of incorporation or bylaws provide otherwise, action required or permitted by this Act to be taken at a board of directors' meeting may be taken without a meeting if the action is taken by all members of the board. The action must be evidenced by one or more written consents describing the action taken, signed by each director, and included in the minutes or filed with the corporate records reflecting the action taken.

(b)   Action taken under this section is effective when the last director signs the consent, unless the consent specifies a different effective date.

(c)   A consent signed under this section has the effect of a meeting vote and may be described as such in any document.

§ 8.22
Notice of Meeting

(a)   Unless the articles of incorporation or bylaws provide otherwise, regular meetings of the board of directors may be held without notice of the date, time, place, or purpose of the meeting.

(b)   Unless the articles of incorporation or bylaws provide for a longer or shorter period, special meetings of the board of directors must be preceded by at least two days' notice of the date, time, and place of the meeting. The notice need not describe the purpose of the special meeting unless required by the articles of incorporation or bylaws.

§ 8.23
Waiver of Notice

(a)   A director may waive any notice required by this Act, the articles of incorporation, or bylaws before or after the date and time stated in the notice. Except as provided by subsection (b), the

waiver must be in writing, signed by the director entitled to the notice, and filed with the minutes or corporate records.

(b)   A director's attendance at or participation in a meeting waives any required notice to him of the meeting unless the director at the beginning of the meeting (or promptly upon his arrival) objects to holding the meeting or transacting business at the meeting and does not thereafter vote for or assent to action taken at the meeting.

§ 8.24
Quorum and Voting

(a)   Unless the articles of incorporation or bylaws require a greater number, a quorum of a board of directors consists of:

  (1)   a majority of the fixed number of directors if the corporation has a fixed board size; or

  (2)   a majority of the number of directors prescribed, or if no number is prescribed the number in office immediately before the meeting begins, if the corporation has a variable-range size board.

(b)   The articles of incorporation or bylaws may authorize a quorum of a board of directors to consist of no fewer than one-third of the fixed or prescribed number of directors determined under subsection (a).

(c)   If a quorum is present when a vote is taken, the affirmative vote of a majority of directors present is the act of the board of directors unless the articles of incorporation or bylaws require the vote of a greater number of directors.

(d)   A director who is present at a meeting of the board of directors or a committee of the board of directors when corporate action is taken is deemed to have assented to the action taken unless: (1) he objects at the beginning of the meeting (or promptly upon his arrival) to holding it or transacting business at the meeting; (2) his dissent or abstention from the action taken is entered in the minutes of the meeting; or (3) he delivers written notice of his dissent or abstention to the presiding officer of the meeting before its adjournment or to the corporation immediately after adjournment of the meeting. The right of dissent or abstention is not available to a director who votes in favor of the action taken.

§ 8.25
Committees

(a)   Unless the articles of incorporation or bylaws provide otherwise, a board of directors may create one or more committees and appoint members of the board of directors to serve on them. Each committee must have two or more members, who serve at the pleasure of the board of directors.

(b)   The creation of a committee and appointment of members to it must be approved by the greater of (1) a majority of all the directors in office when the action is taken or (2) the number of directors required by the articles of incorporation or bylaws to take action under section 8.24.

(c)   Sections 8.20 through 8.24, which govern meetings, action without meetings, notice and waiver of notice, and quorum and voting requirements of the board of directors, apply to committees and their members as well.

(d)   To the extent specified by the board of directors or in the articles of incorporation or bylaws, each committee may exercise the authority of the board of directors under section 8.01.

(e)   A committee may not, however:
   (1)   authorize distributions;
   (2)   approve or propose to shareholders action that this Act requires to be approved by shareholders;
   (3)   fill vacancies on the board of directors or on any of its committees;
   (4)   amend articles of incorporation pursuant to section 10.02;
   (5)   adopt, amend, or repeal bylaws;
   (6)   approve a plan of merger not requiring shareholder approval;
   (7)   authorize or approve reacquisition of shares, except according to a formula or method prescribed by the board of directors; or
   (8)   authorize or approve the issuance or sale or contract for sale of shares, or determine the designation and relative rights, preferences, and limitations of a class or series of shares, except that the board of directors may authorize a committee (or a senior executive officer of the corporation) to do so within limits specifically prescribed by the board of directors.

(f)   The creation of, delegation of authority to, or action by a committee does not alone constitute compliance by a director with the standards of conduct described in section 8.30.

Subchapter C/Standards of Conduct
§ 8.30
General Standards for Directors

(a)   A director shall discharge his duties as a director, including his duties as a member of a committee:
   (1)   in good faith;
   (2)   with the care an ordinarily prudent person in a like position would exercise under similar circumstances; and
   (3)   in a manner he reasonably believes to be in the best interests of the corporation.

(b)   In discharging his duties a director is entitled to rely on information, opinions, reports, or statements, including financial statements and other financial data, if prepared or presented by:
   (1)   one or more officers or employees of the corporation whom the director reasonably believes to be reliable and competent in the matters presented;
   (2)   legal counsel, public accountants, or other persons as to matters the director reasonably believes are within the person's professional or expert competence; or
   (3)   a committee of the board of directors of which he is not a member if the director reasonably believes the committee merits confidence.

(c)   A director is not acting in good faith if he has knowledge concerning the matter in question that makes reliance otherwise permitted by subsection (b) unwarranted.

(d)   A director is not liable for any action taken as a director, or any failure to take any action, if he performed the duties of his office in compliance with this section.

§ 8.31
[Withdrawn][6]

§ 8.32
[Withdrawn][7]

§ 8.33
Liability for Unlawful Distributions

(a)   A director who votes for or assents to a distribution made in violation of section 6.40 or the articles of incorporation is person-

---

[6]See sections 8.60–8.63. The original section 8.31 read as follows:
§ 8.31
Director Conflict of Interest
(a)   A conflict of interest transaction is a transaction with the corporation in which a director of the corporation has a direct or indirect interest. A conflict of interest transaction is not voidable by the corporation solely because of the director's interest in the transaction if any one of the following is true:
   (1)   the material facts of the transaction and the director's interest were disclosed or known to the board of directors or a committee of the board of directors and the board of directors or committee authorized, approved, or ratified the transaction;
   (2)   the material facts of the transaction and the director's interest were disclosed or known to the shareholders entitled to vote and they authorized, approved, or ratified the transaction; or
   (3)   the transaction was fair to the corporation.
(b)   For purposes of this section, a director of the corporation has an indirect interest in a transaction if (1) another entity in which he has a material financial interest or in which he is a general partner is a party to the transaction or (2) another entity of which he is a director, officer, or trustee is a party to the transaction and the transaction is or should be considered by the board of directors of the corporation.
(c)   For purposes of subsection (a) (1), a conflict of interest transaction is authorized, approved, or ratified if it receives the affirmative vote of a majority of the directors on the board of directors (or on the committee) who have no direct or indirect interest in the transaction, but a transaction may not be authorized, approved, or ratified under this section by a single director. If a majority of the directors who have no direct or indirect interest in the transaction vote to authorize, approve, or ratify the transaction, a quorum is present for the purpose of taking action under this section. The presence of, or a vote cast by, a director with a direct or indirect interest in the transaction does not affect the validity of any action taken under subsection (a)(1) if the transaction is otherwise authorized, approved, or ratified as provided in that subsection.
(d)   For purposes of subsection (a)(2), a conflict of interest transaction is authorized, approved, or ratified if it receives the vote of a majority of the shares entitled to be counted under this subsection. Shares owned by or voted under the control of a director who has a direct or indirect interest in the transaction, and shares owned by or voted under the control of an entity described in subsection (b)(1), may not be counted in a vote of shareholders to determine whether to authorize, approve, or ratify a conflict of interest transaction under subsection (a)(2). The vote of those shares, however, shall be counted in determining whether the transaction is approved under other sections of this Act. A majority of the shares, whether or not present, that are entitled to be counted in a vote on the transaction under this subsection constitutes a quorum for the purpose of taking action under this section.
[7]The original section 8.32 read as follows:
§ 8.32
Loans to Directors
(a)   Except as provided by subsection (c), a corporation may not lend money to or guarantee the obligation of a director of the corporation unless:
   (1)   the particular loan or guarantee is approved by a majority of the votes represented by the outstanding voting shares of all classes, voting as a single voting group, except the votes of shares owned by or voted under the control of the benefited director; or
   (2)   the corporation's board of directors determines that the loan or guarantee benefits the corporation and either approves the specific loan or guarantee or a general plan authorizing loans and guarantees.
(b)   The fact that a loan or guarantee is made in violation of this section does not affect the borrower's liability on the loan.
(c)   This section does not apply to loans and guarantees authorized by statute regulating any special class of corporations.

ally liable to the corporation for the amount of the distribution that exceeds what could have been distributed without violating section 6.40 or the articles of incorporation if it is established that he did not perform his duties in compliance with section 8.30. In any proceeding commenced under this section, a director has all of the defenses ordinarily available to a director.

(b) A director held liable under subsection (a) for an unlawful distribution is entitled to contribution:

(1) from every other director who could be held liable under subsection (a) for the unlawful distribution; and

(2) from each shareholder for the amount the shareholder accepted knowing the distribution was made in violation of section 6.40 or the articles of incorporation.

(c) A proceeding under this section is barred unless it is commenced within two years after the date on which the effect of the distribution was measured under section 6.40(e) or (g).

Subchapter D/Officers
§ 8.40
Required Officers

(a) A corporation has the officers described in its bylaws or appointed by the board of directors in accordance with the bylaws.

(b) A duly appointed officer may appoint one or more officers or assistant officers if authorized by the bylaws or the board of directors.

(c) The bylaws or the board of directors shall delegate to one of the officers responsibility for preparing minutes of the directors' and shareholders' meetings and for authenticating records of the corporation.

(d) The same individual may simultaneously hold more than one office in a corporation.

§ 8.41
Duties of Officers

Each officer has the authority and shall perform the duties set forth in the bylaws or, to the extent consistent with the bylaws, the duties prescribed by the board of directors or by direction of an officer authorized by the board of directors to prescribe the duties of other officers.

§ 8.42
Standards of Conduct for Officers

(a) An officer with discretionary authority shall discharge his duties under that authority:

(1) in good faith;

(2) with the care an ordinarily prudent person in a like position would exercise under similar circumstances; and

(3) in a manner he reasonably believes to be in the best interests of the corporation.

(b) In discharging his duties an officer is entitled to rely on information, opinions, reports, or statements, including financial statements and other financial data, if prepared or presented by:

(1) one or more officers or employees of the corporation whom the officer reasonably believes to be reliable and competent in the matters presented; or

(2) legal counsel, public accountants, or other persons as to matters the officer reasonably believes are within the person's professional or expert competence.

(c) An officer is not acting in good faith if he has knowledge concerning the matter in question that makes reliance otherwise permitted by subsection (b) unwarranted.

(d) An officer is not liable for any action taken as an officer, or any failure to take any action, if he performed the duties of his office in compliance with this section.

§ 8.43
Resignation and Removal of Officers

(a) An officer may resign at any time by delivering notice to the corporation. A resignation is effective when the notice is delivered unless the notice specifies a later effective date. If a resignation is made effective at a later date and the corporation accepts the future effective date, its board of directors may fill the pending vacancy before the effective date if the board of directors provides that the successor does not take office until the effective date.

(b) A board of directors may remove any officer at any time with or without cause.

§ 8.44
Contract Rights of Officers

(a) The appointment of an officer does not itself create contract rights.

(b) An officer's removal does not affect the officer's contract rights, if any, with the corporation. An officer's resignation does not affect the corporation's contract rights, if any, with the officer.

Subchapter E/Indemnification
§ 8.50
Subchapter Definitions

In this subchapter:

(1) "Corporation" includes any domestic or foreign predecessor entity of a corporation in a merger or other transaction in which the predecessor's existence ceased upon consummation of the transaction.

(2) "Director" means an individual who is or was a director of a corporation or an individual who, while a director of a corporation, is or was serving at the corporation's request as a director, officer, partner, trustee, employee, or agent of another foreign or domestic corporation, partnership, joint venture, trust, employee benefit plan, or other enterprise. A director is considered to be serving an employee benefit plan at the corporation's request if his duties to the corporation also impose duties on, or otherwise involve services by, him to the plan or to participants in or beneficiaries of the plan. "Director" includes, unless the context requires otherwise, the estate or personal representative of a director.

(3) "Expenses" include counsel fees.

(4) "Liability" means the obligation to pay a judgment, settlement, penalty, fine (including an excise tax assessed with respect to an employee benefit plan), or reasonable expenses incurred with respect to a proceeding.

(5)   "Official capacity" means: (i) when used with respect to a director, the office of director in a corporation; and (ii) when used with respect to an individual other than a director, as contemplated in section 8.56, the office in a corporation held by the officer or the employment or agency relationship undertaken by the employee or agent on behalf of the corporation. "Official capacity" does not include service for any other foreign or domestic corporation or any partnership, joint venture, trust, employee benefit plan, or other enterprise.

(6)   "Party" includes an individual who was, is, or is threatened to be made a named defendant or respondent in a proceeding.

(7)   "Proceeding" means any threatened, pending, or completed action, suit, or proceeding, whether civil, criminal, administrative, or investigative and whether formal or informal.

§ 8.51
Authority to Indemnify

(a)   Except as provided in subsection (d), a corporation may indemnify an individual made a party to a proceeding because he is or was a director against liability incurred in the proceeding if:

(1)   he conducted himself in good faith; and

(2)   he reasonably believed:

(i)   in the case of conduct in his official capacity with the corporation, that his conduct was in its best interests; and

(ii)   in all other cases, that his conduct was at least not opposed to its best interests; and

(3)   in the case of any criminal proceeding, he had no reasonable cause to believe his conduct was unlawful.

(b)   A director's conduct with respect to an employee benefit plan for a purpose he reasonably believed to be in the interests of the participants in and beneficiaries of the plan is conduct that satisfies the requirement of subsection (a)(2)(ii).

(c)   The termination of a proceeding by judgment, order, settlement, conviction, or upon a plea of nolo contendere or its equivalent is not, of itself, determinitive that the director did not meet the standard of conduct described in this section.

(d)   A corporation may not indemnify a director under this section:

(1)   in connection with a proceeding by or in the right of the corporation in which the director was adjudged liable to the corporation; or

(2)   in connection with any other proceeding charging improper personal benefit to him, whether or not involving action in his official capacity, in which he was adjudged liable on the basis that personal benefit was improperly received by him.

(e)   Indemnification permitted under this section in connection with a proceeding by or in the right of the corporation is limited to reasonable expenses incurred in connection with the proceeding.

§ 8.52
Mandatory Indemnification

Unless limited by its articles of incorporation, a corporation shall indemnify a director who was wholly successful, on the merits or otherwise, in the defense of any proceeding to which he was a party because he is or was a director of the corporation against reasonable expenses incurred by him in connection with the proceeding.

§ 8.53
Advance for Expenses

(a)   A corporation may pay for or reimburse the reasonable expenses incurred by a director who is a party to a proceeding in advance of final disposition of the proceeding if:

(1)   the director furnishes the corporation a written affirmation of his good faith belief that he has met the standard of conduct described in section 8.51;

(2)   the director furnishes the corporation a written undertaking, executed personally or on his behalf, to repay the advance if it is ultimately determined that he did not meet the standard of conduct; and

(3)   a determination is made that the facts then known to those making the determination would not preclude indemnification under this subchapter.

(b)   the undertaking required by subsection (a)(2) must be an unlimited general obligation of the director but need not be secured and may be accepted without reference to financial ability to make repayment.

(c)   Determinations and authorizations of payments under this section shall be made in the manner specified in section 8.55.

§ 8.54
Court-Ordered Indemnification

Unless a corporation's articles of incorporation provide otherwise, a director of the corporation who is a party to a proceeding may apply for indemnification to the court conducting the proceeding or to another court of competent jurisdiction. On receipt of an application, the court after giving any notice the court considers necessary may order indemnification if it determines;

(1)   the director is entitled to mandatory indemnification under section 8.52, in which case the court shall also order the corporation to pay the director's reasonable expenses incurred to obtain court-ordered indemnification; or

(2)   the director is fairly and reasonably entitled to indemnification in view of all the relevant circumstances, whether or not he met the standard of conduct set forth in section 8.51 or was adjudged liable as described in section 8.51(d), but if he was adjudged so liable his indemnification is limited to reasonable expenses incurred.

§ 8.55
Determination and Authorization of Indemnification

(a)   A corporation may not indemnify a director under section 8.51 unless authorized in the specific case after a determination has been made that indemnification of the director is permissible in the circumstances because he has met the standard of conduct set forth in section 8.51.

(b)   The determination shall be made:

(1)   by the board of directors by majority vote of a quorum consisting of directors not at the time parties to the proceeding;

(2)   if a quorum cannot be obtained under subdivision (1), by majority vote of a committee duly designated by the board of directors (in which designation directors who are parties may participate), consisting solely of two or more directors not at the time parties to the proceeding;

    (3) by special legal counsel:

        (i) selected by the board of directors or its committee in the manner prescribed in subdivision (1) or (2); or

        (ii) if a quorum of the board of directors cannot be obtained under subdivision (1) and a committee cannot be designated under subdivision (2), selected by majority vote of the full board of directors (in which selection directors who are parties may participate); or

    (4) by the shareholders, but shares owned by or voted under the control of directors who are at the time parties to the proceeding may not be voted on the determination.

(c) Authorization of indemnification and evaluation as to reasonableness of expenses shall be made in the same manner as the determination that indemnification is permissible, except that if the determination is made by special legal counsel, authorization of indemnification and evaluation as to reasonableness of expenses shall be made by those entitled under subsection (b)(3) to select counsel.

§ 8.56
Indemnification of Officers, Employees, and Agents

Unless a corporation's articles of incorporation provide otherwise:

    (1) an officer of the corporation who is not a director is entitled to mandatory indemnification under section 8.52, and is entitled to apply for court-ordered indemnification under section 8.54, in each case to the same extent as a director;

    (2) the corporation may indemnify and advance expenses under this subchapter to an officer, employee, or agent of the corporation who is not a director to the same extent as to a director; and

    (3) a corporation may also indemnify and advance expenses to an officer, employee, or agent who is not a director to the extent, consistent with public policy, that may be provided by its articles of incorporation, bylaws, general or specific action of its board of directors, or contract.

§ 8.57
Insurance

A corporation may purchase and maintain insurance on behalf of an individual who is or was a director, officer, employee, or agent of the corporation, or who, while a director, officer, employee, or agent of the corporation, is or was serving at the request of the corporation as a director, officer, partner, trustee, employee, or agent of another foreign or domestic corporation, partnership, joint venture, trust, employee benefit plan, or other enterprise, against liability asserted against or incurred by him in that capacity or arising from his status as a director, officer, employee, or agent, whether or not the corporation would have power to indemnify him against the same liability under section 8.51 or 8.52.

§ 8.58
Application of Subchapter

(a) A provision treating a corporation's indemnification of or advance for expenses to directors that is contained in its articles of incorporation, bylaws, a resolution of its shareholders or board of directors, or in a contract or otherwise, is valid only if and to the extent the provision is consistent with this subchapter. If articles of incorporation limit indemnification or advance for expenses, indemnification and advance for expenses are valid only to the extent consistent with the articles.

(b) This subchapter does not limit a corporation's power to pay or reimburse expenses incurred by a director in connection with his appearance as a witness in a proceeding at a time when he has not been made a named defendant or respondent to the proceeding.

Subchapter F/Directors' Conflicting Interest Transactions
§ 8.60
Subchapter Definitions

In this subchapter:

    (1) "Conflicting interest" with respect to a corporation means the interest a director of the corporation has respecting a transaction effected or proposed to be effected by the corporation (or by a subsidiary of the corporation or any other entity in which the corporation has a controlling interest) if

        (i) whether or not the transaction is brought before the board of directors of the corporation for action, the director knows at the time of commitment that he or a related person is a party to the transaction or has a beneficial financial interest in or so closely linked to the transaction and of such financial significance to the director or a related person that the interest would reasonably be expected to exert an influence on the director's judgment if he were called upon to vote on the transaction; or

        (ii) the transaction is brought (or is of such character and significance to the corporation that it would in the normal course be brought) before the board of directors of the corporation for action, and the director knows at the time of commitment that any of the following persons is either a party to the transaction or has a beneficial interest in or so closely linked to the transaction and of such financial significance to the person that the interest would reasonably be expected to exert an influence on the director's judgment if he were called upon to vote on the transaction: (A) an entity (other than the corporation) of which the director is a director, general partner, agent, or employee; (B) a person that controls one or more of the entities specified in subclause (A) or an entity that is controlled by, or is under common control with, one or more of the entities specified in subclause (A); or (C) an individual who is a general partner, principal, or employer of the director.

    (2) "Director's conflicting interest transaction" with respect to a corporation means a transaction effected or proposed to be effected by the corporation (or by a subsidiary of the corporation or any other entity in which the corporation has a controlling interest) respecting which a director of the corporation has a conflicting interest.

    (3) "Related person" of a director means (i) the spouse (or a parent or sibling thereof) of the director, or a child, grandchild, sibling, parent (or spouse of any thereof) of the director, or an individual having the same home as the director, or a trust or estate of which an individual specified in this clause

(i) is a substantial beneficiary; or (ii) a trust, estate, incompetent, conservatee, or minor of which the director is a fiduciary.

(4) "Required disclosure" means disclosure by the director who has a conflicting interest of (i) the existence and nature of his conflicting interest, and (ii) all facts known to him respecting the subject matter of the transaction that an ordinarily prudent person would reasonably believe to be material to a judgment about whether or not to proceed with the transaction.

(5) "Time of commitment" respecting a transaction means the time when the transaction is consummated or, if made pursuant to contract, the time when the corporation (or its subsidiary or the entity in which it has a controlling interest) becomes contractually obligated so that its unilateral withdrawal from the transaction would entail significant loss, liability, or other damage.

§ 8.61
Judicial Action

(a) A transaction effected or proposed to be effected by a corporation (or by a subsidiary of the corporation or any other entity in which the corporation has a controlling interest) that is not a director's conflicting interest transaction may not be enjoined, set aside, or give rise to an award of damages or other sanctions, in a proceeding by a shareholder or by or in the right of the corporation, because a director of the corporation, or any person with whom or which he has a personal, economic, or other association, has an interest in the transaction.

(b) A director's conflicting interest transaction may not be enjoined, set aside, or give rise to an award of damages or other sanctions, in a proceeding by a shareholder or by or in the right of the corporation, because the director, or any person with whom or which he has a personal, economic, or other association, has an interest in the transaction, if:

(1) directors' action respecting the transaction was at any time taken in compliance with section 8.62;

(2) shareholders' action respecting the transaction was at any time taken in compliance with section 8.63;

(3) the transaction, judged according to the circumstances at the time of commitment, is established to have been fair to the corporation.

§ 8.62
Directors' Action

(a) Directors' action respecting a transaction is effective for purposes of section 8.61(b)(1) if the transaction received the affirmative vote of a majority (but no fewer than two) of those qualified directors on the board of directors or on a duly empowered committee of the board who voted on the transaction after either required disclosure to them (to the extent the information was not known by them) or compliance with subsection (b); provided that action by a committee is so effective only if (1) all its members are qualified directors, and (2) its members are either all the qualified directors on the board or are appointed by the affirmative vote of a majority of the qualified directors on the board.

(b) If a director has a conflicting interest respecting a transaction, but neither he nor a related person of the director specified in section 8.60(3)(i) is a party to the transaction, and if the director has a duty under law or professional canon, or a duty of confidentiality to another person, respecting information relating to the transaction such that the director may not make the disclosure described in section 8.60(4)(ii), then disclosure is sufficient for purposes of subsection (a) if the director (1) discloses to the directors voting on the transaction the existence and nature of his conflicting interest and informs them of the character and limitations imposed by that duty before their vote on the transaction, and (2) plays no part, directly or indirectly, in their deliberations or vote.

(c) A majority (but no fewer than two) of all the qualified directors on the board of directors, or on the committee, constitutes a quorum for purposes of action that complies with this section. Directors' action that otherwise complies with this section is not affected by the presence or vote of a director who is not a qualified director.

(d) For purposes of this section, "qualified director" means, with respect to a director's conflicting interest transaction, any director who does not have either (1) a conflicting interest respecting the transaction, or (2) a familial, financial, professional, or employment relationship with a second director who does have a conflicting interest respecting the transaction, which relationship would, in the circumstances, reasonably be expected to exert an influence on the first director's judgment when voting on the transaction.

§ 8.63
Shareholders' Action

(a) Shareholders' action respecting a transaction is effective for purposes of section 8.61(b)(2) if a majority of the votes entitled to be cast by the holders of all qualified shares were cast in favor of the transaction after (1) notice to shareholders describing the director's conflicting interest transaction, (2) provision of the information referred to in subsection (d), and (3) required disclosure to the shareholders who voted on the transaction (to the extent the information was not known by them).

(b) For purposes of this section, "qualified shares" means any shares entitled to vote with respect to the director's conflicting interest transaction except shares that, to the knowledge, before the vote, of the secretary (or other officer or agent of the corporation authorized to tabulate votes), are beneficially owned (or the voting of which is controlled) by a director who has a conflicting interest respecting the transaction or by a related person of the director, or both.

(c) A majority of the votes entitled to be cast by the holders of all qualified shares constitutes a quorum for purposes of action that complies with this section. Subject to the provisions of subsections (d) and (e), shareholders' action that otherwise complies with this section is not affected by the presence of holders, or the voting, of shares that are not qualified shares.

(d) For purposes of compliance with subsection (a), a director who has a conflicting interest respecting the transaction shall, before the shareholders' vote, inform the secretary (or other officer or agent of the corporation authorized to tabulate votes) of the number, and the identity of persons holding or controlling the vote, of all shares that the director knows are beneficially owned (or the voting of which is controlled) by the director or by a related person of the director, or both.

(e)   If a shareholders' vote does not comply with subsection (a) solely because of a failure of a director to comply with subsection (d), and if the director establishes that his failure did not determine and was not intended by him to influence the outcome of the vote, the court may, with or without further proceedings respecting section 8.61(b)(3), take such action respecting the transaction and the director, and give such effect, if any, to the shareholders' vote, as it considers appropriate in the circumstances.

CHAPTER 9/[RESERVED]

. . . .

CHAPTER 10/AMENDMENT OF ARTICLES OF INCORPORATION AND BYLAWS
Subchapter A/Amendment of Articles of Incorporation
§ 10.01
Authority to Amend

(a)   A corporation may amend its articles of incorporation at any time to add or change a provision that is required or permitted in the articles of incorporation or to delete a provision not required in the articles of incorporation. Whether a provision is required or permitted in the articles of incorporation is determined as of the effective date of the amendment.

(b)   A shareholder of the corporation does not have a vested property right resulting from any provision in the articles of incorporation, including provisions relating to management, control, capital structure, dividend entitlement, or purpose or duration of the corporation.

§ 10.02
Amendment by Board of Directors

Unless the articles of incorporation provide otherwise, a corporation's board of directors may adopt one or more amendments to the corporation's articles of incorporation without shareholder action:
   (1)   to extend the duration of the corporation if it was incorporated at a time when limited duration was required by law;
   (2)   to delete the names and addresses of the initial directors;
   (3)   to delete the name and address of the initial registered agent or registered office, if a statement of change is on file with the secretary of state;
   (4)   to change each issued and unissued authorized share of an outstanding class into a greater number of whole shares if the corporation has only shares of that class outstanding;
   (5)   to change the corporate name by substituting the word "corporation," "incorporated," "company," "limited," or the abbreviation "corp.," "inc.," "co.," or "ltd.," for a similar word or abbreviation in the name, or by adding, deleting, or changing a geographical attribution for the name; or
   (6)   to make any other change expressly permitted by this Act to be made without shareholder action.

§ 10.03
Amendment by Board of Directors and Shareholders

(a)   A corporation's board of directors may propose one or more amendments to the articles of incorporation for submission to the shareholders.

(b)   For the amendment to be adopted:
   (1)   the board of directors must recommend the amendment to the shareholders unless the board of directors determines that because of conflict of interest or other special circumstances it should make no recommendation and communicates the basis for its determination to the shareholders with the amendment; and
   (2)   the shareholders entitled to vote on the amendment must approve the amendment as provided in subsection (e).

(c)   The board of directors may condition its submission of the proposed amendment on any basis.

(d)   The corporation shall notify each shareholder, whether or not entitled to vote, of the proposed shareholders' meeting in accordance with section 7.05. The notice of meeting must also state that the purpose, or one of the purposes, of the meeting is to consider the proposed amendment and contain or be accompanied by a copy or summary of the amendment.

(e)   Unless this Act, the articles of incorporation, or the board of directors (acting pursuant to subsection (c)) require a greater vote or a vote by voting groups, the amendment to be adopted must be approved by:
   (1)   a majority of the votes entitled to be cast on the amendment by any voting group with respect to which the amendment would create dissenters' rights; and
   (2)   the votes required by sections 7.25 and 7.26 by every other voting group entitled to vote on the amendment.

§ 10.04
Voting on Amendments by Voting Groups

(a)   The holders of the outstanding shares of a class are entitled to vote as a separate voting group (if shareholder voting is otherwise required by this Act) on a proposed amendment if the amendment would:
   (1)   increase or decrease the aggregate number of authorized shares of the class;
   (2)   effect an exchange or reclassification of all or part of the shares of the class into shares of another class;
   (3)   effect an exchange or reclassification, or create the right of exchange, of all or part of the shares of another class into shares of the class;
   (4)   change the designation, rights, preferences, or limitations of all or part of the shares of the class;
   (5)   change the shares of all or part of the class into a different number of shares of the same class;
   (6)   create a new class of shares having rights or preferences with respect to distributions or to dissolution that are prior, superior, or substantially equal to the shares of the class;
   (7)   increase the rights, preferences, or number of authorized shares of any class that, after giving effect to the amendment, have rights or preferences with respect to distributions or to dissolution that are prior, superior, or substantially equal to the shares of the class;

(8) limit or deny an existing preemptive right of all or part of the shares of the class; or

(9) cancel or otherwise affect rights to distributions or dividends that have accumulated but not yet been declared on all or part of the shares of the class.

(b) If a proposed amendment would affect a series of a class of shares in one or more of the ways described in subsection (a), the shares of that series are entitled to vote as a separate voting group on the proposed amendment.

(c) If a proposed amendment that entitles two or more series of shares to vote as separate voting groups under this section would affect those two or more series in the same or a substantially similar way, the shares of all the series so affected must vote together as a single voting group on the proposed amendment.

(d) A class or series of shares is entitled to the voting rights granted by this section although the articles of incorporation provide that the shares are nonvoting shares.

§ 10.05
Amendment Before Issuance of Shares

If a corporation has not yet issued shares, its incorporators or board of directors may adopt one or more amendments to the corporation's articles of incorporation.

§ 10.06
Articles of Amendment

A corporation amending its articles of incorporation shall deliver to the secretary of state for filing articles of amendment setting forth:

(1) the name of the corporation;

(2) the text of each amendment adopted;

(3) if an amendment provides for an exchange, reclassification, or cancellation of issued shares, provisions for implementing the amendment if not contained in the amendment itself;

(4) the date of each amendment's adoption;

(5) if an amendment was adopted by the incorporators or board of directors without shareholder action, a statement to that effect and that shareholder action was not required;

(6) if an amendment was approved by the shareholders:

   (i) the designation, number of outstanding shares, number of votes entitled to be cast by each voting group entitled to vote separately on the amendment, and number of votes of each voting group indisputably represented at the meeting;

   (ii) either the total number of votes cast for and against the amendment by each voting group entitled to vote separately on the amendment or the total number of undisputed votes cast for the amendment by each voting group and a statement that the number cast for the amendment by each voting group was sufficient for approval by that voting group.

§ 10.07
Restated Articles of Incorporation

(a) A corporation's board of directors may restate its articles of incorporation at any time with or without shareholder action.

(b) The restatement may include one or more amendments to the articles. If the restatement includes an amendment requiring shareholder approval, it must be adopted as provided in section 10.03.

(c) If the board of directors submits a restatement for shareholder action, the corporation shall notify each shareholder, whether or not entitled to vote, of the proposed shareholders' meeting in accordance with section 7.05. The notice must also state that the purpose, or one of the purposes, of the meeting is to consider the proposed restatement and contain or be accompanied by a copy of the restatement that identifies any amendment or other change it would make in the articles.

(d) A corporation restating its articles of incorporation shall deliver to the secretary of state for filing articles of restatement setting forth the name of the corporation and the text of the restated articles of incorporation together with a certificate setting forth:

   (1) whether the restatement contains an amendment to the articles requiring shareholder approval and, if it does not, that the board of directors adopted the restatement; or

   (2) if the restatement contains an amendment to the articles requiring shareholder approval, the information required by section 10.06.

(e) Duly adopted restated articles of incorporation supersede the original articles of incorporation and all amendments to them.

(f) The secretary of state may certify restated articles of incorporation, as the articles of incorporation currently in effect, without including the certificate information required by subsection (d).

§ 10.08
Amendment Pursuant to Reorganization

(a) A corporation's articles of incorporation may be amended without action by the board of directors or shareholders to carry out a plan of reorganization ordered or decreed by a court of competent jurisdiction under federal statute if the articles of incorporation after amendment contain only provisions required or permitted by section 2.02.

(b) The individual or individuals designated by the court shall deliver to the secretary of state for filing articles of amendment setting forth:

   (1) the name of the corporation;

   (2) the text of each amendment approved by the court;

   (3) the date of the court's order or decree approving the articles of amendment;

   (4) the title of the reorganization proceeding in which the order or decree was entered; and

   (5) a statement that the court had jurisdiction of the proceeding under federal statute.

(c) Shareholders of a corporation undergoing reorganization do not have dissenters' rights except as and to the extent provided in the reorganization plan.

(d) This section does not apply after entry of a final decree in the reorganization proceeding even though the court retains jurisdiction of the proceeding for limited purposes unrelated to consummation of the reorganization plan.

§ 10.09
Effect of Amendment

An amendment to articles of incorporation does not affect a cause of action existing against or in favor of the corporation, a proceeding to which the corporation is a party, or the existing rights of persons other than shareholders of the corporation. An amendment changing a corporation's name does not abate a proceeding brought by or against the corporation in its former name.

Subchapter B/Amendment of Bylaws
§ 10.20
Amendment by Board of Directors or Shareholders

(a) A corporation's board of directors may amend or repeal the corporation's bylaws unless:
    (1) the articles of incorporation or this Act reserve this power exclusively to the shareholders in whole or part; or
    (2) the shareholders in amending or repealing a particular bylaw provided expressly that the board of directors may not amend or repeal that bylaw.

(b) A corporation's shareholders may amend or repeal the corporation's bylaws even though the bylaws may also be amended or repealed by its board of directors.

§ 10.21
Bylaw Increasing Quorum or Voting Requirement for Shareholders

(a) If expressly authorized by the articles of incorporation, the shareholders may adopt or amend a bylaw that fixes a greater quorum or voting requirement for shareholders (or voting groups of shareholders) than is required by this Act. The adoption or amendment of a bylaw that adds, changes, or deletes a greater quorum or voting requirement for shareholders must meet the same quorum requirement and be adopted by the same vote and voting groups required to take action under the quorum and voting requirement then in effect or proposed to be adopted, whichever is greater.

(b) A bylaw that fixes a greater quorum or voting requirement for shareholders under subsection (a) may not be adopted, amended, or repealed by the board of directors.

§ 10.22
Bylaw Increasing Quorum or Voting Requirement for Directors

(a) A bylaw that fixes a greater quorum or voting requirement for the board of directors may be amended or repealed:
    (1) if originally adopted by the shareholders, only by the shareholders;
    (2) if originally adopted by the board of directors, either by the shareholders or by the board of directors.

(b) A bylaw adopted or amended by the shareholders that fixes a greater quorum or voting requirement for the board of directors may provide that it may be amended or repealed only by a specified vote of either the shareholders or the board of directors.

(c) Action by the board of directors under subsection (a)(2) to adopt or amend a bylaw that changes the quorum or voting requirement for the board of directors must meet the same quorum

requirement and be adopted by the same vote required to take action under the quorum and voting requirement then in effect or proposed to be adopted, whichever is greater.

CHAPTER 11/MERGER AND SHARE EXCHANGE
§ 11.01
Merger

(a) One or more corporations may merge into another corporation if the board of directors of each corporation adopts and its shareholders (if required by section 11.03) approve a plan of merger.

(b) The plan of merger must set forth:
    (1) the name of each corporation planning to merge and the name of the surviving corporation into which each other corporation plans to merge;
    (2) the terms and conditions of the merger; and
    (3) the manner and basis of converting the shares of each corporation into shares, obligations, or other securities of the surviving or any other corporation or into cash or other property in whole or part.

(c) The plan of merger may set forth:
    (1) amendments to the articles of incorporation of the surviving corporation; and
    (2) other provisions relating to the merger.

§ 11.02
Share Exchange

(a) A corporation may acquire all of the outstanding shares of one or more classes or series of another corporation if the board of directors of each corporation adopts and its shareholders (if required by section 11.03) approve the exchange.

(b) The plan of exchange must set forth:
    (1) the name of the corporation whose shares will be acquired and the name of the acquiring corporation;
    (2) the terms and conditions of the exchange;
    (3) the manner and basis of exchanging the shares to be acquired for shares, obligations, or other securities of the acquiring or any other corporation or for cash or other property in whole or part.

(c) The plan of exchange may set forth other provisions relating to the exchange.

(d) This section does not limit the power of a corporation to acquire all or part of the shares of one or more classes or series of another corporation through a voluntary exchange or otherwise.

§ 11.03
Action on Plan

(a) After adopting a plan of merger or share exchange, the board of directors of each corporation party to the merger, and the board of directors of the corporation whose shares will be acquired in the share exchange, shall submit the plan of merger (except as provided in subsection (g)) or share exchange for approval by its shareholders.

(b) For a plan of merger or share exchange to be approved:

(1) the board of directors must recommend the plan of merger or share exchange to the shareholders, unless the board of directors determines that because of conflict of interest or other special circumstances it should make no recommendation and communicates the basis for its determination to the shareholders with the plan; and

(2) the shareholders entitled to vote must approve the plan.

(c) The board of directors may condition its submission of the proposed merger or share exchange on any basis.

(d) The corporation shall notify each shareholder, whether or not entitled to vote, of the proposed shareholders' meeting in accordance with section 7.05. The notice must also state that the purpose, or one of the purposes, of the meeting is to consider the plan of merger or share exchange and contain or be accompanied by a copy or summary of the plan.

(e) Unless this Act, the articles of incorporation, or the board of directors (acting pursuant to subsection (c)) require a greater vote or a vote by voting groups, the plan of merger or share exchange to be authorized must be approved by each voting group entitled to vote separately on the plan by a majority of all the votes entitled to be cast on the plan by that voting group.

(f) Separate voting by voting groups is required:

(1) on a plan of merger if the plan contains a provision that, if contained in a proposed amendment to articles of incorporation, would require action by one or more separate voting groups on the proposed amendment under section 10.04;

(2) on a plan of share exchange by each class or series of shares included in the exchange, with each class or series constituting a separate voting group.

(g) Action by the shareholders of the surviving corporation on a plan of merger is not required if:

(1) the articles of incorporation of the surviving corporation will not differ (except for amendments enumerated in section 10.02) from its articles before the merger;

(2) each shareholder of the surviving corporation whose shares were outstanding immediately before the effective date of the merger will hold the same number of shares, with identical designations, preferences, limitations, and relative rights, immediately after;

(3) the number of voting shares outstanding immediately after the merger, plus the number of voting shares issuable as a result of the merger (either by the conversion of securities issued pursuant to the merger or the exercise of rights and warrants issued pursuant to the merger), will not exceed by more than 20 percent the total number of voting shares of the surviving corporation outstanding immediately before the merger; and

(4) the number of participating shares outstanding immediately after the merger, plus the number of participating shares issuable as a result of the merger (either by the conversion of securities issued pursuant to the merger or the exercise of rights and warrants issued pursuant to the merger), will not exceed by more than 20 percent the total number of participating shares outstanding immediately before the merger.

(h) As used in subsection (g):

(1) "Participating shares" means shares that entitle their holders to participate without limitation in distributions.

(2) "Voting shares" means shares that entitle their holders to vote unconditionally in elections of directors.

(i) After a merger or share exchange is authorized, and at any time before articles of merger or share exchange are filed, the planned merger or share exchange may be abandoned (subject to any contractual rights), without further shareholder action, in accordance with the procedure set forth in the plan of merger or share exchange or, if none is set forth, in the manner determined by the board of directors.

§ 11.04
Merger of Subsidiary

(a) A parent corporation owning at least 90 percent of the outstanding shares of each class of a subsidiary corporation may merge the subsidiary into itself without approval of the shareholders of the parent or subsidiary.

(b) The board of directors of the parent shall adopt a plan of merger that sets forth:

(1) the names of the parent and subsidiary; and

(2) the manner and basis of converting the shares of the subsidiary into shares, obligations, or other securities of the parent or any other corporation or into cash or other property in whole or part.

(c) The parent shall mail a copy or summary of the plan of merger to each shareholder of the subsidiary who does not waive the mailing requirement in writing.

(d) The parent may not deliver articles of merger to the secretary of state for filing until at least 30 days after the date it mailed a copy of the plan of merger to each shareholder of the subsidiary who did not waive the mailing requirement.

(e) Articles of merger under this section may not contain amendments to the articles of incorporation of the parent corporation (except for amendments enumerated in section 10.02).

§ 11.05
Articles of Merger or Share Exchange

(a) After a plan of merger or share exchange is approved by the shareholders, or adopted by the board of directors if shareholder approval is not required, the surviving or acquiring corporation shall deliver to the secretary of state for filing articles of merger or share exchange setting forth:

(1) the plan of merger or share exchange;

(2) if shareholder approval was not required, a statement to that effect:

(3) if approval of the shareholders of one or more corporations party to the merger or share exchange was required:

(i) the designation, number of outstanding shares, and number of votes entitled to be cast by each voting group entitled to vote separately on the plan as to each corporation; and

(ii) either the total number of votes cast for and against the plan by each voting group entitled to vote separately on the plan or the total number of undisputed votes cast for the plan separately by each voting group and a statement that the number cast for the plan by each voting group was sufficient for approval by that voting group.

(b) Unless a delayed effect date is specified, a merger or share exchange takes effect when the articles of merger or share exchange are filed.

§ 11.06
Effect of Merger or Share Exchange

(a) When a merger takes effect:

(1) every other corporation party to the merger merges into the surviving corporation and the separate existence of every corporation except the surviving corporation ceases;

(2) the title to all real estate and other property owned by each corporation party to the merger is vested in the surviving corporation without reversion or impairment;

(3) the surviving corporation has all liabilities of each corporation party to the merger;

(4) a proceeding pending against any corporation party to the merger may be continued as if the merger did not occur or the surviving corporation may be substituted in the proceeding for the corporation whose existence ceased;

(5) the articles of incorporation of the surviving corporation are amended to the extent provided in the plan of merger; and

(6) the shares of each corporation party to the merger that are to be converted into shares, obligations, or other securities of the surviving or any other corporation or into cash or other property are converted and the former holders of the shares are entitled only to the rights provided in the articles of merger or to their rights under chapter 13.

(b) When a share exchange takes effect, the shares of each acquired corporation are exchanged as provided in the plan, and the former holders of the shares are entitled only to the exchange rights provided in the articles of share exchange or to their rights under chapter 13.

§ 11.07
Merger of Share Exchange With Foreign Corporation

(a) One or more foreign corporations may merge or enter into a share exchange with one or more domestic corporations if:

(1) in a merger, the merger is permitted by the law of the state or country under whose law each foreign corporation is incorporated and each foreign corporation complies with that law in effecting the merger;

(2) in a share exchange, the corporation whose shares will be acquired is a domestic corporation, whether or not a share exchange is permitted by the law of the state or country under whose law the acquiring corporation is incorporated;

(3) the foreign corporation complies with section 11.05 if it is the surviving corporation of the merger or acquiring corporation of the share exchange; and

(4) each domestic corporation complies with the applicable provisions of sections 11.01 through 11.04 and, if it is the surviving corporation of the merger or acquiring corporation of the share exchange, with section 11.05.

(b) Upon the merger or share exchange taking effect, the surviving foreign corporation of a merger and the acquiring foreign corporation of a share exchange is deemed:

(1) to appoint the secretary of state as its agent for service of process in a proceeding to enforce any obligation or the rights of dissenting shareholders of each domestic corporation party to the merger or share exchange; and

(2) to agree that it will promptly pay to the dissenting shareholders of each domestic corporation party to the merger or share exchange the amount, if any, to which they are entitled under chapter 13.

(c) This section does not limit the power of a foreign corporation to acquire all or part of the shares of one or more classes or series of a domestic corporation through a voluntary exchange or otherwise.

CHAPTER 12/SALE OF ASSETS
§ 12.01
Sale of Assets in Regular Course of Business and Mortgage of Assets

(a) A corporation may, on the terms and conditions and for the consideration determined by the board of directors:

(1) sell, lease, exchange, or otherwise dispose of all, or substantially all, of its property in the usual and regular course of business,

(2) mortgage, pledge, dedicate to the repayment of indebtedness (whether with or without recourse), or otherwise encumber any or all of its property whether or not in the usual and regular course of business, or

(3) transfer any or all of its property to a corporation all the shares of which are owned by the corporation.

(b) Unless the articles of incorporation require it, approval by the shareholders of a transaction described in subsection (a) is not required.

§ 12.02
Sale of Assets Other Than in Regular Course of Business

(a) A corporation may sell, lease, exchange, or otherwise dispose of all, or substantially all, of its property (with or without the good will), otherwise than in the usual and regular course of business, on the terms and conditions and for the consideration determined by the corporation's board of directors, if the board of directors proposes and its shareholders approve the proposed transaction.

(b) For a transaction to be authorized:

(1) the board of directors must recommend the proposed transaction to the shareholders unless the board of directors determines that because of conflict of interest or other special circumstances it should make no recommendation and communicates the basis for its determination to the shareholders with the submission of the proposed transaction; and

(2) the shareholders entitled to vote must approve the transaction.

(c) The board of directors may condition its submission of the proposed transaction on any basis.

(d) The corporation shall notify each shareholder, whether or not entitled to vote, of the proposed shareholders' meeting in accordance with section 7.05. The notice must also state that the purpose, or one of the purposes, of the meeting is to consider the sale, lease, exchange, or other disposition of all, or substantially all, the property of the corporation and contain or be accompanied by a description of the transaction.

(e) Unless the articles of incorporation or the board of directors (acting pursuant to subsection (c)) require a greater vote or a vote by voting groups, the transaction to be authorized must be approved by a majority of all the votes entitled to be cast on the transaction.

(f) After a sale, lease, exchange, or other disposition of property is authorized, the transaction may be abandoned (subject to any contractual rights) without further shareholder action.

(g) A transaction that constitutes a distribution is governed by section 6.40 and not by this section.

CHAPTER 13/DISSENTERS' RIGHTS
Subchapter A/Right to Dissent and Obtain Payment for Shares
§ 13.01
Definitions

In this chapter:

(1) "Corporation" means the issuer of the shares held by a dissenter before the corporate action, or the surviving or acquiring corporation by merger or share exchange of that issuer.

(2) "Dissenter" means a shareholder who is entitled to dissent from corporate action under section 13.02 and who exercises that right when and in the manner required by sections 13.20 through 13.28.

(3) "Fair value," with respect to a dissenter's shares, means the value of the shares immediately before the effectuation of the corporate action to which the dissenter objects, excluding any appreciation or depreciation in anticipation of the corporate action unless exclusion would be inequitable.

(4) "Interest" means interest from the effective date of the corporate action until the date of payment, at the average rate currently paid by the corporation on its principal bank loans or, if none, at a rate that is fair and equitable under all the circumstances.

(5) "Record shareholder" means the person in whose name shares are registered in the records of a corporation or the beneficial owner of shares to the extent of the rights granted by a nominee certificate on file with a corporation.

(6) "Beneficial shareholder" means the person who is a beneficial owner of shares held in a voting trust or by a nominee as the record shareholder.

(7) "Shareholder" means the record shareholder or the beneficial shareholder.

§ 13.02
Right to Dissent

(a) A shareholder is entitled to dissent from, and obtain payment of the fair value of his shares in the event of any of the following corporate actions:

    (1) consummation of a plan of merger to which the corporation is a party (i) if shareholder approval is required for the merger by section 11.03 or the articles of incorporation and the shareholder is entitled to vote on the merger or (ii) if the

corporation is a subsidiary that is merged with its parent under section 11.04;

    (2) consummation of a plan of share exchange to which the corporation is a party as the corporation whose shares will be acquired, if the shareholder is entitled to vote on the plan;

    (3) consummation of a sale or exchange of all, or substantially all, of the property of the corporation other than in the usual and regular course of business, if the shareholder is entitled to vote on the sale or exchange, including a sale in dissolution, but not including a sale pursuant to court order or a sale for cash pursuant to a plan by which all or substantially all of the net proceeds of the sale will be distributed to the shareholders within one year after the date of sale;

    (4) an amendment of the articles of incorporation that materially and adversely affects rights in respect of a dissenter's shares because it:

        (i) alters or abolishes a preferential right of the shares;

        (ii) creates, alters, or abolishes a right in respect of redemption, including a provision respecting a sinking fund for the redemption or repurchase, of the shares;

        (iii) alters or abolishes a preemptive right of the holder of the shares to acquire shares or other securities;

        (iv) excludes or limits the right of the shares to vote on any matter, or to cumulate votes, other than a limitation by dilution through issuance of shares or other securities with similar voting rights; or

        (v) reduces the number of shares owned by the shareholder to a fraction of a share if the fractional share so created is to be acquired for cash under section 6.04; or

    (5) any corporate action taken pursuant to a shareholder vote to the extent the articles of incorporation, bylaws, or a resolution of the board of directors provides that voting or nonvoting shareholders are entitled to dissent and obtain payment for their shares.

(b) A shareholder entitled to dissent and obtain payment for his shares under this chapter may not challenge the corporate action creating his entitlement unless the action is unlawful or fraudulent with respect to the shareholder or the corporation.

§ 13.03
Dissent by Nominees and Beneficial Owners

(a) A record shareholder may assert dissenters' rights as to fewer than all the shares registered in his name only if he dissents with respect to all shares beneficially owned by any one person and notifies the corporation in writing of the name and address of each person on whose behalf he asserts dissenters' rights. The rights of a partial dissenter under this subsection are determined as if the shares as to which he dissents and his other shares were registered in the names of different shareholders.

(b) A beneficial shareholder may assert dissenters' rights as to shares held on his behalf only if:

    (1) he submits to the corporation the record shareholder's written consent to the dissent not later than the time the beneficial shareholder asserts dissenters' rights; and

    (2) he does so with respect to all shares of which he is the beneficial shareholder or over which he has power to direct the vote.

Subchapter B/Procedure for Exercise of Dissenters' Rights
§ 13.20
Notice of Dissenters' Rights

(a) If proposed corporate action creating dissenters' rights under section 13.02 is submitted to a vote at a shareholders' meeting, the meeting notice must state that shareholders are or may be entitled to assert dissenters' rights under this chapter and be accompanied by a copy of this chapter.

(b) If corporate action creating dissenters' rights under section 13.02 is taken without a vote of shareholders, the corporation shall notify in writing all shareholders entitled to assert dissenters' rights that the action was taken and send them the dissenters' notice described in section 13.22.

§ 13.21
Notice of Intent to Demand Payment

(a) If proposed corporate action creating dissenters' rights under section 13.02 is submitted to a vote at a shareholders' meeting, a shareholder who wishes to assert dissenters' rights (1) must deliver to the corporation before the vote is taken written notice of his intent to demand payment for his shares if the proposed action is effectuated and (2) must not vote his shares in favor of the proposed action.

(b) A shareholder who does not satisfy the requirements of subsection (a) is not entitled to payment for his shares under this chapter.

§ 13.22
Dissenters' Notice

(a) If proposed corporate action creating dissenters' rights under section 13.02 is authorized at a shareholders' meeting, the corporation shall deliver a written dissenters' notice to all shareholders who satisfied the requirements of section 13.21.

(b) The dissenters' notice must be sent no later than 10 days after the corporate action was taken, and must:
(1) state where the payment demand must be sent and where and when certificates for certificated shares must be deposited;
(2) inform holders of uncertificated shares to what extent transfer of the shares will be restricted after the payment demand is received;
(3) supply a form for demanding payment that includes the date of the first announcement to news media or to shareholders of the terms of the proposed corporate action and requires that the person asserting dissenters' rights certify whether or not he acquired beneficial ownership of the shares before that date;
(4) set a date by which the corporation must receive the payment demand, which date may not be fewer than 30 nor more than 60 days after the date the subsection (a) notice is delivered; and
(5) be accompanied by a copy of this chapter.

§ 13.23
Duty to Demand Payment

(a) A shareholder sent a dissenters' notice described in section 13.22 must demand payment, certify whether he acquired benefi-

cial ownership of the shares before the date required to be set forth in the dissenter's notice pursuant to section 13.22(b)(3), and deposit his certificates in accordance with the terms of the notice.

(b) The shareholder who demands payment and deposits his shares under section (a) retains all other rights of a shareholder until these rights are cancelled or modified by the taking of the proposed corporate action.

(c) A shareholder who does not demand payment or deposit his share certificates where required, each by the date set in the dissenters' notice, is not entitled to payment for his shares under this chapter.

§ 13.24
Share Restrictions

(a) The corporation may restrict the transfer of uncertificated shares from the date the demand for their payment is received until the proposed corporate action is taken or the restrictions released under section 13.26.

(b) The person for whom dissenters' rights are asserted as to uncertificated shares retains all other rights of a shareholder until these rights are cancelled or modified by the taking of the proposed corporate action.

§ 13.25
Payment

(a) Except as provided in section 13.27, as soon as the proposed corporate action is taken, or upon receipt of a payment demand, the corporation shall pay each dissenter who complied with section 13.23 the amount the corporation estimates to be the fair value of his shares, plus accrued interest.

(b) The payment must be accompanied by:
(1) the corporation's balance sheet as of the end of a fiscal year ending not more than 16 months before the date of payment, an income statement for that year, a statement of changes in shareholders' equity for that year, and the latest available interim financial statements, if any;
(2) a statement of the corporation's estimate of the fair value of the shares;
(3) an explanation of how the interest was calculated;
(4) a statement of the dissenter's right to demand payment under section 13.28; and
(5) a copy of this chapter.

§ 13.26
Failure to Take Action

(a) If the corporation does not take the proposed action within 60 days after the date set for demanding payment and depositing share certificates, the corporation shall return the deposited certificates and release the transfer restrictions imposed on uncertificated shares.

(b) If after returning deposited certificates and releasing transfer restrictions, the corporation takes the proposed action, it must send a new dissenters' notice under section 13.22 and repeat the payment demand procedure.

§ 13.27
After-Acquired Shares

(a) A corporation may elect to withhold payment required by section 13.25 from a dissenter unless he was the beneficial owner of the shares before the date set forth in the dissenters' notice as the date of the first announcement to news media or to shareholders of the terms of the proposed corporate action.

(b) To the extent the corporation elects to withhold payment under subsection (a), after taking the proposed corporate action, it shall estimate the fair value of the shares, plus accrued interest, and shall pay this amount to each dissenter who agrees to accept it in full satisfaction of his demand. The corporation shall send with its offer a statement of its estimate of the fair value of the shares, an explanation of how the interest was calculated, and a statement of the dissenter's right to demand payment under section 13.28.

§ 13.28
Procedure if Shareholder Dissatisfied With Payment or Offer

(a) A dissenter may notify the corporation in writing of his own estimate of the fair value of his shares and amount of interest due, and demand payment of his estimate (less any payment under section 13.25), or reject the corporation's offer under section 13.27 and demand payment of the fair value of his shares and interest due, if:
> **(1)** the dissenter believes that the amount paid under section 13.25 or offered under section 13.27 is less than the fair value of his shares or that the interest due is incorrectly calculated;
> **(2)** the corporation fails to make payment under section 13.25 within 60 days after the date set for demanding payment; or
> **(3)** the corporation, having failed to take the proposed action, does not return the deposited certificates or release the transfer restrictions imposed on uncertificated shares within 60 days after the date set for demanding payment.

(b) A dissenter waives his right to demand payment under this section unless he notifies the corporation of his demand in writing under subsection (a) within 30 days after the corporation made or offered payment for his shares.

Subchapter C/Judicial Appraisal of Shares
§13.30
Court Action

(a) If a demand for payment under section 13.28 remains unsettled, the corporation shall commence a proceeding within 60 days after receiving the payment demand and petition the court to determine the fair value of the shares and accrued interest. If the corporation does not commence the proceeding within the 60-day period, it shall pay each dissenter whose demand remains unsettled the amount demanded.

(b) The corporation shall commence the proceeding in the [name or describe] court of the county where a corporation's principal office (or, in if none in this state, its registered office) is located. If the corporation is a foreign corporation without a registered office in this state, it shall commence the proceeding in the county in this state where the registered office of the domestic corporation merged with or whose shares were acquired by the foreign corporation was located.

(c) The corporation shall make all dissenters (whether or not residents of this state) whose demands remain unsettled parties to the proceeding as in an action against their shares and all parties must be served with a copy of the petition. Nonresidents may be served by registered or certified mail or by publication as provided by law.

(d) The jurisdiction of the court in which the proceeding is commenced under subsection (b) is plenary and exclusive. The court may appoint one or more persons as appraisers to receive evidence and recommend decision on the question of fair value. The appraisers have the powers described in the order appointing them, or in any amendment to it. The dissenters are entitled to the same discovery rights as parties in other civil proceedings.

(e) Each dissenter made a party to the proceeding is entitled to judgment (1) for the amount, if any, by which the court finds the fair value of his shares, plus interest, exceeds the amount paid by the corporation or (2) for the fair value, plus accrued interest, of his after-acquired shares for which the corporation elected to withhold payment under section 13.27

§ 13.31
Court Costs and Counsel Fees

(a) The court in an appraisal proceeding commenced under section 13.30 shall determine all costs of the proceeding, including the reasonable compensation and expenses of appraisers appointed by the court. The court shall assess the costs against the corporation, except that the court may assess costs against all or some of the dissenters, in amounts the court finds equitable, to the extent the court finds the dissenters acted arbitrarily, vexatiously, or not in good faith in demanding payment under section 13.28.

(b) The court may also assess the fees and expenses of counsel and experts for the respective parties, in amounts the court finds equitable:
> **(1)** against the corporation and in favor of any or all dissenters if the court finds the corporation did not substantially comply with the requirements of sections 13.20 through 13.28; or
> **(2)** against either the corporation or a dissenter, in favor of any other party, if the court finds that the party against whom the fees and expenses are assessed acted arbitrarily, vexatiously, or not in good faith with respect to the rights provided by this chapter.

(c) If the court finds that the services of counsel for any dissenter were of substantial benefit to other dissenters similarly situated, and that the fees for those services should not be assessed against the corporation, the court may award to these counsel reasonable fees to be paid out of the amounts awarded the dissenters who were benefited.

CHAPTER 14/DISSOLUTION
Subchapter A/Voluntary Dissolution
§ 14.01
Dissolution by Incorporators or Initial Directors

A majority of the incorporators or initial directors of a corporation that has not issued shares or has not commenced business may dissolve the corporation by delivering to the secretary of state for filing articles of dissolution that set forth:

(1) the name of the corporation:

(2) the date of its incorporation;

(3) either (i) that none of the corporation's shares has been issued or (ii) that the corporation has not commenced business;

(4) that no debt of the corporation remains unpaid;

(5) that the net assets of the corporation remaining after winding up have been distributed to the shareholders, if shares were issued; and

(6) that a majority of the incorporators or initial directors authorized the dissolution.

§ 14.02
Dissolution by Board of Directors and Shareholders

(a) A corporation's board of directors may propose dissolution for submission to the shareholders.

(b) For a proposal to dissolve to be adopted:

(1) the board of directors must recommend dissolution to the shareholders unless the board of directors determines that because of conflict of interest or other special circumstances it should make no recommendation and communicates the basis for its determination to the shareholders; and

(2) the shareholders entitled to vote must approve the proposal to dissolve as provided in subsection (e).

(c) The board of directors may condition its submission of the proposal for dissolution on any basis.

(d) The corporation shall notify each shareholder, whether or not entitled to vote, of the proposed shareholders' meeting in accordance with section 7.05. The notice must also state that the purpose, or one of the purposes, of the meeting is to consider dissolving the corporation.

(e) Unless the articles of incorporation or the board of directors (acting pursuant to subsection (c)) require a greater vote or a vote by voting groups, the proposal to dissolve to be adopted must be approved by a majority of all the votes entitled to be cast on that proposal.

§ 14.03
Articles of Dissolution

(a) At any time after dissolution is authorized, the corporation may dissolve by delivering to the secretary of state for filing articles of dissolution setting forth:

(1) the name of the corporation;

(2) the date dissolution was authorized;

(3) if dissolution was approved by the shareholders:

(i) the number of votes entitled to be cast on the proposal to dissolve; and

(ii) either the total number of votes cast for and against dissolution or the total number of undisputed votes cast for dissolution and a statement that the number cast for dissolution was sufficient for approval.

(4) If voting by voting groups is required, the information required by subparagraph (3) shall be separately provided for each voting group entitled to vote separately on the plan to dissolve.

(b) A corporation is dissolved upon the effective date of its articles of dissolution.

§ 14.04
Revocation of Dissolution

(a) A corporation may revoke its dissolution within 120 days of its effective date.

(b) Revocation of dissolution must be authorized in the same manner as the dissolution was authorized unless that authorization permitted revocation by action by the board of directors alone, in which event the board of directors may revoke the dissolution without shareholder action.

(c) After the revocation of dissolution is authorized, the corporation may revoke the dissolution by delivering to the secretary of state for filing articles of revocation of dissolution, together with a copy of its articles of dissolution, that set forth:

(1) the name of the corporation;

(2) the effective date of the dissolution that was revoked;

(3) the date that the revocation of dissolution was authorized;

(4) if the corporation's board of directors (or incorporators) revoked the dissolution, a statement to that effect;

(5) if the corporation's board of directors revoked a dissolution authorized by the shareholders, a statement that revocation was permitted by action by the board of directors alone pursuant to that authorization; and

(6) if shareholder action was required to revoke the dissolution, the information required by section 14.03(3) or (4).

(d) Unless a delayed effective date is specified, revocation of dissolution is effective when articles of revocation of dissolution are filed.

(e) When the revocation of dissolution is effective, it relates back to and takes effect as of the effective date of the dissolution and the corporation resumes carrying on its business as if dissolution had never occurred.

§ 14.05
Effect of Dissolution

(a) A dissolved corporation continues its corporate existence but may not carry on any business except that appropriate to wind up and liquidate its business and affairs, including:

(1) collecting its assets;

(2) disposing of its properties that will not be distributed in kind to its shareholders;

(3) discharging or making provision for discharging its liabilities;

(4) distributing its remaining property among its shareholders according to their interests; and

(5) doing every other act necessary to wind up and liquidate its business and affairs.

(b) Dissolution of a corporation does not:

(1) transfer title to the corporation's property;

(2) prevent transfer of its shares or securities, although the authorization to dissolve may provide for closing the corporation's share transfer records;

(3) subject its directors or officers to standards of conduct different from those prescribed in chapter 8;

(4) change quorum or voting requirements for its board of directors or shareholders; change provisions for selection, resignation, or removal of its directors or officers or both; or change provisions for amending its bylaws;

(5) prevent commencement of a proceeding by or against the corporation in its corporate name;

(6) abate or suspend a proceeding pending by or against the corporation on the effective date of dissolution; or

(7) terminate the authority of the registered agent of the corporation.

§ 14.06
Known Claims Against Dissolved Corporation

(a) A dissolved corporation may dispose of the known claims against it by following the procedure described in this section.

(b) The dissolved corporation shall notify its known claimants in writing of the dissolution at any time after its effective date. The written notice must:

(1) describe information that must be included in a claim;

(2) provide a mailing address where a claim may be sent;

(3) state the deadline, which may not be fewer than 120 days from the effective date of the written notice, by which the dissolved corporation must receive the claim; and

(4) state that the claim will be barred if not received by the deadline.

(c) A claim against the dissolved corporation is barred:

(1) if a claimant who was given written notice under subsection (b) does not deliver the claim to the dissolved corporation by the deadline;

(2) if a claimant whose claim was rejected by the dissolved corporation does not commence a proceeding to enforce the claim within 90 days from the effective date of the rejection notice.

(d) For purposes of this section, "claim" does not include a contingent liability or a claim based on an event occurring after the effective date of dissolution.

§ 14.07
Unknown Claims Against Dissolved Corporation

(a) A dissolved corporation may also publish notice of its dissolution and request that persons with claims against the corporation present them in accordance with the notice.

(b) The notice must:

(1) be published one time in a newspaper of general circulation in the county where the dissolved corporation's principal office (or, if none in this state, its registered office) is or was last located;

(2) describe the information that must be included in a claim and provide a mailing address where the claim may be sent; and

(3) state that a claim against the corporation will be barred unless a proceeding to enforce the claim is commenced within five years after the publication of the notice.

(c) If the dissolved corporation publishes a newspaper notice in accordance with subsection (b), the claim of each of the following claimants is barred unless the claimant commences a proceeding to enforce the claim against the dissolved corporation within five years after the publication date of the newspaper notice:

(1) a claimant who did not receive written notice under section 14.06;

(2) a claimant whose claim was timely sent to the dissolved corporation but not acted on;

(3) a claimant whose claim is contingent or based on an event occurring after the effective date of dissolution.

(d) A claim may be enforced under this section:

(1) against the dissolved corporation, to the extent of its undistributed assets; or

(2) if the assets have been distributed in liquidation, against a shareholder of the dissolved corporation to the extent of his pro rata share of the claim or the corporate assets distributed to him in liquidation, whichever is less, but a shareholders' total liability for all claims under this section may not exceed the total amount of assets distributed to him.

Subchapter B/Administrative Dissolution
§14.20
Grounds for Administrative Dissolution

The secretary of state may commence a proceeding under section 14.21 to administratively dissolve a corporation if:

(1) the corporation does not pay within 60 days after they are due any franchise taxes or penalties imposed by this Act or other law;

(2) the corporation does not deliver its annual report to the secretary of state within 60 days after it is due;

(3) the corporation is without a registered agent or registered office in this state for 60 days or more;

(4) the corporation does not notify the secretary of state within 60 days that its registered agent or registered office has been changed, that its registered agent has resigned, or that its registered office has been discontinued; or

(5) the corporation's period of duration stated in its articles of incorporation expires.

§14.21
Procedure for and Effect of Administrative Dissolution

(a) If the secretary of state determines that one or more grounds exist under section 14.20 for dissolving a corporation, he shall serve the corporation with written notice of his determination under section 5.04.

(b) If the corporation does not correct each ground for dissolution or demonstrate to the reasonable satisfaction of the secretary of state that each ground determined by the secretary of state does not exist within 60 days after service of the notice is perfected under section 5.04, the secretary of state shall administratively dissolve the corporation by signing a certificate of dissolution that recites the ground or grounds for dissolution and its effective date. The secretary of state shall file the original of the certificate and serve a copy on the corporation under section 5.04.

(c) A corporation administratively dissolved continues its corporate existence but may not carry on any business except that necessary to wind up and liquidate its business and affairs under section 14.05 and notify claimants under sections 14.06 and 14.07.

(d) The administrative dissolution of a corporation does not terminate the authority of its registered agent.

§14.22
Reinstatement Following Administrative Dissolution

(a) A corporation administratively dissolved under section 14.21 may apply to the secretary of state for reinstatement within two years after the effective date of dissolution. The application must:

(1) recite the name of the corporation and the effective date of its administrative dissolution;

(2) state that the ground or grounds for dissolution either did not exist or have been eliminated;

(3) state that the corporation's name satisfies the requirements of section 4.01; and

(4) contain a certificate from the [taxing authority] reciting that all taxes owed by the corporation have been paid.

(b) If the secretary of state determines that the application contains the information required by subsection (a) and that the information is correct, he shall cancel the certificate of dissolution and prepare a certificate of reinstatement that recites his determination and the effective date of reinstatement, file the original of the certificate, and serve a copy on the corporation under section 5.04.

(c) When the reinstatement is effective, it relates back to and takes effect as of the effective date of the administrative dissolution and the corporation resumes carrying on its business as if the administrative dissolution had never occurred.

§14.23
Appeal From Denial of Reinstatement

(a) If the secretary of state denies a corporation's application for reinstatement following administrative dissolution, he shall serve the corporation under section 5.04 with a written notice that explains the reason or reasons for denial.

(b) The corporation may appeal the denial of reinstatement to the [name or describe] court within 30 days after service of the notice of denial is perfected. The corporation appeals by petitioning the court to set aside the dissolution and attaching to the petition copies of the secretary of state's certificate of dissolution, the corporation's application for reinstatement, and the secretary of state's notice of denial.

(c) The court may summarily order the secretary of state to reinstate the dissolved corporation or may take other action the court considers appropriate.

(d) The court's final decision may be appealed as in other civil proceedings.

Subchapter C/Judicial Dissolution
§ 14.30
Grounds for Judicial Dissolution

The [name or describe court or courts] may dissolve a corporation:

(1) in a proceeding by the attorney general if it is established that:

    (i) the corporation obtained its articles of incorporation through fraud; or

    (ii) the corporation has continued to exceed or abuse the authority conferred upon it by law;

(2) in a proceeding by a shareholder if it is established that:

    (i) the directors are deadlocked in the management of the corporate affairs, the shareholders are unable to break the deadlock, and irreparable injury to the corporation is threatened or being suffered, or the business and affairs of the corporation can no longer be conducted to the advantage of the shareholders generally, because of the deadlock;

    (ii) the directors or those in control of the corporation have acted, are acting, or will act in a manner that is illegal, oppressive, or fraudulent;

    (iii) the shareholders are deadlocked in voting power and have failed, for a period that includes at least two consecutive annual meeting dates, to elect successors to directors whose terms have expired; or

    (iv) the corporate assets are being misapplied or wasted;

(3) in a proceeding by a creditor if it is established that:

    (i) the creditor's claim has been reduced to judgment, the execution on the judgment returned unsatisfied, and the corporation is insolvent; or

    (ii) the corporation has admitted in writing that the creditor's claim is due and owing and the corporation is insolvent; or

(4) in a proceeding by the corporation to have its voluntary dissolution continued under court supervision.

§ 14.31
Procedure for Judicial Dissolution

(a) Venue for a proceeding by the attorney general to dissolve a corporation lies in [name the county or counties]. Venue for a proceeding brought by any other party named in section 14.30 lies in the county where a corporation's principal office (or, if none in this state, its registered office) is or was last located.

(b) It is not necessary to make shareholders parties to a proceeding to dissolve a corporation unless relief is sought against them individually.

(c) A court in a proceeding brought to dissolve a corporation may issue injunctions, appoint a receiver or custodian pendente lite with all powers and duties the court directs, take other action required to preserve the corporate assets wherever located, and carry on the business of the corporation until a full hearing can be held.

§ 14.32
Receivership or Custodianship

(a) A court in a judicial proceeding brought to dissolve a corporation may appoint one or more receivers to wind up and liquidate, or one or more custodians to manage, the business and affairs of the corporation. The court shall hold a hearing, after notifying all parties to the proceeding and any interested persons designated by the court, before appointing a receiver or custodian. The court appointing a receiver or custodian has exclusive jurisdiction over the corporation and all its property wherever located.

(b) The court may appoint an individual or a domestic or foreign corporation (authorized to transact business in this state) as a receiver or custodian. The court may require the receiver or custodian to post bond, with or without sureties, in an amount the court directs.

(c) The court shall describe the powers and duties of the receiver or custodian in its appointing order, which may be amended from time to time. Among other powers:

    (1) the receiver (i) may dispose of all or any part of the assets of the corporation wherever located, at a public or private sale, if authorized by the court; and (ii) may sue and defend in his own name as receiver of the corporation in all courts of this state;

(2) the custodian may exercise all of the powers of the corporation, through or in place of its board of directors or officers, to the extent necessary to manage the affairs of the corporation in the best interests of its shareholders and creditors.

(d) The court during a receivership may redesignate the receiver a custodian, and during a custodianship may redesignate the custodian a receiver, if doing so is in the best interests of the corporation, its shareholders, and creditors.

(e) The court from time to time during the receivership or custodianship may order compensation paid and expense disbursements or reimbursements made to the receiver or custodian and his counsel from the assets of the corporation or proceeds from the sale of the assets.

§14.33
Decree of Dissolution

(a) If after a hearing the court determines that one or more grounds for judicial dissolution described in section 14.30 exist, it may enter a decree dissolving the corporation and specifying the effective date of the dissolution, and the clerk of the court shall deliver a certified copy of the decree to the secretary of state, who shall file it.

(b) After entering the decree of dissolution, the court shall direct the winding up and liquidation of the corporation's business and affairs in accordance with section 14.05 and the notification of claimants in accordance with sections 14.06 and 14.07.

Subchapter D/Miscellaneous
§ 14.40
Deposit With State Treasurer

Assets of a dissolved corporation that should be transferred to a creditor, claimant, or shareholder of the corporation who cannot be found or who is not competent to receive them shall be reduced to cash and deposited with the state treasurer or other appropriate state official for safekeeping. When the creditor, claimant, or shareholder furnishes satisfactory proof of entitlement to the amount deposited, the state treasurer or other appropriate state official shall pay him or his representative that amount.

CHAPTER 15/FOREIGN CORPORATIONS
Subchapter A/Certificate of Authority
§ 15.01
Authority to Transact Business Required

(a) A foreign corporation may not transact business in this state until it obtains a certificate of authority from the secretary of state.

(b) The following activities, among others, do not constitute transacting business within the meaning of subsection (a):

    (1) maintaining, defending, or settling any proceeding;

    (2) holding meetings of the board of directors or shareholders or carrying on other activities concerning internal corporate affairs;

    (3) maintaining bank accounts;

    (4) maintaining offices or agencies for the transfer, exchange, and registration of the corporation's own securities or maintaining trustees or depositaries with respect to those securities;

    (5) selling through independent contractors;

    (6) soliciting or obtaining orders, whether by mail or through employees or agents or otherwise, if the orders require acceptance outside this state before they become contracts;

    (7) creating or acquiring indebtedness, mortgages, and security interests in real or personal property;

    (8) securing or collecting debts or enforcing mortgages and security interests in property securing the debts;

    (9) owning, without more, real or personal property;

    (10) conducting an isolated transaction that is completed within 30 days and that is not one in the course of repeated transactions of a like nature;

    (11) transacting business in interstate commerce.

(c) The list of activities in subsection (b) is not exhaustive.

§ 15.02
Consequences of Transacting Business Without Authority

(a) A foreign corporation transacting business in this state without a certificate of authority may not maintain a proceeding in any court in this state until it obtains a certificate of authority.

(b) The successor to a foreign corporation that transacted business in this state without a certificate of authority and the assignee of a cause of action arising out of that business may not maintain a proceeding based on that cause of action in any court in this state until the foreign corporation or its successor obtains a certificate of authority.

(c) A court may stay a proceeding commenced by a foreign corporation, its successor, or assignee until it determines whether the foreign corporation or its successor requires a certificate of authority. If it so determines, the court may further stay the proceeding until the foreign corporation or its successor obtains the certificate.

(d) A foreign corporation is liable for a civil penalty of $____ for each day, but not to exceed a total of $____ for each year, it transacts business in this state without a certificate of authority. The attorney general may collect all penalties due under this subsection.

(e) Notwithstanding subsections (a) and (b), the failure of a foreign corporation to obtain a certificate of authority does not impair the validity of its corporate acts or prevent it from defending any proceeding in this state.

§ 15.03
Application for Certificate of Authority

(a) A foreign corporation may apply for a certificate of authority to transact business in this state by delivering an application to the secretary of state for filing. The application must set forth:

    (1) the name of the foreign corporation or, if its name is unavailable for use in this state, a corporate name that satisfies the requirements of section 15.06;

    (2) the name of the state or country under whose law it is incorporated;

    (3) its date of incorporation and period of duration;

    (4) the street address of its principal office;

(5) the address of its registered office in this state and the name of its registered agent at that office; and

(6) the names and usual business addresses of its current directors and officers.

(b) The foreign corporation shall deliver with the completed application a certificate of existence (or a document of similar import) duly authenticated by the secretary of state of other official having custody of corporate records in the state or country under whose law it is incorporated.

§ 15.04
Amended Certificate of Authority

(a) A foreign corporation authorized to transact business in this state must obtain an amended certificate of authority from the secretary of state if it changes:

(1) its corporate name;

(2) the period of its duration; or

(3) the state or country of its incorporation.

(b) The requirements of section 15.03 for obtaining an original certificate of authority apply to obtaining an amended certificate under this section.

§ 15.05
Effect of Certificate of Authority

(a) A certificate of authority authorizes the foreign corporation to which it is issued to transact business in this state subject, however, to the right of the state to revoke the certificate as provided in this Act.

(b) A foreign corporation with a valid certificate of authority has the same but no greater rights and has the same but no greater privileges as, and except as otherwise provided by this Act is subject to the same duties, restrictions, penalties, and liabilities now or later imposed on, a domestic corporation of like character.

(c) This Act does not authorize this state to regulate the organization or internal affairs of a foreign corporation authorized to transact business in this state.

§ 15.06
Corporate Name of Foreign Corporation

(a) If the corporate name of a foreign corporation does not satisfy the requirements of section 4.01, the foreign corporation to obtain or maintain a certificate of authority to transact business in this state:

(1) may add the word "corporation," "incorporated," "company," or "limited," or the abbreviation "corp.," "inc.," "co.," or "ltd.," to its corporate name for use in this state; or

(2) may use a fictitious name to transact business in this state if its real name is unavailable and it delivers to the secretary of state for filing a copy of the resolution of its board of directors, certified by its secretary, adopting the fictitious name.

(b) Except as authorized by subsections (c) and (d), the corporate name (including a fictitious name) of a foreign corporation must be distinguishable upon the records of the secretary of state from:

(1) the corporate name of a corporation incorporated or authorized to transact business in this state;

(2) a corporate name reserved or registered under section 4.02 or 4.03;

(3) the fictitious name of another foreign corporation authorized to transact business in this state; and

(4) the corporate name of a not-for-profit corporation incorporated or authorized to transact business in this state.

(c) A foreign corporation may apply to the secretary of state for authorization to use in this state the name of another corporation (incorporated or authorized to transact business in this state) that is not distinguishable upon his records from the name applied for. The secretary of state shall authorize use of the name applied for if:

(1) the other corporation consents to the use in writing and submits an undertaking in form satisfactory to the secretary of state to change its name to a name that is distinguishable upon the records of the secretary of state from the name of the applying corporation; or

(2) the applicant delivers to the secretary of state a certified copy of a final judgment of a court of competent jurisdiction establishing the applicant's right to use the name applied for in this state.

(d) A foreign corporation may use in this state the name (including the fictitious name) of another domestic or foreign corporation that is used in this state if the other corporation is incorporated or authorized to transact business in this state and the foreign corporation:

(1) has merged with the other corporation;

(2) has been formed by reorganization of the other corporation; or

(3) has acquired all or substantially all of the assets, including the corporate name, of the other corporation.

(e) If a foreign corporation authorized to transact business in this state changes its corporate name to one that does not satisfy the requirements of section 4.01, it may not transact business in this state under the changed name until it adopts a name satisfying the requirements of section 4.01 and obtains an amended certificate of authority under section 15.04.

§ 15.07
Registered Office and Registered Agent of Foreign Corporation

Each foreign corporation authorized to transact business in this state must continuously maintain in this state:

(1) a registered office that may be the same as any of its places of business; and

(2) a registered agent, who may be:

(i) an individual who resides in this state and whose business office is identical with the registered office;

(ii) a domestic corporation or not-for-profit domestic corporation whose business office is identical with the registered office; or

(iii) a foreign corporation or foreign not-for-profit corporation authorized to transact business in this state whose business office is identical with the registered office.

§ 15.08
Change of Registered Office or Registered
Agent of Foreign Corporation

(a) A foreign corporation authorized to transact business in this state may change its registered office or registered agent by delivering to the secretary of state for filing a statement of change that sets forth:

(1) its name;

(2) the street address of its current registered office;

(3) if the current registered office is to be changed, the street address of its new registered office;

(4) the name of its current registered agent;

(5) if the current registered agent is to be changed, the name of its new registered agent and the new agent's written consent (either on the statement or attached to it) to the appointment; and

(6) that after the change or changes are made, the street addresses of its registered office and the business office of its registered agent will be identical.

(b) If a registered agent changes the street address of his business office, he may change the street address of the registered office of any foreign corporation for which he is the registered agent by notifying the corporation in writing of the change and signing (either manually or in facsimile) and delivering to the secretary of state for filing a statement of change that complies with the requirements of subsection (a) and recites that the corporation has been notified of the change.

§ 15.09
Resignation of Registered Agent of Foreign Corporation

(a) The registered agent of a foreign corporation may resign his agency appointment by signing and delivering to the secretary of state for filing the original and two exact or conformed copies of a statement of resignation. The statement of resignation may include a statement that the registered office is also discontinued.

(b) After filing the statement, the secretary of state shall attach the filing receipt to one copy and mail the copy and receipt to the registered office if not discontinued. The secretary of state shall mail the other copy to the foreign corporation at its principal office address shown in its most recent annual report.

(c) The agency appointment is terminated, and the registered office discontinued if so provided, on the 31st day after the date on which the statement was filed.

§ 15.10
Service on Foreign Corporation

(a) The registered agent of a foreign corporation authorized to transact business in this state is the corporation's agent for service of process, notice, or demand required or permitted by law to be served on the foreign corporation.

(b) A foreign corporation may be served by registered or certified mail, return receipt requested, addressed to the secretary of the foreign corporation at its principal office shown in its application for a certificate of authority or in its most recent annual report if the foreign corporation:

(1) has no registered agent or its registered agent cannot with reasonable diligence be served;

(2) has withdrawn from transacting business in this state under section 15.20; or

(3) has had its certificate of authority revoked under section 15.31.

(c) Service is perfected under subsection (b) at the earliest of:

(1) the date the foreign corporation receives the mail;

(2) the date shown on the return receipt, if signed on behalf of the foreign corporation; or

(3) five days after its deposit in the United States Mail, if mailed postpaid and correctly addressed.

(d) This section does not prescribe the only means, or necessarily the required means, of serving a foreign corporation.

Subchapter B/Withdrawal
§ 15.20
Withdrawal of Foreign Corporation

(a) A foreign corporation authorized to transact business in this state may not withdraw from this state until it obtains a certificate of withdrawal from the secretary of state.

(b) A foreign corporation authorized to transact business in this state may apply for a certificate of withdrawal by delivering an application to the secretary of state for filing. The application must set forth:

(1) the name of the foreign corporation and the name of the state or country under whose law it is incorporated;

(2) that it is not transacting business in this state and that it surrenders its authority to transact business in this state;

(3) that it revokes the authority of its registered agent to accept service on its behalf and appoints the secretary of state as its agent for service of process in any proceeding based on a cause of action arising during the time it was authorized to transact business in this state;

(4) a mailing address to which the secretary of state may mail a copy of any process served on him under subdivision (3); and

(5) a commitment to notify the secretary of state in the future of any change in its mailing address.

(c) After the withdrawal of the corporation is effective, service of process on the secretary of state under this section is service on the foreign corporation. Upon receipt of process, the secretary of state shall mail a copy of the process to the foreign corporation at the mailing address set forth in its application for withdrawal.

Subchapter C/Revocation of Certificate of Authority
§ 15.30
Grounds for Revocation

The secretary of state may commence a proceeding under section 15.31 to revoke the certificate of authority of a foreign corporation authorized to transact business in this state if:

(1) the foreign corporation does not deliver its annual report to the secretary of state within 60 days after it is due;

(2) the foreign corporation does not pay within 60 days after they are due any franchise taxes or penalties imposed by this Act or other law;

(3) the foreign corporation is without a registered agent or registered office in this state for 60 days or more;

(4) the foreign corporation does not inform the secretary of state under section 15.08 or 15.09 that its registered agent or registered office has changed, that its registered agent has resigned, or that its registered office has been discontinued within 60 days of the change, resignation, or discontinuance;

(5) an incorporator, director, officer, or agent of the foreign corporation signed a document he knew was false in any material respect with intent that the document be delivered to the secretary of state for filing;

(6) the secretary of state receives a duly authenticated certificate from the secretary of state or other official having custody of corporate records in the state or country under whose law the foreign corporation is incorporated stating that it has been dissolved or disappeared as the result of a merger.

§ 15.31
Procedure for and Effect of Revocation

(a) If the secretary of state determines that one or more grounds exist under section 15.30 for revocation of a certificate of authority, he shall serve the foreign corporation with written notice of his determination under section 15.10.

(b) If the foreign corporation does not correct each ground for revocation or demonstrate to the reasonable satisfaction of the secretary of state that each ground determined by the secretary of state does not exist within 60 days after service of the notice is perfected under section 15.10, the secretary of state may revoke the foreign corporation's certificate of authority by signing a certificate of revocation that recites the ground or grounds for revocation and its effective date. The secretary of state shall file the original of the certificate and serve a copy on the foreign corporation under section 15.10.

(c) The authority of a foreign corporation to transact business in this state ceases on the date shown on the certificate revoking its certificate of authority.

(d) The secretary of state's revocation of a foreign corporation's certificate of authority appoints the secretary of state the foreign corporation's agent for service of process in any proceeding based on a cause of action which arose during the time the foreign corporation was authorized to transact business in this state. Service of process on the secretary of state under this subsection is service on the foreign corporation. Upon receipt of process, the secretary of state shall mail a copy of the process to the secretary of the foreign corporation at its principal office shown in its most recent annual report or in any subsequent communication received from the corporation stating the current mailing address of its principal office, or, if none are on file, in its application for a certificate of authority.

(e) Revocation of a foreign corporation's certificate of authority does not terminate the authority of the registered agent of the corporation.

§ 15.32
Appeal From Revocation

(a) A foreign corporation may appeal the secretary of state's revocation of its certificate of authority to the [name or describe] court within 30 days after service of the certificate of revocation is perfected under section 15.10. The foreign corporation appeals by petitioning the court to set aside the revocation and attaching to the petition copies of its certificate of authority and the secretary of state's certificate of revocation.

(b) The court may summarily order the secretary of state to reinstate the certificate of authority or may take any other action the court considers appropriate.

(c) The court's final decision may be appealed as in other civil proceedings.

CHAPTER 16/RECORDS AND REPORTS
Subchapter A/Records
§ 16.01
Corporate Records

(a) A corporation shall keep as permanent records minutes of all meetings of its shareholders and board of directors, a record of all actions taken by the shareholders or board of directors without a meeting, and a record of all actions taken by a committee of the board of directors in place of the board of directors on behalf of the corporation.

(b) A corporation shall maintain appropriate accounting records.

(c) A corporation or its agent shall maintain a record of its shareholders, in a form that permits preparation of a list of the names and addresses of all shareholders, in alphabetical order by class of shares showing the number and class of shares held by each.

(d) A corporation shall maintain its records in written form or in another form capable of conversion into written form within a reasonable time.

(e) A corporation shall keep a copy of the following records at its principal office:

(1) its articles or restated articles of incorporation and all amendments to them currently in effect;

(2) its bylaws or restated bylaws and all amendments to them currently in effect;

(3) resolutions adopted by its board of directors creating one or more classes or series of shares, and fixing their relative rights, preferences, and limitations, if shares issued pursuant to those resolutions are outstanding;

(4) the minutes of all shareholders' meetings, and records of all action taken by shareholders without a meeting, for the past three years;

(5) all written communications to shareholders generally within the past three years, including the financial statements furnished for the past three years under section 16.20;

(6) a list of the names and business addresses of its current directors and officers; and

(7) its most recent annual report delivered to the secretary of state under section 16.22.

§ 16.02
Inspection of Records by Shareholders

(a) Subject to section 16.03(c), a shareholder of a corporation is entitled to inspect and copy, during regular business hours at the corporation's principal office, any of the records of the corporation described in section 16.01(e) if he gives the corporation written notice of his demand at least five business days before the date on which he wishes to inspect and copy.

older of a corporation is entitled to inspect and
gular business hours at a reasonable location spec-
poration, any of the following records of the corpo-
the shareholder meets the requirements of subsection (c)
and gives the corporation written notice of his demand at least
five business days before the date on which he wishes to inspect
and copy:

(1) excerpts from minutes of any meeting of the board of
directors, records of any action of a committee of the board
of directors while acting in place of the board of directors on
behalf of the corporation, minutes of any meeting of the
shareholders, and records of action taken by the shareholders or board of directors without a meeting, to the extent not
subject to inspection under section 16.02(a);

(2) accounting records of the corporation; and

(3) the record of shareholders.

(c) A shareholder may inspect and copy the records identified in
subsection (b) only if:

(1) his demand is made in good faith and for a proper purpose;

(2) he describes with reasonable particularity his purpose
and the records he desires to inspect; and

(3) the records are directly connected with his purpose.

(d) The right of inspection granted by this section may not be
abolished or limited by a corporation's articles of incorporation or
bylaws.

(e) This section does not affect:

(1) the right of a shareholder to inspect records under section 7.20 or, if the shareholder is in litigation with the corporation, to the same extent as any other litigant;

(2) the power of a court, independently of this Act, to compel the production of corporate records for examination.

(f) For purposes of this section, "shareholder" includes a beneficial owner whose shares are held in a voting trust or by a nominee on his behalf.

§ 16.03
Scope of Inspection Right

(a) A shareholder's agent or attorney has the same inspection
and copying rights as the shareholder he represents.

(b) The right to copy records under section 16.02 includes, if
reasonable, the right to receive copies made by photographic, xe-
rographic, or other means.

(c) The corporation may impose a reasonable charge, covering
the costs of labor and material, for copies of any documents provided to the shareholder. The charge may not exceed the estimated cost of production or reproduction of the records.

(d) The corporation may comply with a shareholder's demand to
inspect the record of shareholders under section 16.02(b)(3) by
providing him with a list of its shareholders that was compiled no
earlier than the date of the shareholder's demand.

§ 16.04
Court-Ordered Inspection

(a) If a corporation does not allow a shareholder who complies
with section 16.02(a) to inspect and copy any records required by

that subsection to be available for inspection, the [name or describe court] of the county where the corporation's principal office (or, if none in this state, its registered office) is located may
summarily order inspection and copying of the records demanded
at the corporation's expense upon application of the shareholder.

(b) If a corporation does not within a reasonable time allow a
shareholder to inspect and copy any other record, the shareholder
who complies with section 16.02(b) and (c) may apply to the
[name or describe court] in the county where the corporation's
principal office (or, if none in this state, its registered office) is located for an order to permit inspection and copying of the records
demanded. The court shall dispose of an application under this
subsection on an expedited basis.

(c) If the court orders inspection and copying of the records demanded, it shall also order the corporation to pay the shareholder's costs (including reasonable counsel fees) incurred to
obtain the order unless the corporation proves that it refused inspection in good faith because it had a reasonable basis for doubt
about the right of the shareholder to inspect the records demanded.

(d) If the court orders inspection and copying of the records demanded, it may impose reasonable restrictions on the use or distribution of the records by the demanding shareholder.

Subchapter B/Reports
§ 16.20
Financial Statements for Shareholders

(a) A corporation shall furnish its shareholders annual financial
statements, which may be consolidated or combined statements
of the corporation and one or more of its subsidiaries, as appropriate, that include a balance sheet as of the end of the fiscal year,
an income statement for that year, and a statement of changes in
shareholders' equity for the year unless that information appears
elsewhere in the financial statements. If financial statements are
prepared for the corporation on the basis of generally accepted
accounting principles, the annual financial statements must also
be prepared on that basis.

(b) If the annual financial statements are reported upon by a
public accountant, his report must accompany them. If not, the
statements must be accompanied by a statement of the president
or the person responsible for the corporation's accounting
records:

(1) stating his reasonable belief whether the statements
were prepared on the basis of generally accepted accounting
principles and, if not, describing the basis of preparation;
and

(2) describing any respects in which the statements were
not prepared on a basis of accounting consistent with the
statements prepared for the preceding year.

(c) A corporation shall mail the annual financial statements to
each shareholder within 120 days after the close of each fiscal
year. Thereafter, on written request from a shareholder who was
not mailed the statements, the corporation shall mail him the latest financial statements.

§16.21
Other Reports to Shareholders

(a) If a corporation indemnifies or advances expenses to a director under section 8.51, 8.52, 8.53, or 8.54 in connection with a proceeding by or in the right of the corporation, the corporation shall report the indemnification or advance in writing to the shareholders with or before the notice of the next shareholders' meeting.

(b) If a corporation issues or authorizes the issuance of shares for promissary notes or for promises to render services in the future, the corporation shall report in writing to the shareholders the number of shares authorized or issued, and the consideration received by the corporation, with or before the notice of the next shareholders' meeting.

§ 16.22
Annual Report for Secretary of State

(a) Each domestic corporation, and each foreign corporation authorized to transact business in this state, shall deliver to the secretary of state for filing an annual report that sets forth:

(1) the name of the corporation and the state or country under whose law it is incorporated;

(2) the address of its registered office and the name of its registered agent at that office in this state;

(3) the address of its principal office;

(4) the names and business addresses of its directors and principal officers;

(5) a brief description of the nature of its business;

(6) the total number of authorized shares, itemized by class and series, if any, within each class; and

(7) the total number of issued and outstanding shares, itemized by class and series, if any, within each class.

(b) Information in the annual report must be current as of the date the annual report is executed on behalf of the corporation.

(c) The first annual report must be delivered to the secretary of state between January 1 and April 1 of the year following the calendar year in which a domestic corporation was incorporated or a foreign corporation was authorized to transact business. Subsequent annual reports must be delivered to the secretary of state between January 1 and April 1 of the following calendar years.

(d) If an annual report does not contain the information required by this section, the secretary of state shall promptly notify the reporting domestic or foreign corporation in writing and return the report to it for correction. If the report is corrected to contain the information required by this section and delivered to the secretary of state within 30 days after the effective date of notice, it is deemed to be timely filed.

CHAPTER 17 / TRANSITION PROVISIONS
. . . .

Appendix E

The Constitution of the United States of America
(Selected Provisions)

...

ARTICLE I

...

Section 8

The Congress shall have Power to lay and collect Taxes, Duties, Imposts and Excises, to pay the Debts and provide for the common Defence and general Welfare of the United States; but all Duties, Imposts and Excises shall be uniform throughout the United States;

To borrow Money on the credit of the United States;

To regulate Commerce with foreign Nations, and among the several States, and with the Indian Tribes;

To establish an uniform Rule of Naturalization, and uniform Laws on the subject of Bankruptcies throughout the United States;

To coin Money, regulate the Value thereof, and of foreign Coin, and fix the Standard of Weights and Measures;

To provide for the Punishment of counterfeiting the Securities and current Coin of the United States;

To establish Post Offices and post Roads;

To promote the Progress of Science and useful Arts, by securing for limited Times to Authors and Inventors the exclusive Right to their respective Writings and Discoveries;

To constitute Tribunals inferior to the supreme Court;

To define and punish Piracies and Felonies committed on the high Seas, and Offenses against the Law of Nations;

To declare War, grant Letters of Marque and Reprisal, and make Rules concerning Captures on Land and Water;

To raise and support Armies, but no Appropriation of Money to that Use shall be for a longer Term than two Years;

To provide and maintain a Navy;

To make Rules for the Government and Regulation of the land and naval Forces;

To provide for calling forth the Militia to execute the Laws of the Union, suppress Insurrections and repel Invasions;

To provide for organizing, arming, and disciplining, the Militia, and for governing such Part of them as may be employed in the Service of the United States, reserving to the States respectively, the Appointment of the Officers, and the Authority of training the Militia according to the discipline prescribed by Congress;

To exercise exclusive Legislation in all Cases whatsoever, over such District (not exceeding ten Miles square) as may, by Cession of particular States, and the Acceptance of Congress, become the Seat of the Government of the United States, and to exercise like Authority over all Places purchased by the Consent of the Legislature of the State in which the Same shall be, for the Erection of Forts, Magazines, Arsenals, dock-Yards, and other needful Buildings;—And

To make all Laws which shall be necessary and proper for carrying into Execution the foregoing Powers, and all other Powers vested by this Constitution in the Government of the United States, or in any Department or Officer thereof.

Section 9

The Migration or Importation of such Persons as any of the States now existing shall think proper to admit, shall not be prohibited by the Congress prior to the Year one thousand eight hundred and eight, but a Tax or Duty may be imposed on such Importation, not exceeding ten dollars for each Person.

The Privilege of the Writ of Habeas Corpus shall not be suspended, unless when in Cases of Rebellion or Invasion the public Safety may require it.

No Bill of Attainder or ex post facto Law shall be passed.

No Capitation, or other direct, Tax shall be laid, unless in Proportion to the Census or Enumeration herein before directed to be taken.

No Tax or Duty shall be laid on Articles exported from any State.

No Preference shall be given by any Regulation of Commerce or Revenue to the Ports of one State over those of another: nor shall Vessels bound to, or from, one State, be obliged to enter, clear, or pay Duties in another.

No Money shall be drawn from the Treasury, but in Consequence of Appropriations made by Laws; and a regular Statement and Account of the Receipts and Expenditures of all public Money shall be published from time to time.

No Title of Nobility shall be granted by the United States: And no Person holding any Office of Profit or Trust under them, shall, without the Consent of the Congress, accept of any present, Emolument, Office, or Title, of any kind whatever, from any King, Prince, or foreign State.

Section 10

No State shall enter into any Treaty, Alliance, or Confederation; grant Letters of Marque and Reprisal; coin Money; emit Bills of Credit; make any Thing but gold and silver Coin a Tender in Payment of Debts; pass any Bill of Attainder, ex post facto Law, or Law impairing the Obligation of Contracts, or grant any Title of Nobility.

No State shall, without the Consent of the Congress, lay any Imposts or Duties on Imports or Exports, except what may be absolutely necessary for executing its inspection Laws: and the net Produce of all Duties and Imposts, laid by any State on Imports or Exports, shall be for the Use of the Treasury of the United States;

and all such Laws shall be subject to the Revision and Controul of the Congress.

No State shall, without the Consent of Congress, lay any Duty of Tonnage, keep Troops, or Ships of War in time of Peace, enter into any Agreement or Compact with another State, or with a foreign Power, or engage in War, unless actually invaded, or in such imminent Danger as will not admit of delay.

ARTICLE II [OMITTED]

...

ARTICLE III
Section 1

The judicial Power of the United States, shall be vested in one supreme Court, and in such inferior Courts as the Congress may from time to time ordain and establish. The Judges, both of the supreme and inferior Courts, shall hold their Offices during good Behaviour, and shall, at stated Times, receive for their Services, a Compensation, which shall not be diminished during their Continuance in Office.

Section 2

The judicial Power shall extend to all Cases, in Law and Equity, arising under this Constitution, the Laws of the United States, and Treaties made, or which shall be made, under their Authority;—to all Cases affecting Ambassadors, other public Ministers and Consuls;—to all Cases of admirality and maritime Jurisdiction;—to Controversies to which the United States shall be a Party;—to Controversies between two or more States;—between a State and Citizens of another State;—between Citizens of different States;—between Citizens of the same State claiming Lands under Grants of different States, and between a State, or the Citizens thereof, and foreign States, Citizens or Subjects.

In all Cases affecting Ambassadors, other public Ministers and Consuls, and those in which a State shall be Party, the supreme Court shall have original Jurisdiction. In all the other Cases before mentioned, the supreme Court shall have appellate Jurisdiction, both as to Law and Fact, with such Exceptions, and under such Regulations as the Congress shall make.

The Trial of all Crimes, except in Cases of Impeachment, shall be by Jury; and such Trial shall be held in the State where the said Crimes shall have been committed; but when not committed within any State, the Trial shall be at such Place or Places as the Congress may by Law have directed.

...

ARTICLE IV
Section 1

Full Faith and Credit shall be given in each State to the public Acts, Records, and judicial Proceedings of every other State. And the Congress may by general Laws prescribe the Manner in which such Acts, Records and Proceedings shall be proved, and the Effect thereof.

Section 2

The Citizens of each State shall be entitled to all Privileges and Immunities of Citizens in the several States.

A Person charged in any State with Treason, Felony, or other Crime, who shall flee from Justice, and be found in another State, shall on Demand of the executive Authority of the State from which he fled, be delivered up, to be removed to the State having Jurisdiction of the Crime.

No Person held to Service or Labour in one State, under the Laws thereof, escaping into another, shall, in Consequence of any Law or Regulation therein, be discharged from such Service or Labour, but shall be delivered up on Claim of the Party to whom such Service or Labour may be due.

Section 3

New States may be admitted by the Congress into this Union; but no new State shall be formed or erected within the Jurisdiction of any other State; nor any State be formed by the Junction of two or more States, or Parts of States, without the Consent of the Legislatures of the States concerned as well as of the Congress.

The Congress shall have Power to dispose of and make all needful Rules and Regulations respecting the Territory or other Property belonging to the United States; and nothing in this Constitution shall be so construed as to Prejudice any Claims of the United States, or of any particular State.

Section 4

The United States shall guarantee to every State in this Union a Republican Form of Government, and shall protect each of them against Invasion; and on Application of the Legislature, or of the Executive (when the Legislature cannot be convened) against domestic Violence.

ARTICLE V [OMITTED]

...

ARTICLE VI

All Debts contracted and Engagements entered into, before the Adoption of this Constitution, shall be as valid against the United States under this Constitution, as under the Confederation.

This Constitution, and the Laws of the United States which shall be made in Pursuance thereof; and all Treaties made, or which shall be made, under the Authority of the United States, shall be the supreme Law of the Land; and the Judges in every State shall be bound thereby, any Thing in the Constitution or Laws of any State to the Contrary notwithstanding.

The Senators and Representatives before mentioned, and the Members of the several State Legislatures, and all executive and judicial Officers, both of the United States and of the several States, shall be bound by Oath or Affirmation, to support this Constitution; but no religious Test shall ever be required as a Qualification to any Office or public Trust under the United States.

ARTICLE VII [OMITTED]

. . .

AMENDMENT I [1791]

Congress shall make no law respecting an establishment of religion, or prohibiting the free exercise thereof; or abridging the freedom of speech, or of the press; or the right of the people peaceably to assemble, and to petition the Government for a redress of grievances.

AMENDMENT II [1791]

A well regulated Militia, being necessary to the security for a free State, the right of the people to keep and bear Arms, shall not be infringed.

AMENDMENT III [1791]

No Soldier shall, in time of peace be quartered in any house, without the consent of the Owner, nor in time of war, but in a manner to be prescribed by law.

AMENDMENT IV [1791]

The right of the people to be secure in their persons, houses, papers and effects, against unreasonable searches and seizures, shall not be violated, and no Warrants shall issue, but upon probable cause, supported by Oath or affirmation, and particularly describing the place to be searched, and the persons or things to be seized.

AMENDMENT V [1791]

No person shall be held to answer for a capital, or otherwise infamous crime, unless on a presentment or indictment of a Grand Jury, except in cases arising in the land or naval forces, or in the Militia, when in actual service in time of War or public danger; nor shall any person be subject for the same offense to be twice put in jeopardy of life or limb; nor shall be compelled in any criminal case to be a witness against himself, nor be deprived of life, liberty, or property, without due process of law; nor shall private property be taken for public use, without just compensation.

AMENDMENT VI [1791]

In all criminal prosecutions, the accused shall enjoy the right to a speedy and public trial, by an impartial jury of the State and district wherein the crime shall have been committed, which district shall have been previously ascertained by law, and to be informed of the nature and cause of the accusation; to be confronted with the Witnesses against him; to have compulsory process for obtaining witnesses in his favor, and to have the Assistance of counsel for his defence.

AMENDMENT VII [1791]

In Suits at common law, where the value in controversy shall exceed twenty dollars, the right of trial by jury shall be preserved, and no fact tried by a jury, shall be otherwise reexamined in any Court of the United States, than according to the rules of the common law.

AMENDMENT VIII [1791]

Excessive bail shall not be required, no excessive fines imposed, nor cruel and unusual punishments inflicted.

AMENDMENT IX [1791]

The enumeration in the Constitution, of certain rights, shall not be construed to deny or disparage others retained by the people.

AMENDMENT X [1791]

The powers not delegated to the United States by the Constitution, nor prohibited by it to the States, are reserved to the States respectively, or to the people.

AMENDMENT XI [1798]

The Judicial power of the United States shall not be construed to extend to any suit in law or equity, commenced or prosecuted against one of the United States by Citizens of another State, or by Citizens or Subjects of any Foreign State.

AMENDMENT XII [1804]

The Electors shall meet in their respective states and vote by ballot for President and Vice-President, one of whom, at least, shall not be an inhabitant of the same state with themselves; they shall name in their ballots the person voted for as President, and in distinct ballots the person voted for as Vice-President, and they shall make distinct lists of all persons voted for as President, and of all persons voted for as Vice-President, and of the number of votes for each, which lists they shall sign and certify, and transmit sealed to the seat of the government of the United States, directed to the President of the Senate;—The President of the Senate shall, in the presence of the Senate and House of Representatives, open all the certificates and the votes shall then be counted;—The person having the greatest number of votes for President, shall be the President, if such number be a majority of the whole number of Electors appointed; and if no person have such majority, then from the persons having the highest numbers not exceeding three on the list of those voted for as President, the House of Representatives shall choose immediately, by ballot, the President. But in choosing the President, the votes shall be taken by states, the representation from each state having one vote; a quorum for this purpose shall consist of a member or members from two-thirds of the states, and a majority of all the states shall be necessary to a choice. And if the House of Representatives shall not choose a President whenever the right of choice shall devolve upon them, before the fourth day of March next following, then the Vice-President shall act as President, as in the case of the death or other constitutional disability of the President. The person having the greatest number of votes as Vice-President, shall be the Vice-President, if such number be a majority of the whole number of Electors appointed, and if no person have a majority, then from the two highest numbers on the list, the Senate shall choose the Vice-President; a quorum for the purpose shall consist of two-thirds of the whole number of Senators, and a majority of the whole number shall be necessary to a choice. But no person constitutionally ineligible to the office of President shall be eligible to that of the Vice-President of the United States.

AMENDMENT XIII [1865]
Section 1

Neither slavery nor involuntary servitude, except as a punishment for crime whereof the party shall have been duly convicted, shall exist within the United States, or any place subject to their jurisdiction.

Section 2

Congress shall have power to enforce this article by appropriate legislation.

AMENDMENT XIV [1868]
Section 1

All persons born or naturalized in the United States, and subject to the jurisdiction thereof, are citizens of the United States and of the State wherein they reside. No State shall make or enforce any law which shall abridge the privileges or immunities of citizens of the United States; nor shall any State deprive any person of life, liberty, or property, without due process of law; nor deny to any person within its jurisdiction the equal protection of the laws.

Section 2

Representatives shall be appointed among the several States according to their respective numbers, counting the whole number of persons in each State, excluding Indians not taxed. But when the right to vote at any election for the choice of electors for President and Vice President of the United States, Representatives in Congress, the Executive and Judicial officers of a State, or the members of the Legislature thereof, is denied to any of the male inhabitants of such State, being twenty-one years of age, and citizens of the United States, or in any way abridged, except for participation in rebellion, or other crime, the basis of representation therein shall be reduced in the proportion which the number of such male citizens shall bear to the whole number of male citizens twenty-one years of age in such State.

Section 3

No person shall be a Senator or Representative in Congress, or elector of President and Vice President, or hold any office, civil or military, under the United States, or under any State, who, having previously taken an oath, as a member of Congress, or as an officer of the United States, or as a member of any State legislature, or as an executive or judicial officer of any State, to support the Constitution of the United States, shall have engaged in insurrection or rebellion against the same, or given aid or comfort to the enemies thereof. But Congress may by a vote of two-thirds of each House, remove such disability.

Section 4

The validity of the public debt of the United States, authorized by law, including debts incurred for payment of pensions and bounties for services in suppressing insurrection or rebellion, shall not be questioned. But neither the United States nor any State shall assume or pay any debt or obligation incurred in aid of insurrection or rebellion against the United States, or any claim for the loss or emancipation of any slave; but all such debts, obligations and claims shall be held illegal and void.

Section 5

The Congress shall have power to enforce, by appropriate legislation, the provisions of this article.

AMENDMENT XV [1870]
Section 1

The right of citizens of the United States to vote shall not be denied or abridged by the United States or by any State on account of race, color, or previous condition of servitude.

Section 2

The Congress shall have power to enforce this article by appropriate legislation.

AMENDMENT XVI [1913]

The Congress shall have power to lay and collect taxes on incomes, from whatever source derived, without apportionment among the several States, and without regard to any census or enumeration.

AMENDMENT XVII [1913]

The Senate of the United States shall be composed of two Senators from each State, elected by the people thereof, for six years; and each Senator shall have one vote. The electors in each State shall have the qualifications requisite for electors of the most numerous branch of the State legislatures.

When vacancies happen in the representation of any State in the Senate, the executive authority of each State shall issue writs of election to fill such vacancies; *Provided*, That the legislature of any State may empower the executive thereof to make temporary appointments until the people fill the vacancies by election as the legislature may direct.

This amendment shall not be so construed as to affect the election or term of any Senator chosen before it becomes valid as part of the Constitution.

AMENDMENT XVIII [1919]
Section 1

After one year from the ratification of this article the manufacture, sale, or transportation of intoxicating liquors within, the importation thereof into, or the exportation thereof from the United States and all territory subject to the jurisdiction thereof for beverage purposes is hereby prohibited.

Section 2

The Congress and the several States shall have concurrent power to enforce this article by appropriate legislation.

Section 3

This article shall be inoperative unless it shall have been ratified as an amendment to the Constitution by the legislatures of the several States, as provided in the Constitution, within seven years from the date of the submission hereof to the States by the Congress.

AMENDMENT XIX [1920]

The right of citizens of the United States to vote shall not be denied or abridged by the United States or by any State on account of sex.

Congress shall have power to enforce this article by appropriate legislation.

AMENDMENT XX [1933]
Section 1

The terms of the President and Vice President shall end at noon on the 20th day of January, and the terms of Senators and Representatives at noon on the 3d day of January, of the years in which such terms would have ended if this article had not been ratified; and the terms of their successors shall then begin.

Section 2

The Congress shall assemble at least once in every year, and such meeting shall begin at noon on the 3d day of January, unless they shall by law appoint a different day.

Section 3

If, at the time fixed for the beginning of the term of the President, the President elect shall have died, the Vice President elect shall become President. If a President shall not have been chosen before the time fixed for the beginning of his term, or if the President elect shall have failed to qualify, then the Vice President elect shall act as President until a President shall have qualified; and the Congress may by law provide for the case wherein neither a President elect nor a Vice President elect shall have qualified, declaring who shall then act as President, or the manner in which one who is to act shall be selected, and such person shall act accordingly until a President or Vice President shall have qualified.

Section 4

The Congress may by law provide for the case of the death of any of the persons from whom the House of Representatives may choose a President whenever the right of choice shall have devolved upon them, and for the case of the death of any of the persons from whom the Senate may choose a Vice President whenever the right of choice shall have devolved upon them.

Section 5

Sections 1 and 2 shall take effect on the 15th day of October following the ratification of this article.

Section 6

This article shall be inoperative unless it shall have been ratified as an amendment to the Constitution by the legislatures of three-fourths of the several States within seven years from the date of its submission.

AMENDMENT XXI [1933]
Section 1

The eighteenth article of amendment to the Constitution of the United States is hereby repealed.

Section 2

The transportation or importation into any State, Territory, or possession of the United States for delivery or use therein of intoxicating liquors, in violation of the laws thereof, is hereby prohibited.

Section 3

This article shall be inoperative unless it shall have been ratified as an amendment to the Constitution by conventions in the several States, as provided in the Constitution, within seven years from the date of the submission hereof to the States by the Congress.

AMENDMENT XXII [1951]
Section 1

No person shall be elected to the office of the President more than twice, and no person who has held the office of President, or acted as President, for more than two years of a term to which some other person was elected President shall be elected to the office of the President more than once. But this Article shall not apply to any person holding the office of President when this Article was proposed by the Congress, and shall not prevent any person who may be holding the office of President, or acting as President, during the term within which this Article becomes operative from holding the office of President or acting as President during the remainder of such term.

Section 2

This article shall be inoperative unless it shall have been ratified as an amendment to the Constitution by the legislatures of three-fourths of the several States within seven years from the date of its submission to the States by the Congress.

AMENDMENT XXIII [1961]
Section 1

The District constituting the seat of Government of the United States shall appoint in such manner as the Congress may direct:

A number of electors of President and Vice President equal to the whole number of Senators and Representatives in Congress to which the District would be entitled if it were a State, but in no event more than the least populous State; they shall be in addition to those appointed by the States, but they shall be considered, for the purposes of the election of President and Vice President, to be electors appointed by a State; and they shall meet in the District and perform such duties as provided by the twelfth article of amendment.

Section 2

The Congress shall have power to enforce this article by appropriate legislation.

AMENDMENT XXIV [1964]
Section 1

The right of citizens of the United States to vote in any primary or other election for President or Vice President, for electors for President or Vice President, or for Senator or Representative in Congress, shall not be denied or abridged by the United States or any State by reason of failure to pay any poll tax or other tax.

Section 2

The Congress shall have power to enforce this article by appropriate legislation.

AMENDMENT XXV [1967]
Section 1

In case of the removal of the President from office or of his death or resignation, the Vice President shall become President.

Section 2

Whenever there is a vacancy in the office of the Vice President, the President shall nominate a Vice President who shall take office upon confirmation by a majority vote of both Houses of Congress.

Section 3

Whenever the President transmits to the President pro tempore of the Senate and the Speaker of the House of Representatives his written declaration that he is unable to discharge the powers and duties of his office, and until he transmits to them a written declaration to the contrary, such powers and duties shall be discharged by the Vice President as Acting President.

Section 4

Whenever the Vice President and a majority of either the principal officers of the executive departments or of such other body as Congress may by law provide, transmit to the President pro tempore of the Senate and the Speaker of the House of Representatives their written declaration that the President is unable to discharge the powers and duties of his office, the Vice President shall immediately assume the powers and duties of the office as Acting President.

Thereafter, when the President transmits to the President pro tempore of the Senate and the Speaker of the House of Representatives his written declaration that no inability exists, he shall resume the powers and duties of his office unless the Vice President and a majority of either the principal officers of the executive department or of such other body as Congress may by law provide, transmit within four days to the President pro tempore of the Senate and the Speaker of the House of Representatives their written declaration that the President is unable to discharge the powers and duties of his office. Thereupon Congress shall decide the issue, assembling within forty-eight hours for that purpose if not in session. If the Congress, within twenty-one days after receipt of the latter written declaration, or, if Congress is not in session, within twenty-one days after Congress is required to assemble, determines by two-thirds vote of both Houses that the President is unable to discharge the powers and duties of his office, the Vice President shall continue to discharge the same as Acting President; otherwise, the President shall resume the powers and duties of his office.

AMENDMENT XXVI [1971]
Section 1

The right of citizens of the United States, who are eighteen years of age or older, to vote shall not be denied or abridged by the United States or by any State on account of age.

Section 2

The Congress shall have power to enforce this article by appropriate legislation.

Glossary

abandoned property Property that is unowned because the owner has given up dominion and control with the intent to relinquish all claim or rights to it.

ab initio From the very beginning (Latin).

abstract In real property law, a summary compilation of the official records relating to a particular parcel of land.

abuse of discretion The failure of a judge or administrator to use sound or reasonable judgment in arriving at a decision.

acceleration clause In commercial paper, a statement in a time instrument (where payment is to be made at a prescribed time or times) that permits the entire debt to become due immediately upon the occurrence of some event, such as failure to pay one installment when due.

acceptance In contract law, the agreement of the offeree to the proposal or offer of the offeror.

acceptor In commercial paper, a drawee who agrees by his or her signature to honor a draft as presented.

accession An addition to, product of, or change in personal property; depending on the circumstances, either the owner of the original property or another person responsible for the accession might be the owner of the altered property.

accommodated party The person who benefits by having another party lend his or her name (credit) on an instrument.

accommodation party A person who signs an instrument for the purpose of lending his or her name (credit) to another party on that instrument.

accord and satisfaction A form of discharge in contract law by which an agreement between the parties of a contract permits a substituted performance in lieu of the required obligation under the existing contract. The contract can be effectively terminated (satisfied) by performance as originally agreed upon or by the substitute performance.

account receivable A record of a debt owed to a person but not yet paid.

accredited investor An investor who is deemed not to need protection and, thus, can be sold securities exempt from SEC regulation.

accretion The gradual adding of land by natural causes, such as a deposit of soil by the action of a river.

acid rain Polluting precipitation caused by rain falling through the air and absorbing sulfur dioxide emissions from industrial plants.

acknowledgment A formal declaration or admission before a designated public official, such as a notary public, that something is genuine or that a particular act has taken place.

action at law A suit in which the plaintiff is seeking a legal remedy (such as damages), as distinguished from an equitable remedy (such as an injunction).

action in equity A civil suit in which the plaintiff is seeking an equitable remedy, such as an injunction or decree of specific performance.

action *in personam* A suit to hold a defendant personally liable for a wrong committed.

action *in rem* A suit to enforce a right against property of the defendant.

act of state doctrine In international law, a rule that a foreign government's public acts committed in its territory are beyond review or inquiry by a domestic court.

actual authority The express and implied authority of an agent.

actus reus An act or conduct which the law seeks to prohibit or preclude.

adjudication The legal process of resolving a dispute.

adjudicatory power In administrative agency law, the right of an administrative agency to initiate actions as both prosecutor and judge against those thought to be in violation of the law (including agency rules and regulations) under the jurisdiction of the administrative agency—referred to as the quasi-judicial function of an agency.

adjustment case A procedure under Chapter 13 of the Bankruptcy Act which allows an individual to pay his or her debts from future income over an extended period of time.

administrative agency A board, commission, agency, or service authorized by a legislative enactment to implement specific laws on either the local, state, or national level.

administrative law Public law administered and/or formulated by a government unit such as a board, agency, or commission to govern the conduct of an individual, association, or corporation.

administrator In probate law, a person appointed by a probate court to supervise the distribution of a deceased person's property. This title is usually given when there is no will or when the person named as executor or executrix in the will cannot serve.

adverse possession The acquisition of title to real property by actually taking possession of the land without the owner's consent and retaining such possession openly for a prescribed statutory period.

affidavit A written sworn statement made before a person officially authorized to administer an oath.

affirmative action The granting of preferences based on race or gender to minority or women employees.

affirmative defense A defendant's claim to dissolve himself or herself of liability even if the plaintiff's claim is true.

after-acquired property Property received or added after a specific event has taken place. For example, in secured transactions law, an after-acquired property clause in a security agreement means that property received by the debtor after the security agreement is made will be subject to the same security interest as the existing property referred to therein.

agency A relationship created by contract, agreement, or law between a principal and an agent whereby the principal is bound by the authorized actions of the agent.

agency coupled with an interest A relationship in which an agent, with consideration, has the right to exercise authority or is given an interest in the property of the principal subject to the agency.

agent One who is authorized to act for another, called a principal, whose acts bind the principal to his or her actions.

aggregate theory An approach under which associations or organizations are treated as a collection of persons, each with individual rights and liabilities.

agreement A meeting of the minds between two or more parties, which may or may not constitute a contract.

air rights A landowner's rights to the air space above his or her real property.

alien corporation A corporation chartered or incorporated in another country but doing business in the United States.

alteration (material) In commercial paper, the modification of the terms of an instrument that results in a change of the contract of any party on that instrument.

amendment The changing of a law, right, or interest that usually becomes binding upon fulfillment of a required act or action.

ancillary covenant A covenant that is a subsidiary or auxiliary part of a larger agreement; to be valid, a covenant not to compete must be ancillary as well as reasonably limited in time and area.

annual percentage rate The total of the items making up the finance charge, or cost of borrowing money or buying on credit, expressed as a yearly percentage rate that the consumer can use to "shop around" for the best credit terms.

answer In pleadings, the defendant's response to the plaintiff's complaint or petition.

anticipatory breach The repudiation of a contract by a party before the time of performance has arrived, allowing the nonbreaching party the opportunity to seek a remedy.

anticipatory repudiation Breaching a contract by refusing to perform before it is actually time to perform.

apparent authority Authority created by the words or conduct of the principal that leads a third person to believe the agent has such authority.

apparent intent The establishment of a person's motive from his or her actions and/or words as interpreted by a reasonable person.

appellant The party who appeals a decision of a lower court, usually that of a trial court.

appellee The party against whom an appeal is made (sometimes referred to as a respondent—a person who defends on an appeal).

appraisal right The right of a dissenting shareholder to sell back his or her shares to the corporation for cash.

arbitration The submission of a dispute to a third party or parties for settlement.

arson At common law, the act of willfully and maliciously burning the dwelling of another.

articles of incorporation A legal document, meeting the legal requirements of a given state, filed with a designated state official as an application for a certificate of incorporation.

articles of partnership The agreement of the partners that forms and governs the operation of the partnership.

artisan's lien A possessory lien held by one who has expended labor upon or added value to another's personal property as security for the work performed (labor and/or value added).

ascendants The heirs of a decedent in the ascending line—parents or grandparents.

assault The intentional movement or exhibition of force that would place a reasonable person in fear of physical attack or harm.

assault and battery Any intentional physical contact by a person on another without consent or privilege.

assignee The one to whom an assignment has been made.

assignment The transfer of rights or a property interest to a third person, who can receive no greater rights than those possessed by the transferor.

assignment for the benefit of creditors The voluntary transfer by a debtor of some or all of his or her property to an assignee or trustee, who sells or liquidates the debtor's assets and tenders to the creditors (on a pro rata basis) payment in satisfaction of the debt.

assignor The one who makes an assignment.

association The voluntary act or agreement by which two or more persons unite together for some special purpose or business.

assumed name statute A law in most states which requires any firm, including a partnership, to register with a state official the fictitious name under which the firm is doing business; also called fictitious name statute.

attachment (1) A legal proceeding provided by statute that permits a plaintiff in an existing court action to have nonexempt property of the defendant seized and a lien placed on the property as security of a judgment that may be rendered in the plaintiff's favor (this action being independent of plaintiff's suit and exercisable only on grounds provided by statute). (2) In secured transactions law, a method of perfecting a security interest without the secured party taking possession of the collateral or making a proper filing (which in most states applies only to a purchase money security interest in consumer goods).

attestation   The act of witnessing a document, such as a will, and signing to that effect.

attorney-at-law   A lawyer.

attorney-in-fact   An agent.

auction with reserve   An auction in which the auctioneer, as agent for the owner of the goods, has the right to withdraw the goods from sale at any time prior to accepting a particular bid (such acceptance usually being signified by the fall of the hammer).

auction without reserve   An auction where once the goods are placed on the auction block (for sale) they must be sold to the highest bidder.

award   In arbitration proceedings, the decision or determination rendered by an arbitrator on a controversy submitted for settlement. For example, the arbitrator's award was unfair. In general usage, to grant some type of remedy. For example, the court awards an injunction.

bailee   The person to whom a bailor has entrusted or transferred personal property without transferring title.

bailee's lien   Usually a possessory lien held by a bailee on bailed property for which the bailee is entitled to compensation or reimbursement.

bailment   The creation of a legal relationship through delivery or transfer of personal property (but not title) by one person, called the bailor, to another person, called the bailee, usually for a specific purpose as directed by the bailor.

bailor   A person who entrusts or transfers personal property (but not title) to another, called the bailee, usually for the accomplishment of a specific purpose.

bank draft   A draft by one bank on funds held by another bank.

bankruptcy   A court procedure by which a person who is unable to pay his or her debts may be declared bankrupt, have nonexempt assets distributed to his or her creditors, and thereupon be given a release from any further payment of the balance due on most of these debts.

battery   The wrongful intentional physical contact by a person (or object under control of that person) on another.

bearer   In commercial paper, the person possessing an instrument either payable to anyone without specific designation or one indorsed in blank.

bearer instrument   An instrument either payable to anyone without specific designation or one indorsed in blank.

beneficiary   A person for whose benefit a will, trust, insurance policy, or contract is made.

benefit test   A test through which the law determines whether a promise has consideration by seeing if the promisor has received an advantage, profit, or privilege in return for his or her promise.

bequest   In a will a gift by the testator of specific personal property other than money.

bilateral contract   A contract formed by the mutual exchange of promises of the offeror and the offeree.

bilateral mistake   A mistake in which both parties to a contract are in error as to the terms of or performance expected under the contract. Also called mutual mistake.

bill of lading   A negotiable or nonnegotiable document of title evidencing the receipt of goods for shipment, with shipping instructions to the carrier. A negotiable bill of lading is both a receipt and evidence of title to the goods shipped.

binder   A temporary insurance contract formed when the insurance agent or broker accepts a prospective policyholder's application.

blank indorsement   An indorsement that specifies no particular indorsee and that usually consists of a mere signature of the indorser.

blue sky laws   Laws enacted for the protection of investors that regulate the sales of stocks and bonds, and that also regulate other activities of investment companies related to such sales.

board of directors   A body composed of persons elected by the corporation's shareholders and entrusted with the responsibility of managing the corporation.

bona fide occupational qualification (BFOQ)   A defense in Title VII discrimination suits in which an employer must demonstrate a connection between the protected classification and job performance, and must prove that the performance affected is of the "essence" of the job and not merely tangential to the fundamental job function.

bona fide purchaser   A purchaser who acts in good faith and gives something of value for the goods received.

bonds   In corporate financing, secured or unsecured debt obligations of a corporation in the form of securities (instruments).

boycott   In antitrust law, an agreement between two or more parties not to deal with a third party. When the purpose is to exclude a firm or firms from a market, such an agreement is per se illegal under Section 1 of the Sherman Act. In labor law, action by a union to prevent others from doing business with the employer. A primary boycott, directed at the employer with whom the union has a labor dispute, is usually legal. A secondary boycott, aimed at an employer with whom the union does not have a labor dispute, is usually an unfair labor practice.

breach of duty   Failure to fulfill a legal obligation.

broker   In real property law, an agent employed by a landowner to find an acceptable buyer for his or her real property or employed by a prospective buyer to find a landowner willing to sell such property.

bubble concept   EPA air pollution plan allowing large plants with multiple emission points (stacks) to place the entire plant under a "bubble" in order to meet a single allowable emission level, rather than requiring each stack to meet a particular level.

bulk transfer   A transfer of goods—such as materials, supplies, merchandise, or inventory (including equipment)—in such quantity or under such circumstances that the transfer is considered not to be in the ordinary course of the transferor's business.

burden of proof The duty of a party to prove or disprove certain facts.

burglary The act of entering, with or without force, in daytime or nighttime, any dwelling or other building with the intent to commit a felony or larceny.

business judgment rule A rule which protects corporate managers from responsibility for honest errors of judgment.

business trust A business association created by agreement in which legal ownership and management of property is transferred, in return for trust certificates, to trustees who have the power to operate the business for the benefit of the original owners or certificate holders. It is usually treated in the same manner as a corporation if certificate holders do not control the management activities of the trustees.

bylaws The internal rules made to regulate and govern the actions and affairs of a corporation.

capacity The legal ability to perform an act—especially an act from which legal consequences flow, such as the making of a contract.

case law Essentially synonymous with "common law."

cashier's check A check drawn by a bank on itself.

cause of action A person's right to seek a remedy when his or her rights have been breached or violated.

caveat emptor In sales law, "let the buyer beware."

Celler-Kefauver Act A 1950 congressional enactment amending Section 7 of the Clayton Act. The act prohibits a firm from acquiring all or part of the stock or assets of another firm where, in any line of commerce in any section of the country, the effect of such acquisition may be substantially to lessen competition.

certificate of authority A foreign corporation's permission to do business in the state of issuance.

certificate of deposit An instrument (essentially a note) that is an acknowledgment by a bank that it has received money and promises to repay the amount upon presentment when due.

certificate of incorporation A document of a state that grants permission to do business in that state in the corporate form—sometimes called a charter.

certificate of origin A document that designates the country from which goods originate.

certificate of title A written opinion by an attorney as to the validity of a title.

certified check A bank's guaranty (acceptance) by an appropriate signature that it will pay the check upon presentment.

challenge for cause In jury selection, an objection to a prospective juror hearing a particular case, stating a reason that questions the impartiality of the juror.

charging order An action by a creditor which requires that a partner's share of partnership profits be paid to the creditor until the debt is fully discharged.

chattel Any property or interest therein other than real property. The more modern term is "personal property."

chattel paper Any writing or writings that evidence both a monetary obligation for and a security interest in (or a lease of) specific goods.

check A draft drawn on a bank (drawee) payable on demand.

CIF Cost, insurance, and freight; that is, the price charged by the seller includes not only the cost of the goods but also the cost of freight and insurance charges on the goods to the named destination.

circumstantial context In the process of statutory interpretation, a court's examination of the problem or problems that caused the enactment of the statute.

civil law As compared to criminal law, rules for establishing rights and duties between individuals whereby an individual can seek personal redress for a wrong committed by another individual. As compared to common law, codified rules reduced to formal written propositions as the law of a state or country. The written code serves as the basis of all decisions.

Civil Rights Act A comprehensive 1964 congressional enactment that prohibits discrimination in housing, public accommodations, education, and employment.

civil rights law The body of statutory and constitutional law defining and enforcing the privileges and freedoms belonging to every person in the United States. The objective of civil rights law is to secure equality of opportunity for all persons.

class action A legal proceeding initiated by one or more members of a similarly situated group or class of persons on behalf of themselves and other group members.

classified board A board of directors divided into classes with only one class elected each year; the result is directors who serve staggered terms.

Clayton Act A 1914 congressional enactment to generally prohibit price discrimination by a seller of goods, exclusive dealing and tying of a seller's products, mergers and consolidations of corporations that result in a substantial lessening of competition or tend to create a monopoly, and certain interlocking directorates. The act also provides an exemption from the antitrust laws for the organization and normal activities of labor unions.

close corporation A corporation that has a limited number of outstanding shares of stock, usually held by a single person or small group of persons, with restrictions on the right to transfer those shares to others.

closing In real property law, a meeting between the seller and buyer and any other interested parties at which passage of title and matters relating thereto are executed.

COD Collect on delivery; that is, the buyer must pay for the goods before he or she can inspect or receive possession of them.

codicil An addition to or change in a will executed with the same formalities as the will itself.

coinsurance clause A provision in a property insurance policy specifying that the property owner must bear a proportionate part of a casualty loss if he or she does not insure the property in an amount equal to a stated percentage of the property's value.

collateral In secured transactions law, the property subject to a security interest.

collateral note A note secured by personal property.

collective bargaining The term for negotiations between an employer and the union representative.

collusion Joint conduct by two or more independent entities for a common purpose. A prerequisite to finding a violation of Section 1 of the Sherman Act.

co-makers Two or more persons who create or execute a note or certificate of deposit.

comity In international law, the recognition that one nation or sovereign gives to the judicial or legislative acts of another nation or sovereign.

Commerce Clause A clause contained in Article I, Section 8, of the U.S. Constitution, which permits Congress to control trade among the several states (and with foreign nations).

commercial contract A contract between two or more persons (merchants) engaged in trade or commerce.

commercial impracticability A legal doctrine which excuses a seller of goods from performance because an unforeseen occurrence has caused performance to be extremely burdensome.

commercial paper Instruments that are written promises or obligations to pay sums of money (called drafts, checks, certificates of deposit, or notes). When used in Article 3 of the UCC, the term refers only to negotiable instruments; when used elsewhere, to negotiable and nonnegotiable instruments.

commercial speech Expressions that primarily convey a commercial message (i.e., advertising); recently recognized by the Supreme Court as being protected by the First Amendment to the U.S. Constitution.

commingle To blend or mix together.

common carrier A carrier that holds itself out for hire to the general public to transport goods.

common law Rules that have been developed from custom or judicial decisions without the aid of written legislation, and subsequently used as a basis for later decisions by a court—also referred to as judgemade or case law.

common stock A class of stock that carries no rights or priorities over other classes of stock as to payment of dividends or distribution of corporate assets upon dissolution.

community property A system of marital property ownership recognized in eight states under which property acquired after marriage (except by gift or inheritance) is co-owned by the husband and wife, regardless of which person acquired it.

comparable worth The theory that jobs having comparable worth should receive comparable pay.

comparative negligence The rule used in negligence cases in many states that provides for computing both the plaintiff's and the defendant's negligence, with the plaintiff's damages being reduced by a percentage representing the degree of his or her contributing fault. If the plaintiff's negligence is found to be greater than the defendant's, the plaintiff will receive nothing and will be subject to a counterclaim by the defendant.

compensatory damages A monetary sum awarded for the actual loss a person has sustained for a wrong committed by another person.

complaint In an action at law, the initial pleading filed by the plaintiff in a court with proper jurisdiction. In an action in equity, it is frequently referred to as a *petition*.

composition of creditors An agreement between a debtor and his or her creditors that each creditor will accept a lesser amount than the debt owed as full satisfaction of that debt.

conclusions of law Answers derived by applying law to facts.

concurrent jurisdiction Where more than one court of a different name or classification has the right to hear a particular controversy.

condemnation The process by which the government either exercises its power of eminent domain to take private property or officially declares property unfit for use.

condition In contract law, a provision or clause in a contract which, upon the occurrence or nonoccurrence of a specified event, either creates, suspends, or terminates the rights and duties of the contracting parties.

condition concurrent A condition in a contract that both parties' performances are to take place at the same time.

condition precedent A condition that must take place before the parties are bound to their contractual obligations.

condition subsequent A condition that terminates the rights and obligations of the parties under an existing contract.

conditional indorsement An indorsement whereby the indorser agrees to be liable on the instrument only if a specified event takes place.

confession of judgment An agreement whereby a debtor allows a creditor to obtain a court judgment without legal proceedings in the event of nonpayment or other breach by the debtor. Usually not permissible today.

conflict of laws The body of rules specifying the circumstances in which a state or federal court sitting in one state shall, in deciding a case before it, apply the rules of another state (rather than the rules of the state in which the court is sitting).

confusion of goods An intermingling of the goods of different persons such that the property of each can no longer be distinguished.

conglomerate merger A merger between two companies which are not competitors and do not occupy a supplier-customer relationship.

consent A defense in an assault and battery action where it is alleged that the plaintiff expressly or implicitly agreed to expose himself to certain physical dangers.

consent decree   A court injunction, the terms of which are arrived at by agreement of the parties.

consent order   An administrative agency order, the terms of which are arrived at by agreement between the agency and the charged party.

consideration   In contract law, a detriment to the promisee or benefit to the promisor, bargained for and given in exchange for a promise.

consolidation   A transaction in which two corporations combine to form an entirely new corporation, thereby losing their former identities.

construction (of contracts)   The use of considerations outside of the expressed or stated language of a contract to ascertain the true intent and purpose of the parties at the time they entered into the agreement.

constructive annexation   The situation existing when personal property not physically attached to real property is adapted to the use to which the realty is designed so that the law considers it a fixture.

constructive bailment   A bailment created when a bailee comes into possession of personal property without the consent of the owner. (An example is lost property found by a person—a bailee.)

constructive delivery   A legal substitute for actual delivery of property which is the subject of a gift; consists of delivery of something which represents an item of intangible property or which gives control over an item of tangible property; also called symbolic delivery.

constructive eviction   Legally justified abandonment of leased property by a tenant because of a landlord's action which has caused the property to be unsuitable for the purpose for which it was leased.

constructive trust   A trust imposed by law to correct or rectify a fraud or to prevent one party from being unjustly enriched at the expense of another.

consumer goods   Goods that are used or bought primarily for personal, family, or household purposes.

Consumer Product Safety Act   A congressional enactment that created the Consumer Product Safety Commission, which has the responsibility of establishing and enforcing rules and standards to insure that products covered under the Act are safe for consumers' use.

continuation statement   In secured transactions law, a document filed with a proper public official to continue public notice of the priority of an existing security interest in collateral upon the expiration of a previous filing.

contract   An agreement that establishes enforceable legal relationships between two or more persons.

contract, combination, or conspiracy   Express or tacit agreement required for a violation of the Sherman Act.

contract carrier   A carrier who transports goods only for those under individual contract.

contributory negligence   The fault (negligence) of a plaintiff, the result of which contributed to or added to his or her injury (used as a defense by a defendant against whom the plaintiff has filed a negligence action).

controlling shareholders   Usually the majority shareholders or those with sufficient voting power to elect a majority of the directors, pass motions, or make binding decisions.

conversion   An action which unlawfully injures the personal property of another or unlawfully interferes with the owner's right to possess and enjoy such property.

conveyance   A transfer of an interest in property.

corporate opportunity   A doctrine that prohibits directors, officers, or any other corporate managers from personally taking advantage of business situations that belong solely to or should be given to the corporation.

corporate stock   Shares of stock, each representing an ownership interest in the business, issued by a corporation for the purpose of raising capital.

corporation   An association of persons created by statute as a legal entity (artificial person) with authority to act and to have liability separate and apart from its owners.

counterclaim   A pleading by the defendant in a civil suit against the plaintiff, the purpose being to defeat or sue the plaintiff so as to gain a judgment favorable to the defendant.

counteroffer   A proposal made by an offeree in response to the offer extended him or her, the terms varying appreciably from the terms of the offer. Such a proposal by the offeree usually constitutes a rejection of the offer.

course of dealing   The situation in which past conduct between two parties in performing a prior contract is used as a basis for interpreting their present conduct or agreement.

course of performance   When a contract for the sale of goods involves repeated occasions for performance known by both parties and not objected to by either, the performance is considered interpretive of the remaining obligations of the contract.

covenant against encumbrances   A guaranty by a grantor that there are no outstanding liens, easements, or liabilities held by a third party on the real property he or she is conveying, except as stated in the deed.

covenant not to compete   A clause within a contract legally permitting a restraint of trade where such is a legitimate protection of a property interest and the restraint as to area and time is reasonable under the circumstances. An example is a clause in a sale of business contract where the seller agrees not to start up a competing business within a reasonable time and within the area where the said business has been operating.

covenant of quiet enjoyment   A guaranty by a grantor of real property that the grantee or those who hold the property in the future will not be evicted or disturbed by a person having a better title or a right of foreclosure of a lien. Also, a guaranty by a landlord to a tenant that the tenant's right to possession will not be disturbed substantially.

covenant of seisin   A guaranty by a grantor that he or she has good title to the real property being conveyed.

covenants of title   The guarantees given by the grantor in a warranty deed.

cover   In response to a seller's failure to deliver goods, the buyer's purchase of the goods from someone else in a commercially reasonable manner; the buyer's basic measure of damages for breach of contract in such a case is the difference between the contract price and the cover price.

creditor beneficiary   A creditor who has rights in a contract (of which he or she is not a party) made by the debtor and a third person, where the terms of said contract expressly benefit the creditor.

crime   Any wrongful action by an individual or persons for which a statute prescribes redress in the form of a death penalty, imprisonment, fine, or removal from an office of public trust.

cross-elasticity of demand   The extent to which the quantity of a commodity demanded responds to changes in price of a related commodity. Used to help define a relevant market.

cross-elasticity of supply   The extent to which the quantity of a product supplied responds to changes in price of a related commodity. Used to help define a relevant market.

cumulative dividend preference   A characteristic of most preferred stock whereby all dividends in arrears must be paid to the preferred shareholders before any dividends can be paid to owners of common stock.

cumulative preferred stock   A type of preferred stock on which dividends not paid in any given year are accumulated to the next succeeding year. The total amount accumulated must be paid before common shareholders can receive a dividend.

cumulative voting   Where permitted, the procedure by which a shareholder is entitled to take his or her total number of shares, multiply that total by the number of directors to be elected, and cast the multiplied total for any director or directors to be elected.

currency control   In international law, restrictions by a government on the transfer of currency from one country to another.

curtesy   The common-law right of a surviving husband to a life estate in a portion of his deceased wife's real property.

cy pres   So near or as near. The doctrine by which the courts will find a substitute purpose when the stated purpose of a charitable trust is not possible to accomplish.

damages   The monetary loss suffered by a party as a result of a wrong.

deadlock   A situation in a corporation where two equally divided factions exist in opposition to each other, thus bringing the affairs of the corporation to a virtual standstill.

debenture   In securities regulation law, a debt security; a written promise by a corporation to repay borrowed money. Usually refers to a corporate bond or promissory note that is not secured by specific assets of the firm (i.e., is not secured by a mortgage on corporate assets).

debit   A charge of indebtedness to an account (for example, a charge against a bank deposit account).

debt securities   Instruments representing the bonded indebtedness of a corporation (they may be secured by corporate property or simply by a general obligation debt of the corporation).

debtor   A person who owes payment of a debt and/or performance on an obligation.

decedent   A person who has died.

deceit   A false statement, usually intentional, that causes another person harm.

deed   The document representing ownership of real property.

deed of bargain and sale   A deed without warranties.

de facto corporation   A corporation not formed in substantial compliance with the laws of a given state but which has sufficiently complied to be a corporation in fact, not right. Only the state can challenge the corporation's existence.

de facto merger   A less formal means of merger where the results are achieved through asset or stock acquisition. Also called a practical merger.

defamation   Injury of a person's character or reputation, usually by publication of a false statement about that person.

default   The failure to perform a legal obligation.

defendant   The party against whom a civil lawsuit has been instituted by a plaintiff, or against whom a criminal prosecution has been instituted by the government.

defense   Any matter which is advanced or put forth by a defendant as a reason in law or fact why the plaintiff is not entitled to recover the relief he seeks.

defensive merger   A merger sought by management in order to avoid consequences it does not feel will be in its best interests.

deficiency judgment   A personal judgment given by a court against a debtor in default where the value of the property placed as security for the debt is less than the debt owed.

de jure corporation   A corporation formed in substantial compliance with the laws of a given state; a corporation by right.

delegated powers   The constitutional right of the federal government to pass laws concerning certain subjects and fields, thereby keeping the states from passing laws in these areas (sometimes referred to as enumerated powers).

delegation   In contract law, the transfer of the power or right to represent or act for another; usually referred to as the delegation of duties to a third party, as compared to the assignment of rights to a third party.

delegation of authority   In administrative law, a grant of authority from a legislative body to an administrative agency.

demand instrument   An instrument which is payable immediately when the holder decides to present it.

demurrer   A pleading by a defendant in the form of a motion denying that plaintiff's complaint or petition states a cause of action.

de novo   To start completely new. A trial *de novo* is a completely new trial requiring the same degree of proof as if the case were being heard for the first time.

depositary bank   The first bank to which an instrument is transferred for collection.

deposition   Testimony of a witness, under oath and subject to cross examination, which is taken outside of court; an important discovery procedure.

descendants   The lineal heirs of a decedent in a descending line—children and grandchildren.

destination contract   In sales law, a contract whereby the seller is required to tender goods to the buyer at a place designated by the buyer.

detriment test   A test to determine whether a promise is supported by consideration. The law requires the promisee to have done something not otherwise legally required or to have refrained from doing something he or she had a right to do.

devise   A term of conveyance in real estate transactions. In a will, a gift of real estate by the testator is a devise.

direct collection   The collection by the assignee (of an assignor-creditor) of a debt originally owed the creditor.

directed verdict   A verdict that is directed by the court because reasonable persons could not differ as to the result.

disaffirmance   The legal avoidance, or setting aside, of an obligation.

discharge in bankruptcy   A release granted by a bankruptcy court to a debtor who has gone through proper bankruptcy proceedings; the release frees the person from any further liability on provable claims filed during the proceedings.

disclaimer   A provision in a sales contract which attempts to prevent the creation of a warranty.

discovery   Full disclosure of the evidence in a particular case before it comes to trial; various procedures are available to accomplish this disclosure.

dishonor   In commercial paper, a refusal to pay or accept an instrument upon proper presentment.

disparagement of goods   Making malicious and false statements of fact as to the quality or performance of another's goods.

dissolution   The termination of a partnership's or corporation's right to exist as a going concern.

diversity of citizenship   The condition that exists when the plaintiff and defendant are citizens of different states.

dividend   A payment made by a corporation in cash or property from the income or profit of the corporation to a shareholder on the basis of his or her investment.

documents of title   Bills of lading, dock warrants, dock receipts, warehouse receipts, and any other paper that, in the regular course of business or financing, is evidence of the holder's right to obtain possession of the goods covered.

domestic corporation   A corporation chartered or incorporated in the state in which the corporation is doing business.

dominant estate   The land that benefits from an easement appurtenant.

donee   The person to whom a gift is made or a power is given.

donee beneficiary   A person who has rights in a contract (to which he or she is not a party) made between two or more parties for his or her express benefit.

donor   The person making a gift or giving another the power to do something.

double jeopardy   A constitutional prohibition against trying a person a second time for the same crime for which he or she was convicted or acquitted at an earlier trial.

dower   The common-law right of a widow to a life estate in a specific portion of her deceased husband's real property.

draft   An instrument created by a party (the drawer) that orders another (the drawee) to pay the instrument to a third party (the payee); also called a bill of exchange.

drawee   The person on whom a draft or check is drawn and who is requested (ordered) to pay the instrument.

drawee bank   A bank on which a draft or check is drawn, such bank being ordered to pay the instrument when it is duly presented.

drawer   The person creating (drafting) a draft or check.

due process   The right of every person not to be deprived of life, liberty, or property without a fair hearing and/or just compensation.

duress   The overcoming of a person's free will through the use of threat, force, or actions whereby the person is forced to do something he or she otherwise would not do.

earnest money   A deposit paid by a buyer to hold a seller to a contractual obligation. Frequently this amount also serves as liquidated damages in the event of the buyer's breach. Historically, the deposit was said to show the buyer's good faith in entering into the contract with the seller.

easement   A nonpossessory interest in real property that gives the holder the right to use another's land in a particular way.

easement appurtenant   An easement created specifically for use in connection with an adjoining tract of land.

easement in gross   An easement that is not used in connection with another tract of land.

economic duress   The overcoming of a person's free will by means of a threat or other action involving the wrongful use of economic pressure, whereby the person is forced to do something he or she otherwise would not do.

election   A principle of law whereby a third person who learns of the identity of the undisclosed principal prior to receiving a judgment must choose to receive the judgment against either the agent or the undisclosed principal. Election of one releases the other from liability to the third party.

embezzlement   The act of expropriating from the true owner property entrusted to the wrongdoer through a fiduciary relationship.

eminent domain The power of the government to take private property for public use by paying just compensation.

employment at will A common-law doctrine under which workers are hired for an indefinite period of time. Either party can terminate the employment contract at any time, with no reason being given. In recent years, courts and legislatures have created a number of exceptions to the employer's absolute right to terminate an employment-at-will relationship.

endowment insurance Life insurance which is payable either to the insured when he or she reaches a specified age or to the named beneficiary if the insured dies before reaching the specified age.

entity theory The view that a partnership is a legal entity separate from the individual partners.

entrapment The act by a government official of encouraging or inducing a person to commit a crime that he or she would not otherwise commit for the sole purpose of instituting a criminal prosecution against him or her.

entry barrier A condition that makes entry into a market by a new competitor more costly and risky.

environmental impact statement A statement required by the National Environmental Policy Act (NEPA) for any major federal action that might significantly affect the quality of the environment. The statement must assess the action's environmental impact and analyze possible alternatives.

Environmental Protection Agency The federal agency charged with the responsibility for establishing and enforcing environmental standards and for continuing research on pollution and measures to eliminate or control it.

equal protection clause A provision in the Fourteenth Amendment to the U.S. Constitution that prohibits states from making distinctions among persons or firms without a reasonable, rational basis.

equipment Goods that are used or bought for use primarily in business.

equitable action An action brought in a court seeking an equitable remedy, such as an injunction or decree of specific performance.

equity securities Shares of capital stock representing an ownership interest in the corporation.

escheat The process by which a decedent's property passes to the state when he or she did not leave a valid will and there are no legal heirs.

escrow agent An agent who, by agreement, holds property, documents, or money of one party with the authority to transfer such property to a designated person upon the occurrence of a specified event.

establishment of religion clause The clause in the First Amendment to the U.S. Constitution which prohibits the federal government from "establishing" a religion. This restriction has also been applied to the states under the due process clause.

ethics The study and application of moral principles.

eviction Action by the landlord which physically bars the tenant from entering the leased premises.

exclusive agency In real property law, the arrangement by a seller of real property with a broker whereby only that broker is entitled to a commission if a sale of the real property is made through the efforts of anyone other than the seller.

exclusive dealing agreement An agreement which commits a buyer to purchase a certain product only from one seller, or a seller to sell only to one buyer.

exclusive right to sell In real property law, the arrangement by a seller of real property with a broker whereby the broker is entitled to his or her commission if a sale of the real property is made through the effort of anyone, including the seller.

exculpatory clause A contract clause providing that one party agrees to free the other of all liability in the event he or she suffers a physical or monetary injury in a particular situation, even if the loss is caused by the negligence of the other party to the contract.

excusing conditions Conditions affecting a person's knowledge or freedom of action and eliminating or reducing a moral obligation.

executed contract A contract wholly performed by both parties to the contract, as opposed to an executory contract, which is wholly unperformed by both parties.

execution of a judgment The process by which a judgment creditor obtains a writ directing the sheriff or other officer to seize nonexempt property of the debtor and sell it to satisfy the judgment.

executive committee In a corporation, a certain number of the members of the board of directors appointed by the board as a committee with the delegated authority to make decisions concerning ordinary business matters that come up during intervals between regular board meetings.

executive order An order by the president of the United States or governor of a state that has the force of law.

executor (female, executrix) The personal representative in a testator's will to dispose of an estate as the will has directed.

executory contract A contract wholly unperformed by both parties to the contract, as opposed to an executed contract, where both parties have fully performed their obligations under the contract.

executory interest A future interest held by a third party.

exempt property Real or personal property of a debtor that cannot by law be seized to satisfy a debt owed to an unsecured creditor.

ex parte On one side only. For example, an *ex parte* proceeding is held on the application of one party only, without notice to the other party; and an *ex parte* order is made at the request of one party when the other party fails to show up in court, when the other party's presence is not needed, or when there is no other party.

export license A license to ship goods or articles of commerce from a particular country.

express authority Authority specifically given by the principal to the agent.

express contract A contract formed from the words (oral and/or in writing) of the parties, as opposed to an implied contract, which is formed from the conduct of the parties.

express warranty In sales law, a guarantee or assurance as to the quality or performance of goods that arises from the words or conduct of the seller.

ex-ship From the carrying vessel; a delivery term indicating that the seller's risk and expense for shipment of goods by vessel extends until the goods are unloaded at the port of destination.

extension clause A clause in a time instrument providing that under certain circumstances the maturity date can be extended.

extraordinary bailment A bailment in which the bailee is given by law greater duties and liabilities than an ordinary bailee. Common carriers and innkeepers are the most common examples of extraordinary bailees.

Fair Labor Standards Act (FLSA) A 1938 congressional enactment regulating minimum wages, overtime, and child labor.

false imprisonment The wrongful detention or restraint of one person by another.

false pretenses A material misrepresentation of a fact or circumstance calculated to mislead.

family purpose doctrine The doctrine under which (in a few states) the head of a household is liable for the negligent acts of any members of his or her family that occur while they are driving the family car.

farm products Goods that are crops, livestock, or supplies used or produced in farming operations, or goods that are products or livestock in their unmanufactured state (such as ginned cotton, maple syrup, milk, and eggs). For secured transactions law these goods must be in the possession of a debtor engaged in raising, fattening, grazing, or other farm operations.

FAS Free alongside ship; a delivery term indicating that the seller must deliver goods to the designated dock alongside the vessel on which the goods are to be loaded and must bear the expenses of delivery to the dock site.

fault Breach of a legal duty.

Federal Communications Commission (FCC) A seven-member commission established in 1934 by congressional enactment of the Federal Communications Act. The commission is empowered to regulate all interstate communication by telephone, telegraph, radio, and television.

federal preemption A legal principle which grants the Congress, the federal courts, and federal agencies exclusive authority in certain matters of law where the need for a uniform national body of law is great. Labor relations law, for example, is almost exclusively the domain of the federal government.

federal question A question presented by a case in which one party, usually the plaintiff, is asserting a right (or counterclaim, in the case of the defendant) which is based upon a federal rule of law—e.g., a provision of the U.S. Constitution, an act of Congress, or a U.S. treaty.

Federal Trade Commission (FTC) A five-member commission established in 1914 by congressional enactment of the Federal Trade Commission Act. The commission enforces prohibitions against unfair methods of competition and unfair or deceptive acts or practices in commerce; it also enforces numerous federal laws (particularly federal consumer protection acts, such as "Truth in Lending" and "Fair Packaging and Labeling").

fee simple The absolute ownership of real property.

fee simple defeasible An ownership interest in real property subject to termination by the occurrence of a specific event.

felony A criminal offense punishable by death or imprisonment for a period exceeding one year.

fictitious payee A payee on an instrument who is either nonexistent or an actual person not entitled to payment. (Usually the fraud is perpetrated by a dishonest employee in charge of payroll or payment of accounts who drafts an instrument with intent to defraud his or her employer.)

fiduciary A position of trust in relation to another person or his or her property.

financing statement An instrument filed with a proper public official that gives notice of an outstanding security interest in collateral.

finding of fact The process whereby from testimony and evidence a judge, agency, or examiner determines that certain matters, events, or acts took place upon which conclusions of law can be based.

firm offer In sales law, an irrevocable offer dealing with the sale of goods made by a merchant offeror in a signed writing and giving assurance to the offeree that the offer will remain open. This offer is irrevocable without consideration for the stated period of time or, if no period is stated, for a reasonable period, neither period to exceed three months.

fixture A piece of personal property that is attached to real property in such a manner that the law deems the item to be part of the real property.

floating lien concept In secured transactions law, the concept whereby a security interest is permitted to be retained in collateral even though the collateral changes in character and classification. For example, a security interest in raw materials is retained even if the raw materials change character in the manufacturing process and end up as inventory.

FOB Free on board; a delivery term indicating that the seller must ship the goods and bear the expenses of shipment to the FOB point of designation (which can be either the seller's or the buyer's place of business).

forbearance The refraining from doing something that a person has a legal right to do.

foreclosure The procedure or action taken by a mortgagee, upon default of the mortgagor, whereby the mortgagee satisfies his or her claim by some action (usually by selling off the mortgaged property).

foreign corporation A corporation chartered or incorporated in one state but doing business in a different state.

forgery   The act of making a false instrument and/or passing an instrument known to be false with the intent to perpetrate a fraud or injury to another. Also, the false instrument itself. Also, a signature of another made without authorization.

formal contract   A contract that derives its validity only from compliance with a specific form or format required by law. Examples are contracts under seal (where a seal is required), negotiable instruments, and recognizances (formal acknowledgments of indebtedness made in a court of law).

franchise   (1) A business conducted under someone else's trademark or tradename. The owner of the business, which may be a sole proprietorship, partnership, corporation, or other form of organization, is usually referred to as the *franchisee*. The owner of the trademark or tradename, who contractually permits use of the mark or name, in return for a fee and usually subject to various restrictions, is ordinarily referred to as the *franchisor*. The permission to use the mark or name, which is part of the franchising agreement, is called a *trademark license*. (2) The term can also be used to refer to a privilege granted by a governmental body, such as the exclusive right granted to someone by a city to provide cable TV service in that city.

fraud   An intentional or reckless misrepresentation of a material fact that causes anyone relying on it injury or damage.

fraud implied in law   A presumption of fraud which exists when a debtor transfers property without receiving fair consideration in return and the debtor has insufficient assets remaining to satisfy creditors; burden of proof falls to debtor to show absence of fraud.

fraud in fact   An action by a debtor in which he transfers property with the specific intent of defrauding creditors.

fraud in the execution   In commercial paper, inducing a person to sign an instrument, the party signing being deceived as to the nature or essential terms of the instrument.

fraud in the inducement   In commercial paper, the use of deceit in inducing a person to sign an instrument, although the deceived party knows what he or she is signing and the essential terms of the instrument. This knowledge is what distinguishes fraud in inducement from fraud in the execution.

fraudulent conveyance   The transfer of property in such a manner that the conveyance is deemed either in fact or by law to defraud creditors.

free speech clause   The clause in the First Amendment to the U.S. Constitution which prohibits the federal government from abridging the freedom of speech. This restriction has also been applied to the states under the Due Process Clause.

frustration of purpose doctrine   A legal doctrine followed in many states which excuses a party from a contract because of an occurrence which undermines the basic purpose of the contract.

FTC holder in due course rule   An FTC rule which states that it is illegal for a seller to execute a sales contract or arrange a direct loan unless the contract includes a clause which informs the holder of the contract that he or she is subject to all claims and defenses against such contract.

full faith and credit clause   The provision in the U.S. Constitution which requires the courts of one state to recognize judgments and other public actions of its sister states.

fungible   In sales or securities law, goods or securities of which any unit is, by nature or usage of trade, the equivalent of any other like unit.

future advance   In secured transactions law, the concept whereby an outstanding security interest applies to future loans made by the secured party. If the security interest is properly perfected, the future loan, for priority purposes, dates back to the time the original security interest was created.

future interest   An interest in real property, the use or enjoyment of which is postponed until a later date or the occurrence of a designated event.

futures contract   A contract to buy or sell standard commodities (such as rice, coffee, or wheat) at a future date and a specified price. (The seller is agreeing to sell goods he or she does not own at the time of making the contract.)

garnishee   A person who holds money owed to or property of a debtor subject to a garnishment action.

garnishment   The legal proceeding of a judgment creditor to require a third person owing money to the debtor or holding property belonging to the debtor to turn over to the court or sheriff the property or money owed for the satisfaction of the judgment. State and federal laws generally permit only a limited amount of a debtor's wages to be garnished.

general warranty deed   A deed to real property which guarantees that the title is a good, marketable one.

gift   A voluntary transfer of property to another without consideration.

gift *causa mortis*   A gift made by a donor in contemplation of his or her death from some existing affliction or impending peril.

gift *inter vivos*   A gift made during the lifetime of a donor and not in contemplation of his or her death.

Golden Rule, The   A rule of ethical conduct stating that one should do to others as one would have others do to oneself.

good faith   Honesty in fact on the part of a person in negotiating a contract, or in the carrying on of some other transaction.

goods   Tangible and movable personal property except for money used as medium of exchange.

grand jury   An inquisitional body of citizens charged with the duty of conducting its own investigation into a crime to determine if sufficient evidence exists to warrant the issuance of an indictment against an alleged offender.

grantee   The person to whom an interest in real property is conveyed by deed.

grantor   The person conveying an interest in real property by deed.

Green River ordinances   State and municipal laws that regulate door-to-door sales on private premises. So called after the Green River, Wyoming, case in which such laws were held to be valid and enforceable.

guaranty A promise to pay an obligation of a debtor if the debtor is in default.

hazardous waste Defined in the Resource Conservation and Recovery Act (RCRA) as a solid waste or combination of solid wastes which may cause or significantly contribute to an increase in mortality or serious diseases or pose a substantial hazard to human health when improperly handled.

holder Any person in possession of a document, security, or instrument that is drawn, issued, or indorsed to him or her.

holder in due course (HDC) A holder who takes an instrument for value, in good faith, and without notice that the instrument is overdue or has been dishonored or that any defense or claim by any person exists against it.

holder through a holder in due course A holder who fails to qualify as a holder in due course but has the rights of one (by law of assignment) if he or she can show that a prior holder of the instrument qualified as a holder in due course. This is referred to as the "shelter provision."

holding company A company whose main function is to own other companies through control of their stock. Also called an investment company.

holographic will A will entirely in the handwriting of the testator. Witnesses are not required for its execution but are necessary at probate to prove the handwriting of the testator.

horizontal merger A merger of two competing firms at the same level in the production or distribution of a product.

horizontal price fixing Price fixing among competitors. *Per se* illegal under Section 1 of the Sherman Act.

horizontal restraint of trade An arrangement between two or more competitors that suppresses or limits competition.

hostile environment harassment In employment discrimination law, unwelcome requests for sexual favors made to an employee by the employer or by someone for whose actions the employer is responsible, under circumstances in which the requests have created an intimidating, hostile, or offensive environment.

illusory contract An agreement of the parties that, on examination, lacks mutuality of obligation—i.e., one in which consideration is found to be lacking on the part of one party. The result is that neither party is bound by the agreement.

immunity The right of a witness to be free from indictment or arrest in exchange for particular or general testimony offered to a court.

implied authority Authority inferred for an agent to carry out his or her express authority and/or authority inferred from the position held by the agent to fulfill his or her agency duties.

implied contract A contract in which the parties' manifestation of assent or agreement is inferred, in whole or in part, from their conduct, as opposed to an express contract formed by the parties' words.

implied warranties Assurances or guarantees of certain standards or actions imposed by law.

implied warranty of habitability An obligation imposed on the landlord to keep residential property in a liveable condition.

import license A license allowing the importation of goods or articles of commerce into a particular country.

impostor One who poses as another person or as an agent for another person.

incidental beneficiary One who benefits from a contract between others but who cannot legally enforce the contract because his or her benefit is a secondary effect, not an intended result of the contract.

incorporated partnership A close corporation with more than one shareholder.

incorporation The act or process of forming or creating a corporation.

indemnification Where allowed, the right to reimbursement for expenses, losses, or costs incurred.

independent contractor One who is hired by another to perform a given task in a manner and method independent from the control of employer.

indirect collection The creditor's collection of payment(s) of a debt, even though the debt has been assigned by the creditor to an assignee.

indorsee The person who receives an indorsed instrument.

indorsement The signature of the indorser (usually on the back of an instrument) for the purpose of transferring an instrument and establishing the limits of his or her liability.

indorsement for deposit A type of restrictive indorsement that requires the depositary bank to place into the account of the restrictive indorser the amount of the instrument.

indorsement in trust A type of restrictive indorsement whereby the amount on the instrument is to be paid to the indorsee, who in turn is to use or hold the funds for the benefit of the indorser or a third party.

indorser The person who indorses an instrument, usually for the purpose of transferring it to a third person.

informal contract Any contract that does not depend on a specified form or formality for its validity.

injunction A decree issued by a court hearing an equity action either prohibiting a person from performing a certain act or acts or requiring the person to perform a certain act or acts.

innocent misrepresentation A false statement of fact, not known to be false, that causes another harm or damage.

insider trading The buying or selling of corporate securities of a particular firm by persons having business knowledge about such firm that is not available to the general public, with the expectation of making a personal profit in such transactions.

insolvency In bankruptcy law, the financial condition of a debtor when his or her assets at fair market value are less than his or her debts and liabilities.

installment contract In sales law, a contract that authorizes or requires the delivery and acceptance of goods in separate lots.

installment note   An instrument (note) in which the principal (plus interest usually) is payable in specified partial amounts at specified times until the full amount is paid.

insurable interest   The rights of a person who will be directly or financially affected by the death of a person or the loss of property. Only these rights can be protected by an insurance policy.

intermediary bank   Any bank to which an instrument is transferred in the course of collection and which is not the depositary or payor bank.

interpretation (of statutes)   An analysis of the expressed words of a statute to ascertain their meaning and significance.

interrogatories   In a lawsuit, a discovery procedure involving the submission of written questions by one party to the other, which the other party must answer under oath.

interstate commerce   The carrying on of commercial activities or the commercial transportation of persons or property between points lying in different states.

Interstate Commerce Commission (ICC)   An administrative agency established in 1887 by congressional enactment of the Interstate Commerce Act regulating the licensing and rates of common carriers in interstate commerce.

inter vivos   "Between the living," as an *inter vivos* gift (one made during the life of the donor) or an *inter vivos* trust.

inter vivos trust   A trust established and effective during the life of the settlor.

intestate   The situation in which a person dies without leaving a valid will.

inventory   Goods held by a person or firm for sale or lease in the ordinary course of business; also refers to raw materials (and work in process on them) where held by a manufacturing company.

investment company   Any corporation organized for the purpose of owning and holding the stock of other corporations.

involuntary case   In bankruptcy, a liquidation proceeding that is brought about by the unpaid creditors.

irrevocable offer   An offer or proposal that by law cannot be withdrawn by an offeror without liability.

issue   The first delivery of an instrument to a holder.

joint stock company   An unincorporated association that closely resembles a corporation but for most purposes is treated as a partnership.

joint tenancy   A co-ownership of property by two or more parties in which each owns an undivided interest that passes to the other co-owners on his or her death (known as the "right of survivorship").

joint tortfeasors   Two or more persons who in concert commit a tort; also two or more persons whose independent torts are so linked to an injury that a court will hold either or both liable.

joint venture   Collaboration by two or more firms involving a pooling of resources, integration of some aspect of the firms' operations, and an intent to accomplish a defined business objective that could not be accomplished as efficiently (or at all) by a single firm.

judgment notwithstanding the verdict (judgment n.o.v.)   The entry of a judgment by a trial judge in favor of one party even though the jury returned a verdict in favor of the other party.

judicial review   The process by which the courts oversee and determine the legitimacy or validity of executive, legislative, or administrative agency action.

junior security interest   A security interest or right that is subordinate to another security interest or right.

jurisdiction of a court   The power of a court to hear and decide a particular dispute and to issue a judgment that is legally binding on the parties in the dispute.

justice   The application of rules to arrive at what is recognized as a fair and reasonable result; also a title given to a judge.

landlord's lien   The right held by the landlord to seize, hold, or sell a tenant's personal property for nonpayment of rent.

Landrum-Griffin Act   A 1959 congressional amendment of the 1935 NLRA which established a bill of rights for union members, required public financial disclosures by unions and union leaders, and regulated election procedures for union officials by union members.

larceny   The unlawful taking and carrying away of property of another with the intent to permanently deprive the owner of its use.

latent defect   In sales law, an imperfection in a good that cannot be discovered by ordinary observation or inspection.

law   Enforceable rules governing the relationship of individuals and persons, their relationship to one another, and their relationship to an organized society.

lease   A conveyance to another of the right to possess property in return for a payment called rent.

leasehold   The interest acquired by the lessee under a lease.

leasehold estate   The real property held by the lessee who has been given temporary possession in return for payment of rent.

legacy   In a will, a specific gift of money.

legal detriment   A required element of contractual consideration; exists when the promisee does or promises to do something he or she is not legally obligated to do, or refrains or promises to refrain from doing something he or she has a legal right to do.

legal entity   An association recognized by law as having the legal rights and duties of a person.

legal impossibility of performance   An event that takes place after a contract is made, rendering performance under the contract, in the eyes of the law, something that cannot be done. Also referred to as objective impossibility, it legally discharges a party's obligation; it can be compared to subjective impossibility, which makes the contractual obligation more difficult to perform but does not discharge it.

legal rate of interest The rate of interest applied by statute where there is an agreement for interest to be paid but none is stated, or where the law implies a duty to pay interest irrespective of agreement. In the latter case, this may be referred to as a *judgment rate*, a rate of interest applied to judgments until paid by the defendant.

legal tender Any currency recognized by law as the medium of exchange that must be accepted by a creditor in satisfaction of a debtor's debt.

legal title That which represents ownership of property.

legislative history The history of the legislative enactment used by the court as a means of interpreting the terms of a statute. It consists primarily of legislative committee reports and the transcripts of committee hearings and floor debates.

lessee The person who leases or rents property from a lessor. If the lease involves an interest in real property, the lessee is frequently referred to as the tenant.

lessor The person who leases property to the lessee. If the lease involves an interest in real property, the lessor is frequently referred to as the landlord.

letter of credit A letter authorizing one person to pay money, to extend credit, or to supply a commodity to a third person on the credit of the writer.

libel Written defamation of one's character or reputation.

license In real property law, the landowner's permission for another to come upon his or her land. In intellectual property law, a contract by which the owner grants permission to another to use a patent, copyright, trademark, or trade secret, usually in return for payment of a royalty.

licensee In real property and tort law, a person who enters upon the property of another for his or her own convenience, pleasure, or benefit with the knowledge or consent of the owner. In other contexts, such as intellectual property law, one to whom a license is granted.

lien An interest held by a creditor in property of the debtor for the purpose of securing payment of the debt.

lien creditor In secured transactions law, any creditor who is able to legally attach the property of the debtor. This includes an assignee for the benefit of creditors, a trustee in bankruptcy, or an appointed receiver in equity.

life estate An interest in real property for the duration of the life of some designated person, who may be the life tenant or a third person.

life tenant The person holding (owning) a life estate in designated property.

limitation of remedies A provision in a sales contract which attempts to limit the remedies available to a party; usually employed by a seller to limit a buyer's remedies for breach of warranty.

limited defense See *personal defense*.

limited partnership A partnership created under statute with at least one limited and one general partner. The limited partner's liability to third persons is restricted to his or her capital contributions.

liquidated damages An amount of, or a method for computing, breach of contract damages that is agreed upon by the parties to a contract before a dispute actually arises.

liquidated debt An undisputed debt; that is, a debt about which there is no reasonable basis for dispute as to its existence or amount.

liquidating partner After an act of dissolution of the partnership, any partner who has authority to wind up the partnership, thereby terminating it.

liquidation Conversion of the assets of a corporation to cash and the subsequent distribution of the cash to creditors and shareholders.

liquidation preference Preferred shareholders' priority over common shareholders to the distribution of corporate assets upon the corporation's dissolution.

liquidation proceeding Under the Bankruptcy Act, a proceeding in which the debtor's assets are sold to pay off creditors insofar as it is possible to do so and the debtor is discharged from further responsibility.

lobbying contract A contract made by one person with another under the terms of which the former agrees to represent the latter's interest before legislative or administrative bodies by attempting to influence their votes or decisions on legislative, quasi-legislative, or related proceedings.

long-arm statutes Laws that permit a plaintiff to bring a certain action and recover a judgment in a court in his or her home state against a defendant who resides in another state.

lost property Property located at a place where it was not put by its owner, which place is unknown by the owner.

Magnuson-Moss Warranty Act A congressional enactment designed to prevent deceptive warranty practices, make warranties easier to understand, and create procedures for consumer enforcement of warranties. The act applies only to written warranties given in a consumer sales transaction and can be enforced by the Federal Trade Commission, attorney general, or an aggrieved party.

mail fraud The use of the mails for the purpose of executing a fraudulent scheme.

maker The person who creates or executes a promissory note or certificate of deposit.

marital deduction An estate planning device that can be used by the surviving husband or wife to effect substantial estate tax savings.

market (1) An area over which buyers and sellers negotiate the exchange of a well-defined commodity. (2) From the point of view of the consumer, the firms from which he or she can buy a well-defined product. (3) From the point of view of a producer, the buyers to whom it can sell a well-defined product. Market definition is crucial in determining the market shares of firms under antitrust scrutiny.

market division arrangements Any concerted action among actual or potential competitors to divide *geographic* markets, to assign particular *customers*, or to market particular *products* among themselves so as to avoid or limit competition. Such market divisions are treated as *per se* violations of Section 1 of the Sherman Act.

market power   The ability of a firm to raise its price without losing most of its customers.

market share   A firm's percentage of the production or sales in a relevant market; an important measure of market power.

maturity   In commercial paper, the time when a debt or obligation is due.

maximum rate of interest   A statutory limit on the amount of interest that can be charged on a given transaction.

mechanic's lien   A statutory lien against real property for labor, services, or materials used in improving the real property.

mens rea   The evil mental state required to attach criminal liability to a person for his or her conduct.

merchant   In sales law, a person who customarily deals in goods of the kind that are involved in a transaction, or who otherwise by occupation holds himself or herself out as having knowledge or skill peculiar to the goods involved in the transaction.

merger   The purchase of either the physical assets or the controlling share ownership of one company by another. As a business combination, a merger can come under antitrust review if the Justice Department or the FTC have reason to believe it might lessen competition.

metes and bounds   A term used to describe the exterior lines of a parcel of land where metes means measure of length and bounds refers to the boundaries of the property.

ministerial power   In administrative agency law, the routine day-to-day administration of the law, as opposed to discretionary powers, which involve the power to exercise judgment in the rendering of decisions.

minor   Any person under the age of majority. In most states the age of majority is eighteen years; in some it is 21.

minority shareholders   Those shareholders whose voting power is not sufficient to elect a majority of the directors, pass motions, or make binding decisions.

mirror image rule   A principle used in contract law where the acceptance must adhere exactly to the offer in order for it to be valid.

misdemeanor   Any crime or offense which is punishable by fine or imprisonment for less than a year. Less serious than a felony.

mislaid property   Property located at a place where it was put by the owner, who has now forgotten the location.

mistake   An unintentional error.

mitigation of damages   A duty imposed on an injured party to minimize his or her losses or injuries through the exercise of reasonable diligence and ordinary care after the injury has been inflicted.

Model Business Corporation Act   Uniform rules governing the incorporation and operation of corporations for profit recommended by the American Bar Association for enactment by the various states.

money   In commercial paper, any medium of exchange authorized or adopted by a domestic or foreign government as part of its currency.

monopoly   According to the economic model, a market having only one seller, high barriers to entry, and no close substitutes for the product being sold. The courts generally define a monopolist as a firm possessing such an overwhelming degree of market power that it is able to control prices or exclude competition.

moral agent   A person or organization capable of having moral obligations.

moral dilemmas   Situations involving two distinct moral obligations that are in conflict.

moral minimum   The minimum obligations of moral responsibility.

mortgage   The agreement by which a lien on a debtor's property is conveyed to a creditor.

mortgagee   The creditor in a mortgage agreement.

mortgagor   The debtor in a mortgage agreement.

motion to dismiss   Motion filed by the defendant in which he alleges that the complaint does not state a cause of action, in other words, that the complaint fails to state a legally recognizable claim.

mutual-benefit bailment   A nongratuitous bailment frequently formed by contract through which both parties benefit.

mutuality of obligation   The principle in contract law that both parties must obligate themselves in order for either to be obligated.

National Labor Relations Act (NLRA)   A 1935 congressional enactment regulating labor-management relations. This act (1) established methods for selecting a labor union that would represent a particular group of employees, (2) required the employer to bargain with that union, (3) prescribed certain fundamental employee rights, (4) prohibited several "unfair labor practices" by employers, and (5) created the National Labor Relations Board to administer and enforce the NLRA. Also known as the Wagner Act.

natural monopoly   Unusual market structure resulting from unique characteristics of the product or service offered. Some goods (e.g., electricity) or services (e.g., local telephone system) require large capital outlays and/or require uniformity in delivery systems so that only one firm can efficiently provide them at a profit.

necessaries   In contract law, items contracted for which the law deems essential to a person's life or health (usually such items as food, clothing, shelter, medical services, and primary and secondary education).

negligence   The failure to exercise reasonable care required under the circumstances, which failure is the proximate or direct cause of damage or injury to another.

negotiability   The status of an instrument that meets the requirements under the UCC for an instrument to be negotiable.

negotiable document of title   A document of title in which the terms state the goods are to be delivered to "bearer" or to the "order" of a named person. The person who is in legal possession of the document is entitled to the goods described therein.

negotiable instrument A signed written document that contains an unconditional promise or order to pay a sum certain in money on demand or at a definite time to the order of a specific person or to bearer. The document can be either a draft, a check, a certificate of deposit, or a note.

negotiation The transfer of an instrument in such form that the transferee becomes a holder.

nominal damages A monetary award by a court where there is a breach of duty or contract but where no financial loss has occurred or been proven.

nonexempt property The property of a debtor subject to the claims of unsecured creditors.

nonexistent principal A principal not recognized by law.

nonnegotiable document of title A document of title which states that the goods are to be delivered to a specific person or entity. Legal possession of this document is not tantamount to ownership of the goods.

nonnegotiable instrument An instrument that does not meet the requirements of negotiability under the UCC.

nonprice predation Conduct by a dominant firm that is aimed at increasing the costs of competitors or increasing entry barriers for potential competitors.

nonprofit corporation A private corporation formed to perform a religious, charitable, educational, or benevolent purpose without a profit-oriented goal.

nonstock corporation A corporation in which capital stock is not issued; usually occurs only in the case of a nonprofit corporation.

nontrading partnership A partnership formed primarily for the production (but not sale) of commodities or for the providing of services.

no-par value stock Stock issued by a corporation with no amount stated in the certificate. The amount a subscriber pays is determined by the board of directors.

note In commercial paper, an instrument whereby one party (the maker) promises to pay another (the payee or bearer) a sum of money on demand or at a stated date.

notice A fact that a person actually knows, or one he or she should know exists based on all facts and circumstances.

novation The substitution, by agreement, of a new contract for an existing one, thereby terminating the old contract. This is usually accomplished by a three-sided agreement of the parties that a third person's performance be substituted for that of one of the original parties to the contract.

nuisance Action by a defendant that impinges upon or interferes with the rights of others. The remedy for plaintiff is an injunction compelling abatement.

nuncupative will An oral will permitted by some states but on which significant restrictions and conditions are imposed by statute.

obligee The person to whom a duty is owed.

obligor A person who owes a duty to another.

occupation In personal property law, the acquisition of unowned property by the first person to take possession with an intent to become the owner.

Occupational Safety and Health Act (OSHA) A 1970 congressional enactment creating the Occupational Safety and Health Administration as part of the Labor Department, and requiring that agency to develop and enforce occupational safety and health standards for American industries.

offer In contract law, a proposal made by an offeror which manifests a present intent to be legally bound and expresses the proposed terms with reasonable definiteness.

offeree The person to whom an offer is made.

offeror A person who makes a proposal to another, with the view in mind that if it is accepted, it will create a legally enforceable agreement between the parties.

oligopoly A market structure in which a small number of firms dominate the industry.

open listing The arrangement by a seller of real property whereby the seller's obligation to pay a commission to a broker arises only if he or she is the first broker to procure an acceptable buyer (a buyer who is ready, willing, and able to buy at the stated price).

option An irrevocable offer formed by contract and supported by consideration.

option contract A contract in which consideration is given to the offeror from the offeree in return for the promise to keep the offer open.

order instrument An instrument payable to a designated payee or payees, or whomever they so direct, and requiring for its negotiation the indorsement of those persons.

ordinary bailment Any bailment not classified as an extraordinary bailment.

output contract An enforceable agreement for the sale of all the goods produced by a seller (the exact amount of which is not set or known at the time of the agreement) or all those produced at a given plant of the seller during the term of the contract; a contract in which the seller agrees to sell and the buyer agrees to buy all or up to a stated amount that the seller produces.

owner-consent statute A legislative enactment in a few states whereby the owner is liable for the negligence of any person driving the owner's car with his or her permission.

ownership in place The rights to oil, gas, and other minerals while they are still in the ground.

pari delicto Parties equally at fault.

parol evidence rule A rule that in some instances prohibits the introduction of evidence, oral or written, that would, if admitted, vary, change, alter, or modify any terms or provisions of a complete and unambiguous written contract.

partially-disclosed principal In agency law, a principal who is known to exist but whose identity is unknown by third persons dealing with the agent.

participating preferred stock A type of preferred stock giving its holders the right to share with common shareholders in any dividends remaining after the preferred shareholders have received their preferred dividend and common shareholders have received their specified dividend.

partition The dividing of land co-owned by several persons into specific designated pieces (sections) of property.

partnership An association of two or more persons who by agreement as co-owners carry on a business for profit.

par value stock Stock that has been assigned a specific value by the board of directors; the amount is stated in the certificate, and the subscriber to the corporation must pay at least this amount.

payee The person to whom an instrument is made payable.

payment against documents A term in a contract that requires payment for goods upon receipt of their documents of title, even though the goods have not as yet arrived.

payor bank The bank (drawee) on which an instrument is drawn (payable).

per capita "By heads," in descent and distribution of a decedent's estate where the heirs are of one class (such as children) and take equal shares.

peremptory challenge The right to exclude a prospective juror without having to state a reason or cause.

perfection In secured transactions law, the concept whereby a secured party obtains a priority claim on the collateral of his or her debtor as against other interested parties by giving some form of notice of his or her outstanding security interest.

perfect tender rule In sales law, a rule of law providing that it is a seller's obligation to deliver or tender delivery of goods that are in strict conformance with the terms of the sales contract.

performance Carrying out of an obligation or promise according to the terms agreed to or specified. In contract law, complete performance by both parties discharges the contract.

periodic tenancy The interest created by a lease for an indefinite duration where rent is paid at specified intervals and a prescribed time for giving notice of termination is required.

per se **rule** Antitrust doctrine wherein certain types of group business behavior are inherently anticompetitive and are therefore automatically illegal. Horizontal price fixing and boycotts are examples of *per se* illegal activities.

personal defense In commercial paper, any defense by a party that cannot be asserted against a holder in due course or against a holder through a holder in due course. A personal defense (often referred to as a limited defense) is effective only against ordinary holders.

personal property All property not classified as real property; "movables." May be tangible (e.g., cars and gasoline) or intangible (e.g., shares of corporate stock and other contractual rights).

per stirpes "By roots or stocks," in descent and distribution of a decedent's estate, where a class of heirs take the share their predeceased ancestor would have taken.

piercing the corporate veil The action of a court in disregarding the separate legal entity (identity) of the corporation, thereby subjecting the owners to possible personal liability.

plain meaning rule The rule under which a court applies a particular statute literally, where it feels the wording of the statute is so clear as to require no interpretation (that is, no resort to outside factors).

plaintiff The party who initiates a civil lawsuit.

plat A map showing how pieces of real property are subdivided.

pledge In secured transactions law, a transfer of personal property from the debtor to the creditor, as security for a debt owed.

pledgee A person to whom personal property is pledged by a pledgor.

pledgor A person who makes a pledge of personal property to a pledgee.

police power The inherent power of a government to regulate matters affecting the health, safety, morals, and general welfare of its citizens; usually used to refer to such power possessed by the state governments, as distinguished from the federal police power.

possibility of reverter A future interest retained by the grantor when he or she conveys real property subject to a condition that upon the occurrence of a designated event the title will automatically be returned to the grantor or his or her heirs.

power of attorney An instrument or document authorizing one person to act as an agent for another (the principal), who is issuing the instrument or document. The agent does not have to be an attorney-at-law.

precatory Expressive of a wish or desire, as in a devise by a testator of real estate expressing the "hope" that the devisee will pass it on to another named party. Such language may not be legally binding.

precedent A rule of a previously decided case that serves as authority for a decision in a current controversy—the basis of the principle of *stare decisis*.

predatory pricing Below-cost pricing by a dominant firm for the purpose of suppressing competition.

preemption The federal regulation of an area of law which is so complete that any state statutes or other regulations affecting that area are, as to such area, completely void.

preemptive right The right of a shareholder to purchase shares of new stock issues of a corporation equal in number to enable the shareholder to maintain his or her proportionate interest in the corporation.

preexisting obligation A legal duty for performance previously contracted or imposed by statute. A later promise to perform an existing contractual obligation or a promise to perform a duty imposed by law is a promise without consideration and therefore unenforceable.

preference The transfer of property or payment of money by a debtor to one or more creditors in a manner that results in favoring those creditors over others. This is an act of bankruptcy, and the trustee can set aside the transfer if the creditors knew or had reason to know that the debtor was insolvent and if the transfer took place within four months of filing the petition in bankruptcy.

preferred stock A class of stock that has a priority or right over common stock as to payment of dividends and/or distribution of corporate assets upon dissolution.

preliminary negotiations In contract law, usually an invitation to a party to make an offer—not the offer itself but only an inquiry.

preponderance of the evidence The greater weight and degree of the credible evidence; this is the burden of proof in most civil lawsuits.

prescriptive easement An easement acquired without consent of the owner by continuous and open use for a prescribed statutory period.

presentment In commercial paper, the demand by a holder for payment or acceptance of an instrument.

presumption Upon introduction of certain proof, a fact that is assumed even though direct proof is lacking. Presumptions of fact usually are rebuttable while presumptions of law usually are not.

price discrimination Under the Robinson-Patman Act, the practice of charging different prices to different buyers for goods of like grade and quality.

price fixing Any action or agreement which tampers with the free market pricing mechanism of a product or service.

prima facie At first sight (Latin); on the face of it; a fact that will be considered as true unless disproved.

prima facie **case** In employment discrimination law, the situation that exists when the plaintiff has proved facts which make it logical to infer that intentional discrimination probably has occurred.

primary party The maker of a note or the acceptor of a draft or check.

principal One who agrees with another (called an *agent*) that that person will act on his or her behalf.

prior restraint Government action which prevents a rally, assembly, or expressive activity from taking place because of the probability of violence or other unlawful conduct. A prior restraint usually is unconstitutional.

private corporation A corporation formed by individuals, as compared to one formed by the government.

private law Rules of laws that determine rights and duties between private parties, that is, between individuals, associations, and corporations.

privilege An advantage or right granted by law. Using it as a defense, a person is permitted to perform an act that is not ordinarily permitted to others without liability. In some cases the defense of privilege is absolute, resulting in complete immunity from liability, while in other cases it is qualified, resulting in immunity only if certain factors are proven.

privileges and immunities clause A provision in the U.S. Constitution which usually prohibits a state from discriminating against the citizens of another state because of their out-of-state residency.

privity of contract Relationship of contract; a relationship that exists between two parties by virtue of their having entered into a contract.

probate The legal procedure by which a deceased person's property is inventoried and appraised, claims against the estate are paid, and remaining property is distributed to the heirs under the will or according to state law if there is no will.

procedural due process The constitutional requirement that government action be preceded by fair procedures, including notice and an opportunity to be heard.

procedural law The rules for carrying on a lawsuit (pleading, evidence, jurisdiction), as opposed to substantive law.

proceeds The money or property received from a sale.

professional corporation Where permitted, the formation of a corporation by persons engaged in a particular profession, such as medicine, law, or architecture.

profit Under real property law, a nonpossessory right to go upon the land of another and take something from it—sometimes referred to as "profit à prendre" (French), particularly when the interest involves the right to take growing crops from another's land.

promise In commercial paper, an undertaking to pay an instrument. The promise must be more than a mere acknowledgment of an obligation, such as an IOU.

promisee The person who has the legal right to demand performance of the promisor's obligation. In a bilateral contract both the offeror and the offeree are promisees. In a unilateral contract only the offeree is the promisee.

promisor The person who obligates himself or herself to do something. In a bilateral contract both offeror and offeree are promisors. In a unilateral contract only the offeror is the promisor.

promissory estoppel A doctrine whereby a promise made by a promisor will be enforced, although not supported by consideration, if such promise would reasonably induce the promisee to rely on that promise and thereby so change his or her position that injustice can be avoided only by enforcement of the promise.

promissory note A note containing the promise of the maker to pay the instrument upon presentment when due.

promoter A person who makes necessary arrangements and/or contracts for the formation of a corporation. Promoters are the planners for the creation of a corporation.

prospectus A document provided by a corporation that sets forth the nature and purposes of an issue of stock, bonds, or other securities being offered for sale, usually including additional financial data about the issuing corporation.

protest A formal certification of an instrument's notice of dishonor, under the seal of an authorized person or a notary public (required only for notice of dishonor of foreign drafts).

proximate cause   The foreseeable or direct connection between the breach of duty and an injury resulting from that breach.

proxy   An authorization by one person to act for another; usually refers to the exercise of a shareholder's voting rights by another person or group.

public corporation   A corporation formed by the government, as distinguished from one formed by private parties.

public law   Rules that deal with either the opinion of government or the relationship between a government and its people.

public policy   Any conduct, act, or objective that the law recognizes as being in the best interest of society at a given time. Any act or conduct contrary to the recognized standard is illegal, even if there is no statute expressly governing such act or conduct.

punitive damages   A monetary sum awarded as a punishment for certain wrongs committed by one person against another. The plaintiff must prove his or her actual out-of-pocket losses directly flowing from the wrong before punitive damages will be awarded.

purchase money security interest   A security interest taken or retained by a seller to secure all or part of the price of the collateral; also a security interest taken by a secured party who lends money specifically to allow the debtor to acquire the collateral (where the acquisition does subsequently take place).

qualified indorsement   An indorsement whereby the indorser does not guarantee payment but does extend warranties to subsequent holders; usually a blank or special indorsement accompanied by the words *without recourse*.

qualified indorser   An indorser who only guarantees that he or she has no knowledge of any defense against him or her.

quasi-contract   A contract imposed upon the parties by law to prevent unjust enrichment, even though the parties did not intend to enter into a contract (sometimes referred to as an *implied-in-law contract*).

quasi-judicial   The case-hearing function of an administrative agency.

quasi-legislative   The rule-making power of an administrative agency.

quid pro quo   Something given or received for something else.

quid pro quo **harassment**   In employment discrimination law, unwelcome requests for sexual favors made to an employee by the employer or by someone for whose actions the employer is responsible, under circumstances indicating that the request is tied to tangible job benefits.

quitclaim deed   A deed by a grantor that passes to the grantee only those rights and interests (if any) the grantor has in the real property. This deed does not purport to convey any particular interest.

quorum   The number of qualified persons whose presence is required at a meeting for any action taken at the meeting to be valid. Unless otherwise specified, a majority.

ratification   The affirmance of a previous act.

rational basis test   The usual test applied by the courts in determining the constitutionality of a statute that is challenged on the ground that it violates the equal protection clause; under this test, if the classification of subject-matter in the statute is found to be reasonably related to the purposes of the statute, the statute is not a violation of the equal protection clause.

real defenses   In commercial paper, certain defenses listed in the UCC that can be asserted against any holder, including a holder in due course (sometimes referred to as universal defenses).

real estate mortgage note   A note secured by a parcel or parcels of the maker's real property.

real property   Land and most things attached to the land, such as buildings and vegetation.

reasonable definiteness   In contract law, the requirement that a contract possess sufficient certainty to enable a court to determine the rights and obligations of the parties (especially to determine whether a breach has occurred).

receiver   A person appointed and supervised by the court to temporarily manage a business or other assets for the benefit of creditors or others who ultimately may be entitled to the assets. The business or other property is said to be placed in *receivership*.

recording   The filing of a document with a proper public official, which serves as notice to the public of a person's interest.

redemption   The exercise of the right to buy back or reclaim property upon the performance of a specified act.

reformation (of contract)   An equitable remedy that modifies the actual words of the existing contract to reflect the true intentions or agreement of the contracting parties at the time of the making of the contract.

registration statement   A document setting forth certain corporate financial and ownership data, including a prospectus, that is generally required by the SEC to be filed with it before the corporation can offer its securities for sale.

rejection   In contract law, a refusal by the offeree of proposal or offer of the offeror, such refusal being known to the offeror.

release   The voluntary relinquishing of a right, lien, interest, or any other obligation.

relevant market   In antitrust law, the geographic area and/or product or products determined by a court or government agency to measure whether an antitrust violation has taken place.

remand   To send back a case from an appellate court to the lower court with instructions (usually to hold a new trial).

remedy   Generally, the means by which a right is enforced or a wrong is prevented; in a narrower sense, a court order addressed to the defendant, in proper circumstances, requiring the defendant to do a particular act requested by plaintiff (e.g., payment of damages) or to refrain from a particular act (e.g., prohibition of specified conduct on the part of defendant by the issuance of an injunction).

renunciation In commercial paper, the action of a holder who gives up his or her rights against a party to an instrument either by giving a signed writing or by surrendering the instrument to that party.

reorganization case A procedure under Chapter 11 of the Bankruptcy Act which reorganizes a company and restructures its debt in order to allow for the continuance of a business.

replevin A legal remedy that permits recovery of possession of personal property.

repossession The taking back or regaining of possession of property, usually on the default of a debtor. Repossession can take place peaceably (without breach of the peace) or by judicial process.

requirements contract An enforceable agreement for a supply of goods, the exact amount of which is not set or known at the time of the agreement but which is intended to satisfy the needs of a buyer during the term of the contract; a contract in which the seller agrees to sell and the buyer agrees to buy all (or up to a stated amount) of the goods that the buyer needs.

res In law a thing or things; property (corpus) made subject to a trust.

resale price maintenance An agreement by which a seller and buyer agree on the price at which the buyer will resell to others. The agreement may be explicit or implicit and may be completely voluntary or forced upon one party by the other. Also called vertical price fixing.

rescission In contract law, the cancellation of a contract by a court, the effect being as if the contract had never been made.

reserved powers The constitutional rights of states to pass laws under powers that are not specifically delegated to the federal government.

respondeat superior The doctrine under which a master or employer can be held liable for the actions of his or her subordinate.

restitution An equitable remedy that places the nonbreach or injured party in his pre-contracting position or returns him or her to the status quo.

restraint of trade Any contract, agreement, or combination which eliminates or restricts competition (usually held to be against public policy and therefore illegal).

restrictive indorsement An indorsement that either is conditional or purports to prohibit the further transfer of an instrument, or an indorsement that states a particular purpose to be fulfilled before the restrictive indorser can be held liable on the instrument.

resulting trust A trust created by law, when none was intended, to carry out the intentions of the parties to a transaction where one of the parties is guilty of wrongdoing.

reversion A future right to possession kept by a person who has transferred land; an example is the landlord's right to possession after termination of a lease.

revocation In contract law, the withdrawing of an offer by the offeror.

risk of loss The financial burden for damage or destruction of property.

robbery The felonious taking of things of value from the person of another or in his or her presence, by force or intimidation.

Robinson-Patman Act A 1936 congressional enactment that substantially amended Section 2 of the Clayton Act, basically making it illegal for a seller in interstate commerce to so discriminate in price that the likely result would be competitive injury.

rule-making power The statutory right of an administrative agency to issue rules and regulations governing both the conduct and the activities of those within the agency's jurisdiction (referred to as an agency's *quasi-legislative function*).

sale Passage of a title from a seller to a buyer for a price.

sale of control A transfer by sale of a sufficient number of a corporation's shares of stock to allow the purchaser to control the corporation.

sale on approval A bailment of goods coupled with an offer to sell the goods to the bailee.

sale or return A sale of goods with possession and title passing to the buyer but with the buyer given the right, by agreement, to retransfer both possession and title to the seller without liability for doing so.

sanction A penalty used as a means of coercing obedience with the law or with rules and regulations.

scienter The intent to deceive, manipulate, or defraud.

scope of employment The range of activities of a servant for which the master is liable to third persons. These actions may be expressly directed by the master or incidental to or foreseeable in the performance of employment duties.

secondary party The drawer or indorser of an instrument.

secured party The lender, seller, or other person in whose favor there is a security interest.

securities In securities regulation law, primarily stocks and bonds; also includes such items as debentures, investment contracts, and certificates of interest or participation in profit sharing agreements.

Securities Act of 1933 A federal statute establishing requirements for the registration of securities sold in interstate commerce or through the mails (prior to sale). The statute basically requires that pertinent financial information be disclosed to both the Securities and Exchange Commission and to the prospective purchaser. A misleading failure to make such disclosure renders directors, officers, accountants, and underwriters severally and jointly liable.

Securities and Exchange Commission A federal agency given the responsibility to administer and enforce federal securities laws.

Securities Exchange Act of 1934 A federal statute designed to strengthen the Securities Act of 1933 and expand regulation in the securities business. This Act deals with regulation of national stock exchanges and over-the-counter markets. Numerous provisions were enacted to prevent unfair practices in trading of stock, to control bank credit used for speculation, to compel publicity as to the affairs of corporations listed on these exchanges, and to prohibit the use of inside information. This Act created the Securities and Exchange Commission (SEC).

security agreement The contractual arrangement made between a debtor and a secured party.

security interest The right or interest in property held by a secured party to guarantee the payment or performance of an obligation.

separation of powers The result of the U.S. Constitution, which created and balanced the powers of three branches of government (executive, legislative, and judicial) by giving each separate duties and jurisdictions.

service mark A name or mark used to distinguish one provider of services from others; under proper circumstances a service mark may receive the same protection that a trademarked good receives.

servient estate The land that gives up or is subject to an easement.

settlor The party who establishes a trust by transferring property to a trustee to be managed for the benefit of another.

severable In contract law, the portion of a contract that, in the eyes of the law, is capable of possessing an independent legal existence separate from other parts of the same contract. Thus certain obligations of a severable contract may be construed as legally valid even though a clause or part of the contract purporting to create other obligations is declared illegal.

sexual harassment Harassment or intimidation of an employee based on the employee's sex.

shareholder The owner of one or more shares of capital stock in a corporation.

shareholder agreement A binding agreement made prior to a meeting by a group of shareholders as to the manner in which they will cast their votes on certain issues.

shares of capital stock Instruments in the form of equity securities representing an ownership interest in a corporation.

shelf registration A SEC rule which allows a company to file one registration statement for the future sale of securities and, thus, enables the company to react quickly to favorable market conditions and raise capital on short notice.

Sherman Antitrust Act An 1890 congressional enactment that (1) made illegal every contract, combination in the form of trust or otherwise, or conspiracy in restraint of trade or commerce among the several states, and (2) made it illegal for any person to monopolize, or attempt to monopolize, or combine or conspire with any other person or persons to monopolize any part of the trade or commerce among the several states.

shipment contract In sales law, a contract whereby the seller is authorized or required to ship goods to the buyer by delivery to a carrier.

short-swing profits In securities law, any profits made on a sale and purchase or purchase and sale of securities where both took place within a six-month period.

sight draft A draft payable on demand; that is, upon presentment to the drawee.

slander Oral defamation of one's character or reputation.

sole proprietorship A person engaged in business for himself or herself without creating any form of business organization.

sovereign compulsion The doctrine under which a domestic court will refuse to hold a defendant liable for actions that it was required to take by the law of a recognized foreign sovereign.

sovereign immunity The doctrine that bars a person from suing a government body without its consent.

special indorsement An indorsement that specifies the person to whom or to whose order the instrument is payable and that requires a proper indorsement of the indorsee for further negotiation.

special warranty deed A deed containing a warranty by the grantor that the title being conveyed has not been impaired by the grantor's own act; in other words, the grantor's liability is limited to his or her own actions.

specific performance A decree issued by a court of equity that compels a person to perform his or her part of the contract where damages are inadequate as a remedy and the subject matter of the contract is unique.

spendthrift trust A provision in a private, express trust to prevent the beneficiary from squandering the principal or income of the trust.

stale check Any noncertified check that is over six months old.

standing The right to sue.

stare decisis Literally "stand by the decision"—a principle by which once a decision has been made by a court, it serves as a precedent or a basis for future decisions of similar cases.

statute of frauds The requirement that certain types of contracts be in writing (or that there be written evidence of the existence of the oral contract) in order for the contract to be enforceable in a lawsuit.

statute of limitations A law that sets forth a maximum time period, from the happening of an event, for a legal action to be properly filed in or taken to court. The statute bars the use of the courts for recovery if such action is not filed during the specified time.

statutes of descent and distribution State laws that specify to whom and in what proportions the estate of an intestate decedent will be distributed.

statutory law Enforceable rules enacted by a legislative body.

stock Equity securities that evidence an ownership interest in a corporation; shares of ownership in a corporation.

stock certificate A formal document that provides evidence of the ownership of particular shares of stock.

stock dividend   A dividend which consists of the issuance of additional shares of the corporation's own stock to be given to the current shareholders.

stock subscription   An offer by a prospective investor to buy shares in a corporation.

stop payment order   A bank customer's direction (order) to his or her bank to refuse to honor (pay) a check drawn by him or her upon presentment.

strict liability   A legal theory under which a person can be held liable for damage or injury even if not at fault or negligent. Basically, any seller of a defective product that is unreasonably dangerous is liable for any damage or injury caused by the product, provided that the seller is a merchant and the product has not been modified or substantially changed since leaving the seller's possession. This rule applies even if there is no sale of the product and even if the seller exercised due care.

strike   A cessation of work by employees for the purpose of coercing their employer to accede to some demand. A strike is legal only if it consists of a complete work stoppage by a participating majority of employees for a legally recognized labor objective.

S corporation   A corporation with only one class of stock held by thirty-five or fewer individual stockholders who all agree in writing that the corporation will be taxed in the same manner as a partnership.

sublease   The transfer by the lessee (tenant) of a portion of the leasehold to a third party, as compared to an assignment of a lease, where the lessee transfers the entire unexpired term of the leasehold to a third party.

subrogation   The substitution of one person in another's place, allowing the party substituted the same rights and claims as the party being substituted.

subsidiary corporation   A corporation that is controlled by another corporation (called a *parent corporation*) through the ownership of a controlling amount of voting stock.

substantial performance   The doctrine that a person who performs his or her contract in all major respects and in good faith, with only slight deviation, has adequately performed the contract and can therefore recover the contract price less any damages resulting from the slight deviation.

substantive due process   The constitutional requirement that government action must be fair and reasonable in substance.

substantive law   The basic rights and duties of parties as provided for in any field of law, as opposed to procedural law, under which these rights and duties are determined in a lawsuit.

subsurface rights   The right of a landowner to use or own minerals, oil, gas, and the like beneath the land's surface.

summary judgment   A court's judgment for one party in a lawsuit, before trial, on the ground that there are no disputed issues of fact which would necessitate a trial. The court's conclusion is based upon the motion of that party, the pleadings, affidavits, depositions, and other documentary evidence.

summons   A writ by a court that is served on the defendant, notifying that person of the cause of action claimed by the plaintiff and of the requirement to answer.

surety   A person or business entity that insures or guarantees the debt of another by becoming legally liable for the debt upon default.

symbolic delivery   The delivery of something that represents ownership of or control over an item of property in a case where actual physical delivery of the property itself is not feasible because of its bulk or because it is intangible (often referred to as constructive delivery).

Taft-Hartley Act   A 1947 congressional amendment of the 1935 NLRA which (1) prohibited certain "unfair labor practices" by unions, (2) outlawed closed shop agreements, (3) established the Federal Mediation and Conciliation Service for the purpose of assisting employers and unions in reaching compromises, (4) granted employers and unions the power to file lawsuits to enforce collective bargaining agreements, and (5) gave the president authority to intervene in industry-wide disputes when, in the president's opinion, the occurrence or continuance of the dispute would "imperil the national health or safety." This Act is also known as the Labor-Management Relations Act.

tellers   Impartial individuals used to supervise an election (sometimes referred to as judges or inspectors).

tenancy at sufferance   The interest held by a tenant who remains on the land beyond the period of his or her rightful tenancy and without permission of the landlord.

tenancy at will   The interest created by a lease for an indefinite duration that either party can terminate at any time.

tenancy by the entirety   A joint tenancy between husband and wife. In some states neither of the spouses can convey their interest without the consent of the other.

tenancy for years   The interest created by a lease for a specific period of time.

tenancy in common   A co-ownership of property by two or more parties in which each owns an undivided interest that passes to his or her heirs at death.

tenants in partnership   The legal interest of partners in partnership property.

tender   An offer by a contracting party to pay money, or deliver goods, or perform any other act required of him or her under the contract.

tender of delivery   In sales law, where the seller places or holds conforming goods at the buyer's disposition and gives the buyer notification sufficient to enable that person to take possession of the goods.

tender offer   In securities regulation law, an offer to buy a certain amount of a corporation's stock at a specified price per share; usually made with the intention of obtaining the controlling interest in the corporation.

tenor   In commercial paper, the exact copy of an instrument. If the amount of an instrument has been altered, the holder in due course can recover only the original amount on the instrument, called the original tenor.

termination   The ending of an offer, contract, or legal relationship (usually an ending without liability).

term insurance   Life insurance which is effective only for a specified period of time, and which does not build up a cash surrender value or include a borrowing privilege.

testamentary capacity   The state of mind of a testator in knowing what property is owned and how he or she wants to dispose of it.

testamentary trust   A trust created by the settlor's will, to be effective on his or her death.

testate   The situation in which a person dies leaving a valid will.

testator (female, testatrix)   A person who makes a will.

textual context   The court's reading of a statute in its entirety rather than a single section or part; a principle of statutory interpretation.

time instrument   An instrument which is payable at a specific future date.

time is of the essence   In contract law, a phrase in a contract that requires performance within a specified time as a condition precedent to liability.

title   A person's right of ownership in property. The extent of this right is dependent on the type of title held.

title examination   The buyer's investigation of a seller's title to real property.

title insurance   A policy issued by an insurance company to compensate a buyer of real property for any loss he or she will suffer if the title proves to be defective.

Title VII   That portion of the Civil Rights Act of 1964 that prohibits discrimination in employment on the basis of race, color, religion, sex, or national origin.

title warranty   In sales law, an assurance or guarantee given by the seller, expressly or impliedly, to the buyer that he or she has good title and the right to transfer that title, and that the goods are free from undisclosed security interests.

tort   A noncontractual wrong committed by one against another. To be considered a tort, the wrong must be a breach of a legal duty directly resulting in harm.

tortfeasor   A person who commits a noncontractual wrong (sometimes referred to as a *wrongdoer*).

tort of conversion   One's unlawful interference with the right of another to possess or use his or her personal property.

trade acceptance   A draft or bill of exchange drawn by a seller of goods on the purchaser and obligating the purchaser to pay the instrument upon acceptance.

trade dress   The distinctive packaging of a product that may earn protection similar to that granted the trademark of the product itself.

trade fixture   A piece of personal property affixed by a tenant to the real property that is necessary for carrying on the tenant's business.

trademark   A distinctive mark, sign, or motto that a business can reserve by law for its exclusive use in identifying itself or its product.

trade name   The name of a business; under proper circumstances it may earn the same protection as a trademark for goods that are sold. Examples include Sears and Macy's.

trade secret   Valuable, confidential data or know-how developed and possessed by a business firm; can be legally protected.

trading partnership   A partnership formed primarily for the purpose of buying and selling commodities.

transferee   A person to whom a transfer is made.

transferor   A person who makes a transfer.

treasury stock   Shares of stock that were originally issued by a corporation and that subsequently were reacquired by it.

trespass   In realty and personalty, the wrongful invasion of the property rights of another.

trust   Two or more companies that have a monopoly. In the law of property, a relationship whereby a settlor transfers legal ownership of property to a trustee to be held and managed for a beneficiary who has equitable title to the property.

trustee   One who administers a trust.

trustee in bankruptcy   A person elected or appointed to administer the estate of the bankrupt person.

trust indorsement   A restrictive indorsement that by its terms shows an intent to benefit the indorser or some third party.

tying agreement   Any arrangement in which one party agrees to supply a product or service only on the condition that the customer also take another product or service.

ultra vires   Any acts or actions of a corporation that are held to be unauthorized and beyond the scope of the corporate business as determined by law or by the articles of incorporation.

unconscionable contract   A contract or a clause within a contract which is so grossly unfair that a court will refuse to enforce it.

underwriter   The person or entity who markets a security offering from the issuer to dealers; analogous to a wholesaler.

undisclosed principal   In agency law, a principal whose identity and existence are unknown by third parties, leading them to believe that the agent is acting solely for himself or herself.

undue influence   The overcoming of a person's free will by misusing a position of confidence or relationship, thereby taking advantage of that person to affect his or her decisions or actions.

unenforceable contract   Generally a valid contract that cannot be enforced in a court of law because of a special rule of law or a failure to meet an additional legal requirement (such as a writing).

unfair labor practices   Certain practices, including employer domination of unions, interference with employee organizing, discrimination against union members, and refusal to bargain collectively, which were prohibited by the National Labor Relations Act (NLRA).

Uniform Commercial Code (UCC) Uniform rules dealing with the sale of goods, commercial paper, secured transactions in personal property, and certain aspects of banking, documents of title, and investment securities. Recommended by the National Conference of Commissioners on Uniform State Laws for enactment by the various states, it has been adopted by forty-nine states (and Louisiana has adopted parts of it).

Uniform Limited Partnership Act (ULPA) Uniform rules governing the organization and operation of limited partnerships recommended by the National Conference of Commissioners on Uniform State Laws for enactment by the various states. The ULPA was substantially modified in 1976 by the Revised Uniform Limited Partnership Act (RULPA).

Uniform Partnership Act (UPA) Uniform rules governing the partnership operation, particularly in the absence of an agreement, recommended by the National Conference of Commissioners on Uniform State Laws for enactment by the various states.

unilateral contract An offer or promise of the offeror which can become binding only by the completed performance of the offeree; an act for a promise, whereby the offeree's act is not only his or her acceptance but also the completed performance under the contract.

unilateral mistake A mistake in which only one party to a contract is in error as to the terms or performance expected under the contract.

universal defenses See *real defenses.*

unliquidated debt A disputed debt; a debt about which there is a reasonable basis for dispute as to its existence or amount.

unqualified indorsement A special or blank indorsement that guarantees payment upon proper presentment, dishonor, and notice of dishonor.

unqualified indorser An indorser who guarantees that no defense of any party is good against him or her.

usage of trade Any practice or method repeated with such regularity in a vocation or business that it becomes the legal basis for expected performance in future events within that vocation or business.

usury An interest charge exceeding the maximum amount permitted by statute.

U.S. Code The full and complete compilation of all federal statutes.

Utilitarianism An ethical theory that is committed solely to the purpose of promoting "the greatest good for the greatest number."

valid contract A contract that meets the four basic requirements for enforceability by the parties to it.

venue A designation of the right of the defendant to be tried in a proper court within a specific geographic area.

vertical integration A condition that exists when one firm operates at more than one level of the distribution chain for a product.

vertical merger A merger of two firms, one of which is a supplier or customer of the other.

vertical nonprice restriction An arrangement between a seller and buyer that places limitations on the area within which, location from which, or customers to whom the buyer can resell.

vertical price fixing See *resale price maintenance.*

vertical restraint of trade An arrangement among firms at different levels of the distribution chain that suppresses or limits intrabrand competition.

vicarious liability The liability of a person, not himself or herself at fault, for the actions of others.

voidable contract A contract from which one or both parties can, if they choose, legally withdraw without liability.

voidable transfer In bankruptcy law, a transfer by a bankrupt debtor that can be set aside by a trustee in bankruptcy.

void contract A contract without legal effect.

voir dire The examination of prospective jurors by lawyers in a particular case to determine their fitness (i.e., to discover whether they have an interest in the outcome of the suit, a bias or prejudice against a party, or are otherwise unlikely to exercise the objectivity necessary in jury deliberations).

voluntary case Under the Bankruptcy Act, a proceeding that is instituted by the debtor, not the creditors.

voting trust A trust whereby shareholders transfer their shares of stock to a trustee for the sole purpose of voting those shares. The shareholders, through trust certificates, retain all other rights as they pertain to the transferred shares.

wagering agreement Any agreement, bet, or lottery arrangement the performance of which is dependent primarily upon chance, such agreement usually being prohibited by statute. These agreements are in contrast to risk-shifting (insurance) contracts and speculative bargaining (commodity market) transactions, which are usually legal by statute.

waiver The voluntary giving up of a legal right.

warehouseman A person engaged in the business of storing the property of others for compensation.

warehouse receipt A document of title issued by a person engaged in the business of storing goods for hire and containing the terms of the storage agreement. A negotiable warehouse receipt acts as both receipt and evidence of title to the goods stored.

warranty An assurance or guaranty, expressly or impliedly made, that certain actions or rights can take place, that information given is correct, or that performance will conform to certain standards.

warranty deed A deed with covenants, express or implied, that the title to real property is good and complete.

warranty of fitness for a particular purpose In sales law, an implied warranty imposed by law on a seller, who has reason to know of the buyer's intended use of the goods (where the buyer relies on the seller's skill and judgment), that the goods are suitable for the buyer's intended use.

warranty of merchantability   In sales law, an implied warranty imposed by law upon a merchant seller of goods that the goods are fit for the ordinary purposes for which goods of that kind are used.

waste   A term used to describe a tenant's duty not to damage a landlord's reversionary interest.

watered stock   Shares of stock issued by a corporation for a consideration less than the par value or stated value of the stock.

whole life insurance   Life insurance which continues in effect during the entire life of the insured; this type of life insurance also builds up a cash surrender value over time, and often includes the privilege of borrowing money from the insurance company.

will   A document by which a person directs the disposition of his or her property (estate) upon his or her death.

winding up   The actual process of settling the affairs of a partnership or corporation after dissolution.

wire fraud   Fraud committed by use of telephone or telegraph or other such electronic means.

workers' compensation laws   State statutory provisions calling for payments to employees for accidental injuries or diseases arising out of and in the course of employment. These payments, for medical expenses and lost income, are made regardless of whether anyone is at fault.

writ of certiorari   An order issued by an appellate court directing a lower court to remit to it the record and proceedings of a particular case so that the actions of the lower court may be reviewed.

writ of execution   In a civil lawsuit in which the plaintiff has won, a court order directing an enforcement agent to sell the defendant's nonexempt property in order to pay the judgment against him or her.

Case Index*

Subject Index

Council on Environmental
Quality (CEQ), 1008
Counterclaim, 39
Counteroffer, 256
Course of dealing, 384
Course of performance,
384–385
Court-annexed arbitration, 60
Courts
of equity, 32
federal, 20–21
of law, 32
of limited jurisdiction, 20
state, 19–20
system of, 19–20
Covenant, 867
against encumbrances, 855
ancillary, 296
of quiet enjoyment, 855, 868
restrictive, 296
of seisin, 855
Cover, by buyer, 470–473
Credit cards, 1031–1032
case, 1033
Credit reports, 1032
Creditor beneficiaries, 349
Creditors
assignment for benefit of, 600
composition of, 600
general, 609
priorities among, 586–587
satisfaction of claims by (in
partnerships), 685–687
case, 686
secured, 602, 609
Creditors' composition agreement, 283
Creeping contract, 251
Crime. See also Computer
crime; Federal crime; White
collar crime
defined, 137
degree of moral turpitude,
138–139
degree of seriousness of, 138
elements of responsibility for,
142–144
general intent, 142
international, 156
jurisdiction over, 139
punishment for, 139–140
specific intent, 142
strict liability, 144
Criminal cases, jurisdiction
over, 23
Criminal law, 9, 160
defenses, 145–146
defenses negating intent,
144–145
international crime and, 156
as public law, 10
v. civil law, 137–138
Criminal liability
in agency relationship,
655–656
in partnerships, 685
Cross elasticity of demand, 952

Cross elasticity of supply, 953
Cross-examination, 45
Cruel and unusual punishment,
142
Cumulative voting (by share-
holders), 741
Currency controls, 1062
Curtesy, 852, 916

D

Damages, 9, 324
compensatory, 385–391
liquidated, 393–394
mitigation of, 391
money, 385–395
nominal, 393
punitive, 394
trademark infringement and,
191
Damages. See also Punitive
damages
Documents of title, 574–575
DDT, 1017
De facto discrimination,
108
Death, termination of agency
relationship by, 633
Debit instruments, 566
Debt
adjustment of, 617–619
nondischargeable, 612–613
liquidated, 282–283
settlement of, 282–283
statute of limitations and,
287
unliquidated, 282
Debt securities, 733
Debtor, 573
default of, 591–593
discharge of, 610–611
case, 611–612
distribution of estate of, 609
duties of, 602–603
estate of, 603–604
examination of, 602
right to request status of debt,
591
Debtor default, 1038–1039
Debtor-in-possession, 613
Decedent, 910
descendants of, 917
Deceptive trade practices, 248,
1023
Deceptive trade practices acts,
81, 201–202
Decree of specific performance,
32
Deed, 855–856, 858–859
of bargain and sale, 855
case, 857–858
general warranty deed, 855
quitclaim, 855
special warranty, 855
Defamation, 102, 171–173.
See also Commercial
defamation
Default judgment, 40

Defendants, 9
failure to respond of, 40
Defense, 39
Defensive merger, 785
Delectus personae, 673
Delegatee, 355
Delegation of duties under con-
tracts, 355–356
Delegator, 355
Demand instruments, 486, 497
Denial, 39
Deposition, 41
Deregulation, 133–134
Descent and distribution,
statutes of, 916–918
Destination contract, 462
Destruction of subject matter,
370–371
Detainer, 881
Deterrence, 139–140
Direct examination, 45
Directors of corporations,
761–762, 767–768
case, 765–767
Disclaimer, 821
Disclaimers
by custom or usage, 444
by examination, 443
by language, 443
of warranties, 443–444
Disclose or abstain rule, 806
Disclosure statement, in elec-
tronic banking, 564–565
Discovery proceedings, 41
case, 41–42
Discretionary powers, of administrative agencies, 121
Discrimination
gender, protection from,
109–110
racial, protection from,
108–109
Dishonor
damages for wrongful, 552
notice of, 537
Disparagement. See Injurious
falsehood
District courts. See General trial
courts
Diversity of citizenship, 24
Dividends
illegal, 746
right to, 743–744
Doctrine of equivalents,
195–196
Doctrine of incorporation,
97–98
Doctrine of substantial performance, 11
Documents, requests for production of, 41
Documents of title, 412–413
nonnegotiable, 413
Domestic corporation, 723
Domestic relations courts. See
Courts of limited jurisdiction
Dominant estate, 847

Donaldson, Thomas, 225
Double jeopardy, 140
Dower, 852, 916
Drafts, 482–483
dishonor of, 536
Drawee bank, 549
Drawers
forged signature of, 557–560
case, 559–560
negligent, 557–559
promissory liability of,
536–537
Due care, for corporate managers, 763–768
cases, 764–767
during takeover, 783
case, 784–785
Due process, 110–113
adjudicative-legislative distinction of, 112–113
deprivation of life, liberty, or
property, 111–112
Fourteenth Amendment,
97–98
procedural, 24, 111–113
requirements of, case,
113–115
significant contact and, 27
procedural requirements of,
112
and protection of criminal
defendant, 140–141
Duress, 327–328
case, 328–329
Duress defense, 144
Durham rule, 144
Duty, 160
of candor, 196
of care (in partnership), 677
fiduciary (in partnership),
677–679
case, 678
of loyalty during corporate
takeover, 782
moral, 213–214
negligence and, 161–163
nondelegable, 648
not to commit waste, 869
of obedience (in partnership),
677
to account, in agency relationship, 630
to notify, in agency relationship, 630
to render service (to partnership), 677
to speak, 320–321
case, 322–323
to warn, 447

E

Earnest money, 853
Easement, 335, 847–848
appurtenant, 847
by express grant or reservation, 848
by implication, 848